South American Handbook

Ben Box

If your system is jaded, South America will uplift your senses with the tropical sun rising over a palm-fringed beach, or a bracing wind blowing off the southern ice fields. Light can be blinding on the high altitude salt flats, or dense and green in the rainforest. The gentle scent of ripe guava fills the countryside, but the fire of chili from that innocent-looking jar will electrify your taste buds.

As capybara wade through wetland shallows in the Pantanal, the spectacled bear struggles for survival in secret places in the Andes. Penguins congregate in the lee of glaciers, while tiny swifts dart through mighty waterfalls and their eternal rainbows. Volcanoes come to life and the earth trembles, yet elsewhere there are ancient, immovable tabletop plateaux. But surpassing all is the Amazon Basin, the earth's greatest jungle, where the immensity of the trees and the smallest details of the wildlife are truly amazing.

You can explore the cities of prehispanic civilizations and the churches of colonial times, or you can immerse yourself in the present with its celebrations and its social dilemmas. Where past and present mix, there are festivals, crafts and gastronomy, from the humble potato in its umpteen varieties to the most sophisticated of wines.

If you are looking for something more active, throw yourself off a giant sand dune into a lake, or climb the highest mountain. Walk in the treetops of the rainforest, at eye level with birds and monkeys. Help homeless street kids gain a better life, or learn the martial arts of slaves. Dance in an Andean village square to a solo violin, or to techno brega in a warehouse-sized club in Belém. Whatever South America inspires you to do, you will find that there is no limit to the passion that it fires within you.

In this era of countless websites which bring images and information from every barrio and pueblito, the *South American Handbook* gives the details on how to navigate between each place, big or small. It is a celebration of the spirit of adventure and independence that characterizes travel in this part of the world. Drawing on the expertise of correspondents in the region and the experiences of travellers, the Handbook provides the thread from Acandí to Ushuaia and everywhere you may wish to stop off in between.

THIS PAGE Catedral Metropolitana, Brasília
PREVIOUS PAGE Scarlet macaw wing

Iguaçu Falls, Brazil

Where to go in South America

South America is a magnificently varied part of the world and tremendously hospitable. It is a tantalizing mixture of enticing images and ambiguous press reports, inspiring an air of mystery and a certain amount of trepidation. In common with many other places, South America suffers from meteorological, geological and social uncertainties. Within that context you will find some of the most dramatic landscapes on earth, biological diversity in a range of habitats, historical monuments of strength and elegance and a deep cultural resilience.

Salar de Uyuni, Bolivia

The Andes

Down the length of South America runs the Andean mountain chain, which starts in the north overlooking the Caribbean and ends in the south in the fabulous towers and spires of the Chaitén Massif and the Torres del Paine National Park. Condors patrol its deep canyons and strata of rocks display colours you never knew existed in stone. Out of Lake Titicaca, the highest navigable lake in the world, strode the Inca dynasty, founding Cuzco, which has metamorphosed into the gringo capital of South America. Further south, beautiful lakes in Chile and Argentina shelter beneath snowcapped peaks. On their shores are resorts for summer watersports, fishing and winter skiing. Unlike its treeless Argentine counterpart, Chilean Patagonia is a wet and windy confusion of fjords, channels and ancient woodlands.

Forests and wetlands

In the heart of the continent, the Amazon Basin contains 20% of the world's plant and bird species, 10% of the mammals and an inestimable number of insects. In the waters live some 2000 species of fish, plus shy giant otters, caiman and two species of freshwater dolphin. There are trees that strangle their neighbours, palms with a million thorns, plants that heal and vines that will blow your mind. Stalking in the undergrowth is the mythical jaguar, whose influence has spread through almost every religion that has come into contact with the rainforest. On its perimeter, cattle and cowboys share the land with wild birds and animals in the llanos of the Orinoco and the wetlands of the Brazilian/Bolivian Pantanal, while mysterious ecosystems hide on table-top mountains on the Venezuela/Brazil border and in Bolivia.

Islands and beaches

On the Pacific, at islands such as the Ballestas (Peru) and Isla de la Plata (Ecuador) you can see much marine life, but the destination par excellence is the Galápagos. On the peaks of massive volcanoes, which jut into the ocean, albatross, boobies, giant tortoises and iguanas have evolved with little instinctive fear of man, a paradise for naturalists. Meanwhile, the Atlantic coast of Brazil, all 7408 km of it, is an endless succession of beaches, in wooded coves, dotted with islands in the south, palm tree and dune-fringed in the north.

Football on Ipanema beach, Brazil

Paria Peninsula, Venezuela

Itineraries for South America

South America is a big place, so it's important not to be too ambitious on a first visit. Decide what type of holiday you want and research which countries offer what you are interested in. Then work out an itinerary in which the places you want to see and the distance between them coincides with the amount of time you have available. Over the years a Gringo Trail has become firmly established, a network of places to which foreigners tended to gravitate for reasons of shared interests, lower prices, safety in numbers and so on. Some of these places have passed into legend, others are still going strong. New places are added as fashions change or transport links are opened.

By plane you can visit many places and airpasses, both regional and domestic, will reduce the cost of flying a little, but if your travel budget (or carbon consciousness) prohibits air tickets, bus is the best alternative. Buses are rarely the stand-in-the-aisle with the chickens and the soldiers bone-shakers of lore. Many are comfortable and mechanically sound, easing the passage of long or mountainous journeys, but you should build the length of the ride into your schedule. Trains cannot be relied on as a main means of transport as most are for tourists and are highly priced at that. Car hire is also expensive and driving can be tiring, but those who enjoy the independence can do well and many bring their own cars or motorcycles. Cycling is also popular.

ITINERARY ONE: 3-4 weeks
Rivers, waterfalls and lakes

While three to four weeks will give plenty of time to do some exploration in any of the countries of South America, there are many itineraries covering more than one. Starting in Buenos Aires, where you will want to spend a couple of days to attune yourself, you can head west to the wine and adventure sports region of Mendoza, then cross the Andes to Valparaíso on the Pacific. Alternatively, go north to Iguazú Falls and venture into Brazil or Paraguay. Across the Río de la Plata is Uruguay, with its beaches and estancias. If you fly south there are many options for flitting between Argentina and Chile, in the Lake District, in the magnificent trekking territory of Torres del Paine and the Chaitén Massif and Tierra del Fuego. Northwest Argentina, with Salta as a base, opens up opportunities for crossing the Altiplano into Chile's Atacama or into southwest Bolivia with its multi-coloured lakes and volcanoes. Another ideal base is Cuzco, for Machu Picchu and Peru's southeastern jungle, the circuit around Arequipa and the Nazca Lines and the route around or across Lake Titicaca to Bolivia. Further up the Andean chain, northern Peru, with its pre-Inca archaeological sites and beaches, combines well with Ecuador's avenue of volcanoes and easily reachable Amazonian jungles and Pacific beaches. Brazil, often dubbed a continent in itself, has more than enough for a month-long trip: combinations of Rio de Janeiro, Salvador, the beaches north and south, the dunes of the Lençóis Maranhenses, the Amazon, the Pantanal wetlands. But just as Iguazú fits with Argentina, so it does with southeastern Brazilian trips. At the other extreme, from Manaus on the Amazon a road heads north to the Sabana Grande of Venezuela, with its table top mountains and waterfalls, and on to the Caribbean. Caracas and Maracaibo are further gateways, for Venezuela's coast and the northernmost reaches of the Andean chain, leading into Colombia and its colonial jewel on the sea, Cartagena.

Guambiano women, Silvia, Colombia

ITINERARY TWO: 6 - 8 weeks
Treks and wildlife tours

To see a variety of South American destinations in less than a month, some flights will be inevitable because of the distances involved. With more time, you need not leave the ground for the above suggestions and you can add on more destinations, particularly those that require a set number of days. For instance, to appreciate fully wildlife-watching in the Iberá marshes in northeast Argentina, or staying on an estancia in the Pampas, Patagonia or Uruguay, allow a couple of days. Climbing in the Andes (eg Aconcagua) and long-distance trekking in the Lake District or Patagonia will take up a good four days minimum (and may require acclimatization). Likewise, the many trails in the Inca heartland. Other good trekking options include many national parks in Ecuador, the Andes in Colombia and Venezuela, and the Chapada Diamantina in Brazil. Any boat journey on the Amazon takes a few days, while trips to jungle lodges, with accompanying river journeys, also require about four days. Shorter wildlife tours can be found in the Venezuelan Llanos. The basic Salar de Uyuni tour in Bolivia is three days. From the highlands of Bolivia heading east, the steep valleys of the Yungas offer welcome warmth before the Amazonian lowlands and an array of national parks: Madidi, Amboró and Noel Kempff Mercado. From the eastern city of Santa Cruz, take the train to Brazil and the Pantanal, or the new roads across the Chaco into Paraguay. From Asunción, Iguazú and the neighbouring Jesuit missions are not too far. In the north, the Guianas have some of the least spoiled swathes of rainforest, as well as savannahs and waterfalls. On their own they can be visited in under a month, but they fit well with northern Brazil, especially Belém and the mouth of the Amazon. Don't forget that if your Spanish or Portuguese needs some encouragement, a week's intensive course is a good introduction to your trip.

Gauchos at work, Argentina

Climbers on Cotopaxi, Ecuador

ITINERARY THREE: 3 months
Jungle, desert and mountains

In three months you can travel the length of the Andes, with plenty of side trips along the way. Some highlights might include San Agustín and Popayán in Colombia; Otavalo in northern Ecuador, with visits to birdwatching lodges; Quito and the volcanoes to the south, plus the Quilotoa circuit. Preferable crossings into Peru are at Macará for Piura and on to the fascinating archaeological and bird watching zone at Chiclayo, or south of Loja and Vilcabamba through to Chachapoyas, another area of prehispanic riches. It is simplest to take the coastal Panamerican Highway to Trujillo, then head up into the mountains and the trekking mecca of Huaraz. Spend a few days recharging your batteries in Lima then take the train up to Huancayo and the Central Andes, or the coast road to Nazca. Either way, your goal will be Cuzco, the Sacred Valley and a rainforest trip to Manu or Tambopata, before heading into Bolivia via Lake Titicaca. An Andean journey would then pass the Salar de Uyuni before descending to Northwest Argentina or the Chilean Pacific deserts. By the time you reach the far south (time this for the warmer months) meandering through channels and fjords, boating on lakes in ancient forests, scaling mountain passes and taking remote border crossings between Chile and Argentina will easily fill the three months. You can also cross South America from east to west. The Amazon river is a major transport route as far as Iquitos in Peru, from where you can head further via Pucallpa to the Central Highlands and over to the Pacific at Pisco or Lima, or to the Cordillera Blanca via La Unión. Alternatively boats from Iquitos go to Yurimaguas for the climb up to Chachapoyas and on to Chiclayo. A more southerly route would take in some of the new Interoceánica road through the far western state of Acre, to Puerto Maldonado in Peru (for Tambopata) and then to Cuzco.

Mount Fitz Roy, Argentina

Sucre, Bolivia

Contents

The *South American Handbook* 2015 is accompanied by exclusive website content, to help you get the most out of your travels without weighing you down. The site includes a wealth of background information on South America; accompanying photographs; special features; and topical travel tips from expert author Ben Box.

Enter the site at www.footprinttravelguides.com/guide, where you can register to get access to the exclusive areas of the website. You will need a copy of the book to answer password questions the first time you log in.

Contents

Footprint features

Essentials

Planning your trip

Best time to travel in South America

Making the best choice of when to visit South America depends on latitude as much as on the weather. For example, the far south of Argentina and Chile is busiest in the southern hemisphere summer, December-February; in winter, June-August, it is cold and snow and rain can disrupt transport. The further north you go the more the seasons fall into wet and dry. The Peruvian and Bolivian Andes are dry (and very cold at night) April-October, the rest of the year is rainy. The sierras of Ecuador and Colombia are wet February-May and October-November. East of the Andes is wet November-April, wettest March-May in the Amazon Basin. Each chapter details the intricacies of the weather, but changes in world climate and periodic phenomena such as El Niño can play havoc with the general rules.

Getting to South America

Air

Most South American countries have direct flights from **Europe**; only Paraguay does not. In many cases, though, the choice of departure point is limited to Madrid and one or two other cities (Paris or Amsterdam, for instance). Argentina and Brazil have the most options: France, Germany, Italy, Spain and the UK. Brazil also has flights from Lisbon to a number of cities. Where there are no direct flights connections can be made in the USA (Miami, or other gateways), Buenos Aires, Rio de Janeiro or São Paulo. **Main US gateways** are Miami, Houston, Dallas, Atlanta and New York. On the west coast, Los Angeles has flights to several South American cities. If buying airline tickets routed through the USA, check that US taxes are included in the price. Flights from **Canada** are mostly via the USA, although there are direct flights from Toronto to Bogotá. Likewise, flights from **Australia** and **New Zealand** are best through Los Angeles, except for the **LAN** route from Sydney and Auckland to Santiago, and **Qantas'** non-stop route Sydney-Santiago, from where connections can be made. From **Japan** and from **South Africa** there are direct flights to Brazil. Within **Latin America** there is plenty of choice on local carriers and some connections on US or European airlines. For airpasses, see below. To Guyana, the main routes are via the Caribbean (Port of Spain, Trinidad and Barbados) or New York, Miami and Toronto. Suriname is served by flights from Amsterdam and Port of Spain, while Guyane has flights from Paris and the French-speaking Caribbean. All three have air connections with northern Brazil.

Prices and discounts

Most airlines offer discounted fares on scheduled flights through agencies who specialize in this type of fare; some are listed in Tour operators, below. If you buy discounted air tickets always check the reservation with the airline concerned to make sure the flight still exists. Also remember the IATA airlines' schedules change in March and October each year, so if you're going to be away a long time it's best to leave return flight coupons open. Peak times are 7 December-15 January and 10 July-10 September. If you intend travelling during those times, book as far ahead as possible. Between February and May and September and November special offers may be available. **Note** Using the internet for booking flights, hotels and other services directly can give you some good deals. But don't forget that a travel agent can find the best flights to suit your itinerary, as well as providing advice on documents, insurance, safety, routes, lodging and times of year to travel. A reputable agent will also be bonded to give you some protection if things go wrong.

Air passes

Various airpasses are available, normally bought in conjunction with an international flight to South America. As well as its Brazil airpass, **TAM** has an airpass linking Brazil with South American countries except Colombia, Ecuador and the Guianas. You must include at least two of those countries with a maximum of two stops per country (four in Brazil) not including origin and destination; maximum number of countries is five; minimum stay five days, maximum 30; maximum eight coupons, which range from US$339-1236. Prices do not include taxes or surcharges (prices are higher if you arrive on an international carrier other than TAM).

The **One World Visit South America** air pass links all South American countries except the Guianas for passengers arriving and leaving on airlines in the One World Alliance and flights within South America must be with **American Airlines, British Airways, LAN or TAM**. Prices are mileage-based; minimum three flights, maximum stay one year.

LAN has an airpass valid for travel on any of its routes in South America, on any part of its network in South America (except the Falklands/Malvinas), available to anyone who has purchased an international ticket with LAN/TAM, Iberia, or a One World Alliance and certain other airlines (eg United). It's valid for 12 months and must be bought outside South America (except

Packing for South America

Everybody has their own preferences, but a good principle is to take half the clothes, and twice the money, that you think you will need. Listed here are those items most often mentioned. These include an inflatable travel pillow and strong shoes (footwear over 9½ English size, or 42 European size, is difficult to find in South America). Always take out a good travel insurance policy. You should also take waterproof clothing and waterproof treatment for leather footwear and wax earplugs, vital for long bus trips or in noisy hotels. Also important are flip flops, which can be worn in showers to avoid athlete's foot, and a sheet sleeping bag to avoid sleeping on dirty sheets in cheap hotels. Other useful things include: a clothes line, a nailbrush, a vacuum flask, a water bottle, a universal sink plug of the flanged type that will fit any waste-pipe, string, a Swiss Army knife, an alarm clock, candles (for power cuts), a torch/flashlight, pocket mirror, a padlock for the doors of the cheapest hotels (or for tent zip if camping), a small first-aid kit, sun hat, lip salve with sun protection, contraceptives, waterless soap, dental floss (which can also be used for repairs), wipes and a small sewing kit. Always carry toilet paper, especially on long bus trips. The most security conscious may also wish to include a length of chain and padlock for securing luggage to bed or bus/train seat, and a lockable canvas cover for your rucksack. Don't forget cables and adaptors for recharging phones, laptops and other electrical equipment. Contact lens wearers note that lens solution can be difficult to find in Bolivia and Peru. Ask for it in a pharmacy, rather than an opticians.

Brazil). The cost of coupons is given on the LAN website. Coupons cost more for those not arriving on LAN/TAM or Iberia. See the respective countries for air passes operated by national airlines.

Gol's Mercosul airpass covers flights in Argentina, Bolivia, Brazil, Chile, Paraguay and Uruguay. It is valid for five to 30 days, allows three to nine coupons and must include at least two countries in the area with a maximum of three stopovers and five flight coupons per country. Fares range from US$632-1252, based on the number of destinations.

Boat

Travelling as a passenger on a cargo ship to South America is not a cheap way to go, but if you have the time and want a bit of luxury, it makes a great alternative to flying. There are sailings from Europe to the Caribbean, east and west coasts of South America. Likewise, you can sail from US ports to east and west coast South America. In the main, passage is round trip only. Agencies which specialize in this type of travel include: **Cargo Ship Voyages Ltd**, 10 Westway, Cowes, Isle of Wight, PO31 8QP, T01983-303314, www.cargoshipvoyages.com. **Globoship**, Neuengasse 30, CH-3001, Bern, Switzerland, T031-313 0004, www.globoship.ch. **Strand Voyages**, Unit 695 The Chandlery, 50 Westminster Bridge Rd, London SE1 7QY, T020-7953 7607, www.strandtravelltd. co.uk. **The Cruise People**, 88 York St, London W1H 1QT, T020-7723 2450, and 1252 Lawrence Avenue East, Suites 210-214, Toronto, Canada, M3A 1C3, T416-900 0889, www.cruisepeople. co.uk or www.thecruisepeople.ca. **Travltips Cruise and Freighter Travel Association**, 25-37 Francis Lewis Blvd, Flushing, NY 11358, T800-872 8584, www.travltips.com.

Transport in South America

→ See Getting to South America for details of air transport.

Boat

Because air services have captured the lucrative end of the passenger market, passenger services on the rivers are in decline. Worst hit have been the upper reaches of rivers. The situation has been aggravated for the casual traveller by a new generation of purpose-built tugs (all engine-room and bridge), that can handle up to a dozen freight barges but have no passenger accommodation. In Peru passenger boats must now supplement incomes by carrying cargo, and this lengthens journeys. In the face of long delays, travellers might consider shorter 'legs' involving more frequent changes of boat; though the more local the service, the slower and more uncomfortable it will be. The introduction of fast boats on some major Amazon routes has speeded up journeys, but they cost a lot more than the regular passenger boats.

Hammocks, mosquito nets (not always good quality), plastic containers for water storage, kettles and cooking utensils can be purchased in any sizeable riverside town, as well as tinned food. Fresh bread, cake, eggs and fruit are available in most villages. Cabin bunks are provided with thin mattresses but these are often foul. Replacements can be bought locally but rolls of plastic foam that can be cut to size are also available and much cheaper. Eye-screws for securing washing lines and mosquito nets are useful, and tall passengers who are not taking a hammock and who may find insufficient headroom on some boats should consider a camp-chair.

In Venezuelan Amazonas hitching rides on boats is possible if you camp at the harbour or police post where all boats must register. Take any boat going in your direction as long as it reaches the next police post. See the special section on the Brazilian Amazon.

Bus and train

The continent has an extensive road system with frequent bus services. The buses are often comfortable; the difficulties of Andean terrain affect the quality of vehicles. In mountainous country do not expect buses to get to their destination after long journeys anywhere near on time. Do not turn up for a bus at the last minute; if it is full it may depart early. Tall travellers are advised to take aisle rather than window seats on long journeys as this allows more leg room. When the journey takes more than three or four hours, meal stops at roadside restaurants (usually with toilets), good and bad, are the rule. Usually, no announcement is made on the duration of a stop; ask the driver and follow him, if he eats, eat. See what the locals are eating and buy likewise, or make sure you're stocked up well on food and drink at the start. For drinks, stick to bottled water or soft drinks or coffee (black). The food sold by vendors at bus stops may be all right; watch if locals are buying, though unpeeled fruit is, of course, reliable.

Where they still run, trains are slower than buses. They tend to provide finer scenery and you can normally see much more wildlife than from the road – it is less disturbed by one or two trains a day than by the more frequent road traffic.

Car

The car A normal car will reach most places, but high ground clearance is useful for badly surfaced or unsurfaced roads and for fording rivers. For greater flexibility in mountain and jungle

Carnet de passages

There are two recognized documents for taking a vehicle through customs in South America: a *carnet de passages* issued jointly by the **Fedération Internationale de l'Automobile (FIA** – Paris) and the **Alliance Internationale de Tourisme (AIT** – Geneva), and the *Libreta de Pasos por Aduana* issued by the **Federación Interamericana de Touring y Automóvil Clubs (FITAC)**. The *carnet de passages* is recognized by all South American customs authorities but is not required by any. The *libreta*, a 10-page book of three-part passes for customs, should be available from any South American automobile club member of FITAC, but in practice it is only available to non-residents from the Touring y Automóvil Club de Venezuela. At US$400, it is not worth the effort or expense, nor is it needed to enter Venezuela. If you wish to purchase one of these documents, get a *carnet de passages*, issued in the country where the vehicle is registered. In the UK it costs £190, £195 or £200 for 5, 10 or 25 pages respectively, available from the **RAC**, www.rac.co.uk. In the USA the AAA does not issue the *carnet*, but both US and Canadian motorists can purchase it from the **Canadian Automobile Association** (CAA), with offices throughout Canada, www.caa.ca, who can give full details. In Canada the fee is CA$775 for CAA and AAA members, US$975 for non members. Also from the AAA of Australia, for a fee of AU$400, see www.aaa.asn.au/touring/overseas.htm. In all cases you have to add on administration fees, deposits and insurance premiums, which can take the cost into the thousands, depending on the value of the car. Ask the motoring organization in your home country about availability of the *carnet*.

territory 4WD vehicles are recommended. In Patagonia, main roads are gravel rather than paved: perfectly passable without 4WD. Consider fitting wire guards for headlamps, and for windscreens too. Diesel cars are cheaper to run than petrol ones and the fuel is easily available, although in Venezuela you may have to look hard for it outside Caracas. Standard European and Japanese cars run on fuel with a higher octane rating than is commonly available in North, South or Central America, and in Brazil petrol (*gasolina*) is in fact gasohol, with a 12% admixture of alcohol.

Security Spare no ingenuity in making your car secure, inside and out (even wing mirrors, spot lamps, wheels without locking nuts can be stolen). Try never to leave the car unattended except in a locked garage or guarded parking space. Lock the clutch or accelerator to the steering wheel with a heavy, obvious chain or lock. Street children will generally protect your car for a tip.

Documents To drive your own vehicle in South America, you must have an international driver's license. You must also have the vehicle's registration document in the name of the driver, or, in the case of a car registered in someone else's name, a notarized letter of authorization. Be very careful to keep **all** the papers you are given when you enter, to produce when you leave (see box, above).

Insurance Insurance for the vehicle against accident, damage or theft is best arranged in the country of origin. In Latin American countries it is very expensive to insure against accident and theft, especially as you should take into account the value of the car increased by duties calculated in real (ie non-devaluing) terms. If the car is stolen or written off you will be required to pay very high import duty on its value. Third-party insurance can be very difficult to find. Some countries may insist that it be bought at the border (Venezuela seems to be the only country where it is easy to obtain). If you can get the legally required minimum cover, so much the better. If not, drive with extreme caution and very defensively. If involved in an accident and you're uninsured, your car could be confiscated. If anyone is hurt, do not pick them up (you may become liable). Try to seek assistance from the nearest police station or hospital.

Car hire The main international car hire companies operate in all countries, but they tend to be very expensive, reflecting the high costs and accident rates. Hotels and tourist agencies will tell you where to find cheaper rates, but you will need to check that you have such basics as spare wheel, toolkit and functioning lights, etc. You'll probably have more fun if you drive yourself, although it's always possible to hire a car with driver. If you plan to do a lot of driving and will have time at the end to dispose of it, investigate the possibility of buying a second-hand car locally; since hiring is so expensive it may well work out cheaper and will probably do you just as well.

Car hire insurance Check exactly what the hirer's insurance policy covers. In many cases it only protects you against minor bumps and scrapes, not major accidents, nor 'natural' damage (eg flooding). Ask if extra cover is available. Also find out, if using a credit card, whether the card automatically includes insurance. Beware of being billed for scratches which were already on the vehicle. Also check the windscreen and ask what procedures are involved if a new one is needed.

Cycling

Unless you are planning a journey almost exclusively on paved roads – when a touring bike would suffice – a mountain bike is strongly recommended. The good quality ones (and the cast-iron rule is **never** to skimp on quality) are incredibly tough and rugged, with low gear ratios for difficult terrain, wide tyres with plenty of tread for good road-holding, V brakes, sealed hubs and bottom bracket and a low centre of gravity for improved stability. A chrome-alloy frame is better than aluminium as it can be welded. Although touring bikes, and to a lesser extent mountain bikes and spares are available in the larger Latin American cities, remember that most locally manufactured goods are shoddy. Where imported components can be found, they are very expensive. (Shimano parts are the easiest to find.) Buy everything you can before leaving home.

Remember that you can always stick your bike on a bus, canoe or plane to get yourself nearer to where you want your wheels to take you. This is especially useful when there are long stretches of major road ahead. In almost any country it is possible to rent a bike for a few days, or join an organized tour for riding in the mountains. You should check, however, that the machine you are hiring is up to the conditions you will be encountering, or that the tour company is not a fly-by-night outfit without back-up, good bikes or maintenance.

Visit www.warmshowers.org for a hospitality exchange for touring cyclists.

Motorcycling

The motorcycle The bike should be off-road capable. Buying a bike in the USA and driving down works out cheaper than buying one in the UK. Get to know the bike before you go, ask the dealers in your country what goes wrong with it and arrange to get parts flown out to you.

Security Try not to leave a fully laden bike on its own. An Abus D or chain will keep the bike secure. A cheap alarm gives you peace of mind if you leave the bike outside a hotel at night. Most hotels will allow you to bring the bike inside. Look for hotels that have a courtyard or more secure parking and never leave luggage on the bike overnight. Also take a cover for the bike.

Documents A passport, international driving licence and bike registration document are necessary. Riders fare much better with a *carnet de passages* (see box, opposite) than without.

Border crossings If you do not have a *carnet*, do not try to cross borders on a Sunday or a holiday as a charge is levied on the usually free borders. Customs and immigration inspectors are mostly friendly, polite and efficient. If in doubt ask to see the boss and/or the rule book.

Maps and guidebooks

Those from the **Institutos Geográficos Militares** or **Nacionales** in the capitals are often the only good maps available in Latin America. It is therefore wise to get as many as possible in your home country before leaving, especially if travelling by land. A recommended series of general maps is that published by **International Travel Maps** (ITM) ① *12300 Bridgeport Rd, Richmond, Vancouver BC, V6V 1J5, Canada, T604-273 1400, www.itmb.ca*. As well as maps of South America Southern, North East and North West (1:4M), there are maps of most countries, the Amazon Basin, Easter Island, the Galápagos and several cities. Another map series that has been mentioned is that of **New World Edition** ① *Bertelsmann, Neumarkter Strasse 18, 81673 München, Germany*, Mittelamerika, Südamerika Nord, Südamerika Sud, Brasilien (all 1:4M). **Stanford's** ① *12-14 Long Acre, Covent Garden, London WC2E 9LP, T020-7836 1321, www.stanfords.co.uk (another branch at 29 Corn St, Bristol, T0117-929 9966)*, also sells a wide variety of maps.

Where to stay in South America

Hotels Sleeping accommodation for independent travellers can be roughly divided into two types: hotels and hostels. Within each group there is wide variation of type and price. Choice is greater, and costs often higher, in big cities and popular tourist destinations. A decent hotel room may cost US$25-50, but can be more than this, especially when you get into the self-styled "boutique" range. Hostel prices also vary, from US$12-25 per person in a shared room, but most also have dearer private rooms. For those on a really tight budget, it is a good idea to ask for a boarding house – *casa de huéspedes, hospedaje, pensión, casa familial* or *residencial* (according to country) – they are normally to be found in abundance near bus and railway stations and markets. There are often great seasonal variations in hotel prices in resorts. Remember, cheaper hotels don't always supply soap, towels and toilet paper; in colder (higher) regions they may not supply enough blankets, so take a sleeping bag. To avoid price hikes for gringos, ask if there is a cheaper room.

Unless otherwise stated, all places to stay listed in this edition have shower and toilet, phone, TV and luggage storage. They are clean and friendly and offer breakfast. All but the most basic places have Wi-Fi and internet in common areas if not rooms. Hostels aimed at the backpacker market have a communal kitchen. In any class, hotel rooms facing the street may be noisy: always ask for the best, quietest room. The electric showers used in many hotels should be checked for obvious flaws in the wiring; try not to touch the rose while it is producing hot water. **Cockroaches** are ubiquitous and unpleasant, but not dangerous. Take some insecticide powder if staying in cheap hotels.

Alternatives to hotels and hostels are popular in South America. For bed-and-breakfast accommodation, see the website www.bedandbreakfast.com. The long-established **Experiment in International Living Ltd** ① *17 Graham Rd, Malvern, Worcestershire WR14 2HR, T01684-562577, and offices worldwide, http://eiluk.org*, can arrange stays with families from one to four weeks in Argentina, Brazil, Chile, Ecuador and Brazil, an excellent way to meet people and learn the language. They also offer volunteering opportunities. Many language schools offer lodging with families as part of the course. Short-term room rentals can be found on **AirBnB**, www.airbnb.com. **Travel networking** is widespread. Visit **www.couchsurfing.org**, **www.tripping.com, www.stay4free.com**, or one of many similar sites. **Tripbod**, www.tripbod.com, is a service linking travellers and local experts, to find the best local choices. A similar idea for eating, is **EatWithALocal**, www.eatwithalocal.com. The overall concept works, but don't go with

Price codes

Where to stay

$$$$	over US$150	$$$	US$66-150
$$	US$30-65	$	under US$30

Price of a double room in high season, including taxes.

Restaurants

$$$	over US$12	$$	US$7-12	$	US$6 and under

Prices for a two-course meal for one person, excluding drinks or service charge.

a contact on the first site you look at; check the security measures and that the interests of the site's other users coincide with yours.

Note If using a site like Booking.com to reserve a room in a hotel or hostel and it says "no rooms available", it is worth checking the establishment's own website because they may keep a few rooms off the general booking site and at a better price (direct payments avoid the booking site's commission charges).

Toilets Many hotels, restaurants and bars have inadequate water supplies. **Almost without exception used toilet paper should not be flushed down the pan, but placed in the receptacle provided**. This applies even in expensive hotels. Failing to do this will block the pan or drain, a considerable health risk. It is common to stand on the toilet seat (facing the wall, easier to balance).

Youth hostels Organizations affiliated to the Youth Hostels movement exist in Argentina, Brazil, Colombia, Chile, Peru and Uruguay. There is an associate organization in Ecuador. More information in individual countries and from **Hostelling International**. Independent sites on hostelling are the **Internet Guide to Hostelling**, www.hostels.com, **www.hosteltrail.com**, geared to hostels and budget lodging in South America, **www.hostelworld.com**, www.hostelsclub.com and **Ho.La Hostels**, www.holahostels.com, with an extensive list of hostels in South America.

Camping Organized campsites are referred to in the text immediately below hotel lists, under each town. If there is no organized site in town, a football pitch or gravel pit might serve. See the tips in Responsible Travel below and obey the following rules for 'wild' camping: (1) arrive in daylight and pitch your tent as it gets dark; (2) ask permission to camp from the parish priest, or the fire chief, or the police, or a farmer regarding his own property; (3) never ask a group of people – especially young people; (4) never camp on a beach (because of sandflies and thieves). If you can't get information from anyone, camp in a spot where you can't be seen from the nearest inhabited place, or road, and make sure no one saw you go there. In Argentina and Brazil, it is common to camp at gas/petrol stations. As Béatrice Völkle of Gampelen, Switzerland, adds, camping wild may be preferable to those organized sites which are treated as discos, with only the afternoon reserved for sleeping.

If taking a cooker, the most frequent recommendation is a multifuel stove (eg MSR International, Coleman Peak 1), which will burn unleaded petrol or, if that is not available, kerosene, benzina blanca, etc. Alcohol-burning stoves are simple, reliable, but slow and you have to carry a lot of fuel: for a methylated spirit-burning stove, the following fuels apply, *alcohol desnaturalizado, alcohol metílico, alcohol puro (de caña)* or *alcohol para quemar*. Ask for 95%, but 70% will suffice. In all countries fuel can usually be found in chemists/pharmacies. Gas cylinders and bottles are usually exchangeable, but if not can be recharged; specify whether you use butane or propane. Gas canisters are not always available. The **Camping Clube do Brasil** gives 50% discounts to holders of international campers' cards.

Food and drink in South America

Food in South America is enticingly varied and regionally based. Within one country you cannot guarantee that what you enjoyed on the coast will be available in the sierras. It is impossible to list here what is on offer in each country and there is a section on food and drink in each chapter's Planning your trip section. Chinese restaurants tend to offer good value and where there are large immigrant communities you'll find excellent Japanese or Italian restaurants. Pizza is ubiquitous, sometimes genuine, sometimes anything but. Then there's fruit, fruit and more fruit in all the tropical regions, eaten fresh or as ice cream, or as a juice.

In all countries except Brazil and Chile (where cold meats, cheese, eggs, fruit, etc, generally figure) breakfast usually means coffee or tea with rolls and butter, and anything more costs extra. In Colombia and Ecuador breakfast usually means eggs, a roll, fruit juice and a mug of milk with coffee. **Vegetarians** should be able to list all the foods they cannot eat; saying "*soy vegetariano/a*" (I'm a vegetarian) or "*no como carne*" (I don't eat meat) is often not enough. Most restaurants serve a daily special meal, usually at lunchtime, which is cheap and good.

Shopping in South America

Handicrafts, like food, enjoy regional distinctiveness, especially in items such as textiles. In the Andes, weaving has a spiritual significance, as well as a practical one. Each region, even every village, has its own distinct pattern or style of cloth, so the choice is enormous. Reproductions of pre-Columbian designs can be found in pottery and jewellery and many artisans make delightful gold and silver items. Musical instruments (eg from Bolivia), gaucho wear, the *mate* drinking gourd and silver straw (*bombilla*), soapstone carvings and ceramics are just some things you take home. Remember that handicrafts are almost invariably cheaper away from the capital. **Gemstones** are good in Brazil; emeralds in Colombia. Leather goods are best in Argentina, Uruguay, Brazil and Colombia, while Peru markets native cotton. Buy **beachwear** in Brazil; it is matchless. **Bargaining** seems to be the general rule in most street markets, but don't make a fool of yourself by bargaining over what, to you, is a small amount of money.

What to do in South America

Bird and wildlife watching

At least 980 of the 2926 species of birds registered in South America exist in **Argentina**. Enthusiasts head for Península Valdés, Patagonia (to see marine mammals as well as birds), the subtropical forests in the northwest, or the Iberá Marshes and Chaco savanna in the northeast. The pampas, too, have rich birdlife, characterized by the oven birds, horneros, which build oven-shaped nests six times as big as themselves on the top of telegraph and fence posts. Contact www.avesargentinas.org.ar.

Bolivia has more than 40 well-defined ecological regions and the transition zones between them. On a trip to the Salar de Uyuni you will see Andean birdlife but also landscapes of unmatched, stark beauty. For lowland birds and animals, the main options are Rurrenabaque in the lowlands of the river Beni and the Parque Nacional Amboró, three hours west of Santa Cruz, containing ecosystems of the Amazon basin, Andean foothills and the savannahs of the Chaco plain. For table-top mountains, forests, cerrado, wetlands and a stunning array of wildlife, make the effort to get to Parque Nacional Noel Kempff Mercado.

Brazil's habitats include Amazonian rainforest, the Pantanal wetlands, the subtropical forest at Iguaçu, the cerrado of the central plateau, the arid northeast, the Lagoa dos Patos of Rio Grande do Sul and the few remaining pockets of Mata Atlântica of the east coast. None is difficult to get to and a variety of birds can be seen, including many endemics. National parks and protected areas, including those offshore (Abrolhos, Fernando de Noronha), are designed to allow access to Brazil's areas of outstanding beauty. Whales, eg off Santa Catarina, can be seen May-November. For serious birdwatching, contact **Pantanal Bird Club** ① *www.pantanal birdclub.org*, and **Birding Brazil Tours** ① *www.birdingbraziltours.com*.

In **Chile** birdwatching opportunities vary from the flamingos and wildfowl of the altiplano, as in the Parque Nacional Lauca in the far north, to the birds of the forests in the south, to the condors, geese and other species in the Torres del Paine. See www.avesdechile.cl (in Spanish). Mammals include llama, alpaca, vicuña and guanaco, and the rare deer, pudú and huemul. The trees of Chile are another attraction: many deciduous varieties, the araucaria, or monkey-puzzle tree, and areas of very ancient forest. Also, the flowering of the desert is a sight to look out for.

Colombia claims to have more birds than any other country in a wide variety of habitats. Some of the more easily accessible areas are the Parque Nacional Tayrona, the marshes between Santa Marta and Barranquilla, several good spots around the capital, Parque Nacional Los Nevados, the Laguna de Sonso, near Buga, and the road from Cali to Buenaventura, around Popayán, Puracé and San Agustín, La Planada Reserve near Pasto, some routes into the eastern Llanos (eg Garzón to Florencia and Pasto to Mocoa) and around Leticia (eg the Parque Nacional Amacayacu). Contact www.proaves.org. For migratory species, not just birds, but also whales and turtles, visit the Pacific coast between July and October.

Ecuador The Galápagos Islands are the top destination for reliably seeing wildlife close-up, but a number of the species from the Galápagos may also be seen in the Parque Nacional Machalilla and on other parts of the coast. An added bonus on the mainland coast is the opportunity to watch whales from June to September. A huge number of bird species in a great variety of habitats and microclimates may easily be seen. There are five general regions: western lowlands and lower foothills, western Andes, Inter-Andean forests and páramos, eastern Andes and Oriente jungle. The **Jocotoco Foundation** ① *www.fjocotoco.org*, specializes in buying up critical bird habitat in Ecuador.

Paraguay's main asset is its wildlife. It's a birdwatcher's paradise, with 687 species, many of them endangered. National parks and reserves are the best places to go. Those in the Chaco have the rarest wildlife, but they are hard to get to. For details of NGOs and foundations working for the conservation of birds, and of national parks and reserves, see Paraguay, Planning your trip.

Peru Nearly 19% of all the bird species in the world and 45% of all neotropical birds are found in Peru. A birding trip is possible during any month as birds breed all year round. The peak in breeding activity occurs just before the rains come in October. The key sites, out of many, are the Manu Biosphere Reserve, Tambopata National Reserve, Abra Málaga, Iquitos, Paracas, Lomas de Lachay, the Colca Canyon, the Huascarán Biosphere Reserve and northern Peru, with its Tumbesian dry forest and Pacific slopes of the Andes. Before arranging any trip, consult **PromPerú** ① *www.peru.info*, and www.perubirdingroutes.com *(Spanish and English)*.

Birdwatching is possible throughout **Uruguay**, but is best in the east where a number of national parks have been set up in the coastal zones: the sand dunes at Cabo Polonio, lakes, marshes and forest reserves on the Atlantic, Santa Teresa and offshore islands. Some also include marine mammals. As most Uruguayan land is farmed, nature reserves are small, but many estancias offer wildlife-watching otions. For birdwatching information, contact **Aves Uruguay** ⓘ *www.avesuruguay.org.uy (in Spanish)*, or the Ministry of Tourism.

Venezuela's llanos are a prime wildlife destination, but you should plan the timing carefully to make the most of your trip. Amazonas and the Orinoco delta offer wildlife possibilities, but in the latter case tours can be expensive and poorly organized. The Gran Sabana does not have quite the extent of wildlife that you will find in the llanos, but is unmatched for open landscapes. In the Andes, too, the scenery is the key, and throughout the páramo the unusual frailejón plant (felt-leaved and with a yellow bloom) is a common sight. You may also be lucky enough to see the condor. Another significant birdwatching site is the Parque Nacional Henri Pittier in the coastal mountains between Maracay and the Caribbean.

In **Guyana**, habitats range from undisturbed rain- and other types of forest to savannahs, wetlands and coastal areas. The country's checklist of birds numbers over 815, including a fantastic range of Guianan Shield endemics and Amazon species including Harpy Eagle, Red Siskin and Guianan cock-of-the-rock. See **Guyana Birding Tourism Program** ⓘ *www.guyana birding.com*, for comprehensive lists and details. Birding sites include Iwokrama (which also has a high incidence of jaguar sightings), Surama, various ranches in the Rupununi, Woweta Cock-of-the-Rock Trail, Kaieteur Falls and Shell Beach, famous for its marine turtle nesting grounds and colonies of scarlet ibis. The 1.6 million-ha Central **Suriname** Nature Reserve has a variety of pristine ecosystems with a high diversity of plant life, significant populations of jaguar, giant armadillo, giant river otter, tapir, sloths, eight species of primates, and 400 of the 576 bird species recorded in the country.

On the **Falkland Islands/Islas Malvinas** five types of penguins are the main attraction, but albatross, giant petrels, geese, ducks and many other species (total 227) can be seen close to. Marine mammals, too, are easy to see: sea lions and elephant seals on the beaches, orca and other whales and dolphins off shore. See **Falklands Conservation** ⓘ *www.falklandsconservation.com*.

Climbing
ⓘ *Climbing operators are listed in the relevant places throughout the book.*

Among the most popular peaks in **Argentina** are Aconcagua, in Mendoza province, Pissis in Catamarca, and Lanín and Tronador, reached from the Lake District. The northern part of Los Glaciares National Park, around El Chaltén, has some spectacular peaks with very difficult mountaineering. There are climbing clubs in Mendoza, Bariloche, Esquel, Junín de los Andes, Ushuaia and other cities, and in some places equipment can be hired.

Some of the world's best mountaineering can be found in **Bolivia**. With a dozen peaks at or above 6000 m and almost a thousand over 5000 m, most levels of skill can find something to tempt them. The season is May to September, with usually stable conditions June to August. The Cordillera Real has 600 mountains over 5000 m, including six at 6000 m or above (Huayna Potosí is the most popular). Quimza Cruz, southeast of La Paz, is hard to get to but offers some excellent possibilities. The volcanic Cordillera Occidental contains Bolivia's highest peak, Sajama (6542 m). The Apolobamba range, northwest of La Paz, has many peaks over 5000 m.

The most popular form of climbing in **Brazil** is rock-face climbing *escalada*. In the heart of Rio, you can see, or join, climbers scaling the rocks at the base of Pão de Açúcar and on the Sugar Loaf itself. Not too far away, the Serra dos Órgãos provides plenty of challenges, not least the Dedo de Deus (God's Finger).

In **Chile**, some volcanoes and high mountains are difficult to get to. Others, like Villarrica and Osorno are popular excursions, although access is controlled by CONAF (see Tourist information in Essentials A-Z of the Chile chapter) and you need permission to climb.

The best climbing in **Colombia** is in the national parks of Los Nevados (eg Nevado del Ruiz, Nevado de Tolima) and Sierra Nevada del Cocuy (check conditions before setting out). For rock and ice climbing, the Nevados and Cocuy offer some technical challenges and Suesca, north of Bogotá near Nemocón, is considered the most important centre for rock climbing in the country.

Ecuador offers some exceptional high-altitude climbing, with 10 mountains over 5000 m – most with easy access. The four most frequently climbed are Cotopaxi, Chimborazo and Iliniza Norte. The other six, Iliniza Sur, Antisana, El Altar, Sangay, Carihuairazo and Cayambe vary in degree of difficulty and/or danger. Sangay is technically easy, but extremely dangerous from the falling rocks being ejected from the volcano. Many other mountains can be climbed and climbing clubs, guiding agencies and tour operators will give advice. There are two seasons: June to August for the western cordillera and December to February for the eastern cordillera.

In **Peru**, the Cordillera Blanca, with Huaraz as a base, is an ice climber's paradise. Over 50 summits are between 5000 and 6000 m and over 20 exceed 6000 m. There is a wide range of difficulty and no peak fees are charged (although national park entrance has to be paid in the Cordillera Blanca). The Cordillera Huayhuash, southeast of Huaraz, is a bit more remote, with fewer facilities, but has some of the most spectacular ice walls in Peru. In the south of the country, the Cordilleras Vilcabamba and Vilcanota are the main destinations, but Cuzco is not developed for climbing. Climbing equipment can be hired in Huaraz but the quality can be poor.

The heart of **Venezuelan** mountaineering and trekking is the Andes, with Mérida as the base. A number of important peaks can be scaled and there are some superb hikes in the highlands.

Fishing

① *Fishing operators are listed in the relevant places throughout the book.*

The main areas for fishing in **Argentina** are in the Lake District, around Junín de los Andes (south to Bariloche), and around Esquel, and further south around Río Gallegos and Río Grande. The best time for fishing is at the beginning of the season, in November and December (the season runs from early November to the end of March).

There is enormous potential for fishing in **Brazil**. Freshwater fishing can be practised in so many places that the best bet is to make local enquiries on arrival. Favoured rivers include tributaries of the Amazon, those in the Pantanal and the Rio Araguaia, but there are many others. Agencies can arrange fishing trips.

In **Chile**, the lakes and rivers of Araucanía, Los Lagos and Aisén offer great opportunities for trout and salmon fishing. The season runs from mid-November to the first Sunday in May (or from mid-September on Lago Llanquihue). Some of the world's best fishing is in the Lake District, which is a very popular region. Less heavily fished are the lakes and rivers south of Puerto Montt. Sea fishing is popular between Puerto Saavedra (Araucanía) and Maullín (Los Lagos).

In **Colombia**, fishing is particularly good at Girardot, Santa Marta and Barranquilla; marlin is fished off Barranquilla. There is trout fishing, in season, in the lakes in the Bogotá area and at Lago de Tota in Boyacá. Travel agencies in Bogotá and Medellín can arrange fishing trips.

Deep-sea fishing, mainly for white and blue marlin, is exceptional in the **Venezuelan** Caribbean, but there is also good fishing closer to shore. Here again, Los Roques is a good destination, while Macuto and Río Chico on the mainland are popular. Freshwater fishing is possible in the lakes in the Andes and in the rivers in the Llanos.

Horse riding

ⓘ Horse riding operators are listed in the relevant places throughout the book.

In **Argentina**, many estancias offer horse riding, as well as fishing, canoeing, walking and birdwatching. Since estancias fall into four main categories, there is much variety in the type of country you can ride through. In the pampas, estancias tend to be cattle ranches extending for thousands of hectares; in the west they often have vineyards; northeastern estancias border swamps; those in Patagonia are sheep farms at the foot of the mountains or beside lakes. There is also horse riding on estancias in **Uruguay**.

In **Brazil** some of the best trails for horse riding are the routes that used to be taken by the mule trains that transported goods between the coast and the interior.

Treks in the mountains of **Chile** can be organized in Santiago, but south of Concepción and north, the Elqui and Hurtado valleys, there are more opportunities and a number of companies organize riding holidays.

In **Ecuador** horse rentals are available in many popular resort areas including Otavalo, Baños and Vilcabamba. Throughout the country, *haciendas* also usually offer horse riding.

Mountain biking

ⓘ Mountain biking operators are listed in the relevant places throughout the book.

There are lots of opportunities in the mountains and Lake Districts of **Argentina** and **Chile**. The Carretera Austral is also a great ride. Bikes are manufactured locally, but quality is variable.

In **Bolivia**, hard-core, experienced, fit and acclimatized riders can choose from a huge range of possibilities. Either take a gamble and figure it out from a map, or find a guide and tackle the real adventure rides. Some popular rides in the La Paz region, achievable by all levels of riders, are La Cumbre to Coroico, down the so-called 'world's most dangerous road'; the Zongo Valley descent into the Yungas; Chacaltaya to La Paz, down from the (ex) world's highest ski-slope; Hasta Sorata, to the trekking paradise of Sorata. If you plan on bringing your own bike and doing some hard riding, be prepared for difficult conditions, an almost complete absence of spare parts and very few good bike mechanics. There are now a number of operators offering guided mountain biking tours, but only a few rent good quality, safe machines. Choose a reputable company, guides who speak your language and only opt for the best, US-made bikes.

In **Colombia**, cycling is a major sport, but because some remote parts are unsafe, it is not wise to venture off the beaten track and you should enquire locally about the security situation before setting out. A good specialist agency in Bogotá can give details, or ask at popular travellers' hotels.

Ecuador is growing in popularity as there are boundless opportunities in the Sierra, on coastal roads and in the upper Amazon basin. Agencies which offer tours, rent equipment and can help plan routes are listed under Quito and other cities.

This is a relatively new sport in **Peru**, but dedicated cyclists are beginning to open up routes which offer some magnificent possibilities. Peru has many kilometres of trails, dirt roads and single track, but very few maps to show you where to go. There is equipment for hire and tours in the Huaraz and Cuzco areas or join an organized group to get the best equipment and guiding.

Surfing

ⓘ Surf schools and organizations are listed in the relevant places throughout the book.

In **Brazil** the best waves are at Cacimba do Padre beach, Fernando de Noronha (the archipelago, 345 km out in the Atlantic). International surf championships are held here annually. Other good waves are found in the south, where long stretches of the Atlantic, often facing the swell head-on, give some excellent and varied breaks. Many Brazilian mainland surf spots are firmly on the international championship circuit, including Saquarema, in Rio de Janeiro state. Best waves in

Rio de Janeiro city are at Joatinga, Prainha or Grumari beaches. One of the best states for surfing is Santa Catarina (for information visit www.brazilsurftravel.com).

In **Ecuador** there are a few, select surfing spots, such as Mompiche, San Mateo, Montañita and Playas, near Guayaquil. Surf is best December to March, except at Playas where the season is June to September. In the Galápagos there is good surfing at Playa Punta Carola, outside Puerto Baquerizo Moreno on San Cristóbal.

Peru is a top international surfing destination. Its main draws are the variety of waves and the year-round action. The main seasons are September to February in the north and March to December in the south, though May is often ideal south of Lima. The biggest wave is at Pico Alto (sometimes 6 m in May), south of Lima, and the largest break is 800 m at Chicama, near Trujillo.

Trekking

South American Explorers ① *www.saexplorers.org*, have good information and advice on trekking and sell books.

There is ample scope for short and long-distance trekking in **Argentina**. The best locations are in the foothills and higher up in the Andes. Some suggestions are the valleys around Salta; San Juan and La Rioja; Mendoza and Malargüe; and in the national parks of the Lake District. Around El Chaltén in Los Glaciares National Park there is some of the best trekking on the continent.

There are many opportunities for trekking in **Bolivia**, from gentle one-day hikes in foothills and valleys to challenging walks of several days from highlands to lowlands on Inca or gold diggers trails. The best known are: the Choro, Takesi and Yunga Cruz hikes, all of whose starting points can be reached from La Paz; the Illampu Circuit from Sorata; and the Apolobamba treks in the northwest. Various treks are outlined in the text, especially near La Paz and from Sorata.

In **Brazil** trekking is very popular, especially in Rio de Janeiro, São Paulo, Minas Gerais, Paraná and Rio Grande do Sul. There are plenty of hiking agencies which handle tours. Trails are frequently graded according to difficulty; this is noticeably so in areas where *trilhas ecológicas* have been laid out in forests or other sites close to busy tourist areas. Many national parks and protected areas provide good opportunities for trekking (eg the Chapada Diamantina in Bahia). The latest area to come under the trekker's gaze is Jalapão in Tocantins.

In **Chile**, trekking possibilities are endless, from short, signposted trails in national parks to hikes of several days, such as the world-renowned circuit of the Parque Nacional Torres del Paine.

Trekking is popular in **Colombia** with walks ranging from one-day excursions out of Bogotá, or at San Agustín, to three- to four-day hikes. Good places for longer treks include the national parks of Los Nevados (from Ibagué, Manizales or Pereira), Sierra Nevada del Cocuy in the northeast, and Puracé (between Popayán and San Agustín). Well-trodden is the path to the Ciudad Perdida in the Sierra Nevada de Santa Marta, which has one of the country's main archaeological sites. In the departments of Boyacá and Santander there are many colonial *caminos reales*. Sources of information include tourist offices and Ministerio del Medio Ambiente (see Tourist information, in Colombia chapter). See also Bogotá, What to do.

In **Ecuador**, the varied landscape, diverse environments and friendly villages make travelling on foot a refreshing change from crowded buses. Hiking in the Sierra is mostly across high elevation *páramo*, through agricultural lands and past indigenous communities. There are outstanding views of glaciated peaks in the north and pre-Columbian ruins in the south. In the tropical rainforests of the Oriente, local guides are often required because of the difficulty in navigation and because you will be walking on land owned by local indigenous tribes. The Andean slopes are steep and often covered by virtually impenetrable cloud forests and it rains a lot. Many ancient trading routes head down the river valleys. Some of these trails are still used. Others may be overgrown and difficult to follow but offer the reward of intact ecosystems.

In **Peru** there are some fabulous circuits around the peaks of the Cordillera Blanca (eg Llanganuco to Santa Cruz, and the treks out of Caraz) and Cordillera Huayhuash. The Ausangate trek near Cuzco is also good. A second type of trek is walking among, or to, ruins. The prime example is the Inca Trail to Machu Picchu, but others include those to Vilcabamba (the Incas' last home) and Choquequirao, and the treks in the Chachapoyas region. The Colca and Cotahuasi canyons also offer superb trekking.

In **Venezuela** there are popular treks in the Sierra Nevada de Mérida, Roraima and other national parks, even in the Parque Nacional El Avila, just outside Caracas.

Volunteering in South America

There is some overlap between volunteering and gap-year or career-break tourism as many people who make this type of trip do some form of work. There is an increasing amount of help for students on a gap year and, in the UK at least, a well-planned and productive gap year can be an advantage when it comes to university and job application. The career-break market is growing fast and there is help online to guide you. See www.gapyear.com, www.goabroad.com (studying, volunteering, internships and much more), www.lattitude.org.uk, www.yearoutgroup.org and www.thecareerbreaksite.com. A site worth looking at for older gap years is www.inspiredbreaks. co.uk. For a range of options, try www.gvi.co.uk (**Global Vision International**) or www.i-to-i.com. More specific (but not limited to South America) are www.raleighinternational.org (**Raleigh International**), www.rainforestconcern.org (**Rainforest Concern**), www.handsupholidays.com, www.madventurer.com, www.questoverseas.com (**Quest Overseas**, which also organizes expeditions), www.outreachinternational.co.uk (**Outreach**, in Ecuador and the Galápagos), www.projects-abroad.co.uk, located in Argentina, Bolivia, Ecuador and Peru, www.visions serviceadventures.com (international community service summer programmes in Ecuador, Galápagos and Peru) and www.vso.org.uk (**Voluntary Service Overseas**), working in Guyana. An excellent place to start for low- and zero-cost volunteer programmes in South America is Steve McElhinney's website, www.volunteersouthamerica.net. See also www.volunteerlatinamerica.com.

In **Argentina**, consider the MAPU Association in Esquel, www.patagoniavolunteer.org.

In **Bolivia**, see www.volunteerbolivia.org.

In **Brazil**, for a website with information on volunteering, see http://portaldovoluntario. v2v.net, in Portuguese. For a different approach to B&B in Rio de Janeiro, see **Casa 579**, http:// casa579.com, a house in Santa Teresa where lodging is strongly linked to volunteering.

In **Colombia**, Peace Brigades International, www.peacebrigades.org/index.php, which protects human rights and promotes non-violent transformation of conflicts, employs foreign nationals who often work as human rights' monitors and observers. Fluent Spanish is essential.

In **Ecuador**, 'voluntourism' attracts many visitors. Several language schools operate volunteering schemes in conjunction with Spanish classes. **Fundación Arcoiris** (www.arcoiris. org.ec) works with a variety of nature conservation and sustainable community development projects in the far south of the country; **Fundación Jatun Sacha** (www.jatunsacha.org) has many different sites at which volunteers can work, all in exceptional natural areas.

In **Peru**, in Cuzco the **HoPe Foundation** at Hostal Marani accepts volunteers (www.hopeperu. org), as does the **Amauta Spanish School** (www.amautaspanish.com). In Huanchaco, near Trujillo, **Otra Cosa Network** (www.otracosa.info) arranges a wide range of volunteer placements in the north of the country. Projects which aim to get children away from the street and into education include **Seeds of Hope** in Huaraz (www.peruseeds.org) and **Luz de Esperanza** in Huancayo (www.peruluzdeesperanza.com).

For other options in the continent, contact, **South American Explorers**, see page 33 and see the projects supported by the **LATA Foundation** (www.latafoundation.org).

If looking for paid work, visit the **International Career and Employment Center**, www. internationaljobs.org. To teach in international Baccalaureate (IB) schools, you need to be a qualified subject teacher (primary or secondary level) with one to two years' experience. See www.ibo.org for a list of bilingual schools. You don't have to speak Spanish to work in a bilingual school. Most schools offer private health care packages and annual flights home. See also www. thelajoblist.blogspot.com for information on teaching English in Latin America. Other resources are books by Susan Griffith, including: *Work your Way around the World*, 16th edition, 2014, and *Gap Years for Grown Ups*, 4th edition, 2011.

Whitewater rafting
ⓘ *Rafting operators are listed in the relevant places throughout the book.*

In **Argentina** there are some good whitewater rafting runs in Mendoza province, near the provincial capital, and near San Rafael and Malargüe. In the Lake District there are possibilities in the Lanín, Nahuel Huapi and Los Alerces national parks.

In **Brazil** companies offer whitewater rafting trips in São Paulo state (eg on the Rios Juquiá, Jaguarí, do Peixe, Paraibuna), in Rio de Janeiro (also on the Paraibuna, at Três Rios in the Serra dos Órgãos), Paraná (Rio Ribeira), Santa Catarina (Rio Itajaí) and Rio Grande do Sul (Três Coroas). The Rio Novo, Jalapão, Tocantins, is an excellent, new destination.

In **Chile** over 20 rivers between Santiago and Tierra del Fuego are excellent for whitewater rafting. Some run through spectacular mountain scenery, such as the Río Petrohué, which flows through temperate rainforest beneath the Osorno and Calbuco volcanoes. Rafting is generally well organized and equipment is usually of a high standard. Access to headwaters of most rivers is easy. For beginners, many agencies in Santiago, Puerto Varas and Pucón offer half-day trips on grade III rivers. The best grade IV and V rafting is in Futaleufú, near Chaitén.

In **Colombia** whitewater rafting is growing in popularity and is at present based at San Gil (Santander), Villeta and Utica (Cundinamarca) and less developed in San Agustín (Huila).

Ecuador is a whitewater paradise with dozens of accessible rivers, warm waters and tropical rainforest; regional rainy seasons differ so that throughout the year there is always a river to run. The majority of Ecuador's whitewater rivers share a number of characteristics. Plunging off the Andes, the upper sections are very steep creeks offering, if they're runnable at all, serious technical grade V, suitable for experts only. As the creeks join on the lower slopes they form rivers that are less steep, with more volume. Some of these rivers offer up to 100 km of continuous grade III-IV whitewater, before flattening out to rush towards the Pacific Ocean on one side of the ranges or deep into the Amazon Basin on the other. Of the rivers descending to the Pacific coast, the Blanco and its tributaries are the most frequently run. They are within easy reach of Quito, as is the Quijos on the eastern side of the Sierra. In the Oriente, the main rivers are the Aguarico and its tributary the Dué, the Napo, Pastaza and Upano.

Peru has some of the finest whitewater rivers in the world. Availability is almost year-round and all levels of difficulty can be enjoyed. Cuzco is probably the rafting capital and the Río Urubamba has some very popular trips. Further afield is the Río Apurímac, which has some of the best whitewater rafting, including a trip at the source of the Amazon. In the southeastern jungle, a trip on the Río Tambopata to the Tambopata-Candamo Reserved Zone involves four days of white-water followed by two of drifting through virgin forest; an excellent adventure which must be booked up in advance. Around Arequipa is some first-class, technical rafting in the Cotahuasi and Colca canyons and some less-demanding trips on the Río Majes. Other destinations are the Río Santa near Huaraz and the Río Cañete, south of Lima.

Responsible travel in South America

Since the early 1990s there has been a phenomenal growth in tourism that promotes and supports the conservation of natural environments and is also fair and equitable to local communities. In South America, this 'ecotourism' segment provides a vast and growing range of destinations and activities, for which there is a huge demand. While the authenticity of some ecotourism operators' claims needs to be interpreted with care, there are a great many whose aims and credentials are laudable and we try to highlight these in the book.

10 ways to be a responsible traveller

There are some aspects of travel that you have to accept are going to have an impact, but try to balance the negatives with positives by following these guidelines:

Cut your emissions Plan an itinerary that minimizes carbon emissions whenever possible. This might involve travelling by train, hiring a bike or booking a walking or canoeing tour rather than one that relies on vehicle transport. See below for details of carbon offset programmes. Visit www.seat61.com for worldwide train travel.

Check the small print Choose travel operators that abide by a responsible travel policy (it will usually be posted on their website). Visit www.responsibletravel.com.

Keep it local If travelling independently, try to use public transport, stay in locally owned accommodation, eat in local restau- rants, buy local produce and hire local guides.

Cut out waste Take biodegradable soap and shampoo and leave excess packaging, particularly plastics, at home. The countries you are visiting may not have the waste collection or recycling facilities to deal with it.

Get in touch Find out if there are any local schools, charities or voluntary conservation organizations that you could include in your itinerary. If appropriate, take along some useful gifts or supplies. For a list of projects that could benefit from your support, see www.stuffyourrucksack.com.

Learn the lingo Practice some local words, even if it's just to say 'hello', 'thank you' and 'goodbye'. Respect local customs and dress codes and always ask permission before photographing people – including your wildlife tour guide. Once you get home, remember to honour any promises you've made to send photographs.

Avoid the crowds Consider travelling out of season to relieve pressure on popular destinations, or visit a lesser-known alternative.

Take only photos Resist the temptation to buy souvenirs made from animals or plants. Not only is it illegal to import or export many wildlife souvenirs, but their uncontrolled collection supports poaching and can have a devastating impact on local populations, upsetting the natural balance of entire ecosystems. **CITES**, the Convention on International Trade in Endangered Species (www.cites.org) bans international trade in around 900 species of animals and plants, and controls trade in a further 33,000 species. Several organizations, including **WWF**, **TRAFFIC** and the **Smithsonian Institution** have formed the Coalition Against Wildlife Trafficking (www.cawtglobal.org).

Use water wisely Water is a precious commodity in many countries. Treating your own water avoids the need to buy bottled water which can contribute to the build-up of litter. If you don't carry water treatment equipment, support places that encourage the reuse of plastic bottles.

Don't interfere Avoid disturbing wildlife, damaging habitats or interfering with natural behaviour by feeding wild animals, getting too close or being too noisy. Leave plants and shells where you find them.

Code green for hikers and campers

• Take biodegradable soap, shampoo and toilet paper, long-lasting lithium batteries and plastic bags for packing out all rubbish.
• Use a water filter instead of buying bottled water.
• Keep to trails to avoid erosion and trampling vegetation. Don't take short cuts, especially at high altitude where plants may take years to recover.
• If possible, use an existing campsite.
• Before setting up camp, contact land-owners for area restrictions and permit requirements. Seek advice on sensitive areas. Always register with the appropriate authorities and advise friends or relatives of your itinerary and expected return date.
• Try to pitch your tent on non-vegetated areas, avoid particularly sensitive habitats, such as wildflower meadows and wetlands.
• When choosing a campsite, avoid disturbing wildlife or livestock, and avoid areas where access would cause unnecessary erosion.
• Avoid damaging historical, archaeological and palaeontological sites.
• Do not dig trenches around your tent unless flash flooding is a real threat.
• For cooking use a camp stove. If you need to build a fire, use only fallen timber. Allow the fire to burn down to a fine ash which can be raked out and disposed of. Aim to leave no trace of your fire. Be sure to observe any fire-use restrictions in place.
• If toilets, portable latrines or composting toilets are not available, dig latrines at least 50 m from water sources, trails and camp sites. Cover the hole with natural materials and either burn or pack out your toilet paper.
• Wash clothing and cooking items well away from water sources and scatter grey water so that it filters through soil. If you must wash in streams, rivers or lakes, use biodegradable, phosphate-free soap.
• Pack out all rubbish and unused food, plus litter left by others.

Code green for animal and ecological welfare

• Do not hire any mule or horse that is lame or has open sores from badly fitting tack.
• Avoid handling, feeding or riding on marine life or aquatic mammals. This Handbook does not support the keeping of marine mammals (eg dolphins) in captivity.
• Choose resorts and lodges that treat sewage and support protected areas.
• Help conserve underwater and riverine environments by taking part in local clean-ups, or in diving areas collecting data for Project AWARE (www.projectaware.org).
• Choose dive operators that use mooring buoys or drift diving techniques, rather than anchors that can damage fragile habitats.
• Never touch coral. Practice buoyancy control skills and tuck away trailing equipment.

How should I offset my carbon emissions?

Carbon offsetting schemes allow you to offset greenhouse gas emissions by donating to various projects, from tree planting to renewable energy schemes. Although some conservation groups are concerned that carbon offsetting is being used as a smoke-screen to delay the urgent action needed to cut emissions and develop alternative energy solutions, it remains an important way of counterbalancing your carbon footprint.

How does carbon offsetting work?

For every tonne of CO_2 you generate through a fossil fuel-burning activity such as flying, you pay for an equivalent tonne to be removed elsewhere through a 'green' initiative. There are numerous online carbon footprint calculators (such as www.carbon footprint. com). Alternatively, book with a travel operator that supports a carbon offset provider like TICOS (www.ticos.co.uk) or **Reduce my Footprint** (www.reducemy footprint.travel).

Where does my money go?

It's not all about tree-planting schemes. Support now goes to a far wider range of climate-friendly technology projects, ranging from the provision of energy-efficient light bulbs and cookers to large-scale renewable energy schemes such as wind farms.

Essentials A-Z

Children → *For health matters, see page 23.*
Travel with children can bring you into closer contact with South American families and, generally, presents no special problems. In fact the path is often smoother for family groups as officials tend to be more amenable where children are concerned.

Food
Food can be a problem if the children are picky eaters. It is easier to take food such as biscuits, drinks and bread on longer trips than to rely on meal stops. Avocados are safe and nutritious for babies as young as 6 months and most older children like them too. A small immersion heater and jug for making hot drinks is invaluable, but remember that electric current varies. Try and get a dual-voltage one (110v and 220v).

Hotels
In all hotels, try to negotiate family rates. If charges are per person, always insist that 2 children will occupy 1 bed only, therefore counting as 1 tariff. If rates are per bed, the same applies. You can often get a reduced rate at cheaper hotels. Sometimes when travelling with a child you will be refused a room in a hotel that is 'unsuitable'. On river boat trips, unless you have large hammocks, it may be more comfortable and cost effective to hire a 2-berth cabin for 2 adults and a child.

Transport
People contemplating overland travel in South America with children should remember that a lot of time can be spent waiting for public transport. Even then, buses can be delayed on the journey. Travel on trains allows more scope for moving about, but trains are few and far between these days. In many cases trains are luxurious and much more expensive than buses. If hiring a car, check that it has rear seat belts.

On all long-distance buses you pay for each seat, and there are no half-fares if the children occupy a seat each. For shorter trips it is cheaper, if less comfortable, to seat small children on your knee. There may be spare seats which children can occupy after tickets have been collected. In city and local excursion buses, small children generally do not pay a fare, but are not entitled to a seat when paying customers are standing. On sightseeing tours you should always bargain for a family rate – often children can go free. All civil airlines charge half for children under 12, but some military services don't have half-fares, or have younger age limits. Note that a child travelling free on a long excursion is not always covered by the operator's travel insurance; it is advisable to pay a small premium to arrange cover.

Disabled travellers
In most of South America, facilities for the disabled are severely lacking. For those in wheelchairs, ramps and toilet access are limited to some of the more upmarket, or most recently built hotels. Pavements are often in a poor state of repair or crowded with street vendors. Most archaeological sites, even Machu Picchu, have little or no wheelchair access. Visually or hearing-impaired travellers are also poorly catered for, but there are experienced guides in some places who can provide individual attention. There are also travel companies outside South America who specialize in holidays which are tailor-made for the individual's level of disability. Some moves are being made to improve the situation and Ecuador's former vice-president (until 2013) Lenín Moreno, himself a paraplegic, made huge strides in providing assistance at all levels to people with disabilities. At street level, Quito's trolley buses are supposed to have wheelchair access, but they are often too crowded to make this practical. In Chile all new public buildings are supposed to provide access for the disabled by law. PromPerú has initiated a programme to provide facilities at airports, tourist sites, etc. While disabled South Americans have to rely on others to get around, foreigners will find that people are generally very helpful. The **Global**

Access – Disabled Travel Network website, www.globalaccessnews.com, is useful. Another informative site, with lots of advice on how to travel with specific disabilities, plus listings and links belongs to the **Society for Accessible Travel and Hospitality**, www.sath.org.

Health → *Hospitals/medical facilities are listed in the Directory sections of each chapter.* See your GP or travel clinic at least 6 weeks before departure for general advice on travel risks and vaccinations. Try phoning a specialist travel clinic if your own doctor is unfamiliar with health in the region. Make sure you have sufficient medical travel insurance, get a dental check, know your own blood group and, if you suffer a long-term condition such as diabetes or epilepsy, obtain a **Medic Alert** bracelet (www.medicalert.org.uk).

Vaccinations and anti-malarials
Confirm that your primary courses and boosters are up to date. It is advisable to vaccinate against polio, tetanus, typhoid, hepatitis A and, for more remote areas, rabies. Yellow fever vaccination is obligatory for most areas. Cholera, diphtheria and hepatitis B vaccinations are sometimes advised. Specialist advice should be taken on the best antimalarials to take before you leave.

Health risks
The major risks posed in the region are those caused by insect disease carriers such as mosquitoes and sandflies. The key parasitic and viral diseases are malaria, South American trypanosomiasis (Chagas' disease) and dengue fever. Be aware that you are always at risk from these diseases. **Malaria** is a danger throughout the lowland tropics and coastal regions. **Dengue fever**, which is widespread, is particularly hard to protect against as the mosquitoes can bite throughout the day as well as night (unlike those that carry malaria). In May 2014 it was confirmed that the chikungunya virus, transmitted by the same mosquito that carries dengue and hitherto common in Africa and Asia, had reached Guyana. Try to wear clothes that cover arms and legs and also use effective mosquito repellent. Mosquito nets dipped in permethrin provide a good physical and chemical barrier at night. **Chagas' disease** is spread by faeces of the triatomine, or assassin bugs, whereas sandflies spread a disease of the skin called **leishmaniasis**.

Some form of **diarrhoea** or intestinal upset is almost inevitable, the standard advice is always to wash your hands before eating and to be careful with drinking water and ice; if you have any doubts about the water then boil it or filter and treat it. In a restaurant buy bottled water or ask where the water has come from. Food can also pose a problem, be wary of salads if you don't know whether they have been washed or not.

There is a constant threat of **tuberculosis** (TB) and although the BCG vaccine is available, it is still not guaranteed protection. It is best to avoid unpasteurized dairy products and try not to let people cough and splutter all over you.

One of the major problems for travellers in the region is **altitude sickness**. It is essential to get acclimatized to the thin air of the Andes before undertaking long treks or arduous activities. The altitude of the Andes means that strong protection from the sun is always needed, regardless of how cool it may feel.

Another risk, especially to campers and people with small children, is that of the **hanta virus**, which is carried by some forest and riverine rodents. Epidemics have occurred in Argentina and Chile, but do occur worldwide. Symptoms are a flu-like illness which can lead to complications. Try as far as possible to avoid rodent-infested areas, especially close contact with rodent droppings.

Websites
www.cdc.gov Centres for Disease Control and Prevention (USA).
www.nhs.uk/nhsengland/Healthcareabroad/pages/Healthcareabroad.aspx Department of Health advice for travellers.
www.fitfortravel.scot.nhs.uk Fit for Travel (UK), a site from Scotland providing a quick A-Z of vaccine and travel health advice requirements for each country.
www.itg.be Institute for Tropical Medicine, Antwerp.

www.nathnac.org National Travel Health Network and Centre (NaTHNaC).
www.who.int World Health Organisation.

Books

Dawood, R, editor, *Travellers' health*, 5th ed, Oxford: Oxford University Press, 2012.
Johnson, Chris, Sarah Anderson and others, *Oxford Handbook of Expedition and Wilderness Medicine*, OUP 2008.
Wilson-Howarth, Jane. *The Essential Guide To Travel Health: don't let Bugs Bites and Bowels spoil your trip*, Cadogan 2009, and *How to Shit around the World: the art of staying clean and healthy while travelling*, Travelers' Tales, US, 2011.

Internet

Email is common and public access to the internet is widespread. In large cities an hour in a cyber café will cost between US$0.50 and US$2, with some variation between busy and quiet times. Speed varies enormously, from city to city, café to café. Away from population centres service is slower and more expensive. Remember that for many South Americans a cyber café provides their only access to a computer, so it can be a very busy place and providers can get overloaded.

Language

The official language of the majority of South American countries is Spanish. The exceptions are Brazil (Portuguese), Guyana and the Falklands/Malvinas (English), Suriname (Dutch) and Guyane (French). English is often spoken by wealthy and well-educated citizens, particularly in Colombia, but otherwise the use of English is generally restricted to those working in the tourism industry. The basic Spanish of Hispanic America is that of south-western Spain, with soft 'c's' and 'z's' pronounced as 's', and not as 'th' as in the other parts of Spain. There are several regional variations in pronunciation, particularly in the River Plate countries; see box, opposite. Differences in vocabulary also exist, both between peninsular Spanish and Latin American Spanish, and between the usages of the different countries.

Without some knowledge of Spanish (or Portuguese) you will become very frustrated and feel helpless in many situations. English, or any other language, is absolutely useless off the beaten track. Some initial study, to get you up to a basic vocabulary of 500 words or so, and a pocket dictionary and phrase-book, are most strongly recommended: your pleasure will be doubled if you can talk to the locals. Not all the locals speak Spanish (or Portuguese); you will find that in the more remote highland parts of Bolivia and Peru, and lowland Amazonia, some people speak only their indigenous languages, though there will usually be at least one person in each village who can speak Spanish (or Portuguese).

Language courses

If you are going to Brazil, you should learn some Portuguese. Spanish is not adequate: you

Second languages and anomalies

Argentina English is the second most common language; French and Italian (especially in Patagonia) may be useful. In Spanish, the chief variant pronunciations are the replacement of the 'll' and 'y' sounds by a soft 'j' sound, as in 'azure' (though rarely in Mendoza or the northwest), the omission of the 'd' sound in words ending in '-ado', the omission of final 's' sounds, the pronunciation of 's' before a consonant as a Scottish or German 'ch', and the substitution in the north and west of the normal rolled 'r' sound by a hybrid 'rj'. In grammar the Spanish 'tú' is replaced by 'vos' and the second person singular conjugation of verbs has the accent on the last syllable eg *vos tenés, podés*, etc. In the north and northwest, the Spanish is closer to that spoken in the rest of Latin America.

Bolivia Outside the cities, especially in the highlands, Aymara and Quechua are spoken by much of the indigenous population. In the lowlands, some Tupi Guaraní is spoken.

Chile The local pronunciation of Spanish, very quick and lilting, with the 's' dropped and final syllables cut off, can present difficulties to the foreigner.

Colombia Colombia has arguably the best spoken Spanish in Latin America, clearly enunciated and not too fast. This is particularly true in the highlands. There are several indigenous languages in the more remote parts of the country.

Ecuador Quichua is the second official language, although it is little used outside indigenous communities in the highlands and parts of Oriente.

Paraguay Guaraní is the second official language. Most people are bilingual and, outside Asunción, speak Guaraní. Many people speak a mixture of the two languages known as *jopara*.

Peru Quechua, the Andean language that predates the Incas, has been given some official status and there is much pride in its use. It is spoken by millions of people in the Sierra who have little or no knowledge of Spanish. Aymara is used in the area around Lake Titicaca. The Jungle is home to a plethora of languages but Spanish is spoken in all but the remotest areas.

Suriname The native language, called Sranan Tongo, originally the speech of the Creoles, is now a lingua franca understood by all groups, and English is widely used.

Guyane Officials do not usually (or deliberately not) speak anything other than French, but Créole is more commonly spoken.

In the Guianas, the Asians, Maroons and Amerindians still speak their own languages among themselves.

---

may be understood but you will probably not understand the answers. Language classes are cheap in a number of centres in South America, for instance Quito. For details, see below and also in the main text under Language courses.
Academia Buenos Aires, C Hipolito Yrigoyen 571, p 4, CP 1086, T+54 11-4345 5954, www.academiabuenosaires.com. Also has partner schools in Bariloche and Montevideo.
AmeriSpan, T215-531 7917 (worldwide), T1-800-511 0179 (USA), www.amerispan.com, offers Spanish immersion programmes, educational tours, volunteer and internship positions throughout Latin America. Language programmes are offered in Argentina, Bolivia, Brazil, Chile, Colombia, Ecuador, Peru and Uruguay.
Cactus, T0845-130 4775 (UK), +44-1273-359010 (international), www.cactuslanguage.com.
Spanish Abroad, 3219 East Camelback Rd No 806, Phoenix, AZ 85339, USA, T1-888-722 7623, or T602-778 6791, www.spanish abroad.com, also run courses.

LGBT (Lesbian, Gay, Bisexual, Transgendered) travellers

South America is hardly well known for its gay-friendliness, but recent years have seen a slight shift in public opinion and attitudes. There is still a definite divide between the countryside and the city, but at least in the latter there are now more gay bars, organizations and social networks springing up. The legal framework has also been changing and homosexuality is now legal across South America, with the exception of Guyana, where male homosexuality is still a crime. Many countries have anti-discrimination laws, civil partnerships are becoming more common and recognized, as are same-sex marriages in Argentina, Brazil and Uruguay. There is also a slowly increasing acceptance and knowledge of transgender issues, particularly in Uruguay, Colombia and Brazil. That said, it is wise to use caution and avoid overt displays of affection in public, particularly in rural areas, where the population tends to be more conservative. In the often macho Latin culture, gay men are more likely to experience trouble or harassment than gay women, but men also have a much better developed support network of bars, clubs and organizations, while lesbian culture and communities remain more hidden.

Some of the best cities for gay life are Buenos Aires (Argentina), Santiago (Chile), Bogotá (Colombia), Rio de Janeiro and other cities in Brazil, Lima (Peru) and Quito (Ecuador). Useful websites include: www.gaytravel.com, www.globalgayz.com, www.iglta.org (International Gay and Lesbian Travel Association), www.lghei.org (Lesbian and Gay Hospitality Exchange International) and www.passportmagazine.com. Argentina: www.theronda.com.ar, www.nexo.org (in Spanish). Brazil: www.riogayguide.com and http://gayguide.net/South_America/Brazil/. Chile: http://santiago.gaycities.com and the sites of movements such as www.acciongay.cl, www.mums.cl (Movimiento por la Diversidad Sexual) and www.movilh.org (Movimiento de Integración y Liberación Homosexual). Colombia: www.guiagaycolombia.com. Ecuador: www.quitogay.net. Peru: www.gayperu.com (in Spanish). Uruguay: www.gaysylesbianasdeuruguay.com.

Local customs and laws
Appearance
There is a natural prejudice in all countries against travellers who ignore personal hygiene and have a generally dirty and unkempt appearance. Most Latin Americans, if they can afford it, devote great care to their clothes and appearance; it is appreciated if visitors do likewise. Buying clothing locally can help you to look less like a tourist. In general, clothing requirements in Brazil are less formal than in the Hispanic countries. As a general rule, it is better not to wear shorts in official buildings, upmarket restaurants or cinemas. Also, for Brazilians, it is normal to stare and comment on women's appearance, and if you happen to look different or to be travelling alone, you will attract attention. Single women are very unlikely to be groped or otherwise molested (except at Carnaval), but nonetheless Brazilian men can be very persistent, and very easily encouraged.

Courtesy
Remember that politeness – even a little ceremoniousness – is much appreciated. Men should always remove any headgear and say "con permiso" ("com licença" in Brazil) when entering offices, and be prepared to shake hands (this is much more common in Latin America than in Europe or North America); always say "Buenos días" (until midday) or "Buenas tardes" ("Bom dia" or "Boa tarde" in Brazil) and wait for a reply before proceeding further. Always remember that the traveller from abroad has enjoyed greater advantages in life than most Latin American minor officials and should be friendly and courteous in consequence. Never be impatient. Do not criticize situations in public; the officials may know more English than you think and they can certainly interpret gestures and facial expressions. Be judicious about talking politics with strangers. Politeness can be a liability, however, in some situations; most Latin Americans are disorderly queuers. In commercial transactions (eg buying goods in a shop), politeness should be accompanied by firmness, and always ask the price first (arguing about money in a foreign language can be difficult).

Politeness should also be extended to street traders. Saying "*No, gracias*" or "*Não, obrigado/a*" with a smile is better than an arrogant dismissal. Whether you give money to beggars is a personal matter, but your decision should be influenced by whether a person is begging out of need or trying to cash in on the tourist trail. In the former case, local people giving may provide an indication. On giving money to children, most agree don't do it. There are times when giving food in a restaurant may be appropriate, but find out about local practice.

Money → *See each country's Money section in Planning your trip for exchange rates.*
Cash
The main ways of keeping in funds while travelling are with cash, either US dollars or, in a growing number of places, euros; credit cards/debit cards; US dollars traveller's cheques (TCs, increasingly hard to exchange – see below). Sterling and other currencies are not recommended. Though the risk of loss is greater, the chief benefit of US$ notes is that better rates and lower commissions can usually be obtained for them. In many countries, US$ notes are only accepted if they are in excellent, if not perfect condition (likewise, do not accept local currency notes in poor condition). Low-value US$ bills should be carried for changing into local currency if arriving in a country when banks or *casas de cambio* (exchange shops) are closed (US$5 or US$10 bills). They are very useful for shopping: shopkeepers and *casas de cambio* tend to give better exchange rates than hotels or banks (but see below). If you are travelling on the cheap it is essential to keep in funds. At weekends, on public holidays and when travelling off the beaten track always have plenty of local currency, preferably in small denominations. When departing by air, make sure you can pay the airport departure tax which, unless included in your ticket price, is never waived.

Approximate costs of travelling are given in the Planning your trip section of each chapter.

Plastic
It is straightforward to obtain a cash advance against a credit card. Many banks are also linked to one, if not both of the main international **ATM** acceptance systems, Plus and Cirrus. Coverage is not uniform throughout the continent, though, so it may be wise to take 2 types of cards. Moreover, do not rely on one card, in case of loss. Frequently, the rates of exchange on ATM withdrawals are the best available. Find out before you leave what ATM coverage there is in the countries you will visit and what international 'functionality' your card has. Check if your bank or credit card company imposes handling charges. With a credit card, obtain a credit limit sufficient for your needs, or pay money in to put the account in credit. If travelling for a long time, consider a direct debit to clear your account regularly. Transactions using credit cards are normally at an officially recognized rate of exchange. They are often subject to tax.

By using a debit card rather than a credit card you incur fewer bank charges, although a credit card is needed as well for some purchases and with a credit card you are better protected in cases of fraud, overcharging, etc. Obviously you must ensure that the account to which your debit card refers contains sufficient funds. Before travelling, it may be worth setting up two bank accounts: one with all your funds but no debit card, the other with no funds but which does have a debit card. As you travel, use the internet to transfer money from the full account to the empty account when you need it and withdraw cash from an ATM. That way, if your debit card is stolen, you won't be at risk of losing all your capital. If you do lose a card, immediately contact the 24-hr helpline of the issuer in your home country (keep this number in a safe place).

Another option is to take a prepaid currency card. There are many on offer, but it pays to check their fees and charges carefully.

Exchange
When changing money on the street if possible, do not do so alone. If unsure of the currency of the country you are about to enter, check rates

with more than one changer at the border, or ask locals or departing travellers. Whenever you leave a country, exchange any local currency before departing, because the further away you get, the less the value of a country's money.

Post → *Local post offices are listed in the Directory sections of each chapter.*

Postal services vary in efficiency and prices are quite high; pilfering is frequent. All mail, especially packages, should be registered. Some countries have local alternatives to the post office. Check before leaving home if your embassy will hold mail, and for how long, in preference to the Poste Restante/General Delivery (Lista de Correos) department of a country's Post Office. If there seems to be no mail at the Lista under the initial letter of your surname, ask them to look under the initial of your forename or your middle name. Remember that there is no W in Spanish; look under V, or ask. To reduce the risk of misunderstanding, use title, initial and surname only. If having items sent to you by courier (such as DHL), do not use poste restante, but an address such as a hotel: a signature is required on receipt.

Safety → *For specific local problems, see under the individual countries in the text.*
Drugs
Users of drugs, even of soft ones, without medical prescription should be particularly careful, as some countries impose heavy penalties -- up to 10 years' imprisonment -- for even possession of such substances. The planting of drugs on travellers, by traffickers or police, is not unknown. If offered drugs on the street, make no response at all and keep walking. Note that people who roll their own cigarettes are often suspected of carrying drugs and subjected to intensive searches. Note that the sale of marijuana in Uruguay, which became legal in 2014, applies to Uruguayan citizens and permanent residents only.

Keeping safe
Generally speaking, most places in South America are no more dangerous than any major city in Europe or North America. In provincial towns, main places of interest, on daytime buses and in ordinary restaurants the visitor should be quite safe. Nevertheless, in large cities (particularly in crowded places, eg bus stations, markets), crime exists, most of which is opportunistic. If you are aware of the dangers, act confidently and use your common sense, you will lessen many of the risks. The following tips are all endorsed by travellers. Keep all documents secure; hide your main cash supply in different places or under your clothes: extra pockets sewn inside shirts and trousers, pockets closed with a zip or safety pin, moneybelts (best worn under rather than outside your clothes at the waist), neck or leg pouches, a thin chain for attaching a purse to your bag or under your clothes and elasticated support bandages for keeping money above the elbow or below the knee. Be extra vigilant when withdrawing cash from an ATM: ensure you are not being watched; never give your card to anyone, however smart he may look or plausible he may sound as a 'bank employee' wishing to swipe your card to check for problems. Keep cameras in bags; take spare spectacles (eyeglasses); don't wear expensive wristwatches or jewellery. If you wear a shoulder-bag in a market, carry it in front of you.

Ignore mustard smearers and paint or shampoo sprayers, and strangers' remarks like "what's that on your shoulder?" Furthermore, don't bend over to pick up money or other items in the street. These are all ruses to distract your attention and make you easy prey for an accomplice. Take local advice about being out at night and, if walking after dark, walk in the road, not on the pavement/sidewalk.

It is worth knowing that genuine police officers only have the right to see your passport (not your money, tickets or hotel room). Before handing anything over, ask why they need to see it and make sure you understand the reason. Insist on seeing identification and on going to the police station by main roads. On no account take them directly back to your lodgings. Be even more suspicious if he seeks confirmation of his status from a passer-by. A related scam is for a 'tourist' to gain your confidence, then accomplices create a reason to check your documents. If someone tries to bribe you, insist on a receipt. If attacked, remember your assailants may be armed, and try not to resist.

Leave any valuables you don't need in safe-deposit in your hotel when sightseeing locally. Always keep an inventory of what you have deposited. If there is no safe, lock your bags and secure them in your room. Hostels with shared rooms should provide secure, clean lockers for guests. If you lose valuables, always report to the police and note details of the report – for insurance purposes.

When you have all your luggage with you, be careful. From airports take official taxis or special airport buses. Take a taxi between bus station/railway station and hotel. Keep your bags with you in the taxi and pay only when you and your luggage are safely out of the vehicle. Make sure the taxi has inner door handles and do not share the ride with a stranger. Avoid night buses; never arrive at night; and watch your belongings whether they are stowed inside or outside the cabin (roof top luggage racks create extra problems, which are sometimes unavoidable – make sure your bag is waterproof). Major bus lines often issue a luggage ticket when bags are stored in the hold of the bus. Finally, never accept food, drink, sweets or cigarettes from unknown fellow travellers on buses or trains. They may be drugged, and you would wake up hours later without your belongings.

Police

Law enforcement in Latin America is often achieved by periodic campaigns, for example a round-up of criminals in the cities just before Christmas. At such times, you may well be asked for identification and, if you cannot produce it, you will be jailed. If a visitor is jailed his or her friends should provide food every day. This is especially important for people on a diet, such as diabetics. In the event of a vehicle accident in which anyone is injured, all drivers involved are automatically detained until blame has been established, and this does not usually take less than 2 weeks. Never offer a bribe unless you are fully conversant with the customs of the country.

(In Chile, for instance, it would land you in serious trouble if you tried to bribe a *carabinero*.) Wait until the official makes the suggestion, or offer money in some form which is apparently not bribery, for example "In our country we have a system of on-the-spot fines (*multas de inmediato*). Is there a similar system here?" Do not assume that an official who accepts a bribe is prepared to do anything else that is illegal. You bribe him to persuade him to do his job, or to persuade him not to do it, or to do it more quickly or slowly. You do not bribe him to do something which is illegal. The mere suggestion would make him very upset. If an official suggests that a bribe must be paid before you can proceed on your way, be patient (assuming you have the time) and he may relent.

Student travellers

Student cards must carry a photo if they are to be of any use in Latin America for discounts. If you are in full-time education you will be entitled to an International Student Identity Card, which is distributed by student travel offices and travel agencies in 77 countries. The ISIC gives you special prices on all forms of transport such as air, sea, rail, and access to a variety of other concessions and services. If you need to find the location of your nearest ISIC office contact the ISIC Association, www.isic.org, which has offices worldwide.

Telephone → *Local dialling codes are listed at the beginning of each town entry.*

The most common method of making phone calls is with a pre-paid card. These are sold in a variety of denominations in, or just outside, phone offices. Phone offices (*centros de llamadas, locutorios*) are usually private, sometimes with lots of cabins, internet and other services, at other times just a person at a table offering national and international calls, mobile phone calls through various providers and phone cards. Public phone booths are also operated with phone cards, very rarely with coins or tokens. With privatization, more and more companies are competing on the market, so you can shop around. SKYPE can also be used. If you want to use a mobile phone, either take your own if your provider has an agreement with a local operator (these vary from country to country), or buy a local SIM card. Phones must be tri- or quad-band; again, this varies. Rental (not cheap) and buying a pay-as-you-go phone is possible, but you will have to check the range of the phone. The area covered is often small and rates rise dramatically once you leave it.

Tour operators

Amazing Peru and Beyond, Av Petit Thouars 5356, Lima, T1-800-704 2915, www.amazing peru.com. Wide selection of tours throughout Latin America.

Andean Trails, 33 Sandport Street, Leith, Edinburgh, EH6 6EP, UK, T0131-467 7086, www. andeantrails.co.uk. Small group trekking, mountain biking and jungle tours in the Andes and Amazon.

Aston Garcia, Salters House, Salters Lane Industrial Estate, Sedgefield, Co Durham, TS21 3EE, UK, T01740-582007, www.astongarcia tours.com. Escorted, private and tailor-made tours in Brazil, Chile, Ecuador and Peru.

Audley Travel, New Mill, New Mill Lane, Witney, Oxfordshire, OX29 9SX, UK, T01993-838650, www.audleytravel.com. Tailor-made holidays to South America (and elsewhere).

Chile Tours, Suite 2, 56 Sloane Sq, London, SW1W 8AX, T020-7730 5959, www.chiletours.org.

Chimu Adventures, 1st Floor, 16 Winchester Walk, London, SE1 9AQ, T020-74038265, www.chimuadventures. com. Providing tours,

treks, active adventures and accommodation throughout South America and the Antarctic.

Condor Travel, Armando Blondet 249, San Isidro, Lima 27, T01-615 3000, www.condor travel.com. In USA T1-877-236 7199. A full range of tours, including custom-made, and services in Argentina, Bolivia, Brazil, Chile, Colombia, Ecuador and Peru (offices in each country), with a strong commitment to social responsibility.

Discover South America, T01273-921655 (UK), www.discoversouthamerica.co.uk. British/ Peruvian-owned operator offering tailor-made and classic holidays in South America. Specialist in off-the-beaten track destinations in Peru.

Discover the World, Artic House, 8 Bolters Lane, Banstead, Surrey SM7 2AR, T01737-214250, www.discover-the-world.co.uk. Includes Antarctica and the Falklands/ Malvinas in its portfolio of destinations.

Dragoman, Camp Green, Debenham, Suffolk IP14 6LA, UK, T01728-862211, www.dragoman.co.uk. Overland adventures.

Exodus Travels, Grange Mills, Weir Rd, London SW12 0NE, T0845-287 3647, www.exodus.co.uk.

Experience Chile, Clarendon House, 20-22 Aylesbury End, Beaconsfield, Bucks, HP9 1LW, UK, T020-8133 6057, and Padre Mariano 236, of 102, Providencia, Santiago, T02-570 9436, www.experiencechile.org.

Explore, Nelson House, 55 Victoria Rd, Farnborough, Hampshire, GU14 7PA, UK, T0843-636 8548, www.explore.co.uk.

Galápagos Classic Cruises with Classic Cruises and World Adventures, 6 Keyes Rd, London NW2 3XA, T020-8933 0613, www.

galapagoscruises. co.uk, specialize in individual and group travel including cruises, diving and land-based tours to the Galápagos, Ecuador, the Amazon, Peru, Venezuela and Antarctica.

Geodyssey, 116 Tollington Park, London N4 3RB, UK, T020-7281 7788, www.geodyssey.co.uk. For tours to Latin America and the Caribbean.

HighLives, 48 Fernthorpe Rd, London, SW16 6DR, T020-8144 2629, www.highlives.co.uk. Organized luxury, tailor-made tours in Latin America.

Journey Latin America, 12-13 Heathfield Terrace, London W4 4JE, UK, T020-3432 5923, www.journeylatinamerica.co.uk. The specialists.

Last Frontiers, The Mill, Quainton Rd, Waddesdon, Bucks, HP18 0LP, UK, T01296-653000, www.lastfrontiers.com. South American specialists offering tailor-made itineraries plus family holidays, honeymoons, Galápagos and Antarctic cruises.

Latin America for Less, 203 Valona Drive Round Rock, TX 78681, USA, T1-877-269 0309 (USA toll free), T020-3202 0571 (UK), www.latinamericaforless.com. Specialize in travel packages.

Latin American Travel Association, www.lata. org. For useful country information and listings of all UK tour operators specializing in Latin America. Also has the LATA Foundation, www. latafoundation.org, supporting charitable work in Latin America.

Metropolitan Touring, Av de las Palmeras N45-74 y de las Orquídeas, Quito, T02-298 8300, with offices in Bogotá, Lima, Santiago de Chile and Córdoba, Argentina, www.metropolitan-touring.com. Long-established Ecuadorean company offering tours in Ecuador, Colombia, Peru, Chile and Argentina.

Neblina Forest Tours, Puembo PO Box 17 17 12 12 Quito, Ecuador, T+539-2-239 3014, www. neblinaforest.com. Birdwatching and cultural tours in Ecuador, Peru, Bolivia, Brazil, Costa Rica, Guyana and Colombia with a fully South American staff.

Oasis Overland, The Marsh, Henstridge, Somerset, BA8 0TF, UK, T01963-363400, www.oasisoverland.co.uk. Small group trips to Peru and Bolivia and overland tours throughout South America.

Rainbow Tours, Layden House, 2nd Floor, 76-86 Turnmill St, London EC1M 5QU, UK, T020-7666 1260, www.rainbowtours.co.uk/latinamerica. Tailor-made travel throughout Latin America.

Reef and Rainforest Tours Ltd, Dart Marine Park, Steamer Quay, Totnes, Devon TQ9 5AL, UK, T01803-866965, www.reefandrainforest.co.uk. Tailor-made and group wildlife tours.

Select Latin America, 3.51 Canterbury Court, 1-3 Brixton Rd, Kennington Park Business Centre, London SW9 6DE, UK, T020-7407 1478, www.selectlatinamerica.co.uk. Tailor-made holidays and small group tours.

South America Adventure Tours, 336 Kennington Lane, Suite 25, Vauxhall, London SE11 5HY, T0845-463 3389, www.southamericaadventuretours.com. Specialize in personalized adventure tours in Argentina, Costa Rica, Ecuador and Peru.

South America Adventure Travel, JA Cabrera 4423/29, C1414BGE, Buenos Aires, Argentina, T512-592 3877, US Toll Free T877-275 4957, with offices in Texas, Lima and São Paulo, www.southamericaadventure.travel. Specialize in budget adventure tours.

SouthAmerica.travel, www.SouthAmerica.travel, internet-based tour company with offices in Buenos Aires, Lima and Rio de Janeiro, UK T0800-011 2959 or T020-3026 9287, in Germany T0800-747 4540, US and Canada T1-800-747 4540, Australia T1-800-269979, worldwide phone T+1-206-203 8800. Experienced company offering 4- and 5-star luxury tours to South America (except Venezuela and the Guianas), with discount flights to South America from anywhere.

Steamond, 23 Eccleston St, London, SW1W 9LX, T020-7730 8646, www.steamondtravel.com. Organizing all types of travel to Latin America since 1973, very knowledgeable and helpful.

Steppes Latin America, 51 Castle St, Cirencester, Glos GL7 1QD, T0843-636 8412, www.steppestravel.co.uk. Tailor-made itineraries for destinations throughout Latin America.

Swoop Patagonia, Old Market Studios, 68 Old Market Street, Bristol, BS2 0EJ, UK, T0117-369 0196, www.swoop-patagonia.co.uk. Specialists in adventure tours to Patagonia.

Tambo Tours, USA, T1-888-2-GO-PERU (246-7378), www.tambotours.com. Long-established adventure and tour specialist with offices in Peru and the US. Customized trips to the Amazon and archaeological sites of Peru, Bolivia and Ecuador.

Trailfinders, 194 Kensington High Street, London, W8 7RG, T020-7368 1200, www.trailfinders.com. 28 branches throughout the UK and in Ireland.

Tribes Travel, The Old Dairy, Wood Farm, Ipswich Rd, Otley, Suffolk, IP6 9JW, UK, T01473-890499, www.tribes.co.uk. Tailor-made tours from ethical travel specialists.

Tucan, 316 Uxbridge Rd, Acton, London W3 9QP, T020-8896 1600, Av del Sol 616, of 202, AP 0637, Cuzco T51-84-241123, www.tucantravel.com.

Vaya Adventures, 1525 Shattuck Ave, Suite J, Berkeley, CA 94709, USA, T888-310 3374, www.vayaadventures.com. Customized, private itineraries throughout South America.

Tourist information → *Local sources of information are given in the country chapter*s
South American Explorers, 126 Indian Creek Rd, Ithaca, New York 14850, www.saexplorers. org, is a non-profit educational organization staffed by volunteers, widely recognized as the best place to go for information on South America. Highly recommended as a source for specialized information, trip reports, maps, lectures, library resources. SAE publishes a 64-page quarterly journal, helps members plan trips and expeditions, stores gear, holds post, hosts book exchanges, provides expert travel advice, etc. Annual membership fee US$60 individual (US$90 couple) includes subscription to its quarterly journal, The South American Explorer (overseas postage extra). The SAE membership card is good for many discounts throughout Ecuador, Peru, Argentina and, to a lesser extent, Bolivia and Uruguay. The Clubhouses in Quito, Lima, Cuzco and Llmache are attractive and friendly. SAE will sell used equipment on consignment (donations of used equipment, unused medicines, etc, are welcome).

Finding out more

It is better to seek security advice before you leave from your own consulate than from travel agencies. You can contact:
British Foreign and Commonwealth Office, Travel Advice Unit, www.fco.gov.uk/en/travel-and-living-abroad. Footprint is a partner in the Foreign and Commonwealth Office's **Know before you go** campaign, www.gov.uk/knowbeforeyougo.

US State Department's Bureau of Consular Affairs, Overseas Citizens Services, T1-888-407 4747 (from overseas: T202-501 4444), www.travel.state.gov.
Australian Department of Foreign Affairs, T+61-2-6261 3305, www.smartraveller.gov.au/.

Useful websites

Website addresses for individual countries are given in the relevant chapter's Planning your trip sections and throughout the text.
www.bootsnall.com/South-America An online travel guides for South America, which is updated monthly.
http://gosouthamerica.about.com/ Articles and links on sights, planning, countries, culture, gay and lesbian travel.
http://lanic.utexas.edu The Latin American Network Information Center: loads of information on everything.
www.lata.org Lists tour operators, hotels, airlines, etc. Has a useful (free) guide which can also be ordered by phoning T020-8715 2913.
www.oas.org The Organization of American States site, with its magazine *Americas*.
http://newworldreview.com An entertaining journal of food, drink and travel in the Americas.
http://planeta.wikispaces.com/ Ron Mader's website contains masses of useful information on ecotourism, conservation, travel and news.
www.rainforest-alliance.org Rainforest Alliance works for conservation and sustainability in South America and worldwide,

including information on tour operators who promote sustainability.
www.virtualtourist.com/f/4/ South America travel forum, which can take you down some interesting alleyways, lots of links, trips, etc; good exploring here.

Visas and documentation → *See each country's Planning your trip section for specific visa requirements.*
Passports and other important documents

You should always carry your passport in a safe place about your person, or if not going far, leave it in the hotel safe. If staying in a country for several weeks, it is worthwhile registering at your embassy or consulate. Then, if your passport is stolen, the process of replacing it is simplified and speeded up. Keep photocopies of essential documents, including your flight ticket, and some additional passport-sized photographs, or send yourself before you leave home an email with all important details, addresses, etc, which you can access in an emergency. It is your responsibility to ensure that your passport is stamped in and out when you cross borders. The absence of entry and exit stamps can cause serious difficulties; seek out the proper immigration offices if the stamping process is not carried out as you cross. Also, do not lose your entry card; replacing one causes a lot of trouble and possibly expense. If planning to study in Latin America for a long period, get a student visa in advance.

Contents

Argentina

At a glance

⏱ **Time required** 2-6 weeks.
☀ **Best time** Buenos Aires, Sep-Nov, Mar-May; autumn in the Lake District. Oct-May in Patagonia; Sep-Dec for whale watching on the Atlantic coast; Jun-Aug skiing in Tierra del Fuego, but passes can be snowbound.
✖ **When not to go** Holiday season, Jan-Feb, is very crowded on the beaches, in the Lake District and in Patagonia.

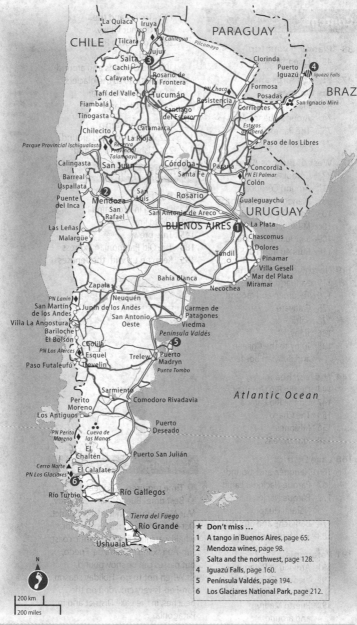

★ **Don't miss ...**
1 A tango in Buenos Aires, page 65.
2 Mendoza wines, page 98.
3 Salta and the northwest, page 128.
4 Iguazú Falls, page 160.
5 Península Valdés, page 194.
6 Los Glaciares National Park, page 212.

Argentina is a hugely varied country, from the blistering heat of the Chaco in the north to the storms of Tierra del Fuego in the south. In between these extremes, there is so much to enjoy – from nights tangoing in the chic quarters of Buenos Aires to long days riding with *gauchos* in the grasslands of the pampas. You can climb to the roof of the Americas and raft Andean rivers. You can visit the birthplace of Che Guevara and the resting place of a dinosaur known to have been bigger than T Rex. In the northwest, canyons of rocks eroded into unimaginable shapes lead to sleepy villages and staging posts on the colonial trade routes. At the northern border with Brazil, 275 waterfalls cascade into a great gorge at Iguazú. Swifts dart behind the torrents of water and birds and butterflies are easy to see in the surrounding forest. Endangered mammals, giant storks and anacondas live side-by-side in the Iberá marshes. In the dried-up river beds of San Juan, there are exotic rockforms at Talampaya and Ischigualasto. On the Patagonian coast, at Península Valdés, Southern right whales and elephant seals come to breed in the sheltered bays, while estuaries are home to colonies of penguins and pods of dolphin. Lonely roads cross the empty plateau inland, leading to the Andes' jagged finale at the peaks and glaciers of the Chaltén Massif. To set the taste buds tingling, the vineyards of Mendoza and the Welsh tearooms of the Chubut valley hang out the welcome sign. And (vegetarians look away), don't forget the meat, barbecued on an open wood fire at the end of the day.

Planning your trip

Where to go in Argentina

The capital, **Buenos Aires**, has a distinctly European feel, its architecture mostly 20th-century, though earlier buildings can be found in San Telmo district. The central docklands have been reclaimed as an upmarket restaurant zone and the Palermo district, with its large parks and its cobbled streets, has become increasingly sought after. Across the Río de la Plata is Uruguay; just northwest is Tigre, on the Paraná delta, a popular spot for escaping the city; to the southeast are coastal resorts which lead round to the most famous, Mar del Plata. West and south of Buenos Aires stretch the grasslands of the pampas, home of the *gaucho* (cowboy) and large estancias.

Through **Northwest Argentina** a string of cities gives access to the Andean foothills and the higher peaks. On the way to the mountains are Córdoba, an important industrial centre close to resorts in the Sierras de Córdoba, and Santiago del Estero, Argentina's oldest city. From Tucumán, surrounded by sugar cane but in view of the Andes, there is a beautiful route through desert foothills around Cafayate and the Valles Calchaquíes to the fine city of Salta. This is the ideal centre for exploring this wonderful part of the country with its remote valleys and high-altitude communities. From Salta there are routes to Bolivia, through an area of isolated villages, to Chile over lonely passes and to Paraguay across the Chaco.

In the **Northeast**, the wetlands of Mesopotamia have some interesting wildlife zones, such as the Iberá Marshes, and in Misiones province, sandwiched between Brazil and Paraguay, are ruined Jesuit missions, principally San Ignacio Miní. The highlight of this region are the magnificent Iguazú Falls, usually included on any itinerary to the country.

Back in the Northwest, **Ruta 40** starts its long, frequently remote journey beside the Andes to the far south. Among the many attractions it passes are the city of Mendoza, on the main Buenos Aires-Santiago road, with its vineyards, climbing and skiing centres, and the strange lunar landscapes of San Juan province. It traverses the **Lake District**, renowned for its lovely scenery and good fishing. The main centres are San Martín de los Andes and Bariloche, but there are many smaller places to visit, like Esquel, the terminus of the Old Patagonian Express. From Bariloche and other points, there are crossings to Chile. Ruta 40 continues south to the stunning peaks and glaciers of Los Glaciares national park.

On the Atlantic side of **Patagonia**, a good place to break the journey is Puerto Madryn and the Península Valdés. Here you can see whales, elephant seals and guanaco at close quarters. Just south of here are the Welsh communities of the Chubut Valley and, south again, three areas of petrified forest. Río Gallegos is the most southerly town of any size on the mainland. One road goes west to the most visited part of Los Glaciares, El Calafate, near where the Perito Moreno glacier tumbles into Lago Argentino. Just north of here, El Chaltén at the foot of the jagged FitzRoy massif has some of the most spectacular trekking in the country. This increasingly popular area now forms part of the circuit which includes the Torres del Paine national park in Chile. Beyond Río Gallegos is the Argentine side of Tierra del Fuego. Ushuaia, on the shores of the Beagle Channel, is the best base for boat trips, hikes in the mountains and skiing in winter.

Best time to visit Argentina

Climate ranges from sub-tropical in the north to cold temperate in Tierra del Fuego. The densely populated central zone is temperate. From mid-December to the end of February, Buenos Aires can be oppressively hot and humid, with temperatures of 27-35°C (80-95°F) and an average humidity of 70%. The city virtually shuts down in late December and early January as people escape on holiday. Autumn (March-May) can be a good time to visit and spring in Buenos

Aires (September-October) is often very pleasant. The Northeast is best visited in winter (June-August) when it is cooler and drier. Corrientes and Misiones provinces are increasingly wet from September. The winter is also a good time to visit the Northwest, but routes to Chile across the Andes may be closed by snow at this time so spring and autumn may be better. In the winter establishments may close in the far south, transport can be restricted and routes across the Andes to Chile may be blocked by snow. Spring and autumn are the best seasons for visiting the Lake District. Ideally Patagonia should be visited in December or February-April, avoiding the winter months when the weather is cold and many services are closed. There are also school holidays in July when some facilities such as youth hostels may be heavily booked. Note that Bariloche is very popular with school groups in July and December/early January.

National parks Argentina has 39 protected areas, covering most of the country's natural environments. Best-represented are the northwestern highlands and Patagonia forests. **Administración de Parques Nacionales** (APN) ① *Santa Fe 690, opposite Plaza San Martín, T011 4311 0303, www.parquesnacionales.gov.ar, Mon-Fri 1000-1700*, has information and advice. The website **www.patrimonionatural.com** has information on Argentina's national parks, natural reserves, UN-recognized and RAMSAR sites.

Transport in Argentina

Air Internal air services are run by **Aerolíneas Argentinas** (AR) ① *T0810-222 86527, www.aerolineas.com.ar*, **Austral** (part of AR), **LAN** ① *T0810-999 9526, within Chile T600-526 2000, www.lan.com*, and the army airline **LADE** (in Patagonia, Buenos Aires, Córdoba and Paraná) ① *T0810-810 5233, www.lade.com.ar*; its flights are always heavily booked. **Sol** ① *T0810-444 4765,*

Driving in Argentina

Roads Only 30% of Argentina's roads are paved and a further 17% improved. Most main roads are rather narrow but roadside services are good. To avoid flying stones on gravel roads (called *ripio* on maps) and dirt roads, don't follow trucks too closely, overtake with plenty of room, and pull over and slow down for oncoming vehicles. Most main roads have private tolls about every 100 km, US$0.30-1.50. Unprivatized secondary roads are generally poor. Internal checkpoints prevent food, vegetable and meat products entering Patagonia, Mendoza, San Juan, Catamarca, Tucumán, Salta and Jujuy provinces.

Safety All motorists are required to carry two warning triangles, a fire-extinguisher, a tow rope or chain, and a first aid kit. The handbrake must be fully operative and seat belts must be worn if fitted. Headlights must be on in the daytime on roads in Buenos Aires province.

Documents Full car documentation must be carried (including an invoice for the most recently paid insurance premium) together with international driving licence (for non-residents). For drivers of private vehicles entering Argentina from Chile, there is a special *salida y admisión temporal de vehículos* form.

Organizations Automóvil Club Argentino (ACA), Av Libertador Gen San Martín 1850, Buenos Aires, T011-4808 4000 or T0800-888 9888/3777, www.aca.org.ar, has a travel documents service, car service facilities, and road maps (including online). Foreign automobile clubs with reciprocity with ACA are allowed to use ACA facilities and discounts (with a membership card). ACA accommodation comprises: Motel, Hostería, Hotel, Centro Recreativo, and campsites. All have meal facilities.

Car hire The minimum age for renting is usually 21-25 (private arrangements may be possible). A credit card is required. Prices range from US$55-110 a day; highest prices are in Patagonia. Discounts available for weekly rental. 4WD vehicles offered in some agencies. At tourist centres such as Salta, Posadas, Bariloche or Mendoza it may be more economical to hire a taxi with driver, which includes a guide, fuel, insurance and a mechanic.

Fuel Petrol/gasoline (*nafta*) costs on average US$1.60-2 per litre and diesel US$1.25. Octane ratings: regular petrol (*común*) 85; *súper* 93-95, *premium* 98-100 (oil companies have different grades). Unleaded fuel is widely available. Cars are being converted to *gas natural comprimido* (GNC), which costs about 25% of *nafta*, but filling stations are further apart. Always refuel when you can in less developed areas like Chaco and Formosa and in parts of Patagonia as even petrol stations are infrequent.

www.sol.com.ar, flies to cities in the centre of the country and, seasonally, to coastal destinations, the far south and Uruguay. **Andes** ⓘ *T0810-777-26337, www.andesonline.com*, based in Salta, flies between Buenos Aires and Salta, Jujuy and Puerto Madryn. Some airlines operate during the high season, or are air taxis on a semi-regular schedule. Children under three travel free. Seats on all domestic flights are reserved well in advance, especially for travel during December and January. Reconfirmation of all flights 24 hours in advance (online if possible) is essential. Check in at least two hours before the flight.

Aerolíneas Argentinas has a **Visite Argentina** airpass which offers domestic flights at cheaper rates than those bought individually. Details can be found on *www.aerolineas.com.ar*: go to Cheap flights menu. You can buy from three to 12 coupons for a maximum of 90 days. Coupons cost from US$150 to US$220 each, depending on whether for North and Central Argentina, or for Patagonia. It is unwise to set too tight a schedule because of delays caused by bad weather, or flight cancellations or postponements.

Bus Long-distance buses are the cheapest way to get around. *Coche cama* or *semi cama* buses between cities are more expensive than the *comunes*, but well worth the extra money for the comfort of reclining seats and fewer stops. Fares vary according to time of year: advance booking is essential Dec-Mar, Easter, Jul and long weekends. The biggest bus companies are: **Andesmar** ⓘ *T0261-405 0600/0810-122 1122, www.andesmar.com*; **Chevallier** ⓘ *T011-4000 5255, www. nuevachevallier.com.ar*; **Flecha Bus** ⓘ *T011-4000 5200, www.flechabus.com.ar*; **Vía Bariloche** ⓘ *T0810-333 7575, www.viabariloche.com.ar*. Long-distance tickets can be bought online or over the phone. At www.plataforma10.com and www.omnilineas.com.ar (also in English) you can check bus prices and times and book tickets throughout the country. Student discounts of 20% are sometimes available – always ask. Buses have strong a/c, even more so in summer; take a sweater for night journeys. On long-distance journeys, meals are included. They can vary from a sandwich to a full meal, so take your own food and drink for longer journeys. Note that luggage is handled by *maleteros*, who expect a tip (US$0.35 or less is acceptable) though many Argentines refuse to pay.

Taxi Licensed taxis known as *Radio Taxi* can be hired on the street, or can be called in advance and are safer. Remise is a system common, where car and driver are booked from an office and operate with a fixed fare (more than a regular taxi).

Maps Several road maps are available including those of the **ACA** (best and most up-to-date), **Firestone** (also accurate and detailed), and **Automapa**, www.automapa.com.ar (regional maps, Michelin-style, high quality). Topographical maps are issued by the **Instituto Geográfico Nacional** ⓘ *Av Cabildo 381, Buenos Aires, T011-4576 5576, Mon-Fri 0800-1400, www.ign.gob.ar*. Some maps may be bought online, others only at the office. Take passport if buying maps there. For walkers, the **Sendas y Bosques** series is recommended: 1:200,000, laminated and easy to read, with good books containing English summaries; www.guiasendasybosques.com.ar.

Where to stay in Argentina → *See Essentials for our hotel price guide.*
Hotels Bills in four- and five-star hotels are normally quoted without 21% VAT. It is often cheaper to book a room at reception, rather than over the internet. If you pay in cash (pesos) you may get a discount, but more expensive hotels sometimes have more expensive rates for non-Argentines.

Camping Camping is very popular in Argentina and there are many superbly situated sites, most with good services, whether municipal or private. Some are family-oriented, others are livelier and frequented by younger people (often near beaches), with partying till the small hours. Prices vary widely, from US$5 to US$10 per tent. Camping is almost impossible in Buenos Aires and many sites are closed off-season. Camping is allowed at the side of major highways (not recommended) and in most national parks (not at Iguazú Falls). Many ACA and YPF service stations have an area for campers (usually free) and owners are generally friendly, but ask first. Most service stations have hot showers. A list of camping sites is available from ACA (for members, but easily available) and from the national tourist office in Buenos Aires. See **www. acampante.com** and **www.solocampings.com.ar** for lists of campsites and other information.

If you are planning a long trip, renting a motorhome is a good idea. A recommended company is **Andean Roads Motorhome Rentals**, see www.andeanroads.com for contact details and rates (starting at US$110-195 per day for three weeks or more).

Estancias An estancia is, generally speaking, a farm, but the term covers a wide variety of establishments. Accommodation for visitors is often pricey but most estancias are extremely comfortable and offer an insight into traditional country life. In the pampas, they tend to be cattle ranches extending for thousands of hectares; in the west they often have vineyards; northeastern estancias border swamps; those in Patagonia are sheep farms at the foot of the mountains or beside lakes. Many also offer horse riding, fishing, canoeing or birdwatching. The national tourist board website lists all estancias: www.turismo.gov.ar (rural tourism page).

Youth hostels Hostelling International Argentina ① *Florida 835 pb, Buenos Aires, T011-4511 8723, www.hostels.org.ar,* offers discounts to cardholders at their 66 hostels throughout Argentina, buses and backpacker tours. An HI card in Argentina costs US$20 (US$30 for two years). Also has its own travel agency, www.hitravel.com.ar. See www.hostelsuites.com for a chain of HI-affiliated hostels. Very few Argentine hostels have laundry facilities, which may be tricky if you have expensive trekking gear to wash carefully.

Food and drink in Argentina → *See Essentials for our restaurant price guide.*

Restaurants The cheapest option is always to have the set lunch as a main meal of the day and then find cheap, wholesome snacks for breakfast and supper. Also good value are *tenedor libre* restaurants – eat all you want for a fixed price. Most Argentines have lunch around 1300; restaurants open 1200-1500. Out of Buenos Aires, offices close for lunch and a siesta 1200-1700. Around 1700, many people go to a *confitería* for tea, sandwiches and cakes, but cafés are open all day except 0200-0600 and get busy from 2400. Dinner is generally eaten between 2000 and 2300. Nightclubs open at 2400, but usually only get busy around 0200.

Food National dishes are based upon plentiful supplies of beef. Many dishes are distinctive and excellent; the *asado*, a roast cooked on an open fire or grill; *puchero*, a stew, very good indeed; *bife a caballo*, steak topped with a fried egg; the *carbonada* (onions, tomatoes, minced beef), particularly good in Buenos Aires; *churrasco*, a thick grilled steak; *parrillada*, a mixed grill (usually enough for two or more people), mainly roast meat, offal, and sausages; *chorizos* (including *morcilla*, blood sausage), though do not confuse this with *bife de chorizo*, which is a rump steak (*bife de lomo* is fillet steak). A *choripán* is a roll with a *chorizo* inside. *Empanada* is a tasty meat pie; *empanadas de humita* are filled with a thick paste of cooked corn/maize, onions, cheese and flour *Milanesa de pollo* (breaded, boneless chicken) is usually good value. Also popular is *milanesa*, a breaded veal cutlet. *Ñoquis* (gnocchi), potato dumplings normally served with meat and tomato sauce, are tasty and often the cheapest item on the menu; they are also a good vegetarian option when served with either *al tuco* or Argentine roquefort (note that a few places only serve them on the 29th of the month, when you should put a coin under your plate for luck). *Locro* is a thick stew made of maize, white beans, beef, sausages, pumpkin and herbs. Pizzas come in all sorts of exotic flavours, both savoury and sweet. **Note** Extras such as chips, *puré* (mashed potato) are ordered and served separately. A popular sweet is *dulce de leche* (especially from Chascomús), milk and sugar evaporated to a pale, soft fudge. Other popular desserts are *almendrado* (ice cream rolled in crushed almonds), *dulce de batata* (sweet potato preserve), *dulce de membrillo* (quince preserve), *dulce de zapallo* (pumpkin in syrup); these *dulces* are often eaten with cheese. *Postre Balcarce*, a cream and meringue cake and *alfajores*, wheat-flour biscuits filled with *dulce de leche* or apricot jam, are very popular. Note that *al natural* in reference to fruit means canned without sugar (fresh fruit is *al fresco*). Croissants (known as *media lunas*) are in two varieties: *de grasa* (dry) and *de manteca* (rich and fluffy).

Drink It is best not to drink tap water; in the main cities it is safe, but often heavily chlorinated. Never drink tap water in the northwest, where it is notoriously poor. It is usual to drink soda or mineral water at restaurants, and many Argentines mix it with cheap wine and with ice. Argentine wines (a subject in themselves) are sound in all price ranges. The ordinary *vinos de la casa*, or *comunes* are wholesome and relatively cheap; the reds are better than the whites. In restaurants wines are quite expensive. *Clericó* is a white-wine *sangría* drunk in summer. **Vineyards** can be visited in Mendoza and San Juan provinces and Cafayate (in the south of Salta province). The local beers, mainly lager, are quite acceptable. If invited to drink *mate* (pronounced 'mattay'), always accept; it's the essential Argentine drink, usually shared as a social ritual between friends or colleagues. *Mate* is a stimulating green tea made from the yerba mate plant, slightly bitter in taste, drunk from a cup or seasoned gourd through a silver, perforated straw.

Essentials A-Z

Accident and emergency
Police T101 or 911. If robbed or attacked, call the tourist police, **Comisaría del Turista**, Av Corrientes 436, Buenos Aires, T011-4346 5748 (24 hrs) or T0800-999 5000, turista@ policiafederal.gov.ar, English, Italian, French, Portuguese, Japanese and Ukrainian spoken. **Fire department**, T100. **Urgent medical service** T107.

Electricity
220 volts (and 110 too in some hotels), 50 cycles, AC, European Continental-type plugs in old buildings, Australian 3-pin flat-type in the new. Adaptors can be purchased locally for either type (ie from new 3-pin to old 2-pin and vice-versa).

Embassies and consulates
For all Argentine embassies and consulates abroad and for all foreign embassies and consulates in Argentina, see http://embassy.goabroad.com.

Festivals in Argentina
No work may be done on the national holidays (1 Jan, Good Fri, 1 May, 25 May, 10 Jun, 20 Jun, 9 Jul, 17 Aug, 12 Oct and 25 Dec) except where specifically established by law. There are limited bus services on 25 and 31 Dec. On Holy Thu and 8 Dec employers decide whether their employees should work, but banks and public offices are closed. Banks are also closed on 31 Dec. There are gaucho parades in San

Antonio de Areco (110 km from Buenos Aires) and throughout Argentina, with fabulous displays of horsemanship and with traditional music, on the days leading up to the Día de la Tradición, 10 Nov. On 30 Dec there is a ticker-tape tradition in downtown Buenos Aires: it snows paper and the crowds stuff passing cars and buses with long streamers.

Money → *US$1 = 8.00 pesos, €1 = 11.08 pesos (May 2014).*
The currency is the Argentine peso (ARS or $, we use ARS), divided into 100 centavos. Peso notes in circulation: 2, 5, 10, 20, 50 and 100. Coins in circulation: 5, 10, 25 and 50 centavos, 1 and 2 pesos. Restrictions on Argentines buying US dollars has created a free, or "blue" market rate for dollars (mercado azul). Before Jan 2014, when the official rate was devalued to ARS8 = US$1, the advantages of using the blue market were significant; since the devaluation the gap between the 2 rates has narrowed a little, with the blue rate at ARS10.80 = US$1 in May 2014. The blue market is not legally available to tourists, but there are ways round this and its use is common (2014). Ask a trusted local resident for advice on the safest places to change money. Use dollars in cash whenever possible; some establishments may accept them at near the blue rate (some may also take euros). Alternatively, find better rates at www.exchangeinargentina.com or by wiring US dollars from a US bank account via www.xoom.com, which allows transfers to

its Argentine outlet, **More Argentina** (www.moreargentina.com.ar), at a rate close to the blue rate. Note: the exchange rate changes on a daily basis. Inflation is also high. Prices therefore fluctuate on a daily basis. Prices given in this edition are calculated at the official exchange rate at the time of research. Always pay the exact amount of a bill as small change is in short supply. Transactions at ATMs (known as *cajeros automáticos*), exchange houses (*casas de cambio)* and banks are at the official rate. Foreigners can use credit cards to withdraw cash and for making payments. You will need to show your passport with your card. ATMs can be found in every town and city. They are usually Banelco or Link, accepting international cards, but they dispense only pesos, impose withdrawal and daily limits and a charge per transaction (limits change, check on arrival). You will also have to add any commission imposed by your card's issuing company. Note that fake notes circulate, mostly AR$100, 20 and 10. Check that the green numbers showing the value of the note (on the left hand top corner) shimmer; that there is a watermark; that there is a continuous line from the top of the note to the bottom about ¾ of the way along. US dollar bills are often scanned electronically for forgeries. Remember that Uruguay has no foreign exchange restrictions so, if you need dollars, you can get them there. For information on travellers' cheques, see Essentials at the front of the book.

Credit cards
Visa, MasterCard, American Express and Diners Club cards are all widely accepted in the major cities and provincial capitals, though less so outside these. There is a high surcharge on credit card transactions in many establishments; many hotels offer reductions for cash.

Cost of travelling
You can find comfortable accommodation with a private bathroom and breakfast for around US$45-60 for 2 people, while a good dinner in the average restaurant will be around US$12-20 pp. Prices are cheaper away from the main

touristy areas: El Calafate, Ushuaia and Buenos Aires can be particularly pricey. For travellers on a budget, hostels usually cost between US$10-20 pp in a shared dorm. A cheap breakfast costs US$4-5 and set meals at lunchtime about US$8, US$10 in Buenos Aires. Fares on long-distance buses increase annually and very long journeys are quite expensive. Even so it's worth splashing out an extra 20% for coche cama service on overnight journeys. The average cost of internet use is US$0.50-2 per hr.

Opening hours
There is much variation nationally, but banks, government offices and businesses are not open on Sat. Office hours are usually 0800 or 0900 to between 1700 and 2100, with an hour break for lunch. **Banks**: opening hours vary according to city and sometimes according to the season. **Shops**: 0900-1800, many close at 1300 on Sat. Outside the main cities many close for at 1300 the daily afternoon siesta, reopening at about 1700. Shopping malls usually open 1000-2200.

Postal services
Post offices Correo Central, Correos Argentinos, T4891 9191 for enquiries, www.correoargentino. com.ar, Mon-Fri 0800-2000, Sat 1000-1300. **Centro Postal Internacional**, for all parcels over 2 kg for mailing abroad, at Av Comodoro Py y Antártida Argentina 1100, near Retiro station, Buenos Aires, helpful, many languages spoken, packing materials available, Mon-Fri 1000-1700.

Safety
Argentina is generally a safe country. All travellers should, however, remain on their guard in big cities, especially Buenos Aires, where petty crime is a problem. Robbery, sometimes violent, and trickery do occur.

Tax
Airport taxes By law airport taxes must be included in the price of your air ticket. When in transit from one international flight to another, you may be obliged to

pass through immigration and customs, have your passport stamped. There is a 5% tax on the purchase of air tickets.

VAT/IVA 21%; VAT is not levied on medicines, books and some foodstuffs.

Telephone → *Country code +54.*
Ringing: equal tones with long pauses. Engaged: equal tones with equal pauses. To call a mobile phone in Argentina, dial the city code followed by 15, then the mobile's number (eg 011-15-xxxx xxxx in Buenos Aires). To call a mobile from abroad, dial the country code, then 9, then the city code and number, omitting 15 (eg+54-9-11-xxxx xxxx). Note that area phone codes are constantly being modified.

Time
GMT -3.

Tipping
10% in restaurants and cafés. Porters and ushers are usually tipped.

Tourist information
The national office of the **Secretaría de Turismo**, Av Santa Fe 883, Buenos Aires, T011-4312-2232, www.turismo.gov.ar. For tourist information abroad, contact Argentine embassies and consulates.
Tourist offices Each province has a tourist office, Casa de Provincia, in Buenos Aires. Prefix all phone numbers: 011.
Buenos Aires Province, Av Callao 237, T5300 9500, www.casaprov.gba.gov.ar, www.turismo.buenosaires.gob.ar (official site of city of Buenos Aires tourism).
Catamarca, Av Córdoba 2080, T4374 6891, www.cata.gov.ar.
Chaco, Av Callao 322, T4372 3045/5209, casa.del.chaco@ecomchaco.com.ar.
Chubut, Sarmiento 1172, T4382 2009, www.chubutpatagonia.gob.ar.
Córdoba, Av Callao 332, T4371 1668, casadecordoba@cba.gov.ar.
Corrientes, Maipú 271, T4394 7418, casadecorrientes@argentina.com.

Entre Ríos, Suipacha 844, T4328 5985, www.casadeentrerios.gob.ar.
Formosa, Hipólito Yrigoyen 1429, T4384 8443, www.casadeformosa.gov.ar.
Jujuy, Av Santa Fe 967, T4393 1295, see Facebook page.
La Pampa, Suipacha 346, T4326 0511, www.casa.lapampa.gov.ar.
La Rioja, Av Callao 745, T4816 7068, www.turismolarioja.gov.ar.
Mendoza, Av Callao 441, T4371 7301, http://casa.mendoza.gov.ar.
Misiones, Santa Fe 989, T4317 3700, www.turismo.misiones.gov.ar.
Neuquén, Maipú 48, T4343 2324, casanqn_turismoycultura@neuquen.gov.ar.
Río Negro, Tucumán 1916, T4371 7273, casarionegro@sion.com.
Salta, Av Roque Saenz Peña 933, T4326 2456, www.casadesalta.gov.ar.
San Juan, Sarmiento 1251, T4382 9241, sarmientina@ciudad.com.ar.
San Luis, Azcuénaga 1087, T5778 1621, cslsecretaria@sanluis.gov.ar.
Santa Cruz, 25 de Mayo 279, T4343 8478, www.casadesantacruz.gov.ar.
Santa Fé, 25 de Mayo 178, T4342 0408, delegacionsantafe@ciudad.com.ar.
Santiago del Estero, Florida 274, p 1, T4322 1389.
Tierra del Fuego, Esmeralda 783, T4328 7040, www.tierradelfuego.org.ar.
Tucumán, Suipacha 140, T4322 0564, casaenbsas@tucumanturismo.gov.ar.

For **Patagonia**, see www.patagonia.com.ar or www.patagonia-argentina.com.

Websites
www.argentina.ar Promotional website of the various bureaux and ministries covering tourism, culture, economy, education and science.
www.buenosairesherald.com *Buenos Aires Herald*, English language daily.
www.argentinaindependent.com Online newspaper covering cultural, economic, social, political and environmental topics, also promoting tourism.

www.guiaypf.com.ar Site of the YPF fuel company, with travel and tourist information.
http://america.infobae.com An Argentine online newspaper, in Spanish.
www.smn.gov.ar Useful web site for forecasts and weather satellite images.
www.tageblatt.com.ar *Argentinisches Tageblatt*, German-language weekly, very informative.
www.welcomeargentina.com and **www.interpatagonia.com** Online travel guides to the whole country.

Visas and immigration

Passports are not required by citizens of South American countries who hold identity cards issued by their own governments. No visa is necessary for British citizens, nationals of western European countries, Central American and some Caribbean countries, plus citizens of Australia, Canada, Croatia, Hong Kong, Israel, Japan, Malaysia, New Zealand, Russia, Singapore, South Africa, Turkey and USA, who are given a tourist card ('tarjeta de entrada') on entry and may stay for 3 months, which can be renewed only once for another 3 months (fee AR$300/US$37.50) at the Dirección Nacional de Migraciones, Av Antártida Argentina 1355 (Retiro), Buenos Aires, T4317 0234, open Mon-Fri 0800-1400, or any other delegation of the Dirección Nacional de Migraciones (www.migraciones.gov.ar). For all others there are 3 forms of visa: a tourist visa (multiple entry, valid for 3 months; onward ticket and proof of adequate funds must be provided; fees vary depending on the country of origin; can be extended 90 days), a business visa and a transit visa. If leaving Argentina on a short trip, check on re-entry that border officials look at the correct expiry date on your visa, otherwise they will give only 30 days. Carry your passport at all times; backpackers are often targets for thorough searches – just stay calm; it is illegal not to have identification to hand.

At land borders if you don't need a visa, 90 days' permission to stay is usually given without proof of transportation out of Argentina. Make sure you are given a tourist card, otherwise you will have to obtain one before leaving the country. If you need a 90-day extension for your stay then leave the country (eg at Iguazú), and 90 further days will be given on return. Visa extensions may also be obtained from the address above, ask for 'Prórrogas de Permanencia'. No renewals are given after the expiry date. To authorize an exit stamp if your visa or tourist stamp has expired, go to Dirección Nacional de Migraciones and a 10-day authorization will be given for AR$300, providing a proof of transportation out of the country. If you leave the country with a tourist card or visa that has expired, you will be fined US$50.

Reciprocal fees: in 2010 Argentina introduced entry fees for citizens of countries which require Argentines to obtain a visa and pay an entry fee, namely Australia (US$100, valid one year), Canada (CAD$100, valid 10 years) and the US (US$160, valid 10 years). This fee is only payable by credit card online before arrival. You must print the receipt and present it to immigration wherever you enter the country. Go to www.migraciones.gov.ar or www.provinciapagos.com.ar for instructions.

Weights and measures
Metric.

Buenos Aires and the Pampas

With its elegant architecture and fashion-conscious inhabitants, Buenos Aires is often seen as more European than South American. Among its fine boulevards, neat plazas, parks, museums and theatres, there are chic shops and superb restaurants. However, the enormous steaks and passionate tango are distinctly Argentine and to understand the country, you have to know its capital. South and west of Buenos Aires the flat, fertile lands of the pampa húmeda stretch seemingly without end, the horizon broken only by a lonely windpump or a line of poplar trees. This is home to the gaucho, whose traditions of music and craftsmanship remain alive.

Arriving in Buenos Aires → *Phone code: 011. Colour map 8, B5. Population: Greater Buenos Aires 12.8 million (includes the Federal District and 24 neighbouring districts in the province of Buenos Aires); rest of the province of Buenos Aires 5.7 million (2010 census).*

Orientation Buenos Aires has two **airports**, **Ezelza**, for international and few domestic flights, and **Aeroparque**, for domestic flights, most services to Uruguay and some to Brazil and Chile. Ezeiza is 35 km southwest of the centre, while Aeroparque is 4 km north of the city centre on the riverside. All international and interprovincial buses use the Retiro **bus terminal** at Ramos Mejía y Antártida Argentina, which is next to the Retiro **railway station**.

The commercial heart of the city, from Retiro station and Plaza San Martín through Plaza de Mayo to San Telmo, east of Avenida 9 de Julio, can be explored on foot, but you'll probably want to take a couple of days to explore its museums, shops and markets. Many places of interest lie outside this zone, so you will need to use public transport. City **buses** (*colectivos*) are plentiful, see below for city guides, and the **metro**, or Subte, is fast and clean; see Transport for fares. Yellow and black **taxis** can be hailed on the street, but if possible, book a radio or a remise taxi by phone. Again, see Transport for details. Street numbers start from the dock side rising from east to west, but north/south streets are numbered from Avenida Rivadavia, one block north of Avenida de Mayo rising in both directions. Avenida Roque Sáenz Peña and Avenida Julio A Roca are commonly referred to as Diagonal Norte and Diagonal Sur respectively. ▸▸ *See also Transport, page 68.*

Tourist offices   National office ① *Av Santa Fe 883, T4312 2232 or T0800-555 0016, info@turismo. gov.ar, Mon-Fri 0900-1700,* maps and literature covering the whole country. There are kiosks at Aeroparque and Ezeiza airports, daily 0800-2000. **City information** ① *www.turismo.buenosaires. gob.ar, in Spanish only.* There are tourist kiosks open daily downtown at Plaza Roberto Arlt (Esmeralda y Rivadavia), in Recoleta (Avenida Quintana 596, junction with Ortiz), in Puerto Madero (Dock 4, T4315 4265), and at Retiro bus station (ground floor, T4313 0187).

Guided tours are organized by the city authorities, including a Pope Francis tour throughout the city and bike tours in Palermo parks, both on weekends and holidays only: free leaflet from city-run offices and other suggested circuits on city website.

Those overcharged or cheated can go to the **Defensoría del Turista** ① *Defensa 1250 (San Telmo), T15-2017 6845, turistasantelmo@defensoria.org.ar, Mon-Fri 1000-1800, Sat-Sun and holidays 1100-1800.*

Information   A good guide to bus and subway routes is *Guía T*, available at newsstands. There is also the interactive map at http://mapa.buenosaires.gob.ar. Also handy is Auto Mapa's pocket-size *Plano* of the Federal Capital, US$8.50, or the more detailed *City Map* covering La Boca to Palermo, both available at newsstands, US$3.80; otherwise it is easy to get free maps of the centre from tourist kiosks and most hotels. The daily press has useful supplements, such as the Sunday tourism section in *La Nación* (www.lanacion.com.ar), *Sí* in *Clarín* (www.si.clarin.com), and the equivalent *No* of *Página 12* (www.pagina12.com.ar). The *Buenos Aires Herald* also has information on what's on at www.buenosairesherald.com. For entertainments, see www.agendacultural. buenosaires.gob.ar, www.vuenosairez.com, www.wipe.com.ar and www.whatsupbuenosaires. com. Also very useful are www.gringoinbuenosaires.com and www.discoverbuenosaires.com. Blogs worth exploring include http://baexpats.com and www.goodmorningba.com.

Places in Buenos Aires

The capital has been virtually rebuilt since the beginning of the 20th-century and its oldest buildings mostly date from the early 1900s, with some elegant examples from the 1920s and 1930s. The centre has maintained the original layout since its foundation and so the streets are often narrow and mostly one way. Its original name, 'Santa María del Buen Ayre' was a recognition of the favourable winds which brought sailors across the ocean.

1 Federal District of Buenos Aires

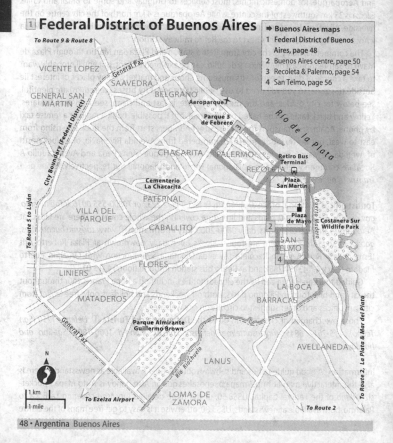

➡ **Buenos Aires maps**
1 Federal District of Buenos Aires, page 48
2 Buenos Aires centre, page 50
3 Recoleta & Palermo, page 54
4 San Telmo, page 56

Around Plaza de Mayo

The heart of the city is the **Plaza de Mayo**. On the east side is the **Casa de Gobierno**. Called the *Casa Rosada* because it is pink, it contains the offices of the President of the Republic. It is notable for its statuary and the rich furnishing of its halls. The **Museo del Bicentenario** ① *Paseo Colón 100, T4344 3802, www.museobicentenario.gob.ar, Wed-Sun and holidays 1000-1800 Dec-Mar 1100-1900), free*, in the Fuerte de Buenos Aires and Aduana Taylor, covers the period 1810-2010 with historical exhibits and art exhibitions, permanent and temporary. **Antiguo Congreso Nacional** (Old Congress Hall, 1864-1905) ① *Balcarce 139, Thu, 1500-1700, closed Jan-Feb, free*, on the south of the Plaza, is a National Monument. The **Cathedral** ① *San Martín 27, T4331 2845, www.catedralbuenosaires.org.ar, Mon-Fri 0800-1900, Sat-Sun 0900-1930; guided visits to San Martín's Mausoleum and Crypt, religious artefacts, and Temple and Crypt; Mass is held daily, check times*, on the north of Plaza, stands on the site of the first church in Buenos Aires. The current structure dates from 1753-1822 (its portico built in 1827), but the 18th-century towers were never rebuilt. The imposing **tomb** (1880) of the Liberator, Gen José de San Martín (Monday-Saturday 0930-1300, 1500-1700, Sunday 0900-1100, 1500-1900), is guarded by soldiers in fancy uniforms. A small exhibition to the left of the main nave displays items related to Pope Francis, former archbishop of Buenos Aires. **Museo del Cabildo y la Revolución de Mayo** ① *Bolívar 65, T4334 1782, www.cabildonacional.gob.ar, Wed-Fri 1030-1700, Sat-Sun and holidays 1130-1800, free*, is in the old Cabildo where the movement for independence from Spain was first planned. It's worth a visit for the paintings of old Buenos Aires, the documents and maps recording the May 1810 revolution, and memorabilia of the 1806 British attack; also Jesuit art. In the patio is a café and restaurant and stalls selling handicrafts (Thursday-Friday 1100-1800). Also on the Plaza is the Palacio de Gobierno de la Ciudad (City Hall). Within a few blocks north of the Plaza are the main banks and business houses, such as the **Banco de la Nación**, opposite the Casa Rosada, with an impressively huge main hall and topped by a massive marble dome 50 m in diameter.

On the Plaza de Mayo, the **Mothers of the Plaza de Mayo** march in remembrance of their children who disappeared during the 'dirty war' of the 1970s (their addresses are H Yrigoyen 1584, T4383 0377, www.madres.org, and Piedras 153, T4343 1926, www.madresfundadoras. org.ar). The Mothers march anti-clockwise round the central monument every Thursday at 1530, with photos of their disappeared loved-ones pinned to their chests.

West of Plaza de Mayo

Running west from the Plaza, the Avenida de Mayo leads 1.5 km to the **Palacio del Congreso** (Congress Hall) ① *Plaza del Congreso, Av Rivadavia 1864, T6310 7222 for guided visits, Mon, Tue, Thu, Fri 1000, 1200, 1600, 1800, www.congreso.gov.ar; passport essential*. This huge Greco-Roman building houses the seat of the legislature. Avenida de Mayo has several examples of fine architecture of the early 20th-century, such as the sumptuous **La Prensa** building (No 575, tree guided visits at weekends), the traditional **Café Tortoni** (No 825, www.cafetortoni.com. ar), or the eclectic **Palacio Barolo** (No 1370, www.pbarolo.com.ar), and many others of faded grandeur. Avenida de Mayo crosses the **Avenida 9 de Julio**, one of the widest avenues in the world, which consists of three major carriageways with heavy traffic, separated in some parts by wide grass borders. Five blocks north of Avenida de Mayo the great **Plaza de la República**, with a 67-m obelisk commemorating the 400th anniversary of the city's founding, is at the junction of Avenida 9 de Julio with Avenidas Roque Sáenz Peña and Corrientes. **Teatro Colón** ① *Cerrito 628, entrance for guided visits Tucumán 1171, T4378 7127, www.teatrocolon.org.ar*, is one of the world's great opera houses. The interior is resplendent with red plush and gilt; the stage is huge and salons, dressing rooms and banquet halls are equally sumptuous. Consult the website for details of performances, tickets and guided visits. Close by is the **Museo Judío** ① *Libertad 769,*

To Palermo Parks & Aeroparque

To Recoleta

➡ Buenos Aires maps
1 Federal District of Buenos
Aires, page 48
2 Buenos Aires centre, page 50
3 Recoleta & Palermo, page 54
4 San Telmo, page 56

Quintana

Arroyo

Guido

Juncal

Palacio
San Martín

Av del Libertador

Basavilbaso

Maip...

Gral
San Martín

Arenales

Av Santa Fe

Palacio
Paz

Esmeralda

Maipú

MT de Alvear

Plaza
Libertad

Montevideo

Pizzurno

Paraguay

Av Callao

Av Córdoba

Cerrito

C Pellegrini

Suipacha

Viamonte

Callao

Uruguay

Talcahuano

Libertad

Plaza
Lavalle

Teatro
Colón

Delleplane

Paraná

Tucumán

Lavalle

Tribunales

Plaza de la
República &
Obelisk

Rodríguez Peña

Montevideo

Callao

Uruguay

Av Corrientes

Av Corrientes

Carlos
Pellegrini

To La Chacarita
Cemetery

9 de Julio

Diagonal
Norte

Sarmiento

Av R S Peña

Carabelas

Juan D Perón

Bartolomé Mitre

Av Callao

Rivadavia

Congreso

Plaza del
Congreso

Saenz
Peña

Av de Mayo

Lima

Av de
Mayo

Piedras

Palacio del
Congreso

H Yrigoyen

Lima

Av 9 de Julio

B de Irigoyen

Piedras

Alsina

Av Entre Ríos

Solís

Virrey Cebalos

L Saenz Peña

San José

Moreno

Santiago del Estero

Salta

Moreno

Tacuari

Belgrano

Roca

Chacabuco

To 16

To 10

200 metres

200 yards

Where to stay

1 06 Central D3
2 BA Stop D2
3 Bisonte Palace B3
4 Casa Calma B3
5 Castelar E2
6 Colón C3
7 Dolmen B3
8 Dorá B3
9 El Cóndor y el Aguila
   Hostel D1
10 El Conquistador D3
11 Faena Universe C5
12 Goya C3
14 Hispano D3
15 Hostel Suites Obelisco D3
16 Kilca Hostel &
   Backpacker E1
17 La Argentina E3
18 Limehouse D2
19 Marbella E2
20 Milhouse Hostel E3
21 Moreno E4
23 Panamericano &
   Tomo 1 restaurant C3
25 Plaza San Martín Suites B3
26 Portal del Sur E3
27 St Nicholas D1
28 V&S C3
29 Waldorf B4

Restaurants

1 Al paso y algo más C4
2 Cabaña Las Lilas D5
3 Café Tortoni D3
4 Clásica y Moderna B1
5 Confitería Ideal D3
6 Dadá B4
7 El Gato Negro C1
8 Fiká E3
9 Florida Garden B4

10 Gijón E2
11 Güerrín D2
12 Gianni's B4/C4
13 Las Cuartetas D3
14 Le Grill D5
15 Sam Bucherie C4
16 Sorrento C4
17 Tancat B3

Bars & clubs

18 Bahrein C4
19 Druid In B4
20 La Cigale C4

Museums

2 Museo de Armas B3
3 Museo de Arte
   Hispanoamericano
   Isaac Fernández
   Blanco A3
4 Museo de la Ciudad E4
5 Museo del Bicentenario E5
6 Museo del Cabildo
   y la Revolución
   de Mayo E4
7 Museo del Holocausto B1
8 Museo Etnográfico
   JB Ambrosetti E4
9 Museo Judío C2
10 Museo Nacional
   Ferroviario A3
11 Museo y Biblioteca
   Mitre D4

T4123 0832, www.judaica.org.ar; for visits make an appointment with the rabbi (take identification), which has religious objects relating to Jewish presence in Argentina in a 19th-century synagogue. Not far away is **Museo del Holocausto** (Shoah Museum) ① *Montevideo 919, T4811 3588, www.museodelholocausto.org.ar, Mon-Thu 1100-1900, Fri 1100-1600, US$1.70 (ID required)*, a permanent exhibition of pictures, personal and religious items with texts in Spanish on the Holocaust, antisemitism in Argentina and the lives of many Argentine Jews in the pre- and post-war periods. **La Chacarita** ① *Guzmán 670, daily 0700-1700, take Subte Line B to the Federico Lacroze station*. This well-known cemetery has the lovingly tended tomb of Carlos Gardel, the tango singer.

North of Plaza de Mayo

The city's traditional shopping centre, Calle Florida, is reserved for pedestrians, with clothes and souvenir shops, restaurants and the elegant **Galerías Pacífico** ① *Florida entre Córdoba y Viamonte, www.galeriaspacifico.com.ar, guided visits from the fountain on lower ground floor, Mon-Fri, 1130, 1630*, a beautiful mall with fine murals and architecture, many exclusive shops and good food outlets. More shops are to be found on Avenida Santa Fe, which crosses Florida at Plaza San Martín. Avenida Corrientes, a street of theatres, bookshops, restaurants and cafés, and nearby Calle Lavalle (partly reserved for pedestrians), used to be the entertainment centre, but both are now regarded as faded. Recoleta, Palermo and Puerto Madero have become much more fashionable (see below). The **Basílica Nuestra Señora de La Merced** ① *J D Perón y Reconquista 207, Mon-Fri 0800-1800*, founded 1604, rebuilt for the third time in the 18th century, has a beautiful interior with baroque and rococo features. In 1807 it was a command post against the invading British. **Museo y Biblioteca Mitre** ① *San Martín 336, T4394 8240, www.museomitre. gov.ar, Mon-Fri 1300-1730, US$1.70*, preserves intact the household of President Bartolomé Mitre; has a coin and map collection and historical archives.

The **Plaza San Martín** has a monument to San Martín at the western corner of the main park and, at the north end, a memorial with an eternal flame to those who fell in the Falklands/ Malvinas War of 1982. On the plaza is **Palacio San Martín** ① *Arenales 761, T4819 8092, www. mrecic.gov.ar, Thu 1500 free tours in Spanish and English*. Built 1905-1909, it is three houses linked together, now the Foreign Ministry. It has collections of prehispanic and 20th-century art. On the opposite side of the plaza is the opulent **Palacio Paz** (Círculo Militar) ① *Av Santa Fe 750, T4311 1071, www.circulomilitar.org, guided tours Wed-Fri 1100, 1500, Tue 1500, Sat 1100, US$7.50 (in English Wed 1530, US$9,20)*. The Círculo Militar includes **Museo de Armas** ① *Av Santa Fe 702, Tue-Fri 1300-1900, Sat 1400-1900, US$1.70*. It has all kinds of weaponry related to Argentine history, including the 1982 Falklands/Malvinas War, plus Oriental weapons.

Plaza Fuerza Aérea Argentina (formerly Plaza Británica) has the clock tower presented by British and Anglo-Argentine residents, while in the **Plaza Canadá** (in front of the Retiro Station) there is a Pacific Northwest Indian totem pole, donated by the Canadian government. Behind Retiro station is **Museo Nacional Ferroviario** ① *Av del Libertador 405, T4318 3343, daily 1030-1800 (closed on holidays), free*. For railway fans: locomotives, machinery, documents of the Argentine system's history; the building is in very poor condition. In a warehouse beside is the workshop of the sculptor Carlos Regazzoni who recycles refuse material from railways.

Museo de Arte Hispanoamericano Isaac Fernández Blanco ① *Suipacha 1422 (3 blocks west of Retiro), T4327 0228, www.museos.buenosaires.gob.ar/mifb.htm, Tue-Fri, 1400-1900, Sat, Sun and holidays 1100-1900, Thu free, US$0.85*, is one of the city's best museums. It contains a fascinating collection of colonial art, especially paintings and silver, also temporary exhibitions of Latin American art, in a beautiful neocolonial mansion (Palacio Noel, 1920s) with Spanish gardens; weekend concerts.

Recoleta and Palermo

Nuestra Señora del Pilar, Junín 1898, is a jewel of colonial architecture dating from 1732 (renovated in later centuries), facing onto the public gardens of Recoleta. A fine wooden image of San Pedro de Alcántara, attributed to the famous 17th-century Spanish sculptor Alonso Cano, is preserved in a side chapel on the left, and there are stunning gold altars. Upstairs is an interesting museum of religious art. Next to it, the **Cemetery of the Recoleta** ⓘ *entrance at Junín 1790, near Museo de Bellas Artes (see below), www.cementeriorecoleta.com.ar, 0700-1700, tours in Spanish and English are available (visitasguiadasrecoleta@buenosaires.gob.ar),* is one of the sights of Buenos Aires. With its streets and alleys separating family mausoleums built in every imaginable architectural style, La Recoleta is often compared to a miniature city. Among the famous names from Argentine history is Evita Perón who lies in the Duarte family mausoleum: to find it from the entrance go to the first tree-filled plaza; turn left and where this avenue meets a main avenue (go just beyond the Turriaca tomb), turn right; then take the third passage on the left. On Saturday and Sunday there is a good craft market in the park on Plaza Francia outside the cemetery (1000-1800), with street artists and performers. Next to the cemetery, the **Centro Cultural Recoleta** ⓘ *T4803 1040, www.centroculturalrecoleta.org, Tue-Fri 1400-2100, Sat, Sun, holidays 1200-2100,* specializes in contemporary local art.

Museo de Bellas Artes (National Gallery) ⓘ *Av del Libertador 1473, T5288 9999, www.mnba. org.ar, Tue-Fri 1230-2030, Sat-Sun 0930-2030, free.* This excellent museum gives a taste of Argentine art, as well as a fine collection of European works, particularly post-Impressionist. Superb Argentine 19th and 20th-century paintings, sculpture and wooden carvings; also films, classical music concerts and art courses. **Biblioteca Nacional** (National Library) ⓘ *Av del Libertador 1600 y Agüero 2502, T4808 6000, www.bn.gov.ar, Mon-Fri 0900-2100, Sat and Sun 1200-1900, closed Jan.* Housed in a modern building, only a fraction of the extensive stock can be seen. Art gallery, periodical archives; cultural events held. Next to it is **Museo del Libro y de la Lengua** ⓘ *Av Las Heras 2555, T4808 0090, Tue-Sun 1400-1900, free,* whose exhibitions illustrate singularities of the Spanish (castellano) spoken in Argentina and the local publishing industry. **Museo Nacional de Arte Decorativo** ⓘ *Av del Libertador 1902, T4802 6606, www.mnad.org.ar, Tue-Sun 1400-1900 (closed Sun in Jan), US$1.70, Tue free, guided visits US$2.50 in Spanish, English and French, check times.* It contains collections of painting, furniture, porcelain, crystal, sculpture exhibited in sumptuous halls, once a family residence.

Palermo Chico is a delightful residential area with several houses of once wealthy families, dating from the early 20th-century. The predominant French style of the district was broken in 1929 by the rationalist lines of the **Casa de la Cultura** ⓘ *Rufino de Elizalde 2831, T4808 0553, www.fnartes.gov.ar, Tue-Sun 1500-2000 (Jan closed).* The original residence of the writer Victoria Ocampo was a gathering place for artists and intellectuals and is now an attractive cultural centre with art exhibitions and occasional concerts.

Museo de Arte Popular José Hernández ⓘ *Av del Libertador 2373, T4803 2384, www. museohernandez.buenosaires.gob.ar, Wed-Fri 1300-1900, Sat-Sun and holidays 1000-2000, US$0.20, free Sun; see website for exhibitions, events and workshops.* The widest collection of Argentine folkloric art, with rooms dedicated to indigenous, colonial and Gaucho artefacts; handicraft shop and library. **Museo de Arte Latinoamericano (MALBA)** ⓘ *Av Figueroa Alcorta 3415, T4808 6500, www.malba.org.ar, Thu-Mon and holidays 1200-2000, US$5.50, students and seniors US$2.75 (Wed half price, students free, open till 2100); Tue closed.* One of the most important museums in the city houses renowned Latin American artists' works: powerful, moving and highly recommended. It's not a vast collection, but representative of the best from the continent. Good library, cinema (showing art house films as well as Argentine classics), seminars and shop, also has an elegant café, serving delicious food and cakes. Of the fine **Palermo Parks**, the largest is Parque Tres de Febrero, famous for its extensive rose garden, Andalusian Patio, and delightful

Recoleta & Palermo

Where to stay
1 Alvear Palace
2 Art
3 Back in BA
4 Bo Bo
5 Casa Esmeralda
7 Hostal El Candil
8 Hostel Suites Palermo
9 Krista
10 Legado Mítico
11 Magnolia
12 Querido
13 Solar Soler

Restaurants
1 Arkakao
2 Bröet
3 Clásico y Moderna
4 Como e Casa
5 El Mirasol de la Recova
6 Juana M
7 La Madeleine
8 María de Bambi
9 Milion
10 Notorious
11 Persicco
12 Rodi Bar
13 Sirop & El Folie
14 The Shamrock

Bars & clubs
15 Buller Brewing Company
16 Casa Bar

Buenos Aires maps
1 Federal District of Buenos Aires, page 48
2 Buenos Aires centre, page 50
3 Recoleta & Palermo, page 54
4 San Telmo, page 56

Jardín Japonés (with café) ⓘ *T4804 4922, www.jardinjapones.org.ar, daily 1000-1800, US$4, seniors free*. It is a charming place for a walk, delightful for children, and with a good café serving some Japanese dishes. Close by is the **Hipódromo Argentino** (Palermo racecourse) ⓘ *T4778 2800, www.palermo.com.ar, races 10 days per month, free*. Opposite the parks are the Botanical and Zoological Gardens. At the entrance to the **Planetarium** ⓘ *just off Belisario Roldán, in Palermo Park, T4771 6629, www.planetario.gov.ar, 3 presentations Tue-Fri, 5 at weekends, US$4.20; small museum*, are several large meteorites from Campo del Cielo. **Museo de Artes Plásticas Eduardo Sívori** ⓘ *Av Infanta Isabel 555 (Parque Tres de Febrero), T4774 9452, www.museosivori.org.ar, Tue-Fri 1200-2000, Sat-Sun and holidays 1000-2000 (1800 in winter), US$1.70, Wed free*. Emphasis on 19th and 20th-century Argentine art, sculpture and tapestry. The **Botanical Gardens** ⓘ *Santa Fe 3951, T4831 4527, www.jardinbotanico.buenosaires.gob.ar entrance from Plaza Italia (take Subte, line D) or from C República Arabe Siria, Mon-Fri 0800-1800, Sat-Sun 0930-1800 (closes at 1900 in summer), free guided visits Sat-Sun and holidays 1030, 1500*, contain characteristic specimens of the world's vegetation. The trees native to the different provinces of Argentina are brought together in one section; see also yerba mate section. One block beyond is **Museo Evita** ⓘ *Lafinur 2988, T4807 0306, www.museoevita.org, Tue-Sun 1100-1900, US$3.50 for non-residents*. In a former women's shelter run by Fundación Eva Perón, the exhibition of dresses, paintings and other items is quite interesting though lacks the expected passion; also a library and a café-restaurant.

In Belgrano is the **Museo de Arte Español Enrique Larreta** ⓘ *Juramento 2291, T4784 4040, Mon-Fri, 1300-1900, Sat-Sun 1000-2000, guided visits Sat-Sun 1600, 1800, US$0.35, Thu free*. The home of the writer Larreta, with paintings and religious art from the 14th to the 20th century; also has a beautiful garden. See www.mibelgrano.com.ar/museos.htm for two other museums in this district: **Museo Histórico Sarmiento** ⓘ *Juramento 2180, T4782 2354, www.museosarmiento. gov.ar*, and **Museo Casa de Yrurtia** ⓘ *O'Higgins 2390, T4781 0385*.

South of Plaza de Mayo

The church of **San Ignacio de Loyola**, begun 1664, is the oldest colonial building in Buenos Aires (renovated in 18th and 19th centuries). It stands in a block of Jesuit origin, called the **Manzana de las Luces** (Enlightenment Square – Moreno, Alsina, Perú and Bolívar). Also in this block are the **Colegio Nacional de Buenos Aires** ⓘ *Bolívar 263, T4331 0734*, formerly the site of the Jesuits' Colegio Máximo, the Procuraduría de las Misiones (today the Mercado de las Luces, a crafts market) and 18th-century **tunnels** ⓘ *T4343 3260, www.manzanadelasluces.gov.ar, guided tours from Perú 272, Mon-Fri 1500, Sat and Sun 1500, 1630, 1800 in Spanish (in English by prior arrangement), arrive 15 mins before tour, US$2.50; the tours explore the tunnels and visit the buildings on C Perú*. For centuries the whole block was the centre of intellectual activity, though little remains today but a small **cultural centre** with art courses, concerts, plays and film shows. The **Museo de la Ciudad** ⓘ *Alsina 412, T4343 2123, Mon-Fri 1100-1900, Sat, Sun 1000-2000, US$0.20, free on Mon and Wed*. Permanent exhibition covering social history and popular culture, special exhibitions on daily life in Buenos Aires changed every two months, and a reference library open to the public.

Santo Domingo ⓘ *Defensa y Belgrano, Mon-Fri 0900-1300, Sun 1000-1200*, was founded in 1751. During the British attack on Buenos Aires in 1806 some of Whitelocke's soldiers took refuge in the church. The local forces bombarded it, the British capitulated and their regimental colours were preserved in the church. General Belgrano is buried here. The church holds occasional concerts.

Museo Etnográfico JB Ambrosetti ⓘ *Moreno 350, T4345 8196, see Facebook, Tue-Fri 1300-1900, Sat-Sun 1500-1900 (closed Jan), US$0.50, guided visits Sat-Sun 1600*. Anthropological and ethnographic collections from Patagonian and Argentina's northwest cultures (the latter a rich collection displayed on the first floor); also a small international room with a magnificent Japanese Buddhist altar.

San Telmo and La Boca

One of the few places which still has late colonial and Rosista buildings (mostly renovated in the 20th century) is the *barrio* of **San Telmo**, south of Plaza de Mayo. It's an atmospheric place, with lots of cafés, antique shops and little art galleries. On Sundays, it has a great atmosphere, with an antiques market at the Plaza Dorrego (see page 67), free tango shows (1000-1800) and live music. **Museo de Arte Moderno de Buenos Aires (MAMBA)** ① *Av San Juan 350, T4342 3001, Tue-Fri 1100-1900, Sat, Sun and holidays 1100-2000, US$0.85, Tue free*, has temporary art exhibitions from local and foreign artists. Next door is **Museo de Arte Contemporáneo de Buenos Aires (MACBA)** ① *T5299 2010, www.macba.com.ar, Mon-Fri 1200-1900, Sat, Sun 1100-1930, US$3.50 (Wed US$1.70)*, focusing on geometric abstraction.

East of the Plaza de Mayo, behind the Casa Rosada, a broad avenue, Paseo Colón, runs south towards San Telmo and as Av Almirante Brown on to the old port district of **La Boca** ① *take a radio taxi from the centre or San Telmo and, to return, call for a taxi from any café, US$7 one way*, where the Riachuelo flows into the Plata. The much-photographed, brightly painted tin and

San Telmo

➡ **Buenos Aires maps**
1 Federal District of Buenos Aires, page 48
2 Buenos Aires centre, page 50
3 Recoleta & Palermo, page 54
4 San Telmo, page 56

Where to stay
1 Art Factory
2 Axel
3 Circus
4 Garden House
5 Hostal de Granados
6 Hostel-Inn Buenos Aires
7 Kilca Hostel & Backpacker
8 La Casita de San Telmo
9 La Cayetana Historic House
10 Lola House
11 Lugar Gay de Buenos Aires
12 Mansión Dandi Royal
13 Ostinatto
14 Sabatico Travelers Hostel
16 Telmho

Restaurants
1 Brasserie Petanque
2 Británico
3 Dorrego
4 Dylan
5 Gran Parilla del Plata
6 La Brigada
7 La Poesía
8 Naturalisa Sabia
9 Nonna Bianca
10 Pride Café

Bars & clubs
11 Bar Seddon

wooden houses cover one block of the pedestrianized Caminito. As La Boca is the poorest and roughest area within central Buenos Aires, tourists are limited to this little street running from the Plaza La Vuelta de Rocha. You can also visit **Fundación Proa** ① *Av Pedro de Mendoza 1929, T4104 1000, www.proa.org, Tue-Sun 1100-1900,* for varied art exhibitions, cultural events and for its café-restaurant with a view, and the **Museo de Bellas Artes Benito Quinquela Martín** ① *Av Pedro de Mendoza 1835, T4301 1080, www.museoquinquela.gov.ar, Tue-Fri 1000-1800, Sat, Sun and holidays 1100-1800 (Tue-Sun 1100-1730 in summer), US$1.70,* with over 1000 works by Argentine artists, particularly Benito Quinquela Martín (1890-1977), who painted La Boca port life. Also sculptures and figureheads rescued from ships. Do not go anywhere else in La Boca and avoid it at night. The area is especially rowdy when the Boca Juniors football club is playing at home. At Boca Juniors stadium is **Museo de la Pasión Boquense** ① *Brandsen 805, T4362 1100, www. museoboquense.com, daily 1000-1800, US$9, guided tour of the stadium in Spanish or English, 1100-1700, plus ticket to the museum, US$12.*

Docks and Costanera Sur

Fragata Presidente Sarmiento ① *dock 3, Av Alicia Moreau de Justo 980, Puerto Madero, T4334 9386, daily 1000-1900, US$0.35.* A naval training ship until 1961; now a museum. Nearby, in dock 4, is the **Corbeta Uruguay** ① *T4314 1090, daily 1000 1900, US$0.35, for both ships see www. ara.mil.ar,* the ship that rescued Otto Nordenskjold's Antarctic expedition in 1903. The **Puerto Madero** dock area has been renovated; the 19th-century warehouses are restaurants and bars, an attractive place for a stroll and popular nightspot. In dock 4 there is also **Colección Fortabat** ① *Olga Cossettini 141, T4310 6600, www.coleccionfortabat.org.ar, Tue-Sun 1200-2000, US$6,* which houses a great art collection. East of San Telmo on the far side of the docks, the Avenida Costanera runs as a long, spacious boulevard. A stretch of marshland reclaimed from the river forms the interesting **Costanera Sur Wildlife Reserve** ① *entrances at Av Tristán Achával Rodríguez 1550 (take Estados Unidos east from San Telmo) or next to the Buquebús ferry terminal (take Av Córdoba east), T4315 4129; for pedestrians and bikers only, Tue-Sun 0800-1800 (in summer, closes at 1900), free, take colectivos 4, 130 or 152,* where over 150 species of birds have been spotted over the past few years. Free guided tours at weekends and holidays 0930, 1600, from the administration next to the southern entrance, but much can be seen from the road before then (binoculars useful). Also free nocturnal visits every month on the Friday closest to the full moon (book Monday before, T4313 4275). It's half an hour walk from the entrance to the river shore and about three hours to walk the whole perimeter. In summer it's very hot with little shade. For details (particularly birdwatching) contact **Aves Argentinas/AOP** (see page 73), or see www.reservacostanera.com.ar (English version).

◉ Buenos Aires listings

For hotel and restaurant price codes, and other relevant information, see Essentials.

● Where to stay

Shop around for hotels offering discounts on multi-night stays. The tourist offices at Ezeiza and Aeroparque airports book rooms. A/c is a must in high summer. Finding hotels for Fri, Sat, Sun nights can be difficult and hostels can get very busy, resulting in pressure on staff. A bed in a hostel dorm costs US$10-20. The range of 'boutique' hotels and hostels is impressive, especially in Palermo and San Telmo. The same applies to restaurants, bars and clubs. There are far more than we can list here. There are fine examples of the Four Seasons (www. fourseasons.com/buenosaires), Hilton (www. hilton.com), Hyatt (www.buenosaires.park. hyatt.com), Marriott (www.marriott.com),

NH (www.nh-hoteles.com), **Pestana** (www.
pestana.com), **Sofitel** (www.sofitel.com) and
Unique Hotels (www.uniquehotels.com.ar)
chains. Hotels will store luggage, and most
have English-speaking staff.

Centre *p48, map p50*
$$$$ Alvear Palace, Av Alvear 1891, T4808
2100, www.alvearpalace.com. The height of
elegance, an impeccably preserved 1920s
Recoleta palace, sumptuous marble foyer, with
Louis XV-style chairs, and a charming orangery
where you can take tea with superb patisseries.
Antique-filled bedrooms. Recommended.
$$$$ Casa Calma, Suipacha 1015, T5199 2800,
www.casacalmahotel.com. A relaxing haven in
a downtown setting, homely yet luxurious, with
a wellness centre and honesty bar.
$$$$ Faena Universe, Martha Salotti 445
(Puerto Madero), T4010 9000, www.faena.com.
Set in a 100-year-old silo, renovated by Philippe
Starck, this is not for all budgets or tastes.
Eclectic decoration, staff trained to be perfect,
the whole place is unique.
$$$$-$$$ Castelar, Av de Mayo 1152, T4383
5000, www.castelarhotel.com.ar. A wonderfully
elegant 1920s hotel which retains all the
original features in the grand entrance and bar.
Cosy bedrooms, charming staff, and excellent
value. Also a spa with turkish baths and
massage. Highly recommended.
$$$$-$$$ Dolmen, Suipacha 1079, T4315
7117, www.hoteldolmen.com.ar. Good location,
smart spacious entrance lobby, with a calm
relaxing atmosphere, good professional service,
modern, comfortable well-designed rooms,
small pool.
$$$$-$$$ El Conquistador, Suipacha 948,
T4328 3012, www.elconquistador.com.ar.
Stylish '70s hotel, which retains the wood and
chrome foyer, but has bright modern rooms,
and a lovely light restaurant on the 10th floor
with great views. Well situated, good value.
$$$$-$$$ Panamericano, Carlos Pellegrini
551, T4348 5000, www.panamericano.us. Very
smart and modern hotel, with luxurious and
tasteful rooms, covered rooftop pool, and
superb restaurant, **Tomo 1**. Excellent service

too. Also has properties in Bariloche (www.
panamericanobariloche.com) and El Calafate
(www.casalossauces.com).
$$$ Art, Azcuénaga 1268, T4821 6248,
www.arthotel.com.ar. Charming boutique
hotel on a quiet residential street, only a few
blocks from Recoleta or Av Santa Fe, simply
but warmly decorated, good service, solarium,
compact standard rooms.
$$$ Bisonte Palace, MT de Alvear 902, T4328
4751, www.hotelesbisonte.com. Charming,
with calm entrance foyer, which remains
gracious thanks to courteous staff. Plain
but spacious rooms, ample breakfast, good
location. Very good value.
$$$ Colón, Carlos Pellegrini 507, T4320 3500,
www.exehotelcolon.com. Splendid location
overlooking Av 9 de Julio and Teatro Colón,
extremely good value. Charming bedrooms,
comfortable, gym, great breakfasts, and perfect
service. Highly recommended.
$$$ Dorá, Maipú 963, T4312 7391, www.dora
hotel.com.ar. Charming and old-fashioned with
comfortable rooms, good service, attractive
lounge with paintings. Warmly recommended.
$$$ Goya, Suipacha 748, T4322 9269,
www.goya hotel.com.ar. Welcoming and
central, worth paying more for superior
rooms, though all are comfortable.
Good breakfast, English spoken.
$$$ Hispano, Av de Mayo 861, T4345 2020,
www.hhispano.com.ar. Plain but comfortable
rooms in this hotel which has been welcoming
travellers since the 1950s, courtyard and small
garden, central.
$$$ Marbella, Av de Mayo 1261, T4383 3573,
www.hotelmarbella.com.ar. Modernized,
and central, though quiet, multi-lingual.
Recommended.
$$$ Moreno, Moreno 376, T6091 2000,
www.morenobuenosaires.com. 150 m from
the Plaza de Mayo, decorated in dark, rich
tones, large rooms, good value, jacuzzi,
gym and chic bar, winery and restaurant.
$$$ Plaza San Martín Suites, Suipacha 1092,
T5093 7000, www.plazasanmartin.com.ar. Neat
modern self-contained apartments right in
the city centre, comfortable and attractively

decorated, with lounge and little kitchen. Pet friendly, room service. Good value.

$$$ Waldorf, Paraguay 450, T4312 2071, www.waldorf-hotel.com.ar. Welcoming staff and a comfortable mixture of traditional and modern in this centrally located hotel. Good value, with a buffet breakfast, English spoken. Recommended.

$ La Argentina, Av de Mayo 860, T4342 0078. Cheap, central and rickety, but it stands the test of time. Amazing old building, bringing new meaning to "high-ceilinged", can be noisy if your room is near the "slam-the-door-shut" elevator. Good, cheap and cheerful restaurant attached, doing very affordable menú del día. Recommended.

Youth hostels

$ pp 06 Central, Maipú 306, T5219 0052, www.06centralhostel.com. A few metres from the Obelisco and Av Corrientes, simple, spacious dorms, nicely decorated doubles (**$$**), cosy communal area.

$ pp BA Stop, Rivadavia 1194, T4382 7406, www.bastop.com. In a converted 1900s corner block, dorms, private rooms (**$$** double), large screen TV, table tennis, bar, English spoken, safe, very helpful staff. Repeatedly recommended.

$ El Cóndor y el Aguila Hostel, Espinosa 1628, near junction Av San Martín and Av Juan B Justo, T4581 6663, www.elcondoryelaguila.com.ar. 5 private rooms and 4 dorms. Terrace, laundry and internet access. Free transfer from Retiro and Aeroparque, and free tea and coffee.

$ pp Hostel Suites Obelisco, Av Corrientes 830, T4328 4040, www.hostelsuites.com. Elegant hostel built in a completely restored old building in the heart of the city. Dorms, **$$** doubles and private apartments, DVD room, laundry service. Free transfer from Ezeiza airport. HI discount.

$ pp Limehouse Hostel, Lima 11, T4383 4561, www.limehouse.com.ar. Dorms for up to 12 and doubles with and without bath (**$$**), popular, typical city hostel with bar, roof terrace, "chilled", great if you like the party atmosphere, efficient staff. Recommended.

$ pp Milhouse Hostel, Hipólito Yrigoyen 959, T4345 9604, www.milhousehostel.com. In 1890 house, lovely rooms (**$$$** in double)

and dorms, comfortable, laundry, tango lessons, very popular so reconfirm bookings at all times.

$ pp Portal del Sur, Hipólito Yrigoyen 855, T4342 8788, www.portaldelsurba.com.ar. Nice dorms and especially lovely doubles (**$$$**) and singles in a converted 19th-century building. Recommended for single travellers.

$ pp St Nicholas, B Mitre 1691, T4373 5920, www.snhostel.com. Beautifully converted old house, now a party hostel with spotless rooms, large roof terrace and a pub with daily live shows; also **$$** double rooms.

$ pp V&S, Viamonte 887, T4322 0994, www.hostelclub.com. Central popular hostel (**$$$** in attractive double room, bath), café, tango classes, tours, warm atmosphere, welcoming. Recommended.

Palermo *p53, map p54*

$$$$ Legado Mítico, Gurruchaga 1848, T4833 1300, www.legadomitico.com. Stylish small hotel with 11 rooms named after Argentine cultural legends. They use local designs and products. Luxurious and recommended.

$$$$ Magnolia, Julián Àlvarez 1746, T4867 4900, www.magnoliahotelboutique.com. Lovely boutique hotel in a quiet area. This refurbished early 20th-century house has attractively designed rooms opening onto the street or to inner courtyards and a perfect retreat on its rooftop terrace.

$$$$ Querido, Juan Ramírez de Velazco 934, T4854 6297, www.queridobuenosaires.com. Purposed-built, designed and cared for by a Brazilian-English couple. 7 rooms, 4 of which have balconies, for a comfortable stay in Villa Crespo area, few blocks from Palermo Soho and from the subway.

$$$$-$$$ Bo Bo, Guatemala 4882, T4774 0505, www.bobohotel.com. On a leafy street, 15 rooms decorated in contemporary style, some with private balconies, excellent restaurant.

$$$$-$$$ Krista, Bonpland 1665, T4771 4697, www.kristahotel.com.ar. Intimate, hidden behind the plain façade of an elegant townhouse, well placed for restaurants. Good value, comfortable, individually designed spacious rooms, wheelchair access.

$$$ **Solar Soler**, Soler 5676, T4776 3065, www.solarsoler.com.ar. Welcoming B&B in Palermo Hollywood, excellent service. Recommended.

Youth hostels

$ pp **Back in BA**, El Salvador 5115, T4774 2859, www.backinba.com. Small hostel with dorms for up to 6 and private rooms ($$), lockers with charging points, patio, bar, information, tours and classes can be arranged, good Palermo Soho location.

$ pp **Casa Esmeralda**, Honduras 5765, T4772 2446, www.casaesmeralda.com.ar. Laid-back, dorms and $$ doubles, neat garden with hammocks. Offers basic comfort with great charm.

$ pp **Hostal El Candil**, Lerma 476, T4899 1547, www.hostalelcandil.com. Argentine/Italian-owned hostel with shared rooms and doubles ($$), international atmosphere, quiet, comfortable, welcoming, rooftop terrace, tours arranged.

$ pp **Hostel Suites Palermo**, Charcas 4752, T4773 0806, www.suitespalermo.com. A beautiful century-old residence with the original grandeur partially preserved and a quiet atmosphere. Comfortable renovated dorms and private rooms with bath ($$ doubles), good service, small travel agency, free internet, Wi-Fi, cooking and laundry facilities, DVD room and breakfast included. Free transfer from Ezeiza airport. HI discount.

San Telmo and around *p56, map p56*

$$$$ **Mansión Dandi Royal**, Piedras 922, T4361 3537, www.hotelmansiondandiroyal.com. A wonderfully restored 1903 residence, small upmarket hotel with an elegant tango atmosphere, small pool, good value. Daily tango lessons and *milonga* every Fri at 2130.

$$$$-$$$ **Axel Hotel**, Venezuela 649, T4136 9393, www.axelhotels.com. Stunning gay hotel with 5 floors of stylishly designed rooms, each floor with a cosy living area, rooftop pool, gourmet restaurant. Recommended.

$$$$-$$$ **La Cayetana Historic House**, México 1330, T4383 2230, www.lacayetana hotel.com.ar. 11 suites in a beautifully restored 1820s house, each room individually designed, quiet, buffet breakfast, parking. Recommended.

$$$ **La Casita de San Telmo**, Cochabamba 286, T4307 5073, www.lacasitadesantelmo.com. 7 rooms in restored 1840's house, most open onto a garden with a beautiful fig tree, owners are tango fans; rooms rented by day, week or month.

$$$ **Lola House**, Castro Barros 1073, Boedo, T4932 2139, www.lolahouse.com.ar. Small boutique hotel in a nicely refurbished house, welcoming owners, comfortable, safe; 10 mins from centre on Subte E, also on bus routes.

$$$ **Lugar Gay de Buenos Aires**, Defensa 1120 (no sign), T4300 4747, www.lugargay.com.ar. A men-only gay B&B with 8 comfortable rooms, video room, jacuzzi, a stone's throw from Plaza Dorrego.

$$$ **Telmho**, Defensa 1086, T4116 5467, www.telmho-hotel.com.ar. Smart rooms overlooking Plaza Dorrego, huge beds, modern bathrooms, lovely roof garden, helpful staff.

Youth hostels

$ pp **Art Factory**, Piedras 545, T4343 1463, www.artfactoryba.com.ar. Large, early 1900s house converted into a hostel, informal atmosphere with individually designed and brightly painted private rooms (some with bath, $$), dorms, halfway between the centre and San Telmo.

$ pp **Circus**, Chacabuco 1020, T4300 4983, www.hostelcircus.com. Stylish rooms for 2 ($$) to 4 people, tastefully renovated building, small heated swimming pool, bar and restaurant.

$ pp **Garden House**, Av San Juan 1271, T4304 1824, www.gardenhouseba.com.ar. Small, welcoming independent hostel for those who don't want a party atmosphere; good barbecues on the terrace. Dorms and some $$ doubles. Recommended.

$ pp **Hostal de Granados**, Chile 374, T4362 5600, www.hostaldegranados.com.ar. Small, light, well-equipped rooms in an interesting building on a popular street, rooms for 2 ($$), dorms for 4 to 8, laundry.

$ pp **Hostel-Inn Buenos Aires**, Humberto Primo 820, T4300 7992, www.hibuenosaires.com.

An old 2-storey mansion with dorms for up to 8 people and also private rooms (**$$**), activities, loud parties, individual lockers in every room. HI discount.

$ pp Kilca Hostel & Backpacker, Mexico 1545, between Saenz Peña and Virrey Cevallos, T4381 1966, www.kilcabackpacker.com. In a restored 19th-century house with attractive landscaped patios. A variety of rooms from dorms to doubles; all bathrooms shared, but one double with bath (**$$**).

$ pp Ostinatto, Chile 680, T4362 9639, www.ostinatto.com. Shared rooms, also has double rooms with and without bath (**$$**), and apartments for rent. Minimalist contemporary design in a 1920s building, very nice, promotes the arts, music, piano bar, movie room, tango lessons, arranges events, rooftop terrace.

$ pp Sabatico Travelers Hostel, México 1410, T4381 1138, www.sabaticohostel.com.ar. Dorms and double rooms with and without bath (**$$**), full range of services and information, rooftop BBQ, mini pool and bar. Good location.

Apartments/self catering/homestays

B&T Argentina, T4876 5000, www.byt argentina.com. Accommodation in student residences and host families; also furnished flats.

Bahouse, www.bahouse.com.ar. Very good flats, by the week or month, all furnished and well-located in San Telmo, Retiro, Recoleta, Belgrano, Palermo and the centre.

Casa 34, Nicaragua 6045, T4775 0207, www.casa34.com. Helpful, with a big range.

Tu Casa Argentina, Fitzroy 2179, T4773 5544, www.tucasaargentina.com. Furnished flats by the day, week, month (from US$55 per day). Credit cards not accepted, deposit and rent payable in dollars. Efficient and helpful.

🍴 Restaurants

Eating out in Buenos Aires is one of the city's great pleasures, with a huge variety of restaurants from the chic to the cheap. To try some of Argentina's excellent steak, choose from one of the many *parrillas*, where your huge slab of lean meat will be expertly cooked over a wood fire. If in doubt about where to eat, head for Puerto Madero, the revamped docks area, an attractive place to stroll along the waterfront before dinner. There are good places here, generally in stylish interiors, serving international as well as local cuisine, with good service if a little overpriced. Take a radio taxi to Palermo or Las Cañitas for a wide range of excellent restaurants all within strolling distance. For more information on the gastronomy of Buenos Aires see: www.guiaoleo.com.ar, restaurant guide in Spanish.

There is a growing interest in less conventional eating out, from secret, or *puerta cerrada*, restaurants, to local eateries off the normal restaurant circuit, exploring local markets and so on. 2 fantastic food-oriented blogs in English are: www.saltshaker.net, chef Dan Perlman who also runs a highly recommended private restaurant in his house, see website for details; and www.buenosairesfoodies.com. Another highly-regarded closed door option can be found at The Argentine Experience, http://theargentineexperience.com, while tours are run by Parrilla Tour Buenos Aires, http://parrillatour.com/.

Some restaurants are *tenedor libre*: eat as much as you like for a fixed price. Most cafés serve tea or coffee plus facturas, or pastries, for breakfast.

Centre *p48, map p50*

$$$ Dadá, San Martín 941. A restaurant and bar with eclectic decoration. Good for gourmet lunches.

$$$ Sorrento, Av Corrientes 668 (just off Florida). Intimate, elegant atmosphere, one of the most traditional places in the centre for very good pastas and seafood.

$$$ Tancat, Paraguay 645. Delicious Spanish food, very popular at lunchtime.

$$$-$$ Gijón, Chile y San José. Very good value *parrilla* at this popular *bodegón*, south of Congreso district.

$$ Al paso y algo más, San Martín 487. Open till 1630. Recommended choice for *choripan* and *churrasquito* sandwiches plus other meat dishes, cramped at lunchtime.

$$ Las Cuartetas, Av Corrientes 838. A local institution open early to very late for fantastic pizza, can be busy and noisy as it's so popular.

$$ Fikä, Hipólito Yrigoyen 782. Mon-Fri open till 1900, Sat closes at 1600. Popular at lunchtime with a varied menu, is also attractive for a coffee break or a drink.

$$ Gianni´s, San Martín 430 and Reconquista 1028. The set menu with the meal-of-the-day makes an ideal lunch. Good risottos and salads. Slow service; open till 1700.

$$ Güerrín, Av Corrientes 1368. A Buenos Aires institution. Serves filling pizza and *faina* (chick pea polenta) which you eat standing up at a bar, or at tables, though you miss out on the colourful local life that way. For an extra service fee, upstairs room is less crowded or noisy.

$$ Sam Bucherie, 25 de Mayo 562. Open till 1800. The most imaginative sandwiches and salads downtown.

Cafés
Café Tortoni, Av de Mayo 825-9. This most famous Buenos Aires café has been the elegant haunt of artists and writers for over 100 years, with marble columns, stained glass ceilings, old leather chairs, and photographs of its famous clientele on the walls. Live tango. Packed with tourists, pricey, but still worth a visit.

Confitería Ideal, Suipacha 384. One of the most atmospheric cafés in the city. Wonderfully old-fashioned 1930s interior, serving good coffee and excellent cakes with good service. See Tango shows, below. Highly recommended.

El Gato Negro, Av Corrientes 1669. A beautiful tearoom, serving a choice of coffees and teas, and good cakes. Delightfully scented from the wide range of spices on sale.

Florida Garden, Florida y Paraguay. Another well-known café, popular for lunch, and tea.

Ice cream
The Italian ice cream tradition has been marked for decades by '*heladerías*' such as **Cadore**, Av Corrientes 1695, or **El Vesuvio**, Av Corrientes 1181, the oldest of all.

North of Plaza de Mayo *p52, map p54*
3 blocks west of Plaza San Martín, under the flyover at the northern end of Av 9 de Julio, between Arroyo and Av del Libertador in La Recova, are several recommended restaurants.

$$$ El Mirasol de la Recova, Posadas 1032. Serves top-quality *parrilla* in an elegant atmosphere.

$$$ Juana M, Carlos Pellegrini 1535 (downstairs). Excellent choice, popular with locals for its good range of dishes, and its very good salad bar.

Recoleta *p53, map p54*
$$$ Sirop & Folie, Pasaje del Correo, Vte Lopez 1661, T4813 5900. Delightful chic design, delicious French-inspired food, superb patisserie too. Highly recommended.

$$$ Rodi Bar, Vicente López 1900. Excellent *bife* and other dishes in this typical *bodegón*, welcoming and unpretentious.

$$$-$$ La Madeleine, Av Santa Fe 1726. Bright and cheerful choice, quite good pastas.

$$$-$$ María de Bambi, Ayacucho 1821 (with a small branch at Arenales 920). Open till 2130, closed on Sun. This small, quiet place is probably the best value in the area, serving very good and simple meals, also salon de té and patisserie.

Tea rooms, café-bars
Bröet, Azcuénaga 1144, www.broet.com.ar. Austrian-owned artisanal bakery with traditionally-made bread from around the world.

Clásica y Moderna, Av Callao 892, T4812 8707, www.clasicaymoderna.com. One of the city's most welcoming cafés, with a bookshop, great atmosphere, good breakfast through to drinks at night, daily live music and varied shows.

Como en casa, Av Quintana 2, Riobamba 1239, Laprida 1782 and at San Martín y Viamonte (former convent of Santa Catalina). Very popular in the afternoon for its varied and delicious cakes and fruit pies.

Milion, Paraná 1048. Stylish bar and café in an elegant mansion with marble stairs and a garden, good drinks, mixed clientèle. Recommended Fri after midnight.

Ice cream
Arkakao, Av Quintana 188. Great ice creams at this elegant tea room.
Freddo, and **Un'Altra Volta**, both with several branches in the city.

Palermo *p53, map p54*
This area of Buenos Aires is very popular, with many chic restaurants and bars in Palermo Viejo (referred to as 'Palermo Soho' for the area next to Plaza Cortázar and 'Palermo Hollywood' for the area beyond the railways and Av Juan B Justo) and the Las Cañitas district. It's a sprawling district, so you could take a taxi to one of these restaurants, and walk around before deciding where to eat. It's also a great place to stop for lunch, with cobbled streets, and 1900s buildings, now housing chic clothes shops. The Las Cañitas area is fashionable, with a wide range of interesting restaurants mostly along Báez, and most opening at around 2000, though only open for lunch at weekends:
$$$ Bio, Humboldt 2192, T4774 3880. Open daily. Delicious gourmet organic food, on a sunny corner.
$$$ La Cabrera, Cabrera 5127 and 5099. Superb *parrilla* and pasta, huge portions, with 2 branches; very popular. They offer a sparkling white wine while you wait.
$$$ Campobravo, Báez y Arévalo and Honduras y Fitz Roy. Stylish, minimalist, superb steaks and vegetables on the *parrilla*. Popular and recommended, can be noisy.
$$$ El Manto, Costa Rica 5801, T4774 2409. Genuine Armenian dishes, relaxed, good for a quiet evening.
$$$ El Preferido de Palermo, Borges y Guatemala, T4774 6585. Very popular *bodegón* serving both Argentine and Spanish-style dishes.
$$$ Janio, Malabia 1805, T4833 6540. Open for breakfast through to the early hours. One of Palermo's first restaurants, sophisticated Argentine cuisine in the evening.
$$$ Morelia, Baez 260 and Humboldt 2005. Cooks superb pizzas on the *parrilla*, and has a lovely roof terrace for summer.
$$$ Siamo nel forno, Costa Rica 5886. Excellent true Italian pizzas, recommended tiramisu.

$$$ Social Paraíso, Honduras 5182. Closed Sun evening and Mon. Simple delicious dishes in a relaxed chic atmosphere, with a lovely patio at the back. Good fish and tasty salads.
$$ Krishna, Malabia 1833. A small, intimate place serving Indian-flavoured vegetarian dishes.

Tea rooms, café-bars and ice cream
Palermo has good cafés opposite the park on Av del Libertador.
Cusic, El Salvador 6016, T4139 9173, www. cusic.com.ar. Closed Mon. For breakfast and lunches, breads, sandwiches, wraps, puddings.
Persicco, Honduras 4900, Salguero y Cabello, Av Santa Fe 3212, Maure y Migueletes, Tucumán y Reconquista (Centre) and Av Rivadavia 4933 (Caballito). The grandsons of **Freddo**'s founders also offer excellent ice cream.

San Telmo *p56, map p56*
$$$ Brasserie Petanque, Defensa y Mexico. Very attractive, informal French restaurant offering a varied menu with very good, creative dishes. Excellent value for their set lunch menus.
$$$ La Brigada, Estados Unidos 465, T4361 5557. Excellent *parrilla*, serving Argentine cuisine and wines. Very popular, expensive. Always reserve.
$$$ Gran Parrilla del Plata, Chile 594, T4300 8858, www.parrilladelplata.com. Popular, good value *parrilla* on a historic corner.
$$$-$$ Naturaleza Sabia, Balcarce 958. Tasty vegetarian and vegan dishes in an attractive ambience.

Tea rooms, café-bars and ice cream
Británico, Brasil y Defensa 399. Open 24 hrs. A historic place with a good atmosphere at lunchtime.
Dorrego, Humberto Primo y Defensa. Bar/café with great atmosphere, seating on plaza outside, good for late-night coffee or drinks.
La Poesía, Chile y Bolívar. Ideal for a coffee break on the sunny sidewalk.
Pride Café, Balcarce y Giuffra. Wonderful sandwiches, juices, salads and brownies, with lots of magazines to read.
Dylan, Perú 1086. Very good ice cream.

Nonna Bianca, Estados Unidos 425. For ice cream in an internet café.

Puerto Madero (Docks) *p57, map p48*
$$$ Cabaña Las Lilas, Av Moreau de Justo 516, T4313 1336. Reputedly one of the finest *parrillas* in town, pricey and popular with foreigners and business people.
$$$ Le Grill, Av Moreau de Justo 876, T4331 0454. A gourmet touch at a sophisticated *parrilla* which includes dry-aged beef, pork and lamb on its menu.

🟠 Bars and clubs

Generally it is not worth going to clubs before 0230 at weekends. Dress is usually smart. Entry can be from US$10-15, sometimes including a drink. A good way to visit some of the best bars is to join a pub crawl, eg **The Buenos Aires Pub Crawl**, www.buenosairespubcrawl.com, whose daily crawls are a safe night out.

Bars
Buller Brewing Company, Roberto M Ortiz 1827, Recoleta, www.bullerpub.com. Brew pub which also serves international food.
Casa Bar, Rodríguez Peña 1150, Recoleta. Beers from around the world in a restored mansion, good place to watch international sports matches, also serves food.
La Cigale, 25 de Mayo 597, Centre, T4893 2332. Popular after office hours, good live music.
Mundo Bizarro, Serrano 1222. Famous for its weird films, cocktails, American-style food, electronic and pop music.
Seddon, Defensa y Chile. Traditional bar open till late with live music on Fri.
Sugar, Costa Rica 4619. Welcoming bar with cheap beer and drinks, happy hour nightly, shows international sports.

The corner of Reconquista and Marcelo T de Alvear in Retiro is the centre of the small 'Irish' pub district, overcrowded on St Patrick's Day, 17 Mar. **Druid In**, Reconquista 1040, Centre, is by far the most attractive choice there, open for lunch and with live music weekly. The **Shamrock**, Rodríguez Peña 1220, in Recoleta, is

another Irish-run, popular bar, happy hour for ISIC holders.

Clubs
Bahrein, Lavalle 345, Centre, www.bahreinba. com. Funky and electronic.
L'Arc, Niceto Vega 5452, Palermo. Hosts The X Club weekly, with a cocktail bar and live bands.
Niceto Club, Niceto Vega 5510, Palermo, T4779 9396, www.nicetoclub.com. Early live shows and dancing afterwards. Club 69 weekly parties for house, electronic, hip hop and funk music.

Gay clubs Most gay clubs charge from US$10 entry. **Amerika**, Gascón 1040, Almagro, www.ameri-k.com.ar. Fri-Sun, attracting over 2000 party-goers over 3 floors. **Bach Bar**, Cabrera 4390, www.bach-bar.com.ar. Friendly lesbian bar in Palermo Viejo, Wed-Sun. **Sitges**, Av Córdoba 4119, Palermo, T4861 3763, www. sitges online.com.ar. Gay and lesbian bar.

Jazz clubs Notorious, Av Callao 966, T4813 6888, www.notorious.com.ar. Live jazz at a music shop with bar and restaurant. **Thelonious**, Salguero 1884, www.thelonious. com.ar, T4829 1562. Live jazz and DJs. **Virasoro Bar**, Guatemala 4328, www.virasorobar.com.ar, T4831 8918. Live jazz in a 1920's Art Deco house.

Salsa clubs La Salsera, Yatay 961, T4866 1829, www.lasalsera.com. Highly regarded.

🟠 Entertainment

At carnival time, look for the **Programa Carnaval Porteño** (it's on Facebook).

Cinemas
The selection of films is excellent, ranging from new Hollywood releases to Argentine and world cinema; details are listed daily in main newspapers. Films are shown uncensored and most foreign films are subtitled. Tickets best booked early afternoon to ensure good seats (average price US$9, discount on Wed and for 1st show daily).

Independent foreign and national films are shown during the **Festival de Cine Independiente** (BAFICI), held every Apr, more information on the festival at www.bafici.gov.ar.

Cultural events

Centro Cultural Borges, Galerías Pacífico, Viamonte y San Martín, p 1, T5555 5359, www.ccborges.org.ar. Art exhibitions, concerts, film shows and ballet; some student discounts.

Ciudad Cultural Konex, Sarmiento 3131 (Abasto), T4864 3200, www.ciudadcultural konex.org. A converted oil factory hosts this huge complex holding plays, live music shows, summer film projections under the stars, modern ballet, puppet theatre and, occasionally, massive parties.

Usina del Arte, Caffarena y Av Pedro de Mendoza (La Boca), www.usinadelarte.org. Temporary art exhibitions, plays, live music, film shows at an impressive 1910s converted power station which also offers guided visits.

Villa Ocampo, Elortondo 1811, Beccar, Partido de San Isidro, T4732 4988, www.villaocampo. org. Former residence of writer and founder of Revista Sur Victoria Ocampo, now owned by UNESCO, in northern suburbs, Thu-Sun and holidays 1230-1800, US$2.50 (weekends and holidays US$4) entry, open for visits, courses, exhibitions and meals at its café-restaurant.

See also the programmes of the **Alliance Française**, www.alianzafrancesa.org.ar, **British Arts Centre**, www.britishartscentre.org.ar, **Goethe Institut**, www.goethe.de/ins/ar/bue/esindex.htm, and **Instituto Cultural Argentino Norteamericano**, www.icana.org.ar.

Tango shows

There are 2 ways to enjoy tango: you can watch the dancing at a tango show. Most pride themselves on very high standards and although they are not cheap (show only US$50-90, show and dinner US$75-150), this is tango at its best. Most prices include drinks and hotel transfers. Or you can learn to dance at a class and try your steps at a *milonga* (tango club). The Tango page on www.turismo.buenosaires.gob.ar lists *tanguerías* for tango shows, classes and *milongas*.

See also the websites www.tangocity.com and www.todotango.com.

Every Aug there is a tango dancing competition, **Festival y Mundial de Baile**, open to both locals and foreigners.

Bar Sur, Estados Unidos 299, T4362 6086, www.bar-sur.com.ar. Open 2000-0200. Price with or without dinner. Good fun, public sometimes join the professional dancers.

El Querandí, Perú 302, T5199 1770, www.querandi.com.ar. Daily shows, with or without dinner, also open for lunch. Tango show restaurant, dating back to 1920s.

El Viejo Almacén, Independencia y Balcarce, T4307 7388, www.viejoalmacen.com.ar. Daily, dinner from 2000, show 2200. Impressive dancing and singing. Recommended.

Esquina Carlos Gardel, Carlos Gardel 3200 y Anchorena, T4867 6363, www.esquinacarlos gardel.com.ar. Opposite the former Mercado del Abasto, this is the most popular venue in Gardel's own neighbourhood; dinner at 2030, show at 2230. Recommended.

Esquina Homero Manzi, Av San Juan 3601 (Subte Boedo), T4957 8488, www.esquina homeromanzi.com.ar. Traditional show at 2200 with excellent musicians and dancers, dinner (2100) and show available, tango school. Recommended.

Piazzolla Tango, Florida 165 (basement), Galería Güemes, T4344 8201, www.piazzolla tango.com. A beautifully restored belle époque hall hosts a smart tango show; dinner at 2045, show at 2215.

Milongas are very popular with younger *porteños*. You can take a class and get a feel for the music before the dancing starts a couple of hours later. Both tango and *milonga* (the music that contributed to the origins of tango and is more cheerful) are played. Cost is from US$8; even beginners are welcome.

Centro Cultural Torquato Tasso, Defensa 1575, T4307 6506, www.torquatotasso.com.ar. See web for programme and prices (daily lessons), English spoken.

Confitería Ideal, Suipacha 384, T4328 7750, www.confiteriaideal.com. Very atmospheric ballroom for daily milongas at this old central café. Most days dancing starts as early as 1500; lessons start 1230 on some days, 1530 on others (not on Sun). Also evening tango shows.

La Viruta (at Centro Armenio), Armenia 1366, Palermo Viejo, T4774 6357, www.lavirutatango.

com. Very popular, classes every day except Mon, entry US$7 (check website for times), also salsa and rock dancing classes, with restaurant.

Theatre

About 20 commercial theatres play all year and there are many amateur theatres. The main theatre street is Av Corrientes.

Complejo Teatral de Buenos Aires, Corrientes 1530, T4371 0111/8, http://complejoteatral.gob. ar, is a group of 5 theatres with many cultural activities. Book seats for theatre, ballet and opera as early as possible. Tickets for most popular shows (including rock and pop concerts) are sold also through **Ticketek**, T5237 7200, www. ticketek.com.ar. See also www.alternativateatral. com and www.mundoteatral.com.ar. For live Argentine and Latin American bands, best venues are: **La Trastienda**, Balcarce 460, San Telmo, www.latrastienda.com, theatre/café with lots of live events, also serving meals and drinks from breakfast to dinner, great music, or **ND Teatro**, Paraguay 918, www.ndteatro.com.ar.

O Shopping

The main, fashionable shopping streets are Florida and Santa Fe (from Av 9 de Julio to Av Pueyrredón). Palermo is the best area for chic boutiques and well-known international fashion labels; head for C Honduras and C El Salvador, between Malabia and Serrano. C Defensa in San Telmo is known for its antique shops. It also has a few craft stalls around C Alsina, Fri 1000-1700. **Pasaje de la Defensa**, Defensa 1179, is a beautifully restored 1880s house containing small shops.

Bookshops

Buenos Aires is renowned for its bookshops and was UNESCO's World Book Capital in 2011. Many shops are along Florida, Av Corrientes (from Av 9 de Julio to Callao) or Av Santa Fe, and in shopping malls. Second hand and discount bookshops are mostly along Av Corrientes and Av de Mayo. Rare books are sold in several specialized stores in the Microcentro (the area enclosed by Suipacha, Esmeralda, Tucumán and Paraguay). The main chains of bookshops, usually selling a small selection of foreign books are: **Cúspide, Distal, Kel** (imported books, mostly in English) and **Yenny-El Ateneo**, whose biggest store is on Av Santa Fe 1860, in an old theatre, there is café where the stage used to be.

Eterna Cadencia, Honduras 5574, T4774 4100, www.eternacadencia.com. Has an excellent selection and a good café.

Walrus Books, Estados Unidos 617, San Telmo, T4300 7135, www.walrus-books.com.ar. Sells secondhand books in English, including Latin American authors, good children's section.

Handicrafts

Arte y Esperanza, Balcarce 234 and Suipacha 892, www.arteyesperanza.com.ar. Crafts made by indigenous communities, sold by a Fair Trade organization.

Artesanías Argentinas, Montevideo 1386, www.artesaniasargentinas. org. Aboriginal crafts and other traditional items sold by a Fair Trade organization.

El Boyero, Florida 753 (Galerías Pacífico) and 953, T4312 3564, http://es.elboyero.com. High quality silver, leather, woodwork and other typical Argentine handicrafts.

Martín Fierro, Santa Fe 992. Good handicrafts, stonework, etc. Recommended.

Plata Nativa, Galería del Sol, Florida 860, local 41, www.platanativa.com. For Latin American folk handicrafts and high quality jewellery.

In Dec there is a **Feria Internacional de Artesanías**.

Leather goods

Several shops are concentrated along Florida next to Plaza San Martín and also in Suipacha (900 block).

Aida, Galería de la Flor, local 30, Florida 670. Quality, inexpensive leather products, can make a leather jacket to measure in the same day.

Dalla Fontana, Reconquista 735, www. dalla-fontana.com.ar. Leather factory, fast, efficient and reasonably priced for madeto-measure clothes.

Casa López, MT de Alvear 640/658, www.
casalopez.com.ar. The most traditional and
finest leather shop, expensive but worth it.
Galería del Caminante, Florida 844. Has a
variety of good shops with leather goods,
arts and crafts, souvenirs, etc.
Prüne, Florida 963 and in many shopping
centres, www.prune.com.ar. Fashionable
designs for women, many options in leather
and not very expensive.

Markets and malls

Markets can be found in many of the city's parks
and plazas, which hold weekend fairs. You will
find pretty much the same sort of handicrafts.
The following offer something different.
Feria de Mataderos, Lisandro de la Torre y
Av de los Corrales, T4342 9629, www.feriade
mataderos.com.ar, subte E to end of line then
taxi (US$7), or buses 55, 63, 80, 92, 103, 117,
126, 141, 155, 180. Sat from 1700 (Jan-Feb),
Sun 1100-2000 (Mar-Dec). Long way but few
tourists, fair of Argentine handicrafts and
traditions, music and dance festivals, gaucho
horsemanship skills; nearby **Museo Criollo de
los Corrales**, Av de los Corrales 6436, T4687
1949, Sun 1200-1830, US$0.20.
Mercado de las Luces, Manzana de las Luces,
Perú y Alsina. Mon-Fri 1030-1930, Sun 1400-1930.
Handicrafts, second-hand books, plastic arts.
Parque Centenario, Av Díaz Vélez y L Marechal.
Sat-Sun and holidays 1100-2000, local crafts,
cheap handmade clothes, used items of all sorts.
Parque Rivadavia, Av Rivadavia 4900. Sun
0900-1300. Second-hand books, stamps, coins,
records, tapes, CDs and magazines.
Plaza Dorrego, San Telmo. Sun 1000-1700.
For souvenirs, antiques, etc, with free tango
performances and live music, wonderfully
atmospheric, and an array of 'antiques'.
Plaza Italia, Santa Fe y Uriarte (Palermo). Sat 1200-
2000, Sun 1000-2000. Second hand textbooks
and magazines (daily), handicrafts market.

The city has many fine shopping
malls, including **Abasto de Buenos Aires**,
Av Corrientes 3247, T4959 3400, nearest Subte:
Carlos Gardel, line B, in the city's impressive,
Art Deco former fruit and vegetable market

building, and **Patio Bullrich**, Av Del Libertador
750 and Posadas 1245, T4814 7400, nearest
Subte: 8 blocks from Plaza San Martín, line C,
the most upmarket mall in the city.

⊙ What to do

Cricket Asociación Argentina de Cricket,
Juan María Gutiérrez 3829, T3974 9593,
www.cricketargentina.com, for information.
Cricket is played Sep-Apr.
Cycle hire and tours La Bicicleta Naranja,
Pasaje Giuffra 308, San Telmo and Nicaragua
4825, Palermo, T4362 1104, www.labicicle
tanaranja.com.ar. Bike hire and tours to all
parts of the city, 3-4 hrs. **Lan&Kramer Bike
Tours**, San Martín 910 p 6, T4311 5199, www.
biketours.com.ar. Daily at 0930 and 1400 next
to the monument of San Martín (Plaza San
Martín), 3½- to 4-hr cycle tours to the south
or the north of the city; also to San Isidro and
Tigre, 4½-5 hrs and full day tours, plus summer
evening tours downtown; also, bike rental.
Urban biking, Maipú 971, T4314 2325, www.
urbanbiking.com. 4½-hr tours either to the
south or to the north of the centre, starting
daily 0900 and 1400 from Av Santa Fe y Maipú;
night city tours, 3½-4 hrs, full day tours to San
Isidro and Tigre (including kayak in the Delta),
or occasionally, to the pampas. Also rents bikes.
Football and rugby Football fans should
see **Boca Juniors**, matches every other Sun at
their stadium (La Bombonera, Brandsen 805,
La Boca, www.bocajuniors.com.ar, tickets for
non-members only through tour operators, or
the museum – see the murals), or their arch-
rivals, **River Plate**, Av Figueroa Alcorta 7597,
T4789 1200, www.cariverplate.com.ar. Football
season Feb-Jun, and Aug-Dec, most matches
on Sun. Buy tickets from stadiums, sports stores
near the grounds, ticket agencies or hostels
and hotels, which may arrange guide/transport
(don't take a bus if travelling alone, phone
a radio taxi; see also **Tangol**, below). Rugby
season Apr-Oct/Nov. For more information,
Unión de Rugby de Buenos Aires, www.urba.
org.ar, or **Unión Argentina de Rugby**, T4898
8500, www.uar.com.ar.

Polo The high handicap season is Sep-Dec, but it is played all year round. Argentina has the top polo players in the world. A visit to the national finals at Palermo in Nov and Dec is recommended. For information, **Asociación Argentina de Polo**, T4777 8005, www.aapolo.com.

Tour operators and travel agents

An excellent way of seeing Buenos Aires is by a 3-hr tour. Longer tours may include dinner and a tango show, or a boat trip in the Delta, or a gaucho *fiesta* at a ranch (great food and dancing). Bookable through most travel agents. See also **BA Free Tour**, www.bafreetour.com, www.buenosaireslocaltours.com and **City Walkers**, www.citywalkers.com.ar for free walking tours. For another type of walking tour, see **BA Street Art**, http://buenosairesstreetart.com, and **Graffitimundo**, http://graffitimundo.com, who offer tours of the city's best graffiti, see websites for prices and times.

Anda, T3221 0833, www.andatravel.com.ar. Operator specializing in socially and environmentally responsible tourism in Buenos Aires and around the country, including volunteering opportunities.

Argentina Excepción, Costa Rica 5546, T4772 6620, www.argentina-excepcion.com. French/Argentine agency offering tailor-made, upper end tours, fly-drives, themed trips and other services. Also has a Santiago branch, www.chile-excepcion.com.

BAT, Buenos Aires Tur, Lavalle 1444 of 10, T4371 2304, www.buenosairestur.com. City tours, twice daily; Tigre and Delta, daily, 5 hrs.

Buenos Aires Bus (Bus Turístico), www.buenosairesbus.com. Open yellow double-decker buses follow 2 routes every 10-20 mins covering main sights from La Boca to Núñez with multilingual recorded tours. 1-day (US$27) and 2-day (US$33) hop-on/hop-off tickets can be purchased online or onboard. Find bus stops on website or on map provided at city's tourist offices.

Buenos Aires Vision, Esmeralda 356, p 8, T4394 4682, www.buenos-aires-vision.com.ar. City tours, Tigre and Delta, Tango (cheaper without dinner) and **Fiesta Gaucha**.

Cultour, T156-365 6892 (mob), www.cultour.com.ar. A highly recommended walking tour of the city, 3-4 hrs led by a group of Argentine history/tourism graduates. In English and Spanish.

Eternautas, Av Julio A Roca 584 p 7, T5031 9916, www.eternautas.com. Historical, cultural and artistic tours of the city and Pampas guided in English, French or Spanish by academics from the University of Buenos Aires, flexible.

Flyer Lufthansa City Center, Av Fondo De La Legua 425, San Isidro, T4512 8100, www.lcc-flyer.com. English, Dutch, German spoken, repeatedly recommended, especially for estancias, fishing, polo, motorhome rental.

Kallpa, Tucumán 861, p 2, T5278 8010, www.kallpatour.com. Tailor-made tours to natural and cultural destinations throughout the country, with an emphasis on adventure, conservation and golf.

Mai10, Av Córdoba 657, p 3, T4314 3390, www.mai10.com.ar. High-end, personalized tours for groups and individuals, covers the whole country, special interests include art, cuisine, estancias, photo safaris, fishing and many more.

Say Hueque, Viamonte 749, p 6 of 1, and other branches in Palermo and San Telmo, T5258 8740, www.sayhueque.com. Recommended travel agency offering good-value tours aimed at independent travellers, friendly English-speaking staff.

Tangol, Florida 971, ground floor, shop 31, and Defensa 831, T4363 6000, www.tangol.com. Friendly, independent agency specializing in football and tango, plus various sports, such as polo and paragliding. Can arrange tours, plane and bus tickets, accommodation. English spoken. Discounts for students. Overland tours in Patagonia Oct-Apr.

● Transport

Air

Ezeiza (officially Ministro Pistarini, T5480 6111, www.aa2000.com.ar), the international airport, is 35 km southwest of the centre (also handles some domestic flights). The airport has 3 terminals: 'A', 'B' and 'C'. There are duty free shops (expensive), ATM and exchange facilities at Banco Nación (terminal 'A') (only change the very minimum to get you into the city), a **Ministerio de Turismo** desk, and a post office (Mon-Fri 0900-1700, Sat 0900-1200). No hotels nearby, but there is an attractive B&B 5 mins away with transfer included: **$$$ Bernie's**, Estrada 186, Barrio Uno, T4480 0420, www. posadabernies.com, book in advance. There is a **Devolución IVA/Tax Free** desk (return of VAT) for purchases over the value of AR$70 (ask for a Global Refund check plus the invoice from the shop when you buy). Hotel booking service at Tourist Information desk – helpful, but prices are higher if booked in this way.

Airport buses A display in immigration shows choices and prices of transport into the city. A good dual carriageway links with the General Paz highway which circles the city. The safest way between airport and city is by an airport bus service run every 30 mins by **Manuel Tienda León** (office in front of you as you arrive), company office and terminal at Av Madero 1299 y San Martín, behind Sheraton Hotel in Retiro (take a taxi from the terminal; do not walk outside), T4315 5115, www.tiendaleon.com.ar. The bus costs US$14 one way, pay by pesos, dollars, euros or credit card. **Manuel Tienda León** will also collect passengers from addresses in centre for a small extra fee, book the previous day. Bus from Ezeiza to Aeroparque, 1½ hrs, US$14. Remise taxis for up to 4 passengers (**Manuel Tienda León**, **Taxi Ezeiza**, www.taxiezeiza.com.ar, and other counters at Ezeiza) charge US$50 airport to town, but less from city to airport. Radio taxis charge US$45 (make sure you pay for your taxi at the booth and then wait in the queue), see Taxis below for more details. On no account take an unmarked car at Ezeiza, no matter how attractive the fare may sound. Drivers are adept at separating you from far more money than you can possibly owe them. Always ask to see the taxi driver's licence. If you take an ordinary taxi the Policía de Seguridad Aeroportuaria on duty notes down the car's licence and time of departure.

Aeroparque (Jorge Newbery Airport), 4 km north of the centre, T5480 6111, www.aa2000. com.ar, handles all internal flights, and some flights to neighbouring countries. On the 1st floor there is a *patio de comidas* and many shops. At the airport also tourist information, car rental, bus companies, ATM, public phones and luggage deposit (ask at information desk in sector B). **Manuel Tienda León** buses to Aeroparque (see above for address), more-or-less hourly; from Aeroparque, 0900-2330, 30-min journey, US$5. Local bus 45 run from outside the airport to the Retiro railway station. No 37 goes to **Palermo** and **Recoleta** and No 160 to **Palermo** and **Almagro**. If going to the airport, make sure it goes to Aeroparque by asking the driver. Remise taxis to **Ezeiza**, operated by **Manuel Tienda León**, US$50; to the city centre US$16. Taxi to centre US$8. **Manuel Tienda León** operates buses between Ezeiza and Aeroparque airports, US$14.

Bus
Local City buses are called *colectivos* and cover a very wide radius. They are clean, frequent, efficient and very fast. Colectivo fares are calculated in 3-km sections, US$0.50-0.60, but fares are cheaper if you have a pre-paid smart card called *Sube* (see www.xcolectivo.com.ar for details). If not using a smart card, have coins ready for ticket machine as drivers do not sell tickets, but may give change. The bus number is not always sufficient indication of destination, as each number may have a variety of routes, but bus stops display routes of buses stopping there and little plaques are displayed in the driver's window. A rapid transit system, **Metrobús**, incorporating existing bus routes, is being implemented, including along Av 9 de Julio. See www.omnilineas.com.ar and page 47, above, for city guides listing bus routes.

Long distance Bus terminal for all international and interprovincial buses is at Ramos Mejía y Antártida Argentina (Subte Line C), behind Retiro station, T4310 0700, www. tebasa.com.ar. The terminal is on 3 floors. Bus information is at the Ramos Mejía entrance on the middle floor. Ticket offices are on the upper floor, but there are hundreds of them so you'll need to consult the list of companies and their office numbers at the top of the escalator. They are organized by region and are colour coded. Buenos Aires city information desk is on the upper floor. It is advisable to go to the bus station the day before you travel to get to know where the platforms are so that when you are fully laden you know exactly where to go. At the basement and ground levels there are leftluggage lockers, tokens sold in kiosks; for large baggage, there's a *guarda equipaje* on the lower floor. For further details of bus services and fares, look under proposed destinations. There are no direct buses to either of the airports. **International buses** International services are run by both local and foreign companies; heavily booked Dec-Mar (especially at weekends), when most fares usually rise sharply. Do not buy Uruguayan bus tickets in Buenos Aires; wait till you get to Colonia or Montevideo. To **Montevideo**, Bus de la Carrera, Cauvi and Cóndor Estrella, US$51-59, 8 hrs; see Ferries, below. To **Bolivia**, most Argentine companies only reach the border, where you can change buses at **La Quiaca** or **Aguas Blancas**. Alternatively change buses at **San Salvador de Jujuy** or at **Orán**, busier transport hubs. Some companies go across the border to **Santa Cruz de la Sierra**, 39 hrs via **Yacuiba**. Direct buses to **Brazil** by Pluma, T4313 3880, and Crucero del Norte, T5258 5000, eg to **Porto Alegre**, 20 hrs, **Florianópolis**, 27 hrs, **Curitiba**, 34 hrs, **São Paulo,** 34-38 hrs and **Rio de Janeiro**, 40 hrs. Crucero del Norte and Flecha Bus operate summer services to southern Brazil beach resorts. The route across the Río de la Plata and through Uruguay is a bit cheaper and offers a variety of transport and journey breaks.

Direct buses to **Santiago** (Chile), 1400 km, with Ahumada, CATA and **Pullman del Sur** daily, 20 hrs. To **Asunción** (Paraguay), 1370 km via Clorinda (toll bridge): several bus companies, around 18 hrs. Also to **Ciudad del Este** (16½ hrs), **Encarnación** (13 hrs) and other destinations in Paraguay. To **Peru**: 4 companies including Ormeño (T4313 2259), direct service to **Lima** (only stops for meals, not included in the price), 3 days. If you need a visa for Chile, get one before travelling.

Driving
Driving in Buenos Aires is no problem, provided you have eyes in the back of your head and good nerves. Traffic fines are high and police look out for drivers without the correct papers. Car hire is cheaper if you arrange it when you arrive rather than from home. Sixt, Cerrito 1314, www.sixt.com.ar, and national rental agencies, such as **Dietrich**, Cerrito 1575, T0800-999 2999, www.localizadietrich.com. **Ruta Sur**, Av General Paz 1260, T5238 4071, www.rutasur.eu. Rents 4WDs and motorhomes. Motoring Associations: see **ACA**, page 40.

Ferry
To **Montevideo** and **Colonia** from Terminal Dársena Norte, Av Antártida Argentina 821 (2 blocks from Av Córdoba y Alem). **Buquebus**, T4316 6500, www.buquebus.com (tickets from Terminal, Retiro bus station, from offices at Av Córdoba 867 and Posadas 1452, by phone or online): **1)** Direct to **Montevideo**, 1-4 a day, 3 hrs, from US$105 tourist class, one way, also carries vehicles and motorcycles. **2)** To **Colonia**, services by 3 companies: Buquebus: minimum 5 crossings a day, from 1-3 hrs, US$53 tourist class one way on slower vessel, US$72 tourist class on faster vessel, with bus connection to **Montevideo**. (Buquebus also offers flights to Uruguay and Brazil with onward connections, www.flybqb.com.uy.) **Colonia Express**, www.coloniaexpress.com, makes 2-3 crossings a day between Buenos Aires and Colonia in a fast catamaran (no vehicles carried), 50 mins, prices range from US$18 to US$35 one way, depending on type of service and where bought. Office is at Av Córdoba 753, T4317 4100; Terminal Fluvial is at Av Pedro de Mendoza 330. You must go there by taxi, US$8 from Retiro. **Seacat**, www.seacatcolonia. com, 3 fast ferries to Colonia, 1 hr, US$-42 one way, from the same terminal as Buquebus, with bus to Montevideo (US$40-52) and Punta del Este (US$58-66) on most crossings. Office:

Av Córdoba 772, T4322 9555, phone sales: T4314 5100. See under Tigre, page 75, for services to Carmelo and Nueva Palmira.

Metro (Subte)

Seven lines link the outer parts of the city to the centre. **Line 'A'** runs under Av Rivadavia, from Plaza de Mayo to San Pedrito (Flores). **Line 'B'** from central Post Office, on Av L N Alem, under Av Corrientes to Federico Lacroze railway station at Chacarita, ending at Juan Manuel de Rosas (Villa Urquiza). **Line 'C'** links Plaza Constitución with the Retiro railway station, and provides connections with all the other lines but 'H'. **Line 'D'** runs from Plaza de Mayo (Catedral), under Av Roque Sáenz Peña (Diagonal Norte), Córdoba, Santa Fe and Palermo to Congreso de Tucumán (Belgrano). **Line 'E'** runs from Plaza de Mayo (Cabildo, on C Bolívar) through San Juan to Plaza de los Virreyes (connection to Line 'P' or Premetro train service to the southwest end of the city). **Line 'H'** runs from Corrientes, via Once to Hospitales (Parque Patricios), under Av Jujuy and Av Almafuerte. Note that 3 stations, 9 de Julio (Line 'D'), Diagonal Norte (Line 'C') and Carlos Pellegrini (Line 'B') are linked by pedestrian tunnels. The fare is US$0.45, the same for any direct trip or combination between lines, magnetic cards (for 1, 2, 5, 10, or 30 journeys) must be bought at the station before boarding; only pesos accepted. Trains are operated by **Metrovías**, T0800-555 1616, www.metrovias.com.ar, and run Mon-Sat 0500-2220 (Sun 0800-2200). Line A, the oldest was built in 1913, the earliest in South America. Backpacks and luggage allowed. Free map (if available) from stations and tourist office.

Taxi

Taxis are painted yellow and black, and carry Taxi flags. Fares are shown in pesos. The meter starts at US$1.50 when the flag goes down; make sure it isn't running when you get in. A fixed rate of US$0.15 for every 200 m or 1-min wait is charged thereafter. The fare from 2200 to 0600 starts at US$1.80, plus US$0.18 for every 200 m or 1-min wait. A charge is sometimes made for each piece of hand baggage (ask first). About 10% tip expected. For security, take a remise or radio taxi booked by phone or at the company's office. Check that the driver's licence is displayed. Lock doors on the inside. The 2 airports and Retiro bus station are notorious for unlicensed taxi crime; use the airport buses and remises listed above, and taxis from the official rank in the bus terminal which are registered with police and safe.

Radio taxis are managed by several different companies; extra fee US$0.90. Phone a radio taxi from your hotel (they can make recommendations), a phone box or *locutorio*, giving the address where you are, and you'll usually be collected within 10 mins. **City**, T4585 5544; **Porteño**, T4566 5777; **Premium**, T5238 0000; **Tiempo**, T4854 3838.

Remise taxis operate all over the city, run from an office and have no meter. The companies are identified by signs on the pavement. Fares are fixed and can be cheaper than regular taxis, can be verified by phoning the office, and items left in the car can easily be reclaimed. **Universal**, T4105 5555.

Tram

Old-fashioned street cars operate Mar-Nov on Sat and holidays 1600-1930 and Sun 1000-1300, 1600-1930 and Dec-Feb on Sat and holidays 1700-2030, Sun 1000-1300, 1700-2030, free, on a circular route along the streets of Caballito district, from C Emilio Mitre 500, Subte Primera Junta (Line A) or Emilio Mitre (Line E), no stops en route. Operated by **Asociación Amigos del Tranvía**, T4431 1073, www.tranvia.org.ar.

Train

There are 4 main terminals: **1) Retiro** (3 lines: **Mitre**, **Belgrano** and **San Martín** in separate buildings. The state of services changes all the time, owing largely to poor maintenance. The independent website, www.sateliteferroviario. com.ar, is a good source of information on all services. Urban and suburban services include: Mitre line (T0800-222 8736) to **Belgrano**, **Mitre** (connection to Tren de la Costa, see page 75), **Olivos**, **San Isidro**, and **Tigre** (see page 74); long-distance services to **Rosario Norte**, 7½ hrs, US$3-7; to **Tucumán** via Rosario, Mon and Fri, 0728 (return Wed 1552, Sat 1900), an extra weekly service is added in summer, 26½ hrs, US$50 sleeper (for 2, breakfast included), US$17 pullman, US$9 1st class, US$5 *turista* (run by **Ferrocentral**, T0800-1221 8736, www.ferrocentralsa.com.ar). To **Córdoba** via Rosario, Mon and Thu 2035 (return Wed and Sun 1439), 17 hrs, US$38 sleeper (for 2, breakfast included), US$11.50 pullman, US$6.50 1st class, US$4 *turista* (run by **Ferrocentral**). Belgrano line to northwestern suburbs, including Villa Rosa, run by **Ferrovías**, T0800-777 3377. San Martín line for services to Pilar and long-distance services to Junín and Alberdi (see www.ferrobaires.gba.gov.ar).

2) Constitución, Roca line urban and suburban services to La Plata, Ezeiza, Ranelagh and Quilmes. Long-distance services (run by **Ferrobaires**, T4304 0028, www.ferrobaires.gba. gov.ar): **Bahía Blanca**, 5 a week 1945, 14 hrs, US$15-22. Also services to **Mar del Plata** (3 a week in early 2014, US$21-26) and Tandil.

3) Federico Lacroze, Urquiza line and Metro headquarters (run by **Metrovías**, T0800-555 1616, www.metrovias.com.ar). Suburban services: to General Lemos.

4) Once, Sarmiento line, urban and suburban services to Moreno and Luján. Long-distance services to Lincoln (run by **Ferrobaires**).

❶ Directory

Banks ATMs are widespread for MasterCard or Visa. The financial district lies within a small area north of Plaza de Mayo, between Rivadavia, 25 de Mayo, Av Corrientes and Florida. In non-central areas find banks/ ATMs along the main avenues. Banks open Mon-Fri 1000-1500. *Casas de cambio* include **Banco Piano**, San Martín 345, T4321 9200, www.banco piano.com.ar, changes all TCs (commission 2%). **Forex**, MT de Alvear 540, T4010 2000. Other South American currencies can only be exchanged in *casas de cambio*.
Embassies and consulates For all foreign embassies and consulates in Buenos Aires, see http://embassy.goabroad.com.
Language schools Academia Buenos Aires, Hipólito Yrigoyen 571, p 4, T4345 5954, www.academiabuenosaires.com. **All-Spanish**, Talcahuano 77 p 1, T4832 7794, www.all-spanish.com.ar. One-to-one classes. **Amauta Spanish School**, Federico Lacroze 2129, T4777 2130, www.amautaspanish. com. Spanish classes, one-to-one or small groups, centres in Buenos Aires, Bariloche and at an estancia in the Pampas. **Argentina I.L.E.E**, T4782 7173, www.argentinailee. com. Recommended by individuals and organizations alike, with a school in Bariloche. **Cedic**, Reconquista 715, p 11 E, T4312 1016, www.cedic.com.ar. Recommended. **Elebaires**,

Av de Mayo 1370, of 10, p 3, T4383 7706, www.elebaires.com.ar. Small school with focused classes, also offers one-to-one lessons and excursions. Recommended. **Expanish**, Perón 698, T5252 3040, www.expanish.com. Well-organized courses which can involve excursions, accommodation and Spanish lessons in sister schools in Peru and Chile. Highly recommended. IBL (**Argentina Spanish School**), Florida 165, p 3, of 328, T4331 4250, www.ibl.com.ar. Group and one-to-one lessons, all levels, recommended. **Bue Spanish School**, Av Belgrano 1431, p 2, apt18, T4381 6347, www.buespanish.com.ar. Intensive and regular Spanish courses, culture programme, free materials. **Laboratorio de Idiomas** (**Universidad de Buenos Aires**), 25 de Mayo 221 (also other branches), T4334 7512 or 14343 1196, www.idiomas. filo.uba.ar. Offers cheap, coherent courses, including summer intensive courses. For other schools teaching Spanish, and for private tutors look in *Buenos Aires Herald* in the classified advertisements. Enquire also at *Asatej* (see Useful addresses).

Medical services Urgent medical service: for free municipal ambulance service to an emergency hospital department (day and night) **Casualty ward**, Sala de guardia, 1107 or T4923 1051/58 (SAME). Inoculations: **Hospital Rivadavia**, Av Las Heras 2670, T4009 2000, Mon-Fri, 0700-1200 (bus 10, 37, 59, 60, 62, 92, 93 or 102 from Plaza Constitución), or **Dirección de Sanidad de Fronteras y Terminales de Transporte**, Ing Huergo 690, T4343 1190, Mon-Fri 1000-1500, bus 20 from Retiro, no appointment required (yellow fever only; take passport). If not provided, buy the vaccines in **Laboratorio Biol**, Uriburu 153, T4953 7215, or in larger chemists. Many chemists have signs indicating that they give injections. Any hospital with an infectology department will give hepatitis A. **Centros Médicos Stamboulian**, 25 de Mayo 464, T4515 3000, Pacheco de Melo 2941, also in Belgrano, Villa Crespo, Villa Urquiza and Flores, www.stamboulian.com.ar. Private health advice for travellers and inoculations centre. Public

Hospitals: **Hospital Argerich**, Almte Brown esq Py y Margall 750, T4121 0700. **Hospital Juan A Fernández**, Cerviño y Bulnes, T4808 2600/2650, probably the best free medical attention in the city. **British Hospital**, Perdriel 74, T4309 6400, www.hospital britanico.org.ar. **German Hospital**, Av Pueyrredón 1640, between Beruti and Juncal, T4827 7000, www.hospitalale man.com.ar. Both have first-aid centres (*centros asistenciales*) as do other main hospitals. Dental treatment: excellent dental treatment centre at **Croid**, Vuelta de Obligado 1551 (Belgrano), T4781 9037, www.croid.com.ar. **Dental Argentina**, Laprida 1621, p 2 B, T4828 0821, www.dental-argentina.com.ar. **Useful addresses** Migraciones. (Immigration), Antártida Argentina 1355, edif 4, T4317 0234, www.migraciones.gov.ar, 0800-1400 (for renovation of tourist visas or '*prórrogas*' – see Visas and immigration, page 46). **Central Police Station**. Moreno 1550, Virrey Cevallos 362, T4346 5700 (emergency, T101 or 911 from any phone, free) See page 43 for **Comisaría del Turista** (tourist police). **Aves Argentinas/AOP** (a BirdLife International partner), Matheu 1246, T4943 7216, www.avesargentinas.org.ar. For information on birdwatching and specialist tours, good library, open Mon-Fri 1030-1330, 1430-2030 (closed Jan). Student organizations: **Asatej**: Helpful Argentine Youth and Student Travel Organization, runs a Student Flight Centre, Florida 835, p 3, oficina 320, T4114 7528, www.asatej.com, Mon-Fri 1000-1900 (with many branches in BA and around the country). Booking for flights (student discounts) including cheap 1-way flights (long waiting lists), hotels and travel; information for all South America, notice board for travellers, ISIC cards sold (giving extensive discounts; Argentine ISIC guide available here), English and French spoken. Cheap fares also at **TIJE**, San Martín 601, T5272 8480 or branches at Av Santa Fe 898, T5272 8450, and elsewhere in the city, Argentina, Uruguay and Chile, www.tije.com. **YMCA**: (Central), Reconquista 439, T4311 4785, www.ymca.org.ar. **YWCA**: Humberto 1° 2360, T4941 3776, www.ywca.org.ar.

Around Buenos Aires

Tigre → *Population: 42,000 (Partido de Tigre –Tigre county – 376,000).*
This touristy little town, 32 km northwest of Buenos Aires, is a popular weekend destination lying on the lush jungly banks of the Río Luján, with a fun fair and an excellent fruit and handicrafts market (Puerto de Frutos, Monday-Friday 1000-1800, Saturday-Sunday and holidays 1000-1900 with access from Calles Sarmiento or Perú). There are restaurants on the waterfront in Tigre across the Río Tigre from the railway line, along Lavalle and Paseo Victorica; cheaper places can be found on Italia and Cazón on the near side, or at the Puerto de Frutos. North of the town is the delta of the Río Paraná: innumerable canals and rivulets, with holiday homes and restaurants on the banks and a fruit-growing centre. The fishing is excellent and the peace is only disturbed by motor-boats at weekends. Regattas are held in November. Take a trip on one of the regular launch services (*lanchas colectivas*) which run to all parts of the delta, including taxi launches – watch prices for these – from the wharf (*Estación Fluvial*). Tourist catamarans, many companies with daily services, one- to two-hour trips, eg US$13-17, from Lavalle 499 on Río Tigre, T4731 0261/63, www.tigreencatamaran.com.ar, and three to seven services daily, 1½-hour trips, US$15, from Puerto de Frutos, **Río Tur** (T4731 0280, www.rioturcatamaranes. com.ar). **Sturla** (Estación Fluvial, oficina 10, T4731 1300, www.sturlaviajes.com.ar) runs four one-hour trips a day, US$15 (includes a ride on **Bus Turístico**); they also have trips with lunch, night-time boat trips, full-day excursions from the centre of Buenos Aires, commuting services to Puerto Madero, and more. You can also hire kayaks, canoes or rowing boats, rent houses, or visit *recreos*, little resorts with swimming pools, tennis courts, bar and restaurant. **Bus Turístico** (T4731 1300, www.busturisticotigre.com.ar) runs one-hour tours, US$5, every hour on an open-top bus with 10 stops, starting 1040 at the railway station. **Tigre tourist office** ① *by the Estación Fluvial, Mitre 305, T0800-888 84473, www.tigre.gov.ar/turismo, also at Juncal 1600 and the Puerto de Frutos,* with a full list of houses to rent, activities, etc. **Centro de Guías de Tigre y Delta** ① *Estación Fluvial of 2, T4731 3555, www.guiastigreydelta.com.ar.* For guided walks and launch trips.

Museo Naval ① *Paseo Victorica 602, T4749 0608, Tue-Fri 0830-1730, Sat-Sun* and holidays *1030-1830, US$1.70 (voluntary fee).* Worth a visit to see the displays on the Argentine navy. There are also relics of the 1982 Falklands/Malvinas War. **Museo de Arte** ① *Paseo Victorica 972, T4512 4528, www.mat.gov.ar, Wed-Fri 0900-1900, Sat-Sun 1200-1900, US$2.50,* hosts a collection of Argentine figurative art in the former Tigre Club Casino, a beautiful belle époque building.

Museo del Mate ① *Lavalle 289, T4506 9594, www.elmuseodelmate.com, Wed-Sun 1100-1800 (1100-1900 in summer), US$2.50,* tells the history of mate and has an interesting collection of the associated paraphernalia.

Isla Martín García
This island in the Río de la Plata (Juan Díaz de Solís' landfall in 1516) used to be a military base. Now it is an ecological/historical centre and an ideal excursion from the capital, with many trails through the cane brakes, trees and rocky outcrops – interesting birds and flowers. Boat trips: four weekly from Tigre at 0900, returning 2000, three-hour journey, US$55 return including lunch, *asado* and guide; US$90 pp including weekend overnight at inn, full board. Reservations only through Cacciola (address under Tigre, Transport, below), who also handle bookings for the inn and restaurant on the island. There is also a campsite.

For hotel and restaurant price codes, and other relevant information, see Essentials.

⬤ Where to stay

Tigre *p74*

$$$$ La Becasina, Arroyo Las Cañas (Delta islands second section), T4328 2687, www. labecasina.com. One of Argentina's most delightful places to stay, an hour by launch from Tigre, buried deep from the outside world, with 15 individual lodges on stilts in the water, connected by wooden walkways, all comforts and luxuries provided and tasteful décor, with intimate dining room, jacuzzi and pool amidst the trees. Full board, excellent food and service. Recommended.

$$$$ Villa Julia, Paseo Victorica 800, in Tigre itself, T4749 0642, www.villajulia.com.ar. A 1906 villa converted into a chic hotel, beautifully restored fittings, comfortable, good restaurant open to non-residents.

$$$ Los Pecanes, on Arroyo Felicaria, T4728 1932, www.hosterialospecanes.com. On a secluded island visited regularly by hummingbirds. Ana and Richard offer a few comfortable rooms and delicious food. Ideal base for boat excursions and birdwatching. Cheaper Mon-Fri.

$$$ Posada de 1860, Av Libertador 190, T4749 4034, www.tigrehostel.com.ar. A beautiful stylish villa with suites and an associated **Hostel Tigre** at No 137 (same phone and website) with dorms for up to 6 at **$** pp, and private rooms (**$$$** double).

$$ TAMET, Río Carapachay Km 24, T4728 0055, www.tamet.com.ar. For a relaxing stay on an island with sandy beaches and quite comfortable premises, with breakfast, games and canoes. Also has camping.

⊖ Transport

Tigre *p74*

Bus From central **Buenos Aires**: take No 60 from Constitución: the 60 'bajo' is a little longer than the 60 'alto' but is better for sightseeing.

Ferry To **Carmelo** (Uruguay) from Terminal Internacional, Lavalle 520, Tigre. **Cacciola**, T4749 0931, www.cacciolaviajes.com (in Buenos Aires at Florida 520, p 1, of 113, T4393 6100), 2 a day, 2½ hrs, US$42. To Montevideo (bus from Carmelo), 5½ hrs, US$52. To **Nueva Palmira** (Uruguay) from Terminal Internacional. **Líneas Delta Argentino**, oficina 6 at Estación Fluvial, T4731 1236, www.lineasdelta.com.ar. Daily at 0730, 3 hrs, US$30, US$47 return. To **Carmelo** US$35, US$53 return, and **Colonia**, 4½ hrs from Tigre, US$45, US$63 return, both daily 0730. **Note** Argentine port taxes are generally included in the fares for Argentine departures.

Train From **Buenos Aires**: Mitre line from Retiro. Alternatively **Tren de la Costa**, T3220 6300, US$3.35 one way from Maipú station (reached by Mitre line from Retiro) to Delta station (Tigre) every 30 mins. (Buses to Tren de la Costa are 60 from Constitución, 19 or 71 from Once, 152 from centre.) Terminus, Estación Delta, has the huge fun fair, El Parque de la Costa, and a casino.

The Pampas

South and west of Buenos Aires the flat, fertile lands of the pampa húmeda stretch seemingly without end, the horizon broken only by a lonely windpump or a line of poplar trees. This is home to the gaucho, whose traditions of music and fine craftsmanship remain alive. Argentina's agricultural heartland is punctuated by quiet pioneer towns, like Chascomús, and the houses of grand estancias. Argentina's former wealth lay in these splendid places, where you can stay as a guest, go horse riding, and get a great insight into the country's history and gaucho culture.

Luján ➔ *Phone code: 02323. Population: 65,000.*

This is a place of pilgrimage for devout Catholics throughout Argentina. In 1630 an image of the Virgin brought by ship from Brazil was being transported to its new owner in Santiago del Estero by ox cart, when the cart got stuck, despite strenuous efforts by men and oxen to move it. This was taken as a sign that the Virgin willed she should stay there. A chapel was built for the image, and around it grew Luján. The chapel has long since been superseded by an impressive neo-Gothic basilica and the Virgin now stands on the High Altar. Luján is a very popular spot at weekends, and there are huge pilgrimages on the last weekend of September (**La Peregrinación Gaucho**), the first weekend of October (**Peregrinación Juvenil**), 8 May (the saint's day) and 8 December (**Inmaculada Concepción**), when the town is completely packed.

Complejo Museográfico Provincial Enrique Udaondo ① *T420245, museoudaondo on Facebook, Wed 1230-1630, Thu-Fri 1130-1630, Sat-Sun 1030-1730, US$1*, in the old Cabildo building, is one of the most interesting museums in the country. Exhibits illustrate its historical and political development. General Beresford, the commander of the British troops which seized Buenos Aires in 1806, was a prisoner here, as were Generals Mitre, Paz and Belgrano in later years. Next to it are museums devoted to transport and to motor vehicles. Behind the Cabildo is the river, with river walks, cruises and restaurants.

Some 20 km before Luján, near General Rodríguez, is **Eco Yoga Park** ① *T011-156-507 0577, www.ecoyogapark.com.ar*, a spiritual centre and farm with volunteering opportunities, yoga, meditation, organic gardens and vegetarian food. See website for day and weekend packages. Take Luján bus (see Transport, below), get off at La Serenísima, then take taxi US$10.

San Antonio de Areco ➔ *Phone code: 02326. Colour map 8, B5. Population: 18,000.*

San Antonio de Areco, 113 km northwest of Buenos Aires, is a completely authentic, late 19th-century town, with single-storey buildings around a plaza filled with palms and plane trees, streets lined with orange trees, and an attractive *costanera* along the river bank. There are several estancias and a couple of villages with accommodation nearby and the town itself has historical *boliches* (combined bar and provisions store, eg **Los Principios**, Moreno y Mitre). The gaucho traditions are maintained in silver, textiles and leather handicrafts of the highest quality, as well as frequent gaucho activities, the most important of which is the **Day of Tradition** in the second week of November (book accommodation ahead), with traditional parades, gaucho games, events on horseback, music and dance. Ricardo Güiraldes, the writer whose best-known book, *Don Segundo Sombra*, celebrates the gaucho, lived in the **Estancia La Porteña** ① *8 km from town, T9-11-5626 7347, www.laporteniadeareco.com*, which dates from 1823. It is a national historic monument and offers day visits and accommodation in three different houses (**$$$$**, huge banquets with lots of meat). Superb gaucho silverwork for sale at the workshop and **museum of Juan José Draghi** ① *Lavalle 387, T454219, www.draghiplaterosorfebres.com, 0900-1300, 1530-2000 (Sun 1000-1300 only), US$1.70 for a guided visit*. Excellent chocolates at **La Olla de Cobre** ① *Matheu 433, T453105, www.laolladecobre.com.ar*, with a charming little café for drinking chocolate and the most amazing home-made *alfajores*. There is a large park spanning the river near the **tourist information centre**. The **Centro Cultural y Museo Usina Vieja** ① *Alsina 66, Tue-Sun 1100-1700, US$0.50*, is the city museum. There are ATMs on the plaza, but nowhere to change TCs. The **tourist office** ① *Zerboni y Arellano, T453165, www.san antoniodeareco.com*, is by the river.

La Plata, Chascomús and Dolores

La Plata (*Phone code: 0221. Colour map 8, B5. Population: 642,000*), near the shores of the Río de la Plata, was founded in 1882 as capital of Buenos Aires province and is now an important administrative centre, with an excellent university. It's a well-planned city, with the French-style **legislature** and the elegant **Casa de Gobierno** on **Plaza San Martín**, central in a series of plazas along the spine of the city. On **Plaza Moreno** to the south there's an impressive Italianate palace housing the **Municipalidad**, and the **Cathedral**, a striking neo-Gothic brick construction. North of Plaza San Martín is La Plata's splendid park, the **Paseo del Bosque**, with mature trees, a zoo and a botanical garden, a boating lake and the **Museo de La Plata** ① *T425 7744, www.fcnym. unlp.edu.ar, Tue-Sun 1000-1800 and holiday Mon, closed 1 Jan, 1 May, 24, 25, 31 Dec, US$1.20,* which is highly recommended. This museum houses an outstanding collection of stuffed animals, wonderful dinosaur skeletons and artefacts from pre-Columbian peoples throughout the Americas. The **Parque Ecológico** ① *Camino Centenario y San Luis, Villa Elisa, T473 2449, www. parquecologico.laplata.gov.ar, 0900-1930, free, getting there: take bus 273 D or 6,* is a good place for families, with native *tala* forest and plenty of birds.

Municipal tourist offices ① *Diagonal 79 entre 5 y 56, Palacio Campodónico, T422 9764, Mon-Fri 0900-1700, and Pasaje Dardo Rocha, T427 1535, daily 1000-2000, www.laplata.gov.ar.* The latter, in an Italianate palace, also houses a gallery of contemporary **Latin American art** ① *C 50 entre 6 y 7, T427 1843, www.macla.laplata.gov.ar, Tue-Fri 1000-2000, Sat-Sun 1400-2100 (1600-2200 in summer), free.*

To get to the heart of the pampas, stay in one of many estancias scattered over the plains. There are several accessible from the main roads to the coast, fast Ruta 2 (be prepared for tolls) and Ruta 11, near two well-preserved historic towns, Chascomús and Dolores.

Chascomús is a beautifully preserved town from the 1900s, with a rather Wild West feel to it. Built on a huge lake, it is perfect for fishing and water sports. There's a great little museum **Museo Pampeano** ① *Av Lastra y Muñiz, T430982, Tue-Fri 0800-1400, Sat-Sun 1000 1400, 1700-1900 (Tue Fri 0900-1500, Sat-Sun 1030-1630 in winter), US$0.50,* with gaucho artefacts, old maps and fabulous antique furniture. **Tourist office** ① *Av Costanera by the pier, T02241-430405, 0900-1900 daily, www.chascomus.gov.ar.* **Dolores** is a delightful small town, like stepping back in time to the 1900s, very tranquil. **Museo Libres del Sur** ① *daily 1000-1700,* is an old house in Parque Libres del Sur, full of gaucho silver, plaited leather *talero*, branding irons, and a huge cart from 1868.

⊚ The Pampas listings

For Where to stay and Restaurants price codes and other relevant information, see Essentials.

⊜ Where to stay

San Antonio de Areco *p76*
Most hotels offer discounts Mon-Thu or Fri.
$$$ Antigua Casona, Segundo Sombra 495, T02325-15-416030, www.antiguacasona.com. Charmingly restored 1897 house with 5 rooms opening onto a delightful patio and exuberant garden, relaxing and romantic. Bikes to borrow.
$$$ Paradores Draghi, Lavalle 387, T455583, www.paradoresdraghi.com.ar. Traditional-style, comfortable rooms face a manicured lawn with a pool. Just metres away Draghi family has its silversmith workshop. Recommended.

$$$ Patio de Moreno, Moreno 251, T455197, www.patiodemoreno.com. The top hotel in town is a stylish place with spacious, minimalist rooms, a large patio with a pool and great service.
$$ Hostal de Areco, Zapiola 25, T456118, www.hostaldeareco.com.ar. Popular, with a warm welcome, good value.
$$ Los Abuelos, Zerboni y Zapiola T456390 (see Facebook). Very good, welcoming, small pool, plain but comfortable rooms, facing riverside park.

Estancias
Some of the province's finest estancias are within easy reach for day visits, offering horse riding, an *asado* lunch, and other activities. Stay overnight

to really appreciate the peace and beauty of these historical places. See **Estancia La Porteña**, above. Look online at: www.sanantoniodeareco.com/turismo/estancias/index.htm.

$$$$ El Ombú, T492080, T011-4737 0436 (Buenos Aires office), www.estanciaelombu.com. Fine house with magnificent terrace dating from 1890, comfortable rooms, horse riding, English-speaking owners; price includes full board and activities but not transfer. Recommended.

$$$$ La Bamba, T454895, www.la-bamba.com.ar. Dating from 1830, in grand parkland, charming rooms, English-speaking owners who have lived here for generations, superb meals, price is for full board. Recommended.

La Plata, Chascomús and Dolores *p76*
La Plata

$$$ La Plata Hotel, Av 51 No 783, T422 9090, www.weblaplatahotel.com.ar. Modern, well furnished, comfortable, spacious rooms and nice bathrooms. Price includes a dinner (drinks extra).

$ pp La Plata Hostel, C 50 No 1066, T457 1424, www.laplata-hostel.com.ar. Well-organized, convenient hostel in a historic house, high ceilings, small garden, simple but comfortable dorms for 4 or 8.

Estancias: **$$$$ Casa de Campo La China**, 60 km from La Plata on Ruta 11, T0221-421 2931, www.casadecampolachina.com.ar. A charming 1930s adobe house set in eucalyptus woods, with beautifully decorated spacious rooms off an open gallery, day visits (US$45) to ride horses, or in carriages, eat *asado*, or stay the night, guests of Cecilia and Marcelo, who speak perfect English. Delicious food, meals included in price. Highly recommended.

Chascomús

For a full list see www.chascomus.com.ar.
$$$ Chascomús, Av Lastra 367, T422968, www.chascomus.com.ar (under 'hoteles'). The town's most comfortable hotel, atmospheric, welcoming, with stylish turn-of-the-century public rooms and lovely terrace.
$$$ La Posada, Costanera España 18, T423503, www.chascomus.com.ar (under 'cabañas').

On the laguna, delightful, very comfortable cabañas with cooking facilities.
$$$ Roble Blanco, Mazzini 130, T436235, www.robleblanco.com.ar. A very good choice, in a refurbished 100-year-old house, modern comfortable rooms, a large heated pool with attractive deck and welcoming common areas. Also has a spa. Recommended.
$$ Laguna, Libres del Sur y Maipú, T426113, www.lgnhotel.com.ar. Old fashioned, sleepy hotel by the station. Pleasant, quiet rooms.
Estancias: Both estancias will collect you from Chascomús.
$$$$ Haras La Viviana, in Castelli, 65 km from Chascomús, T011-4702 9633, www.harasla viviana.com.ar. Perfect for horse riding, since fine polo ponies are bred here. Tiny cabins in gardens by a huge *laguna* where you can kayak or fish, very peaceful, good service, wonderful welcome from lady novelist owner, fluent English spoken, also French, Italian, Portuguese.
$$$ La Horqueta, 3 km from Chascomús on Ruta 20, T011-4777 0150, www.lahorqueta. com. Full board, mansion in lovely grounds with laguna for fishing, horse riding, bikes to borrow, English-speaking hosts, safe gardens especially good for children, plain food.

Dolores

$$$$ Estancia Dos Talas, 10 km from Dolores, T02245-443020, www.dostalas.com.ar. One of the oldest and most beautiful estancias, you are truly the owners' guests here. The rooms and the service are impeccable, the food exquisite; stay for days and relax completely. Pool, riding, English spoken.

🍴 Restaurants

San Antonio de Areco *p76*

Many *parrillas* on the bank of the Río Areco.
$$ Almacén de Ramos Generales, Zapiola 143, T456376 (best to book ahead). Perfect place, popular with locals, very atmospheric, superb meat, very good pastas and a long wine list.
$$ Café de las Artes, Bolívar 70, T456398 (better book ahead). In a hidden spot, this

cosy place serves delicious pastas with a large wine selection.

$$ La Costa, Zerboni y Belgrano (on the riverside park). A very good traditional *parrilla* with an attractive terrace.

$$ La Ochava de Cocota, Alsina y Alem. Relaxing, attractive, excellent service, superb *empanadas* and vegetable pies. It is also a café.

$ La Esquina de Merti, Arellano y Segundo Sombra. The ideal place for a beer on the main plaza. Go early to get a table outside.

La Plata *p76*
$$ Cervecería Modelo, C 54 y C5. Traditional German-style *cervecería*, with good menu and beer.

$$ Don Quijote, Plaza Paso. Delicious food in lovely surroundings, well known.

$$ El Chaparral Platense, C 60 y C 116 (Paseo del Bosque). Good *parrilla* in the park, great steaks.

$$ La Aguada, C 50 entre 7 y 8. The oldest restaurant in town, good for *minutas* (light meals), famous for its *papas fritas*.

Confitería París, C 7 y 48. The best croissants, and a lovely place for coffee.

Chascomús *p76*
$$ Colonial, Estados Unidos y Artigas. Great food, pastas and cakes are recommended.

⊙ What to do

The Pampas *p75*
Horse riding All estancias offer horse riding. Other operators can be contacted from the hotels in the Pampas towns.

⊖ Transport

Luján *p76*
Bus From **Buenos Aires** Bus 57 Empresa Atlántida either from Plaza Once, route O (the fastest), or from Plaza Italia, routes C and D; US$3. To **San Antonio de Areco**, several a day, US$4.50, Empresa Argentina, 1 hr.

San Antonio de Areco *p76*
Bus From **Buenos Aires** (Retiro bus terminal), 1½-2 hrs, US$8, every hour with Chevallier or Pullman General Belgrano.
Remise taxis Sol, San Martín y Alsina, T455444.

La Plata *p76*
Bus Terminal at Calle 42 entre 3 y 4 T427 3198. To **Buenos Aires**, very frequent during the day, hourly at night, **Costera Metropolitana** and Plaza, 1 hr 10 mins either to Retiro terminal or to Centro (stops along Av 9 de Julio), US$1.80. To **Mar del Plata** US$41 with **El Rápido**.
Train To/from **Buenos Aires** (Constitución), frequent, US$1.15, 1 hr 20 mins.

Chascomús *p76*
Bus Frequent service, several per day to **Buenos Aires**, 2 hrs, US$9, **La Plata**, **Mar del Plata**, and daily to **Bahía Blanca** and **Villa Gesell**; terminal T422595.
Train Station T422220. 3 a week with Ferrobaires, www.ferrobaires.gba.gov.ar, to **Buenos Aires** (Constitución) and to **Mar del Plata**, passing Dolores en route, erratic service.

Atlantic Coast

Among the 500 km of resorts stretching from to San Clemente de Tuyú to Monte Hermoso, the most attractive is upmarket Pinamar, with the chic Cariló next door. Villa Gesell is relaxed and friendly but past its best, while, next to it are the quiet, beautiful Mar Azul and Mar de las Pampas. Mar del Plata, Argentina's most famous resort, is a huge city with packed beaches, popular for its lively nightlife and casino; much more appealing in winter. Next to it, tranquil Miramar is great for young families, and Necochea has wild expanses of dunes to explore. Near the port of Bahía Blanca is the Sierra de la Ventana, the highest range of hills in the pampas, a great place for hiking.

Pinamar and Cariló → *Phone code: 02254.*

The two most desirable resorts on the coast, 340 km from Buenos Aires, via Ruta 11, are next to each other. **Pinamar** is one of the most attractive resorts on the whole coast, with stylish architecture and mature trees lining its avenues. It is great for young people and families, with smart *balnearios* ranging from chic, quiet places with superb restaurants, to very trendy spots with loud music, beach parties and live bands at night. There are golf courses and tennis courts, and fine hotels and smart restaurants all along the main street, Avenida Bunge. Explore the dunes at **Reserva Dunícola**, 13 km north, by horse or 4WD. **Tourist office** ① *Av Shaw 18, T491680, www.pinamar.gov.ar, www.pinamarturismo. com.ar,* English spoken, helpful, can book accommodation. **Cariló**, the most exclusive beach resort in Argentina, has a huge area of mature woodland, where its luxury apart-hotels and *cabañas* are all tastefully concealed. The *balnearios* are neat and exclusive and there are good restaurants and shops around the tiny centre. See www.carilo.com and www.parquecarilo.com.

Villa Gesell, Mar de las Pampas and Mar Azul → *Phone code: 02255.*

In contrast to elite Cariló, **Villa Gesell**, 22 km south of Pinamar, is set amid thousands of trees planted by its German founder. It has grown from an ecological tourist retreat into a thriving tourist town, with dated holiday homes and a highly commercialised main street, Avenida 3. In January, it's overrun by Argentine youth, far quieter in late February and March. The main **tourist office** ① *Paseo 107 entre 2 y 3, T478042, www.gesell.gov.ar, daily 0800-2400, also in bus terminal and 3 other locations,* is on the right as you drive into town, very helpful, English spoken. Some 5 km south are two of the most tranquil and charming beach retreats: idyllic and wooded **Mar de las Pampas** and **Mar Azul**. The beach here is broad and uncrowded, so although there is less to do than in Pinamar or Mar del Plata and no nightlife to speak of, you can completely relax and enjoy the sea in peace. In January you'll find traffic jams and queues at restaurants. Mar de las Pampas has a **tourist office** ① *Mercedes Sosa y El Lucero, T452823, summer 0800-0000.* See also www.mardelaspampas.com.ar, for more information.

Mar del Plata → *Phone code: 0223. Colour map 8, C5. Population: 560,000.*

The oldest and most famous Argentine resort has lost much of its charm since it was built in 1874. It's now a huge city offering great nightlife in summer, but if you like some space on the beach, it's best to go elsewhere as there are plenty of better beaches on this stretch of coast. There are hundreds of hotels, all busy (and double the price) in January-February; winter can be pleasantly quiet. **Tourist offices** ① *next to the Casino Central on Blvd Marítimo 2270, T495 1777, 0800-2000 (1000-1700 on Sun), at the airport and bus terminal, www.turismomardelplata. gov.ar.* English spoken, good leaflets on daily events with bus routes. Also lists of hotels and apartment/ chalet letting agents. See also www.puntomardelplata.com.

The city centre is around **Playa Bristol**, with the huge casino, and **Plaza San Martín**, with pedestrian streets Rivadavia and San Martín, busy in summer with shoppers. Some 10 blocks southwest, the area of Los Troncos contains some remarkable mansions dating from Mar del Plata's heyday, from mock Tudor **Villa Blaquier** to **Villa Ortiz Basualdo** (1909), inspired by Loire chateaux, now the **Museo Municipal de Arte** ① *Av Colón 1189, T486 1636, daily in summer 1700-2200, winter Wed-Mon 1200-1700, US$1, including guided tour.* Rooms furnished in period style. The **Centro Cultural Victoria Ocampo** ① *Matheu 1851, T492 0569, daily in summer, off season closed Tue and mornings, US$1.* This beautiful 1900's wooden house in lovely gardens was where the famous author entertained illustrious literary figures; concerts held in grounds in summer. Nearby is the **Villa Mitre** ① *Lamadrid 3870, T495 1200, Mon-Fri 0800-1800, Sat-Sun 1400-1800, US$1.25.* Donated by a descendent of Bartolomé Mitre to the municipality, it contains the Historical Archive, is a museum and holds cultural events.

Beaches include fashionable **Playa Grande**, where the best hotels and shops are, as well as the famous golf course, with private balnearios for wealthy *porteños*, a small area open to the public; **Playa La Perla**, now packed and pretty grim, but **Playa Punta Mogotes**, further west, and beaches stretching along the road to Miramar are by far the most appealing. The **port area**, south of Playa Grande, is interesting when the old orange fishing boats come in, and at night, for its seafood restaurants. A sea lion colony basks on rusting wrecks by the Escollera Sur (southern breakwater) and fishing is good all along the coast. There are one-hour **boat trips** ① *from Dársena B, Muelle de Guardacostas in the port, US$19, T489 0310, www.cruceroanamora. com.ar,* along the city coast on the *Anamora,* several times daily in summer, weekends only in winter. Lively festivals are **Fiesta del Mar**, in mid December, the national fishing festival in mid to late January, and the international film festival in November, www.mardelplatafilmfest.com.

Miramar → *Phone code: 02291. Colour map 8, C5. Population: 24,500.*
Miramar, 47 km southwest of Mar del Plata, along the coast road, is a charming small resort, known as the 'city of bicycles', and oriented towards families. It has a big leafy plaza at its centre, a good stretch of beach with soft sand and a relaxed atmosphere; a quieter, low-key alternative to Mar del Plata. The most attractive area of the town is away from the high rise buildings on the sea front, at the **Vivero Dunícola Florentino Ameghino**, a 502-ha forest park on the beach, with lots of walks, restaurants and picnic places for *asado* among the mature trees. In town there are lots of restaurants along Calle 21, and good cafés at *balnearios* on the seafront. **Tourist office** ① *Av Costanera y 21, T02291-420190, www.turismodemiramar.com.ar, Mon-Fri 0700-2100, Sat-Sun in summer 0900-2100.* Helpful, listings and maps.

Necochea → *Phone code: 02262. Colour map 8, C5. Population: 92,933.*
Necochea is a well-established resort, famous for its long stretch of beach, and while the central area is built up and busy in the summer, further west there are beautiful empty beaches and high sand dunes. There's also a fine golf club and rafting nearby on the river Quequén. **Tourist offices** ① *on the beach front at Av 79 y Av 2, T438333, www.necochea.tur.ar,* English spoken, list of apartments for rent. See also www.necocheanet.com.ar. There are banks with ATMs and *locutorios* along the pedestrianized Calle 83.

The **Parque Miguel Lillo** (named after the Argentine botanist) starts three blocks west of Plaza San Martín and stretches along the seafront, a wonderful dense forest of over 600 ha. There are lovely walks along paths, many campsites and picnic spots, a train ride (www.trendelparque. com.ar), lots of restaurants, and places to practise various sports. West of Necochea, there's a natural arch of rock at the **Cueva del Tigre**, and beyond it stretches a vast empty beach, separated from the land by sand dunes up to 100 m high, the **Médano Blanco**. This is an exhilarating area for walking or horse riding and the dunes are popular for 4WD riding and sandboarding. Vehicles and buses stop where the road ends at **Parador Médano Blanco** (a good place for lunch) where you can rent 4WDs, T155 68931.

Bahía Blanca and around → *Phone code: 0291. Colour map 8, C4. Population: 301,572.*
The province's most important port and naval base, Bahía Blanca is a quiet, attractive city. It's a good starting point for exploring **Sierra de la Ventana**, 100 km north, or relaxing on beaches an hour to the east. The architecture is remarkable with many fine buildings especially around the central **Plaza Rivadavia**, notably the ornate, Italianate **Municipalidad** of 1904 and the French-style **Banco de la Nación** (1927). Three blocks north on the main shopping street, at Alsina 425, is the classical **Teatro Municipal** (1922). The **Museo Histórico** ① *at the side of the Teatro Municipal, Dorrego 116, T456 3117, Tue-Fri 0800-1200, 1600-2000, Sat-Sun 1600-2000,* has

sections on the pre-Hispanic period and interesting photos of early Bahía Blanca. Not to be missed, though, is the **Museo del Puerto** ① *Torres 4121, T457 3006, 7 km away in the port area at Ingeniero White, Mon-Fri 0830-1230, weekends 1530-1930, free; getting there: bus 500A or 504 from plaza, taxi US$5.* It houses entertaining and imaginative displays on immigrant life in the early 20th century, and a quaint *confitería* on Sunday. **Tourist office** ① *Drago 1800, T481 8944, Mon-Fri 0700-1300, information posts at Av Colón y Drago and bus terminal; municipal site www. bahiablanca.gov.ar.* Very helpful.

At **Pehuén-Có**, 84 km east of Bahía Blanca, there's a long stretch of sandy beaches, with dunes, relatively empty and unspoilt (beware of jellyfish when wind is in the south), signposted from the main road 24 km from Bahía Blanca. It has a wild and untouristy feel, with very few hotels, several campsites well shaded (eg http://campingpehuen-co.com.ar), and a couple of places to eat. See www.visitapehuenco.com.ar. There's a more established resort at **Monte Hermoso**, 106 km east, with more hotels and a better organized campsite and wonderful beaches. One of the few places on the coast where the sun rises and sets over the sea. **Tourist office** ① *Faro Recalada y Pedro de Mendoza, T02921-481123, http://montehermoso.porinternet.com.ar.*

Sierra de la Ventana → *Phone code: 0291.*

The magnificent Sierra de la Ventana, the highest range of hills in the pampas, lies within easy reach of Bahía for a day or weekend visit (100 km north of Bahía Blanca). They hills are accessible for long hikes, with stunning views from their craggy peaks. There are daily buses and *combis* from Bahía Blanca, or stop at **Tornquist**, 70 km north of Bahía Blanca by Ruta 33, a quaint, non-touristy place.

The sierras are reached within the **Parque Provincial Ernesto Tornquist**, 25 km northeast of Tornquist on Ruta 76. There are two main points of entry, one at the foot of Cerro Ventana and the other, further east, at the foot of Cerro Bahía Blanca. To enter the Cerro Ventana section, turn left (signposted) after the massive ornate gates from the Tornquist family home. Nearby is **Campamento Base** ① *T0291-156 495304,* camping, basic dormitory, hot showers. At the entrance to the park itself, there's a car park and a **guardaparques station** ① *Dec-Easter 0800-1700,* where you register for longer walks, they also give advice. From here it's a three-hour walk to the summit of **Cerro de la Ventana**, which has fantastic views from the 'window' (which gives the range its name), in the summit ridge; clearly marked path but with no shade; ascents only permitted till 1200 and in good weather. There are also easier walks to waterfalls. To enter the Cerro Bahía Blanca section, continue 4 km further along Ruta 76. There's a car park and **interpretation centre** ① *T491 0039, Dec-Easter 0800-1800,* with *guardaparques,* who can advise on walks. From here you can go on a guided visit (only with own vehicle, four to five hours), to natural caves, and the **Cueva de las Pinturas**, which contains petroglyphs. Also from here, an hour-long trail goes to Cerro Bahía Blanca. **Villa Ventana**, 10 km further, is a pretty, wooded settlement with excellent teashop, **Casa de Heidi**, and good food at **Las Golondrinas**. Helpful **tourist office** ① *entrance to Villa Ventana, T491 0001, www.sierradelaventana.org.ar.*

The town of **Sierra de la Ventana**, further east, is a good centre for exploring the hills, with a greater choice of hotels than Villa Ventana, and wonderful open landscapes all around. Excellent **tourist office** ① *Av Roca 19, just before railway track, T491 5303 (same website as Villa Ventana).*

For hotel and restaurant price codes, and other relevant information, see Essentials.

Where to stay

Atlantic Coast *p79*

Since accommodation is plentiful all along the coast, only a small selection is listed here. All the resorts also have a wide selection of campsites, most are well-equipped and many have *cabañas* as well as tent sites. Most resorts have *balnearios*, private beaches, where you pay US$25-50 per day for family/group use of a sunshade or beach hut, showers, toilets and restaurants. Avoid Jan when the whole coast is packed out.

Pinamar *p80*

There are plenty of hotels in Pinamar, of a high standard, all 4-stars have a pool. Some hotels are a long way from the beach. Book ahead in Jan and Feb. All those listed are recommended.
$$$$-$$$ Del Bosque, Av Bunge 1550 y Júpiter, T11-4394 9605, www.hotel-delbosque. com. Very attractive, in woods, not on the beach, a smart 4-star with a wide range of rooms and seasonal prices, pool, tennis courts, nice restaurant, good service.
$$$ La Posada, Del Tuyú y Del Odiseo, T482267, www.laposadapinamar.com.ar. Very comfortable, small, quiet, with spacious rooms, next to sea and town centre, pretty gardens where breakfast is served. An excellent choice.
$$$ Viejo Hotel Ostende, Biarritz y El Cairo, T486081, www.hotelostende.com.ar. Attractive, smallish hotel, open since 1913. Although it has been renovated, it retains some historic flavour in the old wing, comfortable in a simple way, excellent service. There's a pool and private balneario. Breakfast, dinner and a beach hut are all included. Open summer only.

Estancias

$$$ Estancia La Unión, Ruta 56, 45 km from Pinamar, outside Gral Madariaga, T02267-156 37983, estancialaunion@telpin.com.ar. An early 19th-century estancia offering fine hospitality and excellent riding, including polo ponies; good birdwatching too. Swimming pool and other activities, good food, children welcome.

Villa Gesell *p80*

$$$ De la Plaza, Av 2 entre 103 y 104, T468793, www.delaplazahotel.com. Small, spotless, with excellent service, open all year round. Rooms are plain but very comfortable, good value.
$$ Hostería Gran Chalet, Paseo 105 No 447 entre Av 4-5, T462913, www.gesell.com.ar/ granchalet. Closed off season. Warm welcome, comfortable large rooms, good breakfast.
$ pp Hostel El Galeón, Av 5 No 834 (entre Paseos 108 y 109), T453785, www.galeongesell. com.ar. Popular hostel, can accommodate from singles to groups of 8 but no dorms, some rooms have kitchen, DVDs, laundry service, cooking facilities, good communal areas, convenient.

Mar del Plata *p80*

Busy traffic makes it impossible to move along the coast in summer: choose a hotel near the beach you want.
$$$$ Costa Galana, Bv Marítimo 5725, T410 5000, www.hotelcostagalana.com. The best by far, a 5-star modern tower, all luxury facilities, at Playa Grande.
$$$ Dos Reyes, Av Colón 2129, T491 0383, www.dosreyes.com.ar. Long-established but modernized town centre hotel with smart, well-equipped rooms. Guests have access to a *balneario*. Good value off season, big breakfast.
$$$-$$ Selent, Arenales 2347, T494 0878, www.hotelselent.com.ar. Quiet with neat rooms, warm welcome, great value. Open all year. Recommended.
$$ Abra Marina, Alsina 2444, T486 4646, http:// users.copetel.com.ar/abramarinacafehotel. A good budget choice open all year round, simple rooms, all services, café/bar, central.
$$ Los Troncos, Rodríguez Peña 1561, T451 8882, www.hotellostroncos.com.ar. Small, chalet-style hotel in quiet residential area, handy for Güemes bars and restaurants, garden.

Miramar *p81*

Dozens of hotels and apartments between Av 26 and the sea. For a full list see http://turismodemiramar.com.

$$ Brisas del Mar, C 29 No 557, T420334, www.brisasdelmarhotel.com.ar. Sea front, family-run, neat rooms, cheery restaurant, attentive, good value. Open in summer only.

Necochea *p81*

Most hotels are in the seafront area just north of Av 2. There are at least 100 within 700 m of the beach. Many close off season, when you can bargain with those still open.

$$$ Hostería del Bosque, C 89 No 350, T420002, www.hosteria-delbosque.com.ar. 5 blocks from beach, quiet, comfortable, lovely atmosphere in this renovated former residence of an exiled Russian princess, great restaurant.

$$$ Presidente, C 4 No 4040, T423800, www.presinec.com.ar. A 4 star large hotel recommended for excellent service, comfortable rooms and pool, price depends on room category and season, closed in winter.

$$ Bahía, Diagonal San Martín 731, T423353, hotelbahia@necocheanet.com.ar. Really kind owners, comfortable rooms, pool in neat gardens. Recommended.

$$ San Miguel, C 85 No 301, T521433, www.hotel-sanmiguel.com.ar. Good service and value, comfortable, open all year.

Bahía Blanca and around *p81*

$$$ Argos, España 149, T455 0404, www.hotelargos.com. 3 blocks from plaza, 4-star business hotel, smart, Wi-Fi, good breakfast, restaurant.

$$ Bahía Blanca, Chiclana 251, T455 3050, www.bahia-hotel.com.ar. Business hotel, good value, well-equipped comfortable rooms, bright bar and *confitería*. Recommended.

$$ Barne, H Yrigoyen 270, T453 0294, www.hotelbarne.bvconline.com.ar. Family-run, low-key, good value, welcoming.

$ Hostel Bahía Blanca, Soler 701, T452 6802, www.hostelbahiablanca.com. Light, spacious dorms from US$12 and doubles with and without bath in this old building. Close to town, offers lots of travel advice.

Monte Hermoso

$$ Petit Hotel, Av Argentina 244, T02921-481818, www.petitfrentealmar.com.ar. Simple, modernized 1950s style, family-run, on the beach, restaurant, breakfast extra, cooking facilities. Recommended.

Sierra de la Ventana *p82*
Tornquist

$ La Casona, Rawson 232, T0291-494 0693, http://com-tur.com.ar/lacasona/. A renovated house with plain rooms.

$ San José, Güemes 138, T0291-494 0152, www.sanjose-hotel.com.ar. Small, central, with plain, faded rooms.

Villa Ventana

Lots of accommodation in *cabañas*; municipal campsite by river with all facilities. See www.sierralaventana.org.ar.

$$$ El Mirador, on RP 76 Km 226, T0291-494 1338, www.complejoelmirador.com.ar. Great location right at the foot of Cerro de la Ventana, comfortable rooms, some with tremendous views, very peaceful, good restaurant.

$$ San Hipólito, on RP 76 Km 230, T0291-156 428281, campoequino@celt.com.ar. Fully furnished, comfortable, small cabins on a large ranch, welcoming owners, Polito and his wife. Ideal for families with kids. Enjoyable horse rides in the hills.

Sierra de la Ventana town

$$$ Cabañas La Caledonia, Los Robles y Ombúes in Villa Arcadia, a couple of blocks over the railway track, T0291-491 5268, www.lacaledonia.com.ar. Well-equipped, comfortable small cabins in pretty gardens with a pool. Price is for a cabin for up to 4 people.

$$$ Las Vertientes, RP 76, Km 221, signposted just west of the turning to Villa Ventana, T011-4773 6647, http://com-tur.com.ar/lasvertientes/. Very welcoming ranch with a house for rent (price is for 6 people; breakfast extra) in lovely surroundings, relaxing, horse riding, mountain biking, trekking, day visits.

$$ Alihuen, Tornquist y Balneario, T491 5074, http://com-tur.com.ar/alihuen. A delightful old place near the river, dining room, garden, pool, good value.

Camping Yamila, access on C Tornquist, T0291-154 189266, www.campingyamila.8m.com. Camping and small cabins with bunks, $. Lovely shady site by river, hot showers, food shop.

🍴 Restaurants

Mar del Plata *p80*

2 areas have become popular for smaller shops bars and restaurants: Around C Güemes:

$$ Almacén El Condal, Alsina y Garay. Charming old street-corner bar, serving *picadas* and drinks, popular with young crowd.

$$ Tisiano, San Lorenzo 1332. Good pasta restaurant in leafy patio.

Around Alem, next to cemetery, lots of pubs and bars. Traditional favourites:

$$ Manolo, Rivadavia 2371 and on the coast at Bv Marítimo 4961. Famous for *churros* and hot chocolate in the early hours. popular with post-party people.

$$ Pehuén, Bernardo de Irigoyen 3666. Very good and popular parrilla.

Seafood restaurants in the Centro Comercial Puerto, many brightly lit and not atmospheric.

$$ El Viejo Pop. The best place, ship design, candlelit, superb paella.

$$ Taberna Baska, 12 de Octubre 3301. Seafood and Basque country dishes, next to the port.

Necochea *p81*

There are some excellent seafood restaurants.

$$ Chimichurri, C 83 No 345, T420642. Recommended for *parrilla*.

$$ Parrilla El Loco, Av 10 y 65, T437094. A classic *parrilla*, deservedly popular for superb steaks.

$$ Sotavento, Av Costanera y Pinolandia. On the beach, varied menu, can get very busy but good value.

$ Pizzería Tempo, Calle 83 No 310, T425100. A lively traditional place serving good pizzas.

Bahía Blanca and around *p81*

$$ Micho, Guillermo Torres 3875, T457 0346. A superb chic fish restaurant at the port (take bus 500 or 501, but go there by taxi at night, as it's in an insalubrious area).

$$ Santino, Dorrego 38. Italian-influenced, quiet sophisticated atmosphere, good value. Recommended.

$ El Mundo de la Pizza, Dorrego 55. Fabulous pizzas, lots of choice, the city's favourite.

$ For You, Belgrano 69. Good *tenedor libre*.

Cafés

Café del Angel, Paseo del Angel, entrances at O'Higgins 71 and Drago 63. Good value lunches, friendly place.

Muñoz, O'Higgins y Drago. Sophisticated café, good for reading the papers.

Piazza, on the corner of the plaza at O'Higgins y Chiclana. Great coffee, buzzing atmosphere, good salads, and cakes too.

Monte Hermoso

$$ Marfil, Valle Encantado 91. The smartest, delicious fish and pastas.

$ Pizza Jet, Valle Encantado e Int Majluf. Hugely popular for all kinds of food, arrive before 2130 to get a table.

🚌 Transport

Pinamar *p80*

Bus Terminal 20 mins' walk from the beach at Av Bunge e Intermédanos, T403500. To **Buenos Aires**, US$39-43, 4-5hrs, several companies.

Villa Gesell *p80*

Bus Direct to **Buenos Aires**, many companies, 5 hrs, US$41-46. To **Mar del Plata** see below. Terminal at Av 3 y Paseo 140.

Mar del Plata *p80*

Air Camet airport, T478 3990, 10 km north of town. Several flights daily to **Buenos Aires**, and LADE to many Patagonian towns once or twice a week. Remise taxi from airport to town, US$10, also bus 542 (signed Aeropuerto) US$1 (payable with a magnetic card).

Bus For information T561 3743. The new combined bus and train station, Terminal Ferroautomotora, is Av Luro y San Juan. To **Buenos Aires**, 5-6 hrs, US$41-54, many companies. El Rápido (T494 2507, www.el-rapido.com.ar) run several services a day to most coastal towns: to **Villa Gesell**, 1½ hrs, US$10; to **Pinamar**, 2 hrs, US$12.50; to **Miramar**, 40 mins, US$2.50; to **Necochea**, US$11 (also Río Paraná, T561 1907, Cóndor Estrella, T561 3999); to **Bahía Blanca**, 7 hrs, US$42. To **Bariloche**, Via Bariloche, El Rápido Argentino, 18-20 hrs, US$176. To all Patagonian towns along RN 3, ending at **Comodoro Rivadavia**, 23 hrs, US$130-170, with Transportadora Patagónica. To **Mendoza**, Andesmar, daily, 19-22 hrs, US$120-153.
Train To/from **Buenos Aires** (Constitución), enquire beforehand if any trains are running. See www.nuevaterminalmardel.com.ar for train and bus information.

Miramar *p81*
Bus Terminals at C 34 y Av 23, T423359, at Fortunato de la Plaza y C 19, and a few others. To **Buenos Aires**, 6½-7 hrs, US$49-60. To **Necochea**, Cóndor Estrella, 1½ hrs, US$3.50.

Necochea *p81*
Bus Terminal at Av 58 y Jesuita Cardiel, T422470, 3 km from the beach area; bus 513 from outside the terminal to the beach. Taxi to beach area US$5. To **Buenos Aires**, 6½-8½ hrs, US$54-60. To **Bahía Blanca**, US$20.

Bahía Blanca and around *p81*
Air Airport Comandante Espora, lies 11 km northeast of centre, US$10 in a taxi. Airport information T486 0300. Daily flights to **Buenos Aires**. LADE (T452 1063) has weekly flights to **Buenos Aires**, **Necochea**, **Mar del Plata** and Patagonian coastal towns.
Bus Terminal in old railway station 2 km from centre, at Estados Unidos y Brown, T481 9615, connected by buses 512, 514, or taxi US$5, no hotels nearby; information office Mon-Fri

0700-1300. To **Buenos Aires** frequent, several companies, 8-10 hrs, US$74-80, shop around. Most comfortable by far is Plusmar suite bus, with flat beds, US$91 (T456 0616). To **Mar del Plata**, see above. To **Córdoba**, 13-15 hrs, US$89-105. To **Bariloche**, El Valle, Vía Bariloche, 11-13 hrs, US$70-85. To **Mendoza**, Andesmar, 16 hrs, US$112-132. To **Puerto Madryn**, Andesmar, Don Otto, Cóndor Estrella, 8½-10½ hrs, US$50-57. To **Tornquist**, US$6, Cóndor Estrella, T481 4846, www.condorestrella.com. ar, 1 hr 20 min; to **Sierra de la Ventana** (town) Cóndor Estrella and Expreso Cabildo, 2 hr 20 mins, US$9. Also minibus to Tornquist with Cerro, T494 1129.
Train Station at Av Gral Cerri 750, T452 9196. To/from **Buenos Aires**, see page 72.

Pehuén-Có and Monte Hermoso
Bus From Monte Hermoso either to **Buenos Aires** or **Bahía Blanca** (US$7) with Cóndor Estrella. Several combis or minibuses also to **Bahía Blanca**. From Pehuén-Có to Bahía Blanca, with La Patagonia, T0291-4553215.

Sierra de la Ventana *p82*
Bus Geotur, San Martín 193, T491 5355. Operates a minibus a few times a day along RP 76 from Sierra de la Ventana to Tornquist, dropping off hikers at the entrance to the park. Also specializes in mountain biking, trekking and horse riding trips.

❶ Directory

Mar del Plata *p80*
Banks Many ATMs all around the central area, along Peatonal San Martín, at Santa Fe y Rivadavia and by the casino. **Useful addresses** Immigration office: San Lorenzo 3449, T475 5707, Mon-Fri 0800-1400.

Bahía Blanca *p81*
Banks Many ATMs on plaza for all major cards. **Useful addresses** Immigration office: Brown 963, T456 1529, Mon-Fri 0900-1300.

West of Buenos Aires

Rising out of the flat arid Pampa, the Sierras of Córdoba and San Luis provide a dramatic backdrop to popular holiday towns and mountain retreats. Beyond the plains, fertile valleys stretch along the length of the Andean precordillera and climb up to the heights of Aconcagua and its neighbours. The western provinces of Mendoza, San Juan, La Rioja and Catamarca cover extreme contrasts, but Mendoza and the surrounding area to the south is popular for its excellent wines, climbing and superb ski and adventure resorts such as Malargüe.

Córdoba → *Phone code: 0351. Colour map 8, A3. Population: 1.5 million. Altitude: 484 m.*

Córdoba, the capital Córdoba Province and the second largest city in the country, was founded in 1573 and has some fine historic buildings as well as a lively university population. In fact, it was the Jesuits in Córdoba who established the first university in the whole country in 1613. (Today, the city boasts two universities.) Córdoba is also an important route centre and vital industrial hub, as it is the home of Argentina's motor industry. It is also a busy modern metropolis with a flourishing shopping centre.

Arriving in Córdoba

Orientation Pajas Blancas airport is 12 km northwest of city and the bus terminal is at Boulevard Perón 250, eight blocks east of main Plaza. ▶▶ *See Transport, page 91.*

Tourist offices **Agencia Córdoba Turismo** ① *old Cabildo, Pasaje Santa Catalina, T434 1200, www. cordoba.gov.ar and www.cordobaturismo.gov.ar, daily 0800-2000. Also at the bus terminal, T433 1982, daily 0700-2100, and at the airport, T434 8390, daily 0800-2000.* All have useful city maps and information on guided walks and cycle tours. The municipality runs good, daily city tours leaving from the Centro Obispo Mercadillo, T434 1215, some free, some US$10 (US$5 extra in English).

Places in Córdoba

At the city's heart is **Plaza San Martín**, with a statue of the Liberator. On the west side is the old **Cabildo** ① *Independencia 30, free, except for entry to exhibitions, 0900-2100 (Mon 1400-2100).* Built around two internal patios, the building now houses the tourist office, a small gallery and a bookshop. Next to it stands the **Cathedral** ① *T422 3446, 0800-1300, 1630-2000,* the oldest in Argentina (begun 1640, consecrated 1671), with attractive stained glass windows and a richly decorated ceiling. Look out for statues of angels resembling Native Americans. Behind the cathedral is the pleasant Plaza del Fundador, with a statue to the city founder Jerónimo Luis de Cabrera. One of the features of this part of the city is its old churches. Near Plaza San Martín at Independencia 122 is the 16th-century **Carmelo Convent** and chapel of **Santa Teresa** ① *Mon-Sat, 0700-1430, 1730-1930,* whose rooms and beautiful patio form the **Museo de Arte Religioso Juan de Tejeda** ① *Wed-Sat 0930-1230, US$0.75, guided visits also in English and French.* This houses one of the finest collections of religious art in the country. The **Manzana Jesuítica** ① *contained within Av Vélez Sarsfield, Caseros, Duarte Quirós and Obispo Trejo,* has been declared a World Heritage Site by UNESCO. **La Compañía** (Obispo Trejo y Caseros, built between 1640 and 1676) has a vaulted ceiling reminiscent of a ship's hull. Behind it, on Caseros, is the beautiful **Capilla Doméstica**, a private 17th-century Jesuit chapel (guided visits only). Next to it are two former Jesuit institutions: the main building of the **Universidad Nacional de Córdoba** ① *T433 2075, Tue-Sun 0900-1300, 1600-2000, US$2,* housing one of the most valuable libraries in the country; and the **Colegio Nacional de Montserrat**. **Guided tours** ⓘ *Mon-Sun 1000, 1100, 1700 and 1800, available in English,* of the church, chapel, university (called Museo Histórico) and school leave from Obispo Trejo 242. The **Basílica de La Merced** ⓘ *25 de Mayo 83,* was built in the early 19th century, though its fine gilt wooden pulpit dates from the colonial period. On its exterior, overlooking Rivadavia, are fine murals in ceramic by local artist Armando Sica. Further east, at Boulevard J D Perón, is the magnificent late 19th-century **Mitre railway station** ⓘ *daily 0900-1700,* with its beautiful tiled *confitería*, still used for Sunday evening tango shows.

Museo Marqués de Sobremonte ⓘ *Rosario de Santa Fe 218, 1 block east of San Martin, T433 1661, Mon-Fri 0900-1400, US$1.50, texts in English and German.* Formerly the house of Rafael Núñez, governor of Córdoba, and now the only surviving colonial family residence in the city, the museum displays 18th- and 19th-century provincial history. **Museo Municipal de Bellas**

Córdoba

Where to stay 🛏
1 Aldea *A1*
2 Alex *B3*
3 Amerian Córdoba Park *B1*
4 Baluch Backpackers Hostel *A2*
5 Córdoba B&B *A1*
6 Córdoba Hostel *C2*
9 Palenque Hostel *B2*
11 Sussex *A2*
12 Tango Hostel *C1*
13 Windsor *B2*

Restaurants 🍴
1 Alfonsina *B2*
2 El Arrabal *C1*
3 Farro de Garrido *A1*
5 Juan Griego *A2*
8 Mandarina *A2*
9 Sol y Luna *A2, B1*
10 Sorocabana *A2*
11 Sushi Man *C1*

Artes ① *Av General Paz 33, T433 1512, Tue-Sun 0900-2100, US$0.40*, has a permanent collection of contemporary art by celebrated Argentine artists in an early 20th-century mansion. South of Plaza San Martín, in the hip **Nuevo Córdoba** district are two more fine art museums: **Bellas Artes Palacio Ferreyra** ① *Av H Yrigoyen 511, T434 3636, Tue-Sun 1000-2000, US$1.50, Wed free*, with 12 salons of Argentine and international works, and **Museo Caraffa** ① *Av H Yrigoyen 651, T433 3412, Tue-Sun 1000-2000, US$1.50, Wed free (near 50% discount when buying tickets for both Bellas Artes and Museo Caraffa)*, showing art from Córdoba. Also in this district is the **Paseo del Buen Pastor** ① *Av H Yrigoyen 325*, on the site of a women's prison, which now has a cultural centre, art gallery, fountains, book shop and café.

⊙ Córdoba listings

For hotel and restaurant price codes, and other relevant information, see Essentials.

⊙ Where to stay

Córdoba *p87, map p88*
$$$ Amerian Córdoba Park, Bv San Juan 165, T420 7000, www.amerian.com. Swish, modern hotel with marbled foyer and professional service. Comfortable, superb breakfast, convenient and reliable. Also has a business centre, gym, spa and pool.
$$$ Windsor, Buenos Aires 214, T422 4012, www.windsortower.com. Small, smart, warm, large breakfast, sauna, gym, pool. Excellent white tablecloth dining at the expensive Sibaris restaurant.
$$ Alex, Bv Illia 742, 1421 4350, www.alexhotel.com.ar. Good value, modern, cosy despite a slightly off-putting exterior. All rooms include a mate kit, helpful staff, close to the bus station.
$$ Córdoba B&B, Tucumán 440, T423 0973, www.cordobabyb.com.ar. Sparsely decorated but pleasant doubles and triples, central, parking, good value.
$$ Sussex, San Jerónimo 125, T422 9070, www.hotelsussexcba.com.ar. Well kept, with family welcome, small pool, buffet breakfast.
$ pp Aldea, Santa Rosa 447, T426 1312, www.aldeahostel.com. Nicely designed and decorated, welcoming, terrace with sofas, games, dorm prices depend on number sharing, quite central.
$ pp Baluch Backpackers Hostel, San Martin 338, T422 3977, www.baluchbackpackers.com. Inviting dorms for 4-6 (US$10.50-11.50) and nice doubles (**$$**). Owned and run by backpackers,

central, information and bus tickets, many services, organizes various activities.
$ pp Córdoba Hostel, Ituzaingó 1070, T468 7359, www.cordobahostel.com.ar. In Nueva Córdoba district, small rooms (US$13-14 in dorms, **$$** in double), quite noisy, private lockers in rooms. Small discount for HI members.
$ pp Palenque Hostel, Av Gral Paz 371, T423 7588, www.palenquehostel.com.ar. Lovely hostel in a 100-year-old building, spacious common areas, small dorms, doubles with TV.
$ pp Tango Hostel, Fructuoso Rivera 70, T425 6023, http://tangohostelcordoba.com. Good hostel in Nueva Córdoba student district, clubs and bars all around. rooms for 2-5 (US$10.50-11.50, double **$$**), library, free coffee/*mate*, local trips arranged.

Estancias
Estancia Los Potreros, Sierras Chicas, Casilla de Correo 64, 5111 Rio Ceballos, T011-4313 1410, www.estancialospotreros.com. An exclusive 2428-ha working cattle farm in the wild and scenic Córdoba hills. High standard of accommodation, with warm hospitality and attention to detail in keeping with a time past. The "riders' estancia", unrivalled in its fabulous horses (impeccably trained and calm polo horses). Even for non-equestrians you can relax by the pool, go birdwatching or just enjoy the peaceful hilltop setting and savour the delicious food and wines – all included in the price. 3 nights minimum stay (US$1080). Highly recommended (either take a bus to the nearest town, Río Ceballos, or the owners, Kevin and Louisa, will arrange a taxi from Córdoba city or airport, 1 hr).

🍴 Restaurants

Córdoba *p87, map p88*

$$$-$$ Juan Griego, Obispo Trejo 104, T1557 39760, www.juangriegorestobar.com. Mon-Fri 0800-1600. On the 7th floor of the Colegio de Escribanos with a view of the Manzana Jesuítica, this modern Argentine restaurant is unmissable. Open for breakfast and lunch.

$$ Faro de Garrido, Av Figueroa Alcorta 366, T1565 30247. Succulent grilled meats are the order of the day at this traditional, high-quality *parrilla*. Great for lunch or dinner.

$$ Sushi Man, Independencia1181, Nuevo Córdoba, T4603586, www.sushimanweb.com. Those who have had their fill of meat and would like to order in can opt for this chain restaurant offering decent sushi options; several branches.

$$-$ Sol y Luna, Gral Paz 278, T425 1189, www.solylunaonline.com.ar. Mon-Sat 1200-1530. Vegetarian with a change of menu daily, fresh food, lunchtime specials, good desserts. 2nd branch at Montevideo 66, Nuevo Córdoba, T421 1863.

$ Alfonsina, Duarte Quirós 66, T427 2847. Daily 0800-0200. Rural style in an old house, simple meals, pizzas and *empanadas* or breakfasts with homemade bread, piano and guitar music, popular.

Cafés

Mandarina, Obispo Trejo 171, T426 4909. Central, welcoming, leafy, lots of great breakfasts, good for lunch and dinner. Highly recommended.

Sorocabana, San Jerónimo 91, T422 7872. Daily 24 hrs. Great breakfasts, popular, good views of Plaza San Martín.

🍸 Bars and clubs

Córdoba *p87, map p88*

As one young Argentine reveler put it: "'Disco' is an outdated word. These days, we go out to *boliches*." No matter the term, there are plenty of bars, pubs and *boliches* in which to wet one's whistle and dance the night away

in Córdoba. See www.nochecordobacapital.com.ar. In **Nuevo Córdoba** head to Calles Rondeau, Larrañaga or Cañada.

El Abasto district, on the river (about 8 blocks north of Plaza San Martín) has several good, cheap places.

Another popular nightlife area lies further northwest in **Chateau Carreras**. C Buenos Aires between Centro and Nuevo Córdoba has many trendy nightspots as well.

🎭 Entertainment

Córdoba *p87, map p88*

See free listings in the local newspaper *La Voz del Interior* (www.vos.com.ar), and **www.cordoba.net**, for events.

Cinema Many including **Cineclub Municipal**, Bv San Juna 49, **Teatro Córdoba**, 27 de Abril 275, both showing independent and foreign language films, and the theatre in **Shopping Patio Olmos** (a mall in a wonderful old palace with a stylish food area), with new releases.

Music *Cuarteto* is a Cordobés style with an enthusiastic following. See www.kuarteto.com for groups, news and shows.

Tango. There are free tango shows in Plaza San Martin Sat, 2100, and at the plaza of Shopping Patio Olmos, Sun, 2000. **El Arrabal**, Belgrano y Fructuoso Rivera, www.elarrabalconcert.com.ar, restaurant offers dinner and a tango show at 2330, Fri and Sat. Ask here about private lessons.

Theatre **Teatro del Libertador**, Av Vélez Sarsfield 365, T433 2323, is traditional and sumptuous, with a rich history. Several other smaller theatres.

🛍 Shopping

Córdoba *p87, map p88*

Handicrafts **Mundo Aborigen**, Rivadavia 155, see Facebook. NGO promoting indigenous communities. **Paseo de las Artes**, Achával Rodríguez y Belgrano. Handicraft market, Sat-Sun 1600-2100 (in summer 1700-2300), ceramics, leather, wood and metalware.

⊖ Transport

Córdoba *p87, map p88*

Air Pajas Blancas airport is 12 km northwest of city, T475 0874, has shops, post office, a good restaurant and a *casa de cambio* (open Mon-Fri 1000-1500). The bus service can be unreliable; a regular or remise taxi charges around US$10. AR/Austral run a shuttle service several times a day to/from **Buenos Aires**, about 2 hrs. LAN also flies to Buenos Aires. Most major Argentine cities are served, usually via Buenos Aires. Sol flies to **Rosario** on weekdays, connection to **Punta del Este** in summer. International flights to **Peru**, **Brazil** and **Chile** direct, others via Buenos Aires.

Bus Municipal buses and electric buses (trolleys) do not accept cash. You have to buy cards from kiosks, normal US$0.50.

Minibuses to nearby towns stop at the main terminal and then stop at the minibus terminal, Bv. Illia 155, T425 2854.

The terminal at Bvd Perón 250, T434 1700, has restaurants, supermarket, internet, left-luggage lockers, ATM, remise taxi desk and tourist office. Taxi US$4 to Plaza San Martín. To **Buenos Aires**, several companies, 9-11 hrs, US$50 *semi-cama*, US$56-68 *ejecutivo/cama*. To **Salta**, 12 hrs, US$62-86 (*semi cama* and *ejecutivo*). To **Mendoza**, 9-12 hrs, frequent, US$54-72 (*semi cama* and *ejecutivo*). To **La Rioja**, 6-7 hrs, US$31-35. To **Catamarca**, 6 hrs, US$31-35. TAC and Andesmar have connecting services to several destinations in **Patagonia**. See towns below for buses to the Sierras de Córdoba.

⊕ Directory

Córdoba *p87, map p88*

Banks Open in the morning (0800-1300). There are many Link and Banelco ATMs; all accept international credit cards.
Consulates Bolivia, Vélez Sarsfield 56, T411 4489. Chile, Buenos Aires 1386, T469 2010.
Language schools Espanex, Av General Paz 55, p 18, T421 8954, www.espanex.org. Large organization with schools in Bariloche and Buenos Aires too, can arrange accommodation.
Medical services Hospital Córdoba, Libertad 2050, T433 9022. Hospital Clínicas, Santa Rosa 1564, T433 7014. For both, www.fcm.unc.edu.ar.
Useful addresses Dirección Nacional de Migraciones, Caseros 676, T422 2740.

Around Córdoba

Sierras de Córdoba

The Sierras de Córdoba offer beautiful mountain landscapes with many rivers and streams, plus the advantage of good infrastructure and accessibility. Adventure tourism has really taken off here, so there's something for everyone in the hills and valleys. Popular for tourism among the upper classes in the late 19th century, the Sierras de Córdoba were opened up for mass tourism in the 1940s with the building of lots of hotels. The most visited sights lie along the valleys of **Punilla**, Traslasierra and **Calamuchita**, and on the east side of the **Sierra Chica**, north of Córdoba, all forming itineraries of about 70 km long each. There's a useful network of dirt roads (usually used for rally competitions!). In all towns, municipal websites have lists of accommodation and places to eat. There are campsites at all the main tourist centres, but summer rainstorms may cause sudden floods along riversides so choose a pitch with care.

Punilla Valley

Villa Carlos Paz is a large modern town (*Phone code: 03541; Population: 86,000; Altitude: 642 m*), the nearest resort to Córdoba (36 km west). It is crammed with hotels. Trips on artificial Lago San Roque are offered in all kinds of water-vehicles and a chair-lift runs to the summit of Cerro de la Cruz for splendid views. **Municipal tourist office** ① *Av San Martín 400, T421624, www.villacarlospaz.gov.ar.*

On the banks of the Río Cosquín, 26 km north of Villa Carlos Paz, **Cosquín** (*Phone code: 03541; Population: 18,800; Altitude: 708 m*) is the site of the most important **folklore festival**, in the last two weeks in January (www.aquicosquin.org). A popular rock festival is held in early February in Santa Maria, the next town over (www.cosquinrock.net), so that accommodation is almost impossible to find between 10 January and 10 February. **Tourist office** ① *Av San Martín 590, Plaza Nacional del Folclore, T454644, www.cosquinturismo.gob.ar,* has full details of services and activities and organizes tours to local *quintas*.

La Falda *(Phone code: 03548; Population: 16,000; Altitude: 934 m)*, 82 km north of Córdoba, is a good base for walking, if not an attractive town. The **tourist office** ① *Av Edén 93, T423007, www. turismolafalda.gob.ar,* has information on several circuits and all related services.

To the west, an 80-km rough winding road goes to La Higuera, across the Cumbres de Gaspar. It crosses the vast **Pampa de Olaén**, a 1100-m-high grass-covered plateau with the tiny, 18th-century chapel of **Santa Bárbara** (20 km from La Falda) and the **Cascadas de Olaén**, with three waterfalls, 2 km south of the chapel.

North of La Falda is **La Cumbre** *(Phone code: 03548; Population: 7200; Altitude: 1141 m, www. alacumbre.com.ar)*, at the highest point in the Punilla Valley. Founded by British engineers and workers who built the railway here in 1900, it is an attractive place with tree-lined avenues. It has classy shops, good places to eat and have tea, a golf course and, nearby, the paragliding centre of **Cuchi Corral** (see What to do, below). It's the best place to visit if you want to avoid the major resorts to the south; it's a 1½-hour drive from Córdoba. Located 11 km from La Cumbre is the **Centro de Rescate, Rehabilitación y Conservación de Primates** (Center for Rescue, Rehabilitacion and Care of Primates) ① *www.proyectocaraya.com, Mon-Sun 0900-2030, US16,* where visitors can see a wide array of howler monkeys in their natural environment. Guided tours available. To arrive, take a taxi from La Cumbre. (US$16.00)

About 106 km north of Córdoba and set in the heart of the Sierras, **Capilla del Monte** *(Phone code: 03548; Altitude: 979 m)* is a good centre for trekking, paragliding and exploring. Excursions in the hills, particularly to Cerro Uritorco, 1979 m, a four-hour climb (no shade, entry US$2.50) via La Toma where there are medicinal waters and from where there are further walking opportunities. There is horse riding and tours to meditation and 'energy' centres: the location of many sightings of UFOs, the area is popular for 'mystical tourism' and holds an annual Festival Alienígena in February. **Tourist office** ① *RN 38 y F Alcorta, daily 0830-2030, T482200, www.capilladelmonte.gov.ar.*

Jesús María *(Colour map 8, A3. Population: 27,000. Altitude: 533 m. www.jesusmaria.gov.ar)*, 51 km north of Córdoba on Ruta 9, the town holds a popular gaucho and folklore festival each January, lasting 10 nights from second week. Mainly it is associated with the former Jesuit **Estancia de Jesús María** ① *T420126, Tue-Sun 1000-1300, 1400-1800 winter (1430-1900 summer), US$1.75, easy 15-min walk from bus station.* Dating from the 17th century, the estancia has the remains of its once famous winery, reputed to have produced the first wine in the Americas, which was served to the Spanish royal family. In the cloister is an excellent **Museo Jesuítico**, where Cuzco-style paintings, religious objects and a curious collection of plates are exhibited. It is a UNESCO World Heritage site, along with six other estancias including the splendid **Estancia de Santa Catalina** ① *70 km northwest of Jesús María, T0351-15-5503752, www.santacatalina.info, US$1.25,* which is still in private hands. Some 4 km from Jesús María is **Sinsacate**, a fine colonial posting inn, now a museum, with chapel attached.

An unpaved road branches off Ruta 9 at Santa Elena, 104 km north of Jesús María, to **Cerro Colorado**, 157 km north of Córdoba, the former home of the late Argentine folklore singer and composer Atahualpa Yupanqui. His house is a **museum** ① *daily 0900-1300, 1600-2000, US$2.50, at the end of the winding road to Agua Escondida, also offers guided tours,* lush grounds, with chance of spotting armadillos. For more information contact the **Fundación Atahualpa Yupanqui** ① *T(549)0-11-15-6685 3900, www.atahualpayupanqui.org.ar*. There are about 35,000 rock paintings by the indigenous Comechingones in the nearby **Reserva Natural y Cultural Cerro Colorado** ① *at the foot of Cerro Intihuasi, daily in summer, winter daily 0800-1900, US$2, only with guide, 1- to 1½-hr tour*, and a small **archaeological museum** ① *daily 0700-1300, 1400-2000, tours at 0830, 1030, 1600 and 1800.*

Traslasierra

A scenic road southwest from Villa Carlos Paz passes **Icho Cruz**, before climbing into the Sierra Grande and crossing the Pampa de Achala, a huge granite plateau at 2000 m. At La Pampilla, 55 km from Villa Carlos Paz, is the entrance to the **Parque Nacional Quebrada del Condorito** ① *administration at Resistencia 30, T433371, Villa Carlos Paz, www.parquesnacionales.gov.ar*, covering 37,344 ha of the Pampa de Achala and surrounding slopes. This is the easternmost habitat of the condor and an ideal flying school for the younger birds. Sightings are not guaranteed, but there's great trekking on the *pastizal de altura* (sierran grassland). **Balcón Norte**, 7 km on foot from the car park at the visitors centre, has a marked trail and is linked to Balcón Sur viewpoint. Tours go from Villa Carlos Paz. Ciudad de Córdoba and **TAC** buses can stop at La Pampilla on their way to Mina Clavero (from Villa Carlos Paz: one hour, US$5).

Mina Clavero *(Phone code: 03544; Colour map 8, A3; Population: 6800; Altitude: 915 m)* This is a good centre, 40 km west of Córdoba, for exploring the high *sierra* and the Traslasierra Valley. There is an intriguing museum, **Museo Rocsen** ① *13 km south and about 5 km east of the village of Nono, T498218, www.museorocsen.org, daily 0900 till sunset, US$5.50, free entry for students, take a taxi.* The personal collection of Sr Bouchón, it is a wonderfully bizarre mix of subjects, including furniture, minerals, instruments, archaeology and animals ('by far the best natural history and cultural museum, a whole day is needed to visit' – Federico Kirbus). There are many hotels, *hosterías, hospedajes*, campsites and restaurants in and around Mina Clavero. **Tourist office** (with ATM) ① *Plazoleta Merlo, T470171, www.minaclavero.gov.ar, open 0900 till 2200.*

Calamuchita

Alta Gracia *(Colour map 8, A3; Phone code: 03547; Population: 42,600; Altitude: 580 m)*. Beside Lago Tajamar, Alta Gracia, 39 km southwest of Córdoba, has an interesting **Estancia Jesuítica Alta Gracia** ① *T421303, www.museoliniers.org.ar, winter Tue-Fri 0900-1300, 1500-1900, Sat-Sun 0930-1230, 1530-1830 (summer Tue-Fri 0900-2000, Sat-Sun opens 30 mins later), closed 1 Jan, 1 May, 25 Dec, US$1.75, free Wed, 4 guided visits a day (8 per day Jan-Mar), phone in advance for English tours*, a UNESCO World Heritage Site. If you visit only one Jesuit estancia in the Córdoba region, make it this one. The main buildings of the estancia are situated around the plaza. The church, completed in 1762, with a baroque façade but no tower, is open for services only. To the north of the church is the former Residence, built round a cloister and housing the **Museo Casa del Virrey Liniers**. **Tourist office** ① *El Molino y Av del Tajamar, T428128, www.altagracia.gov.ar*.

Che Guevara grew up in Alta Gracia after his parents left Rosario to live in the more refreshing environment in the foothills of the Andes. He had started to suffer from asthma, which would plague him for the rest of his life. See page 148. **Museo Casa de Ernesto Che Guevara** ① *in Villa Nydia, Avellaneda 501, T428579, summer daily 0900-2000, winter daily 0900-1900, Mon 1400-1900, US$12 (US$7 for students), from the Sierras Hotel, go north along C Vélez Sarsfield-Quintana and turn left on C Avellaneda.* Che lived here between 1935-1937 and 1939-1943 before going to Córdoba: plenty of personal belongings from his childhood and youth, also the letter addressed to Fidel Castro where Che resigns from his position in Cuba. Texts in Spanish and other languages.

Villa General Belgrano (*Phone code: 03546*) This completely German town 85 km south of Córdoba, was founded by the surviving interned seamen from the *Graf Spee*, some of whom still live here. It is a good centre for excursions in the surrounding mountains. Genuine German cakes and smoked sausages are sold, there is an Oktoberfest, a **Fiesta de la Masa Vienesa** in Easter week, for lovers of Viennese-style pastries, and the **Fiesta del Chocolate Alpino** during July holidays. **Tourist office** ① *Av Roca 168, T461215, www.vgb.gov.ar, 0900-2100, helpful German-and English-speaking staff.* **La Cumbrecita** is a charming German village 30 km west, from where lots of outdoor excursions can be made; see www.lacumbrecita.gov.ar.

◉ Around Córdoba listings

For hotel and restaurant price codes, and other relevant information, see Essentials.

◉ Where to stay

Punilla Valley *p91*
Cosquín
$$$ La Puerta del Sol, Perón 820, T452045, www.lapuertadelsolhotel.com.ar. **$$$$** in high season. A decent choice, pool, car hire, half board available.
$$ Siempreverde, Santa Fe 525, behind Plaza Molina, T450093, http://hosteriasiempreverde. com. Spotless, welcoming and informative owner, some rooms small, comfortable, gorgeous garden.

La Falda
All 80 hotels are full in Dec-Feb.
$$$ L'Hirondelle, Av Edén 861, T422825, www.lhirondellehostal.com. Lovely building, some rooms retain their original parquet floor and there's a large garden with a pool, and a restaurant. Welcoming owners.
$$ La Asturiana, Av Edén 835, T422923, hotellaasturiana@yahoo.com.ar. Simple, comfortable rooms, pool, superb breakfast.

La Cumbre
There are plenty of hotels but *cabañas* here are high quality and in attractive settings, ideal for larger groups who want the flexibility of self-catering. Cruz Chica is a lovely place to stay, but you'll need a car or taxi to get there.
$$ Hotel La Viña, Caraffa 48, T03548-451388, www.hotellavina.com.ar. Nice budget option, with cosy flowery rooms, a large pool and pleasant gardens.

$ pp Hostel La Cumbre, Av San Martín 282, T03548-451368, www.hostellacumbre.com. Dorms, rooms for up to 6 and doubles (**$$**). Family-owned, HI member, historic building with garden and pool, occasional *asados*, laundry, information and activities. Recommended.

Capilla del Monte
$$$ Montecassino, La Pampa 107, T482572, www.hotelmontecassino.com. Beautiful building from 1901, with lovely rooms, cable TV, jacuzzi and pool with stunning views.
$$$ Petit Sierras, Pueyrredón 622 y Salta, T481667, www.hotelpetitsierras.com.ar. Renovated hotel with comfortable rooms. See Facebook page for packages and promotions..

Traslasierra *p93*
Mina Clavero
Several close in low season.
$ pp Hostel Andamundos, San Martín 554, T470249, www.andamundoshostel.com.ar. Doubles **$$**, dorms US$13-17. Centrally located, well-maintained and bright, great atmosphere, HI discount. They can organize local excursions.
$ pp Oh La La!! Hostel, Villanueva 1192, T472634, www.ohlalahostel.com.ar. Youth hostel (double rooms **$$**), shared bathrooms, tourist information, pool and gardens.

Calamuchita *p93*
Alta Gracia
$$$$-$$$ El Potrerillo de Larreta, on the road to Los Paredones, 3 km from Alta Gracia, T423804, www.potrerillodelarreta.com. Old-fashioned, fabulous 1918 resort and country club in gorgeous gardens with wonderful

views. Tennis courts, 18-hole golf course, swimming pool. Great service.

$$$ 279 Boutique Bed & Breakfast, Giorello 279, T424177, www.279altagracia.com. This small, immaculate bed and breakfast is the best place to stay in town. A short stroll to the centre of town, quiet. Recommended.

$ pp Alta Gracia Hostel, Paraguay 218, T428810, www.altagraciahostel.com.ar. Family-run hostel, with dorm beds, nice bathrooms and kitchen. 3 blocks from the main street. Highly recommended.

Villa General Belgrano

Many *cabaña* complexes, chalet-style hotels, often family-oriented. Book ahead Jan-Feb, Jul and Easter.

$$ La Posada de Akasha, Los Manantiales 60, T462440, www.laposadadeakasha.com. Extremely comfortable, spotless chalet-style house, with small pool, welcoming.

$ pp El Rincón, Fleming 347, T461323, www.hostelelrincon.com.ar. The only hostel in town is beautifully set in dense forests and green clearings 10-min walk from bus terminal. Dorms (US$13-14), doubles or singles with bath (**$** pp) and camping (US$8-9 pp). US$3.50 for superb breakfasts. HI discounts, half price for children under 16. In high season rates are higher and the hostel is usually full. 10-min walk from terminal. Recommended.

Camping Camping Granja Ecológica Veilchental, Ruta Provincial 201 Camino a La Cumbrecita Km 7, T03546-15-513449, http://facebook.com/veilchental. 5 mins from town, tent rental available, showers, meals.

La Cumbrecita

Various hotels and cabañas, prices **$$$-$$**.

$$ El Ceibo, T481060, www.hosteriaelceibo.com. Neat rooms for 2-4, near the entrance to the town, great views, access to the river.

⚙ What to do

Punilla Valley *p91*

Climbing Club Andino Córdoba, 27 de Abril 2050, Barrio Alto Alberdi, Córdoba, T0351-480 5126, www.clubandinocordoba.com.ar. Information on climbing and trekking

throughout the region. It has refugios in the Tanti area, northwest of Villa Carlos Paz.

For Cerro Champaquí (2790m), near Villa General Belgrano, see operators like **Alto Rumbo** in Córdoba, www.champaqui.com.ar, or ask at the information offices in Villa Alpina, T03547-15-595163, www.villaalpinacordoba.com.ar, or Villa Yacanto, T03546-485007, www.villayacanto.gov.ar.

La Cumbre

Paragliding The world-renowned paragliding site of Cuchi Corral is 9 km west of La Cumbre on an unpaved road; **Escuela de Parapentes**, Ruta 38, Km 65, T03548-403580, www.cordobaserrana.com.ar/parapente.htm. Several local companies offer flights, which start at US$85 for your 1st flight, the *Vuelo Bautismo*, 20 mins, accompanied by a trained paragliding instructor in tandem.

⊖ Transport

Sierras de Córdoba *p91*

Bus From **Córdoba** to some of the main towns in the Sierras: **Villa Carlos Paz** (a transport hub with frequent buses to **Buenos Aires** and other main destinations, as well as to the towns in the Punilla and Traslasierra valleys), CoataCórdoba, 45 mins, US$2. There are also buses from Córdoba and Villa Carlos Paz to Cosquín, La Falda and Capilla del Monte. **Villa Carlos Paz** same company to Mina Clavero, 2¼ hrs, US$6. **Córdoba** to Mina Clavero, same company, 3 hrs US$7.50, and to **Villa General Belgrano**, 2 hrs, US$5.50. **Córdoba** to Alta Gracia, Sierras de Calamuchita, 1 hr 5 mins, US$1.50.

Cosquín

Train A tourist *Tren de las Sierras* runs 52 km between Cosquín and Rodríguez del Busto, via La Calera, 2 a day Mon-Fri, 3 a day Sat, Sun, 2¼ hrs, US$1. It is planned to extend the line from Córdoba to Cruz del Eje; see www.ferrocentralsa.com.ar.

Villa General Belgrano

Bus To **La Cumbrecita** with Pájaro Blanco, Av San Martín 105, T461709, every 2-4 hrs, 1 hr 20 mins, US$7 return.

Mendoza and around → Phone code: 0261. Colour map 8, B2. Population: city 115,000; greater Mendoza 1 million (estimated). Altitude: 756 m.

At the foot of the Andes, Mendoza is a dynamic and attractive city, surrounded by vineyards and *bodegas*. The city was colonized from Chile in 1561 and it played an important role in gaining independence from Spain when the Liberator José de San Martín set out to cross the Andes from here, to help in the liberation of Chile. Mendoza was completely destroyed by fire and earthquake in 1861, so today it is essentially a modern city of low buildings and wide avenues (as a precaution against earthquakes), thickly planted with trees and gardens.

Arriving in Mendoza

Orientation El Plumerillo airport is 8 km northeast of the centre and the bus terminal is on Av Videla, 15 minutes' walk from the centre. Main **tourist office** ① *Garibaldi y San Martín, T420 1333, www.ciudaddemendoza.gov.ar, open 0900-2100,* very helpful, English and French spoken. Also at **Las Heras y Perú** ① *T429 6298, open Mon-Sat 0900-2000;* at the **Municipalidad** ① *9 de Julio 500, 7th floor, T449 5185, Mon-Fri 0900-1300;* at bus station and at airport. All hand out maps and accommodation lists, private lodgings in high season, also lists of bodegas and advice on buses. The city runs also free walking tours and the **Bus Turístico. Provincial tourist office** ① *Av San Martín 1143, T413 2101, www.turismo.mendoza.gov.ar.*

Places in and around Mendoza

In the centre of the city is the **Plaza Independencia**, in the middle of which is the small **Museo Municipal de Arte Moderno** ① *T425 7279, Tue-Fri 0900-2000, Sat, Sun and holidays 1400-2000, US$2 (valid also 24 hrs for Museo del Area Fundacional and Aquarium),* with temporary exhibitions, and on the east side, leafy streets lined with cafés. Among the other pleasant squares nearby is **Plaza España**, attractively tiled and with a mural illustrating the epic gaucho poem, *Martín Fierro.* **Plaza Pellegrini** (Avenida Alem y Avenida San Juan) is a beautiful small square where wedding photos are taken on Friday and Saturday nights, and a small antiques market (Thursday-Saturday). By the Plaza San Martín is the **Basílica de San Francisco** (España y Necochea), 1893, in which is the mausoleum of the family of General San Martín.

On the west side of the city is the great **Parque San Martín** ① *information office next to the gates, the entrance is 10 blocks west of the Plaza Independencia, reached by bus 3 (line 112) from Plaza Independencia, or the trolley 'Parque' from Sarmiento y 9 de Julio, 0900-1800.* It is beautifully designed, with a **zoo** ① *Tue-Sun 0900-1700 (0900-1800 in summer), US$3.75,* many areas for sports and picnics, and a large lake, where regattas are held. **Bike rental** ① *www.lasbicisdelparque.com. ar,* next to lake's north end. The **Museo de Ciencias Naturales y Antropológicas** ① *T428 7666 (closed in 2014),* has a female mummy among its fossils and stuffed animals. There are views of the Andes rising in a blue-black perpendicular wall, topped off in winter with dazzling snow, into a china-blue sky. On a hill in the park is the **Cerro de la Gloria**, crowned by an astonishing monument to San Martín, with bas-reliefs depicting various episodes in the equipping of the Army of the Andes and the actual crossing. **Bus Turístico** and **El Oro Negro** tourist buses run to the top of the Cerro de la Gloria from the city centre, otherwise it's a 45-minute walk from park's gates.

Mendoza's interesting history can be traced in two good museums: **Museo del Pasado Cuyano** ① *Montevideo 544, T423 6031, Tue-Sat 1000-1400 (0900-1300 in summer), US$1.25,* housed in a beautiful 1873 mansion (city's oldest building), with San Martín memorabilia in one of its rooms and an exquisite Spanish 17th-century carved altarpiece; excellent tours. Also recommended is **Museo del Area Fundacional** ① *Beltrán y Videla Castillo, T425 6927, Tue-Sat 0800-2000 (Jun-Aug 0900-1900), Sun 1500-2000, holidays 1000-1900, US$2 (valid also 24 hrs for*

Museo Municipal de Arte Moderno and Aquarium), getting there: from C Chile buses 5 (line 54) and 3 (line 112); it is also one of the Bus Turístico stops. It has displays of the city pre-earthquake, with original foundations revealed, and the ruins of Jesuit church **San Francisco** opposite; informative free tour includes museum, an interesting underground chamber and church.

In the nearby suburb of Luján de Cuyo, the city's best art gallery, with a small collection of Argentine paintings, is in the house where Fernando Fader painted decorative murals, at the **Museo Provincial de Bellas Artes, Casa de Fader** ① *Carril San Martín 3651, Mayor Drummond, T496 0224, Tue-Fri 0830-1300, Sat-Sun 1400-1800, US$1.25, getting there: bus 1 (line 19) from C La Rioja, between Catamarca and Garibaldi, 40 mins,* in the gardens are sculptures.

Mendoza

200 metres
200 yards

Where to stay 🛌
1 Alamo Hostel & Suites *B1*
2 Campo Base *B1*
3 Chimbas Hostel *C3*
4 Confluencia *A2*
5 Damajuana *C1*
6 Hostel Internacional Mendoza *C2*
7 Hostel Suites Mendoza *A2*
8 InterContinental *C3*
9 Mendoza Backpackers *C2*
10 Mendoza Inn *C1*
11 NH *B1*
12 Nutibara *C1*
13 Park Hyatt *B1*
14 Sheraton *B2*

Restaurants 🍴
1 Anna Bistro *A1*
2 Azafrán *B1*
3 Facundo *B1*
4 Ferruccio Soppelsa *A2*
5 Francesco Barbera *B1*
7 La Marchigiana *A2*
9 Las Tinajas *B2*
10 Liverpool *B2*
12 Mesón Español *C2*
13 Montecatini *A1*
15 Por Acá & Tres con Noventa *C1*
16 Quinta Norte *B1*
17 Vía Civit *B1*

Bars & clubs 🍸
18 Gio Bar *B1*

Wine tours Many bodegas welcome visitors and offer tastings without pressure to buy (grape harvesting season March/April). Rent a bicycle and make a day of it. If you've only time for one, though, make it **Bodega La Rural (San Felipe)** ① *at Montecaseros 2625, Coquimbito, Maipú, T497 2013, www.bodegala rural.com.ar; getting there: bus 10 (subnumber 173) from La Rioja y Garibaldi*. Traditional, but recently modernized, with a **Museo del Vino** ① *Mon-Sat 0900-1300, 1400-1700, closed Sun*. South of Maipú is **Carinae** ① *Videla Aranda 2899, Cruz de Piedra, T499 0470, www.carinaevinos.com, daily 1000-1800*. French owners with an interest in astronomy as well as producing fine wines. (In Maipú itself, 15 km south of Mendoza, see the plaza and eat good simple food at the Club Social.) In the suburb of Godoy Cruz are **Bodegas Escoríhuela Gascón** ① *Belgrano 1108, T424 2282, www.escorihuela.com.ar, Mon-Fri 0930-1730, getting there: bus 9 (line 151) or bus 10 (lines 173 and 174) from C La Rioja between Garibaldi and Catamarca*, with an excellent restaurant (see below).

In or near **Luján de Cuyo** ① *RS Peña 1000, T498 1912, www.lujandecuyo.gov.ar, for tourist information*, there are several bodegas (booking a visit is advisable; a fee is charged in most cases). Larger ones include **Norton** ① *T490 9700 ext 4, www.norton.com.ar, 6 visits a day Mon-Fri, reserve the same day*, **Catena Zapata** ① *T413 1100, www.catenawines.com*, and **Séptima** ① *T498 9558, www.bodegaseptima.com, Mon-Fri 1000-1800, Sat 1000-1400, with sunset tastings on Thu in summer*. **Tapiz** ① *C Pedro Molina, Russell, T490 0202, www.tapiz.com.ar*, is not only a winery, but also a 1890s house converted into a superb hotel (**$$$$**) with restaurant to match. (See also **Cavas Wine Lodge**, below.) Also with a hotel, **La Posada**, is **Carlos Pulenta-Vistalba** ① *RS Peña 3135, Vistalba, T498 9400, www.carlospulentawines.com*. Famed for its Malbec is **Renacer** ① *Brandsen 1863, Perdriel, T524 4416, www.bodegarenacer.com.ar*. Also in Perdriel is **Achával Ferrer** ① *C Cobos 2601, T15-553 5565, www.achaval-ferrer.com*, a boutique bodega which has won many prizes. **El Lagar de Carmelo Patti** ① *Av San Martín 2614, Mayor Drummond, T498 1379, Mon-Sat 1100-1300, 1500-1700*, has tours and tastings led by the owner (by appointment and in Spanish only). For general information on wines of the region, visit: www.turismo.mendoza.gov.ar; www.vendimia.mendoza.gov.ar on the annual wine festival; www.welcometomendoza.com.ar (expat site, more than just wine); and www.welcome argentina.com/vino/index_i.html.

The vineyards of Uco valley around the towns of Tupungato and Tunuyán, about 80 km south of Mendoza, are increasingly relevant as producers of high-altitude wines. Several wineries welcome visitors, of which **Bodegas Salentein** ① *Ruta 89 Km 14, Los Árboles, Tunuyán, T02622-429500 ext 3200, www.bodegasalentein.com*, and **The Vines of Mendoza** ① *Ruta 94 Km 11, Tunuyán, T632 1768, www.vinesofmendoza.com*, are among the finest examples.

◉ Mendoza and around listings

For hotel and restaurant price codes, and other relevant information, see Essentials.

● Where to stay

Mendoza and around *p96, map p97*
Hostels advertise themselves outside tourist office in town, offering free transfers and lots of extras; don't be pressurized into something you don't want. The Hyatt (www.mendoza.park.hyatt.com), InterContinental (www.intercontinental.com), Sheraton (www.

starwoodhotels.com) and NH (www.nh-hotels.com) chains have good hotels in the city. Hostels about US$12-18 pp; including **Hostel Suites Mendoza**, Patricias Mendocinas 1532 (at Av Heras), T423 7018, www.hostelsuites.com.
$$$$ Cavas Wine Lodge, Costaflores, Alto Agrelo, Luján de Cuyo, T410 6927, www.cavaswinelodge.com. A pricey but heavenly experience, ideal for a romantic and wonderfully relaxing stay. Spacious rooms in a beautifully restored rural mansion, with restaurant and spa. Each room has a fireplace

and terrace, swimming pool, wonderful views. Highly recommended.

$$$ Nutibara, Mitre 867, T429 5428, www.nutibara.com.ar. In the need of renovation of its small rooms, but still a good choice for its central though quiet location and its pool.

$$$ Parador del Ángel, 100 m from main plaza, Chacras de Coria, Luján de Cuyo, T496 2201, www.paradordelangel.com.ar. Restored 100-year old house, tastefully decorated, very relaxing, gardens, pool, owner is an experienced mountain climber.

$$$ Tikay Killa Lodge & Wines, Montecaseros 3543, Coquimbito, Maipú, T542 3232, www.tikaykilla.com.ar. Small lodge in the Ruta del Vino, white rooms, parking, garden, wine tours and other activities organized, helpful English-speaking manager.

$ pp Alamo Hostel & Suites, Necochea 740, T429 5565, www.hostelalamo.com. Beautiful hostel in a very well-kept 1940s residence with dorms for 4 to 8 and doubles with or without bath (**$$**). Bike rental and tiny pool in a pleasant patio. Recommended for a quiet, yet sociable stay.

$ pp Campo Base, Mitre 946, T429 0707, www.hostelcampobase.com.ar. A lively place, discounts for HI members, cramped rooms and private doubles (**$$**), lots of parties and barbecues, popular with mountain climbers, excursions run by YTA agency.

$ pp Chimbas Hostel, Cobos 92 y Acceso Este, T431 4191, www.chimbashostel.com.ar. Cheaper without bath and in triples, also private doubles with bath (**$$**), close to bus station (phone in advance for pick-up), 20 mins walk to centre, swimming pool, gym, pleasant, quiet atmosphere.

$ pp Confluencia, España 1512, T429 0430, www.hostalconfluencia.com.ar. Slightly more expensive than other hostels, but a convenient choice for groups who care for tidiness and a central location. Rooms for 2 to 4 (private doubles **$$**),some ensuite.

$ pp Damajuana, Arístides Villanueva 282, T425 5858, www.damajuanahostel.com.ar. A great hostel, comfortable stylish dorms with bath, also double rooms (**$$**), pool and garden. Recommended.

$ pp Hostel Internacional Mendoza, España 343, T424 0018, www.hostelmendoza.net. A comfortable hostel, HI discount, 15 min walk south of Plaza Independencia, small rooms for 4 and 6 with bath (cheaper without a/c), doubles with bath (**$$**), warm atmosphere, good value dinners on offer, barbecues on Fri, bike rental, huge range of excursions run by YTA agency. Warmly recommended.

$ pp Mendoza Backpackers, San Lorenzo 19, T429 4941, www.mendozabackpackers.com. Well-run central hostel with an attractive lounge and terrace bar, dorms for 4 and 6, some with bath. HI discounts. Excursions run by YTA agency.

$ pp Mendoza Inn, Arístides Villanueva 470, T420 2486, www.mendozahostel.com. In the lively bar area, small dorms for 4 to 8, some with bath, and a private double (**$$**), large garden with a tiny pool, dinner extra, HI discounts. Excursions run by YTA agency.

Camping Camping Suizo, Av Champagnat, El Challao, 8 km from city, www.campingsuizo.com.ar, modern, shady, with pool, barbecues, hot showers and cabañas for 4 and 6. Recommended.

Restaurants

Mendoza and around *p96, map p97*
There are many open-air cafés for lunch on Peatonal Sarmiento and restaurants around Las Heras. The atmospheric indoor market on Las Heras, Mon-Sat 0830-1300, 1700-2100; Sun 0930-1300, has cheap pizza, *parrilla* and pasta. A few food stalls remain open 0830-2300.

$$$ 1884 Francis Mallman, Bodega Escorihuela, Belgrano 1188, Godoy Cruz, T424 2698. Open for dinner only, reservation is advisable. The place to go for a really special dinner. Mallman is one of the country's great chefs, exotic and imaginative menu. Highly recommended.

$$$ Anna Bistró, Av Juan B Justo 161, T425 1818. One of the most attractive restaurants in town, informal, French-owned, very welcoming, good food and drink, French and Italian flavours, open from breakfast to a late dinner, excellent value. Recommended

$$$ **Azafrán**, Sarmiento 765, T429 4200.
A fine-wine lover's heaven, with an extensive
range from all the best bodegas, expert
advice on wines and a fabulous delicatessen
where you can enjoy superb *picadas*. Its menu
changes with the season. Recommended.
$$$ **El Mesón Español**, Montevideo 244,
T429 6175. Spanish food, including great
paella, live music Wed-Sat.
$$$ **Facundo**, Sarmiento 641, T420 2866.
Good modern *parrilla*, lots of other choices
including Italian, good salad bar.
$$$ **Francesco Barbera**, Chile 1268, T425
3912. Smart old town house with a wonderful
garden, excellent Italian food, choose from over
350 different wines.
$$$ **La Marchigiana**, Patricias Mendocinas
1550, T423 0751. One of Mendoza's best
restaurants and great value. Italian food served
in spacious surroundings with charming old-
fashioned service.
$$ **Las Tinajas**, Lavalle 38, T429 1174, www.
lastinajas.com. Large buffet-style/all-you-can-
eat at very reasonable prices, wide selection
of pastas, grills, Chinese, desserts and so on.
Cheap wine, too.
$$$ **Montecatini**, Gral Paz 370, T425 2111,
Good Italian food, seafood and *parrilla*, more
tourist oriented, popular with families.
$$ **Gio Bar**, Chile 1288. Attractively set
and casual, a good choice for Italian-style
sandwiches, pizzas and salads.
$$ **Quinta Norte**, Mitre 1206. Cheap deals and
generous portions in an elegant mansion on
Plaza Independencia.
$$ **Vía Civit**, Emilio Civit 277. Open from
breakfast onwards. For first-class sandwiches,
tarts and pastries in a relaxed, elegant
traditional bakery.

Calle Arístides Villanueva, the extension of
Colón heading west, has good restaurants and
bars (as well as hostels).
$$$-$$ **3 90 (Tres con Noventa)**, Arístides
Villanueva 451, T429 8686. Delicious pastas,
good value, studenty, warm cosy atmosphere.
Highly recommended.
$$ **Por Acá**, Arístides Villanueva 557. 2100 till
late. Bar for pizzas and drinks, popular, noisy.

Ferruccio Soppelsa, Espejo y Patricias
Mendocinas, with several branches. The best
place for ice cream (even wine flavours!).
Recommended.
La Alameda (Av San Martín, north of
C Córdoba) is another pleasant bar area with
some basic restaurants open also for lunchtime.
Liverpool, San Martín y Rivadavia. Pub food,
sandwiches, burgers, Beatles memorabilia and
European football matches on the screen.

⊛ Festivals

Mendoza and around *p96, map p97*
The riotous wine harvesting festival, **Fiesta de
la Vendimia**, is held in the amphitheatre of
the Parque San Martín in early **Mar**. Local wine
festivals start in **Dec**. A parallel event is the
less-promoted but equally entertaining **Gay
Vendimia Festival**, featuring parties, shows and
the crowning of the Festival Queen. Much more
modest is the **Vendimia Obrera** in **mid-Mar**,
when vineyard workers, many of whom are
of Bolivian origin, recover the roots of the
original celebration with live music, wine and
food in Cordón del Plata, a village in the Uco
valley. Hotels fill up fast and prices rise; also in
Easter, Jul (the ski season) and around **mid-Sep**
(Chilean holidays).

⊙ Shopping

Mendoza and around *p96, map p97*
Handicrafts The main shopping area is along
San Martín and Las Heras, with good clothes,
souvenir, leather and handicraft shops as well
as vast sports emporia. **Mercado Artesanal**, San
Martín 1133, Mon-Fri 0900-1900 (Jan mornings
only), Sat 0900-1300, for traditional leather,
baskets, weaving; also weekend market on
Plaza Independencia. Cheap shops include:
El Turista, Las Heras 351, and **Las Viñas**, Las
Heras 399. For higher quality head to **Raíces**,
Peatonal Sarmiento 162, or **Alpataco**, next
door. Good choice of wines at *vinotecas*,
eg **Winery**, Chile 898, T420 2840; **The Vines of
Mendoza**, Belgrano 1194, T438 1031, www.
vinesofmendoza.com, Mon-Sat 1500-2200,

tasteful, pricey, wine-tasting and shopping experience, presenting the best of the region's boutique bodegas, international orders only.

⚫ What to do

Mendoza and around *p96, map p97*
Climbing Club Andinista Mendoza, F L Beltrán 357, Guaymallén, T431 9870, www.clubandinista. com.ar. See page 107 for Aconcagua.

Cycling For bike tours and rentals: **Internacional Mendoza**, Pedro Molina 63, T423 2103, www.intermza.com. See also **YTA** below for bike tours and rentals as well, or shop around a handful of agencies along C Urquiza in the wine region of Coquimbito, Maipú, such as **Mr Hugo**, Urquiza 2288, Coquimbito, Maipú, T497 4067, www.mrhugobikes.com. Good.

Whitewater rafting Popular on the Río Mendoza; ask agencies for details, eg **Argentina Rafting**, office in Mendoza at Amigorena 86, T429 6325, www.argentinarafting.com. Varied activities from its base camp in Potrerillos, or **Ríos Andinos**, 5 km north of Potrerillos, T0261-517 4184, www.riosandinos.com, also offers horse riding, trekking and combinations.

Tour operators
Many agencies, especially on Peatonal Sarmiento, run trekking, riding and rafting expeditions, as well as traditional tours to Alta Montaña and bodegas.
Aconcagua Spirit, Rivadavia 345, Maipú, T0261-559 2819, www.aconcaguaspirit.com.ar. Recommended for their 11-day horseback expeditions across the Andes.
Bus Turístico, www.mendozacitytour.com. Open double-decker bus for city's sightseeing with 15 stops including Cerro de la Gloria. Hourly departures from Peatonal Sarmiento y Av San Martín, tickets (US$10, hop on/hop off) sold at city's tourist offices.
Bus Vitivinícola, www.busvitivinicola.com. 4 weekly departures from top hotels and Av San Martín y Garibaldi for visiting Luján de

Cuyo's main wineries in 2 alternative circuits, half or full day tours, hop on/hop off, US$20.
El Oro Negro, T498 0510, www.bateatour. com.ar. Open bus for 2½ hrs bilingual city tours (US$8) including Cerro de la Gloria, 3 daily departures from Plaza Independencia (on C Chile), or 1½ hrs Parque San Martín and Cerro de la Gloria bilingual tours (US$5), 3-4 daily departures from same point.
The Grapevine, T429 7522, www.the grapevine-winetours.com. British-owned and run, it organizes personalized tours in the wine region, including flights combined with visits and lunch and summer full-moon wine tours, among a great diversity of choices.
Huentata, Las Heras 529, T425 7444, www.huentata.com.ar. Conventional tours including Villavicencio and Cañón del Atuel. Recommended.
Inka Expediciones, Juan B Justo 345, T425 0871, www.inka.com.ar. Climbing expeditions, including Aconcagua, highly professional, fixed departure dates, mules for hire.
Kahuak, Rivadavia 234, T423 8409, www. kahuak.com.ar. Mainly focused on a wide range of wine tours. Recommended.
Mendoza Viajes, Peatonal Sarmiento 129, T461 0210, www.mendozaviajes.com. Imaginative tours in comfortable coaches, professional, cheap deals available.
Trekking Travel, Adolfo Calle 4171, Villa Nueva, Guaymallén, T421 0450, www.trekking-travel. com.ar. From easy horseback riding to the Andes crossing; trekking in the Aconcagua and Cordón del Plata.
YTA, Peatonal Sarmiento 231, T425 5511, www.youthtravelargentina.com. All bilingual excursions starting from half-day wine tours (US$20 pp) to full-day Alta Montaña circuit (US$38 pp), offering also varied activities such as paragliding, trekking, horse riding, rafting, delightful bike rides through vineyards (US$35 pp) and exclusive Harley-Davidson wine tours in Uco valley. Occasional treks in Aconcagua area. Discounts for HI members and own hostel network guests. Make sure about extra costs.

⊖ Transport

Mendoza and around *p96, map p97*

Air El Plumerillo airport, 8 km northeast of centre, T520 6000, has money exchange, tourist information, shops, restaurant and *locutorio*, but no left luggage. Reached from the centre along San Juan. Av Alem and Salta by bus 6 (line 63 'Mosconi'), hourly, 40 mins journey. Taxi to/from centre US$8. Daily flights to **Buenos Aires** and **Santiago de Chile**. Also to **Córdoba**, **Bariloche**, **Iguazú** and a few other national destinations.

Bus Most local services have 2 numbers, a general number and a 'subnumber' in brackets which indicates the specific route. Buses within and near the city are paid with Red Bus magnetic cards (trips from US$0.45), which are topped up. They are sold for US$1.25 at designated outlets, where you can also top up. There are 6 trolley bus routes, plus a streetcar 'Metrotranvía' that runs along Av Belgrano in the centre from Mendoza station to Gutiérrez station, in Maipú, in 30 mins, US$0.45, and a tourist bus decorated as a streetcar runs along the main commercial avenues (US$0.40).

Long distance The huge bus terminal is on the east side of Av Videla, 15 mins' walk from centre (go via Av Alem, which has pedestrian tunnel to gates opposite platforms 38-39), with shops, *locutorio*, tourist information, ATMs, a good café, left luggage (opposite platform 53) and toilets. It's not a place to linger at night. Taxi to/from centre US$2.50. To **Buenos Aires**, 13-17 hrs, US$76-108, many companies. To **Bariloche**, 17 hrs, US$90-102, with Cata. To **Córdoba**, 9-12 hrs, US$54-72, several companies.To/from **San Juan**, US$13-14, 2-2½ hrs. To **La Rioja**, US$42-60, 8-9½ hrs. To **Catamarca** 10-11½ hrs, US$52-74. To **Tucumán**, 13-20 hrs, US$68-96. To **Salta**, 18 hrs, US$109-124, with Andesmar. To **Potrerillos**, 1 hr, US$2.25 with Buttini (opposite platform 56), which goes on to Uspallata, US$5.75, 2¼ hrs and up to Las Cuevas, twice a day, US$7, 4 hrs. To **Tupungato**, US$4.50-5.50, 1½-2 hrs, with TBMitre/Cata. To **San Rafael**, US$7.50-9.50, 3-3½ hrs, with Buttini, Cata and Iselin. To **Malargüe**, direct with Viento Sur minibuses,

US$15, 5 hrs, or with Cata, 6½ hrs, US$15; alternatively with Buttini, Cata or Iselin, for connection in San Rafael.

Transport to Santiago, Chile Minibuses (US$32, 6-7 hrs) run by Chi-Ar, Nevada and Radio Móvil daily Buses to Santiago daily, Cata Internacional US$42-57, 8 hrs, from *semi-cama* without service to **Royal Suite**. Also with Andesmar and El Rápido Internacional. Most buses and minibuses are comfortable enough, but it's worth paying for a good service as waiting time at the border can be several hours. Buses also go daily to **Viña del Mar** and **Valparaíso**. Information at Mendoza bus terminal: shop around. Book at least 1 day ahead. Passport required, tourist cards given on bus. The ride is spectacular.

There are also direct services, though not daily, to **Lima** (Perú) with Ormeño and El Rápido Internacional, to **Santa Cruz de la Sierra** (Bolivia) with Quirquincho, and to **Montevideo** (Uruguay), with El Rápido Internacional.

Car hire Most companies have their offices along C P de la Reta (900 block), next to Plaza Pellegrini.

⊙ Directory

Mendoza and around *p96, map p97*

Banks Open 0800-1245. Many ATMs on and around Plaza San Martín taking all cards. Many *casas de cambio* along San Martín, corner of Espejo/Catamarca. Most open till 2000 Mon-Fri (closing during siesta), and some open Sat morning. **Consulates** Chile, Belgrano 1080, T425 5024, cgchilmen@itcsa.net. **Language schools** Intercultural , República de Siria 241, T429 0269, www.spanishcourses.com.ar. **Medical facilities** Central hospital near bus terminal at Alem y Salta, T420 0600. Lagomaggiore, public general hospital (with good reputation) at Timoteo Gordillo s/n, T425 9700. Children's Hospital Notti, Bandera de los Andes 2603 (Guaymallén), T445 0045. **Useful addresses** Migraciones, San Juan 211, T424 3512. Unidad Policial de Asistencia al Turista, Av San Martín 1143, T413 2135, 24 hrs.

South of Mendoza

San Rafael → *Phone code: 0260. Colour map 8, B2. Population: department 191,323.*

San Rafael, 236 km south of Mendoza, is a tranquil, leafy town in the heart of fertile land which is irrigated by snow melt from the Andes to produce fine wines and fruit. A road runs southwest over El Pehuenche or Maule pass to Talca (Chile). Several bodegas and olive oil factories can be visited (check opening times at tourist office), including the impressive champagnerie at **Bianchii** ① *Ruta 143, 9 km west of centre, T444 9600, www.vbianchi.com.* Famiglia Bianchi's Reserva Malbec 2012 was awarded as the world's best red wine in the 'Vinalies Internationales 2014'. Some 3 km west is the more intimate **Jean Rivier** ① *H Yrigoyen 2385, T443 2675, www.jeanrivier.com.* Excellent wine. At a walking distance from town is **La Abeja** ① *Av H Yrigoyen 1900, T443 9804, www.bodegalaabeja.com.ar,* San Rafael's oldest winery. On the way out to Malargüe, around 20 km southwest of San Rafael is **Algodón Wine Estates** ① *on Ruta 144, Cuadro Benegas, T442 9020, www.algodonwineestates.com* A state-of-the-art winery with pricey accommodation, restaurant, tennis courts and a golf course. A small but interesting **natural history museum** ① *daily 0800-1900, US$0.70; Iselin bus along Av JA Balloffet,* is 6 km southwest of town at Isla Río Diamante. **Tourist office** ① *Av H Yrigoyen 775 y Balloffet, T443 7860, www.sanrafaelturismo.gov.ar, and in bus terminal (mornings only).*

Southwest of San Rafael, 35 km, is the **Cañón del Atuel**, a spectacular gorge 55 km long with strange polychrome rock formations, home of the Andean condor. It is famous as a rafting centre. Daily buses, **Iselin** (see Transport), go to the Valle Grande dam at the near end of the canyon, returning in the evening, US$2.50. Remise taxis from San Rafael to Valle Grande charge about US$20. Here there is plenty of accommodation, campsites, river rafting, zip lining, paragliding and horse riding. The only public transport through the entire gorge up to El Nihuil is **Iselin** bus at weekends in summer.

Las Leñas → *Altitude: 2240 m. Ski season: mid-Jun to end-Oct. T011-4819 6060, or T0800-222 5362, www.laslenas.com.*

At 154 km southwest of San Rafael, Route 222 heads west into the Andes from RN 40 to the chic (ie expensive) ski resort of Las Leñas. It passes **Los Molles**, at Km 30, where there is an increasing number of accommodation and eating choices, and thermal springs. Further along the Las Leñas road is the **Pozo de las Animas**, two natural pits filled with water where the wind makes a ghostly wail, hence the name (Well of the Spirits). At the end of Valle de Los Molles is Las Leñas, in a spectacular setting with excellent skiing over 170 sq km on 29 pistes, with a maximum drop of 1200 m. It offers many summer adventure activities, too. Beyond Las Leñas the road continues into Valle Hermoso, accessible December to March only.

Malargüe → *Phone code: 0260. Colour map 8, B2. Population: department 27,660.*

Further south on Ruta 40, Malargüe is developing as a base for excursions and several outdoor activities in stunning open landscape nearby. Most remarkable and one of Argentina's most dramatic landscapes, **La Payunia Reserve** ① *access only by guided tour from La Pasarela, 120 km south,* has vast grasslands and stark volcanoes where thousands of guanacos roam. After snowy winters, **Laguna Llancanelo**, 75 km southeast, is usually filled with a great variety of birdlife in spring, when Chilean flamingos come to nest. In addition, **Caverna de las Brujas** has extraordinary underground cave formations. Other impressive sights include a handful of magnificent high Andean valleys and the unusual rock formations of **Volcán Malacara** and **Castillos de Pincheira**. Furthermore, Malargüe has gained the interest of astrophysicists by hosting the world's largest **Pierre Auger Cosmic Ray Observatory** ① *Av San Martín (Norte) 304,*

T447 1562, www.auger.org, free lectures Mon-Fri 1700 (ask in advance for English presentations). A visit is recommended together with the excellent **Planetarium** ① *Cdte Rodríguez (Oeste) 207, T447 2116, www.planetariomalargue.com.ar, free guided visits and daily shows (US$4)*. At the northern access and by a large park with beautiful shade (site of the first estancia) is the helpful **tourist office** ① *Ruta 40 Norte, T447 1659, www.malargue.gov.ar, 0800-2130*, also at the bus station.

◉ South of Mendoza listings

For hotel and restaurant price codes, and other relevant information, see Essentials.

◉ Where to stay

San Rafael *p103*
$$$ Nuevo Mundo, Av Balloffet 725, T444 5666, www.hnmsanrafael.com. Small business hotel, a little out of town, with pool, restaurant and spa.
$$ San Rafael, C Day 30, T443 0127, www.hotelsanrafael.com.ar. A decent and reasonably priced option with plain rooms yet in need of renovation.
$$ Francia, Francia 248, T442 9351, www.alojamientofrancia.com.ar. A lovely place on a quiet street in town with simple, functional rooms in a manicured garden; excellent value.
$$ Regine, Independencia 623, T442 1470, www.hotelregine.com.ar. Some 8 blocks from centre, a comfortable choice with good rooms, restaurant and a large pool in an attractive garden. Very good value.
$ pp Tierrasoles Hostel, Alsina 245, T443 3449, www.tierrasoles.com.ar. 5 blocks from bus station, small dorms for 6 to 8 and doubles (**$$**) in a nice residence with a backyard. HI discounts.
$ pp Trotamundos Hostel, Barcala 298, T443 2795, www.trotamundoshostel.com.ar. On a quiet area next to main streets, a lively hostel with a nice patio, small dorms for 3 to 6 and a private double (**$$**).

Las Leñas *p103*
There are several plush hotels, all **$$$$-$$$**, and most with pool (see www.laslenas.com). Plus a disco, shop renting equipment

and several restaurants. For cheaper accommodation stay in Los Molles or Malargüe.

Los Molles
Cheaper options than Las Leñas.
$$$ Complejo Los Molles, T15-459 1654, www.complejolosmolles.com. Wood and stone detached houses, plain and comfortable, for 4 up to 8 people with breakfast. Restaurant and ski rental.
$$$ Hotel Termas Lahuen-Có, T449 9700, www.hotellahuenco.com. Dating from 1930s, and now rather kitsch, with thermal baths, meals.
$$$ La Valtellina, T15-440 2761, www.la valtellina.com.ar. Attractively rustic Alpine cottages, Italian owned and run, with an excellent restaurant and tea house.

Malargüe *p103*
$$$ Malargüe, Av San Martín (Norte) 1230, T447 2300, www.hotelmalarguesuite.com. On the northern access to town, this comfortable 4-star hotel has a new wing with slightly bigger rooms, an indoor pool, restaurant, spa and a casino to open in 2015.
$$ Rioma, Fray Inalicán (Oeste) 127, T447 1065, www.hotelrioma.com.ar. Small, family-run and spotless place with basic facilities. Convenient for its pool and proximity to bus station.
$ pp Eco Hostel Malargüe, Prol Constitución Nacional (Finca No 65), Colonia Pehuenche, 5 km from centre, T447 0391, www.hostel malargue.com. Eco-hostel built with an enhanced traditional quincha method, in rural surroundings, on dairy farm with organic fruit and veg, good meals, basic, comfortable dorms and rooms (**$$**), cheaper without bath and HI discount, Choique travel agency.

🍴 Restaurants

San Rafael p103

$$$ El Rey del Chivo, Av H Yrigoyen 651.
A good and basic place for the regional
speciality, *chivito* (kid).

$$$ Pettra, Av H Yrigoyen 1750. Very good
choice for a great range of meals in an area
full of restaurants.

$$ Nina, Av San Martín y Olascoaga. A casual place
on a central corner for a light meal, including
fine salads, and an open-air café open till late.

An area of attractive open-air cafés and
small restaurants lies along C Pellegrini
between Chile and Day in town

$$$-$$ Las Duelas, Pellegrini 190. For tasty
sandwiches and salads.

La Delicia del Boulevard, Av H Yrigoyen 1594.
Very good ice cream on the way to wineries.

Malargüe p103

$$$ La Cima, Av San Martín (Norte) 886.
Parrilla and more elaborate meals, including
fish. Good value.

$$$-$$ El Chuma, Illescas (Oeste) 155.
The place for trying *chivito*.

$$ Bonafide, Av San Martín (Sur) 364.
Very good café open till late, serving
also simple meals, including good pizza

$$ La Posta, Av Roca (Este) 174. Popular
parrilla, offering pastas and pizza too.

⚙ What to do

San Rafael p103

Tour operators charge similar prices for same
conventional excursions, including the most
popular day-tour to Cañón del Atuel for about
US\$35 pp (lunch and extra activities are not
included). Ask in advance for tours in English.

Atuel Travel, Buenos Aires 31, T4429282, www.
atueltravel.com.ar. A recommended agency.

Raffeish, In Valle Grande, T443 6996,
www.raffeish.com.ar. Recommended
as most professional rafting company.

Renta Bike, Day 487, T15-440 1236, www.
renta-bike.com.ar. Bike rental, wine tours and
excursions along Cañón del Atuel.

Malargüe p103

Tour operators charge similar rates for same
excursions (eg Payunia for about US\$70 pp),
which take a full day in most cases and may
include a light meal. 2-day trekking in Payunia,
fly-fishing, rafting and several-day horse rides
in the Andes, including the approach to the
remains of the crashed Uruguayan airplane
(described in the film *Alive*) are also available,
though some activities are in summer only.
Ask in advance for tours in English.

A recommended range of tours is offered
by **Choique**, Av San Martín (Sur) 33, T447
0391, www.choique.com, and **Karen
Travel**, Av San Martín (Sur) 54, T447 2226,
www.karen travel.com.ar.

Some 30 km south of Malargüe, in the
Cuesta del Chihuido area on Ruta 40, are
Manqui Malal, T447 2567, and **Turcará**, T15-
453 5908, where trekking, zip lining, camping
and meals are offered.

🚌 Transport

San Rafael p103

Air Airport 7 km west of town. Buttini bus,
US\$1.20. Remise taxis, US\$7. To/from **Buenos
Aires** with Aerolíneas Argentinas/Austral.

Bus Terminal at General Paz y Paunero, 10-min
walk to centre. To/from **Mendoza**, 3-3½ hrs,
many daily, US\$7.50-9.50; **Neuquén**, US\$37-48,
7-9½ hrs. To **Buenos Aires**, 12½-14 hrs, US\$74-
98. To **Valle Grande**, 1-1½ hrs, US\$2.50, with
Iselin. To **Las Leñas** and **Malargüe**, see below.
To **Talca** (Chile), via Paso Pehuenche or Maule,
once weekly (snow may occasionally block the
road), 9 hrs, US\$37.50, with Cata.

For wineries west of town, take **Buttini** bus
(destination 25 de Mayo) along C Avellaneda
and then Av H Yrigoyen, and tell the driver the
bodega you want to visit.

Las Leñas p103

Bus From **Mendoza**, change bus in **San
Rafael**. From San Rafael, 1 a day in winter
holidays (3 weekly rest of year) with Iselín,
US\$8.50, and **Cata** buses and several transfer
services from Malargüe in winter holidays only.

Malargüe *p103*

Air Only chartered flights from Buenos Aires and São Paulo (Brazil) in the skiing season.

Bus Terminal at Aldao y Beltrán. To **Mendoza**, direct daily with **Viento Sur** minibuses, 5 hrs, US$15; or with **Cata**, 6½ hrs, US$15; alternatively with bus connection in San Rafael. To **San Rafael**, 2½-3 hrs, US$7.50, with

Buttini, Cata or Iselin. Cata leaves twice weekly either to **Agua Escondida**, on La Pampa border (across Payunia), and to **Barrancas**, on Neuquén border (along Ruta 40).

To **Neuquén** (via Ruta 40 and Rincón de los Sauces), Sun-Fri 2115, with **Leader/Rincón** from Los Amigos bar, Av San Martín (Sur) 765, by the clock tower.

Mendoza to Chile

From Mendoza to the Chilean border is 210 km on Ruta 7, the only route for motorists. Leave the city south by Avenida Pedro Molina/Rondeau, Acceso Este, Acceso Sur/Ruta 40, to the junction where Ruta 7 turns west and follow signs to Potrerillos, Uspallata and Chile. In the mountains, the road may blocked by snow and ice in winter: if travelling by car in June to October enquire about road conditions and requirements for snow chains and a shovel in Mendoza before setting out (www.vialidad.mendoza.gov.ar and www.gendarmeria.gov.ar).

Potrerillos and Uspallata → *Phone code: 02624. Colour map 8, A1.*

Potrerillos is a pretty village for horse riding, walking and rafting. In summer a two-day hike passing from desert steppe to scenic peaks goes from Potrerillos to **Vallecitos** ① *Refugio San Bernardo, T15-454 9099, www.alpes-andes-location.com*, French-run mountain hut at 2800 m. Vallecitos is a tiny ski resort 26 km from Potrerillos along a winding *ripio* road (season July-September). **Los Penitentes** ① *187 km west of Mendoza, on the road to Chile, T420356, www. penitentesweb.com*, is a much better ski resort at 2600 m, named after its majestic mass of pinnacled rocks, looking like a horde of cowled monks. Both Vallecitos and Los Penitentes are used as acclimatization areas before attempting the ascent of Aconcagua.

Another recommended stopping point is the picturesque village of **Uspallata** ① *52 km from Potrerillos, www.turismo.lasheras.gov.ar*. From here you can explore the mysterious white, egg-shaped domes of Las Bóvedas (2 km on RN 149 north; entry US$2), built in the early 19th-century to smelt metals, where there is a small, interesting museum. The RN 149 leads north to Barreal and Calingasta (see page 110), unpaved for its first part, rough and tricky when the snow melts and floods it in summer. The tourist office in Uspallata keeps unreliable hours.

Puente del Inca → *Colour map 8, B2. Altitude: 2,718 m.*

The road that leads from Uspallata to cross the border to Chile is one of the most dramatic in Argentina, climbing through a gorge of richly coloured rock. Surrounded by mountains of great grandeur, Puente del Inca, 72 km west of Uspallata, is a good base for trekking or exploring on horseback. The natural bridge after which the place is named is one of the wonders of South America. Bright ochre yellow, it crosses the Río de las Cuevas at a height of 27 m, has a span of 48 m, and is 28 m wide, and seems to have been formed by sulphur-bearing hot springs. The bridge itself cannot be crossed. There are the remains of a thermal bath complex at the river just under the bridge. Horse treks go to Los Penitentes. Los Horcones, the Argentine customs post (dealing with all Argentine entry formalities), is 1 km west. Some 2 km further west is the access to Parque Provincial Aconcagua, from where a road leads over 1 km north to a ranger station: from here you can walk to the green lake of Laguna de Horcones (US$2.50 entry), excellent views of Aconcagua, especially morning. The trail continues either to Confluencia, Plaza de Mulas or Plaza Francia base camps. Five kilometres west from Puente del Inca is **Los Puquios**

① www.lospuquios.com.ar, a small family-oriented ski centre, which in summer provides assistance to climbing expeditions, including a camping ground.

Aconcagua → *Colour map 8, B1. Altitude: 6962 m.*

West of Puente del Inca on the right, there is a good view of Aconcagua, the highest peak in the Americas, sharply silhouetted against the blue sky. In 1985, a complete Inca mummy was discovered at 5300 m on the mountain. The best time for climbing Aconcagua is from mid-November to mid-February. For camping, trekking or climbing it is first necessary to obtain a **permit**. These have several price ranges with fees modified with every year: for summer (high, mid or low season) and winter (1 March to 30 April and 1 May to 14 November), the chosen access route and whether you are going alone or with a guide. Permits allow climbing, 20 days from the date that is stamped at the park entrance: long treks, seven days, and short treks, three days. A permit for foreigners to climb Aconcagua cost from US$438 to US$975 in 2013-14. In winter, climbing cost US$813. Seven-day treks were US$175-263 (summer), US$263 (winter); short treks cost US$88-138 (summer and winter). Treks may not go beyond base camps. Permits must be bought, in person only at **Centro de Visitantes (Subsecretaría de Turismo)** ① *Av San Martín 1143, p 1, Mendoza, T425 8751, Mon-Fri 0800-1800, Sat-Sun and holidays 0900-1300 from Nov-Apr (Mon-Fri 0800-1300 May-Oct).* All information, regulations and advice can be found on the official website: www.aconcagua.mendoza.gov.ar.

There are two access routes: Río Horcones and Río Vacas, which lead to the two main base camps, Plaza de Mulas and Plaza Argentina respectively. Río Horcones starts a few kilometres west from Puente del Inca, at the Horcones ranger station (open 0800-2000). About 70% of climbers use this route. From here you can go to Plaza de Mulas (4370 m) for the North Face, or Plaza Francia (4200 m) for the South Face. The intermediate camp for either is Confluencia (3300 m), four hours from Horcones. Río Vacas is the access for those wishing to climb the highly risky Polish Glacier. The Plaza Argentina base camp (4200 m) is three days from Punta de Vacas and the intermediate camps are Pampa de Leñas and Casa de Piedra. From Puente del Inca, mules are available (US$90-360 per mule for 60 kg of gear, price is one way only and varies according to destination base camp). This only takes you to Plaza de Mulas, where are an accident prevention and medical assistance service (climbing season only), and a camping area (crowded in summer). The same service is offered at Plaza Argentina in high season. Climbers should make use of this service to check for early symptoms of mountain sickness and oedema. Take a tent able to withstand 100 mph/160 kph winds, and clothing and sleeping gear for temperatures below 40°C. Allow at least eight to 10 days for acclimatization at lower altitudes before attempting the summit (four days ideally from Plaza de Mulas).

In Mendoza you can book programmes, which include trekking, or climbing to the summit, with all equipment and camping included (see Tour operators, above). A full list of authorized guides and agencies is published on Aconcagua's official website.

Treks and climbs are also organized by the famous climber **Sr Fernando Grajales** ① *T1-800-516 6962 (US toll free), www.grajales.net.*

Border with Chile

The road to the Chilean border, fully paved, goes through the 3.1-km Cristo Redentor toll road tunnel to Chile (open 24 hours; US$2 for cars, cyclists are not allowed to ride through, ask the officials to help you get a lift). The last settlement before the tunnel is tiny forlorn **Las Cuevas**, 16 km from Puente del Inca, with hostel accommodation, two restaurants, a basic café and a *kiosko*. In summer you can take the old road over La Cumbre pass to the statue of El Cristo Redentor (Christ the Redeemer), a 7-m statue erected jointly by Chile and Argentina in 1904 to celebrate the settlement of their boundary dispute. Take an all day excursion from Mendoza, drive in a 4WD, after snow has melted, or walk from Las Cuevas (4½ hours up, two hours down – only to be attempted by the fit, in good weather).

The Chilean border is beyond Las Cuevas, and all Argentine exit formalities for cars and buses are dealt with at the Chilean customs post, open 24 hours (0800-2000 in winter).

⦿ Mendoza to Chile listings

For hotel and restaurant price codes, and other relevant information, see Essentials.

⦿ Where to stay

Potrerillos and Uspallata *p106*
Potrerillos
$$$ Silver Cord B&B, Valle del Sol, T02624-481083, www.silvercordbb.com.ar. With breakfast, internet, laundry service, lots of outdoor activities and 4WD trips, guides speak English.
Camping Excellent ACA site, T482013. Shady, hot water after 1800, pool, clean.

Los Penitentes
$$ pp Hostería Penitentes, Villa Los Penitentes, T0261-524 4708, www.hosteria penitentes.com.Cheery place near ski slopes, with breakfast, good café, cheaper for several nights. Recommended.
$ pp Campo Base Penitentes, T0261-425 5511, www.penitentes.com.ar. A cheap ski resort option, lively, slightly cramped dorms, shared bath, restaurant, bar, minibus service to Mendoza. Hostel is open all year, offers ski programmes in season. HI discounts.

Uspallata
$$$ Gran Hotel Uspallata, on RN 7, Km 1149, towards Chile, T02624-420449, www.granhotel uspallata.com.ar. Lovely location, spacious and modern in big gardens away from the centre, pool, good value, restaurant.
$$$ Los Cóndores, Las Heras s/n, T02624-420002, www.loscondoreshotel.com.ar. Low season prices, bright, neat rooms, good restaurant (dinners only), heated pool.

$$$ Valle Andino, Ruta 7, T02624-420095, www.hotelvalleandino.com. Modern airy place, good rooms, heated pool, restaurant, breakfast included.
$ pp Mountain Chill Out Hostel (officially Hostel Internacional Uspallata), RN 7, Km 1141.5, T0261-575 9204, www.hosteluspallata.com.ar. Dorms for 4 to 6 with or without bath, private rooms sleep 1-6, with bath (**$$$-$$**), also comfortable cabins for up to 5, discounts for HI members, bar, restaurant, tours arranged, bike and ski rental, attractive surroundings.

Puente del Inca *p106*
$$$ Hostería Puente del Inca, RN7, Km 175, T0261-423 4848, http://hosteriapuentedelinca. onlinetravel.com.ar. Next to the small ski centre at Los Puquios. Full-board available, huge cosy dining room, advice on Aconcagua, helpful owners, great atmosphere.
Camping At Los Puquios.

Border with Chile *p107*
$ pp Arco de las Cuevas, Las Cuevas, T0261-516 6034, arcodelascuevas@gmail.com. Above the old road to Cristo Redentor. Spartan but comfortable dorms, use of kitchen extra, restaurant and bar. Transfer to Aconcagua park US$8.

⦿ Restaurants

Potrerillos and Uspallata *p106*
Potrerillos
$$$-$$ Tomillo, Av Los Cóndores, El Salto, T02624-483072, www.tomillorestaurant. com.ar. Open all day (closed Tue and Wed in low season). Excellent homemade cooking, including trout. Also simple and warm accommodation in private doubles (**$$**).

Uspallata

$$$ La Estancia de Elías, Km 1146. Opposite petrol station, a good and crowded *parrilla*.

$$$-$$ Lo de Pato, RN7 Km 1148. The town's classic, popular *parrilla* and also pasta; take away food plus bakery.

❹ What to do

Potrerillos and Uspallata *p106*
Potrerillos
Argentina Rafting, base camp at Ruta Perilago, T02624-482037 (office at Amigorena 86, T0261-429 6325, Mendoza), www.argentina rafting.com. Reliable company, organizes good trips with climbing, hiking, kayaking and other adventure sports.

Uspallata

Desnivel Aventura, on route 7 by the YPF petrol station, T0261-15-589 2935, www. desnivelaventura.com. Offers rafting, riding, mountain biking, trekking, climbing, skiing.

❺ Transport

Puente del Inca *p106*
Bus Buttini (T0261-431 5932) from Mendoza several a day for **Potrerillos**, 1 hr, US$2.25 and **Uspallata**, 2¼ hrs, US$5.75, and **Puente del Inca** (3 a day), US$7, 4 hrs. Uspallata-Puente del Inca, US$3.75. Buttini continues twice a day from Puente del Inca to **Las Cuevas**, US$9 return. Buses going to Chile do not pick up passengers on the way.

San Juan and La Rioja

San Juan → *Phone code: 0264. Colour map 8, A2. Population: city 109,123; greater San Juan 480,000 (estimated). Altitude: 650 m.*

San Juan, 177 km north of Mendoza, was founded in 1562 and is capital of its namesake province. Nearly destroyed by a 1944 earthquake, the modern centre is well laid-out, but lacks Mendoza's charm and sophistication. **Tourist office** ① *Sarmiento Sur 24 y San Martín, T421 0004, turismo@ sanjuan.gov.ar, Mon-Fri 0700-2030, Sat-Sun and holidays 0900-2000, and at bus station*. See www. sanjuanlaestrelladelosandes.com.

Places in and around San Juan You're most likely to visit on the way to the national parks further north, but there are some *bodegas* worth visiting. See www.travelsanjuan.com.ar/vino. html for some suggestions of bodegas to visit. **Museo Casa Natal de Sarmiento** ① *Sarmiento Sur 21, T422 4603, Tue-Fri and Sun 0900-1900, Mon and Sat 0900-1500, US$2 (free Sun)*. This is the birthplace of Domingo Sarmiento (President of the Republic, 1868-1874). **Museo Histórico Celda de San Martín** ① *Laprida 57 Este, daily 1000-1300, 1600-1900, US$2*, includes the restored cloisters and two cells of the Convent of Santo Domingo. San Martín slept in one of these cells on his way to lead the crossing of the Andes. Opposite Plaza 25 de Mayo, take the lift to the top of Cathedral's campanile (53 m) for city views, daily 0930-1300, 1830-2130, US$1.25.

The University of San Juan's **Museo Arqueológico** ① *Acceso Sur entre C 5 y Progreso, Rawson, a few km south of the centre, T424 1424, www.ffha.unsj.edu.ar/gambier.htm, Mon-Fri 0800-1400, US$2, getting there: buses 15, 49, 50 from centre*, contains an outstanding collection of prehispanic indigenous artefacts, including several well-preserved mummies. **Vallecito**, 64 km east, has a famous shrine to the **Difunta Correa**, Argentina's most loved unofficial saint whose infant, according to legend, survived at her breast even after the mother's death from thirst in the desert. At roadsides everywhere you'll see mounds of plastic bottles left as offerings to ask for safe journeys, and during Holy Week 100,000 pilgrims visit the site. There is a remarkable collection of personal items left in tribute in several elaborate shrines; also cafés, toilets and souvenir stalls. Buses from San Juan to La Rioja stop here for five minutes, or **Vallecito** runs a couple of services a day.

West of San Juan → *Phone code: 02648.*

Calingasta, 170 km west of San Juan, is an idyllic, secluded village in a green valley with stunning striped rocks (cider festival in April). To reach Calingasta you go north of San Juan towards Talacasto, then take the paved Quebrada de las Burras road (Rutas 436, then 149) to Pachaco, where a bridge crosses the Río San Juan. Cyclists should note that there is no shade on these roads, fill up with water at every opportunity. Consult the police before cycling from Calingasta to San Juan. **Tourist information** ⓘ *Av Argentina s/n, T441066, www.calingastaturismo.gob.ar.*

Barreal (*phone code: 02648*), 40 km south of Calingasta on the road to Uspallata, is a tranquil place between the Andes and the precordillera. It has become a very attractive base for exploring the nearby mountains on foot, horseback or 4WD vehicles, including Cerro Mercedario (6770 m), Ansilta and Tontal mountain ranges plus a handful of over 6000 m peaks. The village itself is ideal for delightful bike riding along its peaceful rural roads, where dogs rarely bark, beneath the shade of willow and poplar trees, and with views of distant Aconcagua from higher sites. As well as visits to a small winery (www.entretapias.com) and a herb farm (www.demicampo.com.ar), rafting and fishing there is an additional wonderful experience: blokart sailing in the vast plain of Leoncito, 20 km south of Barreal. **Tourist office** ⓘ *Av Roca y Las Heras, T441066, daily 0900-2100.*

At **Parque Nacional El Leoncito**, access 26 km from Barreal, there are two observatories: **Cesco** ⓘ *T441087, centrohugomira@yahoo.com.ar, daily visits 1000-1200, 1600-1800 (US$2.50) and nocturnal visits with small telescopes observation, from sunset (US$6.25),* and **CASLEO** ⓘ *T441088, www.casleo.gov.ar, US$1.25, daily 1000-1200, 1500-1730 mid-Sep to mid-Mar (1000-1200, 1430-1700 mid-Mar to mid-Sep), phone in advance for night visits from 1700 with observation with small telescopes (US$13), also with dinner and accommodation (US$65 pp); no buses; tours from Barreal*

San Juan

To Calingasta, Barreal, Jáchal & La Serena (Chile)

To Airport, Difunta Correa, Valle Fértil, San Luis & La Rioja

Museo de Ciencias Naturales
Mercado Artesanal Tradicional

Maipú
Pedro Echagüe
25 de Mayo
San Luis
Av Libertador Gral San Martín
Plaza Laprida
Laprida
Rivadavia
Av José Ignacio de la Roza
Mitre
Santa Fe
Córdoba
Gral Paz

Museo Casa Natal de Sarmiento
Museo Histórico Celda de San Martín
Cathedral
Plaza 25 de Mayo

Maipú
Safra
Alem
Catamarca
Sarmiento
Entre Ríos
Mendoza
Gral M Acha
Tucumán
Rioja
Jujuy
Aberastain
Caseros
Güemes
Rawson
Santiago del Estero

Plaza Gertrudis Funes
Cambio Santiago
Plaza Aberastain
Palacio Municipal

To Calingasta
To 3
To 5

To Bus Terminal
To 3

9 de Julio

To Mendoza & Museo Arqueológico

N
300 metres
300 yards

Where to stay 🛏
1 Albertina
2 Alkázar
3 América
4 Gran Hotel Provincial
5 San Juan Hostel
6 Zonda

Restaurants 🍴
1 Club Sirio Libanés 'El Palito'
2 Las Leñas
3 Remolacha
4 Soychú
5 Tagore

or San Juan, and a **nature reserve** ① *office in Barreal at Cordillera de Ansilta s/n, T441240, www.elleoncito.gob.ar, free*, with an arid environment, an easy 2-km trail, a small waterfall, a four-hour trek to El Leoncito peak and interesting wildlife (including pumas), ranger post and a basic site for free camping with toilets at visitor's centre (take food and water).

Ischigualasto and Talampaya parks → *Phone code: 02646. Colour map 8, A2.*

Ruta 141 runs across the south of the province towards La Rioja province and Córdoba. Just after Marayes (133 km), paved Ruta 510 (poor in parts) goes north 114 km to **San Agustín del Valle Fértil**, the best base for exploring Ischigualasto. **Tourist information** ① *on plaza, T420104, www.vallefertilsanjuan.gob.ar.*

North of San Agustín, at a police checkpoint, 56 km by paved road, a side road goes northwest for 17 km to the 62,000 ha **Parque Provincial Ischigualasto** ① *Apr-Sep 0900-1600 (Oct-Mar 0900-1700), US$20, with reduced rates for Argentines; US$13 for full-moon entry,* (a UNESCO World Heritage Site), also known as **Valle de la Luna**. The site occupies an immense basin, which was once filled by a lake, between the scarlet red Barrancas Coloradas to the east and the green, black and grey rocks of Los Rastros to the west. The vegetation is arid scrub and bushes. For many, the attraction lies in the bizarre sculptural desert landforms dotted throughout the park's other-worldly terrain. They have been named after things that they resemble. The park's other fascination lies in the 250 million years of strata that you can see in the eroded cliffs where fossils from the Triassic period have been found. Here the skeletons of the oldest known dinosaurs have been discovered (230 million years), though you'll have to visit the museum at San Juan to see their bones and fossils. (**Museo de Ciencias Naturales** ① *España y Maipú, T421 6774, closed in 2014.*)

Tours and access to Ischigualasto park There is one tour route, lasting three hours, visiting part of the park but encompassing the most interesting sites. You have to follow a ranger in your own vehicle and it can be crowded at holiday times. There are also three to four-hour treks and full-moon visits. Full-day tours from San Juan (food and entry fee extra); tours also from San Agustín (in both towns, ask at tourist office). You can camp opposite the ranger station, US$6, which has a small museum, but bring all food and water; expensive *confitería* next to ranger station. More information on tours and fees at www.ischigualasto.gob.ar. ▶ *See also What to do, page 115.*

Just beyond the police checkpoint, near Los Baldecitos, paved Ruta 150 heads east to Patquía (through the attractive rock formations of El Chiflón park) and then to La Rioja or Chilecito. From the junction Ruta 76 heads north to Villa Unión (see page 116.) Some 61 km north of Los Baldecitos a paved road goes 14 km east to the 215,000-ha **Parque Nacional Talampaya** ① *office in Villa Unión, T03825-470356, www.talampaya.gov.ar, mid-Sep to Apr 0800-1800 (May to mid-Sep 0830-1730), US$7 for foreigners (valid 2 days)*, another collection of spectacular desert landforms and a UNESCO World Heritage Site. The park occupies the site of an ancient lake, where sediments have been eroded by water and wind for some 200 million years, forming a dramatic landscape of pale red hills. Numerous fossils have been found and some 600 year-old petroglyphs can be seen not far from the access to the gorge. Along the *cañón* of the Río Talampaya, extraordinary structures have been given popular names and, at one point, the gorge narrows to 80 m and rises to 143 m. A refreshing leafy spot in the centre of the gorge, 'the botanical garden', has amazingly diverse plants and trees. The end of the *cañón* is marked by the imposing cliffs of 'the cathedral' and the curious 'king on a camel'. 'The chessboard' and 'the monk', 53 m high, lie not far beyond the gorge, marking the end of the **Cañón de Talampaya**. The **Circuito Los Cajones** continues in the same direction up to '*los pizarrones*', an enormous wall of rock, covered with petroglyphs, and then to '*los cajones*', a narrow pass between rock walls. El Sendero del Triásico includes 16 life-sized replicas of dinosaurs. **Circuito Ciudad Perdida**, an area of high cliffs and a large number of breathtaking rock formations, and **Circuito Arco Iris**, a multi-coloured canyon, are other routes covered by organized tours, from Ruta 76 Km 133 (south of the main access).

Tours and access to Talampaya park Tour operators in San Agustín combine Talampaya with Ischigualasto. Those from La Rioja and Chilecito sometimes combine a visit with Ischigualasto (check if guide's fee and entrance is included). Independent access is possible: buses/combis linking La Rioja and Villa Unión stop at the park entrance (a 14-km walk to the *administración*), or better, at Pagancillo (village 30 km north), as most of the park wardens live there and offer free transfer to the park early in the morning. No private vehicles allowed beyond the administration. The park can only be visited on tours arranged at the *administración*: guided walks to Quebrada Don Eduardo, a secondary gorge, next to the canyon (three hours, US$16 pp) and the canyon itself (five hours, US$38 pp), also full-moon walks; guided bike rides (2½ hours, US$20 pp, cycle/helmet provided); combined bike and trekking, 4½ hours, US$32 pp, all run by **Asociación de Guías** ① *T03825-15-410288, talampaya@hotmail.com.ar*. Vehicle guided visits for Cañón de Talampaya (2½ hours, US$23 pp), Cañón de Talampaya and Los Cajones (4½ hours, US$37 pp), Cañón de Talampaya and Cajones de Shimpa (three hours, US$27 pp), and Cañón de Talampaya from a truck top (three hours, US$29 pp), are run by **Rolling Travel** ① *T0351-570 9909, www.talampaya.com*. From Ruta 76 Km 133, excursions to Ciudad Perdida and Arco Iris (both 4½ hours, US$45 for two people) are run by **Runacay** ① *www.runacay.com*. Best time to visit is in the morning, for natural light and avoiding strong afternoon winds. *Administración* has small restaurant, toilets, public telephones.

La Rioja → *Phone code: 0380. Colour map 8, A2. Population: department 180,995.*

Founded 1591, at the edge of the plains, with views of Sierra de Velasco, La Rioja can be oppressively hot from November to March. But the town comes alive after the daily siesta and during the annual carnival, **Chaya** (in February), and the **Tinkunaco** festival (beginning on New Year's Eve and lasting four days). The city's main buildings and plazas date from the late 19th century. The **Church and Convent of San Francisco** ① *25 de Mayo y Bazán y Bustos, Tue-Sun 0900-1200, 1830-2100, free*, contains the Niño Alcalde, a remarkable image of the infant Jesus. You can also see the cell (*celda*) in which San Francisco Solano lived and the orange tree, now dead, which he planted in 1592 (25 de Mayo 218). San Francisco helped to bring peace between the Spaniards and the indigenous people in 1593, an event celebrated at Tinkunaco. The **Convent of Santo Domingo** ① *Luna y Lamadrid*, dates from 1623, said to be the oldest surviving church in Argentina. **Museo Arqueológico Inca Huasi** ① *Alberdi 650, Tue-Fri 0900-1230, 1600-2000, Sat 0900-1300, US$1*, owned by the Franciscan Order, contains a huge collection of fine Diaguita Indian ceramics, considered among the most important pre-Hispanic artefacts in the country. The **Mercado Artesanal** ① *Luna 782, Tue-Sat 0900-1230, 1600-2000*, has expensive handicrafts. In a beautiful and well-kept house, the **Museo Folklórico** ① *Luna 802, T442 8500, Tue-Sat 0900-1230, 1600-2000, US$1.25, free guided visits*, gives a fascinating insight into traditional La Rioja life, with a superb collection of native deities, rustic wine-making machinery and delicate silver *mates*. Well worth a visit too for its leafy patio. **Tourist offices: municipal** ① *Av Perón 401, T447 0000 ext 337, Mon-Fri 0800-1300, 1600-2100, and on plaza opposite the Cathedral Mon-Fri 0800-1300, 1600-2100; Sat, Sun and holidays 0800-2100*; **provincial** ① *Av Ortiz de Ocampo y Av Félix de la Colina (opposite bus terminal), T442 6345, daily 0800-2100, www.turismolarioja.gov.ar*.

For hotel and restaurant price codes, and other relevant information, see Essentials.

◉ Where to stay

San Juan *p109, map p110*

$$$ Alkázar, Laprida 82 Este, T421 4965, www.alkazarhotel.com.ar. Comfortable rooms, sauna, pool, gym, well run, central, excellent restaurant.

$$$ América, 9 de Julio 1052 Este, T427 2701, www.hotel-america.com.ar. A good, quite comfortable choice if you need to be next to bus station.

$$$ Gran Hotel Provincial, Av J I de la Roza 132 Este, T430 9999, www.granhotelprovincial.com. Large, central, good rooms, pool, gym, restaurant.

$$$-$$ Albertina, Mitre 31 Este, T421 4222, www.hotelalbertina.com. Next to cinema on plaza, a small hotel with comfortable rooms, restaurant and jacuzzi in the Junior suites, no parking. Very good value.

$ pp San Juan Hostel, Av Córdoba 317 Este, T420 1835, www.sanjuanhostel.com. Kindly run by its owner, central, with dorms for 4 to 10, and private rooms with and without bath (**$$ $**), barbecues on rooftop, bike rental, tours arranged.

$ pp Zonda, Caseros 486 Sur, T420 1009, www.zondahostel.com.ar. Simple, light rooms, for 2-6, shared bath, room for 4 with bath (**$$**). Trips and Spanish lessons arranged. HI member discount.

West of San Juan *p110*
Barreal

$$$ Eco Posada El Mercedario, Av Roca y C de los Enamorados (Las Tres Esquinas), T0264-15-509 0907 or 02648-441167, www.elmercedario.com.ar. Built in 1928 on the northern edge of town, this lovely adobe building preserves a traditional atmosphere with renovated comfort in its good rooms; solar heated water, good value restaurant, a tiny pool in a large garden, bicycles and excursions arranged through their own agency **Ruta Sur**. Recommended.

$$$ El Alemán, Los Huarpes s/n, T441193, elalemanbarreal@gmail.com. Run by Perla, Bernhard and their daughter, very functional apartments for 2 to 4 (with solar heated water) facing a neat garden in a rural area next to the river. Restaurant with some German specialities.

$$$ Posada de Campo La Querencia, T0264-15-436 4699, www.laquerenciaposada.com. A few spotless comfortable rooms in a homely place south of town run by very attentive owners. Delicious breakfast, manicured park with a pool and magnificent views of the Andes.

$$$ Posada Paso de los Patos, Patricias Mendocinas y Gualino, T0264-463 4727, www.posadapasolospatos.com.ar. In a lovely location south of town with grand views, a stylish building with 10 well-equipped rooms facing the Andes, restaurant, pool, full and half-day bike rides to the nearby mountains.

$$$-$$ Posada San Eduardo, Av San Martín s/n, T441046, saneduardobarreal@yahoo.com.ar. Charming colonial-style house, simple rooms around a courtyard, superior rooms with fireplace, relaxing, beautiful park with a large pool, restaurant, horse rides.

$ pp Hostel Barreal, Av San Martín s/n, T441144, www.hostelbarreal.com. Neat, rooms with bath, lovely garden. Rafting, kayaks and excursions organized.

$ pp Hostel Don Lisandro, Av San Martín s/n, T0264-15-5059122, www.donlisandro.com.ar. In a house built in 1908, a few dorms in rustic style for 3 and 4 and doubles with or without bath (**$$-$**). Its table football is a gem. Trekking and excursions organized, including blokarting.

Camping Municipal site in C Belgrano, T0264-15-672 3914, shady, well-maintained, pool, open all year.

Ischigualasto and Talampaya parks *p111*
San Agustín del Valle Fértil

$$$ Hostería Valle Fértil, Rivadavia s/n, T420015, www.hosteriavallefertil.com. Good, a/c, smart, very comfortable, with fine views, also has *cabañas*, pool and good restaurant open to non-residents.

$ pp **Campo Base**, Tucumán entre Libertador y San Luis, T420063, www.hostelvalledelaluna.com.ar. HI affiliated, cheerful, private doubles ($$), small basic dorms for 4 to 8 (cheaper without a/c), shared bath, backyard with small pool, tours combining the 2 parks.

$ pp **Los Olivos**, Santa Fe y Tucumán, T420115, posada_losolivos@hotmail.com. Welcoming and simple hostel accommodation in dorms and a private double ($$), tours arranged.

Camping Municipal campsite, Calle Rivadavia, 10 blocks from plaza, T0264-15-470 3525, US$3.25 per tent.

Parque Nacional Talampaya

Several basic places in **Pagancillo**, many more and better options in Villa Unión (see below)

Camping Basic site next to *administración*, US$4.

La Rioja p112

A/c or fan are essential for summer nights. High season is during Jul winter holidays.

$$$ **King's**, Av Quiroga 1070, T442 2122, www.k-hotellarioja.com.ar. 4-star in need of renovation, buffet breakfast included, a/c, gym, pool.

$$$ **Plaza**, San Nicolás de Bari y 9 de Julio (on Plaza 25 de Mayo), T443 6290, www.plazahotel-larioja.com. Functional 4-star, pool on top floor, breakfast included, a/c. Superior rooms have balconies on plaza.

$$$ **Vincent Apart Hotel**, Santiago del Estero 10, T443 2326, www.vincentaparthotel.com.ar. Spotless flats for up to 4, a/c, with dining room, kitchen and fridge, breakfast included, excellent value.

$$ **Savoy**, San Nicolás de Bari y Roque A Luna, T442 6894, www.hotelsavoylarioja.com.ar. In a quiet residential area, tidy, comfortable, a/c, 2nd floor is best.

$ pp **Apacheta Hostel**, San Nicolás de Bari 669, T15-444 5445, www.apachetahostel.com.ar. Cheerfully decorated, well-run central hostel with dorms for 5 to 8 and a private double ($$).

Restaurants

San Juan p109, map p110

$$$ **Club Sirio Libanés ' Restaurant Palito'**, Entre Ríos 33 Sur. Pleasant, long-established, tasty food, some Middle Eastern dishes, including its 'arab potpourri', buffet. Recommended.

$$ **Remolacha**, Av de la Roza y Sarmiento, T422 7070. Stylish, warm atmosphere, great terrace on C Sarmiento, superb Italian-inspired menu, delicious steaks and pastas. Recommended.

$$ **Soychú**, Av de la Roza 223 Oeste, T422 1939. Great value vegetarian food. Highly recommended.

A lively area of bars and restaurants lies along Av San Martín Oeste (west of 1500 block) including:

$$$ **Las Leñas**, Av San Martín 1670 Oeste. Huge, popular parrilla.

$$ **Tagore**, Av San Martín 1556. Vegetarian meals for take away.

West of San Juan p111
Barreal

$$ **Isidoro**, Pres Roca s/n. In the middle of the village, for local dishes and wines, good value.

La Rioja p112

$$$ **El Nuevo Corral**, Av Quiroga y Rivadavia. Traditional rustic *comidas de campo* and good local wines.

$$$ **La Vieja Casona**, Rivadavia 425. Smart *parrilla*, offering *chivito* (kid).

$$ **La Aldea de la Virgen de Luján**, Rivadavia 756. Lively atmosphere, cheap and popular small place, including some Middle Eastern dishes.

Shopping

San Juan p109, map p110

San Juan is known for its fine bedspreads, blankets, saddle cloths and other items made from sheep and llama wool, fine leather, wooden plates and mortars and, of course, its wines. **Mercado Artesanal** Tradicional, Av España 330 Norte, sells woven blankets/saddlebags, knives and ponchos.

● What to do

San Juan *p109, map p110*
CH Travel, General Acha 714 Sur, T427 4160,
www.chtraveltur.com. Recommended for its
tours to Barreal, Valle de la Luna and 4-day
expeditions to Parque Nacional San Guillermo,
in the remote northern San Juan high plateau.
All great experiences at full moon.
Nerja Tours, Mendoza 353 Sur, T421 5214,
www.nerja-tours.com.ar. Good for local day trips
and adventure tourism inside the national parks.

West of San Juan *p110*
Barreal
Baho, T0264-524 3234 or 473 7283, baho
aventura@gmail.com and on Facebook.
4WD trips, trekking and quad bikes.
Don Lisandro Expediciones, Av San Martín
s/n, T0264-15-5059122, www.donlisandro.
com.ar. Full-day to several-day high altitude
treks in the Andes, including Laguna Blanca
and Balcón de los Seis Mil. Combined visit to
astronomical observatories and blokarting on
Pampa del Leoncito. Check available activities
in winter. Recommended.
Fortuna Viajes, Av Roca s/n (at Posada Don
Ramón, northern outskirts), T0264-15-404 0913.
1-week horseback crossing of the Andes led by
expert Ramón Ossa. Also trekking in the Andes
and 4WD excursions in Precordillera.
Ruta Sur, Av Roca y C de los Enamorados (at Eco
Posada El Mercedario), T441167 or T0264-15-
6619057. Bike tours and rental, 4WD excursions
to the Andes foothills and Precordillera.

Ischigualasto and Talampaya parks *p109*
Paula Tur, Tucumán s/n, San Agustín, T420096,
www.paula-tour.com.ar. Combined visits to
Ischigualasto, Talampaya and El Chiflón parks.

La Rioja *p112*
Corona del Inca, PB Luna 914, T445 0054,
www.coronadelinca.com.ar. Wide range of tours
to Talampaya, Valle de la Luna, Laguna Brava,
Corona del Inca crater, horse riding in Velasco
mountains and further afield, English spoken.

● Transport

San Juan *p109, map p110*
Air Chacritas Airport, 11 km southeast
on RN 20. Daily to/from **Buenos Aires** with
Aerolíneas Argentinas/Austral. Radio taxi
to centre, about US$10.
Bus Terminal at Estados Unidos y Santa Fe,
9 blocks east of centre (with almost all buses
going through the centre). T422 1604. **La Rioja**,
5½-7 hrs, US$30-43, many daily. **Chilecito**,
8 hrs, US$26, daily with Vallecito. **Tucumán**,
many daily, 11-14 hrs, US$55-80. **Córdoba**,
many daily, 8-14 hrs, US$40-49. **Buenos Aires**,
14-17 hrs, US$79-113 (Autotransportes San
Juan, San Juan Mar del Plata). **San Agustín** with
Vallecito, 3 a day (2 on Sun), 4 hrs, US$12. Hourly
departures to and from **Mendoza**, fares above.
Also to **Barreal** (3½ hrs, US$13) and **Calingasta**
(3 hrs, US$12), 2 a day with El Triunfo, T421 4532
(tell the driver your accommodation in Barreal,
as the bus stops en route).
Car hire Tréhol, Laprida 82 Este, T422 5935,
trebolrentacar@live.com.ar

West of San Juan *p110*
Barreal
Bus See above for San Juan; El Triunto bus
stops en route along main road (Av Roca); tickets
sold at YPF station, return to San Juan at 0300
(not on Sun), 1600 (and 1700 Mon and Fri only).

Ischigualasto and Talampaya parks *p111*
San Agustín del Valle Fértil
Bus Vallecito runs 3 services a day (2 on Sun)
to **San Juan**, see above. 3 buses a week to
La Rioja, 4 hrs, US$11.

La Rioja *p112*
Air Airport 5 km northeast, via San Nicolás
de Bari, RP5, T443 9211. To **Buenos Aires** daily
with Austral.
Bus Terminal is several km from the centre,
T442 5453; Minibus and bus No 2 takes 15 mins,
US$0.40, taxi US$4, or 45 mins' walk. To **Buenos
Aires**, Urquiza and Chevallier US$81-108,
13½-17 hrs. To **Mendoza**, US$42-60, 8-9½ hrs,
many companies, and **San Juan** (see above).

To **Tucumán**, US$26-31, 5-7 hrs. To **Villa Unión**, 4 companies daily, 4 hrs, US$12. To **Chilecito**, several daily, 3 hrs, US$8. Minibuses run provincial services, faster and more frequent than buses, but costing a little more. They have their own terminal at Artigas y España.

⊙ Directory

San Juan p109, map p110
Banks Banks 0800-1300. Banelco and Link ATMs in town.

La Rioja p112
Banks ATMs on San Nicolás de Bari.

Ruta 40 north of San Juan

Ruta 40, the principal tourist route on the east Andean slope, heads north from San Juan towards Cafayate and Salta. At Talacasto, 57 km from San Juan, Ruta 436 branches toward Las Flores (joining Ruta 149 23 km after Talacasto). From Las Flores, 180 km from San Juan, Ruta 150 goes up to the Chilean border at Agua Negra pass (4765 m; 0800-1800, but frequently closed by snow, immigration, customs and ACA at Las Flores, T02647-497047).

Villa Unión → *Phone code: 03825. Colour map 8, A2.*

San José de Jachal, 99 km north of Talacasto is a wine- and olive-growing centre with many adobe buildings. From here, the undulating Ruta 40, mostly paved, crosses dozens of dry watercourses. It continues paved to **Villa Unión** (www.turismovillaunion.gov.ar), an alternative base for visiting Parque Nacional Talampaya. The town has hotels, a campsite behind the ACA station and places to eat. From here excursions can be made by four-wheel drive vehicle to the remote **Reserva Provincial Laguna Brava**, 180 km north. The road goes through **Vinchina** and Jagüe (both have basic facilities). As you climb the Portezuelo del Peñón, the salt lake of Laguna Brava becomes visible with some of the mightiest volcanoes on earth in the background. Vicuña and flamingos may be seen in the reserve. Tours are run by Runacay ⓘ *in Villa Unión, T03825-470368, www.runacay.com (also has Hostel Laguna Brava in town)*, and La Rioja and Chilecito operators.

Ruta 40 heads east from Villa Unión through the Cuesta de Miranda (2020 m) before descending through a deep narrow canyon in a series of hairpins to Nonogasta (92 km from Villa Unión).

Chilecito → *Phone code: 03825. Colour map 8, A2. Population: department 49,432.*

Chilecito, 16 km north of Nonogasta, is La Rioja province's second town. Founded in 1715, it has good views of Sierra de Famatina, especially from the top of El Portezuelo, an easy climb from the end of Calle El Maestro. The region is famous for its wines, olives and walnuts. **Finca Samay Huasi** ⓘ *3 km south, T422629, Mon-Fri 0800-1900, Sat-Sun 0800-1200, 1400-1800 (closed 22 Dec-6 Jan), US$1.25*, was the house of Joaquín V González, founder of La Plata University. He designed the gardens with native trees and strange stone monoliths expressing his love of ancient cultures; there's also a small natural history museum. It's an attractive place for a relaxing day; overnight guests welcome (book in advance). **Molino San Francisco y Museo de Chilecito** ⓘ *J de Ocampo 50, Mon-Fri 0800-1200, 1600-1930, Sat-Sun 0800-2000, US$1.25*, has archaeological, historical and artistic exhibits. At the **Cooperativa La Riojana** ⓘ *La Plata 646, T423150, www.lariojana.com.ar*, there are free guided visits (45 minutes), you can watch local grapes being processed to make a wide variety of wines, including organic products; also a smart wine shop open in the mornings. At **Santa Florentina** (8 km northwest), there are the impressive remains of a huge early 20th century foundry, linked to Chilecito and La Mejicana mine by cable car. **Tourist office** ① *Castro y Bazán 52, T422688, www.emutur.com.ar, daily 0800-1230, 1530-2100*, also at the bus station.

North of Chilecito

From Chilecito it's 126 km to the junction with Ruta 60 at the Catamarca/La Rioja border. Beyond, the desert is spectacular, with a distinct culture and remote untouristy towns. From La Rioja city it's most easily reached by the paved Ruta 75 to **Aimogasta** (41 km south of the Ruta 40 junction) and on to the small settlements of Tinogasta and Fiambalá, useful staging posts if taking the Paso San Francisco to Chile, or north on Ruta 40 to Belén. The *Zonda*, a strong, dry mountain wind, can cause dramatic temperature increases.

Tinogasta (*Phone code: 03837*) is in an oasis of vineyards, olive groves, and poplars. It is the starting point for expeditions to Ojos del Salado (6891 m) and **Pissis** (6795 m), the second and third highest mountains in the Western hemisphere.

Fiambalá is 49 km north of Tinogasta, a peaceful place in a vine-filled valley, with **Termas de Fiambalá**, hot springs, situated 16 km east (take a taxi; make sure fare includes wait and return). 4WD vehicles may be hired for approaching the Pissis-Ojos del Salado region; ask at the Intendencia.

Border with Chile – Paso San Francisco

Fiambalá is the starting point for the crossing to Chile via Paso San Francisco (4726 m), 203 km northwest along a paved road. In summer the border is open 24 hours, T498001. On the Chilean side roads run to El Salvador and Copiapó. This route is closed by snow June to October; take enough fuel for at least 400 km as there are no service stations from Fiambalá to just before Copiapó.

Belén → *Phone code: 03835. Colour map 6, C3. Population: department 28,000. Altitude: 1255 m.*
Back on Ruta 40, the road is paved via **Londres**, a quiet, pretty village, to Belén. There are important prehispanic ruins at **El Shincal** (0700-1900), 7 km from Londres. The setting is superb, in a flat area between a crown of mountains and the river. Tours are run by **Ampujaco Tur** (General Roca 190, Belén, T461189), or at **Hotel Belén**. **Cóndor** buses, several times daily from Belén, stop 100 m from the ruins, US$2.50. Taxi from Belén about US$30 with wait.

Belén is an intimate little town, famous for its ponchos, saddlebags and rugs, which you can see being woven. The museum, **Cóndor Huasi** ① *San Martín y Belgrano, 1st floor, daily*, contains fascinating Diaguita artefacts, and there is a newly constructed Virgen (the last one was struck by lightning) on the Cerro de Nuestra Señora de Belén above town; good views. Important festival: **Nuestra Señora de Belén**, 24 December-6 January. **Tourist information** ① *bus terminal, near plaza, Rivadavia y Lavalle, T461304, http://belencunadelponchoturismo.blogspot.co.uk.*

North of Belén Ruta 40 runs another 176 km, partially paved, to Santa María at the provincial border with Tucumán (see page 122), and on to Cafayate (page 125). From El Eje, on Ruta 40 north of Belén, a paved road branches off north, then becoming Ruta 43 that heads 222 km north, mostly paved, through the Puna de Catamarca, past the breathtaking **Reserva Natural Laguna Blanca** (a Ramsar site), the distant enormous crater of Volcán Galán and **El Peñón** (Hostería del Altura El Peñón, www.hosteriaelpenon.com, **$$$** with bath, breakfast, restaurant, bar, Wi-Fi) to tiny remote **Antofagasta de la Sierra** (also with a *hostería*) and onwards to San Antonio de los Cobres in Salta. Trips to this region are run by **Socompa**, see page 134.

⊚ Ruta 40 north of San Juan listings

For hotel and restaurant price codes, and other relevant information, see Essentials.

⊜ Where to stay

Villa Unión *p116*

$$$ Cañón de Talampaya, on Ruta 76 Km 202 (on southern access), T470753, www.hotelcanontalampaya.com. Comfortable rooms in rustic style with a/c, restaurant serving some organic products, and a pool.

$$$ Hotel Pircas Negras, on Ruta 76 (on southern access), T470611, www.hotelpircas negras.com. Large modern building, comfortable rooms, restaurant and pool, excursions organized.

$$ Chakana, in Banda Florida, T03825-15-51 0168, chakanahospedaje@yahoo.com.ar. In rural surroundings across the river from Villa Unión, this charming little hotel is carefully run by Natalia and Martín, who also prepare very good meals.

$$ Hotel Noryanepat, JVGonzález 150, T470133, www.hotelnoryanepat.com.ar. Small rooms with a/c, good.

See also **Hostel Laguna Brava** of Runacay, page 116.

Chilecito *p116*

$$$ Chilecito (ACA), TGordillo y A G Ocampo, T422201, acachilecito@hotmail.com. Comfortable, renovated rooms, parking, pool, cheap set menus.

$$$ Hotel Ruta 40, Libertad 68, T422804, www.hotelruta40.com.ar. Family-run hotel with all services, including kitchen and laundry, bicycles, local produce for breakfast.

$$$ Posada del Sendero, Pasaje Spilimbergo, San Miguel, T03825-15-414041, www.posada delsendero.com.ar. In peaceful Chilecito's rural suburbs, a pleasant family-run place with simple rooms with a/c on a lovely park with pool. Excursions with own **Salir del cráter** agency.

$$ Hostal Mary Pérez, Florencio Dávila 280, T423156, hostal_mp@hotmail.com. Good value, comfortable, welcoming atmosphere, good breakfast. Recommended.

North of Chilecito *p117*
Tinogasta

$$$ Hotel de Adobe Casagrande, Moreno 801, T421140, www.casagrandetour.com. Individually designed rooms, bar, restaurant, pool, jacuzzi, can arrange tours and activities.

$$ Hotel Nicolás, Perón 231, T420028, www. nicolastinogasta.com.ar. Small, long-established hotel with breakfast, a/c, Wi-Fi, laundry, parking.

Fiambalá

$$ Hostería Municipal, Almagro s/n, T03837-496291. Good value, also restaurant.

$ pp Complejo Turístico, at the Termas, bookings at tourist office T03837-496250. With cabins, restaurant, also camping.

Belén *p117*

$$$ Belén, Belgrano y Cubas, T461501, www. belen cat.com.ar. Comfortable, restaurant, prices depend on day of arrival and excursions taken.

$$ Samai, Urquiza 349, T461320. Old fashioned but welcoming, homely little rooms with bath and fan.

⊘ Restaurants

Chilecito *p116*

$$$-$$ El Rancho de Ferrito, PB Luna 647, T422481. Popular *parrilla*, with local wines.

$$ La Rosa, Ocampo 149, T424693. Relaxing atmosphere, huge variety of pizzas, more extensive menu Fri and Sat.

⊙ What to do

Chilecito *p116*

This is an excellent base for amazing treks in the Famatina mountains and 1-day trips to Talampaya and Valle de la Luna.

Inka Ñan, 25 de Mayo 37, T422418, www.inkananturismo.tur.ar

Salir del cráter, contact at **Posada del Sendero** (see above) or T423854, www.salirdelcrater.com. ar. Trekking and 4WD trips around Chilecito, plus excursions to neighbouring provinces.

⊖ Transport

Chilecito *p116*
Bus Terminal on Av Perón, on south access to town. To **San Juan** with **Vallecito**, 8 hrs, US$26; to **La Rioja**, several times daily, US$8, 3 hrs. To **Córdoba**, US$35-39, 7-8 hrs, and **Buenos Aires**, US$84-92, 17 hrs, **Urquiza** (T423279).

North of Chilecito *p117*
Tinogasta
Bus To **Catamarca**, Empresa Gutiérrez (connection to Buenos Aires) and **Robledo**, 4-5 hrs, US$16.

Fiambalá
Bus Empresa Gutiérrez to **Catamarca** via Tinogasta. For Belén, change at Aimogasta.

Belén *p117*
Bus From Belén to **Santa María**, San Cayetano and Parra (connections there to Cafayate and Salta), daily, 4-5 hrs, US$11. **Tinogasta**, Robledo, 4 weekly, 2-3 hrs, US$8. To **El Peñón** and **Antofagasta de la Sierra**, El Antofagasteño, T03837-461152, Mon-Tue, return Mon, Fri, minimum 6 hrs to El Peñón, US$12, 11 hrs to Antofagasta, US$19. For more frequent services to **Catamarca** or **La Rioja**, take bus to Aimogasta, 2½ hrs, US$5.

Northwest Argentina

Two of the oldest cities in Argentina, Santiago del Estero and Tucumán, are at the start of the route to the fascinating Northwest. Both have some good museums and other sites of interest, but the summer heat may urge you to press on to the mountains. Of the two routes to the atmospheric city of Salta, the more beautiful is via Tafí del Valle, the wine-producing town of Cafayate and the dramatic canyon of the Quebrada de las Conchas or the equally enchanting Valles Calchaquíes. Pretty towns in arid landscapes, archaeological remains and the Andes in the distance make for a memorable journey.

Santiago del Estero → *Phone code: 0385. Colour map 6, C4. Population: 267,125. Altitude: 200 m, 395 km north of Córdoba, 159 km southeast of Tucumán*

Founded in 1553 by conquistadores pushing south from Peru, this is the oldest Argentine city, though little of its history is visible today. It's rather run down, but the people are relaxed and welcoming. On the **Plaza Libertad** stand the **Municipalidad** and the **Cathedral** (the fifth on the site, dating from 1877), with the Cabildo-like Prefectura of Police. In the convent of **Santo Domingo**, Urquiza y 25 de Mayo, is one of two copies of the 'Turin Shroud', given by Philip II to his 'beloved colonies of America'. On Plaza Lugones is the church of **San Francisco**, the oldest surviving church in the city, founded in 1565, with the cell of San Francisco Solano, patron saint of Tucumán, who stayed here in 1593. Beyond it is the pleasant **Parque Francisco de Aguirre**. A highly recommended museum, **Museo de Ciencias Antropológicas** ① *Avellaneda 353, T421 1380, www.wagnermuseo.gov.ar, Tue-Sun 0800-2000, free*, has an eclectic collection of prehispanic artefacts, exquisitely painted funerary urns, flattened skulls, anthropomorphic ceramics and musical instruments; fascinating, if poorly presented. Also interesting is the **Museo Histórico Provincial** ① *Urquiza 354, Mon-Fri 0700-1300, 1400-2000, Sat-Sun 1000-1200, free*. In a 200-year-old mansion, it has 18th- and 19th-century artefacts from wealthy local families. **Centro Cultural del Bicentenario de Santiago del Estero** ① *Libertad 439, T422 4858, www.ccbsantiago.gov.ar, 0900-1300, 1800-2200*, acts as an umbrella organization for all cultural activities in the city. **Carnival** is in February. **Tourist office** ① *Plaza Libertad 417, T421 4243, www.turismosantiago.gov.ar*.

⊕ Santiago del Estero listings

For hotel and restaurant price codes, and other relevant information, see Essentials.

⊟ Where to stay

Santiago del Estero *p119*
$$$ Carlos V, Independencia 110, T424 0303, www.carlosvhotel.com. Corner of the plaza, the city's most luxurious hotel, elegant rooms, pool, good restaurant, still good value for its range.
$$$ Centro, 9 de Julio 131, T421 9502, www.hotelcentro.com.ar. Nice décor, very comfortable, airy restaurant. Recommended.
$$$ Libertador, Catamarca 47, T421 9252, www.hotellibertadorsrl.com.ar. Smart and relaxing, spacious lounge, plain rooms, patio with pool (summer only), elegant restaurant, 5 blocks south of plaza in the better part of town.
$$$ Savoy, Peatonal Tucumán 39, T421 1234, www.savoysantiago.com.ar. Good option, characterful, art nouveau grandeur, swirling stairwell, large airy rooms, small pool.

$ pp Res Emaus, Av Moreno Sur 675, T421 5893. Good cheap choice, with bath and TV, helpful.

⊕ Restaurants

Santiago del Estero *p119*
$$ Mia Mamma, on the main plaza at 24 de Septiembre 15. A cheery place for *parrilla* and tasty pastas, with good salad for starters.

⊖ Transport

Santiago del Estero *p119*
Air Airport on northwest outskirts, T434 3654. Flights to **Buenos Aires** and **Tucumán**.
Bus At Perú y Chacabuco, bus information, T422 7091, www.tosde.com.ar. Terminal has toilets, *locutorio*, café, bar and kiosks. **Córdoba**, 6 hrs, US$28-35; **Salta**, 6-7 hrs, US$30-45.

Tucumán and around → *Phone code: 0381. Colour map 6, C4. Population: 548,866. Altitude: 450 m.*

San Miguel de Tucumán was founded by Spaniards coming south from Peru in 1565. Capital of a province rich in sugar, tobacco and citrus fruits, it is the biggest city in the north. It stands on a plain and is sweltering hot in summer (a 1230-1630 siesta is strictly observed); so retreat to the cooler mountain town of **Tafí del Valle** in the Sierra de Aconquija. **Tourist office** ⓘ *on the plaza, 24 de Septiembre 484, T422 2199/430 3644, www.tucumanturismo.gov.ar, Mon-Fri 0800-2200, Sat-Sun 0900-2100.* Also in the bus terminal.

Places in Tucumán
On the west side of the main Plaza Independencia is the ornate **Casa de Gobierno** and the **Museo Casa Padilla** ⓘ *25 de Mayo 36, Mon-Sat 0900-1230, 1600-1900, US$0.50*, with a small collection of art and antiques. Nearby, the church of **San Francisco**, has a picturesque façade. On the south side of Plaza Independencia is the **Cathedral**. A block south, the **Museo de Bellas Artes Timoteo Navarro** ⓘ *9 de Julio 36, T422 7300*, in a wonderfully restored building, has a large collection local and national art. Two blocks south is the interesting **Casa Histórica** ⓘ *Congreso 151, T431 0826, daily 1000-1800, US$1.20; son et lumière show in garden nightly (not Thu, not when raining) at 2030, US$2.50*, tickets also from tourist office on Plaza Independencia, no seats. Here, in 1816, the country's Declaration of Independence was drawn up.

East of the centre is the **Parque de Julio**, one of the finest urban parks in Argentina. Extending over 400 ha, it contains a wide range of sub-tropical trees as well as a lake and sports facilities.

The **Museo de la Industria Azucarera** ① *daily 0830-1800, free*, traces the development of the local sugar industry.

Tafí del Valle → *Phone code: 03867. Population: 15,000. Altitude: 1976 m.*

South of Tucumán at Acheral on RN38, Ruta 307 heads northwest out of the sugar cane fields to zigzag up through forested hills to a treeless plateau, before El Mollar and the Embalse La Angostura. Here the valley is greener and you descend gradually to Tafí del Valle, a small town and popular weekend retreat from the heat of Tucumán in the summer (106 km). It has a cool microclimate, and makes a good base for walking, with several peaks of the Sierra de Aconquija providing satisfying day-hikes. There's some excellent, if pricey, accommodation and a **cheese festival** in early February, with live music. **Tourist information** ① *Peotonal Los Farores, T0381-156 438337, www.tafidelvalle. com, daily 0800-2200. Map US$1.40.* Visit the **Capilla Jesuítica y Museo de La Banda** ① *T421685, Mon-Sat 0900-1900, Sun 0900-1600 (closing early off season), US$1, includes a guided tour,* southwest of town across bridge over Río Tafí, 500 m on left, an 18th-century chapel and 19th-century estancia, with museum of archaeology and religious art. **Museo de Mitos y Leyendas Casa Duende** ① *R 307, Km 58 T0381-156 408500, daily 1000-1900, US$2 for guided visit,* is a private museum concentrating on the gods, beliefs and environment of the people of the Valles Calchaquíes.

Tucumán

To Airport

To ⑥ (2 blocks)

To Train Station (2 blocks)

To Fundación Miguel Lillo

To San Javier

Corrientes
Honduras
Santiago del Estero
Haiti
San Juan
Guatemala
Cuba
Córdoba
Mercado del Norte
Mendoza
A Jacques
Río de Janeiro
Norte Supermarket
San Francisco
Francia
San Martín
Casa de Gobierno
Museo Casa Padilla
Plaza Independencia
Cathedral
24 de Septiembre
C Alvarez
Museo de Bellas Artes Timoteo Navarro
Ayacucho
Casa Histórica
San Lorenzo

Maipú
Muñecas
25 de Mayo
Junín
Salta
Lapríd
Rivadavia
Montegudo
Balcarce
Av Avelaneda
Pasaje Celedo Río Gutiérrez
Soldati
Parque 9 de Julio
9 de Julio
Buenos Aires
Chacabuco
Congreso
Las Heras
Entre Ríos
Moreno
Av Saenz Peña
Charcas
Díaz Velez
Av B Aráoz
Ruta 9 To Santiago del Estero & Buenos Aires
Shopping del Jardín

To ⑦

To ⑪

200 metres
200 yards

N

Amaicha, Quilmes and Santa María

From Tafí the road runs 56 km northwest over the 3040 m Infiernillo Pass (Km 85) with spectacular views and through grand arid landscape to **Amaicha del Valle** (*Population: 5000; Altitude: 1997 m; tourist information T03892 421198*) with the popular **Complejo Pachamama museum** ① *T421004, daily 0830-1200, 1400-1830 (closed Sun off season), US$2.50,* highly recommended, with overview of the Calchaquí culture, geology, tapestry for sale by Héctor Cruz, well-known Argentine sculptor and artist. From Amaicha the paved road continues north 15 km to the junction with Ruta 40.

Some 35 km north, and 5 km off the main road, are the striking ruins of **Quilmes** ① *0800-1800, US$2, includes guided tour and museum, with café, huge gift shop (museum and hotel closed in 2014)*. The setting is amazing, an intricate web of walls built into the mountain side, where 5000 members of a Diaguita tribe lived, resisting Inca, and then Spanish domination, before being marched off to Córdoba and to the Quilmes in Buenos Aires where the beer comes from. For a day's visit take 0600 Aconquija bus from Cafayate to Santa María, alight after an hour at stop 5 km from site, or take 0700 **El Indio** bus (not on Thursday) from Santa María; take 1130 bus back to Cafayate, US$3; otherwise tours run from Cafayate.

Santa María (department population: 22,548), 22 km south of Amaicha by paved road, is a delightful, untouristy small town with an interesting archaeology museum at the **Centro Cultural Yokavil** ① *corner of plaza, 0830-1300, 1700-2100, donation requested,* pleasant hotels and a municipal campsite. A helpful tourist kiosk is on the plaza, T03838-421083, with map and list of accommodation; also a *locutorio* and internet places, ATM on Mitre at Banco de la Nación (only one for miles). South of Santa María, Ruta 40 goes to Belén, see page 117.

Tucumán to Salta

The speedy route to Salta is via Rosario de la Frontera and Güemes. **Rosario de la Frontera** (*Phone code: 03876; Altitude: 769 m*), 130 km north of Tucumán, is a convenient place for a stop, with thermal springs 8 km away (www.hoteltermasalta.com.ar; also **ACA** *hostería*, www.aca.org.ar). About 20 km north is the historical post house, **Posta de Yatasto**, with museum, 2 km east of the main road; campsite. About 70 km north of Rosario de la Frontera, at Lumbreras, a road branches off Ruta 9 and runs 90 km northeast to the **Parque Nacional El Rey** ① *park office in Salta, España 366, T431 2683, www.parquesnacionales.gov.ar*, one of three cloudforest parks in the northwest. Stretching from heights of over 2300 m through jungle to the flat arid Chaco in the east, it contains a variety of animal and plant life. **Norte Trekking** ① *T0387-431 6616, www.nortetrekking.com*, and **Clark Expediciones** ① *T0387-497 1024, www.clarkexpediciones.com*, are licensed to run expeditions to the park; both are recommended as there is no public transport to the park. Although drier in winter, the access road is poor, not recommended for ordinary vehicles. Park roads are impassable in the wet, November to May.

◉ Tucumán and around listings

For hotel and restaurant price codes, and other relevant information, see Essentials.

◉ Where to stay

Tucumán *p120, map p121*
$$$$ Catalinas Park, Av Soldati 380, T450 2250, www.catalinaspark.com. The city's most comfortable, good value, luxurious hotel, overlooking Parque 9 de Julio, outstanding food and service, pool (open to non-residents), sauna, gym. Highly recommended.
$$$ Carlos V, 25 de Mayo 330, T431 1666, www.hotelcarlosv.com.ar. Central, good service, with elegant restaurant.

$$$ **Dallas**, Corrientes 985, T421 8500, www.
dallashotel.com.ar. Welcoming, nicely furnished
large rooms, good bathrooms. Recommended,
though far from centre.

$$$ **Mediterráneo**, 24 de Septiembre 364,
T431 0025, www.hotelmediterraneo.com.ar.
Good rooms, TV, a/c. 20-30% discount for
Footprint owners.

$$$ **Suites Garden Park**, Av Soldati 330, T431
0700, www.gardenparkhotel.com.ar. Smart,
welcoming 4-star, views over Parque 9 de Julio,
pool, gym, sauna, restaurant. Also apartments.

$$$-$$ **Miami**, Junín 580, 8 blocks from plaza,
T431 0265, www.hotelmiamitucuman.com.ar.
Good modern hotel, refurbished rooms, pool.

$$$-$$ **Versailles**, Crisóstomo Alvarez 481,
T422 9760, www.hotelversaillestuc.com.ar.
Comfortable beds though rooms a bit small,
good service, price depends on season.
Recommended.

$ pp **Backpacker's Tucumán**, Laprida 456,
T430 2716, www.backpackerstucuman.com.
Youth hostel with HI discounts in restored
house with quiet atmosphere, lovely patio,
basic dorms (US$10-12), English spoken,
good. Plus $$-$ double room without bath.

$ **Hostel OH!**, Santa Fé 930, T430 8849,
www.hosteloh.com.ar. Neat, modern hostel
with shared (US$12-14 pp) or private rooms,
quiet, *parrilla*, pool, games, garden.

$ **Tucumán Hostel**, Buenos Aires 669, T420
1584, www.tucumanhostel.com. HI hostel in a
refurbished building. Large, high-ceiling dorms
(US$10-12), double rooms with and without
bath. Slightly unkempt but chilled garden.
Recommended.

Tafí del Valle *p121*

Many places, including hotels, close out of season.

$$$ **Hostería Tafí del Valle**, Av San Martín y
Gdor Campero, T421027, www.soldelvalle.com.ar.
Right at the top of the town, with splendid views,
good restaurant, luxurious small rooms, pool.

$$$ **La Rosada**, Belgrano 322, T421323,
http://larosadatafi.com. Spacious rooms, well
decorated, plenty of hot water, comfortable,
excellent breakfast included, helpful staff, lots
of expeditions on offer and free use of cycles.

$$$ **Lunahuana**, Av Critto 540, T421330, www.
lunahuana.com.ar. Stylish comfortable rooms
with good views, spacious duplexes for families.

$$$ **Mirador del Tafí**, R 307, Km 61.2, T421219,
www.miradordeltafi.com.ar. Warm attractive
rooms and spacious lounge, superb restaurant,
excellent views, look for midweek offers.
Highly recommended.

$ pp **La Cumbre**, Av Perón 120, T421768,
www.lacumbretafidelvalle.com. Basic, cramped
rooms, but central, helpful owner is a tour
operator with wide range of activities.

Estancias

$$$ **Estancia Las Carreras**, R 325, 13 km
southwest of Tafí, T421473, www.estancialas
carreras.com. A fine working estancia with
lodging and a restaurant serving its own
produce (including cheeses). It offers many
activites such as riding, trekking, mountain
biking and farm visits.

$$ **Los Cuartos**, Av Gob Critto y Av Juan
Calchaquí s/n, 10381-155 874230, www.
estancialoscuartos.com. Old estancia in town,
rooms full of character, charming hosts.
Recommended. Also offer a day at the estancia,
with lunch. Delicious *té criollo*, US$7-9, lunch,
US$16, and farm cheese can be bought here.

⑦ Restaurants

Tucumán *p120, map p121*

Many popular restaurants and cafés along
25 de Mayo, north from Plaza Independencia,
and on Plaza Hipólito Yrigoyen.

$$$-$$ **El Fondo**, San Martín 848, T422 2161.
Superb renowned steak house.

$$$-$$ **La Leñita**, 25 de Mayo 377.
Recommended for *parrilla*, superb salads,
live folk music at weekends.

$$ **Il Postino**, 25 de Mayo y Córdoba.
Attractive buzzing pizza place, plus tapas and
tortillas too, stylish décor. Recommended.

$ **Sir Harris**, Laprida y Mendoza. A Tucumán
institution, cosy with good quality *tenedor libre*,
some veggie dishes. Recommended.

Cafés

Café de París, Santiago del Estero 502 y 25 de Mayo. *Tapas* bar and stylish little restaurant.
Cosas del Campo, Lavalle 857 (south of centre, next to Plaza San Martín), T420 1758. Renowned for its *empanadas*, also for take-away.
Panadería Villecco, Corrientes 749. Exceptional bread, also wholemeal (*integral*) and pastries.

Tafí del Valle *p121*
Many places along Av Perón.
$$ Parrilla Don Pepito, Av Perón 193. Very good food, excellent *empanadas*.

🍷 Bars and clubs

Tucumán *p120, map p121*
Costumbres Argentinos, San Juan 666 y Maipú. An intimate place with a good atmosphere, for late drinks.

🎉 Festivals

Tucumán *p120, map p121*
9 Jul, Independence Day and **24 Sep**, Battle of Tucumán, both with huge processions/parties. **Sep**, Fiesta Nacional de la Empanada, in Famaillá, 35 km from Tucumán, 3 days of baking, eating and folk music, usually in 1st half of the month.

🛒 Shopping

Tucumán *p120, map p121*
Handicrafts Mercado Artesanal, 24 de Septiembre 565. Small, but nice selection of lace, wood and leatherwork. Daily 0800-1300, 1700-2200 (in summer, mornings only).
Mercado del Norte, Maipú between Mendoza and Córdoba, Mon-Sat 0900-1400, 1630-2100. Indoor market and bazaar featuring cheap regional foods, meat and local produce.
Regionales del Jardín, Congreso 18. Good selection of local jams, *alfajores*, etc.

🔵 What to do

Tafí del Valle *p121*
La Cumbre, see Where to stay, above. Energetic and helpful company, offering full day walks to nearby peaks, waterfalls and ruins, or to Cerro Muñoz, with an *asado* at the summit (4437 m), has open-sided truck.

⊖ Transport

Tucumán *p120, map p121*
Air Airport at Benjamín Matienzo, 10 km east of town. Bus No 120 from terminal (pre-paid cards required, sold in kiosks). Taxi US$10. Minibus transfer from airport to Plaza Independencia, US$2, to hotel US$7. Flights to **Buenos Aires** via **Córdoba**.
Bus Local buses use pre-paid cards, US$0.50 per journey, which you have to buy in advance in kiosks.

Bus terminal Av Brig Terán 250, T400 2000/5000, www.terminaltuc.com, 7 blocks east of Plaza Independencia. For long-distance buses. Has a shopping complex, left luggage lockers, excellent tourist information office (by *boletería* 1), lots of *locutorios*, toilets and banks (with ATM). Bus 4 from outside terminal to San Lorenzo y 9 de Julio in centre. Taxi to centre US$3.75. To **Buenos Aires**, many companies, 14-16 hrs, US$75-100. To **Salta** direct (not via Cafayate), 4-4½ hrs, several companies US$19-25. To **Cafayate** from Tafí del Valle: see below. To **Mendoza**, 13-14 hrs, US$68-96, via Catamarca, La Rioja, and San Juan. To **Córdoba**, 8 hrs, US$43-49. To/from **Santiago del Estero**, 2 hrs, US$10-13.
Train For train from Buenos Aires, see under Buenos Aires, Transport.

Tafí del Valle *p121*
Bus Smart Aconquija terminal on Av Critto, with café, toilets, helpful information, T421025. To/from **Tucumán**, Aconquija (http://transporte aconquija.com.ar), 10 daily (6 on Sun), 2½ hrs, US$6. To **Cafayate**, 4 a day, 2½ hrs, US$11.

Tucumán p120, map p121
Banks Most banks along San Martín especially 700 block between Junín and Maipú.

Bicycle shop Bike Shop, San Juan 984, T431 3121. Good. **Car hire** Movil Renta, San Lorenzo 370, T431 0550, www.movilrenta.com. ar, and at airport. 20% discount for *Footprint* book owners.

Cafayate → Phone code: 03868. Colour map 6, C3. Population: 14,850. Altitude: 1660 m.

Cafayate is a popular town for daytrippers and tourists, attracted by its dry sunny climate, its picturesque setting against the backdrop of the Andes and its excellent wines, of which the fruity white *Torrontés* is unique to Argentina. **Cerro San Isidro** (five hours return) gives you a view of the Aconquija chain in the south and Nevado de Cachi in the north. Six **bodegas** can be visited, including: **El Esteco** ① *at the junction of Rutas 68 and 40*, T54 11 5198 8000, www.elesteco. com. Superb wines and a splendid setting. Next door is the sumptuous **Patios de Cafayate** hotel (**$$$$**, T422229), formerly part of the bodega and now with luxury spa. It's also a great place for lunch. **Etchart** ① *2 km south on Ruta 40*, T421310, www.bodegasetchart.com. More modest but also famous for good wine. Offers tours, but ring first to book. The boutique bodega, **San Pedro de Yacochuya** ① T4319439, www.sanpedrodeyacochuya.com.ar, also has tours, beautiful hillside setting. **Vasija Secreta** ① *on outskirts*, T421850, www.vasijasecreta.com *(next to ACA hostería, 1421296, www.aca.tur.ar)*, is one of the oldest in the valley, English spoken. One block from the plaza is **Nanni** ① *Chavarría 151*, T421527, www.bodegananni.com, US2.50, very traditional, family-owned, with good tastings of organic wines and a restaurant. There are more vineyards at Tombolón, to the south. In all cases check visiting times as they vary and can be quite precise. The quality of tours and tastings also varies. The **tourist office** ① *20 de Febrero*, T422442/422223, www.cafayate.todowebsalta.com.ar, daily 0800-2200, is at the northeast corner of the plaza. They have a basic map showing bodegas and an accommodation list.

The **Museo de la Vid y El Vino** ① *Güemes Sur y F Perdiguero*, www.museodelavidyelvino. gov.ar, Tue-Sun 1000-1930, US$4, in a new building, tells the history of wine through old wine-making equipment. The tiny **Museo Arqueológico Rodolfo I Bravo** ① *Calchaquí y Colón 191*, T421054, Mon-Fri 1130-2100, Sat 1130-1500, free, has beautiful funerary urns, worth seeing if you haven't come across them elsewhere, and some Inca items. Two banks have ATMs.

Ruta 68 goes northeast from Cafayate to Salta; 6 km out of town is the rather unexpected landscape of Los Médanos (dunes), whose sand is constantly moving through thickets. The road then goes through the dramatic gorge of the Río de las Conchas (also known as the **Quebrada de Cafayate**) with fascinating rock formations of differing colours, all signposted. The road goes through wild and semi-arid landscapes. The vegetation becomes gradually denser as you near Salta, a pretty river winding by your side with tempting picnic spots.

Valles Calchaquíes
A longer alternative to Salta is to take the RN40 north of Cafayate through the stunningly varied landscape of the Valles Calchaquíes to Cachi. The mainly *ripio* road (difficult after rain) winds from the spectacular rock formations of the arid **Quebrada de las Flechas** up through Andean-foothills with lush little oases and tiny unspoilt villages at **San Carlos** (helpful tourist office on plaza); **Angastaco**, a small, modern, smart town with a petrol station, bus service and lodging options at the main plaza; and **Molinos** (all with limited bus services). The church of **San Pedro de Nolasco** in Molinos, mid-18th century, has a cactus-wood ceiling.

Cachi → *Phone code: 03868. Colour map 6, C3. Population: 7315. Altitude: 2280 m.*

Cachi is a beautiful town, in a valley made fertile by pre-Inca irrigation, set against a backdrop of arid mountains and the majestic Nevado del Cachi (6380 m). Its rich Diaguita history, starting long before the Incas arrived in 1450, is well presented in the **Museo Arqueológico** ① *T491080, Mon-Fri 1000-1900, Sat 1000-1800, Sun 1000-1300, US$1.50*, next to the Iglesia San José with painted funerary urns and intriguing petroglyphs. The simple church next door has a roof and lecterns made of cactus wood. There are panoramic views from the hill-top cemetery, 20 minutes' walk from the plaza, and satisfying walks to **La Aguada** (6 km southwest), or to the ruins at **Las Pailas**, 16 km northwest, barely excavated. The view is breathtaking, with huge cacti set against snow-topped Andean peaks. It's a four-hour walk each way to Las Pailas (12-km track from the main road, the last part for a car is slow and rough; it leads to a farmstead from where it's 15 minutes on foot to the ruins; young man at the farm will offer to guide you). Cachi **tourist office** ① *T491902, www.cachi.todowebsalta.com.ar, Mon-Fri 0900-2100, Sat-Sun 0900-1300, 1700-2100, and Mercado de Artesanías on the plaza.* ATM at the bank at Güemes y Ruiz de los Llanos.

From Cachi to Salta follow Ruta 40 for 11 km north to Payogasta (*Hostería*), then turn right to Ruta 33. The road climbs continuously up the Cuesta del Obispo passing a dead-straight stretch of 14 km known as La Recta del Tin-Tin through the magnificent **Los Cardones National Park** ① *administration office in Payogasta, 11 km from Cachi, T496005, loscardones@apn.gov.ar*, with huge candelabra cacti, up to 6 m in height. Paving ends at the end of national park. The road reaches the summit at Piedra de Molino (3347 m) after 43 km. Then it plunges down through the Quebrada de Escoipe, a breathtaking valley between olive green mountains, one of Argentina's great routes. The road rejoins Ruta 68 at El Carril, from where it is 37 km to Salta.

⊚ Cafayate listings

For hotel and restaurant price codes, and other relevant information, see Essentials.

● Where to stay

Cafayate *p125*
Accommodation is hard to find at holiday periods (Jan, Easter, late Jul), but there are many places to stay. Off season, prices are much lower. All those listed are recommended.
$$$$-$$$ Viñas de Cafayate, R21, Camino al Divisadero, T422272/282, www.cafayatewineresort.com. On a hillside above Cafayate, colonial style, calm, welcoming with pretty, spacious bedrooms, some with views. Excellent restaurant with local delicacies, open to non-residents with reservation, full buffet breakfast.
$$$ Killa, Colón 47, T422254, www.killacafayate.com.ar. A delightfully restored colonial house with pleasing views. Delightful owner, who has a fascinating garden, tranquil, comfortable, good breakfasts.

$$$ Portal del Santo, Silvero Chavarria 250, T422400, www.portaldelsanto.todowebsalta.com.ar. Family-run hotel with lovely large rooms overlooking a beautiful pool and garden.
$$$ Villa Vicuña, Belgrano 76, T422145, www.villavicuna.com.ar. Half a block from the main plaza, 2 colourful patios, bright rooms, pleasant and calm. Afternoon tea with home-made pastries served on demand.
$$ Hostal del Valle, San Martín 243, T421039. Well-kept big rooms around leafy patio, charming owner. New living room at the top has superb views over the valley (as do upper floor rooms).
$ El Balcón, Pasaje 20 de Febrero, T421739, www.hosteltrail.com/hostels/elbalcon. The cheapest option. Basic rooms, very central, the views from the roof are wonderful.
$ pp El Hospedaje, Quintana de Niño y Salta, T421680, www.elhospedaje.todowebsalta.com.ar. Simple but pleasant rooms in colonial-style house, wonderful pool, good value, heater in room, HI discount.

$ Hostel Ruta 40, Güermes Sur 178, T421689, www.hostel-ruta40.com. Very sociable place to stay, dorms US$18, private room **$$**. Discount for HI members.

$ Rusty K Hostal, Rivadavia 281, T422031, www.rustykhostal.todowebsalta.com.ar. Neat, basic rooms and a great garden with BBQ. 2 blocks from the main plaza. Lots of activities to enjoy by bike.

Camping Luz y Fuerza, Ruta Nacional 40, T421568, camping with pool, games, grills showers and a buffet.

Valles Calchaquíes p125

$$$$ Colomé, 20 km west of Molinos, T0387-421 9132, www.bodegacolome.com. Leave town via the vicuña farm and follow signs, or phone for directions from Cafayate. Recommended as one of the best places to stay in Argentina, winery in a beautiful setting with delightful rooms, horse riding, tastings of excellent wines, all food is organic, power is hydroelectric.

$$$$-$$$ Hacienda de Molinos, A Cornejo (by the river), T494094, www.haciendade molinos.com.ar. Open all year round. Stunning 18th-century hacienda, with rooms around a courtyard. Great attention to detail, the rooms are an oasis of calm. Swimming pool with a view of the Cachi mountains.

Also in Molinos: **$** pp Hostal San Agustín, Sarmiento y A Cornejo at the Colegio Infantil, T494015. Small but spotless rooms, some with private bath, run by nuns (who don't like to advertise the place, ask around discreetly for "las monjas" and someone will come and give you a key).

Cachi p126

$$$$ El Molino de Cachi, T491094, www. bodegaelmolino.com.ar. 4 km on the road to La Aguada, in restored 300-year-old mill, only 5 rooms, superb food, exquisite in every way, pool; has its own bodega.

$$$$-$$$ Finca Santana, take the road to Cachi Adentro, and ask for Camino to Finca San Miguel, on right at top, T0387-432 1141, fincasantana@fibertel.com.ar. 2 rooms in boutique B&B in the heart of the valley,

spectacular views, and complete sense of privacy and silence. Welcoming, spacious living room, terrace and garden, gourmet breakfast, trekking can be arranged. Wonderful.

$$$ ACA Hostería Cachi, at the top of Juan Manuel Castilla, T491904. Smart modern rooms (with wheelchair access), great views, pool, good restaurant, non-residents can use the pool if they eat lunch.

$$$ Casa de Campo La Paya, 12 km south of Cachi at La Paya, clearly signposted from the road, T491139. A restored 18th-century house, pool, elegant rooms, excellent dinners, hospitable. Recommended

$$$ El Cortijo, opposite the ACA hotel, on Av Automóvil Club s/n, T491034, www. elcortijohotel.com. Lovely peaceful rooms, each with its own style, warm hospitality, original art works. Recommended.

$$$ Llaqta Mawk'a, Ruiz de Los Llanos s/n, up from Plaza, T491016. Traditional frontage hides modern block, garden/terrace, view of the Nevado de Cachi, pool. Comfy rooms, ample breakfast, good value, popular with tourists (street parking). Horse riding with Ariel Villar arranged.

$$ Hospedaje Don Arturo, Bustamante s/n, T491087, www.hospedajedonarturo. blogspot.com. Homely, small rooms, quiet street, charming owners.

$ Hospedaje El Nevado de Cachi, Ruiz de los Llanos y F Suárez, T491912. Impeccable small rooms around a courtyard, hot water, *comedor*.

$ Viracocha Art Hostel, Ruiz de los Llanos s/n, T15-442 2371. Good central option offering bike hire, private and shared rooms.

Camping Municipal campsite at Av Automóvil Club Argentina s/n, T491902, with pool and sports complex, also *cabañas* and *albergue*.

🍴 Restaurants

Cafayate p125

$$ Baco, Güemes Norte y Rivadavia. *Parrilla*, *pasta casera*, pizzas, regional dishes, *empanadas* and *picadas*. Seating inside and on street, attractive corner, lively atmosphere. Good selection of local wines and beers.

$$ El Rancho, Toscano 4, T421256.
Traditional restaurant on plaza, serving
meats, regional dishes.
$$ El Terruño, Güemes Sur 28, T422460, www.
terruno.todowebsalta.com.ar. Meat and fish
dishes, including local specialities, good service.
$$ La Carreta de Don Olegario, Güemes,
on Plaza, T421004. Huge and brightly lit,
good set menus including the usual meat
dishes and pastas.
$$-$ La Casa de Las Empanadas, Mitre 24,
T15-454111, www.casadelaempanada.com.ar.
Cosy place with exposed brick and wooden
tables featuring local specialties like *humitas*
and the titular *empanadas*.

Cafés
Helados Miranda, Güemes Norte 170. Fabulous
homemade ice cream, including wine flavour.

Cachi *p126*
$$-$ Ashpamanta, Bustamante – Cachi 4417,
T15-578 2244. Just off the main plaza, this little
restaurant serves traditional Argentine favorites
like pizza and pasta, plus some regional gems
such as quinoa risotto.
$ Oliver Café, Ruiz de Los Llanos 160, on
the plaza. Tiny café for ice creams, coffee,
breakfasts, fruit juices, sandwiches and pizza.

O Shopping

Cafayate *p125*
Handicrafts Apart from the rather general
souvenir shops, there are some fine handicrafts.
Visit Calchaquí tapestry exhibition of **Miguel
Nanni**, Güemes 65 on the main plaza, silver work at
Jorge Barraco, Colón 157, T421244. Local pottery,
woollen goods, etc are sold in the **Mercado de
Artesanos Cafayetanos** on the plaza (small, pricey).

O What to do

Cafayate *p125*
Turismo Cordillerana, Güemes Sur 178,
T421689. Tours, trekking, horses, bike hire.
Cycle hire Many places, ask tourist
office for list.

Cachi *p126*
Local guides: **Fernando Gamarra**,
Benjamín Zorrilla y Güemes, T155 005471,
fg_serviciosturisticos@yahoo.com.ar.
For more conventional trips around
Cachi. **Santiago Casimiro**, T03868-15
638545, santiagocasimiro@hotmail.com.
Recommended for mountain hikes;
he's a nurse trained in mountain rescue.
Tourism Urkupiña, Benjamin Zorrilla s/n,
T03868 491317, uk_cachi@hotmail.com.
Local agency for tours and bus tickets.

O Transport

Cafayate *p125*
Bus El Indio on Belgrano, ½ block from plaza,
to **Santa María** (for Quilmes) 4 daily, US$5;
also to **Salta**. To **Angastaco**, El Indio, 1 daily
Mon-Fri, US$5, 1½ hrs (but does not continue
to Molinos and Cachi). To/from **Tucumán**,
Aconquija at Güemes Norte y Alvarado,
T421052 (open 1000-1200, 1900-2100, Sun
1100-1300, 1930-2100 and 20 mins before
bus is due), 4 daily, 5½ hrs, US$17.50; to **Tafí
del Valle**, 4 daily, US$11, 3 hrs (more via **Santa
María**, 5½ hrs); and to **Salta** US$29-32.50.

Cachi *p126*
Bus To **Salta**, Ale, T0387-423 1811, daily
at 0400, 0700, 1600, 4 hrs, US$9.

Salta → *Phone code: 0387. Colour map 6, C3. Population: 536,113. Altitude: 1190 m.*

Founded in 1582, Salta, 1600 km north of Buenos Aires, is an atmospheric city, with many
fine 19th-century buildings, elegant plazas, stirring folkloric music and fabulous food. It lies in
the broad Lerma valley, surrounded by steep and forested mountains, and is a good base for
exploring the Andean regions, Cachi in the Calchaquí valleys to the south (described above) and
the Quebrada de Humahuaca north of Jujuy (described in the next section).

Salta is a fascinating city to explore on foot; in a couple of hours you can get a feel for its wonderful architecture. Good maps are available from the **provincial tourist office** ⓘ *Buenos Aires 93 (1 block from main plaza), T431 0950, www.turismosalta.gov.ar, weekdays 0800-2100, weekends 0900-2000*. Very helpful, gives advice on tours and arranges accommodation in private houses in high season (July), only when hotels are fully booked. The **municipal tourist office** ⓘ *Caseros*

Salta

Where to stay 🛏
1 Apart Ilusión *D3*
2 Ayres de Salta *B1*
4 Backpackers Home *D2*
3 Backpackers Suites *D1*
6 Bloomers Bed & Brunch *C2*
7 Carpe Diem *D2*
8 Correcaminos Hostel *B2*
9 Del Antiguo Convento *C2*
10 El Lagar *A1*
11 Hostal Quara *B2*
13 Las Marías *D2*
14 Las Rejas *B1*
15 Legado Mítico *B1*
16 Munay *D1*
18 Posada de las Nubes *A1*
19 Salta *C1*
20 Solar de la Plaza *B1*

Restaurants 🍴
1 Doña Salta *C2*
2 El Churrúa *C2*
3 El Corredor de las Empanadas *C2*
4 El Solar del Convento *C1*
6 La Casa de Güemes *C1*
7 La Criollita *B1*
9 Mama Paca *B2*

Bars & clubs 🍸
11 Gauchos de Güemes *A3*
12 La Casona del Molino *C1*
13 La Vieja Estación *A1*

711, T0800-777 0300, Mon-Fri 0800-2100, Sat-Sun 0900-2100, is for Salta city only, small but helpful. Other websites: www.turismoensalta.com of the **Cámara de Turismo** ① *Gral Güemes 15 y Av Virrey Toledo, T15-500 4431*; www.saltalalinda.gov.ar and www.saltaciudad.com.ar.

Places in Salta

The heart of Salta, is **Plaza 9 de Julio**, planted with tall palms and surrounded by colonial buildings. On the plaza, the **Cabildo**, 1783, one of the few to be found intact in the country, houses the impressive **Museo Histórico del Norte** ① *Caseros 549, Tue-Fri 0900-1900, Sat-Sun 0900-1330, US$2, free Wed*. The museum has displays on pre-Columbian and colonial history, independence wars, and a fine 18th-century pulpit. Opposite the Cabildo, is the 19th-century **Cathedral** (open mornings and evenings), painted pink and cream and reflected in the blue plate glass of a bank next door. It contains a huge late baroque altar (1807) and the much venerated images of the Virgin Mary and of the Cristo del Milagro, sent from Spain in 1592. The miracle was the sudden cessation of a terrifying series of earthquakes when the images were paraded through the streets on 15 September 1692. They still are, each September. The **Museo de Arqueología de Alta Montaña** (MAAM) ① *Mitre 77, T437 0592, http://maam.culturasalta. gov.ar, Tue-Sun 1100-1930, US$5*, has a collection of exhibits from high-altitude shrines, including mummies of child sacrifices, video material in Spanish and English, also temporary exhibits. Controversy surrounds the discovery of the mummies and their display. They are exhibited with sensitivity; visitors can choose whether or not to view them. A block southwest of the Plaza is the **Museo de la Ciudad 'Casa de Hernández'** ① *Florida 97 y Alvarado, T437 3352, Mon-Fri 0900-1300, 1600-1800, Sat 0900-1300, free*. This fine 18th-century mansion includes furniture and portraits, but a marvellous painting of Güemes. The magnificent façade of **San Francisco** church ① *on Caseros, 0800-1200, 1700-2100*, rises above the skyline with its splendid tower, ornately decorated in plum red and gold. Further along Caseros, the Convent of **San Bernardo**, rebuilt in colonial style in the mid-19th century, has a beautifully carved wooden portal of 1762, but is not open to visitors as nuns still live there. They will open up the small shop for you, selling quaint handicrafts.

At the end of Caseros is the **Cerro San Bernardo** (1458 m) ① *accessible by cable car (teleférico from Parque San Martín), daily 1000-1900, US$4.50 each way, US$4.50 children return, fine views, 30-40 mins' walk to return*. At the summit are gardens, waterfalls, a café, a silver collection and playground. Further along Avenida H Yrigoyen is an impressive **statue to General Güemes**, whose *gaucho* troops repelled seven powerful Spanish invasions from Bolivia between 1814 and 1821.

Up beyond the Güemes statue is the **Museo Antropológico** ① *Paseo Güemes, T422 2960, www.antropologico.gov.ar, Mon-Fri 0800-1900, Sat and holidays 1000-1800, knowledgeable staff, US$0.75*. Fascinating displays on pre-Inca cultures include painted urns, intriguing board-flattened skulls (meant to confer superiority), a mummy discovered high in the Andes and many objects from Tastil (see below). **Museo de Ciencias Naturales** ① *Parque San Martín, T431 8086, Tue-Sun 1530-1930, US$0.25*, displays a bewildering number of stuffed animals and birds; the armadillo collection is interesting.

San Antonio de los Cobres → *Phone code: 0387, Population: 4000, Altitude: 3775 m.*

Sitting in the vast emptiness of the *puna*, San Antonio de los Cobres, 168 km by road from Salta, is a simple, remote mining town of adobe houses with a friendly Coya community. Ruta 51 leads to La Polvorilla railway viaduct (see below), 20 km, ask in town for details and beware sudden changes in the weather. Try the *quesillo de cabra* (goat's cheese) from Estancia Las Cuevas. The **Huaira Huasi** restaurant, used by tour groups, has a good menu. At **Santa Rosa de Tastil** there are important prehispanic ruins and a small **museum** ① *Tue-Sun 0900-1900, Mon 0900-1500, free*, recommended. Take El Quebradeño bus (see Transport, below), a tour from Salta, or share a taxi.

Cloud line

One of the great railway journeys of South America is the *Tren a las Nubes* (Train to the Clouds). Engineered by Richard Maury, of Pennsylvania (who is commemorated by the station at Km 78 which bears his name) this remarkable project was built in stages between 1921 and 1948, by which time developments in road and air transport had already reduced its importance. The line includes 21 tunnels, 13 viaducts, 29 bridges, 2 loops and 2 zig-zags. From Salta the line climbs gently to Campo Quijano (Km 40, 1520 m), where it enters the Quebrada del Toro, an impressive rock-strewn gorge. At El Alisal (Km 50) and Chorrillos (Km 66) there are zig-zags as the line climbs the side of the gorge before turning north into the valley of the Río Rosario near Puerto Tastil (Km 101, 2675 m), missing the archaeological areas around Santa Rosa de Tastil. At Km 122 and Km 129 the line goes into 360° loops before reaching Diego de Almagro (3304 m). At Abra Muñano (3952 m) the road to San Antonio can be seen zig-zagging its way up the end-wall of the Quebrada del Toro below. From Muñano (3936 m) the line drops slightly to San Antonio, Km 196. The spectacular viaduct at La Polvorilla is 21 km further at 4190 m, just beyond the branch line to the mines at La Concordia. The highest point on the line is reached at Abra Chorrillos (4475 m, Km 231). From here the line runs on another 335 km across a rocky barren plateau 3500-4300 m above sea level before reaching Socompa (3865 m).

This is a comfortable ride, but a long day out (see page 135). The train leaves Salta to the cheerful accompaniment of musicians on the platform, then enters the Quebrada del Toro. As you climb through the gorge the landscape changes from forested mountains to farmland to arid red rock dotted with giant cactii. Eventually you reach the beautiful *puna*. On the seven-hour ascent there are chats from bilingual guides (English spoken, but French and Portuguese too on request), and lunch is served. If altitude sickness hits, oxygen is on hand. At La Polvorilla viaduct, you can get out briefly to admire the construction and buy locally made llama-wool goods. Don't bother haggling: the shawls and hats are beautifully made and the people's only source of income. At San Antonio, the Argentine flag is raised to commemorate those who worked on the railway and the national anthem is sung. Passengers may be given the option of returning from San Antonio by bus or in a Movitrak vehicle, allowing more time at San Antonio and a visit to the ruins at Santa Rosa de Tastil, thus avoiding the more tedious descent by train.

The famous **Tren a las Nubes** is a 570 km, narrow gauge railway running from Salta through the town of San Antonio de los Cobres to Socompa, on the Chilean border (see box). San Antonio can also be reached by Ruta 51 from Salta. From **Campo Quijano**, the road runs along the floor of the Quebrada del Toro before climbing to Alto Blanco (paved section).

Ruta 51 from San Antonio de los Cobres to **San Pedro de Atacama**, Chile uses the **Sico** Pass (4079 m). It's a spectacular route, crossing white salt lakes dotted with flamingos and vast expanses of desert. The first 110 km are paved; the route has been replaced by that over Paso de Jama (see page 138). There is a customs post at Paso Sico (you may be allowed to spend the night here), open 24 hours: check first in San Antonio de los Cobres if it is open, T0387-498 2001. On the Chilean side continue via Mina Laco and Socaire to Toconao (road may be bad between these two points). Customs and immigration are in San Pedro de Atacama. Note that fruit, vegetables and dairy products may not be taken into Chile (search 20 km after Paso Sico). Gasoline is available in San Pedro and Calama. Obtain sufficient drinking water for the trip in San Antonio and do not underestimate the effects of altitude.

Salta listings

For hotel and restaurant price codes, and other relevant information, see Essentials.

Where to stay

Salta *p128, map p129*

All hotels and hostels listed are recommended. Book ahead in Jul holidays and around 10-16 Sep during celebrations of Cristo del Milagro.

$$$$ Legado Mítico, Mitre 647, T422 8786, www.legadomitico.com. This small, welcoming hotel is absolutely lovely, luxurious rooms each with its own personality, the personalized pre-ordered breakfasts are a fantastic way to start the day.

$$$$ Solar de la Plaza, Juan M Leguizamon 669, T431 5111, www.solardelaplaza.com.ar. Elegant old former Salteño family home, faultless service, sumptuous rooms, great restaurant and a pool.

$$$$-$$$ Ayres de Salta, Gral Güemes 650, T422 1616, www.ayresdesalta.com.ar. Spacious, central 4-star hotel near Plaza Belgrano, everything you would expect in this price-range: spacious rooms, heated pool, great views from roof terrace.

$$$ Apart Ilusión (Sweet Dreams), José Luis Fuentes 743, Portezuelo Norte, T432 1081, www.aparthotelilusion.com.ar. On the slopes of Cerro San Bernardo, beautiful views, well-equipped self-catering apartments for 2-4, decorated with local handicrafts, English-speaking owner Sonia Alvarez, welcoming, breakfast and parking available, good value.

$$$ Bloomers Bed & Brunch, Vicente López 129, T422 7449, www.bloomers-salta.com.ar. Closed mid-May to mid-Jun. In a refurbished colonial house, 5 spacious non-smoking rooms individually decorated, and one apartment, use of kitchen, library. The brunch menu, different each day, is their speciality.

$$$ Carpe Diem, Urquiza 329, T421 8736, www.bedandbreakfastsalta.com. Welcoming B&B, beautifully furnished, convenient, several languages spoken, no children under 14.

$$$ El Lagar, 20 de Febrero 877, T431 9439, www.ellagarhotel.com.ar. An intimate boutique hotel owned by wine-making Etchart family, beautifully furnished rooms full of fine paintings, excellent restaurant, gardens.

$$$ Salta, Buenos Aires 1, in main plaza, T426 7500, www.hotelsalta.com. A Salta institution with neo-colonial public rooms, refurbished bedrooms, marvellous suites overlooking plaza, *confitería* and honorary membership of the Polo and Golf Club.

$$ Del Antiguo Convento, Caseros 113, T422 7267, www.hoteldelconvento.com.ar. Small, convenient, with old-fashioned rooms around a neat patio, very helpful, a good choice.

$$ Las Marías, Lerma 255, T422 4193, www.saltaguia.com/lasmarias. Central hostel, $ pp in shared rooms, close to Parque San Martín.

$$ Las Rejas, General Güemes 569, T421 5971, www.lasrejashostel.com.ar. 2 houses converted into a small B&B and a hostel (US$15-17 pp), comfortable, central, helpful owners.

$$ Munay, San Martín 656, T422 4936, www.munayhotel.com.ar. Good choice, smart rooms for 2-5 with good bathrooms, warm welcome. Also have hotels of the same standard in Cafayate, Humahuaca, Jujuy and La Quiaca.

$$ Posada de las Nubes, Balcarce 639, T432 1776, www.posadadelasnubes.com.ar. Charming, small, with simply decorated rooms around a central patio. Great location for Balcarce nightlife, might be a little too loud on weekends.

$ Backpackers Home, Buenos Aires 930, T423 5910, **Backpackers Suites**, Urquiza 1045, T431 8944, www.backpackerssalta.com. HI-affiliated hostels, both well run, with dorms and private rooms (**$$**, cheaper for HI members), with laundry and budget travel information. Crowded and popular.

$ Correcaminos Hostel, Vicente López 353, T422 0731. 4 blocks from plaza, modern dorms, 2 doubles, shared bath, laundry, pleasant garden, good, lively.

$ Hostal Quara, Santiago del Estero 125, T422 0392, www.hostalquara.com.ar. Dorms US$13-

14, also doubles with and without bath, with heating, TV room, drinks for sale, helpful staff, can organize tours.

Estancias
Among Salta's most desirable places to stay are its colonial-style estancias, known locally as *fincas*. All those listed are recommended for their individual style, setting, comfort, food and activities, especially horse riding. All are in the **$$$$-$$$** price range, mostly pp.
Finca El Bordo de las Lanzas, 45 km east of Salta, T490 3070, www.turismoelbordo.com.ar.
Finca El Manantial del Milagro, La Silleta, 25 km from Salta, T490 8080, www.hotelmanantial.com.ar.
Finca Los Los, Chicoana, 40 km from Salta at the entrance to the Valles Calchaquíes, T0387-156 833121, www.redsalta.com/loslos. Mar-Dec.
Finca Santa Anita, Coronel Moldes, 60 km from Salta, on the way to Cafayate, T490 5050, www.santaanita.com.ar.
Finca Valentina, Ruta 51, Km 11, La Merced Chica, T15 415 3490, www.finca-valentina.com.ar. Associated with recommended tour operator **Socompa**, below.
Hostal Selva Montana, C Alfonsina Storni 2315, San Lorenzo, T492 1184, www.hostal-selvamontana.com.ar.

San Antonio de los Cobres *p130*
$$$ Hostería de las Nubes, T490 9059, www.hoteldelasnubes.com, edge of San Antonio on Salta road. Smart, comfortable, modern and spacious. Recommended.
$$-$ Hospedaje Belgrano, Belgrano s/n, T490 9025. Welcoming, basic, hot showers, evening meals.
   There are other lodgings. Ask at the Municipalidad, Belgrano s/n, T490 9045, about dorm and double room at the tourist information office (**$**) and minibus tours to salt flats and Purmamarca.

Campo Quijano
$$$ Hostería Punta Callejas, T0387-490 4086, www.puntacallejas.com.ar. Very comfortable, pool, tennis, riding, excursions.

Camping Several sites, including municipal campsite, at entrance to Quebrada del Toro gorge, lovely spot with good facilities, hot showers, bungalows.

🍴 Restaurants

Salta *p128, map p129*
Salta has delicious and distinctive cuisine: try the *locro*, *humitas* and *tamales*, served in the municipal market at San Martín y Florida.
$$$ El Solar del Convento, Caseros 444, half a block from plaza, T421 5124. Elegant and not expensive, champagne when you arrive, delicious steaks. Recommended.
$$ Chirimoya, España 211, T431 2857. Those looking to get away from the *carne* can opt for this café a few blocks off the main plaza. It offers veggie twists on pastas, sandwiches and *milanesas*. There's even a "raw ravioli".
$$ Doña Salta, Córdoba 46 (opposite San Francisco convent library), T432 1921. Excellent regional dishes and pleasant, rustic atmosphere, good value.
$$ El Charrúa, Caseros 221, T432 1859, www.parrillaelcharrua.com.ar. A good, brightly lit family place with a reasonably priced and simple menu where *parrilla* is particularly recommended.
$$ La Casa de Güemes, España 730. Popular, local dishes and *parrilla*, traditionally cooked in the house where General Güemes lived.
$ El Corredor de las Empanadas, Caseros 117 and Zuviría 913. Delicious *empanadas* and tasty local dishes in airy surroundings.
$ La Criollita, Zuviría 306. Small and unpretentious, a traditional place for tasty *empanadas*.
$ Mama Paca, Gral Güemes 118. Recommended by locals, traditional restaurant for seafood from Chile and homemade pastas.

🍸 Bars and clubs

Salta *p128, map p129*
Visit a *peña* to hear passionate folklore music live. There are many bars, called *peñas*, with excellent live bands on Balcarce

towards railway station, a great place to go at weekends (taxi US$1.50). **Los Cardones** (no 885, T432 0909, www.cardonessalta.com.ar) has good food and a good nightly show. **La Vieja Estación** (no 877, T431 7191), great atmosphere, good food. **La Casona del Molino**, Luis Burela 1, T434 2835. Most authentic, in a crumbling old colonial house, good food and drink. **Gauchos de Güemes**, Uruguay 750, T421 7007, popular, delicious regional food.

❀ Festivals

Salta *p128, map p129*
16-17 Jun, commemoration of the death of General Martín Güemes: folk music in evening and *gaucho* parade in morning around the Güemes statue. Salta celebrates **Carnival** with processions and dancers on the 4 weekends before Ash Wednesday at the *corsódromo*, located on Av Gato Mancha near the convention center (US$4).
15 Sep, Cristo del Milagro (see above);
24 Sep, Battles of Tucumán and Salta.

○ Shopping

Salta *p128, map p129*
Handicrafts Arts and handicrafts are often cheaper in surrounding villages. **Mercado Artesanal** on the western outskirts, in the Casa El Alto Molino, San Martín 2555, T434 2808, daily 0900-2100, take bus 2, 3, or 7 from Av San Martín in centre and get off as bus crosses the railway line. Excellent range and high quality in lovely 18th-century mansion. Opposite is a cheaper tourist market for similar items, but factory-made.
Markets Mercado Municipal, San Martín y Florida, for meat, fish, vegetables and other produce and handicrafts, closed 1300-1700 and Sun.

○ What to do

Salta *p128, map p129*
There are many tour operators, mostly on Buenos Aires, offering adventure trips and excursions; staff give out flyers on the street. Out of season, tours often run only if there is sufficient demand; check carefully that tour will run on the day you want. All agencies charge similar prices for tours (though some charge extra for credit card payments). City tour US$20; Valles Calchaquíes US$115 (2 days); Cachi US$46; Puna and salt lakes US$83. The tourist office gives reports on agencies and their service.

Clark Expediciones, Mariano Moreno 1950, T497 1024, www.clarkexpediciones.com. Specialist birding tours, eco-safaris and treks. English spoken.
Movitrack, Caseros 468, T431 6749, www.movitrack.com.ar. Entertaining safaris in a 4WD truck, to San Antonio de los Cobres, Humahuaca, Cafayate, adventure trips, German, English spoken, expensive. They also have an OxyBus for high-altitude journeys.
New Sendas, in Chicoana, 47 km south, T490 7009, www.newsendas.com. Expert guide Martín Pekarek offers adventure excursions and horses for hire, English and German spoken. Also with lodging at Hostería de Chicoana.
Norte Trekking, Gral Güemes 265, T431 6616, www.nortetrekking.com. Mon-Fri 0900-1400, 1500-1900. Excellent tours in 4WDs and minivans all over Salta and Jujuy, to Iruya, over Jama Pass to San Pedro de Atacama, hiking, horse riding, excursions to El Rey national park with experienced guide Federico Norte, knowledgeable, speaks English. Tailors tours to your interest and budget.
Puna Expediciones, Agustín Usandivaras 230, T416 9313, www.punaexpeditions.com.ar. Qualified and experienced guide Luis H Aguilar organizes treks in remote areas of Salta and Jujuy and safaris further afield. Recommended.
Sayta, Chicoana, 49 km from Salta, T0387-15 683 6565, www.saltacabalgatas.com.ar. An estancia specializing in horse riding, for all levels of experience, good horses and attention, great *asados*, also has lodging for overnight stays, adventure and rural tourism. Recommended.
Socompa, Balcarce 998, p 1, T577 0444, www.socompa.com. Excellent company

specializing in trips to salt flats and volcanoes in the puna, 3 days to the beautiful, remote hamlet of Tolar Grande; can be extended to 12 days to include Atacama and Puna of Catamarca; 4 days to Puna of Catamarca. English and Italian spoken, knowledgeable guides. Highly recommended.

⊖ Transport

Salta *p128, map p129*
Air The airport (T424 7356, www.aa2000.com. ar) is 12 km southwest, served by vans run by Transfer del Pino, US$4. Bus on Corredor 8A to airport from San Martín, US$0.30. Taxi from bus station, US$6-9. Flights to **Buenos Aires** (2¼ hrs) and **Córdoba**.
Bus Local buses in the city charge US$0.30 (www.saetasalta.com.ar).

Long distance terminal is 8 blocks east of the main plaza, T431 5022 for information. Taxi to centre US$2. Toilets, *locutorio*, café, *panadería*, kiosks. To **Buenos Aires**, several companies daily, US$75-90, 20-22 hrs. To **Córdoba**, several companies daily, 12 hrs, US$50-65. To **Santiago del Estero**, 6-7 hrs, US$30-45. To **Tucumán**, 4 hrs, several companies, US$19-25. To **Mendoza** via Tucumán, 2 companies daily, US$85-105, 18-20 hrs. To **La Rioja**, US$50, 10-11 hrs. To **Jujuy**, frequent service, US$6.50, 2-2½ hrs. To **San Antonio de Los Cobres**, 5 hrs, El Quebradeño, daily, US$7.

To **Cachi** 0700, 1330, US$6.50, 4 hrs, with Ale Hnos, T421 1588. To **Cafayate**, US$13-14, with El Indio, T422 9393, and Aconquija.

International buses To **Paraguay**: travel to **Resistencia**, daily, 12 hrs, US$57, La Veloz del Norte or Flecha Bus, or to **Formosa**, US$64-73, 16 hrs, then change to a direct bus to Asunción. To **Chile**: Services to **Calama** and **San Pedro de Atacama** with Andesmar, T431 0263, Géminis, T431 7778, and Pullman, T422 1366, each 3 a week, but check days as they change, via Jujuy and the Jama Pass, US$60-70, 11 hrs.

Géminis and Pullman offices are at booths 15 and 16 in the terminal. To **Bolivia**: to **La Quiaca**, on Bolivian border, Balut, Andesmar, Flecha, 7½ hrs, US$25. To **Aguas Blancas** US$21, 5 hrs, or **Pocitos** (both on the Bolivian border, see page 140), US$26, 8 hrs, 2 companies daily.
Car hire Avis, Caseros 420 and, T421 2181 and at the airport, Ruta 51, T424 2289, salta@avis.com.ar. Efficient and very helpful, recommended. NOA, Buenos Aires 1, T431 7080, www.noarentacar.com, in Hotel Salta, helpful, also mountain bike, US$13 per day. Many others.
Train Station at 20 de February y Ameghino, 9 blocks north of Plaza 9 de Julio. The only train service is the **Tren a las Nubes** (see box, page 131), which usually runs end-Mar to early Dec on Sat, with extra trains in high season (Semana Santa and July) between Salta and La Polvorilla viaduct departing 0705, arriving back in Salta 2348, weather permitting. The regular route is train to La Polvorilla and back to San Antonio de los Cobres, where passengers change to a bus to Salta by 2300. There are also several multi-day tours to the region which include the train (see website). The basic fare (train up, bus back) is US$182, 50% discount for minors and seniors. Contact T422 3033, or Buenos Aires T011-5258 3000, www.trenalasnubes.com.ar.

⊕ Directory

Salta *p128, map p129*
Banks Banks, open 0900-1400, all have ATMs (many on España, also casas de cambio). **Consulates** Bolivia, Mariano Boedo 34, T421 1040, coliviansalta@yahoo.com.ar, Mon-Fri, 0900-1400. Chile, Santiago del Estero 965, T431 1857, Mon-Fri 0830-1330. **Medical services** Hospital San Bernardo, Tobias 69, T432 0300, www.hospitalsanbernardo.com.ar. **Useful addresses** Immigration, Maipú 35, T422 0438, 0730-1230.

Though it lacks Salta's elegance, since there are few colonial buildings remaining, the historical city of Jujuy is the starting point for some of the country's most spectacular scenery and it has a distinctly Andean feel, evident in its food and music. With extremely varied landscapes, the area is rich in both contemporary and ancient culture, with prehispanic ruins at Tilcara, delightful villages and excursions. The **tourist office** ⓘ *Gorriti 295, on the plaza, T422 1325, www.turismo. jujuy.gov.ar, Mon-Fri 0700-2200, Sat-Sun 0900-2100*, has an accommodation leaflet and a map. Also at bus terminal, 0700-2100.

Places in Jujuy

San Salvador de Jujuy (pronounced Choo-Chooey, with *ch* as in Scottish loch) often referred to by locals as San Salvador, is the capital of Jujuy province and sits in a bowl ringed by lushly wooded mountains. The city was finally established in 1593, after earlier attempts met resistance from local indigenous groups, but the city was plagued by earthquakes, sacking and the Calchaquíes Wars for the next 200 years. It struggled to prosper, then in August 1812 General Belgrano, commanding the republican troops, ordered the city to be evacuated and destroyed before the advancing Spanish army. This extraordinary sacrifice is marked on 23-24 August by festivities known as **El Exodo Jujeño** with gaucho processions and military parades.

Away from the busy shopping streets, in the eastern part of the city, is the **Plaza Belgrano**, a wide square planted with tall palms and orange trees. It's lined with impressive buildings, including the elaborate French baroque-style **Casa de Gobierno** ⓘ *daily 0800-2100*, containing the famous flag Belgrano presented to the city. On the west side is the late 19th-century **Cathedral** (the original, 1598-1653, was destroyed by earthquake in 1843) containing one of Argentina's finest colonial treasures: a gold-plated wooden pulpit, carved by *indígenas* in the Jesuit missions, depicting gilded angels mounting the stairs. The modern church of **San Francisco** ⓘ *Belgrano y Lavalle, 2 blocks west of the plaza, daily 0730-1200, 1700-2100*, contains another fine gilded colonial pulpit, with ceramic angels around it, like that at Yavi. The **Museo Histórico Franciscano** ⓘ *Mon-Fri 0900-1300, 1700-2100*, at the church, includes 17th-century paintings and other artefacts from Cuzco. There are several other museums; don't miss the **Museo Arqueológico Provincial** ⓘ *Lavalle 434, Mon-Fri 0800-2000, US$1*, with beautiful ceramics from the Yavi and Humahuaca cultures, haphazardly displayed, a mummified infant, and a 2500-year-old sculpture of a goddess giving birth.

There are hot springs 19 km west at **Termas de Reyes** ⓘ *1 hr by bus Etap (línea 1C) from bus terminal or corner of Gorriti and Urquiza, US$0.75, municipal baths and pool US$3.25*; also cabins with thermal water. This resort (**Hotel Termas de Reyes** *T0388-492 2522, www.termasdereyes. com*) is set among magnificent mountains. Day use costs US$63, various treatments, and there are packages from one to seven nights.

⊙ Jujuy listings

For hotel and restaurant price codes, and other relevant information, see Essentials.

⊖ Where to stay

Jujuy *p136*
$$$ El Arribo, Belgrano 1263, T422 2539, www.elarribo.com. Attractive, well-located

posada set in a restored colonial house with swimming pool, smiling staff. Highly recommended.
$$$ Gregorio I, Independencia 829, T424 4747, www.gregoriohotel.com. Wonderful, small boutique hotel with 20 rooms. Smart, modern style, with local art scattered throughout. Recommended.

$$ **Sumay**, Otero 232, T423 5065, www.
sumayhotel.com.ar. Rather dark, but clean,
very central, helpful staff.
$ pp **Aldea Luna**, Tilquiza, 1 hr from Jujuy,
3 hrs from Salta, T0388-155 094602, www.aldea
luna.com.ar. Very peaceful, set in the Yungas
reserve. Dorm US$9 pp (food not included),
private room US$13 pp (food not included).
Restaurant with vegetarian food.
$ pp **Club Hostel**, San Martín 134, 2½ blocks
from plaza, T423 7565, www.clubhosteljujuy.
com.ar. Dorms and doubles $$; with jacuzzi,
patio, lots of information, welcoming, has a
good travel agency.
$ pp **Hostal Casa de Barro**, Otero 294,
T422 9578, www.hostalcasadebarro.com.ar.
Lovely double, triple and quadruple rooms
from US$11.50 pp, whitewashed with
simple decorations, shared bathrooms and
a fantastic area for eating and relaxing. The
wonderful staff provide dinner on demand.
Highly recommended.
$ pp **Yok Wahi/Dublin Hostel and Bar**,
Independencia 946, T422 9608, www.yokwahi.
com. Hostel and Irish pub 6 blocks from bus
station, with dorms (US$12 pp) and doubles
with and without bath ($$), heating, *parrilla*,
book exchange, information.
Camping $ pp El Refugio is closest, Yala,
Km 14, Av Libertador 2327, T490 9344,
www.elrefugiodeyala.com.ar. Pretty spot on
riverbank 14 km north of city, also has youth
hostel, pool, and restaurant, horse riding and
treks organized. Highly recommended, great
place to relax.

❶ Restaurants

Jujuy *p136*
$$$ **Krysys**, Balcarce 272. Popular bistro-style
parrilla, excellent steaks.
$$ **Chung King**, Alvear 627. Closed Sun.
Atmospheric, serving regional food for
over 60 years; with pizzería at No 631.
$$ **Manos Jujeños**, Sen Pérez 381. Daily
1200-1500, 2000-2400, closed Mon. Regional
specialities, the best *humitas*, charming, good
for the *peña* at weekends.

$$ **Ruta 9**, Belgrano 743 and Costa Rica 968.
Great places for regional dishes such as *locro*
and *tamales*, also a few Bolivian dishes.
$ **Madre Tierra**, Belgrano 619. Mon-Sat 1130-
1430. Vegetarian café, behind a wholemeal
bakery, delicious food.
$ **Tío Bigote**, Pérez y Belgrano. Closed Mon and
Sun evening. Very popular café and pizzería.

Cafés
Following Lavalle across the bridge to the bus
terminal (where it becomes Dorrego) there are
lots of cheap *empanada* places.
Sociedad Española, Belgrano y Sen Pérez.
Closed Sun. Good cheap set menus with a
Spanish flavour.

⊙ Shopping

Jujuy *p136*
Handicrafts There are stalls near the
cathedral. Centro de Arte y Artesanías, Balcarce
427. Paseo de las Artesanías, on the west side
of the plaza.
Markets For food, you can't beat the
Municipal market at Dorrego y Alem, near the
bus terminal. Outside, women sell home-baked
empanadas and *tamales*, delicious goat's
cheese and all kinds of herbal cures.

❹ What to do

Jujuy *p136*
Siete Colores, Gorriti 291, T422 6998.
Organizes trips to the Yungas and the
Quebrada including Iruya.

⊖ Transport

Jujuy *p136*
Air Airport at El Cadillal, 32 km southeast,
T491 1505, taxi US$10. Flights to **Salta** and
Buenos Aires.
Bus Bus terminal at Iguazú y Dorrego, 6 blocks
south of the centre, T422 1373. There are
services to **Buenos Aires**, 21-24 hrs, **Tucumán**,
6 hrs, and **Córdoba**. To **Salta**, see above.
To **La Quiaca**, 5-6 hrs, US$11, **Balut**. Several

rigorous luggage checks en route for drugs, including coca leaves. To **Humahuaca**, Balut, US$5, 2½ hrs, several daily, via Tilcara 1½ hrs, US$3.50. To **Orán** and **Aguas Blancas** (border with Bolivia), US$17-21, daily with Balut and others, via San Pedro. To **Purmamarca**, take buses to Susques or to Humahuaca (those calling at Purmamarca village). To **Susques**, Purmamarca and Andes Bus, US$11, 4-6½ hrs, daily (except Mon). To **Calilegua**: various companies to Libertador Gral San Martín almost every hour, eg Balut, US$4.50, from there take Empresa 23 de Agosto or Empresa 24 de Setiembre, leaving 0830 to **Valle Grande**, across Parque Nacional Calilegua. All Pocitos or Orán buses pass through Libertador San Martín.

To Chile: via the **Jama** pass (4400 m), the route taken by most traffic, including trucks, crossing to northern Chile; hours 0800-2200. **Géminis** bus tickets sold at **Paisajes del Noroeste**, San Martín 134, www.paisajesdelnoroeste.tur.ar.

⊙ Directory

Jujuy p136

Banks ATMs at banks of Alvear. **Consulates** Bolivia, Independencia1098, T424 0501, Mon-Fri 0830-1300. **Useful addresses** Immigration, 19 de Abril 1057, T423 5658.

Jujuy to the Chilean and Bolivian borders

Ruta 9, the Pan-American Highway, runs through the beautiful **Quebrada de Humahuaca**, a vast gorge of vividly coloured rock, with giant cactii in the higher parts, and emerald green oasis villages on the river below. (January-March ask highway police about flooding on the roads.) The whole area is very rich culturally: there are pre-Inca ruins at Tilcara (see below), and throughout the Quebrada there are fine 16th-century churches and riotous pre-Lent carnival celebrations. In Tilcara, pictures of the Passion are made of flowers and seeds at Easter and a traditional procession on Holy Wednesday at night is joined by thousands of pan-pipe musicians.

For drivers heading off main roads in this area, note that service stations are far apart: at Jujuy, Tilcara, Humahuaca, Abra Pampa and La Quiaca. Spare fuel and water must be carried.

Jujuy to Chile
Beyond Tumbaya, where there's a restored 17th-century church, Ruta 52 runs 3 km west to **Purmamarca**, a quiet, picturesque village, much visited for its spectacular mountain of seven colours, striped strata from terracotta to green (best seen in the morning), a lovely church with remarkable paintings and a good handicrafts market. (Buses to Jujuy 1½ hours, US$6; to Tilcara US$1. Salta–San Pedro de Atacama buses can be boarded here, book at **Hotel Manantial del Silencio** a day ahead.) It's worth staying the night in Purmamarca to appreciate the town's quiet rhythm. There's a helpful, tiny tourist office on the plaza with list of accommodation, maps and bus tickets, open 0700-1800.

From Purmamarca paved Ruta 52 leads through another *quebrada* over the 4164 m Abra Potrerillos to the Salinas Grandes salt flats at about 3400 m on the Altiplano (fantastic views especially at sunset). From here roads lead southwest past spectacular rock formations along the east side of the salt flats to San Antonio de los Cobres, and west across the salt flats via Susques to the Jama Pass (4400 m) and Chile. The only place with lodging beyond Purmamarca is **Susques**, which has an outstanding church (**Complejo Turístico Pastos Chicos**, T0387-15-487 4709, info@pastoschicos.com.ar, and others). There are no services or money exchange at the border, which is open 0700-2000. This is the route taken by most passenger and truck traffic from Salta or Jujuy to San Pedro de Atacama.

Jujuy to Bolivia

About 7 km north of the Purmamarca turning is **La Posta de Hornillos** ① *open, in theory, Wed-Mon 0830-1800, free*, a museum in a restored colonial posting house where Belgrano stayed, also the scene of several battles. About 2 km further is **Maimará** with its brightly striped rock, known as the 'Artist's Palette', and huge cemetery, decorated with flowers at Easter.

Tilcara → *Phone code: 0388. Colour map 6, C3. Population: 5600. Altitude: 2460 m.*

Tilcara lies 22 km north of the turn-off to Purmamarca. It's the liveliest Quebrada village, the best base for exploring the area. It has an excellent handicrafts market around its pleasant plaza and plenty of places to stay and to eat. The little **tourist office** ① *Belgrano 590, T0388 4955720, www.tilcara.com.ar, daily 0800-2100*, has very helpful staff. Visit the **Pucará** ① *daily 0900-1800*, a restored prehispanic hilltop settlement, with panoramic views of the gorge, and the superb **Museo Arqueológico** ① *Belgrano 445, daily 0900-1230, 1400-1800, US$1 for both and the Jardín Botánico*, with a fine collection of pre-Columbian ceramics, masks and mummies. There are four art museums in town and good walks in all directions. There are fiestas throughout January, carnival and Holy Week. There's an ATM on the plaza, taking most international cards.

The road continues through **Huacalera** and **Uquía**, which has one of the most impressive churches in the valley (from 1691), with extraordinary Cuzqueño paintings of angels in 17th-century battle dress and other works of art.

Humahuaca → *Phone code: 03887. Colour map 6, B3. Population: 11,300. Altitude: 2940 m.*

Although Humahuaca, 129 km north of Jujuy, dates from 1591, it was almost entirely rebuilt in the mid-19th century. Now it is visited by daily coach trips. It still has a distinctive culture of its own, though, and is a useful stopping point for travelling north up to the puna, or to Iruya. On 1-2 February is **La Candelaria** festival. **Jueves de Comadres, Festival de las Coplas y de la Chicha**, at the Thursday before carnival is famously animated, lots of drinking and throwing flour and water around. Book accommodation ahead. ATM on main plaza, all major credit cards. On the little plaza is the church, **San Antonio**, originally of 1631, rebuilt 1873-80, containing a statue of the Virgen de la Candelaria, gold retables and 12 fine Cuzqueño paintings. Also on the plaza, tourists gather to watch a mechanical figure of San Francisco Solano blessing the town from **El Cabildo**, the neo-colonial town hall, at 1200 daily. Overlooking the town is the massive **Monumento a la Independencia Argentina**, commemorating the heaviest fighting in the country during the Wars of Independence. At **Coctaca**, 10 km northeast, there is an impressive and extensive (40 ha) series of pre-colonial agricultural terraces. Tourist information available from the **Cabildo** ① *Tucumán y Jujuy, office hours, donations accepted.*

Iruya → *Colour map 6, B3. Population: 5500. Altitude: 2600 m.*

A rough *ripio* road 25 km north of Humahuaca runs northeast from the Panamericana (RN9) 8 km to Iturbe (also called Hipólito Irigoyen), and then up over the 4000 m Abra del Cóndor before dropping steeply, around many hairpin bends, into the Quebrada de Iruya. The road is very rough and unsuited to small hire cars, but is one of Argentina's most amazing drives. Iruya, 66 km from Humahuaca, is a beautiful hamlet wedged on a hillside. Its warm, friendly inhabitants hold a colourful **Rosario** festival on first Sunday in October and at Easter. It is worth spending a few days here to go horse riding or walking: the hike (seven hours return) to the remote **San Isidro** is unforgettable. At Titiconte 4 km away, there are unrestored pre-Inca ruins (guide necessary). Iruya has no ATM. The tourist office is on San Martín (irregular hours), and there is a *locutorio*, post office and a few food and handicraft shops. See www.iruyaonline.com.

Tres Cruces and Abra Pampa

Some 62 km north of Humahuaca on the Panamericana is Tres Cruces, where customs searches are made on vehicles from Bolivia. **Abra Pampa** (*Population: 6000*), 91 km north of Humahuaca, is a mining town. In the third week of January is the important Huancar folklore festival.

Monumento Natural Laguna de los Pozuelos ① *50 km northwest of Abra Pampa, park office, Rivadavia 339, Abra Pampa, T03887-491349, altitude: 3650 m; temperatures can drop to -25°C in winter*, is a nature reserve with a lake at its centre visited by huge colonies of flamingos. There is a ranger station at the southern end of the park, with a campsite nearby. There is no bus transport, so it's best to go with a guide; the Laguna is 5 km from the road, very tough, high clearance recommended, walk last 800 m to reach the edge of the lagoon. Check with the park office before going, the lake can be dry with no birds, eg in September.

From a point 4 km north of Abra Pampa roads branch west to Cochinoca (25 km) and southwest to **Casabindo** (62 km). On 15 August at Casabindo, the local saint's day, the last and only *corrida de toros* (running with bulls) in Argentina is held, amidst a colourful popular celebration. **El Toreo de la Vincha** takes place in front of the church, where a bull defies onlookers to take a ribbon and medal which it carries. The church itself is a magnificent building, with twin bell towers, and inside a superb series of 16th century angels in armour paintings. Most visitors arrive on day-trips from Tilcara.

La Quiaca and Yavi → *Phone code: 03885. Altitude: 3442 m. 5121 km from Ushuaia. Colour map 6, B3.*

On the border with Bolivia, a concrete bridge links this typical border town with Villazón on the Bolivian side. Warm clothing is essential particularly in winter when temperatures can drop to -15°C, though care should be taken against sunburn during the day. In mid-October, villagers from the far reaches of the remote *altiplano* come to exchange ceramic pots, sheepskins and vegetables, in the colourful three-day **Fiesta de la Olla**, which also involves much high-spirited dancing and drinking. Two ATMs, but no facilities for changing cash or TCs, but plenty of *cambios* in Villazón. **Yavi** is 16 km east of La Quiaca. Its **church of San Francisco** (1690) ① *Mon 1500-1800, Tue-Fri 0900-1200, 1500-1800, Sat-Sun 0900-1200*, is one of Argentina's treasures, with a magnificent gold retable and pulpit and windows of onyx. Caretaker Lydia lives opposite the police station and will show you round the church.

Border with Bolivia → *Do not photograph the border area.*

The border bridge is 10 blocks from La Quiaca bus terminal, 15 minutes walk (taxi US$2). Argentine office open 0700-2400. If leaving Argentina for a short stroll into Villazón, show your passport, but do not let it be stamped by Migración, otherwise you will have to wait 24 hours before being allowed back into Argentina. Formalities on entering Argentina are usually brief at the border but thorough customs searches are made 100 km south at Tres Cruces. Leaving Argentina is very straightforward, but if you need a visa to enter Bolivia, it is best to get it before arriving in La Quiaca. The **Bolivian consulate** is at 9 de Julio 100 y República Arabe Siria, T422283, open 0700-1600 weekdays (in theory). Argentine time is one hour later than Bolivia, two hours when Buenos Aires adopts daylight saving.

Parque Nacional Calilegua → *Colour map 6, C3.*

① *Park office: San Lorenzo s/n, Calilegua, T03886-422046, calilegua@apn.gov.ar. See also www.calilegua.com. Reached by Ruta 83, via Ruta 34, from just north of Libertador, the park entrance is at Aguas Negras, 12 km along the dirt road (4WD essential when wet), which climbs through the park and beyond to Valle Grande (basic accommodation and shops), 90 km from Libertador.*

Libertador General San Martín, a sugar town 113 km northeast of Jujuy on Ruta 34 to southeastern Bolivia, is the closest base for exploring the park, an area of peaks over 3000 m and deep valleys covered in cloud forest, with a huge variety of wildlife, including 300-400 species of bird (estimates vary) and 60 species of mammals (you may spot tapirs, pumas, tarucas, Andean deer and even jaguars here) There are six marked trails of various lengths, five starting at or near Aguas Negras. There are also cycling routes. Rangers are stationed at Aguas Negras, with a campsite nearby, and at Mesada de las Colmenas. Best time for visiting is November-March, the warmest but also the wettest. **Tourist office** ① *at the bus terminal*.

Routes to Bolivia

From Libertador, Ruta 34 runs northeast 244 km, to the Bolivian border at **Pocitos** (also called **Salvador Mazza**) and Yacuiba (see Yacuiba in southeastern Bolivia). It passes through **Embarcación** and **Tartagal** (good regional museum). In Pocitos, the border town, is **Hotel Buen Gusto**, just tolerable. There are no *casas de cambio* here. The border is open 24 hours. From Yacuiba, across the border, buses go to Santa Cruz de la Sierra and Tarija. **Bolivian consulate** ① *Av San Martín 446, T471336, Mon-Fri 0900-1400*. Several bus companies have services from the border to Salta and Tucumán.

Another route is via Aguas Blancas. At Pichanal, 85 km northeast of Libertador, Ruta 50 heads north via **Orán** (*Population: 138,000*), an uninteresting place.

Aguas Blancas on the border is 53 km from Orán (open 24 hours, restaurants, shops, no accommodation, nowhere to change money and Bolivianos are not accepted south of Aguas Blancas, fill up with fuel here, or in Orán). **Bolivian consulate** ① *Av San Martín 134, Orán, T421969, Mon-Fri 0830-1300, 1600-1900*. Buses run from Bermejo, across the river by bridge, to Tarija, three to four hours, US$3 (US$6 by shared taxi). See above for time differences.

ⓖ Jujuy to the Chilean and Bolivian borders listings

For hotel and restaurant price codes, and other relevant information, see Essentials.

● Where to stay

Jujuy to Chile *p138*
Purmamarca
$$$$ El Manantial del Silencio, Ruta 52 Km 3.5, T0388-490 8081, www.hotelmanantial.com.ar. Signposted from the road into Purmamarca. Luxurious rooms, modern building, wonderful views, spacious living rooms with huge fire, charming hosts, includes breakfast, heating, riding, pool, superb restaurant (guests only).
$$$ Casa de Piedra, Pantaleon Cruz 6, T490 8092, www.postadelsol.com. Well-situated new hotel made of stone and adobe with very comfortable rooms.
$$$ La Posta, C Santa Rosa de Lima 4 blocks up from plaza, T490 8029, www.postade purmamarca.com.ar. Beautiful setting by the

mountain, comfortable rooms, helpful owner. Highly recommended.
$$ El Viejo Algarrobo, C Salta behind the church, T490 8286, www.hotelviejoalgarrobo. com.ar. Small but pleasant rooms, cheaper with shared bath, helpful, good value and quality regional dishes in its restaurant (**$**).
$ El Pequeño Inti, C Florida 10 m from plaza, T490 8089, elintidepurmamarca@hotmail. com. Small, modern rooms around a little courtyard, breakfast, hot water, good value. Recommended.

Susques
$$ El Unquillar, R52, Km 219 (1 km west of Susques), T03887-490201,www.hotelel unquillar.com.ar. Attractive, with local weavings, good rooms. Restaurant open to public. Phone for pick-up.
$ Res La Vicuñita, San Martín 221, Susques, T03887-490207, opposite the church.

Without bath, hot water, breakfast available, simple and welcoming.

Jujuy to Bolivia: Maimará *p139*

$$$ Posta del Sol, Martín Rodríguez y San Martín, T499 7156, www.postadelsol.com. Comfortable, rooms and cabins, with good restaurant, owner is tourist guide and has helpful information.

Tilcara *p139*

Book ahead in carnival and around Easter when Tilcara is very busy. All those listed are recommended.

$$$ Alas de Alma, Dr Padilla 437, T495 5572, www.alas.travel. Central, relaxed atmosphere, spacious doubles, and *cabañas* for up to 4 people. 2 mins from the main street.

$$$ Posada con los Angeles, Gorriti 156 (sign-posted from access to town), T495 5153, www.posadaconlosangeles.com.ar. A much-recommended favourite with charming rooms, each in a different colour, all with fireplace and door to the garden with beautiful views.

$$$ Quinta La Paceña, Padilla 660 at Ambrosetti, T495 5098, www.quintalapacena.com.ar. This architect-designed traditional adobe house is a peaceful haven. The garden is gorgeous and wonderfully kept.

$ Casa los Molles, Belgrano 155, T495 5410, www.casalosmolles.com.ar. Not really a hostel, this affordable *casa de campo* offers simple dorms in a friendly atmosphere (US$12-13 pp), as well as a charming double (**$$-$**) and 2 comfortable *cabañas* (**$$$** for up to 4 people). Small and central, book in advance.

$ pp Malka, San Martín s/n, 5 blocks from plaza up steep hill, T495 5197, www.malkahostel.com.ar. A superb youth hostel, one of the country's best. It has beautifully situated rustic *cabañas* (**$$$** up to 8), dorms for 5 people, US$18 pp, and doubles with bath (**$$$**). Catch a taxi from town or walk for 20 mins.

$ Tilcara Hostel, Bolivar 166, T15-507 4372, www.tilcarahostel.com. This hostel is welcoming with dorms at US$9 pp. Also offer doubles and comfortable cabins (**$$**).

Camping Camping El Jardín, access on Belgrano, T495 5128, www.eljardintilcara.com.ar. Hot showers, also hotel and basic hostel.

Huacalera

$$$ Solar del Trópico, T0388-154 785021, www.solardeltropico.com. 2 km from Huacalera, Argentine/French-owned B&B who will cook fusion food on request. Rustic, spacious bedrooms, organic gardens, artist's studio; workshops are run regularly. Tours offered. Call to arrange a pick-up beforehand.

Humahuaca *p139*

$$$$-$$$ Hotel Huacalera, Ruta 9 km 1790, T54388, 15 581 3417. www.hotelhuacalera.com. Upscale resort situated in the *puna*, it offers colourful rooms with terraces, spa, swimming pool and nature excursions.

$$ Hostal Azul, B Medalla Milagrosa, La Banda, T421107. Across the river, smart, welcoming, pleasant, simple rooms, good restaurant and wine list, parking. Recommended.

$ pp Posada El Sol, Medalla Milagrosa s/n, over bridge from terminal, then 520 m, follow signs, T421466, www.posadaelsol.com.ar. Quiet rural area, shared rooms or private (**$$**) in a warm welcoming place, laundry, horse riding, owner will collect from bus station if called in advance. HI affiliated. Recommended.

Iruya *p139*

$$$ Hostería de Iruya, San Martín 641, T03887-482002, www.hoteliruya.com. A special place, extremely comfortable, with good food, and great views from the top of the village. Highly recommended.

$$$-$$ Mirador de Iruya, La Banda s/n, T03887-421463, www.elmiradordeiruya.com.ar. Cross the river and climb a little to this hostal. Doubles, triples and quads available. Fantastic views from the terrace.

$ Hospedaje Asunta, Belgrano s/n (up the hill), T0387-154 045113. Friendly hostel with 28 beds. Fantastic views. Recommended.

Abra Pampa *p140*
$ Residencial El Norte, Sarmiento 530,
T491315. Private or shared room, hot water,
good food. Also **Res y restaurante Cesarito**,
Pérez 200, T491125,1 block from main plaza.

La Quiaca *p140*
$$ Munay, Belgrano 51-61, T423924, www.
munayhotel.com.ar. In same group as Munay
in Salta, rooms with heating and fan, parking.
$ Hostel Copacabana, Pellegrini 141, T423875,
www.hostelcopacabana.com.ar. Only a few
blocks from the bus terminal and the plaza. Clean
dorms, and doubles and comfortable living areas.

Yavi *p140*
$$ Hostal de Yavi, Güemes 222, T03541 15-
633522, www.hostaldeyavi.blogspot.com.
Simple bedrooms with bath, and some hostel
space. Cosy sitting room, good food. Tours also
arranged: to see cave paintings; moonlight
walks; trekking; and trips to the Laguna de los
Pozuelos. Recommended.
$ La Casona, Sen Pérez y San Martín,
T03887-422316. Welcoming, with and
without bath, breakfast.

Parque Nacional Calilegua *p140*
$$$ Finca Portal de Piedra, Villa Monte, Santa
Bárbara, T03886-156 820564, www.ecoportalde
piedra.com. 17 km north of Libertador General
San Martín. Eco-run finca in its own reserve (Las
Lancitas), convenient for PNs Calilegua and El Rey,
guesthouse and cabin, simple food, horse riding,
trekking, birdwatching and other excursions,
from Jujuy take a bus via San Pedro and Palma
Sola (which is 12 km north of the finca).
$$$ Posada del Sol, Los Ceibos 747 at Pucará,
Libertador General San Martín, T03886-424900,
www.posadadelsoljujuy.com.ar. Comfortable,
functional hotel, with gardens and pool, has
advice on local trips.

Restaurants

Tilcara *p139*
$$ El Patio, Lavalle 352, T495 5044. Great range,
lovely patio at the back, popular, very good.

$$ Pucará, up the hill towards the Pucará,
T495 5721. Imaginative, posh Andean food and
hearty puddings, intimate, rustic atmosphere.
$ Música Esperanza (Bar del Centro),
Belgrano 547, T495 5462. Small restaurant/café
serving local dishes in the patio. Not always
open. Both the restaurant and crafts shop next
door sustain an NGO that organizes free art and
music workshops for local children.

Cafés
El Cafecito de Tukuta, Rivadavia, on the
plaza. For a taste of Tilcara's culture, don't
miss this place, good coffee and locally
grown herbal teas, *peña* at weekends from
celebrated local musicians.
La Peña de Carlitos, Lavalle 397, on the plaza,
www.lapeniadecarlitos.com.ar. With music from
the charismatic and delightful Carlitos, also
cheap *menú del día*, *empanadas*, and drinks.

Humahuaca *p139*
$$-$ El Portillo, Tucumán 69. A simply
decorated room, serving slightly more
elaborate regional meals than the usual.

Transport

Tilcara *p139*
Bus El Quiaqueno combines with Andesmar/
Brown, passes Tilcara en route to **Jujuy** 4 times
a day from 1340, and en route to **La Quiaca** 6
times a day from 1110. **Jama Bus** runs between
Tilcara, Humahuaca and La Quiaca.

Humahuaca *p139*
Bus To all places along the Quebrada from the
terminal (toilets, *confitería*, fruit and sandwich
sellers outside), to **Iruya** (see below) and to
La Quiaca, with **Balut** and **La Quiaqueña**
(more comfortable), several daily, 2½ hrs, US$6.

Iruya *p139*
Bus Daily from **Humahuaca** Iruya SA, 0820,
1030 daily, and Sun-Fri 1600, 3-3½ hrs, US$5
one way, returning 0600 (not on Sun) and
1300, 1515, 1600, 1800. Also **Panamericano
de Jujuy**, daily 0830, return from Iruya 1400,

US$5. Also trips of several days organized by tour operators.

La Quiaca *p140*
Bus Terminal, España y Belgrano, luggage storage. Several buses daily to **Salta** (US$24) with **Balut** (7½ hrs) and others. Several daily to **Humahuaca** and **Jujuy**, schedules above. Take own food, as sometimes long delays. Buses are stopped for routine border police controls and rigorous searches for drugs. **Note** If your bus arrives in the early morning when no restaurants are open and it is freezing cold outside, wrap up warm and stay in the terminal until daylight as the streets are unsafe in the dark.

Yavi *p140*
No buses go to Yavi. You can hitchhike from the exit to R5 (US$1 pp is expected) or take a remise taxi for US$17 return, including ½-hr

stay. **Remiseria Acuario**, España y 25 de Mayo s/n, T03885-423333.

Parque Nacional Calilegua *p140*
Bus From Libertador daily at 0830 going across the park to **Valle Grande** (US$4, 5 hrs), returning the same day. Remise charges about US$7-10 from Libertador to Park entrance. All Pocitos or Orán buses pass through Libertador General San Martín.

Routes to Bolivia: Aguas Blancas *p141*
Bus Between Aguas Blancas and **Orán** buses run every 45 mins, US$1, luggage checks on bus. See under Salta for through buses to **Salta**. Or go to **Güemes**, 3 a day, US$17 and change. To **Jujuy** with **Balut**, 2 daily, US$17-21. Some services from Salta and Jujuy call at **Orán** en route to **Tartagal** and **Pocitos**. Note that buses are subject to searches for drugs and contraband.

The Northeast

The river systems of the Paraná, Paraguay and Uruguay, with hundreds of minor tributaries, small lakes and marshlands, dominate the Northeast. Between the Paraná and Uruguay rivers is Argentine Mesopotamia containing the provinces of Entre Ríos, Corrientes and Misiones, this last named after Jesuit foundations, whose red stone ruins have been rescued from the jungle. The great attraction of this region is undoubtedly the Iguazú Falls, which tumble into a gorge on a tributary of the Alto Paraná on the border with Brazil. But the region offers other opportunities for wildlife watching, such as the flooded plains of the Esteros del Iberá. This is also the region of mate tea, sentimental chamamé music and tiny chipá bread.

Up the Río Uruguay

This river forms the frontier with Uruguay and there are many crossings as you head upstream to the point where Argentina, Uruguay and Brazil meet. On the way, you'll find riverside promenades, sandy beaches, hot springs and palm forests.

Gualeguaychú → *Phone code: 03446. Colour map 8, B5. Population: 109,461 (department).*
On the Río Gualeguaychú, 19 km above its confluence with the Río Uruguay and 236 km north of Buenos Aires, this is a pleasant town with a massive **pre-Lenten carnival**. Parades are held in the Corsódromo (see www.carnavaldelpais.com.ar or www.grancarnaval.com.ar for details of participating groups, prices of tickets, etc). Some 33 km southeast the Libertador Gral San Martín Bridge (5.4 km long) provides the most southerly route across the Río Uruguay, to Fray Bentos (vehicles US$6; pedestrians and cyclists may cross only on vehicles, officials may arrange lifts). **Tourist office** ⓘ *Paseo del Puerto, T422900, www.gualeguaychuturismo.com, 0800-2000 (2200 in summer, 2400 Fri-Sat).* **Uruguayan consulate** ⓘ *B Rivadavia 510, T426168, conuruguale@entrerios.net.*

True brew

Yerba mate (*ilex paraguayensis*) is made into a tea which is widely drunk in Argentina, Paraguay, Brazil and Uruguay. Traditionally associated with the gauchos, the modern *mate* paraphernalia is a common sight anywhere: the gourd (*un mate*) in which the tea leaves are steeped, the straw (usually silver) and a thermos of hot water to top up the gourd. It was the Jesuits who first grew *yerba mate* in plantations, inspiring one of the drink's names: *té de jesuitas*. Also used has been *té de Paraguay*, but now just *mate* or *yerba* will do. In southern Brazil it is called *ximarão*; in Paraguay *tereré*, when drunk cold with digestive herbs.

Nice walks can be taken along the *costanera* between the bridge and the small port, from where short boat excursions and city tours leave (some also from the *balneario norte*). **El Patio del Mate** ① *G Méndez y Costanera, T4243/1, www.elpatiodelmate.com.ar, daily 0800-2000 (2200 in summer),* is a workshop dedicated to the *mate* gourd. On the outskirts are thermal pools at **Termas del Guaychú** ① *Ruta 14 Km 63.5, www.termasdelguaychu.com.ar,* and **Termas del Gualeguaychú** ① *Ruta 42 Km 2.5, T499167.*

Concepción del Uruguay → Phone code: 03442. Colour map 8, B5. Population: 100,728 (department).

The first Argentine port of any size on the Río Uruguay was founded in 1783. Overlooking Plaza Ramírez is the church of the Immaculate Conception which contains the remains of Gen Urquiza. **Palacio San José** ① *32 km west of town, T432620, www.palaciosanjose.com.ar, Mon-Fri 0800-1900, Sat-Sun 0900-1800, US$2, free guided visits throughout the day, and night visits at Easter, Jan-Feb (on Fri) and Oct-Dec (1 Sat a month).* Urquiza's former mansion, set in beautiful grounds with a lake, is now a museum, with artefacts from his life and a collection of period furniture. Take Ruta 39 west and turn right after Caseros train station. Buses to Paraná or Rosario del Tala stop at El Cruce or Caseros, 4 or 8 km away respectively, so it's best to take a remise. **Tourist office** ① *Galarza y Supremo Entrerriano, 1425820, and Galarza y Daniel Flías, T440812, 0800-2000 (0700-2200 in high season).*

Colón → Phone code: 03447. Colour map 8, A5. Population: 62,160 (department).

Founded in 1863, Colón is 45 km north of Concepción del Uruguay. It has shady streets, an attractive *costanera* and long sandy beaches. The Artigas Bridge (US$6 toll, open 24 hrs) crosses the river to Paysandú; all formalities are dealt with on Uruguayan side. *Migraciones* officials board the bus, but non-Argentines/Uruguayans should get off bus for stamp. **Tourist office** ① *Av Costanera Quirós y Gouchón, T421233, www.colonturismo.gov.ar, 0600-2000 (2200 in high season).* **Uruguayan consulate** ① *San Martín 417, T421999, crou@ciudad.com.ar.*

Parque Nacional El Palmar

① *58 km north of Colón, T493049, www.pnelpalmar.com.ar. US$10.*

This park of 8500 ha is on the Río Uruguay, entrance gates off Ruta 14, where you'll be given a map and information on walks. The park contains varied scenery with a mature palm forest, sandy beaches on the Uruguay river, indigenous tombs and the remains of an 18th-century quarry and port, a good museum and many rheas and other birds. The Yatay palms grow up to 12 m and some are hundreds of years old. It is best to stay overnight as wildlife is more easily seen in the early morning or at sunset. There are **camping facilities** ① *www.campingelpalmar.com.ar, US$3.75 plus US$5.75 pp,* a restaurant and shop. Very popular at weekends in summer.

Refugio de Vida Silvestre La Aurora del Palmar ① *T0345-490 5725, www.auroradelpalmar. com.ar, free,* is opposite the Parque Nacional El Palmar, 3 km south of Ubajay at Km 202 Ruta 14. A private reserve protecting a similar environment to that of its neighbour, La Aurora covers 1300 ha, of which 200 are covered with a mature palm forest. There are also gallery forests along the streams and patches of *espinal* or scrub. Birds are easily seen, as are capybaras along the streams. The administration centre is only 500 m from Ruta 14 and services are well organized. There are guided excursions on horseback, by 4WD and on foot combined, or canoe. Camping is permitted and there are private rooms at $$$ **Casona La Estación** (rate for four people) or $$$-$$ in doubles or dorms in old railway carriages.

Concordia → *Phone code: 0345. Colour map 8, A5. Population: 170,033 (Department).*

Just downriver from Salto, Uruguay, Concordia, 120 km north of Colón, is a large city with few fine turn-of-the-20th century buildings and a beautiful 70-ha riverside park, northeast of town. About 20 km upriver Salto Grande international hydroelectric dam provides road and railway crossings to Uruguay. **Tourist office** ① *Pellegrini y Bartolomé Mitre, T4213905, daily 0800-2100.* **Uruguayan consulate** ① *Asunción 131, T422 1426, conurucon@arnet.com.ar.*

Upstream from Concordia in the province of Corrientes is the port of **Monte Caseros**, with the Uruguayan town of Bella Unión, on the Brazilian border, almost opposite. An international bridge is planned; in the meanwhile, small launches provide the border crossing (four a day, not on Sunday). Less adventurous, there are two international bridges at Paso de los Libres and Santo Tomé, the former being very busy and used by most bus companies crossing to Uruguaiana and Brazilian tourist destinations.

⊚ Up the Río Uruguay listings

For hotel and restaurant price codes, and other relevant information, see Essentials.

● Where to stay

Gualeguaychú *p144*
Accommodation is scarce during carnival. Prices 25% higher Dec-Mar, Easter and long weekends. The tourist office can contact estate agents for short stays in private flats.
$$$ **Puerto Sol**, San Lorenzo 477, T434017, www.hotelpuertosol.com.ar. Good rooms, next to the port, has a small resort on a nearby island (transfer included) for relaxing drink.
$$$ **Tykuá**, Luis N Palma 150, T422625, www.tykuahotel.com.ar. 3 blocks from the bridge, with all services including safe.
Camping Several sites on riverside, others next to the bridge and north of it. El Ñandubaysal, T423298. The smartest, on the Río Uruguay, 15 km southeast.

Concepción del Uruguay *p145*
$$$$-$$ **Grand Hotel Casino**, Eva Perón 114, T425586, www.grandhotelcasino.com.ar. Originally a French-style mansion with adjacent theatre, superior rooms have a/c and TV, VIP rooms have new bathrooms.
$$$ **Antigua Posta del Torreón**, España y Almafuerte, T432618, www.postadeltorreon. com.ar. 9 confortable rooms in a stylish boutique hotel with a pool.
$$ **Nuevo Residencial Centro**, Moreno 130, T427429, www.nuevorescentro.com.ar. One of the cheapest options in town. Basic rooms, some with a/c, in a traditional 19th-century building with a lovely patio, 1.5 blocks from the plaza. No breakfast.

Colón *p145*
$$$ **Holimasú**, Belgrano 28, T421305, www.hotelholimasu.com.ar. Nice patio, a/c extra, $$ in low season.
$$$ **Hostería Restaurant del Puerto**, Alejo Peyret 158, T422698, www.hosteriadecolon.

com.ar. Great value, lovely atmosphere in old house, pool, no credit cards.

$$ La Posada de David, Alejo Peyret 97, T423930, www.colonentrerios.com.ar/ posadadedavid. Nice family house, garden, welcoming, good double rooms, great value.

Camping Several sites, some with cabins, on river bank, from US$5 daily.

❶ Restaurants

Concepción del Uruguay *p145*
$$$ El Conventillo de Baco, España 193, T433809. A refined choice with some outside tables and a chance to try fish from the river.

Colón *p145*
$$$ Chiva Chiva, Gral Urquiza y Brown. An artist's refuge; her inspiration is in the meals and drinks and in the pottery on display.

$$$ La Cosquilla del Angel, Alejo Peyret 180. The smartest place in town, meals include fish, set menu, live piano music in evenings.

$$$ Viejo Almacén, Gral Urquiza y Paso. Cosy, very good cooking and excellent service.

❷ Transport

Gualeguaychú *p144*
Bus Bus terminal at Bv Artigas y Bv Jurado, T440688 (30 min walk to centre, remise taxi US$3). To **Concepción del Uruguay**, 1 hr, US$3. To **Buenos Aires**, US$18, 3½ hrs, several daily. To **Fray Bentos**, US$5, 1½ hrs, and **Mercedes**, US$7, 2 hrs, Ciudad de Gualeguay and ETA CUT (not Sun). To **Montevideo**, from US$35, 6½ hrs, Plus Ultra.

Concepción del Uruguay *p145*
Bus Terminal at Rocamora y Los Constituyentes (remise, US$2). To **Buenos Aires**, frequent, 4-4½ hrs, US$20. To **Colón**, 1 hr, US$3.

Colón *p145*
Bus Terminal at Paysandú y Sourigues (10 blocks north of main plaza), T421716, left luggage at **Remises Base** (opposite Terminal) on 9 de Julio. Not all long distance buses enter Colón. **Buenos Aires**, US$21-26, 5-6 hrs. **Mercedes** (for Iberá), several companies, 7-8 hrs, US$18. **Paraná**, 4-6 hrs, US$10. To **Uruguay** Bus to **Paysandú**, Copay and Río Uruguay, US$4, 1 hr.

Parque Nacional El Palmar *p145*
Bus Buses from Colón, 1 hr, will drop you at the entrance and it may be possible to hitch the 12 km to the park administration. For **Refugio de Vida Silvestre La Aurora del Palmar** tell the bus driver you are going to La Aurora del Palmar (ask for Ruta 14 Kilómetro 202), to avoid confusion with the national park. Nearest town is Ubajay, 6 km, where buses stop; local services by **JoviBus**. Remise taxis can be taken from there, about US$10; ask at Parador Gastiazoro where buses stop. Remises also from Colón and Concordia. Otherwise take a tour.

Concordia *p146*
Bus Terminal at Justo y Yrigoyen, T4217235, 15 blocks northwest of Plaza 25 de Mayo (reached by No 2 bus). **Buenos Aires**, US$32-37, 5-7½ hrs. **Paraná** US$13.50, 4½ hrs.

To Uruguay By **ferry** to Salto, US$3, 15 mins, 4 a day, not Sun. Port is 15 blocks southeast of centre. The **bus** service via the Salto Grande dam, US$4, 1½ hrs, is run by Flecha Bus and Chadre, 2 day each, not Sun; all formalities on the Argentine side, open 24 hrs. Passengers have to get off the bus to go through immigration. **Bikes** are not allowed to cross the international bridge but officials will help cyclists find a lift.

Up the Río Paraná

Several historic cities stand on the banks of the Paraná, which flows south from its confluence with the Río Paraguay. National parks protecting endangered marshes, especially at Iberá, are the highlight of the zone.

Rosario → *Phone code: 0341. Colour map 8, B5. Population: 1.2 million.*

The largest city in the province of Santa Fe and the third largest city in Argentina, Rosario, 295 km northwest of Buenos Aires, is a great industrial and export centre. It has a lively cultural scene with several theatres and bars where there are daily shows. At weekends (daily in summer) boats go to dozens of riverside resorts on the islands and sandbars opposite the city. The **tourist office**ⓘ *Av Belgrano y Buenos Aires, T480 2230, www.rosarioturismo.com*, is on the riverside park next to the Monumento a la Bandera. See www.viarosario.com, for the latest events information.

The old city centre is Plaza 25 de Mayo. Around it are the **cathedral** and the **Palacio Municipal**. On the north side is the **Museo de Arte Decorativo**ⓘ *Santa Fe 748, T480 2547, museo@museoestevez. gov.ar, Wed-Sun 0900-1400, in winter to 1700, US$0.50*. This sumptuous former residence houses a valuable private collection of paintings, furniture, tapestries sculptures and silverwork, brought mainly from Europe. Left of the cathedral, the **Pasaje Juramento** opens the pedestrian way to the imposing **Monumento a la Bandera** ⓘ *T480 2238, www.monumentoalabandera.gov.ar, Mon 1400-1800, Tue-Fri 0900-1800, Sat-Sun 0900-1230, 1400-1800, US$0.65 (tower), free (Salón de las Banderas)*. This commemorates the site on which, in 1812, General Belgrano, on his way to fight the Spaniards in Jujuy, raised the Argentine flag for the first time. A 70-m tower has excellent panoramic views. In the first half of November in the Parque a la Bandera (opposite the monument) **Fiesta de las Colectividades** lasts 10 nights, with folk music, dances and food stalls. From Plaza 25 de Mayo, Córdoba leads west towards Plaza San Martín and beyond, the Boulevard Oroño. These 14 blocks, the **Paseo del Siglo,** have the largest concentration of late 19th- and early 20th-century buildings in the city. **Museo de Bellas Artes J B Castagnino** ⓘ *Av Pellegrini 2202, T480 2542, www.museocastagnino.org.ar, closed Tue, open 1400-2000, US$1*. Just outside the 126-ha Parque Independencia, it has an impressive collection of French impressionist, Italian baroque and Flemish works, and one of best collections of Argentine paintings and sculpture. Upriver is the **Museo de Arte Contemporáneo** (MACRO) ⓘ *Blvd Oroño on the river shore, T480 4981, www.macromuseo.org.ar, Thu-Tue 1400-2000, US$1*. Inside a massive old silo, this remarkable museum is 10 levels high with a small gallery on each level, and at the top is a viewing deck.

Che Guevara was born here in 1928. The large white house at Entre Ríos y Urquiza where he lived for the first two years of his life before his family moved to Alta Gracia, near Córdoba (see page 93), is now an insurance company office.

Paraná → *Phone code: 0343. Colour map 8, A5. Population: 339,930 (department).*

About 30 km southeast of Santa Fe, the capital of Entre Ríos was, from 1854-1861, capital of the Republic. The centre is on a hill offering views over the Río Paraná and beyond to Santa Fe. Around **Plaza Primero de Mayo** are the **Municipalidad**, the **Cathedral** and the Colegio del Huerto, seat of the Senate of the Argentine Confederation between 1854 and 1861. Take pedestrianized San Martín and half block west of the corner with 25 de Junio is the fine **Teatro 3 de Febrero** (1908). Two blocks north is the **Plaza Alvear**; on the west side of which is the **Museo de Bellas Artes** ⓘ *Buenos Aires 355, T420 7868, Tue-Fri 0700-1300, 1500-1900, Sat 1000-1400, 1700-2000, Sun 1000-1300, US$0.75*. It houses a vast collection of Argentine artists' work, with many by painter Cesario Bernaldo de Quirós. The city's glory is **Parque Urquiza**, along the cliffs above the Río Paraná. **Tourist offices**: in the centreⓘ *Buenos Aires 132, T423 0183*; at **Parque Urquiza**ⓘ *Av Laurencena y Juan de San Martín, T420 1837*; at the **bus terminal**ⓘ *T420 1862*; and at the Hernandarias tunnel. **Provincial office**ⓘ *Laprida 5, T0810-444 8874, www.unatierradiferente.com.*

Santa Fe → *Phone code: 0342. Colour map 8, A4. Population: 525,093.*

From Paraná to Santa Fe, the road goes under the Río Paraná by the Herandarias tunnel (toll) and then crosses a number of bridges (bus service, US$3, 50 minutes). Santa Fe, capital of its province, was founded by settlers from Asunción in 1573, though its present site was not occupied until 1653. The south part of the city, around the **Plaza 25 de Mayo** is the historic centre. On the Plaza itself is the majestic **Casa de Gobierno**, built in 1911-1917 in French style on the site of the historic Cabildo, in which the 1853 constitution was drafted. Opposite is the **Cathedral**. Across San Martín is the extensive Parque General Belgrano. **Museo Histórico Provincial** ① *San Martín 1490, T457 3529, all year 0830-1230, afternoon hours change frequently, closed Mon, free.* The building, dating from 1690, is one of the oldest surviving civil buildings in the country. About 100 m south is the **Iglesia y Convento de San Francisco** (1673 to 1695), with fine wooden ceilings, built from timber floated down the river from Paraguay, carved by indigenous craftsmen and fitted without the use of nails. On the opposite side of the park is the superb **Museo Etnográfico y Colonial** ① *25 de Mayo 1470, Tue-Fri 0830-1200, 1530-2030, Sat-Sun from 1530, 1600 or 1730 depending on season, US$0.50,* with a chronologically ordered exhibition of artefacts from 2000 BC to the first Spanish settlers of Santa Fe la Vieja. **Tourist offices**: at the **bus terminal** ① *T457 4124, 0700-2000 (0800 at weekends),* and opposite the **Teatro Municipal** ① *San Martín 2020; also at Bulevar Gálvez 1150 and Santiago del Estero 3100, T0800-777 5000, www.santafeturismo.gov.ar,* all good. **Provincial office** ① *San Martín 1399, T458 9475, turismo@santafe.gov.ar.*

Esteros del Iberá

The **Reserva Natural del Iberá** protects nearly 13,000 sq km of wetlands known as the **Esteros del Iberá**, similar to the Pantanal in Brazil. Over sixty small lakes, no more than a few metres deep, cover 20-30% of the protected area, which is rich in aquatic plants. Like islands in the *lagunas*, *embalsados* are floating vegetation, thick enough to support large animals and trees. Wildlife includes black caiman, marsh deer, capybara and about 370 species of bird, among them the *yabirú* or *Juan Grande*, the largest stork in the western hemisphere. More difficult to see are the endangered maned wolf, the 3-m-long yellow anaconda, the *yacaré* ñato and the river otter. There is a visitors' centre by the bridge at the access to Carlos Pellegrini (see below), open 0730-1200, 1400-1800, helpful and informative park rangers. **Mercedes** *(Phone code: 03773; Population: 47,425)*, 250 km southeast of Corrientes, gives access to the eastern side, with regular transport to Carlos Pellegrini. There are a few restaurants, ATMs and a small tourist office at Sarmiento 650, T420100. The surrounding countryside is mostly grassy *pampas*, where rheas can be seen, with rocks emerging from the plains from time to time. **Carlos Pellegrini**, 120 km northeast of Mercedes (rough road), stands on beautiful **Laguna Iberá** ① *www.ibera.gov.ar, T03773-15-459110*. A one-day visit allows for a three-hour boat excursion (US$20 per person if not included in hotel rates), but some hotels offer more activities for longer stays.

The western side of Iberá, some two hours from Corrientes by road, has several access points, including Portal San Nicolás, which is on the reserve owned by the **Conservation Land Trust** (CLT) ① *www.proyectoibera.org*. The Trust's aim is integrate its lands into the publicly-owned national reserve. San Nicolás, reached from San Miguel (160 km from Corrientes) has a *guardaparques* post and a campsite. From the jetty it's 45 minutes by boat to CLT's **San Alonso** lodge ($$$$, two-night programme including rustic rooms, criollo food and all excursions; see Rincón del Socorro, under Where to stay below, for contact details). **San Alonso** can be reached by boat, or by a two-day, one-night ride.

Another access point is Portal Yahaveré, southwest of San Nicolás. Between here and Corrientes is **Parque Nacional Mburucuyá** ① *12 km east of the town of Mburucuyá, T03782-498907, www.pnmburucuya.gob.ar, free.* Buses San Antonio from Corrientes go daily to Mburucuyá, 2½ hours, US$4; remises to the park, US$15. Covering 17,660 ha, it stretches north from the marshes of the Río Santa Lucía and includes savanna with *yatay* palms, 'islands' of wet Chaco forest, and *esteros*. Wildlife is easy to see. The land was donated by Danish botanist Troels

Pedersen, who identified 1300 different plants here. Provincial route 86 (unpaved) crosses the park for 18 km to the information centre and free campsite.

Corrientes → *Phone code: 0379. Colour map 6, C6. Population: 356,310.*

Corrientes, founded in 1588 is some 30 km below the confluence of the Ríos Paraguay and Alto Paraná. The 2.75-km General Belgrano bridge crosses the Río Paraná (toll) to Resistencia (25 km). The river can make the air moist and oppressive, but in winter the climate is pleasant. The city, known as the capital of Carnaval in Argentina, is the setting for Graham Greene's novel, *The Honorary Consul*. **Tourist offices: city tourist office** ① *Carlos Pellegrini 542, T442 3779, daily 0700-2100, good map*. **Provincial office** ① *25 de Mayo 1330, T442 7200, province and city information, Mon-Fri 0700-1300*, and in the **bus station** ① *T441 4839, www.corrientes.gov.ar, 0700-2200*.

On the **Plaza 25 de Mayo**, one of the best preserved in Argentina, are the **Jefatura de Policía**, built in 19th-century French style, the Italianate **Casa de Gobierno** and the church of **La Merced**. The **Museo de Artesanías** ① *Quintana 905, Mon-Fri 0800-1200, 1600-2000, free*, is a large old house with an exhibition of handicrafts made from the most diverse materials imaginable, by indigenous groups and contemporary urban and rural artisans. Six blocks south is the leafy Plaza de la Cruz, on which the church of **La Cruz de los Milagros** (1897) houses a cross, the Santo Madero, placed there by the founder of the city, Juan Torres de Vera – *indígenas* who tried to burn it were killed by lightning from a cloudless sky. The **Museo de Ciencias Naturales 'Amadeo Bonpland'** ① *San Martín 850, Mon-Sat 0900-1200, 1600-2000*, contains botanical, zoological, archaeological and mineralogical collections including 5800 insects and huge wasp nest. A beautiful walk eastwards, along the Avenida Costanera, beside the Paraná river leads to **Parque Mitre**, from where there are views of sunset.

⊙ Up the Río Paraná listings

For hotel and restaurant price codes, and other relevant information, see Essentials.

● Where to stay

Rosario *p148*
Rosario has a good range of business hotels (eg 4 in the **Solans** group, www.solans.com) and a number of hostels at the budget end.
\$\$\$ Esplendor Savoy Rosario, San Lorenzo 1022, T448 0071, www.esplendorsavoyrosario. com. Early 20th-century mansion, once Rosario's best, now completely remodelled as a luxury hotel with all modern services. Gym, business centre, Wi-Fi, etc.
\$\$\$ Merit Majestic, San Lorenzo 980, T440 5872, www.amerian.com. Modern, inviting 3-star, well designed rooms in an ornate turn-of-the-century building, stylish.
\$\$\$-\$\$ Boulevard, San Lorenzo 2194, T447 5795, www.hotelboulevard.com.ar. Small 1920s house, tastefully renovated as a charming B&B with doubles and triples. Recommended.

\$ Hostel Point, Catamarca 1837, T440 9337, www.hostelpoint.com.ar. Central, nicely designed, brightly coloured dorms (US\$10.55-11.25) and a lovely double. Recommended.
\$ pp La Lechuza, San Lorenzo 1786, T424 1040, www.lalechuzahostel.com.ar. Welcoming, sociable hostel with helpful owner, dorms from US\$10.55, private rooms **\$\$**, with bar, central.
\$ pp Passers Hostel, 1 Mayo 1117, T440 4590, www.passershostel.com.ar. Funky wallpaper and furniture, spacious dorms. Only a few metres from the Monumento a la Bandera.
\$ pp Punto Clave, Ituzaingó 246, T481 9569, www.puntoclavehostel.com.ar. A fun, cheerful hostel with large dorms, a comfortable common area with big bean bags and helpful owners. Recommended.

Paraná *p148*
\$\$\$ Gran Hotel Paraná, Urquiza 976, T422 3900, www.hotelesparana.com.ar. Overlooking Plaza Primero de Mayo, 3 room categories, smart restaurant La Fourchette, gym.

$$ San Jorge, Belgrano 368, T422 1685, www.
sanjorgehotel.com.ar. Renovated house, helpful
staff, older rooms are cheaper than the modern
ones at the back.
$$-$ Paraná Hostel, Andrés Pazos 159, T422
8233, www.paranahostel.com.ar. Small, central,
nice living room with cable TV and comfy sofas.
Smart dorms and private rooms. Best budget
option in the area.

Santa Fe *p148*
$$$-$$ Hostal Santa Fe de la Veracruz, San
Martín 2954, T455 1740, www.hostalsf.com.
Traditional favourite, 2 types of room, both good
value, large breakfast, restaurant, sauna (extra).
$$ Castelar, 25 de Mayo 2349, T456 0999,
www.castelarsantafe.com.ar. On a small plaza,
1930's hotel, good value, comfortable, breakfast
included, restaurant.

Esteros del Iberá *p149*
Mercedes
$$ Sol, San Martín 519 (entre Batalla de Salta
y B Mitre), T420283, www.corrientes.com.ar/
hotelsolmercedes/. Comfortable rooms around
a wonderful patio with black and white tiles,
and lots of plants. Lovely.
$$ La Casa de China, Mitre y Fray L Beltrán,
call for directions, T156 27269, lacasadechina@
hotmail.com. A delightful historical old
house with clean rooms and a lovely patio.
Recommended.

Carlos Pellegrini
Rates are generally full board and include
water and/or land-based excursions.
$$$$ pp Posada Aguapé, T03773-499412,
www.iberawetlands.com. On a lagoon with
a garden and pool, comfortable rooms,
attractive dining room. Recommended.
$$$$ pp Posada de la Laguna, T03773-
499413, www.posadadelalaguna.com.
A beautiful place run by Elsa Güiraldes
(grand-daughter of famous Argentine novelist,
Ricardo Güiraldes) and set on the lake, very
comfortable, large neat garden and a swimming
pool, English and some French spoken, excellent
country cooking. Highly recommended.

$$$$ pp Rincón del Socorro, T03773-475114,
www.rincondel socorro.com (Conservation Land
Trust). Incredibly luxurious, beautifully set in its
own 12,000 ha 35 km south of Carlos Pellegrini,
with 6 spacious bedrooms, each with a little
sitting room, 1 double bungalow, and elegant
sitting rooms and dining rooms. Delicious
home-produced organic food, bilingual guides,
asados at lunchtime, night safaris and horse
riding. Gorgeous gardens, pool with superb
views all around. Highly recommended.
$$$$-$$$ Ecoposada del Estero, T03773-
15-443602, www.ecoposadadelestero.com.ar.
2-room bungalows and restaurant, associated
with Iberá Expediciones, Yaguarete y Pindó,
www.iberaexpediciones.com, who run guided
treks, horse riding, 4WD trips, birdwatching,
lots of information.
$$$$-$$$ Irupé Lodge, T03752-438312 or
03773-402193, www.ibera-argentina.com.
Rustic, simple rooms, great views of the laguna
from dining room, offers conventional and
alternative trips, camping on islands, diving,
fishing, several languages spoken. Offers
combined Iberá and Iguazú tours.
$$$ pp Hostería Ñandé Retá, T03773-
499411, www.nandereta.com. Large old
wooden house in a shady grove, play room,
full board, home cooking.
$$$ pp Posada Ypá Sapukai, Sarmiento 212,
T03773-1551 4212, www.ypasapukai.com.ar.
Private rooms and shared single rates **$** pp.
Good value, nice atmosphere, excellent staff.
$$$ Rancho Iberá, Caraguatá y Aquará,
T03783-1531 8594, www.posadaranchoibera.
com.ar. Designed like an old Argentine
country house, *posada* with double and triple
bedrooms and a well-maintained garden.
Also has a cottage for 5.
$$$ Rancho Inambú, T03773-1543 6159,
Yeruti, entre Aguapé y Pehuajó, www.rancho
inambu.com.ar. Nice rustic rooms set in lush
garden, lovely common area and a great bar
(open to non-guests).
$$$ pp San Lorenzo, at Galarza, T03756-
487084, www.rincontreslagunas.com. Next to
2 lakes on the northeast edge of the region,
splendid for wildlife watching, only 3 rooms. •

Access from Gob Virasoro (90 km), via Rutas 37 and 41. Transfer can be arranged to/from Virasoro or Posadas for an extra charge. Closed Jan-Feb. See also associated tour company, Rincón Tres Lagunas, T03756-15-511931, same website, for birdwatching, nighttime boat excursions, tours to Misiones and more.

$ pp Don Justino Hostel, Curupí y Yaguareté, T03773-15-628823. Small hostel 3 blocks from the lake, 2 from the plaza. Organizes tours and boat trips.

Camping Municipal campsite, T03773-15-629656, with hot showers, jetty for boat trips, also riding and other guided tours.

Corrientes *p150*
$$$ La Alondra, 2 de abril 827, T443 0555, www.laalondra.com.ar. The best place to stay in town. 7 beautiful rooms and a wonderful communal area. Antique furniture throughout, exquisite styling and a homely feel. Lovely patio and 12-m pool.

$ pp Bienvenida Golondrina, La Rioja 455, T443 5316, http://bvngolondrina.blogspot.com. The only hostel in the city. Half a block from the port, in a carefully remodelled old building. Bright dorms, cheaper with fan, private rooms (**$$**), a roof-top terrace and lots of internal patios to relax in.

🍴 Restaurants

Rosario *p148*
$$$ Escauriza, Bajada Escauriza y Paseo Ribereño, La Florida, 30 mins' drive from centre, near bridge over the Paraná, T454 1777. Said to be the "oldest and best" fish restaurant, with terrace overlooking the river.
$$ Amarra, Av Belgrano y Buenos Aires, T447 7550. Good food, including fish and seafood, quite formal, cheap set menus Mon-Fri noon.
$$ La Estancia, Av Pellegrini 1510 y Paraguay. Typical good *parrilla* popular with locals a few blocks east of Parque Independencia.
$ New Taipei, Laprida 1121. Decent Chinese food for a change from the usual Argentine fare.

Cafés and bars
Antares, Callao 286, T437 0945. Daily 1830. A good choice of their own label beers, happy hour, serves food.
El Born, Pellegrini 1574. Daily 0800-0300, from 1800 Sat-Sun. Tapas bar, also has a clothes shop.
Kaffa, Córdoba 1473. Good coffee served inside the large bookshop El Ateneo Yenny.
La Maltería del Siglo, Santa Fé 1601. Daily for food, drinks and background music. Livens up when major football matches are on.
Rock'n'Feller's, Oroño y Jujuy. Popular restobar, upmarket, international fare including Tex-Mex options. Popular at night too.
Verde que te quiero Verde, Córdoba 1358. Open 0800-2100, closed Sun. Great vegetarian café, serving a fantastic brunch and lots of good veggie options. Recommended.

Santa Fe *p148*
Many places in the centre close on Sun.
$$ El Quincho de Chiquito, Av Almirante Brown y Obispo Príncipe (Costanera Oeste). Classic fish restaurant, excellent food, generous helpings and good value.
$$ España, San Martín 2644. An elegant place, specializing in seafood and fish.
$ El Brigadier, San Martín 1670. This colonial-style place next to the Plaza 25 de Mayo serves superb *surubí al paquete* (stuffed fish) and many *parrilla* dishes.
$ Club Sirio Libanés, 25 de Mayo 2740. Very good Middle Eastern food, popular Sun lunch for families.

Corrientes *p150*
$ Martha de Bianchetti, 9 de Julio y Mendoza. Smart café and bakery.
Panambí, Junín near Córdoba. A traditional, central *confitería*, serving good pastries and regional breads.

🚌 Transport

Rosario *p148*
Air Airport at Fisherton, 15 km west of centre, T451 3220. Remises charge US$25. Daily flights to **Buenos Aires**.

Bus Terminal at Santa Fe y Cafferata, about 30 blocks west of the Monumento de la Bandera, T437 3030, www.terminalrosario.gov.ar. For local buses you must buy a rechargeable magnetic card sold at kiosks in the centre or near bus stops (US$1.50 for card and 1st journey), several bus lines to centre with stops on Córdoba (eg 101, 103, 115); from centre, take buses on Plaza 25 de Mayo, via C Santa Fe. Remise US$6. **Buenos Aires**, 4 hrs, US$22-26. **Córdoba**, 6 hrs, US$30-33.50. **Santa Fe**, 2½ hrs, US$10-11.

Train Rosario Norte station, Av del Valle 2750. To/from **Buenos Aires**, operated by Ferrocentral, T436 1661, www.ferrocentralsa.com.ar, ticket office at the station open daily except Wed (different times each day). To **Buenos Aires** Wed 1115 and Sat 1408, US$2.75, 3.75 and 6.75; to **Tucumán** Mon and Fri 1455.

Paraná p148

Bus Terminal at Av Ramírez 2598 (10 blocks southeast of Plaza Primero de Mayo), T422 1202. Buses 1, 6 to/from centre, US$1. Remise US$8. To **Colón** on Río Uruguay, 4-5 hrs, US$10. To **Buenos Aires**, 7-8 hrs, US$34.50-40.

Santa Fe p148

Air Airport at Sauce Viejo, 17 km south, T499 5064. Taxi US$6 from bus terminal. Daily flights to and from **Buenos Aires**.

Bus Terminal near the centre, Gen M Belgrano 2910, T457 4124. To **Córdoba**, US$25-32, 5 hrs. Many buses to **Buenos Aires** US$31-36, 6 hrs; to **Paraná** frequent service US$4.50, 50 mins.

Esteros del Iberá p149

Bus Mercedes to **Carlos Pellegrini**: Itatí II combis Mon-Sat 1230 (schedules change frequently) from Pujol 1166, T420184, T156 29598, 4-5 hrs, US$11. Combi spends an hour picking up passengers all around Mercedes after leaving the office. Returns from Pellegrini at 0430, book by 2200 the night before at the local grocery (ask for directions). Mercedes to **Buenos Aires**, 9-10 hrs, US$50-64. Mercedes to **Corrientes**, 3 hrs, US$12. To **Puerto Iguazú**, best to go via Corrientes, otherwise via any important town along Ruta 14, eg Paso de los Libres, 130 km southeast. There is a direct bus from Carlos Pellegrini to **Posadas**.

Corrientes p150

Air Camba Punta Airport, 10 km east of city, T445 8684. (Remise US$5.) Flights to/from **Buenos Aires**.

Bus Terminal: Av Maipú 2400, 5 km southeast of centre, bus No 103 (ask the driver if it goes to terminal as same line has many different routes), 20 mins, US$1. To **Resistencia**, 1 hr, US$3-5. To **Posadas** US$16-27, 3½-4 hrs, several companies. To **Buenos Aires**, several companies, 11-12 hrs, US$63-71. Sol, NS de la Asunción and El Pulqui run Corrientes-Resistencia-**Asunción** (Paraguay), US$25.

❶ Directory

Rosario p148

Banks Many banks along C Córdoba, east of plaza San Martín. **Bike hire and repair** Bike House, San Juan 973, T424 5280, info@bikehouse.com.ar. **Bike Rosario**, Zeballos 327, T155 713812, www.bikerosario.com.ar, Sebastián Clérico. Bike rental (US$11.50 per day), bike tours, also kayak trips. **Speedway Bike Center**, Roca 1269, T426 8415, info@speedwaybikecenter.com.ar.

Santa Fe p148

Banks Banking district around San Martín y Tucumán.

The Chaco

Much of the Chaco is inaccessible because of poor roads (many of them impassable during summer rains) and lack of public transport, but it has two attractive national parks which are reachable all year round. Resistencia and Formosa are the main cities at the eastern rim, from where Rutas 16 and 81 respectively go west almost straight across the plains to the hills in Salta province. Buses to Salta take Ruta 16. Presidencia Roque Sáenz Peña, 170 km northwest of Resistencia, is a reasonable place to stop over. The Chaco has two distinct natural zones. The Wet Chaco spreads along the Ríos Paraná and Paraguay covered mainly by marsh-lands with savanna and groves of caranday palms, where birdwatching is excellent. Further west, as rainfall diminishes, scrubland of algarrobo, white quebracho, palo borracho and various types of cactii characterize the Dry Chaco, where South America's highest temperatures, exceeding 45°C, have been recorded. Winters are mild, with only an occasional touch of frost in the south. The Chaco is one of the main centres of indigenous population in Argentina: the Qom/Toba are settled in towns by the Río Paraná and the semi-nomadic Wichí live in the western region. Less numerous are the Mocoví in Chaco and the Pilagá in central Formosa. For introductory articles see http://pueblos-originarios-argetnina. wikispaces.com/, http://pocnolec.blogspot.co.uk/ and www.chacolinks.org.uk.

Resistencia → *Phone code: 0362. Colour map 6, C6. Population: 386,390.*

The hot and energetic capital of the Province of Chaco, Resistencia is 6.5 km up the Barranqueras stream on the west bank of the Paraná and 544 km north of Santa Fe. It is known as the 'city of the statues', there being over 200 of these in the streets. Four blocks from the central Plaza 25 de Mayo is the **Fogón de los Arrieros** ① *Brown 350 (between López y Planes and French), T442 6418, open to non-members Mon-Sat 0900-1200, Mon-Fri 2100-2300, US$2.* This famous club and informal cultural centre deserves a visit, for its occasional exhibitions and meetings. The **Museo Del Hombre Chaqueño** ① *Juan B Justo 280, Mon-Fri 0800-1200, 1600-2000, free,* is a small anthropological museum with an exhibition of Wichí, Toba and Mocoví handicrafts. It has a fascinating mythology section in which small statues represent Guaraní beliefs. There are banks and *cambios* in the centre for exchange. **Tourist office** ① *Plaza 25 de Mayo, T445 8289, Mon-Fri 0800-2000.* **Provincial tourist office** ① *Av Sarmiento 1675, T443 8880, www.chaco.travel, Mon-Fri 0800-1300, 1400-2000, Sat 0800-1200.*

Parque Nacional Chaco

① *T03725-499161, chaco@apn.gov.ar, 24 hrs, free, 115 km northwest of Resistencia, best visited between Apr-Oct to avoid intense summer heat and voracious mosquitoes.*

The park extends over 15,000 ha and protects one of the last remaining untouched areas of the Wet Chaco with exceptional *quebracho colorado* trees, *caranday* palms and dense riverine forests with orchids along the banks of the Río Negro. Some 340 species of bird have been sighted in the park. Mammals include *carayá* monkeys and, much harder to see, collared peccary, puma and jaguarundi. 300 m from the entrance is the visitors' centre and a free campsite with hot showers and electricity. The paved Ruta 16 goes northwest from Resistencia and after about 60 km Ruta 9 branches off, leading north to Colonia Elisa and Capitán Solari, 5 km east of the park entrance, via a dirt road. **La Estrella** run daily buses Resistencia-Capitán Solari, where a minibus runs to the park. Tour operators run day-long excursions to the park from Resistencia.

Formosa → *Phone code: 0370. Colour map 6, C6. Population: 233,028.*

The capital of Formosa Province, 186 km above Corrientes, is the only Argentine port of any note on the Río Paraguay. It is oppressively hot from November to March. **Tourist office** ① *José M Uriburu 820 (Plaza San Martín), T442 5192, www.formosa.gob.ar/turismo.* Ask about guided excursions and accommodation at estancias.

Border with Paraguay

The easiest crossing is by road via the Puente Loyola, 4 km north of **Clorinda** (*Phone code: 03718, Colour map 6, C6*). From Puerto Falcón, at the Paraguayan end of the bridge, the road runs 40 km northeast to Asunción, crossing the Río Paraguay. **Immigration** formalities for entering

Argentina are dealt with at the Argentine end, those for leaving Argentina at the Paraguayan end. Crossing, open 24 hours. Bus from Clorinda to Asunción, US$5, one a day, or to Puerto Falcón US$1 and from Falcón to Asunción, **Empresa Falcón** every hour, US$1.50, last bus to the centre of Asunción 1830.

Parque Nacional Río Pilcomayo

ⓘ *Access to the park is free, 24 hrs, administration centre in Laguna Blanca, Av Pueyrredón y Ruta 86, T03718-470045, riopilcomayo@apn.gov.ar, Mon-Fri 0700-1430.*

Some 48,000 ha, 65 km northwest of Clorinda, this natural wetland has lakes, marshes and low-lying parts which flood in the rainy season. The remainder is grassland with caranday palm forests and Chaco woodland. Among the protected species are aguará-guazú, giant anteaters and coatis. Caimans, black howler monkeys, rheas and a variety of birds can also be seen. The park has two entrances: Laguna Blanca, where there is an information point and a free campsite with electricity and cold water. From there, a footpath goes to the Laguna Blanca, the biggest lake in the park. A bit further is the area of Estero Poí, with another information point and a campsite without facilities. **Godoy** buses run from Formosa or Resistencia to the small towns of Laguna Naineck, 5 km from the park (for Laguna Blanca) and Laguna Blanca, 8 km from the park (for Estero Poí). Remise taxis from both towns should charge no more than US$5 for these short journeys. There are police controls on the way to the park.

⦿ The Chaco listings

For hotel and restaurant price codes, and other relevant information, see Essentials.

⦿ Where to stay

Resistencia *p154*
$$$ Covadonga, Güemes 200, T444 4444, www.hotelcovadonga.com.ar. Comfortable, swimming pool, sauna and gym.
$$$-$$ Niyat Urban Hotel, Hipólito Yrigoyen 83, T444 8451, www.niyaturban.com.ar. The newest and best hotel in town. Modern, spacious and stylish rooms overlooking the park, efficient staff.
$$-$ Bariloche, Obligado 239, T442 1412, jag@cpsarg.com. Good budget choice, welcoming owner, decent rooms with a/c. No breakfast, but there's a nearby café at Gran Hotel Royal.

Formosa *p154*
$$ Colón, Belgrano 1068, T442 6547, www.hotelcolonformosa.com. Central, comfortable rooms, all regular services.
$$ Plaza, José M Uriburu 920, T442 6767, plaza_formosa@hotmail.com. On Plaza, pool, very helpful, some English spoken, secure parking.

$ El Extranjero, Av Gutnisky 2660, T452276. Opposite bus terminal, OK, with a/c.

⦿ Festivals

Resistencia *p154*
Fiesta Nacional de Pescado de los Grandes is celebrated **10-12 Oct**, Río Antequeros, 14 km away.

Formosa *p154*
The world's longest **Via Crucis** pilgrimage with 14 stops along Ruta 81 (registered in the Guinness Book of Records) takes place every Easter week, starting in Formosa and ending at the border with the province of Salta, 501 km northwest. **Festival de la caña con ruda** is held on the last night of **Jul**, when Paraguayan *caña* flavoured by the *ruda* plant is drunk as a protection against the mid-winter blues. A good chance to try regional dishes. **Nov** Festival Provincial de Folclore. Held at Pirané (115 km northwest), the major music festival in the northeast, attracting national stars.

⊖ Transport

Resistencia *p154*

Air Airport 8 km west of town (taxi US$3), T444 6009. Flights to/from **Buenos Aires**, 1¼ hrs.

Bus Modern terminal on Av Malvinas Argentinas y Av Maclean in western outskirts (bus 3 or 10 from Oro y Perón, 1 block west of plaza, 20 mins, US$1; remise US$5). To **Buenos Aires** 12-13 hrs, US$63-71 several companies. To **Formosa** 2-2½ hrs, US$9-12. To **Iguazú**, 8-10½ hrs, US$47-57, several companies, some require change of bus in **Posadas**, 5½ hrs, US$26-33. To **Salta**, FlechaBus and La Veloz del Norte, 12½ hrs, US$57. To **Asunción** 3 companies, 6 hrs, US$15.

Formosa *p154*

Air El Pucu airport, 5 km southwest, T445 2490; remise, US$3. Flights to/from **Buenos Aires**, 1½ hrs.

Bus Terminal at Av Gutnisky 2615, 15 blocks west of Plaza San Martín, T445 1766 (remise US$3). **Asunción**, 3 hrs, US$14. **Buenos Aires** 15-17 hrs, US$74-80.

Misiones

While Posadas is one of the main crossing points to Paraguay, most people will head northeast, through the province of the Jesuit Missions, towards Iguazú. This is a land of ruined religious establishments, gemstones and waterfalls.

Posadas → *Phone code: 0376. Population: 324,756 (department).*

This is the main Argentine port on the south bank of the Alto Paraná, 377 km above Corrientes, and the capital of the province of Misiones. On the opposite bank of the river lies the Paraguayan town of Encarnación, reached by the San Roque bridge. The city's centre is **Plaza 9 de Julio**, on which stand the Cathedral and the **Gobernación**, in imitation French style. The riverside and adjacent districts are good for a stroll. Follow Rivadavia or Buenos Aires north to Avenida Andrés Guaçurarí (referred also to as Roque Pérez), a pleasant boulevard, lively at night with several bars. Immediately north of it is the small and hilly **Bajada Vieja** or old port district. There is a good **Museo Regional Aníbal Cambas** ① *Alberdi 600 in the Parque República del Paraguay, 11 blocks north of Plaza 9 de Julio, T444 7539, Mon-Fri 0700-1900*, its permanent exhibition of Guaraní artefacts and pieces collected from the nearby Jesuit missions is worth seeing. **Tourist office** ① *Colón 1985, T444 7539, daily 0800-2000.*

Border with Paraguay

Argentine immigration and customs are on the Argentine side of the bridge to Encarnación. Buses across the bridge (see Transport, page 159) do not stop for formalities; you must get exit stamps. Get off the bus, keep your ticket and luggage, and catch a later bus. Pedestrians and cyclists are not allowed to cross; cyclists must ask officials for assistance. Boats cross to Encarnación, 15 minutes, hourly Monday to Friday 0800-1700, US$2.50. Formalities and ticket office at main building. Port access from Avenida Costanera y Avenida Andrés Guaçurarí, T442 5044 (*Prefectura*).

San Ignacio Miní → *Phone code: 0376. Colour map 7, C1.*

① *0700-1900, US$14 with tour (ask for English version), leaves from entrance every 20 mins. Allow 1½ hrs. Go early to avoid crowds and the best light for pictures (also late afternoon); good birdwatching. Son et lumière show at the ruins, daily 1900 autumn and winter, 2000 spring and summer, in 5 languages, cancelled if raining, US$10, T447 0186.*

The little town of San Ignacio is the site of the most impressive Jesuit ruins in the region, 63 km northeast of Posadas. It is a good base for visiting the other Jesuit ruins and for walking. San Ignacio, together with the missions of Santa Ana and Loreto, is a UNESCO World Heritage Site.

There are heavy rains in February. Mosquitoes can be a problem. The local festival is 30-31 July. **Tourist office** ① *Independencia 605, T447 0130.*

San Ignacio Miní was founded on its present site in 1696. The 100-sq-m, grass-covered plaza is flanked north, east and west by 30 parallel blocks of stone buildings with four to 10 small, one-room dwellings in each block. The roofs have gone, but the massive metre-thick walls are still standing except where they have been torn down by the *ibapoi* trees. The public buildings, some of them 10 m high, are on the south side of the plaza. In the centre are the ruins of a large church finished about 1724. The masonry, sandstone from the Río Paraná, was held together by mud. Inside the entrance, 200 m from the ruins, is the **Centro de Interpretación Jesuítico-Guaraní**, with displays on the lives of the Guaraníes before the arrival of the Spanish, the work of the Jesuits and the consequences of their expulsion, as well as a fine model of the mission. **Museo Provincial** contains a small collection of artefacts from Jesuit reducciones.

The ruins of two other Jesuit missions are worth visiting. **Loreto** ① *with ticket to San Ignacio within 15 days, 0700-1830,* can be reached by a 3-km dirt road (signposted) which turns off Ruta 12, 10 km south of San Ignacio. Little remains other than a few walls; excavations are in progress. There are no buses to Loreto; the bus drops you off on Ruta 12, or take a tour from Posadas or a remise. **Santa Ana** ① *with San Ignacio ticket, 16 km south of San Ignacio, 0730-1930 (1830 in winter), buses stop on Ruta 12,* was the site of the Jesuit iron foundry. Impressive high walls still stand and beautiful steps lead from the church to the wide open plaza. The ruins are 700 m along a path from Ruta 12 (signposted).

Near San Ignacio, is the **Casa de Horacio Quiroga** ① *1470124, 0800-1900, US$1 (includes 40-min guided tour; ask in advance for English). Take Calle San Martín (opposite direction to the ruins) to the Gendarmería HQ. Turn right and on your right are 2 attractive wood and stone houses. After 200 m the road turns left and 300 m later, a signposted narrow road branches off.* The house of this Uruguayan writer, who lived part of his tragic life here as a farmer and carpenter between 1910 and 1916 and in the 1930s, is worth a visit. Many of his short stories were inspired by the subtropical environment and its inhabitants.

San Ignacio to Puerto Iguazú

Ruta 12 continues northeast, running parallel to Río Alto Paraná, towards Puerto Iguazú. With its bright red soil and lush vegetation, this attractive route is known as the Región de las Flores. You get a good view of the local economy: plantations of *yerba mate*, manioc and citrus fruits, timber yards, manioc mills and *yerba mate* factories. The road passes through several small modern towns including Eldorado, with accommodation, campsites, places to eat and regular bus services. Just outside Eldorado, **Estancia Las Mercedes** ① *T03751-1541 8224, www.estancialasmercedes.com,* is an old *yerba mate* farm with period furnishings, open for day visits with activities like riding, boating, and for overnight stays with full board (**$$$**). **Wanda**, 50 km north of Eldorado, was named after a Polish princess and is famous as the site of open-cast amethyst and quartz mines which sell gems. There are guided tours to two of them, **Tierra Colorada** and **Compañía Minera Wanda** ① *daily 0700-1900.*

Gran Salto del Moconá

For 3 km the waters of the Río Uruguay in a remote part of Misiones create magnificent falls (known in Brazil as Yucumã) up to 20 m high. They are surrounded by dense woodland protected by the Parque Estadual do Turvo (Brazil) and the Parque Provincial Moconá, the Reserva Provincial Esmeralda and the Reserva de la Biósfera Yabotí (Argentina – one of the last remaining areas of Selva Paranaense). Moconá has roads and footpaths, accommodation where outdoor activities can be arranged, such as excursions to the falls, trekking in the forests, kayaking, birdwatching and 4WD trips. Alternative bases are El Soberbio (70 km southwest) or San Pedro (92 km northwest). From the former a paved road runs to the park entrance; from the latter the road is impassable after heavy rain. If the river is high (May-October) the falls may be under water. Regular bus service from Posadas to El Soberbio or San Pedro, and from Puerto Iguazú to San Pedro. **Eldorado** bus company has a direct Puerto Iguazú-Moconá service, once a day, leaving Iguazú at 0700, returning 1800, three hours 40 minutes journey.

◉ Misiones listings

For hotel and restaurant price codes, and other relevant information, see Essentials.

◉ Where to stay

Posadas *p156*

$$$ Julio César, Entre Ríos 1951, T442 7930, www.juliocesarhotel.com.ar. 4-star hotel, pool and gym, spacious reasonably priced rooms, some with river views. Recommended.

$$ City, Colón 1754, T433901, citysa@arnet. com.ar. Good rooms, some overlooking plaza, restaurant on 1st floor, parking.

$$ Le Petit, Santiago del Estero 1630, T443 6031, www.hotellepetit.com.ar. Good value, small, a short walk from centre on a quiet street.

$$ Residencial Colón, Colón 2169, T442 5085, www.residencialcolon.blogspot.com. Small but affordable rooms, parking. Also apartments for up to 6 people.

$ pp Hostel Posadeña Linda, Bolívar 1439, T443 9238, www.hostelposadasmisiones.com. Central, good value, very pleasant, with all hostel facilities and tourist information.

San Ignacio Miní *p156*

$$ La Toscana, H Irigoyen y Uruguay, T447 0777, www.hotellatoscana.com.ar. Family-run, 12-bedroom hotel with rustic, inviting rooms and a wonderful pool with a terrace. It's an easy 10-min walk from the tourist office and main plaza. Highly recommended.

$$ San Ignacio, San Martín 823, T447 0047, www.hotelsanignacio.com.ar. Good if not dated rooms with a/c and self-catering apartments for 4-5 people. Breakfast extra. Phone booths and an interesting view of town from the reception.

$ pp Adventure Hostel, Independencia 469, T447 0955. Large hostel with a fantastic pool and a games area. Spacious communal areas, comfortable double rooms (**$$**). Camping available. Short walk to centre of town.

$ Hostel El Jesuita, San Martín 1291, T447 0542, http://eljesuitahostelycamping.blogspot. co.uk. Welcoming owners, spacious double rooms with their own exit to the garden, small comfortable dorm (US$10), 1½ blocks from the ruins. Call when you arrive to be picked up. Lots of travel advice. Camping, US$4.50. Recommended.

Camping Complejo Los Jesuitas, C Emilia Mayer, T446 0847, www.complejolosjesuitas. com.ar. Campsite and cabins for 4 people.

Gran Salto del Moconá *p157*

$$$ pp El Refugio Moconá, 3 km from access to the reserve, 8 km from the falls (or contact at Bolívar 1495, in Posadas), T0376-442 1829, www.refugiomocona.com.ar. Price for 3-day package. Rustic rooms for 4-5 with shared bath, campsite, tents for rent, meals available. Many activities, boat trips and excursions. Transfer with sightseeing to and from San Pedro, 2 hrs.

$$ Hostería Puesta del Sol, C Suipacha s/n, El Soberbio, T03755-495161 (T011-4300 1377 in Buenos Aires). A splendid vantage point overlooking town, with a swimming pool and restaurant. Comfortable rooms, full board available. They also run boat excursions to the falls, 7-8 hrs, landing and meal included (minimum 4 people), via Brazil or on the Argentine side.

There are other lodges in the vicinity, for example: www.donenriquelodge.com.ar, www. lodgelamision.com.ar, www.posadalabonita.net

🍴 Restaurants

Posadas *p156*
Most places offer *espeto corrido*, eat as much as you can *parrilla* with meat brought to the table.
$$ El Mensú, Fleming y Cnel Reguera (in the Bajada Vieja district). Closed Mon. Attractive house with a varied menu of fish and pasta, large selection of wines.
$$ La Querencia, Bolívar 1849 (on Plaza 9 de Julio). A large traditional restaurant offering *parrilla*, *surubí* and pastas.
$$ Plaza Café, Bolívar 1979 just outside the shopping centre. Great salads and large mains. Busy during the day and busier at night. Highly recommended.
$ Bar Español, Bolívar 2085. Open since 1958, this restaurant has tasty Spanish-influenced food. Have an ice cream for dessert next door at Duomo.
$ La Nouvelle Vitrage, Colón y Bolívar. Good pizzas, sandwiches and coffee, nice view of the plaza.

San Ignacio Miní *p156*
There are several restaurants catering for tourists on the streets by the Jesuit ruins.

⚙ What to do

Posadas *p156*
Abra, Salta 1848, 1442 2221, www.abratours. com.ar. Tours to San Ignacio, including Santa Ana Jesuit ruins, also those in Paraguay and in Brazil, plus tours to waterfalls.
Guayrá, San Lorenzo 2208, T443 3415, www. guayra.com.ar. Tours to Iberá, to Saltos del Moconá, to both sites in a 5-day excursion, and to other sites in Misiones, also car rental and transfer to Carlos Pellegrini (for Iberá).

⊖ Transport

Posadas *p156*
Air Gen San Martín Airport, 12 km west, T445 7413, reached by remise US$8. To

Buenos Aires, direct or via Corrientes or Formosa, 1 hr 50 mins.
Bus Terminal about 5 km out of the city at Av Santa Catalina y Av Quaranta (T445 6106, municipal tourist office), on the road to Corrientes. Remise US$6. For bus into town, cross the street from the terminal and look for Nos 15, 21 or 8 to the centre, US$1. Travel agencies in the centre can book bus tickets in advance. To **Buenos Aires**, 12-13 hrs, US$77-88. Frequent services to **San Ignacio Miní**, 1 hr, US$4.75-6, and **Puerto Iguazú**, US$18-20, 5-6 hrs.
International To **Encarnación** (Paraguay), Servicio Internacional, 50 mins, US$1.25, leaving at least every 30 mins from platforms 11 and 12 (lower level), tickets on bus.

To **Brazil** and the Jesuit Missions in Rio Grande do Sul, take an **Aguila Dorada** or **Horianski** bus from Posadas to **San Javier**, 124 km, then a ferry, US$5, to Porto Xavier, from where buses run to Santo Ângelo, 4 hrs (see Rio Grande do Sul in the Brazil chapter). Immigration is at either end of the ferry crossing

San Ignacio Miní *p156*
Bus Stop in front of the church, leaving almost hourly to **Posadas** or to **Puerto Iguazú** (US$17). Do not rely on bus terminal at the end of Av Sarmiento, only a few stop there. More buses stop on Ruta 12 at the access road (Av Sarmiento).

To **Paraguay**, a ferry crosses the Río Paraná at **Corpus** to **Bella Vista**, foot passengers US$1.50 (for cars weekdays only), which is a good route to the Paraguayan Jesuit missions. There are immigration and customs facilities.

ⓘ Directory

Posadas *p156*
Consulates Paraguay, San Lorenzo 1561, T442 3858. Mon-Fri 0800-1400. Same-day visas. **Immigration** Dirección Nacional de Migraciones, Buenos Aires 1633, T442 7414, 0630-1330.

Iguazú Falls → *Colour map 7, C1.*

The mighty Iguazú Falls are the most overwhelmingly magnificent in all of South America. So impressive are they that Eleanor Roosevelt remarked "poor Niagara" on witnessing them (they are four times wider). In 2012 they were confirmed as one of the New7Wonders of Nature. Viewed from below, the tumbling water is majestically beautiful in its setting of begonias, orchids, ferns and palms. Toucans, flocks of parrots and cacique birds and great dusky swifts dodge in and out along with myriad butterflies (there are at least 500 different species). Above the impact of the water, upon basalt rock, hovers a perpetual 30-m-high cloud of mist in which the sun creates blazing rainbows.

Visiting Iguazú Falls Entry is US$27 (children US$18.75), payable in pesos only. Argentines, Mercosur and Misiones inhabitants pay less. Entry next day is half price with same ticket, which you must get stamped at the end of the first day. Open daily 0800-1800. Visitor Centre includes information and photographs of the flora and fauna, as well as books for sale. There are places to eat, toilets, shops and a *locutorio* in the park. In the rainy season, when water levels are high, waterproof coats or swimming costumes are advisable for some of the lower catwalks and for boat trips. Cameras should be carried in a plastic bag. **Tourist offices** ① *Aguirre 311,*

1 Around the Iguazú Falls

➡ Iguazú Falls maps
1 Around the Iguazú Falls, page 160
2 Puerto Iguazú, page 163

Where to stay 🛏
1 Camping e Pousada Internacional
2 Hostel Inn Iguazú
4 Hostel Natura & Paudimar Campestre
5 Hotel Das Cataratas
6 Posada 21 Oranges
7 Pousada Evelina
8 Sheraton Internacional Iguazú Resort
9 Pousada Cataratas

Puerto Iguazú, T420800, and **municipal office** ① *Av Victoria Aguirre y Balbino Brañas, T422938, 0900-2200, www.iguazuturismo.gov.ar; at the falls, T0800-266 4482, www.iguazuargentina.com.* **National park office** ① *Victoria Aguirre 66, T420722, iguazu@apn.gov.ar.*

The falls, on the Argentina-Brazil border, are 19 km upstream from the confluence of the Río Iguazú with the Río Alto Paraná. The Río Iguazú (*I* is Guaraní for water and *guazú* is Guaraní for big), which rises in the Brazilian hills near Curitiba, receives the waters of some 30 rivers as it crosses the plateau. Above the main falls, the river, sown with wooded islets, opens out to a width of 4 km. There are rapids for 3.5 km above the 74 m precipice over which the water plunges in 275 falls over a frontage of 2470 m, at a rate of 1750 cu m a second (rising to 12,750 cu m in the rainy season).

Around the falls → *In Oct-Mar (daylight saving dates change each year) Brazil is 1 hr ahead.*

On both sides of the falls there are national parks. Transport between the two parks is via the Ponte Tancredo Neves as there is no crossing at the falls themselves. The Brazilian park offers a superb panoramic view of the whole falls and is best visited in the morning when the light is better for photography. The Argentine park (which requires at least a day to explore properly) offers closer views of the individual falls in their forest setting with its wildlife and butterflies, though to appreciate these properly you need to go early and get well away from the visitors

areas. Busiest times are holidays and Sundays. Both parks have visitors' centres and tourist facilities on both sides are constantly being improved, including for the disabled.

Parque Nacional Iguazú covers an area of 67,620 ha. The fauna includes jaguars, tapirs, brown capuchin monkeys, collared anteaters and coatimundis, but these are rarely seen around the falls. There is a huge variety of birds; among the butterflies are shiny blue morphos and red/black heliconius. From the Visitor Centre a small gas-run train (free), the **Tren de la Selva**, whisks visitors on a 25-minute trip through the jungle to the Estación del Diablo, where it's a 1-km walk along catwalks across the Río Iguazú to the park's centrepiece, the **Garanta del Diablo**. A visit here is particularly recommended in the evening when the light is best and the swifts are returning to roost on the cliffs, some behind the water. Trains leave on the hour and 30 minutes past the hour. However, it's best to see the falls from a distance first, with excellent views from the two well-organized trails along the **Circuito Superior** and **Circuito Inferior**, each taking around an hour and a half. To reach these, get off the train at the **Estación Cataratas** (after 10 minutes' journey) and walk down the **Sendero Verde**. The Circuito Superior is a level path which takes you along the easternmost line of falls, Bossetti, Bernabé Mandez, Mbiguá (Guaraní for cormorant) and San Martín, allowing you to see these falls from above. This path is safe for those with walking difficulties, wheelchairs and pushchairs, though you should wear supportive non-slippery shoes. The Circuito Inferior takes you down to the water's edge via a series of steep stairs and walkways with superb views of both San Martín falls and the Garganta del Diablo from a distance. Wheelchair users, pram pushers, and those who aren't good with steps should go down by the exit route for a smooth and easy descent. You could then return to the Estación Cataratas to take the train to Estación Garganta, 10 and 40 minutes past the hour, and see the falls close up. Every month on the five nights of full moon, there are 1½-hour guided walks (bilingual) that may include or not a dinner afterwards or before the walk, at the Restaurant La Selva, depending on the time of departure. See www.iguazuargentina.com for dates, times and email booking form; reservations also in person at the park, T03757-491469, or through agencies: US$68 with dinner; US$50 without.

At the very bottom of the Circuito Inferior, a free ferry crosses 0930-1530 on demand to the small, hilly **Isla San Martín** where trails lead to miradores with good close views of the San Martín falls (boats go 0930-1530). The park has two further trails: **Sendero Macuco**, 7 km return (the park says two to three hours, allow much more), starting from near the Visitor Centre and leading to the river via a natural pool (El Pozón) fed by a slender waterfall, **Salto Arrechea** (a good place for bathing and the only permitted place in the park). **Sendero Yacaratiá** starts from the same place, but reaches the river by a different route, and ends at Puerto Macuco, where you could take the *Jungle Explorer* boat to the see the Falls themselves (see below). This trail is really for vehicles (30 km in total) and is best visited on an organized safari.

Puerto Iguazú → *Phone code: 03757. Colour map 7, C1. Population: 82,227.*

This modern town is 18 km northwest of the falls high above the river on the Argentine side near the confluence of the Ríos Iguazú and Alto Paraná. It serves mainly as a centre for visitors to the falls. The port lies to the north of the town centre at the foot of a hill: from the port you can follow the Río Iguazú downstream towards Hito-Tres Fronteras, a *mirador* with views over the point where the Ríos Iguazú and Alto Paraná meet and over neighbouring Brazil and Paraguay. There are souvenir shops, toilets and pubs are here; bus US$0.50. **La Aripuca** ① *T423488, www.aripuca. com.ar, US$3, turn off Ruta 12 just after Hotel Cataratas, entrance after 250 m, 0900-1800, English and German spoken*, is a large wooden structure housing a centre for the appreciation of the native tree species and their environment. **Güirá Oga** ① *Casa de los Pájaros, US$2, daily 0830-1830 (0900-1645 in winter), turn off Ruta 12 at Hotel Orquídeas Palace, entrance is 800 m further along the road from Aripuca; T423980, www.guiraoga.com.ar*, is a sanctuary for birds that have been injured, where they are treated and reintroduced to the wild; exquisite parrots and magnificent birds of prey. There is also a trail in the forest and a breeding centre for endangered species.

⦿ Iguazú Falls listings

For hotel and restaurant price codes, and other relevant information, see Essentials.

⦿ Where to stay

Puerto Iguazú *p162, maps p160 and p163*
$$$$ Panoramic, Paraguay 372, T0800-999 4726, www.panoramic-hoteliguazu.com. On a hill overlooking the river, this hotel is stunning.

Serene outdoor pool with great views, large well-designed rooms and all 5-star inclusions.
$$$$ Posada Puerto Bemberg, Fundadores Bemberg s/n, Puerto Libertad (some 35 km south of Iguazú), T03757-496500, www. puertobemberg.com. Wonderful luxury accommodation and gourmet cuisine in **Casa Bemberg**, dating from 1940s, surrounded by lush gardens. Huge living areas, beautifully

decorated rooms and helpful staff. Good birdwatching with resident naturalist. Highly recommended.

$$$$ Sheraton Internacional Iguazú Resort, T491800, www.sheraton.com/iguazu. Fine position overlooking the falls, excellent, good restaurant and breakfast, sports facilities and spa. Taxi to airport available. Recommended.

$$$$ Yacutinga Lodge, 30 km from town, pick up by jeep, www.yacutinga.com. A beautiful lodge in the middle of the rainforest, with 2-4 night packages, learning about the bird and plant life and Guaraní culture. Accommodation is in rustic adobe houses in tropical gardens, superb food and drinks included, as well as boat trips and walks.

$$$ Iguazú Jungle Lodge, Hipólito Iyrigoyen y San Lorenzo, T420600, www. iguazujunglelodge.com. A well-designed complex of lofts and family suites, 7 blocks from the centre, by a river, with lovely pool. Comfortable and stylish, DVDs, great service, restaurant. Warmly recommended.

$$$ Posada 21 Oranges, C Montecarlo y Av los Inmigrantes, T494014, www.21oranges.com. 10 simple but comfortable rooms set around a pool, lovely garden, welcoming. US$5 taxi ride or 20-min walk to town.

$$$ Secret Garden, Los Lapachos 623, T423099, www.secretgardeniguazu.com. Small B&B with attentive owner, fern garden surrounding the house. Spacious

2 Puerto Iguazú

➡ **Iguazú Falls maps**
1 Around the Iguazú Falls, page 160
2 Puerto Iguazú, page 163

Where to stay 🛏
1 Garden Stone
2 Hostería Casa Blanca
3 Iguazú Jungle Lodge
4 Marco Polo Inn
5 Panoramic
6 Peter Pan
8 Noelia
10 Secret Garden

Restaurants 🍴
1 Aqva
2 El Quincho del Tío Querido
5 La Rueda
6 Pizza Color
8 Tango Bar Iguazú

rooms, good breakfast and cocktails, relaxing atmosphere.

$$$-$$ Hostería Casa Blanca, Guaraní 121, near bus station, T421320, www. casablancaiguazu.com.ar. Family run, large rooms, good showers, beautifully maintained.

$ pp Garden Stone, Av Córdoba 441, T420425, www.gardenstonehostel.com. Lovely hostel with a homely feel set in nice gardens, with a large outdoor eating area, swimming pool. Recommended for a tranquil stay.

$ pp Hostel Inn Iguazú, R 12, Km 5, T421823, http://hiiguazu.com. 20% discount to HI members and 10% discount on long-distance buses, dorms US$13, a/c doubles **$$**. Large, well-organized hostel which used to be a casino. Huge pool, games and a range of free DVDs to watch. They also organize package tours to the falls, which include accommodation. No guests under 18.

$ pp Marco Polo Inn, Av Córdoba 158, T425559, www.hostel-inn.com. The biggest and most central hostel in town, right in front of the bus station, a/c doubles **$$**. Nice pool, fun bar at night (open to non-residents). It gets busy so reserve in advance. Recommended.

$ pp Noelia, Fray Luis Beltrán 119, T420729, www.hostelnoelia.com. Cheap, well-kept and helpful, good breakfast, family-run, good value.

$ pp Peter Pan, Av Córdoba 267, T423616, www.peterpanhostel.com. Just down the hill from the bus station, spotless, central pool and large open kitchen. The doubles (**$$**) are lovely. Helpful staff.

🍴 Restaurants

Puerto Iguazú p162, maps p160 and p163

$$ Aqva, Av Córdoba y Carlos Thays, T422064. Just down from the bus station, this lovely restaurant serves dishes made with ingredients from the area.

$$ El Quincho del Tío Querido, Bompland 110, T420151. Recommended for parrilla and local fish, very popular, great value.

$$ La Rueda, Córdoba 28, T422531. Good food and prices, fish, steaks and pastas, often with mellow live music. Highly recommended.

$$ Pizza Color, Córdoba 135. Popular for pizza and parrilla.

$$ Tango Bar Iguazú, Av Brasil 1, T422008. Bar which serves pizzas and pastas. It turns into a milonga with tango classes and dancing at night.

⏱ What to do

Iguazú Falls p160, map p160

Explorador Expediciones, Perito Moreno 217, T491469, www.rainforestevt.com.ar. Offers small-group safaris, 3-day packages, birdwatching trips, adventure tours, tours to Moconá. Recommended.

Jungle Explorer, T421696, www.iguazujungle. com. Run a series of boat trips, all highly recommended, eg: **Aventura Náutica**, an exhilarating journey by launch along the lower Río Iguazú, from opposite Isla San Martín right up to the San Martín falls and then into the Garganta del Diablo, completely drenching passengers in the mighty spray. Great fun; not for the faint-hearted, 12 mins. On **Paseo Ecológico** you float silently for 2½ km from Estación Garganta to appreciate the wildlife on the river banks, 30 mins.

Puerto Iguazú p162, maps p160 and p163

Agencies arrange day tours to the Brazilian side (lunch in Foz), Itaipú and Ciudad del Este. Some include the Duty Free mall on the Argentine side. Tours to the Jesuit ruins at San Ignacio Miní also visit a gem mine at Wanda (you don't see as much of the ruins as you do if staying overnight). There are also horse riding trips.

Agroturismo Sombra de Toro, Ruta Nacional 101, Bernardo de Yrigoyen, T03757-15-449425. By the Parque Provincial Urugua-í, which adjoins the Iguazú national park, this farm owned by the Mackoviak family offers tours and accommodation on their private reserve, which contains Selva Paranaense and examples of the rare sombra de toro tree.

Aguas Grandes, Entre Ríos 66, T425500. Tours to both sides of the falls and further afield, activities in the forest, abseiling down waterfalls, good fun.

⊖ Transport

Iguazú Falls *p160, map p160*

Bus A public *Cataratas/Waterfalls* bus runs every 30 mins from Hito Tres Fronteras, 0730-1830. It stops at Puerto Iguazú bus terminal 10 mins after departure, at the park entrance for the purchase of entry tickets, then continues to the Visitor Centre, US$4. Journey time 45 mins; return buses from the park: 0815-1915. You can get on or off the bus at any point en route.

Cars are not allowed beyond visitor centre.

Puerto Iguazú *p162, maps p160 and p163*

Air Airport is 20 km southeast of Puerto Iguazú near the Falls, T422013. **Four Tourist Travel** bus service between airport and bus terminal, US$4, will also drop off/collect you from your hotel. Taxi US$15. Direct flights to **Buenos Aires**, 1½ hrs.

Bus The bus terminal, at Av Córdoba y Av Misiones, T423006, has a phone office, restaurant, various tour company desks and bus offices. To **Buenos Aires**, 16-18 hrs, US$99-115, 5 companies. To **Posadas**, stopping at San Ignacio Miní, frequent, 5-6 hrs, US$18-20; to **San Ignacio Miní**, US$17.

Taxi T420973/421707. Fares in town US$2.50-4.

Border with Brazil

Crossing via the Puente Tancredo Neves is straightforward. When leaving Argentina, Argentine immigration is at the Brazilian end of the bridge. Border open 0700-2300. **Brazilian consulate**, Av Córdoba 264, T420192.

Bus Buses leave Puerto Iguazú terminal for **Foz do Iguaçu** every 15 mins, 0730-1830, US$4.

The bus stops at the Argentine border post, but not the Brazilian. Both Argentine and Brazilian officials stamp you in and out, even if only for a day visit. Whether you are entering Brazil for the first time, or leaving and returning after a day in Argentina, you must insist on getting off the bus to get the required stamp and entry card. Buses also stop at the Duty Free mall. The bus does not wait for those who need stamps, just catch the next one, of whatever company.

Taxis Between the border and Puerto Iguazú US$30.

Border with Paraguay

Crossing to Paraguay is via Puente Tancredo Neves to Brazil and then via the Puente de la Amistad to Ciudad del Este. Brazilian entry and exit stamps are not required unless you are stopping in Brazil.

The **Paraguayan consulate** is at Perito Moreno 236, T424230, Mon-Fri 0800-1600.

Bus Direct buses (non-stop in Brazil) leave Puerto Iguazú terminal every 40 mins, US$4.50, 45 mins, liable to delays especially in crossing the bridge to Ciudad del Este. Only one bus on Sun, no schedule, better to go to Foz and change buses there.

⊕ Directory

Puerto Iguazú *p162, maps p160 and p163*

Banks ATMs at Macro, Misiones y Bonpland, and **Banco de la Nación**, Av Aguirre 179. Sheraton has an ATM. Good exchange rates at the Brazilian border.

Lake District

The Lake District contains a series of great lakes strung along the foot of the Andes from above 40°S to below 50°S in the Parque Nacional Los Glaciares area. This section covers the northern lakes; for convenience the southernmost lakes, including those in the Los Glaciares park area, are described under Patagonia (see page 191). The area is dramatic, beautiful and unspoilt, offering superb trekking, fishing, watersports, climbing and skiing. See the Chilean Lake District chapter, for map and details of the system of lakes on the far side of the Andes. These can be visited through various passes. Off season, from mid-April to June and mid-August to mid-November, many excursions, boat trips, etc run on a limited schedule, if at all. Public transport is also limited.

Neuquén and around → *Phone code: 0299. Colour map 8, C2.*
Population: Greater Neuquén: 362,673.

Founded in 1904 on the west side of the confluence of the Ríos Limay and Neuquén, Neuquén is a pleasant provincial capital and a major stop en route from the east coast to the northern lakes and Bariloche. It serves both the oilfields to the west and the surrounding fruit orchards. There are also wine bodegas nearby. In the centre is the Parque Central, where the railway station used to be, with open spaces, museums and cultural activities (annual **Feria Artesanal** in November). Avenida Argentina, the main commercial street, with ATMs and a weekend handicrafts market, runs north to Plaza de las Banderas and Parque Centenario. **Regional tourist office** ① *Félix San Martín 182, T442 4089, www.neuquentur.gob.ar, Mon-Sun 0700-2100.* **Municipal office** ① *Av Argentina y Roca, T449 1200, http://turismo.neuquen.wpengine.com.* Also at the airport. See also www.neuquen.com.

Dinosaurs The area west of Neuquén is rich in dinosaur fossils. The city was home to the **Museo Paleontológico de la Universidad Nacional del Comahue** ① *now closed indefinitely.* Consult the tourist office regarding exhibitions of dinosaur fossils found in the region. The research project at the **Lago Barreales reservoir** ① *Ruta 51, Km 65, northwest of the city, T0299-155-490784, www. proyectodino.com.ar,* has displays of the finds and offers a hands-on experience of the digs.

Villa El Chocón
Red sedimentary rocks here have preserved, in relatively good condition, bones and footprints of the animals that lived in this region during the Cretaceous period about 100 million years ago. The **Museo Paleontológico Ernesto Bachmann** ① *civic centre, T0299-490 1223, daily 0700-2100, US$4,* displays the fossils of a giant carnivore (*Giganotosaurus carolinii*), guides in museum give good tours. 'Cretaceous Valley', 18 km south of Villa El Chocón, near the Embalse Ezequiel Ramos Mexía, has pedestals of eroded pink rock coming out of the blue water. There are two walks beside the lake to see dinosaur footprints. **Tourist office** ① *Club Chocón, T490 1242, www.chocon.gov.ar.*

Zapala → *Phone code: 02942. Colour map 8, C2. Population: 36,550.*
Just over 100 km west of Neuquén, at Plaza Huincul, **Museo Carmen Funes** ① *RN 22 y RP 17, T0299-496 5486, Mon-Fri 0900-1900, Sat-Sun 1030-2030, US$1.75,* has, among its exhibits, remains of the largest herbivore ever found. In Zapala itself, 185 km west of Neuquén, the excellent geology museum, **Museo Mineralógico Dr Juan Olsacher** ① *Etcheluz 52 (by bus terminal), T422928, Mon-Fri 0900-1930, free,* has collections of minerals, fossils, shells, rocks and a complete crocodile jaw, believed to be 80 million years old. **Tourist office** ① *Ruta Nacional 22, Km 1392, T02942-424296.*

For hotel and restaurant price codes, and other relevant information, see Essentials.

⊕ Where to stay

Neuquén *p166*

$$$$ Del Comahue, Av Argentina 377, T443 2040, www.hoteldelcomahue.com. 4-star, extremely comfortable, spa, pool, good service, wine bar and excellent restaurant specializing in Patagonian fare, **1900 Cuatro**.

$$$ Hostal del Caminante, JJ Lastra (Ruta 22, Km 1227), 13 km southwest of Neuquén, towards Zapala, T444 0118, www.hostaldel caminante.com. A comfortable suburban place set among fruit plantations with garden, swimming pool and restaurant.

$$$ Royal, Av Argentina 143, T448 8902, www.royalhotel.com.ar. Central hotel with all services, free continental breakfast, parking.

$ Hostel Punto Patagónico, Periodistas Neuquinos 94, T447 9940, www.punto patagonico.com. A bit out of the centre, good hostel, reductions for HI members, breakfast, rustic furniture. Recommended.

Villa El Chocón *p166*

$$$ La Posada del Dinosaurio, lakeshore, Villa El Chocón, Costa del Lago, Barrio 1, T0299-490 1201, www.posadadinosaurio.com.ar. Comfortable, modern, all rooms have lake view.

Zapala *p166*

$$$ Hue Melén, Brown 929, T422407, www. hotelhuemelen.com. Good value, decent rooms and restaurant with the best food in town. Try your luck in the downstairs casino.

$$ Coliqueo, Etcheluz 159, opposite bus terminal, T421308. Convenient and fair.

$$ Pehuén, Elena de la Vega y Etcheluz, 1 block from bus terminal, T423135. Comfortable and recommended.

⊕ Restaurants

Neuquén *p166*

$$ El Ciervo, Argentina 219. Good central option featuring an abundance of fresh seafood dishes.

$ La Birra, Santa Fe 19. Lots of choice, welcoming, chic, modern.

⊖ Transport

Neuquén *p166*

Air Airport 7 km west of centre, T440 0245. Taxi US$11; also served by city buses. Flights to **Buenos Aires** and **Comodoro Rivadavia**; LADE flies to **Bariloche**. Schedules change frequently.

Bus City buses, Indalo, take rechargeable magnetic cards, sold at bus terminal and elsewhere, from US$1. Terminal at Ruta 22 y Solalique, on Ruta 22, 4 km west of town, T445 2300. Taxi US$7. Many companies to **Buenos Aires**, daily, 15-19 hrs, US$120-135. To **Zapala** daily, 3 hrs, US$12. To **Junín de los Andes**, 5-6 hrs, US$28-55, Albus. To **San Martín de los Andes**, 7 hrs, US$23-56, Albus. To **Bariloche**, many companies, 5-6 hrs, US$43-50, sit on left. To **Mendoza**, TAC, daily, 12-13 hrs, US$75-87. **To Chile**: several companies run to **Temuco**, 12-14 hrs, also from Zapala. Buy Chilean pesos before leaving.

Zapala *p166*

Bus To **San Martín de los Andes**, 4 hrs, US$17-23, via Junín de los Andes. To **Bariloche**, change at San Martín.

Parque Nacional Lanín

ⓘ *US$9 to enter park (discount with student/teacher card). Helpful advice on walks from guardaparques at the entrance and at Puerto Canoa. Park office, Perito Moreno y Elordi, San Martín de los Andes, T427233, servicioslanin@apn.gov.ar, Mon-Fri 0800-1300, helpful but maps poor. Bus* *transport into the park is tricky, with services usually running to Lago Huechulafquen from San Martín de los Andes with Ko Ko Bus, but the timetable varies from year to year.*

This beautiful, large park has sparkling lakes, wooded mountain valleys and one of Argentina's most striking peaks, the snow capped Lanín Volcano. The lakes of **Huechulafquen** and **Paimún** are unspoilt, beautiful, and easily accessible for superb walking and fishing, with *hosterías* and camping all along the lakeside. From Puerto Canoa there is a boat excursion to **Lago Epulafquen** on the catamaran **José Julián** ① *T429264, www.catamaranjosejulian.com.ar, 4 trips a day in summer (Dec-Mar), for other months ask locally, US$30, coffee and chocolate on board.* Geologically, Lanín Volcano is one of the youngest of the Andes; it is extinct and one of the world's most beautiful mountains. It's a challenging and popular climb, starting near **Seccional de Guardaparques** (VHF 155675 or T491270) at Mamuil Malal pass where you must register and all climbing equipment and experience are checked. Crampons and ice axes are essential, as is protection against strong, cold winds. There are three *refugios*, the first of which is a five-hour walk. It's a six- to seven-hour walk to the base of the volcano and back. Before setting off, seek advice from the Lanin National Park office.

Border with Chile: the Mamuil Malal

Formalities are carried out at the Argentine side of the Mamuil Malal Pass (it used to be called Tromen). This route runs through glorious scenery to Pucón (135 km) on Lago Villarrica (Chile). It is open 0800-2000, but is closed in winter and during heavy rain or snow (phone to check: *gendarmería*, T491270, or customs, T492163). Parts are narrow and steep. (Details of the Chilean side are given under Puesco, The Lake District.) The international bus may not pick up passengers at the pass or on the Chilean part of the route.

Junín de los Andes → *Phone code: 02972. Colour map 8, B4. Population: 10,300.*

Known as the trout capital of Argentina, Junín de los Andes is a relaxed, pretty town on the broad Río Chimehuín, a less touristy option than San Martín, with many trout-filled rivers and lakes nearby, and the best base for trekking in Parque Nacional Lanín. Its small **Museo Mapuche** ① *Ginés Ponte y Nogueira, Mon-Fri 0900-1400, 1600-1930,* has a collection of items from the Mapuche culture and there are impressive sculptures at **Vía Christi** ① *on the hill opposite, free entry.* **Tourist office** ① *Plaza at Col Suárez y Padre Milanesio, T02972-491160, 0800-2100.*

San Martín de los Andes → *Phone code: 02972. Colour map 8, C1. Population: 25,000.*

This picturesque and upmarket tourist town, 40 km southwest of Junín, with its chocolate-box, chalet-style architecture, is spectacularly set at the east end of Lago Lacar. Mirador Bandurrias, 45-minute walk from the centre offers good views. There is excellent skiing on Cerro Chapelco (with varied summer activities for kids), and facilities for water skiing, windsurfing and sailing on Lago Lácar. The **tourist office** ① *Roca y Rosas, T427347, www.sanmartindelosandes.gov. ar/turismo, 0800-2100 all year,* has maps, accommodation lists, prices, very busy in summer. Surrounded by lakes and mountains to explore, the most popular excursions are south along the **Seven Lakes Drive** (see below), north to the thermal baths at **Termas de Lahuen-Co** (also reached on foot after two days from Lagos Huechulafquen and Paimún) and to **Lagos Lolog** and **Lácar**. There's a *ripio* track along the north side of Lago Lácar with beaches and rafting at **Hua Hum**, and along the south to quieter and beautiful **Quila Quina**. Two good walks from Quila Quina: along a nature trail to a lovely waterfall, or a two-hour walk to a quiet Mapuche community in the hills above the lake. Boats from San Martín's pier, T428427, to Hua Hum three daily in season, US$72 return; to Quila Quina, hourly, 30 minutes, US$24. Cyclists can complete a circuit around Lago Lácar, or take the cable car up to Chapelco and come back down the paths.

Border with Chile: the Hua Hum Pass

A *ripio* road along the north shore of Lago Lácar through the Lanín National Park crosses the border to Puerto Pirihueico, where a boat crosses Lago Pirihueico; bikes can be taken (foot passengers US$2; for information, www.barcazas.cl). Border open 0800-2000. **Ko Ko** Bus goes to the pass (usually open all year round), two hours, and **Lafit** continues to Panguipulli (Chile), T427422 at *Ko Ko* office in terminal for schedule. For connections from Puerto Pirihueico to Panguipulli and beyond, see Chile chapter.

⊚ Parque Nacional Lanín listings

For hotel and restaurant price codes, and other relevant information, see Essentials.

⊜ Where to stay

Lago Huechulafquen *p167*

$$$ Hostería Paimun, Ruta 61, T02972-491758, www.hosteriapaimun.com.ar. Basic, comfortable rooms, private beach, fly fishing guide, lake excursions, cosy restaurant, stunning views all around

$$$ Huechulafquen, Ruta 61, Km 55, T02972-427590, www.hosteriahuechulafquen.com. Nov-May. Half board, comfortable cabin-like rooms, gardens, expert fly fishing guide, restaurant open to non-residents in high season.

Camping Several sites in beautiful surroundings on Lagos Huechulafquen and Paimún in Parque Nacional Lanín. The most recommended are: Bahía Cañicul (48 km from Junín), **Camping Lafquen-co** (53 km from Junín) and **Piedra Mala** (65 km from Junín); last 2 US$7 pp. There are 3 more campsites beyond Hostería Paimún, including Mawizache (Raúl and Carmen Hernández, both very knowledgeable), just beyond the picturesque little chapel. Offers fishing trips with expert, good restaurant. Open all year.

Junín de los Andes *p168*

$$$$ Río Dorado Lodge & Fly shop, Pedro Illera 378, T492451, www.riodorado.com.ar. Comfortable rooms in log cabin-style fishing lodge, big American breakfast, good fly shop, fishing excursions to many rivers and lakes, lovely gardens, attentive service.

$$$ Caleufu Travel Lodge, JA Roca 1323 (on Ruta 234), T492757, www.caleufutravellodge.

com.ar. Excellent value, welcoming, very good, homey rooms, neat garden, also comfortable apartments for up to 5 people, 3-6 night packages and fly fishing. Owner Jorge speaks English. Recommended.

$$ Hostería Chimehuín, Col Suárez y 25 de Mayo, T491132, www.hosteriachimehuin.com.ar. Closed May. Cosy, quaint fishing lodge by the river, fishing and mountain guides. Recommended.

$$ Res Marisa, JM de Rosas 360 (on Ruta 234), T491175, residencialmarisa@hotmail.com. A simple place with helpful owners, breakfast extra, very good value.

$ pp La Casa de Marita y Aldo, 25 de Mayo 371, T491042, casademaritayaldo@hotmail.com. A cheery and popular family house with basic accommodation. Very helpful owners.

$ pp Tromen, Lonquimay 195, T491498, www.hosteltromen.com.ar. Small house with dorms and private rooms for up to 4 people. At night take a taxi from the bus station as the streets in the area have no signs or lights.

San Martín de los Andes *p168*

Single rooms are expensive. There are 2 high seasons, when rates are much higher: Jan/Feb and Jul/Aug. *Cabañas* are available in 2 main areas: up Perito Moreno on the hill to the north of town, and down by the lakeside. Prices increase in high season but are good value for families or groups. When everywhere else is full, tourist office provides a list of private addresses in high season. See www.sanmartindelosandes.gov.ar for a full list of places to stay. All listed are recommended.

$$$$ La Casa de Eugenia, Coronel Díaz 1186, T427206, www.lacasadeeugenia.com.ar. B&B

in a beautifully renovated 1900s house, very welcoming and relaxing, cosy rooms, huge breakfast, charming hosts.

$$$$ Le Châtelet, Villegas 650, T428294, www.lechatelethotel.com. Chic and luxurious, beautiful chalet-style hotel with excellent service to pamper you. Wood-panelled living room, gorgeous bedrooms and suites, buffet breakfast, spa and pool with massage and facial treatments. Also, welcome glass of wine.

$$$ Arco Iris, Los Cipreses 1850, T428450, www.arcoirisar.com. Comfortable, well-equipped cabañas in a quiet area of town, each has a cosy living room, spacious kitchen, Wi-Fi and cable TV. Own access to the river, so you can fish before breakfast or enjoy a drink on the water side in the evening.

$$$ Hostería Bärenhaus, Los Alamos 156, Barrio Chapelco (8370), T422775, www.baerenhaus.com.ar. 5 km outside town, pick-up from bus terminal and airport arranged. Welcoming young owners, very comfortable rooms with heating, English and German spoken.

$$$ Hostería Walkirias, Villegas 815, T428307, www.laswalkirias.com. A lovely place, smart, tasteful rooms with big bathrooms. Sauna and pool room. Buffet breakfast. Great value off season and for longer stays, open all year.

$$$ Plaza Mayor, Cnel Pérez 1199, T427302, www.hosteriaplazamayor.com.ar. A chic and homely hostería in a quiet residential area, with traditional touches in the simple elegant rooms, excellent home-made breakfast, heated pool with solarium, BBQ, parking.

$$ Crismalú, Rudecindo Roca 975, T427283, www.interpatagonia.com/crismalu. Simple rooms in attractive chalet-style converted home, good value.

$$ Hostería Las Lucarnas, Cnel Pérez 632, T427085, www.hosterialaslucarnas.com.ar. Great value, centrally located, pretty place with simple comfortable rooms, English-speaking owner, breakfast included. Discounts for more than 5 nights, open all year.

$ pp Bike Hostel, Av Koessler 1531, T424117, www.hosteltrail.com/bikehostel. Rooms for 4-6 in a split-level alpine house, US$12-15, well cared-for, good, includes bike rental.

$ pp Puma, A Fosbery 535 (north along Rivadavia, 2 blocks beyond bridge), T422443, www.pumahostel.com.ar. Discount for HI and ISIC members, small dorms with bath and a double room with view, laundry, bikes for hire, very well run by mountain guide owner, good value.

$ pp Rukalhue, Juez del Valle 682 (3 blocks from terminal), T427431, www.rukalhue.com.ar. Large camp-style accommodation with 1 section full of dorm rooms (US$13-22) and 1 section with doubles, triples and apartments (**$$$-$$**). Also has apartments with private bath and kitchenette.

Camping ACA Camping, Av Koessler 2175, T429430, www.interpatagonia.com/aca, with hot water and laundry facilities, also *cabañas*. Camping Quila Quina, T411919. Lovely site on a stream near Lago Lácar, 18 km from San Martín, with beaches, immaculate toilet blocks, restaurant and shop, access to boats and treks. Open only in summer and Easter.

🍽 Restaurants

Junín de los Andes *p168*
$$$ Ruca Hueney, Col Suárez y Milanesio, T491113. Good steak, trout and pasta dishes, popular, great atmosphere.

$ La Nueva Posta de Junín, JM de Rosas 160 (on Ruta 234), T492080. *Parrilla* with good service and wine list; also trout, pizza and pastas.

San Martín de los Andes *p168*
$$$ 54 La Vaca, Rivadavia y San Martín, T422564. A traditional Argentine *parilla*, great atmosphere.

$$ El Regional, Mascardi 822, T425326. Popular for regional specialties – smoked trout, venison, wild boar, pâtés and hams, El Bolsón's homemade beer, cheerful German-style decor.

$$ La Costa del Pueblo, Costanera opposite pier, T429289. Overlooking the lake, huge range of pastas, chicken and trout dishes, generous portions, good service, cheerful.

$$ La Tasca, Mariano Moreno 866, T428663. Good for venison, trout and home made pastas, varied wine list.

Cafés

Beigier, Av Costanera 815. Hidden cottage with views of the bay serving a fantastic home-made afternoon tea with home-made goodies.
Deli, Villegas y Juez del Valle, T428631. Affordable place with views of the bay and nice salads, pastas and pizzas.

O Shopping

San Martín de los Andes *p168*
Abuela Goye, San Martín 807, sells delicious chocolates and runs a good café serving gorgeous cakes and delicious ice creams.
Mamusia, San Martín 601. Recommended chocolate shop, also sells home-made jams.
There are also many clothing, camping and handicraft shops along San Martín.

O What to do

San Martín de los Andes *p168*
Cycling
Many places in the centre rent mountain and normal bikes, US$10-20 per day, maps provided. **HG Rodados**, San Martín 1061, T427345, hgrodados@smandes.com.ar. Arranges trips, rents mountain bikes, also spare parts and expertise.

Fishing
Licence, US$30 for a day, to US$120 for a season, with extra charges for trolling. Contact the tourist office for a list of fishing guides or the national park office.
Jorge Cardillo Pesca, Villegas 1061, T428372, www.jorgecardillo.com. Fly shop, sells equipment, fishing licences and offers excursions.

Skiing
Chapelco has 29 km of pistes, many of them challenging, with an overall drop of 730 m. Very good slopes and snow conditions from Jul to Sep make this a popular resort with foreigners and wealthier Argentines. Details, passes, equipment hire from office at San Martín y Elordi, T427845; see www.chapelco.com.ar. At the foot of the mountain are a restaurant and

a café, with 4 more restaurants and a lodge on the mountain and a café at the top.

Tours
Prices for conventional tours are similar in most agencies. Most tours operate from 2 Jan: eg Villa la Angostura via Seven Lakes; Lakes Huechulafquen and Paimún. 1 day's rafting at Hua Hum, US$60-70; many other options.
El Claro, Col Díaz 751, T428876, www.el claroturismo.com.ar. For conventional tours, horse riding, mountain biking and trekking.
El Refugio, Pérez 830, just off San Martín, upstairs, T425140, www.elrefugioturismo.com. ar. Bilingual guides, conventional tours, boat trips, also mountain bike hire, rafting, horse riding and trekking. Recommended.
Lanín Expediciones, San Martín 851, oficina 5, T429799, www.laninexpediciones.com. Adventure tourism for beginners or experts, from a 3-hr walk near San Martín, winter night walks in the forest, rafting in Aluminé, trekking in Lanín area, a 3-day ascent of the volcano, and climbs to 4700-m Domuyo peak.

O Transport

Junín de los Andes *p168*
Air Chapelco airport 19 km southwest towards San Martín, served by AR from **Buenos Aires**. LADE office in bus terminal, San Martín de los Andes, T427672.
Bus Terminal at Olavarria y F San Martín, T492038. To **San Martín**, Centenario, Castelli and others, 50 mins, US$1.75-3. To **Buenos Aires**, 20-21 hrs, US$160-175. To **Chile** (via Paso Mamuil Malal), see below. Castelli goes daily in Jan-Feb (Sun, Mon, Wed, Fri in Dec) to **Lago Paimún** (Parque Nacional Lanín), 2 hrs, US$8.

San Martín de los Andes *p168*
Air Chapelco airport, 23 km away, transfer US$25-30. See under Junín de los Andes above.
Bus Terminal at Villegas 251 y Juez del Valle, T427044. Café, left luggage, toilet facilities, *kiosko, locutorio*. To **Buenos Aires**, 21-22 hrs, US$120-150, daily, 4 companies. To **Villa La Angostura**, Albus 4 a day, US$9. To **Bariloche**,

3½-4 hrs, US$16 (not via 7 Lagos), Vía Bariloche and Ko Ko. **To Chile**: **Pucón**, **Villarrica** and **Valdivia** via Junín de los Andes and Mamuil Malal, US$23, 5 hrs to Pucón with San Martín, heavily booked in summer. See above for route via Hua Hum Pass.

Ⓘ Directory

San Martín de los Andes *p168*
Banks ATMs on San Martín. **Medical services** Hospital Ramón Carrillo, San Martín y Coronel Rodhe, T427211. **Police station** Belgrano 635, T427300, or T101.

Parque Nacional Nahuel Huapi

Ⓘ *US$8 payable at any of the 3 park entrances. More info at the Nahuel Huapi national park office, San Martín 24, Bariloche, T0294-442 3111, www.nahuelhuapi.gov.ar, daily 0900-1400.*
Covering 709,000 ha and stretching along the Chilean border, this is the oldest national park in Argentina. With lakes, rivers, glaciers, waterfalls, torrents, rapids, valleys, forest, bare mountains and snow-clad peaks, there are many kinds of wild animals living in the region, including the pudú, the endangered huemul (both deer) as well as river otters, cougars and guanacos. Bird life, particularly swans, geese and ducks, is abundant. The outstanding feature is the splendour of the lakes. The largest is **Lago Nahuel Huapi** (*Altitude: 767 m*), 531 sq km and 460 m deep in places, particularly magnificent to explore by boat since the lake is very irregular in shape and long arms of water, or *brazos*, stretch far into the land. On a peninsula in the lake is exquisite **Parque Nacional Los Arrayanes** (see below). There are many islands: the largest is **Isla Victoria**, with its idyllic hotel. Trout and salmon have been introduced.

North of Villa La Angostura, Lagos Correntoso and Espejo both offer stunning scenery, and tranquil places to stay and walk. Navy blue Lago Traful, a short distance to the northeast, can be reached by a road which follows the Río Limay through the Valle Encantado, with its fantastic rock formations or directly from Villa La Angostura. **Villa Traful** is the perfect place to escape to, with fishing, camping, and walking. There's a **tourist office** Ⓘ *Ruta Provincial 65, T0294-4479-018 9099.* Spectacular mountains surround the city of Bariloche, great trekking and skiing country. The most popular walks are described in the Bariloche section. South of Lago Nahuel Huapi, Lagos Mascardi, Guillelmo and Gutiérrez offer horse riding, trekking and rafting along the Río Manso. See page 186 for accommodation along their shores.

The well-maintained *ripio* road known as the '**Seven Lakes Drive**' runs south from San Martín to Bariloche via Lago Hermoso and Villa La Angostura and passes beautiful unspoilt stretches of water, framed by steep, forested mountains. There are several places to stay, open summer only. An alternative route, fully paved and faster, but less scenic is via Junín de los Andes and **Confluencia** on Ruta 40 (ACA service station and a hotel). Round-trip excursions along the Seven Lakes route, five hours, are operated by several companies, but it's better in your own transport.

Villa La Angostura → *Colour map 8, C1. Phone code: 0294. Population: 13,000.*
This pretty town, 80 km northwest of Bariloche on Lago Nahuel Huapi, is a popular holiday resort with wealthier Argentines and there are countless restaurants, hotels and *cabaña* complexes around the centre, **El Cruce** and along Ruta 231 between Correntoso and Puerto Manzano. The picturesque port, known as **La Villa**, is 3 km away at the neck of the Quetrihué Peninsula. At its end is **Parque Nacional Los Arrayanes** Ⓘ *entry US$8*, with 300-year-old specimens of the rare *arrayán* tree, whose flaky bark is cinnamon coloured. The park can be reached on foot or by bike (12 km each way; for a return walk start from 0900 to 1400, 1500 for cycling), or you could take the boat back. Catamarans run at least twice daily in summer from Bahía Mansa and Bahía Brava in La Villa, US$38-42 (plus the national park entry fee); go to the national parks office by the Bahía Mansa

jetty. See also below for tours by boat from Bariloche. There is a small ski resort at **Cerro Bayo** (www.cerro bayoweb.com) with summer activities too. **Tourist office** ① *Av Arrayanes 9, T0294-449 4124, www.villalaangostura.gov.ar. Also opposite the bus terminal, Av Siete Lagos 93. Open high season 0830-2230, low season 0900-2100.* Good maps with accommodation marked.

◉ Parque Nacional Nahuel Huapi listings

For hotel and restaurant price codes, and other relevant information, see Essentials.

● Where to stay

Parque Nacional Nahuel Huapi *p172*
Villa Traful
$$$ Hostería Villa Traful, T447 9005, www.hosteriavillatraful.com. A cosy house with a tea room by the lake, also *cabañas* for 4-6 people, pretty gardens, good value. The owner's son, Andrés organizes fishing and boat trips.
$$ Cabañas Aiken, T0294-447 9048, www.aiken.com.ar. Well-decorated *cabañas* in beautiful surroundings near the lake (close to the tourist office), each with its own *parrillada*, also has a restaurant. Recommended.
$ pp Vulcanche Hostel, Los Sorbus 67, T154-692314, www.vulcanche.com. Chalet-style hostel in gardens with good views, with good dorms and **$$** doubles, breakfast extra, large park for camping.

Villa La Angostura *p172*
$$$$ La Escondida, Av Arrayanes 7014, T447 5313, www.hosterialaescondida.com.ar. Wonderful setting, right on the lake, 14 rooms, heated pool, offers mid-week, weekend and long-stay specials. Recommended.
$$$$ La Posada, R 231, Km 65, C Las Balsas s/n, T449 4450, www.hosterialaposada.com. In a splendid elevated position off the road with clear views over the lake, welcoming, beautifully maintained hotel in lovely gardens, with pool, spa, fine restaurant; a perfect place to relax.
$$$$ Las Balsas, on Bahía Las Balsas (signposted from Av Arrayanes), T449 4308, www.lasbalsas.com. One of the best small hotels in Argentina, with fabulous cosy rooms, warm relaxed public areas, fine cuisine, impeccable service, and a wonderfully intimate

atmosphere in a great lakeside location with its own secluded beach. Lakeside heated swimming pools, spa, trips and excursions arranged. Highly recommended.
$$$ Hostería ACA al Sur, Av Arrayanes 8 (behind the petrol station), T448 8413, www.acavillalaangostura.com.ar. Modern, attractive single-storey hotel with well-designed rooms in the centre of town. Recommended.
$$$ Hostería Le Lac, Av de los 7 Lagos 2350, T448 8029, www.hosterialelac.com.ar. 3 star, 8 rooms, some with jacuzzi and DVD, gardens, lake view, can arrange lots of activities, several languages spoken by owner.
$$$ Hotel Angostura, Nahuel Huapi 1911, at La Villa, T449 4224, www.hotelangostura.com. Built in 1938, this traditional hotel has a lovely lakeside setting and a good restaurant and tea room, **Viejo Coihue**. Also has 3 cabins for 6 (**$$$$**). Boat excursions along the nearby shore are arranged.
$$ Bajo Cero, Av 7 Lagos al 1200, T449 5454, www.bajocerohostel.com. Well-situated, rooms for 2-6, can arrange trekking, cycling and other excursions.
$ pp Hostel La Angostura, Barbagelata 157, 150 m up road behind tourist office, T449 4834, www.hostellaangostura.com.ar. A warm, luxurious hostel, all small dorms have bathrooms (US$18), good doubles (US$50), HI discounts, welcoming owners organize trips and rent bikes. Recommended.
$ pp Italian Hostel, Los Maquis 215 (5 blocks from terminal), T449 4376, www.italianhostel.com.ar. Welcoming, small, with dorms (US$18) and doubles (**$$**), rustic, functional and nice, run by a biker who closes the place in Apr-Oct. Fireplace and orchard from where you can pick berries and herbs for your meals. Recommended.
Camping Osa Mayor, signposted off main road, close to town, T449 4304, www.camping

osamayor.com.ar. Well-designed leafy and level site, US$8-13, all facilities, also rustic *cabañas* $$$ for 2 people, and dorms $$ for 2 people, helpful owner.

$ **TemaTyCo**, Ruta 231 y Mirlo, T447 5211. Chic tearoom with a wide range of teas and delicious cakes.

⊙ Restaurants

Parque Nacional Nahuel Huapi *p172*
Villa Traful
$$ **Ñancu Lahuen**, Villa Traful. A chocolate shop, tea room, and restaurant serving local trout. Delightful and cosy, with big open fire, delicious food and reasonably priced.

Villa La Angostura *p172*
$$$ **Cocina Waldhaus**, Av Arrayanes 6330, T447 5323. Very recommended, this is 'auteur cuisine' with gorgeous local delicacies created by Chef Leo Morsea, served in a charming chalet-style building.
$$ **El Esquiador**, Las Retamas 146 (behind the bus terminal), T449 4331. Good, popular *parrilla* has an all-you-can-eat choice of cold starters, a main meal and a dessert.
$$ **Los Pioneros**, Av Arrayanes 267, T449 5525. Famous for fine local dishes in a chalet-style building and great Argentine steaks. Great pizza place next door run by the same owners. They also serve locally brewed beers.
$ **Hora Cero**, Av Arrayanes 45, T449 5800 Hugely popular, this serves a big range of excellent pizzas.

⊙ What to do

Villa La Angostura *p172*
There is lots to do here: bicycle hire, US$15-20 per day, and mountain biking (**Bayo Abajo**, Av Siete Lagos 94, bayoabajo@argentina.com, bike hire), boat trips (US$550-600, 2 people, includes lunch and national park entrance fee), canopying (US$25), climbing, fishing, horse riding (US$55-60) and trekking (**Alma Sur**, T154-564724, www.almasur.com).

⊙ Transport

Villa La Angostura *p172*
Bus Terminal at Av 7 Lagos y Av Arrayanes, opposite ACA service station. Urban buses, 15 de Mayo, US$1, link El Cruce (main bus stop on main road, 50 m from tourist office), La Villa, Correntoso and Puerto Manzano, and go up to Lago Espejo (US$1-2) and Cerro Bayo (US$3) in high season. To/from **Bariloche**, 1 hr, US$6-8, several companies. If going on to **Osorno** in Chile, 3½ hrs, you can arrange for the bus company to pick you up in La Angostura.

Bariloche and around → *Phone code: 0294. Colour map 8, C1. Population: 133,500.*

Beautifully situated on the south shore of Lago Nahuel Huapi, at the foot of Cerro Otto, San Carlos de Bariloche is an attractive tourist town and the best centre for exploring the national park. There are many good hotels, restaurants and chocolate shops among its chalet-style stone and wooden buildings. Others along the lake shore have splendid views.

Tourist information **Oficina Municipal de Turismo** ⓘ *Centro Cívico p 6, T442 2484, www. barilochepatagonia.info, daily 0800-2100. Municipal site: www.bariloche.gov.ar.* List of city buses, details of hikes and campsites and helpful in finding accommodation. Very useful for information on hiking is **Club Andino Bariloche (CAB)** ⓘ *20 de Febrero 30, T442 2266, www.clubandino.org, Mon-Fri 0900-1300, plus 1500-1930 high season.* You can also contact the **Association of Guides**, all of whom are trained, and know the geography, flora and fauna. They sell excellent maps showing walks, with average walking times, and *refugios*, and can advise on which have room. Ask for the *Sendas y Bosques* (walks and forests) series, which are 1:200,000, laminated and easy to read, with good books containing English summaries of the walks, www.guiasendasybosques. com.ar, the detailed *Active Patagonia* map and the *Carta de Refugios, Senderos y Picadas* for Bariloche. They can also tell you about transport, which varies from year to year and between high and low season. **Note** At peak holiday times (July and December to January), Bariloche is heaving with holidaymakers and students. The best times to visit are in the spring (September to November) and autumn (March to April), when the forests are in their glory, or February for camping and walking and August for skiing.

Places in Bariloche

At the heart of the city is the **Centro Cívico**, built in 'Bariloche Alpine style' and separated from the lake by Avenida Rosas. It includes the **Museo de La Patagonia** ① *T442 2309, Tue-Fri 1000-1230, 1400-1900, Sat 1000-1700, entry by donation*, which, apart from the region's fauna (stuffed), has indigenous artefacts and material from the lives of the first white settlers. The **cathedral**, built in 1946, lies six blocks east of here, with the main commercial area on Mitre in between. Opposite the main entrance to the cathedral there is a huge rock left in this spot by a glacier during the last glacial period. On the lakeshore is the **Museo Paleontológico** ① *12 de Octubre y Sarmiento, T15-461 1210, Mon-Sat 1600-1900, US$1.25, children US$0.75*, which displays fossils mainly from Patagonia, including an ichthyosaur and replicas of a giant spider and shark's jaws.

Around Bariloche

One of South America's most important ski centres is just a few kilometres southwest from Bariloche, at **Cerro Catedral** (see What to do, page 181). You can take a boat trip from Puerto Pañuelo (Km 25.5, bus 10, 20/21, or transfer arranged with tour operator, US$47 50 return) across

1 Bariloche

Lago Nahuel Huapi

Puerto San Carlos

Where to stay
1 Below 41 A1
2 Antiguo Solar B2
4 Familia Arko B1
5 Hostel Inn Bariloche A1
6 Hostería Güemes B1
7 La Bolsa B2
8 Penthouse 1004 A1
9 Periko's B1
10 Premier A2
11 Pudu A1
12 Ruca Hueney B2
13 Tres Reyes A2

Restaurants
1 Chez Philippe B1
2 Covita A3
3 El Boliche de Alberto B2
4 Huang Ji A2
5 Jauja B2
6 Kandahar B1
7 La Alpina A2
10 Vegetariano B1

Bars & clubs
11 Cerebro A1
12 Wilkenny A1

➡ **Bariloche maps**
1 Bariloche, page 175
2 Bariloche – the road to Llao Llao, page 176

200 metres
200 yards

Lago Nahuel Huapi to **Isla Victoria** and **Bosque de Arrayanes**, on the Quetrihué Peninsula; full- or half-day excursion (fewer options in low season), with **Turisur** ① *T442 6109 www.turisur. com.ar*, on the 1937 boat *Modesta Victoria* or with **Espacio** ① *T443 1372, www.islavictoriayarrayanes. com, US$47-50 plus transfer to port and park entry, take picnic lunch if you don't want to buy food sold on board*, on modern *Cau Cau*. The all-day boat trip to **Puerto Blest**, in native Valdivian rainforest, is highly recommended, also US$47-50 with **Turisur**. From Puerto Pañuelo, sail down to Puerto Blest (hotel, restaurant), continuing by short bus ride to Puerto Alegre and again by launch to Puerto Frías. From Puerto Blest, walk through forest to the Cascada and Laguna de los Cántaros (1½ hours). Another boat trip goes from Puerto Pañuelo to Brazo Tristeza, at the southwest tip of the lake, one of several trips on the *Kaikén Patagonia* (www.kaikenpatagonia.com.ar).

Avenida Bustillo runs parallel to the lakeshore west of Bariloche, with access to the mountains above. At Km 5, a cable car (*teleférico*) goes up to **Cerro Otto** (1405 m) with its revolving restaurant and splendid views. Transport and other details under What to do (page 180). At Km 17.7 a chairlift goes up to **Cerro Campanario** (1049 m) ① *daily 0900-1800, 7 mins, US$6*, with fine views of Isla Victoria and Puerto Pañuelo. At Km 18.3 **Circuito Chico** begins – a 60-km circular route around Lago Moreno Oeste, past Punto Panorámico and through Puerto Pañuelo to **Llao Llao**, Argentina's most famous hotel (details on this and others on Avenida Bustillo in Where to stay, below). Take bus No 20 (no 21 for return), 45 minutes, US$1, a half-day drive or tour with agency, or full day's cycle. You could also extend this circuit, returning via **Colonia Suiza** and **Cerro Catedral** (2388 m) one of South America's most important ski centres. Whole-day trip to **Lagos Gutiérrez** and **Mascardi** and beautiful **Pampa Linda** at the base of mighty **Cerro Tronador** (3478 m), visiting the strange **Ventisquero Negro** (black glacier), highly recommended.

② Bariloche – the road to Llao Llao

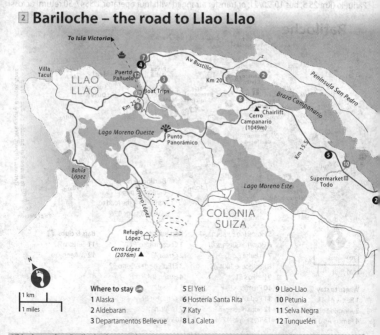

Where to stay 🛏	5 El Yeti	9 Llao-Llao
1 Alaska	6 Hostería Santa Rita	10 Petunia
2 Aldebaran	7 Katy	11 Selva Negra
3 Departamentos Bellevue	8 La Caleta	12 Tunquelén
4		

Border with Chile

The Samoré (formerly Puyehue) Pass A spectacular six-hour drive through the pass 125 km northwest of Bariloche. A good broad paved road, RN 40 then RN 231, goes around the east end of Lago Nahuel Huapi, then follows the north side of the lake through Villa La Angostura. The road is rough *ripio* from there on, with the occasional paved stretch. It passes the junction with 'Ruta de Los Siete Lagos' for San Martín at Km 90, Argentine customs at El Rincón, Km 105, and the pass at Km 122 at an elevation of about 1314 m. Chilean customs is at Pajarito, Km 145, in the middle of a forest. The border is open 0800-2000 but liable to be closed after snowfalls (*Gendarmería* in Bariloche, T442 2711). In early 2013 it was closed because of fire at the border complex. There is an absolute ban in Chile on importing any fresh food from Argentina. You are strongly advised to get rid of all your Argentine pesos before leaving Argentina; it is useful to have some Chilean pesos before you cross into Chile from Bariloche, though you can buy them at a reasonable rate at the Chilean border post. Since the government lifted restrictions on foreign currency in 2014, it is possible to buy Chilean Pesos at official exchange houses. Further information on border crossings in the Lake District will be found in the Chile chapter.

Via Lake Todos Los Santos The route is Bariloche to Puerto Pañuelo by road (30 minutes, departure 0900), Puerto Pañuelo to Puerto Blest by boat (one hour), Puerto Blest to Puerto Alegre on Lago Frías by bus (15 minutes), cross the lake to Puerto Frías by boat (20 minutes), then two hours by road to Peulla (lunch not included in price). Leave for Petrohué in the afternoon by boat (one hour 40 minutes), cross Lago Todos Los Santos, passing the Osorno volcano, then by bus to Puerto Varas (two hours). This route is beautiful, but the weather is often wet. The journey

➡ **Bariloche maps**
1 Bariloche, page 175
2 Bariloche – the road to Llao Llao, page 176

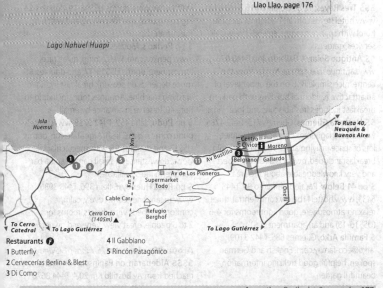

Lago Nahuel Huapi

Restaurants ❼
1 Butterfly
2 Cervecerías Berlina & Blest
3 Di Como
4 Il Gabbiano
5 Rincón Patagónico

can be done in one day, US$280, two days with an overnight stop in Peulla (breakfast is included, but not supper or lodging, see under Peulla, Chile), or with more stops if you prefer. From 1 May to 31 August, only two-day crossings run. **Cruce Andino** ① *in Bariloche see Turisur, below, www. cruceandino.com*, has the monopoly on this crossing. Book in advance during the high season. The only day the trip does not run is the 1 May.

⦿ Bariloche and around listings

For hotel and restaurant price codes, and other relevant information, see Essentials.

⦿ Where to stay

Bariloche *p174, maps p175 and p176*
Prices rise in 2 peak seasons: Jul-Aug for skiing, and mid-Dec to Mar for summer holidays. If you arrive in the high season without a reservation, consult the listing published by the tourist office (address above). This selection gives lake-view, high-season prices where applicable. In low season you pay half of these prices in most cases. All those listed are recommended.

$$$ Premier, Rolando 263, T442 6168, www. hotelpremier.com. Good central choice (very good value in low season), small 'classic' rooms and larger superior rooms, English spoken.

$$$ Tres Reyes, 12 de Octubre 135, T442 6121, www.hotel3reyes.com.ar. Traditional lakeside hotel with spacious rooms, splendid views, all services, gardens.

$$ Antiguo Solar, A Gallardo 360, T440 0337, www.antiguosolar.com.ar. Not far from the centre, nice simple B&B on the upper level of an attractive residential building, with parking, breakfast includes fresh biscuits and local jams.

$$ Hostería Güemes, Güemes 715, T442 4785, www.hosteriaguemes.com.ar. Lovely, quiet, lots of space in living areas, very pleasant, big breakfast included, owner is a fishing expert and very knowledgeable about the area.

$ pp 41 Below, Pasaje Juramento 94, T443 6433, www.hostel41below.com. Central, quiet, relaxing atmosphere, good light rooms for 4-6 (US$16-18) and an apartment (**$$**).

$ Familia Arko, Güemes 685, T442 3109, arko@eco-family.com. English and German spoken, helpful, good trekking information, beautiful garden.

$ pp Hostel Inn Bariloche, Salta 308, T442 6084,www.hostelbariloche.com. Large, well-designed hostel with great views of the lake from the communal areas and rooms. Comfortable beds; in dorm US$15 pp); also doubles (**$$**), discount for HI members. The best feature is the great deck with a view in the garden. Neighbouring **Marco Polo Inn**, T440 0105, is in the same group.

$ pp La Bolsa, Palacios 405 y Elflein, T442 3529, www.labolsadeldeporte.com.ar. Relaxed atmosphere, rustic rooms with duvets, 1 double with bath, some rooms with views, deck to sit out on.

$ pp Penthouse 1004, San Martín 127, 10th floor, T443 2228, www.penthouse1004. com.ar. Welcoming hostel at the top of a block of apartments with amazing views. Helpful staff, cosy rooms, dorms US$18-19, doubles **$$**. Big communal area for chilling and watching the sunset.

$ pp Periko's, Morales 555, T452 2326, www.perikos.com. Welcoming, quiet, nice atmosphere, dorms US$13-17, and doubles **$$** (price depends on season), breakfast included, washing machine. Arranges tours, including to Ruta 40. Reserve in advance by email.

$ pp Pudu, Salta 459, T442 9738, www.hostel pudu.com. "A gem". Irish/Argentine-run, dorms US$17 and doubles **$$** with spectacular lake views, downstairs is a small garden and a bar. Long term rates available.

$ pp Ruca Hueney, Elflein 396, T443 3986, www.rucahueney.com. Lovely, calm, comfortable beds with duvets, rooms for 2 to 6 people, great view, very kind owners.

Around Bariloche *p175, maps p175 and p176*
$$$$ Aldebaran, on Península San Pedro, reached from Av Bustillo Km 20.4, T444 8678,

www.aldebaranpatagonia.com. Not in chalet style, but tasteful rooms in this modern boutique hotel on the lake shore, superb views. Rustic-style restaurant, sauna and spa with outdoor pool, so you can bask under the stars. Great service from helpful bilingual staff.

$$$$ Llao-Llao, Av Bustillo Km 25, T444 5700/8530, www.llaollao.com. Deservedly famous, superb location, complete luxury, golf course, pool, spa, water sports, restaurant.

$$$$ Tunquelén, Av Bustillo, Km 24.5, T444 8400/8600, www.tunquelen.com. 4-star, comfortable, splendid views, feels quite secluded, superb restaurant, attentive service.

$$$ Departamentos Bellevue, Av Bustillo, Km 24.6, T444 8389, www.bellevue.com.ar. Open year-round. A famous tea room with beautiful views also offers accommodation with high-quality furnishings, very comfortable, well-equipped self-catering *cabañas*, delicious breakfast included. Access to beaches on Lake Moreno, lovely gardens.

$$$ Hostería Santa Rita, Av Bustillo, Km 7.2, T446 1028, www.santarita.com.ar. Bus 10, 20/21 to Km 7.5. Peaceful lakeside views, comfortable, lovely terrace, great service.

$$$ Katy, Av Bustillo, Km 24.3, T444 8023, www.gringospatagonia.com. Delightful, peaceful, garden full of flowers, charming Slovenian family Kastelic (also half-board, **$$$$**). Also offers adventure tourism.

$$$ La Caleta, Av Bustillo, Km 1.95, T154 607727, www.bungalows-bariloche.com.ar. *Cabañas* sleep 4, open fire, excellent value, minimum booking 3 nights (7 in high season). Also owns San Isidro *cabañas* at Km 5.7, further west.

$ pp Alaska, Lilinquen 328 (buses 10, 20/21, get off at La Florida, Av Bustillo Km 7.5), T446 1564, www.alaska-hostel.com. Well run, cosy with shared rustic rooms for 4, US$14 pp, also doubles **$$** (cheaper without bath), nice garden, washing machine, organizes horse riding and rafting, rents mountain bikes. Recommended.

Camping List of sites from tourist office. These are recommended among the many along Bustillo. **Petunia**, Km 13.5, T446 1969,

www.campingpetunia.com. A lovely shady site going down to lakeside with all facilities. Shops and restaurants on most sites; these are closed outside Jan-Mar. **Selva Negra**, Km 2.95, T444 1013, www.campinglaselvanegra.alojar.com. ar. Very good, discounts for long stay. **El Yeti**, Km 5.7, T444 2073, www.elyeti.alojar.com.ar. All facilities, *cabañas*.

❼ Restaurants

Bariloche *p174, maps p175 and p176*
Bariloche is blessed with superb food, much of it locally produced, including smoked trout and salmon, wild boar and other delicacies, not least fine chocolate and, in season, delicious berries. There are many good delicatessens.

$$$ Chez Philippe, Primera Junta 1080, T442 7291. Delicious local delicacies and fondue, fine French-influenced cuisine.

$$$ Jauja, Elflein 148, T442 2952. Recommended for delicious local dishes, quiet and welcoming, good value.

$$$ Kandahar, 20 de Febrero 698, T442 4702. Atmospheric, warm and intimate, with exquisite food, run by ski champion Marta Peirono de Barber, superb wines and pisco sour. Dinner only, reserve in high season. Highly recommended.

$$ Covita, Rolando 172, T442 1708. Mon-Sat for lunch, Thu-Sat for dinner. Vegetarian restaurant (also serves fish), offering curries, masalas and pastas.

$$ El Boliche de Alberto, Villegas 347, T443 1433, www.elbolichedealberto.com. Very good pasta, huge portions, popular after 2000 (queues in summer). There is a 2nd location at Bustillo Km 8800 that specializes in grilled meats.

$$ Vegetariano, 20 de Febrero 730, T442 1820, www.vegetarianpatagonia.com.ar. Also fish, excellent food, beautifully served, warm atmosphere, take-away available. Highly recommended.

$ Huang Ji, Rolando 268, T442 8168. Good Chinese, next to a bowling alley.

La Alpina, Moreno 98. Old-fashioned café serving delicious cakes, good for tea, Wi-Fi, charming.

Around Bariloche *p175, maps p175 and p176*
\$\$\$ Butterfly, Hua Huan 7831, just off
Av Bustillo Km 7.9, T446 1441, www.the
butterflygroup.com.ar. 2 seatings: 1945 and
2130. German/Argentine/Irish-owned, an elite
dining experience, tasting menus using only
local ingredients, carefully selected wines, art
exhibitions, only 6 tables. Reserve in advance
and discuss the menu with the chef
\$\$\$ Il Gabbiano, Av Bustillo Km 24.3, T444
8346, www.gabbiano.com.ar. Closed Wed.
Delicious Italian lunches and dinners. Booking
essential (no credit cards).
\$\$\$ Rincón Patagónico, Av Bustillo, Km 14,
Paraje Laguna Fantasma, T446 3063, www.
rinconpatagonico.com.ar. Traditional *parrilla*
with Patagonian lamb cooked *al palo*, huge
menu but service can be minimal at busy times.
\$\$ Di Como, Av Bustillo, Km 0.8, T452 2118.
A 10-min walk from town. Good pizza and
pasta, terrace and great views of the lake.

🄽 Bars and clubs

Cerebro, JM de Rosas 406, www.cerebro.com.ar.
Jun-Dec. The party starts at 0130, Fri best.
Cervecería Berlina, Ruta 79 y F Goye, T445 4393,
www.cervezaberlina.com. Open 1200-0100 (until
last person has left). 3 good brews. They have a
diverse menu (**\$\$**) at their restaurant at Av Bustillo
Km 11.750, with a deck for watching the sunset.
Cervecería Blest, Av Bustillo Km 11.6, T446
1026, www.cervezablest.com.ar. Wonderful
brewery with delicious beers, serving
imaginative local and German dishes and steak
and kidney pie (**\$\$\$-\$\$**). Recommended.
Cerveza Artesanal Gilbert, Km 24, Barrio Las
Cartas, Circuito Chico, T445 4292. Daily 1100-
2300. Popular beers and simple meals (**\$\$**).
Wilkenny, San Martín 435, T442 4444. Lively Irish
pub with expensive food but it really gets busy
around 2400. Great place to watch televised sports.

O Shopping

Bariloche *p174, maps p175 and p176*
The main shopping area is on Mitre between the
Centro Cívico and Beschtedt, also on San Martín.

Chocolate The local stuff is excellent: several
shops on Mitre. Local wines, from the Alto Río
Negro, are also good. **Abuela Goye**, Mitre 258
and Quaglia 219, www.abuelagoye.com. First rate
chocolatier, also with café in the Quaglia branch
(2 other branches and outlets nationwide).
Fenoglio, Av Bustillo 1200, Mitre 76 and others.
Daily 1100-1900. Chocolate production with
tastings and a good shop. **Mamuschka**, Mitre y
Rolando, www.mamuschka.com. Considered
the best chocolate here, also with café.
Handicrafts Feria Artesanal Municipal,
Moreno y Villegas.

🄽 What to do

Bariloche *p174, maps p175 and p176*
Climbing
Note that at higher levels, winter snow
storms can begin as early as Apr, making
climbing dangerous.
Club Andino Bariloche, see Tourist
information, above. The club can contact
mountain guides and provide information.

Cycling
Bikes can be hired at many places in high season.
Circuito Chico, Av Bustillo 18300, T459 5608,
www.circuitochicobikes.com. Rents mountain
bikes, with road assistance service, and kayaks.
Dirty Bikes, Lonquimay 3908, T444 2743,
www.dirtybikes.com.ar. Very helpful for repairs,
tours and bike rentals (US\$6-45 per day).

Fishing
Martín Pescador, Rolando 257, T442 2275.
Fishing, camping and skiing equipment.

Horse riding
Ariane Patagonia, T452 3488, www.ariane
patagonia.com.ar. Horse-riding trips, visits to
farms and estancias, personalized service.
Bastion del Manso, Av Bustillo 13491, T445
6111, www.bastiondelmanso.com. Relaxed
place with tuition and full-day's riding offered,
including rafting and longer treks.
See also **Estancia Peuma Hue**, under Bariloche
to El Bolsón, Where to stay, below.

Kayaking

Patagonia Infinita, T15-455 3954, www.patagoniainfinita.com.ar. Kayaking and trekking trips in Parque Nacional Nahuel Huapi.
Pura Vida Patagonia, T154 414053, www.puravidapatagonia.com. Informative, attentive guides, good value, trips from 1-9 days in Nahuel Huapi.

Paragliding

There are several paragliding schools. Take-offs are usually from Cerro Otto, but there are other starting points, 10- to 40-min tandem flights.

Skiing

Cerro Catedral, T440 9000, www.catedralaltapatagonia.com. Mid-Jun to end-Sep, busiest from mid-Jun to mid-Aug for school holidays, ski lifts: 0900-1630. It has 120 km of slopes of all grades, allowing a total drop of 1010 m, and 52 km of cross country (Nordic) skiing routes. There are also snowboarding areas and a well-equipped base with hotels, restaurants and equipment hire, ski schools and nursery care for children. Bus, labelled 'Catedral' (3 de Mayo company), leaves from the bus terminal and Moreno entre Beschtedt y Palacios every 90 mins, 35 mins, US$3, taxi US$25. The cable car for Catedral costs US$25 round trip.
Cerro Otto, T444 1035, www.telefericobariloche.com.ar. Cable car and funicular passengers can take a bus leaving from Mitre y Villegas, hourly 1000-1930 in summer, returning hourly.

Tours

Check what your tour includes; cable cars and chair lifts usually extra. Tours get booked up in season. Most travel agencies will pick you up from your hotel and charge roughly the same prices: Circuito Chico US$19, half-day; Isla Victoria and Bosque de Arrayanes, full-day boat trip (see above); Tronador, Ventisquero Negro and Pampa Linda, US$40 plus National Park entry via Lago Mascardi by boat; El Bolsón US$35, full-day, including Lago Puelo; several other tours.
Aguas Blancas, Morales 564, T443 2799, www.aguasblancas.com.ar. Rafting on the Río Manso, all grades, with expert guides, and all

equipment provided, also 'duckies' – inflatable kayaks for beginners.
Canopy, Colonia Suiza, Cerro López, T440 0286, www.canopybariloche.com. Zip line adventure in the forest, including 4WD ride to get there and night descents.
Eco Family, 20 de Junio 728, T442 8995, www.eco-family.com. Riding, walking, skiing, other adventures, bilingual guides. Highly recommended.
Senza Limiti Adventures, J Cortázar 5050, T452 0597, www.slimiti.com. Adventure travel company, including kayaking, mountain-biking, hut-to-hut treks and much more, licensed by National Parks Administration.
Tronador Turismo, Quaglia 283, T442 5644, www.tronadorturismo.com.ar. Conventional tours, trekking and rafting. Also to Refugio Neumeyer and to Chilean border. Great adventurous wintersports options.
Turisur, Mitre 219, T442 6109, www.turisur.com.ar. Boat trips to Bosque de Arrayanes, Isla Victoria on a 1937 ship and to Tronador via Lago Mascardi. Licensee for the Cruce Andino trip to Puerto Montt. Always reserve 1 day ahead.

Trekking

There's a network of paths in the mountains, and several *refugios* allowing for treks over several days. *Refugios* are leased by **Club Andino Bariloche**. On treks to *refugios* remember to add costs of ski lifts, buses, food at *refugios* and lodging (in **Club Andino** *refugios*. US$10-20 per night, plus US$8-20 for food. Take a good sleeping bag. Horseflies (*tábanos*) infest the lake shores and lower areas in summer. Among the many great treks available are: from Llao Llao a delightful, easy circuit in Valdivian (temperate) rainforest (2 hrs), also climb the small hill for wonderful views. Up to privately-owned **Refugio López** (2076 m, bus 10 to Colonia Suiza and López, check return times), 5 hrs return, from southeastern tip of Lago Moreno up Arroyo López, for fabulous views. From Cerro Catedral to **Refugio Frey** (1700 m), beautiful setting on small lake, via Arroyo Piedritas (4 hrs each way), or via cable car to **Refugio Lynch** and via Punta Nevada (only experienced walkers). To beautiful Lago Gutiérrez, 2 km downhill from Cerro Catedral, along lake shore to the road from El Bolsón and walk back to Bariloche (4 hrs), or Bus 50. From **Pampa Linda**, idyllic (*hosterías*, campsite), walk up to **Refugio Otto Meiling** (5 hrs each way), to tranquil Laguna Ilon (5½ hrs each way), or across Paso de las Nubes to Puerto Frías, boat back to Bariloche (2 days: closed when boggy). Bus to Pampa Linda from outside **Club Andino Bariloche** 0830 in summer, **Expreso Meiling**, T452 9875, or from **Transitando lo Natural**, 20 de Febrero 25, T452 7926, 2¼ hrs. Contact **CAB** for maps, guidebooks and to check if walks are open (see under Tourist information, above). **Andescross**, T15-463 3581, www.andescross. com. Expert guides, all included. Trekking to Chile across the Andes, via Pampa Linda, Lago Frías, Peulla.

⊖ Transport

Bariloche *p174, maps p175 and p176*
Air Airport is 15 km east of town, with access from Ruta 40, 7 km east of centre, T440 5016; bus service 72 from town centre; also colectivos and taxis. If staying on the road to Llao Llao, west of town, expect to pay more for transport to your hotel. Car rental agencies, internet, exchange, ATM, café at the airport. Many flights a day to **Buenos Aires**. AR also flies to **El Calafate** in summer only. LADE to **Buenos Aires**, **Comodoro Rivadavia**, **Esquel** and several other destinations in Patagonia.
Bus Station 3 km east of centre; urban buses 'Mascardo', 'Manso', 20, 21, 22, to/ from centre; also bus 10, 11, 72. City buses run by **3 de Mayo**, Moreno 480, also at terminal, http://3demayobariloche.com. ar. Buy rechargeable ticket before travelling. Taxi US$6-8. Bus info at terminal T443 2860, http://terminaldebariloche.com.ar. Toilets, small *confitería, kiosko, locutorio* with internet, tourist information desk. Bus company offices in town (purchase tickets there or at terminal): **Vía Bariloche/El Valle/Don Otto/ TAC**, Mitre 321, T442 9012, terminal T443 2444;

Chevallier/Flechabus, Moreno 107, T442 3090. At terminal: **Andesmar/Tramat**, T443 0211; **Ko Ko**, T443 1135. **Buenos Aires**, 7 companies daily, 19-22 hrs, US$118-131. To **Bahía Blanca**, 5 companies, 14 hrs, US$70-85. To **Mendoza**, US$90-102, **Andesmar** and **Tramat**, 17-19 hrs. To **Esquel**, via **El Bolsón**, fares and schedules given below. To **San Martín de los Andes**, and **Villa La Angostura**, see above. To **Comodoro Rivadavia**, US$56-63, Don Otto, Andesmar, 14 hrs, and Marga who continue to **Río Gallegos**, US$55-65, 23 hrs. In Río Gallegos make other onward connections to El Calafate and Ushuaia. **Taqsa** (T0800-333-1188, www. taqsa.com.ar) run to **El Chaltén** and **El Calafate** via El Bolsón, Esquel, Perito Moreno and Los Antiguos on Ruta 40, US$108, 27 hrs. Or take **Chaltén Travel's** 3-day trip on Ruta 40, www. chaltentravel.com (page 198), depart 0645 on odd-numbered days from **Turacción**, Quaglia 262. **To Chile**: Vía Bariloche runs daily services via Samoré pass to **Osorno**, 5 hrs, US$30, and **Puerto Montt** (6-7½ hrs, same fare); Andesmar goes to **Valdivia** via Osorno, US$35, US$50 *cama*, not daily. Take passport when booking. Sit on left side for best views.
Car hire Rates are from US$60-130 per day. Lagos, Mitre 83, T442 8880, www.lagosrentacar. com.ar, among many others. To enter Chile, a permit is necessary; it's generally included in the price. State when booking car, allow 24 hrs.

⊙ Directory

Bariloche *p174, maps p175 and p176*
Banks ATMs at many banks on Mitre, Moreno and San Martín. Cambio Sudamérica, Mitre 63, has good rates. **Consulates** Chile, España 275, T442 3050, Mon-Fri 0900-1300, 1400-1730, helpful. **Language schools** ILEE, www. argentinailee.com, arranges classes and home stay. La Montaña, Elflein 251, T452 4212, www. la montana.com. Spanish courses, family lodging, activities and volunteering. **Medical facilities** Emergencies: Dial 107. Clinic: Hospital Zonal, Moreno 601, T442 6119. **Useful addresses** Immigration office: Libertad 191, T442 3043. Police: T442 2772, or 101.

South of Bariloche

More wild and beautiful scenery can be explored along the Andes, with a few tourist centres like El Bolsón and Esquel giving access to lakes and national parks. There is trekking, rafting, skiing and fishing on offer, a train ride on the famous La Trochita and the magnificent Los Alerces national park to explore.

Bariloche to El Bolsón

Ruta 258, the paved road from Bariloche to El Bolsón, 126 km south, passes the beautiful lakes Gutiérrez, Mascardi and Guillelmo. From the southern end of Lago Mascardi, 35 km south of Bariloche, a *ripio* road (note one-way system) runs west towards Cerro Tronador and **Pampa Linda**, the starting point for excellent trekking including the two-day walk over Paso de los Nubes to Laguna Frías (see Trekking, page 181, and Where to stay, page 186). **Río Villegas**, about 70 km south of Bariloche, is very beautiful, and there's world class rafting to be done on the **Río Manso**.

El Bolsón and around → *Population: 40,000. Phone code: 0294. Colour map 8, C1.*

El Bolsón is an attractive town in a broad fertile valley, surrounded by the mountains of the cordillera and dominated by the dramatic peak of Cerro Piltriquitrón 2284 m (hence its name: the big bag). It's a magical setting which attracted thousands of hippies to create an ideological community here in the 1970s; they now produce the handicrafts, beers, fruit and jams, sold at the market on Tuesday, Thursday, Saturday, 0900-1800. There are many mountain walks and waterfalls nearby, and good fishing at Lagos Puelo (see below) and Epuyén (15 km off Ruta 40, picnic ground, Centro Cultural, campsites at Puerto Patriada, 25 km south of El Bolsón via El Hoyo) – both within easy access. **Tourist office** ① *Av San Martín y Roca, T449 2604, www. elbolson.gov.ar, 0900-2100 all year, until 2400 in high summer, they are extremely helpful with maps, treks to refugios and accommodation, English spoken.*

There are waterfalls at **Cascada Escondida**, 10 km northwest of town (two-hour dusty walk, ask for short-cut through woods), a good place for a picnic. There are fine views from **Cerro Piltriquitrón** – drive or taxi 10 km, then walk one hour through the sculptures of the **Bosque Tallado** (or six- to seven-hour round trip walk), food and shelter at *refugio* (1400 m), then three-hour walk from there to the summit. Views of the valley from **Cabeza del Indio**, a good 6 km drive or bike ride from the centre, and a pleasant one hour walk up to **Cerro Amigo**: follow Gral Roca east until it becomes Islas Malvinas and continue up the hill. There is wonderful trekking in the mountains and valleys west of town on an excellent network of trails with well-equipped and staffed *refugios* in superb locations; some 10 shelters are operational, most open October-March. Most shelters offer simple accommodation (US$10-12 per person, sleeping bag required), a hearty breakfast (US$3.75), other meals (US$5-7.50), basic supplies including home-baked bread and home-brewed beer, camping and hot showers. They have radio communication with each other and with town. Additional information and compulsory registration at the **Club Andino Piltriquitrón** ① *Sarmiento y Roca, T449 2600, www.capiltriquitron.com.ar, Mon-Fri 1800-2000* or tourist office in El Bolsón. In high season there are minibuses to the trailheads, at other times hitch or take a remise taxi.

At **Lago Puelo** in the **Parque Nacional Lago Puelo** there are gentle walks on marked paths, boat trips across the lake on a 1931 boat and canoes for rent. Wardens at the park entrance (US$3.50) can advise on these and a three-day trek through magnificent scenery to Chilean border. Gorgeous homemade *alfajores* in fairy tale setting at **El Bolsonero** on the old road to Lago Puelo. Buses, US$1-2, from Avenida San Martín y Dorrego in El Bolsón go to the lake via

Villa Lago Puelo. **Boats:** *Juana de Arco* (T449 8946, www.interpatagonia.com/juanadearco). Information in summer from hut in Avenida San Martín y Pellegrini, from 30-minute trip, US$15, to the Chilean border, with interpreted trail, US$38.

Cholila and around → *Phone code: 02945. Population: 3000.*

A peaceful sprawling village, 76 km south of El Bolsón, with superb views at Lago Cholila (17 km west), crowned by the Matterhorn-like mountains of Cerros Dos and Tres Picos (campsite and expensive **Hostería El Pedregoso**). Excellent fishing, canoeing and kayaking on rivers nearby. Along Valle de Cholila (Ruta 71) are several lovely old brick and wooden houses and barns. Among them are the **wooden cabins**, where Butch Cassidy, the Sundance Kid and Etta Place lived between 1901 and 1905; the cabins have been renovated, controversially (officially US$1.50 entry, if anyone's around to charge you). They are 13 km north, east of the road, opposite a police station. One kilometre west of the road is the **Casa de Piedra** teahouse serving *té galés* and offering basic accommodation. **Villa Lago Rivadavia**, 15 km south of Cholila lies next to the northern gates of Parque Nacional Los Alerces, with an increasing number of *cabañas*. Tourist information hut open in summer only, opposite petrol station at El Rincón; also basic information at Municipalidad in Cholila, T498040.

Esquel → *Phone code: 02945. Colour map 9, A1. Population: 30,000.*

Esquel, 293 km south of Bariloche, was originally an offshoot of the Welsh colony at Chubut, 650 km to the east, and still has a pioneer feel. A breezy open town in a fertile valley, with a backdrop of mountains, Esquel is the base for visiting the Parque Nacional Los Alerces and for skiing at **La Hoya** in winter (15 km, good 6½-hour trek in summer). Good walks from the town to Laguna La Zeta, 5 km, and to Cerro La Cruz, two hours (one way). It's also the departure point for the famous narrow gauge railway, **La Trochita** (see box, opposite, and Transport). **Tourist office** ① *Av Alvear y Sarmiento, T451927, www.esquel.gov.ar, daily 0800-2200.* ATMs at **Banco de la Nación** ① *Av Alvear y Roca, and on 25 de Mayo 739.*

Trevelin → *Colour map 9, A1. Population: 5000.*

An offshoot of the Welsh Chubut colony (see box, opposite), where Welsh is still spoken, the pretty village of Trevelin, 24 km southwest of Esquel, has a Welsh chapel (built 1910, closed) and tea rooms. The **Museo Regional** ① *US$4, 1100-2000,* in the old mill (1918) includes artefacts from the Welsh colony. The **Museo Cartref Taid** ① *US$4, 1600-2000 (ask for directions in the tourist office),* is the house of John Evans, one of Trevelin's first pioneers, full of his belongings, another great insight into the local Welsh history. There's also a touching memorial of Evans' life at **El Tumbo del Caballo Malacara**, 200 m from the main plaza; a private garden containing the remains of Evans' horse, Malacara, who once saved his life; guided tours US$4. **Nant-y-fall Falls** ① *17 km southwest on the road to the border, US$38 pp including guide to the falls,* are a series of impressive cascades in lovely forest. **Tourist office** ① *in the central plaza, T480120, www.trevelin. gob.ar.* Has maps, accommodation booking service, helpful, English spoken.

Parque Nacional Los Alerces → *Colour map 9, A1.*

① *33 km west of Esquel, US$8.*

One of the most appealing and untouched expanses of the Andes region, this national park has several lakes including **Lago Futalaufquen**, with some of the best fishing in the area, **Lago Menéndez** which can be crossed by boat to visit rare and impressive *alerce* trees (Fitzroya cupressoides), some of which are over 2000 years old, and the green waters of **Lago Verde**. Relatively undeveloped, access is possible only to the east side of the park, via

The Old Patagonian Express

Esquel is the terminus of a 402-km branch-line from Ingeniero Jacobacci, a junction on the old Buenos Aires-Bariloche mainline, 194 km east of Bariloche. This narrow-gauge line (0.75 m wide) took 23 years to build, being finally opened in 1945. It was made famous outside Argentina by Paul Theroux who described it in his book *The Old Patagonian Express*. The 1922 Henschel and Baldwin steam locomotives (from Germany and USA respectively) are powered by fuel oil and use 100 litres of water every kilometre. Water has to be taken on at least every 40 km along the route. A replica is used when there are strong winds. Most of the coaches are Belgian and also date from 1922. If you want to see the engines, go to El Maitén where the workshops are.

Until the Argentine government handed responsibility for railways over to the provincial governments in 1994, regular services ran the length of the line. Since then, tourist services have been maintained out of Esquel and El Maitén by the provincial government of Chubut.

a *ripio* road (which is an alternative way from Esquel to El Bolsón) with many camping spots and *hosterías*. Helpful *guardaparques* give out maps and advice on walks at the visitor centre (T471020) in Villa Futalaufquen (southern end of Lago Futulaufquen); also a service station, two food shops, *locutorio* and a restaurant **El Abuelo Monje**. Fishing licences from food shops, the *kiosko* or **Hosterías Cume Hué** and **Futalaufquen**, or petrol stations in Esquel. See http://losalercesparquenacional.blogspot.com/, or T471015.

Trekking and tours The west half of the park is inaccessible, but there are splendid walks along footpaths on the southern shore of Lago Futalaufquen, with several waterfalls, and near Lago Verde further north. Treks at Los Alerces range from an hour to two or three days. All long treks require previous registration with the *guardaparques*; some paths are closed in autumn and winter. At Lago Futalaufquen's northern end, walk across the bridge over Río Arrayanes to Lago Verde. A longer more difficult trek is to **Cerro El Dedal** (1916 m), either returning the way you came from Villa Futalaufquen, eight hours, or making an eight- to 10-hour loop through Puerto Limonao. Walkers must register with the *guardaparques* and you're required to start before 1000. Carry plenty of water. Also a two- to three-day hike through *coihue* forest to the tip of beautiful, secluded **Lago Krügger**. (Check with the visitor centre or *guardaparques' office* beforehand, as Lake Krügger was closed during the 2014 season.) On Lago Futalaufquen is a free campsite at Playa Blanca. **Cerros Alto El Petiso** and **La Torta** can be climbed and there is a trekkers' shelter at the base of **Cerro Cocinero**. **Boat trips** go to El Alerzal, from Puerto Limonao, across Lago Futalaufquen along the pea-green Río Arrayanes, lined with extraordinary cinnamon-barked trees, to Puerto Mermoud on Lago Verde. A short walk leads to Puerto Chucao, on Lago Menéndez, where another boat makes the unforgettable trip to see the majestic 2600-year-old alerce trees, walking to silent Lago Cisne, past the white waters of Río Cisne. A cheaper alternative is to get to Puerto Chucao on your own and take the boat there. Boats run frequently in high season; fare from Puerto Limonao US$64, from Chucao US$54. Book through **Patagonia Verde**, see Esquel, Tours, below.

Border with Chile: Paso Futaleufú → *Colour map 9, A1.*

There is a campsite (**Camping Puerto Ciprés**) on the Argentine side of river, 70 km southwest of Equel, via Trevelin. Cross the border river by the bridge after passing Argentine customs; Chilean customs is 1 km on the other side of river (one hour for all formalities). The Chilean town of Futaleufú is 9 km from the border. See page 190 for buses to the border.

South of Esquel, Ruta 40 is paved through the towns of **Tecka** and **Gobernador Costa** in Chubut province (the latter has a couple of hotels and *cabañas* and a municipal campsite). At 38 km south of Gobernador Costa, gravelled Ruta 40 forks southwest through the town of Alto Río Senguer, while provincial Ruta 20 heads almost directly south for 141 km, before turning east towards Sarmiento and Comodoro Rivadavia. At La Puerta del Diablo, in the valley of the lower Río Senguer, Ruta 20 intersects provincial Ruta 22, which joins with Ruta 40 at the town of Río Mayo (see page 208). This latter route is completely paved and preferable to Ruta 40 for long-distance motorists; good informal campsites on the west side of the bridge across the Río Senguer.

⊚ South of Bariloche listings

For hotel and restaurant price codes, and other relevant information, see Essentials.

⊜ Where to stay

Bariloche to El Bolsón *p183*
$$$$ El Retorno, Villa Los Coihues, on the shore of Lago Gutiérrez, T446 7333, www. hosteriaelretorno.com. Stunning lakeside position, comfortable hunting lodge style, family run, with a beach, tennis, very comfortable rooms (**$$$** in low season) and self-catering apartments (Bus 50, follow signs from the road to El Bolsón).
$$$$ Estancia Peuma Hue, Ruta 40, Km 2014, T54-9-294-450 1030, www.peuma-hue.com. Best comfort in a homely environment, on the southern shores of Lago Gutiérrez, below Cerro Catedral Sur. Charming owner Evelyn Hoter and dedicated staff make it all work perfectly, tasty home-made food, superb horse riding and other activities, health treatments, yoga, meditation, etc, candlelit concerts. All inclusive, varied accommodation. Highly recommended.
$$$ Hostería Pampa Linda, T449 0517, www. hosteriapampalinda.com.ar. A comfortable, peaceful base for climbing Tronador and many other treks (plus horse riding, trekking and climbing courses), simple rooms, all with stunning views, restaurant, full board optional, packed lunches available for hikes. Charming owners, Sebastián de la Cruz is one of the area's most experienced mountaineers. Highly recommended. Nearby is **Refugio Pampa Linda** (see below) and **Camping Río Manso**.
$$$ pp **Hotel Tronador**, T449 0556, www. hoteltronador.com. 60 km from Bariloche, on

the narrow road from Villa Mascardi to Pampa Linda (there are restricted times for going in each direction: check with tourist office), open Nov-Apr, full board, lakeside paradise, lovely rooms with lake view, beautiful gardens, charming owner, also riding, fishing and lake excursions. Also camping **La Querencia**.
Camping Camping **La Cascada**, at Mallín Ahogado, near La Cascada Escondida, T483 5304, Camping-La-Cascada on Facebook. Lovely setting, helpful owner, camping and *cabañas*, organic vegetables, homemade bread and beer. Recommended. **Camping Las Carpitas**, RN 40, 33 km from Bariloche, T449 0527, www.campinglascarpitas.com.ar, great location, all facilities, also *cabañas*. **Camping Los Rápidos**, after crossing the Río Manso to Pampa Linda, T15-431 7028, www.losrapidos. com.ar. All facilities, attractive shaded site going down to lake, *confitería*, open all year. **Camping Los Vuriloches**, Pampa Linda, T446 2131, www. pampalindatere@hotmail.com. Idyllic spacious lakeside site with trees, good meals, food shop.

El Bolsón *p183*
Difficult to find accommodation in the high season: book ahead.
$$$ Amancay, Av San Martín 3207, T449 2222, www.hotelamancayelbolson.com. Good, comfortable and light rooms, though small and a bit old-fashioned, breakfast included.
$$$ La Posada de Hamelin, Int Granollers 2179, T449 2030, www.posadadehamelin.com. ar. Charming rooms, welcoming atmosphere, huge breakfasts with homemade jams and cakes, German spoken. Highly recommended.

$$ El Refugio del Lago, T02945-499025, www.elrefugiodellago.com.ar. Buses between El Bolsón and Esquel stop (briefly) at Lago Epuyén, though some don't enter the village itself. Transfers available on request. Relaxed, comfortable rooms in a lovely wooden house a short walk from the lakeshore, also cabins, dorms (US$19), with breakfast, good meals. Camping US$6-7 pp. Recommended.

$$ La Casona de Odile, Barrio Luján, T449 2753, www.odile.com.ar. Private rooms and 3-6-bed dorms (US$17 pp) by stream, delicious home cooking, bicycle rental. Recommended.

$ pp Altos del Sur, Villa Turismo, T449 8730, www.altosdelsur.bolsonweb.com. Peaceful hostel in a lovely setting, HI member, shared rooms and private doubles, dinner available, will collect from bus station if you call ahead.

$ pp El Pueblito, 4 km north in Barrio Luján, 1 km off Ruta 40 (take bus from Plaza Principal, US$0.50), T449 3560, www.elpueblitohostel. com.ar. Wooden building in open country, dorms (US$12-15 depending on season and if with breakfast), also has cabins (**$$**), laundry facilities, shop, open fire. Recommended.

$ pp Hostel La Casa del Viajero, Liberdad y Las Flores, Barrio Usina, T449 3092, www. lacasadelviajero.com.ar. A little out of the centre, in a beautful setting. Surrounded by organic gardens, simple, comfortable rooms (dorms – US$15, and private – US$25). Call them for pick up from the centre of town.

$ pp Refugio Patagónico, Islas Malvinas y Pastorino, T448 3628,www.refugiopatagonico. com. Basic hostel, with small dorms (US$12.50) and doubles (**$$**), in a spacious house set in open fields, views of Piltriquitrón, 5 blocks from the plaza.

Camping La Chacra, Av Belgrano 1128, T449 2111, www.campinglachacra.com.ar. 15 mins' walk from town, well shaded, good facilities, lively atmosphere in season. Quem-Quem, on river bank Río Quemquemtreu, T449 3550, www.quem-quem.com.ar. Lovely site, hot showers, good walks, free pickup from town.

There are many *cabañas* in picturesque settings with lovely views in the Villa Turismo, about US$60-100 for 2 people.

Cholila and around *p184*

$$$ Frontera, Ruta Nacional 40, 9 km from Lago Puelo, isolated in woodland, off the main road heading for Esquel, T0294-447 3092, www.frontera-patagonia.com.ar. *Cabañas* for 4 and *hostería*, in native forest, furnished to a very high standard, delicious breakfasts and dinner if required.

$$$ Lodge Casa Puelo, R16, Km 10, T0294-449 9539, www.casapuelo.com.ar. *Cabañas* for up to 6. Beautifully designed rooms and self-catering cabins right against forested mountains where you can walk, good service, English-speaking owner Miguel, who knows the local area intimately. Very comfortable, dinner offered. Recommended.

$$$-$$ La Yoica, just off R16, Km 5, T0294-449 9200, www.layoica.com.ar. Charming Scottish owners make you feel at home in these traditional *cabañas* set in lovely countryside with great views. Price for up to 4 people.

$$$-$$ Cabañas Cerro La Momia, Ruta 71, Villa Lago Rivadavia T011-4964 2586. Very good *cabañas* for up to 6, picturesque setting among fruit orchards and wooded slopes. Restaurant, excursions arranged.

$ pp La Pasarela, 2 km from town, T449 9061, www.lpuelo.com.ar. Dorms (US$10 pp), cabins and camping US$7.50, shops, fuel.

Esquel *p184*

Ask at tourist office for lodgings in private houses.

$$$ Angelina, Av Alvear 758, T452763, www.hosteriaangelina.com.ar. Good value, welcoming, big breakfast, English and Italian spoken, open high season only.

$$$ Canela, Los Notros y Los Radales, Villa Ayelén, on road to Trevelin, T453890, www.canelaesquel.com. Bed and breakfast and tea room in a lovely, quiet residential area, English spoken, owner knowledgeable about Patagonia.

$$$ Cumbres Blancas, Av Ameghino 1683, T455100, www.cumbresblancas.com.ar. Attractive modern building, a little out of centre, very comfortable, spacious rooms, sauna, gym, airy restaurant. Recommended.

$$$-$$ La Chacra, Km 5 on Ruta 259 towards Trevelin, T452802, www.lachacrapatagonia. com. Relaxing, spacious rooms, huge breakfast, Welsh and English spoken.

$$ La Posada, Chacabuco 905, T454095, www.laposadaesquel.blogspot.com.ar. Tasteful B&B in quiet part of town, lovely lounge, very comfortable, excellent value.

$$ La Tour D'Argent, San Martín 1063, T454612, www.latourdargent.com.ar. Bright, comfortable, family-run, very good value.

$ pp Anochecer Andino, Av Ameghino 482, T450498. 4 blocks from the commercial centre and 2 from the mountains, basic, helpful, can organize ski passes and excursions. They also can provide dinner and have a bar.

$ pp Casa del Pueblo, San Martín 661, T450581, www.esquelcasadelpueblo.com.ar. Smallish rooms but good atmosphere (**$$** double), laundry, HI discounts, organizes adventure activities.

$ pp Hospedaje Rowlands, behind Rivadavia 330, T452578, gales01@hotmail.com. Warm family welcome, Welsh spoken, breakfast extra, basic rooms with shared bath and a double with bath (**$**), good value.

$ pp Planeta Hostel, Roca 458, T456846, www.planetahostel.com. 4-6 bed dorms (US$15-18), doubles **$$**, shared bath, specialize in snowboarding, climbing and mountain biking, English spoken.

$ Res El Cisne, Chacabuco 778, T452256. Basic small rooms, hot water, quiet, well kept, good value, breakfast extra.

Camping Millalen, Av Ameghino 2063 (5 blocks from bus terminal), T456164, good services and cabins.

Trevelin *p184*
$$$ Casa de Piedra, Almirante Brown 244, T480357, www.casadepiedratrevelin.com. Stone and wood cottage in the suburbs. King-size beds, heating and a charming common area, popular.

$$ Pezzi, Sarmiento 351, T480146, hpezzi@ intramed.net. Charming family house with a beautiful garden, English spoken. Recommended.

$ pp Casa Verde Hostal, Los Alerces s/n (9203), T480091, www.casaverdehostel.com.ar. Charming owners, spacious log cabin with panoramic views, comfortable dorms for 4-6 and doubles (**$$**), laundry, HI member, breakfast extra. English and Welsh spoken, excursions into Los Alerces, bikes for hire. Highly recommended.

Camping Many sites, especially on the road to Futaleufú and Chile; also many *cabañas*; ask for full list at tourist office.

Parque Nacional Los Alerces *p184*
East side of Lago Futalaufquen
$$$$ El Aura, Lago Verde Wilderness Resort, T011-4816 5348 (Buenos Aires), www.elaura patagonia.com. Exquisite taste in these 3 stone cabins and a guest house on the shore of Lago Verde. Luxury in every respect, attention to detail, ecologically friendly. Impressive place.

$$$ Hostería Quime Quipan, T425 423, www.hosteriaquimequipan.com.ar. Comfortable rooms with lake views, dinner included. Recommended.

$$ Bahía Rosales, T15-403413, www.bahia rosales.com. Comfortable *cabaña* for 6 with kitchenette and bath, **$** pp in small basic cabin without bath, and camping in open ground, hot showers, restaurant, all recommended.

$$ Cabañas Tejas Negras, next to Pucón Pai, T471046, www.tejasnegras.com.ar. Really comfortable *cabañas* for 4, also good camp site, and tea room.

$$ Motel Pucón Pai, T451425. Slightly spartan rooms, but good restaurant, recommended for fishing; basic campsite with hot showers.

Camping Several campsites at Villa Futalaufquen (eg **Nahuel Pan**), Lagos Rivadavia, Verde and Río Arrayanes.

❼ Restaurants

El Bolsón *p183*
$$$ Pasiones Argentinas, Av Belgrano y Berutti, T448 3616, www.facebook.com/ pasiones.restaurant. Traditional Argentine food, in a wonderful cosy setting.

$$ Amancay, San Martín 3217, T449
2222, see hotel, above. Good *parrilla*
and homemade pastas.
$$ Arcimbaldo, Av San Martin 2790, T449
2137. Good value *tenedor libre*, smoked fish
and draft beer, open for breakfast.
$$ Jauja, Av San Martín 2867, T449 2448.
Great meeting place, delicious fish and pasta,
outstanding ice cream, English spoken.
$$ Martin Sheffield, Av San Martín 2760,
T449 1920. Central, good food, Patagonian
specialities, menu of the day, with or without
a drink.

Cafés
Cerveza El Bolsón, RN 258, Km 123.9,
T449 2595, www.cervezaselbolson.com.
Microbrewery where you can see how the
beer is made and sample the 18 varieties.
Picadas served with beer, sitting outside
in the gardens. Highly recommended.
El Rey de Sandwich, Roca 345. Good value
sandwiches at this *rotisería*, next to **Vía
Bariloche** bus terminal.

Esquel *p184*
$$ Don Chiquino, behind Av Ameghino 1641,
T450035. Delicious pastas in a fun atmosphere
with plenty of games brought to the tables by
magician owner Tito. Recommended.
$$ La Española, Rivadavia 740, T451509.
Excellent beef, salad bar and tasty pasta.
Recommended.
$$ Vascongada, 9 de Julio y Mitre, T452229.
Traditional style, trout and other local specialities.
$ La Tour D'Argent, San Martín 1063, T454612,
www.latourdargent.com.ar. Delicious local
specialities, good-value set meals and a warm
ambience in this popular, traditional restaurant.

Cafés
María Castaña, Rivadavia y 25 de Mayo.
Popular, good coffee.

Trevelin *p184*
$$ Parrilla Oregon, Av San Martín y JM
Thomas, T480408, www.oregontrevelin.
com.ar/restaurante.html. Large meals

(particularly breakfasts), set menus based on
parrilla and pastas.
$ Nain Maggie, Perito Moreno 179, T480232,
www.nainmaggie.guiapatagonia.net. Tea room,
offering *té galés* and *torta negra*, expensive
but good.
**Heladería Artesanal Serenata y
Chocolatería Mizke**, Rotonda 28 de
Julio 190, T48012. Decent chocolates
and ice cream on thecentral plaza.

○ What to do

El Bolsón *p183*
Grado 42, Av Belgrano 406, T449 3124,
www.grado42.com. Tours to El Maitén to
take La Trochita, 7 hrs; also short excursions
in the surroundings and day trips to Parque
Nacional Los Alerces, as well as wide range of
adventure activities. Sells **Chaltén Travel** bus
tickets (see page 198). Recommended.

Esquel *p184*
Fishing Tourist office has a list of guides and
companies hiring out equipment.
Skiing One of Argentina's cheapest, with
laid back family atmosphere, **La Hoya**, 15 km
north, has 22 km of pistes, 8 ski-lifts. For
skiing information ask at **Club Andino Esquel**,
Pellegrini 787, T453248; travel agencies run
3 daily minibuses to La Hoya from Esquel.
Details of facilities, lifts and passes can be found
on www.patagoniaexpress.com/la_hoya.html,
or phone CAM, La Hoya, T451927.

Tour operators
Brazo Sur, Rivadavia 891, T456359, www.
brazosur.com.ar. For *Safari Lacustre* boat trips,
adventure activities and regional tours.
Frontera Sur, Sarmiento 784, T450505,
www.fronterasur.net. Good company
offering adventure tourism of all sorts,
as well as more traditional excursions,
ski equipment and trekking.
Patagonia Verde, 9 de Julio 926, T454396,
www.patagonia-verde.com.ar. Boat trips to
El Alerzal on Lago Menéndez, rafting on Río
Corcovado, tickets for *La Trochita* and for Ruta

40 to El Calafate. Also range of adventure activities, horse riding, short local excursions and ski passes. Ask about lodging at **Lago Verde**. English spoken. Excellent company, very professional.

⊖ Transport

El Bolsón p183

Bus Several daily from **Bariloche** and **Esquel**, with **Don Otto, TAC, Via Bariloche**. Check with **Vía Bariloche**, T0800-333 7575, www. viabariloche.com.ar, for timings. Heavily overbooked in high season. US$9.50-11, 2 hrs to Bariloche; US$13.50 El Bolsón-Esquel, 2½-3 hrs. Other destinations from these 2 towns. Buses to **Lago Puelo** with Vía Bariloche every 2 hrs, 4 on Sun, 45 mins, US$5. To **Parque Nacional Los Alerces** (highly recommended route), with **Transportes Esquel** (from ACA service station), once a day, US$10, 4-5 hrs, via Cholila and Epuyen.

Esquel p184

Air Airport, 20 km east of Esquel, T451676, by paved road, US$19 by taxi. To **Buenos Aires, Comodora Rivadavia** and **Trelew**. LADE (Av Alvear 1085, T452124) to **Bariloche, Comodoro Rivadavia, El Calafate, Mar del Plata** and several other destinations in Patagonia; weekly departures.

Bus Terminal at Av Alvear 1871, T451584, US$2.50 by taxi from centre, it has toilets, *kiosko*, *locutorio* with internet, café, tourist information desk, left luggage. To **Buenos Aires** change in Bariloche, with **Andesmar**, T450143, or Via Bariloche, T454676. To **Bariloche** (via El Bolsón, 2½ hrs), 4-5 hrs, US$13-15, **Don Otto** (T453012), Vía Bariloche, TAC and others. To **Puerto Madryn**, 9 hrs, US$54, Ejecutivo de Chubut. To **Trelew**, US$50-60, 8-9 hrs overnight, Don Otto and Ejecutivo de Chubut. To **Río Gallegos** (for connections to El Calafate

or Ushuaia), take a bus to Trelew and change there. To **Trevelin**, Vía Trevelin (T455222) and **Jacobsen** (T454676, www.transportejacobsen. com.ar), Mon-Fri, hourly 0600-2300, every 2 hrs weekends, 30 mins, US$1. To **Paso Futaleufú** (Chilean border) via Trevelin, Jacobsen 0800, 1800 Mon, Wed and Fri (Tue and Thu 1800 only), return 0930, 1930, US$7. Buses connect there for Chaitén.

Car hire Los Alerces, Sarmiento 763, T456008, www.losalercesrentacar.com.ar. Good value, good cars, top service.

Train *La Trochita* (which Paul Theroux called the Old Patagonian Express) generally runs from Esquel to **Nahuel Pan** (19 km) daily Mon-Fri and twice a day on Sat and in high season (much less frequent in winter), taking 2½ hrs, US$32 return, children under 5 free. At remote Nahuel Pan, there is just a small terrace of houses, home to a Mapuche community, who sell delicious cakes and display their knitwear, some of it very fine quality. In high season a service runs from El Maitén at the northernmost end of the line to Desvío Thomae (55 km), also US$32. Information, in English including schedules in El Maitén, T02945-495190, and in Esquel T02945-451403. See www.patagoniaexpress.com/el_trochita.htm. Tickets from tour operators, or from Esquel station office, Urquiza y Roggero.

Parque Nacional Los Alerces p184

Bus From **Esquel** (Jacobsen, see above) runs daily at 0700 and 1330 from Esquel to Lago Puelo, US$15, along the east side of Lago Futalaufquen. It returns at 1500. From **Trevelin**, Jacobsen, at 0830, return 2100, and Martín at 1730, return 2030, US$15-20.

Border with Chile: Paso Futaleufú p185

Buses from Esquel via Trevelin to **Paso Futaleufú** (La Balsa), see above. Very little traffic for hitching.

Patagonia

Patagonia is the vast, windy, mostly treeless plateau covering all of southern Argentina south of the Río Colorado. The Atlantic coast is rich in marine life; penguins, whales and seals can all be seen around Puerto Madryn. The far south offers spectacular scenery in the Parque Nacional Los Glaciares, with the mighty Perito Moreno and Upsala glaciers, as well as challenging trekking around Mount Fitz Roy. The contrasts are extreme: thousands of prehistoric handprints can be found in the Cueva de las Manos, but in most of Patagonia there's less than one person to each square kilometre; far from the densely wooded Andes, there are petrified forests in the deserts; and one legacy of brave early pioneers is the over-abundance of tea and cakes served up by Argentina's Welsh community in the Chubut valley.

Patagonia's appeal lies in its emptiness. Vegetation is sparse, since a relentless dry wind blows continually from the west, raising a haze of dust in summer, which can turn to mud in winter. Rainfall is high only in the foothills of the Andes, where dense virgin beech forests run from Neuquén to Tierra del Fuego. During a brief period in spring, after the snows melt, there is grass on the plateau, but in the desert-like expanses of eastern Patagonia, water can be pumped only in the deep crevices which intersect the land from west to east. This is where the great sheep estancias lie, sheltered from the wind. There is little agriculture except in the north, in the valleys of the Colorado and Negro rivers, where alfalfa is grown and cattle are raised. Centres of population are tiny and most of the towns are small ports on the Atlantic coast. Only Comodoro Rivadavia has a population over 100,000, thanks to its oil industry. Patagonia has attracted many generations of people getting away from it all, from Welsh religious pioneers to Butch Cassidy and the Sundance Kid, and tourism is an increasingly important source of income.

Arriving in Patagonia

Getting there

Air There are daily flights from Buenos Aires to Viedma, Trelew, Puerto Madryn, Comodoro Rivadavia, Río Gallegos, Río Grande, El Calafate's airport, Lago Argentino, and Ushuaia. **Aerolíneas Argentinas** (AR) and **LADE** fly these routes and it is vital that you book flights well ahead in the summer (December to February) and the winter ski season for Ushuaia (July and August). At other times of year, flights can be booked with just a few days' notice. The Chilean airline, **LAN**, flies to Ushuaia from Argentine destinations as well as Punta Arenas (for connections to Puerto Montt and Santiago) in summer. Even if a flight is sold out, check again on the day of departure.

Flying between Patagonian towns is complicated without flying all the way back to Buenos Aires, since there are often only weekly flights with **LADE**. The baggage allowance is 15 kg. Overnight buses may be more convenient.

Road The principal roads in Patagonia are the Ruta 3, which runs down the Atlantic coast, and the Ruta 40 on the west. One of Argentina's main arteries, Ruta 3 runs from Buenos Aires to Ushuaia, interrupted by the car ferry crossing through Chilean territory across the Magellan Strait to Tierra del Fuego. It is paved in Argentine territory, but sections on Chilean Tierra del Fuego (Cerro Sombrero to San Sebastán) are *ripio*. Regular buses run along the whole stretch, more frequently between October and April, and there are towns with services and accommodation every few hundred km. Ruta 40, which was at the time of writing slowly being paved, zigzags across the moors from Zapala to Lago Argentino, near El Calafate, ending at Cabo Vírgenes. It's by far the more interesting road, lonely and bleak, offering fine views of the Andes and plenty of wildlife as well as giving access to many national parks. A number of companies run daily tourist bus services in summer between Los Antiguos and El Chaltén. The east-west road across Patagonia, from south of Esquel in the Lake District to Comodoro Rivadavia, is paved, and there's a good paved highway running from Bariloche through Neuquén to San Antonio Oeste.

Although increasingly being paved, many of the roads in southern Argentina are still *ripio* – gravelled – limiting maximum speeds to 60 kph, or less where surfaces are poor, very hard on low-clearance vehicles. Strong winds can also be a hazard. Windscreen and headlight protection is a good idea (expensive to buy, but can be improvised with wire mesh for windscreen, strips cut from plastic bottles for lights). There are cattle grids (*guardaganados*), even on main highways, usually signposted; cross them very slowly. Always carry plenty of fuel, as service stations may be as much as 300 km apart and as a precaution in case of a breakdown, carry warm clothing and make sure your car has anti-freeze. Petrol prices in Chubut, Santa Cruz and Tierra del Fuego provinces are 40% cheaper than in the rest of the country (10-15% for diesel).

In summer hotel prices are very high, especially in El Calafate and El Chaltén. From November onwards you must reserve hotels a week or more in advance. Camping is increasingly popular and estancias may be hospitable to travellers who are stuck for a bed. Many estancias, especially in Santa Cruz province, offer transport, excursions and food as well as accommodation: see www. estanciasdesantacruz.com and www.interpatagonia.com/estancias. **ACA** establishments, which charge roughly the same prices all over Argentina, are good value in Patagonia.

Viedma, Carmen de Patagones and around → *Phone code: 02920. Colour map 8, C4.*

These two pleasant towns lie on opposite banks of the Río Negro, about 27 km from its mouth and 270 km south of Bahía Blanca. Patagones is older and charming, but most services are in **Viedma** (*Population: 80,000*), capital of Río Negro Province. A quiet place, its main attraction is the perfect bathing area along the shaded south bank of the river. **El Cóndor** is a beautiful beach 30 km south of Viedma, three buses a day from Viedma in summer, with hotels open January-February, restaurants and shops, free camping on beach 2 km south. And 30 km further southwest is the sealion colony, **Lobería Punta Bermeja**, daily bus in summer from Viedma; hitching easy in summer. **Provincial tourist office** ① *Av Caseros 1425, T422150, www.rionegrotur. gob.ar (Spanish only), Mon-Fri 0700-1400, 1800-2000.* **Municipal tourist office** ① *Av Francisco de Viedma 51, T427171, www.viedma.gov.ar, daily 0900-2100,* helpful. Another office is open daily 0900-2200 at Balneario El Cóndor.

Carmen de Patagones (*Population: 18,190*) was founded in 1779 and many early pioneer buildings remain in the pretty streets winding down to the river. There's a fascinating museum, **Museo Histórico Regional "Emma Nozzi"** ① *JJ Biedma 64, T462729, Mon-Fri 1000-1200, 1500-1700, Sat-Sun and bank holidays 1700-1900,* with artifacts of the indigenous inhabitants, missionaries and gauchos; good guided tours. Helpful **tourist office** ① *Mitre 84, T464819.* On 7 March the Battle of Patagones (1827) is celebrated in a week-long colourful fiesta of horse displays and fine food. The two towns are linked by two bridges and a four-minute frequent ferry crossing (US$1).

Bahía San Blas is an attractive small resort and renowned shark fishing area, 100 km from Patagones (tourist information at www.bahiasanblas.com in Spanish); plentiful accommodation. Almost due west and 180 km along the coast, on the Gulf of San Matías, is **San Antonio Oeste** (*Phone code: 02934*), and 17 km south, the popular beach resort, **Las Grutas**. The caves themselves are not really worth visiting; but the water is famously warm. Las Grutas is closed in the winter, but very crowded in the summer; accessible by hourly bus from San Antonio. San Antonio is on the bus routes north to Bahía Blanca and south as far as Río Gallegos and Punta Arenas.

For hotel and restaurant price codes, and other relevant information, see Essentials.

⊜ Where to stay

Viedma *p192*
$$$ Nijar, Mitre 490, T422833, www. hotelnijar.com. Most comfortable, smart, modern, good service.
$$ Peumayen, Buenos Aires 334, T425222, www.hotelpeumayen.com.ar. Old-fashioned friendly place on the plaza.
$$ Res Roca, Roca 347, T431241. A cheap option with comfortable beds, helpful staff, breakfast included.

⊝ Transport

Viedma *p192*
Air Airport 5 km south. LADE (Saavedra 576, T424420, www.lade.com.ar) fly to **Buenos Aires**, **Mar del Plata**, **Bahía Blanca**, **Comodoro Rivadavia** and other Patagonian destinations.
Bus Terminal in Viedma at Av Pte Perón y Guido, 15 blocks from plaza (www.terminal patagonia.com.ar); taxi US$3.50. To **Buenos Aires** 13 hrs, daily, US$65-88, **Don Otto** and others. To **Puerto Madryn**, 6½ hrs, several daily, US$35-41, **Don Otto** and others. To **Bahía Blanca**, 4 hrs, many daily, US$21-25.

Puerto Madryn and around → *Phone code: 0280. Colour map 9, A3. Population: 74,000.*

Puerto Madryn is a seaside town 250 km south of San Antonio Oeste. It stands on the wide bay of Golfo Nuevo, the perfect base for the Península Valdés and its extraordinary array of wildlife, just 70 km east. It was the site of the first Welsh landing in 1865 and is named after the Welsh home of the colonist, Jones Parry. Popular for skin diving and the nature reserves, the town's main industries are a huge aluminium plant and fish processing plants. There is a popular beach in the town itself and you can often spot whales directly from the coast at the long beach of **Playa El Doradillo**, 16 km northeast (October-December). **EcoCentro** ① *Julio Verne 3784, T445 7470, www.ecocentro.org.ar, daily 1500-2000 (2100 high season) (closed Tue), US$9.* An inspired interactive sea life information centre, art gallery, reading room and café, it is perched on a cliff at the south end of town, with fantastic views of the whole bay. **Museo de Ciencias Naturales y Oceanográfico** ① *Domecq García y J Menéndez, T445 1139, Mon-Fri 0900-2000, Sat 1600-2000, US$1.50.* This informative museum has displays of local flora and fauna. Run by the same museum, and at the time of writing in the process of opening, is a small museum of the history of Puerto Madryn, housed in the old railway station, next door to the current bus station (Dr Ávila 350). There is a handicraft market on the main plaza. The **tourist office** ① *Av Roca 223, T445 3504, www.madryn.travel, daily 0700-2100 (Dec-Feb 2200),* is extremely helpful. Also at the bus station, daily 0700-2100.

Around Puerto Madryn

With **elephant seal** and **sea lion** colonies at the base of chalky cliffs, breeding grounds for **Southern right whales** in the sheltered Golfo Nuevo and the Golfo San José, and **guanacos**, **rheas**, **maras** (a large rodent, sometimes called the **patagonian hare**) and **armadillos** everywhere on land, the area around Puerto Madryn, especially the Península Valdés, is a spectacular region for wildlife. Whales can be seen from June to mid-December, particularly interesting with their young September-October. The sea lion breeding season runs from late December to late January, but visiting is good up to late April. Bull elephant seals begin to claim their territory in the first half of August and the breeding season is late September/early October. Orcas can be seen attacking seals at Punta Norte in February/March. Conservation officials can be found at the main viewpoints, informative but only Spanish spoken. The **EcoCentro** in Puerto Madryn, studies the marine ecosystems. **Punta Loma** ① *0900-1700; US$8, children US$4, information and video, many companies offer tours*. This is a sea lion reserve 15 km southeast of Puerto Madryn, best visited at low tide; sea lions can even be seen in Puerto Madryn harbour. See also Puerto Deseado, page 203 and Punta Tombo, page 201.

Península Valdés

① *Entry US$21 for foreigners, children US$10.50; administration T445 0489, www.peninsulavaldes. org.ar, daily 0800-2100 (2000 in low season).*

The Península Valdés, near Puerto Madryn, in Chubut province, has an amazing array of wildlife: marine mammals including Southern right whales, penguins and guanacos. The best way to see the wildlife is by car/on a guided tour. See Puerto Madryn for car hire. Take your time, roads are

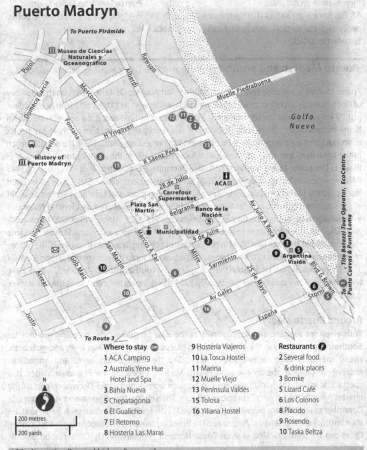

Puerto Madryn

Where to stay 🛏️
1 ACA Camping
2 Australis Yene Hue Hotel and Spa
3 Bahía Nueva
5 Chepatagonia
6 El Gualicho
7 El Retorno
8 Hostería Las Maras
9 Hostería Viajeros
10 La Tosca Hostel
11 Marina
12 Muelle Viejo
13 Península Valdés
15 Tolosa
16 Yiliana Hostel

Restaurants 🍽️
2 Several food & drink places
3 Bomke
5 Lizard Café
6 Los Colonos
8 Plácido
9 Rosendo
10 Taska Beltza

Keeping up with the Joneses

On 28 July 1865, 153 Welsh immigrants landed at Puerto Madryn, then a deserted beach deep in *indígena* country. After three weeks they pushed, on foot, across the parched pampa and into the Chubut river valley, where there is flat cultivable land along the riverside for a distance of 80 km upstream. Here, maintained in part by the Argentine government, they settled, but it was three years before they realized the land was barren unless watered. They drew water from the river, which is higher than the surrounding flats, and built a fine system of irrigation canals. The colony, reinforced later by immigrants from Wales and from the US, prospered, but in 1899 a great flood drowned the valley and some of the immigrants left for Canada. The last Welsh contingent arrived in 1911. The object of the colony had been to create a 'Little Wales beyond Wales', and for four generations they kept the Welsh language alive. The language has, however, been dying out from the fifth generation. There is an offshoot of the colony of Chubut at Trevelin, at the foot of the Andes nearly 650 km to the west, settled in 1888 (see page 184). It is interesting that this distant land gave to the Welsh language one of its most endearing classics: *Dringo'r Andes* (Climbing the Andes), written by one of the early women settlers.

mostly unpaved except the road from Puerto Madryn to Puerto Pirámides. In summer there are several shops, but take sun protection and drinking water.

The Golfos Nuevo and San José are separated by the Istmo Carlos Ameghino, which leads to **Península Valdés**, a bleak, but beautiful treeless splay of land, dotted with large estancias, 56 in total, mostly dedicated to sheep farming, some have accommodation and rural tourism activities (see where to stay). In depressions in the heart of the peninsula are large salt flats; Salina Grande is 42 m below sea level. At the entrance to the peninsula, on the isthmus, there is an interesting visitors' centre with a wonderful whale skeleton. Five kilometres from the entrance, Isla de los Pájaros can be seen in Golfo San José, though its seabirds can only be viewed through fixed telescopes (at 400 m distance); best time is September to April. The main tourist centre of the Peninsula is **Puerto Pirámides** (*Population: 700*), much smaller than Puerto Madryn, but pretty and lively, located on a pleasant stretch of beach. It lies 107 km east of Puerto Madryn and boat trips leave from here to see the whales in season (sailings controlled by Prefectura – Naval Police, according to weather). There is accommodation and eating places here. **Tourist information** ⓘ *1ra Bajada al Mar, near the beach, T449 5044, www. puertopiramides.gov.ar*. A 3-km track (beware incoming tide) or 15-km *ripio* road goes to a mirador at Punta Pardelas where you can see whales.

Punta Norte (176 km) at the north end of the Valdés Peninsula has elephant seals and penguins (September-March) below its high, white cliffs, best seen at low tide, also, occasionally, orcas. There is a basic café here, selling sandwiches and *empanadas*. At Punta Cantor, overlooking **Caleta Valdés**, 45 km south of Punta Norte, you can see huge colonies of elephant seals at close quarters, as well as plenty of landbased wildlife, including mara, *ñandú petiso* (Darwin's rhea) and guanacos. There are three marked walks. **Estancia La Elvira** has a restaurant and other facilities here (see Where to stay listings). At **Punta Delgada** (at the south of the peninsula) elephant seals and other wildlife can be seen. The beach on the entire coast is out of bounds; this is strictly enforced.

⊙ Puerto Madryn and around listings

For hotel and restaurant price codes, and other relevant information, see Essentials.

⊚ Where to stay

Puerto Madryn *p193, map p194*
Book ahead in summer, and whale season.
$$$$ Australis Yene Hue Hotel and Spa, Roca 33, T447 1214, www.hotelesaustralis. com.ar. Luxury hotel on the beachfront with a small spa, modern rooms, and nice buffet breakfast. Ask for a room with a view.
$$$$-$$$ Península Valdés, Av Roca 155, T447 1292, www.hotelpeninsula.com.ar. Luxurious seafront hotel with great views. Spa, sauna, gym.
$$$ Bahía Nueva, Av Roca 67, T445 1677, www.bahianueva.com.ar. One of the best sea front hotels, quite small but comfortable rooms, professional staff, cheaper in low season.
$$$ Hostería Las Maras, Marcos A Zar 64, T445 3215, www.hosterialasmaras.com.ar. Nice modern place, well-decorated rooms with large beds, cheaper with fan, parking.
$$$ Tolosa, Roque Sáenz Peña 253, T447 1850, www.hoteltolosa.com.ar. Extremely comfortable, modern, great breakfasts. Disabled access. Recommended.
$$ Hostería Viajeros, Gob Maíz 545, T445 6457, www.hostelviajeros.com.ar. Rooms for 2, 3 and 4 people, big kitchen/dining room, lawn, parking, new superior rooms on 2nd floor (**$$$**), helpful, family-run.
$$ Marina, Roca 7, T447 1429, marina1985 2011@hotmail.com. Good-value seafront apartments for up to 6 people, book ahead.
$$ Muelle Viejo, H Yrigoyen 38, T447 1284, www.muelleviejo.com. Ask for the comfortable modernized rooms in this funny old place. Rooms for 4 are excellent value.
$ pp Chepatagonia, Alfonsina Storni 16, T445 5783, www.chepatagoniahostel.com.ar. Good view of the beach (and whales in season), helpful owners, mixed and single dorms, doubles with shared bath (**$$**), lockers, bicycle hire and many other services. A good choice.

$ pp El Gualicho, Marcos A Zar 480, T445 4163, www.elgualicho.com.ar. Best budget option, some double rooms (**$$**), HI discounts, nicely designed, enthusiastic owner, English-speaking staff, heating, free pick up from bus terminal, *parrilla*, garden, bikes for hire, runs tours with good guides and value, parking, pool table. Highly recommended.
$ El Retorno, Bartolomé Mitre 798, T445 6044, www.elretornohostel.com.ar. 3 blocks from beach, hot water, lockers, cosy common area, free bus terminal pick-up. Double rooms available (**$$**). Also rents apartments with seaview (**$$$**).
$ pp La Tosca Hostel, Sarmiento 437, T445 6133, www.latoscahostel.com. Dorms have bathrooms, free pick-up from bus station if you call them, helpful. Also has small but cosy doubles (**$$**).Organizes tours. Welcoming. Recommended.
$ pp Yiliana Hostel, Av Gales 268, T447 5956, www.yilianahostel.com.ar. Family-run, dorms and private rooms (**$$** with bath), nice patio area, hot showers, laundry arranged, bike hire.
Camping ACA, Blvd Brown 3860, 4 km south of town at Punta Cuevas, T445 2952, www. acamadryn.com.ar. Open year-round, hot showers, café, shop, also duplexes for 4-6, no kitchen facilities, shady trees, close to the sea. Cheaper rates Apr-Nov.

Península Valdés *p194*
Puerto Pirámide
$$$$-$$$ Las Restingas, 1ra Bajada al Mar, T449 5101, www.lasrestingas.com. Exclusive, 8 rooms with sea views, very comfortable, with sophisticated regional restaurant. Good deals available in low season.
$$$ ACA Motel, Julio A Roca s/n, T449 5004, www.motelacapiramides.com. Welcoming, handy for the beach, with good seafood restaurant (you might spot whales from its terrace). There is also an ACA service station (daily) with good café and shop.
$$$ Cabañas en el Mar, Av de las Ballenas y 1ra Bajada al Mar, T449 5049, www.piramides.

net. Comfortable, well-equipped 2-6 bed *cabañas* with sea view.

$$$ Del Nómade, Av de las Ballenas s/n, T449 5044, www.ecohosteria.com.ar. Eco lodge using solar power and water recycling, buffet breakfast, heating, café, specializes in wildlife watching, nature and underwater photography, kayaking, scuba diving, adventure sports, courses offered.

$$$ The Paradise, 2da Bajada al Mar, T449 5030, www.hosteriaparadise.com.ar. Large comfortable rooms, suites with jacuzzis, fine seafood restaurant.

$$ La Nube del Angel, 2da Bajada al Mar, T449 5070. Open all year. Lovely owners, small cabañas for 2-6 people, quiet, 5 mins' walk from the beach.

Camping Municipal campsite by the black sand beach, T449 5084. Hot showers in evening, good, get there early to secure a place. Do not camp on the beach: people have been swept away by the incoming tide.

Estancias

$$$$ El Pedral, Punta Ninfas, T011-5272 0342, www.elpedral.com. By a pebble beach, with lots of wildlife-watching opportunities, farm activities, horse riding, zodiac trips (extra), guesthouse with en suite rooms, restaurant and bar, swimming pool.

$$$$ Faro Punta Delgada, Punta Delgada, T445 8444, www.puntadelgada.com. Next to a lighthouse, amazing setting, half and full board, excellent food, very helpful. Recommended; book in advance, no credit cards.

$$$ La Elvira, Caleta Valdés, near Punta Cantor, T420 1482 (office in Puerto Madryn Av Roca 835, local 3, T445 8820), www.laelvira. com.ar. Traditional Patagonian dishes and comfortable accommodation (B&B, half and full board available).

$$$ San Lorenzo, on RP3, 20 km southwest of Punta Norte, T445 8444 (contact through **Argentina Visión** in Puerto Madryn, see Tour operators). Great for day excursions to a beautiful stretch of coast to see penguins, fossils, birdwatching and horse treks

🍴 Restaurants

Puerto Madryn *p193, map p194*
Excellent seafood restaurants, mostly charging similar prices, but quality varies. There are also less-touristy take-aways.

$$$ Placido, Av Roca 506, T445 5991, www. placido.com.ar. On the beach, great location and service, but food can be hit and miss. Seafood and vegetarian options, also cheaper pasta dishes.

$$$ Taska Beltza, 9 de Julio 461, T447 4003. Excellent food, with Basque influence – book ahead, closed Mon. Highly recommended.

$$ Los Colonos, Av Roca y A Storni, T445 8486. Quirky restaurant built into the wooden hull of a boat, plenty of maritime heritage, cosy, *parrilla*, seafood and pastas.

$ Rosendo, Av Roca 549, 1st floor. Open lunchtime and evenings in high season, from 1700 in low season. Snack bar/café overlooking the main street. Excellent homemade *empanadas*, snacks, cocktails and wines. Reading and games room. Recommended.

One block in 9 de Julio between 25 de Mayo and Mitre has an interesting mix of food and drink places, including a winebar, a craft beer pub and several restaurants.

Cafés

Bomke, Av Roca 542. Popular ice cream place with outdoor seating at the back. Excellent ice creams. Recommended.

Lizard Café, Av Roca y Av Galés, near the seafront. Lively funky place with friendly people. Good for plentiful pizzas or for late night drinks.

Puerto Pirámides

Towanda, 1ra Bajada al Mar s/n, T447 3806. Quirky café and snack bar with outside seating overlooking the main street and beach. Friendly staff, recommended.

⚙ What to do

Puerto Madryn *p193, map p194*
Diving
Puerto Madryn is a diving centre, with several shipwrecked boats in the Golfo Nuevo.

A 1st dive ('bautismo') for beginners costs about US$60-70 pp.

Aquatours, Av Roca 550, T445 1954, www.aquatours.com.ar. A variety of options, including PADI courses, good value.

Lobo Larsen, Roca 885, loc 2 (also Bv Brown 860), T447 0277, www.lobolarsen.com. Friendly company that specializes in diving with the sea lion colony at Punta Lomas. Wide variety of courses offered.

Puerto Madryn Buceo, Blvd Brown, 3rd roundabout in Balneario Nativo Sur, T154 564422, www.madrynbuceo.com. Courses of all kinds from beginners' dives to a week-long PADI course, around US$190, or US$60 for a day excursion.

Scuba Duba, Blvd Brown 893, T445 2699, www.scubaduba.com.ar. Professional and good fun, diving with sea lions at Punta Loma, pick-up from hotel, offer a hot drink and warm clothes after the dive, good equipment, instructor Javier A Crespi is very responsible.

Mountain bike hire

From US$10. At **El Gualicho**, see Where to stay, above.

Tours

Many agencies do similar 7- and 9-hr tours to the Península Valdés, about US$55-70 pp, plus the entrance to the Peninsula. They include the interpretation centre, Puerto Pirámides (the whales boat trip is US$65 extra), Punta Delgada and Caleta Valdés. Shop around to find out how long you'll spend at each place, how big the group is, and if your guide speaks English. On all excursions take binoculars. Most tour companies stay about 1 hr on location. Tours to see the penguins at Punta Tombo and Welsh villages are better from Trelew. Tours do not run after heavy rain in the low season. Many of the agencies below also have offices at the bus terminal (Dr Avila 350). Recommended for Península Valdés:

Alora Viaggio, Av Roca 27, T445 5106, www.aloraviaggio.com. Helpful company, also has an office in Buenos Aires (T011-4827 1591, 0800-1300).

Argentina Visión, Av Roca 536, T445 5888, www.argentinavision.com. Also 4WD adventure trips and estancia accommodation, English and French spoken.

Chaltén Travel, Av Roca 115, T445 4906, www.chaltentravel.com. Runs a tourist bus service to Perito Moreno on Ruta 40, every other day, for conections north to Bariloche and south to El Chaltén and El Calafate.

Cuyun Có, Av Roca 165, T445 1845, www.cuyunco.com.ar. Offers a friendly, personal service and a huge range of conventional and more imaginative tours: guided walks with biologists, 4WD expeditions, and can arrange estancia accommodation. Bilingual guides.

Tito Botazzi, Blvd Brown y Martín Fierro, T447 4110, www.titobottazzi.com, and at Puerto Pirámide (T449 5050). Particularly recommended for small groups and well-informed bilingual guides; very popular for whale watching.

Península Valdés: Puerto Pirámides *p194*

Hydrosport, 1ra Bajada, al Mar, T449 5065, www.hydrosport.com.ar. Rents scuba equipment and boats, and organizes land and sea wildlife tours to see whales and dolphins.

Whales Argentina, 1ra Bajada al Mar, T449 5015, www.whalesargentina.com.ar. Recommended for whale watching.

⊖ Transport

Puerto Madryn *p193, map p194*

Air El Tehuelche Airport 8 km west, T445 6774; taxi US$17. Daily flights from **Buenos Aires** in high season, with more flights to **Bariloche**, Buenos Aires, and El Calafate from Trelew. Limited LADE flights to **Buenos Aires**, **Bahía Blanca**, **Viedma**, **Trelew**, **Comodoro Rivadavia** and other Patagonian airports (in low season Mon and Fri departures only). Buses to Trelew stop at entrance to airport if asked.

Bus Terminal at Av Dr Ávila, entre Necochea e Independencia, T445 1789. To **Buenos Aires**, 18-19 hrs, several companies, US$98-115. To **Bahía Blanca**, 9½ hrs with Don Otto and others, US$50-57. To **Comodoro**

Rivadavia, 6 hrs, US$35-42 with Don Otto and Transportadora Patagónica. To **Río Gallegos**, 18 hrs, US$98-112, Andesmar. To **Trelew**, 1 hr, every hour, US$4 with **28 de Julio/ Mar y Valle.**
Car hire Expensive, US$75 per day, and note large excess for turning car over. Drive slowly on unpaved *ripio* roads; best to hire 4WD. Many agencies on Av Roca. **Dubrovnik**, Av Roca 19, head office Moreno 941 Comodoro Rivadavia, T0297-444 1844, http://rentacardubrovnik. com. Also in El Calafate and Bariloche. Reliable company. **Wild Skies**, Morgan 2274, p 1, Depto 6 B Sur, T154 676233, www.wildskies.com.ar. Efficient service, English spoken, recommended.

Taxi There are taxis outside the bus terminal, T445 2966/447 4177, and on the main plaza.

Península Valdés *p194*
Bus Mar y Valle bus company from Puerto Madryn to Puerto Pirámides, daily at 0855, returns 1800, US$8 each way, 1½ hrs.

Directory

Puerto Madryn *p193, map p194*
Banks Lots of ATMs at banks. **Medical services** For emergencies call 107 or SEP, Sarmiento 125, 445 4445.

Trelew and the Chubut Valley → *Phone code: 0280. Colour map 9, A3. Population: 98,000.*

Pronounced 'Trel e Oo', Trelew is a busy town, with an excellent museum and a shady plaza, which hosts a small handicraft market at weekends. Visit mid-October to see the **Eisteddfod** (Welsh festival of arts – five of them are held throughout Welsh Patagonia, September-October). Evidence of Welsh settlement still remains in a few brick buildings: the 1889 **Capilla Tabernacl**, on Belgrano, between San Martín and 25 de Mayo, and the **Salón San David**, a 1913 Welsh meeting hall. The latter has a **mini-museum** ① *Mon-Fri 0900 1300 (all day during Sep Oct)*, of objects donated by descendants of the Welsh settlers, also organizes Welsh language and traditional dance classes. On the road to Rawson, 3 km south, is one of the oldest standing Welsh chapels, **Capilla Moriah**, from 1880, with a simple interior and graves of many original settlers in the cemetery. **Museo Paleontológico Egidio Feruglio** ① *Fontana 140, T442 0012, www.mef.org.ar, Sep-Mar daily 0900-1900, otherwise Mon-Fri 1000-1800, Sat-Sun 1000-1900, US$8, full disabled access and guides for the blind.* This is an excellent museum, which presents the origins of life and dynamically poised dinosaur skeletons. It has good information in Spanish and free tours in English, German and Italian; also a café and shop, as well as information about **Parque Paleontológico Bryn-Gwyn**, 8 km from Gaiman (see below). **Museo Regional Pueblo de Luis** ① *Fontana y Lewis Jones 9100, T442 4062, Mon-Fri 0800-2000, Sat-Sun 1400-2000, US$2.* In the old 1889 railway station, it has displays on indigenous societies, failed Spanish attempts at settlement and on Welsh colonization. The **Museo Municipal de Artes Visuales (MMAV)** ① *Mitre 350, T443 3774, Mon-Fri 0800-2000, Sat-Sun 1400-1900*, is in an attractive wooden building, with exhibitions of local artists. **Tourist office** ① *on the plaza, Mitre 387, T442 0139, Mon-Fri 0800-2000, Sat-Sun 0900-2100*, map available; also at bus station (same opening times) and at the airport when flights arrive. www.trelewturismo.wordpress.com (in Spanish only). See also **Entretur**, www.trelewpatagonia.gov.ar.

Gaiman and around → *Colour map 9, A3. District population: 12,947.*
A small pretty place with old brick houses retaining the Welsh pioneer feel, Gaiman hosts the annual Eisteddfod (Welsh festival of arts) in September-October. It's renowned for delicious Welsh teas and its fascinating tiny museum, **Museo Histórico Regional Galés** ① *Sarmiento y 28 de Julio, T449 1007, US$0.65, Tue-Sun 1500-1900*, revealing the spartan lives of the idealistic Welsh pioneers. There are also several Welsh chapels here, on the banks of the Río Chubut. **Geoparque Bryn Gwyn** ① *8 km south of town, T443 2100, www.mef.org.ar, Tue-Sun 1000-1600*

US$2.50, getting there: taxi from Gaiman US$7. Fossil beds 40 million years old are shown on a good guided tour; there is a visitor centre offering try-outs in paleontology fieldwork. **Tourist office** ⓘ *Belgrano 574, T449 1571, www.gaiman.gov.ar, Mon-Sat 0900-2000, Sun 1100-1800* (shorter hours in low season), very helpful and knowledgeable, good map of the area, marking all the Welsh sites.

Dolavon, founded in 1919, is a quiet settlement, with a few buildings reminiscent of the Welsh past. The main street, Avenida Roca, runs parallel to the irrigation canal built by the settlers, where willow trees now trail into the water, and there's a Welsh chapel, **Capilla Carmel** at one end. The **old flour mill** ⓘ *T08015-468 1212 (mobile phone, Mirna), Tue-Sun 1100-1600, US$2*, at Maipú y Roca dates from 1927 and can be visited. There's **Autoservicio Belgrano** at the far end of San Martin, for food supplies, one tea room, **El Molienda** ⓘ *Maipú 61, US$10*, but nowhere to stay. The municipal campsite, two blocks north of the river, is free, with good facilities.

In the irrigated valley between Dolavon and Gaiman, you'll see more Welsh chapels tucked away among fringes of tall *alamo* (poplar) trees and silver birches (best if you're in your own transport). The **San David chapel** (1917) is a beautifully preserved brick construction, with an elegant bell tower, and sturdy oak-studded door, in a quiet spot surrounded by birches.

Paved Ruta 25 runs from Dolavon west to the upper Chubut Valley, passing near the **Florentino Ameghino** dam, a leafy spot for a picnic. From Ameghino to Tecka on Ruta 40 (south of Trevelín) is one of the most beautiful routes across Patagonia to the Andes, lots of wildlife to see. It goes through Las Plumas (mind the bridge if driving), Los Altares, which has an **ACA** motel

Trelew

Where to stay 🛏
1 Galicia
2 Libertador
3 Rayentray
4 Rivadavia

5 Touring Club

Restaurants 🍴
1 Café de mi Ciudad
2 Café Verdi

5 La Bodeguita
6 La Casona
7 Miguel Angel

(**$$**, Ruta 25, km 321, dep_6076@aca.org.ar, restaurant, bar), camping 400 m behind service station (very basic), fuel and some shops, and Paso de Indios.

South of Trelew
Punta Tombo ① *park entrance US$10, 0800-1800 (high season). Tours from Trelew and Puerto Madryn, US$70; 45 mins at the site, café and toilets, usually include a stop at Gaiman. Access from Ruta 1, a ripio road between Trelew and Camarones. Best visited Sep-Mar.* This nature reserve is 125 km south of Trelew, open from September, when huge numbers of Magellanic penguins come here to breed, the largest single penguin colony on the South American subcontinent. Chicks can be seen from mid-November; they take to the water January to February. It's fascinating to see these creatures up close, but to avoid tourist crowds, go in the afternoon. You'll see guanacos, hares and rheas on the way. Another large **penguin colony** ① *all year, US$6* – with lots of other marine life, including whales and orcas – is at Cabo Dos Bahías, easily reached from the town of **Camarones**, 275 km north of Comodoro Rivadavia. The Guarda Fauna is 25 km from town.

Some 90 km south of Camarones along the coast is **Bahía Bustamante**, a settlement of seaweed harvesters and sheep ranchers on Golfo San Jorge (180 km north of Comodoro Rivadavia). It is in the first marine national park in Argentina and has an award-winning resort with full-board and self-catering accommodation (T011-4778 0125, www.bahiabustamante.com, electricity dusk to 2300; closed April to August). Its main attractions are the coastal and steppe landscapes of the Patagonia Austral Marine National Park, exceptional birdwatching (including 100,000 penguins), marine and land mammals, hiking and cycling. Horse riding and kayaking are extra. Guides are on hand. Phone or email in advance for pick-up from **ACA** in Garayalde.

⦿ Trelew and the Chubut Valley listings

For hotel and restaurant price codes, and other relevant information, see Essentials.

⦿ Where to stay

Trelew *p199, map p200*
$$$ Galicia, 9 de Julio 214, T443 3802, www.hotelgalicia.com.ar. Central, grand entrance, comfortable rooms, excellent value. Recommended.
$$$ La Casona del Río, Chacra 105, Capitán Murga, T443 8343, www.lacasonadelrio.com.ar. **$$$$** Feb-Jul, 5 km from town, pick-up arranged, attractive, family-run B&B with heating, TV, meals available, bicycles, massage, laundry, tennis and bowls, English and French spoken.
$$$ Libertador, Rivadavia 31, T442 0220, www.hotellibertadortw.com. Modern hotel, highly recommended for service and comfortable bedrooms.
$$$ Rayentray, Belgrano 397, at San Martín, T443 4702, www.cadenarayentray.com.ar.

Large, modern, comfortable rooms, professional staff, pool.
$$ Rivadavia, Rivadavia 55, T443 4472, www.rivadaviahotel.com.ar. Simple, comfortable rooms, breakfast extra.
$$ Touring Club, Fontana 240, Peatonal Luis Gazín, T443 3997, www.touringpatagonia. com.ar. Gorgeous 1920s bar, faded elegance, simple rooms, great value, breakfast included. Open from breakfast to the small hours for sandwiches and drinks. Wi-Fi in rooms and bar. Recommended.

Gaiman *p199*
$$$$-$$$ Posada Los Mimbres, Chacra 211, 6 km west of Gaiman, T449 1299, www. posadalosmimbres.com.ar. Rooms in the old farmhouse or in modern building, good food, very relaxing, **$$$** in Apr-Aug.
$$$-$$ Ty Gwyn, 9 de Julio 111, T449 1009, tygwyn@tygwyn.com.ar. Neat, comfortable, above the tea rooms, excellent value.

\$\$ Hostería Ty'r Haul, Sarmiento 121, T449 1880, www.hosteriatyrhaul.com.ar. Historic building, rooms are comfortable and well-lit.
\$\$ Plas y Coed, Yrigoyen 320, T449 1133, www.plasycoed.com.ar. Marta Rees' delightful tea shop has double and twin rooms in an annex next door. Highly recommended.
Camping Municipal site, Camping de los Bomberos (fire brigade).

🍴 Restaurants

Trelew *p199*, *map p200*
\$\$ La Bodeguita, Belgrano 374, T443 7777. Delicious pastas and pizzas. Reasonable wine list. Recommended.
\$\$ La Casona, Pasaje Jujuy and Lewis Jones, near Plaza Centenario. Patagonian lamb, *parrilla*; good lunchtime venue.
\$\$ Miguel Angel, next door to **Touring Club** (see Where to stay), in Peatonal Luis Gazín, Av Fontana. Good standard fare of meat and pasta dishes.

Cafés
Café de mi Ciudad, Belgrano 394. Smart café serving great coffee; read the papers here. Also has Wi-Fi.
Café Verdi, attached to Teatro Verdi, San Martín 130. Home-made waffles, pizzas and pasta, drinks.

Gaiman *p199*
Siop Bara, Tello y 25 de Mayo, sells Welsh cakes and ice creams.

Welsh teas
Served from about 1500, US\$16, by several Tea Rooms.
Plas Y Coed (see Where to stay, above). The best, and oldest; Marta Rees is a wonderful raconteur and fabulous cook.
Ty Gwyn, 9 de Julio 111. Opens 1400. Large tea room, more modern than some, welcoming; generous teas. Recommended.
Ty Nain, Yrigoyen 283. The prettiest house and full of history (mini museum inside), owned by the charming Mirna Jones (her grandmother was the first woman to be born in Gaiman).

❶ What to do

Trelew *p199*, *map p200*
Agencies run tours to Punta Tombo, Chubut Valley (half- and full-day). Tours to Península Valdés are best done from Puerto Madryn.
Nieve Mar, Italia 20, T443 4114, www.nievemar tours.com.ar. Punta Tombo and Valdés, bilingual guides (reserve ahead), organized and efficient. Has a branch in Puerto Madryn (Av Roca 493).

❷ Transport

Trelew *p199*, *map p200*
Air Flights to/from **Buenos Aires**, **Bariloche**, **El Calafate** and **Ushuaia**. LADE (Italia 170, T443 5740) flies to Patagonian airports and Buenos Aires once a week. Airport 5 km north of centre; taxis about US\$7. Local buses to/from Puerto Madryn stop at the airport entrance if asked, turning is 10 mins' walk, US\$8.
Bus The terminal is on the east side of Plaza Centenario in Urquiza y Lewis Jones, T442 0121.
Local 28 de Julio goes frequently to **Gaiman**, 30-45 mins (buy tickets from Mar y Valle, buses take different routes, some on unpaved roads); US\$1, US\$2 return, and **Dolavon** 1 hr, US\$4, to **Puerto Madryn**, 1hr, US\$4. To **Puerto Pirámides**, 2½ hrs, US\$11, daily, Mar y Valle and 28 de Julio.
   Long distance Buenos Aires, 19-20 hrs; US\$110-150, several companies go daily; to **Comodoro Rivadavia**, 5 hrs, US\$30-37, many departures; to **Río Gallegos**, 17 hrs, US\$93-107 (with connections to El Calafate, Puerto Natales, Punta Arenas), many companies. To **Esquel**, 9-10 hrs, US\$50-60, 2 companies.
Car hire Expensive. Airport desks are staffed only at flight arrival times and cars are snapped up quickly. All have offices in town.

South of Trelew: Camarones *p201*
Bus Ñandú buses from **Trelew**, Mon, Wed and Fri, 3½ hrs, departs 0800, returns same day 1600, US\$17 one-way, US\$23 return.

Comodoro Rivadavia and inland → *Phone code: 0297. Colour map 9, A2.*
District population: 182,630.

The largest city in the province of Chubut, 375 km south of Trelew, oil was discovered here in 1907. It looks rather unkempt, reflecting changing fortunes in the oil industry, the history of which is described at the **Museo del Petroleo** ⓘ *3 km north, San Lorenzo 250, T455 9558, Tue-Fri 0900-2000, Sat-Sun 1500-2000, getting there: taxi US$4.* There's a beach at Rada Tilly, 8 km south (buses every 30 minutes); walk along beach at low tide to see sea lions. **Tourist office:** CEPTur ⓘ *Av H Yrigoyen y Moreno, T444 0664, www.comodoroturismo.gob.ar, Mon-Fri 0900-1400,* English spoken. Also in **bus terminal** ⓘ *daily 0800-2100,* very helpful, English spoken.

Sarmiento → *Colour map 9, A2. Population: 10,000. Phone code: 0297.*
If you're keen to explore the petrified forests south of Sarmiento and the Cueva de las Manos near Perito Moreno, take the road to Chile running west from Comodoro Rivadavia. It's 156 km to Colonia Sarmiento (known as Sarmiento), a quiet relaxed place, sitting just south of two large lakes, Musters and Colhué Huapi. This is the best base for seeing the 70 million-year-old **petrified forests** of fallen araucaria trees. Most accessible is the **Bosque Petrificado José Ormachea** ⓘ *32 km south of Sarmiento on a ripio road, warden T489 8047, US$7.* Less easy to reach is the bleaker **Víctor Szlapelis** petrified forest, some 40 km further southwest along the same road (follow signposts, road from Sarmiento in good condition). From December to March a *combi* service runs twice daily: contact Sarmiento tourist office. Taxi Sarmiento to forests, US$20 (three passengers), including one-hour wait. Contact Sr Juan José Valero, the park ranger, for guided tours, Uruguay 43, T0297-489 8407 (see also the Monumento Natural Bosques Petrificados). **Tourist office** ⓘ *Pietrobelli 388, T489 2105,* is helpful, has map of town, arranges taxi to forests.

Comodoro Rivadavia to Río Gallegos
Caleta Olivia (*Population: 40,000*) lies on the Bahía San Jorge, 74 km south of Comodoro Rivadavia, with hotels (one opposite bus station, good) and a municipal campsite near beach (tourist information: Güemes y San Martín, T485 0988). A convenient place to break long bus journeys, see the sound sculptures, **Ciudad Sonora** ⓘ *at Pico Truncado (a few simple hotels, campsite, tourist information T499 2202), daily bus service,* 58 km southwest, where the wind sings through marble and metal structures.

In a bizarre lunar landscape surrounding the Laguna Grande, **Monumento Natural Bosques Petrificados** ⓘ *access by Ruta 49 which branches off 91 km south of Fitz Roy, no facilities, nearest campsite at Estancia La Paloma, on Ruta 49, 24 km before the entrance, T0297-444 3503,* is the country's largest area of petrified trees. The araucarias, 140 million years old, lie in a desert which was once, astonishingly, a forest. There is a museum and a well-documented 1-km trail that passes the most impressive specimens. No charge but donations accepted; please do not remove 'souvenirs'. Tours from Puerto Deseado with **Los Vikingos** (address on page 205).

Puerto Deseado (*Colour map 9, B3; Phone code: 0297; Population: 10,200*) is a pleasant fishing port on the estuary of the Río Deseado, which drains, strangely, into the Lago Buenos Aires in the west. It's a stunning stretch of coastline and the estuary is a wonderful nature reserve, with Magellanic penguins, cormorants, and breeding grounds of the beautiful Commerson's dolphin. **Cabo Blanco**, 72 km north, is the site of the largest fur seal colony in Patagonia, breeding season December-January. **Tourist office** ⓘ *vagón histórico, San Martín 1525, T487 0220.*

The quiet **Puerto San Julián** (*Colour map 9, B2; Phone code: 02962; Population: 7150*) is the best place for breaking the 778 km run from Comodoro Rivadavia to Río Gallegos. It has a fascinating history, little of which is visible today. The first Mass in Argentina was held here in 1520 after

Magellan had executed a member of his mutinous crew. Francis Drake also put in here in 1578, to behead Thomas Doughty, after amiably dining with him. There is much wildlife in the area: red and grey foxes, guanacos, wildcats in the mountains, rheas and an impressive array of marine life in the coastal Reserva San Julián. Recommended zodiac boat trip run by **Excursiones Pinocho** ① *T454600, www.pinochoexcursiones.com.ar*, to see Magellanic penguins (September-March), cormorants and Commerson's dolphins (best in December). Ceramics are made at the **Escuela de Cerámica**; good handicraft centre at Moreno y San Martín. There is a regional museum at the end of San Martín on the waterfront. **Tourist office** ① *Av San Martín entre Rivadavia y M Moreno, T452009, www.sanjulian.gov.ar, and in the bus station.*

Piedrabuena (*Population: 4900*) on Ruta 3 is 125 km south of San Julián on the Río Santa Cruz. On Isla Pavón, south of town on Ruta 3 at the bridge over Río Santa Cruz, is a tourist complex, with popular wooded campsite and wildlife park, T497498, liable to get crowded in good weather. **Hostería Municipal Isla Pavón**, is a four-star catering for anglers of steelhead trout. National trout festival in March. **Tourist office** ① *Av G Ibáñez 157 (bus station), T02962-1557 3065*. See Transport, page 221, for **Las Lengas** bus Piedrabuena-El Chaltén bus service. **Santa Cruz** (turn off 9 km south of Piedrabuena) has the **Museo Regional Carlos Borgialli**, with a range of local exhibits. There is a **tourist information centre** ① *Av Piedra Buena y San Martin, T02962-498700*, and Municipal campsite. Some 24 km further south, a dirt road branches 22 km to **Parque Nacional Monte León** ① *office at Belgrano y 9 de Julio, Puerto de Santa Cruz, T02962-489184, monteleon@ apn.gov.ar*, which includes the Isla Monte León, an important breeding area for cormorants and terns, where there is also a penguin colony and sea lions. There are impressive rock formations and wide isolated beaches at low tide. The **Hostería Estancia Monte León** ① *Ruta 3, Km 2399, T011-4621 4780 (Buenos Aires), www.monteleon-patagonia.com*, is a good base for visiting the park (open November to April, four tasteful rooms, **$$$$**, library, living room and small museum).

⊙ Comodoro Rivadavia and inland listings

For hotel and restaurant price codes, and other relevant information, see Essentials.

● Where to stay

Comodoro Rivadavia *p203*
$$$ Lucania Palazzo, Moreno 676, T449 9300, www.lucania-palazzo.com. Most luxurious business hotel, superb rooms, sea views, good value, huge American breakfast, sauna and gym included. Recommended.
$$ Azul, Sarmiento 724, T446 7539, info@ hotelazul.com.ar. Breakfast extra, quiet old place with lovely bright rooms, kind, great views from the *confitería*.
$$ Hospedaje Cari Hue, Belgrano 563, T447 2946, Hospedaje-Cari-Hue on Facebook. Sweet rooms, with separate bathrooms, very nice owners, breakfast extra. The best budget choice.

Sarmiento *p203*
$$$ Chacra Labrador, 10 km from Sarmiento, T0297-489 3329, agna@coopsar.com.ar. Excellent small estancia, breakfast included, other meals extra and available for non-residents, English and Dutch spoken, runs tours to petrified forests at good prices, will collect guests from Sarmiento (same price as taxi).
$ Colón, Perito Moreno 645, T489 4212. One of the better cheap places in town.
$ Los Lagos, Roca y Alberdi, T489 3046. Good, heating, restaurant.
Camping Club Deportivo Sarmiento, 25 de Mayo y Ruta 20, T489 3101. **Río Senguer**, Ruta Provincial 24, 1 km from centre, T489 8482.

Comodoro Rivadavia to Río Gallegos *p203*
Puerto Deseado
$$ Isla Chaffers, San Martín y Mariano Moreno, T487 2246, administracion@hotelislachaffers. com.ar. Modern, central.

$$ Los Acantilados, Pueyrredón y España, T487 2167, www.hotellosacantilados.com. Beautifully located, good breakfast.

Puerto San Julián
$$$ Bahía, San Martín 1075, T453144, hotelbahia@yahoo.com.ar. Modern, comfortable, good value. Recommended.
$$$ Estancia La María, 150 km northwest of Puerto San Julián, offers transport, lodging, meals, visits to caves with paintings of human hands, guanacos, etc, 4000-12,000 years old, less visited than Cueva de las Manos. Contact Fernando Behm in San Julián, Saavedra 1163, T452328.
$$ Municipal Costanera, 25 de Mayo y Urquiza, T452300, www.costanerahotel.com. Very nice, well run, good value, no restaurant.
$$ Sada, San Martín 1112, T452013, www.hotelsada.com.ar. Fine, on busy main road.
Camping Good municipal campsite, Magallanes 650, T454506. Repeatedly recommended, all facilities.

Restaurants

Comodoro Rivadavia p203
$$ Cayo Coco, Rivadavia 102. Bistro with excellent pizzas, good service. Also Cayo Coco del Mar, Av Costanera 1051.
$$ Maldito Peperoni, Sarmiento 581. Cheerful, modern, pastas.

Comodoro Rivadavia to Río Gallegos p203
Puerto Deseado
$$ Puerto Cristal, España 1698, T487 0387. Panoramic views of the port, a great place for Patagonian lamb, *parrilla* and seafood.

Puerto San Julián
Also bars and tearooms.
$$ La Rural, Ameghino 811. Good, but not before 2100.

What to do

Comodoro Rivadavia to Río Gallegos p203
Puerto Deseado
Darwin Expediciones, España 2551, T15-624 7554, www.darwin-expeditions. com. Excursions by boat to Ría Deseado reserve and trips to the Monumento Natural Bosques Petrificados.
Los Vikingos, Estrada 1275, T15-624 5141/ 487 0020, www.losvikingos.com.ar. Excursions by boat to Ría Deseado reserve and Reserva Provincial Isla Pingüino, bilingual guides, customized tours.

Transport

Comodoro Rivadavia p203
Air Airport, 13 km north. Bus No 6 from bus terminal, hourly (45 mins), US$0.75. Taxi to airport, US$6. Regular flights to **Buenos Aires**. LADE flies to all Patagonian destinations once or twice a week, plus **Bariloche**, **El Bolsón** and **Esquel**.
Bus Terminal in centre at Pellegrini 730, T446 7305; has luggage store, *confitería*, toilets, excellent tourist information office 0800-2100, some kiosks. In summer buses usually arrive full; book ahead. Services to **Buenos Aires** several daily, 24-28 hrs, US$121-136. To **Bariloche**, 14½ hrs, US$56-63, **Don Otto**, T447 0450, **Marga**, **Andesmar**. To **Esquel** (paved road) 9 hrs direct with **EETAP**, T447 4841, **Marga** and **Don Otto**, US$44-50. To **Río Gallegos**, daily, 10-12 hrs, US$63-73. To **Puerto Madryn** and **Trelew**, see above. To/from **Sarmiento** and **Caleta Olivia**, see below. To **Puerto Deseado**, Sportman, 2 a day, US$27.

Sarmiento p203
Bus 3 daily to/from **Comodoro Rivadavia**, US$11, 2½ hrs. From Sarmiento you can reach **Esquel** (448 km north along Rutas 20 and 40); overnight buses on Sun stop at Río Mayo, take food for journey.

Comodoro Rivadavia to Río Gallegos *p203*

Caleta Olivia

Bus To **Río Gallegos**, Andesmar, Sportman and others, US$57-66, 9½ hrs. Many buses to/from **Comodoro Rivadavia**, 1 hr, US$9, and 2 daily to **Puerto Deseado**, 2½-3 hrs, US$20, Sportman. To **Perito Moreno** and **Los Antiguos**, 5-6 hrs, US$24-26, Sportman, 2 a day.

Puerto Deseado

Air LADE (Don Bosco 1519, T487 2674) flies weekly to **Comodoro Rivadavia**, **El Calafate**, **Río Gallegos** and **Ushuaia**.

Puerto San Julián

Bus Many companies to both **Comodoro Rivadavia**, US$34-39, and **Río Gallegos**, 6 hrs, US$28-32.

❶ Directory

Comodoro Rivadavia *p203*

Banks Many ATMs and major banks along San Martín. Change money at **Thaler**, Mitre 943, Mon-Fri 0900-1300, or at weekends **ETAP** in bus terminal. **Consulates** Chile, Almte Brown 456, entrepiso, of 3, T446 2414.

Río Gallegos and around → *Phone code: 02966. Colour map 9, C2. Population: 98,000.*

The capital of Santa Cruz Province, 232 km south of Piedrabuena, on the estuary of the Río Gallegos, this pleasant open town was founded in 1885 as a centre for the trade in wool and

Río Gallegos

Where to stay	7 Punta Arenas	2 El Club Británico &
2 Comercio	8 Santa Cruz	Café Central
3 Covadonga	9 Sehuen	4 La Ría
4 Nevada		7 RoCo
5 Oviedo	Restaurants ❼	
6 París	1 El Chino	

200 metres
200 yards

sheepskins, and boasts a few smart shops and some excellent restaurants. The delightful Plaza San Martín, two blocks south of the main street, Avenida Roca, has an interesting collection of trees, many planted by the early pioneers, and a tiny corrugated iron cathedral, with a wood-panelled ceiling in the chancel and stained glass windows. The small **Museo de los Pioneros** ① *Elcano y Alberdi, daily 1000-1900, free,* is worth a visit. Interesting tour given by the English-speaking owner, a descendent of the Scottish pioneers; great photos of the first sheep-farming settlers, who came here in 1884 from the Malvinas/Falkland Islands. **Museo de Arte Eduardo Minichelli** ① *Maipú 13, Mon-Fri 0800-1900, Sat-Sun and holidays 1400-1800 (closed Jan/Feb),* has work by local artists. **Museo Malvinas Argentinas** ① *Pasteur 74, Mon and Thu 0800-1300, Tue and Fri 1300-1730, 3rd Sun of month 1530-1830.* Quite stimulating, it aims to inform visitors, with historical and geographical reasons, why the Malvinas are Argentine. **Provincial tourist office** ① *Av Pres Kirchner 863, T437412, Mon-Fri 0900-1600.* At Kirchner y San Martín is the **Carretón Municipal**, an information caravan open till 2100 in summer. Helpful, English spoken, has list of estancias, and will phone round hotels for you. **Municipal office** ① *Av Beccar 126, T436920.* At the airport, an information desk operates in high season. Small desk at **bus terminal** ① *T442159, daily till 2030.*

Cabo Vírgenes ① *134 km south of Río Gallegos, US$3,* is where a nature reserve protects the second largest colony of Magellanic penguins in Patagonia. There's an informative self-guided walk to see nests among the *calafate* and *mata verde* bushes. Good to visit from November, when chicks are born, to January. Great views from Cabo Vírgenes lighthouse. *Confitería* close by with snacks and souvenirs. Access from *ripio* Ruta 1, 3½ hours. Tours with tour operators cost US$60. About 13 km north of Cabo Vírgenes is **Estancia Monte Dinero** ① *T428922, www.montedinero. com.ar,* where the English-speaking Fenton family offers accommodation ($$$$ per person), food, day visits and excursions; excellent.

◉ Río Gallegos and around listings

For hotel and restaurant price codes, and other relevant information, see Essentials.

🛏 Where to stay

Río Gallegos *p206, map p206*
$$$ Santa Cruz, Kirchner 701, T420601, www.hotelsantacruzrgl.com.ar. Good value, spacious rooms with good beds, full buffet breakfast. Recommended.
$$$-$$ Sehuen, Rawson 160, T425683, www.hotelsehuen.com. Good, cosy, helpful.
$$ Comercio, Kirchner 1302, T420209, www.hotelcomerciorgl.com. Good value, including breakfast, nice design, comfortable, cheap *confitería*.
$$ Covadonga, Kirchner 1244, T420190, hotelcovadongargl@hotmail.com. Small rooms, attractive old building, breakfast extra.
$$ Nevada, Zapiola 480, T425990. Good budget option, nice simple rooms, no breakfast.

$$ París, Kirchner 1040, T420111, www. hotelparisrg.com.ar. Simple rooms, shared bath, good value.
$$ Punta Arenas, F Sphur 55, T427743, www.hotelpuntaarenas.com. Rooms with shared bath cheaper. Smart, rooms in new wing cost more. Something Café attached.
$ Oviedo, Libertad 746, T420118. A cheaper budget option, breakfast extra, laundry facilities, café, parking.
Camping Club Pescazaike, Paraje Guer Aike, Ruta 3, 30 km west, T423442, info@pescazaike. com.ar, also *quincho* and restaurant.

🍴 Restaurants

Río Gallegos *p206, map p206*
$$ El Club Británico, Kirchner 935, T432668. Good value, excellent steaks, "magic".
$$ La Ría, Sarmiento y Gob Lista, T444114, near the river, looking across Plaza de la República. Patagonian dishes.

$$ RoCo, Kirchner 1157. Large, smart restaurant, popular, with a varied menu of meat, fish, pasta and other dishes.
$ El Chino, 9 de Julio 27. Varied *tenedor libre*.
Café Central, Kirchner 923. Smart and popular.

⚙ What to do

Río Gallegos *p206, map p206*
Macatobiano Turismo, Av San Martín 1093, T422466, macatobiano@macatobiano.com. Air tickets and tours to Pingüinero Cabo Vírgenes (see above) and to Estancia Monte León, as well as tickets to El Calafate and Ushuaia. Recommended.

⊖ Transport

Río Gallegos *p206, map p206*
Air Airport 10 km from centre. Taxi (remise) to/from town US$8, see below. Regular flights to/from **Buenos Aires**, **Ushuaia** and **Río Grande** direct. LADE flies to many Patagonian destinations between **Buenos Aires** and **Ushuaia**, including **El Calafate** and **Comodoro Rivadavia**, but not daily. Book as far in advance as possible.
Bus Terminal, T442159, at corner of Ruta 3 and Av Eva Perón, 3 km from centre (small, so can get crowded, left luggage, *confitería*, toilets, kiosk, ATM); taxi to centre US$4, bus Nos 1 and 12 from posted stops around town. For all long distance trips, turn up with ticket 30 mins before departure. Take passport when buying ticket; for buses to Chile some companies give out immigration and customs forms. To **El Calafate**, 4-5 hrs, US$19-25, **Sportman**, and **Taqsa** (T442194, and at airport, www.taqsa.com.ar). To **Comodoro Rivadavia**, Andesmar,

Don Otto/ Transportadora Patagónica, **Sportman** and others, 10-12 hrs, US$63-73. For **Bariloche**, Marga, daily, 24 hrs, US$55-65, change in Comodoro Rivadavia.

To **Buenos Aires**, 36 hrs, several daily with Andesmar, US$184-241. To **Río Grande** US$55, 9 hrs, Marga and Tecni Austral, and to **Ushuaia** US$72.

To Chile **Puerto Natales**, Pacheco, T442765, www.busespacheco.com, and Bus Sur, T457047, www.bus-sur.cl, 2 weekly each, 4½ hrs, US$28. To **Punta Arenas**, Pacheco, 4 a week, and Ghisoni, T457047, www.busesbarria.cl, 5 a week, 5½ hrs, US$24. **By car** make sure your car papers are in order (go first to tourist office for necessary documents, then to the customs office at the port, at the end of San Martín, very uncomplicated). For road details, see Tierra del Fuego sections in Argentina and Chile.
Car hire Localiza, Sarmiento 245, T436717. **Cristina**, Libertad 123, T425709. Hertz at the airport. Essential to book rental in advance in season.
Taxi Taxi ranks plentiful, rates controlled, remise slightly cheaper. **Note**: Remise meters show metres travelled, refer to card for price; taxi meters show cost in pesos.

ⓘ Directory

Río Gallegos *p206, map p206*
Banks 24-hr ATMs for all major international credit and debit cards all over town. Change TCs here if going to El Calafate, where it is even more difficult. **Cambio El Pingüino**, Zapiola 469, and **Thaler**, San Martín 484. Both will change Chilean pesos as well as US$.
Consulates Chile, Mariano Moreno 148, T422364. Mon-Fri 0900-1300, 1400-1730.

Ruta 40 to the glaciers

Río Mayo (*Phone code: 02903*; **tourist office** ⓘ *Av Argentina s/n, T420058, www.turismoriomayo.gob.ar;* fuel and hotels **$$-$**), is reached by Ruta 22 (paved) which branches southwest 74 km west of Sarmiento. During the second half of January, it holds the **Fiesta Nacional de la Esquila** (national sheep-shearing competition). From Río Mayo, a road continues west 140 km to the Chilean border at Coyhaique Alto for Coyhaique in Chile. Ruta 40 was at the time of writing in the process of being paved, but this project may take some time, consequently high-clearance vehicles are still advised.

There is no public transport and very few other vehicles even in mid-summer, but several tour operators cover the whole route (eg **Chaltén Travel**, see What to do section, El Calafate). At Km 31 on this road a turning leads west to Lago Blanco, to Chile via Paso Huemules and Balmaceda (border open 0800-2200 in summer, 0900-2000 in winter, www.gendarmeria.gov.ar).

Perito Moreno *(Phone code: 02963; Colour map 9, B2; Population: 6000; Altitude: 400 m)*, not to be confused with the famous glacier of the same name near El Calafate, nor with nearby Parque Nacional Perito Moreno, is a provincial town with some interesting historical houses and plenty of character, 25 km east of Lago Buenos Aires, the second largest lake in South America. Southwest is Parque Laguna, with varied bird life and fishing. The town calls itself the 'archaeological capital of Santa Cruz' because of the **Cueva de las Manos** (see below). To see that you'll probably stop off here for at least one night, but if staying longer consider going the extra 56 km west to Los Antiguos (see below), especially if heading for Chile Chico. Two ATMs; traveller's cheques and US$, euros and Chilean pesos can be changed at **Banco Santa Cruz**, Avenida San Martín 1385, T432028. **Tourist office** ① *Av San Martín 2005, http://peritomoreno.tur. ar, low season Mon-Fri 0700-2400, Sat-Sun1000-2000, high season 0700-2400*, can advise on tours. Also has information on Patagonian estancias, in English.

Some 88 km south, a new marked road runs 28 km east to the famous **Cueva de las Manos** ① *US$10 for foreigners, US$6 for locals, under 12 free, compulsory guided tours with rangers who give information 0900-1900 (1000-1800 May-Oct)*. In a beautiful volcanic canyon is an intriguing series of galleries containing an exceptional assemblage of cave art, executed between 13,000 and 9500 years ago; paintings of human hands and animals in red, orange, black, white and green. It was declared a World Heritage Site in 1999. The best time to visit is early morning or evening. There is another access road, 46 km long, at Km 124. Tours run from Perito Moreno (eg with **Zoyen**, San Martín y Saavedra, T432207, zoyenturismo@yahoo.com.ar).

After hours of spectacular emptiness, even tiny **Bajo Caracoles** *(Population: 100)* is a relief: a few houses with an expensive grocery store selling uninspiring *empanadas* and very expensive fuel. From here Ruta 41 goes 99 km northwest to **Paso Robballos**, continuing to Cochrane in Chile. The website www.rutanacional40.com has good information in Spanish.

Parque Nacional Perito Moreno

① *Free. Park office in Gobernador Gregores, Av San Martín 883, T02962-491477. Accessible only by own transport, Nov-Mar.*

South of Bajo Caracoles, 101 km, is a crossroads. Ruta 40 heads southeast while the turning northwest goes to remote Parque Nacional Perito Moreno, at the end of a 90-km *ripio* track. There is trekking and abundant wildlife among the large, interconnected system of lakes below glaciated peaks, though much of the park is dedicated to scientific study only. Lago Belgrano, the biggest lake, is a vivid turquoise, its surrounding mountains streaked with a mass of differing colours. Ammonite fossils can be found. The park ranger, 10 km beyond the park entrance, has maps and information on walks and wildlife, none in English. Camping is free: no facilities, no fires. There is no public transport into the park. The website www.turismoruta40.com.ar/ pnperitomoreno.html has good information on the park in Spanish.

From the Parque Moreno junction to Tres Lagos, Ruta 40 improves considerably. East of the junction (7 km) is **Hotel Las Horquetas** (closed) and 15 km beyond is Tamel Aike village (police station, water). After another 34 km Ruta 40 turns sharply southwest, but if you need fuel before Tres Lagos, you must make a 72 km detour to Gobernador Gregores (always carry spare). **Estancia La Siberia**, between Ruta 40 and Lago Cardiel some 90 km from the turning, is a lunch stop on the El Calafate–Bariloche bus route, but also has rooms (**$$**), open October-April, no phone, see Facebook). At **Tres Lagos** a road turns off northwest to Lago San Martín. From Tres

Lagos Ruta 40 deteriorates again and remains very rugged until the turnoff to the Fitz Roy sector of Parque Nacional Los Glaciares. 21 km beyond is the bridge over Río La Leona, with delightful **Hotel La Leona Roadhouse and Country Lodge**, a great place to stay and sample local cuisine. Near here are petrified tree trunks 30 m long, protected in a natural reserve.

Border with Chile: Los Antiguos From Perito Moreno Ruta 43 (paved) runs south of Lago Buenos Aires to **Los Antiguos** (*Phone code: 02963*), an oasis set on the lake, in the middle of a desert, 2 km from the Chilean border. Blessed by a lovely climate and famous for its cherries and great views, Los Antiguos is an increasingly popular tourist town. It is developing fast, with new hotels, restaurants, bus terminal, internet and other services, ideal for a couple of days' rest and for stocking up on the basics before journeying on. **Tourist office** ⓘ *Av 11 de Julio 446, T491261, 0800-2400 Dec-Easter, 0800-2000 rest of year.*

⊚ Ruta 40 to the glaciers listings

For hotel and restaurant price codes, and other relevant information, see Essentials.

⊜ Where to stay

Río Mayo *p208*
$$$$ Estancia Don José, 3 km west of Río Mayo, T420015 or T0297-156 249155, www.turismoguenguel.com.ar. Excellent estancia, with superb food, 2 rooms and 1 cabin. The family business involves sustainable production of guanaco fibre.

Perito Moreno
$$ Americano, San Martín 1327, T432074, www.hotelamericanoweb.com.ar. 12 pleasant rooms, some superior, decent restaurant.
$$ Belgrano, San Martín 1001, T432019. This hotel is often booked by Ruta 40 long-distance bus companies, basic, not always clean, 1 key fits all rooms, helpful owner, breakfast extra, excellent restaurant.
$$ Hotel El Austral, San Martín 1381, T432605, hotelaustral@speedy.com.ar. Similar to others on the main street, but clean.
$ Alojamiento Dona María, 9 de Julio 1544, T432452. Basic but well-kept.
$ pp Santa Cruz, Belgrano 1565, T432133. Simple rooms.
Camping Municipal site 2 km at Paseo Roca y Mariano Moreno, near Laguna de los Cisnes, T432072. Also 2 *cabaña* places.
Estancias 2 estancias on RN40: 28 km south:

$$$$ pp Telken, sheep station of the Nauta family, T02963-432079, telkenpatagonia@ argentina.com or jarinauta@yahoo.com.ar. Oct-Apr. Comfortable rooms, all meals available shared with family, English and Dutch spoken, horse treks and excursions (Cueva de las Manos US$80). Highly recommended.
$$$ Hostería Cueva de Las Manos, 20 km from the cave at Estancia Los Toldos, 60 km south, 7 km off the road to Perito Moreno,' T02963-432207 or T0297-156-23 8811, www. cuevadelasmanos.net. 1 Nov-5 Apr, closed Christmas and New Year. Private rooms and dorms, runs tours to the caves, horse riding, meals extra and expensive.
$$ Estancia Turística Casa de Piedra, 80 km south of Perito Moreno on Ruta 40, in Perito Moreno ask for Sr Sabella, Av Perón 941, T02963-432199. Price is for rooms, camping, hot showers, homemade bread, use of kitchen, excursions to Cueva de las Manos and volcanoes by car or horse.

Bajo Caracoles
$$ Hotel Bajo Caracoles, T490100. Old-fashioned but hospitable, meals.

Parque Nacional Perito Moreno *p209*
Nearest accommodation is **$$$ Estancia La Oriental**, T02962-452196, laorientalpatagonia@ yahoo.com.ar. Full board. Splendid setting, with comfortable rooms. Nov-Mar. With horse riding, trekking.

See www.cielospatagonicos.com for other estancias in Santa Cruz: **Menelik** near PN Perito Moreno, and **El Cóndor**, on the southern shore of Lago San Martín, 135 km from Tres Lagos.

Tres Lagos
$ Restaurant Ahoniken, Av San Martín. Has rooms.
Camping At Estancia La Lucia, US$2.50, water, barbecue, 'a little, green paradise'; supermarket, fuel.

Border with Chile: Los Antiguos *p210*
$$$ Antigua Patagonia, Ruta 43, T491038, www.antiguapatagonia.com.ar. Luxurious rooms with beautiful views, excellent restaurant. Tours to Cueva de las Manos and nearby Monte Zevallos.
$$$-$ Mora, Av Costanera 1064, T154 207472, www.hotelmorapatagonia.com. Rooms range from dorms to 1st class with private bath, parking, lake views, corporate rates, multi-purpose room.
$$ Sol de Mayo, Av 11 de Julio, Chacra 133 'A', T491232, chacrasoldemayo@hotmail.com. Basic rooms with shared bath, kitchen, central, also has cabins for rent.
$ pp Albergue Padilla, San Martín 44 (just off main street), T491140. Comfortable dorms, doubles (**$$**); *quincho* and garden. Also camping. El Chaltén travel tickets.
Camping An outstanding **Camping Municipal**, 2 km from centre on Ruta Provincial 43, T491387, with hot showers, US$4 pp, also has cabins for 4 (no linen).

● Restaurants

Border with Chile: Los Antiguos *p210*
Viva El Viento, 11 de Julio 477, T491109, www.vivaelviento.com. Open daily in high season 0900-2100. Dutch-owned, good atmosphere, food and coffee, also has Wi-Fi internet, lots of information, boats on the lake arranged, horse riding, trips to Cueva de Las Manos. Live music Tue. Recommended.
Several other places in town.

● Transport

Río Mayo *p208*
Bus To **Sarmiento** once a day (2115) with Etap, US$13, 2 hrs.

Perito Moreno
Road distances: Bariloche 823 km, El Chaltén 582 km, El Calafate 619 km. It is nearly impossible to hitchhike between Perito Moreno and El Calafate. Hardly any traffic and few services.
Bus Terminal on edge of town next to petrol station, T432072, open only when buses arrive or depart. If crossing from Chile at Los Antiguos, 2 buses daily in summer, 1 hr, US$3.35, La Unión, T432133. To **El Chaltén** and **El Calafate**, Chaltén Travel, see next paragraph, at 1015. Chaltén Travel also runs a tourist service at 0630 from Hotel Belgrano every other day to **Puerto Madryn**.
Car Several mechanics on C Rivadavia and Av San Martín, good for repairs.
Taxi Parada El Turista, Av San Martín y Rivadavia, T432592.

Border with Chile: Los Antiguos *p210*
Bus Bus terminal on Av Tehuelches with large café/restaurant, free Wi-Fi. Most bus companies will store the luggage. Minibuses from Chile arrive at this terminal. To **Comodoro Rivadavia**, Sportman (at Terminal, T0297-15-405 3769) 2 daily, US$37. To **El Chaltén** (10 hrs) and **El Calafate** (12 hrs), via Perito Moreno, every other (even) day at 0800, US$80 and 106 respectively, also north to **Bariloche**, every even day, US$80, Chaltén Travel (open only in high season, at Hotel Belgrano, www.chalten travel.com), mid-Nov-Apr. Also **Marga** all year round at 0700, US$90 to El Calafate, 16½ hrs, and **Cal-Tur** (www.caltur.com.ar). **To Chile:** 4 companies to **Chile Chico**, 8 km west, US$4, 45 mins including border crossing (for routes from Chile Chico to Coyhaique, see Chile chapter).

● Directory

Border with Chile: Los Antiguos *p210*
Banks ATM on Av 11 de Julio. **Medical services** Hospital and medical emergency: Patagonia, Argentina 68, T491303. Pharmacy: Rossi Abatedaga, Av 11 Julio 231, T491204.

Parque Nacional Los Glaciares

This park, the second largest in Argentina and a UNESCO World Heritage Site, extends over 724,000 ha. 40% of it is covered by ice fields (*hielos continentales*) from which 13 major glaciers descend into two great lakes, Lago Argentino and, further north, Lago Viedma, linked by the Río La Leona, flowing south from Lago Viedma. The only accessible areas of the park are the southern area around Lago Argentino, accessible from El Calafate, and the northern area around Cerro El Chaltén (Fitz Roy). Access to the central area is difficult and there are no tourist facilities.

Arriving at Parque Nacional Los Glaciares

Access to the southern part of the park is 50 km west of El Calafate, US$27.50 for non-Argentines. **National Park Office** ① *Av del Libertador 1302, in Calafate, T491005, www.losglaciares.com, helpful, English spoken, Dec-Mar 0800-2000, Apr-Nov 0800-1800;* in **El Chaltén** ① *across the bridge at the entrance to the town, T493004 (opening times as above). The park itself is open Jan-Feb 0800-2100, rest of the year 0800-1600*. An informative talk about the national park and its paths is given to all incoming bus passengers. Both hand out helpful trekking maps of the area, with paths and campsites marked, distances and walking times. Note that the hotel, restaurant and transport situation in this region changes greatly between high and low season.

El Calafate and around → *Phone code: 02902. Colour map 9, B1. Population: 8000.*

This town sits on the south shore of **Lago Argentino** and exists almost entirely as a tourist centre for the **Parque Nacional los Glaciares**, 50 km away. In both El Calafate and El Chaltén most of the inhabitants hail from Buenos Aires and other provincial cities. With the recent decline in tourism as a result of global recession, many people have returned north and the local population has fallen. The town has been known to get packed out in January and February, but it is empty and quiet all winter. It's certainly not cheap, but pleasant enough, with picturesque wooden architecture and a bustling main drag. Lago Argentino's stunning turquoise waters nearby add further charm. The shallow part at Bahía Redonda is good for birdwatching in the evenings. **Tourist office** ① *in the bus station, T491476, open 0800-2000, and Rosales y Av del Libertador, T491090, open 0800-2000, www.elcalafate.tur.ar*. Very helpful staff speak several languages. **Provincial office** ① *1 de Mayo 50, T492353*.

For the main excursions to the glaciers, see below. At **Punta Gualicho** (or Walichu) on the shores of Lago Argentino 7 km east of town, there are cave paintings (badly deteriorated); six-hour horse ride (US$40 pp). A recommended 15-minute walk is from the Intendencia del Parque, following Calle Bustillo up the road towards the lake through a quiet residential area to **Laguna Nímez** ① *US$6, 2½-km self-guided trail with multilingual leaflets, high season 0900-2000, low season 1000-1700)*, a bird reserve (fenced in), with flamingos, ducks, black-necked swans and abundant birdlife. **Centro de Interpretación Histórica** ① *Av Brown y Bonarelli, US$8*, has a very informative anthropological and historical exhibition about the region, with pictures and bilingual texts, also a very relaxing café/library. The **Glaciarium** ① *6 km from town on R 11, http://glaciarium.com, daily 0900-2000, US$18, US$10 (6-12s), free bus from provincial tourist office hourly*, is a modern museum dedicated to Patagonian ice and glaciers, with an ice-bar (US$15 entrance for 25 minutes, includes beverage, 1100-2000), café and shop. There are several estancias within reach, offering a day on a working farm, *asado al palo*, horse riding and accommodation. **Estancia Alice 'El Galpón del Glaciar'** ① *T497503, Buenos Aires, T011-5217 6719, www.elgalpondelglaciar. com.ar*. **Estancia Nibepo Aike** ① *on Brazo Sur of Lago Argentino in the national park, 55 km southwest (book at Av Libertador 1215 p 1A, T02902-492797, Buenos Aires T011-5272 0341, www. nibepoaike.com.ar)*, beautiful setting in a more remote area, traditional 'estancia' style with original furniture, largely self-sustainable, delightful meals served, trekking, riding and other rural pursuits. **Cerro Frías** ① *25 km west, T492808, www.cerrofrias.com*, excursion includes one meal and an ascent of Cerro Frías (1030 m) for great views; options are by horse, on 4WD vehicles or on foot, US$63 (US$45 without lunch). See also **Helsingfors**, in Where to stay below.

Glaciar Perito Moreno

At the western end of Lago Argentino (80 km from El Calafate) the major attraction is the Glaciar Perito Moreno, one of the few glaciers in the world that is both moving and maintaining in size, despite climate change. It descends to the surface of the water over a 5-km frontage and a height of about 70 m. Several times in the past, it advanced across the lake, cutting the Brazo Rico off from the Canal de los Témpanos; then the pressure of water in the Brazo Rico broke through the ice and reopened the channel. This spectacular rupture last occurred in January 2013. The glacier can be seen close up from a series of walkways descending from the car park. Weather may be rough. The vivid blue hues of the ice floes, with the dull roar as pieces break off and float away as icebergs from the snout, are spectacular, especially at sunset. ▸▸ *See also Transport, page 220.*

El Calafate

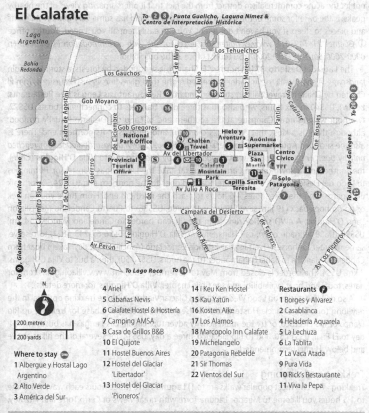

		Restaurants ❼
4 Ariel	**14** i Keu Ken Hostel	**1** Borges y Alvarez
5 Cabañas Nevis	**15** Kau Yatún	**2** Casablanca
6 Calafate Hostel & Hostería	**16** Kosten Aike	**4** Heladería Aquarela
7 Camping AMSA	**17** Los Alamos	**5** La Lechuza
8 Casa de Grillos B&B	**18** Marcopolo Inn Calafate	**6** La Tablita
10 El Quijote	**19** Michelangelo	**7** La Vaca Atada
11 Hostel Buenos Aires	**20** Patagonia Rebelde	**9** Pura Vida
Where to stay 🛏	**12** Hostel del Glaciar 'Libertador'	**21** Sir Thomas	**10** Rick's Restaurante
1 Albergue y Hostal Lago Argentino	**13** Hostel del Glaciar 'Pioneros'	**22** Vientos del Sur	**11** Viva la Pepa
2 Alto Verde		
3 América del Sur		

N

200 metres
200 yards

Glaciar Upsala

At the northwest end of Lago Argentino, 60 km long and 4 km wide, Upsala Glacier is a stunning expanse of untouched beauty. The glacier itself, unlike its cousin Perito Moreno, is suffering badly from the changing climate. When large parts break from the main mass of ice, access by lake may be blocked. Normally it can be reached by motor-boat from Punta Bandera, 50 km west of El Calafate, on a trip that also goes to Lago Onelli and Spegazzini glaciers. Small Lago Onelli is quiet and very beautiful, beech trees on one side, and ice-covered mountains on the other. The lake is full of icebergs of every size and sculpted shape.

El Chaltén and around → *Phone code: 02962.*

This small tourist town lies 217 km northwest of El Calafate in the north of the park (road paved), at the foot of the jagged peaks of the spectacular Fitz Roy massif, which soars steeply from the Patagonian steppe, its sides too steep for snow to stick. Chaltén is the Tehuelche name meaning the 'smoking mountain', and occasionally at sunrise the mountains are briefly lit up bright red for a few seconds, a phenomenon known as the 'sunrise of fire', or '*amanecer de fuego*'. The town is windy, with an Alpine feel. It's a neat place, but incredibly expensive. Nevertheless you should not let the acute commercialism detract from the fact that it offers amazing views of the nearby peaks, is the base for some of the country's finest trekking and has some very good restaurants and places to sleep. If you haven't got a tent, you can easily rent all you'll need. **Tourist office** ① *Güemes 21, T493011, www.elchalten.com, excellent site with accommodation listed, Mon-Fri 0900-2000, Sat-Sun 1300-2000.* Also tourist office at the bus station

The **Lago del Desierto**, 37 km north of El Chaltén, is surrounded by forests, a stunning virgin landscape. A short walk to a mirador at the end of the road gives fine views. Excursions from El Chaltén by **Chaltén Travel** daily in summer, and from **Restaurant Las Lengas** (see Restaurants, below), US$40 for six hours, who also runs three daily transfers to connect with boats, US$27, two-hour waiting time. Campsite at the southern end of Lago del Desierto (usually no food, although there is a kiosk that advertizes *choripán*), and refugios at its northern end. There is also the secluded **Aguas Arriba Lodge** ① *T011-4152 5697, www.aguasarribalodge.com, reached only by boat, or by a 2- to 3-hr walk (luggage goes by boat).* To get to **Villa O'Higgins** (Chile), the southernmost town on the Carretera Austral, take the Las Lengas transfer, or **JR** minibus to Lago del Desierto, then a 45-minute boat trip goes to the northern end (US$24.50), or walk up a path along the east shores 4½ hours to reach the northern end. From there you can trek or go on horseback (19 km, seven hours with guide, US$36) to Puerto Candelario Mancilla on Lago O'Higgins. A 4WD service runs from the Chilean border to Candelario Mancilla, 14 km: US$18 (US$9 luggage only), call Hans Silva in Villa O'Higgins, T+56-67-243 1821, to reserve, same number for horses. Overnight at Estancia Candelario Mancilla. Next day, take a boat from Candelario Mancilla to Bahía Bahamóndez (three hours, US$76.50), then a bus to Villa O'Higgins, 7 km, US$4. The border is closed from May to November (check at www.villaohiggins.com for dates, tours and boat availability and see Chile chapter, **Villa O'Higgins**, for more details).

Also daily boat trips on Lago Viedma to pass Glaciar Viedma, with ice trekking optional in the day-long tour. The estancia **Hostería El Pilar** (see Where to stay) is a base for trekking up Río Blanco or Río Eléctrico, or try the multi activity adventure circuit. **Las Lengas** has buses twice a day to El Pilar, US$11.50, and to Río Eléctrico, three a day, US$14, for several of the hikes above and below. Highly recommended.

Trekking and climbing

Trekking The two most popular walks are to **1) Laguna Torre** (three hours each way). After one to 1½ hours you'll come to Mirador Laguna Torre with great views of Cerro Torre and Fitz Roy, and 1¼ hours more to busy **Camping De Agostini** near the lake, where you have fantastic views. **2) Laguna de Los Tres** (four hours each way). Walk 1¾ hours up to Camping Capri, great views of Fitz Roy, then another hour to **Camping Poincenot**. Just beyond it is **Camping Río Blanco** (only for climbers, registration at the national park office required). From Río Blanco you can walk another hour, very steep, to Laguna de los Tres where you'll get a spectacular view (not a good walk if it's cloudy). You can connect the two paths by taking one that takes about two hours and branches off south, northwest of Laguna Capri, passes by Lagunas Madre e Hija and reaches the path to Laguna Torre, west of the Mirador. This may be too long for a day. From El Chaltén to Laguna Torre along this route takes about seven hours. **3) Loma del Pliegue Tumbado** (four hours each way). To a viewpoint where you can see both cordons and Lago Viedma: marked path from Park Ranger's office, a good day walk, best in clear weather. **4) Laguna Toro** (seven hours each way). For more experienced trekkers, to wild glacial lake across the ice cap. **5) Up Río Blanco to Piedra del Fraile** (seven hours each way, two hours each way from the road to Lago del Desierto). A beautiful walk out of the national park to campsite with facilities, and Refugio Piedra del Fraile, neither is free. Recommended. The best day walks are Laguna Capri, Mirador Laguna Torre, both of which have great views after an hour or so. A one-hour hike is to Chorillo del Salto, a small but pristine waterfall; take the road to Lago del Desierto for about 30 minutes, then follow the marked path. No guide is necessary.

Most paths are very clear and well worn, but a map is essential, even on short walks: the park information centre gives helpful maps of treks, as do the tourist office and hotels. If you wish to buy maps, the best are by *Zagier and Urruty*, www.patagoniashop.net, 1:50,000 (US$6-15), updated quite regularly and available in shops in El Calafate and El Chaltén.

Climbing Base camp for Fitz Roy (3405 m) is Campamento Río Blanco (see above). Other peaks include Cerro Torre (3102 m), Torre Egger (2900 m), Cerro Solo (2121 m), Poincenot (3002 m), Guillaumet (2579 m), Saint-Exupery (2558 m), Aguja Bífida (2394 m) and Cordón Adela (2938 m): most of these are for very experienced climbers. Generally the best time is mid February to end March; November-December is very windy; January is fair; winter is extremely cold, but weather is unpredictable and it all depends on the specific route being climbed. Permits for climbing are available at the national park information office. Guides are available in El Chaltén.

El Calafate to Chile

If travelling from El Calafate to Torres del Paine by car or bike, you'll cross this bleak area of steppe. About 40 km before reaching the border there are small lagoons and salt flats with flamingos (between El Calafate and Punta Arenas it is also possible to see guanacos and condors). From Calafate you can take the paved combination of Ruta 11, RN 40 and RN 5 to La Esperanza (165 km), where there's fuel, a campsite and a large but expensive *confitería* (lodging $$ with bath). From La Esperanza, Ruta 7 heads west (not completely paved) along the valley of the Río Coyle. A shorter route (closed in winter) missing La Esperanza, turns off at El Cerrito and joins Ruta 7 at **Estancia Tapi Aike**. Ruta 7 continues to the border crossing from Cancha Carrera to Cerro Castillo, meeting the good road between Torres del Paine (20 km north) and Puerto Natales (63 km south). For bus services along this route see under El Calafate.

Río Turbio → *Phone code: 02902. Colour map 9, C2. Population: 6650.*

A charmless place, 267 km west of Río Gallegos, 30 km from Puerto Natales (Chile), you're most likely to visit en route to or from Torres del Paine in Chile. The site of Argentina's largest coalfield hasn't recovered from the depression hitting the industry in the 1990s. It has a cargo railway, connecting it with Punta Loyola; Mina 1 is where the first mine was opened. There is a ski centre:

Valdelén has six pistes and is ideal for beginners, also scope for cross-country skiing between early June and late September (contact Club Andino Río Turbio for more info T421900). **Tourist information** ① *in the municipality, Plazoleta Castillo, T421950.*

Border with Chile

1) Paso Mina Uno/Dorotea is 5 km south of Río Turbio. Open all year, 0900-2300. On the Chilean side this runs south to join the main Puerto Natales-Punta Arenas road. **2) Paso Casas Viejas/Laurita** is 33 km south of Río Turbio via 28 de Noviembre. Open all year, 0900-0100. On the Chilean side this runs west to join the main Puerto Natales-Punta Arenas road. **3) Paso Río Don Guillermo (or Cancha Carrera)** is 48 km north of Río Turbio, this is the most convenient crossing for Parque Nacional Torres del Paine. Open all year, 0900-2300. Argentine customs are fast and friendly. On the Chilean side the road continues 7 km to the border post at Cerro Castillo, where it joins the road from Puerto Natales to Torres del Paine. All crossings may have different hours in winter; see www.gendarmeria.gov.ar.

⦿ Parque Nacional Los Glaciares listings

For hotel and restaurant price codes, and other relevant information, see Essentials.

⚈ Where to stay

Parque Nacional Los Glaciares *p212*

$$$$ Estancia Helsingfors, 73 km northwest of La Leona, on Lago Viedma, in BsAs: T011-5277 0195, reservations T02966-675753, www.helsingfors.com.ar. Nov-Apr. Fabulous place in splendid position on Lago Viedma, stylish rooms, welcoming lounge, delicious food (full board), and excursions directly to glaciers and to Laguna Azul, by horse or trekking, plus boat trips.

$$$$ Los Notros, 70 km west of Calafate on the road to the Moreno glacier, T499510 (in BA: T011-4813 7285), www.losnotros.com. Exclusive retreat with wonderful views of the glacier, spacious rooms, all-inclusive packages.

El Calafate *p212, map p213*

Prepare to pay more for accommodation here than elsewhere in Argentina. El Calafate is very popular in Jan-Feb, so book all transport and accommodation in advance. Best months to visit are Oct, Nov and Mar, Apr when it is less crowded and less overpriced. Many hotels open only from Sep/Oct to Apr/May.

$$$$ El Quijote, Gob Gregores 1191, T491017, www.quijotehotel.com.ar. A very good hotel, spacious, well designed with traditional touches,

tasteful rooms with TV, restaurant *Sancho*, stylish lobby bar, English and Italian spoken.

$$$$ Kau Yatún, Estancia 25 de Mayo (10 blocks from centre, east of arroyo Calafate), T491059, www.kauyatun.com. Renovated main house of a former estancia, well-kept grounds, 2 excellent restaurants, only half board or all inclusive packages that include excursions in the national park.

$$$$ Kosten Aike, Gob Moyano 1243, T492424, www.kostenaike.com.ar. Relaxed yet stylish, elegant spacious rooms (some superior), jacuzzi, gym, excellent restaurant, **Ariskaiken** (open to non residents), cosy bar, garden, English spoken. Open year-round. Recommended.

$$$$ Los Alamos, Gob Moyano y Bustillo, T491144, www.posadalosalamos.com. Cheaper in low season. Very comfortable, charming rooms, good service, lovely gardens, good bar and without doubt the best restaurant in town, La Posta.

$$$ Alto Verde, Zupic 138, T491326, www.welcomeargentina.com/altoverde. Top quality, **$$** in low season, spotless, spacious, helpful, also with apartments for 4.

$$$ Cabañas Nevis, Av del Libertador 1696, T493180, www.cabanasnevis.com.ar. Owner Mr Patterson offers very nice cabins for 5 and 8 (price quoted is for 5), some with lake view, great value.

$$$ Casa de Grillos B&B, Los Cóndores 1215, T491160, www.casadegrillos.com.ar. Welcoming B&B in the calm green area, next to Nímez nature reserve. It has all the comfort and charm of a family house, **$$** low season.

$$$ Michelangelo, Espora y Gob Moyano, T491045, www.michelangelohotel.com. ar. Lovely, quiet, welcoming, restaurant. Recommended.

$$$ Patagonia Rebelde, José Haro 442, T494495 (in Buenos Aires T015-5890 1276), www.patagoniarebelde.com. Charming new building in traditional Patagonian style, like an old inn with rustic decor, good comfort with well-heated bedrooms and comfy sitting-rooms.

$$$ Vientos del Sur, up the hill at Río Santa Cruz 2317, T493563, www.vientosdelsur.com. Very hospitable, calm, comfortable, good views, kind family attention.

$$$-$$ Ariel, Av Libertador 1693, T493131, www.hotelariel.com ar. Modern, functional, well maintained. Breakfast included.

$$ Hostel Buenos Aires, Buenos Aires 296, 200 m from terminal, T491147, www.glaciarescalafate.com. Quiet, kind owner, helpful, comfortable with doubles, cheaper without bath, good hot showers, laundry service, luggage store, bikes for hire.

$$ Sir Thomas, Espora 257, T492220, www.sirthomas.com.ar. Modern, comfortable wood-lined rooms, breakfast included.

$$-$ pp Albergue y Hostal Lago Argentino, Campaña del Desierto 1050-61 (near bus terminal), T491423, www.hostallagoargentino. com.ar. **$** pp shared dorms, too few showers when full, nice atmosphere, good flats, cabañas and **$$** doubles on a neat garden and also in building on opposite side of road.

$$-$ pp Calafate Hostel & Hostería, Gob Moyano 1226, T492450, www.calafatehostels. com. A huge log cabin with good rooms: dorms with or without bath, breakfast extra, **$$** doubles with bath and breakfast. Book a month ahead for Jan-Feb, HI discounts, travel agency, **Always Glacier**, and restaurant **Isabel** on premises.

$$-$ pp Marcopolo Inn Calafate, C 405, T493899, www.marcopoloinncalafate.com.

Part of Hostelling International. **$** pp in dorms. Laundry facilities, various activities and tours on offer.

$ pp América del Sur, Puerto Deseado 153, T493525, www.americahostel.com.ar. Panoramic views from this comfortable, relaxed hostel, welcoming, well-heated rooms (dorms for 4, **$$** doubles with views, 1 room adapted for wheelchair users), chill-out area, fireplace. Warmly recommended, but can be noisy.

$ pp Hostel del Glaciar 'Libertador', Av del Libertador 587 (next to the bridge), T492492, www.glaciar.com. HI discounts, open Sep-May. Smaller and pricier than 'Pioneros', rooms are good and well-heated, all with own bath (US$20 pp dorms for 4 and **$$$-$$** doubles), breakfast included. Free transfer from bus terminal, laundry service. Owners run **Patagonia Backpackers** (see below under What to do). Recommended.

$ pp Hostel del Glaciar 'Pioneros', Los Pioneros 255, T491243, www.glaciar.com. Discount for HI members, open mid-Sep to mid-Mar. Accommodation for all budgets: standard **$$** doubles (also for 3 and 4) with bath, superior **$$$** doubles with bath, shared dorms up to 4 beds, US$16.50 pp. Many languages spoken, lots of bathrooms, no breakfast in dorms, only for guests in private rooms, free shuttle from bus terminal, laundry service, movie rental. Very popular, so book well in advance and double-check.

$ pp i Keu Ken Hostel, F M Pontoriero 171, T495175, www.patagoniaikeuken.com.ar. On a hill, very helpful, flexible staff, hot water, heating, luggage store, good.

Camping AMSA, Olavarría 65 (50 m off the main road, turning south at the fire station), T492247. Hot water, open in summer, US$6.50 pp. **El Huala**, 42 km from El Calafate, on the road to Lago Roca. Free with basic facilities, open all year round. **Lago Roca**, 50 km from El Calafate, T499500, www. losglaciares. com/campinglagoroca, beautifully situated, US$6 pp, bike hire, fishing licences, restaurant/ *confitería*, Oct-Apr. (**Ferretería Chuar**, 1 block from bus terminal, sells camping gas.)

El Chaltén p214

In high season places are full: you must book ahead. Most places close in low season.

$$$$ Hostería El Puma, Lionel Terray 212, T493095, www.hosteriaelpuma.com.ar. A little apart, splendid views, lounge with log fire, tasteful stylish furnishings, comfortable, transfers and big American breakfast included. Recommended.

$$$$ Los Cerros, Av San Martín 260, T493182, www.loscerrosdelchalten.com. Stylish and sophisticated, in a stunning setting with mountain views, sauna, whirlpool and massage. Half-board and all-inclusive packages with excursions available.

$$$$ Senderos, Perito Moreno 35, T493336, www.senderoshosteria.com.ar. 4 types of room and suite in a new, wood-framed structure, comfortable, warm, can arrange excursions, excellent restaurant.

$$$ El Pilar, R23, Km 17, T493002, www.hosteriaelpilar.com.ar. Country house in a spectacular setting at the meeting of Ríos Blanco and de las Vueltas, with clear views of Fitz Roy. A chance to sample the simple life with access to less-visited northern part of the park. Simple comfortable rooms, great food, breakfast and return transfers included.

$$$ Lunajuim, Trevisán 45, T493047, www.lunajuim.com. Stylish yet relaxed, comfortable (duvets on the beds), lounge with wood fire. Recommended.

$$$ Nothofagus, Hensen y Riquelme, T493087, www.nothofagusbb.com.ar. Cosy bed and breakfast, simple rooms, cheaper without bath and in low season, Oct and Apr (**$$**), good value. Recommended.

$$ Hospedaje La Base, Av Lago del Desierto 97, T493031. Good rooms for 2, 3 and 4, tiny kitchen, self service breakfast, great video lounge. Recommended.

$$-$ Ahonikenk Chaltén, Av Martín M de Güemes 23, T493070. Nice simple rooms, some dorms, restaurant/pizzería attached, good pastas.

$ pp Albergue Patagonia, Av San Martín 493, T493019, www.patagoniahostel.com.ar. HI-affiliated, cheaper for members, small and cosy with rooms for 2 with own bath (**$$**) or for 2

(**$$**), 4, 5 or 6 with shared bath, also has cabins, video room, bike hire, laundry, luggage store and lockers, restaurant, very welcoming. Helpful information on Chaltén, also run excursions to Lago del Desierto. Closed Jun-Sep.

$ pp Albergue Rancho Grande, San Martín 724, T493005, www.ranchograndehostel.com. HI-affiliated, in a great position at the end of town with good open views and attractive restaurant and lounge, rooms for 4, with shared bath, breakfast extra. Also **$$** doubles, breakfast extra. Helpful, English spoken. Recommended. Reservations in Calafate Hostel/Chaltén Travel, Calafate.

$ pp Cóndor de los Andes, Av Río de las Vueltas y Halvorsen, T493101, www.condordelosandes.com. Nice little rooms for up to 6 with bath, sheets included, breakfast extra, also doubles with bath (**$$$-$$**), laundry service, library, quiet, HI affiliated.

Camping del Lago, Lago del Desierto 135, T493010, centrally located with hot showers. Several others. A gas/alcohol stove is essential for camping as open fires are prohibited in campsites in the national park. Take plenty of warm clothes and a good sleeping bag. It is possible to rent equipment in El Chaltén, ask at park office or Rancho Grande.

In the national park Poincenot, Capri, Laguna Toro, Laguna Torre. None has services, all river water is drinkable. Pack up all rubbish and take it back to town, do not wash within 70 m of rivers. **Camping Los Troncos/Piedra del Fraile** on Río Eléctrico is beyond park boundary, privately owned, has facilities.

Río Turbio p215

$$ Nazó, Gob Moyano 464, T421800. Modern building, rooms for 2-4, laundry service, restaurant and bar.

$ Hostería Capipe, Paraje Julia Dufour, 9 km from town, T482935. Simple, with restaurant.

❼ Restaurants

El Calafate p212, map p213

$$ La Lechuza, Av del Libertador 1301, www.lalechuzapizzas.com.ar. Good-quality pizzas, pasta, salad and meat dishes. Excellent wine list. Has another branch up the road at No 935.

$$ La Tablita, Cnel Rosales 28 (near the bridge). Typical *parrilla*, generous portions and quality beef. Recommended.

$$ La Vaca Atada, Av del Libertador 1176. Good homemade pastas and more elaborate and expensive dishes based on salmon and king crab.

$$ Mi Viejo, Av del Libertador 1111. Closed Tue. Popular *parrilla*.

$$ Pura Vida, Av Libertador 1876, near C 17. Open 1930-2330 only, closed Wed. Comfortable sofas, homemade Argentine food, vegetarian options, lovely atmosphere, lake view (reserve table). Recommended.

$$ Rick's Restaurante, Av del Libertador 1091. Lively *parrilla* with good atmosphere.

$$ Viva la Pepa, Emilio Amado 833. Mon-Sat 1100-2300. A mainly vegetarian café with great sandwiches and crêpes filled with special toppings. Wi-Fi, craft beers. Child-friendly.

Cafés

Borges y Alvarez, Av del Libertador 1015 (Galería de los Gnomos). A lively, friendly book-bar open daily till 0400. Excellent place to hang out. Recommended.

Casablanca, 25 de Mayo y Av del Libertador. Jolly place for omelettes, hamburgers, vegetarian, 30 varieties of pizza.

Heladería Aquarela, Av del Libertador 1197. The best ice cream – try the *calafate*. Also homemade chocolates and local produce.

El Chaltén *p214*
$$ Estepa, Cerro Solo y Antonio Rojo. Small, intimate place with good, varied meals, friendly staff.

$$ Fuegia, San Martín 342. Dinner only. Pastas, trout, meat and vegetarian dishes. Recommended.

$$ Josh Aike, Lago de Desierto 105. Excellent *confitería*, homemade food, beautiful building. Recommended.

$$ Pangea, Lago del Desierto 330 y San Martín. Open for lunch and dinner, drinks and coffee, calm, good music, varied menu. Recommended.

$$ Patagonicus, Güemes y Madsen. Midday to midnight. Lovely warm place with salads, *pastas caseras* and fabulous pizzas for 2, US$3-8. Recommended.

$$ Ruca Mahuida, Lionel Terray 55, T493018. Widely regarded as the best restaurant with imaginative and well-prepared food.

$$ Zaffarancho (behind **Rancho Grande**), music bar-restaurant, good range and reasonably priced. Film nights 3 times a week.

$ Domo Blanco, San Martín 164. Delicious ice cream.

$ Las Lengas, Viedma 95, opposite tourist office, T493023, laslengaselchalten@yahoo.com.ar. Cheaper than most. Plentiful meals, basic pastas and meat dishes. US$3 for meal of the day. Lots of information. See Lago del Desierto, above, and Transport, below, for owner's minibus services.

Bars and clubs

El Chaltén *p214*
Cervecería Bodegón El Chaltén, San Martín 564, T493109. Brews its own excellent beer, also local dishes and pizzas, coffee and cakes, English spoken. Recommended.

Shopping

El Calafate *p212, map p213*
Plenty of touristy shops in main street Av del Libertador. Recommended for homemade local produce, especially Patagonian fruit teas, sweets and liqueurs, **Estancia El Tranquilo**, Av del Libertador 935, www.eltranquilo.com.ar.

El Chaltén *p214*
Several outdoor shops. Also supermarkets, all expensive, and little fresh food available: **El Gringuito**, Av Antonio Rojo, has the best choice. Fuel is available next to the bridge.

What to do

El Calafate *p212, map p213*
Most agencies charge the same rates and run similar excursions. Note that in winter boat

trips can be limited by bad weather, even cancelled.

Calafate Mountain Park, Av del Libertador 1037, T491446, www.calafatemountainpark.com. Excursions in 4WD to panoramic views, 3-6 hrs. Summer and winter experiences including kayaking, quad biking, skiing and more.

Chaltén Travel, Av del Libertador 1174, T492212, also Av Güemes 7, T493092, El Chaltén, www.chaltentravel.com. Huge range of tours (has a monopoly on some): glaciers, estancias, trekking, and bus to El Chaltén. Sell tickets along the Ruta 40 to Perito Moreno, Los Antiguos and Bariloche, departures 0800 on odd-numbered days (0900 from El Chaltén) mid-Nov to Apr, overnight in Perito Moreno (cheaper to book your own accommodation), 36 hrs, English spoken.

Hielo y Aventura, Av del Libertador 935, T492205, www.hieloyaventura.com. Mini-trekking includes walk through forests and 2½-hr trek on Moreno glacier (crampons included); Big Ice full-day tour includes a 4-hr trek on the glacier. Also half-day boat excursion to Brazo Sur for a view of stunning glaciers, including Moreno. Recommended.

Lago San Martín, Av del Libertador 1215, p 1, T492858, www.lagosanmartin.com. Operates with Estancias Turísticas de Santa Cruz, specializing in arranging estancia visits, helpful.

Mar Patag, 9 de Julio 57, of 4, T492118, www.crucerosmarpatag.com. Exclusive 2-day boat excursion to Upsala, Spegazzini and Moreno glaciers, with full board. Also does a shorter full-day cruise with gourmet lunch included.

Mundo Austral, 9 de Julio 2427, T492365, www.mundoaustral.com.ar. For all bus travel and cheaper trips to the glaciers, helpful bilingual guides.

Patagonia Backpackers, at Hosteles del Glaciar, T491792, www.patagonia-back packers.com. Alternative glacier tour, entertaining, informative, includes walking, US$45. Recommended constantly.

Solo Patagonia, Av del Libertador 867, T491155, www.solopatagonia.com. This company runs 2 7-hr trips taking in Upsala, Onelli and Spegazzini glaciers, US$92.

El Chaltén *p214*
For trekking on horseback with guides: El Relincho, T493007, www.elrelincho patagonia.com.ar. Also offer trekking, accommodation and rural activities.

In summer **Restaurant Las Lengas**, see above, runs a regular minibus to Lago del Desierto passing by some starting points for treks and by **Hostería El Pilar**, see above (www.transportelaslengas.com).

Casa De Guías, Av San Martín s/n, T493118, www.casadeguias.com.ar. Experienced climbers who lead groups to nearby peaks, to the Campo de Hielo Continental and easier treks.

Fitz Roy Expediciones, San Martín 56, T436424, www.fitzroyexpediciones.com.ar. Organizes trekking and adventure trips including on the Campo de Hielo Continental, ice climbing schools, and fabulous longer trips. Climbers must be fit, but no technical experience required; equipment provided. Email with lots of notice to reserve. Ecocamp with 8 wilderness cabins recently opened. Highly recommended.

Patagonia Aventura, T493110, www.patagonia-aventura.com. Has various ice trekking and other tours to Lago and Glaciar Viedma, also to Lago del Desierto.

⊖ Transport

El Calafate *p212, map p213*
Air Airport, T491220, 23 km east of town, Transpatagonia Expeditions, T493766, runs service from town to meet flights, US$10 open return. Taxi (T491655/491745), US$13. Daily flights to/from **Buenos Aires**. Many more flights in summer to **Bariloche**, **Ushuaia** and **Trelew**. LADE flies to **Ushuaia**, **Comodoro Rivadavia**, **Río Gallegos**, **Esquel** and other Patagonian airports (office at J Mermoz 160, T491262). Note that a boarding fee of US$21, not included in the airline ticket price, has to be paid at El Calafate.

Bike hire US$17 per day.
Bus Terminal on Roca 1004, 1 block up stairs from Av del Libertador. Terminal fee US$0.65, always included in bus ticket price. Some bus companies will store luggage for

a fee. To **Perito Moreno** glacier see below. To **Río Gallegos** daily with 4-5 hrs, US$19-25, **Sportman** (T02966-15 464841) and **Taqsa** (T491843). To **El Chaltén** daily with Taqsa, US$26, **Chaltén Travel** (T492212, at 0800, 1300, 1830), **Los Glaciares, Cal-Tur** (T491368, www. caltur.com.ar, who run many other services and tours), 3 hrs, US$30. To **Bariloche**, see page 198 for **Chaltén Travel**'s buses via Los Antiguos and Perito Moreno, also Cal-Tur. Taqsa runs a bus to Bariloche via Los Antiguos, 36 hrs, US$108 (frequency depends on demand). To **Ushuaia** take bus to Río Gallegos for connections.

Direct bus services to Chile (Take passport when booking bus tickets to Chile.) To **Puerto Natales**, daily in summer with Cootra (T491444), via Río Turbio, 7 hrs, with Pacheco, Mon, Wed, Fri 1100, or with Turismo Zaahj (T491631), 3-9 a week depending on season, 5 hrs, US$25 (advance booking recommended, tedious customs check at border). **Note** Argentine pesos cannot be exchanged in Torres del Paine.
Car hire Average price under US$100 per day for small car with insurance but usually only 200 free km. Localiza, Av del Libertador 687, T491398, localiza calafate@hotmail.com. Nunatak, Gob Gregores 1075, T491987, www.nunatakrentacar. com.ar. ON Rent a Car, Av del Libertador 1831, T493788 or T02966-156 29985, onrentacar@ cotecal.com.ar. All vehicles have a permit for crossing to Chile, included in the fee, but cars are poor.

Glaciar Perito Moreno *p213*
Boat A 45-mins catamaran trip departs from near the entrance to the walkways and gets closer to the glacier's face, US$18; can be arranged independently through **Solo Patagonia** (see above) or is offered with the regular excursions. Another boat trip with a mini-trek on the glacier is organized by tour operators.
Bus From El Calafate with Taqsa, Interlagos, US$25 return; also guided excursions. Many agencies in El Calafate also run minibus tours

(park entry not included), US$36. Minitrekking tours (transport plus a 2½-hr walk on the glacier, US$128. Out of season trips to the glacier may be difficult to arrange. Taxis about US$75 for 4 passengers round trip including wait of 3-4 hrs at the glacier. A reliable driver is Ruben, T498707. There is small taxi stand outside the bus terminal.

El Chaltén *p214*
Bus Tax of US$1.15 is charged at the terminal. In summer, buses fill quickly: book ahead. Fewer services off season. Daily buses to **El Calafate**, 4-5 hrs (most stop at El Calafate airport), companies and price given above, El Chaltén phone numbers: **Chaltén Travel** see above for address, **Cal Tur** T493079. See page 198 for Chaltén Travel to Los Antiguos and Bariloche. To **Piedrabuena** on Ruta 3, for connections to Los Antiguos, Puerto Madryn, etc, **Las Lengas** (see Restaurants, above, www.transporte laslengas.com.ar), 6 hrs, once a day, US$37. **Las Lengas** also run to El Calafate airport 3 times a day, 3 hrs, US$28, reserve in advance.
Taxi Servicio de Remís El Chaltén, Av San Martén 430, T493042, reliable.

Río Turbio *p215*
Bus To **Puerto Natales**, 2 hrs, US$8, hourly with Cootra (Tte del Castillo 01, T421448), and other companies. To **El Calafate**, Cootra, 4 hrs, US$20. **Río Gallegos**, 5 hrs, US$23 (Taqsa/Marga, T421422).

ⓘ Directory

El Calafate *p212, map p213*
Banks Best to take cash as high commission is charged on exchange, but there are ATMs at airport and banks. **Thaler**, Av del Libertador 963, loc 2, changes money and TCs.

El Chaltén *p214*
Banks 24-hr ATM next to the gas station at the entrance to town. Credit cards are accepted in all major hotels and restaurants.

Tierra del Fuego

The island at the extreme south of South America is divided between Argentina and Chile, with the tail end of the Andes cordillera providing dramatic mountain scenery along the southern fringe of both countries. There are lakes and forests, mostly still wild and undeveloped, offering good trekking in summer and downhill or cross-country skiing in winter. Until a century ago, the island was inhabited by four ethnic groups, Selk'nam (or Ona), Alacaluf (Kaweskar), Haush (Manekenk) and Yámana (Yahgan). They were removed by settlers who occupied their land to introduce sheep and many died from disease. Their descendants (except for the extinct Haush) are very few in number and live on the islands. Many of the sheep farming estancias which replaced the indigenous people can be visited. Ushuaia, the island's main city, is an attractive base for exploring the southwest's small national park, and for boat trips along the Beagle channel to Harberton, a fascinating pioneer estancia. There's good trout and salmon fishing, and a tremendous variety of bird life in summer. Autumn colours are spectacular in March and April.

Arriving in Tierra del Fuego → *Colour map 9, C3.*

Getting there There are no road/ferry crossings between the Argentine mainland and Argentine Tierra del Fuego. You have to go through Chilean territory. (Accommodation is sparse and planes and buses fill up quickly from November to March. Essential to book ahead.) From Río Gallegos, Ruta 3 reaches the Chilean border at Monte Aymond (67 km; open 24 hours summer, 0900-2300 April to October), passing Laguna Azul. For bus passengers the border crossing is easy, although you have about a 30-minute wait at each border post as luggage is checked and documents are stamped (it's two more hours to Punta Arenas). Hire cars need a document for permission to cross the border. Some 30 km into Chile is **Kamiri Aike**, with a dock 16 km east at **Punta Delgada** for the 20-minute Magellan Strait ferry-crossing over the Primera Angostura (First Narrows) to **Bahía Azul**. At Punta Delgada is **Hostería El Faro** for food and drinks. Three boats work continuously, 0830-0100, US$25 per vehicle, foot passengers US$3, www.tabsa. cl. The road is paved to Cerro Sombrero, from where *ripio* (unsurfaced) roads run southeast to Chilean San Sebastián (130-140 km from ferry, depending on route taken). Chilean San Sebastián is just a few houses with **Hostería La Frontera** 500 m from the border. It's 15 km east, across the border (24 hours, 0800-2200 April to October), to Argentine San Sebastián, not much bigger, with a seven-room **ACA hostería ($$)**, T02964-425542; service station open 0700-2300. From here the road is paved to Río Grande (see below) and Ushuaia.

The other ferry crossing is **Punta Arenas-Porvenir**. RN255 from Kamiri Aike goes southwest 116 km to the intersection with the Punta Arenas-Puerto Natales road, from where it is 53 km to Punta Arenas. The ferry dock is 5 km north of Punta Arenas centre, at Tres Puentes. The ferry crosses to Bahía Chilota, 5 km west of Porvenir Tuesday to Sunday (subject to tides, **Transportadora Austral Broom**, www.tabsa.cl, publishes timetable a month in advance), 2½ hours, US$67 per vehicle, foot passengers US$10. From Porvenir a 234 km *ripio* road runs east to Río Grande (six hours, no public transport) via San Sebastián. **Note** Fruit and meat may not be taken onto the island, nor between Argentina and Chile. ▶▶ *See also Transport, page 224. For details of transport and hotels on Chilean territory, see the Chile chapter.*

Río Grande and around → *Phone code: 02964. Colour map 9, C2. Population: 67 000.*

Río Grande is a sprawling modern town in windy, dust-laden sheep-grazing and oil-bearing plains. (The oil is refined at San Sebastián in the smallest and most southerly refinery in the world.) Government tax incentives to companies in the 1970s led to a rapid growth in population. Although incentives were withdrawn, it continues to expand, most recently into mobile phone and white goods assembly. The city was founded by Fagnano's Salesian mission in 1893; you can visit the original building **La Candelaria** ① *11 km north, T421642, Mon-Sat 1000-1230, 1500-1900, US$2, afternoon teas, US$3, getting there: taxi US$8 with wait.* The museum has displays of indigenous artefacts and natural history. Río Grande's **Museo Virginia Choquintel** ① *Alberdi 555, T430647, Mon-Fri 0900-1700, Sat 1500-1900,* is also recommended for its history of the Selk'nam, the pioneers, missions and oil. Next door is a handicraft shop called **Kren** ("sun" in Selk'nam), which sells good local products. Nearby estancias can be visited, notably **María Behety** (15 km), with a vast sheep-shearing shed, but the area's main claim to fame is sport-fishing, especially for trout. **Local festivals**: Sheep shearing in January. Rural exhibition and handicrafts 2nd week February. Shepherd's day, with impressive sheepdog display first week March. **Tourist office** ① *Rosales 350, on the plaza, T431324, Mon-Fri 0900-1700.* **Provincial office** ① *Av Belgrano 319, T422887, infuerg1@tierradelfuego.org.ar.*

Tolhuin → *Colour map 9, C2.*

About 20 km south of Río Grande, trees begin to appear on the steppe while the road, Ruta 3, runs parallel to the seashore. On Sunday people drive out to the woods for picnics, go fishing or look for shellfish on the mudflats. The road is mostly very good as it approaches the mountains to the south. Tolhuin, "la corazón de la isla" at the eastern tip of Lago Fagnano, is 1¼ hours from Río Grande. The small town caters for horse riders, anglers, mountain bikers and trekkers. There are cabins, hostels and campsites. On Sunday it is crammed full of day-trippers. The **Panificadora La Unión** in the centre is renowned for its breads, pastries and chocolate and is an obligatory stop. Líder and Montiel minibuses break the Río Grande-Ushuaia journey here. **Tourist office** ① *Av de los Shelknam 80, T02901-492125, tolhuinturismo@tierradelfuego.org.ar.*

The road leaves Lago Fagnano and passes *lenga* forest destroyed by fire in 1978 before climbing into healthier forests. After small Lago Verde and fjord-like Lago Escondido, the road crosses the cordillera at Paso Garibaldi. It then descends to the Cerro Castor winter sports complex and the Tierra Mayor recreation area (see Ushuaia What to do, below). There is a police control just as you enter the Ushuaia city limits; passports may be checked.

◉ Río Grande and around listings

For hotel and restaurant price codes, and other relevant information, see Essentials.

● Where to stay

Río Grande *p222*
Book ahead, as there are few decent choices. Several estancias offer full board and some, mainly on the northern rivers, have expensive fishing lodges, others offer horse riding.
See www.tierradelfuego.org.ar for a full list.
$$$$ pp Estancia Viamonte, 40 km southeast on the coast, T430861, www.estanciaviamonte. com. For an authentic experience of Tierra del Fuego, built in 1902 by pioneer Lucas Bridges,

writer of *Uttermost Part of the Earth*, to protect the Selk'nam/Ona people, this working estancia has simple and beautifully furnished rooms in a spacious cottage. Price is for full board and all activities: riding and trekking; cheaper for dinner, bed and breakfast only. Delicious meals. Book a week ahead.
$$$ Posada de los Sauces, Elcano 839, T430868, www.laposadadelossauces. ar. Best by far, with breakfast, beautifully decorated, comfortable, good restaurant (trout recommended), cosy bar, very helpful staff.
$$$ Villa, Av San Martín 281, T424998, hotelvilla@live.com. Central, modern, restaurant/ confitería, parking, discount given for cash.

Tolhuin p223
$$$ Cabañas Khami, on Lago Fagnano, 8 km from Tolhuin, T156-11243, www.cabanias khami.com.ar. Well-equipped, rustic cabins, good value with linen. Price given for 6 people, 3-night weekend rates available.

🍴 Restaurants

Río Grande p222
$$ El Rincón de Julio, next to Posada de los Sauces, Elcano 800 block. For excellent *parrilla*.
$$ La Nueva Colonial, Av Belgrano 489. Delicious pasta, warm family atmosphere.

Cafés
El Roca (sic), Espora 643, ½ block from Plaza. Confitería and bar in historic premises (the original cinema), good and popular.
Tío Willy, Alberdi 279. Serves *cerveza artesanal* (micro brewery).

🚌 Transport

Río Grande p222
Air Airport 4 km west of town, T420600. Taxi US$3. To **Buenos Aires**, daily, 3½ hrs direct. LADE flies to **Río Gallegos**.

Bus To **Punta Arenas**, Chile, via Punta Delgada, 7-9 hrs, **Pacheco** (Finocchio 1194, T425611, daily except Sun) and **Tecni Austral** (Moyano 516, T430610), US$42. To **Río Gallegos**, Tecni Austral, Mon-Sat, 8 hrs; **Marga/Taqsa** (Mackinley 545, T434316), daily, 0815, US$55, connection to El Calafate and Comodoro Rivadavia. To **Ushuaia**, 3½-4 hrs, **Montiel** (25 de Mayo 712, T420997) and **Líder** (Perito Moreno 635, T420003, www.lidertdf. com.ar), US$25. Both use small buses, frequent departures. They stop en route at **Tolhuin**, US$15. Also **Tecni Austral**, about 1600 (bus has come from Punta Arenas), **Marga** and **Pacheco**, US$18-20.

ℹ️ Directory

Río Grande p222
Banks ATMs: several banks on San Martín by junction with Av 9 de Julio. **Link** ATM at YPF station at river end of Belgrano. **Thaler** cambio, Espora 631, Mon-Fri 1000-1500. **Consulates** Chile, Belgrano 369, T430523, Mon-Fri 0830-1330.

Ushuaia and around → *Phone code: 02901. Colour map 9, C2. Population: 57,000.*

Situated 212 km southwest of Río Grande, the most southerly town in Argentina and growing fast, Ushuaia is beautifully positioned on the northern shore of the Beagle Channel, named after the ship in which Darwin sailed here in 1832. Its streets climb steeply towards snow-covered Cerro Martial and there are fine views to neighbouring peaks and over the Beagle Channel to the jagged peaks of Isla Navarino (Chile). **Tourist offices** at the **Muelle Turístico** ① *T437666, 0800-1700 (daily, Oct-Mar, closed Apr-Sep, has free Wi-Fi and toilets)*; **San Martín** ① *674, esq Fadul, T424550, www.turismoushuaia.com; 1700-2100, daily, Oct-Mar, 0900-2000, Apr-Sep; helpful English-speaking staff, who find accommodation in summer; information available in English, French, Portuguese and German*. There is a tourist desk at the airport, open when there are flights arriving. **Oficina Antártica** ① *Laserre y Prefectura Naval, at entrance to port, T430015, antartida@tierradelfuego.org.ar, Mon-Fri 0900-1700, has information on Antarctica and a small library with navigational charts*. Ushuaia is the main centre for Antarctic trips with occasional good last-minute deals to be had (see What to do listings). **Provincial tourist office** ① *Maipú 505, T423423, info@tierradelfuego.org.ar*.

Best time to visit March to April is a good time because of the autumn colours and the most stable weather. November, spring, has the strongest winds (not good for sailing to Antarctica). Most visitors arrive in January. Summer temperatures average at about 15ºC, but exceed 20º more frequently than in the past. Likewise, there has been a reduction in snowfall in winter (average temperature 0ºC). Lots of Brazilians come to ski, so there is a mini high season in July-August. European skiers also come to train in the northern hemisphere summer.

Places in Ushuaia

First settled in 1884 by missionary Thomas Bridges, whose son Lucas became a great defender of the indigenous peoples here, Ushuaia's fascinating history is still visible in its old buildings and at **Estancia Harberton**, 85 km west (see below). A penal colony for many years, the old prison, **Presidio** ① *Yaganes y Gob Paz, at the back of the Naval Base, Mon-Sun 0900-2000, US$14 for foreigners, tours in Spanish 1130, 1630, 1730, English 1400,* houses the small **Museo Marítimo**, with models and artefacts from seafaring days, and, in the cells of most of the huge five wings, the **Museo Penitenciario**, which details the history of the prison and of the pioneers who came to the area. There are also temporary exhibitions, a shop and a café. Highly recommended. **Museo del Fin del Mundo** ① *Maipú y Rivadavia, T421863, Mon-Fri 1000-1900, Sat, Sun and bank holidays 1400-2000, US$9, guided tours 1100, 1400, 1700, fewer in winter.* In the 1912 bank building, it has small displays on indigenous peoples, missionaries and first settlers, as well as nearly all the birds of Tierra del Fuego (stuffed). Recommended. The building also contains an excellent library with helpful staff. On the same ticket is the **Antigua Casa de Gobierno** ① *Maipú 465, same hours,* with an exhibition on the history of the city and temporary exhibitions. **Museo Yámana** ① *Rivadavia 56, T422874, www.tierradelfuego.org.ar/mundoyamana, daily 0900-2000, US$7.50.* Scale models depicting the geological evolution of the Island and the everyday life of Yamana people, texts in English, also recommended. Also, recently opened, is the **Galería Temática** ① *San Martín 152, PB, 1er y 2do p, T422245, www.historiafueguina.com, Mon-Sat 1100-2100, Sun 1700-2100, US$10,* where numerous lifesized displays take you through an informative history of Tierra del Fuego with a useful audioguide in different languages. There is also a themed garden at the back, reached through a huge souvenir shop with good knitwear and other goods. **Local events**: first half of April, **Classical Music Festival** (www.festivaldeushuaia.com); winter solstice, the longest night with a torch-light procession and fireworks, 20-21 June; August, annual sled dog race and Marcha Blanca, a ski trek from Lago Escondido to Tierra Mayor valley (www.marchablanca.com).

Cerro Martial, about 7 km behind the town, offers fine views down the Beagle Channel and to the north. Take a chairlift (*aerosilla*), daily, year-round, first up 1000, last up 1615, last down 1730, US$10, tariffs change in winter, closed for repair for a time in April. To reach the chairlift, follow Magallanes out of town, allow 1½ hours. Several companies run minibus services from the corner of Maipú and Fadul, frequent departures daily in summer, US$4. Taxis charge US$7.50 9 to the base, from where you can walk down all the way back. There are several marked trails, leaflet given out at the lower platform, including to a viewpoint and to **Glaciar Martial** itself, from 600 m to 1 km. Possible to walk up ski slope to viewpoint, 1 hour. Splendid tea shop at the **Cumbres de Martial cabañas** at the base; basic *refugio* with no electricity up at the Cerro. Also by the lower platform is the **Canopy** ① *T02901-1551 0307, www.canopyushuaia.com.ar, US$35, US$25 for a shorter run, US$28 and US$20 under 12s,* a series of zip lines and bridges in the trees, eleven stretches in all. All visitors are accompanied by staff, safe, good fun. The café at the entrance, **Refugio de Montaña**, serves hot chocolate and coffee, cakes, pizzas and has a warm stove.

The **Estancia Harberton** ① *T422742, www.estanciaharberton.com, US$7.50, daily 1000-1900 15 Oct-15 Apr, except 25 Dec, 1 Jan and Easter,* the oldest on the island and run by descendants of British missionary, Thomas Bridges, whose family protected the indigenous peoples here, is 85 km from Ushuaia on Ruta J. It's a beautiful place, offering a wide variety of guided walks through protected forest. Also does delicious teas, US$6.60, or lunch, US$30 (reserve ahead), in the *Mánakatush casa de té* overlooking the bay. The impressive **Museo Acatushún**

① *www.acatushun.org*, has skeletons of South American sea mammals and birds, the result of 25 years' scientific investigation in Tierra del Fuego, with excellent tours in English. You can camp free, with permission from the owners, or stay in cottages. Access is from a good unpaved road which branches off Ruta 3, 40 km east of Ushuaia and runs 45 km through forest before the open country around Harberton; marvellous views, about two hours (no petrol outside of Ushuaia and Tolhuin). The road passes Laguna Victoria, where there is a good chance of seeing condors, and the turning to Puerto Almansa fishing port.

Short boat excursions from Ushuaia are highly recommended, though the Beagle Channel can be very rough. These can be booked through most agencies. They leave from the **Muelle Turístico**, where all operators have ticket booths and representatives (**Tolkeyen** and **Rumbo Sur** also have offices on San Martín). All passengers must pay US$1.25 port tax; this is not included in tickets. Operators offer slight variations on a basic theme of trips to Isla de los Lobos, Isla de los Pájaros, Les Eclaireurs lighthouse and Harberton. See under What to do below for details of these and of longer sea trips.

Tren del Fin del Mundo ① *T431600, www.trendelfindelmundo.com.ar, 4-5 departures daily, US$36.50 tourist, US$60 1st class return, US$82 premium and US$126 special, cheaper in winter, plus US$14 park entrance and cost of transport to the station, tickets at station, the port, or travel agencies, sit on left outbound for the best views*, is the world's southernmost steam train, running new locomotives and carriages on track first laid by prisoners to carry wood to Ushuaia. A totally touristy experience with commentary in English and Spanish (written material in other languages), 50-minute ride from the Fin del Mundo station, 8 km west of Ushuaia, into Tierra del Fuego National Park (one way of starting a hike). There is one stop at Estación Macarena, 15 minutes, for a view of the river and a walk up to Macarena waterfall. In 1st class you can buy food and drinks at the station *confitería* to eat at your table. At the same entrance as the train station is Ushuaia's nine-hole golf course.

Ushuaia

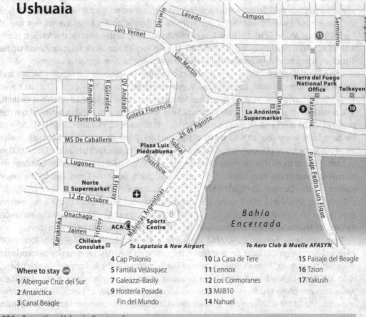

Where to stay ●
1 Albergue Cruz del Sur
2 Antarctica
3 Canal Beagle
4 Cap Polonio
5 Familia Velásquez
7 Galeazzi-Basily
9 Hostería Posada Fin del Mundo
10 La Casa de Tere
11 Lennox
12 Los Cormoranes
13 Mil810
14 Nahuel
15 Paisaje del Beagle
16 Tzion
17 Yakush

Parque Nacional Tierra del Fuego

ⓘ *US$14. Tierra del Fuego National Park Office, San Martín 1395, Ushuaia, T421315, tierradelfuego@ apn.gov.ar, Mon-Fri 0900-1600. Tourist office and National Park office have details and a map of park, with walks. For buses see Transport, page 233.*

Covering 63,000 ha of mountains, lakes, rivers and deep valleys, this small but beautiful park stretches west to the Chilean border and north to Lago Fagnano, though large areas are closed to tourists. Public access is allowed from the park entrance 12 km west of Ushuaia, where you'll be given the basic map with marked walks. **1) Senda Costera**, 8 km, three hours each way. Along the shore from Ensenada. From Lago Acigami (formerly known as Lago Roca), continue along to Río Lapataia, crossing the broad green river, where there are more short paths to follow. From Ensenada a boat goes to Isla Redonda, a provincial Reserva Natural, first at 1000, last back at 1700, US$52 return, US$65 to Isla Redonda and on to Lapataia. There are four trails on island, two hours, a refugio for sleeping, hot water, and a post office, open end-October to beginning of April. **2) Senda Hito XXIV**, along the northeast shore of Lago Acigami to the Chilean frontier, 3.5 km, 90 minutes one way, lots of birdlife. **3) Cerro Guanaco** (1106 m), 4 km, four hours one way. Challenging hike up through forest to splendid views. **4) Senda Pampa Alta**, 4.9 km via a *mirador* (look out), or 3.7 km via the road, to Río Pipo. The main campsite is in a good spot at Lago Acigami: see below for details of this and other sites. It's best to go in the early morning or afternoon to avoid the tour buses. You'll see geese, the torrent duck, Magellanic woodpeckers and austral parakeets. There are no legal crossing points to Chile. Helpful *guardaparque* (ranger) at Lago Acigami. Remember that the weather can be cold, damp and unpredictable, even in summer; winter days are short.

Restaurants 🍴
1 137 Pizzas & Pastas
2 Bodegón Fueguino
3 Café Bar Banana
5 Café Tante Sara
6 Chicho's
8 El Bambú
9 El Turco
10 Gadget Café
11 Kaupé
12 Laguna Negra
13 Martinica
14 Moustacchio
16 Parrilla La Rueda
17 Ramos Generales
18 Sandwichería Kami
7 Tante Sara
19 Tía Elvira
20 Volver

For hotel and restaurant price codes, and other relevant information, see Essentials.

● Where to stay

Ushuaia *p224, map p226*
The tourist office has a comprehensive list of all officially registered accommodation and will help with rooms in private homes, campsites, etc. An excellent choice is to stay with Ushuaia families on a B&B basis. The range of lodging is growing at all budget levels, from the very chic, to cabañas, to the basic B&B, in the centre and the suburbs. There are too many to list here. Despite the expansion, you must book in advance in high season.

Cabañas and places outside town
The following all are recommended.
$$$$ Cabañas del Beagle, Las Aljabas 375, T432785, www.cabanasdelbeagle.com. 3 rustic-style cabins 1.3 km above the city, fully equipped with kitchen, hydromassage, fireplace, heating, phone, self-service breakfast, very comfortable, personal attention.
$$$$ Cumbres del Martial, Luis F Martial 3560, 7 km from town, T424779, www.cumbres delmartial.com.ar. At the foot of the *aerosilla* to Glaciar Martial, 4 *cabañas* and 6 rooms, beautifully set in the woods, charming, very comfortable, cabins have whirlpool baths. Small spa (massage extra) with saunas and gym. The tearoom, with disabled access, is open all year, restaurant with traditional fondues.
$$$$ Finisterris Lodge Relax, Monte Susana, Ladera Este, 7 km from city, T156 12121, www. finisterrislodge.com. In 17 ha of forest, 5-star luxury in individual cabins, with top-of-the-range fittings, hydromassage and private spa (massage arranged, extra), rustic style but spacious, 'home-from-home' atmosphere, 24-hr attention from owner, given mobile phone on arrival. Meals can be ordered in, or private chef and sommelier can be booked for you.
$$$$ Las Hayas, Luis Martial 1650 (road to Glaciar Martial), T430710, www.lashayashotel. com. 4 standards of room, all very good with TV, safe, 3 types of view, channel, mountains or forest. 2 restaurants: **Martial** for lunch and dinner, **Drake** for breakfast. Everything is included in room price except massages and hairdresser. A fine hotel. Just beyond is the same family company's
$$$$ Los Acebos, Luis F Martial 1911, T442200, www.losacebos.com.ar. All rooms with channel view, safe, games room, **Rêve d'Orange** restaurant independent of hotel. Golf days organized.Very comfy, as expected, but less characterful than Las Hayas.
$$$$ Los Cauquenes, at Bahía Cauquen, De La Ermita 3462, T441300, www.loscauquenes. com. High-quality 5-star hotel overlooking Beagle Channel, price varies according to size and view, spa, very tastefully decorated, prize-winning restaurant, regional food on dinner menu, wine bar with over 100 Argentine wines.
$$$$ Los Yámanas, Costa de los Yámanas 2850, western suburbs, T446809, www.hotel yamanas.com.ar. In the same group as Canoero tour operator, all rooms with Channel view, spacious, well-decorated, hydromassage, fitness centre, spa and conference centre outside in wooded grounds, shuttle to town. Very pleasant.
$$$$ Tierra de Leyendas, Tierra de Vientos 2448, T446565, www.tierradeleyendas.com. ar. In the western suburbs. 5 very comfortable rooms with views of the Beagle Channel, or the mountains at the back, 1 room with jacuzzi, all others with shower, excellent restaurant serving regional specialties, open only for guests for breakfast and dinner. No cable TV, but DVDs, living room with games, library, deck overlooking Río Pipo's outflow. Only for non smokers. Recommended and award-winning.
$$$ pp Estancia Harberton, T422742, www.estanciaharberton.com. Mid-Oct to mid-Apr. 2 restored buildings on the estancia (see above), very simple rooms, wonderful views, heating. Price includes walking tour and entry to museum; 2 rooms with bath, 1 room with 2 beds, shared bath, 1 room with bunks, shared bath. Kitchenette for tea and coffee. Lunch and dinner extra. No credit cards.

In town

$$$$ Canal Beagle, Maipú y 25 de Mayo, T432303, www.hotelcanalbeagle.com.ar. ACA hotel (discounts for members), **$$$** Apr-Oct, comfortable and well-attended, with a small pool, gym, spa, business centre, some rooms with channel views (others overlook the container dock), good restaurant.

$$$$ Cap Polonio, San Martín 746, T422140, www.hotelcappolonio.com.ar. Smart, central, modern, comfortable, popular restaurant/café **Marcopolo**.

$$$$ Lennox, San Martín 776, T436430, www.lennoxhotels.com. Boutique hotel on the main street, with breakfast, services include hydromassage, minibar, restaurant and confitería on 4th floor. Laundry service.

$$$$ Mil810, 25 de Mayo 245, T437714, www.hotel1810.com. City hotel with 30 standard rooms, 1 with disabled access, no restaurant but breakfast and *confitería*, all rooms with minibar, safe, quite small but cosy, calm colours, good views, business centre and multiple use room where you can hang out while waiting for flight.

$$$ Galeazzi-Basily, Gob Valdez 323, T423213, www.avesdelsur.com.ar. Among the best, beautiful family home, incredible welcome, in pleasant area 5 blocks from centre, 4 rooms with shared bath. Also excellent *cabañas* in the garden. Highly recommended.

$$$ Hostería Posada Fin del Mundo, Rivadavia 610, T437345, www.posadafin delmundo.com.ar. Family atmosphere, comfortable rooms, good value, has character.

$$$ Paisaje del Beagle, Gob Paz 1347, T421214, www.paisajedelbeagle.com.ar. Family-run, quiet, with a cosy dining area for good breakfast, laundry service. Recommended.

$$$ Tzion, Gob Valdez 468, T432290, tzion_byb@hotmail.com. B&B with 3 rooms, 1 with bath, high above town, 10 mins' walk from centre, nice family atmosphere, cheaper low season, laundry service, English and French spoken. Great views, highly recommended.

$$ pp La Casa de Tere, Rivadavia 620, T422312, www.lacasadetere.com.ar. Shared or private bath, use of kitchen facilities, freshly baked bread, open fire, singles, doubles and triples, hot water, helpful owner.

$$ Nahuel, 25 de Mayo 440, T423068, www. bybnahuel.com.ar. Charming Sra Navarrete has a comfortable B&B with channel views from the upper rooms and the terrace, good value, but noisy street.

$$-$ Familia Velásquez, Juana Fadul 361, T421719, losnokis_figueroa@hotmail.com. Cosy, welcoming house of a pioneer, with basic rooms, breakfast, cooking and laundry facilities, good.

$ pp Albergue Cruz del Sur, Deloqui 242, T434099, xdelsur@yahoo.com. Cosy, free tea, coffee and mate, book in advance.

$ pp Antártica, Antártida Argentina 270, T435774, www.antarcticahostel.com. Central, welcoming, spacious chill-out room, excellent 24-hr bar, dorms for 6 and large doubles, breakfast included, game night Thu with good prizes. Recommended.

$ pp Los Cormoranes, Kamshén 788 y Alem, T423459, www.loscormoranes.com. Large hostel, with good views, cosy rooms, with lockers, OK bathrooms. Doubles (**$$**) available. They can book tours. HI member discount.

$ pp Yakush, Piedrabuena 118 y San Martín, T435807, www.hostelyakush.com.ar. Very well-run, central with spacious dorms, also doubles (**$$**, cheaper without bath), book exchange and library, dining room, steep garden with views. In-house tour op organizes excursions.

Camping La Pista del Andino, Leandro N Alem 2873, T435890. Set in the Club Andino ski premises in a woodland area, it has wonderful views over the channel. Electricity, hot showers, tea room and grocery store, very helpful. Recommended.

Parque Nacional Tierra del Fuego *p227*
Camping

Camping Lago Roca, T433313, 21 km from Ushuaia, by forested shore of Lago Acigami (Roca), a beautiful site with good facilities, reached by bus Jan-Feb. It has a backpackers' *refugio*, toilets, showers, restaurant and confitería, expensive small shop; camping equipment for hire with deposit. There are also campsites with facilities at **Río Pipo** 16 km from Ushuaia and at **Laguna Verde**, 20 km, near Lapataia, and **Bahía Ensenada** with no facilities.

❶ Restaurants

Ushuaia *p224, map p226*
Lots of restaurants along San Martín and Maipú. Be aware that most open 1200-1500 and again from 1900 at the earliest. Several cafés are open all the time. Ask around for currently available seafood, especially *centolla* (king crab) and *cholga* (giant mussels). Much cheaper if prepare your own meal. **Note** *centolla* may not be fished Nov-Dec. Beer drinkers should try the handcrafted brews of the **Cape Horn** brewery, Pilsen, Pale Ale and Stout.

$$$ Bodegón Fueguino, San Martín 859. Open 1230-1500, 2000-2400, closed Mon. Snacks, homemade pastas and good roast lamb with varied sauces in a renovated 1896 *casa de pioneros*.
$$$ Tía Elvira, Maipú 349. Mon-Sat 1200-1500, 1900-2300. Excellent seafood.
$$$ Volver, Maipú 37. Delicious seafood and fish in atmospheric 1896 house, with ancient newspaper all over the walls. Recommended.
$$$-$$ Moustacchio, San Martín 298. Long established, good for seafood and meat, all-you-can-eat branch US$13.
$$$-$$ Parrilla La Rueda, San Martín y Rivadavia. Good *tenedor libre* (US$24 with dessert) for beef, lamb and great salads. Recommended for freshness.
$$ 137 Pizzas and Pastas, San Martín 137. Tasty filling versions of exactly what the name says, plus excellent *empanadas*, elegant decor.
$$ Chicho's, Rivadavia 72, T423469. Bright, cheerful place just off the main street, friendly staff, kitchen open to view. Fish, meat and chicken dishes, pastas, wide range of *entradas*.
$$ El Turco, San Martín 1410. A very popular place, serving generous milanesas, pastas, pizzas, seafood and meat. Very tasty *empanadas*.
$$-$ Martinica, San Martín entre Antártida Argentina y Yaganes. Cheap, small, busy, sit at the bar facing the *parrilla* and point to your favourite beef cut. Takeaway (T432134) and good meals of the day, also pizzas and *empanadas*.

Cafés
Café Bar Banana, San Martín 273, T424021. Quite small, always busy, pool table, offers good fast food, such as burgers, small pizzas, puddings, breakfasts and an all-day *menú* for US$7.50.
Café Tante Sara, San Martin 701. Opposite the tourist office, is very good, smart, good coffee, tasty sandwiches, always busy. Also has restaurant and *panadería* at San Martín 175, selling breads, sandwiches, chocolates, *empanadas* and snacks, coffee, lots of choice.
El Bambú, Piedrabuena 276. Open 1100-1700. One of few purely vegetarian places in town, take-away only, homemade food, delicious and good value.
Gadget Café, Av San Martín 1256, www. gadgettugelateria.com.ar. The best ice cream parlour in town, multiple flavours, friendly. Recommended.
Laguna Negra, San Martín 513. Mainly a shop selling chocolate and other fine produce, catering to the cruise ship passengers, but has a good little café at the back for hot chocolate and coffee. Also has a bigger branch at Libertador 1250, El Calafate. Sells postcards and stamps, too.
Ramos Generales, Maipú 749, T424317. Daily 0900-2400 in high season. An old warehouse, with wooden floor and a collection of historic objects. Sells breads, pastries, wines and drinks, also cold cuts, sandwiches, salads, ice cream, Argentine mate and coffee. Not cheap but atmospheric. Recommended.
Sandwichería Kami, San Martín 54. Open 0800-2100. Friendly, simple sandwich shop, selling rolls, baguettes and *pan de miga*.

❍ Shopping

Ushuaia *p224, map p226*
Ushuaia's tax free status doesn't produce as many bargains as you might hope. Lots of souvenir shops on San Martín and several offering good quality leather and silver ware. In comparison, the **Pasaje de Artesanías**, by the Muelle Turístico, sells local arts and crafts.
Atlántico Sur, San Martín 627, is the (not especially cheap) duty free shop. **Boutique**

del Libro, San Martín 1120, T424750, www.
boutiquedellibro.com.ar. Mon-Sat 1000-1300
and 1530-2030 year-round. Has an excellent
selection of books, including several in English
and other languages on Tierra del Fuego. CDs
and DVDs upstairs. (Branches throughout
Argentina, see website for details)

❍ What to do

Ushuaia p224, map p226
Boat trips and cruises
All short boat trips leave from the Muelle
Turístico. Take your time to choose the size
and style of boat you want. Representatives
from the offices are polite and helpful. All
have a morning and afternoon sailing and
include Isla de los Lobos, Isla de los Pájaros
and Les Eclaireurs lighthouse, with guides and
some form of refreshment. Note that weather
conditions may affect sailings, prices can
change and that port tax is not included.
Canoero, T433893, www.catamaranescanoero.
com.ar. Catamarans for 130 passengers
(Ushuaia's biggest fleet), 2½- to 3-hr trips to the
3 main sites and Isla Bridges, US$54. They also
have a 4½-hr trip almost daily to the Pingüinera
on Isla Martillo near Estancia Harberton (Oct-
Mar only), boats stay for 1 hr, but you cannot
land on Martillo, US$80 (US$90 including
Harberton – entry extra). Also longer tours
to Estancia Harberton and Lapataia Bay.
Patagonia Adventure Explorer, T15-465842,
www.patagoniaadvent.com.ar. Has a sailing
boat and motor boats for the standard trip, plus
Isla Bridges: US$60 sailing boat. Good guides.
Pira-Tour, T435557, www.piratour.com.ar
and www.piratour.net. Runs 2-3 buses a day
to Harberton, from where a boat goes to the
Pingüinera on Isla Martillo: 15 people allowed
to land (maximum 45 per day – the only
company licensed to do this). US$110 with
entrance to Harberton.
Tres Marías, T436416, www.tresmariasweb.
com. The only company licensed to visit Isla H,
which has archaeological sites, cormorants,
other birds and plants. Departures 1000 and
1500, 4 hrs. Also has sailing boat, no more than

10 passengers; specialist guide, café on board,
US$60 on Tres Marías, US$80 on sailing boat.
Highly recommended.
Also **Rumbo Sur** and **Tolkeyen**; see Tour
operators, below.

Sea trips
Ushuaia is the starting point, or the last stop,
en route to Antarctica for several cruises from
Oct-Mar that usually sail for 9 to 21 days along
the western shores of the Antarctic peninsula
and the South Shetland Islands. Other trips
include stops at Falkland/Malvinas archipelago
and at South Georgia. Go to Oficina Antártica
for advice (see page 224). Agencies sell
'last minute tickets', but the price is entirely
dependent on demand. Coordinator for trips
is **Turismo Ushuaia**, Gob Paz 865, T436003,
www.ushuaiaturismoevt.com.ar, which
operates with IAATO members only. See the
website for prices for the upcoming season.
Port tax is US$15 per passenger and an exit
tax of US$10 is also charged.
Freestyle Adventure Travel, Gob Paz 866, T15-
609792, www.freestyleadventuretravel.com.
Organizes trips to Antarctica, particularly good
for last-minute deals. 7- to 22-day cruises, wide
variety of itineraries. Cape Horn expeditions
also available.
Polar Latitudes, sales@polar-latitudes.com,
www.polar-latitudes.com Antarctic cruises
aboard small expedition vessels, some itineraries
take in the Falklands/Malvinas and South
Georgia All-suite accommodation onboard.
To Chile Australis Expedition Cruises,
www.australis.com, operates 2 luxury cruise
ships between Ushuaia and **Punta Arenas**,
with a visit to Cape Horn, highly recommended.
Full details are given under Punta Arenas, Tour
operators. Check-in at Comapa (see below).
Fernández Campbell have a 1½-hr crossing
to **Puerto Williams**, Fri, Sat, Sun 1000, return
1500, US$125 for foreigners, tickets sold at
Zenit Explorer, Juana Fadul 126, Ushuaia,
T433232, and Naviera RFC in Puerto Williams.
Ushuaia Boating, Gob Paz 233, T436193 (or
at the Muelle Turístico), www.ushuaiaboating.
com.ar. Operates all year round a channel

crossing to Puerto Navarino (Isla Navarino), 30-90 mins depending on weather, and then bus to Puerto Williams, 1 hr, US$120 one way, not including taxes. At **Muelle AFASYN**, near the old airport, T435805, ask about possible crossings with a club member to Puerto Williams, about 4 hrs, or if any foreign sailing boat is going to Cabo de Hornos or Antarctica. From Puerto Williams a ferry goes once a week to Punta Arenas.

Fishing

Trout season is Nov to mid-Apr, licences US$21 per day (an extra fee is charged for some rivers and lakes). **Asociación de Caza y Pesca** at Maipú 822, T423168, cazaypescaushuaia@ speedy.com.ar.com.ar, Mon-Fri 1600-2000, sells licences, with list on door of other places that sell it.

Hiking and climbing

Club Andino, Fadul 50, T422335. For advice, Mon-Fri 0930-1230, 1600-2000. Sells maps and trekking guidebooks; free guided walks once in a month in summer; also offers classes, eg yoga, dancing, karate-do and has excercise bikes. The winter sports resorts along Ruta 3 (see below) are an excellent base for summer trekking and many arrange excursions.
Nunatak, 25 de Mayo 296, T430329, www. antartur.com.ar. Organizes treks, canoeing, mountain biking and 4WD trips to Lagos Escondido and Fagnano. Good winter excursions.

Horse riding

Centro Hípico, Ruta 3, Km 3021, T155 69099, www.horseridingtierradelfuego.com. Rides through woods, on Monte Susana, along coast and through river, 2 hrs, US$40; 4-hr ride with light lunch, US$80; 7-hr ride with asado, US$105. Gentle horses, well-cared for, all guides have first-aid training. Very friendly and helpful. All rides include transfer from town and insurance. Hats provided for children; works with handicapped children. They can arrange long-distance rides of several days, eg on Península Mitre.

Winter sports

Ushuaia is becoming popular as a winter resort with 11 centres for skiing, snowboarding and husky sledging. The **Cerro Castor** complex, Ruta 3, Km 26, T499301, www.cerrocastor.com, is the only centre for Alpine skiing, with 24 km of pistes, a vertical drop of 800 m and powder snow. Attractive centre with complete equipment rental, also for snowboarding and snowshoeing. The other centres along Ruta 3 at 18-36 km east of Ushuaia offer excellent cross country skiing (and alternative activities in summer). **Tierra Mayor**, 20 km from town, T437454, the largest and most recommended, lies in a beautiful wide valley between steep-sided mountains. It offers half and full day excursions on sledges with huskies, as well as cross country skiing and snowshoeing. Equipment hire and restaurant. **Kawi Shiken** at Las Cotorras, Ruta 3, Km 26, T444152, 155 19497, www.tierradelfuego.org.ar/hugoflores, specializes in sled dogs, with 100 Alaskan and Siberian huskies, with winter rides on snow and summer rides in a dog cart.

Tours operators

Lots of companies offer imaginative adventure tourism expeditions. All agencies charge the same fees for excursions; ask tourist office for a complete list: Tierra del Fuego National Park, 4 hrs, US$50 (entry fee US$14 extra, entrance fee valid for 48 hrs); Lagos Escondido and Fagnano, 7 hrs, US$70 without lunch. With 3 or 4 people it might be worth hiring a remise taxi.
All Patagonia, Juana Fadul 58, T433622, www. allpatagonia.com. Trekking, ice climbing, and tours; trips to Cabo de Hornos and Antarctica.
Canal, Roca 136, T435777 www.canalfun.com. Huge range of activities, trekking, canoeing, riding, 4WD excursions. Recommended.
Comapa, San Martín 409, T430727, www. comapa.tur.ar. Conventional tours and adventure tourism, bus tickets to Punta Arenas and Puerto Natales, trips to Antarctica, agents for **Australis Expedition Cruises**. Recommended.
Compañía de Guías de Patagonia, San Martín 628, T437753, www.companiadeguias. com.ar. The best agency for walking guides,

expeditions for all levels, rock and ice climbing (training provided), also diving, sailing, riding, 7-day crossing of Tierra del Fuego on foot and conventional tours. Recommended.

Rumbo Sur, San Martín 350, T421139, www.rumbosur.com.ar. Flights, buses, conventional tours on land and sea, including to Harberton, plus Antarctic expeditions, mid-Nov to mid-Mar, English spoken.

Tolkar, Roca 157, T431412, www.tolkarturismo.com.ar. Flights, bus tickets to Argentina and Punta Arenas/Puerto Natales, conventional and adventure tourism, canoeing and mountain biking to Lago Fagnano.

Tolkeyen, San Martín 1267, T437073, www.tolkeyenpatagonia.com. Bus and flight tickets, catamaran trips (50-300 passengers), including to Harberton (Tue, Thu, Sat-Sun, US$94) and Parque Nacional, large company.

Travel Lab, San Martín 1444, T436555, www.travellab.com.ar. Conventional and unconventional tours, mountain biking, trekking etc, English and French spoken, helpful

⊝ Transport

Ushuaia *p224, map p226*

Air Airport 4 km from town T431232. Book ahead in summer; flights fill up fast. In winter flights often delayed. Taxi to airport US$5-7 (no bus). Schedules tend to change from season to season. Airport tourist information only at flight times, T423970. To **Buenos Aires** (Aeroparque or Ezeiza), 3½ hrs, **El Calafate**, 1 hr, and **Río Gallegos**, 1 hr; also to **Río Grande**, 1 hr, several a week (but check with agents). In summer LAN flies to **Punta Arenas** twice a week. The **Aeroclub de Ushuaia** flies to **Puerto Williams** and organizes flight tours of Tierra del Fuego from the downtown airport, www.aeroclubushuaia.com.

Bus Urban buses from west to east across town, most stops along Maipú, US$0.50. Tourist office provides a list of minibus companies that run daily from town (stops along Maipú) to nearby attractions. To the **national park**:

in summer buses and minibuses leave from the bus stop on Maipú at the bottom of Fadul. **Transporte Lautaro** and **Transporte Santa Lucía**, 3 a day each (hourly from 0900), last return 1900, US$19 return (US$12.50 one way). From same bus stop, many other colectivos go to the *Tren del Fin del Mundo* (0900 and 1400, return 1200, 1700 and 1745), Lago Escondido, Lago Fagnano (1000 and 1100, return 1400 and 2200) and Glaciar Martial (1000 and 1200, return 1400 and 1600). For **Harberton**, check the notice boards at the station at Maipú y Fadul. The only regular bus is run by Pira-Tur, see What to do, above.

Passport needed when booking international bus tickets. Buses always booked up Nov-Mar; buy your ticket to leave as soon as you arrive. To **Río Grande**, 3½-4 hrs, combis **Líder** (Gob Paz 921, T436421), and **Montiel** (Gob Paz 605, T421366), US$25. Also buses en route to Río Gallegos and Punta Arenas.

To **Río Gallegos**, Tecni Austral, 0500, 13 hrs, US$72 (through Tolkar), and **Marga/Taqsa**, Gob Godoy 41, daily at 0500. To **Punta Arenas**, US$68-81, Tecni Austral, Mon, Wed, Fri, 0500, 11-12 hrs (through Tolkar); Pacheco, 0700 Mon, Wed, Fri, 12-13 hrs (through Tolkeyen, San Martín 1267, T437073), **Bus Sur** (at Comapa) Tue, Thu, Sat, Sun 0800; Bus Sur also goes to **Puerto Natales**, US$70, Tue, Sat 0800.

Car hire Most companies charge minimum US$60-70 per day, including insurance and 200 km per day, special promotions available. Localiza, Sarmiento 81, T437780, www.localizadietrich.com. Cars can be hired in Ushuaia to be driven through Chile and then left in any Localiza office in Argentina, but you must buy a one-off customs document for US$50, to use as many times as you like to cross borders. Must reserve well in advance and pay a drop-off fee. **Budget**, Godoy 49, T437373.

Taxi Cheaper than remises, T422007, T422400. Taxi stand by the Muelle Turístico. **Remises Carlitos y Bahía Hermosa**, San Martín y Rosas, T422222.

ⓘ Directory

Ushuaia *p224, map p226*

Banks Banks open 1000-1500 in summer. ATMs are plentiful all along San Martín, using credit cards is easiest (but Sat, Sun and holidays machines can be empty). **Agencia de Cambio Thaler**, San Martín 209, T421911, www.cambio-thaler.com, Mon-Fri 1000-1500, in high season Mon-Sat 1000-2000. **Consulates** Chile, Jainén 50, T430909, Mon-Fri 0900-1300.

Useful addresses Dirección Nacional de Migraciones, Fuegia Basket 187, T422334. Biblioteca Popular Sarmiento, San Martín 1589, T423103. Mon-Fri 1000-2000, library with a good range of books about the area.

Contents

Footprint features

At a glance

⊛ **Time required** 2-4 weeks, but don't try to do too much; distances are long and land transport is slow.

☀ **Best time** Altiplano: all year is good, Jun and Jul are clearest and coldest at night, and busiest. Feb-Apr are good for festivals, but this is wet season. Alasitas in La Paz in late Jan should not be missed. For climbing May-Sep.

✖ **When not to go** Nov-Mar is the rainy season, heaviest in lowlands but check road conditions everywhere at this time of year.

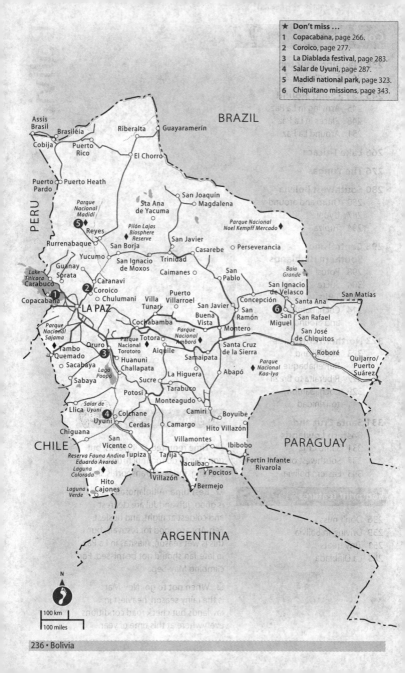

★ Don't miss ...
1 Copacabana, page 266.
2 Coroico, page 277.
3 La Diablada festival, page 283.
4 Salar de Uyuni, page 287.
5 Madidi national park, page 323.
6 Chiquitano missions, page 343.

BRAZIL

Assis
Brasuco
Brasiléia
Cobija
Puerto
Rico
Riberalta
Guayaramerín
Puerto
Pardo
Puerto Heath
El Chorro

PERU

Parque
Nacional
Madidi
Reyes
San Joaquín
Sta Ana
de Yacuma
Magdalena
Pilón Lajas
Biosphere
Reserve
Parque Nacional
Noel Kempff Mercado
Rurrenabaque
San Borja
San Javier
Casarebe
Perseverancia
Yucumo
San Ignacio
de Moxos
Trinidad
Guanay
Lake
Titicaca
Sorata
Caranavi
Caimanes
San
Pablo
Baia
Grande
Carabuco
Coroico
Villa
Tunari
Puerto
Villarroel
San Ignacio
de Velasco
Santa Ana
San Matías
Copacabana
Chulumani
San Javier
Concepción
LA PAZ
Cochabamba
Buena
Vista
San
Ramón
San Rafael
Parque
Nacional
Sajama
Parque Totora
Nacional
Torotoro
Parque
Nacional
Amboró
Montero
San
Miguel
San José
de Chiquitos
Tambo
Quemado
Oruro
Aiquile
Samaipata
Santa Cruz
de la Sierra
Roboré
Sacaba
Huanuni
Challapata
La Higuera
Abapó
Parque
Nacional
Kaa-Iya
Quijarro/
Puerto
Suárez
Sabaya
Lago
Poopó
Sucre
Tarabuco
Potosí
Monteagudo
Camiri
Boyuibe
Llica
Salar de
Uyuni
Colchane
Cerdas
Camargo
Hito Villazón
Chiguana
Uyuni
Villamontes
Ibibobo
PARAGUAY
Reserva Fauna Andina
Eduardo Avaroa
San
Vicente
Tupiza
Tarija
Yacuiba
Fortín Infante
Rivarola
Laguna
Colorada
Villazón
Pocitos
Laguna
Verde
Hito
Cajones
Bermejo

CHILE

ARGENTINA

N

100 km
100 miles

On Bolivia's Altiplano you are so far up it will make your head spin. Every day in La Paz, one of the highest seats of government in the world transforms itself from a melée of indigenous markets and modern business into a canyon of glittering stars as the lights come on at nightfall.

Bolivia has some of the most bio-diverse conservation areas in South America: Amboró, Kaa-Iya (the continent's largest), Madidi and Noel Kempff Mercado, all with an incredible range of habitats and variety of flora and fauna. If you fancy a trek, there are adventurous trails within a day of the capital, while anyone nostalgic for the revolutionary days of the 1960s can follow the Che Guevara Trail. For an exhilarating bike ride, head for Coroico, where in less than an hour you can go from mountain heights to the lush Yungas valleys, through waterfalls and round hairpin bends – but do go with an expert.

In Bolivia you learn to expect the unexpected. On the largest salt flat on earth, a vast blinding-white expanse, you lose track of what is land and what is sky. At Carnaval in Oruro, dancers wear masks of the scariest monsters you could ever dream of. To visit the mines at Potosí, once the silver lode for the Spanish Empire, you should buy coca leaves and other gifts for the miners. In the surreal Reserva Nacional de Fauna Andina Eduardo Avaroa, volcanoes overlook lakes of blue, white, green and red, where flamingos feed, and Dalí-esque rock structures dot the Altiplano. In the Bolivian Amazon you can swim with pink river dolphins or fish for piranhas.

Before you go home, you can fill your bags with everything from the beautiful autumnal colours of the textiles, to packs of dried llama foetuses. The latter are said to protect homes from evil spirits but are unlikely to ingratiate you with most customs and agriculture officers.

Planning your trip

Where to go in Bolivia

La Paz is a good place to start, as many international flights land here and it is closest to the well-travelled overland routes from Peru and Chile. The city is easy to explore, but you do need time to adjust to the altitude. This is, after all, one of the highest seats of government in the world (Sucre, not La Paz, is Bolivia's official capital). There are some good museums and churches in La Paz, and many indigenous market areas. Daytrips include the pre-Inca city of **Tiwanaku**, which is close to beautiful **Lake Titicaca**, where a night or more on its shores is recommended. Northeast of La Paz, over the cordillera, are the **Yungas**, subtropical valleys rich in vegetation, where a town like **Coroico** can provide welcome relief from the chill of the Altiplano. Equally pleasant and also lower than La Paz is **Sorata**, a good base for climbing, trekking and biking.

South of La Paz is the mining city of **Oruro**, which hosts famous carnival celebrations, including the **Diablada** devil-dance, usually held in mid- to late February. Southeast are the colonial cities of **Potosí**, where Spain garnered much of its imperial wealth from abundant silver deposits and present-day miners scour the mountain for meagre pickings; and **Sucre**, one of Bolivia's finest colonial cities and a centre for language study and volunteering. **Uyuni** and **Tupiza**, further south again, are the jumping-off places for trips to high-altitude puna with salt flats, coloured lakes, flamingos and volcanoes. **Tarija**, southeast of Potosí, is best known for its fruits and wine, and delightful climate.

East of La Paz is **Cochabamba**, Bolivia's fourth largest city and centre of one of the country's main agricultural zones. Reached from Cochabamba, **Parque Nacional Torotoro** (in Potosí department), with its dinosaur tracks, rock paintings, canyons and waterfalls, is a tough but excellent excursion. Further east is **Santa Cruz de la Sierra**, Bolivia's largest city, from where you can visit **Amboró**, **Noel Kempff Mercado** and other unique national parks, as well as follow in the footsteps of Che Guevara. Also reached from Santa Cruz, **Samaipata** is a particularly pleasant resort town with an important archaeological site. In the far east of the country, don't miss the fabulous **Jesuit missions** of Chiquitania, or the lovely **Reserva Valle de Tucavaca** along the road and railway to Brazil.

From La Paz you can fly or ride (when roads are passable) into the Beni region, in the heart of the Bolivian Amazon. **Rurrenabaque** is the chief destination and starting point for **Parque Nacional Madidi**, which claims a greater bio-diversity than anywhere else on earth. Outside of Rurrenabaque, the further north you go the fewer tourists you will meet. The dry season (May to September) is the best time to visit.

National parks Administered by the **Servicio Nacional de Areas Protegidas (SERNAP)** ⓘ *Francisco Bedregal 2904 y Victor Sanjinés, Sopocachi, T02-242 6268/6272, www.sernap.gob.bo*, an administrative office with limited tourist information. Better are Sernap's regional offices, addresses given in the travelling text. Involved NGOs include: **Fundación para el Desarrollo del Sistema Nacional de Areas Protegidas** ⓘ *Prolongación Cordero 127, across from US Embassy, La Paz, T02-211 3364/243 1875, www.fundesnap.org*; **Fundación Amigos de la Naturaleza (FAN)** ⓘ *Km 7.5 Vía a La Guadria, Santa Cruz, T03-355 6800, www.fan-bo.org*; **Probioma** ⓘ *Calle 7 Este 29, Equipetrol, Santa Cruz, T03-343 1332, www.probioma.org.bo*. See also www.biobol.org, a portal with information on Bolivia's protected areas, and the World Conservation Society's site with information on the Gran Chaco and on northwestern Bolivia, www.wcs.org/international/latinamerica/amazon_andes. See also Ramsar's site, www.ramsar.org, for protected wetlands, including the Llanos de Moxos (Ríos Blanco, Matos and Yata), at 6.9 million ha the largest protected wetland in the world.

Driving in Bolivia

Road A relatively small (but growing) percentage of Bolivian roads are paved, the rest are gravel-surfaced or earth. Any road, whatever its surface, may be closed in the rainy season (December-March). Road tolls vary from US$0.50 to US$2.10 for journeys up to 100 km. On toll roads you are given a receipt at the first toll; keep it at hand as it is asked for at subsequent toll posts. The **Administradora Boliviana de Carreteras** (ABC, Av Mcal Santa Cruz, Edif Centro de Comunicaciones p 8, T237 5000) maintains a useful website, www.abc.gob.bo, with daily updates of road conditions, including any roadblocks due to social unrest. ABC also has a toll-free phone for emergencies and to report road hazards, T800 107222.

Safety Always carry spare petrol/gas and supplies and camping equipment if going off major roads. Your car must be able to cope with high altitude and below-freezing temperatures. Take great care on the roads, especially at night. Too many truck drivers are drunk and many vehicles drive with faulty headlights. Stalled trucks without lights are a common cause of accidents.

Documents To bring a private vehicle into Bolivia you need an International Driving Permit, the vehicle's registration document (in your name or with a notarized letter of authorization from the owner) and your passport. On entry you get temporary admission from customs (free of charge) and surrender the document on departure; maximum 90 days. A *carnet de passages en douane* is not required, but insurance is compulsory. It is called **SOAT** and can be bought locally. Generally the police are helpful to foreign motorists, but stop you often and ask to see your documents, a complete first aid kit, triangle and fire extinguisher.

Organizations **Automóvil Club Boliviano**, Av 6 de Agosto 2993 y Arce, La Paz, T279 1755.

Car hire The minimum age for hiring a car is 25. Rental companies may only require your licence from home, but police ask to see an international licence. Rental of a small car costs about US$350 per week; a 4WD vehicle US$600 per week or more.

Fuel *Especial*, 85 octane containing lead, US$0.54 per litre (may cost more in remote areas). Diesel costs about the same. Higher octane *premium*, US$0.84 per litre, is only available in La Paz, if at all. There may be fuel shortages, especially in border areas, so keep your tank full. **Note** There are restrictions on which vehicles may drive in La Paz, depending on license plate number and day of the week.

Best time to visit Bolivia

The dry season is May to September, July and August see the most tourists, while some of the best festivals, eg Carnaval and Holy Week, fall during the wet season – generally December to March. The country has four climatic zones: (1) The Puna and Altiplano; average temperature, 10°C, but above 4000 m may drop as low as -30°C at night from June to August. By day, the tropical sun raises temperatures to above 20°C. Rainfall on the northern Altiplano is 400-700 mm, much less further south. Little rain falls upon the western plateau between May and November, but the rest of the year can be wet. (2) The Yungas north of La Paz and Cochabamba, among the spurs of the Cordillera; altitude, 750-1500 m; average temperature 24°C. Rainfall in the Yungas is 700-800 mm a year, with high humidity. (3) The Valles, or high valleys and basins gouged out by the rivers of the Puna; average temperature 19°C. (4) The tropical lowlands; altitude 150m to 750 m; rainfall is high but seasonal (heaviest November to March, but can fall at any time); large areas suffer from alternate flooding and drought. The climate is hot, ranging from 23° to 25°C in the south and to 30°C in the north. Occasional cold winds from the south, the *surazos*, can lower the temperature suddenly and considerably.

Transport in Bolivia

Air All of the following offer internal air services. **Boliviana de Aviación (BoA)**, *www.boa.bo*; also flies to São Paulo and Buenos Aires and Amaszonas, www.amaszonas.com, to Cuzco, Arequipa and Asunción. TAM, the civilian branch of the Bolivian Air Force, flies to main cities as well as Uyuni and several smaller and more remote destinations. **Aerocon** ① *T03-351 1010, www.aerocon.bo*, based in Trinidad, serves mostly the northern jungle and Potosí; note that Aerocon has had a few accidents since 2010. **Amaszonas** ① *T02-222 0848*, flies to all main cities and between La Paz and Rurrenabaque, Trinidad and Uyuni. **Ecojet** ① *T901-105055*, based in Cochabamba flies from Cochabamba to Sucre, Trinidad and Riberalta and from Sucre to Santa Cruz. Many flights radiate from La Paz, Santa Cruz or Cochabamba. Make sure you have adequate baggage insurance.

Bus Buses ply most of the main roads. Inter-urban buses are called *flotas*, urban ones *micros* or *minibuses* (vans); *trufis* are shared taxis. Larger bus companies run frequent services and offer a/c, TV and other mod cons. You can usually buy tickets with reserved seats a day or two in advance. Alternatively, savings may sometimes be obtained by bargaining for fares at the last minute, although not at peak travel times like national holidays. A small charge is made for use of bus terminals; payment is before departure.

In the wet season, bus travel is subject to long delays and detours, at extra cost, and cancellations are not uncommon. On all journeys, take some food, water and toilet paper. It is best to travel by day, not just to enjoy the scenery and avoid arriving at night, but also for better road safety (also see Road safety, page 243). Bus companies are responsible for any items packed in the luggage compartment or on the roof, but only if they give you a ticket for each bag.

Train The western highland railway is operated by **Ferroviaria Andina (FCA)** ① *T02-241 6545, www.fca.com.bo*. There are passenger trains to Villazón from Oruro, via Atocha, Tupiza and Uyuni. There are plans to reopen to passengers the La Paz to Arica line (2014). The eastern lowland line is run by **Ferroviaria Oriental** ① *www.fo.com.bo*, with services from Santa Cruz east to the Brazilian border and south to the Argentine border at Yacuiba.

Maps Good maps of Bolivia are few and far between, and maps in general can be hard to find. **Instituto Geográfico Militar** (IGM, see page 259). Many IGM maps date from the 1970s and their accuracy is variable; prices also vary, US$4.50-7 a sheet. **Walter Guzmán Córdova** makes several travel and trekking maps, available from some bookshops in La Paz. The **German Alpine Club (Deutscher Alpenverein)** ① *www.alpenverein.de*, produces two maps of Sorata-Ancohuma-Illampu and Illimani, but these are not usually available in La Paz.

Where to stay in Bolivia → *See Essentials for our hotel price guide.*

Hotels and hostales Hotels must display prices by law, but often do not. The number of stars awarded each hotel is also regulated, but not always accurate. The following terms likewise reflect the size and quality of an establishment (from largest and best, to smallest and simplest): *hotel, hostal, residencial, alojamiento* and *casa de huéspedes*. A *pensión* is a simple restaurant and may double as a place to sleep in smaller towns.

Camping Camping is best suited to the wilderness areas of Bolivia, away from towns, and people. Organized campsites, car or trailer camping does not exist here. Because of the abundance of cheap hotels you should never have to camp in populated areas

Youth hostels Youth hostels or self-styled 'backpackers' are not necessarily cheaper than hotels. A number of mid-range *residenciales* are affiliated to **Hostelling International (HI)** ① *www. hostellingbolivia.org*; some others just say they are. Another website listing hostels is www. boliviahostels.com, but they are not necessarily affiliated to HI.

Food and drink in Bolivia → *See Essentials for our restaurant price guide.*

Restaurants in Bolivia Most restaurants do not open early but many hotels include breakfast, which is also served in markets (see below). In *pensiones* and cheaper restaurants a basic lunch (*almuerzo* – usually finished by 1300) and dinner (*cena*) are normally available. The *comida del día* is the best value in any class of restaurant. Breakfast and lunch can also be found in markets, but eat only what is cooked in front of you. Dishes cooked in the street are not safe. Llama meat contains parasites, so make sure it has been properly cooked, and be especially careful of raw salads as many tourists experience gastrointestinal upsets.

Food Bolivian highland cooking is usually tasty and *picante* (spicy). Recommended local specialities include *empanadas* (cheese pasties) and *humintas* (maize pies); *pukacapas* are *picante* cheese pies. Recommended main dishes include *sajta de pollo*, hot spicy chicken with onion, fresh potatoes and *chuño* (dehydrated potatoes), *parrillada* (mixed grill), *fricase* (juicy pork with *chuño*), *silpancho* (very thin fried breaded meat with eggs, rice and bananas), and *ají de lengua*, ox-tongue with hot peppers, potatoes and *chuño* or *tunta* (another kind of dehydrated potato). *Pique macho*, roast meat, sausage, chips, onion and pepper is especially popular with Bolivians and travellers alike. Near Lake Titicaca fish becomes an important part of the local diet and trout, though not native, is usually delicious. Bolivian soups are usually hearty and warming, including *chairo* made of meat, vegetables and *chuño*. *Salteñas* are very popular meat or chicken pasties eaten as a mid-morning snack, the trick is to avoid spilling the gravy all over yourself.

In the lowland Oriente region, the food usually comes with cooked banana, yucca and rice. This area also has good savoury snacks, such as *cuñapés* (cheese bread made with manioc flour). In the northern lowlands, many types of wild meat are served in tourist restaurants and on jungle tours. Bear in mind that the turtles whose eggs are eaten are endangered and that other species not yet endangered soon will be if they stay on the tourist menu.

Ají is hot pepper, frequently used in cooking. *Rocoto* is an even hotter variety (with black seeds), sometimes served as a garnish and best avoided by the uninitiated. *Llajua* is a hot pepper sauce present on every Bolivian table. It's potency varies greatly so try a little bit before applying dollops to your food.

Bolivia's temperate and tropical fruits are excellent and abundant. Don't miss the luscious grapes and peaches in season (February-April). Brazil nuts, called *almendras* or *castañas*, are produced in the northern jungle department of Pando and sold throughout the country.

The popular tourist destinations have a profusion of cafés and restaurants catering to the gringo market. Some offer decent international cuisine at reasonable prices, but many seem convinced that foreigners eat only mediocre pizza and vegetarian omelettes. There must be a hundred 'Pizzerías Italianas' in Bolivia's tourist towns.

Drink The several makes of local lager-type **beer** are recommendable; *Paceña*, *Huari*, *Taquiña* and *Ducal* are the best-known brands. There are also micro-brews in La Paz (see page 254). *Singani*, the national spirit, is distilled from grapes, and is cheap and strong. *Chuflay* is *singani* and a fizzy mixer, usually 7-Up. Good **wines** are produced by several vineyards near Tarija (tours are available, see page 312). *Chicha* is a fermented maize drink, popular in Cochabamba. The hot maize drink, *api* (with cloves, cinnamon, lemon and sugar), is good on cold mornings. **Bottled water** is readily available. Tap, stream and well water should never be drunk without first being purified.

Essentials A-Z

Accident and emergency
Ambulance T165 in La Paz, T161 in El Alto. **Police** T110 nationwide. Robberies should be reported to the *Policía Turística*, they will issue a report for insurance purposes but stolen goods are rarely recovered. In cities which do not have a *Policía Turística* report robberies to the **Fuerza Especial de Lucha Contra el Crimen (FELCC)**, Departamento de Robos. In La Paz, see page 248.

Electricity
220 volts 50 cycles AC. Sockets usually accept both continental European (round) and US-type (flat) 2-pin plugs. Also some 110-volt sockets, when in doubt, ask.

Embassies and consulates
For all Bolivian embassies abroad and all foreign embassies and consulates in Bolivia, see http://embassy.goabroad.com.

Festivals in Bolivia
2 Feb: Virgen de la Candelaria, in rural communities in Copacabana, Santa Cruz departments. **Carnaval**, especially famous in Oruro, is celebrated throughout the country in Feb or Mar. There are parades with floats and folkloric dances, parties, much drinking and water throwing even in the coldest weather and nobody is spared. Many related festivities take place around the time of Carnaval. 2 weeks beforehand is **Jueves de Compadres** followed by **Jueves de Comadres**. In the Altiplano Shrove Tuesday is celebrated as **Martes de Challa**, when house owners make offerings to Pachamama and give drinks to passers-by. **Carnaval Campesino** usually begins in small towns on Ash Wednesday, when regular Carnaval ends, and lasts for 5 days, until **Domingo de Tentación**. Palm Sunday (**Domingo de Ramos**) sees parades to the church throughout Bolivia; the devout carry woven palm fronds, then hang them outside their houses. **Semana Santa** in the eastern Chiquitania is very interesting, with ancient processions, dances, and games not found outside the region. **Corpus Christi** is also a colourful festival. **3 May**: Fiesta de la Invención de la Santa Cruz, various parts. **2 Jun**: Santísima Trinidad in Beni Department. **24 Jun**: San Juan, bonfires throughout all Bolivia. **29 Jun**: San Pedro y San Pablo, at Tiquina, Tihuanaco and throughout Chiquitania. **25 Jul**: Fiesta de Santiago (St James), Altiplano and lake region. **14-16 Aug**: Virgen de Urkupiña, Cochabamba, a 3-day Catholic festivity mixed with Quechua rituals and parades with folkloric dances. **16 Aug**: San Roque, patron saint of dogs; the animals are adorned with ribbons and other decorations. **1** and **2 Nov**: All Saints and All Souls, any local cemetery. Cities may be very quiet on national holidays, but celebrations will be going on in the villages. Hotels are often full at the most popular places, for instance Copacabana on Good Friday; worth booking in advance.

Public holidays Some dates may be moved to the nearest weekend. 1 Jan, New Year's Day; Carnaval Week, Mon, Shrove Tuesday, Ash Wednesday; Holy Week: Thu, Fri and Sat; 1 May, Labour Day; Corpus Christi (movable May-Jun); 16 Jul, La Paz Municipal Holiday; 5-7 Aug, Independence; 24 Sep, Santa Cruz Municipal Holiday; 2 Nov, Day of the Dead; Christmas Day.

Money → *US$1 = Bs6.9. €1 = Bs9.5 (May 2014)*
The currency is the boliviano (Bs), divided into 100 centavos. There are notes for 200, 100, 50, 20 and 10 bolivianos, and 5, 2 and 1 boliviano coins, as well as 50, 20 and (rare) 10 centavos. Bolivianos are often referred to as pesos; expensive items, including hotel rooms, may be quoted in dollars.

Many *casas de cambio* and street changers (but among banks only **Banco Nacional de Bolivia**, BNB, www.bnb.com.bo) accept cash euros as well as dollars. Large bills may be hard to use in small villages, always carry some 20s and 10s. ATMs (**Enlace** network T800-103060) are common in all departmental capitals and some other cities but not in all small towns, including several important tourist destinations. Samaipata and Sorata, among others, have no ATM. **Banco Unión**, has most ATMs in small towns, see www.bancounion.com.bo for locations. ATMs are not always reliable and, in addition to plastic, **you must always carry some cash**. Most ATMs dispense both Bs and US$. Debit cards and Amex are generally less reliable than Visa/MC credit cards at ATMs. Note that Bolivian ATMs dispense cash first and only a few moments later return your card. In small towns without banks or ATMs, look for **Prodem**, which changes US$ cash at fair rates, and gives cash advances at tellers on Visa/MC credit – not debit – cards for about 5% commission. (Prodem ATMs do not accept international cards.) **Banco Fie** is also found throughout the country, changes US$ cash at all branches and gives cash advances at some locations. ATM scams are worst in La Paz, but may occur elsewhere. For lost Visa cards T800 100188, MasterCard T800-100172. For travellers' cheques, see Essentials at front of book

Cost of travelling Bolivia is cheaper to visit than most neighbouring countries. Budget travellers can get by on US$15-20 per person per day for 2 travelling together. A basic hotel in small towns costs as little as US$5 pp, breakfast US$1.50, and a simple set lunch (*almuerzo*) around US$2.50-3.50. For around US$35, though, you can find much better accommodation, more comfortable transport and a wider choice in food. Prices are higher in the city of La Paz; in the east, especially Santa Cruz and Tarija; and in Pando and the upper reaches of the Beni. The average cost of using the internet is US$0.50 per hr.

Opening hours
Banks and offices: normally open Mon-Fri 0900-1600, Sat 0900-1300, but may close for lunch in small towns. **Shops**: Mon-Fri 0830-1230, 1430-1830 and Sat 0900-1200. Opening and closing in the afternoon are later in lowland provinces.

Post and couriers
The main branches of post offices in La Paz, Santa Cruz and Cochabamba are best for sending parcels. DHL and FedEx have offices in major cities.

Safety
Violent crime is less common in Bolivia than some other parts of South America. Tricks and scams abound however. Fake police, narcotics police and immigration officers – usually plain-clothed but carrying forged ID – have been known to take people to their 'office' and ask to see documents and money; they then rob them. Legitimate police do not ask people for documents in the street unless they are involved in an accident, fight, etc. If approached, walk away and seek assistance from as many bystanders as possible. Never get in a vehicle with the 'officer' nor follow them to their 'office'. Many of the robberies are very slick, involving taxis and various accomplices. Take only radio taxis, identified by their dome lights and phone numbers. Always lock the doors, sit in the back and never allow other passengers to share your cab. If someone else gets in, get out at once. Also if smeared or spat-on, walk away, don't let the good Samaritan clean you up, they will clean you out instead.

The largest cities (Santa Cruz, El Alto, La Paz and Cochabamba) call for the greatest precautions. The countryside and small towns throughout Bolivia are generally safe. Note however that civil disturbance, although less frequent in recent years, remains part of Bolivian life. It can take the form of strikes, demonstrations in major cities and roadblocks (*bloqueos*), some lasting a few hrs, others weeks. Try to be flexible in your plans if you encounter disruptions and make the most of nearby attractions if transport is not running. You can often find transport to the site of a roadblock, walk across and get onward transport on the other side. Check with locals first to find out how tense the situation is.

Road safety
This should be an important concern for all visitors to Bolivia. Precarious roads, poorly maintained vehicles and frequently reckless drivers combine to cause many serious, at times fatal, accidents. Choose your transport judiciously and don't hesitate to pay a little more to travel with a better company. Look over the vehicle before you get on; if it doesn't feel right, look for another. If a driver is drunk or reckless, demand that he stop at the nearest village and let you off. Also note that smaller buses, although less comfortable, are often safer on narrow mountain roads.

Tax

Airport tax International departure tax of US$24 is payable in dollars or bolivianos, cash only. Airport tax for domestic flights, US$2. **IVA/VAT** 13%.

Telephone → *Country code +591.*

Equal tones with long pauses: ringing. Equal tones with equal pauses: engaged. IDD prefix: 00. Calls from public *cabinas* are expensive. Cellular numbers have no city code, but carry a 3-digit prefix starting with 7.

Time

GMT-4 all year.

Tipping

Up to 10% in restaurants is very generous, Bolivians seldom leave more than a few coins. Tipping is not customary for most services (eg taxi driver) though it is a reward when service has been very good. Guides expect a tip as does someone who has looked after a car or carried bags.

Tourist information

The Viceministerio de Turismo, C Mercado, Ed Ballivián, p 18, has an informative website, www.bolivia.travel.
InfoTur offices are found in most departmental capitals (addresses given under each city), at international arrivals in El Alto airport (La Paz) and Viru Viru (Santa Cruz). In La Paz at Mariscal Santa Cruz y Colombia.

Useful websites

www.bolivia.com (Spanish) News, tourism, entertainment and information on regions.
www.bolivia-online.net (Spanish, English and German) Travel information about La Paz, Cochabamba, Potosí, Santa Cruz and Sucre.
www.presidencia.gob.bo Presidential website.
http://lanic.utexas.edu/la/sa/bolivia Excellent database on various topics

indigenous to Bolivia, maintained by the University of Texas, USA.
www.noticiasbolivianas.com All the Bolivian daily news in one place.
www.chiquitania.com Detailed information in English about all aspects of Chiquitania.

Visas and immigration

A passport only, valid for 6 months beyond date of visit, is needed for citizens of almost all Western European countries, Israel, Japan, Canada, South American countries, Australia and New Zealand. Nationals of all other countries require a visa. US citizens can obtain a visa in advance at a Bolivian consulate or on arrival at the airport or border post. Requirements include a fee of US$135 cash (subject to change), proof of sufficient funds (eg showing a credit card) and a yellow fever vaccination certificate. Only the fee is universally enforced. Some nationalities must gain authorization from the Bolivian Ministry of Foreign Affairs, which can take 6 weeks. Other countries that require a visa do not need authorisation (visas in this case take 1-2 working days). It is best to check current requirements before leaving home. Tourists are usually granted 90 days stay on entry at airports, less at land borders. You can apply for a free extension (*ampliación*) at immigration offices in all departmental capitals, up to a maximum stay of 90 days per calendar year (180 days for nationals of Andean nations). If you overstay, the current fine is Bs20, roughly US$3 per day. Be sure to keep the green paper with entry stamp inside your passport, you will be asked for it when you leave.

Weights and measures

Metric, but some old Spanish measures are used for produce in markets.

La Paz and around

The minute you arrive in La Paz, the highest seat of government in the world, you realize this is no ordinary place. El Alto airport is at a staggering 4061 m above sea level. The sight of the city, lying hundreds of metres below, at the bottom of a steep canyon and ringed by snow-peaked mountains, takes your breath away – literally – for at this altitude breathing can be a problem.

The Spaniards chose this odd place for a city on 20 October 1548, to avoid the chill winds of the plateau, and because they had found gold in the Río Choqueyapu, which runs through the canyon. The centre of the city, Plaza Murillo, is at 3636 m, about 400 m below the level of the Altiplano and the sprawling city of El Alto, perched dramatically on the rim of the canyon.

Arriving in La Paz → *Phone code: 02. Population: La Paz: 912,512, El Alto: 1,079,698.*

Orientation La Paz has the highest commercial **airport** in the world, high above the city at El Alto. A taxi from the airport to the centre takes about 30 minutes. There are three main **bus terminals**; the bus station at Plaza Antofagasta, the cemetery district for Sorata, Copacabana and Tiwanaku, and Minasa bus station in Villa Fátima for the Yungas, including Coroico, and northern jungle. A system of cable cars (*teleféricos*) is under construction. The red line, between El Alto and Vita, west of the main bus station, is scheduled to open in mid-2014. There are three types of city bus: *puma katari* (a fleet of new buses operating since March 2014), *micros* (small, old buses) and faster, more plentiful minibuses. *Trufis* are fixed-route collective taxis, with a sign with their route on the windscreen. Taxis come in three types: regular honest taxis, fake taxis and radio taxis, the safest, which have a dome light and number.

The city's main street runs from **Plaza San Francisco** as Avenida Mariscal Santa Cruz, then changes to Avenida 16 de Julio (more commonly known as El Prado) and ends at **Plaza del Estudiante**. The business quarter, government offices, central university (UMSA) and many of the main hotels and restaurants are in this area. Banks and exchange houses are clustered on Calle Camacho, between Loayza and Colón, not far from **Plaza Murillo**, the traditional heart of the city. From the Plaza del Estudiante, Avenida Villazón splits into Avenida Arce, which runs southeast towards the wealthier residential districts of **Zona Sur**, in the valley, 15 minutes away; and Avenida 6 de Agosto which runs through **Sopocachi**, an area full of restaurants, bars and clubs. Zona Sur has shopping centres, supermarkets with imported items and some of the best restaurants and bars in La Paz (see page 258). It begins after the bridge at La Florida beside the attractive Plaza Humboldt. The main road, Avenida Ballivián, begins at Calle 8 and continues up the hill to San Miguel on Calle 21 (about a 20-minute walk).

Sprawled around the rim of the canyon is **El Alto**, Bolivia's second-largest city (after Santa Cruz, La Paz is third). Its population of more than one million is mostly indigenous migrants from the countryside and its political influence has grown rapidly. El Alto is connected to La Paz by motorway (toll US$0.25) and by a road to Obrajes and the Zona Sur. Minibuses from Plaza Eguino leave regularly for Plaza 16 de Julio, El Alto, more leave from Plaza Pérez Velasco for La Ceja, the edge of El Alto. Intercity buses to and from La Paz always stop at El Alto in an area called *terminal*, off Avenida 6 de Marzo, where transport companies have small offices. If not staying in La Paz, you can change buses here and save a couple of hours. There is accommodation nearby, but the area is not safe, especially at night.➤➤ *See Transport, page 263, for full details.*

Best time to visit La Paz Because of the altitude, nights are cold the year round. In the day, the sun is strong, but the moment you go into the shade or enter a building, the temperature falls. From December-March, the summer, it rains most afternoons, making it feel colder than it actually is. Temperatures are even lower in winter, June-August, when the sky is always clear.

1 La Paz

To ①②⑬, Bus Station, El Alto, Airport,
Titicaca, Tiwanaku & Oruro

Plaza Riosinio ⑤

Museo Costumbrista
& other museums

Where to stay

1 Adventure Brew B&B *A2*
2 Adventure Brew Hostel *A2*
3 Arthy's Guesthouse *A2*
4 Bacoo *A3*
5 Casa Fusión *E5*
6 El Rey Palace *D4*
7 Estrella Andina *B2*
8 Europa & Café El Consulado *C4*
9 Hostal Copacabana *B2*
10 Hostal República *B4*
11 La Joya *B1*
12 La Loge & La Comedie Restaurant *E5*
13 Mitru La Paz *E5*
14 Onkel Inn 1886 *C3*
15 Radisson Plaza *D5*
16 Rosario *B2*
17 Stannum *E5*
18 Tambo de Oro *A3*
19 Wild Rover Backpackers Hostel *B4*

Restaurants

1 Alexander Coffee *C4, E5*
2 Arco Iris *E4*
3 Armonía *E5*
4 Beatrice *E4*
5 Café Soho *A3*
6 Fridolín *E5*
7 Ken-Chan *D4*
8 Kuchen Stube *E5*
9 La Terraza *C4, E5*
10 Maphrao On *E6*
11 Mongo's *E5*
12 Olive Tree *E6*
13 Reineke Fuchs *E5*
14 Rendezvous *E5*
15 Sancho Panza *E5*
16 Vienna *D4*

Bars & clubs

17 Equinoccio *E4*
18 Marka Tambo & Etno Café *A3*
19 Tetekos *C4*
20 Thelonius Jazz Bar *E4*

N

100 metres
100 yards

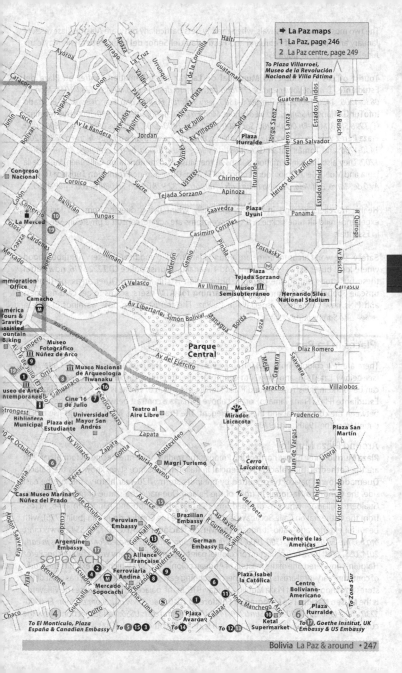

To Plaza Villarroel,
Museo de la Revolución
Nacional & Villa Fátima

Congreso
Nacional

La Merced

Immigration
Office

Camacho

américa
Tours &
Gravity
assisted
mountain
Biking

Museo
Fotográfico
Núñez de Arco

Museo Nacional
de Arqueología
Tiwanaku

Museo de Arte
Contemporáneo

Cine 16
de Julio

strongest

Biblioteca
Municipal

Universidad
Mayor San
Andrés

Plaza del
Estudiante

Teatro al
Aire Libre

Casa Museo Marina
Núñez del Prado

Magri Turismo

SOPOCACHI

Peruvian
Embassy

Brazilian
Embassy

Argentine
Embassy

Alliance
Française

German
Embassy

Puente de las
Américas

Ferroviaria
Andina

Mercado
Sopocachi

Plaza Isabel
la Católica

Centro
Boliviano-
Americano

Plaza
Iturralde

To El Montículo, Plaza
España & Canadian Embassy

Plaza
Avaroa

Ketal
Supermarket

To Goethe Institut, UK
Embassy & US Embassy

Plaza
Iturralde

Plaza
Central

Plaza
Uyuni

Plaza
Tejada Sorzano

Museo
Semisubterráneo

Hernando Siles
National Stadium

Parque
Central

Mirador
Laicacota

Plaza San
Martín

Cerro
Laicacota

The two most important festivals, when the city gets particularly busy, are **Alasitas** (last week of January and first week of February) and **Festividad del Señor del Gran Poder** (end May/early June). ▶▶ *See Festivals, page 259.*

Tourist offices The **Gobierno Municipal de La Paz** has information centres at: **Plaza del Estudiante** ① *at the lower end of El Prado between 16 de Julio and México, T237 1044, Mon-Fri 0830-1200, 1430-1900, Sat-Sun 0900-1300, very helpful, English and French spoken;* **El Prado InfoTur** ① *Mariscal Santa Cruz y Colombia, Mon-Fri 0830-1900, Sat-Sun 0930-1300;* **Bus terminal** ① *T228 5858, Mon-Fri 0600-2200, Sat 0800-1600, Sun 1400-2200, holidays 0800-1200, 1600-2000;* **Plaza Pérez Velasco** ① *opposite San Francisco, under the pedestrian walkway, Mon-Fri 0830-1200, 1430-1700;* and **Tomás Katari** ① *Av Bautista y José María Aliaga, by the cemetery, Mon-Fri 0900-1700.* They also have information booths at the Museo Costumbrista on Calle Jaén, Valle de la Luna and Muela del Diablo. Tourist office for **El Alto: Dirección de Promoción Turística** ① *C 5 y Av 6 de Marzo, Edif Vela, p 5, also at arrivals in airport, T282 9281, Mon-Fri 0800-1200, 1400-1800.*

Health Travellers arriving in La Paz, especially when flying directly from sea level, may experience mild altitude sickness. If your symptoms are severe, consult a physician. See Health in Essentials.

Safety The worst areas for crime are around Plaza Murillo and the Cemetery neighbourhood where local buses serve Copacabana and Tiwanaku. **Tourist police** ① *T222 5016,* now patrol these bus stops during the daytime, but caution is still advised. Other areas, particularly upscale Sopocachi, are generally safer. **Warning for ATM users**: scams to get card numbers and PINs have flourished, especially in La Paz. The tourist police post warnings in hotels. ▶▶ *See also Safety, page 243.*

Places in La Paz

There are few colonial buildings left in La Paz; probably the best examples are in **Calle Jaén** (see below). Late 19th- and early 20th-century architecture, often displaying European influence, can be found in the streets around Plaza Murillo, but much of La Paz is modern. The **Plaza del Estudiante** (Plaza Franz Tamayo), or a bit above it, marks a contrast between old and new styles, between the commercial and the more elegant. The **Prado** itself is lined with high-rise blocks dating from the 1960s and 1970s.

Around Plaza Murillo

Plaza Murillo, three blocks north of the Prado, is the traditional centre. Facing its formal gardens are the **Cathedral**, the **Palacio Presidencial** in Italian renaissance style, known as the **Palacio Quemado** (burnt palace) twice gutted by fire in its stormy 130-year history, and, on the east side, the **Congreso Nacional**. In front of the Palacio Quemado is a statue of former President Gualberto Villarroel who was dragged into the plaza by a mob and hanged in 1946. Across from the Cathedral on Calle Socabaya is the **Palacio de los Condes de Arana** (built 1775), with beautiful exterior and patio. It houses the **Museo Nacional de Arte** ① *T240 8542, www.mna. org.bo, Tue-Fri 0900-1230, 1500-1900, Sat 1000-1700, Sun 0900-1330, closed for renovations in early 2014, US$1.50.* It has a fine collection of colonial paintings including many works by Melchor Pérez Holguín, considered one of the masters of Andean colonial art, and which also exhibits the works of contemporary local artists. Calle Comercio, running east-west across the Plaza, has most of the stores and shops. West of Plaza Murillo, at Ingavi 916, in the palace of the Marqueses de Villaverde is the **Museo Nacional de Etnografía y Folklore** ① *T240 8640, www.musef.org.bo, Mon-Fri 0900-1230, 1500-1900, Sat 0900-1630, Sun 0900-1430, US$3, filming costs US$6.* Various sections show the cultural richness of Bolivia by region through textiles and other items. It has a *videoteca*.

Northwest of Plaza Murillo is **Calle Jaén**, a picturesque colonial street with a restaurant/peña, a café, craft shops, good views and four museums (known as **Museos Municipales** ① *Tue-Fri 0930-1230, 1500-1900, Sat 1000-1900, Sun 0900-1330, US$1.50 each*) housed in colonial buildings. **Museo Costumbrista Juan de Vargas** ① *on Plaza Riosinio, at the top of Jaén, T228 0758, US$0.60,*

② La Paz centre

➜ La Paz maps
1 La Paz, page 246
2 La Paz centre, page 249

N

100 metres
100 yards

Where to stay 🛏
1 Arcabucero *C1*
2 El Solario *B1*
3 Fuentes *C1*
4 Gloria *B2*
5 Hosp Milenio *A3*

6 Hostal Naira *C2*
7 La Casona *B2*
8 La Posada de la
   Abuela Obdulia *C1*
9 Loki *A1, C3*
10 Milton *D1*
11 Muzungu *B1*
12 Posada El Carretero *A3*
13 Presidente &
    La Kantuta Restaurant *B2*
14 Sagárnaga *C1*
15 Torino *B3*

Restaurants 🍴
1 100% Natural *C1*
2 Alexander Coffee *B3*
3 A Lo Cubano *C1*
4 Angelo Colonial *C1*
5 Banais *B2*
6 Café del Mundo *C1*
7 Café Illampu *C1*
8 Colonial Pot *C1*
9 La Cueva *C2*
10 Pepe's *C1*
11 Pizzería Italia *C1*

12 Sol y Luna *C2*
13 Star of India *C2*
14 Steakhouse *C1*

Bars & clubs 🍸
15 Hard Rock Café *B1*
16 Oliver's English Tavern *C2*
17 Peña Parnaso *C2*

has miniature displays depicting incidents in the history of La Paz and well-known Paceños, as well as miniature replicas of reed rafts used by the Norwegian Thor Heyerdahl, and the Spaniard Kitin Muñoz, to prove their theories of ancient migrations. **Museo del Litoral Boliviano** ① *T228 0758*, has artefacts of the War of the Pacific, and interesting selection of old maps. **Museo de Metales Preciosos** ① *T228 0329*, is well set out with Inca gold artefacts in basement vaults, also ceramics and archaeological exhibits, and **Museo Casa Murillo** ① *T228 0553*, the erstwhile home of Pedro Domingo Murillo, one of the martyrs of the La Paz independence movement of 16 July 1809, has a good collection of paintings, furniture and national costumes. **Museo Tambo Quirquincho** ① *C Evaristo Valle, south of Jaén, Plaza Alonso de Mendoza, T239 0969, Tue-Fri, 0930-1230, 1500-1900, Sat-Sun, 0900-1300, US$1.20*, displays modern painting and sculpture, carnival masks, silver, early 20th-century photography and city plans, and is recommended.

Plaza San Francisco up to the cemetery district

At the upper end of Avenida Mcal Santa Cruz is the **Plaza San Francisco** with the **church and monastery of San Francisco** ① *open for Mass at 0700, 0900, 1100 and 1900, Mon-Sat, and also at 0800, 1000 and 1200 on Sun*. Dating from 1549, this is one of the finest examples of colonial religious architecture in South America and well worth seeing. The **Centro Cultural Museo San Francisco** ① *Plaza San Francisco 503, T231 8472, Mon-Sat 0900-1800, US$2.80, allow 1½-2 hrs, free guides available but tip appreciated, some speak English and French*, offers access to various areas of the church and convent including the choir, crypt (open 1400-1730), roof, various chapels and gardens. Fine art includes religious paintings from the 17th, 18th and 19th centuries, plus visiting exhibits and a hall devoted to the works of Tito Yupanqui, the indigenous sculptor of the Virgen de Copacabana. There is a pricey but good café at entrance. Behind the San Francisco church a network of narrow cobbled streets rise steeply up the canyon walls. Much of this area is a street market. Handicraft shops, travel agencies, hotels and restaurants line the lower part of **Calle Sagárnaga** (here you find the highest concentration of tourists and pick-pockets). The **Mercado de Brujas**, 'witchcraft market', on Calles Melchor Jiménez and Linares, which cross Santa Cruz above San Francisco, sells charms, herbs and more gruesome items like llama foetuses. The excellent **Museo de la Coca** ① *Linares 914, T231 1998, Mon-Sat 1000-1900, Sun 1000-1600, US$2, www.cocamuseum.com, shop with coca products for sale*, is devoted to the coca plant, its history, cultural significance, medical values and political implications, with explanations in five languages. Nearby is the recommended **Museo de Arte Texil Andino Boliviano** ① *Linares 906, daily 1000-1900, Sun 1000-1700, US$1.20*, a small collection of old traditional weavings (not to be confused with the larger **Museo de Textiles Andinos Bolivianos** in Miraflores.

Further up, from Illampu to Rodríguez and in neighbouring streets, is the produce-based **Rodríguez market** ① *daily, but best on Sun morning*. Turning right on Max Paredes, heading north, is **Avenida Buenos Aires**, where small workshops turn out the costumes and masks for the Gran Poder festival, and with great views of Illimani, especially at sunset. Continuing west along Max Paredes towards the **cemetery district**, the streets are crammed with stalls selling every imaginable item. Transport converges on the cemetery district (for more information see page 263). See also Safety, page 248.

The Prado, Sopocachi, Miraflores and Zona Sur

Museo de Arte Contemporáneo Plaza ① *Av 16 de Julio 1698, T233 5905, daily 0900-2100, US$2.20*. In a 19th-century house which has been declared a national monument, there is a selection of contemporary art from national and international artists. Just off the Prado (down the flight of stairs near the Maria Auxiliadora church) is **Museo Nacional de Arqueología** or **Tiahuanaco** (Tiwanaku) ① *Tiwanacu 93 entre Bravo y F Zuazo, T231 1621, www.bolivian.com/arqueologia, closed for renovation in 2014*. It contains good collections of the arts and crafts of ancient Tiwanaku and items from the eastern jungles. It also has an exhibition of gold statuettes and objects found in Lake Titicaca. On Avenida Libertador Simón Bolívar, from where there are views of Mount Illimani,

Tiny treats

One of the most intriguing items for sale in Andean markets is *Ekeko*, the god of good fortune and plenty and one of the most endearing of the Aymara folk legends. He is a cheery, avuncular little chap, with a happy face, a pot belly and short legs. His image, usually in plaster of Paris, is laden with various household items, as well as sweets, confetti and streamers, food, and with a cigarette dangling cheekily from his lower lip. Believers say that these statues only bring luck if they are received as gifts. The *Ekeko* occupies a central role in the festival of Alacitas, the Feast of Plenty, which takes place in La Paz at the end of January. Everything under the sun can be bought in miniature: houses, trucks, buses, suitcases, university diplomas; you name it, you'll find it here. The idea is to have your mini-purchase blessed by a *Yatiri*, an Aymara priest, and the real thing will be yours within the year.

is the modern **Mercado Camacho** produce market. In Sopocachi district, by Plaza España, is **El Montículo**, a park with great views of the city and Illimani. In the residential district of Miraflores, east of the centre, on Plaza Tejada Sorzano, outside the Hernán Siles national football stadium is the **Museo Semisubterráneo**, a sunken garden full of replicas of statues and artefacts from Tiwanaku, but difficult to get to because of the traffic. At the north end of Avenida Busch are Plaza Villarroel and **Museo de la Revolución Nacional** ① *Tue-Fri 0930-1200, 1500-1800, Sat-Sun 1000-1200, US$0.15,* a memorial of the 1952 revolution and a mausoleum with tombs of former presidents.

Around La Paz

South of La Paz

To the south of the city are dry hills of many colours, topped by the **Muela del Diablo**, a striking outcrop. Here is the **Valle de la Luna**, or 'Valley of the Moon' (US$3), with impressive eroded hills; the climate in this valley is always much warmer than in the city. For transport details see page 263. About 3 km from the bridge at Calacoto the road forks, get out of the minibus at the turning and walk a few minutes east to the Valle entrance, or get out at the football field which is by the entrance. Take good shoes and water, but do not go alone, armed robbery has occurred. Just past the Valle de la Luna is **Mallasa** where there are several small roadside restaurants and cafés and the **Hotel Oberland** (see page 256). To the southeast of La Paz and best accessed from the La Paz–Oruro road are the **Yungas de Inquisivi** and **Quime**, see page 280.

Tiwanaku

① *The site is open 0900-1700, US$12, including entry to museums. Allow 4 hrs to see the ruins and village. See also Transport, page 263.*

This remarkable archaeological site, 72 km west of La Paz, near the southern end of Lake Titicaca, takes its name from one of the most important pre-Columbian civilizations in South America. It is the most popular excursion from La Paz, with facilities being improved as a result. Many archaeologists believe that Tiwanaku existed as early as 1600 BC, while the complex visible today probably dates from the eight to the 10th centuries AD. The site may have been a ceremonial complex at the centre of an empire which covered almost half Bolivia, southern Peru, northern Chile and northwest Argentina. It was also a hub of trans-Andean trade. The demise of the Tiwanaku civilization, according to studies by Alan Kolata of the University of Illinois, could have been precipitated by the flooding of the area's extensive system of raised fields (*Sukakollu*), which were capable of sustaining a population of 20,000. The Pumapunku section, 1 km south of the main complex may have been a port, as the waters of the lake used to be much higher than they are today. The raised field system is once again being used in parts of the Titicaca area.

One of the main structures is the **Kalasasaya**, meaning 'standing stones', referring to the statues found in that part: two of them, the Ponce monolith (centre of inner patio) and the Fraile monolith (southwest corner), have been re-erected. In the northwest corner is the Puerta del Sol, originally at Pumapunku. Its carvings, interrupted by being out of context, are thought to be either a depiction of the creator god, or a calendar. The motifs are exactly the same as those around the Ponce monolith. The **Templo Semisubterráneo** is a sunken temple whose walls are lined with faces, all different, according to some theories depicting states of health, the temple being a house of healing; another theory is that the faces display all the ethnicities of the world. The **Akapana**, originally a pyramid (said to have been the second largest in the world, covering over 28,000 sq m), still has some ruins on it. Plastering of the Akapana's walls was halted in 2009 when UNESCO, among others, declared it inappropriate. At **Pumapunku**, some of whose blocks weigh between 100 and 150 tonnes, a natural disaster may have put a sudden end to the construction before it was finished. There is a small **Museo Lítico** at the ticket office, with several large stone pieces and, at the site, the **Museo Regional Arqueológico**, containing a well-illustrated explanation of the raised field system of agriculture. Many other artefacts are in the **Museo Nacional de Arqueología** in La Paz.

Written guide material is difficult to come by; hiring a guide costs US$20 for two hours, some speak English but don't be bullied into taking one if you prefer to go on your own. Locals sell copies of Tiwanaku figures; cheaper here than in La Paz.

Nearby **Tiwanaku village**, with several basic hotels and eateries, still has remnants from the time of independence and the 16th-century church used pre-Columbian masonry. In fact, Tiwanaku for a long while was the 'quarry' for the altiplano. For the **Willkakuti**, winter solstice festival on 21 June, there is an all-night vigil and colourful dances. There is also a colourful local festival on the Sunday after Carnaval.

By road to Chile
The main route to Chile is via Tambo Quemado (see page 282), but an alternative route, on which there are no trucks, is to go by good road direct from La Paz via Viacha to **Santiago de Machaco** (130 km, petrol); then 120 km on a very bad road to the border at **Charaña** (basic **Alojamiento Aranda**; immigration behind railway station). From Visviri, on the Chilean side of the frontier (no services), a regular road runs to Putre. A motorized railway car also runs from Viacha to Charaña on Monday and Thursday at 0800 (four hours, US$4.30), returning Tuesday and Friday at 1200. There is no train service on the Chilean side.

Trekking and climbing near La Paz
Three so-called 'Inca Trails' link the Altiplano with the Yungas, taking you from the high Andes to the sub-tropics, with dramatic changes in weather, temperature and vegetation. Each has excellent sections of stonework and they vary in difficulty from relatively straightforward to quite hard-going. In the rainy season going can be particularly tough. ➤➤ *For details of how to reach the starting point of each trail, see Transport sections on page 263.*

Takesi Trail Start at **Ventilla** (see below), walk up the valley for about three hours passing the village of Choquekhota until the track crosses the river and to the right of the road, there is a falling-down brick wall with a map painted on it. The Takesi and Alto Takesi trails start here, following the path to the right of the wall. The road continues to Mina San Francisco. In the first hour's climb from the wall is excellent stone paving which is Inca or pre-Inca, depending on who you believe, either side of the pass at 4630 m. There are camping possibilities at Estancia Takesi and in the village of Kakapi you can sleep at the simple **Kakapi Tourist Lodge**, 10 beds with good mattresses, solar shower and toilet. It is run by the local community and sponsored by Fundación Pueblo. It is also possible to camp. You also have to pass the unpleasant mining settlement of Chojlla, between which and Yanakachi is a gate where it is necessary to register and often pay a small 'fee'. Yanakachi has a number of good places to stay, several good hikes and an orphanage you can help at. The Fundación Pueblo office on the plaza has information. Buy a minibus ticket on arrival in Yanakachi or walk 45 minutes down to the La Paz–Chulumani road for transport. The trek can be done in one long day, especially if you organize a jeep to the start of the trail, but is more relaxing in two or three. If you take it slowly, though, you'll have to carry camping kit. Hire mules in Choquekhota for US$10 per day plus up to US$10 for the muleteer. A two- to three-day alternative is from Mina San Francisco to El Castillo and the village of Chaco on the La Paz–Chulumani road. This trek is called La Reconquistada and has the distinction of including a 200-m disused mining tunnel.

Choro Trail (La Cumbre to Coroico) Immediately before the road drops down from La Cumbre to start the descent to Las Yungas, there is a good dirt road leading up to the *apacheta* (narrow pass) where the trail starts properly. Cloud and bad weather are normal at La Cumbre (4660 m): you have to sign in at the Guardaparque post on the way to the pass. The trail passes Samaña Pampa (small shop, sign in again, camping US$0.60), Chucura (pay US$1.50 fee, another shop, camping), Challapampa (camping possible, US$1.20, small shop), the Choro bridge and the Río Jacun-Manini (fill up with water at both river crossings). At Sandillani is a lodge ($$-$). There is good paving down to Villa Esmeralda, after which is Chairo (lodging and camping), then to Yolosa. It takes three days to trek from La Cumbre to Chairo, from where you can take a truck to Puente Yolosita, the turn-off for Cocoico on the new road. From Puente Yolosita trucks run uphill to Coroico when they fill, US$0.80, 15 minutes. The Choro Trail has a reputation for unfriendliness and occasional robbery, take care.

Huayna Potosí Huayna Potosí (6088 m) is normally climbed in two days, with one night in a basic shelter at 5300 m or camped on a glacier at 5600 m. Acclimatization and experience on ice are essential, and the mountain is dangerous out of season. There are four shelters: a community-run shelter 10 minutes up from the pass, one by the lake, very cold; **Refugio Huayna Potosí** at 4780 m, with toilets and shower, run by the tour operator of the same name, and a basic shelter at 5300 m owned by the same operator. Average cost is US$120 per person for two-day tour for three people (US$200 for one) including all equipment except sleeping bag. The starting point for the normal route is at Zongo. A three-day trek in the area is also offered. See Climbing, hiking and trekking, page 260, for tour operators.

◉ La Paz and around listings

For hotel and restaurant price codes, and other relevant information, see Essentials.

● Where to stay

El Alto *p245*
$$ Alexander Palace, Av Jorge Carrasco 61 y C 3, Ceja, Zona 12 de Octubre, T282 3376, www.bit.ly/alexanderpalacehotel. Modern, with breakfast, **$** pp in dorm, parking, disco.
$ Orquídea, C Dos 22 y Av 6 de Marzo, Villa Bolívar A, near bus terminals, T282 6487. Comfortable heated rooms, cheaper with shared bath, electric showers, good value. Better than others in the area.

Around Plaza Murillo *p248, maps p246 and p249*
$$$ Gloria, Potosí 909, T240 7070, www.hotel gloria.com.bo. Modern, central, includes buffet breakfast, 2 restaurants (1 is vegetarian), good food and service, runs **Gloria Tours** (www.gloria tours.com.bo) and also owns **Gloria Urmiri** resort, 2 hrs from La Paz. Recommended.
$$$ Presidente, Potosí 920 y Sanjines, T240 6666, www.hotelpresidente-bo.com. The 'highest 5-star in the world'. Excellent service, comfortable, heating, good food, gym and sauna, pool, all open to non-residents, bar. See also **Urban Rush**, under What to do, below.
$$-$ Hostal República, Comercio 1455, T220 2742, www.hostalrepublica.com. Old house of

former president, more expensive in apartment, with and without bath, hot water, good café, quiet garden, book ahead and ask for room on upper floor.

$ Adventure Brew Bed & Breakfast, Av Montes 533, T246 1614, www.theadventure brewbedandbreakfast.com. Mostly private rooms with bath, cheaper in dorms for 8, includes pancake breakfast, use of kitchen, free beer from microbrewery every night, rooftop bar with great views and spa, nightly BBQs, good value, popular meeting place.

$ Adventure Brew Hostel, Av Montes 504, T291 5896, www.theadventurebrewhostel.com. More economical than B&B above, 8 to 12-bed dorms, with shared hot showers, includes pancake breakfast and a free beer every night, rooftop terrace with great views of the city and Illimani, basement bar, travel agency and bank, lively young crowd, convenient to the bus station, associated with **Gravity Bolivia** (see What to do).

$ Arthy's Guesthouse, Montes 693, T228 1439, http://arthyshouse.tripod.com. Shared bath, warm water, safe, helpful, popular with bikers, English spoken, 2400 curfew.

$ Bacoo, Calle Alto de la Alianza 693, T228 0679, www.bacoohostel.com. Some rooms with private bath, cheaper in dorm, jacuzzi, restaurant and bar, garden, ping pong and pool, arrange tours.

$ Hosp Milenio, Yanacocha 860, T228 1263, hospedajemilenio@hotmail.com. Economical, shared bath, electric shower, basic, family house, homely and welcoming, popular, helpful owner, quiet, kitchen, breakfast extra, security boxes, great value.

$ Loki, Loayza 420, T211 9024 and Av América 120, esq Plaza Alonso de Mendoza, T245 7300, www.lokihostel.com. Members of a chain of popular party hostels. The Loayza location has a more subdued atmosphere with double rooms, more dorms at América, TV room, computer room, bar (meals available), tour operator.

$ Posada El Carretero, Catacora 1056, entre Yanacocha y Junín, T228 5271, elcarreteroposada@gmail.com. Very economical single and double rooms (cheaper with shared bath), also dorms, hot showers, helpful staff, good atmosphere and value.

$ Tambo de Oro, Armentia 367, T228 1565. Near bus station, cheaper with shared bath, hot showers, good value if a bit run down, safe for luggage.

$ Torino, Socabaya 457, T240 6003, www. hoteltorino.com.bo. Ask for better rooms in new section, older ones are run-down, cheaper without bath. Old backpackers' haunt, free book exchange, cultural centre, travel agency, good service. Restaurant next door for breakfast and good-value lunch (Mon-Fri 1200-1500).

$ Wild Rover Backpackers Hostel, Comercio 1476, T211 6903, www.wildroverhostel.com. Party hostel in renovated colonial-style house with courtyard and high-ceilings, dorms with 6-10 beds and doubles with shared bath, bar, TV room, book exchange, meals available, helpful staff speak English.

Plaza San Francisco up to the cemetery district *p250, maps p246 and p249*

$$$ La Casona, Av Mcal Santa Cruz 938, T290 0505, www.lacasonahotelboutique.com. Boutique hotel in beautifully restored former San Francisco convent dating to 1860, nice rooms (those in front get street noise), suites have jacuzzi, includes buffet breakfast and some museum entry fees, heating, safe box, terrace and cupola with nice views, very good restaurant, new in 2012.

$$$ Rosario, Illampu 704, T245 1658, www.hotelrosario.com. Sauna, laundry, internet café (free for guests, great view), good restaurant with buffet breakfast, stores luggage, no smoking, very helpful staff. Highly recommended. **Turisbus** travel agency downstairs (see Tour operators, page 262), Cultural Interpretation Centre explains items for sale in nearby 'witches' market'.

$$ Estrella Andina, Illampu 716, T245 6421, juapame_2000@hotmail.com. Cheaper in low season, all rooms have a safe and are decorated individually, English spoken, family run, comfortable, tidy, helpful, roof terrace, heaters, money exchange, very nice. Also owns **$ Cruz de los Andes**, Aroma 216, T245 1401, same style but shares premises with a car garage.

$$ Fuentes, Linares 888, T231 3966. Cheaper without bath, hot water, variety of rooms and prices, nice colonial style, comfortable, sauna, good value, family run.

$$ Hostal Naira, Sagárnaga 161, T235 5645, www.hostalnaira.com. Hot water, comfortable but pricey, rooms around courtyard, some are dark, price includes good buffet breakfast in Café Banais, safety deposit boxes.

$$ La Posada de la Abuela Obdulia, C Linares 947, T233 2285, http://hostalabuelaposada.com. Very pleasant inn.

$$ Milton, Illampu 1126-1130, T236 8003, www.hotelmiltonbolivia.com. Hot water, psychedelic 1970s style wallpaper in many rooms, restaurant, laundry, excellent views from roof, popular.

$ Arcabucero, C Viluyo 307 y Linares, T231 3473, arcabucero-bolivia@hotmail.com. Price rises in high season, pleasant new rooms in converted colonial house, excellent value but check the beds, breakfast extra.

$ El Solario, Murillo 776, T236 7963. Central, shared bath medical services, taxi and travel agency, good value, gets crowded.

$ La Joya, Max Paredes 541, T245 3841, www.hotelajoya.com. Cheaper without bath, modern and comfy, lift, area unsafe at night but provides transfers.

$ Muzungu Hostel, Illampu 441, T2451640, muzunguhostel@hotmail.com. Rooms with 1-4 beds, with and without bath and cheaper rate for dorms, several common areas, good restaurant (closed Sun) and bar, breakfast and 1 drink per day included.

$ Onkel Inn 1886, Colombia 257, T249 0456, onkelinn@gmail.com. Hostel in a remodelled 19th-century house, rooms with and without bath, doubles, triples and bunks. Jacuzzi, laundry facilities, café and bar, HI affiliated. Also in Copacabana.

$ Sagárnaga, Sagárnaga 326, T235 0252, www.hotel-sagarnaga.com. Cheaper in plain rooms without TV, solar hot water, 2 ATMs, English spoken, *peña*, popular with tour groups, helpful owner.

The Prado, Sopocachi, Miraflores and Zona Sur *p250, map p246*

$$$$ Casa Grande, Av Ballivián 1000 y C 17, T279 5511, and C 16 8009, T277 4000, both in Calacoto, www.casa-grande.com. bo. Beautiful, top quality apartments on Ballivian and hotel suites under a greenhouse dome on C16, buffet breakfast, pool and spa,

airport transfers at night only, restaurants, very good service.

$$$$ Europa, Tiahuanacu 64, T231 5656, www.hoteleuropa.com.bo. Next to the Museo Nacional de Arqueología. Excellent facilities and plenty of frills, health club, several restaurants, parking. Recommended.

$$$$ Stannum, Av Arce 2631, Torre Multicine, p 12 , T214 8393, www.stannumhotels.com. Boutique hotel on the 12th floor of an office building with lovely views of Illimani and the city, above mall and cinema complex. Comfortable rooms with minimalist decor, includes breakfast, bathtub, heating, a/c, fridge, restaurant, bar, gym, spa, airport transfers, no smoking anywhere on the premisies, new in 2013.

$$$$-$$$ Radisson Plaza, Av Arce 2177, T244 1111, www.radisson.com/lapazbo. 5-star hotel with all facilities, includes breakfast, gym, pool and sauna, excellent buffet in restaurant (see Restaurants, below).

$$$ El Rey Palace, Av 20 de Octubre 1947, T241 8541, www.hotelreypalace.com. Large suites with heating, excellent restaurant, stylish.

$$$ Mitru La Paz, 6 de Agosto 2628, Edif Torre Girasoles, T243 2242, www.hotelmitrulapaz. com. Modern hotel on the 1st 3 floors of the highest building in La Paz (37 storeys). Includes breakfast and complimentary hot drinks, bright ample rooms most with bathtubs, heating, safe boxes, fridge, convenient location for Sopocachi dining, good value for its price category, new in 2013.

$$$-$$ La Loge, Pasaje Medinacelli 2234, Sopocachi, T242 3561, www.lacomedie-lapaz.com/es/loge. Above, and owned by, La Comedie restaurant, elegant apart-hotel rooms, a good option with all services.

$$ Sopocachi, T214 0933, www.casafusion. com.bo. Lovely hotel with modern comfortable rooms, includes buffet breakfast, heating, good value, new in 2013.

South of La Paz *p251*

$$ Allkamari, near Valle de las Animas, 30 mins from town on the road to Palca, T279 1742, www.casalunaspa.com. Reservations required, cabins for up to 8 in a lovely valley between the Palca and La Animas canyons, a place to relax and star-gaze, **$** pp in dorm, solar heating, jacuzzi included, meals on request, horse and bike rentals, massage, shamanic rituals, taxi from Calacoto US$7, bus No 42 from the cemetery to within 1 km.

$$ Oberland, Mallasa, El Agrario 3118, near main road, 12 km from La Paz centre, T274 5040, www.h-oberland.com. A Swiss-owned, chalet-style restaurant (excellent, not cheap) and hotel (also good) with older resort facilities, lovely gardens, spa, sauna, covered pool (open to public – US$2 – very hot water), volleyball, tennis. Permit camping with vehicle, US$4 pp. Recommended.

$$-$ Colibrí Camping, C 4, Jupapina, near Mallasa, 30 mins from La Paz, T7629 5658, www.colibricamping.com. Cabins, teepee, tents and sleeping bags for hire or set up your own tent for US$7 pp, nice views, details about transport in their website.

🍴 Restaurants

Around Plaza Murillo *p248, maps p246 and p249*

$$ La Kantuta, in Hotel Presidente, Potosí 920, T240 6666. Excellent food, good service. La Bella Vista on the top floor is fancier.

Cafés
Alexander Coffee, Potosí 1091. Part of a chain, sandwiches, salads, coffee, pastries.
Café Soho, Jaén 747. Mon-Sun 0930-2300. Cosy café with small courtyard, inside and outside seating, local artwork.

Plaza San Francisco up to the cemetery district *p250, maps p246 and p249*

$$$-$$ Steakhouse, Tarija 243B, T231 0750, www.4cornerslapaz.com. Daily 1500-2300. Good cuts of meat, large variety of sauces and a great salad bar in a modern environment.

$$ La Cueva, Tarija 210B, T231 4523, www.4cornerslapaz.com. Daily 1130-late. Small cosy mexican restaurant, quick service, wide selection of tequilas.

$$ Pizzería Italia, Illampu 840, T246 3152, and 809, 2nd floor, T245 0714. Thin-crust pizza, and pasta.

$$-$ A Lo Cubano, Sagárnaga 357, entre Linares y Illampu, T245 1797. Mon-Sat 1200-2200. *Almuerzo* for US$3.65, but it runs out fast, also other choices of good Cuban food, good value.

$$-$ Angelo Colonial, Linares 922, T215 9633. Open early for breakfast. Vegetarian options, good music, internet, can get busy with slow service. Has a *hostal* at Av Santa Cruz 1058.

$$-$ Colonial Pot, Linares 906 y Sagárnaga. Bolivian dishes and a variety of main courses including vegetarian, set meal US$4.35 and à-la-carte, pastries, snacks, hot and cold drinks, quiet, homey, music, exceptional value.

$$-$ Sol y Luna, Murillo 999 y Cochabamba, T211 5323, www.solyluna-lapaz.com. Mon-Fri 0900-0100, Sat-Sun 1700-0100. Dutch run, breakfast, *almuerzo* and international menu, coffees and teas, full wine and cocktail list, live music Mon and Thu, movies, Wi-Fi, guide books for sale, book exchange, salsa lessons.

$$-$ Star of India, Cochabamba 170, T211 4409. British-run Indian curry house, will deliver, including to hotels.

$$-$ Tambo Colonial, in Hotel Rosario (see above). Excellent local and international cuisine, good salad bar, buffet breakfast, peña at weekend.

$ 100% Natural, Sagárnaga 345. Range of healthy, tasty fast foods ranging from salads to burgers and llama meat, good breakfasts.

Cafés
Banais, Sagárnaga 161, same entrance as Hostal Naira. Coffee, sandwiches and juices, buffet breakfast, set lunch, laid-back music and computer room.
Café del Mundo, Sagárnaga 324, www.cafe-delmundo.com. Swedish-owned, breakfasts, pancakes, waffles, sandwiches, coffees, teas and chocolate.
Café Illampu, Linares 940, upstairs. Mon-Sat 0800-2000, Sun 0930-1700. La Paz branch of the Swiss-run Sorata café known for its sandwiches, bread and cakes. Also salads, llama sausages, and European specialties like *roesti* and *spaetzle*. Recommended.
Pepe's, Pasaje Jiménez 894, off Linares. All-day breakfasts, sandwiches, omelettes, tables outside, cards and dominoes, magazines and guidebooks.

The Prado, Sopocachi, Miraflores and Zona Sur *p250, map p246*

$$$ Chalet la Suisse, Av Muñoz Reyes 1710, Cota Cota, T279 3160, www.chaletlasuisse.com.

Open 1900-2400, booking is essential on Fri. Serves excellent fondue, steaks.

$$$ Gustu, C 10 No 300, Calacoto, T211 7491, www.restaurantgustu.com. Upmarket restaurant with remarkable food and cookery school. Part of the Nordic cuisine pioneers, aimed at stimulating Bolivian gastronomy and giving opportunities to vulnerable people through the MeltingPot Foundation, www. meltingpot-bolivia.org.

$$$-$$ La Comedie, Pasaje Medinacelli 2234, Sopocachi, T242 3561. Mon-Fri 1200-1500, 1900-2300, Sat-Sun from 1900. 'Art café restaurant', contemporary, French menu, good salads, wine list and cocktails. See also La Loge under Where to stay.

$$ Beatrice, Guachalla y Ecuador, opposite Sopocachi market. Open 1200-2200, closed Tue. Excellent homemade pasta, good value and very popular with locals.

$$ El Consulado, Bravo 299 (by Hotel Europa), T211 7706. Open 0900-2000. Serves lunch and coffee and drinks in the evening. In gorgeous setting with outdoor seating and covered terrace, includes high-end handicraft store, book exchange, Wi-Fi, photo gallery, organic coffee and food, pricey but worth it.

$$ Maphrao On, Hnos Manchego 2586, near Plaza Isabela la Católica, T243 4602. Open 1200-1400, 1900-2400. Thai and Southeast Asian food, warm atmosphere, good music.

$$ Reineke Fuchs, Pje Jáuregui 2241, Sopocachi, T244 2979, and Av Montenegro y C 18, San Miguel, T277 2103, www.reineke fuchs.com. Mon-Fri 1200-1430 and from 1900, Sat from 1900 only. German-style bar/restaurant, many imported German beers, also set lunch from US$5.

$$ Suma Uru, Av Arce 2177 in Radisson Plaza Hotel, T244 1111. *Almuerzo* Mon-Fri for US$8 and excellent buffet, in 5-star setting on Sun 1200-1500, US$11.60. Friendly to backpackers.

$$-$ Ken-Chan, Bat Colorado 98 y F Suazo, p 2 of Japanese Cultural Center, T244 2292. Open 1800-2300. Japanese restaurant with wide variety of dishes, popular.

$$-$ Mongo's, Hnos Manchego 2444, near Plaza Isabela la Católica, T244 0714. Open 1830-0300, live music Tue, club after midnight. Excellent Mexican fare and steaks, open fires,

bar (cocktails can be pricey), popular with gringos and locals.

$$-$ Rendezvous, Sargento Carranza 461, end of Sánchez Lima, Sopocachi, T291 2459. Mon-Sat 1900-2200. Mediterranean cuisine, excellent variety and quality, best to book as usually full. Also has a very nice small hotel above the restaurant.

$$-$ Sancho Panza, Av Ecuador 738 y Gutiérrez, T242 6490, Sopocachi. Tue-Sat 1200-1500, 1900-2300, Sun 1200-1500. Mediterranean and Spanish tapas, also good value set lunches.

$$-$ Vienna, Federico Zuazo 1905, T244 1660, www.restaurantvienna.com. Mon-Fri 1200-1400, 1830-2200, Sun 1200-1430. Excellent German, Austrian and local food, great atmosphere and service, live piano music, popular.

$ Armonía, Av Ecuador 2286, above bookstore. Mon-Sat 1230-1400. Nice varied vegetarian buffet with organic produce from proprietors' farm. Recommended.

$ Como en Casa, Av del Ejercito 1115, on the road through the Parque Urbano towards Miraflores. Open 1100-1500. Good value set meals, meat and vegetable options, good service and atmosphere.

$ Olive Tree, Campos 334, Edificio Iturri, T243 1552. Mon-Fri 1100-2200, Sat 1100-1500. Good salads, soups and sandwiches, attentive service.

Cafés

Alexander Coffee (Café Alex), Av 16 de Julio 1832, also at 20 de Octubre 2463 Plaza Avaroa, Av Montenegro 1336, Calacoto, and the airport. Open 0730-2400. Excellent coffee, smoothies, muffins, cakes and good salads and sandwiches, Wi-Fi. Recommended.

Arco Iris, F Guachalla 554 y Sánchez Lima, Sopocachi. Also in Achumani, C 16 by the market. Bakery and handicraft outlet of Fundación Arco Iris (www.arcoirisbolivia.org), which works with street children, good variety of breads, pastries, meats and cheeses.

Fridolín, Av 6 de Agosto 2415; and Prolongación Montenegro, San Miguel. Daily 0800-2200. *Empanadas, tamales,* savoury and sweet (Austrian) pastries, coffee, breakfast, Wi-Fi.

Kuchen Stube, Rosendo Gutiérrez 461, Sopocachi. Mon-Fri 0800-2000, Sat-Sun

0800-1900. Excellent cakes, coffee and German specialities, also *almuerzo* Mon-Fri.

La Terraza, 16 de Julio 1615, 0630-0030; 20 de Octubre 2171 y Gutiérrez; and Av Montenegro 1576 y C 8, Calacoto, both 0730-2400. Excellent sandwiches and coffee, pancakes, breakfasts, Wi-Fi.

🍸 Bars and clubs

The epicentre for nightlife in La Paz is currently Plaza Avaroa in Sopocachi. Clubs are clustered around here and crowds gather Fri and Sat nights.

Around Plaza Murillo *p248, maps p246 and p249*
Etno Café, Jaén 722, T228 0343. Mon-Sat 1930-0300. Small café/bar with cultural programmes including readings, concerts, movies, popular, serves artisanal and fair trade drinks (alcoholic or not).

San Francisco up to the cemetery district *p250, maps p246 and p249*
Hard Rock Café, Santa Cruz 399 e Illampu, T211 9318, www.hardrockcafebolivia.lobopages.com. Serves Hard Rock fair, turns into nightclub around 2400, popular with locals and tourists, especially on Sun.
Oliver's English Tavern, Murillo y Cochabamba. Fake English pub serving breakfast from 0600, curries, sandwiches, fish and chips, pasta, sports channels, music, dress up parties and more. Pub crawl tours (see What to do, below) start here.

The Prado, Sopocachi, Miraflores and Zona Sur *p250, map p246*
Equinoccio, Sánchez Lima 2191, Sopocachi. Thu-Sat, cover charge US$2.10, or more for popular bands. Top venue for live rock music and bar.
Glam, Sánchez Lima 2237, next to Ferroviaria Andina. Thu-Sat from 2100. Good place to go dancing, live salsa on Fri.
Hallwrights, Sánchez Lima 2235, next to Glam. Mon-Sat 1700-0000. The only wine bar in La Paz.
Tetekos, C México 1553. Loud music, cheap drinks, popular with locals and backpackers.
Thelonius Jazz Bar, 20 de Octubre 2172, Sopocachi, T242 4405. Wed-Sat shows start at 2200. Renowned for jazz, cover charge US$3-5.

🎭 Entertainment

For current information on cinemas and shows, check *La Prensa* or *La Razón* on Fri, or visit www.laprensa.com.bo or www.la-razon.com. Also look for *Bolivian Express* (in English) and *Mañana*, both free monthly magazines with listings of concerts, exhibits, festivals, etc.

Around Plaza Murillo *p248, maps p246 and p249*
Bocaisapo, Indaburo 654 y Jaén. Thu-Fri 1900-0300. Live music in a bar; no cover charge, popular.
Marka Tambo, Jaén 710, T228 0041. Thu-Sat 2100-0200, also Mon-Sat 1230-1500 for lunch. US$6 for evening show, food and drinks extra, live shows with traditional dancing and music (*peña*), touristy but recommended.

Plaza San Francisco up to the cemetery district *p250, maps p246 and p249*
Peña Parnaso, Sagárnaga 189, T231 6827. Daily starting at 2030, meals available, purely for tourists but a good way to see local costumes and dancing.
Cinemas Films mainly in English with Spanish subtitles cost around US$3.50-4. See www. cinecenter.com.bo, http://megacenter.irpavi. com and www.multicine.com.bo; the latter has the most comfortable halls. **Cinemateca Boliviana**, Oscar Soria (prolong Federico Zuazo) y Rosendo Gutiérrez, T244 4090, www. cinematecaboliviana.org. Municipal theatre with emphasis on independent productions.
Theatre Teatro Municipal Alberto Saavedra Pérez has a regular schedule of plays, opera, ballet and classical concerts, at Sanjinés e Indaburo, T240 6183. The National Symphony Orchestra is very good and gives inexpensive concerts. Next door is the **Teatro Municipal de Cámara**, which shows dance, drama, music and poetry. **Casa Municipal de la Cultura 'Franz Tamayo'**, almost opposite Plaza San Francisco, hosts a variety of exhibitions, paintings, sculpture, photography, etc, mostly free. Free monthly guide to cultural events at information desk at entrance. The **Palacio Chico**, Ayacucho y Potosí, in old Correo, operated by the Secretaría Nacional de Cultura, also has free exhibitions (good for modern art), concerts and ballet, Mon-Fri 0900-1230, 1500-1900.

⚙ Festivals

La Paz *p245, maps p246 and p249*
Starting **24 Jan** Alasitas, in Parque Central up
from Av del Ejército, also in Plaza Sucre/San
Pedro, recommended. **Carnaval** in **Feb** or **Mar**.
End May/early Jun Festividad del Señor del
Gran Poder, the most important festival of the
year, with a huge procession of costumed and
masked dancers on the 3rd Sat after Trinity.
Jul Fiestas de Julio, a month of concerts and
performances at the Teatro Municipal, with
a variety of music, including the University
Folkloric Festival. **8 Dec**, festival around Plaza
España, colourful and noisy. On **New Year's**
Eve there are fireworks displays; view from
higher up. See page 242 for national holidays
and festivals outside La Paz.

⚙ Shopping

La Paz *p245, maps p246 and p249*
Camping equipment Kerosene for
pressure stoves is available from a pump in
Plaza Alexander, Pando e Inca. **Ayni Sport
Bolivia**, Jiménez 806, open Mon-Sun 1030-
2100. Rents and sometimes sells camping
equipment and mountain gear (trekking shoes,
fleeces, climbing equipment etc). **Caza y Pesca**,
Edif Handal Center, No 9, Av Mcal Santa Cruz
y Socabaya, T240 9209. English spoken. **The
Spitting Llama**, Linares 947 (inside Hostal
La Posada de la Abuela), T7039 8720, www.
thespittingllama.com. Sell camping gear
including GPS units, used books, guidebooks,
issue ISIC cards, English spoken, helpful;
branches in Cochabamba and Copacabana.
Tatoo Bolivia, Illampu 828, T245 1265, www.
tatoo.ws. Tatoo clothing plus outdoor
equipment including backpacks, shoes, etc.
English and Dutch spoken. For camping stove
fuel enquire at **Emita Tours** on Sagárnaga.
Handicrafts Above Plaza San Francisco
(see page 250), up Sagárnaga, by the side of
San Francisco church (behind which are many
handicraft stalls in the Mercado Artesanal), are
booths and small stores with interesting local
items of all sorts. The lower end of Sagárnaga
is best for antiques. **Galería Dorian**, Sagárnaga
177, is an entire gallery of handicraft shops;
includes **Tejidos Wari**, unit 12, for high-quality

alpaca goods, will make to measure, English
spoken. On Linares, between Sagárnaga and
Santa Cruz, high quality alpaca goods are
priced in US$. Also in this area are many places
making fleece jackets, gloves and hats, but
shop around for value and service. **Alpaca
Style**, C 22 No 14, T271 1233, Achumani.
Upmarket shop selling alpaca and leather
clothing. **Arte y Diseño**, Illampu 833. Makes
typical clothing to your own specifications
in 24 hrs. **Artesanía Sorata**, Linares 900,
T245 4728, and Sagárnaga 363. Specializes in
dolls, sweaters and weavings. **Ayni**, Illampu
704, www.aynibolivia.com. Fair trade shop
in Hotel Rosario, featuring Aymara work.
Comart Tukuypaj, Linares 958, T231 2686, and
C 21, Galería Centro de Moda, Local 4B, San
Miguel, www.comart-tukuypaj.com. High-
quality textiles from an artisan community
association. **Incapallay**, Linares 958, p 2, www.
incapallay.org. A weavers' cooperative from
Tarabuco and Jalq'a communities, near Sucre.
Jiwitaki Art Shop, Jaén 705, T7725 4042. Run
by local artists selling sketches, paintings,
sculptures, literature, etc. Open Mon-Fri 1100-
1300, 1500-1800. **LAM** shops on Sagárnaga.
Good quality alpaca goods. **Millma**, Sagárnaga
225, T231 1338, and Claudio Aliaga 1202,
Bloque L-1, San Miguel, closed Sat afternoon
and Sun. High-quality alpaca knitwear and
woven items and, in the San Miguel shop, a
permanent exhibition of ceremonial 19th and
20th century Aymara and Quechua textiles
(free). **Mother Earth**, Linares 870, T239 1911.
0930-1930 daily. High-quality alpaca sweaters
with natural dyes. **Toshy** on Sagárnaga. Top-
quality knitwear.
Jewellery Good jewellery stores with native
and modern designs include **King's**, Loayza 261,
between Camacho and Mercado also at Torre
Ketal, C 15, Calacoto and Mi Joyita, Av Mariscal
Santa Cruz 1351, El Prado.
Maps IGM: head office at Estado Mayor, Av
Saavedra 2303, Miraflores, T214 9484, Mon-Thu
0900-1200, 1500-1800, Fri 0900-1200, take
passport to buy maps. Also office in Edif Murillo,
Final Rodríguez y Juan XXIII, T237 0116, Mon-Fri
0830-1230, 1430-1830, some stock or will get
maps from HQ in 24 hrs. **Librería IMAS**, Av Mcal
Santa Cruz entre Loayza y Colón, Edif Colón,
T235 8234. Ask to see the map collection. Maps

are also sold in the Post Office on the stalls opposite the Poste Restante counter.

Markets In addition to those mentioned in the Plaza San Francisco section (page 250), the 5-km sq **Feria 16 de Julio, El Alto** market is on Thu and Sun (the latter is bigger). Take any minibus that says La Ceja and get off at overpass after toll booth (follow crowd of people or tell driver you're going to La Feria), or take 16 de Julio minibus from Plaza Eguino. Arrive around 0900; most good items are sold by 1200. Goods are cheap, especially on Thu. Absolutely everything imaginable is sold here. Be watchful for pickpockets, just take a bin liner to carry your purchases. **Mercado Sopocachi**, Guachalla y Ecuador, a well-stocked covered market selling foodstuffs, kitchen supplies, etc.

Musical instruments Many shops on Pasaje Linares, the stairs off C Linares, also on Sagárnaga/Linares, for example **Walata 855**.

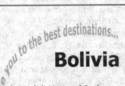

La Paz *p245, maps p246 and p249*

City tours
The **Teleférico**, scheduled to start operating in mid-2014, promises a spectacular overview of La Paz (see Transport). **Sightseeing**, T279 1440, city tours on a double-decker bus, 2 circuits, downtown and Zona Sur with Valle de la Luna (1 morning and 1 afternoon departure to each), departs from Plaza Isabel la Católica and can hop on at Plaza San Francisco, tour recorded in 7 languages, US$9 for both circuits, Mon-Fri at 0830 and 1430, Sat-Sun at 0900 and 1430. Free walking tours of La Paz are given by Red C&P, www.redcapwalkingtours.com, 1100 and 1400 every day from Plaza San Pedro, 2½ hrs; they also offer pub crawl and local food tours. See also **La Paz On Foot** tour operator, below.

Climbing, hiking and trekking
Guides must be hired through a tour company. There is a mountain rescue group, **Socorro Andino Boliviano**, Calle 40 Villa Aérea, T246 5879. **Andean Summits**, Muñoz Cornejo 1009 y Sotomayor, Sopocachi, T242 2106, www.andean summits.com. For mountaineering and other trips off the beaten track, contact in advance. **Bolivian Mountains**, Rigoberto Paredes 1401 y Colombia, p 3, San Pedro, T249 2775, www.bolivianmountains.com (in UK T01273-746545). High-quality mountaineering with experienced guides and good equipment, not cheap. **Climb On**. Brand new outfit (ask at **Gravity** or **Kanoo** – see below) offering all-inclusive tours, ½ day or longer, routes for beginners and experts. **Climbing South America**, Murillo 1014 y Rodríguez, Ed Provenzal PB, of 1, T215 2232, www.climbingsouthamerica.com. Climbing and trekking in Bolivia, Argentian and Chile, equipment rental, Australian run. **Refugio Huayna Potosí**, Sagárnaga 308 e Illampu, T245 6717, www.huayna-potosi.com. Climbing and trekking tours, run 2 mountain shelters on Huayna Potosí and climbing school.

Football
Popular and played on Wed and Sun at the **Siles Stadium** in Miraflores (Micro A), which is shared by both La Paz's main teams, Bolívar and The Strongest. There are reserved seats.

Golf

Mallasilla is the world's highest golf course, at 3318 m. Non-members can play here on weekdays, US$85.

Tour operators

America Tours, Av 16 de Julio 1490 (El Prado), Edificio Avenida pb, No 9, T237 4204, www. america-ecotours.com. Cultural and ecotourism trips to many parts of the country, rafting, trekking and horse riding, English spoken. Highly professional and recommended.

Andean Base Camp, Illampu 863, T246 3782. Overland tours throughout Bolivia, Swiss staff, good reports.

Andean Secrets, General Gonzales 1314 y Almirante Grau, San Pedro (Mon Fri 1500-1900, Sat 0900-1730, Sun 1000-1400), T7729 4590, quimsacruz_bolivia@hotmail.com, www. andean-secrets.com. Female mountain guide Denys Sanjines specializes in the Cordillera Quimsa Cruz.

Barracuda Biking Company, Illampu 750, inside Hostal Gloria, of 4, T245 9950, info@ barracudabiking.com. Bike trips to Coroico at a lower price than the upmarket companies.

Bolivian Journeys, Sagárnaga 363, p 2, T235 7848, www.bolivianjourneys.org. Camping, mountain bike tours, equipment rental, maps, English and French spoken, helpful.

Crillon Tours, Camacho 1223, T233 7533, www.titicaca.com. A company with over 50 years' experience. Joint scheduled tours with Lima arranged. Fixed departures and luxury camper service to Salar de Uyuni (www.uyuni. travel), trips throughout Bolivia, including the Yungas, Sajama and Lauca, community and adventure tourism and much more. ATM for cash. Recommended. Full details of their Lake Titicaca services on page 273. See www.alwa. travel for their deluxe overlanding scheme.

Deep Rainforest, Galería Dorian, Sagárnaga 189, of 9A, T215 0385, www.deep-rainforest. com. Off the beaten track trekking, climbing, canoe trips from Guanay to Rurrenabaque, rainforest and pampas trips.

Enjoy Bolivia, Plaza Isabel La Católica, Edif Presidente Bush, of 2, T243 5162, www.njbol travel.com. Wide selection of tours and transport service. Airport and bus terminal transfers, van service to Oruro (US$13 pp shared, US$90 private).

Fremen Tours, Av 20 de Octubre 2396, Edif María Haydee, p 10, T242 1258, www.andes-amazonia.com. Customized tours and special interest travel throughout Bolivia, including **Tayka** hotels around Salar de Uyuni and Reina de Enín riverboat.

Gloria Tours, Potosí 909, T240 7070, www.gloriatours.com.bo. Good service. See Hotel Gloria, page 253.

Gravity Bolivia, Av 16 de Julio 1490 (El Prado), Edif Avenida, Ground Floor Office 10, T231 3849, www.gravitybolivia.com. A wide variety of mountain biking tours throughout Bolivia, including the world-famous downhill ride to Coroico. They offer a zipline at the end of the ride, or independently (www.ziplinebolivia. com). Also bike rides more challenging than Coroico, including single-track and high-speed dirt roads, with coaching and safety equipment. Also have cycle spares, very knowledgeable service. Book on website in advance or by phone until 2200, T7721 9634. Recommended.

Kanoo Tours, Illampu 832 entre Sagárnaga y Santa Cruz, T246 0003, www.kanootours.com. Also at **Adventure Brew Hostel**. Sells **Gravity Bolivia** tours (see above), plus Salar de Uyuni, Rurrenabaque jungle trips and Perú.

La Paz On Foot, Prol Posnanski 400, Miraflores, T224 8350/7154 3918, www. lapazonfoot.com. Walking city tours, walking and sailing trips on Titicaca, tours to Salar de Uyuni, multi-day treks in the Yungas and Apolobamba and regional tours focused on Andean food and biodiversity which also include Peru, northern Chile and Argentina. Recommended.

Lipiko Tours, Av Mariscal Santa Cruz 918 y Sagárnaga, Galería La República, T214 5129, www.travel-bolivia.co.uk. Tailor-made tours for all budgets, 4WD tours, trekking, climbing and adventure sport, trips to Amazon and national parks. Also cover Peru, Chile and Argentina.

Magri Turismo, Capitán Ravelo 2101, T244 2727, www.magriturismo.com. Recommended for tours throughout Bolivia, flight tickets. Own La Estancia hotel on the Isla del Sol.

Moto Andina, Urb La Colina N°6 Calle 25, Calacoto, T7129 9329, www.moto-andina. com (in French). Motorcycle tours of varying difficulty in Bolivia, contact Maurice Manco.

Mundo Quechua, Av Circunvalación 43, Achumani, Zona Sur, T279 6145, www.mundo quechua.com. Daily tours to the Cordillera Real, private transport in and around La Paz, custom made climbing, trekking and 4WD tours throughout Bolivia. Also extensions to Peru and Argentina. English and French spoken, good service.

Peru Bolivian Tours, Calle Capitán Ravelo 2097, esquina Montevideo, Edif Paola Daniela, 1st piso, oficina 1-A, T244 5732, www.perubolivian.com. More than 20 years' experience, arranges special programmes throughout Bolivia and Peru.

Topas Travel, Carlos Bravo 299 (behind **Hotel Plaza**), T211 1082, www.topas.bo. Joint venture of Akhamani Trek (Bolivia), Topas (Denmark) and the Danish embassy, offering trekking, overland truck trips, jungle trips and climbing, English spoken, restaurant and *pensión*.

Transturin, Av Arce 2678, Sopocachi, T242 2222, www.transturin.com. Full travel services with tours in La Paz and throughout Bolivia.

Details of their Lake Titicaca services on page 274.

Tupiza Tours, Villalobos 625 y Av Saavedra, Edif Girasoles, ground floor, Miraflores, T224 5254, www.tupizatours.com. La Paz office of the Tupiza agency. Specialize in the Salar and southwest Bolivia, but also offer tours around La Paz and throughout the country.

Turisbus, Av Illampu 704, T245 1341, www. turisbus.com. Lake Titicaca and Isla del Sol, Salar de Uyuni, Rurrenbaque, trekking and Bolivian tours. Also tours and tickets to Puno and Cuzco.

Turismo Balsa, Av 6 de Agosto 3 y Pinilla, T244 0620, www.turismobalsa.com. City and tours throughout Bolivia. Owns **Hotel Las Balsas**, in beautiful lakeside setting at Puerto Pérez on Lake Titicaca, T02-289 5147, 72 km from La Paz, with excellent restaurant.

Urban Rush, T240 6666, www.urbanrush bolivia.com. Go to **Hotel Presidente** 1300-1700 for abseiling or rap jumping from one of the tallest buildings in La Paz, gaining popularity quickly.

⊙ Transport

La Paz *p245, maps p246 and p249*

Air

La Paz has the highest commercial **airport** in the world, at El Alto (4061 m); T281 0240. Cotranstur minibuses, T231 2032, white with 'Cotranstur' and 'Aeropuerto' written on the side and back, go from Plaza Isabel La Católica, stopping all along the Prado and Av Mcal Santa Cruz to the airport, 0615-2300, US$0.55 (allow about 1 hr), best to buy an extra seat for your luggage, departures every 4 mins. Shared transport from Plaza Isabel La Católica, US$3.50 pp, carrying 4 passengers, also private transfers from **Enjoy Bolivia**, see Tour operators, page 261. Radio-taxi is US$9 to centre, US$14 to Zona Sur. Prices are displayed at the airport terminal exit. There is an **Info Tur** office in arrivals with a *casa de cambio* next to it (dollars, euros cash and TCs, poor rates; open 0530-1300, 1700-0300, closed Sun evening – when closed try the counter where departure taxes are paid). Several ATMs in the departures hall. The international and domestic departures hall is the main concourse, with all check-in desks. There are separate domestic and international arrivals. Bar/restaurant and café upstairs in departures. For details of air services, see under destinations.

Bus

City buses There are 3 types of city bus: the modern puma katari, introduced in Mar 2014, with 3 lines along different routes, mostly from El Alto through the centre to the Zona Sur, US$0.25-0.30 depending on route, additional lines will be added; *micros* (small, old buses), which charge US$0.20 a journey; and minibuses (small vans), US$0.20-0.35 depending on the journey. *Trufis* are fixed-route collective taxis, with a sign with their route on the windscreen, US$0.45 pp in the centre, US$0.55 outside.

Long distance For information, T228 5858. Buses to: **Oruro**, **Potosí**, **Sucre**, **Cochabamba**, **Santa Cruz**, **Tarija**, **Uyuni**, **Tupiza**, and **Villazón**, leave from the main terminal at Plaza Antofagasta (micros 2, M, CH or 130), see under each destination for details. Taxi to central hotels, US$1.40. The terminal (open 0400-2300) has a tourist booth by the main entrance, ATMs, internet, a post office, **Entel**, restaurant, luggage store and travel agencies. Touts find passengers the most convenient bus and are paid commission by the bus company. To **Oruro** van service with **Enjoy Bolivia**, see Tour operators, page 261, US$13 pp shared, US$90 private.

To **Copacabana**, several bus companies (tourist service) pick-up travellers at their hotels (in the centre) and also stop at the main terminal, tickets from booths at the terminal (cheaper) or agencies in town. They all leave about 0800 (**Titicaca Bolivia** also at 1400), 3½ hrs, US$3.60-4.50 one way, return from Copacabana about 1330. When there are not enough passengers for each company, they pool them. **Diana Tours**, T235 0252, **Titicaca Bolivia**, T246 2655, **Turisbus**, T245 1341 (more expensive), many others. You can also book this service all the way to Puno, US$7.

Public buses to **Copacabana**, **Tiwanaku**, **Desaguadero** (border with Peru) and **Sorata**, leave from the Cemetery district. To get there, take any bus or minibus marked 'Cementerio' going up C Santa Cruz (US$0.15-0.22). On Plaza Reyes Ortiz are **Manco Capac**, and 2 de Febrero for **Copacabana** and **Tiquina**. From the Plaza go up Av Kollasuyo and at the 2nd street on the right (Manuel Bustillos) is the terminal for minibuses to **Achacachi**, **Huatajata** and **Huarina**, as well as Trans Unificada and Flor del Illampu minibuses for **Sorata**. Several micros (20, J, 10) and minibuses (223, 252, 270, 7) go up Kollasuyo. Taxi US$2 from downtown, US$4.30 from Zona Sur. Buses to **Coroico, the Yungas and northern jungle** leave from Terminal Minasa in Villa Fátima (25 mins by micros B, V, X, K, 131, 135, or 136, or *trufis* 2 or 9, which pass Pérez Velasco coming down from Plaza Mendoza, and get off at Minasa terminal, Puente Minasa). See Safety, page 248.

International buses From main bus terminal: to **Buenos Aires**, US$102, 2 a week with Ormeño, T228 1141, 54 hrs via Santa Cruz and Yacuiba; via Villazón with **Río Paraguay**, 3 a week, US$75, or **Trans Americano**, US$85. Alternatively, go to Villazón and change buses in Argentina. To **Arica** via the frontier at Tambo Quemado and Chungará, **Pullmanbus** at

0630 (good), **Cuevas** at 0700, **Zuleta** at 0600, **Nuevo Continente** at 1230 except Sat, **Litoral**, T228 1920, Sun-Thu 1230, US$26. Connecting service for Iquique or Santiago. To **Puno** and **Cuzco**, luxury and indirect services, see under Lake Titicaca, page 275. Direct to Cuzco, 12 hrs with **Litoral**, US$23 via Desaguadero and Puno (5 hrs, US$8). To **Lima**, Ormeño daily at 1430, US$90, 27 hrs; **Nuevo Continente** at 0830, US$88, 26 hrs, via Desaguadero, change to Cial in Puno.

Cable car
Teleférico A system of 3 lines of cable cars joining neighbourhoods along the edge of the altiplano, including El Alto, with the centre of the city and the Zona Sur, are under construction in 2014. The red line from La Ceja, El Alto, to the old train station, 3 blocks above Plaza Eguino, in an area known as Vita in the northwest of the city, is due to start operating in mid-2014.

Car hire
Imbex, C11, No 7896, Calacoto, T212 1012, www.imbex.com. Wide range of well-maintained vehicles; Suzuki jeeps from US$60 per day, including 200 km free for 4-person 4WD. Also office in Santa Cruz, T311001. Recommended. **Kolla Motors**, Rosendo Gutierrez 502 y Ecuador, Sopocachi, T241 9141, www.kollamotors.com. 6-seater 4WD Toyota jeeps, insurance and gasoline extra. **Petita Rent-a-car**, Valentín Abecia 2031, Sopocachi Alto, T242 0329, www.rentacarpetita.com. Swiss owners Ernesto Hug and Aldo Rezzonico. Recommended for personalized service and well-maintained 4WD jeeps, minimum rental 1 week. Their vehicles can also be taken outside Bolivia. Also offer adventure tours (German, French, English spoken). Ernesto has a highly recommended garage for VW and other makes, Av Jaimes Freyre 2326, T241 5264.

Taxi
Taxis are often, but not always, white. Taxi drivers are not tipped. There are 3 types: standard taxis which may take several passengers at once (US$0.45-1.75 for short trips within city limits), fake taxis which have been involved in robberies, and radio taxis which take only one group of passengers at a time. Since it is impossible to distinguish between the first two, it is best to pay a bit more for a radio taxi, especially at night. These have a dome light, a unique number (note this when getting in) and radio communication (eg Gold T241 1414 in the centre, 272 2722 in Zona Sur, Servisur T271 9999). They charge US$1.40-2.20 in centre, more to suburbs and at night.

Train
Ferroviaria Andina (FCA), Sánchez Lima 2199 y Fernando Guachalla, Sopocachi, T241 6545, www.fca.com.bo, Mon-Fri 0800-1600. Sells tickets for the **Oruro-Uyunui-Tupiza-Villazón** line; see schedule and fares under Oruro Transport (page 286). Tickets for *ejecutivo* class sold up to 2 weeks in advance, for *salón* 1 week. Must show passport to buy tickets. Also operate a **tourist train** from **El Alto** station, C 8, Villa Santiago I, by Cuartel Ingavi, the 2nd Sun of each month at 0800, to **Guaqui** via Tiwanaku; returning from Guaqui at 1500; US$4.35 *ejecutivo*, US$2.90 *popular*, confirm all details in advance.

South of La Paz *p251*
For Valle de la Luna, Minibuses 231, 273 and 902 can be caught on C México, the Prado or Av 6 de Agosto. Alternatively take Micro 11 ('Aranjuez' large, not small bus) or ones that say 'Mallasa' or 'Mallasilla' along the Prado or Av 6 de Agosto, US$0.65, and ask driver where to get off. Most of the travel agents organize tours to the Valle de la Luna. There are brief, 5-min stops for photos in a US$15 tour of La Paz and surroundings; taxis cost US$6, US$10 with a short wait.

Tiwanaku *p251*
To get to Tiwanaku, tours booked through agencies cost US$12 (not including entry fee or lunch). Otherwise take any **Micro** marked 'Cementerio' in La Paz, get out at Plaza Félix Reyes Ortiz, on Mariano Bautista (north side of cemetery), go north up Aliaga, 1 block east of Asín to find Tiwanaku micros, US$2, 1½ hrs, every 30 mins, 0600 to 1500. Tickets can be bought in advance. **Taxi** costs US$30-55 return (shop around), with 2 hrs at site. Some **buses** go on from Tiwanaku to Desaguadero; virtually all Desaguadero buses stop at

the access road to Tiwanaku, 20-min walk from the site. Return buses (last back 1700) leave from south side of the Plaza in village. Minibuses (vans) to **Desaguadero**, from José María Asín y P Eyzaguirre (Cemetery district) US$2, 2 hrs, most movement on Tue and Fri when there is a market at the border.
Note When returning from Tiwanaku (ruins or village) to La Paz, do not take an empty minibus. We have received reports of travellers being taken to El Alto and robbed at gun point. Wait for a public bus with paying passengers in it.

Takesi Trail *p252*
Take a **Líneas Ingavi** bus from C Gral Luis Lara esq Venacio Burgoa near Plaza Líbano, San Pedro, going to **Pariguaya** (2 hrs past Chuñavi), daily at 0800, US$3, 2 hrs. On Sun, also mini-buses from C Gral Luis Lara y Boquerón, hourly 0700-1500. To **Mina San Francisco**: hire a **jeep** from La Paz; US$85, takes about 2 hrs. **Veloz del Norte** (T02-221 8279) leaves from Ocabaya 495 in Villa Fátima, T221 8279, 0900 daily, and 1400 Thu-Sun, US$3, 3½ hrs, continuing to Chojlla. From Chojlla to La Paz daily at 0500, 1300 also on Thu-Sun, passing **Yanakachi** 15 mins later.

Choro Trail *p253*
To the *apacheta* pass beyond **La Cumbre**, take a **taxi** from central La Paz for US$20, 45 mins, stopping to register at the Guardaparque hut. Buses from Villa Fátima to Coroico and Chulumani pass La Cumbre. Tell driver where you are going, US$2.80. The trail is signed.

Huayna Potosí *p253*
The mountain can be reached by transport arranged through tourist agencies (US$100) or the refugio, **taxi** US$45. **Minibus** Trans Zongo, Av Chacaltaya e Ingavi, Ballivián, El Alto, daily 0600, 2½ hrs, US$1.80 to Zongo, check on return time. Also minibuses from the Ballivián area that leave when full (few on Sun). If camping in the Zongo Pass area, stay at the site near the white house above the cross.

ⓘ Directory

La Paz *p245, maps p246 and p249*
Embassies and consulates For all foreign embassies and consulates in La Paz, see http://embassy.goabroad.com. **Language schools** Instituto Exclusivo, Av 20 de Octubre 2315, Edif Mechita, T242 1072, www.instituto-exclusivo.com. Spanish lessons for individual and groups, accredited by Ministry of Education. **Instituto de La Lengua Española**, María Teresa Tejada, C Aviador esq final 14, No 180, Achumani, T279 6074, T7155 6735. One-to-one lessons US$7 per hr. Recommended. Speak Easy Institute, Av Arce 2047, between Goitia and Montevideo, T244 1779, speakeasyinstitute@yahoo.com. US$6 for one-to-one private lessons, cheaper for groups and couples, Spanish and English taught. **Private Spanish lessons** from: Isabel Daza, Murillo 1046, p 3, T231 1471, T7062 8016. US$4 per hr. Enrique Eduardo Patzy, Méndez Arcos 1060, Sopocachi, T241 5501 or T776-22210, epatzy@hotmail.com. US$6 an hr one-to-one tuition, speaks English and Japanese. Recommended.
Medical services For hospitals, doctors and dentists, contact your consulate or the tourist office for recommendations. Health and hygiene: Ministerio de Desarollo Humano, Secretaría Nacional de Salud, Av Arce, near Radisson Plaza, yellow fever shot and certificate, rabies and cholera shots, malaria pills, bring own syringe. Centro Piloto de Salva, Av Montes y Basces, T245 0026, 10 mins walk from Plaza San Francisco, for malaria pills, helpful. Laboratorios Illimani, Edif Alborada p 3, of 304, Loayza y Juan de la Riva, T231 7290, open 0900-1230, 1430-1700, fast, efficient, hygienic. Tampons may be bought at most *farmacias* and supermarkets. Daily papers list pharmacies on duty (de turno). For contact lenses, **Optalis**, Comercio 1089. **Useful addresses** Immigration: to renew a visa go to **Migración Bolivia**, Camacho 1468, T211 0960. Mon-Fri 0830-1230, 1430-1830, go early. Allow 48 hrs for visa extensions. **Tourist Police**: C Hugo Estrada 1354, Plaza Tejada Sorzano frente al estadio, Miraflores, next to Love City Chinese restaurant, T800-140081, 0900-1800, or in office hours T222 5016. Open 0830-1800, for police report for insurance claims after theft.

Lake Titicaca

Lake Titicaca is two lakes joined by the Straits of Tiquina: the larger, northern lake (Lago Mayor, or Chucuito) contains the Islas del Sol and de la Luna; the smaller lake (Lago Menor, or Huiñamarca) has several small islands. The waters are a beautiful blue, reflecting the hills and the distant cordillera in the shallows of Huiñamarca, mirroring the sky in the rarified air and changing colour when it is cloudy or raining. A boat trip on the lake is a must.

Arriving at Lake Titicaca

Getting there A paved road runs from La Paz to the southeastern shore of the lake. One branch continues north along the eastern shore, another branch goes to the Straits of Tiquina (114 km El Alto-San Pablo) and Copacabana. A third road goes to Guaqui and Desaguadero on the southwestern shore. ▶▶ *See also Transport, page 274.*

La Paz to Copacabana

Huatajata Along the northeast shore of the lake is Huatajata, with Yacht Club Boliviano and **Crillon Tours' International Hydroharbour** and **Inca Utama Hotel** (see below). Reed boats are still built and occasionally sail here for the tourist trade. There are several small but interesting exhibits of reed boats that were used on long ocean voyages. Beyond here is **Chúa**, where there is fishing, sailing and **Transturin's** catamaran dock (see below).

Islands of Lake Huiñamarca

On **Suriqui** (one hour from Huatajata) in Lake Huiñamarca, a southeasterly extension of Lake Titicaca, you can see reed *artesanías*. The late Thor Heyerdahl's *Ra II*, which sailed from Morocco to Barbados in 1970, his *Tigris* reed boat, and the balloon gondola for the Nazca (Peru) flight experiment (see the Nazca Lines in the Peru chapter), were also constructed by the craftsmen of Suriqui. Reed boats are still made on Suriqui, probably the last place where the art survives. On **Kalahuta** there are *chullpas* (burial towers), old buildings and the uninhabited town of Kewaya. On **Pariti** there is Inca terracing and the **Museo Señor de los Patos**, with weavings and Tiwanku-era ceramics.

From Chúa the main road reaches the east side of the Straits at **San Pablo** (clean restaurant in blue building, toilets at both sides of the crossing). On the west side is San Pedro, the main Bolivian naval base, from where a paved road goes to Copacabana and the border. Vehicles are transported across on barges, US$5. Passengers cross separately, US$0.20 (not included in bus fares) and passports may be checked. Expect delays during rough weather, when it can get very cold.

Copacabana → *Phone code: 02. Colour map 6, A2. Population: 5515. Altitude: 3850 m.*

A popular little resort town on Lake Titicaca, 158 km from La Paz by paved road, Copacabana is set on a lovely bay and surrounded by scenic hills. **Municipal tourist office** ⓘ *16 de Julio y 6 de Agosto, Wed-Sun 0800-1200, 1400-1800*. There are two unreliable ATMs in town, best bring some cash.

Red de Turismo Comunitario ⓘ *6 de Agosto y 16 de Julio, T7729 9088, Mon-Sat 0800-1230, 1300-1900*, can arrange tours to nearby communities. At major holidays (Holy Week, 3 May, 6 August), the town fills with visitors.

Copacabana has a heavily restored, Moorish-style **basilica** ⓘ *open 0700-2000; minimum 5 people at a time to visit museum, Tue-Sat 1000-1100, 1500-1600, Sun 1000-1100, US$1.50, no photos allowed*. It contains a famous 16th-century miracle-working Virgen Morena (Dark Lady), also known as the Virgen de Candelaria, one of the patron saints of Bolivia. The basilica is clean, white, with coloured tiles decorating the exterior arches, cupolas and chapels. It is notable for its spacious atrium with four small chapels; the main chapel has one of the finest gilt altars in Bolivia. There are 17th- and 18th-century paintings and statues in the sanctuary. Vehicles decorated with flowers and confetti are blessed in front of the church.

On the headland which overlooks the town and port, **Cerro Calvario**, are the Stations of the Cross (a steep 45-minute climb – leave plenty of time if going to see the sunset). On the hill behind the town is the **Horca del Inca**, two pillars of rock with another laid across them; probably a sun clock, now covered in graffiti. There is a path marked by arrows, boys will offer to guide you: fix price in advance if you want their help.

There are many great hikes in the hills surrounding Copacabana. North of town is the **Yampupata Peninsula**. It is a beautiful 17 km (six hours) walk to the village of Yampupata at the tip of the peninsula, either via Sicuani on the west shore or Sampaya on the east shore, both picturesque little towns. There are also minibuses from Copacabana to Yampupata, where you can hire a motorboat or rowboat to Isla del Sol or Isla de la Luna; boats may also be available from Sampaya to Isla de la Luna.

Isla del Sol
The site of the main Inca creation myth (there are other versions) is a place of exceptional natural beauty and spiritual interest. Legend has it that Viracocha, the creator god, had his children, Manco Kapac and Mama Ocllo, spring from the waters of the lake to found Cuzco and the Inca dynasty. A sacred rock at the island's northwest end is worshipped as their birthplace. Near the rock are the impressive ruins of **Chincana**, the labyrinth, a 25-minute walk from the village of Challapampa, with a basic **museum** ① *US$1.45 includes landing fee and entry to Chincana*. Near the centre of the island is the community of Challa with an **ethnographic museum** ① *US$2.15, includes trail fees*. Towards the south end of the island is the **Fuente del Inca**, a spring reached by Inca steps leading up from the lake and continuing up to the

Copacabana

Where to stay
1 Chasqui del Sol
2 Ecolodge
3 Emperador
4 Gloria Copacabana
5 Kantutas
6 Kotha Kahuaña
7 La Cúpula
8 Las Olas
9 Leyenda
10 Pacha
11 Rosario del Lago
12 Sonia
13 Utama

Restaurants
1 Aransaya
2 Café Bistrot Copacabana
3 La Orilla
4 Puerta del Sol
5 Snack 6 de Agosto
6 Sujna Wasi

village of Yumani. Near the southeast tip of the island, 2 km from the spring, are the ruins of **Pilcocaina** ① *US$0.70 include landing fees*, a two storey building with false domes and nice views over the water. You must pay the fees even if you don't visit the museums or ruins. Keep all entry tickets, you may be asked for them at other locations. Several restored pre-Columbian roads cross the island from north to south.

The three communities are along the east shore of the island. All have electricity (Yumani also has internet), accommodation and simple places to eat. The island is heavily touristed and gets crowded in high season. Touts and beggars can be persistent, especially in Yumani. Tour operators in Copacabana offer half- and full-day 'tours' (many are just transport, see page 275) but an overnight stay at least is recommended to appreciate fully the island and to enjoy the spectacular walk from north to south (or vice-versa) at a comfortable pace. In a day trip, you will barely have time for a quick look at Chincana and you will see Pilcocaina from the boat. Note that it is a steep climb from the pier to the town of Yumani. Local guides are available in Challapampa and Yumani.

Southeast of Isla del Sol is the smaller **Isla de la Luna**, which may also be visited. The community of Coati is located on the west shore, an Inca temple and nunnery on the east shore.

Border with Peru

West side of Lake Titicaca The road goes from La Paz 91 km west to the former port of **Guaqui** (at the military checkpoint here, and other spots on the road, passports may be inspected). The road crosses the border at **Desaguadero** 22 km further west and runs along the shore of the lake to Puno. Bolivian immigration is just before the bridge, open 0830-2030 (Peru is one hour earlier than Bolivia). Get exit stamp, walk 200 m across the bridge then get entrance stamp on the other side. Get Peruvian visas in La Paz. There are a few hotels and restaurants on both sides of the border; very basic in Bolivia, slightly better in Peru. Money changers on Peruvian side give reasonable rates. Market days are Friday and Tuesday: otherwise the town is dead.

Via Copacabana From Copacabana a paved road leads 8 km south to the frontier at Kasani, then to Yunguyo, Peru. Do not photograph the border area. For La Paz tourist agency services on this route see International buses, page 263, and What to do, page 273. The border is open 0730-1930 Bolivian time (one hour later than Peruvian time). International tourist buses stop at both sides of the border; if using local transport walk 300 m between the two posts. Do not be fooled into paying any unnecessary charges to police or immigration. Going to Peru, money can be changed at the Peruvian side of the border. Coming into Bolivia, the best rates are at Copacabana.

East side of Lake Titicaca

From Huarina, a road heads northwest to Achacachi (market Sunday; fiesta 14 September). Here, one road goes north across a tremendous marsh to **Warisata**, then crosses the altiplano to Sorata (see below). At Achacachi, another road runs roughly parallel to the shore of Lake Titicaca, through **Ancoraimes** (Sunday market, the church hosts a community project making dolls and alpaca sweaters, also has dorms), **Carabuco** (with colonial church), **Escoma**, which has an Aymara market every Sunday morning, to **Puerto Acosta**, 10 km from the Peruvian border. It is a pleasant, friendly town with a large plaza and several simple places to stay and eat. The area around Puerto Acosta is good walking country. From La Paz to Puerto Acosta the road is paved as far as Escoma, then good until Puerto Acosta (best in the dry season, approximately May to October). North of Puerto Acosta towards Peru the road deteriorates and should not be attempted except in the dry season. There is a smugglers' market at the border on Wednesday and Saturday, the only days when transport is plentiful. You should get an exit stamp in La Paz before heading to this border (only preliminary entrance stamps are given here). There is a Peruvian customs post 2 km from the border and 2 km before Tilali, but Peruvian immigration is in Puno.

Sorata → *Phone code: 02. Colour map 6, A2. Population: 2523. Altitude: 2700 m. See map, page 269.*

Sorata, 163 km from La Paz along a paved road, is a beautiful colonial town nestled at the foot of Mount Illampu; all around it are views over steep lush valleys. The climate is milder and more humid compared to the altiplano. Nearby are some challenging long-distance treks as well as great day-hikes. The town has a charming plaza, with views of the snow-capped summit of Illampu on a clear day. The main fiesta is 14 September. There is no ATM in Sorata, take cash.

A popular excursion is to **San Pedro cave** ⓘ *0800-1700, US$3, toilets at entrance*, beyond the village of San Pedro. The cave has an underground lake (no swimming allowed) and is lit. It is reached either by road, a 12 km walk (three hours each way), or by a path high above the Río San Cristóbal (about four hours, impassable during the rainy season and not easy at any time). Get clear directions before setting out and take sun protection, food, water, etc. Taxis and pick-ups from the plaza, 0600-2200, US$11 with a 30-minute wait. The **Mirador del Iminiapi** (Laripata) offers excellent views of town and the Larecaja tropical valleys. It is a nice day-walk or take a taxi, US$11 return.

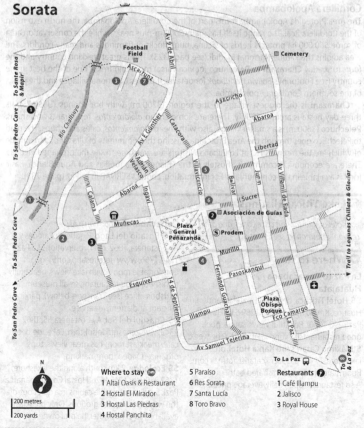

Sorata

Where to stay
1 Altai Oasis & Restaurant
2 Hostal El Mirador
3 Hostal Las Piedras
4 Hostal Panchita
5 Paraíso
6 Res Sorata
7 Santa Lucía
8 Toro Bravo

Restaurants
1 Café Illampu
2 Jalisco
3 Royal House

200 metres
200 yards

Trekking and climbing from Sorata

Sorata is the starting point for climbing **Illampu** and **Ancohuma**. All routes out of the town are difficult, owing to the number of paths in the area and the very steep ascent. Experience and full equipment are necessary. You can hire trekking guides and mules (see What to do, page 274). The three- to four-day trek to **Lagunas Chillata and Glaciar** is the most common and gets busy during high season. Laguna Chillata can also be reached by road or on a long day-hike with light gear, but mind the difficult navigation and take warm clothing. Laguna Chillata has been heavily impacted by tourism (remove all trash, do not throw it in the pits around the lake) and groups frequently camp there. The **Illampu Circuit**, a six- to seven-day high-altitude trek (three passes over 4000 m, one over 5000 m) around Illampu, is excellent. It can get very cold and it is a hard walk, though very beautiful with nice campsites on the way. Some food can be bought in Cocoyo on the third day. You must be acclimatized before setting out. Another option is the Trans-Cordillera Trek, 10-12 days from Sorata to Huayna Potosí, or longer all the way to Illimani at the opposite (south) end of the Cordillera Real. Some communities charge visitors fees along the way.

Cordillera Apolobamba

The Area Protegida Apolobamba forms part of the Cordillera Apolobamba, the north extension of the Cordillera Real. The range itself has many 5000 m-plus peaks, while the conservation area of some 560,000 ha protects herds of vicuña, huge flocks of flamingos and many condors. The area adjoins the Parque Nacional Madidi (see page 323). This is great trekking country and the four- to six-day **Charazani to Pelechuco** (or vice versa) mountain trek is one of the best in the country (see Footprint's *Bolivia Handbook* for details). It passes traditional villages and the peaks of the southern Cordillera Apolobamba.

Charazani is the biggest village in the region (3200 m), with hot springs (US$0.75). Its three-day fiesta is around 16 July. There are some cheap *alojamientos*, restaurants and shops. **Pelechuco** (3600 m) is a smaller village, also with cheap *alojamientos*, cafés and shops. The road to Pelechuco goes through the Area Protegida, passing the community of Ulla Ulla, 5 km outside of which are the reserve's HQ at La Cabaña. Visitors are welcome to see the orphaned vicuñas. There are economical community hostels at the villages of Lagunillas and Agua Blanca. Basic food is available in the communities. For information, contact SERNAP in La Paz (page 238).

◉ Lake Titicaca listings

For hotel and restaurant price codes, and other relevant information, see Essentials.

● Where to stay

La Paz to Copacabana *p266*
Huatajata
$$ Hotel Titicaca, between Huatajata and Huarina, Km 80 from La Paz, T289 5180 (in La Paz T290 7000). Beautiful views, sauna, pool, good restaurant. It's very quiet during the week.
$ Máximo Catari's Inti Karka Hotel, on the lakeshore, T7197 8959, erikcatari@hotmail.com. Rooms are cheaper with shared bath. Also restaurant, open daily, average prices.

Copacabana *p266, map p267*
$$$ Rosario del Lago, Rigoberto Paredes y Av Costanera, T862 2141, reservations La Paz T244 1756, www.hotelrosario.com/lago. Comfortable rooms with lake views, beautifully furnished, good restaurant, small museum, Turisbus office (see Transport below), parking. Efficient and attentive service.
$$ Chasqui del Sol, Av Costanera 55, T862 2343, www.chasquidelsol.com. Lakeside hotel, café/breakfast room has great views, trips organized, video room, parking.
$$ Ecolodge, 2 km south along the lakeshore, T862 2500 (or T245 1626, **Hostal Copacabana**, La Paz). Small comfortable cabins in a quiet out-of-the-way location, nice grounds. Only breakfast available, solar hot water, helpful owner.

$$ Gloria Copacabana, 16 de Julio y Manuel Mejía, T862 2094, La Paz T240 7070, www.hotelgloria.com.bo. Full board available, bar, café and restaurant with international and vegetarian food, gardens, parking. Same group as **Gloria** in La Paz.

$$ Las Olas, lake-end of Pje Michel Pérez past La Cúpula, T7250 8668, www.hostallasolas.com. Tastefully decorated suites, each in its own style. All have kitchenettes, heaters, lovely grounds and views, outdoor solar-heated jacuzzi, a special treat. Warmly recommended.

$$ Utama, Michel Pérez, T862 2013, www.utamahotel.com. Comfortable rooms, hot water, good showers, restaurant, book exchange.

$$-$ La Cúpula, Pje Michel Pérez 1-3, 5 mins' walk from centre, T6708 8464, www.hotelcupula.com. Variety of rooms and prices from suite with jacuzzi to comfortable rooms with shared bath, reliable hot water, sitting room with TV and video, fully equipped kitchen, library, book exchange, attentive service,

excellent restaurant (**$$** with vegetarian options, great breakfast). Popular, advance booking advised. Highly recommended.

$ Emperador, C Murillo 235, T862 2083. Very economical, even cheaper without bath, electric showers, newer rooms at the back, popular, helpful, tours arranged.

$ Kantutas, Av Jaúregui esquina Bolívar, on Plaza Sucre, T862 2093. Good rooms, a decent option in the middle price range, convenient location for transport.

$ Kotha Kahuaña, Av Busch 15, T862 2022. Very economical, cheaper without bath, simple kitchen facilities, quiet, hospitable, basic but good value.

$ Leyenda, Av Costanera y Germán Busch, T7067 4097, hostel.leyenda@gmail.com. Lakeshore hotel with eclectic decor, rooms elaborately decorated with local motifs, electric shower.

$ Sonia, Murillo 253, T7196 8441. Rooms are cheaper without bath, good beds, big

windows, roof terrace, laundry facilities, breakfast in bed on request, very helpful, good value. Recommended.

Isla del Sol p267
Yumani
Most of the *posadas* on the island are here. Quality varies; ignore the touts and shop around for yourself. Please conserve water, it is hauled up the steep hill by donkeys.

$$ Palla Khasa, 600 m north of town on the main trail to Challapampa, T7321 1585, pallakhasa@gmail.com. Includes good breakfast, nice cabins, large rooms, good beds, restaurant with fine views, nice location and grounds, family run, solar electricity, changes US$ and other currencies. Book in advance.

$ Imperio del Sol, on the way up to town, 500 m below the Casa Cultural, about the middle of the steps, T7196 1863, www.hotel imperiodelsol.com. Nice hotel, comfortable rooms, small garden. Recommended.

$ Inti Kala, at the top of the hill, T7194 4013, javierintikala@hotmail.com. Cheaper without bath, electric shower, fantastic views, could use a coat of paint, serves good meals.

$ Templo del Sol, at the top of the hill, T7400 5417. Comfortable rooms, cheaper without bath, electric shower, great views, comfy beds, could use a coat of paint, good restaurant.

Challa
Located mid-island on the east shore, about 200 m below the main north-south trail. Most hostels are on the beach, the town is uphill.

$ Inca Beach, on the beach, T7353 0309. Simple rooms with bath, electric shower, kitchen and laundry facilities, meals available, nice common area, camping possible, good value.

$ Qhumpuri, on hillside above beach, T7472 6525. Simple 2-room units with nice views, private toilet, shared electric shower, tasty meals available.

Challapampa
$ Cultural, 1 block from beach, T7190 0272. Clean rooms, cheaper without bath, nice terrace, does not include breakfast.

$ Manco Kapac, by the dock, T7128 8443. Basic clean rooms, shared bath, electric shower, camping possible, does not include breakfast.

$ Wipala, 1 km north on trail to Chincana, T7257 0092. Simple rooms, electric shower, lovely quiet location, does not include breakfast.

Tour group accommodation
La Posada del Inca, a restored colonial hacienda, owned by **Crillon Tours**, only available as part of a tour with Crillon, see page 261. **Magri Turismo** also owns a hotel on the island, **La Estancia**, www.ecolodge-laketiticaca.com. See La Paz, Tour operators on page 261. See also **Transturin's** overnight options on page 274.

Sorata p269, map p269
$$ Altai Oasis, T213 3895, www.altaioasis. com. At the bottom of the valley in a beautiful setting, 15-min steep downhill walk from town, or taxi US$2. Cabins, rooms with bath (cheaper with shared bath), dorms and camping (US$5 pp). Very good restaurant (**$$**), bar, lovely grounds, pool, peaceful, very welcoming, family-run by the Resnikowskis, English and German spoken. Warmly recommended.

$ Hostal El Mirador, Muñecas 400, T7350 5453. Cheaper with shared bath, hot water, kitchen, laundry facilities, terrace.

$ Hostal Las Piedras, just off Ascarrunz, T7191 6341, laspiedras2002@yahoo.de. Rooms with and without bath, good mattresses, electric shower, very nice, good breakfast with home-made products available, very helpful, English and German spoken. Recommended.

$ Hostal Panchita, on plaza, T213 4242. Simple rooms, shared bath, electric shower, sunny courtyard, washing facilities, does not include breakfast, good value.

$ Paraíso, Villavicencio 117. With electric shower, basic rooms, terrace, breakfast available.

$ Res Sorata, on plaza, T213 6672. Cheaper without bath, electric shower, restaurant, large but scruffy grounds, poor beds, a bit run down overall but still adequate.

$ Santa Lucía, Ascarrunz, T213 6686. Rooms are cheaper with shared bath, electric shower, carpeted rooms, patio, does not include breakfast, not always open.

$ Toro Bravo, below petrol station at entrance to town, T7725 5255. With electric shower, ample grounds and rooms (upstairs rooms are better), small pool, restaurant, a bit faded but good value.

🍴 Restaurants

La Paz to Copacabana *p266*
Huatajata
$$-$ Inti Raymi, next to Inca Utama hotel.
With fresh fish and boat trips. There are other
restaurants of varying standard, most lively at
weekends and in the high season.

Copacabana *p266, map p267*
Excellent restaurants at hotels **Rosario del Lago**
and **La Cúpula**. Many touristy places on Av 6 de
Agosto toward the lakeshore, all similar.
$$ Café Bistrot Copacabana, Cabo Zapana y
6 de Agosto, upstairs. Daily 0730-2100. Varied
menu, international dishes, vegetarian options,
French and English spoken.
$$-$ La Orilla, Av 6 de Agosto, close to lake.
Daily 1000-2200 (usually). Warm, atmospheric,
tasty food with local and international choices.
$ Aransaya, Av 6 de Agosto 121. Good
restaurant and café.
$ Puerta del Sol, Av 6 de Agosto. Good trout.
$ Snack 6 de Agosto, Av 6 de Agosto, 2
branches. Good trout, big portions, some
vegetarian dishes, serves breakfast.
$ Sujna Wasi, Jaúregui 127. Daily 0730-2300.
Serves breakfast, vegetarian lunch, wide range
of books on Bolivia, slow service.

Sorata *p269, map p269*
There are several **$$-$ Italian** places on the
plaza, all quite similar.
$$-$ Café Illampu, 15 min walk on the way
to San Pedro cave. Closed Tue and Dec-Mar.
Excellent sandwiches, bread and cakes,
camping possible. Offers tours with own 4WD
vehicle, Swiss-run, English and German spoken.

$$-$ Jalisco, on plaza. Mexican and Italian
dishes, sidewalk seating.
$ Royal House, off Muñecas by the market.
Decent set lunch, friendly.

🎉 Festivals

Copacabana *p266, map p267*
Note: At these times hotel prices quadruple.
1-3 Feb Virgen de la Candelaria, massive
procession, dancing, fireworks, bullfights.
Easter, with candlelight procession on Good
Friday. **23 Jun**, San Juan, also on Isla del Sol.
4-6 Aug, La Virgen de Copacabana.

Sorata *p269, map p269*
14 Sep, Fiesta Patronal del Señor de la
Columna, is the main festival.

⚙ What to do

Lake Titicaca *p266*
Crillon Tours, La Paz, see page 261.
Run a hydrofoil service on Lake Titicaca
with excellent bilingual guides. Tours stop
at their Andean Roots cultural complex at
Inca Utama. Very experienced company. The
Inca Utama Hotel and Spa ($$$) has a health
spa based on natural remedies and Kallawaya
medicine; the rooms are comfortable, with
heating, electric blankets, good service, bar,
restaurant, Wi-Fi, reservations through Crillon
Tours in La Paz. Crillon is Bolivia's oldest travel
agency and is consistently recommended.
Also at **Inca Utama** is an observatory
(*alajpacha*) with 2 telescopes and retractable
roof for viewing the night sky, an Altiplano
Museum, a floating restaurant and bar on the

lake (**La Choza Náutica**), a 252-sq m floating island and examples of different Altiplano cultures. Health, astronomical, mystic and ecological programmes are offered. The hydrofoil trips include visits to Andean Roots complex, Copacabana, Islas del Sol and de la Luna, Straits of Tiquina and the Cocotoni community. See Isla del Sol, Where to stay, for **La Posada del Inca**. Crillon has a sustainable tourism project with Urus-Iruitos people from the Río Desaguadero area on floating islands by the Isla Queweya. Trips can be arranged to/from Puno and Juli (bus and hydrofoil excursion to Isla del Sol) and from Copacabana via Isla del Sol to Cuzco and Machu Picchu. Other combinations of hydrofoil and land-based excursions can be arranged (also highland, Eastern lowland, jungle and adventure tours). See www.titicaca.com and www.uyuni.travel for details. All facilities and modes of transport connected by radio.

Transturin (see also La Paz, Tour operators, page 262) run catamarans on Lake Titicaca, either for sightseeing or on the La Paz-Puno route. The catamarans are more leisurely than the hydrofoils of **Crillon** so there is more room and time for on-board meals and entertainment, with bar, video and sun deck. From their dock at Chúa, catamarans run 2-day/1-night cruises starting either in La Paz or Copacabana. Puno may also be the starting point for trips. Overnight cruises involve staying in a cabin on the catamaran, moored at the Isla del Sol, with lots of activities. On the island, Transturin has the Inti Wata cultural complex which has restored Inca terraces, an Aymara house, the underground Ekeko museum and cultural demonstrations and activities. There is also a 30-passenger totora reed boat for trips to the Pilcocaina Inca palace. All island-based activities are community-led and for catamaran clients only. Transturin runs through services to Puno without many of the formalities at the border. Transturin offers last-minute programmes with 40% discount rates in Puno, Cuzco and La Paz, if booked 6 days prior to departure only. You can book by phone or by email, but ask first, as availability depends on date.

Turisbus (www.turisbus.com, see La Paz, Tour operators page 262 and **Hoteles Rosario**,

La Paz, and **Rosario del Lago**, Copacabana) offer guided tours in the fast launches *Titicaca Explorer I* (28 passengers) and *II* (8 passengers) to the Isla del Sol, returning to Copacabana via the Bahía de Sicuani for trips on traditional reed boats. Also La Paz-Puno, with boat excursion to Isla del Sol, boxed lunch and road transport, or with additional overnight at **Hotel Rosario del Lago**.

Copacabana *p266, map p267*
Town is filled with tour agencies, all offering excursions to floating islands on imitation reed vessels, and tours to Isla del Sol (see Transport, below). Kayak and pedal-boat rentals on the beach, US$3 per hr.

Sorata *p269, map p269*
Trekking guides
It may be cheaper to go to Sorata and arrange trekking there than to book a trek with an agency in La Paz. Buy necessary foods and supplies in La Paz, Sorata shops have basic items. **Asociación de Guías**, Sucre 302 y Guachalla, leave message at **Res Sorata** (T213 6672); hires guides, porters and mules. Prices vary: guides approximately US$30 per day, mules US$15 per day. Porters take maximum 2 mules, remember you have to feed your guide/porter.
Eduardo Chura, T7157 8671, guiasorata@yahoo.com, is an independent local trekking guide.

⊖ Transport

La Paz to Copacabana *p266*
Huatajata
Bus La Paz-Huatajata, US$1, frequent minibuses from Bustillos y Kollasuyo, Cementerio district, daily 0400-1800, continuing to Tiquina.

Islands of Lago Huiñamarca *p266*
Boat Máximo Catari (see **Huatajata**, Where to stay, above) and Paulino Esteban (east end of town, T7196 7383) arrange trips to the islands in Lago Huiñamarca for US$15 per hr.

Copacabana *p266, map p267*
If arriving in Bolivia at Copacabana and going to La Paz, be sure to arrive there before dark. See also Safety on page 248.

Bus To/from **La Paz**, US$2.15 plus US$0.30 for Tiquina crossing, 4 hrs, throughout the day with **Manco Capac, 2 de Febrero**. Both have offices on Copacabana's main plaza (but leave from Plaza Sucre) and in La Paz at Plaza Reyes Ortiz, opposite entrance to cemetery. Buy ticket in advance at weekends and on holidays. **Diana Tours** and others daily at 1330, from Plaza Sucre, 16 de Julio y 6 de Agosto, US$3.50-4.50, take you to Sagárnaga e Illampu in the tourist district, but will not drop you off at your hotel. (See also Border with Peru via Copacabana, below.)

Isla del Sol *p267*
Boat Boat companies have ticket booths at the beach, by the bottom of Av 6 de Agosto; there are also agencies selling boat and bus tickets along Av 6 de Agosto. All departures are at 0830, unless otherwise noted, and boats arrive back at Copacabana around 1730. The crossing from Copacabana to Yumani takes about 1½ hrs, to Challpampa 2 hrs. Return tickets are only valid on the same day, get a one way fare if you plan to stay overnight. **Andes Amazonía** run full-day trips Copacabana-Challapampa-Yumani-Copacabana, US$5. If you wish to walk, you can be dropped off at Challapampa around 1030-1100 and picked up at Yumani at 1530 (boats leave punctually, so you will have to walk quickly to see the ruins in the north and then hike south to Yumani and down to the pier). They also have a 1330 departure to Yumani, returning 1600, with a 10-min stop at Pilcocaina on the way back. Unión Marinos, run Copacabana–Challapampa–Copacabana, US$4.30; they depart Challapampa at 1330. Titicaca Tours run Copacabana–Coati (Isla de la luna)–Yumani–Copacabana, US$4.30; they stop for 1 hr at Coati and depart Yumani at 1530. One way fares from Copacabana to Yumani US$2.85, to Challapampa US$3.60. Boats also run from Challa to Copacabana Wed, Sat, Sun at 0700, returning 1330, US$1.50 one way.

From **Yampupata**: to Yumani by motorboat, US$13 per boat (US$3 pp by rowboat); to Isla de la Luna, US$26 per boat.

Border with Peru *p268*
Via Guaqui and Desaguadero
Bus Road paved all the way to Peru. Buses from La Paz to Guaqui and Desaguadero depart from J M Asín y P Eyzaguirre, Cementerio, from 0500, US$1.50, shared taxi US$3, 2 hrs. From Desaguadero to **La Paz** buses depart 4 blocks from bridge, last vehicle 2000.

Via Copacabana
Bus Several agencies go from La Paz to **Puno**, with a change of bus and stop for lunch at Copacabana, or with an open ticket for continuing to Puno later. They charge US$8 and depart La Paz 0800, pick-up from hotel. From Copacabana they continue to the Peruvian border at Kasani and on to Puno, stopping for immigration formalities and changing money (better rates in Puno). Both **Crillon Tours** (page 261) and **Transturin** (page 262) have direct services to Puno without a change of bus at the border. From Copacabana to Puno, **Trans Titicaca** (www.titicacabolivia.com) at 0900, 1330, 1830 and other agencies at 1330, offices on 6 de Agosto, US$4-5, 3 hrs. Also **Turisbus** (www.turisbus.com) to Puno from Hotel Rosario del Lago at 1330, US$9. To go to **Cuzco**, you will have to change in Puno where the tour company arranges connections, which may involve a long wait, check details (US$14-22 La Paz–Cuzco). In high season, book at least a day in advance. It is always cheaper, if less convenient, to buy only the next segment of your journey directly from local bus companies and cross the border on your own. *Colectivo* Copacabana (Plaza Sucre)–**Kasani** US$0.60 pp, 15 mins, Kasani–**Yunguyo**, where Peruvian buses start, US$0.30 pp.

East side of Lake Titicaca *p268*
Bus **La Paz** (Reyes Cardona 772, Cancha Tejar, Cementerio district, T238 2239)–**Puerto Acosta**, 5 hrs, US$4, Tue-Sun 0500. Transport past Puerto Acosta only operates on market days, Wed and Sat, and is mostly cargo trucks. Bus Puerto Acosta–La Paz at about 1500. There are frequent minivans to La Paz from **Escoma**, 25 km from Puerto Acosta; trucks from the border may take you this far.

Sorata *p269, map p269*

Bus Minibuses throughout the day from **La Paz** with Trans Unificada (C Manuel Bustillos 683 y Av Kollasuyo in the Cementerio district, T238 1693); also Perla del Illampu (Manuel Bustillos 615, T238 0548), US$2.50, 3½ hrs. Booking recommended on Fri. In Sorata they leave from C Samuel Tejerina, near the exit to La Paz. To or from **Copacabana** and **Peru**, change buses at Huarina but they are often full so start early and be prepared for a long wait.

Jeeps run from La Paz (C Chorolque y Tarapacá, T245 0296, often full), via Sorata to **Santa Rosa** (US$15, 13 hrs), on the road to **Mapiri** and **Guanay**, a rough route with interesting vegetation and stunning scenery. Onward transport can be found in Santa Rosa. From Guanay private boats may be arranged to **Rurrenabaque** (see page 279), and vehicles run to Caranavi and thence to Coroico. Sorata–Coroico by this route is excellent for offroad motorcycling. If travelling by public transport it is easier to go La Paz–Coroico–Caranavi–Guanay–Santa Rosa–Sorata–La Paz, than vice versa.

Cordillera Apolobamba *p270*

Charazani

Bus From Calle Reyes Cardona 732, off Av Kollasuyo, Cemetery district, La Paz, daily with Trans Altiplano, 0600-0630, 7 hrs, US$3.50, very crowded. Return to La Paz at 1800; also has 0900 on Sat and 1200 Mon and Fri.

Pelechuco

Bus From **La Paz** Trans Provincias del Norte leaves daily 0600-0700 from Ex Tranca de Río Seco in El Alto, passing through Qutapampa, Ulla Ulla and Agua Blanca to Pelechuco, 10-12 hrs, US$5, sometimes on sale 24 hrs before departure at the booking office in Calle Reyes Cardona. Return to La Paz between 0300 and 0400 most days.

The Yungas

Only a few hours from La Paz are the subtropical valleys known as the Yungas. These steep, forested slopes, squeezed in between the Cordillera and the Amazon Lowlands, provide a welcome escape from the chill of the capital. The warm climate of the Yungas is also ideal for growing citrus fruit, bananas, coffee and especially coca.

La Paz to the Yungas

The roads from La Paz to Nor- and Sud-Yungas go via **La Cumbre**, a pass at 4725 m about one hour northeast of the city. The road out of La Paz circles cloudwards over La Cumbre; all around are towering snowcapped peaks. The first village after the pass is **Unduavi**, where there is a check point, a petrol station, and roadside stalls. Beyond Unduavi an unpaved road branches right 75 km to Chulumani and the Sud-Yungas. Beyond Sud-Yungas, to the southeast, are the Yungas de Inquisivi, see Quime, page 280. The paved road contnues to Cotapata, where it again divides: right is the old unpaved road to Yolosa, the junction 8 km from Coroico (this is the popular cycling route). To the left, the new paved road goes via Chuspipata and Puente Yolosita, where an unpaved road climbs steeply to Coroico. Between Yolosita and Yolosa (see below) is Senda Verde (www.sendaverde.com), an animal refuge, eco-lodge and restaurant with opportunities for volunteering. In addition, from Puente Villa on the Unduav–Chulumani road, an unpaved road runs to Coripata and Coroico. For the La Cumbre–Coroico hike (Choro), see page 253.

All roads to Coroico drop some 3500 m to the green subtropical forest in 70 km. The best views are in May to June, when there is less chance of fog and rain. The old road, the so-called "World's Most Dangerous Road", is steep, twisting, clinging to the side of sheer cliffs, and it is slippery in the wet. It is a breathtaking descent (best not to look over the edge if you don't like heights) and its reputation for danger is more than matched by the beauty of the scenery. Many tourists go on a mountain-bike tour: it is your responsibility to choose top quality bikes (with hydraulic disc brakes) and a reputable company which offers bilingual guides, helmet, gloves, vehicle support throughout the day (see La Paz, Tour operators, page 261). Many bike companies take riders back to La Paz the same day, but Coroico is worth more of your time. In Yolosa, at the end of the bike ride, is a three-segment zipline (total 1555 m) operated by **Gravity Bolivia**; see page 261 and www.ziplinebolivia.com. The road is especially dangerous when it is raining (mid-December to mid-February), be sure the bike is in top shape and be extra cautious.

Coroico → *Phone code: 02. Colour map 6, A3. Population 2903. Altitude: 1750 m*

The little town of Coroico, capital of the Nor-Yungas region, is perched on a hill amid beautiful scenery. The hillside is covered with orange and banana groves and coffee plantations. Coroico is a first-class place to relax with several good walks. A colourful four-day festival is held 19-22 October. On 2 November, All Souls' Day, the cemetery is festooned with black ribbons. A good walk is up to the waterfalls, starting from **El Calvario**. Follow the stations of the cross by the cemetery, off Calle Julio Zuazo Cuenca, which leads steeply uphill from the plaza. Facing the chapel at El Calvario, with your back to the town, look for the path on your left. This leads to the falls which are the town's water supply (Toma de Agua) and, beyond, to two more falls. **Cerro Uchumachi**, the mountain behind El Calvario, can be climbed following the same stations of the cross, but then look for the faded red and white antenna behind the chapel. From there it's about two hours' steep walk to the top (take water). A third walk goes to the pools in the **Río Vagante**, 7 km off the road to Coripata; it takes about three hours. The **tourist information** is at the Prefectura ① *Monsey Julio Zuazo Cuenca, corner of the main plaza*. In the interests of personal safety, women in particular should not hike alone in this area.

Caranavi → *Phone code: 02. Colour map 6, A2. Population 21,883. Altitude: 600 m.*

From the junction at Puente Yolosita the paved road follows the river 11 km to Santa Bárbara, then becomes gravel for 65 km to Caranavi, an uninspiring town 156 km from La Paz. From here the road continues towards the settled area of the Alto Beni, at times following a picturesque gorge. Market days are Friday and Saturday. There is a range of hotels and *alojamientos* and buses from La Paz (Villa Fátima) to Rurrenabaque pass through. Beyond Caranavi, 70 km, is **Guanay** at the junction of the Tipuani and Mapiri rivers (basic lodging).

Chulumani and Sud-Yungas → *Phone code: 02. Colour map 6, A2. Population 3650. Altitude: 1750 m.*

The road from Unduavi to Chulumani goes through **Puente Villa**, where a branch runs north to Coroico through Coripata. The capital of Sud Yungas is **Chulumani** is a small town with beautiful views, 124 km from La Paz. There are many birds in the area and good hiking. The 24 August **fiesta** lasts 10 days and there is a lively market every weekend. **Tourist office** ① *in the main plaza, open irregular hours, mostly weekends*. There is no ATM in Chulumani, take cash. **Irupana** (*altitude 1900 m*), 31 km east of Chulumani (mini-bus or shared taxi US\$2), is a friendly little place with a lovely location, delightful climate, more good walking and birdwatching, and a couple of very nice places to stay. The 500-ha **Apa Apa Reserve** ① *5 km from Chulumani on the road to Irupana (see Where to stay, page 278)*, is the one of the last areas of original Yungas forest with lots of birds, other wildlife, hiking trails and pleasant accommodation.

◉ The Yungas listings

For hotel and restaurant price codes, and other relevant information, see Essentials.

● Where to stay

Coroico *p277*
Hotel rooms are hard to find at holiday weekends and prices are higher.

\$\$\$-\$\$ El Viejo Molino, 1279 7329, www.hotelviejomolino.com. 2 km on road to Caranavi. Upmarket hotel and spa with pool, gym, jacuzzi, games room, restaurant, etc.
\$\$ Gloria, C Kennedy 1, T289 5554, www.hotelgloria.com.bo. Traditional resort hotel, full board, pool, restaurant with set lunches and à la carte, internet, free transport from plaza. •

$$-$ Bella Vista, C Héroes del Chaco 7 (2 blocks from main plaza), T213 6059, www.coroicobellavista.blogspot.com. Beautiful rooms and views, includes breakfast, cheaper without bath, 2 racquetball courts, terrace, bike hire, restaurant, pool.

$$-$ Esmeralda, on the edge of town, 10 mins uphill from plaza (see website for transport), T213 6027, www.hotelesmeralda.com. Most rooms include breakfast, cheaper in dorms, hot showers, satellite TV and DVD, book exchange, good buffet restaurant, sauna, garden, pool, can arrange local tours and transport to/from La Paz and Coroico bus stop.

$$-$ Hostal Kory, at top of steps leading down from the plaza, T7156 4050, info@ hostalkory.com. Rooms with shared bath are cheaper, electric showers, restaurant, huge pool, terrace, good value, helpful.

$ Don Quijote, 500 m out of town, on road to Coripata, T213 6007, www.donquijote. lobopages.com. Economical, electric shower, pool, quiet, nice views.

$ El Cafetal, Miranda, 10-min walk from town, T7193 3979. Rooms with and without bath, very nice, restaurant with excellent French/ Indian/ vegetarian cuisine, French-run.

$ Los Silbos, Iturralde 4043, T7350 0081. Cheap simple rooms with shared bath, electric showers, good value.

$ Matsu, 1 km from town (call for free pick-up, taxi US$2), T7069 2219. Economical, has restaurant, pool, views, quiet, helpful.

$ Residencial de la Torre, Julio Zuazo Cuenca, ½ block from plaza. Welcoming place with courtyard, cheap sparse rooms, no alcoholic drinks allowed.

$ Sol y Luna, 15-20 mins beyond **Hotel Esmeralda**, La Paz contact: Maison de la Bolivie, 6 de Agosto 2464, Ed Jardines, T244 0588, www.solyluna-bolivia.com. Excellent accommodation in fully equipped cabins, apartments and rooms with and without bath, splendid views, restaurant (vegetarian specialities), camping US$3 pp (not suitable for cars), garden, pool, shiatsu massage (US$15-20), good value, Sigrid (owner) speaks English, French, German, Spanish.

Chulumani and Sud-Yungas *p277*
Chulumani suffers from water shortages, check if your hotel has a reserve tank.

$ Apa Apa, 5 km from town on road to Irupana, then walk 20 mins uphill from turnoff, or taxi from Chulumani US$3.50, T7254 7770, La Paz T213 9640, apapayungas@hotmail.com. A lovely old hacienda with simple rooms, private bath, hot water, delicious meals available, home-made ice-cream, pool, large campsite with bathrooms and grills, tours to Apa Apa Reserve, family run by Ramiro and Tildy Portugal, English spoken.

$ Country House, 400 m out of town on road to cemetery, T7528 2212, La Paz T274 5584. With electric shower, lovely tranquil setting, pool and gardens, library, breakfast and other home-cooked meals available, family run. Enthusiastic owner Xavier Sarabia is hospitable and offers hiking advice and tours, English spoken.

$ Hostal Familiar Dion, Alianza, ½ block below plaza, T289 6034. Cheaper without bath, electric shower, very well maintained, restaurant, attentive.

$ Huayrani, Junín y Cornejo, uphill from centre near bus stops, T213 6351. Electric shower, nice views, pool, parking.

Irupana

$ Bougainville Hotel, near the centre of town, T213 6155. Modern rooms, electric shower, pizzería, pool, family run, good value.

$ Nirvana Inn, uphill at the edge of town past the football field, T213 6154. Comfortable cabins on beautiful grounds with great views, pool, parking, flower and orchid gardens lovingly tended by the owners. Includes breakfast, other meals on request.

❼ Restaurants

Coroico *p277*
$$ Bamboos, Iturralde y Ortiz. Good Mexican food and pleasant atmosphere, live music some nights with cover charge. Happy hour 1800-1900.

$$-$ Back-stube, Pasaje Adalid Linares, 10 m from the main square. Mon 0830-1200, Wed-Fri 0830-1430, 1830-2200, Sat-Sun 0830-2200. National and international food, vegetarian options, à la carte only, breakfasts, pastries, top quality, terrace with panoramic views, nice atmosphere.

$$-$ Carla's Garden Pub, Pasaje Adalid Linares, 50 m from the main plaza. Open lunch until late. Sandwiches, snacks, pasta and international food, BBQ for groups of 5 or more. Lots of music, live music at weekends. Garden, hammocks, games, nice atmosphere.

$ Pizzería Italia, 2 with same name on the plaza. Daily 1000-2300. Pizza, pasta, snacks.

Chulumani and Sud-Yungas *p277*
$ La Cabaña Yungeña, C Sucre 2 blocks below plaza. Tue-Sun. simple set lunch and dinner.

Couple of other places around plaza, all closed Mon. Basic eateries up the hill by bus stops.

● What to do

Coroico *p277*
Cycling
CXC, Pacheco 79, T7157 3015, www.cxccoroico.lobopages.com. Good bikes, US$20 for 6 hrs including packed lunch, a bit disorganized but good fun and helpful, English and German spoken.

Horse riding
El Relincho, Don Reynaldo, T7191 3675, 100 m past **Hotel Esmeralda** (enquire here), US$25 for 4 hrs with lunch.

● Transport

Coroico *p277*
Bus From La Paz all companies are Minasa terminal, Puente Minasa, in Villa Fátima. buses

and minibuses leave throughout the day US$4.25, 2½ hrs on the paved road. **Turbus Totaí**, T221 6592, and several others. Services return to La Paz from the small terminal down the hill in Coroico, across from the fooball field. All are heavily booked at weekends and on holidays.

Pick-ups from the small mirador at Pacheco y Sagárnaga go to **Puente Yolosita**, 15 mins, US$0.70. Here you can try to catch a bus to **Rurrenabaque**, but there's more chance of getting a seat in **Caranavi**, where La Paz-Rurre buses pass through in the evening, often full. Caranavi-Rurre 12 hrs, US$6-7, **Flota Yungueña**, at 1800-1900, **Turbus Totaí** 2100-2200, and others. See also **Deep Rainforest**, La Paz (page 261). For Guanay to **Sorata** via **Mapiri** and **Santa Rosa**, see page 276.

Chulumani and Sud-Yungas *p277*
Bus From **La Paz**, several companies from Villa Fátima, leave when full, US$3.60, 4 hrs: eg **San Cristóbal**, C San Borja 408 y 15 de Abril, T221 0607. In Chulumani most buses leave from the top of the hill by the petrol station; minibuses and taxis to local villages from plaza.

● Directory

Coroico *p277*
Language classes Siria León Domínguez, T7195 5431. US$5 per hr, also rents rooms and makes silver jewellery, excellent English. **Medical services** Hospital is the best in the Yungas.

Southwest Bolivia

The mining town of Oruro, with one of South America's greatest folkloric traditions, shimmering salt flats, coloured lakes and surrealistic rock formations combine to make this one of the most fascinating regions of Bolivia. Add some of the country's most celebrated festivals and the last hide-out of Butch Cassidy and the Sundance Kid and you have the elements for some great and varied adventures. The journey across the altiplano from Uyuni to San Pedro de Atacama is a popular route to Chile and there are other routes south to Argentina.

Oruro and around → *Phone code: 02. Colour map 6, A2. Population: 240,996. Altitude: 3725 m.*

The mining town of Oruro is the gateway to the altiplano of southwest Bolivia. It's a somewhat drab, dirty, functional place, which explodes into life once a year with its famous carnival, symbolized by La Diablada. To the west is the national park encompassing Bolivia's highest peak: Sajama. The **tourist office** ① *Bolívar y Montes 6072, Plaza 10 de Febrero, T525 0144, Mon-Fri 0800-1200, 1430-1830,* is helpful and informative. The Prefectura and the Policía de Turismo jointly run information booths in front of the **Terminal de Buses** ① *T528 7774, Mon-Fri 0800-1200, 1430-1830, Sat 0830-1200*; and opposite the **railway station** ① *T525 7881, same hours.*

Although Oruro became famous as a mining town, there are no longer any working mines of importance. It is, however, a railway terminus and the commercial centre for the mining communities of the altiplano, as well as hosting the country's best-known carnival (see La Diablada, page 283). The Plaza 10 de Febrero and surroundings are well maintained and several buildings in the centre hint at the city's former importance. The **Museo Simón Patiño** ① *Soria Galvarro 5755, Mon-Fri 0830-1130, 1430-1800, Sat 0900-1500, US$1,* was built as a mansion by the tin baron Simón Patiño, it is now run by the Universidad Técnica de Oruro and contains European furniture and temporary exhibitions. There is a view from the Cerro Corazón de Jesús, near the church of the Virgen del Socavón, five blocks west of Plaza 10 de Febrero at the end of Calle Mier.

The **Museo Sacro, Folklórico, Arqueológico y Minero** ① *inside the Church of the Virgen del Socavón, entry via the church daily 0900-1145, 1500-1730, US$1.50, guided tours every 45 mins,* contain religious art, clothing and jewellery and, after passing through old mining tunnels and displays of mining techniques, a representation of *El Tío* (the god of the underworld). **Museo Antropológico** ① *south of centre on Av España y Urquidi, T526 0020, Mon-Fri 0900-1200, 1400-1800, Sat-Sun 1000-1200, 1500-1800, US$0.75, guide mandatory, getting there: take micro A heading south or any trufi going south.* It has a unique collection of stone llama heads as well as impressive carnival masks.

The **Museo Mineralógico y Geológico** ① *part of the University, T526 1250, Mon-Fri 0800-1200, 1430-1700, US$0.70, getting there: take micro A south to the Ciudad Universitaria,* has mineral specimens and fossils. **Casa Arte Taller Cardozo Velásquez** ① *Junín 738 y Arica, east of the centre, T527 5245, Mon-Sat 1000-1200, 1500-1800, US$1.* Contemporary Bolivian painting and sculpture is displayed in the Cardozo Velásquez home, a family of artists.

There are thermal baths outside town at **Obrajes** ① *23 km from Oruro, minibuses leave from Caro y Av 6 de Agosto, US$1, 45 min; baths open 0700-1800, US$1.50, Oruro office: Murgía 1815 y Camacho, T525 0646.*

Quime → *Population: 3000.*
North of Oruro, one hour by bus (two to three hours south of La Paz) is the junction at Conani, where there are several places to eat and stay. From here a road, mostly paved, runs over the altiplano to the Tres Cruces pass (over 5000 m) before dropping 2000 m on a spectacular road to Quime, a town in the Yungas de Inquisivi, at the southern edge of the Cordillera Quimsa

Cruz. It can also be reached along scenic secondary roads from Chulumani in Sud-Yungas and Cochabamba. It's an increasingly popular escape from La Paz, to relax or hike in the cordillera. Excursions include to Aymara mining communities and waterfalls and mountain biking trips, including a downhill from Tres Cruces. The main festival is from 23 July (Santiago). There are basic services, but no ATMs.

Oruro

Where to stay 🛏
1 Alojamiento La Paz II C3
2 El Lucero A3
3 Flores Plaza C2
4 Gran Sucre D2
5 La Fontana D2
6 Repostero D3

7 Res Gloria D2
8 Res Gran Boston C3
9 Villa Real San Felipe D2

Restaurants 🍴
1 Ardentía C2
2 Café Sur D2

3 Govinda D2
4 La Cabaña C2
5 La Casona C2
6 Las Retamas D1
7 Nayjama D3
8 Panadería Doña Filo D2
9 Sergio's C2

200 metres
200 yards

Parque Nacional Sajama

A one-day drive to the west of Oruro is the **Parque Nacional Sajama** ① *park headquarters in Sajama village, T02-513 5526 (in La Paz SERNAP T02-242 6303), www.biobol.org, US$4.25 payable to community of Sajama,* established in 1939 and covering 100,230 ha. The park contains the world's highest forest, consisting mainly of the rare queñual tree (Polylepis tarapacana) which grows up to an altitude of 5500 m. The scenery is wonderful with views of several volcanoes, including Sajama – Bolivia's highest peak at 6542 m – Parinacota and Pomerape (jointly called Payachatas). The road is paved and leads across the border into the Parque Nacional Lauca in Chile. You can trek in the park, with or without porters and mules, but once you move away from the Río Sajama or its major tributaries, lack of water is a problem. There is basic accommodation in Sajama village (see below) as well as a more comfortable and expensive option at **Tomarapi** on the north side of the mountain; see page 285.

Sajama village → *Population: 500. Altitude: 4200 m.*

In Sajama village, visitors are billeted in basic family-run *alojamientos* on a rotating basis (about US$4.50 per person). All are basic to very basic, especially the sanitary facilities; no showers or electricity, solar power for lighting only. Alojamientos may provide limited food, so take your own supplies. It can be very windy and cold at night; a good sleeping bag, gloves and hat are essential. Crampons, ice axe and rope are needed for climbing the volcanoes and can be hired in the village. Maps are hard to find. Local guides charge US$50-70 per day. Pack animals can be hired, US$8 per day including guide. Good bathing at the Manasaya thermal complex, 6 km northwest of village, entry US$4.25; jeeps can be rented to visit, US$8-16. Many villagers sell alpaca woolen items.

By road to Chile

The shortest and most widely used route from La Paz to Chile is the road to **Arica** via the border at **Tambo Quemado** (Bolivia) and **Chungará** (Chile). From La Paz take the highway south towards Oruro. Immediately before Patacamaya, turn right at green road sign to Puerto Japonés on the Río Desaguadero, then on to Tambo Quemado. Take extra petrol (none available after Chilean border until Arica), food and water. The journey is worthwhile for the breathtaking views.

Bolivian **customs and immigration** are at Tambo Quemado, where there are a couple of very basic places to stay and eat. Border control is open daily 0800-2000. Shops change bolivianos, pesos chilenos and dollars. From Tambo Quemado there is a stretch of about 7 km of 'no-man's land' before you reach the Chilean frontier at Chungará. Here the border crossing, which is set against the most spectacular scenic backdrop of Lago Chungará and Volcán Parinacota, is thorough but efficient; open 0800-2000. Expect a long wait at weekends and any day behind lines of lorries. Drivers must fill in 'Relaciones de Pasajeros', US$0.25 from kiosk at border, giving details of driver, vehicle and passengers. Do not take any livestock, plants, fruit, vegetables, coca or dairy products into Chile.

An alternative crossing from Oruro: several bus companies travel southwest to Iquique, via the border posts of **Pisiga** (Bolivia) and **Colchane** (Chile). The road is paved from Oruro to Toledo (32 km) and from Opoquari to Pisiga via Huachachalla (about 100 km). The rest of the 170 km road in Bolivia is unpaved; on the Chilean side it's paved all the way to Iquique, 250 km. There is also service from Oruro to Arica via Patacamaya and Tambo Quemado.

South of Oruro

Machacamarca, about 30 minutes south of Oruro, has a good **railway museum** ① *Wed and Fri 0900-1200, 1500-1700.* Further south, the road runs between the flat plain of Lago Poopó and the Cordillera Azanaque, a very scenic ride. There are thermal baths at **Pazña**, 91 km from Oruro. About 65 km south is the **Santuario de Aves Lago Poopó** (a Ramsar site), an excellent bird reserve on the lake of the same name. The lake dries up completely in winter. The closest place to

La Diablada

Starting on the **Saturday before Ash Wednesday**, Los Carnavales de Oruro include the famous **Diablada** ceremony in homage to the miraculous Virgen del Socavón, patroness of miners, and in gratitude to Pachamama, the Earth Mother. The **Diablada** was traditionally performed by indigenous miners, but several other guilds have taken up the custom. The carnival is especially notable for its fantastically elaborate and imaginative costumes.

The **Sábado de Peregrinación** starts its 5 km route through the town at 0700, finishing at the Sanctuary of the Virgen del Socavón, and continues into the early hours of Sunday. There the dancers invoke blessings and ask for pardon.

At dawn on Sunday, **El Alba** is a competition of all participating musicians at Plaza del Folklore near the Santuario, an amazing battle of the bands. The **Gran Corso** or **La Entrada** starts at 0800 on the Sunday, a more informal parade (many leave their masks off) along the same route.

Monday is **El Día del Diablo y del Moreno** in which the Diablos and Morenos, with their bands, bid farewell to the Virgin. Arches decorated with colourful woven cloths and silverware are set up on the road leading to the Santuario, where a mass is held. In the morning, at Avenida Cívica, the Diablada companies participate in a play of the Seven Deadly Sins. This is followed by a play about the meeting of the Inca Atahualpa with Pizarro, performed by the Fraternidad Hijos del Sol. At night, each company has a private party.

On Tuesday, **Martes de Chall'a**, families get together, with ch'alla rituals to invoke ancestors, unite with Pachamama and bless personal possessions. Throughout Carnaval everyone throws water and sprays foam at everyone else (plastic tunics are sold for US$0.20 by street vendors).

The Friday before Carnaval, traditional miners' ceremonies are held at mines, including the sacrifice of a llama. Visitors may only attend with advance permission.

Preparations for Carnaval begin four months before the actual event, on the first Sunday of November, and rehearsals are held every Sunday until one week before Carnaval, when a plain clothes rehearsal takes place, preceded by a mass for participants. In honour of its syncretism of ancestral Andean traditions and Catholic faith, the Oruro Carnaval has been included on UNESCO's Heritage of Humanity list.

Seating Stands are erected along the entire route and must be purchased from the entrepreneurs who put them up. Tickets are for Saturday and Sunday, there is no discount if you stay only one day. A prime location is around Plaza 10 de Febrero where the companies perform in front of the authorities, seats run US$35-55, some are sold at the more expensive hotels. Along Av 6 de Agosto seats cost US$20-25, good by the TV cameras, where performers try their best.

Where to stay During Carnaval, accommodation costs two to three times more than normal and must be booked well in advance. Hotels charge for Friday, Saturday and Sunday nights. You can stay for only one night, but you'll be charged for three. Locals also offer places to stay in their homes, expect to pay at least US$10 per person per night.

Transport The maximum fare is posted at the terminal, but when demand is at its peak, bus prices from La Paz can triple. Buses get booked up quickly, starting Friday and they do not sell tickets in advance. There's usually no transport back to La Paz on Tuesday, so travel on Monday or Wednesday. Many agencies organize day trips from La Paz on Saturday, departing 0430, most will pick you up from your hotel. They return late, making for a tiring day. Trips cost US$45-60, and include breakfast, a snack and sometimes a seat for the parade.

Oruro to see flamingos and other birds is **Lago Uru Uru** (the northern section of the Poopó lake system), go to Villa Challacollo on the road to Pisiga (minibuses 102, 10, 5 or blue micros) and walk from there. Birds start arriving with the first rains in October or November. Further along, at Km 10 is Chusakeri, where chullpas can be seen on the hillside.

Access to the lake is a little closer from **Huari**, 15 minutes south of Challapata. Huari (124 km south of Oruro, paved) is a pleasant little town with a large brewery; there is a small museum and Mirador Tatacuchunita, a lookout on nearby Cerro Sullka. Sunsets over the lake are superb. There are a couple of basic *alojamientos*, eg **25 de Mayo**, two blocks from the plaza towards Challapata, shared bath, cold water in morning only. It is about an 8 km walk from Huari to the lake, depending on the water level. Near the lake is the Uru-Muratos community of **Llapallapani** with circular adobe homes, those with straw roofs are known as *chillas* and those with conical adobe roofs are *putukus*. Cabins in putuku style form part of a community tourism programme. Boats can be hired when the water level is high, at other times Poopó is an unattainable mirage. There is good walking in the Cordillera Azanaque behind Huari; take food, water, warm clothing and all gear. **Challapata** (*fiesta* 15-17 July) has several places to stay, eg **Res Virgen del Carmen**, by main plaza, and a gas station.

Atlantis in the Andes Jim Allen's theory of Atlantis (www.atlantisbolivia.org) is well known around Oruro. **Pampa Aullagas**, the alleged Atlantis site, is 196 km from Oruro, southwest of Lago Poopó. Access is from the town of **Quillacas** along a road that branches west from the road to Uyuni just south of Huari, or from the west through Toledo and Andamarca. A visit here can be combined with visits to the Salar de Coipasa.

Southwest of Lago Poopó, off the Oruro-Pisiga-Iquique road (turn off at **Sabaya**), is the **Salar de Coipasa**, 225 km from Oruro. It is smaller and less visited than the Salar de Uyuni, and has a turquoise lake in the middle of the salt pan surrounded by mountains with gorgeous views and large cacti. Coipasa is northwest of the Salar de Uyuni and travel from one to the other is possible with a private vehicle along the impressive **Ruta Intersalar**. Along the way are tombs, terracing and ancient irrigation canals at the archaeological site of **Alcaya** ① *US$1.25*, gradually being developed by the local community (near **Salinas de Garci Mendoza**, locally known as Salinas). At the edge of the Salar de Uyuni is **Coquesa** (lodging available), which has a mirador and tombs with mummies ① *US$1.25 entry to each site*. Nearby are the towering volcanic cones of Cora Cora and Tunupa. Access to the north end of the Salar de Uyuni is at **Jirira**, east of Coquesa, with a salt hotel (see Where to stay) and airstream camper vans run by **Crillon Tours** (www.uyuni.travel).

Note: Getting stranded out on the altiplano or, worse yet on the salar itself, is dangerous because of extreme temperatures and total lack of drinking water. It is best to visit this area with a tour operator that can take you, for example, from Oruro through the salares to Uyuni. Travellers with their own vehicles should only attempt this route following extensive local inquiry or after taking on a guide to avoid becoming lost or bogged. The edges of the salares are soft and only established entry points or ramps (*terraplenes*) should be used to cross onto or off the salt.

◉ Oruro and around listings

For hotel and restaurant price codes, and other relevant information, see Essentials.

● Where to stay

Oruro *p280, map p281*

$$ Flores Plaza, Adolfo Mier 735 at Plaza 10 de Febrero, T525 2561, www.floresplazahotel.com. Comfortable carpeted rooms, central location.

$$ Gran Sucre, Sucre 510 esq 6 de Octubre, T527 6800, hotelsucreoruro@entelnet.bo. Refurbished old building (faded elegance), rooms and newer suites, heaters on request, internet in lobby, helpful staff.

$$ Samay Wasi, Av Brasil 232 opposite the bus terminal, T527 6737, www.hotelessamaywasi.com. Carpeted rooms, discount for IYHF members, has a 2nd branch in Uyuni.

$$ Villa Real San Felipe, San Felipe 678 y La Plata, south of the centre, T525 4993, www.hotelvillarealsanfelipe.com. Quaint hotel, nicely furnished but small rooms, heating, buffet breakfast, sauna and whirlpool, restaurant, tour operator.

$ El Lucero, 21 de Enero 106 y Brasil, opposite the terminal, T528 5884. Multi-storey hotel, reliable hot water, front rooms noisy, good value.

$ La Fontana, off Bakovic, opposite the bus terminal, T527 9412. Simple rooms, does not include breakfast, restaurant, good service, helpful owner.

$ Repostero, Sucre 370 y Pagador, T525 8001. Hot water, parking, restaurant serves set lunch. Renovated carpeted rooms are more expensive but better value than their old rooms.

$ Res Gran Boston, Pagador 1159 y Cochabamba, T527 4708. Refurbished house, rooms around a covered patio, cheaper with shared bath, good value.

Quime *p280*

$ Hostal Rancho Colobrí, 4 blocks from main plaza (ask directions), http://rancho colibri.wordpress.com. 8 rooms with shared bath, breakfast extra but has a fully-equipped kitchen. Owner Marko Lewis has masses of information on the area (website is also helpful).

2 other basic, slightly cheaper *alojamientos* in town: Santiago and Quime.

Parque Nacional Sajama *p282*

$$ Tomarapi Ecolodge, north of Sajama in Tomarapi community, near Caripe, T02-241 4753, represented by **Millenarian Tourism & Travel**, Av Sánchez Lima 2193, La Paz, T02-241 4753, www.boliviamilenaria.com. Including full board (good food) and guiding service with climbing shelter at 4900 m, helpful staff, simple but comfortable, with hot water, heating.

South of Oruro *p282*

$ Alojamiento Paraíso, Sabaya. Take sleeping bag, shared bath, cold water, meals on request or take own food, sells petrol.

$ Doña Wadi, Salinas de Garci Mendoza, C Germán Busch, near main plaza, T513 8015. Shared bath, hot water, basic but clean, meals available.

$ Posada Doña Lupe, Jirira. Partly made of salt , hot water, cheaper without bath, use of kitchen but bring your own food, no meals available, caters to tour groups, pleasant, comfortable.

$ Zuk'arani, on a hillside overlooking Salinas de Garci Mendoza and the Salar, T2513 7086, zukarani@hotmail.com. 2 cabins for 4, with bath, hot water, cheaper in rooms with shared bath, hot water, meals on request.

Restaurants

Oruro *p280, map p281*

$$ La Cabaña, Junín 609. Sun and Mon 1200-1530 only, Comfortable, smart, good international food, bar.

$$ Nayjama, Aldana 1880. Good regional specialties, very popular for lunch, huge portions.

$$-$ Las Retamas, Murguía 930 esq Washington. Mon-Sat 0930-2330, Sun 0930-1430. Excellent quality and value for set lunches (**$**), Bolivian and international dishes à la carte, very good pastries at Kuchen Haus, pleasant atmosphere, attentive service, a bit out of the way but well worth the trip. Recommended.

$ Ardentia, Sorria Galvarro y Junín, open 1900-2200. Home cooking, tasty pasta and meat dishes.

$ La Casona, Pres Montes 5970, opposite Post Office. *Salteñas* in the morning, closed midday. Good *pizzería* at night.

$ Govinda, 6 de Octubre 6071. Mon-Sat 0900-2130. Excellent vegetarian.

$ Sergio's, La Plata y Mier, at Plaza 10 de Febrero. Very good pizza, hamburgers, snacks; also pastries in the afternoon, good service.

Cafés

Café Sur, Arce 163, near train station. Tue-Sat. Live entertainment, seminars, films, good place to meet local students.

Panadería Doña Filo, 6 de Octubre esq Sucre. Closed Sun. Excellent savoury snacks and sweets, takeaway only.

Bars and clubs

Oruro *p280, map p281*

Bravo, Montesinos y Pagador. Open 2100-0300. Varied music.

Imagine, 6 de Octubre y Junín. Open 2200-0400. Latin and other music.

○ Shopping

Oruro *p280, map p281*

Camping equipment Camping Oruro, Pagador 1660, T528 1829, camping_oruro@ hotmail.com.

Crafts On Av La Paz the blocks between León and Belzu are largely given over to workshops producing masks and costumes for Carnaval. Artesanías Oruro, A Mier 599, esq S Galvarro. Lovely selection of regional handicrafts produced by 6 rural community cooperatives; nice sweaters, carpets, wall-hangings.

Markets Mercado Campero, V Galvarro esq Bolívar. Sells everything, also *brujería* section for magical concoctions. Mercado Fermín López, C Ayacucho y Montes. Food and hardware. C Bolívar is the main shopping street. Global, Junín y La Plata. Well stocked supermarket. Irupana, S Galvarra y A Mier. Natural food and snacks.

○ What to do

Oruro *p280, map p281*

Asociación de Guías Mineros, contact Gustavo Peña, T523 2446. Arranges visits to San José mine.

Freddy Barrón, T527 6776, lufba@hotmail. com. Custom-made tours and transport, speaks German and some English.

○ Transport

Oruro *p280, map p281*

Bus Bus terminal 10 blocks north of centre at Bakovic and Aroma, T525 3535, US$0.25 terminal use fee, luggage store, ATMs. Micro 2 to centre, or any saying 'Plaza 10 de Febrero'. To **Challapata** and **Huari**: several companies go about every hour, US$1, 1¾ hrs, and Huari, US$1.25, 2 hrs, last bus back leaves Huari about 1630. You can also take a bus to Challapata and a shared taxi from there to Huari, US$0.30. Daily services to: **La Paz** at least every hour 0400-2200, US$2-3.40, 4 hrs; also tourist van service with **Enjoy Bolivia**, see La Paz Tour operators, page 261. Note that in 2014, work was in progress to widen the La Paz to Oruro highway

to 4 lanes, causing travel delays. **Cochabamba**, US$3.35-4, 4 hrs, frequent. **Potosí**, US$2.70-4, 5 hrs, several daily. **Sucre**, all buses around 2000, US$7, 9 hrs. **Tarija**, 2 departures at 2030, US$9.30-14.50, 14 hrs. **Uyuni**, several companies, all depart 1900-2100, US$4.35 regular, US$7.25 *semi-cama*, 7-8 hrs. **Todo Turismo**, offers a tourist bus departing from La Paz at 2100, arrange ahead for pick-up in Oruro at midnight, US$27. To **Tupiza**, via Potosí, **Boquerón** at 1230, **Illimani** at 1630 and 2000, US$9.75-12.40, 11-12 hrs, continuing to Villazón, US$10-13, 13-14 hrs. **Santa Cruz**, **Bolívar** at 2000, US$8.70, *bus cama* at 2130, US$14, 11 hrs. To **Pisiga** (Chilean border), Trans Pisiga, Av Dehene y España, T526 2241, at 2000 and 2030, or with Iquique bound buses, US$3.75, 4-5 hrs. **International buses** (US$2 to cross border): to **Iquique** via Pisiga, US$13-14, 8 hrs, buses leave around 1200 coming from Cochabamba. **Arica** via Patacamaya and Tambo Quemado, several companies daily around 1100-1300 and 2300, US$22 normal, US$26-29 *semi-cama*, US$33 *cama*, 8 hrs, some continue to Iquique, 12 hrs.

Train The station is at Av Velasco Galvarro y Aldana, T527 4605, ticket office Mon-Fri 0800-1200, 1430-1800, Sun 0830-1120, 1530-1800. Tickets for *ejecutivo* class are sold up to 2 weeks in advance, 1 week for *salón*. Tickets can also be purchased in La Paz, see page 264. Ferroviaria Andina (FCA, www.fca.com.bo), runs services from Oruro to **Uyuni**, **Tupiza** and **Villazón**. Expreso del Sur runs Tue and Fri at 1530, arriving in Uyuni at 2220, and Wara Wara on Sun and Wed at 1900, arriving in Uyuni at 0220.

Fares: Expreso del Sur to **Uyuni**: *Ejecutivo* US$17, *Salón* US$8.60; **Tupiza**, 12½ hrs: US$34, US$15.30 respectively; **Villazón**: 15½ hrs, US$40, US$18 respectively. **Wara Wara del Sur to Uyuni**: *Ejecutivo* US$14.60, *Salón* US$6.70; **Tupiza**, 13½-14 hrs: US$26, US$11.40 respectively; **Villazón**, 17 hrs: US$31.40, US$14.30 respectively.

Quime *p280*

To get to Quime, take any bus from La Paz to Oruro or Cochabamba and get out at Conani, 2-3 hrs (likewise get out at Conani coming from Oruro or Cochabamba). Change to a bus, minibus or taxi (wait till full) to Quime, 1½ hrs,

US$3.55. Direct buses from La Paz to Quime, 5 hrs, are Inquisivi from the bus terminal (T282 4734) and Apóstol Santiago from El Alto (T259 7544), US$3.55.

Parque Nacional Sajama *p282*
To get to the park, take a La Paz-Oruro bus and change at Patacamaya. Mini-vans from Patacamaya to Sajama Sun-Fri 1200, 3 hrs, US$2.50. Sajama to **Patacamaya** Mon-Fri 0600, some days via **Tambo Quemado**, confirm details and weekend schedule locally. From Tambo Quemado to Sajama about 1530 daily, 1 hr, US$0.65. Or take a La Paz-Arica bus, ask for Sajama, try to pay half the fare, but you may be charged full fare.

South of Oruro *p282*
To **Coipasa** ask if **Trans Pisiga**, address above, is running a fortnightly service. If not, you can take one of the buses for Iquique and get off at the turnoff, but it's difficult to hire a private vehicle for onward transportation in this sparsely populated area. Salinas de Garci Mendoza from **Oruro**, **Trans Cabrera**, C Tejerina y Caro, daily except Sat (Mon, Wed Fri, Sun 1900, Tue, Thu 0830, Sun also at 0730). Return to Oruro same days, US$3.40, 7 hrs.

❶ Directory

Oruro *p280, map p281*
Useful addresses Immigration, S Galvarro 5744 entre Ayacucho y Cochabamba, across from Museo Simón Patiño, T527 0239, Mon-Fri 0830-1230, 1430-1830.

Uyuni → *Phone code: 02. Colour map 6, B3. Population: 18,000. Altitude: 3670 m.*

Uyuni lies near the eastern edge of the Salar de Uyuni and is one of the jumping-off points for trips to the salt flats, volcanoes and lakes of southwest Bolivia. With the arrival of regular flights to Uyuni and the paving of the Uyuni-Potosí road, tourism in the area is changing fast, with new hotels and new packages being offered. Still a commercial and communication centre, Uyuni was, for much of the 20th century, important as a major railway junction. Two monuments dominate Avenida Ferroviaria: one of a railway worker, erected after the 1952 Revolution, and the other commemorating those who died in the Chaco War. Most services are near the station. **Museo Arqueológico y Antropológico de los Andes Meridionales** ① *Arce y Potosí, Mon-Fri 0830-1200, 1400-1800, Sat-Sun 0900-1300, US$0.35*, is small museum with local artefacts. The market is at Potosí y Bolívar. Fiesta 11 July. There is a Railway Cemetery of sorts outside town with engines from 1907 to the 1950s, now rusting hulks. **Pulacayo**, 25 km from Uyuni on the road to Potosí, is a town at the site of a 19th-century silver mine. The train cemetery here is more interesting and contains the first locomotive in Bolivia and the train robbed by Butch Cassidy and the Sundance Kid.

Tourist office Dirección de Turismo Uyuni ① *at the clock tower, T693 2060, Mon-Sat 0800-1200, 1430-1830, Sun 0900-1200.* **Subprefectura de Potosí** ① *Colón y Sucre, Mon-Fri 0800-1200, 1430-1830, Sat 0800-1200*, departmental information office, the place to file complaints in writing. There is only one ATM in Uyuni which does not always work, take cash.

Salar de Uyuni

Crossing the Salar de Uyuni, the largest and highest salt lake in the world, is one of the great Bolivian trips. Driving across it is a fantastic experience, especially during June and July when the bright blue skies contrast with the blinding white salt crust. Farther south, and included on most tours of the region, is the **Reserva Eduardo Avaroa** (REA, see below) with the towering volcanoes, multi-coloured lakes with abundant birdlife, weird rock formations, thermal activity and endless puna that make up some of most fabulous landscapes in South America. For information on the north shore of the salar, see South of Oruro, page 282.

Trips to the Salar de Uyuni originating in Uyuni enter via the *terraplén* (ramp) at **Colchani** (**Museo de la Llama y de la Sal**; see also Where to stay, below) and include stops to see traditional salt mining techniques and the Ojos del Agua, where salt water bubbles to the surface of the slat flat, perhaps a call at a salt hotel (see Where to stay, below) and a visit to the **Isla Incahuasi** ⓘ *entry US$5*. This is a coral island, raised up from the ocean bed, covered in tall cactii. There is a walking trail with superb views, a café, basic lodging and toilets. If on an extended tour (see below), you may leave the Salar by another *terraplén*, eg Puerto Chuvica in the southwest. Some tours also include **Gruta de la Galaxia**, an interesting cave at the edge of the Salar.

The Salar de Uyuni contains what may be the world's largest lithium deposits and the Bolivian government has announced plans to build large-scale extraction facilities. A pilot plant was recently operating (away from usual tourist routes) and concern has been expressed about the impact of more extensive lithium mining.

San Cristóbal
The original village of San Cristóbal, southwest of Uyuni, was relocated in 2002 to make way for a huge open-pit mine, said to be one of the largest silver deposits in South America. The original church (1650) had been declared a national monument and was therefore rebuilt in its entirety. Ask at the Fundación San Cristóbal Office for the church to be opened as the interior artwork, restored by Italian techniques, is worth seeing. The fiesta is 27-28 July.

Reserva Nacional de Fauna Andina Eduardo Avaroa
ⓘ *SERNAP office at Colón y Avaroa, Uyuni, T693 2225, www.biobol.org, Mon-Fri 0830-1230, 1430-1800; entry to reserve US$22 (Bs150, not included in tour prices; pay in bolivianos). Park ranger/entry points are near Laguna Colorada, Lagunas Verde and Blanca, close to the Chilean border, and at Sol de Mañana, near Quetena Chico.*

In the far southwest of Bolivia, in the López region, is the 714,745-ha Reserva Nacional Eduardo Avaroa (REA). There are two access routes from Uyuni (one via the Salar) and one from Tupiza.

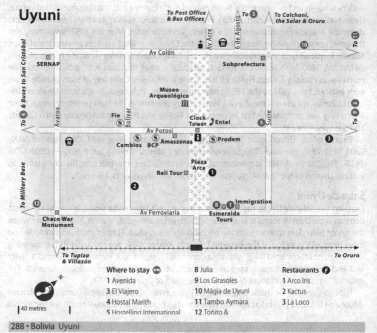

Uyuni

Where to stay
1 Avenida
3 El Viajero
4 Hostal Marith
5 Hostelling International
8 Julia
9 Los Girasoles
10 Mágia de Uyuni
11 Tambo Aymara
12 Toñito &

Restaurants
1 Arco Iris
2 Kactus
3 La Loco

This is one of Bolivia's prime attractions and tour vehicles criss-cross the puna every day, many on the route from Uyuni to San Pedro de Atacama (Chile). Roads are still unmarked rugged tracks, however, and may be impassable in the wet season. **Laguna Colorada** at 4278 m, 346 km southwest of Uyuni, is just one of the highlights of the reserve, its shores and shallows encrusted with borax and salt, an arctic white counterpoint to the flaming red, algae-coloured waters in which the rare James flamingos, along with the more common Chilean and Andean flamingos, breed and live. **Laguna Verde** (lifeless because it is laden with arsenic) and its neighbour **Laguna Blanca**, near the Chilean border, are at the foot of Volcán Licancábur, 5868 m. Between Lagunas Colorada and Verde there are thermal pools at Laguna Blanca (blissful water, a challenge to get out into the bitter wind – no facilities) and at Polques, on the shores of Río Amargo/Laguna Salada by the Salar de Chalviri. A *centro comunal* at Polques has dining room, changing room and toilets. All these places are on the 'classic' tour route, across the Salar de Uyuni to **San Juan**, which has a museum of local *chullpas*, and is where most tour companies stop: plenty of lodgings. Other tours stop at **Culpina K**. Then you go to the Salar de Chiguana, Mirador del Volcán de Ollagüe, Cinco Lagunas, a chain of small, flamingo-specked lagoons, the much-photographed Arbol de Piedra in the Siloli desert, then Laguna Colorada (spend the second night here. **Hospedaje Laguna Colorada**, the newer and better **$ Don Humberto** in Huayllajara, and **Campamento Ende**). From Colorada you go over the Cuesta del Pabellón, 4850 m, to the Sol de Mañana geysers (not to be confused with the Sol de Mañana entry point), the Desierto de Dalí, a pure sandy desert as much Daliesque for the spacing of the rocks, with snow-covered peaks behind, as for the shape of the rocks themselves, and Laguna Verde (4400 m).

Jurisdiction of the reserve belongs to the villages of **Quetena Chico** and Quetena Grande, to the east of Laguna Colorada. The villagers run lodging in the reserve: Quetena Chico runs *hospedajes* at Laguna Colorada. Quetena Grande runs La Cabaña at Hito Cajónes (see below). In Quetena Chico is the reserve's visitors information centre, **Centro Ecológico Ch'aska** ① *daily 0730-1800*, informative displays about the region's geology, vulcanology, fauna, flora and human history; a worthwhile stop. The village has two cheap *hospedajes* (**Piedra Preciosa** and **Hostal Quetena**, hot water extra), and places to eat.

Sadly, lakes in the reserve are gradually drying up, most noticeably Laguna Verde. This has been attributed to global climate change but the real reason may be massive underground water consumption by Bolivian, Chilean and Argentine mines.

From Tupiza Tour operators in Tupiza run trips to the REA and Salar de Uyuni and go to places not included on tours from Uyuni. These include the beautiful **Lagunas Celeste** and **Negra** below Cerro Uturunco, which is near Quetena Chico; the **Valle de las Rocas**, 4260 m, between the villages of **Alota** and **Villa Mar** (a vast extension of rocks eroded into fantastic configurations, with polylepis trees in sheltered corners); and isolated communities in the puna. The high altitude scenery is out of this world. With the exception of Quetena Chico, *alojamientos* in the villages on the tour routes cannot be booked. You turn up and search for a room. All provide kitchen space for the tour's cook or independent traveller to prepare meals, take your own stove, though. See also **Tayka** in Salar de Uyuni, Where to stay, below. There is public transport from Uyuni into the region, but rarely more than one bus a week, with several hours rough travelling. If travelling independently, note that there are countless tracks and no signposts.

Crossing into Chile

There is a REA ranger station near Lagunas Blanca and Verde: if going from Bolivia, have your park entry receipt at hand, if crossing from Chile pay the entry fee here. Alongside is a *refugio, La Cabaña*; US$5 pp in comfortable but very cold dorms, solar-powered lighting, hot water seldom works, cooking facilities but take your own food (in high season book in advance – tour agencies can do this by radio). There is good climbing and hiking in the area with outstanding views. You must register at the ranger station before heading out and they may insist that you take a guide (eg to climb Licancábur, US$30 for guide plus US$40 for transport). Mind the altitude, intense solar radiation and lack of drinking water.

From the ranger station it's 5 km to the border at Hito Cajones (on the Chilean side called Hito Cajón), 4500 m. Bolivian immigration open 0800-2100, charges US$2 in any currency. If you plan to cross to Chile here, you should first go to the immigration office in Uyuni (see Directory, page 293). There are no services or facilities at the border. A further 6 km along a good dirt road into Chile is the intersection with the fully paved road from San Pedro de Atacama to Paso de Jama, the border between Chile and Argentina. From here it's 40 km (2000 m downhill) to San Pedro. Chilean customs and immigration are just outside San Pedro and can take 45 minutes at busy times. ▶▶ *See Transport, page 292.*

⊙ Uyuni listings

For hotel and restaurant price codes, and other relevant information, see Essentials.

● Where to stay

Uyuni *p287, map p288*
Many hotels fill early, reservations are advised in high season, but new hotels are opening (eg **Samay Wasi**, Av Potosí 965, www.hoteles samaywasi.com). Be conservative with water use, this is a very dry area, water is scarce and supplied at limited hours (better hotels have reserve tanks).

$$$ Jardines de Uyuni, Potosí 113, T693 2989, www.hotelesrusticosjardines.com. Tastefully decorated, comfortable, heating, open fire in the lounge, small pool, parking.

$$$ Mágia de Uyuni, Av Colón 432, T693 2541, www.hostalmagiauyuni.com. Nice ample rooms and suites upstairs with heating, cheaper in older colder rooms downstairs (ask for a heater), parking.

$$ Los Girasoles, Santa Cruz 155, T693 3323, www.girasoleshotel.hostel.com. Buffet breakfast, bright and warm (especially 2nd floor), comfortable, nice decor, heaters, cheaper in old section, internet extra.

$$ Tambo Aymara, Camacho s/n y Colón, T693 2227, www.tamboaymara.com. Lovely colonial-style modern hotel, large comfortable rooms, heating, Belgian/Bolivian owned, operate their own tours.

$$-$ Toñito, Av Ferroviaria 48, T693 3186, www.bolivianexpeditions.com. Spacious rooms with good beds, solar-powered showers and heating in new wing, cheaper in old section with electric showers, parking, book exchange, tours.

$ Avenida, Av Ferroviaria 11, near train station, T693 2078. Simple but well maintained, cheaper with shared bath, hot water (shared showers 0700-2100), long patio with laundry facilities, family run, helpful, good value, popular and often full.

$ El Viajero, Cabrera 334 y 6 de Agosto, near bus terminals, T02-693 3549. Basic rooms, cheaper with shared bath, electric shower, parking.

$ Hostal Marith, Av Potosí 61, T693 2174. Basic, cheaper with shared bath and in dorm, electric showers from 0830, patio with laundry facilities, tours (have salt hotel at Atulcha near the salar).

$ Hostelling International, Potosí y Sucre, T693 2228 (listed on www.hihostels. com). Cheaper with shared bath, hot water, modern and popular but poor beds, discount for IYHF members.

$ Julia, Ferroviaria 314 y Arce, T693 2134, www.juliahoteluyuni.com. Spacious rooms, cheaper with shared bath, electric showers, internet extra.

Salar de Uyuni and Reserva Eduardo Avaroa *p287 and p288*
These *hoteles de sal* are generally visited on tours, seldom independently.

$$$$-$$$ Luna Salada, 5 km north of Colchani near the edge of the salar, T7242 9716, La Paz T02-278 5438, www.lunasaladahotel. com.bo. Lovely salt hotel, comfortable rooms, hot water, ample common areas with lovely views of the Salar, salt floors, skylights make it warm and cosy, reserve ahead.

$$$$-$$$ Palacio de Sal, on the edge of the salar, near the ramp outside Colchani, www. palaciodesal.com.bo. Book through **Hidalgo**

Tours, Potosí, T02-622 9512. Spacious, luxury salt hotel, decorated with large salt sculptures, heating, sauna, lookout on 2nd storey with views of the salar.

$$$ Mallku Cueva, outside Villa Mar, along the route from Tupiza to the reserve, T617 9014, www.hotelesrusticosjardines.com. Nicely decorated upmarket hotel with all services, including Wi-Fi.

$$$ Tayka, Uyuni office: Sucre 7715 entre Uruguay y México, T693 2987, La Paz T7205 3438, www.taykahoteles.com. A chain of 4 upmarket hotels in Salar de Uyuni-REA area, operating in conjunction with local communities. The hotels have comfortable rooms with bath, hot water, heating, restaurant, price includes breakfast, discounts in low season. The Hotel de Sal (salt hotel) is in Tahua, on the north shore of the Salar; the Hotel de Piedra (stone hotel) is in San Pedro de Quemes, on the south shore of the Salar; the Hotel del Desierto (desert hotel) is in Ojo de Perdiz in the Siloli Desert, north of Laguna Colorada; the Hotel del Volcán (volcano hotel) is in San Pablo de Lípez, between Uturunco Volcano and Tupiza.

$ Alojamiento del Museo de Sal, on the road to the Salar from Colchani, by the *tranca*, T7272 0834. Simple cheap salt hotel, shared bath, kitchen facilities, dining area used by groups, has a small museum with salt sculptures, reserve ahead, good value.

San Cristóbal *p288*
$$ Hotel San Cristóbal, in centre, T7264 2117. Purpose-built and owned by the community. The bar is inside a huge oil drum, all metal furnishings. The rest is comfortable if simple, hot water, good breakfast, evening meal extra.

There are also a couple of inexpensive *alojamientos* in town.

🍴 Restaurants

Uyuni *p287, map p288*
Plaza Arce has various tourist restaurants serving mostly mediocre pizza.
$$-$ Kactus, Bolívar y Ferrovaria. Daily 0830-2200. Set lunches and international food à la carte, also sells pastries and whole-wheat bread, slow service.

$$-$ La Loco, Av Potosí y Camacho, T693 3105. Mon-Sat 1600-0200 (food until about 2130), closed Jan-Feb. International food with a Bolivian and French touch, music and drinks till late, open fire, popular, reserve in Jul-Aug. Also run a small exclusive guest-house: **La Petite Porte** (**$$$** www.hotel-lapetiteporte-uyuni.com).

$ Arco Iris, Plaza Arce. Daily 1600-2230. Good Italian food, pizza, and atmosphere, occasional live music.

$ Extreme Fun Pub, Potosí 9. Restaurant/pub, pleasant atmosphere, good service, videos, friendly owner is very knowledgeable about Bolivia.

$ Minuteman, pizza restaurant attached to Toñito Hotel (see above), good pizzas and soups, also breakfast.

⚙ What to do

Uyuni *p287, map p288*
There are over 70 agencies in Uyuni offering salar tours and quality varies greatly. You generally get what you pay for but your experience will depend more on your particular driver, cook and companions than the agency that sells you the tour. Travel is in 4WD Landcruisers, cramped for those on the back seat, but the staggering scenery makes up for any discomfort. Always check the itinerary, the vehicle, the menu (especially vegetarians), what is included in the price and what is not. Trips are usually 3-4 days: Salar de Uyuni, Reserva Eduardo Avaroa, and back to Uyuni or on to San Pedro de Atacama (Chile); or Tupiza to Uyuni, San Pedro de Atacama or back to Tupiza. Prices range from US$50-350 pp plus park fee of Bs 150 (US$22) The cheapest tours are not recommended and usually involve crowding, insufficient staff and food, poor vehicles (fatal accidents have taken place) and accommodation. The best value is at the mid- to high-end, where you can assemble your own tour for a total of 4-5 passengers, with driver, cook, good equipment and services. Three factors often lead to misunderstandings between what is offered and what is actually delivered by the tour operator: 1) agencies pool clients when there are not enough passengers to fill a

vehicle. 2) Agencies all over Bolivia sell Salar tours, but booking from far away may not give full information on the local operator. 3) Many drivers work for multiple agencies and will cut tours short. If the tour seriously fails to match the contract and the operator refuses any redress, complaints can be taken to the **Subprefectura de Potosí** in Uyuni (see above) but don't expect a quick refund or apology. Try to speak to travellers who have just returned from a tour before booking your own, and ignore touts on the street and at the rail or bus stations.

Tour operators

Andes Travel Office (ATO), in Hotel Tambo Aymara (see above), T693 2227, tamboaymara@gmail.com. Upmarket private tours, Belgian-Bolivian owned, English and French spoken, reliable.

Atacama Mística, Av Ferroviaria s/n, T693 3607, www.atacamamistica.cl. Chilean-Bolivian company, daily tours with transfer to San Pedro de Atacama, also transfers between San Pedro and Uyuni, good service.

Creative Tours, Sucre 362, T693 3543, www.creativetours.com.bo. Long-established company, partners in the **Tayka** chain of hotels, see below. Premium tours in the region and throughout the country, with offices in Uyuni, Cochabamba and Trinidad, and representatives in the main cities.

Esmeralda, Av Ferroviaria y Arce, T693 2130, esmeraldaivan@hotmail.com. Economical end of market.

Hidalgo Tours, Av Potosí 113 at Hotel Jardines de Uyuni, www.salardeuyuni.net. Well

established Salar/REA operator, runs Palacio de Sal and Mallku Cueva hotels, also in Potosí.
Oasis Odyssey, Av Ferroviaria, T693 3175, www.oasistours-bo.com. Also have office in Sucre.
Reli Tours, Av Arce 42, T693 3209.

San Cristóbal *p288*

Llama Mama, T7240 0309. 60 km of exclusive bicycle trails descending 2-3 or 4 hrs, depending on skill, 3 grades, US$20 pp, all inclusive, taken up by car, with guide and communication.

⊙ Transport

Uyuni *p287, map p288*
Air To/from **La Paz** , Amazonas, Potosí y Arce, T693 3333, 1 or 2 daily, US$143, also TAM 3 times a week.
Bus Most offices are on Av Arce and Cabrera. To **La Paz**, US$12-17, 11 hrs, daily at 2000 (La Paz-Uyuni at 1900) with Panasur, www.uyunipanasur.com, **Cruz del Norte**, and **Trans Omar**, www.transomar.com; or transfer in Oruro. Tourist buses with **Todo Turismo**, T693 3337, daily at 2000, US$33 (La Paz office, Plaza Antofagasta 504, Edif Paola, p1, opposite the bus terminal, T02-211 9418, daily to Uyuni at 2100), note this service does not run if the road is poor during the rainy season. **Oruro**, several companies 2000-2130, US$6, 7 hrs; **Todo Turismo** (see above), US$20. To **Potosí** several companies around1000 and 1900, US$5.50, 6 hrs, spectacular scenery. To **Sucre**, 6 de Octubre and **Emperador** at 1000, US$10, 9 hrs; or transfer in Potosí. To **Tupiza** US$7.50, 8 hrs, via **Atocha**, several companies daily

at 0600 and 2030 (from Tupiza at 1000 and 1800), continuing to **Villazón** on the Argentine border, US$10, 11 hrs. For **Tarija** change in Potosí or Tupiza. Regional services to villages in **Nor- and Sud-Lípez** operate about 3 times a week, confirm details locally. To **Pulacayo** take any bus for Potosí.

Road and train A road and railway line run south from Oruro, through Río Mulato, to Uyuni (323 km, each about 7 hrs). The road is sandy and, after rain, very bad, especially south of Río Mulato. The train journey is more comfortable. **Expreso del Sur** leaves for **Oruro** on Wed and Sat at 2350, arriving 0710 the next day. **Wara Wara del Sur** leaves on Tue and Fri at 0115, arriving 0910 (prices for both under Oruro, page 286). To **Atocha**, **Tupiza** and **Villazón** Expreso del Sur leaves Uyuni on Tue and Fri at 2220, arriving, respectively, at 0045, 0400 and 0705. **Wara Wara** leaves on Mon and Thu at 0220, arriving 0500, 0835 and 1205. The ticket office (T693 2320) opens Mon-Fri 0900-1200, 1430-1800, Sat-Sun 1000-1100, and 1 hr before the trains leave. It closes once tickets are sold – get there early or buy through a tour agent (more expensive).

Advance preparations are required to drive across the salar and REA. Fuel is not easily available in the Lípez region, so you must take jerrycans. A permit from the Dirección General de Substancias Controladas in La Paz is required to fill jerrycans; you will be authorized to fill only two 60 l cans. Fuel for vehicles with foreign plates may be considerably more expensive than for those with local plates.

Travelling to Chile Chile is 1 hr ahead of Bolivia from mid-Oct to Mar. Chile does not allow coca, dairy produce, tea bags, fruit or vegetables to be brought in.

The easiest way is to go to San Pedro de Atacama as part of your tour to the Salar and REA (see above). **Colque Tours** runs 2 mini-buses daily from near the ranger station at Hito Cajones to San Pedro de Atacama, departing 1000 and 1700, US$6.50, 1 hr including stop at immigration. At other times onward transport

to San Pedro must be arranged by your agency, this can cost up to US$60 if it is not included in your tour. The ranger station may be able to assist in an emergency. **Hostal Marith** (see Uyuni, Where to stay) and Atacama Mística tour operator run transport service from Uyuni to San Pedro de Atacama, US$30, confirm details in advance.

From Uyuni to **Avaroa** and on to **Calama**, **Centenario**, Cabrera y Arce, Sun, Mon, Wed, Thu at 0330, transfer at the border to **Intertrans** (daily from Calama to Ollagüe) or Atacama, Thu, Mon 2000 . To Avaroa, US$6, 4½ hrs; to Calama US$15, 4 hrs; allow 2 hrs at the border.

If driving your own vehicle, from **Colchani** it is about 60 km across to the southern shore of the Salar. Follow the tracks made by other vehicles in the dry season. The salt is soft and wet for about 2 km around the edges so only use established ramps. It is 20 km from the southern shore to Colcha K military checkpoint. From there, a poor gravel road leads 28 km to San Juan then the road enters the Salar de Chiguana, a mix of salt and mud which is often wet and soft with deep tracks which are easy to follow; 35 km away is Chiguana, another military post, then 45 km to the end of this Salar, a few kilometres before border at Ollagüe. This latter part is the most dangerous; very slippery with little traffic. Or take the route that tours use to Laguna Colorada and continue to Hito Cajones. **Atacama Mística** of Uyuni will let you follow one of their groups if you arrange in advance. There is no fuel between Uyuni and Calama (Chile) if going via Ollagüe, but expensive fuel is sold in San Pedro de Atacama. Keep to the road at all times; the road is impassable after rain.

⑥ Directory

Uyuni *p287, map p288*
Useful addresses Immigration: Av Ferroviaria entre Arce y Sucre, T693 2062, Mon-Fri 0830-1230, 1430-1830, Sat-Sun 0900-1100, for visa extensions, also register here before travel to Chile.

Set in a landscape of colourful, eroded mountains and stands of huge cactii (usually flowering December-February), Tupiza, 200 km south of Uyuni, is a pleasant town with a lower altitude and warmer climate, making it a good alternative for visits to the Reserva Eduardo Avaroa and the Salar. Several Tupiza operators offer Salar, REA and local tours. Beautiful sunsets over the fertile Tupiza valley can be seen from the foot of a statue of Christ on a hill behind the plaza.

There is good hiking around Tupiza but be prepared for sudden changes of climate including hailstorms, and note that dry gullies are prone to flash flooding. A worthwhile excursion is to **Quebrada Palala** with the nearby 'Stone Forest'; here is the hamlet of Torre Huayco, part of a community tourism project, Circuitos Bioculturales. **Oploca**, a small town 17 km northwest of Tupiza with a lovely colonial church, is also part of the project, as is Chuquiago, 30 km south of Tupiza, along the rail line. Each has a small eco-albergue (**$** pp, with breakfast, simple comfortable rooms, kitchen) and guides. A circuit can be done in one to three days by bicycle, horse, trekking, jeep, or a combination of these (US$35-50 per day, ask tour operators in Tupiza). The routes are very scenic and the villages are tranquil. You can arrange to spend a couple of days relaxing there.

Tupiza is the base for **Butch Cassidy and the Sundance Kid tours**. The statue in the main plaza is to **Victor Carlos Aramayo** (1802-1882), of the 19th century mining dynasty. Butch and

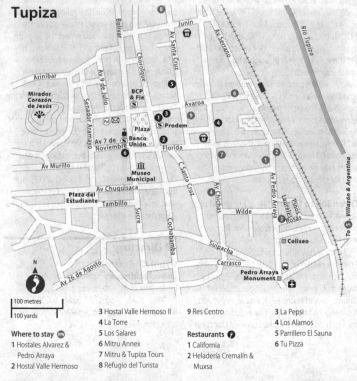

Tupiza

Where to stay 🛌
1 Hostales Alvarez & Pedro Arraya
2 Hostal Valle Hermoso
3 Hostal Valle Hermoso II
4 La Torre
5 Los Salares
6 Mitru Annex
7 Mitru & Tupiza Tours
8 Refugio del Turista
9 Res Centro

Restaurants 🍴
1 California
2 Heladería Cremalín & Muxsa
3 La Pepsi
4 Los Alamos
5 Parrillero El Sauna
6 Tu Pizza

Sundance's last holdup was of an Aramayo company payroll at Huaca Huañusca on 4 November 1908. They are believed (by some, see *Digging Up Butch and Sundance*, by Anne Meadows, Bison Books, 2003) to have died soon afterwards at the hands of a police patrol in **San Vicente**, a tiny mining camp at 4500 m, but no grave in the San Vicente cemetery has yet to be positively identified as theirs. There is a small museum with local artifacts but no lodging or other services. Visits can be arranged by Tupiza agencies.

There are two ATMs in Tupiza, beside Tu Pizza restaurant and at Banco FIE. Don't rely on them, though; take cash.

South to Argentine border

Villazón The Argentine border is at Villazón (*Phone code: 02; Population: 37,133; Altitude: 3443 m*), 81 km south of Tupiza. There is a museum about the Chicha culture at the plaza. Of traditional villages in the surroundings, those to the west, like Berque, are known for their pottery. Many *casas de cambio* on Av República de Argentina, leading to the border, change US$, pesos and euros, all at poor rates. There are banks and an ATM in town. The border area must not be photographed.

Border with Argentina The Bolivian Immigration office is on Avenida República de Argentina just before bridge, open daily 0600-2000, taxi from Villazón bus terminal US$0.50 pp. Queuing begins at 0500 and there may be long delays. Argentine Immigration (open 0700-2400 Argentine time, see below) is on the other side of the bridge, 10 blocks from La Quiaca bus terminal, taxi US$1. Change all your bolivianos in Villazón as there is nowhere to do so in La Quiaca or beyond. Entering Bolivia, boys offer to wheel your bags uphill to the bus stations, US$1, but they will ask for more. The Argentine consulate is at Plaza 6 de Agosto 121, T597 2011, Monday-Friday 0800-1300. **Note** Argentine time is one hour later than Bolivia, two hours when Buenos Aires adopts daylight saving.

◉ Tupiza listings

For hotel and restaurant price codes, and other relevant information, see Essentials.

● Where to stay

Tupiza *p294, map p294*
$$-$ Mitru, Av Chichas 187, T694 3001, www.hotelmitru.com. Pleasant ample grounds with pool, nice atmosphere, a variety of rooms and prices, the more expensive rooms have king-size beds, a/c and hair driers, cheaper in older section with private bath and even cheaper with shared bath. All include good buffet breakfast with bread made on the premises, reliable solar hot water, parking, luggage store, book exchange, Wi-Fi. Very helpful and knowledgeable, popular, reserve ahead in high season. Warmly recommended.
$ Hostal Alvarez, Av P Arraya 492, T694 5327. Near the bus and train stations, Small 10-room hostel, brighter rooms on 2nd storey, cheaper with shared bath, extra charge for a/c and breakfast, new in 2013.

$ Hostal Pedro Arraya, Av P Arraya 494, T694 2734, www.hostalpedroarraya.com. Convenient to bus and train stations, small rooms, cheaper with shared bath, hot water, breakfast available, laundry facilities, terrace, family run.
$ Hostal Valle Hermoso, Av Pedro Arraya 478, T694 2592, www.vallehermosotours.com. Breakfast available, cheaper with shared bath, cheaper in dorm. TV/breakfast room, book exchange, motorbike parking. Second location, Valle Hermoso II, Av Pedro Arraya 585, T694 3441, near the bus station, 3 simple rooms with bath, several dorms with bunk beds, same prices as No 1, 10% discount for IYHF members in both locations.
$ La Torre, Av Chichas 220, T694 2633, www.latorretours-tupiza.com. Lovely refurbished house, newer rooms at back, comfortable, cheaper with shared bath and no TV, great service, good value. Recommended.
$ Los Salares, C Ecuador s/n, Zona Chajrahuasi, behind petrol station, T694 5813,

www.lossalares.hostel.com. 9 rooms, 1 without bath (cheaper), continental breakfast and kitchen, parking, a bit out of town.
$ Mitru Annex, Avaroa 20, T694 3002, www.tupizatours.com. Nicely refurbished older hotel, buffet breakfast, cheaper with shared bath, good hot showers, Wi-Fi, use of pool and games room at Hotel Mitru.
$ Refugio del Turista, Av Santa Cruz 240, T694 3155, www.tupizatours.com. Refurbished home with garden, shared bath, reliable hot water, well-equipped kitchen, laundry facilities, parking and electric outlet for camper-vans, popular budget option, good value.
$ Res Centro, Av Santa Cruz 287, T694 2705. Nice patio, couple of rooms with private bath, most shared, basic but clean, hot water, parking, helpful owner, good value.

Villazón *p295*
$ Hostal Plaza, Plaza 6 de Agosto 138, T597 3535. Adequate rooms, cheaper without bath, electric shower, includes simple breakfast, good restaurant, **La Perla**, underneath hotel, also internet below.
$ Olimpo, Av República Argentina y Chorolque 116, T5972219. Among the better hotels in town, cheaper with shared bath, includes simple breakfast.
$ Tierra Andina, 25 de Mayo 52, T594 5133. Another good option, with and without bath and most economical in 4-bed dorms, includes a very basic breakfast.

🍴 Restaurants

Tupiza *p294, map p294*
Several touristy pizza places on C Florida are mediocre to terrible, also watch your belongings here. The best options are just outside town (all **$$-$**), they serve grilled meat and good regional specialties like *picante de cabrito* (spicy goat) but open only Sat or Sun midday – go early. These include: La Campiña, in Tambillo Alto, 45 mins' walk north along the river; and La Estancia, 2 km north in Villa Remedios. There are food stalls upstairs in the market but mind the cleanliness.
$$-$ Café Muxsa, Cochabamba 133 y Florida, on Plaza, Tue-Sun 1700-2200. A variety of good quality sandwiches, tacos and salads, nicely served, good coffee, pastries, Wi-Fi, popular.

$ California, Cochabamba 413, 2nd floor. Set lunches, hamburguers and snacks in the evening when service is slow.
$ Los Alamos, Av Chichas 157. Open 0800-2400. Local and international dishes, good atmosphere, average food, good juices, large portions, popular with tourists.
$ Parrillero El Sauna, Av Santa Cruz entre Avaroa y Junín. Tue-Sun from 1700. Very good parrilladas with Argentine meat, salad buffet.
$ Tu Pizza, Sucre y 7 de Noviembre, on Plaza. Mon-Sat 1830-2300. Cute name, variety of pizzas, very slow service.
Heladería Cremalín, Cochabamba y Florida, on Plaza, ice cream, juices and fruit shakes.
La Pepsi, Avaroa s/n, Mon-Sat 0830-1830. *Salteñas* in the morning, also very good sweet and savoury pastries, sandwiches, juices, cappuccino.

ⓞ What to do

Tupiza *p294, map p294*
1-day jeep tours US$35 pp for group of 5; horse riding 3-, 5- and 7-hr tours, the latter includes lunch, US$10 per hr, multi-day tours US$70 per day; 2-day San Vicente plus colonial town of Portugalete US$80 pp (plus lodging); Salar de Uyuni and REA, 4 days with Spanish speaking guide, US$200 pp for a group of 5, plus Bs150 (US$22) park fee. Add US$23 pp for English speaking guide.
La Torre Tours, in Hotel La Torre (see above), Salar/REA tours and local trips on jeep, bicycle, walking or horse riding.
Tupiza Tours, in Hotel Mitru (see above), www.tupizatours.com. Highly experienced and well organized for Salar/REA and local tours. Also offer 1-day 'triathlon' of horse riding, biking and jeep, US$50 pp for group of 5, a good way to see the area if you only have 1 day; Butch Cassidy tours; paseos bioculturales, and extensions to the Uyuni tour. Have offices in La Paz and Tarija, and offer tours in all regions of Bolivia. Highly recommended.
Valle Hermoso Tours, in Hostal Valle Hermoso 1 (see above), www.vallehermosotours.com. Offers similar tours on horse or jeep, as do several other agencies and most Tupiza hotels.

✈ Transport

Tupiza *p294, map p294*
Bus There is small, well-organized, bus terminal at the south end of Av Pedro Arraya. To **Villazón** several buses daily, USUS2.75, 2 hrs; also ATL mini-buses from opposite terminal, leave when full, US$4. To **Potosí**, several companies around 1000 and 2100, US$5, 8 hrs. To **Sucre**, Expreso Villazón at 1500, Trans Illimani at 2030 (more comfortable but known to speed), US$11, 12 hrs; or transfer in Potosí. To **Tarija**, several around 1930-2030, US$9, 6 hrs (change here for **Santa Cruz**). To **Uyuni**, several companies around 1000 and 1800, US$8, 8 hrs. To **Oruro**, Trans Illimani at 1300, 1800, US$15, 12 hrs; continuing to **Cochabamba**, US$19, 17 hrs. To **La Paz** several at 1200 and 1730-2030, US$19, 16-17 hrs. Agent for the Argentine company **Balut** at terminal sells tickets to Jujuy, Salta, Buenos Aires or Córdoba (local bus to the border at Villazón, then change to Balut), but beware overcharging or buy tickets directly from local companies once in Argentina.
Train Train station ticket office open Mon-Sat 0800-1100, 1530-1730, and early morning half an hour before trains arrive. To **Atocha**, **Uyuni** and **Oruro**: Expreso del Sur Wed and Sat at 1815; Wara Wara Mon and Thu at 1825. Fares are given under Oruro, page 286.

Villazón *p295*
Bus Bus terminal is near plaza, 5 blocks from the border. Lots of company offices. Taxi to border, US$0.50 or hire porter, US$1, and walk. From **La Paz**, several companies, 18 hrs, US$16-28 (even though buses are called 'direct', you may have to change in Potosí), depart La Paz 1630, depart **Villazón** 0830-1000 and 1830-1900. To **Potosí** several between 0800-0900 and 1830-1900, US$9, 10 hrs. To **Tupiza**, several daily, US$2.75. To **Tarija**, US$5.50, 7 hrs. Tickets for buses in **Argentina** are sold in Villazón but beware of scams and overcharging. Buy only from company offices, never from sellers in the street. Safer still, cross to La Quiaca and buy onward tickets there.
Road The road north from Villazón through Tupiza, Potosí and Sucre, to Cochabamba or Santa Cruz is paved. About 30% of the scenic road to Tarija is paved. A second road from Tupiza to Tarija is mostly paved.
Train Station about 1 km north of border on main road, T597 2565. To Tupiza, Atocha, Uyuni and Oruro: Expreso del Sur Wed and Sat at 1530; Wara Wara Mon and Thu at 1530. Fares are given under Oruro, page 286.

✆ Directory

Tupiza *p294, map p294*
Useful addresses Public Hospital, on Suipacha opposite the bus terminal. IGM office, Bolívar y Avaroa, on Plaza, p 2.

Central and Southern Highlands

This region boasts two World Cultural Heritage sites, the mining city of Potosí, the source of great wealth for colonial Spain and of indescribable hardship for many Bolivians, and Sucre, the white city and Bolivia's official capital. In the south, Tarija is known for its fruit and wines and its traditions which set it apart from the rest of the country.

Potosí → *Phone code: 02. Colour map 6, B3. Population: 175,562. Altitude: 3977 m.*

Potosí is the highest city of its size in the world. It was founded by the Spaniards on 10 April 1545, after they had discovered indigenous mine workings at Cerro Rico (4824 m), which dominates the city. Immense amounts of silver were once extracted. In Spain 'es un Potosí' (it's a Potosí) is still used for anything superlatively rich.

By the early 17th century Potosí was the largest city in the Americas, but over the next two centuries, as its lodes began to deteriorate and silver was found elsewhere, Potosí became little more than a ghost town. It was the demand for tin – a metal the Spaniards ignored – that saved the city from absolute poverty in the early 20th century, until the price slumped because of over-supply. Mining continues in Cerro Rico (mainly tin, zinc, lead, antimony and wolfram) to this day.

Arriving in Potosí

Orientation The bus terminal (Nueva Terminal) is on Av de las Banderas at the north end of the city. The airport, 5 km out of town on the Sucre road, has no scheduled flights. ▶▶ *See also Transport, page 302.*

Tourist office InfoTur Potosí ① *C Ayacucho, behind the façade of Compañia de Jesús church, T623 1021, Mon-Fri 0830-1230, 1430-1800, Sat 0900-1200.* Also a kiosk on Plaza 6 de Agosto, staffed sporadically by tourist police; and information office at bus terminal, Mon-Fri 0800-1200, 1430-1800. Beware scams involving fake plainclothes policemen. The official police wear green uniforms and work in pairs. ▶▶ *See also Safety, pages 243 and 248.*

Places in Potosí

Large parts of Potosí are colonial, with twisting streets and an occasional great mansion with its coat of arms over the doorway. The city is a UNESCO World Heritage site. Some of the best buildings are grouped round the Plaza 10 de Noviembre. The old Cabildo and the Royal Treasury – Las Cajas Reales – are both here, converted to other uses. The massive Cathedral faces Plaza 10 de Noviembre.

The **Casa Nacional de Moneda**, or Mint, ① *on C Ayacucho, T622 2777, www.bolivian.com/cnm, Tue-Sat 0900-1230, 1430-1830, Sun 0900-1230, entry US$3, plus US$3 to take photos, US$6 for video, entry by regular, 2-hr guided tour only (in English or French if there are 10 or more people, at 0900, 1030, 1430 and 1630),* is nearby. Founded in 1572, rebuilt 1759-1773, it is one of the chief monuments of civil building in Hispanic America. Thirty of its 160 rooms are a museum with sections on mineralogy, silverware and an art gallery in a splendid salon on the first floor. One section is dedicated to the works of the acclaimed 17th- to 18th-century religious painter Melchor Pérez de Holguín. Elsewhere are coin dies and huge wooden presses which made the silver strips from which coins were cut. The smelting houses have carved altar pieces from Potosí's ruined churches. You can't fail to notice the huge, grinning mask of Bacchus over an archway between two principal courtyards. Erected in 1865, its smile is said to be ironic and aimed at the departing Spanish. Wear warm clothes; it's cold inside.

Potosí has many outstanding colonial churches. **Convento y Museo de Santa Teresa** ① *Santa Teresa y Ayacucho, T622 3847, http://museosantateresa.blogspot.co.uk, only by guided* *tour in Spanish or English, Mon-Sat 0900-1230, 1500-1800; Sun 0900-1200, 1500-1800, museum is closed Tue and Sun morning; US$3, US$1.50 to take photos, US$25 for video*, has an impressive amount of giltwork inside and an interesting collection of colonial and religious art. Among Potosí's baroque churches, typical of 18th-century Andean or 'mestizo' architecture, are the Jesuit **Compañía church and bell-gable** ① *Ayacucho entre Bustillos y Oruro*, whose beautiful façade hides the modern tourist office building, and whose tower has a **mirador** ① *0800-1200,*

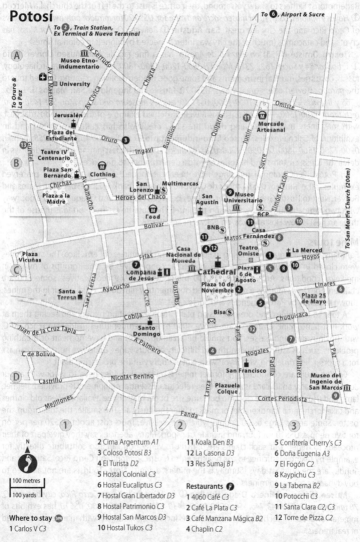

Potosí

To ②, Train Station, Ex Terminal & Nueva Terminal

To ⑥, Airport & Sucre

Museo Etno-indumentario

University

To Oruro & La Paz

Jerusalén

Plaza del Estudiante

Teatro IV Centenario

Plaza San Bernardo

Clothing

Plaza a la Madre

San Lorenzo

Multimarcas

Héroes del Chaco

Food

San Agustín

Museo Universitario

Mercado Artesanal

RCP

BNB

Casa Doña Eugenia

Matos Fernández

Casa Nacional de Moneda

Teatro Omiste

La Merced

Compañía de Jesús

Cathedral

Plaza 6 de Agosto

Plaza Vicuñas

Santa Teresa

Plaza 10 de Noviembre

Plaza 25 de Mayo

Bisa

Santo Domingo

San Francisco

Museo del Ingenio de San Marcos

Plazuela Colque

To San Martín Church (200m)

N

100 metres
100 yards

1400-1800, 30 mins later Sat-Sun, US$1.40. **San Francisco** ① *Tarija y Nogales, T622 2539, Mon-Fri 0900-1100, 1430-1700, Sat 0900-1100, US$2.15*, with a fine organ, worthwhile for the views from the tower and roof, museum of ecclesiastical art, underground tunnel system. **San Lorenzo** (1728-1744) ① *Héroes del Chaco y Bustillos, Mass 0700-1000*, with a rich portal and fine views from the tower. **San Martín** ① *on Hoyos, T622 3682, Mon-Fri 1000-1200, 1500-1830, Sat 1500-1800, free*, with an uninviting exterior, is beautiful inside, but is normally closed for fear of theft. Ask the German Redemptorist Fathers to show you around; their office is just to the left of the church. **La Merced** ① *Hoyos y Millares, US$1.40 for museo sacro and mirador, US$0.70 for mirador only (with café)*, views of Cerro Rico and the city are great. **San Agustín** ① *Bolívar y Quijarro, open only for Mass*, has crypts and catacombs (much of the city was interconnected by tunnels in colonial times).

Teatro Omiste (1753) *on Plaza 6 de Agosto*, has a fine façade. The **Museo Universitario** ① *C Bolívar 54 y Sucre, T622 7310, Mon-Fri 0800-1200, 1400-1800, US$0.70*, displays archaeology, fossils, costumes, musical instruments and some good modern Bolivian painting. Guided tour to the *mirador* (tower) offers great views, US$0.70. **Museo del Ingenio de San Marcos** ① *La Paz 1565 y Betanzos, T622 6717, 1000-1500, US$1.40; textiles museum and shop Mon-Sat 1430-2200; restaurant 1200-1500, 1900-2200*. This is a well-preserved example of the city's industrial past, with machinery used in grinding down the silver ore. It also has cultural activities and an exhibition of Calcha textiles. **Museo Etno-indumentario** ① *Av Serrudo 152, T622 3258, Mon-Fri 0900-1200, 1500-1800, Sat 0900-1200, US$1.40, includes tour.* This fascinating museum displays in detail the dress, customs and histories of Potosí department's 16 provinces.

In Potosí, 2000 colonial buildings have been catalogued. Among the better preserved examples is the house of the Marqués de Otaví, now the BNB bank, on Junín between Matos and Bolívar. Next to Hostal Gran Libertador, Millares between Nogales and Chuquisaca, is a doorway with two rampant lions in low relief on the lintel. The Casa de las Tres Portadas (house of the three arches) is now Hostal Tukos, on Bolívar near La Paz.

Mine tours

For many, the main reason for being in Potosí is to visit the mines of Cerro Rico. The state mines were closed in the 1980s and are now worked as cooperatives by small groups of miners in medieval conditions. An estimated 14,000 miners work in 49 cooperatives, some 800 are children. *The Devil's Miner* is a recommended documentary film about child labour in the mines, shown regularly by Potosí agencies and Sucre cafés.

A tour to the mines and ore-processing plant involves meeting miners and seeing them at work first-hand. Mine entrances are above 4000 m and temperatures inside can reach 40ºC, with noxious dust and gasses. You should be acclimatized, fit and have no heart or breathing problems, such as asthma. The length and difficulty of tours varies, up to five hours; you can ask for a shorter, less gruelling, visit if you wish. Not all tours visit the processing plant.

Guided tours are conducted by former miners; by law all guides have to work with a tour agency and carry an ID card issued by the Prefectura. Essential equipment is provided: helmet, lamp and usually protective clothing but large size boots may not be available. Wear old clothes and take torch and a handkerchief or mask to filter the dusty air. The smaller the tour group, the better. Some are as large as 20 people, which is excessive. Tours cost about US$20 per person for two people, US$10 for four, and include transport. Many agencies say they give part of their proceeds to miners but such claims are difficult to verify. You can also contribute directly, for example by taking medicines to the health centre (*Posta Sanitaria*) on Cerro Rico. Saturday and Sunday are the quietest days (Sunday is the miners' day off). **Note** Tourists are not allowed to buy dynamite to give to miners.

Museo Histórico Minero Diego Huallpa ① *by Mina Pailaviri on Cerro Rico, city buses P, Q, 70 and others, T623 1143, Mon-Sat 0900-1200, 1430-1800, Sun 0900-1500, US$10*, has exhibits of minerals and mining techniques, two-hour visits include mine tunnels with mannequins instead of real miners.

Tarapaya

A good place to freshen up after visiting the mines (or to spend a day relaxing) is Tarapaya, 21 km on the road to Oruro, where there are **thermal baths** ① *public pools US$0.60, private baths US$1.20 per hr, family baths US$2.80*, and cabins for rent. On the other side of the river from Tarapaya is a 60-m diameter crater lake, whose temperature is 30-34°C; take sun protection. Below the crater lake are boiling ponds, not fit for swimming. **Balneario Miraflores** (25 km) ① *pools US$0.35, private baths US$2.80*, has hotter water than Tarapaya, but is not as clean. Minibuses run to both balnearios from outside Chuquimia market on Avenida Universitaria, 0600-1800, US$0.55; taxi US$8.50. Last vehicle back to Potosí from Miraflores at 1800.

⊙ Potosí listings

For hotel and restaurant price codes, and other relevant information, see Essentials.

● Where to stay

Potosí *p298, map p299*
Unless otherwise stated hotels have no heating.
$$$ Coloso Potosi, Bolivar 965, 1622 2627, www.potosihotel.com. Comfortable modern rooms with frigo-bar, heating, bath tubs and nice views. Has a small indoor pool and sauna, parking.
$$$-$$ Hostal Patrimonio, Matos 62, T622 2659, www.hostalpatrimonio.com. Bright, warm, modern hotel. Heating, frigo-bar and safe in each room, sauna and jacuzzi (suites each have their own).
$$ Cima Argentum, Av Villazón 239, T622 9538, www.hca-potosi.com. Modern comfortable rooms and suites, warm and bright, heating, frigo-bar and safe in each room.
$$ El Turista, Lanza 19, T622 2492. Older place but well maintained, heating, nice common areas, helpful staff, great view from top rooms.
$$ Hostal Colonial, Hoyos 8, T622 4809, www.hostalcolonialpotosi.com. Older place but well located, carpeted, heating, bathtubs, frigo-bar.
$$ Hostal Gran Libertador, Millares 58, T622 7877. Colonial-style hotel, good buffet breakfast, cafeteria, comfortable rooms, central heating, quiet, helpful, parking.
$$-$ Hostal Tukos (Las Tres Portadas), Bolívar 1092, T623 1025. Old colonial house with spacious rooms, skylights, warm and nice.
$ Carlos V, Linares 42, T623 1010, frontdesk@hostalcarlosv.com. Cheaper rooms without bath, hot water, kitchen facilities.
$ Hostal Eucalyptus, Linares 88, T622 3738, www.koalabolivia.com. Pleasant bright rooms,

cheaper with shared bath, heating, good breakfast, 350 m from the main plaza.
$ Hostal San Marcos, La Paz y Periodista, T623 001, hostalsanmarcos@hotmail.com. Colonial house, nice comfortable rooms, heating, cooking facilities.
$ Koala Den, Junín 56, T622 6467, papamilla@hotmail.com. Private rooms with bath and breakfast (cheaper in dorm), heating, TV and video, use of kitchen, popular and often full.
$ La Casona, Chuquisaca 460, T623 0523, www.hotelpotosi.com. Cheaper with shared bath and in dorm, courtyard, kitchen facilities.
$ Res Sumaj, Gumiel 12, T622 2336, hoteljer@entelnet.bo. Basic, small dark rooms with shared bath, helpful, 10% IYHF discount.

● Restaurants

Potosí *p298, map p299*
$$ 4060 Café, Hoyos y Sucre. Open 1600-late, food until 2300. Restaurant/bar serving good meals, varied menu, large portions, nice atmosphere, heating. Recommended.
$$ El Fogón, Frías 58 y Ururo. Daily 1200-2300. Restaurant/grill, good food and atmosphere.
$$-$ Kaypichu, Millares 16. Tue-Sun 0700-1300, 1700-2300. Breakfast, vegetarian options, *peña* in high season.
$$-$ La Taberna, Junín 12, open all day. Bolivian and international food, set lunch and à la carte in the evening, good service.
$$-$ Potocchi, Millares 24, T622 2759. Open 0800-2230. International and local dishes, can accommodate special diets with advance notice, *peña* in high season.
$ Doña Eugenia, Santa Cruz y Ortega. Open 0900-1300. Typical food such as the warming kalapurca soup with corn and meat

(be careful it is hot) and chicharrón de cerdo, fried pork rinds.

$ Torre de Pizza, Matos 14. Open 0700-2200. Pizza, pasta, vegetarian options, also breakfast, family run, attentive service.

Cafés

Café La Plata, Tarija y Linares at Plaza 10 de Noviembre. Mon-Sat 1000-2200. Upmarket place for coffee, sweets and drinks. Nice atmosphere, English and French spoken.
Café Manzana Mágica, Oruro 239. Meat-free meals only, a popular, small café.
Chaplin, Matos y Quijarro. Mon-Fri 0830-1200. Breakfasts and excellent *tucumanas* (fried empanadas).
Confitería Cherry's, Padilla 8. Open 0800-2230. Small economical place, good cakes, breakfast.
Santa Clara, Quijarro 32 y Matos, also Sucre 33 y Bolívar and other locations. Mon-Sat 0700-2300. Popular with locals for afternoon snacks.

⊛ Festivals

Potosí *p298, map p299*
Fiesta de Manquiri: on 3 consecutive Sat at the end of **May**/beginning of **Jun** llama sacrifices are made at the cooperative mines in honour of *Pachamama*. **Carnaval Minero**, 2 weeks before Carnaval in Oruro, includes Tata Ckascho, when miners dance down Cerro Rico and El Tío (the *Dios Minero*) is paraded. **San Bartolomé**, or **Chutillos**, is held from the middle of **Aug**, with the main event being processions of dancers on the weekend closest to the **24th-26th**; Sat features Potosino, and Sun national, groups. Costumes can be hired in *artesanía* market on C Sucre. Hotel and transport prices go up by 30% for the whole of that weekend.
10 Nov, Fiesta Aniversario de Potosí. Potosí is sometimes called the 'Ciudad de las Costumbres', especially at Corpus Cristi, Todos Santos and Carnaval, when special sweets are prepared, families go visiting friends, etc.

⊙ Shopping

Potosí *p298, map p299*
Mercado Artesanal, at Sucre y Omiste. Mon-Sat 0830-1230, 1430-1830. Sells handwoven cloth and regional handicrafts. Several craft shops on C Sucre between Omiste and Bustillos.

Mercado Central, Bustillos y Bolívar, sells mainly meat and some produce. There are several other markets around town.

⊙ What to do

Potosí *p298, map p299*
All agencies offer mine tours (see page 300), trips to the Salar de Uyuni and REA (see page 291 for advice on booking a trip), as well as trekking at Kari-Kari lakes.
Claudia Tours, Ayacucho 7, T622 5000, turismoclaudiabolivia@gmail.com. City tours, mines and trekking; also in Uyuni, Av Ferroviaria opposite Hotel Avenida.
Hidalgo Tours, La Paz 1133, T622 9512, www.salardeuyuni.net; also Av Potosí 113, Uyuni. Specialized services in Potosí and to Salar de Uyuni. Guide Efraín Huanca has been recommended for mine tours. Pioneering tour operator for the Uyuni salt flats and the lagoons, having the first salt hotel in the world, the **Palacio de Sal Hotel**.
Koala Tours, Ayacucho 5, T622 2092, www.koalabolivia.com. Owner Eduardo Garnica speaks English and French. Their mine tours are popular and have been recommended.
Silver Tours, Quijarro 12, T622 3600, www.silvertours.8m.com. Economical mine tours.
Sin Fronteras, Ayacucho 17 y Bustillos, T622 4058, frontpoi@entelnet.bo. Owner Juan Carlos Gonzales speaks English and French and is very helpful. Also hires camping gear.
Turismo Potosí, Lanza 12 y Chuquisaca, T622 8212. Guide and owner Santos Mamani has been recommended.

⊖ Transport

Potosí *p298, map p299*
Air The airport is about 7 km from Potosí on the road to Sucre. Aerocon, Plaza del Estudiante, Edif 4° Centenario, T6960 7526, Mon-Sat from La Paz at 0615, to La Paz at 0800, 1 hr, US$139 one way.
Bus Large modern bus terminal (Nueva Terminal, use fee US$0.30) with ATMs, luggage store, information office, Tourist Police and food court. **Note** it is far from the centre: taxi US$2; city buses F, I, 150, US$0.20, but there are no city buses or taxis late at night; not safe

to go out on the street, try to arrive by day or wait inside until morning. Daily services: **La Paz** several companies 1900-2230, US$7, 10 hrs by paved road; *bus cama* US$16 (departures from La Paz 1830-2030). To travel by day, go to **Oruro**, San Miguel and others, all day, US$4.50, 5 hrs. **Cochabamba** several companies · 1830-2030, US$7.50, 10 hrs; San José at 0500 and 1530. **Sucre** frequent service 0630-1800, US$2.50, 3 hrs; also shared taxis from behind the old bus terminal, Cielito Lindo, T624 3381, 2½ hrs, US$6 pp, drop-off at your hotel. For **Santa Cruz** change in Sucre or Cochabamba. **Tupiza** several companies around 0730 and 2000, US$5, 8 hrs; continuing to **Villazón**, US$9, 10 hrs. **Tarija** several companies 1800-1830, US$8.50, 11 hrs, spectacular journey. To go

by day take a bus to **Camargo**, 6 hrs, US$6, then change. Buses to **Uyuni** leave from either side of the railway line at Av Toledo y Av Universitaria, 1000-1200 and 1800-2000, US$5, 5-6 hrs on a new road, superb scenery; book in advance.

Train Station is at Av Sevilla y Villazón, T622 3101, www.fca.com.bo. A 25-passenger railcar to **Sucre** Tue, Thu, Sat 0800, 6 hrs, US$3.60; confirm details in advance.

ⓘ Directory

Potosí *p298, map p299*
Useful addresses Migración: Calama 188 entre Av Arce y Av Cívica, T622 5989. Mon-Fri 0830-1230, 1430-1830. Police station: on Plaza 10 de Noviembre.

Sucre → *Phone code: 04. Colour map 6, B3. Population: 338,281. Altitude: 2790 m.*

Founded in 1538 as La Plata, it became capital of the Audiencia of Charcas in 1559. Its name was later changed to Chuquisaca before the present name was adopted in 1825 in honour of the second president of the new republic. Sucre is sometimes referred to as La Ciudad Blanca, owing to the tradition that all buildings in the centre are painted in their original colonial white. This works to beautiful effect and in 1991 UNESCO declared the city a World Heritage Site. There are two universities, the older dating from 1624. From 1825 to 1899 Sucre was the only capital of Bolivia; it remains the constitutional capital as it is home to Bolivia's judicial branch although La Paz is the administrative one. *La capitalidad* remains an emotionally charged issue among *sucrenses*, who strive to see Sucre regain its status as the only capital.

Arriving in Sucre
Orientation Airport is 5 km northwest of town. The bus terminal is on north outskirts of town, 3 km from centre.▸▸ *See also Transport, page 310.*

Tourist office Dirección de Turismo de la Alcaldía ⓘ *Argentina 65, p 2, Casa de la Cultura, T643 5240, www.sucreturistico.gob.bo, Mon-Fri 0800-1200, 1400-1800,* some English spoken; also have information kiosks at the airport, bus terminal, **Plazuela Libertad** ⓘ *Destacamento 111 y Arenales* and **La Recoleta** ⓘ *Polanco e Iturrichia.* **Tourist office** ⓘ *Estudiantes 25, T644 7644, open Mon-Fri 0900-1200, 1500-1830,* staffed by university students (open only during term). **Safety** Caution is advised after 2200 and in market areas.

Places in Sucre centre
Plaza 25 de Mayo is large, spacious, full of trees and surrounded by elegant buildings. Among these are the **Casa de la Libertad** ⓘ *T645 4200, Tue-Sat 0900-1230, 1430-1800, US$2.15 with tour; US$5.80 video.* Formerly the Assembly Hall of the Jesuit University, where the country's Declaration of Independence was signed, this house contains a famous portrait of Simón Bolívar by the Peruvian artist Gil de Castro, admired for its likeness. Also on the Plaza are the beautiful 17th century **Cathedral** and **Museo Eclesiástico** ⓘ *Ortiz 61, T645 2257, Mon-Fri 1000-1200, 1500-1700, US$1.45.* Worth seeing are the famous jewel-encrusted Virgin of Guadalupe, 1601, and works by Viti, the first great painter of the New World, who studied under Raphael.

San Felipe Neri ① *entrance through school, Ortiz 165 y Azurduy, T645 4333, Mon-Sat 1400-1800, US$1.45 (extra charge for photos).* Visits include the neoclassical church with its courtyard, the crypt and the roof (note the penitents' benches), which offers fine views over the city. The monastery is used as a school. Diagonally opposite is the church of **La Merced** ① *T645 1338,*

Sucre

Where to stay 🛌
1 Austria *B3*
2 Casa de Huéspedes Finita *D3*
3 Casa Kolping *D3*
4 El Hostal de Su Merced *D2*
5 Forastero *C1*
6 Grand *C2*
7 Hostal Charcas *C2*
8 Hostal Colón 220 *D1*
9 Hostal Los Pinos *D1*
10 Hostal San Francisco *B2*
11 Hostal Santa Teresa de Jesús *D3*
12 Hostelling International Sucre *B3*
13 ICBA Wasi *D3*
14 Independencia *C2*
15 La Posada *D2*
16 La Selenita *D3*
17 Monasterio *D3*
18 Pachamama Hostal *A3*
19 Parador Santa María La Real *D2*
20 San Marino Royal *C2*
21 Villa Antigua *D3*
22 Villa de la Plata *B3*

Restaurants 🍴
1 Amsterdam *C3*
2 Bibliocafé *D2*
3 Café Florín *D2*
4 Café Mirador *D3*
5 El Germen *C3*
6 El Patio *C2*
7 El Tapado *C1*
8 Joy Ride Café, tour agency & shop *D2*
9 La Patisserie *D2*
10 La Taverne *C2*
11 Locot's Café Aventura *C3*
12 Los Balcones & Abis *C2*
13 Metro Café *C2*
14 Nouvelle Cuisine *D3*

which is notable for its gilded central and side altars. **San Miguel** ① *Arenales 10, T645 1026, Mass Mon-Sat 0800 and 1915, Sun 1100, no shorts, short skirts or short sleeves allowed*, completed in 1628, has been restored and is very beautiful with Moorish-style carved and painted ceilings, *alfarjes* (early 17th century), pure-white walls and gold and silver altar. In the Sacristy some early sculpture can be seen. Santa Mónica, Arenales y Junín, is perhaps one of the finest gems of Spanish architecture in the Americas, but has been converted into the theatre and hall for Colegio Sagrado Corazón. **San Francisco** (1581) ① *Ravelo y Arce, Mass daily 0700 and 1900, Sun also 1030 and 1700*, has altars coated in gold leaf and 17th century ceilings; one of its bells summoned the people of Sucre to struggle for independence. **San Lázaro** (1538) ① *Calvo y Padilla, Mass daily 0700, Sun also 1900*. This is regarded as the first cathedral of La Plata (Sucre). On the nave walls are six paintings attributed to Zurbarán; it has fine silverwork and alabaster in the Baptistery. San Miguel, San Francisco and San Lázaro are only open during mass. **Monasterio de Santa Clara** ① *Calvo 212, Mass daily 0730, museum open Mon-Fri 1400-1800, Sat 1400-1730, US$2, good guided tours in Spanish*, Displays paintings by Bitti, sculptures, books, vestments, some silver and musical instruments (including a 1664 organ). Small items made by the nuns on sale.

The excellent **Museo de Arte Indígena ASUR** (Museo Téxtil Etnográfico) ① *Pasaje Iturricha 314, opposite Casa Kolping in La Recoleta, T645 6651, www.asur.org.bo, Mon-Fri 0830-1200, 1430-1800, Sat from 0930, US$2.25, English and French-speaking guides*, displays regional textiles and traditional techniques, shop sells crafts. Near the main plaza is the **Museo Nacional de Etnografía y Folklore (MUSEF)** ① *España 74 y San Alberto, T645 5293, Tue-Fri 0930-1230, 1430-1830, Sat 0930-1230, free*, with an impressive exhibit of masks. The **Museo Universitario Charcas** ① *Bolívar 698, T645 3285, Mon-Fri 0800-1200, 1400-1800, Sat 0800-1200, US$0.50, photos extra*, has anthropological, archaeological and folkloric exhibits, and colonial collections and presidential and modern-art galleries.

Four blocks northwest of Plaza 25 de Mayo is the **Corte Suprema de Justicia** ① *Luis Paz Arce 352, Mon-Fri 1000-1200, 1500-1800, free*, the seat of Bolivia's national judiciary and what remains of the city's official status as capital of Bolivia. To enter you must be smartly dressed and leave your passport with the guard; guides can be found in the public relations office. The nearby **Parque Bolívar** contains a monument and a miniature of the Eiffel Tower and Arc de Triomphe in honour of one of Bolivia's richest 20th-century tin barons, Francisco Argandoña, who created much of Sucre's splendour. At the downhill-end of the park is Fuente del Bicentenario, where a **sound and light show** ① *Thu-Sun 1900-2100*, is displayed. The **obelisk** opposite the Teatro Gran Mariscal, in Plazuela Libertad, was erected with money raised by fining bakers who cheated on the size and weight of their bread. Also on this plaza is the Hospital Santa Bárbara (1574).

Around Sucre

Southeast of the city, at the top of Dalence is **La Recoleta**, a lookout with arches, offering good views over the city. Here, within the Franciscan convent of La Recoleta is the **Museo de la Recoleta** ① *Plaza Pedro de Anzúrez, T645 1987, Mon-Sat 0900-1130, 1500-1800, US$1.45 for entrance to all collections, guided tours only*. It is notable for the beauty of its cloisters and gardens; the carved wooden choir stalls above the nave of the church are especially fine (see the martyrs transfixed by lances). In the grounds is the Cedro Milenario, a 1400-year-old cedar. Behind Recoleta monastery a road flanked by Stations of the Cross ascends an attractive hill, **Cerro Churuquella**, with large eucalyptus trees on its flank, to a statue of Christ at the top.

About 5 km south on the Potosí road is the **Castillo de la Glorieta** ① *Mon-Sat 0830-1200, 1300-1700, US$4.30, take Micro 4 marked Liceo Militar*. The former mansion of the Argandoña family, built in a mixture of contrasting European styles with painted ceilings, is in the military compound. Ask to see the paintings of the visit of the pope, in a locked room. Some 3 km north of Sucre is **Cal Orcko**, considered the world's largest paleontological site, where tracks from eight types of dinosaur have been identified (inside the Fancesa cement works, not open to the public). Nearby is **Parque Cretácico** ① *T645 7392, Mon-Thu 0900-1700, Fri-Sat 1000-2000, Sun*

1000-1700, US$4.35, children US$0.75, crowded at weekends, with fibreglass dinosaurs, recorded growls, a 30-minute guided tour and binoculars through which (for an extra US$0.30) you can look at the prints on Cal Orcko, 300 m away. The **Sauro Tours** bus leaves daily 0930, 1200, 1430 from corner of cathedral, US$1.75 return, or take Micro 4 from C Junín.

Tarabuco → *Colour map 6, B4. Altitude: 3295 m.*
Tarabuco, 64 km southeast of Sucre, is best known for its colourful indigenous market on Sunday, with local people in traditional dress. It starts around 0930-1000 and is very popular with tourists. Textiles are sold in a purpose-built market on Calle Murillo. Next to the market is a small museum, **Incapallay** ⓘ *Murillo 25, T646 1936, www.incapallay.org, Sun 0930-1400,* run by a weavers' association. The *Pujllay* independence celebration on the third Sunday in March is very vibrant. No one sleeps during this fiesta but basic accommodation and meals are available. The market is not held at Carnaval (when all Tarabuco is dancing in Sucre), Pujllay, Easter Sunday or All Saints' Day.

◉ Sucre listings

For hotel and restaurant price codes, and other relevant information, see Essentials.

● Where to stay

Sucre *p304, map p305*
$$$ Parador Santa María La Real, Bolívar 625, T643 9630, www.parador.com.bo. Tastefully restored and upgraded colonial house, bathtub, safety box, frigobar, heating.
$$$ Refugio Andino Bramadero, 30 km from the city towards Ravelo, details from Raúl y Mabel Cagigao, Avaroa 472, T645 5592, bramader@yahoo.com, or **Restaurant Salamandra** (Avaroa 510, good food). Cabins or rooms, well-furnished, full board, drinks and transport included, excellent value, owner Raúl can advise on hikes and astronomy, book in advance. Recommended.
$$$ Sky Hacienda, in Mosoj Llacta, by Yotala, 19 km south of Sucre along the road to Potosí, T643 0045, www.skyhacienda.com. Upmarket hotel in a rural setting, nice views from the rooms with heating, jacuzzi, restaurant, nice patio and garden, pool, horse riding, bicycles, minimum stay 2 nights, no children under 12. Transfers to airport and bus station are extra.
$$$ Villa Antigua, Calvo 237, T644 3437, www.villaantiguahotel.com. Tastefully restored colonial house with garden, internet room, gym, large rooftop terrace has great views, some suites with kitchenette, airport transfers.
$$$-$$ Monasterio, Calvo 140, T644 0181, www.hotelmonasteriosucre.com. Beautiful 16th century house with colonial and neoclassic architecture. Elegant common areas, heated rooms and suites, restaurant serves international dishes, quiet terrace, airport transfers.
$$ Casa Kolping, Pasaje Iturricha 265, La Recoleta, T642 3812. Pleasant, lovely location with nice views, good **Munay Pata** restaurant (**$$-$**),internet lounge, wheelchair access, parking.
$$ El Hostal de Su Merced, Azurduy 16, T644 2706, www.desumerced.com. Beautifully restored colonial building, lots of character, owner and staff speak French and English, good breakfast buffet, sun terrace, restaurant. Recommended.
$$ Hostal Santa Teresa de Jesús, San Alberto 431, T645 4189, santateresadejesushostal@ hotmail.com. Refurbished colonial house, restaurant, comfortable, garage. Recommended.
$$ Independencia, Calvo 31, T644 2256, www.independenciahotel.com. Historic colonial house, opulent salon, spiral stairs, lovely garden, comfortable, some rooms with bathtub, café, attentive service.
$$ La Posada, Audiencia 92, T646 0101, www.hotellaposada.com.bo. Smart, colonial-style, good restaurant. Recommended.
$$ La Selenita, J Mostajo 145, T643 4239, laselenitasucre@yahoo.fr. Pleasant guesthouse with 4 cabins for 2-3 persons, 2 types of breakfast with home-made bread and jam available, nice gardens, quiet, panoramic views of the colonial city, French-Belgian run, new in 2012.

$$ San Marino Royal, Arenales 13, T645 1646, www.sanmarinoroyalhotel.com.bo. Nicely converted colonial house, frigobar, cafeteria, **$$$** for suite with jacuzzi.

$$-$ Hostelling International Sucre, G Loayza 119 y Ostria Gutiérrez, T644 0471, www.hostellingbolivia.org. Functional hostel 1½ blocks from bus terminal, cheaper without bath and in dorms, breakfast available, garden, internet extra, parking, discount for HI members.

$$-$ ICBA Wasi, Avaroa 326, T645 2091, www.icba-sucre.edu.bo. Part of Insituto Cultural Boliviano-Alemán, imaginatively designed, spotless rooms with solar hot water, some with kitchenette. Recommended.

$ Austria, Av Ostria Gutiérrez 506, by bus station, T645 4202, www.hostalaustria.com.bo. Hot showers, good beds and carpeted rooms, cafeteria, parking, cheaper with shared bath and no breakfast, parking extra.

$ Casa de Huéspedes Finita, Padilla 233 (no sign), T645 3220, delfi_eguez@hotmail. com. Some rooms with bath, good breakfast, hot water, heaters, tasty lunch available on request, garden, terrace, also apartments with fully equipped kitchens for longer stays. Good value and recommended for warm family atmosphere.

$ Forastero, Destacamento 111 No 394, T7181-3654, pichicamichel@hotmail.com. 2 adjacent houses, one with comfortable rooms with and without bath, the second with economical dorms with 3 to 7 beds, bath and individual safety boxes, good hot showers, kitchen facilities, common areas, restaurant (quinoa specialties) in nice garden, tours, discounts for groups and long stays, helpful, enthusiastic owner, English spoken. Recommended.

$ Grand, Arce 61, T645 2461. Older hotel but well maintained, comfortable (ask for room 18), ground floor at the back is noisy, some rooms dark, electric showers, good value lunch in **Arcos** restaurant, Wi-Fi in patio, motorcycle parking.

$ Hostal Charcas, Ravelo 62, T645 3972, hostalcharcas@yahoo.com. Cheaper without bath or TV, good value, huge breakfast extra, hot showers, at times runs bus to Tarabuco on Sun.

$ Hostal Colón 220, Colón 220, T645 5823, colon220@bolivia.com. Very nice guesthouse, cheaper with shared bath, laundry, helpful owner speaks English and German and has tourist information, coffee room.

$ Hostal los Pinos, Colón 502, T645 5639. Comfortable, hot showers, garden, quiet, peaceful, parking.

$ Hostal San Francisco, Av Arce 191 y Camargo, T645 2117. Colonial building, electric showers, breakfast available, quiet, patio, good value.

$ Pachamama Hostal, Arce 450, T645 3673, hostal_pachamama@hotmail.com. Simple rooms with bath, electric shower, pleasant patio, parking, good value.

$ Villa de la Plata, Arce 369, T645 6849, villadelaplata888@gmail.com. Good value apartments with kitchenette, discounts for long stays, popular.

⊕ Restaurants

Sucre *p304, map p305*
Sausages and chocolates are among the locally produced specialties.

$$ El Huerto, Ladislao Cabrera 86, San Matías, T645 1538. Daily 1130-1600 and Thu-Sun 1830-2100. International food with salad bar, good *almuerzo*, in a beautiful garden. Take a taxi there at night.

$$ El Tapado, Olañeta 165 y Loa, T643 8778. Open daily, all day. Extensive breakfast and dinner menu, llama dishes, sandwiches, a choice of drinks including micro brews, parties in the patio on Fri and Sat night.

$$ La Taverne of the **Alliance Française**, Arce 35. Mon-Sat 1200-1500, 1800-2230, Sun 1900-2200. Lovely terrace seating, weekly lunch specials, international food, also regular cultural events.

$$-$ El Germen, San Alberto 231. Mon-Sat 0800-2200. Mostly vegetarian, set lunches, excellent breakfast, German pastries, book exchange, German magazines. Recommended.

$$-$ Los Balcones, Plaza 25 de Mayo 33, upstairs. Open 1200-2400. Good food, popular with locals, set lunch with salad bar, views over plaza.

$$-$ Nouvelle Cuisine, Avaroa 537. Daily 1100-2300. Excellent *churrasquería* (grill), good value.

Cafés

Abis, Plaza 25 de Mayo 32. Belgian-owned café and heladería, with coffees, breakfasts, sandwiches, light meals, ice cream.

Amsterdam, Bolívar 426. Mon-Fri from 1200, Sun from 1530. Drinks, snacks and meals, book exchange, Wi-Fi, live music Wed-Thu. Dutch run, works with a programme for migrant children from the countryside.

Bibliocafé, N Ortiz 38, near plaza. Pasta and light meals. *Almuerzo* 1200-1500, 1800-0200, Sun 1900-2400. Music and drinks, Wi-Fi.

Café Florín, Bolívar 567. Daily 0730-0200, weekends to 0300. Breakfast, sandwiches, snacks and international meals (**$$**), large portions, micro brews. Sunny patio, Wi-Fi, tour bookings, cosy atmosphere. Dutch run, popular.

Café Mirador, Pasaje Iturricha 297, La Recoleta. Open 0930-2000. Very good garden café, fine views, good juices, snacks and music, popular.

El Patio, San Alberto 18. Small place for delicious *salteñas/empanadas*.

Joy Ride Café, N Ortiz 16, www.joyridebol. com. Daily 0730-2300. Great international food and drink, music, Wi-Fi, very popular, upstairs lounge shows films, also cultural events.

La Patisserie, Audiencia 17. 0830-1230, 1530-2030. French-owned, popular for crêpes, salads and puddings.

Locot's Café Aventura, Bolívar 465, T691 5958. Mon-Sat 0800-0000, Sun 1100-2300. Bar serving international and Mexican food, live music and theatre, Wi-Fi, also offer many types of adventure sports: mountain biking, hiking, riding, paragliding.

Metro Café, Calvo 2 on Plaza 25 de Mayo. A variety of coffees, sandwiches, breakfasts, pastries, desserts, juices; delicious and good service.

Bars and clubs

Sucre *p304, map p305*

Mitos, Pje Tarabuco y Junín. Thu-Sat 2200-0300, Disco, popular with travellers.

Stigma, Bolívar y Camargo. Varied music, young crowd.

Tabaco's, Eduardo Berdecio, east of centre. Varied music, popular with university students.

Festivals

Sucre *p304, map p305*

24-26 May: Independence celebrations, most services, museums and restaurants closed on 25. **8 Sep**: Virgen de Guadalupe, 2-day fiesta. **21 Sep**: Día del Estudiante, music around main plaza. **Oct/Nov**: Festival Internacional de la Cultura, 2nd week, shared with Potosí.

Shopping

Sucre *p304, map p305*

Handicrafts ASUR, opposite Casa Kolping in La Recoleta. Weavings from around Tarabuco and from the Jalq'a. Weavings are more expensive, but of higher quality than elsewhere. **Artesanías Calcha**, Arce 103, opposite San Francisco church. Recommended, knowledgeable proprietor. Several others nearby. **Bolsa Boliviana**, Calvo 64, non-profit with many nice items, especially bags. **Casa de Turismo**, Bustillos 131, several craft shops and tour operators under one roof. **Centro Cultural Masis**, Bolívar 561, T645 3403, www. losmasis.com. Teaches local youth traditional music and culture and has items for sale; visitors welcome at events and exhibitions. **Incapallay**, Audiencia 97 y Bolívar, T646 1936, www.incapallay.org. Fair trade shop selling textiles by Tarabuco and Jalq'a weavers; also in Tarabuco and La Paz. Artisans sell their wares at the La Recoleta lookout. **Chocolates Para Tí**, Arenales 7, Audiencia 68, at the airport and bus terminal. One of the best chocolate shops in Sucre. **Taboada**, Arce y Arenales, at airport and bus terminal, www.taboada.com.bo. Also very good.

Markets The central market is colourful with some stalls selling *artesanía*, but beware of theft and crafty vendors.

What to do

Sucre *p304, map p305*

Bolivia Specialist, N Ortiz 30, T643 7389, www.boliviaspecialist.com. Dutchman Dirk Dekker's agency for local hikes, horse riding and 4WD trips, all sorts of tours throughout Bolivia and Peru, bus and plane tickets, loads of information and connections.

Candelaria Tours, JJ Pérez 303-305 y Colón, T646 0289, www.candelariatours.com. Hikes around Sucre, tours to weaving communities, English spoken.

Cóndor Trekkers, Loa 457, T7289 1740, www.condortrekkers.org. Not-for-profit trekking company using local guides supported by volunteers, city walks and treks around Sucre, proceeds go to social projects, first aid carried.

Joy Ride Tourism, N Ortiz 2, at corner of Plaza, T645 7603, www.joyridebol.com. Mountain- and motor-biking, hiking, climbing, horse riding, paragliding, tours to Potosí and Salar de Uyuni.

L y D, final Panamá 127 y Comarapa, Barrio Petrolero, T642 0752, turismo_lyd@hotmail.com. Lucho and Dely Loredo and son Carlos (who speaks English) offer custom-made tours using private or public transport, to regional communities and attractions, and further afield.

Oasis Tours, Arce 95, of 2, T643 2438, www.oasistours-bo.com. City walking tour, indigenous communities, Chataquila, Inca Trail. Also sell bus tickets and have their own office in Uyuni for Salar trips. Very helpful owner.

Seatur, Plaza 25 de Mayo 24, T646 2425. Local tours, hiking trips, English, German, French spoken.

⊖ Transport

Sucre *p304, map p305*

Air **Juana Azurduy de Padilla** airport is 5 km northwest of town (T645 4445). **BoA** (Calvo 94, T691 2325) 3 per week to Cochabamba. **TAM** (Arenales 217, T646 0944) daily to **La Paz**, **Santa Cruz** and **Cochabamba**, 5 weekly to **Tarija** and 2 weekly to **Yacuiba**. Aerocon (at airport, T645 0007) flies to **Trinidad**. Ecojet (T901-105055), daily to **Santa Cruz**. Airport tax US$1.60. Micros 1, D and F go from entrance to Av Hernando Siles, a couple of blocks from main plaza, US$0.20, 25 mins. Taxi US$3.50.

Bus Bus terminal is on north outskirts of town, 3 km from centre on Ostria Gutiérrez, T644 1292; taxi US$1.15; Micro A or 3. Daily to/from **La Paz** several companies at 1700-2000, 12 hrs, regular US$7-10, *semi-cama* US$12-13, *cama* US$18-20. To **Cochabamba**: several companies daily at 1830-1930, 9 hrs via Aiquile; at 2100 via Oruro, 12 hrs, US$6-7.50. To **Potosí**: frequent

departures between 0630 and 1800, US$2.15-2.50, 3 hrs. Shared taxis with pick up service: **Cielito Lindo**, at Casa de Turismo, Bustillos 131, T643 2309, **Cielito Express**, T643 1000 and **Expreso Dinos**, T643 7444, both outside the bus terminal, 2½ hrs, US$6 pp. To **Oruro**: 2000-2200, 4 companies via Potosí, 8 hrs, US$7-8.70. To **Tarija**: 4 companies, at 1500-1600, 14 hrs, US$9-14 via Potosí. To **Uyuni**: direct at 0830, **6 de Octubre**, 9 hrs, **Emperador** 0700, 1230, with change and 2-hr wait in Potosí, US$7.25-10. Or catch a bus to Potosí and change; try to book the connecting bus in advance. To **Villazón** via Potosí and Tupiza: at 1330, 1730, **6 de Octubre**, 12 hrs, US$11.60; to **Tupiza**, 9 hrs, US$9.50. To **Santa Cruz**: many companies 1600-1730, 15 hrs, US$10-12; *semi cama* US$15.

To **Tarabuco** Mini-vans leave when full from C Túpac Yupanqui (Parada de Tarabuco), daily starting 0630, US$1, 1¼ hrs on a good paved road. To get to the Parada take a micro "C" or "7" from the Mercado Central. Also buses to Tarabuco from Av de las Américas y Jaime Mendoza, same fare and times. Tourist bus from the Cathedral on Sun at 0830, US$5 round-trip, reserve at Oasis Tours (address above); also **Real Audiencia**, depart San Alberto 181 y España, T644 3119, at 0830, return 1330; you must use the same bus you went in on. Shared taxi with **Cielito Lindo** (see transport to Potosí above), Sun at 0900, US$5 return.

Car hire Imbex, Serrano 165, T646 1222, www.imbex.com. Recommended.

Road 164 km from **Potosí** (fully paved), 366 km to **Cochabamba** (mostly paved except for some segments in the Puente Arce-Aiquile-Epizana segment, which are being paved in 2014).

Taxi US$0.60 per person within city limits.

Train Station at El Tejar, 1 km south on Potosí road, take Micro 4, T644 0751, www.fca.com.bo. A 25-passenger railcar to **Potosí**, Mon, Wed, Fri at 0800, US$3.60, 6 hrs; tickets go on sale at 0600, confirm details in advance.

⊙ Directory

Sucre *p304, map p305*

Language classes The Instituto Cultural Boliviano-Alemán (ICBA, Goethe Institute),

Avaroa 326, T645 2091, www.icba-sucre.edu. bo, runs Spanish, German, Portuguese and Quechua courses. **Alianza Francesa**, Aniceto Arce 35, T645 3599, sucre.alianzafrancesa.org. bo, also offers Spanish and French classes. **Centro Boliviano Americano**, Calvo 301, T644 1608, www.cbasucre.org, is also recommended for language courses. These centres run cultural events, have libraries and branches in La Paz. **Academia Latinoamericana de Español**, Dalence 109, T646 0537, www.latinoschool. com. Professional, good extracurricular activities, US$90 for 20 hrs per week (US$120 for private teacher – higher prices if you book by phone or email). **Bolivian Spanish School**, C Kilómetro 7 250, T644 3841, www. bolivianspanishschool.com. Near Parque Bolívar, pleasant school, good value, excellent teachers. **Continental Spanish School**, Olañeta 224,

T643 8093, www.schoolcontinental.com. Good teachers and fun activities. **Fox Academy**, San Alberto 30, T644 0688, www.foxacademysucre. com. Spanish and Quechua classes, US$5 per hr, non-profit, proceeds go to teaching English to children, volunteering arranged. **Casa Andina de Lenguas**, Loayza 119, T644 0471, www. spanish-viva-online.net. At HI Hostelling Sucre, www.hostellingbolivia.org, US$6 per hr. **Sucre Spanish School**, Calvo 350, T643 6727, www. sucrespanishschool.com, US$6 per hr, salsa and cooking classes, friendly and flexible. **Medical services** Hospital Santa Bárbara, Ayacucho y R Moreno, Plazuela Libertad, T646 0133, public hospital. Hospital Cristo de las Américas, Av Japón s/n, T644 3269, private hospital. **Useful addresses** Immigration: Bustlllos 284 entre La Paz y Azurduy, T645 3647, Mon-Fri 0830-1230, 1430-1830.

Tarija → *Phone code: 04. Colour map 6, B4. Population: 234,422. Altitude: 1840 m.*

Tarija has a delightful climate and streets and plazas planted with flowering trees. Still known for its fruit, wines and strong cultural heritage which sets it apart from the rest of the country, it has also experienced an economic boom and rapid growth since 2005 due to natural gas development in the department. The best time to visit is from January to April, when the fruit is in season. Founded 4 July 1574 in the rich valley of the Río Guadalquivir, the city declared itself independent of Spain in 1807, and for a short time existed as an independent republic before joining Bolivia. In Plaza Luis de Fuentes there is a statue to the city's founder, Capitán Luis de Fuentes Vargas. The **Dirección de Turismo** ① *Ingavi y Gral Trigo, T667 2633, Mon-Fri 0800-1200, 1500-1900,* is helpful, city and departmental map. **Dirección Municipal de Turismo** ① *C 15 de Abril y Mcal Sucre, 1663 3581, Mon-Fri 0800-1200, 1430-1830,* helpful, city map, some English spoken; also have a booth at the Terminal de Buses ① *T666 7701, 0700-1100, 1430-2200.* In the wine producing area of **Valle de la Concepción**, **Información Turística** ① *Plaza Principal, T667 2854, Mon-Sat 0800-1600,* offer maps and pamphlets. Note that blocks west of C Colón have a small O before number (oeste), and all blocks east have an E (este); blocks are numbered from Colón outwards. All streets north of Av Las Américas are preceded by N (norte).

Places in Tarija The oldest and most interesting church in the city is the **Basílica de San Francisco** ① *corner of La Madrid y Daniel Campos, 0700-1000, 1800-2000, Sun 0630-1200, 1800-2000.* It is beautifully painted inside, with praying angels depicted on the ceiling and the four evangelists at the four corners below the dome. The library is divided into old and new sections, the old containing some 15,000 volumes, the new a further 5000. To see the library, go to the door in Ingavi O-0137. Behind the church is the **Museo Fray Francisco Miguel de Mari** ① *Colón y La Madrid, T664 4909, www.franciscanosdetarija.com/pag/ced/museo.htm, 1000-1100, 1600-1700, US$2.85,* with colonial and contemporary art collections, colonial books, the oldest of which is a 1501 *Iliad*, 19th-century photograph albums and other items. **Casa Dorada** ① *Trigo e Ingavi (entrance on Ingavi), http://casadelaculturatarija.com, guided tours Mon-Fri at 0900, 1000, 1100, 1500, 1600, and 1700, US$0.70.* Begun in 1886 and also known as the Maison d'Or, it is now part of Casa de la Cultura. It belonged to importer/exporter Moisés Narvajas and his wife Esperanza Morales and has been beautifully restored inside and out. Tarija's **Museo de Arqueología y Paleontología** ① *Trigo y Lema, Mon-Fri 0800-1200, 1500-1800, Sat 0900-1200, 1500-1800, US$0.45*, contains a palaeontological collection (fossils, remains of several Andean elephants of the Pleistocene), as well as smaller mineralogical, ethnographic and anthropological collections. The outskirts of the city can be a good place to look for **fossils**, but report any finds to the university.

About 15 km north of the centre is the charming village of **San Lorenzo**. Just off the plaza is the **Museo Méndez** ① *0900-1230, 1500-1830, minimum US$0.30 entry*, the house of the independence hero Eustaquio Méndez, 'El Moto'. The small museum exhibits his weapons, his bed, his 'testimonio'. At lunchtime on Sunday, many courtyards serve cheap meals. Minibuses from Domingo Paz y J.M Saracho, every five minutes, US$0.30. The road to San Lorenzo passes **Tomatitas** (5 km) a popular picnic and river bathing area, from where good day trips include the waterfalls at **Coimata** and the valley at **Rincón de la Victoria**. There is a spectacular one- to two-day Camino del Inca from Tajzara in **Reserva de Sama** to Pinos Sud, from where public transport can take you back to the city (for information contact **SERNAP** ① *Av Jaime Paz 1171, T665 0605*, or the NGO **Prometa** ① *Alejando del Carpio 659, T664 1880, www.prometa.org.bo*).

Tarija is proud of its **wine and singani** (brandy) production. Not all wineries receive visitors. To visit a *bodega*, contact its shop in town beforehand to make arrangements or, better yet, take a tour (see What to do, page 314) which provides transport and allows you to visit several different bodegas on the same day. **Campos de Solana** ① *15 de Abril E-0259 entre Suipacha y Méndez, T664 5498*. Increasingly recognized for their selection of fine wines (the Malbec is highly regarded), as well as the popular Casa Real brand of singani. The Campos de Solana bodega is in El Portillo, 6 km on road to Bermejo and the Casa Real bodega is in Santa Ana, about 15 km off the road to Bermejo. **Casa Vieja** ① *15 de Abril 540, T667 2349*, a traditional *bodega artesanal*, small-scale winery, located in Valle de la Concepción, 25 km from Tarija. Interesting and recommended. **El Potro** ① *C José María Villena, San Gerónimo near the airport, T7298 8832, daily 1000-1900*. Guided tours and wine-tasting. **La Concepción** ① *Colón y La Madrid, T665 1514*. Wines (try their Cabernet Sauvignon) and Rujero singani, bodega in Valle de Concepción. Wine shops (*vinotecas*) include: **Las Duelas Calamuchita** ① *opposite the sports field in village of Calamuchita, T666 8943, daily 0900-1700*. Small winery, *vinos artesanales*, wine-tasting and regional preserves. **La Vinoteca** ① *Ingavi O-0731 y Gral Trigo, Mon-Sat 0900-1900*. For wine, cheese and ham.

To Argentina → *Bolivia is 1-2 hrs behind Argentina, depending on the time of year.*

The road to Villazón (see page 295) is the shortest route to Argentina; 189 km, but a tiring trip along a winding, scenic mountain road. The alternative route via Bermejo is the most easily reached from Tarija; 210 km all paved, the views are also spectacular (sit on right). **Bermejo** (Population: 13,000, Altitude: 415 m) is well supplied with places to sleep and eat, there are many *casas de cambio*. Be prepared for up to four hours at customs and immigration here; it's very hot. An international bridge crosses the river from Bermejo to Aguas Blancas, Argentina. A third option, from Tarija to the Yacuiba/Pocitos border (see page 340), is 290 km away.

◉ Tarija listings

For hotel and restaurant price codes, and other relevant information, see Essentials.

● Where to stay

Tarija *p311*
Some hotels may offer low-season discounts, May-Aug.

$$$$-$$$ Los Parrales Resort, Urb Carmen de Aranjuez Km 3.5, T664 8444 , www.los

parraleshotel.com. Large luxury hotel offering fine views over the city and surrounding hills. Includes buffet breakfast, pool, spa, gym, Wi-Fi in communal areas. Non-guests can pay to use the pool and other facilities.
$$$ Terravina, Bolívar E 525 y Santa Cruz, T666 8673, terravinatarija@gmail.com. Modern boutique hotel with a wine theme, rooms with fridge and heating and fully furnished

1-2 bedroom apartments, two rooms on the ground floor are equipped for handicapped guests, includes buffet breakfast.

$$ Hostal Carmen, Ingavi O-0784, T664 3372, www.hostalcarmentarija.com. Older place but well maintained, excellent buffet breakfast, hot water, heating, airport transfers available. Often full, advance booking advised, very helpful, good value. Recommended.

$$ La Pasarela, 10 km north of Tarija near the village of Coimata, T666 1333, www.lapasarelahotel.com. Belgian-owned hotel with good restaurant/bar, country views, tranquil, family atmosphere, living room, jacuzzi, swimming pool, mountain bikes, laundry and camping.

$$ Mitru Tarija, Avaroa 450, entre Isaac Attie y Delgadillo, 1664 3930, www.hotelmitru.com. Modern hotel, comfortable rooms with a/c, heating, garden with hammocks, new in 2014.

$ Alojamiento Familiar, Rana S 0231 y Navajas, T664 0832. Shared bath, hot shower, cheap, helpful, close to bus terminal, traffic noise.

$ Miraflores, Sucre 920, T664 3355. Hot water, cheaper rooms with shared bath are simple, popular place but indifferent service.

$ Res Rosario, Ingavi O-0777, T664 2942. Simple rooms, cheaper with shared bath, hot water, good budget option, family atmosphere, helpful.

⑨ Restaurants

Tarija *p311*
Many restaurants (and much else in town) close between 1400 and 1600.

$$$ Carnes y Tintos, Av España 1788 y Juan José Echalar, half a block from Av Las Américas, T666 0815. Grill, very good for prime local and Argentine meat and an extensive list of local wines.

$$ Don Pepe Rodizio, D Campos N-0138, near Av Las Américas. Stylish restaurant serving tasty daily set lunch, all-you-can-eat *rodizio* on weekends for US$10. Recommended.

$$ El Fogón del Gringo, La Madrid O-1053, Plaza Uriondo. Mon-Sat 1900-2300, on Fri-Sun also 1200-1430. Upmarket *parillada* includes excellent salad bar.

$$ La Taberna Gattopardo, on main plaza. Daily 0800-2100. Pizza, *parrillada* with

Argentine beef, local wines, deserts, snacks, excellent salads, popular meeting place, Wi-Fi.

$ Miiga Comida Coreana, Cochabamba 813 y Ballivian. Open every night except Tue. Sushi with salmon and a small but tasty range of Korean dishes

$ El Molino, Ingavi O-550 entre Saracho y Campero. Midday only. Tasty and healthy vegetarian set lunch.

$ El Patio, Sucre N-0458. Mon-Sat. Good set lunch with small salad bar, pleasant seating in patio, also great *tucumanas al horno*.

DeliGelato, Colón N-0421, Plaza Sucre. Daily until 2130. Good ice-cream.

Nougat Café-Bar, Gral Trigo corner 15 de Abril. Daily 0800-2400. Nicely decorated. European-style café. Breakfast, à la carte dishes, snacks and sweets, Wi-Fi.

Pastelería Jenny, 15 de Abril 0215. Good coffee and cakes.

⑧ Festivals

Tarija *p311*
Tarija is known for its fiestas. **Carnaval Chapaco** in Feb/Mar is lively and colourful; **Compadres and Comadres**, celebrated on the Thursdays preceding carnival, are an important part of the tradition. **Fiesta de la Vendimia**, held Feb/Mar in Valle de la Concepción, 25 km from Tarija, is a week-long vintage and art festival. During Easter week, Mar/Apr, communities such as San Lorenzo and Padcaya welcome visitors with colourful arches and flowers to La Pascua Florida processions. **Abril en Tarija**: cultural events are held throughout Apr. 15 Aug-14 Sep **La Virgen de Chaguaya**, 45 km pilgrimage from the city to the Santuario Chaguaya, south of El Valle. For less devoted souls, Línea P *trufi* from Plaza Sucre, Tarija, to Padcaya, US$1; bus to Chaguaya and Padcaya from terminal daily, 0700, returns 1700, US$1.35. San Roque,16 Aug-1st week Sep, is Tarija's main festival. A procession on the 1st Sun takes the richly dressed saint's statue around the various churches. Chunchos, colourfully attired male devotees of the saint, dance in processions and women throw flowers from the balconies. No alcohol is consumed. On 2nd Sun in Oct the flower festival

commemorates the **Virgen del Rosario** (celebrations in the surrounding towns are recommended, eg San Lorenzo and Padcaya).

☀ What to do

Tarija *p311*
Bolivian Wine Tours, Méndez entre Avaroa y Av Las Américas, T7022 5715. Speciality tours to vineyards and wine cellars (*bodegas*) focusing not only on the production of high-altitude wines but also on local culture.
Educación y Futuro, at the Ecosol shop, Virgino Lema y Suipacha, Plazuela Sucre, T666 4973, www.educacionyfuturo.com. An NGO offering homestays with rural families, cheese making and guided trekking.
Sur Bike, Ballivián 601 e Ingavi, T7619 4200. Cycling trips in the countryside outside Tarija US$27-41, for a day trip including snack. Bike rentals US$16.50 per day.
Tupiza Tours, at hotel **Mitru**, T7022 5715, www.tupizatours.com. Tarija contact of the Tupiza agency.
VTB, at **Hostal Carmen** (see Where to stay above), T663 3281, www.vtbtourtarija. com. All tours include a free city tour; 4-6 hr trips including bodegas, US$23 pp; comprehensive 10 hr "Tarija and surroundings in 1 Day", US$35; can also try your hand at excavation with palaeontology specialist! Good vehicles, recommended.
Viva Tours, Bolivar 251, Edif Ex-Hansa, of 6, T663 8325, auriventur@hotmail.com. Vineyard tours US$30 with lunch.

⊖ Transport

Tarija *p311*
Air BoA (General Trigo 327, T611 1389) flies Mon-Sat to **Cochabamba**, Sun to **La Paz**. TAM (La Madrid O-0470 entre Trigo y Campero, T662 2734), to either **La Paz, Sucre**, **Santa Cruz** or **Yacuiba**, depending on day of week. Aerocon (Ballivián 525, T665 8634) flies to **Santa Cruz**. Shared taxi from airport to centre, US$0.75 pp, or *micro* A from Mercado Central which drops you 1 block away. Some hotels have free transport to town, you may have to call them. Airport information T664 3135.
Bus The bus station is southeast of centre on Av Las Américas (30-min walk from centre), T666 6701. Note that the **Copa Moya** bus company has a poor safety record. To **La Paz** several buses at 0700-0800 and 1700 (935 km) 17 hrs, US$14, via Potosí and **Oruro** (US$12.50); check which company operates the best buses. To **Potosí**, several additional departures 1630-1800, 10 hrs, US$10. To **Sucre** at 1630 and 1800, US$12.50. To **Tupiza**, Diamante, 1930, and Juárez, 2030, US$9.50, 6 hrs. To **Santa Cruz** via Villamontes, several companies at 1830, US$14, 17 hrs. To get to Villamontes in daylight, take a **La Guadalupana** or **La Entreriana** bus from Parada del Chaco (east end of Av Las Américas) to **Entre Ríos**, US$3, 3½ hrs, some continue to Villamontes (spectacular route), mostly in daylight.
To Argentina: to **Villazón**, several companies daily, 1930-2030, 8 hrs, US$5.50. To **Bermejo**, shared taxis leave when full from opposite the bus station, US$5.50, 3 hrs; bus US$3, 4 hrs. Buses to **Yacuiba** US$7, 9 hrs, most depart in the evening.

❶ Directory

Tarija *p311*
Useful addresses Immigration, Ingavi O-0789, T664 3450, Mon-Fri 0830-1230, 1430-1830. Visa renewals in 48 hrs.

Cochabamba and around → *Phone code: 04. Colour map 6, A3. Population: 650,038. Altitude: 2570 m.*

Set in a bowl of rolling hills at a comfortable altitude, Cochabamba enjoys a wonderfully warm, dry and sunny climate. Its parks and plazas are a riot of colour, from the striking purple of the bougainvillaea to the subtler tones of jasmine, magnolia and jacaranda. Bolivia's fourth largest city was founded in 1574 and in colonial times it was the 'breadbasket' of Bolivia, providing food for the great mining community of Potosí. Today it is an important commercial centre.

Cochabamba

To ⑨ · Immigration · To Palacio Portales & ①⑦④⑤⑧⑩ ⑪⑬

Pedro Borda

La Paz

José de la Reza

México

M Rocha

Convent of Santa Teresa

Ecuador

Departmental Tourist Office **i**

La Compañía ✝

General Achá

Casona Santiváñez

Santiváñez

Santo Domingo

Exprintbol

Museo Arqueológico

BNB

BoA

Plazuela de San Sebastián

Colina de San Sebastián

La Coronilla

To Airport

To Incallacta Market, Local Buses for Tarata, Cliza & Punata

Av Ballivián (El Prado)

Av Salamanca

Paccieri

Plaza Colón **i**

Venezuela

Bolivia Cultura

Ecuador

Colombia

Av Las Heroínas

Bolívar

San Francisco

Plaza 14 de Septiembre

Cathedral

Sucre

IGM

Cnl Jordán

Calama

Cabrera

Uruguay

Av Aroma

Brasil

Brasil

Montes

To La Cancha Market & Local Buses for Totora & Torotoro (at Av 6 de Agosto, approx 6 blocks)

Av República

Av 9 de Abril

Micros to Villa Tunari

José Martí

To ⑤

Hamiraya

Junín

Av Ayacucho

Baptista

España

Lanza

Antezana

Tô de Julio

Aguirre

Esteban Arze

25 de Mayo

Av San Martín

To La Paz & Oruro

To Cerro de San Pedro & Cristo de la Concordia

To La Paz

A López

Av Ayacucho

N

100 metres
100 yards

Where to stay 🛏	Restaurants 🍴	Bars & clubs 🍸
1 Aranjuez A3	1 Brazilian Coffee A2	12 Cocafé A2
2 Gina's A2	2 Café París B2	13 La Muela del Diablo A3
3 Gran Hotel Cochabamba A3	3 Casablanca A2	14 Na Cunna A3
4 Hostal Florida C2	4 Churrasquería Tunari A3	
5 Hostal Maya B1	5 Doña Alcira A3	
6 Hostal Nawpa House B2	6 Ganesha A2	
7 Monserrat A2	7 La Cantonata A2	
8 Regina A2	8 La Estancia A3	
9 Res Familiar C2	9 Los Castores A2	
10 Res Familiar Annex B2	10 Paprika A3	
	11 Sole Mio A3	

Many visitors particularly enjoy La Cancha market, one of the largest in Bolivia, as well as Cochabamba's very good dining and nightlife.

Fertile foothills surrounding the city still provide much of the country's grain, fruit and coca. Markets, colonial towns and archaeological sites are all close by too. Conquering the challenging Cerro Tunari is a must for all adventurers. Further afield, the dinosaur tracks and great scenery at Torotoro National Park are worth the trip. The paved lowland route to Santa Cruz de la Sierra has much more transport than the rough old road over the mountains via Comarapa and Samaipata. Both offer access to Carrasco and Amboró national parks. There is an animal refuge by Villa Tunari, along the lowland road.

Arriving in Cochabamba

Orientation The city is served by paved roads from La Paz and Santa Cruz. Neither airport, nor bus station are far from the centre. Buses and taxis serve both. The city is divided into four quadrants based on the intersection of Avenida Las Heroínas running west to east, and Avenida Ayacucho running north to south. In all longitudinal streets north of Heroínas the letter N (Norte) precedes the four numbers. South of Heroínas the numbers are preceded by S (Sur). In all transversal streets west of Ayacucho the letter O (Oeste) precedes the numbers and all streets running east are preceded by E (Este). The first two numbers refer to the block, 01 being closest to Ayacucho or Heroínas; the last two refer to the building's number. ▸▸ *See also Transport, page 322.*

Tourist information Dirección de Turismo de la Alcaldía ① *Plaza Colón 448, T425 8030-8035, Mon-Fri 0800-1200, 1430-1830,* is the best option. Other offices at the bus station and Jorge Wilstermann airport (0700-1100, 1500-2200). The **departmental tourist office** is at ① *Colombia E-0340, entre 25 de Mayo y España, T450 5392, Mon-Fri 0800-1200, 1430-1830.* **Tourist police** ① *Plaza 14 de Septiembre, north side, T450 3880.* The unofficial web resource for the city: **www.bolivia-online.net.**

Safety Both Cochabamba city and department have public safety issues. Do not venture into any of the hills around town on foot (including San Pedro with the Cristo de la Concordia, San Sebastián and La Coronilla), take only radio taxis (marked with stickers on the back doors) at night, and mind your belongings in markets, on public transport, and other crowded places where you should wear your bag in front. In the main towns in the coca growing region of Chapare tourists are reasonably safe. ▸▸ *See also Safety, page 243.*

Places in Cochabamba

At the heart of the old city is the arcaded **Plaza 14 de Septiembre** with the **Cathedral** ① *Mon-Fri 0800-1200, 1700-1900, Sat-Sun 0800-1200,* dating from 1571, but much added-to. Of the colonial churches nearby, the **Convent and Museum of Santa Teresa** ① *Baptista y Ecuador, T422 1252, Mon-Fri 0830-1200, 1430-1800, Sat 1430-1700, US$3, camera US$ 3.50 extra, guides included,* original construction 1760-90, has a beautiful interior.

Museo Arqueológico ① *Aguirre y Jordán, T425 0010, www.museo.umss.edu.bo, Mon-Fri 0800-1800, Sat 0830-1200, US$3, free student guide in Spanish (English Mon-Fri 1300-1600).* Part of the Universidad de San Simón, one of the most complete museums in Bolivia, displaying artefacts including Amerindian hieroglyphic scripts, mummies, and pre-Inca textiles, through to the colonial era. **Casona Santiváñez** ① *Santiváñez O-0156, Mon-Fri 0800-1200, 1430-1800, free,* has a nice colonial patio, and exhibition of paintings and historic photographs.

From Plaza Colón, at the north end of the old town, the wide **Avenida Ballivián** (known as **El Prado**) runs northwest to the wealthy modern residential areas; along it you can find restaurants and bars. Also in the north is the Patiño family's **Palacio Portales** ① *Av Potosí 1450, T448 6414, guided tours in Spanish Tue-Fri 1530, 1630, 1730, in English 1600, 1700, 1800, Sat in*

Spanish at 0930, 1000, 1100, English 1100, 1130, Sun Spanish 1100, English 1030, 1130, US$1.50.
The gardens are open Tue-Fri 1500-1830, Sat-Sun 0930-1130. Built in French renaissance style, furnished from Europe and set in 10 ha of gardens inspired by Versailles, the Patiño mansion was finished in 1927 but never occupied. It is now the **Centro Cultural Simón I Patiño**① *http://portal. fundacionpatino.org*, with an excellent art gallery in the basement. Take a taxi (five minutes from the centre) or micro G from Avenida San Martín. Next to Palacio Portales is the very nice **Museo de Historia Natural Alcide d'Orbigny** ① *Av Potosí 1458 y Av América, T448 6969, Mon-Fri 0900-1230, 1500-1830, free*, named after the famous 19th-century French naturalist. It houses natural history collections of international importance.

To the south of the old town lie the bus and train stations and one of the best markets in Bolivia. The huge and fascinating **La Cancha market**① *between Esteban Arze, Punata, República and Pulacayo,* is open all week but best on Wednesday and Saturday when it is packed with campesinos and trading spills over into surrounding streets. It has a vast array of foodstuffs and local goods. Souvenirs can be found at San Antonio on Avenida Esteban Arze y Punata, well worth a visit, but watch your valuables.

Around Cochabamba

Parque Nacional Tunari, 300,000 ha, is just outside the city (see www.biobol.org). Despite this proximity, it remains a beautiful unspoilt natural area and a good place for acclimatization to altitude. There are llamas and alpacas above 4000 m and even the occasional condor. The highest point in the park, Cerro Tunari (5035 m), offers magnificent views, even as far as Illimani. It can be climbed in a day trip; going with a local operator is recommended. **Note** Armed attacks of visitors have taken place along the marked trail from the park entrance in the north of the city. Safer alternatives, although not signposted, are along the south flank of the mountain, either reached from above Hacienda Pairumani (see below) or from Berghotel Carolina, which arranges tours with pack animals (see page 319).

Quillacollo, 13 km west of the city, has a produce Sunday market and a famous festival (see page 321). Take any micro or trufi marked "Quillacollo" along Av Heroínas. Some 8 km beyond town is the turn-off to the beautiful **Hacienda Pairumani**① *T426 0083 to check if it is open, Mon Fri 1500-1600, Sat 0900-1130,* centre of the Patiño agricultural foundation, also known as **Villa Albina**, built in 1925-1932, furnished from Europe and inhabited by Patiño's wife, Albina. Pairumani can be reached from Avenida Aroma in Cochabamba or by Trufi 211 from Plaza Bolívar in **Quillacollo**.

Some 27 km west of Cochabamba are **Inka-Rakay** ruins, with fine views of the Cochabamba valley and the mountains around the ruins. A day trip to the ruins can end at the plaza in nearby Sipe Sipe or one of its local restaurants with a bowl of *guarapo* (wine-based drink) and a plate of *charque* (sun-dried beef), served with potatoes, eggs and corn; best at weekends. Or take trufi "Sipe Sipe" from Plaza Bolivar in Quillacollo and get off at the church on the main square, then ask for the way up to the ruins.

Tarata, 33 km southeast of Cochabamba, is a colonial town with a traditional arcaded plaza on which stand the church (daily 0800-1300) and the Casa Consistorial. In the plaza, the **clock tower** ① *Mon-Fri 0800-1200, 1330-1700, Sat-Sun 0800-1200,* houses a German timepiece with chimes. Inside the **Franciscan Convent** ① *Mon-Sat 0930-1130, 1430-1800, US$0.30, guided visits from Casa de Cultura y Turismo, main square, T457 8727,* overlooking the town, are the remains of the martyr, San Severino, patron saint of the town, more commonly known as the 'Saint of Rain'; festival, on the last Sunday of November, attracts thousands of people. Large procession on 3 May, day of La Santa Cruz, with fireworks and brass band. Market days Thursday and Sunday (bus US$0.65, one hour, last returns 1900). For fine alpaca products, visit **Doña Prima Fernández Prado**① *Arce E-0115, opposite the convent,* who sells sweaters, bags and textiles from two rooms off a beautiful colonial patio. The local sausages are nationally famous. Beyond Tarata are Cliza, Mizque and Aiquile, along a scenic rail line. A *ferrobus,* a bus running on train tracks, has irregular service on this route; enquire if it is running (T455 6208).

Parque Nacional Torotoro

ⓘ *Entry US$15, payable at the Oficina de Turismo, Calle Cochabamba, Main Plaza, T7227 0968, 04-413 5736, www.biobol.org.* In the department of Potosí, but best reached from Cochabamba (136 km), is **Torotoro**, a small village, set amid beautiful rocky landscape in the centre of the Parque Nacional Torotoro, covering an area of 21,693 ha. It can also be reached along a dusty road from Sucre. Attractions include caves, a canyon, waterfalls, ruins, rock paintings, and thousands of incredible fossilized dinosaur tracks, some of which can be seen by the Río Torotoro just outside the village. Near the community of **Wayra K'asa**, about 8 km northwest of Torotoro, **Umajalanta cave**, the largest in Bolivia, has many stalactites, stalagmites and a lake with endemic blind fish; 7 km have been explored and are open to caving (head torch and helmet are required and for hire at the entrance). In the Cañón de Torotoro, 4 km from the village, are the fantastic **El Vergel** waterfalls and the walk along the river bed is great fun if you like rock-hopping and skipping over pools. The views over the canyon from the observation lookout are amazing and you can also see a number of endemic birds; on the way to the lookout are dinosaur prints. Fossils can be seen at Siete Vueltas, 5 km from the village. Itas, in the community of Ovejerías, 21 km from Torotoro, offers lovely views of the surrounding ridges and canyons, interesting rock formations (some resemble gothic cathedrals), rock paintings and, with a little luck, condors. By the community of Molle Cancha is a turtle cemetery.

Tours or day trips can be organized by the **Asociación de Guías** ⓘ *Main Plaza across from the Oficina de Turismo.* Every visitor gets a map and a personal guide; Mario Jaldín, T7141 2381, is excellent. Going with a local guide is compulsory. Four wheel drive tours are also offered by **El Mundo Verde Travel** (www.elmundoverdetravel.com), which can also provide transport from Sucre, and other Cochabamba agencies.

Cochabamba to Santa Cruz

The lowland road from Cochabamba through Villa Tunari to Santa Cruz is fully paved but prone to landslides after heavy rain. **Villa Tunari** is a relaxing place and holds an annual Fish Fair the first weekend of August, with music, dancing and food. **Parque Ecoturístico Machía**, just outside town, is managed by **Inti Wara Yassi** ⓘ *T04-413 6572, www.intiwarayassi.org, entrance US$0.90, US$2 for camera, US$3.60 for video, donations welcome, open daily 0900-1600.* This 36-ha park includes a well-signposted 3-km interpretive trail, which explains the park's ecology and other good trails through semi-tropical forest. There are panoramic lookouts, waterfalls and a wide variety of wildlife. The park is run by an animal rescue organization, which attempts to rehabilitate captive animals and return them to the wild. They also operate two other parks, one about half way between Santa Cruz and Trinidad and another near Rurrenabaque. For volunteer opportunities, contact them in advance.

Parque Nacional Carrasco South of Villa Tunari, this park covers 622,600 ha between 300 and 4500 m. It has 11 ecological life zones, superb birdwatching and many rivers, waterfalls, canyons and pools. Access is from Villa Tunari, Totora and Monte Punku – Sehuencas. From the park entrance closest to Villa Tunari, a cable car takes you across the river for a 2½-hour walking circuit to the Cavernas de Repechón (Oil-bird caves). Guides may be hired from the **Kawsay Wasi community** ⓘ *T7939 0894, www.tusoco.com.* Julián (T7480 9714) has been recommended. See www.biobol.org.

The highland road to Santa Cruz The 500 km highland road from Cochabamba to Santa Cruz is very scenic. Some sections are unpaved and the newer lowland route is preferred by most transport. Between Monte Punku (Km 119) and Epizana is the turnoff to Pocona and Inkallajta. To reach the ruins follow the road for 13 km as far as the village of Collpa, then take the left fork for a further 10 km. The Inca ruins of **Inkallajta** (1463-1472, rebuilt 1525), on a flat spur of land at the mouth of a steep valley, are extensive and the main building of the fortress is said to have been the largest roofed Inca building. There are several good camping sites near the river and some basic facilities and services. The mountain road continues to **Epizana**, junction for the road to Sucre (being paved in 2014) via the beautiful colonial village of **Totora** and the more modern town of **Aiquile**. Past Epizana the road from Cochabamba goes on to **Pojo**, Comarapa and Samaipata (see page 337).

⊛ Cochabamba and around listings

For hotel and restaurant price codes, and other relevant information, see Essentials.

● Where to stay

Cochabamba *p314, map p315*
However attractive their prices, places to stay south of Av Aroma and near the bus station are unsafe at all times.
$$$ Aranjuez, Av Buenos Aires E-0563, T428 0076, www.aranjuezhotel.com. The most beautiful of the luxury hotels with a nice garden and lots of style, 4-star, small, good restaurant, jazz in the bar Fri-Sat night, small pool open to public (US$1). Recommended.
$$$ Gran Hotel Cochabamba, Plaza de la Recoleta E-0415, T448 9520, www.granhotelcochabamba.com. One of the best hotels in Cochabamba, pool, tennis courts, business centre, airport transfers, parking.
$$ Ginas, México 346 entre España y 25 de Mayo, T422 2925, www.ginashostal.web.bo. Has a variety of rooms for 1-5 persons, includes breakfast, safe box in rooms, convenient location in the heart of the city, monthly rates available.
$$ Monserrat, España 0342, T452 1011, http://hotelmonserrat.com. In the bohemian zone with bars and restaurants, sauna, cafetería, buffet breakfast.
$$ Regina, Reza 0359, T425 4629, www.hotelreginabolivia.com/regina. Spacious, efficient, with breakfast, restaurant.
$ Hostal Florida, 25 de Mayo S-0583, T425 7911. Cheaper with shared bath, hot water, noisy, popular, safe deposit box, breakfast.
$ Hostal Maya, Colombia 710 y Suipacha, T425 9701. Includes breakfast, private bath, hot water, central.
$ Hostal Ñawpa House, España 250, T452 7723. Simple rooms with electric shower, large courtyard, laundry facilities, book exchange.

$ Res Familiar, Sucre E-0554, T422 7988. Very pleasant, secure, cheaper without bath, good showers, sunny courtyard. Its annex at 25 de Mayo N-0234 (entre Colombia y Ecuador), T422 7986, is also pleasant, with a big courtyard, shared bath, hot water, comfortable.

Around Cochabamba *p317*
$$$-$$ Berghotel Carolina, Palrumani, at the foot of the Cerro Tunari, T7213 0003, www.berghotelcarolina.com. Arranges private transport (25 mins) from Plaza Bolívar in Quillacollo. Mountain lodge with 5 comfortable rooms with private bath and 2 with shared bath, restaurant, bar, living room with fireplace, sauna and large terrace. Organizes guided 2-day walking tours with tent to the Laguna Cajón (4100 m), Cerro Tunari and other peaks in Parque Tunari. Walking trails start right from the lodge.
$$ El Poncho Eco Center, Marquina, Quillacollo, T439 2283, T7648 6666, www.elponcho.org. Ecological cabins, restaurant and pool.

Parque Nacional Torotoro *p318*
An upmarket community run hotel is under construction in Wayra K'asa, by the cave, due to open in late 2014. The following are in the village of Torotoro:
$$ Hostal Asteria, in the centre of the village, T6707 3401, La Paz office T02-211 6552. Colonial-style hotel, restaurant serving all meals, living room with books and DVDs, beautiful patio, parking.
$$ Villa Etelvina, 15-min walk from plaza, T7073 7807, www.villaetelvina.com. Bungalow for 4 with private bath, cheaper in rooms with shared bath, includes breakfast, beautiful garden, parking.
$ El Molino, 1.5 km from the village, T7647 5999, Cochabamba office T04-402 6172, www.elmolinotorotoro.com. Beautiful Spanish-style

country house surrounded by mountains and a river, comfortable rooms with private bath, nice common areas, fireplace, bar, pool table, indoor patio.

$ Hostal Las Hermanas, on main road from Cochabamba, 1 block before plaza on the left, T7221 1257. Basic rooms, cheaper with shared bath, Doña Lily serves delicious food and is very attentive.

Cochabamba to Santa Cruz: Villa Tunari
p318

$$ Victoria Resort, on the road to Santa Cruz, 4 km before Villa Tunari on the right, T413 6538, www.victoria-resort.com. Modern, cabaña style, 500 m from the main road in the middle of the forest, quiet, large pool, breakfast buffet.

$ El Puente Jungle Lodge, Av de la Integración, 4 km from town, T458 0085, www.hotelelpuente.com.bo (or book in advance through **Salar Amazon Tours**, see below). Cabins from 2 persons to family-size surrounded by tropical vegetation, with breakfast and bath, pool, zip-line, stream and natural pools.

$ Hostal Mirador, on road to Santa Cruz, before first bridge, T7795 5766, boborgne36@ yahoo.fr. With bath, small pool and tower with views of river San Mateo.

The highland road to Santa Cruz: Totora
p318

$ Casa de Huespedes Villa Eva, on main road, T7437 1530. Well furnished country house with large living room, fully equipped kitchen, and comfortable rooms with private bath.

● Restaurants

Cochabamba *p314, map p315*
The restaurant and nightlife district is on España, Ecuador, Mayor Rocha and Av Ballivian (El Prado), and north of the Río Rocha on the Pasaje Boulevard de la Recoleta and Av Pando. Those on very tight budgets can find an edible lunch at the **Mercado 25 de Mayo** at 25 de Mayo entre Sucre y Jordán.

$$ Churrasquería Tunari, Pasaje Boulevard de la Recoleta, T448 8153. The most delicious meat you can find in Cochabamba.

$$ La Cantonata, España y Mayor Rocha, T425 9222. Good Italian restaurant. Recommended.

$$ La Estancia, Pasaje Blvd de la Recoleta 786, T424 9262. Best steak in town, salads and international food in this traditional restaurant.

$$ Sole Mio, Av América 826 y Pando, T428 3379. A smart Neapolitan pizza restaurant, delicious, also good for desserts. Attentive service.

$$-$ Ganesha, Mayor Rocha E-0375. Closed Sun. Good filling vegetarian food, buffet lunch and breakfast, mostly soy-protein based dishes.

$$-$ Paprika, Chuquisaca 688 y Antezana, www.paprika.com.bo. Opens in the evening. Nice atmosphere, international food, good cocktails and desserts.

Cafés
Brazilian Coffee, Av Ballivián 537 just off Plaza Colón. Open 24 hrs. Upmarket, tables on pavement.

Café París, Bolívar, corner of Plaza 14 de Septiembre. Serves good coffee and crêpes.

Casablanca, 25 de Mayo entre Venezuela y Ecuador. Attractive, buzzing, good food and a wide selection of coffee, popular for wine and cocktails in the evening.

Doña Alcira, Plazuela La Recoleta. Serves traditional *empanaditas* and *helados de canela* (cinnamon ice-cream).

Los Castores, Ballivián y Oruro. Popular, good for *salteñas*.

Parque Nacional Torotoro *p318*
Several small restaurants in town including **Pensión La Huella**, and **El Comedor**, at the food market 2 blocks above the main plaza, good local food, cheap but clean.

Cochabamba to Santa Cruz: Villa Tunari
p318
There are several eating places on both sides of the main road to Santa Cruz. The more expensive ones are on the riverside. The more popular food stalls 1 block from the bus terminal serve different fish dishes and have also a cheap daily menu. Upstairs at the market (breakfast and lunch) is a very cheap option.

● Bars and clubs

Cochabamba *p314, map p315*
Cocafé, Antezana y Ecuador. Caring, family atmosphere, good place for foreigners to meet.

Street musicians always pass by to show off their skills.
La Muela del Diablo, Potosí 1392 y Portales, next to Palacio Portales. Bolivian rock music, theatre groups, German beer.
Na Cunna, Av Salamanca 577, T452 1982. Opens in the evenings, Fri live music. Irish pub and restaurant. They also serve Guinness.

⊕ Entertainment

Cochabamba *p314, map p315*
Theatre mARTadero, Av 27 de Agosto entre Ollantay y Ladislao Cabrera, T458 8778, www.martadero.org. Cultural and artistic centre for local and international artists, exhibitions, and events, in a refurbished slaughterhouse. Daily 1500-1800. Micros/trufis P, Q, and 212 to Plaza de los Arrieros. **Teatro Achá**, España 280 y Plaza 14 de Septiembre, T425 8054. The city's oldest cultural centre, with monthly presentations. **Teatro Hecho a Mano**, Venezuela 0655 entre Lanza y Antezana, T452 9790. Theatre school. For cinema, see www.cinecenter.com.bo.

⊕ Festivals

Cochabamba *p314, map p315*
Carnaval is celebrated 15 days before Lent. Rival groups (*comparsas*) compete in music, dancing, and fancy dress, culminating in El Corso on the last Sat of the Carnaval. Mascaritas balls also take place in the carnival season, when the young women wear long hooded satin masks. **14 Sep**: Día de Cochabamba.

Around Cochabamba *p317*
Fiesta de la Virgen de Urkupiña (www.urcupina.com), in Quillacollo, 14-15 Aug. Plenty of transport from Cochabamba, hotels all full. Be there before 0900 to be sure of a seat, as you are not allowed to stand in the street. The 1st day is the most colourful with all the groups in costumes and masks, parading and dancing in the streets till late at night. Many groups have left by the 2nd day and dancing stops earlier. The 3rd day is dedicated to the pilgrimage.

⊙ Shopping

Cochabamba *p314, map p315*
Camping gear, maps, etc The Spitting Llama, España N-301 y Ecuador, T489 4540, www.thespittingllama.com. IGM, 16 de Julio S-237, T425 5503, Mon-Thu 0800-1200, 1430-1800, Fri 0800-1200, sells topographic maps of Cochabamba department.
Handicrafts Artesanos Andinos, Pasaje Catedral, T450 8367. An artisans' association selling textiles. **Fotrama**, Bolivar 0349, entre San Martín y 25 de Mayo, www.fotrama.com. High quality alpaca clothing.

⊙ What to do

Cochabamba *p314, map p315*
Adventure sports
Cochabamba is growing in popularity for parapenting, with several outfits offering tamdem jumps and courses more cheaply than other places, starting at US$30-35 and US$200-250 respectively.
AndesXtremo, La Paz 138 entre Ayacucho y Junín, T452 3392, www.andesxtremo.com. Adventure sports company offering parapenting, climbing, rafting and trekking, good value, professional staff. Recommended.
Bolivia Cultura, Ecuador 342 entre 25 de Mayo y España, T452 7272, www.boliviacultura.com Tours to Torotoro. They run year round tours for 3 and 4 days to all the major sites and can arrange longer trips.
D'Orbigny Travel, Pasaje de la Promotora 344 entre España y Heroínas, T451 1367. Run by an enthusiastic Bolivian couple, excursions in Cochabamba department and throughout Bolivia. Recommended.
El Mundo Verde Travel, no storefornt, T653 44272, www.elmundoverdetravel.com. Great for local information, regional experts offer tours to Torotoro, Pico Tunari and Chapare and throughout Bolivia; day trips and adventure tours. Dutch-Bolivian run. English, Dutch and Spanish spoken. Recommended.
Fremen Tours, Tumusla 245 entre Ecuador y Colombia, T425 9392, www.frementours.com. Offers tours throughout the country, including their own facilities at Villa Tunari and on the *Reina de Enín* riverboat.

Salar Amazon Tours, Condominio Los Faros 4 en Pasaje la Sevillana (Zona Templo Mormón), T458 0085, www.salaramazon.com. Offer salar and jungle tours and Reina de Enín cruises, also run Hotel El Puente in Villa Tunari.

⊜ Transport

Cochabamba *p314, map p315*
Air Jorge Wilstermann airport, T412 0400. Airport bus is Micro B from Heroínas y Ayacucho, US$0.40; taxis from airport to centre US$4. Arrive 2 hours aheadfor international flights. Cochabamba is an air transport hub with several daily flights to/from **La Paz** (35 mins) and **Santa Cruz** (40 mins) with **Amaszonas**, Av Libertador Bolívar 1509, Edif El Solar, PB, T479 4200, **Boliviana de Aviacion**, Jordán 202 y Nataniel Aguirre, T901-105010 and **TAM** Militar, Buenos Aires entre Av Santa Cruz y América, T441 1545). **Aerocon**, Ancieto Padilla 755, T448 9210 (see note on page 240), **Ecojet**, Plazuela Constitucion 0879 entre 16 de Julio y Chuquisaca, T901-105055, and **TAM** have flights to **Trinidad**, with connections to other northern cities.

Bus *Micros* and *colectivos*, US$0.25; *trufis*, US$0.30. Anything marked 'San Antonio' goes to the market. *Trufis* C and 10 go from bus terminal to the city centre. **Long distance** The main bus terminal is on Av Aroma y Ayacucho, 600-700 m south of Plaza 14 de Septiembre (T155). To **Santa Cruz**, almost hourly 0600-2130, 12 hrs, US$7.50; Trans Copacabana semi cama, 2130, US$10; Bolívar buscama, US$15; all via the paved lowland road through Villa Tunari. See page 318. To **Mairana, Samaipata** and **Santa Cruz**, along the old mountain road via Epizana and Comarapa, a beautiful ride, **Trans Carrasco**, 6 de Agosto y República, T456-9348, daily at 0730 to Santa Cruz (14 hrs), 1200 to Mairana (11 hrs), US$6. **El Mundo Verde Travel** offers 4x4 tours from Cochabamba to **Samaipata**. To/from **La Paz** almost hourly 0530-2300, 7 hrs, US$6 (**Trans Copacabana** semi cama, 2230, US$8.50, **Bolívar** buscama, 2230, 2300, US$12.50). To **Oruro**, 0600-1730 (Sun last bus at 2100), 4 hrs, US$3.35-4. To **Potosí**, departures at 2000 (US$7), 2100 (semi cama, US$11) with **Bolívar** and Trans Copacabana, 10 hrs. Daily to

Sucre, 8 hrs, several companies (Bolívar and Trans Copacabana at 1930, 2000 US$7, 2030 semi cama, US$8.50). To **Sucre** by day; go to Aiquile by bus (several from Av 6 de Agosto entre Av República y Av Barrientos, none before 1200) or **ferrobus** (see page 317), then a bus at 0200-0300 passing en route to Sucre, or Fri and Sun, 2000. **Regional** Local buses leave from Av Barrientos y Av 6 de Agosto, near La Coronilla for **Tarata, Punata** and **Cliza**. From Av 6 de Agosto y Av República to **Totora**. Av Oquendo y 9 de Abril (be careful in this area), to **Villa Tunari**, US$4.50, 4-5 hrs, several daily; **Puerto Villarroel**, US$7.75, 6 hrs (from 0800 when full, daily).

Taxi About US$0.75 from anywhere to the Plaza, more expensive to cross the river; double after dark.

Parque Nacional Torotoro *p318*
Bus Buses and minivans from the end of Av República y Vallegrande, daily at 1800; return to Cochabamba Mon-Sat at 0600; Sun at 1300 and 1500; US$3, 4-5 hrs in the dry season, 7-8 hrs in the wet season, on a cobbled road. There is no bus service from Sucre, it takes 14 hrs in a private vehicle along a road opened in 2013.

The highland road to Santa Cruz: Inkallajta *p318*
Take a trufi from 0500 onwards from 6 de Agosto y Manuripi (Av República) in Cochabamba (ask for the "Parada Pocona"). For 3 people the trufi will drop you off at the entrance to the Inca ruins (US$3 pp). Arrange with the driver to pick you up at a specific time to return to Cochabamba. If alone, ask to get off after arriving in Collpa at a big green sign, where the road to the ruins turns off to the right. Walk along the cobbled road for approximately 10 km to the ruins. Trufis return from Pocona to Cochabamba when full till 1600. Taxis from Pocona charge around US$14 one way to the ruins.

⊙ Directory

Cochabamba *p314, map p315*
Language classes Beyond Bolivia, www. beyondsouthamerica.com. Dutch organization which offers language classes Spanish/

Portuguese, homestays and recommended volunteer programmes and interships. **Bolivia Sostenible**, Julio Arauco Prado 230, Zona Las Cuadras, T423 3786, www.boliviasostenible. org. Offers home stays and paid placements for volunteers. **Centro de Idiomas Kori Simi**, Lanza 727, entre La Paz y Chuquisaca, T425 7248, www.korisimi.com. Spanish and Quechua school run by staff from Switzerland, Germany and Bolivia, also offers activity programme, homestays and volunteer placements. **Runawasi**, Maurice Lefebvre 0470, Villa Juan XXIII, Av Blanco Galindo Km 4.5, T424 8923,

www.runawasi.org. Spanish, Quechua and Aymara, also has accommodation. **Volunteer Bolivia**, Ecuador E-0342, T452 6028, www. volunteerbolivia.org. Bolivian/US-run organization which offers language classes, homestays and a recommended volunteer programme. There are many qualified language teachers in the city. **Medical facilities** For hospitals, doctors and dentists, contact your consulate or the tourist office for advice.
Useful addresses Immigration Office: Av Ballivián 720 y La Paz, T452 4625, Mon-Fri 0830-1230, 1430-1830.

Northern Lowlands

Bolivia's Northern Lowlands account for about 70% of national territory. Flat savannahs and dense tropical jungle stretch northwards from the great cordilleras, sparsely populated and, until recently, rarely visited by tourists. Improved roads and frequent flights, particularly to Rurrenabaque and Trinidad, are opening up the area and wildlife and rainforest expeditions are becoming increasingly popular. Most people head to Rurrenabaque. If seeking hard travel off the beaten track, try Cobija, Riberalta or Guayaramerín, all near the border with Brazil. Beni department has 53% of the country's birds and 50% of its mammals, but destruction of forest and habitat by loggers and colonists is proceeding at an alarming rate.

Madidi and Rurrenabaque

Caranavi to San Borja
From Caranavi, a road runs north to Sapecho, where a bridge crosses the Río Beni. Beyond Sapecho (7 km from the bridge), the road passes through Palos Blancos (several cheap lodgings). The road between Sapecho and Yucumo, three hours from Sapecho *tránsito*, is a good all-weather gravel surface. There are basic *hospedajes* and restaurants in **Yucumo** where a road branches northwest, fording rivers several times on its way to Rurrenabaque. Taking the eastern branch from Yucumo it is 50 km (one to two hours) to **San Borja**, a small, relatively wealthy cattle-raising centre with simple hotels and restaurants clustered near the plaza. From San Borja the road goes east to Trinidad via **San Ignacio de Moxos** (see page 329). The road passes through part of the Pilón Lajas Reserve (see below).

Parque Nacional Madidi
① *Headquarters in San Buenaventura, about 4 blocks upriver from the plaza, T03-892 2540. US$18 entry is collected near the dock in San Buenaventura. Insect repellent and sun protection are essential. See www.biobol.org.*
Parque Nacional Madidi is quite possibly the most bio-diverse of all protected areas on the planet. It is the variety of habitats, from the freezing Andean peaks of the Cordillera Apolobamba in the southwest (reaching nearly 6000 m), through cloud, elfin and dry forest to steaming tropical jungle and pampas (neo-tropical savannah) in the north and east, that account for the array of flora and fauna within the park's boundaries. In an area roughly the size of Wales or El Salvador (1,895,740 ha) are an estimated 900 bird species, 10 species of primate, five species of cat (with healthy populations of jaguar and puma), giant anteaters and many reptiles. Madidi is at the

centre of a bi-national system of parks that spans the Bolivia-Peru border. The Heath river on the park's northwestern border forms the two countries' frontier and links with the Tambopata National Reserve in Peru. To the southwest the Area Protegida Apolobamba protects extensive mountain ecosystems. It is easiest to visit the lowland areas of Madidi through Rurrenabaque.

Pilón Lajas Biosphere Reserve and Indigenous Territory

ⓘ *HQ at Campero y Germón Busch, Rurrenabaque, T892 2246, crtmpilonlajas@yahoo.com, entrance fee US$25.*

Beyond the Beni River in the southeast runs the Pilón Lajas Biosphere Reserve and Indigenous Territory (400,000 ha), home to the Tsimane and Mosetene peoples. Together with Madidi, it constitutes approximately 60,000 sq km, one of the largest systems of protected land in the neotropics. Unfortunately, much of this land is under pressure from logging interests, especially along the western border of the reserve. Set up under the auspices of UNESCO, Pilón Lajas has one of the continent's most intact Amazonian rainforest ecosystems, as well as an incredible array of tropical forest animal life. NGOs have been working with the people of La Unión, Playa Ancha, Nuevos Horizontes and El Cebú to develop sustainable forestry, fish farming, cattle ranching and *artesanía*.

Rurrenabaque → *Phone code: 03. Population: 15,197. Altitude: 200 m.*

The charming, picturesque jungle town of Rurre (as the locals call it), on the Río Beni, is the main jumping off point for tours in the Bolivian Amazon and pampas, from 2-4 day trips through to full expeditions. Across the river is the smaller town of San Buenaventura (canoe US$0.15). Despite its growth as a trading, transport and ecotourism centre, Rurre is a pleasant town to walk around, although the climate is usually humid. Market day is Sunday. **Dirección Regional de Turismo** ⓘ *Avaroa y Vaca Díez, Mon-Fri 0800-1200, 1400-1800, Sat 0900-1100,* has general information and a bulletin board for posting comments on tours; read this before booking a tour and write your own feedback. Bicycles rented at US$2 per hour. There are two ATMs, both on Comercio near the intersection with Aniceto.

Forty minutes upstream from Rurre is **San Miguel del Bala**, in a beautiful setting, 3 km from the entrance to Madidi. This community lodge gives a good taste of the jungle, offers day trips, well-laid out trails and has en suite cabins where you can stay, bar and a pool fed by a waterfall. It is owned and operated by the indigenous Tacana community. Community tourism is also being developed at **Santa Rosa de Yacuma**, 100 km northeast of Rurre, for information contact **FAN** (page 238).

◉ Madidi and Rurrenabaque listings

For hotel and restaurant price codes, and other relevant information, see Essentials.

● Where to stay

Madidi *p323*

Chalalán Ecolodge is 5 hrs upriver from Rurrenabaque, at San José de Uchupiamonas, in Madidi National Park. La Paz office: Sagárnaga 189, Edif Shopping Doryan, of 22, T02-231 1451; in Rurrenabaque, C Comercio entre Campero y Vaca Díez, T892 2419, www. chalalan.com. This is Bolivia's top ecotourism project, founded by the local Quechua-Tacana community, Conservation International and the Interamerican Development Bank, and now has a well-deserved international reputation. Accommodation is in thatched cabins, and activities include fantastic wildlife-spotting and birdwatching, guided and self-guided trails, river and lake activities, and relaxing in pristine jungle surroundings. 3 day/2 night packages cost US$350 pp (US$320 with shared bath), plus transport to Rurre and national park fees.

San Miguel del Bala, 40-min boat trip upriver from Rurre (office at C Comercio entre Vaca Díez y Santa Cruz), T892 2394, www. sanmigueldelbala.com. 7 cabins in a delightful setting, good bathrooms, nice public areas, good restaurant, attentive staff, 3 days/2 nights cost US$240 pp. Advance booking required. Highly recommended.

Pilón Lajas *p324*
Mapajo, Mapajo Ecoturismo Indígena, Santa Cruz entre Avaroa y Comercio, Rurrenabaque, T892 2317, http://mapajo-ecoturismo-indigena.blogspot.co.uk. A community-run ecolodge 3 hrs by boat from Rurrenebaque has 6 *cabañas* without electricity (take a torch), shared cold showers and a dining room serving traditional meals. 3 days/2 nights cost US$250 pp. You can visit the local community, walk in the forest, go birdwatching, etc. Take insect repellent, wear long trousers and strong footwear. Recommended.

Rurrenabaque *p324*
In high season hotels fill up very quickly.
$$ El Ambaibo, Santa Cruz entre Bolívar y Busch, T892 2107. Includes breakfast and airport transfer, large pool (US$3 for non-guests), parking, a step up from the average in Rurre.
$$ Safari, Comercio on the outskirts downriver (can be a hot walk), T892 2410. A peaceful spot with beautiful garden and comfortable rooms, pool, terrace and a good restaurant. Recommended.
$ Asaí, Vaca Díez y Busch, T892 2439. Electric showers, cheap, quiet, laundry area, courtyard and hammocks, breakfast extra.
$ Beni, Comercio y Arce, along the river, T892 2408. Best rooms have a/c and TV, hot showers, cheaper with fan and without bath, kitchen facilities. Spacious, good service.
$ El Curichal, Comercio 1490, T892 2647, elcurichal@hotmail.com. Nice courtyard, hammocks, laundry and small kitchen facilities, helpful staff, will change cash and TCs. Popular economy option.
$ Hostal Pahuichi, Comercio y Vaca Díez, T892 2558. Some big rooms with electric shower, fan, rooftop views, cheap and good.
$ Mirador del Lobo, upstream end of Comercio, contact through El Lobo in La Paz, T02-245 1640. Cheap rooms in large breezy building overlooking the river, some rooms with electric shower.

$ Oriental, on plaza, T892 2401. Hot showers, fan, small breakfast included, quiet, hammocks in peaceful garden, family-run. A good option.
$ Res Jislene, C Comercio entre La Paz y Beni, T892 2526. Erlan Caldera and family are very hospitable, hot water, fan, hammock area, cheap basic rooms, good breakfast if booked in advance, information, helpful.
$ Santa Ana, Avaroa entre Vaca Díez y Campero, T892 2399. Cheap basic rooms, laundry, pleasant hammock area in garden.

❼ Restaurants

Rurrenabaque *p324*
$$ Camila's, Avaroa y Campero. Daily 0800-0130. International food, *parrillada* on Sun, drinks.pool tables, fast service.
$$ Casa del Campo, Vaca Díez y Avaroa. Daily 0700-2100. Good sandwices, juices, fresh organic food, great salad selection, breakfast, delicious desserts, garden, friendly staff but very slow service.
$$ Juliano's, Santa Cruz entre Bolívar y Avaroa. Daily 1200-1430, 1800-late. French and Italian food, good presentation and service. Recommended.
$$-$ Luna Café, Comercio entre Santa Cruz y Vaca Díez. Open 0800-2200. International meals, pizza, snacks and drinks.
$$-$ Pizzería Italia & Monkey's Bar, Avaroa entre Santa Cruz y Vaca Díez. Open 0900-0100. Big pizzas, imaginative pastas, lively crowd, big screen TV, pool tables.
$ La Cabaña, Santa Cruz, by the river. Mon-Sat 0800-2200, Sun 0800-1600. Wide selection of international and Bolivian food.

Cafés
French Bakery, Vaca Díez entre Avaroa y Bolívar. Mon-Sat 0600-1200. Run by Thierry. Delicious croissants and *pain au chocolat*, get there early.
Moskkito Bar, Vaca Díez y Avaroa. Cool bar for tall jungle tales. Burgers, pizzas, rock music and pool tables.
Pachamama, south end of Avaroa. Open 1200-2230. English/Israeli café/bar, snacks, films (US$3), board games and a book exchange.
Ron, an American expat, drives round town in a kit car offering banana bread, cinnamon rolls,

granola bars and his views on the sad state of the world. Catch him while they're hot, at the corner of Santa Cruz and Avaroa.

❹ What to do

Rurrenabaque *p324*

There are 2 types of tours, jungle or pampas. Both cost about US$80 pp plus US$13.50 park fee for a typical 3-day tour. Prices and quality both vary but booking in Rurre is usually cheaper than in La Paz. Jungle tours normally involve travelling by boat on the Río Beni. Lodging is either in purpose-built camps on higher-end tours, or tents at the budget end. Tours are long enough for most people to get a sense of life in the jungle. In the rainy season the jungle is very hot and humid with many more biting insects and far fewer animals to be seen. In the more open terrain of the Pampas you will see a lot more wildlife. Pampas tours involve 4-hr jeep ride to the Río Yacuma at either end, and a series of boat trips. You may have to wade through knee-deep water; wear appropriate shoes. You might see howler, squirrel and capuchin monkeys, caiman, capybara, pink dolphins, possibly anacondas and a huge variety of birds. You will not see jaguars. One-day trips are not recommended as they spend most of the time travelling, unless going to San Miguel del Bala.

Rurrenabaque has thrived on its steadily increasing number of visitors but also suffered the consequences of haphazard growth in tourism. Not all of the many tour operators here are reputable nor do all tourists in Rurre behave responsibly. Many agencies offer ecologically unsound practices such as fishing, feeding monkeys, catching caiman or handling anaconda. Before signing up for a tour, check the bulletin board at the Dirección Municipal de Turismo and try to talk to other travellers who have just come back. Post your own comments after you return. Go with an established company as competition has been forcing down prices and, consequently, the quality of tours. Some operators pool customers, so you may not go with the company you booked with. There are many more agencies in town than those listed below. Shop around and choose carefully.

Tour operators

Aguilar Tours, Av Avaroa, T892 2478, www.aguilar.lobopages.com. Jungle and pampas tours.

Bala Tours, Av Santa Cruz y Comercio, T3892 2527, www.balatours.com. Arranges Pampas and jungle tours, with their own lodge in each (with bath and solar power). English-speaking guides. Combined trips to Pampas and jungle arranged. Recommended.

Donato Tours, Avaroa entre Pando y Arce, T892 2571, http://donatotours.com. Regular tours plus the opportunity to stay in a community in Pilón Lajas for 1 to 20 days.

Lipiko Tours, Av Santa Cruz s/n, between Bolívar and Avaroa, T892 2221, www.travel-bolivia.co.uk.

Madidi Travel, Comercio y Vaca Díez, T892 2153, in La Paz, Linares 968, T02-231 8313, www.madidi-travel.com. Specializes in tours to the private Serere Sanctuary in the Madidi Mosaic (details on website), minimum 3 days/2 nights, good guiding.

Mashaquipe Tours, Avaroa y Arc,e http://mashaquipe.com.bo. Jungle and pampas tours run by an organization of indigenous families with a lodge in Madidi National Park.

❺ Transport

Caranavi to San Borja *p323*

Bus See page 279 for buses in Caranavi. **Yucumo** is on the La Paz-Caranavi-Rurrenabaque and San Borja bus routes. Rurrenabaque-La Paz bus passes through about 1800. If travelling to Rurrenabaque by bus take extra food in case there is a delay (anything from road blocks to flat tyres to high river levels). **Flota Yungueña** daily except Thu at 1300 from San Borja to **La Paz**, 19 hrs via Caranavi. Also San Borja to **Rurrenabaque**, **Santa Rosa**, **Riberalta**, **Guayaramerín** about 3 times a week. Minibuses and *camionetas* normally run daily between San Borja and **Trinidad** throughout the year, US$15, about 7 hrs including 20 mins crossing of Río Mamoré on ferry barge (up to 14 hrs in wet season). Gasoline available at Yolosa, Caranavi, Yucumo, San Borja and San Ignacio.

Rurrenabaque *p324*
Air Several daily flights to/from **La Paz** with
Amaszonas, Comercio entre Santa Cruz y Vaca
Diez, T892 2472, US$95; and 3 a week with
TAM, Santa Cruz y Avaroa, T892 2398, US$68.
Amaszonas also flies to **Trinidad** and **Santa
Cruz**. Book flights as early as possible and buy
onward ticket on arrival. Check flight times in
advance; they change frequently. Delays and
cancellations are common. Airport taxes US$2.
Airlines provide transport to/from town, US$1.
Bus To/from **La Paz** via Caranavi with
Flota Yungueña, Totaí and Vaca Díez; 18-
20 hrs, US$8.50, daily at 1030 and Sat-Mon
also at 1900. Some continue to **Riberalta**

(US$17, 13 hrs from Rurre), **Guayaramerín**
(US$18, 15 hrs) or **Cobija** (US$32, 30 hrs).
Rurrenebaque-**Riberalta** may take 6 days or
more in the wet season. Take lots of food, torch
and be prepared to work. To **Trinidad**, with
Trans Guaya (buses) or Trans Rurrenabaque
(minibuses) daily, **Flota Yungueña** Mon, Wed,
via **Yucumo** and **San Borja**, US$18, check that
the road is open.

ⓘ Directory
Rurrenabaque *p324*
Immigration Arce entre Bolívar y Busch,
T892 2241, Mon-Fri 0830-1230, 1430-1830,
same-day extensions.

Riberalta to Brazil

Riberalta → *Phone code: 03. Colour map 3, B6. Population: 97,982. Altitude: 175 m.*
This town, at the confluence of the Madre de Dios and Beni rivers, is off the beaten track and
a centre for brazil nut production. It's very laid back, but take care if your bus drops you in the
middle of the night and everything is closed. There are places to eat on the plaza and near the
airport. Change cash in shops and on street.

Guayaramerín and border with Brazil → *Phone code: 03. Colour map 4, C1.*
Population: 39,010.
Guayaramerín is a cheerful, prosperous little town on the bank of the Río Mamoré, opposite
the Brazilian town of Guajará-Mirim. There are several restaurants and cafés around the plaza. It
has an important *Zona Libre*. Passage between the two towns is unrestricted; boat trip US$1.65
(more at night).

Bolivian immigration Avenida Costanera near port; open 0800-1100, 1400-1800. Passports
must be stamped here when leaving, or entering Bolivia. On entering Bolivia, passports must
also be stamped at the Bolivian consulate in Guajará-Mirim. For Brazilian immigration, see
Guajará Mirim, and the Border with Brazil, in the Brazil chapter. The Brazilian consulate is on
24 de Septiembre, Guayaramerín, T855 3766, open 0900-1300, 1400-1700; visas for entering
Brazil are given here. To enter Brazil you must have a yellow fever certificate, or be inoculated at
the health ministry (free). Exchange cash at the dock on the Bolivian side where rates are written
up on blackboards (no traveller's cheques), although there is an ATM at the Banco do Brasil in
Guajará-Mirim; no facilities for cash.

Cobija → *Phone code: 03. Colour map 3, B5. Population: 55,692.*
The capital of the lowland Department of Pando lies on the Río Acre which forms the frontier
with Brazil. A new, single-tower suspension bridge crosses the river to Brasiléia. As a duty-free
zone, shops in centre have a huge selection of imported consumer goods at bargain prices.
Brazilians and Peruvians flock here to stock up. As this is a border area, watch out for scams and
cons. **Bolivian immigration** ⓘ *Av Internacional 567, T842 2081, open daily 0900-1800*. **Brazilian
consulate** ⓘ *Av René Barrientos s/n, T842 2110, , Mon-Fri 0830-1230*. There are *casas de cambio* on
Av Internacional and Av Cornejo. Most shops will accept dollars or reais, and exchange money.

⊙ Riberalta to Brazil listings

For hotel and restaurant price codes, and other relevant information, see Essentials.

● Where to stay

Riberalta *p327*
Ask for a fan and check the water supply.
$$ Colonial, Plácido Méndez 1, T852 3018.
Charming colonial casona, large, well-furnished rooms, no singles, nice gardens and courtyard, comfortable, good beds, helpful owners.
$ Alojamiento Comercial Lazo, NG Salvatierra.
With a/c, cheaper with fan, comfortable, laundry facilities, good value.
$ Res Los Reyes, near airport, T852 2628.
With fan, cheap, safe, pleasant, but noisy disco nearby on Sat and Sun.

Guayaramerín *p327*
$$ San Carlos, 6 de Agosto, 4 blocks from port, T855 3555. With a/c, hot showers, changes dollars cash, TCs and reais, swimming pool, reasonable restaurant.
$ Santa Ana 25 de Mayo, close to airport, T855 3900. With bath, fan, cheap and recommended.

Cobija *p327*
$$ Diana, Av 9 de Febrero 123, T842 3653, www.dianahotel.boliviafull.com. A/c, TV, safe, buffet breakfast, pool.
$$ Nanijos, Av 9 de Febrero 147, T842 2230.
Includes breakfast, a/c, TV, *comedor* does good lunch, helpful.
$$ Triller, Av Internacional 640, T842 2024. With a/c (cheaper with fan) and bath, restaurant.

◑ What to do

Riberalta *p327*
Riberalta Tours, Av Sucre 634, T852 3475, www.riberaltatours.com. Multi-day river and jungle tours, airline tickets, very helpful.

● Transport

Riberalta *p327*
Air Flights to **Trinidad** and **Cobija** with Aerocon (at airport, T852 4679). TAM (Av Suárez Chuquisaca, T852 3924) to **Trinidad, Santa Cruz, Cochabamba** and **La Paz**. Expect cancellations in the wet season.

Bus Roads to all destinations are appalling, even worse in the wet season. Several companies (including **Yungueña**) to **La Paz**, via **Rurrenabaque** and **Caranavi** daily, 35 hrs to 3 days or more, US$27. To **Trinidad** via Rurrenabaque and San Borja, 25-35 hrs. To **Guayaramerín** 7 daily, US$5, 2 hrs. To **Cobija** several companies, none with daily service, 10-11 hrs.
River Cargo boats carry passengers along the **Río Madre de Dios**, but they are infrequent. There are no boats to Rurrenabaque.

Guayaramerín *p327*
Air Daily flights to **Trinidad**, with onward connections, with Aerocon (25 de Mayo y Beni, T855 5025). TAM has same services as for Riberalta.
Bus Buses leave from General Federico Román. Same long-haul services as Riberalta, above. To **Riberalta** 2 hrs, US$5, daily 0700-1730.
River Check the notice of vessels leaving port on the Port Captain's board, prominently displayed near the immigration post on the riverbank. Boats sailing up the Mamoré to **Trinidad** are not always willing to take passengers.

Cobija *p327*
Air Daily flights to **Riberalta** and **Trinidad**, with onward connections, with Aerocon, Leoncio Justiniano 43, T842 4575. TAM (Av 9 de Febrero 49, T842 2267), to **La Paz** or **Trinidad** on alternating days.
Bus Flota Yungueña and Flota Cobija to **La Paz** via Riberalta and Rurrenabaque, 2-3 days or more, US$30-40. To **Riberalta** with several bus companies, depart from 2 de Febrero, most on Wed, Fri, Sun at 0600; good all-weather surface; 2 river crossings on pontoon rafts, takes 10-11 hrs.
Taxi US$0.60 in centre, but more expensive beyond, charging according to time and distance, expensive over the international bridge to Brasiléia. Besides taxis there are motorbike taxis (US$0.60). **Brasiléia** can also be reached by **canoe**, US$0.35. The bridge can be crossed on foot as well, although one should be dressed neatly in any case when approaching

Brazilian customs. Entry/exit stamps (free) are necessary and yellow fever vaccination certificate also, when crossing into Brazil. From Brasiléia **Real Norte**, has buses to **Rio Branco**, US$7.60, and **Assis Brasil**, US$4, and Taxis **Brasileiros** run to Rio Branco, US$10.

Cochabamba to Trinidad

Villa Tunari to the Lowlands
Another route into Beni Department is via the lowland road between Cochabamba and Santa Cruz. At Ivirgazama, east of Villa Tunari, the road passes the turn-off to **Puerto Villarroel**, 27 km further north, from where cargo boats ply irregularly to Trinidad in about four to 10 days. You can get information from the Capitanía del Puerto notice board, or ask at docks. There are only a few basic places to sleep in Villarroel and very few stores.

Trinidad → *Phone code: 03. Colour map 6, A3. Population: 101,293. Altitude: 327 m.*
The hot and humid capital of the lowland Beni Department is a dusty city in the dry season, with many streets unpaved. Primarily a service centre for the surrounding ranches and communities, most travellers find themselves in the area for boats up and down the Río Mamoré. There are two ports, Almacén and Varador, check at which one your boat will be docked. Puerto Varador is 13 km from town on the Río Mamoré on the road between Trinidad and San Borja; cross the river over the main bridge by the market, walk down to the service station by the police checkpoint and take a truck, US$1.70. Almacén is 8 km from the city. The main mode of transport in Trinidad is the motorbike (even for taxis, US$0.40 in city); rental on plaza from US$2 per hour, US$8 per half day. Transport can be arranged from the airport. **Tourist office** ⓘ *in the Prefectura building at Joaquín de Sierra y La Paz, ground floor, T462 4831, www.trinidad.gob.bo; also at Centro de Informacion Turistica, 6 de Agosto, next to Hotel Campanario.*

About 5 km from town is the Laguna Suárez, with plenty of wildlife; swimming is safe where the locals swim, near the café with the jetty (elsewhere there are stingrays and alligators). Motorbike taxi from Trinidad, US$1.30.

San Ignacio de Moxos → *Electricity is supplied in town from 1200-2400.*
San Ignacio de Moxos, 90 km west of Trinidad, is known as the folklore capital of the Beni Department. It's a quiet town with a mainly indigenous population; 60% are *Macheteros*, who speak their own language. San Ignacio still maintains the traditions of the Jesuit missions with big *fiestas*, especially during Holy Week and the **Fiesta del Santo Patrono de Moxos**, the largest festival in the Beni, at the end of July.

ⓒ Cochabamba to Trinidad listings

For hotel and restaurant price codes, and other relevant information, see Essentials.

● Where to stay

Trinidad *p329*
$$$$ Flotel Reina de Enín, river cruise, see What to do, below.
$$ Campanario, 6 de Agosto 80, T462 4733. Rooms with a/c and frigobar, meeting room, restaurant, bar, pool.
$$ Jacaranda Suites, La Paz entre Pedro de la Rocha y 18 de Noviembre, T462 2446.

Good services, restaurant, pool, meeting rooms, internet.
$ Copacabana, Tomás Villavicencio, 3 blocks from plaza, T462 2811. Good value, some beds uncomfortable, cheaper with shared bath, helpful staff.
$ Monteverde, 6 de Agosto 76, T462 2750. With a/c (cheaper with fan), frigobar, owner speaks English. Recommended.
$ Res 18 de Noviembre, Av 6 de Agosto 135, T462 1272. With and without bath, welcoming, laundry facilities.

San Ignacio de Moxos *p329*
There are some cheap *alojamientos* on and around the main plaza.

Restaurants

Trinidad *p329*
$$ Club Social 18 de Noviembre, N Suárez y Vaca Díez on plaza. Good value lunch, lively, popular with locals.
$$ El Tábano, Villavicencio entre Mamore y Nestor Suarez. Good fish and local fare, relaxed atmosphere.
$$ La Estancia, Barrio Pompeya, on Ibare entre Muibe y Velarde. Excellent steaks.
$$ Pescadería El Moro, Bolívar 707 y 25 de Diciembre. Excellent fish. Also several good fish restaurants in Barrio Pompeya, south of plaza across river.
$ La Casona, Plaza Ballivián. Good pizzas and set lunch, closed Tue.
Heladería Oriental, on plaza. Good coffee, ice-cream, cakes, popular with locals.

What to do

Trinidad *p329*
Most agents offer excursions to local *estancias* and jungle tours. Most *estancias* can also be reached independently in 1 hr by hiring a motorbike.
Flotel Reina de Enín, Av Comunidad Europea 624, T 7391 2965, www.amazoncruiser.com. bo. Cruises on the Mamoré River within in the Ibaré-Mamoré Reserve. Comfortable berths with bath, US$445 pp for 3 day/2 night cruise includes all activities: dolphin watching, horse riding, visiting local communities, jungle walks, swimming and piranha fishing.
La Ruta del Bufeo, T462 7739, www.laruta delbufeo.blogspot.com. Specializes in river tours for seeing dolphins.
Moxos, 6 de Agosto 114, T462 1141. Multi-day river and jungle tours with camping. Recommended.
Paraíso Travel, 6 de Agosto 138, T462 0692. Offers excursions to Laguna Suárez, Rio Mamoré, camping and birdwatching tours.

Transport

Villa Tunari to the Lowlands: Puerto Villarroel *p329*
From Cochabamba you can get a bus to **Puerto Villarroel** (see Cochabamba Transport, Bus), **Puerto San Francisco**, or **Todos Santos** on the Río Chapare.

Trinidad *p329*
Air Daily flights with **Aerocon** (6 de Agosto y 18 de Noviembre, T462 4442) and **TAM** (Bolívar 42, T462 2363) to La Paz, Santa Cruz, Cochabamba, Cobija, Riberalta and Guayaramerín (Aerocon also to Sucre).
Amazonas (18 de Noviembre 267, T462 2426) Mon, Wed, Fri to **Rurrenabaque**. Airport, T462 0678. Mototaxi to airport US$1.20.
Bus Bus station is on Rómulo Mendoza, between Beni and Pinto, 9 blocks east of main plaza. Motorbike taxis will take people with backpacks from bus station to centre for US$0.45. To **Santa Cruz** (10 hrs on a paved road, US$8-18) and **Cochabamba** (US$12-17, 20 hrs), with **Copacabana**, **Mopar** and **Bolívar** mostly overnight (*bus cama* available). To **Rurrenabaque**, US$18, 12-20 hrs. Enquire locally what services are running to San Borja and **La Paz**. Similarly to **Riberalta** and **Guayaramerín**.
River Cargo boats down the Río Mamoré to **Guayaramerín** take passengers, 3-4 days, assuming no breakdowns, best organized from Puerto Varador (speak to the Port Captain). **Argos** is recommended as friendly, US$22 pp, take water, fresh fruit, toilet paper and ear-plugs; only for the hardy traveller.

San Ignacio de Moxos *p329*
Bus The Trinidad to San Borja bus stops at the **Donchanta** restaurant for lunch, otherwise difficult to find transport to San Borja. Minibus to Trinidad daily at 0730 from plaza, also *camionetas*, check road conditions and times beforehand.

Santa Cruz and Eastern Lowlands

In contrast to the highlands of the Andes and the gorges of the Yungas, eastern Bolivia is made up of vast plains stretching to the Chaco of Paraguay and the Pantanal wetlands of Brazil. Agriculture is well developed and other natural resources are fully exploited, bringing a measure of prosperity to the region. There are a number of national parks with great biodiversity, such as Amboró and Noel Kempff Mercado. Historical interest lies in the pre-Inca ceremonial site at Samaipata, the beautiful Jesuit Missions of Chiquitos and, of much more recent date, the trails and villages where Che Guevara made his final attempt to bring revolution to Bolivia.

Santa Cruz → *Phone code: 03. Colour map 6, A4. Population: 1,566,000. Altitude: 416 m.*

A little over 50 years ago, what is now Bolivia's largest city was a remote backwater, but rail and road links ended its isolation. The exploitation of oil and gas in the Departments of Santa Cruz and Tarija, and a burgeoning agribusiness sector, helped fuel rapid development. Since the election of Evo Morales in 2006 however, *Cruceños* have been concerned about the impact of his economic policies, perceived as favouring the highlands. There is considerable local opposition to the national government and Santa Cruz has spearheaded the eastern lowland departments' drive for greater autonomy from La Paz. The city is modern and busy, far removed from most travellers' perceptions of Bolivia. The centre still retains a bit of its former air, however, and the main plaza – 24 de Septiembre – is well cared for and a popular meeting place. During the extended lunchtime hiatus locals (who call themselves *cambas*) take refuge in their homes from the heat or rain, and the gridlock traffic eases. December to March is the hottest and rainiest time of the year.

Arriving in Santa Cruz

Orientation The International **airport** is at **Viru-Viru**, 13 km from the centre, reached by taxi or micro. Regional flights operate from **El Trompillo** airport, south of the centre on the Segundo Anillo. Long distance and regional **buses** leave from the combined bus/train terminal, **Terminal Bimodal**, Avenida Montes on the Tercer Anillo. The city has eight ring roads, Anillos 1, 2, 3, 4 and so on, the first three of which contain most sites of interest to visitors. The neighbourhood of Equipetrol, where many upscale hotels, restaurants and bars are situated, is northwest of the centre in the Tercer (3rd) Anillo.

Tourist information There is a **departmental tourist office** ① *Junín 22 on main plaza, T334 6776, Mon-Fri 0800-1200, 1500-1800; also a desk at Viru-Viru airport, 0700-2000.* **InfoTur** ① *Sucre y Potosí, inside the Museo de Arte, T339 9581, Mon-Fri 0800-1200, 1500-1900.* **APAC** ① *Av Busch 552 (2nd Anillo), T333 2287, www.festivalesapac.com,* has information about cultural events in the department of Santa Cruz. See also **www.destinosantacruz.com**.

Health and safety Dengue fever outbreaks are common during the wet season (Jan-Mar), take mosquito precautions. Take great care in crowds and market areas and take only radio taxis at night. ▶▶ *See also Safety, page 243.*

Places in Santa Cruz

The Plaza 24 de Septiembre is the city's main square with the huge **Cathedral** (also a basilica) ① *museum, T332 4683, Mon-Fri 1500-1800, US$1.50.* You can climb to a mirador in the cathedral **bell tower** ① *daily 0800-1200, 1500-1900, US$0.50,* with nice views of the city. **Manzana Uno**, the block behind the Cathedral, has been set aside for rotating art and cultural exhibits. **El Casco Viejo**, the heart of the city, with its arcaded streets and buildings with low, red-tiled roofs and overhanging eaves, retains a slight colonial feel, despite the profusion of modern, air-conditioned shops and restaurants. The **Museo de Historia** ① *Junín 141, T336 5533, Mon-Fri 0800-1200, 1500-1830, free* has several displays including archaeological pieces from the Chané and Guaraní cultures and explorers' routes. **Museo de Arte Contemporáneo** ① *Sucre y Potosí,*

Santa Cruz

To ⑥⑨, Av San Martín & Barrio Equipetrol

To ③④⑩, Av Monseñor Rivero & Viru-Viru Airport

Where to stay ⬤
1 Bibosi *B1*
2 Copacabana *B1*
3 Cortez *A2*
4 Hostal Río Magdalena *B3*
5 Jodanga *D3*
6 Los Tajibos *A1*
7 Milan *B2*
8 Res Bolívar *B2*
9 Royal Lodge *A1*
10 Sarah *B1*
11 Senses *B2*
12 Villa Magna *B3*

Restaurants ⑦
1 Alexander Coffee *B2*
2 Café 24 & Café Lorca *B2*
3 El Chile *D3*
4 Freddo *A2*
5 Fridolín *B2*
6 Horno Caliente *D2*
7 Ken *B3*
8 La Casona *B2*
9 La Creperie *B2*
10 Los Hierros *A2*
11 Los Lomitos *B3*
12 Michelangelo *C2*
13 Pizzería Marguerita *B2*
14 Rincón Brasilero *B2*
15 Su Salud *B3*
16 Tapekuá *C2*
17 Vegetarian Center *B3*

Bars & clubs ⑦
18 Café Irlandés *B2*

T334 0926, Mon-Fri 0900-1200, 1500-2000, Sat-Sun 1500-1900, free, houses contemporary Bolivian and international art in a nicely restored old house.

Some 12 km on the road to Cotoca are the **Botanical Gardens** ① *micro or trufi from C Suárez Arana, 15 mins, open daily 0800-1700, entry US$0.50,* a bit run-down but with many walking trails, birds and several forest habitats. **Parque Ecológico Yvaga Guazu** ① *Km 12.5 Doble Vía a La Guardia, taxi US$5, T352 7971, www.parqueyvagaguazu.org, daily 0800-1600, US$9 for 2-hr guided tour in Spanish (more for English-speaking guide),* 14 ha of tropical gardens with native and exotic species, plants for sale, restaurant serves Sunday buffet lunch. **Biocentro Güembé** ① *Km 7 Camino a Porongo, taxi US$7, T370 0700, www.biocentroguembe.com, daily 0830-1800, US$13 includes guided tour in Spanish or English,* is a resort with accommodation (**$$$** range), restaurant, butterfly farm, walk-in aviary, swimming pools and other family recreation.

◉ Santa Cruz listings

For hotel and restaurant price codes, and other relevant information, see Essentials.

◉ Where to stay

Santa Cruz *p331, map p332*

$$$$ Los Tajibos, Av San Martín 455, Barrio Equipetrol, 1342 1000, www.lustajiboshotel. com. Set in 6 ha of lush gardens, one of several hotels in this price bracket in the city and the most traditional, all facilities including business centre, art gallery, restaurants and spa. Weekend discounts.

$$$ Cortez, Cristóbal de Mendoza 280 (Segundo Anillo), T333 1234, www.hotelcortez. com. Traditional tropical hotel with restaurant, pool, gardens, meeting rooms, parking, good location for dining and nightlife.

$$$ Royal Lodge, Av San Martín 200, Equipetrol, T343 8000. With restaurant and bar, pool, airport transfers. Excellent option for its location and price range.

$$$ Senses, Sucre y 24 de Septiembre, just off main plaza, 1339 6666, www.sensescorp.com. Self-styled boutique hotel in the heart of the city, minimalist decor, includes all services.

$$$ Villa Magna, Barrón 70, T339 9700, www. villamagna-aparthotel.com. Fully furnished apartments with small pool, Wi-Fi, parking, attentive owner and staff, English and German spoken, from daily to monthly rates.

$$-$ Hostal Río Magdalena, Arenales 653 (no sign), T339 3011, www.hostalrio magdalena.com. Comfortable rooms, downstairs ones are dark, with a/c or fan, small yard and pool, popular.

$$ Bibosi, Junín 218, T334 8548, htlbibosi@ hotmail.com. Includes breakfast, private bath, electric shower, a/c, cheaper with fan, Wi-Fi in lobby, good value.

$$ Copacabana, Junín 217, T336 2770, hotelcopacabanascz@hotmail.com. Very good, popular with European tour groups, rooms cheaper without a/c, restaurant.

$$ Jodanga, C El Fuerte 1380, Zona Parque Urbano, Barrio Los Chóferes, T339 6542, www.jodanga.com. Good backpacker option 10 mins' walk from Terminal Bimodal, cheaper with fan and without bath, cheaper still in dorm, kitchen, bar, swimming pool, billiards, DVDs, nice communal areas, laundry, helpful owner and multilingual staff.

$ Milán, René Moreno 70, T339 7500, www.hotelmilan.web.bo. Some rooms with a/c, hot water, central location.

$ Res Bolívar, Sucre 131, T334 2500, www.residencialbolivar.com. Includes good breakfast, cheaper with shared bath and in dorm, lovely courtyard with hammocks, rooms can get hot, alcohol prohibited, popular.

$ Sarah, C Sara 85, T332 2425, hotel.sarah@ hotmail.com. Simple rooms which cost less without a/c, screened windows, small patio, good value.

❶ Restaurants

Santa Cruz *p331, map p332*

Santa Cruz has the best meat in Bolivia, try a local *churrasquería* (grill). Av San Martín in Barrio Equipetrol, and Av Monseñor Rivero are the areas for upmarket restaurants and nightlife. Both are away from the centre, take a taxi at night. Some restaurants close Mon.

$$$-$$ La Creperie, Arenales 135. Mon-Sat 1900-2400. Serves good crêpes, fondues and salads.

$$$-$$ Los Hierros, Av Monseñor Rivero 300 y Castelnau. Daily 1200-1500, 1900-2400. Popular upmarket grill with salad bar.

$$$-$$ Michelangelo, Chuquisaca 502. Mon-Fri 1200-1430, 1900-2330, Sat evenings only. Excellent Italian cuisine, a/c.

$$ Ken, Uruguay 730 (1er Anillo), T333 3728. 1130-1430, 1800-2300, closed Wed. Sushi and authentic Japanese food, popular.

$$ La Casona, Arenales 222, T337 8495. Open 1130-1500, 1900-2400. German-run restaurant, very good food.

$$ Pizzería Marguerita, Junín y Libertad, northwest corner of the plaza. Open 0830-2400. A/c, good service, coffee, bar. Popular with expats, Finnish owner speaks English and German.

$$ Rincón Brasilero, Libertad 358. Daily 1130-1430,1930-2330. Brazilian-style buffet for lunch, pay by weight, very good quality and variety, popular; pizza and à la carte at night. Recommended.

$$ Tapekuá, Ballivián y La Paz, T334 5905. French and international food, good service, live entertainment some evenings.

$$-$ El Chile, Av Las Américas 60. Daily 1200-1500, 1700-2400. Mexican and Bolivian food, good set lunch with salad bar, à la carte at night.

$$-$ Los Lomitos, Uruguay 758 (1er Anillo), T332 8696. Daily 0800-2400. Traditional *churrasquería* with unpretentious local atmosphere, excellent Argentine-style beef.

$$-$ Vegetarian Center, Aroma 64, entre Bolívar y Sucre. Mon-Sat 1200-1500. Set lunch or pay-by-weight buffet.

$ Pizzería El Horno, 3er Anillo, frente a Hospital Oncológico, Equipetrol, T342 8042; also Av Roque Aguilera 600, Las Palmas; and Lagunillas 134, Braniff. Daily 1100-2300. True Italian pizza, very popular.

$ Su Salud, Quijarro 115. Mon-Thu 0800-2100, Fri and Sun 0800-1700. Tasty vegetarian food, filling lunches, sells vegetarian products.

Cafés
There are lots of very pleasant a/c cafés where you can get coffee, ice cream, drinks, and snacks.

Alexander Coffee, Junín y Libertad near main plaza, and Av Monseñor Rivero 400 y Santa Fe. For good coffee and people watching.

Café 24, downstairs at René Moreno y Sucre, on the main plaza. Daily 0830-0200. Breakfast, juices, international meals, wine rack, nice atmosphere, Wi-Fi.

Café Lorca, upstairs at René Moreno y Sucre, on the main plaza. Mon-Thu 0900-0100, Fri-Sat 0900-0300, Sun 1800-2400. Meals and drinks, Spanish wines, small balcony with views over plaza, live music Tue-Sat from 2100, part of a cultural project, see www.lorcasantacruz.org.

Freddo, Monseñor Rivero 245. Good expensive ice cream imported from Argentina.

Fridolín, 21 de Mayo 168, Pari 254, Av Cañoto y Florida, and Monseñor Rivero y Cañada Strongest. All good places for coffee and pastries.

Horno Caliente, Chuquisaca 604 y Moldes, also 24 de Septiembre 653. Salteñas 0730-1230, traditional local snacks and sweets 1530-1930. Popular and very good.

🕐 Bars and clubs

Santa Cruz *p331, map p332*
Bar Irlandés Irish Pub, 3er Anillo Interno 1216 (between Av Cristo Redentor and Zoológico). Irish-themed pub, food available, Irish owner, live music Wed, Fri and Sat evenings. Also *Café Irlandés*, Plaza 24 de Septiembre, overlooking main plaza. Popular.

Kokopelli, Noel Kempff Mercado 1202 (3er Anillo Interno), bar with Mexican food and live music.

⊛ Festivals

Santa Cruz *p331, map p332*
Cruceños are famous as fun-lovers and their music, the *carnavalitos*, can be heard all over South America. Of the various festivals, the brightest is **Carnaval**, renowned for riotous behaviour, celebrated for the **15 days before Lent**: music in the streets, dancing, fancy dress and the coronation of a queen. Water and

paint throwing is common – no one is exempt. **24 Sep** is the local holiday of Santa Cruz city and department.

The Festival de Música Renacentista y Barroca Americana "Misiones de Chiquitos" is held in late Apr through early May every even year (next in 2014) in Santa Cruz and the Jesuit mission towns of the Chiquitania. It is organized by Asociación Pro Arte y Cultura (APAC), Av Busch 552, Santa Cruz, T333 2287, www.festivalesapac.com, and celebrates the wealth of sacred music written by Europeans and indigenous composers in the 17th and 18th centuries. APAC sells books, CDs, and videos and also offers – in both Santa Cruz and the mission towns – a schedule of musical programmes. The festival is very popular: book hotels at least 2-3 weeks in advance. Every odd year the city of Santa Cruz APAC holds a Festival Internacional de Teatro, and every Aug and Dec a Festival de la Temporada in Santa Cruz and major towns of Chiquitania, featuring *musica misional* with local performers.

Cultural centres with events and programmes: Centro Cultural Santa Cruz, René Moreno 369, T335 6941, www.culturabcb.org.bo. Centro Simón I Patiño, Independencia y Suárez de Figueroa 89, T 337 2425, www.fundacionpatino.org. Exhibitions, galleries, and bookstore on Bolivian cultures. See also Centro Boliviano Americano, Cochabamba 66, T334 2299, www.cba.com.bo; Centro Cultural Franco Alemán, 24 de Septiembre on main plaza, T335 0142, www.ccfrancoaleman.org; Centro de Formación de la Cooperación Española, Arenales 583, T335 1311, www.aecid-cf.bo. For cinema, Cine Center, Ave El Trompillo (2do Anillo) entre Monseñor Santiesteban y René Moreno, www.cinecenter.com.bo.

O Shopping

Santa Cruz *p331, map p332*
Handicrafts Bolivian Souvenirs, Shopping Bolívar, loc 10 & 11, on main plaza, T333 7805; also at Viru-Viru airport. Expensive knitwear and crafts from all over Bolivia. Paseo Artesanal La Recova, off Libertad, ½ block from Plaza. Many different kiosks selling crafts. Vicuñita Handicrafts, Ingavi e Independencia, T333

4711. Wide variety of crafts from the lowlands and the altiplano, very good.
Jewellery Carrasco, Velasco 23, T336 2841, and other branches. For gemstones. RC Joyas, Bolívar 262, T333 2725. Jewellery and Bolivian gems.
Markets Los Pozos, between Quijarro, Campero, Suárez Arana and 6 de Agosto; is a sprawling street market for all kinds of produce. Siete Calles, Isabel la Católica y Vallegrande, mainly clothing. Mercado Nuevo, at Sucre y Cochabamba.

O What to do

Santa Cruz *p331, map p332*
Bird Bolivia, T358 2674, www.birdbolivia com. Specializes in organized birding tours, English spoken
Forest Tour, Galeria Casco Viejo, upstairs, No 115, T337 2042, www.forestbolivia.com. Environmentally sensitive tours to Refugio los Volcanes, bird watching, national parks, Chiquitania and Salar de Uyuni. English spoken.
Magri Turismo, Velarde 49 y Irala, T334 4559, www.magriturismo.com. Long-established agency for airline tickets and tours.
Misional Tours, Los Motojobobos 2515, T360 1985, www.misionaltours.com. Covers all of Bolivia, specializing in Chiquitania, Amboró, and Santa Cruz. Tours in various languages.
Ruta Verde, 21 de Mayo 318, T339 6470, www.rutaverdebolivia.com. Offers national parks, Jesuit missions, Amazonian boat trips, Salar de Uyuni, and tailor-made tours, Dutch/ Bolivian owned, English and German also spoken, knowlegdeable and helpful.

⊖ Transport

Santa Cruz *p331, map p332*
Air Viru-Viru, open 24 hrs, airline counters from 0600; *casa de cambio* changing cash US$ and euros at poor rates, 0630-2100; various ATMs; luggage lockers 0600-2200, US$5.50 for 24 hrs; ENTEL for phones and internet, plus a few eateries. Taxi US$10, micro from Ex-Terminal (see below), or El Trompillo, US$1, 45 min. From airport take micro to Ex-Terminal then taxi to centre. Domestic flights with Boliviana de Aviación (BoA) and TAM (Bolivia),

to **La Paz**, **Cochabamba**, **Sucre**, **Tarija** and **Cobija**. International flights to **Asunción**, **Buenos Aires**, **Salta**, **Lima**, **Madrid**, **Miami**, **Washington**, **Santiago** and **São Paulo**.

El Trompillo is the regional airport operating daily 0500-1900, T352 6600, located south of the centre on the Segundo Anillo. It has a phone office and kiosk selling drinks, but no other services. Taxi US$1.50, many micros. **TAM** has flights throughout the country, different destinations on different days. **Aerocon** flies via **Trinidad** to various towns in the northern jungle.

Bus Most long distance buses leave from the combined bus/train terminal, **Terminal Bimodal**, Av Montes on the Tercer Anillo, T348 8382; police check passports and search luggage here; taxi to centre, US$1.50. Terminal fee, US$0.50, left luggage US$0.50, there are ATMs and cambios. Regional buses and vans leave either from behind the Terminal Bimodal (use pedestrian tunnel under the rail tracks) or from near the Ex-Terminal (the old bus station, Av Irala y Av Cañoto, 1er Anillo, which is no longer functioning). To **Cochabamba**, via the lowland route, many depart 0600-0930 and 1630-2130, US$8-16, 8-10 hrs, also Trans Carrasco vans leave when full across the street from the Terminal Bimodal, US$15; via the old highland route, **Trans Carrasco**, depart from the main plaza in El Torno, 30 km west of Santa Cruz, daily at 1200 (from Mairana daily at 0800 and 1500), US$6, 14 hrs. Direct to **Sucre** via Aiquile, around 1600, US$7.50-15, 12-13hrs. To **Oruro**, US$11-20, 14-15 hrs, and **La Paz** between 1630-1900, US$11-25, 15-16 hrs; change in Cochabamba for daytime travel. To **Camiri** (US$4, 4-5 hrs), **Yacuiba** (border with Argentina), US$7-16, 8 hrs and **Tarija**, US$13-26, 17-24 hrs. To **Trinidad**, several daily after 2000, 9 hrs, US$7-15. To **San José de Chiquitos**, US$7-10, 5 hrs, **Roboré**, US$7-10, 7 hrs, and **Quijarro** (border with Brazil), at 1030 and between 1700-2000, US$12-22, 8-10 hrs. Also vans to San José, leave when full, US$10, 4½ hrs. To **San Ignacio de Velasco**, US$10, 10 hrs; **Jenecherú** bus-cama US$18; also **Expreso San Ignacio** vans leave when full, US$20, 8 hrs.

International: Terminal fee US$1.50. To **Asunción**, US$52-64, 20-24 hrs via Villamontes and the Chaco, at 1930, with **Yacyretá**,

T362 5557, Mon, Tue, Thu, Sat; **Stel Turismo**, T349 7762, daily; **Pycazú**, daily, and **Palma Loma**. Other companies are less reliable. See page 339 for the route to Paraguay across the Chaco. To **Buenos Aires** daily departures around 1900, US$70-90, 36 hrs, several companies. To São Paulo via Puerto Suárez, with **La Preferida**, T364 7160, Mon, Wed, Fri, US$140, 2 days.

Taxi About US$1-1.50 inside 1er Anillo (more at night), US$2 inside 3er Anillo, fix fare in advance. Use radio-taxis at night (eg **Matico**, T335 6666).

Train Ferroviaria Oriental, at Terminal Bimodal, T338 7300, www.fo.com.bo, runs east to **San José de Chiquitos**, **Roboré** and **Quijarro** on the Brazilian border. The **Ferrobus** (a rail-car with the fastest most luxurious service) leaves Santa Cruz Tue, Thu, Sun 1800, arriving Quijarro 0700 next day, US$33.60; **Expreso Oriental** (an express train), Mon, Wed, Fri 1450, arriving 0729, US$14.30; There is also little-used weekly train service south to **Yacuiba** on the Argentine frontier; buses are much faster.

ⓘ Directory

Santa Cruz p331, map p332
Car hire Avis, Av Cristo Redentor Km. 3.5, T343 3939, www.avis.com.bo. **Barron's**, Av Alemana 50 y Tajibos, T342 0160. Outstanding service and completely trustworthy. IMBEX, C El Carmen 123, entre Av Suárez Arana y Av Charcas, T311 1000, www.imbex.com. Localiza, Cristo Redentor entre 2do y 3er Anillo, T341 4343; also at airport, T341 4343; www. localiza.com. **Medical services** Santa Cruz is an important medical centre with many hospitals and private clinics. Clínica Foianini, Av Irala 468, www.clinicafoianini.com, is among the better regarded and more expensive; San Juan de Dios, Cuellar y España, is the public hospital. **Useful addresses** Immigration, Av El Trompillo (2do Anillo) near El Deber newspaper, T351 9574, Mon-Fri 0830-1200, 1430-1800; busy office, give yourself extra time. Fundación Amigos de la Naturaleza (FAN), Km 7.5 Vía a La Guadria, T355 6800, www.fan-bo.org. SERNAP, Calle 9 Oeste 138, frente a la Plaza Italia, Barrio Equipetrol, T339 4310, Mon-Fri 0800-1200, 1400-1800.

Southwest of Santa Cruz

The highlights of this area known as Los Valles Cruceños, are southwest of Santa Cruz: the Inca site of El Fuerte by the pleasant resort town of Samaipata, nearby Parque Nacional Amboró and the Che Guevara Trail, on which you can follow in the final, fatal footsteps of the revolutionary.

Samaipata → *Phone code: 03. Colour map M6, A4. Population 3000. Altitude: 1650 m.*

From Santa Cruz the old mountain road to Cochabamba runs along the Piray gorge and up into the highlands. Some 100 km from Santa Cruz is Samaipata, a great place to relax midweek, with good lodging, restaurants, hikes and riding, and a growing ex-pat community. A two-hour walk takes you to the top of Cerro de La Patria, just east of town, with nice views of the surrounding valleys. Local *artesanías* include ceramics, paintings and sculpture. At weekends the town bursts into life as crowds of Cruceños come to escape the city heat and to party. See www.samaipata. info and www.guidetosamaipata.com.

The **Museo de Arqueología** houses the tourist information office and a collection of ceramics with anthropomorphic designs, dating from 200 BC to AD 300, and provides information on the nearby pre-Inca ceremonial site commonly called **El Fuerte** ① *daily 0900-1630, museum Mon-Fri 0830-1200, 1400-1800, Sat-Sun 0830-1600, US$8 for El Fuerte and Museum, US$0.85 for museum only, ticket valid 4 days, Spanish- and English-speaking guides available at El Fuerte, US$12.* This sacred structure (altitude 1990 m) consists of a complex system of channels, basins, high-relief sculptures, etc, carved out of one vast slab of rock. Some suggest that Amazonian people created it around 1500 BC, but it could be later. There is evidence of subsequent occupations and that it was the nethermost outpost of the Incas' Kollasuyo (their eastern empire). Behind the rock are poorly excavated remains of a city. It is not permitted to

Samaipata

To Mairana, Mataral, Comarapa, Vallegrande, Sucre & Cochabamba

*To El Fuerte (9 km),
Bermejo & Santa Cruz*

To Cerro de la Patria

Cornejo · Arteaga · Perez · Muñilo · Terrazas · Bolívar · Campero · Sucre · Aranales · 27 de Mayo · Talamas · Saldías · El Comandante · Av Jumbari · Espejos · Warnes · Saavedra · Arce

Parque Aeronáutico

Museo Arqueológico

Jumbari Tours

Road Runners

Michael Blendinger Tours

To Santa Cruz Plaza

Ben Verhoef Tours

Tucandera Tours

Taxis to Santa Cruz

To ⑤ & Valleabajo

To La Pajcha Waterfall (40 km)

N
Not to scale

Where to stay 🛌
1 Andoriña
2 El Jardín
3 El Pueblito Resort
4 Hostal Siles
5 Landhaus
6 La Posada del Sol
7 La Víspera
8 Res Kim
9 Res Paola

Restaurants 🍴
1 Café 1900
2 Chakana & La Cocina
3 El Descanso en Las Alturas
4 El Nuevo Turista
5 La Bohème
6 La Mexicana
7 Latina Café
8 Tierra Libre

walk on the rock, so visit the museum first to see the excellent model. El Fuerte is 9 km from Samaipata; 3 km along the highway to Santa Cruz, then 6 km up a rough, signposted road (taxi US$6 one way, US$13 return with two hours wait); two to three hours' walk one way. Pleasant bathing is possible in a river on the way to El Fuerte.

In addition to tours to El Fuerte and the Ruta del Che (see below), many other worthwhile excursions can be made in the Samaipata area. Impressive forests of giant ferns can be visited around **Cerro La Mina** and elsewhere in the Amboró buffer zone. Also **Cuevas**, 20 km east of town, with waterfalls and pools, often visited together with El Fuerte. Further east are forest and sandstone mountains at **Bella Vista/Codo de los Andes**. There is a wonderful hike up to the **Mirador de Cóndores**, with many condors and nearby the the 25-m-high **La Pajcha** waterfall, 40 km south of Samaipata. **Postrervalle** is a quaint hamlet with many interesting walks and mountain bike trails. There is good birdwatching throughout the region, especially around Mataral (see below), and tour operators in Samaipata can arrange all of the above trips.

The little village of **Bermejo**, 40 km east of Samaipata on the road to Santa Cruz, provides access to the strikingly beautiful **Serranía Volcanes** region, abutting on Parque Nacional Amboró. Here is the excellent **Refugio Los Volcanes** ① *T03-337 2042, www.refugiovolcanes.net*, a small lodge with a 15-km trail system, with good birdwatching, orchids and bromeliads. Ginger's Paradise, some 2 km from Bermejo (www.gingersparadise.com), offers an organic, communal alternative, popular with backpackers (you can work to offset some room costs).

Comarapa and the highland road to Cochabamba

Past Samaipata the road from Santa Cruz continues west 17 km to **Mairana**, a hot dusty roadside town where long-distance buses make their meal stops and there is daily service to Cochabamba (see Santa Cruz transport, page 336). It is 51 km further to **Mataral**, where there are petroglyphs and the road to Vallegrande branches south. Another 57 km west is **Comarapa** (altitude 1800 m), a tranquil agricultural centre half-way between Santa Cruz and Cochabamba. The town provides access to several lovely natural areas including **Laguna Verde** (12 km, taxi US$11.50 with two hours wait, or walk back over the hills), surrounded by cloud forest bordering Parque Nacional Amboró; and the **Jardín de Cactáceas de Bolivia**, where the huge *carpari* cactus and 25 other endemic species may be seen (entry US$0.75, take a *trufi* from Comarapa to Pulquina Abajo, US$1). The Jardín itself is run-down but there are many more impressive cactii, good walking and birdwatching throughout the area. The tourist office at El Parquecito in Comarapa can arrange local guides. Beyond Comarapa the road is unpaved and very scenic. It climbs through cloud forest past the village of **La Siberia** to the pass at El Churo and enters the department of Cochabamba (see page 318).

Parque Nacional Amboró

This vast (442,500 ha) protected area lies only three hours west of Santa Cruz. Amboró encompasses four distinct major ecosystems and 11 life zones and is home to thousands of animal, plant and insect species (it is reputed to contain more butterflies than anywhere else on earth). The park is home to over 850 species of birds, including the blue-horned curassow, quetzal and cock-of-the-rock, red and chestnut-fronted macaws, hoatzin and cuvier toucans, and most mammals native to Amazonia, such as capybaras, peccaries, tapirs, several species of monkey, and jungle cats like the jaguar, ocelot and margay, and the spectacled bear. There are also numerous waterfalls and cool, green swimming pools, moss-ridden caves and large tracts of virgin rainforest. The park itself is largely inaccessible, but there is good trekking in the surrounding 195,100-ha buffer zone which is where most tours operate. The best time of year to visit the park is during April to October. There are two places to base yourself: Samaipata (see above) to access the southern highland areas of the park, and Buena Vista (see below) for northern lowland sections. You cannot enter the park without a guide, either from a tour operator, or from a community-based project. The park is administered by **SERNAP**, for their Santa Cruz office see page 336. There are also park offices in Samaipata and Buena Vista. Note that there are many biting insects so take repellent, long-sleeved shirts, long trousers and good boots. See www.biobol.org.

Buena Vista → *Phone code: 04. Colour map 6, A4.*

This sleepy little town is 100 km northwest of Santa Cruz by paved road (see www.buenavistabolivia.com). No ATM in town, but US$ cash can be changed. There is an interpretation office one block from the plaza, T932 2055. Three kilometres from town is **Eco-Albergue Candelaria** ① *T7781 3238 or contact in advance through Hacienda El Cafetal (page 341)*, a community tourism project offering cabins in a pleasant setting, activities and tours. From Buena Vista there are five tourist sites for entering the national park: **Villa Amboró** ① *T03-343 1332, www.probioma.org.bo*, good for hiking; the community can arrange horse riding. Get there either by 4WD, or take a taxi-trufi to Las Cruces (35 km from Buena Vista) and then hike to the refuge (about two hours). **Macuñucu**, about 2 km from Villa Amboró, is an entrance favoured by tour operators. **La Chonta** ① *T6773 5333, www.lachontaamboro.wordpress.com*, a community-based ecotourism lodge, offers tours to the forest and to farming communities with local guides. Take a taxi-trufi via Haytú to the Río Surutú and from there walk or horse ride 2½ hours. Further along the road to Cochabamba is **Mataracú**, used by the operators, with natural pools, waterfalls and dinosaur fossils. It has the private **Mataracú Tent Camp** ① *T03-342 2372*, and other camping options. At **Cajones de Ichilo** ① *T0763 02581, 0600 0900, 1800-2200*, a community lodge 70 km west from Buena Vista in Cochabamba department in mountainous scenery with a large river, there are trails which offer a good chance of seeing mammals and, with luck, the horned currassow, one of the most endangered species of bird in Bolivia.

Vallegrande and La Higuera

Some 115 km south of the Santa Cruz-Cochabamba road is La Higuera, where Che Guevara was killed. On 8 October each year, visitors, most from outside Bolivia, gather there to celebrate his memory. La Higuera is reached through the town of Vallegrande where, at **Hospital Nuestro Señor de Malta** ① *no fee, but voluntary donation to the health station*, you can see the old laundry building where Che's body was shown to the international press on 9 October 1967. Near Vallegrande's air strip you can see the results of excavations carried out in 1997 which finally unearthed his physical remains (now in Cuba), ask an airport attendant to see the site. Vallegrande has a small archaeological museum US$1.50, above which is the **Che Guevara Room** ① *free*.

The schoolhouse in La Higuera (60 km south of Vallegrande) where Che was executed is now a museum. Another **museum** ① *T03-942 2003*, owned by René Villegas, is open when he is in town. Guides, including Pedro Calzadillo, headmaster of the school, will show visitors to the ravine of El Churo (or Yuro), where Che was captured on 8 October 1967.

Tours organized by agencies in Santa Cruz and Samaipata follow some of the last movements of Che and his band.

To Paraguay and Argentina

South of Santa Cruz a good paved road passes through Abapó, Camiri (**Hotel Premier**, Av Busch 60, T952 2204, is a decent place to stay), Boyuibe, Villamontes – access for the Trans-Chaco route to Paraguay – and Yacuiba, on the border with Argentina.

Villamontes → *Phone code: 04. Colour map 6, B4.*

Villamontes, 500 km south of Santa Cruz, is renowned for fishing. It holds a Fiesta del Pescado in August. It is a hot, friendly, spread-out city on the north shore of the Río Pilcomayo, at the base of the Cordillera de Aguaragüe. The river cuts through this range (Parque Nacional Aguaragüe) forming **El Angosto**, a beautiful gorge. The road to Tarija, 280 km west, is cut in the cliffs along this gorge. At Plaza 6 de Agosto is the **Museo Héroes del Chaco** ① *Tue-Sun 0800-1200, 1400-1800, US$0.30*, with photographs, maps, artefacts, and battle models of the 1932-1935 Chaco War. There is no ATM, but banks, **Prodem** and various *cambios* are on Av Méndez Arcos.

From Villamontes, the road to Paraguay runs east to **Ibibobo** (70 km). The first 30 km is paved, thereafter it's gravel and further paving is in progress. Motorists and bus travellers should carry extra water and some food, as climatic conditions are harsh and there is little traffic in case of a breakdown. Bolivian exit stamps are given at Ibibobo. If travelling by bus, passports are collected by driver and returned on arrival at Mcal Estigarribia (Paraguay), with Bolivian exit stamp. Paraguayan immigration and thorough drugs searches take place in Mcal Estigarribia. See Santa Cruz Transport (page 336) for international bus services. From Ibibobo to the Bolivian frontier post at Picada Sucre is 75 km, then it's 15 km to the actual border and another 8 km to the Paraguayan frontier post at **Fortín Infante Rivarola**. There are customs posts, but no police, immigration nor any other services at the border.

Yacuiba → *Colour map 6, B4. Population: 11,000.*

Yacuiba is a prosperous city (reported less-than-safe due to drug running) at the crossing to Pocitos in Argentina. Hotels include **Valentín**, San Martín 1153, www.valentinhotelbolivia.com, and **París**, Comercio 1175 y Campero, T04-682 2182 (both **$$**). The train service from Santa Cruz is slow and poor, road travel is a better option, or **Aerocon** flights to Santa Cruz (Santa Cruz 1336, T468 3841). In Yacuiba, there are ATMs on Campero. Argentine consul at Comercio y Sucre. Passengers leaving Bolivia must disembark at Yacuiba, take a taxi to Pocitos on the border (US$0.40, beware unscrupulous drivers) and walk across to Argentina.

● Southwest of Santa Cruz listings

For hotel and restaurant price codes, and other relevant information, see Essentials.

● Where to stay

Samaipata *p337, map p337*
Rooms may be hard to find at weekends in high season.

$$$$-$$$ El Pueblito Resort, camino a Valle Abajo, 20 mins' walk uphill from town, T944 6383, www.elpueblitoresort.com. Fully-equipped cabins and rooms, pool, restaurant and bar set around a mock colonial plaza, with shops and meditation chapel.

$$ Landhaus, C Murillo uphill from centre, T944 6033, www.samaipata-landhaus.com. Cabins and rooms in nice ample grounds, small pool, hammocks, parking, sauna (extra), craft shop, good breakfast available. Older rooms are cheaper and good value.

$$ La Posada del Sol, C Arteaga, 3 blocks north of plaza, T7211 0628, www.laposadadel sol.net. Most rooms with bath, electric shower, nice grounds, restaurant, views, US-Bolivian run.

$$ La Víspera, 1.2 km south of town, T944 6082, www.lavispera.org. Dutch-owned organic farm with accommodation in 4 cosy cabins with kitchen, camping US$4-7 pp, breakfast and lunch available in Café-Jardín (0800-1500 daily),

book exchange, maps for sale. A peaceful slow-paced place; owners Margarita and Pieter are very knowledgeable and can arrange excursions and horse riding. They also sell medicinal and seasoning herbs. Highly recommended.

$ Andoriña, C Campero, 2½ blocks from plaza, T944 6333, www.andorinasamaipata.com. Tastefully decorated hostel, cheaper without bath, good breakfast, kitchen, bar, good views, volunteer opportunites. Dutch-Bolivian run, enthusiastic owners Andrés and Doriña are very knowledgeable, English spoken.

$ El Jardín, C Arenales, 2 blocks from market, T7311 4461. With electric shower, cheaper in dorm, ample grounds, camping US$3 pp, kitchen facilities, Belgian-Bolivian run.

$ Hostal Siles, C Campero, T944-6408. Simple rooms, cheaper with shared bath electric shower, kitchen and laundry facilities, good value.

$ Paola, C Terrazas, diagonal to the plaza, T944 6093. Simple rooms, cheaper without bath, electric shower, restaurant serves set meals, internet (extra), kitchen and laundry facilities.

$ Res Kim, C Terrazas, near plaza, T944 6161. Cheaper with shared bath, family-run, spotless, good value.

Comarapa *p338*
$ El Paraíso, Av Comarapa 396 (main road to Cochabamba), T946 2045. Pleasant economical hotel, electric shower, nice garden, parking, decent restaurant, popular.

Buena Vista *p339*
$$$-$$ Hacienda El Cafetal, 5.5 km south of town (taxi from plaza US$3), T935 2067. Comfortable suites for up to 5 people, double rooms, restaurant, bar, birdwatching platform, on a working coffee plantation (tours available), with shade forest.
$$ Buenavista, 700 m out of town, T03-932 2104, www.buenavistahotel.com.bo. Pretty place with rooms, suites and cabins with kitchen, viewing platform, pool, sauna, very good restaurant, horse riding.
$ La Casona, Av 6 de Agosto at the corner of the plaza, T03-932 2083. Small simple rooms with fan, shared bath, electric shower, courtyard in hammocks, plants and birds, good value.
$ Quimori, 1 km east of Buena Vista, T03-932 2001. Includes breakfast, other meals with advance notice, pool, nice grounds, tours in dry season, family-run.
$ Res Nadia, T03-932 2049. Cheaper without bath, simple, small, family run.

Vallegrande and La Higuera *p339*
$ Hostal Juanita, M M Caballero 123, Vallegrande, T942 2231. Cheaper without bath, electric shower, good value, Doña Juanita is kind.
$ La Casa del Telegrafista, La Higuera, T6773 3362, casadeltelegrafista@gmail.com. Small, welcoming French-owned posada, rooms with shared bath, lovely garden, great views, meals on request, camping (US$2), horseback and mountain bike tours, US$15, also bikes for hire.
$ Res Vallegrande, on the plaza, Vallegrande. Basic accommodation.

Villamontes *p339*
$$ El Rancho, Av Méndez Arcos opposite the train station, 15 blocks from the centre, T672 2059, rancho@entelnet.bo. Lovely rooms, frigobar, nice grounds and pool, parking, excellent restaurant.
$ Gran Hotel Avenida, Av Méndez Arcos 3 blocks east of Plaza 15 de Abril, T672 2106. Helpful owner, parking.

$ Res Raldes, Cap Manchego 171, 1½ blocks from Plaza 15 de Abril, T672 2088, fernandoarel@gmail.com. Well maintained, family run, electric shower, cheaper with shared bath and fan, nice courtyard, small pool, parking.

● Restaurants

Samaipata *p337, map p337*
$$ El Descanso en Las Alturas, C Arteaga, uphill from plaza, opens mostly on weekends. Wide choice including good steaks and pizzas.
$$ La Mexicana, C Rubén Terrazas near the plaza. Tue-Sun 1100-1500 and 1800-2300. Nice restaurant/bar with very good Mexican food. Also serves breakfast Sat-Sun.
$$ Latina Café, Bolívar, 3 blocks from plaza. Fri-Tue 1800-2200, Sat-Sun also 1200-1430. Nice upmarket restaurant/bar with very good Bolivian and international food including vegetarian. French-Bolivian run and recommended.
$$-$ Chakana, Terrazas on plaza. Daily 0800-2300. Bar/restaurant/café serving *almuerzos*, good snacks, salads, cakes and ice cream, outside seating, book exchange, Dutch-owned.
$$-$ Tierra Libre, Sucre ½ block from plaza. Open 1200-2200, Sun 1200-1500, closed Wed. Nice terrace with outdoor seating, good meat and vegetarian, pleasant atmosphere.
$ Café 1900, Sucre on plaza. Daily 0800-2300. Good set lunch, sandwiches and crepes.
$ El Nuevo Turista, opposite the gas station on the highway. Good local dishes.
$ La Boheme, Sucre y Terrazas, diagonal to plaza. Daily 1200-2400. Trendy Australian-run bar for drinks and snacks.
$ La Cocina, Sucre by the plaza. Tue-Sat 1900-2200. Middle Eastern and Mexican fast food with home-made breads.

Buena Vista *p339*
$$-$ La Plaza, on the plaza. Elegant restaurant/bar with a terrace, wide range of international dishes, good service.
$ El Patujú, on the plaza. The only café in town, serving excellent local coffee, teas, hot chocolate and a range of snacks. Also sells local produce and crafts.

● What to do

Samaipata *p337, map p337*
Cycling
Club de Ajedrez, Bolivar near the museum, rents bikes.

Massage
Samaipata spa, at the end of C Bolivar, T7263 6796, www.samaipataspa.com. Daily 0900-1200, 1500-2000. Offers massage, yoga and alternative therapies.

Wine tasting
Two bodegas located outside Samaipata are Uvairenda (www.uvairenda.com) and Vargas (www.vitivinicolavargas.com).

Tour operators
Samaipata has many tour operators, more than we can list. Except as noted, all are on C Bolívar near the museum. Most day-trips cost about US$20-25 pp in a group of 4.
Ben Verhoef Tours, Campero 217, T944 6365, www.benverhoeftours.com. Dutch-owned, English, German and Spanish also spoken. Offer tours along La Ruta del Che and throughout the area.
Jucumari Tours, T944 6129, erwin-am@ hotmail.com. Run by Edwin Acuña, who has a 4WD vehicle.
Michael Blendinger, T944 6227, www. discoveringbolivia.com. German guide raised in Argentina who speaks English, runs fully equipped 4WD tours, short and long treks, horse rides, specialist in nature and archaeology.
Road Runners, T944 6193. Olaf and Frank speak English, German and Dutch, enthusiastic, lots of information and advice.
Tucandera Tours, T7316 7735, tucandera. tours@hotmail.com. Saul Arias and Elva Villegas are biologists, excellent for nature tours and birdwatching, English spoken, competitive prices. Recommended.

Buena Vista *p339*
Amboró Travel & Adventure on the plaza, T7160 0691, amborotravel@hotmail.com. Prices include transport to and from the park, guide and meals. Recommended.
Puertas del Amboró, corner of the plaza, T03-932 2059. They also offer full packages.

● Transport

Samaipata *p337, map p337*
Bus From **Santa Cruz** to Samaipata, only Sucre-bound buses leave from the Terminal Bimodal. Taxis **Expreso Samaipata** in Santa Cruz at Av Omar Chávez 1147 y Soliz de Holguín, T333 5067 (Samaipata T944 6129), leave when full Mon-Sat 0530-2030 (for Sun book in advance), US$4.50 per person shared; or US$20 in private vehicle, 2½ hrs. Returning to Santa Cruz, they pick you up from your hotel in Samaipata. Buses leaving Santa Cruz for **Sucre** and other towns pass through Samaipata between 1800 and 2100; tickets can be booked with 1 day's notice through **Hotel El Nuevo Turista**, at main road opposite petrol station. To get to **Samaipata** from **Sucre**, buses leave at night and arrive 0500-0600 (set your alarm in case the driver forgets to stop for you), stopping in Mataral or Mairana for breakfast, about half an hour before Samaipata.

Comarapa *p338*
To/from **Santa Cruz** with **Turismo Caballero** (T350 9626) and **Trans Comarapa** (T7817 5576), both on Plazuela Oruro, Av Grigotá (3er Anillo), 3 daily each, US$4.50, 6 hrs. To **Cochabamba**, 2 buses a day pass through from Mairana.

Buena Vista *p339*
Sindicato 10 de Febrero in Santa Cruz at Izozog 668 y Av Irala, 1er Anillo behind ex-terminal, T334 8435, 0730-1830, US$3 pp (private vehicle US$15), 2½ hrs. Also another shared taxi company nearby, and 'Linea 102' buses from regional section of Terminal Bimodal. From Buena Vista, the access to the park is by gravel road, 4WD jeep or similar recommended as rivers have to been crossed. All operators and community eco-lodge coordinators offer transport.

Vallegrande and La Higuera *p339*
Bus Flota Vallegrande has 2 daily buses morning and afternoon from Santa Cruz to **Vallegrande** via **Samaipata** (at 1130 and 1630), 5 hrs, US$5. Best to book in advance. From Vallegrande market, a daily bus departs 0815 to **Pucará** (45 km), from where there is transport (12 km) to **La Higuera**. Taxi Vallegrande-La Higuera US$25-30.

Villamontes *p339*

Bus To **Yacuiba**, Coop El Chaco, Av Méndez Arcos y Ismael Montes, hourly 0630-1830, US$1.35, 1½ hrs. Cars from Av Montenegro y Cap Manchego, hourly or when full, 0630-1830, US$2, 1½ hrs. Long distance buses from terminal on Av Méndez Arcos, 13 blocks east of Plaza 15 de Abril (taxi US$0.40 pp). To **Tarija** via Entre Ríos, mostly unpaved (sit on the right for best views), US$5-6, 10-11 hrs, several companies 1730-1930; for day travel, **Copacabana** may depart at 1030, 2-3 per week from the terminal; Guadalupana, Wed and Sat at 0930, from Coop El Chaco office. To **Santa Cruz**, several companies daily, US$4.50-8.50, some bus cama, 7-8 hrs.

To **Asunción**, buses from Santa Cruz pass through 0200-0300, reserve a day earlier, US$35, about 15 hrs. 5 companies, offices all on Av Montenegro, either side of Av Méndez Arcos. Best are **Stel**, T672 3662, or Vicky Vides T7735 0934; **Yaciretá**, T672 2812, or Betty Borda, T7740 4111.

Yacuiba *p340*

Bus To **Santa Cruz**, about 20 companies, mostly at night, 14 hrs, US$8-15. To **Tarija**, daily morning and evening.

Eastern Bolivia

The vast and rapidly developing plains to the east of the Eastern Cordillera are Bolivia's richest area in natural resources. For the visitor, the beautiful churches and rich traditions of the former Jesuit missions of Chiquitos are well worth a visit. Here too are some of the country's largest and wildest protected natural areas. This combination of natural beauty, living indigenous culture and Jesuit heritage make the region one of Bolivia's hidden gems.

Jesuit Missions of Chiquitos

Nine Jesuit missions survive east of Santa Cruz, six of which – San Javier, Concepcion, San Rafael, Santa Ana, San Miguel and San José de Chiquitos – have churches which are UNESCO World Heritage Sites. Many of these were built by the Swiss Jesuit, Padre Martin Schmidt and his pupils. Besides organizing *reducciones* and constructing churches, Padre Schmidt wrote music (some is still played today on traditional instruments) and he published a Spanish-Chiquitano dictionary based on his knowledge of all the dialects of the region. He worked in this part of the then-Viceroyalty of Peru until the expulsion of the Jesuits in 1767 by order of Charles III of Spain. One of the best ways to appreciate this region is at the bi-annual **Festival de Música Renacentista y Barroca Americana**, held every even year (next in 2014, see page 335), but the living legacy of the missions can be appreciated year-round. Church services are exceptionally well attended, with Chuiquitano musicians and choirs sometimes performing at Sunday mass. The centres of the towns have been beautifully refurbished and are a pleasure to stroll around.

Access to the mission area is by bus or train from **Santa Cruz**: a paved highway runs north to San Ramón (180 km) and on north, to San Javier (40 km further), turning east here to Concepción (60 km), then to San Ignacio de Velasco (160 km, of which the first 30 are paved). A newly paved road runs south from San Ignacio either through San Miguel, or Santa Ana to meet at San Rafael for the continuation south to San José de Chiquitos. Access is also possible by the paved Santa Cruz-Puerto Suárez highway, which goes via San José de Chiquitos. By rail, leave the Santa Cruz-Quijarro train at San José and from there travel north by bus. The most comfortable way to visit is by jeep, in about five days. The route is straightforward and fuel is available. For information see **www.chiquitania.com** for extensive historical and practical information.

San Javier (or San Xavier) The first Jesuit mission in Chiquitos (1691), its church built by Padre Schmidt between 1749 and 1752. Some of the original wooden structure has survived more or less intact and restoration was undertaken between 1987 and 1992 by the Swiss Hans Roth, himself a former Jesuit. Subtle designs and floral patterns cover the ceiling, walls and carved columns. One of the bas-relief paintings on the high altar depicts Martin Schmidt playing the piano for his indigenous choir. It is a fine 30 minute walk (best in the afternoon light) to **Mirador El Bibosi** and the small **Parque Piedra de Los Apóstoles**. There is also good walking or all-terrain cycling in the surrounding countryside (no maps, ask around), thermal swimming holes at **Aguas Calientes**, and horse riding from several hotels. Patron saint's *fiesta*, 3 December, but 29 June, Feast of Saints Peter and Paul, is best for viewing traditional costumes, dances and music. Tourist guides' association has an office in the **Alcaldía** ① *T7761 7902, or 7763 3203 for a guide.* Information also from the **Casa de Cultura** ① *on the plaza, T963 5149.*

Concepción The lovely town is dominated by its magnificent **cathedral** ① *0700-2000, tours 1000, 1500, donation invited,* completed by Padre Schmidt and Juan Messner in 1756 and totally restored by Hans Roth (1975-1986). The interior of this beautiful church has an altar of laminated silver. In front of the church is a bell-cum-clock tower housing the original bells and behind it are well-restored cloisters. On the plaza, forming part of the Jesuit complex, is the **Museo Misional** ① *Mon-Sat 0800-1200, 1430-1830, Sun 1000-1230, US$3.50,* which has an *artesanía* shop. The ticket also gives entry to the **Hans Roth Museum**, dedicated to the restoration process. Visit also the **Museo Antropológico de la Chiquitania** ① *16 de Septiembre y Tte Capoblanco, 0800-1200, 1400-1800, free,* which explains the life of the indigenous peoples of the region. It has a café and guesthouse. Fiesta de la Inmaculada Concepción: 8 December. An orchid festival is held in the second week of October. The **Municipal tourist office** ① *Lucas Caballero y Cabo Rodríguez, one block from plaza, T964 3057,* can arrange trips to nearby recreational areas, ranches and communities. An **Asociación de Guías Locales** ① *south side of plaza, contact Ysabel Supepi, T7604 7085; or Hilario Orellana, T7534 3734,* also offers tours to local communities many of which are developing grass-roots tourism projects: eg **Santa Rita**, **San Andrés** and **El Carmen**. With a week's advance notice, they can also organize private concerts with 30 to 40 musicians. Various restaurants in town. Many places sell wood carvings, traditional fabrics and clothing.

San Ignacio de Velasco This is the main commercial and transport hub of the region, with road links to Brazil. A lack of funds for restoration led to the demolition of San Ignacio's replacement Jesuit church in 1948, the original having burnt down in 1808. A modern replica contains the elaborate high altar, pulpit and paintings and statues of saints. Tourist information office at **Casa de la Cultura** ① *La Paz y Comercio, on the plaza, T962 2056 ext 122, culturayturismo.siv@ gmail.com, Mon-Fri 0800-1200, 1430-1830,* can help organize guides and visits to local music schools. The **Centro Artesanal** ① *Santa Cruz entre Bolívar y Oruro, Mon-Sat 0800-1930, Sun 0800-1200,* sells lovely textile and wood crafts. There is community tourism in the villages of **San Juancito**, 18 km from San Ignacio, where organic coffee is grown, and **San Rafael de Sutuquiña**, 5 km; both have artisans. **Laguna Guapomó** reservoir on the edge of San Ignacio is good for swimming and fishing. Patron saint's day, preceded by a cattle fair, 31 July. There is only one ATM in town, best take some cash.

Santa Ana, San Rafael and San Miguel de Velasco These three small towns are less visited than some others along the missions circuit. Allow at least two days if travelling independently from San Ignacio: you can take a bus to Santa Ana in the afternoon, stay overnight, then continue to San Rafael the next afternoon and return to San Ignacio via San Miguel on Tuesday, Thursday or Sunday (see Transport, page 349). A day trip by taxi from San Ignacio costs about US$65 or an all-inclusive tour can be arranged by **Parador Santa Ana** (see Where to stay, page 348). Local guides are available, US$10.

The church in Santa Ana (town founded 1755, church constructed 1773-80, after the expulsion of the Jesuits), is a lovely wooden building. It is the most authentic of all the Jesuit *templos* and Santa Ana is a particularly authentic little village. The tourist office on the plaza can provide guides. Simple economical accommodation at **Comunidad Valenciana**, T980 2098. Fiesta de Santa Ana: 26 July.

San Rafael's church was completed by Padre Schmidt in 1748. It is one of the most beautifully restored, with mica-covered interior walls and frescoes in beige paint over the exterior. Patron saint's day, with traditional dancing, 24 October. $ **Hotel Paradita**, T962 4008, and others; restaurants near the plaza; tourist information office T962 4022.

The frescoes on the façade of the church (1752-1759) at San Miguel depict St Peter and St Paul; designs in brown and yellow cover all the interior and the exterior side walls. The mission runs three schools and a workshop; the sisters are very welcoming and will gladly show tourists around. There is a **Museo Etnofolclórico**, off the Plaza at Calle Betania; next door is the Municipalidad/ Casa de la Cultura, with a tourist information office, T962 4222. San Miguel has many worksops and rivals San Ignacio for the quality of its Jesuit-inspired art. Patron saint's day: 29 September.

San José de Chiquitos → *Phone code: 03. Colour map 6, B5.*

One complete side of the plaza is occupied by the superbly restored frontage of the Jesuit mission complex of four buildings and a bell tower, begun in the mid-1740s. Best light for photography is in the afternoon. The stone buildings, in Baroque style, are connected by a wall. They are the workshops (1754); the church (1747) with its undulating façade; the four-storey bell-tower (1748) and the mortuary (*la bóveda* – 1750), with one central window but no entrance in its severe frontage. The complex and **Museo** ① *Mon-Fri 0800-1200, 1430-1800, Sat-Sun 0900-1200, 1500-1800, entry US$3*, are well worth visiting. Behind are the *colegio* and workshops, which house the **Escuela Municipal de Música**, visits to rehearsals and performances can be arranged by the tourist office. **InfoTur** ① *in the Municipio, C Velasco, ½ block from plaza, T972 2084, Mon-Fri 0800-1200, 1430-1830*, has information and arranges various tours; there is internet upstairs. On Mondays, Mennonites bring their produce to San José and buy provisions. The colonies are 50 km west and the Mennonites, who speak English, German, plattdeutsch and Spanish, are happy to talk about their way of life. Fiesta de San José is 1 May, preceded by a week of folkloric and other events. There is only one ATM in town, best take some cash.

About 2 km south from San José is the 17,000 ha **Parque Nacional Histórico Santa Cruz la Vieja** ① *www.biobol.org*. It has a monument to the original site of Santa Cruz (founded 1561) and a *mirador* with great views. The park's heavily forested hills contain much animal and bird life. There are various trails for hiking; guides can be organized by the tourist office in San José. It gets very hot so start early, allow over one hour to get there on foot (or hire a vehicle) and take plenty of water and insect repellent. There is also good walking with lovely views at **Cerro Turubó** and the **Serranía de San José**, both outside San José.

East of San José de Chiquitos

Paving of the highway from Santa Cruz east to Brazil in 2011 opened up this once isolated region of friendly villages surrounded by natural wonders. The **Serranía de Chiquitos** is a flat-topped mountain range running east-west, north of the highway and railroad. It is filled with rich vegetation, caves, petroglyphs, waterfalls, birds and butterflies. These hills are part of the 262,000-ha **Reserva Valle de Tucavaca** (www.biobol.org) which protects unique Chiquitano dry forest and offers great hiking opportunities. Various community tourism projects are underway in the area and local guides are available in the towns.

The village of **Chochís**, 80 km east of San José de Chiquitos, is known for its sanctuary of the Virgen Asunta built by Hans Roth in 1988 (one of his few major works not connected with restoring Jesuit missions). The large sanctuary is built at the foot of an impressive red sandstone outcrop called **La Torre,** 2 km from town. Along the rail line from Chochís toward La Torre is a signed trail leading to the **Velo de Novia** waterfall, a pleasant one- to two-hour walk. A much more challenging hike climbs 800 m to the flat top of **Cerro de Chochís**, where you can camp or return to town in a long day; guide required.

Sixty kilometers east of Chochís is **Roboré**, the regional centre and transport hub. The **Oficina Municipal de Turismo** ① *Rubén Terrazas, one block from plaza, T974 2276*, has information about local excursions including **Los Helechos** and **Totaisales**, two lovely bathing spots in the forest. Roboré is an old garrison town dating back to the Chaco War and retains a strong military presence. The local fiesta is 25 October.

Seven kilometres east of Roboré, a paved road branches northeast and in 14 km reaches the particularly friendly village of **Santiago de Chiquitos**. Founded in 1754, Santiago was one of the last missions built in Chiquitania. There are good accommodations and more good walking to a fine *mirador*, natural stone arches and caves with petroglyphs; guides available in town. A poor road continues 150 km past Santiago to **Santo Corazón**, a still-isolated Jesuit mission town (the last one built, 1760) inside **Area Natural de Manejo Integrado San Matías** ① *www.biobol.org*.

Aguas Calientes is 32 km east of Roboré along the rail line and highway to Brazil. The hot little village is unimpressive but nearby is a river of crystal-clear thermal water, teeming with little fish and bird life. There are several spots with facilities for bathing and camping, which is preferable to the basic accommodations in town. There are many tiny biting sand-flies, so your tent should have good netting. Soaking in the thermal water amid the sights and sounds of the surrounding forest at dawn or on a moonlit night is amazing.

Parque Nacional Noel Kempff Mercado

In the far northeast corner of Santa Cruz Department, **Parque Nacional Noel Kempff Mercado** (named after a Bolivian conservation pioneer who was killed while flying over the park) ① *park office in San Ignacio de Velasco, C Oruro y Cochabamba, T962 2747, Mon-Fri 0830-1200, 1430-1800; additional information from SERNAP and FAN, both in Santa Cruz (page 336), also www.biobol.org*, is one of the world's most diverse natural habitats. This World Heritage Site covers 1,523,446 ha and encompasses seven ecosystems, within which are 139 species of mammals (including black jaguars), 620 species of birds (including nine types of macaw), 74 species of reptiles and 110 species of orchids. Highlights include the **Huanchaca** or **Caparú Plateau**, which with its 200-500 m sheer cliffs and tumbling waterfalls is a candidate for Sir Arthur Conan Doyle's *Lost World* (Colonel Percy Fawcett, who discovered the plateau in 1910, was a friend of Conan Doyle).

This outstanding natural area received about 40 visitors in 2012-2013. Organizing a trip requires time, money and flexibility; there is no infrastructure, visitors must be self-sufficient and take all equipment including a tent. The authorities sometimes restrict access, enquire in advance. Operators in Santa Cruz (see page 335) may be able to arrange all-inclusive tours. Otherwise, the best base is San Ignacio (page 332), which has some provisions but more specialized items should be brought from Santa Cruz.

The southwestern section of the park is reached from the village of **Florida**, where there is a ranger station and a community tourism project offering basic accommodation and guides (guide compulsory, US$25 per day, www.parquenoelkempffmercado.blogspot.com). It is 65 km from Florida to the trailhead (pickup US$60 one way), which provides access to the 80-m high **El Encanto** waterfall and the climb to the plateau; allow five to six days for the return excursion. To reach Florida from San Ignacio, either hire a 4WD (US$100 per day), or there is one bus a week in the dry season (June to November, see Transport page 350).

In the northeastern section of the park are the great **Arco Iris** and **Federico Ahlfeld** waterfalls, both on the Río Paucerna and accessible mid-Dec to May when water levels are sufficiently high. Access is either from the Bolivian village of **Piso Firme** or the Brazilian town of **Pimenteiras do Oeste**; in all cases you must be accompanied by a Bolivian boatman/guide, available in Piso Firme and organized by the park office in San Ignacio. It is six to seven hours by motorized canoe from Piso Firme to a shelter near the Ahlfeld waterfall, and a full day's walk from there to Arco Iris. There is, in principle, one bus a week to Piso Firme from Santa Cruz and another from San Ignacio in the dry season (see Transport page 350).

To Brazil

There are four routes from Santa Cruz: by air to Puerto Suárez, by rail or road to Quijarro (fully paved except for 40 km between Santa Cruz and San José de Chiquitos), by road to San Matías (a busy border town reported unsafe due to drug smuggling), and via San Ignacio de Velasco to either Vila Bela or Pontes e Lacerda (both in Brazil). Puerto Suárez is near Quijarro and this route leads to Corumbá on the Brazilian side, from where there is access to the southern Pantanal. The San Matías and Vila Bela/Pontes roads both link to Cáceres, Cuiabá and the northern Pantanal in Brazil. There are immigration posts of both countries on all routes except Vila Bela/Pontes. If travelling this way get your Bolivian exit stamp in San Ignacio (immigration office near Jenecherú bus station) and Brazilian entry stamp in Cáceres or Vilhena. There may be strict customs and drugs checks entering Brazil, no fresh food may be taken from Bolivia.

Quijarro and Puerto Suárez → *Phone code: 03. Colour map 6, B6.*

The eastern terminus of the Bolivian road and railway is **Quijarro**. It is quite safe by day, but caution is recommended at night. The water supply is often unreliable. Prices are much lower than in neighbouring Brazil and there are some decent places to stay. **Rossy Tours**, C Costa Rica, four blocks toward river from train station, T978 2022, offers 4WD tours to **Parque Nacional Otuquis** in the Bolivian Pantanal, and various boat trips. ATMs and bank are at the border, see below.

On the shores of Laguna Cáceres, 8 km west of Quijarro, is **Puerto Suárez**, with a shady main plaza. There is a nice view of the lake from the park at the north end of Avenida Bolívar.

Border with Brazil

The neighbourhood by the border is known as Arroyo Concepción. You need not have your passport stamped if you visit Corumbá for the day. Otherwise get your exit stamp at Bolivian immigration (see below), entry stamp at Brazilian border complex. Yellow Fever vaccination is compulsory to enter Bolivia and Brazil, have your certificate at hand when you go for your entry stamp, otherwise you may be sent to get revaccinated. Bolivian immigration is at the border at Arroyo Concepción (0800-1200, 1400-1730 daily), or at Puerto Suárez airport, where Bolivian exit/entry stamps are also issued. There is one ATM at Arroyo Concepción, at the Hotel Pantanal. Money changers right at the border offer the worst rates, better to ask around in the small shops past the bridge. There are Brazilian consulates in Puerto Suárez and Santa Cruz. See Transport, below, for taxis from the border.

⊙ Eastern Bolivia listings

For hotel and restaurant price codes, and other relevant information, see Essentials.

⊙ Where to stay

Jesuit Missions of Chiquitos *p343*
San Javier
$ Alojamiento San Xavier, C Santa Cruz, T963 5038. Cheaper without bath, electric shower, garden, nice sitting area. Recommended.
$ Residencial Chiquitano, Av Santa Cruz (Av José de Arce), ½ block from plaza, T963 5072. Simple rooms, fan, large patio, good value.

Concepción
$$ Gran Hotel Concepción, on plaza, T964 3031. Excellent service, buffet breakfast, pool, gardens, bar, very comfortable. Highly recommended.
$$ Hotel Chiquitos, end of Av Killian, T964 3153, hotel_chiquitos@hotmail.com. Colonial style construction, ample rooms, frigobar,

pool, gardens and sports fields, orchid nursery, parking. Tours available. Recommended.
$ Colonial, Ñuflo de Chávez 7, ½ block from plaza, T964 3050. Economical place, hammocks on ample veranda, parking, breakfast available.
$ Las Misiones, C Luis Caballero, 1 block from church, T964 3021. Small rooms, nice garden, small pool, also has an apartment, good value.
$ Oasis Chiquitano, C Germán Bush, 1½ blocks from plaza. Buffet breakfast, pool, nice patio with flowers.
$ Residencial Westfalia, Saucedo 205, 2 blocks from plaza, T964 3040. Cheaper without bath, German-owned, nice patio, good value.

San Ignacio de Velasco
$$$ La Misión, Libertad on plaza, T962 2333, www.hotel-lamision.com. Upmarket hotel, restaurant, meeting rooms, pool, parking, downstairs rooms have bath tubs.
$$ Apart Hotel San Ignacio, 24 de Septiembre y Cochabamba, T962 2157, www.

aparthotel-sanignacio.com. Comfortable rooms, nice grounds, pool, hammocks, parking. Despite the name, no apartments or kitchenettes.

$$ Parador Santa Ana, Libertad entre Sucre y Cochabamba, T962 2075, www.paradorsanta ana.blogspot.com. Beautiful house with small patio, tastefully decorated, 5 comfortable rooms, good breakfast, knowledgeable owner arranges tours, credit cards accepted. Recommended.

$$ San Ignacio, Libertad on plaza, T962 2283. In a beautifully restored former episcopal mansion, non-profit (run by diocese, funds support poor youth in the community), breakfast.

$ Res Bethania, Velasco y Cochabamba, T962 2367. Simple rooms with shared bath, electric shower, small patio, economical and good value.

San José de Chiquitos *p345*

$$$ Villa Chiquitana, C 9 de Abril, 6 blocks from plaza, T7315 5803, www.villachiquitana. com. Charming hotel built in traditional style, restaurant open to public, frigobar, pool (US$3 for non-guests), garden, parking, craft shop, tour agency. French run.

$ Turubó, Bolívar on the plaza, T972 2037, hotelturubo@hotmail.com. With a/c or fan, electric shower, variety of different rooms, ask to see one before checking-in, good location.

East of San José de Chiquitos *p345*
Chochís

$ Ecoalbergue de Chochís, 1 km west of town along the rail line, T7263 9467; Santa Cruz contact: Probioma, T343 1332, www.probioma. org.bo. Simple community-run lodging in 2 cabins, shared bath, cold water, small kitchen, screened hammock area, camping US$3.50 pp, meals on advance request.

$ El Peregrino, on the plaza, T7313 1881. Simple rooms in a family home, some with fan and fridge, shared bath, electric shower, ample yard, camping possible.

Roboré

$$ Anahí, Obispo Santiesteban 1½ blocks from plaza, T974 2362. Comfortable rooms with electric shower, nice patio, parking, kitchen and washing facilities, owner runs tours.

$$ Choboreca, C La Paz, T974 2566. Nice hotel, rooms with a/c.

Several other places to stay in town.

Santiago de Chiquitos

$$ Beula, on the plaza, T337 7274, pachecomary @hotmail.com. Comfortable hotel in traditional style, good breakfast, frigobar. Unexpectedly upmarket for such a remote location.

$ El Convento, on plaza next to the church, T7890 2943. Former convent with simple rooms, one has private bath, lovely garden, hot and no fan but clean and good value.

$ Panorama, 1 km north of plaza, T313 6286, katmil@bolivia.com. Simple rooms with shared bath and a family farm, friendly owners Katherine and Milton Whittaker sell excellent home-made dairy products and jams, they are knowledgeable about the area and offer volunteer opportunities.

There are also various *alojamientos familiares* around town, all simple to basic.

Aguas Calientes

$$ Cabañas Canaan, across the road from Los Hervores baths, T7467 7316. Simple wooden cabins, cold water, fan, restaurant, rather overpriced but better than the basic places in town.

$ Camping Miraflores, 1 km from town on the road to Los Hervores baths, T7262 0168, www.aguascalientesmiraflores.com.bo. Lovely ample grounds with clean bathrooms, electric showers, barbeques, small pier by the river.

Quijarro *p347*

$$$-$$ Bibosi, Luis Salazar s/n, 4½ blocks east of train station, T978 2044. Variety of rooms and prices, some with a/c, fridge, cheaper with fan and shared bath, breakfast, pool, patio, restaurant, upscale for Quijarro.

$$ Tamengo, Costa Rica 57, Barrio Copacabana, 6 blocks toward river from train station, T978 3356, www.hosteltrail.com/hostels/tamengo resort. Located by the river, all rooms with a/c (cheaper with shared bath and in dorm), restaurant and bar, pool, sports fields, book exchange. Day-use of facilities by visitors US$8.50. Arranges tours and volunteer opportunities.

$ Gran Hotel Colonial, Av Luis de la Vega, 2 blocks east of train station, T978 2037. With a/c (cheaper with fan and private bath; even cheaper with shared bath). Restaurant serves good set lunch.

Willy Solís Cruz, Roboré 13, T7365 5587, wiland_54@hotmail.com. For years Willy has helped store luggage and offered local information and assistance. His home is open to visitors who would like to rest, take a shower, do laundry, cook or check the internet while they wait for transport; a contribution in return is welcome. He speaks English, very helpful.

Puerto Suárez *p347*
$ Beby, Av Bolívar 111, T976 2270. Private bath, a/c, cheaper with shared bath and fan.
$ Casa Real, Vanguardia 39, T976 3335, www.hotelenpuertosuarez.com. A/c, frigobar, Wi-Fi, parking, tours.

⊕ Restaurants

Jesuit Missions of Chiquitos *p343*
San Javier
$$ Ganadero, in Asociación de Ganaderos on plaza. Excellent steaks. Other eateries around the plaza.

Concepción
$ El Buen Gusto, north side of plaza. Set meals and regional specialties.

San Ignacio de Velasco
$ Club Social, Comercio on the plaza. Daily 1130-1500. Decent set lunch.
Panadería Juanita, Comercio y Sucre. Good bakery.
Mi Nonna, C Velasco y Cochabamba. 1700-2400, closed Tue. Café serving cappuccino, sandwiches, salads and pasta.

San José de Chiquitos *p345*
$$ Sabor y Arte, Bolívar y Mons Santisteban, by the plaza. Tue-Sun 1800-2300. International dishes, for innovation try their coca-leaf ravioli, nice ambience, French-Bolivian run.
$$-$ Rancho Brasilero, by main road, 5 blocks from plaza. Daily 0900-1530. Good Brazilian-style buffet, all you can eat grill on weekends.

East of San José de Chiquitos *p345*
Roboré
$ Casino Militar, on the plaza, daily for lunch and dinner. Set meals and à la carte. Several other restaurants around the plaza.

Santiago de Chiquitos
$ Churupa, ½ block from plaza. Set meals (go early or reserve your meal in adavance) and à la carte. Best in town.

❀ Festivals

The region celebrates the **Festival de Música Renacentista y Barroca Americana** every even year (next in 2014). Many towns have their own orchestras, which play Jesuit-era music on a regular basis. **Semana Santa** (Holy Week) celebrations are elaborate and interesting throughout the region.

⊖ Transport

Jesuit Missions of Chiquitos *p343*
San Javier
Trans Guarayos, T346 3993, from Santa Cruz Terminal Bimodal regional departures area, 7 a day, 4 hrs, US$4.50, some continue to **Concepción**. Several others including **Jenecherú**, T348 8618, daily at 2000, US$6, bus-cama US$10, continuing to Concepción and **San Ignacio**. Various taxi-*trufi* companies also operate from regional departures area, US$5, 3½ hrs.

Concepción
Bus To/from **Santa Cruz**, Trans Guarayos, US$5, 5 hrs, and Jenecherú, as above, US$6; various others. To **San Ignacio de Velasco**, buses pass though from Santa Cruz (many at night); also **Flota 31 del Este** (poor buses) from C Germán Busch in Concepción, daily at 1700, 5-6 hrs, US$4.25. Concepción to **San Javier**, 1 hr, US$1.50.

San Ignacio de Velasco
Bus From **Santa Cruz**, many companies from Terminal Bimodal depart 1900-2000, including Jenecherú (most luxurious buses, see above), US$10, bus cama US$17-30, 11 hrs; returning 1800-1900. For daytime service **31 del Este** (slow and basic) at 1100. Also *trufis* from regional departures area 0900 daily (with minimum 7 passengers), US$17, 8 hrs. To **San José de Chiquitos**, see San José Transport, below. To **San Rafael** (US$3, 2½ hrs) via **Santa Ana** (US$1.50, 1 hr) Expreso Baruc, 24 de Septiembre y Kennedy, daily at 1400; returning 0600. To **San Miguel**, *trufis* leave when full from Mercado de Comida, US$1.75, 40 min. To **San Matías** (for Cáceres, Brazil) several daily passing through from Santa Cruz starting 0400, US$12, 8 hrs. To **Pontes e Lacerda** (Brazil), Rápido Monte Cristo, from Club Social on the plaza, Wed and Sat 0900, US$22, 8-9 hrs; returning Tue and Fri, 0630. All roads to Brazil are poor. The best option to

Pontes e Lacerda is via Vila Bela (Brazil), used by **Amanda Tours** (T7608 8476 in Bolivia, T65-9926 8522 in Brazil), from **El Corralito** restaurant by the market, Tue, Thu, Sun 0830, US$28; returning Mon, Wed, Fri 0600.

San José de Chiquitos *p345*

Bus To **Santa Cruz** many companies pass through starting 1700 daily, US$6. Also *trufis*, leave when full, US$10, 4 hrs. To **Puerto Suárez**, buses pass through1600-2300, US$10, 4 hrs. To **San Ignacio de Velasco** via San Rafael and San Miguel, **Flota Universal** (poor road, terrible buses), Mon, Wed, Fri, Sat at 0700, US$7, 5 hrs, returning 1400; also **31 de Julio**, Tue, Thu, Sun from San Ignacio at 0645, returning 1500.

Train Westbound, the **Ferrobus** passes through San José Tue, Thu, Sat at 0150, arriving Santa Cruz 0700; **Expreso Oriental**, Mon, Wed, Fri 0109, arriving 0740. Eastbound, the **Ferrobus** passes through San José Tue, Thu, Sun 2308, arriving Quijarro 0700 next day; **Expreso Oriental** Mon, Wed, Fri 2100, arriving 0729 next day. See Santa Cruz Transport (page 336) and www. fo.com.bo for fares and additional information.

East of San José de Chiquitos *p345*

Bus To **Chochís** from San Jose de Chiquitos, with **Perla del Oriente**, daily 0800 and 1500, US$3.50, 2 hrs; continuing to **Roboré**, US$1, 1 hr more; Roboré to San José via Chochís 0815 and 1430. Roboré bus terminal is by the highway, a long walk from town, but some buses go by the plaza before leaving; enquire locally. From **Santiago de Chiquitos** to Roboré, Mon-Sat at 0700, US$1.50, 45 min; returning 1000; taxi Roboré-Santiago about US$15. Buses to/from Quijarro stop at **Aguas Calientes**; taxi Roboré-Aguas Calientes about US$22 return. From Roboré to **Santa Cruz**, several companies, US$7-20, 7-9 hrs; also *trufis* 0900, 1400, 1800, US$14.50, 5 hrs. From Roboré to **Quijarro** with Perla del Oriente, 4 daily, US$4.50, 4 hrs; also *trufis* leave when full, US$8, 3 hrs.

Train All trains stop in Roboré (see www.fo. com.bo), but not in Chochís or Aguas Calientes. Enquire in advance if they might stop to let you off at these stations.

Parque Nacional Noel Kempff Mercado *p346*

Road/us All overland journeys are long and arduous, take supplies. The following are subject to frequent change and cancellation, always enquire locally. **San Ignacio-Florida**, Trans Velasco, Av Kennedy y 24 de Septiembre, T7602 3269, dry season only (Jun-Nov), Sat 0900, US$10, at least 10 hrs; same company runs **San Ignacio-Piso Firme**, dry season only, Fri 1000, US$18, 24 hrs or more, returning Sun 1400. **Santa Cruz-Piso Firme** (via Santa Rosa de la Roca, not San Ignacio), **Trans Bolivia**, C Melchor Pinto entre 2do y 3er Anillo, T336 3866, Thu morning, US$24, 24 hrs or more; returning Sun. For **Pimenteiras do Oeste** (Brazil) see San Ignacio Transport (above) to Pontes e Lacerda and make connections there via Vilhena.

Quijarro and Puerto Suárez *p347*

Air **Puerto Suárez** airport is 6 km north of town, T976 2347; airport tax US$2. Flights to **Santa Cruz** with TAM, 3 times a week, US$85. Don't buy tickets for flights originating in Puerto Suárez in Corumbá, these cost more.

Bus Buses from Quijarro pick up passengers in Puerto Suárez on route to **Santa Cruz**, many companies, most after 1800 (**Trans Bioceánico** at 1030), US$12-22, 8-10 hrs.

Taxi Quijarro to the border (**Arroyo Concepción**) US$0.70 pp; to **Puerto Suárez** US$1 pp, more at night. If arriving from Brazil, you will be approached by Bolivian taxi drivers who offer to hold your luggage while you clear immigration. These are the most expensive cabs (US$5 to Quijarro, US$15 to Puerto Suárez) and best avoided. Instead, keep your gear with you while your passport is stamped, then walk 200 m past the bridge to an area where other taxis wait (US$0.70 pp to Quijarro). Colectivos to Puerto Suárez leave Quijarro when full from Av Bolivar corner Av Luiz de la Vega, US$1.

Train With paving of the highway from Santa Cruz train service is in less demand, but it remains a comfortable and convenientoption-. Ticket office in Quijarro station Mon-Sat 0730-1200, 1430-1800, Sun 0730-1100. Purchase tickets directly at the train station (passport required;do not buy train tickets for Bolivia in Brazil). The **Ferrobus** leaves Quijarro Mon, Wed, Fri 1800, arriving Santa Cruz 0700 next day; **Expreso Oriental**, Tue, Thu, Sun 1450, arriving 0740 next day. See Santa Cruz Transport (page 336) and www.fo.com.bo for fares and additional information.

Contents

Footprint features

At a glance

⏳ **Time required** 3-4 weeks for northeast or south, up to a year.

☀ **Best time** Feb/Mar for Carnival, also Jun and New Year's Eve. Apr-Jun and Aug-Oct are generally best.

✖ **When not to go** Dec-Feb and Jul school holidays. In Amazon Mar-May are wettest, in the south it's Nov-Mar.

Brazil

VENEZUELA

GUYANA

COLOMBIA

SURINAME

GUYANE

Boa Vista

Caracaraí

Al Içana
Xié

PN do Pico
da Neblina

Rio Branco

Parque Indígena
Tumucumaque

Macapá

Óbidos

Amazonas

Ilha do
Marajó

Belém

Benjamin
Constant

Manaus

Santarém

Itaituba

Vitória

Alcântara

São
Luís

PN Lençóis
Maranhenses

Parnaíba

Fortaleza

Canoa
Quebrada

Japim

Feijó

Humaitá

Democracia

Esteito

Colinas

Teresina

Natal

Porto Velho

Arapuanã

Alta
Floresta

Peixoto de
Azevedo

Balsas

João
Pessoa

Rio
Branco

Guajará-Mirim

Cocoal

Juína

Sinop

Miranorte

Petrolina

Caruaru

Recife

PERU

Vilhena

PN da Chapada
dos Guimarães

São Félix

Monte Santo

Maceió

BOLIVIA

Cáceres

Cuiabá

Goiás
Velho

Goiânia

BRASILIA

Chapada
Diamantina

Aracaju

Salvador

Itaparica

Ilhéus

PN do Pantanal
Matogrossense

Corumbá

Paraíso

Anápolis

Diamantina

Caravelas

Porto Seguro

Arraial de Ajuda

PN Marinho de Abrolhos

Bonito

Campo
Grande

São José do
Rio Preto

Belo Horizonte

Ouro Preto

Vitória

CHILE

PARAGUAY

Ponta Porã

Foz do
Iguaçu

São Paulo

Petrópolis

Rio de
Janeiro

Búzios

Curitiba

Iguape

Paranaguá

São
Joaquim

Florianópolis

Caxias
do Sul

Laguna

ARGENTINA

Torres

Porto Alegre

Atlantic
Ocean

URUGUAY

Rio Grande

Curral Alto

Chuy/Chuí

N

300 km

300 miles

There are few countries as beautiful and vibrant as Brazil with nature so exuberant and people so welcoming. Thousands of kilometres of pristine and deserted beaches line the coast, some pounded by superb surf, others lapped by gentle sea. They are backed by dunes the size of deserts or forests of coconut palms. Offshore, jewel-like islands offer some of the best snorkelling and diving in the South Atlantic. In the warm shallows humpback whales gather to calf and spinner dolphins cavort in the waves.

The table-top mountains of the interior are covered in medicinal plants and drained by mineral-rich rivers that tumble through gorges and rush over tiered waterfalls. In the Amazon, virgin forest stretches unbroken for more than 2500 km in every direction and the earth is a tapestry of green broken by a filigree of rivers. There are islands here too: the largest bigger than Denmark, wilder and more forested than Borneo. The Pantanal, the world's biggest wetland, offers some of the best wildlife-watching in the western hemisphere.

The cobble and whitewash gold-mining towns of Minas Gerais and Goiás contrast with the busy metropolises of São Paulo, Salvador and Recife, each of which have a thrilling urban culture. And then there is Rio de Janeiro, the jewel in the country's urban crown, with its bays and islands, boulder mountains, beaches and beautiful people.

Best of all, though, are the Brazilians themselves, in all their joyful diversity. Portugal, France, Ireland, Holland and Britain all laid claims here and left their cultures to mingle with the indigenous inhabitants. Brazil is now home to the greatest numbers of Africans, Arabs and Japanese in the Americas, and bierfests, sushi, bauhaus, rock music and rodeos are as much a part of the culture as bossa nova and football. As yet, the country is undiscovered beyond the clichés, but Brazil is becoming big news, with a thriving economy, the 2014 Football World Cup and the Olympics to host in 2016.

Planning your trip

Where to go in Brazil

Rio de Janeiro was for a long time *the* image of Brazil, with its beautiful setting – the Sugar Loaf and Corcovado overlooking the bay and beaches, its world renowned carnival, the nightlife and its *favelas* (slums – which are now being incorporated into tourism). It is still a must on many itineraries, but Rio de Janeiro state has plenty of other beaches, national parks and colonial towns (especially **Paraty**) and the imperial city of Petrópolis. **São Paulo** is the country's industrial and financial powerhouse; with some fine museums and its cultural life and restaurants are very good. All the São Paulo coast is worth visiting and inland there are hill resorts and colonial towns. The **state of Minas Gerais** contains some of the best colonial architecture in South America in cities such as Ouro Preto, Mariana, São João del Rei and Diamantina. All are within easy reach of the state capital, Belo Horizonte. Other options in Minas include national parks with good hill scenery and birdwatching and hydrothermal resorts.

The atmosphere of the South is dominated by its German and Italian immigrants. The three states, Paraná, Santa Catarina and Rio Grande do Sul have their coastal resorts, especially near Florianópolis, capital of Santa Catarina. **Rio Grande do Sul** is the land of Brazil's *gaúchos* (cowboys) and of its vineyards, but the main focus of the region is the magnificent **Iguaçu Falls** in the far west of Paraná, on the borders of Argentina and Paraguay.

The Northeast is famous for beaches and colonial history. Combining both these elements, with the addition of Brazil's liveliest African culture, is **Salvador de Bahia**, one of the country's most famous cities and a premier tourist destination. Huge sums of money have been lavished on the restoration of its colonial centre and its carnival is something special. Inland, Bahia is mostly arid sertão, in which a popular town is **Lençóis**, a historical monument with a nearby national park. The highlight of the southern coast of Bahia is the beach and party zone around **Porto Seguro**, while in the north the beaches stretch up to the states of Sergipe and Alagoas and on into Pernambuco. **Recife**, capital of Pernambuco, and its neighbour, the colonial capital **Olinda**, also mix the sea, history and culture, while inland is the major handicraft centre of Caruaru. Travelling around to the north-facing coast, there are hundreds of beaches to choose from, some highly developed, others less so. You can swim, surf or ride the dunes in buggies. Last stop before the mouth of the Amazon is **São Luís**, in whose centre most of the old houses are covered in colonial tiles. East of São Luís are the extraordinary dunes and lakes of the **Lençóis Maranhenses** and the labyrinthine **Parnaíba delta**.

Through the North flows the **Amazon**, along which river boats ply between the cities of Belém, Santarém and Manaus. From **Manaus** particularly there are opportunities for exploring the jungle on adventurous expeditions or staying in lodges. North of Manaus is the overland route through Boa Vista to Venezuela. The forest stretches south to the central tableland which falls to the **Pantanal** in the far west. This seasonal wetland, the highlight of the Centre West, is one of the prime areas for seeing bird and animal life in the continent. At the eastern end of the Centre West is **Brasília**, built in the 1960s and now a World Heritage Site in recognition of its superb examples of modern architecture. Also in this region is one of the largest river islands in the world (Bananal – a mecca for fishing) and the delightful hill and river landscapes of **Bonito** in Mato Grosso do Sul.

Best time to visit Brazil

Brazil is a tropical country, but the further south you go the more temperate the winters become and there are places in the coastal mountains which have gained a reputation for their cool climate and low humidity. The heaviest rains fall at different times in different regions: November to March in the southeast, December to March in the centre west and April to August on the northeast coast around Pernambuco (where irregular rainfall causes severe droughts). The rainy season in the north and Amazônia can begin in December and is heaviest March to May, but it is getting steadily shorter, possibly as a result of deforestation. It is only in rare cases that the rainfall can be described as either excessive or deficient. Few places get more than 2,000 mm: the coast north of Belém, some of the Amazon Basin, and a small area of the Serra do Mar between Santos and São Paulo, where the downpour has been harnessed to generate electricity.

May to September is usually referred to as winter, but this is not to suggest that this is a bad time to visit. On the contrary, April to June and August to October are recommended times to go to most parts of the country. One major consideration is that carnival falls within the hottest, wettest time of year (in February), so if you are incorporating carnival into a longer holiday, it may be wet wherever you go. Also bear in mind that mid-December to February is the national holiday season, which means that hotels, planes and buses may be full and many establishments away from the holiday areas may be shut.

The average annual temperature increases steadily from south to north, but even on the Equator, in the Amazon Basin, the average temperature is not more than 27°C. The highest recorded was 44.6°C (2006), in the dry northeastern states. From the latitude of Recife south to Rio, the mean temperature is from 23° to 27°C along the coast, and from 18° to 21°C in the Highlands. From a few degrees south of Rio to the border with Uruguay the mean temperature is from 17° to 19°C. Humidity is relatively high in Brazil, particularly along the coast.

Transport in Brazil

Air Because of the great distances, flying is often the most practical option. All state capitals and larger cities are linked several times a day and all national airlines offer excellent service. Deregulation of the airlines has reduced prices on some routes and low-cost airlines offer fares that can often be as cheap as travelling by bus (when booked through the internet). Paying with an international credit card is not always possible online; but it is usually possible to buy an online ticket through a hotel, agency or willing friend without surcharge. Most airlines' websites provide full information, including a booking service, although not all are in English. The dominant airlines are **GOL** ① *T0300-115 2121, www.voegol.com.br*, **TAM** ① *T0800-570 5700/4002 5700, www.tam.com.br* and **TRIP/Azul** (code share) ① *T4003-1118, or T0800-887 1118 outside main cities, www.voetrip.com.br, www.voeazul.com.br*. Many other airlines operate, some regional, others nationwide. **Avianca** (formerly Oceanair) ① *T4004 4040/T0300-789 8160, www.avianca. com.br*, and **Pantanal** ① *T0800-602 5888, www.voepantanal.com.br*, have extensive routes. Small scheduled domestic airlines fly to virtually every city and town with any semblance of an airstrip. Internal flights often have many stops and can be quite slow. Most airports have left-luggage lockers. Seats are often unallocated on internal flights; board in good time.

TAM offers a 30-day **air pass** covering all Brazil on TAM and/or Pantanal flights, starting at US$538 for four coupons (more expensive if you arrive on an airline other than TAM). Additional coupons, up to a maximum of nine, may be bought. All sectors must be booked before the start of the journey. Two flights forming one connection count as two coupons. The airpass must be purchased outside Brazil, no journey may be repeated. Remember domestic airport tax has to be paid at each departure. Converting the voucher can take some hours, do not plan an onward flight immediately. Cost and restrictions on the airpass are subject to change.

GOL has a similar 30-day **airpass**, from four to nine coupons, starting at US$538 (plus tax), which must be bought outside Brazil. If you have to change planes on a route, this counts as one coupon if the stop-over is less than four hours. A maximum of two connections may

Driving in Brazil

Road Around 13% of roads are paved and several thousand more all-weather. The best highways are heavily concentrated in the southeast; those serving the interior are being improved to all-weather status and many are paved. Some main roads are narrow and therefore dangerous. Many are in poor condition.

Safety Try to never leave your car unattended except in a locked garage or guarded parking area.

Documents To drive in Brazil you need an international licence. A national driving licence is acceptable as long as your home country is a signatory to the Vienna and Geneva conventions. (See Motoring, Essentials.) There are agreements between Brazil and all South American countries (but check in the case of Bolivia) whereby a car can be taken into Brazil (or a Brazilian car out of Brazil) for a period of 90 days without any special documents. For cars registered in other countries, you need proof of ownership and/or registration in the home country and valid driving licence (as above). A 90-day permit is given by customs and procedure is very straightforward. Make sure you keep all the papers you are given when you enter, to produce when you leave.

Car hire Renting a car in Brazil is expensive: the cheapest rate for unlimited mileage for a small car is about US$55-65 per day. Minimum age for renting a car is 21 and it is essential to have a credit card. Companies operate under the terms *aluguel de automóveis* or *autolocadores*.

Fuel Fuel prices vary from week to week and according to region. *Gasolina común* costs about US$1.35 per litre with *gasolina maxi* and *maxigold* a little more. *Alcool común* costs US$1; *alcool maxi* costs US$1.40. Diesel costs US$1.10. There is no unleaded fuel. Fuel is only 85 octane. It is virtually impossible to buy premium grades of petrol anywhere. With alcohol fuel you need about 50% more than regular gasoline. Larger cars have a small extra tank for 'gasolina' to get the engine started; remember to keep this topped up.

be made in the same city. Dates maybe changed, but routes cannot once the ticket has been bought. GOL also sells a **Northeast Brazil airpass**, minimum three coupons (US$390), maximum six (US$690), covering all the states between Bahia and Maranhão.

Bus There are three standards of **bus**: *comum* or *convencional*, which are quite slow, not very comfortable and fill up quickly; *executivo* (executive), which are a few reais more expensive, comfortable, but don't stop to pick up passengers en route and are therefore safer; and *semi-leito* or *leito* (literally, bed), which run at night between the main centres, offering reclining seats with foot and leg rests, toilets, and sometimes refreshments, with a higher ticket price. For journeys over 100 km, most buses have chemical toilets. A/c can make leito buses cold at night, so take a blanket or sweater (and toilet paper); on some services blankets are supplied. Some companies have hostess service. Ask for a window seat (*janela*) if you want the view.

Buses stop frequently (every two to four hours) for snacks at *postos*. Bus stations for interstate services and other long-distance routes are called *rodoviárias*. They are normally outside the city centres and offer snack bars, lavatories, left-luggage (*guarda volume*), local bus services and information centres. The bus companies themselves are the best source of reliable information, at *rodoviárias* or online (most take credit and Visa debit cards). See **www.buscaonibus.com.br** or **http://rodoviaria online.com.br** (which also has details of bus stations) for one-stop sources of services and fares between major cities. Buses usually arrive and depart in good time, although loading luggage, ID checks and, in some cities such as São Paulo, metal detector checks can slow things up.

Taxi Taxi meters measure distance/cost in reais. At the outset, make sure the meter is cleared and shows tariff '1', except Sunday 2300-0600, and in December when '2' is permitted. Check the meter works, if not, fix price in advance. Radio taxi service costs about 50% more but cheating is less likely. Taxis outside larger hotels usually cost more than ordinary taxis. If you are seriously cheated, note the taxi number and insist on a signed bill, threatening to go to the police; it can work.
Note Be wary of Mototaxis. Many are unlicensed and a number of robberies have been reported.

Boat The only area where boat travel is practical (and often necessary) is the Amazon region. There are some limited transport services along the São Francisco River and through the Pantanal.

Train There are 30,379 km of railway track which are not combined into a unified system; almost all run goods trains only. Brazil has two gauges and there is little transfer between them. Two more gauges exist for the isolated Amapá Railway and the tourist-only São João del Rei and Ouro Preto-Mariana lines. Other tourist services run from Curitiba to the Paraná coast and the Trem do Pantanal between Campo Grande and Miranda. There are suburban passenger services in Rio de Janeiro, São Paulo and other cities and long-distance services in the state of São Paulo and between Belo Horizonte and Vitória.

Maps and guides Editora Abril publishes the magazines *Quatro Rodas* and *Viagem e Turismo*, as well as a wide range of other publications. Its *Guia Brasil* is a type of Michelin Guide to hotels, restaurants (not the cheapest), sights, facilities and general information on hundreds of cities and towns in the country, including good street maps (we acknowledge here our debt to this publication). All are available at news stands and bookshops all over the country and online: www.abril.com.br. For the group's travel blog, see http://viajeaqui.abril.com.br.

Where to stay in Brazil → *See Essentials for our hotel price guide.*

Hotels Usually hotel prices include breakfast: rolls, ham, eggs, cheese, cakes, fruit. There is no reduction if you don't eat it. Normally an *apartamento* is a room with sleeping and living areas and sometimes cooking facilities. A *quarto* is a standard room: com banheiro is en suite, sem banheiro is with shared bathroom. A *pousada* is either the equivalent of bed-and-breakfast, often small and family-run, or a sophisticated and often charming small hotel. A *hotel* is the same as anywhere in the world. The star rating system (five-star hotels are not price-controlled) is not the standard used in North America or Europe. Many of the older hotels can be cheaper than hostels. Business visitors are strongly recommended to book in advance. It is also a good idea to book in advance in small towns that are popular at weekends with city dwellers (eg near São Paulo and Rio de Janeiro) and it is essential to book at peak times. If staying more than three nights in a place in low season, ask for a discount. A *motel* is specifically intended for guests who are not intending to sleep: there is no stigma attached and they usually offer good value (the rate for a full night is called the *pernoite*), though the decor can be a little garish.

Roteiros de Charme This is a private association of hotels and *pousadas* in the southeast and northeast, which aims to give a high standard of accommodation in establishments typical of the town they are in. Visit www.roteirosdecharme.com.br. They are equivalent to international hotel associations such as **Small Luxury Hotels of the World** (www.slh.com), **Leading Hotels of the World** (www.lhw.com) and **Relais et Chateaux** (www.relaischateaux.com), all of which have members in Brazil. There are, however, many fine hotels and *pousadas* listed in our text that are not included in these associations.

Youth hostels For information contact **Federação Brasileira de Albergues da Juventude** ① *R os Andrades 1137, sala 2018, Porto Alegre, CEP 90020-007, T051-3228 3802, www.albergues.com. br.* Its annual book and website provide a full list of good-value accommodation. Also see the *Internet Guide to Hostelling*, which has list of Brazilian youth hostels: www.hostels.com/brazil.

Camping Members of the Camping Clube do Brasil or those with an international campers' card pay only half the rate of a non-member. The club has 43 sites around the country. See **Camping Clube do Brasil**, www.campingclube.com.br. It may be difficult to get into some Clube campsites during the high season (January/February). Private campsites charge about US$8-15 per person. For those on a very low budget and in isolated areas where there is no camp site, service stations can be used as camping sites; they have shower facilities, watchmen and food; some have dormitories; truck drivers are a mine of information. There are also various municipal sites. Campsites often tend to be some distance from public transport routes and are better suited to those with their own transport. Never camp at the side of a road; wild camping is generally not possible. Good camping equipment may be purchased in Brazil and there are several rental companies. Camping gas cartridges are easy to buy in sizeable towns in the south. Most sizeable towns have laundromats with self service. *Lavanderias* do the washing for you but are expensive.

Food and drink in Brazil → *See Essentials for our restaurant price guide.*

The main meal is usually taken in the middle of the day; cheap restaurants tend not to be open in the evening. The most common dish is *bife (ou frango) com arroz e feijão*, steak (or chicken) with rice and the excellent Brazilian black beans. The most famous dish with beans is the *feijoada completa*: several meat ingredients (jerked beef, smoked sausage, smoked tongue, salt pork) along with spices, herbs and vegetables, are cooked with the beans. Manioc flour is sprinkled over it, and it is eaten with kale (*couve*) and slices of orange, and accompanied by glasses of *cachaça* (see below). Almost all restaurants serve the *feijoada completa* for Saturday lunch (until about 1630).

Throughout Brazil, a mixed grill, including steak, served with roasted manioc flour (*farofa*; raw manioc flour is known as *farinha*) goes under the name of *churrasco* (originally from the cattlemen of Rio Grande do Sul), served in specialized restaurants known as churrascarias or *rodízios*; good places for large appetites.

Brazil's best cooking is regional. For instance, Bahia has some excellent fish dishes (see note on page 527); some restaurants in most of the big cities specialize in them. Minas Gerais has two splendid special dishes involving pork, black beans, farofa and kale; they are *tutu á mineira* and *feijão tropeiro*. A white hard cheese (*queijo prata*) or a slightly softer one (*queijo Minas*) is often served for dessert with bananas, or guava or quince paste. *Comida mineira* is quite distinctive and very wholesome and you can often find restaurants serving this type of food in other parts of Brazil.

Meals are extremely large by European standards; portions are usually for two and come with two plates. Likewise beer is brought with two glasses. If you are on your own and in a position to do so tactfully, you may choose to offer what you can't eat to a person with no food. Alternatively you could ask for an *embalagem* (doggy bag) or get a take away called *a marmita* or *quentinha*, most restaurants have this service but it is not always on the menu. Many restaurants serve *comida por kilo*, usually at lunchtime, where you serve yourself and pay for the weight of food on your plate: good for vegetarians. Unless you specify to the contrary many restaurants will lay a *coberto opcional*, olives, carrots, etc, costing US$0.65-1. **Warning** Avoid mussels, marsh crabs and other shellfish caught near large cities: they are likely to have lived in a highly polluted environment. In a restaurant, always ask the price of a dish before ordering.

For **vegetarians**, there is a growing network of restaurants in the main cities. In smaller places where food may be monotonous try vegetarian for greater variety. Most also serve fish. Alternatives in smaller towns are the Arab and Chinese restaurants. And don't forget that there are myriad unusual, delicious fruits from all over Brazil, especially the Amazon and the cerrado.

Lanchonetes are cheap eating places where you generally sit on a stool at the counter to eat. *Salgados* (savoury pastries, also *pastel* – plural *pasteis*), *coxinha* (a pyramid of manioc filled with meat or fish and deep fried), *kibe* (deep-fried or baked mince with onion, mint and flour), *esfiha* (spicey hamburger inside an onion-bread envelope), *empadão* (a filling – eg chicken – in sauce in a pastry case), *empadas* and *empadinhas* (smaller fritters of the same type), are the usual fare. In Minas Gerais, *pão de queijo* is a hot roll made with cheese. A *bauru* is a toasted sandwich which, in Porto Alegre, is filled with steak, while further north it has tomato, ham and cheese filling. *Cocada* is a coconut and sugar biscuit.

The national alcoholic **drink** is *cachaça* (also known as *pinga*), which is made from sugar-cane, and ranging from cheap fire-water, to boutique distillery and connoisseur labels from the interior of Minas Gerais. Mixed with fruit juice, sugar and crushed ice, *cachaça* becomes the principal element in a *batida*, a refreshing but deceptively powerful drink. Served with pulped lime or other fruit, mountains of sugar and smashed ice it becomes *caipirinha*. A less potent caipirinha made with vodka is called a *caipiroska* and with *saikirinha* or *caipisake*.

Some genuine Scotch whisky brands are bottled in Brazil; they are cheaper even than duty free. Teacher's is the best. Locally made gin, vermouth and campari are good. Wine is becoming increasingly popular, with good-value Portuguese and Argentinean bottles and some reasonable national table wines. The wine industry is mainly concentrated in the south of the country where the conditions are most suitable, with over 90% of wine produced in Rio Grande do Sul. There are also vineyards in Pernambuco.

Brazilian beer is generally lager, served ice-cold. Draught beer is called *chope* or *chopp* (after the German Schoppen, and pronounced 'shoppi'). There are various national brands of bottled beers, which include Brahma, Skol, Cerpa, Antarctica and the best Itaipava and Bohemia. There are black beers too, notably Xingu. They tend to be sweet. The best beer is from the German breweries in Rio Grande do Sul and is available only there.

Brazil's fruits are used to make fruit juices or *sucos*, which come in a delicious variety. *Açai, acerolacaju* (cashew), *pitangagoiaba* (guava), *genipapograviolachirimoyamaracujá* (passion fruit), *sapoti, umbu* and *tamarindo* are a few of the best. *Vitaminas* are thick fruit or vegetable drinks with milk. *Caldo de cana* is sugar-cane juice, sometimes mixed with ice. *Água de côco* or *côco verde* is coconut water served straight from a chilled, fresh, green coconut. The best known of many local soft drinks is *guaraná*, which is a very popular carbonated fruit drink, completely unrelated to the Amazon nut. The best variety is *guaraná Antarctica*. Coffee is ubiquitous and good tea entirely absent.

Essentials A-Z

Accident and emergency
Ambulance T192. Directory enquiries T102. Police T190.

Electricity
Generally 110 V 60 cycles AV, but in some areas 220 V 60 cycles. Sockets also vary, often combination sockets for twin flat and twin round pin.

Embassies and consulates
For Brazilian embassies abroad and for all foreign embassies and consulates in Brazil, see http://embassy.goabroad.com.

Festivals in Brazil

See also Carnival box page 390. National holidays are 1 Jan (New Year); 3 days up to and including Ash Wednesday (Carnival); 21 (Tiradentes); 1 May (Labour Day); Corpus Christi (Jun); 7 Sep (Independence Day); 12 Oct (Nossa Senhora Aparecida); 2 (All Souls' Day); 15 Nov (Day of the Republic); and 25 Dec (Christmas). Local holidays in the main cities are given in the text.

Money → *US$1 = R$2.20; €1 = R$3.02 (May 2014).*

The unit of currency is the real, R$ (plural reais). It floats freely against the dollar. Any amount of foreign currency and 'a reasonable sum' in reais can be taken in; residents may only take out the equivalent of US$4000. Notes in circulation are: 100, 50, 10, 5 and 1 real; coins 1 real, 50, 25, 10, 5 and 1 centavo.

Credit cards Credit or debit cards are the most convenient way of withdrawing money. ATMs are common and frequently offer the best rate of exchange. Note, though, that Banco 24 Horas ATMs give a long list of cards that they accept, but often do not take international cards. The same is true of Banco do Brasil. In some places you may have to hunt long and hard for an ATM that will accept a foreign card. During banking hours you should be able to withdraw cash against a credit card, eg at branches of Banco do Brasil and Bradesco. Credit cards will be charged interest, debit cards should not, but machines that take debit cards are harder to find. The lobbies in which machines are placed usually close 2130-0400. Bradesco and HSBC are the best for ATM service. Some BBV branches have Visa and MasterCard ATMs. Emergency phone numbers: MasterCard T0800-891 3294; Visa T0800-891-3680.

Banks In major cities banks will change cash and TCs. If you keep the exchange slips, you may convert back into foreign currency up to 50% of the amount you exchanged. Take US dollars in cash, or euros.

Cost of travelling Owing to the strength of the real against other currencies, Brazil is expensive for the traveller. It is hard to find a hostel bed for less than US$15 pp. Budget hotels have rooms with few frills for US$30, but you can find a good double room for US$45 in any part of the country. Hostels can be a good choice when travelling alone. For 2 or more people, however, a room in a simple hotel may cost less than several dorm beds in a hostel. Hotels and even restaurants in resort areas may offer discounts mid-week, be sure to ask. Conversely, prices rise during holidays and festivals. Eating out can be expensive, too. À la carte and *comida a kilo* (pay by weight) places can both be costly. In higher class restaurants you should expect to pay around US$20 a head minimum and, in larger cities, US$40. There are many more moderately priced restaurant options at lunchtime than in the evening. If travelling on a tight budget, ask for the *refeição* (buffet), or *prato feito* (single serving), both money-saving options. The *prato comercial* is similar but rather better and a bit more expensive. Vegetarians should ask the price without meat, it may be lower. Some supermarkets have economical cafeterias. Shopping for food in supermarkets is cheaper than eating out and hostels usually have kitchen facilities. Most hotels have a small kitchen where they make breakfast and you may be allowed to prepare simple meals there. Long-haul bus routes are generally better value than several short journeys with intermediate stops. Flying may be less expensive than bus travel when airfares are booked online at least 21 to 28 days in advance. Taxis are very expensive, but city buses run to most airports and all *rodoviárias*. Note however that large luggage will not pass bus turnstiles and watch your belongings on crowded public transport. Hourly rate for use of internet, US$2.

Opening hours

Banks: 1000-1600, but closed on Sat.
Businesses: Mon-Fri 0900-1800, closing for lunch some time between 1130 and 1400.
Government offices: Mon-Fri 1100-1800.
Shops: open on Sat until 1230 or 1300.

Postal services

Postal services are handled by **Correios do Brasil**, whose website lists all agencies and services offered (in Portuguese), www.correios.com.br. It offers services for traditional letters, fax and transmission of documents by internet. Poste Restante is available nationwide; there is a charge of US$0.40 for letters addressed to Poste Restante. **Federal Express** and other courier services operate within Brazil.

Safety

Although Brazil's big cities suffer high rates of violent crime, this is mostly confined to the *favelas* (slums), which should be avoided unless accompanied by a tour leader, or NGO. If the worst does happen and you are threatened, try not to panic, but hand over your valuables. Do not resist, but report the crime to the local tourist police, who should be your first port of call in case of difficulty. The situation is much more secure in smaller towns and in the country. Also steer well clear of areas of drug cultivation and red light districts. In the latter drinks are often spiked with a drug called 'Goodnight Cinderella'.

Police There are several types of police: Polícia Federal, civilian dressed, who handle all federal law duties, including immigration. A subdivision is the **Polícia Federal Rodoviária**, uniformed, who are the traffic police. **Polícia Militar** are the uniformed, street police force, under the control of the state governor, handling all state laws. They are not the same as the Armed Forces' internal police. **Polícia Civil**, also state-controlled, handle local laws; usually in civilian dress, unless in the traffic division. In cities, the Prefeitura controls the **Guarda Municipal**, who handle security. Tourist police operate in places with a strong tourist presence.

Identification You must always carry identification when in Brazil; it is a good idea to take a photocopy of the personal details in your passport, plus that with your Brazilian immigration stamp, and leave your passport in the hotel safe deposit. See the Safety section

in Essentials at the beginning of the book for general advice.

Tax

Airport tax The amount of tax depends on the class of airport. The international departure tax is usually included in the ticket price. If not, you will have to pay on leaving Brazil. At the time of writing there were 4 categories of domestic airport for tax purposes, but changes to airport ownership and upgrading may mean that rates will change for the World Cup in 2014. Tax must be paid on checking in, in reais or US dollars. Tax is waived if you are in Brazil less than 24 hrs.

VAT Rate varies from 7 to 25% at state and federal level; average 17-20%.

Telephones

International phone code +55. Ringing: equal tones with long pauses. Engaged: equal tones, equal pauses. Dialling: it is necessary to dial a 2-digit telephone company code before the area code for all calls. Phone numbers are now printed: 0XX21, where the XX stands for the company code (we do not show the XX in the text below). To dial internationally dial 00 + company code without the zero, then the country code and number. Operating **company codes: Embratel**, 21 (nationwide); **Telefônica**, 15 (state of São Paulo); **Oi**, 31 (Alagoas, Amazonas, Amapá, Bahia, Ceará, Espírito Santo, Maranhão, most of Minas Gerais, Pará, Paraíba, Pernambuco, Piauí, Rio de Janeiro, Rio Grande do Norte, Roraima, Sergipe); **Brasil Telecom**, 14 (Acre, Goiás, Mato Grosso, Mato Grosso do Sul, Paraná, Rondônia, Santa Catarina, Rio Grande do Sul, Tocantins and the city of Brasília); **CTBC-Telecom**, 12 (some parts of Minas Gerais, Goiás, Mato Grosso do Sul and São Paulo state); **Intelig**, 23.

Telephone booths, or *orelhões* (big ears) are easy to find and normally take phone cards, which can be bought at newsstands, post offices and some chemists/pharmacies. They cost from US$4 for 30 units. International phone cards, *cartões telefônicas internacionais*, are also available in tourist areas and are often sold at hostels. Local calls from private phones are often free. International calls may be made from telephone company offices.

Mobile phones These are widespread and coverage is excellent even in remote areas, but prices are among the highest in the world and users pay to receive calls outside the metropolitan area where their phone is registered. SIM cards are hard to buy as users require a Brazilian social security number (CPF), but phones can be hired. Generally a mobile phone's 8-digit number begins with 8 or 9. When using a mobile phone you do not drop the zero from the area code as you have to when dialling from a fixed line.

NB Cyber-cafés are plentiful and are usually called **Lan house** or **ciber-café**.

Stop press From 2014 many 8-digit mobile phone numbers in Brazil will change, with an extra digit, usually a '9', inserted at the beginning of the number after the area code. So, for example, mobile number 1234 5678 will become 91234 5678.

Time

Official time Brazil has 3 time zones: Brasília standard time, which is GMT -3. States in this zone are divided into 2 groups: those with daylight saving (GMT -2, 3rd Sun in Oct to 3rd Sun in Feb), which are Brasília (Federal District), Espírito Santo, Goiás, Minas Gerais, Paraná, Rio de Janeiro, Rio Grande do Sul, Santa Catarina, São Paulo and Tocantins; and those without daylight saving, Alagoas, Amapá, Bahia, Ceará, Maranhão, Pará, Paraíba, Pernambuco, Piauí, Rio Grande do Norte, Rondônia, Sergipe. Amazon standard time (GMT -4) is used in Acre, Amazonas and Roraima, while Mato Grosso and Mato Grosso do Sul use Amazon time, plus daylight saving (as above, GMT -3). Fernando do Noronha is GMT -2.

Tipping

Tipping is not usual, but is always appreciated. Restaurants, 10% of bill if no service charge but small tip if there is; taxi drivers, none; cloakroom attendants, small tip; hairdressers,

10-15%; porters, fixed charges but tips as well; unofficial car parkers on city streets should be tipped 2 reais.

Tourist information

Ministério do Turismo, Esplanada dos Ministérios, Bloco U, 2nd and 3rd floors, Brasília, www.turismo.gov.br or www.visit brazil.com (in many languages). **Embratur**, the Brazilian Institute of Tourism, SCN Quadra 02 bloco G, Ed Embratur, Brasília, is in charge of promoting tourism abroad, T061-2023 8537. Tourist information bureaux are not usually helpful with information on cheap hotels and it is difficult to get information on neighbouring states. Expensive hotels provide tourist magazines for their guests. Telephone directories (not Rio) contain good street maps.

National parks are run by the Instituto Chico Mendes de Conservação da Biodiversidade, ICMBio, EQSW 103/104, Bloco C, Complexo Administrativo, Setor Sudoeste, Brasília, DF, T061-3341 9101, www.icmbio.gov.br. National parks are open to visitors, usually with a permit issued by ICMBio. See also the Ministério do Meio Ambiente website, www.mma.gov.br.

Useful websites

See tourist office sites under individual cities.
www.abeta.tur.br The Brazilian Association of Adventure Tourism Companies' website, with a list of memebers by state and types of activity available (in Portuguese); Abeta, Av C Colombo 550, s 505, Savassi, Belo Horizonte, T031-3261 5707.
http://washington.itamaraty.gov.br (USA).
www.brazil.org.uk (UK).
www.brazilmax.com Bill Hinchberger's *Hip Gringo's Guide* to Brazil with loads of news, cultural articles and travel information and a strong ecological angle.
www.gringo-rio.com Guide to all things about Rio, city and state, by a gringo, for gringos, also apartment rentals.
www.gringoes.com Information on all things Brazilian for visitors and ex-pats.

www.guiadasemana.com.br Weekly guide to entertainment, bars and restaurants to most of the main cities, in Portuguese.

www.ipanema.com Insider's guide to Rio in English.

www.maria-brazil.org A fun site with a blog, info, tips, recommendations, mostly about Rio.

www.socioambiental.org Accurate informa-tion on environmental and indigenous issues.

www.survival-international.org The world's leading campaign organization for indigenous peoples with excellent info on various Brazilian indigenous groups.

www.wwf.org.br World Wide Fund in Brazil.

Visas and immigration

Consular visas are not required for stays of up to 90 days by tourists from EU countries, Israel, Norway, South Africa, Switzerland, South and Central American countries and some Caribbean, Asian and African countries. For them, only the following documents are required at the port of disembarkation: a passport valid for at least 6 months; and a return or onward ticket, or adequate proof that you can purchase your return fare, subject to no remuneration being received in Brazil and no legally binding or contractual documents being signed. Visas are required by US and Canadian citizens, Japanese, Australians, New Zealanders and people of other nationalities, and those who cannot meet the requirements above, must get a visa before arrival, which may, if you ask, be granted for multiple entry. Visas are valid from date of issue. Visa fees vary from country to country, so apply to the Brazilian consulate, in the country of residence of the applicant. The consular fees range start at US$20, rising to US$25 (Japanese citizens), US$35 (Australians), US$65 (Canadians), to a US$140 processing fee for US citizens (the visa itself is free). In all cases there is a US$20 handling fee if you do not apply in person. Do not lose the emigration permit given to you when you enter Brazil. If you leave the country without it, you may have to pay a fine.

Foreign tourists may stay a maximum of 180 days in any one year. 90-day renewals (*pedido de prorrogação de prazo de estada*) are easily obtainable, but only at least 30 days before the expiry of your 90-day permit, from and at the discretion of the Polícia Federal. You will have to obtain a copy of the GRU tax form online at www.dpf.gov.br, or at the Polícia Federal, take it to a branch of Banco do Brasil, pay the required fee and then return to the Polícia Federal (www.dpf.gov.br lists all offices, but check in good time as offices change often). You will then be given the extension form to fill in and be asked for your passport to stamp in the extension. Regulations state that you should be able to show a return ticket, cash, cheques or a credit card, a personal reference and proof of an address of a person living in the same city as the office (in practice you simply write this in the space on the form). Some points of entry, such as the Colombian border, refuse entry for longer than 30 days, renewals are then for the same period, insist if you want 90 days. For longer stays you must leave the country and return (not the same day) to get a new 90-day permit. If your visa has expired, getting a new visa can be costly (US$40 for a consultation, plus the cost of a new visa) and may take up to 45 days. If you overstay your visa you will be fined a minimum of US$4.55, maximum US$455. After paying the fine, you will be issued with an exit visa and must leave within 8 days. **Note** Officially, if you leave Brazil within the 90-day permission to stay and then re-enter the country, you should only be allowed to stay until the 90-day permit expires. If, however, you are given another 90-day permit, this may lead to charges of overstaying if you apply for an extension. For UK citizens a joint agreement allows visits for business or tourism of up to 6 months a year from the date of first entry.

Weights and measures
Metric.

Rio de Janeiro

Brazilians say: God made the world in six days; the seventh he devoted to Rio (pronounced 'Heeoo' by locals). Rio has a glorious theatrical backdrop of tumbling wooded mountains, stark expanses of bare rock and a deep blue sea studded with rocky islands. From the statue of Christ on the hunchbacked peak of Corcovado, or from the conical Pão de Açúcar (Sugar Loaf), you can experience the beauty of a bird's-eye view over the city which sweeps along a narrow alluvial strip on the southwestern shore of the vast Baía de Guanabara. Although best known for the curving Copacabana beach, for Ipanema – home to the Girl and beautiful sunsets, and for its swirling, reverberating, joyous Carnival, Rio also has a fine artistic, architectural and cultural heritage from its time as capital of both imperial and republican Brazil. But this is first and foremost a city dedicated to leisure: sport and music rule and a day spent hang gliding or surfing is easily followed by an evening of jazz or samba. Rio has another cultural heart, its favelas (slums), where the poor and mostly black communities live. It was here that carnival, samba and Brazilian football were born. This joyful Brazilian spirit coexists with great misery and shocking violence, something that the authorities have confronted for the 2014 Football World Cup and in preparation for the 2016 Olympics and Para-Olympics. The city has been declared a UNESCO World Heritage Landscape site.

Arriving in Rio de Janeiro → *Phone code: 021. Colour map 4, C3.*

Orientation **Aeroporto Internacional Tom Jobim** (Galeão) is on the Ilha do Governador, about 16 km on the Petrópolis highway. The air shuttle from São Paulo and a few domestic flights end at Santos Dumont airport in the city centre. Taxis from here are much cheaper than from the international airport. There are also frequent buses. International buses and those from other parts of Brazil arrive at the **Rodoviária Novo Rio** (main bus station) near the docks.

As the city is a series of separate districts connected by urban highways and tunnels, you need to take public transport. An underground railway, the **Metrô**, runs from west and northwest under the centre to the south. Buses run to all parts, treat them with caution at night when taxis are better. ▸▸ *See Transport, page 395.*

Climate Rio has one of the healthiest climates in the tropics. Trade winds cool the air. June, July and August are the coolest months with temperatures ranging from 22°C (18° in a cold spell) to 32°C on a sunny day at noon. December to March is hotter, from 32°C to 42°C. Humidity is high. October to March is the rainy season. Annual rainfall is about 1120 mm and heavy rains tend to cause mud-slides in the early part of the year.

Tourist offices **Riotur**① *Praça Pio X, 119, 9th floor, Centro, T2271 7000, www.rioguiaoficial.com. br and www.rio.rj.gov.br/riotur*, is the city's government tourist office. There are also booths or offices in **Copacabana**① *Av Princesa Isabel 183, T2541 7522, Mon-Fri 0900-800*, and **Copacabana Quiosque 15**① *Av Atlântica opposite R Hilário Gouveia, daily 0800-2000*. The helpful staff speak English, French and German and have good city maps and a useful free brochure. There are information stands at the international airport, Terminals 1 and 2, and Novo Rio bus station. There is also a free telephone information service, *Alô Rio*, in Portuguese and English, T021-2542 8004 or T021-2542 8080.

The state tourism organization is **Turisrio**① *R da Ajuda 5, 6th floor, Centro, T2333 1037, www. turisrio.rj.gov.br, Mon-Fri 0900-1800*. The private sector **Rio Convention and Visitors Bureau**① *R Guilhermina Guinle 272, 6th floor, T2266 9750, www.rcvb.com.br*, also offers information and assistance in English. *Trilhas do Rio*, by Pedro da Cunha e Meneses (Editora Salamandra, 2nd edition), US$30, describes walking trips around Rio. The guide *Restaurantes do Rio*, by Danusia Bárbara, published annually, is worth looking at for the latest ideas on where to eat in both the city and state of Rio. Many hotels provide guests with the quarterly *Guia do Rio*. ▸▸ *See also Tours, page 394.*

Safety The majority of visitors enjoy Rio's glamour and rich variety without any problems. It is worth remembering that, despite its beach culture, carefree atmosphere and friendly people, Rio is one of the world's most densely populated cities. If you live in London, Paris, New York or LA and behave with the same caution in Rio that you do at home, you will be unlucky to encounter any crime. The tourist police, **BPTur** ① *R Figueiredo Magalhães 550, Copacabana, T2332 7949, T8596 7676, bptur@policiamilitar.rj.gov.br,* patrols the main tourist sites and gives safety tips. Tourist police officers are helpful, efficient and multilingual. If you have any problems, contact the tourist police first, or ring emergency line 190. **DEAT, Delegacia Especial de Apoio ao Turismo** ① *Av Afrânio de Melo Franco 159, Leblon, T2332 2924, or R Bambina 37, Botafogo, T2536 2466,* should be contacted in case of fraudulent or criminal activities against tourists.

Extra vigilance is needed on the beaches at night. Don't walk on the sand. Likewise in the back streets between the Copacabana Palace and Rua Figueiredo de Magalhães. Santa Teresa

Rio de Janeiro

Where to stay
1 Alpha, El Misti & Sun Rio Hostels

Metrô lines / stations
Ⓜ Linha 1 Ⓜ Linha 2

is now far safer and better policed than before, but caution is needed walking between Santa Teresa and Lapa at night and around the small streets near the Largo das Neves. A number of *favelas* were "pacified" in the run up to the 2014 and 2016 mega sporting events. Even so, you should never enter a *favela* on your own or without a person you know well and trust. A tour with a reputable operator (see Tours, page 394), or a stay in an established hostel (see for example **The Maze** in Tavares Bastos, http://jazzrio.com/en/bed-and-breakfast), can be a worthwhile experience. Otherwise *favelas* remain very dangerous places.

Background

The Portuguese navigator, Gonçalo Coelho, arrived at what is now Rio de Janeiro on 1 January 1502. Thinking that the Baía de Guanabara (the name the local *indígenas* used) was the mouth of a great river, they called the place the January River. Although the bay was almost as large and as safe a harbour as the Baía de Todos Os Santos to the north, the Portuguese did not take of advantage of it. In fact, it was first settled by the French, who, under the Huguenot Admiral Nicholas Durand de Villegagnon, occupied Lage Island on 10 November 1555, but later transferred to Seregipe Island (now Villegagnon), where they built the fort of Coligny.

In early 1559-1560, Mem de Sá, third governor of Brazil, mounted an expedition from Salvador to attack the French. The Portuguese finally took control in 1567. Though constantly attacked by *indígenas*, the new city grew rapidly and when King Sebastião divided Brazil into two provinces, Rio was chosen capital of the southern captaincies. Salvador became sole capital again in 1576, but Rio again became the southern capital in 1608 and the seat of a bishopric.

Rio de Janeiro was by the 18th century becoming the leading city in Brazil. Not only was it the port out of which gold was shipped, but it was also the focus of the export/import trade of the surrounding agricultural lands. On 27 January 1763, it became the seat of the Viceroy. After independence, in 1834, it was declared capital of the Empire and remained so for 125 years.

Main areas of the city

The city is usually divided into north and south zones, Zona Norte and Zona Sul, with the historical and business centre, O Centro, in between. The parts that most interest visitors are the centre itself and the Zona Sul, which has the famous districts of Flamengo, Botafogo, Urca, Copacabana, Ipanema, Leblon and then out to the newer suburb of Barra de Tijuca.

The city's main artery is the Avenida Presidente Vargas, 4½ km long and over 90 m wide. It starts at the waterfront, divides to embrace the famous Candelária church, then crosses the Avenida Rio Branco in a magnificent straight stretch past the Central do Brasil railway station, with its imposing clock tower, until finally it incorporates a palm-lined, canal-divided avenue. The second principal street in the centre is the Avenida Rio Branco, nearly 2 km long, on which only a few ornate buildings remain, by Cinelândia and the Biblioteca Nacional. Some of the better modern architecture is to be found along the Avenida República do Chile, such as the conical new Cathedral.

City centre and Lapa

Around Praça 15 de Novembro

Praça 15 de Novembro (often called Praça XV or Quinze, Metrô Carioca) has always been one of the focal points in Rio. Today it has one of the greatest concentrations of historic buildings in the city. The last vestiges of the original harbour, at the seaward end of the Praça, have been restored. The steps no longer lead to the water, but a new open space leads from the Praça to the seafront which gives easy access to the ferry dock for Niterói. Stage shows, music and dancing are held in the Praça and at weekends an antiques, crafts, stamp and coin fair is held from 0900-1900.

The **Paço Imperial** (former Royal Palace) ① *T2215 2622, Tue-Sun 1200-1800*, is on the southeast corner of the Praça 15 de Novembro. This beautiful colonial building was built in 1743 as the residence of the governor of the Capitania. It later became the Paço Real when the Portuguese court moved to Brazil. After Independence it became the Imperial Palace. It has an exhibition space, a small display at the west end on the history of the building and the Bistro do Paço and Atrium restaurants.

Across the Rua da Assembléia is the neoclassical **Palácio Tiradentes** ① *T2588 1000, www. alerj.rj.gov.br, Mon-Sat 1000-1700, Sun and holidays 1200-1700, guided visits T2588 1251*, the state legislative assembly, built 1922-26. It is named after the dentist Joaquim José da Silva Xavier, the symbolic father of Brazilian independence.

On Rua 1 de Março, across from Praça 15 de Novembro, there are three buildings related to the Carmelite order. The convent of the **Ordem Terceira do Monte do Carmo**, started in 1611, is now used as the Faculdade Cândido Mendes. The order's present church, the **Igreja da Ordem Terceira do Carmo** ① *R Primeiro de Março, Mon-Fri 0800-1400, Sat 0800-1200*, is the other side of the old cathedral (see below) from the convent. It was started in 1755, consecrated in 1770 and its towers added in 1849-50. It has strikingly beautiful portals by Mestre Valentim, the son of a Portuguese nobleman and a slave girl. He also created the main altar of fine moulded silver, the throne and its chair and much else.

Between the former convent and the Igreja da Ordem Terceira do Carmo is the old cathedral, the **Igreja de Nossa Senhora do Carmo da Antiga Sé**, separated from the Carmo Church by a closed passageway. It was the chapel of Convento do Carmo from 1590 until 1754 and has a beautiful baroque interior. A new church was built in 1761, which became the city's cathedral. In the crypt are the alleged remains of Pedro Alvares Cabral, the Portuguese explorer (though Santarém, Portugal, also claims to be his last resting place).

On the northwest side of Praça 15 de Novembro, you go through the Arco do Teles and the Travessa do Comércio to Rua do Ouvidor. The **Igreja Nossa Senhora da Lapa dos Mercadores** ① *R do Ouvidor 35, Mon-Fri 0800-1400*, was consecrated in 1750, remodelled 1869-1872 and has been fully restored. Across the street, with its entrance at Rua 1 de Março 36, is the church of **Santa Cruz dos Militares**, built 1770-1811. It is large, stately and beautiful and has the first neoclassical façade in Brazil; the altar is by Mestre Valentim.

The Church of **Nossa Senhora da Candelária** (1775-1810) ① *on Praça Pio X (Dez), at the city end of Av Pres Vargas where it meets R 1 de Março, Mon-Fri 0800-1600, Sat 0800-1200, Sun 0900-1300*, has beautiful ceiling decorations and romantic paintings. It has long been the church of 'society Rio'.

The **Centro Cultural Banco do Brasil (CCBB)** ① *entrances on Av Pres Vargas and R 1 de Março 66, Metrô Uruguaiana, T3808 2020, www.bb.com.br/cultura, Tue-Sun 0900-2100*, is highly recommended for good exhibitions. It has a library, multimedia facilities, a cinema, concerts (US$6 at lunchtime) and a restaurant. Opposite is the **Centro Cultural Correios** ① *R Visconde de Itaboraí 20, T2253 1580, Tue-Sun 1200-1900*, which holds temporary exhibitions and a postage stamp fair on Saturdays. **Casa França-Brasil** ① *R Visconde de Itaboraí 78, T2332 5120, www.fcfb. rj.gov.br, Tue-Sun 1000-2000*, dates from the first French Artistic Mission to Brazil and it was the first neoclassical building in Rio. **Espaço Cultural da Marinha** ① *Av Alfredo Agache at Av Pres Kubitschek, T2104 6025, www.mar.mil.br/dphdm/, Tue-Sun 1200-1700 and every 3rd weekend of the month 1300-1500, museum, free*, was given to the navy to become a museum containing displays on underwater archaeology and navigation and the *Galeota*, the boat in which the royal family was rowed around the Baía de Guanabara. Moored outside are the tug *Laurindo Pitta* ① 1 hr 20 min trips Thu-Sun 1315 and 1515, US$6.25, the warship *Bauru* and the submarine *Riachuelo* (both can be visited). Boats give access to **Ilha Fiscal** ① T2233 9165, boats to Ilha

② Rio de Janeiro centre

➡ **Rio de Janeiro maps**
1 Rio de Janeiro, page 365
2 **Rio de Janeiro centre, page 368**
3 Glória, Santa Teresa, Catete, Flamengo, page 374
4 Copacabana, page 376
5 Ipanema and Leblon, page 378

Restaurants 🍴
1 Adega Flor de Coimbra
2 Albamar
3 Bar das Artes
4 Bar Luiz
5 Café da Moda
6 Confeitaria Colombo
7 Eça
8 Republique
9 Sabor Saúde
10 Travessa do Comércio

Bars & clubs 🍸
11 Carioca da Gema
12 Clube dos Democráticos
13 Club Six
14 Estudantina Musical
15 Mercado 32
16 Rio Scenarium
17 Sacrilégio
18 The Week

Fiscal, Thu-Sun, 1300, 1430, 1600 Sep-Mar, 30 mins earlier Apr-Aug, US$6.25, in bad weather access is by minibus, with its beautiful neo-Gothic palace. The **Museu Naval** ① *just south (off Praça XV, R Dom Manuel 15, Tue-Sun 1200-1700,* is good, with English summaries.

Praça Mauá, which lies north of Avenida Presidente Vargas, marks the end of Centro and the beginning of the port zone, which is being completely reinvented and revitalised in preparation for the 2016 Olympics, under the Porto Maravilha programme (www. portomaravilha.com.br – check on the website for the latest openings). Empty warehouses will be replaced by leisure areas, accommodation and a series of new museums and galleries. These include the **Museu de Arte do Rio (MAR)** ① *Praça Mauá, T2203 1235, www.museude artedorio.org.br, Tue-Sun 1000-1800, US$4, half price under 21 and students, free for over 60s and for all on Tue,* which opened in 2013. The museum showcases artists responsible for the establishment of the Brazilian style (including Burle Marx, Castagneto, Di Cavalcánti, Goeldi, Ismael Nery and Lygia Clark) and those who are shaping Brazilian art today through some of the city's most exciting temporary exhibitions.

Just north of Candelária, on a promontory overlooking the bay, is the **Mosteiro** (monastery) **de Sao Bento** ① *T2206 8100, www.osb.org.br, daily 0700-1800, free, guided tours Mon-Sat 0900-1600, shorts not allowed.* Every Sunday at 1000, Mass is sung with plainsong, which is free, but arrive an hour early to get a seat. On other days, Mass is at 0715. It contains much of what is best in the 17th- and 18th-century art of Brazil. São Bento is reached either by a narrow road from Rua Dom Gerardo 68, or by a lift whose entrance is at Rua Dom Gerardo 40 (Metrô Uruguaiana or taxi from centre US$6). The main body of the church is adorned in gold and red. The carving and gilding is remarkable, much of it by Frei Domingos da Conceição. The paintings, too, should be seen. The Chapels of the Immaculate Conception (Nossa Senhora da Conceição) and of the Most Holy Sacrament (Santíssimo Sacramento) are masterpieces of colonial art. The organ, dating from the end of the 18th century, is very interesting.

Southeast of Praça 15 de Novembro, by the Largo da Misericórdia, is the **Museu Histórico Nacional** ① *Praça Mcal Âncora, T2550 9224, Tue-Fri 1000-1700, Sat, Sun and holidays 1400-1800, US$3, free Sun,* has excellent displays on Brazil's history (starting with indigenous peoples), coins, a collection of beautiful carriages and temporary shows. It's a big complex, including a 16th-17th century fortress, the Caso de Trem (artillery store, 1760) and arsenal (1764). There are good English summaries and a restaurant. **Museu da Imagem e do Som (MIS)** ① *Praça Rui Barbosa, T2332 9068 and at R Visconde de Maranguape 15, Largo da Lapa, T2332 9508, www. mis.rj.gov.br, Mon-Fri 1100-1700 by appointment only, due to move to Copacabana in 2013,* has photographs of Brazil and modern Brazilian paintings; also collections and recordings of Brazilian classical and popular music and a small cinema.

Around Largo da Carioca

The second oldest convent in the city is the **Convento de Santo Antônio** ① *T2262 0129, Mon, Wed, Thu, Fri 0730-1900, Tue 0630-2000, Sat 0730-1100 and 1530-1700, Sun 0900-1100, free,* on a hill off the Largo da Carioca, built 1608-1615. Santo Antônio is an object of devotion for women looking for a husband and you will see them in the precincts. The church has a marvellous sacristy adorned with blue tiles and paintings illustrating the life of St Anthony. In the church itself, the baroque decoration is concentrated in the chancel, the main altar and the two lateral altars.

Separated from this church only by some iron railings is the beautiful church of the Ordem Terceira de **São Francisco da Penitência** ① *T2262 0197, Mon-Fri 0900-1200, 1300-1600, free.* Its Baroque carving and gilding of walls and altar, much more than in its neighbour, is considered among the finest in Rio. Behind the church is a tranquil, catacomb-filled garden.

Across Ruas da Carioca and 7 de Setembro are the churches of **São Francisco de Paula** ① *upper end of R do Ouvidor, Mon-Fri 0900-1300*, containing some of Mestre Valentim's work, and **Nossa Senhora do Rosário e São Benedito dos Pretos** ① *R Uruguaiana 77 e Ouvidor, Mon-Fri 0700-1700, Sat 0700-1300*, the centre of African Christian culture in Rio, with a museum devoted to slavery. One long block behind the Largo da Carioca and São Francisco de Paula is the **Praça Tiradentes**, old and shady, with a statue to Dom Pedro I. At the northeast corner of the praça is the **Teatro João Caetano** ① *T2221 0305*, while the **Centro de Arte Hélio Oiticica** ① *R Luís de Camões 68, Mon-Fri 1000-1800*, a contermporary exhibition space, has a bookshop and air-conditioned café. Also on R Luís de Camões is the **Real Gabinete Português de Leitura** ① *No 30, T2221 3138, www.realgabinete.com.br, Mon-Fri 0900-1800, free*, an architectural gem with a magnificent reading hall and some 120,000 books. Shops nearby specialize in selling goods for umbanda, the Afro-Brazilian religion. Combine any of these with a drink at the **Confeitaria Colombo**, see Restaurants below.

South of the Largo da Carioca are the modern buildings on Avenida República do Chile including the new cathedral, the **Catedral Metropolitana** ① *www.catedral.com.br, 0700-1900, Mass Mon-Fri 1100, Sun 1000*, dedicated in November 1976. It is an oblate concrete cone, whose most striking feature is four enormous 60-m-high stained-glass windows. Crossing Avendia República do Paraguai from the cathedral is the station, with museum, for the tram to Santa Teresa (see below).

Avenida Rio Branco and Cinelândia

The area around Praça Floriano, Cinelândia, was the city's liveliest zone in the 1920s and 1930s. **Theatro Municipal** ① *Praça Floriano, T2332 9191, www.theatromunicipal.rj.gov.br, Mon-Fri 1300-1700, guided visits T2332 9220, US$6.25, 4 a day Mon-Fri, 3 a day Sat. The box office is open 1000-1800*. One of the most magnificent buildings in Brazil in the eclectic style, it was built in 1905-1909, in imitation of the Opéra in Paris. The decorative features inside and out represent many styles, all lavishly executed. Opera and orchestral performances are given here. The **Biblioteca Nacional** ① *Av Rio Branco 219, T3095 3879, www.bn.br, Mon-Fri 0900-2000, Sat 0900-1500, free*, dates from 1905-1910. The monumental staircase leads to a hall, off which lead the fine internal staircases of Carrara marble. It houses over nine million volumes and documents. The **Museu Nacional de Belas Artes** ① *Av Rio Branco 199, T2219 8474, www.mnba.gov.br, Tue-Fri 1000-1800, Sat, Sun and holidays 1200-1700, US$4*, was built between 1906 and 1908, in eclectic style. It has 800 original paintings and sculptures and 1000 direct reproductions. One gallery, dedicated to works by Brazilian artists from the 17th century onwards, includes paintings by Frans Janszoon Post (Dutch 1612-1680), who painted Brazilian landscapes in classical Dutch style, and Frenchmen Debret and Taunay. It has one of the best collections of Brazilian modernism in the country, with important works by artists like Cândido Portinári and Emiliano Di Cavalcánti. The **Centro Cultural Justiça Federal** (1905-1909) ① *Av Rio Branco 241, T3261 2550, www.ccjf.trf2 .gov.br, Tue-Sun 1200-1900*, in the former Supreme Court, has excellent eclectic architecture; you can see the court chamber and good temporary exhibitions.

Just south of the Catedral Metropolitana is **Lapa**, an area slowly rediscovering its belle-époque, artistic past. After 40 years of neglect, streets with a reputation for extreme danger have revived; town houses have been renovated, antiques markets, cafés and music venues have opened and the area has become the heart of Bohemian Rio. You still need to be a bit vigilant here, but it's one of *the* places to go for a night out.

West of the centre

About 3 km west of the public gardens of the Praça da República (beyond the Sambódromo – see box, Carnival, page 390) is the **Quinta da Boa Vista** ① *daily 0700-1800*, formerly the emperor's private park, from 1809 to 1889. If you are comfortable in crowds, a good time to visit is Saturday or Sunday afternoon. It is full of locals looking for fun and relaxation and therefore more police are on hand. **Note** Beware of thieves by the park entrance and in the park itself on weekdays.

In the entrance hall of the **Museu Nacional** ① *Quinta da Boa Vista, T2562 6900, www.museunacional.ufrj.br, Tue-Sun 1000-1600, US$1.50*, is the famous Bendegó meteorite, found in the State of Bahia in 1888; its original weight, before some of it was chipped, was 5360 kg. The museum also has important collections which are poorly displayed. The building was the principal palace of the Emperors of Brazil, but only the unfurnished Throne Room and ambassadorial reception room on the second floor reflect past glories. The museum contains collections of Brazilian indigenous weapons, costumes, utensils, etc, of minerals and of historical documents. There are also collections of birds, beasts, fishes and butterflies. Despite the need for conservation work, the museum is still worth visiting. The safest way to reach the museum is by taking a taxi to the main door. Having said that, it can be reached by Metrô to São Cristóvão, then cross the railway line and walk five minutes to the park. This is safer than taking a bus. Also in the park is the **Jardim Zoológico** ① *T3878 4200, Tue-Sun 0900-1630, US$3, young children free, students with ID pay half*, with a captive breeding programme for some endangered animals, such as golden lion tamarins.

Maracanã Stadium ① *T2334 1705, www.maracanaonline.com.br, daily 0900-1700; independent visit Gate 15, guided tours of the renovated stadium available*. Highly recommended for football fans. This is one of the largest sports centres in the world. Its original capacity of 200,000 has been cut to about 80,000 in the complete and hugely expensive remodelling for the 2014 World Cup. Matches are worth going to if only for the spectators' samba bands. There are three types of ticket, but prices vary according to the game. Agencies charge much more for tickets than at the gate or on the internet. It is cheaper to buy tickets from club sites on the day before the match. Seats in the white section have good views. Maracanã is now used only for major games; Rio teams play most matches at their home grounds (still a memorable experience, about US$2 per ticket). Maracanã can be visited most safely during a game with www.bealocal.com, T9643 0366: all is organized including transport from hotel/hostel, tickets and a safe area from which to watch the game.

Santa Teresa → See map, page 374.

Known as the coolest part of Rio, this hilly inner suburb southwest of the centre, boasts many colonial and 19th-century buildings, set in narrow, curving, tree-lined streets. Today the old houses are lived in by artists, intellectuals and makers of handicrafts. As Rio's up-and-coming place to stay, it has hostels, hotels and homestays (including the upper floor of the former home of Ronnie Biggs, the British, 1960s great train robber). At the end of the tram line (see below), Largo das Neves, you will be able to appreciate the small-town feel of the place. There are several bars here. The essential stop is the Largo do Guimarães, which has some not-to-be-missed eating places (see Restaurants). **Chácara do Céu** ① *R Murtinho Nobre 93, T3970 1126, www.museuscastro maya.com.br, Wed-Mon 1200-1700, US$1, take the Santa Teresa tram to Curvelo station, walk along R Dias de Barros, following the signposts to*

Parque das Ruínas. Also called Fundação Raymundo Ottoni de Castro Maia, it has a wide range of art objects and modern painters, including Brazilian; exhibitions change through the year. The **Chalé Murtinho** ① *R Murtinho 41, daily 1000-1700*, was in ruins until it was partially restored and turned into a cultural centre called **Parque das Ruínas**. There are exhibitions, a snack bar and superb views.

Santa Teresa is best visited on the traditional open-sided **tram**, the *bondinho*. A serious accident has closed the line until 2014. The route runs from Rua Profesor Lélio Gama, near the Largo da Carioca (Metrô to Carioca or Cinelândia), over the **Arcos da Lapa** aqueduct and then winds its way up to the district's historic streets, ending either at Paula Mattos or Dois Irmãos. Buses number 434 and 464 run from Leblon (via Ipanema, Copacabana and the Guanabara Bay suburbs) to Avenida Riachuelo in Lapa, a few hundred metres north of the arches, from where minibus 014 Castelo (US$1.35) runs to the Largo do Guimarães. Taxis from Glória metro to Santa Teresa cost around US$5; at night, only take a taxi.

Zona Sul → *See map, page 374.*

The commercial district ends where Avenida Rio Branco meets Avenida Beira Mar. This avenue, with its royal palms and handsome buildings, coasting the Botafogo and Flamengo beaches, makes a splendid drive, Avenida Infante Dom Henrique, along the beach over re-claimed land (the Aterro), leading to Botafogo and through two tunnels to Copacabana.

Glória, Catete and Flamengo

On the Glória and Flamengo waterfront, with a view of the Pão de Açúcar and Corcovado, is the **Parque do Flamengo**, designed by Burle Marx, opened in 1965 during the 400th anniversary of the city's founding and landscaped on 100 ha reclaimed from the bay. It is a popular recreation area. (**Note** Be careful after dark.) **Museu de Arte Moderna** ① *Av Infante Dom Henrique 85, city end of Parque Flamengo, T2240 4944, www.mamrio.com.br, Tue-Fri 1200-1800, 1900 weekends and holidays, US$6.* This spectacular building houses works by many well-known Europeans and collections of Brazilian contemporary art, the best modern art in Brazil outside São Paulo.

The **Monumento aos Mortos da Segunda Guerra Mundial/National War Memorial** ① *Av Infante Dom Henrique 75, opposite Praça Paris, crypt and museum Tue-Sun 1000-1700, mausoleum Tue-Sun 1000-1600; free, beach clothes and rubber-thonged sandals not permitted,* to Brazil's dead in the Second World War. The Memorial is two slender columns supporting a slightly curved slab, representing two palms uplifted to heaven. In the crypt are the remains of Brazilian soldiers killed in Italy in 1944-1945 and on ships torpedoed by U-boats. The beautiful little church on the Glória Hill, overlooking the Parque do Flamengo, is **Nossa Senhora da Glória do Outeiro** ① *Mon-Fri 0900-1200, 1300-1700, Sat-Sun 0900-1200, buses 119 from the centre and 571 from Copacabana.* It was the favourite church of the imperial family; Dom Pedro II was baptized here. The building is polygonal, with a single tower. It contains excellent examples of blue-faced Brazilian tiling. Its main wooden altar, was carved by Mestre Valentim. The adjacent museum of religious art keeps the same hours.

The charming **Parque do Catete** ① *0800-1800*, is a small park with birds and monkeys between Praia do Flamengo and the Palácio do Catete, which contains the fine **Museu da República** ① *R do Catete 153, T3235 3693, www.museudarepublica.org.br, Tue-Fri 1000-1700, Sat, Sun and holidays 1400-1800, US$3.75. Take bus 571 from Copacabana, or the Metrô to Catete station.* The palace was built in 1858-1866. In 1887 it was converted into the presidential seat, until the move to Brasília. The first floor is devoted to the history of the Brazilian republic.

Museu do Folclore Edison Carneiro ① *R do Catete 181, T2285 0441, Tue-Fri 1100-1800, Sat-Sun 1500-1800, free, signs in Portuguese, take bus 571 from Copacabana, or the Metrô to Catete station.* This museum has an exhibit of small ceramic figures representing everyday life in Brazil, some very funny, some scenes animated by electric motors. There are fine Candomblé and Umbanda costumes, religious objects, ex-votos and sections on many of Brazil's festivals. It has a small, but excellent library, with helpful staff for finding books on Brazilian culture, history and anthropology.

The **Museu Carmen Miranda** ① *Rui Barbosa 560, Parque do Flamengo (in front of the Morro da Viúva), T2334 4293, Tue-Fri 1100-1700, Sat-Sun 1400-1700, US$1,* houses over 3000 items related to the famous Portuguese singer who emigrated to Brazil, then Hollywood, and is forever associated with Rio. These include her famous gowns, fruit-covered hats, jewellery and reviews, recordings and occasional showings of her films.

Botafogo

Museu Villa-Lobos ① *R Sorocaba 200, T2266 3845, www.museuvillalobos.org.br, Mon-Fri 1000-1700, free.* Such was the fame and respect afforded to Latin America's most celebrated composer that Rio de Janeiro founded this museum only a year after his death in 1960. Inside the fine 19th-century building is the collection Includes instruments, scores, books and recordings. The museum has occasional shows and concerts, and supports a number of classical music projects throughout Brazil. **Museu do Índio** ① *R das Palmeiras 55, T3214 8702, www.museudoindio.org.br, Tue-Fri 0900-1730, Sat and Sun 1300-1700, US$1.85, Sun free. It's a 10-min walk from Botafogo Metrô; from rodoviária, Bus 136 passes Rua São Clemente, also 172, 178, from Zona Sul 511, 512, 522 (to Botafogo Metrô).* The museum houses 12,000 objects from many Brazilian indigenous groups. There is also a small, well-displayed handicraft shop.

Pão de Açúcar (Sugar Loaf mountain)

The Pão de Açúcar, or Sugar Loaf, is a massive volcanic cone at the entrance to Guanabara Bay that soars to 396 m. Below it, halfway up the cable car ride, is the **Morro da Urca**, with the **Abençoado** restaurant (see page 385). You can get refreshments at the top. The sea-level cable car station is in a military area, so it is safe to visit. At Praia Vermelha, the beach to the south of the rock, is the Círculo Militar da Praia Vermelha restaurant. From here, the Pista Cláudio Coutinho runs part-way round the foot of the rock. It is a 1.2-km paved path for walking, jogging and access to climbing places. It is open 0700-1800. Here you have mountain, forest and sea side-by-side, right in the heart of the city. If you go early you may see marmosets and tanagers. You can also use the Pista Coutinho as a way of getting up the Pão de Açúcar more cheaply than the US$27 **cable car ride** ① *Av Pasteur 520, T2546 8400, www.bondinho. com.br, 0800-1950, last car down 2100, every 20 mins, children 6-12 half price, under 6 free.* About 350 m from the path entrance is a track to the left, open 0800-1800, which leads though the forest (go left at the ridge) to Morro de Urca, from where the cable car can be taken for US$8 (you can come down this way, too, but if you take the cable car from sea level you must pay full fare). You can save even more money, but use more energy, by climbing the Caminho da Costa, the continuation of the Pista Coutinho, to the summit of the Pão de Açúcar. Only one stretch, of 10 m, requires climbing gear, but if you wait at the bottom of the path for a group going up, they will let you tag along. This way you can descend to Morro de Urca by cable car for free and walk down from there. There are 35 rock routes up the mountain, with various degrees of difficulty. The best months for climbing are April to August. A permit to climb costs US$97; ask at the Tourist Office. See What to do, page 394, for climbing clubs; there is also a book on climbing routes. ▶▶ *For getting there, see Transport, page 397.*

Corcovado

Corcovado is a hunchbacked peak, 710 m high, surmounted by a 38-m-high statue of Christ the Redeemer, O Cristo Redentor, which was completed in 1931. There is a superb view from the top (sometimes obscured by mist), to which there are a cog railway and road; taxis, cooperative minivans and train put down their passengers behind the statue. Private cars are only allowed as far as Paineiras, from where you can catch train or cabs. The 3.8-km railway

3 Glória, Santa Teresa, Catete, Flamengo

Where to stay
1 Casa Áurea C2
2 Casa Cool Beans C1
3 Casa da Gente A3
3 Glória Palace C5
4 Hotel Santa Teresa C2
5 Imperial D4
6 Mama Ruisa C3
7 Novo Mundo D5
8 Rio Forest Hostel A3
9 Rio Hostel B3
10 Um Meia Três D2

Restaurants
1 Adega do Pimenta C2
2 Alcaparra E5
3 Aprazível D2
4 Bar do Arnaudo C2
5 Espírito Santa C2
6 Estação República D4
7 Lamas F4
8 Portella C2
9 Sobrenatural C2

Bars & clubs
10 Bar do Mineiro C2
11 Goya Beira A1
12 Semente D1

itself offers fine views. Average speed is 15 kph on the way up and 12 kph on the way down. There is an exhibition of the history of the railway. From the upper terminus there is a system of escalators, one with a panoramic view, to the top, near which is a café (alternatively you can climb 220 steps up). To see the city by day and night ascend at 1500 or 1600 and descend on the last train, approximately 1815. Mass is held on Sunday in a small chapel in the statue pedestal. To reach the vast statue of Cristo Redentor at the summit of Corcovado, you have to go through Laranjeiras and Cosme Velho. The road through these districts heads west out of Catete. ▶▶ *See Transport, page 397.*

Those who want to see what Rio was like early in the 19th century should go to the **Largo do Boticário** ① *R Cosme Velho 822*, a charming small square in neo-colonial style. Much of the material used in creating the effect of the square came from old buildings demolished in the city centre. The square is close to the terminus for the Corcovado cog railway. The **Museu Internacional de Arte Naïf do Brasil (MIAN)** ① *R Cosme Velho 561, T2205 8612, Tue-Fri 1000-1800, US$6*, which re-opened in 2012 after renovation, is one of the most comprehensive museums of naïf and folk paintings in the world with a permanent collection of 8000 works by naïf artists from 130 countries. The museum also hosts temporary exhibitions, has a café and a souvenir shop.

Copacabana → *Tourist police patrol*
Copacabana beach until 1700. See map, page 376.
Built on a narrow strip of land (only a little over 4 sq km) between mountain and sea, Copacabana has one of the highest population densities in the world: 62,000 per sq km, or 250,000 in all. Copacabana began to develop when the Túnel Velho (Old Tunnel) was built in 1891 and an electric tram service reached it. Weekend villas and bungalows sprang up; all have now gone. In the 1930s the **Copacabana Palace Hotel** was the only tall building; it is now one of the lowest on the beach. The opening of the Túnel Novo (New Tunnel) in the 1940s led to an explosion of population which shows no sign of having spent its force. Unspoilt art deco blocks towards the Leme (city) end of Copacabana are now under preservation order.

After a brief period of decline, new beach cafés, paving and targeted policing have

National War Memorial

Marina de Glória

Parque do Flamengo

ossa Senhora da Glória

ad De Nossa Senhora

Russel

veira Martins
eu da Catete
ública   Parque do
eu do Folclore
són Carneiro

erreira Viana

acedo

Belga Mar

Praia do Flamengo   Aterro do Flamengo

NGO
iandaré

ão do
nengo

⟶ **Rio de Janeiro maps**
1 Rio de Janeiro, page 365
2 Rio de Janeiro centre, page 368
3 Glória, Santa Teresa, Catete, Flamengo, page 374
4 Copacabana, page 376
5 Ipanema and Leblon, page 378

To Museu Carmen Miranda 6

made the beach pleasant again and safer. While the water can be dirty when the currents wash shoreward, Copacabana and Leme are now as attractive places to relax in the sun as neighbouring Ipanema. And they're a good deal cheaper. The shops are mostly in Avenida Nossa Senhora de Copacabana and Rua Barata Ribeiro, but the more stylish shops remain in Ipanema, Leblon and in the various large shopping centres in the city. At the far end of the beach, is **Museu Histórico do Exército e Forte de Copacabana** ① *Av Atlântica at Francisco Otaviano, T2521 1032, www.fortedecopacabana.com, Tue-Sun and bank holiday 1000-1800, US$5*, which charts the history of the army in Brazil. There are good views out over the beaches and a small restaurant.

The world-famous beach is divided into numbered *postos*, where the lifeguards are based. They will advise on the water quality for swimming. Different sections attract different types of people, eg young people, artists and gays. ▶▶ *See also Transport, page 398.*

4 Copacabana

Where to stay 🛌
1 Angrense
2 Atlantis Copacabana
3 Benidorm Palace
4 CabanaCopa Hostel
5 Che Lagarto Copacabana

6 Copacabana Palace & Cipriani Restaurant
7 Copacabana Rio
8 Copacabana Sol
9 Copinha Hostel
10 El Misti Hostel

11 Pestana Rio Atlântica
12 Rio Backpackers
13 Rio Design
14 Santa Clara
15 Sofitel

Ipanema and Leblon → *See map, page 378.*

Beyond Copacabana are the seaside suburbs of Ipanema and Leblon. The two districts are divided by a canal from the Lagoa Rodrigo de Freitas to the sea, beside which is the Jardim de Alá. Ipanema and Leblon are a little less built-up than Copacabana, but they are more sophisticated. The sea is good for swimming. Praia de Arpoador at the Copacabana end of Ipanema is a peaceful spot to watch surfers, with the beautiful backdrop of Morro Dois Irmãos (on the slopes is Vidigal favela). A permanent cycle track runs all the way from the north end of Flamengo to Barra de Tijuca via Ipanema and Copacabana. The seaward lane of the road running beside the beach is closed to traffic until 1800 on Sundays and holidays; this makes it popular for rollerskating and cycling.

Lagoa, Jardim Botânico and Gávea

Backing Ipanema and Leblon are the residential districts of Lagoa and Jardim Botânico, beside the **Lagoa Rodrigo de Freitas**, a saltwater lagoon on which Rio's rowing and small-boat sailing clubs are active. The lake is too polluted for bathing, but parks and extensive leisure areas surround it. Avenida Epitácio Pessoa, on the eastern shore, leads to the Túnel Rebouças which runs beneath Corcovado and Cosme Velho.

Well worth a visit is the **Jardim Botânico** (Botanical Gardens) ① *T3874 1808, www.jbrj. gov.br, 0800-1700, US$3.50,* 8 km from the centre (see Transport, page 398). These were founded in 1808. The most striking features are the transverse avenues of 30 m high royal palms. Among the more than 7000 varieties of plants from around the world are examples of the pau brasil tree, now endangered, and many other threatened species. There is a herbarium, an aquarium, a library and a botanical museum. A new pavilion contains sculptures by Mestre Valentim transferred from the centre. Many improvements were carried out before the 1992 Earth Summit, including a new Orquidário and an enlarged bookshop.

The **Planetário** ① *Padre Leonel Franco 240, Gávea, T2274 0096, www.rio.rj.gov. br/planetario, by appointment, shows for children on weekends at 1630, 1800 and 1930, free; getting there: buses 176 and 178 from the centre, Flamengo, 591 and 592 from Copacabana.* Inaugurated in 1979, the planetarium has a sculpture of the Earth and Moon by Mario Agostinelli. There are occasional *chorinho* concerts on Thursday or Friday.

To Botafogo

Tunel Novo

Praça Demétrio Ribeiro

Villa Lobos Theatre

(Princes Isabel)

LEME

Prado Jnr

Copacabana

Praça Lido Weekend Fair

Gustavo Sampaio

Av Atlântica

Praça Júlio de Noronha

Praia do Leme

MORRO DO LEME

Restaurants 🍽
1 Aipo and Aipim
2 Apetite Café
3 Cafeina
4 Cervantes
5 Chon Kou
6 Churrascaria Palace
7 Eclipse
8 La Tratoria
9 Nomangue
10 Siri Mole & Cia
11 Traiteurs de France

The flat-topped **Pedra da Gávea** can be climbed or scrambled up for magnificent views, but beware of snakes. Behind the Pedra da Gávea is the Pedra Bonita. A road, the Estrada das Canoas, climbs up past these two rocks on its way to the Parque Nacional Tijuca. There is a spot on this road which is one of the chief hang-glider launch sites in the area (see page 393). On the slopes of the Pedra da Gávea is Rocinha, reportedly the largest favela in Rio. It was declared "pacified" in 2011 and it has the full range of urban amenities, but still faces health, sanitation and security problems. Tourism is one of many long-running initiatives here and property speculation is creeping in. The neighbourhood's website is www.rocinha.org. See also http://lifeinrocinha.blogspot.co.uk and for some tourist options, see Tour operators, page 394 and Carlinhos' www.terracetourist.com. ▸▸ *See also Transport, page 398.*

5 Ipanema & Leblon

500 metres
500 yards

Where to stay
1 Arpoador Inn
2 Best Western Sol Ipanema
3 Casa 6, Harmonia & Karisma
4 Dolphin Inn
5 Fasano Rio
6 Ipanema Beach House
7 Ipanema Hostel
8 Ipanema Inn
9 Marina All Suites & Bar D'Hotel
10 Marina Palace
11 Mar Ipanema
12 San Marco

Restaurants
1 Alessandro & Frederico
2 Árabe da Gávea
3 Bistrô ZaZá
4 Casa da Feijoada
5 Celeiro
6 CT Boucherie
7 Esplanada Grill & Gero
8 Fellini
9 Forneria
10 Guimas
11 Manekineko
12 New Natural
13 Porção
14 Roberta Sudbrack
15 Satyricon
16 Zuka

Bars & clubs
17 00
18 Académia da Cachaça
19 A Garota de Ipanema
20 Empório
21 Melt

➡ **Rio de Janeiro maps**
1 Rio de Janeiro, page 365
2 Rio de Janeiro centre, page 368
3 Glória, Santa Teresa, Catete, Flamengo, page 374
4 Copacabana, page 376
5 Ipanema and Leblon, page 378

Southern suburbs

Leblon to Barra da Tijuca

From Leblon, two inland roads take traffic west to the outer seaside suburb of Barra da Tijuca: the Auto Estrada Lagoa-Barra, which tunnels under Dois Irmãos, and the Estrada da Gávea, which goes through Gávea. Beyond Leblon the coast is rocky. A third route to Barra da Tijuca is the Avenida Niemeyer, which skirts the cliffs on the journey past Vidigal, a small beach where the Sheraton is situated. It passes São Conrado and has two tunnels under the Pedra da Gávea.

Barra da Tijuca

This rapidly developing residential area is also one of the principal recreation areas of Rio, with its 20-km sandy beach and good waves for surfing. At the westernmost end is the small beach of Recreio dos Bandeirantes, where the ocean can be very rough. The channels behind the Barra are popular with jetskiers. It gets very busy on Sundays. There are innumerable bars and restaurants, clustered at both ends, campsites, motels and hotels: budget accommodation tends to be self-catering. The main 2016 Olympic village facilities will be here, so more and more buildings are going up. Although buses do run as far as Barra, getting to and around here is best by car. A bit further out is the **Museu Casa do Pontal** ① *Estrada do Pontal 3295, Recreio dos Bandeirantes, www.museucasadopontal.com.br, Tue-Sun 0930-1700*, a collection of Brazilian folk art. Recommended.

Parque Nacional da Tijuca

① *Entry US$14.55 (US$10.15 low season). Open 0800-1700, 1800 in summer. National park information, T2492 2252, parnatijuca@icmbio.gov.br. See also www.amigosdoparque.org.br. See Transport page 398.*

The Pico da Tijuca (1022 m) gives a good idea of the tropical vegetation of the interior and a fine view of the bay and its shipping. A two- to three-hour walk leads to the summit: on entering the park at Alto da Boa Vista (0600-2100), follow the signposts (maps are displayed) to Bom Retiro, a good picnic place (1½ hours' walk). At Bom Retiro the road ends and there is another hour's walk up a fair footpath to the summit (take the path from the right of the Bom Retiro drinking fountain; not the more obvious steps from the left). The last part consists of steps carved out of the solid rock; look after children at the summit as there are several sheer drops, invisible because of bushes. The route is shady for almost its entire length. The main path to Bom Retiro passes the Cascatinha Taunay (a 30-m waterfall) and the Mayrink Chapel (built 1860). Beyond the Chapel is the restaurant A Floresta. Other places of interest not passed on the walk to the peak are the Paulo e Virgínia Grotto, the Vista do Almirante and the Mesa do Imperador (viewpoints). Allow at least five to six hours for the excursion. Maps of the park are available; walking is safest at weekends and holidays. If hiking in the national park other than on the main paths, a guide may be useful if you do not want to get lost: a list of registered guides is available at the **Visitors Centre** ① *T2492 2252/2492 2253, open 0900-1700.*

Parque Estadual da Pedra Branca ① *Núcleo Camorim, Camorim, Jacarepaguá, T3417 3642, www.inea.rj.gov.br/unidades/pqpedra_branca.asp*, the second largest urban forest in the world after the Serra da Cantareira in São Paulo, is also in Rio, though few Cariocas are aware of it. Pedra Branca is the city's best kept natural secret, protecting an astounding 12,500 ha of pristine rainforest, lakes and mountains, which are home to over 500 animal species. A number are threatened or critically endangered. There are many trails in the park, including one leading to the highest peak in Rio de Janeiro, the Pedra Branca (1024 m).

⊚ Rio de Janeiro listings

For hotel and restaurant price codes, and other
relevant information, see Essentials.

⊚ Where to stay

The best places to stay in Rio are Santa Teresa,
for nightlife, culture and easy access to Lapa,
the Sambódromo and carnival; Copacabana,
Ipanema, Leblon and the Arpoador for the
beach. Ipanema is probably the safest area in
the city. Backpackers are well catered for, with
hostels opening all the time. Hostelling sites
(www.hostels.com, www.hostelworld.com) list
the latest options. Economy hotels, however,
are usually dubious establishments in equally
dubious areas. Guest houses and B&Bs are
a better-value and better-run option, even
for those on a medium budget. Self-catering
apartments are available at all levels and are a
popular form of accommodation; see below.
   Prices rise astronomically over New Year
and Carnaval. Reserve well in advance.

Homestays
$$$$-$$$ Hidden Pousadas Brazil,
www.hiddenpousadasbrazil.com, have
great accommodation options in carefully
selected small mid- to upper-end hotels and
homes throughout Rio and beyond. These
include lovely properties in Leblon, Ipanema,
Copacabana and Santa Teresa.
$$$$-$$ Cama e Café, R Laurinda Santos
Lobo 124, T2225 4366 (T9638 4850, 24 hrs),
www.camaecafe.com and www.riohome stay.
com. One of the best accommodation options
in Rio with a range of some 50 homestays in
Santa Teresa, Cosme Velho and Ipanema from
the simple to the luxurious. They provide the
opportunity to get to know locals and see
Rio from the inside. Rooms can be treated as
impersonally as those in a hotel, or guests can
fit in as part of the household; good value.
Cama e Café work hard to match guests with
hosts who share similar interests.

Santa Teresa *p371, map p374*
Santa Teresa is hilly and offers views out over
Rio but is inconvenient for transport. Boutique
hotels range from the **$$$$ Hotel Santa
Teresa**, R Almte Aelxandrino 660, T3380 0200,
www.santateresahotel.com (French-owned,
chic and exclusive 5-star, restaurant and spa
behind high walls), and **Mama Ruisa**, R Santa
Cristina 132, T2242 1281, www.mamaruisa.com
(also French-run, simple, elegant).
$$$$-$$$ Um Meia Três, R Aprazível 163,
T2232 0034, www.hotelinrio.net. Small, lovely
views, book online for best rates.
$$$ Casa Áurea, R Áurea 80, Santa Teresa,
T2242 5830, www.casaaurea.com.br. Small
hotel in a converted colonial house. Rooms
are bright and airy and service attentive.
Breakfast is served in a little garden visited
by marmosetš in the mornings.
$$$ Casa Cool Beans, R Laurinda Santos
Lobo 136, T2262 0552, www.casacoolbeans.
com, with another branch in Ipanema. In a
large Santa Teresa town house on a quiet back
street, decorated with art and graffiti by local
artists, with a small pool, spacious wood-
floored rooms and a generous breakfast,
American-run.
$$$ Casa da Gente, R Gonçalves Fontes 33,
www.casadagente.com. French/Brazilian
run, inspired by fair trade and sustainability
principles, excellent accommodation, double
and shared rooms (**$$**), helpful staff, convenient
location, nice atmosphere, good value.
$ Rio Forest Hostel, R Joaquim Murtinho
517, T3563 1021, www.rioforesthostel.com.br.
Bright, airy hostel with dorms and rooms with
a view. Decent showers, welcoming.
$ pp Rio Hostel, R Joaquim Murtinho 361,
T3852 0827, www.riohostel.com.br. Dorms
(**$$** in double room), with breakfast, excellent
facilities include kitchen, bar, pool, internet,
laundry service, hot water, airport pick-up
US$17, relaxed, English spoken, events and
trips organized. Owner loves all things British
and Australian.

Glória, Catete and Flamengo p372, map p374

These are mainly residential areas between the centre and Copacabana. Catete, and Glória to the north and Flamengo to the south, lie next to a park landscaped by Burle Marx and a beautiful beach lapped by a filthy sea. They have good bus and Metrô links.

$$$$ Glória Palace, R do Russel 632, Glória, www.hotelgloriario.com.br. Rio's other stylish and elegant 1920s hotel. Refurbished as a super-luxury hotel in 2013.

$$$$ Novo Mundo, Praia Flamengo 20, Catete, T2105 7000, www.hotelnovomundo-rio.com.br. Renovated 4-star rooms with some 3-star fittings, suites with balcony views of the Sugar Loaf, a good business choice.

$$ Imperial, R do Catete 186, T2556 5212, Catete, www.imperialhotel.com.br. One of the city's very first grand hotels (late 19th century). Rooms either in the grander, older main building, or the modern annexe (modern, US motel-style), better equipped but overlooking the parking lot.

Botafogo p373

Another middle-class neighbourhood with a great beach lapped by dirty water. Convenient for public transport and mall shopping but care should be taken at night.

$$$ O Veleiro, T2554 8980, Praia de Botafogo, www.oveleiro.com. Address given only with reservation. B&B with a great breakfast, Canadian/Carioca-owned, transfers to/from airport or bus station, tours, guiding, helpful staff. Recommended.

$$-$ pp El Misti Hostel, R Praia de Botafogo 462, casa 9, T2226 0991, www.elmistihostel rio.com. Converted colonial house with dorms, shared bath, private rooms with shared bath (**$$**), capoeira classes, tour service. Popular with party-goers. Convenient for public transport. Free pick-up for all bookings. Has other branches in Copacabana and around Brazil.

$$-$ Sun Rio Hostel, R Praia de Botafogo 462, casa 5, T2226 0461, www.sunriohostel.com.br, next door to El Misti. A/c dorms, doubles and

en-suites, all very well kept. Shared kitchen, bike rental and tours organized. Owner Daniela is very welcoming.

At the same address, casa 9, is another hostel **$$-$ pp Alpha Hostel**, T2286 7799, www.alphahostel.com, with private rooms and cheaper dorms, breakfast, tours, airport and bus terminal transfer.

Copacabana p375, map p376

$$$$ Copacabana Palace, Av Atlântica 1702, T2548 7070, www.copacabanapalace.com.br. Justifiably world famous hotel with distinguished guest list, dripping in 1920s elegance, superb facilities and effortless service. Go for cocktails and dinner if you can't afford to stay. Cipriani (**$$$**), is the best restaurant for formal evening dining in Rio with standards similar to its sister restaurants in New York and Venice.

$$$$ Copacabana Rio, Av N S de Copacabana 1256, T2267 9900, www.copacabanariohotel.com.br. Quiet, efficiently run 1970s tower with simple but well-maintained 3-star rooms, small pool and generous breakfasts. Safe area at Ipanema end of beach, 1 block from the sand.

$$$$ Pestana Rio Atlântica, Av Atlântica 2964, T2548 6332, www.pestana.com. Part of the Portuguese Pestana group, an excellent choice, spacious bright rooms and a rooftop pool and terrace with sweeping views, very high standards. Recommended.

$$$$ Rio Design, R Francisco Sá 17, T3222 8800, www.riodesignhotel.com. Comfortable mock-boutique suites in a great location at the Arpoador end of Copacabana. Decent breakfast with a view on the top floor, small spa. Good service.

$$$$ Sofitel, Av Atlântica, 4240, T2525 1232, www.sofitel.com. One of the best beachfront options, at the safer Arpoadoar end, an easy walk to Ipanema. Airy rooms (best on the upper floors), sauna, pool and Le Pré Catelan restaurant, with one of the best kitchens in the city.

$$$ Angrense, Travessa Angrense 25, T2548 0509, www.angrensehotel.com.br.

Well-kept rooms in a little art deco block on a quiet street, English-speaking staff, reliable tour agency and good carnival rates.

$$$ Atlantis Copacabana, Av Bulhões de Carvalho 61, T2521 1142, www.atlantishotel. com.br. Renovated Arpoador hotel in a quiet, safe street close to the beach. Small rooftop pool, sauna, good value.

$$$ Benidorm Palace, R Barata Ribeiro 547, T2548 8880, www.benidorm.com.br. Modern rooms decked out in light wood in a tower, best and quietest at the back with small marble bathrooms. Sauna and internet in the lobby.

$$$ Copacabana Sol, R Santa Clara 141, T2549 4577, www.copacabanasolhotel.com.br. Safe, helpful, quiet, with good breakfast.

$$$ Santa Clara, R Décio Vilares, 316, T2256 2650, www.hotelsantaclara.com.br. Quiet, central location, attentive service, tours arranged.

$$-$ Copinha Hostel, R Felipe de Oliveira 11, T2275 8520, www.copinhahostel.com.br. Well-run, lemon-yellow hostel with a range of dorms and doubles, some with bath, kitchen, transport services.

$ pp Cabana Copa Hostel, Travessa Guimarães Natal 12, T3988 9912, www. cabanacopa.com.br. Dorms of various sizes, including one for women only, a/c, also private rooms (**$$$**), tours, good reputation.

$ pp Che Lagarto Copacabana, R Barata Ribeiro 111, T3209 0348, www.chelagarto. com. Several dorms and doubles (**$$**). Helpful, young party atmosphere, several languages spoken, organizes tours, bar.

$ pp El Misti Hostel, Travessa Frederico Pamplona 20, T2547 0800, www.elmisti copacabana.com. 500 m from Copacabana beach, 200 m from metro and buses. Dorms and doubles (**$$$**). Tour services, open bar, meals. Free pick-up for all bookings.

$ pp Rio Backpackers, Trav Santa Leocádia 38, at corner of R Rompeu Loureiro, T2236 3803, www.riobackpackers.com.br. Dorms and private rooms **$$$** with fan or a/c, 24-hr security, laundry, free bikes, tours and other services.

Ipanema, Leblon and further west
p377, map p378

$$$$ Best Western Sol Ipanema, Av Vieira Souto 320, T2525 2020, www.bestwestern. com. Huge breakfast, good member of US chain, popular.

$$$$ Fasano Rio, Av Vieira Souto 80, Ipanema, T3202 4000, www.fasano.com.br. Phillippe Starck-designed luxury hotel with rooftop terrace, fitness centre, etc, good bar and superior restaurant, Fasano Al Mare.

$$$$ La Maison, R Sergio Porto 58, Gávea, T3205 3585, www.lamaisonario.com. In a period town house on a quiet backstreet. Bright spacious rooms tastefully decorated in primary colours, wonderful views of Corcovado from the open-sided breakfast area and the little pool. The beach is a taxi ride away.

$$$$ La Suite, R Jackson de Figueiredo 501, Joá, T2484 1962, www.lasuiterio. com. Distinguished boutique hotel with 8 individually themed rooms in a wealthy suburb between Leblon and Barra de Tijuca. Fabulous location – the pool sits eyrie-like over the exclusive beach at Joá with sweeping views out towards São Conrado. Every room has a terrace, view and a marble bathroom.

$$$$ Marina Palace and Marina All Suites, Av Delfim Moreira 630 and 696, T2294 1794, www.hotelmarina.com.br. Two 1980s towers almost next door to each other. The former has smart, modern but standard rooms and a rooftop pool; the latter is a luxury boutique with 'designer' suites, with the excellent Bar D'Hotel (**$$$**), serving light but well-flavoured fish dishes in cool surroundings. Excellent breakfasts and cocktails.

$$$ Arpoador Inn, Francisco Otaviano 177, T2523 0060, www.arpoadorinn.com.br. Well-maintained. Seafront restaurant Azul Marinho, off-season special offers are a good deal.

$$$ Dolphin Inn, R Bulhões de Carvalho 480, Casa 6, T9672 0025, www.bedandbreakfast. com/brazil-rio-de-janeiro-riodolphininn-page.html. Delightful private house in a safe, quiet street, may be rented whole or in part, convenient, welcoming US/Carioca surfer owners, kitchen, reserve in advance.

$$$ Ipanema Inn, Maria Quitéria 27, behind Caesar Park, T2523 6092, www.ipanemainn. com.br. Popular package tour and small business hotel less than 100 m from beach. Good value and location.

$$$ Mar Ipanema, R Visconde de Pirajá 539, T3875 9190, www.maripanema.com. 1 block from the beach, simple, smart, modern rooms.

$$$ San Marco, R Visconde de Pirajá 524, T2540 5032, www.sanmarcohotel.net. Renovated 2-star 2 blocks from beach, with simple rooms and a free caipirinha for every internet booking, very helpful. Recommended.

$$-$ Casa 6, R Barão da Torre 175, casa 6, T2247 1384, www.casa6ipanema.com. Charming, colourful but simple French-owned B&B in a townhouse 3 blocks from the beach. Also has doubles (**$$$**), good long stay rates.

$$-$ Harmonia, R Barão da Torre 175, casa 18, T2523 4905, www.hostelharmonia.com. 3 blocks from beach, doubles or dorms, cheaper without breakfast, kitchen facilities, English, Spanish, German and Swedish spoken.

$$-$ Ipanema Beach House, R Barão da Torre 485, T3202 2693, www.ipanemahouse.com. Dorms (US$27) and doubles (**$$$**) all with shared baths. Great little hostel with rooms arranged around a garden and small pool. Small bar, kitchen, internet and tours, good service.

$$-$ Ipanema Hostel, R Canning, casa 1, Ipanema, T2287 2928, www.riohostelipanema. com. Sister hostel to the Rio Hostel in Santa Teresa, range of small rooms and dorms, tour operator, lively crowd.

$$-$ Karisma, R Barão da Torre 177, T2523 1372, www.karismahostel.com. Tranquil little hostel 3 blocks from the beach, small but well-kept dorms and pokey doubles, all up a steep flight of stairs. English spoken.

$$ Rio Surf n Stay, R Raimundo Veras 1140, Recreio dos Bandeirantes, T3418 1133, www. riosurfnstay.com. Hostel and surf camp with dorms and private rooms, camping, surf lessons, equipment rental.

Self-catering apartments
Renting a small flat, or sharing a larger one, can be much better value than a hotel room.

All price levels are available. Copacabana, Ipanema and Leblon prices range from about US$25 a day for a simple studio (US$500-600 a month) up to US$2000 a month for a luxurious residence sleeping 4-6. Always get a written agreement when renting and check the building's (usually excellent) security arrangements.

See websites including www.alugue temporada.com.br, www.riotemporada.net and www.vivareal.com.br for more details. Also adverts in *Balcão*, twice weekly, *O Globo* or *Jornal do Brasil* (daily); under 'Apartamentos – Temporada'; advertisements are classified by district and size of apartment: *vagas e quartos* means shared accommodation; *conjugado* (or *conj*) is a studio with limited cooking facilities; *3 Quartos* is a 3-bedroom flat.

Copacabana Holiday, R Barata Ribeiro 90A, Copacabana, T2542 1525, www. copacabanaholiday.com.br. Recommended, well-equipped apartments from studios to 3-bedroom, starting at US$500 per month, minimum 30 days.

Fantastic Rio, Av Atlântica 974, Suite 501, Copacabana, T/F2543 2667, http://fantasticrio. br.tripod.com. All types of furnished accommodation, owned by Peter Corr, good service.

❼ Restaurants

The best of Rio's many restaurants are in Copacabana, Ipanema or Leblon. Expect to pay US$30-40+ per person in the better restaurants. You can eat well for an average US$5 per person, less if you choose the *prato feito* at lunchtime (US$2-7.50), or eat in a place that serves food by weight (starting at about US$10 per kg).

Galetos are lunch counters specializing in chicken and grilled meat, very reasonable. In the shopping centres there is usually a variety of restaurants and snack bars grouped around a central plaza where you can shop around for a good meal. Rio lacks that almost ubiquitous Brazilian institution, the corner bakery, and a decent breakfast can be hard to find. But there are plenty of stand-up juice bars serving fruit juices made from as many as 25 different fruits, all of which are wonderful.

City centre and Lapa *p366, map p368*
Many restaurants in the business district are open only for weekday lunch. Many lanchonetes in this area offer good, cheap meals. Travessa do Comércio has many informal street restaurant after 1800, especially on Fri. R Miguel Couto (opposite Santa Rita church) is called the Beco das Sardinhas because on Wed and Fri in particular is full of people eating sardines and drinking beer. There are several Arab restaurants on Av Senhor dos Passos, which are also open Sat and Sun. In addition to those listed there are plenty of cafes, including a few new chic options on R Lavradio in Lapa, where the lively Sat antiques market is held.
$$$ Adega Flor de Coimbra, R Teotônio Regadas 34, Lapa, T2224 4582. Founded in 1938, Portuguese food and wines, speciality *bacalhau* (salt cod). Very good.
$$$ Albamar, Praça Marechal Âncora 184-6, T2240 8378. Mon 1130-1600, Tue-Sat 1130-2200. Popular, long-established fish and seafood, with lovely views of the bay.
$$$ Eça, Av Rio Branco 128, T2524 2300. The best business lunch in the centre, classic French cooking with worldwide influences from chef Frédéric de Maeyer.
$$$ Republique, Praça da República 63 (2nd floor), T2532 9000. Designed by architect Chicô Gouveia. Chef Paulo Carvalho cooks Portuguese, Italian and French dishes.
$$ Bar Luiz, R da Crioca 39, T2262 6900. A little bar in a colonial house in the centre, famous as much for its clientèle as its tapas and *chope* in the evening, good for a quiet snack lunch, too.
$$ Café da Moda, R Gonçalves Dias 49, 3rd floor, Centro, T2222 0610, www.folic. com.br. An a/c café devoted to the narrow waistline, located in the Folic shop. Salads are named after famous models, or have more macho names for men. Light meals without hip names also available.

$$-$ Bar das Artes, Praça 15 de Novembro 48 (Paço Imperial), T2215 5795. Salads, sandwiches and light meals in a neat, peaceful café in the former Imperial Palace.
$$-$ Confeitaria Colombo, R Gonçalves Dias 32, near Carioca Metrô station. Recommended for atmosphere and the only one of its kind in Rio. Over 100 years old, it has the original belle époque decor, open 0900-1800, no service charge so tip the excellent waiters. More modern but similar establishments in some of the main hotels.
$ Sabor Saúde, R da Quitanda 21, T2252 6041. Breakfast and lunch only, vegetarian and wholefood dishes and sandwiches, also light meals (not always vegetarian).

Santa Teresa *p371, map p374*
$$$ Aprazível, R Aprazível 62, T3852 4935. Decent but unspectacular Brazilian dishes and seafood with tables outdoors in a tropical garden overlooking Guanabara Bay. This is a good Sun lunch spot when they have Choro and Samba performed by Rio's equivalent of the Buena Vista Social Club.
$$ Adega do Pimenta, R Almte Alexandrino 296. Daily 1130-2200, Sun 1100-1800, closed Sat, Tue. A very small German restaurant in the Largo do Guimarães with excellent sausages, sauerkraut and cold beer.
$$ Bar do Arnaudo, Largo do Guimarães, R Almte Alexandrino 316, T2252 7246. A modest-looking restaurant decorated with handicrafts but serving generous portions of wonderful Northeast Brazilian cooking.
$$ Espírito Santa, R Almte Alexandrino 264, T2507 4840, www.espiritosanta.com.br. Closed Mon, lunch only Tue, Wed, Sun. Upstairs is a chic Mediterranean restaurant with a wonderful sweeping view of the city, downstairs is a weekend basement club, good cocktails.
$$ Portella, R Paschoal Carlos Magno 139, Largo do Guimarães, T2507 5181, www. portellabar.com.br. São Paulo-style corner restaurant-bar with good picanha steaks, award-winning *petiscos* (bar snacks). Live music most weekends.

$$ Sobrenatural, R Almirante Alexandrino 432, T2224 1003, www.restaurantesobre natural.com.br. Open lunch and evening, closed Mon. A charming rustic restaurant serving fish caught daily on owner's boat. For a light lunch, order a mix of excellent appetizers. Recommended.

Glória, Catete and Flamengo p372, map p374

There are many cheap and mid-range eating places on R do Catete.

$$$ Alcaparra, Praia do Flamengo 144, Flamengo, T2557 7236. Elegant traditional Italian popular with politicians and business people. Overlooking the sea.

$$ Lamas, Marquês de Abrantes 18A, Flamengo, T2556 0799. Steak, seafood and general Brazilian fare have been served here for over 130 years. Excellent value, great atmosphere, opens late, popular with Brazilian arts/media people. Recommended.

$ Estação República, R do Catete 104, Catete, in the Palácio do Catete. More than 40 dishes in this per kilo restaurant, soups, sushi, salads and stews.

Botafogo p373

In Baixo Botafogo, those on a budget will find a number of enticing bars and restaurants, eg Botequim, R Visconde de Caravelas 184, one of several on this street, or Aurora, R Capitão Salomão 43.

$$$ Abençoado, on the summit of Morro de Urca, T2275 8925, www.abencoadorio. com.br. For Brazilian comfort snacks given a gourmet twist, caipirinhas and *batidas* and breathtaking views.

$$$ Miam Miam, Gen Goes Monteiro 34, T2244 0125, www.miammiam.com.br. Closed Mon. Retro chic and highly fashionable, where the alternative fashion set go for cocktails and light Mediterranean food.

$$$ Oui Oui, R Conde de Irajá 85, Botafogo, T2527 3539, www.restauranteouioui.com.br. Equally fashionable, for tapas-style *petiscos* and cocktails.

$$ Raajmahal, R Gen Polidoro 29, Baixo Botafogo, T2542 6242, www.raajmahal. com.br. One of the few restaurants offering authentic Indian food. A 2nd branch in Lapa is due to open.

$$ Yorubá, R Arnaldo Quintela 94, Botafogo (no sign), T2541 9387. Evenings only except weekends, closed Mon, Tue. Award-winning Bahian cooking.

Copacabana, Ipanema and Leblon p375, maps p376 and p378

$$$$ Esplanada Grill, R Barão de Torre 600, Ipanema, T2239 6028, www.esplanadagrill. com.br. Formal atmosphere for the best steak and other cuts of meat in Rio.

$$$ Alessandro & Frederico, R Garcia D'Ávila, 134 loja D, Ipanema, T2521 0828, www. alessandroefrederico.com.br. Upmarket café with decent café latte and breakfasts.

$$$ Bistrô ZaZá, R Joana Angélica 40, Ipanema, www.zazabistro.com.br. Hippy-chic, pseudo Moroccan/French restaurant, good fish dishes and cocktails and good fun. Evenings are best for intimate dining when the tables are lit by candles.

$$$ CT Boucherie, R Dias Ferreira 636, Leblon, T2543 1050, www.ctboucherie.com.br. Elegant, unpretentious meat restaurant, with a focus on the superb cuts of meat, accompanied by sauces of choice and delectable side dishes.

$$$ Forneria, R Aníbal de Mendonça 112, Ipanema, T2540 8045. Serves superior bar snacks and supreme burgers in pizza dough to the elegant, after-beach crowd.

$$$ Gero, R Aníbal de Mendonça 157, Ipanema, T2239 8158. Light Italian fare and excellent fish in a beautiful, minimalist space.

$$$ Manekineko, R Dias Ferreira, 410, Leblon, T2540 7641, www.manekineko.com.br. Exquisite Japanese and Japanese fusion cooking served in an intimately designed modern dining room.

$$$ Nomangue, R Sá Ferriera 25, lj B, Copacabana, T2521 3237, www.nomangue.com.br. Excellent northeast Brazilian and seafood.

$$$ Porcão, Barão de Torre 218, Ipanema, T2522 0999 (also on Av NS de Copacabana). One of the city's best *churrascarias*, serving all manner of meat in unlimited quantities for a set price.

$$$ Satyricon, R Barão da Torre 192, Ipanema, T2521 0627. The best seafood in Rio; especially the squid. Lively crowd in a large dining room. Avoid Sat when there is a seafood buffet.

$$$ Siri Mole & Cia, R Francisco Otaviano 90. Good Bahian seafood and Italian coffee in elegant a/c. At the upper end of this price bracket.

$$$ Zuka, R Dias Ferreira 233, Leblon, T3205 7154. One of the most fashionable restaurants in Rio with an eclectic fusion of everything – French and Japanese, American fast food and Italian.

$$$-$$ Churrascaria Palace, R Rodolfo Dantas 16B, Copacabana, T2541 5898. 20 different kinds of barbecued meat served on a spit at your table with buffet salads to accompany. Good value.

$$ Casa da Feijoada, Prudente de Morais 10, Ipanema, T2247 2776. Serves an excellent *feijoada* all week. Generous portions.

$$ Celeiro, R Dias Ferreira 199, Leblon, T2274 7843. Some of the best salads in the city, and light food by weight.

$$ Chon Kou, Av Atlântica 3880, T2287 3956. A traditional Chinese restaurant which also offers an extensive sushi menu, a/c; sit upstairs for good views over Copacabana beach.

$$ Fellini, R General Urquiza 104, Leblon, T2511 3600. The best per kilo in the city with delicious buffet options and plenty for vegetarians.

$$ New Natural, R Barão da Torre 173, T2287 0301. One of Ipanema's most popular vegetarian and wholefood restaurants; large range of hot dishes and desserts served per kilo. Home delivery. Natural products shop next door.

$$-$ Aipo and Aipim, Av Nossa Senhora de Copacabana 391b and 920, Copacabana, and R Visconde de Pirajá 145, Ipanema, T2267 8313. Popular chain, plentiful tasty food sold by weight.

$$-$ Eclipse, Av N S de Copacabana 1309, T2287 1788. Spruce, well-run and very popular 24-hr restaurant offering good-value *prato feito* lunches and a generous range of meats, pastas, snacks and sandwiches served in the cool interior or on streetside tables.

$ Apetite Café, R Souza Lima 78, T2247 3319. One of Copa's few bakery cafes. Offers a range of breakfasts, respectable coffee, snacks, options for kids and an a/c interior for when it gets too hot.

$ Cafeina, C Ramos 44, T2547 8651. Very popular breakfast spot with good coffee, tasty pastries and other snacks and ice cold juices

$ Cervantes, Barata Ribeiro 07-B e Prado Júnior 335B, Copacabana, T2275 6147. Stand-up bar or sit-down, a/c restaurant, open all night, queues after 2200. Said to serve the best sandwiches in town, a local institution.

$ La Tratoria, R Fernando Mendes 7A, Copacabana, T2255 3319, opposite **Hotel Excelsior**. Italian, good food and service, very reasonable. Recommended.

$ Traiteurs de France, Av NS de Copacabana 386, Copacabana, T2548 6440. Delicious tarts and pastries, not expensive.

Gávea, Lagoa and Jardim Botânico
p377

Gávea is the heartland of trendy 20-something Rio, while Jardim Botânico and Lagoa appear, at first sight, to offer no end of exciting upmarket dining opportunities. They're mostly all show and poor value. Here are a few exceptions:

$$$ Roberta Sudbrack, Av Lineu de Paula Machado 916, Jardim Botânico, T3874 0139. Celebrated for her European-Brazilian fusion cooking, Roberta was the private chef for President Henrique Cardoso.

$$ Árabe da Gávea, Gávea shopping mall, R Marquês de São Vicente 52, T2294 2439. By far the best Arabic restaurant in Rio.

$$ Guimas, R José Roberto Macedo Soares 5, Baixo Gávea, T2259 7996. One of the places where the under 30s come to be seen, especially after 2200 towards the end of the week and on Mon, before moving down the street to the two tatty bars on the corner of the street and Praça Santos Dumont. The restaurant serves simple, traditional Portuguese food, at only a handful of tables.

⏵ Bars and clubs

Rio nightlife is young and vivacious. The current hotspots are **Lapa** at weekends, with a string of clubs along Mem de Sá, Lavradio and the Beco do Rato, with dance steps from samba and forró to techno and hip hop. **Santa Teresa** is increasingly lively and is often used as a drinking spot before moving onto Lapa, or a night spot in its own. There is a cluster of bars around the Largo das Neves. Similarly busy, even on Sun and Mon is **Baixa Gávea**, where beautiful 20 somethings gather around Praça Santos Dumont. In **Ipanema/Leblon**, there is always activity on and around Av General San Martin and Rua Dias Ferreira.

Bars Wherever you are, there's one near you. Beer costs around US$2.50 for a large bottle, but up to US$7 in the plusher bars; where you are often given an entrance card which includes 2 drinks and a token entrance fee. A cover charge of US$3-7 may be made for live music, or there might be a minimum consumption charge of around US$3, sometimes both. Snack food is always available. Copacabana, Ipanema and Leblon have many beach barracas, several open all night. The seafront bars on Av Atlântica are great for people-watching. The big hotels have good cocktail bars.

Centre, Lapa and Santa Teresa *p366 and p371, maps p368 and p374*
Lapa is without doubt the centre of Rio nightlife and should not be missed if you are in Rio over a weekend. Ideally arrive early on Sat for the afternoon market and live street tango, eat and stay for a bar and club crawl. Always be wary of pickpockets around Lapa. See also Samba schools.
Bar do Mineiro, on the Largo dos Guimarães, R Paschoal Carlos Magno 99, T2221 9227. A very popular Santa Teresa bar.

Carioca da Gema, Av Mem de Sá 79, Centro, T2221 0043, www.barcariocadagema.com.br. Great samba club café, second only to Rio Scenarium, good food too.
Club Six, R das Marrecas 38, Lapa, T2510 3230, www.clubsix.com.br. Huge pounding European/NYC dance club with everything from hip-hop to ambient house.
Clube dos Democráticos, R do Riachuelo 91, T2252 4611, www.clubedosdemocraticos. com.br. An old dance hall where bands play Gafieira or dance hall samba. If you're 20- or 30-something at heart and a samba lover it's the place to be.
Estudantina Musical, Praça Tiradentes 79, 3rd floor, T2232 1149. Closed Mon-Wed. A famous old-school *gafieira* hall, busiest on Thu when hundreds gather to dance samba.
Goya Beira, Largo das Neves 13, Santa Teresa, T2232 5751. One of several restaurant bars on this pretty little square, attracts an arty crowd after 2100. Decent *petiscos* and a range of aromatic vintage *cachaças*.
Mercado 32, R do Mercado 32, Centro, T2221 2327, www.mercado32.com.br. Closed weekends. In the heart of the centre in a converted 19th-century building, this little restaurant and bar offers live MPB on most nights during the week and live chorinho every Thu from 2030.
Rio Scenarium, R do Lavradio 20, Lapa, T3147 9005, www.rioscenarium.com.br. 3-storey Samba club in a colonial house used as a movie prop warehouse. Overflowing with Brazilian exuberance and joie de vivre, with people dancing furiously, to the bizarre backdrop of a 19th-century apothecary's shop or a line of mannequins wearing 1920s outfits. This is Rio at its Bohemian best. Buzzes with beautiful people of all ages on Fri. Arrive after 2300.
Sacrilégio, Av Mem de Sá 81, next to Carioca da Gema, Lapa, T2507 3898. Samba, chorinho, pagode and occasional theatre. Close to many other bars.
Semente, R Joaquim Silva 138, T2242 5165. Popular for Samba, Choro and Salsa from 2200 Mon-Sat, US$8 cover; minimum consumption US$7. Book a table at weekends. Great

atmosphere both inside and in the streets outside. Recommended.

The Week, R Sacadura Cabral 154, Zona Portuária, T2253 1020, www.theweek.com.br. Heaving with a gay and straight crowd and with state of the art spaces, DJs and sound systems. But don't expect any Brazilian sounds, it's strictly international dance here.

Glória, Flamengo and Botafogo *p372, map p374*

Look out for the frequent free live music performances at the Marina da Glória and along Flamengo beach during the summer.

Casa da Matriz, R Enrique de Novais 107, Botafogo, T2226 9691, www.matrizonline.com.br. Great little grungy club with a bar, Atari room, small cinema and 2 dance floors. Full of Rio students.

Porão, under the Anglican church hall, R Real Grandeza 99, Botafogo, T2537 6695, www.bcsrio.org.br. British expats meet here on Fri night.

Copacabana and Ipanema *p375, maps p376 and p378*

There is frequent live music on the beaches of Copacabana and Ipanema, and along the Av Atlântica throughout the summer; especially around New Year.

A Garota de Ipanema, R Vinícius de Morais 49, Ipanema. Where the song *Girl from Ipanema* was written. Now packed with foreigners on the package Rio circuit listening to Bossa. For the real thing head up the street to Toca do Vinícius on Sun afternoon (see below).

Académia da Cachaça, R Conde de Bernadotte 26-G, Leblon; with another branch at Av Armando Lombardi 800, Barra da Tijuca, www.academiadacachaca.com.br. The best *cachaças*, great caipirinhas and traditional Brazilian dishes. Good on Fri.

Barril 1800, Av Vieira Souto 110, Ipanema, T2523 0085, www.barril1800.com.br. Nice place to watch the sunset. Highly recommended.

Devassa, R Rainha Guilhermina 48, Leblon. A 2-floor pub/restaurant/bar which is

always heaving. Brews its own beer. Also at Av Visconde de Pirajá 539, Ipanema.

Empório, R Maria Quitéria 37, Ipanema. Street bar which attracts hordes. Mon is busiest.

Melt, R Rita Ludolf 47, T2249 9309, www.melt-rio.com.br. Downstairs bar and upstairs sweaty club. Occasional performances by the cream of Rio's new samba funk scene, usually on Sun. Always heaving on Thu.

Shenanigans, R Visconde de Pirajá 112, Ipanema, T2267 5860, www.shenanigans.com.br. Obligatory mock-Irish bar with Guinness and Newcastle Brown. Not a place to meet the locals.

Vinícius, R Vinícius de Morais 39, Ipanema, 2nd floor, http://viniciusbar.com.br. Mirror image of the Garota de Ipanema with slightly better acts and food.

Gávea, Jardim Botânico and Lagoa *p377*

00 (Zero Zero), Av Padre Leonel Franca 240, Gávea, T2540 8041, www.00site.com.br. Mock LA bar/restaurant/club with a small outdoor area, very trendy. Gay night on Sun.

Bar Lagoa, Av Epitácio Pessoa 1674, Lagoa, T2523 1135, www.barlagoa.com.br. Slightly older, arty crowd on weekday evenings.

Belmonte IV, R Jardim Botânico 617, T2239 1649. An unpretencious little bakery and snack bar, open all hours for beer and delicious *empanadas*, pies stuffed with crabs, prawns or chicken.

Garota da Gávea, Praça Santos Dumont 148, T2274 2347. Closed Mon-Wed. Corner bar/restaurant, informal meeting place, very popular for *petiscos* and a cold beer on Thu and at weekends.

Barra da Tijuca *p379*

Nuth, R Armando Lombardi 999, Barra da Tijuca, www.nuth.com.br. Barra's slickest club; mock Miami with snacks. Mix of tacky Brazilian and Eurotrash music and some samba funk live acts. Expensive.

Pepê, at Posto 2, Barra da Tijuca beach. Very popular with surfers.

⊕ Entertainment

Rio de Janeiro *p364, maps p365 and p368*
Cinemas
There are cinemas serving subtitled
Hollywood films and major Brazilian releases
on the top floor of almost all the malls. The
normal seat price is US$10, discounts on Wed
and Thu (students pay half price any day of
the week).
Centro Cultural do Banco do Brasil, see
page 367, T2808 2020. One of Rio's better
arts centres with the best art films and
exhibitions from fine art to photography
(Metro: Uruguaiana).
Cinemateca do MAM, Infante Dom Henrique
85, Aterro do Flamengo, T2210 2188. Cinema
classics, art films and roving art exhibitions
and a good café with live music. Views of
Guanabara Bay from the balconies.
Estação Ipanema, R Visconde de Pirajá 605,
Ipanema. European art cinema, less mainstream US and Brazilian releases.

Live music
Many Cariocas congregate in Lapa from
Thu-Sat for live music. There are free
concerts throughout the summer, along
the Copacabana and Ipanema beaches, in
Botafogo and at the parks: mostly samba,
reggae, rock and MPB (Brazilian pop): there
is no advance schedule, information is given
in the local press (see below). Rio's famous
jazz, in all its forms, is performed in lots of
enjoyable venues, see the press. See www.
samba-choro. com.br, for more information.
Centro Cultural Carioca, R do Teatro 37, T2242
9642, www.centroculturalcarioca.com.br. An
exciting venue that combines music (mostly
samba) and dance, 1830-early morning.
This restored old house with wrap-around
balconies and exposed brick walls is a dance
school and music venue that attracts a lovely
mix of people. Professional dancers perform
with musicians; after a few tunes the audience
joins in. Thu is impossibly crowded; Sat is
calmer. Bar food available. US$12 cover charge.
Highly recommended.

Circo Voador, R dos Arcos s/n, Lapa, T2533
0354, www.circovoador.com.br. Lapa's
recuperation began with this little concert
hall under the arches. Some of the city's best
smaller acts still play here, including Seu Jorge
who first found fame playing with Farofa
Carioca at the Circo.
Praia Vermelha at Urca. Residents bring
musical instruments and chairs onto beach for
an informal night of samba from 2130-2400,
free. Bus No 511 from Copacabana.
Toca do Vinícius, Vinícius de Moraes 129C,
Ipanema, www.tocadovinicius.com.br. Rio's
leading bossa nova and choro record shop
with live concerts from some of the finest past
performers every Sun lunchtime.

⊕ Festivals

Rio de Janeiro *p364, maps p365 and p368*
Less hectic than Carnival, see box, page 390,
but very atmospheric, is the festival of **Iemanjá**
on the night of **31 Dec**, when devotees of the
orixá of the sea dress in white and gather on
Copacabana, Ipanema and Leblon beaches,
singing and dancing around open fires and
making offerings. The elected Queen of the
Sea is rowed along the seashore. At midnight
small boats are launched as offerings to
Iemanjá. The religious event is dwarfed,
however, by a massive New Year's Eve party,
called **Reveillon** at Copacabana. The beach
is packed as thousands of revellers enjoy free
outdoor concerts by big-name pop stars,
topped with a lavish midnight firework display.
It is most crowded in front of Copacabana
Palace Hotel. Another good place to see
fireworks is in front of R Princesa Isabel,
famous for its fireworks waterfall at about
10 mins past midnight.
Note Many followers of Iemanjá are now
making their offerings on 29 or 30 Dec and at
Barra da Tijuca or Recreio dos Bandeirantes
to avoid the crowds and noise of Reveillon.
The festival of **São Sebastião**, patron saint of
Rio, is celebrated by an evening procession on
20 Jan, leaving Capuchinhos Church, Tijuca,
and arriving at the cathedral of São Sebastião.

Carnival in Rio

Carnival in Rio is spectacular. On the Friday before Shrove Tuesday, the mayor of Rio hands the keys of the city to Rei Momo, the Lord of Misrule, signifying the start of a five-day party. Imagination runs riot, social barriers are broken and the main avenues, full of people and children wearing fancy dress, are colourfully lit. Areas throughout the city such as the Terreirão de Samba in Praça Onze are used for shows, music and dancing. *Bandas* and *blocos* (organized carnival groups) seem to be everywhere, dancing, drumming and singing.

There are numerous samba schools in Rio divided into two leagues, both of which parade in the Sambódromo. The Carnival parades are the culmination of months of intense activity by community groups, mostly in the city's poorest districts. Every school presents 2500-6000 participants divided into *alas* (wings) each with a different costume and 5-9 *carros alegóricos*, beautifully designed floats. Each school chooses an *enredo* (theme) and composes a *samba* (song) that is a poetic, rhythmic and catchy expression of the theme. The *enredo* is further developed through the design of the floats and costumes. A *bateria* (percussion wing) maintains a reverberating beat that must keep the entire school, and the audience, dancing throughout the parade. Each procession follows a set order with the first to appear being the *comissão de frente*, a choreographed group that presents the school and the theme to the public. Next comes the *abre alas*, a magnificent float usually bearing the name or symbol of the school. Schools are given between 65 and 80 minutes and lose points for failing to keep within this time. Judges award points to each school for components of their procession, such as costume, music and design, and make deductions for lack of energy, enthusiasm or discipline.

The Sambódromo is a permanent site at Rue Marquês de Sapucai, Cidade Nova, is 600 m long with seating for 43,000 people. Designed by Oscar Niemeyer and built in 1983-1984, it handles sporting events, conferences and concerts during the rest of the year. It has been remodelled and will hold certain events at the 2016 Olympics. A Cidade de Samba (Samba City), Rivadávia Corréa 60, Gamboa, T2213 2503, http://cidadedosambarj.globo.com (closed in 2014), is a theme park bringing a number of the larger schools together in one location. There is a permanent carnival production centre of 14 workshops; visitors can watch floats and costumes being prepared, visit the gift shop or watch one of the year-round carnival-themed shows.

Rio's *bailes* (fancy-dress balls) range from the sophisticated to the wild. The majority of clubs and hotels host at least one. The Copacabana Palace hotel's is elegant and expensive whilst the Scala club has licentious parties. It is not necessary to wear fancy dress; just join in, although you will feel more comfortable if you wear a minimum of clothing to the clubs. The most famous are the Red & Black Ball (Friday) and the Gay Ball (Tuesday) which are both televised.

Bandas and *blocos* can be found in all neighbourhoods and some of the most popular and entertaining are Cordão do Bola Preta (meets at 0900 on Saturday in Rua 13 de Maio 13, Centro), Simpatia é Quase Amor (meets at 1600 Sunday in Praça General Osório, Ipanema) and the transvestite Banda da Ipanema (meets at 1600 on Saturday and Tuesday in Praça General Osório, Ipanema). It is necessary to join a *bloco* in advance to receive their distinctive T-shirts, but anyone can join in with the *bandas*.

On the same evening, an umbanda festival is celebrated at the Caboclo Monument in Santa Teresa. **Carnival 13-17 Feb** 2015, **5-9 Feb** 2016 (see box, above). Festas Juninas: Santo Antônio on **13 Jun**, whose main event is a mass, followed by celebrations at the Convento do Santo Antônio and the Largo da Carioca. Throughout the state of Rio, the

Tickets The Sambódromo parades start with the Grupo de Acesso (Série A) schools on Friday and Saturday while Grupo Especial schools (the higher league) parade on Sunday and Monday. There are *cadeiras* (seats, US$62) at ground level closest to the parade, *arquibancadas* (terraces, prices vary according to sector, from US$88-140, unnumbered seats except section 9, US$220), *frisas* (open boxes, US$440-3,160), and *camarotes* (VIP boxes for 4-8, from about US$2,000 pp – schedule and prices 2014, http://liesa.globo.com). The terraces, while uncomfortable, house the most fervent fans, tightly packed; this is where to soak up the atmosphere but not take pictures (too crowded). Tickets are sold at travel agencies as well as the Maracanã Stadium box office. Tickets are usually sold out well before Carnaval weekend. Samba schools have an allocation of tickets which members sometimes sell, if you are offered one of these check its date. Tickets for the champions' parade on the Saturday following Carnival are much cheaper. Taxis to the Sambódromo are negotiable and will find your gate. The nearest metrô is Praça Onze and this can be an enjoyable ride in the company of costumed samba school members. You can follow the participants to the *concentração*, the assembly and formation on Avenida Presidente Vargas, and mingle with them while they queue to enter the Sambódromo.

Sleeping and security Reserve accommodation well in advance. Virtually all hotels raise their prices during Carnival, although it is usually possible to find a room. Your property should be safe inside the Sambódromo, but the crowds outside can attract pickpockets; only take the money you need for fares and food.

Taking part Most samba schools accept a number of foreigners and you will be charged for your costume (the money helps fund poorer members of the school). You should be in Rio for at least two weeks before carnival. Attend fittings and rehearsals on time and show respect for your section leaders – enter into the competitive spirit of the event.

Rehearsals *Ensaios* are held at the schools' *quadras* from October on and are well worth seeing. (Go by taxi, as most schools are based in poorer districts.)

Samba Schools Acadêmicos de Salgueiro, R Silva Teles 104, Andaraí, T2238 9226, www.salgueiro.com.br. Beija Flor de Nilópolis, Pracinha Wallace Paes Leme 1025, Nilópolis, T2791 2866, www.beija-flor.com.br. Imperatriz Leopoldinense, R Prof. Lacê 235, Ramos, T2560 8037, www.imperatrizleopoldinense.com.br. Mocidade Independente de Padre Miguel, Av Brasil 31.146, Padre Miguel, T3332 5823, www.mocidadeindependente.com.br. Portela, R Clara Nunes 81, Madureira, T2489 6440, www.gresportela.com.br. Primeira Estação de Mangueira, R Visconde de Niterói 1702, Mangueira, T2567 4737, www.mangueira.com.br. Unidos da Tijuca, Av Francisco Bicalhao 47, Santo Cristo, T2263 9679, www.unidosdatijuca.com.br. Vila Isabel, Boulevard 28 de Setembro 382, Vila Isabel, T2578 0077, www.gresunidosdevilaisabel.com.br.

Useful information Riotur's website, www.rioguiaoficial.com.br, and guide booklet give information on official and unofficial events (in English). The entertainment sections of newspapers and magazines such as *O Globo*, *Jornal do Brasil*, *Manchete* and *Veja Rio* are worth checking. Liga Independente das Escolas de Samba do Rio de Janeiro, T3213 5151, http://liesa. globo.com, for schools' addresses and rehearsal times, ticket prices and lots more information.

festival of São João is a major event, marked by huge bonfires on the night of **23-24 Jun**. It is traditional to dance the quadrilha and drink quentão, cachaça and sugar, spiced

with ginger and cinnamon, served hot. The Festas Juninas close with the festival of São Pedro on **29 Jun**. Being the patron saint of fishermen, his feast is normally accompanied by processions of boats. **Oct** is the month of the feast of **Nossa Senhora da Penha**.

O Shopping

Rio de Janeiro *p364, maps p365 and p368*
Bookshops Da Vinci, Av Rio Branco 185, lojas 2, 3 and 9. All types of foreign books. **Folha Seca**, R do Ouvidor 37, T021-2507 7175. Next to NS de Lapa church, good range of Brazilian photography and art books difficult to find elsewhere. Ask here about **Samba do Ouvidor**, a samba show outside, or check http://sambadaouvidor.blogspot.com for dates. **Livraria da Travessa**, R Visconde de Pirajá 572, Ipanema, T021-3205 9002. Classy little bookshop, good choice of novels, magazines and guidebooks in English. Great café upstairs too. **Saraiva**, R do Ouvidor 98, T021-2507 9500. A massive (megastore) bookshop which also includes a music and video shop and a café; other branches in **Shopping Iguatemi** and **Shopping Tijuca**.
Fashion Fashion is one of the best buys in Brazil; with a wealth of Brazilian designers selling clothes of the same quality as European or US famous names at a fraction of the price. Rio is the best place in the world for buying high-fashion bikinis. The best shops in Ipanema are at the **Forum de Ipanema** arcade, R Visconde de Pirajá 351, Garcia D'Ávila and R Nascimento Silva, which runs off it, in Ipanema. This is where some of the best Brazilian designers, together with international big name stalwarts like Louis Vuitton and Cartier. Most of the international names, as well as all the big Brazilian names like Lenny (Brazil's best bikinis), Alberta, Salinas, Club Chocolate and so on are also housed in the **Fashion Mall** in São Conrado.

Saara, www.saarario.com.br, is a multitude of little shops along R Alfândega, dos Andradas, Praça da República and Buenos Aires, where clothing bargains can be found (as well as costume jewellery, toys, perfume and other items). Little shops on Aires Saldanha, Copacabana (1 block back from beach), are good for bikinis and cheaper than in shopping centres.
Jewellery Amsterdam Sauer, R Garcia D'Ávila 105, with10 shops in Rio and others throughout Brazil. They offer free taxi rides to their main shop. **Antônio Bernardo**, R Garcia d'Ávila 121, Ipanema, T2512 7204, and in the Fashion Mall. Brazil's foremost jeweller who has been making beautifully understated jewellery with contemporary designs for 30 years. Internationally well known, but available only in Brazil. **H Stern**, next door to Amsterdam Sauer at R Visconde de Pirajá 490/R Garcia Dávila 113, Ipanema, has 10 outlets, plus branches in major hotels.

There are several good jewellery shops at the Leme end of Av NS de Copacabana.
Markets Northeastern market at Campo de São Cristóvão, with music and magic, on Sun 0800-2200 (bus 472 or 474 from Copacabana or centre), www.feiradesaocristovao.org.br. A recommended shop for northeastern handicrafts is **Pé de Boi**, R Ipiranga 55, Laranjeiras, www.pedeboi.com.br. Sat antiques market on the waterfront near Praça 15 de Novembro, 1000-1700. Also in Praça 15 de Novembro is **Feirarte II**, Thu-Fri 0800-1800. **Feirarte I** is a Sun open-air handicrafts market (everyone calls it the Feira Hippy) at Praça Gen Osório, Ipanema, www.feirahippieipanema.com, 0800-1800, items from all over Brazil. **Babilônia Feira Hype** is held every other weekend at the Jockey Club, 1400-2300, selling clothes, crafts, massage, live music and dance, popular. A **stamp, coin and postcard market** is held in the Passeio Público on Sun 0800-1300. Markets on Wed 0700-1300 on R Domingos Ferreira and on Thu, same hrs, on Praça do Lido, both Copacabana (Praça do Lido also has a Feirarte on Sat-Sun 0800-1800). **Sunday market** on R da Glória, colourful, cheap fruit, vegetables and flowers; **early-morning food market**, 0600-1100, R Min Viveiros de Castro, Ipanema. Excellent food and household-goods markets at various places in the city and suburbs (see newspapers for times and places).

Music Arlequim, Paço Imperial, Praça XV de Novembro 48, loja 1, www.arlequim.com.br. Mon-Fri 1000-2000, Sat 1000-1800. A good selection of music and film in the same space as the Livraria Imperial, which sells used books. **Bossa Nova & Companhia**, R Duvivier 37a, www.bossanovaecompanhia.com.br. Excellent selection of bossa nova, chorinho and jazz, small museum in the basement.

Shopping malls Rio Sul, at the Botafogo end of Túnel Novo, has almost everything the visitor may need. Some of the services in Rio Sul are: international phone office; Câmbio; post office at G2, a good branch of Livraria Saraiva, a gym and a cinema. A US$5 bus service runs as far as the Sheraton passing the main hotels, every 2 hrs between 1000 and 1800, then 2130.

Other shopping centres, which include a wide variety of services, include **Shopping Leblon** (Av Afrânio Melo Franco 290, www.shoppingleblon.com.br) and **The Fashion Mall** in São Conrado (www.scfashionmall.com.br), see above, undoubtedly the most fashionable in the city. **Shopping Cidade Copacabana** (www.shoppingcidadecopacabana.com.br), **Norte Shopping** (Todos os Santos), **Barra** and the brand new, mega **Shopping Village Mall** (Av das Américas 3900, www.shoppingvillagemall.com.br), in Barra da Tijuca (see page 379).

☼ What to do

Rio de Janeiro *p364, maps p365 and p368*
Boat trips Several agencies offer trips to Ilha de Paquetá (to which there is also a US$2.50, 45-min ferry), and day cruises, including lunch, to Jaguanum Island (see under Itacuruçá) and a sundown cruise around Guanabara Bay.
Cycling Mobilicidade Bike Rio, see www.mobilicidade.com.br or T4063 3999 for the city's bicycle hire scheme. There are dozens of cycle hire stations and bikes cost US$6. There are some 140 km of cycle paths in Rio, over 6 km in Parque Nacional Tijuca (see www.ta.org.br/site2/index.htm for a map). Some hostels rent bicycles.

Dancing Rio Samba Dancer, Hélio Ricardo is a Rio native and Samba and Forró dancer. He speaks English and Spanish and teaches and accompanies individuals in dance; http://riosambadancer.com.
Football See Maracanã stadium, page 371.
Helicopter rides Helisight, R Visconde de Pirajá 580, loja 107, Térreo, Ipanema, T2511 2141, www.helisight.com.br. Prices from US$105 pp for 6/7-min overflights.
Horse racing and riding Jockey Club Racecourse, by Jardím Botânico and Gávea, meetings on Mon and Thu evenings and Sat and Sun 1400, US$1-2, long trousers required. Take any bus marked 'via Jóquei'. Sociedade Hípico Brasileiro, Av Borges de Medeiros 2448, T2156 0156, www.shb.com.br, Jardim Botânico. For riding.
Parapenting and hang-gliding For the Brazilian Association, see www.abvl.com.br, the website of the Associação Brasileira de Vôo Livre, which oversees all national clubs and federations. **Barra Jumping**, Aeroporto de Jacarepaguá, Av Ayrton Senna 2541, T3151 3602, www.barrajumping.com.br. Tandem jumping (Vôo duplo). **Rio Tandem Fly**, instructor Paulo Falcão T2422 6371/9966 3416, pilot Roni Falcão, T9963 6623, www.riotandemfly.com.br. Several others offer tandem jumping; check that they are accredited with the Associação Brasileira de Vôo Livre. Ask for the **Parapente Rio Clube** at São Conrado launch site. Basic cost US$120 for a tandem flight. **Delta Flight** and **Rio by Jeep**, T3322 5750/9693 8800, www.deltaflight.com.br. Tandem flight tours above Rio from Pedra Bonita Mountain with instructors licensed by the Brazilian Hang-Gliding Association. Contact Ricardo Hamond. **Just Fly**, T2268 0565, T9985 7540, www.justfly.com.br. Tandem flights with Paulo Celani (licensed by Brazilian Hang Gliding Association), pick-up and drop-off at hotel included, in-flight pictures US$15 extra, flights all year, best time of day 1000-1500 (5% discount for Footprint South American and Brazil Handbook readers on presentation of book at time of reservation). **Pedro Beltrão**, T7822 4206, pedrobeltrao@gmail.com. Highly

regarded, experienced hang-gliding operator with flights from the Pedra Bonita. Some 20 years flying experience. Excellent prices.

Rock climbing and hill walking Clube Excursionista Carioca, R Hilário Gouveia 71, room 206, T2255 1348, www.carioca.org.br. Recommended for enthusiasts, meets Wed and Fri. Jungle Me, T4105 7533, www.jungle me.com.br. Hikes in Rio off the beaten track including the three peaks in Tijuca national park (an 8-hr circuit), wild beaches and Pedra Bonita. Rio Hiking, T2552 9204/ 9721 0594, www.riohiking.com.br. Hiking tours to the top of mountains in Rio city and state, friendly, fun, English spoken. Also offers many other activities including kayaking, cycling, birdwatching, surfing and horse riding.

Tours

Be A Local, T9643 0366, www.bealocal.com. Guided tours to football matches, see under Maracanã stadium, page 371, and recommended visits to favelas and baile funk parties.

Brazil Expedition, R Visconde Piraja 550 lj 201, Ipanema, T9998 2907, www.brazilexpedition. com. Backpacker bus trips south to Paraty and Ilha Grande with stops along the Costa Verde. Day trips and Rio 'starter packs', accommodation advice. Recommended.

Favela Santa Marta, T9177 9459, www. favelasantamartatour.blogspot.co.uk. Visits with locals to a beautifully situated favela with stunning views of Corcovado and Sugar Loaf, with insights into local community life.

Favela Tour, Estr das Canoas 722, Bl 2, apt 125, São Conrado, T3322 2727, T99989-0074, www.favelatour.com.br. Safe, interesting guided tours of Rio's favelas in English, Spanish, Italian, German or French, 3 hrs. Ask Marcelo Armstrong, the owner, about eco tours and river rafting. For the best price call Marcelo direct rather than through a hotel. Recommended.

Jeep Tour, T2108 5800, www.jeeptour. com.br. Among their tours are escorted groups to favelas.

Metropol, R São José 46, T2533 5010, www.metropolturismo.com.br. Eco, adventure and culture tours to all parts of Brazil.

Rio Extreme, T8806 0235, www.rioextreme. com. Broad range of excursions from city tours, sights and nightlife excursions to hikes to the Pedra da Gávea, Itatiaia National Park and Ilha Grande.

Rio G, R Prudente de Morais 167C, Ipanema, T3813 0003, www.riogtravel.com. Very helpful, English spoken, specialists in the GLBT market.

Rio Walks, T2516 5248, www.riowalks. com.br. Guided walks around the old centre, the bay, the boroughs (eg Santa Teresa), bars and botequins.

Guides

Cultural Rio, R Santa Clara 110/904, Copacabana, T3322 4872, T9911 3829, www.culturalrio.com.br. Tours escorted personally by Professor Carlos Roquette, English/French spoken, almost 200 options available, entirely flexible to your interests.

Luiz Amaral Tours, R Visc de Pirajá 550, office 215, Ipanema, T2259 5532, T9637 2522, www.travelrio.com/tours.htm. Good company offering personalized tours run by Luiz Felipe Amaral who speaks good English.

⊖ Transport

Rio de Janeiro *p364, maps p365 and p368*
Air
Rio has 2 airports: **Tom Jobim International Airport** (T3398 4527, www.aeroportogaleao.net), previously called Galeão, and the **Santos Dumont** airport on Guanabara Bay (T3814 7246, www.aeroportosantosdumont.net), for domestic flights. Jobim international airport is situated on Governador Island some 16 km north of the centre of Rio. It is in 2 sections: international and domestic. There is a **Pousada Galeão ($$$)**, comfortable, good value, and **Luxor Aeroporto**, in Terminal 1, T3222 9700, www.luxorhoteis.com.br, if you need an early start, follow signs in airport

Taxis can be booked from within the airports or picked up at the stands outside the terminals. Fixed-rate taxis charge around US$33 from Jobim to Copacabana and Ipanema and US$33 to the city centre and Santa Teresa; buy a ticket at the counter. **Aerotaxi** cabs (T021-2467 1500), available outside both terminals at Tom Jobim airport cost US$25 (plus US$0.75 per item of luggage). Metered taxis cost around US$30 from Jobim to Copacabana, but beware of pirate taxis, which are unlicensed. Fixed-price taxis leave from the first floor of both terminals and have clearly marked booths selling tickets.

The a/c **Real Auto** bus, (T0800-240850, www.realautoonibus.com.br), runs frequently from the 1st floor of both terminals, 0500-2400, fares from US$3.50. There are 2 routes: *Linha 2018 via Orla da Zona Sul*, runs every 30 mins, to the Terminal Alvorada bus station in Barra da Tijuca and back again, stopping at the *rodoviária*, Av Rio Branco in the centre, Santos Dumont airport, Flamengo, Copacabana, Ipanema, São Conrado and Barra's Av das Américas. (This should not

be confused with the *Linha 2018 via Linha Vermelha*, which runs a sporadic circular route via Barra and nowhere else of any use to foreign tourists.) *Linha 2145* runs every 25 mins to Santos Dumont airport and back again, calling at Av Rio Branco along the way. Buses can be flagged down anywhere along their route and passengers can request to jump off at any time. There is also a standard Rio bus running along the 2018 line with similar frequency, US$2. Ordinary city buses also run from the airport to various locations in Rio, from the first floor of both terminals. These are far less secure and are not recommended.

There are *câmbios* in the airport departure hall. There is also a *câmbio* on the 1st floor of the international arrivals area, but it gives worse rates than the Banco do Brasil, 24-hr bank, 3rd floor, which has Visa ATMs (may not accept foreign cards) and gives cash advances against Visa. Duty-free shops are well stocked, but not cheap. Only US dollars or credit cards are accepted on the air-side of the departure lounge. There is a better choice of restaurants outside passport control. Left luggage only in Terminal 1.

The **Santos Dumont** airport on Guanabara Bay, right in the city, is used for Rio-São Paulo shuttle flights, other domestic routes, air taxis and private planes. The shuttle services operate every 30 mins from 0630 to 2230. Sit on the right-hand side for views to São Paulo, the other side coming back, book in advance. Taxi to the centre US$16, to Copacabana US$25, Ipanema US$33.

Metro
The Metrô, www.metrorio.com.br, provides good service, clean, a/c and fast; a better option to city buses. Line 1 runs between the inner suburb of Tijuca (station Uruguai) and Ipanema/General Osório, Line 2 from Pavuna, passing Engenho da Rainha and the Maracanã stadium, to Botafogo. Line 2 joins Line 1 at Central and the two run together as far as Botafogo. It operates 0500-2400 Mon-Sat, 0700-2300 Sun and holidays, 24 hrs during Carnaval. Stations often have a number of

different access points, some close earlier than the main ones. On Mon-Fri 0600-0900 and 1700-2000, the last carriage of each train is for women only; it has a pink stripe. The fare is US$1.50 single and for the metro with the connecting *Metrô na superfície Gávea/Barra* express bus which passes through Ipanema and Leblon. Other integrated systems include *Integração Expressa* between certain stations (eg Estácio and *rodoviária*) and *Barra Expresso* from Ipanema/General Osório to Barra da Tijuca. There is also a pre-paid card, *Cartão Pré-Pago*, initial payment US$2.25. Work continues on the expansion of the Metrô to Rocinha, São Conrado and Barra da Tijuca in time for the 2016 Olympics.

Bus

Local There are good services, but buses are very crowded and not for the aged or infirm during rush hours; buses have turnstiles which are awkward if you are carrying luggage. Hang on tight, drivers live out Grand Prix fantasies. Buses run to all parts, but should be treated with caution at night, when taxis are a better bet. They are usually marked with the destination and any going south of the centre will call at Copacabana and generally Ipanema/Leblon. At busy times allow about 45 mins to get from Copacabana to the centre by bus, less if you take a bus on the *aterro* expressway on the reclaimed waterfront. The fare on standard buses is US$1.35; suburban bus fares are up to US$3 depending on the distance. Bus stops are often not marked. The route is usually written on the front of the bus. See www.rioonibus.com for all routes. Private companies operate a/c (*frescão*) buses which can be flagged down practically anywhere: **Real, Pegaso, Anatur**. They run from all points in Rio Sul to the city centre, *rodoviária* and the airports. Fares are from US$3.50. **City Rio** is an a/c tourist bus service with security guards which runs between all the major parts of the city. Good maps show what sites of interest are close to each bus stop, marked by grey poles and found where there are concentrations of hotels. **Minivans** run from Av Rio Branco in the centre as far as Barra da Tijuca and have the destination written on the window. They are fast, frequent and by far the cheapest way of getting along the beaches, fare US$1.25. These vans also run along the sea front from Leme to Rocinha and can be hailed from the kerb. **Note** Rio's public transport systems are being integrated by **Fetranspor**, www.fetranspor.com.br. A number of unified, pre-paid ticket options are available, for instance the *bilhete único*, US$2.30, which can be used on buses, Metrô, ferries, etc, under certain conditions (see www.cartaoriocard.com.br for the full range).

Long distance Rodoviária Novo Rio, Av Rodrigues Alves, corner with Av Francisco Bicalho, just past the docks, T3213 1800, www.novorio.com.br. Buses run from Rio to all parts of the country. It is advisable to book tickets in advance at the *rodoviária* or with one of the booking agencies listed below; timetables are on the web site. The *rodoviária* has a **Riotur** information centre, which is very helpful, T2263 4857. Left luggage costs US$5. There are ATMs and *câmbios* for cash only. A local bus terminal is just outside the *rodoviária*: turn right as you leave and run the gauntlet of taxi drivers – best ignored. The main bus station is reached by buses 326, Bancários/Castelo, from the centre and the airport; 136, *rodoviária*/Copacabana via Glória, Flamengo and Botafogo; 127, *rodoviária*/Copacabana via Túnel do Pasmado; 128, *rodoviária*/Leblon, via Copacabana and Ipanema; 170, *rodoviária*/Gávea, via Glória, Botafogo and Jardim Botânico; 172, *rodoviária*/Leblon, via Joquei and Jardim Botânico. The a/c Real bus (opposite the exit) goes to the airport and along the beach to São Conrado and will secure luggage. From the *rodoviária* it is best to take a taxi to your hotel or to the nearest metrô station (Estácio). Taxis can be booked at the booth on the ground floor, which ensures against overcharging. Fare to Flamengo US$15. Booking agencies include: **Dantur Passagens e Turismo**, Av Rio Branco 156, subsolo, loja 134, Metro Carioca, T2262 3424, www.dantur.com.br; **Guanatur**, R Dias

da Rocha 16A, Copacabana, T2235 3275, www.
guanaturturismo.com.br; **Paxtur Passagens**,
R República do Líbano 61, loja L, Center, T3852
2277. They charge about US$3 for bookings.

International bus Asunción, 1511 km
via Foz do Iguaçu, 30 hrs (**Pluma**, T0800-646
0300, www.pluma.com.br), US$100; **Buenos
Aires** (Crucero del Norte, www.crucero
delnorte.com.ar), via Porto Alegre and Santa
Fe, 48 hrs, US$200, book 2 days in advance.

Car
Service stations are closed in many places
Sat and Sun. Road signs are notoriously
misleading in Rio and you can easily end up in
a favela. Take care if driving along the Estrada
Gávea to São Conrado as it is possible to enter
unwittingly Rocinha.

Taxi
Official taxis are yellow with a blue stripe and
have meters. Smaller ones are marked TAXI
on the windscreen or roof. Only use taxis
with an official identification sticker on the
windscreen. Make sure meters are cleared
and on tariff 1 (starting at R$4.40), except
between 2100 and 0600 and on Sun and
holidays, when tariff 2 applies (starting at
R$5.85). The websites www.tarifadetaxi.com/
rio-de-janeiro and www.taxisimples.com.br/
?cidade=rio-de-janeiro have a map and allow
you to calculate the approximate taxi price.
Print the map and don't hesitate to argue if the
route is too long or the fare too much. The fare
between Copacabana and the centre is about
US$30. It is safer to use taxis from pontos – taxi
ranks or Radio Taxis, but the latter are more
expensive, eg **Cootramo**, T3976 9944, www.
cootramo.com.br, **Coopertramo**, T2209 9292,
www.radio-taxi.com.br, **Central Táxi**, T2195
1000, www.centraltaxi.com.br, **Transcoopass**,
T2209 1555, www.transcoopass.com.br.

Pão de Açúcar *p373*
Bus Bus 107 (from the centre, Catete or
Flamengo) and 511 from Copacabana (512
to return) take you to the cable-car station,
Av Pasteur 520, at the foot.

Cable car T2461 2700, open 0800-1950
(last one down at 2200, quietest before
1000), US$27 return, free for children under
6, aged 6-12 half price, every 30 min or when
full. There are two sections, Praia Vermelha
to Morro de Urca and from Urca to Sugar Loaf
(US$8 Morro da Urca to the top). Termini are
ample and efficient and the present Italian
cable cars carry 75 passengers. Even on the
most crowded days there is little queuing.
See main text for walking options.

Corcovado *p374*
Bus Take a Cosme Velho bus to the cog
railway station at R Cosme Velho 513: from
the centre or Glória/Flamengo No 180, 422,
498, get off at Igreja São Jesus Tadeo; from
Copacabana take No 583, 584, from Botafogo
or Ipanema/Leblon No 583 or 584; from Santa
Teresa Microônibus Santa Teresa. From Largo
do Machado Metrô station take a Cosme Velho
integração bus to the train station.
Car If driving to Corcovado, the entrance
fee is US$5 for the vehicle, plus US$5 pp. The
car park is half-way up, from which you have
to take a van, US$10-13.50, or walk. Coach
trips tend to be rather brief and special taxis,
which wait in front of the station, offer tours of
Corcovado and Mirante Dona Marta for US$25.
Train Every 20-30 mins between 0830 and
1900, journey time 15 mins (US$23 return;
single tickets available; children aged 6-12 half
price); go early to avoid long queues. Trem do
Corcovado, R Cosme Velho 513, T2558 1329,
www.corcovado.com.br. Ignore touts for tours
who say that the train is not running. Climb
the 220 steps or take the escalator to the top.
Taxis and minivans from Paineiras charge
US$6.50 pp. Also, a 206 bus does the very
attractive run from Praça Tiradentes (or a
407 from Largo do Machado) to Silvestre (the
railway has no stop here now), where the
active walk of 9 km will take you to the top. For
safety reasons go in company, or at weekends
when more people are about.

Copacabana *p375, map p376*
Bus/Metrô Cardeal Arcoverde, Siqueira Campos and Cantagalo Metrô stations are a few blocks inland from the beach. There are many buses to and from the city centre, US$1.50. Take numbers 119, 154, 413, 415, 455, 474 from Av Nossa Senhora de Copacabana. If you are going to the centre from Copacabana, look for 'Castelo', 'Praça 15', 'E Ferro' or 'Praça Mauá' on the sign by the front door. From the centre to Copacabana is easier as all buses in that direction are marked. 'Aterro' means the expressway between Botafogo and downtown Rio (closed Sun). The 'Aterro' bus does the journey in 15 mins.

Ipanema and Leblon *p377, map p378*
Bus/Metrô The Ipanema/General Osório Metrô station is at Praça General Osório, from where 'Metrô do superfície' buses run to Gávea along Rua Visconde de Pirajá in Ipanema and Av Ataulfo de Paiva in Leblon. Many buses and minivans from the centre and/or Leme run to Ipanema and Leblon along the seafront roads.

Jardim Botânico *p377*
Bus Take bus No 170 from the centre, or any bus to Leblon, Gávea or São Conrado marked 'via Jóquei'; from Glória, Flamengo or Botafogo take No 571, or 172 from Flamengo, or the Metrô na Superfície from Botafogo or Ipanema/Gral Osório; from Copacabana, Ipanema or Leblon take No 572 (584 back to Copacabana).

Barra da Tijuca *p379*
Bus From the city centre to Barra, 1 hr, are Nos 175, 176; from Botafogo, Glória or Flamengo take No 179; Nos 591 or 592 from Leme; and from Copacabana via Leblon No 523 (45-60 mins). A taxi from the centre costs US$25 (US$35 after 2400), from Ipanema US$15. A comfortable bus, Pegasus, goes along the coast from the Castelo bus terminal to Barra da Tijuca and continues to Campo Grande or Santa Cruz, or take the free 'Barra Shopping' bus. Bus 700 from Praça São Conrado (terminal of bus 553 from Copacabana) goes the full length of the beach to Recreio dos Bandeirantes.

Parque Nacional Tijuca *p379*
Bus For the park entrance, take bus No 221 from Praça 15 de Novembro, No 233 'Barra da Tijuca' or 234 from the *rodoviária*, or No 454 from Copacabana to Alto da Boa Vista. There is no public transport within the park, best explore by trail, tour, bicycle or car.

ⓘ Directory

Rio de Janeiro *p364, maps p365 and p368*
Banks Banco do Brasil at the International Airport is open 0800-2200. The international airport is probably the only place to change TCs at weekends. Banco 24 horas ATMs around town and in airports, also at main branches of banks. **Money changers:** Most large hotels and reputable travel agencies will change currency and TCs. Copacabana (where rates are generally worse than in the centre) abounds with câmbios and there are many also on Av Rio Branco. **Câmbio Belle Tours**, Rio Sul Shopping, ground floor, loja 101, parte A-10, Mon-Fri 1000-1800, Sat 1000-1700, changes cash. In the gallery at Largo do Machado 29 are **Câmbio Nick** at loja 22 and, next door but one, **Casa Franca**. **Car hire** Many agencies on Av Princesa Isabel, Copacabana; **Telecar**, R Figueiredo Magalhães 701, Copacabana, T2548 6778, www.telecar. com.br. A credit card is essential for hiring a car. **Embassies and consulates** For foreign embassies and consulates in Brazil, see http://embassy.goabroad.com. **Language courses** Instituto Brasil-Estados Unidos, Av Copacabana 690, 5th floor, lots of branches and courses, www.ibeu. org.br. Good English library at Copacabana address. **Medical services** Vaccinations at Saúde de Portos, Praça Mcal Âncora, T2240 8628/8678, Mon-Fri 1000-1100, 1500-1800 (international vaccination book and ID required). **Policlínica**, Av Nilo Peçanha 38, www.pgrj.org.br. Recommended for diagnosis and investigation. A good public hospital

for minor injuries and ailments is Hospital Municipal Rocha Maia, R Gen Severiano 91, Botafogo, T2295 2295/2121, near Rio Sul Shopping Centre. Free, but there may be queues. Hospital Miguel Couto, Mário Ribeiro 117, Gávea, T3111 3800. Has a free casualty ward. Dentist: English-speaking, Amílcar Werneck de Carvalho Vianna, Av Visc de Pirajá 550, Ipanema, T2512 7512. Dr Mauro Svartz, R Visconde de Pirajá 414, room 509, T2521 5196. Speaks English and Hebrew,

helpful. Useful addresses Immigration: Federal Police, Praça Mauá (passport section), Av Rodrigues Alves 1, 3rd floor, T2203 4000. To renew a 90-day permit to stay you may have to go to the international airport; check in advance. Student Travel Bureau, Av Nilo Peçanha 50, sala 3103, Centro, T3526 7700, and R Visconde de Pirajá 550, lj 201, Ipanema, T2512 8577, www.stb.com.br (offices throughout Brazil) has details of discounts and cultural exchanges for ISIC holders.

East of Rio

It is not only the state capital that is blessed with beautiful beaches, forests and mountains. There are chic resorts, surfing centres and emerald green coves, national parks in rainforest-clad hills and strange rocky mountains, and fine historical towns dating from both the colonial and imperial epochs. Within easy reach of Rio are the popular coastal resorts of Cabo Frio and Búzios and the imperial city of Petrópolis.

Niterói → Phone code: 021. Colour map 7, B5. Population: 459,451.

This city is reached across Guanabara Bay by bridge and by ferries which carry some 200,000 commuters a day. Founded in 1573, Niterói has various churches and forts, plus buildings associated with the city's period as state capital (until 1960). Many of these are grouped around the Praça da República. The Capela da Boa Viagem (1663) stands on an island, attached by a footbridge to the mainland. Museu de Arte Contemporânea-Niterói ① Mirante da Praia da Boa Viagem, T2620 2400, www.macniteroi.com, Tue-Sun 1000-1800, Sat 1300-1900, US$2, Wed free; the bistro below is open Tue-Sun 0900-1800; midibus 47A or 47B, is an Oscar Niemeyer project. It is best seen at night, especially when there is water in the pond beneath the building (which Niemeyer envisaged as a flower emerging from the water, but which is generally seen as a spaceship). There are other Niemeyer buildings near the port, when it's all done Niterói will be second to Brasília for Niemeyer buildings.

The most important historical monument is the Fortaleza da Santa Cruz ① T2710 7840, daily 0900-1600, US$1.50, go with guide. Dating from the 16th century and still a military establishment, it stands on a promontory which commands a fine view of the entrance to the bay. It is about 13 km from the centre of Niterói, on the Estrada Gen Eurico Gaspar Dutra, by Adão e Eva beach (taxi 30 minutes). The Museu de Arqueologia de Itaipu ① 20 km from the city, T2709 4079, Wed-Sun 1300-1800, is in the ruins of the 18th-century Santa Teresa Convent and also covers the archaeological site of Duna Grande on Itaipu beach. Tourist office: Neltur ① Estrada Leopoldo Fróes 773, São Francisco, T2710 2727, or T0800-282 7755, 5 km from ferry dock, www.niteroiturismo.com.br, has a useful map. Office also at the Museu de Arte Contemporânea.

Local beaches Take bus No 33 from the dock, passing Icaraí and São Francisco, both with polluted water but good nightlife, plenty of eating places and superb sunset views, to the fishing village of Jurujuba, with simple bars at the water's edge. About 2 km further along a narrow road are the twin beaches of Adão and Eva just before the Fortaleza da Santa Cruz (see above). At weekends and holidays a tourist bus runs from the Praça Arariboia in the centre around the bay to Fortaleza da Santa Cruz at 1000, 1230, 1430, US$5.50. To get to the ocean beaches, take buses from the street directly ahead of the ferry entrance, at right angles to the coast road to Piratininga, Camboinhas (bus 39 for both), Itaipu (see the archaeology museum, above, buses 38 or 770D) and Itacoatiara (bus 38). These are fabulous stretches of sand, the best in the area, about 40 minutes' ride through picturesque countryside.

Lagos Fluminenses

To the east of Niterói lie a series of salt-water lagoons, the Lagos Fluminenses. The first major lakes, Maricá and Saquarema are muddy, but the waters are relatively unpolluted and wildlife abounds in the surrounding scrub and bush. An unmade road goes along the coast between Itacoatiara and Cabo Frio, giving access to the long, open beaches of Brazil's **Costa do Sol**.

In the holiday village of **Saquarema**, the little white church of Nossa Senhora de Nazaré (1675) is on a green promontory jutting into the ocean. Saquarema is a fishing town and one of the top spots for quality consistent pumping surf in Brazil.

The largest lake is **Araruama** (220 sq km), famous for its medicinal mud. The salinity is extremely high, the waters calm, and almost the entire lake is surrounded by sandy beaches, making it popular with families looking for safe, unpolluted bathing. The almost constant breeze makes the lake perfect for windsurfing and sailing. There are many hotels, youth hostels and campsites in the towns by the lakes and by the beaches. All around are saltpans and the wind pumps used to carry water into the pans. At the eastern end of the lake is **São Pedro de Aldeia**, which, despite intensive development, still retains some of its colonial charm.

Cabo Frio → *Phone code: 022. Colour map 7, B5. Population: 140,000.*

Cabo Frio, 156 km from Rio, is a popular holiday and weekend haunt of Cariocas because of its cooler weather, white sand beaches, sailing, surfing and good underwater swimming. **Forte São Mateus** (1616) is now a ruin at the mouth of the Canal de Itajurú, which connects the Lagoa Araruama and the ocean. A small headland at its mouth protects the nearest beach to the town, Praia do Forte, which stretches south for about 7½ km to Arraial do Cabo. The canal front, Av dos Pescadores, is pretty, lined with palm trees, restaurants and schooners tied up at the dock. It leads around to the bridge, which crosses to the Gamboa district. **Convento Nossa Senhora dos Anjos** (1696), Largo de Santo Antônio in the town centre, houses the **Museu de Arte Religiosa e Tradicional** ① *Wed-Fri 1400-2000, Sat-Sun 1600-2000*. Above the Largo de Santo Antônio is the **Morro da Guia**, which has a look-out and an 18th-century chapel (access on foot only). The beaches of **Peró** and **Conchas** ① *'São Cristovão' (with 'Peró' on its notice board) or 'Peró' bus, US$0.65, 15-20 mins, has lots of condos, but not many places to stay*, are lovely (a headland, Ponta do Vigia, separates the two and you can walk from one to the other). **Tourist office** ① *Av do Contorno s/n, Algodoal, T2643 0949, www.cabofriotur.com.br, daily 0830-1800, and at Pier do Cabo Frio, Av do Contorno s/n, Passagem, daily 0900-1700.*

Búzios → *Phone code: 024. Colour map 7, B5. Population: 27,700. www.buzioschannel.com.br.*

Known as a lost paradise in the tropics, this village, 192 km from Rio, found fame in the 1964 when Brigite Bardot was photographed sauntering barefoot along the beach. The world's press descended on the sophisticated, yet informal resort, following the publicity. Originally a small fishing community, founded in 1740, Búzios remained virtually unknown until the 1950s when its natural beauty started to attract the Brazilian jet-set who turned the village into a fashionable summer resort. The city gets crowded at all main holidays, the price of food, accommodation and other services rises substantially and the traffic jams are long and stressful.

During the daytime, the best option is to head for one of the 25 beaches. The most visited are Geribá (many bars and restaurants), Ferradura (blue sea and calm waters), Ossos (the most famous and close to the centre), Tartaruga and João Fernandes. Schooner trips of two to three hours pass many of the beaches: many companies offer the trip from the pier in the centre, US$30. Water sports include diving, snorkelling, surfing on Geribá and Brava beaches, wind surfing, kite surfing, jet ski and stand-up paddleboarding. Some of the world's best sailing waters are found around the Búzios peninsula, which will be the venue for the sailing competitions in the 2016 Olympics. On land there are **Radical Parque** ① *Estrada da Usina 1, www.radicalparque.com.br,* with karting, bowling, rock climbing walls and other adventure sports, and a first-class **golf course** ① *www.buziosgolf.com.br.* **Tourist office**: at Manguinhos, T2633 6200, www.buziosturismo.com, on the western edge of the peninsula, and at Praça Santo Dumont, T2623 2099, 0800-2200. See also www.buziosonline.com.br.

Petrópolis → *Phone code: 024. Post code: 25600. Colour map 7, B5. Population: 286,537.*

A steep scenic mountain road from Rio leads to this summer resort, 68 km north of Rio, known for its floral beauty and hill scenery, coupled with adventure sports. Until 1962 Petrópolis was the 'summer capital' of Brazil. Now it combines manufacturing (particularly textiles) and tourism. Whitewater rafting, hiking, climbing, riding and cycling are possible in the vicinity. Petrópolis celebrates its foundation on 16 March. Patron saint's day, São Pedro de Alcântara, 29 June. **Tourist office**: Petrotur ① *Praça Liberdade, T0800-024 1516, Mon-Sun 0900-1700. See* www.petropolis.rj.gov.br and http://destinopetropolis.com.br. Very helpful, good English; map not to scale. There are five other kiosks in and around the city, including Pórtico Quitandinha, 300 m from *rodoviária*.

The **Museu Imperial** (Imperial Palace) ① *R da Imperatriz 220, T2237 8000, Tue-Sun 1100-1800, US$4,* is Brazil's most visited museum. It is an elegant building, neoclassical in style, fully furnished and equipped. It is so well kept you might think the imperial family had left the day before, rather than in 1889. It's worth a visit just to see the Crown Jewels of both Pedro I and Pedro II. In the palace gardens is a vehicle museum and a pretty French-style tearoom, the

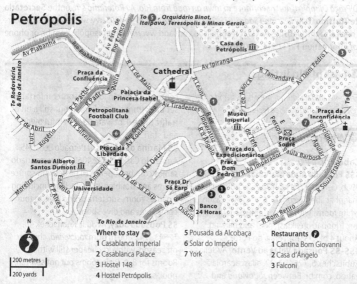

Petrópolis

To ⑤, Orquidário Binot, Italpava, Teresópolis & Minas Gerais

Where to stay			
1 Casablanca Imperial		5 Pousada da Alcobaça	**Restaurants** ⑦
2 Casablanca Palace		6 Solar do Império	1 Cantina Bom Giovanni
3 Hostel 148		7 York	2 Casa d'Ângelo
4 Hostel Petrópolis			3 Falconi

Petit Palais. The Neo-Gothic **Catedral de São Pedro de Alcântara** ① *Tue-Sat 0800-1200, 1400-1800, Sun 0800-1300, 1500-1930, Mon 0800-1200*, completed in 1925, contains the tombs of the Emperor and Empress in the Imperial Chapel to the right of the entrance. The summer home of air pioneer **Alberto Santos Dumont** ① *R do Encanto 22, T2247 3158, Tue-Sun 0930-1700, US$2.50*, is known as 'A Encantada' and is worth a visit. The interior of the **Casa de Petrópolis** ① *R Ipiranga 716, T2231 6197, Fri-Tue 1300-1830*, is completely original and over-the-top, but has been lovingly restored. It holds art exhibitions and classical concerts. A charming restaurant in the old stables is worth a stop for coffee, if not for lunch. **Orquidário Binot** ① *R Fernandes Vieira 390, T2248 5665, Mon-Fri 0800-1100, 1300-1600, Sat 0700-1100, take bus to Vila Isabel*, has a huge collection of orchids from all over Brazil (plants may be purchased).

Serra dos Órgãos

① *0800-1700, entry US$12, best months for trekking Apr-Sep, US$18 for first day's trekking in the park, US$1.80 thereafter, but US$9 at weekends. For information from ICMBio, Av Rotariana s/n, Alto Teresópolis, T2152 1100, www.icmbio.gov.br.*

The Serra dos Órgãos, so called because their strange shapes are said to recall organ-pipes, is an 11,000-ha national park (created in 1939, the second oldest in the country). The main attraction is the precipitous Dedo de Deus ('God's Finger') Peak (1692 m). The highest point is the 2263 m Pedra do Sino ('Bell Rock'), up which winds a 14-km path, a climb of five to six hours (11 km). The west face of this mountain is one of the hardest climbing pitches in Brazil. Another well-known peak is the Pedra do Açu (2245 m) and many others have names evocative of their shape. Near the Sub-Sede Guapimirim (Km 98.5, off BR-116, just outside the park) is the **Von Martius natural history museum** ① *0800-1700*. Near the headquarters (Sede) entrance is the Mirante do Soberbo, with views to the Baía de Guanabara. To climb the Pedra do Sino, you must sign a register (under 18s must be accompanied by an adult and have authorization from the park authorities).

Further information on the area from the Teresópolis **tourism information centres** ① *Praça Olímpica; and at entrance to town on road from Rio, Av Rotariano s/n*, or the **Secretaria de Turismo** ① *Av Feliciano Sodré, 675, 2nd floor, Várzea, T2644-4095, www.teresopolis.rj.gov.br* . Check also the websites www.teresopolison.com and www.visiteteresopolis.com.br, or phone for information T2742 9149, ext 4015.

⊙ East of Rio listings

For hotel and restaurant price codes, and other relevant information, see Essentials.

⊙ Where to stay

Cabo Frio *p400*
$$$ Pousada Água Marinha, R Rui Barbosa 996b, Centro, T2643 8447, www.pousadaagua marinhacabofrio.com.br. **$$** in low season, white rooms with comfortable beds, a/c or fan, frigobar, breakfast, pool and parking. About 4 blocks from Praia do Forte.
$$$-$$ Pousada Velas ao Vento, Av Júlia Kubitschek 5, T2645 3312, eliascacarola@ yahoo. com.br. Between *rodoviária* and

centre. Cheaper in low season, comfortable, set back from the main road but still a bit of traffic noise. Hot water, a/c, helpful owner and staff.
$$ Marina dos Anjos, R Bernado Lens 145, Arraial do Cabo, T2622 4060, www.marinado sanjos.com.br. Superior HI hostel with spruce dorms and doubles (**$$$**), facilities including a games room, sun terrace and links to tour companies and dive shops.
$$ Pousada Suzy, Av Júlia Kubitschek 48, T2643 1742. 100 m from *rodoviária*, cheaper off season, with a/c, cheaper still with fan. Rooms for 8, **$**. Plain rooms but not spartan, pool, sauna, garage.

Peró

$$$ La Plage, R das Badejos 40, T2647 1746, www.laplage.com.br. Rates rise in high season when minimum stay of 7 days; fully equipped suites, those upstairs have sea view, excellent for families. Right on the beach, services include pool and bar, à la carte restaurant, hydro-massage, sauna, 24-hr cyber café, garage.

$$$ Pousada Espírito do Mar, R Anequim 122, T2644 3077, www.espiritodomar.com.br. **$$** in low season. Orange building with central pool around which the rooms are built. Good, spacious but simple rooms, extra bed available. Frigobar, a/c, TV and fan. Cabo Frio bus passes outside.

$$-$ Peró Hostel, R Coutrin 13, T2643 7431. Smart modern HI hostel, doubles and dorms, many with own terraces, some with fridge, good services including tours and Tai Chi.

Camping Clube do Brasil, Av Wilson Mendes 700, 2 km from town, T9861 5742. **Dunas do Peró**, Estr do Guriri 1001, T2629 2323, www.pousadadunasdopero.com.br. Small *pousada* with a campsite on Praia do Peró.

Búzios *p400*
Reservations needed in summer, holidays such as Carnival and New Year's Eve, and weekends. For cheaper options and more availability, try Cabo Frio.

There are good, including luxury hotels on Praia da Ferradura and on Morro do Humaitá,

superb views, 10 mins' walk from the town centre. Hire a buggy to get around town. Several private houses rent rooms, especially in summer and holidays. Look for the signs: 'Alugo Quartos'.

$$$$ Casas Brancas, Alto do Humaitá 8, T2623 1458, www.casasbrancas.com.br. A series of rooms perched on the hill in mock-Mykonos buildings with separate terraces for the pool and spa areas, wonderfully romantic at night when all is lit by candlelight. Very good. If you can't afford to stay go for dinner.

$$$$ El Cazar, Alto do Humaitá 6, T2623 1620. Next door to Casas Brancas and almost as luxurious; though a little darker inside. Beautiful artwork, tasteful and relaxing.

$$$$ Insólito, Rua E1 Lotes 3 e 4, Praia da Ferradura, T2623 2172, www.insolitos.com.br. Mediterranean-style boutique hotel with individually themed rooms each with a deck affording sea views, some have jacuzzis, very expensive. The restaurant offers a fusion of contemporary French and Brazilian cuisine, sea view and sophisticated atmosphere.

$$$$ Pousada Byblos, Alto do Humaitá 14, T2623 1162, www.byblos.com.br. Wonderful views over the bay, bright, light rooms with tiled floors and balconies.

$$$$ Pousada Pedra Da Laguna, Rua 6, lote 6, Praia da Ferradura, T2623 1965, www.pedradalaguna.com.br. Spacious rooms, the best with a view 150 m from the beach. Part of the Roteiros do Charme.

$$$$ Pousada Saint Germain, Alto do Humaitá 5, T2623 1044, www.saintgermain-buzios.com.br. Nice views, verandas, a/c, mosquito nets, pool, Brazilian/American run.

$$$ Pousada Hibiscus Beach, R 1 No 22, Quadra C, Praia de João Fernandes, T2623 6221, www.hibiscusbeach.com. A peaceful spot, 15 pleasant bungalows, garden, pool, light meals available, help with car/buggy rentals and local excursions. One of the best beach hotels.

$$$ Pousada Santorini, R 9, Lote 28, Quadra C, Praia João Fernandes, T2623 2802, www.pousadasantorini.com.br. Good service, lovely beach views, mock-Greek island design with spacious rooms and public areas, popular, book well ahead. Pool, restaurant, bar and massage.

$$-$ Nomad Hostel, R das Pedras 25, T2620 8085, www.nomadbuzios.com.br. Popular hostel with a/c, mixed and female dorms (US$27-38), private suites (**$$$**), a beach bar, lockers and a travel desk.

$$-$ Ville Blanche, R Turibe de Farias 222, T2623 1644, http://villeblanchebuzios. blogspot.co.uk. Simple *pousada*, central, dorms for up to 10, and bright, tiled floor doubles with balcony.

$ Country Camping Park, R Maria Joaquina Justiniano 895 (off Praça da Rasa), Praia Rasa, Km 12, T2629 1155, www.macamp.com.br. Chalets and a well-run, shady campsite 1 km from the beach.

Petrópolis *p401, map p401*

$$$$ Pousada da Alcobaça, R Agostinho Goulão 298, Correas, T2221 1240, www. pousadadaalcobaca.com.br. Delightful, family-run country house in flower-filled gardens, pool and sauna. Worth stopping by for tea on the terrace, or dinner at the restaurant. Recommended.

$$$$ Solar do Império, Av Koeler 276, T2103 3000, www.solardoimperio.com.br. Converted neo-classical colonial mansion set in gardens on Petrópolis's grandest street. Fittings evoke the imperial era but modern facilities include a pool, sauna and ofuro hot tub.

$$$ Casablanca Imperial, R da Imperatriz 286, T2242 6662, www.casablancahotel. com.br. Most atmospheric in this chain, cheaper rooms in modern extension, good restaurant, pool. Also **$$$ Casablanca Palace**, R 16 de Março 123, T2231 0818.

$$$ York, R do Imperador 78, T2243 2662, www.hotelyork.com.br. Convenient, helpful, the fruit and milk at breakfast come from the owners' farm. Recommended.

$$ Hostel Petrópolis, R Santos Dumont 345, Centro, T2237 3811, www.hostelpetropolis oficial.com.br. Well-run hostel in a red town house, central. Double rooms and dorms are a little small, no breakfast. The owner has dogs.

$$-$ Hostel 148, R Alberto Torres 148, T2246 5848, www.hostel148.com.br. Dorms for 5-8, rooms for 3-7 with bath and a suite, lockers, kitchen for guests' use other than at breakfast time, tours and adventure sports arranged. New in 2013.

Serra dos Órgãos/Teresópolis *p402*
ICMBio allows camping, US$3.50 pp. There is also lodging at the **Abrigo Quatro da Pedra do Sino**, T2152 1120.

$$$$ Reserva Eclógica Guapiaçu (Guapi Assu Bird Lodge), c/o Regua, Nicholas and Raquel Locke, Caixa Postal 98112, Cachoeiras de Macacu, T2745 3998, www.regua. co.uk. Private rainforest reserve with very comfortable accommodation in a spacious wooden house and guided walks through pristine forest, price is full board. Families of South America's largest and rarest primate, the muriqui (woolly spider monkey) live here, excellent birding. Bookable in the UK through www.telltaletravel.com as part of a tour.

$$$$ Serra dos Tucanos, Caixa Postal 98125, Cachoeiras do Macacu, T2649 1557, www.serra dostucanos.com.br. British-run lodge in the Parque Estadual Três Picos near Teresópolis, with some of the very best birdwatching, guiding and facilities in the Atlantic coast forest. Cabins around a spring-water swimming pool. Airport transfers.

$ Recanto do Lord, R Luiza Pereira Soares 109, Teresópolis, T2742 5586, www.teresopolis

hostel.com.br. Big, well-equipped HI hostel, dorms and doubles, wonderful mountain views and 'adventure' trips in the Serra dos Órgãos.

❼ Restaurants

Cabo Frio *p400*

There's a neat row of restaurants on Av dos Pescadores, mostly fish, local meats, or pasta. There is seating on the pavement under awnings, French-style. Upstairs are a number of bars/clubs.

$$$-$$ Picolino, R Mcal F Peixoto 319, T2647 6222. In a nice old building, very smart, mixed menu but mostly local fish and seafood.

$$ Galeto do Zé, Av dos Pescadores e Trav Maçonica. For seafood and snacks. Also **Do Zé**, Av dos Pescadores 100, T2643 4277, serving Brazilian specialities.

$$ Hippocampus, R Mcal F Peixoto 283, T2645 5757. Mostly seafood, generally good, international and regional dishes.

$$ "In" Sônia, Av dos Pescadores 140 loja 04. Good service and tasty fish, many dishes for 2.

$$ Tonto, Av dos Pescadores 140 loja 01, next to "In" Sônia. Serves pizza and local dishes (T2645 1886 for delivery), has a bar too.

$$-$ Chico's, Av Teixeira e Souza 30, upstairs in Centro Comercial Víctor Nunes da Rocha, T2647 2735. Smart, does breakfast, self-service.

$ Branca, Praça Porto Rocha 15. Lunches à kilo 1100-1700, also fast food, pizza after 1800, coffee, pastries and cakes, good, a big, popular place.

Búzios *p400*

There are many restaurants along Av José Bento Ribeiro Dantas/R das Pedras and Orla Bardot (too many to mention here); one of the charms of Búzios is browsing. In Manguinhos is the **Porto da Barra** gastronomic centre, with a collection of sophisticated and informal restaurants on the waterfront, as popular as the main drag. There are plenty of beachside barracas on the peninsula (closed out of season) and cheaper places away from the sea front. A few places on Praça Santos Dumont off R das Pedras offer sandwiches and self-service food.

$$$ Aquarium, Av José Bento Ribeiro Dantas 412, Orla Bardot, T2623 0937. Smart a/c seafood restaurant with a mixture of influences.

$$$ Cigalon, R das Pedras 199, T2623 0932. Good French and Italian restaurant in the Pousada do Sol, where Bardot once stayed. Exgtensive wine list.

$$$ Parvati, R das Pedras 144, T2623 1375. Top class Italian restaurant, with a romantic air.

$$$ Satyricon, Av José Bento Ribeiro Dantas 500, Oral Bardot, T2623 2691. Another illustrious Italian specializing in seafood. Decent wine list.

$$ O Barco, Av Jose Bento Ribeiro Dantas, Orla Bardot, 12629 8307. Good value for fresh sea food from the owner's fishmonger. Very popular with locals. Hard to find a table in high season.

$ Bananaland, R Manoel Turíbio de Farias 50, T2623 0855. Cheap and cheerful per kilo buffet.

$ Chez Michou, R das Pedras, 90, Centro, T2623 2169. An open-air bar with videos, music and dozens of choices of pancakes accompanied by ice cold beer. Always crowded.

Petrópolis *p401, map 401*

$$ Falconi, R do Imperador 757. Traditional Italian. Recommended.

$ Cantina Bom Giovanni, R do Imperador 729, upstairs. Popular, Italian, lunch and dinner.

$ Casa d'Ángelo, R do Imperador 700, by Praça Dom Pedro II. Traditional tea house with self service food that doubles as a bar at night.

❶ Bars and clubs

Búzios *p400*

In season Búzios nightlife is young, beautiful and buzzing. Many of the bars and clubs are on R das Pedras. There are plenty of others including more upscale wine bar-style options.

Anexo, Av José Bento Ribeiro Dantas 392, Orla Bardot, T2623 4966. Daily from 2000, chill-out lounge with electronica. Open bar with tables on the streets overlooking Praia da Armação beach. Has another branch at Porto da Barra.

House of Rock and Roll, R Maria Joaquina 01, loja 8, Centro. Daily live band plays music ranging from 70's Rock to Brazilian pop music.
Pachá, R das Pedras 151, T2633 0592, www. pachabuzios.com. Electronic music Fri and Sat only from 2200 until late. Young crowd, 1000 people capacity. Packed full in high season.
Pátio Havana, R das Pedras 101, T2623 2169. Has live jazz, blues and Brazilian music on Fri and Sat, also a 5-star restaurant with international cuisine.
Privelège, Av José Bento Ribeiro Dantas 550, Orla Bardot. One of Brazil's best European-style dance clubs with pumping techno, house and hip hop and 5 rooms including a cavernous dance floor, sushi bar and lounge.

⊖ Transport

Niterói *p399*
Bus No 751-D Aeroporto-Galeão-Charitas, 761-D Galeão-Charitas, 740-D and 741 Copacabana-Charitas, US$3.
Car The toll on the Rio-Niterói bridge is US$2.50.
Ferry From the 'barcas' at Praça 15 de Novembro (ferry museum at the terminal), ferry boats and launches cross every 20 mins (30 mins Sat-Sun) to Niterói (15 mins, US$1.70). Catamarans (*aerobarcas*) leave every 10 mins Mon-Fri (US$4). They also go to Charitas, near São Francisco beach. Of the frequent ferry and catamaran services from Praça 15 de Novembro, Rio, ferries are slower, cheaper and give better views than catamarans.

Lagos Fluminenses: Saquarema *p400*
Bus Mil e Um (1001) Rio-Saquarema, every 2 hrs 0730-1800, 2 hrs, US$10.

Cabo Frio *p400*
Air Flights from **Belo Horizonte**, **Rio de Janeiro**, **São Paulo** and other cities.

Bus Urban Salineira and Montes Brancos run local services. US$2 to **Búzios, São Pedro da Aldeia, Saquarema, Araruama** and **Arraial do Cabo**. The urban bus terminal is near Largo de Santo Antônio, opposite the BR petrol station.
Long distance: the *rodoviária* is well within the city, but a 2-km walk from centre and beaches. City buses stop nearby. To **Belo Horizonte** US$47-65. To **Petrópolis** US$30. 1001 to **Rio de Janeiro**, Niterói US$14, to **São Paulo** US$45-80.

Búzios *p400*
Bus Mil e Um from Novo Rio, T021-2516 1001, US$23, 2½ hrs (be at the bus terminal 20 mins before departure). Departures every 2 hrs, 0700 to 1900 daily. You can also take any bus to **Cabo Frio** (many more during the day), from where it's 30 mins to Búzios. Buy return tickets well in advance in high season. At any other time buy return ticket 1 day in advance. Búzios' *rodoviária* is a few blocks' walk from centre. Some *pousadas* are within 10 mins on foot, while others need a local bus (US$1) or taxi. Buses from Cabo Frio run the length of the peninsula and pass several *pousadas*.
Car Via BR-106 takes about 2½ hrs from Rio.

Petrópolis *p401, map p401*
Bus New *rodoviária* 3 km north beyond Bingen by the highway; bus No 100 to centre, US$1.10. From **Rio** every 15 mins throughout the day (US$10) with **Única Fácil**, Sun every hr, 1½ hrs, sit on the left hand side for best views. Buses leave from the Novo Rio *rodoviária*; also a/c buses, hourly from 1100, from Av Nilo Peçanha, US$12. To **Teresópolis** for the Serra dos Órgãos, **Viação Teresópolis**, 8 a day, US$7.

Serra dos Órgãos *p402*
Bus Rio-Teresópolis: Viação Teresópolis buses leave hourly from the Novo Rio *rodoviária*. *Rodoviária* at R 1 de Maio 100. Fare US$11.

One of the main attractions near the inland highway to São Paulo is the Itatiaia National Park, a good area for climbing, trekking and birdwatching. For a really beautiful route, though, take the Rio de Janeiro-Santos section of the BR101, which hugs the forested and hilly Costa Verde southwest of Rio.

Dutra Highway

The Dutra Highway, BR-116, heads west from Rio towards São Paulo. It passes the steel town of **Volta Redonda** and some 30 km further west, the town of **Resende**. In this region, 175 km from Rio, is **Penedo** (five buses a day from Resende) which in the 1930s attracted Finnish settlers who brought the first saunas to Brazil. There is a Finnish museum, a cultural centre and Finnish dancing on Saturday. This popular weekend resort also provides horse riding, and swimming in the Portinho River. There are plenty of mid-range and cheap hotels in town. For tourist information, T024-3351 1876.

Parque Nacional de Itatiaia

① *Entry per day is US$11 per person, half price for each succeeding day at weekends, 90% discount midweek. Open 0800-1700, 0700-1400 for the higher section (you can stay till 1700). Information can be obtained from ICMBio, Estrada Parque Km 8.5, T024-3352 1292 or T3352 2288, www4. icmbio.gov.br/parna_itatiaia/. Avoid weekends and holidays if you want to see wildlife.*

This park, being so close to Rio and São Paulo, is a must for those with limited time who wish to see some of world's rarest birds and mammals in a whole range of different ecosystems. Trails from one hour to two days go through deep valleys shrouded in pristine rainforest, hiding icy waterfalls and clear-water rivers. The 30,000-ha mountainous park is Brazil's oldest, founded in 1937 to protect Atlantic Coast Rainforest in the Serra de Mantiqueira. It is divided into two parts, the lower, with the administration, reached from the town of Itatiaia (Km 316 on the Dutra Highway), and the upper section, reached from the Engenheiro Passos-Caxambu road (Circuito da Águas). Important species include jaguar, puma, brown capuchin and black-face titi monkeys. The park is particularly good for birds with a list of 350+, with scores of spectacular tanagers, hummingbirds, cotingas and manakins. The best trails head for Pedra de Taruga and Pedra de Maçã and the Poranga and Véu de Noiva waterfalls. The Pico das Agulhas Negras and the Serra das Prateleiras (up to 2540 m) offer decent rock climbing.

Information and maps can be obtained at the park office. The **Administração do Parque Nacional de Itatiaia** operates a refuge in the park, which acts as a starting point for climbs and treks. Although buses do run through the park calling at the hotels, hiring a car to visit Itatiaia is the best option.

Costa Verde (Emerald Coast)

The Rio de Janeiro-Santos section of the BR101 is one of the world's most beautiful highways, running along the aptly called Emerald Coast, which is littered with islands, beaches, colonial settlements and mountain fazendas. It is complete through to Bertioga (see page 434), which has good links with Santos and São Paulo. Buses run from Rio to Angra dos Reis, Paraty, Ubatuba, Caraguatatuba and São Sebastião, where you may have to change for Santos or São Paulo.

Mangaratiba, 116 km from Rio, has muddy beaches, but the surroundings are pleasant and better beaches can be found outside town. These include Ibicuí (2 km) and Brava to the east, Saco, Guiti and Cação at the head of the bay, and São Brás further west. Boats sail from Mangaratiba to Ilha Grande (see below).

Angra dos Reis → *Phone code: 024. Post code: 23900. Colour map 7, B4. Population: 119,247.*
Said to have been founded on 6 January 1502 (O Dia dos Reis – The Day of Kings/Epiphany), this is a port, 151 km southwest of Rio, with an important fishing and shipbuilding industry. It has several small coves with good bathing within easy reach and is situated on an enormous bay full of islands. Of particular note are the church and convent of **Nossa Senhora do Carmo**, built in 1593 (Praça Gen Osório), the **Igreja Matriz de Nossa Senhora da Conceição** (1626) in the centre of town, and the church and convent of **São Bernardino de Sena** (1758-1763) on the Morro do Santo Antônio. On the Largo da Lapa is the church of **Nossa Senhora da Lapa da Boa Morte** (1752), with a **sacred art museum** ① *Thu-Sun 1000-1200, 1400-1800*. On the Península de Angra, just west of the town, is the **Praia do Bonfim**, a popular beach, and a little way offshore the island of the same name, on which is the hermitage of Senhor do Bonfim (1780). The **TurisAngra tourist office** is at ① *Av Júlio Maria 10, T3367 7866, www.turisangra.com.br, www.angra.rj.gov.br, open 0800-2000; with kiosks at Praia do Anil, Av Ayrton Senna 580, T3367 7826, open 0800-2000, Estação Santa Luiza, T3365 6421, and at the* rodoviária; good information.

Ilha Grande → *Phone code: 021. Colour map 7, B5.*
Ilha Grande is a mountain ridge covered in tropical forest sticking out of an emerald sea and fringed by some of the world's most beautiful beaches. As there are no cars and no roads either, just trails through the forest, the island is still relatively undeveloped. Much of it forms part of a State Park and Biological Reserve, and cannot even be visited (INEA visitors centre, T3361 5553, Mon-Sun 0900-1800). The island was a notorious pirate lair, then a landing port for slaves. By the 20th century it had become the site of an infamous prison for the country's most notorious criminals (closed in 1994 and now overgrown rubble). The weather is best from March to June and, like everywhere along the coast, the island is overrun during the Christmas, New Year and Carnaval period. There is a tourist office at the ferry port on arrival, T021-2220 4323, Mon-Sat 0800-1800, Sun 0900-1300, but it is best to visit **TurisAngra** (see above) first. Information at www.ilhagrande.org; also www.ilhagrande.com.br.

The beach at **Vila do Abraão** may look beautiful to first arrivals but those further afield are far more spectacular. The two most famous are **Lopes Mendes**, two hours' walk from Abraão, and **Aventureiro**, six hours (ask about access, boat transport and where to stay if you want to spend the night here at **TurisAngra** in Angra dos Reis in advance). Good beaches closer to Abraão include the half moon bay at **Abraãoozinho** (15 minutes' walk) and **Grande das Palmas** which has a delightful tiny whitewashed chapel (one hour 20 minutes' walk), both east of town. Lagoa Azul, Freguesia de Santana and Saco do Céu are all boat trips. Good treks include over the mountains to Dois Rios, where the old jail was situated (13 km one way, about three hours), Pico do Papagaio (980 m) through forest, a stiff, three-hour climb (guide is essential) and Pico da Pedra d'Água (1031 m).

Paraty → *Phone code: 024. Post code: 23970. Colour map 7, B4. Population: 29,544.*
Paraty, 98 km from Angra dos Reis, is one of Brazil's prettiest colonial towns, whose centre has been declared a national historic monument in its entirety. It was the chief port for the export of gold in the 17th century and a coffee-exporting port in the 19th century. At the weekend Paraty buzzes with tourists who browse in the little boutiques and art galleries, or buy souvenirs from the indigenous Guaraní who sell their wares on the cobbles. Many of the numerous little bars and restaurants, like the *pousadas*, are owned by expat Europeans and Paulistanos, who are determined to preserve Paraty's charm. During the week, especially off season, the town is quiet and intimate. Much of the accommodation available is in colonial buildings, some sumptuously decorated, with flourishing gardens or courtyards. The town centre is out of bounds for motor

vehicles; heavy chains are strung across the entrance to the streets. In spring the roads are flooded, while the houses are above the water level. **Centro de Informações Turísticas** ① *Av Roberto Silveira, near the entrance to the historical centre, T3371 6553/1897, daily 0900-1600.* More information is available at www.paraty.com.br and www.paraty.tur.br (Portuguese).

There are four churches: **Santa Rita** (1722), built by the 'freed coloured men' in elegant Brazilian baroque, faces the bay and the port. It houses an interesting **Museum of Sacred Art** ① *Wed-Sun 0900-1200, 1300-1800, US$1.* **Nossa Senhora do Rosário e São Benedito** (1725, rebuilt 1757) ① *R do Comércio, Tue 0900-1200,* built by black slaves, is small and simple. **Nossa Senhora dos Remédios** (1787-1873) ① *Mon, Wed, Fri, Sat 0900-1200, Sun 0900-1500,* is the town's parish church, or Matriz, the biggest in Paraty. **Capela de Nossa Senhora das Dores** (1800) ① *Thu 0900-1200,* is a small chapel facing the sea that was used mainly by the wealthy whites in the 19th century. There is a great deal of distinguished Portuguese colonial architecture in delightful settings. **Rua do Comércio** is the main street in the historical centre. The **Casa da Cadeia**, close to Santa Rita church, is the former jail and is now a public library and art gallery. The **Casa da Cultura** ① *at the junction of R Samuel Costa and R Dona Geralda, Wed-Mon 1000-1930, winter to 1830, US$2.50,* houses an excellent multimedia history display (also in English, though this option can be hidden).

The town's environs are as beautiful as Paraty itself. Just a few kilometres away lie the forests of the Ponta do Juatinga peninsula, fringed by wonderful beaches, washed by little waterfalls and still home to traditional fishing communities (beware of dangerous currents at Playa Brava). At **Fazenda Murycana**, an old sugar estate and 17th-century cachaça distillery, you can taste and buy the different types of cachaça. It has an excellent restaurant. Mosquitoes can be a problem, take repellent and don't wear shorts. If short of time, the one must is a boat trip round the bay; some of its islands are home to rare animals. Boats also go to wonderful beaches like **Praia da Conçeicao, Praia Vermelha** and **Praia da Lula**, all of which have simple restaurants and are backed by forest and washed by gentle waves. Further south are **Saco da Velha**, protected by an island, and **Paraty Mirim** (17 km, also reached by bus, four a day, three on Sunday). The **Gold Trail**, hiking on a road dating from the 1800s, can be done on foot or horseback. Many other adventure sports are available (see What to do, page 414).

Trindade

Trindade, 27 km south of Paraty, may not be as beautiful in its own right but its setting, sandwiched between rainforested slopes and emerald sea, is spectacular. It has a long, broad beach and has long been a favourite for surf hippies from São Paulo and Rio who come in droves over Christmas and New Year. It is finding its place on the international backpacker circuit as the campsites, *pousadas* and restaurants are cheap and cheerful. See www.paratytrindade.com.br.

Note If travelling along the coast into São Paulo state as far as Guarujá, do not drive or go out alone after dark.

⊚ West of Rio listings

For hotel and restaurant price codes, and other relevant information, see Essentials.

⊜ Where to stay

Parque Nacional de Itatiaia *p407*
There is accommodation in hotels and cabins inside and outside the national park.

$$$$-$$$ Hotel Donati, T3352 1110, www. hoteldonati.com.br. Delightful, mock-Swiss chalets and rooms, set in tropical gardens visited by animals every night and early morning. A series of trails lead off from the main building and the hotel can organize professional birding guides. Decent restaurant and 2 pools. Highly recommended.

$$$-$$ Aldeia dos Pássaros, Estrada do Parque Nacional, Km 6, T3352 1152, www.aldeiadospassaros.com. Simple chalets in forest in park's lower reaches, with pool, riverside sauna, restaurant, organic garden and bar. Helpful staff, good breakfasts and reasonable off-season rates.

$$ Pousada Esmeralda, Estrada do Parque, T3352 1643, www.pousadaesmeralda.com.br. Comfortable chalets set around a lake in a lawned garden, wooden furnishings and log fires. Be sure to book a table for a candlelit dinner.

$ Ypê Amarelo, R João Maurício Macedo Costa 352, Campo Alegre, T3352 1232, www.pousadaypeamarelo.com.br. IYHA youth hostel with annexes set in an attractive garden visited by hummingbirds.

Angra dos Reis *p408*

$$ Caribe, R de Conceição 255, T3365 0033, www.angra2reis.com.br/caribe. Central, in a 1970s tower, well-kept, a reasonable option.

Ilha Grande *p408*

There are many *pousadas* in Abraão and reservations are only necessary in peak season or on holiday weekends. Prices vary considerably from month to month. Ignore dockside hotel touts who lie about hotel closures and flash pictures of their lodgings to unsuspecting tourists. Numerous eating places serve the usual fish/chicken, beans and rice options.

Abraão

$$$ Aratinga Inn, Vila do Abraão, www.aratingailhagrande.com.br or through www.hiddenpousadasbrazil.com. Simply furnished rooms, but lovely location in a tropical garden dotted with boulders right under the brow of Papagaio peak. Excellent service which includes Anglo-Australian afternoon tea.

$$$-$$ Ancoradouro, R da Praia 121, T3361 5153, www.pousadancoradouro.com.br. Simple rooms with en suites in a beach front building, 10 mins' walk east of the jetty.

$$$-$$ Porto Girassol, R do Praia 65, T9918 7293, www.portogirassol.com.br. Simple

rooms in a mock-colonial beach house 5 mins east of the jetty, best rooms have balconies, small garden.

$$ Pousada Sanhaço, R Santana 120, T3361 5102, www.pousadasanhaco.com. A range of a/c rooms, the best of which have balconies with sea views and cosy en suites. The *pousada* is decorated with paintings by local artists, generous breakfast.

$$-$ Pousada Cachoeira, Rua do Bicão, T3361 9521, www.cachoeira.com. Lovely little *pousada* with a dining room palapa and living area, cabins and a terrace of rooms nestled in a forest garden next to a fast-flowing stream. Good breakfasts and boat tours. English and German spoken. **$$** in high season.

$ pp Albergue Holdandés, R Assembléia de Deus, T3361 5034, www.holandeshostel.com.br. Dormitories and four little chalets (**$$**) lost in the forest, great atmosphere, be sure to reserve, HI affiliated.

Paraty *p408*

Over 300 hotels and *pousadas*; in mid-week look around and find a place that suits you best. Browse through www.paraty.com.br for yet more options. For luxury, see www.hiddenpousadasbrazil.com and www.pontadocorumbe.com.br.

$$$$ Bromelias Pousada & Spa, Rodovia Rio-Santos, Km 562, Graúna, T3371 2791, www.pousadabromelias.com.br. Asian-inspired with its own aromatherapy products and massage treatments, tastefully decorated chalets in the Atlantic coastal forest. Pool, sauna and restaurant.

$$$$ Casa Cairuçu, a 10-25 minute boat ride from Paraty, www.casa-cairucu.com. Luxurious self-catering beach villa in a beautiful, secluded location, 3 en suite double rooms, boat transfer, maid service, internet and local phone included. A professional chef and concierge are available at extra cost, fridge can be pre-stocked. Activities include kayaking and trekking.

$$$$ Pousada do Ouro, R Dr Pereira (or da Praia) 145, T3371 4300, www.pousadaouro.com.br. Near Paraty's eastern waterfront, once

Geko Hostel + Pousada + Beach Bar – Paraty. This is a small, cool Hostel, full of character, located right in front of "Pontal" Beach, right in Town. The atmosphere is good, with a **great Beach Bar**, tasty meals, and all the services backpackers should need. Private bedrooms, dorms **all with A/C and en-suite bathrooms**. Beds from R$29/U$14, Free breakfast on the beach, and **Free Pick Up** from the bus station.

paraty@gekohostel.com   +55 (0) 24 3371-7504 | From São Paulo (011) 3042 8854

Av. Orlando Spinelli, 5 - Praia do Pontal -

* Breakfast on the Beach, Parties, Live Music BBQs and dinners every Night!

Geko Chill Bar Paraty

Chill Inn Hostel Paraty, Pousada & Beach Bar. Fun hostel, run by an international team of cool people. It is located right in front of the beach, 2 minutes from the Historic Center. Full Brazilian Breakfast is served on the Beach, **free internet** and **free taxi** from the bus station. The bar serves a tasty caipirinha, perfect for a chill out session in hammock or to be shared amongst new friends. Priv. bedrooms and shared dorms **all with A/C and en-suite bathrooms** start at R$29/U$14 p/p.

bookings@chillinnhostel.com   +55 (0) 24 3373-1302 - Rio (0)21 4042-6350

Orlando Carpinelli, 3 - Praia do Pontal - Paraty, RJ | Skype: *chillinnparaty*

Chill Inn Eco-Suites Paraty - Bed & Breakfast. For those looking for something off the beaten track, this charming *Jungle Lodge* is located 5km from Paraty's Historical Center and offers Cozy accommodation in the middle of Brazilian nature. Surround yourself by lush Tropical Rainforest and enjoy a refreshing swim in the natural pools of the property's stunning river. Prices start at $26/R$60 p/person for a Private bedroom with en-suite bathroom, Wi-Fi, breakfast and a Free Taxi ride.

paraty@chillinnsuites.com | +55 (0) 24 3373-1302 (from Rio (21) 4042-6350 | from São Paulo (11) 3230-7111) Skype: *chillinnparaty*
Estrada Paraty-Cunha km2. Rua do Bananal, Ponte Branca, Paraty, RJ

POUSADA
CHILL INN
ECO SUITES - PARATY
+55 (0) 24 3373-1302

Bed & Breakfast
Jungle Lodge

www.chillinnsuites.com

a private home built from a gold fortune, suites in the main building, plainer rooms in an annexe, open-air poolside pavilion in a tropical garden. Has had many famous guests.

$$$$ Pousada Pardieiro, R do Comércio 74, T3371 1370, www.pousadapardieiro.com.br. Quiet, with a calm, sophisticated atmosphere, a colonial building with lovely gardens, delightful rooms facing internal patios and a small pool. Always full at weekends, no children under 15.

$$$$ Pousada Picinguaba, T12-3836 9105, www.picinguaba.com. Stylish French-owned hotel some 30 km from Paraty; with superior service, an excellent restaurant and simple, elegant (fan-cooled) rooms. Marvellous views out over a bay of islands. Booking ahead essential.

$$$$ Pousada do Sandi, Largo do Rosário 1, T3371 2100, www.pousadadosandi.com. br. 18th-century building with a grand lobby, comfortable, adjoining restaurant and pool.

$$$$-$$$ Le Gite d'Indaitiba, Rodovia Rio-Santos (BR-101) Km 562, Graúna, T3371 7174, www.legitedindaiatiba.com.br. French-owned chalets set in gardens on a hillsidewhich has views of the bay. French restaurant in tropical surroundings.

$$$ Morro do Forte, R Orlando Carpinelli, T3371 1211, www.pousadamorrodoforte.com. br. Out of the centre, lovely garden, good breakfast, pool, German owner Peter Kallert offers trips on his yacht. Recommended.

$$$ Pousada Arte Colonial, R da Matriz 292, T3371 7231, www.pousadaartecolonial.com.br. Some rooms **$$$$** in high season. One of the best deals in Paraty: colonial building in the centre decorated with style and genuine personal touch by its French owner. Helpful, breakfast included. Highly recommended.

$$$ Pousada do Corsário, Beco do Lapeiro 26, T3371 1866, www.pousadacorsario.com. br. New building with a pool and its own gardens; next to the river and 2 blocks from

the centre, simple but stylish rooms, most with hammocks outside. Highly recommended.
$$$ Pousada Eclipse, R das Ingás 4, T3371 2168, www.pousadaeclipse.com.br. Just outside the old town, Good rooms, comfortable, excellent service, good breakfast, with pool, parking, bar.
$$$ Vivenda & Maris, R Beija Flor 9 and 11, Caboré, www.vivendaparaty.com and www.maris paraty.com.br. Identical *pousadas* with lovely garden chalet rooms around a pool, personal service, quiet, intimate, 10-min walk from centre.
$$$-$ Chill Inn Hostel and Pousada, R Orlando Carpinelli 3, Praia do Pontal, T3373 1302, www.chillinnhostel.com. Beachfront accommodation, dorms (US$16-25), all with bathrooms and a/c. Breakfast at beach bar, free taxi and internet.
$$ Geko Hostel, R Orlando Carpinelli 5, Praia do Pontal, T3371 7504, www.gekohostel.com. Private rooms and dorms (US$16 24, all with a/c), free pick-up from bus station, breakfast on the beach, free internet café, free Wi-Fi.
$$ Solar dos Gerânios, Praça da Matriz, T3371 1550, www.paraty.com.br/geranio. Beautiful colonial family house on main square in traditional rustic style, excellent value and English spoken. Warmly recommended.
$$-$ Pousada do Careca, Praça Macedo Soares, T3371 1291, www.pousadadocareca. com. Very simple rooms in the historic centre, those without street windows are musty.
$ pp Casa do Rio, R Antônio Vidal 120, T3371 2223, www.paratyhostel.com. Peaceful little hostel with riverside courtyard and hammock, HI discount, kitchen, breakfast included, private rooms (**$$**). Offers jeep and horse riding trips. Recommended.
Camping Camping Beira-Rio, just across the bridge, before the road to the fort, T3371 1985. Camping Club do Brasil, Av Orlando Carpinelli, Praia do Pontal, T3371 1050. Small, good, very crowded in Jan and Feb, US$8 pp. Also at Praia Jabaquara, T3371 7364.

Trindade *p409*
$$$ Garni Cruzeiro do Sul, R Principal (first on the right as you enter the village), T3371

5102, www.hotelgarnicruzeirodosul.com.br. Smart little beachside *pousada* with duplex rooms, most of which have sea views, **$$$$** at highest season.
$$-$ Ponta da Trindade Pousada & Camping, T3371 5113. Simple rooms with fan, sand-floored campsite with cold water showers and no power.
$$-$ Pousada Marimbá, R Principal, T3371 5147. Simple colourful rooms and a little breakfast area.

🍴 Restaurants

Paraty *p408*
The best restaurants in Paraty are in the historic part of town and are among the best in the southeast outside Rio or São Paulo. The less expensive restaurants, those offering *comida a quilo* (pay by weight) and the fast-food outlets are outside the historical centre, mainly on Av Roberto Silveira. Paraty has some plates unique to the region, like *peixe à Parati* – local fish cooked with herbs, green bananas and served with *pirão*, a mixture of manioc flour and the sauce that the fish was cooked in.
$$$ Bartolomeu, R Samuel Costa 176, T3371 3052, www.bartholomeuparaty.com.br. Brazilian-European fusion dishes, good atmosphere and cocktails. Has an associated *pousada* (see website).
$$$ Caminho do Ouro, R Samuel Costa 236, T3371 1689. Gourmet food using locally-produced ingredients. The restaurant becomes a samba club on weekend nights.
$$$ Punto Divino, R Mcal Deodoro 129, T3371 1348, http://puntodivino.com. Wood-fired pizza and calzoni served with live music and a good selection of wine.
$$$ Thai Brasil, R Dona Geralda 345, 3371 0127, www.thaibrasil.com.br. Beautiful restaurant ornamented with handicrafts and hand-painted furniture, the cooking loosely resembles Thai, without spices.
$$ Café Paraty, R da Lapa and Comércio. Open 0900-2400. Sandwiches, appetizers, light meals, also bar with live music nightly (cover charge), a local landmark.

\$\$ Dona Ondina, R do Comércio 2, by the river. Closed Mon, Mar and Nov. Family restaurant with well-prepared simple food, good value.
\$ Sabor da Terra, Av Roberto Silveira, next to Banco do Brasil. Closes 2200. Reliable, if not bargain-priced, self service food.

🍸 Bars and clubs

Paraty *p408*
Armazem Paraty, R Samuel Costa 18, T3371 2082. Arty shop by day, samba club by night.
Bar Dinho, Praça da Matriz at R da Matriz. Good bar with live music at weekends, sometimes mid-week.
Coupé, Praça Matriz, T3371 6008, www.casa coupe.com.br. A popular hang-out, outside seating, good bar snacks and breakfast.
Teatro Espaço, The Puppet Show, R Dona Geralda 327, T3371 1575, www.ecparaty.org.br. Wed, Sat 2100, US\$12: a silent puppet theatre for adults only which has toured throughout the USA and Europe. Not to be missed.

✳️ Festivals

Paraty *p408*
Feb/Mar Carnival, hundreds of people cover their bodies in black mud and run through the streets yelling like prehistoric creatures (anyone can join in). **Mar/Apr** Semana Santa, with religious processions and folk songs.
Mid-Jul Semana de Santa Rita, traditional foods, shows, exhibitions and dances.
Aug Festival da Pinga, the cachaça fair at which local distilleries display their products and there are plenty of opportunities to over-indulge. **Sep** (around the 8th) Semana da Nossa Senhora dos Remédios, processions and religious events. **Sep/Oct** Spring Festival of Music, concerts in front of Santa Rita church. The city is decorated with lights for Christmas. **31 Dec** New year's, a huge party with open-air concerts and fireworks (reserve accommodation in advance). As well as the Dança dos Velhos, another common dance in these parts is the ciranda, in which everyone,

young and old, dances in a circle to songs accompanied by guitars.

The **Festa Literária Internacional de Parati** (FLIP, www.flip.org.br) occurs every northern summer and is one of the most important literary events in Latin America. It is always attended by big name writers.

🎯 What to do

Parque Nacional de Itatiaia *p407*
Information on treks can be obtained from **Clube Excursionista Brasileira**, Av Almirante Barroso 2, 8th floor, Rio de Janeiro, T021-2220 3695.
Wildlife guides Edson Endrigo, T3742 8374, www.avesfoto.com.br. Birding trips in Itatiaia and throughout Brazil. English spoken. Ralph Salgueiro, T3351 1823, www.ecoralph.com.

Angra dos Reis *p408*
Boat trips Trips around the bay are available, some with a stop for lunch on the island of Gipóia (5 hrs). Several boats run tours from the Cais de Santa Luzia and there are agencies for saveiros in town, boats depart between 1030-1130 daily (during Jan and Feb best to reserve in advance).

Ilha Grande *p408*
Boat trips These are easy to organize on the quay in Abraão. Ask about trips to good scuba diving sites around the coast.
Cycling Bikes can be hired and tours arranged; ask at *pousadas*.

Paraty *p408*
Angatu, T011-3872 0945, www.angatu.com. Private tours and diving trips around the bay in luxury yachts and motor cruisers. Also offers entry to exclusive private parties and private villa rental. Book well ahead.
Antígona, Praça da Bandeira 2, Centro Histórico, T3371 2199. Daily schooner tours, 5 hrs, bar and lunch on board. Recommended.
Paraty Tours, Av Roberto Silveira 11, T3371 1327, www.paratytours.com.br. Good range of trips. English and Spanish spoken.

⊖ Transport

Parque Nacional de Itatiaia *p407*

Bus Itatiaia lies just off the main São Paulo-Rio highway. There are connections to Itatiaia town or nearby Resende from both **Rio** and **São Paulo**. There is only one way into the park from Itatiaia town and one main road within it – which forks off to the various hotels, all of which are signposted. Four times a day (variable hours), a bus marked '504 Circular' leaves Itatiaia town for the Park, calling at the hotels. Coming from Resende this may be caught at the crossroads before Itatiaia. Through tickets to São Paulo are sold at a booth in the large bar in the middle of Itatiaia main street.

Costa Verde: Mangaratiba *p407*

Bus From Rio Rodoviária with **Costa Verde**, several daily, US$16.

Angra dos Reis *p108*

Bus To **Angra** at least hourly from Rio's *rodoviária* with **Costa Verde**, www.costa verdetransportes.com.br, several direct, comfortable buses take the 'via litoral', sit on the left, US$22, 2½ hrs. From Angra to **São Paulo**, Reunidas, www.reunidaspaulista.com. br, 4 buses daily (3 on Sat), US$35, 7 hrs. To **Paraty**, many buses leave from the local bus station on Largo da Lapa near the Ilha Grande jetty, then go to the *rodoviária*; **Colitur** every 30-40 mins (Sun, holidays hourly) US$5.50, 2 hrs; **Costa Verde** (from Rio) roughly every 3 hrs, faster and pricier.

Ilha Grande *p408*

Ferry Fishing boats and ferries (Barcas SA; T021-2533 7524) leave from **Angra dos Reis, Conceição de Jacareí** and **Mangaratiba**, taking 2 hrs or so to reach Vila do Abraão. From Angra there are 4 daily yachts and catamarans and 1 ferry (at 1000) leaving between 0730 and 1600, and an extra ferry at 1330 at weekends and public holidays. From Conceição de Jacareí there are 7 yacht

sailings daily between 0900 and 1815, with an occasional late boat at 2100 on busy Fri. From Mangaratiba there is a ferry at 0800 and a yacht at 1400. Schedules change frequently and it's well worth checking for the latest on www.ilhagrande.org, which details the names and phone numbers of all boats currently sailing. Ferries cost US$4 on weekdays and double that at weekends, yachts US$8 and catamarans US$30. All the towns are served by **Costa Verde** buses from the *rodoviária* in Rio. **Easy Transfer**, T021-7753 2190, www. easytransferbrazil.com, offer a van and boat service from Rio to Ilha Grande; door to door from the city (US$32.50) and from the airport (price depends on flight times and numbers); and from Ilha Grande to Paraty (US$25). There are discounts on multi-trips (eg Rio–Ilha Grande–Paraty–Rio).

Paraty *p408*

Bus To **Fazenda Murycana** take a Penha/Ponte Branca bus from the *rodoviária*, 4 a day; alight where it crosses a small white bridge and then walk 10 mins along a signed, unpaved road.

Rodoviária at the corner of R Jango Padua and R da Floresta. 9 buses a day go to **Rio** (241 km), 4½ hrs, US$31, Costa Verde – see under Angra dos Reis for details; to Angra dos Reis (98 km, 1½ hrs, more expensive than Colitur, T3371 1224, every 30-40 mins). 3 a day to **Ubatuba** (75 km), just over 1 hr, US$7.50, Colitur, who also go to **Trindade**. To **São Paulo**, Reunidas and São José, 5½ hrs, US$25, booked up quickly, very busy at weekends. To **São Sebastião**, change in Caraguatatuba. On holidays and in high season, the frequency of bus services increases.

⊕ Directory

Paraty *p408*

Banks Banco do Brasil, Av Roberto Silveira, not too far from the bus station, with ATM. One other in town for Visa and MasterCard, 0600-2200.

São Paulo

The city of São Paulo is vast and can feel intimidating at first. But this is a city of separate neighbourhoods, only a few of which are interesting for visitors and, once you have your base, it is easy to negotiate. Those who don't flinch from the city's size and who are prepared to spend money and time here, and who get to know Paulistanos, are seldom disappointed. (The inhabitants of the city are called Paulistanos, to differentiate them from the inhabitants of the state, who are called Paulistas.) Nowhere in Brazil is better for concerts, clubs, theatre, ballet, classical music, all round nightlife, restaurants and beautifully designed hotels.

Arriving in São Paulo → *Phone code: 011. Population: 10 million, 20 million in greater São Paulo. Colour map 7, B4.*

Orientation There are air services from all parts of Brazil, Europe, North and South America to the international **airport** at Guarulhos, also known as Cumbica, 30 km northeast of the city. The local airport of Congonhas, 14 km south of the city centre on Avenida Washington Luiz, is used for the Rio-São Paulo shuttle, and some flights to Belo Horizonte and Vitória. The **main rodoviária** is Tietê, which is very convenient and has its own Metrô station, as do the other three bus stations for inter-state bus services.

Much of the city centre is pedestrianized, so walking is the only option if you wish to explore it. The best and cheapest way to get around São Paulo is on the integrated Metrô and CPTM urban light railway system, which is clean, safe, cheap and efficient, and being expanded. Bus routes can be confusing and slow due to frequent traffic jams, but buses are safe, clean and only crowded at peak hours. If travelling with luggage, take a taxi. ▶▶ *See Transport, page 430.*

The **Old Centre** (Praça da República, Sé, Santa Cecília) is a place to visit but not to stay. The central commercial district, containing banks, offices and shops, is known as the Triângulo, bounded by Ruas Direita, 15 (Quinze) de Novembro, São Bento and Praça Antônio Prado, but spreading as far as the Praça da República. **Jardins**, the city's most affluent inner neighbourhood, is a good place to stay and to visit, especially if you want to shop and eat well. Elegant little streets hide hundreds of wonderful restaurants and accommodation ranges from the luxurious to the top end of the budget range. You are safe here at night. The northeastern section of Jardins abuts one of São Paulo's grandest modern avenues, **Paulista**, lined with skyscrapers, shops and a few churches and museums including MASP (Museu de Arte de São Paulo). There are metro connections from here and a number of good hotels. Between Jardins and the centre, **Consolação**, with R Augusta at its heart, is undergoing a renaissance at the cutting edge of the city's underground live music and nightlife scene. **Ibirapuera Park and around**: the inner city's largest green space is home to a handful of museums, running tracks, a lake and frequent free live concerts on Sun. The adjoining neighbourhoods of Moema and Vila Mariana have a few hotels, but **Moema Itaim Vila Olímpia** are among the nightlife centres of São Paulo with a wealth of streetside bars, designer restaurants and European-style dance clubs. Hotels tend to be expensive as they are near the new business centre on Avenidas Brigadeiro Faria Lima and Luis Carlos Berrini. **Pinheiros and Vila Madalena** are less chic, but equally lively at night and with the funkiest shops.

Avoid the Centro after dark, especially the areas around Luz station and Praça da República and do not enter favelas.

Tourist offices There are tourist information booths with English speaking staff in international and domestic arrivals Guarulhos (Cumbica) airport, 0600-2200; and tourist booths in the Tietê bus station (0600-2200) and in the following locations throughout the city: **Olido** ① *Av São João 473, Mon-Fri 0900-1800*; at **Parque Prefeito Mário Covas** ① *Av Paulista 1853, daily 000-2000*; at the **Mercado Municipal** ① *R da Cantareira 306, Mon-Sat 0900-1800, Sun 0700-1600*. An excellent map is available free at all these offices, as well as free maps and pamphlets in English. Visit www.cidadedesaopaulo.com (Portuguese, English and Spanish), also www.guiadasemana. com.br/ sao-paulo and http://vejasp.abril.com.brfor what's on and where to go.

Climate São Paulo sits on a plateau at around 800 m and the weather is temperamental. Rainfall is ample and temperatures fluctuate greatly: summer averages 20-30°C (occasionally peaking into the high 30s or 40s), winter temperatures are 15-25°C (occasionally dropping to below 10°C). The winter months (April-October) are the driest, with minimal precipitation in June/July. Christmas and New Year are wet. When there are thermal inversions, air pollution can be troublesome.

Background

Until the 1870s São Paulo was a sleepy, shabby little town known as 'a cidade de barro' (the mud city), as most buildings were made of clay and packed mud. It was transformed in the late 19th century when wealthy landowners and Santos merchants began to invest. From 1885 to 1900 the coffee boom and arrival of large numbers of Europeans transformed the state. By the late 1930s São Paulo state had one million Italians, 500,000 each of Portuguese and immigrants from the rest of Brazil, 400,000 Spaniards and 200,000 Japanese. It is the world's largest Japanese community outside Japan. Nowadays, it covers more than 1500 sq km, three times the size of Paris.

Centro Histórico

A focal point of the centre is the **Parque Anhangabaú**, an open space between the Triângulo and the streets which lead to Praça da República (Metrô Anhangabaú is at its southern end). Beneath Anhangabaú, north-south traffic is carried by a tunnel. Crossing it are two viaducts: **Viaduto do Chá**, which is open to traffic and links Rua Direita and Rua Barão de Itapetininga. The **Viaduto Santa Ifigênia**, an iron bridge for pedestrians only, connects Largo de São Bento with Largo de Santa Ifigênia.

On **Largo de São Bento** there is the **Igreja e Mosteiro de São Bento** ① *T3328 8799, www.mosteiro.org.br for details of all services, including Gregorian chant*, an early 20th-century building (1910-22) on the site of a 1598 chapel. Due south of São Bento is the **Martinelli building** ① *on R Líbero Badaró at Av São João, closed*, the city's first skyscraper (1922). It was surpassed by the **Edifício Banespa** (officially Altino Arantes, or Santander Cultural, finished 1947) ① *R João Brícola 24, T3249 7180, Mon-Fri 1000-1700*, with 360° views from the top, up to 40 km, smog permitting. South of these two buildings is the **Centro Cultural Banco do Brasil** ① *R Álvares Penteado 112, T3113 3651, www.bb.com.br*, an art nouveau building with a diverse programme in its exhibition spaces, cultural centre, concert halls and galleries in the old vaults. The **Pateo do Collégio (Museu de Anchieta)** ① *Praça Pátio do Colégio, T3105 6899, www.pateodocollegio.com.br, Metrô Sé, with a café, Tue-Sun 0900-1700, US$3* is an exact replica of the original Jesuit church and college, but dates from 1950s. Most of the buildings are occupied by the Museu de Anchieta, named after the Jesuit captain who led the first mission. This houses, amongst other items a 17th-century font that was used to baptize *indígenas* and a collection of Guaraní art and artefacts from the colonial era and a modernist painting of the priest, by Italian Albino Menghini.

São Paulo

➡ **Sao Paulo maps**
1 São Paulo, page 418
2 São Paulo centre, page 420
3 Jardins & Avenida Paulista, page 423

Where to stay ⬤
1 Blue Tree Towers E3
2 Casa Club C2
3 Formule 1 Paraíso D5
4 Global Hostel D5
5 Grand Hyatt E2
6 Hilton E2
7 Paradiso Hostel D5
8 Praça da Árvore Hostel E5
9 Sampa Hostel C2
10 Vergueiro Hostel C5

Restaurants ⬤
1 AK Vila C2
2 Goshala C3
3 La Mar D3
4 Peixeria C2

Bars & clubs ⬤
5 A Marcenaria C2
6 Bambu C2
7 Genial C2
8 Grazie a Dio C2
9 Ó de Borogodó C2
10 Posto 6 C2

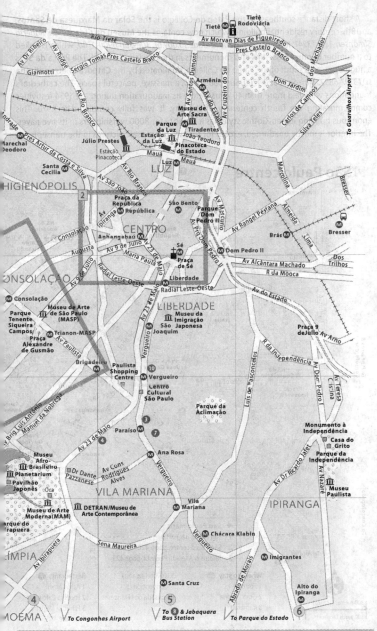

A short distance southeast of the Pateo do Collégio is the **Solar da Marquesa de Santos**, an 18th-century residential building, which now contains the **Museu da Cidade** ⓘ *R Roberto Simonsen 136, T3241 1081, www.museudacidade.sp.gov.br, Tue-Sun 0900-1700*, which is linked to a number of other museums and monuments in the city (see website). The **Praça da Sé** is a huge open area south of the Pateo do Collégio, dominated by the **Catedral Metropolitana** ⓘ *T3107 6832, Mon-Sat 0800-1700, Sun 0800-1830*, a massive, peaceful space. The cathedral's foundations were laid more than 40 years before its inauguration during the 1954 festivities commemorating the fourth centenary of the city. It was fully completed in 1970. This enormous building in neo-Gothic style has a capacity for 8000 worshippers in its five naves. The interior is mostly unadorned, except for the two gilt mosaic pictures in the transepts: on

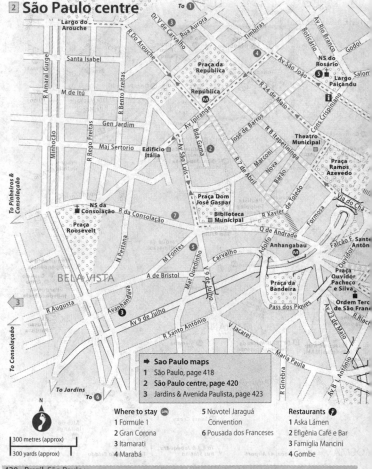

2 São Paulo centre

➡ Sao Paulo maps
1 São Paulo, page 418
2 São Paulo centre, page 420
3 Jardins & Avenida Paulista, page 423

Where to stay
1 Formule 1
2 Gran Corona
3 Itamarati
4 Marabá
5 Novotel Jaraguá Convention
6 Pousada dos Franceses

Restaurants
1 Aska Lámen
2 Efigênia Café e Bar
3 Famiglia Mancini
4 Gombe

300 metres (approx)
300 yards (approx)

the north side is the Virgin Mary and on the south Saint Paul. Just off the northeastern corner of the Praça da Sé is **Igreja da Ordem Terceira do Carmo** ①*R Rangel Pestana 230, Tue-Sun 0900-2100, free*. This peaceful church dates from 1632 and was built by lay brothers, many of whom were bandeirantes or their children. It preserves much of its baroque interior, including an impressive ceiling painting and an 18th-century gilt altarpiece.

West of the Praça da Sé, the Viaduto do Chá leads to the **Theatro Municipal** ①*T3297 0300, www.prefeitura.sp.gov.br/cidade/secretarias/cultura/theatromunicipal*, one of the few distinguished early 20th-century survivors that São Paulo can boast. Its interior is most impressive, with stained glass, opulent hallways and public areas together with its stage and auditorium, thoroughly renovated and modernised in late 2011.

To Luz, Pinacoteca Museum & Tietê

To Mercado Municipal

5 Ponto Chic
6 Sushi Yassu

Bars & clubs 🍸
7 Royal Club

To ❶❹❺ & Liberdade

Historic buildings walk ~ ◄ ~ ~

Praça da República

In Praça da República the trees are tall and shady. Near the Praça is the city's tallest building, the **Edifício Itália** ①*Av Ipiranga 344, 12189 2929, US$5*. There is a restaurant on top and a sightseeing balcony. If you walk up Avenida São Luís, which has many airline offices and travel agencies (especially found in the Galeria Metrópole), you arrive at Praça Dom José Gaspar, in which is the **Biblioteca Municipal Mário de Andrade**, surrounded by a pleasant shady garden.

North of the centre

About 10 minutes' walk from the centre is the old **Mercado Municipal** (see Shopping, page 430). **Parque da Luz** on Avenida Tiradentes (110,000 sq m) was formerly a botanical garden. It is next to the Luz railway station. There are two museums: in the park is the **Pinacoteca do Estado** (State Art Collection) ①*Praça da Luz 2, T3224 1000, www.pinacoteca.org.br, Tue-Wed 1000-1730, Thu 1000-2200, Fri-Sun 1000-1730, US$3, free on Sat (closes 1730)*. It and its neighbouring sister gallery, the **Estação Pinacoteca** ①*Largo General Osório 66, T3335 4990, Tue-Sun 1000-1730, US$3, Sat free*, preserve the best collection of modernist Brazilian art outside the Belas Artes in Rio, together with important works by Europeans like Picasso and Chagall. Both have good cafés, the Pinacoteca has a very good art bookshop. Nearby, the **Museu de Arte Sacra** ①*Av Tiradentes 676, T3326 1373, www.museu artesacra.org.br, Tue-Sun 1000-1800, US$3*, is modern and tasteful, housed in the serene

Mosteiro da Luz (1774), still partially occupied. It has a priceless, beautifully presented collection including works by many of Brazil's most important Baroque masters. The convent is one of the few colonial buildings left in São Paulo; the chapel dates from 1579.

Liberdade

Directly south of the Praça da Sé, and one stop on the Metrô, is Liberdade, the central Japanese district, now also home to large numbers of Koreans and Chinese. The Metrô station is in Praça da Liberdade, in which there is an oriental market every Sunday (see Shopping). The Praça is one of the best places in the city for Japanese food. **Museu da Imigração Japonesa** ① *R São Joaquim 381, exhibition on 7th, 8th and 9th floors, T3209 5465, www.nihonsite.com.br/muse, Tue-Sun 1330-1730, US$3,* is excellent, with a roof garden; captions have English summaries.

West of the centre

Jardins and Avenida Paulista

Avenida Paulista has been transformed since the 1930s from the city's most fashionable promenade into six lanes of traffic lined with banks' and multinationals' headquarters. Its highlight is undoubtedly MASP, the common name for the **Museu de Arte de São Paulo** ① *Av Paulista 1578 (above the 9 de Julho tunnel); T3251 5644, www.masp.art.br, Metrô Trianon-MASP; open 1000-1800, except Thu 1000-2000, closed Mon, US$7.50.* The museum has the finest collection of European masters in the southern hemisphere with works by artists like Raphael, Bellini, Bosch, Rembrandt, Turner, Constable, Monet, Manet and Renoir. Also some interesting work by Brazilian artists, including Portinari. Temporary exhibitions are also held and when a popular show is on, it can take up to an hour to get in. There is a very good art shop.

Opposite MASP is **Parque Tenente Siqueira Campos** ① *daily 0700-1830,* which covers two blocks on either side of Alameda Santos; a bridge links the two parts of the park. It is block of subtropical forest in the busiest part of the city. The **Museu da Imagem e do Som** (**MIS**) ① *Av Europa 158, T2117 4777, www.mis.sp.gov.br, Tue-Fri 1200-2200, Sat-Sun 1100-2100, free, exhibitions US$3,* has an arts cinema, sound labs, archives of Brazilian cinema and music, weekly club nights and a good restaurant. Next to MIS is the **Museu Brasiliero da Escultura** (MuBE); free to temporary exhibitions and recitals in the afternoons. Avenida Europa continues to Avenida Brigadeiro Faria Lima, on which is the **Casa Brasileira** ① *Av Faria Lima 2705, T3032 3727, www.mcb.sp.gov.br, Tue-Sun 1000-1800, US$2, Sun free,* a museum of Brazilian furniture. It also holds temporary exhibitions.

Cidade Universitária

The Cidade Universitária is on the west bank of the Rio Pinheiros, opposite the district of Pinheiros. The campus also contains the famous **Instituto Butantan** (Butantan Snake Farm and Museum) ① *Av Dr Vital Brasil 1500, T011-2627 9536, Tue-Sun 0900-1645, www.butantan.gov. br, US$2.50, children half price, under 7 free, Metrô Butanta.* The insituto's collection of preserved snakes, spiders and scorpions was destroyed by fire in May 2010. The museum and vivarium are open to visitors. The **Museu de Arte Contemporâneo** (**MAC**) ① *T3091 3039, www.mac. usp.br, Tue-Thu 1000-2000, Fri-Sun 1000-1800, free,* with an important collection of Brazilian and European modern art, is in the Prédio Novo da Reitoria. Also the **Museu de Arqueologia e Etnologia** (MAE) ① *R Reitoria 1466, T3812 4001,* with Amazonian and ancient Mediterranean collections. Not far from the Butantan Institute, just inside Cidade Universitária, is the **Casa do Bandeirante** ① *Praça Monteiro Lobato, T3031 0920, Tue-Sun 0900-1700,* the reconstructed home of a 17th-century pioneer.

On the west bank of the Rio Pinheiros, just southeast of the Cidade Universitária, is the palatial **Jóquei Clube/Jockey Club** ① *Av Lineu de Paula Machado 1263, T2161 8300, www. jockeysp.com.br*, racecourse in the Cidade Jardim area. Take Butantã bus from República. Race meetings are held Monday and Thursday at 1930 and weekends at 1430. It has a **Museu do Turfe** ① *Tue-Sun, closed Sat-Sun mornings.*

③ Jardins & Avenida Paulista

➡ Sao Paulo maps
1 São Paulo, page 418
2 São Paulo centre, page 420
3 Jardins & Avenida Paulista, page 423

500 metres (approx)
500 yards (approx)

Where to stay 🛏
1 Dona Ziláh *A2*
2 Emiliano *B2*
3 Fasano hotel & restaurant *B2*
4 Guest 607 *A1*
5 Ibis São Paulo Paulista *A3*
6 Paulista Garden *C2*
7 Pousada dos Franceses *C3*
8 Renaissance *B3*
9 Unique *C2*
10 Vila Madalena Hostel *A1*

Restaurants 🍴
1 A Mineira *C3*
2 Casa Nero & Vento Haragano *A2*
3 Charlô Bistrô & Dalva e Dito *B2*
4 Cheiro Verde *B2*
5 DOM *B2*
6 Dui *A2*
7 Figueira Rubaiyat *B1*
8 Fran's Café *B2/C3*
9 Gero *B2*
10 Jun Sakamoto *A1*
11 Mani *B1*
12 MASP *B3*
13 Sattva *A2*
14 Sujinho *A3*
15 Tavares *A2*
16 Tordesilhas *B2*

Bars & clubs 🍸
16 Bar Balcão *A2*
17 Beco 203 *B3*
18 Caos *B3*
19 Casa de Francisca *C3*
20 Finnegan's Pub *A1*
21 Kabul *A3*
22 Outs Club *A3*
23 Studio SP *A3*
24 Volt *A3*

South of the centre

Ibirapuera

The **Parque do Ibirapuera** ① *entrance on Av Pedro Álvares Cabral, daily 0500-2400 but unsafe after dark, www.parquedoibirapuera.com*, was designed by Oscar Niemeyer and landscape artist Roberto Burle Marx for the city's fourth centenary in 1954. Within its 160 ha are many public buildings and monuments. These include the state-of-the-art **Planetarium** ① *T5575 5206, Sat, Sun 1200-1800, US$5*, the **Museu de Arte Moderna (MAM)** ① *T5085 1300, www.mam.org.br, Tue-Sun 1000-1730, US$3*, with temporary art exhibitions, a great café restaurant and art shop. The MAM overlooks a sculpture garden located between the **Oca** (Pavilhão Lucas Nogueira Garcez), a brilliant white dome which stages exhibitions, and the **Fundação Bienal**. Every even-numbered year the **Bienal Internacional de São Paulo** (São Paulo Biennial) has the most important show of modern art in Latin America, usually in September. Also in the park: **Museu Afro-Brasil** ① *T3320 8900, www.museuafrobrasil.com.br, Tue-Sun 1000-1700, US$5*: temporary exhibitions, theatre, dance and cinema spaces, photographs and panels devoted to exploring African Brazil. **Pavilhão Japonês** ① *T5081 7296, www.bunkyo.bunkyonet.org.br, Wed, Sat, Sun 1300-1700, free except for exhibitions*, exhibition space showing works from Japanese and Japanese-Brazilian artists, designed by Japanese and built exclusively with materials from Japan. It is set in Japanese gardens and has a traditional tea house upstairs. Bicycles can be hired in the park, US$3 per hour. To get to Ibirapuera: Metrô Ana Rosa is a 15-minute walk, but Ibirapuero metro is under construction; bus 5164-21 every 30 minutes from Metrô Santa Cruz; any bus (eg 175T-10, 477U-10, 675N-10) to DETRAN, a Niemeyer building opposite the park which has reopened as the new headquarters of **Museu de Arte Contemporânea de São Paulo** ① *Av Pedro Álvares Cabral 1301, T5573 9932, Tue-Sun 1000-1800*. At present only the ground floor functions as a gallery, showing sculptures by the likes of Henry Moore. From DETRAN cross Av 23 de Maio by footbridge.

Parque da Independência

In the suburb of Ipiranga, 5.5 km southeast of the city centre, the Parque da Independência contains the **Monumento à Independência**. Beneath the monument is the **Imperial Chapel** ① *Tue-Sun 1300-1700*, with the tomb of the first emperor, Dom Pedro I, and Empress Leopoldina. **Casa do Grito** ① *Tue-Sun 0930-1700*, the little house in which Dom Pedro I spent the night before his famous cry of Ipiranga, 'Independence or Death', is preserved in the park. The **Museu Paulista** ① *T2065 8000, www.mp.usp.br, Tue-Sun 0900-1700, US$3*, contains old maps, traditional furniture, collections of old coins, religious art and *indígena* ethnology. Behind the Museum is the **Horto Botânico** (**Ipiranga Botanical Garden**) and the **Jardim Francês** ① *Tue-Sun 0900-1700, getting there: take bus 478-P (Ipiranga-Pompéia for return) from Ana Rosa, or take bus 4612 from Praça da República*.

Parque do Estado (Jardim Botânico)

This large park, a long way south of the centre, at **Água Funda** ① *Av Miguel Estefano 3031-3687, T5073 6300, www.ibot.sp.gov.br, Tue-Sun 0900-1700, US$1.50, getting there: take Metrô to São Judas on the Jabaquara line, then take bus 4742*, contains the Jardim Botânico, with lakes and trees and places for picnics, and a very fine orchid farm worth seeing during November-December (orchid exhibitions in April and November).

Excursions

Paranapiacaba is a tiny 19th-century town in the cloudforest of the Serra do Mar, 50 km southeast of São Paulo. It was built by British railway workers. There is a small railway museum and a handful of *pousadas* and restaurants. A frequent train runs on the Turquoise Line (Linha Turquesa) from Luz station to Rio Grande da Serra, US$2.50, 55 mins, from where bus No 424 runs to Paranapiacaba in the week, every 30 minutes at weekends, about one hour. A tourist train, the *Expresso Turístico*, runs from Luz at 0830 or Estação Prefeito Celso Daniel-Santo André at 0900 on Sundays direct to Paranapiacaba, returning 1630, 1½ hours, US$15. See www.cptm. sp.gov.br/e_operacao/exprtur/parana.asp for details.

⊙ São Paulo listings

For hotel and restaurant price codes, and other relevant information, see Essentials.

● Where to stay

For both business and leisure, São Paulo has by far the best hotels in Brazil. The best area to stay is northeastern Jardins (also known as Cerqueria César), which is safe and well connected to the Metrô via Av Paulista. Both **Novotel** (www.novotel.com) and **Accor** (www.accorhotels.com.br – Formule 1 and Ibis) are well-represented in the Centro Histórico and Jardins and Avenida Paulista areas. There are cheapies in the centre, but this is an undesirable area at night.

Centro Histórico *p417, map p420*
$$$ Gran Corona, Basílio da Gama 101, T3214 0043, www.grancorona.com.br. In a small street. Comfortable if a bit dated, good services, good restaurant. Warmly recommended.
$$$ Marabá, Av Ipiranga 757, T2137 9500, www.hotelmaraba.com.br. Good small hotel in the centre, refurbished, colourful rooms, small bar, restaurant and gym.
$$ Itamarati, Av Dr Vieira de Carvalho 150, T3474 4133, www.hotelitamarati.com.br. Good location, safe, cheaper at weekends. Highly recommended and very popular.

Jardins, Avenida Paulista and around *p422, map p423*
$$$$ Emiliano, R Oscar Freire 384, T3069 4369, www.emiliano.com.br. Bright and

beautifully designed, attention to every detail and the best suites in the city. No pool but a relaxing small spa. Excellent Italian restaurant, location and service.
$$$$ Fasano, R Vittorio Fasano 88, T3896 4077, www.fasano.com.br. One of the world's great hotels with decor like a modernist gentleman's club designed by Armani, a fabulous pool and the best formal haute cuisine restaurant in Brazil. Excellently positioned in Jardins.
$$$$ Renaissance, Al Santos 2233 (at Haddock Lobo), T3069 2233, http://marriott. com. The best business hotel off Av Paulista with standard business rooms, a good spa, gym, pool and 2 squash courts.
$$$$ Unique, Av Brigadeiro Luis Antônio 4700, Jardim Paulista, T3055 4700, www.hotel unique.com. The most ostentatious hotel in the country, an enormous half moon on concrete uprights with curving floors, circular windows and beautiful use of space and light. The bar on the top floor is São Paulo's answer to the LA Sky Bar and is always filled with the rich and famous after 2130.
$$$ Dona Ziláh, Al França 1621, Jardim Paulista, T3062 1444, www.zilah.com. Little *pousada* in a renovated colonial house, well maintained, decorated with a personal touch. Excellent location, bike rental and generous breakfast included.
$$$ Paulista Garden, Al Lorena 21, T3885 8498, www.paulistagardenhotel.com.br. Small, simple if dated rooms with small workspaces and tiny bathrooms with electric showers,

quieter on upper floors, uninspiring but good location close to Ibirapuera Park.

$$$-$$ Guest 607, R João Moura 607, Pinheiros, T2619 6007, www.guest607.com.br. Simple but colourfully painted guest house a stroll from the Benedito Calixto weekend market, cosy, suites, rooms with shared bath and a shared room, decent little café/restaurant.

$$$-$$ Pousada dos Franceses, R dos Franceses 100, Bela Vista, T3288 1592, www.pousadadosfranceses.com.br. Plain little *pousada* 10 mins' walk from Brigadeiro Metrô. Dorms, doubles and singles, TV room.

$$$-$ Paradiso Hostel, R Chuí 195, T97587 0747, www.paradisohostel.com. Studio rooms and dorms in 2 modest town houses in a quiet street just behind the Orthodox cathedral, spacious, well-kept, no breakfast, but there's a very good padaria round the corner.

$$$-$ Vergueiro Hostel, R Vergueiro 434, Liberdade, T2649 1323, www.hostelvergueiro. com. Simple rooms, some with balconies, studio apartments and shared rooms for up to 6.

$$$-$ Vila Madalena Hostel, R Francisco Leitão 686, T3034 4104, www.vilamadalena hostel.com. Prices for double bed through todorms for 4 or 8. 15 mins from Clínicas Metrô, well-run, popular, arty hostel with good services, bikes for rent.

$$-$ Casa Club, R Mourata Coelho 973, Vila Madalena, T3798 0051, www.casaclub. com.br. Tiny hostel with shared rooms that can be booked privately, one for women only. Previously a bar and retains its party atmosphere, restaurant.

$$-$ Sampa Hostel, R Girassol 519, Vila Madalena, T3031 6779, www.sampahostel. com.br. Dorms and 2 private rooms which need booking in advance, convenient, with fan, breakfast.

South of the centre *p424*

The area known as the New Centre, around Av Brigadeiro Faria Lima and Av Luis Carlos Berrini, has no sights of interest for the tourist, however it has the plushest, most expensive hotels, including **Grand Hyatt**, www.saopaulo. hyatt.com, and the **Hilton**, www.hilton.com, both as good as you would expect.

$$$$ Blue Tree Towers, Av Brigadeiro Faria Lima 3989, Vila Olímpia, T3896 7544, www. bluetree.com.br. Modern business hotel with excellent service, ideally positioned for Faria Lima, Vila Olímpia and Itaim, pool, massage, gym, sauna and business centre. There are several other **Blue Trees** around the city.

$$ Praça da Árvore Hostel, R Pageú 266, Saúde, T5071 5148, www.spalbergue.com.br. Well-kept *pousada* in a quiet street, cheaper for HI members, helpful, 2 mins from Praça do Árvore metro, private rooms with shared bath and dorms for 4 to 8, kitchen, laundry.

$ pp Global Hostel, Eça de Queiroz 560, Vila Mariana, 5-min walk from Paraíso Metro station, T2308 7401, www.globalhostel.com. br. Near Parque Ibirapuera, 6- to 10-bed dorms with fans and lockers which fit backpacks, kitchen and laundry facilities.

Associação Paulista de Albergues da Juventude, R 7 de Abril 404, 12th floor, Conj 124, T3258 0388, www.alberguesp.com.br.

🍴 Restaurants

Centro Histórico *p417, map p420*
There are plenty of restaurants and cafés in the centre, most open lunchtime only. There are many per kg options and *padarias*.

$$$-$$ Famiglia Mancini, R Avanhandava, Bela Vista, www.famigliamancini.com. br. A group of Italian restaurants and delicatessens, most owned by the same family, on a pretty pedestrianized street in Bela Vista, can be very busy.

$$-$ Café da Pinacoteca, Pinacoteca Museum, Praça da Luz 2, T3326 0350. Portuguese-style café with marble floors and mahogany balconies. Great coffee, sandwiches and cakes.

$$-$ Efigênia Café e Bar, Largo São Bento s/n, T3311 8800. A perfect pit stop while exploring the city centre. Tables under the Viaduto Santa Ifigênia and a good-value buffet of hot and cold plates of Brazilian standards.

$$-$ Ponto Chic, Largo do Paiçandu 27, T3222 6528. A corner café where the *bauru* sandwich (cheese, salad and roast beef) was born. An unpretentious place, very popular.

Liberdade *p422, map p420*
$$ Aska Lámen, R Galvã Bueno 466, Liberdade, T3277 9682. Traditional Japanese restaurant with a bar overlooking an open kitchen serving lunchtime noodle dishes.
$$ Gombe, R Tomás Gonzaga 22, T3209 8499. Renowned for grilled tuna and noodle dishes.
$$ Sushi Yassu, R Tomás Gonzaga 98, T3288 2966. The best of Liberdade's traditional Japanese restaurants. Excellent sushi/sashimi combinations.

Jardins, Avenida Paulista and around
p422, map p423
Those on a budget can eat to their stomach's content in per kg places or, cheaper still, bakeries (*padarias*) There's one on almost every corner and they serve sandwiches, delicious Brazilian burgers made from decent meat and served with ham, egg, cheese or salad. They always have good coffee, juices, cakes and set lunches (*almoços*) for a very economical price. Most have a designated sitting area – either at the *padaria* bar or in an adjacent room. Juices are made from mineral or filtered water.
$$$ AK Vila, R Fradique Coutinho 1240, Vila Madalena, T3231 4496. New York-style deli with a broad menu including light seafood dishes, *petiscos* and steaks, as well as sandwiches and bagels from the deli counter.
$$$ Casa Nero, Al Lorena 2101, Jardins, T3081 2966. A very fashionable, chic steakhouse with a moody interior and choice-cuts of Brazilian and Argentinean meat.
$$$ Charlô Bistrô, R Barão de Capanema 440, T3088 6790 (with another branch at the Jockey Club, Av Lineu de Paula Machado 1263, Cidade Jardim, T3034 3682). One of the premier VIP and old family haunts in the city run by a scion of one of the city's establishment families.

Decked out in tribute to a Paris brasserie and with food to match.
$$$ Dalva e Dito, R Padre João Manoel 1115, T3064 6183. Brazilian home cooking with a gourmet twist from chef Alex Attala. The soaring dining room is split by a long open kitchen.
$$$ DOM, R Barão de Capanema 549, T3088 0761. Jardins' evening restaurant of the moment. Alex Attala has won the coveted Veja best chef of the year award twice. Contemporary food, fusing Brazilian ingredients with French and Italian styles and served in a large modernist dining room.
$$$ Dui, Alameda Franca 1590, T2649 7952. Brazilian-Asian-Mediterranean fusion cuisine, with great cocktails in the downstairs bar.
$$$ Figueira Rubaiyat, R Haddock Lobo 1738, T3063 3888. The most interesting of the Rubaiyat restaurant group. Very lively for Sun lunch, light and airy and under a huge tropical fig tree.
$$$ Gero, R Haddock Lobo 1629, T3064 0005. Fasano's version of a French Bistrô a Côté, but serving pasta and light Italian. Ever so casual design; be prepared for a long wait at the bar alongside people who are there principally to be seen. Reservations are not accepted.
$$$ Jun Sakamoto, R Lisboa 55, Pinheiros, T3088 6019. Japanese with a touch of French; superb fresh ingredients (some of it flown in especially from Asia and the USA).
$$$ Mani, R Joaquim Antunes 210, Pinheiros, T3085 4148. A menu of light Mediterranean dishes using Brazilian ingredients, highly regarded. Helena Rizzo was voted the world's best female chef in 2014 (www.theworlds50best.com).
$$$ Vento Haragano, Av Rebouças 1001, T3083 4265. One of the best *rodízios* in the city.
$$$-$$ Tordesilhas, Al Tietê 489, Consolação, T3107 7444, www.tordesilhas.com. Informal, with shady plants, polished floor tiles and plenty of natural light, serving Brazilian home comfort fare, with a contemporary touch.
$$ A Mineira, Al Joaquim Eugénio de Lima 697, T3283 2349. Self-service Minas

food by the kilo. Lots of choice. Cachaça and pudding included.

$$ Fran's Café, Av Paulista 358, and throughout the city. Open 24 hrs, the Brazilian equivalent of Starbuck's but with proper coffee and light meals.

$$ Goshala, R dos Pinheiros 267, Pinheiros, T3063 0367. 100% Vegetarian, Brazilian food with an Indian face, plenty of choice and variety.

$$ Peixeria, R Inácio Pereira da Rocha 112, T2859 3963. This rustic-chic fish restaurant with raw brick walls, wood tables, culinders for lampshades and a giant model tarpon suspended from the ceiling draws a fashionable crowd sick of the inflated prices of gourmet São Paulo and seduced by the ultra-fresh fish, seafood petiscos and modest bills.

$$ Sattva, Alameda Itu 1564, T3083 6237. Vegetarian dishes, pizzas and pastas, all made with organic ingredients, good value lunchtime dish of the day, often has live music at night.

$$ Sujinho, R da Consolação 2068, Consolação, T3256 8026. South American beef in large portions, other carnivorous options also available.

$$ Tavares, R da Consolação 3212, T3062 6026. Good-value breakfasts and prato feito lunches and an à la carte menu ranging from pasta and pizzas to steaks and bacalhau.

$ Cheiro Verde, R Peixoto Gomide 1413. Lunch only. Hearty veggie food, like vegetable crumble in gorgonzola sauce and pasta with buffalo mozarella and sun-dried tomato.

South of the centre *p424*
Vila Olímpia and Itaim

Restaurants here are ultra, ultra trendy; full of the beautiful posing in beautiful surroundings. We include only a handful of the best.

$$$ Kosushi, R Viradouro 139, Itaim Bibi, T3167 7272. The first of São Paulo's chic Japanese restaurants which began life in Liberdade and is now housed in a beautifully designed Asian modernist space. Great sushi combinations. Also in Cidade Jardim Shopping.

$$$ La Mar, R Tapabuã 1410, Itaim, T3073 1213. Peruvian seafood dishes adapted for the Brazilian palate, also Japanese fusion.

$$$ Parigi, R Amauri 275, Itaim, T3167 1575. One of the city's premier evening places to be seen; Franco-Italian dining in a beautiful dining room.

⊙ Bars and clubs

The best places for nightlife are Itaim, Moema and Vila Olímpia, and Vila Madalena/Pinheiros. Jardins' best bars are in the top hotels. Vila Olímpia, Itaim and Moema have a series of funky, smart bars overflowing onto the street, filled with an eclectic mix of after-workers, clubbers, singles and couples; all united by being under 40 and having money. These sit alongside imitation US and European club/lounge bars playing techno, hip hop and the like. The busiest streets for a bar wander are R Atilio Inocenti near the junction of Av Juscelino Kubitschek and Av Brigadeiro Faria Lima, Av Hélio Pellegrino and R Araguari, which runs behind it. Vila Madalena is younger still, more hippy-chic, but is the best part of town to hear live, Brazilian music and uniquely Brazilian close dances like Forró, as opposed to international club sounds. The liveliest streets are Aspicuelta and Girassol.

West of the centre *p422*
Consolação

Beco 203, R Augusta 609, T2339 0351, www.beco203.com.br. Cutting edge alternative rockers from Brazil and the world over play here.

Caos, Rua Augusta 584, T2365 1260. One of the area's newer and most popular bars with an astonishing variety of music.

Kabul, R Pedro Taques 124, T2503 2810, www.kabul.com.br. Live misic ranging from Brazilian jazz to samba, rock and alternative acts.

Outs Club, R Augusta 486, T6867 6050, www.clubeouts.com. One of the bastions of alternative, rock and hard rock, from UK indie to Brazilian metal.

Royal Club, R Consolação 222, T3129 9804, www.royalclub.com.br. Highly fashionable funk and rare groove club playing non-Brazilian music.

Studio SP, R Augusta 591, T3129 7040, www.studiosp.org. Many different styles of live music at this show hall.

Volt, R Haddock Lobo 40, T2936 4041, www.barvolt.com.br. A hip favourite as a pre- and post-club stop, Brazilian drum and bass and Chicago house.

Jardins

Bar Balcão, R Dr Melo Alves 150, T3063 6091. After work meeting place, very popular with young professionals and media types who gather on either side of the long low wooden bar which winds its way around the room like a giant snake.

Casa de Francisca, R José Maria Lisboa 190, T3493 5717, www.casadefrancisca.art.br. Intimate bar/restaurant with refined live music.

Finnegan's Pub, R Cristiano Viana 358, Pinheiros, www.finnegan.com.br. One of São Paulo's various Irish bars, this one actually run by an Irishman, popular with ex-pats.

Vila Madalena/Pinheiros

A Marcenaria, R Fradique Coutinho 1378, T3032 9006, www.amarcenaria.com.br. The bar of choice for the young and single who gather around 2130, until the dance floor fills up around 2300.

Bambu, R Purpurina 272, T3031 2331, www.bambubrasilbar.com.br. For dancing *forró* and other northeastern styles and drinking *caipirinhas*.

Genial, R Girassol 374, T3812 7442. Music-themed bar which serves good *petiscos* and a popular *feijoada* on Sun.

Grazie a Dio, R Girassol 67, T3031 6568, www.grazieadio.com.br. The best bar in Vila Madalena for live music, different band every night. Great for dancing, always packed.

Ó de Borogodó, R Horácio Lane 21, T3814 4087. An intimate club, hard to find as it is unmarked (next to a hairdresser), open Wed-Sat for samba, choro and *forró*.

Posto 6, R Aspicuelta 644, Vila Madalena, T3812 7831. An imitation Rio de Janeiro Boteco with an attractive crowd and a backdrop of Bossa Nova and MPB. Busy from 2100 onwards.

South of the centre p424
Itaim, Moema and Vila Olímpia

The area just south of Ibirapuera and north of the new centre is packed with lively bars, each with its own atmosphere. The busiest streets are Atilio Inocenti, near the junction of Av Kubitschek and Av Brig Faria Lima, Av Hélio Pellegrino and Araguari, which runs behind it.

Bourbon Street Music Club, R dos Chanés 127, Moema, T5095 6100, www.bourbon street.com.br. Great little club with emerging local acts and international stars, too.

Na Mata Café, R da Mata 70, Itaim, T3079 0300, www.namata.com.br. Popular flirting and pick-up spot with a dark dance room, varied Brazilian and European dance tunes and select live bands.

⊕ Entertainment

São Paulo *p416, maps p418, p420 and p423*
See www.guiasp.com.br, the 'Guia da Folha' section of *Folha de São Paulo* and *Veja São Paulo* of the weekly news magazine Veja for listings.

Cinema Entrance is usually half price on Wed; normal seat price is US$10. Cine clubs: **Cine SESC**, R Augusta 2075, and cinemas at: **Museu da Imagem e do Som**, **Centro Cultural Itaú** and **Centro Cultural São Paulo**.

Theatre The Theatro Municipal (see page 421) is used by visiting theatrical and operatic groups, as well as the City Ballet Company and the Municipal Symphony Orchestra who give regular performances. There are several other 1st-class theatres: **Aliança Francesa**, R General Jardim 182, Vila Buarque, T3017 5699, www.alianca francesa.com.br. **Paiol**, R Amaral Gurgel 164, Vila Buarque, T221 2462; among others. Free concerts at Teatro Popular do Sesi, Av Paulista 1313, T3284 9787, at midday, under MASP (Mon-Sat). **Centro Cultural São**

Paulo, R Vergueiro 1000, T3397 4002, www. centrocultural.sp.gov.br. Arts centre and concert halls with regular classical music and ballet, library, theatres and exhibition spaces.

⊛ Festivals

São Paulo *p416, maps p418, p420 and p423*
Foundation of the City **25 Jan**. Carnival in **Feb** (most attractions and businesses are closed). This includes the parades of the escolas de samba in the Anhembi sambódromo – the São Paulo special group parades on the Fri and Sat and the Rio group on the Sun and Mon to maximize TV coverage. In Jun there are the **Festas Juninas** and the **Festa de São Vito**, the patron saint of the Italian immigrants. **Festa da Primavera** in **Sep**. In Dec there are Christmas and New Year festivities. All year, there are countless anniversaries, religious feasts, international fairs and exhibitions, look in the press or the monthly tourist magazines to see what is on while you are in town. See page 424 for the São Paulo Biennial.

⊘ Shopping

São Paulo *p416, maps p418, p420 and p423*
Handicrafts Casa dos Amazonas, Al dos Jurupis 460, Moema, www.arteindigena. com.br. Huge variety from all over Brazil. **Galeria Arte Brasileira**, Al Lorena 2163. Good value, stock from all over Brazil. **Sutaco**, R Boa Vista 170, Edif Cidade I, 3rd floor, Centro, T3241 7333. Handicrafts from São Paulo state.
Jewellery There are many shops selling Brazilian stones, including branches of H Stern.
Markets The Mercado Municipal, R da Cantareira 306, T3326 3401, www.mercado municipal.com.br, in an art deco building, with foodstalls below and restaurants on the upper gallery. **Antiques market**, below the Museu de Arte de São Paulo. Sun, 1000-1700. **Flea markets**, in Praça Benedito Calixto in Pinheiros, www.pracabeneditocalixto.com. br, on Sat, and in the main square of the Bixiga district (Praça Don Orione) on Sun. There is a Sunday market in the Praça da República

in the city centre. **Ceasa flower market**, Av Doutor Gastão Vidigal 1946, Jaguaré. Tue and Fri 0700-1200, should not be missed. '**Oriental**' fair, Praça de Liberdade. Sun 1000-1900, good for Japanese snacks, plants and some handicrafts, very picturesque, with remedies on sale, tightrope walking, gypsy fortune tellers, etc.

⊙ What to do

São Paulo *p416, maps p418, p420 and p423*
Adventure tourism
Pure Brazil by Venturas, R Minerva 268, Perdizes, T3872 0362, www.purebrasil.net. Customized itineraries to well-known and remote destinations, specialists in wildlife and adventure tourism.
SPin Brazil Tours, T5904 2269/9185 2623, www.spintours.com.br. Tailor-made services and private tours of São Paulo city and state with options on destinations further afield. These include bilingual 3- and 4-hr tours of the city of São Paulo, bilingual tours tailored to visitor interest and coordinated visits to football matches, the Brazilian Grand Prix and so on.
Trip on Jeep, R Arizona 623, Brooklin, T5543 5281, www.triponjeep.com. Land Rover expeditions in the state of São Paulo, birdwatching, ecotourism and trips elsewhere in Brazil and South America. English-speaking guides.
Football The most popular local teams are Corinthians, Palmeiras and São Paulo who play in the Morumbi and Pacaembu stadiums. The latter has a Museu do Futebol, Praça Charles Miller, T3664 3848, www.museudofutebol. org.br, Tue-Sun 1000-1700, US$3.

⊖ Transport

São Paulo *p416, maps p418, p420 and p423*
Air From the international airport **Guarulhos** (Cumbica), Av Monteiro Lobato 1985, T2445 2945, www.aeroportoguarulhos.net, there are airport taxis which charge US$60-75 on a ticket system (the taxi offices are outside Customs, 300 m down on the left; go to get

your ticket then take your bags right back to the end of the taxi queue). Fares from the city to the airport are slightly less and vary from cab to cab. The best service between the airport and city is on the fast, a/c **Airport Bus Service** (www.airportbusservice.com. br) leaving from outside international arrivals (where it has a ticket office). Its routes are: to the Tietê bus terminal (40 mins), Praça da República (US$17.50, 1 hr), Av Paulista (US$17.50, 1¼ hrs), Itaim Bibi (1 hr 20 mins), Av Luís Carlos Berrini (1½ hrs), Aeroporto Congonhas (1 hr 10 mins), to all destinations US$17.50, except Tietê US$18.50. Most buses leave at least once an hour, 0530-2400 and every 90 mins thereafter, though there are fewer services to Berrini and Itaim. If you have a flight connection to Congonhas, your airline will provide a courtesy bus. Allow plenty of time for getting to the airport and for checking in. In rush hour transfer times can double and the airport is often overcrowded. A new, fast road between airport and city is due to open in 2015. If looking for a hotel near the airport, **$$$ Monreale**, www.monreale hotels.com, has been recommended. From Congonhas airport, T5090 9000, there are about 400 flights a week to Rio. To get to Congonhas, take a bus or Metrô and bus (see www.sptrans.com.br), or a taxi, about US$20 from the centre, Vila Madalena or Jardins.

Airport information Money exchanges, in the arrivals hall, Guarulhos, 0800-2200 daily. See Arriving in São Paulo, page 416, for the tourist office.

Bus City buses are run by **SP Trans**, www.sptrans.com.br. You can work out your route on the planner on the bus company's website and on Google maps, which mark bus stops. These maps, plus those on the Metrô and CPTM websites (see below) will give you a good coverage of the city. Even if you do not speak Portuguese they are fairly self-explanatory. Local transport maps are also available at stations and depots. Some city bus routes are run by trolley buses. City bus fare is US$1.30 using the *bilhete único*, which integrates bus, metro and light railway

in a single, rechargeable plastic swipe card available from thousands of authorized outlets, including SP Trans' own shops (eg Praça da Sé 188, R Augusta 449), metro stations, newsstands, lottery shops, *padarias*, etc.

The main *rodoviária* for long-distance buses is **Tietê**, T2223 7152, which handles buses to the interior of São Paulo state, all state capitals (but see also under Barra Funda and Bresser below) and international buses. Taxi from Jardins US$13.75. The left luggage charges US$6 per day per item.

Buses from Tietê: To **Rio**, 6 hrs, every 30 mins, US$35-65, special section for this route in the *rodoviária*, ask how to take the coastal route via Santos ('via litoral') unless you wish to go the direct route. To **Florianópolis**, 11 hrs, US$48-61 (leito 90). **Porto Alegre**, 18 hrs, US$90. **Curitiba**, 6 hrs, US$35-65. **Salvador**, 30 hrs, US$150. **Recife**, 40 hrs, US$180. **Cuiabá**, 24 hrs, US$95. **Porto Velho**, 40 hrs, US$140. **Brasília**, 16 hrs, US$83. **Foz do Iguaçu**, 16 hrs, US$50-82 (leito 115). **São Sebastião**, 4 hrs US$25 (say 'via Bertioga' if you want to go by the coast road, beautiful journey but few buses take this route).

International buses from Tietê: to **Montevideo**, via Porto Alegre, with TTL, once a week, plenty of meal stops, bus stops for border formalities, passengers disembark only to collect passport and tourist card on the Uruguayan side. To **Buenos Aires**, **Pluma**, 36 hrs, US$165. To **Asunción** (1044 km), US$80, 18 hrs with **Pluma**, stopping at Ciudad del Este. **Cometa del Amambay**, T6221 1485, runs to **Pedro Juan Caballero** and **Concepción**.

There are 3 other bus stations: **Barra Funda**, T3666 4682, with Metrô station, for buses from cities in southern São Paulo state and many places in Paraná. **Bresser**, T6692 5191, on the Metrô, is for destinations in Minas Gerais, eg **Cometa** (T4004 9600, www.viacao cometa.com.br) or **Gontijo** (T3392 6890, www.gontijo.com.br) go to Minas Gerais: **Belo Horizonte**, 9 hrs, US$45. Buses from **Santos** and the southern coast of São Paulo state arrive at **Jabaquara**, T5012 2256, at the southern end of the Metrô. Buses leave here for Santos every 10-30 mins, taking about 70 mins, last bus at midnight, US$10.50.

Car The *rodízio*, restriction on car use by licence plate number, to curb traffic pollution, may be extended beyond the winter months. Check.

Metrô The best and cheapest way to get around São Paulo is on the excellent metrô system, daily 0500-2400, www.metro. sp.gov.br, with a clear journey planner and information in Portuguese and English. It is clean, safe, cheap and efficient and has 5 main lines. It is integrated with the overground CPTM (Companhia Paulista de Trens Metropolitanos), www.cptm.sp.gov.br, an urban light railway which extends the metrô along the margins of the Tietê and Pinheiros rivers and to the outer city suburbs. There are 6 lines, numbers 7 to 12, which are colour-coded like the Metrô. Information T0800-055 0121. Basic fare US$1.50 with the *bilhete único* (see above); backpacks are allowed.

Taxi Taxis display cards of actual tariffs in the window (starting price R$3.60). From 2000-0600 fares rise by 65 cents per km. There are ordinary taxis, which are hailed on the street, or at taxi stations such as Praça da República, radio taxis and deluxe taxis. For **Radio Taxis**, which are more expensive but involve fewer hassles, **Central Radio Táxi**, T3035 0404, www.centralradiotaxi.com; **São Paulo Rádio Táxi**, T5073 2814; **Vermelho e Branco**, T3146 4000, www.radiotaxivermelhoebranco. com.br; visit www.taxisp.com.br for a list, or look in the phone book; calls are not accepted from public phones.

Train São Paulo has 2 stations: 1) **Estação da Luz** the hub for three CPTM suburban lines which operate at Metrô frequencies and with free transfers to the Metrô; 2) **Júlio Prestes** station, for services to the west.

❶ Directory

São Paulo *p416, maps p418, p420 and p423*
Banks There are many national and international banks; most can be found either in the Triângulo, downtown, or on Av Paulista, or Av Brigadeiro Faria Lima. Hours 1000-1600; but some vary. All have different times for foreign exchange transactions (check at individual branches). Many **Banco 24 Horas** ATMs in the city. Money changers: there are many *câmbios* on or near Praça da República. At the Tietê *rodoviária* there's a *câmbio*, Mon-Fri 1000-1800, Sat 1000-1600, and ATMs. Most travel agents on Av São Luís change TCs and cash at good rates, but very few are open on Sat, let alone Sun. **Car hire** Interlocadora, several branches, São Luís, T255 5604, Guarulhos T6445 3838, Congonhas T240 9287. **Consulates** For foreign consulates in São Paulo, see http://embassy.goabroad. com. **Language courses** Universidade de São Paulo (USP) in the Cidade Universitária has courses available to foreigners, including a popular Portuguese course, registry is through the **Comissão de Cooperação Internacional**, R do Anfiteatro 181, Bloco das Colméias 05508, Cidade Universitária.
Medical services Hospital Samaritano, R Conselheiro Brotero 1486, Higienópolis, T824 0022. Recommended. **Emergency and ambulance** T192, no charge. **Fire**: T193.
Useful addresses Police: Deatur, special tourist police, R da Consolação 247, T3151 4167; Guarulhos airport T2611 2686; Congonhas airport T5090 9032 (they are on Facebook). Radio Patrol, T190. **Federal Police**, R Hugo d'Antola 95, Lapa de Baixo, T3538 5000, at Guarulhos airport T2445 2212, www.dpf. gov.br, 1000-1600 for visa extensions.

On the coast there are fine beaches, although pollution is sometimes a problem. The further you go from the port of Santos, the more unspoilt the beaches become, with some areas of special natural interest.

Santos → *Phone code: 013. Post code: 11000. Colour map 7, C4. Population: 417,983.*

Santos, on an island about 5 km from the open sea, is the most important Brazilian port. Over 40% by value of all Brazilian imports and about half the total exports pass through it. Santos is also a holiday resort with magnificent beaches and views. The scenery on the routes crossing the Serra do Mar is superb. The roadway includes many bridges and tunnels. From Rio the direct highway, the Linha Verde is also wonderful for scenery. The port is approached by the winding Santos Channel; at its mouth is an old fort (1709). The centre of the city is on the north side of the island. Due south, on the Baía de Santos, is **Gonzaga**, where hotels and bars line the beachfront. Between these two areas, the eastern end of the island curves round within the Santos Channel. **Tourist offices** ⓘ *at the* rodoviária; *Ilha de Conveniência, Av Bartolomeu de Gusmão (opposite Av Cons Nébias); Orquidário Municipal; and other points in the city (details on http://santosturismo.wordpress.com); information by phone T0800-173887. Head office: Estação do Valongo, Largo Marquês de Monte Alegre s/n, T3201 8000, www.santos.sp.gov.br.*

Places in Santos The best way get around the centre of Santos is by the newly restored Victorian trams which leave on guided tours from in front of the Prefeitura Municipal on Praça Visconde de Mauá. The tram passes in front of most of the interesting sights, including the *azulejo*-covered houses on Rua do Comércio. The streets around **Praça Mauá** are very busy in the daytime. **Museu do Café** ⓘ *R 15 de Novembro 95, T3213 1750, www.museudocafe.com.br, Tue-Sat 0900-1700, Sun 1000-1700, US$2.50.* The old Bolsa Oficial de Café was closed to all but rich men up until the mid-20th century, but is now a delightful museum, with large wall paintings by Benedito Calixto and a very impressive art deco stained-glass ceiling. Upstairs is a small but very well-presented collection of displays. The lobby café serves some of the best coffee in Brazil. The only colonial church regularly open to the public in the centre is **Santo Antônio do Valongo** (17th century, but restored) ⓘ *T3219 1481, www.portalvalongo.com, Tue-Sun 0800-1700*, which is by the railway station on Largo Marquês de Monte Alegre. **Fundação Pinacoteca** ⓘ *Av Bartolomeu de Gusmão 15, T3288 2260, www.pinacotecadesantos.org.br, Tue-Sun 0900-1800, free*, features a large collection of ecclesiastical paintings and landscapes by one of Brazil's most distinguished early 19th-century artists.

At **Santos Football Stadium and Museum** ⓘ *Princesa Isabel 77, Vila Belmiro, T3257 4000, www.santosfc.com.br, tour US$3*, the ground floor houses a collection of trophies and photographs chronicling the history of Pele's club, including several cabinets devoted to him and containing his shirts, boots and other memorabilia. **Monte Serrat**, just south of the city centre, has at its summit a semaphore station and look-out post which reports the arrival of all ships in Santos harbour. There is also a church, dedicated to Nossa Senhora da Monte Serrat. The top can be reached on foot or by **funicular** (every 30 minutes, US$12 return). In the western district of José Menino is the **Orquidário Municipal** ⓘ *daily 0800-1700, bird enclosure 0800-1800, US$1.50*, the municipal orchid gardens, in the **Praça Washington**. The flowers bloom October to February; the orchid show is in November.

The **Ilha Porchat**, a small island reached by a bridge at the far end of Santos/São Vicente bay, has beautiful views of the high seas on one side and of the city and bay on the other. The lookout was designed by Oscar Niemeyer and, in summer, there is lively nightlife here.

São Sebastião → *Phone code: 012. Post code: 11600. Colour map 7, B4. Population: 58,038.*

East of Santos, a vehicle ferry (free for pedestrians) crosses from Ponta da Praia to **Guarujá**, from where a road (SP-061) runs to **Bertioga**. The coastal road beyond Bertioga is paved, and the Rio-Santos highway, 1-2 km inland, provides a good link to São Sebastião. Beyond Praia Boracéia are a number of beaches, including **Camburi**, surrounded by the Mata Atlântica, into which you can walk on the Estrada do Piavu (bathing in the streams is permitted, but use of shampoo is forbidden). There are several good hotels and restaurants in Camburi and at Praia de Boracéia. The road carries on from Camburi, past clean beach **Maresias**, a fashionable place for surfers.

From Maresias it is 21 km to São Sebastião. There are 21 good beaches and an adequate, but not overdeveloped, tourist infrastructure. The natural attractions of the area include many small islands offshore and a large portion of the **Parque Estadual da Serra do Mar** on the mainland, with other areas protected for their ecosystems (www.oescafandro. com.br/natureza/parque-estadual-da-serra-do-mar/). There are forest trails and old sugar plantations. In the colonial centre is **Museu de Arte Sacra** ⓘ *R Sebastião Neves 90*, in the 17th-century chapel of São Gonçalo. The town's parish church on Praça Major João Fernandes dates from the early 17th century and rebuilt in 1819. The **tourist office** ⓘ *Av Dr Altino Arantes 174, T3892 2620*, is in the historic **Casa Esperança**.

The beaches within 2-3 km of São Sebastião harbour are polluted; others to the south and north are clean. Ilhabela is expensive in season, when it is cheaper to stay in São Sebastião.

Ilhabela → *Phone code: 012. Population: 21,000; rising to 100,000 in high season.*

The island of São Sebastião, known popularly as Ilhabela, is of volcanic origin, roughly 390 sq km in area. The four highest peaks are Morro de São Sebastião, 1379 m, Morro do Papagaio, 1309 m, Ramalho, 1205 m, and Pico Baepi, 1025 m. All are often obscured by mist. Rainfall on the island is heavy, about 3000 mm a year. The slopes are densely wooded and 80% of the forest is protected by the Parque Estadual de Ilhabela. The only settled district lies on the coastal strip facing the mainland, the Atlantic side being practically uninhabited except by a few fisherfolk. The island abounds with tropical plants, flowers, and wild fruits, whose juice mixed with *cachaça* and sugar makes a delicious cocktail. The terraced **Cachoeira da Toca** ⓘ *US$4, includes insect repellent*, waterfalls amid dense jungle close to the foot of the Baepi peak give cool freshwater bathing; lots of butterflies. You can walk on a signed path, or go by car; it's a few kilometres from the ferry dock. The locals claim there are over 300 waterfalls on the island, but only a few can be reached on foot. In all shady places, especially away from the sea, there thrives a species of midge known locally as *borrachudo*. Those allergic to insect bites should remain on the inhabited coastal strip. There is a small hospital (helpful) by the church in town. **Secretaria Municipal de Turismo** ⓘ *Praça José Leite dos Passos 14, Barra Velha, T3895 7220, www.ilhabela.sp.gov.br. Also www.ilhabela.com.br.*

No alterations are allowed to the frontage of the main township, **Ilhabela**. It is very popular during summer weekends, when it is difficult to find space for a car on the ferry. It is, however, a nice place to relax on the beach, with good food and some good value accommodation.

Visit the old **Feiticeira** plantation, with underground dungeons. The road is along the coast, sometimes high above the sea, towards the south of the island (11 km from the town). You can go by bus, taxi, or horse and buggy. A trail leads down from the fazenda to the beautiful beach of the same name. Another old fazenda is **Engenho d'Água**, which is nearer to the town, which gives its name to one of the busiest beaches (the fazenda is not open to the public).

Beaches and watersports On the mainland side the beaches 3-4 km either side of the town are polluted: look out for oil, sandflies and jellyfish on the sand and in the water. There are some three dozen beaches around Ilhabela, only about 12 of them away from the coast facing the mainland. **Praia dos Castelhanos**, reached by the rough road over the island to the Atlantic side (no buses), is recommended. Several of the ocean beaches can only be reached by boat. The island is considered the **Capital da Vela** (of sailing) because its 150 km of coastline offers all types of conditions. There is also plenty of adventure for divers.

Ubatuba → *Phone code: 012. Post code: 11680. Colour map 7, B4. Population: 66,861.*

This is one of the most beautiful stretches of the São Paulo coast with a whole range of watersports on offer. In all, there are 72 beaches, some large, some small, some in coves, some on islands. They are spread out over a wide area, so if you are staying in Ubatuba town, you need to use the buses which go to most of them. The commercial centre of Ubatuba is at the northern end of the bay. Here are shops, banks, services, lots of restaurants (most serving pizza and fish), but few hotels. These are on the beaches north and south and can be reached from the Costamar bus terminal. The **tourist office** ① *Av Iperoig 214, T3833 9123, www.ubatuba. sp.gov.br; also www.ubatuba.com.br*, is very helpful.

Saco da Ribeira, 13 km south, is a natural harbour which has been made into a yacht marina. Schooners leave from here for excursions to **Ilha Anchieta** (or dos Porcos), a popular four-hour trip. On the island are beaches, trails and a prison, which was in commission from 1908-1952. Agencies run schooner trips to Ilha Anchieta and elsewhere. Trips leave Saco da Ribeira at 1000, returning 1500, four-hour journey, US$26 per person. A six-hour trip can be made from Praia Itaguá, but in winter there is a cold wind off the sea in the afternoon, same price. The Costamar bus from Ubatuba to Saco da Ribeira (every 20 minutes, 30 minutes, US$1.50) drops you at the turn off by the Restaurante Pizzaria Malibu.

Straddling the border of São Paulo and Rio de Janeiro states is the **Parque Nacional Serra da Bocaina** ① *visit in advance ICMBio, T012-3117 2143, in São José do Barreiro, the nearest town, www4.icmbio.gov.br/parna_bocaina*. It rises from the coast to its highest point at Pico do Tira (or Chapéu) at 2200 m, encompassing three strata of vegetation.

Southwest from Santos → *Phone code: 013.*

Itanhaém, 61 km from Santos, has a pretty colonial church of Sant'Ana (1761), Praça Narciso de Andrade, and the Convento da Nossa Senhora da Conceição (1699-1713, originally founded 1554), on a small hill. There are several good seafood restaurants along the beach, hotels and camping. There are more beaches 31 km south of Itanhaém at **Peruíbe**, where the climate is said to be unusually healthy owing to a high concentration of ozone in the air. Local rivers have water and black mud which has been proven to contain medicinal properties. There are plenty of places to stay and to eat in Peruíbe (none close to the bus station, some close out-of-season). Peruíbe marks the northernmost point of the **Estação Ecológico Juréia-Itatins** ① *contact the Instituto Florestal, Estrada do Guaraú 4164, CEP 11750-000, Peruíbe, T013-3457 9243, for permission to visit the ecological station, www.jureia.com.br*. The station was founded in 1986 and protects 820 sq km of Mata Atlântica, "as it was when the Portuguese arrived in Brazil". The four main ecosystems are restinga, mangrove, Mata Atlântica and the vegetation at 900 m on the Juréia mountain range.

Iguape → *Phone code: 013. Colour map 7, C3. Population: 27,427.*

At the southern end of Juréia-Itatins is the town of Iguape founded in 1538. Typical of Portuguese architecture, the small **Museu Histórico e Arqueológico** ① *R das Neves 45, Tue-Sun 0900-1730*, is housed in the 17th-century Casa da Oficina Real de Fundição. There is also a **Museu de Arte Sacra** ① *Sat-Sun 0900-1200, 1330-1700*, in the former Igreja do Rosário, Praça Rotary. **Tourist office** ① *9 de Julho 63, T3841 3358, www.iguape.sp.gov.br*.

Rodeo Romeos

Some 422 km northwest of São Paulo and 115 km northwest of the city of Ribeirão Preto, is **Barretos**, where, in the third week in August, the **Festa do Peão Boiadeiro** is held. This is the biggest annual rodeo in the world. The town is taken over as 600,000 fans come to watch the horsemanship, enjoy the concerts, eat, drink and shop in what has become the epitome of Brazilian cowboy culture. See www.osindependentes.com.br/festadopeao/.

Opposite Iguape is the northern end of the **Ilha Comprida** with 86 km of beaches (some dirty and disappointing). This **Área de Proteção Ambiental** ① *the ICMBio office of the Area de Proteção Ambiental Cananéia-Iguape-Peruíbe is at R da Saúde s/n, Canto do Morro, Iguape, T3841 2388, www.icmbio.gov.br/apacip*, is not much higher than sea level and is divided from the mainland by the Canal do Mar Pequeno. The northern end is the busiest and on the island there are good restaurants, hotels, supermarkets – fresh fish is excellent. There is also accommodation.

Cananéia and Ilha do Cardoso → *Colour map 7, C3. Population: 12,298.*
At the southern end of Ilha Comprida, across the channel, is Cananéia, 270 km from São Paulo. The colonial centre, around Praça Martim Afonso de Souza and neighbouring streets, contains the 17th-century church of **São João Batista** and the **Museu Municipal**. To the south are good beaches. For guides, contact Manoel Barroso, Avenida Independencia 65, T013-3851 1273, Portuguese only. Recommended. Cananéia has several hotels, starting in price range **$$**.

For the densely wooded Ilha do Cardoso, a protected area, take a ferry from the dock at Cananéia, four hours, three daily (T3851 1268/3841 1122, see www.cananeiatur.com/barcos.htm). Or drive 70 km along an unpaved road, impassable when wet, to **Ariri**, 10 minutes by boat to the island. The tiny village of Marujá, no electricity, has rustic *pousadas* and restaurants. There is camping and idyllic beaches; best for surfing is Moretinho.

⊚ São Paulo coast listings

For hotel and restaurant price codes, and other relevant information, see Essentials.

⊟ Where to stay

Santos *p433*
Many beachfront hotels on Av Pres Wilson, cheap hotels are near the Orquidário Municipal (Praça Washington), 1-2 blocks from the beach.
$$$$ Ville Atlântico, No 1, T3289 4500, www.atlantico-hotel.com.br. Good, on the seafront, sauna, restaurant, bar.
$$$ Hotel Natal, Av Marechal Floriano Peixoto 104, T3284 2732, www.hotelnatalsantos.com.br. Safe, comfortable, cheaper with shared bath, fridge, full breakfast.

Ilhabela *p434*
Several in the **$$$$-$$$** range and some in the **$$$-$$** range, mostly on the road to the left of the ferry.
$$$ Ilhabela, Av Pedro Paulo de Morais 151, T3896 1083, www.hotelilhabela.com.br. Family-oriented, gym, pool, good breakfast. Recommended.
$$$ Pousada dos Hibiscos, Av Pedro Paulo de Morais 714, T3896 1375, www.pousadados hibiscos.com.br. Good atmosphere, swimming pool. Recommended.
$$$ Vila das Pedras, R Antenor Custódio da Silva 46, Cocaia, T3896 2433, www.viladas pedras.com.br. 11 chalets in a forest garden, tastefully decorated, nice pool.

$$$-$ **Bonns Ventos Hostel**, R Benedito Serafim Sampaio 371, Perequê, T3896 2725, www.bonnventoshostel.com.br. Well-kept and well-run hostel with basic dorms and spacious doubles with and without bath, prices rise at weekends and high season, garden, pool, HI affiliated.

Camping Pedras do Sino, at Perequê, near ferry dock, www.campingpedradosino. com.br, and at Praia Grande, 11 km south, www.cantogrande.com.br.

Ubatuba p435

At all holiday times it is expensive, with no hotel less than US$40. On many of the beaches there are hotels and *pousadas*, ranging from luxury resorts to more humble establishments.

$$$$-$$$ **Saveiros**, R Lucian Strass 65, Praia do Lázaro, 14 km from town, T3842 0172, www.hotelsaveiros.com.br. Pretty *pousada* with pool, restaurant, English spoken.

$$$ **Coquille**, R Praia Grande 405, T3835 1611, www.hotelcoquille.com. On the edge of the forest and 250 m on the beach, pool, bike rental and surfing lessons.

$$$ **São Charbel**, Praça Nóbrega 280, T3832 1090, www.saocharbel.com.br. Helpful, comfortable, restaurant, bar, swimming pool, etc.

$$$ **São Nicolau**, R Conceição 213, T3832 5007, www.hotelsaonicolau.com.br. Good, fridge, good breakfast.

$$$ **Xaréu**, R Jordão Homem da Costa 413, T3832 1525, www.hotelxareubatuba.com.br. Pleasant, quiet. Recommended.

$$$-$ **Tribo Hostel**, R Amoreira 71, Praia do Lázaro, 14 km from Ubatuba, T3842 0585, www.ubatubahostel.com. On a very pretty beach, great value, dorms (price depends on season) with fan and shared bath, also suites, pool, restaurant, party atmosphere at weekends, quiet in the week.

Camping There are about 10 sites in the vicinity, including 2 Camping Clube do Brasil sites at Lagoinha (25 km from town) and Praia Perequê-Açu, 2 km north. Robbery at campsites occurs at weekends.

Southwest from Santos p435
Peruíbe

$$$-$$ **Waldhaus Ecopousada**, R Gaivota 1201, Praia do Guaraú, T3457 9170, www. jureiaecoadventure.com.br. In lovely gardens with views acorss the beach to Juréia, comfortable, plain rooms, with breakfast (other meal available in Guaraú), offers trips on foot, by jeep or canoe.

Iguape p435

$$ **Solar Colonial Pousada**, Praça da Basílica 30, T3841 1591. A range of rooms in a converted 19th-century house.

Camping At Praia da Barra da Ribeira, 20 km north. Wild camping is possible at Praia de Juréia, the gateway to the ecological station.

⊖ Transport

Santos p433

Bus In Santos US$1; to **São Vicente**, US$2. To **São Paulo** (50 mins, US$10) every 15 mins, from the *rodoviária* near the city centre, José Menino or Ponta da Praia (opposite the ferry to Guarujá). (The 2 highways between São Paulo and Santos can get very crowded, especially at rush hours and weekends.) To **Guarulhos/ Cumbica airport**, 11 daily, US$10, allow plenty of time as the bus goes through Guarulhos, 2-3 hrs. To **Rio**, many daily, 8 hrs, US$58; to São Sebastião, US$22, 6 daily, to Caraguatatuba, US$25, change here for Ubatuba and Paraty.

Taxi All taxis have meters. The fare from Gonzaga to the bus station is about US$15.

São Sebastião p434

Bus 2 buses a day from **Rio** (more on Fri and Sun), heavily booked in advance, US$30 (US$12 from Paraty); from **Santos**, see above; 11 buses a day also from **São Paulo**, US$26, which run inland via São José dos Campos, unless you ask for the service via Bertioga, only 2 a day.

Ilhabela p434

Bus A bus runs along the coast. **Litorânea** from **São Paulo** connects with a service right through to Ilhabela; office in Ilhabela at R Dr Carvalho 136.

Ferry At weekends and holidays the 15-20 min ferry between São Sebastião and Perequê runs non-stop day and night. During the week it does not sail 0130-0430. Free for foot passengers; cars US$15 weekdays, US$23 at weekends.

Ubatuba *p435*

Bus There are 3 bus terminals: 1) Rodoviária Costamar, R Hans Staden e R Conceição, serves all local destinations; 2) Rodoviária at R Profesor Thomaz Galhardo 513 for buses to **Paraty**, US$7.50; services to **Rio**, US$35, and **São Paulo**, 17 daily, US$28; 3) Rodoviária Litorânea, the main bus station: go up **Conceição** for 8 blocks

from Praça 13 de Maio, turn right on R Rio Grande do Sul, then left into R Dra Maria V Jean.
Taxi In town are very expensive.

Iguape *p435*

Bus To Iguape: from **São Paulo, Santos,** or **Curitiba,** changing at Registro.

Ferry A continuous ferry service runs from Iguape to **Ilha Comprida** (free but small charge for cars); buses run until 1900 from the ferry stop to the beaches. From Iguape it is possible to take a boat trip down the coast to **Cananéia** and **Ariri.** Tickets and information from Dpto Hidroviário do Estado, R Major Moutinho 198, Iguape. It is a beautiful trip, passing between the island and the mainland.

Minas Gerais and Espírito Santo

Minas Gerais was once described as having a heart of gold and a breast of iron. Half the mineral production of Brazil comes from the state, including most of the iron ore. Minas Gerais also produces 95% of all Brazil's gemstones. All this mineral wealth has left the state a legacy of sumptuous colonial cities built on gold and diamond mining. Streets of whitewashed 18th-century houses with deep blue or yellow window frames line steep and winding streets leading to lavishly decorated churches with rich gilt interiors. The colonial gold mining towns of Minas Gerais are the highlights of any visit. There are also other attractions: rugged national parks, which are great for trekking, lots of festivals and a famous cuisine, the comida mineira. The state of Minas Gerais, larger than France, is mountainous in the south, rising to the 2787 m peak of Agulhas Negras in the Mantiqueira range, and in the east, where there is the Parque Nacional Caparaó containing the Pico da Bandeira (2890 m). The capital, Belo Horizonte is culturally very active. From Belo Horizonte north are undulating grazing lands, the richest of which are in the extreme west: a broad wedge of country between Goiás in the north and São Paulo in the south, known as the Triângulo Mineiro. The coastal state of Espírito Santo is where mineiros head to for their seaside holidays. The most popular beaches are south of Vitória, the state capital, while north of the city are several turtle-nesting beaches. Inland are immigrant towns.

Belo Horizonte → *Phone code: 031. Post code: 30000. Colour map 7, B5.*

Belo Horizonte (*Population: 4.8 million; Altitude: 800 m*) is surrounded by mountains and enjoys an excellent climate (16°-30°C) except for the rainy season (December-March). It was founded on 12 December 1897 and is one of Brazil's fastest growing cities, now suffering from atmospheric pollution. The third largest city in Brazil is hilly, with streets that rise and fall and trees lining many of the central avenues. The large **Parque Municipal** is an oasis of green in the heart of downtown; closed at night and on Monday, except for a small section in the southwest corner (the Parque Municipal is not too safe, so it's best not to go alone). The main commercial district is around Avenida Afonso Pena; at night the movimento shifts to Savassi, southwest of the centre, where all the good eating places are.

Arriving in Belo Horizonte

Tourist offices The municipal information is **Belotur** ①*R Pernambuco 284, Funciários, T3277 9797, www.belohorizonte.mg.gov.br*. Very helpful, with lots of useful information and maps. The monthly *Guia Turístico* for events, opening times, etc, is freely available. Belotur has offices also at Tancredo Neves/Confins and Pampulha airports, at the *rodoviária* (particularly polyglot), at the Mercado Central and the Mercado das Flores (Av Afonso Pena 1055). See also www.guiabh. com.br. **Setur** ① *Rodovia Prefeito Américo Gianetti s/n, Prédio Gerais, 11th floor, Bairro Serra Verde, T3915 9454, www.turismo.mg.gov.br or www.minasgerais.com.br*, the tourism authority for the state of Minas Gerais, is helpful.

① Belo Horizonte & Pampulha

➡ **Belo Horizonte maps**
1 Belo Horizonte & Pampulha, page 439
2 Belo Horizonte centre, page 440

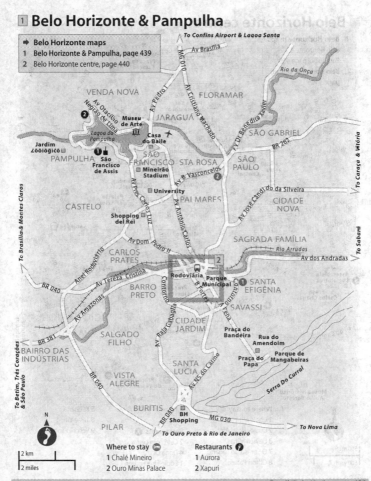

Where to stay
1 Chalé Mineiro
2 Ouro Minas Palace

Restaurants
1 Aurora
2 Xapuri

Places in Belo Horizonte

The principal building in the Parque Municipal is the **Palácio das Artes** ① *Afonso Pena 1537, T3237 7234, 1000-2200, Sun 1400-2200*, which contains the **Centro de Artesanato Mineiro** (with craft shop), exhibitions, cinema and theatres. On the stretch of Avenida Afonso Pena outside the Parque Municipal an open-air market operates each Sunday (0800-1430). The avenue is transformed by thousands of coloured awnings covering stalls selling every conceivable type of local handicraft. Six blocks up Avenida João Pinheiro from Avenida Afonso Pena is the **Praça da Liberdade**, which is very attractive, with trees, flowers and fountains which are lit at night. It is surrounded by fine public buildings, some in eclectic, fin-de-siècle-style, others more recent. Some house museums, others cultural centres and they form part of the **Circuito Cultural Praça da Liberdade** (see www.memorialvale.com.br/site/circuito-

② Belo Horizonte centre

➡ Belo Horizonte maps
1 Belo Horizonte & Pampulha, page 439
2 Belo Horizonte centre, page 440

Where to stay 🛌
1 Chalé Mineiro
2 Quality Hotel Afonso Pena
3 Dayrell Minas
7 O Sorriso do Lagarto
8 Othon Palace
9 Pousadinha Mineira

Restaurants 🍴
2 Café com Letras
4 Dona Derna
1 Eddie Fine Burger
5 Kauhana
8 Taste Vin
9 Vecchio Sogno

cultural). The new **Museu Clube da Esquina** ① *Av Cristóvão Colombo at Praça da Liberdade, www.museuclubedaesquina.org.br,* devoted to a group of artists and musicians (including Milton Nascimento, Lo Borges and Beto Guedes) is due to open in 2014.

The Praça itself The **railway station** is part of a complex that includes buildings dating from the 1920s around the **Praça da Estação** (also called Praça Rui Barbosa). Here is the **Museu de Artes e Ofícios** ① *Praça Rui Barbosa s/n, T3248 8600, open 1200, at 1100 Sat, Sun, closed Mon,* telling the story of various public and private professions in Minas.

Museu Mineiro ① *Av João Pinheiro 342, T3269 1168, www.cultura.mg.gov.br, Tue-Fri 1000-1700, Sat-Sun 1000-1600,* houses religious and other art. **Museu Histórico Abílio Barreto** ① *Av Prudente de Morais 202, Cidade Jardim, T3277 8573, www.amigosdomhab.com.br, bus 2902 from Av Afonso Pena,* in an old fazenda, is the last reminder of Belo Horizonte's predecessor, the village of **Arraial do Curral d'el Rey.** It has historical exhibits.

About 8 km northwest from the centre is the picturesque suburb of **Pampulha,** famous for its modern buildings and the artificial lake, created in the 1930s by Brasília architect Oscar Niemeyer and landscaped by Roberto Burle Marx. The **Igreja São Francisco de Assis** ① *Av Otacílio Negrão de Lima Km 12, T3427 1644, Tue-Sat 0900-1700, Sun 1200-1700, US$1.50,* was inaugurated in 1943. The painter Cândido Portinari installed beautiful blue and white tiles depicting Saint Francis' life on the exterior. On the wall behind the altar is a powerful composition also by Portinari. On the opposite shore is the glass and marble **Museu de Arte de Pampulha (MAP)** ① *Av Octacílio Negrão de Lima 16585, T3443 4533, Tue-Sun 0900-1900, free.* It has a fine collection of modern art from Minas Gerais. The **Casa do Baile** ① *Av Octacílio Negrão de Lima 751, T3277 7433, Tue-Sun 0900-1900, free,* is a perfect example of Niemeyer's fascination with the curved line. Just south of the lake is the **Mineirão** football stadium, about 750 m away. This is the second largest stadium in Brazil after the Maracanã stadium in Rio.

Inhotim ① *Rua B, 20, Inhotim, Brumadinho, T3571 9700, www.inhotim.org.br, Tue-Fri 0930-1630, Sat-Sun 0930-1730, US$10, US$14 weekends, free Tue, take your own food, restaurants are expensive,* is a captivating contemporary art complex set in 1255 hectares of beautiful tropical gardens. It contains dozens of purpose-built galleries showing the work of Brazilian and international artists. Allow a day for a full, leisurely visit, which can be organized through a tour operator, or hire a car as there is only one coletivo a day, 1½ hours, US$12.50.

⑦ Belo Horizonte listings

For hotel and restaurant price codes, and other relevant information, see Essentials.

⑧ Where to stay

Belo Horizonte *p438, maps p439 and p440*
$$$$ Dayrell Minas, R Espírito Santo 901, T3248 1000, www.dayrell.com.br. One of the best business hotels in the centre, full business facilities, rooftop pool.
$$$$ Ouro Minas Palace, Av Cristiano Machado 4001, T3429 4001 (toll free T0800-314000), www.ourominas.com.br. The most luxurious hotel in the city with palatial suites, including several for women-only on the top

floors, excellent service, pool, sauna, gym, excellent business facilities, not central but within easy reach of the centre and airports.
$$$$ Quality Hotel Afonso Pena, Av Afonso Pena 3761, T2111 8900, www.atlanticahotels. com.br. Good business hotel with spacious, practical modern rooms and, on the upper floor, city views, decent business facilities, helpful staff, generous breakfast, a pool and a pocket-sized gym.
$$$$-$$$ Othon Palace, Av Afonso Pena 1050, T2126 0000, www.hoteis-othon.com. br. 1980s hotel, glass-fronted, excellent, safe, good restaurant, pool, helpful staff, lower floors can be noisy.

$ pp **Chalé Mineiro**, R Santa Luzia 288, Santa Efigênia, T3467 1576, www.chalemineiro hostel.com.br. Attractive, HI affiliated, with a small pool, dorms and private rooms (**$$**), a shared kitchen, TV lounge and telephones. Towels, breakfast and use of internet are extra.

$ pp **O Sorriso do Lagarto**, R Cristina 791, São Pedro, T3283 9325, www.osorrisodolagarto. com.br. Simple, small hostel in a converted town house with kitchen, breakfast, lockers, washing machines and a living area with DVD player. Has other branchces in Ouro Preto and Salvador da Bahia.

$ pp **Pousadinha Mineira**, R Espírito Santo 604, Centro, T3273 8156, www.pousadinhamineira. com.br. Large central hostel with separate men's and women's wings, shared bath, breakfast extra, take your own bed linen or hire it.

❼ Restaurants

Belo Horizonte *p438, maps p439 and p440*
Mineiros love their food and drink and Belo Horizonte has a lively café dining and bar scene. Savassi and Lourdes districts overflow with street cafés, bars and restaurants. There is a lively, cheap food market on R Tomé de Souza, between Pernambuco and Alagoas, in Savassi every Thu night between 1900 and 2300. Pampulha has the best of the fine dining restaurants; which are well worth the taxi ride. There are plenty of cheap per kilo restaurants and *padarias* near the budget hotels in the city centre and the Mercado Central is a good place for lunch or a snack.

$$$ Aurora, R Expedicionário Mário Alves de Oliveira 421, São Luís, T3498 7567. Closed Mon-Tue. One of the best restaurants in town, garden setting next to Lago da Pampulha. Imaginative menu fusing Mineira and Italian techniques and making use of unusual Brazilian fruits.

$$$ Taste Vin, R Curitiba 2105, Lourdes, T3292 5423. Excellent French, soufflés and provençale seafood. The wine list includes decent Brazilian options. Recommended.

$$$ Vecchio Sogno, R Martim de Carvalho 75 and R Dias Adorno, Santo Agostinho, under the Assembléia Legislativo, T3292 5251. Lunch only on Sun. The best Italian in the city with an inventive menu fusing Italian and French cuisine with Brazilian ingredients, excellent fish.

$$$ Xapuri, R Mandacaru 260, Pampulha, T3496 6198. Closed Mon. Great atmosphere, live music, very good food, a bit out of the way but recommended.

$$ Dona Derna, R Tomé de Souza 1380, Savassi, T3223 6954. A range of restaurants in one. Upstairs is Italian fine dining with excellent dishes and a respectable wine list. Downstairs on weekdays is traditional Italian home cooking and by night a chic pizzeria called Memmo.

$$-$ Café com Letras, R Antônio de Albuquerque 781, Savassi, T2555 1610, www. cafecomletras.com.br. Arty little a/c café bar and bookshop with live music on Mon and Sun; varied menu of healthy, well-prepared petiscos, sandwiches, salads and light lunches.

$$-$ Eddie Fine Burger, 4 branches including R da Bahia 2652, Lourdes, Pátio Savassi, BH Shopping, www.eddieburger.com.br. US-style diner serving North American and Brazilian burgers, all made with prime Brazilian beef.

$$-$ Kauhana, R Tomé de Souza, Savassi, T3284 8714. Tasty wood-fire cooked pizzas both savoury and sweet, pleasant open-air dining area.

$ Mala e Cuia, a chain of restaurants serving good *comida mineira* at R Gonçalves Dias 874, Savassi, T3261 3059, Av Antônio Carlos 8305, Pampulha, T3441 2993, Av Raja Gabaglia 1617, São Bento.

❼ Bars and clubs

Belo Horizonte *p438, maps p439 and p440*
Rua Tomé de Souza in Savassi has umpteen lively bars, particularly between Paraíba and Sergipe. The beer and caipirinhas are cheap and plentiful. Also try Santa Teresa neighbourhood for lively nightlife. A useful blog for finding out the latest and best openings is www.baresbh.com.

Marilton's Bar, R Quimberlita 205, Santa Teresa, T3467 7824. Popular for live music, attracts a good crowd. Serves hearty steaks, pastas and petiscos.

A Obra, R Rio Grande do Norte 1168, Savassi, T3215 8077, www.aobra.com.br. The leading alternative music venue in the city. Great for DJs and new Minas acts.
Vinnil, R dos Incofidentes 1068, Savassi, T3261 7057, www.vinnil.com.br. Funky retro club bar in a 1940s building decorated with art and hosting great live acts at weekends.

⊛ Festivals

Belo Horizonte *p438, maps p439 and p440*
The city celebrates **Maundy Thursday**; Corpus Christi; **15 Aug**, Assunção (Assumption); **8 Dec**, Conceição (Immaculate Conception).

○ Shopping

Belo Horizonte *p438, maps p439 and p440*
Markets See above for the Sun handicraft fair on Av Afonso Pena. **Mercado Central**, Av Augusto de Lima 744. "A temple to Minas produce", open every day.

⊙ What to do

Belo Horizonte *p438, maps p439 and p440*
Minas Golden Tours, R da Bahia 1345, T3023 1451, www.minasgoldentours.com.br. Offers a broad range of tours throughout the state (and connections with Rio, São Paulo, Brasília and Bahia) and around Belo Horizonte, including to Inhotim, Caraça and the colonial towns. Recommended.

⊖ Transport

Belo Horizonte *p438, maps p439 and p440*
Air The international airport, Tancredo Neves, is near Lagoa Santa, at Confins, 39 km from Belo Horizonte, T3689 2700, www.aeroportoconfins. net. Taxi to centre, US$60, cooperative taxis have fixed rates to different parts of the city. Airport bus, **Unir** (www.conexaoaeroporto.com. br), *executivo* US$11, or *normal* Nos 5250 or 5270, US$4.65, both go to/from the *rodoviária*.

Closer to the city is the national airport, **Carlos Drummond de Andrade**, at Pampulha,

which has shuttle services from Rio, São Paulo and Salvador, T3490 2001. Urban transportation to/from this airport is cheaper than from Confins. From Pampulha airport to town, take blue bus 1202, 25 mins, US$1.50, passing the *rodoviária* and the cheaper hotel district.
Bus The city has a good public transport system (www.bhtrans.pbh.gov.br): red buses run on express routes; yellow buses have circular routes around the Contorno; blue buses run on diagonal routes. All charge US$1.50. There are also buses which integrate with the regional, overground Metrô. A new BRT rapid transit bus system is expected to open for the World Cup in 2014, linking the centre to the Mineirão stadium. It will be further extended by 2016, but not to the airport.

The *rodoviária* is by Praça Rio Branco at the northwest end of Av Afonso Pena, T3271 3000/8933. The bus station has toilets, post office, phones, left-luggage lockers (US$2.50, open 0700-2200), shops and is clean and efficient. Buses leave from the rather gloomy platforms beneath the ticket hall. Taxi to centre US$8.50.

To **Rio** at least 6 a day, 6-7 hrs, US$33. To **Vitória** many daily, 8½ hrs, US$43. To **Brasília**, 3 every night, 12 hrs, US$63. To **São Paulo** at least once an, 9-10 hrs, US$45. To **Salvador**, US$108, 24 hrs, once a night. To **Porto Seguro**, 17 hrs, direct, via Nanuque and Eunápolis, US$80, twice nightly. All major destinations served. For buses in Minas Gerais, see under destination.
Train To **Vitória**, see page 458. Ticket office, R Aarão Reis 423, Praça da Estação, is open daily 0600-1730; closes 1530 Sat and 1200 Sun.

ⓘ Directory

Belo Horizonte *p438, maps p439 and p440*
Banks ATMs at central banks. **Medical services** Mater Dei, R Gonçalves Dias 2700, T3339 9000. Recommended. **Post offices** Av Afonso Pena 1270, with fax, philatelic depart ment and small museum, closes 1800; poste restante is behind the main office at R de Goiás 77. The branch office on R da Bahia is less busy.

East and south of Belo Horizonte

Most of the colonial cities lie southeast and south of Belo Horizonte and many people choose to visit them on the way to or from Rio as they make for the most charming and restful of stopping places. Ouro Preto is the most famous and a much more pleasant place to stay than the state capital. Mariana is a good day trip from Ouro Preto. Further south are Congonhas, with its remarkable statuary, São João del Rei, with some beautiful colonial architecture, and Tiradentes, the most heavily visited of the Minas colonial towns after Ouro Preto. In the far south of the state, closer to the road to São Paulo, is one of Brazil's main New Age sites, São Tomé das Letras.

Sabará → *Colour map 7, B5. Population: 115,352.*

East of the state capital by 23 km is the colonial gold-mining (and steel-making) town of Sabará, strung along the narrow steep valleys of the Rio das Velhas and Rio Sabará. **Secretaria de Turismo** ① *R Pedro II 200, T3672 7690, www.sabara.org.br.*

Rua Dom Pedro II is lined with beautiful 18th-century buildings. Among them is the **Solar do Padre Correa** (1773) at No 200, now the **Prefeitura**; the **Casa Azul** (also 1773), No 215; and the **Teatro Municipal**, former Opera House (1770 – the second oldest in Brazil). At the top of Rua Dom Pedro II is the Praça Melo Viana, in the middle of which is **Nossa Senhora do Rosário dos Pretos** ① *church and museum Tue-Sun 0800-1100, 1300-1700.* The church was left unfinished at the time of the slaves' emancipation. There is a museum of religious art in the church. To the right of the church as you face it is the **Chafariz do Rosário** (the Rosário fountain). In Rua da Intendência is the museum of 18th-century gold mining in the **Museu do Ouro** ① *Tue-Sun 1200-1730, US$1.30.* It contains exhibits on gold extraction, plus religious items and colonial furniture. Another fine example is the **Casa Borba Gato** ① *R Borba Gato 71;* the building currently belongs to the Museu do Ouro.

The church of **Nossa Senhora do Carmo** (1763-1774) ① *US$1.30 (includes a leaflet about the town)*, with doorway, pulpits and choirloft by Aleijadinho (see box, page 445) and paintings by Athayde, is on Rua do Carmo. **Nossa Senhora da Conceição** ① *Praça Getúlio Vargas, free,* built 1701-1720, has much visible woodwork and a beautiful floor. The carvings have much gilding, there are painted panels and paintings by 23 Chinese artists brought from Macau. The clearest Chinese work is on the two red doors to the right and left of the chancel. **Nossa Senhora do Ó**, built in 1717 and showing Chinese influence, is 2 km from the centre of the town at the Largo Nossa Senhora do Ó (take local bus marked 'Esplanada' or 'Boca Grande').

If you walk up the Morra da Cruz hill from the Hotel do Ouro to a small chapel, the Capela da Cruz or Senhor Bom Jesus, you can get a wonderful view of the whole area.

Caeté → *Colour map 7, B5. Population: 36,299.*

A further 25 km is Caeté, which has several historical buildings and churches. On the Praça João Pinheiro are the **Prefeitura** and **Pelourinho** (both 1722), the **Igreja Matriz Nossa Senhora do Bom Sucesso** (1756 rebuilt 1790) ① *daily 1300-1800,* and the **Chafariz da Matriz**. Also on the Praça is the tourist information office in the Casa da Cultura (T6511855). Other churches are **Nossa Senhora do Rosário** (1750-1768), with a ceiling attributed to Mestre Athayde, and **São Francisco de Assis**. The **Museu Regional** ① *R Israel Pinheiro 176, Tue-Sun 1200-1700,* in the house of the Barão de Catas Altas, or Casa Setecentista, contains 18th- and 19th-century religious art and furniture.

O Aleijadinho

Antônio Francisco Lisboa (1738-1814), the son of a Portuguese architect and a black slave woman, was known as O Aleijadinho (the little cripple) because in later life he developed a maiming disease (possibly leprosy) which compelled him to work in a kneeling (and ultimately a recumbent) position with his hammer and chisel strapped to his wrists. His finest work, which shows a strength not usually associated with the sculpture in the 18th century, is probably the set of statues in the gardens and sanctuary of the great Bom Jesus church in Congonhas do Campo, but the main body of his work is in Ouro Preto, with some important pieces in Sabará, São João del Rei and Mariana.

Parque Natural de Caraça

ⓘ *The entrance is 11 km from the seminary, T3837 2698, www.santuariodocaraca.com.br, 0800-1700; if staying overnight you cannot leave after 2000, US$10 per vehicle.*

The Parque Natural de Caraça is a remarkable reserve about 120 km east of Belo Horizonte. It has been preserved so well because the land belongs to a seminary, part of which has been converted into a hotel. The rarest mammal in the park is the maned wolf; the monks feed them on the seminary steps in the evening. Also endangered is the southern masked titi monkey. Other primates include the common marmoset and the brown capuchin monkey. Some of the bird species at Caraça are endemic, others rare and endangered. The trails for viewing the different landscapes and the wildlife are marked at their beginning and are quite easy to follow.

Ouro Preto → *Phone code: 031. Post code: 35400. Colour map 7, B5. Population: 66,277.*

Founded in 1711, this famous former state capital has cobbled streets that wind up and down steep hills, crowned with 13 churches. Mansions, fountains, terraced gardens, ruins, towers shining with coloured tiles, all blend together to maintain a delightful 18th-century atmosphere. October-February is the wettest time, but the warmest month of the year is February (average 30°C). The coldest months are June-August, with the lowest temperatures in July (10°C).

Tourist offices ⓘ *Praça Tiradentes 41, T3559 3269, and R Cláudio Manoel 61, T3559 3287, www.ouropreto.org.br,* Portuguese only spoken, very helpful; also has a desk at the *rodoviária*, Monday-Friday 0700-1300. The R Cláudio Manoel 61 office is in the Centro Cultural e Turístico mini-mall, with the town's best exhibition space, as well as shops and cafés. An accredited local guide, **Associação de Guias de Turismo (AGTOP)**, can be obtained through the tourist office, or at the *rodoviária*. Do not use unaccredited guides. See also www.circuitodoouro.org.br and www.ouropreto.com.br (in Portuguese).

Most churches charge a conservation tax of US$1.50-5; bags and cameras are taken at the entrance and guarded in lockers (visitors keep the key). Churches are all closed Monday.

Places in Belo Horizonte In the central **Praça Tiradentes** is a statue of the leader of the **Inconfidentes**, Joaquim José da Silva Xavier. Another Inconfidente, the poet Tomás Antônio Gonzaga lived at Rua Cláudio Manoel 61, close to São Francisco de Assis church. On the north side of the praça (at No 20) is a famous **Escola de Minas** (School of Mining), founded in 1876, in the fortress-like **Palácio dos Governadores** (1741-1748); it has the interesting **Museu de Ciencia e Técnica** ⓘ *Tue-Sun 1200-1700, US$2,* with a fine display of rocks, minerals, semi-precious and precious stones. On the south side of the Praça, No 139, is the **Museu da Inconfidência** ⓘ *T3551 1121, Tue-Sun 1200-1730, US$3,* a fine historical and art museum in the former **Casa de Câmara e Cadeia**, which has some drawings by Aleijadinho and the studio of

Manoel da Costa (Mestre) Athayde, in an annex. In the Casa Capitular of NS do Carmo is **Museu do Oratório** ① *T3551 5369, daily 0930-1730, US$1*, a collection of beautiful 18th- and 19th-century prayer icons and oratories including many made of egg and sea shell. **Casa dos Contos** ① *R São José 12, T3551 1444, Tue-Sat 1230-1730, Sun and holidays 0900-1500, US$0.65*. Built between 1782-1784, it is the Centro de Estudos do Ciclo de Ouro (Centre for Gold Cycle Studies) and a museum of money and finance. The **Casa Guignard** ① *R Conde de Bobadela 110, T3551 5155, Tue-Fri 0900-1200, 1300-1800, free*, displays the paintings of Alberto da Veiga Guignard. The **Teatro Municipal** ① *in R Brigadeiro Musqueiro, Mon-Fri 1200-1800*, is the oldest functioning theatre in Latin America. It was built in 1769.

São Francisco de Assis (1766-1796) ① *Largo de Coimbra, T3551 3282, Tue-Sun 0830-1200, 1330-1700, US$4*; the ticket also permits entry to NS da Conceição (keep your ticket for admission to the museum). This church is considered to be one of the masterpieces of Brazilian baroque. Aleijadinho worked on the general design and the sculpture of the façade, the pulpits and many other features. Mestre Athayde (1732-1827) was responsible for the painted ceiling. **Nossa Senhora da Conceição** (1722) ① *closed for renovation until 2016*, is heavily gilded and contains Aleijadinho's tomb. It has a museum devoted to him (works are currently in the São Francisco de Assis museum). **Nossa Senhora das Mercês e Perdões** (1740-1772) ① *R das Mercês, 1000-1400*, was rebuilt in the 19th century. Some sculpture by Aleijadinho can be seen in the main chapel. **Santa Efigênia** (1720-1785) ① *Ladeira Santa Efigênia e Padre Faria, 0800-1630, US$1.50*; Manuel Francisco Lisboa (Aleijadinho's father) oversaw the construction and much of the carving is by Francisco Xavier de Brito (Aleijadinho's mentor). It has wonderful panoramic views of the city. **Nossa Senhora do Carmo** (1766-1772) ① *R Brigadeiro Mosqueira, 1330-1700*, has a museum of sacred art with Aleijadinho sculptures. **Nossa Senhora do Pilar** (1733) ① *Praça Mons Castilho Barbosa, Tue-Sun 0900-1045, 1200-1645, US$ 4*, also contains a religious art museum. Entry is shared with São Francisco de Paula, Ladeira de São José (1804). **Nossa Senhora do Rosário** ① *Largo do Rosário*, dated from 1785, has a curved façade. The interior is much simpler than the exterior, but there are interesting side altars.

The **Mina do Chico Rei** ① *R Dom Silvério, 0800-1700, US$5*, is not as impressive as some other mines in the area, but is fun to descend on the pulley, crawl through the narrow tunnels and learn how the gold was mined. Between Ouro Preto and Mariana is the **Minas de Passagem** ① *T3557 5000, www.minasdapassagem.com.br, Mon-Tue 0900-1700, Wed-Sun 0900-1730*, gold mine, dating from 1719. It's an exciting place to visit with a thrilling descent on an old mining cart followed by a guided wander through gloomy passages and large artificial caverns to a dark crystal-clear lake. Much of the machinery dates from the early 18th century.

Mariana → *Phone code: 031. Post code: 35420. Colour map 7, B5. Population: 46,710.*

Streets are lined with beautiful, two-storey 18th-century houses in this old mining city, which is much less hilly than Ouro Preto. Mariana's historical centre slopes gently uphill from the river and the Praça Tancredo Neves, where buses from Ouro Preto stop. **Tourist office**: Secretaria de Cultura e Turismo de Mariana ① *R Direita 93, T3558 2315, www.mariana.mg.gov.br*. The tourist office will help with guides and tours and offers a map and other informative publications.

Places in Mariana The first street parallel with the Praça Tancredo Neves is Rua Direita, and is home to the 300-year-old houses. At No 54 is the **Casa do Barão de Pontal** ① *Tue 1400-1700*, whose balconies are carved from soapstone, unique in Minas Gerais. The ground floor of the building is a museum of furniture. At No 35 is the **Museu-Casa Afonso Guimarães** (or Alphonsus de Guimaraens) ① *free*, the former home of a symbolist poet: photographs and letters. At No 7 is the **Casa Setecentista**, which now belongs to the Patrimônio Histórico e Artístico Nacional.

Rua Direita leads to the Praça da Sé, on which stands the **Cathedral** ① *Basílica de Nossa Senhora da Assunção, organ concerts are given on Fri at 1100 and Sun at 1200, US$10*. The portal and the lavabo in the sacristy are by Aleijadinho. The painting in the beautiful interior and side altars is by Manoel Rabello de Sousa. Also in the cathedral is a wooden German organ (1701), a gift to the first diocese of the Capitania de Minas do Ouro in 1747. The **Museu Arquidiocesano** ① *R Frei Durão, Tue-Sun 0900-1200, 1300-1700, US$2*, has fine church furniture, a gold and silver collection, Aleijadinho statues and an ivory cross. Opposite is the **Casa da Intendência/Casa de Cultura** ① *R Frei Durão 84, 0800-1130, 1330-1700*, which holds exhibitions and has a museum of music. On the south side of Praça Gomes Freire is the **Palácio Arquiepiscopal**, while on the north side is the **Casa do Conde de Assumar**, who was governor of the Capitania from 1717 to 1720.

From Praça Gomes Freire, Travessa São Francisco leads to Praça Minas Gerais and one of the finest groups of colonial buildings in Brazil. In the middle of the Praça is the **Pelourinho**, the stone monument to Justice, at which slaves used to be beaten. On one side of the square is the fine **São Francisco church** (1762-1794) ① *daily 0800-1700*, with pulpits designed by Aleijadinho, paintings by Mestre Athayde, who is buried in tomb No 94, a fine sacristy and one side-altar by Aleijadinho. At right angles to São Francisco is **Nossa Senhora do Carmo** (1784) ① *daily 1400-1700*, with steatite carvings, Athayde paintings, and chinoiserie panelling. Across Rua Dom Silvério is the **Casa da Câmara e Cadeia** (1768), at one time the Prefeitura Municipal. On Largo de São Pedro is **São Pedro dos Clérigos** (begun in 1753), one of the few elliptical churches in Minas Gerais. Restoration is under way.

Capela de Santo Antônio, on Rua Rosário Velho, is wonderfully simple and the oldest in town. It is some distance from the centre. Overlooking the city from the north, with a good viewpoint, is the church of **Nossa Senhora do Rosário**, Rua do Rosário (1752), with work by Athayde and showing Moorish influence.

Parque Nacional Caparaó

① *US$6. Contact R Vale Verde s/n, Alto do Caparaó, CEP 36979-000, T3747 2086, www.icmbio.gov.br/parna_caparao.*

This is one of the most popular parks in Minas (on the Espírito Santo border), with good walking through stands of Atlantic rainforest, páramo and to the summits of three of Brazil's highest peaks: Pico da Bandeira (2890 m), Pico do Cruzeiro (2861 m) and Pico do Cristal (2798 m). The park, surrounded by coffee farms, features rare Atlantic rainforest in its lower altitudes and Brazilian alpine on top. Loss of forest and floral biodiversity has adversely affected wildlife, but there are nonetheless a number of Atlantic coast primates, like the brown capuchins, together with a recovering bird population. From the park entrance (where a small fee has to be paid) it is 6 km on a good unpaved road to the car park at the base of the waterfall. From the hotel (see page 451) jeeps run to the car park at 1970 m (2½ hours' walk), then it's a three to four hour walk to the summit of the Pico da Bandeira, marked by yellow arrows; plenty of camping possibilities, the highest being at Terreirão (2370 m). This is good walking country. It is best to visit during the dry season (April-October). It can be quite crowded in July and during Carnival. ⏵⏵ *See Transport, page 454, for how to get there.*

Congonhas → *Phone code: 031. Post code: 36404. Colour map 7, B5. Population: 41,256.*

This hill town is connected by a paved 3.5 km road with the Rio-Belo Horizonte highway. Most visitors spend little time in the town, but go straight to **O Santuário de Bom Jesus de Matosinhos** ① *Tue-Sun 0700-1900, there are public toilets on the Alameda das Palmeiras, the information desk at the bus station will guard luggage and you can visit the sanctuary between bus changes*, which dominates Congonhas. The great pilgrimage church was finished in 1771;

below it are six linked chapels, or pasos (1802-1818), showing scenes with life-size Passion figures carved by Aleijadinho and his pupils in cedar wood. These lead up to a terrace and courtyard. On this terrace (designed in 1777) stand 12 prophets, sculpted by Aleijadinho between 1800 and 1805. Carved in soapstone with dramatic sense of movement, they constitute one of the finest works of art of their period in the world. Inside the church, there are paintings by Athayde and the heads of four sainted popes (Gregory, Jerome, Ambrose and Augustine) sculpted by Aleijadinho for the reliquaries on the high altar. To the left of the church, as you face it, the third door in the building alongside the church is the Room of Miracles, which contains photographs and thanks for miracles performed.

On the hill are souvenir shops, the Colonial Hotel and Cova do Daniel restaurant (both are good). From the hotel the Alameda das Palmeiras sweeps round to the **Romarias**, which contains the Espaço Cultural, the headquarters of the local tourist office, workshops, the museums of mineralogy and religious art and the Memória da Cidade. To get there take bus marked 'Basílica' which runs every 30 minutes from the centre of the rodoviária to Bom Jesus, 5 km, US$1. A taxi from the rodoviária costs US$6, US$12.50 return including the wait while you visit the sanctuary. In town, the bus stops in Praça JK. You can walk up from Praça JK via Praça Dr Mário Rodrigues Pereira, cross the little bridge, then go up Ruas Bom Jesus and Aleijadinho to the Praça da Basílica. **Tourist office**: Diretoria de Turismo ⓘ Alameda Cidade Matozinhos de Portugal 153, Basílica, T3731 2077, with a help point at Av Júlia Kubistchek 2039, T3731 7394, www.congonhas.org.br.

São João del Rei → Phone code: 032. Post code: 36300. Colour map 7, B5. Population: 78,616.

This colonial city is at the foot of the Serra do Lenheiro. A good view of the town and surroundings is from Alto da Boa Vista, where there is a Statue of Christ (Senhor dos Montes). São João del Rei is very lively at weekends, but feels far less of a tourist museum piece than nearby Tiradentes (see below). Through the centre of town runs the Corrego do Lenheiro (sadly a winding stream no more); across it are two fine stone bridges, A Ponte da Cadeia (1798) and A Ponte do Rosário (1800). **Tourist office**: Secretaria da Cultura e Turismo ⓘ in the house of Bárbara Heliodora, Praça Frei Orlando 90, T3372 7338, 0900-1700, free map, www.cultura.saojoaodelrei.mg.gov.br; also www.guiadelrei.com.br.

There are five 18th-century churches in the town, three of which are splendid examples of Brazilian colonial building. **São Francisco de Assis** (1774) ⓘ Praça Frei Orlando, 0830-1700, closed Mon, US$1.50. The façade, with circular towers, the doorway intricately carved and the greenish stone framing the white paint to beautiful effect was designed by Francisco de Lima Cerqueira and his disciple Aniceto de Souza Lopez. Inside are two sculptures by the same artists, about whom nothing is known beyond their names in the church's records and that they carried out the work in 1774. The six side altars are in wood; restoration has removed the plaster from the altars, revealing fine carving in sucupira wood.

Basílica de Nossa Senhora do Pilar (the Cathedral) ⓘ R Getúlio Vargas (formerly R Direita), open afternoons, built 1721, has a 19th-century façade which replaced the 18th-century original. It has rich altars and a brightly painted ceiling. In the sacristy are portraits of the Evangelists. **Nossa Senhora do Carmo** ⓘ Praça Dr Augusto Viegas (Largo do Carmo), open afternoons, very well restored, is all in white and gold. Construction commenced in 1733. Almost opposite São Francisco is the house of **Bárbara Heliodora** which contains the **Museu Municipal Tomé Portes del Rei**, with historical objects and curios, and, downstairs, the tourist office (see above). The **Museu Ferroviário** (railway museum) ⓘ Av Hermílio Alves 366, T3371 8485, Tue-Sun 0900-1100, 1300-1700, US$2.50 (included in the train ticket to Tiradentes, see below), is well worth exploring. The museum traces the history of railways in general and in Brazil in brief. You can walk along the tracks to the round house, in which are several working engines in superb condition, an engine shed and a steam-operated machine shop, still working. It is here that the engines get up steam before going to couple with the coaches for the run to Tiradentes. On days when the trains are running, you can get a good, close-up view of operations even if not taking the trip; highly recommended.

Tiradentes → *Phone code: 032. Post code: 36325. Population: 5759.*

This charming little town, 15 km from São João, with its nine streets and eight carefully restored, baroque churches, is at the foot of the green Serra São José. Neat whitewashed cottages trimmed in yellow and blue hide art galleries, restaurants, souvenir shops and *pousadas*, all busy with tourists even during the week. It is especially busy during Holy Week, when there are numerous religious processions. It was founded as São José del Rei on 14 January 1718. After the ousting of the emperor in 1889 the town was renamed in honour of the martyr of the Inconfidência. **Tourist office** ① *R Resende Costa 71, T3355 1212, www.tiradentes.mg.gov.br and www.tiradentes.net*, is in the Prefeitura.

Places in Tiradentes The **Igreja Matriz de Santo Antônio** (1710-1736) ① *daily 0900-1700, US$1.30, no photos*, contains some of the finest gilded wood carvings in the country. The church has a small but fine organ brought from Porto in the 1790s. The upper part of the reconstructed façade is said to follow a design by Aleijadinho. In front of the church are also a cross and a sundial by him. **Santuário da Santíssima Trindade**, on the road which leads up behind the Igreja Matriz de Santo Antônio, is 18th century, while the room of miracles associated with the annual Trinity Sunday pilgrimage is modern.

The charming **Nossa Senhora do Rosário** church (1727) ① *on a small square on R Direita, Wed-Mon 1200-1600, US$0.65*, has fine statuary and ornate gilded altars. **São João Evangelista** ① *Largo do Sol, Wed-Mon 0900-1700*, is in a lovely open space. It is a simple church, built by the Irmandade dos Homens Pardos (mulattos). Beside Igreja São João Evangelista is the **Museu Padre Toledo**, the house of one of the leaders of the Inconfidência Mineira. It exhibits some handsome colonial furniture and a painted roof depicting the Five Senses. At the junction of Rua da Câmara and Rua Direita is the **Sobrado Ramalho**, said to be the oldest building in Tiradentes. It has been beautifully restored as a cultural centre. **Nossa Senhora das Mercês** (18th century) ① *Largo das Mercês, Sun 0900-1700*, has an interesting painted ceiling and a notable statue of the Virgin. The magnificent **Chafariz de São José** (public fountain, 1749) is still used for drinking, clothes washing and watering animals. You can follow the watercourse into the forest of the Serra de São José (monkeys and birds can be seen).

The **steam train** ① *runs on Fri, Sat, Sun and holidays, 1000 and 1500 from São João del Rei, returning from Tiradentes at 1300 and 1700, US$20 one way, T3371 8485*, on the line between São João del Rei and Tiradentes (13 km) has been in continuous operation since 1881, using the same locomotives and rolling stock, running on 76 cm gauge track, all lovingly cared for. The maximum speed is 20 kph.

São Tomé das Letras and around → *Phone code: 035. Colour map 7, B4. Population: 6204.*

A beautiful hilltop town in southern Minas, one of the five highest places in Brazil, São Tomé has attracted many new age visitors and its hotels are graded in UFOs instead of stars. It is said to be a good vantage point for seeing UFOs, which draw crowds at weekends. Nearby are caves with inscriptions, which some say are extraterrestrial in origin. It is believed that there are many places with special energies. Behind the town are rocky outcrops on which are the Pyramid House, the Cruzeiro (Cross, 1430 m, with good 360° views), the Pedra da Bruxa and paths for walking or, in some parts, scrambling. A quarry town since the beginning of the 20th century, there is evidence of the industry everywhere you look. **Tourist office** ① *R José Cristiano Alves 4, T3237 1226, www.saotomedasletras.cam.mg.gov.br and www.saothomedasletras.net*.

On the main Praça is the frescoed 18th-century **Igreja Matriz** beside the fenced cave in which are the faded red rock paintings (*letras*) of the town's name. A second church, the **Igreja das Pedras** (Nossa Senhora do Rosário – 18th century) is on a Praça to the left as you enter town (Rua Ernestina Maria de Jesus Peixoto). It is constructed in the same style as many of the charming old-style buildings, with slabs of the local stone laid on top of each other without mortar.

In the surrounding hills are many caves, waterfalls and rapids. Some of these places make a good hike from the town, but you can also visit several in a day on an organized tour. Call T3237 1283 or enquire at Néctar shop on Rua José Cristiano Alves. Tours run on weekends and holidays from the Praça at 1000 and 1400 to waterfalls, caves, etc. The Carimbado cave is especially rich in myths and legends. Shangri-lá, which is a beautiful spot, is also called the Vale do Maytréia.

⊙ East and south of Belo Horizonte listings

For hotel and restaurant price codes, and other relevant information, see Essentials.

● Where to stay

Parque Natural de Caraça *p445*
$$$ Pousada do Caraça, the seminary hotel, for reservations T031-3837 2698 Mon-Fri 0800-1700, or pousadadocaraca@gmail.com. It has pleasant rooms in a variety of wings and individual houses; room rates vary; price is full board. There is a restaurant serving good food which comes from farms within the seminary's lands. Lunch is served 1200-1400, US$7.60. Lodging also available at the **$$$ Pousada Fazenda do Engenho**, T3809 4004, faz. engenho@gmail.com, on a farm 10 km from the seminary B&B only, Wi-Fi available but no mobile phone reception. Details for both places on www.santuariodocaraca.com.br.

Ouro Preto *p445*
Prices indicated here are for high season; many hotels offer, or will negotiate, lower prices outside holiday times or when things are quiet.
Ask at the tourist office for accommodation in *casas de família*, reasonably priced. Avoid touts who greet you off buses and charge higher prices than those advertised in hotels; it is difficult to get hotel rooms at weekends and holiday periods.

$$$$ Pousada do Mondego, Largo de Coimbra 38, T3551 2040, www.mondego. com.br. Beautifully kept colonial house in a fine location by São Francisco church, room rates vary according to view, small restaurant, Scotch bar, popular with groups. Recommended (a Roteiro de Charme hotel, see page 357), the hotel runs a jardineira bus tour of the city, 2 hrs, minimum 10 passengers, US$10 for non-guests.

$$$$ Pousada Solar de NS do Rosário, Av Getúlio Vargas 270, T3551 5200, www.hotel solardorosario.com.br. Fully restored historic building with a highly recommended restaurant, bar, sauna, pool; all facilities in rooms.

$$$ Pousada Casa Grande, R Conselheiro Quintiliano, 96, T3551 4314, www.hotelpousada casagrande.com.br. In a large colonial town-house, smart, safe, good views. Recommended.

$$$ Pousada Mirante do Café, Fazenda Alto das Rubiáceas, Santo Antônio do Leite, 25 km west of Ouro Preto, T3335 8478, www. mirantedocafe.com.br. Price varies with season and weekend. Coffee farm with full board available, visits allowed during coffee harvest, pool, trails, horse riding and other leisure activities.

$$$ Pousada Nello Nuno, R Camilo de Brito 59, T3551 3375, www.pousadanellonuno. com.br. Cheaper rooms have no bath, friendly owner Annamélia speaks some French. Highly recommended.

$$$-$$ Colonial, Trav Padre Camilo Veloso 26, close to Praça Tiradentes, T3551 3133, www.hotelcolonial.com.br. With new rooms and refurbished older rooms, but check for size, pleasant.

$$ Pousada São Francisco de Paula, Padre JM Pen 202, next to the São Francisco de Paula church, 100 m from *rodoviária*, T3551 3156, www.pousadasaofranciscodepaula.com.br. One of the best views of any in the city, from the rooms or from a hammock in the garden. Rooms with and without bath or breakfast, dormitory, use of a kitchen, multilingual staff, excursions. Snacks are available. Recommended (book in after 1200).

$$ Pousada Tiradentes, Praça Tiradentes 70, T3551 2619, www.pousadatiradentesop. com.br. Spartan rooms, but well kept and moderately comfortable, fridge, conveniently located.

$$ Pouso Chico Rey, R Brig Musqueira 90, T3551 1274, www.pousodochicorei.com.br. Fascinating old house with Portuguese colonial furnishings, very small and utterly delightful (but plumbing unreliable), book in advance.

$ Brumas, R Antônio Pereira 43 (next to the Museu da Inconfidência), T3551 2944, www. brumashostel.com.br. Small well-kept double rooms and dorms with parquet floors, those on the upper corridor have mountain views. Excellent location in the heart of the colonial town overlooking São Francisco church.

$ Ouro Preto Hostel, Trav das Lajes 32, Antônio Dias, T3551 6011, www.ouropretohostel.com. Also HI-affiliated, dorms, also suites (**$$**), some with balcony, near Mina do Chico Rei.

Camping Camping Clube do Brasil, Rodovia dos Inconfidentes Km 91, 2 km north, T3551 1799. Expensive but good.

Students may be able to stay, during holidays and weekends, at the self-governing student hostels, known as *repúblicas* (very welcoming, 'best if you like heavy metal music' and 'are prepared to enter into the spirit of the places'). The Prefeitura has a list of over 50 repúblicas with phone numbers, available at the Secretaria de Turismo. Many are closed Christmas to Carnival.

Mariana *p446*

$$$ Faísca, R Antônio Olinto 48, T3557 1206, www.hotelfaisca.com.br. Up the street from the tourist office, rooms with fan and fridge, breakfast room.

$$$ Pousada Solar dos Corrêa, R Josefá Macedo 70 and R Direita, T3557 2080. Central, restored 18th-century town house with spacious a/c rooms, with fridge, parking.

$$$ Pouso da Typographia, Praça Gomes Freire 220, T3557 1577. Much the best in town with fan-cooled rooms in an attractive colonial house which once was a printing works.

$$$-$$ Pousada do Chafariz, R Cônego Rego 149, T3557 1492, www.pousadado chafariz.com.br. Converted colonial building, fridge, parking.

$$ Providência, R Dom Silvério 233, T3557 1444, www.hotelprovidencia.com.br. Along the road that leads up to the Basílica: has use of the neighbouring school's pool when classes finish at noon, small rooms, quiet.

Parque Nacional Caparaó *p447*

$$$ Caparaó Parque, T3747 2559, 2 km from the park entrance, 15 mins' walk from the town of Alto Caparaó, nice. Ask where camping is permitted.

$$ São Luiz, in Manhumirim. Good value, but **Cids Bar**, next door, Travessa 16 do Março, has better food.

São João del Rei *p448*

$$$ Beco do Bispo, Beco do Bispo 93, 2 mins west of São Francisco de Assis, T3371 8844, www.becodobispo.com.br. The best in town, bright rooms with firm mattresses, hot showers, pool, convenient, very helpful English speaking staff. Organizes tours. Highly recommended.

$$$ Lenheiros Palace, Av Pres Tancredo Neves 257, T3371 8155, www.hotellenheiros. com.br. A modern hotel with good facilities, parking, **Lenheiros Casa de Chá** tea house, breakfast, no restaurant.

$$$ Ponte Real, Av Eduardo Magalhães 254, T3371 7000, www.hotelpontereal.com.br. Modern, comfortable, sizeable rooms, good restaurant.

$$$ Pousada Casarão, opposite São Francisco church, Ribeiro Bastos 94, T3371 7447, www.pousadacasarao.com. In a delightful converted mansion house, firm beds, fridge, swimming pool, games room.

Tiradentes p449

$$$$ Solar da Ponte, Praça das Mercês (proprietors John and Anna Maria Parsons), T3355 1255, www.solardaponte.com.br. Country house atmosphere, 12 rooms, price includes breakfast and afternoon tea, fresh flowers in rooms, bar, sauna, lovely gardens, swimming pool, light meals for residents only, restaurants nearby (it is in the Roteiros de Charme group, see page 357). For horse-riding treks, contact John Parsons here. Recommended.

$$$ Pousada Mãe D'Água, Largo das Forras 50, T3355 1206, www.pousadamaedagua.com.br. Including breakfast but not tax, very nice, outdoor pool in garden.

$$$ Pousada Três Portas, R Direita 280A, T3355 1444, www.pousadatresportas.com.br. Charming, central, in restored town house, has sauna, thermal pool, hydromassage, heating.

$$$ Pouso das Gerais, R dos Inconfidentes 109, T3355 1234, www.pousodasgerais.com.br. Fresh fan-cooled rooms, marble basins, central, quiet, pool. Recommended.

$$ Pousada do Laurito, R Direita 187, T3355 1268. Central, good value, very popular with international backpackers.

São Tomé das Letras p449

Streets are hard to follow because their names seem to change almost from one block to the next; numbering is also chaotic. There are lots of pousadas and rooms to let all over town.

$$$ dos Sonhos II, R Prefeito Elias da Silva Guedes 8, T3237 1235, www.hsonhos.com.br. Very nice, restaurant, swimming pool, sauna.

$$$ Pousada Arco-Iris, R João Batista Neves 19, T3237 1212, www.pousarcoiris.com.br. Rooms and chalets, sauna, swimming pool.

$$$-$$ Pousada Harmonia, Estrada para Sobradinho s/n, Bairro do Canta Galo, T3237 1280. 4 km from town, but shop on the main Praça. The community emphasizes

several disciplines for a healthy lifestyle, for mind and body, 'new age', workshops, massage, excursions, vegetarian food, clean accommodation.

$$ Pousada Souza Reis, Praça do Rosário 540, T3237 1264, www.hospedagemsouzareis.com. Next to Igreja de Pedra, with bath and breakfast, good value, helpful.

❼ Restaurants

Ouro Preto p445

Try the local liquor de jaboticaba.

$$ Adega, R Teixeira Amaral 24, T3551 4171. Vegetarian smorgasbord, all you can eat, 1130-1530. Highly recommended.

$$ Casa do Ouvidor, R Conde de Bobadela 42, T3551 2141, www.casadeouvidor.com.br. Traditional Minas fare served in a lovely old mansion 2 mins' walk from the Praça Tiradentes, very good.

$$ Forno de Barro, Praça Tiradentes 54. Decent Mineira cooking.

$$ O Sotão, R São José 201, T8725 9434. Great value pancake and crepe restaurant with some 40 different flavours, lively at weekends. Also in Mariana on Praça Gomes Freire.

$$ Taverna do Chafariz, R São José 167, T3551 2828. Good local food. Recommended.

$ Beijinho Doce, R Direita 134A. Delicious pastries and cakes, try the truffles.

$ Café & Cia, R São José 187, T3551 0711. Closes 2300, very popular, comida por kilo at lunchtime, good salads, juices.

$ Pasteleria Lampião, Praça Tiradentes. Best at lunchtime; good views at the back.

Mariana p446

$$ Bistrô, R Salomão Ibrahim da Silva 61, T3557 4138. Comida mineira, decent steaks, pasta, pizza and petiscos, German-Brazilian beers. Open at night.

$$ Lua Cheia, Dom Viçoso.58, T3557 3232. Good-value lunchtime buffet with Minas food, pasta, salads and juices.

$$ Rancho da Praça, Praça Gomes Freire 108, T3557 3444. Buffet of well-prepared Minas dishes served in traditional iron pots and pans.

São João del Rei p448

$$$ Churrascaria Ramón, Praça Severiano de Resende 52. One of the better *churrascarias* with generous portions and plenty of side dishes.

$$$ Quinto do Ouro, Praça Severiano de Rezende 04, T3371 7577. Tasty and well-prepared regional food. Said to be the best Mineira cooking in town.

$ Restaurant 611, R Tome Portes del Rei 511, Vila Santo Antônio, T3371 5590. Very cheap but great Mineira cooking. Lots of choice, popular. Also **611 Centro**, R Getulio Vargas 145, Centro, T3371 8793.

Tiradentes p449

There are many restaurants, snack bars and *lanchonetes* in town and it is a small enough place to wander around and see what takes your fancy.

$$$ Estalagem, R Ministro G Passos 280. Excellent and generous traditional Mineira meat dishes.

$$$ Quartier Latin, R São Francisco de Paula 46, Praça da Rodoviária, T3355 1552. French, cordon bleu chef, excellent.

$$$ Quinto de Ouro, R Direita 159. Mineira and international dishes. Recommended.

$$$ Theatro da Vila, R Padre Toledo 157, T3355 1275. Inventive and delicious Franco-Brazilian fusion cooking served in intimate rustic-chic dining room. Views over the Serra across the garden, small theatre that holds performances in summer.

$$$ Virados do Largo, Largo do Ó. Good Mineira food and service.

$ Maria Luísa Casa de Chá, Largo do Ó 1, diagonally opposite Aluarte, T3355 1502. Tea, cakes and sandwiches in an arty Bohemian atmosphere. Great for breakfast.

🍷 Bars and clubs

Tiradentes p449

Aluarte, Largo do Ó 1, is a bar with live music in the evening, nice atmosphere, cover charge, garden, sells handicrafts.

🎉 Festivals

Ouro Preto p445

Ouro Preto is famous for its **Holy Week** processions, beginning on the Thu before Palm Sunday and continuing (but not every day) until Easter Sunday. The most famous is that commemorating Christ's removal from the Cross, late on Good Friday. Many shops close then, and on winter weekends. Attracting many Brazilians, **Carnival** here is also memorable. **Jun**, **Corpus Christi** and the **Festas Juninas** are celebrated. Every **Jul** the city holds the **Festival do Inverno da Universidade Federal de Minas Gerais** (UFMG), the Winter Festival, about 3 weeks of arts, courses, shows, concerts and exhibitions. Also in **Jul**, on the 8th, is the anniversary of the city. **15 Aug**: Nossa Senhora do Pilar, patron saint of Ouro Preto. **12-18 Nov**: Semana de Aleijadinho, a week-long arts festival.

Congonhas p447

Congonhas is famous for **Holy Week** processions at Bom Jesus church. The most celebrated ceremonies are the **meeting of Christ and the Virgin Mary** on the **Tue**, and the dramatized **Deposition from the Cross** late on **Good Friday**. The pilgrimage season, first half of **Sep**, draws thousands. **8 Dec**, Nossa Senhora da Conceição.

São João del Rei p448

Apr, Semana Santa **15-21 Apr**, Semana da Inconfidência. **May or Jun**, Corpus Christi. **First 2 weeks of Aug**, Nossa Senhora da Boa Morte, with baroque music (novena barroca). Similarly, **12 Oct**, Nossa Senhora do Pilar, patron saint of the city. **8 Dec**, founding of the city. FUNREI, the university (R Padre José Maria Xavier), holds Inverno Cultural in **Jul**.

🛍 Shopping

Ouro Preto p445

Gems are not much cheaper from sellers in Praça Tiradentes than from the shops, and in the shops, the same quality of stone is offered at the same price. If buying on the street, ask for the seller's credentials. Buy soapstone carvings at roadside stalls and bus stops rather than in cities; they are much cheaper. Many artisans sell jewellery and semi-precious stones in Largo de Coimbra in front of São Francisco de Assis church. Recommended is **Gemas de Minas**, Conde de Bobadela 63.

⊖ Transport

Sabará *p444*
Bus Viação Cisne from separate part of **Belo Horizonte** *rodoviária*, US$2.50, 30 mins.

Parque Natural de Caraça *p445*
Turn off the BR-262 (towards Vitória) at Km 73 and go via Barão de Cocais to Caraça (120 km). There is no public transport to the seminary. **Buses** go as far as **Santa Bárbara** (6 a day, fewer at weekends, 3 hrs, US$25), then take a taxi, US$35 one way. You must book the **taxi** to return for you, or else **hitch** (not easy). The park entrance is 10 km before the seminary. Or hire a **car**, or take a tour from Belo Horizonte, which will work out cheaper than going under your own steam if you can join a tour.

Ouro Preto *p445*
Bus Don't walk from the *rodoviária* to town at night; robberies have occurred. The *rodoviária* is at R Padre Rolim 661, near São Francisco de Paula church, T3559 3252. A 'Circular' bus runs from the *rodoviária* to Praça Tiradentes, US$1.15. Taxi US$8 at least. Hourly buses 0600-2300 from Belo Horizonte 2 hrs, US$14. Day trips are run. Book your return journey to **Belo Horizonte** early if returning in the evening; buses get crowded. Bus to/from **Rio**, 4 a day, US$33, 8 hrs. To **Congonhas** you will need to change bus in **Ouro Branco**: 3 daily to Ouro Branco from Ouro Preto, first at 0715 (US$2.50, 1 hr), 7 daily from Ouro Branco to Congonhas (US$5, 90 mins). Take the 1615 bus from Congonhas to Ouro Branco for the last bus back to Ouro Preto. Direct buses to **São Paulo**, 1 at night, 10 hrs, US$57.

Train The Maria Fumaça Trem da Vale is now a diesel train, not a steam locomotive, Praça Cesário Alvim, s/n, T3551 7310, www.tremdavale.org. It leaves Fri-Sun at 1000, returning from Mariana at 1400, with an extra train leaving Ouro Preto at 1530 and from Mariana at 0800 on public holidays, US$20/US$25 return. For the best views for 18-km, 40-min journey, sit on the right side and in the back carriages.

Mariana *p446*
Bus Mariana is only 12 km from Ouro Preto and can easily be visited as a side trip. Buses run between the Escola de Minas near Praça Tiradentes in Ouro Preto and the Secretaria de Cultura e Turismo de Mariana, Praça Tancredo Neves, every 30 mins, US$2.50.

Parque Nacional Caparaó *p447*
Bus The park is 49 km by paved road from Manhuaçu (about 190 km south of Governador Valadares) on the Belo Horizonte-Vitória road (BR-262). There are buses from **Belo Horizonte** (twice daily), Ouro Preto or Vitória to **Manhumirim**, 15 km south of Manhuaçu. From Manhumirim, take a Rio Doce bus direct to Alto Caparaó, 7 a day, US$2.25. From Alto Caparaó walk 4 km to the park, or hire a jeep. By **car** from the BR-262, go through Manhumirim, Alto Jaquitibá and Alto Caparaó, then 1 km to Hotel Caparaó Parque.

Congonhas *p447*
Bus The *rodoviária* is 1½ km outside town, Av Júlia Kubitschek 1982, T3731 3886; bus to town centre US$1; for 'Basílica', see above. To **Belo Horizonte**, 1½ hrs, US$12, 2 buses direct, otherwise go to the main road where many more pass. To **São João del Rei**, 2½ hrs, US$13, direct Sat and Sun only, otherwise flag down bus on main BR-040 road, 7 daily, or go to **Conselheiro Lafaiete**, 20 mins, US$2.50, from where 7 buses a day go to São João del Rei. Bus to **Ouro Preto**: see above.

São João del Rei *p448*
Bus *Rodoviária* is 2 km west of the centre. To **São Paulo**, 8 hrs, 8 a day, US$40. **Belo Horizonte**, 7 daily, 4 hrs, US$25. To **Tiradentes**, 8 a day, 7 on Sat, Sun and holidays, US$5.

Tiradentes *p449*
Bus Last bus back to **São João del Rei** is 1815, 2230 on Sun.

São Tomé das Letras *p449*
Bus There are 3 daily buses (2 on Sun) to São Tomé from **Tres Corações**, the birthplace of Pelé, the legendary football star (to whom there is a statue in Praça Col José Martins), US$5, 1½ hrs (paved road). Tres Corações has hotels and regular buses to **Belo Horizonte**, US$30, 5½ hrs, and **São Paulo**, US$20.

Espírito Santo

The coastal state of Espírito Santo is where mineiros head to for their seaside holidays. The most popular beaches are south of Vitória, the state capital, while north of the city are several turtle-nesting beaches. Inland are immigrant towns.

Vitória and around → *Phone code: 027. Post code: 29000. Colour map 7, B6.*
Five bridges connect the island on which Vitória stands with the mainland. The state capital is beautifully set, its entrance second only to Rio's, its beaches quite as attractive, but smaller, and the climate is less humid. Port installations at Vitória and nearby Ponta do Tubarão have led to some beach and air pollution at places nearby. It is largely a modern city: The upper, older part of town, reached by steep streets and steps, is less hectic than the lower harbour area, but both are full of cars. The car-parking boys have their work cut out to find spaces. **Tourist offices**: in the *rodoviária*, at the airport, T3235 6350 (helpful, with map and leaflets) and at the Curva da Jurema beach, Módulo 18, T3382 3053. The **Postos de Informações Turísticas** are staffed by students. For the **Superintendência de Turismo** ① *13315 5540.* **Fala Vitória** ① *T156, www.vitoria.es.gov.br.* For the state see www.descubraoespiritosanto.es.gov.br.

On Avenida República is the large **Parque Moscoso**, an oasis of quiet, with a lake and playground. Of the few colonial buildings still to be seen in the upper city, the **Capela de Santa Luzia** (1551) ① *R José Marcelino, Mon-Fri 0800-1800* has a painted altar, otherwise a small open space. In the **Palácio Anchieta**, or **do Governo** ① *Praça João Climaco (upper city)*, is the tomb of Padre Anchieta, one of the founders of São Paulo. Praça João Climaco has some restored buildings around it, including the Casa do Cidadão. The **Teatro Carlos Gomes** ① *Praça Costa Pereira*, often presents plays, also jazz and folk festivals.

Urban beaches such as **Camburi** can be affected by pollution, but it is pleasant, with a fair surf. Several buses run from the centre to Camburi, look for one with Av Beira Mar on the destination board. Buses pass Praia do Canto, a smart district with good restaurants and shops, then cross A Ponte de Camburi.

Vila Velha, reached by A Terceira Ponte (the Third Bridge) across the bay, is a separate municipality from Vitória. The Third Bridge, a toll road, is a sweeping structure and one of the symbols of the city. It has an excellent series of beaches: Praia da Costa is the main one, with others, including Itaparica, heading south. The second main symbol of Vila Velha is the monastery of **Nossa Senhora da Penha** (1558) ① *daily 0515-1645, http://conventodapenha.org. br*, on a high hill with superb views of the bay, bridge and both cities. The Dutch attacked it in 1625 and 1640. Minibuses take the infirm and not-so-devout up the hill for US$1 return, 0630-1715 (you have to use the phone in the upper car park if you want a ride down). A museum in the convent costs US$0.50. From here you will see that Vila Velha is neither old, nor a small town. It's a built up beachfront city, noisy at times, but the sea suffers less from pollution than Camburi. Vila Velha is the place of origin of Garoto chocolates, whose factory can be visited on weekdays (T3320 1709 for times). **Tourist information** ⓘ *T3139 9015, www.vilavelha.es.gov.br.*

Some 14 km south of Vila Velha is **Barra do Jucu**, which has bigger waves, and the **Reserva de Jacarenema**, which preserves coastal ecosystems.

Inland from Vitória

Santa Leopoldina or **Domingos Martins**, both around 45 km from Vitória, are less than an hour by bus (Pretti to Santa Leopoldina five a day, four on Sunday; Aguia Branca to Domingos Martins, Friday 1700 only). Both villages preserve the architecture and customs of the first German and Swiss settlers who arrived in the 1840s. Domingos Martins (also known as Campinho) has a Casa de Cultura with some items of German settlement. Santa Leopoldina has an interesting **museum** ⓘ *Tue-Sun 0900-1100, 1300-1800,* which covers the settlers' first years in the area. Domingos Martins is on the route of a tourist train that runs on Saturday and Sunday from the town of Viana, outside Vitória, to Domingos Martins, Marechal Floriano and Araguaya. The railcar of the **Trem das Montahas Capixabas** ⓘ *US$75 return, US$52 one way, http://serraverdeexpress.com.br, ticket office in Vitória: Av Nossa Senhora dos Navegantes 451, T2123 0229,* leaves at 1030, getting back to Viana at 1700; Domingos Martins is 1 hour 10 minutes into the journey and Araguaya is reached at 1300. The line climbs over 500 m from the coastal plain into Mata Atlântica.

Along the BR-262 west towards Minas Gerais, most of the hills are intensely worked, with very few patches of Mata Atlântica remaining. A significant landmark is the **Pedra Azul**, a huge granite outcrop, with a sheer face (a bit like a massive tombstone). From the side you can see a spur which looks like a finger pointing to the summit. It's a Parque Estadual, whose entrance is on the BR-262. The Pedra Azul bus stop is at the turn-off to the town of Alonso Cláudio ('region of waterfalls'). There are many *pousadas* here. The next town, **Venda Nova do Imigrante**, some 10 km, is a pretty place to stop, with well-tended flower beds along the main street, plenty of eating places, handicrafts and local Italian produce and at least one hotel.

Santa Teresa is a charming hill town two hours, 78 km by bus from Vitória. A brochure from the Prefeitura lists local sites of interest including waterfalls, valley views and some history. It also lists where to stay and eat. Fazendas also offer accommodation, days out and rural pursuits. See Santa Teresa's website, www.santateresa-es.com.br. In the Galeria de Arte, just past the *rodoviária*, shops sell handicrafts and honey, jams, liqueurs, sweet wines and biscuits. Stalls on the side of the main road also sell local products. There is a museum, botanical garden and small zoo for study of Mata Atlântica wildlife at the **Museu Mello Leitão** ⓘ *Av José Ruschi 4, T3259 1182, 0800-1200, 1300-1700 (closed Mon morning), US$1.* Its library includes the works of the hummingbird and orchid scientist, Augusto Ruschi. Hummingbird feeders are hung outside the admin building.

Guarapari and beaches south of Vitória → *Colour map 7, B6. Population: 88,400.*

South of Vitória (54 km) is Guarapari, whose beaches are the closest to Minas Gerais, so they get very crowded at holiday times. The beaches also attract many people seeking cures for rheumatism, neuritis and other complaints, from the radioactive monazitic sands. Information about the sands can be found at **Setuc** ⓘ *in the Casa de Cultura, Praça Jerônimo Monteiro, T3261 3058,* and at the **Antiga Matriz** church on the hill in the town centre, built in 1585.

Further south (28 km) is **Anchieta** with nearby beaches at Praia de Castelhanos (5 km east, on a peninsula) and **Iriri**. The next spot down the coast, 5 km, is **Piúma**, a calm place, renowned for its craftwork in shells. About 3 km north of the village is Pau Grande beach, where you can surf. The resort town of **Marataízes**, with good beaches, hotels and camping, is 30 km south of Piúma. It is just north of the Rio state border. Planeta buses go to Mataraízes and Piúma from Vitória.

Turtle beaches

The **Reserva Biológica Comboios** ① *open 0800-1200, 1300-1700, for information, contact Projeto Tamar, Regência, T027-3274 1209, www.projetotamar.org.br*, 104 km north of Vitória via Santa Cruz, is designed to protect the marine turtles which frequent this coast. **Regência**, at the mouth of the Rio Doce, 65 km north of Santa Cruz, is part of the reserve and has a regional base for Tamar, the national marine turtle protection project.

Linhares, 143 km north of Vitória on the Rio Doce, has good hotels and restaurants. It is a convenient starting place for the turtle beaches.

Itaúnas and around → *Colour map 7, B6. Population: 26,494. Pleasant beach hotels.*

The most attractive beaches in the state are around **Conceição da Barra**. Corpus Christi (early June) is celebrated with an evening procession for which the road is decorated with coloured wood chips.

Itaúnas, 27 km north by road, or 14 km up the coast, has been swamped by sand dunes, 30 m high. From time to time, winds shift the sand dunes enough to reveal the buried church tower. Itaúnas has been moved to the opposite river bank. The coast here is a protected turtle breeding ground. There are a few *pousadas* and a small campsite at Itaúnas and other hotels 3 km further north at Guaxindiba. Take a bus from the bakery in Conceição da Barra at 0700; it returns at 1700.

① Espírito Santo listings

For hotel and restaurant price codes, and other relevant information, see Essentials.

⊛ Where to stay

Vitória *p455*
Many hotels belonging to chains such as Bristol (www.britolhotels.com.br) and Accor (www.accorhotels.com).
$$$ Slaviero Slim Alice Vitória, R Cnel Vicente Peixoto 95, Praça Getúlio Vargas, T3331 1144, www.gruponeffa.com.br. In the busy lower city, good rooms with comfy beds, typical business hotel. With 2 restaurants.
$$ Vitória, R Cais de São Francisco 85, T3223 0222, hotelsolemar-es@hotmail.com.br. Near Parque Moscoso. Comfortable rooms, some with round beds, rambling building, good restaurant Mar e Sol.

Adequate hotels can be found opposite the *rodoviária* and a couple in the city centre.

Camburi
$$$ Aeroporto, R Ary Ferreira Chagas 30, T2127 3100, www.hotelaeroportovitoria.com.br. Large rooms, well-furnished, good breakfast, on way to airport from Camburi beach.

$$$-$$ Minuano, Av Dante Michelini 337, 12121 7877, www.hotelminuano.com.br. Hotel and churrascaria at the Canal end of Camburi, 3 standards of room.

Vila Velha
$$$ Itaparica Praia, R Itapemirim 30, Coqueiral de Itaparica, Vila Velha, T3320 4000, www.hotelitaparica.com.br. More pricey in high season, rooms with sea view cost a bit more. Huge rooms, pool, garage, quiet, safe and good.

Inland from Vitória: Santa Teresa *p456*
$$$-$$ Pierazzo, Av Getúlio Vargas 115, T3259 1233, www.hotelpierazzo.com.br. Central, nice rooms with frigobar, comfortable, helpful, small pool, sauna. Recommended.

Itaúnus and around: Conceição da Barra *p457*
$$$ Pousada Mirante, Av Atlântica 566, T3762 1633, http://pousadamirante.com.br. With a/c, spotless, English spoken.
$$$ Pousada Porto Márlin, Praia Guaxindiba, T3762 1800, www.redemarlin.com.br. With a/c, fridge, seaview, waterpark, restaurant and bar.

Camping Camping Clube do Brasil, full facilities, Rodovia Adolfo Serra, Km 16, T3762 1346.

🍴 Restaurants

Vitória *p455*

A local speciality is *moqueca capixaba*, a seafood dish served in an earthenware pot. It is a variant of the moqueca which is typical of Bahia. Note that it's big enough for 2 people, but you can get half portions. It is served with rice and *siri desfiado*, crab and shrimp in a thick sauce, very tasty. Several places on R Joaquim Lírio, Praia do Canto, from breads to pastas to seafood. Lots of lanches, etc, on R G Neves at Praça Costa Pereira, in the city centre, and pizzas and others on R 7 de Setembro.

$$$ Pirão, R Joaquim Lírio 753, Praia do Canto. Specializes in *moqueca*, also fish, seafood and a couple of meat dishes. Well-established and rightly highly regarded. Ask for a bib to keep your front clean. Closed in the evening.

$ Restaurante Expresso, G Neves 22, T3223 1091. A better class of self-service for lunch, good choice and puddings, a/c, clean, popular.

Cafés/padarias

Cheiro Verde, R Prof Baltazar, next to Pão Gostoso. *Churrascaria* and *comida caseira*, self-service.

Expressa, as above, next door and open later in afternoon, on G Neves. For good breads, cakes, savouries and cold stuffs.

Pão Gostoso, R Prof Baltazar. Also selling breads, cakes, savouries and cold stuffs.

🍸 Bars and clubs

Vitória *p455*

The junction of Joaquim Lírio and João da Cruz in Praia do Canto is known as O Triângulo. 2 bars at the junction, **Bilac** and **Búfalo Branco** are very popular Fri and Sat with young crowd. Another bar is **Apertura**, J Lírio 811, quieter. All serve food. Many other places in the area. From centre take any bus going to Camburi and get out opposite São José supermarket just before Ponte de Camburi.

🚌 Transport

Vitória *p455*

Air Eurico Salles airport is at Goiaberas, 11 km from the city. Several buses go there eg Nos 162, 163, 122, 212. Taxi from centre US$20.

Bus City buses are mostly green, US$1. No 212 is a good route, from *rodoviária* to airport, marked Aeroporto; make sure it says Via Av Beira Mar: it goes right along the waterfront, past the docks (ask to be let off for Av Princesa Isabel in centre), Shopping Vitória opposite the State Legislative Assembly, by the Third Bridge, São José supermarket just before Ponte de Camburi, all along Camburi beach, then turns left to airport.

To Vila Velha: from Vitória take a yellow 500 bus marked 'Vilha Velha' from Praça Getúlio Vargas, or a 514 from Av Mal Mascarenhas de Moraes. No 508 connects Camburi and Vila Velha. Buses back to Vitória leave from the *rodoviária*, or a stop on Champagnat, almost opposite Carone supermarket, fare US$1. For NS da Penha, ask to be let off the yellow bus into Vila Velha on Av Henrique Moscoso at or near R Antônio Ataíde, which you go down (right from direction of bus) to R Vasco Coutinho then turn right.

The *rodoviária* is a 15-min walk west of the centre; many buses go there and there is a city bus stop just outside. It has good lanches, sweet shops and toilets. **Rio**, 8 hrs, US$40-44. **Belo Horizonte**, see above. **Ouro Preto**, US$33, 7 hrs. **São Paulo**, US$54-80, 16 hrs. **Alvorada** bus from Vitória to **Guarapari**, 1½ hrs, several daily, US$5.

Train Daily passenger service to **Belo Horizonte**, departs 0700, arrives Belo Horizonte at 2010, returns 0730, arrives 2030; US$44 executivo (very comfortable), US$28 econômico. Tickets from **Estrela Loterias**, Av Nossa Senhora da Penha 2150, Loja 28, Supermercado Carrefour, Barro Vermelho, Mon-Fri 0800-1900, www.vale.com. The station is called Pedro Nolasco, Cariacica, Km 1 BR-262: take a yellow bus saying 'Ferroviária', best is No 515 going to Campo Grande; to the city (cross the main road outside the station), Praia do Canto and Camburi, take a 'T Laranjeiras via Beira Mar' bus.

Inland from Vitória: Santa Teresa *p456*
Bus Several buses daily from **Vitória**
rodoviária with **Lirio dos Vales**, US$10, most

go via Fundão on the BR-101 going north, all
paved. Fewer via Santa Leopoldina, not all
paved, a beautiful journey.

North of Belo Horizonte

Diamantina, the most remote of the colonial cities to the north of the State capital is reached from Belo Horizonte by taking the paved road to Brasília (BR-040). Turn northeast to **Curvelo**, beyond which the road passes through the impressive rocky country of the Serra do Espinhaço. Equally remote is the town of Serro, while in the Serra do Espinhaço itself is the Cipó national park, protecting high mountain grassland and rare species.

Diamantina → *Phone code: 038. Post code: 39100. Colour map 7, A5. Population: 44,259.*

This centre of a once-active diamond industry Diamantina has excellent colonial buildings. Its churches are not as grand as those of Ouro Preto, but it is the least spoiled of all the colonial mining cities, with carved overhanging roofs and brackets. This very friendly, beautiful town is in the deep interior, amid barren mountains. It is lively at weekends. **President Juscelino Kubitschek**, the founder of Brasília, was born here. His **house** ① *R São Francisco 241, Tue-Sun 1000-1200, 1400-1800, US$2*, is now a museum. Festivals include Carnival, 12 September, which is O Dia das Serestas, the Day of the Serenades, for which the town is famous; this is also the anniversary of Kubitschek's birth. **Departamento de Turismo** ① *Praça Antônio Eulálio 53, 3rd floor, T3531 1636/9527, www.diamantina. mg.gov.br;* pamphlets, reliable map, friendly and helpful, free tour of churches with guide (tip guide).

Places in Diamantina The oldest church in Diamantina is **Nossa Senhora do Rosário** ① *Largo Dom Joaquim, Tue-Sat 0800-1200, 1400-1800, Sun 0800-1200*, built by slaves in 1728. **Nossa Senhora do Carmo** ① *R do Carmo, Tue-Sat 0800-1200, 1400-1800, Sun 0800-1200*, dates from 1760-1765 and was built for the Carmelite Third Order. It is the richest church in the town, with fine decorations and paintings and a pipe organ, covered in gold leaf, made locally.

São Francisco de Assis ① *R São Francisco, just off Praça JK, Sat 0800-1200, 1400-1800, Sun 0900-1200*, was built between 1766 and the turn of the 19th century. It is notable for its paintings. Other colonial churches are the **Capela Imperial do Amparo** (1758-1776), **Nossa Senhora das Mercês** (1778-1784) and **Nossa Senhora da Luz** (early 19th century). The **Catedral Metropolitana de Santo Antônio**, on Praça Correia Rabelo, was built in the 1930s in neo-colonial style to replace the original cathedral.

After repeated thefts, the diamonds of the **Museu do Diamante** ① *R Direita 14, Tue-Sat 1200-1730, Sun 0900-1200, US$1*, are now kept in the Banco do Brasil. The museum houses an important collection of materials used in the diamond industry, plus oratories and iron collars used to shackle slaves. **Casa de Chica da Silva** ① *Praça Lobo Mesquita 266, Tue-Sat 1200-1730, Sun 0900-1200, free*. Chica da Silva was a slave in the house of the father of Padre Rolim (one of the Inconfidentes). She became the mistress of João Fernandes de Oliveira, a diamond contractor. Chica, who died 15 February 1796, has become a folk-heroine among Brazilian blacks.

Behind the 18th-century building which now houses the **Prefeitura Municipal** (originally the diamonds administration building, Praça Conselheiro Matta 11) is the **Mercado Municipal** or **Mercado dos Tropeiros** (muleteers) ① *Praça Barão de Guaicuí*. The **Casa da Glória** ① *R da Glória 297, Tue-Sun 1300-1700*, is two houses on either side of the street connected by an enclosed bridge. It contains the Instituto Eschwege de Geologia.

Walk along the **Caminho dos Escravos**, the old paved road built by slaves between the mining area on Rio Jequitinhonha and Diamantina. A guide is essential (ask at the Casa de Cultura), and beware of snakes and thunderstorms. Along the river bank it is 12 km on a dirt road to **Biribiri**, a pretty village with a well-preserved church and an abandoned textile factory. It also has a few bars and at weekends it is a popular, noisy place. About halfway, there are swimming pools in the river; opposite them, on a cliff face, are animal paintings in red. The age and origin are unknown. The plant life along the river is interesting and there are beautiful mountain views.

At **São Gonçalo do Rio das Pedras** and **Milo Verde** (35 and 42 km south of Diamantina on an unsealed road), there are trails for hiking and riding, waterfalls and some colonial buildings in the towns. Simple lodging is available.

The sleepy little town of **São Gonçalo do Rio Preto**, which sits next to a beautiful mountain river, is famous for its traditional festivals. It lies some 60 km from Diamantina on the edge of the **Parque Estadual de São Gonçalo do Rio Preto**, an area of pristine *cerrado* filled with flowering trees and particularly rich in birdlife. There are *pousadas* in São Gonçalo and cabins in the park (accessible by taxi). Guides are also available.

Serro → *Phone code: 038. Post code: 39150. Colour map 7, B5. Population: 21,012.*

From Diamantina, 92 km by paved road and reached by bus from there or from Belo Horizonte, is this unspoiled colonial town on the Rio Jequitinhonha. It has six fine baroque churches, a museum and many beautiful squares. It makes queijo serrano, one of Brazil's best cheeses, being in the centre of a prosperous cattle region. The most conspicuous church is **Santa Rita** on a hill in the centre of town, reached by a long line of steps. On the main Praça João Pinheiro, by the bottom of the steps, is **Nossa Senhora do Carmo**, arcaded, with original paintings on the ceiling and in the choir. The town has two large mansions: those of the **Barão de Diamantina** ① *Praça Presidente Vargas*, now in ruins, and of the **Barão do Serro** ① *across the river on R da Fundição, Tue-Sat 1200-1700, Sun 0900-1200*, beautifully restored and used as the town hall and Casa de Cultura. The **Museu Regional Casa dos Ottoni** ① *Praça Cristiano Ottoni 72*, is an 18th-century house with furniture and objects from the region. There are hotels in town.

Parque Nacional da Serra do Cipó

① *Entry US$1.50, 0800-1700, headquarters in Jaboticatubas, T031-3718 7151, www.icmbio.gov.br; www.guiaserradocipo.com.br.*

About 105 km northeast of Belo Horizonte, **Parque Nacional da Serra do Cipó**, 33,400 sq km of the Serra do Espinhaço, covers important cerrado and gallery forest habitats, which provide a home for rare bird species like the Cipó Canastero and Grey-backed Tachuri, as well as endangered mammals such as maned wolf and monkeys such as the masked titi and brown capuchin. There are a number of carnivorous plants. The predominant habitat is high mountain grassland, with rocky outcroppings. As infrastructure in the park is not fully developed, ICMBio recommend employing a local guide.

◉ North of Belo Horizonte listings

For hotel and restaurant price codes, and other relevant information, see Essentials.

◉ Where to stay

Diamantina *p459*
All are within 10 mins' walking distance of the centre unless otherwise stated.

$$$ Pousada do Garimpo, Av da Saudade 265, T3532 1040, www.pousadadogarimpo. com.br. Plain, well-kept rooms in a smart hotel on the outskirts, pool, sauna, restaurant serving some of the city's best Minas cooking.
$$$ Relíquias do Tempo, R Macau de Baixo 104, T3531 1627, www.pousadareliquias dotempo. com.br. Cosy rooms in a pretty 19th-

century house just off Praça JK, decorated like a colonial family home, generous breakfasts.
$$$ Tijuco, R Macau do Melo 211, T3531 1022, www.hoteltijuco.com.br. A deliciously dated Niemeyer building with tastefully renovated plush wood interior and rooms which retain their 60s feel, great views.
$$$-$$ Montanhas de Minas, R da Roman 264, T3531 3240, www.grupomontanhasde minas.com.br. Spacious rooms with stone floors, some with balconies, decent breakfasts.
$$ Pousada Ouro de Minas, R do Amparo 90A, T3531 2306, www.grupomontanhas deminas.com.br. Simple well-kept rooms with tiny bathrooms in a converted colonial house. In the same group is Pousada Acayaca, R Acaiaca 65.
$$ Santiago, Largo Dom João 133, T3531 3407. Next to municipal bus station, plain, small but tidy rooms, reasonable breakfast.

Parque Nacional da Serra do Cipó *p460*
$$$$ Cipó Veraneio, Rodovia MG-10, Km 95, Jaboticatubas, T3718 7000, www. cipoveraneiohotel.com.br. Comfortable a/c rooms with cable TV, fridge, in terraces of stone cabins, pool, sauna, very good tour operator and a *cachaça* distillery just up the road which produces some of Minas's finest.

🍴 Restaurants

Diamantina *p459*
$$$ Cantina do Marinho, R Direita 113, T3531 1686. Formal, decorated with bottles of wine, black-tie waiters. Good value set lunch.
$$ Caipirão, R Campos Carvalho 15, T3531 1526. Minas cooking with buffet lunch cooked over a traditional wood-fired clay oven, evening à la carte.
$$ Grupiara, R Campos Carvalho 12, T3531 3887. Decent regional cooking, convivial atmosphere, good value per kilo options at lunch.

$$ Recanto do Antônio, Beco da Tecla 39, T3531 1147. Minas food and decent steaks, chic rustic dining room in a colonial house.
$ Sisisi, Beco da Mota 89, T3531 3071. Pasta, Minas cooking and good value *prato feito* at lunchtime.

🍸 Bars and clubs

Diamantina *p459*
Apocalipse Point, Praça Barão de Guaicuí 78, T3531 9296. Sertaneja and Axe music. Lively.
Café a Baiuca, R da Quitanda. Coffee bar by day, funky bar by night with music DVDs and a crowd spilling out into the street.
Espaço B, R Beco da Tecla. A bookshop café serving crêpes and draught beer until late.

⚙ Festivals

Diamantina *p459*
Vesperatas, musicians and singers serenade from balconies along the colonial streets and drum troupes and bands parade every other Sat.

🚌 Transport

Diamantina *p459*
Bus To **São Gonçalo do Rio Preto**, one bus per day. 8 buses a day to **Belo Horizonte**, via Curvelo, with **Pássaro Verde**: 2½ hrs to **Curvelo**, US$16.50, to **Belo Horizonte**, US$37, 5 hrs. To **Bahia**, 2 buses to **Araçuaí** per day (4 hrs); from here combis and buses run to **Itaubim** from where there are connections to Porto Seguro and other destinations in Bahia. For **Brasília**: connect in **Curvelo** to **Montes Claros** (2 a day, US$16), then make connections onwards.

Parque Nacional da Serra do Cipó *p460*
Bus Take bus to Serro (2 daily) for Santa Ana do Riacho and the Serra do Cipó.

Southern Brazil

Southern Brazil comprises three states: Paraná, Santa Catarina and Rio Grande do Sul. Paraná has one of the premier tourist sites in South America, the Iguaçu Falls, described in its own section (see page 491). The Paraná coastline, albeit short, has a large area of coastal rainforest and little beach-fringed islands, like Ilha do Mel. Its main port, Paranaguá, is connected with the capital, Curitiba, by one of the most impressive railways in South America. It is the coast, however, from which Santa Catarina gains most of its reputation, with highly regarded surfing beaches and a growing interest in whale watching. Inland, the state has a distinctive European feel, including frosty and snowy winters in the highest parts. The culture of the region has been heavily influenced by large immigrant communities from Japan, Germany, Poland, Italy, Syria and Ukraine. In Rio Grande do Sul this can be seen (and tasted) in the Italian communities, well known for their wines. The southernmost state, as well as having yet more beaches, has some beautiful national parks, the remnants of Jesuit missions and the south's largest industrial centre, Porto Alegre. But above all, this is the land of the gaúcho, the Brazilian cowboy.

Curitiba

Where to stay
1 Bourbon Batel Express
2 Bourbon Curitiba
3 Curitiba Eco Hostel
4 Del Rey
5 Deville Rayon
6 Estação Palace
7 Hostel Roma
9 O'Hara

Restaurants
1 Bar do Victor
2 Durski
3 Jardins Grill
4 Madalosso
5 Porcini Trattoria
6 Salmão
7 Trattoria Barolo

Situated in the Serra do Mar, Curitiba is regarded as one of Brazil's model cities for quality of life. It has something of a European feel, with leafy squares and a street that is open 24 hours. It makes a pleasant base for exploring the coast and the surrounding mountains, and is the start of one of the world's most spectacular railway journeys.

Arriving in Curitiba

Tourist offices Setu ① *R Deputado Mário de Barros 1290, Centro Cívico, T3313 3500, www.turismo.pr.gov.br.* Municipal office at ① *R da Glória 362, Centro Cívico, T3250 7729, Mon-Fri 0800-1200, 1400-1800.* **Disque Turismo** ① *T3254 1516 (state), T3352 8000 (city); also booth at the Rodoferroviária (T3320 3121, 0800-1800).* **Kiosks** at ① *Palacete Wolf and cultural centre, Praça Garibaldi 7, T3321 3206, and Torre Panorâmica Brasil Telecom, R Professor Lycio de Castro Vellozo 191, T3339 7613.* ➤➤ *See Transport, page 466, for the city's integrated transport system.*

Teatro Guaíra
R Benjamin Constant
R Cons Macedo
Itararé
R Nilo Cairo
R Tibagi
R Conselheiro Laurindo
R João Negrão
Guarapuava
R Gen Carneiro
Jf Faivre
R Francisco Torres
R Mariano Torres
To Paranaguá
To Jardim Botânico Fanchette Rischbieter
Wholesale
Av 7 de Setembro
Av Pres A Camargo
Rodoferroviária
To ⑦ & Shopping Curitiba

Places in and around Curitiba

One of the cleanest cities in Latin America, the capital of Paraná state has extensive open spaces and some exceptionally attractive modern architecture. The commercial centre is the busy Rua 15 de Novembro, part of which is a pedestrian area called **Rua das Flores**. The **Boca Maldita** is a particularly lively part where local artists exhibit. On Praça Tiradentes is the **Cathedral** ① *R Barão do Serro Azul 31, T3324 5136*, built in neo-Gothic style and inaugurated in 1893 (restored in 1993). Behind the cathedral, near Largo da Ordem, is a pedestrian area with a flower clock and old buildings, very beautiful in the evening when the old lamps are lit; nightlife is concentrated here. The oldest church in Curitiba is the **Igreja de Ordem Terceira da São Francisco das Chagas**, built in 1737 in Largo da Ordem. Its most recent renovation was in 1978-1980. In its annex is the **Museu de Arte Sacra** ① *T3321 3265.* The **Igreja de Nossa Senhora do Rosário de São Benedito** was built in the Praça Garibáldi in 1737 by slaves and was the Igreja dos Pretos de São Benedito. It was demolished in 1931 and a new church was inaugurated in 1946. A mass for tourists, Missa do Turista, is held on Sunday at 0800.

Museu Paranaense ① *in the Palácio São Francisco, R Kellers 289, T3304 3300, www. museupr.pr.gov.br, Tue-Fri 0900-1800, Sat-Sun 1000-1600, US$1*, holds permanent and temporary exhibitions, including documents, manuscripts, ethnological and historical material, stamps, works of art, photographs and archaeological pieces. **Museu de Arte Contemporânea** ① *R Desembargador Westphalen 16, Praça Zacarias, T3222 5172, Tue-Fri 1000-1900, Sat-Sun 1000-1600*, displays Brazilian contemporary art in its many forms, with an emphasis on artists from Paraná.

North of the centre, the **Solar do Barão** ① *R Presidente Carlos Cavalcanti 53, T3321 3240*, built in 1880-1883, is used for concerts in the auditorium and exhibitions. The **Passeio Público**, in the heart of the city (closed Monday), inaugurated in 1886. It has three lakes, each with an island, and playground. The **Centro Cívico** is at the end of Avenida Dr Cândido de Abreu, 2 km from the centre: a monumental group of buildings dominated by the **Palácio Iguaçu**, headquarters of the state and municipal governments. In a patio behind it is a relief map to scale of Paraná. The **Bosque de João Paulo II** behind the Civic Centre on Rua Mateus Leme, was created in December 1980 after the Pope's visit to Curitiba. It also contains the **Memorial da Imigração Polonesa no Paraná** (Polish immigrants memorial). The **Museu Oscar Niemeyer (MON)** ① *R Mal Hermes 999, T3350 4400, www. museuoscarniemeyer.org.br, Tue-Sun 1000-1800, US$3*, was designed by, and is devoted to the famous Brazilian modernist architect who designed Brasília and was a disciple of Le Corbusier (he died in 2012), together with other Paranense artists. The stunning principal building is shaped like a giant eye. An underground passage, lined with exhibits and photographs, links it to a sculpture garden.

Close to the rodoferroviária is the market, where there are a couple of lanchonetes. **Shopping Estação** ① *Av 7 de Setembro 2775*, in the old railway station, has a railway museum and exhibitions on perfume and Brazil's natural environments, as well as shops and restaurants, etc. About 4 km east of the rodoferroviário, the **Jardim Botânico Fanchette Rischbieter** has a fine glass house, inspired by Crystal Palace in London. The gardens are in the French style and there is also a **Museu Botânico** ① *R Ostoja Roguski (Primeira Perimetral dos Bairros), T3362 1800 (museum), 0600-2000*. Take the orange Expreso buses from Praça Rui Barbosa.

Parque Nacional Vila Velha → *Colour map 7, C2.*

① *The park office (phone, toilets, lanchonete, tourist information) is 300 m from the highway and the park a further 1½ km (entrance US$3.50, 0800-1900). Allow all day if visiting all 3 sites (unless you hitch, or can time the buses well, it's a lot of walking).*

West of Curitiba on the road to Ponta Grossa is the **Museu Histórico do Mate** ① *T3555 1939, free, BR 277 at Km 17, www.museuparanaense.pr.gov.br*, an old water-driven mill where mate was prepared. On the same road is Vila Velha, 91 km from Curitiba: the sandstone rocks have been weathered into most fantastic shapes. About 4 km away are the **Furnas** ① *US$2*, three water holes, the deepest of which has a lift (US$1.30 – not always working) which descends almost to water level. Also in the park is the Lagoa Dourada (surrounded by forest) whose water level is the same as that in the Furnas.

⊙ Curitiba and around listings

For hotel and restaurant price codes, and other relevant information, see Essentials. For important phone changes, see Telephone, page 361.

⊙ Where to stay

Curitiba *p463, map p462*
There are good hotels southeast of the centre in the vicinity of the Rodoferroviária, but the

cheaper ones are close to the wholesale market, which operates noisily through the night.
$$$$ Bourbon Curitiba, R Cândido Lopes 102, T3221 4600, www.bourbon.com.br. Good modern hotel in the centre with a mock old-fashioned charm, rooms have jacuzzis, business centre.
$$$$ Deville Rayon, R Visconde de Nácar 1424, T2108 1100, www.deville.com.br. Central, much the best option for business travellers

with all the expected services, pool, saunas, well-equipped gym and travel agency.

$$$ Bourbon Batel Express, Av Visconde de Guarapuava 4889, T3342 7990, www.bourbon.com.br. Modern and comfortable, good breakfast, Wi-Fi in rooms US$3 per day, attentive service, good value.

$$$ Del Rey, R Ermelino de Leão 18, T2106 0099, www.hoteldelrey.com.br. Central, upmarket yet relaxed, large rooms, good restaurant, gym, good value. Recommended.

$$$-$$ O'Hara, R 15 de Novembro 770, T3778 6044, www.hotelohara.com.br. Good location, fan, excellent breakfast, parking.

$$ Curitiba Eco Hostel, R Luiz Tramontin 1693, Campo Comprido, T3274 7979, www.curitibaecohostel.com.br. Cheaper for HI members, the youth hostel association for Paraná is in this suburb – catch a bus from the *rodoviária* to Praça Rui Barbosa, marked Expreso Centenário, then change to a Tramontina bus to the door.

$$ Estação Palace, R Des Westphalen 126, T3322 9840, www.hotel-curitiba.com.br/estacao. Excellent for price, 24-hr room service, rather stark but immaculate. Recommended.

$ pp Hostel Roma, R Barão do Rio Branco 805, T3322 2838, www.hostelroma.com.br. Smart HI hostel with single-sex dorms, also family rooms (**$$**), TV room, members' kitchen.

Camping Camping Clube do Brasil, BR-116, Km 84, 16 km towards São Paulo, T358 6634.

🍴 Restaurants

Curitiba *p463, map p462*
The shopping malls have good food courts, eg include Shopping Crystal Plaza, R Com Araújo, Batel, Shopping Curitiba, R Brig Franco at Praça Osvaldo Cruz, and largest of all, Barigüi, R Prof Pedro Viriato Parigot de Souza 600, Ecoville. Hot sweet wine sold on the streets in winter helps keep out the cold.

$$$ Bar do Victor, R Lívio Moreira 284, São Lourenço, T3353 1920. Tue-Sat 1200-1450, 1830-2330, Sun 1130-1430. Excellent fish restaurant.

$$$ Durski, R Jaime Reis 254, T3225 7893. Open 1930-2300, closed Tue, Sat 1200-1600,

1930-2300, Sun 1200-1600. Good variety of Eastern European cuisine, with top quality.

$$$ Jardins Grill, Av Silva Jardim 1477 e Lamenha Lins, Rebouças, T3232 4717, www.jardinsgrill.com.br. Very good for, meats, salad and sushi buffets and pastas.

$$$ Madalosso, Av Manoel Ribas 5875, Santa Felicidade, T3372 2121. Closed Sun evening. The largest Italian *rodízio* in Brazil, 4600 seats!

$$$ Porcini Trattoria, R Buenos Aires 277, Batel, T3022 5115, www.porcini.com.br. Open daily for lunch and dinner, except Mon lunch. Mainly Italian food, good salads and vegetables, superb quality, fantastic wine list Recommended.

$$$ Terra Madre Ristorante, R Des Otávio do Amaral 515, Bigorrilho, T3335 6070, www.terramaderistorante.com.br. Superb Italian cuisine at better prices than others in its category. Also run a wine store.

$$$ Trattoria Barolo, Av Silva Jardim 2487, Água Verde, T3243 3430. Closed Sun evening. Excellent Italian for fish and meat dishes and pizza, huge wine list, good prices.

$$ Salmão, R Emiliano Perneta 924. Open until 0100. In historic house, delicious fish and pizza, special offers, live music every night. Short taxi ride from centre.

🍸 Bars and clubs

Curitiba *p463, map p462*
A cluster of bars at the Largo da Ordem have tables and chairs on the pavement, music, and bar food, while Av do Batel (or Batel district) has good bars and restaurants.

🎭 Entertainment

Curitiba *p463, map p462*
Look in the newspaper for music and what's on in the bars, clubs and theatres; Gazeta do Povo has a what's on section called *Caderno G*, www.gazetadopovo.com.br/cadernog.

Theatres Theatre festival in Mar. Teatro Guaíra, R 15 de Novembro, T3304 7999, www.tguaira.pr.gov.br. For plays and revues (also has free events – get tickets early in the day).

Teatro Positivo, R Prof Pedro Viriato Parigot de Souza 5300, Campo Comprido, T3317 3000, www.teatropositivo.com.br. An impressive theatre attracting international and Brazilian stars, on the magnificent campus of the Universidade Positivo, www.up.edu.br. Good exhibitions are held here, too (bus lines Linha Expresso Centenário and Linha Ligeirinho Pinhais from centre).

O Shopping

Curitiba *p463, map p462*
Handicrafts Feira de Arte e Artesanato, Praça Garibáldi, Sun 0900-1400.
Lojas de Artesanato, Casa de Artesanato Centro, R Mateus Leme 22, T3352 4021.

O Transport

Curitiba *p463, map p462*
Air Afonso Pena (21 km away) for international and national flights, T3381 1515, www.aeroportocuritiba.net; good services: ATMs, left luggage, hotel booking desk, and cafés. Daily flights from Rio, São Paulo, Buenos Aires, Asunción, and cities in the interior of Paraná state. 2 types of bus run from the Rodoferroviária to the airport, making several stops: Aeroporto Executivo, www. aeroportoexecutivo.com.br, daily 0500-2330, 20 mins, US$6; regular city bus, 40 mins, US$2.
Bus There are several route types on the integrated transport system and you are advised to pick up a map with details. **Express** are red and connect the transfer terminals to the city centre, pre-paid access through the silver 'tubo' bus stops; conventional orange **Feeder** buses connect the terminals to the surrounding neighbourhoods; **Interdistrict** green buses run on circular routes connecting transfer terminals and city districts without passing through the centre; **Direct or speedy** silver grey buses use the 'tubo' stations to link the main districts and connect the surrounding municipalities with Curitiba; **Conventional** yellow buses operate on the normal road network between the surrounding municipalities, the Integration Terminals and the city centre; **City circular** white mini buses, **Linha Turismo**, circle the major transport terminals and points of interest in the traditional city centre area. US$16 (multi-ticket booklets available), every 30 mins from 0900-1700, except on Mon. First leaves from R das Flores, in front of McDonald's. 5 stops allowed.

Short-distance bus services within the metropolitan region (up to 40 km) begin at Terminal Guadalupe at R João Negrão s/n. The Terminal Rodoviário/Estação Rodoferroviária is on Av Afonso Camargo s/n, T3320 3000, for other cities in Paraná and other states. Banks, restaurants, bookshops, shops, phones, postoffice, pharmacy, tourist agency, tourist office and public services are all here. Frequent buses to **São Paulo** (6 hrs, US$35-65) and **Rio** (12 hrs, US$68-85, leito 100). To **Foz do Iguaçu**, 8 a day, 10 hrs, US$62, leito 113. **Porto Alegre**, 10 hrs, US$52-56, leito 82. **Florianópolis**, US$25-35, 4½ hrs; **Blumenau** 4 hrs, US$18; 8 daily with **Catarinense**. Good service to most destinations in Brazil. International services to **Buenos Aires** (change buses at Foz do Iguaçu), **Asunción** and **Montevideo**, not daily.
Train Rodoferroviária, Av Affonso Camargo s/n. There are 2 trains running on the line from Curitiba to **Morretes** and **Paranaguá**: the **Litorina**, a modern a/c railcar with on-board service with bilingual staff, which stops at Morretes, with a halt at Marumbi Park station; hand luggage only; weekends only; tickets can be bought 2 days in advance; departs 0915 Sat and holidays, 0730 on Sun, US$135 to Morretes, 3 hrs. On Sun a **Litorina** runs to Paranaguá, 0730, US$42. Also the **Trem Classe Convencional**, which runs daily to Morretes, with a stop at Marumbi, buy tickets 2 days in advance, departs daily 0815, returns 1500: turístico, US$42 (US$33 back), executivo US$62 (US$43 back), a US$33/US$23 econômico fare is available from the ticket office only, best bought 2 weeks in advance. Schedules change frequently; check times in advance; delays to be expected. For information and reservations, **Serra Verde Express**, T3888 3488,

www.serraverde express.com.br. Tickets sold at the Rodoferro viária, Portão 8, 0700-1830 (till 1200 on Sun). Sit on the left-hand side on journey from Curitiba. On cloudy days there's little to see on the higher parts. The train is usually crowded on Sat and Sun. Serra Verde Express also gives information about trips by car on the Estrada de Graciosa and sells various packages to the coast.

Parque Nacional Vila Velha *p464*
Bus Take a bus from **Curitiba** to the park, not to the town of Ponta Grossa 26 km away. Princesa dos Campos bus from Curitiba 0745, 1415, 1715, 1½ hrs, US$13. One bus from Vila Velha between 1530-1600, US$1.10, 4½ km to turn-off to Furnas (another 15 mins' walk) and Lagoa Dourada. Bus Mon-Sat 1330 to **Furnas** –

Ponta Grossa that passes the car park at the top of the park. On Sun, 1200,1620,1800. It may be advisable to go to Ponta Grossa and return to Curitiba from there (114 km, many buses a day, US$14, **Princesa dos Campos**, www.princesadoscampos.com.br.

❶ Directory

Curitiba *p463, map p462*
Consulates Uruguay, Av Carlos Cavalho 417, sala 3101 A, T3225 5550.
Medical services Emergency: T190 for Police and T193 for ambulance or fire. The Cajuru Hospital is at Av São José 738, T3362 1121, and the Evangélico is at Al Augusto Stellfeld 1908, T3322 4141, both of which deal with emergencies.

The Paraná coast

The railway to the coast winds its way around the slopes of the Marumbi mountain range, across rushing rivers and through the forest to the sea. There are pretty colonial towns en route. The coast itself only has a few beaches, but in compensation has some of the richest biodiversity in Brazil.

Curitiba to Paranaguá

Two roads and a railway run from Curitiba to Paranaguá. The railway journey is the most spectacular in Brazil. There are 13 tunnels and sudden views of deep gorges and high peaks and waterfalls as the train rumbles over dizzy bridges and viaducts. Near Banhado station (Km 66) is the waterfall of Véu da Noiva; from the station at Km 59, the mountain range of **Marumbi** can be reached. See page 466 for schedules and fares. Of the roads, the older, cobbled Estrada da Graçiosa, with numerous viewpoints and tourist kiosks along the way, is much more scenic than the paved BR277.

Parque Nacional Marumbi

Marumbi Park is a large area of preserved Atlantic rainforest and is a UNESCO World Heritage Site and Biosphere Reserve. The forest in the 2343-ha park is covered in banana trees, palmito and orchids. There are rivers and waterfalls and among the fauna are monkeys, snakes and toucans. A climbing trail reaches 625 m to Rochedinho (two hours). Hands need to be free to grasp trees, especially during the rainy season (December to March), when trails are muddy. The last five minutes of the trail is a dangerous walk along a narrow rock trail. At the park entrance, notify administration of your arrival and departure. There is a small museum, video, left luggage and the base for a search and rescue unit at weekends. Volunteer guides are available at weekends. Wooden houses can be rented for US$55 a night; take torch. Camping is free. To get there take the train from Curitiba at 0815, arriving Marumbi at 1020. Return at 1540 to Curitiba. If continuing the next day to Morretes your Curitiba-Marumbi ticket is valid for the onward journey.

Morretes → *Colour map 7, C3. www.morretes.com.br.*

Morretes, founded in 1721, is one of the prettiest colonial towns in southern Brazil. Whitewashed colonial buildings with painted window frames straddle the pebbly river and church spires stick up from a sea of red tiled roofs against the backdrop of forested hills. The Estrada da Graciosa road passes through Morretes and the train stops here too. Most of the numerous restaurants serve the local speciality, Barreado, a meat stew cooked in a clay pot – originally a day in advance of Carnaval in order to allow women to escape from their domestic chores and enjoy the party. There are a handful of *pousadas* too and a series of walks into the mountains. **Antonina**, 14 km from Morretes is as picturesque, less touristy, and sits on the Baía do Paranaguá. It can be reached by local bus from Morretes.

Paranaguá → *Phone code: 041. Colour map 7, C3. Population: 128,000.*

In the centre of Paranaguá colonial buildings decay in the heat and humidity; some are just façades encrusted with bromeliads. The **Museu de Arqueologia e Etnologia** ① *R 15 Novembro 575, T041-3721 1200, www.proec.ufpr.br, Tue-Fri 0900-1200, 1330-1800, Sat-Sun 1200-1800, US$1,* is housed in a formidable 18th-century Jesuit convent. Other attractions are a 17th-century fountain, the church of **São Benedito**, and the shrine of **Nossa Senhora do Rocio**, 2 km from town. **Tourist information** ① *Av Arthur de Abreu 44, next to station, T3420 2940, www.fumtur. com.br.* Boat schedules, toilet, and left-luggage available.

The Paranaguá region was an important centre of indigenous life. Colossal shell middens, called **Sambaquis**, some as high as a two-storey building, protecting regally adorned corpses, have been found on the surrounding estuaries. They date from between 7000 (possibly earlier) and 2000 years ago, built by the ancestors of the Tupinguin and Carijo people who encountered the first Europeans to arrive here. The Spanish and Portuguese disputed the bay and islands when gold was found in the late 16th century. More important is the area's claim to be one of Latin America's biodiversity hotspots and the best place on the Brazilian coast to see rare rainforest flora and fauna. Mangrove and lowland subtropical forests, islands, rivers and rivulets here form the largest stretch of Atlantic coast rainforest in the country and protect critically endangered species (see below). Most of the bay is protected by a series of national and state parks, but it is possible to visit on an organized tour from Paranaguá. The **Barcopar** cooperative ① *access from Praça 29 de Julho (Palco Tutóia), T3425 4325,* offers a range of excellent trips in large and small vessels ranging from two hours to two days, US$20 per person to US$100.

At the mouth of the Baia de Guaratuba are two towns connected by ferry, **Caiobá** on the north shore (50 km from Paranaguá) and **Guaratuba** on the south. A few km north of Caiobá is **Matinhos**, a popular beach resort, especially in October when Paraná's surf championships are held here. A recommended restaurant here is **La Bodeguita**, Av Paranaguá, Betaras, T3452 6606, mainly fish, huge helpings.

Ilha do Mel

① *Limit of 5,000 visitors a day. An entrance fee is included in the boat fare (see Transport, below); foreigners must show passport and fill in a form before boarding the boat.*

Ilha do Mel sits in the mouth of the Baía de Paranaguá and was of strategic use in the 18th century. On this popular weekend escape and holiday island there are no roads, no vehicles, limited electricity, no banks or ATMs, and no chemists. Outside of Carnaval and New Year it is a laid back little place. Bars play Bob Marley and Maranhão reggae; surfers lounge around in hammocks and barefooted couples dance forró on the wooden floors of simple beachside shacks. Much of the island is forested, its coastline is fringed with broad beaches, broken in the south by rocky headlands.

The rugged eastern half, where most of the facilities are to be found is fringed with curving beaches and capped with a lighthouse, Farol das Conchas, built in 1872 to guide shipping into the bay. The flat, scrub forest-covered western half is predominantly an ecological protection area, its northern side watched over by the Fortaleza Nossa Senhora dos Prazeres, built in 1767 on the orders of King José I of Portugal, to defend what was one of the principal ports in the country. The best surf beaches are Praia Grande and Praia de Fora. Both are about 20 minutes' walk from the Nova Brasilia jetty. Fortaleza and Ponta do Bicho on the north shore are more tranquil and are safe for swimming. They are about 45 minutes' walk from the jetty or five minutes by boat. Farol and Encantadas are the liveliest and have the bulk of the accommodation, restaurants and nightlife. A series of well-signposted trails, from 20 minutes to three hours, cover the island and its coast. It is also possible to take a long day walking around the entire island, but the stretch along the southern shore between Encantadas and Nova Brasilia has to be done by boat. For information see www. ilhadomel.net.

Superagüi National Park

The island of Superagüi and its neighbour, Peças, are the focus for the Guaraqueçaba Environmental Protection Area. They also form a national park and UNESCO World Heritage Site. Access to the park and accommodation can be arranged through the village on Superagüi beach, just north of Ilha do Mel. Many endangered endemic plants and animals live in the park, including hundreds of endemic orchids, Atlantic rainforest specific animals like brown howler monkeys and large colonies of red-tailed Amazons (a parrot on the red list of critically endangered species and which can be seen nowhere else). There are also jaguarundi, puma and jaguar. The *indígena* village is one of several Guarani villages in the area; other inhabitants are mostly of European descent, living off fishing. There is superb swimming from deserted beaches, but watch out for stinging jelly fish. Contact **ICMBio** ⓘ *R Paula de Miranda s/n, Guaraqueçaba, T041-3482 7146, www.icmbio.gov.br,* for information.

ⓔ The Paraná coast listings

For hotel and restaurant price codes, and other relevant information, see Essentials. For important phone changes, see Telephone, page 361.

ⓔ Where to stay

Morretes *p468*
$$$ Hotel Nhundiaquara, R General Carneiro 13, T3462 1228; www.nundiaquara.com.br. Smart, beautifully set on the river, excellent restaurant but small, plain rooms.
$$$ Pousada Cidreira, R Romulo Pereira 61, T3462 1604, www.pousadacidreira.com.br. Central, plain tiled rooms, TV, most with balcony.
$$$ Pousada Graciosa, Estrada da Graciosa Km 8 (Porto da Cima village), T3462 1807, www.pousadagraciosa.com. Much the best in the area; some 10 km north of Morretes with

simple but comfortable wooden chalets set in rainforest. Promotes cycling tours. No children under 12.

Paranaguá *p468*
$$$ Camboa, R João Estevão (Ponta do Caju), T3420 5200, www.hotelcamboa. com.br. Full- or half-board available. Family resort, tennis courts, large pool, saunas, trampolines, restaurant, out of town near the port. Book ahead. Also has **$$$ Camboa Capela**, in an 18th-century house in Antonina, T3432 3267, same website.
$$$ San Rafael, R Julia Costa 185, T3423 2123, www.sanrafaelhotel.com.br. Business hotel with plain rooms, restaurants, pool and jacuzzis.
$$ Ponderosa, R Pricilenco Corea 68 at 15 Novembro, T3423 2464. A block east and

north of the boat dock, some rooms with a view, basic.

$$ Pousada Itiberê, R Princesa Isabel 24, T3423 2485, www.ilhadomelpreserve.net/itibere.htm. Very smart spartan rooms, some with sea views, helpful service, shared bath, 3 blocks east of the boat dock.

Ilha do Mel *p468*

All rooms are fan cooled unless otherwise stated.

$$$$ Astral da Ilha, Praia da Fora, T3426 8916, www.astraldailha.com.br. Themed suites and chalets (some suites **$$$** in low season) 30 m from beach, with a/c, mezzanine, solar-heated water, gardens, restaurant, excursions by boat and bike.

$$$$-$$$ Pôr do Sol, Nova Brasilia, T3426 8009, www.pousadapordosol.com.br. Simple, elegant rooms around a shady garden, large deck with cabins and hammocks by the beach. Breakfast.

$$$ Aconchego, Nova Brasilia, T3426 8030, www.cwb.matrix.com.br/daconchego. Very clean, beachside deck with hammocks, TV and breakfast area, charming. Includes breakfast. **$$** low season.

$$$ Enseada das Conchas, Farol, T3426 8040, www.pousadaenseada.com.br. 4 en suite rooms with TVs and fridge, charmingly decorated. Lots of rescued cats.

$$$ Long Beach, Praia Grande, T3426 8116, LongBeachIlhaDoMel on Facebook. Best on the beach, chalets for up to 6, very popular with surfers. Book ahead.

$$$-$$ D'Lua, Farol, T3426 8031, www.pousadalua.com.br. Another feline-friendly place, basic and hippy with a helpful owner, Maria José (cheaper in low season).

$$$-$$ Plancton, Farol at Fora, T3426 8061, www.pousadaplancton.com.br. A range of wooden buildings in a hummingbird-filled garden, cheaper with shared bath, fresh atmosphere, Italian food in high season.

$$$-$$ Recanto do Frances, Encantadas, T3426 9105, www.recantodofrances.com.br. Full of character, with each chalet built in a different style to represent a different French

city. 5 mins from Prainha or Encantadas. Good crêpe restaurant. Recommended.

$$ Recanto da Fortaleza, Ponta do Bicho, T3426 8000, www.pousadarecantodafortaleza.com.br. The best of the 2 next to the Fort, basic cabins, free pick-up by boat from Nova Brasilia (ring ahead), bike rental. Price includes breakfast and dinner.

Camping There are mini campsites with facilities at Encantadas, Farol and Brasília. Camping is possible on the more deserted beaches (good for surfing). If camping, watch out for the tide, watch possessions and beware of the *bicho de pé* which burrows into feet (remove with a needle and alcohol) and the *borrachudos* (discourage with repellent).

❼ Restaurants

Morretes *p468*

$$$ Armazém Romanus, R Visc Do Rio Branco 141. Family-run restaurant with the best menu and wine list in the region, dishes from home-grown ingredients, including *barreado* and desserts.

$$ Terra Nossa, R 15 de Novembro 109. *Barreado*, pasta, pizzas and fish, generous portions.

$ Madalozo, R Alm Frederico de Oliveira 16, overlooking the river. Good *barreado*, generous salads.

Ilha do Mel *p468*

Many *pousadas* serve food, some only in season (Christmas-Carnaval). Many have live music or dancing (especially in high season) after 2200.

$$ Fim da trilha, Prainha (Fora de Encantadas), T3426 9017. Spanish seafood restaurant, one of the best on the island. Also has a *pousada*.

$ Colmeia, Farol. Seafood, snacks, crêpes, juices and good cakes and puddings. Also has a *pousada*, www.pousadacolmeia.com.br.

$ Mar e Sol, Farol. Huge portions of fish, chicken with chips and rice and a small selection of more adventurous dishes.

$ Toca do Abutre, Farol. Live music and huge plates of fish or chicken with rice, beans and chips.

⊖ Transport

Ilha do Mel *p468*

Ferry By ferry from Paranaguá to **Encantadas** and **Brasília**, at 0930 and 1530 (1400 Sat-Sun) with **Abaline**, T3425 6325/2616, 1 hr 40 mins, US$8 each way, boats leave from R Gen Carneiro (R da Praia). Also ferry from Pontal do Paraná/Pontal do Sul, T3455 1144, daily from 0800 to 1800 (1900 Fri-Sat) every hr, every 30 mins Sat-Sun, US$13.50 return. From **Paranaguá**, take the **bus** to Pontal do Sul (many daily, 1½ hrs, US$2). There are handicraft stalls at the ferry point. The last bus back to Paranaguá leaves at 2200.

Superagüi National Park *p469*

Ferry To/from **Paranaguá** Mon, Thu, Fri leaving **Superagüi** 0700, returning from Paranaguá 1430, more frequent at holiday times, 2½-3½ hrs, US$15 one way, T3482 7150, or T3482 7131. Boats sail daily Paranaguá–Guaraqueçaba, 2½-3 hrs, then take another boat to Superagüi on Mon, Thu or Fri, 2½-3 hrs. The road Paranaguá-Guaraqueçaba is unmade.

Santa Catarina

Famous for its beaches and popular with Argentine and Paraguayan holidaymakers in high summer, this is one of the best stretches of Brazilian coast for surfing, attracting 1½ million visitors to the 170 beaches just in the summer months of January and February. For the rest of the year they are pleasant and uncrowded. Immigrant communities, such as the German, give a unique personality to many towns and districts with the familiar European pattern of mixed farming. Rural tourism is important and the highlands, which are 100 km from the coast, are among the coldest in Brazil, giving winter landscapes reminiscent of Europe, or Brazil's southern neighbours.

Florianópolis → *Phone code: 048. Colour map 7, C3. Population: 345,000.*

Halfway along the coast of Santa Catarina is the state capital and port of Florianópolis, founded in 1726 on the Ilha de Santa Catarina. The island is joined to the mainland by two bridges, one of which is Ponte Hercílio Luz, the longest steel suspension bridge in Brazil (closed for repairs). The newer Colombo Machado Salles bridge has a pedestrian and cycle way beneath the roadway. The natural beauty of the island, beaches and bays make Florianópolis a magnet for holidaymakers in summer. The southern beaches are usually good for swimming, the east for surfing, but be careful of the undertow. **Tourist offices: Setur**, head office at ① *R Teniente Silveira 60, T3952 7000, www.pmf.sc.gov.br*, with information posts at **Portal Turístico** ① *mainland end of the bridge, Av Eng Max de Souza 236, Coqueiros, open Mon-Sat 0800-1800, the* rodoviária *Mon-Fri 0800-1800, and Praça Fernando Machado daily 0800-1800, T156 for all.* For information on the island see www.guiafloripa.com.br, and for the state www.guiasantacatarina.com.br. The state's **Secretaria de Estado de Turismo, Cultura e Esporte** is at ① *R Eduardo Gonçalves D'avila 303, Itacorubi, T3212 1900, www.sol.sc.gov.br*, and the tourism promotion office, **Santur**, has an information office at ① *R Felipe Schmidt 249, 8th floor, T3212-6328, www.santur.sc.gov.br.*

In the 1960s Florianópolis port was closed and the aspect of the city's southern shoreline was fundamentally changed, with land reclaimed from the bay. The two main remnants of the old port area are the late 19th-century **Alfândega** and **Mercado Público**, both on Rua Conselheiro Mafra, fully restored and painted ochre. In the Alfândega is a handicraft market ① *Mon-Fri 0900-1900, Sat 0900-1200.* The market is divided into boxes, some are bars and restaurants, while others are **shops** ① *T3224 0189, Mon-Fri 0600-1830, Sat 0600-1300,* a few fish stalls open on Sunday. The **Cathedral** *on Praça 15 de Novembro,* was completed in 1773.

Forte Sant'ana (1763), beneath the Ponte Hercílio Luz, houses a **Museu de Armas Major Lara Ribas** ⓘ *Mon 1400-1800, Tue-Sun 0830-1200, 1400-1800, free*, with a collection of guns and other items, mostly from the 19th and 20th centuries. **Museu Histórico** ⓘ *in the 18th-century Palácio Cruz e Souza, Praça 15 de Novembro, Tue-Fri 1000-1800, Sat-Sun 1000-1600, US$1.50*, has

Florianópolis

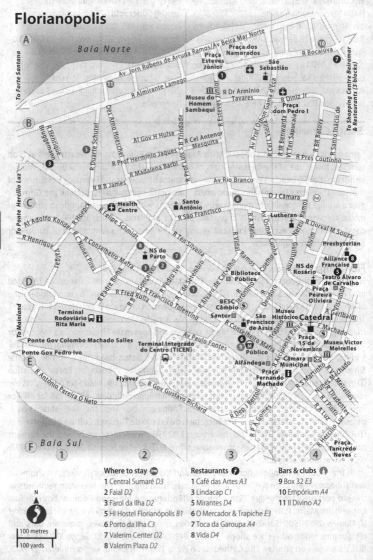

Where to stay 🛏
1 Central Sumaré *D3*
2 Faial *D2*
3 Farol da Ilha *D2*
5 HI Hostel Florianópolis *B1*
6 Porto da Ilha *C3*
7 Valerim Center *D2*
8 Valerim Plaza *D2*

Restaurants 🍴
1 Café das Artes *A3*
3 Lindacap *C1*
5 Mirantes *D4*
6 O Mercador & Trapiche *E3*
7 Toca da Garoupa *A4*
8 Vida *D4*

Bars & clubs 🍸
9 Box 32 *E3*
10 Empórium *A4*
11 Il Divino *A2*

a beautiful Art Nouveau interior, a display on the poet Cruz e Sousa and other documents and objects. **Museu de Antropologia** ① *UFSC Campus, Trindade, T3331 8821, Mon-Fri 0900-1200, 1300-1700*, has a collection of stone and other archaeological remains from the cultures of the coastal *indígenas*. **Museu do Homem Sambaqui** ① *R Esteves Júnior 711, Mon-Fri 1330-1630, closed Jan*, exhibits pieces from the sambaqui culture and fossils. The **Museu Victor Meirelles** ① *R Victor Meirelles 59, T3222 0692, Tue-Fri 1300-1800, US$1 donation*, was the home of Imperial Brazil's most prominent painter, with examples of his work and temporary exhibitions.

Ilha de Santa Catarina → *Colour map 7, C3.*

There are 42 beaches around the island. All have their own characteristics and attractions and are popular, especially in high season. Besides the sand and surf, there are watersports on the Lagoa de Conceição, walking in the forest reserves, hang gliding or paragliding from the Morro da Lagoa and sandboarding. **Note** Surfing is prohibited 30 April-30 July because of the migration of the island's largest fish, the tainha. ▶▶ *See Transport, page 480, for bus services around the island.*

The island, from north to south: northern beaches tend to have calmer waters, eg Daniela, Jurerê and Canasvieiras. Near Jurerê **Forte São José da Ponta Grossa** is beautifully restored with a small **museum** ① *US$2*. Jurerê Internacional is the favourite haunt of the very wealthy. There is a pleasant fishing village at **Ponta das Canas**, 1 km from which is Praia Brava for good surfing. Also in the north of the island is Praia dos Ingleses, very built up, but popular with families.

On the northeast coast, **Praia do Moçambique**, the longest on the island, is good for surfing. At its southern end is **Barra da Lagoa**, formerly a fishing village, lively in the summer, with lots of good restaurants and surfing. Next are the beaches at Galheta (naturist) and Mole, good walking and surfing, lively at night. Inland from here the **Lagoa da Conceição** has the whole range of watersports, from wind and kite surfing to jet skiing. In the town is the church of NS da Conceição (1730), lots of bars and a few guesthouses. From the Marina da Conceição there are daily boat trips to **Costa da Lagoa** which run until 1830, check when you buy your ticket. Other than by boat the only way to the nature trail of Costa da Lagoa is on foot. Above the lake the Canto da Lagoa is a very upmarket area.

Sandboarding is the thing on the dunes of Joaca between Lagoa de Conceição and the surf beach of Joaquina (championships in January). From Campeche there is a great view of the entire southeast coast. Ilha de Campeche has petroglyphs on the Atlantic side (national heritage site). Boats go to the island in summer from Armação village at south end of Campeche beach (it's difficult from Campeche because of surf); they leave when full, giving four hours on the island. Just inland from Armação, **Lagoa do Peri** is a protected area. Further south is **Pântano do Sul**, a fishing village with a long, curved beach, lovely views, several *pousadas*, bars and restaurants. From here it's a good 4-km walk over rocks and a headland to beautiful Lagoinha do Leste. For **Praia dos Naufragados** at the southernmost tip, go to Caieira da Barra do Sul (beyond Ribeirão da Ilha) and then a one hour walk through fine forests. **Forte Nossa Senhora da Conceição** is on a small island just offshore. It can be seen from the lighthouse near Praia dos Naufragados.

Porto Belo Beaches → *Phone code: 047. Population: 10,704.*

On the coast north of Florianópolis there are many resorts. They include Porto Belo, a fishing village on the north side of a peninsula settled in 1750 by Azores islanders, with a calm beach and a number of hotels and restaurants. Around the peninsula are wilder beaches reached by rough roads: Bombas, Bombinhas, Quatro Ilhas (quieter, 15 minutes' walk from Bombinhas), Mariscal, and, on the southern side, Zimbros (or Cantinho). Many of the stunning beaches around **Bombinhas** are untouched, accessible only on foot or by boat. The clear waters are good for diving.

Blumenau → *Phone code: 047. Post code: 89100. Colour map 7, C3. Population: 261,808.*
The BR-101 heads north, parallel to the coast, passing **Camboriú** (Phone code: 047. Colour map 7, C3. Population: 41,445), the most concentrated beach development on Brazil's southern coast. From 15 December to February it is very crowded and expensive.

Inland, some 47 km up the Rio Itajaí-Açu, is the prosperous city of **Blumenau**, where high-tech and electronics industries are replacing textiles as the economic mainstay. The surrounding district was settled mostly by Germans and this is reflected in the clean, orderly street scene and some almost caricatured Germanic architectureture. See the **German Evangelical Church**, the **Museu da Família Colonial** ① *Av Duque de Caxias 78, Tue-Fri 0900-1700, Sat-Sun 1000-1600* and, among other museums, the **Museu da Cerveja** *R 15 de Novembro 160, Tue-Fri 0900-1800, Sat-Sun 0900-1700.* Eleven local breweries offer tours. Details of these and other attractions and events from the **tourist office** ① *R Itajaí 3435, T3222 3176, www.blumenau.sc.gov.br.*

Oktoberfest, second largest street party in Brazil, is usually held in the first half of October, with hundreds of thousands packing into the Vila Germânica Park for live music, draught beer and events such as drinking competitions and the 'sausage Olympics'. There is also a fun fair and folk dancing shows (www.oktoberfestblumenau.com.br). Weekends can be very crowded. It is repeated, but called Sommerfest, in the three weeks preceding Carnival.

At **Pomerode**, 33 km west of Blumenau, the north German dialect of Plattdeutsch is still spoken and there are several folkloric groups keeping alive the music and dance of their ancestors. There is an excellent **zoo** ① *R Herman Weege 180, daily 0800-1800, US$5.* Next door, **Cevejaria Schornstein** ① *R Herman Weege 60* serves beers from its own onsite microbrewery, with German-influenced snacks and main meals, huge portions, high quality ingredients. The **Museu Pomerano** ① *Rodovia SC 418, Km 3,* tells the story of the colonial family. **Festa do Pomerania** is in January, www.pomerode.sc.gov.br.

São Francisco do Sul → *Phone code: 047. Colour map 7, C3. Population: 32,300.*
www.saofranciscodosul.com.br.
Some 80 km up the coast at the mouth of the Baia de Babitonga, São Francisco do Sul is the port for the town of Joinville, 45 km inland at the head of the Rio Cachoeira. There is an interesting **Museu Nacional do Mar** reflecting Brazil's seafaring history. The centre has over 150 historical sites and has been protected since 1987. There are some excellent **beaches** nearby.

Joinville itself is the state's largest city. It lies 2 km from the main coastal highway, BR-101, by which Curitiba and Florianópolis are less than three hours away. The industry does not spoil the considerable charm of the city. The **Alameda Brustlein**, better known as the **Rua das Palmeiras**, is an impressive avenue of palm trees leading to the **Palácio dos Príncipes**. The trees have been protected since 1982. The futuristic **cathedral** ① *on Av Juscelino Kubitscheck with R do Príncipe,* has spectacular windows recounting the story of man. The **Casa da Cultura** (Galeria Municipal de Artes 'Victor Kursancew') ① *R Dona Fransisca 800, Mon-Fri 0900-1800, Sat 0900-1300,* also contains the School of Art 'Fritz Alt', the School of Music 'Vila Lobos' and the Municipal School of Ballet (not to be confused with the Bolshoi Ballet School, Av José Vieira 3185). A number of museums and exhibition centres reflect the history of the area and the city's artistic achievements. In July, Joinville hosts the largest dance festival in the world, attracting around 4000 dancers over 12 days. Styles include jazz, folklore and classical ballet. There is also a large **Festa das Flores** (flower festival) in November. There are many good restaurants and good air and road links to other parts of Brazil. **Tourist office** at the **Fundação Turística** ① *Pórtico, R 15 de Novembro s/n, T3433 5007, the airport, Rodovia SC301, Km 0, and R Ottakar Doerffel s/n, 0800-1900, http://turjoinville.com.br,* which has information posts at four access points.

Southern Santa Catarina

At **Praia do Rosa**, 101 km south of Florianópolis, is the headquarters of the **Right Whale Institute** ①*Instituto Baleia Franca*. This is one of Brazil's prime whale-watching sites. The southern right whales come to the bays to calve from May to November. The institute's base is **Turismo Vida, Sol e Mar** ①*Praia do Rosa, Imbituba, Santa Catarina, CEP 88780-000, T3254 4199, www.vidasolemar.com.br*, which has over ten years' experience in right whale watching and dolphin watching, US$49, US$76 at weekends. Boats leave from Garopaba, Imbituba or Itapirubá, not Rosa itself. The **$$$$-$$$Vida, Sol e Mar** eco-resort and beach village, T3355 61111, same web address, has villas and suites, pool, good restaurant, horse riding, snorkelling, surf school and other activities. There are many other *pousadas* in the town (eg the tasteful, luxury **Quinta do Bucanero**, Praia do Rosa, T3355 6056, www.bucanero.com.br), and a good **youth hostel** ①*Albergue de Juventude Dinda Rosa, Estrada Geral do Rosa s/n, T3355 6614*. The hostel has its own (expensive) convenience store. Praia do Rosa is listed as one of the 29 most beautiful bays in the world by the French-based organization Les Plus Belles Baies du Monde. The town is confusing to walk around, with few signs and poor access to the beach as hotels block the way (even though they shouldn't). If lodging is hard to find, try 14 km north in **Garopaba** (www.garopaba.sc.gov.br), where there are other beaches to visit and many more places to stay, eg **Pousada do Morro** (T51-3388 4605, http://pousadadomorro.com.br, same owners as **Casa da Lagoa**, see below).

Laguna → *Phone code: 048. Colour map 7, C3. Population: 47,568.*

Some 27 km from Tubarão is the fishing port of Laguna. The town, founded in 1676, was the capital of the Juliana Republic in 1839, a short-lived separatist movement led by Italian idealist Guiseppe Garibáldi. In the centre of historic Laguna is an Azorean church (1696), **Santo Antônio dos Anjos**, light blue and white inside, with features picked out in gold. Across the street is birthplace of Garibáldi's wife, Anita, a simple house, now a small museum (US$2.75), with pieces from the period of her life. Behind, in a similar house, is a handicraft shop. There is also a Museu Anita Garibáldi on the Praça da República Juliana and a number of other colonial buildings, mostly around the main square and neighbouring streets. The **Fonte do Carioca** is still the spring from which people collect drinking water. Beside it is a tiled building, **Pinto D'Ulysséu**, with a private collection on Garibáldi.

Some 5 km from the centre of town, beyond the town's main beach resort, **Mar Grosso** (Laguna Internacional – many hotels abd *pousadas*), is the Molhes da Barra channel to Santo Antônio lagoon on which Laguna stands. Here you can watch fishermen with cast nets fishing with bottle-nosed dolphins. You can see dolphins at almost any time, but most frequently in May-July, the red mullet season. They are more active in the mornings. A little ferry crosses to Ponta da Barra which has several restaurants, the best being **Boião**, T3644 5065. (Taxis at the Rodoviária Municipal will go to Molhes da Barra.)

Serra Catarinense → *Colour map 7, C2.*

From Florianópolis to the southern highlands BR-282 first passes **Termas de Imperatriz**, a popular rafting area. The road climbs to the **Costa da Serra** (about 800 m), which has *mata atlântica* and several community tourism farms. Some 700 m higher still is the **Serra Geral**. The university town and regional centre of **Lages** (229 km) has no tourist attractions but has pioneered rural tourism. It has some 2-star hotels. Outside town is the **Fazenda Boqueirão** ①*Rodovia BR 282, Km 228, T049-3221 9900, www.fazendaboqueirao.com.br*, a working cattle farm since 1896 now offering accommodation (**$$$$**, cheaper midweek when it's quieter), Gaucho entertainment and food, good riding, outdoor sports, very busy at weekends. 74 km south of Lages is **São Joaquim** (Population: 22,836. Altitude: 1360 m), the *Capital Nacional da Maçã* (apples). For information contact **Secretaria de Turismo de São Joaquim** ① *T049-3233 2790, www.serracatarinense.com*. It claims to be the coldest place in Brazil, but that honour goes to **Urubici**, 60 km away. Surrounded by natural beauty spots and with an excellent tourist infrastructure, this is the place to go for adventure: trekking and riding, homestays and guesthouses in town (www.urubici-sc.com.br). From the coast the road up the Serro do Corvo Branco goes to Urubici. It separates a proposed new national park, Campo dos Padres from the **Parque Nacional de São Joaquim** (33,500 ha, T3278 4002), which has canyons containing sub-tropical vegetation, araucaria forest at higher levels and puma, ocelot, wild cat and wild dog. From São Joaquim to the coast SC-438 passes **Bom Jardim da Serra** (43 km) then descends the **Serra do Rio do Rastro**. The first 12 bends, about 5 km, are very sharp. There are plenty of stopping places for the view and street lamps for night driving. At the top viewpoint are coatis – don't feed them, they attack. Once out of the cloud forest (and the ceiling of clouds) the jagged mountains can be appreciated, with the plain to the Costa da Serra stretching away below. Continue to Lauro Müller, the junction with the Corvo Branco road and Gravatal, before rejoining the BR-101 at the coalfield town of Tubarão (27 km from Laguna).

◉ Santa Catarina listings

For hotel and restaurant price codes, and other relevant information, see Essentials.

◉ Where to stay

Florianópolis *p471, map p472*
$$$$-$$$ Valerim Plaza, R Felipe Schmidt 705, T2106 0200, www.hotelvalerim.com.br. More modern than Valerim Center, buffet restaurant open till 2300.
$$$ Faial, R Felipe Schmidt 603, T3203 2766, www.hotelfaial.com.br. Comfortable and traditional hotel with good restaurant. Also owns the Farol da Ilha, R Bento Gonçalves 163, T3203 2760, www.hotel faroldailha.com.br, which is good too, convenient for the bus station.
$$$ Porto da Ilha, R Dom Jaime Câmara 43, T3229 3000, www.portodailha.com.br. Central, comfortable, cheaper at weekends. Recommended.
$$$ Valerim Center, R Felipe Schmidt 554, T3225 1100. Large rooms, hot water, hard beds.
$$ Central Sumaré, R Felipe Schmidt 423, T3222 5359, www.hotelcentralsumare.com.br. With breakfast, simple rooms, cheaper with shared bath, central.
$ pp HI Hostel Florianópolis, R Duarte Schutel 227, T3225 3781, www.floripahostel.

com.br. HI, good breakfast included, cooking facilities, some traffic noise, luggage store. Prices rise in Dec-Feb; more expensive for non-members, private rooms **$$**.
Camping Camping Clube do Brasil, São João do Rio Vermelho, north of Lagoa da Conceição, 21 km out of town; also at Barra da Lagoa, Lagoa da Conceição, Praia da Armação, Praia dos Ingleses, Praia Canasvieiras.

Ilha de Santa Catarina *p473*
There are many *pousadas* and apartments to rent on the island, also many resorts and top-end hotels. Prices rise steeply for Reveillon/New Year and Carnaval. Agencies have offices in Florianópolis *rodoviária*, where you can shop around.

Lagoinha
$$$$ Pousada da Vigia, R Cônego Walmor Castro 291, T3284 1789, www.pousadavigia. com.br. A Roteiros do Charme hotel at the northern tip of the island, above a calm bay, suites and rooms with sea or garden view, terrace restaurant, very good.

Canasvieiras
$ pp HI Hostel Canasvieiras, R Dr João de Oliveira 517, T3266 3066, www.floripahostel.

com.br. Open mid-Dec to mid-Mar, 2 blocks from the sea with well-kept dorms and doubles (**$$**), cheaper for HI members.

Praia dos Ingleses
$$$-$$ Companhia Inglesa, R Dom João Becker 276, T3269 1350, www.hotelciainglesa. com.br. Little beach hotel with pool and helpful staff. Recommended for families.

Barra da Lagoa
$$$-$$ Pousada 32, R Angelina Joaquim dos Santos 300, by beach, T3232 1886, www. pousada32.com.br. Apartments for 4 to 8 with kitchen and fan, double rooms without kitchen, comfortable, trips arranged, surf school, diving.
$ pp The Backpackers Sharehouse, Estr Geral, across hanging bridge, T3232 7606. Good hostel, free surfboard hire, English spoken. Recommended.
$ Banana Beach, Servidão da Prainha 20 (across hanging bridge at bus station, take bus 320 or 330 from TICEN terminal, then change to no 360), T3232 3193, http://banana-beach.com. Book in advance, female and mixed dorms and doubles, shared bath, kitchen, tours by boat and car on island. Recommended.
$ pp HI Hostel Barra da Lagoa, R Inelzyr Bauer Bertolli s/n, T3232 4491, www. floripahostel.com.br. Modern hostel with kitchen, rooms with fan, private rooms **$$$**.
Camping Fortaleza da Barra, Estr Geral 3317, T3232 4235. Basic facilities, helpful owner. Looks after valuables.

Lagoa da Conceição
$$$ Casa da Lagoa, Servidão Palmeiras Nativas 500, T3269 9569, http://casalagoa. com.br. Close to the lake and the centre of town, rooms for 2-4 with a/c, frigobar, safe, breakfast included, garden, a good choice.
$$$-$$ Pousada Pau de Canela, R Pau de Canela 606, Rio Tavares, T3233 4989, www. pousadadecanela.com.br. Pleasant *pousada* between Lagoa da Conceição and Campeche. Restaurant, bar and swimming pool.

Joaquina
$$$-$$ Joaquina Beach, R A Garibaldi Santiago, T3232 5059, www.joaquinabeach hotel.com.br. Pleasant hotel with 3 standards of room, those with sea views, safe and a/c are more expensive, buffet breakfast, pool.
$ Pousada Dona Zilma, R Geral da Praia da Joaquina 279, T3232 5161. Quiet, safe. Recommended.

Praia do Campeche
$$$$ Pousada Natur Campeche, Servidão Família Nunes 59, T3237 4011, www.natur campeche.com.br. Lovely *pousada* with tasteful rooms, some with Jacuzzi, gardens, quiet, pool, close to the beach.
$$$$-$$$ Pousada Vila Tamarindo, Av Campeche 1836, 1323/ 3464, www. tamarindo.com.br. Tranquil setting with lovely views, gardens, helpful staff, good buffet breakfast.
$$$ São Sebastião da Praia, Av Campeche 1373, T3338 2020, www.hotelsaosebastiao. com.br. Resort hotel on splendid beach, chalets, rooms, suites, a/c, buffet breakfast, restaurant, good value.

Near Pântano do Sul
$$$ Pousada Sítio dos Tucanos, Estrada Geral da Costa de Dentro 2776, T3237 5084, www.pousadasitiodostucanos.com. Prices rise in high season. English, German, Spanish spoken, suites and 1 chalet in garden setting, excellent organic food, transport to beach. Highly recommended. Take bus 410 from TICEN to Rio Tavares, 'phone the *pousada* then change to 563 Costa do Dentro bus and await pick-up at end of line.
$ Albergue do Pirata, Estrada Geral da Costa de Dentro, 4973, near Pântano do Sul, T3389 2727, www.frankville.com.br/por/hostel_ florianopolis_albergue_do_pirata.php. Dorms with and without bath, and doubles (**$$$-$$**), with breakfast, in natural surroundings with lots of trails. Also has camping, US$8.75 pp without breakfast.

Blumenau *p474*

Reservations are essential during Oktoberfest.

$$$-$$Glória, R 7 de Setembro 954, T3326 1988, www.hotelgloria.com.br. German-run, modern, excellent coffee shop.

$$Hermann, Floriano Peixoto 213, T3322 4370, www.hotelhermann.com.br. One of the oldest houses in Blumenau, cheaper rooms with shared bath, excellent big breakfast, German spoken.

Pomerode

There are a couple of good mid-range hotels in the **$$$-$$**range: Pousada Max, R 15 de Novembro 257, T3387 3070, www.pousada max.com.br, and **Schroeder**, R 15 de Novembro 514, T3387 0933, www.hotelschroeder.com.br.

São Francisco do Sul *p474*

$$$Zibamba, R Fernandes Dias 27, T3444 2020, www.hotelzibamba.com.br. Central, good, restaurant.

Joinville

$$$$Tannenhof, Visconde de Taunay 340, T3145 6700, www.tannenhof.com.br. 4-star, pool, gym, traffic noise, excellent breakfast, restaurant.

$$$Germânia, Ministro Calógeras 612, T3433 9886, www.hotelgermania.com.br. Colourful modern building with pretty garden, pool, fitness centre, reading room.

$$Mattes, 15 de Novembro 801, T3422 3582, www.hotelmattes.com.br. Good facilities, big breakfast, German spoken. Recommended.

$$-$Pousada Flor do Brasil, R Paraíba 919, T3027 2152. Opposite bus station, clean rooms with fan, private bath.

Serra Catarinense *p475*

In the Lages area there are a number of farms which take guests, as well as the Fazenda do Boqueirão mentioned above. Likewise in the São Joaquim, Urubici and other areas, there are many Turismo Rural and more conventional places to stay, with too many *pousadas* to list here: see www.serra catarinense.com. Two upmarket options are:

$$$$Rio do Rastro Eco Resort, Rodavia SC-438, Km 130, near Bom Jardim da Serra, T48-9931 6100, www.riodorastro.com.br (a Roteiros do Charme hotel). Built around lakes that feed into one another, nice cabins with good facilities, TV, some with jacuzzi. Good restaurant, games room, outdoor Jacuzzi, sauna, pool, gym. Views of valley and escarpments, trails (not signed – guides are provided).

$$$Urubici Park, Av Adolfo Konder 2278, T3278 5300, Urubici, www.uph.com.br. Cosy and attractive mountain lodge hotel with pool and excellent breakfast, helpful staff, good value. Highly recommended.

⑦ Restaurants

Florianópolis *p471, map p472*

On Rua Bocaiúva, east of R Almte Lamego, there are several Italian restaurants and BBQ places.

$$$Lindacap, R Felipe Schmidt 1162 (closed Mon, Sun lunch only). Recommended for its varied range of dishes, good buffet.

$$$Toca da Garoupa, R Alves de Brito 178. A very good seafood restaurant in a rustic, wood slat house.

$$O Mercador, Box 33/4 in the Mercado Público. Excellent self-service specializing in seafood.

$$Trapiche, Box 31 in the Mercado Público. Self-service fish and seafood (see Bars, below).

$$Vida, R Visc de Ouro Preto 298, next to Alliance Française. Decent value vegetarian lunches served in an attractive colonial building.

$Café das Artes, R Esteves Junior 734 at north end. Nice café with excellent cakes.

$Mirantes, R Alvaro de Carvalho 246, Centro. Self-service, good value. Other branches in the city.

Ilha de Santa Catarina *p473*
Barra da Lagoa

On R Altimiro Barcelos Dutra are several snackbars selling excellent wholemeal pastries stuffed with tasty, fresh ingredients. Good vegetarian options.

$$ Ponta das Caranhas, R Jornalista M de Menezes 2377. Excellent seafood, lovely location on the lake.

Pântano do Sul
$$ Bar do Vadinho, Praia do Pântano do Sul. Set lunch of the day's fish catch, with rice, chips, salad, *pirão* and beans, set price US$11 for all you can eat. Open daily in summer, weekends only in winter. Recommended.

🎧 Bars and clubs

Florianópolis *p471, map p472*
To find out about events and theme nights check the Beiramar centre for notices in shop windows, or ask in surf shops. The Mercado Público in the centre, which is alive with fish sellers and stalls during the day, has a different atmosphere at night; the stall, **Box 32**, serves good, if expensive, seafood, and at night becomes a busy bar specializing in cachaça, including its own brand.
Empórium, Bocaiúva 79, www.emporium bocaiuva.com.br. A delicatessen by day and popular bar at night.
Il Divino, Av Beira Mar Norte, T3225 1266, www.ildivinobrasil.com.br. Open Wed-Sun from 1900, bar, lounge, restaurant, sushi bar, dancing to DJs, sophisticated. Also has clubs in Jurerê.

Ilha de Santa Catarina *p473*
Throughout high summer the beaches open their bars day and night. The beach huts of Praia Mole invite people to party all night (bring a blanket). Any bars are worth visiting in the Lagoa area, especially the **Confraria Chopp da Ilha**, packed at weekends, good for watching football matches, or **The Black Swan** pub.

🎉 Festivals

Florianópolis *p471, map p472*
In **Dec** and **Jan** the whole island dances to the sound of the Boi-de-Mamão, a dance which incorporates the puppets of Bernunça, Maricota (the Goddess of Love, a puppet with long arms to embrace everyone) and Tião, the monkey. Around **Easter** is the Festival of the Bull, **Farra de Boi**. It is only in the south that, controversially nowadays, the bull is killed on Easter Sunday. The festival arouses fierce local pride.

⏱ What to do

Florianópolis *p471, map p472*
Brazil Ecojourneys, Estrada Rozália Paulina Ferreira, 1132 Armação, T3389 5619, http://brazilecojourneys.com. Small group guided tours in Southern Brazil covering many interests: adventure, wildlife, farm stays, community-based tourism, gay and lesbian tourism and volunteering, English spoken, very professional. Warmly recommended.

Serra Catarinense *p475*
In July there is a long horse ride between Santa Catarina and Rio Grande do Sul, the direction changes each year. Thousands of riders participate; it's open to anyone, camp on the way.
Caminhos da Serra, Av Adolfo Konder 2628, Urubici, T49-3278 4273, www.caminhos daserra.tur.br. Trekking, riding, information and reservations for places to stay.
Gaúcho do Brasil, T24-9919 0634, www. gauchodobrasil.com. Paul Coudenys, Belgian-owned company offering 6-day rides in the Serra from fazenda to fazenda, "be a gaúcho for a week". Operates out of Lages.The riding season is Oct-May.
Tribo da Serra, Praça Joao Ribeiro 204, sala 1, São Joaquim, T49-3233 4117, tribodaserra. ecoturismo on Facebook. Trekking, horse riding and 4WD trips.

⊖ Transport

Florianópolis *p471, map p472*
Air International and domestic flights arrive at Hercílio Luz airport, Av Deomício Freitas, 12 km south of town, on the island. Take 'Corredor Sudoeste' bus No 183 or 186 from TICEN.

Bus Regular buses from the city to destinations on the island leave from the Terminal Integrado do Centro (TICEN), Av Paulo Fontes, immediately east of the *rodoviária* Rita Maia. For most destinations, buses go from TICEN to another Terminal Integrado (eg TICAN – Canasvieiras; TILAG – Lagoa de Conceição), where you change to another bus for the final point. You do not have to pay for the onward bus as long as you don't leave the platform. For instance, from Florianópolis to Jurerê, take a bus from TICEN to TICAN, then change buses. The bus fare to any point on the island is US$1.60. Yellow micro buses (Transporte Ejecutivo), starting from the south end of Praça 15 de Novembro and other stops, charge US$2. International and buses from other Brazilian cities arrive at the *rodoviária* Rita Maia, at the east (island) end of the Ponte Colombo Machado Salles.

Several buses daily with **Catarinense** to **Porto Alegre** (US$35-48, 7 hrs, road being made into a dual carriageway), **São Paulo**, 10 hrs (US$49-61, leito US$91), **Rio**, 20 hrs (US$100 convencional); to **Foz do Iguaçu** (US$69-75), to **Curitiba** US$25-35. **International buses** Montevideo, US$115, by TTL, not daily. **Buenos Aires**, US$150, Pluma, buses very full in summer, book 1 week in advance. **Asunción**, US$86 (Pluma). To **Ciudad del Este**, Pluma, Wed, Fri, Sat, Sun 1500, arrive 0700, US$57.

Porto Belo Beaches *p473*
Bus **Florianópolis** to Porto Belo, several daily with **Rainha**, fewer at weekends, more frequent buses to **Tijuca**, **Itapema** and **Itajaí**, all on the BR-101 with connections. Buses from Porto Belo to the beaches on the peninsula.

Blumenau *p474*
Bus *Rodoviária* is 7 km from town (get off at the bridge over the river and walk 1 km to centre). Bus to the *rodoviária* from Av Presidente Castelo-Branco (Beira Rio). There are connections in all directions from Blumenau. To **Florianópolis** US$18, 3 hrs. To **Curitiba**, US$18, 4 hrs, frequent. To **Pomerode** Coletivos **Volkmann** (T3395 1400) daily US$2.50, 1 hr; and others; check schedules at tourist offices.

São Francisco do Sul *p474*
Bus Terminal is 1½ km from centre. 2 buses daily with **Catarinense** to **Curitiba**, US$14, 3½ hrs.

Laguna *p475*
Bus To/from **Porto Alegre**, 5½ hrs, US$27, with Eucatur and Santo Anjo; **Florianópolis**, 2 hrs, US$19, 6 daily.

Serra Catarinense *p475*
Bus **Florianópolis** to/from **Lages**, 3½ hrs, US$25, 4-5 a day. **São Joaquim** to/from **Florianópolis** 2 a day with Reunidos, 5½ hrs, US$20.

Directory

Florianópolis *p471, map p472*
Banks Money changers on R Felipe Schmidt outside Banco Estado de Santa Catarina (BESC). **Car hire** There are many car hire companies on the island; see www.guiafloripa.com.br for listings. Promotional rates in low season can be about US$45 a day.

Rio Grande do Sul → *Population: 10.2 million.*

Rio Grande do Sul is gaúcho country; it is also Brazil's chief wine producer. The capital, Porto Alegre, is the most industrialized city in the south, but in the surroundings are good beaches, interesting coastal national parks and the fine scenery of the Serra Gaúcha. On the border with Santa Catarina is the remarkable Aparados da Serra National Park. In the far west are the remains of Jesuit missions. In southern Rio Grande do Sul there are great grasslands stretching as far as Uruguay to the south and Argentina to the west. In this distinctive land of the gaúcho, or cowboy (pronounced ga-oo-shoo in Brazil), people feel closer to Uruguay and Argentina than Brazil (except where football is concerned).

The gaúcho culture has developed a sense of distance from the African-influenced society of further north. This separationist strain was most marked in the 1820s and 1830s when the Farroupilha movement, led by Bento Gonçalves, proclaimed the República Riograndense in 1835.

Porto Alegre → Phone code: 051. Colour map 7, inset. Population: 1,360,590.

The capital of Rio Grande do Sul is where cowboy culture meets the bright lights. It lies at the confluence of five rivers (called Rio Guaíba, although it is not a river in its own right) and thence into the great freshwater lagoon, the Lagoa dos Patos, which runs into the sea. The freshwater port is one of the most up-to-date in the country and Porto Alegre is the biggest commercial centre south of São Paulo. It is also one of the richest and best-educated parts of Brazil and held the first three World Social Forums (2001-2003), putting the city in a global spotlight. Standing on a series of hills and valleys on the banks of the Guaíba, it has a temperate climate through most of the year, though the temperature at the height of summer can often exceed 40°C and drop below 10°C in winter. The city has a good tourist infrastructure, interesting cultural centres and lively nightlife. Football is also a great source of local pride, with Porto Alegre's two major sides, **Grêmio** and **Internacional**, both making the spurious claim to be 'world champions'.

Arriving in Porto Alegre
Tourist offices Prefeitura de Porto Alegre ① *T0800-517686, www2.portoalegre.rs.gov.br/ turismo.* **Porto Alegre Turismo** ① *Travessa do Carmo 84, Cidade Baixa, T3289 0176, daily 0800- 1800; also at airport 0800-2200; Usina do Gasômetro, Tue-Sun 0900-1800; Mercado Público, Mon- Sat 0900-1800; Mercado do Bom Fim, Loja 11, daily 0900-1800.* For the state: **SETUR** ① *R General Câmara 156, 4th floor, T3288 5400, www.turismo.rs.gov.br.* The market area in Praça 15 de Novembro and the bus terminal are dangerous at night. Thefts have been reported in Voluntários da Pátria and Praça Parcão.

Places in Porto Alegre
The older residential part of the town is on a promontory, dominated previously by the **Palácio Piratini** (Governor's Palace) and the imposing **cathedral** (1921-45 and 1972, but very neoclassical) on the **Praça Marechal Deodoro** (or da Matriz). Also on, or near this square, are the neoclassical **Theatro São Pedro** (1858), the **Solar dos Câmara** (1818, now a historical and cultural centre), the **Biblioteca Pública** – all dwarfed by the skyscraper of the **Assembléia Legislativa** – and the **Museu Júlio de Castilhos** ① *Duque de Caxias 1231, T3221 3959, Tue-Sun 1000-1800,* which has an interesting collection on the history of the state. Down Rua General Câmara from Praça Marechal Deodoro is the **Praça da Alfândega**, with the old customs house and the Museu de Arte de Rio Grande do Sul (see below). A short walk east of this group, up Rua 7 de Setembro, is Praça 15 de Novembro, on which is the neoclassical **Mercado Público**, selling everything from religious artefacts to spices and meat. There are some good cafés and bars here and the Chalé da Praça XV, which has a large restaurant serving local food. For art from the state, visit the **Museu de Arte do Rio Grande do Sul** ① *Praça Senador Florêncio (Praça da Alfândega), T3227 2311, Tue-Sun 1000-1900, free.* **Museu de Comunicação Social** ① *R dos Andradas 959, T3224 4252, Mon-Fri 0900-1800, Sat 0900-1200, free,* in the former A Federação newspaper building (1922), deals with the development of the media in Brazil since the 1920s.

A large part of **Rua dos Andradas** (Rua da Praia) has been pedestrianised and gets very busy in the afternoons. Going west along Rua dos Andradas, you pass the wide stairway that leads up to the two high white towers of the church of **Nossa Senhora das Dores**, the oldest in the city. At the end of the promontory, the **Usina do Gasômetro** has been converted from a thermoelectric station into a cultural centre and good café. Its enormous chimney is a city landmark and there is a stunning view of sunset from the balcony. In the **Cidade Baixa** quarter are the colonial **Travessa dos Venezianos** (between Ruas Lopo Gonçalves and Joaquim Nabuco) and the **house of Lopo Gonçalves**, which houses the **Museu de Porto Alegre Joaquim José Felizardo** ⓘ *R João Alfredo 582, T3226 7570, Tue-Sun 0900-1200, 1330-1800, free*, a collection on the history of the city.

The central **Parque Farroupilha** (called Parque Redenção) has many attractions and on Sundays there is an antiques and handicrafts fair at the José Bonifácio end.

Porto Alegre beach resorts

The main beach resorts of the area are to the east and north of the city. Heading east along the BR-290, 112 km from Porto Alegre is **Osório**, a pleasant lakeside town with a few hotels. From

Porto Alegre

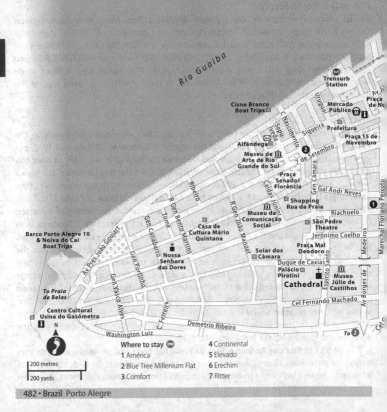

Where to stay
1 América
2 Blue Tree Millenium Flat
3 Comfort
4 Continental
5 Elevado
6 Erechim
7 Ritter

here it is 18 km southeast to the rather polluted and crowded beach resort of **Tramandaí** (daily buses from Porto Alegre). The beaches here are very popular, with lots of hotels, bars, restaurants, and other standard seaside amenities. Extensive dunes and lakes in the region provide an interesting variety of wildlife and sporting opportunities. The beach resorts become less polluted the further north you travel, and the water is clean by the time you reach the well-developed resort of **Torres**. Dolphins visit Praia dos Molhes, north of town, year round; whales can occasionally be seen in July.

There is a paved road running south from Tramandaí along the coast to **Quintão**, giving access to many beaches, including **Cidreira**. Bus from Porto Alegre US$10.

⊙ Porto Alegre listings

For hotel and restaurant price codes, and other relevant information, see Essentials.

⊜ Where to stay

Porto Alegre *p481, map p482*
Hotels in the area around R Garibáldi and Voluntários da Patria between Av Farrapos and *rodoviária* are overpriced and used for short stays.

$$$$ Blue Tree Millenium Flat, Av Borges de Medeiros 3120, Praia de Belas, T3026 2200, www.bluetree.com.br. Smart mini-apartments with microwave, study and breakfast bar. The rooftop pool, gym and bar have stunning sunset views. Recommended.

$$$ Comfort, R Loureiro da Silva 1660, Cidade Baixa, T2117 9000, www.atlanticahotels.com. br. Good value 3-star with gym, breakfast. Handy for Cidade Baixa nightlife.

$$$ Continental, Lg Vespasiano Júlio Veppo 77, T3027 1900, www.hoteiscontinental. com.br. High standards, cheaper at weekends, pool, gym.

$$$ Ritter, Lg Vespasiano Júlio Veppo 55, opposite *rodoviária*, T3228 4044, www.ritter hoteis.com.br. 4-star and 3-star wings, English, French, German spoken, bar, small pool, sauna.

$$ América, Av Farrapos 119, T3226 0062, www.hotelamerica.com.br. Bright, large rooms with sofas, garage, HI-affiliated. Recommended.

$$ Elevado, Av Farrapos 65, T3224 5250, www.hotelelevado.com.br. YHA member, big rooms, microwave and coffee, good value.

$$ Erechim, Av Júlio de Castilhos 341, near *rodoviária*, T3228 7044, www.hotelerechim.

To Guaíba Bridge
Footbridge

Garibáldi

Mauá
Cel Vicente
Carlos Chaves Barcelos
Corredio
Comendador Pereira
Pátria
To ⑤ & Airport

Farrapos

...ntários da Pátria
Pinto Bandeira

Av Alberto Blns

Av Independencia
R dos Andradas

Dr Flores

...al Vitorino
Salgado Filho

To 3: Moinhos de Vento district, restaurants & Av Goethe

Osvaldo Aranha
Sarmento Leite
Paulo Gama

University

Luis Englert

...des André da Rocha
Av Loureira da Silva
Av João Pessoa
Sarmento Leite
Setembrina

Parque
Farroupilha

seu de Porto Alegre Joaquim José Felizardo
Restaurants 🍴   3 Chopp Stübel
1 Atelier de Massas
2 Café do Cofre &
  Santander Cultural

com.br. A good option among several cheap places in this area, 2 standards of room, accredited by Brazilian YHA.

❼ Restaurants

Porto Alegre *p481, map p482*
The Central Market along the Praça is lined with lancherias. As well as restaurants serving gaucho cooking, there are many German, Italian and Japanese places. Vegetarians might try some of the campeiro soups and casseroles or visit one of the many health food lunch buffet spots.
$$$ Al Dente, R Mata Bacelar 210, Auxiliadora, T3342 8534. Good, if expensive northern Italian cuisine. Closed Sun, reservations needed Fri-Sat.
$$$ Chopp Stübel, R Quintino Bocaiúva 940, Moinhos de Vento, T3332 8895. Mon-Sat 1800-0030. German food and beers. Recommended.
$$ Atelier de Massas, R Riachuelo 1482, T3225 1125. Lunch and dinner, Italian, closed Sun, fantastic pastas and steaks, excellent value.
$$ Komka, Av Bahia 1275, San Geraldo, T3222 1881. Open 1130-1430, 1930-2300, closed Sun, for churrasco. Recommended.
$$ Nova Vida, R Demétrio Ribeiro 1182, T3226 8876.1100-1500, closed Sun. Vegetarian, good lasagne.

Cafés
Café do Cofre, 7 de Setembro 1028 (below Santander Cultural), T3227 8322. Lunch only. Good light meals, including salads and sushi.
Café Dos Cataventos, in Casa de Cultura Mário Quintana, R dos Andrades 736, in courtyard. Also **Restaurant Majestic** on roof, T3226 0153. Both serve good drinks, snacks and meals. Fantastic rooftop sunsets. 1200-2300.
   The café in **Usina do Gasômetro** is good for sandwiches and speciality coffee.

❶ Bars and clubs

Porto Alegre *p481, map p482*
Bars
On weekend nights, thousands head for the Cidade Baixa and spill out of the bars

and clubs along Rua da República and José do Patrimônio.
Bar do Goethe, R 24 de Outubro 112, Moinhos de Vento, T8404 9356, www.bardogoethe.com.br. Mon-Fri 1400-2200, Sat 0900-1500, excellent range of artisan beers and German snacks, Wi-Fi.

❿ Entertainment

Porto Alegre *p481, map p482*
Exhibitions and theatres
Casa de Cultura Mário Quintana, R dos Andradas 736, T3221 7147. A lively centre for the arts, with exhibitions, theatre, pleasant bar, Sat-Sun 0900-2100, 1200-2100.
Santander Cultural, R 7 de Setembro 1028, T3287 5718. Cultural centre with a beautiful interior (a former bank), good value art house cinema and a café, holds some interesting exhibitions. Mon-Fri 1000-1900, Sat-Sun 1100-1900.
Theatro São Pedro, Praça Mal Deodoro, T3227 5100. Free noon and late afternoon concerts Sat, Sun, art gallery, café.

✷ Festivals

Porto Alegre *p481, map p482*
On **2 Feb** (a local holiday) is the festival of Nossa Senhora dos Navegantes (Iemanjá), whose image is taken by boat from the central quay in the port to the industrial district of Navegantes. **Semana Farroupilha** celebrates gaúcho traditions with parades in traditional style, its main day being **20 Sep**. The Carnival parade takes place in Av A do Carvalho, renamed Av Carlos Alberto Barcelos (or Roxo) for these 3 days only, after a famous Carnival designer. **Feira do Livro** in Praça da Alfândega, **Oct-Nov**.

⚙ Shopping

Porto Alegre *p481, map p482*
Markets Street market (leather goods, basketware, etc) in area around the central Post Office. Good leather goods are sold

on the streets. Sun morning handicraft and bric-a-brac market (plus sideshows) Av José Bonifácio (next to Parque Farroupilha). There is a very good food market.

☉ What to do

Porto Alegre *p481, map p482*
Ask at the tourist office, Travessa do Carmo 84, Cidade Baixa, about tours of the city, on foot, or by open-top bus, twice a day Tue-Sun. Several boats trips around islands in estuary: **Barco Porto Alegre 10**, from the Usina do Gasômetro, T3211 7665, www.barcoporto alegre10.com.br. Daily trips at 1630, 2-3 at weekends (no sailings on Mon), US$10.
Cisne Branco, from Cais do Porto, near Museu de Arte de Rio Grande do Sul, T3224 5222, www.barcocisnebranco.com.br. Several sailings on Sun, fewer mid-week, 1 hr, US$12.50.
Noiva do Caí, from the Usina do Gasômetro, T3211 7662. Several on Sun, fewer mid-week, one hr, US$10 (check winter schedules).

☉ Transport

Porto Alegre *p481, map p482*
Air The international airport is on Av dos Estados, 8 km from the city, T3358 2000.
Bus The city's integrated transport system (*Tri*, www.tripoa.com.br) operates with pre-paid cards. There are normal buses and 1st-class minibuses (*Lotação*), painted in a distinctive red, blue and white pattern. One journey costs US$1.50.

International and interstate buses arrive at the *rodoviária* at Largo Vespasiano Júlio Veppo, on Av Mauá with Garibáldi, T3210 0101, www.rodoviaria-poa.com.br. There are 2 sections to the terminal; the ticket offices for interstate and international destinations are together in 1 block, beside the municipal tourist office (very helpful). The intermunicipal (state) ticket offices are in another block; for travel information within the state, ask at the very helpful booth on the station concourse.

To **Rio**, US$135, 26 hrs; **São Paulo**, US$90, 18 hrs; **Florianópolis**, US$35-48, 7 hrs (take an executivo rather than a convencional, which is much slower); **Curitiba**, from US$52-56, coastal and Serra routes, 11 hrs. **Foz do Iguaçu**, US$65-74, 13 hrs. To **Uruguaiana**, US$63-81, 8 hrs. Many other destinations.
International buses Note Take your passport and tourist card when purchasing international bus tickets. To **Montevideo**, with TTL (www.ttl.com.br), or take an ordinary bus to border town of Chuí, 7 hrs, US$46-54, walk or taxi across the border, then bus to Montevideo. There are services to **Buenos Aires**, 19 hrs with **Pluma**, 1730 daily, US$113, route is Uruguaiana, Paso de los Libres, Entre Ríos and Zárate.
Metrô Trensurb, www.trensurb.com.br, to the Mercado Público, one stop from the *rodoviária*, US$1; integrated tickets with city buses available.
Road Good roads radiate from Porto Alegre, and Highway BR-116 is paved to Curitiba (746 km). To the south it is paved (mostly in good condition), to Chuí on the Uruguayan border, 512 km, and to Rio Branco, also on the border. In summer visibility can be very poor at night owing to mist; unfenced cows are a further hazard. The paved coastal road to Curitiba via Itajaí (BR-101), the first 100 km is the 4-lane Estrada General Osório highway, is being dualled to Florianópolis, so a rough ride while work progresses. Nevertherless it's a better journey than the BR-116 via Caxias and Lajes. The road to Uruguaiana is entirely paved but bumpy.

☉ Directory

Porto Alegre *p481, map p482*
Banks ATMs can be found at central banks. Exprinter, R Hilário Ribeiro 292 (best for cash). For other addresses consult tourist bureau brochure. **Consulates** Argentina, R Coronel Bordini 1033, Moinhos de Vento, T3321 1360. Uruguay, Av Cristóvão Colombo 2999, Higienópolis, T3325 6197.

Rio Grande do Sul state

Mountains, vineyards, cowboys, waterfowl and ruined Jesuit missions are all part of the mix that makes up Brazil's southernmost state.

Serra Gaúcha → *Population: Canela, 33,625; Gramado, 29,593.*

The Serra Gaúcha boasts stunningly beautiful scenery, some of the best being around the towns of Gramado and Canela, about 130 km north of Porto Alegre. There is a distinctly Swiss/Bavarian flavour to many of the buildings in both towns. In December the Christmas displays are genuinely impressive, and in winter it can snow. This is excellent walking and climbing country among hills, woods, lakes and waterfalls. For canoeists, the Rio Paranhana at Três Coroas is renowned, especially for slalom (**$$$-$$** pp **Refúgio do Pomar**, Estrada do Laticínio 1330, Rodeio Bonito, T051-9668 6463, http://pousada-refugiodopomar.blog spot. com, is recommended for peace and quiet, Buddhist temple nearby, good food and rafting and walking options, HI affiliated). Local crafts include knitted woollens, leather, wickerwork, and chocolate.

Gramado, at 850 m on the edge of a plateau with views, provides a summer escape from the 40°C heat of the plains. It lives almost entirely by tourism and the main street, Avenida Borges de Medeiros, is full of kitsch artisan shops and fashion boutiques. In December the Christmas displays draw hordes of visitors and throughout the summer, thousands of hydrangeas (hortênsias) bloom. For a good walk/bike ride into the valley, take the dirt road Turismo Rural 28, Um Mergulho no Vale (A Dive into the Valley), which starts at Avenida das Hortênsias immediately before Prawer. **Tourist office** ① *Av das Hortênsias 2029, T3286 0200, www.gramadosite.com.br.*

A few kilometres along the plateau rim, **Canela** is less tourism and shopping-oriented than its neighbour (frequent bus service from Gramado, 10 minutes). **Tourist office** ① *R Largo da Fama 77, T3282 1287, turismo@canela.com.br, see also www.canelaturismo.com.br.* The **Mundo a Vapor** museum ① *RS 235 Rodovia Canela-Gramado, T3282 1115, daily 0915-1700, US$5, children US$2.50,* is an interesting museum dedicated to steam power. The main attraction is the dramatic reconstruction of the famous 1895 rail disaster in Montparnasse, Paris. Kids and adults clamour to have their picture taken alongside a giant steam train that appears to have burst through the front of the building.

About 7 km away is the **Parque Estadual do Caracol** ① *T3278 3035, 0830-1800, US$6,* with a spectacular 130-m high waterfall where the Rio Caracol tumbles out of thick forest. A 927-step metal staircase leads to the plunge pool. There is an 18-km circular bike route continuing on to **Parque Ferradura** (US$4), with good views into the canyon of the Rio Cai. From the Ferradura junction, take the right to continue to the **Floresta Nacional** ① *T3282 2608, 0800-1700, US$17 to visit and stay overnight.* From here, the dirt road continues round to Canela. Another good hike or bike option is the 4-km track southeast of Canela past Parque das Sequóias to **Morro Pelado**. At over 600 m, there are spectacular views from the rim edge.

Parque Nacional de Aparados da Serra → *Colour map 7, inset.*

① *Wed-Sat 0900-1800, US$3, T3251 1277/1262, parnaaparadosdaserra@icmbio.gov.br.*

The major attraction at the Parque Nacional de Aparados da Serra is a canyon, 7.8 km long and 720 m deep, known locally as the Itaimbezinho. Here, two waterfalls cascade 350 m into a stone circle at the bottom. For experienced hikers (and with a guide) there is a difficult path to the bottom of Itaimbezinho. One can then hike 20 km to Praia Grande in Santa Catarina state. The park is 80 km from São Francisco de Paula (18 km east of Canela, 117 km north of Porto

Alegre). With similar scenery but no tourist infrastructure is the neighbouring **Parque Nacional da Serra Geral** ① *open daily 0800-1700, same phone and email as above, free.*

Tourist excursions, mostly at weekends, from **São Francisco de Paula** (a few hotels and *pousadas*; tourist information at southern entrance to town, T3244 1602). At other times, take a bus to Cambará do Sul (0945, 1700, 1¼ hours, US$5): several *pousadas* (see www.cambara online.com.br for a list). Also near Cambará is **Campofora** ① *T3244 2993, www.campovfora. com.br,* for riding expeditions in national park.

Caxias do Sul and around

➔ *Phone code: 054. Post code: 95000. Colour map 7, inset. Population: 360,419.*

This expanding modern city's population is principally of Italian descent and it is the centre of the Brazilian wine industry. The church of **São Pelegrino** has paintings by Aldo Locatelli and 5 m-high bronze doors sculptured by Augusto Murer. There is a good **Museu Municipal** ① *R Visconde de Pelotas 586, T3221 2423, Tue-Sat 0830-1130, 1330 1700, Sun 1400-1700,* with displays of artefacts of the Italian immigration. Italian roots are again on display in the **Parque de Exposições Centenário**, 5 km out on Rua Ludovico Cavinato. January-February is the best time to visit. There is a tourist information kiosk in Praça Rui Barbosa and another at the **rodoviária** ① *R Ernesto Alves 1341, T3218 3000,* a 15-minute walk from the main praça (but many buses pass through the centre). **Tourist office** ① *R Ludovico Cavinatto, 1431, T3222 1875, www.caxias.tur.br.*

Caxias do Sul's festival of grapes is held February to March. Good tour and tasting at **Adega Granja União**, R Os 18 de Forte 2346. Visit also the neighbouring towns and sample their wines: **Farroupilha** 20 km from Caxias do Sul. **Nova Milano**, 6 km away (bus to Farroupilha, then change – day trip). **Bento Gonçalves**, 40 km from Caxias do Sul, www.bentogoncalves. rs.gov.br. **Garibáldi**, which has a dry ski slope and toboggan slope. A restored steam train leaves Bento Gonçalves for a 2-hour trip to **Carlos Barbosa**; called 'a rota do vinho' (the wine run), it goes through vineyards in the hills. US$35-37, including wines, with live band; reserve in advance through **Giordani Turismo** ① *railway station, R Duque de Caxias, Bento Gonçalves, T3455 2788, www.giordaniturismo.com.br.* Another worthwhile trip is to **Antônio Prado**, 1½ hours by Caxiense Bus. The town is now a World Heritage Site because of the large number of original buildings built by immigrants in the Italian style.

Jesuit Missions ➔ *Colour map 7, C1. Colour map 8, A6.*

West of **Passo Fundo**, 'the most gaúcho city in Rio Grande do Sul', are the **Sete Povos das Missões Orientais**. The only considerable Jesuit remains in Brazilian territory (very dramatic) are at **São Miguel das Missões**, some 50 km from **Santo Ângelo**. At São Miguel, now a World Heritage Site, there is a church, 1735-1745, and small **museum** ① *0900-1800, US$2.50.* The ruins are not well signposted, it is best to ask for directions at the *rodoviária*. A son et lumière show in Portuguese is held daily, in winter at 2000, and later in summer, although times depend on how many people there are. The show ends too late to return to Santo Ângelo but is worth sticking around for; book a room at the lovely hostel next to the ruins. Gaúcho festivals are held on some Sunday afternoons, in a field near the Mission.

Border with Argentina ➔ *Colour map 7, C1.*

From Santo Ângelo it is a four-hour bus ride to the border town of **Porto Xavier** and an easy crossing (short ferry ride across the Río Uruguay) into Argentina. For exit and entry stamps, visit the federal police at the ferry stations on either side. The five-minute crossing (US$3.75) takes passengers to San Javier, from where there are regular buses, via Posadas, to Iguazú. From the Argentine ferry station it is a short bus or taxi ride to the town centre, with cashpoints, shops, and the bus station.

South of Porto Alegre → *Colour map 7, inset.*

The Rio Guaíba enters the Lagoa dos Patos, which is protected from the Atlantic by a long peninsula. About midway along, 208 km from Porto Alegr, is the charming town of **Mostardas** (www.mostardas.rs.gov.br, with a list of hotels and *pousadas*), a good base for visiting the national park **Lagoa do Peixe** ① *information: Praça Luís Martins 30, Mostardas, T3673 1464, free,* park has no infrastructure. This is one of South America's top spots for migrating birds. The main lake (which has highest bird concentration) is about 20 km from Mostardas and the town of **Tavares**. The park is, however, under threat from invasive planting of trees. The poor road along the peninsula continues 152 km to São José do Norte, opposite Rio Grande (see below).

São Lourenço do Sul On the landward side of the Lagoa dos Patos, **São Lourenço** (*Phone code: 053; Population: 43,691*) is a good place to enjoy the lake, the beaches, fish restaurants and watersports. The town hosts a popular four-day festival in March. On the BR-116, **Pelotas** is the second largest city in the State of Rio Grande do Sul, 271 km south of Porto Alegre, on the Rio São Gonçalo which connects the Lagoa dos Patos with the Lagoa Mirim. There are many good hotels and transport links to all of the state and the Uruguay border at Chuí.

Some 59 km south of Pelotas, at the entrance to the Lagoa dos Patos, is the city **Rio Grande** (*Phone code: 053; Population: 186,544; www.riogrande.rs.gov.br*). It is the distribution centre for the southern part of Rio Grande do Sul, with significant cattle and meat industries. During the latter half of the 19th century Rio Grande was an important centre, but today it is a rather poor town, notable for the charm of its old buildings. The tourist kiosk is at junction of Rua Duque de Caxias and Rua General Becaleron. **Cassino**, a popular seaside town on the ocean, is 24 km away over a good road. There are more beaches further south, all with surf. Across the inlet from Rio Grande is the settlement of **São José do Norte**, founded in 1725. There are frequent passenger ferries and fewer **car ferries** ① *T3503 3151, Estação Ecológica do Taim, BR-471, Km 492, a permit from ICMBio is needed to visit.* Many protected species, including black swans and the quero-quero (the Brazilian lapwing). There are trails outside the reserve.

Border with Uruguay: coastal route → *Colour map 7, inset. Population: 5,167.*

South of Pelotas the BR-471 passes the **Taim** water reserve between the Lagoa Mirim and the ocean on its way to the Brazilian border town of **Chuí**. The highway skirts the town and carries straight through to Uruguay, where it becomes Ruta 9. The main street crossing west to east, Avenida Internacional (Avenida Uruguaí on the Brazilian side, Avenida Brasil in Uruguay) is lined with clothes and household shops in Brazil, duty free shops and a casino in Uruguay. São Miguel fort, built by the Portuguese in 1737, now reconstructed with period artefacts, is worth a visit. A lighthouse 10 km west marks the Barro do Chuí inlet, which has uncrowded beaches and is visited by sea lions. Brazilian immigration is about 2½ km from the border, on BR-471. Make sure that your bus will stop at customs and immigration on both sides of the border. If you not get your passport stamped, you will have trouble leaving either country later on. International buses make the crossing straightforward: the company holds passports; hand over your visitor's card on leaving Brazil and get a Uruguayan one on entry. Have luggage available for inspection. **Uruguayan consulate** ① *Av Venezuela 311, T3265 1151.*

Entering Brazil From Uruguay, on the Uruguayan side, the bus will stop if asked, and wait while you get your exit stamp (with bus conductor's help); on the Brazilian side, the appropriate form is completed by the *rodoviária* staff when you purchase your ticket into Brazil. The bus stops at Polícia Federal (BR-471) and the conductor completes formalities while you sit on the bus.

Border with Uruguay: inland routes → *Colour map 8, A6.*

At **Aceguá**, 60 km south of Bagé, where Brazilian immigration is located, there is a crossing to the Uruguayan town of Melo, and further east, **Jaguarão** with the Uruguayan town of **Rio Branco**, linked by the 1½ km long Mauá bridge and approach road across the Rio Jaguarão. Uruguayan consulate ① *R 27 de Janeiro 701, Jaguarão, T3261 1411.*

Entering Uruguay Before crossing into Uruguay, you must visit Brazilian Polícia Federal in Bagé (R Barão de Triunfo 1572) to get an exit stamp; if not, the Uruguayan authorities will send you back. The crossing furthest west is **Barra do Quaraí** to Bella Unión, via the Barra del Cuaraim bridge. This is near the confluence of the Rios Uruguai and Quaraí. Thirty kilometres east is another crossing from **Quaraí** to **Artigas** in a cattle-raising and agricultural area. Uruguayan consulate ① *R Bento Gonçalves 180, 2nd floor, Quaraí, T3423 1802.*

The southern interior of the state is the region of the real gaúcho. Principal towns of this area include **Santana do Livramento**. Its twin Uruguayan city is Rivera. All one need do is cross the main street to Rivera, but by public transport this is not a straightforward border. The town has hotels and a youth hostel. Uruguayan consulate ① *Av Tamandaré 2080, 5th floor, T3242 1416.*

⊙ Rio Grande do Sul state listings

For hotel and restaurant price codes, and other relevant information, see Essentials.

⊙ Where to stay

Serra Gaúcha *p486*
Gramado
Plenty of hotels and restaurants (mostly pricey).
$$$ Chalets do Vale, R Arthur Reinhelmer 161 (off Av das Hortênsias at about 4700), T3286 4151, www.chaletsdovale.com.br. 3 homely chalets in lovely setting, kitchen, good deal f or groups of 4 or families.
$ pp Albergue Internacional de Gramado, Av das Hortênsias 3880, T3295 1020, www.gramadohostel.com.br. Cosy, dorms, doubles, cheaper for HI members.

Canela
$$$$ Serra Verde, Av Osvaldo Aranha 610, T3278 9700, www.serraverdehotel.com.br. Thermal pools, sauna, massage, parking, very good.
$$$ Vila Suzana Parque, R Col Theobaldo Fleck 15, T3282 2020, www.hotelvilasuzana. com.br. Tiled cabins in a sub-tropical garden, heated pool, welcoming.
$ pp Hostel Viajante, R Ernesto Urbani 132, T3282 2017, www.pousadadoviajante.com.br.

Kitchen facilities, dormitories and double rooms (**$$**).
Camping Camping Clube do Brasil, 1 km from waterfall in Parque do Caracol, 1 km off main road, signposted (8 km from Canela), T3282 4321. Sells excellent honey and chocolate. Sesi, camping or cabins, R Francisco Bertolucci 504, 2½ km outside Canela, T3282 1311. Lovely parkland setting, good facilities. Recommended.

Caxias do Sul *p487*
$$$-$$ Somensi, R Siba Paes 367, Bento Gonçalves, T3453 3111, www.hotelsomensi. com.br. Near the Pipa Pórtico and Cristo Rei church in the upper town. Rooms with a/c or fan, breakfast, garage.
$$-$ Pousada Casa Mia, Irav Niterói 71, Bento Gonçalves, T3451 1215, www.pousada casamia.com.br. HI youth hostel with 2 branches (Av Osvaldo Aranha 381, T3454 4936).

Jesuit Missions *p487*
São Miguel
There is a pizza restaurant next to the *rodoviária* and several snack bars selling decent burgers.
$$$ Pousada das Missões, São Nicolau 601, next to the ruins, T3381 1202,

www.pousadatematica.com.br. Private rooms with or without a/c and TV, youth hostel, lovely site with swimming pool, cheaper for HI members. Highly recommended.
$$ Hotel Barichello, Av Borges do Canto 1567, T3381 1272. Nice and quiet, restaurant with churrasco for lunch.

Santo Ângelo
$$ Turis, R Antônio Manoel 726, T3313 5255. Good value rooms with a/c and fridge, good breakfast, internet.
$$-$ Hotel Nova Esperança, R Sete Povos 463, T3312 1173, www.hotelnovaesperanca.com.br. Simple hotel behind bus station.

Rio Grande p488
$$$ Atlântico Rio Grande, R Duque de Caxias 55, T3231 3833, www.hoteisatlantico.com.br. Reasonable value, restaurant and all services.

Border with Uruguay: coastal route
p488
Chuí
$$$ Bertelli Chuí, BR-471, Km 648, 2 km from town, T3265 1266, www.bertellichuihotel.com.br. Comfortable, with pool.
$$ Rivero, Colômbia 163-A, T3265 1271. With bath, without breakfast.
$$ San Francisco, Av Colombia e R Chile. Shower, restaurant.

⊝ Transport

Jesuit Missions p487
Bus from **Porto Alegre** to **São Miguel das Missões** Sat at 0645 with **Ouro e Prata**, 9½ hrs, US$52. Same company runs many more buses a day to **Santo Ângelo** (T3313 2618), 6½-8 hrs,

US51-59. Buses between São Miguel and Santo Ângelo with **Antonello**, 4 a day.

South of Porto Alegre: Lagoa do Peixe
p488
Bus **Porto Alegre-Mostardas**, 4½ hrs, US$19 with **Palmares**. From Mostardas you can hop off the 1045 bus which passes through the northern end of the park on its way to the beach (basic hotels and restaurants). 3 buses a week between Mostardas/Tavares and São José do Norte (130 km, terrible in the wet), via Bojuru, US$20, 5 hrs in theory.

São Lourenço do Sul p488
Bus From **Porto Alegre**, US$20, several daily.

Rio Grande p488
Bus Frequent daily to and from **Pelotas** (56 km), 1 hr, US$5 and **Porto Alegre** (5 a day, US$28-42, 4½ hrs). Road to Uruguayan border at **Chuí** is paved, but the surface is poor (5 hrs by bus, at 0700 and 1430).

Border with Uruguay: coastal route
p488
Chuí
Bus *Rodoviária* on R Venezuela. Buses run from Chuí to **Pelotas** (6-7 daily, US$21, 4 hrs), **Rio Grande** (0700, 1400, 5 hrs, US$19.50) and **Porto Alegre** (1200, 2330, 7¾ hrs, US$46-54).

Border with Uruguay: inland routes
p489
Santana do Livramento
Bus *Rodoviária* at Gen Salgado Filho e general Vasco Alves. Bus to **Porto Alegre**, 4 daily, 7 hrs, US$37-49.

Foz do Iguaçu

The Iguaçu Falls are the most stunning waterfalls in South America. Their magnitude, and the volume of water that thunders over the edge, has to be seen to be believed. They are 28 km from the city of Foz do Iguaçu. For a description of the falls, maps and an account of road links between Argentina, Brazil and Paraguay, see the Argentina chapter.

Arriving at Foz do Iguaçu

There are good communications by air and road with the main cities of southern Brazil, plus frequent cross-border links to Argentina and Paraguay, see Transport, below. **Tourist offices** In Foz do Iguaçu: **Secretaria Municipal de Turismo** ① *Av das Cataratas 2330 (midway between town and the turn-off to Ponte Tancredo Neves), T2105 8100, 0700-2300, www.pmfi.pr.gov.br.* Very helpful, English spoken. There is a 24-hour tourist help line number, T0800-451516. Airport tourist information is also good, open 0830-2200, gives map and bus information, English spoken. Helpful office, free map, at the *rodoviária*, daily 0700-1800, English spoken. Also at the Terminal de Transporte Urbano, daily 0730-1800.

Parque Nacional Foz do Iguaçu → *Colour map 7, C1.*

① *T3521 4400, www.cataratasdoiguacu.com.br, US$21, payable in reais, Argentine pesos, euros, dollars or credit card, or online by credit card, includes obligatory transport within the park (discounts for Mercosur, Brazilian and local residents). The park is open daily, 0900-1700.*

The Brazilian national park was founded in 1939 and the area was designated a World Heritage Site by UNESCO in 1986. Fauna most frequently encountered are little and red brocket deer, South American coati, white-eared opossum and a sub-species of the brown capuchin monkey. The endangered tegu lizard is common. Over 100 species of butterflies have been identified, among them the electric blue Morpho, the poisonous red and black heliconius and species of Papilionidae and Pieridae. The bird life is rewarding for birdwatchers; five members of the toucan family can be seen.

Take a bus or taxi to the park's entrance, Km 21 from Foz. There's a smart modern **visitor centre** here, with toilets, ATMs, a small café, a large souvenir shop and a Banco Itaú *câmbio* (1000-1500). An **Exposição Ecológica** has information about the natural history of the falls and surrounding park (included in entry fee; English texts poor). Nature lovers are advised to visit first thing in the morning or late in the afternoon, preferably in low season, as crowds can significantly detract from the experience of the falls and surrounding park (at peak times like Semana Santa up to 10,000 visitors a day arrive). From the entrance, shuttle buses leave every 10-15 minutes, stopping first at Park Administration. Next is the start of the **Poço Preto** trail (9 km through the forest to the river, walking or by bicycle), then the **Bananeiras** trail and **Macuco Safari** (see page 495). After 10 km the bus stops at the start of the Cascadas Trail and the Hotel das Cataratas, and finally at the end of the road, Porta Canoas. There are Portuguese, Spanish and English announcements of the five stops. The 1.5-km paved Cascadas Trail is an easy walk, taking you high above the Rio Iguaçu, giving splendid views of all the falls on the Argentine side from a series of galleries. At the end of the path, you can walk down to a boardwalk at the foot of the Floriano Falls which goes almost to the middle of the river to give a good view of and a light spraying from the Garganta del Diablo. There is also a viewing point almost under the powerful Floriano Falls, a dramatic view. From here, there are 150 steps up to the **Porto Canoas** complex (there is a lift for those who find stairs difficult); you can also return the way you came, and walk a little further along the road. The complex consists of a big souvenir shop, toilets, a smart buffet **restaurant**, a café and *lanchonete*, all with good view of the river above the falls. Return to the visitor centre and entrance by free shuttle bus. The whole visit will take around two hours, plus time for lunch. Never feed wild animals and keep your distance when taking photos; coatis have been known to attack visitors with food.

Foz do Iguaçu and around → *Phone code: 045. Population: 301,400.*

A small, modern city, 28 km from the falls, Foz has a wide range of accommodation. The **Parque das Aves bird zoo** ① *Rodovia das Cataratas Km 16, 100 m before the entrance to the falls, T3529 8282, www.parquedasaves.com.br, 0830-1730, US$15,* has received frequent good reports. It contains Brazilian and foreign birds, many species of parrot and beautiful toucans, in huge aviaries through which you can walk, with the birds flying and hopping around you. There are other birds in cages and a butterfly and hummingbird house.

The **Itaipu dam** ① *on the Río Paraná 12 km north, a short film is shown at the visitor centre 10 mins before each guided visit, there are short bus tours, US$12, full tours including the interior*

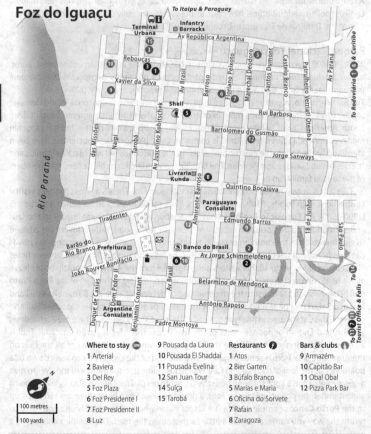

Foz do Iguaçu

Where to stay		Restaurants	Bars & clubs
1 Arterial	9 Pousada da Laura	1 Atos	9 Armazém
2 Baviera	10 Pousada El Shaddai	2 Bier Garten	10 Capitão Bar
3 Del Rey	11 Pousada Evelina	3 Búfalo Branco	11 Oba! Oba!
5 Foz Plaza	12 San Juan Tour	5 Marias e Maria	12 Pizza Park Bar
6 Foz Presidente I	14 Suíça	6 Oficina do Sorvete	
7 Foz Presidente II	15 Tarobá	7 Rafain	
8 Luz		8 Zaragoza	

of the dam: 8 departures daily between 0800 and 1600, US$30 and night views, Fri-Sat 2000, US$7, children and seniors half price for all visits, check times with tourist office, take passport and wear long trousers and sensible shoes, best light for photography in the morning, T0800-645 4645, www. itaipu.gov.br, www.turismoitaipu.com.br, is the site of the largest single power station in the world, built jointly by Brazil and Paraguay. Construction of this massive scheme began in 1975 and it became operational in 1984. The main dam is 8 km long, creating a lake which covers 1400 sq km. The 18 turbines have an installed capacity of 12,600,000 Kw and produce about 75 bn Kwh a year, providing 80% of Paraguay's electricity and 25% of Brazil's. The Paraguayan side may be visited from Ciudad del Este. Several beaches can be visited around the lake. A large reforestation project is underway and six biological refuges have been created on the lakeshore in both countries. There is also the **Ecomuseu de Itaipu** ① *Av Tancredo Neves, Km 11, T0800-645 4645, Tue-Sun 0830-1730, US$5,* and **Refúgio Bela Vista** ① *closed Tue, 4 visits a day from the visitor centre, US$10,* animal rescue centre and home to the fauna displaced by the dam, both geared to educate about the preservation of the local culture and environment, or that part which isn't underwater. Recommended. In addition there is the **Polo Astronômico** ① *T3576 7203, Wed-Sun at 0930 and 1530, Fri-Sat also 1900, US$9,* a planetarium and astronomical observatory.

Border with Argentina

All foreigners must get exit and entry stamps both in Brazil and Argentina every time they cross the border, even if it is only for the day. It is your responsibility to get the stamps, if riding a taxi make shure it stops at both border posts, if riding a city bus, ask for a transfer, get off at the Brazilian border post and get on the next bus through without paying again. If entering Brazil, be sure you also get the entry card stamped.

Between October-February Brazil is one hour ahead of Argentina. It takes about two hours to get from Foz to the Argentine falls, very tiring when the weather is hot.

Border with Paraguay → *Brazil is 1 hr ahead of Paraguay.*

The Ponte de Amizade/Puente de Amistad (Friendship Bridge) over the Río Paraná, 6 km north of Foz, leads straight into the heart of Ciudad del Este. Paraguayan and Brazilian immigration formalities are dealt with at opposite ends of the bridge. Ask for relevant stamps if you need them. The area is intensively patrolled for contraband and stolen cars; ensure that all documentation is in order.

⊙ Foz do Iguaçu listings

For hotel and restaurant price codes, and other relevant information, see Essentials.

● Where to stay

Foz do Iguaçu *p491, map p492*
Note Check hotels' websites for internet prices and special offers. Av Juscelino Kubitschek and the streets south of it, towards the river, are unsafe at night. Many prostitutes around R Rebouças and Almirante Barroso. Taxis are only good value for short distances when you are carrying all your luggage.

$$$$ Suíça, Av Felipe Wandscheer 3580, T3025 3232, www.hotelsuica.com.br. Some way out of the city, rooms, suites and lodges, comfortable, Swiss manager, helpful with tourist information, attractive pools, gym.
$$$$-$$$ Luz, Av Gustavo Dobrandino da Silva 145, near *rodoviária*, T3522 3535, www.luzhotel.com.br. Buffet restaurant, pool. Recommended.
$$$ Baviera, Av Jorge Schimmelpfeng 697, T3523 5995, www.hotelbavieraiguassu.com.br. Chalet-style exterior, on main road, central for bars and restaurants, comfortable, renovated.

$$$ Del Rey, R Tarobá 1020, T2105 7500, www.hoteldelreyfoz.com.br. Nothing fancy, but perennially popular, little pool, great breakfasts. Recommended.

$$$ Foz Plaza, R Marechal Deodoro 1819, T3521 5500, www.fozplazahotel.com.br. Serene and very nice, restaurant, pool. Also has a new annex.

$$$ Foz Presidente I, R Xavier da Silva 1000 and **II** at R Mcal Floriano Peixoto 1851, T3572 4450, www.fozpresidentehoteis.com.br. Good value, decent rooms, restaurant, pool, Number 1 is convenient for buses.

$$$ San Juan Tour, R Marechal Deodoro 1349, T2105 9100, www.sanjuanhoteis.com. br. Cheaper if booked on-line. Comfortable, excellent buffet breakfast, popular, good value. Recommended. The more expensive San Juan Eco is on the road to the falls.

$$$ Tarobá, R Tarobá 1048, T2102 7770, www.hoteltaroba.com.br. In Best Western chain, bright and welcoming, small pool, nice rooms, helpful, good breakfast (extra), good value. Recommended.

$$ Pousada Cataratas, R Parigot de Sousa 180, T3523 7841, www.pousadacataratas.com.br. Well-maintained modern rooms with decent hot showers, small pool, good value with regular discounts and promotions through the website. Can organize tours and transfers to and from the airport and *rodoviária*.

$$ Pousada da Laura, R Naipi 671, T3572 3374. **$** pp in shared dorm with good breakfast. Secure, kitchen, laundry facilities, a popular place to meet other travellers.

$$ Pousada El Shaddai, R Rebouças 306, near Terminal Urbana, T3025 4493, www.pousada elshaddai.com.br. Rooms are cheaper with fan and shared bath, **$** pp in dorm, pool.

$$ Pousada Evelina, R Irlan Kalichewski 171, Vila Yolanda, T3574 3817, www.pousada evelina.com.br. Lots of tourist information, English, French, Italian, Polish and Spanish spoken, good breakfast and location, near Muffato Supermarket, near Av Cataratas on the way to the falls. Warmly recommended.

$$-$ Arterial, Av José Maria de Brito 2661, T3573 1859, hotelarterial@hotmail.com.

Near *rodoviária*. Good value, huge breakfast, opposite is a 24-hr buffet restaurant.

Camping **Camping e Pousada Internacional**, R Manêncio Martins 21, 1½ km from town, T3529 8183, www. campinginternacional.com.br. For vehicles and tents, half price with International Camping Card, also basic cabins (**$**), helpful staff, English, German and Spanish spoken, pool, restaurant. **Note** Camping is not permitted by the Hotel das Cataratas and falls.

Outside Foz do Iguaçu

$$$$ Hotel das Cataratas, directly over-looking the falls, Km 32 from Foz, T2102 7000, www.hoteldascataratas.com. Generally recommended, caters for lots of groups, attractive colonial-style building with pleasant gardens (where wildlife can be seen at night and early morning) and pool. Non-residents can eat here, midday and evening buffets; also à-la-carte dishes and dinner with show. Member of the Orient Express group. An environmental fee of about US$10 is added to the room rate.

On the road to the falls (Rodovia das Cataratas) are several expensive modern hotels with good facilities (eg Bristol Viale Cataratas, www.vialecataratas.com.br, Carimã, www.hotelcarima.com.br, San Martin, www.hotelsanmartin.com.br), but for budget travellers, check out:

$$ Hostel Natura, Rodovia das Cataratas Km 12.5, Remanso Grande, T3529 6949, www.hostelnatura.com (near the Paudimar). Rustic hostel with a small pool set in fields. Rooms with fan, **$** pp in dorm, camping, pool table, TV lounge, small kitchen, arrange visits to the falls; website has detailed instructions for how to reach them.

$$-$ Paudimar Campestre, Av das Cataratas Km 12.5, Remanso Grande, near airport, T3529 6061, www.paudimar.com.br. In high season HI members only. From airport or town take Parque Nacional bus (0525-0040) and get out at Remanso Grande bus stop, by Hotel San Juan Eco, then take the free alimentador shuttle (0700-1900) to the hostel, or 1.2 km walk from main road. Camping as well ($), pool, soccer pitch, quiet, kitchen and communal meals, breakfast. Highly recommended. Tours run to either side of the falls (good value). **Paudimar** desk at *rodoviária*.

🍴 Restaurants

Foz do Iguaçu *p491, map p492*
$$$ Búfalo Branco, R Rebouças 530, T3523 9744. Superb all you can eat *churrasco*, includes filet mignon, bull's testicles, salad bar and desert. Sophisticated surroundings and attentive service. Highly recommended.
$$$ Rafain, Av das Cataratas 1749, 13523 1177, www.rafainchurrascaria.com.br, closed Sun evening. Out of town, take a taxi or arrange with travel agency. Set price for excellent buffet with folkloric music and dancing (2100-2300), touristy but very entertaining. Recommended.
$$$ Zaragoza, R Quintino Bocaiúva 882, T3574 3084. Large and upmarket, for Spanish dishes and seafood. Recommended.
$$ Atos, Av Juscelino Kubitschek 865, T3572 2785. Per kilo buffet with various meats, salads, sushi and puddings. Lunch only.
$$ Bier Garten, Av Jorge Schimmelpfeng 550, T3523 3700. Bustling pizzeria, *churrascaria* and *choperia*.

Cafés
Marias e Maria, Av Brasil 505. Good confeitaria.
Oficina do Sorvete, Av Jorge Schimmelpfeng 244. Daily 1100-0100. Excellent ice creams, a popular local hang-out.

🍸 Bars and clubs

Foz do Iguaçu *p492, map p492*
Bars, all doubling as restaurants, concentrated on Av Jorge Schimmelpfeng for 2 blocks from Av Brasil to R Mal Floriano Peixoto. Wed to Sun are best nights; crowd tends to be young.
Armazém, R Edmundo de Barros 446, T3572 7422. Intimate and sophisticated, attracts discerning locals, good atmosphere, mellow live music. Recommended.

Capitão Bar, Av Jorge Schimmelpfeng 288 and Almte Barroso, T3572 1512. Large, loud and popular, nightclub attached.
Oba! Oba!, Av Mercosul 400, T3529 9070, www.obaobasambashow.com.br. At Churrascaria Bottega. Daily 1200-1530 for lunch, Mon-Sat 2000-2200, with live samba show at 2200.
Pizza Park Bar, R Almirante Barroso 993. Specializes in vodka and whisky brands. Wi-Fi zone.

🎯 What to do

Foz do Iguaçu *p491, map p492*
Tours
There are many travel agents on Av Brasil. Lots of companies on both sides organize conventional tours to the falls, useful more for convenience rather than information, since they collect you from your hotel. Confirm whether all entrance fees are included. Beware of overcharging by touts at the bus terminal.

Parque Nacional Foz do Iguaçu *p491*
Tours
Guayi Travel, R Irian Kalichewiski 265, Vila Yolanda, T3027 0043, www.guayitravel.com. Excellent tours to both sides of the falls, Ciudad del Este, Itaipu and around, including options for birders and wildlife enthusiasts. English and Spanish spoken.
Macuco Safari, T3529 6262, or T9963 3857, www.macucosafari.com.br, 2 hrs, US$70, involves a ride down a 1½-km path through the forest in open jeeps and an optional walk. Then a fast motor boat whisks you close to the falls themselves (in the same vein as Jungle Explorer on the Argentine side). Portuguese, English and Spanish spoken, take insect repellent and waterproof camera bag.

🚌 Transport

Parque Nacional Foz do Iguaçu *p491*
Bus Leave from the Terminal Urbana in Foz, Av Juscelino Kubitschek and República Argentina, every 40 mins from 0730-1800, and are clearly marked 'Parque Nacional'.

You can get on or off at any point on the route past the airport and Hotel das Cataratas, 40 mins, US$1.50 one way, payable in reais or pesos (bus route ends at the park entrance where you purchase entry tickets and change to a park bus).

Foz do Iguaçu p491, map p492

Air Aeroporto Internacional de Cataratas, BR 469, Km 16.5, 13 km east of the centre and 12 km from the falls, T3521 4200. In Arrivals are ATMs and Caribe Tours e Câmbio, car rental offices, tourist office and an official taxi stand, US$25 to town centre. All buses marked Parque Nacional pass the airport in each direction, US$1.50, 0525-0040, does not permit large amounts of luggage but backpacks OK. Many hotels run minibus services for a small charge. Daily flights to Rio, São Paulo, Curitiba and other Brazilian cities.
Bus For transport to the falls see above under Parque Nacional Foz do Iguaçu. *rodoviária* long distance terminal , Av Costa e Silva, 4 km from centre on road to Curitiba, T3522 3633; bus to centre from next to the taxis, US$1.20. Taxi US$10. Book departures as soon as possible. As well as the tourist office, there is Guarda Municipal (police), Visa ATM, and luggage store. To Curitiba, 9-10 hrs, paved road, US$62. To Florianópolis, US$72-76, 14 hrs. Unesul to Porto Alegre, US$65-74. To São Paulo, 16 hrs, US$85. To Campo Grande, US$53. Local buses leave from the Terminal de Transporte Urbano, TTU on Av Juscelino Kubitscheck and passengers can buy pre-paid cards, US$1.20 per journey (it costs more if you don't have a card). Services called *alimentador* in the suburbs are free.

Foz do Iguaçu and around: Itaipu dam p492

Bus Take bus lines Conjunto C Norte or Conjunto C Sul from Foz do Iguaçu Terminal de Transporte Urbano, US$1.50.

Border with Argentina: Foz do Iguaçu/ Puerto Iguazú p493

Bus Marked 'Puerto Iguazú' run every 30 mins Mon-Sat, hourly on Sun, from the Terminal Urbana, crossing the border bridge; 30 mins' journey, 3 companies, US$2.50. See above for procedures regarding entry stamps.
Note Be sure you know when the last bus departs from Puerto Iguazú for Foz (usually 1900); last bus from Foz 1950. If visiting the Brazilian side for a day, get off the bus at the Hotel Bourbon, cross the road and catch the bus to the Falls, rather than going into Foz and out again. Combined tickets to Puerto Iguazú and the falls cost more than paying separately.

Border with Paraguay: Foz do Iguaçu/ Ciudad del Este p493

Bus (Marked Cidade-Ponte) leave from the Terminal Urbana, Av Juscelino Kubitschek, for the Ponte de Amizade (Friendship Bridge), US$1.20. To Asunción, Pluma (0700), Nuestra Señora de la Asunción, from *rodoviária*, US$20-22 (cheaper from Ciudad del Este).
Car If crossing by private vehicle and only intending to visit the national parks, this presents no problems. Another crossing to Paraguay is at Guaíra, at the northern end of the Itaipu lake. It is 5 hrs north of Iguaçu by road and can be reached by bus from Campo Grande and São Paulo. Ferries cross to Saltos del Guaira on the Paraguayan side.

ⓘ Directory

Foz do Iguaçu p491, map p492

Banks It is difficult to exchange on Sun but quite possible in Paraguay where US dollars can be obtained on credit cards. There are plenty of banks with ATMs, câmbios and travel agents on Av Brasil. **Consulates** Argentina, Travessa Eduardo Bianchi 26, T3574 2969. Mon-Fri 1000-1500. Paraguay, R Marechal Deodoro 901, T3523 2898, Mon-Fri 0830-1630. **Medical services** Free 24-hr clinic, Av Paraná 1525, opposite Lions Club, T3521 1850. Few buses: take taxi or walk (about 25 mins).

Salvador de Bahia

Salvador, the third largest city in Brazil, is capital of the state of Bahia, dubbed 'Africa in exile' for its mixture of the African and the European. Often referred to as Bahia, rather than Salvador, the city is home to a heady mix of colonial buildings, beautiful beaches, African culture and pulsating musical rhythms. It stands on the magnificent Baía de Todos os Santos, a sparkling bay dotted with 38 islands. The bay is the largest on the Brazilian coast covering an area of 1,100 sq km. Rising above the bay on its eastern side is a cliff which dominates the landscape and, perched on top, 71 m above sea level, are the older districts with buildings dating back to the 17th and 18th centuries. Beyond the state capital are many fine beaches, particularly in the south around Porto Seguro, while inland is the harsh sertão, traversed by the Rio São Francisco.

Arriving in Salvador → *Phone code: 071. Post code: 40000. Colour map 5, C5.*
Population: 3.2 million.

Orientation Luis Eduardo Magalhães airport is 32 km from city centre. The **Rodoviária** is 5 km from the city with regular bus services to the centre and Campo Grande; the journey can take up to one hour especially at peak periods.

The broad peninsula on which the city is built is at the mouth of the Baía de Todos Os Santos. On the opposite side of the bay's entrance is the Ilha de Itaparica. The commercial district of the city and its port are on the sheltered, western side of the peninsula; residential districts and beaches are on the open Atlantic side. The point of the peninsula is called Barra, which is itself an important area. The centre of the city is divided into two levels, the Upper City (or Cidade Alta) where the Historical Centre lies, and the Lower City (Cidade Baixa) which is the commercial and docks district. The two levels are connected by a series of steep hills called *ladeiras*. The easiest way to go from one level to the other is by the 74-m-high **Lacerda** lift which connects Praça Cairu in the lower city with Praça Municipal in the upper, US$0.05. There is also the **Plano Inclinado Gonçalves**, a funicular railway which leaves from behind the Cathedral going down to Comércio, the commercial district (US$0.05, closes 1300 on Saturday and all Sunday). Most visitors limit themselves to the Pelourinho and historical centre, Barra, the Atlantic suburbs (notably Rio Vermelho which has lively nightlife) and the Itapagipe peninsula, which is north of the centre. The roads and avenues between these areas are straightforward to follow and are well served by public transport. Other parts of the city are not as easy to get around, but have less of a tourist interest. If going to these areas a taxi may be advisable until you know your way around. ▶▶ *See Transport, page 512.*

Best time to visit Salvador Temperatures range from 25°C to 32°C, never falling below 19°C in winter. Humidity can be high, which may make the heat oppressive. It rains somewhat all the year but the main rainy season is between May and September.

Tourist offices Bahiatursa ① *Av Simon Bolivar s/n, Centro de Convenções da Bahia, 1st floor, T3117 3000, www.bahiatursa.ba.gov.br,* has lists of hotels and accommodation in private homes. Other offices at: **Pelourinho** ① *R das Laranjeiras 12, T3321 2133, daily 0830-2100,* English and German spoken; **Rodoviária** ① *T3450 3871, daily 0730-2100,* good, English spoken; and **airport** ① *T3204 1244, daily 0730-2300.* See also www.bahia.com.br.

Safety As in all large cities, use your common sense and be careful of your possessions at all times and in all districts. The authorities have made efforts to police the old part of the city and Barra, which are now well lit at night. The civil police are reported to be very sympathetic and helpful. Police are little in evidence after 2300, however, and at night you should leave valuables securely in your hotel. Also at night, the areas around and in the lifts and buses are unsafe. Do not walk down any of the links between the old and new city, especially the Ladeira de Misericórdia, which links the Belvedere, near the Lacerda Lifts, with the lower city. Nor should you walk around the forts in Porto da Barra at night. Avoid using communal washrooms in popular venues on show nights since thieves target such places; use a restaurant loo instead. Should a local join you on the street or at your table for a chat, leave at once if drugs are mentioned.

Background

On 1 November 1501, All Saints' Day, the navigator Amérigo Vespucci sailed into the bay. As the first European to see it, he named it after the day of his arrival. The first Governor General, Tomé de Sousa, arrived on 23 March 1549 to build a fortified city to protect Portugal's interest from constant threats of Dutch and French invasion. Salvador was formally founded on 1 November 1549 and remained the capital of Brazil until 1763. By the 18th century, it was the most important city in the Portuguese Empire after Lisbon, ideally situated in a safe, sheltered harbour along the trade routes of the 'New World'.

The city's first wealth came from the cultivation of sugar cane and tobacco, the plantations' workforce coming from the West coast of Africa. For three centuries Salvador was the site of a thriving slave trade. Even today, Salvador is described as the most African city in the Western Hemisphere and the University of Bahia boasts the only chair in the Yoruba language in the Americas. The influence permeates the city: food sold on the street is the same as in Senegal and Nigeria, Bahian music is fused with pulsating African polyrhythms, men and women nonchalantly carry enormous loads on their heads, fishermen paddle dug-out canoes in the bay, the pace of life is a little slower than elsewhere. The pulse of the city is candomblé, an Afro-Brazilian religion in which the African deities of Nature, the Goddess of the sea and the God of creation are worshipped. These deities (or orixás) are worshipped in temples (terreiros) which can be elaborate, decorated halls, or simply someone's front room with tiny altars to the orixá. Candomblé ceremonies may be seen by tourists – but not photographed – on Sunday and religious holidays. Contact the tourist office, Bahiatursa, or see their twice-monthly calendar of events. Salvador today is a city of 15 forts, 166 Catholic churches, 1,000 candomblé temples and a fascinating mixture of old and modern, rich and poor, African and European, religious and profane. It is still a major port exporting tropical fruit, cocoa, sisal, soya beans and petrochemical products. Its most important industry, though, is tourism. Local government has done much to improve the fortunes of this once rundown, poor and dirty city and most visitors feel that the richness of its culture is compensation enough for any problems they may encounter. The Bahianas (black women who dress in traditional 18th-century costumes) are street vendors who sit behind their trays of delicacies, savoury and seasoned, made from the great variety of local fish, vegetables and fruits. Their street food is one of the musts for visitors.

Places in Salvador

Centro Histórico

There is much more of interest in the Upper than in the Lower City. From Praça Municipal to the Carmo area 2 km north along the cliff is the Centro Histórico (Historical Centre), now a national monument and also protected by UNESCO. It was in this area that the Portuguese built their fortified city and where today stand some of the most important examples of colonial architecture in the Americas. This area is undergoing a massive restoration programme funded by the Bahian state government and UNESCO. Colonial houses have been painted in pastel colours. Many of the bars have live music which spills out onto the street on every corner. Patios have been created in the open areas behind the houses with open air cafés and bars. Artist ateliers, antique and handicraft stores have brought new artistic blood to what was once the bohemian part of the city. Many popular traditional restaurants and bars from other parts of Salvador have opened branches here. Its transformation has also attracted many tourist shops and the area can get crowded.

Praça Municipal, Praça de Sé and Terreiro de Jesus

Dominating the Praça Municipal is the old Casa de Câmara e Cadeia or **Paço Municipal** (Council Chamber – 1660), while alongside is the **Palácio Rio Branco** (1918), once the

1 Salvador centre

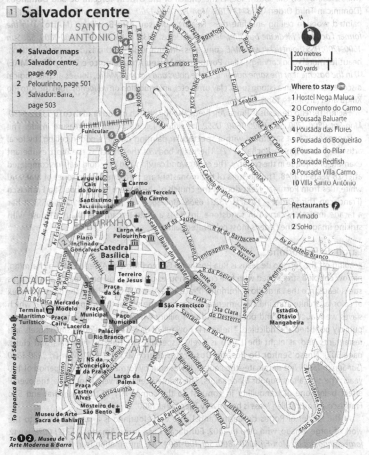

➡ **Salvador maps**
1 Salvador centre, page 499
2 Pelourinho, page 501
3 Salvador: Barra, page 503

200 metres
200 yards

Where to stay
1 Hostel Nega Maluca
2 O Convento do Carmo
3 Pousada Baluarte
4 Pousada das Flores
5 Pousada do Boqueirão
6 Pousada do Pilar
7 Pousada Redfish
8 Pousada Redfish
9 Pousada Villa Carmo
10 Villa Santo Antônio

Restaurants
1 Amado
2 SoHo

Governor's Palace. Leaving it with its panoramic view of the bay, Rua da Misericórdia goes north passing the **Santa Casa Misericórdia** ① *Rua da Misericórdia 6, T3322 7666, Mon-Fri 1000-1730, Sun 1300-1700,* (1695 – see the high altar and painted tiles), to Praça da Sé. This praça with its mimosa and flamboyant trees leads into Terreiro de Jesus, a picturesque praça named after the church which dominates it. Built in 1692, the **church of the Jesuits** became the property of the Holy See in 1759 when the Jesuits were expelled from all Portuguese territories. The façade is one of the earliest examples of baroque in Brazil, an architectural style which was to dominate the churches built in the 17th and 18th centuries. Inside, the vast vaulted ceiling and 12 side altars in baroque and rococo frame the main altar completely leafed in gold. The tiles in blue, white and yellow in a tapestry pattern are also from Portugal. The church is now the **Catedral Basílica** ① *0900-1200, 1400-1800.* On the eastern side of the square is the church of **São Pedro dos Clérigos** ① *Mon-Fri 0900-1200, 1400-1800,* which is beautifully renovated, while close by, on the south-side, is the church of the **Ordem Terceira de São Domingos** (Dominican Third Order) ① *T3242 4185, Mon-Fri, 0900-1200, 1400-1700,* which has a beautiful painted wooden ceiling and fine tiles. Nearby is **Museu Afro-Brasileiro (MAfro)** ① *in the former Faculty of Medicine building, Terreiro de Jesus, T3321 2013, Mon-Fri 0900-1800, Sat-Sun 1000-1700, US$3, joint ticket with MAE,* compares African and Bahian Orixás (deities) celebrations, beautiful murals and carvings, all in Portuguese. **Museu Arqueológico e Etnográfico (MAE)** ① *in the basement of the same building, same hours and ticket as MAfro,* houses archaeological discoveries from Bahia (stone tools, clay urns, etc), an exhibition on *indígenas* from the Alto Rio Xingu area (artefacts, tools, photos).

Facing Terreiro de Jesus is Praça Anchieta and the church of **São Francisco** ① *T3322 6430, Mon-Sat 0800-1700, Sun 0800-1600, US$2.* Its simple façade belies the treasure inside. The entrance leads to a sanctuary with a spectacular painting on the wooden ceiling, by local artist José Joaquim da Rocha (1777). The main body of the church is the most exuberant example of baroque in the country. The cedar wood carving and later gold leaf was completed after 28 years in 1748. The cloisters of the monastery are surrounded by a series of blue and white tiles from Portugal. Next door is the church of the **Ordem Terceira de São Francisco** (Franciscan Third Order – 1703) ① *T3321 6968, Mon-Sat 0800-1700 (Sun to 1600), US$2.* It has a façade intricately carved in sandstone. Inside is a quite remarkable Chapter House with striking images of the Order's most celebrated saints.

Largo do Pelourinho

Leading off the Terreiro de Jesus is Rua Portas do Carmo (formerly Alfredo Brito), a charming, narrow cobbled street lined with fine colonial houses painted in different pastel shades. This street leads into the Largo do Pelourinho (Praça José Alencar). Considered the finest complex of colonial architecture in Latin America, it was once the site of the whipping post at which slaves were auctioned and punished and of a pillory where unscrupulous tradesmen were publicly punished and ridiculed. The area is now full of galleries, boutiques, small hotels and restaurants and at night the Largo is lively, especially on Tuesday (see Bars and clubs, page 507). **Nosso Senhor Do Rosário Dos Pretos church** ① *T3241 5781, Mon-Fri 0830-1800 (Sat-Sun to 1500), free* dominates the square. It was built by former slaves over a period of 100 years. The side altars honour black saints. The painted ceiling is very impressive, the overall effect being one of tranquillity in contrast to the complexity of the Cathedral and São Francisco. Afro-Brazilian Mass is held every Tuesday at 1800.

At the corner of Portas do Carmo and Largo do Pelourinho is a small museum to the work of Jorge Amado, who died in 2002, **Fundação Casa Jorge Amado** ① *T3321 0070, www. jorgeamado.org.br, Mon-Fri 1000-1800, Sat 100-1600, free.* Information is in Portuguese only, but the café walls are covered with colourful copies of his book jackets. The Carmo Hill is at the top of the street leading out of Largo do Pelourinho. **Museu Abelardo Rodrigues** ① *Solar Ferrão, Pelourinho, R Gregório de Mattos 45, 1300-1800 except Mon, US$2*, is a religious art museum, with objects from the 17th, 18th and 19th centuries, mainly from Bahia, Pernambuco

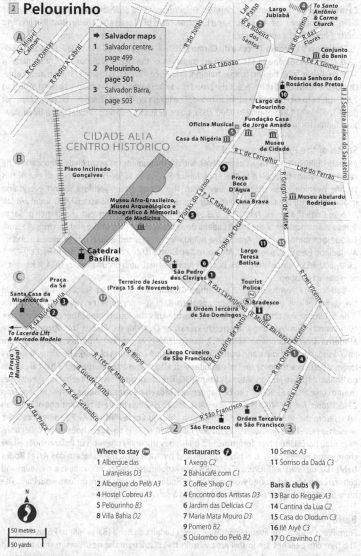

2 Pelourinho

Salvador maps
1 Salvador centre, page 499
2 Pelourinho, page 501
3 Salvador: Barra, page 503

CIDADE ALTA
CENTRO HISTÓRICO

Where to stay
1 Albergue das Laranjeiras D3
2 Albergue do Pelô A3
4 Hostel Cobreu A3
5 Pelourinho B3
8 Villa Bahia D2

Restaurants
1 Axego C2
2 Bahiacafé.com C1
3 Coffee Shop C1
4 Encontro dos Artistas D3
6 Jardim das Delícias C2
9 Pomerô B2
5 Quilombo do Pelô B2
7 Maria Mata Mouro D3
10 Senac A3
11 Sorriso da Dadá C3

Bars & clubs
13 Bar do Reggae A3
14 Cantina da Lua C2
15 Casa do Olodum C3
16 Ilê Aiyê C3
17 O Cravinho C1

50 metres
50 yards

N

and Maranhão. **Museu da Cidade** ① *Largo do Pelourinho, Tue-Fri 0900-1830, Sat 1300-1700, Sun 0900-1300*, has exhibitions of arts and crafts and old photographs. From the higher floors of the museum you can get a good view of the Pelourinho. The **Conjunto do Benin** ① *R Padre Agostinho Gomes 17, Pelourinho, T3241 5679, Mon-Fri 1200-1800, below NS do Rosario dos Pretos*, has diverse exhibitions and shows African crafts, photos and videos on Benin and Angola. The **Casa da Nigéria** ① *R Portas do Carmo 26, Pelourinho, T3328 3782*, offers a similar programme orientated more to Yoruba culture and has showcases of African and African Brazilian arts and crafts, photographs and a library.

The **Igreja da Ordem Terceira do Carmo** (1709) ① *Mon-Sat 0800-1130, 1330-1730, Sun 1000-1200, US$1*, houses one of the sacred art treasures of the city, a sculpture of Christ made in 1730 by a slave who had no formal training, Francisco Xavier das Chagas, known as O Cabra. One of the features of the piece is the blood made from whale oil, ox blood, banana resin and 2,000 rubies to represent the drops of blood. The **Igreja do Carmo** ① *Morro do Carmo, Mon-Sat 0800-1200, 1400-1800, Sun 0800-1200, US$1*, has a beautiful ceiling painted by the freed slave José Teófilo de Jesus.

South of the Praça Municipal

Avenida Chile leads to **Praça Castro Alves**, with its monument to Castro Alves, who started the campaign which finally led to the Abolition of Slavery in 1888. Two streets lead out of this square, Avenida 7 de Setembro, busy with shops and street vendors selling everything imaginable, and, parallel to it, Rua Carlos Gomes. **Museu de Arte Sacra** ① *R do Sodré 276 (off R Carlos Gomes), Mon-Fri 1130-1730, US$2*, is in the 17th-century convent and church of Santa Teresa, at the bottom of the steep Ladeira de Santa Teresa. Many of the 400 carvings are from Europe, but some are local. Among the reliquaries of silver and gold is one of gilded wood by Aleijadinho (see box, page 445). **Mosteiro São Bento** ① *Av 7 de Setembro, Mon-Fri 0900-1200, 1300-1600, US$3*, dates from 1582, but was rebuilt after Dutch occupation in 1624. It houses a religious art musuem.

Both streets eventually come to **Campo Grande** (also known as Praça Dois de Julho). In the centre of the praça is the monument to Bahian Independence, 2 July 1823. Avenida 7 de Setembro continues out of the square towards the Vitória area. There are some fine 19th-century homes along this stretch, known as Corredor da Vitória. The **Museu de Arte Moderna** ① *off Av Contorno, T3117 6139, Tue-Fri 1300-1900, Sat 1300-2100, free*, converted from an old sugar estate house and outbuildings, has a fine collection of works by some of Brazil's foremost artists and holds special exhibitions. It also has an arts cinema and a bar/café (Solar do Unhão) with live jazz on Saturday from 1830. The buildings are worth seeing for themselves (best to take a taxi as access can be dangerous). **Museu de Arte da Bahia** ① *Av 7 de Setembro 2340, Vitória, Tue-Fri 1400-1900, Sat-Sun 1430-1900, US$2*, has interesting paintings of Brazilian artists from the 18th to the early 20th century. **Museu Costa Pinto** ① *Av 7 de Setembro 2490, weekdays 1430-1900, but closed Tue, Sat-Sun 1500-1800, US$2*, is a modern house with collections of crystal, porcelain, silver, furniture, etc. It also has the only collection of balangandãs (slave charms and jewellery). It also has a garden and pleasant café. The **Palacete das Artes Rodin Bahia** ① *R da Graça 289, Graça, T3117 6987, www.palacetedasartes.ba.gov.br*, is a museum and cultural centre based around work by Auguste Rodin. Many works were on loan from Paris. The museum also holds temporary exhibitions, has a café/bar and gardens.

Barra

From Praça Vitória, the avenue continues down Ladeira da Barra (Barra Hill) to Porto da Barra. The best city beaches are in this area. Also in this district are the best bars, restaurants and nightlife. The Barra section of town has received a facelift with a new lighting system. The pavements fill with people day and night and many sidewalk restaurants and bars are open along the strip from Porto da Barra as far as the Cristo at the end of the Farol da Barra beach. Great attention to security is given. A little further along is the **Forte de Santo Antônio da Barra** and **lighthouse**, 1580, built on the spot where Amérigo Vespucci landed in 1501. It is right at the mouth of the bay where Baía de Todos Os Santos and the South Atlantic Ocean meet and is the site of the first lighthouse built in the Americas. The interesting **Museu Hidrográfico** ① *Tue-Sat 1300-1800, US$2*, which has a good café for watching the sunset, is housed in the upper section of the Forte de Santo Antônio; fine views of the bay and coast, recommended.

Atlantic beach suburbs

The promenade leading away from the fort and its famous lighthouse is called Avenida Oceânica, which follows the coast to the beach suburbs of **Ondina**, Amaralina and Pituba. The road is also called Avenida Presidente Vargas and, confusingly, has different numbering. Beyond Pituba are the **best ocean beaches** at Jaguaripe, **Piatã** and Itapoã. En route the bus passes fishing colonies and surf centres at Amaralina and Pituba where jangadas can be seen. A jangada is a small raft peculiar to the northeastern region of Brazil used extensively as well as dug-out canoes. Near Itapoã is the **Lagoa do Abaeté**, surrounded by brilliant, white sands. This is a deep, freshwater lake where local women traditionally come to wash their clothes and then lay them out to dry in the sun. The road leading up from the lake offers a panoramic view of the city in the distance, the coast, and the contrast of the white sands and fresh water less than 1 km from the sea and its golden beaches. (Do not go there alone.) Beyond the lighthouse at **Itapoã** are the magnificent ocean beaches of Stella Maris and Flamengo, both quiet during the week but very busy at the weekends. Beware of strong undertow at these beaches.

Salvador: Barra
3

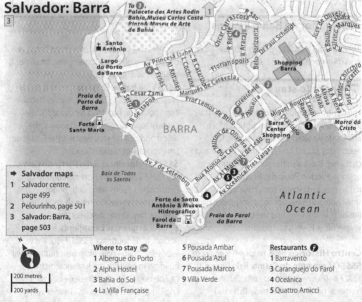

➡ **Salvador maps**
1 Salvador centre, page 499
2 Pelourinho, page 501
3 Salvador: Barra, page 503

200 metres
200 yards

Where to stay 🛏
1 Albergue do Porto
2 Alpha Hostel
3 Bahia do Sol
4 La Villa Française
5 Pousada Ambar
6 Pousada Azul
7 Pousada Marcos
9 Villa Verde

Restaurants 🍴
1 Barravento
3 Caranguejo do Farol
4 Oceânica
5 Quattro Amicci

Bonfim and Itapagipe

See also the famous church of **Nosso Senhor do Bonfim** on the Itapagipe peninsula in the suburbs north of the centre, whose construction began in 1745. It draws endless supplicants (particularly on Friday and Sunday) offering favours to the image of the Crucified Lord set over the high altar; the number and variety of ex-voto offerings is extraordinary. The processions over the water to the church on the third Sunday in January are particularly interesting. Also on the Itapagipe peninsula is a colonial fort on **Monte Serrat** point, and at Ribeira the church of **Nossa Senhora da Penha** (1743). The beach here has many restaurants, but the sea is polluted.

Itaparica

Across the bay from Salvador lies the island of Itaparica, 29 km long and 12 km wide. The town of Itaparica has many fine residential buildings from the 19th century, plus the church of **São Lourenço**, one of the oldest in Brazil. During the summer months the streets are ablaze with the blossoms of the beautiful flamboyant trees. Take a bus or kombi by the coast road (Beira Mar) which passes through the villages of Manguinhos, Amoureiras and Ponta de Areia, which has one of the best beaches on the island with many *barracas*.

The beaches at **Mar Grande** are fair but can be dirty at times. There are many *pousadas* in Mar Grande and at Penha, to the south. The further south you go, the better the beaches.

From Bom Despacho there are many buses, combis and taxis to all parts of the island. Combis and taxis can be rented for trips but be prepared to bargain, US$40-50 for half a day. There are also buses to other towns such as Nazaré das Farinhas, Valença (see page 517) and also **Jaguaribe**, a small, picturesque colonial port. Both of these towns are on the mainland connected by a bridge on the southwest side of the island, turn off between Mar Grande and Cacha Pregos (bus company, **Viazul**). There are good beaches across the bay on the mainland, but a boat is needed to reach these (US$16).

⊙ Salvador de Bahia listings

For hotel and restaurant price codes, and other relevant information, see Essentials.

⊙ Where to stay

The Centro Histórico is the ideal place to stay; the Pelourinho if you're on a tight budget and Santo Antônio if you are looking for reasonably priced hotels with real charm and character. Barra also has some reasonable options. **Hidden Pousadas Brazil**, www. hiddenpousadasbrazil.com, have a network of small hotels in Salvador and throughout Bahia. Business visitors will find the best hotels in Rio Vermelho, a 10-min taxi ride from the centre.

Centro Histórico *p498, maps p499 and p501*
$$$$ O Convento do Carmo, R do Carmo 1, T3327 8400, www.pestana.com. Outstanding historical hotel in the centre with a range of suites in a beautifully converted baroque convent, excellent restaurant, spa, small pool, business services.
$$$$ Villa Bahia, Largo do Cruzeiro de São Francisco 16-18, T3322 4271, www.villabahia. com. Boutique hotel in a renovated 18th-century town house, themed rooms, the airiest and brightest of which is the Goa room. Small pool, hot tub on the roof.
$$$-$$ Pelourinho, R das Portas do Carmo 20, T3243 2324, www.hotelpelourinho.com. Refurbished 1960s hotel with bright decorations, some rooms with great views over the bay, some special offers.
$ pp Albergue das Laranjeiras, R Inácio Acciolli 13, Pelourinho, T3321 1366, www. laranjeirashostel.com.br. In beautiful colonial building in heart of the historical district, can be noisy, café and crêperie downstairs, English spoken. **$$** double, cheaper with

shared bath, for HI members and in low season. Good for meeting other travellers. Warmly recommended.

$ pp Albergue do Pelô, R do Passo 5, T3242 8061, www.alberguedopelo.com.br. Bright reception area, simple freshly painted dorms for 4-12. All are single sex. Breakfast included.

$ pp Hostel Cobreu, Ladeira do Carmo 22, T3117 1401, www.hostelcobreu.com. Good value, US-run, convenient for Pelourinho nightlife, simple but attractive dorms and rooms (**$$**).

Santo Antônio

$$$$-$$$ Pousada das Flores, R Direita de Santo Antônio 442, near Santo Antônio fort, T3243 1836, www.pflores.com.br. Brazilian/French owners, excellent breakfast, beautiful old house.

$$$$-$$$ Villa Santo Antônio, R Direita de Santo Antônio 130, T3326 1270, www.hotel-santoantonio.com. Bright and comfortable converted colonial house, best rooms with views over the bay, all rooms different, good service.

$$$ Pousada do Pilar, R Direita do Santo Antônio 24, T3241 6278, www.pousadadopilar.com. Same owners as Morro do São Paulo's Vila Guaiamu, verandas with excellent bay views, good breakfast, helpful manager, pleasant roof terrace bar.

$$$ Pousada Redfish, Ladeira do Boqueirão 1, T3243 8473, www.hotelredfish.com. English-owned stylish little boutique with plain, large rooms, some with terraces and open-air showers.

$$$-$$ Pousada Baluarte, Lad Baluarte 13, T3327 0367, www.pousadabaluarte.com. Bohemian household, lovely owners, 5 rooms, cheaper without bath, excellent home-made breakfasts.

$$$-$$ Pousada do Boqueirão, R Direita do Santo Antônio 48, T3241 2262, www.pousada boqueirao.com.br. Family-run, beautiful remodelled house overlooking bay, relaxed atmosphere, most European languages spoken, great food, first class in all respects. Highly recommended.

$$$-$$ Pousada Villa Carmo, R do Carmo 58, T3241 3924, www.pousadavillacarmo. com.br. Italian/Brazilian owned, many European languages spoken, very comfortable, rooms with fan or a/c.

$ pp Hostel Nega Maluca, R dos Marchantes 15, T3242 9249, www.negamaluca.com. Popular party hostel, good dorms and private rooms (**$$**), well-equipped, good breakfast.

Campo Grande/Vitória

Upmarket residential area, between Barra and city centre, convenient for museums.

$$$ Bahia do Sol, Av 7 de Setembro 2009, T3338 8800, www.bahiadosol.com.br. Comfortable, safe and frigobar in room, family run, good restaurant, bureau of change. Ask for a room on the upper floors.

Barra *p502, map p503*

$$$ Pousada Azul, R Dra P Fróes 102, T3011 9798, www.pousadaazul.com.br. A quiet place in a semi-residential street, a/c or fan, generous breakfast, self-service laundry.

$$$ Villa Verde, R da Palmeira 190, T3011 3597/8854 6601, www.pousadavillaverde.com. A/c studios with kitchen and double room with fan, garden, terrace, hammocks, safe, very good. Recommended.

$$ Pousada Ambar, R Afonso Celso 485, T3264 6956, www.ambarpousada.com.br. Also has albergue at **$**. Good service, breakfast, convenient, French owner also speaks English.

$ pp Albergue do Porto, R Barão de Sergy 197, T3264 6600, www.alberguedoporto. com.br. One block from beach, short bus ride or 20 mins on foot from historical centre. HI hostel in beautiful turn-of-the-century house, cheaper for members, breakfast, convenient, English spoken, en suite double rooms **$$**, laundry facilities, safe, TV lounge, games room, courtyard. Highly recommended.

$ pp Alpha Hostel, R Eduardo Diniz Gonçalves 128, T3237 6282, www.alphahostel.com. Barra branch if the Rio hostel, bright, colourful dorms and rooms with fan, helpful staff, hammocks in public areas. The backstreets in the area should be treated with caution at night.

$ Pousada Marcos, Av Oceânica 281, T3264 5117, www.pousadamarcos.com.br. Youth hostel-style, great location near the lighthouse, very busy, notices in Hebrew for potential travelling companions, efficient.
$ La Villa Francaise, R Recife 222, Jardim Brasil, T3245 6008, www.lavilafrancaise.com. Small guesthouse behind Shopping Barra, bright, colourful, well run, quieter than many others, helpful French-Brazilian owners, sumptuous breakfast.

Atlantic beach suburbs *p503*
$$$$ Pestana Bahia, R Fonte de Boi 216, Rio Vermelho, T2103 8000, www.pestana.com. One of the best in Salvador, all comfort and facilities including for the disabled. No access to the sea.
$$$ Catharina Paraguaçu, R João Gomes 128, Rio Vermelho, T3334 0089, www.hotel catharinaparaguacu.com.br. Charming, small, colonial-style, tastefully decorated.
$$$ Ibis, R Fonte do Boi 215, T3330 8300, www.accorhotels.com.br. Large hotel in this budget business chain, safe, sea views from the upper floors. Great value.
Camping Note that sea bathing is dangerous off shore near the campsites.
Camping Clube do Brasil, R Visconde do Rosário 409, Rosário, T3242 0482. **Ecológica**, R Alameida da Praia, near the lighthouse at Itapoã, take bus from Praça da Sé direct to Itapoã, or to Campo Grande or Barra, change there for Itapoã, about 1 hr, then 30 mins' walk, T3374 3506. Bar, restaurant, hot showers. Highly recommended.

Itaparica *p504*
$$$-$$ Sonho do Verão, R São Bento 2, opposite Pousada Arco Iris, Mar Grande, T3633 1316, http://hotelsonhodeverao.com. br. Chalets and apartments, cooking facilities, French and English spoken, jazz club and art gallery. Like other *pousadas* they rent bicycles; they also rent horses.
$$ Pousada Zimbo Tropical, Estrada de Cacha Pregos, Km 3, Rua Yemanjá, Aratuba, T3638 1148, www.zimbo-tropical.com.

French/Brazilian-run, bungalows in tropical gardens, good breakfast, evening meals and tours available. Recommended.

Restaurants

Local specialities
The main dish is *moqueca*, seafood cooked in a sauce made from coconut milk, tomatoes, red and green peppers, fresh coriander and *dendê* (palm oil). It is traditionally cooked in a wok-like earthenware dish and served piping hot at the table. Served with *moqueca* is *farofa* (manioc flour) and a hot pepper sauce which you add at your discretion, it's usually extremely hot so try a few drops before venturing further. The dendê is somewhat heavy and those with delicate stomachs are advised to try the *ensopado*, a sauce with the same ingredients as the *moqueca*, but without the palm oil.

Nearly every street corner has a Bahiana selling a wide variety of local snacks, the most famous of which is the *acarajé*, a kidney bean dumpling fried in palm oil which has its origins in West Africa. To this the Bahiana adds *vatapá*, a dried shrimp and coconut milk pâté (also delicious on its own), fresh salad and hot sauce (*pimenta*). For those who prefer not to eat the palm oil, the *abará* is a good substitute. Abará is steamed, wrapped in banana leaves. Seek local advice on which are most hygienic stalls to eat from. Two good Bahianas are Chica, at Ondina beach (on the street to the left of Mar A Vista Hotel) and Dinha in Rio Vermelho (who serves acarajé until midnight, extremely popular), and Regina at Largo da Santana (very lively in the late afternoon). Bahians usually eat *acarajé* or *abará* with a chilled beer on the way home from work or on the beach at sunset. Another popular dish with African origins is *Xin-Xin de Galinha*, chicken on the bone cooked in dendê, with dried shrimp, garlic and squash.

Centro Histórico *p498, maps p499 and p501*
$$$ Maria Mata Mouro, R da Ordem Terceira 8, Pelourinho, T3321 3929. International menu, good service, relaxing ambience, closed Sun night.

$$$ **Sorriso da Dadá**, R Frei Vicente 5, T3321 9642, www.dada.com.br. Bahia's most famous chef has had many illustrious clients, but Dadá herself is not always in attendance.

$$$-$$ **Axego**, R João de Deus1, T3242 7481. Celebrated for its seafood, *feijoada* at Sun lunch.

$$$-$$ **Encontro dos Artistas**, R das Laranjeiras 15, T3321 1721. Very good seafood and *moquecas* served in a little street-side restaurant.

$$$-$$ **Jardim das Delícias**, R João de Deus 12, Pelourinho, T3321 1449. Elegant restaurant and antiques shop with tropical garden, very reasonable for its setting, classical or live music.

$$ **Quilombo do Pelô**, R das Portas do Carmo 13, T3322 4371. Rustic Jamaican restaurant, open daily from 1100, good food with relaxed, if erratic service, vegetarian options. Also has hotel.

$$ **Senac**, Praça José Alencar 13-15, Largo do Pelourinho, T3324 4557. State-run catering school, with typical Bahian cooking upstairs and per kilo lunches downstairs, both a/c. Upstairs is better but lots of choice, including vegetarian, downstairs.

$$-$ **Pomerô**, R Portas do Carmo 33, Pelourinho, T3321 5556, www.pomero.com.br. Closed Mon. Good value, simple grilled meats, fish steaks, bar snacks, *moquecas*, popular

$ **Bahiacafé.com**, Praça da Sé 20, T3322 1266. Smart, Belgian-run internet café, good breakfasts, excellent food, English spoken.

$ **Coffee Shop**, Praça da Sé 5, T3322 7817. Cuban-style café serving sandwiches; main attraction is excellent coffee, and tea served in china cups, doubles as cigar shop.

Between Historical Centre and Barra

$$$ **Amado**, Av Lafayete Coutinho 660, Comércio, Campo Grande, T3322 3520, www.amadobahia.com.br. The best of Salvador's top-end restaurants, set on a deck overlooking the bay. The menu is strong on seafood.

$$$ **SoHo**, Av Contorno 1010, Píer D, Bahia Marina, T3322 4554. One of the city's most fashionable restaurants. Excellent Japanese food. Great cocktails and sea views, dinner only. Bus connections poor, go by taxi.

Barra *p502, map p503*

$$$ **Barravento**, Av Oceânica 814, T3247 2577. Popular, upmarket beach bar restaurant, seafood, steaks, cocktails and *chope*.

$$ **Oceánica**, Pres Vargas 1, T3264 3561. Long-established, popular seafood restaurant, open late.

$$ **Quatro Amicci**, R Dom Marcos Teixeira 35. Excellent pizzas from wood-fired oven, bright, lively at weekends.

$ **Caranguejo do Farol**, Av Oceânica 235, above the road, T3264 7061. Specializing in crab, extremely busy, also a buzzing bar.

Many medium-priced a/c restaurants in Shopping Barra and Barra Center Shopping.

Itaparica *p504*

$$$ **Philippe's Bar and Restaurant**, Largo de São Bento, Mar Grande. French and local cuisine, information in English and French.

$$ **Volta ao Mundo**, Largo de São Bento 165, Mar Grande. Good value, buffet lunches, all-you-can-eat.

There are many Bahianas selling *acarajé* in the late afternoon and early evening in the main praça by the pier at Mar Grande.

Bars and clubs

Nightlife is concentrated on and around the Pelourinho where there is always a free live street band on Tue and at weekends. The Pelourinho area is also good for a bar browse; though be wary after 2300. There are many bars on the Largo de Quincas Berro d'Água, especially along R Portas do Carmo. R João de Deus and its environs are dotted with simple pavement bars with plastic tables. The most famous Salvador musicians are the *maracatú* drum orchestras like **Olodum** and **Ilê Aiyê** (see below). There is live music all year round but the best time to hear the most frenetic performers, particularly the *axê* stars, is during Carnaval.

Largo do Pelourinho *p500, map p501*
Bar do Reggae and **Praça do Reggae**, Ladeiro do Pelourinho, by Nossa Senhora dos

Rosarios dos Pretos. Live reggae bands every Tue and more frequently closer to carnival.

Cantina da Lua, Praça 15 de Novembro 2, Terreiro de Jesus, T3322 4041. Daily, popular, good place to meet, outdoor seating, but the food isn't great.

O Cravinho, Praça 15 de Novembro 3, T3322 6759. Dark little bar with occasional live music, *cachaça* made on the premises and bar food.

Barra *p502, map p503*

Most Barra nightlife happens at the Farol da Barra (lighthouse). R Marquês de Leão is very busy, with lots of bars with tables on the pavement. Like the Pelourinho, the whole area is good for a browse, but be wary of pickpockets.

Habeas Copos, R Marquês de Leão 172. Famous and traditional street side bar, very popular.

Atlantic beach suburbs *p503*

Once the bohemian section of town the nightlife in **Rio Vermelho** rivals the Pelourinho. There are a number of lively bars around the Largo de Santana, a block west of the Hotel Catharina Paraguaçu.

⊕ Entertainment

Salvador de Bahia *p497, maps p499 and p501*
The Fundação Cultural do Estado da Bahia edits *Bahia Cultural*, a monthly brochure listing monthly cultural events. These can be found in most hotels and Bahiatursa information centres. Local newspapers *A Tarde* and *Correio da Bahia* have good cultural sections listing all events in the city.

Cinema

The main shopping malls at Barra, Iguatemi, Itaigara and Brotas, and **Cineart** in Politeama (Centro), run more mainstream movies. See www.saladearte.art.br for film shows in various cinemas and other locations. The impressive Casa do Comércio building near Iguatemi houses the **Teatro do SESC** with a mixed programme of theatre, cinema and music Wed-Sun.

Music

During the winter (Jul-Sep) ring the blocos to confirm that free rehearsals will take place.

Ara Ketu, T3264 8800, hails from the sprawling Periperi suburb in the Lower City. Once a purely percussion band Ara Ketu has travelled widely and borrowed on various musical forms (samba, candomblé, soukous, etc) to become a major carnival attraction and one of the most successful bands in Bahia. Rehearsals take place on Thu nights at 1930 on Trapiche Barnabé, Comércio. As these get very full, buy tickets in advance from Pida kiosks, the Central do Carnaval, Ticketmix and at the bloco's HQ, R Afonso Celso, 161, Barra.

Banda Olodum, R Gregório de Mattos 22, T3321 5010, http://olodum.uol.com.br. Olodum's headquarters where the drumming troupe made famous by their innovative power-house percussion and involvement with Paul Simon, Michael Jackson and Branford Marsalis perform live every Tue and Sun at 1930 to packed crowds.

Didá, Neguinho do Samba was the musical director of Olodum until he founded Didá, an all-woman drumming group based along similar lines to Olodum. They rehearse on Fri nights in the Praça Teresa Batista, Pelourinho. Starts 2000, US$10.

Filhos de Gandhi, the original and largest African drumming group, formed by striking stevedores during the 1949 carnival. The hypnotic shuffling cadence of Filhos de Gandhi's afoxé rhythm is one of the most emotive of Bahia's carnival.

Ilê Aiyê, R do Curuzu 197, Liberdade, T3256 8800, www.ileaiye.com.br. Established in the largest suburb of the city, Ilê Aiyê is a thriving cultural group dedicated to preserving African traditions which under the guidance of its president Vovô is deeply committed to the fight against racism. Rehearsals take place mid-week at Boca do Rio and on Sat nights in front of their headquarters (address above, details of live performances throughout Salvador are published here).

Timbalada, T3355 0680, www.timbalada. com. Carlinhos Brown is a local hero. He has become one of the most influential musical composers in Brazil today, mixing great lyrics, innovative rhythms and a powerful stage presence. He played percussion with many Bahian musicians, until he formed his own percussion group, Timbalada. He has invested heavily in his native Candeal neighbourhood: the Candy All Square, a centre for popular culture, is where the Timbalada rehearsals take place every Sun night, 1830, from Sep to Mar. Not to be missed. Brown opened the **Museu du Ritmo**, R Torquato Bahia 84, Edif Mercado do Ouro, T3353 4333, www.carlinhosbrown. com.br/universo/museu-du-ritmo,and the **International Centre for Black Music**, a complex built around a 1000-sq-m concert arena in a giant courtyard formed from the walls of a former colonial mansion house which once was home to the gold exchange.

Artists and bands using electronic instruments and who tend to play in the *trios eléctricos* draw heavily on the rich rhythms of the drumming groups creating a musical genre known as **Axé**. The most popular of such acts are **Chiclete com Banana**, www. chicletecombanana.com.br, and **Ivete Sangalo**. Also look out for the internationally famous **Daniela Mercury**. **Gerónimo** was one of the first singer/songwriters to use the wealth of rhythms of the Candomblé in his music and his song *E d'Oxum* is something of an anthem for the city. **Mariene de Castro** is Bahia's most exciting new artist and one of the few singing traditional Bahian samba.

All the above have albums released and you can find their records easily in most record stores. See Shopping in the Pelourinho. Also try Flashpoint in Shopping Iguatemi.

Theatre
Castro Alves, at Campo Grande (Largo 2 de Julho), T3339 8000, www.tca.ba.gov.br, seats 1400 and is considered one of the best in Latin America. It also has its own repertory theatre, the **Sala de Coro**, for more experimental productions. The theatre's Concha Acústica is an open-air venue used

frequently in the summer, attracting the big names in Brazilian music.
Teatro Gregório de Matos in Praça Castro Alves, T3322 2646, offers space to new productions and writers.
Theatro XVIII, R Frei Vicente, T3332 0018, www.theatroxviii.com.br, an experimental theatre in the Pelourinho.
Vila Velha, Passéio Público, Gamboa da Cima, T3336 1384. A historically important venue where many of the *tropicalistas* first played. Nowadays it has an eclectic programme of modern dance, theatre and live music.

⊛ Festivals

Salvador de Bahia *p497, maps p499 and p501*
6 Jan (Epiphany); **Ash Wednesday** and **Maundy Thursday**, half-days; **2 Jul** (Independence of Bahia); **30 Oct**; Christmas Eve, half-day. An important local holiday is Festa do Nosso Senhor do Bonfim; it takes place on the 2nd Sun after Epiphany, but the washing or *lavagem* of the Bonfim church, with its colourful parade, takes place on the preceding Thu (usually mid-Jan). The Festa da Ribeirav is on the following Mon. Another colourful festival is that of the fishermen of Rio Vermelho on **2 Feb**; gifts for Yemanjá, Goddess of the Sea, are taken to sea in a procession of sailing boats to an accompaniment of candomblé instruments. The Holy Week processions among the old churches of the upper city are also interesting. For **Carnival**, see box, page 510.

⊙ Shopping

Largo do Pelourinho *p497, map p501*
Handicrafts Artesanato Santa Bárbara, R Portas do Carmo 7. Excellent handmade lace products. **Atelier Portal da Cor**, Ladeira do Carmo 31. Run by a co-operative of local artists, Totonho, Calixto, Raimundo Santos, Jô, good prices. Recommended. **Instituto Mauá**, R Gregório de Matos 27. Open Tue-Sat 0900-1800, Sun 1000-1600, good-quality Bahian handicrafts at fair prices, better value and

Carnival in Bahia

Carnival officially starts on Thursday night at 2000 when the keys of the city are given to the Carnival King 'Rei Momo'. The unofficial opening though is on Wednesday with the Lavagem do Porto da Barra, when throngs of people dance on the beach. Later on in the evening is the Baile dos Atrizes, starting at around 2300 and going on until dawn, very bohemian, good fun. Check with Bahiatursa for details on venue, time, etc (carnival dates in 2015 12-17 February, in 2016 4-9 February); see also http://home.centraldocarnaval.com.br and www.carnaval.bahia.com.br.

Carnival in Bahia is the largest in the world and it encourages active participation. It is said that there are 1½ million people dancing on the streets at any one time.

There are two distinct musical formats. The Afro Blocos are large drum-based troupes (some with up to 200 drummers) who play on the streets accompanied by singers atop mobile sound trucks. The first of these groups was the Filhos de Gandhy (founded in 1949), whose participation is one of the highlights of Carnival. Their 6000 members dance through the streets on the Sunday and Tuesday of Carnival dressed in their traditional costumes, a river of white and blue in an ocean of multicoloured carnival revellers. The best known of the recent Afro Blocos are Ilê Aiye, Olodum, Muzenza and Malê Debalé. They all operate throughout the year in cultural, social and political areas. Not all of them are receptive to foreigners among their numbers for Carnival. The basis of the rhythm is the enormous *surdo* (deaf) drum with its bumbum bumbum bum anchor- beat, while the smaller *repique*, played with light twigs, provides a crack-like overlay. Ilê Aiye take to the streets around 2100 on Saturday night and their departure from their headquarters at Ladeira do Curuzu in the Liberdade district is not to be missed. The best way to get there is to take a taxi to Curuzu via Largo do Tanque thereby avoiding traffic jams. The ride is a little longer in distance but much quicker in time. A good landmark is the Paes

---

quality for crafts than the Mercado Modelo. **Loja de Artesanato do SESC**, Largo Pelourinho. Mon-Fri 0900-1800 (closed for lunch), Sat 0900-1300, similar store to Instituto Mauá.

Jewellery In the Pelourinho are: **Casa Moreira**, Ladeira da Praça, just south of Praça da Sé. Exquisite jewellery and antiques, most very expensive, but some affordable charms. **Scala**, Praça da Sé. Handmade jewellery using locally mined gems (eg. Acquamarine, amethyst and emerald), workshop at back.

Markets Mercado Modelo, at Praça Cairu, lower city, offers many tourist items such as wood carvings, silver-plated fruit, leather goods, local musical instruments. Lace items for sale are often not handmade (despite labels), are heavily marked up and are much better bought at their place of origin (for example Ilha de Maré, Pontal da Barra and Marechal Deodoro). Bands and dancing, especially Sat (but for money from tourists taking photos), closed at 1200 Sun. The largest and most authentic market is the **Feira de São Joaquim**, 5 km from Mercado Modelo along the sea front: trucks, burros, horses, boats, people, mud, very smelly, every day (Sun till 1200 only), busiest on Sat morning; interesting African-style pottery and basketwork; very cheap. (The car ferry terminal for Itaparica is nearby.) Every Wed from 1700-2100 is a **handicrafts fair** in the 17th-century fort of Santa Maria at opposite end of Porto da Barra beach.

Music in the Pelourinho The major carnival afro blocos have boutiques selling T-shirts, etc: **Boutique Olodum**, on Praça José Alencar, **Ilê Aiyê**, on R Francisco Muniz Barreto 16. **Cana Brava**, R João de Deus 22, T3321 0536. CD shop with knowledgeable American owner. **Oficina de Investigação Musical**, R das Portas do Carmo 24, T3322 2386. Handmade traditional percussion instruments (and lessons, US$15 per hr), Mon-Fri 0800-1200 and 1300-1600. Best place to buy berimbaus in Bahia.

Mendonça supermarket on the corner of the street from where the *bloco* leaves. From there it's a short walk to the departure point.

The enormous *trios eléctricos* 12-m sound trucks, with powerful sound systems that defy most decibel counters, are the second format. These trucks, each with its own band of up to 10 musicians, play songs influenced by the afro blocos and move at a snail's pace through the streets, drawing huge crowds. Each Afro Bloco and *bloco de trio* has its own costume and its own security personnel who cordon off the area around the sound truck. The *bloco* members can thus dance in comfort and safety.

There are three official Carnival routes. The oldest is Osmar, from Campo Grande to Praça Castro Alves near the old town. The *blocos* go along Avenue 7 de Setembro and return to Campo Grande via the parallel R Carlos Gomes. The best night at Praça Castro Alves is Tuesday (the last night of Carnival) when the famous '*Encontro dos trios*' (Meeting of the Trios) takes place. Trios jostle for position in the square and play in rotation until dawn (or later!) on Ash Wednesday. It is not uncommon for major stars from the Bahian (and Brazilian) music world to make surprise appearances.

The second route is Dodô, from Farol da Barra to Ondina. The *blocos alternativos* ply this route. These are nearly always *trios eléctricos* connected with the more traditional *blocos* who have expanded to this now popular district. The third and newest route is Batatinha, in the historic centre and the streets of Pelourinho. No *trios eléctricos* take part on this route, but marching bands, folkloric groups and fancy-dress parades.

Day tickets for these are available the week leading up to Carnival. Check with Bahiatursa on where the tickets are sold for the stands. There is little or no shade from the sun so bring a hat and lots of water. Best days are Sunday to Tuesday. Or just go it alone; find a *barraca* in the shade and watch the *blocos* go by.

● What to do

Salvador de Bahia *p497, maps p499 and p501*
Boat and bus tours Available from several companies. All-day boat trip on Baía de Todos Os Santos last from 0800-1700 including a visit to Ilha dos Frades, lunch on Itaparica (not included). There are also city tours.
Capoeira A martial art, often said to have developed from the traditional foot-fighting technique introduced from Angola by African slaves, but latterly claimed to be have originated with the indigenous people of Brazil and then modified by slaves. The music is by drum, tambourine and berimbau; there are several different kinds of the sport. If you want to attempt Capoeira, the best school is **Mestre Bimba**, R das Laranjeiras, T3322 0639, www.capoeiramestre bimba.com.br. It has male and female teachers. Exhibitions take place in the Largo do Pelourinho every Friday evening around 2000. You can also see capoeiristas in public spaces like the Pelourinho, outside the Mercado Modelo and at Campo Grande. Genuine capoeiristas do not expect a contribution, but if you wish to take pictures ask first. At the Casa da Cultura at **Forte de Santo Antônio Alem do Carmo**, there are several capoeira schools, usually giving classes in the evening.

Tour operators and guides
Ben Paris, T8812 4576, bt_paris@yahoo.com. A US resident in Salvador who can take you around the sights. Good access to musicians, candomblé terreiros and fascinating spots in the Recôncavo.
Tatur Turismo, Av Tancredo Neves 274, Centro Empresarial Iguatemi, Sala 222-224, Bloco B, T3114 7900, www.tatur.com.br. Run by Irishman, Conor O'Sullivan. English spoken. Specializes in Bahia, arranges private guided tours and can make any travel, hotel and accommodation arrangements. Highly recommended.

⊝ Transport

Salvador de Bahia *p497, maps p499 and p501*
Air An a/c bus service every 30-40 mins between **Luis Eduardo Magalhães Airport** and the centre, a distance of 32 km, costs US$2. It takes the coast road to the city, stopping at hotels en route. Service runs 0500-2200 (0600 at weekends) and 0630-2100 from the Praça da Sé to the airport. Also ordinary buses, US$1.50. 'Special' taxis to both Barra and centre (buy ticket at the airport desk next to tourist information booth), US$35-45; normal taxis (from outside airport), US$30. Allow plenty of time for travel to the airport and for check-in. ATMs are in a special area to the extreme right as you arrive, a good place to get money. **Banco do Brasil** is to the extreme left, open Mon-Fri 0900-1500. **Jacarandá** exchange house is in front of international arrivals, open 24 hrs a day, but poor rates and only good for changing a small amount (count your money carefully). Tourist information booth, English spoken, has list of hotels and useful map.

Daily flights to all the main cities.
Bus Local buses US$1.50, executivos, a/c, US$2 to US$4 depending on the route. On buses and at the ticket-sellers' booths, watch your change and beware pickpockets. To get from the old city to the ocean beaches, take a 'Barra' bus from Praça da Sé to the Barra point and walk to the nearer ones; the Aeroporto executivo leaves Praça da Sé, passing Barra, Ondina, Rio Vermelho, Amaralina, Pituba, Costa Azul, Armação, Boca do Rio, Jaguaripe, Patamares, Piatã and Itapoã, before turning inland to the airport. The glass-sided Jardineira bus goes to Flamengo beach (30 km from the city) following the coastal route; it passes all the best beaches; sit on the right hand side for best views. It leaves from the Praça da Sé daily 0730-1930, every 40 mins, US$3.50. For beaches beyond Itapoã, take the executivo to Stella Maris and Flamengo beaches. These follow the same route as the Jardineira.

Long distance buses leave from the *rodoviária*, near Shopping Iguatemi, T3460 8300. Bus RI or RII, 'Centro-Rodoviária-Circular';

in the centre, get on in the Lower City at the foot of the Lacerda lift; buses also go to Campo Grande (US$1.50). A quicker executive bus from Praça da Sé or Praça da Inglaterra (in front of McDonald's), Comércio, run to Iguatemi Shopping Centre, US$2, weekdays only, from where there is a walkway to the *rodoviária* (take care in the dark, or a taxi, US$13.50-19). Itapemirim, T3358 0037, www.itapemirim.com.br, buses to **Recife**, US$80, 13 hrs. To **Fortaleza**, 19 hrs, US$103 at 1900. An d to **Rio**, 27 hrs, US$140, good stops, clean toilets. **São Paulo**, 30 hrs, US$154, with São Geraldo, www.saogeraldo.com.br. **Belo Horizonte**, 22 hrs, Gontijo, T3358 7448, www.gontijo.com.br, US$106. There are daily bus services to **Brasília** along the fully paved BR-242, via Barreiras, 23 hrs, Paraíso, US$90. **Ilhéus**, 7 hrs, Aguia Branca, US$35, *leito* US$75. **Porto Seguro**, Aguia Branca, overnight at 2000, US$75. To **Lençóis** 3 a day, 6½ hrs, US$29 with **Real Expresso**, www.realexpresso.com.br, quickest and safest is early morning bus. Frequent services to the majority of destinations; a large panel in the main hall lists destinations and the relevant ticket office.
Taxi Taxi meters start at US$1.50 for the 'flagdown' and US$0.70 per 100 m. They charge US$30 per hr within city limits, and 'agreed' rates outside. Taxi Barra-Centro US$10 daytime; US$15 at night. Watch the meter, especially at night; the night-time charge should be 30% higher than daytime charges.

Itaparica *p504*
Ferry The main passenger ferry leaves for Bom Despacho from São Joaquim (buses for Calçada, Ribeira stop across the road from the ferry terminal; the 'Sabino Silva – Ribeira' bus passes in front of the Shopping Barra). First ferry from Salvador at 0540 and, depending on demand, at intervals of 45 mins thereafter; last ferry from Salvador at 2230. Returning to Salvador the 1st ferry is at 0515 and the last at 2300. In summer ferries are much more frequent. Information from COMAB/Ferry Fácil, open 0700-2300 at terminal. A one way ticket for foot passengers Mon-Fri

is US$1.75, Sat-Sun US$2. Catamarans depart for Bom Despacho twice daily, US$3 (US$3.75 at weekends). **Mar Grande** can be reached by a smaller ferry (**Lancha**) from the Terminal Marítimo in front of the Mercado Modelo in Salvador. The ferries leave every 45 mins and the crossing takes 50 mins, US$3 return.

ⓘ Directory

Salvador de Bahia *p497, maps p499 and p501*
Banks Banks are open 1000-1600. Selected branches of major banks have ATMs for Visa, also **Banco 24 Horas**. Don't change money on the street especially in the Upper City where

higher rates are usually offered. **Shopping Tour** in Barra Shopping centre changes dollars, as will other tour agencies. If stuck, all the big hotels will exchange, but at poor rates.
Language classes Diálogo, R Dr João Pondé 240, Barra, T3264 0053, www.dialogo-brazilstudy.com. Accommodation with host families, optional dance, *capoeira* and cookery classes. **Useful addresses** Immigration: (for extensions of entry permits), **Policia Federal**, Av O Pontes 339, Aterro de Água de Meninos, Lower City, T3319 6000, open 1000-1600. Show an outward ticket or sufficient funds for your stay. **Tourist Police**: R Gregório de Matos 16, T3321 1092.

Inland from Salvador

There are strong historical associations inland from Salvador, seen in the colonial exploitation of sugar and diamonds. Lençóis, famous for the latter, also has some beautiful countryside, which is ideal for trekking.

The Recôncavo
The area around Salvador, known as the Recôncavo Baiano, was one of the chief centres of sugar and tobacco cultivation in the 16th century. Some 73 km from Salvador is **Santo Amaro da Purificação**, an old sugar centre sadly decaying, noted for its churches (often closed because of robberies), municipal palace (1769), fine main praça, birthplace of the singers Caetano Veloso and his sister Maria Bethânia and ruined mansions including Araújo Pinto, former residence of the Barão de Cotegipe. Other attractions include the splendid beaches of the bay, the falls of Vitória and the grotto of Bom Jesus dos Pobres. The festivals of **Santo Amaro**, 24 January-2 February, and **Nossa Senhora da Purificação** on 2 February itself are interesting. There is also the **Bembé do Mercado** festival on 13 May. Craftwork is sold on the town's main bridge. There are no good hotels or restaurants.

Cachoeira and São Félix
At 116 km from Salvador and only 4 km from the BR-101 coastal road are the towns of **Cachoeira** (Bahia's 'Ouro Preto', *Population: 30,416*) and **São Félix** (*Population: 13,699*), on either side of the Rio Paraguaçu below the Cachoeira dam. Cachoeira was twice capital of Bahia: once in 1624-1625 during the Dutch invasion, and once in 1822-1823 while Salvador was still held by the Portuguese. There are beautiful views from above São Félix.

Cachoeira's main buildings are the **Casa da Câmara e Cadeia** (1698-1712), the **Santa Casa de Misericórdia** (1734 – the hospital, someone may let you see the church), the 16th-century **Ajuda** chapel (now containing a fine collection of vestments), and the Convent of the **Ordem Terceira do Carmo**, whose church has a heavily gilded interior. Other churches are the **Matriz** with 5-m-high azulejos, and **Nossa Senhora da Conceição do Monte**. There are beautiful lace cloths on the church altars. All churches are either restored or in the process of restoration. The **Museu Hansen Bahia** ⓘ *R Ana Néri*, houses fine engravings by the German artist who made the Recôncavo his home in the 1950s. There is a great wood-carving tradition in Cachoeira.

The artists can be seen at work in their studios. A 300 m railway bridge built by the British in the 19th century spans the Rio Paraguaçu to São Felix where the Danneman cigar factory can be visited to see hand-rolling. **Tourist office** ① *R Ana Néri 4, Cachoeira, T3425 1123.*

Lençóis → *Phone code: 075. Colour map 5, C4. Population: 8,910.*

This historical monument and colonial gem was founded in 1844 to exploit the diamonds in the region. While there are still some *garimpeiros* (gold prospectors), it is not precious metals that draw most visitors, but the climate, which is cooler than the coast, the relaxed atmosphere and the wonderful trekking and horse riding in the hills of the Chapada Diamantina. A few of the options are given below under Excursions, and *pousadas* and tour operators offer guiding services to point you in the right direction. This is also a good place for buying handicrafts. **Tourist office** ① *Praça Otaviano Alves 01, Antiga Prefeitura, T3334 1380, daily 0800-1200, 1700-2100.*

Parque Nacional da Chapada Diamantina → *Colour map 5, C4.*

Palmeiras, 50 km from Lençóis, is the headquarters of the Parque Nacional da Chapada Diamantina (founded 1985), which contains 1500 sq km of mountainous country. There is an abundance of endemic plants, waterfalls, large caves (almost all of which can only be visited with a guide), rivers with natural swimming pools and good walking tours. Parque Nacional da Chapada Diamantina information, **ICMBio** ① *R Barão do Rio Branco 25, Palmeiras, T075-3332 2418, entry US$2.75.* See also www.parnachapadadiamantina.blogspot.co.uk and www.infochapada.com.

Excursions near Lençóis and in the Chapada Diamantina

There are more than 24 tour operators in Lençóis and visiting even the most distant sights on a tour (or an extended hike) is straightforward. Most tours tend to be car-based and rather sedentary as these are more profitable. As there are plenty of great sights and hikes around Lençóis, be sure to take a good look at all the options before making a choice. The most impressive sights in the Chapada are included in the standard packages. Most have an entrance fee. These include the extensive **Gruta do Lapa Doce**, US$5, and **Pratinha** caves, US$5 (the latter are cut through by glassy blue water). The table-top mountains at the **Morro de Pai Inácio**, US$2, 30 km from Lençóis, offer the best view of the Chapada, especially at sunset. The 384-m-high **Cachoeira da Fumaça** (Smoke Waterfall, also called **Glass**) is the second highest in Brazil and lies deeper within the park, 2½ hours hike from the village of **Capão**. The view is astonishing; the updraft of the air currents often makes the water flow back up creating the 'smoke' effect. The **Rio Marimbus** flows through an area of semi-swamp reminiscent of the Pantanal and very rich in birdlife while the **Rio Mucugezinho** plunges over the blood-red **Cachoeira do Diabo** in an extensive area of *cerrado* just below the craggy **Roncador** (snorer) waterfall. Near Lençóis, visit the **Serrano** with its wonderful natural pools in the river bed, which give a great hydromassage, or the **Salão de Areia**, where the coloured sands for the bottle paintings come from. **Ribeirão do Meio** is a 45-minute walk from town; here locals slide down a long natural water chute into a big pool (it is best to be shown the way it is done and to take something to slide in). Also near Lençóis are two very pretty waterfalls, the **Cachoeira da Primavera** and the **Cachoeira Sossego**, a 'picture postcard' cascade plunging into a swimming pool.

⊚ Inland from Salvador listings

For hotel and restaurant price codes, and other relevant information, see Essentials.

⊜ Where to stay

Lençóis *p514*

$$$$ Canto das Águas, Av Senhor dos Passos, T3334 1154, www.lencois.com.br. Riverside hotel with a/c or fan, pool, efficient, best rooms are in the new wing. A Roteiro de Charme hotel.

$$$ Casa da Geleia, R Gen Viveiros 187, T3334 1151, www.casadageleia.com.br/. 6 smart chalets in a huge garden at the entrance to the town, English spoken, good breakfast, home-made jam, information on birdwatching and hikes.

$$$ Hotel de Lençóis, R Altinha Alves 747, T3369 5000, www.hoteldelencois.com.br. Rooms organized in terraces set in a grassy garden on the edge of the park. Good breakfast, pool and restaurant.

$$$ Pousada Vila Serrano, R Alto do Bonfim 8, T3334 1486, www.vilaserrano.com.br. Great little mock-colonial *pousada* in a small garden 5 mins from town centre. Excellent service, welcoming, excursions organized.

$$$-$$ Estalagem de Alcino, R Gen Viveiros 139, T3334 1171, www.alcinoestalagem.com. An enchanting, beautifully restored house furnished with 19th-century antiques. Most have shared bathrooms. Superb breakfast served in hummingbird-filled garden. Highly recommended.

$$ Casa de Hélia, R da Muritiba 3, T3334 1143, www.casadehelia.com.br. Attractive little guesthouse, English and some Hebrew spoken, good facilities, legendary breakfast. Recommended.

$$-$ Pousada dos Duendes, R do Pires, T3334 1229, www.pousadadosduendes.com. English-run *pousada*, shared hot showers, breakfast and other meals (vegetarians and vegans catered for), welcoming, comfortable. Their tour agency (H2O Expeditions) arranges

tours and treks from 1-11 days and more, Olivia Taylor is very helpful.

$ pp Hostel Lençóis, R Boa Vista 121, T3334 1497, www.hostelchapada.com.br. A large, well-run hostel with an adventure sports agency in one of the town's grand old houses. Singles, en suite doubles (**$$**) and single-sex 4-6 room dorms (US$17); shared kitchen and a large garden with hammocks.

Camping Camping Lumiar, near Rosário church in centre, T3334 1241, with popular restaurant. Recommended.

⊘ Restaurants

Cachoeira *p513*

$ Café com Arte Sebo Ana Néri, R 13 de Maio 16. *Petiscos*, good coffee, beer and art from local and international artists.

$ Casa Comercial NS Rosário o Recanto do Misticismo, Praça da Aclamação s/n. Typically 'Cachoeira', pizza café and restaurant with 2 candomblé-inspired shrines, occasional live music.

$ Pouso da Palavra, Praça da Aclamação s/n. Arty little café in a cosy period house, owned by poet Damário Da Cruz, exhibitions of local artists' work, CDs, souvenirs and beautiful mandala candle shades for sale.

Lençóis *p514*

$$$ Cozinha Aberta, Rui Barbosa 42, T3334 1309, www.cozinhaaberta.com.br. The best in town with organic and slow food from Paulistana chef Deborah Doitschinoff. Just east of main praça.

$$ Neco's, Praça Maestro Clarindo Pachêco 15, T3334 1179. Neco and his wife offer a set meal of local dishes of the kind eaten by the *garimpeiros*.

$ Gaya, Praça Horácio Matos s/n, T3334 1167. Organic and wholefood with generous salads, juices and sandwiches. Runs trips into the Chapada.

🍸 Bars and clubs

Lençóis *p514*
Fazendinha e Tal, Rua das Pedras 125. Very popular bar with rustic garimpeiro decoration serving hundreds of different cachacas and with occasional live music.

🎉 Festivals

Cachoeira *p513*
São João (**24 Jun**), 'Carnival of the Interior' celebrations include dangerous games with fireworks. **Nossa Sehora da Boa Morte early Aug**) is also a major festival. A famous candomblé ceremony at the Fonte de Santa Bárbara is held on **4 Dec**.

🛍 Shopping

Lençóis *p514*
The Mon morning market is recommended. There is a local craft market just off the main praça every night.
Instrumentos, R das Pedras 78, T3334 1334. Unusual faux-Brazilian and African musical instruments by quirky ex-pat Argentine Jorge Fernando.
Zambumbeira, R das Pedras at Tamandare, T3334 1207. Beautiful ceramics by renowned artisans like Zé Caboclo, jewellery, walking sticks and arty bric-a-brac.

🏄 What to do

Lençóis *p514*
Body and soul
The Chapada is a centre for alternative treatments and there are many practitioners. Ask on arrival for recommendations.

Guides
Each *pousada* generally has a guide attached to it to take residents on tours, about US$20-30. The following are recommended:
Edmilson (known locally as Mil), R Domingos B Souza 70, T3334 1319. Knows the region extremely well, knowledgeable and reliable.

Roy Funch, T3334 1305, funchroy@ yahoo. com, www.fcd.org.br. The ex-director of the Chapada Diamantina National Park is an excellent guide and has written a visitor guide to the park in English. (Recommended as the best information on history, geography and trails of the Chapada.) Highly recommended. He can be booked through www.elabrasil.com from the USA or UK.
Luiz Krug, contact via **Vila Serrano**, T3334 1102. An independent, English-speaking guide specializing in geology and caving.
Trajano, contact via **Vila Serrano** or **Casa da Hélia**, T3334 1143, Speaks English and some Hebrew and is a good-humoured guide for treks to the bottom of the Cachoeira da Fumaça.
Zé Carlos, T3334 1151, through **Casa da Geleia** or **Vila Serrano**. The best guide for birding.

Tour operators
Chapada Adventure, Av 7 de Setembro 7, T3334 2037, www.chapadaadventure.com. br. A small operator offering good value car-based tours and light hiking throughout the Chapada.
Fora da Trilha, R das Pedras 202, www. foradatrilha.com.br. Longer hikes and light adventures, from canyoning to rapelling.
Venturas e Aventuras, Praça Horácio de Matos 20, T3334 1304. Excellent trekking expeditions, up to 6 days.

⊖ Transport

Cachoeira *p513*
Bus From **Salvador** (Camurjipe) every hr or so from 0530; **Feira Santana**, 2 hrs, US$6.

Lençóis *p514*
Air Airport, Km 209, BR-242, 20 km from town T3625 8100. (T0300-789 8747, www. voetrip.com.br) from **Salvador** weekly, otherwise air taxi.
Bus Terminal, T3334 1112. **Real Expresso** from **Salvador** 3 a day, US$29, *comercial* via Feira de Santana. Book in advance, especially at weekends and holidays. For the rest of

Bahia state change at Feira de Santana; it is not necessary to go via Salvador. Buses also from **Recife**, **Ibotirama**, **Barreiras** or **Palmas** (for Jalapão), **Chapada dos Veadeiros** and **Brasília**, 16 hrs (all with transfer in Seabra, several buses daily).

❶ Directory

Lençóis *p514*
Banks Bradesco with ATM on the main square.

South of Salvador

On the coast south of Salvador is a whole string of popular resorts. It was on this part of what is now Brazil that the Portuguese first made landfall. Bahia's north coast runs from the Coconut Highway onto the Green Line, to give of an idea of how the shore looks, and don't forget the beaches there.

Tinharé, Morro de São Paulo and Boipeba → *Phone code: 075.*

Valença (*Phone code: 075. Colour map 7, A6. Population: 77,509*), a town 271 km south of Salvador, is at the mouth of the Rio Una, which enters an enormous region of mangrove swamps. The river estuary and the swamps separate Tinharé, 1½ hours south of Valença by boat, from the mainland and it is hard to tell which is land and which is water. Some say that Tinharé is a mini archipelago rather than a large island. The most popular beaches are at Morro de São Paulo, a tourism hotspot. Immediately south is the island of **Boipeba**, separated from Tinharé by the Rio do Inferno. Accommodation is split between Velha Boipeba, the little town where the riverboat ferry arrives, the adjacent beach, Boca da Barra, which is more idyllic and the fishing village Moreré. This is a two-hour walk or half an hour's boat ride south, US$30 minimum (high tide only). Boipeba's community tourism association is at www.ilhaboipeba.org.br.

Morro de São Paulo is on the headland at the northernmost tip of Tinharé, lush with ferns, palms and birds of paradise. The village is dominated by the lighthouse and the ruins of a colonial fort (1630), built as a defence against European raiders. It has a landing place on the sheltered landward side, dominated by the old gateway of the fortress. From the lighthouse a path leads to a ruined look out with cannon, which has panoramic views. The fort is a good point to watch the sunset from. Dolphins can be seen in August. Fonte de Ceu waterfall is reached by walking along the beach to **Gamboa** then inland. Watch the tide; it's best to take a guide, or take a boat back to Morro (US$10-15). The beaches, numbered Primeira to Quinta (First to Fifth) are progressively quieter the further south you go. From town to Quarta Praia is 40 minutes on foot, but VW buses, motorbikes and buggies run to the beaches and there is a service to Boipeba. On 7 September there's a big festival with live music on the beach. **Tourist office**① *Praça Aureliano Lima, T3652 1083, www.morrosp.com.br,* or visit *www.morrodesaopaulo.com.br.* **Note** There is a port tax of US$4 payable at the prefeitura on arrival, and US$1 on leaving the island.

Itacaré → *Phone code: 073.*

This picturesque fishing village sits in the midst of remnant Atlantic Coast rainforest at the mouth of the Rio de Contas. Some of Bahia's best beaches stretch north and south. A few are calm and crystal clear, the majority are great for surfing. There are plenty of beaches within walking distance of town. Itacaré is a surf resort for Paulistanos and is very busy with Brazilian tourists in high season. Much of the accommodation here is tasteful, blending in with the natural landscape and there are many excellent restaurants and lively if still low key nightlife. *Pousadas* are concentrated in town and around the Praias da Coroinha and Concha, the first beaches to the north and south of the town centre. Besides surfing, operators are now offering trekking and mountain biking trips in the Mata Atlântica, off-roading, rafting, waterfall-climbing and other adrenalin activities. North of Itacaré is the **Peninsula de Maraú**, fringed with beautiful beaches to its tip at **Barra Grande**. To explore the area fully you will need a car or to take a tour. **Secretaria Municipal de Turismo de Itacaré** ① *R João de Souza, T3251 2134; see www.itacare.com.br.*

Ilhéus → *Phone code: 073. Post code: 45650. Colour map 7, A6. Population: 222,127.*

At the mouth of the Rio Cachoeira, 462 km south of Salvador, the port serves a district which produces 65% of all Brazilian cocoa. A bridge links the north bank of the river with Pontal, where the airport is located. Ilhéus is the birthplace of Jorge Amado (1912-2002) and the setting of one of his most famous novels, *Gabriela, cravo e canela* (Gabriela, Clove and Cinnamon). The church of **São Jorge** (1556), the city's oldest, is on the Praça Rui Barbosa; it has a small museum. **Secretária de Turismo** ① *on the beach opposite Praça Castro Alves; see www.brasilheus.com.br.*

North of Ilhéus, two good beaches are Marciano, with reefs offshore and good surfing, and Barra, 1 km further north at the mouth of the Rio Almada. South of the river, Pontal beaches can be reached by 'Barreira' bus; alight just after Hotel Jardim Atlântico. Between Ilhéus and **Olivença** are more fine beaches. At nearby **Una** there is an important wildlife sanctuary and ecopark devoted to protecting the Golden-face Tamarin, the **Reserva Biológica de Una** ① *www.ecoparque.org.br.* Further south, 52 km, is **Canavieiras**, a former cocoa port, now a fishing port with a colonial centre and restaurants at the harbour. Its beach, Ilha de Atalaia, with barracas, surfing and kite-surfing is getting onto the tourist map. There are *pousadas* in town and a 5-star resort some 40 km away.

Porto Seguro and the Discovery Coast → *Phone code: 073. Post code: 45810.*
Colour map 7, A6. Population: 95,721.
About 400 km south of Ilhéus on the coast is the old town of Porto Seguro. In 1500, Pedro Álvares Cabral sighted land at Monte Pascoal south of Porto Seguro. As the sea here was too open, he sailed north in search of a secure protected harbour, entering the mouth of the Rio Burnahém to find the harbour he later called Porto Seguro (safe port). Where the first mass was celebrated, a cross marks the spot on the road between Porto Seguro and Santa Cruz Cabrália. A rather uncoordinated tourist village, **Coroa Vermelha**, has sprouted at the site of Cabral's first landfall, 20 minutes by bus to the north of Porto Seguro.

Porto Seguro itself is Bahia's second most popular tourist destination, with charter flights from Rio and São Paulo and plenty of hustle and bustle. Contact the **Secretária de Turismo de Porto Seguro** ① *Praça dos Pataxós, T3288 3708. Information desk at Praça Manoel Ribeiro Coelho 10.*

To its historical quarter, **Cidade Histórica**, take a wide, steep, unmarked path uphill from the roundabout at the entrance to town. Three churches (Nossa Senhora da Misericórdia (1530), Nossa Senhora do Rosário (1534), and Nossa Senhora da Pena (1718), the former jail, Casa de Câmara e Cadêia (now a sacred art museum) and the monument marking the landfall of Gonçalo Coelho comprise a small, peaceful place with lovely gardens and panoramic views.

Only 10 minutes north of Coroa Vermelha, **Santa Cruz Cabrália** is a delightful small town at the mouth of the Rio João de Tiba, with a splendid beach, river port, and a 450-year-old church with a fine view. A good trip from here is to Coroa Alta, a reef 50 minutes away by boat, passing along the tranquil river to the reef and its crystal waters and good snorkelling. A 15-minute river crossing by ferry to a new road on the opposite bank gives easy access to the deserted beaches of **Santo André** and **Santo Antônio**.

Arraial da Ajuda → *Colour map 7, A6. www.arraialdajuda.tur.br.*

Immediately across the Rio Buranhém south from Porto Seguro is the village of Arraial da Ajuda, the gateway to the idyllic beaches of the south coast. Set high on a cliff, there are great views of the coastline from behind the church of Nossa Senhora da Ajuda in the main praça. Each August there is a pilgrimage to the shrine of Nossa Senhora da Ajuda. Ajuda has become more popular than Porto Seguro with younger tourists and independent travellers and there are many *pousadas*, from the very simple to the very sophisticated, restaurants, bars and small shops. In high season there are frequent parties on the road to the beach. At Brazilian holiday times it is very crowded. The town has a famous Capoeira school (with classes for foreigners).

The **beaches**, several protected by a coral reef, are splendid. The nearest is 15 minutes' walk away. During daylight hours those closest to town (take 'R da Praia' out of town to the south) are extremely busy; excellent barracas sell good seafood, drinks, and play music. The best beaches are Mucugê, Pitinga and Taipé.

Trancoso → *Phone code: 073.*

Some 15 km from Ajuda, 25 km south of Porto Seguro by paved road, is Trancoso. This pretty, peaceful town, with its beautiful beaches (Praia dos Nativos is the most famous), has become very chic, with the rich and famous from home and abroad buying properties and shopping in the little boutiques. In summer it can get packed. Trancoso has an historic church, São João Batista (1656). From the end of Praça São João there is a fine coastal panorama.

Caraíva and around → *Phone code: 073. www.caraiva.com.br.*

This atmospheric, peaceful fishing village on the banks of the Rio Caraíva, 65 km south of Porto Seguro, has marvellous beaches and is a real escape from the more developed Trancoso and Porto Seguro. Despite the difficulty of getting there, it is becoming increasingly popular. Good walks are north to Praia do Satu (Sr Satu provides an endless supply of coconut milk) and, acorss a headland, Praia Espelho (9 km), or 6 km south to a rather sad Pataxó Indian village, Barra Velha (watch the tides). The high season is December-February and July; the wettest months are April June and November. Use flip-flops for walking the sand streets and take a torch. There are no medical facilities and only rudimentary policing. There are a series of super-luxurious isolated resorts 10 km south of Caraíva at the Ponta do Corumbau.

Parque Nacional de Monte Pascoal → *Entry US$2.65. Colour map 7, A6.*

① *Office: R D Pedro 1358, Itamaraju, 93 km south of Eunápolis, T073-3294 1870, parquemontepascoal @icmbio.gov.br.*

Caraíva is the northern entrance to the Parque Nacional de Monte Pascoal, set up in 1961 to preserve the flora and fauna of the coastal area in which Europeans made landfall in Brazil. Another 14 km paved access road leaves the BR-101 at Km 796. To walk the trails costs US$21 for a group of 10 with guide).

Caravelas and around → *Colour map 7, A6. Population: 20,103.*

Further south still, 107 km from Itamaruju, is this charming town, rapidly developing for tourism, but a major trading town in 17th and 18th centuries. Caravelas is in the mangroves; the beaches are about 10 km away at Barra de Caravelas (hourly buses), a fishing village. There are food shops, restaurants and bars.

The **Parque Nacional Marinho dos Abrolhos** is 70 km east of Caravelas. Day trips leave from Caravelas and take about 2½ hours to reach the archipelago. Humpback whales are invariably seen between July and November. Abrolhos is an abbreviation of Abre os olhos: 'Open your eyes' from Amérigo Vespucci's exclamation when he first sighted the reef in 1503. Established in 1983, the park consists of five small islands (Redonda, Siriba, Guarita, Sueste, Santa Bárbara), which are volcanic in origin, and several coral reefs. The warm current and shallow waters (8-15 m deep) make for a rich undersea life (about 160 species of fish) and good snorkelling. The park is best visited in October-March, entry is US$27. Diving is best December to February. The archipelago is administered by ICMBio and a navy detachment mans a lighthouse on Santa Bárbara, which is the only island that may be visited. Permission from **Parque Nacional Marinho dos Abrolhos** ⓘ *Praia do Kitongo s/n, Caravelas, Bahia 45900, T073-3297 2258, www.icmbio.gov.br/ parnaabrolhos*. Visitors can't stay on the islands, but may stay overnight on schooners. Visits and permits can be organized through **Portomondo** in Porto Seguro, or in Caravelas (see page 523).

ⓔ South of Salvador listings

For hotel and restaurant price codes, and other relevant information, see Essentials.

ⓦ Where to stay

Tinharé, Morro de São Paulo and Boipeba *p517*
Morro de São Paulo
There are many cheap *pousadas* and rooms to rent near the fountain (Fonte Grande) but this part of town is very hot at night. The beaches are backed by hotels for about 20 km south of town.
$$$$-$$$ Pousada Farol do Morro, Primeira Praia, T3652 1036, www.faroldomorro.com.br. Little huts running up the hill all with a sea view and served by a private funicular railway, pool.
$$$ Pousada Vista Bela, R da Biquinha 15, T3652 1001, www.vistabelapousada.com. Owner Petruska is extremely welcoming, good rooms, those to the front have good views and are cooler, all have fans, hammocks. Price depends on season and type of room.
$$$-$$ Pousada Colibri, R do Porto de Cima 5, T3652 1056. 6 apartments up some steep steps. Cool, always a breeze blowing, excellent views, Helmut, the owner, speaks English and German.
$$ Pousada Ilha do Sol, Primeira Praia, T3652 1576. Modest but scrupulously clean, good views.

Terceira Praia (3rd beach)
$$$ Fazenda Vila Guaiamú, T3652 1035, www.vilaguaiamu.com.br. 7 tastefully

decorated chalets set in tropical gardens visited by marmosets, tanagers and rare cotingas, excellent food. The hotel has a spa and the Italian photographer-owner runs an eco-tourism project protecting a rare species of crab which lives in the fazenda's river. Guided walks available. Highly recommended.
$$$ Pousada Fazenda Caeira, T3652 1042, www.fazendacaeira.com.br. Spacious, airy chalets in a coconut grove overlooking the sea, good breakfasts, library, games room.
$$$-$$ Village do Dendê, Gamboa, T3653 7104, www.morrobahiabrazil.com.br. Close to centre, dock and beach, self-contained 2-room chalets (prices are higher according to season, breakfast and cleaning extra), gardens, restaurant.

Boipeba
$$$ Pousada Tassimirim, ½-hr walk south of town, T3653 6030, or T9981 2378 (R Com Madureira 40, 45400-000 Valença), www.ilha boipeba.org.br/pousadas.html. Bungalows, bar, restaurant, including breakfast and dinner.
$$$ Santa Clara, Boca da Barra, T3653 6085, www.santaclaraboipeba.com. Californian-owned, with the island's best restaurant, large, tasteful cabins and a good-value room for 4 at **$** pp. Therapeutic massages available.
$$ Horizonte Azul, Boca da Barra, T3653 6080, www.ilhaboipeba.org.br/pousadas.html. Next to Santa Clara, a range of chalets in a hillside garden visited by hundreds of rare birds. Owners speak English and French. Lunch available. Recommended.

$$ Pousada do Canto, Moreré, T3653 6131, morerecantosul@yahoo.com.br. A variety of rooms and cabins, some thatched, prices rise in high season, lovely surroundings.

Itacaré *p517*

$$$ Art Jungle, T9975 1083, www.artjungle. org. 6 tree houses in a modern sculpture garden in the middle of forest, great views. A favourite with celebrities, yet relatively unpretentious.
$ pp Pedra Bonita, R Lodônio Almeida 120, T9141 4372, www.itacarehostel.com.br. Pleasant little HI hostel with small doubles **$$**) and dorms (US$13-21 pp, price depends on season and a/c) in an annexe, small pool, internet and TV area.

Ilhéus *p518*

Plenty of cheap hotels near the municipal *rodoviária* in centre and *pousadas* along the coast to Olivença.
$$ Britânia, R Jorge Amado 16, T3634 1722, www.brasilheus.com.br/britania_por.htm. The best value in the town centre with large rooms in an early 20th-century wooden hotel just west of the Cathedral square.

Porto Seguro *p518*

Prices rise steeply Dec-Feb and Jul. Off-season rates can drop by 50%, for stays of more than 3 nights negotiate. Outside Dec-Feb rooms with bath and hot water can be rented for US$150 per month.
$$$ Estalagem Porto Seguro, R Marechal Deodoro 66, T3288 2095, hotelestalagem@ hotelestalagem.com.br. In an old colonial house, relaxing atmosphere, pool, good breakfast. Highly recommended.
$$ Pousada dos Navegantes, Av 22 de Abril 212, T3288 2390, www.portonet.com.br/ navegantes. A/c, pool, conveniently located.
Camping Camping Mundaí Praia, T3679 2287, www.campingmundai.com.br. Good value.

Santa Cruz Cabrália

$$$-$$ Victor Hugo, Villa de Santo Antônio, Km 3, T3671 4064, www.pousadavictorhugo. com.br. Smart, tasteful, right on the beach.

Arraial da Ajuda *p519*

At busy times, don't expect to find much under US$20 pp in a shared room for a minimum stay of 5-7 days. Camping is best at these times.
$$$$ Pousada Pitinga, Praia Pitinga, T3575 1067, www.pousadapitinga.com.br. Bold architecture amid Atlantic forest, a hideaway, great food and pool, a Roteiros de Charme hotel.
$$$ Pousada Erva Doce, Estrada do Mucugê 200, T3575 1113, www.ervadoce.com.br. Good restaurant, well-appointed chalets (more expensive in high season).
$$ Pousada Flamboyant, Estrada do Mucugê 89, T3575 1025, www.flamboyant.tur.br. Pleasant courtyard, pool, good breakfast.
$$ O Cantinho, Praça São Bras, T3575 1131, www.pousadacantinho.com.br. Terraces of smart rooms, a/c or fan, nice courtyard, excellent breakfast, discounts off season.
$$ Pousada do Roballo, T3575 1053, www.pousadadoroballo.com.br. Welcoming with a tiny pool and rooms with little verandas in gardens.
$ pp Hostel Arraial, R do Campo 94, T3575 1192, www.arraialdajudahostel.com.br. Backpacker hostel with HI discounts, more expensive in Jan, with breakfast, snack bar, pool, good location at the top of town.

Trancoso *p519*

$$$$ Etnia, Estrada Velha do Arraial (just west of the Quadrado), T3668 1137, www. etniabrasil.com.br. Very chic, well-run and beautifully kept *pousada* set in shady, hilly lawned gardens. Fashionable.
$$$$-$$$ Mata N'ativa, Estrada Velha do Arraial (next to the river on the way to the beach), T3668 1830, www.matanativa pousada.com.br. The best in town, a series of elegant cabins in a lovingly maintained garden by the riverside, cheaper in low season. Owners Daniel and Daniela are very hospitable and run one of the few hotels to adopt environmental best practice. Good English, Spanish and Italian. Recommended.
$$$ Capim Santo, T3668 1122, to the left of the main praça, www.capimsanto.com.br.

With breakfast and the best restaurant in Trancoso. Recommended.

$ pp Café Esmeralda, on the Quadrado (main praça), T3668 1527, www.trancosonatural.com. Small rooms with fan at a locally-owned café which serves good breakfast and lunch.

Caraíva *p519*
$$$ Vila do Mar, R 12 de Outubro s/n, T3668 5111, www.pousadaviladomar.com.br. The plushest hotel in town, with spacious, stylish airy, wooden cabanas overlooking the beach set on a lawn around an adult and children's pool.

$$$-$$ Pousada San Antonio, Praia de Caraíva, T9999 9552, www.pousadasan antonio.com.br. Pleasant, simple, colourful rooms in a garden, by the beach, breezy public areas, with breakfast. Has 2 properties.

Caravelas *p519*
$$$ Pousada Liberdade, Av Ministro Adalicio Nogueira 1551, T3297 2076. www. pousadaliberdade.com.br. Spacious chalets in a large garden, just outside town centre. Diving excursions to Abrolhos arranged.
$$ Pousada Caravelense, Praça Teófilo Otoni 2, T3297 1182. TV, fridge, good breakfast, excellent restaurant. Recommended.

Restaurants

Tinharé, Morro de São Paulo and Boipeba *p517*
There are plenty of restaurants in Morro de São Paulo town and on the 2nd and 3rd beaches. Most are OK though somewhat overpriced. For cheap eats stay in a *pousada* which includes breakfast, stock up at the supermarket and buy seafood snacks at the *barracas* on the 2nd beach.
$$ Belladonna on the main street. Good Italian restaurant with great music, a good meeting point, owner Guido speaks Italian, English and French, open evenings only.
$$ Chez Max, 3rd beach. Simple but decent seafood in a pretty restaurant overlooking the sea.

$ Comida Natural, on the main street. Good breakfasts, *comida a kilo*, good juices.

Itacaré *p517*
There are lots of restaurants in Itacaré, mostly on R Lodônio Almeida. Menus here are increasingly chic and often include a respectable wine list.
$$$ Casa Sapucaia, R Lodônio Almeida, T251 3091. Sophisticated Bahian food with an international twist.
$$$ Dedo de Moça, R Plínio Soares (next to the São Miguel Church), T3251 3391. One of Bahia's best restaurants, with dishes which combine Brazilian ingredients with French and Oriental techniques. Lovely little bar.
$$ Boca de Forno, R Lodônio Almeida 134, T3251 2174. The busiest restaurant in Itacaré, serving good wood-fired pizzas in tastefully decorated surroundings.
$$ La In, R Lodônio Almeida 116, T3251 3054. Great little Bahian and seafood restaurant, colourful, very good value lunches and dinners. Right next to the youth hostel.
$ O Restaurante, R Pedro Longo 150, T3251 2012. One of the few restaurants with a *prato feto*, and a mixed seafood menu.

Porto Seguro *p518*
Several restaurants on the town's streets and many snack bars along the waterfront and river.
$$ da Japonêsa, Praça Pataxós 38. Excellent value with varied menu, open 0800-2300. Recommended.
$$-$ Portinha, R Saldanha Marinho 33, T3288 2743. Lively little self-service restaurant in a square near the river. Good variety and great puddings.

Arraial da Ajuda *p519*
$$$ Don Fabrizio, Estrada do Mucugê 402, T575 1123. The best Italian in town, in an upmarket open air restaurant with live music and reasonable wine.
$$$ Manguti, Estrada do Mucugê, T575 2270, www.manguti.com.br. Reputed by some to be the best in town, meat, pasta,

fish alongside other Brazilian dishes.
Very popular and informal.
$$ Pizzaria do Arraial, Praça São Bras 28.
Basic pizzeria and pay by weight restaurant.
$ Mineirissima, Estrada do Mucugê, T575
3790. Good value pay by weight with very
filling Minas Gerais food and *moquecas*.
Opens until late but menu service only
after 1800.
$ Paulinho Pescador, Praca São Bras 116.
Open 1200-2200, closed Mon, excellent
seafood, also chicken and meat, one price
(US$5), English spoken, good service, popular,
there are often queues for tables.
    Recommended *barracas* are Tem Q Dá
and Agito on Mucugê beach and Barraca de
Pitinga and Barraca do Genésio on Pitinga.

Trancoso *p519*
Food in Trancoso is expensive. Those on a
tight budget should shop at the supermarket
between the main square and the new part of
town. There are numerous fish restaurants in
the *barracas* on the beach. None is cheap.
$$$ Cacau, Praca São João, Quadrado,
T3668 1266. One of the best in town with
a varied international and Brazilian menu.
Pleasant surrounds.
$$$ Capim Santo, Praca São João,
Quadrado, T3668 1122. Wonderful Brazilian-
European fusion cooking in intimate garden
surroundings. Great caipirinhas.
$$$ Japaiano, Praca São João, Quadrado,
T3668 2121. Japanese-Brazilian fusion cooking
from acclaimed Carioca and ex-Nobu chef
Felipe Bronze.
$ Portinha, on the main square. The only
place serving food at a reasonable price.
Excellent pay by weight options and good if
overpriced juices.

Caraíva *p519*
There is forró dancing 0100-0600 at Pelé and
Ouriços on alternate nights in season.
$$ Boteco do Pará, by the river, just east of
the 'port'. Serves the best fish in the village.
Also has simple lodging, Pousada da Canoa.

🍸 Bars and clubs

**Tinharé, Morro de São Paulo and
Boipeba** *p517*
Morro de São Paulo
There is always plenty going on in Morro.
The liveliest bars are 87 and Jamaica, both on
the 2nd beach. These tend to get going after
2300 when the restaurants in town empty.

Itacaré *p517*
There is frequent extemporaneous forró and
other live music all over the city and most
restaurants and bars have some kind of music
between Oct and Apr.

Porto Seguro *p518*
Porto Seguro is famous for the lambada. There
are lots of bars and street cafés on Av Portugal.
Porto Prego on R Pedro Álvares Cabral. A good
bar for live music, small cover charge.

Arraial da Ajuda *p519*
The lambada is danced at the Jatobar bar
(summer only), by the church on the main
square (opens 2300 – pensão at the back is
cheap, clean and friendly). Limelight has raves
all year round. Many top Brazilian bands play
at the beach clubs at Praia do Parracho during
the summer, entry is about US$20. Entry to
other beach parties is about US$10. There is
also a capoeira institute; ask for directions.

✳ Festivals

Ilhéus *p518*
Festa de São Sebastião, **17-20 Jan**, Carnival,
Festa de São Jorge, **23 Apr**, Foundation day,
28 Jun, and Festa do Cacau throughout **Oct**.

⏱ What to do

Trancoso *p519*
Tour operators
Portomondo, Trancoso, T3575 3686, www.
portomondo.com. The best operator in
southern Bahia with tours around Trancoso,
Caraíva and Corumbau and to Monte Pascoal

and Abrolhos. Excellent diving and ecotourism itineraries and car or helicopter transfers to hotels in Trancoso and further south.

⊖ Transport

Tinharé, Morro de São Paulo and Boipeba p517

Air Air taxi from Salvador airport US$100 1-way, 20 mins, **Addey** T3377 1393, www. addey.com.br, and **Aerostar** T3377 4406, www.aerostar.com.br.

Ferry From Salvador, several companies operate a catamaran (1½ hrs) service from the Terminal Marítimo in front of the Mercado Modelo to Morro de São Paulo, US$27. Times vary according to the weather and season. **Catamara Gamboa do Morro**, T9975 6395. Part of the trip is on the open sea, which can be rough. Boats leave every day from **Valença** for Gamboa (1½ hrs) and Morro de São Paulo (1½ hrs) from the main bridge in Valença 5 times a day (signalled by a loud whistle). The fare is US$5. A *lancha rápida* taking 25 mins travels the route between Valença and Morro, US$15. Only buses between 0530-1100 from Salvador to Valença (5 hrs, US$19) connect with ferries. For the shortest route to Valença, take the ferry from São Joaquim to Bom Despacho on Itaparica island, from where it is 130 km to Valença via Nazaré das Farinhas by **Camarujipe** bus, 2 hrs, US$7. If not stopping in Valença, get out of the bus by the main bridge in town, don't wait till you get to the *rodoviária*, which is a long way from the ferry. Private boat hire can be arranged if you miss the ferry schedule. There is a regular boat from Valença to Boipeba Mon-Sat 1230 (check tide), return 1500-1700, 4 hrs, US$7; speedboats charge US$18. The Salvador-Morro catamaran at 0900 connects with a boat to Boipeba at 1200, US$77 total fare. Also, Mon-Sat bus Valença-Torrinha at 1100 (plus 1400 in summer) connects with a boat to Boipeba, 2½ hrs.

Itacaré p517

Bus The *rodoviária* is a few mins' walk from town. Porters are on hand with barrows to help with luggage. Frequent buses 0700-1900 to **Ilhéus** (the nearest town with an airport), 45 mins, US$7 along the paved road. To **Salvador**, change at **Ubaitaba** (3 hrs, US$5) or Ilhéus; Ubaitaba-Salvador, 6 hrs, US$16, several daily.

Ilhéus p518

Air Daily flights to **Salvador** in high season with **Gol** and **TAM**.

Bus *Rodoviária* is 4 km from the centre on Itabuna road. Several daily to **Salvador**, 8 hrs, US$35, **Expresso São Jorge**. To **Eunápolis**, 4 hrs, US$25. Local buses leave from Praça Cairu.

Porto Seguro p518

Air Airport T3288 1880. Regular flights from **Rio**, **São Paulo**, **Salvador** and **Belo Horizonte**. Taxi airport-Porto Seguro, US$15. Also buses.

Bus From Porto Seguro: **Salvador** Aguia Branca, once daily, 12 hrs, US$75. **Eunápolis**, 1 hr, US$6. For **Rio** direct bus (**São Geraldo**), leaving at 1700, US$102, 18 hrs, from Rio direct at 2015, or take bus for Ilhéus and change at Eunápolis. To **Belo Horizonte** daily, direct, US$75-82 (São Geraldo). Other services via Eunápolis (bus to/from Salvador 10-11 hrs, US$40, 100 leito) or Itabuna (5 hrs, US$25).

The *rodoviária* has reliable luggage store and lounge on the 3rd floor, on the road to Eunápolis, 2 km from the centre, regular bus service (30 mins) through the city to the old *rodoviária* near the port. Local buses US$0.50. Taxis charge US$7 from the *rodoviária* to the town (negotiate at quiet times).

Arraial da Ajuda p519

Ferry Across the Rio Buranhém from Porto Seguro take 15 mins to the south bank, US$1 for foot passengers, US$6 for cars, every 30 mins day and night. It is then a further 5 km to Arraial da Ajuda, US$1 by bus; combis charge US$1.50 pp; taxis US$10.

Trancoso p519

Bus Buses run regularly on the paved road between Porto Seguro, Ajuda and Trancoso, at least every hour in high season: US$5 Porto Seguro-Trancoso, US$3 Ajuda-Trancoso. Arriving from the south, change buses at Eunápolis from where the newly paved Linha Verde road runs, several buses daily.

Caraíva and around p519

Caraíva can only be reached by canoe across the river, US$3.25 return. Access roads are poor and almost impossible after heavy rain. There are services several times a day from Trancoso, which is the easiest point of access. **Aguia Azul** bus company takes this route from Porto Seguro at 0700 and 1500, via Trancoso, US$8. If arriving by bus from the south, change to **Aguia Azul** bus in Itabela, departs at 1500, or take a taxi, about 50 km. Heading south take the bus to Eunápolis at 0600, 3 hrs.

Parque Nacional de Monte Pascoal
p519

From Caraíva there is a river crossing by boats which are always on hand. Buses run from **Itamaraju** 16 km to the south, at 0600 Fri-Mon.

Caravelas p519

Bus To **Texeira de Freitas** (on the BR-101, 4 a day), **Eunápolis** and **Prado**. Also twice weekly to/from **Porto Seguro**.

Parque Nacional Marinho dos Abrolhos

The journey to the islands takes about 3-4 hrs depending on the sea conditions. Between Jul and early Dec humpback whale sightings are almost guaranteed. Boats leave at 0700 from the Marina Porto Abrolhos just north of Caravelas town centre (around US$50 depending on numbers) and they return at dusk. It is possible to dive or snorkel at Abrolhos. If you are coming from Porto Seguro everything including transfers can be arranged by Portomondo (see above). Other options are given on www.ilhasdeabrolhos.com.br.

O Directory

Porto Seguro p518
Banks ATMs at a couple of banks and at airport. **Bicycle hire** Oficina de Bicicleta, Av Getúlio Vargas e R São Pedro, about US$13 for 24 hrs. Also at Praça de Bandeira and at 2 de Julho 242. **Car hire** Several companies at the airport.

Arraial da Ajuda p519
Banks ATMs at banks in small shopping centre on Estrada do Mucugê.

North of Salvador

The paved BA-099 coast road from near Salvador airport is known as the Estrada do Coco (Coconut Highway, because of the many plantations) and for 50 km passes some beautiful beaches. The best known from south to north are **Ipitanga** (with its reefs), **Buraquinho**, **Jauá** (with reefs, surfing, pools at low tide, clean water), **Arembepe** (famous hippy village in 1960s with a Tamar turtle protection project, T071-3624 3694, cv.arembepe@tamar.org.br), **Guarajuba**, **Itacimirim**, **Castelo Garcia D'Ávila** (with its 16th-century fort) and **Forte**. Regular buses serve most of these destinations.

Praia do Forte

The former fishing village, 80 km north of Salvador, takes its name from the castle built by a Portuguese settler, Garcia D'Ávila, in 1556 to warn the city to the south of enemy invasion. Praia do Forte is now a pleasant resort town with lovely beaches and all but one of the streets of sand. Inland from the coast is a restinga forest, which grows on sandy soil with a very delicate ecosystem. Near the village is a small *pantanal* (marshy area), which is host to a large number of birds, caimans and other animals. Birdwatching trips on the pantanal are rewarding. The

Tamar Project ① *Av Farol Garcia D'Ávila s/n, T071-3676 0321, www.projetotamar.org.br*, preserves the sea turtles which lay their eggs in the area. Praia do Forte is now the headquarters of the national turtle preservation programme and is funded by the Worldwide Fund for Nature.

The coast road north

The Linha Verde (the extension of the Estrada do Coco) runs for 142 km to the border of Sergipe, the next state north; the road is more scenic than the BR-101, especially near Conde. There are very few hotels or *pousadas* in the more remote villages. The most picturesque are **Imbassaí**, **Subaúma**, **Baixio** (very beautiful, where the Rio Inhambupe meets the sea) and **Conde**. Sítio do Conde on the coast, 6 km from Conde, has many *pousadas*, but the beaches are not very good. Sítio do Conde is an ideal base to explore other beaches at Barra do Itariri, 12 km south, at the mouth of a river (fine sunsets). The last stop on the Linha Verde is **Mangue Seco**. A steep hill rising behind the village to tall white sand dunes offers superb view of the coastline. There are plenty of small cheap places to stay along the seafront from the jetty, none with addresses or phone numbers (the village is tiny). There are simple restaurants around the main square next to the church. The beach has a handful of *barracas* serving cheap fish. Access from Sergipe is by boat on the Rio Real from Pontal (10-minute crossing). Buses run between Pontal and Estância twice a day. The ferry across the river usually leaves before 1000 in the morning. There are private launches as well; it is usually possible to find someone to share the ride.

ⓝ North of Salvador listings

For hotel and restaurant price codes, and other relevant information, see Essentials.

ⓦ Where to stay

North of Salvador: Jauá *p525*
$$$-$$ Lagoa e Mar, Praia de Jauá, T3672 1573, www.hotellagoaemar.com.br. Very good breakfast, spacious bungalows, swimming pool, 350 m to beach, restaurant, helpful, transport to airport, 10% discount to Footprint owners.

Praia do Forte *p525*
The town's main street had its name changed from Alameda do Sol to Av ACM. This street doesn't have numbers marked, so you just have to walk along to find the place you want. Prices rise steeply in the summer season. It may be difficult to find cheap places to stay.
$$$$ Aloha Brasil Pousada, R da Aurora, T3676 0279, www.pousadaalohabrasil.com.br. Relaxing tropical garden and pool, charming rooms with king size beds and verandas.
$$$$ Praia do Forte EcoResort, Av do Farol, T3676 4000, www.tivolihotels.com. Large

scale family resort set in tropical gardens on the beach and with programmes to visit the nearby protected areas. Room are spacious, well appointed and comfortable. Service, which includes a spa and entertainment, is excellent. Beautiful pool.
$$$ Ogum Marinho, Av ACM, T3676 1165, www.ogummarinho.com.br. A/c, cheaper with fan, nice little courtyard garden, good restaurant and service. It has an art gallery with work by Brazilian artists.
$$$ Sobrado da Vila, Av ACM, T3676 1088, www.sobradodavila.com.br. Best in the village itself with a range of individually decorated rooms with balconies and a good-value restaurant, convenient for restaurants.
$$$-$$ Pousada Casa de Praia, Praça dos Artistas 08-09, T3676 1362, www.casadepraia.tur.br. Good value and location rooms, with and without a/c, popular.
$$ Pousada João Sol, R da Corvina, T3676 1054, www.pousadajoaosol.com.br. 6 well-appointed chalets. The owner speaks English, Spanish and German. Great breakfast.
$$ Pousada Tatuapara, Praça dos Artistas 1, T3676 1466, www.tatuapara.com.br. Spacious

and well-maintained, fan, fridge, good breakfast, pool.

$ pp Albergue da Juventude, Praia do Forte, R da Aurora 3, T3676 1094, www.albergue. com.br. Smart youth hostel with decent shared rooms and rooms with en suites (**$$**), a large breakfast, fan, kitchen and shop, cheaper for HI members.

$ Cafe Tango, Av ACM, T3676 1637. Pleasant open-air tea and coffee bar with great pastries and cakes.

$ Casa da Nati, Av ACM, T3676 1239. Per kilo and Bahian food.

$ Point do Ivan, Av ACM. T99971711. Bahian food, good *moquecabobo de* and cheap *prato feito*.

🍴 Restaurants

Praia do Forte *p525*
$$ Bar Do Souza, Av ACM, on the right as you enter the village. Best seafood in town, open daily, live music at weekends. Recommended.
$$ O Europeu, Av ACM, T3676 0232. Anglo-Brazilian owned, with the most adventurous menu in town with well-prepared dishes. The owners, William and Vera, are very knowledgeable about the area. Recommended.

☀ What to do

Praia do Forte *p525*
Praia do Forte is ideal for windsurfing and sailing owing to constant fresh Atlantic breezes.

⊖ Transport

Praia do Forte *p525*
Bus To **Salvador** (US$6): Linha Verde from 0530 to 1800 daily, 1½ hrs.

Recife and the northeast coast

The eight states north of Bahia are historically and culturally rich, but generally poor economically. Steeped in history are, for instance, Recife, Olinda, or São Luís and cultural heritage abounds (eg 'Forró' and other musical styles, many good museums, lacework, ceramics). There is a multitude of beaches: if established resorts aren't your thing, you don't have to travel far for somewhere more peaceful, while off the beaten track are some which have hardly been discovered.

Pernambuco was the seat of Dutch Brazil in the 17th century. Its capital, Recife, and close neighbour, Olinda, have the most creative music scene in the northeast and their famous wild carnival draws thousands of visitors.

Recife → *Phone code: 081. Post code: 50000. Colour map 5, B6. Population: 1.42 million.*

The capital of Pernambuco State, 285 km north of Maceió and 839 km north of Salvador, was founded on reclaimed land by the Dutch prince Maurice of Nassau in 1637 after his troops had burnt Olinda, the original capital. The city centre consists of three portions, always very busy by day; the crowds and the narrow streets, especially in the Santo Antônio district, can make it a confusing city to walk around. Recife has the main dock area, with commercial buildings associated with it. South of the centre is the residential and beach district of Boa Viagem, reached by bridge across the Bacia do Pina. Olinda, the old capital, is 7 km to the north but now absorbed by the conurbation (see page 537).

Arriving in Recife

Tourist offices The main office for the Pernambuco tourist board, **Setur** ① *Centro de Convenções, Complexo Rodoviário de Salgadinho, Av Professor Andrade Bezerra s/n, Salgadinho, Olinda, T3182 8300, www.setur.pe.gov.br*, is between Recife and Olinda. There are other

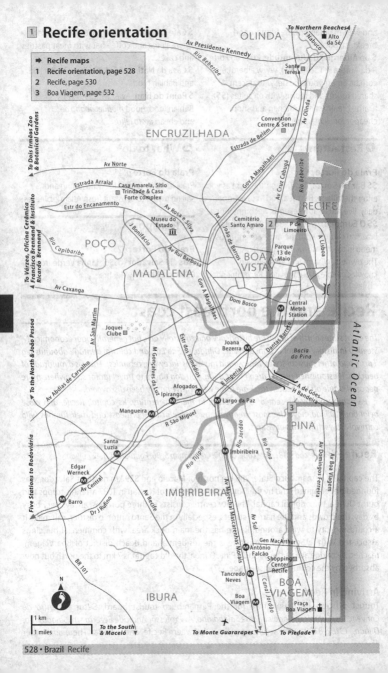

Recife orientation

Recife maps
1 Recife orientation, page 528
2 Recife, page 530
3 Boa Viagem, page 532

branches in Boa Viagem (T3463 3621), at the *rodoviária*, and at the airport (T3224 2361, open 24 hours); they cannot book hotels, but the helpful staff speak English and can offer leaflets and decent maps.

Hours of opening of museums, art galleries, churches, etc are published in the *Diário de Pernambuco* and *Jornal do Comércio*. The former's website has lots of tourist information, www.dpnet.com.br.

Opportunistic theft is unfortunately common in the streets of Recife and Olinda (especially on the streets up to Alto da Sé, Olinda). Prostitution is less common than it once was in Boa Viagem, as the police have taken strict measures against sex tourism. Any problems, contact the **Tourist Police**, T3326 9603/3464 4088.

Places in central Recife

Recife Antigo is the 2-km-long island between the ocean and the Rio Beberibe, the heart of old Recife and recently rehabilitated as the spiritual heart of the city, with great nightlife at weekends. **Marco Zero** on Praça Rio Branco is the official centre and focal point for Recife's carnival. Just north is the **Kahal Zur Israel synagogue** (Centro Cultural Judaico) ① *R de Bom Jesus 197, T3224 2178, www.kahalzurisrael.com, Tue-Fri 0900-1600, Sun 1400-1730, US$3*, on the old R dos Judeus, has been redeveloped with a museum telling the story of the Jewish presence in Dutch-held Recife in 16th century until Portuguese persecution. On the Praça do Arsenal da Marinha is the **Torre da Malakoff**, with a good view of the city from the observatory. Continuing north, the church of **Nossa Senhora do Pilar** ① *R de São Jorge* is undergoing extensive refurbishment after years of neglect. **Forte do Brum** ① *Praça Comunidade Lusa Brasileira, Tue-Fri 0800-1600, Sat-Sun 1400-1700, US$1*, (built by the Dutch in 1629) is an army museum.

The island just south of Recife Antigo contains the neighbourhoods of **Santo Antônio and São José**. Here are many historical monuments, including the church of **Santo Antônio do Convento de São Francisco** (1606) ① *R do Imperador, www.ordemterceiradesaofranciscodorecife. blogspot.co.uk*, which has beautiful Portuguese tiles, and adjoining it, one of the finest baroque buildings in northeast Brazil, the **Capela Dourada** (Golden Chapel, 1697) ① *Mon-Fri 0800-1130, 1400-1700, Sat morning only, US$1.50, no flash photography*. It is through the Museu Franciscano de Arte Sacra. The church is immediately south of **Praça da República**, on which stands the **Palácio do Campo das Princesas**, a neoclassical former Governor's Palace, with an interior garden designed by Burle Marx. **Teatro de Santa Isabel** ① *Praça da República, T3355 3323, www.teatrosantaisabel.com.br, guided visits Sun 1400, 1700*, built in 1851, is one of three traditional theatres in the city. The others are **Apolo** ① *R do Apolo 121*, and **Parque** ① *R do Hospício 81, Boa Vista*, restored and beautiful.

The **Museu de Arte Moderna Aloisio Magalhães** ① *R da Aurora, 265, Boa Vista, T3355 6870, www.mamam.art.br, Tue-Fri 1200-1800, Sat-Sun 1300-1700, free* shows modern Brazilian and contemporary art (much of it from Recife and the Northeast), in a series of galleries set in a beautiful 19th century town house overlooking the Capibaribe river.

A couple of blocks south, close to the central post office, is the **Praça do Sebo**, where the city's second-hand booksellers concentrate; this Mercado de Livros Usados is off the Rua da Roda, behind the Edifício Santo Albino, near the corner of Avenida Guararapes and Rua Dantas Barreto. The first Brazilian printing press was installed in 1706 and Recife claims to publish the oldest daily newspaper in South America, Diário de Pernambuco, founded 1825 (see above). The distinctive lilac building is on the Praça da Independência. Head down Av Dantas Barreto to **São Pedro dos Clérigos** (1782) ① *T3224 2954, Mon-Fri 0800-1200, 1400-1600, being restored in 2014*, which should be seen for its façade, its fine wood sculpture and a splendid trompe-

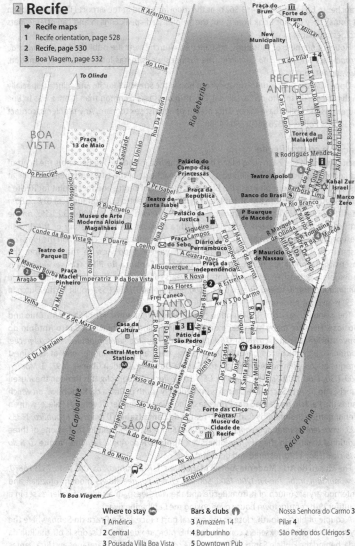

2 Recife

➡ Recife maps
1 Recife orientation, page 528
2 Recife, page 530
3 Boa Viagem, page 532

Where to stay
1 América
2 Central
3 Pousada Villa Boa Vista

Restaurants
1 Leite
2 Gelattos

Bars & clubs
3 Armazém 14
4 Burburinho
5 Downtown Pub
6 Estação Pirata
7 Metropole

Churches
Capela Dourada 1
Nossa Senhora de Penha 2
Nossa Senhora do Carmo 3
Pilar 4
São Pedro dos Clérigos 5

Buses
To Itamaracá & Igarassu 1
To Porto da Galinhas 2
To Boa Viagem 3

200 metres
200 yards

l'oeil ceiling. The **Pátio de São Pedro**, the square round the church, has sporadic folk music and poetry shows on Wednesday to Sunday evenings (T3426 2728) and there are atmospheric bars and restaurants. Not far away, is **Nossa Senhora do Carmo** (1663) ① *Praça do Carmo, Mon-Fri 0800-1200, 1400-1900, Sat 0700-1200, Sun 0700-1000*. The former municipal prison is now the **Casa da Cultura** ① *T3224 0557, www.casadeculturape.com.br, Mon-Fri 0900-1900, Sat 0900-1800, Sun 0900-1400*. The cells have been converted into a gallery of hundreds of shops and stalls selling arts and souvenirs from all over Pernambuco. Southeast of the Casa da Cultura is the Dutch **Forte das Cinco Pontas** (with **Museu da Cidade do Recife**) ① *T3224 8492, www.recife.pe.gov/cultura/museucidade.php, Mon-Fri 0900-1800, Sat-Sun 1300-1700, US$1.50 donation* (1630 with Portuguese alterations, 1677), which has a cartographic history of the settlement of Recife. This, and Forte do Brum, jointly controlled access to the port at the southern and northern entrances respectively. A few blocks north of Cinco Pontas is **Nossa Senhora de Penha** ① *Praça Do Vital, Tue-Thu 0800-1200, 1500-1700, Fri 0600-1800, Sat 1500-1700, Sun 0700-0900*, an Italianate church which holds a traditional blessing of São Felix on Friday, attended by the sick seeking miracles. There are many other colonial churches.

West of the centre is the **Museu do Estado** ① *Av Rui Barbosa 960, Graças, Tue-Fri 0900-1700, Sat-Sun 1400-1700*, has excellent paintings by the 19th-century landscape painter, Teles Júnior.

Oficina Cerâmica Francisco Brennand ① *Av Caxangá, Várzea, T3271 2466, www.brennand.com.br, Mon-Thu 0800-1700, Fri 0800-1600, US$5. Take the metrô to Camaragibe and a taxi from there US$7.50 one way*. A museum and 19th-century ceramics factory set in mock-Moorish gardens and filled with Brennand's extraordinary Gaudiesque ceramic sculptures and paintings. The artist, who is one of Brazil's most illustrious, can sometimes be seen walking here, cane in hand looking like an old Sigmund Freud. **Instituto Ricardo Brennand** ① *Alameda Antônio Brennand s/n, Várzea, T2121 0365, www.institutoricardobrennand.org.br, Tue-Sun 1300-1700, last admission 1630, US$7.50*. Another scion of the Brennand family has built this fantasy castle on the outskirts of the city to house his art collection. This is one of the most important in the country and includes the largest assemblage of New World Dutch paintings in the world (with many Franz Posts), as well as Brazilian modern art, armoury and medieval maps.

Boa Viagem

Boa Viagem, the main residential and hotel quarter, is about 6 km south of the city. The 8-km promenade commands a striking view of the Atlantic, but the beach is backed by a busy road, is crowded at weekends and not very clean. Sadly the beach is plagued by bull sharks (*Carcharhinus leucas*) who lost their mangrove habitat to the south to ill-considered coastal development. You can go fishing on jangadas at Boa Viagem with a fisherman at low tide. The main praça has a small food and crafts market at weekends. Boa Viagem's fine church dates from 1707. Take any bus marked 'Boa Viagem'; from Nossa Senhora do Carmo, take buses marked 'Piedade', 'Candeias' or 'Aeroporto' – they go on Avenida Domingos Ferreira, two blocks parallel to the beach, all the way to Praça Boa Viagem (at Avenida Boa Viagem 500). Back to the centre take buses marked 'CDU' or 'Setubal' from Avenida Domingos Ferreira.

South of Recife

About 60 km south of Recife, beyond the city of Cabo and the beaches of Gaibu and Itapuama, is **Porto de Galinhas**, a beautiful beach which has been growing as a resort since the 1990s. It has upmarket hotels, *pousadas*, restaurants and shops to north and south. Because of a reef close to the shore, swimming is only possible at high tide. Porto de Galinhas information centre, T3552 1728.

Boa Viagem detail

➡ Recife maps
1 Recife orientation, page 528
2 Recife, page 530
3 Boa Viagem, page 532

Atlantic Ocean

200 metres
200 yards

Where to stay 🛏
1 Aconchego
2 Coqueiral
8 Cosmopolitan Hostel
3 Hostel Boa Viagem
4 Maracatus do Recife
5 Pousada da Julietá
6 Pousada da Praia
7 Recife Monte

Restaurants 🍴
2 Chica Pitanga
3 Churrascaria Porcão
4 Ilha da Kosta
5 La Capannina
6 La Maison
7 Parraxaxá
11 Sushimi
12 Picanha do Tio Dadá

Bars & clubs 🍸
13 Baltazar
14 O Boratcho

For hotel and restaurant price codes, and other relevant information, see Essentials.

Where to stay

Boa Viagem is the main tourist district and the best area to stay. All hotels listed in this area are within a block or two of the beach. There is not much reason to be in the city centre and accommodation here is of a pretty low standard. During Carnival and for longer stays at other times, private individuals rent rooms and houses in Recife and Olinda; listings can be found in the classified ads in *Diário de Pernambuco*, or on www.recife.olx.com.br. This accommodation is generally cheaper, safer and quieter than hotels. See www.hiddenpousadasbrazil.com for the best of the more charming *pousada* accommodation.

Recife *p527, map p530*

$$$ Pousada Villa Boa Vista, R Miguel Couto 81, Boa Vista, T3223 0666, www.pousadavilla boavista.com.br. Only modern hotel in town, 5-min cab ride from centre, plain, comfortable rooms (with powerful showers), around a courtyard. Quiet, safe.

$$ Central, Av Manoel Borba 209, Boa Vista, T3222 4001, hotelcentralrecife@hotmail.com. A splendid and recently renovated 1920s listed building with original French-style open-lifts and plain, but freshly painted rooms, enormous old iron bathtubs, upper floors have wonderful views.

$ América, Praça Maciel Pinheiro 48, Boa Vista, T3221 1300, www.hotelamericarecife.com.br. Frayed, very simple rooms with low foamy beds, the best of which are on the upper floors and offer a good view out over the city.

Boa Viagem *p531, map p532*

$$$ Aconchego, Félix de Brito e Melo 382, T3464 2960, www.hotelaconchego.com.br. Motel style rooms around pleasant pool area, sitting room, restaurant, bar, English-speaking owner, will collect from airport. Sister hotel in Porto de Galinhas.

$$$ Coqueiral, R Petrolina, 43, T3326 5881, www.hotelcoqueiral.com.br. Dutch-owned, small and homely with pretty breakfast room. Recommended.

$$$ Pousada da Praia, Alcides Carneiro Leal 66, T3326 7085, www.hpraia.com. A/c, TV, safe, a/c, rooms vary (some tiny), very helpful, popular with Israelis. Roof-top breakfast room.

$$$ Recife Monte, R Petrolina e R dos Navegantes 363, T2121 0909, www.recife montehotel.com.br. Very smart and good value for category, caters to business travellers. Offers internet discounts.

$$ Maracatus do Recife, R Maria Carolina 185, T3326 1221, www.alberguemaracatus.com.br. Hostel with good breakfast, no hot water, simple, cooking facilities, pool, safe, recently renovated.

$$ Pousada da Julieta, R Prof Jose Brandão 135, T3326 7860. 1 block from beach, very good value, albeit with dated furnishings.

$$-$ Cosmopolitan Hostel, R Paulo Setubal 53, T3204 0321, www.cosmopolitanhostel. com. Simple mixed and sex-segregated dorms, doubles and singles in a decent location near the beach.

$ pp Hostel Boa Viagem, R Aviador Severiano l ins 455, T3326 9572, www.hostelboaviagem. com.br. From doubles (**$$**) and singles with a/c to dormitories, well-located HI hostel, excellent value, good bathrooms, pool, owners speak French and are from Caruaru so can arrange trips. Call ahead to arrange transport from airport or bus station.

Restaurants

Recife *p527, map p530*
Lanchonetes abound in the city, catering to office workers, but tend to close in evening.
$$$ Leite (lunches only), Praça Joaquim Nabuco 147/53 near Casa de Cultura, T3224 7977, www.restauranteleite.com.br. Old and famous, good service, smart (another branch in Boa Viagem, at Prof José Brandão 409).

$ Gelattos, Av Dantas Barreto 230, Santo
Antônio, T3224 6072, www.gelattos.com.br
(2 other branches). Great juices (sucos) and
snacks, including, hamburgers and sandwiches.

Boa Viagem p531, map p532
Restaurants on the main beach road of
Av Boa Viagem are pricey; venture a block
or two inland for cheaper deals. Be careful
of eating the local small crabs, known as
guaiamum; they live in the mangrove
swamps which take the drainage from
Recife's mocambos (shanty towns).
$$$ Churrascaria Porção, Av Eng Domingos
Ferreira 4215. Good for meat and salad, popular.
$$$ É, R do Atlântico 147, Pina. Between centre
and Boa Viagem. Fusion-cooking, romantic
contemporary surroundings, one of the best
in city.
$$$ La Maison, R Capitão Rebelinho 106,
T3325 1158. Fondue restaurant in low-lit
basement, with rosé wine and peach melba
on menu.
$$ La Capannina, Av Cons Aguiar 538, T3465
9420. Italian, pizzas, salad, pasta and sweet
and savoury crêpes, delivery service.
$$ Chica Pitanga, R Petrolina, 19, T3465
2224, www.chicapitanga.com.br. Upmarket,
excellent food by weight.
$$ Ilha da Kosta, R Pe Bernardino Pessoa, 50,
T3466 2222. Self-service seafood, sushi, pizza
and Brazilian cuisine, open 1100 to last client
and all afternoon.
$$ Parraxaxá, Av Fernando Simões Barbosa
1200, T3463 7874, www.parraxaxa.com.br.
Rustic-style, award-winning, northeastern
buffet, including breakfast. Recommended.
$$ Sushimi, Shopping Center Recife, T3463
6500, www.sushimi.com.br. Classic, Japanese
fast-food in suitably sterile surroundings. One
of a range of options in this Mall (open 1000-
2200, T3464 6000).
$ Picanho do Tio Dadá, R Baltazar Pereira
100, T3465 0986. Loud, TV screens, good value
portions of beef.

🍸 Bars and clubs

Recife centre p527, map p530
In both Recife and Olinda there is frequent
live music, in public spaces and in bars and
theatres. The historic centre of Recife Antigo
has been restored and is now an excellent
spot for nightlife. Bars around R do Bom Jesus
are the result of a scheme to renovate the
dock area. Also try the bars and clubs around
R Tomazino (R do Burburinho) and the Marco
Zero (the epicentre of Recife carnival). Always
take a taxi at night. Others include **Armazém
14**, Av Alfredo Lisboa s/n, Cais do Porto, for big
name acts; **Burburinho**, R Tomazina 106, T3224
5854, a live music and comedy club, good
starting place for the bars on this street; and
Estação Pirata, R do Apolo, good live bands.
Try to visit a northeastern forró where couples
dance to typical music, very lively especially
Fri and Sat, several good ones at Candeias.
See www.reciferock.com and www.guiada
semana.com.br for what's on where.
    The 2 most popular nightclubs (both huge,
2300 to dawn) are **Downtown Pub**, R Vigário
Tenório 105, T3424 6317, www.downtownpub.
com.br, live international and Brazilian rock
music and dance club, US$15, and **Metropole**,
R das Ninfas 125, Boa Vista, T3423 0123, www.
boatemetropole.com.br, US$15-20. European-
style dance club with big-name Brazilian DJs.

Boa Viagem p531, map p532
Baltazar, R Baltazar Pereira 130, T3327 0475.
Live music nightly, bar snacks, large and
popular. Open 1600 to early hours.
O Boratcho, Galeria Joana D'arc, Av Herculano
Bandeira, Pina T3327 1168, www.boratcho.
com.br. Tex Mex restaurant and live music
venue for alternative mangue beat bands.

🎉 Festivals

Recife p527, maps p528, p530 and p532
See www.agendadorecife.com.br for a
weekly calendar of events. **1 Jan**, Universal
Brotherhood. **Carnival** in Recife features a
pre-carnavalesca week of shows, processions

and balls, before the Galo da Madrugada, with up to a million participants officially opens Carnaval on the Sat morning. The festival continues until Tue with trios elétricos, samba and the distinctive local maracatu and frevo dances and rhythms. **12-15 Mar**, parades to mark the city's foundation. **Mid-Apr, Pro-Rock Festival**, a week-long celebration of rock, hip-hop and manguebeat at Centro de Convenções, Complexo de Salgadinho and other venues. Check Diário de Pernambuco or Jornal do Comércio for details. **Jun, Festas Juninas**. The days of Santo Antônio (13 Jun), São João (24 Jun), São Pedro and São Paulo (29 Jun), form the nuclei of a month-long celebration whose roots go back to the Portuguese colony. Intermingled with the Catholic tradition are Indian and African elements. The annual cycle begins on **São José's day, 19 Mar**, historically the 1st day of planting maize; the harvest in Jun then forms a central part of the festas juninas. During the festivals the forró is danced. This dance, now popular throughout the Northeast, is believed to have originated when the British builders of the local railways held parties that were 'for all'. **11-16 Jul**, Nossa Senhora do Carmo, patron saint of the city. **Aug** is the Mes do Folclore. **1-8 Dec** is the festival of Iemanjá, with typical foods and drinks, celebrations and offerings to the goddess; also **8 Dec**, Nossa Senhora da Conceição.

O Shopping

Recife *p527, maps p528, p530 and p532*
Handicrafts Centro do Artesanato de Pernambuco, Av Alfredo Lisboa, Armazém 11, Recife Antigo, T3181 3151, www.artesanat odepernambuco.pe.gov.br. A big complex of small shops and stalls selling typical Pernambuco art, including ceramic figurines, knitwear and clothing. **Casa da Cultura**, R Floriano Peixoto, Santo Antônio, T3184 3151, www.casadaculturape.com.br. Some 150 arts and crafts shops selling contemporary and antique figurines, prints and art work. Prices for ceramic figurines are lower than Caruaru.

Markets Cais de Alfândega, Recife Barrio, market of local work, 1st weekend of every month. **Domingo na Rua**, Sun market in Recife Barrio, with stalls of local artesanato and performances. **Feira do Recife Antigo**, Altura do Centro Judaico, every Sun 1400-2000, arts and crafts, foodstuffs and miscellany. **Hippy fair** at Praça Boa Viagem, on the sea front, wooden statues of saints, weekend only. **Mercado São José** (1875) for local products and handicrafts. **Sítio Trindade**, Casa Amarela. Sat craft fair. On 23 Apr, here and in the Pátio de São Pedro, you can see the *xangô* dance.

O What to do

Recife *p527, maps p528, p530 and p532*
Diving Offshore are some 20 wrecks, including the remains of Portuguese galleons, with diverse marine life.
Seagate, Av Herculano Bandeira 287, Boa Viagem, T3426 1657/9972 9662, www. seagaterecife.com.br. Daily departures and night dives.

O Transport

Recife *p527, maps p528, p530 and p532*
Air The Gilberto Freyre international airport, T3464 4188, www.aeroportorecife.com, 12 km from the city in Boa Viagem, is one of the best and most modern in Brazil; with plenty of places for coffees and magazines and boutiques of elegant little tourist shops. There is a bank desk before customs which gives much the same rate for dollars as the moneychangers in the lobby. Internal flights to all major cities and international flights to Portugal and the US. Airport taxis cost US$7.50 to the seafront and US$26 to Olinda. The Aeroporto metrô station (on Rua Dez de Junho in front of Praça Ministro Salgado Filho, just outside the airport terminal) connects to Shopping Recife and Recife Central station in the city centre (US$1) via the blue Linha Sul line. You can change for a metrô to the *rodoviária* (on the Camaragibe branch of the Linha Centro) at Joana Bezerra or Central. The a/c

bus No 42 runs (Mon-Fri 0530-1920, Sat 0615-1850, no bus Sun, US$1.20) from the airport to Shopping Recife, then along the entire length of Avs Cons Aguiar and Domingos Ferreira, Boa Viagem, to Recife Antigo, returning to the airport through Boa Vista. The non a/c bus 33 takes a similar route (daily 0400-2310, US$1.20). To Olinda, take bus 42 or 33 to Boa Viagem and change to bus 910 (daily 0330-2225, US$1.75) which runs from both Praça Nossa Senhora da Boa Viagem and Av Boa Viagem to Praça do Varadouro in Olinda, the closest bus stop to the colonial centre. Bus 370 (TIP/TI Aeroporto, US$1.20, daily 0400-2250) connects the airport and the *rodoviária*.

Bus City buses cost US$1.20; they are clearly marked and run frequently until about 2300 weekdays, 0100 weekends. Many central bus stops have boards showing routes. See www.granderecife.pe.gov.br for details. On buses, especially at night, look out for landmarks as street names are written small and are hard to see. Integrated bus-metrô (see Train, below) routes and tickets (US$1.50) are available. Urban transport information, T158. See below for buses to Olinda and other destinations outside the city. Taxis are plentiful; fares double on Sun, after 2100 and on holidays; number shown on meter is the fare; don't take the taxi if a driver tells you it is km. **Porto de Galinhas** can be reached by frequent buses and minivans from Av Dantas Barreto and R do Peixoto and from outside the *rodoviária*. Buses leave for **Igarassu** from Av Martins de Barros, in front of Grande Hotel, Recife, 45 mins, US$1.65.

The *rodoviária*, mainly for long-distance buses, is 20 km outside the city at Jaboatão dos Guararapes (it is called Terminal Integrado dos Passageiros, or TIP). T3452 1999. There is a 30-min metrô connection to the central railway station, opposite the Casa da Cultura. From Boa Viagem a taxi all the way costs US$30, or go to Central or Joanna Bezerra metrô stations and change there. To Olinda from the *rodoviária*, take the metrô to Recife Central and then bus No 983 (Rio Doce/Princesa Isabel, daily 0400-2250) to Largo do Varadouro.

To **Salvador**, daily 1930, 12 hrs, US$80. To **Rio**, 2 daily, 44 hrs, US$180. To **São Paulo**, 2 daily, 50 hrs, US$180. To **João Pessoa**, every 20-30 mins, 2 hrs, US$10. To **Caruaru**, see below. Buses to Olinda, see below; to beaches beyond Olinda from Av Dantas behind the post office. To **Cabo** (every 20 mins) and beaches south of Recife from Cais de Santa Rita.

Train Commuter services, known as the Metrô (overground light rail), leave from the central station. It has 2 lines: Linha Centro (which has two branches, one of which, the Camaragibe branch connects to the *rodoviária*) and the Linha Sul which runs to Shopping Recife, Tancredo Neves and the airport, all of which stations are close to Boa Viagem.

❶ Directory

Recife *p527, maps p528, p530 and p532*
Banks Banks open 1000-1600, hours for exchange vary 1000-1400, sometimes later. **Exchange: Anacor**, Shopping Center Recife, loja 52, also at Shopping Tacaruna, loja 173. **Norte Câmbio Turismo**, Av Boa Viagem 5000, and at Shopping Guararapes, Av Barreto de Menezes. **Medical services** Unimed, Av Bernardo Vieira de Melo 1496, Guararapes, T3462 1955/3461 1530, general medical treatment.

Around Recife

'Around Recife' is a bit of literary licence because this section deals with not only fine colonial towns not far from the state capital, but also the Fernando de Noronha archipelago, way out in the Atlantic. Of the former, Olinda is one of the best examples in Brazil and only minutes from Recife. In the drier interior is Caruaru, a fascinating market town. Fernando de Noronha, best reached from Recife (hence its inclusion here), has a wonderful marine environment and is ideal for those who are seeking a remote destination.

Olinda → *Phone code: 081. Post code: 53000. Colour map 5, B6. Population: 367,902.*

The old capital of Brazil founded in 1537 and named a World Heritage Site by UNESCO in 1982 is about 7 km north of Recife. A programme of restoration, partly financed by the Netherlands government, was initiated in order to comply with the recently conferred title of National Monument, but many of the buildings are still in need of repair. The compact network of cobbled streets is steeped in history and invites wandering. This is a charming spot to spend a few relaxing days and a much more appealing base than Recife.

Many of the historic buildings have irregular opening hours, but can be viewed from the outside. The **tourist office** ① *Praça do Carmo, T3429 9279, daily 0900-2100,* provides a complete list of all historic sites with a useful map, *Sítio Histórico*. Guides with identification cards wait in Praça do Carmo. Some are former street children and half the fee for a full tour of the city (about US$20) goes to a home for street children.

The **Basílica e Mosterio de São Bento** ① *R São Bento, Mon-Fri 0830-1130, 1430-1700, Mass Sat 0630 and 1800; Sun 1000,* with Gregorian chant. Monastery closed except with written

Olinda

São Francisco

Cathedral Alto da Sé

Museu de Arte Sacra

Praça da Sé

Bispo Chutinho

Misericórdia

das Bertiogas

Bernardo do Bonfim

Museu Regional

Amparo

4 Cantos

Cel Joaquim Cavalcanti

Museu do Mamulengo

Beato do Muto

Prudente de Morais

Porta Seguro

13 de Maio

Henrique Dias

Museu de Arte Contemporânea

Av Joaquim Nabuco

Bica de São Pedro

Travessa de São Francisco

São Francisco

Sol

Ladeira da Sé

Bonfim

Alfredo

Tiberato

Liberdade

Dr J Gonçalves

7 de Setembro

4 de Janeiro

São Bento

10 de Novembro

13 de Novembro

São Bento

Eufrásio Barbosa

Av Sigismundo Gonçalves

Manoel Borba

Praia de São Francisco

Beira Mar

Atlantic Ocean

Bus Stops

Praça João Alfredo

Carmo

To Recife

200 metres

200 yards

N

Where to stay
1 7 Colinas
2 Casa de Chica
3 Olinda Hostel
4 Pousada Baobá
5 Pousada Bela Vista
6 Pousada do Amparo
7 Pousada d'Olinda
8 Pousada dos Quatro Cantos
9 Pousada São Francisco
10 São Pedro

Restaurants
1 Creperie
2 Maison do Bomfim
3 Mourisco
4 Oficina do Sabor

Bars & clubs
7 Bodega do Véio
5 Farândola
6 Marola

permission. Founded 1582 by the Benedictine monks, burnt by the Dutch in 1631 and restored in 1761, this is the site of Brazil's first law school and the first abolition of slavery. The magnificent gold altar is one of the finest pieces of baroque carving in the Americas. Despite its weathered exterior, the **Convento de Franciscano de NS das Neves** (1585) ⓘ *Ladeira de São Francisco, Tue-Fri 0800-1200, 1400-1700, Sat 0800-1200, US$2.50, Mass Tue 1900, Sat 1700 and Sun 0800*, has splendid woodcarving and paintings, superb gilded stucco, and azulejos showing scenes from the life of St Francis and from Lisbon before the 1755 earthquake. The Capela de São Roque within the church of **Nossa Senhora das Neves** has a glorious painted ceiling. Make the short, but very steep, climb up to the **Alto da Sé** for memorable views of the city and the coastline stretching all the way to Recife. Here, the simple **Igreja da Sé** (1537) ⓘ *Mon-Fri 0800-1200, 1400-1700*, a cathedral since 1677, was the first church to be built in the city. Nearby, the **Igreja da Misericórdia** (1540) ⓘ *R Bispo Coutinho, daily 1145-1230, 1800-1830*, has fine tiling and gold work. On a small hill overlooking Praça do Carmo, the **Igreja do Carmo** church (1581) is also impressive.

There are some houses of the 17th century with latticed balconies, heavy doors and brightly painted stucco walls. The local colony of artists means excellent examples of regional art, mainly woodcarving and terracotta figurines, may be bought in the Alto da Sé, or in the handicraft shops at the **Mercado da Ribeira** ⓘ *R Bernardo Vieira de Melo*, (Vieira de Melo gave the first recorded call for independence from Portugal, in Olinda in 1710). Handicrafts are also sold at good prices in the Mercado Eufrásio Barbosa, by the junction of Avenida Segismundo Gonçalves and Santos Dumont, Varadouro. There is a **Museo de Arte Sacra** ⓘ *R Bispo Coutinho 726, Tue-Fri 0900-1300*, in the former Palacío Episcopal (1696). At Rua 13 de Maio 149, in the 18th-century jail of the Inquisition, is the **Museu de Arte Contemporânea** ⓘ *same hours as Museu Regional*. The **Museu Regional** ⓘ *R do Amparo 128, Tue-Fri 0900-1700, Sat and Sun 1000-1800, US$0.50*, is excellent.

The **beaches** close to Olinda are polluted. Those further north from Olinda, beyond Casa Caiada, are beautiful, palm-fringed, seldom crowded; at **Janga**, and **Pau Amarelo**, the latter can be dirty at low tide (take either a 'Janga' or 'Pau Amarela' bus, Varodouro bus to return). At many simple cafés you can eat sururu (clam stew in coconut sauce), agulha frita (fried needle-fish), miúdo de galinha (chicken giblets in gravy) and casquinha de carangueijo (seasoned crabmeat). Visit the Dutch fort on Pau Amarelo beach; small craft fair here on Saturday nights.

Igarassu → *Colour map 5, B6. Population: 82,277.*

Igarassu, 39 km north of Recife on the road to João Pessoa, has the first church ever built in Brazil (SS Cosme e Damião, built in 1535) and the convent of Santo Antônio with a small museum next door.

Caruaru → *Colour map 5, C6. Population: 253,634. Altitude: 554 m.*

The paved road from Recife passes through rolling hills, with sugar cane and large cattle fazendas, before climbing an escarpment. As the road gets higher, the countryside becomes drier, browner and rockier. Caruaru, 134 km west of Recife, is a busy, modern town, one of the most prosperous in the agreste in Pernambuco. It is also culturally very lively, with excellent local and theatre and folklore groups.

Caruaru is most famous for its markets. The Feira da Sulanca is basically a clothes market supplied mostly by local manufacture, but also on sale are jewellery, souvenirs, food, flowers and anything else that can go for a good price. The most important day is Monday. There is also the Feira Livre or do Troca-Troca (free, or barter market). On the same site, Parque 18 de Maio, is the Feira do Artesanato, leather goods, ceramics, hammocks and basketware, all the popular crafts of the region. It is tourist-oriented but it is on a grand scale and is open daily 0800-1800.

The little clay figures (*figurinhas* or *bonecas de barro*) originated by Mestre Vitalino (1909-1963), and very typical of the Nordeste, are the local speciality; most of the local potters live at **Alto da Moura**, 6 km away (a bumpy 30-minute bus ride, US$0.65), where a house once owned by Vitalino is open (the **Casa Museu Mestre Vitalino**, US$2.50), with personal objects and photographs, but no examples of his work.

Fernando de Noronha → *1 hr ahead of Brazilian Standard Time.*

This small archipelago 345 km off the northeast coast was declared a Marine National Park in 1988. There are many unspoilt beaches and interesting wildlife and excellent scuba-diving and snorkelling. Only one island is inhabited and is dominated by a 321-m peak. It is part of the state of Pernambuco administered from Recife. The islands were discovered in 1503 by Amérigo Vespucci and were for a time a pirate lair. In 1738 the Portuguese built the Forte dos Remédios (begun by the Dutch), later used as a prison in this century, and a church to strengthen their claim to the islands. Remains of the early fortifications still exist.

Vila dos Remédios, near the north coast, is where most people live and socialize. At Baía dos Golfinhos is a lookout point for watching the spinner dolphins in the bay. On the south side there are fewer beaches, higher cliffs and the coastline and islands are part of the marine park.

All development is rigorously controlled by ICMBio, to prevent damage to the nature reserve. Many locals are dependent on tourism and most food is brought from the mainland; prices are about double. Entry to the island is limited to two plane-loads per day. There is a daily tax of US$22.80, to be paid on arrival. An additional tax of US$5 is payable for walking the trails. Take sufficient reais as dollars are heavily discounted. For information, contact the national park office and **Tamar information centre** ⓘ *Al do Boldró s/n, Fernando de Noronho, T081-3619 1171, infonoronha@tamar.org.br, open 0900-2200.* See also www.fernandodenoronha.com.br or www.ilhadenoronha.com.br. The rains are from February-July; the island turns green and the sea water becomes lovely and clear. The dry season is August-March, but the sun shines all year round. No repellent available for the many mosquitoes.

ⓘ Around Recife listings

For hotel and restaurant price codes, and other relevant information, see Essentials.

● Where to stay

Olinda *p537, map p537*
Prices at least triple during Carnival when 5-night packages are sold. Rooms at regular prices can often be found in Boa Viagem during this time. If you can afford it, staying in a beautiful converted mansion (*pousada*) is the ideal way to absorb the colonial charm of Olinda.
$$$ 7 Colinas, Ladeira de São Francisco 307, T3439 7766, www.hotel7colinas.com.br. Spacious hotel with delightful, light rooms in beautiful private gated grounds with a large swimming pool, restaurant and bar. Helpful staff.

$$$ Pousada Baobá, R do Sol 147, T3429 0459, www.pousadabaobadeolinda.com.br. New, modestly sized and simply decorated rooms, with or without en suite bathrooms. Public areas are bright and colourful, staff attentive, small pool.
$$$ Pousada do Amparo, R do Amparo 199, T3439 1749, www.pousadoamparo.com.br. Olinda's best hotel is a gorgeous, 18th-century house, full of antiques and atmosphere in the Roteiros do Charme group. Rooms have 4-poster beds and each is decorated differently. The public areas include a spacious, art-filled foyer, a pool and sauna area surrounded by a little garden and an excellent, delightfully romantic restaurant.
$$ Casa de Chica, R 27 de Janeiro 43, T9963 3337, www.casadechica.com.br. Boxy but well-

kept rooms in a bright little *pousada* next to São Pedro church. Attractive public areas.

$$ Olinda Hostel, R do Sol 233, T3429 1592, www.alberguedeolinda.com.br. HI hostel, 8-bed rooms with fan and shared bath, tropical garden, TV room, hammocks, small pool.

$$ Pousada Bela Vista, R Amparo 215, T3429 3930, www.hotelbelavista.tur.br. Renovated *pousada* with brightly painted rooms, sparsely furnished. Public areas are decorated with giant carnival puppets and a tiny pool is due for mid-2014.

$$ Pousada d'Olinda, P João Alfredo 178, T3494 2559, www.pousadadolinda.com.br. Basic but well-kept dorms and doubles around a pool, garden, communal breakfast area, good breakfast, lunchtime restaurant, 10% off for owners of Footprint Handbooks in low season, English, French, German, Arabic and Spanish spoken.

$$ Pousada dos Quatro Cantos, R Prudente de Morais 441, T3429 0220, www.pousada4 cantos.com.br. A large converted town house with a little walled garden and terraces, bright rooms and suites decorated with Pernambuco arts and crafts, furnished mostly with antiques, welcoming and full of character.

$$ Pousada São Francisco, R do Sol 127, T3429 2109, www.pousadasaofrancisco.com. br. Well-kept and airy rooms with terraces and pokey bathrooms. Pool and bar in pleasant gardens visited by hummingbirds in the early morning, restaurant, parking. Within walking distance of the historic centre.

$$ São Pedro, R 27 de Janeiro 95, T3439 9546, www.pousadapedro.com. Quiet, walled garden, small shaded pool, delightful breakfast area and lobby decorated with art and antiques. Rustic rooms are tiny, especially on the lower floors.

Caruaru *p538*
Cheap *hospedarias* are around the central Praça Getúlio Vargas. Lots of cheap lunch restaurants.

$$$ Grande Hotel São Vicente de Paulo, Av Rio Branco 365, T3721 5011, www.grande hotelcaruaru.com.br. Good, a/c, central, laundry, garage, bar, restaurant, pool, TV.

$$ Centenário, 7 de Setembro 84, T3722 4011, F3721 1033. Also suites, good breakfast, pool, central, can be noisy, otherwise recommended.

$$ Central, R Vigário Freire 71, T3721 5880, www.hotelcentralcaruaru.com.br. Suites or rooms, all with a/c, TV, good breakfast, in the centre. Has a similar sister hotel. Recommended.

Fernando de Noronha *p539*
$$$$ Pousada do Vale, T3619 1293, w ww.pousadadovale.com. Well-run *pousada*, comfortable rooms, best are the duplex wooden bungalows. 300 m from Vila dos Remedios town centre.

$$$$ Zé Maria, R Eunice Cordeiro 1, T3619 1258, www.pousadazemaria.com.br. Spacious bungalows with generous beds, verandas with hammocks and views to the Morro do Pico, small deep-blue half-moon pool.

$$$$-$$$ Solar dos Ventos, T3619 1347, www.pousadasolardosventos.com.br. Next to the Maravilha, shares the same spectacular view, but not in the sameleague, well-appointed bungalows, no pool.

$$$ Pousada dos Corais, Residencial Floresta Nova, Quadra "D" Casa 07, T3619 1147, www. pousadacorais.com.br. 8 small, plain a/c rooms around a little pool. Good breakfast.

$$ Verde Livre, Vila Remédios, T3619 1312. With a/c, TV, fridge and breakfast, simple but good.

⑦ Restaurants

Olinda *p537, map p537*
Several *lanchonetes* and fast-food options along the seafront. The traditional Olinda drinks, **Pau do Índio** (contains 32 herbs) and **Retetel**, are both made on the R do Amparo. Also try tapioca, a manioc pancake stuffed with cheese, fruit or syrup.

$$$ Oficina do Sabor, R do Amparo 355, T3429 3331, www.oficinadosabor.com. Consistently wins awards, pleasant terrace overlooking city, food served in hollowed-out pumpkins and lots of vegetarian options.

$$ Creperia, R Prudente de Morais 168, T3429 2935. Savoury and sweep crêpes, pizzas and petiscos (bar snacks) served in an open-plan dining area.

$$ Maison do Bomfim, R do Bonfim 115, www.maisondobomfim.com.br. Serene, fan-cooled, rustic-style restaurant, French cuisine, as well as Brazilian and Italian.

$ Mourisco, Praça João Alfredo 7. Excellent, good value food by weight in lovely, part-covered, garden, delicious deserts. Warmly recommended.

Fernando de Noronha *p539*

$$$ Ecologiku's, Estr Velha do Sueste, T3619 1807. Opened sided restaurant with a little garden, great Bahian food, delicious *moqueca*. Good *caipirinhas*.

$$$ Porto Marlin, Porto de Santo Antônio, T3619 1452. Good Japanese food à la carte with an all you can eat buffet on Thu and Sat from 1800.

$ Açai e Raizes, BR363, Floresta Velha, T3619 0058. Roadside sandwich bar with good snacks, puddings and delicious cream of *cupuaçu* and *açai*.

$ Cia da Lua, Bosque dos Flamboyantes, T3619 1631. Decent coffee, snacks, sandwiches, internet access and car and buggy rental.

$ Jacaré, Praça Pres Eurico Dutra (next to the Banco Real), T3619 1947. Best value on the island with lunchtime seafood and general Brazilian buffet.

🌙 Bars and clubs

Olinda *p537, map p537*

Every Fri night bands of wandering musicians walk the streets serenading passers-by. Each Sun from 1 Jan to Carnival there is a mini Carnival in the streets.

Beginning at dusk, but best after 2100, the Alto da Sé becomes the scene of a street fair, with arts, crafts, makeshift bars and barbecue stands, and impromptu traditional music; even more animated at Carnival. Plenty of funky bars on R do Sol.

Bodega do Véio, R do Amparo 212, T3429 0185. An Olinda institution, live music Thu-Sun. Great petiscos and caipirinhas, vibrant crowd.

Cantinho da Sé, Ladeira da Sé 305. Lively, good view of Recife, food served.

Farândola, R Dom Pedro Roeser 190, behind Carmo church. Mellow bar with festival theme and 'big-top' style roof. Warmly recommended.

Marola, Trav. Dantas Barreto 66. Funky wooden *barraca* on rocky shoreline specializing in seafood, great *caiprifrutas* (frozen fruit drink with vodka – try the cashew), can get crowded. Recommended.

Pernambucanamente, Av Min Marcos Freire 739, Bairro Novo. Live, local music every night.

Preto Velho, Alto da Sé. Live samba at weekends, most lively on Sat.

Fernando de Noronha *p539*

Vila dos Remédios town has several bars; including a pizzeria with lively weekend forró from 2200 on weekends, and a bar with live reggae nightly in high season.

🎉 Festivals

Olinda *p537, map p537*

At Olinda's **carnival** thousands of people dance through the narrow streets of the old city to the sound of the frevo, the brash energetic music which normally accompanies a lively dance performed with umbrellas. The local people decorate them with streamers and straw dolls, and form themselves into costumed groups to parade down the R do Amparo; **Pitombeira** and **Elefantes** are the best known of these groups. **Foundation Day** is celebrated with 3 days of music and dancing, **12-15 Mar**, night time only.

Caruaru *p538*

17 Dec-2 Jan, Festas Natalinas; Semana Santa, Holy Week, with lots of folklore and handicraft events; **18-22 May**, city's anniversary. **13 Jun** Santo Antônio and **24 Jun** São João, the latter a huge forró festival, are part of Caruaru's Festas Juninas. **Sep**, Micaru, a street carnival; also in **Sep**, Vaquejada (a Brazilian cross between rodeo and bull fighting), biggest in the northeast.

Fernando de Noronha *p539*
Boat trips and jeep tours are available; it is also possible to hire a beach buggy. You can hitch everywhere as everyone stops. There are good hiking, horse riding and mountain biking possibilities, but you must either go with a guide or ranger in many parts.

Diving Diving is organized by **Atlantis Divers**, T081-3619 1371, www.atlantisdivers.com.br, **Águas Claras**, T3619 1225, www.aguasclaras-fn.com.br, and **Noronha Divers**, T3619 1112, www.noronhadivers.com.br. Diving costs between US$75-150 for 2 tanks. This is the diving mecca for Brazilian divers with a great variety of sites to explore and fish to see. **Trip Noronha**, T019-3808 5265, www.trip noronha.com.br. Offers tours around the island, attractive *pousada* packages and dive trips, good.

⊙ Transport

Olinda *p537, map p537*
Bus See **Recife** Transport, page 536, for buses from airport and *rodoviária* to Olinda. From Recife take a Rio Doce (Princesa Isabel) bus, No 981, which runs from Recife Central metrô (useful for connections to Boa Viagem, the airport and the *rodoviária*); or Jardim Atlântico No 974 (0430-2330), which leaves from the R do Sol and Ponte Duarte Coelho in Recife. From Boa Viagem take bus No 910 (Piedade/Rio Doce, daily 0330-2225), which runs through Recife to the Praça do Varadouro, the closest stop to the historical centre of Olinda. All fares US$1.20. Taxi drivers between Olinda and Recife try to put meters onto *bandeira* (rate) 2 – only meant for Sun, holidays, after 2100 and when an Olinda taxi is operating in Recife or vice versa – but should change it back to 1 if queried (taxi to Boa Viagem US$23, US$26 at night).

Caruaru *p538*
Bus The *rodoviária* is 4 km from town; buses from Recife stop in the centre. Bus from centre, at the same place as Recife bus stop, to *rodoviária*, US$1.20. Many buses from TIP in **Recife**, 2 hrs, US$12.75.

Fernando de Noronha *p539*
Air Daily flights from **Recife** with , 1 hr 20 mins, about US$400 return. From Natal , 1 hr, US$475 return.

South of Recife

Two small states, Alagoas and Sergipe, are wedged between Pernambuco and Bahia. For no good reason, most people pass through, but there are some good examples of colonial architecture and, like the entire northeast coast, some fine beaches.

South to Alagoas
There are many interesting stopping points along the coast between Recife and Maceió. The main highway, BR-101, heads a little inland from the coast, crossing the state border near Palmares. It then continues to Maceió. On the coast the Pernambuco-Alagoas border is by São José da Coroa Grande, after which a coastal road, unpaved in parts, runs to Barra do Camaragibe. Mid-way between Recife and Maceió is **Maragogi**, www.maragogionline.com.br (with a list of places to stay). Although it is becoming increasingly popular and crowded in high season, this little beach town has preserved something of its local character. The beach is glorious and some 6 km offshore, a reef reveals a series of deep swimming pools at low tide. Trips out there are easy to organize (expect to pay around US$15). **Real Alagoas** buses run daily from both Recife and Maceió, three hours from either; there are also combis from Maceió.

Near the mouth of the Rio Camaragibe, 38 km south of Maragogi, is **São Miguel dos Milagres**, a tiny colonial town with a crumbling Portuguese church, close to some of the best beaches in northeastern Brazil. Some, such Praias do Patacho, do Toque and do Riacho, are becoming popular with the São Paulo jetset and 'boutique' *pousadas* are springing up (see www.hiddenpousadasbrazil.com). The Tatuamunha river near São Miguel is the best place in the world to see West Indian manatees. The **Santuário do Peixe Boi** ① *Projeto Aribama, R Luiz Ferreira Dorta, s/n, Porto de Pedras, T9108 0906, daily 1000-1600, US$15*, on the river is devoted to the rehabilitation of the mammals, which are subsequently released into the estuary. *Pousadas* can organize visits. They can also arrange transfers from Maceió or Recife (US$60 or US$80 respectively); alternatively take a combi from Maceió's *rodoviária* or a taxi from Maragogi (US$35).

Maceió and around → *Phone code: 082. Post code: 57000. Colour map 5, C6. Population: 797,759*

The capital of Alagoas state is mainly a sugar port, but for tourism it's friendly, safe and good value. Two of its old buildings, the **Palácio do Governo**, which also houses the **Fundação Pierre Chalita** (Alagoan painting and religious art) and the church of **Bom Jesus dos Mártires** (1870, covered in tiles), are particularly interesting. Both are on the Praça dos Martírios (or Floriano Peixoto). The **cathedral**, Nossa Senhora dos Prazeres (1840), is on Praça Dom Pedro II. The helpful **tourist office** is at Setur ① *R Boa Vista 453, Centro, T3315 5700, www.turismo.al.gov.br,* (also at airport and *rodoviária*). The municipal tourist authority is Maceió Turismo ① *R Firmino de Vasconcelos 685, Pajuçaru, T3327 7711, www.maceio turismo.com.br;* information post on Pajuçara beach, by Sete Coqueiros artisan centre. Also visit www.turismomaceio.com.br.

Lagoa do Mundaú, a lagoon whose entrance is 2 km south at **Pontal da Barra**, limits the city to the south and west: excellent shrimp and fish are sold at its small restaurants and handicraft stalls; a nice place for a drink at sundown. Boats make excursions in the lagoon's channels. Beyond the city's main dock the beachfront districts begin; within the city, the beaches are smarter the further from the centre you go. The first, going north, is **Pajuçara** where there is a nightly craft market. At weekends there are wandering musicians and entertainers. Further out, **Jatiúca**, **Cruz das Almas** and **Jacarecica** (9 km from centre) are all good for surfing. The beaches, some of the finest and most popular in Brazil, have a protecting coral reef a kilometre or so out. Bathing is much better three days before and after full or new moon, because tides are higher and the water is more spectacular. Jangadas take passengers to a natural swimming pool 2 km off Pajuçara beach (**Piscina Natural de Pajuçara**), at low tide you can stand on the sand and rock reef (beware of sunburn). You must check the tides, there is no point going at high tide. Jangadas cost US$20 per person per day (about US$35 to have the jangada to yourself). On Sunday or local holidays in the high season it is overcrowded (at weekends lots of jangadas anchor at the reef selling food and drink).

By bus (22 km south), past Praia do Francês, the attractive colonial town and former capital of Alagoas, **Marechal Deodoro**, overlooks the Lagoa Manguaba. The 17th-century **Convento de São Francisco**, Praça João XXIII, has a fine church (Santa Maria Magdalena) with a superb baroque wooden altarpiece, badly damaged by termites. You can climb the church's tower for views. Adjoining it is the **Museu de Arte Sacra** ① *Mon-Fri 0900-1300, US$1.50, guided tours available, payment at your discretion.* Also open to visitors is the **Igreja Matriz de Nossa Senhora da Conceição** (1783). The town is the birthplace of Marechal Deodoro da Fonseca, founder of the Republic; the modest **house** ① *Mon-Sat 0800-1700, Sun 0800-1200, free,* where he was born is on the Rua Marechal Deodoro, close to the waterfront. On a day's excursion, it is easy to visit the town, then spend some time at beautiful **Praia do Francês**. The northern half of the beach is protected by a reef, the southern half is open to the surf. Along the beach there are many barracas and bars selling drinks and seafood; also several *pousadas*.

Penedo → *Phone code: 082. Post code: 57200. Colour map 5, C6. Population: 56,993.*
This charming town, some 35 km from the mouth of the Rio São Francisco, with a nice waterfront park, Praça 12 de Abril, was originally the site of the Dutch Fort Maurits (built 1637, razed to the ground by the Portuguese). The colonial town stands on a promontory above the river. Among the colonial architecture, modern buildings on Av Floriano Peixoto do not sit easily. On the Praça Barão de Penedo is the neoclassical **Igreja Matriz** (closed to visitors) and the 18th-century **Casa da Aposentadoria** (1782). East and a little below this square is the Praça Rui Barbosa, on which are the **Convento de São Francisco** (1783 and later) and the church of **Santa Maria dos Anjos** (1660). As you enter, the altar on the right depicts God's eyes on the world, surrounded by the three races, one Indian, two negroes and the whites at the bottom. The church has fine trompe-l'oeil ceilings (1784). The convent is still in use. Guided tours are free. The church of **Rosário dos Pretos** (1775-1816), on Praça Marechal Deodoro, is open to visitors. **Nossa Senhora da Corrente** (1764), on Praça 12 de Abril, and **São Gonçalo Garcia** (1758-1770) ① *Av Floriano Peixoto, Mon-Fri 0800-1200, 1400-1700.* Also on Avenida Floriano Peixoto is the pink **Teatro 7 de Setembro** (No 81) of 1884. The **Casa de Penedo** ① *R João Pessoa 126 (signs point the way up the hill from F Peixoto), Tue-Sun 0800-1800,* displays photographs and books on, or by, local figures. **Tourist information** at Praça Barão de Penedo 2, T3551 3907.

An interesting crossing into Sergipe can be made by frequent ferry (car and foot passengers, US$5 and US$1 respectively) from Penedo to **Neópolis**.

The canyons and beaches of the **Rio São Francisco** make a good excursion. The river courses its way through the hills of Minas Gerais and the desert backlands of Bahia before cutting through a series of dramatic gorges near the Xingó dam and subsequently through windswept dunes before entering the Atlantic in northern Sergipe. A number of tour operators in Atalaia (see below) run day-trips to the river mouth stopping at deserted beaches along the way; US$50-60 per person, depending on numbers.

Aracaju → *Phone code: 079. Post code: 49000. Colour map 5, C5. Population: 461,534.*
Capital of Sergipe founded 1855, it stands on the south bank of the Rio Sergipe, about 10 km from its mouth, 327 km north of Salvador. In the centre is a group of linked, beautiful parks: **Praça Olímpio Campos**, in which stands the cathedral, **Praça Almirante Barroso**, with the Palácio do Governo, and **Praças Fausto Cardoso** and **Camerino**. Across Avenida Rio Branco from these two is the river. There is a handicraft centre, the **Centro do Turismo** ① *in the restored Escola Normal, on Praça Olímpio Campos, Rua 24 Horas, 0900-1300, 1400-1900*; the stalls are arranged by type (wood, leather, etc). The city's beaches are at **Atalaia**, 16-km by road (taxi US$22), and the 30-km-long **Nova Atalaia**, on Ilha de Santa Luzia across the river. It is easily reached by boat from the Hidroviária (ferry station), which is across Avenida Rio Branco from Praça Gen Valadão. Ask at the tourist office, **Turismo Sergipe**, Travessa Baltazar Góes 86, Edifício Estado, T3179 7553, www.turismosergipe.net, about local tours, or look for leaflets in hotels.

São Cristóvão is the old state capital, 17 km southwest of Aracaju on the road to Salvador; bus US$3.50 from *rodoviária* and the old bus station at Praça João XXIII (taxi US$50-60 round trip from Aracaju). It was founded in 1590 by Cristóvão de Barros. It is the fourth oldest town in Brazil. Built on top of a hill, its colonial centre is unspoiled: the **Museu de Arte Sacra e Histórico de Sergipe** contains religious and other objects from the 17th to the 19th centuries; it is in the **Convento de São Francisco** ① *Tue-Fri 1000-1700, Sat-Sun 1300-1700, US$2.50.* Also worth visiting (and keeping the same hours) is the **Museu de Sergipe** in the former **Palácio do Governo** both are on Praça de São Francisco. Also on this square are the churches of **Misericórdia** (1627) and the **Orfanato Imaculada Conceição** (1646, permission to visit required from the Sisters). On Praça Senhor dos Passos are the churches **Senhor dos Passos** and **Terceira Ordem do Carmo** (both 1739), while on the Praça Getúlio Vargas (formerly Praça Matriz) is the 17th-century **Igreja Matriz Nossa Senhora da Vitória** ① *Tue-Fri 1000-1700, Sat-Sun 1500-1700.*

Estância → *Colour map 5, C5*

On the BR-101, almost midway between Aracaju and the Sergipe-Bahia border, and 247 km north of Salvador, is Estância, one of the oldest towns in Brazil. Its colonial buildings are decorated with Portuguese tiles. The month-long festival of **São João** in June is a major event. There are pleasant hotels, but most buses stop at the *rodoviária*, which is on the main road (four hours from Salvador).

ⓦ South of Recife listings

For hotel and restaurant price codes, and other relevant information, see Essentials.

ⓦ Where to stay

Maceió *p543*
It can be hard to find a room during the Dec-Mar holiday season, when prices go up. There are many hotels on Praia Pajuçara, mostly along Av Dr Antônio Gouveia and R Jangadeiros Alagoanos.
$$$$ Ponta Verde Praia, Av Alvaro Otacílio 2933, Ponta Verde, T2121 0040, www.hotel pontaverde.com.br. The best option on the beach, convenient for clubs, restaurants and Pajuçara, comfortable, good buffet breakfast.
$$$ Coqueiros Express, R Deportista H Guimarães 830, Ponta Verde, T4009 4700, www.coqueirosexpress.com.br. Smart, well-run, best rooms on upper floors, small pool, good breakfast.
$$$ Pousada Estalagem, R Eng D Sarmento Barroca 70, T3327 6088, www.pousadaes talagem.com.br. Flats for up to 6, with little cookers in a quiet backstreet above a photo shop.
$$$ Ritz Praia, R Eng Mário de Gusmão 1300, Laranjeiras, T2121 4600, www.ritzpraia.com.br. 1 block from beach, sun deck and tiny pool on top floor, bright and airy rooms.
$$$-$$ Gogá da Ema, R Laranjeiras 97, T3327 0329, www.hotelgogodaema.com.br. Close to beach on a quiet backstreet, good breakfast, simple rooms.

$$$-$ Alagamar Hostel, R Prefeito Abdon Arroxelas 327, T3231 2246, www. maceiopraiaalbergue.com. Always book in advance here (2 months for high season), good location and value but rooms vary, single-sex dorms. HI affiliated.

Penedo *p544*
$$$ São Francisco, Av Floriano Peixoto 237, T3551 2273, www.hotelsaofrancisco. tur.br. Standard rooms have no a/c, fridge. Recommended except for poor restaurant.
$$ Pousada Colonial, Praça 12 de Abril 21, T3551 2355, www.pousadacolonialde penedo.com.br. Luxo and suite have phone, TV and fridge, suites have a/c, spacious, good cheap restaurant, front rooms with view of the river.
$$ Pousada Estylos I, Praça Jacome Calheiros 79, T3551 2465. Also Estylos II, R Damaso do Monte 86, T3551 2429. Modest, modern, rooms with a/c or fan, quiet, river views, nice, not always open out of season.
$$ Turista, R Siqueira Campos 143, T3551 2237. With bath, fan, hot water. Recommended.

Aracaju *p544*
The centre is best avoided at night. Stay at Atalaia beach, just 10 mins from the city.
$$$-$$ San Manuel, R Niceu Dantas 75, Atalaia, T3218 5200, www.sanmanuelpraia hotel.com.br. Pleasant, modern, business facilities, best rooms have sea view.

$$ Oceânica, Av Santos Dumont 413, Atalaia, T3243 5950, www.pousadaoceanica-se.com.br. Facing the beach, spotless rooms, simple.

$$ Raio de Sol, R François Hoald 89, Atalaia, T3212 8600, www.pousadaraiodesol.com.br. Well-kept, bright rooms in a block 50 m back from the beach, quieter than on the sea front. Courteous, efficient staff.

🍴 Restaurants

Maceió p543
Local specialities include oysters, *pitu*, a crayfish (now becoming scarce), and *sururu*, a kind of cockle. Local ice cream, Shups, recommended. The best restaurants, bars and clubs are on and around R Egenheiro Paulo B Nogueira on Jatiúca beach. Many others in Pajuçara, eg on Av Antônio Gouveia. The beaches for 5 km from the beginning of Pajuçara to Cruz das Almas in the north are lined with barracas (thatched bars), providing music, snacks and meals until 2400 (later at weekends). Vendors on the beach sell beer and food during the day: clean and safe. There are many other bars and barracas at Ponto da Barra, on the lagoon side of the city.

$$$ Divina Gula, R Eng Paulo B Nogueira 85, Jatiúca, T3235 1016. Closed Mon. Wide-ranging menu, lively atmosphere and busy, large portions.

$$ Barrica's, Av Álvaro Calheiros 354, Ponta Verde. Lively waterfront bar with a menu that includes pasta, pizza, grilled meat and fish and some vegetarian options.

🎉 Festivals

Maceió p543
27 Aug: Nossa Senhora dos Prazeres; **16 Sep**: Freedom of Alagoas; **8 Dec**: Nossa Senhora da Conceição; **15 Dec**: Maceiofest,'a great street party with trios elêctricos'; Christmas Eve; New Year's Eve, half-day.

🚌 Transport

Maceió p543
Air 20 km from centre, taxi US$25. **Transporte Tropical Bus** from airport to Ponta Verde/

Pajuçara, every 30 mins 0630-2100, US$1.15; allow 45 mins.

Bus Taxis from town go to all the northern beaches, but buses run as far as Ipioca (23 km). The Jangadeiras bus marked 'Jacarecica-Center, via Praias' runs past all the beaches as far as Jacarecica. From there you can change to 'Riacho Doce-Trapiche', 'Ipioca' or 'Mirante' buses for Riacho Doce and Ipioca. To return take any of these options, or take a bus marked 'Shopping Center' and change there for 'Jardim Vaticana' bus, which goes through Pajuçara. Combis to Marechal Deodoro, Praia do Francês and Barra de São Miguel leave from opposite the Hospital Santa Casa in front of the Texaco station. Combi US$2.50 to Marechal Deodoro, 30 mins, calling at Praia do Francês in each direction. Last bus back from Praia do Francês to Maceió at 1800. Taxi US$25.

The *rodoviária* is 5 km from centre, on a hill with good views. Taxi, US$10 to Pajuçara. To Ponte Verde/ Pajuçara take buses No 711 or 715, or buses marked Ouro Preto p/Centro; they run every few minutes. To the *rodoviária*, Ponte Verde/ Jacintinho bus runs via Pajuçara from the centre, also take 'Circular' bus (25 mins Pajuçara to bus station). Bus to **Recife**, 10 a day, 3½ hrs express (more scenic coastal route, 5 hrs) US$15-28. **Maceió-Aracaju**, 5 hrs, US$20. To **Salvador**, 10 hrs, 4 a day, US$46-70.

Penedo p544
Bus To **Aracaju**, 2 a day, US$8.50, 4½ hrs, book in advance. It is quicker to take the ferry to **Neópolis**, then a minibus to Aracaju from there, 3½ hrs, US$8. 115 km from **Maceió**, 4 buses a day, US$12.50, 3-4 hrs. *Rodoviária*: Av Beira Rio, near service station.

Aracaju p544
Bus Interstate *rodoviária* is 4 km from centre, linked by local buses from adjacent terminal, US$1.15 (buy a ticket before going on the platform), T3259 2848. To **Salvador**, 6-7 hrs, several daily, US$25-35.

João Pessoa ➔ *Phone code: 083. Post code: 58000. Colour map 5, B6. Population: 597,934.*

It is a bus ride of two hours through sugar plantations over a good road from Recife (126 km) to João Pessoa, capital of the State of Paraíba on the Rio Paraíba. It's a pleasant, historical town with a rich cultural heritage. The beaches, beside the turquoise waters of the Atlantic, are wonderful. At Ponta do Seixas is the most easterly point in Brazil; near here the Transamazônica highway begins its immense, if not controversial, route west into the heart of the country. The city tourist office is **SETUR** ① *Av Odon Bezerra 367, Tambaú, T3218 9850, www.joaopessoa. pb.gov.br/secretarias/setur*, with information offices (Monday-Friday 0800-1200, 1400-1800) at São Francisco church, Estação Cabo Branco and at **PBTur's Centro Turístico** ① *Av Almte Tamandaré 100, Tambaú, T3214 8206, http://pbtur.blogspot.co.uk*, also at the airport, T3041 4200, and *rodoviária*.

Places in João Pessoa

João Pessoa is a capital that retains a small town atmosphere. In the **Centro Histórico** is the São Francisco Cultural Centre (Praça São Francisco 221), one of the most important baroque structures in Brazil, with the beautiful church of **São Francisco** which houses the **Museu Sacro e de Arte Popular** ① *Tue-Sun 0800-1200, 1400-1700*. Other tourist points include the **Casa da Pólvora**, now the **Museu Fotográfico Walfredo Rodríguez** (Ladeira de São Francisco) ① *Tue-Sun 0800-1200, 1400-1700*. Also the **Teatro Santa Roza** (1886) ① *Praça Pedro Américo, Varadouro, 1400-1700* **Casa do Artesão** ① *Praça da Independência 56, Centro, Tue-Fri 0900-1700, Sat-Sun 1000-1800*, where popular artists exhibit their work, with more than a thousand items on display, has been nominated as the best popular museum in Brazil.

João Pessoa's parks include the 17-ha **Parque Arruda Câmara**, north of the centre, and **Parque Solon de Lucena** or **Lagoa**, a lake surrounded by impressive palms in the centre of town, the city's main avenues and bus lines go around it.

The beachfront stretches for some 30 km from Ponta do Seixas (south) to the port of **Cabedelo** (north), on a peninsula between the Rio Paraíba and the Atlantic Ocean. This is Km 0 of the Transamazônica highway. The ocean is turquoise green and there is a backdrop of lush coastal vegetation. About 7 km from the city centre, following Avenida Presidente Epitáceo Pessoa is the beach of **Tambaú** (take bus No 510 'Tambaú' from outside the *rodoviária* or the city centre, alight at Hotel Tropical Tambaú), which has many hotels and restaurants. Regional crafts, including lace-work, embroidery and ceramics are available at Mercado de Artesanato, Centro de Turismo, Almte Tamandaré 100. The town's main attractions are its beaches, where most tourists stay. About 14 km south of the centre is the Cabo Branco lighthouse at Ponta do Seixas, the most easterly point of continental Brazil and South America; there is a panoramic view from the cliff top. **Cabo Branco** is much better for swimming than **Tambaú**. Take bus 507 'Cabo Branco' from outside the *rodoviária* to the end of the line; hike up to the lighthouse.

The best known beach of the state is **Tambaba**, the only official nudist beach of the Northeast, 49 km south of João Pessoa in a lovely setting. Two coves make up this famous beach: in the first bathing suits are optional, while the second one is only for nudists. Strict rules of conduct are enforced. Between Jacumã (many hotels, restaurants) and Tambaba are several nice beaches such as **Tabatinga** which has summer homes on the cliffs and **Coqueirinho**, surrounded by coconut palms, good for bathing, surfing and exploring caves.

For hotel and restaurant price codes, and other relevant information, see Essentials.

⊜ Where to stay

João Pessoa *p547*
All those listed are at Tambaú, unless indicated otherwise:

$$$$ Tropical Tambaú, Av Alm Tamandaré 229, T2107 1900, www.tropicaltambau.com.br. An enormous round building on the seafront which looks like a military bunker and has motel-style rooms around its perimeter. Comfortable and with good service. Recommended.

$$$$-$$$ Caiçara, Av Olinda 235, T2106 1000, www.hotelcaicara.com. A slick, business orientated place (Best Western) with a pleasant restaurant attached.

$$$ Nobile Inn Royal, Coração de Jesus, T2106 3000, www.royalhotel.com.br. Comfortable rooms with fridges around a pool.

$$$ Xênius, Av Cabo Branco 1262, T3015 3535, www.xeniushotel.com.br. Popular standard 4-star with a pool, good restaurant and well-kept but standard rooms (low-season reductions).

$$ Solar Filipéia, R Isidro Gomes 44, behind Centro de Turismo, T3219 3744, www.solar filipeia.com.br. Very smart hotel with large, bright rooms with bathrooms in tile and black marble and excellent service.

$$ Teiú Hotel Pousada, R Carlos Alverga 36, T3247 5475, www.teiupraia.webnode.pt. Centrally located and 1 block from the beach. Intimate, with balconies and sea view. Recommended.

$ Hostel Manaíra, R Major Ciraulo 380, Manaíra, T3247 1962, www.manairahostel. com.br. Friendly, brand new hostel close to the beach, with a pool, barbecue, cable TV and breakfast, good value.

$ Pousada Mar Azul, Av João Maurício 315, T3226 2660. Very clean large rooms, the best are on the upper level, right on the oceanfront road. Some have a/c and private bathrooms, others have fans. Well kept, safe and a real bargain.

⊘ Restaurants

João Pessoa *p547*
There are few options in the centre, other than the stalls in Parque Solon de Lucena next to the lake, beside which are some simple restaurants. Every evening on the beachfront, stalls are set up selling all kinds of snacks and barbecued meats. At Cabo Branco there are many straw huts on the beach serving cheap eats and seafood.

$$$ Adega do Alfredo, Coração de Jesus s/n, T3226 4346, www.adegadoalfredo.com.br. Very popular traditional Portuguese restaurant in the heart of the club and bar area.

$$$ Gulliver, Av Olinda 590, Tambaú, T3226 2504, www.restaurantegulliver.com.br. Fashionable French/Brazilian restaurant frequented by João Pessoa's upper middle classes.

$$ Cheiro Verde, R Carlos Alverga 43, Manaíra, T3226 2700. Self service, well established, regional food.

$$ Mangaí, Av General Édson Ramalho 696, Manaíra, T3226 1615, www.mangai.com.br. This is one of the best restaurants in the northeast to sample the region's cooking, with almost 100 hot dishes to choose from, sitting in copper tureens over a traditional wood-fired stove some 20 m long. Has branches in Brasília and Natal.

$$ Sapore d'Italia, Av Cabo Branco 1584, T3247 3322, www.saporeonline.com. Standard Italian fare including pizza.

$$ Toca do Caju, Av N S dos Navegantes 750, T2107 8700, www.pousadadocaju.com.br. Self service, price by kilo, good value. international food and barbecue. Has an adjoining *pousada*.

⊘ Bars and clubs

João Pessoa *p547*
There are many open bars on and across from the beach in Tambaú and Cabo Branco. The area known as Feirinha de Tambaú, on Av Tamandaré by the **Tambaú Hotel** and

nearby streets, is very lively, with R Coração do Jesus being the centre. There are numerous little bars and *forró* places here.

⊛ Festivals

João Pessoa *p547*
Pre-carnival celebrations are renowned: the *bloco* Acorde Miramar opens the celebrations the Tue before Carnival and on Wed, known as Quarta Feira de Fogo, thousands join the Muriçocas de Miramar. Celebrations for the patroness of the city, Nossa Senhora das Neves, take place for 10 days around 5 Aug.

○ Shopping

João Pessoa *p547*
Mercado Central, Centro. Bus 513, 511. Basic, big, dirty, but interesting. All fruit and spices of the region are sold there. Supermercado Pão de Açúcar, Av Epitácio Pessoa 1200-1400. Also good value lunches. Minimarket O Canto do Galeto, Av Ruy Carneiro 183, next to fruit market, serves take-away grilled chicken.

○ What to do

João Pessoa *p547*
City tours and trips to beaches are available. For nighttime folklore dances, ask at Tropical Tambaú for details. Buggy tours go to places where buses do not go. English-speaking driver Orlando, T9984 8010, has car for sightseeing, very helpful, takes 3.

○ Transport

João Pessoa *p547*
Air Aeroporto Presidente Castro Pinto, Bayeux, 11 km from centre, T3232 1200; national flights. Taxi to centre costs US$15, to Tambaú US$25.

Bus Most city buses stop at the *rodoviária* and go by the Lagoa (Parque Solon de Lucena). Take No 510 for Tambaú, No 507 for Cabo Branco.

Rodoviária is at R Francisco Londres, Varadouro, 10 mins from the centre, T3221 9611; luggage store; PBTUR information booth is helpful. Taxi to the centre US$5, to Tambaú US$12. To Recife, every 30 mins, US$10, 2 hrs. To Natal with Nordeste, every 2 hrs, US$14-20, 3 hrs. To Fortaleza with Nordeste, 2 a day, 12 hrs, US$50-75. To Salvador, US$60, 14 hrs.

○ Directory

João Pessoa *p547*
Banks Banco 24 Horas ATMs in Tambaú, the centre and Manaíra. Câmbios at Action Câmbio, Manaíra Shopping, cash and TCs. Mondeo Tour, Av Nego 46, near Posto Select, no TCs. **Useful addresses** Tourist police, Delegacia de polícia ao turista, Centro de Turismo, Tambaú, T3214 8022, open 0800-1800. The Centro de Turismo has internet, phones and, behind it, a post office.

Natal → *Phone code: 084. Colour map 2, B6. Population: 713,000.*

Natal, capital of Rio Grande do Norte, located on a peninsula between the Rio Potengi and the Atlantic Ocean, is one of the most attractive cities of Brazil's northeast coast, as well as a popular destination for those seeking sun and good beaches. The air is said by NASA to be the second purest in the world, after Antarctica. The inventors of the beach-buggy must have had Rio Grande do Norte in mind as the dunes and strand that surround the city are ideal for daredevil stunts and whizzing along the open sands.

Arriving in Natal
Tourist offices Secretaria de Turismo do Estado (SETUR) ① *R Mossoró 359, Petrópolis, T3232 2516, http://turismo.natal.rn.gov.br* is the government agency responsible for tourism in the

state. Information booths at **Centro de Turismo** ① *T3211 6149 (see Shopping, page 555)*, at the municipal tourist office, **SETURDE** ① *Av Pres Café Filho 746, Praia do Meio, T3232 9073, www.natal.rn.gov.br/seturde*, on Erivan Franca in Ponta Negra, **rodoviária** ① *T3232 7310*, and **airport** ① *T3643 1043*. For information T0800-841516, or, for the **Polícia Federal** ① *T3204 5500*, and for the **Tourist Police** ① *Av Engenheiro Roberto Freire 8790, Ponta Negra, T3232 7404 (Delegacia do Turista)*.

Places in Natal

The oldest part is the **Ribeira** along the renovated riverfront. The **Cidade Alta**, or Centro, is the main centre and Avenida Rio Branco its principal artery. The main square is made up by the adjoining **praças**: **João Maria**, **André de Albuquerque**, **João Tibúrcio** and **7 de Setembro**. At Praça André de Albuquerque is the old cathedral (inaugurated 1599, restored 1996). The small church of **Santo Antônio** ① *R Santo Antônio 683, Cidade Alta, Tue-Fri 0800-1700, Sat 0800-1400*, dates from 1766. It has a blue and white façade, a fine, carved wooden altar and a sacred art museum.

On a hill overlooking Ribeira is the **Centro do Turismo** ① *R Aderbal de Figueiredo 980, off R Gen Gustavo C Farias*, Petrópolis (see Bars and clubs, and Shopping, page 555). A converted prison with a wide variety of handicraft shops, art gallery, antique shop and tourist information booth, it offers good view of the Rio Potengi and the sea. At Praia do Forte, the tip of Natal's peninsula, is the **Forte dos Reis Magos** ① *T3221 0342, 0800-1630 daily except Christmas Day, New Year and Carnaval, US$3*. The star-shaped fort was begun in 1598 and is now the city's main historical monument. Its blinding white walls contrast with the blue of sea and sky. You can wander round the interior rooms, mostly empty although the former military prison now houses a lanchonete, and there are guides. The easiest way to get there is by taxi or on a tour; no buses go to the entrance, from where you have to walk along a causeway to the fort. Between it and the city is a military installation.

The **Museu Câmara Cascudo** ① *Av Hermes de Fonseca 1398, Tirol, T3342 4912, www.mcc.ufrn.br, Tue-Fri 0800-1700, US$1*, has exhibits on archaeological digs, Umbanda rituals and the sugar, leather and petroleum industries.

A large ecological zone, the **Parque das Dunas**, separates the commercial centre from Ponta Negra, 12.5 km away, the beach and nightlife spot where most visitors stay.

Beaches

Natal has excellent beaches, some of which are also the scene of the city's nightlife. East of the centre, from north to south are: **Praia do Forte**, **do Meio**, **dos Artistas de Areia Preta** and **Mãe Luzia**. The first two have reefs offshore, therefore little surf, and are appropriate for windsurfing. The others are urban beaches and local enquiries regarding pollution are recommended before bathing. Mãe Luzia marks the start of the **Via Costeira**, which runs south along the ocean beneath the towering sand dunes of **Parque das Dunas** (access restricted to protect the 9 km of dunes), joining the city to the neighbourhood and popular beach of Ponta Negra. A cycle path parallels this road and provides great views of the coastline. Lining Mãe Luzia and Barreira d'Água (the beach across from Parque das Dunas) are the city's four and five-star hotels.

Furthest south is vibrant and pretty **Ponta Negra**, justifiably the most popular beach. The seafront, Avenida Erivan França, is a car-free promenade for much of its length; the remainder is the busiest part of town. It has many hotels, from albergues up to three- and four-star, restaurants and bars. The northern end of the beach is good for surfing, while the southern end is calmer and suitable for swimming. At the south end of the beach is **Morro do Careca**, a 120-m-high protected dune surrounded by vegetation. Although no longer used for sand-skiing, it remains one of the 'postcards' of the city.

Around Natal

The coast south of the city is referred to as **Litoral Sul**, to the north as **Litoral Norte**. While there are buses south (leaving from the *rodoviária* in Natal), notably to Tibau and Pipa along the coastal road, agencies in Ponta Negra also offer dune buggy day trips along the beaches (see page 555).

Pirangi do Norte, 25 km from Natal, has calm waters, is popular for watersports and offshore bathing (500 m out) when natural pools form between the reefs. In the town is the world's largest cashew-nut tree (*maior cajueiro do mundo*, entry US$1.80); branches springing from a single trunk cover an area of some 8400 sq m, a whole city block. A guide on site offers a brief explanation and there is a look-out for seeing the tree from above. Outside are handicraft stalls, tourist information and musicians.

Beyond Barreta is the long, pristine beach of **Malembar**, access on foot or by a five-minute boat ride across the mouth of the **Lagoa Guaraíra** from Tibau do Sul at the south end. The ferries to/from Tibau do Sul costs US$10 return; buggy drivers should not add this fee to a day tour. Crossings are determined by the state of the tide (times are critical and you should follow the buggy driver's instructions regarding departure times). Around **Tibau do Sul** the lovely beaches circled by high cliffs, the lagoons, Atlantic forest and the dolphins

Ponta Negra

Atlantic Ocean

Not to scale

Where to stay 🛏
1 Hotel e Pousada
   O Tempo e o Vento
2 Ingá Praia
3 Lua Cheia Hostel,
   Taverna Pub &
   Rastapé Bar
4 Manary Praia
5 Manga Rosa
6 Maria Bonita 2
7 Pousada América do Sol
8 Pousada Castanheira
9 Pousada Lilly-jo
10 Pousada Maravista
11 Pousada Porta do Sol
12 Verdes Mares

Restaurants 🍴
1 Açaí do Pará
2 Barraca do Caranguejo
3 Camarões
4 Casa de Taipa
5 Cipó Brasil
6 Curva do Vento
7 Old Five

Bars & clubs 🍸
8 Decky

are some of the attractions that make this one of the most visited stretches of the southern coast (it can get crowded during holiday periods and weekends). South of town there are fine, wide, white-sand beaches, separated by rocky headlands, set against high cliffs and coconut groves.

At Praia do Madeiro and neighbouring **Baía dos Golfinhos**, the ocean is calm and clear and dolphins can often be seen (ask locally for the best time and swim from Madeiro beach to see them, rather than take an expensive tour from Pipa). Between Praia do Madeiro and Pipa, on a 70-m high dune, is the **Santuário Ecológico de Pipa** ① *0800-1600, US$4*. This 60-ha park was created in 1986 to conserve the mata atlântica forest; there are 17 trails and lookouts over the cliffs which afford an excellent view of the ocean and dolphins.

Praia da Pipa, 3 km further south (85 km from Natal), is the busiest beach resort in the state after Ponta Negra, popular with Brazilians and foreigners alike, for its beautiful beaches and charming restaurants.

The coast **north of Natal** is known for its many impressive, light-coloured sand dunes, some reaching a staggering 50 m in height. A 25-minute ferry crossing on the Rio Potengi takes you from Natal to **Redinha**, an urban beach, with ocean and river bathing, and buggies to hire.

Genipabu, 30 km north of the city, has effectively become a suburb of Natal. Its major attractions are very scenic dunes and the Lagoa de Genipabu, a lake surrounded by cashew trees and dunes where tables are set up on a shoal in the water and drinks served. There are also many hotels, bars and restaurants on the sea shore and the area can feel overwhelmingly crowded at weekends. The dunes are a protected **Parque Ecológico** ① *T9974 8265*, and only authorized buggy drivers are allowed to enter. All buggy tours go through the dunes and make the most of the vehicles' manoeuvrability on the fantastic slopes and hollows: prepare yourself for 'emoção'. At the top of a dune overlooking the lake and coast are lots of colourful umbrellas and handicraft stalls. **Camel rides** ① *dromedários, T3225 2053, www.dromedunas. com.br*, start from here.

North of Genipabu is **Jacumã**, 49 km from Natal. At Lagoa de Jacumã, a lake surrounded by dunes, you can aerobunda, sit in a sling and fly on a cable into the water. Really refreshing. To get back up to the top of the dune you take the fusca funicular, a 'cable car' made from a trolley on a rail, powered by a wheel-less VW Beetle. Lovely beaches continue along the state's coastline; as you get further away from Natal the beaches are more distant from the main highways and access is more difficult.

⊙ Natal listings

For hotel and restaurant price codes, and other relevant information, see Essentials.

⊙ Where to stay

Natal *p549*
The **Via Costeira** is a strip of enormous, upmarket beachfront hotels, which are very isolated, with no restaurants or shops within easy walking distance. **Ponta Negra** is the ideal place to stay, with its attractive beach and concentration of restaurants. Economical hotels are easier to find in the city proper but

there is otherwise not much reason to stay there (no nightlife and a long way from the action). Prices of beach hotels below are for the high season (Dec-Feb and Jul), unless otherwise stated.

In the centre
$$$$ Maine, Av Salgado Filho 1791, Lagoa Nova, T4005 5774, www.hotelmaine. com.br. On the principal avenue leading from the centre to Ponta Negra. Full service in this 4-star hotel, restaurant with panoramic views.

$$$ Golden Tulip Interâtlantico, Av Getúlio Vargas 788, Petropólis, T3087 4800, www.goldentulipinteratlantico.com. Business hotel in the city centre, restaurant, gym and pool.

Beaches p550, map p551
Praia do Meio, Praia dos Artistas and Praia de Areia Preta

The distinction between these first 2 beaches is often blurred. Most hotels here are on the beachfront Av Pres Café Filho, the numbering of which is illogical. Many *pousadas* open for just 1 season, then close for good. There are better budget options in Ponta Negra.

$$$ Bruma, Av Pres Café Filho 1176, Praia dos Artistas, T2202 4303, www.hotelbruma.com.br. Slick, intimate, 2 rooms per floor beachfront balconies, also has more expensive suites, tiny pool, terrace. Recommended.

Ponta Negra
Here, too, the street numbering is pretty chaotic.

$$$$ Manary Praia, R Francisco Gurgel 9067, T3204 2900, www.manary.com.br. Price depends on view from room; phone in advance as prices vary greatly according to month. This is a very stylish hotel on a quiet corner, some rooms overlook the pool/terrace and beach, all are very comfortable, 'neocolonial' design using local materials, spa, member of the Roteiros de Charme group, see page 357. Recommended.

$$$ Hotel e Pousada O Tempo e o Vento, R Elias Barros 66, T3219 2526, www.otempoeovento.com.br. **$$** in low season, fridge, safe in room, pool and wet bar, luxo rooms are very comfortable, good breakfast. Recommended.

$$$ Ingá Praia, Av Erivan França 17, T3219 3436, www.ingapraiahotel.com.br. **$$** without sea view, cheaper in low season (service tax not included). Very comfortable, cosy, rooms have all the expected facilities. Recommended.

$$$ Manga Rosa, Av Erivan França 240, T3219 0508, www.mangarosanatal.com.br. Well-appointed small rooms with attractive wooden fittings, colourful bedspreads and sea views.

$$$-$$ Pousada Castanheira, Rua da Praia 221, T3236 2918, www.pousadacastanheira.com.br. English/Brazilian owners, **$$** in low season, comfortable spacious rooms with fridge and safe, small pool, breakfast room with sea view, room service, parking, very helpful staff. Recommended.

$$ Maria Bonita 2, Estrela do Mar 2143, Arabaiana, T3236 2941, www.mariabonita2.com.br. With a/c, cheaper with fan, not as close to the beach as most, but near the Broadway and its nightlife.

$$ Pousada Lilly-jo, Estrela do Mar 2183, T3236 2278, www.pousadalillyjo.com. Nice place, with pool, helpful, owner speaks English, good breakfast.

$$ Pousada Maravista, R da Praia 223, T3236 4677, www.hotelpousadamaravista.com.br. One of the cheaper options, next to Pousada Castanheira, high-ceilinged rooms, hot showers, fan, good breakfast, simple, English spoken, Marilyn is very welcoming. Recommended.

$$ Pousada Porta do Sol, R Francisco Gurgel 9057, T3236 2555, www.pousadaportadosol.com.br. Clean and tidy, good seafront location, fridge, a/c except in rooms with sea breeze, some fans, good mattresses, excellent breakfast, pool, good value, English and French spoken (ask for Patrick or Suerda). Recommended.

$ pp Lua Cheia, R Dr Manoel Augusto Bezerra de Araújo 500, Ponta Negra, T3236 3696, www.tavernapub.com.br. HI hostel in 'castle' with 'medieval' **Taverna Pub** in basement (see Bars and clubs below). Includes breakfast. Highly recommended.

$ Pousada América do Sol, R Erivan França 35, T3219 2245, www.pousadaamericadosol.com.br. Price per person in albergue-style rooms with bath, hot water, lockers, cheaper without a/c, popular, simple, use of kitchen, breakfast included. Also has *pousada* rooms at **$$** (half-price in low season), a/c, frigobar, parking.

$ pp Verdes Mares, R das Algas 2166, Conj Algamar, Ponta Negra, T3236 2872, www.hostelverdesmares.com.br. HI hostel,

$$ in nicely decorated doubles, discount in low season, quiet, comfortable, pool. Recommended.

Around Natal: Praia da Pipa p552

In Pipa more than 30 *pousadas* and many private homes offer accommodation. See www.pipa.com.br for some listings.

$$$$ Toca da Coruja, Av Baía dos Golfinhos, T3246 2226, www.tocadacoruja.com.br. Comfortable chalets and cheaper suites in a separate block, with all facilities including safe in room, in gardens with lots of trees, 2 spring-water swimming pools, bar, quiet, member of the Roteiros de Charme group, see page 357.

$$$ Ponta do Madeiro, Rota do Sol, Km 3, Tibaú do Sul, T3246 4220, www. pontadomadeiro.com.br. Beautifully set in Mata Atlântica, views of and access to Madeiro beach, between Pipa and Tibaú, 3 types of chalet in gardens, pool, restaurant, trips on land and sea and hourly transfers to Pipa, US$4.

$$$ Pousada da Bárbara, Largo de São Sebastião s/n, 1st right after church in centre, T3246 2351, www.pousadadabarbara.com. **$$** in low season, 20 m from town beach, a/c, hot shower and veranda, pool, very good.

$$$ Sombra e Água Fresca, R Praia do Amor 1000, T3246 2258, www.sombraeagua frescaresort.com.br. A/c, fridge, pools, restaurant with beautiful view especially at sunset. Cheaper in low season, rooms of varying size and standard.

$$$ Tartaruga, Av Baía dos Golfinhos 508, T3246 2385, www.pousadatartaruga.com.br. Rooms around a pretty little pool, nicely decorated, shady bar and restaurant area.

$$$-$ Pousada Pomar da Pipa, R da Mata, T3246 2256, www.pomardapipa.com. 150 m from praça, quiet, beautiful garden, very helpful, good value.

$$ Pousada Aconchego, R do Ceu s/n, Praia da Pipa, T3246 2439, www.pousada-aconchego. com. Family-run *pousada* with simple chalets, in a garden filled with cashew and palm trees, tranquil, central, good breakfast.

$$-$ Vera-My house, R da Mata 17, T3246 2295, www.praiadapipa.com/veramyhouse. With bath, about US$10 pp in dormitory, use of kitchen, cheaper without breakfast. Good value, friendly. Recommended.

❼ Restaurants

Natal p549

Prawns feature heavily on menus here as Natal is the largest exporter in Brazil. The city centre area of Petrópolis is well known locally for having the best restaurants in the state.

$$ Mangaí, Av Amintos Barros 3300, Lagoa Nova, www.mangai.com.br. Very good regional food (*carne do sol*, tapioca and many other *sertaneja* dishes) in rustic atmosphere, open 0600-2200, closed Mon. Recommended.

$ A Macrobiótica, Princesa Isabel 524, vegetarian, shop, lunch only. Next door is **Neide**, at No 530, for coffee and sweets.

Beaches p550, map p551
Ponta Negra

$$ Barraca do Caranguejo, Av Erivan França 1180. Live music nightly from 2100. 12 different types of prawn dish for US$6.75, *rodízio* style.

$$ Camarões, Av Eng Roberto Freire 2610. Also at Natal Shopping Centre. Touristy, but very good seafood.

$$ Cipó Brasil, Av Erivan França 3 and Rua Aristides Porpino Filho 3111. Jungle theme, 4 levels, sand floors, lantern-lit, dishes and rinks well-presented. Serves pizzas and crêpes (house speciality), good for cocktails, live music nightly after 2100. In the same group is **Casa de Taipa**, R Dr Manoel A B de Araújo 130A, by Taverna Pub (see below), serving tapioca, salads, juices and coffee.

$$ Curva do Vento, R Dr Manoel A B de Araújo 396, T2010 4749. Some of the best pizzas in Ponta Negra, together with all manner of Rosti (stuffed with curry, lobster or stroganoff) and a broad selection of ice-cold beers. Lively.

$$ Old Five, Av Erivan França 230, T3236 2505. Romantic and rustic chic beach bar/restaurant, next to the dunes with outdoor candles, low-light, decent cocktails and a menu of seafood, fish and chicken standards and bar snacks.

$$-$ Açaí do Pará, R das Algas 2151, T3219 3024. Pará dishes including delicious *takaka*, *frango no tucupi* and *maniçoba*, snacks and a superb selection of juices including *camu camu* and *açaí*.

🍸 Bars and clubs

Natal *p549*
Natal's nightlife hot spot lies in the streets around Dr Manoel A B de Araújo (behind Ponta Negra beach on the other side of Av Eng Roberto Freire).
Centro de Turismo (see Shopping, below) has Forró com Turista, a chance for visitors to learn this fun dance, Thu at 2200; many other enjoyable venues where visitors are encouraged to join in.
Decky, Av Roberto Freire 9100, Ponta Negra, T3219 2471. Models of Mick Jagger and John Lennon greet you at the entrance of this al fresco rock bar, where live bands play to a buzzing crowd at weekends. Also serves food.
Rastapé, R Aristides Porpino 2198, Ponta Negra, T3219 0181, www.rastapenatal.com.br. Lively faux-rustic forró bar with 3 live bands a night and areas for eating, chatting and dancing. Very popular.
Taverna Pub, R Dr Manoel A B de Araújo 500, Ponta Negra, T3236 3696, www.tavernapub. com.br. Medieval-style pub in youth hostel basement. Eclectic (rock, Brazilian pop, jazz, etc.) live music Tue-Sun from 2200, best night Wed, singles night Mon. Recommended. This street and the one that joins it by Taverna/Lua Cheia is known as 'Broadway', with lots of bars and cafés.

🎉 Festivals

Natal *p549*
In **Jan** is the Festa de Nossa Senhora dos Navegantes when numerous vessels go to sea from Praia da Redinha, north of town. **Dec** sees Carnatal, the Salvador-style out of season carnival, a lively 4-day music festival in the first week of the month, with dancing in the streets.

🛍 Shopping

Natal *p549*
Handicrafts Centro Municipal de Artesanato, Av Pres Café Filho, Praia do Meio. Daily 1000-2200. Sand-in-bottle pictures are very common in Natal. **Centro de Turismo**, R Aderbal de Figueiredo, 980, off R Gen Gustavo C Farias, Petrópolis. A converted prison with a wide variety of handicraft shops, art gallery, antique shop, café, restaurant and tourist information booth, offers good view of the Rio Potengi and the sea, daily 0900-1900, Thu at 2200 is *Forró com Turista* (see Bars and clubs, above).
Shopping centres Natal Shopping, Av Senador Salgado Filho 2234, Candelária, between Ponta Negra and the centre. Large mall with restaurants, ATMs, cinemas and 140 shops. Free shuttle bus service to major hotels. Praia Shopping, Av Eng Roberto Freire 8790, Ponta Negra. Smart shops, food hall. There are more restaurants outside, mostly fast food, on R Praia de Genipabu. It also has exchange (see Directory, below) and the Central do Cidadão. This facility has a post office, federal police office and Banco do Brasil with ATM; open Tue-Fri 1000-2200, Sat 1000-1800.

⚡ What to do

Natal *p549*
Boat tours To natural swimming pools at Pirangi do Norte, 25 km south of Natal, and to the nearby beaches of the Litoral Sul are available from **Marina Badauê**, Pirangi do Norte, T3238 2066, www.marinabadaue.com.br. A 2-hr tour includes hotel pick-up, a snack (or breakfast if you take an early tour), and allows time for a swim, US$42 per person. The company has a restaurant and bar at the seashore.

Tour operators
Buggy tours are by far the most popular, around US$30 for a dune buggy trip. If you

book direct with the buggy owner, rather than through a hotel or agency, there will be a discount. The price should include all commissions and ferry crossings. Buggy drivers (*bugueiros*) have an association (APCBA, R Projetada 405, Praia de Genipabu, Extremoz, T3225 2061) and all members must be approved by Setur and Detran. Look for the sign 'Autorizado Setur' plus a number on the buggy.

Cariri Ecotours, R Francisco Gurgel 9067, Ponta Negra, T9600 1818, www.caririeco tours.com.br. Mainly 4WD tours throughout Rio Grande do Norte, Ceará, the Sertão, Paraíba and Pernambuco, beach safaris along the coast to Fortaleza or Paraíba, to natural monuments, national parks and archaeological sites, with a strong ecological emphasis. Trustworthy, excellent guides. Good English, will also begin/end tours in Recife or Fortaleza.

Around Natal: Praia da Pipa *p552*
Several agencies run buggy trips, offer boat trips for dolphin watching or lunch/dinner cruises, kayaking, surfing and kitesurfing. There is also horse riding and walking in the Santuário Ecológico.

⊖ Transport

Natal *p549*
Air Aeroporto Augusto Severo, Parnamirim, T3087 1200. The airport has a tourist office, VIP Câmbio, ATMs, car hire, restaurants and shops. Trampolim da Vitória micro-buses from airport to Petrópolis and the city centre via Shopping Natal, US$1.30, from where there are connections to Ponta Negra on bus No 66.

Bus *Rodoviária*, Av Capitão Mor Gouveia 1237, Cidade da Esperança. Regional tickets are sold on street level, interstate on the 2nd floor. To **Recife**, 9 daily, convencional and more comfortable executive both US$31, 4 hrs. With **Nordeste** to **Mossoró**, US$19-24, 4 hrs. To **Aracati**, US$28, 5½ hrs. To **Fortaleza**, US$39-55, 7½ hrs. To **João Pessoa**, see page 549. To **Teresina**, US$78 convencional, 17-20 hrs.

Taxi Taxis are expensive compared to other cities; US$12 for 10-min journey. Standard US$25 fare from airport or *rodoviária* to centre, US$17-20 to Ponta Negra.

Around Natal *p551*
Pirangi do Norte
Bus From Natal, new *rodoviária*, many daily, US$4 to Pirangi, 1 hr.

Tibau do Sul and Pipa
Bus From Natal 12 a day (6 at weekends) to Tibau do Sul and on to Pipa, US$6, 2½ hrs. Combis go to **Goianinha**, US$4, from where buses run south to João Pessoa.

⊖ Directory

Natal *p549*
Banks Banco 24 horas, Natal Shopping. Natal Câmbio, in Natal Shopping, open Mon-Sat 1000-2200. Ponta Negra Câmbio, Av Erivan França 91, cash and TCs, Mon-Fri 0900-2200, Sat 1000-2100, Sun 0900-2000. Praia Câmbio in Praia Shopping, open Mon-Sat 0900-2200, Sun 0900-1700. **Car hire** There are many rental agencies on Av Eng Roberto Freire for cars and buggies. Buggy rental about US$50 a day, price depends on make.

Fortaleza and the north coast

→ *Phone code: 088 outside metropolitan Fortaleza, but prefix numbers beginning with 3 with 085.*
The state of Ceará has been dubbed A Terra da Luz, Land of Light. It has some of the finest beaches in Brazil, scenic dunes and almost constant sunshine. The sophisticated capital, Fortaleza, is still home to jangadas (traditional fishing boats), while its nightlife is famous throughout the country. As well as the mysterious Parque Nacional de Sete Cidades, Piauí shares with Maranhão the remarkable Parnaíba delta, which is beginning to be recognized as a major ecological site with great tourist potential. The Parque Nacional Lençóis Maranhenses, across the delta, is a landscape of fabulous sand dunes and crystal lakes. Maranhão's capital, São Luis, is one of Brazil's UNESCO sites of worldwide cultural importance, because of its colonial centre.

Fortaleza → *Phone code: 085. Post code: 60000. Colour map 5, B5. Population: 2.1 million.*

Fortaleza, the fourth largest city in Brazil, is a busy metropolis with many highrise buildings, an important clothes manufacturing industry, many hotels and restaurants and a lively nightlife. Fishermen's *jangadas* still dot the turquoise ocean across from the beach and transatlantic cruise ships call in for refuelling. The mid-day sun is oppressive, tempered somewhat by a constant breeze; evening temperatures can be more pleasant, especially by the sea. The wettest months are March to July, known locally as 'winter'.

Arriving in Fortaleza

Tourist offices Setur, state tourism agency ① *Av General Afonso Albuquerque s/n, Cambeba, T3101 4639, www.ceara.gov.br.* Information booths at *rodoviária*, airport, the Centro de Turismo and Farol de Mucuripe (0700-1730). Posta Telefônica Beira Mar, on Beira Mar almost opposite Praiano Palace, information, sells Redenção tickets to Jericoacoara, good range of postcards and clothes, papers and magazines.

Safety In Fortaleza avoid the Serviluz favela between the old lighthouse (Avenida Vicente de Castro), the favela behind the railway station, the Passeio Público at night, Avenida Abolição at its eastern (Nossa Senhora da Saúde church) and western ends. Also be careful at Mucuripe and Praia do Futuro. Generally, though, the city is safe for visitors.

Places in Fortaleza

Praça do Ferreira, from which pedestrian walkways radiate, is the heart of the commercial centre. The whole area is dotted with shady squares. **Fortaleza Nossa Senhora da Assunção** ① *Av Alberto Nepomuceno, daily 0800-1100, 1400-1700,* originally built in 1649 by the Dutch, gave the city its name. Near the fort, on Rua Dr João Moreira, is the 19th-century **Passeio Público** or Praça dos Mártires, a park with old trees and statues of Greek deities. West of here, a neoclassical former prison (1866) houses the **Centro de Turismo do Estado** ① *Av Senador Pompeu 350, near the waterfront, T0800-991516, closed Sun,* with museums, theatre and high-quality craft shops (bargaining expected). It houses the **Museu de Arte e Cultura Populares** and the **Museu de Minerais**. Further west along Rua Dr João Moreira, at **Praça Castro Carreira** (commonly known as Praça da Estação), is the nicely refurbished train station **Estação João Felipe** (1880).

The **Teatro José de Alencar** ① *on praça of the same name, T229 1989, Mon-Fri 0800-1700, hourly tours, English speaking guides, US$1.50, Wed free,* was inaugurated in 1910. This magnificent iron structure was imported from Scotland and is decorated in neo-classical and art nouveau styles. It also houses a library and art gallery. The new **cathedral**, completed in 1978, in gothic style but concrete, stands beside the new, **Mercado Central** with beautiful stained glass windows. Both are on Praça da Sé, at Avenida Alberto Nepomuceno. The **Museu do Maracatu** ① *Rufino de Alencar 231, at Teatro São José*, houses costumes of this ritual dance of African origin.

The **Centro Dragão do Mar de Arte e Cultura** ① *R Dragão do Mar 81, Praia de Iracema*, hosts music concerts, dance, and art and photography exhibitions. It has various entrances, from Ruas Almirante Barroso, Boris and from junction of Monsenhor Tabosa, Dom Manuel and Castelo Branco. This last one leads directly to three museums: on street level, the **Memorial da Cultura Cearense**, with changing exhibitions; on the next floor down is an art and cultural exhibit; in the basement is an excellent audio-visual museum of **El Vaqueiro**. Also at street level is the Livraria Livro Técnico. There is a planetarium with a whispering gallery underneath. The centre also houses a contemporary art museum **Museu de Arte Contemporânea do Ceará** ① *T3488 8600, www.dragaodomar.org.br, Tue-Fri 0830-2130, Sat and Sun 1430-2130, US$1 for entry to each museum/gallery, free on Sun*. This area is very lively at night.

Fortaleza has 25 km of beaches, many of which are the scene of the city's nightlife; those between **Barra do Ceará** (west) and **Ponta do Mucuripe** (east) are polluted. **Praia de Iracema**

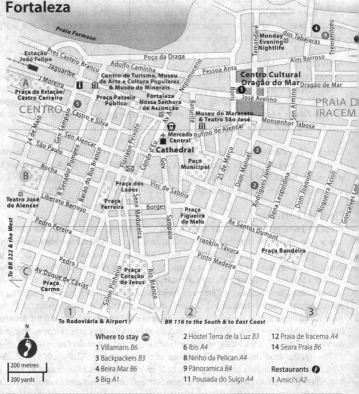

Fortaleza

Where to stay
1 Villamaris *B6*
3 Backpackers *B3*
4 Beira Mar *B6*
5 Big *A1*

2 Hostel Terra de la Luz *B3*
6 Ibis *A4*
8 Ninho da Pelican *A4*
9 Pânoramica *B4*
11 Pousada do Suíço *A4*

12 Praia de Iracema *A4*
14 Seara Praia *B6*

Restaurants
1 Amici's *A2*

is one of the older beach suburbs with some original turn-of-the-century houses. East of Iracema, the **Avenida Beira Mar** (Avenida Presidente Kennedy) connects **Praia do Meireles** with Volta da Jurema and **Praia do Mucuripe**, 5 km from the centre. Fortaleza's main fishing centre, jangadas, bring in the catch here. **Praia do Futuro**, 8 km southeast of the centre, is the most popular bathing beach, 8 km long, unpolluted, with strong waves, sand dunes and fresh-water showers, but no natural shade; there are many vendors and barracas serving local dishes. Thursday night, Saturday and Sunday are very busy. A city bus marked 'P Futuro' from Praça Castro Carreira, 'Praia Circular', does a circular route to Praia do Futuro; a bus marked 'Caça e Pesca' passes all southeast beaches on its route. About 29 km southeast of the centre is **Praia Porto das Dunas**, popular for watersports including surfing.

Northwest of the centre is **Praia Barra do Ceará**, 8 km, where the Rio Ceará flows into the sea. Here are the ruins of the 1603 Forte de Nossa Senhora dos Prazeres, the first Portuguese settlement in the area. The beaches west of the Rio Ceará are cleaner, lined with palms and have strong waves. A new bridge across this river gives better access to this area, for example, **Praia de Icaraí**, 22 km, and **Tabuba**, 5 km further north. Beyond Tabuba, 37 km from Fortaleza, is **Cumbuco**, a lively beach, dirty in high season, chaotic bars, horse riding, dunes which you can sandboard down into a rainwater lake, palm trees.

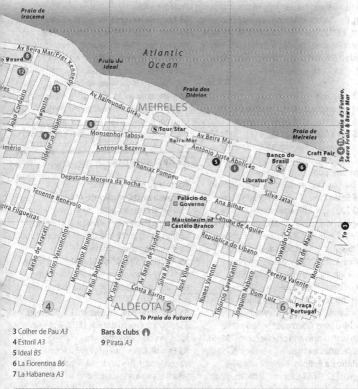

3 Colher de Pau *A3*
4 Estoril *A3*
5 Ideal *B5*
6 La Fiorentina *B6*
7 La Habanera *A3*

Bars & clubs 🎧
9 Pirata *A3*

⊙ Fortaleza listings

For hotel and restaurant price codes, and other relevant information, see Essentials.

⊙ Where to stay

Fortaleza *p557, map p558*
Almost all hotels offer reduced prices in the low season. There are many *pousadas* in the Iracema/Meireles area, but they change frequently.

Centre

$ Backpackers, R Dom Manuel 89, T3091 8997, www.backpackersce.com.br. Lively central hostel with basic rooms, dorms and private, no breakfast, but use of kitchen, helpful, English spoken, bike and car parking, information.
$ Big, Gen Sampaio 485, on Praça da Estação in centre, T3212 2066. All rooms with fan, cheaper without TV, even cheaper without bath, simple breakfast, OK, but caution needed at night, right in thick of the central scrum.

By the beach

There are several business-oriented hotels on Av Beira Mar, all of a similar standard.
$$$$ Beira Mar, Av Beira Mar 3130, T3242 5000, Meireles, www.hotelbeiramar.com.br. Some rooms seafront, others side view, comfortable rooms, safe, pool, 24-hr business centre, parking, good value, especially in low season.
$$$$ Seara Praia, Av Beira Mar 3080, Meireles, T4011 2200, www.hotelseara.com.br. 30% cheaper in low season, smart, comfortable hotel with pool, gym, cyber café, French cuisine.
$$$ Ibis, Atualpa Barbosa de Lima 660, Iracema, T3052 2450, www.accorhotels. com.br. Breakfast extra, in Accor style, with usual facilities, pool.
$$ Hostel Terra da Luz, R Rodrigues Júnior 278, Iracema, T3082 2260, www.hostel terradaluz.com. Good quality backpacker hostel with dorms and private rooms (**$$-$**), good facilities and garden, very helpful staff.
$$ Ninho da Pelican, Av Beira Mar 934, Iracema, T3219 0871. Rooms with fan, great

value for location, convenient for everything, French owner.
$$ Panorâmica, R Ildefonso Albano 464, Meireles, T3219 8347, www.portaldehospedagem.com.br. Simple rooms, best of which are on the top floor, some have terraces, quiet location.
$$ Pousada do Suiço, R Antônia Augusto 133, Iracema, T3219 3873, www.pousadadosuico. com.br. Must reserve mid-Oct to Feb. Very private, no sign, quiet street, variety of rooms, some with kitchens, small pool, fridge, Swiss run, changes cash and TCs. Recommended.
$$ Pousada Salinas, Av Zezé Diogo 3300, Praia do Futuro, T3234 3626, www.pousada salinas.com.br. **$** in low season, popular, fridge, parking, just across from sea, some English spoken.
$$ Praia de Iracema, Raimundo Girão 430, Iracema, T3219 2299, www.hotelpraiade iracema.com. 20% discount in low season, fridge, safe in room, coffee shop, pool, brightly coloured bed covers, on corner so traffic outside, but OK for value and comfort.
$$ Villamaris, Av Abolição 2026, Meireles, T3248 0112, www.hotelvillamaris.com.br. Cheaper in low season, cosy, security guard, fridge, small rooftop pool, 1 block from beach.

❼ Restaurants

Fortaleza *p557, map p558*
Iracema and Dragão do Mar
Two good areas for places to eat, with plenty of variety. There are many eating places of various styles at the junction of Tabajaras and Tremembés, mostly smart.
$$ Amici's, R Dragão do Mar 80. Pasta, pizza and lively atmosphere in music-filled street, evenings only. Some say it's the best at the cultural centre.
$$ Colher de Pau, Ana Bilhar 1178, Meireles, T3267 6680. Opens daily at 1830, *sertaneja* food, seafood, very pleasant.
$$ Estoril, R dos Tabajaras 397, Iracema. Varied food in this landmark restaurant, which is also a restaurant school.

Urban beaches

Several good fish restaurants at Praia de Mucuripe, where the boats come ashore between 1300 and 1500. R J Ibiapina, at the Mucuripe end of Meireles, 1 block behind beach, has pizzerias, fast food restaurants and sushi bars.

$$$-$$ La Fiorentina, Osvaldo Cruz 8, corner of Av Beira Mar, Meireles. Some seafood expensive, but fish, meats, pasta, unpretentious, attentive waiters, good food, frequented by tourists and locals alike.

$$-$ Ideal, Av Abolição e José Vilar, Meireles. Open 0530-2030, bakery serving lunches, small supermarket and deli, good, handy.

$ La Habanera, Praça da Igreja in Iracema, Av Beira Mar e Ararius 6. Café, wicker chairs, marble tables, old photos of Fidel, Che, et al, coffee and cigars.

O Bars and clubs

Fortaleza p557, map p558
Fortaleza is renowned for its nightlife and prides itself with having the liveliest Mon night in the country. Forró is the most popular dance and there is a tradition to visit certain establishments on specific nights. **Mon** Forró is danced at the **Pirata Bar**, Iracema, US$15, open-air theme bar, from 2300, and other establishments along R dos Tabajaras and its surroundings. **Tue** Live golden oldies at **Boate Oásis**, Av Santos Dumont 6061, Aldeota. **Wed** Regional music and samba-reggae at **Clube do Vaqueiro**, city bypass, Km 14, by BR-116 south and E-020, at 2230. **Thu** Live music, shows and crabspecialities at the beach shacks in Praia do Futuro. **Fri** Singers and bands play regional music at **Parque do Vaqueiro**, BR-020, Km 10, past city bypass. **Sat** Forró at **Parque Valeu Boi**, R Trezópolis, Cajueiro Torto, **Forró Três Amores**, Estrado Tapuio, Eusébio and **Cantinho do Céu**, CE-04, Km 8. **Sun** Forró and *música sertaneja* at **Cajueiro Drinks**, BR-116, Km 20, Eusébio.

The streets around Centro Cultural Dragão do Mar on R Dragão do Mar are lively every night of the week. Brightly painted, historic buildings house restaurants where musicians play to customers and the pavements are dotted with cocktail carts.

Caros Amigos, R Dragão do Mar, 22. Live music at 2030: Tue, Brazilian instrumental; Wed, jazz; Thu, samba; Sun, Beatles covers, US$1 (also shows music on the big screen).

Restaurant e Crêperie Café Crème, R Dragão do Mar 92, live music on Tue.

⊛ Festivals

Fortaleza p557, map p558
6 Jan, Epiphany; Ash Wednesday; **19 Mar**, São José; Christmas Eve; New Year's Eve, half-day. The Festas Juninas in Ceará are much livelier than carnival. A festival, the **Regata Dragão do Mar**, takes place at Praia de Mucuripe on the last Sun in **Jul**, during which the traditional jangada (raft) races take place. Also during the last week of Jul, the out-of-season Salvador-style carnival, **Fortal**, takes place along Avs Almte Barroso, Raimundo Giro and Beira Mar. On **15 Aug**, the local Umbanda terreiros (churches) celebrate the **Festival of Iemanjá** on Praia do Futuro, taking over the entire beach from noon till dusk, when offerings are cast into the surf. Well worth attending (members of the public may 'pegar um passo' – enter into an inspired religious trance – at the hands of a pai-de-santo). For 4 days in **mid-Oct** Ceará Music, a festival of Brazilian music, rock and pop, is held Marina Park.

O Shopping

Fortaleza p557, map p558
Handicrafts Fortaleza has an excellent selection of locally manufactured textiles, which are among the cheapest in Brazil, and a wide selection of regional handicrafts. The local craft specialities are lace and embroidered textile goods; also hammocks (US$15 to over US$100), fine alto-relievo wood carvings of northeast scenes, basket ware, leatherwork and clay figures (bonecas de barro). Bargaining is OK at the **Mercado Central**, Av Alberto Nepomuceno (closed Sun), and the **Centro de Turismo** in the old prison

(see above). Crafts also available in shops near the market, while shops on R Dr João Moreira 400 block sell clothes. Every night (1800-2300) there are stalls along the beach at Praia Meireiles. Crafts also available in the commercial area along Av Monsenhor Tabosa.

⚡ What to do

Fortaleza *p557, map p558*
Surfing Surfing is popular on a number of Ceará beaches.
Windsurfing A number of Ceará beaches are excellent for windsurfing and kite surfing (see www.kite-surf-brazil.com). Equipment can be rented in some of the popular beaches such as Porto das Dunas and in the city. **Bio Board**, Av Beira Mar 914, T3242 1642, www. bioboard.com.br. Looks after equipment for you, windsurf school, Açaizeiro Café with açai, juices, sandwiches upstairs (opens 1000 till 2000, 1900 Sat, 1800 Sun), also travel agency.

Tour operators
Many operators offer city and beach tours. Others offer adventure trips further afield, most common being off-road trips along beaches from Natal in the east to the Lençóis Maranhenses in the west.

⊖ Transport

Fortaleza *p557, map p558*
Air Aeroporto Pinto Martins, Praça Eduardo Gomes, 6 km south of centre, T3392 1200, www.infraero.gov.br. Airport has a tourist office, car hire, food hall upstairs, Banco do Brasil. Direct flights to major cities. Buses 64 (Corujão/Aeroporto/Centro/Rodoviária) and 404 (Aeroporto/Benfica/Rodoviária) from airport to Praça José de Alencar in the centre and the *rodoviária*, US$1. Taxis charge US$11-15 to centre, Av Beira Mar or Praia do Futuro, US$23 at night. Use Cooperativa Taxi Comum or Taxi Especial Credenciado.
Bus *Rodoviária* at Av Borges de Melo 1630, Fátima, 6 km south from centre. For city transport information look up www.fortaleza.

ce.gov.br/etufor/ and www.fortalbus.com. Many city buses to the centre (US$1); if in doubt the tourist kiosk will point you in the right direction. Taxi to Praia de Iracema, or Av Abolição US$10. There is a luggage store. Opposite the *rodoviária* is Hotel Amuarama, which has a bar and restaurant; there's also a lanchonete.

To **Mossoró**, 6 a day, US$20, **Natal**, 8 daily, US$44, 7½ hrs. **João Pessoa**, 2 daily, US$50-75, 10 hrs. **Guanabara**, www.expressoguanabara. com.br, to **Recife**, 5 daily, US$46-89, 12 hrs. Guanabara, to **Teresina**, several daily, US$27.50 (leito US$56), 10 hrs; to **Parnaíba** US$20 (leito US$50); to **Belém**, 3 daily, US$80-92, 23 hrs. Piripiri, for **Parque Nacional de Sete Cidades**, US$25-33, 9 hrs, a good stop en route to Belém, also **Guanabara**, who go to **São Luís**, 3 daily, US$73-78, 18 hrs.

In **Ceará**: Guanabara to **Sobral** US$11-14, **Ubajara** 0800, 1800, return 0800, 1600, 6 hrs, US$20. **Fretcar**, T3242 2911, www.fretcar. com.br, to the west of the state, including **Camocim** US$18.

ⓘ Directory

Fortaleza *p557, map p558*
Banks ATM for Cirrus/MasterCard and Visa outside cinema at Centro Cultural Dragão do Mar. Also at Av Antonio Sales and Iguatemi Shopping. Exchange at **Tropical Viagens**, R Barão do Rio Branco 1233, **Libratur**, Av Abolição 2194, open 0900-1800 Mon-Fri, 0800-1200 Sat; also has kiosk outside Othon hotel on Av Beira Mar which is open every day till 2300. Recommended. More *câmbios* on Av Mons Tabosa: eg TourStar, No 1587, **Sdoc**, No 1073. **Car hire** Many car hire places on Av Monsenhor Taboso, and at its junction with Ildefonso Albano. **Brasil Rent a Car**, Av Abolição 2300, T085-3242 0868. There are also many buggy rental shops. **Note** When driving outside the city, have a good map and be prepared to ask directions frequently as road signs are non-existent, or placed after junctions. **Medical services** Instituto Dr José Frota (IJF), R Barão do Rio Branco 1618, T255 5000. Recommended public hospital.

Coast east of Fortaleza

Aquiraz, 31 km east of Fortaleza, first capital of Ceará which conserves several colonial buildings and has a religious art museum, is the access point for the following beaches: **Prainha**, 6 km east, a fishing village and 10 km long beach with dunes, clean and largely empty. You can see jangadas coming in daily in the late afternoon. The village is known for its lacework: you can see the women using the bilro and labirinto techniques at the **Centro de Rendeiras**. 18 km southeast of Aquiraz is **Praia Iguape**, another fishing and lacework village, 3 km south of which is **Praia Barro Preto**, wide, tranquil, with sand dunes, palms and lagoons. All these beaches have accommodation.

Cascavel, 62 km southeast of Fortaleza (Saturday crafts fair), is the access point for the beaches of **Caponga** and **Águas Belas**, where traditional fishing villages coexist with fancy weekend homes and hotels.

Some 4 km from **Beberibe**, 78 km from Fortaleza, is **Morro Branco**, with a spectacular beach, coloured craggy cliffs and beautiful views. Jangadas leave the beach at 0500, returning at 1400-1500, lobster is the main catch in this area. The coloured sands of the dunes are bottled into beautiful designs and sold along with other crafts such as lacework, embroidery and straw goods. Jangadas may be hired for sailing (one hour for up to six people US$60). Beach buggies are also for hire. There are *pousadas*, or you can rent fishermen's houses. Meals can also be arranged at beachfront bars. South of Morro Branco and 6 km from Beberibe is **Praia das Fontes**, which also has coloured cliffs with sweet-water springs; there is a fishing village and a lagoon. South of Praia das Fontes are several less developed beaches including **Praia Uruaú** or **Marambala**. The beach is at the base of coloured dunes, there is a fishing village with some accommodation. Just inland is Lagoa do Uruaú, the largest in the state and a popular place for watersports. Buggy from Morro Branco US$50 for four.

Canoa Quebrada → *Colour map 5, B5. Visit www.canoa-quebrada.com.*

On the shores of the Rio Jaguaribe, **Aracati** is the access point to the southeastern-most beaches of Ceará; it is along the main BR-304. The city is best known for its Carnival and for its colonial architecture.

About 10 km from Aracati is Canoa Quebrada on a sand dune, famous for its labirinto lacework and coloured sand sculpture, for sand-skiing on the dunes, for the sunsets, and for the beaches. There are many bars, restaurants and forró establishments. To avoid biting insects (bicho do pé), wear shoes. In the second half of July the Canoarte Festival takes place, it includes a jangada regatta and music festival.

South of Canoa Quebrada and 13 km from Aracati is **Majorlândia**, an attractive village, with many-coloured sand dunes and a wide beach with strong waves, good for surfing; the arrival of the fishing fleet in the evening is an important daily event; lobster is the main catch. It is a popular weekend destination with beach homes for rent and Carnaval here is lively.

Community tourism Some 120 km east of Fortaleza, in the district of Beberibe, is **Prainha do Canto Verde**, a small fishing village on the vast beach, which has an award-winning community tourism project. There are guesthouses (eg **$ Dona Mirtes**, with breakfast, will negotiate other meals), houses for rent (**Casa Cangulo**, or **Chalé Marésia**), restaurants (good food at **Sol e Mar**), a handicraft cooperative, jangada and catamaran cruises, fishing and walking trails. Each November there is a Regata Ecológica, with jangadas from up and down the coast competing. (For the regatta, Christmas and Semana Santa, add 30% to prices.) This is a simple place, which lives by artesanal fishing (ie no big boats or industrial techniques) and has built up its tourism infrastructure without any help from outside investors (they have been fighting the speculators since 1979). It's a very friendly place and foreigners are welcome to get to know how the fisher folk live; knowledge of Portuguese is essential. To get to Prainha do Canto Verde, take a São Benedito bus to Aracati or Canoa Quebrada, buy a ticket to Quatro Bocas and ask to be let off at Lagoa da Poeira, two hours from Fortaleza. If you haven't booked a transfer in advance, Márcio at the Pantanal restaurant at the bus stop will take you, US$4. A truck from the village goes to Aracati for US$5 return.

Ponta Grossa is near Icapuí, the last municipality before Rio Grande do Norte (access from Mossoró), from where you then head to Redonda. Ponta Grossa is down a sand road just before Redonda. Both Ponta Grossa and Redonda are very pretty places, nestled at the foot of the cliffs, but Ponta Grossa has its own community tourism development. One of the main attractions of Ponta Grossa is that, offshore, is one of the few places where manatees (*peixe boi marinho*) visit. There's a good lookout from the cliffs and a delightful walkway extending over the ocean into an area of pristine mangrove forest. Beach trips go from Canoa Quebrada to Ponta Grossa for lunch, but if you want to stay here, contact **Tucum, Rede Cearense de Turismo Comunitário** ⓘ *R Pinho Pessoa 86, Joaquim Távora, Fortaleza, T085-3226 2476, www.tucum.org*, who can give information on all community tourism and the preservation of traditional ways of life in Ceará.

◉ Coast east of Fortaleza listings

For hotel and restaurant price codes, and other relevant information, see Essentials.

◉ Where to stay

Canoa Quebrada *p563*
There are many *pousadas* in town, see www.portalcanoaquebrada.com.br.
$$$-$$ Pousada Califôrnia, R Nascer do Sol 136, T3421 7039, www.californiacanoa.com. Prices vary according to room and season, a/c, TV, pool, bar, internet, buggy tours, horse riding, kite surfing, book exchange, several languages spoken, use of kitchen.
$$$-$$ Pousada Via Láctea, R Descida da Praia e Av Beira Mar, T3241 7103, www.pousadavialactea.com. Rooms and chalets, nive views, 50 m from the sea, pool, English spoken, tours organized. Recommended.
$$ Hostel Ibiza, R Dragão do Mar (Broadway) 360, T088-3421 7262, www.hostelpousada ibiza.com/htm. Tiny, boxy but cheap and fairly spruce doubles and dorms in a bright, hostel decorated with dozens

of international flags, party atmosphere, 200 m from the beach.
$$ Pousada Alternativa, R Francisco Caraço, T3421 7278, www.pousada-alternativa. com.br. Rooms with a/c and bath, cheaper with fan and without fridge, central, safe.
$$ Pousada Oasis do Rei, R Nascer do Sol 110, T3421 7082, www.pousadaoasisdorei.com.br. Simple rooms with a/c, safe, around a pool in a small garden, some with sea view.

◉ Transport

Coast east of Fortaleza *p563*
Bus For the eastern beaches near Fortaleza (**Prainha, Iguape, Barro Preto**) and towns such as **Aquiraz** or **Aracati**, take São Benedito buses (www.gruposaobenedito.com.br) from the *rodoviária*. To **Beberibe**, 10 a day US$10. To **Morro Branco** 4 daily US$12.50. To **Canoa Quebrada** 4 daily, US$15, 3 hrs, more via Aracati. There are regular buses to the western beaches near Fortaleza, including Cumbuco, from the *rodoviária*.

Paracuru, a fishing port which has the most important Carnaval on the northwest coast, is two hours by bus from Fortaleza (**$$ Villa Verde**, near the main square, is a good place to stay). West of Paracuru, about 120 km from Fortaleza and 12 km from the town of Paraipaba, is **Lagoinha**, a very scenic beach, with cliffs, dunes and palms by the shore; a fishing village is on one of the hills.

Some seven hours by bus and 230 km from Fortaleza is the sleepy fishing village of **Almofala**, home of the Tremembés Indians who live off the sea and some agriculture. There is electricity, but no hotels or restaurants, although locals rent hammock space and cook meals. Bathing is better elsewhere, but the area is surrounded by dunes and is excellent for hiking along the coast to explore beaches and lobster-fishing communities. In Almofala, the church with much of the town was covered by shifting sands and remained covered for 50 years, reappearing in the 1940s; it has since been restored. There is also a highly praised turtle project.

Jijoca de Jericoacoara (Gijoca) is near the south shore of scenic Lagoa Paraíso (or Lagoa Jijoca), the second largest in the state. There are *pousadas* on its shore. It is excellent for windsurfing as it has a 'comfortable' wind, very good for beginners and those gaining experience (Jericoacoara is for 'professionals'). There is also good for kite surfing. **Note** The low season, August to November, is the windy season.

Jijoca is one of the access points for **Jericoacoara**, or 'Jeri' (*Phone code: 088, www. portaljericoacoara.com*). One of the most famous beaches of Ceará and all Brazil (if not the world), it has towering sand dunes, deserted beaches with little shade, cactus-covered cliffs rising from the sea and interesting rock formations. The most famous is the **Pedra Furada**, a rock arch by the sea. Its atmosphere has made it popular with Brazilian and international travellers and developers, with crowds at weekends mid-December to mid-February, in July and during Brazilian holidays. Many places full in low season, too. Jericoacoara is part of an environmental protection area which includes a large coconut grove, lakes, dunes and hills covered in caatinga vegetation. **ICMBio** ① *R Praia da Malhada s/n, Jericoacoara, T3669 2140, parnajericoacoara.ce@icmbio.gov.br*. The village east of Jeri, **Preá**, is much quieter, with simple fish restaurants.

Parnaíba → *Phone code: 086. Post code: 64200. Colour map 5, A4. Population: 132,282.*

Parnaíba makes a good break in the journey north or south. It's a relaxed, friendly place, with a pretty colonial centre by the river and connections to Jericoacoara and Tutóia (and onward to São Luís and the Lençóis Maranhenses). Tours into the Delta do Parnaíba can be arranged from here (see page 570). They leave from Porto das Barcas (Tatus), a pleasant shopping and entertainment complex, with several good restaurants and a large open-air bar on the riverside. Buses between Parnaíba and Porto das Barcas leave every hour and take 10 minutes. There is a tourist office, **Piemtur** ① *Terminal Turístico Porto das Barcas and at R Dr Oscar Clark 575, T3321 1532.*

Delta do Parnaíba and the Parque Nacional Lençóis Maranhenses
→ *Colour map 5, A3.*

These twin parks comprise two of Brazil's most extraordinary landscapes. The **Delta do Parnaíba** is one of the largest river deltas in the world, a labyrinth of mangroves, rivers and unspoilt tropical islands with largely unstudied wildlife and traditional Caiçara fishing communities. The adjacent **Lençóis Maranhenses** (ICMBio contact T098-3349 1155) is a 155,000-ha coastal desert of vast shifting dunes and isolated communities cut by broad rivers and, in the rainy season (June-September), pocked with lakes, whose clear reflective waters are a vivid sky blue against brilliant white sand. Crossing the Parnaíba delta, which separates Piauí from Maranhão, can only be done by chartered boat for up to 12 people from either **Tutóia** or Porto das Barcas (see page 571). Trips into the Lençóis Maranhenses all the way from São Luís to Jericoacoara are easy to organize from São Luís or **Barreirinhas** with **EcoDunas** (see page 570). As well as Barreirinhas – the main centre – there is accommodation in the little beach towns of Caburé, Atins and Vassouras up the Rio Preguiças. Rural Maranhão and Piauí have a big problem with wind- and ocean-borne plastic waste.

São Luís → *Phone code: 098. Post code: 65000. Colour map 5, A3. Population: 870,028.*

The capital of Maranhão state, 1070 km west of Fortaleza, founded in 1612 by the French and named after St Louis of France, is in a region of heavy tropical rains, but the surrounding deep forest has been cut down to be replaced by babaçu palms. It stands upon São Luís island between the bays of São Marcos and São José. The urban area extends to São Francisco island, connected with São Luís by three bridges. An old slaving port, the city has a large black population, and has retained much African culture with, these days, lots of music including

São Luís historic centre

To São Francisco

Where to stay
2 Grand São Luís
3 HI Solar das Pedras
5 Portas da Amazônia
6 Pousada Colonial

Restaurants
1 Antigamente
2 Armazen Estrela
3 Padaria Frances Valery
4 Papagaio Amarelo

Bars & clubs
6 Reggae Bar do Porto
7 Reggae (Roots)

200 metres
200 yards

good reggae. São Luís tourist offices, **Viva Cidadão** ① *Av Jamie Tavares 26B, T3231 2000, www. turismo.ma.gov.br,* **municipal tourist office** ① *R da Palma 53, T3212 6215,* **state tourist office** ① *R Portugal 165, T3231 4696,* and at Lagoa da Jansen (Ponta d'Areia), the airport and *rodoviária*. Also see www.turismo-ma.com.br and www.saoluis.ma.gov.br.

The old part, on very hilly ground with many steep streets, is full of colonial and art deco buildings. The historical centre is being restored with UNESCO support. The damp climate stimulated the use of ceramic tiles for exterior walls, and São Luís shows a greater variety of such tiles than anywhere else in Brazil, in Portuguese, French and Dutch styles. The commercial quarter (R Portugal, also called Rua Trapiche) is still much as it was in the 17th century. One house on this street has been renovated as the **Casa do Maranhão** ① *Tue-Fri 0900-1900, Sat-Sun 0900-1800, free,* a showcase for the Bumba-Meu-Boi festival and the music of the state, with displays of costumes and video presentations. The progress of the renewal of the historical centre can be seen in the 19th-century **Solar dos Vasconcelos** ① *R da Estrela 462, T3231 9075, Tue-Sun 0900-1900, free.*

The **Palácio dos Leões** (Governor's Palace) ① *Av Dom Pedro II, T3214 8638, Mon, Wed, Fri 1500-1800, US$3,* has beautiful floors of dark wood (jacarandá) and light (cerejeira), European furniture and great views from terrace. The **Centro de Cultura Popular Domingos Vieira Filho** (**Casa da Festa**) ① *R do Giz 225, T3218 9924,* has exhibitions on the Festa do Divino, the African-Brazilian *Tambor-de-Mina* spirit religion (similar to *candomblé*) and Christmas festivities.

The best colonial churches are the **Cathedral** (1629), on Praça Dom Pedro II, and the churches of **Carmo** (1627), Praça João Lisboa, **São João Batista** (1665), Largo São João, **Nossa Senhora do Rosário** (1717), on Rua do Egito, and the 18th-century **Santana**, Rua de Santana. On Largo do Desterro is the church of **São José do Desterro**, finished in 1863, but with some much older parts.

The **Cafua das Mercês** ① *R Jacinto Maia 43, Mon-Fri 0800-1900,* is a museum of Afro-Brazilian culture housed in the old slave market. **Museu de Artes Visuais** ① *R Portugal 293, Praia Grande, T3231 6766, Tue-Fri 0900-1900, Sat-Sun 0900-1800, free,* has a collection of tiles, rare photographs, Marahnense artists and holds temporary exhibitions. **Casa de Nhozinho** ① *R Portugal 185, T3218 9951, Tue-Sun 0900-1900, free* is a fine, tiled colonial building with exhibitions devoted to Maranhão *caboclo* life. The **Casa das Minas** ① *R São Pantaleão 857, T3218 9920, T3221 6856, open sporadically and during festivals,* is one of the oldest sacred spaces in Brazil for African-Brazilian religions and is an important centre of black culture in São Luís.

The **Museu Histórico e Artístico do Maranhão** ① *R do Sol 302, T3221 4537, Tue-Sun 0900-1530, US$1.25,* in a 19th-century mansion, has displays of costumes, a theatre and exhibition space.

Alcântara → *Colour map 5, A3. Population: 21,291.*
Some 22 km away by boat is Alcântara the former state capital, on the mainland bay of São Marcos. Construction of the city began at the beginning of the 17th century and it is now a historical monument. There are many old churches, such as the ruined **Matriz de São Matias** – 1648, and colonial mansions (see the **Casa**, and **Segunda Casa, do Imperador**, also the old cotton barons' mansions with their blue, Portuguese tiled façades). On the grassy **Praça da Matriz**, which retains a pillory at its centre, is the **Museu Histórico** ① *daily 0900-1400* with some fine tiles and colonial miscellanea. Another small museum, the **Casa Histórica** ① *Praça da Matriz, Mon-Fri 1000-1600,* has some 18th-century English furniture and porcelain imported by the Alcântara aristocracy. Canoe trips go to **Ilha do Livramento**, good beaches, good walking around the coast (can be muddy after rain), mosquitoes after dark.

For hotel and restaurant price codes, and other relevant information, see Essentials.

⚫ Where to stay

Coast west of Fortaleza *p565*
Jijoca de Jericoacoara
$$$ Pousada do Paulo, Córrego do Urubu s/n, T088-3669 1181. Has a windsurf school. It's also a good place to stay (prices depends on season and cabin, lovely location with lake views, garden, beach, hammocks and various sizes of cabin, all very nice, some with TV and a/c; excellent restaurant, bar.

Jericoacoara
4-5-day packages for Reveillon are available, but prices rise steeply. Many *pousadas* can be found on www.portaljericoacoara.com. Ask around for families who take in guests.
$$$$ Recanto do Barão, R do Forró 433, T3242 0685, www.recantodobarao.com. 21 rooms mostly for 3 to 5 (ie families, groups), nicely decorated with hibiscus theme, lots of hammocks, fridge, hot shower, big rooms, upper balcony for sunset, pool, Land Rover tours. Good reputation.
$$$-$$ Casa Nostra, R das Dunas, T3669 2035, www.portaljericoacoara.com/casanostra.htm. Nice rooms, good breakfast, money exchange, Italian spoken. Recommended.
$$$-$$ Pousada da Renata, T3669 2109, www.pousadadarenata.com. Owned by the sister of Fernanda at **Pousada do Paulo** at Jijoca. Patio with hammocks, breakfast, English, Italian and German spoken.
See also **Pousada do Serrote**, R da Igerja, T3669 2061, www.pousadadoserrote.com.br. With 4 chalets.
$$$-$ Pôr do Sol, R das Dunas 50, T3669 2099, www.pousadapordosoljeri.com. Family atmosphere, lovely place to stay, with a/c or fan, buggy trips arranged. Recommended.

$$ Calanda, R das Dunas (across from Casa do Turismo, by setting sun dune), T3669 2285, www.pousadacalanda.com. With solar energy, good rooms, good breakfast, restaurant with varied menu, good views, helpful, German, English and Spanish spoken, full moon party every month. Warmly recommended.
$$ Chalé dos Ventos, R São Francisco 50, T3669 2023, www.portaljericoacoara.com/pousada_chale_dos_ventos_jericoacoara.htm. Price depends on room, chalet on 2 floors, good views, great breakfast, nice atmosphere.
$$-$ Pousada Tirol, R São Francisco 202, T3669 2006. HI-affiliated, non-members pay more, has dorms and double rooms, with breakfast, hot water, safe, helpful, great fun. Recommended.

Parnaíba *p565*
$$$ Pousada dos Ventos, Av São Sebastião 2586, Universidade, T3323 2555, www.pousadadosventos.com.br. The best business hotel in town, 10 mins taxi ride from the centre, spacious, simple rooms and an attractive breakfast area next to the pool.
$$ Pousada Chalé Suiço, Av Padre R J Vieira 448, Fátima, T3321 3026, www.chalesuico.com.br. Cheaper without a/c or breakfast, bar, laundry, pool, tours arranged, wind-surfing, sandboarding, buggies and bikes.
$ Residencial, R Almirante Gervásio Sampaio 375, T3322 2931, www.residencialpousada.com.br. Very plain, simple doubles, dorms and plusher en-suites with cold water showers gathered around a plant-filled courtyard. There are many other basic hotels nearby.

Delta do Parnaíba and Parque Nacional Lençóis Maranhenses *p565*
Delta do Parnaíba
$ pp Ilha das Canarias, Morro do Meio Caiçara Comunidade. Bring a hammock and ask at **Raimundo Aires** restaurant (good for fish), idyllic beaches nearby. Simple, no showers, just the river.

Barreirinhas

Most hotels can organize tours.

$$ Belo Horizonte, R Joaquim Soeiro de Carvalho 245, T3499 0054, www.bhmirante. com.br. Near the central square, well-kept tiled and whitewash rooms, quietest at the front, welcoming owner, pleasant rooftop breakfast area. Also owns **Pousada do Mirante** in Caburé, with restaurant.

$$ Pousada Igarapé, R Coronel Godinho 320, Centro, T3349 0641. Small, boxy rooms, a/c or fan, opposite the Assembleia de Deus church (noisy hellfire sermons at weekends).

$ Tia Cota, R Coronel Godinho 204, T3349 1237. Simple rooms, fan or a/c, decent beds and mattresses, ranging from phone box-sized with shared baths to more spacious en-suite doubles.

Caburé

$$ Pousada do Paulo, T9143 4668. Rooms for up to 4, well-kept. The owner was the first to settle here and named the town after a local bird. Best food in the village. Watch out for glass on the vast, sweeping Atlantic beach.

São Luís p566, map p566

Many cheap hotels can be found in R da Palma, very central, and R Formosa.

$$$ Grand São Luís, Praça Dom Pedro II 299, T2109 3500, www.grandsaoluis.com.br. 1960s 'grand dame' with plainly decorated rooms, the best of which have sweeping sea views. Business facilities, pool and gym.

$$$ Portas da Amazônia, R do Giz 129, T3222 9937, www.portasdaamazonia.com. br. Tastefully converted rooms in a colonial building in the the heart of the centre. Smart and well run.

$$$ Pousada Colonial, R Afonso Pena 112, T3232 2834, www.clickcolonial.com.br. Well kept rooms in a beautiful restored, tiled house, a/c, comfortable, quiet. Recommended.

$ pp HI Solar das Pedras, R da Palma 127, T3232 6694, www.ajsolardaspedras.com.br. By far the best backpacker option in town. Well-run with a range of tidy 4-6 person dorms and doubles (**$$**), internet, large lockers and a little garden out back.

Alcântara p567

$$$ Pousada dos Guarás, Praia da Baronesa, T3337 1339. A beach front *pousada* with bungalows, good restaurant, canoe hire and advice on excursions around the town.

$$ Pousada Bela Vista, Vila Jerico s/n, Cema, T3337 1569, daniloalcantara80@gmail.com. Cabins and pretty suites with breathtaking views over the bay and forest; good restaurant. Excellent tours in the environs of Alcântara: a real adventure.

$ Pousada da Josefa, R Direita, T3337 1109. A family-run restaurant and *pousada* right in the centre with a range of very simple, plain rooms. Look at several.

$ Sítio Tijupá, R de Baixo s/n at the Post Office, T3337 1291. Tiny simple *pousada* with small but well-kept rooms, with fan.

⑦ Restaurants

Coast west of Fortaleza p565
Jericoacoara

There are several restaurants serving vegetarian and fish dishes.

$$ Bistrogonoff, Beco do Guaxelo 60. Fish and meat combinations, stroganoffs and a healthy selection of pastas. Convivial atmosphere, very popular in the evenings.

$$ Carcará, R do Forró. Restaurant and bar, northeastern specialities, seafood and pastas, said to be "o mais fino" in town.

$$ Espaço Aberto, R Principal. Meat dishes, delicious seafood, salads, pleasant atmosphere.

$$ Na Casa Dela, R Principal. Northeastern Brazilian and Bahian cooking in an intimate setting.

$$ Naturalmente On the beach. Nice atmosphere, wonderful crêpes.

$$ Pizzaria Dellacasa, R Principal, next to phone office. Good variety of pizza, pasta, salads, art gallery.

$$ Taverna, R Principal. Cantina and restaurant, lovely pasta and pizza, crêpes, expresso coffee. Drinks.

$$ Tudo na Brasa, R Principal. Particularly recommended for the *churrascaria*.
$$ Do Sapão, R São Francisco s/n. Good-value prato feito, set meals including vegetarian pizzas and pastas. Live music. Named in homage to the giant toads that appear everywhere in Jeri after dark.

São Luís *p566, map p566*
R da Estrela has many eating places with good food and outdoor terraces (eg **Antigamente**, No 220, T3232 3964, which has live music Thu-Sat, and adjacent **Papagaio Amarelo**, No 210, both of which have live music). Good food also in the Mercado Praia Grande. R dos Afogados has many places for lunch. There is further choice in the São Francisco district, just across bridge. The centre is very lively on Fri and Sat. On Sun it is largely closed and most people go to Praia Calhau to eat and relax.
$$ Armazen Estrela, R da Estrela 401, T3254 1274. Fine dining upstairs and a great little *botequin* downstairs, in a cool room with Romanesque brick arches. Good food and live music at weekends.
$ Padaria Frances Valery, Rua do Giz 164. Delicious cakes, quiches and good coffee.

🌙 Bars and clubs

Coast west of Fortaleza *p565*
Jericoacoara
Forró nightly in high season at R do Forró, Wed and Sat in low season, 2200. Action moves to bars when forró has stopped about 0200. There are also frequent parties to which visitors are welcome. Once a week in high season there is a folk dance show which includes capoeira. **Sky**, R Principal on the beach. A popular sunset bar and evening chill-out space with tables under the stars.

São Luís *p566, map p566*
There is *cacuriá* dancing, drum parades and buzzing nightlife every Fri and Sat along the north end of R do Giz and along **R João Gualberto**. For cultural events see www.cultura.ma.gov.br.

Reggae Bar do Porto, R do Portugal 49, T3232 1115. One of the best reggae bars in the city with a broad range of live acts and DJs.
Reggae (Roots) Bar, R da Palma 86, T3221 7580. Live reggae and Maranhão roots music most nights. Especially lively at weekends.

✷ Festivals

São Luís *p566, map p566*
On **24 Jun** (São João) is the **Bumba-Meu-Boi**. For several days before the festival street bands parade, particularly in front of the São João and São Benedito churches. There are dances somewhere in the city almost every night in Jun. In **Aug**, São Benedito, at the Rosário church.

Alcântara *p567*
Principal festivals: Festa do Divino, at Pentecost (Whitsun); **29 Jun**, São Pedro **early Aug**, São Benedito.

⚙ What to do

Coast west of Fortaleza *p565*
Jericoacoara
Clube dos Ventos, R das Dunas, T3669 2288, www.clubedosventos.com. With restaurant and bar, windsurf equipment hire; windsurf and kitesurf courses. Kite surfing at Preá and Lagoa Jijoca.
Jeri Off Road, T088-3669 2268, T9958 5457, www.jeri.tur.br. Adventure trips in the area, transfers, buggy rides and kitesurf. Recommended, but popular.
Buggy tours Associação de Bugueiros, ABJ, R Principal. Run buggy to all the local sites.

Delta do Parnaíba and Parque Nacional Lençóis Maranhenses *p565*
Eco Dunas, R Inácio Lins 164, Barreirinhas, T098-3349 0545, also at São Luís airport, www.ecodunas.com.br. The best option for tours of Lençóis Maranhenses, the Delta and options all the way from São Luís to Jericoacoara, or vice versa. Excellent guides,

infrastructure and organization. Some English spoken and flights arranged.

São Luís *p566, map p566*
Phylipi, T8118 1710, phylipi@hotmail. com. Knowledgeable city guide, reliable, personable and good value at US$30 for a 3-hr tour of the city centre for up to 10 people. Speaks English and French.

⊖ Transport

Coast west of Fortaleza *p565*
Paracuru and Lagoinha
Bus from **Fortaleza**, Fretcar (www.fretcar. com.br) to Paracuru, 2 hrs, US$4. To **Lagoinha**, 3 hrs, US$5.50.

Almofala
Bus From **Fortaleza** to Almofala Fretcar, US$13.

Jijoca and Jericoacoara
Bus Fretcar buses, see above, run from Fortaleza to destinations throughout western Ceará, including **Jijoca** (T088-3669 1143), may daily, US$13-18, and **Jericoacoara** (T088-9900 2109), 2 a day direct at 0800, 1500, US$30. The journey takes 6-7 hrs all told. A *jardineira* (open-sided 4WD truck) meets the bus from Fortaleza at Jijoca, US$5, 20 mins. Buses return from Jeri twice daily. There are also faster a/c combis which can be booked through hotels and *pousadas* in Jeri.
  If coming from Belém or other points north and west, go via Sobral (from Belém US$101, 20 hrs), where you change for Cruz, 40 km east of Jijoca, a small pleasant town with basic hotels (there is only one bus a day Sobral-Cruz, US$15, 3-4 hrs, but Fretcar runs to **Cruz** from Fortaleza 4 times a day, US$17.50. Either continue to Jijoca the next day (Cruz-Jijoca, daily, US$2, meets *jardineira* for Jeri) or take an horário pick-up Cruz-Jijoca.
  An alternative from the west, especially if going through Parnaíba, is by buggy or jardineira from **Camocim** (a pleasant town at the mouth of the Río Coreaú separating

Piauí and Ceará, facing the dunes on the eastern shore), which is 1½-2 hrs by road from Parnaíba, 0715, US$10, with **Guanabara**. It has several hotels and eating places. You take a ferry across the river, US$1 per passenger, then the vehicle at 1100 to Jericoacoara (2 hrs, US$10). You can break the journey from Camocim to Jericoacoara at villages such as **Nova Tatajuba** (on the west margin of the outflow of Lagoa Grande; the beach is wide, dunes follow the shore, the ocean is clear and calm and there is a fishing village with a few basic *pousadas*), or **Guriú** where hammock space can be found. There is good bird watching here. Walk 4 hrs, or take a boat across the bay to Jericoacoara. The journey along the beach has beautiful scenery. In Jericoacoara ask around for buggy or jardineira rides to Camocim, about US$20 pp.

Parnaíba *p565*
Bus *Rodoviária* is 5 km south of the centre on BR-343. Taxi from centre US$6. To **Fortaleza**, 10 hrs, US$20-50 (leito); **São Luís**, 10 hrs, US$38; **Teresina**, 6 hrs, US$30-42.

Delta do Parnaíba and Lençóis Maranhenses *p565*
Bus Parnaíba-Tutóia: bus, 2½ hrs, US$8, with Nazaré at 0700, 1200 and 1400. Tutóia-**Barreirinhas** by Toyota pick-up, leave when full from the dock area for **Paulinho Neves** (1 hr, US$6); pick-ups leave from here to Barreirinhas (2 hrs, US$10). Frequent buses from Tutóia to São Luís. **São Luis-Barreirinhas**, with Cisne Branco, 3-3½ hrs on a new road, US$20, 4 a day. Hotels in São Luís can book minivan trips, same price as bus.
Ferry Up the Parnaíba delta to the crab-fishing village of **Morro do Meio** on Ilha das Canarias, boats on Mon at high tide (usually in the small hours) from Porto das Barcas (Tatus), 12 km from Parnaíba. It is sometimes possible to hitch a lift from Ilha das Canarias to Tutóia with a crab fisherman. Charter boat to Tutóia from Parnaíba, Porto das Barcas, for 12 people for about US$200(eg **Capitão Báu**, T086-3323 0145, 8831 9581), or contact

Clip Turismo (Av Presidente Vargas 274, Parnaíba, T3323 9838, and at Porto das Barcas, T3322 2072, www.clipecoturismo. com. br) for boat trips, minimum 4 people. Also **Morais Brito** Porto das Barcas 13, Parnaíba, T3321 1969, www.deltadorioparnaiba.com. br (they offer excursions to other locations in Piauí and Maranhão states, too). To **Caburé**, **Mandacuru** (with a lighthouse offering sweeping views) and **Atins**: daily boat service from end of the Orla in Barreirinhas (3-4 hrs). There is accommodation in Caburé and Atins and in the tiny riverside dune community at Vassouras (bring hammock).

São Luís *p566, map p566*
Air Flights with Gol and TAM from most state capitals via Fortaleza or Belém, also from Parnaíba and Teresina. Airport 13 km from centre, T3217 6100; buses ('São Cristovão') to city until midnight, US$1. Minivans every 40 mins until 2200 stop at Praça Deodoro (1 hr), US$1.50. Taxi US$20.

Bus *Rodoviária* is 12 km from the centre on the airport road, 'Rodoviária via Alemanha' bus to centre (Praça João Lisboa), US$1. Bus to **Fortaleza**, US$73-78, 3 a day, 18 hrs. To **Belém**, 13 hrs, US$60 (leito 138). Also to **Recife**, 26 hrs, US$110, and all other major cities and local towns.

Alcântara *p567*
Ferry Ferries cross the bay daily, leaving São Luís dock (Terminal Hidroviário Campos Melo, west end of R Portugal, T098-3222 8431): check time and buy the ticket the day before as departure depends on the tides. The journey takes 60 mins, US$5 on foot, US$25 for car. The sea can be rough between Sep and Dec. Sometimes catamaran tours can be booked through tour operators in São Luís, meals are not included.

West of Fortaleza

Western Ceará and Piauí
At 340 km from Fortaleza and at 840 m is **Ubajara** ⓘ *T3634 1300 ext 231 for information; www.portalubajara.com.br*, with an interesting Sunday morning market selling produce of the sertão.

About 3 km from town is **Parque Nacional Ubajara** ⓘ *the ICMBio office is at the park entrance, 5 km from the caves, T085-3634 1388, US$2 for entry and guide to the bottom, there is bar by the entrance serving juices, snacks, refrigerantes, etc*, with 563 ha of native highland and caatinga brush. The park's main attraction is the Ubajara cave on the side of an escarpment. Fifteen chambers totalling 1120 m have been mapped, of which 360 are open to visitors. Access is along a 6-km footpath and steps (two to three hours, take water) or with a **cable car** ⓘ *T3634 1219, Tue-Sun 0900-1430, last up at 1500, US$2 each way for descent and ascent*, which descends the cliff to the cave entrance. Lighting has been installed in nine caverns of the complex. A guide leads visitors in the cave, which is completely dry and home to 14 types of bat. At one point the lights are turned out to appreciate total blackness. Several rock formations look like animals: horse's head, jacaré, snake. The views of the sertão from the upper cablecar platform are superb. In the national park there is a new easy walkway through the woods with stunning views at the end. Start either to the left of the Park entrance, or opposite the snack bar near the cable car platform.

Teresina → *Phone code: 086. Post code: 64000. Colour map 5, B3. Population: 715,360.*
About 435 km up the Rio Parnaíba is the state capital. The city is reputed to be the hottest after Cuiabá (temperatures rise to 42°C). **Praça Pedro II** lies at the heart of the city and is the hub of Teresina life. See the **Museu do Piauí** ⓘ *Praça Marechal Deodoro, Tue-Fri 0800-1730, Sat-Sun 0800-1200, US$1.50*. The **Casa da Cultura** ⓘ *Praça Saraiva, Centro, T086-3215 7849, www.fcmc.*

pi.gov.br, Mon-Fri 0800-1900, Sat 0900-1300, Sun 1300-1600, is devoted to the history of the city and to the lives of famous ex-residents. The website has lots of cultural information. The **Central do Artesanato** ① *Praça Dom Pedro II, T3222 5772, Mon-Fri 0800-2200*, is a handicraft market and cultural centre. Local handicrafts include carved wood, leather and hammocks. There is an interesting **open market** by the Praça Marechal Deodoro and the river is picturesque. Every morning along the river bank there is the **troca-troca** where people buy, sell and swap. Most of the year the river is low, leaving sandbanks known as coroas (crowns). **Tourist office**: municipal tourist office **Turismo Teresina** ① *contact the Prefeitura Municiapl, Av Campos Sales 1292, T3215 9426, www.turismoteresina.com*. The state tourist office website is www.turismo.pi.gov.br. **Sindicato dos Guias de Turismo do Piauí** ① *R Eliseu Martins 2029 at Magalhães Filho, T3226 1622, singtur-pi@bol.com.br.*

Parque Nacional de Sete Cidades → *Colour map 5, B4.*

① *0800-1700, T086-3343 1342, www.icmbio.gov.br, US$7.50-15 compulsory fee for a guide guide, prices vary for group size and if on foot or in car.*

Unusual eroded rock formations decorated with mysterious inscriptions are to be found in the Parque Nacional de Sete Cidades, 12 km from Piracuruca, 190 km northeast of Teresina. The rock structures are just off the Fortaleza-Teresina road. From the ground it looks like a medley of weird monuments. The inscriptions on some of the rocks have never been deciphered; one theory suggests links with the Phoenicians, and the Argentine Professor Jacques de Mahieu considers them to be Nordic runes left by the Vikings. There is plenty of birdlife, and iguanas, descending from their trees in the afternoon. There are places to stay near the park including **$$$ Hotel Fazenda Sete Cidades**, BR-222, Km 63, T3276 2222, www.hotelfazendasetecidades. com.br, with pool, hammocks, restaurant and information on the park. **Piripiri** is a cheap place to break the Belém-Fortaleza journey; several good hotels.

ⓦ West of Fortaleza listings

For hotel and restaurant price codes, and other relevant information, see Essentials.

ⓔ Where to stay

Western Ceará: Ubajara *p572*
$$ Pousada Gruta de Ubajara, 50 m from the park entrance, T3634 1375, grutade ubajara@hotmail.com. Rooms in chalets of various sizes, restaurant, owner makes his own cachaça.
$$ Sítio do Alemão, take Estrada do Teleférico 2 km from town, after the Pousada da Neblina turn right, signposted, 1 km to Sítio Santana, in the coffee plantation of Herbert Klein, T088-9961 4645, www.sitio-do-alemao.20fr.com. Here, down a path, there are 3 small chalets, with full facilities, and 2 older ones with shared bath, **$**, view from breakfast/hammock area to Sertão, excursions, bicycle hire offered,

if chalets are full Mr Klein may accommodate visitors at the house (Caixa Postal 33, Ubajara, CE, CEP 62350-000). No meals other than breakfast but Casa das Delícias in Ubajara will send lasagne if necessary. Warmly recommended. **Note** Camping not allowed in the national park.

Teresina *p572*
Many cheap hotels and dormitórios around Praça Saraiva. Many other cheap ones in R São Pedro and in R Alvaro Mendes.
$$$ Formula Flat Europa, R José Olímpio de Melo 3330, Ilhotas, T3223 7100, www. formulaflateuropa.com.br. Bright, modern and well-appointed flats with microwaves, kitchenettes and living areas. Space for up to 3 people making this an **$** option pp.
$$$ Real Palace, R Areolino de Abreu 1217, T2107 2700, www.realpalacehotel.com.br.

Business oriented hotel with a range of no-frills rooms and suites and a small business centre.
$$$ Sambaíba, R Gabriel Ferreira 230-N, T3222 6712, hotelsambaiba@bol.com.br. 2-star, central, good.
$$ Santa Teresinha, Av Getúlio Vargas 2885, opposite *rodoviária*, T3221 0919. A/c, cheaper with fan, helpful.

🍴 Restaurants

Teresina *p572*
Many places for all pockets around Praça Dom Pedro II; diners are frequently serenaded by *violeiros* (itinerant musicians).
$$ Camarão do Elias, Av Pedro Almeida 457, T232 5025. Good seafood.
$$ Pesqueirinho, R Domingos Jorge Velho 6889, in Poty Velho district. For fish dishes.
$ Sabores Rotisserie, R Simplício Mendes 78, Centro. By kg, good quality and variety.

✳ Festivals

Teresina *p572*
Teresina is proud of its **Carnival**, which is then followed by **Micarina**, a local carnival in **Mar**. There is much music and dancing in **Jul** and **Aug**, when there is a **Bumba-meu-Boi**, the Teresina dance festival, **Festidanças**, and a convention of itinerant guitarists.

🚌 Transport

Western Ceará: Ubajara *p572*
Bus Guanabara bus from **Fortaleza**, 0800, 1800, return 0800, 1600, 6 hrs, US$15.

Teresina *p572*
Air Senador Petrônio Portela airport is 5 km from the centre, T3133 6270. Flights to **Fortaleza, Brasília, Rio, São Paulo, São Luís, Belém, Manaus**. Buses from outside the airport run straight to town and to the *rodoviária*.
Bus *Rodoviária*, 4 km from the centre, T3229 9047. The bus trip from **Fortaleza** is scenic and takes 9 hrs (US$27.50, leito US$56). There are direct buses to **Belém** (13 hrs, US$63-70), **Recife** (16 hrs, US$72-82) and to **São Luís** (6 hrs, US$29-33) and **Salvador** (18 hrs, US$86).

Parque Nacional de Sete Cidades and Piripiri *p573*
Bus **ICMBio** staff bus leaves the Praça da Bandeira in Piripiri (26 km away, *rodoviária* T3276 2333), at 0700, ask for a lift. It passes Hotel Fazenda Sete Cidades at 0800, reaching the park 10 mins later. If you miss the bus, take a mototaxi. Return at 1630, or hitchhike (to walk takes all day, very hot, start early). Taxi from Piripiri, US$35, or from Piracuruca, US$50. Bus Teresina-Piripiri and return, throughout the day 2½ hrs, US$10. Bus São Luís-Piripiri, 3 a day, 10 hrs, US$35. Several daily buses Piripiri-**Fortaleza**, 9 hrs, US$35. Bus Piripiri-**Ubajara**, marked 'São Benedito', or 'Crateús', 2½ hrs; US$10, first at 0700 (a beautiful trip).

🛈 Directory

Teresina *p572*
Banks There are ATMs for both Visa and MasterCard, eg Banco 24 Horas – TecBan, Av João XXIII 2220.

The Amazon

The area is drained by the mighty Amazon, which in size, volume of water – 12 times that of the Mississippi – and number of tributaries has no equal in the world. At the base of the Andes, far to the west, the Amazonian plain is 1300 km wide, but east of the confluences of the Madeira and Negro rivers with the Amazon, the highlands close in upon it until there is no more than 80 km of floodplain between them. Towards the river's mouth – about 320 km wide – the plain widens once more and extends along the coast southeastwards into the state of Maranhão and northwards into the Guianas.

Brazilian Amazônia, much of it still covered with tropical forest, is 56% of the national area. Its jungle is the world's largest and densest rain forest, with more diverse plants and animals than any other jungle in the world. It has only 8% of Brazil's population, and most of this is concentrated around Belém (in Pará), and in Manaus, 1600 km up the river. The population is sparse because other areas are easier to develop.

Northern Brazil consists of the states of Pará, Amazonas, Amapá and Roraima. The states of Rondônia and Acre are dealt with under Southern Amazônia, see page 606.

Climate

The rainfall is heavy, but varies throughout the region; close to the Andes, up to 4000 mm annually, under 2000 at Manaus. Rains occur throughout the year but the wettest season is between December and May, the driest month is October. The humidity can be extremely high and the temperature averages 26°C. There can be cold snaps in December in the western reaches of the Amazon basin. The soil, as in all tropical forest, is poor.

Travel up the Amazon River

Rivers are the arteries of Amazônia for the transport of both passengers and merchandise. The two great ports of the region are Belém, at the mouth of the Amazon, and Manaus at the confluence of the Rio Negro and Rio Solimões. Manaus is the hub of river transport, with regular shipping services east to Santarém and Belém along the lower Amazon, south to Porto Velho along the Rio Madeira, west to Tabatinga (border with Colombia and Peru) along the Rio Solimões and northwest to São Gabriel da Cachoeira along the Rio Negro. There is also a regular service connecting Belém and Macapá, on the northern shore of the Amazon Delta, and Santarém and Macapá.

The size and quality of vessels varies greatly, with the largest and most comfortable ships generally operating on the Manaus-Belém route. Hygiene, food and service are reasonable on most vessels but **overcrowding** is a common problem. Many of the larger ships offer air-conditioned berths with bunkbeds and, for a higher price, 'suites', with a private bathroom (in some cases, this may also mean a double bed instead of the standard bunkbed). The cheapest way to travel is 'hammock class'; on some routes first class (upper deck) and second class (lower deck) hammock space is available, but on many routes this distinction does not apply. Some new boats have air-conditioned hammock space. Although the idea of swinging in a hammock may sound romantic, the reality is you will probably be squeezed in with other passengers, possibly next to the toilets, and have difficulty sleeping because of **noise** and an aching back.

Riverboat travel is no substitute for visiting the jungle. Except for a few birds and the occasional dolphin, little wildlife is seen. However, it does offer an insight into the vastness of Amazônia and a chance to meet some of its people. Extensive local inquiry and some flexibility in one's schedule are indispensable for river travel. **Agencies** on shore can inform you of the arrival and departure dates for several different ships, as well as the official (highest) prices for each, and they are sometimes amenable to bargaining. Whenever possible, **see the vessel** yourself (it may mean a journey out of town) and have a chat with the captain or business manager to confirm departure time, length of voyage, ports of call, price, etc. Inspect cleanliness in the kitchen, toilets and showers. All boats are cleaned up when in port, but if a vessel is reasonably clean upon arrival then chances are that it has been kept that way throughout the voyage. You can generally arrange to sleep on board a day or two before departure and after arrival, but be sure to secure carefully your belongings when in port. If you take a berth, lock it and keep the key even if you will not be moving in right away. If you are travelling hammock class, board ship at least 6-8 hours before sailing in order to secure a good spot (away from the toilets, tables where people eat and the engine and check for leaks in the deck above you). Be firm but considerate of your neighbours as they will be your intimate companions for the duration of the voyage. Always keep your gear locked and, if possible, don't leave it unattended. Take some light warm clothing, it can get very chilly at night.

Compare fares for different ships and remember that prices may fluctuate with supply and demand. Most ships sail in the evening and the first night's supper is not provided. **Payment** is usually in advance. Insist on a signed ticket indicating date, vessel, class of passage, and berth number if applicable.

All ships carry cargo as well as passengers and the amount of cargo will affect the length of the voyage because of weight (especially when travelling upstream) and loading/unloading at intermediate ports.

The following are the **major shipping routes** in Amazônia, indicating main intermediate ports, average trip durations, and basic fares. Facilities in the main ports are described in the appropriate city sections, see below. There are many other routes and vessels providing extensive local service. All **fares shown are one-way only** and include all meals unless otherwise stated.

Boat services

Belém–Manaus Via Santarém, Óbidos and Parintins on the lower Amazon. Five to six days upriver, four days downriver, including 18-hour stop in Santarém, US$225 upriver, US$190 down; suites also available, US$500-380, hammock space US$95-82. Vehicles are also carried. The Belém–Manaus route is very busy. Try to get a cabin.

Belém–Santarém 2½ days upriver, 1½ days downriver, berth US$170, suite US$190, hammock space US$57 up, US$48 downriver. All vessels sailing Belém–Manaus will call in Santarém.

Santarém–Manaus Same intermediate stops as above. Two days upriver, 1½ days downriver, US$219 cabin, US$44 hammock. All vessels sailing Belém–Manaus will call in Santarém and there are many others operating only the Santarém–Manaus. Speedboats (*lanchas*) on this route take 11 hours sitting, US$115 (US$82, nine hours, to Parintins).

Belém–Macapá (Porto Santana) Non-stop, 24 hours on large ships, double berth US$164, hammock space US$46 pp, meals not included but can be purchased onboard (expensive). Also non-stop fast catamaran *Atlântica*, eight hours, three a week, US$46. Same voyage via Breves, 36-48 hours on smaller riverboats, hammock space US$40 pp including meals. See page 585.

Macapá (Porto Santana)–Santarém Via Boca do Jari, Prainha, and Monte Alegre on the lower Amazon, two days upriver, 1½ days downriver, berth US$200, hammock US$60.

Manaus–Porto Velho Via Humaitá on the Rio Madeira (from where there are buses to Porto Velho, saving about 24 hours). Tuesday and Saturday, five days upriver, 3½ days downriver (up to seven days when the river is low), US$274, hammock space US$82.

Manaus–Tefé 36 hours, US$95 double berth, US$27 hammock space. Jet boats US$121, daily 0600-0700 except Tuesday and Sunday, 13 hours, continuing to Tabatinga (flights Manaus– Tefé–Tabatinga).

Manaus–Tabatinga (see page 600) Via Fonte Boa (three days), Tonantins (four days), São Paulo de Olivença (five days) and Benjamin Constant along the Rio Solimões. Six days upriver (depending on cargo), three to four days downriver, US$164 upriver, US$100 downriver (hammock, US$400 berth for two, negotiable). The better boats on this run include: *M Monteiro*, *Oliveira V* and *Voyager III* and *IV* (a *Voyager V* is under construction and nearing completion). Jet boat, *Puma*, Tuesday 0700, 38 hours, US$274.

Manaus–São Gabriel da Cachoeira Leaving from Porto Raimundo in Manaus not the main boat port, three days by slow boat, 24 hours by fast boat, along the Rio Negro (see page 601).

What to take

A hammock is essential on all but the most expensive boats, it is often too hot to lie down in a cabin during day. Light cotton hammocks seem to be the best solution. Buy a wide one on which you can lie diagonally; lying straight along it leaves you hump-backed. A climbing carabiner clip is useful for fastening hammocks to runner bars of boats. It is also useful for securing baggage, making it harder to steal.

Health → *See also Health, in Essentials.*

There is a danger of malaria in Amazônia. Mosquito nets are not required when in motion as boats travel away from the banks and too fast for mosquitoes to settle, though repellent is a boon for night stops. A yellow-fever inoculation is strongly advised; it is compulsory in some areas and may be administered on the spot with a pressurized needle gun. The larger ships must have an infirmary and carry a health officer. Drinking water is generally taken on in port (ie city tap water), but taking your own mineral water is a good idea.

Food

Ample but monotonous, better food is sometimes available to cabin passengers. Meal times can be chaotic. Fresh fruit is a welcome addition; also take plain biscuits, tea bags, seasonings, sauces and jam. Non-meat eaters should take vegetables and tinned fish. Fresh coffee is available. Most boats have some sort of rooftop bar serving expensive drinks and snacks. Plates and cutlery may not be provided. Bring your own plastic mug as drinks are served in plastic beakers which are jettisoned into the river.

In Amazônia Inevitably fish dishes are very common, including many fish with indengous names, eg matrinchã, jaraqui, pacu, tucunaré, and tambaqui, which are worth trying. Pirarucu is another delicacy of Amazonian cuisine, but because of overfishing it is in danger of becoming extinct. Also shrimp and crab dishes (more expensive). Specialities of Pará include duck, often served in a yellow soup made from the juice of the root of the manioc (*tucupi*) with a green vegetable (*jambu*), the famous pato no tucupi. Also *tacaca* (shrimps served in tucupi), vatapá (shrimps served in a thick sauce, highly filling, simpler than the variety found in Salvador), *maniçoba* (made with the poisonous leaves of the bitter cassava, simmered for eight days to render it safe – tasty). *Caldeirada*, a fish and vegetable soup, served with *pirão* (manioc puree) is a speciality of Amazonas. There is also an enormous variety of tropical and jungle fruits, many unique to the region. Try them fresh, or in ice creams or juices. Avoid food from street vendors.

Belém and around

From Belém, the great city near the mouth of the Amazon, to Parintins, site of a renowned annual festival, on the border with Amazonas state, it is 60 hours by boat. This section deals with the first few stops on the river, plus the route through Amapá state to the frontier with French Guiane.

Belém → *Phone code: 091. Post code: 66000. Colour map 5, A1. Population: 1.3 million.*

Belém (do Pará) is the great port of the Amazon. It is hot (mean temperature, 26°C), but frequent showers freshen the streets. There are fine squares and restored historic buildings set along broad avenues. Belém used to be called the 'City of Mango Trees' and there are many such trees remaining.

Tourist offices Belém Paratur ① *Praça Maestro Waldemar Henrique s/n, T3224 9493, www.paraturismo.pa.gov.br.* Helpful, some staff speak English.

Safety Belém has its share of crime and is prone to gang violence. Take sensible precautions especially at night. Police for reporting crimes, Rua Santo Antônio e Trav Frei Gil de Vila Nova.

Places in Belém The largest square is the **Praça da República** where there are free afternoon concerts; the main business and shopping area is along the wide Av Presidente Vargas leading to the river and the narrow streets which parallel it. The neoclassical **Theatro da Paz** (1868-1874) ① *Tue-Fri 0900-1800, tours at set times US$2*, is one of the largest theatres in the country. It has its own orchestra and stages performances by national and international stars and also gives free concert and theatre shows. An opera festival is staged, usually each August or September. Visit the **Cathedral** (1748) ① *Mon 1500-1800, Tue-Fri 0800-1100, 1530-1800*, another neoclassical building which contains several remarkable paintings. It stands on Praça Frei Caetano Brandão, opposite the 18th-century **Santo Aleixandre** church, which is noted for its wood carving. The 17th-century **Mercês** church (1640), near the market, is the oldest church in Belém; it forms part of an architectural group known as the Mercedário, the rest of which was heavily damaged by fire in 1978 and is being restored.

The **Basílica of Nossa Senhora de Nazaré** (1909) ① *Praça Julho Chermont on Av Magalhães Barata, Mon-Sat 0500-1130, 1400-2000, Sun 0545-1130, 1430-2000*, built from rubber wealth in romanesque style, is an absolute must for its stained-glass windows and beautiful marble. A museum at the basilica describes the Círio de Nazaré religious festival. The **Palácio Lauro Sodré** or **Museu do Estado do Pará** ① *Praça Dom Pedro II, T3225 3853, Mon-Fri 0900-1800, Sat-Sun 1900-1200*, a gracious 18th-century Italianate building, contains Brazil's largest framed painting, 'The Conquest of Amazônia', by Domenico de Angelis. The **Palácio Antônio Lemos, Museu da Cidade** ① *Tue-Fri 0900-1200, 1400-1800, Sat-Sun 0900-1300*, which houses the **Museu de Arte de Belém** and is now the **Prefeitura**, was originally built as the Palácio Municipal between 1868 and 1883. In the downstairs rooms there are old views of Belém; upstairs the historic rooms, beautifully renovated, contain furniture, paintings etc, all well explained.

The Belém market, known as '**Ver-o-Peso**' was the Portuguese Posto Fiscal, where goods were weighed to gauge taxes due (hence the name: 'see the weight'). It now has lots of gift shops selling charms for the local African-derived religion, umbanda; the medicinal herb and natural perfume stalls are also interesting. It is one of the most varied and colourful markets in South America; you can see giant river fish being unloaded around 0530, with frenzied wholesale buying for the next hour; a new dock for the fishing boats was built just upriver from the market in 1997. The area around the market swarms with people, including many armed thieves and pickpockets.

In the old town, too, is the **Forte do Castelo** ① *Praça Frei Caetano Brandão 117, T4009 8828, Tue-Fri 1000-1800, Sat-Sun 1000-1400.* The fort overlooks the confluence of the Rio Guamá and the Baía do Guajara and was where the Portuguese first set up their defences. It was rebuilt in 1878. The excellent museum (**Museu do Forte do Presépio**) has interesting displays on indigenous archaeology and some artefacts. The site also contains the **Boteca Onze** restaurant (entry US$2; drinks and *salgadinhos* served on the ramparts from 1800 to watch the sunset). At the square on the waterfront below the fort the açaí berries are landed nightly at 2300, after picking in the jungle (açaí berries ground up with sugar and mixed with manioc are a staple food in the region).

At the **Estação das Docas**, the abandoned warehouses of the port have been restored into a complex with an air-conditioned interior and restaurants outside. The Terminal Marítimo has an office of **Valverde Tours**, which offers sunset and nighttime boat trips. The Boulevard

Belém

To Armazém 10 dock
Armazém 3 dock
To ⑨ & Airport
To ⑬
To Souzamar

Baía do Guajará

Estação das Docas

Praça (Maestro) Waldemar Henrique & Handicraft Maiket

Ver-O-Peso

Sanave

Forte do Castelo

Santo Aleixandre

Cathedral

Praça Dom Pedro II

Palácio Lauro Sodré

Joaquim Távora

Praça do Carmo

Prefeitura

Mercês

Praça da República

Amazon Star

Theatro da Paz

Praça D Henrique

To ⑱ & Mangal das Garças

To Basílica NS de Nazaré, Museu Goeldi, Bosque Rodrigues Alves, BR 116 & Brasília

Shopping Iguatemi

To ⑬

300 metres
300 yards

Where to stay
1 Amazônia Hostel
2 Grão Pará
3 Itaoca

4 Le Massilia
5 Machado's Plaza
6 Novo Avenida
8 Unidos
9 Vila Rica

Restaurants
1 Açaí at Hilton Hotel
2 Boteca Onze

3 Cantina Italiana
4 Churrascaria Rodeio
6 Doces Bárbaros
7 Govinda
8 Lá em Casa
9 Mãe Natureza
10 Sabor Paraense

Bars & clubs
11 A Pororó & Carousel
12 Café Com Arte
13 do Gilson
14 Mormoço
15 São Mateus

das Artes contains the **Cervejaria Amazon** brewery, with good beer and simple meals, an archaeological museum and arts and crafts shops. The Boulevard de Gastronomia has smart restaurants and the five-star Cairu ice cream parlour (try açaí or the Pavê de Capuaçu). Also in the complex are ATMs, internet café, phones and good toilets.

The **Mangal das Garças** ⓘ *end of Av Tamandaré, on the waterfront, 10 mins' walk east of cathedral*, is a good new park with flora of the state, including mangroves, a butterfly and hummingbird house, colourful birds, a museum, viewing tower and the **Manjar das Garças** restaurant (good for all-you-can-eat meals).

The **Bosque Rodrigues Alves** ⓘ *Av Almte Barroso 2305, T3226 2308, 0900-1700, closed Mon*, is a 16-ha public garden (really a preserved area of original flora), with a small animal collection; yellow bus marked 'Souza' or 'Cidade Nova' (any number) 30 minutes from 'Ver-o-Peso' market, also the bus from the Cathedral. The **Museu Emílio Goeldi** ⓘ *Av Magalhães Barata 376, www. museu-goeldi.br, Tue-Thu 0900-1200, 1400-1700, Fri 0900-1200, Sat-Sun 0900-1700, US$1.30, additional charges for specialist area*, takes up a city block and consists of the museum proper (with a fine collection of Marajó Indian pottery, an excellent exhibition of Mebengokre Indian lifestyle) and botanical exhibits including Victoria Régia lilies. Take a bus from the Cathedral.

A return trip on the ferry from Ver-o-Peso to **Icaoraci** provides a good view of the river. Several restaurants here serve excellent seafood; you can eat shrimp and drink coconut water and appreciate the breeze coming off the river. Icaoraci is 20 km east of the city and is well-known as a centre of ceramic production. The pottery is in Marajoara and Tapajonica style. Take the bus from Av Presidente Vargas to Icaoraci (one hr). Open all week but best on Tuesday to Friday. Artisans are friendly and helpful, will accept commissions and send purchases overseas.

The nearest beach is at **Outeiro** (35 km) on an island near Icaoraci, about an hour by bus and ferry (the bus may be caught near the Maloca, an *indígena*-style hut near the docks which serves as a nightclub). A bus from Icaoraci to Outeiro takes 30 minutes. Further north is the island of **Mosqueiro** (86 km) ⓘ *buses Belém-Mosqueiro every hour from rodoviária, US$2, 80 mins*, accessible by an excellent highway. It has many beautiful sandy beaches and jungle inland. It is popular at weekends when traffic can be heavy (also July) and the beaches can get crowded and polluted. Many hotels and weekend villas are at the villages of Mosqueiro and Vila; recommended (may be full weekends and July). Camping is easy and there are plenty of good places to eat.

Ilha do Marajó → *Colour map 5, A1.*

At almost 50,000 sq km, the world's largest island formed by fluvial processes is flooded in rainy December to June and provides a suitable habitat for water buffalo, introduced from India in the late 19th century. They are now farmed in large numbers (try the cheese and milk). It is also home to many birds, crocodiles and other wildlife, and has several good beaches. It is crowded at weekends and in the July holiday season. The island was the site of the pre-Columbian Marajoaras culture.

Ponta de Pedras

Boats leave Belém (near Porto do Sal, five hours) most days for Ponta de Pedras (**$$ Hotel Ponta de Pedras**, good meals, buses for Soure or Salvaterra meet the boat). Bicycles for hire to explore beaches and the interior of the island. Fishing boats make the eight-hour trip to Cachoeira do Arari (one *pousada*, **$$-$**) where there is a Marajó museum. A 10-hour boat trip from Ponta de Pedras goes to the Arari lake where there are two villages, Jenipapo built on stilts, forró dancing at weekends, and Santa Cruz which is less primitive, but less interesting (a hammock and a mosquito net are essential). There is a direct boat service to Belém twice a week.

Soure → *Colour map 5, A1. Population: 20,000.*
The 'capital' of the island has fine beaches: Araruna (2 km – take supplies and supplement with coconuts and crabs, beautiful walks along the shore), do Pesqueiro (bus from Praça da Matriz, 1030, returns 1600, eat at Maloca, good, cheap, big, deserted beach, 13 km away) and Caju-Una (15 km). Small craft await passengers from the river boats, for **Salvaterra** village (good beaches and bars: seafood), 10 minutes, or trips are bookable in Belém from Mururé, T3241 0891. There are also 17th-century Jesuit ruins at **Joanes** as well as a virgin beach. Changing money is only possible at very poor rates. Take plenty of insect repellent.

Macapá → *Phone code: 096. Post code: 68900. Colour map 2, C6. Population: 283,308.*
The capital of Amapá State is situated on the northern channel of the Amazon Delta and is linked to Belém by boat and daily flights. Along with Porto Santana it was declared a Zona Franca in 1993 and visitors flock to buy cheap imported electrical and other goods. Each brick of the **Fortaleza de São José do Macapá**, built between 1764 and 1782, was brought from Portugal as ballast; 50 iron cannons remain. Today it is used for concerts, exhibits, and colourful festivities on the anniversary of the city's founding, 4 February. In the handicraft complex, **Casa do Artesão** ① *Av Azárias Neto, Mon-Sat 0800-1900,* craftsmen produce their wares onsite. A feature is pottery decorated with local manganese ore, also woodcarvings, leatherwork and indigenous crafts. **São José Cathedral**, inaugurated by the Jesuits in 1761, is the city's oldest landmark.

The riverfront is a very pleasant place for an evening stroll. The **Complexo Beira-Rio** has food and drink kiosks, and a nice lively atmosphere. The pier (trapiche) has been rebuilt and is a lovely spot for savouring the cool of the evening breeze, or watching sunrise over the Amazon. There is a monument to the equator, **Marco Zero** (take Fazendinha bus). The equator also divides the nearby enormous football stadium in half, aptly named O Zerão. South of here, at Km 12 on Rodovia Juscelinho Kubitschek, are the **botanical gardens**. **Fazendinha** (16 km from the centre) is a popular local beach, very busy on Sunday. **Curiarú**, 8 km from Macapá, was founded by escaped slaves, and is popular at weekends for dancing and swimming.

Tourist offices: Setur ① *R Bingo Uchôa 29, Centro, T3212 5335, www.setur.ap.gov.br.*

Border with Guyane → *Colour map 2, B6.*
The main road crosses the Rio Caciporé and continues to the border with Guyane at **Oiapoque** (*Population: 13,000*), on the river of the same name. It is 90 km inland from the Parque Nacional Cabo Orange (**ICMBio** contact T096-3521 2706), Brazil's northernmost point on the Atlantic coast. About 7 km to the west is Clevelândia do Norte, a military outpost and the end of the road in Brazil. Oiapoque is remote, with its share of contraband and prostitution. It is also the gateway to gold fields in the interior of both Brazil and Guyane. Prices here are high, but lower than in neighbouring Guyane. The **Cachoeira Grande Roche** rapids can be visited, upstream along the Oiapoque River, where it is possible to swim, US$30 per motor boat. The road north to the Guyane border (BR-156) is unpaved from Tatarugalzinho and is difficult in parts, especially during the wet season (but open throughout the year). It is being paved. It is advisable to carry extra fuel, food and water from Macapá onwards. Immigration officers will stamp you out the day before if you want to make an early start to Guyane. A bridge linking Guyane and Amapá is under construction and the road is asphalted all the way to Cayenne. As combis to Cayenne leave before lunch it is best to get to St-Georges before 1000. There is already much deforestation along the Brazilian side of the road and many Brazilian *garimpeiros* and hunters are causing havoc in Guyane.

⊕ Belém and around listings

For hotel and restaurant price codes, and other relevant information, see Essentials.

⊜ Where to stay

Belém *p578, map p579*
There are now a few decent mid-range hotels in the city and a few clean, well-kept bargains in the upper budget category. The cheapest rooms are still very scruffy in Belém: consider an upgrade, this is a place where US$3-4 can make an enormous difference.
$$$$ Machado's Plaza, R Henrique Gurjão 200, T4008 9800, www.machadosplazahotel.com.br. Bright hotel with smart and tastefully decorated rooms, a small business centre, plunge pool and a pleasant a/c breakfast area. Good value.
$$$ Itaoca, Av Pres Vargas 132, T4009 2400, www.hotelitaoca.co.br. Well kept, bright rooms, the best are on the upper floors away from the street noise, and with river views. Decent breakfast.
$$$ Le Massilia, R Henrique Gurjão 236, T3224 2834, www.massilia.com.br. Intimate, French owned boutique hotel with chic little duplexes and more ordinary doubles. Excellent French restaurant (**$$$**) and a tasty French breakfast.
$$$ Vila Rica, Av Júlio César 1777, T3210 2000, www.hotelvilarica.com.br/hotel_belem.htm. 5 mins from airport, helpful with transfers, very good.
$$ Grão Pará, Av Pres Vargas 718, T3224 9600, www.hotelgraopara.com.br. Contemporary fittings, smart, hot water, the best have superb river views, excellent breakfast, great value.
$$ Unidos, Ó de Almeida 545, T3229 0600. Simple, spacious rooms with clean en suites.
$$-$ Novo Avenida, Av Pres.Vargas 404, T3242 9953, www.hotelnovoavenida.com.br. Slightly frayed but spruce rooms with decent breakfast. Groups of can sleep in large rooms for **$** pp. Very good value.
$ pp Amazônia Hostel, Av Gov José Malcher 592, Nazaré (between Quintino Bocaiúva and Rui Barbosa), T4008 4800, www.amazonia

hostel.com.br. Good hostel. (Don't confuse with **Amazônia**, R Ó de Almeida 548, which is not recommended.)

Soure *p581*
$$ Ilha do Marajó, 2a Travessa 10, 15 mins' walk from centre, T3741 1315. A/c, bath, pool, popular with package tours.
$$ Marajó, Praça Inhangaíba 351, Centro, T3741 1396. A/c, bath, clean, helpful owner.

Salvaterra
$$$ Pousada das Guarãs, Av Beira Mar, Salvaterra, T4005 5656, www.pousada dosguaras.com.br. Well-equipped, tour programme, on beach.

Joanes
$$ Pousada Ventania do Rio-Mar, take bus, US$1.20 from Foz do Câmara, T3646 2067, 9992 5716, www.pousadaventania.com. Near the beach, fan, hammocks, laundry service, arranges tours on horseback or canoe, Belgian and Brazilian owners. Ask about their social integration projects with locals.

Macapá *p581*
$$$ Atalanta, Av Coracy Nunes 1148, T3223 1612. 10 mins' walk from the river. The best business-style hotel in town with a rooftop pool and comfortable, modern rooms, includes generous breakfast.
$$$ Ceta Ecotel, R do Matodouro 640, Fazendinha, T3227 3396, www.ecotel.com.br. 20 mins from town centre by taxi. All furniture made on site, sports facilities, gardens with sloths and monkeys, ecological trails. Highly recommended.
$$$ Pousada Ekinox, R Jovino Dinoá 1693, T3223 0086, www.ekinox.com.br. Nice atmosphere, book and video library, excellent meals and service, riverboat tours available. Recommended.
$$-$ Santo Antônio, Av Coriolano Jucá 485, T3222 0226, 1 block south and half a block east of Praça da Bandeira. Best rooms are on

upper floors, cheaper with fan, good breakfast extra; in dorm.

Border with Guyane: Oiapoque *p581*
Plenty of cheap, poorly maintained hotels along the waterfront.

🍴 Restaurants

Belém *p578, map p579*
All the major hotels have good restaurants.
$$$ Açaí, Hilton Hotel, Av Pres Vargas 882, T3242 6500. Recommended for regional dishes and others, Sun brunch or daily lunch and dinner.
$$$ Boteco Onze, Praça F C Brandão s/n, T3224 8599. The best regional cooking in Belem with live music every night and river views.
$$$ Churrascaria Rodeio, Trav Padre Eutíquio 1308 and Rodovia Augusto Montenegro Km 4, T3248 2004. A choice of 20 cuts of meat and 30 buffet dishes for a set price. Well worth the short taxi ride to eat all you can.
$$$ Lá em Casa, Av Governador José Malcher 247 (also in Estação das Docas). Try menu paraense, good cooking, fashionable.
$$ Cantina Italiana, Trav Benjamin Constant 1401. Very good Italian, also delivers.
$$ Mãe Natureza, Manoel Barata 889, T3212 8032. Vegetarian and wholefood dishes in a bright clean dining room. Lunch only.
$$ Sabor Paraense, R Sen Manoel Barata 897, T3241 4391. A variety of fish and meat dishes served in a bright, light dining room.
$ Doces Bárbaros, Benjamin Constant 1658, T3224 0576. Cakes, snacks, sandwiches and decent coffee. Lunch only.
$ Govinda, Ó de Almeida 198. Basic but tasty vegetarian food. Lunch only.
$ Good snack bars serving *vatapá* (Bahian dish), tapioca rolls, etc, are on Assis de Vasconcelos on the eastern side of the Praça da Republica.

Macapá *p581*
$$$ Chalé, Av Pres Vargas 499. Nice atmosphere and good food.
$$ Cantinho Baiano, Av Beira-Rio 1, Santa Inês. Good seafood. 10 mins' walk south of the

fort. Many other restaurants along this stretch about 1½ km beyond the Cantino Baiano.
$$ Martinho's Peixaria, Av Beira-Rio 810. Another good fish restaurant.
$ Bom Paladar Kilo's, Av Pres Vargas 456. Good pay-by-weight buffet.
$ Sorveteria Macapá, R São José 1676, close to centre. Excellent ice cream made from local fruit.

🍸 Bars and clubs

Belém *p578, map p579*
Belém has some of the best and most distinctive live music and nightlife in northern Brazil.
A Pororó. Vast warehouse jam packed with techno *brega* acts playing a kind of up tempo disco driven 2/4 dance to thousands of people every Fri and Sat.
Bar do Gilson, Travessa Padre Eutíquio 3172, T3272 1306. A covered courtyard decorated with black and white photography, live samba and *choro* at weekends.
Café com Arte, Av Rui Barbosa 1436. Good after 2300. A colonial house with 3 floors devoted to live rock and DJs.
Carousel, Av Almte Barroso at Antônio Baena. Live *aparelhagem* – a kind of up-tempo techno with twanging guitars played by DJs on a sound stage that looks like the flight control gallery for a 1970s starship. Has to be seen to be believed. Every Fri.
Mormoço, Praça do Arsenal s/n, Mangal das Garças. A warehouse-sized building on the waterfront, some of the best live bands in Belém at weekends, playing local rhythms like *carimbó* and Brazilianized reggae and rock.
São Mateus, Travessa Padre Eutíquio 606. A mock Carioca *boteco* street bar, Belém rock and Brazilian soul most nights.

✷ Festivals

Belém *p578, map p579*
Círio (Festival of Candles) in **Oct**, is based on the legend of the Nossa Senhora de Nazaré, whose image was found on the site of her

Basílica around 1700. On the 2nd Sun in Oct, a procession carries a copy of the Virgin's image from the Basílica to the cathedral. On the Mon, 2 weeks later, the image is returned to its usual place. There is a Círio museum in the Basílica crypt, enter at the right side of the church; free. (Hotels are fully booked during Círio.)

Macapá p581

Marabaixo is the traditional music and dance of the state of Amapá; a festival held 40 days after Easter. The sambódromo, near Marco Zero, is used by Escolas de Samba during Carnaval and by Quadrilhas during the São João festivities.

O Shopping

Belém p578, map p579
A good place to buy hammocks is the street parallel to the river, 1 block inland from Ver-o-Peso, starting at US$5-7.50.
Arts and crafts market, Praça da República every weekend. Seed and bead jewellery, whicker, hammocks and raw cotton weave work, toys and knic-knacs. Mostly predictable but the odd gem.
Complexo São Brás, Praça Lauro Sodré. Handicraft market and folkloric shows in a building dating from 1911.
Parfumaria Orion, Trav Frutuoso Guimarães 268. Sells a variety of perfumes from Amazonian plants, much cheaper than tourist shops.

O What to do

Belém p578, map p579
Larger hotels organize city and 1-day boat tours.
Amazon Star, R Henrique Gurjão 236, T3241 8624, www.amazonstar.com.br. City and river tours, Ilha de Marajó hotel bookings and tours, very professional, good guides, jungle tours, books flight tickets. Repeatedly recommended.
Amazônia Sport & Ação, Av 25 de Setembro 2345, T3226 8442. Extreme sports, diving and climbing.

O Transport

Belém p578, map p579
Air Bus 'Perpétuo Socorro-Telégrafo' or 'Icoaraci', every 15 mins from the Prefeitura, Praça Felipe Patroni, to the airport, 40 mins, US$1.50. Taxi to airport, US$18 (ordinary taxis are cheaper than Co-op taxis, buy ticket in advance in Departures side of airport). ATMs for credit cards in the terminal. Airport T3210 6272.

Daily flights south to **Brasília** and other Brazilian cities, and west to **Santarém** and **Manaus** with TAM. To **Paramaribo** (and Cayenne twice a week) with **Surinam Airways**, R Gaspar Viana 488, T3212 7144, airport T211 6038, English spoken, helpful with information and documentation.

Bus The rodoviária is at the end of Av Governador José Malcher 5 km from the centre (T3246 8178). Take Aeroclube, Cidade Novo, No 20 bus, or Arsenal or Canudos buses, US$1, or taxi, US$10 (day), US$12 (night) (at rodoviária you are given a ticket with the taxi's number on it, threaten to go to the authorities if the driver tries to overcharge). Good snack bar, showers (US$0.15) and 2 agencies with information and tickets for riverboats. Regular bus services to all major cities. To **Santarém**, via Marabá (on the Trans-amazônica) once a week (US$100, can take longer than boat, goes only in dry season). **Transbrasiliana** go direct to Marabá, 16 hrs, US$44. To **São Luís**, 2 a day, US$60, 13 hrs, interesting journey through marshlands. To **Fortaleza**, US$80-92 (24 hrs), many companies.
Ferry To **Santarém, Manaus**, and intermediate ports (see Boat services, page 576). All larger ships berth at Portobrás/ Docas do Pará (the main commercial port) at Armazém (warehouse) No 10 (entrance on Av Marechal Hermes, corner of Av Visconde de Souza Franco). The guards will sometimes ask to see your ticket before letting you into the port area, but tell them you are going to speak with a ship's captain. Ignore the touts who approach you and avoid a boat called Amazon Star: it has a deservedly bad reputation. **Macamazónia**, R Castilho Franca,

sells tickets for most boats, open Sun. There are 2 desks selling tickets for private boats in the *rodoviária*; some hotels recommend agents for tickets. Purchase tickets from offices 2 days in advance. Smaller vessels (sometimes cheaper, usually not as clean, comfortable or safe) sail from small docks along Estrada Nova (not a safe part of town). Take a Cremação bus from Ver-o-Peso.

To **Macapá (Porto Santana)**, the quickest (12 hrs) are the catamaran *Atlântico I* or the launches *Lívia Marília* and *Atlântico II* (slightly slower), all leaving at 0700 on alternate days. Other boats take 24 hrs: *Silja e Souza* (Wed) of Souzamar, Trav Dom Romualdo Seixas corner R Jerônimo Pimentel, T3222 0719, and *Almirante Solon* (Sat) of Sanave (Serviço Amapaense de Navegação, Castilho Franca 234, opposite Ver-o-Peso, T3222 7810), slightly cheaper, crowded, not as nice. Via Breves, ENAL, T3224 5210 (see Boat services, page 576). Smaller boats to Macapá also sail from Estrada Nova.

Ilha do Marajó p580
Ferry From Belém docks the ferry sails to Soure on Fri at 2000 (4 hrs). There are daily boats to Foz do Cámara at 0630, 0700 and 1300 (1½-3 hrs U$$7.50). Then take a bus to Salvaterra and a ferry to Soure. Boats return from Foz do Cámara at 0800 and 1100. There is a 'taxi-plane' service to Soure leaving Belém at 0630 returning 1600, US$60.

Macapá p581
Air TAM (T223 2688), fly to Belém and other Brazilian cities. GOL fly to Belém (at night), Brasília and São Paulo.
Bus *Rodoviária* on BR-156, north of Macapá. To **Amapá**, **Calçoene** and **Oiapoque** (15-17 hrs, U$$45), at least 2 daily. The road is from Amapá to the border is due to be paved; before then you may have to get out and walk up hills, bus has no a/c.
Ferry Ships dock at Porto Santana, 30 km from Macapá (frequent buses US$2.50, or share a taxi US$30). To **Belém**, *Silja e Souza* of Souzamar, Cláudio Lúcio Monteiro 1375,

Santana, and *Almirante Solon* of Sanave, Av Mendonça Furtado 1766. See under Belém, Ferry, for other boats. Purchase tickets from offices 2 days in advance. Also smaller and cheaper boats. The faster (12 hrs) catamaran *Atlântico I* or launches leave for Belém most days. *São Francisco de Paula I* sails to **Santarém** and **Manaus**, not going via Belém.

Border with Guyane: Oiapoque p581
Bus At least 2 a day for **Macapá**, 12-15 hrs (dry season), 14-24 hrs (wet season), US$45. Also shared jeepscheaper in the back than in the cabin. You may be asked to show your Polícia Federal entry stamp and Yellow Fever vaccination certificate either when buying a ticket from the offices on the waterfront or at the bus station when boarding for Macapá.
Ferry Crossing to Guyane: motorized canoes cross to St-Georges de L'Oyapock, 10 mins downstream, US$5 pp, bargain for return fare. A vehicle ferry will operate until the bridge is completed.

ⓘ Directory

Belém *p578, map p579*
Banks Money can only be changed at banks during the week. At weekends hotels will only exchange for their guests, while restaurants may change money, but at poor rates. Exchange rates are generally the best in the north of the country.
Consulates Venezuela, Ferreira Cantão 331, T3222 6396, http://belemdopara.consulado. gob.ve (check website before arriving if you need a Venezuelan visa for entering overland; it takes 3 hrs and costs US$30). **Medical services** Health: a yellow fever certificate or inoculation is mandatory. It is best to get a yellow fever vaccination at home (always have your certificate handy) and avoid the risk of recycled needles. Medications for malaria prophylaxis are not sold in Belém pharmacies. Bring an adequate supply from home. **Clínica de Medicina Preventativa**, Av Bras de Aguiar 410 (T3222 1434), will give injections, English spoken, open 0730-1200, 1430-1900 (Sat 0800-

1100). Hospital Ordem Terceira, Trav Frei Gil de Vila Nova 2, doctors speak some English, free consultation but it's a bit primitive. Surgery open Mon 1300-1900, Tue-Thu 0700-1100, 24 hrs for emergencies.

Macapá *p581*
Banks ATMs at banks. **Casa Francesa**, Independência 232, changes euros (euros can be bought in Macapá and Belém).
Consulates For the French honorary consul, ask at **Pousada Ekinox**, visas for Guyane have to be obtained from Brasília which can take a while.

Border with Guyane: Oiapoque *p581*
Banks **Exchange**: It is possible to exchange US$ and reais to euros, but dollar rates are low and TCs are not accepted anywhere.
Banco do Brasil, Av Barão do Rio Branco, open 1000-1500, and **Bradesco**, have Visa facilities to withdraw reais which can be changed into euros. **Casa Francesa**, on the riverfront, and one câmbio in the market sell reais for US$ or euros. Rates are worse in St-Georges. Best to buy euros in Belém, or abroad. **Useful addresses** Immigration: Polícia Federal, for Brazilian exit and entry stamps, is at Av Rio Branco 500, T3521 1380.

Belém to Manaus

A few hours up the broad river from Belém, the region of the thousand islands is entered. The passage through this maze of islets is known as 'The Narrows' and is perhaps the nicest part of the journey. The ship winds through 150 km of lanes of yellow flood with equatorial forest within 20 m or 30 m on both sides. On one of the curious flat-topped hills after the Narrows stands the little stucco town of **Monte Alegre**, an oasis in mid-forest (airport; some simple hotels, **$$-$**). There are lagoon cruises to see lilies, birds, pink dolphins; also village visits (US$40 per day).

Santarém → *Phone code: 093. Post code: 68000. Colour map 4, A5. Population: 262,538.*
The third largest city on the Brazilian Amazon is small enough to walk around. It was founded in 1661 as the Jesuit mission of Tapajós; the name was changed to Santarém in 1758. There was once a fort here and attractive colonial squares overlooking the waterfront remain. Standing at the confluence of the Rio Tapajós with the Amazon, on the southern bank, Santarém is halfway (two or three days by boat) between Belém and Manaus. Most visitors breeze in and out on a stopover by boat or air. **Tourist office**: **Comtur** ① *R Floriano Peixoto 777, T3523 2434*, has good information available in English. See also www.paraturismo.pa.gov.br.

The yellow Amazon water swirls alongside the green-blue Tapajós; the **meeting of the waters**, in front of the market square, is nearly as impressive as that of the Negro and Solimões near Manaus. A small **Museu dos Tapajós** in the old city hall on the waterfront, now the **Centro Cultural João Fona** ① *open 0900, closed weekend, free*, downriver from where the boats dock, has a collection of ancient Tapajós ceramics, as well as various 19th-century artefacts. The unloading of the fish catch between 0500 and 0700 on the waterfront is interesting. There are good beaches nearby on the Rio Tapajós.

Alter do Chão

Some 34 km west of Santarém is this friendly village on the Rio Tapajós, at the outlet of Lago Verde. Of particular interest is the **Centro do Preservação de Arte Indígena** ① *R Dom Macedo Costa, T527 1110, 0800-1200, 1300-1700*, which has a varied collection of artefacts from tribes of Amazônia and Mato Grosso. Good swimming in the Tapajós from the beautiful, clean beach.

Óbidos and around → *Phone code: 093. Population: 46,500.*

At 110 km up-river from Santarém (five hours by boat), Óbidos is located at the narrowest and deepest point on the river. It is a picturesque and clean city with many beautiful, tiled buildings and some nice parks. Worth seeing are the **Prefeitura Municipal** ① *T3547 1194*, the cuartel and the **Museu Integrado de Óbidus** ① *R Justo Chermont 607, Mon-Fri 0700-1100, 1330-1730*. There is also a **Museu Contextual**, a system of plaques with detailed explanations of historical buildings throughout town. The airport has flights to Manaus, Santarém and Parintins.

Just across the Pará-Amazonas border, between Santarém and Manaus, is **Parintins** (*Phone code: 092. Post code: 69150-000, www.parintins.am.gov.br*), 15 hours by boat upriver from Óbidos. Here, on the last three days of June each year, the **Festa do Boi** draws over 50,000 visitors. Since the town has only two small hotels, everyone sleeps in hammocks on the boats that bring them to the festival from Manaus and Santarém. The festival consists of lots of folkloric dancing, but its main element is the competition between two rival groups, the Caprichoso and the Garantido, in the bumbódromo, built in 1988 to hold 35,000 spectators.

⦿ Belém to Manaus listings

For hotel and restaurant price codes, and other relevant information, see Essentials.

⦿ Where to stay

Santarém *p586*
$$$ Mirante, Trav Francisco Correa, 115, T3067 7100, www.mirantehotel.com. Homely, fridge, some rooms with balcony, individual safes, good value. Recommended.
$$ Brasil, Trav dos Mártires 30, T3523 6665. Nice, family-run, includes good breakfast, communal bath, good food, good service.
$$ New City, Trav Francisco Correia 200, T3523 2351. A/c, frigobar, good, will collect from airport.
$$-$ Rios, R Floriano Peixoto 720, T522 5701. Large rooms, comfortable.

Alter do Chão *p586*
$$$ Pousada Tupaiulândia, Pedro Teixeira 300, T093-3527 1157. A/c, OK, very helpful, good breakfast extra, next to telephone office opposite bus stop.
$$ Pousada do Tapajós, R Lauro Sodré 100, T9210 2166, www.pousadadotapajos.com.br. Cheaper for HI members. Private and shared rooms (**$**), hammock area, TV room, outdoor living room, kitchen and laundry, convenient location and a few steps from Praia do Cajueiro.

$$ Pousada Villa Praia, first on the right as you enter the village, T3527 1130. Large rooms, very helpful staff, good value.

Óbidos *p587*
$$ Braz Bello, R Correia Pinto, on top of the hill. Shared bath, full board available.

⦿ Restaurants

Santarém *p586*
$$ Mascote, Praça do Pescador 10. Open 1000-2330, restaurant, bar and ice cream parlour.
$$ Mascotinho, Praça Manoel de Jesus Moraes, on riverfront. Bar/pizzeria, popular, outside seating, good view.
$ Lucy, Praça do Pescador. Good juices and pastries. Recommended.

Alter do Chão *p586*
Lago Verde, Praça 7 de Setembro. Good fresh fish, huge portions.

⦿ Festivals

Santarém *p586*
29 Jun, São Pedro, with processions of boats on the river and boi-bumbá dance dramas.

Alter do Chão *p586*
2nd week in Sep, Festa do Çairé, religious processions and folkloric events.

○ What to do

Santarém *p586*
Amazon Dream, www.amazon-dream.com. For 5, 6 and 10-day cruises out of Santarém, on a traditional-style river boat.
Gil Serique, Av Adriano Pimentel 80, T9123 4567/9179 0678, www.gilserique.com. English-speaking guide. Recommended.
Santarém Tur, in Amazon Park, and at R Adriano Pimental 44, T3522 4847, www. santaremtur.com.br. Owned by Perpétua and Jean-Pierre Schwarz (speaks French), friendly, helpful, also group tours (group of 5, US$65 per day pp). Recommended.

● Transport

Santarém *p586*
Air 15 km from town, T3522 4328. Internal flights only. Buses run to the centre or waterfront. From the centre the bus leaves in front of the cinema in Rui Barbosa every 80 mins from 0550 to 1910, or taxis (US$15 to waterfront). The hotels Amazon Park and New City have free buses for guests; you may be able to take these.
Bus *Rodoviária* is on the outskirts, take 'Rodagem' bus from the waterfront near the market, US$0.50. Santarém to **Marabá** on the Rio Tocantins with **Transbrasiliana**. From Marabá there are buses east and west on the Transamazônica. Enquire at the *rodoviária* for

other destinations. Road travel during rainy season is always difficult, often impossible.
Ferry To **Manaus**, **Belém**, **Macapá**, **Itaituba**, and intermediate ports (see Boat services, page 576). Boats to Belém and Manaus dock at the Cais do Porto, 1 km west, take 'Floresta-Prainha', 'Circular' or 'Circular Externo' bus; taxi US$7.50. Boats to other destinations, including Macapá, dock by the waterfront by the centre of town. Local service to **Óbidos**, US$20, 4 hrs, Oriximiná US$25, Alenquer, and **Monte Alegre** (US$20, 5-8 hrs).

Alter do Chão *p586*
Bus Tickets and information from the bus company kiosk opposite Pousada Tupaiulândia. From **Santarém**: bus stop on Av São Sebastião, in front of Colégio Santa Clara, US$2, about 1 hr.

Óbidos and around: Parintins *p587*
Air There is a small airport with flights to **Manaus** and **Óbidos** ; taxi to town US$10.
Ferry Apart from boats that call on the **Belém-Manaus** route, there are irregular sailings from **Óbidos** (ask at the port). Journey times are about 12-15 hrs from **Manaus** and 20 hrs from **Santarém**.

● Directory

Santarém *p586*
Banks Cash withdrawals on Visa at Banco do Brasil, Av Rui Barbosa 794. It is very difficult to change dollars (impossible to change TCs anywhere), try travel agencies.

Manaus → *Phone code: 092. Post code: 69000. Colour map 4, A3. Population: 1.9 million.*

The next city upriver is Manaus, capital of Amázonas State – the largest in Brazil. Once an isolated urban island in the jungle, it now sprawls over a series of eroded and gently sloping hills divided by numerous creeks (igarapés). The city is growing fast and 20-storey modern buildings are rising above the traditional flat, red-tiled roofs. An initiative in 2001 saw the start of a restoration programme in which historic buildings have been given a new lease of life and theatres, cultural spaces and libraries created. Further expansion is bound to come now that a new 3.5-km road bridge has been built over the Rio Negro connecting Manaus with Iranduba. More development has resulted from Manaus being a Football World Cup venue, for instance a new airport. Manaus is an excellent port of entry for visiting the Amazon. Less than a day away are river islands and tranquil waterways. The opportunities for trekking in the forest, canoeing and meeting local people should not be missed and, once you are out of reach of the urban influence, there are plenty of animals to see. There is superb swimming in the natural pools and under falls of clear water in the little streams which rush through the woods, but take locals' advice on swimming in the river (both for nature's animal hazards and man's pollution).

Arriving in Manaus → *Manaus is 1 hr behind Brazilian standard time (2 hrs Oct-Feb, Brazil's summer time).*

Orientation Boats dock at different locations depending on where they have come from. The **docks** are quite central. The **airport** is 18 km from the centre, the **bus terminal** 9 km. Both are served by local buses and taxis. All city bus routes start below the cathedral in front of the port entrance; just ask someone for the destination you want. The city centre is easily explored on foot (although bear in mind an average temp of 27°C). ▶▶ *See Transport, page 598, for further details.*

Tourist office AmazonasTur (state tourism office) ① *Av Eduardo Ribeiro 666, near Teatro Amazonas, T3182 6250, Mon-Fri 0800-1700, Sat 0800-1200, www.visitamazonas.am.gov.br, open 0800-1700. Limited English and information.* City tour from here daily 0930, 1430, US$33, 2½ hours. Offices at the **airport** ① *T3182 9850, daily 24 hrs.* Also in **Amazonas Shopping Center** ① *Av Djalma Batista 482, Chapada, Mon-Sat 0900-2200, Sun and holidays 0300-2100*, and in the **PAC at the Estação Hidroviária** (the docks) ① *T3182 7950, Mon-Fri 0800-1700.* Weekend editions of *A Crítica*, newspaper, list local entertainment and events.

Safety Manaus is a friendly, if busy city and a good deal safer than the big cities of southern Brazil. As in any city, the usual precautions against opportunist crime should be taken, especially when arriving at night. Bars and streets in the working heart of port area, south of Rua Quintino Bocaiuva, are not places to hang around after dark. ▶▶ *See page 592 for advice on choosing a jungle tour.*

Places in and around Manaus

Dominating the centre is a **Cathedral** built in simple Jesuit style on a hillock; very plain inside or out. Nearby is the main shopping and business area, the tree-lined Avenida Eduardo Ribeiro; crossing it is Avenida 7 de Setembro, bordered by ficus trees. **Teatro Amazonas** ① *Largo de São Sebastião, T3232 1768 for information on programmes, www.culturadoam. blogspot.com, Mon-Sat 0900-1700, compulsory guided tour US$5.50, students and over-60s half price, tours in languages other than Portuguese on demand (you may see a rehearsal). Recommended.* This opulent theatre was completed in 1896 during the great rubber boom following 15 years of construction. It has been restored four times and should not be missed. There are ballet, theatre and opera performances several times a week, many of them free. The opera season is April-May. **Igreja São Sebastião** (1888), on the same praça, has an unusual altar of two giant ivory hands holding a water lily of Brazil wood. Largo de São Sebastião is surrounded by shady trees, several galleries and eating places. At night there is usually music, some live, some recorded.

Museu Casa de Eduardo Ribeiro ① *R José Clemente e Joaquim Saremtno, T3234 8755, Tue-Sat 0900-1700, Sun 1600-2000* was the house of the state governor from 1890 to 1900. Inside are old maps of Manaus, a modest collection of period furniture and Ribeiro's bedroom, lovingly re-created. On Thursdays actors dressed in Belle Epoque costumes guide visitors through the museum and re-enact moments from a typical day in the life of the house during the rubber boom. It has a pretty garden.

On the waterfront in the heart of the docks, the **Mercado Adolfo Lisboa**, Rua dos Barés 46, was built in 1902 as a miniature copy of the now demolished Parisian Les Halles. The wrought ironwork which forms much of the structure was imported from Europe and is said to have been designed by Eiffel. It was restored in 2013. Just to the east of it are the fish and banana and fruit markets. A short distance to the west the remarkable **Floating Harbour installations**, completed in 1902, were designed and built by a Scottish engineer to cope with the up to 14 m annual rise and fall of the Rio Negro. The large passenger ship floating dock is connected to street level by a 150 m-long floating ramp, at the end of which, on the harbour wall, can be seen the high water mark for each year since it was built. When the water is high, the roadway

Manaus

Where to stay		Restaurants
1 10 de Julho & Restaurant Marlene	5 Go Inn	1 Africa House & Casa do Pensador
4 Casa Teatro & Restaurant Himawari	6 Hostel Amazonas	2 Alemã Gourmet
	7 Hostel Manaus	3 Bar do Armando
	9 Lider	4 Búfalo
	10 Manaós	5 Canto da Peixada
	11 Manaus Hostel	6 Fiorentina
	13 Park Suites	7 Pizzaria Scarola
	12 Taj Mahal Continental	8 Senac
		9 Skina dos Sucos
		10 Sorveteria Glacial

floats on a series of large iron tanks measuring 2½ m in diameter. The large beige **Alfândega** (Customs House) ① *R Marquês de Santa Cruz, Mon-Fri 0800-1200, 1400-1600*, is at the entrance to the city if your boat arrives to dock at the passenger port. It was entirely prefabricated in England, and the tower once acted as lighthouse. The entire **Conjunto Arquitetônico do Porto de Manaus** was declared a national heritage site in 1987.

The **Biblioteca Pública Estadual** (Public Library) ① *R Barroso 57, Mon-Fri 0730-1730*, inaugurated in 1871, features an ornate European cast iron staircase. It is well stocked with 19th-century newspapers, rare books and old photographs, and worth a visit. The **Palacete Provincial** ① *Praça Heliodoro Balbi (also called Praça da Polícia), T3635 5832, Tue-Sat 0900-1900, Sun 1600-2000, free*, is a stately, late 19th-century civic palace, housing six small museums: **Museu de Numismática** (Brazilian and international coins and notes), **Museu Tiradentes** (history of the Amazon police and Brazilian military campaigns), **Museu da Imagem e do Som** (with free internet, cinema showings and a DVD library), **Museu de Arqueologia** (preserving a few Amazon relics), a **restoration atelier** and the **Pinacoteca do Estado**, one of the best art galleries in northern Brazil. There are guides in every room. It has a decent air-conditioned café, **Café do Pina**, which also has a stand in the nicely-laid out park outside.

The **Instituto Geográfico e Histórico do Amazonas** ① *R Frei José dos Inocentes 132 (near Prefeitura), T3622 1260, Mon-Fri 0900-1200, 1300-1600, US$1.50*, located in a fascinating older district of central Manaus, houses a museum and library of over 10,000 books which thoroughly document Amazonian life through the ages. The **Centro Cultural dos Povos da Amazônia** ① *Praça Francisco Pereira da Silva s/n, Bola da Suframa, T2125 5300, www.ccpa. am.gov.br*, is a large cultural complex devoted to Amazonian indigenous peoples, with a large, well curated museum whose artefacts including splendid headdresses, ritual clothing and weapons; explanatory displays in Portuguese and passable English. There are also play areas for the kids, a library and internet.

Botanic Gardens, **Instituto Nacional de Pesquisas Amazonas** (INPA) ① *Estrada do Aleixo, at Km 3, not far from the Museu de Ciências Naturais da Amazônia, T3643 3377, www.inpa.gov.br, Mon-Fri 0900-1100, 1400-1630, Sat-Sun 0900-1600, US$2, take any bus to Aleixo*. At the centre for scientific research in the Amazon, labs (not open to the public) investigate farming, medicines and tropical diseases in the area. There is a small museum and restaurant, lots of birds, named trees and manatees (best seen Wednesday and Friday mornings when the water is changed), caimans and giant otters; worth a visit. INPA also manages what is probably the largest urban rainforest reserves in the world, on the northeastern edge of Manaus. The **zoo** ① *Estrada Ponta Negra 750 (look for the life-size model jaguar), T3625 2044, Tue-Sun 0900-1630, US$0.65, plus US$1 for trail, getting there: take bus 120 or 207, 'Ponta Negra', from R Tamandaré, US$1*. It is run by CIGS, the army jungle-survival unit. It has been expanded and improved and has a 800-m trail which leads into the zoo itself.

There is a curious little church, **Igreja do Pobre Diabo** ① *at the corner of Av Borba and Av Ipixuna in the suburb of Cachoeirinha*; it is only 4 m wide by 5 m long, and was built by a tradesman, the 'poor devil' of the name. Take Circular 7 Cachoeirinha bus from the cathedral to Hospital Militar.

Excursions About 15 km from Manaus is the confluence of the yellow-brown Solimões (Amazon) and the blue-black Rio Negro, which is itself some 8 km wide, commonly known as the **'meeting of the waters'**. The two rivers run side by side for many kilometres without their waters mingling. You can see this natural phenomenon in a range of ways depending on time and budget. Tourist agencies' day trips, including a boat trip to this spot and visits to other sites, cost about US$110 including lunch. The simplest route is to take a taxi or No 713 'Vila

Buriti' bus to the CEASA ferry dock, and take the car ferry across. The ferry (very basic, with no shelter on deck and no cabins) runs all day until 1800 (approximately). Passenger ferries commute the crossing and you'll skim over the meeting of the waters for US$2 each way. Small private launches cross, 40 minutes' journey, US$15-20 per seat, ask for the engine to be shut off at the confluence, you should see dolphins especially in the early morning. Alternatively, hire a motor boat from near the market (US$17 per person, US$95 per boat, up to eight people), or take a boat from **Fontur** Ponta Negra, T3658 3052, www.fontur.com.br, at the **Hotel Tropical/Park Suites** (US$75 for 5 people); allow three to four hours to experience the meeting properly. A 2-km walk along the Porto Velho road from the CEASA ferry terminal will lead to a point from which Victoria Regia water lilies can be seen in April/May-September in ponds, some way from the road. Agencies can arrange tours.

Museu do Seringal ① *Igarapé São João, 15 km north of Manaus up the Rio Negro, Tue-Sun 0800-1600, T3234 8755, US$2.50, US$22 round trip on a private launch from the Hotel Tropical/ParkSuites, access only by boat*, is a full-scale reproduction of an early 20th-century rubber-tapping mansion house, serf quarters, factory and shop complete with authentic products. A guided tour, especially from one of the former rubber tappers, brings home the full horror of the system of debt peonage which enslaved Brazilians up until the 1970s. The museum can be visited with **Amazon Eco Adventure** or **Amazon Gero Tours**.

The small town of **Presidente Figueiredo** is set in forest and savannah rich in waterfalls and cut by many clear-water rivers. Numerous threatened and endangered bird species live here, including Guianan Cock of the Rock. Presidente Figueiredo is 117 km north and can easily be visited in a day trip from Manaus (bus US$25).

Arquipélago de Anavilhanas, the largest archipelago in a river in the world, is in the Rio Negro, from about 80 km upstream from Manaus, near the town of Novo Airão, four hours by boat. There are hundreds of islands, covered in thick vegetation. Tour companies arrange day visits to the archipelago for US$200-300 per person (see page 597). Most Rio Negro lodges and Rio Negro safari cruises visit the archipelago.

Mamirauá ① *4-day, 3-night package US$360 all inclusive ("worth every penny"). Reservations through T097-3343 4672, www.mamiraua.org.br. Book well in advance. All profits go to local projects and research. Daily flights Manaus-Tefé, then 1½ hours by boat to lodge.* This sustainable development reserve, at the confluence of the Rios Solimões, Japurá and Auti-Paraná, is one of the best places to see the Amazon. It protects flooded forest (várzea) and is listed under the Ramsar Convention as an internationally important wetland. In the reserve **Uakari** (www.uakarilodge.com.br) is a floating lodge with 10 suites. Lots of mammals and birds to see, including cayman, dolphin and harpy eagles, also the endangered pirarucu fish. Visitors are accompanied by guides the whole time.

Tours from Manaus

There are two types of tours: those based at **jungle lodges** and **river boat trips**. Most tours, whether luxury or budget, combine river outings on motorized canoes with piranha fishing, caiman spotting, visiting local families and short treks in the jungle. Specialist tours include fishing trips and those aimed specifically at seeing how the people in the jungle, caboclos, live. Booking in advance on the internet is likely to secure you a good guide (who usually works for several companies and may get booked up). Be sure to ascertain in advance the exact itinerary of the tour, what the price includes (are drink and tips extra?), that guides are knowledgeable and will accompany you themselves and that there will be no killing or capture of anything. Ensure that others in your party share your expectations and are going for the same length of time. Choose a guide who speaks a language you understand. A shorter tour may be better than a long, poor one. Packaged tours, booked overseas, are usually of the same price and quality as those negotiated locally.

Note There are many hustlers on the street, even at the hotels. Freelance guides not permitted to operate at the airport. The tourist police (**Politur**) work with a group of agencies called **Agencol**, T3213 8891, who meet incoming flights, 1300-1500. Check for official and ABAV (Brazilian Association of Travel Agents) credentials personally and don't go with the first friendly face you meet. Investigate a few operators and make enquiries at your own pace. **Secretaria de Estado da Cultura e Turismo** is not allowed by law to recommend guides, but can provide you with a list of legally registered companies. Unfortunately, disreputable operations are rarely dealt with in any satisfactory manner and most continue to operate. When you are satisfied that you have found a reputable company, book direct with the company itself and ask for a detailed, written contract if you have any doubts.

Flights over the jungle give a spectacular impression of the extent of the forest. Bill Potter, resident in Manaus, writes: "opposite Manaus, near the junction of the Rio Negro and the Rio Solimões, lies the **Lago de Janauri**, a small nature reserve. This is where all the day or half-day trippers are taken, usually combined with a visit to the 'meeting of the waters'. Although many people express disappointment with this area because so little is seen and/or there are so many 'tourist-trash' shops, for those with only a short time it is worth a visit. You will see some birds and with luck dolphins. In the shops and bars there are often captive parrots and snakes. The area is set up to receive large numbers of tourists, which ecologists agree relieves pressure on other parts of the river. Boats for day trippers leave the harbour constantly throughout the day, but are best booked at one of the larger operators." If you take a tour in a canoe early in the morning away from the main lake area, you will see a lot of birds. Remember, though, that here as elsewhere throughout the region there is a great difference between high water (June) and low water (November). Water level falls between these two months and channels are increasingly difficult to navigate. The rainy season starts in December.

Those with more time can take the longer cruises and will see various ecological environments. To see virgin rainforest, a five-day trip by boat is needed. Most tour operators operate on both the Rio Solimões and the Rio Negro. The Rio Negro is considered easier to navigate, generally calmer and with fewer biting insects, but as it is a black water river with forest growing on poor soil and the tannin-filled waters are acidic, there are fewer frutiferous trees and fish and therefore fewer animals. The tributaries of the Solimões have higher concentrations of wildlife; including biting insects. Currently most Solimões tours go to the Rio Mamori and Rio Juma areas via the Port Velho highway. There is plenty of deforestation along the initial stages of Rio Mamori. The best lodges for wildlife are the furthest from Manaus but don't expect to see lots of animals. This is difficult anywhere in the Amazon, but you should see caiman, macaws, boa constrictors and river dolphins. It is the immensity of the forest and rivers and the seemingly limitless horizons, as well as a glimpse of the extraordinary way of life of the Amazon people, which make these tours exciting. For the best wildlife options in the Brazilian Amazon head for Alta Floresta, the Mamirauá reserve near Tefé (see above), or the little visited forests of northern Roraima.

Generally, between April and September excursions are only by boat; in the period October to March the Victoria Regia lilies virtually disappear.

Prices vary, but usually include lodging, guide, transport, meals and activities. The recommended companies charge approximately the following (per person, per day): US$77 for hammock accommodation; US$87 in a shared room; US$98 in a private room. All transport, meals and English-speaking guides are included. Longer, specialized, or more luxurious excursions will cost significantly more. Most river trips incorporate the meeting of the waters on the first day, so there is no need to make a separate excursion. For Lodges, see under Where to stay, below.

What to take Leave luggage with your tour operator or hotel in Manaus and only take what is necessary for your trip. Long sleeves, long trousers, shoes and insect repellent are advisable for treks where insects are voracious. Take a mosquito net (and a hammock mosquito net if going on a cheaper tour) for trips in February-June. A hat offers protection from the sun on boat trips. Bottled water and other drinks are expensive in the jungle, so you may want to take your own supplies.

◉ Manaus listings

For hotel and restaurant price codes, and other relevant information, see Essentials.

● Where to stay

Manaus *p588, map p590*

10% tax and service must be added to bills. Hotel booking service at airport (see Transport, below, on taxi drivers' ruses). The best option is the area around the Teatro Amazonas, where the Italianate colonial houses and cobbled squares have been refurbished. Av Joaquim Nabuco and R dos Andradas have many cheap hotels, most of which charge by the hour and all of which are in an area which is undesirable after dark. Similarly risky at night is the Zona Franca around the docks. Improvements are expected to be made in the run-up to the World Cup.

$$$$ Park Suites, Av Coronel Teixeira 1320, Ponta Negra, T3306 4500, www.atlanticahotels. com.br. The best appointed and most modern hotel in the city in the upmarket suburb of Ponta Negra, beside the old Hotel Tropical. Suites are well appointed, housed in a large tower block with great views over the river from the upper floors. The hotel has the best business facilities in the city and has a lovely infinity pool set in gardens overlooking the beach.

$$$$ Taj Mahal Continental, Av Getúlio Vargas 741, T3627 3737, www.grupotajmahal. com.br. Large, impressive central hotel, popular, tour agency for flights, revolving restaurant, massage and high level of service.

$$$ Casa Teatro, 10 de Julho 632, T3633 8381, www.casateatro.com.br. A self-styled boutique hotel in the historic zone, nicely decorated rooms, café for breakfast, but no restaurant, a good central choice.

$$$ Go Inn, R Mons Coutinho 560, T3306 2600, www.atlanticahotels.com.br. Modern, central, no-nonsense style, café, Wi-Fi extra, disabled facilities, gym.

$$$ Lider, Av 7 de Setembro 827, T3621 9700, www.liderhotelmanaus.com.br. Small, modern rooms with little breakfast tables. The best are at the front on the upper floors. Very well kept.

$$$ Manaós, Av Eduardo Ribeiro 881, T3633 5744, www.hotelmanaos.brasilcomercial. com. Smart rooms with marble floors, decent breakfast, close to Teatro Amazonas.

$$ 10 de Julho, R 10 de Julho 679, T3232 6280, www.hoteldezdejulho.com.br. Near opera house, much the best cheap option, English speaking, simple rooms (some with a/c and hot water), efficient, laundry, good tour operators in the lobby (see What to do below), which also assist with boat transport arrangements.

$ Hostel Amazonas, R Ramos Ferreira 922, T3342 6406, www.hostelamazonas.com. br. Shared rooms US$15 (cheaper for HI members), also triples, double (**$$**), and family apartments. Towels are not included.

$ pp Hostel Manaus, R Lauro Cavalcante 231, Centro, T3233 4545, www.hostelmanaus.com. "The original", Australian-owned. Cheaper for HI members. Fine restored old house, with excellent value dorms and private rooms (**$$**), best to confirm bookings, kitchen, laundry, airport pick-up. Good location 1 block from Museu do Homem do Norte, reasonably central and quiet. (Not to be confused with another hostel using a similar name.) Also here is **Amazon Antônio Jungle Tours**, www. antonio-jungletours.com. Ask here about the Rio Negro route to São Gabriel da Cachoeira, where **Pousada Pico da Neblina** has accommodation and tours; see page 601.

$ pp **Manaus Hostel**, R Costa Azevedo 63, T3231 2139, www.manaushostel.com.br. Not to be confused with the above. All rooms with shared bath, private doubles have a/c, $$, dorms with fan and with a/c.

Lodges near Manaus

There are several lodges within a few hrs boat or car journey from Manaus. Most emphasize comfort (although electricity and hot water is limited) rather than a real jungle experience, but they are good if your time is limited and you want to have a brief taste of the Amazon rainforest. It is not possible just to turn up at a jungle lodge, you will need the lodge to take you there through its own designated transport, or to arrive with a tour company. Agencies for reservations are also listed. Very few of the lodges are locally owned and only a small percentage of labour is drawn from local communities. For Homestays in the jungle, see Amazon Gero Tours, below.

$$$$ **Amazon Ecopark Lodge**, Igarapé do Tarumã, 20 km from Manaus, 15 mins by boat, jungle trails; 60 apartments with shower, bar, restaurant, T9146 0594, www.amazonecopark. com.br. Comfortable lodge with 60 apartments and a decent restaurant. 1- to 4-day packages. Pleasant guided walks but poor for wildlife.

$$$$ **Anavilhanas Jungle Lodge**, Edif Manaus Shopping Center, Av Eduardo Ribeiro 520, sala 304, T3622 8996, www.anavilhanas lodge.com. Small, elegant lodge on the Anavilhanas Archipelago, 3- to 6-day packages, comfortable, trips to see river dolphins included. In the Roteiros do Charme group.

$$$$ **Ariaú Amazon Towers**, Rio Ariaú, 2 km from Archipélago de Anavilhanas, Manaus office at R Leonardo Malcher 699, T2121 5000, www. ariautowers.com.br. 60 km and 2 hrs by boat from Manaus on a side channel of the Rio Negro. Complex of towers connected by walkways, beach (Sep-Mar), trips to the Anavilhanas islands in groups of 10-20. Highly recommended.

$$$$ **Juma Lodge**, T3232 2707, www. jumalodge.com. Small lodge on the Rio Juma, idyllic location near the Rio Mamori, 2½ hrs south of Manaus by road and boat,

all-inclusive 3- to 6-day packages. One of best options for wildlife and birdwatching.

$$$$ **Malocas Lodge**, 160 km northeast of Manaus on the Rio Preto (80 km by road then canoe, 3 hrs total), T3648 0119, www.malocas. com. Simple rooms with bath plus 1 suite, includes good food and activities, 1- to 7-day packages, French-Brazilian run.

$$$ **Aldeia dos Lagos Lodge**, Silves Project, T3248 9988, www.aldeiadoslagos.com. Simple floating lodge on a lake, run in conjunction with the local community and an NGO. Good for birds and caiman.

$$$ **Amazon Antônio's Lodge**, through Antônio Jungle Tours, www.antonio-jungle tours.com. A thatched roof wooden lodge, rooms with fan, 6 new chalets, observation tower. In a beautiful location overlooking a broad curve in the river Urubu some 200 km from Manaus.

$$$ **Ararinha Lodge**, exclusively through Amazon Gero Tours, www.amazongerotours. com. One of the more comfortable lodges in Paraná do Araça on the Lago Mamori. Smart wooden chalets with suites of individual rooms, beds with mosquito nets. One of the best areas for wildlife in the Mamori region.

🍴 Restaurants

Manaus *p588, map p590*
Many restaurants close on Sun nights and Mon. City authorities grade restaurants for cleanliness: look for A and B.

$$$ **Himawari**, R 10 de Julho 618, T3233 2208. Swish, sushi and Japanese food, attentive service, opposite Teatro Amazonas, open Sun night, when many restaurants close. Recommended.

$$ **Búfalo**, churrascaria, Av Joaquim Nabuco 628. Best in town, all-you-can-eat Brazilian barbecue with a vast choice of meat.

$$ **Canto da Peixada**, R Emílio Moreira 1677 (Praça 14 de Janeiro). Superb fish dishes, lively atmosphere, unpretentious, close to centre, take a taxi.

$$ **Fiorentina**, R José Paranaguá 44, Praça Heliodoro Balbi. Fan-cooled, traditional Italian,

including vegetarian dishes, average food but one of best options in centre, dishes served with mugs of wine! Great feijoada on Sat, half-price on Sun. **Bob's Shakes** is in the same building.
$$ Marlene, 10 de Julho 625, Tue-Sun 1100-2300. Good Brazilian food per kg at lunch, also grill and desserts at night when prices are higher, a/c inside, plus sidewalk seating, popular.
$$ Pizzaria Scarola, R 10 de Julho 739, corner with Av Getúlio Vargas. Standard Brazilian menu, pizza delivery, popular.
$ Alemã Gourmet, R José Paranaguá, Praça Heliodoro Balbi. Food by weight, good for lunch, great pastries, hamburgers, juices, sandwiches.
$ Casa do Pensador, J Clemente 632. Open 1600-2300. For drinks and good, reasonably priced food, at night has tables on the street. **Africa House**, next door, serves mainly juices.
$ Senac, R Saldanha Marinho 644. Cookery school, self-service, open daily, lunch only. Highly recommended.
$ Skina dos Sucos, Eduardo Ribeiro e 24 de Maio. Regional fruit juices and snacks.
$ Sorveteria Glacial, Av Getúlio Vargas 161 and other locations. Recommended for ice cream.

O Bars and clubs

Manaus p588, map p590
The city has very lively nightlife and the scene is constantly changing. Clubs and bars are often far from the centre.
Bar do Armando, 10 de Julho e Tapajós, near the Teatro. Bohemian atmosphere, good place for drinking outside.
Djalma Oliveira, R 10 de Julho 679, T9185 4303, djalmatour@hotmail.com. Nightlife tours throughout Manaus and private car hire. Manaus clubs are often far from the centre. Djalma is far better value for a night out than a taxi. He also offers day tours and transfers.

⊕ Entertainment

Manaus p588, map p590
Performing arts For Teatro Amazonas, see page 589.

Teatro da Instalação, R Frei José dos Inocentes, T/F3622 2840. Performance space in recently restored historic buildings with free music and dance (everything from ballet to jazz), Mon-Fri May-Dec at 1800. Charge for performances Sat and Sun. Recommended.

⊛ Festivals

Manaus p588, map p590
6 Jan: Epiphany; **24 Jun**: São João; **14 Jul**; **5 Sep**; **30 Oct**; **1 Nov**, All Saints' Day, half-day. **Feb**: Carnival dates vary – 5 days of Carnival, culminating in the parade of the Samba Schools. 3rd week in **Apr**: Week of the Indians, indigenous handicraft. In **Jun**: Festival do Amazonas; a celebration of all the cultural aspects of Amazonas life, indigenous, Portuguese and from the northeast, especially dancing; **29 Jun**: São Pedro, boat processions on the Rio Negro. In **Sep**: Festival da Bondade, last week, stalls from neighbouring states and countries offering food, handicrafts, music and dancing, SESI, Estrada do Aleixo Km 5. **Oct**: Festival Universitário de Música – FUM, the most traditional festival of music in Amazonas, organized by the university students, on the University Campus. **8 Dec**: Processão de Nossa Senhora da Conceição, from the Igreja Matriz through the city centre and returning to Igreja Matriz for a solemn mass.

O Shopping

Manaus p588, map p590
Since Manaus is a free port, the whole area a few blocks off the river front is full of electronics shops. All shops close at 1400 on Sat and all day Sun.
Handicrafts There are many handicrafts shops in the area around the Teatro Amazonas.
Central de Artesanato Branco e Silva, R Recife 1999, T3642 5458. A gallery of arts and crafts shops and artists studios selling everything from indigenous art to wooden carvings by renowned Manaus sculptor Joe Alcantara.
Eco Shop, Largo de São Sebastião, T3234 8870, and Amazonas Shopping, T3642 2026,

www.ecoshop.com.br. Indigenous arts and crafts from all over the Amazon, including Yanomami and Tikuna baskets, Wai Wai necklaces and Baniwa palm work. The souvenir shop at the INPA has some interesting Amazonian products on sale. For hammocks go to R dos Andradas, many shops. **Galeria Amazônica**, R Costa Azevedo 272, Largo do Teatro, T3233 4521, www.galeriamazonica. org.br. A large, modern space filled with Waimiri Atroari indigenous arts and crafts, one of the best places for buying indigenous art in Brazil. In the Praça do Congresso, Av E Ribeiro, there is a very good Sun craftmarket.

☉ What to do

Manaus *p588, map p590*
Swimming For swimming, go to Ponta Negra beach by Soltur bus, US$1, though the beach virtually disappears beneath the water in Apr-Aug; popular by day and at night with outdoor concerts and samba in the summer season. Boats to nearby beaches from **Park Suites** cost US$2.25 pp. Every Sun, boats leave from the port in front of the market to beaches along Rio Negro, US$2.65, leaving when full and returning at end of the day. This is a real locals' day out, with loud music and foodstalls on the sand. Good swimming at waterfalls on the Rio Tarumã, lunch is available, shade, crowded at weekends. Take Tarumã bus from R Tamandaré or R Frei J dos Inocentes, 30 mins, US$1.10 (very few on weekdays), getting off at the police checkpoint on the road to Itacoatiara.

Tour operators
Check agencies' licences from tourist office and ABAV, www.abavam.com.br. If in the least doubt, use only a registered company.
Amazing Tours Agency, Leopoldo Carpinteiro Peres 1570, T8165 1118, UK contact: T07726 115298, www.manausjungletours.com. Leonardo is a local guide who grew up in the jungle and has a good knowledge of flora and fauna. English spoken, and some Dutch. Also trips to Jau National Park.

Amazon Antônio Tours, Hostel Manaus, R Lauro Cavalcante 231, T3234 1294, www. antonio-jungletours.com. Jungle tours on the Rio Urubu, a black water river 200 km northeast of Manaus. Good prices for backpackers.
Amazon Backpacker Tours, R 10 de Julho 679, in Hotel 10 de Julho, T3213 8891, T9168 4543 (24 hrs), www.amazonbackpackes.com. br. Services range from transfers, transport tickets and city tours to boat trips, jungle tours in the Mamori and Juma areas and tours to a new property 225 km from Manaus beyond Tupana, reached by Transamazônica. More than 5 day trip, US$125 per day, hammocks and shared rooms in Indian maloca. Lots of wildlife when water is high; good for fish when water low. Very helpful.
Amazon Clipper Cruises, T3656 1246, www.amazonclipper.com.br. Informed guides, well-planned activities, comfortable cabins and good food on comfortable small boats, traditional and premium classes.
Amazon Eco Adventures, R 10 de Julho 695, T8831 1011, www.amazonecoadventures.com. Some of the best 1-day boat tours of the Solimões and Rio Negro available in Manaus, with options for water sports and fishing. The agency also runs spectacular ultra-light flights over the forest. Good value, excellent guiding.
Amazon Gero Tours, R 10 de Julho 679, sala 2 (outside Hotel 10 de Julho), T9983 6273, www. amazongerotours.com. Backpacker-oriented tours south of the Solimões and bookings made for lodges everywhere. Tours throughout the region are frequently recommended. Gero, the owner is very friendly and dedicated. Operates **Ararinha Lodge** (see above). He can also arrange homestays in a riverine community in the heart of the Amazon, a fascinating, immersive alternative to a jungle lodge offering a real glimpse of the realities of Amazon life. Take a Portuguese phrasebook, your own mosquito net, toiletries, torch (flashlight) and insect repellent.
Amazon Nature Tours, Av 7 de Setembro 188, Manaus, www.amazon-nature.com (in USA T401-423 3377). Excellent expedition cruises on the live-aboard motor yacht *Tucano*, all cabins with a/c and bath, small groups,

experienced guides for trips into the forest, 5 or 8 days on the rivers Negro and Amazon. **Amazon Riders**, R Lauro Cavalcante 214, T8175 9747, www.amazonriders.com. Extended tours in the jungle, wildlife tours, meeting tribes on the Yavari river, 2 days from Manaus, and more.

Iguana Tour, R 10 de Julho 679 in Hotel 10 de Julho, T3633 6507, or 9136 4325, www.amazon brasil.com.br. Short and long tours, plenty of activities, many languages spoken.

Jaguar Adventure Tours R Marciano Armond, Vila Operária 23A, Cachoeirinha, T9155 7185, www.amazontoursbrazil.com. Carlos Jorge Damasceno, multilingual, many years experience, deep jungle explora-tion with an ecological slant and visits to remote historical and indigenous settlements, also arranges boat trips on typical Amazonian craft and on luxury boats.

MV Desafio, T3633 8644, www.mvdesafio. com.br. Schooner offering 4-day, 3-night river cruises, 12 cabins, restaurant and bar, refurbished to a high standard.

Nonato Amazon Tours, R Aticun 37, Cidade Nova I, T9115 5491, nonatoamazontours@ hotmail.com. Specializes in fishing, Raimundo Nonato Monteiro speaks Italian.

Tucunaré Turismo, R Miranda Leão 194, T3234 5071, www.tucunareturismo.com.br. Branch at the airport and a few blocks east of the docks. Good for internal flights and short tours.

Viverde, R das Guariúbas 47, Parque Acarquara, T3248 9988, www.viverde.com.br. Family-run agency acting as a broker for a wide range of Amazon cruises and lodges and running their own city tours and excursions.

Guides Guides are licensed to work through tour agencies, so it is safest to book guides through approved agencies. They do some-times work individually. Advance notice and a minimum of 3 people for all trips offered by these guides:

Cristina de Assis, T9114 2556, amazonflower@ bol.com.br. Offers tours telling the story of the city and the rubber boom with visits to historic buildings and the Museu Seringal, trips to the Rio Negro, to Presidente Figueiredo, the Boi Bumba party in Parintins and the forest. Cristina speaks good English.

Pedro Fernandes Neto, T8831 1011, pedroff neto@hotmail.com. Adventure tour specialist offering light adventure trips to the large INPA rainforest reserve, the forest around Manaus and the waterfalls and rivers of Presidente Figueiredo.

⊖ Transport

Manaus *p588, map p590*
Air Airport T3652 1210, www.infraero.gov.br. International flights to **Miami** and **Panama City**. TAP are starting Lisbon-Manaus-Belém-Lisbon flights in Jun 2014. Internal flights to many Amazonian and northern Brazilian destinations; for other cities change in Brasília or São Paulo. Domestic airport tax US$11.50. The taxi fare to or from the airport is US$25, taxi syndicate price; arrange to be met and, when returning to the airport, ask your hotel for their recommended cheapest option. Bus to town leaves from stop outside terminal on the right. Bus No 306 'Aeroporto Internacional' (or from Praça da Matriz restaurant next to the cathedral), US$1.40, 0500-2300. Many tour agencies offer free transfers without obligation. Check all connections on arrival.
Note Check in time is 2 hrs in advance. Allow plenty of time at Manaus airport, formalities are slow especially if you have purchased duty-free goods. Many flights depart in the middle of the night and while there are many snack bars there is nowhere to rest. In the terminal there are also shops, internet, Banco do Brasil, Confidence câmbio and a tourist office.
Bus Manaus *rodoviária* is 9 km out of town at the intersection of Av Constantino Nery and R Recife, T3642 5805. Take a local bus from centre, US$1.40, marked 'Aeroporto Internacional' or 'Cidade Nova' (or taxi, US$25) and ask the driver to tell you where to get off. Services and fares are given under destinations.
Ferry There are 3 main docks: the westernmost floating docks are for large cargo vessels. The next floating docks, at the end of Av Eduardo Ribeiro below the Praça da Matriz, belonging to the Estação Hidroviária, have a large plaque showing the levels of the Rio Negro. Vessels for major destinations,

Santarém, **Belém**, **Porto Velho**, **Tabatinga** (for Colombia and Peru), and intermediate ports, sail from here. There is a small Porto Ajato, just downstream from the Estação Hidroviária, where the fast boats sail, eg to **Tabatinga**, **Tefé** and **Santarém**; ticket sales are right on this pier, Mon-Fri 0800-1700, Sat 0800-1200. See also Boat services, page 576.

Further downstream along the shore, behind the markets, are various other piers where riverboats sail to smaller destinations such as Tefé. In this area are many agents under umbrellas identified with photo IDs. They claim to sell tickets for all boats. There is another cluster of these agents outside the Estação Hidroviária, between it and the Alfândega. In principle, tickets for major destinations must be purchased from official booths inside the Estação Hidroviária, but these have the highest prices and they are not negotiable. Alternatively, you can buy tickets from one of the agents outside, who may be amenable to discounts (about 10-20%), but shop around and beware tricks and scams. A third option is to approach boat owners directly and try to negotiate the fare with them, but if you have not purchased your ticket at the Estação Hidroviária, you will not be allowed onto their dock to visit boats or embark. Small motorboats provide water taxi service from near the Porto Ajato to the Estação Hidroviária dock (US$3 pp; beware overcharging), circumventing this restriction. Another workaround is to take a taxi (car) to the Estação Hidroviária dock; you will not be asked to show your ticket, but will have to pay a toll of US$7.50; go very early in the morning to avoid traffic and long queues at the port entrance. This plus the taxi fare may be substantially less than the savings for purchasing tickets outside the Estação Hidroviária. **Note** Be careful of people who wander around boats after they've arrived at a port: they are almost certainly looking for something to steal. Also beware of overcharging and theft by porters at all docks.

Immigration For those arriving by boat who have not already had their passports stamped (eg from Letícia), the immigration office is at Polía Federal, address below.

Road The Catire Highway (BR 319) from Manaus to Porto Velho (868 km), has been officially closed since 1990. For over 200 km at each end of the road (Manaus to Careiro-Castanho; Humaitá to Porto Velho), driving is no problem, but the paving of the middle 400 km or so is subject to study and controversy. Enquire locally if the road is passable for light vehicles; some bridges are flimsy. The alternative for drivers is to ship a car down river on a barge, others have to travel by boat.

ⓘ Directory

Manaus *p588, map p590*
Banks AI Ms can be found at central banks and other public locations. **Câmbio Parcam**, R 10 de Julho 651, T3308 2009, Mon-Fri 0800-1700, Sat 0800-1200. Do not change money on the streets. **Embassies and consulates** Colombia, R 24 de Maio 220, Rio Negro Center, T3234 6777, cmanaos@ cancilleria.gov.co, double check whether a Colombian tourist card can be obtained at the border. **Peru**, R Constelação 16A, Morada do Sol, Aleixo, T3236 9607, conpemao@gmail.com, Mon-Fri 0900-1500. **Venezuela**, R Rio Juraí 839, Vieira Alves, T3584 3636/3828, convemao@ vivax.com.br, 0800-1200. Some nationalities entering Venezuela overland need a visa (check in advance with a Venezuelan consulate); all need a yellow fever certificate. **Medical services** Clínica São Lucas, R Alexandre Amorin 470, T3622 3678, reasonably priced, some English spoken, good service, take a taxi. Hospital Tropical, Av Pedro Teixeira (D Pedro I) 25, T3238 1711. Centre for tropical medicine, not for general complaints, treatment free, some doctors speak a little English. Take buses 201 or 214 from Av Sete de Setembro in the city centre. **Pronto Soccoro 28 de Agosto**, R Recife 1581, T3642 4272, free for emergencies. **Useful addresses** Police: for immigration and to extend or replace a Brazilian visa, Polícia Federal, Av Domingos Jorge Velho 40, Bairro Dom Pedro II, Planalto, T3655-1515/1517.

Amazon frontiers

To get to the border with Colombia and Peru, a river boat is the only alternative to flying and this, of course, is the true way to experience the Amazon. On the route to Venezuela, buses and trucks have almost entirely replaced river traffic to Boa Vista, from where roads go to Santa Elena de Uairén and Lethem in Guyana.

Rondônia and Acre, lands which mark not just the political boundaries between Brazil and Peru and Bolivia, but also developmental frontiers between the forest and colonization. Much of Rondônia has been deforested. Acre is still frontier country with great expanses of forest in danger of destruction.

Manaus to Colombia, Peru, Venezuela and Guyana

Benjamin Constant and up the Rio Javari → *Phone code: 097. Colour map 3, A5.*

At the confluence of the Rios Solimões and Javari, is the friendly pleasant town of Benjamin Constant. Some boats between Tabatinga and Manaus call here. The **Museu Magüta** ① *Av Castelo Branco 396, www.museumaguta.com.br, Mon-Fri 0800-1600, Sat 0800-1400, Sun 0800-1600*, displays photographs, costumes, traditional art and music of native indigenous groups. The Rio Javari is the border between Brazil and Peru, upriver on the Peruvian side is the town of **Islandia**. Further upriver is the Brazilian town of **Atalaia do Norte**, 26 km by paved road from Benjamin Constant. Further still are the Território Indígena do Vale do Javari and privately owned nature reserves, with accommodation and facilities for birdwatching, dolphin and caiman spotting. We list two below.

Border with Colombia and Peru

The busy Brazilian port of Tabatinga is upstream and on the opposite shore from Benjamin Constant along the Rio Solimões. Tabatinga is also on the land border with **Leticia** (Colombia), a pleasant city with the best infrastructure in the area. There is no separation between the two and Avenida da Amizade in Tabatinga becomes Avenida Internacional in Leticia. On an island across from Tabatinga and Leticia is the small Peruvian town of **Santa Rosa**, which is prone to severe flooding in the rainy season. All three towns have accommodation and restaurants and people move freely between them with no border formalities. If you are only visiting any of the towns just for the day, there is no need to get stamped-in, but always keep your passport with you. There is drug smuggling throughout the area and Tabatinga is particularly unsafe, do not go out here at night. Reais and pesos colombianos are accepted in all three towns; soles are seldom used. There are ATMs in Tabatinga and Leticia, and the latter is the best place to change cash; TCs are not accepted anywhere. Leticia and Santa Rosa are one hour behind Tabatinga.

Tabatinga → *Phone code: 097.*

Tabatinga has several ports; which one is used depends on the water level at the time. There are about five boats a week to Manaus, *Voyager* boats use their private docks near Rua Santos Dumont. The docks for local boats to Santa Rosa and Benjamin Constant are behind the market by Rua Pedro Teixeira. There are **tourist offices** ① *at the land border and on Av da Amizade, 4 blocks from the border, Mon-Sat 0800-1700.*

Immigration Once you get an exit stamp from one country, you must get the entry stamp at your next destination within 24 hours, there are fines if you are late. Yellow fever vaccination certificates may be requested to enter any of the three countries.

Brazil Entry and exit stamps at **Policia Federal** ①*Av da Amizade 65, about 1 km from the border, Tabatinga, T3412 2180, open daily 0800-1200, 1400-1800.* Proof of US$500 or an onward ticket may be asked for. Taxi to port US$9, to Leticia $12. There are no immigration facilities in Benjamin Constant. **Brazilian Consulate** ①*Cra 10 corner C 10, Leticia, T592 7530, Mon-Fri 0700-1200, 1400-1700; onward ticket, 5x7 photo and yellow fever vaccination certificate needed for visa; allow 36 hrs; efficient, helpful.* There is also a consulate in Iquitos, Peru.

Colombia Entry and exit stamps at **Migración Colombia** ①*Leticia airport, T592 4535, Mon-Fri 0800-1700, Sat-Sun 0800-1500,* taxi from the centre US$4, mototaxi US$2.50. An administrative office at C9 9-62 does not issue entry/exit stamps, go there for extensions and to pay the fine if you have overstayed. The **Colombian Consulate** ①*R Gral Sampaio 623 (1 block from Av da Amizade, behind Canto da Peixada Restaurant, about 10 blocks from the border), Tabatinga, T3412 2104, ctabatin@minrelext.gov.co, Mon-Fri 0800-1330,* issues visas.

Peru Entry and exit stamps at **Migración** in Santa Rosa, 0730-1700. If entering Peru, you may be asked to show your boat ticket in order to get the entry stamp; if taking a *rápido* to Iquitos, get your entry stamp the day before, you cannot get it before departure early in the morning. **Peruvian Consulate** ①*Cra 11 5-32, Leticia, T592-7204, Mon-Fri 0800-1200,* it is a lengthy (one week minimum), involved process to get a visa here. Best get a visa in your home country.

Up the Rio Negro to Colombia or Venezuela Boats go from Manaus to **Sao Gabriel da Cachoeira** (Population: 40,000), from where you can continue to Colombia via San Felipe (fortnightly flights from here to Villavicencio) or to Venezuela via San Felipe or Cucuí. This route goes to Puerto Ayacucho via the Canal de Casaquiare, which links the Amazon and Orinoco river systems. São Gabriel da Cachoeira has the largest indigenous population of any municipality in Brazil. The neighbouring Parque Nacional do Pico da Neblina is closed to visitors. All information and tours at **Pousada Pico da Neblina** ①*R Cap Euclides 322, Bairro da Praia, T097-9168 0047, www.pousadapicodaneblina.com (same owner as Hostel Manaus, see page 594),* **$$** *in a/c double rooms, or* **$** *in dorms,* a big yellow house behind Comercial Carneiro. Four-day guided tours including visits to villages, climbing Bella Adormecida mountain, camping in the jungle and river trips cost US$85 per person per day. Between Manaus and São Gabriel is the town of **Barcelos**, which has **Hotel Barcelos**.

Boats for São Gabriel da Cachoeira (see page 577) go from the Porto Beira Mar de São Raimundo, upriver from the main port. Take bus 101 'São Raimundo', or 112 'Santo Antônio', 40 minutes. Two companies go to São Gabriel: **Tanaka** ①*in Manaus T9239 8024, in São Gabriel opp Maraska internet, T097-3471 1730, Fri 1800 from Manaus, returns Fri 0800, 3 days, US$135, and fast boat, 24 hrs, Tue and Fri 1500, return Tue and Fri 0800, US$165 (take a mattress for the express boat).* **Genesis** ①*in Manaus T8119 8591, in São Gabriel at Hotel Roraima II, T Manuel Felício Braga 3500, T3471 1771,* quicker boats than Tanaka, but smaller and rowdier. No scheduled boats travel beyond São Gabriel, so you have to wait until there are enough passengers and cargo to leave.

Manaus to Venezuela and Guyana

The road which connects Manaus and Boa Vista (BR-174 to Novo Paraíso, then the Perimetral, BR-210, rejoining the BR174 after crossing the Rio Branco at Caracaraí) can get badly potholed. There are service stations with toilets, camping, etc, every 150-180 km, but all petrol is low octane. Drivers should take a tow cable and spares, and bus passengers should prepare for delays in the rainy season. At Km 100 is Presidente Figueiredo, described above. About 100 km further on is a service station at the entrance to the **Uaimiri Atroari Indian Reserve**, which straddles the road for about 120 km. Private cars and trucks are not allowed to enter the Indian Reserve between sunset and sunrise, but buses are exempt from this regulation. Nobody is allowed to stop within the reserve at any time. At the northern entrance to the reserve there are toilets and a spot to hang your hammock (usually crowded with truckers overnight). At Km 327 is the village of Vila Colina with **Restaurante Paulista**, good food, clean, you can use the shower and hang your hammock. At Km 359 there is a monument to mark the **equator**. At Km 434 is the clean and pleasant **Restaurant Goaio**. Just south of Km 500 is **Bar Restaurante D'Jonas**, where you can also camp or sling a hammock. Beyond here, large tracts of forest have been destroyed for settlement, but already many homes have been abandoned.

At **Caracaraí**, a busy port with modern installations on the Rio Branco, a bridge crosses the river for traffic on the Manaus-Boa Vista road. It has hotels in our **$$-$** range. Boa Vista has road connections with the Venezuelan frontier at Santa Elena de Uairén (237 km, paved, the only gasoline 110 km south of Santa Elena) and Bonfim for the Guyanese border at Lethem. Both roads are open all year.

Boa Vista → *Phone code: 095. Post code: 69300. Colour map 2, B2. Population: 200,568.*

The capital of the extreme northern state of Roraima, 785 km north of Manaus, is a pleasant, clean, laid-back little town on the Rio Branco. Tourism is beginning here and there are a number interesting new destinations opening up, many offering a chance to explore far wilder and fauna-rich country than that around Manaus. The landscape is more diverse, too, with a mix of tropical forest, savannah and highlands dotted with waterfalls. The area immediately around the city has been heavily deforested. It has an interesting modern cathedral and a museum of local indigenous culture. There is swimming in the Rio Branco, 15 minutes from the town centre (too polluted in Boa Vista), reachable by bus only when the river is low. **Tourist office**: Detur ⓘ *R Coronel Pinto 267, T2121 2525, www.turismo.rr.gov.br.* Information is available at the *rodoviária*, T3623 1238; see also www.rr.gov.br.

Border with Venezuela

Border searches are thorough and frequent at this border crossing. If entering Brazil, ensure in advance that you have the right papers, including yellow fever certificate, before arriving at this border. Officials may give only two months' stay and car drivers may be asked to purchase an unnecessary permit. Ask to see the legal documentation. Everyone who crosses this border to Venezuela must also have a yellow fever certificate. Check requirements for visas beforehand (some nationalities need one, but not, for example, Western Europeans). See the Directory, below, for the Venezuelan consulate. There is another Venezuelan consulate in Manaus (see above). On the Brazilian side there is a basic hotel, **Pacaraima Palace**, a guesthouse, camping and a bank.

Border with Guyana → *Colour map 2, B3. Population: 9,326.*

The main border crossing between Brazil and Guyana is from **Bonfim**, 125 km (all paved) northeast of Boa Vista, to Lethem. The towns are separated by the Rio Takutu, which is crossed by a new bridge. The river crossing is 2.5 km from Bonfim, 1.6 km north of Lethem. Formalities are strict on both sides of the border: it is essential to have a yellow fever vaccination both to leave Brazil and to enter Guyana The bus passes through Brazilian Immigration where you receive your exit stamp. After the bridge, there are taxis to the Guyana Immigration office (US$5). You are given a visa for the exact amount of time you stipulate staying. The border is open 24 hours, but officials tend to leave immigration after 1800.

There is no Guayanese consul in Boa Vista, so if you need a visa for Guyana, you must get it in Rio de Janeiro or Brasília. Reais can be changed into Guyanese dollars in Boa Vista or near Brazilian immigration in Lethem, where reais are also accepted.

◉ Manaus to Colombia, Peru, Venezuela and Guyana listings

For hotel and restaurant price codes, and other relevant information, see Essentials.

● Where to stay

Benjamin Constant and up the Rio Javari *p600*
There are a number of very cheap, simple *pousadas* in town.
$$-$ Benjamin Constant, R Getulio Vargas 36, near port and market, T3415 5310. Has a variety of rooms with a/c, bath, cold water, helpful owner. Recommended.
$ Amazonas, R Getúlio Vargas 181, T3415 5902. Wooden building with nice porch, a/c, cheaper with fan, bath, cold water, frigobar.

Atalaia do Norte
$$ Itacoaí, Av Pedro Teixeira, T3417 1123. Nice clean rooms with a/c, electric shower, no breakfast, same owner runs another hotel next door.

Up the Rio Javari
$$$$ Heliconia, T+57-311-508 5666 (Leticia), www.amazonheliconia.com. Price, based on 2 people, includes transport from Leticia and all food and activities (except canopy and massage treatments). Up a small tributary of the Javari, 3 hrs by boat from Leticia, isolated, comfortable cabins (with bathrooms open to the forest behind) set around a jungle garden. Night-time caiman-spotting excursions as well as trips to visit local indigenous communities, excellent walks, birdwatching and fishing tours.
$$$$ Palmarí, T+57-1-610 3514 (Bogotá), www.palmari.org. Includes meals, drinks, guiding and all activities (except canopy). The reserve is on terra firme forest, walkable year-round, with both other types of Amazon forest nearby. Various types of accommodation and

prices, starting at US$130 pp per night plus transport from Leticia, Tabatinga or Santa Rosa. The reserve has Wi-Fi and cell phone access, attentive service. German owner Axel Antoine-Feill has set up the Instituto de Desenvolvimiento Socioambiental do Vale do Javarí, www.idsavj.org, to work with local indigenous communities

Tabatinga *p600*
Tabatinga is dangerous at night, do not leave your your hotel after dark. Apart from those listed, there are various other hotels on the streets leading from the port to Av da Amizade.
$$$ Takana, R Osvaldo Cruz, 970, 13412 3557, www.takanahotel.com.br. Comfortable and clean, hot water, frigobar. Upmarket for Tabatinga.
$$$-$$ Tarumã, R da Pátria 70, near Igreja da Matriz, T3412 2083, hoteltaruma@hotmail com. Rooms/suites with electric shower, frigobar. nice.
$$ Vitoria Regia, R da Patria, 820, T3412 2668. Quiet area near Igreja da Matriz, ample rooms, cold water, frigobar.
$ International Backpacker, R Santos Dumont 2, upstairs, T+57-313-219 5121 (Colombian cell phone), amazonasdiscover@ hotmail.com. Cheap basic rooms with bath, fan, cold water, cheaper still in dorm or hang your hammock on the porch, basic kitchen facilities, no breakfast. Right at the port; convenient for night-time arrivals/departures.
$ Pajé, R Pedro Teixeira 367, T3412 2774, hotelpaje@gmail.com. Small rooms, cheaper with fan, bath, cold water, very basic but friendly.

Boa Vista *p602*
Accommodation is generally expensive. Economic hardship has caused an increase in crime, sometimes violent.

$$$ **Aipana Plaza**, Joaquim Nabuco 53, T3224 4116. Best in town with plain rooms decorated with photos of Roraima, hot water, attractive pool area with a shady little bar.

$$$ **Uiramutam Palace**, Av Capt Ene Garcez 427, T3224 9757. Business hotel with modest rooms and large bathrooms. Decent pool.

$$ **Barrudada**, R Araújo Filho 228, T3623 1378. Simple rooms in a modern tower block very close to the centre. The best on the upper floors have views of the river. Breakfast and lunch included.

$$ **Eusêbio's**, R Cecília Brasil 1107, T3623 0300. Spruce, modest rooms with cold water showers. The best are airy and on the upper floors. Pleasant pool and a laundry service. Has a good a/c restaurant (**$$**) and a generous breakfast.

$$-$ **Ideal**, R Araújo Filho 481, T3224 6342. Simple but well-kept rooms, some have a/c, generous breakfast and convenient for the centre.

Border with Guyana: Bonfim *p602*
$$ **Bonfim**, owned by Mr Myers, who speaks English and is very helpful, fan, shower.

❼ Restaurants

Tabatinga *p600*
$$$ **Te Contei?**, Av da Amizade 1813. Closed Tue. International and regional dishes à la carte, excellent pizza.

$$$ **Tres Fronteras Do Amazonas**, R Rui Barbosa, Barrio San Francisco. Excellent mix of Brazilian, Peruvian and Colombian dishes.

$$-$ **Tapioquinha e Taco**, Av da Amizade near Marechal Mallet, 4 blocks from border, daily 0800-2200. Brazilan, Peruvian and Mexican food, economical *prato feito*.

Boa Vista *p602*
There are several restaurants serving snacks and juices on the riverside along R Floriano Peixoto.

$$ **Peixada Tropical**, R Pedro Rodrigues at Ajuricaba. A range of river fish dishes in various styles from Bahian sauces to Milanesa.

$ **1000 Sabores**, R Araújo Filho e Benjamin Constant. Pizzas, snacks and juices. Open early and closes late.

$ **Café com Leite Suiço**, at Santa Cecilia, 15 mins by car on road to Bom Fim. Open 0630-1300 for regional food, good.

$ **Catequeiro**, Araújo Filho e Benjamin Constant. Recommended *prato feito*.

Border with Guyana: Bonfim *p602*
There is a café at the *rodoviária*, opposite the church, whose owner speaks English and gives information. Others nearby.

❾ Bars and clubs

Boa Vista *p602*
R Floriano Peixoto is lively after dark at weekends when there is live music in and around the **Orla Taumanan**, a complex of little bars/restaurants.

❿ What to do

Boa Vista *p602*
Roraima Adventures, R Coronel Pinto 86, sala 106, T3624 9611, www.roraima-brasil.com. br. A range of interesting trips to little known and little visited parts of Roraima including the spectacular Tepequem and Serra Grande mountains and the Rio Uraricoera, which is replete with wildlife. Pre-formed groups get the best prices, which are competitive with Manaus. Helpful with visas for Venezuela.

⓿ Transport

Benjamin Constant and up the Rio Javari *p600*
Shared taxis run all day between Benjamin Constant and **Atalaia do Norte**, US$9, 30 mins. There is no public river transport up the Rio Javari.

Border with Colombia and Peru *p600*
Tabatinga
Air There are separate airports at Tabatinga and Leticia. From Tabatinga, **TAM** and **Trip** fly daily to **Manaus**.

River About 5 sailings a week to **Manaus** and intermediate ports (see Travel up the Amazon River, Boat services, page 576). Buy tickets directly from docked riverboats or at Transtur agency (see below). Expect long queues and thorough drug searches when boarding vessels, have your passport at hand and never accept bags from other passengers. All boats for **Iquitos** leave from Santa Rosa. Tickets for *rápidos* (fast boats) to Iquitos are sold in Tabatinga: **Transtur**, R Marechal Mallet 290, T8113 5239, departures Wed, Fri, Sun; **Golfinho**, office next door, T3412 3186, www.transportegolfinho.com, Tue, Thu. Both leave at 0400 Peruvian time, US$75 including breakfast and lunch, 10-12 hrs. Buy tickets and get your exit and entry stamps the day before, and be at the dock in Santa Rosa at 0300. Canoes cross from Tabatinga to Santa Rosa, US$1.75 during the day, US$3 starting 0230 (Peruvian time) to reach the *rápido*. Take a taxi to the dock in Tabatinga, do not walk; or spend the night in Santa Rosa. There are also *lanchas* (large riverboats) sailing most evenings from Santa Rosa to Iquitos, US$28 in hammock, 3-4 days, tickets sold onboard, conditions vary and may be crowded and dirty. Small ferries run from Tabatinga to Benjamin Constant throughout the day, US$9, 30 mins.
Taxi Charge US$12 to most destinations in Tabatinga or Leticia, payable in reais or pesos colombianos, beware overcharging and negotiate.

Boa Vista *p602*
Air Flights to **São Paulo**, **Rio de Janeiro**, **Belém**, etc. Book through **Aguia**, R Benjamin Constant 1683B, T3624 1516 (owner speaks some English). No left luggage, information or exchange facilities at the airport, which is 4 km from the centre. Bus 'Aeroporto' from the centre is US$1. Taxi to *rodoviária*, US$17, to centre US$20, 45 mins' walk.

Bus (See also Border with Bolivia and Peru, page 608.) *Rodoviária* is 3 km at the end of Av Ville Roy; taxi to centre, US$15, bus US$1, 10 mins (marked '13 de Setembro' or 'Joquey Clube' to centre). The local bus terminal is on Av Amazonas, by R Cecília Brasil, near central praça. It is difficult to get a taxi or bus to the *rodoviária* in time for early morning departures; as it's a 25-min walk, book a taxi the previous evening. To **Manaus**, US$60, with **Eucatur**, 12 hrs, 4 daily. Advisable to book. Buses between Boa Vista and **Caracaraí** take 8 hrs.

Border with Venezuela *p602*
Bus One bus a day goes from Boa Vista *rodoviária* to **Santa Elena de Uairén**, stopping at all checkpoints, US$20, 4 hrs, take water. Or share a taxi, US$10 pp.

Border with Guyana: Bonfim *p602*
Bus Boa Vista-Bonfim 6 a day US$12, 2½ hrs, continues to immigration; colectivos charge US$25.

❶ Directory

Boa Vista *p602*
Banks US$ and Guyanese notes can be changed in Boa Vista. There is no official exchange agency and the local rates for bolívares are low: the **Banco do Brasil**, Av Glaycon de Paiva 56, will not change bolívares, but has an ATM. ATMs at other banks. Best rate for dollars, **Casa PedroJosé**, R Araújo Filho 287, also changes TCs and bolívares; **Timbo's** (gold and jewellery shop), Av B Constant 170, will change money.
Consulates Venezuela, Av Benjamin Constant 968, T3623 9285, Mon-Fri 0830-1300. Visas available, relaxed service, allow 24-48 hrs.
Medical services Yellow fever inoculations are free at a clinic near the hospital.

Porto Velho → *Phone code: 069. Post code: 78900. Colour map 4, B1. Population: 450,000.*

This city stands on a high bluff overlooking a curve of the Rio Madeira. It first prospered during the local gold and timber rush and now is booming as the result of the Madeira Hydroelectric Complex, the first two dams of which are currently one of the largest civil engineering projects in the world. Its sewage treatment system will be one of the most advanced in Brazil. Buildings in the centre are being renovated and a large riverside park dotted with Vitória Régia lily ponds and a new museum devoted to the history of the city are being developed. But it is less of a tourist city than Rio Branco, a far more interesting access point to Brazil from Peru or Bolivia.

At the top of the hill, on Praça João Nicoletti, is the **Cathedral**, built in 1930, with beautiful stained glass windows; the **Prefeitura** is across the street. The principal commercial street is Avenida 7 de Setembro, which runs from the railway station and market hall to the upper level of the city, near the *rodoviária*. The centre is hot, noisy and sprawls from the river to the bus station (1½ km). In the old railway yards known as Praça Madeira-Mamoré are the **Museus Ferroviário** (see below) and **Geológico** ① *both 0800-1800* and a promenade with bars by the river, a wonderful place to watch the sunset. There are several viewpoints over the river and railway yards: **Mirante I** (with restaurant) is at the end of Rua Carlos Gomes; **Mirante II** (with a bar and ice cream parlour), at the end of Rua Dom Pedro II, is the best place to watch the sunset over the river. There is a fruit and vegetable market at the corner of Rua Henrique Dias and Avenida Farquhar and a dry goods market three blocks to the south, near the port. **Tourist office**: Semdestur ① *R José do Patrocínio 852, Centro, T3901 3180*. See also www.portovelho. ro.gov.br, www.rondonia.ro.gov.br and www.turismoderondonia.com. Tourist office at the airport opens when flights arrive. Malaria is common in the area.

The Madeira–Mamoré Railway → *See www.efmm.net.*

Porto Velho was the terminus of the Madeira-Mamoré railway. It was supposed to go as far as Riberalta, on the Rio Beni, above that river's rapids, but stopped short at Guajará Mirim. Over 6000 workers died during its construction (1872-1913). The BR-364 took over many of the railway bridges, leaving what remained of the track to enthusiasts to salvage what they could. The **museum** ① *Praça Madeira-Mamoré, T3901 3186, free,* is open to visitors. The railway itself is undergoing refurbishment and it is hoped that it will reopen in 2014, to run some 10 km through Porto Velho and its suburbs, and that it will be listed as a World Heritage Site by UNESCO. See http://efmm100anos.wordpress.com.

The BR-364 → *Colour map 4, C2.*

The Marechal Rondon Highway, BR-364, is fully paved to Cuiabá, 1,550 km. A result of the paving of BR-364 is the development of farms and towns along it. **Note** At the Mato Grosso state border, proof of yellow-fever inoculation is required: if no proof is presented, a new shot is given.

Parque Nacional Pacaás Novos → *765,800 ha.*

The Parque Nacional Pacaás Novos, lies west of the BR-364; it is a transitional zone between open plain and Amazonian forest. The majority of its surface is covered with cerrado vegetation and the fauna includes jaguar, brocket deer, puma, tapir and peccary. The average annual temperature is 23°C, but this can fall as low as 5°C when the cold front known as the friagem blows up from the South Pole. Details from **ICMBio** ① *R Costa e Silva s/n, Campo Novo, T3239 2031.*

Guajará Mirim → *Phone code: 069. Colour map 4, B1. Population: 38,045.*
From Porto Velho, the paved BR-364 continues 220 km southwest to Abunã (hotels **$**), where the BR-425 branches south to Guajará Mirim. The BR-425 is a fair road, partly paved, which uses the former rail bridges (poor condition). It may be closed March-May. Across the Mamoré from Guajará Mirim is the Bolivian town of Guayaramerín, which is connected by road to Riberalta, from where there are air services to other Bolivian cities. Guajará Mirim is a charming town. The **Museu Municipal** ① *T541 3362, 0500-1200, 1400-1800*, is at the old Guajará Mirim railway station beside the ferry landing; highly recommended. Banco do Brasil only changes money in the morning.

Border with Bolivia
Get Brazilian exit and entry stamps from **Polícia Federal** ① *Av Presidente Dutra 70, corner of Av Quintino Bocaiúva, T3541 2437*. The **Bolivian consulate** is at Avenida Beira Rio 505, 1st floor, T3541 8620, Guajará Mirim; visas are given here.

Rio Branco → *Phone code: 068. Post code: 69900. Colour map 3, B6. Population: 253,059.*
The BR-364 runs west from Porto Velho to Abunã (239 km), then in excellent condition, 315 km to Rio Branco the capital of the State of Acre. This intriguing state is rich in natural beauty, history and the seringueiro culture. During the rubber boom of the late 19th century, many Nordestinos migrated to the western frontier in search of fortune. As a result, the unpopulated Bolivian territory of Acre was gradually taken over by Brazil and formally annexed in the first decade of the 20th century. In compensation, Bolivia received the Madeira–Mamoré railroad, as described above. The chief industries are rubber and *castanha-de-pará* (Brazil nut) extraction and, now that ranching has slowed down, ecotourism. While Rondônia has lost well over 50% of its forest, Acre retains 82% primary forest. It has some of the most exciting ethno-tourism projects in South America.

Rio Branco is clean, well-maintained and orderly with the highest percentage of cycle ways of any city in Brazil. There are attractive green spaces and a lively waterfront promenade, the **Mercado Velho**, which buzzes with bar life in the evenings, especially at weekends. The Rio Acre, navigable upstream as far as the Peru and Bolivia borders, divides the city into two districts, Primeiro (west) and Segundo (east), on either side of the river. In the central, Primeiro district are **Praça Plácido de Castro**, the shady main square; the **Cathedral**, Nossa Senhora de Nazaré, along Avenida Brasil; the neo-classical **Palácio Rio Branco** on Rua Benjamin Constant, across from Praça Eurico Gaspar Dutra. Two bridges link the districts. In the Segundo district is the **Calçadão da Gameleira**, a pleasant promenade along the shore, with plaques and an old tree marking the location of the original settlement. The **Horto Forestal**, in Vila Ivonete (1° distrito), 3 km north of the centre ('Conjunto Procon' or 'Vila Ivonete' city-buses), has native Amazonian trees, a small lake, paths and picnic areas.

Museu da Borracha (Rubber Museum) ① *Av Ceará 1144, T3223 1202, Tue-Fri 0800-1800, Sat-Sun 1600-2100*, in a lovely old house with a tiled façade, has information about the rubber boom, archaeological artefacts, a section about Acreano Indians, memorabilia from the annexation and a display about the Santo Daime doctrine. Recommended. **Casa Povos da Floresta** ① *Parque da Maternidade, Centro, T3224 5667, Wed-Fri 0800-1800, Sat-Sun 1600-2100, free* has displays and artefacts devoted to the forest people of Acre, including various of the indigenous peoples and the *seringueiro* rubber tappers who colonised the state. **Tourist office:** For Acre: **Secretária de Turismo** ① *at the Estádio, Av Chico Mendes, T3901 3024, www.ac.gov.br.*

Xapuri → *Phone code: 068. Colour map 3, B5.*
Xapuri is where **Chico Mendes** lived and worked. Mendes, leader of the rubber tappers and opponent of deforestation, was murdered by landowners in 1988. His legacy is increased

awareness of sustainability in the state and his colleague, Marina Silva, was appointed Environment Minister by President Lula da Silva. Both the rubber-tappers' community and the forest Mendes sought to protect survive. Jaguar, harpy eagle and tapir are still abundant here, as are towering Brazil nut and kapok trees. Besides the functioning rubber tapping community, Xapuri is now an ecotourism venture (see Where to stay, below). Chico Mendes' cousin works as a guide. A stay here for one or two nights is a magical experience, well worth undertaking if en route between Brazil and Peru/Bolivia.

Border with Bolivia and Peru

The BR-317 from Rio Branco heads south and later southwest, parallel to the Rio Acre; it runs to **Brasiléia**, opposite the Bolivian town of Cobija on the Rio Acre. There are lodgings (**$$ La Fronteira**, very helpful), several restaurants – **La Felicitá** is good. Polícia Federal give exit/entry stamps for Bolivia, Banco do Brasil changes dollars, no ATM. A striking, single-tower suspension bridge crosses the river to Cobija. Another crossing is at **Epitaciolândia** (**$$ Hotel Kanda**, five minutes' walk from the police post), just east. Ask the bus driver to let you off near Polícia Federal, open 0700-2200, to get passport stamped. **Cobija** is opposite. The border is open 24 hours on the Brazilian side, 0800-1800 in Cobija. **Bolivian consulate** ⓘ *R Hilário Meireles 236, Brasiléia, T3546 5760, colivian-brasileia@rree.gob.bo*.

The road ends at Assis Brasil (120 km) where the Peruvian, Bolivian and Brazilian frontiers meet. Across the Rio Acre are Iñapari (Peru) and Bolpebra, Bolivia. In **Assis Brasil**, there are three hotels, two restaurants (including a good *churrascaria* on the main street), shops and money changers. Cross to Iñapari from Assis Brasil by another distinctive suspension bridge. The Brazilian border is open daily 0830-1200, 1400-1830, the Peruvian side daily 0930-1300, 1500-1930. There are waits of 20-30 minutes at each border post when taking the international bus. **Note** Take small denomination dollar bills or Peruvian soles as there is nowhere to change money on the Peruvian side.

◉ Southern Amazônia listings

For hotel and restaurant price codes, and other relevant information, see Essentials.

⬤ Where to stay

Porto Velho *p606*
Cheap rooms are hard to come by as many are taken by migrant workers on the twin dams project. There are hotels by the *rodoviária*, or take bus No 301 'Presidente Roosevelt' (outside Hotel Pontes), which goes to railway station at riverside, then along Av 7 de Setembro as far as Av Marechal Deodoro. It passes several hotels.
$$$ Central, Tenreiro Aranha 2472, T2181 2500, www.enter-net.com.br/hcentral. A reliable, place which has been remodelled. Recommended.
$$$ Vila Rica, Av Carlos Gomes 1616, T3224 3433, www.hotelvilarica.com.br. Tower block with restaurant, pool and sauna.

$$ Por do Sol, R Carlos Gomes 3168, behind the *rodoviária* to the northeast, T3222 9161, hotelpordosol@yahoo.com.br. A/c rooms off a corridor, the best are in the middle.
$$ Samauma, R Dom Pedro II 1038, T3224 5300, hotelsamauma@hotmail.com. Best mid-range option in the centre, comfortable rooms, popular restaurant, breakfast, welcoming staff.
$$-$ Tía Carmen, Av Campos Sales 2995, T3221 7910. Very good, honest, good cakes in lanchonette in front of hotel. Recommended.

Guajará Mirim *p607*
$$$$-$$$ Pakaas Palafitas Lodge, Estrada do Palheta Km 18, T/F3541 3058, www.pakaas.com.br. 28 bungalows in a beautiful natural setting, price is per person per day.
$$ Jamaica, Av Leopoldo de Mato 755, T3541 3721, and **$$ Lima Palace**, Av 15 de

Novembro 1613, T3541 3421, both have a/c, fridge, parking.
$ Mamoré, R M Moraes, T3541 5500. Clean, friendly and popular.

Rio Branco *p607*
There are hotels and restaurants by the *rodoviária*.
$$$ Imperador Galvez, R Santa Inés 401, T3223 7027, www.hotelimperador.com.br. Comfortable, quiet, modern rooms, large pool, huge breakfasts.
$$$ Irmãos, R Rui Barbosa 450-69, T3214 7100, www.irmaospinheiro.com.br. Bright, spacious rooms, pool, generous breakfast, some English-speaking staff. There's a *churrascaria* next door.
$$$ Terra Verde, R Marechal Deodoro 221, T3213 6000, www.terraverdehotel.com.br. One of the best in the city, well appointed rooms and more luxurious suites, pool, good breakfast.
$$ Afa, R Franco Ribeiro 108, T3224 1396. Simple rooms, quiet and well-kept but small windows, good breakfast.
$$ Papai, R Floriano Peixoto 849, T3223 2044. Central, simple but garish pink and lime green rooms, best on the upper floors.
$ Ouro Verde, R Uirapuru 326, next to *rodoviária*, T3223 2378. No frills option, rooms only a little larger than the beds they contain, but with bath, tidy, on a sunny terrace.

Xapuri *p607*
$$-$ Pousada Ecologica Seringal Cachoeira, Ramal do Cachoeira, Xapuri, T3901 3023. In the Chico Mendes reserve, a series of comfortable wooden cabanas, with a/c, suites and dorms, open-sided public dining and lounge area, overlooking a small river. Day and night safari walks are US$15.

❼ Restaurants

Porto Velho *p606*
$$$ Caravela do Madeira, R José Camacho 104, T3221 6641. The city's business lunch venue, a/c, international menu.
$$ Café Madeira, Majo Amarantes at Carlos Gomes on the riverfront, T3229 1193.

Overlooking the Madeira, *petisco* bar snack, a favourite spot for a sunset beer.
$$ Emporium, Av Presidente Dutra 3366, T3221 2665. Nice atmosphere, good meats and salads, expensive drinks, open 1800-2400. The street behind Emporium is known as the **Calçada da Fama** and is replete with bars and restaurants. It's very busy at weekends.

Guajará Mirim *p607*
Oasis, Av 15 de Novembro 460. The best place to eat. Recommended (closed Mon).

Rio Branco *p607*
Local specialities *Tacacá*; a soup served piping hot in a gourd (*cuia*) combines manioc starch (*goma*), cooked jambu leaves which numb mouth and tongue, shrimp, spices and hot pepper sauce. Also a delicious Amazonian take on Espírito Santo or Bahia's *moqueca*, rich coconut sauce flavoured with an Amazon leaf, *xicoria*, and fresh coriander and accompanied with rice, *pirão*, *farofa* and delicious chilli and tucupi sauce.
$$ Afa, R Franco Ribeiro 108, T3224 1396. The best-value per kilo restaurant in the city, with a wide choice of dishes. Plenty of veggie options.
$$ Elcio, Av Ceará 2513. Superb fish *moquecas*. Serves 2-3 people.

⦿ Shopping

Porto Velho *p606*
Indian handicrafts Artesanato Indígena Karitiana, R Rui Barbosa 1407 between José Camacho and Calama, T3229 7591, daily 0800-1200, 1400-1700. An indigenous-run cooperative selling art including beads, earrings and necklaces, ritual items and weapons.

⊖ Transport

Porto Velho *p606*
Air Airport 8 km west of town. Take bus marked 'Aeroporto' (last one between 2400-0100). Daily flights to many Brazilian cities.
Bus *Rodoviária* is on Jorge Teixeira between Carlos Gomes and Dom Pedro II. It has

restaurants, snack bars and 24-hr ATM. From town take bus No 407 'Norte Azul', or any 'Esperança da Communidade' or 'Presidente Roosevelt' bus from the cathedral in the centre to the *rodoviária*, 1.5 km. Health and other controls at the Rondônia-Mato Grosso border are strict. To break up a long trip is much more expensive than doing it all in one stretch.

To **São Paulo**, 1000, 40 hrs, US$140. To **Cuiabá**, 24 hrs, US$70. To **Guajará-Mirim**, see below. To **Rio Branco**, Eucatur, 2 daily, 8-10 hrs, US$33. To **Campo Grande**, 27 hrs, US$150. To **Cáceres** for the Pantanal, 18 hrs, US$62-95.

Ferry See River Transport, page 576. Passenger service from **Porto Cai N'Água** (which means 'fall in the water', watch out or you might!), for best prices buy directly at the boat, avoid touts on the shore. Boat tickets for Manaus are also sold in the *rodoviária*. The Rio Madeira is fairly narrow so the banks can be seen and there are several 'meetings of waters'.

Road Road journeys are best done in the dry season, the 2nd half of the year.

Guajará Mirim *p607*
Bus From **Porto Velho** to Guajará Mirim, 5-6 hrs, 6 daily from 0630, fastest at midday, US$22.

Guajará Mirim/Guayaramerín *p607*
Boat Speedboat across the Rio Mamoré (border with Bolivia), US$2 (more at night), 5-min crossing, operates all day, tickets at the waterside; ferry crossing for vehicles, T3541 3811, Mon-Sat 0800-1200, Mon-Fri |1400-1600, 20-min crossing.

Rio Branco *p607*
Air Plácido de Castro, BR-364, Km 18 Sena Madureira, T3211 1003; taxi to centre US$28, or take any bus marked 'Custódio Freire' (US$1) to the urban bus terminal in the city centre. Buses also run to the *rodoviária*. GOL, TAM and TRIP fly to Rio Branco: daily flights to **Campo Grande** and **Cuiabá** (with immediate onward connections to São Paulo, Foz do Iguaçu), to **Cruzeiro do Sul**, **Manaus**, **Porto Velho** and **Tabatinga**.

Bus *Rodoviária* on Av Uirapuru, Cidade Nova, 2° distrito (east bank), T3224 6984, 5 km from centre; city bus 'Norte-Sul' to the centre. Taxi drivers will change money, poor rates. To **Porto Velho**, Viação Rondônia, see above. To **Guajará Mirim**, daily with **Rondônia** at 1130 and 2200, 5-6 hrs, US$20; or take Inácio's Tur shopping trip, 3 per week. From Rio Branco the BR-364 continues west (in principle) to Cruzeiro do Sul and Japim, with a view to reaching the Peruvian frontier further west when completed.

Car Prices for car rentals with the nationwide agencies are higher in Acre than in other states.

Border with Bolivia and Peru *p 608*
At least 4 buses daily with **Real Norte** (US$15) and numerous combi vans (taxi lotação from Calçadão da Gameleira, Segundo district, Rio Branco) to **Brasiléia** and **Epitaciolândia**, whose *rodoviária* is 100 m from the Brazilian border post. Onward transport from Cobija to La Paz (1490 km) only May-Nov, but regular flights to La Paz, Santa Cruz and Trinidad. Three daily buses and numerous shared combi vans (also from Calçadão da Gameleira, US$37) to **Assis Brasil** with Real Norte (4-5 hrs, US$31), and one daily direct bus to **Puerto Maldonado** (8-10 hrs) with **Móvil Tours** (US$40), for direct connections to Cuzco.

⚙ Directory

Porto Velho *p606*
Banks Banks open in the morning only. Marco Aurélio Câmbio, R José de Alencar 3353, T9984 0025, efficient, good rates, Mon-Fri 0900-1500. Parmetal, R Joaquim Nabuco 2265, cash only, good rates, Mon-Fri 0730-1800, Sat 0730-1300. Exchange available at airport (ask tourist office if no one about). It is difficult elsewhere in Rondônia. **Medical services** Hospital Central, R Júlio de Castilho 149, 24 hr emergencies.

Rio Branco *p607*
Useful addresses Polícia Federal, R Floriano Peixoto 874, Centro, T3212 1200. State HQ.

Brasília, Goiás and Tocantins

The Centre West is the frontier where the Amazon meets the central plateau. It is also Brazil's frontier with its Spanish American neighbours. Lastly, it contains the border between the expansion of agriculture and the untouched forests and savannahs. On this region's eastern edge is Brasília, the symbol of the nation's commitment to its empty centre. Although not generally viewed as a tourist attraction, Brasília is interesting as a city of pure invention along the lines of Australia's Canberra and Washington in the United States. Its central position makes it a natural crossroads for visiting the north and interior of Brazil and, when passing through, it is well worth undertaking a city tour to view its innovative modern design.

Goiás is quite a mixture: colonial mining towns, a modern state capital and centres which owe their existence to rapidly expanding agro-industry. There are two fine national parks, Emas and Chapada dos Veadeiros. Pirenópolis is a beautifully restored colonial town surrounded by natural attractions and lively with weekenders from Brasília. An interesting festival, with processions on horseback, is held here during May/June. The former state capital, Cidade de Goiás, also has fine plazas, churches and museums. See also www.goiasturismo.go.gov.br and www.cidadeshistoricasgoias.com.br.

In Tocantins, Brazil's newest state, the incomprehensibly-planned capital of Palmas provides access to the fantastic hinterland of Jalapão, fast-becoming popular with Brazilians but as yet little visited by foreigners. Information from www.turismo.to.gov.br.

Brasília → *Phone code: 061. Post code: 7000. Colour map 7, A3. Population: 2.1 million (2000).*

Arriving in Brasília

Orientation The Eixo Monumental divides the city into Asa Sul and Asa Norte (north and south wings) and the Eixo Rodoviário divides it east and west. Buildings are numbered according to their relation to them. For example, 116 Sul and 116 Norte are at the extreme opposite ends of the city. The 100s and 300s lie west of the Eixo and the 200s and 400s to the east; Quadras 302, 102, 202 and 402 are nearest the centre and 316, 116, 216 and 416 mark the end of the Plano Piloto. Residential areas are made up of six-storey apartment blocks, called 'Super-Quadras'. All Quadras are separated by feeder roads, along which are the local shops. There are also schools, parks and cinemas in the spaces between the Quadras (especially in Asa Sul). The main shopping areas, with more cinemas, restaurants, etc, are situated on either side of the city bus station (*rodoviária*). The private residential areas are west of the Super-Quadras, and on the other side of the lake. At right angles to these residential areas is the 'arrow', the 8-km-long, 250-m-wide **Eixo Monumental**. The main north-south road (Eixo Rodoviário), in which fast-moving traffic is segregated, follows the curve of the bow; the radial road is along the line of the arrow – intersections are avoided by means of underpasses and cloverleaves. Motor and pedestrian traffic is segregated in residential areas. A Metrô has been built from the centre to the southwestern suburbs. The Park Shopping station serves the new interstate *rodoviária*. The Metrô is being extended. It is worth telephoning addresses away from the centre to ask how to get there. ▶▶ *See also Transport, page 625.*

Climate The climate is mild and the humidity refreshingly low, but overpowering in dry weather. The noonday sun beats hard, but summer brings heavy rains and the air is usually cool by night. Altitude: 1171 m.

Tourist offices Setur ① *Centro de Convenções, 3rd floor, T3214 2767*, helpful, English-speaking staff, good map of the city. There are branches at the Rodoviária Interestadual and at the airport; they will book hotels and have maps of the city, but have more limited information. For national tourism entities, see Tourist information in Essentials A-Z, page 362. See also www.aboutbrasilia.com. **Maps** Detailed street maps of the city are impossible to find. Newsagents and the airport sell a map showing the Quadras. Otherwise, see **Setur**'s map.

Background

The purpose-built federal capital of Brazil succeeded Rio de Janeiro (as required by the Constitution) on 21 April 1960. The creation of an inland capital had been urged since the beginning of the 19th century, but it was finally brought into being after President Kubitschek came to power in 1956, when a competition for the best general plan was won by Professor Lúcio Costa, who laid out the city in the shape of a bent bow and arrow. (It is also described as a bird, or aeroplane in flight.) Only light industry is allowed in the city and its population was limited to 500,000; this has been exceeded and more people live in a number of shanty towns, with minimal services, located well away from the main city, which is now a UNESCO World Heritage Site. Brasília is on undulating ground in the unpopulated uplands of Goiás, in the heart of the undeveloped Sertão. The official name for central Brasília is the Plano Piloto.

Places in and around Brasília

At the tip of the arrow is the **Praça dos Três Poderes**, with the Congress buildings, the Palácio do Planalto (the President's office), the Supremo Tribunal Federal opposite it and the Ministério da Justiça and Palácio Itamaraty respectively below them. Nineteen tall Ministry buildings line the Esplanada dos Ministérios, west of the Praça, culminating in two towers linked by a

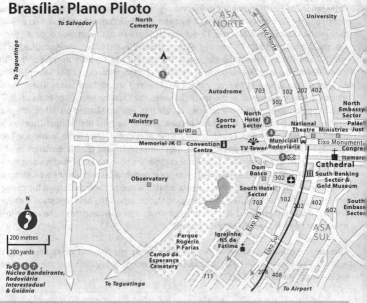

Brasília: Plano Piloto

walkway to form the letter H, representing Humanity. They are 28 storeys high: no taller buildings are allowed in Brasília. Where the bow and arrow intersect is the city bus terminal (Rodoviária Municipal, or do Plano Piloto), with the cultural and recreational centres and commercial and financial areas on either side. There is a sequence of zones westward along the shaft of the arrow; a hotel centre, a radio city, an area for fairs and circuses, a centre for sports, the **Praça Municipal** (with the municipal offices in the Palácio do Buriti) and, lastly (where the nock of the arrow would be), the old combined bus and railway station (rodoferroviária – now closed) with the industrial area nearby. Other than the Santuário Dom Bosco and the JK bridge, the most impressive buildings are all by Oscar Niemeyer.

The **Palácio da Alvorada**, the President's official residence (not open to visitors), is on the lakeshore. The 80-km drive along the road round the lake to the dam is attractive. There are spectacular falls below the dam in the rainy season. Between the Praça dos Três Poderes and the lake are sites for various recreations, including golf, fishing and yacht clubs, and an acoustic shell for shows in the open air. The airport is at the eastern end of the lake. Some 395 ha between the lake and the northern residential area (Asa Norte) are reserved for the Universidade de Brasília, founded in 1961. South of the university area, the Av das Nações runs from the Palácio da Alvorada along the lake to join the road from the airport to the centre. Along it are found all the principal embassies. Also in this area is the attractive vice-presidential residence, the **Palácio do Jaburu** (not open to visitors). This area is very scenic.

A fine initial view of the city may be had from the **television tower**① *West Eixo Monumental, Mon 1400 2000, Tue-Sun 0800-2000*, which has a free observation platform at 75 m; also bar and souvenir shop. If the TV tower is closed, the nearby Alvorada hotel has a panoramic terrace on the 12th floor (lift to 11th only): ask at reception. A good and cheap way of seeing Brasília is by taking a bus from the municipal *rodoviária* at the centre: the destinations are clearly marked.

Lago Do
Paranoá

Palácio da
Alvorada

Palácio do
Jaburu

Palácio do
Planalto

Praça
os Três
oderes

Avenida das Nações

The circular bus routes 106, 108 and 131 go round the city's perimeter. If you go around the lake by bus, you must change at the Paranoá dam; to or from Paranoá Norte take bus 101, 'Rodoviária', and to and from Sul, bus 100, bypassing the airport. Tours 1300-1700, start from the downtown hotel area and municipal *rodoviária* (US$12-20). Many hotels arrange city tours (see also Tour operators). Some buildings are open 1000-1400 Saturday-Sunday, with guided tours in English, well worth it.

Praça dos Três Poderes: **Congress** ① *Mon-Fri 0930-1200, 1430-1630 (take your passport), guides free of charge (in English 1400-1700)*. Visitors may attend debates when Congress is in session (Friday morning). Excellent city views from the 10th floor in Annex 3. The **Palácio do Planalto** ① *Sun 0930-1330, 30-min tours*, may also be visited. The guard is changed ceremonially at the Palácio do Planalto on Friday at 1730. Opposite the Planalto is the Supreme Court building, **Supremo Tribunal Federal. Espaço Lúcio Costa** ① *Tue-Sun 0900-1800, free*, contains a model of Plano Piloto, sketches and autographs of the designer's concepts and gives the ideological background to the planning of Brasília. (Town clothes (not shorts or minis) should be worn when visiting all these buildings.) The **Museu Histórico de Brasília** ① *Tue-Sun and holidays 0900-1800*, is really a hollow monument, with tablets, photos and videos telling the story of the city. The sculpture 'Os Candangos' in front of the Planalto is a symbol of the city. By Bruno Giorgi, it pays homage to the candangos, or pioneer workers who built Brasília on empty ground. The marvellous building of the Ministry of Foreign Affairs, the **Itamarati** ① *guided visits Mon, Wed, Fri 1500-1700, free*, has modern paintings and furniture and beautiful water gardens. Opposite the Itamarati is the **Palácio da Justiça** ① *Mon-Fri 0900-1200, 1500-1700*, with artificial cascades between its concrete columns. The **Panteão Tancredo Neves** is a 'temple of freedom and democracy', built 1985-1986 by Niemeyer. It includes an impressive homage to Tiradentes, the precursor of Brazilian independence.

Niemeyer's **Procuradaria Geral da República**, comprising two glass cylinders, one suspended from a concrete cog, opened in 2002. The **Museu Nacional de Brasília**, on the Conjunto Cultural da República (next to the cathedral), and the adjacent **Biblioteca Nacional** are the last grand projects Niemeyer designed for the capital. The former is particularly impressive, a huge dome of white concrete, blank but for a door halfway up, sitting in a shallow pool of water which reflects it like a mirror. This door is reached by a long sinuous ramp. Inside is a 700-seat auditorium and state-of-the-art galleries.

The **Catedral Metropolitana** ① *0800-1930, T3224 4073*, on the Esplanada dos Ministérios, is a spectacular circular building in the shape of the crown of thorns. Three aluminium angels, suspended from the airy, domed, stained-glass ceiling, are by the sculptor Alfredo Ceschiatti, who also made the five life-sized bronze apostles outside. The baptistery, a concrete representation of the Host beside the cathedral, is connected to the main building by a tunnel (open Sundays only). The outdoor carillon was a gift from the Spanish government: the bells are named after Columbus's ships.

South of the TV tower on Avenida W3 Sul, at Quadra 702, is the Sanctuary of **Dom Bosco** ① *T3223 6542, 0800-1800*, a modernist cube with tall gothic arches filled with stained glass that shades light to dark blue and indigo as it ascends. It is especially striking in late afternoon when shafts of light penetrate the building.

The **Templo da Boa Vontade** ① *Setor Garagem Sul 915, lotes 75/76, T3245 1070, www.tbv. com.br, 24 hrs, getting there: take bus 151 from outside the Centro do Convenções or on Eixo Sul to Centro Médico*. This is a seven-faced pyramid topped by one of the world's largest crystals, a peaceful place dedicated to all philosophies and religions.

A permanent memorial to Juscelino Kubitschek, the '**Memorial JK**' ① *daily 0900-1800, US$1.50*, contains his tomb and his car, together with a lecture hall and exhibits. It has toilets and a lanchonete. The **Monumental Parade Stand** has unique and mysterious acoustic characteristics (the complex is north of the Eixo Monumental, between the 'Memorial JK' and the rodoferroviária). There are remarkable stained glass panels, each representing a state of the Federation, on the ground floor of the Caixa Econômica Federal.

Some 15 km out along the Belo Horizonte road is the small wooden house, known as '**O Catetinho**', in which President Kubitschek stayed in the late 1950s during his visits to the city when it was under construction; it is open to visitors and most interesting. Northwest of Brasília, but only 15 minutes by car from the centre, is the 30,000-ha **Parque Nacional de Brasília** ① *entrance at Rodovia BR 450 Via EPIA; contact the park's office, Rodovia DF 003, Km 8.5, T3233 4553, US$7.15*. Founded in 1961 to conserve the flora and fauna of the Federal Capital, only a portion of the park is open to the public without a permit. There is a swimming pool fed by clear river water, a snack bar and a series of trails through gallery forest (popular with joggers in the early morning and at weekends). The rest of the park is grassland, gallery forest and cerrado vegetation. Large mammals include tapir, maned wolf and pampas deer; birdwatching is good.

For hotel and restaurant price codes, and other relevant information, see Essentials.

● Where to stay

Brasília *p611, map p612*

The best area is the northern hotel zone which has shops and restaurants nearby. Weekend discounts of 30% are often available but must be requested. Most cheap accommodation is in Núcleo Bandeirante, reasonably close to both the Rodoviária Interestadual and the Airport. It can be reached by city bus from either (see Transport, below). The area is reported safe and has a number of economical hotels along Av Central, with more upmarket options on 3ra Av. The tourist office has a list of places to stay.

Asa Norte

$$$$ Kubitschek Plaza, Qd 2, bloco E, T3329 3333, www.kubitschek.com.br. Popular business hotel with modern rooms and excellent facilties; pool, sauna and gym. Sister hotel, the Manhattan Plaza (same website) next door is very similar.

$$$$ Royal Tulip Alvorada, Trecho 1, Lt 1-B, Bl C (Lagoa Norte), T3424 7000, www.royal tulipbrasiliaalvorada.com. The city's newest, most luxurious business hotel, with rooms in a giant red horseshoe overlooking the lake, an enormous pool and excellent, comprehensive business facilities.

$$$ Aristus, Qd 2, bloco O, T3328 8675, www. aristushotel.com.br. Delightfully dated but smart 70s block with simple rooms and breakfast.

$$$ Bittar Inn, Qd 2, bloco N, T3704 3010, www.hoteisbittar.com.br. Simple rooms, a bit cramped, at the cheaper end of this chain's hotels, good value for the area.

$$$ Casablanca, Qd 3, bloco A, T3328 8586, www.casablancabrasilia.com.br. Another 1970s delight; more intimate than most in the area, but some noisy rooms.

$$$-$$ El Pilar, Qd 3, bloco F, T3533 5900, www.elpilar.com.br. Plain, freshly painted, with fan. Avoid rooms below street level as they collect car fumes.

$$-$ Albergue da Juventude de Brasília, Setor Recreativo Parque Norte (SRPN), Qd 02, Lt 02, T3343 0531, www.brasiliahostel. com.br. Cheaper for HI members, dorms and double rooms (**$$**), also cheaper Jan-Feb. Kitchen, laundry, cyber-café, in same grounds as Camping de Brasília. Take bus 143 from municipal *rodoviária*.

Asa Sul

$$$$ Nacional, Qd 1, bloco A, T3321 7575, www.hotelnacional.com.br. Cavernous, frayed old-fashioned and a city landmark with many tour agencies outside.

Núcleo Bandeirante

$$$ Potiguar, 3ra Av, Bl 518, Lt 566, T3552 3032, hotelpotiguar@brturbo.com.br. Ample rooms, cheaper without a/c, frigobar, good breakfast, helpful owner.

$$ El Salvador, Av Central, Lt 605, next to Banco do Brasil, T3386 0021, www. hotelelsalvador.com.br. Functional rooms, cheaper without a/c, breakfast.

$$ Olinda, Av Central, Lts 380/510, above supermarket, Núcleo Bandeirante, T3552 4115. Simple, basic rooms, cheaper without a/c, frigobar, breakfast, rundown but still the best economy option in the area.

● Restaurants

Brasília *p611, map p612*

At weekends, few restaurants in central Brasília are open. Plenty of choice of restaurants in all brackets in the Pier 21 entertainment mall on the lake shore. Other cheaper options along R 405/406. Snack bars can be found all over the city. Places serving *prato feito* or *comercial* can be found all over the city, especially on Av W3 and in the Setor Comercial Sul. Other good bets are the Conjunto Nacional and the Conjunto Venâncio, 2 shopping/office complexes on either side of the municipal *rodoviária*, and

Shopping Brasília, below the southern hotel zone, and Patio Brasília, below the northern. Both have a wide range of boutiques and fast food restaurants. Tropical fruit flavour ice cream can be found in various parlours, eg Av W3 Norte 302. Freshly made fruit juices in all bars.

Asa Norte

All of the large hotels in this area have upmarket restaurants, most catering to business visitors.

$$$ Trattoria da Rosario, SHIS QI 17, bloco H, Loja 215, Lago Sul, Fashion Park, T3248 1672, closed Mon, lunch only on Sun. Northern Italian food and excellent Uruguayan lamb.

$$$ Universal Diner, SCLS 210, bloco B, loja 30, T3443 2089, www.universaldiner. com.br. Lunch only on Sun. One of the city's best contemporary restaurants with strong Asian influences.

$$ Boa Saúde, Av W3 Norte, Qd 702, Edif Brasília Rádio Center. Sun-Fri 0800-2000. Respectable vegetarian with a range of salads, quiches and pies.

$$ Bom Demais, Av W3 Norte, Qd 706. Comfortable, serving fish, beef and rice, etc, live music at weekends.

The municipal *rodoviária* sells the best coffee and pastries in town (bottom departure level).

Asa Sul

There are many cheap places on Av W3 Sul, eg at blocos 502 and 506. Good mid-range options around Av Anhanguera between Tocantins and Goiás and especially around Praça Tamandaré and Av República Líbano.

$$$ La Chaumière, Av W3 Sul, Qd 408, bloco A, loja 13, T3242 7599, www.lachaumiere. com. br; lunch only Sun. The city's favourite French cooking in classical surroundings.

$$$ Le Français, Av W3 Sul, Qd 404, bloco B, loja 27, T3225 4583. French food served in bistro atmosphere, classic and modern dishes.

$$$ O Convento, SHIS, QI 9, conjunto 9, casa 4, T3248 1211. The best for regional and Brazilian cuisine in a mock farmhouse dining room decorated with antiques and arts and crafts.

$$$ Piantella, SCLS 202, bloco A, loja 34, T3224 9408, www.piantella.com.br. A favourite of senior politicians, vast menu combining *feijoada*, Italian food, steaks and seafood, good wines, too.

$$ Oca da Tribo, SCES Trecho 2 m opposite Agenpol, T3226 9880. Wholefood restaurant with vegetarian options and others, good buffet lunch.

$$ Vercelli, SCLS 410, bloco D, loja 34, T3443 0100. Lunch only. Pizzas, pastas and a great deal more on a huge menu.

$ Naturama, SCLS 102, bloco B, loja 9, T3225 5125. Vegetarian and wholefood dishes, lunchtime.

🎵 Bars and clubs

Brasília *p611, map p612*

Arena Café, CA 7, bloco F1, loja 33, T3468 1141. Popular gay bar with DJs from Thu to Sat.

Bar Brasília, SHC/S CR, Qd 506, bloco A, loja 15, parte A, T3443 4323. Little boteco with 1950s decor, draught beer and wooden tables. Lively after 1900, especially Fri.

Bier Fass, SHIS Q 5, bloco E, loja 52/53, T3248 1519. Cavernous bar/restaurant with live music Tue-Sun and 20/30s crowd. Happy hour from 1800.

Café Cancun, Shopping Liberty Mall, SCN, Qd 3, bloco D, loja 52, T3327 1566. Tacky Mexican restaurant by day and teen and 20-something beautiful people club after dark.

Clube de Choro, SDC, Qd 3, bloco G, T3327 0494. Wed-Sat, one of the best clubs in the country devoted to the music which gave rise to samba. Top names from all over Brazil as well as the city itself. Great atmosphere. Tickets sold 9 days in advance.

Frei Caneca, Brasília Shopping, SCN, Qd 5, bloco A, lojas 82s/94s, T3327 0202. Similar to Café Cancun. Dreadful 'flashback' night on Thu, most interesting at weekends.

Gates Pub, Av W3 Sul 403, T3225 4576, www. gatespub.com.br. Great for forró dancing and live music with a young, middle class crowd.

UK Brasil Pub, SCLS 411, bloco B, loja 28, T3346 5214. Some of the best live bands in the city play here. Guinness, sandwiches, all ages.

● Entertainment

Brasília *p611, map p612*
Information about entertainment, etc is available in 2 daily papers, *Jornal de Brasília* and *Correio Brasiliense*. Any student card (provided it has a photograph) will get you into the cinema/ theatre/concert hall for half price.
Cinema Pier 21, SCSS, Trecho 2, Cj 32/33, is an enormous complex with 13 cinema screens, nightclubs, restaurants, video bars and children's theme park.
Theatre There are 3 auditoria of the **Teatro Nacional**, Setor Cultural Norte, Via N 2, next to the bus station, T3325 6109, foyer open 0900-2000, box office open at 1400; the building is in the shape of an Aztec pyramid. The Federal District authorities have 2 theatres, the **Galpão** and **Galpãozinho**, between Quadra 308 Sul and Av W3 Sul. There are several other concert halls.

○ Shopping

Brasília *p611, map p612*
Handicrafts Artíndia, SRTVS, Qd 702, also in the *rodoviária* and at the airport. For Amerindian handicrafts. **Feira hippy** at the base of the TV tower Sat, Sun and holidays. Leather goods, wood carvings, jewellery, bronzes. **Galeria dos Estados**, which runs underneath the eixo from Setor Comercial Sul to Setor Bancário Sul, 10 mins' walk from municipal *rodoviária*, south along Eixo Rodoviário Sul. For handicrafts from all the Brazilian states.

● What to do

Brasília *p611, map p612*
Many tour operators have their offices in the shopping arcade of the Hotel Nacional.
City tours (3-4 hrs) with English commentary can also be booked at the airport by arriving air passengers – a convenient way of getting to your hotel if you have heavy baggage. Some tours have been criticized as too short, others that the guides speak poor English, and for night-time tours, the flood lighting is inadequate on many buildings.
Presmic Turismo, SIA trecho 03, lotes 625/695, Shopping SIA, sala 208C, T3225 0155, www. presmic.com.br. Full-, half-day and night-time city tours (0845, 1400 and 1930 respectively).

● Transport

Brasília *p611, map p612*
Air Airport, 12 km from centre, T3364 9000. Frequent daily flights to **Rio** and **São Paulo** (1½ hrs in both cases) to main cities. From the airport, take Ônibus Executivo to Esplanada dos Ministérios, Rodoviária do Plano Piloto (not the Interestadual), Setores Hoteleiros Norte e Sul, and back to airport every 20 mins 0630-2300, US$5, T3344 2769, www.tcb. df.gov.br. To Núcleo Bandeirante, take bus Nos 129 or 73.1 (small bus) to Candanga, then change to No 80.1, total fare US$2, about 1 hr but allow plenty of extra time; to Rodoviária Interestadual, to Candanga (as above) then take any bus to Park Shopping, or take bus 011 to Metrô station 114 S, then train to Park Shopping station. Taxis: US$18 to Núcleo Bandeirante or Rodoviária Interestadual, US$20 to Rodoviária Municipal, US$23 to hotel sectors.
Bus The terminal, **Rodoviária Interestadual** (or Nova) is southwest of the city opposite Park Shopping. The **Rodoviária Municipal do Plano Piloto** in the centre serves regional destinations in DF and some parts of Goiás; many city buses also stop here. Both *rodoviárias* are on the Metrô, fare between them US$1.75, station for Rodoviária Interestadual is called "Park Shopping". Rodoviária Interestadual to Núcleo Bandeirante: walk first to the Metrô station, then over the large pedestrian overpass toward Park Shopping, then down to the main road where buses stop, No 092 (runs on 3a Av in Núcleo Bandeirante), fare US$1.20, about 30 min but allow plenty of extra time. Taxi fare US$15. From Núcleo Bandeirante to the Rodoviária Municipal, take bus No 160,

which runs on Av Central. If travelling by city us always allow plenty of time as traffic can cause long delays.

To **Rio**: 17 hrs, US$85-90. To **São Paulo**, 16 hrs, US$75-85. To **Belo Horizonte**: 12 hrs, US$59. To **Belém** 36 hrs, with **Transbrasiliana**, US$160. To **Salvador**: 24 hrs, 2 daily, US$93. To **Cuiabá** 17½ hrs, US$70 daily with São Luis. For **Mato Grosso**: generally Goiânia seems to be the better place for buses. All major destinations served. Bus tickets for major companies sold at the city *rodoviária*.
Metro The Metrô, www.metro.df.gov.br, runs from the Central station to the southwest suburbs of Ceilândia and Samambaia and is being extended in each case. A northern line is under construction, as will be an urban light railway linking the airport with the Northern Terminal. A single ticket is US$1.75, but multiple-use smart cards are available. Trains run 0600-2330, 0700-1900 on Sun and holidays.

❶ Directory

Brasília *p611, map p612*
Banks Banco 24 Horas at airport, and all over the city, including at central banks. Good exchange rates at Hotel Nacional and hotels with 'exchange-turismo' sign. **Car hire** All large companies at the airport and the Car Rental Sector. Multinational agencies and Interlocadora, airport, T0800-138000. Unidas, T2365 2266 at airport, Mon-Fri 0800-1800.
Embassies and consulates For all foreign embassies and consulates in Brasília, see http://embassy.goabroad.com.

Goiás

Goiânia ➜ *Phone code: 062. Colour map 4, A1. Population: 1.3 million.*
The state capital is a friendly city with all services and good air and road links to the rest of the country. It has few attractions of its own but provides access to several outstanding areas in the state of Goiás. It is a spacious city, founded in 1933, with well-lit main avenues radiating out from the central **Praça Cívica**, on which stand the Government Palace and main Post office. The city conserves many art-deco buildings dating to the 1930s. Goiânia has more parks and gardens than any other of Brazil's large cities and many are filled with interesting forest and cerrado plants, as well as marmosets and remarkably large numbers of birds. It has the second-highest proportion of green areas of any city in the world and the goal is one tree for each resident. **Bosque dos Buritis**, three blocks east of the Praça Cívica, is pleasant for a stroll, daily 0700-2000. **Tourist office**: There are **Centros de Atendimento ao Turista** (CAT) at the *rodoviária* ① *near food court, T3524 7261, Mon-Sat 1000-2130, Sun 1100-1900*, and airport ① *T3524 5060, daily 0700-2300*, but none in town. The Prefeitura's website is www.goiania.go.gov.br.

The **Memorial do Cerrado Museum** ① *Campus II da Universidade Católica de Goiás, Parque Atheneu, T3946 1723, US$7, Mon-Sat 0700-1930, Sun 0800-1200, 1300-1700*, just outside the city, provides an interesting introduction to Cerrado life, with reconstructions of indigenous villages, quilombos and colonial streets as well as planted cerrado vegetation. The **Museu Zoroastro Artiaga** ① *Praça Cívica 13, T3201 4676, Mon-Fri 0800-1800, Sat-Sun 0900-1500, free*, has a small but interesting collection of indigenous and historical objects, fossils and religious items as well as cases depicting indigenous and early settler life in Goiás. **Museu Antropológico da UFG** ① *Praça Universitária, 1 km east of Praça Cívica, T3209 6010, Tue-Fri 0900-1700, free*, houses wide-ranging ethnographic displays on the *indígenas* of the Centre West. The **Museu de Artes de Goiânia** ① *R 6 605, T3524 1190, Tue-Sun 1000-1200, 1300-1700, free*, in the Bosque dos Buritis has a room showcasing the work of a number of local artists including Siron Franco, who is nationally renowned.

Cidade de Goiás ➔ *Phone code: 062. Colour map 1, C5. Population: 24,000.*

This delightful town, nestled amid cerrado-covered ridges, is one of Central Brazil's hidden gems. Its cobbled streets lined with Portuguese whitewash and brilliant yellow and blue façades and elegantly simple baroque churches have been awarded UNESCO World Heritage status. The town was founded in 1727 as Araial de Santana, later renamed Vila Boa de Goyaz, then Cidade de Goiás. Like its Minas counterparts it became rich on gold, before becoming the capital of Goiás state, which it remained until just before the Second World War. The **tourist office** ① *R Moretti Foggia near the river, T3371 7714, catcidadedegoias@hotmail.com, Mon-Fri 0800-1800, Sat-Sun 0900-1730, Portuguese only,* has knowledgeable, helpful staff. Most churches are closed on Monday.

The most interesting streets in the colonial part of town spread out from the two principal plazas, Praça Brasil Caiado and, immediately below it towards the river, Praça do Coreto. The former is dominated by a lavish baroque fountain which once supplied all the town's water, while on the latter is the imposing **Catedral de Santana** (or Igreja Matriz) ① *Mon-Sat 0700-1100, 1300-1700, free,* built in 1743. The church of **São Francisco de Paula** (1763) ① *Praça Zacheu Alves de Castro, Mon-Fri 1300 1700, Sat-Sun 0900-1200,* sits on a platform overlooking the market and the Rio Vermelho. It has a beautiful 19th-century painted ceiling by André Antônio da Conceição, depicting the life of St Francis. **Nossa Senhora da Abadia** ① *R Abadia s/n, Tue-Sun 0900-1300,* has a similarly understated but impressive painted ceiling, whilst the other 18th-century churches like **Nossa Senhora do Carmo** ① *R do Carmo, on the riverside, Tue-Fri 1300 1700, Sat Sun morning only,* and **Santa Bárbara** ① *R Passo da Pátria, open only during festa in early Dec,* are even simpler. The latter sits on a hill a kilometre or so east of the town affords wonderful sunset views. The **Museu das Bandeiras** ① *Praça Brasil Caiado/Largo do Chafariz, T3371 1087, Tue-Sat 0900-1700, Sun 0900-1400, US$1.75,* was once the centre of local government. Its rooms, furnished with period pieces, sit over a small but forbidding dungeon. Also on Praça Brasil Caiado is the **Museu Quartel do Vinte** ① *US$1.75, Mon-Fri 0800-1800,* a beautiful 18th-century former barracks. The old governor's palace, the **Palacio Conde dos Arcos** ① *Praça do Coreto, T3371 1200, Tue-Sat 0800-1700, Sun 0900-1300, US$1.75,* has a display of 19th-century furniture and plaques describing the town's life in colonial times. The **Museu de Artes Sacras** ① *Igreja da Boa Morte, Praça do Coreto, T3371 1207, Tue-Fri 0800-1700, Sat-Sun 0900-1300, US$1.75,* houses some 18th-century church silverware and a series of painted wooden statues by one of Brazil's most important religious sculptors, José Joaquim da Veiga Valle. A stroll from the Praça do Coreto, downhill and across the river will bring you to the **Museu Casa de Cora Coralina** ① *R do Cândido 20, T3371 1990, Tue-Sat 0900-1645, Sun 0900-1500, US$3, no photography allowed,* the former home of Goiás's most respected writer, with a collection of her belongings. The staff here are extremely helpful and knowledgeable about the city, though they speak only Portuguese. The 18th-century **Mercado Municipal**, next to the old *rodoviária*, 500 m west of the central Praça do Coreto, is a wonderful spot for cheap lunches, breakfasts and photography. Little artisan shops are springing up all over the town.

Pirenópolis ➔ *Colour map 1, C5. Phone code: 062. Population: 23,000. Altitude: 770 m.*

This lovely colonial silver mining town, 150 km due west of Brasília, has a well-preserved centre. It's almost as pretty as Cidade de Goiás and is a National Heritage Site. The city is the nation's unofficial silver capital and is a good place to stock up on presents. It's also a favourite weekend haunt for the capital's middle classes who congregate in the lively restaurants and bars which line the northern end of Rua do Rosário. One of Brazil's most unusual and vibrant festivals takes place here every May/June (see page 624) and at weekends the Praça Central fills with country folk in stetsons and spurs, blasting out Sertanejo music from their souped-up cars. **Tourist office:** Centro de Atendimento ao Turista ① *R do Bonfim 14, Centro Histórico, T3331 2633, daily 0800-1800, Portuguese only, www.pirenopolis.go.gov.br.*

The **Igreja Matriz Nossa Senhora do Rosário** ① *Wed-Sun 0800-1900, US$1.20,* which has been restored after being gutted by a fire in 2002, is the oldest church in the state (1728), but its lavish interior is sadly no more. **Nossa Senhora do Carmo** ① *Wed-Sun 1400-1800,* serves as a museum of religious art. **Museu Família Pompeu** ① *RNova 33, T3331 1102, US$1.20, by appointment only,* displays the best collection of pictures and documents devoted to the history of the city (in Portuguese only). The tiny, private **Museu das Cavalhadas** ① *R Direita 37, daily 0800-1100, 1300-1700, US$1.20,* has a collection of masks and costumes from the Festa do Divino.

The walks and adventure activities in state parks, private reserves and fazendas in the cerrado and hills are as much as a draw as the colonial architecture. The landscape is rugged, with many waterfalls and canyons, birding is good and there is a reasonably healthy population of maned wolf and the various South American cats. **Santuário de Vida Silvestre Vagafogo** ① *6 km from town, T3335 8515, www.vagafogo.com.br, daily 0900-1700, US$9.50; Sat-Sun for brunch (US$21) and adventure sports (US$60); open daily for all activities in Jan and Jun,* 17 ha private reserve of Evandro Engel and family, bathing in the lovely Rio Vagafogo, good birding (200 species), many interesting animals, excellent nature library, local fruits and nuts for sale. Evandro is very knowledgeable, helpful and speaks good English; "a special place". **Mosterio Buddhista** ① *T9643 0452, US$15 plus guide (required),* a simple Zen monastery near eight beautiful cascades on a 3-km path in the heart of pristine cerrado forest. Day visits with light walks or longer term retreats. Particularly magical at sunset. **Parque Estadual Serra dos Pireneus** ① *20 km from town, guide required,* a 2833-ha wilderness area reaching up to 1385 m elevation, offers great views (especially at sunset), walking and climbing, waterfalls and natural pools.

Chapada dos Veadeiros → *Phone code: 062. Entry: free*

This spectacular natural area, about 250 km northeast of Brasília, has eroded mountains drained by countless fast-flowing rivers which rush through deep gorges and plummet over spectacular waterfalls. It was designated a UNESCO World Heritage Site in 2001. The Chapada is covered in cerrado forest, rich in biological diversity. Rare mammals include jaguar, maned wolf, puma, tapir, ocelot and giant anteater; birds feature red shouldered macaw, coal crested finch, helmeted manakin and many king vultures. A 600,000 ha Tombador-Veadeiros biological corridor is being assembled here, encompassing the existing Parque Nacional Chapada dos Veadeiros (65,514 ha), various private reserves including Serra do Tombador (9000 ha), and the **Kalunga ethnic reserve** (262,000 ha), home to several Quilombo communities – the descendants of African slaves who fled to the hinterlands in colonial times.

The main access towns are **Alto Paraíso de Goiás** (altitude 1250 m), closest to Brasília and an alternative lifestyles centre; **São Jorge** (1000 m), a resort village on the park boundary, 36 km west of Alto Paraíso; and **Cavalcante** (825 m), a quiet little place with access to Kalunga, good facilities north of the park and less visited than the others. The most popular attractions are waterfalls, found both inside and outside the national park. The area has a pleasant climate and gets busy at weekends, crowded at major holidays including July. **National park headquarters** ① *1 km outside São Jorge, T3445 1116, www.icmbio.gov.br/parna_veadeiros, Tue-Sun 0800-1200 for entry, trails close 1700, only day-visits permitted.* There are two national park trails, a waterfall circuit (daily limit 250 visitors) and a canyon circuit (limit 200 visitors), entry free but guide required. Guides wait at park headquarters where groups form, they charge US$59 for up to 10 visitors. Guides are not required for most sites outside the park, which are on private land and charge US$6-9 entry per person. A vehicle is an asset but hitching is easy at busy times and some attractions can be reached on foot. Tours throughout the region are offered by operators in Alto Paraíso.

Parque Nacional Emas

ⓘ *US$7. Permission is needed to take photographs, but not to visit, as long as you have a voucher and are accompanied by an authorized guide; apply at least a week in advance. Information from ICMBio, Rod GO 206 Km 27, Caixa postal 115, Chapadão do Céu, GO – CEP75828-000, T064-3929 6000. Tourist office in Mineiros, T064-3661 0006. Day trips are not recommended, but longer visits to the Park can be arranged through agencies (eg Trekking Turismo, Mineiros, T064-3661 2014, www.trekkingturismo.com.br, 4WD, biking and trekking tours in the park and to other attractions, rafting and watersports).*

In the far southwest of the state, covering the watershed of the Araguaia, Taquari and Formoso rivers, is the small Parque Nacional Emas. Access is from Mineiros, 89 km northeast, and Chapadão do Céu, 27 km southeast of the park. Almost 132,868 ha of undulating grasslands and cerrado contain the world's largest concentration of termite mounds. Pampas deer, giant anteater, greater rhea, or 'ema' in Portuguese, and maned wolf are frequently seen roaming the grasses. The park holds the greatest concentration of blue-and-yellow macaws outside Amazônia, and blue-winged, red shouldered and red-bellied macaws can also be seen. (There are many other animals and birds.) Along with the grasslands, the park supports a vast marsh on one side and rich gallery forests on the other. As many of the interesting mammals are nocturnal, a spotlight is a must.

◉ Goiás listings

For hotel and restaurant price codes, and other relevant information, see Essentials.

◉ Where to stay

Goiânia p618

The city is well supplied with hotels, the best hotels being 1 km from the centre in the Setor Oeste. There are several chains including Mercure, Sleep Inn, Best Western and Blue Tree.

$$$$ Address, Av República do Líbano 2526, T3257 1000, www.addresshotel.com. br. Well-equipped business hotel, best in the city, modern rooms with separate living areas, gym, pool, restaurant, bar, good views from the upper floors.

$$$$ Papillon, Av República do Libano 1824, T3608 1500, www.papillonhotel.com.br. Modern rooms and suites, pool, gym, sauna, business facilities, very popular, book ahead.

$$$ Oeste Plaza, 389 Rua 2, Setor Oeste, T3224 5012, www.oesteplaza.com.br. Well-maintained, modern, small rooms, those on higher floors have good views, small pool and gym.

$$$-$$ Goiânia Palace, Av Anhangüera 5195, T3224 4874, www.goianiapalace.com.br. Nicely refurbished art deco building with plenty of character. Good breakfast, French-run, English also spoken, good location and value. Recommended.

$$ Astro, R 68 No 191, T3229 0367, www. astrohotelgoiania.com.br. Simple rooms, cheaper without a/c, electric shower, good breakfast, helpful, family-run, good-value midweek discounts.

$$ Santo Antoninho, R 68 No 41, T3223 1815, www.hotelsantoantoninho.com.br. Small rooms with a/c, cheaper in basic rooms with fan, electric shower, well looked after, includes breakfast, good budget option.

Cidade de Goiás p619

$$$$ Vila Boa, Morro Chapéu do Padre s/n, 1 km southeast of the centre, T3371 1000, www.hotelvilaboa.com.br. The best in town, though inconvenient for the centre, pool, bar, restaurant and good views.

$$$ Casa da Ponte, R Moretti Foggia s/n, T3371 4467, casadapontehotel_@hotmail.com. Art deco building next to bridge across Rio Vermelho, the best rooms overlook the river (cheaper without a/c), nice terrace, parking, mid-week discounts are good value.

$$$ Pousada Goyá, R Sta Barbara 38, T3371 4423. Colonial house set in a little garden with views over the river and Serra, frigobar, good breakfast.

$$ Pousada do Sol, R Americano do Brasil, T3371 1717. Well maintained, fans, central.

$$-$ Pousada Vovó Dú, R 15 Novembro 22, T3372 1224. Simple rooms, some very small (cheaper without a/c), electric shower, basic breakfast, good economy option.

Camping Cachoeira Grande campground, 7 km along the BR-070 to Jussara (near the tiny airport, hard to find). Attractive, well-run, with bathing place and snack bar.

Pirenópolis *p619*

Plenty of places to stay but they fill quickly at holidays. Weekday discounts are usually available. At Festa do Divino (see page 624) it's essential to book ahead or visit from Brasília. Central de Reservas, T3331 3323, www. pirenopolis.com.br, is a hotel booking service.

$$$ Arvoredo, Av Abercio final da R Direita, T3331 3479, www.arvoredo.tur.br. Peaceful, small pool, views over the town. Simple rooms with large beds, hammocks, excellent special rates during the week.

$$$ Casa Grande, R Aurora 41, T3331 1758, www.casagrandepousada.com.br. Chalets and rooms in a tropical garden with a pool set around a large colonial house, Wi-Fi in common areas.

$$$ Pousada O Casarão, R Direita 79, T3331 2662, www.ocasaraopirenopolis.com.br. A converted 1896 town house decorated with antiques, mosquito nets, great breakfast, nice gardens, rooms with a/c, fan and frigobar, lovely place, attentive service. Recommended.

$$$ Pouso do Sô Vigario, R Nova 25, T3331 1206, www.pousadaspirenopolis.com.br. Rooms with a/c and fan, pleasant public areas, good location, decent breakfast in a little garden next to the pool. Same owner runs **Pouso do Frade**, R do Bonfim 37, T3331 1046, same price and facilities.

$$ Recanto da Vila, a 5, across from *rodoviária*, T3331 3162, lulu.siqueira2@hotmail.com. Simple rooms in private home, with fan, electric shower, no breakfast but great *pão de queijo* courtesy of friendly owner, good value.

$$ Rex, Praça da Matriz, T331 1121. In what was the first hotel in town, lots of character, electric shower, parking. Good breakfast and location, helpful owner.

Camping AABB, R Pirineus near Hospital Público, T3331 1106, www.aabbpirenopolis.com. Lawns for tents, toilets, showers and grills, US$15 pp, includes use of pool and sports facilities.

Chapada dos Veadeiros *p620*
Alto Paraíso

Pousadas are scattered around town. Several expensive restaurants on Av Ary Ribeiro Veladão with vegetarian options and organic foods.

$$$ Casa Rosa, R Gumercindo Barbosa 233, T3446 1319, www.pousadacasarosa.com.br. Good rooms, the best in chalets near the pool, nice grounds, discounts mid-week and for long stays.

$$$ Portal da Chapada, 9 km along the road to São Jorge, T3446 1820, www.portaldachapada. com.br. The best choice for birdwatchers, with cabins in the cerrado. Comfortable.

$$$ Recanto da Grande Paz, R de João-de-barro 322, T3446 1452, www.recantodagrande paz.com.br. Small comfortable chalets with porch and hammocks, frigobar, pool, breakfast and cafeteria, massage available.

$$ Pousada do Sol, R Gumercindo Barbosa 911, T3446 1201, www.pousadadosol.org. Small and simple, with a range of rooms, the best with balconies and fridges, nice grounds with fruit trees, good breakfast, good value.

São Jorge

There are some 45 *pousadas* and various campsites in this little village but advance booking is indispensable at holidays. Hotel prices often go up 30% at weekends and food is expensive at all times.

$$$$ Baguá, up the hill on the road to national park, T3455 1046, www.baguapousada.com.br. Gorgeous bungalows, each with its own porch and outdoor jacuzzi, hammocks, fans, lovely ample grounds, all very tasetefully done, a real gem.

$$$$-$$$ Casa das Flores, T3455 1055, www.pousadacasadasflores.com.br. Elegant, tastefully decorated rooms (candle-lit), a/c and fan, hammocks, massage and therapies, sauna, pool, restaurant, great breakfast.

$$$ Bambu, T3455 1004, www.bambu brasil.com.br. Roooms with fan and hammocks, nice grounds, breakfast, restaurant, attentive service.

$$$-$$ Áquas de Março, T9962 2082, www.chapadadosveadeiros.com.br. A range of rooms and prices, older smaller ones are good value, decorations by local artists, pleasant garden, saunas, good breakfast, helpful. Recommended.

$$$-$$ Trilha Violeta, T3455 1088, www.trilhavioleta.com.br. Fan, frigobar, rooms around a bougainvillea filled garden, hammocks, includes breakfast.

$$ Casa Grande, T3446 1388, www.pousada casagrande.com.br. Simple but well looked after, electric shower, fan, breakfast.

Cavalcante

$$$ Aruana, uphill from Praça da Bíblia, T3494 1562, www.aruanacavalcante.com.br. Includes breakfast, rooms with fan and solar hot water, nice common areas, ample grounds, therapies arranged, long-stay discounts.

$$$-$$ Sol da Chapada, 100 m from tourist office at lower end of town, T3494 1372, www.soldachapada.com.br. Comfortable chalets with fan, nice grounds, breakfast and excellent organic restaurant (daily 1300-2000), attentive owner. Recommended.

$$ Pioneiro, at the petrol station on Praça Diogo Cavalcante, T3494 1125. Rooms with a/c, electric shower, helpful, good value but no breakfast.

Parque Nacional Emas *p621*

Mineiros

$$$ Pilões Palace, Praça Alves de Assis, T3661 1547, www.piloeshotel.com.br. Restaurant, comfortable, a/c, fridge.

Other hotels: **$$$ Dallas**, www.dallashotel.com.br, and **$$ América**, R 18, Q 4, Bairra Santa Isabel, T3661 5089. Dorm accommodation at the park headquarters; kitchen and cook available but bring own food.

⑦ Restaurants

Goiânia *p618*

Gioanian specialties include dishes made with *pequi* (a local fruit, careful not to bite the seed which has spines), *guariroba* (a type of palm heart), *pelxe na telha*, and *emapadão* (a savoury pie, best at **Alberto's** and other stalls in the Mercado Central, R 3 No 322). The city has a good range of restaurants and bars, many in the upscale setores Marista and Bueno (see www.curtamais.com.br). Economy options include the **Mercado Central**, and several places near R 55 corner R 68.

$$$ Celson & Cia, R 15 539 at C 22. Very popular Goiás and Mineira meat restaurant with a good cold buffet. Evenings only except at weekends.

$$$ Chão Nativo, Av Rep Líbano 1809, also at Av T11 e T4, Setor Bueno, www.restaurantechaonativo.com.br. The city's most famous Goiânian restaurant also serving local and Mineira food. Lively after 2000 and lunchtime on weekends.

$$$ Piquiras, R 146 No 464, Setor Marista, several other locations, www.piquiras.com. Fine dining with a wide range of Brazilian dishes.

$$$ Walmor, R 3 1062 at R 25-B. Large portions of some of Brazil's best steaks, attractive open-air dining area, best after 2000.

$$$-$$ Pizzaria Cento e Dez, R 3 No 1000, T3225 5070, daily 1100-1400, 1800-2400. Traditional pizzeria and Italian dishes, home delivery.

$$ Bendita Tapioca, Alameda dos Buritis near Palacio Legeslativo. Per kilo lunch and à la carte at night.

$$ Tribo do Açai, R 36 590. Buzzing fruit juice bar with excellent buffet salads and health food.

Cidade de Goiás *p619*
$$$ Dali, R 13 de Maio 26, T3372 1640, Tue-Sun 1200-1330. Riverside restaurant offering a broad range of international and local dishes.
$$$ Flor do Ipê, Praça da Boa Vista 32, T3372 1133, Tue-Sun 1100-1430, 1900-late. The best Goiânian food, enormous variety, buffet lunch and à la carte at night, lovely garden setting. Highly recommended.
$$ O Braseiro, Praça Brasil Caiado 03. In a colonial house, good Goianian specialties, buffet served on a wood stove.
$$-$ Espaço Ouro Fino, Praça do Coreto, lunch only, closed Tue-Wed. Good value for varied Brazilian food.

Pirenópolis *p619*
There are plenty of upmarket options along R do Rosário, serving a surprising range of international food. Many have live music at night (and an undisclosed cover charge – be sure to ask), lively at weekends. For economy, try the cafeteria upstairs in **Casa Melo** supermarket, Av Sizenando Jayme 30, Mon-Sat 1100-1430.
$$$-$$ Deli-Deli, Ruia Barbosa 11. Daily 1230-1700, open later on weekends. Meat and vegetarian options, organic ingredients, international dishes, German-Brazilian run.
$$ Tilapa, R Direita, across from Igreja da Matriz, 1200-1600, closed Wed. Very good buffet with fish specialties, nice fruit juices. Recommended.
Pireneus Café, Praça do Coreto, Mon-Thu 1500-2300, Fri-Sun 0900-0100. Café in a traditional home, also sidewalk seating, pleasant place to watch the world go by.
Sorvetes Naturais, R Nova 16. Daily 0800-2100. Good locally made ice cream.

⊕ Festivals

Goiânia *p618*
Events are listed in www.emgoiania. com. **Goiania Noise** (**Nov-Dec**), www. goianianoisefestival.com.br; and **Bananada**

(**May**) are alternative rock festivals with some international participation.

Cidade de Goiás *p619*
Many festivals here and a very lively arts scene. Three weeks of religious events precede Easter. The streets blaze with torches during the solemn **Fogaréu** procession on the Wed of Holy Week, when hooded figures re-enact Christ's descent from the cross and burial. **Carnaval** is a good deal more joyous and still little known to outsiders.

Pirenópolis *p619*
Festa do Divino Espírito Santo, 50 days after Easter (Pentecost-**May/Jun**), is one of Brazil's most famous and extraordinary folkloric/ religious celebrations. It lasts 3 days, with medieval costumes, tournaments, dances and mock battles between Moors and Christians, a tradition held annually since 1819. The whole city throbs with life.

⊙ Shopping

Goiânia *p618*
Crafts at the **Centro do Artesanato**, R 1 near Praça Cívica; and **Mercado Central**, R 3 No 322.

Cidade de Goiás *p619*
Local ceramics are sold at the tourist information office and next to Igreja do Rosário. Candied fruit is a regional speciality.

Pirenópolis *p619*
There are many jewellers on, R do Rosário. **Craft fair** by Praça do Coreto, Sat evening and Sun daytime. **Municipal craft shop** on R do Bomfim. Many craft shops on R do Rosário and on R Rui Barbosa.

⊙ What to do

Goiânia *p618*
Travel agents in town can arrange day tours. **Ararauna Turismo**, R C-143 No 481, Jardim América, T3932-2277, www.ararauna.tur.br, for city and regional tours.

Cidade de Goiás p619
Serra Dourada Aventura, no fixed office, reachable on T3371 2277 or T9238 5195. Hiking in the Serra Dourada and bespoke trips to the wilds of the Rio Araguaia (with notice). Very good value.

Pirenópolis p619
Cerrado Aventuras, Praça do Coreto 45, T3331 3765, www.cerradoaventuras.com.br. English spoken.
Morro Alto, R Direita 71, T3331 3348, www.morroalto.tur.br. Run by Mauro Cruz.

Chapada dos Veadeiros p620
Most tour operators are in Alto Paraíso, but guides also available in São Jorge, Cavalcante and Engenho II (in the Kalunga Reserve). Prices vary according to season and group number. **Alternativas Ecoturismo**, uphill Av Ary Ribeiro Veladão, T3446 1000, www.alternativas.tur.br. Light adventure activities and treks, run by locals, excellent and really go out of the way to help. English-speaking guides available.
EcoRotas, R das Nascentes 129, T3446 1820, www.ecorotas.com.br. Van-based tours to the principal sights. Suitable for all ages.
Transchapada Ecoturismo, R dos Cristais, T3446 1345, www.transchapada.com.br. Light adventure and visits to the major sights.
Travessia, Av Ary Ribeiro Veladão, T3446 1595, www.travessia.tur.br. Short or long treks, plus adventure sports from one of the country's most respected instructors, Ion David. Little English.

⊙ Transport

Goiânia p618
Air Santa Genoveva, 6 km northeast off Rua 57, T3265 1500. Flights to many state capitals. Taxi to centre US$15, to rodoviária US$12; bus to centre, Linha 258, US$1.50, 30 mins. Note that Setor Aeroporto is a central district nowhere near the airport.
Bus Rodoviária in Araguaia Shopping, Setor Norte Ferroviário, 40-min walk from Praça Cívica (T3240 0000). Taxi to centre US$7.50; many buses to centre (U$1.50) including Linha

002 and 003 along Av Goiás. If arriving from the west, you can get off at the small rodoviaria de Campinas and take the Eixão rapid transit line (U$0.75) to the centre, easier with luggage than a bus from the main rodoviária.

To **Brasília**, 207 km, at least 15 departures a day, 2½ hrs, US$17-24, and **São Paulo**, 900 km via Barretos, US$71-86, 14½ hrs. To **Cidade de Goiás**, 136 km, hourly 0600-1600 with Moreira, direct 1200, 1800, 2000, 2-3 hrs, US$15. **Pirenópolis** with Goianésia, see below. To **Campo Grande**, US$84. To **Porto Velho**, US$160, 36-38 hrs. To **Belo Horizonte**, US$40-70, 13 hrs.

Cidade de Goiás p619
Bus The rodoviária is 1 km out of town. Regular services to **Goiânia** (2½ hrs), **Aruanã**, **Barra do Garças** and **Jussara**. Some buses stop at the old bus station by the market. Ask to get out here. For Pirenópolis, change in Goiânia.

Pirenópolis p619
Bus To/from **Brasília** with Goianésia, 4 a day, US$13, 3 hrs. Same company to **Goiânia** 0915 daily, US$9, 3 hrs, return 1700; or change in Anápolis, frequent service, US$3.25.

Chapada dos Veadeiros p620
Alto Paraíso: to **Brasília** buses pass through around 0740 (to Rodoviária do Plano Piloto), 1330 (to Interestadual), 1600 (to Plano Piloto), US$21, 3-4 hrs, but often delayed. From Brasília some buses (eg Santo Antônio, see São Jorge and Cavalcante below) leave from Rodoviária do Plano Piloto, others from Rodoviária Interestadual. Private shared taxis to Brasília from bakery behind rodoviária leave when full daily 0630-0830, US$24 to either rodoviária, and to other destinations such as the airport. To **São Jorge**, Santo Antônio passes Alto Paraíso around 1630, US$3, 1 hr. To **Cavalcante**, Santo Antônio passes around 1100, US$15, 1½ hrs. To **Palmas** with Real Expresso, 1 daily. **São Jorge**: To **Brasília** (Rodoviária do Plano Piloto) via Alto Paraíso, Santo Antônio passes around 0700, US$24, 6-7 hrs; from Brasília at 1230. **Cavalcante**: To **Brasília** (Rodoviária do Plano

Piloto) via Alto Paraíso, at 1500, US$24, 6-7 hrs; from Brasília at 0700 daily.

Parque Nacional Emas *p621*
Bus Twice weekly from **Mineiros**.
Car 6 hrs' drive from **Campo Grande**, 20 hrs from Goiânia, paved road poor. The road to the park is unpaved.

Directory

Goiânia *p618*
Exchange Daycoval, Av Goiás 971, T3264 8850, Mon-Fri 0830-1700. **Onex**, downstairs at the *rodoviária*, T3922 6263, Mon-Fri 0700-1900, Sat 0700-1200.

Tocantins

To the north of Goiás, and extracted from that state in 1988, is Tocantins, dominated by vast rivers, cerrado forests and, increasingly soya plantations. Early attempts at regional autonomy date from colonial times, but creation of the new state was largely the work of José Wilson Siqueira Campos, who became its first governor. He is prominently featured in many of the state capital's grandiose monuments. Although new to tourism Tocantins has some stunning scenery and is the only state in the country to have Amazonian forest, Pantanal, cerrado forest and sertão.

The greatest draw is **Jalapão**, a Brazilian Outback of vast cerrado-covered plains with massive table top mountains cut by fast-flowing, clear-water rivers and thundering waterfalls. Wind-sculpted dunes form at the base of crumbling sandstone cliffs and plentiful wildlife includes maned wolf, puma, Brazilian merganser, hyacinth- and Spix's-macaw. Here too is the Afro-Brazilian village of Mombuca, whose residents produce unique crafts from *capim dourado*, the golden-sheened flower stalk of an endemic plant. As yet little-known outside Brazil, Jalapão is among the great natural wonders of South America but it is not easy to visit. The closest towns are **Ponte Alta do Tocantins** and **Mateiros**, both have hotels and limited public transport but distances to and between attractions can be over 100 km with no public transport. You must have your own vehicle (carry spare fuel, water and all supplies), or take an excursion from Palmas (see What to do, below) which start around US$1200 per person for three to five days. The area receives a growing number of Brazilian tourists and visitor sites get crowded at major holidays.

In the southeast of Tocantins, 200 km from Palmas along the road to Brasília, is the colonial town of **Natividade**, nestled at the base of the eponymous 500-m-high serra. The town has restored churches and brightly coloured houses set around neat little plazas, a small **Museu Histórico** and a relaxed, authentic atmosphere. Along the western border of the state is **Ilha do Bananal**, the world's largest river island (20,000 sqkm), bounded by the Rios Araguaia and Javaé. The island contains an indigenous reserve in the south and two parks in the north (**Parque Nacional Araguaia** and **Parque Estadual Cantão**) all very rich in birds and other fauna. There are several permanent lakes, marshland areas and seasonally flooded habitats similar to those of the Pantanal. Tours are offered by agencies in Palmas, or you can travel to **Lagoa da Confusão** or **Formoso do Araguaia** and hire guides there (eg **Sra Raimunda**, Lagoa da Confusão, T063-9265 7341; US$325 for an all-inclusive tour).

The capital of Tocantins is **Palmas** (*Phone code: 063; Population: 220,000. Altitude: 250m. Colour map 5, C1; www.palmas.to.gov.br*), a planned city laid out in an utterly incomprehensible mathematical plan on the edge of the dammed and flooded Tocantins river. Brazil's newest state capital can be hot, humid and hard on pedestrians, but sunsets are gorgeous and people very friendly. There are beaches on the Rio Tocantins, 4 km from the centre, and many waterfalls in the Serra de Lajeado reached from Taquaruçu, 32 km from Palmas and busy at weekends. **Tourist offices**: CATUR① *at airport, T3219 3760, daily 1100-1730; and on Av JK corner Theotônio Segurado, Mon-Fri 0800-1800, Sat-Sun 0900-1600, turismo.palmas@gmail.com.*

For hotel and restaurant price codes, and other relevant information, see Essentials.

⦿ Where to stay

Tocantins *p626*
Natividade
$$ Pousada dos Sertões, 1 km from centre on the road to Dianópolis, T3372 1182. Rooms with bath and a/c, cheaper with fan, parking.
$$-$ Pousada do César, downhill from the colonial centre, T9225 8167. Clean simple rooms with bath and a/c, cheaper with fan, breakfast, parking, family run, also has a *churrascaría* nearby.

Palmas
Palmas is well supplied with hotels but cheaper places (many around Quadras 103 Norte and Sul) are often full.
$$$$-$$$ Pousada das Artes, 103 Sul, Av LO-1 No 78, T3219 1500, www.arteshotel.com.br. Very comfortable rooms with marble and mosaic bathrooms, frigobar, small pool, sauna, gym, bar, tasteful decor, good breakfast, other meals available, cash discounts.
$$$ Graciosa Palace, 103 Norte, NO-1 No 19, T3225 8688, www.hotelgraciosa.com.br. Rooms around a small courtyard, breakfast, simple and pleasant.
$$$ Pousada dos Girassóis, 103 Sul, Av NS 1, T3219 4500, www.pousadadosgirassois.com.br. Comfortable rooms, pool, good breakfast, more expensive ones have balconies. 2nd location 3 blocks away, T3212 0200, more modern and expensive, also with pool, gym and restaurant.
$$ Alfredu's, Av JK 103 Sul, Qd 101, lotes 23/24, T3215 3036. Simple rooms around a gardencourtyard, cheaper with fan, breakfast, helpful, good value. Trips arranged.

⦿ Restaurants

Tocantins *p626*
Palmas
Fish specialties are served at river beaches on weekends. For economy options in the centre try kiosks around Av JK corner Theotônio Segurado.
$$ Paço do Pão, 103 Sul, Av JK, T3215 5665, 1900-2400, closed Tue. Wood-oven pizza with home delivery.
$$ Palmas, 103 Sul, Rua SO-01, Lote 43. Daily 1100-1400. Good quality and variety per kilo lunch.
Açaí.com, 103 Norte, Av JK. Daily 1630-2300. Açaí palm fruit in various forms, sidewalk seating, cool and refreshing in the tropical heat.

⦿ What to do

Tocantins *p626*
Most Palmas agencies do not have storefronts, contact in advance by email or phone. **40 Graus no Cerrado**, T3215 8313, www.40grausnocerrado.com.br (Diego Sommer, English and Spanish spoken); **El Dorado**, T3225 4078, www.jalapao-to.com.br; **Ricanato**, Capim Dourado Shopping, T3215 6320, www.ricanato.com.br. Jalapão trips cover a great deal of distance and involve much driving, minimum 4 days recommended.
Korubo Expedicoes, São Paulo T011-4063 1502, www.korubo.com.br. Excellent tours to Jalapão staying in their luxurious purpose-built safari camp, modelled on those in Botswana; whitewater kayaking, trekking, jeep trips and wildlife tours included in the price. Professional,reliable.
Rota da Iguana, Quadra 108 norte, Alameda 02, lote 30, Palmas, T3217 5107, www.rotadaiguana.com.br. Young, enthusiastic and knowledgeable guides offering tours to Jalapão and other Tocantins destinations. Adventure sports and custom itineraries, English, Portuguese and Spanish spoken. 6 years' experience.

⦿ Transport

Tocantins *p626*
Air Airport is 23 km from the centre, taxi US$35 or take 'Eixão' bus from centre and

transfer to Linha 46 which runs hourly, US$2.60 total. Flights to **Brasília**, **Goiânia**, **São Paulo**, **Belo Horizonte** and **Belém**.

Bus *Rodoviária* is very far from centre, taxi US$30, or 'Eixão' and transfer to Linha 23, allow 1-2 hrs. Bus services to Goiânia, São Paulo, Salvador and Belém. To **Brasília** with **Real Express**, daily at 1900, US$55, 12 hrs. The bus passes through **Natividade** at 2200

(US$18.50, US$42 Natividade-Brasília). Several vans run daily to Natividade. Tranbrasiliana passes through Natividade en route to **Goiânia** around 1900, US$48, 12 hrs. Palmas to **Lagoa da Confusão** (for Ilha do Bananal) with **Tocantinense** at 0600 and 1530, US$15, 4 hrs, poor road; also van service daily at 0900, T3215 2111, will pick up from hotel.

The Pantanal

This vast wetland, which covers a staggering 21,000 sq km (the size of Belgium, Portugal, Switzerland and Holland combined), between Cuiabá, Campo Grande and the Bolivian frontier, is one of the world's great wildlife preserves. Parts spill over into Bolivia, Paraguay and Argentina to form an area totalling some 100,000 sq km. Partly flooded in the rainy season (see below), the Pantanal is a mecca for wildlife tourism or fishing. Whether land or river-based, seasonal variations make a great difference to the practicalities of getting there and what you will experience. A road runs across Mato Grosso do Sul via Campo Grande to Porto Esperança and Corumbá, both on the Rio Paraguai; much of the road is across the wetland, offering many sights of birds and other wildlife.

Arriving in the Pantanal

The Pantanal plain slopes some 1 cm in every kilometre north to south and west to east to the basin of the Rio Paraguai and is rimmed by low mountains. One hundred and seventy five rivers flow from these into the Pantanal and after the heavy summer rains they burst their banks, as does the Paraguai itself; to create vast shallow lakes broken by patches of high ground and stands of *cerrado* forest. Plankton then swarm to form a biological soup that contains as many as 500 million microalgae per litre. Millions of amphibians and fish spawn or migrate to consume them. And these in turn are preyed upon by waterbirds and reptiles. Herbivorous mammals graze on the stands of water hyacinth, sedge and savanna grass and at the top of the food chain lie South America's great predators – the jaguar, ocelot, maned wolf and yellow anaconda. In June at the end of the wet when the sheets of water have reduced to small lakes or canals wildlife concentrates and then there is nowhere on earth where you will see such vast quantities of birds or such enormous numbers of crocodilians. Only the plains of Africa can compete for mammals and your chances of seeing a jaguar or one of Brazil's seven other species of wild cat are greater here than anywhere else on the continent. There are over 700 resident and migratory bird species in the Pantanal and birding along the Transpantaneira road in the north or in one of the fazendas in the south can yield as many as 100 species a day; especially between late June and early October. Many species overlap with the Amazon region, the Cerrado and Chaco and the area is particularly rich in waterbirds. Although the Pantanal is often described as an ecosystem in its own right, it is in reality made up of many distinct habitats which in turn have their own, often distinct biological communities. Botanically it is a mosaic, a mixture of elements from the Amazon region including *várzea* and gallery forests and tropical savanna, the *cerrado* of central Brazil and the dry *chaco* of Paraguay.

Only one area is officially a national park, the **Parque Nacional do Pantanal Matogrossense** in the municipality of Poconé, 135,000 ha of land and water, only accessible by air or river.

Obtain permission to visit the park at **ICMBio** ① *R Rubens de Mendonça s/n, Cuiabá, CEP 78055-500, T065-3648 9100*. Hunting in any form is strictly forbidden throughout the Pantanal and is punishable by four years imprisonment. Fishing is allowed with a licence (enquire at travel agents for latest details); it is not permitted in the spawning season or piracema (1 October-1 February in Mato Grosso do Sul, 1 November-1 March in Mato Grosso).

Best time to visit the Pantanal
The Pantanal is good for seeing wildlife year-round. However, the dry season between July and October is the ideal time as animals and birds congregate at the few remaining areas of water. During these months you are very likely to see jaguars. This is the nesting and breeding season, when birds form vast nesting areas, with thousands crowding the trees, creating an almost insupportable cacophony of sounds. The white sand river beaches are exposed, caiman bask in the sun, and capybaras frolic amid the grass. July sees lots of Brazilian visitors who tend to be noisy, decreasing the chances of sightings. From the end of November to the end of March (wettest in February), most of the area, which is crossed by many rivers, floods. At this time mosquitoes abound and cattle crowd on to the few islands remaining above water. In the southern part, many wild animals leave the area, but in the north, which is slightly higher, the animals do not leave.

What to take
Most tours arrange for you to leave your baggage in town, so you need only bring what is necessary for the duration of the tour with you. In winter (June-August), temperatures fall to 10° C, warm clothing and covers or sleeping bag are needed at night. It's very hot and humid during summer and a hat and sun protection, SPF 30 or above, is vital. Wear long sleeves and long trousers and spray clothes as well as skin with insect repellent. Insects are less of a problem July-August. Take insect repellent from home as mosquitoes, especially in the North Pantanal, are becoming immune to local brands. Drinks are not included in the price of packages and tend to be over-priced, so if you are on a tight budget bring your own. Most importantly, make sure you take a pair of binoculars.

Getting there
There are three options for visiting the Pantanal: by tour, through a working ranch (*fazenda*) or by self-drive. Entry into the northern Pantanal comes either via the Transpantaneira road in the north, reached from the city of Cuiabá, which cuts through the wetland and is lined with fazendas, or the town of Barão do Melgaço which is surrounded by large lakes and rivers and is not as good for wildlife. In the south the access points are Campo Grande and Miranda, which offers access to many of the *fazendas*. *Fazendas* in the northern or southern Pantanal can also be booked directly; most now have websites and a tour of them can be taken with a hire car.

Types of tour
Tourist facilities in the Pantanal currently cater to four main categories of visitors. **Sport fishermen** usually stay at one of the numerous speciality lodges scattered throughout the region, which provide guides, boats, bait, ice and other related amenities. Bookings can be made locally or in any of Brazil's major cities. **All-inclusive tours** combining air and ground transportation, accommodation at the most elaborate fazendas, meals, guided river and land tours, can be arranged from abroad or through Brazilian travel agencies. This is the most expensive option. **Moderately priced tours** using private guides, camping or staying at more modest fazendas can be arranged in Cuiabá (where guides await arrivals at the airport) for the

northern Pantanal, and Campo Grande, for budget tours, or Miranda for the southern Pantanal. Corumbá, once the region's backpacker capital, has now reverted to its status as a border town, of dubious repute at that. For those with the minimum of funds, a glimpse of the Pantanal and its wildlife can be had on the bus ride from Campo Grande to Corumbá, by lodging or camping near the ferry crossing over the Rio Paraguai (Porto Esperança), and by staying in Poconé and day-walking or hitching south along the Transpantaneira.

Choosing a tour

Most tours combine 'safari' jeep trips, river-boat trips, piranha fishing and horse riding with accommodation in lodges. Excursions often take place at sunset and sunrise as these are the best times for spotting bird and wildlife. Choose an agency or fazenda with care. Not all act responsibly or professionally. Be aware that cut price operators tend to cut corners and pay their staff very low wages. We list the best operators below and consider those in Cuiabá (for the north) and Miranda (for the south) to be best. Many operators offer an increasingly interesting range of trips, including hard-core camping safaris photo workshops and indigenous culture exchanges.

The Pantanal faces many threats to its integrity, such as illegal hunting, poaching, overfishing and pollution from agrochemicals and goldminers' mercury from the neighbouring planalto. Visitors can make an important contribution to protecting the area by acting responsibly and choosing guides accordingly. Take your rubbish away with you, don't fish out of season, don't let guides kill or disturb fauna, don't buy products made from threatened or endangered species (including macaw-feather jewellery), don't buy live birds or monkeys and report any violation to the authorities. The practice of catching caiman, even though they may then be released, is traumatic for the animals and has potentially disruptive long-term effects.

Campo Grande and around

Campo Grande → *Phone code: 067. Post code: 79000. Colour map 7, 1. Population: 800,000.*
Capital of the State of Mato Grosso do Sul. It was founded in 1899. It is a pleasant, modern city. Because of the terra roxa (red earth), it is called the 'Cidade Morena'. In the centre is a shady park, the **Praça República**, commonly called the Praça do Rádio after the Rádio Clube on one of its corners. Three blocks west is **Praça Ari Coelho**. Linking the two squares, and running through the city east to west, is Avenida Afonso Pena; much of its central reservation is planted with yellow ypé trees. Their blossom covers the avenue, and much of the city besides, in spring.

The municipal tourist secretariat is part of **Sedesc** ① *Av Afonso Pena 3297, T3314 3588, www.pmcg.ms.gov.br*, which has **Centros de Atendimento ao Turista (CAT)** throughout the city, including: **airport** and **rodoviária** ① *T3314 4448, both open daily*; in the historic building and exhibition centre **Morada dos Baís** ① *Av Noroeste 5140, T3314 9968, Tue-Sat 0800-1800, Sun 0900-1200*; at the **Feira Central market** ① *R 14 de Julho 3351, T3314 3872 (see Shopping)*; **Shopping Campo Grande** ① *Av Afonso Pena 4909, T3314 3142, Mon-Sat 1000-2200, Sun 1400-2000*.

Some distance from the centre is the large **Parque dos Poderes**, which contains the Palácio do Governo and other secretariats, paths and lovely trees. Even larger is the 119-ha **Parque das Nações Indígenas**. Despite its name this is almost completely covered with grassy areas and ornamental trees. But it's a pleasant place for a stroll or quiet read and has good birdlife and a couple of museums: **Museu de Arte Contemporânea** ① *R Antônio Maria Coelho 6000, T3326 7449, Mon-Fri 1200-1800, Sat-Sun 1400-1800, US$2*. This preserves the largest collection of modern art in the state; permanent and temporary exhibitions. **Museu Dom Bosco (Indian Museum)** ① *Av Afonso Pena 7000, Parque das Nações Indígenas, T3326 9788, www.mcdb.org.br*,

Tue-Fri 0800-1730, Sat-Sun 1300-1800, US$2.75, contains relics from the various tribes who were the recipients of the Salesians aggressive missionary tactics in the early and mid-20th century. The largest collections are from the Tukano and Bororo people from the Upper Rio Negro and Mato Grosso respectively, both of whose cultures the Salesians were responsible for almost completely wiping out. There is also a rather depressing display of stuffed endangered species (mostly from the Pantanal, though some are from other areas of Brazil or other countries), two-headed calves and seashells from around the world.

Bonito → *Phone code: 067. Post code: 79290. Colour map 6, B6. Population: 17,000.*

The municipality of Bonito, 248 km from Campo Grande, is in the Serra do Bodoquena. It is surrounded by beautiful *cerrado* forest cut by clear-water rivers rich with fish and dotted with plunging waterfalls and deep caves. It has become Brazil's foremost ecotourism destination; which in Brazilian terms means that families come here to romp around in Nature: from light adventure activities like caving to gentle rafting and snorkelling, all with proper safety measures and great even for small children. Despite the heavy influx of visitors plenty of wildlife appears around the trails when it's quiet. The wet season Is January to February; December to February is hottest, July to August coolest. **Tourist office: Comtur** ⓘ *Rodovia Bonito, Guia Lopes da Laguna, Km 1, T3255 2160 (no English spoken), www.bonito-ms.com.br. See also www.portalbonito.com.br.* Bonito is prohibitively expensive for those on a budget. All the attractions in the area can only be visited with prior booking through a travel agent. As taxis are exorbitant, it is best to book with one of the few agencies that offers tours and transport. Bonito is very popular, especially during December to January, Carnival, Easter, and July (advance booking is essential). **Note** Bonito's attractions are nearly all on private land and must by visited with a guide. Owners also enforce limits on the number of daily visitors so, at

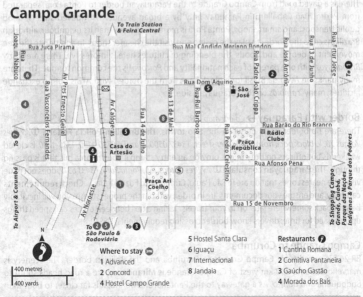

Campo Grande

To Train Station & Feira Central

Rua Juca Pirama

Rua Mal Cândido Mariano Bondon

Rua Joaqu m Nabuco

Rua Pres Ernesto Geisel

Av Vasconcelos Fernandes

Av Calógeras

Rua Dom Aquino

Rua 14 de Julho

Rua Rui Barbosa

Rua 13 de Maio

Rua Pedro Celestino

Rua Padre João Crippa

Rua Padre Antônio

Rua José Antônio

Rua 13 de Junho

Rua rtur Jorge

To 1

São José

Rua Barão do Rio Branco

Rádio Clube

Praça República

Rua Afonso Pena

Rua 15 de Novembro

Casa do Artesão

Praça Ari Coelho

Av Noroeste

To 7

To Airport & Corumbá

To 2 5 São Paulo & Rodoviária

To 3

N

400 metres
400 yards

To Shopping Campo Grande, Cuiabá, Parque das Nações Indígenas & Parque dos Poderes

Where to stay
1 Advanced
2 Concord
4 Hostel Campo Grande
5 Hostel Santa Clara
6 Iguaçu
7 Internacional
8 Jandaia

Restaurants
1 Cantina Romana
2 Comitiva Pantaneira
3 Gaúcho Gastão
4 Morada dos Baís

busy times, pre-booking is essential. Wetsuits are provided for snorkelling and diving, you are not allowed to use sunscreen or insect repellent.

Some 26 km from Bonito is **Lago Azul**. The cave is named after a lake 50 m long and 110 m wide, 75 m below ground level. The water, 20°C, is a jewel-like blue as light from the opening is refracted through limestone and magnesium. Prehistoric animal bones have been found in the lake. The light is at its best January-February, 0700-0900, but is fine at other times. A 25-ha park surrounds the cave. Entry costs US$20. Other caves to visit are **Abismo Anhumas** ① *Fazenda Anhumas, Estrada para Campo dos Indios s/n, T3225 3313, www.abismoanhumas.com. br R$360 (for abseiling and snorkelling) or R$530 (for rapelling and scuba diving), only 20 visitors per day*, with a glassy pool. The ticket, US$180-265, permits abseiling into the cave, followed by three to four hours snorkelling or scuba diving. And **Grutas de São Miguel** ① *Estrada para Campo dos Indios 16 km (12 km from the centre), US$20*, a dry cave with numerous bats, albino owls and impressive cave formations entered along a vertiginous hanging bridge.

The **Balneário Municipal** ① *7 km on road to Jardim, US$7.50*, on the Rio Formoso, with changing rooms, toilets, camping, swimming in clear water, plenty of fish to see (strenuous efforts are made to keep the water and shore clean). **Rafting** on the Rio Formoso: 2½ hours, minimum four people, a mixture of floating peacefully downriver, swimming and shooting four waterfalls, lifejackets available; arranged by many agencies. The **Aquário Natural** ① *8 km on road to Jardim, open 0900-1800, US$60-83 including lunch*, is one of the springs of the Rio Formoso. To visit you must have authorization from the owners; you can swim and snorkel with five types of fish. Do not swim with suntan oil on. Other tours are: from the springs of the Rio Sucuri to its meeting with the Formoso (T3255 1030, US$45 including lunch), about 2 km of crystal-clear water, with swimming or snorkelling, birdwatching, very peaceful.

Ponta Porã → *Phone code: 067. Post code: 79900. Population: 67,000*

There is a paved road from Campo Grande to the Paraguayan border to Ponta Porã, separated from Pedro Juan Caballero in Paraguay only by a broad avenue. With paved streets, good public transport and smart shops, Ponta Porã is more prosperous than its neighbour, although Brazilians cross the border to play the casino and visit the cheaper shops. In addition to the free movement of people and goods, the blending of cultures here is impressive. There are many *Brasiguayos* with one parent of each nationality and *Portoñol* is the common tongue. There are many banks on Avenida Brasil (one block back from the border) with ATMs but no exchange facilities; many *cambiôs* on the Paraguayan side.

Border with Paraguay → *Colour map 7, B2.*

There are no border posts between the two towns. The **Brazilian Polícia Federal** ① *Av Pres Vargas 70, ½ block back from the border street, T3437 0500, Mon-Fri 0730-1130, 1330-1730*, is closed weekends but officers on duty might provide an entry stamp if you are on a bus that is passing through. The **Paraguayan consulate** ① *Av Pres Vargas 130, Ponta Porã, T3431 6312*, does not issue visas, the nearest ones that do are in São Paulo, Curitiba and Foz do Iguaçu. **Check requirements carefully**, and ensure your documents are in order: without the proper stamps you will inevitably be sent back somewhere later on in your travels. Taking a taxi between offices can speed things up if pressed for time; drivers know border crossing requirements; US$10.

Campo Grande to Corumbá

BR-262 is paved from Campo Grande to Corumbá and the Bolivian border. The scenery is marvellous. Some 200 km west of Campo Grande is **Miranda**, where a road heads south to Bodoquena and Bonito. As a gateway to the Pantanal and Bonito, it is far closer to both than either Corumbá or Campo Grande. The best of the southern Pantanal fazendas and tour operators are here, too. There is a cultural and arts centre of the local Terena communities at the entrance to town, open daily.

To the southern Pantanal

Many tours out of Campo Grande and Miranda take a dirt road running off the BR 262 Campo Grande–Corumbá highway called the **Estrada Parque**. It begins halfway between Miranda and Corumbá at a turn off called **Buraco da Piranha** (Piranha hole), heads north into the Pantanal and then, after 51 km, turns west to Corumbá at a point called the **Curva do Leque**. This is the overland access point to **Nhecolândia**, a region rich in wildlife. There are excellent fazendas off the Estrada Parque road with several around Miranda itself open to tourism.

◉ Campo Grande and around listings

For hotel and restaurant price codes, and other relevant information, see Essentials.

● Where to stay

Campo Grande *p630, map p631*
\$\$\$\$ Jandaia, R Barão do Rio Branco 1271, T3316 7700, www.jandaia.com.br. The city's best hotel, aimed at a business market. Modern well-appointed rooms in a tower, pool, gym and some English spoken.
\$\$\$ Advanced, Av Calógeras 1909, T3321 5000, www.hoteladvanced.com.br. Spacious if spartan rooms with hot showers, in an 80s block, very small pool, cheaper with fan.
\$\$\$ Internacional, Allan Kardec 223, T3384 4677. Modern, on a quiet street, comfortable rooms with a/c or fan, some suites, small pool, restaurant.
\$\$ Concord, Av Calógeras 1624, T3321 2999. A renovated town hotel with a small pool and a/c rooms with modern fittings.
\$\$ Iguaçu, R Dom Aquino 761, T3322 4621, www.hoteliguacu.com.br. **\$** with fan. Very popular well-kept hotel with smart, simple a/c rooms. Good breakfast.
\$\$-\$ Hostel Campo Grande, R Joaquim Nabuco 185, T3042 0508. Simple, musty little rooms with saggy foam mattresses and frayed bathrooms. Laundry, kitchen; reception open 24 hrs. **Ecological Expeditions** offer Pantanal trips from their office next door.
\$\$-\$ Hostel Santa Clara, R Vitor Meirelles 125, T3384 0583, www.pantanalsantaclara.com.br.

A pleasant hostel in a converted town house with a/c doubles and dorms, a large garden 5 mins from the new *rodoviária*. Free airport pick-up, kitchen, tour agency.

Bonito *p631*
\$\$\$ Gira Sol, R Pérsio Schamann 710, T3255 2677, www.girasolbonito.com.br. An attractive *pousada* with a small pool in a garden 5 mins' walk from the centre. Bright, spacious rooms with balconies, decent breakfast.
\$\$\$ Pousada Olho d'Água, Rod Três Morros, Km 1, 13255 1430, olhodagua@vip2000.net. Comfortable cabins with fan, set in a garden next to a small lake. Horse riding, bike rental, solar-powered hot water and great food from the vegetable garden. Recommended.
\$\$\$ Tapera, Estrada Ilha do Padre, Km 10, on hill above Shell station on road to Jardim, T3255 1700. Fine views, cool breezes, peaceful, a/c, very comfortable, own transport an advantage.
\$\$ Hostel Beija Flor, Luis da Costa Leite 1028, T3255 4354, www.hostelbeijaflor.com. Private rooms and dorms (**\$** pp), economical, Swiss-owned, English, French and German spoken, runs tours, bikes and underwater cameras for rent.
\$\$-\$ Pousada São Jorge, Av Col Pilad Rebuá 1605, T3255 4046, www.pousadasaojorge.com.br. Clean dorms with bunks and en suites (the best with 2 bathrooms) and a pleasant public dining area with snack bar.

$ Albergue do Bonito, R Lúcio Borralho 716, T3255 1462, www.bonitohostel.com.br. US$21 pp in dorm, **$$** doubles (cheaper with fan), HI affiliated hostel, cheaper for members, English spoken, pool, laundry facilities, use of kitchen, hot showers, secure parking, rents bicycles, camping. Sister hostel to the **Campo Grande Hostel**, also with a branch of **Ecological Expeditions**.

$ pp Pousada Muito Bonito, Pilad Rebuá 1448, T3255 1645, www.muitobonito.com. br. With bath, or rooms with bunkbeds, nice patio, excellent, helpful owners, including breakfast, also with tour company (Mario Doblack speaks English, French and Spanish). Warmly recommended.

Camping There are several campsites in the vicinity, including **Camping Rio Formoso**, Rodovia Bonito/Guia Lopes da Laguna Km 6, T9284 5994, www.campingrioformoso.com.br, US$14 pp, as well as **Albergue do Bonito**, above.

Ponta Porã p632

$$$ Barcelona, R Guia Lopes 45, T3437 2500, www.hotelbarcelona.com.br. Roms with a/c or fan in a tower, bar and sauna.

$$$ Pousada do Bosque, Av Pres Vargas 1151, T3431 1181, www.hotelpousadadobosque. com.br. 'Fazenda style' with lovely grounds and pool, sports fields, restaurant, parking, comfortable rooms.

$$$-$$ Interpark, Av Brasil 3684, T3437 6700, www.grupointerhoteis.com.br. Comfortable modern rooms, small pool, restaurant.

$$ Guarujá, R Guia Lopes 63, T3431 9515. With a/c and fridge, cheaper with fan, parking, faded but functional.

Campo Grande to Corumbá: Miranda
p632

$$$-$$ Águas do Pantanal, Av Afonso Pena 367, T3242 1242, www.aguasdopantanal. com.br. In the town itself, with comfortable a/c rooms and less good backpacker accommodation, attractive pool surrounded by tropical flowers, helpful travel agency. Usually have a rep waiting at the *rodoviária*.

$$$-$$ Pantanal Ranch Meia Lua, BR 262 Km 554, T9686 9064, www.pantanalranch meialua.com. Big, comfortable rooms (and some dorms) in a lemon-yellow farmhouse in extensive wooded gardens, lots of wildlife. It has a big pool, hammocks, bikes for use and hearty Pantanal cooking, welcoming staff, very good. Some of the best tours in the Pantanal; provides information in English.

$$ Pantanal, Av Barão do Rio Branco 609, T3242 1068. Well-maintained a/c rooms with en suites along a gloomy corridor, pool.

$$ Pantanal Ranch Mandovi, BR 262, Km 554, T9638 3520, www.pantanalranchmandovi. com. Lovely rustic guest house set in forested gardens and run by a Kadiweu indigenous Pantaneiro. Lovely atmosphere, many birds (including Hyacinth Macaws) and good tours of the Pantanal. Full board available and camping area ($).

$ Diogo, Av Barão do Rio Branco s/n, T3242 1468. Very simple but well-kept doubles, triples and quadruples, some with a/c.

To the southern Pantanal p633

$$$$ Chácara Anis, Rodoviária Cerá 10, 79200-000 Aquidauana, T067-3241 8312, www.fazenda-pantanal.com. Working cattle ranch, Swiss-owned (Anne-Lyse and Caspar Burn), lovely *pousada* offering up to 7-night stays, several European languages spoken, horse riding expeditions, wildlife watching, tours arranged, swimming pool.

$$$$ Fazenda Xaraés, Estrada Parque, www.xaraes.com.br. One of the most luxurious fazendas, with a pool, tennis court, sauna, air strip and surprisingly plain but well-appointed a/c rooms. The immediate environs have been extensively cleared, but there are some wild areas of savanna and *cerrado* nearby and there are giant otter in the neighbouring Rio Abodrai.

$$$$ Refúgio Ecológico Caiman, 36 km from Miranda, T011-3706 1800 (São Paulo), www. caiman.com.br. The most comfortable, stylish accommodation in the Pantanal. Excellent tours and guiding. Check website for opening times.

$$$ Cacimba de Pedra, Estr Agachi, T9982 4655, cacimbadepedra@terra.com.br. A Jacaré caiman farm and *pousada* in beautiful dry deciduous forest with abundant wildlife. A/c rooms sit in front of an inviting pool.

$$$ Fazenda 23 de Março, T3321 4737, www. fazenda23demarco.com.br. Charming fazenda in pristine wilderness, with a pool, 4 rooms and a Pantanal preservation centre. Visitors can learn to lasso, ride a bronco and turn their hand to other Pantanal cowboy activities.

$$$ Fazenda Baia Grande, Estr La Lima Km 19, T3382 4223, www.fazendabaiagrande. com.br. Very comfortable a/c rooms around a pool in a garden. The fazenda is surrounded by savanna and stands of cerrado. The owner, Alex is very eager to please and enthusiastic.

$$$ Fazenda San Francisco, turn off BR 262 30 km west of Miranda, T3242 3333, www. fazendasanfrancisco.tur.br. Simple rustic a/c cabins around a pool in a garden filled with rheas. Food and guides are excellent, but can be very crowded with tour groups. Several scientific projects take place here, including Gadonça, for the study of wild cats. Birdwatching is also excellent.

$$$ Santa Clara, Estrada Parque s/n, T3384 0583, www.pantanalsantaclara.com.br. A budget option for staying in a ranch house in the Southern Pantanal, on the banks of the Rio Alobrão (where there's a community of giant otters), and with a pool, games areas, double rooms and dorms, full transfers from Campo Grande, full board and tours included.

❶ Restaurants

Campo Grande *p630, map p631*
Local specialities *Caldo de piranha* (soup), *chipa* (Paraguayan cheese bread), sold on streets, delicious when hot, and local liqueur, *pequi com caju*, which contains *cachaça*. There are many cheap restaurants around the *rodoviária* and many other in a/c surrounds in the **Shopping Campo Grande** mall (R Afonso Pena 4909).

$$$ Comitiva Pantaneira, R Dom Aquino 2221, T3383 8799. Hearty, tasty and very meaty regional dishes served by waiters in cowboy gear, or as a buffet, lunchtime only.

$$$ Gaúcho Gastão, R 14 de Julho 775, T3384 4326. The best *churrascaria* in a town, famous for its beef, comfortable, a/c, lunch only.

$$ Cantina Romana, R da Paz, 237, T3324 9777. Over 20 years serving Italian dishes, salads and a lunchtime buffet, good atmosphere.

$$-$ Sabor en Quilo, R Barão do Rio Branco 1118 and R Dom Aquino 1786, T3383 3911/ 3325 5102. Self-service per kilo restaurants with plenty of choice including sushi on Sat, lunchtime only.

$ Morada dos Baís, Av Noroeste, 5140, corner with Afonso Pena, behind tourist office. Brazilian and Italian dishes, snacks and coffee served in a pretty courtyard, lunchtime only.

Bonito *p631*
$$$-$$ Santa Esmeralda, R Cel Pilad Rebuá 1831. Respectable Italian food in one of the few a/c dining rooms.

$$ Cantinho do Peixe, R 31 de Março 1918, T3255 3381. A la carte Pantanal fish dishes including good *pintado na telha* (grilled surubim).

$$ Tapera, R Cel Pilad Rebuá 480, T3255 1110. Good, home-grown vegetables, breakfast, lunch, pizzas, meat and fish dishes, opens 1900 for evening meal.

$ Da Vovó, R Sen F Muller 570, T3255 2723. A great per kilo serving Minas and local food all cooked in a traditional wood-burning stove. Plenty of vegetables and salads.

$ Mercado da Praça, R 15 Novembro 376, T3255 2317. The cheapest in town, a snack bar in the local supermarket offering sandwiches, juices, etc, open 0600-2400.

Campo Grande to Corumbá: Miranda *p632*
$ Zero Hora, Av Barão do Rio Branco at the *rodoviária*, T3242 1330. 24 hr snack bar, provision shop and out the back, with its own private waterfall, a passable, good value per kilo restaurant.

O Shopping

Campo Grande *p630, map p631*
Arts and crafts The Feira Central e
Turística, R 14 de Julho 3351, on Wed-Fri
(16700) and Sat-Sun (1200), has lots of foods
to try, local produce and goods imported
from Bolivia and Paraguay. Local native crafts,
including ceramics, tapestry and jewellery,
are good quality. A local speciality is Os
Bugres da Conceição, squat wooden statues
covered in moulded wax. **Casa do Artesão**,
Av Calógeras 2050, on corner with Av Afonso
Pena. Housed in an historic building, Mon-Fri
0800-2000, Sat 0800-1200.

O What to do

Campo Grande *p630, map p631*
Be wary of the lower-end operators in the
Pantanal. Many cut corners to save money
and services are not always reliable.
**Clube de Observadores de Aves de Campo
Grande**, www.facebook.com/COACGR. The
city's birdwatching club has produced a guide
to birds in Campo Grande's urban parks, *Guia
de aves de Campo Grande, áreas verdes urbanas*.
Ecological Expeditions, R Joaquim Nabuco
185, T3321 0505, www.ecologicalexpeditions.
com.br. Associated with hostels in Campo
Grande, Bonito and on the Rio Paraguai.
Budget camping trips and lodge-based trips
in Nhecolândia (sleeping bag needed for the
former) for 3, 4 or 5 days ending in Corumbá.

Bonito *p631*
There is very little to choose between
agencies in Bonito, who offer the same
packages for the same price, so shop around
to see which you like the feel of best. English
speakers are hard to come by.
Ygarapé, R Cel Pilad Rebuá 1853, T3255 1733,
www.ygarape.com.br. English-speaking
staff, offers transport to the sights. Also PDSE
accredited cave diving.

Campo Grande to Corumbá: Miranda
p632
Explore Pantanal, R Dr Alexandre 305,
Miranda, T3242 4310, or T9638 3520, www.
explorepantanal.com. A good tour agency
with a broad range of standard and more
adventurous bespoke tours, including
live-aboard stays on boats and treks into
the heart of the wetlands. Run by a Kadiweu
indigenous guide, who grew-up in the
Pantanal. Several languages spoken. Great for
small groups who want to get off the beaten
track. Prices are competitive with budget
operators in Campo Grande. See also **Pantanal
Ranch Meia Lua**, above.

O Transport

Campo Grande *p630, map p631*
Air Daily flights to most major cities. Airport
T3368 6000. Take ity bus No 158, or the
designated a/c 015 airport bus which runs from
the centre via Av Afonso Pena, R 26 de Agosto,
Rui Barbosa, Cândido Mariano, Via Parque and
Mato Grosso and costs US$3.50. Taxi to airport,
US$8.50. Airport has car rental offices.
Bus The new *rodoviária* is at Av Gury Marques
1215, about 15 km south of the city on the
road to São Paulo (BR-163), T3026 6789, http://
www.transportal.com.br/rodoviaria-campo-
grande/ (bus 087 leaves every 20 mins form
Praça Ari Coelho in the centre, US$1.50, shuttle
bus to the airport US$5, taxi to the centre
US$10.50, to the airport US$9.25). The terminal
has cafés, internet, a handful of shops and left
luggage. Most Pantanal tour operators will
meet clients off the bus and organize transfers
to destinations further afield.

To **Miranda** and **Bonito**, see below. **São
Paulo**, US$80, 15 hrs, 7 buses daily, 1st at 0600,
last at 2400. **Cuiabá**, US$45, 10-14 hrs, 16
buses daily. To **Goiânia**, with São Luís 4 a day,
US$84, 16-24 hrs, fastest at night; change here
for **Brasília**. **Corumbá**, with Andorinha, T3323
4848, www.andorinha.com, 9 daily from
0515, 6 hrs, US$40, most via Miranda. Campo
Grande-Corumbá buses connect with those
from Rio and São Paulo, similarly those from

Corumbá through to Rio and São Paulo. To **Foz do Iguaçu**, 18 hrs at 1900, US$53, or change at Cascavel, US$40. To **Ponta Porã** for Paraguay, see below.

Train The Trem do Pantanal, (office: Av Afonso Pena 5140 com Av Noroeste, Morada dos Baís, T3043 2233, www.serraverde express.com.br), runs on Sat from Campo Grande to Miranda at 0800, 10 hrs, returning from Miranda on Sun at 0800. It goes via Aquidauana, for lunch, to which a tourist train runs on holidays at 0730. Fares US$65 Campo Grande-Miranda, children US$28, US$52 to Aquidauana, children US$22. Train and fazenda packages, and more, are available. Tickets can be bought through **Serra Verde Express** and travel agencies.

Bonito *p631*
Bus *Rodoviária* is on the edge of town. From **Campo Grande**, US$25, 5½-6 hrs, 5 daily with **Cruzeiro do Sul**, T3312 9710, www.cruzeirodosulms.com.br, or Queiroz, T3042 0224. Bus uses MS-345, with a stop at Autoposto Santa Cruz, Km 60, all types of fuel, food and drinks available.

Ponta Porã *p632*
Bus The *rodoviária* is 3 km out on the Dourados road (Brazilian city buses from the *ponto* in the centre to Rodoviaria, 20 mins, US$1.50; taxi US$10. To/from **Campo Grande**,

4 hrs, US$28. From Ponta Porã to **Bonito**, change at **Jardim** (a friendly town with a good services, offering access to various natural attractions similar to those of Bonito at more modest prices): Ponta Porã-Jardim, 4 a day, fewer on Sun, 4 hrs, US$20; connect the following day at 0500 to Bonito, US$10.50.

Campo Grande to Corumbá: Miranda
p632
Bus **Campo Grande**-Miranda, 9 a day with **Andorinha**, 2-3 hrs, US$20.To **Corumbá**; 9 daily, 3-4 hrs, US$20.

Directory

Campo Grande *p630, map p631*
Banks ATMs at banks in the centre and Banco 24 horas, R Maracaju, on corner with 13 de Junho. Also at R Dom Aquino e Joaquim Nabuco. **Car hire** Agencies on Av Afonso Pena and at airport. **Consulates** Bolivia, R Spipe Calarge 99, T3342 6933, consulado_ cgms04@yahoo.com. **Medical services** Yellow and dengue fevers are both present in Mato Grosso do Sul. Get your immunization at home.

Bonito *p631*
Banks Banco do Brasil, R Luiz da Costa Leite 2279, for Visa. **Bradesco**, Av Coronel Pilão Rebuá 535, Visa ATM.

Corumbá→ *Phone code: 067. Post code: 79,300. Population: 95,701.*

Situated on the south bank by a broad bend in the Rio Paraguai, 15 minutes from the Bolivian border, Corumbá offers beautiful views of the river, especially at sunset. It is hot and humid (70%); cooler in June to July, very hot from September to January. It also has millions of mosquitoes in December to February. Illicit border activity has increased in recent years.

There is a spacious shady **Praça da Independência** and the port area is worth a visit. Avenida Gen Rondon between Frei Mariano and 7 de September has a pleasant palm lined promenade which comes to life in the evenings. The **Forte Junqueira**, the city's most historic building, was built in 1772. It may be visited daily accompanied by a soldier from the base in which it is situated. Most tour operators for the southern part of the Pantanal are in Campo Grande or Miranda, but a few agencies keep offices here and there are a number of upmarket cruise companies along the water front.

Border with Bolivia

Over the border from Corumbá are Arroyo Concepción, Puerto Quijarro and Puerto Suárez. From Puerto Quijarro a 650-km railway and paved road run to Santa Cruz de la Sierra. There are flights to Santa Cruz from Puerto Suárez.

Brazilian immigration Brazilian **Polícia Federal** and **immigration** are at the border complex right at the frontier (Polícia Federal also have an office at Praça da República 51, T3234 7800, dpf.cm.cra.srms@dpf.gov.br, 0800-1130, 1330-1700), there may be queues for entry stamps but much quicker for exit. If leaving Brazil merely to obtain a new visa, exit and entry must not be on the same day. Money changers at the border and in Quijarro offer the same rates as in Corumbá. **Bolivian consulate** ① *R Cabral 1607, Corumbá, T3231 5605, consuladobol@ hotmail.com, Mon-Fri 0800-1600.* A fee is charged to citizens of those countries which require a visa. A yellow fever vaccination certificate is required; go to Rua 7 de Setembro, Corumbá, for an inoculation (preferably get one at home).

⊙ Corumbá listings

For hotel and restaurant price codes, and other relevant information, see Essentials.

⊙ Where to stay

Corumbá *p637*
Although there are hostels around the bus station, this is a 10-min walk to the centre of town on the river bank where most of the hotels, restaurants and tour operators lie.
$$$-$$ Águas do Pantanal, R Dom Aquino Corrêa 1457, T3234 8800, www.aguasdo pantanalhotel.com.br. The smartest in town together with the Nacional Palace, a/c rooms in a 1980s tower, pool and sauna.
$$$-$$ Nacional Palace, R América 936, T3234 6000, www.hnacional.com.br. Smart, modern a/c rooms, a decent pool and parking.
$$-$ Salette, R Delamaré 893, T3231 6246, www.salettehotel.com.br/salette.html. Cheap and cheerful with a range of rooms, the cheapest with fans and shared bathrooms.
$ Corumbá Hostel, R Colombo 1419, T3231 1005. Modern hostel with pool. Fan or a/c rooms and dorms.

⊙ Restaurants

Corumbá *p637*
Local specialities These include *peixadas corumbaenses*, a variety of fish dishes prepared

with the catch of the day; as well as ice cream, liquor and sweets made of *bocaiúva*, a small yellow palm fruit, in season Sep-Feb. There are several good restaurants in R Frei Mariano. Lots of open-air bars on the river front.
$$ Laço de Ouro, R Frei Mariano 556, T3231 7371. Popular fish restaurant with a lively atmosphere and tables spilling out onto the street.
$ Panela Velha, R 15 de Novembro 156, T3232 5650. Popular lunchtime restaurant with a decent, cheap all you can eat buffet.
$ Verde Frutti, R Delamare 1164, T3231 3032. A snack bar with a wide variety of juices and great, ice-cold *acai na tigela*.

⊙ Festivals

Corumbá *p637*
2 Feb, Festa de Nossa Senhora da Candelária, Corumbá's patron saint, all offices and shops are closed. **24 Jun**, Festa do Arraial do Banho de São João, fireworks, parades, traditional food stands, processions and the main event, the bathing of the image of the saint in the Rio Paraguai. **21 Sep**, Corumbá's anniversary, includes a Pantanal fishing festival held on the eve. **Early to mid-Oct**, Festival Pantanal das Águas, with street parades featuring giant puppets, dancing in the street and occasional water fights.

⚙ What to do

Corumbá *p637*
Mutum Turismo, R Frei Mariano 17,
T3231 1818, www.mutumturismo.com.br.
Cruises and upmarket tours (mostly aimed
at the Brazilian market) and airline, train and
bus reservations.

⚙ Transport

Corumbá *p637*
Air Airport, R Santos Dumont, 3 km.
Daily flights to **Campo Grande** and **Brasília**.
Infrequent bus from airport to town, so
take a taxi, US$8.50. Car hire at the airport.
Bus The *rodoviária* is on R Porto Carreiro
at the south end of R Tiradentes, next to
the railway station. City bus to *rodoviária*
from Praça da República, US$1.50; taxis are
extortionate but mototaxis charge US$1.
Andorinha, T3231 2646, services to all points
east. To **Campo Grande**, 6 hrs, US$40, 9 buses
daily, from 0515, connections from Campo
Grande to all parts of Brazil.

Border with Bolivia: Corumbá/Arroyo Concepción *p638*

Bus Leaving Brazil, take Canarinho city bus
marked Fronteira from the port end of R
Antônio Maria Coelho to the Bolivian border
(15 mins, US$1), walk over the bridge to Bolivian
immigration, then take a colectivo to Quijarro
or Puerto Suárez. Taxi from Corumbá *rodoviária*
to Bolivian border US$15, negotiable. Ask to be
taken directly to Bolivian immigration, not to a
Bolivian cab who will hold your luggage while
your passport is stamped. Overcharging and
sharp practices are common. Agencies and
touts at the Corumbá *rodoviária* offer hotels,
Pantanal tours and railway tickets to Santa
Cruz. The latter cost double the fare and are
not recommended. Always buy train or bus
tickets once in Bolivia.

When travelling from Quijarro, take a taxi
or walk to the Bolivian border to go through
formalities. Cross the bridge to Brazilian
immigration. On a small side street to the right
is the bus stop for Corumbá; don't believe taxi
drivers who say there is no bus.
Train Timetables for trains from Puerto
Quijarro to Santa Cruz change frequently,
so check on www.fo.com.bo or on arrival in
Corumbá. If you haven't booked a ticket via
the website, it may be best to stay in Quijarro
to get tickets.

Cuiabá and around

Cuiabá → *Phone code: 065. Post code: 78000. Colour map 7, A1. Population: 543,000. Altitude: 176 m.*
The capital of Mato Grosso state on the Rio Cuiabá, an upper tributary of the Rio Paraguai, is in
fact two cities: Cuiabá on the east bank of the river and Várzea Grande, where the airport is, on
the west. It is very hot; coolest months for a visit are June, July and August, in the dry season.

Cuiabá has an imposing government palace and other fine buildings round the green
Praça da República. On the square is the **Cathedral**, with a plain, imposing exterior, two
clock-towers and, inside, coloured-glass mosaic windows and doors. Behind the altar is a
huge mosaic of Christ in majesty, with smaller mosaics in side chapels. Beside the Cathedral
is the leafy **Praça Alencastro**. On **Praça Ipiranga**, at the junction of Avs Isaac Póvoas and
Tenente Col Duarte, a few blocks southwest of the central squares, there are market stalls
and an iron bandstand from Huddersfield, UK. In front of the Assembléia Legislativa, Praça
Moreira Cabral, is a point marking the **Geogedesic Centre of South America** (see also under
Chapada dos Guimarães). **Museus de Antropologia, História Natural e Cultura Popular**
ⓘ *in the Fundação Cultural de Mato Grosso, Praça da República 151, Mon-Fri 0800-1730, US$0.50,*
displays historical photos, a contemporary art gallery, stuffed Pantanal fauna, indigenous,

archaeological finds and pottery. At the entrance to Universidade de Mato Grosso, 10 minutes by bus from the centre (by pool), is the small **Museu do Índio/Museu Rondon** ① *T3615 8489, Tue-Sun 0800-1100, 1330-1700, US$1*, with artefacts from tribes mostly from the state of Mato Grosso. Particularly beautiful are the Bororo and Rikbaktsa headdresses made from macaw and currasow feathers and also the Kadiwéu pottery. Bus Nos 501 or 505 ('Universidade') to the university museums leave from Av Tenente Col Duarte by Praça Bispo Dom José, a triangular park just east of Praça Ipiranga. **Tourist information** at **Secretaria de Desenvolvimento do Turismo** ① *Sedtur, R Marechal Rondon, Jardim Aeroporto, Várzea Grande and at R Voluntários da Patria 118, T065-3613 9300, Mon-Fri 0900-1800, www.sedtur.mt.gov.br, Mon-Fri 0700-1800*. Good maps, helpful, contact them if you have any problems with travel agencies; also book hotels and car hire, some English and Spanish spoken. .

Cuiabá

To ②, Rodoviária & Chapada dos Guimarães

To ① ② & Praça 8 de Abril

Batista das Neves

Cmte Costa

Br de Melgaço

R C Grande

Cândida Mariano

Voluntários da Patria

Banco do Brasil ⑤

Praça Alencastro

Av Getúlio Vargas

J Dias

R P Celestino

Ricardo Franco

Buses to Rodoviária

Cathedral ✝

Museus do Antropologia, Historia Natural e Cultura Popular

Praça da República

R G Pimentel

To Av CPA, University, Museu do Indio/Museu Rondon & BR 364 to Campo Grande & Goiânia

Joaquim Murtinho

R Antônio Maria

Av Generoso Ponce

R 13 de Junho

Av Ten Col Duarte

R M Coimbra

To University

Praça Ipiranga

To Airport

RMG

R F de Siqueira

To Praça Moreira Cabral & Centro Geodésico

To Casa do Artesão

Com Henrique

Joaquim Leite

Av Gen Mello

N

To Airport & Várzea Grande

Where to stay
1 Amazon Plaza
2 Ipanema
3 Mato Grosso
4 Mato Grosso Pálace
5 Portal do Pantanal
6 Pousada Ecoverde
7 Pousada Safari
8 Ramos

Restaurants 🍴
1 Choppão
2 Getúlio
3 Miranda's

200 metres
200 yards

Cuiabá to Pantanal → *Colour map 6, A6.*

A paved road turns south off the main Cuiabá-Cáceres road to **Poconé** (102 km from Cuiabá, hotels, 24-hour gas station – closed Sunday). From here, the Transpantaneira runs 146 km south to Porto Jofre. The road is of earth, in poor condition, with ruts, holes and many bridges that need care in crossing. Easiest access is in the dry season (July-September), which is also the best time for seeing birds and, in September, the trees are in bloom. In the wet, especially January to February, there is no guarantee that the Transpantaneira will be passable. The wet season, however, is a good time to see many of the shyer animals because more fruit, new growth and other high calorie foods are available, and there are fewer people.

Campos de Jofre, about 20 km north of Porto Jofre, is said to be magnificent between August and October. In Poconé one can hitch to Porto Jofre, or hire a vehicle in Cuiabá. You will get more out of this part of the Pantanal by going with a guide; a lot can be seen from the Transpantaneira in a hired car, but guides can take you into fazendas some 7 km from the Transpantaneira and will point out wildlife. Recommended guides in Cuiabá are under Tour operators. Although there are gas stations in **Pixaim** (a bridge across the Rio Pixaim, two hotels and a tyre repair shop) and Porto Jofre, they are not always well stocked, best to carry extra fuel.

Barão de Melgaço → *Colour map 7, A1.*

On Rio Cuiabá, 130 km from Cuiabá (TUT bus at 0730 and 1500, US$12), Barão de Melgaço is reached by two roads: the shorter, via Santo Antônio de Leverger, unpaved from Santo Antônio to Barão (closed in the wet season), or via São Vicente, longer, but more pavement. The way to see the Pantanal from here is by boat down the Rio Cuiabá. Boat hire, for example from Restaurant Peixe Vivo on waterfront, up to US$100 for a full day; or enquire with travel agencies in Cuiabá. The best time of day would be sunset, but this may mean returning after dark. Initially the river banks are farms and small habitations, but they become more forested, with lovely combinations of flowering trees (best seen September-October). After a while, a small river to the left leads to Chacororó and Sia Mariana lakes, which join each other via an artificial canal which has led the larger of the two lakes to drain into the smaller and begin to dry out. Boats can continue beyond the lakes to the Rio Mutum, but a guide is essential because there are many dead ends. The area is rich in birdlife and the waterscapes are beautiful.

Cáceres → *Phone code: 065. Post code: 78200. Colour map 6, A6. Population: 85,857.*

On the banks of the Rio Paraguai, 200 km west of Cuiabá, Cáceres is very hot but clean and hospitable. It has a number of well-preserved 19th-century buildings, painted in pastel colours.

The **Museu Histórico de Cáceres** ① *R Antônio Maria by Praça Major João Carlos*, is a small local history museum. The main square, Praça Barão de Rio Branco, has one of the original border markers from the Treaty of Tordesillas, which divided South America between Spain and Portugal; it is pleasant and shady during the day. In the evenings, between November and March, the trees are packed with thousands of chirping swallows (andorinhas). The praça is surrounded by bars, restaurants and ice cream parlours and comes to life at night. The city is known for its many bicycles as most people seem to get around on two wheels. Until 1960, Cáceres had regular boat traffic, today It Is limited to a few tour boats and pleasure craft. The town is at the edge of the Pantanal. Vitória Regia lilies can be seen north of town, just across the bridge over the Rio Paraguai along the BR-174. Local festivals are the Piranha Festival, mid-March; International Fishing Festival in mid-September; annual cattle fair.

Border with Bolivia

An unpaved road runs from Cáceres to the Bolivian border at San Matías. Alternatively, go some 300 km north of Cáceres to **Pontes e Lacerda**, from where you can cross to San Ignacio de Velasco. When crossing at San Matías or travelling to/from San Igancio de Velasco, there are thorough drugs and customs searches at all border points but passports are not stamped. Stamps are given at the **Polícia Federal** in either **Cáceres** ① *Av Getúlio Vargas 2125, Bairo COC, 20-min walk from rodoviária in the centre, T3211 6307, daily 0800-1200, 1400-1800*) or perhaps **Vilhena** ① *Av 15 de Novembro 3485*. Do not go directly to Polícia Federal in Cuiabá, you will be sent back to Cáceres. There are Bolivian immigration offices in San Matías and San Ignacio de Velasco.

Along one route to San Ignacio de Velasco is the delightfully friendly and authentic little town of **Vila Bela da Santíssima Trindade** (*Phone code 065, Altitude 210 m*) on the shores of the Rio Guaporé. Once the capital of Mato Grosso state, Vila Bela has a huge crumbling old cathedral and an interesting **Museu Histórico** ① *R Pouso Alegre 668, Mon-Fri 0800-1100, 1300-1700, free*. Dolphins and many birds may be seen by the river and there is bathing by the beautiful 60-m-high Cascata waterfall, 14 km from town in Parque Estadual Ricardo Franco (taxi US$18 each way, or walk and hitch).

Chapada dos Guimarães and Nobres → *Phone code: 065. Post code: 78195.*
Population: 15,755. Colour map 7, A1.

Some 68 km northeast of Cuiabá lies one of the oldest plateaux on earth. It is one of the most scenic areas of Brazil and visitors describe it as an energizing place. The pleasant town of

Chapada dos Guimarães, the main centre, is a base for many beautiful excursions in this area; it has the oldest church in the Mato Grosso, **Nossa Senhora de Santana** (1779), a bizarre blending of Portuguese and French baroque styles, and a huge spring-water public swimming pool (on Rua Dr Pem Gomes, behind the town). Formerly the centre of an important diamond prospecting region, today Chapada is a very popular destination for Cuiabanos to escape the heat of the city at weekends and on holidays. It is a full day excursion from Cuiabá through lovely scenery with many birds, butterflies and flora. There is a post office at Rua Fernando Corrêa 848. The Festival de Inverno is held in last week of July, and Carnival is very busy. Accommodation is scarce and expensive at these times. The **Secretaria de Turismo e Meio Ambiente** ① *Rua Quinco Caldas 100, 4 blocks from the praça*, provides a useful map of the region and organizes tours.

The Chapada is an immense geological formation rising to 700 m, with rich forests, curiously eroded rocks and many lovely grottoes, peaks and waterfalls. A **national park** (T3301 1133, open all year, free) has been established in the area just west of the town, where the **Salgadeira** tourist centre offers bathing, camping and a restaurant close to the Salgadeira waterfall.

The beautiful 85 m **Véu da Noiva** waterfall (Bridal Veil), 12 km before the town near Buriti (well signposted, ask bus from Cuiabá to let you off), is reached by a short route, or a long route through forest. Other sights include the **Mutuca** beauty spot, **Rio Claro**, the viewpoint over the breathtaking 80-m-deep **Portão do Inferno** (Hell's Gate), and the falls of **Cachoeirinha** (small restaurant) and **Andorinhas**.

About 8 km east of town is the **Mirante do Ponto Geodésico**, a monument officially marking the Geodesic Centre of South America, which overlooks a great canyon with views of the surrounding plains, the Pantanal and Cuiabá's skyline on the horizon; to reach it take Rua Fernando Corrêa east. Continuing east, the road goes through agricultural land and later by interesting rock formations including a stone bridge and stone cross. Some 45 km from Chapada you reach the access for **Caverna Arroe-Jari** ('the dwelling of the souls' in the Bororo language), a sandstone cave over 1 km long, the second largest in Brazil; it is a 1-km walk to the cave, in it is Lagoa Azul, a lake with crystalline blue water. Take your own torch/flashlight (guides' lamps are sometimes weak); entry US$4.50. A guide is necessary to get through fazenda property to the cave, but not really needed thereafter.

Some 100 km north of the Chapada is **Nobres** (www.nobres.mt.gov.br), a little town surrounded by caves and clear rivers full of fish. The village of **Bom Jardim** has two-*pousadas*-in-one (**Pousada Bom Jardim**, www.pousadabomjardim.com, **$$$**) and a restaurant. At Lago das Araras, 2 km away, hundreds of blue and yellow macaws roost in the buriti palms and create a raucous dawn chorus. Other attractions such as good snorkelling at the **Reino Encantado** ① *US$55 per day*, **$$** *for overnight stay*, the **Recanto Ecológico Lagoa Azul** ① *US$25 entry* and the **Rio Triste**, both of which offer floating downstream to see the fish. If swimming, beware the sting rays. Buses run Cuiabá-Nobres, with onward buses to Bom Jardim (direct from Cuiabá once a day). Pousada Bom Jardim has a taxi service and agencies in Cuiabá run tours.

For hotel and restaurant price codes, and other relevant information, see Essentials.

⊛ Where to stay

Cuiabá *p639, map p640*

$$$$ Amazon Plaza, Av Getúlio Vargas 600, T2121 2000, www.hotelamazon.com.br. By far the best in the centre with very smart modern rooms, good views over the city, shady pool area, excellent services.

$$$ Mato Grosso Pálace, Joaquim Murtinho 170, T3614 7000, www.hotelmt.com.br. Conveniently located behind the Praça República, standard 3-star rooms with fridge, hot showers.

$$ Ipanema, Jules Rimet 12, T3621 3069. Opposite the front of the *rodoviária*, well-kept rooms, a/c or fan, huge lobby TV for films or football. Many other options in this area.

$$ Mato Grosso, R Comandante Costa 252, T3614 7777, www.hotelmt.com.br. The best value mid-range option in the centre with renovated a/c or fan-cooled rooms, the brightest of which are on the 2nd floor or above, good breakfast, very helpful. Recommended.

$$ pp Portal do Pantanal, Av Isaac Povoas 655, T3624 8999, www.portaldopantanal. com.br. HI hostel, with breakfast, cheaper with fan, internet access US$3 per hr, laundry, use of kitchen.

$$ Pousada Ecoverde, R Pedro Celestino 391, T3624 1386, www.ecoverdetours.com. The best value, if idiosyncratic option, rooms with spacious bathrooms in a converted town house. Facilities include excellent tour agency, laundry service and free airport/bus station pick-up (with 12 hrs notice).

$$ Ramos, R Campo Grande 487, T3624 7472, hotelramos@hotmail.com. A variety of simple a/c and fan-cooled rooms, also has dorms, laundry service. **Pantanal Nature** travel agency is in reception.

$$-$ Pousada Safari, R 24 de Outubro 111, Centro, T9958 2200, www.pantanalecosafari.

com.br. Rooms with shared bath, electric shower, fan, breakfast, laundry facilities, library and book exchange. Owner Laercio Sá is an experienced guide who runs good Pantanal tours.

Cuiabá to Pantanal *p640*

$$$$ Araras Eco Lodge, Km 32, T3682 2800, www.araraslodge.com.br. Book direct or through **Pantanal Explorer**. One of the most comfortable with 14 a/c rooms; pool, excellent tours and food, homemade *cachaça* and a walkway over a private patch of wetland filled with capybara and cayman. Very popular with small tour groups from Europe. Book ahead.

$$$$ Fazenda Piuval, Km 10, T3345 1338, www.pousadapiuval.com.br. The first fazenda on the Transpantaneira and one of the most touristy, with scores of day visitors at weekends. Rustic farmhouse accommodation, pool, excellent horse and walking trails and boat trips on their vast lake.

$$$$ Pousada Rio Clarinho, Km 42, book through **Pantanal Nature**. Charming budget option on the Rio Clarinho which makes up in wildlife what it lacks in infrastructure. The river has rare water birds, as well as river and giant otters and occasionally tapir.

$$$$ Pousada Rio Claro, Km 42, book through **Natureco**. Comfortable fazenda with a pool and simple a/c rooms on the banks of the Rio Claro which has a resident colony of giant otters.

$$$$ Pouso Alegre, Km 33, T3626 1545, www.pousalegre.com.br. Rustic *pousada*, simple accommodation, a/c or fan. One of the largest fazendas and overflowing with wildlife and particularly good for birds (especially on the morning horseriding trail). Many species not yet seen elsewhere in the northern Pantanal have been catalogued here. Their remote oxbow lake is particularly good for water birds. Birding guides provided with advance notice. Best at weekends when the very knowledge-able owner Luís Vicente is there.

$$$-$$ Caranda Fundo, Transpantaneira Km 43, book through **Pantanal Nature**, T3322

0203. One of the best options for budget travellers. Visitors sleep in hammocks in a large room (bring a hammock mosquito net). Tours include horse rides, treks and night safaris; hyacinth macaws nest on the fazenda and there are many mammals, including howler monkeys, peccaries and huge herds of capybara.

Barão de Melgaço *p640*
$$$$ Mutum Pantanal Ecolodge, T3052 7023, www.pousadamutum.com.br. Book through **Pantanal Nature**, or agencies in Cuiabá. Comfortable roundhouses and cabins set on a lawn around a lovely pool. Arranges horse riding, jeep and boat tours.

Cáceres *p641*
$$$ Caiçaras, R dos Operários 745, corner R Gen Osório, T3223 2234. Modern, with a/c rooms and cheaper options without a fridge.
$$$-$$ Riviera Pantanal, R Gen Osório 540, T3223 1177. Simple town hotel with a/c rooms, a pool and a restaurant.
$$ Charm, Col José Dulce 405, T3223 4949. A/c and fan-cooled rooms, with or without a shared bath.
$ União, R 7 de Setembro 340. Near the *rodoviária*. Fan, cheaper with shared bath, basic but good value.

Border with Bolivia: Vila Bela da Santíssima Trindade *p641*
$$ Cascata, R Conde Azambuja 493, T3259 1154, hotel.cascata@terra.com.br. Rooms with breakfast, a/c, some have frigobar, ample grounds, parking.
$$-$ Guaporé, R Pouso Alegre 607, T3259 1030. Simple rooms with a/c and frigobar, cheaper and more basic with fan, breakfast, restaurant, internet, very helpful owner, good value.

Chapada dos Guimarães *p641*
$$$ Pousada Vento Sul, Av Rio da Casca 850, T3301 2706, www.pousadaventosul.tur.br. New *pousada* 1½ km from town centre, spacious rooms with hammock on veranda, very nice, English spoken, birdwatching guide available.

$$$ Solar do Inglês, R Cipriano Curvo 142, T3301 1389, www.solardoingles.com.br. In an old converted house near town centre with 7 rooms. Garden, swimming pool and sauna. Breakfast and afternoon tea included.
$$$ Turismo, R Fernando Corrêa 1065, a block from *rodoviária*, T3301 1176, www.hotel turismo.com.br. Rooms are cheaper without a/c, restaurant, breakfast and lunch excellent, very popular, German-run; Ralf Goebel, the owner, is very helpful in arranging excursions.
$$ Rio's Hotel, R Tiradentes 333, T3301 1126, www.chapadadosguimaraes.com.br/pousadarios. Rooms are cheaper without a/c and with shared bath, good breakfast.
$$-$ São José, R Vereador José de Souza 50, T3301 3013/1574, www.pousadasaojose.tur. br. Fan, cheaper with shared bath and no fan, hot showers, basic, no breakfast, good, owner Mário sometimes runs excursions.
Camping Oásis, 1 block from main praça, T3301 2444, www.campingoasis.com.br. Central, in garden with fruit trees, separate bathrooms for men and women, cooking facilities, car park.

🍴 Restaurants

Cuiabá *p639, map p640*
City centre restaurants only open for lunch. On Av CPA are many restaurants, snack bars, bars and clubs.
$$$ Getúlio, Av Getúlio Vargas 1147, T3264 9992. An a/c haven from the heat with black tie waiters, excellent food, with meat specialities, pizza, good buffet lunch on Sun. Live music upstairs on Fri and Sat from significant cult Brazilian acts.
$$$-$$ Choppão, Praça 8 de Abril, T3623 9101. A local institution, buzzing at any time of the day or night. Go for huge portions of delicious food or just for *chopp* served by fatherly waiters. The house dish of chicken soup promises to give diners drinking strength in the early hours and is a meal in itself. Warmly recommended.
$$-$ Miranda's, R Cmdte Costa 716. Decent self-service per kilo lunchtime restaurant with good value specials.

Cáceres *p641*

$ Gulla's, R Cel José Dulce 250. Buffet by kilo, good quality and variety. Recommended.

O Shopping

Cuiabá *p639, map p640*
Handicrafts in wood, straw, netting, leather, skins, Pequi liquor, crystallized caju fruit, compressed guaraná fruit (for making the drink), indigenous objects on sale at the airport, *rodoviária*, craft shops in centre, and daily market, Praça da República, interesting. Fish and vegetable market, picturesque, at the riverside.
Casa de Artesão, Praça do Expedicionário 315, T321 0603. Sells all types of local crafts in a restored building. Recommended.

O What to do

Cuiabá *p639, map p640*
You should expect to pay US$200-300 per person per day for tours in the Pantanal. All these agencies arrange trips to the Pantanal. Budget trips are marginally more expensive than those in the Southern Pantanal, but accommodation based in fazendas is more comfortable. For longer or special programmes, book in advance.
Natureco, R Benedito Leite 570, T3321 1001, www.natureco.com.br. Tours to remote fazendas in the Pantanal as well as regular trips to north and south Pantanal, to Nobres and Chapada dos Guimarães. Longer 6-night "3-Biome" tours to the Amazon, Pantanal and savannahs. Specialist birding and wildlife tours and trips throughout Brazil. English spoken. Professional and well run.
Pantanal Explorer, R Gov Ponce de Arruda 670, Várzea Grande, T3682 2800, www. pantanalexplorer.com.br. Offers tours to the Pantanal, Amazon, Cerrado and Chapada dos Guimarães, with various packages including birdwatching and riding. Low-impact and responsible, running its own lodge, Araras Eco Lodge (see above) and with connections to others.

Wildlife guides for the Pantanal and Mato Grosso
Recommended birding and wildlife guides for the northern Pantanal and Mato Grosso are listed below. All guides work freelance for other companies as well as employing other guides for trips when busy. Most guides await incoming flights at the airport; compare prices and services in town if you don't wish to commit yourself at the airport. The tourist office recommends guides; this is not normal practice and their advice is not necessarily impartial.
Boute Expeditions, R Getúlio Vargas 64, Várzea Grande, near airport, T3686 2231, www.boute-expeditions.com. Paulo Boute, one of the most experienced birding guides in the Pantanal; works from home and speaks good English and French.
Fabricio Dorileo, fabriciodorileo18@ yahoo. com.br or through Eduardo Falcão, rejaguar@ bol.com.br. Excellent birding guide with good equipment, good English and many years experience in the Pantanal and Chapada dos Guimarães.
Giuliano Bernardon, T8115 6189, giubernardon @gmail.com. Birding guide and photographer with a good depth of knowledge and experience in the Chapada, Pantanal, Mato Grosso Amazon and Atlantic coastal forest.
Joel Souza, owner of Pousada Ecoverde, see Where to stay, above, T9638 1614, www. ecoverdetours.com. Speaks English, German and Italian, knowledgeable and very helpful, checklists for flora and fauna provided, will arrange all transport, accommodation and activities, tends to employ guides rather than guiding himself.
Pantanal Bird Club, T3624 1930, www. pantanalbirdclub.org. Good for even the most exacting clients, PBC are the most illustrious birders in Brazil with many years of experience, owner Braulio Carlos. Tours throughout the area and to various parts of Brazil.
Pantanal Eco Safari, see Pousada Safari, above.
Pantanal Nature Tours, R Campo Grande 487, T3322 0203, or T9955 2632, www. pantanalnature.com.br. Embratur licensed

guide, Ailton Lara, expert wildlife and birding knowledge, frequent jaguar sitings, works with small groups and will customize tours, well organized agency. He also goes to the Chapada dos Guimarães, Nobres (with crystal clear rivers filled with dourado) and Jardim da Amazônia in the north of Mato Grosso. Speaks English. Recommended.

Chapada dos Guimarães *p641*
Chapada Pantanal, Av Fernando Correa da Costa 1022, T065-3301 2757, www.chapadapantanal.tur.br. Tours to all the principal sights in the Chapada and trips further afield to Nobres.
Ecoturismo Cultural, Av Cipriano Curvo 655, T3301 1393, www.chapadadosguimaraes.com.br/ecoturis.htm. Recommended tours, with bilingual guides who know the area well; tours from 1 to 8 days.

⊖ Transport

Cuiabá *p639, map p640*
Air Airport in Várzea Grande; several hotels nearby. Flights to most major cities. ATMs outside; there is a post office and a **Sedtur** office (not always open). Taxi to centre US$12. From the airport to the centre take any white Tuiuiú bus from outside the terminal to Av Tenente Col Duarte, US$1.50. There is a direct Airport–Rodoviária bus, No 007; bus stop is by the farmacia outside airport. A new urban light rail system (VLT) from airport to city centre and new Verdão stadium was built for the 2014 World Cup.
Bus Many bus routes have stops in the vicinity of Praça Ipiranga. *Rodoviária* is on R Jules Rimet, Bairro Alvorada, north of the centre, T3621 3629; town buses stop at the entrance. Bus No 202 from R Joaquim Murtinho behind the cathedral, 20 mins. Comfortable buses (toilets) to **Campo Grande**, 10 hrs, US$45, several daily. Direct to **Brasília**, 24 hrs, US$70. To **Porto Velho**, 9 buses a day, US$65, 26 hrs. Connections to all major cities.

Cáceres *p641*
Bus *Rodoviária*, Terminal da Japonesa. Colibri/União Cascavel buses Cuiabá-Cáceres, US$26, many daily between 0630-2400 (book in advance), 3½ hrs.
Ferry For information on sailings, ask at the **Capitânia dos Portos**, on the corner of the main square at waterfront.

Border with Bolivia *p641*
Bus The bus fare Cáceres-San Matías is US$25 with **Transical-Velásquez**, Mon-Sat at 0630 and 1500, Sun 1500 only (return at same times), 3 hrs. Bus from **Pontes e Lacerda** to **San Ignacio de Velasco** (Bolivia) with **Rápido Monte Cristo**, Tue and Fri 0630, US$22, 8-9 hrs, much longer in rainy season when roads may be impassable; and **Amanda Tours** via Vila Bela, Mon, Wed, Fri 0600, US$28, on slightly better roads. From **Vila Bela** to Cuiabá via Pontes e Lacerda and Cáceres, daily at 0800 and 1930, US$45, 7-8 hrs.

Chapada dos Guimarães *p641*
Bus 7 daily to and from **Cuiabá** (Rubi 0700-1900, last back to Cuiabá 1800), 1½ hrs, US$7.
Car Hiring a car in Cuiabá is the most convenient way to see many of the scattered attractions, although access to several of them is via rough dirt roads which may deteriorate in the rainy season; drive carefully as the area is prone to dense fog. Agencies at the airport.

⊕ Directory

Cuiabá *p639, map p640*
Banks ATMs at banks in the centre. **Incomep Câmbio**, R Gen Neves 155, good rates.
Consulates Bolivia: R Paramaribo 174, Qd 08, lote 06, Jardim das Américas, T3627 4937.

Cáceres *p641*
Banks Casa de Câmbio Mattos, Comandante Bauduino 180, next to main praça, changes cash and TCs at good rates.

Contents

Chile

At a glance

◉ **Time required** 2-4 weeks.

🌣 **Best time** Oct-Dec and Mar-Apr are best; Jun-Aug good for the north. Jan/Feb are busiest holiday months and south can be very crowded. Independence celebrations 18-19 Sep is a busy time.

✖ **When not to go** Jun-Aug in the south. In Santiago air pollution is a problem year round, but it is worst in winter, May-Sep.

PERU

Visviri
PN Lauca
Arica   Putre   Tambo Quemado

Pisagua

Iquique

BOLIVIA

Quillagua   Ollagüe

Tocopilla   Chuquicamata
Calama   El Tatio
        San Pedro de Atacama
Salar de   Toconao
Atacama

Antofagasta   Socompa
Desert of
Atacama

Taltal   Socompa
Parque Nacional
Pan de Azúcar
Chañaral   Potrerillos

Caldera
Copiapó

PARAGUAY

Vallenar

La Serena
Coquimbo   ARGENTINA
Ovalle

Viña   Los Andes
del Mar
Valparaíso   SANTIAGO
        Rancagua   URUGUAY

Talca   Area de
    Protección Vilches
Chillán   Paso Pehuenche
Concepción

Cañete   Los Angeles
    Angol
Temuco   Curacautín
Valdivia   Villarrica
    Pucón
    Panguipulli
Osorno   Lago Ranco
Frutillar   Puerto Montt
Ancud
Castro   Chaitén
Chiloé
Quellón

Puyuguapi
Puerto Cisnes
Coyhaique
Puerto
Aisén

Cochrane
Atlantic
Ocean
Villa O'Higgins

PN Torres
del Paine
PN Bernardo
O'Higgins   Puerto Natales

Punta   Porvenir   Tierra
Arenas   del Fuego
    Puerto Williams

Pacific
Ocean

N

200 km
200 miles

Chile is a ribbon of land squashed between the Pacific and the Andes. Its landscape embraces glacial wilderness and moonscapes, lakes and volcanoes, beaches and salt flats. The north is characterized by the burnt colours of the driest desert in the world. Should rain fall in this barren land, flower seeds that have lain in wait seize the moment to bloom, bringing brilliant colours where no life seemed possible. Snow-capped volcanoes in the Lauca National Park appear close enough to touch in the rarefied air. In one day it is possible to scale a mountain with ice axe and crampons, soak off the exhaustion in a thermal bath and rest beneath the stars of the Southern Cross. Real stargazers will want to visit the astronomical observatories near La Serena, while lovers of mystery will head south for the folklore of Chiloé, Land of Seagulls. The Chilean Lake District is the homeland of the Mapuche, the people who resisted the Spaniards and who proudly maintain their culture and traditions. The lakes themselves are beautiful, set in farmland, overlooked by yet more snow-capped volcanoes. Before the road peters out, blocked by fjords and icefields, the Carretera Austral reveals ancient woodlands, hot springs beside the sea, mountains like castles and raging, emerald rivers – a paradise for fishing and cycling. To reach the ultimate goal of trekkers and birdwatchers, the fabulous granite towers and spires of the Torres del Paine National Park, you have to take a boat, or fly, or make the long haul through Argentina. There are seaports of every size, with their fishing boats, pelicans and sea lions. The most romantic is Valparaíso, described by one observer as "a Venice waiting to be discovered", with its warren of streets and brightly painted houses, its singular lifts up to the clifftops and its old bars.

Planning your trip

Where to go in Chile

A great many of Chile's attractions are outdoors, in the national parks, adventure sports, etc, but the capital, **Santiago**, has a rich cultural life (museums, handicrafts shopping) and is a good base for visiting nearby areas. These include the vineyards of the Maipo Valley, the Andean foothills in the Cajón del Maipo and the ski resorts. The port of Valparaíso and the beach resorts to north and south, principally Viña del Mar, are only a couple of hours away.

North of Santiago is La Serena, a popular seaside resort, from which can be reached the Elqui Valley, where Chilean pisco is made, and several major astronomical observatories. Heading north, the land becomes more barren, but every few years after rain, usually September to October, the flowers that have lain dormant in the desert burst into bloom; if you are in the area, a sight not to be missed. Inland from Antofagasta, the next main city, a road goes to Calama, the huge copper mine at Chuquicamata and the isolated Andean town and popular tourist resort of San Pedro de Atacama. Its attractions are lunar landscapes, hot geysers, salt flats and the way of life at high altitude. Alternatively, from Antofagasta you can take the spectacular coast road to the **far north** and the ports of Iquique, near which are several archaeological sites, thermal springs and abandoned nitrate mines, and Arica, the last main town before Peru. The road route into Bolivia from Arica passes through the magnificent Parque Nacional Lauca, with its wealth of Andean bird and animal life, high lakes and remote volcanoes.

South of Santiago, the longitudinal highway runs through the Central Valley passing through or near a number of cities, such as Rancagua, Talca, Chillán and Concepción (the country's second city). There are national parks which deserve a visit in both the Andean foothills and the coastal range of mountains. You can visit vineyards, thermal springs, unspoilt beaches or simply enjoy Chilean rural life.

The **Lake District** is home to the popular lakes of Villarrica and Llanquihue, but many others are far less developed. Protected areas of great beauty and first-class opportunities for adventure sports and fishing abound. Temuco, at the northern end of this region, is the centre of Mapuche culture and has a huge produce market. Wooded Valdivia, near the coast, is worth a detour for the trip to the rivermouth to see the ruined Spanish forts that protected this outpost of the empire. The southern gateway to the Lake District is Puerto Montt, the starting point for the long haul south. The city's fishing harbour, Angelmó, with its market and food stalls, is not to be missed. From Puerto Montt you can cross to Argentina by road and ferries on Lago Todos los Santos and neighbouring Lagos Frías and Nahuel Huapi on the way to Bariloche.

The island of **Chiloé**, a short bus and ferry ride from Puerto Montt, has a distinctive culture and a green landscape which is the result of its Pacific coastal climate. On the mainland, running south from Puerto Montt, the Carretera Austral has opened up an area of forests, lakes and rivers, linking small communities of settlers. The biggest town is Coyhaique and there are regular excursions by sea to the stunning glacier at the Laguna San Rafael from Puerto Montt and Puerto Chacabuco. Another sea voyage, four days from Puerto Montt, takes you to Puerto Natales in **Chilean Patagonia**, near Chile's most dramatic national park, the Torres del Paine. Hiking around the vertical mountains with their forested slopes, past lakes and glaciers, in the presence of a multitude of southern Andean wildlife is an unforgettable experience (but do allow for the unpredictability of the weather). If you prefer not to venture this far south by ship, there are regular flights to the main city of Chilean Patagonia, Punta Arenas, and there is no problem crossing from Argentina by road or by ferry from **Tierra del Fuego**. The contrast between this southernmost part of the country with the dry, desert north could not be greater.

Best time to visit Chile

The best times to visit vary according to geographical location. For the heartland, any time between October and April is good, but the most pleasant seasons are spring (September to November) and autumn (March to April). In Santiago itself, summers (December to February) are roasting hot and winters (June to August) polluted. The heat of the north is less intense from June to September. In the south December to March, summer, is the best time to visit. Along the Carretera Austral this is the only realistic time to travel because at other times ferry schedules are restricted and in mid-winter many transport services do not run at all. Further south, there is more leeway. The Torres del Paine park is open year round, though snow, fewer hours of daylight and reduced accommodation mean that only day hikes are feasible in winter. Also bear in mind that January to February in the Lake District and further south are the busiest months, with raised prices, hotels and buses full, lots of backpackers on the road and advance booking often essential.

Transport in Chile

Air LAN (www.lan.com) under the banner **Lan Express**, has a modern fleet and good service between Santiago and major towns and cities, but allow plenty of time when checking in. If you didn't print your boarding pass from the internet, there are machines to do so at the airport before you get to the counter to drop luggage. **Sky** (www.skyairline.cl) has a less extensive network than LAN. To the north and Concepción flights are offered by **PAL** (www.palair.cl). Try to sit on the left flying south, on the right flying north to get the best views of the Andes. On long routes with stops, check if it is cheaper to buy each sector separately. LAN's '**South America Air Pass**' can be used on all LAN routes within South America, including the Chilean cities it serves. It must be purchased abroad in conjunction with an international ticket on a LAN flight (or Iberia from Europe) and reservations made well ahead. Domestic single flights cost between US$108 and US$186 each, while flights to Easter Island cost US$442 each way (prices are higher for those arriving on other airlines). Air taxes must be paid on each flight. Route changes and cancellations may be made prior to the flight date on payment of a penalty. Confirm domestic flights at least 24 hours before your departure.

Bus Buses are frequent and on the whole good. Apart from holiday times, there is little problem getting a seat on a long-distance bus. Salón-cama services run between main cities on overnight services. **Tur-Bus** (www.turbus.cl), and **Pullman** (www.pullman.cl), each covering the whole country as far south as Puerto Montt, are among the best companies. Standards on routes vary. *Prémium* buses have six fully reclining seats. *Salón-cama* means 25 seats, *semi-cama* means 34 and salón-*ejecutivo* or *clásico* means 44 seats. Stops are infrequent. Many bus itineraries can be checked online but often a Chilean ID card number is needed for buying tickets online. Since there is lots of competition between bus companies, fares

Driving in Chile

Road Most roads are in good condition and many are paved. The main road is the Panamericana (Ruta 5) from Arica to Chiloé. It is motorway from La Serena to Puerto Montt. A coastal route running much of the length of Chile is being paved. Motorways tolls are very expensive, but the charge includes towing to the next city and free ambulance in case of accident.

Safety In the south (particularly on the Carretera Austral) and in the desert north, always top up your fuel tank and carry spare fuel (you may have to buy a can if renting a car). *Carabineros* (national police) are strict about speed limits (100-120 kph on motorways): *Chiletur Copec* maps mark police posts. Car drivers should have all their papers in order and to hand as there are occasional checks. In suburban areas headlights should be switched on, day and night.

Documents For drivers of private vehicles entering Chile from Argentina, there is a special *salida y admisión temporal de vehículos* form. From Peru or Bolivia, customs type out a *título de importación temporal de vehículos* (temporary admission), valid for the length of stay granted by immigration. Your immigration entry/exit card is stamped 'entrada con vehículo' so you must leave the country with your vehicle (so you cannot go to Bariloche, for example, without your car). Foreigners must have an international driving licence. Insurance is obligatory and can be bought at borders. A *carnet de passages* is not officially required for foreign-owned motorcycles: a temporary import paper is given at the border.

Organizations Automóvil Club de Chile, Av Andrés Bello 1863, Providencia, Santiago, T600-450 6000, www.automovil club.cl. It has a countrywide network and a car hire agency (with discounts for members or affiliates).

Car hire Shop around as there is a lot of competition. Reputable Chilean companies offer much better value than the well-known international ones, although rates may not always include insurance or 19% VAT. The legal age for renting a car is 22. In northern Chile, where mountain roads are bad, check rental vehicles very carefully before setting out. Hire companies charge a large premium to collect the car from another city, so unless making a round-trip it makes economic sense to travel by public transport, then rent a car locally. If intending to leave the country in a hired car, you must obtain authorization from the hire company.

Fuel Gasoline becomes more expensive the further north and further south you go. Unleaded fuel, 93, 95 and 97 octane, US$1.50-1.60, is available in all main cities. Diesel is widely available, US$1.25 a litre. Larger service stations usually accept credit cards, but check before filling up.

may be bargained lower with smaller operators, particularly just before departure. Prices are highest between December and March, and during the Independence celebrations in September. Students with ISIC cards may get discounts, except in high season; discounts are also often available for return journeys. Most bus companies will carry bicycles, but may ask for payment.

Pachamama by Bus ⓘ *Agustinas 2113, Santiago, T02-2688 8018, www.pachamamabybus. com*, is a backpackers' hop-on, hop-off bus service running from Santiago to the north and south weekly, taking scenic routes with frequent stops, with camping where hostel accommodation is not available. English-speaking guides.

Hitchhiking Hitchhiking is generally easy and safe throughout Chile, although you may find that in some regions traffic is sparse, so you are less likely to catch a lift (drivers will sometimes make hand signals if they are only going a short distance beyond – this is not a rude gesture!).

Taxis Taxis have meters, but agree beforehand on fares for long journeys out of city centres or special excursions. In some places a surcharge is applied late at night. Taxi drivers may not know the location of streets away from the centre. There is no need to tip unless some extra service, like the carrying of luggage, is given. Black colectivos in urban areas (collective taxis) operate on fixed routes identified by numbers and destinations. They have fixed charges, often little more expensive than buses, which increase at night and which are usually advertised in the front windscreen. They are flagged down on the street corner (in some cities such as Puerto Montt there are signs). Take small change as the driver takes money and offers change while driving. Yellow colectivos also operate on some inter-urban routes, leaving from a set point when full.

Train There are passenger services from Santiago to Chillán; regional train lines in the Valparaíso and Concepción areas; a scenic line from Talca along the valley of the Río Maule to Constitución and in the far north, only the line from Arica to Tacna (Peru) carries passengers, if it is running. There are plans (2014) to revive the Arica-La Paz line. Trains in Chile are moderately priced. See Santiago, transport, page 675, for rail company offices.

Where to stay in Chile → *See Essentials chapter for our hotel price guide.*

Chile has its share of international chains and some 'historic' establishments. Boutique hotels and characterful B&Bs are becoming more common and in most parts of Chile accommodation is plentiful across the budget ranges. In popular tourist destinations, especially in the south in high season, many families offer rooms: these are advertised by a sign in the window. People often meet buses to offer rooms, which vary greatly in quality and cleanliness; have a look before committing. In summer especially, single rooms can be hard to find.

On hotel bills IVA (VAT) is charged at 19%. The government waives VAT on hotel bills paid in dollars or Euros at authorized hotels only. As a result, larger hotels (but few other establishments) can offer you much lower tariffs if you pay in dollars or Euros than those advertised in pesos. But check the exchange rate: it may be so poor that you end up paying more in dollars than in pesos. Establish clearly in advance what is included in the room price.

Camping Campsites often charge US$18-20 for up to five people, but if a site is not full, owners may give a pitch to a single camper for US$8-10. A few hostels allow camping in their garden and offer good value rates. Cheap gas stoves can be bought in camping shops in Santiago and popular trekking areas and green replaceable cylinders are available. Campsites are very busy in January and February.

Wild camping is easy and safe in remote areas of the far south and in the *cordillera* north of Santiago. In Mapuche and Aymará communities it is courteous and advisable to go to the primary school or some other focal point to meet prominent members of the community first. Camping wild in the north is difficult, because of the lack of water. In much of central and central-southern Chile the land is fenced off and as it is officially illegal to camp on private land without permission, it may be necessary to ask first. Also note that in the Lake District and Chiloé, between mid-December and mid-January, huge horseflies (*tábanos*) can be a real problem when camping, hiking and fishing: do not wear dark clothing.

Youth hostels www.backpackerschile.com focuses on hostels charging around US$15-25 pp of a good standard. There are youth hostels (*albergues*) throughout Chile; average cost about US$12-24 pp. Although some hostels are open only from January to the end of February, many operate all year round. The IH card is usually readily accepted, but YHA affiliated hostels are not necessarily the best. A Hostelling International card costs US$22. These can be obtained from **Asociación Chilena de Albergues Turísticos Juveniles** ⓘ*Hernando de Aguirre 201, of 401, Providencia, Santiago, T2577 1200, www.hostelling.cl.* In summer there are makeshift hostels in many Chilean towns, usually in the main schools; they charge up to US$7 per person and are good meeting places. Don't expect much sleep or privacy, though.

Food and drink in Chile → *See Essentials chapter for our restaurant price guide.*

Restaurants in Chile Breakfast is usually instant coffee or tea with bread, butter and jam. Lunch, served from 1300 to 1530, tends to be the main meal of the day and many restaurants serve a cheaper fixed-price meal at lunch time. When this consists of a single dish it is known as *la colación*, when there is more than one course it is called *el menú*. In more expensive places, this may not be referred to on the menu. Dinner is between 2000 and 2230. *Las onces* (literally elevenses) is the name given to a snack usually including tea, bread, cheese, etc, eaten by many Chileans as their evening meal. The cheapest restaurants in urban areas tend to be by the transport terminals and markets or, in coastal areas, by the port. Also try the *casinos de bomberos* (firemen's canteens) in most towns.

Food A very typical Chilean dish is *cazuela de ave* (or *de vacuno*), a nutritious stew containing large pieces of chicken (or beef), pumpkin potatoes, rice, and maybe onions, and green peppers. *Valdiviano* is another stew, common in the south, consisting of beef, onion, sliced potatoes and eggs. *Empanadas de pino* are turnovers filled with meat, onions, raisins, olives and egg chopped up together. *Pastel de choclo* is a casserole of meat and onions with olives, topped with a maize-meal mash, baked in an earthenware bowl. *Humitas* are mashed sweetcorn mixed with butter and spices and baked in sweetcorn leaves. *Prieta* is a blood sausage stuffed with cabbage leaves. A normal *parrillada* or *asado* is a giant mixed grill served from a charcoal brazier. *Bife/lomo a lo pobre* (a poor man's steak) can be just the opposite: it is a steak topped by two fried eggs, chips and fried onions. The Valparaíso speciality is the *chorrillana*, chips topped with fried sliced steak, fried onions and scrambled eggs, while in Chiloé you can enjoy a *curanto*, a meat, shellfish and potato stew traditionally cooked in a hole in the ground. Many dishes in Mapuche districts are flavoured with *merkén*, a spice blend of smoked red goat's horn pepper, toasted coriander seed and salt. Ready-made packets are sold.

What gives Chilean food its personality is the **seafood**. The delicious congrio fish is a national dish, and *caldillo de congrio* (a soup served with a massive piece of kingclip/ling, onions and potatoes) is excellent. A *paila* can take many forms (the *paila* is simply a kind of dish), but the commonest are made of eggs or seafood. *Paila chonchi* is a kind of bouillabaisse, but has more flavour, more body, more ingredients. *Parrillada de mariscos* is a dish of grilled mixed seafood, brought to the table piping hot on a charcoal brazier. Other excellent local fish are the *cojinova*, the *albacora* (swordfish) and the *corvina* (bass). A range of mussels (*choritos/cholgas*) is available, as are abalone (*locos*), clams (*almejas*) and razor clams (*machas*). Some bivalve shellfish may be periodically banned because they carry the disease **marea roja** (which is fatal in humans). *Cochayuyo* is seaweed, bound into bundles, described as 'hard, leathery thongs'. The *erizo*, or sea-urchin, is also commonly eaten as are *picorocos* (sea barnacles) and the strong flavoured *piure*. *Luche* is dried seaweed, sold as a black cake, like 'flakey bread pudding' to be added to soups and stews. **Avocado** pears (*paltas*) are excellent, and play an important role in recipes. Make sure that vegetables are included in the price for the main dish; menus often don't make this clear. Local **fast food** is excellent. *Completos* are hot dogs with a huge variety of fillings. A *barros jarpa* is a grilled cheese and ham sandwich and a *barras luco* is a grilled cheese and beef sandwich. *Sopaipillas* are cakes made of a mixture including pumpkin, served in syrup. Ice cream is very good; try *lúcuma* and *chirimoya* (custard apple) flavours.

Drink Tap **water** is safe to drink in main cities but bottled water is safer for the north. The local **wines** are very good; the best are from the central areas. The bottled wines cost from US$3 upwards; the very best wines will cost about US$50 in a smart restaurant. **Beer** is quite good and cheap. Draught lager is known as Schop. Chilean brewed beers include Cristal, Escudo and Royal Guard, Austral (good in the far south), Báltica, Brahma and Heineken. Malta, a brown ale, is recommended for those wanting a British-type beer. There are good local breweries in Valparaíso, the Elqui valley (Guayacán), Punta Arenas and Llanquihue near Puerto Varas and an increasing number of microbreweries around the country. In 2014 at least, bars in the capital were giving much greater prominence to beers than to wine.

Pisco, made from grapes, is the most famous spirit. It is best drunk as a 'Pisco Sour' with lime or lemon juice and sugar. Two popular drinks are **vaina**, a mixture of brandy, egg and sugar and **cola de mono**, a mixture of aguardiente, coffee, milk and vanilla served very cold at Christmas. **Chicha** is any form of alcoholic drink made from fruit, usually grapes. **Cider** (*chicha de manzana*) is popular in the south. **Mote con huesillo**, made from wheat hominy and dried peaches, is a soft drink, refreshing in summer. A *vitamina* is a 100% pure fruit juice drink.

Coffee is generally instant except in espresso bars in major cities. Elsewhere specify *café-café* or *expresso*. A *cortado* is an espresso with hot frothed milk served in a glass. Tea is widely available. If you order *café*, or *té, con leche*, it will come with all milk; if you want just a little milk, you must specify that. After a meal, try an *agüita* (infusion) – hot water in which herbs such as mint or aromatics such as lemon peel, have been steeped. There is a wide variety, very refreshing.

Essentials A-Z

Accident and emergency
Air rescue service T138. For earthquake updates and other information see the Ministerio del Interior y Seguridad Pública website, www.onemi.cl, and www.reddeemergencia.cl. **Ambulance** (*ambulancia*)T131. **Fire brigade** (*bomberos*) T132, www.bomberos.cl. **Forest fires** (*incendios forestales*) T130. **Police** (*carabineros*) T133; (detectives, *investigaciones*) T134. **Policía Internacional** head office E Ramírez 852, Santiago, T02-2737 1292, Mon-Fri 0900-1700, handle immigration, lost tourist cards.

Electricity
220 volts AC, 50 cycles. Sockets are 3 round pins in a line, which accept 2-pin plugs.

Embassies and consulates
For all Chilean embassies and consulates abroad and for all foreign embassies and consulates in Chile, see http://embassy.goabroad.com.

Festivals in Chile
Public holidays 1 Jan, New Year's Day; Semana Santa (Fri and Sat); **1 May**, Labour Day; **21 May**, Glorias Navales/Navy Day; **29 Jun**, San Pedro y San Pablo; **16 Jul**, Virgen del Carmen; **15 Aug**, Asunción de la Virgen; **18, 19 Sep**, Independence Days; **12 Oct**, Día de la Raza; **31 Oct**, **Día Nacional de las Iglesias Evangélicas y Protestantes**; **1 Nov**, Todos los Santos; **8 Dec**, Inmaculada Concepción; **25 Dec**, Christmas.

Maps
The Instituto Geográfico Militar, Dieciocho 369, Santiago, T02-2410 9363, www.igm.cl, Mon-Fri 0830-1730, has detailed geophysical and topographical maps of the whole of Chile, useful for climbing; expensive, but the Biblioteca Nacional, Alameda 651, T02-2360 5200, will allow you to photocopy. *Matassi* maps (JLM Mapas), available from www. travelaid.cl, US$6.50, usually with a red cover, are good value but often contain errors. The *Chiletur Copec* guides (see Tourist information, below) are useful for roads and towns, but not all distances are exact. Good road maps are also published by Tur-Bus.

Money → *US$1= 553 pesos, €1– 758 pesos (May 2014)*.
The unit of currency is the peso, its sign is $. Notes are for 1000, 2000, 5000, 10,000 and 20,000 pesos and coins for 1, 5, 10, 50, 100 and 500 pesos. Small shops and bus drivers do not like large notes, especially in the morning and in rural areas.

Plastic/banks (ATMs)
The easiest way to obtain cash is by using ATMs which operate under the sign Redbanc (www.redbanc.cl, for a full list); they take Cirrus (MasterCard), Maestro and Plus (Visa) and permit transactions up to 200,000 pesos chilenos per day. Instructions are available in English. Note, though, that ATMs in Chile charge 4000 pesos commission and 1800 pesos fees (US$10.50 in total) for each

transaction. This charge is not made in ATMs of **BancoEstado** (Banco del Estado) or **Servi-Estado** in **Líder** supermarkets. At BancoEstado ATMs, if you choose the Spanish option, you can opt not to have a receipt and save yourself a further US$2 in charges; in English you don't get this choice. Note also that **Banco del Estado Redbanc** ATMs take only MasterCard. Visa and MasterCard are common in Chile. American Express and Diner's Club are less useful. The best **exchange rates** offered are in Santiago. US dollars cash and euros can be exchanged. Even slightly damaged or marked foreign notes may be rejected. Exchange shops (*casas de cambio*) are open longer hours and often give slightly better rates than banks. It is always worth shopping around. Rates get worse as you go north from Santiago. Official rates are quoted in daily newspapers.

Cost of travelling
The average cost for a traveller on an economical budget is about US$40-45 per day for food, accommodation and land transportation (more for flights, tours, car hire, etc). Breakfast in hotels, if not included, is US$2.50-4. *Alojamiento* in private houses and hostels (bed, breakfast and often use of kitchen) starts at about US$12. Internet costs US$0.60-1 per hr. Southern Chile is much more expensive between 15 Dec and 15 Mar. Santiago tends to be more expensive for food and accommodation than other parts of Chile.

Opening hours
Banks: 0900-1400, closed Sat. **Government offices**: 1000-1230 (the public is admitted for a few hours only). **Other offices**: Mon-Fri 0830-1230, 1400-1800. **Shops** (Santiago) : 1030-1930, Sat 0930-1330.

Postal services
The post office is **Correos Chile**, www.correos.cl. Its branches are usually open Mon-Fri 0900-1800. The main office in the capital is on the Plaza de Armas. Poste restante is well organized (though only kept for 30 days), passport essential to collect letters and parcels; a list of those received in the hall of the central post office (one list for men, another for women), indicate Sr or Sra/Srta on envelope). The central

post office also has philatelic section, 0900-1630, and small stamp museum (ask to see it). If sending a parcel, the contents must first be checked at the post office.

Safety
Chile is one of the safest countries in South America for the visitor. Like all major cities around the world, though, Santiago and Valparaíso do have crime problems. Law enforcement officers are *carabineros* (green military uniforms), who handle all tasks except immigration. *Investigaciones,* in civilian dress, are detective police who deal with everything except traffic.

Taxes
Airport taxes
US$30 for international flights; US$11.80 for international flights under 500 km and domestic flights over 270 km; US$4.65 for domestic flights under 270 km (all taxes included in ticket price).

VAT
VAT/IVA is 19%.

Telephone → *Country code T+56.*
Ringing: a single ring (as in the US). Engaged: equal tones with equal pauses. *Centros de llamadas* (phone centres) are abundant and are the easiest places to make a call. They are much cheaper than main company offices. They have private booths where you can talk as long as you like and pay afterwards. They often have internet, photocopying and fax, too. For international calls use a *centro de llamadas* or a pre-paid phone scratch card, available from *kioskos*.

International roaming is becoming more common, but buying a local pay-as-you-go may be cheaper. Major airports and hotels often have rental desks, can advise on local outlets and how to use mobiles. Mobile numbers are preceded by 09 if calling from a landline.

Time
Official time is 4 hrs behind GMT, 3 hrs behind in summer. Clocks change from mid-Sep or Oct to early Mar.

Tipping

10% in restaurants, if service is not included; tip about 100 pesos in bars. Porters: US$1 or US$0.15 a piece of luggage. Taxi drivers are not tipped.

Tourist information

The national secretariat of tourism, **Sernatur**, www.sernatur.cl, has offices throughout the country (addresses given in the text). The official online guide is www.chile.travel. Look on the website for establishments with the official *Sello de Calidad Turística*. City offices provide town maps and other information. **Copec** publishes a 5-part guide to the country, *Norte, Centro, Sur*, a national route map and a camping guide with road map, with information and a wealth of maps including neighbouring tourist centres in Argentina, in Spanish only, found in bookshops, Copec filling stations and news stands in most city centres. **CONAF** (the Corporacíon Nacional Forestal), Presidente Bulnes 285, Santiago, T02-2663 0000, www.conaf.cl, publishes a number of leaflets (in Spanish and English) and has documents and maps about the national park system. **CODEFF (Comité Nacional Pro-Defensa de la Fauna y Flora)**, Ernesto Reyes 35, Providencia, Santiago, T02-2777 2534, www.codeff.cl, can also provide information on environmental questions. For regulations on sport fishing, see http://pescarecreativa.sernapesca.cl.

South American Explorers has opened a new branch in Chile, at Quinta Escondida, Carrera 013, Limache, V Región, T09-8418 0531, Natascha Scott-Stokes, Mon-Fri 1000-1700, Sat 1000-1300, closed Sun and all bank holidays. See page 691.

Useful websites

www.ancientforests.org/chile.htm Information on Chilean forests.
www.avesdechile.cl Birdwatching site (in Spanish).
www.chile.cl Information in Spanish.
www.dibam.cl Official site for museums, libraries and galleries.
www.pasosfronterizos.gov.cl Details on the border posts between Chile and Argentina.
www.senderodechile.cl About the project for a country-long trekking/mountain biking path.

www.trekkingchile.com Hiking, trekking, mountaineering, culture and travelling in Chile.
www.welcomechile.com Interpatagonia's Chile site with tourist information, in Spanish and English.

Visas and immigration

Passport (valid for at least 6 months) and tourist card only are required for entry by all foreigners except citizens of Kuwait, Egypt, Saudi Arabia and UAE, most African countries, Guyana, Cuba and former Soviet bloc countries not now in the EU, who require visas. It is imperative to check tourist card and visa requirements before travel. National identity cards are sufficient for entry by citizens of all South American countries. Tourist cards are valid in most cases for 90 days, but some are for 60 and others 30 days. Tourist cards can be obtained from immigration offices at major land borders and Chilean airports; you must surrender your tourist card on departure (if you lose it ask immigration for a replacement). If you wish to stay longer than 90 days (as a tourist), you must buy a 90-day extension from the Departamento de Extranjería (head office San Antonio 580, Santiago, T600-486 3000, www.extranjeria. gob.cl, address for extensions in Santiago under Useful addresses, page 676), or any local *gobernación* office. It costs US$100. To avoid the long queue and long-winded bureaucracy, make a day trip to Argentina, Bolivia or Peru and return with a new tourist card (the authorities don't like it if you do this more than 3-4 times). An onward ticket is required. Tourist card holders may change their status to enable them to stay on in employment if they have a contract, they need to contact the Extranjería in whichever province they will be working. On arrival you will be asked where you are staying in Chile. **Note** On arrival by air, US citizens will be charged an administration fee of US$160, Canadians US$132, Australians US$117, Albanians US$30 and Mexicans US$23 (this is a reciprocal tax payable because Chileans have to pay the equivalent amount when applying for visas to enter these countries; rates are posted at arrivals and they do change; can be paid by Visa card). This tax is not charged at land borders. The permission is valid for multiple entry and for the life of the passport. The tax should be paid in cash. For some nationalities a visa will be granted within 24 hrs upon production of an onward ticket, for others, authorization must be obtained from Chile. For other nationalities who need a visa, a charge is made. To travel overland to or from Tierra del Fuego a multiple entry visa is essential since the Argentine-Chilean border is crossed more than once (it is advisable to get a multiple entry visa before arriving, rather than trying to change a single entry visa once in Chile). A student card is useful for getting discounts on transport and access to various concessions and services. They can be obtained from Hernando de Aguirre 201, of 602, Providencia, T2577 1200, and cost US$16.25, photo and proof of status required; www.isic.cl.

Weights and measures
The metric system is obligatory.

Santiago and around

Santiago, the political, economic and financial capital of Chile, is one of the most beautifully set of any city, standing in a wide plain with the magnificent chain of the Andes in full view – rain and pollution permitting. Nearly 40% of Chileans live in and around Santiago, the sixth largest city in South America. It's a modern industrial capital, full of skyscrapers, bustle, noise and traffic, and smog is a problem especially between April and September. Santiago bursts with possibilities, with its parks, museums, shops and hectic nightlife, and is also within easy reach of vineyards, beaches and Andean ski resorts.

Arriving in Santiago → *Phone code: 02. Colour map 8, B1. Population: 6 million. Altitude: 600 m.*

Orientation The airport is 26 km northwest of the centre. The railway station, Estacíon Central, which only serves the south of the country, is on the Alameda, as are the four main bus terminals. The metro (underground railway) has four lines: Line 1 runs west-east, linking the bus and train stations, the centre, Providencia and beyond. City buses are operated under the *Transantiago* system; details under Transport, below. Taxis are abundant, but Radio Taxis, called in advance, tend to be safer.

The centre of the old city lies between the Mapocho and the Avenida O'Higgins, which is usually known as the Alameda. From the Plaza Baquedano (usually called Plaza Italia), in the east of the city's central area, the Mapocho flows to the northwest and the Alameda runs to the southwest. From Plaza Italia the C Merced runs due west to the Plaza de Armas, the heart of the city, five blocks south of the Mapocho. An urban motorway runs the length of Santiago from east to west under the course of the Río Mapocho. Like all large cities, Santiago has problems of theft. Pickpockets and bag-snatchers, who are often well-dressed, operate especially on the metro and around the Plaza de Armas. Avoid the *poblaciones* (shanty towns), notably Pudahuel and parts of the north (such as Conchalí), especially if you are travelling alone or have only recently arrived.

Tourist offices Servicio Nacional de Turismo Sernatur ① *Av Providencia 1550, metro Manuel Montt, next to Providencia Municipal Library, T2731 8310, info@sernatur.cl, Mon-Fri 0900-1900, Sat 0900-1400*, maps, brochures and posters. Good notice board. **Information office** also at the airport daily 0900-2100, T2601 9320. **Municipal Tourist Board** ① *north side of Plaza de Armas, T2713 6745, and at Cerro Santa Lucía, T2664 4206, www.ciudad.cl, Mon-Thu 1000-1800, Fri 1000-1700,* offers free walking tours most days of the week. Almost all museums are closed on Monday and on 1 November.

Best time to visit There is rain during the winter (May-August), but the summers are dry. The rain increases to the south. On the coast at Viña del Mar it is 483 mm a year, but is less inland. Temperatures, on the other hand, are higher inland than on the coast. There is frost now and then, but very little snow. Temperatures can reach 33°C in January, but fall to 13°C (3°C at night) in July. Days are usually hot, the nights cool. There is usually less wind in winter, making smog a more serious problem (smog forecast are published in the daily papers, during television weather forecasts and inside underground stations).

Places in and around Santiago

Around the Plaza de Armas On the eastern and southern sides of the Plaza de Armas there are arcades with shops; on the northern side is the post office and the Municipalidad; and on the western side the Cathedral and the archbishop's palace. The **Cathedral**, much rebuilt, contains a recumbent statue in wood of San Francisco Javier; the chandelier which lit the first meetings of Congress after independence; and an interesting **museum** ① *0930-1230, 1530-1830, free*, of religious art and historical pieces. In the Palacio de la Real Audiencia is the **Museo Histórico Nacional** ① *T2411 7010, www.museonacionalhistorico.cl, Tue-Sun 1000-1730, US$1.15, free on Sun, signs in Spanish*, covering the period from the Conquest until 1925. The Plaza and the Casa Colorada (below) were being remodeled in 2014.

Just west of the Plaza is the **Museo Chileno de Arte Precolombino** ① *in the former Real Aduana, Bandera 361, T2928 1500, www.precolombino.cl, Tue-Sun 1000-1800, US$6.35, students and children free, displays in English*. Its collection of objects from the pre-Columbian cultures of Central America and the Andean region is highly recommended for the quality of the objects and their presentation. At Calle Merced 864, is the **Casa Colorada** (1769), home of the Governor in colonial days and then of Mateo de Toro, first president of Chile. It is now the **Museo de Santiago** ① *T2633 0723, Tue-Sat 1000-1800, Sun and holidays, 1100-1400, US$3, students free*. It covers the history of Santiago from the Conquest to modern times, with excellent displays and models, some signs in English, guided tours. Paseo Ahumada, a pedestrianized street lined with cafés runs south to the Alameda four blocks away, crossing Huérfanos.

Four blocks north of the Plaza de Armas is the interesting **Mercado Central** ① *21 de Mayo y San Pablo*, the best place in Santiago for seafood. The building faces the Parque Venezuela, on which is the Cal y Canto metro station and, at its western end, the **Centro Cultural Estación Mapocho** ① *www.estacionmapocho.cl*, in the old Mapocho station. East of the Mercado Central is the Parque Forestal (see below), through which you come to Plaza Italia.

Along the Alameda The Alameda runs through the heart of the city for over 3 km. It is 100 m wide, and ornamented with gardens and statuary: the most notable are the equestrian statues of Generals O'Higgins and San Martín; the statue of the Chilean historian Benjamín Vicuña MacKenna who, as mayor of Santiago, beautified Cerro Santa Lucía (see below); and the great monument in honour of the battle of Concepción in 1879.

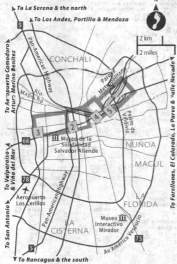

① Santiago orientation

To La Serena & the north
To Los Andes, Portillo & Mendoza

2 km
2 miles

CONCHALI

Pan-American Highway

To Aeropuerto Comodoro Arturo Merino Benítez

Río Mapocho

Parque Metropolitano

Pedro de Valdivia

To Valparaíso & Viña del Mar

III Museo de la Solidaridad Salvador Allende

NUÑOA

MACUL

To Farellones, El Colorado, La Parva & Valle Nevado

Aeropuerto Los Cerrillos

Pan-American Highway

FLORIDA

To San Antonio

LA CISTERNA

Museo III Interactivo Mirador

Av Américo Vespucio

To Rancagua & the south

From the Plaza Italia, where there is a statue of Gen Baquedano and the Tomb of the Unknown Soldier, the Alameda skirts, on the right, Cerro Santa Lucía, and on the left, the Catholic University. Beyond the hill the Alameda passes the neoclassical **Biblioteca Nacional** ① *Av O'Higgins 651, Santa Lucía metro, www.bibliotecanacional.cl, Mon-Fri 0900-1900, Sat 0910-1400 (Jan-Feb, closed Sat), free*, good concerts, temporary exhibitions. Beyond, on the left, between calles San Francisco and Londres, is the oldest church in Santiago: the red-walled church and monastery of **San Francisco** (1618). Inside is the small statue of the Virgin that Valdivia carried on his saddlebow when he rode from Peru to Chile. The **Museo Colonial San Francisco** ① *by Iglesia San Francisco, Londres 4, T2639 8737, http://museosanfrancisco.com, Mon-Fri 0930-1330, 1500-1800, Sat-Sun 1000-1400, US$2*, houses religious art, including 54 paintings of the life of St Francis; in the cloisters is a

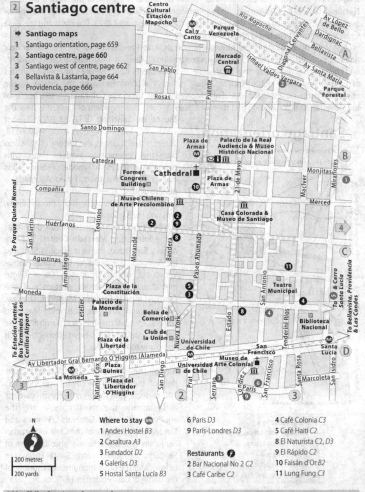

② Santiago centre

→ **Santiago maps**
1 Santiago orientation, page 659
2 **Santiago centre, page 660**
3 Santiago west of centre, page 662
4 Bellavista & Lastarria, page 664
5 Providencia, page 666

Where to stay 🛏
1 Andes Hostel *B3*
2 Casaltura *A3*
3 Fundador *D2*
4 Galerías *D3*
5 Hostal Santa Lucía *B3*
6 París *D3*
9 París-Londres *D3*

Restaurants 🍴
2 Bar Nacional No 2 *C2*
3 Café Caribe *C2*

4 Café Colonia *C3*
5 Café Haití *C2*
8 El Naturista *C2, D3*
9 El Rápido *C2*
10 Faisán d'Or *B2*
11 Lung Fung *C3*

room containing poet Gabriela Mistral's Nobel medal. South of San Francisco is the Barrio París-Londres, built 1923-1929, now restored. Two blocks north of the Alameda is **Teatro Municipal** ① *C Agustinas 794, www.municipal.cl,* under reconstruction in 2014.

A little further west along the Alameda, is the Universidad de Chile; the **Club de la Unión** (www.clubdelaunion.cl), a National Monument, is almost opposite. Nearby, on Calle Nueva York is the **Bolsa de Comercio**; the public may view the trading; passport required. One block further west is Plaza de la Libertad. North of the plaza, hemmed in by the skyscrapers of the Centro Cívico, is the **Palacio de la Moneda** ① *T2690 4000, visitas@presidencia.cl for reservations, Mon-Fri for guided tours of the palace, courtyards are open to the public (access from north side) Mon-Fri 1000-1800 unless important state business is being carried out,* the **Presidential Palace** (1805) containing historic relics, paintings and sculpture, and the elaborate '**Salón Rojo**' used for official receptions. Although the Moneda was damaged by air attacks during the military coup of 11 September 1973 it has been fully restored. Ceremonial changing of the guard every other day, 1000. The large new **Centro Cultural Palacio La Moneda** ① *T2355 6500, www.ccplm. cl, 0900-2100, exhibitions 0900-1930 daily, US$9 for foreigners, US$4.50 for foreign students,* houses temporary exhibitions as well as an arts cinema and an interesting gallery of Chilean handicrafts (both closed Monday).

West of the centre Barrio Brasil, with Plaza Brasil at its heart and the Basílica del Salvador two blocks from the plaza, is one of the earliest parts of the city. It has some fine old buildings, especially around Calle Concha y Toro, but now it's a more bohemian, studenty area with lots of places to stay as well as numerous bars, clubs, cafés and lively restaurants (Metro República). The next barrio west, Yungay, is in much the same vein, with many once elegant buildings, a leafy plaza and, today, a lot of street art. See the historic Peluquería Francesa i Compañía y Libertad, www.boulevardlavaud.cl, which houses a barber's shop dating from 1868, a restaurant, deli and antiques. You can walk from Brasil through Yungay to the Quinta Normal (see below).

Five blocks south of the Alameda is the **Palacio Cousiño** ① *C Dieciocho 438, www.palaciocousino. cl, Metro Toesca, closed due to earthquake damage, but you can tour the grounds.* This large mansion in French rococo style has a superb Italian marble staircase and other opulent rooms.

Parque O'Higgins ① *10 blocks south of Alameda; take Metro Line 2 to Parque O'Higgins station, bus from Parque Baquedano via Av MacKenna and Av Matta.* It has a small lake, tennis courts, swimming pool (open from 5 December), an open-air stage, a club, the racecourse of the Club Hípico and an amusement park, **Fantasilandia** ① *www.fantasilandia.cl, daily in summer, winter weekends only 1200-1900, US$18, US$9 children and seniors, families US$22.55, unlimited rides.* The Alameda continues west to the **Planetarium** ① *Alameda 3349, T2718 2900, www.planetariochile. cl, US$7.* Opposite it on the southern side is the railway station (Estación Central or Alameda). On Avenida Matucana, running north from here, is the popular Parque Quinta Normal (at Avenida D Portales). It was founded as a botanical garden in 1830. Near the park is **Museo Artequín** ① *Av Portales 3530, T2681 8656, www.artequin.cl, Tue-Fri 0900-1700, Sat-Sun 1100-1800, closed Feb, US$1.50.* Housed in the Chilean pavilion built for the 1889 Paris International Exhibition, it contains prints of famous paintings and activities and explanations of the techniques of the great masters. The Quinta Normal metro station has an underground cultural centre with theatres and a free art cinema (part of the Metro Arte project), which shows independent films. 200 m from the station is the Biblioteca de Santiago (public library, www.bibliotecasantiago.cl), in front of which is **Centro Cultural Matucana 100** (www.m100.cl), with several exhibition halls and a theatre. Across Avenida Matucana from Quinta Normal metro station is the **Museo de la Memoria de los Derechos Humanos** ① *Av Matucana 501, T2597 9600, www.museodelamemoria.cl, Tue-Sun 1000-2000, free, audio guide for non-Spanish speakers,* a huge block covered in oxidized copper mesh suspended above an open space. On three floors it concentrates on the events and aftermath of 11 September 1973, with videos, testimonies, documents and other items. It also has information on human rights struggles worldwide and temporary exhibits, a gift shop and café. The **Museo de la Solidaridad Salvador Allende** ① *Av República 475, T2689 8761, www.mssa.cl, Tue-Sun 1000-1800, US$2, Sun free,* houses a highly regarded collection of 20th-century works donated by Chilean and other artists (Picasso, Miró, Matta and many more) who sympathized with the Allende government, plus some personal items of the president himself. The contents were hidden during the Pinochet years.

East of the centre **Cerro Santa Lucía** ① *closes at 2100; visitors must sign a register at the entrance, giving their ID card number,* bounded by Calle Merced to the north, Alameda to the south, calles Santa Lucía and Subercaseaux, is a cone of rock rising steeply to a height of 70 m (reached by stairs and a lift from the Alameda). It can be climbed from the Caupolicán esplanade, on which stands a statue of that Mapuche leader, but the ascent from the northern side, with a statue of Diego de Almagro, is easier. There are striking views of the city from the top, where there is a fortress, the Batería Hidalgo (no public access). It is best to descend the eastern side, to see the small Plaza Pedro Valdivia with its waterfalls and statue of Valdivia. The area is not safe after dark.

③ Santiago west of centre

➡ Santiago maps
1 Santiago orientation, page 659
2 Santiago centre, page 660
3 Santiago west of centre, page 662
4 Bellavista & Lastarria, page 664
5 Providencia, page 666

Where to stay 🛌
2 Conde de Ansúrez
3 Happy House Hostel
4 Hostal de Sammy
6 La Casa Roja

7 La Princesa Insolente
8 Moai Hostel
9 Res Mery
10 Tur Hotel Express

Restaurants 🍴
1 Club Santiago
2 Confitería Torres
3 El Hoyo
4 Fuente Mardoqueo

Parque Forestal lies due north of Santa Lucía hill and immediately south of the Mapocho. **Museo Nacional de Bellas Artes** ⓘ www.mnba.cl (Spanish only), Tue-Sun 1000-1850, US$1, students and seniors US$0.50, free Sun, café, is in an extraordinary example of neoclassical architecture. It has a large display of Chilean and foreign painting and sculpture; contemporary art exhibitions are held several times a year. In the west wing is the **Museo de Arte Contemporáneo** ⓘ www.mac.uchile.cl. **Parque Balmaceda** (Parque Gran Bretaña), east of Plaza Italia, is perhaps the most beautiful in Santiago (the Museo de los Tajamares here, was due to reopen in 2014).

Between the Parque Forestal, Plaza Italia and the Alameda is the **Lastarria** neighbourhood (Universidad Católica Metro). Calle José Victorino Lastarria itself has a number of popular, smart restaurants, while the **Plaza Mulato Gil de Castro** ⓘ C Lastarria 307, has a mural by Roberto Matta and the **Museo Arqueológico de Santiago** and the **Museo de Artes Visuales** ⓘ T2638 3502, Tue-Sun 1030-1830, US$2 for both, free on Sun. The former exhibits Chilean archaeology, anthropology and pre-Columbian art and the latter modern art.

5 Las Vacas Gordas
6 Los Buenos Muchachos
7 Los Chinos Ricos
8 Majestic
9 Ostras Azócar

The **Bellavista district**, on the north bank of the Mapocho from Plaza Italia at the foot of Cerro San Cristóbal, is one of the main eating and nightlife districts in the old city. On its streets are restaurants and cafés, theatres, galleries and craft shops (most selling lapis lazuli on C Bellavista itself). You can cross the Mapocho by bridges from Baquedano or Salvador metro stations, or by a pedestrian bridge between the two which is adorned with hundreds of lovers' eternity padlocks. **La Chascona** ⓘ F Márquez de la Plata 0192, Bellavista, T2777 8741, www.fundacionneruda. org, Tue-Sun 1000-1800, US$7.50 with audio tour. This was the house that the poet Pablo Neruda built for Matilde Urrutia, with whom he lived from 1955. It was wrecked during the 1973 coup, but Matilde restored it and lived there till her death in 1985 (see also page 691).

The sharp, conical hill of **San Cristóbal**, to the northeast of the city, forms the **Parque Metropolitano** ⓘ www.parquemet.cl, daily 0900-2100, the main entrance is at Plaza Caupolicán at the northern end of C Pío Nono in Bellavista, from where a funicular runs to near the summit (daily 1000-1900, Mon 1300-1900, US$3.70 Mon-Fri, US$4.75 weekends return, US$2.75 and US$3.60 one way respectively; on the way up only you can get out at the zoo half way up, reductions for children). Further east is an entrance from Pedro de Valdivia Norte, from where a teleférico used to run (no longer). Taxi-colectivos run to the summit and, in summer, to the swimming pools (see What to do, page 672); to get to Tupahue on foot from Pedro de Valdivia metro station is about 1 km. Vehicles have to pay to enter. It is the largest and most interesting of the city's parks. Souvenirs and snacks are sold at the top of the funicular. On the summit (300 m) stands a colossal statue of the Virgin, which is floodlit at night; beside it is the astronomical observatory of the Catholic University which can be visited on application to the observatory's director. Further east in the Tupahue sector there are terraces, gardens, and paths; nearby is the **Casa de la Cultura Anahuac** which has art exhibitions and free concerts at midday on Sunday. There are two good swimming pools at Tupahue and Antilén. East of Tupahue are the **Botanical Gardens** ① *daily 0900-1800, guided tours available*, with a collection of Chilean native plants.

4 Bellavista & Lastarria

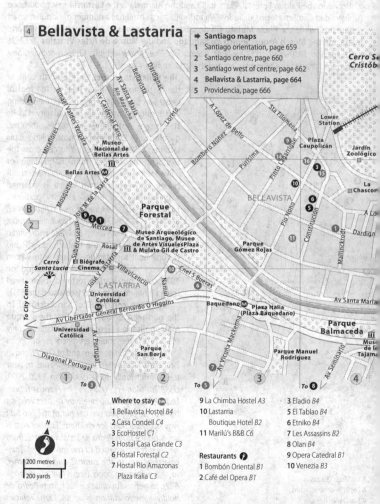

➡ **Santiago maps**

1 Santiago orientation, page 659
2 Santiago centre, page 660
3 Santiago west of centre, page 662
4 **Bellavista & Lastarria, page 664**
5 Providencia, page 666

Where to stay 🛏
1 Bellavista Hostel *B4*
2 Casa Condell *C4*
3 EcoHostel *C1*
5 Hostal Casa Grande *C3*
6 Hostal Forestal *C2*
7 Hostal Río Amazonas
   Plaza Italia *C3*
9 La Chimba Hostel *A3*
10 Lastarria
   Boutique Hotel *B2*
11 Marilú's B&B *C6*

Restaurants 🍴
1 Bombón Oriental *B1*
2 Café del Opera *B1*
3 Eladio *B4*
5 El Tablao *B4*
6 Etniko *B4*
7 Les Assassins *B2*
8 Olan *B4*
9 Opera Catedral *B1*
10 Venezia *B3*

200 metres
200 yards

Providencia East of Plaza Italia, the main east-west axis of the city becomes **Avenida Providencia** which heads out towards the residential areas, such as **Las Condes**, at the eastern and upper levels of the city. It passes through the neighbourhood of Providencia, a modern area of shops, offices, bars and restaurants around Pedro de Valdivia and Los Leones metro stations, which also contains the offices of Sernatur, the national tourist board. At Metro Tobalaba it becomes Avenida Apoquindo. Here, in **El Bosque Norte**, there are lots more good, mid-range and expensive restaurants.

Museo Ralli ① *Sotomayor 4110, Vitacura, T2206 4224 (further east still), www.museoralli.cl, Tue-Sun 1030-1700, Jan weekends only, closed Feb, free,* has an excellent collection of works by modern European and Latin American artists, including Dali, Chagall, Bacon and Miró. **Museo de la Moda** ① *Vitacura 4562, Metro Escuela Militar, T2219 3623, www.museodelamoda.cl, Tue-Fri 1000-1800, Sat-Sun 1100-1900, US$7 including optional guided tour or audio tour, El Garage café Mon-Fri 1000-1800,* is South America's only fashion museum.

Southeast of the centre, in La Florida district, is the excellent **Museo Interactivo Mirador** (MIM) ① *Punta Arenas 6/11, Mirador Metro (Line 5), T2828 8000, www.mim.cl, Tue-Sun 0930-1830, US$7, concessions US$5,* a fun, interactive science and technology museum, perfect for a family outing. There is also an **aquarium** in the grounds.

Cementerio General ① *www.cementerio general.cl, to get there take any Recoleta bus from C Miraflores.* In the *barrio* of Recoleta, just north of the city centre, this cemetery contains the mausoleums of most of the great figures in Chilean history and the arts, including Violeta Parra, Víctor Jara and Salvador Allende. There is also an impressive monument to the victims, known as '*desaparecidos*' (disappeared) of the 1973-1990 military government.

Another memorial to the troubled Pinochet era is in the southeastern suburb of Peñalolén, the **Parque por la Paz** ① *Av Arrieta 8401, http://villagrimaldi.cl; from Tobalaba Metro take any bus marked Peñalolén heading south down Tobalaba, get off at Tobalaba y José Arrieta and catch a bus, or walk 15-20 mins, up Arrieta towards the mountains.* It stands on the site of **Villa Grimaldi**, the most notorious torture centre. Audioguides are available in English (leave passport at reception).

Bars & clubs 🍸

11 Patio Bellavista with
Back Stage Life,
La Casa en el Aire
& many more *B4*
14 Jammin' Club *A3*
15 La Bodeguita de Julio *B4*
16 La Otra Puerta *B3*

Map labels: Statue of the Virgin · Upper Station (Funicular) · Parque Metropolitano · Sofía Concha · Arz Casanova · M Concha · Bellavista · Av Andrés Bello · Av Providencia · Av Salvador · Gral Salvo · Salvador · Av Eliodoro Yáñez · M Infante · To Providencia & Las · & Ñuñoa

For hotel and restaurant price codes, and other relevant information, see Essentials.

🛏 Where to stay

Santiago centre *p659, map p660*
Note Check if breakfast and 19% tax are included in the price quoted. Hostels have double rooms with private or shared bath, **$$**, and dorms for US$13-18pp, **$**.

$$$$-$$$ Fundador, Paseo Serrano 34, T2387 1200, www.hotelfundador.cl. Helpful, charming, stylish, good location, pool, spa, bar, restaurant.

$$$$-$$$ Galerías, San Antonio 65, T2470 7400, www.hotelgalerias.cl.

Excellent, large rooms, generous breakfast, good location, welcoming.

$$$-$$ París-Londres, Londres 54, T2638 2215, www.londres.cl. 1920s mansion with original features in perfect location near San Francisco church, pleasant common rooms, laundry service, usually full, advance bookings in high season.

$$$-$ Andes Hostel, Monjitas 506, T2632 9990, www.andeshostel.com. In Bellas Artes neighbourhood, dorms, rooms or apartments, bar downstairs with pool table, barbeque nights on roof terrace, well run.

$$$-$ Casaltura, San Antonio 811, T2633 5076, www.casaltura.com. 'Boutique hostel', up a long wooden staircase in a renovated house, roof terrace, comfortable and convenient, private rooms and dorms, attentive staff.

5 Providencia

Where to stay 🛏
1 Apart Hotel Santa Magdalena
2 Atton
3 Chilhotel
4 Grand Hyatt Santiago
5 Orly
6 Sheraton Santiago
7 Vilafranca Petit Hotel

Restaurants 🍴
1 A Pinch of Pancho
2 Baco
3 Café El Patio
4 Coppellia & Sveckova

$$ París, París 813, T2664 0921, carbott@
latinmail.com. Great location, good meeting
place, 3 standards of room, breakfast extra,
Wi-Fi available in some parts. Phone in advance
in summer.

West of the centre *p661, map p662*
$$-$ Happy House Hostel, Moneda 1829,
T2688 4849, www.happyhousehostel.cl.
In a restored mansion with all mod-cons. One
of the best hostels in the city, spacious kitchen
and common areas, pool table, bar, spa, free tea
and real coffee all day, book exchange, English
and French spoken, lots of information.
$$-$ La Casa Roja, Agustinas 2113, Barrio Brasil,
T2696 4241, www.lacasaroja.cl. Huge, renovated
mansion, dorms and private rooms, no breakfast,
pool party on Sat, guests can be chef for the
night, live music, 2 bars, cricket net, lots of

> **→ Santiago maps**
> 1 Santiago orientation, page 659
> 2 Santiago centre, page 660
> 3 Santiago west of centre, page 662
> 4 Bellavista & Lastarria, page 664
> 5 Providencia, page 666

5 El Giratorio
6 El Huerto
7 Oriental

Bars & clubs 🍸
8 Brannigan Pub
9 Phone Box Pub

activities and tours, Spanish classes, lively. Shares
services with **La Princesa Insolente**, below.
$ La Princesa Insolente, Moneda 2350, T2671
6551, www.princesainsolentehostel.cl. Shared
rooms and one private room (**$$$**), organic café,
mountain bike rental, has apartments opposite,
travel information. Also has hostels in Pichilemu
and Pucón, surfing with www.deepconnection.
cl. In same group as **La Casa Roja**, above.

Near bus terminals and Estación Central
$$$ Conde de Ansúrez, Av República 25,
T2696 0807, República metro, www.ansurez.cl.
Convenient for airport bus, central station and
bus terminals, helpful, safe.
$$$ Tur Hotel Express, O'Higgins 3750, p 3,
in the Turbus Terminal, T2685 0100, www.
turbus.cl. Comfortable business standard.
Useful if you need to take an early flight
as buses leave for the airport from here.
There is an Ibis hotel here, too.
$$ Res Mery, Pasaje República 36, off 0-100
block of República, T2699 4982, http://
residencialmery.cl. Big green art deco building
down an alley, most rooms without bath, all
with single beds, quiet, breakfast extra.
$$-$ Moai Hostel, Toesca 2335, T2723 6499,
www.moaiviajerohostel.cl. Airport transfer,
book exchange, film library, Spanish classes
arranged, gay-friendly, popular. 5 blocks from
República metro.

South of the Alameda
$$-$ Hostal de Sammy, Toesca 2335, T2689
8772, www.hostaldesammy.com. Good-value
US-run hostel with decent common areas, table
tennis, pool table, big-screen TV with hundreds
of films. Good info, helpful.

East of the centre and Bellavista *p662, map p664*
$$$$ Lastarria Boutique Hotel, Cnel Santiago
Bueras 188, T2840 3700, www.lastarriahotel.
com. In a converted 1927 building, beautifully
decorated, spacious rooms, with personalized
service. Lounge for breakfast and light meals,
cocktails and wines, garden, swimming pool.
$$$ Hostal Río Amazonas, Plaza Italia,
Vicuña Mackenna 47, T2635 1631, www.hostal
rioamazonas.cl. In a restored mansion, good
value, helpful, lots of information, parking.

$$$-$$ Hostal Casa Grande, Vicuña MacKenna 90, T2222 7347, Baquedano metro, www.hostal casagrande.cl. Labyrinthine, old high-ceilinged building, colourful, pleasant patio garden, quiet.
$$ EcoHostel, Gral Jofré 349B, T2222 6833, www. ecohostel.cl. Popular with groups, comfortable beds, well run, smoking patio, tours arranged.
$$-$ Bellavista Hostel, Dardignac 0184, T2899 7145, www.bellavista.hostel.com. European-style, sheets provided but make your own bed, good fun hostel in the heart of this lively area. Guests over 35 not allowed in dorms, only private rooms.
$$-$ Casa Condell, Condell 114, T2209 2343, Salvador metro. Pleasant old house, central, quiet, nice roof-terrace, free local phone calls, English spoken, good but baths shared between rooms can be a problem.

$$-$ Hostal Forestal, Cnel Santiago Bueras 120, T2638 1347, www.hostalforestal.cl. On a quiet side street near the Plaza Italia. Comfy lounge with big screen TV, barbeque area, pool table, information, English spoken.
$ pp La Chimba Hostel, Ernesto Pinto Lagarrigue 262, Bellavista, T2899 7145, www.lachimba.hostel.com. Popular backpacker hostel with good facilities.

Providencia and Las Condes *p665, map p666*
For longer-stay accommodation, contact **Apart Hotel Santa Magdalena**, Helvecia 240 L3, Las Condes, T2374 6875, www.santamagdalena.cl, which has well-serviced apartments.
$$$$ Grand Hyatt Santiago, Av Kennedy 4601, Las Condes, T2950 1234, http:// santiago.grand.hyatt.com. Superb, beautifully decorated, large outdoor pool, gym, 3 restaurants.
$$$$ Sheraton Santiago, Santa María 1742, T2233 5000, www.sheraton.cl. One of the best, good restaurant, good buffet lunch, and all facilities.
$$$$-$$$ Atton, Alonso de Córdova 5199, Las Condes, T2422 7900, www.atton.cl. Comfortable, very helpful, full disabled access. Has 2 other branches.
$$$ Orly, Pedro de Valdivia 027, Metro Pedro de Valdivia, T2231 8947, www.orlyhotel.com. Small, comfortable, convenient, Cafetto café attached with good value meals.
$$$ Vilafranca Petit Hotel, Pérez Valenzuela 1650, T2235 1413, www.vilafranca.cl. Manuel Montt metro. High end B&B, small but impeccable rooms, quiet, cosy, pleasant garden, English spoken.
$$$-$$ Chilhotel, Cirujano Guzmán 103, T2264 0643, metro Manuel Montt, www. chilhotel.cl. Small, comfortable, family-run, airport transfer.
$$ Marilú's Bed and Breakfast, Rafael Cañas 246, T2235 5302, www.bedand breakfast.cl. Comfortable, quiet, convenient, some rooms with shared bath with 1 other room, good beds, English and French spoken, secure, very helpful and welcoming, lots of information.

⑦ Restaurants

For good seafood restaurants go to the **Mercado Central** (by Cal y Canto Metro, lunches only, including **Donde Augusto**, www.dondeaugusto.cl, **El Galeón**, www.elgaleon.cl, and others; www.mercadocentral.cl), or the **Vega Central** market on the opposite bank of the Mapocho, or Av Cumming and C Reyes in Barrio Brasil. It is difficult to eat cheaply in the evening apart from fast food, so if you're on a tight budget, make the lunchtime *almuerzo* your main meal.

Santiago centre *p659, map p660*
$$$-$$ Majestic, Santo Domingo 1526, T2694 9400, In hotel of same name (**$$$**, www.hotelmajestic.cl). Excellent Indian restaurant, with a good range of vegetarian dishes.
$$$-$$ Opera Catedral, Jose Miguel de la Barra 407, Bellas Artes metro, T2664 3038, www.operacatedral.cl. Very good, if expensive, French restaurant on the ground floor. Upstairs is a minimalist pub-restaurant, usually packed at night, serving fusion food at reasonable prices.
$$ Faisán d'Or, Plaza de Armas. Good *pastel de choclo*, pleasant place to watch the world go by.
$$ Lung Fung, Agustinas 715 (downstairs). Delicious oriental food, the oldest Chinese restaurant in Santiago.
$ Bar Nacional No 2, Bandera 317. Popular, local specialities, big portions; also at Huérfanos 1151 (No 1).
$ Confitería Torres, Alameda 1570. Traditional bar/restaurant, good ambience, live music Fri-Sat.
$ El Naturista, Moneda 846 and Huérfanos 1046. Excellent vegetarian, "healthy portions", wide-ranging menu, as well as juices, beer and wine, closes 2100.
$ El Rápido, Bandera 347, next to Bar Nacional No 2. Specializes in *empanadas* and *completos*, good food, good fun.

Cafés
Café Caribe and **Café Haití**, both on Paseo Ahumada and elsewhere in centre and Providencia. Good coffee, institutions for the Santiago business community.
Café Colonia, Maclver 133 and 161. Splendid variety of cakes, pastries and pies, fashionable and pricey.

Café del Opera, Merced 391. For breakfasts, sandwiches, salads, ice creams and breads.

West of the centre *p661, map p662*
$$$-$$ Las Vacas Gordas, Cienfuegos 280, Barrio Brasil, T2697 1066. Good-value grilled steaks, nice wine selection, very popular, book in advance.
$$ Club Santiago, Erasmo Escala 2120, www.clubsantiago.cl. Open 1230-0100, happy hour 1700-2200. Historic restaurant/bar in Concha y Toro district, lunches, snacks, cocktails.
$$ El Hoyo, San Vicente 375, T2689 0339. Closed Sun. Celebrated 100-yr-old *chichería* serving hearty Chilean fare.
$$ Fuente Mardoqueo, Libertad 551, www.fuentemardoqueo.cl. Daily 1200-2300. Simply sandwiches, with a limited choice of fillings, and beer, a wide range, popular.
$$ Los Buenos Muchachos, Cumming 1031, T2566 4660, www.losbuenosmuchachos.cl. Cavernous hall seating over 400 serving plentiful traditional Chilean food, traditional Chilean dance shows at night. Very popular.
$$ Los Chinos Ricos, Brasil 373, www.loschinosricos.cl. Good Chinese, popular with families on Sun lunchtime.
$$ Ostras Azócar, Gral Bulnes 37, www.ostrasazocar.cl. Good prices for oysters. Other seafood places in same street.

East of the centre: Bellavista and Lastarria *p662, map p664*
On C Lastarria are many smart eateries, several in the precinct at Lastarria 70: also **Sur Patagónico**, **Victorino**, **El Callejón de Mesías**, **El Observatorio** and **Zabo**. **El Biógrafo** cinema also has a café. Bellavista is full of restaurants, cafés and bars too, particularly C Dardignac and Patio Bellavista, the block between Dardignac, Pío Nono, Bellavista and Constitución.
$$$ Les Assassins, Merced 297, T2638 4280. Good French cuisine in small, family-run bistro, with decent wine list; good-value set lunches.
$$$-$$ Etniko, Constitución 172, Bellavista, T2732 0119. www.etniko.cl. Fusion restaurant with oriental influences and seafood, also tapas bar/cevichería and dance floor under transparent roof for night sky, live DJs at weekends.
$$$-$$ Los Adobes del Argomedo, Argomedo 411 y Lira, 10 blocks south of the

Alameda, T2222 2104, www.losadobesde argomedo.cl. Long-established traditional restaurant. Good Chilean food, floor show (Mon-Sat) includes *cueca* dancing, salsa and folk.

$$ El Tablao, Constitución 110, T2737 8648. Traditional Spanish restaurant. The food is reasonable but the main attraction is the live flamenco show on Fri-Sat nights.

$$ Eladio, Pío Nono 251. Good steaks, Argentine cuisine, excellent value, also has bingo.

$$ Venezia, Pío Nono, corner of López de Bello. Huge servings of traditional Chilean home-cooked fare (allegedly one of Neruda's favourite haunts), good value.

$$-$ Olan, Seminario 96A-B. Excellent value, tasty Peruvian food in unpretentious surroundings. Another branch at No 67, slightly higher prices.

Bombón Oriental, Merced 333 and 355, Lastarria, T2639 1069. Serves Middle Eastern food, Turkish coffee, arabic snacks and sweets.

Providencia *p665, map p666*
$$$-$$ A Pinch of Pancho, Gral del Canto 45, T2235 1700. Very good fish and seafood on a wide-ranging menu.

$$$-$$ Baco, Nueva de Lyon 113, T231 4444. Metro Los Leones. Sophisticated French restaurant, good food, extensive wine list with many quality wines available by the glass.

$$$-$$ Oriental, Manuel Montt 584. Excellent Chinese, one of the best in Santiago.

$$ El Huerto, Orrego Luco 054, Providencia, T2233 2690. Vegetarian. Open daily, varied menu, very good.

Cafés
For snacks and ice cream there are several good places on Av Providencia including **Coppellia**, No 2211, **Bravissimo**, No 1406. Lots of cafés and some restaurants on the passageways at Metro Los Leones and streets nearby, including **Café di Roma**, **The Coffee Factory**, Sebastián, Fuenzalida 26, very good, **Salón de Té Tavelli**, drugstore precinct, Av Providencia 2124.

Providencia: Las Condes *p665*
This area has many first-class restaurants, including grills, serving Chilean (often with music), French and Chinese cuisine. They tend to be more expensive than central restaurants. Many are located on El Bosque Norte, near Tobalaba metro stop.

$$$-$$ Miguel Torres, Isidora Goyenechea 2874, T2245 7332, http://restaurante migueltorres.cl. Tapas bar owned by the well-known Spanish winery.

$$$-$$ Puerto Marisko, Isidora Goyenechea 2918, T2233 2096, www.restaurantmariscos.cl. Renowned for seafood but also serves pasta and meat dishes, over 20 years of experience.

🔊 Bars and clubs

For all entertainments, nightclubs, cinemas, theatres, restaurants, concerts, *El Mercurio Online* website has all listings and a good search feature, www.emol.com. Listings in weekend newspapers, particularly *El Mercurio* and *La Tercera*. Also *Santiago What's On*. Lively areas to head for are: **Barrio Brasil**, a number of bars and restaurants dotted around the Plaza Brasil and on Avs Brasil and Cumming. Popular with Chilean students (Metro República). **Bellavista**, good selection of varied restaurants, bars and clubs (Metro Baquedano). The first couple of blocks of Román Díaz (between metros Salvador and Manuel Montt) has a collection of bars and eateries, eg **Kleine Kneipe**, No 21, also in Ñuñoa, www.kleinekneipe.cl, and **Santo Remedio**, No 152. Avs Suecia and Gral Holley in **Providencia**, much of it pedestrianized. **Plaza Ñuñoa**, a number of good bars dotted around the Plaza in the middle-class suburb of Ñuñoa. From Av Providencia Condell leads to Ñuñoa, 18 blocks, passing various small bars and restaurants on the way, eg at junctions with Rancagua and Santa Isabel, or take metro to Irrarrázaval. **El Bosque Norte**, chic bars and expensive restaurants for the Chilean jetset (Metro Tobalaba). Also many smart places in Las Condes. For an organized night out, contact **Santiago Pub Crawl**, T09-7165 9977, www.santiagopubcrawl.com, US$20, every Thu, Fri and Sat.

East of the centre: Bellavista *p663, map p664*
Back Stage Life, Patio Bellavista. Good-quality live jazz and blues.

Jammin' Club, Antonia López de Bello 49. Reggae.

La Bodeguita de Julio, Constitución 256. Cuban staff and Cuban cocktails, excellent live music and dancing possible, very popular, free entry before 2300, very good value.

La Casa en el Aire, Patio Bellavista. Pleasant atmosphere, live music.

La Otra Puerta, Pío Nono 348. Lively salsoteca with live music.

Providencia *p665, map p666*

Brannigan Pub, Suecia 35, T2232 7869. Good beer, live jazz, lively.

Golden Bell Inn, Hernando de Aguirre 27. Popular with expats.

Ilé Habana, Bucaré just off Suecia. Bar with salsa music, often live, and a good dance floor.

◉ Entertainment

Santiago *p658, maps p660, p662, p664, p666*
Cinemas There's a good guide to cinema in the free newspaper *publimetro*, given out at metro stations on weekday mornings. 'Ciné Arte' (quality foreign films) is popular. Many multiplex cinemas across the city show mainstream releases, nearly always in the original English with subtitles. Seats cost US$4-7 with reductions on Mon, Tue and Wed (elsewhere in the country the day varies). Some cinemas offer discounts to students and over 60s (proof required).

Theatres Teatro Municipal, Agustinas y San Antonio, www.municipal.cl. Stages international opera, concerts by the Orquesta Filarmónica de Santiago, and the Ballet de Santiago, throughout the year. The full range of events and ticket prices is given on the website. Some cheap seats are often sold on the day of concerts. Free classical concerts are sometimes given in San Francisco church in summer. Arrive early for a seat. Teatro Municipal de Ñuñoa, Av Irarrázaval 1564, T2277 7903, www.ccn.cl. Dance, art exhibitions, cinema, children's theatre. Teatro Universidad de Chile, Plaza Baquedano, T2978 2480, www.ceacuchile.com, is the home of the Orquesta y Coro Sinfónica de Chile and the Ballet Nacional de Chile. There are a great number of theatres which stage plays in Spanish, either in the original language or translations.

✿ Festivals

Santiago *p658, maps p660, p662, p664, p666*
Religious festivals and ceremonies continue throughout **Holy Week**, when a priest washes the feet of 12 men. The image of the Virgen del Carmen (patron of the Armed Forces) is carried through the streets by cadets on **16 Jul**. On Independence Day, **18 Sep**, many families get together or celebrate in *fondas* (small temporary constructions made of wood and straw where people eat traditional dishes, drink *chicha* and dance *cueca*). During **Nov** there is a free art fair in the Parque Forestal on the banks of the Río Mapocho, lasting a fortnight.

◉ Shopping

Santiago *p658, maps p660, p662, p664, p666*
Bookshops Book prices are high compared with neighbouring countries and Europe. There are several bookshops in and around the Drugstore precinct off Av Providencia 2124 between Los Urbinas and Fuen zalida, including Feria Chilena del Libro, www. feriachilenadellibro.cl, with many other branches, good for travel books and maps. For foreign language books: Le Comptoir, www.comptolr.cl, Librería Albers, www.texto. cl, Librería Inglesa. LOM Ediciones, Concha y Toro 23, www.lom.cl, large stock from its own publishing house (literature, history, sociology, art, politics), also bar and reading room with recent Chilean papers and magazines.

Camping and outdoor equipment
There are a number of 'hunting' shops on Bulnes 1-2 blocks south of the Alameda, with a basic range of outdoor equipment. Andes Gear, Helvecia 210, Las Condes, T2245 7076, www. andesgear.cl. Good range of quality clothes and equipment. Imported camping goods from Club Andino and Federación de Andinismo (see below). La Cumbre, Av Apoquindo 5220, T2220 9907, www.lacumbreonline.cl. Mon-Fri 1100-2000, Sat 1100-1600, Dutch-run, very helpful, good climbing and trekking equipment. Lippi, http://lippioutdoor.com. With several branches. Chile's premier outdoor equipment maker. Excellent-quality clothes, boots, tents, etc. Mountain Service, Paseo Las Palmas 2209, Local 016, T2234 3439, Providencia. English

spoken, tents, stoves, clothing, equipment rental. **Parafernalia**, Huérfanos 1973 y Brasil, also in Drugstore precinct, Providencia, http://parafernaliaoutdoor.cl. New and second-hand gear. **Peregrin**, del Arzobispo 0607, Bellavista, T2735 1587, see Facebook. Salvador metro. Decent-quality locally made outdoor clothes. **Tatoo Adventure Gear**, Av Los Leones 81, Providencia, and MallSport, Las Condes 13451, www.tatoo.ws, has all the best brands of outdoor gear.

Crafts For good-quality crafts go to Pomaire (see page 677), where items from all over Chile are for sale at competitive prices. The gemstone, lapis lazuli, can be found in a few expensive shops in Bellavista but is cheaper in the arcades on the south side of the Plaza de Armas. Other craft stalls can be found in an alleyway 1 block south of Av O'Higgins between A Prat and Serrano; on the 600 to 800 blocks of Santo Domingo and at Pío Nono y Av Santa María in Bellavista. **Aldea de Vitacura**, Vitacura 6838, T735 3959. Open 1000-2000. **Centro Artesanal Santa Lucía**, Santa Lucía metro, south exit. Generic *artesanía*. lapis lazuli can be bought here cheaply. Also has a wide variety of woollen goods, jewellery, etc. **Dauvin Artesanía Fina**, Providencia 2169, local 69, www.artesaniasvdauvin.cl. Los Leones metro. **Morita Gil**, Los Misioneros 1991, Pedro de Valdivia Norte, T2232 6853. **Centro Artesanal Los Domínicos**, Apoquindo 9805, Las Condes, www.culturallascondes.cl. Metro Los Domínicos. The best upmarket craft fair in Chile. A good range of modern and traditional Chilean crafts from ceramics to textiles, a pleasant central piazza, places where the artisans can be seen working on wood, silver, glass and so on, cafés, toilets, information.

Markets For food: **Mercado Central**, between Puente y 21 de Mayo by the Río Mapocho (Cal y Canto Metro) is excellent for fish and seafood. There is a cheaper market, the **Vega Central**, on the opposite bank of the river. The **Bío Bío** flea market on C Bío Bío, Metro Franklin (follow crowds), on Sat and Sun morning is huge; everything under the sun, lots of it having fallen off the back of a lorry.

Music Billboard, Providencia 2314 and at La Bolsa 75 (downtown). Good source for rock, jazz and alternative music. **Feria de Disco**, Paseo

Ahumada and in numerous malls. The biggest chain, often sell tickets for rock concerts.
Wine El Mundo del Vino, Isidora Goyenechea 3000, T2584 1173, www.elmundodelvino.cl. For all types of Chilean wines, good selection across the price range; also in the Alto Las Condes, Parque Arauco and Costanera Center malls. **Vinopolis**, El Bosque Norte 038 and Pedro de Valdivia 036. Mon-Fri 0900-2300, Sat 1000-2300, Sun 1000-2200. Also at airport. Sells all types of Chilean wines, good selection across all the prices.

⚙ What to do

Santiago *p658, maps p660, p662, p664, p666*
Cricket There is a burgeoning cricket league based around Santiago, see www.cricketchile.cl for more information. La Casa Roja hostel, see above, has a cricket net on its premises.
Cycling For parts and repairs go to C San Diego, south of the Alameda. The 800 and 900 blocks have scores of bike shops with spare parts, new models and repairs.
Football Main teams including Colo Colo who play at the Estadio Monumental (reached by any bus to Puente Alto; tickets from Av Monumental 5300, Macul, T2294 7300), **Universidad de Chile**, play at Estadio Nacional, Av Grecia 2001, Ñuñoa, Ñuble metro, line 5 (tickets from Av General Miranda 2094, Ñuñoa), and **Universidad Católica** who play at San Carlos de Apoquindo, reached by bus from Metro Escuela Militar, tickets from Andrés Bello 2782, Providencia, T2231 7777.
Horse racing Club Hípico, Blanco Encalada 2540, every Sun and every other Wed afternoon. **Hipódromo Chile**, Av Hipódromo Chile 1715, Independencia, T2270 9237, every Sat.
Skiing and climbing Club Alemán Andino, El Arrayán 2735, T2232 4338, www.dav.cl. Open Tue and Fri, 1800-2000, May-Jun. **Club Andino de Chile**, Av Lib O'Higgins 108, clubandino@ski lagunillas.cl, ski club (open 1900-2100 on Mon and Fri). **Federación de Andinismo de Chile**, Almte Simpson 77 (T2222 0888, www.feach.cl). Open daily (frequently closed Jan/Feb), has the addresses of all the mountaineering clubs in the country and runs a mountaineering school. **Skitotal**, Apoquindo 4900, of 40-46, T2246 0156, www.skitotal.cl, for 1-day excursions and

good value ski hire. Equipment hire is much cheaper in Santiago than in ski resorts. For ski resorts in the Santiago area see below.

Swimming In Parque Metropolitano, Cerro San Cristóbal: **Antilén**, open in summer Wed-Mon 1000-1900, US$11, fine views, and **Tupahue**, large pool with cafés, Tue-Sun 1000-1900, entry US$9 but worth it (check if they are open in winter, one usually is). In **Parque O'Higgins**, T2556 9612, 1330-1830 summer only, US$4. Olympic pool in **Parque Araucano** (near Parque Arauco Shopping Centre, Metro Escuela Militar), open Nov-Mar Tue-Sat 0900-1900.

Tennis Municipal courts in Parque O'Higgins. Estadio Nacional, Av Grecia y Av Marathon, has a tennis club which offers classes.

Tours A number of agencies offer walking tours of the city, others day trips from Santiago. Typical excursions are to the Wine Valleys, US$42-90 (by bike if you wish), Isla Negra (Pablo Neruda's seaside villa) US$72, visits to nearby haciendas and adventure tours such as whitewater rafting, rock climbing or trekking in the Cajón del Maipo, southeast of the city. Many agencies advertise in the Sernatur tourist office (see above).

La Bicicleta Verde, Loreto 6 esq Santa María, T2570 9338, www.labicicletaverde.com. Sightseeing tours around the capital and of vineyards by bike. Also rents bicycles.

Spicy Chile, www.spicychile.cl. 3 walking tours of the city, Mon-Sat, pay by tip, good reputation.

Tours4Tips, T2737 5649, www.tours4tips.com. 2 daily walking tours, pay by tip, also in Valparaíso, popular.

Turismo Reportaje, Candelaria Goyenechea 3983, dpto 503, Vitacura, T09-6551 2429, www.turismoreportaje.com. City walking tours with emphasis on history, pay by tip.

Turistik, T2820 1000, www.turistik.cl. Hop-on, hop-off bus tours of the city, US$47, also offers tours outside the city and tour, dinner and show.

Adventure tours and trekking

Altue, Coyancura 2270, Of 801, Providencia, T2333 1390, www.altue.com. For wilderness trips including tour of Patagonia.

Azimut 360, Gral Salvo 159, Providencia, T2235 3085, www.azimut360.com. Adventure and ecotourism including mountaineering.

Cascada Expediciones, Don Carlos 3227C, Las Condes, www.cascada.travel. Specialize in activity tours in remote areas.

Chile Excepción, T2951 5476, www.chile-excepcion.com. French/Argentine agency offering tailor-made, upper end tours, fly-drives, themed trips and other services.

Chile Off Track, T2979 0251, 9133 4083, www.chileofftrack.com. Customized and tailor-made tours around Santiago and in Patagonia, 6 languages spoken, features include horse riding, mountain excursions, wine tours, visits to hot springs.

Santiago Adventures, T2244 2750, www.santiagoadventures.com. US-run, offering adventure day tours, wine tours, city tours, skiing and Patagonia.

Travel Art, Europa 2081, T2378 3494, http://chile-reise.com. Biking, hiking and multi-active tours throughout Chile. German-run.

⊕ Transport

Santiago *p658, maps p660, p662, p664, p666*
Air

International and domestic flights leave from **Arturo Merino Benítez Airport** at Pudahuel, 26 km northwest of Santiago, off Ruta 68, the motorway to Viña del Mar and Valparaíso. The terminal has most facilities, including Afex *cambio*, ATMs, tourist offices which will book accommodation and a fast-food plaza. Left luggage US$9 per bag per day. Airport information T2690 1752, www.aeropuertosantiago.cl.

Airport taxi: drivers offer rides to the city outside Arrivals, but the official taxi service, T2601 9880, is more reliable, if a little more expensive: US$30 to Pajaritos or Quinta Normal, US$34 to the centre, US$38 to Providencia, up to US$40 to Las Condes. Radio Taxi to airport is cheaper. Many hotels run a transfer service. Frequent bus services to/from city centre by 2 companies: **Tur-Bus** (T2822 7741, from Terminal Alameda), 0615-2400, US$4, every 30 mins; and **Centro puerto** (T2601 9883, from Metro Los Héroes), US$3.50, 0640, 2330, every 15 mins. Buses leave from outside airport terminal and, in Santiago, call at Metro Pajaritos (not 0645-0815), Estación Central, Terminal Santiago and most other regular bus stops. From airport you can take Tur-Bus to Pajaritos, US$3, and take metro from there. Companies that run a good shuttle service are: **Delfos** (T2913 8800, www.transferdelfos.cl) and **Transvip** (T2677 3000, www.transvip.cl), US$10-12 shared vehicle, US$32-42 exclusive, depending on zone, 10% discount if you book return to airport with same company. Otherwise, to go to the airport, book a day ahead. They pick you up from your hotel and, before reaching the terminal, stop at their airport depot where you pay.

Bus

Local The *Transantiago* (www.transantiago.cl) system is designed to reduce congestion and pollution, but has not entirely succeeded. The city is divided into 10 zones lettered A to J. Within each zone, buses (known as *micros*) are the same colour as that given to the zone (eg white for zone A: central Santiago). Zones are linked by trunk lines, run by white *micros* with a green stripe. The system integrates with the metro. Buses display the number and direction of the route within the system. Payment is by prepaid *Bip* card only. A card costs US$2.75, to which you add however much you want to pay in advance. They are most conveniently bought at metro stations. For a day or so it's probably not worth investing in a *Bip* card (just use the metro), but for a few days it's good value. Long-term visitors can buy personalized cards, to prevent theft, etc. There are also *colectivos* (collective taxis) on fixed routes to the suburbs. Routes are displayed with route numbers. Fares vary, depending on the length of the journey, but are usually between US$1.50-2.50 (higher fares at night).

Long distance There are frequent, and good, interurban buses to all parts of Chile. Take a look at the buses before buying the tickets (there are big differences in quality among bus companies); ask about the on-board services, many companies offer drinks for sale, or free, and luxury buses have meals, videos, headphones. Reclining seats are standard and there are also *salón cama* sleeper buses. Fares from/to the capital are given in the text. On Fri evening, when night departures are getting ready to go, the terminals can be chaotic. There are 5 bus terminals: **1)** Terminal

Alameda, which has a modern extension called Mall Parque Estación with good left luggage (US$3.40 per day), ATMs and internet, O'Higgins 3712, Metro Universidad de Santiago, T2776 2424. All **Pullman-Bus** and **Tur-Bus** services go from here, they serve almost every destination in Chile, good quality but prices a little higher than others. **Tur-Bus** also has booking offices at Universidad de Chile and Tobalaba metro stations, at Cal y Canto, at Av Apoquindo 6421, T2212 6435, and in the Parque Arauco and Alto Las Condes malls for those beginning their journeys in Las Condes. **2)** Terminal Santiago, O'Higgins 3878, 1 block west of Terminal Alameda, T2376 1750, www.terminaldebusessantiago.cl, Metro Universidad de Santiago. Services to all parts of southern Chile, including the only service to Punta Arenas (48 hrs). Also international departures. Has a Redbanc ATM. **3)** Terminal San Borja, O'Higgins y San Borja, 1 block west of Estación Central, 3 blocks east of Terminal Alameda, Metro Estación Central (entrance is, inconveniently, via a busy shopping centre, Mall Arauco Estación), T2776 0645. Mainly departures to the Central Valley area, but also to northern Chile. Booking offices and departures organized according to destination. **4)** Terminal Los Héroes, on Tucapel Jiménez, just north of the Alameda, Metro Los Héroes, T2420 0099. A smaller terminal with booking offices of 8 companies, to the north, the south and Lake District and some international services (Lima, Asunción, Montevideo, Buenos Aires, Bariloche, Mendoza). **5)** Metro Pajaritos (Metro Línea 1), to Valparaíso, Viña del Mar and places on the central coast; airport shuttle buses call here. It can be more convenient to take a bus from here than from the central terminals. Some long-distance buses call at Las Torres de Tajamar, Providencia 1108, which is more convenient if you are planning to stay in Providencia. **Note** See the note under Taxis about not taking expensive taxis parked outside bus terminals, but note that official **Tur-Bus** taxis are good and reliable. Also check if student rates are available (even for non-students), or reductions for travelling same day as purchase of ticket; it is worth bargaining over prices, especially shortly before departure and out of summer season.

International buses Most services leave from Terminal Santiago, though there are also departures from Terminal Los Héroes. There are frequent bus and minibus services from Terminal Santiago through the Cristo Redentor tunnel to **Mendoza** in Argentina, 6-7 hrs, US$34-44, many companies, departures around 0800, 1200 and 1600, touts approach you in Terminal Santiago. Minibuses have shorter waiting time at customs. Many of these services continue to **Buenos Aires**, 24 hrs, and many companies in Terminal Santiago have connections to other Argentine cities. For destinations like **Bariloche** or **Neuquén**, it is better make connections in Temuco or Osorno. To **Lima**, **Ormeño** (Terminal Santiago), Tue and Fri 0900, 51 hrs. It is cheaper to take a bus to Arica, a colectivo to Tacna, then bus to Lima.

Car

Car hire Prices vary a lot so shop around first. Tax of 19% is charged, usually included in price quoted. If possible book a car in advance. Information boards full of flyers from companies at airport and tourist office. A credit card is usually asked for when renting a vehicle. Many companies will not hire a car to holders of drivers licences in left hand drive countries unless they have an international licence. Remember that in the capital driving is restricted according to licence plate numbers; look for notices in the street and newspapers. Main international agencies and others are available at the airport (see Essentials for web addresses). Automóvil Club de Chile car rental from head office (see Driving in Chile box, page 652), discount for members and members of associated motoring organizations. **Alameda**, Av Bernardo O'Higgins 4332, T2779 0609, www.alamedarentacar.cl, San Alberto Hurtado metro, line 1, also in the airport, good value. **Rosselot**, call centre T2314 0366, www.rosselot.cl. Reputable Chilean firm with national coverage. **Verschae**, T600 5000 700, www2.verschae.com. Good value, branches throughout country.

Ferry and cruise operators

Navimag, Naviera Magallanes SA, Av El Bosque Norte 0440, p 11, Las Condes, T2442 3120, www.navimag.com. For services from **Puerto** Montt to **Puerto Chacabuco, Puerto Natales** and **Laguna San Rafael**. M/n Skorpios: Augusto Leguía Norte 118, Las Condes, T2477 1900, www.skorpios.cl. For luxury cruise out of Puerto Montt to **Laguna San Rafael** and adventure strips from Puerto Natales to Puerto Edén and the Campo Hielo del Sur.

Metro

See www.metrosantiago.cl. Line 1 runs west–east between **San Pablo** and **Los Dominicos**, under the Alameda; Line 2 runs north-south from **Vesupcio Norte** to **La Cisterna**; Line 4 runs from **Tobalaba** on Line 1 south to **Plaza de Puente Alto**, with a branch (4a) from **V Mackenna** to **La Cisterna**; Line 5 runs north, east and southeast from **Plaza de Maipú** via **Baquedano** to **Vicente Valdés** on Line 4. The trains are modern, fast, quiet, and very full at peak times. The first train is at 0600 (Mon-Sat), 0800 (Sun and holidays), the last about 2300 (2330 on Fri-Sat, 2230 on Sun). Fares vary according to time of journey; there are 3 charging periods, according to demand: the peak rate is US$1.25, the general rate US$1.15 and there is a cheaper rate at unsociable hours, US$1. The simplest solution is to buy a *tarjeta Bip* (see Local buses, above), the charge card from which the appropriate fare is deducted. Transantiago bus services link with the metro.

Taxi

Taxis (black with yellow roofs) are abundant and fairly cheap: minimum charge of US$0.35, plus US$0.20 per 200 m. In every type of taxi always double check the fare (see www.taximetro.cl) Drivers are permitted to charge more at night, but in the daytime check that the meter is set to day rates. At bus terminals, drivers will charge more – best to walk a block and flag down a cruising taxi. Avoid taxis with more than one person in them especially at night. Various Radio Taxi services operate (eg **Radio Taxis Andes Pacífico**, T2912 6000, www.andespacifico. cl); rates are above those of city taxis but they should be more reliable.

Train

Trenes Metropolitanos, T600-585 5000, www. tmsa.cl has details of services. All trains leave from Estación Central (Alameda) at O'Higgins

3322. TerraSur south to **Chillán** with 10 intermediate stops; **Metrotren** suburban route to **San Fernando**; **Expreso Maule** to Talca; Buscarril links **Talca**, **Maule**, **Pencahue** and **Constitución**. Expreso del Recuerdo is a tourist train to **San Antonio**, T2585 5991, www.tren.cl or www.efe.cl, 4 standards of coach, runs on special occasions only. **Booking offices** Alameda O'Higgins 3170, daily 0650-2310; Universidad de Chile metro, loc 10, Mon-Fri 0900-2000, Sat 0900-1400 and others. Left luggage office at Estación Central, open till 2300. **Note** Schedules change with the seasons, so check timetables in advance. Summer services are booked up in a week in advance.

⊙ Directory

Santiago *p658, maps p660, p662, p664, p666*
Banks Open 0900-1400, closed on Sat. Exchange rates are published in *El Mercurio* and *La Nación*. For Cirrus/MasterCard and Visa ATMs just look for the Redbanc sign, most commonly in banks, pharmacies or Copec petrol stations. *casas de cambio* (exchange houses) in the centre are mainly situated on Paseo Ahumada and Huérfanos (metro Universidad de Chile or Plaza de Armas). In Providencia several on Av Pedro de Valdivia. Some *casas de cambio* in the centre open Sat morning (but check first). Avoid street money changers (particularly common on Ahumada, Bandera, Moneda and Agustinas): they pull any number of tricks, or will usually ask you to accompany them to somewhere obscure. The passing of forged notes and muggings are reported. **Embassies and consulates** For all foreign embassies and consulates in Santiago de Chile, see http://embassy.goabroad.com. **Hospitals** Emergency hospital at Marcoleta 377, T2633 2051 (emergency), T2354 3266 (general enquiries). Hospital del Salvador, Av Salvador 334 or J M Infante 551, T2274 0093 emergency, T2340 4000 general, Mon-Thu 0800-1300 and 1330-1645, Fri 0800-1300 and 1330-1545 (has Vacunatoria Internacional at

Salvador 467, 4 blocks south of Salvador metro). Also **Vacunatoria Internacional**, Hospital Luis Calvo, MacKenna, Antonio Varas 360. **Clínica Alemana**, Av Manquehue 1410, p 2, Vitacura, T2210 1301, pacienteinternacional@alemana.cl. Clínica Central, San Isidro 231-243, Santa Lucía metro, T2463 1400, open 24 hrs, German spoken. **Emergency pharmacy**, Portugal 155, Universidad Católica metro, T2631 3005. Consult www.farmaciasahumada.cl for other emergency pharmacies. **Note** If you need to get to a hospital, it is better to take a taxi than wait for an ambulance. **Language schools** Bellavista, C del Arzobispado 0605, Providencia, T2732 3443, www.escuelabellavista.cl. Group and individual classes, lodging with families, free activities. **Escuela de Idiomas Violeta Parra**, Triana 853, Providencia, T2236 4241, www. tandemsantiago.cl. Courses aimed at budget travellers, information programme on social issues, arranges accommodation and visits to local organizations and national parks. **Natalislang Language Centre**, Arturo Bürhle 047, Metro Baquedano, Providencia, T2222 8685, www.natalislang.com. Also has a branch in Valparaíso: Plaza Justicia 45, of 602, T032-225 4849. Many private teachers, including **Lucía Araya Arévalo**, T2749 0706 (home), 2731 8325 (office), lusara5@hotmail.com. Speaks German and English. **Carolina Carvajal**, Av El Bosque Sur 151, dpto Q, Las Condes, T2734 7646, ccarvajal@interactiva.cl. Exchange library, internet access. **Patricio Ríos**, Tobalaba 7505, La Reina, T2226 6926. Speaks English. **Useful addresses** Immigration To extend tourist visa, or any enquiries regarding legal status, go to **Departamento de Extranjería**, San Antonio 580, p 3, T 600-486 3000, Mon-Fri 0900-1600, www.extranjeria.gob.cl. Visit for an extension of tourist visa or any enquiries regarding legal status. Expect long queues. Note that this can also be done at any provincial *extranjería* office. **Policia Internacional**: For lost tourist cards, see Accident and emergency, page 655.

Around Santiago

Pomaire

In this little town 65 km west of Santiago, good-quality handicrafts from all over Chile are for sale at prices cheaper than those in Santiago. The area is rich in clay and pottery can be bought and the artists can sometimes be seen at work. The town is famous for its *chicha de uva* and for its Chilean dishes.

Upper Maipo Valley

Southeast of Santiago is the rugged, green valley of the **Cajón del Maipo**. A road runs past Centros Vacacionales with a variety of activities and through many villages to the main town of San José de Maipo. Its historic centre has a walking route to visit the old station, the church and other sites. There are places to eat, banks and other services; tourist office in the Municipalidad on the Plaza. Some 11 km further is San Alfonso, near which is the Cascada de Ánimas waterfall (entry through a lodge and vacation centre, 60-90 minutes' walk to falls, entry US$9-18 depending on season). Next is San Gabriel (11 km) with a few places selling drinks and snacks and, 2km further, the bridge over the Río Yeso, a scruffy picnic spot with two eating places in dramatic scenery. At **El Volcán** (1400 m), 21 km beyond San Alfonso, there are astounding views, but little else. From El Volcán the road (very poor condition) runs 14 km east to Lo Valdés and the nearby warm natural baths at **Baños Morales** ① *from Oct, US$4.* About 12 km further east up the mountain are **Baños Colina** ① *US$14.50,* hot thermal springs (horses for hire). This area is popular at weekends and holiday times, but is otherwise deserted. If visiting this area or continuing further up the mountain, be prepared for military checks. There are no shops, so take food (local goat's cheese may be sold at the roadside, or at farmhouses). North of Baños Morales, **Parque Nacional El Morado** ① *Oct-Apr, US$3.65, administration near the entrance, check with Conaf which parts of the park are open, T8901 9775, mn.elmorado@yahoo.es, or www.conaf.cl,* covers 3000 ha including several high peaks, an exceptionally secluded and beautiful place with wonderful views.

Ski resorts

There are six main ski resorts near Santiago, four of them around the village of **Farellones**. Farellones, on the slopes of Cerro Colorado at 2470 m, only 32 km from the capital and reached by road in under 90 minutes, was the first ski resort built in Chile. Now it is a service centre for the three other resorts, but it provides accommodation, has a good beginners' area with basic equipment for hire and is connected by lift to El Colorado. Popular at weekends, it has several large restaurants. It offers beautiful views for 30 km across 10 Andean peaks and incredible sunsets. One-day return shuttles are available from Santiago; enquire at **Ski Club Chile** ① *Goyenechea Candelaria 4750, Vitacura (north of Los Leones Golf Club), T2211 7341.*

El Colorado ① *www.elcolorado.cl,* is 8 km further up Cerro Colorado and has a large ski lodge at the base, offering all facilities, and a restaurant higher up. There are 16 lifts giving access to a large intermediate ski area with some steeper slopes. **La Parva** ① *www.laparva.cl,* nearby at 2816 m, is the upper-class Santiago weekend resort with 30 pistes and 14 lifts. Accommodation is in a chalet village and there are some good bars in high season. Good intermediate to advanced skiing, not suitable for beginners.

Valle Nevado ① *T2477 7705, www.vallenevado.com,* is 16 km from Farellones. It offers the most modern ski facilities in Chile with 34 runs, 40 km of slopes and 41 lifts. The runs are well prepared and are suitable for intermediate level and beginners. There is a ski school and heli-skiing. In summer, this is a good walking area, but altitude sickness can be a problem.

Portillo ① *www.skiportillo.cl,* 2855 m, is 145 km north of Santiago and 62 km east of Los Andes near the customs post on the route to Argentina. One of Chile's best-known resorts, Portillo is on the Laguna del Inca, 5.5 km long and 1.5 km wide; this lake, at an altitude of 2835 m, has no outlet, is frozen over in winter, and its depth is not known. It is surrounded on three sides

Vineyards around Santiago

Several vineyards in the Santiago area offer quality tours in English or Spanish, followed by wine tastings. The following are easily accessible. Tours need booking in advance.

Aquitania ① *Av Consistorial 5090, Peñalolén, T2791 4500, www.aquitania.cl, bus D17 or taxi from metro Quilín.*

Concha y Toro ① *Virginia Subercaseaux 210, Pirque, near Puente Alto, 25 km south of Santiago, T2476 5269, www.conchaytoro.cl, metro to Las Mercedes, then taxi or colectivo.*

Cousiño-Macul ① *Av Quilín 7100, Peñalolén, east outskirts of the city, tours Mon-Fri, T2351 4100, www.cousinomacul.com.*

De Martino ① *Camino a Melipilla Km 34, Talagante, T2372 2900, www.demartino.cl, direct bus to Isla de Maipo from Terminal San Borja.*

Undurraga ① *Santa Ana, 34 km southwest of Santiago, T2372 2850, www.undurraga.cl, take a Talagante bus from the Terminal San Borja to the entrance.*

Viña Santa Rita ① *Padre Hurtado 0695, Alto Jahuel, Buin, 45 km south, T2362 2590, www.santa rita.cl, take a bus from Terminal San Borja to Alto Jahuel.*

by accessible mountain slopes. The 23 runs are varied and well prepared, connected by 12 lifts, two of which open up the off-piste areas. This is an excellent family resort, with a highly regarded ski school. Cheap packages can be arranged at the beginning of and out of season, when there are boats for fishing in the lake (afternoon winds can make the homeward pull much longer than the outward pull) and good walking, but get detailed maps before setting out.

Lagunillas ① *www.skilagunillas.cl,* is 67 km southeast of Santiago in the Cajón del Maipo. Accommodation is in the lodges of the **Club Andino de Chile** (see Skiing, page 672). It is more basic than the other ski centres in the region, with less infrastructure, but the skiing is good. Being lower than the other resorts, its season is shorter, but it is also cheaper.

Santiago to Argentina

The route across the Andes via the Cristo Redentor tunnel is one of the major crossings to Argentina. Before travelling check on weather and road conditions beyond Los Andes. See International buses, page 675. Some 77 km north of Santiago is the farming town of **Los Andes**. There is a monument to the Clark brothers, who built the Transandine Railway to Mendoza (now disused). The town has several hotels. The road to Argentina follows the Aconcagua valley for 34 km until it reaches the village of **Río Blanco** (1370 m). East of Río Blanco the road climbs until Juncal where it zig-zags steeply through a series of 29 hairpin bends at the top of which is Portillo (see above).

Border with Argentina Los Libertadores The old pass, with the statue of Christ the Redeemer (**Cristo Redentor**), is above the tunnel on the Argentine side. On the far side of the Andes the road descends 203 km to Mendoza. The 4-km-long tunnel is open 24 hours September to May, 0700-2300 Chilean time June to August, toll US$5. Note that this pass is closed after heavy snowfall, when travellers may be trapped at the customs complex on either side of the border. The Chilean border post of Los Libertadores is at Portillo, 2 km from the tunnel. Bus and car passengers are dealt with separately. Bicycles must be taken through on a pick-up. There may be long delays during searches for fruit, meat and vegetables, which may not be imported into Chile. A *casa de cambio* is in the customs building in Portillo.

ⓐ Around Santiago listings

For hotel and restaurant price codes, and other relevant information, see Essentials.

ⓑ Where to stay

Upper Maipo Valley *p677*

$$$-$$ Cabañas Corre Caminos, Estero Morales 57402, Baños Morales, T9269 2283, www.loscorrecaminos.cl. Cabins sleeping 2-5 people, open all year. Food available, activities including horse riding.

$$ pp Refugio Lo Valdés, 14 km east of El Volcán, Lo Valdés, T9230 5930, refugiolovaldes@dav.cl. Stone-built chalet accommodation or dorm. Good restaurant. Lots of trekking and climbing information, part of Club Alemán Andino.

$$ Res Los Chicos Malos, Baños Morales, T2624 5412, T09-9323 6424, www.banos morales.cl. Comfortable, fresh bread, good meals. There are also *cabañas*, horse riding, open in winter for hot drinks.

Ski resorts *p677*
Farellones

$$$$ Lodge Andes, Camino La Capilla 662, www.lodgeandes.cl. Shared rooms with shared bathrooms or private double rooms, rate includes half board. English spoken. Good value.

$$$$ Posada de Farellones, T2201 3704, www.skifarellones.com. Cosy and warm, Swiss style, transport service to slopes, decent restaurant. Price for half board. Also **Farellones**, www.hotelfarellones.cl, and **La Cornisa**, www.lacornisa.cl.

$$ pp Refugio Universidad de Chile, Los Cóndores 879, T2321 1595, www.uchile.cl. Shared rooms half board. Standard *refugio*, often fills up with university students at weekends.

El Colorado and Valle Nevado
Apartments for daily or weekly rental in El Colorado. Also apartment and resort hotel facilities in **Valle Nevado**, where the 5-star resort has boutique shops, gourmet dining, and backpacker facilities, www.vallenevado.com.

La Parva

$$$$ Condominio Nueva La Parva, reservations in Santiago, El Bosque Norte 0177, piso 2, T2339 8482, www.laparva.cl. Good hotel and restaurant. 3 other restaurants.

Portillo

$$$$-$$$ Hotel Portillo, Renato Sánchez 4270, Las Condes, T2263 0606, www.skiportillo.com. On the shore of Laguna del Inca. From lakeside suites with full board and fabulous views, to bunk rooms without bath. Self-service lunch, open all year, minibus to Santiago. Cinema, nightclub, pool, sauna and medical service.

Lagunillas

$$$ Refugio Club Andino, T07-600 8057, www.skilagunillas.cl. Cabins sleep 2-5, shared bathrooms, room only, B&B or full board.

Santiago to Argentina *p678*
$$$$ Baños El Corazón, at San Esteban, 2 km north of Los Andes, T02-2236 3636, www.termaselcorazon.cl. Full board, with use of pool; also day passes for thermal baths, spa, meals and combinations. Take bus San Esteban/El Carino.

ⓒ Transport

Pomaire *p677*
Bus From Santiago take the Melipilla bus from Terminal San Borja, every few mins, US$2.35-3 each way, 1 hr; alight at side road to Pomaire, 2-3 km from town, colectivos every 10-15 mins. It's easier to visit on a tour, often combined with Isla Negra, see page 691, or by car.

Upper Maipo Valley *p677*
Take line 5 metro to Bellavista La Floridaza, change to Metrobus 72 to the Plaza in San José de Maipo, or take line 4 to Las Mercedes and take bus No 72, to San José, 40 mins, US$1.50, or a colectivo which can go as far as San Gabriel. Colectivo fares: Las Mercedes to San José US$2.35, to San Alfonso US$3, to San Gabriel, US$5. San José to San Alfonso US$1.10, to San Gabriel, US$3. San Alfonso-San Gabriel US$2.35. There is a bus every 30 mins from San

José to San Alfonso, every hr to San Gabriel and at 1400 to El Volcán. In summer only 1 morning bus to Baños Morales, US$14.

Ski resorts *p677*
Bus From Santiago leave from Av Apoquindo 4900 (Escuela Militar Metro), daily from 0800-1000 in season, essential to book in advance, Ski Total, T2246 6881, www.skitotal.cl, and

Ski Van, T2219 2672, www.skivan.cl, offer transport to ski resorts. Reserve in advance; also for hotel or airport pick-up and minibuses to Portillo. It is easy to hitch from the junction of Av Las Condes/El Camino Farellones (YPF petrol station in the middle), reached by a Barnechea bus. **Portillo** is easily reached by any bus from Los Héroes terminal, Santiago, or Los Andes to **Mendoza**. You may have to hitch back.

Valparaíso and around

Sprawling over a crescent of 42 hills (cerros) that rear up from the sea, Valparaíso, the capital of V Región, is unlike any other Chilean city. The main residential areas obey little order in their layout and the cerros have a bohemian, slightly anarchic atmosphere. Here you will find mansions mingling with some of Chile's worst slums and many legends of ghosts and spirits. It is an important naval base and, with the Congress building, it is also the seat of the Chilean parliament. Pacific beaches close to the capital include the international resort of Viña del Mar, Reñaca, Concón and several others. On the same stretch of coast is the port of San Antonio. This coastline enjoys a Mediterranean climate; the cold sea currents and coastal winds produce much more moderate temperatures than in Santiago and the central valley. Rainfall is moderate in winter and the summers are dry and sunny.

Valparaíso → *Phone code: 032. Colour map 8, B1. Population: 300,000.*

First settled in 1542 (but not officially 'founded' until the beginning of the 21st century), Valparaíso became a small port used for trade with Peru. It was raided by corsairs, including Sir Francis Drake, at least seven times in the colonial period. The city prospered from independence more than any other Chilean town. It was used in the 19th century by commercial agents from Europe and the US as their trading base in the southern Pacific and became a major international banking centre as well as the key port for US shipping between the East Coast and California (especially during the gold rush). Its decline was the result of the opening of the trans-continental railway in the United States, and then the Panama Canal in 1914, a decrease in mining activity leading to reduced bank profits, followed by the 1929-1930 Depression, after which British business left. It then declined further owing to the development of a container port in San Antonio, tax breaks encouraging financial institutions to relocate to Santiago and the move of the middle-classes to nearby Viña del Mar, but Valparaíso is now reviving. It is officially the Cultural Capital of Chile and much work is being done to renovate the historical centre and museums and to build new galleries. The historic centre and Cerros Alegre and Concepción are a UNESCO World Cultural Heritage Site.

Arriving in Valparaíso
Orientation The lower city along the waterfront is called El Plan and is connected to the upper city in the 'cerros' by steep winding roads, flights of steps and ascensores or funicular railways as well as taxis, colectivos and certain bus routes. Buses are frequent in El Plan, which is also served by a trolley bus (see below). Pudahuel international airport outside Santiago is 108 km and can be reached by bus with one change. The long-distance bus terminal is on Pedro Montt 2800 block (one of the main streets running east from the Cathedral), corner of Rawson, opposite the Congreso Nacional. ▶▶ *See also Transport, page 688.*

Tourist offices Sernatur ① *in the Consejo Nacional de la Cultura y Las Artes, Prat y Sotomayor, T223 6264, infovalparaiso@sernatur.cl, Mon-Sat 0900-1800.* The **Municipal office** ① *C Condell, opposite Ramírez, Mon-Fri 0830-1400, 1530-1745, www.ciudaddevalparaiso.cl,* is in the old Municipalidad building, with a kiosk in Casa La Sebastiana (see below). There are also two information offices in the bus terminal, but these are privately run on a commission basis and hence do not give impartial advice. There is also a university-run tourist office, **DUOC**, in Edificio Cousiño, Blanco 997.

Safety Robbery is a problem in El Puerto and La Matriz and also around the *ascensores* on Avenida Argentina. The upper outskirts of town, while offering amazing views, are not the safest places, particularly after dark. The poorer and rougher districts tend to be those furthest from the centre. Also, be aware that Calle Chacabuco (on which some hotels are located) is the pick-up point for local rent-boys.

Places in Valparaíso

Little of the city's colonial past survived the pirates, tempests, fires and earthquakes of the period. Most of the principal buildings date from after the devastating earthquake of 1906 (further serious earthquakes occurred in 1971, 1985 and 2010) though some impression of its 19th century glory can be gained from the banking area of **El Plan**. This is the business centre, with once fine office buildings on narrow streets strung along the edge of the bay. Above, covering the hills ('cerros'), is a fantastic, multicoloured agglomeration of fine mansions, tattered houses and shacks, scrambled in oriental confusion along the narrow back streets. Superb views over the bay are offered from most of the 'cerros'. The lower and upper cities are connected by steep winding roads, flights of steps and 15 *ascensores* or funicular railways dating from 1883 1914. For several years there have been problems keeping them running and some operate irregularly for lack of funding for repairs and maintenance. In 2014 seven or eight were open, but the the the municipality was working on more. Sadly, the unusual **Ascensor Polanco** (entrance from Calle Simpson, off Avenida Argentina, a few blocks from the bus station), with its 160 m horizontal tunnel through the rock, then a vertical lift to the summit, is not safe to visit: you have to walk down through a very dangerous area. One of the best ways to see the lower city is on the historic **trolley bus**, which takes a circular route from the Congress to the port (US$0.50). Some of the cars, imported from Switzerland and the US, date from the 1930s. Another good viewpoint is from top of Ascensor Barón, near the bus terminal.

The old heart of the city is the **Plaza Sotomayor**, dominated by the former Intendencia (Government House), now used as the seat of the admiralty. Opposite is a fine monument to the 'Heroes of Iquique'. Bronze plaques on the Plaza illustrate the movement of the shoreline over the centuries and an opening, protected by a glass panel, shows parts of the original quay, uncovered when a car park was being excavated. The passenger quay is one block away (with poor quality, expensive handicraft shops) and nearby is the remodelled Merval railway station and shopping mall for trains to Viña del Mar and Limache. The streets of El Puerto run to the northwest of Plaza Sotomayor. Calle Serrano runs for two blocks to the Plaza Echaurren, the oldest plaza in Valparaíso, once the height of elegance, today the home of sleeping drunks. Nearby stands the stucco church of **La Matriz**, built in 1842 on the site of the first church in the city. Remnants of the old colonial city can be found in the area around La Matriz. **Museo del Mar Almirante Cochrane** ① *Merlet 195, Tue-Sun 1000-1800, free,* has temporary exhibitions and has good views over the port. Take Ascensor Cordillera (if open) from Calle Serrano, off Plaza Sotomayor, to Cerro Cordillera, otherwise the long, steep flight of stairs next to the ascensor; at the top, on Plazuela Eleuterio Ramírez, take Calle Merlet to the left (not a safe area).

Further northwest, along Bustamante, lies the Plaza Aduana from where Ascensor Artillería (closed 2014) rises to **Cerro Artillería**, which is crowned by the huge Naval Academy and the **Museo Naval** ① *www.museonaval.cl, Tue-Sun 1000-1730, US$1.30,* good English signs, with naval history 1810-1880 and exhibitions on Chile's two naval heroes, Lord Cochrane and Arturo Prat, as well as one of the phoenix capsules used to rescue the 33 trapped miners in 2010. Great views are to be had from the Paseo 21 de Mayo at the upper station of the ascensor. Avenida Altamirano runs along the coast at the foot of Cerro Playa Ancha to **Las Torpederas**, a small bathing beach. The **Faro de Punta Angeles** ① *T8621-8728, T250 6100 or T220 8730, contacto@ farosdechile.com, contact for an appointment to visit the lighthouse and attached museum*, on a promontory just beyond Las Torpederas, was the first lighthouse on the West Coast (30-40 minutes' walk from Cerro Artillería).

Both **Cerro Concepción** and **Cerro Alegre** have fine architecture and scenic beauty as well as a thriving street art scene. Artists and students have long lived there, lending them a slightly bohemian feel, and the cerros are becoming deservedly very popular with visitors. A 2-km walk starts at the top of Ascensor Concepción, leading to Paseo Mirador Gervasoni and Calle Pupudo through a labyrinth of narrow streets and stairs. Two museums on these hills are: **Museo Municipal de Bellas Artes** ① *Paseo Yugoslavo 176, Cerro Alegre, T225 2332; take Ascensor El Peral from Plaza de la Justicia, off Plaza Sotomayor; Tue-Sun 1030-1900, US$3.65, concessions US$1.*

⒈ Valparaíso

➡ Valparaíso maps
1 Valparaíso, page 682
2 Cerro Concepción, Cerro Alegre & El Puerto, page 684

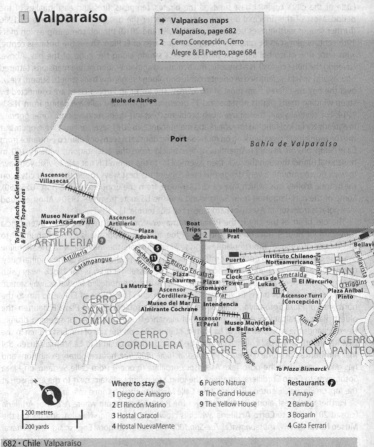

Where to stay 🛏
1 Diego de Almagro
2 El Rincón Marino
3 Hostal Caracol
4 Hostal NuevaMente
6 Puerto Natura
8 The Grand House
9 The Yellow House

Restaurants 🍴
1 Amaya
2 Bambú
3 Bogarín
4 Gata Ferrari

Housed in the impressive Palacio Baburizza, it displays Chilean landscapes and seascapes and some modern paintings. Opposite is the 1920s mansion, **Palacio Astoreca**, newly restored as a luxury hotel (Montealegre 149, www.hotelpalacioastoreca.com). **Casa de Lukas** ① *Paseo Mirador Gervasoni 448, Cerro Concepción, www.lukas.cl, US$2.35, Tue-Sun 1100-1800, closed 1400-1445*, is a beautiful villa dedicated to the work of one of Chile's most famous caricaturists. It has a café.

The *cerro* east of Concepción in Panteón, on which are the cemeteries, founded in the 19th century, of the Catholic families (Cementerio No 1) and the non-Catholic (Cementerio de Disidentes). Both can be visited. Further up Cumming is the Parque Cultural ex-Cárcel de Valparaíso on Cerro Cárcel. The prison has been renovated to hold art exhibitions, theatre, workshops and other events. All over the city, as in Santiago, there is artistic activity, outside as well as indoors, people practising dance moves, circus skills, and so on. The walls of many buildings are decorated; for a study of this art form see *Street Art Chile* by Rod Palmer (**8 Books**); for tours **Valpo Street Art Tours** ① *T312 3014, www.valpostreetart.com*.

Southeast of Plaza Sotomayor Calles Prat, Cochrane and Esmeralda run through the old banking and commercial centre to Plaza Aníbal Pinto, around which are several of the city's

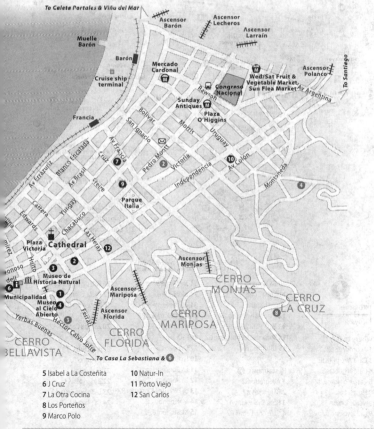

5 Isabel a La Costeñita
6 J Cruz
7 La Otra Cocina
8 Los Porteños
9 Marco Polo
10 Natur-In
11 Porto Viejo
12 San Carlos

oldest bars and cafés. On Esmeralda, just past the Turri Clock Tower and Ascensor Concepción is the building of **El Mercurio de Valparaíso**, the world's oldest Spanish-language newspaper still in publication, first published in 1827. Further east is the Plaza Victoria with the Cathedral. Near Plaza Victoria is the **Museo de Historia Natural** ① *Condell 1546, T254 4840, www.mhnv.cl, Tue-Sat 1000-1800, Sun 1000-1400, open later in summer, free*, in 19th-century Palacio Lyon, redesigned, with library and café. Above Plaza Victoria on Cerro Bellavista is the **Museo al Cielo Abierto**, a collection of 20 street murals on the exteriors of buildings, designed by 17 of Chile's most distinguished contemporary artists. It is reached by the Ascensor Espíritu Santo at the end of Calle Huito (closed 2014), by walking up Huito to Rudolph, or Edwards to Ferrari, or by walking downhill from Casa 'La Sebastiana', former house of **Pablo Neruda** ① *Ferrari 692, Av Alemania,*

② Cerro Concepción, Cerro Alegre & El Puerto

Valparaíso maps
1 Valparaíso, page 682
2 Cerro Concepción, Cerro Alegre & El Puerto, page 684

Where to stay
1 Acontraluz *C2*
3 Casa Aventura *B2*
4 Casa Higueras
6 Catalejo House *B2*
8 Hostal Casa
Verde Limón *B3*
9 La Bicyclette *B2*
10 La Nona *C2*
11 Luna Sonrisa
& El Nidito *C2*
12 Manoir Atkinson *B2*
13 Pata Pata *B2*
14 Somerscales Boutique *C2*
15 Ultramar *B3*

Restaurants
1 Allegretto *B2*
2 Bar Inglés *A2*
3 Bote Salvavidas *A1*
4 Café con Letras *B2*
5 Café Vinilo *B2*
7 Color Café *B2*
8 Delicias Express *B1*
9 El Desayunador *B2*
25 E l Dominó *B3*
26 Fauna *B2*
27 La Cocó *C2*
10 La Colombina *B1*
11 La Concepción *B2*
12 La Rotonda *B1*
13 Le Filou de Montpellier *B2*
14 Malandrino *C2*
15 Mastodonte *A2*
16 Pan de Magia *C2*
17 Pasta e Vino *B2*
18 Pimentón *B3*
19 Turri *B2*
20 Zamba Canuta *A2*

Bars & clubs
28 Cinzano *B3*
21 El Huevo *A3*
22 El Irlandés *A3*
23 La Piedra Feliz *A2*
24 La Playa *B1*

Altura 6900 on Cerro Florida, T225 6606, www.fundacionneruda.org, Tue-Sun 1010-1800, Jan-Feb 1030-1850, US$7.50 including autoguide in several languages, students and seniors US$1.75; getting there: bus 612 (O) from Av Argentina, US$0.65, or colectivo 38 or 39 from Plazuela Ecuador, US$0.65. This has interesting displays, wonderful views and is worth a visit (see also his house at Isla Negra, page 691). It has an art gallery, gardens and a small café. East of Plaza Victoria, reached by following Calle Pedro Montt is Plaza O'Higgins, which is dominated by the huge square arch of the imposing Congreso Nacional. Opposite is the bus terminal, while four blocks north on Errázuriz is the Barón train station and the **Muelle Barón**, near which is the terminal for cruise ships. The end of this pier gives a good view of Valparaíso's amphitheatre-like setting. Just off the pier is a small colony of sea-lions and at the pier's base kayaks and sailing boats can be hired and lessons taken (www.puertodeportivo.cl). A new coastal walkway runs northeast from here past several small beaches as far as **Caleta Portales**, a small fishing harbour with several seafood restaurants almost at the edge of Viña del Mar.

Small boats make 30-minute tours of the harbour from Muelle Prat, near Plaza Sotomayor, US$5.50 pp plus tip for the commentator, wait for boat to fill up.

◉ Valparaíso listings

For hotel and restaurant price codes, and other relevant information, see Essentials.

◉ Where to stay

Valparaíso *p680, maps p682 and p684*
El Plan
$$$ Diego de Almagro, Molina 76, T213 3600, www.dahoteles.com. Comfortable 4-star business standard hotel. Superior rooms look out over the bay.

Cerros Alegre and Concepción
Cerros Alegre, Concepción and, to a lesser extent, Bellavista have many *hostales*, more than we can list. For a selection, see http://hhyr.cl.
$$$$ Acontraluz, San Enrique 473, Cerro Alegre, T211 1320, www.hotelacontraluz.cl. Probably the best of the boutique hotels here. Rooms facing the sea have balconies with tremendous views. Bright, Victorian house with attention to detail and no expense spared. English, French, Russian spoken, most hospitable, 24-hr café, solar power, recycling, no TV.
$$$$ Casa Higueras, Higuera 133, Cerro Alegre, T249 7900, www.hotelcasahigueras.cl. Small, elegant hotel on 5 levels, variety of rooms, good views, fine restaurant, spa, sauna, pool and gardens.
$$$$ Manoir Atkinson, Paseo Atkinson 165, 327 5425, www.hotelatkinson.cl. A boutique hotel, 7 comfortable rooms, terraces with views

of the city and bay, English and French spoken, meals, tours arranged.
$$$$-$$$ Somerscales Boutique, San Enrique 446, Cerro Alegre, T233 1006, www.hotelsomerscales.cl. Spacious rooms in former home of English painter, period furniture. Basic English spoken, top-floor rooms lovely views.
$$$-$$ La Nona, Galos 660, Cerro Alegre, T249 5706, www.bblanona.com. Comfortable, welcoming B&B, some rooms with bath, plenty of information and activities, English spoken.
$$ Hostal Casa Verde Limón, Subida Cumming, Plaza El Descanso 196, Cerro Cárcel, T212 1699, www.casaverdelimon.com. Double, single rooms, dorm and loft, shared bath, breakfast extra, laundry, good budget choice.
$$ La Bicyclette, Almte Montt 213, Cerro Alegre, T222 2215, www.bicyclette.cl. Basic, bright rooms, shared bath, book exchange, lovely patio, French-run, rents bicycles.
$$ Luna Sonrisa, Templeman 833, Cerro Alegre, T273 4117, www.lunasonrisa.cl. Room for 16 guests in doubles, singles or dorm with shared or en suite bath. Bright, comfortable, lots of information, excellent breakfast including wholemeal bread and real coffee, tours arranged, English and French spoken, helpful. Also **El Nidito**, www.elnidito.cl, one classically elegant apartment with 3 en suite bedrooms, large living/dining room with upright piano and spacious balcony, parking. Also 1 smaller apartment, sleeps 2-4.

$$-$ **Casa Aventura**, Pasaje Gálvez 11, off C Urriola, Cerro Concepción, T275 5963, www.casaventura.cl. One of Valparaíso's longest established backpackers' hostels, with rooms and dorms in a traditional house, German and English spoken, tours, helpful, deservedly popular, informative.

$$-$ **Pata Pata**, Templeman 657, T317 3153, www.patapatahostel.com. Family-run, doubles and big dorms ($), shared facilities, lots of movies, good choice.

Other Cerros
$$$ **The Grand House**, Federico Varela 25, Cerro La Cruz, T221 2376, www.thegrand house.cl. Charming house, almost Victorian decor, excellent breakfast, "a true gem".
$$$ **Puerto Natura**, Héctor Calvo 850, Cerro Bellavista, T222 4405, www.puertonatura.cl. Large grounds with fruit trees and small pool, café, excellent views. There is also a holistic centre with sauna, massages, reiki, reflexology and meditation.
$$$ **Ultramar**, Pérez 173, Cerro Cárcel, T221 0000, www.hotelultramar.cl. Italianate building (1907), modern design, buffet breakfast, café, attentive staff. Rooms are spacious with great views but may get stuffy in summer.
$$ **Catalejo House**, Bernardo Vero 870, Cerro San Juan de Dios, T225 9150, www.catalejohouse.com. Rooms with shared bath, good view, good reports.
$$ **Hostal Caracol**, Héctor Calvo 371, Cerro Bellavista, T239 5817, www.hostalcaracol.cl. Rooms or dorm. Pleasant patio and barbeque area, heating. English spoken. A good choice. Offers discounts at **Confieso** restaurant, Rudolph 254, T328 4116, just down the hill.
$$ **The Yellow House**, Capitán Muñoz Gamero 91, Cerro Artillería, T233 9435, www.theyellow house.cl. Tucked away on a cobbled side street. Australian/Chilean-run, rooms and an apartment, some with great views, good showers, non-smoking.

Near the bus terminal
$$-$ **El Rincón Marino**, San Ignacio 454, T222 5815, www.rinconmarino.cl. Uninspiring location, but good-value hostal.
$$-$ **Hostal NuevaMente**, Pocuro 1088, T317 0184, hostalnuevamente.valparaiso on Facebook. Beautiful old hostel with big, light rooms, about 15 mins' walk from centre. Run by a helpful young couple, good local information, some English spoken, movies, tours, bike hire.

⑦ Restaurants

Valparaíso p680, maps p682 and p684
El Plan
$$$ **Zamba & Canuta**, Blanco 1065, T221 6013. Elegant, modern cuisine, wide range of dishes. Excellent views across the bay, also holds events.
$$$-$$ **Bote Salvavidas**, by Muelle Prat. Elegant fish restaurant overlooking the port.
$$$-$$ **Marco Polo**, Pedro Montt 2199, www.marco-polo.cl. Traditional restaurant, pastelería and salon de té, since 1955, good value set lunches, plus mostly Italian dishes.
$$ **Bar Inglés**, Cochrane 851 (entrance also on Blanco Encalada), T221 4625. Historic bar dating from the early 1900s, a chart shows the ships due in port. Good food and drink.
$$ **Isabel a La Costeñita**, Blanco 86. Good seafood, with incredibly kitsch décor.
$$ **La Otra Cocina**, Yungay 2250, near Francia. Good seafood, cosy, good service.
$$ **Los Porteños**, Cochrane 102. A seafood favourite, terse service but good food.
$$ **Porto Viejo**, Cochrane y Valdivia. Good-value set lunch fish dishes, good service.
$ **Bambú**, Independencia 1790, p 2, T223 4216. Closed Sun. Vegetarian lunches only.
$ **El Dominó**, Cumming 67. Traditional, serves empanadas, chorillanas, calagas de pescado (fish nuggets), open till 0500.
$ **J Cruz**, Condell 1466, T221 1225. Valparaíso's most traditional restaurant/museum, famous for its chorillanas, open all night, very popular, queues at lunchtime.
$ **Mastodonte**, Esmeralda 1139. No nonsense, very good value, traditional food in incredibly kitsch surroundings. Excellent service and cheap locally brewed draft beer.
$ **Natur-In**, Colón 2634, www.naturin.cl. Tasty home-made, mostly vegetarian food. Menu changes daily, excellent value, fills up quickly, lunch only.
$ **Pimentón**, Ecuador 27. Homecooked traditional Chilean dishes. Menu changes daily, good value.
$ **San Carlos**, Las Heras y Independencia. Traditional family-run restaurant with lots of

character that hasn't changed in years. Lunch only. Good food guaranteed, always full of locals. Recommended.

There are good cheap seafood lunches upstairs at Mercado Cardonal behind the bus terminal. At Caleta Membrillo, 2 km northwest of Plaza Sotomayor (take any Playa Ancha bus), there are several good fish restaurants including **Club Social de Pescadores**, Altamirano 1480, and **El Membrillo**.

Bogarín, Plaza Victoria 1670. Great juices, ice cream and snacks.

La Rotonda, Prat 701. One of Valparaíso's more traditional cafés, good coffee and breakfast.

Cerros Alegre and Concepción

These *cerros* have a great many places to eat, again more than we can list; wander around to see what takes your fancy.

$$$ La Concepción, Papudo 541, Cerro Concepción, T249 8192. Creative food, beautifully presented and well served, magnificent views.

$$$-$$ Café Vinilo, Almte Montt 448, T223 0665. Inventive lunchtime menus with gourmet interpretations of traditional Chilean dishes. Also a lively bar at night.

$$$-$$ Fauna, Dimalow 166, T212 1408. Varied menu, mostly seafood and fish, Chilean, desserts, large wine list, eat inside or on terrace. Also has a hotel, www.faunahotel.cl.

$$$-$$ La Colombina, Paseo Yugoeslavo 15, Cerro Alegre, T223 6254. The most traditional of the area's restaurants. Good food, wide range of wines, fine views, especially from the top floor.

$$$-$$ Le Filou de Montpellier, Almte Montt 382, T222 4663. French-run, set lunch menu deservedly popular, also open weekday evenings.

$$$-$$ Pasta e Vino, Templeman 352, Cerro Concepción, T249 6187. Wonderfully inventive, tasty pasta dishes, haughty service. Advance booking essential, closed Mon.

$$$-$$ Turri, Templeman 147, Cerro Concepción, T225 9198. Reasonable food, good range of fish dishes, wonderful views, a bit of a tourist trap.

$$ Allegretto, Pilcomayo 529, Cerro Concepción. Lively British owned pizzería, exotic but very tasty toppings, can get busy, closed 1530 (1630 weekends)-2000.

$$ Malandrino, Almirante Montt 532, Cerro Alegre. Wed-Thu 1900-2300, Fri 1300-1600, 1900-2400, Sat 1300-1600, 2000-2400, Sun 1300-1700. Traditional pizzas baked in a clay oven using mostly organic ingredients. Cosy atmosphere. Popular with locals as well as tourists.

Café con Letras, Almte Montt 316, Co Concepción (also on Plaza Sotomayor). Intimate café serving good coffee and snacks, soup in winter, lots of reading material.

Color Café, Papudo 526, Co Concepción. Cosy arty café serving tea and real coffee, fresh juice, good cakes, snacks and all-day breakfasts, regular live music, art exhibits, local art and craft for sale. Upstairs is **La Valija Hostel** (unrelated), good reports.

Delicias Express, Urriola, near Prat. A whole range of fried empanadas, good for a quick snack.

El Desayunador, Almte Montt 399, Cerro Alegre T275 5735. Breakfast bar open early. Wide range of teas, real coffee, cakes, also vegetarian lunches.

La Cocó, Monte Alegre 546, Cerro Alegre. A good selection of sandwiches, including vegetarian, tapas, desserts, teas, coffees and drinks. Live cueca music on Thu 2200.

Pan de Magia, Almte Montt 738 y Templeman, Co Alegre. Cakes, cookies, fantastic empanadas and by far the best wholemeal bread in town, all take away.

Other Cerros

$$ Amaya, Rudolf 112, Cerro Bellavista, T249 3567. Fri-Sun. At the top of the ascensor Espíritu Santo. Peruvian food, mostly seafood-based, friendly service, good views from terrace.

Gata Ferrari, Ferrari 103-A, Bellavista, T320 574. Little café and art gallery with sofas and comfy chairs, at the foot of the *subida* to Museo al Cielo Abierto.

Bars and clubs

Valparaíso *p680, maps p682 and p684*
El Plan
The area around El Puerto can be dangerous at night. There are many bars on Subida Ecuador, but be careful which ones you go into, as in some of them you risk being eaten alive (**El Muro**, for example, is rough and sordid). **El Coyote Quemado** is by far the best.

Cinzano, Plaza Aníbal Pinto 1182, T221 3043. Oldest bar in Valparaíso, also serves food. Flamboyant live music at weekends, noted for tango (no dancing by guests allowed).
El Huevo, Blanco 1386. One of Valparaíso's most popular nightspots with 3 levels of dancing and drinking.
El Irlandés, Blanco 1279. Mon-Sat from 1700 (1800 Thu, Sat). Decent and good fun Irish-run Irish bar with bitter on tap and a good selection of beer, live music at weekend.
La Piedra Feliz, Errázuriz 1054. Wed-Sat from 2000. Every type of music depending on the evening, large pub, live music area, and dance floor, clientele of all ages, entrance US$9.
La Playa, Serrano 567 through to Cochrane 558, near Plaza Sotomayor. Old English-style bar, live music, attracts a student crowd.

⊛ Festivals

Valparaíso *p680, maps p682 and p684*
New Year is celebrated by a spectacular, 40-min firework display launched from the harbour and naval ships, which is best seen from the Cerros. The display is televised nationally and about a million visitors come to the city. Book well in advance; accommodation doubles or trebles in price at this time, but it's well worth it.

⊙ Shopping

Valparaíso *p680, maps p682 and p684*
Markets Large antiques market on Plaza O'Higgins every Sun. Very good selection, especially old shipping items. Along Av Argentina there is a huge, colourful fruit and vegetable market on Wed and Sat and a crowded flea market on Sun. Good locally made handicrafts on Cerros Alegre and Concepción.

⊙ What to do

Valparaíso *p680, maps p682 and p684*
Cooking classes
Chilean Cuisine, T09-6621 4626, www.cookingclasseschile.cl. Fun introduction to Chilean food with English-speaking chef/teacher, can include wine tour, wine tastings.

Horse riding
Ritoque Expediciones, north of Concón, T09-9730 5212, www.ritoqueexpediciones.cl. Excellent day trips over a variety of terrain. Galloping encouraged. Full moon rides. Pickup service from Valparaíso and Viña del Mar.

Skiing
Valposki, T273 4659, or T09-8428 3502, www.valposki.cl. Regular day-trips to El Colorado, Farellones and La Parva ski resorts.

Tours for tips
Free Tour, T09-9236 8789, www.freetour valparaiso.cl. 3-hr walking tour starting from Plaza Aníbal Pinto, daily 1000 and 1500.
La Porteña, valparaisopuertomagia@gmail.com. Tours on foot or by bike.

Wine tours
Wine Tours Valparaíso, T273 4659, or T09-8428 3502, www.wine toursvalparaiso.cl. Small-group tours to the Casablanca Valley with an English-speaking guide.
    Ask at the **Municipal Tourist Office** (see above) about wine tours to the Casablanca Valley (Fri 0930 from Plaza Sotomayor, US$27.50 for 2).

⊙ Transport

Valparaíso *p680, maps p682 and p684*
Air To Valparaíso from the international airport at Pudahuel: take a bus to Pajaritos, US$2.50, cross the platform and take a bus to Valparaíso, US$6-7.50. Return to the airport via the same route. Alternatively, catch any Santiago bus and ask to be let off at the 'paradero de taxis' before the Cruce de Pudahuel. Taxis wait here to go to the airport for US$7.50 (about 7 mins' ride, compared with 1 hr if you go into Santiago). Taxis run 0700-2000. Only take a taxi with an official Airport Taxi sticker (pirates overcharge).
Ascensores Municipal *ascensores* run daily 0700-2300 (US$0.20). Sometimes you pay on entrance, sometimes on exit.
Bus US$0.50 within El Plan, US$0.65 to Cerros, US$0.90 to Viña del Mar from Av Errázuriz. Bus 612, known as the 'O', from Av Argentina near the bus terminal to Plaza Aduana gives fine panoramic views of the city and bay.

Long-distance terminal is on Pedro Montt 2800 block, corner of Rawson, 1 block from Av Argentina, T293 9695; plenty of buses between terminal and Plaza Sotomayor. To **Santiago**, 1¾ hrs, US$11-14.50, frequent (book return in advance on long weekends and public holidays).

Fares are much the same as from Santiago to places such as **Chillán**, 7 hrs, **Concepción**, 8 hrs, **Pucón**, 12 hrs, **Puerto Varas** and **Puerto Montt**, 14 hrs; to **La Serena**, 7 hrs; **Antofagasta**, 17 hrs, **San Pedro de Atacama**, 24 hrs. To **Mendoza** (Argentina) 5 companies, 8 hrs, early morning.

Taxi More expensive than Santiago: a short run under 1 km costs US$2 and a journey across town about US$9-10. Taxi colectivos, slightly more expensive than buses, carry sign on roof indicating route, very convenient.

Train Regular service on **Metro Valparaíso** (Merval), T032-252 7633, www.metro-valparaiso.cl, the line between Valparaíso, **Viña del Mar**, **Quilpué** and **Limache**, with a bus service to **Olmué**; services every 10 mins. A modern system with a similar card system to Santiago. Cards cost US$2.50; fare depends on time of day and distance travelled, lowest fare about US$0.60, to **Viña del Mar** US$0-70-0.80.

ⓘ Directory

Valparaíso *p680, maps p682 and p684*
Banks Banks open 0900 to 1400, closed Sat. Many Redbanc ATMs on Prat, and one at the bus terminal. *Casas de cambio*: best exchange rates from **Marin Orrego**, 3rd floor of the stock exchange building, Prat y Urriola, only changes US$ and euro cash; for other currencies, there are several *casas de cambio* along Cochrane, Prat and Esmeralda.

Viña del Mar and around → *Phone code: 032. Colour map 8, B1. Population: 304,203.*

Northeast of Valparaíso via Avenida España which runs along a narrow belt between the shore and precipitous cliffs is one of South America's leading seaside resorts, Viña del Mar. A mixture of fashionable seaside destinations and fishing communities lines the coast to the north, while south of Valparaíso are more popular resorts at the mouth of the Río Maipo. Pablo Neruda's famous seaside home at Isla Negra is also found here. For a change from the sea visit La Campana national park with its native woodlands, panoramic views and Darwinian associations. For **tourist information** in Viña del Mar try **Sernatur** ⓘ *8 Norte 580 y 2 Poniente, T297 5687, infovalparaiso@sernatur.cl*. Municipal office near Plaza Vergara on Arlegui, by Hotel O'Higgins. See also www.vinadelmarchile.cl and www.vinadelmar.cl.

The older part of Viña del Mar is situated on the banks of an estuary, the Marga Marga, which is crossed by bridges. Around Plaza Vergara and the smaller Plaza Sucre to its south are the **Teatro Municipal** (1930) and the exclusive **Club de Viña**, built in 1910. The municipally owned Quinta Vergara, formerly the residence of the shipping entrepreneur Francisco Alvarez, lies two blocks south. The **Palacio Vergara**, in the gardens, housed the **Museo de Bellas Artes** and the **Academia de Bellas Artes**. It is in poor shape and closed to the public (2014). Part of the grounds is a playground, and there is a modern outdoor auditorium where concerts and events are held throughout the year and, in February, an international music festival. See www.quintavergara.cl.

Calle Libertad runs north from the plaza, lined with banks, offices and shops. At the junction with 4 Norte is the **Palacio Carrasco** and **Museo Fonck** ⓘ *4 Norte 784, www.museofonck.cl, Mon-Fri 1000-1800, Sat and Sun 1000-1400, US$4*, an archaeological and natural history museum, with objects from Easter Island and the Chilean mainland, including Mapuche silver.

On a headland overlooking the sea is **Cerro Castillo**, the summer palace of the President of the Republic. Just north, on the other side of the lagoon is the Casino, built in the 1930s and set in beautiful gardens, US$5 (open all year). **Museo de la Cultura del Mar** ⓘ *in the Castillo Wulff, on the coast near Cerro Castillo, T262 5427, Tue-Sat 1000-1300, 1430-1800, Sun 1000-1400*, contains a collection on the life and work of the novelist and maritime historian, Salvador Reyes. The main beaches, Acapulco and Mirasol are located to the north, but south of Cerro Castillo is

Caleta Abarca, also popular and the best beach for swimming. The coastal route north to Reñaca provides lovely views over the sea.

Jardín Botánico Nacional ① *8 km southeast of the city, www.jardin-botanico.cl, open 1000-1800 (till 1900 Sep-Apr), US$3.75, getting there: take bus No 203 from C Alvarez, or Av Errázuriz in Valparaíso, and get off at the puente El Olivar, cross the bridge and walk 15 mins.* Formerly the estate of the nitrate baron Pascual Baburizza and covering 405 ha, it contains over 3000 species from all over the world and a collection of Chilean cacti, but the species are not labelled. It's a good place for a picnic; there's a canopy adventure trail, with ziplines, and occasional concerts in the summer.

Resorts north of Viña del Mar

North of Viña del Mar the coast road runs through **Las Salinas**, a popular beach between two towering crags, **Reñaca** (long beach, upmarket, good restaurants) and **Cochoa**, where there is a sealion colony 100 m offshore, to **Concón** (18 km). Famous for its restaurants, Concón has six beaches stretching along the bay between Caleta Higuerilla in the west end and, in the east, La Boca (the largest of the six, excellent for beach sports, horses and kayaks for hire). **Tourist office** ① *Maroto 1030, www.concon.cl.* **Quintero**, 23 km north of Concón, is a slightly dilapidated fishing town on a rocky peninsula with lots of small beaches (hotels and *residenciales*).

Horcón is set back in a cove surrounded by cliffs, a pleasant small village, mainly of wooden houses. Packed out in January-February, the rest of the year it is a charming place, populated by fishermen, artists and hippies, with a tumbledown feel unlike the more well-to-do resorts to north and south. Horses still drag the small fishing boats out of the sea. Vegetation is tropical with many cacti on the cliff tops. There are lots of *cabañas*, shop around, especially off season. Further north

Viña del Mar

300 metres	6 Hotel del Mar	3 Café Journal	9 La Flor de Chile
300 yards	8 Offenbacher Hof	4 Cevasco	10 Las Delicias del Mar
		5 Ciboulette	11 Samoiedo
Where to stay	**Restaurants**	6 Enjoy del Mar	13 Wok and Roll
1 Agora	1 Alster	7 Fellini	
3 Cap Ducal	2 Bogarín	8 Jerusalem	

is **Maitencillo** with a wonderful long beach, heaving in high summer but a ghost town off season. Some 14 km beyond is **Zapallar**, an expensive resort with a lovely beach. A hint of its former glory is given by a number of fine mansions along Avenida Zapallar. At **Cachagua**, 3 km south, a colony of penguins on an offshore island may be viewed from the northern end of the beach; take binoculars. **Papudo** (*Phone code: 033*), 10 km further north, was the site of a naval battle in November 1865 in which the Chilean vessel Esmeralda captured the Spanish ship Covadonga. Following the arrival of the railway Papudo rivalled Viña del Mar as a fashionable resort in the 1920s but it has long since declined. With its lovely beach and fishing port, it is an idyllic spot (except in high summer).

Resorts south near the mouth of the Río Maipo

North of the port of **San Antonio** is **Cartagena** (8 km), the most popular resort on this part of the coast. The centre is around the hilltop Plaza de Armas. To the south is the picturesque Playa Chica, overlooked by many of the older hotels and restaurants; to the north is the Playa Larga. Between the two a promenade runs below the cliffs; high above hang old houses, offering spectacular views. Cartagena is packed in summer, when it can have quite an edgy feel, but out of season it is a good centre for visiting nearby resorts of Las Cruces, El Tabo and El Quisco. This stretch of coast is known as the Litoral de los Poetas, since many famous Chilean poets found inspiration here.

North of Cartagena in the village of **Isla Negra** is the beautifully restored **Museo-Casa Pablo Neruda** ① *T035-246 1284, US$7.25 students US$2.75, audio guides in several languages, Jan-Feb Tue-Sun 1000-2000, rest of year Tue-Sun 1000-1800, www.fundacionneruda.org*. Bought by Neruda in 1939, and constantly added to over time, this house, overlooking the sea, was his writing retreat in his later years. It contains artefacts gathered by Neruda from all over the world. Neruda and his last wife, Matilde, are buried here; the touching gravestone is beside the house. The house has a good café specializing in Neruda's own recipes.

Parque Nacional La Campana

① *T33-244 1342, www.conaf.cl, daily 0900-1730, closes 1630 Fri, US$4.55 for foreigners.*
This 8000-ha park includes Cerro La Campana (1828 m) which Darwin climbed in 1834 and Cerro El Roble (2200 m). Some of the best views in Chile can be seen from the top. Near Ocoa there are areas of Chilean palms (*kankán* – which give edible, walnut-sized coconuts in March and April), now found in its natural state in only two locations in Chile. There are three entrances: at Granizo (from which the hill is climbed), reached by paved road from Limache, 4 km west, via Olmué; at Cajón Grande (with natural bathing pools), reached by unpaved road which turns off the Olmué-Granizo road; at Palmar de Ocoa to the north reached by unpaved road (10 km) leading off the Pan-American Highway at Km 100 between Hijuelas and Llaillay.

At **Limache**, on the Merval railway, is the **Quinta Escondida** ① *Carrera 013, T09-8418 0531, www.quintaescondida.com*, a late-19th century house with fruit orchards which offers B&B, self-catering, day visits, access to local sites and activities. This is the Chilean HQ for **South American Explorers** (see page 657). On site is also Rosa Puga's healing centre: the Limache Valley is renowned for its alternative medicine and spiritual retreats, as well as its fruit and vegetable production.

⦿ Viña del Mar and around listings

For hotel and restaurant price codes, and other relevant information, see Essentials.

⦿ Where to stay

Viña del Mar *p689, map p690*
There are lots of places to stay, mostly **$$$**, although many are in the business district and not convenient for the beaches. Out of season agencies rent furnished apartments. In season it's cheaper to stay in Valparaíso.

$$$$ Hotel Del Mar, San Martín 199, T600 700 6000, www.enjoy.cl/enjoy-vina-del-mar. Viña's top hotel, in spacious grounds above the casino overlooking the bay. Gym, spa and several good restaurants.

$$$$-$$$ Cap Ducal, Marina 51, T262 6655, www.capducal.cl. Old mansion charm – a ship-shaped building literally overhanging the ocean, with an elegant restaurant, serving good seafood.

$$$ Agora, 5½ Poniente 253, T269 4669, www.hotelagora.cl. On a quiet side street, brightly coloured rooms, most with full-size bathtub, English spoken, helpful staff (on 4 floors but no lift).

$$$ Offenbacher Hof, Balmaceda 102, T262 1483, www.offenbacher-hof.cl. Large wooden house in a quiet residential street overlooking the city centre, peaceful, helpful.

❼ Restaurants

Viña del Mar *p689, map p690*
Many good bars and restaurants on and around San Martín between 2 and 8 Norte; cuisine including Austrian, Mexican, Chinese and Italian. Cheap bars and restaurants around C Valparaíso and Von Schroeders. Not too safe at night.

$$$ Ciboulette, 1 Norte 191, T269 0084. Intimate Belgian-owned and run bistro serving traditional French cuisine. Good wine list.

$$$-$$ Enjoy del Mar, Av Perú s/n, T250 0785. Modern restaurant serving everything from gourmet dishes to barbecues and fast food, all on an open terrace on the seafront.

$$$-$$ Fellini, 3 Norte 88, T297 5742. Wide range of fresh pasta dishes in delicious sauces, good.

$$$-$$ Las Delicias del Mar, San Martín 459. Traditional Basque seafood restaurant.

$$ La Flor de Chile, 8 Norte 607 y 1 Poniente, T212 3480. Consistently good, typical Chilean food.

$$ Wok and Roll, 5 Norte 476. One of the better sushi restaurants in town. Free delivery service.

$$-$ Cevasco, Av Valparaíso 700, T271 4256. Freshly prepared Chilean fast food. Famous for its oversized hamburgers.

$ Café Journal, Agua Santa y Alvarez. Excellent-value set lunch.

$ Jerusalem, Quinta 259. Authentic middle-eastern fare, including falafel, shawarma and stuffed vine leaves.

Cafés

Alster, Valparaíso 225. Elegant but pricey.

Bogarín, in a mall on Valparaíso between Quinta and Etchevers. For juices and ice cream. Seeral other fast food places in the mall.

Samoiedo, Valparaíso 637. A large modern confitería, ice cream, coffee, popular.

❶ Bars and clubs

Viña del Mar *p689, map p690*
Barlovento, 2 Norte y 5 Poniente, T297 7472. The designer bar in Viña, on 3 floors with a lovely roof terrace, serves tapas, wraps, etc, and good beer. Several other options between San Martín and Perú.

❹ What to do

Viña del Mar *p689, map p690*
Cycling
Bicitours, T09-4094 4506, www.bicitours. cl. 8 cycling tours based in Viña, from 2 to 5 hrs, city tours, to resorts, to Valparaíso, from US$12.75; also bicycle hire, US$9.25 per hr, US$33 per day.

❺ Transport

Viña del Mar *p689, map p690*
Bus 2 blocks east of Plaza Vergara at Av Valparaíso y Quilpué, T275 2000. To **Santiago**, US$11-14.50, 1¾ hrs, frequent, same companies as for Valparaíso from Pajaritos in Santiago, book in advance for travel on Sun afternoons. Long-distance services: prices and itineraries similar to Valparaíso.

Train Services on the Metro Valparaíso line stop at Viña (see under Valparaíso).

Resorts north of Viña del Mar *p690*
Bus From Valparaíso and Viña del Mar: to **Concón**, bus 601, US$1, frequent; to **Quintero** and **Horcón**, **Sol del Pacífico**, every 30 mins, US$3, 2 hrs; to **Zapallar** and **Papudo**, **Sol del Pacífico**, 4 a day, US$6. All from Av Libertad in Viña, or Errázuriz in Valparaíso.

Resorts south near the mouth of the Río Maipo *p691*
Bus Regular bus services to **Isla Negra** from Santiago (Pullman Bus) and **Valparaíso** (Pullman Lago Peñuelas), 1½ hrs, US$6. Many tours go here, too. From Santiago to Cartagena, US$12.50.

Parque Nacional La Campana *p691*
The entrances at **Granizo** (paradero 45) and **Cajón Grande** (paradero 41) are reached by local bus/colectivo from outside Limache train station. No public transport to Ocoa. Get a bus to La Calera and bargain with a taxi or

colectivo driver. Expect to pay around US$30. Bus Santiago-Limache, **Pullman** from Alameda terminal, every 2 hrs, US$8, 2 hrs.

❶ Directory

Viña del Mar *p689, map p690*
Banks Many Redbanc ATMs on Libertad and on Arlegui; also on C Valparaíso (but this is not a safe area at night). Many *casas de cambio* on Arlegui and Valparaíso; shop around for best rates and avoid changing money on the street, especially if alone.

North of Santiago

Along the coast is a mixture of fishing villages, deserted beaches and popular resorts, while inland the scenery is wonderfully dramatic but little visited. The land becomes less fertile as you go further north. Ovalle is a good centre for trips to see petroglyphs and the coastal forests at the Parque Nacional Fray Jorge. The largest resort is La Serena, from where access can be made to the Elqui Valley, one of Chile's major pisco-producing regions and one of the world's major astronomical centres.

From the Río Aconcagua to the Río Elqui is a transitional zone between the fertile heartland and the northern deserts. The first stretch of the Pan-American Highway from Santiago is inland through green valleys with rich blue clover and wild artichokes. North of La Ligua, the highway mainly follows the coastline, passing many beautiful coves, alternately rocky and sandy, with good surf, though the water is very cold. The valleys of the main rivers, the Choapa, Limarí and Elqui, are intensively farmed using irrigation to produce fruit and vegetables. There is a striking contrast between these lush valley floors and the arid mountains with their dry scrub and cactus. In some areas, condensation off the sea provides sufficient moisture for woods to grow. Rainfall is rare and occurs only in winter. On the coast the average temperature is 15°C in winter, 23°C in summer, the interior is dry, with temperatures reaching 33°C in summer, but it is cooler in winter and very cold at night.

Ovalle to La Serena

Ovalle and around → *Phone code: 053. Colour map 8, A1. Population: 53,000.*
This town lies inland, 412 km north of Santiago, in the valley of the Río Limarí, a fruit-growing and mining district. Market days are Monday, Wednesday, Friday and Saturday, till 1600; the market (*feria modelo*) is off Benavente (east of the centre). The town is famous for its *talabarterías* (saddleries), products made of locally mined lapis lazuli, goats cheese and dried fruits. Wine is produced in the Limarí Valley and tours are available to *bodegas* such as **Tamaya** (www.tamaya.cl) and **Tabalí** (www.tabali.cl). **Museo del Limarí** ① *in the old railway station, Covarrubias y Antofagasta, Tue-Fri 0900-1300, 1500-1900, Sat-Sun 1000-1300, US$1, free on Sun*, has displays of petroglyphs and a good collection of Diaguita ceramics and other artefacts. Unofficial tourist information kiosk on the Plaza de Armas.

Monumento Nacional Valle del Encanto ① *about 22 km southwest of Ovalle, open all year, 0800-1800, US$2, getting there: no local bus service; you must take a southbound long-distance bus and ask to be dropped off – 5-km walk to the valley; flag down a bus to return; alternatively, use a tour operator.* This is a most important archaeological site. Artefacts from hunting peoples from over 2000 years ago have been found but the most visible remains date from the Molle culture (AD 700). There are over 30 petroglyphs as well as great boulders, distributed in six sites. There are camping facilities.

Termas de Socos ① *35 km southwest of Ovalle on the Pan-American Highway, US$9, bus US$2,* has a swimming pool and individual tubs fed by thermal springs, as well as sauna, jacuzzi and water massage (very popular). It also boasts a reasonable hotel and a campsite.

Monumento Natural Pichasca ① *47 km northeast of Ovalle, 0800-1800, US$4, getting there: daily buses from Ovalle to Hurtado, the turn-off about 42 km from the city; from here it is 3 km to the park and about 2 km more to sites of interest.* An unpaved and largely winding road leads to the park, which contains petrified tree trunks, archaeological remains, including a vast cave with vestiges of ancient roof paintings, and views of rock formations on the surrounding mountains.

Beyond the village of Pichasca it is 32 km to Hurtado. The road winds along the side of the valley, with the Andes easily visible at its head. Near **Vado Morrillos**, 4 km before Hurtado, is the **Corral Los Andes** (see Where to stay, below). The road continues to **Hurtado** village at 1300 m, near which are the only petroglyphs in Chile depicting the sun, hinting at possible links to the Incas, **Cerro Gigante** (2825 m) and a Diaguita cemetery. From Hurtado a road runs north to Vicuña in the Elqui Valley (see below) only 46 km away. This is a desolate but beautiful road, very poor in places with very little traffic and no public transport. Pickups can be hired in Hurtado for US$35-40.

Parque Nacional Fray Jorge ① *90 km west of Ovalle and 110 km south of La Serena at the mouth of the Río Limarí, T262 0058, Sat, Sun and holidays 0900-1700, last car admitted 1600, US$5; no public transport, take a tour.* Visits closely controlled owing to risk of fire. The park is reached by a dirt road leading off the Pan-American Highway. It contains original forests which contrast with the otherwise barren surroundings. Receiving less than 113 mm of rain a year, the forests survive because of the almost constant covering of fog. Waterproof clothing is essential when you visit.

The good inland road between Ovalle and La Serena makes an interesting contrast to Ruta 5 (Panamericana), with a fine pass and occasional views of the Andes across cacti-covered plains and semi-desert mountain ranges. North of Ovalle 61 km a side road runs 44 km southeast (last 20 km very bad) to **Andacollo** (*Population: 10,216; Altitude: 1050 m*). This old town, in an area of alluvial gold washing and manganese and copper mining, is one of the great pilgrimage sites in Chile. In the enormous **Basilica** (1893), 45 m high and with a capacity of 10,000, is the Virgen del Rosario de Andacollo. The **Fiesta Grande** from 23-27 December attracts 150,000 pilgrims. The ritual dances date from a pre-Spanish past. Colectivos run to the festival from Benavente, near Colocolo, in La Serena, but 'purists' walk (torch and good walking shoes essential). There is also a smaller festival, the **Fiesta Chica** on the first Sunday of October. The tourist office on the Plaza arranges tours to the Basilica and to mining operations.

Coquimbo → *Phone code: 051. Colour map 8, A1. Population: 106,000.*

On the same bay as La Serena, 84 km north of Ovalle, is this important port, with one of the best harbours on the coast and major fish-processing plants. The city is strung along the north shore of a peninsula. On the south shore lies the suburb of Guayacán, with an iron-ore loading port, a steel church designed by Eiffel, an English cemetery and a 83-m-high cross to mark the Millennium (US$2 to climb it). In 1981 heavy rain uncovered 39 ancient burials of humans and llamas which had been sacrificed; they are exhibited in a small **Museo del Sitio** ① *in the Plaza Gabriela Mistral, open Jan-Feb only, Mon-Sat 0930-2030, Sun 0930-1400, free, tourist information*. The **municipal tourist office** is at Las Heras 220, T231 3971. Summer boat trips of the harbour and nearby Punta Lobos cost US$5. Nearby is **La Herradura**, 2.5 km from Coquimbo, slightly more upmarket and with the best beaches. Resorts further south, **Totoralillo** (12 km), **Guanaqueros** (37 km) and **Tongoy** (50 km), have good beaches and can be reached by rural buses or colectivos.

La Serena → *Phone code: 051. Colour map 8, A1. Population: 120,000.*

La Serena, built on a hillside 2 km inland from Bahía de Coquimbo, is an attractive city and tourist centre, 11 km north of Coquimbo (473 km north of Santiago) and is the capital of IV Región (Coquimbo). The city was founded by Juan de Bohón, aide to Pedro de Valdivia, in 1544, destroyed by the Diaguita in 1546 and rebuilt by Francisco de Aguirre in 1549. The city was sacked by the English pirate Sharpe in 1680. In the colonial period the city was the main staging-post on the route north to Peru. In the 19th century the city grew prosperous from copper-mining. While retaining colonial architecture and churches, the present-day layout and style have their origins in the 'Plan Serena' drawn up in 1948 on the orders of President Gabriel González Videla, a native of the city. **Sernatur** ① *Matta 461, of 108, in Edificio de Servicios Públicos (next to post office on the Plaza de Armas), T222 5138, infocoquimbo@sernatur.cl, Mon-Fri 0845-1830 (2030 in summer), Sat-Sun 1000-1400, plus 1600-2000 in summer. Kiosk at bus terminal (summer only)*. See www.laserena.cl.

Around the attractive Plaza de Armas are most of the official buildings, including the Post Office, the **Cathedral** (built in 1844 and featuring a carillon which plays every hour) and the **Museo Histórico Regional** ① *Casa González Videla, www.museohistoricolaserena.cl, Mon-Fri 1000-1800, Sat 1000-1300, US$1.30*, which includes several rooms on the man's life. Tickets are also valid for **Museo Arqueológico** ① *Cordovez y Cienfuegos, T222 4492, www.museo*

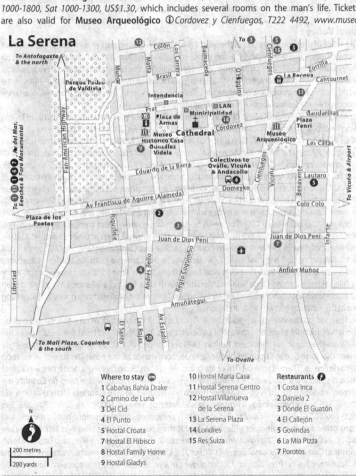

La Serena

To stay
1 Cabañas Bahía Drake
2 Camino de Luna
3 Del Cid
4 El Punto
5 Hostal Croata
7 Hostal El Hibisco
8 Hostal Family Home
9 Hostal Gladys
10 Hostal María Casa
11 Hostal Serena Centro
12 Hostal Villanueva de la Serena
13 La Serena Plaza
14 Londres
15 Res Suiza

Restaurants
1 Costa Inca
2 Daniela 2
3 Donde El Guatón
4 El Callejón
5 Govindas
6 La Mía Pizza
7 Porotos

arqueologicolaserena.cl, Tue-Fri 0930-1750, Sat 1000-1300, 1600-1900, US$1, students free, Sun 1000-1300, free. It has an outstanding collection of Diaguita and Molle exhibits, especially of attractively decorated pottery, also Easter Island exhibits. There are 29 other churches, several of which have unusual towers. **La Recova**, the craft market, at Cienfuegos y Cantournet, includes a large display of handicrafts (some imported) and, upstairs, several good restaurants. One block west of the Plaza de Armas is the **Parque Pedro de Valdivia** ① *daily 1000-2000, US$1.50.* One block south is the delightful **Parque Japonés**.

Avenida Francisco de Aguirre, a pleasant boulevard lined with statues and known as the Alameda, runs from the centre to the coast, terminating at the **Faro Monumental**, a small, neo-colonial mock-castle and lighthouse, now a pub. A series of beaches stretch from here to Coquimbo, 11 km south, linked by the Avenida del Mar. Many apartment blocks, hotels, *cabañas* and restaurants line this part of the bay. The sectors between 4 Esquinas and Peñuelas are probably the best bet for sunbathing or dipping a toe in the water.

Elqui Valley

The valley of the Río Elqui is one of the most attractive oases in this part of northern Chile. There are orchards, orange groves, vineyards and mines set against the imposing, arid mountains. The Elqui Valley is the centre of pisco production with nine distilleries, the largest being Capel in Vicuña. Elqui is also well-known as a centre of mystical energy and is one of the main astronomical centres of the world, with three important observatories. Tour operators in La Serena and Coquimbo arrange tours to the smaller municipal observatory at Mamalluca near Vicuña.

At 2200 m, 89 km southeast of La Serena in the Elqui Valley, 51 km south of Vicuña, **El Tololo** ① *www.ctio.noao.edu, visitors by permit only every Sat 0900-1300; for permits (free) write to Casilla 603, La Serena, T051-220 5200, then pick your permit up before 1200 on the day before (the office is at Colina Los Pinos, on a hill behind the new University – personal applications can be made here for all 3 observatories); they will insist that you have private transport; you can hire a taxi, US$75 for the whole day, but you will require the registration number when you book,* belongs to Aura, an association of US and Chilean universities. It possesses one of the largest telescopes in the southern hemisphere (4-m diameter), six others and a radio telescope. At 2240 m, 150 km northeast of La Serena **La Silla** ① *www.ls.eso.org, registration in advance with online visitor form for free tour every Sat, 1330-1700, except Jul-Aug,* belongs to ESO (European Southern Observatory), and comprises 14 telescopes. From La Serena it is 120 km north along Route 5 to the turn-off, then another 36 km. At 2510 m, 162 km northeast of La Serena, 30 km north of La Silla, **Las Campanas** ① *T220 7301, www.lco.cl, open with permission every Sat 1430-1730,* belongs to the Carnegie Institute, has four telescopes and is a smaller facility than the other two. To get there, follow Route 5 to the same junction as for La Silla, take the turning for La Silla and then turn north after 14 km. La Silla and Las Campanas can be reached without private transport by taking any bus towards Vallenar two hours, US$4, getting out at the junction (*desvío*) and hitch from there.

The road up the valley is paved as far as Pisco Elqui, 37 km beyond **Vicuña**, the valley's capital. This small, friendly town, 66 km east of La Serena, was founded in 1821. On the west side of the plaza are the municipal chambers, built in 1826 and topped in 1905 by a medieval-German-style tower, the Torre Bauer, imported by the German-born mayor of the time. The tourist office is on Plaza de Armas. There is an ATM. There are good views from Cerro La Virgen, north of town. **Capel Pisco distillery**① *1.5 km east of Vicuña, to the right of the main road, guided tours (in Spanish) are offered Dec-May Mon-Sat 1000-1800, free, no booking required.* **Museo Gabriela Mistral**① *Gabriela Mistral 759, www.portaldeelqui.cl/museo-gabriela-mistral, Mon-Fri 1000-1745, Sat 1030-1800, Sun 1000-1300, US$1.20, free Mon Mar-Dec, students ½ price,* contains manuscripts, books, awards and many other details of the poet's life. Next door is the house where the poet was born. There are two observatories near the town which give the public the chance to see the stars: **Observatorio Comunal Cerro Mamalluca**① *Gabriela Mistral 260, Vicuña, T241 1352, www.munivicuna.cl, on Cerro Mamalluca, 6 km north of Vicuña, 1500 m above sea level, several night time tours available, US$10* per person, guides in Spanish and English for groups of 5 or more, book in advance. **Observatorio del Pangue** ⓘ 16 km south of Vicuña on the road to Hurtado, bookings through agencies in La Serena as part of a tour or directly from San Martín 233, Vicuña, T241 2584, www.observatoriodelpangue. blogspot.com, 2 or 3 visits nightly, US$33.50 including transport. Groups are limited to 12 people; tours are informative and in good English and French as well as Spanish, and the telescopes are more powerful than those at Mamalluca. Always book in advance.

From Vicuña the road runs through Paihuano (camping) to **Monte Grande**, where the schoolhouse where Gabriela Mistral lived and was educated by her sister is now a **museum** ⓘ C Principal s/n, T241 5015, Tue-Sun 1000-1300, 1500-1800 (till 1900 in Jan and Feb), US$0.80. The poet's tomb is at the edge of town, opposite the Artesanos de Cochiguaz pisco distillery, which is open to the public. (Buses from the plaza in Vicuña.) Here the road forks, one branch leading to the Cochiguaz valley. There is no public transport. Along this road are several new age settlements; it is said that the valley is an important energy centre. There are several campsites. At night, there is no better place on earth to star gaze. When the moon is new, or below the horizon, the stars seem to be hanging in the air; spectacular shooting stars can be seen every couple of seconds, as can satellites crossing the night sky. Back on the main road, just south of Monte Grande, is the **Cavas del Valle** organic winery with free tastings. The other branch road leads to **Pisco Elqui**, an attractive village with the newly restored church of Nuestra Señora del Rosario on a shady plaza. It's also famous for its night skies and beautiful scenery. At the Hotel Elqui, the **Astropub** has telescopes for stargazing. Horses can be hired, with or without guide (Ramón Luis, T245 1168, is recommended). Its new-age attractions include alternative therapies and massages. More traditional is the **Tres Erres** pisco plant, which is open to the public and gives guided tours in Spanish, US$4. Some 4 km further up the valley at **Los Nichos**, a small *pisco* distillery is open for visits (closed lunchtime) and sells dried fruit and other local products.

Border with Argentina: Paso Agua Negra Paso Agua Negra (4775 m) is reached by a partly paved road from Guanta, 30 km past Rivadavia. The Chilean immigration and customs is at Juntas, 84 km west of the border and 88 km east of Vicuña. The border is open 0800-1700, January to April only, check for the rest of year. There is no public transport beyond Rivadavia. Tell officials if you intend to camp between border posts.

◉ Ovalle to La Serena listings

For hotel and restaurant price codes, and other relevant information, see Essentials.

● Where to stay

Ovalle and around p693
$$$ Hacienda Juntas, near Monte Patria, Km 38, T271 1290, www.haciendajuntas.cl. In 90 ha of vineyards, with pleasant gardens, spectacular views and pool. Restaurant open in high season.
$$$ Plaza Turismo, Victoria 295, T266 2500, www.plazaturismo.cl. Spacious rooms, some overlooking the plaza.
$$$ Termas de Socos, Panamericana Norte Km 370, 35 km southwest of Ovalle, T053-2198 2505, www.termasocos.cl. Reasonable hotel offering full board and access to thermal pools.

$$ Gran Hotel, Vicuña Mackenna 210 (entrance through Galería Yagnam), T262 1084. Decent rooms, good value and service.
$$ Roxy, Libertad 155, T262 0080. Big basic rooms, large colonial-style patio covered in vines in summer, a bit run down, but a good choice.
Camping $ pp Camping y Piscina Los Pumas del Encanto, 10 mins' walk from Valle del Encanto, T262 3667, see Facebook. Nice place with lots of trees and plants, owner Adrián Tello is very knowledgeable.

Río Hurtado
$$$-$ Hacienda Los Andes, Vado Morillos, T269 1822, www.haciendalosandes.com. German/Austrian management at this highly regarded colonial-style hacienda,

all meals use organic local produce, camping, expert horse riding tours.

$$ Tambo de Limarí, Caupolicán 27, Hurtado, T053-2198 2121. Excellent *hospedaje* with wonderful breakfast. Friendly owner, Señora Orieta. There is an interesting collection of ancient riding spurs, stirrups and Spanish padlocks.

Parque Nacional Fray Jorge
1 *cabaña* (**$$$**) sleeping 5. Basic accommodation (**$$**) in an old hacienda and 2 campsites in the national park; 1 at the administration centre, the other 3 km away at El Arrayancito.

La Serena *p694, map p695*
Route 5 from La Serena to Coquimbo is lined with cheap accommodation; as is also Av del Mar, 500 m off the highway (buses run along Route 5, not Av del Mar). Generally accommodation is cheaper in Coquimbo than in La Serena. There are also several hotels in La Herradura. The tourist office in La Serena bus terminal is helpful. Do not be pressurized by touts at the bus station into choosing rooms. Similarly, do not be pressurized to buy tours in hotels: established agencies may give better service and deals.

$$$ Cabañas Bahia Drake, Av del Mar 1300, T222 3367, www.cabanasbahiadrake.cl. Pleasant, fully equipped units for 2 to 6, on the seafront, with swimming pool.

$$$ Del Cid, O'Higgins 138, T221 2692, www.hoteldelcid.cl. Characterful, central, with smallish but spotless rooms around a courtyard. Parking available, English spoken.

$$$ La Serena Plaza, Francisco de Aguirre 0660, T222 5745, www.hotelserenaplaza.cl. Upmarket hotel by the beach with spacious rooms, swimming pool, gym and restaurant.

$$$-$$ Hostal Villanueva de La Serena, Matta 269, T255 0268, www.hostalvillanueva. cl. Large rooms sleeping up to 5, with private or shared bath in colonial house dating from 1800.

$$$-$$ Londres, Cordovez 550, T221 9066, www.hotellondres.cl. Simple, bright rooms with good beds, decent bathrooms.

$$ Hostal Croata, Cienfuegos 248, T222 4997, www.hostalcroata.cl. Small rooms, double or dorms, patio, hospitable.

$$ Hostal El Hibisco, Juan de Dios Peni 636, T221 1407, mauricioberrios2002@yahoo.es. Delightful hosts, welcome drink, lots of information.

$$ Hostal El Punto, Andrés Bello 979, T222 8474, www.hostalelpunto.cl. Dorms and rooms with shared or private bath, tasteful, comfortable, good facilities, café, laundry, parking, book exchange, English and German spoken, tours to Elqui Valley.

$$ Hostal María Casa, Las Rojas 18, T222 9282, www.hostalmariacasa.cl. Very welcoming and helpful, near bus terminal, laundry facilities, garden, camping, book in advance, excellent value.

$$-$ Camino de Luna, Los Carrera 861, T08-889 8962, hostalcaminodeluna@gmail. com. Nice rooms, some with bath. Bright patio. Owner from Valdivia keen to practise English.

$$-$ Hostal Family Home, Av Santo 1056, T221 2099, www.familyhome.cl. Private or shared bath, thin walls and slightly tatty, but it has a 24-hr reception and is close to the bus terminal so useful if you are arriving at night.

$$-$ Hostal Gladys, Gregorio Cordovez 247 (by the Plaza de Armas), T220 324. Shared bath, laundry service, helpful, Gladys works at tourist information in bus terminal (15 mins away).

$$-$ Hostal Serena Centro, Vicuña 431, T252 9581, www.hostalserenacentro.cl. New hostel with private rooms and dorms, family run, convenient location.

$$-$ Res Suiza, Cienfuegos 250, T221 6092, residencial.suiza@terra.cl. With breakfast, good beds, excellent value.

Elqui Valley *p696*
Vicuña
$$$ Hostería Vicuña, Sgto Aldea 101, T241 1301, www.hosteriavicuna.cl. In spacious grounds, pool, tennis court, poor restaurant, parking. Has seen better days.

$$ Halley, Gabriela Mistral 542, T241 2070, turismohalley@yahoo.es. Pleasantly old-fashioned hotel with high-ceilinged rooms, colonial-style courtyard, and a pleasant pool.

$$ Hosp Sundari, C Principal 3, San Isidro (15 mins walk from Vicuña), T241 2072. Delightful bungalows, with breakfast, spotless, bicycles, pool in lovely gardens, aloe and other herbal therapies.

$$ La Elquina, O' Higgins 65, T241 1317, anamorainostroza@terra.cl. Relaxed, quiet, lovely garden, private or shared bath.
$$ Rita Klamt, Condell 443, T241 9611, rita_klamt@yahoo.es. Impeccably kept B&B. Excellent breakfast, pleasant garden with pool, helpful, German and some English spoken.
$$ Sol del Valle, Gabriela Mistral 743, T241 1078, elquisoldelvalle@hotmail.com. Swimming pool, vineyard, restaurant.
$$ Valle Hermoso, Gabriela Mistral 706, T241 1206, nury_alvarez@hotmail.com. Comfortable, parking.
Camping Camping y Piscina Las Tinajas, east end of Chacabuco. Swimming pool, restaurant.

Pisco Elqui

Prices are much lower outside Jan and Feb; if you're heading for Argentina, there is basic, clean accommodation at Huanta (Guanta on many maps), 46 km from Vicuña. *Cabañas* include **$$$$-$$$ Los Misterios de Elqui**, A Prat, T051-245 1126, www.misteriosdeelqui.cl, and **$$$-$$ Los Dátiles**, A Prat s/n, T09-9279 3264, www.losdatileselqui.cl/cabanas.htm.
$$$ Elqui Domos, Sector los Nichos s/n, T09-7709 2879, www.elquidomos.cl. Accommodation in geodesic tent domes or observatory cabins with windows and roofs that open for a direct view of the night sky, English spoken.
$$$ El Tesoro del Elqui, T051-245 1069, www.tesoro-elqui.cl. *Cabañas* for up to 4, shared room for up to 4 with shared bath (**$**), café, pool, pleasant gardens, German and English spoken.
$$ Elqui, O'Higgins s/n by the plaza, T245 1130. Hot shower, central, good restaurant and bar.
$$ Hostal Triskel, Callejón Baquedano, T09-9419 8680, www.hostaltriskel.cl. Single, double, twin, dorm rooms, attractive, bike rental, activities and tours arranged, therapies.
$$ Refugio La Isla, Sector La Isla, T09-7476 9924, refugiolaisla@gmail.com. Idyllic retreat on a hillside overlooking the village. Simple, rustic, pool, meditation room. Access difficult without transport.
Camping $ Campsite behind Camping El Olivo (which is closed). Excellent facilities, cold water, lots of trees by river, helpful owner, laundry facilities, very nice.

⑦ Restaurants

Ovalle *p693*
$$ Club Social Arabe, Arauco 255. Spacious glass-domed premises, limited selection of Arab dishes.
$ Casino La Bomba, Aguirre 364. Run by fire brigade, good value *almuerzos*.
$ El Calamar, in the middle of the Feria Modelo. Good-value lunches. There are many more cheap eateries at the entrance to the market.
El Quijote, Arauco 294. Intimate bar, old-timers' haunt full of socialist posters and memorabilia.

La Serena *p694, map p695*
Most restaurants close off season on Sun; generally more expensive here than in Coquimbo. The best place for seafood is the Sector de Pescadores (**$$**) at Peñuelas, on the coast halfway between La Serena and Coquimbo. Take any bus to Coquimbo and get out at the junction with Los Pescadores; walk 300 m to the coast.
$$$-$$ Donde El Guatón, Brasil 750. *Parrillada*, also good seafood, one of the better places in the town centre.
$$$-$$ Porotos, Av del Mar 900-B, Sector El Faro, T051-210937. Wide variety of well-presented dishes (fish, meat and pasta), decent portions and attentive service.
$$ Costa Inca, Av del Mar 2500, T212802. Good value and a range of delicious Peruvian dishes.
$$ La Mía Pizza, Av del Mar 2100, T212232. Italian, good-value pizzas and also fish dishes, good wine list.
$ Daniela 2, F de Aguirre 335. Good-quality Chilean home cooking.
$ Govindas, Lautaro 841, T224289. Mon-Fri lunchtime. Cheap vegetarian food served in a Hari Krishna yoga centre.
Diavoletto, Prat 565 and O'Higgins 531. Fast food and ice cream, popular. Other cafés on Prat 500 block and Balmaceda 400 block.

Elqui Valley *p696*
Vicuña
$$ Club Social de Elqui, Gabriela Mistral 435. Attractive patio, good value *almuerzo*, real coffee.
$$ Halley, Gabriela Mistral 404. Good meat, with local specialities, goat (huge portion) and rabbit.
$ Michel, Gabriela Mistral 180. Popular, good-value *almuerzo*.

$ Yo Y Soledad, Gabriela Mistral 364. Inexpensive, hearty Chilean food, good value.

🍸 Bars and clubs

La Serena *p694, map p695*
Most clubs are on Av del Mar and in Peñuelas, but in town you could try the following:
El Callejón, O'Higgins 635. Lounge bar and patio, with a relaxed atmosphere, young crowd. Fills up with students at weekends.
El Nuevo Peregrino, Peni y Andrés Bello. Intimate bar with live music at weekends.

🎉 Festivals

Coquimbo *p694*
Coquimbo hosts **La Pampilla**, by far the biggest independence day celebrations in Chile. Between 200-300,000 people come from all over the country for the fiesta, which lasts for a week from **14-21 Sep**. It costs a nominal US$1.50 to enter the main dancing area (*peñas* cost extra); plenty of typical Chilean food and drink.

🎯 What to do

La Serena *p694, map p695*
Responsible operators will not run tours to Mamalluca or Las Damas in bad weather.
Chile Safari, Matta 367, T09-8769 7686, www.chilesafari.com. Biking, surfing.
Delfines, Matta 655, T222 3624, www.turismo delfines.com. Traditional and adventure tours, bike rental, birdwatching and full tourist service.
Elqui Total, Parcela 17, El Arrayan at Km 27 along the road from La Serena to Vicuña, T09-9219 7872, www.elquitotal.cl. Mountain biking, bird-watching, photography, trekking, astronomy tours, also equine tourism, www.mundocaballo.cl.
Elqui Valley Tours, Los Carrera 515, T221 4846, www.elquivalleytour.cl. Good for local tours, enthusiastic guides.
Jeep Tour La Serena, T9454 6000, www.jeep tour-laserena.cl. Private and small group tours (max 6 people) of the area led by Swiss guide Daniel Russ. Apart from the usual tours he also offers trips to the Paso Agua Negra and also a transfer service to San Juan in Argentina (summer only).

Talinay Adventure Expeditions, Prat 470, in the courtyard, T221 8658, www.talinaychile.com. Offers local tours, also trekking and climbing.

🚌 Transport

Ovalle and around *p693*
Bus Most of the many rural buses leave from either of 2 terminals outside the Feria Modelo. The main bus terminal is the Terminal Media Luna (by the rodeo ring on Ariztía Oriente) just south of the city centre. Buses to **Santiago**, several, 6½ hrs, US$17-30; to **Valparaíso**, 6 hrs, US$17; to **Antofagasta**, 14 hrs, US$28; to **La Serena**, 1½ hrs, US$3.50. To **Hurtado**, Buses M&R, T269 1866, T09-9822 0320, has buses on Mon, Wed, Fri at 1200, 1230 and 1500, Sat 1400, Tue and Thu at 1615 and 1645, and Sun 1700 and 1730, US$3.

Taxi
Abel Olivares Rivera, T262 0352. The round trip to **Parque Nacional Fray Jorge** costs US$75.

Andacollo
Colectivo from Ovalle, US$4; **bus**, US$3.

Coquimbo *p694*
Bus Terminal at Varela y Garriga. To **La Serena**, US$1.

La Serena *p694, map p695*
Air Aeropuerto La Florida, 5 km east of the city, T227 1812. To **Santiago** and **Copiapó**, with LAN.
Bus City buses US$0.75. Bus terminal, El Santo y Amunátegui (about 8 blocks south of the centre). **Tur-Bus** office, Balmaceda entre Prat y Cordovez, T221 7126. Buses daily to **Santiago**, a few companies, 7-8 hrs, US$18-33; to **Valparaíso**, 7 hrs. To **Caldera**, 6 hrs, US$14. To **Calama**, US$30-65, 16 hrs. To **Antofagasta**, 12-13 hrs, several companies, US$28-43, and to **Iquique**, 17 hrs, US$35-69, and **Arica**, 20 hrs, US$43-55. To **Vicuña** and **Pisco Elqui**, see below. To **Coquimbo**, bus No 8 from Av Aguirre y Cienfuegos, US$1, every few mins.
Car hire Daire, Balmaceda 3812, T222 6933, good service; **Flota Verschae**, Av Balmaceda 3856, T224 1685, good value; **La Florida** at airport, T227 1947.
Taxi US$0.75 + US$0.25 per every 200 m. Colectivos with fixed rates, destination on roof; also to Coquimbo from Aguirre y Balmaceda.

Elqui Valley: Vicuña *p696*

Bus To **La Serena**, about 10 a day (more in summer), most by Vía Elqui/Megal Bus, first 0800, last 1930, 1 hr, US$3, colectivo from bus terminal US$4. To **Pisco Elqui**, 10 a day with Vía Elqui, 1 hr, US$3.25. Buses from Pisco Elqui to La Serena go via Vicuña, US$3.25.

❶ Directory

La Serena *p694, map p695*
Banks ATMs at most banks and in the bus terminal. Several *casas de cambio*. If heading north note that La Serena is the last place to change TCs before Antofagasta.

North of La Serena

North of the Río Elqui, the transitional zone continues to the mining and agro-industrial centre of Copiapó. Thereafter begins the desert, which is of little interest, except after rain. Then it is covered with a succession of flowers, insects and frogs, in one of the world's most spectacular wildlife events. Rain, however, is rare: there is none in summer; in winter it is light and lasts only a short time. Annual precipitation al Copiapó Is about 115 mm. Drivers must beware of high winds and blowing sand north of Copiapó.

The Huasco valley is an oasis of olive groves and vineyards. It is rugged and spectacular, dividing at Alto del Carmen, 30 km east of Vallenar, into the Carmen and Tránsito valleys. There are pisco distilleries at Alto del Carmen and San Félix. A sweet wine, Pajarete, is also produced.

Reserva Nacional Pingüino de Humboldt

Some 72 km north of La Serena, a road branches west off the Panamericana to **Punta de Choros**. This is the departure point for the Humboldt Penguin Natural Reserve, on Islas Chañaral, Choros and Damas. Besides penguins, there arc seals, sea lions, a great variety of seabirds and, offshore, a colony of grey dolphin. Isla Damas has interesting flora, too. To visit the reserve, tours are available from La Serena and Vallenar or you can hire a boat with local fishermen (around US$80 for up to 10 people). Isla Damas is the only island at which it is possible to disembark (entrance US$4) and camping is allowed, but you must first seek permission from **CONAF** in Punta de Choros, T09-544 3052; toilet but no drinking water.

Vallenar → *Phone code: 051. Colour map 8, A1. Population: 47,000. Altitude: 380 m.*

This is the chief town of the Huasco valley, 194 km north of La Serena. It has a pleasant Plaza de Armas, with marble benches. About seven blocks southeast is the **Museo del Huasco** ① *Sgto Aldea 742, Tue-Fri 1500-1800, US$1*. It contains historic photos and artefacts from the valley. At the mouth of the river, 56 km west, is the pleasant port of Huasco (cheap seafood restaurants near the harbour). There is a tourist kiosk on the plaza in summer.

Copiapó → *Phone code: 052. Colour map 6, C2. Population: 127,000. Altitude: 400 m.*

The valley of the Río Copiapó, generally regarded as the southern limit of the Atacama desert, is an oasis of farms, vineyards and orchards about 150 km long. Copiapó is an important mining centre. Founded in 1744, Copiapó became a prosperous town after the discovery in 1832 of the third largest silver deposits in South America at Chañarcillo (the mine was closed in 1875). The discoverer, Juan Godoy, a mule-driver, is commemorated at Matta y O'Higgins. Opposite is the **Museo Regional del Atacama** ① *Mon 1400-1745, Tue-Fri 0900-1745, Sat 1000-1245, 1500-1745, Sun 1000-1245, US$1 (free Sun)*, with collections on local history, especially the Huentelauquén people, thought to have flourished 10,000 years ago, and the 19th century. **Museo Mineralógico** ① *Colipí y Rodríguez, 1 block east from Plaza Prat, Mon-Fri 1000-1300, 1530-1900, Sat 1000-1300, US$1*. This is the best museum of its type in Chile, with a collection of weird and wonderful minerals and fossils from Chile and around the world. Many ores shown are found only in the Atacama desert. The Museo Ferroviario at the old railway station on Calle Martínez opens irregularly, but the Norris Brothers steam locomotive and carriages used in the inaugural journey between Copiapó and Caldera in 1851 (the first railway in South America) can be seen at the Universidad de Atacama about 2 km north of the centre on Avenida R Freire. Helpful **tourist office** ⓘ *Los Carrera 691, north side of Plaza Prat, T221 2838, infoatacama@sernatur.cl, Mon-Fri 0830-1930, Sat 1030-1430, 1630-1930, Sun 1030-1430; out of season Mon-Fri 0830-1730 only.*

Border with Argentina: Paso San Francisco

Paso San Francisco is reached either by the Camino Internacional northeast from Copiapó, or by an unpaved road southeast from El Salvador: both routes join near the Salar de Maricunga in the **Parque Nacional Tres Cruces**, 96 km west of Paso San Francisco. The road then passes Laguna Verde before entering Argentina, where a paved road continues to Tinogasta. The border post is at Fiambalá, 210 km beyond the border, open 0700-1900, but there is also a police post at La Gruta, 24 km beyond the border. Chilean immigration and customs are near the Salar de Maricunga, 100 km west of the border, open 0900-1900 (24 hours in summer); US$2 per vehicle charge for crossing Saturday, Sunday and holidays. This crossing is liable to closure after snow: T052-2198 1009 for road reports. Always take spare fuel.

North to Antofagasta

From Copiapó the road heads northwest 73 km to the coast at **Caldera**, a port and terminal for the loading of iron ore. **Iglesia de San Vicente de Paul** (1862) on the Plaza de Armas was built by English carpenters working for the railway company. **Bahía Inglesa**, 6 km south of Caldera, named after the visit in 1687 of the English 'corsario', Edward Davis, is popular for its beautiful white sandy beaches and unpolluted sea. Staying in Caldera is cheaper in summer than in Bahía Inglesa, where there are lots of *cabañas* by the beach. A frequent bus service runs between the two in January-February, while colectivos run all year (US$1.50).

Just over 90 km north of Caldera, at the mouth of the Río Salado, is **Chañaral**, a town with old wooden houses perched on the hillside and a base for visits to beaches and the Parque Nacional Pan de Azúcar. There are several *residenciales* and *hostales* in town, some offering tours of the area. The valley of the Río Salado, 130 km in length, less fertile or prosperous than the Copiapó or Huasco valleys, is the last oasis south of Antofagasta. From here to Antofogasta is 420 km and the only town along the way is **Taltal**, where there are simple hotels and restaurants.

Parque Nacional Pan de Azúcar

ⓘ *US$6.25 (US$4 for Chileans). CONAF office in Caleta Pan de Azúcar, 0830-1230, 1400-1800 daily, maps available. There are heavy fines for driving in 'restricted areas' of the park.*

The park, north of Chañaral, consists of the Isla Pan de Azúcar on which Humboldt penguins and other seabirds live, and some 43,769 ha of coastal hills rising to 800 m. There are fine beaches (popular at weekends in summer). Fishermen near the CONAF office offer boat trips round Isla Pan de Azúcar to see the penguins, US$8.50 per person (minimum total US$85). Alternatively, a 2½-hour walk goes from the office to a mirador with extensive views over the south of the park. Vegetation is mainly cacti, of which there are 26 species, nourished by frequent sea mists (*camanchaca*). The park is home to 103 species of birds as well as guanaco and foxes. Pollution from nearby copper mining is a threat. There are two entrances: north by good secondary road from Chañaral, 28 km to Caleta Pan de Azúcar; from the Pan-American Highway 45 km north of Chañaral, along a side road 20 km.

For hotel and restaurant price codes, and other relevant information, see Essentials.

⊜ Where to stay

Reserva Nacional Pingüino de Humboldt: Punta de Choros *p701*
$$ Cabañas Los Delfines, Pilpilen s/n, sitio 33, T09-9639 6678. Cabins for up to 6. There are other sleeping and eating options in the area.

Vallenar *p701*
$$$ Puerto de Vega, Ramírez 201, T261 8534, www.puertodevega.cl. Probably the best in town, 12 individually decorated rooms, pleasant patio and pool.
$$ Hostal Camino del Rey, Merced 943, T261 3184. Good value, private or shared bath.
$ Viña del Mar, Serrano 611, T261 1478. Nice rooms, clean *comedor*, a good choice.

Copiapó *p701*
$$$ Chagall, O'Higgins 760, T235 2900, www.chagall.cl. Executive hotel, central, some rooms with king-size beds and desk, modern fittings, spacious lounge and bar open to public.
$$ La Casona, O'Higgins 150, T221 7278, www.lacasonahotel.cl. More like a home than a hostel, desert colours, good beds, pleasant garden, restaurant, bar, English spoken.
$$ Montecatini, Infante 766, T221 1363, and at Atacama 374, T221 1516, www.montecatini.cl. Helpful, best value in this price bracket. Rooms sleep 1-4, simple but OK for a night or 2 when passing through.
$$ Palace, Atacama 741, T221 2852. Comfortable, parking, central, nice patio. Good value.
$ Res Benbow, Rodríguez 541, T221 7634. Basic rooms, some with bath, but the best value of the many *residenciales* on this part of Rodríguez. Usually full of mine workers. Excellent value full-board deals.
$ Res Eli, Maipú 739, T221 9650. Singles cheaper. Simple rooms, good beds, decent choice.
$ Res Rocío, Yerbas Buenas 581, T221 5360. Singles cheaper. Some rooms with bath and cable TV, patio. Good budget option.

Parque Nacional Pan de Azúcar *p702*
$$$-$$ There are a dozen or so *cabañas* in the park run by **Gran Atacama** in Copiapó (Mall Plaza Real, T221 9271, www.gran atacama.cl). Reservations and advance payment are essential in high season. Perfectly placed on a deserted beach behind the *caleta*, sleep 2 or 6. Some fishermen in the *caleta* let out rooms; quite basic.
Camping Three campsites in the park, one in the Caleta, run by the fishermen, and Camping El Piquero and El Soldado run by Gran Atacama in Copiapó (see above).

⊘ Restaurants

Vallenar *p701*
Cheap eating places along south end of Av Brasil.
$$ Bavaria, Serrano 802. Chain restaurant, good.
$$ Pizza Il Boccato, Plaza O'Higgins y Prat. Good coffee, good food, popular.
$ La Pica, Brasil y Faez. Good cheap meals, seafood, cocktails.

Copiapó *p701*
$$ Bavaria, Chacabuco 487 (Plaza Prat) and on Los Carrera. Good variety, restaurant and café.
$$ Chifa Hao Hwa, Colipí 340 and Yerbas Buenas 334. Good Chinese, one of several in town.
$$ Entre Yuntas, Vallejos 226. Rustic but cosy, Peruvian/Chilean food, live music Fri and Sat.
$$-$ La Vitrola, Cosmocentro Plaza Real, p 2. Self-service lunch buffet, good range, reasonably priced, good views.
$ Benbow, Rodríguez 543. Good value *almuerzo*, extensive menu.
$ Don Elias, Los Carrera e Yerbas Buenas. Excellent seafood, popular.

⊛ Festivals

Copiapó *p701*
1st Sun in Feb Fiesta de la Candelaria, for 9 days. Up to 50,000 pilgrims and 3000 dancers congregate at the Santuario de la Candelaria from all over the north of Chile.

● What to do

Vallenar *p701*
If it rains (Sep-Oct), a tour of the desert in flower can be done with Roberto Alegría, T261 3865. Otherwise ask at the tourist kiosk in Vallenar (if it's open).

Parque Nacional Pan de Azúcar *p702*
Subsole D'Atacama, Merino Jarpa s/n, Chañaral, T09-9972 0077. Sergio and Marcela Molina lead very interesting day tours of the Parque Nacional Pan de Azúcar.

● Transport

Vallenar *p701*
Bus Each company has its own terminal: Tur-Bus, Merced 561; Pullman, opposite (the most frequent buses going north); Tas Choapa, at Vallenar's main terminal. To **La Serena**, 2 hrs, US$6. To **Copiapó**, 2 hrs, US$6. To **Santiago**, 10 hrs, US$29-49.

Copiapó *p701*
Air Desierto de Atacama Airport is 45 km northwest of Copiapó and 15 km east of Caldera. LAN, Colipí 484, T221 3512, airport T221 4360, and Sky, Colipí 526, T221 4640.

Bus Long-distance terminal 2 blocks from centre on Chañarcillo y Chacabuco. TurBus terminal is opposite and **Pullman** is 1 block away on Colipí. To **Santiago** US$34.50-56, 12 hrs. To **La Serena** US$11, 5 hrs. To **Antofagasta**, 7 hrs, US$18-$48. To **Caldera**, US$2, 1 hr, cheapest services on Buses Recabarren and Casther from the street 1 block west of the main bus terminal.

Caldera *p702*
Bus Buses on the Panamericana do not go into Caldera, but stop at Cruce Caldera, outside town (Restaurante Hospedaje Mastique, Km 843, is a good place to eat and stay, **$**). Buses to **Copiapó** and **Santiago**, US$26-58, several daily. To **Antofagasta**, US$17, 7 hrs. To travel north, it may be better to take a bus to **Chañaral** (Inca-bus US$3), then change.

Parque Nacional Pan de Azúcar *p702*
A **taxi** costs US$25 from Chañaral, or hitch a lift from fishermen at sunrise.

● Directory

Copiapó *p701*
Banks Redbanc ATMs at central banks and in Plaza Real shopping mall, including **Cambio Fides**, office B123. **Bicycle repairs** Biman, Los Carrera 998A, T221 7391, excellent.

Far north

Antofagasta, capital of the Second Region, is a major port for the export of copper from La Escondida and Chuquicamata. It is also a major commercial centre and home of two universities. The coast north of Antofagasta is much more picturesque than the aridity surrounding much of the Panamerican Highway. Two possible stops are the fishing port of Mejillones and Tocopilla, beneath towering cliffs. Despite this being the driest region, the climate is delightful. Temperature varies from 16°C in June and July to 24°C in January and February, never falling below 10°C at night.

From the mining service centre of Calama, the route heads up to the altiplano with its saltflats and lunar landscapes. In an oasis on the Río San Pedro is the historic town of San Pedro de Atacama. This has become a popular destination for visitors seeking high altitudes, clear skies, steaming geysers and volcanic horizons. It is also, increasingly, a staging post on the route between Bolivia's Salar de Uyuni and the Pacific Ocean. The Atacama Desert extends over most of the far north to the Peruvian border. The main cities are Iquique and Arica; between them are old mineral workings and geoglyphs. Large areas of the Andean highland have been set aside as national parks; the most visited is Lauca with its volcanoes and lakes.

Antofagasta and around → *Phone code: 055. Colour map 6, C2. Population: 225,316.*

The largest city in Northern Chile, Antofagasta, 1367 km north of Santiago, is not especially attractive in itself, but its setting beside the ocean and in view of tall mountains is dramatic. The **tourist office** ① *Prat 384, p 1, T245 1818, infoantofagasta@sernatur.cl, Mon-Fri 0930-1730, Sat 1000-1400, summer Mon-Fri 0830-1930*, is very helpful. There is also information at the Casa de Cultura, Latorre 2535, and a kiosk at airport (open in the summer only).

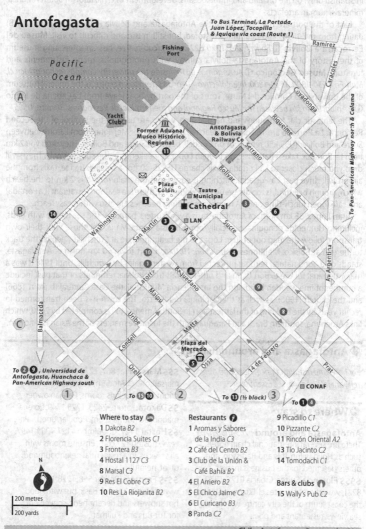

Antofagasta

To Bus Terminal, La Portada,
Juan López, Tocopilla
& Iquique via coast (Route 1)

Pacific Ocean

Fishing Port

Yacht Club

Former Aduana/
Museo Histórico
Regional

Antofagasta
& Bolivia
Railway Co

Plaza Colón

Teatro Municipal

Cathedral

LAN

Plaza del Mercado

CONAF

To ②⑨, Universidad de
Antofagasta, Huanchaca &
Pan-American Highway south

To ⑮⑩

To ⑬ (½ block)

To ①④

To Pan-American Highway north & Calama

Streets: Ramirez, Caracoles, Covadonga, Riquelme, Serrano, Bolívar, Sucre, Av Argentina, Prat, 14 de Febrero, Ossa, Matta, Orella, Uribe, Condell, Balmaceda, Washington, San Martín, Latorre, Maipú, Benjuedano, A Prat

200 metres
200 yards

N

Where to stay
1 Dakota *B2*
2 Florencia Suites *C1*
3 Frontera *B3*
4 Hostal 1127 *C3*
8 Marsal *C3*
9 Res El Cobre *C3*
10 Res La Riojanita *B2*

Restaurants
1 Aromas y Sabores
  de la India *C3*
2 Café del Centro *B2*
3 Club de la Unión &
  Café Bahía *B2*
4 El Arriero *B2*
5 El Chico Jaime *C2*
6 El Curicano *B3*
8 Panda *C2*

9 Picadillo *C1*
10 Pizzante *C2*
11 Rincón Oriental *A2*
13 Tío Jacinto *C2*
14 Tomodachi *C1*

Bars & clubs
15 Wally's Pub *C2*

In the main square, **Plaza Colón**, is a clock tower donated by the British community in 1910 to commemorate 100 years of Chilean independence. It is a replica of Big Ben in London. Calle A Prat, which runs southeast from Plaza Colón, is the main shopping street. Two blocks north of Plaza Colón, at the old port, is the former Aduana, built as the Bolivian customs house in Mejillones and moved to its current site after the War of the Pacific. It houses the **Museo Histórico Regional** ① *Balmaceda 2786, www.museodeantofagasta.cl, Tue-Fri 0900-1700, Sat, Sun, holidays 1100-1400, US$1, children half price*, which has fascinating visual displays (explanations in Spanish only) on life on land and in the oceans, development of civilization in South America, minerals, human artefacts.

East of the port are the buildings of the Antofagasta and Bolivia Railway Company (FCAB) dating from the 1890s and beautifully restored, but still in use and difficult to visit. **Museo del Ferrocarril a Bolivia** ① *Bolívar 280, T220 6221, www.fcab.cl, free*, has an interesting museum of the history of the Antofagasta-Bolivia railway, with photographs, maps, instruments and furniture. **Museo Geológico** ① *Av Angamos 0610, inside the university campus, gchong@ucn.cl, Mon-Fri, 0930-1300, 1530-1800, free, colectivo 114 or 333 from town centre*, is the mineral museum of the Universidad Católica del Norte. Tours of the port by boat leave from **La Cabaña de Mario** ① *C Aníbal Pinto s/n between the Museo Regional and the Terminal de Pescadores, 30 mins, US$5*.

The fantastic cliff formations and natural arch, which are used as the symbol of the Second Region, at **La Portada** are 16 km north, reached by minibus for Mejillones from Latorre, between Sucre and Bolívar (US$4.50 return), or on Condell, between Sucre and Bolívar. They drop you 2 km from La Portada. Take a hat. Buses go to Juan López at weekends in the summer only. These will drop you much closer to La Portada. Taxis charge US$25-30 (for a small extra fee, taxis from the airport will drive past La Portada). Hitching is easy. From the main road it is 2 km to the beach which, though beautiful, is too dangerous for swimming; there is a seafood restaurant (La Portada) and café (open lunch-time only). A number of bathing beaches are also within easy reach.

Juan López, 38 km north of Antofagasta, is a windsurfers' paradise. The sea is alive with birds, including Humboldt penguins, especially opposite Isla Santa María. For those with their own transport, follow the road out of Juan López to the beautiful cove at Conchilla. Keep on the track to the end at Bolsico. **Mejillones** (*Population: 10,100*), a port town 60 km north of Antofagasta, stands on a good natural harbour protected from westerly gales by high hills. Until 1948 it was a major terminal for the export of tin and other metals from Bolivia: remnants of that past include a number of fine wooden buildings: the Intendencia Municipal, the Casa Cultural (built in 1866) and the church (1906), as well as the Capitanía del Puerto. The town has been transformed in recent years by the building of the largest port in South America, to be completed by 2030, which links Argentina, southern Brazil and Paraguay with the lucrative markets of the Asian Pacific Rim.

⊚ Antofagasta and around listings

For hotel and restaurant price codes, and other relevant information, see Essentials.

⊜ Where to stay

Antofagasta and around *p705, map p705*
There are several international chain hotels, such as Holiday Inn, Ibis and Radisson, and others designed for the business market.
$$$$ Florencia Suites, Croacia 0126, T279 8221, www.florenciasuites.cl. Luxury suites on the coast south of the city centre with lovely sea views, restaurant and pool.

$$$ Marsal, Prat 867, T226 8063, www. marsalhotel.cl. Modern, very comfortable, bright and spacious rooms, Catalan owner.
$$ Dakota, Latorre 2425, T225 1749, floreria magnolia@hotmail.com. Popular, good value.
$$ Hostal 1127, Coquimbo 1127, T284 1497, www.hostal1127.com. Ensuite rooms with all services, in a residential neighbourhood, quiet, helpful.
$$-$ Frontera, Bolívar 558, T228 1219, www.fronterahotel.cl. Basic but with good hot showers and decent beds, convenient for Tur-Bus and Pullman.

\$\$-\$ Res El Cobre, Prat 749, T226 7726. Private or shared bath, set around a central courtyard, bright and clean, but tatty.

\$ Res La Riojanita, Baquedano 464, T09-83602796. Basic, very helpful, older rooms have high ceilings but are run-down, newer rooms with bath are smaller. Not a bad budget option.

Camping To the south on the road to Coloso are: **Las Garumas**, Km 6, T263 7395, **\$** per site (ask for lower price out of season), **\$\$** for cabins, cold showers and beach (reservations Av Angamos 601, Av Jaime Guzman s/n).

🍴 Restaurants

Antofagasta and around *p705, map p705*
Many bars and restaurants are closed on Sun.
\$\$\$ Club de la Unión, Prat 474, p 2, T2428 4600, www.clubdelaunion.cl. Open to non-members, traditional atmosphere, excellent *almuerzo* and service.
\$\$\$-\$\$ Picadillo, Av Grecia 1000, T224 7503. Lively atmosphere, serves a wide range of dishes. Good music.
\$\$\$-\$\$ Tomodachi, Balmaceda 2355, Local 21, Mall Plaza, T253 3300, www.tomodachi.cl. The best of the city's sushi restaurants.
\$\$ Aromas y Sabores de la India, Argentina 1294, T278 0280. Indian restaurant and take-away, the only one of its kind in northern Chile.
\$\$ El Arriero, Condell 2644, T226 4371. Grills and traditional hearty criollo food. Good service, cheap set lunch, popular, live music.
\$\$ Panda, Condell 2505, T225 4827. Self-service, Chinese and Chilean, eat all you can for set price.
\$\$ Pizzante, Carrera 1857, T222 3344, www.pizzante.cl. Good pasta, seafood and vegetarian options.
\$\$ Rincón Oriental, Washington 2743, T222 6869. Excellent Cantonese, 'over the top' décor.
\$\$ Tío Jacinto, Uribe 922, T222 8486. Friendly atmosphere, serves good seafood.
\$\$-\$ El Chico Jaime, Mercado Central 2nd floor, local 115, T222 7401. Best of the restaurants in the central market, good food and friendly service.
\$ El Curicano, Simón Bolívar 607. Good value, basic set menu lunches and dinners.
   Above the market are a few good places selling cheap seafood *almuerzos* and super-

cheap set lunches, including **El Mariscal** and **Toledo**. Good fish restaurants in Terminal Pesquero Centro and at Caleta Coloso, which is 18 km south.

Cafés
Café Bahía, Prat 470. Open at 0900 for real coffee.
Café del Centro, Galería, Prat 482. Real coffee.

🍸 Bars and clubs

Antofagasta and around *p705, map p705*
Thanks to Antofagasta's student population, the city's nightlife is buzzing. The most popular bars and clubs are 16 km south of the town in Balneario El Huáscar. Take micro 103 from C Matta to get there. There is also a wide choice on O'Higgins.
Moove, One of the most popular disco options at El Huáscar.
Wally's Pub, Toro 982. British expat-style with darts, pool and beer, closed Sun.

🎭 Entertainment

Antofagasta and around *p705, map p705*
Teatro Municipal, Sucre y San Martín, T259 1732, www.culturaantofagasta.cl. Modern, state-of-the art theatre.
Teatro Pedro de la Barra, Condell 2495. Theatre run by University of Antofagasta, regular programme of plays, reviews, concerts, etc, high standard, details in press.

🎉 Festivals

Antofagasta and around *p705, map p705*
29 Jun, San Pedro, the image of the patron saint of the fishermen is taken out by launch to the breakwater to bless the first catch of the day. On the last weekend of **Oct**, the city's immigrant communities put on a joint festival on the seafront, with national foods, dancing and music.

🛍 Shopping

Antofagasta and around *p705, map p705*
The **Mall Plaza Antofagasta**, Balmaceda y Maipú has a wide variety of shops and a

pleasant promenade on the roof, with colourful flowers and views out to the ocean.

Markets Feria Modelo O'Higgins (next to fish market on Av Pinto). Excellent fruit and veg, also restaurants. Municipal market at Matta y Uribe.

☺ What to do

Antofagasta and around *p705, map p705*
Many tour companies offer packages to the Atacama, but the office of tourism recommends booking tours in San Pedro de Atacama, as it is far cheaper. See www.surfantofagasta.cl for information on surfing in the area.
Buceo Magallanes, Balmaceda 2615, T9-9232 7932, www.buceomagallanes.cl. Regular diving trips and courses.

☺ Transport

Antofagasta and around *p705, map p705*
Air Cerro Moreno Airport, 22 km north. Taxi to airport US$27, but cheaper if ordered from hotel. For airport transfers, **Aerobus**, T226 2727, US$9-10. LAN, PAL and Sky fly daily to **Santiago**, **Copiapó**, **Iquique** and **Arica**. LAN also daily to **La Serena**.
Bus The bus terminal is at Aguirre Cerda 5750, on the northern edge of the city. Bus company phone numbers: **Flota Barrios**, T224 4626; **Géminis** and **Romani**, T256 1021; **Pullman**

Bus, T223 6836; **Tur-Bus**, T600-660 6600. To **Santiago**, many companies: 18 hrs, US$54-78; book in advance in high season. If all seats to the capital are booked, catch a bus to **La Serena** (12 hrs, US$26-42), or **Ovalle**, 14 hrs, and re-book. To **Valparaíso**, US$40-70. To **Copiapó**, 7 hrs, US$18-32. Frequent buses to **Iquique**, US$16-21, 6 hrs. To **Arica**, US$20-37, 11 hrs. To **Calama**, several companies, US$9, 3 hrs; to **San Pedro de Atacama**, Tur-Bus 6 daily, 5 hrs, US$8, or via Calama. Buses for **Mejillones**, 1 hr, US$2, from Corsal terminal, Condell y Sucre; also minibuses Latorre 2730. To **Tocopilla**, 2½ hrs, US$10, many daily.

Juan López
Bus 129 in in the city centre from Condell y Sucre, Antofagasta.

☺ Directory

Antofagasta and around *p705, map p705*
Banks It's difficult to change TCs south of Antofagasta until you reach La Serena. Several with ATMs around the plaza and the rest of the centre. *Casas de cambio* are mainly on Baquedano. **Car hire** First, Bolívar 623, T222 5777. Plus international agencies. **Andrés Ljubetic Romo**, Atacama 2657, T226 8851, is a recommended mechanic. **Consulates** **Argentina**, Blanco Encalada 1933, T222 0440. **Bolivia**, Washington 2675, p 13, T279 4369.

North of Antofagasta

To Iquique

Two routes go north towards Iquique: the Pan-American Highway and the coastal route. At Km 101 on the Pan-American, Carmen Alto (98 km north of Antofagasta, petrol, food), a paved road leads to Calama. To the west of the Highway are the remains of several nitrate towns. Some 107 km north of Carmen Alto is the crossroads to Tocopilla (72 km west) and Chuquicamata (east) and, 81 km beyond, **Quillagua**, officially the driest place in the world (customs post, all southbound vehicles and buses are searched). 111 km further is the first of three sections of the Reserva Nacional del Tamarugal. In this part are the **Geoglyphs of Cerro Pintados**, some 400 figures (humans, animals, geometric shapes) on the hillside (3 km west of the highway). The second part of Tamarugal is near La Tirana (see page 719), the third 60 km north of Pozo Almonte.

The coastal route is more picturesque than the Pan-American Highway. On this road, 187 km north of Antofagasta, is **Tocopilla** (*Phone code: 055; Colour map 6, B2; Population: 24,600*), a useful place to stop with a few *hostales* (**$$**). It has one of the most dramatic settings of any Chilean town, sheltering at the foot of 500-m-high mountains that loom inland. A thermal power station and the port facilities used to unload coal and to export nitrates and iodine from María Elena and Pedro de Valdivia dominate the town. There are some interesting early 20th-century buildings with wooden balustrades and façades, but it was heavily damaged by an earthquake on 14 November 2007 and it's generally a rundown, slightly menacing place. There are two good beaches: Punta Blanca (12 km south) and Caleta Covadonga, 3 km south with a pool.

The coast road from Tocopilla north to Iquique is paved, 244 km, with fantastic views of the rugged coastline and tiny fishing communities. The customs post at **Chipana-Río Loa** (90 km north) searches all southbound vehicles for duty-free goods; 30 minutes' delay. Basic accommodation is available at **San Marcos**, a fishing village, 131 km north. At **Chanaballita**, 184 km north there is a hotel, *cabañas*, camping, restaurant, shops. There are also campsites at **Guanillos**, Km 126, **Playa Peruana**, Km 129 and **Playa El Aguila**, Km 160.

Calama → *Phone code: 055. Colour map 6, B2. Population: 106,970. Altitude: 2265 m.*

Calama lies in the oasis of the Río Loa, 202 km north of Antofagasta. Initially a staging post on the silver route between Potosí and Cobija, it is now an expensive, unprepossessing modern city, serving the nearby mines of Chuquicamata and Radomiro Tomic. Calama can be reached from the south by the paved road from Carmen Alto (see above), or from the north by Route 24 via Chuquicamata. The road passes many abandoned nitrate mines, *oficinas*. **Tourist office** ① *Latorre 1689, T253 1707, www.calamacultural.cl, Mon-Fri 0800-1300, 1400-1800*. Map, tours, helpful staff, English spoken.

Two kilometres from the centre on Avenida B O'Higgins is the **Parque El Loa** ① *daily 1000-1800*, which contains a reconstruction of a typical colonial village built around a reduced-scale reproduction of Chiu Chiu church. The **Museo de Historia Natural** ① *Wed-Sun 1000-1300, 1500-1830, US$1*, with an interesting collection on the *oficinas* and on the region's ecology and palaeontology.

Chuquicamata → *Phone code: 055. Colour map 6, B2. Altitude: 2800 m.*

North of Calama 16 km is the site of the world's largest open-cast copper mine, employing 8000 workers and operated by Codelco (the state copper corporation). The visual spectacle of the site makes for a memorable visit. Everything about Chuquicamata is huge: the pit from which the ore is extracted is 4 km long, 2 km wide and 730 m deep; the giant trucks, with wheels over 3.5 m high, carry 310 ton loads and work 24 hours a day; in other parts of the plant 60,000 tons of ore are processed a day. Guided tours, by bus, in Spanish (although guides usually speak reasonable English) leave from the **Codelco office** ① *Av Central Sur y Av Granaderos, Villa Ayquina, Calama, T232 2122, visitas@codelco.cl, Mon-Fri 1 in 300, make reservation in advance; either call the office in Calama or ask at the tourist office; passport number essential*. Wear covered shoes, long trousers and long sleeves; filming is permitted in certain areas. Tours may be cancelled without notice if there are high winds.

From Calama it is 273 km north to Ollagüe, on the Bolivian border. (There is no petrol between Calama and Uyuni in Bolivia. If really short try buying from the *carabineros* at Ollagüe or Ascotán, the military at Conchi or the mining camp at Buenaventura, 5 km from Ollagüe.) The road follows the Río Loa, passing Chiu Chiu (33 km), one of the earliest Spanish settlements in the area. Just beyond this oasis, a small turning branches off the main road to the hamlet of **Lasana**, 8 km north of Chiu Chiu. Petroglyphs are clearly visible on the right-hand side of the road. There are striking ruins of a pre-Inca *pukará*, a National Monument; drinks are on sale. If arranged in advance, Línea 80 colectivos will continue to Lasana for an extra charge. Pre-book the return trip, or walk back to Chiu Chiu. At **Conchi**, 25 km north of Lasana, the road crosses the Río Loa via a bridge dating from 1890 (it's a military zone, so no photographs of the view are allowed). Beyond Chiu Chiu the road deteriorates, with deep potholes, but, north of Ascotán (*carabinero* checkpoint at 3900 m), it improves as it crosses the Salares de Ascotán and de Carcote and Ollagüe (ask about the conditions on the Salares at Ascotán or Ollagüe before setting out, especially in December/January or August). There are many llama flocks along this road and flamingos on the *salares*.

Ollagüe → *Colour map 6, B2. Altitude: 3690 m.*

This village, on the dry floor of the Salar de Ollagüe, is surrounded by a dozen volcanic peaks of over 5000 m. The **border with Bolivia** is open 0800-2000; US$3 per person charge for entry to Bolivia. There is a municipal hostel and food and drink is available in town. At this altitude the days are warm and sunny, nights cold (minimum -20° C). There are only 50 mm of rain a year, and water is very scarce.

Between Chiu Chiu and El Tatio (see below), **Caspana** (*Population: 400; Altitude: 3305 m*) is beautifully set among hills with a tiny church dating from 1641 and a **museum** ① *Tue-Sun 0900-1400, 1500-1800*, with interesting displays on Atacameño culture. Basic accommodation is available (the nearest to El Tatio). A poor road runs north and east through valleys of pampas grass with llama herds to **Toconce**, which has extensive prehispanic terraces set among interesting rock formations. There are archaeological sites nearby and the area is ideal for hiking. Further information from the tourist office in Calama, who may also help with arranging transport.

⊙ North of Antafagasta listings

For hotel and restaurant price codes, and other relevant information, see Essentials.

● Where to stay

To Iquique: Tocopilla *p708*
$$ Hostal Puerto Caliche, J Montt Salamanca 1040, T281 6286,www.hostalpuertocaliche. co.cl. Several sizes of rooms, comedor, games room and mini gym, parking.

Calama *p709*
$$$$-$$$ Park, Alcalde José Lira 1392, T271 5800, www.parkcalama.cl. On the edge of town by the airport. First class, pool, bar and restaurant, excursions to the salar.
$$$$-$$$ Sonesta, Av Balmaceda 2634, T268 1100, www.sonesta.com. Business hotel at Plaza Sol del Loa, with fitness centre, restaurant, bar, Wi-Fi throughout.
$$$ Hostería Calama, Latorre 1521, T234 1511, www.hosteriacalama.cl. Comfortable heated rooms, good service; gym and small pool. Airport transfer.
$$$ L&S, Vicuña MacKenna 1819, T236 1113, www.lyshotel.cl. Business hotel, upstairs rooms more spacious. Often full Mon-Wed with mining engineers. A good choice.
$$ Hotel Jatata, Sotomayor 1822, T236 1640, jatataexpress.hoteles@gmail.com. Decent rooms with bath, most face onto a corridor, but those with windows onto the street are much better and good value.

$$ Res Alecris, Félix Hoyos 2153, T234 7984. Single, double and triple rooms, private or shared bath, well maintained, very clean, family atmosphere, often fully booked with miners, safe (CCTV, near police station), no breakfast, sunny courtyard. Chatty owner Alejandro.
$$-$ Cavour, Sotomayor 1841, T231 4718. Hot water, TV, no breakfast, rooms off an open-air corridor, simple, hospitable but a bit run-down.
$$-$ Hostal El Arriero, Ramírez 2262, T231 5556, www.hostalelarriero.cl. Family run, spacious doubles and triples (with thin walls) situated around a narrow courtyard, shared bath, Wi-Fi functional most of the time, good value.

❶ Restaurants

Calama *p709*
On pedestrian part of C Eleuterio Ramírez, several cafés, juice bars, *heladerías* and fast food places.
$$ Bavaria, Sotomayor 2095. Good restaurant with cafetería downstairs, real coffee, breakfast 0830-1130 Mon-Fri, very popular, not quiet, also cheaper café at Latorre 1935, upstairs.
$$ Mariscal JP, Félix Hoyos 2127, T231 2559. Closed Mon. Best seafood in town, worth that bit extra (has another branch in the Mercado Central at Latorre 1974).
$$ Mexicano, Vivar 2037. Genuine Mexican cuisine, live music at weekends.

$$-$ Club Croata, Abaroa 1869 at Plaza 23 de Marzo. Excellent value 4-course *almuerzo*, good service.
$ Don Elias, Antofagasta 2029, opposite the Frontera bus station (no sign). Open 1200 for lunch. Cheap, hearty, no-frills Chilean home-cooking. Packed at lunchtime.

Shopping

Calama *p709*
Craft stalls On Latorre 1600 block.
Market Feria El Loa on Antofagasta between Latorre and Vivar, selling fruit juices and crafts.

What to do

Calama *p709*
Several agencies run 1 day and longer tours to the Atacama region, including San Pedro; these are usually more expensive than tours from San Pedro and require a minimum number for the tour to go ahead. Be wary of agencies with poorly maintained vehicles and poor guides; standards here not generally very high. Operators with positive recommendations include: Sol del Desierto, Caur 3486, Villa Lomas Huasi, T233 0428, www.soldeldesierto.cl. A variety of day tours around Chiu Chiu and San Pedro. Also operators listed under San Pedro de Atacama, below.

Transport

To Iquique: Tocopilla *p708*
Bus Bus companies' offices are on 21 de Mayo. Buses to **Antofagasta** many daily, US$10, 2½ hrs. To **Iquique**, along coastal road, 3 hrs, US$11, frequent. To **Calama**, Tur-Bus 3 a day, 3 hrs, US$11.

Calama *p709*
Air Airport is modern and efficient with Redbanc ATM, restaurant upstairs, shop with internet. LAN, daily, to **Santiago**, via **Antofagasta**; also Sky. LAN also flies to **Iquique** and **Arica** twice a week. Transfer services from the airport are offered by **Transfer City Express**, T234 1022, US$11.

Bus Long distance Main terminal, Granaderos 3048, T231 3722, many companies: Tur-Bus, Pullman, Flota Barrios, Géminis, Kenny Bus. To **Santiago** 23 hrs, US$62-120. To **La Serena**, usually with delay in Antofagasta, 16 hrs, US$35-55. To **Antofagasta**, 3 hrs, several companies, US$9. To **Iquique**, 6 hrs, via Tocopilla, US$22, 3 daily with Tur-Bus. To **Arica**, usually overnight, US$25, 9 hrs, or change in Antofagasta. To **Chuquicamata** (see above). To **San Pedro de Atacama**, Tur-Bus several daily, 1½ hrs, US$5.50, Frontera, 6 a day. To Toconao, see below. To **Ollagüe** for **Bolivia**: Intertrans (every day) and **Atacama** (Thu, Mon 2000), US$15, 3 hrs. For **Uyuni**, cross the border, then board bus to Uyuni (Sun, Mon, Wed, Thu). To **Salta**, Argentina, 12 hrs, **Géminis**, Pullman Bus and Andesmar, each 3 a week, US$45-65 (check in advance as days change).
Local Public transport runs on a colectivo system, black cabs with a number on the roof. Just ask which number goes where you want to and flag it down. US$0.75 by day, US$0.85 after 2400.
Car hire A hired car shared between several people is an economic alternative for visiting the Atacama region. A 4WD jeep (necessary for the desert) costs US$100 a day, a car US$40-50. Hire companies include Alamo, T255 6802 (good), Avis, T256 3151, Budget, T236 1072, and Hertz T234 0010. All offices close Sat 1300 till Mon morning. Airport offices only open when flights arrive. If intending to drive in the border area, visit the police in San Pedro to get maps of which areas may have landmines.
Taxi Basic fare US$5.

Directory

Calama *p709*
Banks Exchange rates are generally poor especially for TCs. There are many Redbanc ATMs on Latorre and on Sotomayor. There are several *cambios* for US$, TCs, Argentine pesos and bolivianos.
Consulates Bolivia, León Gallo 1985A, T234 1976, open (in theory anyway) Mon-Fri 0900-1230, helpful.

San Pedro de Atacama → *Phone code: 055. Colour map 6, B2. Population: 2824.*

San Pedro de Atacama (*Altitude: 2436 m*), 103 km southeast of Calama (paved, no fuel, food or water along the way) is a small town, more Spanish/Indian-looking than is usual in Chile. Long before the arrival of the Spanish, the area was the centre of the Atacameño culture. There is a definite sense of history in the shady streets and the crumbling ancient walls, which drift away from the town into the fields, and then into the dust. Owing to the clear atmosphere and isolation, there are wonderful views of the night sky. Lunar landscapes, blistering geysers and salt flats are all close by. Now famous among visitors as the centre for excursions in this part of the Atacama, San Pedro can be overrun with visitors in summer. The **tourist office** ① *Toconao y Gustavo Le Paige, T285 1420, sanpedrodeatacama@gmail.com, Mon-Sun 0900-2100*, is on the plaza. Helpful, has a useful suggestions book, with feedback from other visitors about agencies' tours. See also www.sanpedrochile.com, www.sanpedroatacama.com and www.sanpedro deatacama.net. **Note** The main tourist season October-end February is accompanied by high prices and pressure on resources. ATMs come and go and are out of commission as often as they are working. If coming from inside Chile stock up on pesos before arriving. Dollars, Argentine pesos and bolivianos can be exchanged at bad rates and most companies accept credit cards, but with high charges.

The **Iglesia de San Pedro**, dating from the 17th century, is supposedly the second oldest church in the country. It has been heavily restored (the tower was added in 1964). The roof is made of cactus. Nearby, on the Plaza, is the **Casa Incaica**, the oldest building in San Pedro.

San Pedro de Atacama

Where to stay
1 Altiplánico
2 Awasi
3 Don Raul
4 Elim
6 Hostal Mamatierra
8 Hostal Miskanty
10 Hostal Sonchek
11 Hostelling International

12 Hostería San Pedro
13 Kimal
14 La Casa de Don Tomás
15 Res Chiloé
16 Res Vilacoyo
17 Takha-Takha

Restaurants
1 Adobe & Casa Piedra

2 Bendito Desierto
3 Café Etnico
4 Café Tierra Todo Natural
5 Café y Cia
6 Estrella Negra
7 La Casona
8 La Estaka
9 Milagro

Museo Arqueológico ⓘ *check www.sanpedroatacama.com for updates, Mon-Fri 0900-1200, 1400-1800 (Sat-Sun opens at 1000), US$3.50, children half price.* The collection of Padre Gustave Paige, a Belgian missionary who lived in San Pedro between 1955 and 1980, is now under the care of the Universidad Católica del Norte. It is a fascinating repository of artefacts, well organized to trace the development of prehispanic Atacameño society. Labels on displays (in Spanish and English) are good, and there is a comprehensive booklet in Spanish and English.

Around San Pedro de Atacama

The **Valle de la Luna** ⓘ *US$4.50*, with fantastic landscapes caused by the erosion of salt mountains, is a nature reserve 12 km west of San Pedro. It is crossed by the old San Pedro-Calama road. Although buses on the new Calama-San Pedro road will stop to let you off where the old road branches off 13 km northwest of San Pedro (signposted to Peine), it is far better to travel from San Pedro on the old road, either by bicycle (but difficult after sunset) or by car (a 20-km round trip is possible). The Valle is best seen at sunset (if the sky is clear), although this is also the most crowded time. Do not leave any rubbish behind on desert excursions – the dry climate preserves it perfectly. Take water, hat, camera and torch. Camping is forbidden.

The **Pukará de Quitor** ⓘ *3 km north of San Pedro along the river, US$3*, is a pre-Inca fortress restored in 1981. The fortress, which stands on the west bank, was stormed by the Spanish under Pedro de Valdivia. A further 4 km up the river there are Inca ruins at Catarpe. At **Tulor** ⓘ *12 km southwest of San Pedro, US$5.50*, there is an archaeological site where parts of a stone-age village (dated 800 BC-AD 500) have been excavated; can be visited on foot, or take a tour. Nearby are the ruins of a 17th century village, abandoned in the 18th century because of lack of water.

El Tatio ⓘ *Altitude: 4321 m; entry US$9*, the site of geysers, is a popular attraction. From San Pedro it is reached by a maintained road which runs northeast past the thermal pools at **Puritama** (28 km, US$9, worth a visit). The geysers are at their best 1100-1500, though the spectacle varies: locals say the performance is best when weather conditions are stable. Following recent accidents a series of stone walls and wooden walkways has been built around the geysers, which some say has taken away from the spectacle. A swimming pool has been built nearby (take costume and towel). There is no public transport and hitching is impossible. If going in a hired car, make sure the engine is suitable for very high altitudes and is protected with antifreeze. If driving in the dark it is almost impossible to find your way: the sign for El Tatio is north of the turn off (follow a tour bus). Tours arranged by agencies in San Pedro and Calama; nearest *hospedaje* in Caspana (see above).

Toconao ⓘ *Population: 500, 37 km south of San Pedro de Atacama*, is on the eastern shore of the Salar de Atacama. The 18th-century church and bell tower and all houses are built of bricks of white volcanic stone, *sillar*. There are a few basic residenciales. East of the village is a beautifully green gorge called the Quebrada de Jere, filled with fruit trees and grazing cattle (entry US$2). Worth visiting are the vineyards which produce a sweet wine. The quarry where the *sillar* is worked can be visited, about 1.5 km east (the stones sound like bells when struck).

South of Toconao is one of the main entrances to the **Salar de Atacama** ⓘ *entry is controlled by CONAF in Toconao, US$5.50*. This vast 300,000-ha salt lake (the third largest expanse of salt flats in the world) is home to three of the world's five species of flamingo – the Andean, Chilean and James – and other birds (although some can only be seen when lakes form in winter). The air is so dry that you can usually see right across the Salar. A huge lake half a metre below the surface contributes to a slight haze in the air. The area is also rich in minerals. Three areas of the Salar form part of the **Reserva Nacional de los Flamencos**, which is in seven sectors totalling 73,986 ha and administered by CONAF in San Pedro (Ayllú de Solcor), T285 1608.

From Toconao the road heads south through scenic villages to the mine at Laco (one poor stretch below the mine), before proceeding to Laguna Sico (4079 m), and Paso Sico to Argentina.

Border with Bolivia and Argentina → *Between Oct and Mar, Chilean time is 1 hr later than Bolivian.*

Hito Cajón for the border with Bolivia is reached by road 47 km east of San Pedro. The first 35 km are the paved road to Paso de Jama (see below), then it's unpaved to Hito Cajón. From the border it is 7 km north to Laguna Verde. Chilean immigration and customs are in San Pedro, open 0800-2300 (maybe closed lunchtimes). For the Bolivian consulate, see under Calama. Bolivian immigration only gives one month entry here.

The ride from San Pedro de Atacama to Salta on a fully paved road through the 4400-m **Paso de Jama** is spectacular. It stays high on the puna, going by snow-capped peaks, lakes and salt pans, before reaching the Argentine border post, 160 km from San Pedro. There are no money changing facilities nor any other services here. Be prepared for cold. The road continues paved on the Argentine side to Susques and Jujuy. This is much more popular than the **Paso Sico** route, which is hardly used by any public or heavy traffic (paved to Socaire on the Chilean side, about 40% paved in Argentina to San Antonio de los Cobres, slow going on the unpaved parts). **Chilean immigration** and customs are in San Pedro. When crossing by private vehicle, check the road conditions before setting out as Paso de Jama can be closed by heavy rain in summer and blocked by snow in winter. **Note** At all border crossings, incoming vehicles and passengers are searched for fruit, vegetables, dairy produce and coca leaves, which may not be brought into Chile.

◉ San Pedro de Atacama listings

For hotel and restaurant price codes, and other relevant information, see Essentials.

● Where to stay

San Pedro de Atacama *p712, map p712*
There is electricity, but take a torch (flashlight) for walking at night. Rooms are scarce in Jan/Feb, and pricey all year round. There are unregistered hostels, usually **$** pp, but security is often lax.

$$$$ Altiplánico, Atienza 282, T285 1245, reservations T02-2958 4289, www.altiplanico. com. Comfortable boutique hotel on the edge of town (20-min walk), adobe huts, well designed and spacious.

$$$$ Alto Atacama, Camino Pucara Suchor, T056-2912 3910 (reservations), www.altoatacama.com. In the Catarpe valley, spacious rooms, all with terrace, spa, observatory, packages and excursions offered.

$$$$ Awasi, Tocopilla 4, T285 1460, reservations T02-2233 9641, www.awasi.cl. All-inclusive packages. Just 8 luxury cabins, all built with traditional materials, fine food, excellent customer service, professional tours included.

$$$$ Explora, Atienza y Ayllú de Larache, T02-2395 2800 (head office Av Américo Vespucio Sur 80, 5 piso, Santiago), www.explora.com.

Luxury full board and excursion programme, solar-heated pool, sauna, jacuzzi, massages, the only lodge with its own stables and horses.

$$$$ Hostería San Pedro, Toconao 460, T285 1011, www.dahoteles.com. The town's oldest luxury hotel. Pool (residents only), petrol station, cabins, some rooms with satellite TV, quite comfortable.

$$$$ Kimal, Atienza 452 y Caracoles, T285 1152, www.kimal.cl. Small, intimate, near the centre, room size varies, pool with jacuzzi and spa. Good restaurant (open to the public). Opposite is **Poblado Kimal**, under same ownership.

$$$$ Tierra Atacama, Camino Séquitor s/n, 255 5977 (or 02-2207 8861), www.tierra atacama.com. Modern design, elegant and minimalist, somewhat removed from the village itself. Very good reports, including fine dining, spa, excursions, birdwatching.

$$$ Don Raul, Caracoles 130-B, T285 1138, www.donraul.cl. Pleasant, simple rooms, good value, some with kitchenette, one for the disabled.

$$$ La Casa de Don Tomás, Tocopilla s/n, T285 1055, www.dontomas.cl. Good rooms, bright and spacious lounge, quiet, swimming pool. Late check out/and check in. Decent value.

$$$-$$ Elim, Palpana 6, T285 1567, www. hostalelim.cl. Rooms sleep 1-3, nice hot showers, garden, hammock area, bicycle rental, laundry service.

$$$-$$ Takha-Takha, Caracoles 101, T285 1038, www.takhatakha.cl. Pretty, lovely garden and shady patio rooms with bath are nicer than those without. Also camping under trees, with hot showers.

$$$-$ Hostelling International, Caracoles 360, T256 4683, www.hostellingsanpedro. cl. Lively hostel, cramped shared rooms with lockers, also private rooms. Bicycle rental, tours, sandboarding school.

$$ Haramaksi, Coya, near Tulor, 10 km southwest of San Pedro, T09-9595 7567. Simple accommodation in traditional Atacameño surroundings away from the hubbub of San Pedro. Free transfer from bus station.

$$ Hostal Mamatierra, Pachamama 615, T285 1418, hostalmamatierra@sanpedrodeatacama. com. 5 mins' walk from the centre, will pick you up from the bus terminals. Some rooms with bath, kitchen facilities, peaceful.

$$ Hostal Miskanty, Pasaje Mutulera 141, T285 1430, www.hostalmiskanty.cl. Simple but pleasant rooms with bath, laundry service.

$$ Hostal Sonchek, Le Paige 170, T285 1112, www.hostalsonchek.cl. Decent value hostel, some rooms with bath, café, English and French spoken.

$$ Res Chiloé, Atienza 404, T285 1017, www.residencialchiloe.supersitio.net. Rooms with bath much nicer than those without, good clean bathrooms, good beds, breakfast extra. Sunny veranda, laundry facilities, luggage store, parking.

$$-$ Res Vilacoyo, Tocopilla 387, T285 1006, vilacoyo@sanpedrodeatacama.com. Shared bath, good kitchen facilities, hammock in courtyard, laundry service. One of few good budget options in the centre.

Camping Alberto Terrazas Oasis Camping at Pozo 3, 5 km east of town, T285 1042, has the best facilities including a swimming pool. Camping Los Perales, Tocopilla 481.

🍴 Restaurants

San Pedro de Atacama *p712, map p712*
Few places are open before 1000. Drink bottled water as the local supply has a high mineral content, which may not agree with some.

$$$-$$ Bendito Desierto, Atienza 426. Inventive food served in a kind of grotto.

$$$-$$ La Estaka, Caracoles 259, T285 1164, www.laestaka.cl. Wood fire, cane roof, jazz music, pizzería and other dishes, good food, bar and book exchange, lively after 2300, favoured spot of the local New Age crowd.

$$ Adobe, Caracoles 211, www.cafeadobe.cl. Open fire, internet, good atmosphere, loud music. Described as "like Greenwich Village/ Islington in the Atacama".

$$ Casa Piedra, Caracoles. Open fire, also has a cheap menu, waiters sometimes play live folk music, good food and cocktails.

$$ La Casona, Caracoles. Good food, vegetarian options, cheap *almuerzo*, large portions. Interesting Cubist-style desert paintings. Check bill with care.

$$ Milagro, Caracoles 241. Good food, vegetarian options, attentive service.

$$-$ Café Etnico, Tocopilla 423, T285 1377. Good food, juices and sandwiches, cosy, book exchange, internet (free for diners).

$$-$ Café y Cia, Toconao 568, T285 1506. French run, specializing in salads, omelettes and sandwiches; also has full leaf teas, coffees and ice cream on offer.

$ Café Tierra Todo Natural, Caracoles. Excellent fruit juices, "the best bread in the Atacama", real coffee, yoghurt, best for breakfast, opens earliest.

$ Empanadium, Galería El Peral, Caracoles 317, loc 5. Over 100 varieties of *empanada* fillings.

$ Estrella Negra, Caracoles 362, in patio de comidas. Good cheap vegetarian and some vegan food.

🛍 Shopping

San Pedro de Atacama *p712, map p712*
Handicrafts There are a couple of craft markets, one near the plaza, and the other in the Galería el Peral, Caracoles 317. Very little *artesanía* is produced in San Pedro itself, most comes from Bolivia.

⚙ What to do

San Pedro de Atacama *p712, map p712*
Mountain biking
Bicycles for hire all over town, by the hour or full day: 'professional' model or cheaper

'amateur'. Tracks in the desert can be really rough, so check the bike's condition and carry a torch if riding after dark.

Swimming pools

Piscina Oasis, at Pozo Tres, 3 km southeast but walking there is tough and not recommended. Open all year daily (except Mon) 0500-1730, US$2 to swim, some times empty. Camping, good showers and picnic facilities, very popular Sat-Sun.

Tour operators

Usual tours include: to Valle de la Luna, the Salar de Atacama, Altiplano lakes (including Toconao and Salar de Atacama), El Tatio (begin at 0400) with trekking (take swimming costume and warm clothing). Beware of tours to Valle de la Luna leaving too late to catch sunset – leave before 1600. Before taking a tour, check that the agency has dependable vehicles, suitable equipment (eg oxygen for El Tatio), experienced drivers, a guide who speaks English if so advertised, and that the company is well established. Always get a receipt. Report any complaints to the municipality or Sernatur. There are about 25 agencies, but some are temporary and/or open for only part of the year. Some operators will offer a reduction if you book a series of tours with them.
Atacama Horse Adventure (La Herradura), Tocopilla 406, T285 1956, www.atacama horseadventure.com. Horse-riding tours with good local guides, mountain bike hire.
Atacama Mística, Caracoles 238, T285 1956, www.atacamamistica.cl. Chilean-Bolivian company, daily tours with transfer to San Pedro de Atacama, also transfers between San Pedro and Uyuni, good service.
Azimut 360º, T09-8449 1093, www.azimut. cl. Santiago-based company offers excursions, trekking, private tours with English, German and French-speaking guides.
Cordillera Traveller, Toconao 447-B, T285 1291, www.cordilleratraveller.com. Specializes in tours to Salar de Uyuni.
Cosmo Andino Expediciones, Caracoles s/n, T285 1069, http://cosmoandino-expediciones.cl/. Very professional and experienced, English, French, German, Dutch spoken, good vehicles, drivers and guides, owner Martín Beeris (Martín El Holandés).

Desert Adventure, Caracoles s/n, T285 1067, www.desertadventure.cl. Good guides and range of trips, English spoken, modern fleet of vehicles, mostly good reports.
Rancho Cactus, Toconao 568, T285 1506, www.rancho-cactus.cl. Offers horse riding with good guides to Valle de la Luna and other sites (Farolo and Valerie – speaks French and English), suits inexperienced riders.
Space, Caracoles 166, T256 6278/09-9817 8354, www.spaceobs.com. Run by French astronomer Alain, who speaks 3 languages and has set up a small observatory in the village of Solor, south of San Pedro; gives tours 2000-2330 to study the night sky, hot drink included but wear all your warmest clothes.
Vulcano, Caracoles 317, T285 1023, www. vulcanochile.cl. Mountain climbs, sandboarding and other adventure tours, mountain bike hire, English-speaking guides.

⊖ Transport

San Pedro de Atacama *p712, map p712*
Bus Most buses leave from Licancábur opposite the football field. **Tur-Bus** terminal on Atienza, north of the centre, office Licancábur 294, T285 1549. To **Calama**: US$5.50, **Frontera** (7 daily), 1½ hrs, **Tur-Bus**, several daily. Frequencies vary with more departures in Jan-Feb and some weekends. Book in advance to return from San Pedro on Sun afternoon. **Tur-Bus** to **Arica**, 2030, US$35-55. **Tur-Bus** to **Santiago**, several daily, 23 hrs, US$70-90. **Frontera** to **Socaire**, Mon, Thu, Fri 1930, Sun 1230, 2200, US$3; to **Toconao**, 4 a day (3 on Sun), US$1.50. **To Argentina** Géminis, on Toconao (changes bolivianos), to **Salta**, US$45-65, 9 hrs, reserve in advance.(buses fill up early). Also **Pullman** (Frontera office) and **Andesmar** 3 a week each.
Car Expensive fuel is available in the grounds of Hostería San Pedro. If planning to cross the border to Bolivia, remember that octane ratings are different in the 2 countries, but diesel cars can safely be used.

Border with Bolivia *p714*

As of 2014, there are no buses to the border at Hito Cájon, except by tour. Those who wish to take public transport to the border must do so from Calama. Do not be tempted to hitch to the border and beyond as you risk being stranded without water or shelter at sub-zero temperatures.

San Pedro de Atacama *p712, map p712*
Banks See above for ATMs. The tourist office recommends always changing money at banks; however, Casa de Cambios Mazzetti, on Toconao, Mon-Sat 0730-2230, Sun 0800-1300, is one sturdy option. Some other places change euros; ask around.

Iquique and around

The Cordillera de la Costa slowly loses height north of Iquique, terminating at the Morro at Arica (see page 722): from Iquique north it drops directly to the sea and as a result there are few beaches along this coast. Inland, the central depression (pampa) 1000-1200 m is arid and punctuated by salt-flats south of Iquique. Between Iquique and Arica it is crossed from east to west by four gorges. East of this depression lies the sierra, the western branch of the Andes, beyond which is a high plateau, the altiplano (3500-4500 m) from which rise volcanic peaks. In the altiplano there are a number of lakes, the largest of which, Lago Chungará (see page 725), is one of the highest in the world. The coastal strip and the pampa are rainless; on the coast temperatures are moderated by the Pacific, but in the pampa variations of temperature between day and night are extreme, ranging from 30°C to 0°C. The altiplano is much colder.

Iquique → *Phone code: 057. Colour map 6, B2. Population: 200,000.*
Iquique is an attractive port and city with well-preserved historical buildings. Around it the desert pampa stretches north, south and to the mountains. Several oases also have strong historical associations, either in the form of geoglyphs, the last evidence of peoples long vanished, or the ghost towns of nitrate operations. Mamiña and Pica are thermal resorts within easy reach of Iquique; both are beautiful, tranquil places.

The name of the capital of I Región (Tarapacá) and one of the main northern ports, is derived from the Aymara word *ique-ique*, meaning place of 'rest and tranquillity'. The city, 492 km north of Antofagasta and 47 km west of the Pan-American Highway, is situated on a rocky peninsula at the foot of the high Atacama pampa, sheltered by the headlands of Punta Gruesa and Cavancha. The city, which was partly destroyed by earthquake in 1877, became the centre of the nitrate trade after its transfer from Peru to Chile at the end of the War of the Pacific. A short distance north of town along Amunátegui is the **Free Zone (Zofri)** ① *Mon-Sat 1100-2100, limit on tax free purchases US$1000 for foreigners, getting there: colectivo from the centre US$1*. It is worth visiting this giant shopping centre, which sells all manner of imported items, including electronic goods. It is much better value than its equivalent in Punta Arenas. **Tourist office** ① *Sernatur, Serrano 145, of 303, T242 7686, infoiquige@sernatur.cl, Mon-Fri, 0830-1630*. Masses of information, very helpful. See also www.iquique.cl.

In the centre of the old town is the **Plaza Prat.** On the northeast corner of the Plaza is the Centro Español, built in extravagant Moorish style by the local Spanish community in 1904; the ground floor is a restaurant, on the upper floors are paintings of scenes from Don Quijote and from Spanish history. Three blocks north of the Plaza is the old Aduana (customs house) built in 1871; in 1891 it was the scene of an important battle in the Civil War between supporters of President Balmaceda and congressional forces. Part of it is now the **Museo Naval** ① *Esmeralda 250, www.museonaval.cl, Tue-Sun 1000-1730, US$2*, focusing on the Battle of Iquique, 1879. Along Calle Baquedano, which runs south from Plaza Prat, are the attractive former mansions of the 'nitrate barons', dating from between 1880 and 1903. The finest of these is the **Palacio Astoreca** ① *O'Higgins 350, Tue-Fri 1000-1300, Sat 1000-1330, Sun 1100-1400, US$1*. Built in 1903, it was subsequently the Intendencia and now a museum of fine late 19th-century furniture and shells. The **Museo Regional** ① *Baquedano 951, Mon-Fri 0830-1300, 1530-1830, Sat 1030-1300, Sun (in summer) 1000-1300, 1600-2000, free*, contains an archaeological section tracing the development of prehispanic civilizations in the region; an ethnographical collection of the Isluga culture of the Altiplano (AD 400), and of contemporary Aymara culture; also a section devoted to the nitrate era which includes a model of a nitrate office and the collection of the nitrate entrepreneur, Santiago Humberstone. Sea lions and pelicans can be seen from the harbour. There are **cruises** ① *US$5, 45 mins, minimum 10 people*, from the passenger pier.

The **beaches** at Cavancha just south of the town centre are good; those at Huaiquique are reasonable November-March. There are restaurants at Cavancha. For surfers the better bet is the pounding surf of Playa Brava, further south. Cerro Dragón, the large sand dune behind

Iquique

Where to stay 🛏
1 Arturo Prat
2 Atenas
3 Backpacker's Hostel Iquique
4 Cano
5 Hostal Cuneo
6 Hostal La Casona 1920
7 Hostal Li Ming
8 YMCA

Restaurants 🍴
1 Birimbao
2 Brasileña
3 Casino Español
4 Cioccolata
5 El Rincón del Cachuperto
6 El Tercer Ojito
7 El Wagon
8 Kiru
9 La Picada Curicana
10 Muselina
11 Nan King
12 Peña mi Perú
13 Ruta del Gigante

Iquique, is good for sandboarding; great views too. There are several hills for paragliding, good for beginners.

Around Iquique

Humberstone, a large nitrate town, is now abandoned. It is at the junction of the Pan-American Highway and the road to Iquique. Entry by 'donation', US$3, guided tours Saturday-Sunday, leaflets available, T275 1213. Colectivo from Iquique US$3; phone near site for booking return. Though closed since 1961, you can see the church, theatre, pulpería (company stores) and the pool (built of metal plating from ships' hulls). Nearby are the ruins of other mining towns including Santa Laura. Local tour companies run trips to the area, including Humberstone, Santa Laura, Pisagua and **Pozo Almonte**, 52 km east (*Population: c 5400*). This town was the chief service provider of the nitrate companies until their closure in 1960. The **Museo Histórico Salitrero** ① *on the tree-shaded plaza, Mon-Fri 0830-1300, 1600-1900*, displays artefacts and photos of the nitrate era.

To Cerro Pintados (see page 708) take any bus south, US$4, and walk from the Pan-American Highway then hitch back or flag down a bus. From Pozo Almonte 74 km (paved), **Mamiña** (*Population: c 600; Altitude: 2750 m*) has abundant thermal springs and a mud spring, **Baño Los Chinos** ① *0930-1300*. The therapeutic properties of the waters and mud are Mamiña's main claim to fame. Mineral water from the spring is sold throughout northern Chile. There are ruins of a prehispanic pukará (fortress) and a church, built in 1632, the only colonial Andean church in Chile with two towers. An Aymara cultural centre, Kaspi-kala, has an artesanía workshop and outlet. It is very difficult to find lodging in Mamiña as hotels have exclusive contracts with the nearby mine.

La Tirana (*Population: 550; Altitude: 995 m*) is famous for a religious festival to the **Virgen del Carmen**, held from 10 to 16 July, which attracts some 150,000 pilgrims. Over 100 groups dance night and day, decked out in spectacular colourful masks, starting on 12 July. All the dances take place in the main plaza in front of the church; no alcohol is served. Accommodation is impossible to find, other than in organized camp sites (take tent) which have basic toilets and showers. It is 10 km east of the Pan-American Highway (70 km east of Iquique), turn-off 9 km south of Pozo Almonte. **Pica** (*Population: 1767; Altitude: 1325 m*), 42 km from La Tirana, was the most important centre of early Spanish settlement in the area. Most older buildings date from the nitrate period when it became a popular resort. The town is famous for its pleasant climate, citrus groves and two natural springs, the best of which is **Cocha Resbaladero** ① *0700-2000 all year, US$4, snack bar, changing rooms, beautiful pool, tourist office opposite*.

Many other sites around Iquique, including the Gigante del Atacama (see below) and places to see fossilized dinosaur footprints, are difficult to visit without a car; tours available from Pica.

From Iquique to the Bolivian border

At **Huara**, 33 km north of Pozo Almonte, a paved road turns off the Pan-American Highway to **Colchane**. At 13 km east of Huara are the huge geoglyphs of Cerro Unitas, with the giant humanoid figure of the Gigante del Atacama (86 m tall) and a sun with 24 rays, on the sides of two hills (best seen from a distance). Some buses from Iquique to La Paz and Oruro pass through, or La Paloma at 2300 from Esmeralda y Juan Martínez. 173 km northeast is the **Bolivian border** at Pisiga (open daily 0800-1300, 1500-2000). An unpaved road continues to Oruro, 233 km northeast.

Northwest of Colchane, the **Parque Nacional Volcán Isluga** ① *Park Administration at Enquelga, 10 km north of the entrance, but guardaparques are seldom there, Arica T58-225 0570 for details of hospedaje at the guardería*, covers 174,744 ha at altitudes above 2100 m and has some of the best volcanic scenery in northern Chile. The village of **Isluga**, near the park entrance, 6 km northwest of Colchane, has an 18th-century Andean walled church and bell tower. Wildlife varies according to altitude but includes guanacos, vicuñas, llamas, alpacas, vizcachas, condors and flamingos.

The Pan-American Highway runs across the Atacama desert at an altitude of around 1000 m, with several steep hills which are best tackled in daylight (at night, sea mist, camanchaca, can reduce visibility). At **Zapiga**, 80 km north of Pozo Almonte, there is a crossroads: east through Camiña (*Population: 500; Altitude: 2400 m*), a picturesque village in an oasis, 67 km east of Zapiga along a poor road. Thence mountain roads lead across the Parque Nacional Volcán Isluga to Colchane. The westerly branch runs 41 km to **Pisagua** (*Population: 200*), formerly an important nitrate port, now a fishing village. Several old wooden buildings are National Monuments. The fish restaurants make a pleasant stop for a meal. Mass graves dating from just after the 1973 military coup were discovered near here in 1990. At Km 57 north of Huara there is a British cemetery at Tiliviche dating from 1825. The Geoglyphs of Tiliviche representing a group of llamas (signposted, to left, and easily accessible), Km 127, can be seen from the highway.

⊙ Iquique and around listings

For hotel and restaurant price codes, and other relevant information, see Essentials.

⊛ Where to stay

Iquique *p717, map p718*
Accommodation is scarce in July and also in high summer. There's no campsite in Iquique and wild camping is forbidden on Playa Brava and Playa Cavancha.

$$$ Arturo Prat, Aníbal Pinto 695, Plaza Prat, T252 0000. Under new management and renovated, good location if a bit noisy, good standard, nice pool.

$$$ Atenas, Los Rieles 738, Cavancha, T243 1100, atenashotel2002@yahoo.es. Pleasant, personal, good value, good service and food, pool.

$$$-$$ Cano, Ramírez 996, T247 0277, www.hotelcano.cl. Mostly big rooms, but also some small interior rooms to be avoided. nice atmosphere, brightly coloured, modern décor, parking.

$$ Hostal Cuneo, Baquedano 1175, T242 8654, www.hostalcuneo.cl. Long-established hostel, helpful, piano in the living room, good value.

$$-$ Backpacker's Hostel Iquique, Amunategui 2075 esq Hernán Fuenzalida, T232 0223, www.hosteliquique.cl. Seafront location at Cavancha, all the usual backpacker's services plus surfboard and wetsuit rental, surf classes, sand duning, bicycles, roof terrace with ocean view.

$$-$ Hostal La Casona 1920, Barros Arana 1585, T241 3000, http://casonahostel.com. Fun, in a quiet area of town not far from the beach, English spoken.

$$-$ Hostal Li Ming, Barros Arana 705, T242 1912, www.hostal.cl. Simple, good value,

small rooms, also beachfront apartments to rent.

$ YMCA, Baquedano 964, T241 5551, www. ymcaiquique.org. Impressive façade, modern interior, most rooms are dorm-style with their own bathroom. Basic, but clean and central.

Around Iquique *p719*
Pica
Hotels fill up at weekends, holiday times and during La Tirana's festival 10-16 Jul: book ahead.

$$ Camino del Inca, Esmeralda 14, T057-274 1008, hotelcaminodelinca@hotmail.com. Shady patio, table football, good value.

$$ Los Emilios, Cochrane 201, T274 1126. Interesting old building, nice lounge and patio.

$$-$ O'Higgins, Balmaceda 6, T274 1524, hohiggins@123mail.com. Modern, well furnished.

$ San Andrés, Balmaceda 197, T274 1319, gringa733@hotmail.com. Basic, excellent restaurant, serves good-value 4-course *almuerzos*. Safe parking.

⊙ Restaurants

Iquique *p717, map p718*
The restaurants on the wharf on the opposite side of Av Costanera from the bus terminal are poor value. There are several good, cheap seafood restaurants on the 2nd floor of the central market, Barros Arana y Latorre. There are also many restaurants on the Península Cavancha.

$$$-$$ Casino Español, Plaza Prat, T242 3284. Good meals well served in beautiful Moorish-style 1904 building.

$$$-$$ El Tercer Ojito, P Lynch 1420, T247 1448. Well-presented fish, sushi, pasta and vegetarian options with a Peruvian twist, served in a pleasant courtyard, deservedly popular.

$$$-$$ El Wagon, Thompson 85, T234 1428. Fish and seafood cooked to traditional northern recipes. Regarded as the best eatery in the centre.

$$$-$$ Kiru, Amunátegui 1912, Cavancha, T276 0795, www.kiru.cl. Mon-Sat 1300-1530, 2000-0030, Sun 1300-1600. Half elegant restaurant, half sports bar, Peruvian influenced food, fish and good pasta. Huge *pisco sours*.

$$$-$$ Ruta del Gigante, Baquedano 1288, T247 5215, www.rutadelgigante.cl. Delicious and varied food from the Andes drawn on Aymara family heritage with modern twist. Also has a hostel and can arrange tours.

$$ Brasileña, Vivar 1143, T276 1752. Brazilian run, serves seafood in the week, Brazilian food on Sat.

$$ La Picada Curicana, Pinto y Zegers 204, T276 5830, www.lapicadacuricana.cl. Tue-Sat 1100-1600, 2000-2400, Sun 1200-1700. Good hearty Central Chilean country cooking (such as oven-roasted game, served in clay pots), large portions, good value *menú de la casa*.

$$ Nan King, Amunátegui 533, T242 0434. Large portions, good value, renowned as best Chinese in town.

$ El Rincón del Cachuperto, Valenzuela 125, Península Cavancha, T232 9189. Famed as having the best seafood *empanadas* in Iquique.

$ Peña mi Perú, Bolívar 711. Open 24 hrs. Cheap Chilean and Peruvian staples, good value *menú* on weekdays.

Birimbao, Gorostiaga 419. Opens early for breakfast (0800). Fresh juices.

Cioccolata, Pinto 487, T242 7478 (another branch in the Zofri). Very good coffee and cakes.

Muselina, Baquedano 1406, www.muselina.cl. Mon-Fri 0900-2300, Sun 1800-2200. Café/bistro with good coffee, delicious cakes and smoothies.

Salon de Té Don Luis, Latorre y Vivar. Very popular for *onces*, quite expensive.

Around Iquique *p719*
Pica
Try the local *alfajores*, delicious cakes filled with cream and mango honey.

$$ El Edén, Riquelme 12. 1st class local food in delightful surroundings, fine ice cream, best restaurant in town.

$ La Mía Pappa, Balmaceda, near plaza. Good selection of meat and juices, attractive location.

$ La Palmera, Balmaceda 115. Excellent *almuerzo*, popular with locals, near plaza.

$ La Viña, Ibáñez 70, by Cocha de Resbaladero. Good cheap *almuerzo*.

Bars and clubs

Iquique *p717, map p718*
Most discos are out of town on the road south to the airport.

Siddharta, Mall Las Américas, locales 10-11-193. Sushi.

Taberna Barracuda, Gorostiaga 601, T242 7969. For late night food, drink, nice decor, nice atmosphere.

What to do

Iquique *p717, map p718*
The tourist office maintains a full list of operators. Iquique is a good place for **paragliding**: several agencies offer 30 to 40 min tandem flights from around US$80. It also offers some of the best **surfing** in Chile with numerous reef breaks on Playa Brava, south of the city. Surfboard rental and surf classes are available from a number of agencies.

Altazor, Flight Park, Vía 6, manzana A, sitio 3, Bajo Molle, T230 0110, www.altazor.cl. Parapenting, will pick you up from wherever you are staying. Also offers week long courses including accommodation, as do many other operators.

Avitours, Baquedano 997, T241 3332, www.avitours.cl. Tour to Pintados, La Tirana, Humberstone, Pica, etc, some bilingual guides, day tours start at US$50.

Civet Adventure, Bolívar 684, T242 8483, www.civet-adventure.cl. Adventure tourism in the desert and the High Andes, photography, mountainbiking, landsailing, trekking, English, German and Spanish spoken, contact Sergio Cortez.

Extremo Norte, T276 0997, www.extremo norte.cl. Good tours to the Altiplano and desert, responsible.

Trans Atacama, T02-2620 9620, www.trans atacama.com. A tourist excursion on Sat by train, with historic coaches, from Iquique (pick-up at hotels) to the Pintados geoglyphs.

Includes meals and drinks, 2 classes of carriage: classic or premium.

⊖ Transport

Iquique *p717, map p718*
Air Diego Aracena international airport, 35 km south at Chucumata. Taxi US$16; airport transfer, T231 0800, US$7 for 3 or more passengers, unreliable. **LAN, PAL** and **Sky** fly to **Arica, Antofagasta** and **Santiago**.
Bus Terminal at north end of Patricio Lynch (not all buses leave from here); bus company offices are near the market on Sgto Aldea and B Arana. **Tur-Bus**, Ramírez y Esmeralda, T247 2987 (T242 0634 at terminal), with Redbanc ATM and luggage store. **Pullman**, in terminal T242 6522. Southbound buses are searched for duty-free goods, at Quillagua on the Pan-American Highway and at Chipana on the coastal Route 1. To **Arica**, buses and colectivos, US$11, 4½ hrs. To **Antofagasta**, US$14, 6 hrs. To **Calama**, 6 hrs, US$22. To **San Pedro de Atacama** direct with **Frontera del Norte**, but with a 5-hr layover in Calama 0300-0800. To **Tocopilla** along the coastal road, buses and minibuses, several companies, 3 hrs, US$11. To **La Serena**, 18 hrs, US$35-70. To **Santiago**, 25 hrs, several companies, US$65-92.
International buses To **Bolivia, Litoral**, T242 3670, 2200 daily to **Oruro** and **La Paz**, US$30. **Salvador** and others from Esmeralda near Juan Martínez around 2100-2300, same price (passengers may have a cold wait for customs to open at 0800).

Car hire Econorent, Labbé y O'Higgins, T600-200 0000, weekend specials; IQSA, Labbé 1089, T241 7068. **Procar**, Serrano 796, T241 3470 (airport T241 0920).

Around Iquique *p719*
Mamiña
Bus Transportes Tamarugal, Barros Arana 897, Iquique, daily 0800, 1600, return 1800, 0800, 2½ hrs, US$7, good service. Also with **Turismo Mamiña**, Latorre 779, daily, more-or-less same prices and frequency.

Pica
Bus Minibus **Iquique**-Pica: San Andrés, Sgto Aldea y B Arana, Iquique, daily 0930, return 1800; **Pullman Chacón**, Barros Arana y Latorre, many daily; **Santa Rosa**, Barros Arana 777, daily 0830, 0930, return 1700, 1800. US$4 one-way, 2 hrs.

⊙ Directory

Iquique *p717, map p718*
Banks Numerous Redbanc ATMs in the centre and the Zofri. Best rates for TCs and cash at casas de cambio in the Zofri.
Consulates Bolivia, Gorostiaga 215, Departamento E, T252 7472, colivian-iquique@ entelchile.com. Mon-Fri 0930-1200. Peru, Zegers 570, T241 1466, consulperu-iquique @ rree.gob.pe. **Language schools** Academia de Idiomas del Norte, Ramírez 1345, T241 1827, www.languages.cl. Swiss-run, Spanish classes and accommodation for students.

Arica and Lauca

The Lauca national park, the most northerly in Chile, has some of the country's most stunning scenery: high lakes, snow-capped volcanoes, lava fields and varied bird life. Small Andean villages near the park retain their Aymara culture. Lauca is easily reached from Arica, Chile's northernmost city and capital of the new Arica-Parinacota Region (Región XV). It is the main outlet for Bolivian trade and is even closer to Peru. It's a busy place, dominated by the rocky headland of El Morro.

Arica → *Phone code: 058. Colour map 6, A1. Population: 174,064.*
Arica, 20 km south of the Peruvian border, is built at the foot of the Morro headland and is fringed by sand dunes. The Andes can be clearly seen from the anchorage. Arica used to be the principal route for travellers going overland to Bolivia, via the Parque Nacional Lauca. Now there is competition from the San Pedro de Atacama–Uyuni route. The road route to La Paz via Tambo Colorado is now paved and Arica is a popular seaside destination for landlocked Bolivians, as well

as Chileans. The **Sernatur tourist office** ① *San Marcos 101, T223 3993, infoarica@sernatur.cl, in a kiosk next to the Casa de la Cultura, Mon-Fri 0830-1300, 1500-1830*, is very helpful, English spoken, good map, list of tour companies. Municipal kiosk also on San Marcos, opposite Sernatur, opens at 0830, www.muniarica.cl.

Arica
Arica centre

To ⑥ ⑨
To ⑦
To Airport, Pan-American Highway (North) to Peru, Parque Nacional Lauca & Bolivia
To ③
D Portales
Buses & Colectivos to Tacna
Buses south & to Bolivia
Río San José
N
A

200 metres
200 yards

Where to stay
1 Americano *D2*
2 Arica *E1*
4 Hostal Jardín del Sol *D3*
5 Hostal Pacífico *D2*
6 La Ponderosa Beach House Inn *A1*
7 Maison de France *A1*
8 Res América *D2*
9 Sunny Days *A1*
10 Surf House *C2*

Restaurants
1 Café-Restaurante B *Detail*
2 Chifa El Mesón *B2*
3 Cyclo Public *A3*
4 Don Floro *C3*
5 El Rey del Marisco *Detail*
6 Evergreen *Detail*
7 La Bomba *Detail*
8 Los Aleros del 21 *D3*
9 Maracuyá *E1*
10 Ostión Dorado *E1*

Gral Velásquez
Maipú
Baquedano
Local Colectivos
18 de Septiembre
Thompson
Colón
Bolognesi
Sangra
21 de Mayo
A Prat
Sotomayor
Museo del Mar
Mercado Central
San Marcos

JA Ríos
Av Santa María
M Blanco Encalada
Independencia
J Waidele
Lastu Herrera
Salvo
Angamos

Cemetery

To Playa Chinchorra
Lastarria
Esmeralda
Juan Noe
Charabuco
Av Costanera Norte
Gral Velásquez
Parque Brasil
Parque General C Ibáñez del Campo
Colertivos to Azapa Valley
O' Higgins
Baquedano
Trains to Tacna
Rodríguez
Zambia
To Hospital

La Paz Station
Av Prat
Máximo Lira
6 Montt
18 de Septiembre
Thompson
Colón
Sangra
21 de Mayo
Bolognesi
Sotomayor
Grel Lagos
P Lynch
Maipú
M Blanco Encalada
San Martín
Arturo Gallo
Bolivian Consulate
San Marcos
Casa de la Cultura (Former Aduana)
Plaza Colón
7 de Junio
Cathedral
Yungay
Ejército
Harbour
Plaza Vicuña Mackenna
Morro
Museo Histórico y de Armas
Faldeos El Morro
El Morro
Camino Al Morro
To Poblado Artesanal & Pan-American Highway (South) to Museo Arqueológico de San Miguel & Azapa Valley

To ② ⑨ ⑩, La Lisera, Playa Brava & El Laucho Beaches

To Foblado Artesanal & Pan-American Highway (South) to Museo Arqueológico de San Miguel & Azapa Valley

The **Morro**, with a good view from the park on the top, was the scene of a great victory by Chile over Peru in the War of the Pacific on 7 June 1880. To get there, walk to the southernmost end of Calle Colón, past a small museum displaying a number of Chinchorro mummies, and then follow the pedestrian walkway up to the summit of the hill. Here there is the **Museo Histórico y de Armas** ① *daily 0800-2000, US$1*, contains weapons and uniforms from the War of the Pacific.

At the foot of the Morro is the **Plaza Colón** with the cathedral of San Marcos, built in iron by Eiffel. Though small it is beautifully proportioned and attractively painted. It was brought to Arica from Ilo (Peru) in the 19th century, before Peru lost Arica to Chile, as an emergency measure after a tidal wave swept over Arica and destroyed all its churches. Eiffel also designed the nearby Aduana (customs house) which is now the **Casa de la Cultura** ① *Mon-Fri 0830-2000*. Just north of the Aduana is the La Paz railway station; outside is an old steam locomotive (made in Germany in 1924) once used on this line. In the station is a memorial to John Roberts Jones, builder of the Arica portion of the railway. The **Casa Bolognesi**, Colón y Yungay, is a fine old building painted blue and white. It holds temporary exhibitions. Hidden away on a small side street behind the cathedral is the private **Museo del Mar** ① *Pasaje Sangra 315, www.museodelmardearica.cl, Mon-Sat 1100-1900, US$2*, has over 1000 exhibits from around the world, well-displayed. Just north of the city, the estuary of the Río Lluta is an important stopping place for migrating birds and has been designated a wildlife sanctuary for these and for local birds.

Worthwhile sights outside Arica include the **Museo Arqueológico de San Miguel de Azapa** ① *at Km 12 on the road east to the Azapa valley, T220 5555, www.uta.cl/masma, daily Jan-Feb 0900-2000, Mar-Dec 1000-1800, US$5, getting there: take a yellow colectivo from P Lynch y Chacabuco and 600 block of P Lynch, US$1.50*. Built around an olive press, it contains a fine collection of pre-Columbian weaving, pottery, wood carving and basketwork from the coast and valleys, and also seven mummified humans from the Chinchorro culture (8000-2000 BC), the most ancient mummies yet discovered. Explanations in several languages are loaned free at the entrance. In the museum forecourt are several boulders with pre-Columbian petroglyphs. In San Miguel is an old cemetery and several restaurants. On the road between Arica and San Miguel are several groups of geoglyphs of humans and llamas ('stone mosaics') south of the road (signed to Cerro Sagrado, Cerro Sombrero an Azapa Archaeological Circuit is advertised). North of Arica along Route 11, between Km 14 and Km 16, is the **Lluta valley** where you can see along the hillsides four groups of geoglyphs, representing llamas, an eagle and human giants. The road continues through the Parque Nacional Lauca and on to Bolivia. Take a bus from Mackenna y Chacabuco.

By road to Bolivia

1) Via **Chungará** (Chile) and **Tambo Quemado** (Bolivia). This, the most widely used route, begins by heading north from Arica on the Pan-American Highway (Route 5) for 12 km before turning right (east towards the cordillera) on Route 11 towards Chungará via Putre and Parque Nacional Lauca. The road passes **Termas de Juasi** ① *just after Km 130, look for sign, US$2*, rustic thermal baths, with mud baths and a small swimming pool. This road is now paved to La Paz, estimated driving time six hours. 2) Via **Visviri** (Chile) and **Charaña** (Bolivia), following the La Paz-Arica railway line. This route should not be attempted in wet weather.

Border with Bolivia: Chungará Immigration is open 0800-2000; US$2 per vehicle crossing 1300-1500, 1850-2100 and Saturday, Sunday and holidays. For details of through buses between Arica and La Paz see below under Transport, Arica.

Border with Bolivia: Visviri Immigration is open 0800-2000. Chilean formalities at Visviri, 7 km west of the border, Bolivian formalities at Charaña, just over the border (local barter market every other Friday). When crossing with a private vehicle, US$2 per vehicle is charged between 1300-1500, 1850-2000 and Saturday, Sunday and holidays.

Border with Peru: Chacalluta-Tacna → *Between Oct-Mar Chilean time is 1 hr ahead of Peruvian, 2 hrs.*

Immigration is open Sunday-Thursday 0800-2400, Friday-Saturday 24 hours; it's a fairly uncomplicated crossing. When crossing by private vehicle, US$2 per vehicle is charged between 1300-1500, 1850-2400 and on Saturday, Sunday, holidays. Drivers entering Chile are required to file a form, *Relaciones de Pasajeros*, giving details of passengers, obtained from a stationery store in Tacna, or at the border in a booth near Customs. You must also present the original registration document for your car from its country of registration. The first checkpoints outside Arica on the road to Santiago also require the *Relaciones de Pasajeros* form. If you can't buy the form, details on a piece of paper will suffice or you can get them at service stations. The form is not required for travel south of Antofagasta. Money exchange facilities at the bus terminal in Tacna.

Parque Nacional Lauca

The Parque Nacional Lauca, stretching to the border with Bolivia, is one of the most spectacular national parks in Chile. It is 176 km east of Arica and access is easy as the main Arica-La Paz road runs through the park and is paved. On the way is a zone of giant candelabra cactus, between 2300-2800 m. At Km 90 there is a pre-Inca *pukará* (fortress) above the village of Copaquilla and, a few kilometres further, there is an Inca *tambo* (inn) at Zapahuira. Situated at elevations from 3200 m to 6340 m (beware of soroche unless you are coming from Bolivia), the park covers 137,883 ha and includes numerous snowy volcanoes including three peaks of over 6000 m. At the foot of Volcán Parinacota and its twin, Pomerape (in Bolivia – they are known collectively as Payachatas), is a series of lakes among a jumble of rocks, called Cotacotani. Black lava flows can be seen above Cotacotani. **Lago Chungará** (4517 m, 7 km by 3 km) is southeast of Payachatas, a must for its views of the Parinacota, Sajama and Guallatire volcanoes and for its varied wildlife. At the far end of the lake is the Chile/Bolivia border. The park contains over 120 species of bird, resident or migrant, as well as camelids, vizcacha and puma. A good base for exploring the park and for acclimatization is **Putre** (*Population: 4400; Altitude: 3500 m*), a scenic village, 15 km before the entrance with a church dating from 1670 and surrounded by terracing dating from pre-Inca times, now used for cultivating alfalfa and oregano. From here paths provide easy walking and great views. Festivals: **Pacahayame**, last Sunday in October, festival of the potato: religious celebration and traditional dancing. **Feria de la Voz Andina**, November (check dates and reserve room and transport in advance), with dancing, foods, handicrafts, very popular. **Tourist office** on main plaza, helpful, some English spoken, organizes tours. In town is the **CONAF subadministration office** ⓘ *Teniente del Campo 301, T258 5704, Mon-Fri 0830-1730.*

At **Parinacota** (*Altitude: 4392 m*), at the foot of Payachatas, there is an interesting 17th century church – rebuilt 1789 – with 18th-century frescoes and the skulls of past priests (ask at the stalls outside the church for Senor Sipriani with the key, donations appreciated). Local residents knit alpaca sweaters, US$26 approximately; weavings of wildlife scenes also available. Weavings are sold from stalls outside the church. **CONAF office**, which administers the national park, and visitor centre is also here (open 0830-1730). It's a walk of about one hour from the village to Cotacotani. From here an unpaved road runs north to the Bolivian border at Visviri (see above). You can climb Guane Guane, 5097 m, in two to three hours, ask at the CONAF office. Lago Chungará is 20 km southeast of Parinacota.

During the rainy season (January-February), roads in the park may be impassable; check in advance with CONAF in Arica (see Directory, below). It can be foggy as well as wet in January-March. A map of the park is available from Sernatur in Arica. Maps are also available from the Instituto Geográfico Militar. If driving off the main road, 4WD is necessary.

Reserva Nacional Las Vicuñas → *Altitude: 4300-6060 m.*

South of Lauca is the beautiful Reserva Nacional Las Vicuñas, covering 209,131 ha of altiplano. Many of these beautiful creatures can be seen as well as, with luck, condors, rheas and other birds. Administration is at Guallatiri, reached by turning off the Arica-La Paz road onto the A147, 2 km after Las Cuevas, where there is also a CONAF *refugio* (see Where to stay, below). The same road leads into the **Monumento Natural Salar de Surire**, for which the same weather and road conditions apply. The *salar*, also at 4300 m, is a drying salt lake of 17,500 ha. It has a year-round population of 12,000-15,000 flamingos (Chilean, Andean and James). Administration is in **Surire**, 48 km south of Guallatiri and 129 km south of Putre. A normal car can reach Surire in the dry season, but a high-clearance vehicle is essential for all other roads and, in the summer wet season (January to March, also August), 4WD vehicle: take extra fuel. In the wet, roads may be impassable. There is no public transport to these wildlife reserves, but tours can be arranged in Putre or Arica. All three, Lauca, Las Vicuñas and Salar de Surire are a World Biosphere Reserve. See Footprint's *Chile Handbook*, or ask tour operators such as **Latinorizons** about routes through these parks from Arica to San Pedro de Atacama. Also check with CONAF in Arica about road conditions and whether the parks are closed at any time.

⑥ Arica and Lauca listings

For hotel and restaurant price codes, and other relevant information, see Essentials.

⑤ Where to stay

Arica *p722, map p723*
For apartment rental on the beach, see local newspapers.
$$$$ Arica, San Martín 599, about 2 km along shore (frequent micros and colectivos), T225 4540, www.panamericanahoteles.cl. 4-star, best, price depends on season, decent restaurant, tennis court, pool, lava beach (not safe for swimming).
$$$ Americano, General Lagos 571, T225 7752, www.hotelamericano.cl. Airy, spacious rooms, pleasant patio, rooms on upper floor have views to the Morro. Gym and sauna (extra charge).
$$ Hostal Jardín del Sol, Sotomayor 848, T223 2795, www.hostaljardindelsol.cl. Comfortable, beds with duvets, good value, bike hire. Large kitchen area (US$1 charge).
$$ Sunny Days, Tomás Aravena 161 (a little over halfway along P de Valdivia, 800 m from bus terminal, transport to hotel), T224 1038, www.sunny-days-arica.cl. Run by a New Zealander and his Chilean wife. Rooms with shared or private bath, English spoken, cosy atmosphere, lots of info, book exchange, bike rental. Convenient for the beach. One of the best hostels in the north of Chile.

$$-$ La Ponderosa Beach House Inn, Av Las Dunas, north of town, T09-6539 4445, www.chilloutbeachhouse.com. Ocean-front hotel with surfer dorms and private rooms. Restaurant, laundry service, Wi-Fi, guest kitchen, barbecue areas and rental of sports equipment. Pick-up service from airport, bus terminal and town centre. Camper garage with showers and toilets. All bookings taken online.
$$-$ Maison de France, Aurelio Valdivieso 152, pob Chinchorro, T222 3463, atchumturist@hotmail.com. Owned by Frenchman Cristian, good meals, information on tours and self-guided trips, convenient for beach and nightlife.
$$-$ Res América, Sotomayor 430, T225 4148, www.residencialamerica.com. Variety of room sizes, shared or private bath, hospitable, good value.
$$-$ Surf House, O'Higgins 661, T231 2213, www.aricasurfhouse.cl. Surfers' hostel (the owner also runs a surf school), decent beds and showers, large common areas.
$ Hostal Pacífico, Gen Lagos 672, T225 1616, hostalpacifico672@hotmail.com. Good option in the city centre, private of shared bath.

Parque Nacional Lauca *p725*
The CONAF office at **Lago Chungará** has 4 beds which may be available for visitors. Advance booking in Arica essential, or ask at the Parinacota or Putre offices.

Putre

$$ Kukulí, Canto y Baquedano, T09-9161 4709, www.translapaloma.cl. 10 decent rooms with bath, in town.

$$ La Chakana, Cochrane s/n, T09-9745 9519, www.la-chakana.com. Cabins on the edge of town sleep up to 4, private bath, with pleasant views, English spoken, good breakfast, lots of hiking and mountaineering info, tours, involved with social projects, Aymara museum on site. A good choice.

$$ Terrace Lodge & Tours, Circunvalación, T258 4275, www.terracelodge.com. Small lodge with café, 5 rooms, heating, comfortable, helpful owner, Flavio, runs excellent tours by car, pick-up from Arica can be arranged.

$$-$ Hostal Cali, Baquedano s/n, T09-8536 1242, krlos_team@hotmail.com. Private or shared bath, pleasant, no heating, warm water, good restaurant, supermarket.

$$-$ Hostal Pachamama, Lord Cochrane s/n, Parinacota, T258 5814, www.hostalpacha mama.cl. Rooms sleep up to 3, shared bath, or self-contained cabin sleeps 5. Pleasant inner courtyard, basic rooms.

$$-$ Parinacota Trek, Baquedano 501, T9282 6194, www.parinacotatrek.cl. Hostel rooms and dorm, private or shared bath, washing machine, parking, open all year, near La Paloma and Gutiérrez buses. Also has travel agency for tours and treks throughout the region.

$$-$ Res La Paloma, O'Higgins 353, T09-9197 9319, www.translapaloma.cl. Some rooms with bath, hot showers after 0800 unless requested, no heating but lots of blankets, good food in large, warm restaurant, indoor parking; supermarket opposite.

Camping Sra Clementina Cáceres, blue door on C Lynch, allows camping in her garden and offers lunch.

Parinacota
Accommodation is available with various families, ask at food and artesanía stands. You can camp behind the CONAF office for free, great site.

Reserva Nacional Las Vicuñas: Salar de Surire *p726*
At Surire, the CONAF office has 4 beds available, prior application to CONAF in Arica essential.

🍴 Restaurants

Arica *p722, map p723*
Many good places on 21 de Mayo offering meals, drinks, real coffee, juices and outdoor seating.

$$$ Don Floro, V MacKenna 847, T223 1481. Good seafood, steaks and Peruvian specialities, good service, popular, cosy little place.

$$$ Los Aleros del 21, 21 de Mayo 736, T225 4641. One of the city's longest-established restaurants, specializing in southern Chilean cuisine, large portions, lots of pork dishes.

$$$ Maracuyá, San Martín 0321, at the northern end of Playa El Laucho south of the centre, T222 7600. Arica's premier restaurant specializing in fish and seafood. Expensive, but worth it. Has a sports bar on the top floor.

$$ Chifa El Mesón, Santa María 1364. One of several good-value Chinese restaurants in the area. Generous portions and clean kitchen.

$$ Cyclo Public, Diego Portales 1364 T226 2098. Open from 2030. Fashionable seafood and pasta restaurant, vegetarian options, reasonably priced.

$$ El Rey del Marisco, Colón 565, p 2, T222 9232. Seafood specialities. A timeless sort of place, in business for 35 years, very good.

$$ Mata Rangi, on the pier. Good food in fishy environment, good-value *menú de casa*.

$$-$ Café-Restaurante B, 21 de Mayo 233. Very good, extensive menu including seafood.

$$-$ Ostión Dorado, Playa Corazones. A small shack selling fabulous *empanadas* and other super-fresh seafood.

$ Evergreen, Baquedano entre O'Higgins y Maipú. Lunch only, vegetarian with good menu options and lots of fruit drinks. They also sell tofu and dried mushrooms.

$ La Bomba, Colón 357, at fire station, T225 5626. Good value *almuerzo* and friendly service.

$ Mercado Colón, Maipú y Colón. Several stalls offering tasty good-value lunches and fresh juices.

Parque Nacional Lauca: Putre *p725*
$ Kuchamarka, Baquedano between La Paloma supermarket and Hostal Cali. Popular, good value, specializes in local dishes, including alpaca, as well as vegetarian options.

🎵 Bars and clubs

Arica *p722, map p723*
Chill Out, 18 Sep y Lynch. Open till 0400, but doesn't get going until 2400, popular bar. Also **Bar Central**, next door.
Soho, Buenos Aires 209, Playa Chinchorro, T09-8905 1806. Opens at 1800, closed Wed. Pub, bar, nightclub, see Facebook for special nights.

🎭 Entertainment

Arica *p722, map p723*
Teatro Municipal de Arica, Baquedano 234. Wide variety of theatrical and musical events, as well as exhibitions.

🎉 Festivals

Arica *p722, map p723*
End-Jan or **Feb**, Con la Fuerza del Sol, a festival of Andean dance and music, a slightly more debauched version of the festival at La Tirana, www.aricafuerzadelsol.cl. **Jun**, Festival of Arica and the national *cueca* dance championships.
7 Jun, anniversary of the Chilean victory in the Battle of the Morro, with parties and fireworks.
29 Jun, San Pedro, religious service at fishing wharf and boat parades. First weekend of **Oct**, Virgen de las Peñas, pilgrimage to the site of the Virgin, some 90 km inland near Livilcar.

🛍 Shopping

Arica *p722, map p723*
Calle 21 de Mayo is pedestrianized, with many shops, restaurants and internet cafés.
Crafts Poblado Artesanal, Plaza Las Gredas, Hualles 2825 (take bus 2, 3 or 7). Expensive but especially good for musical instruments, open Tue-Sun 0930-1300, 1530-1930, *peña* Fri and Sat 2130; shop not always open out of season.
Markets Feria Turística Dominical, Sun market, along Chacabuco between Valásquez and Mackenna, mostly bric a brac. **Mercado Central**, Sotomayor y Sangra, between Colón and Baquedano. Mostly fruit and vegetables, mornings only. Smaller fruit and veg market, with food stalls, on Colón between 18 de Septiembre and Maipú.

Parque Nacional Lauca: Putre *p725*
Buy all food for the park in Putre, which has markets where bottled water, fresh bread, vegetables, meat, cheese and canned foods can be obtained. Fuel (both petrol and diesel) is available from the Cali and Paloma supermarkets; expect to pay a premium. **Sra Daria Condori**'s shop on O'Higgins sells locally made *artesanía* and naturally coloured alpaca wool. Other than a small shop with limited supplies in Parinacota, no food is available outside Putre. Take drinking water with you as water in the park is not safe.

⛰ What to do

Arica *p722, map p723*
Surfing There's good surfing at Playa Las Machas (good waves, relatively few people) and Playa Chinchorro, north of the city (good for beginners), and at La Ex Isla Alacrán, see www.arica-info.com. **La Ponderosa Beach House Inn**, see above, north of town near Playa Las Machas and the Lluta estuary, has surf shop, equipment rental, kitesurfing. Also for surfing lessons and equipment rental, **Magic Chile Surf School**, T231 1120, www.surfschool.cl. English spoken, best to call before 0900.
Swimming Olympic pool in **Parque Centenario**, Tue-Sat. Take No 5A bus from 18 de Septiembre. The best beach for swimming is Playa Chinchorro, north of town (bus 24). Buses 7 and 8 run to beaches south of town – the first 2 beaches, La Lisera and El Laucho, are both small and mainly for sunbathing. Playa Brava is popular for sunbathing but not swimming (dangerous currents).

Tour operators
Clinamen Safaris y Expediciones, Sotomayor 361, piso 2, T231 3289, www.clinamen.cl. Bespoke small-group expeditions (maximum 3 people) to the Altiplano. Guide Christian Rolf speaks fluent Spanish, English, German and French.
Latinorizons, Bolognesi 449, T225 0007, www.latinorizons.com. Specializes in tours to Parque Nacional Lauca and the Altiplano, small groups in 4WD; also tourist train rides from Arica, bike rental, not cheap, but good. Also run hostel in Putre.

Parinacota Expeditions, Thompson y Bolognesi, T225 6227, www.parinacota expediciones.cl. One of the oldest operators in Arica for altiplano tours.
Raices Andinas, Héroes del Morro 632, T223 3305, www.raicesandinas.com. Specializes in Altiplano trips, English spoken.
Suma Inti, Gonzalo Cerda 1366, T222 5685, www.sumainti.cl. Tours to the altiplano.

Parque Nacional Lauca *p725*
One-day tours are offered by most tour operators and some hotels in Arica, daily in season, according to demand at other times, but some find the minibuses cramped and dusty. You spend all day in the bus (0730-2030) and you will almost certainly suffer from *soroche*. You can leave the tour and continue another day as long as you ensure that the company will collect you when you want (tour companies try to charge double for this). Much better are 1½-day tours, 1400-1800 next day (eg Latinorizons), which include overnight in Putre and a stop on the ascent at the Aymara village of Socorama. For 5 or more, the most economical proposition is to hire a vehicle.
Alto Andino Nature Tours, Baquedano 299, Putre (Correo Putre) T09-9890 7291, www.birdingaltoandino.com. Specialist private birdwatching tours of the area and also walking tours along the Camino del Inca. All tours personalized and customized, English spoken, owner is an American biologist/naturalist.
Parinacota Trek, see Where to stay, above.
Tour Andino, C Baquedano 340, Putre, T9011 0702, www.tourandino.com. Comfortable 4WD tours from 1 to 4 days with Justino Jirón (owner) to Lauca and other areas, excellent, knowledgeable, flexible.

⊝ Transport

Arica *p722, map p723*
Air Airport 18 km north of city at Chacalluta, T221 1116. Taxi to town US$10, colectivo US$5 per person. Flights to **Santiago**, LAN and Sky (daily) via Iquique and, less frequently, Antofagasta. To **Lima**, LanPerú and others from Tacna (Peru), enquire at travel agencies in Arica.
Bus Local buses run from Maipú, US$0.60. Long distance buses leave from 2 adjacent terminals, both northeast of the centre at Av Portales y Santa María, T224 1390, many buses and colectivos (eg Nos 8, 18) pass (US$0.80), taxi US$2; terminal tax US$0.40. All luggage is carefully searched for fruit 30 mins prior to boarding and at 2 stops heading south. Bus company offices at bus terminal: **Pullman**, T222 3837; **Tur-Bus**, T224 1059.

To **Iquique**, frequent, US$10, 4½ hrs, also collective taxis, several companies, all in the terminal. To **Antofagasta**, US$20-32, 11 hrs. To **Calama**, 10 hrs, US$25, several companies, all between 2000 and 2200. To **San Pedro de Atacama**, 2200, 11½ hrs, US$35-55. To **La Serena**, 23 hrs, US$40-75. To **Santiago**, 30 hrs, a number of companies, US$76-98 (most serve meals of a kind, somewhat better on the more expensive services; student discounts available). To **Viña del Mar** and **Valparaíso**, 29 hrs, US$55. **International buses** See below for transport to Bolivia and Peru.
Car hire **American**, Gen Lagos 559, T225 7752, servturi@entelchile.net. **Cactus**, Baquedano 635, T225 7430, cactusrent@ latinmail.com. **Hertz**, Baquedano 999, T223 1487, and at airport, good service. **Klasse**, Velásquez 760, piso 2, Loc 25, T058-225 4498. good deals. Several others and at Chacalluta airport. Antifreeze is essential for Parque Nacional Lauca, 4WD if going off paved roads.
Taxi Colectivos on fixed routes within city limit line up on Maipú entre Velásquez y Colón (all are numbered), US$2 pp (more after 2000). Taxis are black and yellow and are scarce; hire a colectivo instead, US$2-3.

Border with Bolivia *p724*
Bus To **La Paz**, Bolivia, at least 4 companies from terminal, US$23, most via Chungará (some daily). Buses from Arica to Visviri, **Humire**, T222 0198/226 0164, Tue and Fri, 1030, US$12, also Sun 0830 en route to La Paz; **Martínez**, Tue and Fri 2230 en route to La Paz, both from terminal. Colectivos from Arica US$15. In Visviri take a jeep across the border to Charaña. Buses from Charaña to La Paz, leave before 1000, US$6, 6 hrs.

Border with Peru *p725*
Colectivos Run from the international bus terminal on Diego Portales to **Tacna**, US$4 pp,

1½ hrs. There are many companies and you will be besieged by drivers. For quickest service take a Peruvian colectivo heading back to Peru. Give your passport to the colectivo office where your papers will be filled. After that, drivers take care of all the paperwork. Also buses from the same terminal, US$2, 1 hr longer than journey by colectivo. For Arequipa it is best to go to Tacna and catch an onward bus there.

Train Station at Máximo Lira, by the port. In 2014, no trains were running across the border to **Tacna**.

Parque Nacional Lauca *p725*
Bus La Paloma (Flota Paco) buses leave Germán Riesco 2071, Arica, T222 2710 (bus U from centre) for **Putre** daily at 0700, 3-4 hrs, US$6, returning from La Paloma supermarket 1400 (book in advance – beware overcharging, overworked drivers); also **Guttiérez**, Esteban Ríos 2140, Arica, T222 9338, Mon, Wed, Fri 0700, return same days, 1700. **Jurasi** collective taxi leaves Arica daily at 0700, picks up at hotels, T222 2813, US$12. If you take an Arica–La Paz bus for Putre, it is 3 km from the crossroads to the town at some 4000 m, tough if you've come straight up from sea level. **Humire** buses run to **Parinacota** 1030, Tue and Fri, US$8. Hostal Cali runs buses to Bolivia. Bus to La Paz from Putre crossroads or Lago Chungará can be arranged in Arica (same fare as from Arica).
Hitchhiking Hitching back to Arica is not difficult, with lots of carabineros coming and going; you may be able to bargain on one of the tour buses. Trucks from Arica to La Paz sometimes give lifts, a good place to try is at the Poconchile control point, 37 km from Arica, but to get to this point can cost more than taking a direct bus from the terminal.

⊙ Directory

Arica *p722, map p723*
Banks Many Redbanc ATMs on 21 de Mayo and by Plaza Colón. Money changers on 21 de Mayo and its junction with Colón, some accept TCs. **Consulates** Bolivia, P Lynch 298, T258 3390, colivian_arica@yahoo.es. **Peru**, Av 18 de Setiembre 1554, T223 1020, conperarica@ terra.cl. **Language classes** SW Academia de Artes y Lenguas, 21 de Mayo 483, p 3, T225 8645, www.spanishinchile. blogspot.com. Chilean/British school. **Useful addresses** CONAF, Av Vicuña MacKenna 820, T220 1200, aricayparinacota. oirs@conaf.cl. Mon-Fri 0830-1300, 1430-1630 (take Colectivo 1). Aug-Nov is best season for mountain climbing; permits needed for summits near borders. Either go to the governor's office in Putre, or contact **Dirección Nacional de Fronteras y Límites del Estado** (DIFROL) Bandera 52, p 5, Santiago, T02-2679 4200, in advance, listing the mountains you wish to climb.

Parque Nacional Lauca: Putre *p725*
Banks Bank in Putre changes dollars but commission on TCs is very high. The ATM does not take international cards.

Central Valley

One of the world's most fecund and beautiful landscapes, with snowclad peaks of the Andes to the east and the Cordillera de la Costa to the west, the Central Valley contains most of Chile's population. A region of small towns, farms and vineyards, it has several protected areas of natural beauty. Five major rivers cross the Central Valley, cutting through the Coastal Range to the Pacific: from north to south these are the Rapel, Mataquito, Maule, Itata and Biobío. Some of the river valleys provide ideal conditions for growing grapes and making wine and you can wander between vineyards. As it is the heart of Chilean cowboy country you can see displays of horsemanship at rural shows. It is also a region plagued by earthquakes, most recently on 27 February 2010.

Rancagua to Chillán

Rancagua → *Phone code: 072. Colour map 8, B1. Population: 167,000.*
The capital of VI Región (Libertador Gen Bernardo O'Higgins) lies on the Río Cachapoal, 82 km south of Santiago. Founded in 1743, it is a service and market centre. At the heart of the city is an attractive tree-lined plaza, the Plaza de los Héroes, and several streets of single-storey colonial-style houses. In the centre of the plaza is an equestrian statue of O'Higgins. The main commercial area lies along Avenida Independencia, which runs west from the plaza towards the bus and rail terminals. The **Museo Regional** ① *Estado 685, T222 1524, www.museorancagua.cl, Tue-Fri 1000-1800, Sat-Sun 0900-1300,* has collections on regional history and culture and temporary exhibitions. The **National Rodeo Championships** are held at the end of March in the Complejo Deportivo, north of the centre (plenty of opportunities for purchasing cowboy items). **Tourist office** ① *Germán Riesco 277, T223 0413, inforancagua@sernatur.cl.*

Around **Santa Cruz** and **San Fernando** (51 km south of Rancagua) is the Colchagua Valley, a very successful wine-producing zone. For details of vineyards, hotels, tours and festivals, visit the **Ruta del Vino** ① *Plaza de Armas 298, Santa Cruz, T072-282 3199, www.rutadelvino.cl.* There is a **Museo de Colchagua** ① *Av Errázuriz 145, Santa Cruz, T282 1050, www.museocolchagua.cl, daily 1000-1800, US$11.* For information on the Cachapoal wine producing zone, with details on tours and vineyard visits, enquire at the **Ruta del Vino Cachapoal** ① *109-8232 1399.* On the coast, 126 km west of San Fernando, is **Pichilemu**, Chile's surfing capital, now back in business after the 2010 earthquake. The tourism pages of the online newspaper **www.pichilemunews.cl** are informative; see also **www.pichilemu.cl** and **www.depichilemu.cl** for lodgings. Accommodation ranges from the "boutique" surfers' lodge, **Alaia** (Punta de Lobos 681, www.hotelalaia.com) to **La Sirena Insolente** (Camino Punta de Lobos 169, www.sirenainsolentehostel.cl).

Curicó → *Phone code: 075. Colour map 8, B1. Population: 103,919. Altitude: 200 m.*
Between the Río Lontué and Río Teno, 192 km from Santiago, Curicó is the only town of any size in the Mataquito Valley. It was founded in 1744. Most of the historic centre was destroyed in the February 2010 earthquake. In mid-March is the **Fiesta de la Vendimia** with displays on traditional wine-making. Overlooking the city, the surrounding countryside and with views to the distant Andean peaks is Cerro Condell (100 m); it is an easy climb to the summit from where there are a number of walks. One of the largest bodegas in Chile, **Miguel Torres** ① *5 km south of the city, T256 4100, www.migueltorres.cl, daily 1000-1700 Apr-Oct, daily 1000-1900 Nov-Mar, tours in Spanish only; getting there: take a bus for Molina from the local terminal or outside the railway station and get off at Km 195 on the Pan-American Highway,* is worth a visit. For information on the vineyards of Curicó, see the **Ruta del Vino del Valle de Curicó** ① *Prat 301-A, Curicó, T232 8972, www.rutadelvinocurico.cl, Mon-Fri 0900-1400, 1530-1930.*

Parque Nacional Radal Siete Tazas
① *Entry US$8.*
The park is in two parts, one at Radal, 65 km east of Curicó, the other at Parque Inglés, 9 km further east. At Radal, the Río Claro flows through a series of seven rock cups (*siete tazas*) each with a pool emptying into the next by a waterfall. The river goes through a canyon, 15 m deep but only 1.5 m wide, ending abruptly in a cliff and a beautiful waterfall. There is excellent trekking in the park, through beautiful woods and scenery, similar to what can be found further south, but with a better climate.

Talca → *Phone code: 071. Colour map 8, B1. Population: 175,000.*
At 56 km south of Curicó (258 km from Santiago) this is the most important city between Santiago and Concepción. It is a major manufacturing centre and the capital of VII Región (Maule). Founded in 1692, Talca was destroyed by earthquakes in 1742 and 1928 and was again

heavily damaged in Februry 2010. The colonial mansion in which Bernardo O'Higgins lived as a child, **Museo O'Higginiano** ① *1 Norte 875, T261 5880, www.museodetalca.cl, currently closed to the public*, was later the headquarters of O'Higgins' Patriot Government in 1813-1814 (before his defeat at Rancagua). In 1818 O'Higgins signed the declaration of Chilean independence here. **Paseo peatonal**, Calle 1 Sur entre 3 y 6 Oriente, is a nice place for a stroll, with handicrafts, cafés, bookstalls and shops. The **Maule Valley** ① *Ruta del Vino, Av Circunvalación Oriente 1055, lobby Hotel Casino Talca, T09-8157 9951, www.valledelmaule.cl*, is another wine-producing region. There's a **tourist office** ① *C 1 Poniente 1150 p 1 y 4, T223 3669, infomaule@sernatur.cl, Mon-Fri 0830-1730*. See www.talca.cl, and **CONAF** ① *C 4 Norte 1673, T220 9517, maule.oirs@conaf.cl*.

Constitución and the coast

At the mouth of the Río Maule, 89 km from San Javier on the Pan-American Highway (south of Talca), **Constitución** is an important port and seaside resort. The town and coast were almost completely destroyed in February 2010. The seafront has been remodelled with restaurants open all year. Other services such as banks, ATMs, internet, market and bus station are all working and there is a daily Talca-Constitución train, a lovely 3¼-hour ride beside the river, with halts at villages. Boats trips can be taken on the Río Maule, 5 blocks from the Plaza.

Vilches

This is the starting point for the climb to the volcanoes **Quizapú** (3050 m) and **Descabezado** (3850 m), both of which are in the **Reserva Nacional Altos del Lircay** ① *US$7, entrance 2 km from Alto Vilches bus stop*, which covers 12,163 ha. There are well-signed trails and horses can be hired in Alto Vilches. See www.ecoturismovilches.cl for hiking and horse riding guides, accommodation and other community tourism. Two stand-out treks are to Enladrillado (10 km), a mysterious 800 m by 60 m rock platform, subject to many theories including UFO landings, with fabulous views of Descabezado and Cerro Azul. A further 1.5 km is Laguna del Alto. Allow eight to 10 hours to the lake and back. A second walk goes to Mirador del Venado from where you can descend to the river and the lovely Valle del Venado. From here you can continue to Descabezado Grande and Quizapú (five to six days overall). Near the entrance is CONAF administration with full information on trails and activities.

To the border with Argentina: Paso Pehuenche

From Talca, the international route to the border goes through San Clemente and up the broad valley of the Río Maule to reach the Argentine border at Paso Pehuenche (2553 m). Off this road, beyond the town of Armerillo, is the private **Parque Natural y Refugio Tricahue**. A Belgian/Chilean enterprise, the park is open all year (www.parquetricahue.cl, US$4) for trekking, with snowshoes in winter, cycling, fishing. The beautiful **refugio ($$-$**, www.refugio-tricahue.cl) has cabins, sauna, pool, bicycle hire and kitchen (take your own food – no meals, or walk 500 m to El Fosforito). Bus Talca–Armerillo, US$2, six a day.

An alternative route, south of Talca, is paved for the first 65 km, running southeast from the Panamericana along **Lago Colbún**. At the western end of the lake is the town of Colbún, from where a road goes to Linares on the Panamericana. Thermal springs 5 km south of Colbún at Panimávida, and 12 km, Quinamávida. While in Panimávida, try the local *Bebida Panimávida*, made from spring water, sparkling or still, flavoured with lemon or raspberry. The road southeast from Lago Colbún to the Paso is poor and unpaved. Chilean customs is at La Mina, 106 km from Talca, 60 km from the border. On the Argentine side the road continues to Malargüe and San Rafael. The border is open December-March 0800-2100, April-November 0800-1900.

Chillán → *Phone code: 042. Colour map 8, B1. Population: 146,000. Altitude: 118 m.*
Chillán, 150 km south of Talca, is capital of Ñuble province. Following an earthquake in 1833, the site was moved slightly to the northwest, though the older site, Chillán Viejo, is still occupied. Further earthquakes in 1939, 1960 and 2010, ensured that few old buildings have survived. Chillán was the birthplace of Bernardo O'Higgins and of the world-famous pianist, Claudio Arrau (interactive museum at Arrau 558, T243 3390). The **Fiesta de la Vendimia** is an annual wine festival held in the third week in March. **Tourist office** ① *Centro de Gestión Turística Chillán, Edif Los Héroes, of 324, T243 3349. See www.municipalidadchillan.cl.*

The centre of the city is **Plaza O'Higgins**, on which stands the modern **Cathedral** designed to resist earthquakes. **San Francisco** church, three blocks northeast, has a museum of religious and historical artefacts. Above the main entrance is a mural by Luis Guzmán Molina, a local artist, an interpretation of the life of San Francisco in a Chilean context. Northwest of the Plaza O'Higgins, on the Plaza Héroes de Iquique, is the **Escuela México**. It was donated to the city after the 1939 earthquake. In its library are murals by the great Mexican artists David Alvaro Siqueiros and Xavier Guerrero which present allegories of Chilean and Mexican history. The **Mercado y Feria Municipal** (covered and open markets at Riquelme y Maipón) sell regional arts and crafts, including from the nearby village of Quinchamalí. They also have many cheap, good restaurants, serving regional dishes; open daily, Sunday until 1300. Three blocks further south is the **Museo Naval El Chinchorro** ① *Collin y I Riquelme,* containing naval artifacts and models of Chilean vessels. In Chillán Viejo (southwest of the centre) there is a monument, art gallery and park at **O'Higgins' birthplace** ① *park 0830-2000.*

Termas de Chillán
East of Chillán 82 km by good road (paved for the first 50 km), 1850 m up in the Cordillera, are thermal baths and, above, the largest ski resort in southern Chile. There are two open-air thermal pools (officially for hotel guests only) and a health spa with jacuzzis, sauna, mud baths, etc. Summer activities include horse riding, trekking, canyoning, canopy zip lines, golf and mountain biking. Suitable for families and beginners and cheaper than centres nearer Santiago, the ski resort has 32 runs (the longest is 13 km), 11 lifts, snowboarding and other activities. It also has two hotels (the Gran Hotel and the Pirimahuida) and condominium apartments. Information and reservations from **Termas de Chillán Resort de Montaña** ① *T042 243 4200, www.termaschillan.cl.*

ⓦ Rancagua to Chillán listings

For hotel and restaurant price codes, and other relevant information, see Essentials.

ⓦ Where to stay

Rancagua *p731*
$$$ Aguila Real, Brasil 1045, T222 2047, hotel aguilareal@terra.cl. Modern 3-star, with restaurant. Some English spoken.
$$$ Mar Andino, Bulnes 370, T264 5400, www.hotelmarandino.cl. New, modern, comfortable, decent restaurant, business centre, pool.
$$ Hostal El Parrón, San Martín 135, T275 8550, www.hostalelparron.cl. 2-storey art-deco-style house in the centre, singles, doubles, triples, parking, patio.

Parque Nacional Radal Siete Tazas *p731*
$$ Hostería Flor de la Canela, Parque Inglés, Km 9 al interior de El Radal, T249 1613. Open all year, breakfast extra, good food, good value.

Camping
$$$-$ Valle de las Catas, Camino Radal-Parque Inglés (Fundo Frutillar), T09-1689 7820. Cabins for 4-6 people or camping, hot showers, good service, convenient.
$ Los Robles, Parque Inglés, Km 7 al interior de El Radal, T222 8029. Open all year, toilets, hot showers, tables and benches, good.

Talca *p731*

$$$ Terrabella, 1 Sur 641, T222 6555, terrabella@hotel.tie.cl. Good service, cafetería and swimming pool.

$$$-$$ Casa Chueca, Camino Las Rastras, 4 km from Talca by the Río Lircay, T071-197 0096, T09-9419 0625, www.trekkingchile. com. Closed Jun-Aug. Phone hostal from bus terminal for directions on how to get there. From suites to rooms with shared bath. Vegetarian restaurant, Austrian and German owners, many languages spoken, lovely setting, pool, mountain bikes, good trekking, riding and climbing tours.

$$ Hostal del Puente, 1 Sur 401, T222 0930, www.hostaldelpuente.cl. Family-owned, parking in central courtyard, lovely gardens, English spoken, pleasant atmosphere and surroundings.

$$ Hostal del Río, 1 Sur 407, T251 0218, www.hostaldelrio.cl. Rival to Del Puente next door, a little cheaper, also good.

Constitución *p732*

$$$ Casa Puccllana, Los Hibiscus 1855, Villa Copihue, T267 3393. Sea view, perched above the Piedra de la Iglesia, modern rooms, parking.

$$$ Las Azucenas, Alameda 910, T267 1933, http://lasazucenashotel.com. Colonial style, 6 well-equipped and spacious rooms. Local cuisine and wines offered.

$$ Cabañas Playa el Cable, 3km from Constitución on Playa el Cable, T267 0595, www. playaelcable.cl. Beachfront rooms and restaurant, pool, timber and glass, modern and light.

Vilches *p732*

$$ Refugio Galo, Vilches Altos, www.refugio degalo.com. Open all year for food and lodging, warm welcome, good service, horse riding.

$$-$ pp Refugio Biotamaule, T09-9609 3644, www.biotamaule.blogspot.co.uk. Open in summer only, meals available.

Camping Antahuaras 500 m from Reserva Altos de Lircay administration, at 1300 m, hot showers, good services, light at each site, beautiful location.

Chillán *p733*

$$$ Gran Hotel Isabel Riquelme, Constitución 576, T243 4400, www.

hotelisabelriquelme.cl. Central business hotel, with restaurant, parking.

$$$ Libertador, Libertad 85, T222 3255, www.hlbo.cl. Quite spacious rooms, parking.

$$$-$$ Cordillera, Isabel Riquelme 652, T287 6730, hotelcordillera@hotmail.cl. 3-star, central, small, all rooms with heating, good.

$$ Ventura, O'Higgins 638, T222 7588, www.hotelventura.cl. 3 star, pleasant garden, good home cooked food in restaurant.

Termas de Chillán *p733*

$$$ Cabañas La Piedra, Los Coihues 1143, Km 48 on road to Termas de Chillán, Recinto, T9673 4250, www.cabanaslapiedra. cl. 5 *cabañas* sleep 2, 4 or 8, nestled in forest, "tranquil and rejuvenating", pool, hiking trips to the mountains, music performances outdoors around the pool under stars, good restaurants close by. Manager Jacqueline van Nunen speaks English, German, Dutch, Spanish.

$$$ Robledal, at Las Trancas on the road to the Termas, Km 72 from Chillán, T243 2030, www.hotelrobledal.cl. Pleasant rooms, bar, restaurant, sauna and jacuzzi, tours offered.

$$$-$$ MI Lodge, T09-9321 7567, www.mi snowchile.com. Small lodge with fine views, hot tub and good restaurant. Price depends on season.

There are many *cabañas* in Las Trancas, usually **$$$** pp for up to 6, see www.vallelas trancas.cl. Also **$ Hostelling International**, Km 73.5, T242 3718, hostellinglastrancas@ gmail.com. Camping available, 2 km from the slopes.

🍴 Restaurants

Rancagua *p731*

$ La Cocina Artesanal, O'Carroll 60, T224 1389. Traditional meat and seafood dishes.

Curicó *p731*

Tortas Montero, Prat 669. Salón de té, restaurant and manufacturer of traditional *tortas de manjar* and *dulce de alcayotas*.

Talca *p731*

There are cheap local restaurants and fresh food on sale at the Mercado Municipal, entrance on C 1 Norte.

$ Casino de Bomberos, 2 Sur y 5 Oriente. Good value, open every day. It has the Museo Bomberil Benito Riquelme attached.

⊖ Transport

Rancagua *p731*
Bus The terminal for regional buses is at Doctor Salinas y Calvo, T223 6938, just north of the market. Frequent services to **Santiago** from Tur-Bus terminal at O'Carroll 1175, T223 0482, US$5.45, 1¼ hrs. Main terminal for long-distance buses is at Av O'Higgins 0480, T222 5425.
Train Train station on Av La Marina, T223 8530, T0600-585 5000 for tickets. Main line services between Santiago and Chillán stop here, US$3, 1 hr. Also regular services to/from **Santiago** on Metrotren, 1¼ hrs.

Curicó *p731*
Bus Bus terminal is on Prat, opposite the train station. Local and long distance services leave from here. Tur-Bus stop and office, M de Velasco, 1 block south, T231 2115. Pullman del Sur terminal, Henríquez y Carmen. Many south bound buses bypass Curicó, but can be caught by waiting outside town. To **Santiago** US$7.25, 2½ hrs, several companies, frequent. To **Talca** every 15 mins, US$3.40, 1 hr. To **Temuco**, Alsa and Tur-Bus, US$16-24, 7 hrs.
Train Station is at the west end of Prat, 4 blocks west of Plaza de Armas, T231 0020, tickets from Maipú 657, T0600-585 5000. To/from **Santiago**, 5-6 a day, 2 hrs 20 mins, US$5.

Parque Nacional Radal Siete Tazas *p731*
Take a minibus from Curicó Terminal to **Molina**, 26 km south, US$1; from Molina bus at 1700, return 0800, to **Radal** village, 3 hrs, US$3.20; from 16 Dec to 28 Feb there are 6 daily departures, Buses Hernández and Buses Radal. It's a further 2 km to La Vela de la Novia and 4 km to Siete Tazas. It's 9 km from Radal to Parque Inglés, US$3.40. Access by car is best as the road through the park is paved.

Talca *p731*
Bus Terminal at 12 Oriente y 2 Sur. From **Santiago**, US$6.60. To **Chillán**, frequent,

US$5.40. To **Temuco**, US$13.50, 6 hrs. To **Puerto Montt**, US$22-37, 10½ hrs. To **Alto Vilches** (for Altos del Lircay), bus from platform 23, US$3.40, 6 a day in summer 0715-1730, 3-4 from 0715 (0800 on Sun) Mar-Dec.
Car hire Trekker Ltda, Casilla 143, Talca, T2197 2757, 09-8501 6211, www.trekkerchile. com. Has camper vans, trucks and 4WD vehicles available for routes throughout Chile and into Argentina.
Train Station is at Av 2 Sur y 11 Oriente, T0600-585 5000. To/from **Santiago**, 5-6 a day, 3 hrs, US$6. Talca-**Constitución** daily 0715, return 1615, 3½ hrs, US$4 one way, preference given to local residents.

Constitución *p732*
Bus To **Santiago**, Pullman del Sur, US$12.75.

Chillán *p733*
Bus Two long-distance terminals: Central, Brasil y Constitución (Tur-Bus, Línea Azul); Northern, Ecuador y O'Higgins for other companies. Local buses leave from Maipón y Sgto Aldea. To **Santiago**, 5½ hrs, US$17-36. To **Concepción**, every 30 mins, 1½ hrs, US$4. To **Temuco**, 3½ hrs, US$16.
Train Station, 5 blocks west of Plaza de Armas on Brasil, T0600-585 5000. To/from **Santiago**, 5-6 a day, 5 hrs, US$10.75-23.50.
Note No trains beyond Chillán and no date set for resumption.

Termas de Chillán *p733*
Ski buses run Jun-Sep from Libertador 1042 at 0800 and from Chillán Ski Centre, subject to demand, US$60 (includes lift pass). Bus service Fri, Sat, Sun and holidays 0750, 1320, with **Rem Bus**, Maipón 890, of 15, T222 9377, return 0940, 1650, US$12 return, book in advance. Also **Montecinos**, Sgto Aldea 647, T222 1105. Direct bus from **Santiago** with Nilahue (Porto Seguro 4420, Santiago, T02-2776 1139, www. busesnilahue.cl, in Chillán T270569). At busy periods hitching may be possible from Chillán Ski Centre.

The third biggest city in Chile (516 km from Santiago) and the most important city in southern Chile, is also a major industrial centre. Capital of VIII Región (Biobío), Concepción is 15 km up the Biobío River. Founded in 1550, Concepción became a frontier stronghold in the war against the Mapuche after 1600. Destroyed by an earthquake in 1751, it was moved to its present site in 1764. It was severely damaged again by the February 2010 earthquake.

The climate is very agreeable in summer, but from April to September the rains are heavy; the annual average rainfall, nearly all of which falls in those six months, is from 1250 mm to 1500 mm. **Tourist office: Sernatur** ① *Aníbal Pinto 460, T274 1337, infobiobio@sernatur.cl.* **CONAF** ① *Barros Arana 215, p 2, T262 4000, biobio.oirs@conaf.cl.*

Places in and around Concepción

In the attractive **Plaza de Armas**, or de la Independencia, at the centre are the **Intendencia** and the **Cathedral**. It was here that Bernardo O'Higgins proclaimed the independence of Chile on 1 January 1818. **Cerro Caracol** can easily be reached on foot starting from the statue of Don Juan Martínez de Rozas in the Parque Ecuador, arriving at the Mirador Chileno after 15 minutes. From here it is another 20 minutes' climb to **Cerro Alemán**. The **Biobío** and its valley running down to the sea lie below.

The **Galería de la Historia** ① *Lincoyán y V Lamas by Parque Ecuador*, is a depiction of the history of Concepción and the region; upstairs is a collection of Chilean painting. The **Casa del Arte** ① *Chacabuco y Paicaví, near Plaza Perú, T220 4290*, contains the University art collection; the entrance hall is dominated by La Presencia de América Latina, by the Mexican Jorge González Camerena (1965), a mural depicting Latin American history. Free explanations are given by University Art students.

The **Parque Museo, Pedro del Río Zañartu** ① *16 km from Concepción on the Hualpen peninsula, T241 7386, www.parquepedrodelrio.cl, US$4 per car, Tue-Sun 1000-1900 in summer, 0900-1800 in winter*, is a house built around 1885 (a National Monument) and its gardens. It contains beautiful pieces from all over the world. The park, a nature sanctuary, also contains Playa Rocoto, at the mouth of the Río Biobío. Take a city bus to Hualpencillo from Freire, ask the driver to let you out then walk 40 minutes, or hitch. Go along Avenida Las Golondrinas to the Enap oil refinery, turn left, then right (it is signed).

Costa del Carbón

South of the Biobío is the Costa del Carbón, until recently the main coal producing area of Chile, linked with Concepción by road and two bridges over the Biobío. **Lota** (*Population: 52,000; 42 km south of Concepción*) was, until its closure in 1997, the site of the most important **coal mine** in Chile. The **Parque de Lota Isidora Cousiño**, covering 14 ha on a promontory to the west of the town, was the life's work of Isidora Goyenechea de Cousiño, whose family owned the mine, and is now a national monument. Laid out by an English landscape architect in 1862-1872, it contains plants from all over the world, ornaments imported from Europe, romantic paths and shady nooks overlooking the sea, and peafowl and pheasants roaming freely. South of Lota the road runs past the seaside resort of **Laraquete** where there are miles of golden sand, which is very popular in summer.

Cañete → *Phone code: 041. Colour map 8, C1. Population: 15,642.*

A small town, 130 km south of Concepción, on the site of Fort Tucapel where Pedro de Valdivia and 52 of his men were killed by Mapuche warriors in 1553. **Museo Mapuche** ① *Juan Antonio Ríos, T261 1093, www.museomapuchecanete.cl, 1 km south on the road to Contulmo, in Jan-Feb open Mon-Fri 0930-1730, Sat-Sun 1100-1730, Sun 1300-1730, rest of year Tue-Fri 0930-1730, Sat-Sun 1300-1730, US$1.25*, is housed in a modern building inspired by the traditional Mapuche ruca; includes Mapuche ceramics and textiles. There is nowhere to change dollars in town.

Contulmo → *Population: 2000.*

A road runs south from Cañete along the north side of **Lago Lanalhue** to Contulmo, a sleepy village at the foot of the Cordillera. It hosts a **Semana Musical** (music week) in January. The wooden Grollmus House and Mill are 3 km northwest along the south side of the lake. The house, dating from 1918, has a fine collection of every colour of copihue (the national flower) in a splendid garden. The mill, built in 1928, contains the original wooden machinery. From here the track runs a further 9 km north to the **Posada Campesina Alemana**, an old German-style hotel in a fantastic spot at the water's edge. The **Monumento Natural Contulmo**, 8 km south and administered by **CONAF** ① *Av Pdte Frei 288, Cañete, T261 1241*, covers 82 ha of native forest.

Los Angeles and around → *Phone code: 043. Colour map 8, C1. Population: 114,000.*

On the Pan-American Highway, Los Angeles is 110 km south of Chillán. It is the capital of Biobío province. Founded in 1739 as a fort, it was destroyed several times by the Mapuche. Here, too, severe damage was recorded in February 2010. It has a large Plaza de Armas and a good daily market. **Tourist office**: ① *Caupolicán p 3, of 6, T231 7107*; **CONAF** ① *J Manzo de Velasco 275, T232 1086.* Some 25 km north of Los Angeles is the spectacular **Salto El Laja** where the Río Laja plunges 47 m over the rocks. Numerous tour groups stop here and the place is filled with tourist kiosks. There are hotels in the town centre.

Parque Nacional Laguna de Laja

East of Los Angeles via a 93 km road which runs past the impressive rapids of the Río Laja, this park is dominated by the active Antuco volcano (2985 m) and the glacier-covered Sierra Velluda. The Laguna is surrounded by stark scenery of scrub and lava. There are 46 species of birds including condors and the rare Andean gull. There are several trails. Nearby is the **Club de Esquí de Los Angeles** with two ski-lifts, giving a combined run of 4 km on the Antuco volcano (season May-August).

Angol → *Phone code: 045. Colour map 8, C1. Population: 39,000.*

Capital of the Province of Malleco, Angol is reached from Collipulli and Los Angeles. Founded by Valdivia in 1552, it was seven times destroyed by the *indígenas* and rebuilt. The church and convent of **San Beneventura**, northwest of the attractive Plaza de Armas, built in 1863, became the centre for missionary work among the Mapuche. El Vergel, founded in 1880 as an experimental fruit-growing nursery, now includes an attractive park and the **Museo Dillman Bullock** ① *Mon-Fri 0900-1900, Sat-Sun 1000-1900, US$1, 5 km from town, colectivo No 2*, with pre-Columbian indigenous artefacts. There is a **tourist office** ① *O'Higgins s/n, T045-271 1255*, across bridge from the bus terminal. **CONAF** ① *Prat 191, p 2, T271 1870.*

Parque Nacional Nahuelbuta

Situated in the coastal mountain range at an altitude of 800-1550 m, this beautiful park covers 6832 ha of forest and offers views over both the sea and the Andes. Although the forest includes many species of trees, the monkey puzzle (araucaria) is most striking; some are over 2000 years old, 50 m high and 3 m in diameter. There are over 16 species of orchids as well as pudu deer, Chiloé foxes, pumas, black woodpeckers and parrots. There is a **Visitor Centre** ① *at Pehuenco, 5 km from the entrance, www.conaf.cl or www.parquenahuelbuta.cl, US$8 for foreigners*, camping is near the Visitor Centre (US$24); there are many other campsites along the road from El Cruce to the entrance, at Km 20 and Km 21.

⊙ Concepción and around listings

For hotel and restaurant price codes, and other relevant information, see Essentials.

● Where to stay

Concepción *p736*
$$$$ Sonesta, C A No 809, Brisas del Sol, Talcahuano, T210 9500, www.sonesta.com. Close to airport, attached to casino Marina del Sol, rooms and suites with all facilities, business centre.
$$$ Alborada, Barros Arana 457, T291 1121, www.hotelalborada.cl. Good 4-star with all mod cons, disabled-friendly, tours offered.
$$$ El Dorado, Barros Arana 348, T222 9400, www.hoteleldorado.cl. Comfortable, spacious rooms, central, bar, cafeteria, parking.
$$ Concepción, Serrano 512, T222 8851, www.hotelconcepcion.cl. Central, comfortable, heating, English spoken.
$$ Hostal Antuco, Barros Arana 741, flats 31-33, T223 5485, hostalantuco@ hotmail.com. Entry via Galería Martínez. Some rooms with bath. Simple and spartan, but clean and reasonable value.
$$ Hostal Bianca, Salas 643-C, T225 2103, www.hostalbianca.cl. Private or shared bath, food available, parking, student discounts.
$$ Maquehue, Barros Arana 786, p 7, T221 0261, www.hotelmaquehue.cl. Good services, with restaurant, laundry.

Cañete *p736*
$$ Nahuelbuta, Villagrán 644, T261 1073, hotelnahuelbuta@lanalhueturismo.cl. Private or shared without bath, pleasant, parking.
$$-$ Derby, Mariñán y Condell, T261 1960. Shared bath, basic, restaurant.
$$-$ Gajardo, 7° de la Línea 817 (1 block from plaza). Shared bath, old fashioned, pleasant rooms.

Contulmo *p737*
$ Central, Millaray 131, T261 8089, hotelcentral @lanalhueturismo.cl. Shared bath, no sign, very hospitable.

Lago Lanalhue
$$$ Hostal Licahue, 4 km north of Contulmo towards Cañete, T09-9779 7188, www.licahue.cl. Hotel rooms and cabins, attractively set overlooking lake, pool.
Camping Camping Huilquehue, 15 km south of Cañete on lakeside. Elicura, Contulmo. Playa Blanca, Playa Blanca, 10 km north of Contulmo.

Los Angeles and around *p737*
$$$ Salto del Laja, Salto El Laja, T232 1706, www.saltodellaja.cl. Good rooms, fine restaurant, 2 pools, on an island overlooking the falls.
$$$-$$ El Rincón, Panamericana Sur Km 494 (20 km north of Los Angeles), exit Perales/El Olivo, 2 km east, T09-9441 5019, www.elrincon chile.cl. New English/German owners, private or shared bath. Beautiful, beside a small river, restful, fresh food from organic garden, good base for excursions, English, French, German, Italian and Spanish spoken, cash only.
$$-$ Complejo Turístico Los Manantiales, Salto El Laja, T231 4275, www.losmanantiales. saltosdellaja.com. Hotel rooms, cabins and camping. Private or shared bathrooms, even for tents.

Parque Nacional Laguna de Laja *p737*
$$-$ Cabañas Lagunillas, T232 1086, 2 km from park entrance. Open all year, cabins sleep 6, lovely spot close to the river among pine woods, restaurant, also camping.
$ 2 other *refugios*: Digeder, 11 km from the park entrance, and Universidad de Concepción, both on slopes of Volcán Antuco, for both T041-222 9054, office O'Higgins 740.

❼ Restaurants

Concepción *p736*
$$ La Casa del Cinzano Penquista, Castellón 881. Characterful restaurant, decorated with movie memorabilia and old photos, Chilean food, jazz and blues music.
$ Quick Biss, O'Higgins entre Tucapel y Castellón. Salads, real coffee, good lunches and service.

○ Shopping

Concepción *p736*
The main shopping area is north of Plaza de Armas.
Handicrafts Feria Artesanal, Freire 777. Mercado Municipal, 1 block west of the Plaza de Armas. Seafood, fruit and veg.

○ What to do

Concepción *p736*
Hello Chile, T09-8433 0101, www.hello-chile. com. For tours of the Biobío region and further afield, Austrian/Chilean-run, Spanish courses, car hire arranged, lots of information.

○ Transport

Concepción *p736*
Air Airport north of the city, off the main road to Talcahuano. In summer flights daily to and from **Santiago** (LAN and Sky), fewer in winter; connections to **Temuco**, **Puerto Montt** and **Punta Arenas**.
Bus Terminal Collao, for long distance services (also for **Lota**, **Cañete** and **Contulmo**), is 2 km east, on Av Gral Bonilla, next to football and athletics stadium. (Several buses to city centre, US$0.75, taxi US$5.) Tur-Bus, Línea Azul and Buses Bío Bío services leave from Terminal Camilo Henríquez 2 km northeast of main terminal on J M García, reached by buses from Av Maipú in centre, via Terminal Collao. To **Santiago**, 6½ hrs, US$25-36. To **Los Angeles**, US$4. To **Loncoche**, 5½ hrs, US$12. To **Pucón**, direct in summer only, 7 hrs, US$18. To **Valdivia**, 7 hrs, US$16-34. To **Puerto Montt** several companies, US$21-36, about 9 hrs. Best direct bus to **Chillán** is Línea Azul, 2 hrs, US$3.
Train Station at Prat y Barros Arana, Bío Tren ticket office, Av Padre Hurtado 570, T286 8015, www.biotren.cl, for suburban services in rush hour. Direct long-distance services to Santiago are suspended.

Costa del Carbón: Lota *p736*
Bus Concepción-Lota, 1½ hrs, US$2. Many buses bypass the centre: catch them from the main road.

Cañete *p736*
Bus Leave from 2 different terminals: J Ewert and Inter Sur from Riquelme y 7° de la Línea, Jeldres, Erbuc and other companies from the Terminal Municipal, Serrano y Villagrán. To **Santiago**, 9 hrs, US$36-47. To **Concepción**, 3 hrs, US$6. To **Angol** US$6.

Contulmo *p737*
Bus To **Cañete**, frequent, US$2. To **Concepción**, US$7, 4 hrs; to **Temuco**, Erbuc, US$6.50.

Los Angeles *p737*
Bus Long-distance bus terminal on northeast outskirts of town, local terminal at Villagrán y Rengo in centre, by market. To **Salto de Laja**, every 30 mins with Bus Bío Bío, US$2 return. To **Santiago**, 6½ hrs, US$25-40. To **Viña del Mar** and **Valparaíso**, 8 hrs, US$27. Every 30 mins to **Concepción**, US$4, 2 hrs. To **Temuco**, US$7, hourly. To **Curacautín**, daily at 0945, 1600, 3 hrs, US$9 (otherwise change in Victoria).

Parque Nacional Laguna de Laja *p737*
Bus ERS Bus from Los Angeles (Villagrán 507, by market) to **Abanico**, 20 km past Antuco (6 a day, US$2), then 2 hrs/4 km walk to park entrance (hitching possible). Or bus to **Antuco**, 2 hrs, weekdays 5 daily, 2 on Sun and festivals, last return 1730, US$3, then hitch last 24 km. Details from CONAF in Los Angeles.

Angol *p737*
Bus To **Santiago** US$27-42, **Los Angeles**, US$3. To **Temuco**, Trans Bío-Bío, frequent, US$5.

Parque Nacional Nahuelbuta *p737*
Bus In Dec-Feb there is a direct bus from **Angol**, Sun 0800, return 1700. Otherwise, take the bus to **Vegas Blancas** (27 km west of Angol) 0700 and 1600 daily, return 0900 and 1600, 1½ hrs, US$2, get off at El Cruce, from where it is a steep 7 km walk to park entrance. Sometimes the bus goes to the park entrance, ask first.

Lake District

The Lake District, stretching southwards from Temuco to Puerto Montt, is one of Chile's most beautiful regions. There are some 12 great lakes of varying sizes, as well as imposing waterfalls and snow-capped volcanoes. There are a number of good bases for exploring. Out of season many facilities are closed, in season (from mid-December to mid-March), prices are higher and it is best to book well in advance, particularly for transport. About 20,000 Mapuches live in the area, particularly around Temuco. Although becoming less prevalent, there are possibly 100,000 more of mixed descent who speak the native tongue, Mapudungun, nearly all of them bilingual.

Temuco and around → *Phone code: 045. Colour map 8, C1. Population: 227,000. Altitude: 107 m.*

Although at first sight rather grey and imposing, Temuco is a lively university city and one of the fastest growing commercial centres in the south. Founded in 1881 after the final treaty with the Mapuches and the arrival of the railway, this city is the capital of IX Región (Araucanía), 677 km south of Santiago. Temuco is proud of its Mapuche heritage and it is this that gives it its distinctive character, especially around the outdoor market. The **Sernatur office** ① *Bulnes 590, p 1, T240 6200, infoaraucania@sernatur.cl, Mon-Fri 0900-1900, Sat 0900-1300, 1400-1800, Sun 1100-1500*, has good leaflets in English. Also in the municipal market, T297 3628. See also www.temucochile.com. **CONAF** ① *Bilbao 931, p 2, T229 8100, temuco.oirs@conaf.cl.* **Sernap** ① *Vicuña Mackenna 51, T223 8390*, for fishing permits. North and east of the city are five national parks and reserves, notably Conguillío with its araucaria forests, and flora and fauna found nowhere else. It is great for hiking, or touring by car or even mountain bike. There are also various skiing opportunities.

Places in and around Temuco

The centre is the Plaza Aníbal Pinto, around which are the main public buildings including the cathedral and the Municipalidad. Very little of the old city remains; practically every wooden building burned down following the 1960 earthquake. Temuco is the Mapuches' market town and you may see some, particularly women, in their typical costumes in the huge produce market, the **Feria** ① *Lautaro y Pinto*, one of the most fascinating markets in Chile. Mapuche textiles, pottery, woodcarving, jewellery, etc, are also sold inside and around the **municipal market**, Aldunate y Diego Portales (it also sells fish, meat and dairy produce), but these are increasingly touristy and poor quality. There is a handicraft fair every February in the main plaza. **Agrupación de Mujeres Artesanas** ① *Aldunate 1005, T7790 3676, wanglenzomo@gmail. com, Mon-Fri 1030-1630*, sells many crafts, including textiles made by a Mapuche weavers' co-operative, all with traditional designs. It also offers design classes for traditional dresses (US$73). A couple of kilometres northwest of the centre is the **Museo Regional de la Araucanía** ① *Alemania 84, www.museoregionalaraucania.cl, Tue-Fri 0930-1730, Sat 1100-1700, Sun 1100-1400, US$1 (half price for students and seniors), take bus 1 from the centre.* It is devoted to the history and traditions of the Mapuche nation, with a section on German settlement. For information on visits to Mapuche settlements, eg Chol Chol, go to the main Sernatur office. There are views of Temuco from **Cerro Ñielol** ① *US$1.50, 0800-1900.* This park has a fine collection of native plants in the natural state, including the national flower, the copihue rojo. This is a good site for a picnic with an excellent visitors' centre run by CONAF. A tree marks the spot where peace was made with the Mapuche. Bicycles are only allowed in before 1100. At the top of the hill there is a restaurant, which also has dancing (not always open).

Northeast of the centre, 2 km, is the **Museo Nacional Ferroviario Pablo Neruda** ① *Barros Arana 0565, T297 3941, www.museoferroviariotemuco.cl, Tue-Fri 0900-1800, Sat 1000-1800, Sun 1100-1700 Apr-Sep, 1000-1800 Oct-Mar, US$2, take micro 1 Variante, 9 Directo, 4b, taxi from centre US$2*, the national railway museum. Exhibits include over 20 engines and carriages (including the former presidential carriage) dating from 1908 to 1953, many of which are located outside following earthquake damage to the main building.

Curacautín and around → *Population: 12,500. Altitude: 400 m.*

Curacautín is a small town 84 km northeast of Temuco (road paved) and 56 km southeast of Victoria by paved road is a useful base for visiting the nearby national parks and hot springs (**CONAF** office, Yungay 240, T288 1184).

Some 17 km east of Curacautín are the hot springs of **Termas de Manzanar** ① *www. termasdemanzanar.cl, open all year 1000-2000, US$18 for the swimming pool, discounts for children, reached by bus from Temuco and Victoria.* The building dates from 1954. The road passes the Salto del Indio, where there are 30-m-high falls, park entry US$33 for up to five people (Km 71 from

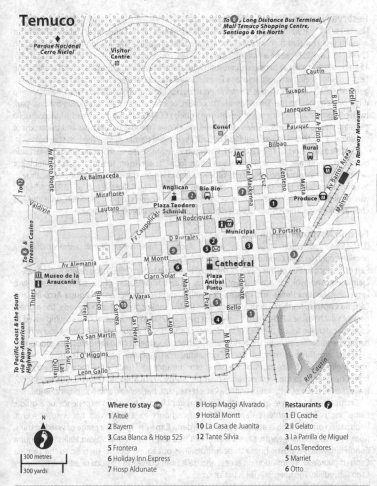

Temuco

Where to stay 🛏
1 Aitué
2 Bayern
3 Casa Blanca & Hosp 525
5 Frontera
6 Holiday Inn Express
7 Hosp Aldunate
8 Hosp Maggi Alvarado
9 Hostal Montt
10 La Casa de Juanita
12 Tante Silvia

Restaurants 🍴
1 El Ceache
2 Il Gelato
3 La Parrilla de Miguel
4 Los Tenedores
5 Marriet
6 Otto

Victoria) and *cabañas*, and Salto de la Princesa, an even more impressive 50-m waterfall, 3 km beyond Manzanar, with a *hostería* and camping.

The beautiful pine-surrounded **Termas Malleco** ① *formerly Tolhuaca, www.termasmalleco.cl, all year, US$18, taxi from Curacautín US$20-30*, are 35 km to the northeast of Curacautín by unpaved road, or 82 km by rough, unpaved road from just north of Victoria (high clearance 4WD vehicle essential). Just 2 km north of the Termas is the **Parque Nacional Tolhuaca** ① *Dec-Apr, taxi from Curacautín US$15-20*, including waterfalls, two lakes, superb scenery and good views of volcanoes from Cerro Amarillo. Park administration is near Laguna Malleco, with a campsite nearby. Much of the park, together with the neighbouring Reserva Nacional Malleco, was severely damaged by forest fires in early 2002. It will take several decades fully to recover, but some half-day trails are open.

Reserva Nacional Nalcas Malalcahuello

Northeast of Curacautín, this 31,305 ha park is on the slopes of the **Lonquimay** volcano (2865 m). It is much less crowded than nearby Parque Nacional Conguillio. The volcano began erupting on Christmas Day 1988; the new crater is called Navidad. To see it, access is made from Malalcahuello, 15 km south and halfway between Curacautín and Lonquimay town. In the park, which is one of the best areas for seeing unspoilt araucaria forest, CONAF has opened several marked trails, from one hour to two days in length. There is a municipal *refugio* at the foot of the volcano. From Malalcahuello it is a one-day hike to the Sierra Nevada mountain, or a two-day hike to Conguillio national park (with equipment and experience, otherwise use a guide). CONAF office on main road in Malalcahuello gives information, as does **La Suizandina** hotel, which gives good access to treks and the ascent of the volcano. Sra Naomi Saavedra at **Res Los Sauces** arranges transport; see Where to stay, below.

Corrolco ski resort ① *T02-2206 0741, www.corralco.com, season Jun-Sep*, on the southeast side of Volcán Lonquimay, this high-end resort offers four lifts servicing 18 runs that are suitable for beginner, intermediate and advanced skill levels. Also in winter, the main route from Malalcahuello to Lonquimay town, goes through the ex-railway tunnel of **Las Raices** ① *toll US$1.50*. At 4.8 km it was, until recently, the longest tunnel in South America. Now it's in poor condition, unlit and has constant filtration. There is talk of repair, but it's unwise to go through by bicycle.

Parque Nacional Conguillio

① *US$8 in high season, US$4 in low season, discounts for children, visitor centre at the park administration by Lago Conguillio, Mon-Sun 0830-1800.*

East of Temuco by 80 km, this is one of the most popular parks in Chile. In the centre is the 3125-m **Llaima volcano**, which is active (eruptions may cause partial closure of the park). There are two large lakes, **Laguna Verde** and **Laguna Conguillio**, and two smaller ones, **Laguna Arco Iris** and **Laguna Captrén**. North of Laguna Conguillio rises the snow-covered **Sierra Nevada**, the highest peak of which reaches 2554 m. This is the best place in Chile to see araucaria forest, which used to cover an extensive area in this part of the country. Other trees include cypresses, lenga and winter's bark (canelo). Birdlife includes the condor and the black woodpecker and there are foxes and pumas.

There are three entrances: from Curacautín, north of the park: see Transport below; from Melipeuco, 13 km south of the southern entrance at Truful-Truful (open all year); and from Cherquenco to the west entrance near the pretty **Araucarias ski resort** ① *T045-223 9999, www.skiaraucarias.cl*, with four ski lifts, a café, restaurant, bar, *refugio* and equipment rental.

Crampons and ice-axe are essential for climbing Llaima, as well as experience or a guide. Climb south from Guardería Captrén. Allow five hours to ascend, two hours to descend. Information on the climb is available from **Guardería Captrén**. There is a range of walking trails, from 1 km to 22 km in length. One is a two- or three-day hike around Volcán Llaima to Laguna Conguillio, which is dusty, but with beautiful views of Laguna Quepe, then on to the Laguna Captrén *guardería*. Information on access and trails from **CONAF** in Temuco or administration by Lago Conguillio. The nearest ATM is in Cunco.

Lake District

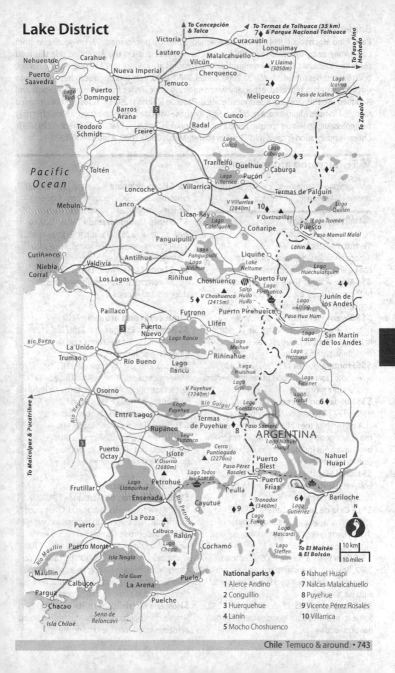

To Concepción & Talca
To Termas de Tolhuaca (35 km) & Parque Nacional Tolhuaca
7
To Paso Pino Hachado

Victoria
Lautaro
Curacautín
Malalcahuello
Lonquimay
Nehuentue
Carahue
Vilcún
V Llaima (3050m)
Nueva Imperial
Cherquenco
2
Lago Icalma
Puerto Saavedra
Temuco
Melipeuco
Paso de Icalma
Lago Budi
Puerto Domínguez
Barros Arana
Cunco
To Zapala
Teodoro Schmidt
Radal
Freire
Lago Colico
Lago Caburga
Trarilelfú
Quelhue
3
Toltén
Villarrica
Pucón
Caburga
4
Lago Villarrica
Loncoche
Lanco
Lican-Ray
V Villarrica (2840m)
10
Termas de Palguín
Mehuin
Lago Calafquén
V Quetrupillán
Lago Quillén
Panguipulli
Coñaripe
Curiñanco
Antilhue
Liquiñe
Puesco
Niebla
Valdivia
Lake Neltume
Paso Mamuil Malal
Corral
Lago Panguipulli
Lanín
Lago Tromén
Los Lagos
Riñihue
Choshuenco
Lago Riñihue
Puerto Fuy
Lago Pirehueico
Lago Huechulafquén
Paillaco
V Choshuenco (2415m)
Salto Huilo Huilo
4
5
Futrono
Puerto Pirehueico
Junín de los Andes
Puerto Nuevo
Llifén
Lago Lolog
Río Bueno
Lago Ranco
Paso Hua Hum
La Unión
Riñinahue
Lago Lácar
San Martín de los Andes
Trumao
Río Bueno
Lago Maihue
Lago Hermoso
Lago Ranco
Lago Huishué
Lago Falkner
Osorno
Lago Gris
Lago Traful
V Puyehue (2240m)
Río Golgol
Lago Puyehue
Lago Constancia
6
Entre Lagos
Termas de Puyehue
Paso Samoré
Rupanco
8
ARGENTINA
Lago Rupanco
Cerro Puntiagudo (2278m)
Lago Nahuel Huapi
Puerto Octay
Islote
Nahuel Huapi
V Osorno (2680m)
Puerto Blest
Frutillar
Lago Todos los Santos
Paso Pérez Rosales
Puerto Frías
Lago Llanquihue
Petrohué
Peulla
Bariloche
Puerto
Ensenada
Tronador (3460m)
6
La Poza
Cayutué
9
Lago Gutiérrez
Río Petrohué
Puerto Montt
V Calbuco
Lago Foneck
Ralún
Lago Chapo
Cochamó
Lago Mascardi
Maullín
Isla Tenglo
Puelo
Lago Steffen
Calbuco
Isla Guar
La Arena
To El Maitén & El Bolsón
Pargua
Puelche
N
Chacao
Seno de Reloncaví
Isla Chiloé

Pacific Ocean

To Maicolpue & Pucatrihue

Río Bueno
Río Negro
Río Maullín

10 km
10 miles

National parks ♦
1 Alerce Andino   6 Nahuel Huapi
2 Conguillío   7 Nalcas Malalcahuello
3 Huerquehue   8 Puyehue
4 Lanín   9 Vicente Pérez Rosales
5 Mocho Choshuenco   10 Villarrica

Border with Argentina

Paso Pino Hachado (1884 m) can be reached either by paved road, 73 km southeast from Lonquimay, or by unpaved road 129 km east from Melipeuco. On the Argentine side this road continues to Zapala. **Chilean immigration** and customs are in Liucura, 22 km west of the border, open September to mid-May 0800-2000, winter 0800-1900. Very thorough searches and two- to three-hour delays reported, especially when entering Chile. Buses from Temuco to Zapala and Neuquén use this crossing: see under Temuco. **Paso de Icalma** (1298 m) is reached by unpaved road, 53 km from Melipeuco, a good crossing for those with their own transport, although it may be impassable in winter (phone Policía Internacional in Temuco, Prat 19, to check: T2293890). Chilean immigration is open mid-October to mid-March 0800-2000, winter 0800-1900.

⊚ Temuco and around listings

For hotel and restaurant price codes, and other relevant information, see Essentials.

● Where to stay

Temuco *p740, map p741*
Accommodation in private houses, category **$**, can be arranged by tourist office.
$$$ Aitué, A Varas 1048, T221 2512, www. hotelaitue.cl. Business standard, central, bar, English spoken, comfortable.
$$$ Bayern, Prat 146, T227 6000, www. hotelbayern.cl. Standard 3-star. Small rooms, helpful staff, buffet breakfast, cafetería/ restaurant, parking.
$$$ Frontera, Bulnes 733-726, T220 0400, www.hotelfrontera.cl. Good business standard, comfortable rooms.
$$$ Holiday Inn Express, Av R Ortega 01800, T222 3300, www.holidayinnexpress. cl. A member of the Chileanized version of this chain, good value, gym, pool, out of town but convenient for the bus terminal, worth considering if driving.
$$ Hostal Montt, M Montt 637, T298 2488. Comfortable if overpriced, some rooms with bath, parking, gym.
$$ La Casa de Juanita, Carrera 735, T221 3203, www.lacasadejuanita.co.cl. Private or shared bath, quiet, good bathrooms, parking, lots of information.
$$-$ Casa Blanca, Montt 1306 y Zenteno, T227 2677, hostalcasablancatemuco@gmail.com. Slightly run-down, but good value for rooms with bath.
$$-$ Hospedaje 525, Zenteno 525, T223 3982. Some rooms with bath, good value, older part has poor beds.

$$-$ Hosp Aldunate, Aldunate 187, T227 0057, cristorresvalenzuela@hotmail.com. Cooking facilities, some rooms with TV and bath.
$$-$ Hosp Maggi Alvarado, Recreo 209, off Av Alemania, T226 3215, cppacl@gmail.com. Small rooms, helpful, nice atmosphere. Also has a good-value *cabaña* sleeping 4.
$$-$ Tante Silvia, Pinto Puelma 259, T248 4442. Rooms or dorms, meals available, for students and groups.

Curacautín and around *p741*
$$ Hostal Las Espigas, Prat 710, T288 1138, rivaseugenia@hotmail.com. Good rooms, dinner available on request.
$$ Plaza, Yungay 157 (main plaza), T288 1256, www.rotondadelcautin.cl. With **La Cabaña** restaurant, pricey. Also has **Hostería La Rotunda del Cautín**, Termas de Manzanar, T2881569. Rooms and good mid-range restaurant.
$ Turismo, Tarapacá 140, T288 1116, hotelturismocuracautin@gmail.com. Good food, hot shower, comfortable, good value if old-fashioned.

Termas de Manzanar
$$$$-$$$ Termas de Manzanar, T045-288 1200, www.termasdemanzanar.cl. Overpriced rooms, also has suites with thermal jacuzzi.
$$$-$ Andenrose, Carr Int Km 68.5, 5 km west of Manzanar, Curacautín, T09-9869 1700, www.andenrose.com. Cosy rooms, cabins and camping, restaurant serving international and Bavarian food, bike, horse, kayak rental, jeep tours arranged, German/Chilean run.
$ Hostería Abarzúa, Km 18, T045-287 0011. Simple, cheaper rooms without bath, full board available (good food), also campsite.

Termas de Tolhuaca
$$$$-$$ Termas Malleco, Km 33 T045-241
9488, www.termasmalleco.cl. With breakfast
or full board, including use of baths and horse
riding, very good; jacuzzi and massage. Camping,
good facilities and unlimited use of pools.
$ Res Rojas, Tarapacá 249, hot water, food,
camping near the river.

Reserva Nacional Nalcas Malalcahuello
p742
Lonquimay
$$$-$ La Suizandina, Km 83 Carretera
Internacional a Argentina, T045-2197 3725 or
T09-9884 9541, www.suizandina.com. Hostel
3 km before Malalcahuello Erbuc bus from
Temuco 2½ hrs). A range of rooms, in main house,
guesthouse, dorm, cabin or camping. Large Swiss
breakfast with home-baked bread, half board
available, credit cards accepted, laundry, book
exchange, bike and ski rental, horse riding, hot
springs, travel and trekking information, German
and English spoken. "Like being in Switzerland".
$$ Hostal Lonquimay, Pinto 555, Lonquimay,
T289 1324. Basic rooms with shared bath.
$$-$ Res Los Sauces, Estación 510, in
Malalcahuello village, T09-7497 8706. Doubles
and singles with shared bath and good-value
cabañas. Full board available.

Parque Nacional Conguillío *p742*
$$$ La Baita, in the park, 3 km south of Laguna
Verde, T258 1073, www.labaitaconguillio.cl.
Cabins with electricity, hot water, kitchen and
wood stoves, charming, lots of information,
Italian/Chilean owned.
$$$-$$ Cabañas Vista Hermosa, 10 km from
the southern entrance, T09-9444 1630, www.
vistahermosaconguillio.cl. Clean but spartan
wooden cabins, each with a wood stove and
fantastic views to the volcano. Electricity in
afternoon only. Run by a horse-riding guide
(former champion rider). Good food.
$$ Adela y Helmut, Faja 16000, Km 5 Norte,
Cunco (on the way to Melipeuco, 16 km from
Cunco, website has directions, phone for pick-
up from bus stop; Nar-Bus, Cruzmar and Inter-
Sur buses from Santiago and Temuco pass the
Faja and will drop passengers who phone the
guesthouse for pick-up), T09-8258 2230, www.
adelayhelmut.com. Guesthouse and restaurant

on a Mapuche/German owned farm, English
spoken, room for families and for backpackers
in 6-bed dorm, breakfast and dinner available,
kitchens, hot showers, solar heating, mountain
bike rental, good reports. Pick-up from Temuco
US$49 for up to 4 people. They run year-round
tours to Conguillío National Park, visiting lakes,
waterfalls, with hikes adapted to physical
ability. They can also arrange fly-fishing
packages and golf.
$ Hosp Icalma, Aguirre Cerda 729, Melipeuco,
T9280 8210, www.melipeucohospedaje.cl.
Spacious, basic rooms.
　　There are other *hostales* and restaurants
in Melipeuco.
Camping Cabañas y Camping La Caseta y
El Hoyón, administered by CONAF, T065-297
2336 (reservas@parquenacionalconguillio.cl)
to reserve.

🍴 Restaurants

Temuco *p740, map p741*
Many good restaurants around Av Alemania
and Mall Mirage, about 10 blocks west of
centre. Make for the Mercado Municipal on
Aldunate y Portales, or the rural bus terminal,
where there are countless restaurants serving
very cheap set meals at lunch.
$$ La Caleta, Mercado Municipal, Aldunate y
Portales, T221 3002. One of the better choices
in the covered market serving fish and seafood.
$$ La Parrilla de Miguel, Montt 1095, T227
5182. Good for meat, large portions, and wine;
one of the better restaurants.
$$ Otto, V MacKenna 530. German food,
sandwiches, cakes, etc.
$ El Ceache, Cruz 231. Simple food such as
chicken and fries, good value set lunch.
$ Los Tenedores, San Martín 827.
Good-value lunch.

Cafés
Il Gelato, Bulnes 420. Delicicious ice cream.
Marriet, Prat 451, loc 9, www.marriet.cl.
Excellent coffee.

Parque Nacional Conguillío *p742*
Buy supplies in Temuco, Curacautín or
Melipeuco: much cheaper than the shop
in the park.

🎭 Entertainment

Temuco *p740, map p741*
Dreams, Av Alemania 945, www.mundo dreams.com. Casino and hotel holds concerts by local and international artists.

🛍 Shopping

Temuco *p740, map p741*
Crafts Best choice in the indoor municipal market at Aldunate y Portales, and in the Agrupación de Mujeres Artesanas (see page 740). **Fundación Chol-Chol**, Sector Rengalil, Camino Temuco–Nueva Imperial Km 16, T261 4007, http://en.cholchol.org. This non-profit organization sells traditional Mapuche textiles, naturally dyed and hand woven by local women. Book in advance to sample some traditional, freshly made Mapuche fare.
Market Temuco Feria, Lautaro y Aníbal Pinto. This is one of the most fascinating markets in Chile, with people bringing excellent fruit and vegetables from the surrounding countryside, including spices, fish, grains, cheese and honey. Also many cheap bars and restaurants nearby. **Frutería Las Vegas**, Matta 274, dried fruit (useful for climbing/trekking).

🚌 Transport

Temuco *p740, map p741*
Air Manquehue Airport 6 km southwest of the city. There is an airport transfer service to the city, **Transfer Temuco**, T233 4033, www. transfertemuco.cl, US$4.25 (book 24 hrs in advance). Also goes to hotels in Villarrica and Pucón, US$15 (may not run out of season). There is no public bus; taxis charge US$9-11. LAN to **Santiago, Concepción, Osorno, Puerto Montt** and **Balmaceda**. Sky to **Santiago, Concepción, Osorno** and **Puerto Montt**.
Bus Long-distance bus terminal (Rodoviária) north of city at Pérez Rosales y Caupolicán, city bus 2, 7 or 10; colectivo 11P; taxi US$3-5. JAC has its own efficient terminal at Balmaceda y Aldunate, T246 5465, www.jac.cl, 7 blocks north of the Plaza, which also serves neighbouring towns. NarBus and Igi-Llaima are opposite. Buses to **Santiago**, many overnight, 8-9 hrs,

US$23-62. To **Concepción**, Bío Bío (Lautaro entre Prat y Bulnes), US$13, 4 hrs. To **Chillán**, 3½ hrs, US$16. Cruz del Sur, 3 a day to **Castro**, 10 a day to **Puerto Montt** (US$11.50-28, 5-6 hrs). To **Valdivia**, JAC, Narbus/Igi Llaima, several daily, US$7, 2½ hrs. To **Osorno**, US$9, 4¼ hrs. To **Villarrica** and **Pucón**, JAC, many between 0705 and 2045, 1½ hrs, and 2 hrs, US$9. Buses to neighbouring towns leave from Terminal Rural, Pinto y Balmaceda, or from bus company offices nearby. To **Coñaripe**, 3 hrs, and **Lican Ray**, 2 hrs. To **Panguipulli**, Power and Pangui Sur 3 hrs, US$6.50. Pangui Sur to **Loncoche**, US$4, **Los Lagos**, US$8, **Mehuin** in summer only. To **Curacautín** via Lautaro, Erbuc, US$6.50, 4 daily, 2½ hrs. To **Lonquimay**, Erbuc, 4 daily, 3½ hrs, US$8. To **Contulmo**, US$6.50, and **Cañete**, US$6, Erbuc and Igi Llaima.
   To Argentina El Valle and Caraza to **Zapala** and **Neuquén**, via Paso Pino Hachado. To **Bariloche** change in Osorno, Tas-Choapa.
Car hire Ace, Carrera 940 (in terminal), T231 8585. Automóvil Club de Chile, San Martín 278, T291 0521. Euro, MacKenna 399, T221 0311, helpful, good value. Full Famas, at airport and in centre T221 5420.

Curacautín *p741*
Bus Terminal on the main road, by the plaza. Buses to/from **Temuco, Los Angeles** and **Santiago**.

Lonquimay
Bus Bus Erbuc from **Temuco** via Lautaro, US$3 to **Malalcahuello**, 4 a day, 2½ hrs, 3½ to Lonquimay town, US$4.

Parque Nacional Conguillio *p742*
For touring, hire a 4WD vehicle in Temuco (essential in wet weather). See also **Adela y Helmut**, under Where to stay, above.
   To the northern entrance, poor *ripio* road: **taxi** from Curacautín to Laguna Captrén, US$70-80 one way. To **Melipeuco** (paved road, stops at **Hospedaje Icalma**), buses every hour from Balmaceda bus terminal, **Temuco** (or flag down at Mackenna y Varas), 2½ hrs, US$7, and once a day to **Icalma** when no snow on road. From May to end-Dec the only access is via Melipeuco. Transport can be arranged from Melipeuco into the park (ask in grocery stores

and *hospedajes*, US$50-60 one way). To **Cunco**, every 20 mins from same terminal. To the western entrance: daily **buses** from Temuco to Cherquenco, from where there is no public transport to the park. Private transport or taking a tour are the best ways to see the area.

⊙ Directory

Temuco *p740, map p741*
Banks Many ATMs at banks on Plaza Aníbal Pinto. Also at the JAC bus terminal (Visa). Many cambios around the plaza, all deal in dollars and Argentine pesos.

Lagos Villarrica, Calafquén and Panguipulli

Wooded Lago Villarrica, 21 km long and about 7 km wide, is one of the most beautiful in the region, with the active, snow-capped Villarrica volcano (2840 m) to the southeast. Villarrica and Pucón, resorts at the lake's southwest and southeast corners, are among the more expensive in the region, but are definitely worth a visit. South of Lago Villarrica, a necklace of six lakes with snowy peaks behind, form picture-postcard views. Calafquén and Panguipulli are the most visited, but there are also hot springs, national parks and interesting routes to Argentina.

Villarrica → *Phone code: 045. Colour map 8, C1. Population: 27,000. Altitude: 227 m.*

The quiet town of Villarrica, pleasantly set at the extreme southwest corner of the lake, can be reached by a 63 km paved road southeast from Freire (24 km south of Temuco on the Pan-American Highway), or from Loncoche, 54 km south of Freire, also paved. Founded in 1552, the town was besieged by the Mapuche in the uprising of 1599: after three years the surviving Spanish settlers, 11 men and 13 women, surrendered. The town was refounded in 1882; the **Museo Leandro Penchulef** ① *O'Higgins 501, T241 1667, Dec-Jan Mon-Fri 1000-1800, Feb 0900 1700, free,* in the striking Universidad Católica, focuses on this event. The **Muestra Cultural Mapuche** ① *Pedro de Valdivia y Zegers, open all summer*, features a Mapuche *ruca* and stalls selling good handicrafts. In January and February Villarrica has a summer programme with many cultural and sporting events (including the **Semana de Chilenidad**) and on 18-19 September the **Gran Fiesta Campestre de Villarrica** is held in the indoor riding arena of the Parque Natural Dos Ríos (see Where to stay), with typical foods, music, dancing, competitions and shows. **Tourist office** ① *Valdivia 1070, T241 1162, open daily in summer 0800-2300, off season 0800-1330, 1430-1800; information and maps.*

Pucón → *Phone code: 045. Colour map 8, C1. Population: 13,000. Altitude: 227 m.*

Pucón, on the southeastern shore of Lago Villarrica, 26 km east of Villarrica, is the major tourist centre on the lake. The black sand beach is very popular for swimming and watersports. Between New Year to end-February it is very crowded and expensive; off season it is very pleasant. Apart from the lake, other attractions nearby include whitewater rafting, winter sports (see Skiing below) and several canopy sites (see Ziplining under What to do). **Tourist office** ① *in the municipal building, O'Higgins 483, T229 3002, ofturismo@municipalidadpucon.cl, sells fishing licences (US$41 per month).* There is also the **Chamber of Tourism** ① *Brazil 315, T244 1671, www.puconturismo.cl.*

There is a pleasant *paseo*, the **Costanera Otto Gudenschwager**, which starts at the lake end of Ansorena (beside Gran Hotel Pucón) and goes along the shore. Walk 2 km north along the beach to the mouth of the Río Trancura (also called Río Pucón), with views of the volcanoes Villarrica, Quetrupillán and Lanín. To cross the Río Pucón: head east out of Pucón along the main road, then turn north on an unmade road leading to a new bridge; from here there are pleasant walks along the north shore of the lake to Quelhue and Trarilelfú, or northeast towards Caburga, or up into the hills through farms and agricultural land, with views of three volcanoes and, higher up, of the lake. The journey to Caburga (see below) is a perfect mountain bike day trip.

Boat trips ① *5 a day, summer only, 2 hrs, US$9,* on the lake leave from the landing stage at La Poza at the western end of O'Higgins. Or take a **boat** ① *summer only, US$15,* to the mouth of the river from near the **Gran Hotel**.

Parque Nacional Villarrica

The park has three sectors: **Volcán Villarrica** ⓘ *entry US$1.75, ascent fee US$7.50*, **Volcán Quetrupillán** and the **Puesco sector** which includes the slopes of the Volcán Lanín on the Argentine border. Each sector has its own entrance and ranger station. A campsite with drinking water and toilets is below the refuge, 4 km inside the park. The Villarrica volcano, 2840 m, 8 km south of Pucón, can be climbed up and down in seven to eight hours, good boots, ice axe and crampons, sunglasses, plenty of water, chocolate and sun block essential. Beware of sulphur fumes at the top – occasionally agencies provide gas masks, otherwise take a cloth mask moistened with lemon juice – but on good days you can see into the crater with lava bubbling at 1250°C. On the descent you toboggan down the snow rather than walk, good fun.

Entry to Volcán Villarrica is permitted only to groups with a guide and to individuals who can show proof of membership of a mountaineering club in their own country. Several agencies take excursions. Entry is refused if the weather is poor. Many guides, all with equipment; ask for recommendations at the tourist office. Take the ski lift for the first part of the ascent as it saves 400 m climbing on scree.

Skiing ⓘ *Ski season is Jul-Sep, occasionally longer. Information on snow and ski-lifts (and, perhaps, transport) from tourist office or Gran Hotel Pucón.* The **Pucón resort** (T244 1901, www.skipucon.cl), owned by the **Gran Hotel Pucón**, is on the eastern slopes of the volcano, reached by a track, 35 minutes. The centre offers equipment rental, ski instruction, first aid, restaurant and bar as well as wonderful views from the terrace. The centre is good for beginners; more advanced skiers can try the steeper areas.

Lagos Caburga and Colico

Lago Caburga (spelt locally Caburgua), a very pretty lake in a wild setting 25 km northeast of Pucón, is unusual for its beautiful white sand beach and has supposedly the warmest water of all the lakes here. The north shore can be reached by a road from Cunco via the north shore of Lago Colico, a more remote lake north of Lago Villarrica. The village of Caburga, at the southern end is reached by a turning off the main road 8 km east of Pucón. The southern end of the lake and around Caburga is lined with campsites. Rowing boats may be hired. Just off the road from Pucón, Km 15, are the Ojos de Caburga, beautiful pools fed from underground, particularly attractive after rain (entry US$1; ask bus driver to let you off). Alternatively, take a mountain bike from Pucón via the Puente Quelhue.

Parque Nacional Huerquehue

ⓘ *The park is open 0800-2000, US$3.50; free parking 1.5 km along the track.*
East of Lago Caburga, the park includes steep hills and at least 20 lakes, some of them very small. Entrance and administration are near Lago Tinquilco, the largest lake, on the western edge of the park. The entrance is 7 km from Paillaco, reached by an all-weather road which turns off 3 km before Caburga. From the entrance there is a well-signed track north to three beautiful lakes, Lagos Verde, Chico and Toro. The track zig-zags up 5 km to Lago Chico, then splits left to Verde, right to Toro. From Toro you can continue to Lago Huerquehue and Laguna los Patos (camping). People in the park rent horses and boats. There is a restaurant at Tinquilco or take your own food.

South of the Huerquehue Park on a turning from the Pucón-Caburga road there are **Termas de Quimey-Co**, about 29 km from Pucón, campsite, cabins and hotel **Termas de Quimey-Co** ⓘ *T09-8775 2113, www.termasquimeyco.com*, and **Termas de Huife Hostería** ⓘ *Pucón, Km 33, T244 1222, www.termashuife.cl*. Beyond Huife are the hot springs of **Los Pozones**, Km 35, set in natural rock pools, basic but popular with travellers. The road there is rough.

Cañi Forest Sanctuary, south of Parque Nacional Huerquehue and covering 500 ha, was the first private forest reserve established in Chile, owned by the non-proft Fundación Lahuén ⓘ *US$3.50*. It contains 17 small lakes and is covered by ancient native forests of coihue, lenga and some of the oldest araucaria trees in the country. From its highest peak, **El Mirador**, five volcanoes can be seen. There is a self-guided trail, US$8 plus transport; for tours with English-speaking guide, contact the Cañi Guides Program ① *see www.ecole.cl.*

Route to Argentina
From Pucón a road runs southeast via Curarrehue to the Argentine border. At Km 18 there is a turning south to the **Termas de Palguín** ① *T244 1968*, with a hotel. There are many beautiful waterfalls within hiking distance: for example, Salto China (entry US$3.50, restaurant, camping); Salto del Puma and Salto del León, both 800 m from the Termas (entry US$3.50 for both). From Pucón take Bus Regional Villarrica from Palguín y O'Higgins at 1100 to the junction (10 km from Termas); last bus from junction to the Termas at 1500, so you may have to hitch back. Taxi from Pucón, US$20.

Near Palguín is the entrance to the Quetrupillán section of the Parque Nacional Villarrica (high clearance vehicle necessary, horses best), free camping, wonderful views over Villarrica Volcano and six other peaks. Ask rangers for the route to the other entrance.

The road from Pucón to Argentina passes turnings north at Km 23 to **Termas de San Luis** ① *T045-241 2880, www.termasdesanluis.cl*, and Km 35 to **Termas de Pangui** (15 km from main road), both with hotels, the latter with teepees (T045-244 2039). It continues to Curarrehue, from where it turns south to Puesco and climbs via **Lago Quellelhue**, a tiny gem set between mountains at 1196 m to reach the border at the **Mamuil Malal**. To the south of the pass rises the graceful cone of Lanín volcano. On the Argentine side the road runs south to Junín de los Andes, San Martín de los Andes and Bariloche.

Chilean immigration and customs Chilean immigration and customs at Puesco, open 0800-1900 (to 2100 December-March), US$2 per vehicle at other times. There are free **CONAF** campsites with no facilities at Puesco and 5 km from the border near Lago Tromén. Daily bus from Pucón, 1800, two hours, US$3. It's a hard road for cyclists, but not impossible.

Lago Calafquén → *Colour map 8, C1. Population: 1700. Altitude: 207 m.*
Dotted with small islands, Lago Calafquén is a popular tourist destination. **Lican-Ray** 30 km south of Villarrica on a peninsula on the north shore, is the major resort on the lake. There are two fine beaches each side of the rocky peninsula. Boats can be hired and there are catamaran trips. Although very crowded in season, most facilities close by the end of March and, out of season, Lican-Ray feels like a ghost town. Some 6 km to the east is the river of lava formed when the Villarrica volcano erupted in 1971. The **tourist office** ① *daily in summer, Mon-Fri off season*, is on the plaza.

Coñaripe (*Population: 1253*), 21 km southeast of Lican-Ray at the eastern end of Lago Calafquén, is another popular tourist spot. Its setting, with a 3 km black sand beach surrounded by mountains, is very beautiful. From here a road (mostly *ripio*) around the lake's southern shore leads to Lago Panguipulli (see below) and offers superb views over Villarrica volcano, which can be climbed from here. Most services are on the Calle Principal. The **tourist office** ① *T063-231 7378, daily 15 Nov-15 Apr, otherwise weekends only*, is on the plaza.

Termas Vergara are 14 km northeast of Coñaripe by a steep *ripio* road which continues to Palguín. There are nice open-air pools here. **Termas Geométricas** ① *3 km beyond Termas Vergara, T09-7477 1708, www.termasgeometricas.cl*. There are 17 pools, geometrically shaped and linked by wooden walkways. There is a small café.

From Coñaripe a road runs southeast over the steep **Cuesta Los Añiques** offering views of tiny Lago Pellaifa. The **Termas de Coñaripe** ① *T045-241 9498, www.termas conaripe.cl, US$30*, are at Km 16. Further south at Km 32 are the **Termas de Liquiñe** ① *T063-197 1301, 8 different thermal centres*. Opposite Liquiñe are the **Termas Río de Liquiñe**. There is a road north to Pucón through Villarrica National Park, high-clearance and 4WD vehicle essential.

The border with Argentina, **Paso Cariñe**, is reached by unpaved road from Termas de Liquiñe. It is open 15 October-31 August. On the Argentine side the road continues to San Martín de los Andes.

Lago Panguipulli and around → *Phone code: 063. Colour map 8, C1. Population: 8000. Altitude: 136 m.*

The lake is reached by paved roads from Lanco and Los Lagos on the Pan-American Highway or unpaved roads from Lago Calafquén. A road leads along the beautiful north shore, wooded with sandy beaches and cliffs. Most of the south shore is inaccessible by road. **Panguipulli**, at the northwest edge of the lake in a beautiful setting, is the largest town in the area. The Iglesia San Sebastián is in Swiss style, with twin towers; its belltower contains three bells from Germany. In summer, catamaran trips are offered on the lake and trips can be made to Lagos Calafquén, Neltume, Pirehueico and to the northern tip of Lago Riñihue. In the last week of January is **Semana de Rosas**, with dancing and sports competitions. **Tourist office** ① *by the plaza, T231 0436, www.sietelagos.cl, also www.municipalidadpanguipulli.cl, daily Dec-Feb, otherwise Mon-Fri.*

Choshuenco (*Population: 622; tourist information T063-231 8305*) lies 45 km east of Panguipulli at the eastern tip of the lake. To the south is the **Reserva Nacional Mocho Choshuenco** (7536 ha) which includes two volcanoes: Choshuenco (2415 m) and Mocho (2422 m). On the slopes of Choshuenco the **Club Andino de Valdivia** has ski-slopes and three *refugios*. This can be reached by a turning from the road which goes south from Choshuenco to Enco at the east end of Lago Riñihue (the lake southwest of Lago Panguipulli). East of Choshuenco a road leads to Lago Pirehueico, via the impressive waterfalls of Huilo Huilo, where the river channels its way through volcanic rock before thundering down into a natural basin. The falls are three hours' walk from Choshuenco, or take the Puerto Fuy bus and get off at Alojamiento Huilo Huilo (see Where to stay, below), from where it is a five-minute walk to the falls. At Huilo Huilo is a biological reserve, lots of outdoor activities and a variety of lodgings in the trees; see www.huilohilo.com.

East of Choshuenco is **Lago Pirehueico**, a long, narrow and deep lake, surrounded by virgin lingüe forest. It is largely unspoilt, although there are plans to build a huge tourist complex in Puerto Pirehueico. There are no roads along the shores of the lake, but two ports. **Puerto Fuy** (*Population: 300*) is at the north end 21 km from Choshuenco, 7 km from Neltume. **Puerto Pirehueico** is at the south end. A ferry runs between the two ports, then a road to the Argentine border crossing at Paso Hua Hum.

The border with Argentina, **Paso Hua Hum** (659 m), is 11 km from Puerto Pirehueico (very hard for cyclists with steep climbs, no public transport to border). On the Argentine side the road leads alongside Lago Lacar to San Martín de los Andes and Junín de los Andes. Chilean immigration is open summer 0800-2000, winter 0800-1900.

⊚ Lagos Villarrica, Calafquén and Panguipulli listings

For hotel and restaurant price codes, and other relevant information, see Essentials.

⊜ Where to stay

Villarrica *p747*
Lodging in private homes in our **$$-$** range can be found on Muñoz blocks 400 and 500, Koerner 300 and O'Higgins 700 and 800. More upmarket accommodation is on the lakefront.
$$$$ Villarrica Park Lake, Km 13 on the road to Pucón, T245 0000, www.starwoodhotels. com. 5-star, all rooms with balconies

overlooking the lake, spa with pools, sauna, solarium, fishing trips.
$$$ El Ciervo, Koerner 241, T241 1215, www. hotelelciervo.cl. Comfortable rooms, pleasant grounds, German-style breakfasts, German and some English spoken, pool, terrace.
$$$ Hostería de la Colina, Las Colinas 115, overlooking town, T241 1503, www. hosteriadelacolina.com. Large gardens, good restaurant (the US owner makes fresh ice cream every day), fine views, very attentive service. Fishing, horse riding and dog sledding can be organized from the *hostería* as well.

$$$ Hotel y Cabañas El Parque, Camino Villarica, Km 2.5, T241 1120, www.hotelel parque.cl. Lakeside with beach, tennis courts, good restaurant set meals.

$$$ Hotel Yachting Kiel, Koerner 153, T241 1631, www.restaurantkiel.cl. Small hotel with 3 rooms, all with views across the lake to the volcano. Spacious bathrooms, heating. German and some English spoken. Good restaurant.

$$$ Parque Natural Dos Ríos, 13 km west of Villarrica, Putue Alto s/n, Casilla 535, T09-9419 8064, www.dosrios.de. B&B rooms or self-catering cabins. Tranquil 40-ha nature park on the banks of the Río Toltén (white-sand beach), birdwatching, child-friendly, German and English spoken.

$$ Bungalowlandia, Prat 749, 1241 1635, www.bungalowlandia.cl. *Cabañas*, dining room, good facilities, pool.

$$ Hostería Bilbao, Henriquez 43, 1241 1186, www.interpatagonia.com/bilbao. Small rooms, pretty patio, good restaurant.

$$ La Torre Suiza, Bilbao 969, 1241 1213, www. torresuiza.com. Rooms and dorms, camping, cycle rental, book exchange, lots of info, reserve in advance. German and English spoken.

$$-$ Hosp Nicolás, Anfion Muñoz 477, T241 2637. Simple rooms with bath. Good value, but thin walls.

$ Chito Fuentes, Vicente Reyes 665, T241 1595. Basic rooms above a restaurant.

Camping Many sites east of town on Pucón road, open in season only and expensive.

Pucón *p747*

In summer (Dec-Feb) rooms may be hard to find. Plenty of alternatives (usually cheaper) in Villarrica. Prices below are Jan-Feb. Off-season rates are 20-40% lower and it is often possible to negotiate. Many families offer rooms, look for the signs or ask in bars/restaurants. Touts offer rooms to new arrivals; check that they are not way out of town.

$$$$ Antumalal, 2 km west of Pucón, T244 1011, www.antumalal.com. Small, luxury, picturesque chalet-type boutique hotel, magnificent views of the lake (breakfast and lunch on terrace), 12 acres of gardens, with meals, open year round, indoor pool, hot tub, sauna, spa, jacuzzis and private beaches.

$$$$ Interlaken, Caupolicán 720, T244 3965, www.hotelinterlaken.cl. Chalets with full facilities, water skiing, pool, no restaurant.

$$$ Cabañas Rucamalal, O'Higgins 770, T244 2297, www.rucamalal.cl. Lovely cabins (with satellite TV) in a pretty garden, spacious, well equipped and decorated, various sizes, pool.

$$$-$$ Hostal Gerónimo, Alderete 665, T244 3762, www.geronimo.cl. Open all year. Quiet, smart, multilingual staff, bar, restaurant.

$$$-$$ Hostería ¡école!, General Urrutia 592, T244 1675, www.ecole.cl. Rooms and dorms, shop, vegetarian and fish restaurant, forest treks (departure for Lahuén Foundation's Cani Forest Sanctuary), rafting and biking, information, language classes, massage.

$$ Donde Germán, Las Rosas 590, T244 2444, www.dondegerman.cl. Single, double or triple rooms with private or shared bath. Fun, organizes tours, book in advance.

$$ El Refugio, Palguín 540, T244 1596, www.hostalelrefugio.cl. Dorm or double room, shared bath, small, convenient, cosy, Dutch/Chilean-owned. Trips sold, but shop around.

$$ Hostal Backpackers, Palguín 695, T244 1417, www.backpackerspucon.com. With or without bath, quiet, next to JAC buses, lots of activities, Navimag reservations, tourist information.

$$ La Tetera, Urrutia 580, T246 4126, www.tetera.cl. 6 rooms, some with bath, English spoken, book swap, information centre, good Spanish classes, car rental, book in advance. Nearby bar music is audible on weekends.

$$-$ Hosp Irma Torres, Lincoyán 545, T244 2226, www.hospedajeirmapucon.es.tl. Private or shared bath, tourist information, bicycle hire.

$$-$ Hosp Víctor, Palguín 705, T244 3525, www.pucon.com/victor. Rooms sleep 2-4 with private or shared bath, laundry. A decent choice.

$$-$ La Bicicleta, Palguín361, T244 4679. Cosy budget hostel offering excursions and bike tours. Owner José can help with all the details.

$$-$ One Way, C Arauco, T7472 3665/6514 5699, onewaypucon@hotmail.com (on Facebook too). Swiss/Chilean-owned backpacker hostel, with a cabaña, breakfast optional, garden, information on treks etc, parking, call or email for information and pick-up.

$ pp Etnico Hostel and Adventures, Colo Colo 36, T244 2305, www.etnico.hostel.com. Owner is mountain guide. Double rooms and mixed dorms, car and bike parking, lots of activities and keen on recycling.

Camping There are many camping and cabin establishments. Those close to Pucón include **La Poza**, Costanera Geis 769, T244 1435, campinglapoza@hotmail.com, hot showers, good kitchen. Several sites en route to volcano, including: **L'Etoile**, Km 2, T244 2188, www.letoilepucon.com, in attractive forest.

Lago Caburga p748

$$$$-$$$ Trailanqui, 20 km west of Lago Colico (36 km north of Villarrica), T257 8219, www.trailanqui.com. Luxurious hotel on the riverbank, with suites and restaurant, also equipped *cabañas*, campsite, horse riding, pool, Sunday lunch buffet.

$$$ Landhaus San Sebastián, Camino Pucón a Caburga, Pucón 2222, T045-2197 2360, www.landhaus.cl. With bath and breakfast, good meals, laundry facilities, English and German spoken, Spanish classes, good base for nearby walks.

Parque Nacional Huerquehue p748

$$$-$$ Puerto Parque Tinquilco, T244 1480, www.parquehuerquehue.cl. Hotel, cabins, camping and motorhome parking, restaurant, kayaks, boats for hire.

$$ Inés Braatz, German speaking family offers accommodation, no electricity, food and camping (US$18-22 depending on season); also rents rowing boats on the lake.

$$ Refugio Tinquilco, 2 km from park entrance, where forest trail leads to lakes Verde and Toro, T02-2278 9831, T09-9539 2728, www.tinquilco.cl. Range of cabins, bunk beds or doubles, cheapest without sheets, bring sleeping bag, private or shared bath, meals available, heating, 24-hr electricity, sauna.

Camping at the park entrance, 2 sites.

$$-$ Camping Olga, T244 1938, camping in the park, 2 km from park entrance, with hot water.

Route to Argentina p749

$$ Kila Leufu/Ruka Rayen, 23 km east on road to Curarrehue, T09-9711 8064, www.kilaleufu.cl. 2 adjacent guesthouses run by the same

Austrian/Mapuche owners. Kila Leufu offers rooms on the Martínez family farm, contact Irma or Margot at **Ruka Rayen** in advance, home-grown food, boat tours. **Ruka Rayen** is on the banks of the Río Palguín, 15 mins' walk from the main road (regular buses to Pucón). Some rooms with bath, English-speaking hosts (Margot's parents own **Kila Leufu**), mountain-bike hire. Both serve meals, offer horse-riding, trekking information and camping. The perfect choice if you want to avoid the hustle and bustle of Pucón. spoken

$$ Rancho de Caballos, Palguín Aito Km 32, T09-8346 1764 (limited signal), www.rancho-de-caballos.com. Restaurant with vegetarian dishes; also *cabañas* and camping, self-guided trails, horse-riding trips ½-7 days, English and German spoken.

Lago Calafquén and around *p749*
Lican-Ray
$$ Cabañas Los Nietos, Manquel 125, Playa Chica, T09-5639 3585, www.losnietos.cl. Self-catering cabins.

$ Res Temuco, G Mistral 517, Playa Grande, T243 1130. Shared bath, with breakfast, good.

$ Camping Las Gaviotas, Km 5 Camino Lican-Ray, T9030 1153, www.campinglas gaviotas.cl. Beach camping with many amenities, such as hot showers, mini market and volleyball area.

Coñaripe
$$-$ Hosp Chumay, Las Tepas 201, on Plaza, T231 7287, turismochumay@hotmail.com. With restaurant, tours, some English spoken, good.

Camping Sites on beach charge US$20, but if you walk 0.5-0.75 km from town you can camp on the beach free. Cold municipal showers on beach, US$0.35. Isla Llancahue, 5 km east, T9562 0437. Campsite with *cabañas* on an island in Río Llancahue.

Termas de Coñaripe
$$$$ Termas de Coñaripe, T241 1111, www.termasconaripe.cl. Excellent hotel with 4 pools, good restaurant, spa with a variety of treatments, cycles and horses for hire. Full board available.

Termas de Liquiñe
$$$ Termas de Liquiñe, T063-2197 1301. Full board, cabins, restaurant, hot pool, small native forest.

$$ Hosp Catemu, Camino Internacional, T8361 9487, neldatrafipan@yahoo.es. Known as much for its restaurant as its cosy, wood-paneled cabins, this option can arrange excursions to the Termas.

Lago Panguipulli *p750*
See www.sietelagos.cl for list of lodgings.
$$ La Casita del Centro, J M Carerra 674, T231 1812, B&B, refurbished, safe, with restaurant, parking.

$ Hosp Familiar, JP Segundo 801, T231 1483. English and German spoken, helpful.

$ pp Hostal Orillas del Lago, M de Rosas 265, T231 1710 (or T231 2499 if no reply, friends have key). From plaza walk towards lake, last house on left, 8 blocks from terminal. Good views, backpacker place.

Camping El Bosque, P Sigifredo 241, T231 1489. Small, good, but not suitable for vehicle camping, hot water. Also 3 sites at Chauquén, 6 km southeast on lakeside.

Choshuenco
$$$ Hostería Ruca Pillán, San Martín 85, T231 8220, www.rucapillan.cl. Family-run hotel rooms and cabins overlooking the lake, restaurant, English spoken, tours.

$$ Cabañas Choshuenco, Bernabé 391, T231 8316, www.choshuencochile.cl. Cabañas, fully-equipped, self-contained, for 6-8 people.

$ pp Cabañas Huilo Huilo, Km 9 east from Choshuenco, on Camino Internacional (1 km before Neltume). Basic but comfortable and well situated for walks, good food.

Lago Pirehueico
$$ Hospedaje y Cabañas Puerto Fuy, Puerto Fuy, www.cabañaspuertofuy.cl. Hot water, good food in restaurant.

$ Hostal Kay Kaen, Puerto Fuy, T063-2197 1632. Meals, use of kitchen, bike rental. One of several private houses offering accommodation.

$ pp Restaurant San Giovani, Puerto Fuy, T2197 1562. Family atmosphere, good rooms.

Camping On the beach (take own food).

🍴 Restaurants

Villarrica *p747*

$$$ El Tabor, S Epulef 1187, T241 1901. Fish and seafood specialities, excellent but pricey.

$$$ La Cava del Roble, Valentín Letelier 658, p 2, T241 6446. Excellent grill, specializes in exotic meat and game, extensive wine list.

$$ La Vecchia Cucina, Pedro de Valdivia 1011, T241 1798. Good Italian serving a range of pizzas and pastas.

$$ The Travellers Resto Bar, Letelier 753, T241 3617. Varied menu including vegetarian and Asian food, bar, English spoken.

$$-$ Juanito, Vicente Reyes 678. Closed Sun. Good, and cheap end of the range.

$ Casa Vieja, Letelier 609. Good-value set lunch, family-run.

$ El Marítimo, Alderete 769, T241 9755. Generally first-rate, unpretentious, serving traditional fish and seafood.

$ El Turismo, Epulef 1201 y Rodriguez. No frills, good Chilean dishes.

Café 2001, Henríquez 379, T241 1470, www.cafebar2001.cl. Best coffee in town. Also good cakes and friendly service at a reasonable price. For ice cream, try the stall next door.

Pucón *p747*

See Where to stay for other recommendations.

$$$ Puerto Pucón, Fresia 246, T244 1592. One of Pucón's older restaurants, Spanish, stylish.

$$$-$$ La Maga, Alderete 276 y Fresia, T244 4277, www.lamagapucon.cl. Uruguayan *parrillada* serving excellent steak. So good that several imitations have opened up nearby to take the overspill.

$$$-$$ Senzo, Fresia 284, T244 9005. Fresh pasta and risotto prepared by a Swiss chef.

$$ Arabian, Fresia 354-B, T244 3469. Arab specialities, including stuffed vine leaves, falafel, etc.

$$ ¡école!, in Hostería of same name, General Urrutia 592, T244 1675. Good vegetarian restaurant.

$$ Il Baretto, Fresia 124, T244 3515. Stone-baked pizzas.

$ Rap Hamburguesa, O'Higgins 625. Open late. Freshly made hamburgers, chips and Chilean fast food.

Cafés

Café de la P, O'Higgins y Lincoyán, T244 3577. Real coffee.

Café Lounge Brasil, Colo Colo 485, T244 4035, www.cafeloungebrasil.com. Gourmet cafeteria which also has a 'boutique' hostel. Meals include vegetarian options, Jamaican coffee.

Cassis, Fresia 223, T244 4715, www.chocolatescassis.com. Chocolates, ice creams, pancakes and snacks as well as coffee.

Mamas and Tapas, O'Higgins y Arauco, T244 9002, www.mamasandtapas.cl. Drink and snacks. There are several others on O'Higgins.

Lago Calafquén: Lican-Ray *p749*

$$ Cábala, Urrutia 201, nice centre location; good pizzas and pastas.

$$-$ The Ñaños, Urrutia 105. Good café, reasonable prices, helpful owner. Service can be patchy.

Panguipulli *p750*

$$-$ Café Central, M de Rosas 750. Fixed menu, good and cheap at lunchtimes, expensive in evenings.

$$-$ El Chapulín, M de Rosas 639. Good food and value. Several cheap restaurants in O'Higgins 700 block.

🛍 Shopping

Pucón *p747*

Camping equipment Eltit supermarket, O'Higgins y Fresia. **Outdoors & Travel**, Lincoyán 36, clothing, equipment, maps.

Handicrafts market Just south of O'Higgins on Ansorena; local specialities are painted wooden flowers.

⚫ What to do

Villarrica *p747*

Fundo Huifquenco, just south of town (500 m) along Av Matta, T241 2200, www.fundohuifquenco.cl. Working farm, trails, horseriding, carriage tours, bicycle hire, meals (book in advance).

Novena Región, Parque Ecológico 3 Esteros, 20 km from Villarrica towards Panguipulli, T09-8901 2574, www.novena-region.com. Mushing and husky trekking on the winter snow and in summer with Siberian Huskies. Unique in Chile.

Ríos Family, T241 2408. Birdwatching and fishing trips.

Rodrigo Puelma, T09-9625 1345. Private guide, speaks basic English.

Villarica Extremo, Valdivia 910, T241-0900, www.villaricaextremo.com. Good excursions featuring the usual suspects like volcano tours, rafting, thermal pools and paintball.

Pucón p747

Climbing Sierra Nevada, O'Higgins 524-A, T244 4210. Offers *Via Ferrata*, a kind of climbing up sheer rock faces for beginners using metal hand- and footholds embedded in the rock.

Fishing Pucón and Villarica are celebrated as centres for fishing on Lake Villarica and in the beautiful Lincura, Trancura and Toltén rivers. Local tourist office will supply details on licenses and open seasons, etc. Two fishing specialists are **Mario's Fishing Zone**, O'Higgins 580, T9760 7280, www.flyfishingpucon.com (expensive but good), and **Off Limits**, O'Higgins 560, T244 3741, www.offlimits.cl (English and Italian spoken).

Horse riding Rancho de Caballos, see Where to stay, above. Average hire costs about US$31 ½ day, US$70 full day (transfer from Pucón extra). **Centro de Turismo Ecuestre Huepilmalal**, Camino a Termas de Huife, Km 25, T09-9643 2673, www.huepilmalal.cl. Rodolfo Coombs and Carolina Pumpin, 40 mins from town, also with lodging; from riding lessons (US$31) to 10-day treks.

Mountain biking Bike hire from US$2.50 per hr to US$200 per day for cross-country excursions with guide. Available from several travel agencies on O'Higgins.

Thermal springs Dozens of thermal springs in the area, ranging from the upmarket to the natural. Transport is provided by tour operators.

Watersports Waterskiing, sailing, rowing boats and windsurfing at Playa Grande beach by Gran Hotel and La Poza beach end of O'Higgins (more expensive than Playa Grande, not recommended).

Whitewater rafting Very popular on the Río Trancura. Many agencies offer trips (see below), Trancura Bajo (grade III), US$30; Trancura Alto (grades 3 and 4), US$50.

Ziplining Called **Canopy** (sliding from platform to platform along a metal cord). Several agencies can arrange this. The best (and most safety conscious) is **Bosque Aventura**, Arauca 611 y O'Higgins, T9325 4795, www.canopypucon.cl.

Tour operators

Tour operators arrange trips to thermal baths, trekking to volcanoes, whitewater rafting, etc. For falls, lakes and termas it's cheaper, if in a group, to flag down a taxi and bargain. Many agencies, so shop around: prices vary at times, quality of guides and equipment variable. In high season, when lots of groups go together, individual attention may be lacking.

Aguaventura, Palguín 336, T244 4246, www.aguaventura.com. French-run, in summer kayaking and rafting specialities, in winter 'snowshop' for ski and snowboard rental, volcano climbing, trekking.

Elementos, Pasaje Las Rosas 640, T244 1750, www.elementos-chile.com. Provider covering the entire country and specializing in sustainable tourism. Has its own **EcoHostel**. Good option for volcano treks.

Kayak Chile, O'Higgins, T09-9184 7529, www.kayakchile.net. Day trips and classes for all levels, all guides are UK or US trained, maximum of 2 students per instructor, responsible. Also sells used equipment.

Mountain Life Adventure, Arauco 265 (at Hostel One Way), T244 4564, mountainlife adventure@hotmail.com. Villarica hike plus treks and climbs up other volcanoes in the region, Chilean/Swiss owned.

Politur, O'Higgins 635, T244 1373, www.politur.com. Well-established and responsible, good for volcano trek and rafting; a little pricier than others.

Pucón Tours, O'Higgins 615, T927 30208. Small group quad-bike excursions US$28, good fun. Also hires out good quality bicycles and offers a wide range of other tours.

Travel Aid, Ansorena 425, loc 4, T244 4040, www.travelaid.cl. Helpful general travel agency, sells trekking maps, guidebooks, lots of information, agents for **Navimag** and other boat trips, English and German spoken.

Volcán Villarica, O' Higgins 555, T900 24587, volcan.villarica@hotmail.com. Specializes in group excursions to Volcán Villarica as well as a number of other activities, including rafting, canyoning and paintball. English spoken, good equipment.

Route to Argentina *p749*
Escape, in Curarrehue, T09-9678 5380, www.patagonia-escape.com. Owned by John 'LJ' Groth, specializing in SUP, private kayak guiding trips and rafting on some beautiful sections of the Río Trancura and around. Safe, responsible, environmentally aware and different.

⊙ Transport

Villarrica *p747*
Bus Terminal at Pedro de Valdivia y Muñoz. JAC at Bilbao 610, T241 1447, and opposite for Pucón and Lican-Ray. Terminal Rural for other local services at Matta y Vicente Reyes. To **Santiago**, 10 hrs, US$27-50, several companies. To **Pucón**, with Vipu-Ray (main terminal) and JAC, in summer every 15 mins, 40 mins' journey, US$1.50; same companies to **Lican-Ray**, US$1.50. To **Valdivia**, JAC, US$8, 5 a day, 2½ hrs. To **Coñaripe** (US$3) and **Liquiñe** at 1600 Mon-Sat, 1000 Sun. To **Temuco**, JAC, US$3-4. To **Loncoche** (Ruta 5 junction for hitching), US$2.25. To **Panguipulli**, go via Lican-Ray, occasional direct buses. Buses to Argentina: buses from Valdivia to **San Martín de los Andes** pass through Villarrica, fares are the same as from Valdivia, T241 2733, book in advance. Note that if the Mamuil Malal pass is blocked by snow buses go via Panguipulli instead of Villarrica and Pucón.

Pucón *p747*
Air Airport 2 km on Caburga road. Check with airlines for summer flights from **Santiago** via Temuco.
Bus No municipal terminal: each company has its own terminal: JAC, Uruguay y Palguín; Tur-Bus, O'Higgins 910, east of town; Igi Llaima and Cóndor, Colo Colo y O'Higgins. JAC to **Villarrica** (very frequent, US$1.50) and **Valdivia** (US$9, 3 hrs). Tur-Bus direct to **Valdivia, Osorno** and **Puerto Montt**, 6 hrs, US$14-17, daily. To **Santiago**, 10 hrs, US$27-50, many companies, early morning and late evening. Colectivos to **Villarrica** from O'Higgins y Palguín. Buses to Argentina: Buses from Valdivia to **San Martín** pass through Pucón.

Car hire Hire prices start at US$35 per day; Avis, Arauco 302, T246 5328, www.avis.cl; Hertz, in the Gran Hotel, T244 1664; Kilómetro Libre, Alderete 480, T244 4399, www.rentacarkilo metrolibre.com; Pucón Rent A Car, Colo Colo 340, T244 3052, www.puconrentacar.cl.
Taxi Araucaria, T244 2323.

Lago Caburga *p748*
Bus Buses Caburga run minibuses every 30 mins from Pucón to **Caburga**, US$1.50; there are colectivos from Ansorena y Uruguay. If walking or cycling, turn left 3 km east of Pucón (sign to Puente Quelhue) and follow the track (very rough) for 18 km through beautiful scenery.

Parque Nacional Huerquehue *p748*
Bus Buses Caburga from **Pucón**, 3 daily, 1½ hrs, US$3.50.

Lago Calafquén and around *p749*
Lican-Ray
Bus Leave from offices around plaza. To **Villarrica**, 1 hr, US$1.50, JAC frequent in summer. In summer, there are direct buses from **Santiago** (Tur-Bus US$20, 10 hrs, salón cama US$45-80) and **Temuco** (2½ hrs, US$7). To **Panguipulli**, Mon-Sat 0730.

Coñaripe
Bus To **Panguipulli**, 7 a day (4 off season), US$3 and 16 daily to **Villarrica**, US$2.75. Nightly bus direct to **Santiago**, Tur-Bus and JAC, 11½ hrs, US$30-60.

Panguipulli *p750*
Bus Terminal at Gabriela Mistral y Portales. To **Santiago** daily, US$21-50. To **Valdivia**, frequent (Sun only 4), several companies, 2 hrs, US$5. To **Temuco** frequent, Power and Pangui Sur, US$6, 3 hrs. To **Puerto Montt**, US$12. To **Choshuenco**, Neltume and Puerto Fuy, 3 daily, 3 hrs, US$7. To **Coñaripe** (with connections for Lican-Ray and Villarrica), 7 daily, 4 off season, 1½ hrs, US$3.

Lago Pirehueico
Bus Daily Puerto Fuy to **Panguipulli**, 3 daily, 3 hrs, US$7.
Ferry The Hua Hum sails from Puerto Fuy to Puerto Pirehueico at 0800, 1300, 1800 (Jan-

Feb), 1400 (rest of year), returns 2 hrs later, foot passengers US$1.50, cars US$30, motorbikes US$9. A beautiful crossing, comparable to the lakes crossing from Puerto Montt to Bariloche, but at a fraction the price (to take vehicles reserve in advance on T063-2197 1871, see Somarco's website, www.barcazas.cl). Buses to **San Martín de los Andes, Argentina**, 50 km, are run by **Ko Ko**, usually all year; T02972-427422 (in San Martín) for schedule.

⊙ Directory

Villarrica *p747*
Banks ATMs at banks on Pedro de Valdivia between Montt and Alderete.

Pucón *p747*
Banks There are 3 or 4 banks with ATMs and several *casas de cambio* on O'Higgins, although *cambio* rates are universally poor. Much better to change money in Temuco.

Valdivia and Osorno

Valdivia is a very pleasant city at the confluence of the Ríos Calle Calle and Cruces, which form the Río Valdivia. It is set in rich agricultural land receiving some 2300 mm of rain a year. To the north of the city is a large island, Isla Teja, where the Universidad Austral de Chile is situated. The student population adds zest to the nightlife. At the mouth of the Río Valdivia are a group of historic forts which make a good day's outing from the city. Osorno, further south, is not such a tourist city, but it is a base for visiting the attractive southern lakes.

Valdivia → *Phone code: 063. Colour map 8, C1. Population: 127,000. 839 km south of Santiago.*
Valdivia was one of the most important centres of Spanish colonial control over Chile. Founded in 1552 by Pedro de Valdivia, it was abandoned as a result of the Mapuche insurrection of 1599 and the area was briefly occupied by Dutch pirates. In 1645 it was refounded as a walled city, the only Spanish mainland settlement south of the Río Biobío. The coastal fortifications at the mouth of the river also date from the 17th century. They were greatly strengthened after 1760 owing to fears that Valdivia might be seized by the British, but were of little avail during the Wars of Independence. overnight on 2 February 1820 the Chilean naval squadron under Lord Cochrane seized San Carlos, Amargos and Corral and turned their guns on Niebla and Mancera, which surrendered the following morning. From independence until the 1880s Valdivia was an outpost of Chilean rule, reached only by sea or by a coastal route through Mapuche territory. From 1849 to 1875 Valdivia was a centre for German colonization of the Lake District. In 2007 it became capital of the newly created Región XIV, Los Ríos. **Tourist offices** ⓘ *Av Prat 675, T223 9060, infolosrios@sernatur.cl*. Good map of region and local rivers, list of hotel prices and examples of local crafts with artisans' addresses. Open daily in summer, weekdays only during off season. Municipal tourist offices on Avenida Prat (Costanera) at the north side of the **Feria Fluvial** ⓘ *T222 0490, www.turismolosrios.cl, Mon-Fri 0900-1800 in winter, 0900-2100 in summer, Sat-Sun 1000-2030*, upstairs in the bus terminal and other locations.

Places in Valdivia The city centre is the tree-lined, shady **Plaza de la República**. A pleasant walk is along **Avenida Prat** (or **Costanera**), which follows the bend in the river, from the bus station to the bridge to **Isla Teja**, the **Muelle Fluvial** (boat dock) and the riverside market. The modern Hotel y Casino Valdivia overlooks the Puente Pedro de Valdivia and the grassy area below it is popular on sunny days. Boats can be hired at the bend per hour. Sealions lounge around the dock. On Isla Teja, near the library in the University, are a **botanic garden** and **arboretum** with trees from all over the world. West of the botanical gardens is the 30-ha **Parque Saval**, with areas of native forest, as well as the **Lago de los Lotos** (beautiful blooms in spring) ⓘ *all open during daylight hours, US$0.75*. On boat trips round the island you can see lots of waterfowl. Also on Isla Teja is the **Museo Histórico y Antropológico** ⓘ *T221 2872, www.museosaustral.cl, Mar-Dec Tue-Sun 1000-1300, 1400-1800, Jan and Feb daily 1000-2000, US$2.75*. Run by the University, it contains exhibits on archaeology, ethnography and the history of German settlement, beautifully housed in the former mansion of Carlos Anwandter, a prominent German immigrant. Next door is the **Museo de Arte Contemporáneo** ⓘ *T222 1968, www.macvaldivia.cl, Tue-Sun 1000-1300, 1400-1900, US$2.25, times change according to the exhibition*.

The surrounding district has lovely countryside of woods, beaches, lakes and rivers. The various rivers are navigable and there are pleasant journeys by rented motor boat on the **Ríos Futa** and **Tornagaleanes** around the **Isla del Rey**. Boat tours go to the **Santuario de la Naturaleza Carlos Anwandter** ⓘ *Embarcaciones Bahía, T234 8727, www.embarcacionesbahia.cl, on the riverfront near the fish market, offers daily tours leaving at 1600 and returning at 2015, 6 hrs, US$18 pp*. The refuge is an area on the Río Cruces which flooded as result of the 1960 earthquake; lots of bird species are visible.

Parque Oncol ⓘ *27 km northwest of Valdivia, T800-370222, www.parqueoncol.cl, park entry US$4.50, students, children and seniors US$1, anyone on a bike US$2*, 754 ha of Valdivian native forest, with several trails and lookouts, zipline (*canopy*) site, US$27 (daily 1130-1600), picnic area, café and campsite.

Coastal resorts near Valdivia

At the mouth of the Río Valdivia there are attractive villages which can be visited by land or river boat. The two main centres are Niebla on the north bank and Corral opposite on the south bank. **Niebla**, 18 km from Valdivia, is a spread-out resort with seafood restaurants and accommodation (also plenty of *cabañas* and campsites on the road from Valdivia). To the west of the resort is the **Fuerte de la Pura y Limpia Concepción de Monfort de Lemus** ⓘ *closed for renovation until May 2014*, on a promontory. It has an interesting museum on Chilean naval history.

Valdivia

Where to stay	6 Hostal Anwandter	12 Melillanca
1 Airesbuenos Central	7 Hostal Arlense House	13 Puerta del Sur
4 Encanto del Río	8 Hostal Casagrande	
5 Hostal Ana María	9 Hostal Torreón	**Restaurants**
	10 Hostal Totem	1 Agridulce
	11 Hostal y Cabañas	2 Café Haussmann
	Internacional	3 Café Moro
		4 Cervecería Kunstmann
		6 Entrelagos
		7 La Baguette
		8 La Calesa
		9 Lomodetoro
		11 Volcán

Corral, quieter than Niebla, is a fishing port with several good restaurants 62 km from Valdivia by road (unsuitable for cars without four-wheel drive or high clearance). The dilapidated but atmospheric **Castillo de San Sebastián** ① *entry US$5, US$3 off season*, with 3-m-wide walls, was defended by a battery of 21 guns. It has a museum and offers a view upriver. In summer there are daily re-enactments of the 1820 storming of the Spanish fort by the Chileans (15 December-15 March, 1600, 1730, 1830). North along the coast are the remains of Castillo San Luis de Alba de Amargos (3 km) and Castillo de San Carlos, with pleasant beaches (4 km). The coastal walks west and south of Corral are splendid. The helpful tourist office on Corral's pier can provide some trekking tips.

In midstream, between Niebla and Corral is **Isla Mancera** a small island, fortified by the Castillo de San Pedro de Alcántara, which has the most standing buildings. The island is a pleasant place to stop, but it can get crowded when an excursion boat arrives.

Osorno and around → *Phone code: 064. Colour map 8, C1. Population: 132,000.*

Founded in 1553, abandoned in 1604 and refounded in 1796, Osorno later became one of the centres of German immigration. On the large Plaza de Armas stands the modern cathedral, while to the east of the plaza along MacKenna are a number of late 19th-century mansions built by German immigrants, now National Monuments. **Museo Histórico Municipal** ① *Matta 809, entrance in Casa de Cultura, www.interpatagonia.com/paseos/museo_osorno/, Mon-Thu 0930-1730, Fri until 1630, Sat from 1400-1900, free,* includes displays on natural history, Mapuche culture, refounding of the city and German colonization. The **Museo Interactivo de Osorno** (MIO) ① *in the former train station, Portales 901, 3 blocks southwest of the plaza, T221 2997, Mon-Thu 0900-1300, 1400 1700, Fri closes 1600, Sat-Sun 1400-1900,* is an interactive science museum designed for both children and adults. **Tourist offices: Sernatur** in provincial government office ① *Plaza de Armas, O'Higgins 667, p 1, Mon-Fri 0900-1800, T223 7575, infosorno@sernatur.cl.* Municipal office in the bus terminal and kiosk on the Plaza de Armas (www.municipalidadosorno.cl).

About 47 km east of Osorno, **Lago Puyehue** (*Colour map 8, C1; Altitude: 207 m*) is surrounded by relatively flat countryside. At the western end is **Entre Lagos** (*Population: 4000*) and the **Termas de Puyehue** ① *all-inclusive resort, day or night passes available, price depends on day and season, from US$74, www.puyehue.cl,* is at the eastern end.

The **Parque Nacional Puyehue**, east of Lago Puyehue, stretches to the Argentine border. On the east side are several lakes and two volcanic peaks: **Volcán Puyehue** (2240 m) in the north (access via private track US$13 belonging to **El Caulle** restaurant, with camping, www.elcaulle.com) and **Volcán Casablanca** (also called Antillanca, 1900 m). Park administration is at Aguas Calientes, 4 km south of the Termas de Puyehue. There is a ranger station at Anticura. Leaflets on attractions are available.

At **Aguas Calientes** ① *www.termasaguascalientes.cl, day passes US$38-45 depending on day of week and season, 0830-2000,* there are indoor and open-air thermal pools with camping, cabins, massages and other therapies.

From Aguas Calientes the road continues 18 km southeast to Antillanca on the slopes of **Volcán Casablanca**, past three small lakes and through forests. This is particularly beautiful, especially at sunrise, with the snow-clad cones of Osorno, Puntiagudo and Puyehue forming a semicircle. The tree-line on Casablanca is one of the few in the world made up of deciduous trees (nothofagus or southern beech). From Antillanca it is possible to climb Casablanca for even better views of the surrounding volcanoes and lakes, no path, seven hours return journey, information from Club Andino in Osorno. Attached to the Hotel Antillanca is one of the smallest ski resorts in Chile; there are three lifts, ski instruction and first aid available. Skiing quality depends on the weather: rain is common. See under Osorno for buses. No public transport from Aguas Calientes to Antillanca; try hitching – always difficult, but it is not a hard walk.

Border with Argentina: Paso Samoré (formerly Puyehue)

The border is normally open 0800-2000. The Chilean border post is at Pajaritos, 4 km east of **Anticura**, which is 22 km west of the border. For vehicles entering Chile, formalities are quick (about 15 minutes), but includes the spraying of tyres, and shoes have to be wiped on a mat. This route is liable to closure after snow. Cyclists should know that there are no supplies between Entre Lagos and La Angostura (Argentina).

◉ Valdivia and Osorno listings

For hotel and restaurant price codes, and other relevant information, see Essentials.

◉ Where to stay

Valdivia *p757, map p758*
Accommodation is often scarce during Semana Valdiviana. In summer, rooms are widely available in private homes, usually **$$**, or **$** singles.
$$$$-$$$ Puerta del Sur, Los Lingües 950, Isla Teja, T222 4500, www.hotelpuerta delsur.com. 5 star, with all facilities and extensive grounds.
$$$ Encanto del Río, Prat 415, T222 4744, www.hotelencantodelrio.cl. Small, comfortable, rooms on the middle floor have balconies and river views, disabled access, heating.
$$$ Melillanca, Alemania 675, T221 2509, www.hotelmelillanca.cl. 4-star, decent business standard, with restaurant, sauna.
$$ Hostal y Cabañas Internacional, García Reyes 660, T221 2015, www.hostalinternacional. cl. Self-catering cabins sleep 5, hostel rooms and dorms with private or shared bath, helpful, English and German spoken, book exchange, excursions to the ocean and rainforest.
$$ Hostal Torreón, P Rosales 783, T221 2622, mrprelle@gmail.com. Old German-style villa, nice atmosphere, rooms on top floor are airy, parking.
$$ Hostal Totem, Anwandter 425, T229 2849, www.turismototem.cl. Simple rooms, French and basic English spoken, tours arranged, credit cards accepted.
$$-$ Airesbuenos Central, García Reyes 550, T222 2202, www.airesbuenos.cl. Eco-conscious hostel. Private rooms and dorms, private or shared bath, garden with friendly duck named Gardel, yoga space, tours, many languages spoken by volunteers, HI affiliated.
$ Hostal Arlense House, Camilo Henríquez 749, Casa 6, T243 1494/9-7984 5597, arlene_ola@ hotmail.com. Charming tumbledown mansion, endearingly wonky floors (after-effect of 1960 earthquake), large rooms, some English spoken.

Around the bus terminal
$$ Hostal Ana María, José Martí 11, 3 mins from terminal, T222 2468, anamsandovalf@ hotmail.com. Good value, also *cabañas*.
$$ Hostal Anwandter, Anwandter 601 and García Reyes 249, T221 8587, www.hostal anwandter.cl. Rooms sleep 1-4, private or shared bathroom, meals available, usual hostel facilities.
$$ Hostal Casagrande, Anwandter 880, T220 2035, www.hotelcasagrande.cl. Heated but small rooms, some gloomy, in attractive house, convenient, great views from breakfast room.
Camping Camping Centenario, in Rowing Club on España. **$** per tent, overlooking river.

Coastal resorts near Valdivia *p758*
$$$ El Castillo, Antonio Ducce 750, Niebla, T228 2061, www.hotelycabanaselcastillo.com. Typical Germanic 1920 mansion, lots of character. Rooms and apartments.parking, playground, pool.
$$ Cabañas Fischer, Del Castillo 1115, Niebla, T228 2007, rosemarief24@gmail.com. Cabins and 2 campsites. Worth bargaining out of season.

Osorno *p759*
$$$ Sonesta, Ejercito 395 Rahue, T255 5000, www.sonesta.com. First-class hotel overlooking river, all amenities, El Olivillo restaurant, attached to Plaza de los Lagos mall and casino.
$$$ Waeger, Cochrane 816, T223 3721, www.hotelwaeger.cl. 4-star, restaurant, comfortable but room sizes vary greatly.
$$$-$$ Eduviges, Eduviges 856, T223 5023, www.hoteleduviges.cl. Spacious, quiet, attractive, gardens; also *cabañas*.
$$ Hostal Riga, Amthauer 1058, T223 2945, resiriga@surnet.cl. Pleasant, good value, quiet area, parking, heavily booked in season.
$ Res Hein's, Errázuriz 1757, T223 4116. Private or shared bath, old-fashioned, spacious, family atmosphere.
There are plenty of cheap options near the bus terminal, for instance on Los Carrera.

Around Osorno p759
Lago Puyehue

$$$$ Hotel Termas de Puyehue, at the Termas de Puyehue, T064-233 1400, www.puyehue.cl. All inclusive: meals, drinks, use of thermal pools and all activities (Spa extra), well maintained, in beautiful scenery, heavily booked Jan-Feb, cheaper May to mid-Dec.

$$ Hosp Millaray, Ramírez 333, Entre Lagos. Very good.

$$ Hostal y Cabañas Miraflores, Ramírez 480, Entre Lagos, T237 1275, www.hostal-miraflores.cl. Pleasant rooms and cabins.

Camping Camping No Me Olvides, Ruta 215, Km 56, on south shore of Lake Puyehue, T9128 3002, www.nomeolvides.cl. Tent site and *cabañas*. Camping Los Copihues, Km 58, T9344 8830, on south shore of Lake Puyehue. Restaurant, spa, camping (US$8) and cabañas.

Aguas Calientes and Antillanca

$$$$ Hotel Antillanca, T02-2946 2900, www.chileanski.com. Full board. Skiing and snowboarding in the winter, outdoor sports in summer, hiking, caving, climbing and rappelling, at foot of Volcán Casablanca, with pool, friendly club-like atmosphere; also has a *refugio*.

Camping See Aguas Calientes, above. CONAF refugio on Volcán Puyehue, but check with CONAF in Anticura whether it is open. Los Derrumbes, 1 km from Aguas Calientes, no electricity.

🍴 Restaurants

Valdivia p757, map p758

$$$-$$ Agridulce, Prat 327, T221 6765, www.agridulcevaldivia.cl. Perfect mix of sophisticated dishes using local produce, tapas and generous sandwiches. Good service and good value.

$$$-$$ Lomodetoro, Los Robles 170, Isla Teja, T234 6423. Probably the best steak in town. Good wine list.

$$ Cervecería Kunstmann, Ruta T350, No 950, T229 2969, www.cerveza-kunstmann.cl. On road to Niebla. German/Chilean food, brewery with 5 types of beer, beautiful interior, museum. Open from 1200 for visits; yellow colectivo from outside the Mercado Municipal.

$$ La Calesa, O'Higgins 160, T222 5467. Elegant, intimate, Peruvian and international cuisine. Good *pisco sours*.

$ Volcán, Caupolicán y Chacabuco, T221 2163. *Pichangas*, *cazuelas*, great food at a good price.

Cafés

Café Haussmann, O'Higgins 394, T221 3878. A Valdivia institution. Good tea, cakes and *crudos*.

Café Moro, Independencia y Libertad, T221 2345. Airy café with a mezzanine art gallery. Good for breakfast, good value lunches, popular bar at night.

Entrelagos, Pérez Rosales 622. Ice cream and chocolates.

La Baguette, Yungay 518, T221 2345. Panadería with French-style cakes, brown bread.

Mi Pueblito, San Carlos 190, T224 5050. Whole-meal bread and vegetarian snacks to take away.

Coastal resorts near Valdivia p758

$$ Las Delicias, Ducce 583, Niebla, T221 3566. With restaurant with 'a view that would be worth the money even if the food wasn't good'. Also *cabañas* and camping.

Osorno p759

Good cheap restaurants in the municipal market

$$$ Atelier, Freire 468. Fresh pasta and other Italian delights, good.

$$ Dino's, Ramírez 898, on the plaza. Restaurant upstairs, bar/cafetería downstairs, good.

$$ Wufehr, Ramírez 1015, T222 6999. Local raw meat specialities and sandwiches. Popular with locals.

$$-$ Club de Artesanos, MacKenna 634. Decent and hearty traditional Chilean fare.

$ Café Literario Hojas del Sur, MacKenna 1011 y Cochrane. More like a living room than a café, cosy, Wi-Fi.

$ La Cabaña, Ramírez 774, T227 2479. Wide variety of cheap lunches ranging from Chinese to home-cooked Chilean. Excellent value.

$ Jano's, Ramírez 977, T221 1828. Bakery with fresh juices and lunch/dinner options. Many vegetarian options as well.

Around Osorno p759
Lago Puyehue

$$$-$$ Jardín del Turista, Ruta 215, Km 46, T437 1214, Entre Lagos, www.interpatagonia.

com/jardindelturista/. Very good, also has *cabañas* and suites.

⊛ Festivals

Valdivia *p757, map p758*
Semana Valdiviana, in **mid-Feb**, culminates in Noche Valdiviana on the Sat with a procession of elaborately decorated boats that sail past the Muelle Fluvial. Accommodation is scarce during festival. In **Sep** there is a film festival.

○ Shopping

Valdivia *p757, map p758*
Markets Colourful riverside market with livestock, fish, etc. The separate **municipal market** building has been restored and is occupied mainly by *artesanía* stalls. On the river-side of the market building several fish restaurants serve cheap, tasty food and have nice atmosphere.

○ What to do

Valdivia *p757, map p758*
To Corral and Niebla and other boat trips along the river, many kiosks along the Muelle Fluvial. Boats will only leave with a minimum of 10 passengers, so off-season organize in advance. Full list of operators in tourist information office. **Tourist House**, Camilo Henríquez 266, T243 3115. Offer range of trips and give good advice.

Sea kayaking
Pueblito Expediciones, San Carlos 188, T224 5055, www.pueblitoexpediciones.cl. Offer classes and trips in sea kayaks in the waters around Valdivia.

○ Transport

Valdivia *p757, map p758*
Air LAN to/from **Santiago** every day via Temuco, or Concepción.
Bus Well-organized terminal at Muñoz y Prat, by the river. To **Santiago**: several companies, 10 hrs, most services overnight, US$30-80; ½-hourly buses to/from **Osorno**, 2 hrs, several companies, US$8. To **Panguipulli**, Empresa Pirehueico, about every 30 mins, US$5. Many daily to **Puerto Montt**, US$9, 3 hrs. To **Puerto**

Varas, 3 hrs, US$10. To **Frutillar**, US$6, 2½ hrs. To **Villarrica**, by JAC, 6 a day, 2½ hrs, US$8, continuing to **Pucón**, US$9, 3 hrs. Frequent daily service to Riñihue via Paillaco and Los Lagos. To **Bariloche** (Argentina) via Osorno, 7 hrs, **Andesmar**, US$35-50.

Coastal resorts near Valdivia *p758*
Ferry The tourist boats to **Isla Mancera** and **Corral** offer a guided ½-day tour (US$25-75, some with meals) from the Muelle Fluvial, Valdivia, or the Marqués de Mancera (behind the tourist office on Av Prat). The river trip is beautiful, but you can also take a **bus** (orange No 20) to Niebla from outside bus station or along Calles Andwander and Carampangue in Valdivia, regular service between 0730 and 2100, 30 mins, US$1.20 (bus continues to Los Molinos), then cross to Corral by **Somarco** vehicle ferry, every 2 hrs, US$1.25. There are occasional buses from Valdivia to Corral.

Osorno *p759*
Air LAN, daily Osorno-**Santiago**, via Concepción and/or Temuco.
Bus Local buses to **Entre Lagos**, **Puyehue** and **Aguas Calientes** leave from the Mercado Municipal terminal, 1 block west of main terminal. Main terminal 4 blocks from Plaza de Armas at Errázuriz 1400. Left luggage open 0730-2030. Bus from centre, US$0.50. To **Santiago**, frequent, US$23, salón cama US$55-64, 11 hrs. To **Concepción**, US$22-33. To **Temuco**, US$9. To **Pucón** and **Villarrica**, frequent, US$13. To **Frutillar**, US$2, **Llanquihue, Puerto Varas** (US$3) and **Puerto Montt** (US$3) services every 30 mins. To **Puerto Octay**, US$3, every 20 mins. To **Bariloche** (Argentina), 4 companies, US$30.

Around Osorno *p759*
Lago Puyehue
Bus To **Entre Lagos** from Osorno, frequent services in summer, Expreso Lago Puyehue and Buses Barria, 1 hr, US$2.75, reduced service off-season. Some buses by both companies continue to **Aguas Calientes** (off-season according to demand) 2 hrs, US$5. Buses that continue to Aguas Calientes do not stop at the lake (unless you want to get off at Hotel Termas de Puyehue and clamber down).

Border with Argentina *p759*

Anticura

Bus To Anticura, 2-3 buses daily from **Osorno**, 3 hrs, US$5-11. Several bus companies run daily services from **Puerto Montt** via Osorno to Bariloche along this route (see under Puerto Montt for details). Although less scenic than the ferry journey across Lake Todos Los Santos and Laguna Verde (see page 764) this crossing is far cheaper, more reliable and still a beautiful trip (best views from the right hand side of the bus).

Southern lakes

This is one of the most beautiful areas in a part of Chile which already has plenty to boast about. Lago Llanquihue, with its views to volcanoes and German-influenced towns, adjoins the Parque Nacional Vicente Pérez Rosales. The oldest national park in the country, this contains another beautiful lake, Todos los Santos, three major volcanoes, waterfalls and a memorable lakes route to Argentina. The region ends at the Seno de Reloncaví, a peaceful glacial inlet, often shrouded in soft rain.

Lago Llanquihue

The lake, covering 56,000 ha, is the second largest in Chile. Across the great blue sheet of water can be seen two snow-capped volcanoes: the perfect cone of Osorno (2680 m) and the shattered cone of Calbuco (2015 m), and, when the air is clear, the distant Tronador (3460 m). The largest towns, Puerto Varas, Llanquihue and Frutillar are on the western shore, linked by the Pan-American Highway. There are roads around the rest of the lake: that from Puerto Octay east to Ensenada is very beautiful, but is narrow with lots of blind corners, necessitating speeds of 20-30 kph at best in places (see below).

Puerto Octay → *Phone code: 064. Colour map 8, C1. Population: 10,000.*

A peaceful, picturesque small town at the north tip of the lake with a backdrop of rolling hills, Puerto Octay was founded by German settlers in 1852. The town enjoyed a boom in the late 19th century when it was the northern port for steamships on the lake. The church and the enormous German-style former convent survive from that period. **Museo el Colono** ⓘ *Independencia 591, T264 3327, http://museoelcolono.jimdo.com, daily 1000-1300, 1500-1900, US$2*, has displays on German colonization. Another part of the museum, housing agricultural tools and machinery for making chicha, is just outside town on the road to Centinela. **Tourist office** ⓘ *P Montt 378, T239 1860*. Some 3 km south along an unpaved road is the Peninsula of Centinela, a beautiful spot with a launch dock and watersports. From the headland are fine views of the volcanoes and the Cordillera of the Andes; a very popular spot in good weather, good for picnics (taxi US$3 one way). Rowing boats and pedalos can be hired.

Frutillar Bajo → *Phone code: 065. Colour map 8, C1. Population: 15,000. Altitude: 70 m.*

About halfway along the west side of the lake, Frutillar is divided into Frutillar Alto, just off the main highway, and Frutillar Bajo beautifully situated on the lake, 4 km away. (Colectivos run between the two towns, five minutes, US$0.60.) Frutillar Bajo is possibly the most attractive – and pricey – town on the lake. At the north end of the town is the **Reserva Forestal Edmundo Winckler**, run by the Universidad de Chile, 33 ha, with a guided trail through native woods, open 1000-1900. **Museo Colonial Alemán** ⓘ *Pérez Rosales s/n, T242 1142, www.museosaustral.cl, daily 0900-1930 summer, 0900-1730, winter, US$4*, includes a watermill, replicas of two German colonial houses with furnishings and utensils of the period, a blacksmith's shop (engravings for US$9), a *campanario* (circular barn with agricultural machinery inside), gardens and shop. In late January to early February there is a highly regarded classical music festival (www.semanasmusicales.cl) and there is a state-of-the-art concert hall on the lakefront, **Teatro del Lago** (www.teatrodellago.cl). Accommodation must be booked well in advance. **Tourist office** ⓘ *on the Costanera, Filippi 753, T242 1261 www.munifrutillar.cl and www.frutillar.com*, helpful.

Puerto Varas and around → *Phone code: 065. Colour map 8, C1. Population: 33,000.*

This beauty spot was the southern port for shipping on the lake in the 19th century. It is infinitely preferable as a centre for visiting the southern lakes to Puerto Montt, 20 km to the south. The Catholic church, built by German Jesuits in 1918, is a copy of the church in Marieenkirche in the Black Forest. North and east of the **Gran Hotel Puerto Varas** (1934) are German-style mansions dating from the early 20th century. **Parque Philippi**, on top of the hill, is pleasant; walk up to **Hotel Cabañas del Lago** on Klenner, cross the railway and the gate is on the right. Puerto Varas is a good base for trips around the lake. On the south shore two of the best beaches are **Playa Hermosa** (Km 7) and **Playa Niklitschek** (Km 8, entry fee charged). **La Poza**, at Km 16, is a little lake to the south of Lago Llanquihue reached through narrow channels overhung with vegetation. **Isla Loreley**, an island on La Poza, is very beautiful (frequent boat trips, US$5); a concealed channel leads to yet another lake, the Laguna Encantada. There's a municipal **tourist office** ⓘ *Del Salvador 320, T236 1194, aboegel@ptovaras.cl, see www.ptovaras.cl.* The information office on the pier belongs to the chamber of tourism and does not give wholly impartial advice. Many places close in the off-season.

Just past the village of Nueva Braunau, 9 km west of Puerto Varas, is the remarkable **Museo Antonio Felmer** ⓘ *T233 0831, www.museoaleman.cl, summer daily 1100-2000, otherwise weekends 1100-1300, 1500-1800 or by appointment, US$4.45,* a huge private collection of machinery, tools and household items used by the first Austrian immigrants to the area, some with English descriptions. On quiet days staff may give demonstrations of the more ingenious objects.

To Argentina via Lago Todos Los Santos

This popular route to Bariloche, involving ferries across Lago Todos Los Santos, Lago Frías and Lago Nahuel Huapi is outstandingly beautiful whatever the season, though the mountains are often obscured by rain and heavy cloud. The route is via Puerto Varas, Ensenada and Petrohué falls (20 minutes stop) to Petrohué, where it connects with catamaran service across Lago Todos Los Santos to Peulla. Lunch stop in Peulla two hours. Chilean customs in Peulla, followed by a two-hour bus ride through the Paso Pérez Rosales to Argentine customs in Puerto Frías, 20 minute boat trip across Lago Frías to Puerto Alegre and 15-minute bus from Puerto Alegre to Puerto Blest. From Puerto Blest it is a beautiful one hour catamaran trip along Lago Nahuel Huapi to Puerto Pañuelo (Llao Llao), from where it's a 30-minute bus journey to Bariloche (bus drops passengers at hotels, campsites or centre). The route is operated by **Cruce Andino**, see Transport, below.

Ensenada

East of Puerto Varas by 47 km, Ensenada is at the southeast corner of Lake Llanquihue, the town's main attraction. Minibuses run from Puerto Varas, frequent in summer (see Transport, below).

Volcán Osorno can be reached from Ensenada, or from a road branching off the Puerto Octay-Ensenada road at Puerto Klocker, 20 km southeast of Puerto Octay. Guided ascents (organized by agencies in Puerto Varas) set out from the *refugio* at **La Burbuja** where there is a small **ski centre** in winter ⓘ *T9-9158 7337, usually open Jun-Sep, www.volcanosorno.com,* and pleasant short walks with great views in summer. From here it is six hours to the summit. The volcano can also be climbed from the north (La Picada); this route is easier and may be attempted without a guide, although only experienced climbers should attempt to climb right to the top as ice climbing equipment is essential and there are many craters hidden below thin crusts of ice. Note that Refugio La Picada, marked on many maps, burned down several years ago.

Parque Nacional Vicente Pérez Rosales

ⓘ *Open 0900-2000 (1830 in winter), US$2.75. The park is infested by horseflies in Dec-Jan: cover up as much as possible with light-coloured clothes which may help a bit.*

Lago Todos los Santos The most beautiful of all the lakes in this part of Chile, this long, irregularly shaped sheet of emerald-green water has deeply wooded shores and several small islands rising from its surface. In the waters are reflected the slopes of Volcán Osorno. Beyond the hilly shores to the east are several graceful snow-capped mountains, with the mighty Tronador in the distance. To the north is the sharp point of Cerro Puntiagudo, and at the northeastern end Cerro Techado rises cliff-like out of the water. The ports of **Petrohué** at its western and **Peulla** at its eastern ends are connected by the **Cruce Andino** service with connections to Bariloche (Argentina). Trout and salmon fishing are excellent in several parts including Petrohué. CONAF has an office in Petrohué with a visitors' centre, small museum and 3D model of the park. There is a *guardaparque* office in Puella. There are no roads round the lake, but private launches can be hired for trips around the lake or to Cayetué on the lake's southern shore (US$110) from where it is a 6 hour hike to Ralún (see below).

Petrohué Petrohué, 16 km northwest of Ensenada, is a good base for walking. The **Salto de Petrohué** *US$3*, is 6 km from Petrohué (unpaved, dusty, lots of traffic; bus US$1), 10 km (paved) from Ensenada. Near the falls is a snackbar; there are also two short trails, the Senderos de los Enamorados and Carileufú. **Peulla**, is a good starting point for hikes in the mountains. The Cascadas Los Novios, signposted above the Hotel Peulla, are stunning.

For crossing the border with Argentina at **Paso Pérez Rosales**, Chilean immigration is in Peulla, 30 km west of the border, open daily, summer 0800-2100, winter 0800-2000.

Seno de Reloncaví and Cochamó

The Reloncaví estuary, the northernmost of Chile's glacial inlets, is recommended for its local colour, its wildlife (including sealions and dolphins) and its peace, although the salmon farming boom of the last decade has left its mark in the shape of hundreds of cages and multicoloured buoys dotted about the fjord. **Ralún**, a small village at the northern end of the estuary, is 31 km southeast from Ensenada by a mostly paved road along the wooded lower Petrohué valley. Roads continue, unpaved, along the east side of the estuary to Cochamó and Puelo and on the west side to Canutillar. In Ralún there is a village shop and post office. Just outside the village there are thermal springs with baths, US$2, reached by boat across Río Petrohué, US$4 pp.

Cochamó, 17 km south of Ralún on the east shore of the estuary, is a pretty village, with a fine wooden church similar to those on Chiloé, in a striking setting, with the estuary and volcano behind. Four km south of the village a road branches inland for about 3 km, following the course of the Cochamó valley. At the end of the road is the trail head up the valley (taxi to start of trail US$12, or ask at your hostal). It is a five hour hike up to La Junta, described as Chile's Yosemite for its imposing granite peaks and now becoming a popular centre for many outdoor activities in and around the alerce forests (trekking, climbing, kayaking, riding, birdwatching and fishing). For more information T235 0271, or see www.cochamo.com.

The **Gaucho Trail** east from Cochamó to **Paso León** on the Argentine border dates from the colonial period and runs along Río Cochamó to La Junta (see above), then along the north side of Lago Vidal, passing waterfalls and the oldest surviving *alerce* trees in Chile at El Arco. The route takes three to four days by horse, five to six days on foot, depending on conditions, which are best December to March. From Paso León it is a three-hour walk to the main road to Bariloche.

Puelo, south of Cochamó, on the south bank of the Río Puelo, is a most peaceful place, with a some expensive fly fishing lodges nearby. Here the road forks. One branch (very rough) continues to Puelche on the Carretera Austral, while the other heads southeast, past Lago Tagua Tagua (ferry 0900, 1300, return 1200, 1630, US$3 one way) to the peaceful village of Llanada Grande, nestled in the Andes, with basic accommodation. The road continues to the village of Primer Corral from where it is a two day trek across to the Argentine village of Puelo and on to El Bolsón.

An alternative route to Argentina starts with a 45-minute walk to Lago Azul from the road between Llanada Grande and Primer Coral. A 25-minute boat trip across Lago Azul leads to a 45-minute hike through pristine forest to Lago Las Rocas, where another 25-minute boat ride ends at the Carabineros de Chile post on Lago Inferior. Go through immigration then navigate Lagos Inferior and Puelo to the pier at Lago Puelo.

For hotel and restaurant price codes, and other relevant information, see Essentials.

◉ Where to stay

Puerto Octay *p763*

Camping wild and barbecues are forbidden on the lakeshore.

$$$$-$$$ Hotel Centinela, Centinela, T239 1326, www.hotelcentinela.cl. Built in 1914 as a summer mansion, Edward VIII once stayed here. Rooms and cabins in idyllic location with superb views, excellent restaurant, bar, open all year.

$$$-$$ Zapato Amarillo, 35 mins' walk north of town, T221 0787, www.zapatoamarillo.cl. **$** pp in dorms. Book in advance in high season, private or shared bath, homemade bread, meals, German/English spoken, mountain bikes, sailboats, tours, house has a grass roof.

$$ Hostería La Baja, Centinela, T9-8218 6897, www.hosterialabaja.cl. Beautifully situated at the neck of the peninsula. Good value.

$ Hostería Irma, 1 km south of Las Cascadas, T239 6227. Very pleasant, good food; also farmhouse accommodation and camping.

Camping El Molino, beside lake, T239 1375. East of Puerto Octay

Frutillar Bajo *p763*

$$$$ Ayacara, Av Philippi 1215, T242 1550, www.hotelayacara.cl. Beautiful rooms with lake view, welcoming, have a pisco sour in the library in the evening.

$$$ Lagune Club, 3 km north of Frutillar Bajo, T233 0033, www.interpatagonia.com/laguneclub. In an old country house in 16 ha of land, private beach, fishing trips, free pickup from terminal. Disabled-visitor friendly, discounts for the over-65s. Also *cabañas*. Good value in dollars.

$$$ Residenz/Café am See, Av Philippi 539, T242 1539, www.hotelamsee.cl. Good breakfast, café has German specialities.

$$$ Winkler, Av Philippi 1155, T242 1388. Much cheaper (**$**) in low season. Also sells cakes from the garage, **Kuchen Laden**.

$$ Hosp Tía Clarita, Pérez Rosales 648, T242 1806, hospedajetiaclarit@hotmail.com. Kitchen facilities, very welcoming, good value.

$$ Hostería Trayén, Av Philippi 963, T242 1346, tttrayen33@hotmail.com. Nice rooms with bath.

North of Frutillar Bajo

$$$$-$$$ Salzburg, Camino Playa Maqui, T242 1589, www.salzburg.cl. Excellent, spa, sauna, restaurant, mountain bikes, arranges tours and fishing.

Frutillar Alto

Several good-value places to stay along Carlos Richter (main street). Cheap accommodation in the school, sleeping bag required.

Camping Los Ciruelillos, 1.5 km south, T242 0163, losciruelillos@surnet.cl. Most services.

Playa Maqui, 6 km north of Frutillar, T233 9139. Fancy, expensive.

Puerto Varas *p764*

$$$$ Cabañas del Lago Luis Welmann 195, T220 0100, www.cabanasdellago.cl. On hill overlooking lake, upper floor rooms have the best view in town. Service not up to much. Also self-catering cabins sleeping 5, heating, sauna, swimming pools and games room. Often full with package groups.

$$$$ Cumbres, Imperial 0561, T222 2000, www.cumbrespatagonicas.cl. Best hotel in town. All rooms look out over the lake, attentive staff, good restaurant. Spa and small pool with great views.

$$$ Bellavista, Pérez Rosales 60, T223 2011, www.hotelbellavista.cl. 4-star hotel, king-size beds; cheerful, restaurant and bar, overlooking lake and main road, sauna, parking.

$$$ Casa Kalfu, Tronador 1134, T275 1261, www.casakalfu.cl. Characterful blue wooden building remodelled in traditional style. Helpful owners, English spoken, good value.

$$$ Weisserhaus, San Pedro 252, T234 6479, www.weisserhaus.cl. Central, cosy, family-run, German-style breakfast, good facilities, very helpful, central heating, very pleasant.

$$$-$$ Amancay, Walker Martínez 564, T223 2201, www.cabanahostalamancay.cl. Nice *cabañas* with log-burning stoves or hostel rooms, good, German spoken.

$$ Canales del Sur, Pérez Rosales 1631A, 1km east of town, T223 0909, www.canalesdel sur.cl.

Pleasantly set on the lakeside. Very helpful, family-run, tours arranged, garden, car hire.
$$ Casa Azul, Manzanal 66 y Rosario, T223 2904, www.casaazul.net. Wooden building, variety of rooms and dorms, heating, beautiful Japanese garden, book exchange, German and English spoken, excursions offered. Reserve in advance in high season.
$$ Casa Margouya, Santa Rosa 318, T223 7640, www.margouya.com. Bright, colourful hostel, lots of information, French-run, English spoken.
$$ Compass del Sur, Klenner 467, T223 2044, www.compassdelsur.cl. Chilean/Swedish-run hostel, all rooms with shared bath, comfy lounge, helpful, German, English, Swedish spoken, excursions offered. Reserve in advance in high season.
$$ Hostería Outsider, San Bernardo 318, T223 1056, www.turout.com. Rooms sleep 1-3, private bath, comfortable, heating, helpful, restaurant, travel agency, English and German spoken, book in advance.
$$-$ Hosp Don Raúl, Salvador 928, T231 0897, www.informatur.com. Shared rooms and bath, hostel facilities, spotless, helpful, camping.
Camping Wild camping and use of barbecues is not allowed on the lake shore. Casa Tronador, Tronador y Manzanal, T09-9078 9631. Expensive but central. CONAF, Km 49, site at Puerto Oscuro, beneath road to volcano, very good. Playa Hermosa, Km 7, T233 8283, fancy (negotiate in low season), take own supplies. Playa Niklitschek, Km 8, T09-8257 0698, www.playaniklitschek.cl. Full facilities.

Ensenada *p764*
$$$$ Hotel Ensenada, Km 45, T221 2028, www.hotelensenada.cl. Olde-worlde, half-board, good food, good view of lake and Osorno Volcano, mountain bikes and tennis for guests.
$$$ Cabañas Brisas del Lago, Km 42, T221 2012, www.brisasdellago.cl. Chalets for up to 6 and rooms for up to 3 on beach, good restaurant nearby, supermarket next door.
$$$-$$ Casa Ko', Km 37, T09-7703 6477, www.casako.com. 3 km off Puerto Varas–Ensenada road, ask bus to drop you at sign and walk or phone in advance for pick-up. Traditional house, helpful owners, lovely surroundings and views, good meals. Plenty of outdoor activities plus programme for artists and photographers.

$$ Hosp Ensenada, Km 43, T221 2050, www.hospedajensenada.cl. Typical old house, rooms sleep 1-4, private or shared bath, beach, parking.
Camping Montaña, central Ensenada, T221 2088. Fully equipped, nice beach sites. Also at Playa Larga, 1 km further east, and at Puerto Oscuro, 2 km north. Trauco, 4 km west, T223 6262. Large site with shops, fully equipped.

Volcán Osorno
There are 2 *refugios* (**$** pp), both of them south of the summit and reached from the southern access road: La Burbuja, the former ski-club centre, 14 km north of Ensenada at 1250 m, and Refugio Teski Ski Club, T09-9700 3700, just below the snowline, with café.

Parque Nacional Vicente Pérez Rosales *p764*
Petrohué
$$$$ Hotel Petrohué, Ruta 225, Km 64, T065-221 2025, www.petrohue.com. Excellent views, half-board available, also has cabins, cosy, restaurant, log fires, sauna and heated pool; hiking, fishing and other activities.
    Albergue in the school in summer. CONAF office can help find cheaper family accommodation.

Peulla
$$$$ Natura Patagonia, T297 2289, www.hotelnatura.cl. Rooms and suites, disabled facilities, lots of activities offered, restaurant.
$$$ Hotel Peulla, T297 2288, www.hotelpeulla.cl. Half-board. Beautiful setting by the lake and mountains, restaurant and bar, cold in winter, often full of tour groups (older partner of Natura).
Camping Camping wild and picnicking in the national park is forbidden. At Petrohué on far side beside the lake, no services, cold showers, locals around the site sell fresh bread (local fishermen will ferry you across). At Peulla, opposite CONAF office. Good campsite 1½ hrs' walk east of Peulla, take food. A small shop in Peulla sells basic goods, including fruit and veg.

Seno de Reloncaví *p765*
Ralún
Lodging is available with families and at restaurant Navarrito (**$**, basic) and **$** pp Posada Campesino (very friendly, clean and simple, without breakfast).

Cochamó

$$$ Cochamó Aventura, San Bernadino 318, Puerto Varas, T09-9289 4314, http://campoaventura.cl. 4 km south of Cochamó in Valle Rio Cochamó, full board available (great breakfast), local food, and very fresh milk from their own cow. Also a renovated mountain house at their other base in the valley of La Junta. They specialize in horse riding and trekking between the Reloncaví Estuary and the Argentine border, 2-10 days.

$$$-$ Refugio Cochamó, La Junta, Cochamó valley, www.cochamo.com. Oct-Apr. The perfect base for outdoor activities in the Cochamó valley, only accessible on foot (4-6 hrs) or horseback. Private rooms have bed linen, bring sleeping bag for dorm beds.

$$ Hostal Cochamó, Av Aeródromo s/n T09-5828 5231, www.hostalcochamo.com. Private rooms and shared dorms, price pp, local meals available, activities arranged as well as transport.

$$ Hostal Maura, JJ Molina 12, T09-9334 9213, www.experienciapatagonia.cl. Beautiful location overlooking the estuary, rooms with shared bath, meals served, kayaks, horse riding, good information, sauna and hot tub (at extra cost).

$$-$ Edicar, Prat y Sgto Aldea, T09-7445 9230, on seafront by the dock/ramp. With breakfast, hot shower, good value.

Also *cabañas* and campsites; for some options see http://cochamo.com. Also a few eating places.

Puelo

$$$ Posada Martín Pescador, Lago Totoral, 2 km from Llanada Grande on road to Primer Corral, www.posadamartinpescador.cl. With bath, hot water, meals, BBQs, horse riding, trekking, fishing, canoeing and rafting.

Basic lodging is available at the restaurant in Puelo, or with families – try Roberto and Olivia Telles, no bath/shower, meals on request, or Ema Hernández Maldona; 2 restaurants.

❷ Restaurants

Puerto Octay *p763*
$$ El Rancho del Espantapajaros, 6 km south on the road to Frutillar, T233 0049, www.espantapajaros.cl. In a converted barn with wonderful views over the lake, serves spit roasted meat. All-you-can-eat, with salad bar and drinks included.

$$ Fogón de Anita, 1 km out of town, T239 1276, www.fogondeanita.blogspot.co.uk. Mid-priced grill. Also German cakes and pastries.

$ Restaurante Baviera, Germán Wulf 582, T2391460. Cheap and good, salmon and *cazuelas*.

Frutillar Bajo *p763*
$$ Andes, Philippi 1057. Good set menus and à la carte.

$ Casino de Bomberos, Philippi 1060. Upstairs bar/restaurant, memorable painting caricaturing the firemen in action (worth studying while awaiting your meal), good value.

Cafés
Many German-style cafés and tea-rooms on C Philippi (the lakefront).

Puerto Varas *p764*
$$$-$$ Mediterráneo, Santa Rosa 068, T223 7268, www.mediterraneopuertovaras.cl. On the lakefront, international and local food, interesting varied menu, often full.

$$$-$$ Xic Dalí, Purísima 690, T223 4424. Intimate Catalan bistro. Inventive menu, top quality preparation and service, good wine list.

$$ Bravo Cabrera, Pérez Rosales s/n, 1 km east of centre, T223 3441, www.bravocabrera.cl. Popular bar/restaurant opposite the lake, big portions, good value, varied menu, lively bar.

$$ Di Carusso, San Bernardo 318. Italian trattoria, good fresh pasta dishes on Fri.

$$ Donde El Gordito, San Bernardo 560, T223 3425, downstairs in market. Good range of meat dishes, no set menu.

$$ La Chamaca Inn, Del Salvador y San Bernard, T223 2876, Good choice for traditional Chilean seafood. Larger than life owner.

$$ La Olla, Ruta 225, 4 km east of town towards Ensenada, T223 4605. Good, popular for seafood, fish and meat, traditional Chilean cuisine.

$ There are a couple of little snack bars along the coast on Santa Rosa at the foot of Cerro Philippi, serving, amongst other things, tasty vegetarian burgers.

Cafés
Café Danés, Del Salvador 441. Coffee and cakes.
Casis, San Juan y San José. Very sweet cakes, generous ice creams and great brownies.
El Barista, Walker Martínez 211A, T223 3130, www.elbarista.cl. Probably the best place for a coffee. Good value set lunches and bar.

Ensenada *p764*
Most eating places close off season. There are a few pricey shops. Take your own provisions.
$$$ Latitude 42, Yan Kee Way Resort, T221 2030. Expensive, excellent and varied cuisine, very good quality wine list. Lake views.
$ Canta Rana for bread and küchen.

⋂ Bars and clubs

Puerto Varas *p764*
Club Orquídea, San Pedro 537, T223 3024, www.cluborquidea.cl. Popular club with tables dotted around several small rooms and alcoves. Occasional live music, huge pizzas.

⋓ What to do

Puerto Varas *p764*
Horse riding Quinta del Lago, Km 25 on road to Ensenada, T233 0193. All levels catered for, US$35-85 for 2-5 hrs, also accommodation. See also Campo Aventura, below.
Kayak Al Sur, Aconcagua e Imperial, T223 2300, www.alsurexpeditions.com. Sea-kayak, rafting and trekking tours, good camping equipment, English spoken, official tour operators to Parque Pumalín.
Ko'kayak, San Pedro 210 and Ruta 225, Km 40, T223 3004, www.kokayak.cl. Kayaking and rafting trips, good equipment and after-trip lunch, French/Chilean-run.
Miralejos, San Pedro 311, T223 4892, www.miralejos.cl. Kayaking in northern Patagonia, also trekking, horse riding and mountaineering. Associated with **Trekking Cochamó**, same address, www.trekkingcochamo.cl, which concentrates on adventure sports in Cochamó. Both are part of the www.secretpatagonia.cl group of operators who specialize in the area.
Yak Expediciones, owner Juan Federico Zuazo (Juanfe), T09-8332 0574, www.yakexpediciones.

cl. Experienced and safe kayaking trips on lakes and sea, in the fjords of Pumalín, enthusiastic and excellent, small groups, also runs courses.
Ziplining (*canopy*), is offered by several operators.

Seno de Reloncaví: Cochamó *p765*
Cabalgatas Cochamó, Cra Principal, T09-7764 5289, http://cabalgatascochamo.wix.com/chile. On a farm by the water, riding trips from 1 to 8 days, also boat trips, climbing and fishing.
Cochamó Aventura Travel Agency, T09-9289 4318, http://campoaventura.cl. Specializes in tailor-made tours and excursions in Chile, including above 1-, 3- and 10-day trips on horseback (see above under Cochamó, Where to stay).
Sebastián Contreras, C Morales, T221 6220, is an independent guide who offers tours on horseback and hires out horses.

In Puelo, fly fishing guides generally charge around US$80 per hour, boat included.

⊖ Transport

Puerto Octay *p763*
Bus To **Osorno** every 20 mins, US$3; to **Frutillar** (1 hr, US$1.50), **Puerto Varas** (2 hrs) and **Puerto Montt** (3 hrs, US$4) Thaebus, 5 a day. Around the east shore: to **Las Cascadas** (34 km), Mon-Fri 1730, returns next day 0700.

Frutillar Bajo *p763*
Bus Most leave from the small bus terminal at Alessandri y Richter in Frutillar Alto. To **Puerto Varas** (US$1.50) and **Puerto Montt** (US$3), frequent, Full Express. To Osorno, Turismosur 1½ hrs, US$2. To **Puerto Octay**, Thaebus, 6 a day, US$1.50.

Puerto Varas *p764*
Bus Pullman is the only long distance company to have its terminal in the town centre (Diego Portales). Other companies have ticket offices dotted around the centre but buses leave from the outskirts of town (Turbus, Jac and Cóndor from Del Salvador 1093 and Cruz del Sur from San Fransisco 1317). To **Santiago**, US$46-63, several companies, 12 hrs. To **Osorno** hourly, US$3, 1 hr. To **Valdivia** US$9, 3 hrs. Minibuses to the following destinations leave from San Bernardo y Walker Martínez: **Puerto Montt**, Thaebus and Full Express

every 15 mins, US$1.70, 30 mins. Same frequency to **Frutillar** (US$1.50, 30 mins). To **Ensenada** hourly. To **Bariloche**, by lakes route, see above.

Ferry Cruce Andino, www.cruceandino.com, operates the bus and ferry crossing from Puerto Varas 0830 to Bariloche, arrive 2015, US$280 one way (low season price), half price on the return. From 1 May to 30 Aug this trip is done over 2 days with overnight stay in Peulla at Hotel Peulla or Hotel Natura. You may break the journey at any point and continue next day.

Parque Nacional Vicente Pérez Rosales p764

Minibuses Every 30 mins to **Petrohué** from Puerto Montt and Puerto Varas in summer (US$4,

1¼ hrs from Puerto Varas), much less frequent off season. Last bus to **Ensenada** at 1800.

Seno de Reloncaví p765

Boat In summer boats sail up the Estuary from Angelmó. The **Sernatur** office in Puerto Montt has details of scheduled trips.

Bus From Puerto Montt to **Ralún**, **Cochamó** and **Puelo**, 3 a day via Puerto Varas and Ensenada, 2 on Sun, with **Transhar** (T225 4187) and **Buses Río Puelo** (T254 4226): US$3 to Ralún, US$4 to Cochamó (2½ hrs). The first bus of the day continues to **Llanada Grande** (5 hrs, US$6). Minibus services from Puerto Montt airport cost between US$12.50 and US$30 pp depending on size of vehicle (see http://cochamo.com).

Puerto Montt and Chiloé

Just 20 minutes south of Puerto Varas, and 1016 km south of Santiago, Puerto Montt is the gateway to the shipping lanes to the south, namely the island of Chiloé and the wilds of Patagonia. It's a rapidly growing, disordered modern city, developing in line with a boom in salmon fishing.

Puerto Montt

Where to stay	6 Hostal Central *C6*	11 Vista al Mar *B1*
2 Casa Perla *B1*	7 Hostal Pacífico *B2*	12 Vista Hermosa *C1*
3 Club Presidente *C4*	8 Hostal Suizo *C1*	
4 Holiday Inn Express *C5*	9 Puerto Sur *C6*	**Restaurants**
5 Hosp Rocco *C1*	10 Tren del Sur *A4*	1 Café Haussman *B5*

200 metres
200 yards

Arriving in Puerto Montt

Tourist offices Puerto Montt: For information and town maps, contact **Sernatur** ① *just southwest of the Plaza de Armas, Antonio Varas 415 y San Martín, T222 3016, infoloslagos@ sernatur.cl, Mon-Fri 0830-1300, 1500-1730.* See www.puertomonttchile.cl for information on the web. There are information desks at the airport and the bus station. **CONAF** ① *Ochogavía 458, T248 6102, loslagos.oirs@conaf.cl* .

Places in Puerto Montt

The capital of X Región (Los Lagos) was founded in 1853 as part of the German colonization of the area. Good views over the city and bay are offered from outside the Intendencia Regional on Avenida X Region. The port is used by fishing boats and coastal vessels, and is the departure point for vessels to Chaitén, Puerto Chacabuco, Laguna San Rafael and for the long haul south to Puerto Natales (if operating – see below). A dual carriageway runs 55 km southwest to Pargua, where there is a ferry service to Chiloé.

The **Iglesia de los Jesuitas** on Gallardo, dating from 1872, has a fine blue-domed ceiling; behind it on a hill is the campanario (clock tower). **Museo Regional Juan Pablo II** ① *Portales 997 near the bus terminal, daily 1030-1800, closed weekends off season, US$1,* documents local history and has a fine collection of historic photos of the city; also memorabilia of the Pope John Paul II's visit in 1988. The **Casa Pauly** ① *Rancagua 210, T248 2611, Mon-Fri 1000-1700,* is one of the city's historic mansions, now in a poor state but which holds temporary exhibitions. Near the plaza, the **Casa del Arte Diego Rivera** ① *Varas y Quillota, www.corporacionculturalpuertomontt.cl,* has a theatre and holds regular exhibitions.

The fishing port of **Angelmó**, 2 km west, has become a tourist centre with seafood restaurants and handicraft shops (reached by Costanera bus along Portales and by colectivos Nos 2, 3, 20 from the centre, US$0.30). The wooded **Isla Tenglo**, reached by launch from Angelmó (US$1 each way), is a favourite place for picnics. Magnificent view from the summit. The island is famous for its curantos, served by restaurants in summer. Boat trips round the island from Angelmó last 30 minutes, US$5.

Parque Provincial Lahuen Ñadi (US$2.65; T248 6101 or 248 6400) contains 200 ha of native forest including probably the most accessible ancient alerce forest in Chile. Take the main road to the airport, which leads off Ruta 5. After 5 km, turn right (north) and follow the signs.

To ⑤ ⑥ , Pelluco,
Chamiza & Carretera
Austral

2 Cafés Central and Real *B4*
3 Club Alemán *B5*
4 Club de Yates *C5*
5 Cotele *C5*
6 Pazos *C5*

Puerto Montt listings

For hotel and restaurant price codes, and other relevant information, see Essentials.

Where to stay

Puerto Montt *p771, map p770*
Accommodation is often much cheaper off season. Check with the tourist office.
$$$$ Club Presidente, Av Portales 664, T225 1666, www.presidente.cl. 4-star, very comfortable, rooms, suites, some with sea view. Often full Mon-Fri with business travellers.
$$$ Holiday Inn Express, Mall Paseo Costanera, T256 6000, www.holidayinn.cl. Good business standard. Spacious rooms with desks and great views, some with balcony. Slightly pokey bathrooms but the best in its category.
$$$ Puerto Sur, Huasco 143, T235 1212, www.hotelpuertosur.cl. Small business oriented hotel in a quiet part of town. 4 floors, no lifts or views but otherwise good value, parking.
$$$ Tren del Sur, Santa Teresa 643, T234 3939, www.trendelsur.cl. 'Boutique' *hostal* with pleasant public areas, objects recycled from the old railway, some rooms without windows, café, heating, helpful English-speaking owner.
$$ Hostal Pacífico, J J Mira 1088, T225 6229, www.hostalpacifico.cl. Comfortable, some rooms a bit cramped. Parking, transfers.
$$ Hostal Suizo, Independencia 231, T225 2640, rossyoelckers@yahoo.es. Private or shared rooms and bath. Painting and Spanish classes, German and Italian spoken. Convenient for Navimag ferry.
$$ House Rocco, Pudeto 233, T227 2897, www.hospedajerocco.cl. Doubles or 4-bed dorms, shared bath. English spoken, quiet residential area, convenient for Navimag.
$$ Vista al Mar, Vivar 1337, T225 5625, hospedajevistaalmar@yahoo.es. Impeccable small guest house, good breakfast, peaceful, great view from the double ensuite.
$$ Vista Hermosa, Miramar 1486, T231 9600, http://hostalvistahermosa.cl/. Simple hostel, ask for front room for best views (10 mins' walk uphill from terminal), also has a fully equipped cabin.

$$-$ Casa Perla, Trigal 312, T226 2104, www.casaperla.com. French, English spoken, helpful, meals, Spanish classes offered off season, pleasant garden, good meeting place.
$$-$ Hostal Central, Huasco 61, T226 3081, hostalcentralpm@hotmail.com. Small, neat rooms in an old wooden house, peaceful neighbourhood, no breakfast, kitchen facilities, midnight curfew. A couple of rooms with nice views. A good choice.
Camping Camping Los Alamos, Chinquihue-Panitao Bajo Km 14.5, T226 4666, losalamos@surnet.cl. Others on this road.

Restaurants

Puerto Montt *p771, map p770*
Local specialities include *picoroco al vapor*, a giant barnacle whose flesh looks and tastes like crab, and curanto.
In Angelmó, there are several dozen small, seafood restaurants in the old fishing port, past the fish market, very popular, lunches only except in Jan-Feb when they are open until late; ask for *té blanco* (white wine – they are not legally allowed to serve wine).
Other seafood restaurants in Chinquihue, west of Angelmó.
$$$ Club Alemán, Varas 264, T229 7000. Old fashioned, good food and wine.
$$$ Club de Yates, Juna Soler s/n, Costanera east of centre, T228 4000. Excellent seafood, fine views from a pier.
$$$-$$ Cotele, Juan Soler 1611, Pelluco, 4 km east, T227 8000. Closed Sun. Only serves beef, but serves it as well as anywhere in southern Chile. Reservations advised.
$$$-$$ Pazos, Pelluco, T225 2552. Serves the best *curanto* in the Puerto Montt area.
$$ Café Haussman, San Martín 185. German cakes, beer and *crudos*.
$ Café Central, Rancagua 117. Spartan décor, generous portions (sandwiches and *pichangas* – savoury salad snack). Giant TV screen.
$ Café Real, Rancagua 137. For *empanadas*, *pichangas, congrío frito*, and lunches.

O Shopping

Puerto Montt *p771, map p770*
Woollen goods and Mapuche-designed rugs can be bought at roadside stalls in Angelmó and on Portales opposite the bus terminal. Prices much the same as on Chiloé, but quality often lower.
Supermarkets Bigger, opposite bus terminal, open 0900-2200 daily. Also in the Paseo del Mar shopping mall, Talca y A Varas. Paseo Costanera, is a big mall on the seafront.

O What to do

Puerto Montt *p771, map p770*
Sailing 2 Yacht Clubs in Chinquihue:
Club de Deportes Náuticas Reloncaví, Camino a Chinquihue Km 7, T225 5022, www.nautico reloncavi.com. Marina, sailing lessons.
Marina del Sur (MDS), Camino a Chinquihue Km 4.5, T225 1958, www.marinadelsur.cl. All facilities, restaurant, yacht charters, notice board for crew (tripulante) requests, specialists in cruising the Patagonian channels.

Tour operators
There are many tour operators. Some companies offer 2-day excursions along the Carretera Austral to Hornopirén, including food and accommodation. Most offer 1-day excursions to Chiloé and to Puerto Varas, Isla Loreley, Laguna Verde, and the Petrohué falls: both are much cheaper from bus company kiosks inside the bus terminal.
Ecosub, Panamericana 510, T226 3939, www.ecosub.cl. Scuba-diving excursions.
Eureka Turismo, Gallardo 65, T225 0412, www.chile-travel.com/eureka.htm.
Helpful, German and English spoken.

O Transport

Puerto Montt *p771, map p770*
Air El Tepual Airport is 13 km northwest of town, T248 6200. It has ATMs and car hire desks. ETM bus to/from terminal (T229 0100, www. etm.cl) 1½ hrs before departure, US$3.75; also meets incoming flights. ETM minibus service to/from hotels, US$11 per person, US$27.50 for 2 to Puerto Varas. Taxi US$22, US$37 to Puerto

Varas. **LAN** and **Sky** have several flights daily to **Santiago**, **Balmaceda** (for Coyhaique) and **Punta Arenas**. Flights to **Chaitén** (or nearby Santa Bárbara) leave from the Aerodromo la Paloma on the outskirts of town. For flight details, see page 787. Charters, sightseeing trips and air taxi services can be arranged with **Aerocord**, La Paloma aerodrome, T226 2300, www.aerocord.cl; **Aerotaxis del Sur**, A Varas 70, T233 0726, www.aerotaxisdelsur.cl; **Cielo Mar Austral**, Quillota 245 loc 1, T226 4010.
Bus Terminal is on sea front at Portales y Lota with rural buses leaving from one side and long distance buses from the other. There are also telephones, restaurants, ATMs, casa de cambio (left luggage, US$1-1.75 per item for 24 hrs); see www.terminalpm.cl. There is an official taxi rank on lev el 1. To **Puerto Varas** (US$1.70), **Llanquihue** (US$2), **Frutillar** (US$3 – minibuses every few mins), **Puerto Octay** (US$4), 5 daily, Expreso Puerto Varas, Thaebus and Full Express. To **Ensenada** and **Petrohué**, Buses JM several daily. To **Cochamó** US$4, 3 hrs. To **Hornopirén**, 5 hrs, US$7.25, **Kémel** (which also runs daily to **Chaitén**) and M&M. To **Osorno** US$3, 2 hrs, to **Valdivia**, US$9, 3½ hrs. To **Pucón**, US$14-17, 6 hrs. To **Temuco** US$11.50-28. **Concepción**, US$21-36. To **Valparaíso**, 14 hrs, US$45-63. To **Santiago**, 12 hrs, US$46-63, several companies including Tur Bus. To **Punta Arenas**, **Pacheco**, **Turibus** and others, 1-3 a week (bus goes through Argentina via Bariloche, take US$ cash for Argentina expenses en route), 32-38 hrs. Also take plenty of food for this "nightmare" trip. Book well in advance in Jan-Feb and check if you need a multiple-entry Chilean visa. Also book any return journey before setting out. For services to **Chiloé**, see page 775.
Buses to Argentina via Osorno and the Samoré pass Daily services to Bariloche on this route via Osorno, 7 hrs, are run by Vía Bariloche and others, US$30. Out of season, services are reduced. Buy tickets for international buses from the bus terminal. Book well in advance in Jan and Feb; ask for a seat on the right hand side for the best views.
Car hire Autovald, Sector Cardenal, Pasaje San Andrés 60, T221 5366, www.autovald.cl. Cheap rates. Full-Car, O'Higgins 525, T223 3055, www.full-car.cl. Hunter, T225 1524 or 9920

6888, office is in Puerto Varas, San José 130, T223 7950, www.interpatagonia.com/hunter/. Good service. **Salfa Sur**, Pilpilco 800, also at Airport, T600-600 4004, or T229 0201, www.salfasur.cl. Good value, several regional offices.

Ferry To **Puerto Natales**, the dramatic 1460-km journey first goes through Seno Reloncaví and Canal Moraleda; from Bahía Anna Pink along the coast and then across the Golfo de Penas to Bahía Tarn it is a 12- to 17-hr sea crossing, usually rough. The journey continues through Canal Messier, Angostura Inglesa and the Concepción, Sarmiento and White channels, taking just under 4 days. If weather conditions permit, the ferry stops at Puerto Edén (pop 180) on Isla Wellington (1 hr south of Angostura Inglesa), a fishing village with *hospedaje* (20 beds, open intermittently), 3 shops, scant provisions, a café. It is the drop-off point for exploring Isla Wellington, which is largely untouched, with stunning mountains. If stopping, take food; maps (not very accurate) available in Santiago. The functional but comfortable passenger and freight (including live animals) roll-on roll-off ferries are run by **Navimag** (Naviera Magallanes SA), Terminal Transbordadores, Angelmó 1735, T243 2360 or T02-2442 3120, www.navimag.com. Sailings to Puerto Montt throughout the year leave Puerto Montt usually on Mon at 2000 (check in 0900-1400, board 1600), arriving Thu. Return is on Fri, arriving Puerto Montt Mon morning. In Puerto Natales check-in is 1500 to 1800 on Thu, board 2000, dep Fri 0600; dinner is not included. Service was resumed in 2014 after several months' hiatus; always confirm times and booking well in advance. In winter especially days and vessels may change. The fare, including meals, ranges from US$400 pp for a bunk in a shared cabin on the Amadeo in low season, to US$1512 for 2 people in AAA double cabin. First class is recommended, but hardly luxurious. Check the website for discounts and special offers. Cars are carried for US$525, motorcycles for US$150. Payment by credit card or foreign currency is accepted in all Navimag offices. On board is a book exchange, bingo is played, video films are shown, bilingual guides give talks on fauna, botany, glaciation and history. Food is good and plentiful and includes vegetarian options at lunch and dinner. Passengers tend to take their own alcohol and extra food. Standards of service and comfort vary, depending on the number of passengers and weather conditions. Take sea-sickness tablets, or buy them on board (you'll be advised when to take them!). **Booking** Tickets can be booked through many travel agencies, **Navimag** offices throughout the country, or direct from www.navimag.com. Book well in advance for departures between mid-Dec and mid-Mar. It is well worth going to the port on the day of departure if you have no ticket. Departures are frequently delayed by weather conditions. **Note** It is cheaper to fly and quicker to go by bus via Argentina.

To **Puerto Chacabuco**: Navimag's ferry sails twice a week to Puerto Chacabuco (80 km west of Coyhaique). The cruise to Puerto Chacabuco lasts about 24 hrs. Cabins sleep 4 or 6 (private bath, window, bed linen and towel) with a berth costing US87-101 in low season. Cars, motorcycles and bicycles are also carried. There is a canteen; long queues if the boat is full. Food is expensive so take your own.

To **Laguna San Rafael**: The m/n *Skorpios 2* of **Skorpios Cruises**, Augusto Leguía Norte 118, Santiago, www.skorpios.cl, T02-2477 1900, leaves Puerto Montt for a luxury cruise to San Rafael, via Chiloé and Puerto Aguirre. The fare varies according to season, type of cabin and number of occupants: double cabin from US$2000 pp. Generally service is excellent, the food superb, and at the glacier, you can chip ice off the face for your whisky. After the visit to San Rafael the ship visits Quitralco Fjord where there are thermal pools and boat trips on the fjord, and Chiloé. From Puerto Montt it's a 6-day/5-night cruise. The *Skorpios 3* sails from Puerto Natales to Glaciar Amalia and Fiordo Calvo in the Campo de Hielo Sur, 4 days, fares from US$1690 pp, double cabin. An optional first day includes a visit to Torres del Paine or the Cueva del Milodón.

To **Chaitén**, via Ayacara, **Naviera Austral** runs this service, as well as Hornopirén–Ayacara, but check with the company for schedules: Angelmó 1673, T227 0430, www.navieraustral. cl. It also has services Chacabuco–Quellón and and Chaitén–Quellón and, in Jan-Feb only, Chaitén–Castro on Chiloé.

Puerto Montt *p771, map p770*
Banks Many ATMs in the city. Commission charges vary widely. **Note** The last city on the mainland with Visa ATM before Coyhaique. Obtain Argentine pesos before leaving Chile. There is a cambio at the bus terminal, **Borex**,

G Gallardo 65. **Consulates** Argentina, Pedro Montt 160, p 6, T225 3996, http://cpmon. cancilleria.gov.ar, quick visa service. **Cycle repairs** Kiefer, Pedro Montt 129, T225 3079. 3 shops on Urmeneta, none very well stocked. **Motorcycle repairs** Miguel Schmuch, Urmeneta 985, T225 8877.

Chiloé → *Colour map 9, A1.*

The island of Chiloé is 250 km long, 50 km wide and covers 9613 sq km. Thick forests cover most of its western side. The hillsides in summer are a patchwork quilt of wheat fields and dark green plots of potatoes. The population is 116,000 and most live on the sheltered eastern side. The west coast, exposed to strong Pacific winds, is wet for most of the year. The east coast and the offshore islands are drier, though frequently cloudy. The culture of Chiloé has been strongly influenced by isolation from Spanish colonial currents, the mixture of early Spanish settlers and indigenous people and a dependence on the sea. Religious and secular architecture, customs and crafts, combined with delightful landscapes, all contribute to Chiloé's uniqueness. The frequent Fiestas costumbistas are good events at which to capture the spirit of the place.

Arriving in Chiloé
Getting there Regular ferries cross the straits of Pargua between Pargua, 55 km southwest of Puerto Montt on the mainland, and Chacao on Chiloé. Sea lions, penguins, birds and occasionally dolphins can be seen. **Buses** Puerto Montt to Pargua, frequent, US$3, one hour, though most buses go through to Ancud (3½ to four hours) and Castro. Transport to the island is dominated by **Cruz del Sur**, who also own Trans Chiloé and have their own ferries (Puerto Montt terminal, Panamericano 500, at end of Avenida Salvador Allende, T248 3127, www.busescruzdelsur.cl). Cruz del Sur run frequent services from Puerto Montt to Ancud and Castro, six a day to Chonchi and Quellón; their fares are highest but they are faster (their buses have priority over cars on Cruz del Sur ferries). **Fares from Puerto Montt**: to Ancud, Cruz del Sur US$10; to Castro, Cruz del Sur US$11.50; to Chonchi, US$11.25, Quellón, US$12.75. Buses drive on to the ferry (passengers may leave the bus). **Ferries** About 24 crossings daily, 30-minute crossing, operated by several companies including **Transmarchilay** and **Cruz del Sur**; all ferries carry buses, private vehicles (cars US$19.50 one way, motorcycles US$14.75, bicycles US$4.20) and foot passengers (US$1.30). An airport outside Castro opened in late 2012; flights from Santiago with **LAN**, via Puerto Montt, Wednesday, Friday, Saturday, Sunday. A bridge to the island across the Chacao channel was approved in 2014; it is scheduled to be built by 2019.

Background
The original inhabitants of Chiloé were the Chonos, who were pushed south by the Huilliches invading from the north. The first Spanish sighting was by Francisco de Ulloa in 1553 and in 1567 Martín Ruiz de Gamboa took possession of the islands on behalf of Spain. The small Spanish settler population divided the indigenous population and their lands between them. The rising of the Mapuche after 1598 which drove the Spanish out of the mainland south of the Río Biobío left the Spanish community on Chiloé (some 200 settlers in 1600) isolated. During the 17th century, for instance, it was served by a single annual ship from Lima.

The islanders were the last supporters of the Spanish Crown in South America. When Chile rebelled the last of the Spanish Governors fled to the island and, in despair, offered it to Britain. Canning, the British Foreign Secretary, turned the offer down. The island finally surrendered in 1826.

The availability of wood and the lack of metals have left their mark on the island. Some of the earliest churches were built entirely of wood, using wooden pegs instead of nails. These early churches often displayed some German influence as a result of the missionary work of Bavarian Jesuits. Two features of local architecture often thought to be traditional are in fact late

Chiloé

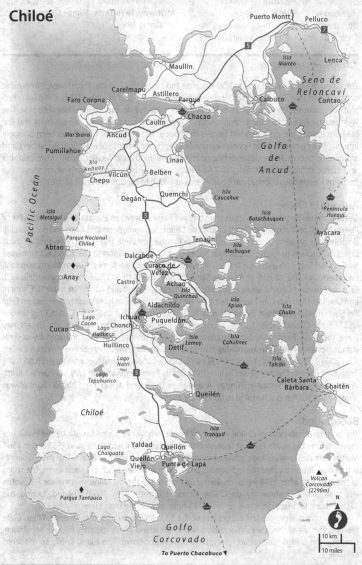

19th century in origin. The replacement of thatch with thin tiles (*tejuelas*) of several distinctive patterns made from alerce (larch) wood, which are nailed to the frame and roof, and *palafitos* or wooden houses built on stilts over the water.

The island is also famous for its traditional handicrafts, notably woollens, basketware and wood, which can be bought in the main towns and on some of the off-shore islands, as well as in Puerto Montt.

Although the traditional mainstays of the economy, fishing and agriculture, are still important, salmon farming has become a major source of employment. Seaweed is harvested for export to Japan. Tourism provides a seasonal income for a growing number of people. Also see www.chiloe.cl.

Ancud and around → *Phone code: 065. Colour map 9, A1. Population: 30,000.*

Ancud lies on the north coast of Chiloé 34 km west of the Straits of Chacao at the mouth of a great bay, the Golfo de Quetalmahue. Founded in 1767 to guard the shipping route around Cape Horn, it was defended by two fortresses, the Fuerte San Antonio and Fuerte Ahui on the opposite side of the bay. The bay is overlooked by the **Fuerte San Antonio** ① *open daily 0800-2100, 0900-2000 at weekends, free*, built in 1770, the site of the Spanish surrender of Chiloé to Chilean troops in 1826. It has a few cannon and surrounding wall. Close to it are the ruins of the **Polvorín del Fuerte**. A lovely 1-km walk north of the fort leads to **Arena Gruesa** beach, where public concerts are held in summer. 2 km east is a **mirador** offering good views of the island and across to the mainland, even to the Andes on a clear day. By the Plaza de Armas is the **Museo Regional** ① *Libertad 370, T262 2413, www.museoancud.cl, Tue-Fri 1000-1730, Sat-Sun 1000-1400, 1000-1900 daily Jan-Feb, US$1.30, half price for seniors and children.* As well as an interesting collection on the early history of Chiloé, it has a replica of the sailing boat that was used on the expedition to take the Straits of Magellan. Beside it is the Centro Cultural, with details of events and handicrafts outside. The modern cathedral stands on the plaza, built anew after the 1960 tsunami. **Tourist office**: Sernatur ① *Libertad 665, on the plaza, T262 2800, infochiloe@ sernatur.cl. Mon-Thu 0830-1800, Fri 0830-1700, in summer Mon-Fri0830-1900, Sat-Sun 0930-1900.* Ask here about the Agro Turismo programme, staying with farming families. CONAF ① *Errázuriz 300 block, Mon-Fri 0830-1400.* **Fundación Amigos de las Iglesias de Chiloé** ① *Errázuriz 227, T262 1046, open daily, suggested donation US$1*, in a precinct off the street, has an exhibition of various churches and styles of construction, a shop and El Convento café.

To **Faro Corona**, the lighthouse on Punta Corona, 34 km west, along the beach, offers good views with birdlife and dolphins (two to three buses daily, though none is the right time for seeing birds). The best time of day to see birds is early morning or late afternoon/evening. The duty officer may give a tour. To **Pumillahue** ① *27 km southwest, 2-3 buses daily, or take a tour (US$26 pp, twice a day, 3½ hrs including short boat trip, several agencies – see below), taxi, or hitch*, where nearby there is a Humboldt and Magellanic penguin colony from October to late March (the birds are seen early morning or late afternoon).

Chepu (*Population: 230*) on the coast southwest of Ancud (38 km, bus Monday, Wednesday, Friday; taxi US$32) is famed for its sea-fishing and the drowned forest (Valley of Dead Trees, devastated by the tsunami in 1960) and environment of its river. There is a wide range of birdlife and good opportunities for horseriding and boat trips here (eg Javier Silva, at Puente Anhuay, T9527 8719, turismo_riochepu@hotmail.com). The **Mirador de Chepu/Chepu Adventures** information centre gives views of the wetlands, information about the flora, fauna and tourist options, has a café, rents (electric) kayaks and has accommodation in cabins or dorms (**$$$-$**, T09-9227 4517, www.chepu.cl – no children under 14). Chepu is also the northern entry for the Parque Nacional Chiloé, see page 779.

Ancud to Castro

There are two routes: direct along Route 5, the Pan-American Highway, crossing rolling hills, forest and agricultural land, or via the east coast, passing through small farming and fishing communities. The road is paved to Huillinco, a few km before Linao, then is ripio to Quemchi. A paved road also branches off Route 5 at Degán to **Quemchi** (*Population: 2000*) which has a small **tourist office** ① *in the plaza open Mon-Fri 0900-2100, Sat-Sun 1000-2000, www.muniquemchi.cl*. At Quemchi the church is of wood, as is the bridge to Isla Aucar (botanical park). Every summer cultural events are held. Boat trips are offered, eg at **Restaurante Barloventos** (barloventos. quemchi@gmail.com). There are other places to eat and basic places to stay (eg **Hostal Backpackers**, beside bus stop, T9764 2038/9440 1321; **Camping La Casona**, T9909 9015).

South of Quemchi is the village of Tenaún, whose church with three towers, like 15 other Chilote churches, is a UNESCO World Heritage Site. Offshore is Isla Mechuque in the Chauques archipelago. It has two small museums of island life and palafito houses in the town. See http://turismoislamechuque.blogspot.co.uk. Boats go from Tenaún (45 minutes), Quicaví and Dalcahue (not daily), but the easiest way to get there is on a tour from Castro, eg with **Turismo Pehuén** (see below) or **Turismo Mi Tierra** (San Martín 473-A, Castro, T9863 2667, www.turismomitierra. cl), which includes a meal of *curanto al hoyo* and a visit to waterfalls at Tocoihue on main island.

Dalcahue (*Population: 4600*), 74 km south of Ancud, is more easily reached from Castro, 30 km further south. The wooden church on the main plaza dates from the 19th century (under repair in 2014). There is a large *artesanía* market on the waterside, near which are several restaurants. The Sunday market, near handicraft market, 0700-1300, is good quality. Tourist kiosk in season. There are various hotels (**$** pp and up).

Quinchao Island A 10-minute ferry crosses the strait between Dalcahue and Quinchao island. The main settlements on this island are Curaco de Vélez (handicrafts sold on the plaza in summer) and **Achao**, a quiet, pretty fishing village with a market. Its wooden church, built in 1730 and saved by a change of wind from a fire which destroyed much of the town in 1784, is a fine example of Chilote Jesuit architecture with a decorated ceiling. The original construction was without use of nails. It has a small museum, US$1. The **tourist office** at Serrano y Progreso is open between December and March only. There are various hotels (**$$-$**) and restaurants.

Between Dalcahue and Castro is the Rilán peninsula, with several traditional villages but also a growing number of upmarket hotels, golf and agrotourism.

Castro → *Phone code: 065. Colour map 9, A1. Population: 30,000.*

The sprawling capital of Chiloé lies on a fjord on the east coast, 88 km south of Ancud. Founded in 1567, the centre is situated on a promontory, from which there is a steep drop to the port. It is far livelier and more commercial than other towns on the island. On the Plaza de Armas is the large **Cathedral**, strikingly decorated in lilac and yellow, with a splendid wood panelled interior, built by the Italian architect, Eduardo Provosoli in 1906. It contains models of other churches on the islands. South of the Plaza on the waterfront is the **Feria**, or Mercado Municipal de Artesanía, where excellent local woollen articles (hats, sweaters, gloves) can be found. Behind it are four traditional restaurants. Palafitos can be seen on the northern side of town and by the bridge over the Río Gamboa (Calle Riquelme, with a number of *hostales*, cafés and handicraft shops). There are good views of the city from **Mirador La Virgen** on Millantuy hill above the cemetery. **Museo Municipal** ① *on Esmeralda, T263 5967*, closed in 2014, contains history, folklore, handicrafts and mythology of Chiloé and photos of the 1960 earthquake. **Museo de Arte Moderno** ① *near the Río Gamboa, in the Parque Municipal, over 3 km northwest of the centre, T263 5454, www.mamchiloe.cl, 1000-1700, to 1800 during exhibitions, donations*, is reached by following Calle Galvarino Riveros up the hill west of town, take bus marked 'Al Parque'. There are good views from the hill. **Tourist information kiosk** ① *on the Plaza de Armas opposite the cathedral*. It has a list of accommodation and prices and other information. On the southern outskirts of town is Nercón, whose UNESCO-recognized church is signed off Ruta 5. From the ceiling of the nave hang models of sailing boats. The community holds its **Fiesta Costumbrista** at the end of January.

Chonchi → *Phone code: 065. Colour map 9, A1. Population: 5000.*

Chonchi is a picturesque fishing village 25 km south of Castro. The wooden church, on the plaza, was built in 1754, remodelled in neoclassical style in 1859 and 1897. The nave roof is painted blue, dotted with stars (key, if closed, from the small handicraft market next door). There is another, undecorated 18th-century church at Vilupulli, 5 km north (sign on Ruta 5, *ripio* road). The woman who has a tiny handicraft stall behind the church holds the key. From Chonchi's plaza Calle Centenario, with several attractive but sadly neglected wooden mansions, drops steeply to the waterfront, Avenida Irarrázabal. The small **Museo de Tradiciones Chonchinas** ⓘ *Centenario 116, T267 2802, US$1, Tue-Sun 1000-1330, 1500-1845*, is housed in a former residence, laid out to give an idea of domestic life in the first decade of the 20th century when Chonchi was the most important port in Chiloé. It shows videos on the churches of Chiloé. The tiny **Museo del Acordeón of Sergio Colivor Barria** ⓘ *Andrade next to Restaurant La Quila, daily*, has some 50 instruments on display. Fishing boats bring in the catch which is carried straight into the modern market; the pier and market are opposite ends of Av Irarrázabal. A tourist information kiosk is open at the crossroads one block uphill from the main plaza in summer; also a desk in the market.

A pleasant excursion is to the **Isla Lemuy** ⓘ *ferry 4 km south on road to Queilén every 30 mins, cars US$5, foot passengers free (micro from Castro)*; lovely walking. At **Puqueldón** there is a small private park, **Parque Yayanes** ⓘ *T09 8861 6462, www.parqueyayanes.cl*, which offers a 30-minute walk across a hanging bridge and through mixed forest, has lodging in cabins and serves traditional food. At Queilén, a fishing village on a peninsula 46 km southeast is **Museo Refugio de Navegantes** ⓘ *Pres Alessandri s/n, T236 7149, Jan and Feb 1100-2000*. Also here are places to stay and several restaurants including **Restaurant Melinka**, Alessandri 126, for good food.

Cucao

From Chonchi a paved road leads west to Cucao, 40 km, one of two settlements on the west coast of Chiloé. At Km 12 is **Huillinco**, a charming village on Lago Huillinco, with *cabañas* and cafés: **de Lago**, 50 m off the road on the lakeshore by **Camping Huillinco**, for teas, coffees, cakes, sandwiches, open January to mid-March and weekends to Semana Santa, and **Los Coihues**, above the village, for more substantial fare.

Cucao is divided by a creek. The landward side is beside the lake and has the small church, a helpful tourist information desk and a couple of traditional restaurants, plus places to stay. Cross the bridge to the newer sector, with hostales, eating places, adventure sports agencies (horse riding, trekking, kayaks, SUP) and the road to the national park. Beyond the park entrance the rough road continues to Canquín, with a bridge shaped like a boat. Over the bridge, on the left, is a track through private property to an immense 20-km beach with thundering Pacific surf and dangerous undercurrents (US$2 to park car). It's about 30 minutes' walk from bridge to bridge. See www.turismocucao.cl.

Parque Nacional Chiloé

ⓘ *US$2.75, open all year 0900-2000 (1800 winter), parque.chiloe@conaf.cl.*

The park is divided into three sections. Much of its 43,057 ha is covered by evergreen forest. The northern sector, covering 7800 ha, is reached by a path which runs south from **Chepu** (see page 777). The second section is a small island, **Metalqui**, off the coast of the north sector. The southern sector, 35,207 ha, is entered 1 km north of Cucao, where there is an administration centre, small museum, restaurant Fogón and cabañas (**$$$** for five to six people) and camping (US$9 per person). There are six trails from 108 m to 1700 m, four lakeside, two to the dunes and beach. Ask at the administration centre or horse riding agencies about excursions further into the park. Horseflies are bad in summer (wear light-coloured clothing).

Quellón → *Phone code: 065. Colour map 9, A1. Population: 13,860. 92 km south of Castro.*
There are pleasant beaches nearby at Quellón Viejo (with an old wooden church), Punta de Lapa and Yaldad. Boat trips go to Isla Cailín in summer from the pier, US$42 for a full day (www. turismochiloe.cl). A trip can also be made to Chaiguao, 11 km east, where there is a small Sunday morning market. Horses can be hired, also kayaks with a guide. **Museo Municipal Amador Cárdenas Paredes** ① *Pedro Montt 309, T268 3452, Mon-Fri 0930-1800*, has an odd collection of antique typewriters and sewing machines. There are amazing views of the mainland on a clear day. The Golfo de Corcovado, between southern Chiloé and the mainland is visited by blue whales from December to April. **Tourist office** ① *Vargas y García*, is often closed, even in summer. See also **Cámara de Turismo Quellón** ① *T9191 2150, www.turismoquellon.cl; see also www. muniquellon.cl*. Note that the street numbering system in Quellón is unfathomable.

From Quellón you can go to **Parque Tantauco** ① *US$6.50, children US$1, information at Av La Paz 034, Quellón, T277 3100, or E Riquelme 1228, Castro, T263 0951, http://parquetantauco.cl.* It covers 120,000 ha of woods and wetlands at the southernmost part of the Island, with many endangered endemic species of mammal. It's a private park, with campsites, *casa de huéspedes* and a refugio. There are 120 km of trails from three hours to five days. Access is by road or by a three-hour boat trip from Quellón to Inio (US$50, Monday, Wednesday, Friday).

◉ Chiloé listings

For hotel and restaurant price codes, and other relevant information, see Essentials.

● Where to stay

Ancud *p777*
$$$ Don Lucas, Salvador Allende (Costanera) 906, T262 0950, www.hoteldonlucas.cl. Nice rooms, some with sea view, disabled access, restaurant. A good choice.
$$$ Galeón Azul, Libertad 751, T262 2567, www.hotelgaleonazul.cl. Small heated rooms, rather basic for the price but excellent views. Bright restaurant.
$$$ Panamericana, San Antonio 30, T262 2340, www.panamericanahoteles.cl. Nice views of the bay, attractive, very comfortable, helpful, restaurant, tours offered, English spoken.
$$ Balai, Pudeto 169, T262 2966, www. hotelbalai.cl. With heating, parking, restaurant, interesting local paintings, models and artefacts on display. Tours arranged.
$$ Hostal Lluhay, Cochrane 458, T262 2656, www.hostal-lluhay.cl. Attentive, sea views, heating, meals, nice lounge, kayak and bicycle rental, tours with Ancud Mágico.
$$ Hostal Vista al Mar, Salvador Allende (Costanera) 918, T262 2617, www.vistaalmar.cl. Close to Cruz del Sur buses, cabins for 2-5, also private rooms with or without bath. Views over the bay, safe, heating, parking.

$$-$ 13 Lunas, Los Carrera 855, T262 2106, www.13lunas.cl. Opposite Cruz del Sur bus terminal, single-sex and mixed dorms, private rooms, wheelchair accessible, very helpful, *asados* and ping pong in the basement, parking, great penguin tour and other activities.
$$-$ Mundo Nuevo, Salvador Allende (Costanera) 748, T262 8383, www. backpackerschile.com. Comfortable hostel, dorms, rooms with and without bath, one room has a boat-bed, great views over the bay, lots of info, heating, good showers, car and bicycle hire, English and German spoken.
$ pp Hosp Austral, A Pinto 1318, T262 4847, www.ancudchiloechile.com. Cosy wooden house, near long-distance bus station, with small breakfast, lots of bathrooms, double room (**$$**), family of Mirta Ruiz, very welcoming and caring, lots of information.
$ pp Hostal Altos de Bellavista, Bellavista 449, T262 2384, cecilia2791@gmail.com. Rooms for 1-5, with or without bath, family atmosphere, long stay available, tatty outside but welcoming inside. Everal other places to stay on Bellavista.
Camping Hostal y Cabañas Arena Gruesa, Av Costanera Norte 290, T262 3428, www. hotelarenagruesa.cl. US$8-9.75 for campsite, also mobile homes, with light, water and services, also cabins for 2-10 and hotel.

Castro *p778*

There is an **Asociación Hospedajes Castro**, approved by the Municipalidad, ask at the tourist office.

$$$$-$$$ Cabañas Trayen, Nercón, 5 km south of Castro, T263 3633, www.trayenchiloe.cl. Lovely views, cabins for 4 to 6.

$$$$-$$$ Hotel de Castro, Chacabuco 202, T263 2301, www.hosteriadecastro.cl. The newer section is spacious and comfortable, with wonderful views and nice suites. Spa, pool. Good restaurant and bar.

$$$ Unicornio Azul, Pedro Montt 228, T263 2359, www.hotelunicornioazul.cl. Striking pink and blue building climbing the hillside from the waterfront, good views over bay, comfortable, restaurant.

$$$-$$ Palafito Hostel, Riquelme 1210, T253 1008. In a restored traditional *palafito* building on stilts over the water, downhill from centre and across bridge. Helpful staff, good breakfast, tours arranged. (On same street are places with similar names: **Palafito Azul**, No 1242, www.palafitoazul.cl, and **Palafito 1326**, No 1326, www.palafito1326.cl.)

$$ Casita Española, Los Carrera 359, T263 5186, www.hosteriadecastro.cl. Heating, parking, good, in same group as **Hostería de Castro**.

$$ Hostal Don Camilo, Ramírez 566, T263 2180, hostaldoncamilo@gmail.com. Pleasant accommodation in functional rooms with all services, good value restaurant, secure parking.

$$-$ Hosp El Mirador, Barros Arana 127, T263 3795, maboly@yahoo.com. Private or shared bath, rooms a bit small, cosy, relaxing, kitchen (shared with family).

$ pp Hosp América, Chacabuco 215, T263 4364, hosameri@telsur.cl. Good location, family welcome, shared bath, comfortable. They offer an evening meal service: you buy, they cook, everyone shares.

$ pp Hosp El Molo, Barros Arana 140, T263 5026, www.elmolochiloe.cl. The oldest hostel in Castro, comfortable, safe, welcoming, good location on steps down to seafront, nice view. Several others on this passageway.

Camping Camping Pudú, Ruta 5, 10 km north of Castro, T263 2286, www.chiloeweb.com/chwb/pudu/. Cabins, showers with hot water, sites with light, water, kids' games. Several sites on road to Chonchi, including Llicaldad, Esmeralda 269, T263 2380, apachecocornejo@gmail.com, also has *cabañas*.

Chonchi *p779*

$$$ Cabañas Treng Treng, José Pinto Pérez 420, T2672532, www.trengtreng.cl. Impeccable fully furnished cabins sleeping 2-7. Splendid views, some English spoken.

$$ Hostal Emarley, Irarrázabal 191, T267 1202. Near market, cheaper rooms with shared bath.

$$ Hostal Esmeralda, Esmeralda con Irarrázabal 267, T235 5035, T9504 4944/9597 9401, abraniff@gmail.com. Beyond market, access from road or beach. Completely renovated, family atmosphere, quiet, suite on top floor, or rooms with and without bath, breakfast extra, small garden, parking, kitchen and Wi-Fi to follow.

$$ Hostal La Tortuga, Pedro Montt 241, T9098 2925, www.hostallatortuga.com. In a historic house on the main plaza, comfortable rooms, cafeteria, laundry.

$$ Huildín, Centenario 102, T2671388, www.hotelhuildin.com. Old fashioned, decent rooms with good beds but windows are onto interior passages, also *cabañas*, garden with superb views.

Cucao *p779*

Most lodgings and restaurants open Jan-Mar, but you can camp all year.

$$$-$$ Hostal Palafito Cucao, T2971164, www.hostelpalafitocucao.cl. Open all year. 300 m from park entrance, built from native timber overlooking lake Cucao. Large windows for great views. Transfers and excursions arranged. Private rooms and a 6-bed dorm, comfortable, good breakfast and kitchen, meals available.

$$ La Paloma, behind the church on lakeshore, T9313 1907. Cabañas and camping (US$6.50 pp) open all year.

$ pp Jostel, T8242 3007/9833 4830, jostle.chiloe@gmail.com. Open summer only for lodging, but also kayaks US$9 per hr, SUP US$18, pedal boats US$14.50.

Camping Campsites, some with restaurants and shops on the road to the national park, others on the road east of Cucao. There are minimarkets on the little street behind Jostel and another before the tourist office.

Quellón p780

$$ El Chico Leo, P Montt 325, T268 1567, www.turismochiloe.cl/hotelelchicoleo. Private or shared bath, heating, games room, restaurant.

There are several other places to stay including cabañas and campsites: see www.muniquellon.cl and www.turismochiloe.cl.

🍴 Restaurants

Ancud p777

$$ La Pincoya, Prat 61, near the dock entrance, T262 2613. Good seafood, service and views.

$$ Quetalmahue, 12 km west of Ancud on the road to Faro Corona and Fuerte Ahui, T09-9033 3930, www.quetalmahue.cl. The best place for traditional *curantos al hoyo* (cooked in the ground, daily in summer).

$ El Cangrejo, Dieciocho 155. Has a good reputation for its seafood.

$ El Embrujo, Maipú 650. Café serving teas, coffees, sandwiches, cakes, beers and tragos.

Above the handicrafts in the Mercado Municipal are 2 restaurants, **Los Artesanos**, loc 71, and **Rincón Sureño**, loc 53, both serving *comida típica*. Walking up Dieciocho towards the Feria Municipal there are many eating places behind the Mercado, including **La Ñaña**, which is cheap and good. All serve much the same local fare. In an alley from Dieciocho to Prat is a row of even cheaper lunch spots, including **El Pingüinito**, decent lunches, but more basic than others. In the Feria Municipal there are 4 restaurants upstairs, all much the same with lunch specials at US$4.50-6.75.

Castro p778

Breakfast before 0900 is difficult to find. There are several eating places and bars on the south side of the Plaza, on Portales and Balmaceda. By the market many places offer set lunch, usually fish dishes. In the market, try *milcaos*, fried potato cakes with meat stuffing. Also *licor de oro* like Galliano.

$$$-$ Donde Eladio, Lillo 97. Meat and seafood specialities on offer.

$$$-$ La Playa, Lillo 41, www.playachiloe.cl. Good seafood, also meat dishes.

$$ Don Octavio, Pedro Montt 261. Good food and nice views over bay, specializes in seafood.

$$ Palafito restaurants near the Feria Artesanía on the waterfront offer good food and good value: **Brisas del Mar**, El Caleuche, El Curanto and La Pincoya.

$$-$ Descarriada, Esmeralda y Blanco, corner of the Plaza. Good local dishes, meat and fish, nice atmosphere, also desserts, tea and coffee, ice cream cart outside.

$$-$ Sacho, Thompson 213. Tue-Sat 1200-1530, 2100-2330, Sun 1200-1530. Good sea views and good food.

Cafés

Café Blanco, Blanco 268. Busy little place for coffee, teas, juices, sandwiches, cakes, piscos, beers and wine. Similar, at No 264, is **Ristretto Caffé**.

Café del Puente, Riquelme 1180-B, T263 4878. Tue-Sun 0900-2100. Smart café over the water serving breakfast, lunches, afternoon tea (30 varieties of tea), coffee, sandwiches, cakes, juices and ice cream.

La Brújula del Cuerpo, O'Higgins 308, Plaza de Armas. Fast food, grill, snacks, drinks and coffee.

Chonchi p779

There are a few places to eat on Av Irrarrázabal. Most places close on Sun, even in summer. **Iscamar**, Centenario 66 y P J Andrade, is open on Sun. **Supermercado Economar**, Irrarrázabal 49, far end of Costanera from Mercado, has a café. Next door is **Chocolatería Pastelería Alejandra**.

$$-$ Tres Pisos, Pedro Andrade 296 y Esmeralda, near the market. Serves good food.

$ Café Sueños de la Pincoya, P J Andrade 135, open daily 1000-2200. For sweet empanadas, cakes, teas and coffee.

Quellón p780

$$ Tierra del Fuego, P Montt 445, T268 2079. For fish, seafood and other local dishes. In hotel of same name.

$ Fogón Onde Agüero, La Paz 307, T268 3653. Good cheap traditional food. Popular at lunchtime.

🛍 Shopping

Ancud p777

Handicrafts Mercado Municipal, at Libertad between Dieciocho and Prat. The Feria Municipal (or Rural) is at Pedro Montt y Pratt, selling local produce, fish and handicrafts on the 2nd floor. Also has a tourist office. Opposite is a huge **Unimarc** supermarket.

Castro *p778*
Handicrafts Mercado Artesanal, Lillo on the wharf, good value woollens at reasonable prices.
Market The municipal market is on Yumbel, off Ulloa, uphill northwest of town: fish and veg.
Supermarket Unimarc, O'Higgins y Aldea. Bakes good bread.

Chonchi *p779*
Handicrafts From Feria artesanal, on the waterfront – woollens, jams, liqueurs, and from the parroquia, next to the church (open Oct-Mar only).

⚙ What to do

Ancud *p777*
Aki Turismo, patio of Mercado Municipal, T254 5253, www.akiturismochiloe.cl. Good value trips to the penguin colony and other tours. Car rental in the same office, www.chiloerentacar.cl.
Austral Adventures, Salvador Allende (Costanera) 904, T262 5977, www.austral-adventures.com. Bespoke small-group tours of the archipelago and northern Patagonia (including Parque Pumalín) on land and sea. Good English-speaking guides, lots of interesting choices; director Britt Lewis.
Mistyk's, Los Carrera 823, T9644 3767, www.turismomistyks.com. For local tours and diving.
Viajes Nativa, in Cruz del Sur bus terminal, T254 6390, www.viajesnativa.cl or www.chiloetour.com. Tours to the penguin colony.

Castro *p778*
Boat trips with **Mar y Magia**, cabin on the dockside or at Chacabuco 202, T253 1048, www.marymagia.cl. Fjord trips US$12.50 pp, longer trips in summer. **Chiloé Nuatural**, P Montt next to Unicornio Azul, T6319 7388, tours@chiloenatural.cl. Offers lots of activities, trips to islands and boat trips.
Turismo Pehuén, Latorre 238, T263 5254, www.turismopehuen.cl. **Naviera Austral** agency, kayak and boat trips, trips to national park, penguin colony, around the island and car hire.

⊟ Transport

Ancud *p777*
Bus Terminal on the east outskirts at Av Prat y Marcos Vera, reached by bus 1, or Pudeto colectivos. **Cruz del Sur** has its own station in centre, Los Carrera 850, T262 2249. To **Castro**, US$3.75, frequent (see below), 1½ hrs. To **Puerto Montt**, frequent services, see Arriving in Chiloé, above. To **Quemchi**, most via Degán, 2 hrs, US$2.75; to **Dalcahue** US$3. Terminal Rural for local services is on Colo Colo, up a ramp behind Unimarc supermarket. Timetables are posted on the door to the admin office and toilet.

Quinchao Island *p778*
Ferry From **Dalcahue**, 10 mins, frequent, in summer it runs till 0100, cars US$4.55, free for pedestrians. San Cristóbal **buses** from **Ancud** and **Castro** (11 a day, 7 at weekends, US$3).

Castro *p778*
Bus There are 2 bus terminals: the crowded Terminal Municipal, San Martín 667, from which all buses and micros to island and long-distance destinations leave; and Cruz del Sur terminal, San Martín 486, T263 5152. Trans Chiloé's office is in Terminal Municipal. Frequent services to **Ancud**, **Chonchi** and **Puerto Montt** by Cruz del Sur, Queilén Bus and others. Cruz del Sur goes as far as Santiago, US$56-76, and all cities in between. Isla de Chiloé and Ojeda both run to **Cucao**, almost hourly in summer, 2-3 a day in winter, 1½ hrs, US$2.75, US$5.40 return to national park. To **Dalcahue** frequent services, US$1.50. To **Achao** via Dalcahue and Curaco de Vélez, see above. To **Puqueldón** on the island of Lemuy, **Gallardo**, 4 daily Mon-Fri fewer Sat-Sun, US$3.50. To **Quemchi**, daily with Queilén Bus, 1½ hrs, US$2.55. To **Queilén**, Queilén Bus and others, 6 a day, US$3.

Chonchi *p779*
Buses and taxis to **Castro**, frequent, US$1.45, from main plaza. Services to **Quellón** (US$2), Cucao and Queilén from Castro and Puerto Montt also call here.

Cucao *p779*

Bus From Castro see above. Buses go via **Chonchi** and **Huillinco**.

Quellón *p780*

Bus To **Castro**, 2 hrs, frequent, Quellón Expreso, US$3, and Cruz del Sur (Pedro Aguirre Cerda 052, T268 1284), US$3.25; also to **Ancud**, US$7.25, and **Puerto Montt**.

Ferries Naviera Austral, Pedro Montt 457, Quellón, T268 2207, www.navieraustral.cl. They run ferries from Quellón to **Chaitén** once a week (more in high season, also from

Castro, office Latorre 238, T263 5254), 5 hrs, seat US$29, bunk US$56-62, US$11 bicycle, US$36 motorbike, US$156 car. To **Puerto Chacabuco**, via Melinka, Raul Marin Balmaceda, Santo Domingo, Melimoyu, Puerto Gala (Isla Toto), Puerto Cisnes, Puerto Gaviota and Puerto Aguirre twice weekly, 28 hrs, reclining seat US$27, bunk US$66-68, cars US$214. All services leave from Castro when Quellón's port is out of commission and schedules are subject to last-minute changes due to inclement weather. Check with the company for schedules and fares for 2014-2015.

Carretera Austral

A third of Chile lies to the south of Puerto Montt, but until recently its inaccessible land and rainy climate meant that it was only sparsely populated and unvisited by tourism. The Carretera Austral, or Southern Highway, has now been extended south from Puerto Montt to Villa O'Higgins, giving access to the spectacular virgin landscapes of this wet and wild region, with its mountains, fjords and islands, hitherto isolated communities, and picturesque ports. Ships were the only means of access and remain important for exporting the timber grown here, and for bringing visitors.

The only settlement of any size is Coyhaique and its nearby airport at Balmaceda and the equally nearby Puerto Chacabuco are the principal entry points. Coyhaique is a good starting point for exploring the Carretera, north to the thermal springs at Puyuhuapi and the unspoilt national park of Queulat, for trekking expeditions and for fishing. Coyhaique is also a good place for booking Parque Nacional Laguna San Rafael glacier trips, for which boats leave from Puerto Chacabuco.

The Carretera extends 575 km from Coyhaique to Villa O'Higgins, beyond which the southern icefields and their glaciers bring the roadway to a halt. This southernmost section of the Carretera is the wildest and most dramatic, with beautiful unspoilt landscapes around Lago General Carrera. The fairy tale peaks of Cerro Castillo offer challenging trekking, and there's world class fishing in the turquoise waters of Río Baker. A road runs off to Puerto Ibáñez for lake crossings to Chile Chico, a convenient border crossing to Argentina, while a more adventurous cross-border route involves road, lake and foot or horseback travel to El Chaltén.

Getting to and travelling on the Carretera Austral

This road can be divided into three major sections: **Puerto Montt-Chaitén**, **Chaitén-Coyhaique**, and **Coyhaique-Villa O'Higgins**. The road is paved south of Chaitén to 32 beyond Villa Santa Lucía, most of the way from La Junta to Coyhaique and south of there to Villa Cerro Castillo and Puerto Ibáñez. Currently, the rest is 'ripio' (loose stones) and many sections are extremely rough and difficult after rain. The Carretera is very popular with cyclists, even though they can't expect to make fast progress. Motorists need to carry sufficient fuel and spares, especially if intending to detour along any of the highway's many side roads, and protect windscreens and headlamps from stones. Unleaded fuel is available all the way to Villa O'Higgins. There is now a road between Puerto El Vagabundo and Caleta Tortel, and the Carretera Austral is connected by a free ferry between Puerto Yungay and Río Bravo, where it continues to Villa O'Higgins. There is little infrastructure for transport or accommodation among the rural hamlets, so allow plenty of time for bus connections, and bring cash, as there are few banks along the whole route. Camping will give you more freedom for accommodation and there are many beautiful sites. Having your own transport here is definitely preferable. If you intend to hitchhike, **note** that it is essential to take up to three days' worth of supplies as you can be stuck for that long, especially in the far south. At the same time (for campers too), food supplies are limited and tend to be expensive. ▶▶ *See also Transport, pages 786, 795 and 801.*

Best time to visit The landscape throughout the region is lushly green because there is no real dry season. On the offshore islands and the western side of the Andes annual rainfall is over 2000 mm, though inland on the steppe the climate is drier and colder. Westerly winds are strong, especially in summer, but there's plenty of sunshine too.Lago General Carrera in particular (described in the Southern section) has a warm microclimate. January and February are the best months.

Puerto Montt to Chaitén

This section of the Carretera Austral, 205 km, should include two ferry crossings. Before setting out, it is imperative to check which ferries are running and when and, if driving, make a reservation: do this in Puerto Montt (not Santiago), on the website of **Transportes Austral**, www. taustral.cl, which is a consortium of the three ferry companies that operate the routes, or at the offices of the ferry companies listed in Transport, below. An alternative route to Chaitén is by ferry from Puerto Montt or Quellón/Castro.

The road (Ruta 7) heads east out of Puerto Montt, through Pelluco, and follows the shore of the beautiful Seno Reloncaví. It passes the southern entrance of the **Parque Nacional Alerce Andlno** ① *US$2.65, T065-248 6101, loslagos.oirs@conaf.cl, has a campsite (no showers) inside the park, 2.7 km from the entrance near Lenca; there's also a private site near this entrance (with showers),* which contains one of the best surviving areas of alerce trees, some over 1000 years old (the oldest is estimated at 4200 years old). Wildlife includes pudú, pumas, vizcachas, condors and black woodpeckers. There are two entrances: 2.5 km from Correntoso (35 km east of Puerto Montt) at the northern end of the park (with ranger station and campsite) and 7 km east of Lenca (40 km south of Puerto Montt) at the southern end. There are three other ranger posts, at Río Chaicas, Lago Chapo and Sargazo. Ranger posts have little information; map is available from CONAF in Puerto Montt.

At 46 km from Puerto Montt (allow one hour), is the first ferry at **La Arena**, across the Reloncaví Estuary to **Puelche**. See Transport, page 801, for ferry details. **Río Negro** Is now called **Hornopirén** after the volcano above it. At the mouth of the fjord is the small Isla Llancahué, with a hotel and thermal springs, good for hiking in the forests amid beautiful scenery. Boat to the island 50 minutes, US$60 one-way shared between passengers, contact hotel, as below; look out for dolphins and fur seals en route. A second ferry sails from Hornopirén to Leptepu, from where a road runs to Fiordo Largo, where another ferry goes to Caleta Gonzalo.

Parque Pumalín
① *Open all year, free. Information centre: Klenner 299, Puerto Varas, T065-225 0079; in USA T415-229-9330, www.parquepumalin.cl (Spanish and English).*
Caleta Gonzalo is the entry point for Parque Pumalín for visitors from the north. The park, created by the US billionaire Douglas Tompkins, is a private reserve of 700,000 ha in two sections which has been given Nature Sanctuary status. Covering large areas of the western Andes, with virgin temperate rainforest, the park is spectacularly beautiful, and is seen by many as one of the most important conservation projects in the world. There are campsites and cabins throughout the park, a number of hot springs and hiking trails.

South of Caleta Gonzalo the Carretera Austral winds through the park's beautiful unspoilt scenery, and there is a steep climb on the ripio road to two lakes, Lago Río Blanco and Lago Río Negro, with panoramic views. After the 2008 eruption of Volcán Chaitén and consequent river flooding, the government decided to abandon Chaitén, cutting off utilities, starting to rebuild the town 10 km north at Santa Barbara and moving the seat of provincial government to Futaleufú. Chaitén, however, survived with running water, generators and fuel and in 2011 the government reversed former decisions and the town is being reestablished in the northern part of the old town. There are shops, *hospedajes* and *cabañas* and all transport links: ferries to Puerto Montt and Chiloé, flights and buses. See www.camaraturismochaiten.cl (in English) and www.munichaiten.cl.

⊙ Puerto Montt to Chaitén listings

For hotel and restaurant price codes, and other relevant information, see Essentials.

0680, hotelschilling@hotmail.com). See www.camaraturismochaiten.cl.

⊛ Where to stay

Puerto Montt to Chaitén *p785*
$$$$ Alerce Mountain Lodge, Km 36
Carretera Austral, T228 6969, www.mountain
lodge.cl. In Los Alerces de Lenca private reserve,
beside Parque Nacional Alerce Andino, remote
lodge, rooms and cabins, all-inclusive 2- to
4-night packages, with hiking, guides speak
English, good food.

Hornopirén
$$$$ Hotel Termas de Llancahué, Isla
Llancahué, T09-9642 4857, www.termasde
llancahue.cl. Full board (excellent food),
hot spring at the hotel, excursions by boat,
fishing, kayaking.
$$ Hornopirén, Carrera Pinto 388, T221
7256, h.hornopiren@gmail.com. Rooms
with shared bath, also *cabañas* and restaurant
at the water's edge.
$$ Hostería Catalina, Ingenieros Militares
s/n, T221 7359, www.hosteriacatalina.cl.
Comfortable rooms and *cabañas*, meals,
excursions, a good place to stay.
For a full list, see www.hornopiren.net.

Chaitén *p785*
Among many places to stay are: **Cabañas
Brisas del Mar** (Corcovado 278, T9115
8808, cababrisas@telsur.cl), **Cabañas Pudú**
(Corcovado 668, T8227 9602, puduchaiten@
hotmail.com), **Casa de Rita** (Riveros y Prat,
T9778 2351, ritagutierrezgarcia@hotmail.
es), **El Refugio** (Corcovado y Juan Todesco),
Hostería Corcovado (Corcovado 408,
T8868 4922), **Hosp Don Carlos** (Riveros 53,
T9128 3328, doncarlos.palena@gmail.com),
Hostería Llanos (Corcovado 378, T8826
0498), and **Shilling** (Corcovado 258, T226

⊙ What to do

Chaitén *p785*
Chaitur, O'Higgins 67, T09-7468 5608,
www.chaitur.com. Nicholas La Penna runs
this agency making bus, boat, plane and
hotel reservations, tours to hot springs,
glaciers, beaches, Carretera Austral,
photography trips. Still *the* place for local
information. English and French spoken,
helpful, book exchange, internet.

⊙ Transport

Puerto Montt to Chaitén *p785*
Parque Nacional Alerce Andino
Bus To the north entrance: take a **Fierro** or **Río
Pato** bus to **Correntoso** (or Lago Chapo bus
which passes through Correntoso), several daily
except Sun, then walk. To the south entrance:
take any bus to **Chaicas, La Arena, Contau**
and **Hornopirén**, US$2.50, getting off at Lenca
sawmill, then walk (signposted).

La Arena to Puelche
Ferry 2 ferries cross the Reloncaví Estuary,
30 mins, every 45 mins, US$17 for a car, US$12.50
for motorcycle, US$5 for bicycle, US$1 for foot
passengers, 0645-0030 daily. Arrive at least
30 mins early to guarantee a place; buses have
priority. Roll-on roll-off type operating all year.
See www.taustral.cl; **Naviera Puelche**, Av Italia
2326, Parque San Andrés, Puerto Montt, T227
0761, www.navierapuelche.cl, or **Naviera
Paredes**, T065-227 6490, www.navieraparedes.cl.

Hornopirén
Bus **Kémel** (4 a day, 2 on Sun, T225 3530)
and **M&M** (2 a day, 1 on Sun) run from **Puerto
Montt**, US$7.25.

Ferry **Hornopirén** to **Chaitén** via Leptepu and Fiordo Largo-Caleta Gonzalo: check on www.taustral.cl, or with **Naviera Puelche**, as above for schedules, normally once a day each way to/from **Leptepu**, twice a day in high season; 2 a day to/from **Caleta Gonzalo**, 4 in high season. If driving your own car, it is essential to reserve a place: cars US$54.50, motorbikes US$13.65, bicycles US$9, passengers in addition to driver US$9, bus passengers US$4.50. One fare covers both ferries. In Hornopirén T065-221 7266, in Ayacara T07-475 1168,

Chaitén *p785*

Air Daily flights (except Sun) from **Puerto Montt** to Santa Bárbara with Aerocord (19 passengers), US$75.
Bus Terminal at Chaitur, O'Higgins 67. **Kémel** (as above) have a daily bus/ferry service from Puerto Montt, 0700, US$25, 9 hrs, return from Chaitén 1200. To **Coyhaique**, Twice a week direct with Becker, also Terraustral, direct in

summer, 12 hrs, otherwise overnight stop in La Junta, to which buses depart Mon, Tue, Fri, Sat 0930. Connections to Puyuhuapi and Coyhaique next day. Minibuses usually travel full, so can't pick up passengers en route. Buses to **Futaleufú**, daily except Thu, 0930; change here for buses to the Argentine border.

Ferry

The ferry port is about 1 km north of town. Schedules change frequently and ferries are infrequent off season. **Naviera Austral**, Corcovado 466, T065-273 1011, www.navier austral.cl. Check website or www.taustral.cl for all future sailings.

To **Chiloé**, Naviera Austral operates ferry services to **Quellón** or **Castro** (Jan-Feb only), once a week, more in summer (Dec-Mar); fares given under Quellón, above.

To **Puerto Montt**, Naviera Austral, Mon-Fri via Ayacara, 10 hrs, passengers US$29, cabin US$55-62, car US$156, motorbike US$36, bicycle US$11.

Chaitén to Coyhaique

This section of the Carretera Austral, runs 422 km through breathtaking and varied scenery, passing tiny villages, most notably the idyllic Puyuhuapi, where there are thermal pools, and good trekking in Parque Nacional Queulat.

Puerto Cárdenas, 44 km south of Chaitén, is on the northern tip of **Lago Yelcho**, a beautiful lake on Río Futaleufú surrounded by hills, much loved by anglers for its salmon and trout (no shops or restaurants in Puerto Cárdenas, but Viola, T09-9884 2946, bungalow opposite yellow house next to old *carabinero* post, offers half board – **$$**, excellent food). Further south at Km 60, a path leads to **Ventisquero Yelcho** (two hours' walk there), a dramatic glacier with high waterfalls. Note that the path passes a campsite whose administrator charges walkers US$3.50 to go to the glacier. Whether he is legally entitled to do this is a contentious issue.

At **Villa Santa Lucía**, an uninspiring modern settlement 76 km south of Chaitén, with basic food and accommodation, a road branches east to the Argentine border. There are two crossings: Futaleufú and Palena, both reached from **Puerto Ramírez** past the southern end of Lago Yelcho, 24 km east of Santa Lucía. Here the road divides: the north branch runs along the valley of the Río Futaleufú to Futaleufú and the southern one to Palena. The scenery is spectacular, but the road is hard going: single track ripio, climbing steeply in places (tough for bikes; allow plenty of time).

Futaleufú → *Phone code: 065.*

The new provincial capital, 8 km west of the border, nestles in a bowl amid steep mountains on the Río Espolón. Its houses are neatly slatted with alerce wood and the wide streets are lined with shrubs and roses. Access to challenging whitewater rafting on the Río Futaleufú has made it into one of the southern hemisphere's prime centres for the sport, and with kayaking, riding, trekking, mountain biking and canyoning on offer Futaleufú now calls itself the capital of adventure tourism. **Lago Espolón**, west of Futaleufú, reached by a turning 41 km northeast of Villa Santa Lucía, is a beautiful lake in an area enjoying a warm microclimate: 30°C in the day in summer, 5°C at night, with excellent fishing at the lake's mouth. The lake is even warm enough for a quick dip, but beware of the currents. **Tourist office** ① *on the plaza at O'Higgins and Prat, T272 1629, www.futaleufu.cl, Oct-Apr, 0900-2100*, for accommodation, maps and fishing licences.

Border with Argentina

Chilean immigration is at the border, 8 km east of Futaleufú. The border is just west of the bridge over the Río Grande: straightforward crossing, open 0800-2000. For Argentinian immigration, see Argentina chapter. Change money in Futaleufú; nowhere to change at the border but you can pay the bus fare to Esquel (Argentina) in US dollars. Alternatively, cross into Argentina further south near **Palena**, which is 8 km west of the border and has a Chilean immigration office. **Note** If entering from Argentina, no fresh produce may be brought into Chile. Check conditions locally before crossing at this border.

XI Región

La Junta in the XI (eleventh) Region is a village 151 km south of Chaitén. La Junta has a service station, where there's a minimarket. From the village you can visit **Lago Rosselot**, surrounded by forest in the **Reserva Nacional Lago Rosselot**, 9 km east of La Junta. The same road continues east, 74 km, to Lago Verde and the Argentine border: open summer 0800-2200, winter 0800-2000. A road leads northwest, with a ferry crossing over the Río Palena (four daily), to the fishing village of **Puerto Raúl Marín Balmaceda** (hostels and camping). Different species of dolphin can be seen and Raúl Marín forms one apex of the blue whale triangle: the giant cetacean may be sighted on the ferry to Quellón in the summer. On clear days there are superb views of Volcán Melimoyu from the beach.

Puyuhuapi → *Phone code: 067. Population: 500.*

With the most idyllic setting along the whole Carretera Austral, Puyuhuapi lies in a tranquil bay at the northern end of the Puyuhuapi fjord, 46 km south of La Junta. The blissful thermal pools at Termas de Puyuhuapi are nearby. The village was founded by four German-speaking Sudeten families in 1935, and handwoven carpets are still made here, now to world renown. **Alfombras de Puyuhuapi** ① *T632 5131, www.puyuhuapi.com, daily in summer 0830-1930, closed lunch, English spoken.* This is the best stopping point between Chaitén and Coyhaique with phone, fuel, shops, but no banks: hotels may change dollars. **Tourist office** ① *by the Municipalidad, main street, www.puertopuyuhuapi.cl, Mon-Sat in season, 1000-1400, 1600-1900,* helpful.

Termas del Ventisqero ① *6 km south of Puyuhuapi beside the Carretera overlooking the fjord, T09-7966 6862, www.termasventisqueropuyuhuapi.cl, entry US$14.50.* In season the baths are open until 2300 and during the day there is a café. See Where to stay, below, for the Termas de Puyuhuapi at the **Puyuhuapi Lodge and Spa**.

South of Puyuguapi, 24 km, is the 154,093-ha **Parque Nacional Queulat** ① *CONAF, La Junta, T221 2225, aysen.oirs@conaf.cl, US$7, reductions for Chileans and children, daily Dec-Mar 0830-2100, rest of year 0830-1830.* It is most visited for the spectacular hanging glacier, **Ventisquero Colgante**. 2.5 km off the road passing the guardeparques' house, you'll find parking and camping areas. Three walks begin from here: a short stroll through the woodland to a viewpoint of the Ventisquero, or cross the river where the path begins to Laguna Tempanos, where boats cross the lake in summer. The third trail, 3.25 km, takes 2½ hours to climb to a panoramic viewpoint of the Ventisquero, where you can watch the ice fall into huge waterfalls like sifted sugar.

Puerto Cisnes

At 59 km south of Puyuhuapi, a winding road branches west and follows the Río Cisnes 33 km to Puerto Cisnes (*Population: 5740, www.municipalidadcisnes.cl*), a fishing village and salmon-farming centre at the mouth of the river on Puyuhuapi fjord, set amongst steep mountains. The Río Cisnes, 160 km in length, is recommended for rafting or canoeing, with grand scenery and modest rapids except for the horrendous drop at Piedra del Gato. Good camping in the forest, and fuel is available in the village.

At 89 km south of Puyuhuapi is **Villa Amengual** and, at Km 92, a road branches east, 104 km to La Tapera and to the Argentine border. Chilean immigration is 12 km west of the border, open summer 0800-2200, winter 0800-2000. On the Argentine side the road continues to meet up with Ruta 40, a section with few services for fuel or food.

Coyhaique → Phone code: 067. Colour map 9, A1. Population: 58,659.

A growing centre for tourism, Coyhaique, 420 km south of Chaitén, is a busy small town perched on a hill between the Ríos Simpson and Coyhaique. It has a cinema and all main services, including stores selling hiking gear and warm clothes. It's a good idea to get cash here as there are no banks along the Carretera Austral. The **Museo Regional de la Patagonia Central** ① *Lillo 23, Tue-Sun winter 0830-1730, summer 0900-2000, US$1 is in the Casa de Cultura*. It traces local history through photos of the first pioneers, as well as sections on archaeology, mineralogy and zoology. From the bridge over the Río Simpson look for the **Piedra del Indio**, a rock outcrop which looks like a face in profile. **Tourist offices**: Sernatur office (very helpful, English spoken) ① *Bulnes 35, 1223 1752, infoaisen@sernatur.cl, Mon-Fri 0830-1730, high season Mon-Fri 0830-2000, Sat-Sun 1000-1800.* CONAF ① *Av Ogana 1060, T221 2109, aysen.oirs@conaf.cl.*

Coyhaique

To Carretera Austral North

To ②④& Puerto Aisén

Military Camp

Reserva Nacional Coyhaique

200 metres
200 yards

Where to stay
1 Belisario Jara
2 Cabañas Baquedano
3 Cabañas Mirador
4 Cabañas Río Simpson
5 Cabañas San Sebastián
6 El Reloj
8 Hostal Bon
9 Hostal Las Quintas
11 Las Salamandras
13 San Sebastián

Restaurants 🍴
1 Café Oriente
2 Casino de Bomberos
3 Club Sandwich Patagonia
4 Donde Ramiro
5 El Mastique
6 Histórico Ricer & Café Ricer
7 La Casona
8 Pizzería La Fiorentina

Bars & clubs 🍸
9 Pepe le Pub
10 Piel Roja

Just outside the town, the **Reserva Nacional Coihaique** ① *0830-1700 Oct-Apr, US$5.50, information from CONAF*, has some trails for walking or biking, with picnic grounds and campsites (US$8). A satisfying walk is up to Cerro Cinchao, and great views from Sendero Los Leñeros to Laguna Verde. Walk to Laguna Verde and Laguna Venus particularly recommended. Follow Baquedano to the end, over bridge, and past the guardeparque's hut where all the trails begin. There are well-marked walks of between 20 minutes and five hours. Ski centre **El Fraile**, 29 km from Coyhaique, is 1599 m above sea level, with five pistes, powder snow, in the middle of ñire (Antarctic beech) and lenga forests (1000-people capacity).

Border with Argentina: Coyhaique Alto
A 43-km road runs east to this crossing. On the Argentine side the road leads through Río Mayo and Sarmiento to Comodoro Rivadavia. **Chilean immigration** is at Coyhaique Alto, 6 km west of the border, open summer 0800-2200, winter 0800-2000.

Puerto Aisén and Puerto Chacabuco → *Phone code: 067. Colour map 9, A1.*
Population: 13,050.
The paved road between Coyhaique and Puerto Aisén passes through **Reserva Nacional Río Simpson**, with beautiful waterfalls, lovely views of the river and excellent fly-fishing. Administration/museum is at the entrance, 32 km west of Coyhaique, no marked trails; campsite opposite turning to Santuario San Sebastián, US$7.

Puerto Aisén is 67 km west of Coyhaique at the meeting of the rivers Aisén and Palos. Formerly the region's major port, it has been replaced by Puerto Chacabuco, 15 km to the west, and though it remains an important centre for services, there's little of interest for the visitor. It's also very wet. **Tourist office** ① *in the Municipalidad, Prat y Sgto Aldea, Dec-Feb only*, gives information on shipping movements.

The Puente President Ibáñez, once the longest suspension bridge in Chile, and a paved road lead to **Puerto Chacabuco** 15 km away; a regular bus service runs between the two. The harbour, rather a charmless place, is a short way from the town.

Balmaceda
From Coyhaique, the Carretera Austral heads south past huge bluffs, through deforested pasture (most dramatically on the slopes of Cerro Galera near El Blanco) and farmsteads edged with *alamo* (poplar) trees, before entering flatter plains and rolling hills. At around Km 41, a paved road runs east past the airport at Balmaceda to the Argentine border at **Paso Huemules** (no accommodation). Chilean immigration is open winter 0800-2000, summer 0800-2200.

Puerto Ibáñez
The Carretera Austral starts to climb again, past the entrance to the Reserva Nacional Cerro Castillo (see below). It winds up through the attractive narrow gorge of Río Horqueta, to a pass between Cerro Castillo and its neighbours, before dropping down a 6-km slalom into the breathtaking valley of Rio Ibáñez. (This is currently the most southerly paved section and the road is safe and wide here.) Here the road forks east to Puerto Ibáñez, a further 31 km away, for the ferry crossing of vast Lago General Carrera.

Puerto Ibáñez (*Population: 828*) is the principal port on the Chilean section of the lake. As such you'll probably just pass through to reach the ferry. It is, however, a centre for distinctive pottery, leather production and vegetable growing (you can buy salad from greenhouses and visit potters). Local archaeology includes rock art and the largest Tehuelche cemetery in Patagonia. There are various hotels, but no other services. Fuel (sold in 5-litre containers) is available at Luis A Bolados 461 (house with five laburnum trees outside). Most shops and restaurants are closed Sunday. There are some fine waterfalls, including the Salto Río Ibáñez, 6 km north.

Villa Cerro Castillo

From the turning to Puerto Ibáñez the Carretera Austral goes through Villa Cerro Castillo (Km 8), a quiet village in a spectacular setting beneath the striking, jagged peaks of **Cerro Castillo**, overlooking the broad valley below. There's a petrol station, public phone, several food shops and a tiny tourist information kiosk by the road side (January and February only), with details of guides offering trekking and horse rides.

The village is a good place to stop for a few days with two appealing attractions. There are truly spectacular treks from one to four or five days in the **Reserva Nacional Cerro Castillo** (179,550 ha, US$3.55), whose entrance is 64 km south of Coyhaique. One goes around the fairytale castle peaks of Cerro Castillo, starting at Las Horquetas Grandes, a bend in the river Río Ibáñez, 8 km south of the park entrance, where any bus driver will let you off. It follows Río La Lima to the gorgeous Laguna Cerro Castillo, then animal trails around the peak itself, returning to the village (accommodation or bus back to Coyhaique). Another equally spectacular five-day trek goes around Lago Monreal. These are challenging walks: attempt only if fit and, ideally, take a guide, as trails are poorly marked (IGM map essential, purchase in advance in Coyhaique).The guardería is on the Senda Ibáñez, 50 m to the left of the main road (as you head south), opposite Laguna Chinguay to the right, with access to walks and campsite (US$9, take equipment – there are no *refugios*). The picnic ground is open summer 0830-2100, winter to 1830. Ask in Villa Cerro Castillo for details.

A few kilometres south of the village is the **Monumento Nacional Alero Las Manos de Cerro Castillo** ① *US$1 charged Dec-Apr.* In a shallow cave, a few handprints have been made on the side of vertical rocks high above the Río Ibáñez. There's no clue to their significance, but they're in a beautiful place with panoramic views. This makes a delightful two hours' walk. The site is accessible all year, signposted clearly from the road. There is also a small local **museum** ① *Dec-Mar 0900-1200*, 2 km south of Villa Cerro Castillo.

⦿ Chaitén to Coyhaique listings

For hotel and restaurant price codes, and other relevant information, see Essentials.

⦿ Where to stay

Chaitén to Coyhaique *p787*
Villa Santa Lucía
$ pp Several places on main street: ask at Nachito, the café where the bus stops, which serves good breakfasts.

Futaleufú *p787*
$$$$ El Barranco, O'Higgins 172, T272 1314, www.elbarrancochile.cl. Elegant rustic rooms, luxurious, pool, sauna, good restaurant, and expert fishing guides, horses and bikes for hire.
$$$ Río Grande, O'Higgins y Aldea, T272 1320, www.pachile.com. Also upmarket, spacious attractive rooms, international restaurant, popular with rafting groups.
$$$ Cabañas Río Espolón, follow Cerda to the end, T272 1423, www.patagoniafutaleufu.cl. Cosy *cabañas* in secluded riverside setting,

restaurant overlooking Río Espolón, *parrilla*, bar. Popular with river-rafting groups, book ahead.
$$-$ Adolfo B&B, O'Higgins 302, T272 1256, lodeva@surnet.cl. Best value in this range, comfortable rooms in family home, shared hot showers.
$ pp **Continental**, Balmaceda 595, T272 1222. Oldest in town, no breakfast, basic, but clean and welcoming.
Camping Aldea Puerto Espolón, Sector La Puntilla, 400 m from town, T272 1509, www.aldeapuertoespolon.blogspot.com. Teepees, dome-tents or your own tent, take sleeping bag, hot showers. Several other campsites.

XI Región: La Junta *p788*
$$$ Espacio y Tiempo, T231 4141, www.espacioytiempo.cl. Spacious rooms, warm and cosy atmosphere, restaurant, attractive gardens, fishing expeditions.
$$ Res Copihue, Varas 611, T231 4184. Some rooms with bath, good meals.

\$\$-\$ Hostería Valdera, Varas s/n, T231 4105, luslagos@hotmail.com. Private bath, meals served. Excellent value.

\$\$-\$ Res Patagonia, Lynch 331, T231 4120. Good meals, small rooms, limited bathrooms.

Puyuhuapi *p788*

\$\$\$\$ Puyuhuapi Lodge and Spa.
Reservations: on the website, or Santiago, T02-2225 6489, www.puyuhuapilodge.com. Splendidly isolated on a nook in the sea fjord, the hotel owns the thermal baths: outdoors by the fjord, or indoor spa complex. Good packages for de-stressing with riding, fishing, kayaking, trekking, mountain biking, yoga and the thermals included.

\$\$\$ El Pangue, 18 km north, Km 240 at end of Lago Risopatrón, Parque Nacional Quelat, T252 6906, www.elpangue.com. Rooms and luxurious *cabañas* for 4 to 7 in splendid rural setting, fishing, horseriding, trekking, mountain bikes, pool, sauna, hot tubs, great views, restful.

\$\$\$-\$\$ Casa Ludwig, Otto Uebel 202, T232 5220, www.casaludwig.cl. Cheaper with shared bath. Open Oct-Mar; enquire in advance at other times. In a beautiful 4-storey house built by first German settlers, wonderful views, a range of rooms, good breakfast, comfortable; charming owner Luisa is knowledgeable about the area, speaks German and English.

\$\$ Aonikenk, Hamburgo 16, T232 5208, aonikenkturismo@yahoo.com. Pleasant heated rooms or *cabañas* (not sound-proofed), good beds, meals, helpful, informative, bike hire.

\$\$ Hostería Alemana, Otto Uebel 450, T232 5118, www.hosteriaalemana.cl. A large traditional wooden house on the main road by the water, very comfortable, lovely lake views and garden.

Camping Campsite behind the general store.

Puerto Cisnes *p788*

\$\$\$-\$\$ Cabañas Río Cisnes, Costanera 101, T234 6404, andromeda346@hotmail.com. Cabins sleep 4 to 8. Owner, Juan Suazo, offers sea fishing trips in his boat.

\$\$ Hostería El Gaucho, Holmberg 140, T234 6514. With bath and breakfast, dinner available. Also various *cabañas* and *residenciales*.

Villa Amengual

\$ pp Hosp El Encanto, Pasaje Plaza 3, T9144 8662, hugomancillaopazo@hotmail.com. With restaurant and café, one of several cheap options in town.

Coyhaique *p789, map p789*

\$\$\$\$-\$\$\$ El Reloj, Baquedano 828, T223 1108, www.elrelojhotel.cl. Tasteful, in a former sawmill, with a good restaurant, charming, comfortable wood panelled rooms, some with wonderful views, nice lounge, the best in town.

\$\$\$ Belisario Jara, Bilbao 662, T223 4150, www.belisariojara.cl. Most distinctive and delightful, an elegant and welcoming small place.

\$\$\$ Cabañas Mirador, Baquedano 848, T223 3191. Attractive, well-equipped *cabañas*, also rooms, in lovely gardens with panoramic views of the Reserva Forestal, and Río Coyhaique below.

\$\$\$ San Sebastián, Baquedano 496, T223 3427. Modern, spacious rooms with great views over the Reserva. Also **Cabañas San Sebastián**, Freire 554, T223 1762, www.cabsansebastian.cl. Central, very good.

\$\$\$-\$\$ Cabañas Río Simpson, 3 km north on road to Pto Aisén, T223 2183, riosimpsoncab@ hotmail.com. Fully equipped cabins for 2-6 people. Horse riding, fishing and tours. Tame alpacas in grounds.

\$\$ Cabañas Baquedano, Baquedano 20, T223 2520, Patricio y Gedra Guzmán, http:// balasch.cl. Welcoming, well-maintained, lovely place, 7 *cabañas* of varying standards, with splendid views over the Reserva Forestal, very helpful hosts who speak English, access to river, great value.

\$\$ Hostal Bon, Serrano 91, T223 1189, hostal_ bon@hotmail.com. Simple but very welcoming place, with multilingual owner. They also have *cabañas* near Reserva Forestal 1 km away.

\$\$ Hostal Las Quintas, Bilbao 1208, T223 1173, nolfapatagonia@hotmail.com. Spartan, but clean and very spacious rooms (some in very bizarre design) with bath.

\$\$-\$ Las Salamandras, Sector Los Pinos, 2 km south in attractive forest, T221 1865, www.backpackerschile.com. Variety of rooms, dorms cabin and camping, kitchen facilities, trekking and other sports and tours.

Many more *hospedajes* and private houses with rooms; ask tourist office for a list.

Camping Tourist office on plaza or Sernatur in Coyhaique has a full list of all sites in XI Región. There are many camping sites in Coyhaique and on the road between Coyhaique and Puerto Aisén, eg **Camping Alborada**, at Km 2, T223 8868, hot shower, and **Camping Río Correntoso**, Km 42, T223 2005, showers, fishing. Camping in Reserva Nacional Río Simpson.

Puerto Aisén and Puerto Chacabuco
p790
Accommodation is hard to find, most is taken up by fishing companies in both ports. There are several places to eat along Tte Merino and Aldea in Puerto Aisén.
$$$$ Loberías del Sur, José Miguel Carrera 50, Puerto Chacabuco, T235 1112, www.loberias delsur.cl. 5-star hotel, whose restaurant serves the best food in the area (handy for meal or a drink before boarding ferry – climb up steps direct from port). Same owner as **Catamaranes del Sur** (see Shipping, below), which also has a nearby nature reserve, Parque Aiken del Sur.
$$$ Patagonia Green, 400 m from bridge (on Pto Chacabuco side), T233 6796, www. patagoniagreen.cl. Nice rooms or cabins for up to 5, kitchen, heating, gardens, arranges tours to Laguna San Rafael, fishing, mountain biking, riding, trekking, etc, English spoken.
$$$-$$ Caicahues, Michimalonco 660, Puerto Aisén, T233 6623, hcaicahues@puertoaysen.cl. Popular business hotel, with heating, book ahead.

Puerto Ibáñez *p790*
$$ Cabañas Shehen Aike, Luis Risopatrón 55, T242 3284, info@aike.cl. Swiss/Chilean-owned, large cabins, lots of ideas for trips, bike rental, organizes tours, fine food, welcoming, English spoken, best to phone in advance.
$ pp Hosp Don Francisco, San Salvador y Lautaro, T8503 3626. Very hospitable, lunch or dinner extra, good food round the clock, camping US$5.50, tents and bikes for hire.
$ Vientos del Sur, Bertrán Dixon 282, T242 3208. Good, nice family, dorms, cheap meals (restaurant open till late); also arranges adventure activities.

Villa Cerro Castillo *p791*
$ Cabañas Don Niba, Los Pioneros 872, T241 9920. Friendly but basic *hospedaje*, good value.
$ Hostería Villarrica, O'Higgins 59, next to Supermercado Villarrica, T241 9500. Welcoming, basic, hot showers, and meals too, kind owners can arrange trekking guides and horse riding. There are other residenciales in town.

🍴 Restaurants

Futaleufú *p787*
$$ Futaleufú, Cerda 407, T272 1295. Serves typical Chilean meat dishes and local foods.
$$ Martín Pescador, Balmaceda y Rodríguez, T272 1279. For fish and meat dishes, rustic.
$$-$ Sur Andes, Cerda 308, T272 1405. Café serving cakes, sweets, light meals and real coffee. Also sells handicrafts.

Puyuhuapi *p788*
$$ Café Rossbach, Costanera. Run by the descendants of the original German settlers, an attractive place by the water for delicious salmon, tea and *küchen*.
$$ Lluvia Marina, next to Casa Ludwig, veronet@entelchile.net. The best café, also selling handicrafts. Superb food in relaxed atmosphere, a great place to just hang out, owner Veronica is very helpful.

Coyhaique *p789, map p789*
$$$ Histórico Ricer, Horn 48 y 40, p 2, T223 2920. Central, warm and cosy, serving breakfast to dinner, regional specialities, with good vegetarian options, historical exhibits. Also has Café Ricer at No 48, serving light food.
$$ La Casona, Obispo Vielmo 77, T223 8894. Justly reputed as best in town, charming family restaurant serves excellent fish, congrio especially, but best known for grilled lamb.
$$-$ Casino de Bomberos next to the fire station, Gral Parra 365, T223 1437. For great atmosphere and a filling lunch, can be slow when serving groups.
$$-$ Donde Ramiro, Freire 319, T225 6885. Good set lunches, big screen TV.
$ Club Sandwich Patagonia, Moraleda 433. 24-hr fast food and huge Chilean sandwiches, a local institution.

$ El Mastique, Bilbao 141. Cheap but good pasta and Chilean food.
$ Pizzería La Fiorentina, Prat 230. Tasty pizzas, good service.

Cafés
Café Oriente, Condell 201. Serves a good lunch and tasty cakes.

🎶 Bars and clubs

Coyhaique *p789, map p789*
El Boliche, Moraleda 380. A beer-drinkers' bar. Many bars on the same street.
Pepe le Pub, Parra 72. Good cocktails and snacks, relaxed, live music at weekends.
Piel Roja, Moraleda y Condell. Good music, laid back, open Wed, Fri, Sat 1000-0500 for dancing, pub other nights.

⊙ Shopping

Coyhaique *p789, map p789*
Handicrafts Artesanía Manos Azules, Riquelme 435. Sells fine handicrafts. **Feria de Artesanía** on the plaza. **Kaienk**, Plaza 219-A, T224 5216, sells good-quality locally made knitwear.

🅾 What to do

Futaleufú *p787*
Tour operators arrange whitewater rafting trips, prices starting from US$75 pp. Local fishing guides can also be found in the village.
Expediciones Chile, Mistral 296, T256 2639 (in US T1-208-629 5032), www.exchile.com. Whitewater rafting, kayaking, etc. Offers the best multi-day trips, book in advance. Day trips can be booked at office.
Futaleufú Explore, O'Higgins 772, T272 1527, www.futaleufuexplore.com. A respected rafting company.
Rancho Las Ruedas, Pilota Carmona 337, T7735 0989, guide.stallion@gmail.com. The best horseriding in the area.

Coyhaique *p789, map p789*
Many tours operate Sep to Apr, some Dec-Mar only. The surrounding area is famous for trout fishing with several *estancias* offering luxury accommodation and bilingual guides. Most tour operators also offer specialist fishing trips.
Andes Patagónicos, Horn 48 y 40, loc 11, T221 6711, www.ap.cl. Trips to local lakes, Tortel, historically based tours and bespoke trips all year round. Good, but not cheap.
Aysen Tour, Pasaje Río Backer 2646, T223 7070, www.aysentour.cl. Tours along the Carretera Austral, also car rental.
Camello Patagón, Carlos Cardell 149, T224 4327, www.camellopatagon.cl. Daily trips to Cavernas de Marmol in Río Tranquilo, among others, also car rental and other services.
Casa del Turismo Rural, Odeón Plaza de Armas, T221 4031, www.casaturismorural.cl, Mon-Fri 1000-1330, 1530-2000 (also weekends in high season). An association of 40 families, mostly in the countryside, who offer activities such as horseriding and fishing. Many do not have telephones or internet, make reservations here.
Expediciones Coyhaique, Portales 195, T223 1783, www.coyhaiqueflyfishing.com. Fly-fishing experts.
Geo Turismo, José de Moraleda 480, T258 3173, www.geoturismopatagonia.cl. Offers wide range of tours, English spoken, professional.
Turismo Prado, 21 de Mayo 417, T223 1271, www.turismoprado.cl. Tours of local lakes and other sights, Laguna San Rafael trips and historical tours.

⊖ Transport

Futaleufú *p787*
Bus Bus to **Chaitén** 6 days a week, information from **Chaitur** in Chaitén. To **Puerto Montt** via Argentina, Mon 0630, 13 hrs, US$38, with **Transporte Patagonia Norte**.

Border with Argentina *p788*
Bus From west side of plaza in Futaleufú, a Jacobsen bus runs to the border, 3 times a week, and Mon-Fri in Jan-Feb, US$4, 30 mins, connecting with services to Trevelin and Esquel.

La Junta

Bus To **Chaitén** 4 a week, information from Chaitur. To **Coyhaique**, with Daniela (T09-9512 3500), Becker (T224 2626), and Aguilas Patagónicas, 7 hrs, US$18.50-22. To **Puerto Cisnes**, with Empresa Entre Verde (T231 4275), US$10.

Puyuhuapi *p788*

Bus Daily to **Coyhaique**, US$14.50-16.50, 6 hrs, plus 2 weekly to **Lago Verde**.

Puerto Cisnes *p788*

Bus To **Coyhaique**, **Aguilas Patagónicas** and **Sao Paulo**, run daily (on Sun only to Coyhaique). US$9-11.

Coyhaique *p789, map p789*

Air Most flights from Balmaceda (see below), although Coyhaique has its own airport, Tte Vidal, about 5 km southwest of town. **Don Carlos**, to **Chile Chico** (Mon-Sat), **Cochrane** (Mon, Thu) and **Villa O'Higgins** (Mon, Thu, for those who like flying, with strong stomachs, or in a hurry).

Bus Full list of buses from tourist information. Terminal at Lautaro y Magallanes, T225 5726, but most buses leave from their own offices.

To **Puerto Aisén**, minibuses run every 45 mins, 1 hr, Alí (Dussen 283, T223 2788, in Puerto Aysén Aldea 1143, T233 3335, www.busesali.cl), Suray (A Prat 265, T223 8387), US$2.75-3.35. Change here for **Puerto Chacabuco**, 20 mins, US$1. To **Puerto Ibáñez** on Lago Gral Carrera, several minibus companies (connect with ferry to Chile Chico) pick up 0530-0600 from your hotel, 1½ hrs, book the day before (eg Yamil Ali, Prat y Errázuriz, T221 9009, **Miguel Acuña**, M Moraleda 304, T225 1579 or 241 1804).

Buses on the **Carretera Austral** vary according to demand, and they are always full so book early. Bikes can be taken by arrangement. North towards **Chaitén**: twice a week direct with Becker (Parra 335, T223 2167), US$44, also Terraustral, otherwise change in La Junta; in winter these stop overnight in La Junta. To **Futaleufú**, with Daniela, 3 a week, US$34. To **Puerto Cisnes**, Sao Paulo (at terminal, T233 2918) and Aguilas Patagónicas (Lautaro 104, T221 1288, www.

aguilaspatagonicas.cl), US$9-11. South to **Cochrane** daily in summer with Don Carlos (Subteniente Cruz 63, T223 1981), **Sao Paulo**, Aguilas Patagónicas or Acuario 13 (at terminal, T255 2143), US$23.50. All buses stop at **Cerro Castillo** (US$8), **Bahía Murta** (US$12), **Puerto Tranquilo** (US$14.50) and **Puerto Bertrand** (US$16).

Car hire If renting a car, a high 4WD vehicle is recommended for Carretera Austral. Buy fuel in Coyhaique, several stations. There are several rental agencies in town, charging at least US$150 a day, including insurance, for 4WD or pick-up. Add another US$50 for paperwork to take a vehicle into Argentina.

Ferry office Navimag, Paseo Horn 47 D, T223 3306, www.navimag.com. Naviera Austral, Horn 40, of 101, T221 0727, www.navieraustral.cl.

Taxi US$7.50 to Tte Vidal airport (US$2 if sharing). Fares in town US$3, 50% extra after 2100. Taxi colectivos (shared taxis) congregate at Prat y Bilbao, average fare US$1.

Puerto Aisén and Puerto Chacabuco *p790*

Bus See under Coyhaique, above.

Ferry Navimag sails twice a week from Puerto Chacabuco to **Puerto Montt**, taking about 24 hrs (for details, see Ferry, page 774). Catamaranes del Sur also have sailings to Laguna San Rafael. Shipping Offices: Agemar, Tte Merino 909, T233 2716, Puerto Aisén. **Catamaranes del Sur**, J M Carrera 50, T235 1115, www.loberiasdel sur.cl. **Naviera Austral**, Terminal de Transbordadores, T235 1493, www.navieraustral.cl. **Navimag**, Terminal de Transbordadores, Puerto Chacabuco, T235 1111, www.navimag.com. It is best to make reservations in these companies' offices in Puerto Montt, Coyhaique or Santiago. For trips to Laguna San Rafael, see page 774.

Balmaceda *p795*

Air Balmaceda airport is used for daily flights to **Santiago** with LAN, mostly via **Puerto Montt**, and Sky, which sometimes makes several stops. Landing can be dramatic owing to strong winds. Sky also flies to **Punta Arenas**, 3 flights weekly. Minibuses to/from hotels in Coyhaique (56 km) US$8, 3 companies who all sell tickets at baggage carousel. Taxi from airport to **Coyhaique**, 1 hr, US$30. Car rental agencies at the airport; very expensive, closed Sun.

Puerto Ibáñez *p790*
Bus Minibus to **Coyhaique**, 1½ hrs, US$7.55. There is a road to **Perito Moreno**, Argentina, but no public transport.
Ferry The *Tehuelche* sails between Puerto Ibáñez and **Chile Chico** daily. It takes passengers and vehicles, fares US$3.75 per adult, US$2.65 for bicycles, US$6.75 for motorbikes, cars US$33, beautiful 2½-hr crossing. It's a new vessel with indoor seating, café and heating. Passports required, reservations essential: in Coyhaique, Baquedano 1198, T223 7958; in Puerto Ibáñez, Gral Carrera 201, T252 6992, in Chile Chico T241 1003, online at http://sotramin.cl. At the quay, Café El Refugio has toilets and sells sandwiches and snacks. Minibuses meet the ferry in Puerto Ibáñez for Coyhaique.

Villa Cerro Castillo *p791*
Bus 6 a week in summer to both **Coyhaique** and **Cochrane**, companies as above under Coyhaique. To **Río Tranquilo**, US$7.

⊙ Directory

Coyhaique *p789, map p789*
Bicycle rental Manuel Iduarte, Parra y Bulnes, check condition first. **Bicycle repairs** Tomás Madrid Urrea, Pasaje Foitzich y Libertad, T225 2132. **Language schools** Baquedano International Language School, Baquedano 20, T223 2520, www.balasch.cl. US$600 per week course including lodging and all meals, or US$40 for 3 classes a day one-to-one tuition, other lodging options and activities can be arranged.

Lago General Carrera and around

Southwest of Villa Cerro Castillo, the Carretera continues to afford stunning views, for instance minty-green Lago Verde and the meandering Río Manso, with swampy vegetation punctuated by the silver stumps of thousands of burnt trees, huge mountains behind. Lago General Carrera (Lago Buenos Aires in Argentina) straddles the border and, at 2240 sq km, is the second largest lake in South America. It's an area of outstanding beauty. Sheltered from the icy west winds by the Campo de Hielo Norte, the region also has the best climate in Southern Chile, with little rain, some 300 days of sunshine and a microclimate at Chile Chico that allows the cultivation of the same crops and fruit as in the Central Valley. Ferries cross the lake (see above), but it is worth taking time to follow the Carretera Austral around the lake's western shores.

Bahía Murta (*Km 198; Population: 586*), 5 km off the Camino, lies at the northern tip of the central 'arm' of the lake. There is a tiny tourist information hut, which opens summer 1000-1430, 1500-1930. Petrol is available from a house with a sign just before Puerto Murta. There's a public phone in the village.

Back on the Carretera Austral, **Puerto Río Tranquilo**, Km 223, is a slightly larger hamlet where the buses stop for lunch: fuel is available. Capilla y Catedral del Marmol, in fact a limestone cliff vaguely resembling sculpted caves, is reached by a wonderful boat ride (ask at petrol station, to hire a boat with guide; tour operators also run trips).

El Maitén, Km 277 south of Coihaique, an idyllic spot at the southwest tip of Lago General Carrera, is where a road branches off east along the south shore of the lake towards Chile Chico, while the Carretera Austral continues south to Puerto Bertand.

South of El Maitén the Carretera Austral becomes steeper and more winding (in winter this stretch, all the way to Cochrane, is icy and dangerous). At Km 294, is the hamlet of **Puerto Bertrand**, lying by the dazzling turquoise waters of Río Baker. As this river is world renowned for fly fishing, good accommodation in Puerto Bertrand is either in one of the luxury *cabañas* that cater for wealthy anglers, or in a simple room in the village.

At **Puerto Guadal**, 13 km east of El Maitén, there are shops, accommodation, restaurants, a post office, petrol and a lovely stretch of lakeside beach. Further east is the village of Mallín

Grande (Km 40), **Paso de las Llaves**, a 30 km stretch carved out of the rock face on the edge of the lake, and **Fachinal** (turn off at Km 74). A further 5 km east is the **Garganta del Diablo**, a narrow gorge of 120 m with a fast-flowing stream below.

Chile Chico → *Population: 4500.*

This is a quiet town in a fruit-growing region, 125 km east of El Maitén. It has an annual fruit festival at end-January and a small museum (open summer only). There are fine views from Cerro de las Banderas. It's 7 km to Los Antiguos, Argentina, where food and accommodation are preferable. **Laguna Jeinimeni**, 52 km from Chile Chico, is a beautiful place with excellent fishing, where you can also see flamingos and black necked swans. The **tourist office** (helpful but usually closed) is in the Casa de la Cultura on O'Higgins, T241 1303, infochilechico@sernatur.cl. An unofficial purple tourist kiosk on the quay where the ferry arrives, sells bus tickets for Ruta 40 (Argentina), but has some accommodation information. Municipal website: www.chilechico.cl.

Border with Argentina: Chile Chico–Los Antiguos Chilean immigration is 2 km east of Chile Chico. Open summer 0730-2200, winter 0800-2000. Argentine side closes for lunch 1300-1400. Remember that you can't take fresh food across in either direction, and you'll need ownership papers if crossing with a car. If entering Argentina here you will not have to fill in an immigration form (ask if you need entry papers).

Cochrane → *Population: 2996.*

From Puerto Bertand heading south, the road climbs up to high moorland, passing the confluence of the Ríos Neff and Baker (there is a mirador here), before winding into Cochrane, 343 km south of Coyhaique. The scenery is splendid all the way; the road is generally rough but not treacherous. Watch out for cattle on the road and take blind corners slowly. Sitting in a hollow on the Río Cochrane, Cochrane is a simple place, sunny in summer, good for walking and fishing. The **Reserva Nacional Lago Cochrane**, 12 km east, surrounds Lago Cochrane. Campsite at Playa Vidal. Boat hire on the lake costs US$15 per person. Northeast of Cochrane is the beautiful **Reserva Nacional Tamango** ① *Dec-Mar 0830-2100, Apr-Nov 0830-1830. Ask in the CONAF office (Río Neff 417, T252 2164, piero.caviglia@conaf.cl) about visiting because some access is through private land and tourist facilities are rudimentary, US$6.30, plus guided visits to see the huemules, Tue, Thu, Sat, US$80 for up to 6 people.* It has lenga forest, a few surviving huemul deer as well as guanaco, foxes and lots of birds including woodpeckers and hummingbirds. Access 9 km northeast of Cochrane, along Río Cochrane. There are marked paths for walks between 45 minutes and five hours, up to Cerro Tamango (1722 m) and Cerro Temanguito (1485 m). Take water and food, and windproof clothing if climbing the Cerros. The views from the reserve are superb, over the town, the nearby lakes and to the Campo de Hielo Norte to the west. It is inaccessible in the four winter months. **Tourist office** ① *on corner of plaza on Dr Steffen, T252 2115, www.cochranepatagonia.cl, summer Mon-Fri 0830-2000, Sat-Sun 1100-2000, off season Mon-Fri 0830-1730.* ATM for MasterCard only.

Caleta Tortel → *Population: 448.*

The Carretera Austral runs south of Cochrane and, after 105 km, at the rather bleak looking Puerto Vagabundo, the road branches west to Caleta Tortel (see Transport, below). This quiet village at the mouth of the river, was until very recently accessible only by water and has no streets, only 7 km of walkways of cypress wood. Surrounded by mountainous land with abundant vegetation, it has a cool, rainy climate, and its main trade is logging, though this is declining as the town looks towards tourism. Located between the Northern and Southern Ice Fields, Tortel is within reach of two glaciers: **Glaciar Steffens** is to the north, a 2½-hour boat journey and three-hour walk, crossing a glacial river in a rowing boat. A boat for 10 people costs US$190. **Glaciar Jorge Montt** is to the southwest, seven to nine hours by boat (depending on wind conditions), through landscapes of pure ice and water, US$650 for 10 people maximum. Another boat trip is to the **Isla de los Muertos**, which has an interesting history, US$70 for 10. At the entrance to the village is a small tourist information office with information on lodging and a useful map. There is a post office, open Monday-Friday 0830-1330. The phone office number is T221 1876. **CONAF**, T294 1980.

Villa O'Higgins

The Carretera Austral runs to Puerto Yungay (122 km from Cochrane), then another 110 km to **Villa O'Higgins**. There is one free ferry (*Padre Antonio Ronchi*) crossing between Yungay (military base) and Río Bravo (1000, 1200, 1800, return to Yungay an hour later, December-March; April-November at 1200, 1500, return 1300,1600; 45 minutes, capacity four to five cars, www.barcazas.cl). The road beyond Río Bravo is very beautiful, but often closed by bad weather (take food – no shops or fuel on the entire route, few people and few vehicles for hitching). Tourist information is available from the Municipalidad, Lago Christie 121.

It is possible to go from Villa O'Higgins to El Chaltén, Argentina. The road continues 7 km south to Bahía Bahamóndez on Lago O'Higgins (bus US$4), from where a boat leaves for Chilean immigration at **Candelario Mancilla** ① *open Nov-Apr 0800-2200, 2¾ hrs, US$76.50; departures vary each year, but usually one a week in Nov, 2 a week in Dec, 4 in Jan, Feb, 2 in Mar. There may be other departures in Nov, even in Apr, but exact dates should be checked in advance.* A detour to Glaciar O'Higgins costs US$48 on the regular crossing or between US$90-150 for a day-long special trip, depending from which side of the lake you start (cheaper from Candelario Mancilla). Sailings may be cancelled if the weather is bad. Then it's 14 km to the Argentine border and a further 5 km to Argentine immigration at Punta Norte on Lago del Desierto. The first part can be done on foot, on horseback, or by 4WD service for US$18 (takes two to four passengers and luggage, US$9 luggage only, call Hans Silva at Villa O'Higgins Expeditions, see below, to reserve car or horses). The next 5 km is a demanding hike, or you can take a horse for US$36 for the whole 19 km, with an extra horse to carry bags (Ricardo is great horseman with an excellent sense of humour).

The route descends sharply towards Lago de Desierto. Bridges are sometimes washed away. Make sure to wear good boots for crossing wetland. Panoramas on the descent are breathtaking, including of Cerro Fritz Roy. A short detour to Laguna Larga (on the right as you walk from the border) is worth it if you have the energy. The 40-minute boat crossing of the lake passes glaciers and ice fields on your right (daily except Monday, US$24.50 if bought in Argentina, US$27 if prepaid in Chile). Finally it takes over an hour by bus or minivan on a gravel road to El Chaltén (37 km). Several companies including Transporte Las Lengas and JR Turismo await the boat (US$27, US$5.50 extra for luggage). There is no food available on either side of the lake, but Argentine immigration at Punta Norte are friendly and, if you are cold, may offer you coffee.

The best combination is to take 4WD from Candelario Mancilla to the border and then continue on horseback. This ensures that the trip can be done in a day (depart Villa O'Higgins 0800, arrive El Chaltén 2115). Allow for delays, though, especially if horses aren't available for hire. It's a good option to pay for each portion of the route separately. The route closes in late April. With the opening of this route it is possible to do the Carretera Austral and go on to Argentina's Parque Nacional Los Glaciares and Chile's Torres del Paine without doubling back on yourself. Full details from **Villa O'Higgins Expeditions**, ① *T067-243 1821, www.villaohiggins. com*), who also own the new **Robinson Crusoe Lodge** in town.

Parque Nacional Laguna San Rafael

① *US$8.50, at the glacier there is a small ranger station which gives information; a pier and 2 paths have been built, one of which leads to the glacier.*

Some 150 nautical miles south of Puerto Aisén is the **Laguna San Rafael**, into which flows a glacier, 30 m above sea level and 45 km in length. The glacier has a deep blue colour, shimmering and reflecting the light. It calves small icebergs, which seem an unreal, translucent blue, and which are carried out to sea by wind and tide. The glacier is very noisy; there are frequent cracking and banging sounds, resembling a mixture of gunshots and thunder. When a hunk of ice breaks loose, a huge swell is created and the icebergs start rocking in the water. The glacier is disintegrating and is predicted to disappear entirely. Some suggest that the wake from tour boats is contributing to the erosion.

The thick vegetation on the shores, with snowy peaks above, is typical of Aisén. The only access is by plane or by boat. The glacier is equally spectacular from the air or the sea. The glacier is one of a group of four that flow in all directions from Monte San Valentín. This icefield is part of the Parque Nacional Laguna San Rafael (1,740,000 ha), regulated by CONAF. In the national park are puma, pudú (miniature deer), foxes, dolphins, occasional sealions and sea otters, and many species of bird. Walking trails are limited (about 10 km in all) but a lookout platform has been constructed, with fine views of the glacier.

◉ Lago General Carrera and around listings

For hotel and restaurant price codes, and other relevant information, see Essentials

● Where to stay

Lago General Carrera *p796*
Bahía Murta
$ Res Patagonia, Pje España 64, Bahía Murta, T241 9600. Comfortable, and serves food. There is free camping by the lake at Bahía Murta.

Puerto Río Tranquilo
$$$ Hostal El Puesto, Pedro Lagos 258, T09-6207 3794, www.elpuesto.cl. No doubt the most comfortable place in Río Tranquilo, with breakfast, also organizes tours.
$$$ Hostal Los Pinos, Godoy 51, Puerto Río Tranquilo, T241 1576. Family-run, well maintained, good mid-price meals.
$$ Cabañas Jacricalor, Carretera Austral 245, Puerto Río Tranquilo, T241 9500 (public phone). Tent-sized *cabañas*, hot shower, good meals, good information for climbers.
$$ Campo Alacaluf, Km 44 on the Río Tranquilo-Bahía Exploradores side road, T241 9500. Wonderful guesthouse hidden away from civilization. Run by very friendly German family.
$$ Hostal Carretera Austral, 1 Sur 223, Río Tranquilo, T241 9500. Also serves meals (**$$-$**).

El Maitén
$$$$ Hacienda Tres Lagos, Carretera Austral Km 274, just west of cruce Maitén, T067-241 1323, T02-2333 4122 (Santiago), www.hacienda treslagos.com. Small, boutique resort on the lake-shore with bungalows, suites and cabins. Good restaurant, wide range of

excursions offered, sauna, jacuzzi, good service. English spoken.
$$$$ Mallín Colorado Ecolodge, Carretera Austral Km 273, 2 km west of El Maitén, T09-7137 6242, www.mallincolorado.cl. Comfortable *cabañas* in sweeping gardens, complete tranquility, charming owners, packages available, including transfers from Balmaceda, horseriding, estancia trip, superb meals, open Oct-Apr.

Puerto Bertrand
$$$ Patagonia Baker Lodge and Restaurant, 3km from Puerto Bertrand, towards the south side of the lake, T241 1903, www.pbl. cl. Stylish *cabañas* in woodland, fishing lodge, birdwatching, fabulous views upriver towards rapids and the mountains beyond.
$$ Hostería Puerto Bertrand, Puerto Bertrand, T241 9900. With breakfast, other meals available, also *cabañas*, activities.
$ Hosp Doña Ester, Casa No 8, Puerto Bertrand, T09-9990 8541. Rooms in a pink house, good.
$ Turismo Hospedaje Campo de Hielo Norte, Ventisquero Neff s/n. Owned by Anselmo Soto, open tourist season only, hospitable, helpful.

Puerto Guadal
$$$ El Mirador Playa Guadal, 2 km from Puerto Guadal towards Chile Chico, T09-9234 9130, www.elmiradordeguadal.com. *Cabañas* near beach, excursions and activities with or without guide, walks to nearby waterfalls, restaurant.
$$$-$$ Terra Luna Lodge, on lakeside, 2 km from Puerto Guadal, T09-8449 1092, www. terra-luna.cl. Welcoming well-run place with lodge, bungalows and camping huts, also

has restaurant, sauna, cinema, private disco, climbing wall, many activities offered.

$$-$ Eco Hostal Un Destino No Turístico, Camino Laguna La Manga, off road to Chile Chico 1.5 km from village, www.destino-noturistico. com. Open from Sep. Private rooms and dorms, also camping, Private rooms, dorms, camping and tent hire, with eco initiatives, workshops, tours and information. Transfers arranged.

$ Hostería Huemules, Las Magnolias 382, Puerto Guadal, T243 1212. Good views, meals.

Camping Camping El Parque, Km 1 on road to Chile Chico, T243 1284.

Chile Chico *p797*

$$ Hosp Don Luis, Balmaceda 175, T8441 4970. Meals available, laundry, helpful.

$$ Hostería de la Patagonia, Camino Internacional s/n, T241 1337. Camping or full-board available. Good food, English, French and Italian spoken, trekking, horse riding, white-water rafting.

Camping Free site at Bahía Jara, 5 km west of Chile Chico, then turn north for 12 km.

Cochrane *p797*

In summer it is best to book rooms in advance.

$$$ Wellmann, Las Golondrinas 36, T252 2171, hotelwellmann@gmail.com. Comfortable, warm, hot water, good meals.

$$$-$$ Cabañas Rogeri, Río Maitén 80, T252 2264, rogeri3@hotmail.cl. *Cabañas* with kitchen for 4.

$$ Res Cero a Cero, Lago Brown 464, T252 2158, ceroacero@hotmail.com. Welcoming.

$$ Res Rubio, Tte Merino 871, T252 2173. Very nice, meals available.

$$ Res Sur Austral, Prat 334, T252 2150. Private or shared bath, hot water, very nice.

$ pp Res Cochrane, Dr Steffen 451, T252 2377, pquintana13@gmail.com. Good meals, hot shower, camping.

Caleta Tortel *p797*

There are several *hospedajes*. All prices are cheaper in the low season. For all T067-223 4815 (public phone) or T2211876 (municipality).

$$$ Entre Hielos Lodge, sector centro, Tortel. T02-2196 0271, www.entrehielostortel.cl. Upmarket place in town, excursions, boat trips.

$$ Estilo, Sector Centro, Tortel, tortelhospe dajeestilo@yahoo.es. Warm and comfortable, good food. Entertaining, talkative host (Spanish).

$$ Hosp Costanera, Sra Luisa Escobar Sanhueza. Cosy, warm, lovely garden, full board available.

Camping There is camping at sector Junquillo at the far end of town.

Villa O'Higgins *p798*

$$ Cabañas San Gabriel, Lago O'Higgins 310. Nice cabins. A good choice for small groups.

$$-$ El Mosco, at the northern entrance to the town, T243 1819, patagoniaelmosco@yahoo.es. Rooms, dorms or camping. Spanish run hostel. English spoken, trekking maps and information. Can help with bike repairs. More expensive than the rest, but nothing else competes in terms of infrastructure.

Restaurants

Chile Chico *p797*

Café Refer, O'Higgins 416. Good, despite the exterior.

Cafetería Loly y Elizabeth, PA González 25, on Plaza. Serves coffee, as well as delicious ice cream and cakes.

Cochrane *p797*

Res El Fogón, San Valentín 65, T09-7644 7914. Its pub is the only eating place open in low season, it's the best restaurant at any time of year. Rooms available.

Caleta Tortel *p797*

Café Celes Salom, bar/restaurant serving basic, cheap meals, disco on Sat, occasional live bands.

What to do

Lago General Carrera and around *p796*
Patagonia Adventure Expeditions, T09-8182 0608, www.adventurepatagonia.com. Professional outfit running exclusive fully supported treks to the Campo de Hielo Norte and the eastern side of Parque Nacional Laguna San Rafael. Expensive but a unique experience. Also rafting on the Río Baker and general help organizing tours, treks and expeditions.

⊖ Transport

Chile Chico *p797*
Bus Several minibuses daily to **Cochrane**, US$23.50, 5 hrs. See above for ferry to Puerto Ibáñez and connecting minibus to Coyhaique. Ferry and minibus tickets from **Miguel Acuña**, Sector Muelle, T223 1579.

Border with Argentina: Chile Chico–Los Antiguos *p797*
Bus In summer, minibuses from Chile Chico to Los Antiguos on the Argentine side 0800-2200, US$4 (in Chilean pesos), ½-1 hr including formalities: 3 companies at B O'Higgins 426, and **La Porteña** at Santiago Ericksen 150. To/from **Coyhaique**, via **Puerto Guadal**, ECA (T243 1224 or T252 8577) on Tue and Fri, **Seguel** (T243 1214 or T224 5237) on Wed.

Cochrane *p797*
Air Don Carlos to **Coyhaique**, Mon, Thu.
Bus Company agencies: **Don Carlos**, Prat 344, T252 2150; **Buses Aldea**, Steffen y Las Golondrinas, T252 2448/2020; **Bus Ale** and **Aguilas Patagónicas**, Las Golondrinas 399, T252 2242 (Ale), 252 2020 (Aguilas); **Acuario 13** and **Sao Paulo**, Río Baker 349, T252 2143. There are buses every day between Coyhaique and Cochrane, check with companies for current timetables, US$23.50. To **Río Tranquilo**, US$11.

To **Villa O'Higgins**, Katalina (T067-252 2020, 243 1823 in O'Higgins), Sun, Thu 0800, return Mon, Fri 1000, 6-7 hrs, US$22. To **Tortel**, Buses Aldea, Tue, Thu, Fri, Sat, 0930, return 1500, US$11. Minibuses, including **Bus Ale**, daily to **Chile Chico**, US$23.50. Petrol is available at the Esso and Copec servicentros.

Caleta Tortel *p797*
Bus From **Cochrane**, see above. On Sun Dec-Mar a bus runs between Tortel and **Villa O'Higgins**, 4 hrs, US$30, 0830 to Tortel, 1630 back to O'Higgins, T067-243 1821.

Parque Nacional Laguna San Rafael *p798*
Ferry Cruises are run by: Skorpios (see under Puerto Montt); Catamaranes del Sur and Compañía Naviera Puerto Montt. Other charters available. Private yachts can be chartered in Puerto Montt.

❶ Directory

Chile Chico *p797*
Banks It's best to change money in Coyhaique. ATM in the middle of O'Higgins for Mastercard and Cirrus, not Visa. Dollars and Argentine pesos can be changed in small amounts in shops and cafés, including **Loly y Elizabeth**, at poor rates. **Hospital** Lautaro s/n, T241 1334.

Far south

This wild and wind-blown area, covering the glacial regions of southern Patagonia and Chilean Tierra del Fuego, is beautiful and bleak, with stark mountains and open steppe. Little vegetation survives here and few people; though it represents 17.5% of Chile's total area, it is inhabited by under 1% of the population. The southernmost city of Punta Arenas and the attractive port of Puerto Natales are the two main centres, the latter being the gateway to the Torres del Paine and Balmaceda national parks. In summer it is a wonderful region for climbing, hiking, boat trips and the southernmost crossings to Argentina.

Summers are sunny and very variable, with highs of 15°C. In winter snow covers the country, except those parts near the sea, making many roads more or less impassable, except on horseback. Cold, piercing winds blow year-round, but are particularly fierce in late spring, when they may exceed 100 kph. Despite chilly temperatures, protection against the sun's ultraviolet rays is essential here all year round and in summer, too, windproof clothing is a must.

Punta Arenas and around → *Phone code: 061. Colour map 9, C2.*
Population: Punta Arenas 123,000, Puerto Natales 20,500.

About 2140 km south of Santiago, Punta Arenas lies on the eastern shore of the Brunswick Peninsula facing the Straits of Magellan at almost equal distance from the Pacific and Atlantic oceans. Founded in 1843, it has grand neoclassical buildings and an opulent cemetery, testimony to its wealthy past as a major port and centre for exporting wool. In the late 19th century, Salesian Missions were established to control the indigenous population so sheep farming could flourish. The city's fortunes slumped when the Panama Canal opened in 1914, but it remains a pleasant place, with attractive, painted wooden buildings away from the centre and good fish and seafood restaurants. Paved roads connect the city with Puerto Natales, 247 km north, and with Río Gallegos in Argentina.

Arriving in Punta Arenas
Tourist office Sernatur ⓘ *Lautaro Navarro 999 y Pedro Montt, T222 5385, infomagallanes@sernatur.cl, Mon-Fri 0830-2000, Sat-Sun 0900-1300 and 1400-1800. See www.patagonia-chile.com (Spanish only).* There is also the **municipal tourist information kiosk** ⓘ *in the plaza, opposite Centro Español, T220 0610, Mon-Fri 0800-2000, Sat-Sun 0900-1800, www.puntaarenas.cl (Spanish only).* Experienced staff, good town map with all hotels marked, English spoken, can book hotels. **CONAF** ⓘ *Av Bulnes 0309, p 4, T223 8554, magallanes.oirs@conaf.cl.*

Places in Punta Arenas
In the centre of the **Plaza Muñoz Gamero** is a striking statue of Magellan with a mermaid and two indigenous Fuegians at his feet. Around the plaza are a number of impressive neoclassical buildings, the former mansions of the great sheep ranching families of the late 19th century. **Palacio Sara Braun** ⓘ *Mon-Sat, 1000-1300, 1700-2030, closed Sun, US$2,* (1895), part of which now houses the Hotel José Nogueira, has several elegant rooms which are open to the public. The fascinating **Museo Regional de Magallanes** ⓘ *Palacio Braun Menéndez, Magallanes 949, T224 4216, www.museodemagallanes.cl, Wed-Mon 1030-1700 (May-Sep closes 1400), US$2, guided tours in Spanish, information in English,* was once the mansion of Mauricio Braun, built in 1905. It has fabulously decorated rooms, with ornate furniture, paintings and marble and crystal imported from Europe. Further north, is the impressive **Cemetery (Cementerio Municipal Sara Braun)** ⓘ *Av Bulnes 029, daily, 0800-1800, 0730-2000 in summer, US$4,* charting a history of European immigration and shipping disasters through the huge mausoleums, divided by avenues of imposing sculpted cypress trees.

The perfect complement to this is **Museo Regional Salesiano Maggiorino Borgatello** ⓘ *in the Colegio Salesiano, Av Bulnes 336 (the entrance is next to church), T222 1001, www.museomaggiorinoborgatello.cl, Tue-Sun 1000-1230, 1500-1730, US$5.* It covers the fascinating history of the indigenous peoples and their education by the Salesian missions, beside an array of stuffed birds and gas extraction machinery. The Italian priest, Alberto D'Agostini, who arrived in 1909 and presided over the missions, took wonderful photographs of the region and his 70-minute film can be seen on video (ask). **Museo del Recuerdo/Museum of Memory** at the **Instituto de la Patagonia** ⓘ *Av Bulnes 01890, Km 4 northeast (opposite the University), T224 4216, outdoor exhibits Mon-Fri 0830-1130, 1430-1830, Sat 0830-1230, US$4,* has an open-air museum with 3000 artefacts used by the early settlers, pioneer homes, research library and botanical gardens.

Museo Naval y Marítimo ⓘ *Pedro Montt 981, T220 5479, www.museonaval.cl/en/museo-de-p-arenas.html, Tue-Sat, 0930-1230, 1400-1700, US$2,* has shipping instruments, maps, photos and relics from the Chilean navy and famous navigators. West of the Plaza Muñoz Gamero on Calle Fagnano is the Mirador Cerro de La Cruz offering a view over the city and the Magellan Straits.

Punta Arenas

To Instituto de la Patagonia, Bus Terminal, Free Port, Airport, Puerto Natales & Ferry to Porvenir

To & Hostels on Calles Caupolicán & Maipú

Cemetery

Where to stay
1 Backpackers' Paradise B3
2 Cabo de Hornos C2
4 Chalet Chapital C1
5 Diego de Almagro C3
7 Ely House A3
8 Hosp Independencia D1
9 Hostal Al Fin del Mundo C3
10 Hostal Ayelen B3
12 Hostal de la Patagonia B3
13 Hostal del Sur B1
14 Hostal Dinka's House A3
16 Hostal La Estancia B3
17 Hostal Sonia Kuscevic A2
18 Hostal Taty's House A3
19 Hostel Keoken A2

20 José Nogueira
   (Palacio Sara Braun) C2
23 Patagonia Pionera C1

Restaurants
1 Café Inmigrante B3
2 Café Montt C3
4 Damiana Elena A2
5 Kisoco Roca C2
6 La Piedra C3
7 Imago Café C3
8 La Luna C3
9 La Marmita B3
10 La Tasca D2
11 Lomit's/Lomito's C2
12 Mercado Municipal D2

13 Remezón D2
15 Sotitos D3

Bars & clubs
16 La Taberna del
   Club de la Unión C2
18 Santino C2
19 Sky Bar at Dreams
   Hotel D3

200 metres
200 yards

The **Parque María Behety**, south of town along 21 de Mayo, features a scale model of Fuerte Bulnes and a campsite, popular for Sunday picnics; ice rink here in winter.

The city's waterfront has been given an extensive face-lift, with public boardwalks and outdoor spaces under special shelters giving protection from the sun's strong ultraviolet rays.

Around Punta Arenas

West of town (7 km) is the **Reserva** Nacional **Magallanes** ① *US$3, taxi US$7.50*, with nature trails from 45 minutes to two days, picnic areas. A recommended walk is a four-hour circuit up to a lookout with beautiful views over town and the surroundings and back down along the Río Minas to Punta Arenas. Nearby is the **Club Andino** (see under skiing below). Some 56 km south, **Fuerte Bulnes**, US$24, is a replica of the wooden fort erected in 1843 by the crew of the Chilean vessel *Ancud* to secure Chile's southernmost territories after Independence. An interesting story, but not that much to see. Nearby is **Puerto de Hambre**, a beautiful, panoramic spot where there are ruins of the church built in 1584 by Sarmiento de Gamboa's colonists. Tours by several agencies. Some 210 km to the northeast on Ruta 255, towards Argentina, is **Parque Nacional Pali Aike** ① *US$2*, near Punta Delgada. One of the oldest archaeological sites in Patagonia (Pali Aike means 'desolate place of bad spirits' in Tehuelche). Evidence of aborigines from 10,000-12,000 years ago, in an extraordinary volcanic landscape pockmarked with countless tiny craters, rocks of different colours and several caves. Tour operators offer full day trips, US$70-80; for more details, ask at CONAF, who manage the park.

Isla Magdalena, US$10, a small island 30 km northeast, is the location of the **Monumento Natural Los Pingüinos**, a spectacular colony of 80,000 pairs of Magellanic penguins, who come here to breed between November and January (also skuas, kelp gulls and other marine wildlife). A small lighthouse on the island gives the best views of the surroundings and the half-hour walk up there gets you close to the all the penguin action. Tread carefully and don't get too close to the nests, protective parent penguins sometimes get a bit fierce. Magdalena is one of a group of three islands (the others are Marta and Isabel), visited by Drake, whose men killed 3000 penguins for food. Boat trips to the island are run by **Comapa** and **Sólo Expediciones**, while the **Australis** cruise ships also call here (see What to do, below). Less spectacular but more easily accessible (70 km north of Punta Arenas by road), **Otway Sound** ① *Oct to mid-Mar, US$11*, has a colony of Magellanic penguins, viewed from walkways and bird hides, best seen in the morning. Rheas can also be seen. It is becoming a popular area for sea-kayaking and other adventure sports.

◉ Punta Arenas and around listings

For hotel and restaurant price codes, and other relevant information, see Essentials.

◉ Where to stay

Punta Arenas *p802, map p803*
Hotel prices are lower during winter months (Apr-Sep). A few streets, in particular Caupolicán and Maipú, some 10-15 mins' walk from the centre have become a "hotbed of hostels", most of them with similar facilities and similar prices (**$$**). These include **Ely House**, **The Pink House**, **Shangri-la**, **Maipú Street** and **Hostal Dinka's House**, the latter painted bright-red and run by the indomitable Dinka herself. The area is also full of car repair places, which

can make it noisy day-time and occasionally at night. For accommodation in private houses, usually **$** pp, ask at the tourist office. No campsites in or near the city.

$$$$-$$$ Cabo de Hornos, Plaza Muñoz Gamero 1025, T271 5000, www.hoteles-australis.com. 4-star, comfy, bright and spacious rooms, with good views from 4th floor up.
$$$$-$$$ Diego de Almagro, Av Colón 1290, T220 8800, www.dahotelespuntaarenas.com. Very modern, good international standard, on waterfront, many rooms with view, heated pool, sauna, small gym, big bright rooms, good value.
$$$$-$$$ José Nogueira, Plaza de Armas, Bories 959 y P Montt, in former Palacio Sara

Braun, T271 1000, www.hotelnogueira.com. Best in town, stylish rooms, warm atmosphere, excellent service. Smart restaurant in the beautiful loggia. A few original rooms now a 'small museum'.

$$$ Chalet Chapital, Sanhueza 974, T273 0100, www.hotelchaletchapital.cl. Small well-run hotel, smallish rooms, helpful staff, a good choice in this price range.

$$$ Hostal de la Patagonia, O'Higgins 730, T224 9970, www.ecotourpatagonia.com. Rooms with heating, good services, dining room, 10 mins' walk from centre. Organizes a variety of tours, including fly fishing.

$$$ Patagonia Pionera, Arauco 786, T222 2045, www.hotelpatagoniapionera.cl. Beautiful 1930s wooden *casona* now a comfortable high-end B&B. Helpful staff, onsite parking.

$$ Hostal Al Fin del Mundo, O'Higgins 1026, T271 0185, www.alfindelmundo.hostel.com. Rooms and dorms, bright, cosy, shared baths, central, helpful, pool table, English spoken.

$$ Hostal Ayelen, Lautarro Navarro 763, T224 2413 www.ayelenresidencial.com. 120-year-old house with some new rooms at the back, bathroom a bit small but super clean, comfy.

$$ Hostal del Sur, Mejicana 151, T222 7249, www.hostaldelsurmag.com. Impeccable old house with modern rooms in residential area, welcoming, with charming reception areas.

$$ Hostel Keoken, Magallanes 209, T224 4086/6376, www.hostelkeoken.cl. Light, wooden, spacious building on 3 floors each with its own entrance up rickety outside staircases. Some rooms with small bath. Good value, some info. Top floor rooms with shared bathroom have paper thin walls. Currently expanding into an even bigger, rambling place.

$$ Hostal La Estancia, O'Higgins 765, T224 9130, www.estancia.cl. Simple but comfortable rooms, some with bath. **$** pp in dorms. English spoken, small shop attached, music and games room recently opened.

$$ Hostal Sonia Kuscevic, Pasaje Darwin 175, T224 8543, www.hostalsk.cl. One of the city's oldest guesthouses, with heating and parking. Better value for longer stays, good discount if you have a Hostelling International card.

$$ Hostal Taty's House, Maipu 1070, T224 1525, www.hostaltatyshouse.cl. Nice rooms with good beds, decent choice in this price bracket, basic English spoken.

$$-$ Backpackers' Paradise, Carrera Pinto 1022, T224 0104, backpackersparadise@ hotmail.com. Popular good kitchen, 1 private and 5 shared rooms. Facilities much improved in recent years.

$ Hostal Independencia, Independencia 374, T222 7572, www.chileaustral.com/ independencia. Rooms, dorms and camping with use of kitchen and bathroom. Trekking equipment rental, parking, fishing and other tours, lots of information.

🍴 Restaurants

Punta Arenas *p802, map p803*
Many eating places close on Sun.
Note *Centolla* (king crab) is caught illegally by some fishermen using dolphin, porpoise and penguin as live bait. There are seasonal bans on *centolla* fishing to protect dwindling stocks; out of season *centolla* served in restaurants will probably be frozen. If there is an infestation of red tide (*marea roja*), a disease which is fatal to humans, bivalve shellfish must not be eaten. Mussels should not be picked along the shore because of pollution and the marea roja. Sernatur and the Centros de Salud have leaflets.

$$$ Remezón, 21 de Mayo 1469, T224 1029. Regional specialities such as krill. Very good, but should be, given the prices.

$$$-$$ Damiana Elena, Magallanes 341, T222 2818. Mon-Sat from 2000. Stylish restaurant serving Mediterranean food with a Patagonian touch, popular with locals, book ahead at weekends.

$$$-$ La Tasca, Plaza Muñoz Gamero 771, above Teatro Cervantes in Casa Español. Large helpings, limited selection, decent set lunch, views over the plaza.

$$$-$$ Sotitos, O'Higgins 1138. Daily (Sun 1200-1500 only). An institution, famous for seafood in elegant surroundings, excellent. Book ahead in season. New second floor serving local specialties and Italian food.

$$ La Luna, O'Higgins 1017, T222 8555. Fish, shellfish and local specialities, huge pisco sours, popular, reasonable. Quirky décor, friendly staff. Recommended.

$$ La Marmita, Plaza Sampiao 678, www.
marmitamaga.cl. Mon-Sat 1230-1500, 1830-
2330. Regional dishes with international twist,
vegetarian options, good sized portions, prettily
presented, chatty owner, generally very good.
$$-$ La Piedra, Lautaro Navarro 1087. Mon-Sat
1200-0100. Meat dishes, fish, soups, salads,
good burgers and sandwiches, daily lunch
specials, housed over 2 floors.
$ Lomit's/Lomito's, Menéndez 722. A fast-food
institution with bar attached, cheap snacks and
drinks (local beers are good), open when the
others are closed, good food.
$ Mercado Municipal, 21 de Mayo 1465.
Wide range of cocinerías offering cheap
empanadas and seafood on the upper
floor of the municipal market.
$ Kiosco Roca, Roca 875, unassuming sandwich
bar, voted best in Punta Arenas. Mon-Fri 0800-
1900, Sat 0800-1300, always packed. Take-away
or a few seats available at the counter.

Cafés

Café Inmigrante, Quillota 599 (esq Mejicana),
T222 2205, www.inmigrante.cl. Daily afternoons
and evenings. Hugely popular cafe run by
3rd generation Croatian expats. Beautifully
prepared sandwiches, daily changing cake
menu, huge portions, family history on menus.
Quirky and popular. Book in advance if possible.
Highly recommended.
Café Montt, Pedro Montt 976. Coffees, teas,
cakes, pastries and snacks, Wi-Fi. Cosy, friendly.
Recommended.
Imago Café, Costanera y Colón. Tiny, laid back
café hidden away in a beachfront bunker
overlooking the straits.

Bars and clubs

Punta Arenas *p802, map p803*
La Taberna del Club de la Unión, on the
plaza in the basement of the Hotel Nogueira.
Mon-Sat from 1830. Atmospheric bar, good for
evening drinks.
Santino, Colón 657, www.santino.cl. Open
1800-0300. Also serves pizzas and other snacks,
large bar, good service, live music Sat.
Sky Bar, O'Higgins 1235. Bar with panoramic
views on the top floor of the luxury **Dreams**
hotel and spa. Open from 1830.

Shopping

Punta Arenas *p802, map p803*
Punta Arenas has certain free-port facilities;
Zona Franca, 3.5 km north of the centre,
opposite Museo del Recuerdo, Instituto de
la Patagonia, is cheaper than elsewhere. The
complex now has over 100 shops and is open
daily from 1000 (www.zonaustral.cl), bus E or
A from Plaza Muñoz Gamero; many colectivos;
taxi US$3.
Handicrafts Chile Típico, Carrera Pinto 1015,
T222 5827. Beautiful knitwear and woollen
ponchos. **Mercado Municipal** (see Restaurants
above). Excellent handicrafts and souvenirs on
the lower floors, recently enlarged.

What to do

Punta Arenas *p802, map p803*
Skiing Cerro Mirador, only 8 km west
of Punta Arenas in the Reserva Nacional
Magallanes, one of the few places in the world
where you can ski with a sea view. Taxi US$8,
local buses at weekends from Punta Arenas
main square. Equipment rental available.
Midway lodge with food, drink and equipment.
Season Jun-Sep, weather and snow permitting.
In summer there is a good 2-hr walk on the hill,
with labelled flora. Contact **Club Andino**, T224
1479, www.clubandino.cl.

Tour operators

Most tour operators organize trips to Torres del
Paine, Fuerte Bulnes, the pingüineras on Isla
Magdalena and Otway Sound and Tierra del
Fuego; shop around.
Adventure Network International, T+1-801
266 4876, www.adventure-network.com.
Antarctic experiences of a lifetime, operating
out of Punta Arenas, flying to the interior of
the Antarctic Continent. Flights to the South
Pole, guided mountain climbing and fully
guided skiing expeditions. Camping with
Emperor Penguins in Nov.
Arka Patagonia, Manuel Señoret 1597, T224
8167, www.arkapatagonia.com. All types of
tours, whale-watching, trekking, etc.
Australis Expedition Cruises, at Comapa,
Magallanes 990, T220 0200, www.australis.com
(in Santiago Av El Bosque Norte 0440, p 11,

T02-2442 3115, in Buenos Aires T011-5199 6697). Runs expedition cruises on the *Vía Australis* and the larger *Stella Australis* between Punta Arenas and Ushuaia, through the Magellan Straits and the 'avenue of glaciers', with stops at Cape Horn and Isla Navarino, glaciers and Isla Magdalena (the itinerary varies according to route). There are plenty of opportunities to disembark and see wildlife. Round trips 3-7 nights, one-ways 3-4 nights, service from Sep-Apr, check website for promotions. Very safe and comfortable, first-class service, fine dining, daily lectures, an unforgettable experience. Advance booking is essential; check-in is at Comapa. Highly recommended.

Turismo Aventour, Patagonia 779, T222 0174, http://aventourpatagonia.cl. Specialize in fishing trips, organize tours to Tierra del Fuego, helpful, English spoken.

Turismo Comapa, Magallanes 990, T220 0200, www.comapa.com. Tours to Torres del Paine (responsible, well-informed guides), Tierra del Fuego and to see penguins at Isla Magdalena. Agents for Australis Expedition Cruises (see above).

Turismo Laguna Azul, Menéndez 786, T222 5200, www.turismolagunaazul.com. Full-day trips to a colony of King Penguins on Tierra del Fuego. Trips run all year round. Also city tours, trips to glaciers and others.

Turismo Yamana, Errázuriz 932, T222 2061, www.yamana.cl. Conventional and deluxe tours, trekking in Torres del Paine, kayaking the fjords of Parque Nacional De Agostini (Tierra del Fuego), multilingual guides.

Whale Sound, Lautaro Navarro 1191, T09-9887 9814, www.whalesound.com. Whale-watching trips in the Magellan Straits.

⊖ Transport

Punta Arenas *p802, map p803*
Most transport is heavily booked from Christmas to Mar: advance booking strongly advised.
Air Carlos Ibáñez del Campo Airport, 20 km north of town. Minibus service by Transfer Austral, Av Independencia 595-B, T272 3358, www.transferaustral.com, US$6. Taxi US$14 to city, US$10 to airport. Note that in most taxis much of the luggage space is taken up by

natural gas fuel tanks. To **Santiago**, LAN, via **Puerto Montt** and Sky (several stops) daily. To **Porvenir**, Aerovías DAP (O'Higgins 891, T261 6100, www.aeroviasdap.cl) 3 times daily Mon-Fri, 2 on Sat, 9 passengers, 12 mins. To **Puerto Williams**, daily except Sun, 1¼ hrs (book a week in advance for Porvenir, 2 in advance for Puerto Williams). **To Argentina** To **Ushuaia**, 1 hr, LAN 3 a week in summer (schedules change frequently). Take passport when booking tickets to Argentina.

Bus The bus terminal is at the northern edge of town by the Zona Franca. At the time of writing bus companies were maintaining their own offices in the city centre. **Cruz del Sur**, **Fernández**, and **Turibus**, Sanhueza 745, T224 2313/222 1429, www.busesfernandez. com. **Pacheco**, Colón 900, T224 2174, www. busespacheco.com; **Pullman**, Colón 568, T222 3359, www.pullman.cl, tickets for all Chile. **Central de Pasajeros**, Colón y Magallanes, T224 5811, office for booking all tickets, also cambio and tour operator. **Bus Sur**, Menéndez 552, T222 2938, www.bus-sur.cl. **Ghisoni** and **Tecni Austral**, Lautaro Navarro 975, T261 3422.

Bus services: To **Puerto Natales**, 3-3½ hrs, Fernández, Bus Sur and Pacheco, up to 8 daily, last departure 2015, US$10, look out for special offers and connections to Torres del Paine. Buses may pick up at the airport with advance booking and payment.

To **Río Grande** and **Ushuaia** via **Punta Delgada** (route is described in Argentina, Arriving in Tierra del Fuego; no buses via Porvenir) Pacheco, Sur, Tecni-Austral and others, 8-10 hrs, US$42, heavily booked; US$70-85 to Ushuaia, 12 hrs. Some services have to change in Río Grande for Ushuaia, others direct. Check companies for frequencies. Book well in advance in Jan-Feb. To **Río Gallegos**, Argentina, via Punta Delgada, Pacheco, Sun, Mon, Tue, Fri; Ghisoni, Mon, Wed, Thu, Fri, Sat. Fares US$24, 5-8 hrs, depending on customs, 15 mins on Chilean side, up to 2 hrs on Argentine side.

To **Otway Sound**: bus with Fernández 1500, return 1900, US$13.50. Tours by several agencies; US$20, entry extra, taxi US$50 return. **Car hire** EMSA, Kuzma Slavic 706, T261 4378, www.emsarentacar.cl. Payne, Menéndez 631, T224 0852, www.payne.cl, also tours, treks, birdwatching, etc. Also multinational companies. **Note** You need a hire company's authorization to take a car into Argentina. This takes 24 hrs (not Sat or Sun) and involves mandatory international insurance at US$30 per week, plus notary fees.

Ferry For services to **Porvenir** (Tierra del Fuego), see page 822. Shipping offices: **Navimag**, at Turismo Comapa, Magallanes 990, T220 0200, www.navimag.com for up to date information on Navimag ferries between Puerto Montt and Puerto Natales; details under Puerto Montt, Transport. For Australis Expedition Cruises to Cape Horn and Ushuaia, see above.

To **Antarctica**: most cruise ships leave from Ushuaia, but a few operators are based in Punta Arenas. See above, **Adventure Network International** or try Antarctica XXI, O'Higgins 1170, T261 4100, www.antarctica xxi.com, flight/cruise packages. See under Santiago Tour operators, page 673. Otherwise, another possibility is with the Chilean Navy. The Navy does not encourage passengers, so you must approach the captain direct. Spanish is essential. 2 vessels, *Galvarino* and *Lautaro*, sail regularly (no schedule); isotop@mitierra.cl, www.armada.cl.

To **Monumento Natural Los Pingüinos**: **Solo Expediciones**, Nogueira 1255, T224 3354, www.soloexpediciones.com, operate their own service on a faster, smaller boat, also passing by Isla Marta, half-day tour, mornings only. **Australis Expedition Cruise** ships (see above) include a morning's excursion to the island.
Taxi Ordinary taxis have yellow roofs. Colectivos (all black) run on fixed routes, pick up from taxi stands around town, US$2 flat fee.

🅾 Directory

Punta Arenas *p802, map p803*
Banks Most banks and some supermarkets have ATMs; many on the Plaza. **Casas de cambio**, many on Lautaro Navarro 1000 block.
Consulates Argentina, 21 de Mayo 1878, T226 1532, F226 1264, cparenas@embargentina. cl, open Mon-Fri 0900-1800, visas take 24 hrs.
Medical services Hospitals: Hospital Regional Lautaro Navarro, Av Los Flamencos 01364, T229 3000. Public hospital, for emergency room ask for La Posta. Has good dentists. **Clínica Magallanes**, Bulnes 01448, T221 1527. Private clinic. **Hospital Naval**, Av Bulnes 200 esq Capitán Guillermos. Open 24 hrs, good, friendly staff.

Puerto Natales and around

Beautifully situated on the calm waters of Canal Señoret fjord, an arm of the Ultima Esperanza Sound, edged with spectacular mountains, Puerto Natales, 247 km north of Punta Arenas, is a quiet town of brightly painted corrugated-tin houses. It's the base for exploring the magnificent O'Higgins and Torres del Paine national parks, and even when inundated with visitors in the summer, it retains an unhurried feel. A lovely place to relax for a few days.

Arriving in Puerto Natales

Tourist office At the **Sernatur office** ① *on the waterfront, Av Pedro Montt 19, T241 2125, infonatales@sernatur.cl, Oct-Mar Mon-Fri 0830-1900, Sat-Sun 1000-1300,1430-1800, Apr-Sep, Mon-Fri 0830-1800, Sat 1000-1300, 1400-1800*, there are good leaflets available on Puerto Natales and Torres del Paine in English, and bus and boat information in the park. **Municipal tourist office** ① *at bus station, Av España 1455.* **CONAF** ① *Baquedano 847, T241 1438, patricio.salinas@conaf.cl.*

Places in Puerto Natales

Museo Histórico Municipal ① *Bulnes 285, T241 1263, Mon, 0800-1700, Tue-Fri, 0800-1900, Sat 1000-1300, 1500-1900, US$2,* has displays and photos of early colonizers, as well as a small collection of archaeological and natural history exhibits. There are lovely walks along the waterfront or up to Cerro Dorotea, which dominates the town, with superb views (watch out for high winds). Take any bus going east and alight at the road for summit (Km 9.5).

Monumento Natural Cueva Milodón ① *25 km north, 0800-2000, US$8 to enter park (US$4 low season), getting there: regular bus from Prat 517, T241 2540, leaves 0945 and 1500, returns*

1200 and 1700. US$8; taxi US$30 return or check if you can get a ride with a tour; some full-day tour buses to Torres del Paine stop at the cave. In this cave (70 m wide, 30 m high and 220 m deep), formed by ice-age glacial lakes, remains were found of a prehistoric ground-sloth, together with evidence of occupation by early Patagonian humans some 11,000 years ago. There is a small, well-presented visitor centre, with restaurant, shop and toilets.

Parque Nacional Bernardo O'Higgins

Usually referred to as the **Parque Nacional Monte Balmaceda** ① *US$10*, the park is at the north end of Ultima Esperanza Sound and can only be reached on boat trips from Puerto Natales. After a three-hour journey up the Sound, the boat passes the Balmaceda Glacier which drops steeply from the eastern slopes of Monte Balmaceda (2035 m). The glacier is retreating; in 1986 its foot was at sea level. The boat docks further north at Puerto Toro, from where it's a 1-km walk to the base of Serrano Glacier on the north slope of Monte Balmaceda. On the trip dolphins, sea-lions (in season), black-necked swans, flightless steamer ducks and cormorants can be seen. The

Puerto Natales

To ㉑ ㉔ , Punta Arenas & Parque Nacional Torres del Paine

Seno Ultima Esperanza

Estero Natales

Pier for Balmaceda Glacier

Pier for Puerto Montt

Museo Municipal

Plaza de Armas

N

200 metres
200 yards

Where to stay
1 Aquaterra *C2*
4 Casa Cecilia *B2*
5 Casa Teresa *C2*
6 Costaustralis *C1*
7 Hosp Casa Lili *B1*
8 Hosp Nancy *C3*
9 Hostal Las Carretas *C3*
10 Hostal Sir Francis Drake *A2*
11 Hostel Natales *B1*
12 Indigo Patagonia *B1*
13 Josmar 2 Camping *C2*
14 Keoken *B1*
16 Lili Patagónico's *C3*
17 Martín Gusinde *B2*
20 Patagonia Adventure *B2*
21 Remota *A2*
23 The Singing Lamb *C3*
24 Weskar Patagonian Lodge *A2*

Restaurants
1 Afrigonia *B2*
3 Angelica's *B2*
4 Cormorán de las Rocas *A2*
5 El Asador Patagónico *B2*
6 El Living *B2*
7 La Mesita Grande *B2*
8 La Picada de Carlitos *C3*
9 Parrilla Don Jorge *B2*
10 Patagonia Dulce *B1*
11 Ultima Esperanza *B2*

Bars & clubs
12 Baguales Brewery *B2*
13 El Bar de Ruperto *B2*

boat then returns to Puerto Natales. There is a route from Puerto Toro on the eastern side of the Río Serrano for 35 km to the Torres del Paine administration centre; guided tours are available on foot or on horseback. It is also possible to travel onwards to the Paine administration centre along the river by boat or zodiac. Better going to the park than from the park (the view suddenly opens up and then just gets better and better).

Border with Argentina

There are three crossing points: **Dorotea**, 16 km east of Puerto Natales. On the Argentine side the road continues to a junction, with alternatives to Río Turbio and north to La Esperanza and Río Gallegos. Chilean immigration is open all year 0800-2400. **Paso Casas Viejas/Laurita**, 16 km northeast of Puerto Natales. On the Argentine side this joins the Río Turbio–La Esperanza road. Chilean immigration is open 0800-2200. **Río Don Guillermo/Cerro Castillo**, 65 km north of Puerto Natales on the road to Torres del Paine, 7 km from the border, open 0800-2200. Cerro Castillo is well-equipped with café, toilets, ATM, tourist information and souvenir shop. On the Argentine side, Paso Río Don Guillermo (Cancha Carrera, 14 km, few facilities), the road leads to La Esperanza and Río Gallegos. All buses from El Calafate go via Cerro Castillo, making it possible to transfer to a bus passing from Puerto Natales to Torres del Paine. The small settlement has several hospedajes and cafeterías. Sheep shearing in December, and rodeo and rural festival third weekend in January. See also www.pasosfronterizos.gov.cl and the Argentina chapter.

⊙ Puerto Natales and around listings

For hotel and restaurant price codes, and other relevant information, see Essentials.

⊝ Where to stay

Puerto Natales and around *p808, map p809*
In season cheaper accommodation fills up quickly. Hotels in the countryside open only in summer months: dates vary. Good deals in upper range hotels may be available; out of season especially and prices may be 50% lower.
$$$$ Costaustralis, Pedro Montt 262, T241 2000, www.hoteles-australis.com. Very comfortable, tranquil, lovely views (but not from inland-facing rooms), lift, English spoken, waterfront restaurant Paine serves international and local seafood.
$$$$ Indigo Patagonia, Ladrilleros 105, T243 26800, www.indigopatagonia.cl. Relaxed atmosphere, on the water front, great views, a boutique hotel with roof-top spa, rooms and suites, café/restaurant serves good seafood and vegetarian dishes. Tours organized.
$$$$ Remota, Ruta 9 Norte, Km 1.5, Huerto 279, T241 4040, www.remota.cl. Modernist design with big windows, lots of trips, activities and treks offered, spa, all-inclusive packages, good food, first-class.

$$$$ The Singular, Km 5 Norte Puerto Bories, T272 2030, www.thesingular.com. Recent converted warehouses, outside the town centre, in a scenic spot overlooking the Ultima Esperanza Sound. Spa, gourmet restaurant and varied excursions offered.
$$$$-$$$ Martín Gusinde, Bories 278, T271 2180, www.hotelmartingusinde.com. Modern 3-star standard, smart, parking, laundry service, excursions organized.
$$$$-$$$ Weskar Patagonian Lodge, Ruta 9, Km 05, T241 4168, www.weskar.cl. Quiet lodge overlooking the fjord, standard or deluxe rooms with good views, 3-course dinners served, lunch boxes prepared for excursions, many activities offered, helpful.
$$$ Aquaterra, Bulnes 299, T241 2239, www.aquaterrapatagonia.com. Good restaurant with vegetarian options, 'resto-bar' downstairs, spa, warm and comfortable but not cheap, very helpful staff. Excursions and tours.
$$$ Hostal Sir Francis Drake, Phillipi 383, T241 1553, www.hostalfrancisdrake.com. Calm and welcoming, tastefully decorated, smallish rooms, good views.
$$$ Keoken, Señoret 267, T241 3670, www.keokenpatagonia.com. Cosy, upmarket B&B, spacious living room, some rooms with views. All rooms have

bathroom but not all are en suite, English spoken, helpful staff, tours.

$$$-$$ **Hostel Natales**, Ladrilleros 209, T241 4731, www.hostelnatales.cl. Private rooms or dorms in this high-end hostel, comfortable, cash only (pesos, dollars or euros).

$$ **Casa Cecilia**, Tomás Rogers 60, T241 2698, www.casaceciliahostal.com. Welcoming, popular, with small simple rooms, private or shared bath. English, French and German spoken, rents camping and trekking gear, tour agency and information for Torres del Paine.

$$ **Hosp Nancy**, Ramírez 540, T241 0022, www.nateslodge.cl. Warm and hospitable, information, tours, equipment rental.

$$ **Ilostal Las Carretas**, Galvarino 745, T241 4584. Tastefully decorated and spotless B&B 15 mins' walk to the centre, comfortable rooms, some with bath, good beds, English spoken.

$$ **Lili Patagónico's**, Prat 479, T241 4063, www.lilipatagonicos.com. $ pp in dorms. Small but pleasant heated rooms, helpful staff. Lots of information, good quality equipment rented. Tours offered. Indoor climbing wall.

$$ **Patagonia Adventure**, Tomás Rogers 179, T241 1028, www.apatagonia.com. Lovely old house, bohemian feel, shared bath, $ pp in dorms, equipment hire, bike and kayak tours and tour arrangements for Torres del Paine.

$$-$ pp **The Singing Lamb**, Arauco 779, T241 0958, www.thesinginglamb.com. Very hospitable New Zealand-run backpackers, dorm accommodation only but no bunks. Home-from-home feel. Good information.

$ **Casa Teresa**, Esmeralda 463, T241 0472, freepatagonia@hotmail.com. Good value, but thin walls and no heating in rooms, tours to Torres del Paine arranged.

$ **Hosp Casa Lili**, Bories 153, T241 4063, lilinatales@latinmail.com. Dorms or private rooms, small, family-run, rents equipment and can arrange tickets to Paine.

Camping Josmar 2, Esmeralda 517, in centre, T241 1685, www.josmar.cl. Family-run, convenient, hot showers, parking, barbecues, electricity, café, tent site or double room.

Border with Argentina *p810*
$ pp **Hosp Loreto Belén**, Km 60, Cerro Castillo, T269 1932 ext 278. Rooms for 4, all with bath, meals, good home cooking.

🍴 Restaurants

Puerto Natales *p808, map p809*
$$$ **Afrigonia**, Eberhard 343, T241 2232. An unexpected mixture of Patagonia meets East Africa in this Kenyan/Chilean-owned fusion restaurant, considered by many to be the best, and certainly the most innovative, in town.

$$$ **Angelica's**, Bulnes 501, T241 0007, www.angelicas.cl. Elegant Mediterranean style, well-prepared pricey food with quality ingredients.

$$$-$$ **Cormorán de las Rocas**, Miguel Sánchez 72, T261 5131-3, www.cormoran delasrocas.com. Patagonian specialities with an innovative twist, wide variety of well-prepared dishes, *pisco sours*, good service and attention to detail, incomparable views.

$$$-$$ **El Asador Patagónico**, Prat 158 on the Plaza. Spit-roast lamb, salads, home-made puddings.

$$$-$$ **Parrilla Don Jorge**, Bories 430, on Plaza, T241 0999, www.parrilladonjorge.cl. Also specializes in spit-roast lamb, but serves fish too, good service.

$$ **La Mesita Grande**, Prat 196 on the Plaza, T241 1571, www.mesitagrande.cl. Fresh pizzas from the wood-burning oven, also pasta and good desserts.

$$ **Ultima Esperanza**, Eberhard 354, T241 1391. One of the town's classic seafood restaurants.

$$-$ **El Living**, Prat 156, Plaza de Armas, www.el-living.com. Comfy sofas, good tea, magazines in all languages, book exchange, good music, delicious vegetarian food, British-run, popular. Wi-Fi, recommended.

$$-$ **La Picada de Carlitos**, Blanco Encalada y Esmeralda. Good, cheap traditional Chilean food, popular with locals at lunchtime, when service can be slow.

Cafés
Patagonia Dulce, Barros Arana 233, T241 5285, www.patagoniadulce.cl. Mon-Sat 1400-2030. For the best hot chocolate in town, good coffee and chocolates.

🍸 Bars and clubs

Puerto Natales *p808, map p809*
Baguales Brewery, Bories 430, on the plaza, www.cervezabaguales.cl. Sep-Mar Mon-Sat

1800-0300. Pub with microbrewery attached. Also serves hamburgers and other snacks.

El Bar de Ruperto, Bulnes 371, T9218 9535. Lively place with DJs, live music, lots of drinks and some food. 2130-0330.

Murciélagos, Bulnes 731. Popular bar with late-night music and dancing.

O Shopping

Puerto Natales *p808, map p809*
Camping equipment Check all camping equipment and prices carefully. (Deposits required.) Camping gas is widely available in hardware stores. See under Where to stay and What to do for places that hire equipment, eg **Casa Cecilia**, **Lili Patagónico's**, Sendero Aventura, **Erratic Rock**. Always check exactly what the price covers.

Supermarkets Several in town. The town markets are also good.

O What to do

Puerto Natales *p808, map p809*
Many agencies along Eberhard. It is better to book tours direct with operators in Puerto Natales than through agents in Punta Arenas or Santiago. Several agencies offer tours to the Perito Moreno glacier in Argentina, 1 day, US$80-100, 14-hr trip, 2 hrs at the glacier, without food or park entry fee. You can then leave the tour in Calafate to continue into Argentina.

Baguales Group, Barros Araña 66, T241 2654, www.baguales group.com. Specialists in the route from the park back to Puerto Natales. Tailor made multi-activity tours that can incorporate zodiacs, horse riding, kayaking and trekking, mostly off the beaten track.

Blue Green Adventures, M Bulnes 1200, T241 1800, www.bluegreenadventures.com. Adventure tour specialist and travel agent, with trekking, riding, kayaking, fishing and multi-activity options, estancia, whalewatching, wine and yoga programmes. Also caters for families.

Comapa, Bulnes 541, T241 4300, www.comapa. com. Large regional operator offering decent day tours to Torres del Paine.

Encuentro Gourmet, Bories 349, T6720 3725, www.encuentrogourmet.com. Patagonian cookery workshops at lunch

and dinner-time, US$44 pp, book at least 24 hrs in advance,

Erratic Rock, Baquedano 719 and Zamora 732, T241 4317, www.erraticrock.com. Trekking experts offering interesting expeditions from half a day to 2 weeks. Also B&B lodge, good-quality equipment hire, daily trekking seminar at 1500.

Estancia Travel, Casa 13-b, Puerto Bories, T241 2221, www.estanciatravel.com. Based at the Estancia Puerto Consuelo, 5 km north of Puerto Natales, offers horse-riding trips from 1 to 10 days around southern Patagonia and Torres del Paine, with accommodation at traditional estancias. Also kayaking trips, British/Chilean run, bilingual, professional guides, at the top end of the price range.

Sendero Aventura, Carlos Bories 349, T6171 3080, www.senderoaventura.com. Adventure tours by land rover, bike or kayak.

Skorpios, www.skorpios.cl. 2- to 3-day cruises up the southern fjords to Puerto Edén and the Pío XI Glacier. No office in Puerto Natales; book online or through an agency.

O Transport

Puerto Natales *p808, map p809*
Air Aerodromo Teniente Julio Gallardo, 7 km north of town. **Sky** airline has services in summer from Santiago via Puerto Montt. Also charter services from Punta Arenas and onward connections to Argentina with **Aerovías DAP**.
Bus In summer book ahead. All buses leave from the new bus terminal 20 mins outside town at Av España 1455, but tickets can be bought at the individual company offices in town. Colectivos leave regularly from the centre US$0.60 (US$0.70 Sun), taxi US$2 flat fee throughout Puerto Natales. **Bus Fernández**, E Ramírez 399, T241 1111, www.busesfernandez. com. **Pacheco**, Ramírez 224, T241 4800, www. busespacheco.com. **Bus Sur**, Baquedano 668, T261 4220, www.bussur.com. **Zaahj**, Prat 236, T241 2260, www.turismozaahj.co.cl.

To **Punta Arenas**, several daily, 3-3½ hrs, US$9.50, **Fernández**, **Pacheco**, **Bus Sur** and others, comfortable **Pullman** service with Zaahj, US$24. To **Argentina**: to **Río Gallegos** direct, **Bus Sur**, and **Pacheco**, 2-3 weekly each, US$28, 4-5 hrs. Hourly to **Río Turbio**, Cootra, and other companies, US$8, 2 hrs (depending on Customs – change bus at border). To **El Calafate**, US$35, **Cootra** via Río Turbio, daily, 4 hrs; **Pacheco**, 3 weekly; or **Zaahj** (3 a week, 4½ hrs) via Cerro Castillo. Otherwise travel agencies run several times a week depending on demand; they do not include Perito Moreno glacier entry fee (12-hr trip), shop around, reserve 1 day ahead. **Bus Sur** also runs 4 buses a week to **Ushuaia** Oct-Apr, 15 hrs, US$70. See Torres del Paine section for buses from Puerto Natales into the park, page 818.

Car hire EMSA, Eberhard 577, T261 4388, www.emsarentacar.cl. **Punta Alta**, Blanco Encalada 244, T241 0115, www.puntaalta.cl. Hire agents can arrange permission to drive into Argentina, takes 24 hrs to arrange, extra insurance is required.

Ferry Details of the Navimag ferries between Puerto Montt and Puerto Natales are given under Puerto Montt, Transport. Navimag, Pedro Montt 308, T241 1642, www.navimag.com, for up to date information.

To **Parque Nacional Bernardo O'Higgins**: Sailings to **Balmaceda Glacier** daily at 0800 in summer, returning 1730, Sun only in winter (minimum 10 passengers), US$125-150. Heavily booked in high season. Take warm clothes, hat and gloves. All agencies can arrange boat trips. **Punta Alta**, see Car hire, above, and **21 de Mayo** (www.turismo21demayo.cl) take the same route, but the former in a faster boat. Both offer the possibility to continue by zodiac to the Pueblito Serrano at the park's southern edge (from US$160 one way from Puerto Natales to the Pueblito Serrano). **Punta Alta** also has an option to return to Natales on the same day by minibus along the southern access road, thus avoiding park entry fees.

ⓘ Directory

Puerto Natales *p808, map p809*
Banks There are several ATMs. Casas de cambio on Blanco Encalada, Bulnes and Prat.
Bicycle repairs El Rey de la Bicicleta, Ramírez 540. Good, helpful.

Parque Nacional Torres del Paine → *Colour map 9, B1.*

Nothing prepares you for the spectacular beauty of Parque Nacional Torres del Paine. World renowned for its challenging trekking, the park's 242,242 ha contain 15 peaks above 2000 m. At its centre is the glacier-topped granite massif Macizo Paine, from which rise the vertical pink granite Torres (Towers) del Paine and, below them, the Cuernos (Horns) del Paine, swooping buttresses of lighter granite under caps of darker sedimentary rock. From the vast Campo de Hielo Sur icecap on its western edge, four main glaciers (ventisqueros), Grey, Dickson, Zapata and Tyndall, drop into vividly coloured lakes formed by their meltwater: turquoise, ultramarine and pistachio expanses, some filled with wind-sculpted royal blue icebergs. Wherever you explore, there are constantly changing views of dramatic peaks and ice fields. The park enjoys a micro-climate especially favourable to wildlife and plants: there are 105 species of birds including condors, ibis, flamingos and austral parakeets, and 25 species of mammals including guanaco, hares, foxes, pumas and skunks. A day tour from Puerto Natales will give a broad overview of the park, but seven to 10 days are needed to see it all properly.

Arriving in Torres del Paine

Information The park is administered by CONAF ⓘ *Administration Centre T061-223 8959/269 1931, magallanes.oirs@conaf.cl, www.parquetorresdelpaine.cl, open 0830-2030 in summer, 0830-1230, 1400-1830 off season,* is in the south of the park at the northwest end of Lago del Toro. There are entrances at Laguna Amarga, Lago Sarmiento, Laguna Azul and the Puente Serrano, and you are required to **register** and show your passport when entering the park, since rangers (*guardaparques*) keep a check on the whereabouts of all visitors. Phone the administration centre for information (in Spanish) on weather conditions. It also has videos and exhibitions with summaries in English of flora and fauna. There are 13 ranger stations (*guarderías*) staffed by rangers, who give help and advice. Entry for foreigners: US$36 (low season US$20, Chilean pesos only; proceeds are shared between all Chilean national parks), includes a reasonable trail map to take with you (not waterproof); climbing the peaks requires two permits, first from DIFROL (can be obtained free online, www.difrol.cl), then from CONAF in the park itself (take passports, DIFROL permit, insurance and route plan). If you are based outside the park and plan on entering

Parque Nacional Torres del Paine

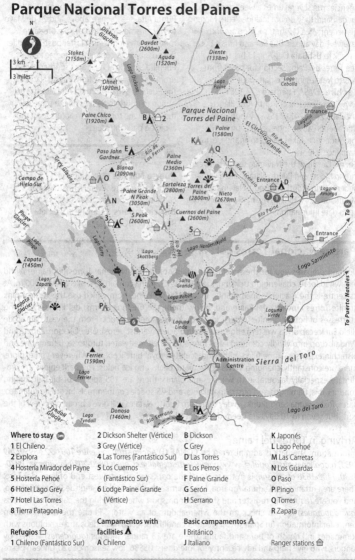

Where to stay

1 El Chileno
2 Explora
4 Hostería Mirador del Payne
5 Hostería Pehoé
6 Hotel Lago Grey
7 Hotel Las Torres
8 Tierra Patagonia

Refugios ⌂

1 Chileno (Fantástico Sur)

2 Dickson Shelter (Vértice)
3 Grey (Vértice)
4 Las Torres (Fantástico Sur)
5 Los Cuernos
  (Fantástico Sur)
6 Lodge Paine Grande
  (Vértice)

Campamentos with facilities ▲

A Chileno

B Dickson
C Grey
D Las Torres
E Los Perros
F Paine Grande
G Serón
H Serrano

Basic campamentos ⚞

I Británico
J Italiano

K Japonés
L Lago Pehoé
M Las Carretas
N Los Guardas
O Paso
P Pingo
Q Torres
R Zapata

Ranger stations ⌂

and leaving several times explain this when you are paying your entrance to be given a multiple entry stamp valid for three consecutive days. The impact of huge numbers of visitors to the park, over 100,000 a year, is often visible in litter around the *refugios* and camping areas. Take all your rubbish out of the park including toilet paper.

Getting around and accommodation The park is well set up for tourism, with frequent bus services running from Puerto Natales through the park, to pick up and drop off walkers at various hotels, to start treks, and to connect with boat trips. For details, see Transport below. Accommodation is available on three levels: there are hotels (expensive, over US$300 for a double room per night), privately run *refugios*, well equipped, staffed, offering meals and free hot water for tea, soup, etc, and campsites with amenities and basic *campamentos*. All options fill up quickly in peak summer months, January and February, so plan your trip and book hotels and *refugios* in advance. Pay in dollars to avoid IVA (VAT). See Where to stay for more details.

Safety warning It is vital to be aware of the unpredictability of the weather (which can change in a few minutes, see Climate below) and the arduousness of some of the stretches on the long hikes. Rain and snowfall are heavier the further west you go and bad weather sweeps off the Campo de Hielo Sur without warning. The only means of rescue are on horseback or by boat; the nearest helicopter is in Punta Arenas and high winds usually prevent its operation in the park. An Argentine visitor disappeared as recently as Christmas 2013 and was not found, despite extensive searches. It is vital to take adequate equipment/clothing and report your route to staff. Mobile phone coverage is erratic.

Forest fires are a serious hazard. Make sure you follow all instructions about lighting fires to the letter. Unauthorized campfires in 2005 and 2011 led to the destruction of 160 sq km and 110 sq km respectively.

Equipment and maps A strong, streamlined, waterproof tent gives you more freedom than crowded *refugios* and is essential if doing the complete circuit. Also essential at all times of year are protective clothing against cold, wind and rain, strong waterproof footwear, a compass, a good sleeping bag, sleeping mat, camping stove and cooking equipment. Most *refugios* will hire camping equipment for a single night. Sun-screen and sunglasses are also necessary, and you'll want shorts in summer. Take your own food: the small shops at the *refugios* and at the **Posada Río Serrano** are expensive and have a limited selection. Maps (US$7), published by Mattassi and (more accurate) Cartografía Digital and Patagonia Interactiva, are obtainable in shops in Punta Arenas or Puerto Natales. All have a few mistakes, however.

Climate Do not underestimate the severity of the weather here. The park is open all year round, although snow may prevent access in the winter. The warmest time is December to March, but also the most unstable; strong winds often blow off the glaciers, and rainfall can be heavy. It is most crowded in the summer holiday season, January to mid-February, less so in December or March. October and November are recommended for wild flowers. In winter there can be good, stable conditions and well-equipped hikers can do some good walking, but some treks may be closed and boats may not be running.

Hikes

There are about 250 km of well-marked trails, and walkers must keep to the paths: cross-country trekking is not permitted. The times indicated should be treated with caution: allow for personal fitness and weather conditions.

El Circuito (Allow at least seven days) The park's emblematic hike is a circuit round the Torres and Cuernos del Paine: it is usually done anticlockwise starting from the Laguna Amarga *guardería*. From Laguna Amarga the route is north along the west side of the Río Paine to Lago Paine, before turning west to follow the Río Paine to the south end of Lago Dickson. From here the path runs along the wooded valley of the Río de los Perros before climbing steeply to Paso John Gardner (1241 m, the highest point on the route), then dropping to follow the Grey Glacier southeast to Lago Grey, continuing to Lago Pehoé and before joining up with the 'W' (see below) back to the Hostería Las Torres or Laguna Amarga. There are superb views, particularly from the top of Paso John Gardner.

Camping gear must be carried. The circuit is often closed in winter because of snow. Walking times between campsites is four to six hours. The most difficult section is the steep slippery slope between Paso John Gardner and Campamento Paso, a poorly signed section exposed to strong westerly winds. The major rivers are crossed by footbridges, which are occasionally washed away.

The 'W' (Allow four to five days) A more popular alternative to El Circuito, it can be completed without camping equipment by staying in *refugios*, and can be done in either direction. It combines several of the hikes described separately below. From Laguna Amarga the first stage runs west via Hotel Las Torres and up the valley of the Río Ascensio via Refugio Chileno to the base of the Torres del Paine (see below). From here return to the Hotel Las Torres and then walk along the northern shore of Lago Nordenskjold via Refugio Los Cuernos to Campamento Italiano. From here climb the Valley of the Río del Francés (see below) before continuing to Lodge Paine Grande. From here you can complete the third part of the 'W' by walking west along the northern shore of Lago Grey to Refugio Grey and Glaciar Grey before returning to Lodge Paine Grande. To do the hike from west to east, either take the scheduled catamaran service across Lago Pehoé to Lodge Paine Grande and start from there, or take the trail to Paine Grande from the administration centre. This precursor to the main hike passes Campamento Las Carretas and for all but the last hour is easy, with views of what you will be undertaking on the 'W'.

The Valley of the Río del Francés (Allow five hours each way) From Lodge Paine Grande this route leads northeast across undulating country along the west edge of Lago Skottberg to Campamento Italiano and then follows the valley of the Río del Francés, which climbs between (to the west) Cerro Paine Grande and the Ventisquero del Francés, and (to the east) the Cuernos del Paine to Campamento Británico. Allow 2½ hours from Lodge Paine Grande to Campamento Italiano, 2½ hours further to Campamento Británico. The views from the mirador, 20 minutes above Campamento Británico, are superb.

To the base of the Torres del Paine (Allow five to six hours each way) From Laguna Amarga the route follows the road west to Hotel Las Torres before climbing along the west side of the Río Ascensio via Campamento Chileno to Campamento Las Torres, close to the base of the Torres and near a small lake. Allow 1½ hours to Hotel Las Torres, then two hours to Campamento Chileno, two hours further to Campamento Torres where there is a fork: the path to the base of the Torres is well-marked, but these last 30 minutes are up the moraine; to see the towers lit by sunrise (spectacular, but you must have good weather), it's well worth humping camping gear up to Campamento Torres and spending the night (no *refugio*). One hour beyond Campamento Torres is the good site at Campamento Japonés (for climbers only).

Up the Río Pingo valley (Allow five hours each way, can only be undertaken with a certified CONAF guide) From Guardería Grey (18 km west by road from the Administration Centre) follow the Río Pingo, via Refugio Pingo and Refugio Zapata (four hours), with views south over Ventisquero Zapata (plenty of wildlife, icebergs in the lake). It is not possible to reach Lago Pingo as a bridge – marked on many maps – has been washed away. Ventisquero Pingo can be seen 3 km away over the lake.

To Laguna Verde (Allow four hours each way) From the administration centre follow the road north 2 km, before taking the path east over the Sierra del Toro and then along the south side of Laguna Verde to the Guardería Laguna Verde. This is one of the easiest walks in the park and may be a good first hike.

To Laguna Azul and Lago Paine (Allow 8½ hours each way) This route runs north from Laguna Amarga to the west tip of Laguna Azul (following the road for 7 km), from where it continues across the sheltered Río Paine valley past Laguna Cebolla to the Refugio Lago Paine (now closed) at the west end of the lake. There are also plenty of shorter walks in the park, see park website www.torresdelpaine.com.

◉ Parque Nacional Torres del Paine listings

For hotel and restaurant price codes, and other relevant information, see Essentials.

● Where to stay

Parque Nacional Torres del Paine *p813, map p814*

All the park's hotels are expensive, many feel overpriced. Agencies in Puerto Natales offer accommodation and transfers or car hire.

$$$$ Explora (Hotel Salto Chico Lodge), T241 1247 (reservations: Av Américo Vespucci Sur 80, p 5, Santiago, T02-2395 2800, www.explora. com). The park's priciest and most exclusive place is nestled into a nook at Salto Chico on edge of Lago Pehoé, superb views. It's all included: pool, gym, horse riding, boat trips, tours. Arrange packages from Punta Arenas.

$$$$ Hostería Mirador del Payne, Estancia Lazo, lovely location on Laguna Verde on east edge of the park, 52 km from Sarmiento entrance, reservations from Fagnano 585, Punta Arenas, T222 8712, www.miradordelpayne.com. Comfortable, meals extra, but inconvenient for park itself, riding, hiking, birdwatching. Private transport essential, or hike there from the park.

$$$$ Hostería Pehoé, T296 1238, www. pehoe.cl, 5 km south of Pehoé ranger station, 11 km north of park administration. Beautifully situated on an island with spectacular view across Lago Pehoé, restaurant.

$$$$ Hotel Lago Grey, head office Lautaro Navarro 1077, Punta Arenas, T271 2100, www.turismolagogrey.com. Great views over Lago Grey, superior rooms worth the extra, glacier walks.

$$$$ Hotel Las Torres, T261 7450, www. lastorres.com. Comfortable rooms, beautiful lounge with wood fire and great views of the Macizo, excellent evening buffet, good service, horse riding, transport from Laguna Amarga ranger station, spa, disabled access. Visitor centre and *confitería* open to non-residents.

$$$$ Tierra Patagonia, T02-2207 8861, www. tierrapatagonia.com. Excellent, environmentally sensitive luxury hotel with spa, pool and outdoor jacuzzi on the edge of the national park overlooking Lago Sarmiento. Full- and half day guided trips by minibus, on foot or on horseback. Gourmet dining in panorama restaurant overlooking the lake and mountains. Highly recommended.

Refugios

Two companies between them run the *refugios* in the park, comfortable dormitory or *cabaña* accommodation (bring your own sleeping bag, or hire sheets for US$8-10 per night). Prices start from US$46pp bed only and go up to US$200pp in a *cabaña* with full board. Meals can be bought individually (US$11, US$15 and US$21), restaurants open to non-residents. *Refugios* have good hot showers and space for camping, US$8-16. All *refugios* hire tents for US$13-15 per night, plus US$3 per sleeping mat (book in advance for **Vértice Refugios** as they have very few tents available). Kitchen facilities are available in some **Vértice Refugios**. **Fantástico Sur** will not let you prepare your own hot food unless you are camping. Most close in winter, although 1 or 2 may stay open, depending on the weather. Advance booking essential in high season.

Fantástico Sur refugios, book in agencies in Puerto Natales or direct at Esmeralda 661, Puerto Natales, T061-261 4184, www.fslodges.com:

Refugio El Chileno, in the Valley of Río Ascencio, at the foot of the Torres.
Refugio Las Torres (Torre Central, Torre Norte), 2 *refugios* next to the Hotel Las Torres (see above), good facilities, especially in the newer Torre Central.
Refugio Los Cuernos, on the northern shore of Lago Nordenskjold. Also has 8 cabins (US$155 double occupancy without board, US$251 full board).
Vértice Refugios (book through agencies in Puerto Natales, or Bulnes 1200, Puerto Natales, T241 2742, via www.verticepatagonia. com) runs: **Mountain Lodges Paine Grande**, on the northwest tip of Lago Pehoé (kitchen facilities, internet) and Vértice Grey. Also the basic **Vértice Dickson Shelter**.

Camping

Fires may only be lit at organized camping sites, not at campamentos. The *guardaparques* expect people to have a stove if camping. In addition to sites at the above *refugios* there are the following sites: **Camping Lago Pehoé**, www.campingpehoe.com, US$16 pp, tent rental US$24 for 2 including sleeping mat, also pre-pitched dome tents, hot showers, shop, restaurant. There are 4 sites run by Vértice Patagonia; **Camping Los Perros, Paine Grande, Dickson** and **Grey** (from US$8 pp). **Camping Serón** and **Camping Las Torres** (by the Refugio Las Torres) both run by **Fantástico Sur** (see above), US$9-11, hot showers. Free camping is permitted in 10 other locations in the park: these sites are known as campamentos and are generally extremely basic. The wind tends to rise in the evening so pitch tent early. Mice can be a problem around camping sites; do not leave food in packs on the ground. Equipment hire in Puerto Natales (see above). Other campsites in or near the park: fixed sites, such as the indigenous Kaweskar-influenced domes of **Ecocamp Patagonia** (Don Carlos 3227C, Las Condes, Santiago, T02-2923 5950, www.ecocamp.travel), the only ISO14001, environmental sustainability-certified hotel in Chile, and the luxury yurts of **Patagonia Camp** at Lago Toro, www.patagonia camp.com. **Camping Río Serrano**, just outside the park's southern entrance on a working estancia, www.campingchile.com, also has horse rides and hikes.

⚫ What to do

Parque Nacional Torres del Paine *p813, map p814*
See under Puerto Natales, What to do, page 812, for recommendations. Before booking a tour, check details carefully and get them in writing.
Experience Chile, T02-2570 9436, www. torresdelpaine.org, www.experiencechile. org. Specializes in tailor-made itineraries for individuals, couples and small groups.
Boat trips From Refugio Lago Pehoé to Refugio Pudeto, US$24 one way with 1 backpack (US$8 for extra backpacks), US$38 return, from Pudeto 0930, 1200, 1800, from Paine Grande 1000, 1230, 1830, 30 mins in high season, reserve in advance at the *refugios* at either end or at **Catamarán Hielos Patagónicos**, Los Arrieros 1517, Puerto Natales, T241 1380, info@hielospatagonicos.cl. Reduced service off season (also Christmas Day and New Year's Day), 1200 only 1 Apr-15 Nov. At all times check in advance that boats are running. See Parque Nacional Bernardo O'Higgins above for entry by 3-hr zodiac trip up the Río Serrano from Balmaceda glacier. Boat to face of glacier from **Hostería Grey**, 2-4 times daily, 3½ hrs, US$90 return. A one-way trip can be made via the glacier face to/from the *hostería* to the **Refugio Grey** for US$60.

⊖ Transport

Parque Nacional Torres del Paine *p813, map p814*
Bus The park administration is 147 km northwest of Puerto Natales by the old road, with a shorter new road, 85 km, opened to the south side of the park in 2007. After mid-Mar there is little public transport and trucks are irregular. There are several companies running daily services into the park, leaving Puerto Natales between 0630 and 0800, and again (Dec-Feb) at 1430, using the old road, with a 20-min stop at Cerro Castillo (3 cafés and some shops), 2½ hrs to Laguna Amarga, 3½ hrs to Guardería Pudeto and 4½ hrs the administration centre. Transport on the new road takes 1½ hrs to park. To go to the Administration centre, all charge US$17 one

way, US$32 open return (return tickets are not interchangeable between different companies). Buses will stop anywhere en route, but all stop at Laguna Amarga entrance, Salto Grande del Paine and the administration centre. Return buses to Puerto Natales stop at Laguna Amarga from 1430 to 2000. Services are provided by **Bus Gómez**, Prat 234, T241 1971; **JBA**, Prat 258, T241 0242; and **Trans Vía Paine**, Bulnes 518, T241 3672. In high season the buses fill quickly so it is best to board at Administration for the return to Puerto Natales. All buses wait at Refugio Pudeto until the 1200 boat from Refugio Paine Grande arrives.

In season there are frequent minibus connections within the park, eg from Laguna Amarga to **Hotel Las Torres**, US$5, and from the administration centre to **Hostería Lago Grey**, US$15. Other than these routes getting around the park without your own transport is difficult and expensive. From Torres del Paine to **El Calafate** (Argentina): take services from Puerto Natales (see above); alternatively take a bus from the park to Cerro Castillo (106 km south of administration centre) then catch a direct service to Calafate (see Puerto Natales Buses). Zaahj has a very comfortable **Super Pullman** service, US$28, Cerro Castillo–El Calafate. Beware that border crossings can take up to several hours in peak season.

Car hire Hiring a pick-up in Punta Arenas is an economical proposition for a group (up to 9 people): US$400-420 for 4 days. A more economical car can cope with the roads if you go carefully; ask the rental agency's advice. If driving there yourself, the shorter new road from Puerto Natales is narrow with lots of blind corners and sudden gusts of wind and can be rough in patches. In the park, the roads are also narrow and winding with blind corners: use your horn a lot. Always fill up with fuel in Puerto Natales.

Tierra del Fuego

The western side of this, the largest island off the extreme south of South America, belongs to Chile and the eastern to Argentina. Here the Andes cordillera runs from west to east, so that the north of the island is flat, covered with vast sheep farms, while the south has mountains, glaciers, lakes and forests. The major population centres, Ushuaia and Río Grande, are on the Argentine side, but Chile has the most southerly town in the world, Puerto Williams, on the island Isla Navarino below Tierra del Fuego. See Argentine Tierra del Fuego for background information.

Porvenir and around → Phone code: 061. Colour map 9, C2. Population: 5100.

Porvenir is a quiet, pleasant place with many inhabitants of Croatian descent. Founded in 1894 in the gold boom, when many people came seeking fortunes from Croatia and Chiloé, it's a quiet, pleasant place with neat, painted tin houses and neatly trimmed yew trees lining the main avenue. There is a small museum, the **Museo Provincial Fernando Cordero Rusque** ⓘ *Zavattaro 402, T581800, www.museoporvenir.cl, Mon-Thu 0900-1700, Fri 0900-1600, Sat-Sun 1030-1330, 1500-1700, US$0.85*, with archaeological and photographic displays on the Selk'nam (Onas); good displays on natural history and the early colonisers. **Mirador de la Ciudad** is a walkable excursion round the bay from Porvenir and uphill to the radio aerials. **Tourist information**: the best information is at the museum. There are tourist notice boards outside the Municipalidad, on seafront and elsewhere. A handicrafts stall in a kiosk on the seafront gives tourist information (opposite Comercial Tuto, No 588).

Porvenir is the base for exploring the wonderfully wild virgin territory of Tierra del Fuego. Trips in the south, the more interesting half, must be totally self-sufficient. There are no hotels, shops, petrol stations or public transport. The only town in the south is Cameron, on the southern shore of Bahía Inútil. In the north, there is fuel and lodging at **Cerro Sombrero**, 46 km south of Primera Angostura, a village built to administrate oil drilling in the area, and a hostal and a place to eat in San Sebastián. There is no car hire on the island and no public transport to Argentina.

North of Porvenir, 6 km, is the **Monumento Natural Laguna de los Cisnes**. Access is across private land; the owner will give permission. Another place to see wildfowl, including black-necked swans from December is **Laguna Santa María**, not far from Porvenir on road to **Bahía Inútil**, a wonderful windswept bay. Cabo Boquerón, the headland at the start of Bahía Inútil, has great views on a clear day, as far as Cabo Froward, Isla Dawson and the distant Cordillera Darwin's snow peaks. Driving east along the bay you pass Los Canelos, with trees, a rare sight, and then the junction for the Cordón Baquedano, on the **Circuito de Oro**. This is a recommended tour, on which you can see gold panning using the same techniques since mining began in 1881, a four-hour, 115-km round trip. Miner Sr Jorge Gesell Díaz is happy to show tourists his workings (very enthusiastic), in summer only. Write in his visitors' book and leave a tip.

The main road east goes to **Onaisin**, 99 km east of Porvenir, and the Argentine border at San Sebastián. A road south at Onaisin passes Caleta Josefina, a handsome ex-estancia built in 1833, where some old buildings remain. To the most southerly point by road, Estancia Lago Fagnano, and the most southerly habitation at Río Azopardo, is four hours. The government is hoping to complete the road to **Yendegaia** with a view to having a summer route, including ferry, to Puerto Navarino, for Puerto Williams; work is underway. This would traverse the new Parque Nacional Yendegaia (created December 2013, www.theconservationlandtrust.org), which adjoins the Parque Naciona Tierra del Fuego in Argentina. Other options are sailing from Porvenir to **Río Cóndor** across Bahía Inútil, south of Cameron, with trekking or riding from Cameron to **Seno Almirantazgo**, a beautiful, wild and treeless place, where mountains sink into blue fjords with icebergs. A large part of the peninsula between Bahía Inútil and Seno Almirantazgo is the **Karukinka** nature reserve (www.karukinkanatural.cl). Also sailing to **Marinelli glacier**, where you can sail, kayak and dive. Fly fishing is world-renowned. The area is rich in brown trout, sea-run brook trout and steelheads, weighing 2-14 kg.

Border with Argentina → *Argentine time is 1 hr ahead of Chilean time, Mar-Oct.*

The only legal border crossing between the Chilean and Argentine parts of Tierra del Fuego is 142 km east of Porvenir at **San Sebastián**; open 0800-2200. On the Argentine side the road continues to Río Grande. **Note** There are two settlements called San Sebastián, on each side of the border but they are 14 km apart; taxis are not allowed to cross. No fruit, vegetables, dairy produce or meat permitted on entry to Chile. For entry to Argentina, see Argentina chapter.

Puerto Williams → *Phone code: 061. Colour map 9, C2. Population: 2300, less than half civilian.*

Puerto Williams is a Chilean naval base on **Isla Navarino**, which is south of the Beagle Channel. About 50 km south east of Ushuaia (Argentina) at 54° 55' 41" south, 67° 37' 58" west, it is small, friendly and remote. The island is totally unspoilt and beautiful, offering great geographical diversity, thanks to **Dientes de Navarino** mountain range, with peaks over 1000 m, covered with southern beech forest up to 500 m, and, south of that, great plains covered in peat bogs, with many lagoons and abundant in flora. The island was the centre of the indigenous Yaganes culture and there are 500 archaeological sites, with the oldest dating from around 3000 years ago. The town is a mixture of neat naval housing and the more haphazard civilian building with some impressive, modern municipal and school buildings. On an inlet at western edge is the Micalvi, an old naval vessel which is now HQ of the yacht club. **Museo Martín Gusinde** ① *www. museoantropologico martingusinde.cl, Nov-Mar Tue-Fri 0930-1300, 1500-1800, Sat-Sun 1430-1830, Apr-Oct Tue-Fri 0930-1330, 1430-1730, Sat 1430-1830, US$1*, is full of information about vanished tribes, local wildlife, and voyages including Charles Darwin and Fitzroy of the *Beagle*, a must. Businesses in town accept US dollars; there is a Centro Comercial, minimarkets and a hospital. **Tourist information** ① *Municipalidad de Cabos de Hornos, O'Higgins 293, T262 1011, www. ptowilliams.cl/Turismo.html, closed in winter.* They may have maps and details on hiking, but it is probably as good, if not better, to get information from agencies, such as Shila (see What to do, below). **CONAF** ① *Carabinero M Leal 106, T262 1303, miguel.gallardo@conaf.cl.*

Around Puerto Williams

For superb views, climb **Cerro Bandera** (three to four hours' round trip, steep, take warm clothes). **Villa Ukika**, 2 km east of town, is where the last descendants of the Yaganes people live, relocated from their original homes at Caleta Mejillones (an old, overgrown cemetery marks the spot on the road to Puerto Navarino). There is excellent trekking around the **Dientes de Navarino**, the southernmost trail in the world, through impressive mountain landscapes, with superb views of Beagle Channel (challenging, 53 km in five days, November to March, snowfall permitting, good level of fitness needed). Also to Laguna Windhond, four days, and others all over island.

Cape Horn

It is possible to catch a boat south from Isla Navarino to Cape Horn (the most southerly piece of land on earth apart from Antarctica). There is one pebbly beach on the north side of the island; boats anchor in the bay and passengers are taken ashore by motorized dinghy. A stairway climbs the cliff above the beach, up to the building where a naval officer and his family run the lighthouse and naval post. A path leads from here to the impressive monument of an albatross overlooking the wild, churning waters of the Drake Passage below. **Australis Expedition Cruises** ships call here (see page 806).

◉ Tierra del Fuego listings

For hotel and restaurant price codes, and other relevant information, see Essentials.

⊖ Where to stay

Porvenir *p819*

$$$ Hostería Yendegaia, Croacia 702, T258 1919, www.hosteriayendegaia.com. Comfortable, family-run inn with good facilities and helpful staff. English-speaking owner runs birdwatching tours and to the king penguins.
$$ Central, Phillipi 298, T258 0077, opposite Rosas. All rooms with bath.
$$ España, Croacia 698, T258 0540, www.hotelespana.cl. Comfortable, well equipped, light and spacious rooms, helpful and friendly. Good restaurant with food all day.
$$ Rosas, Phillipi 296, T258 0088, hotelrosas@chile.com. Heating, restaurant and bar.
$ pp Hostal Kawi, Pedro Silva 144, T258 1638, hostalkawi@yahoo.com. Comfortable, rooms for 3, meals available, offers fly-fishing trips.

Elsewhere in Chilean Tierra del Fuego

$$$-$$ Hostería Tunkelen, Arturo Prat Chacón 101, Cerro Sombrero, T061-221 2757, www.hosteriatunkelen.cl. 3 buildings with rooms of different standards: with private bathrooms, shared bathrooms or backpacker dorms. Restaurant. Good for groups.

Border with Argentina: San Sebastián *p820*

$$-$ Hostería de la Frontera, T061-269 6004, frontera@entelchile.net. Where some buses stop for meals and cakes, cosy, with bath (the annex is much more basic), good food.

Puerto Williams *p820*

$$$$ Lakutaia, 2 km west of town, T8429 6630 (Santiago: T02-946 2703), www.lakutaia.cl. A 'base camp' for a range of activities and packages (riding, trekking, birdwatching, sailing, flights), 24 double rooms in simple but attractive style, lovely views from spacious public areas, bikes for hire, 3 golf 'holes' – most southerly in world!
$$ Forjadores de Cabo de Hornos, Uspashun 58, Plaza B O'Higgins, T262 1140, www.hostalforjadoresdelcabodehornos.cl. Simple place to stay, meals, agency for tours and transport, welcoming.
$$ Hostal Akainij, Austral 22, T262 1173, www.turismoakainij.cl. Comfortable rooms, very helpful, excellent, filling meals, basic English spoken, adventure tours and transfers.
$$ Hostal Coirón, Ricardo Maragaño 168, T262 1227, or through **Ushaia Boating** or **Sim Ltda** (see What to do). Double rooms or dorms, shared bath, helpful, good food, relaxed, quite basic, but OK.
$$ Hostal Pusaki, Piloto Pardo 222, T262 1116, http://hostalpusaki.wix.com/pusaki#!. Double

room or dorms, good meals available, owner Patty is helpful and fun.
$$ Hostal Yagan, Piloto Pardo 260, T262 1118, hostalyagan@hotmail.com (HostalYagan on Facebook). Comfortable, some rooms with bath, meals available, run by Daniel Yevenes, who offers tours and transport to Ushuaia.
$$ Refugio El Padrino, Costanera 276, T262 1136, T8438 0843, ceciliamancillao@yahoo.com.ar. The vivacious Cecilia Mancilla is great fun, good food.

❼ Restaurants

Porvenir *p819*
$$ Club Croata, Señoret entre Phillippi y Muñoz Gamero, next to the bus stop on the waterfront. A lively place with good food.
$$-$ El Chispa, Señoret 202, T258 0054. Good restaurant for seafood and other Chilean dishes.
$$-$ La Picá de Pechuga, Bahía Chilote s/n, by ferry dock. Good fresh seafood and fish. Owner Juan Bahamonde runs **Cordillero de Darwin** tours (see below):
$ Panadería El Paine, Sampaio 368. Shop and tea room, very friendly.

Puerto Williams *p820*
$$-$ Café Angelus, Centro Comercial Norte 151, T262 1080. Also travel agent and transport. Run by Loreto Camino, friendly cheerful atmosphere, small, good simple cooking, coffee (including Irish), beer.
$ Los Dientes de Navarino, Centro Comercial Sur. Popular with locals, limited fare.
Panaderías and minimarkets: **Simón & Simón** and **Temuco** are opposite each other on Piloto Pardo, junction Condell. The former seems to be centre of reference in town.

❹ What to do

Porvenir *p819*
For adventure tourism and trekking activities contact tour operators in Punta Arenas (see What to do, page 806).
Turismo Cordillera de Darwin, run by Juan 'Pechuga' Bahamonde, T09-9888 6380, or T061-258 0167, gerencia@cordilleradarwin.com or jebr_darwin@hotmail.com (cordilleradarwin on Facebook). Runs land, fishing and boating

tours. 4-hr Oro circuit without lunch; with lunch, 0800-1700 including Laguna Santa María. Costs of tours to far south vary according to circumstances. Boat and fishing trips, 6 days allowing a day for unforeseen delays.

Puerto Williams *p820*
Boat trips Victory Adventures, Tte Muñoz 118, Casilla 70, T061-222 7089, www.victory-cruises.com, Captain Ben Garrett and his family run this online travel agency for many tours and expeditions around Tierra del Fuego, Patagonia and the southern oceans to Antarctica. They also have the **$$$-$$ Hostal Bella Vista** B&B, rooms and suites sleep 1-4, internet services and a minimarket. **Australis Expedition Cruises**, Av El Bosque Norte 0440, p 11, Las Condes, Santiago, T02-2442 3115, www.australis.com (see page 806), call at Wulaia Bay on the west side of Isla Navarino after visiting Cape Horn; you can disembark to visit the museum and take a short trek.
Trekking You must register first with Carabineros on C Piloto Pardo, near Brito. Tell them when you get back, too. Sometimes they will not allow lone trekking.

Tour operators
Akainij, see Where to stay.
Sea, Ice and Mountains, Ricardo Maragaño 168, T262 1150, www.simltd.com. Sailing trips, trekking tours and many other adventure activities, including kayaking and wildlife spotting.
Shila, O'Higgins 322 (a hut at entrance to Centro Comercial), T7897 2005, www.turismoshila.cl. Luis Tiznado Gonzales is an adventure guide, trekking and fishing, equipment hire (bikes, tents, sleeping bags, stoves, and more). Lots of trekking information, sells photocopied maps.

❺ Transport

Ferries to Tierra del Fuego
There are 2 crossings. The ferry company accepts no responsibility for damage to vehicles.
Punta Arenas to Porvenir The Crux Australis, sails from Tres Puentes (5 km north of Punta Arenas, bus A or E from Av Magallanes, or colectivo 15, US$1; taxi US$5) at 0900 or 1500-

1600, no service Mon in season; less frequent sailings off season. **Tabsa/Transboradora Austral Broom**, Bulnes 5075 (Tres Puentes), T272 8100, www.tabsa.cl or through **Comapa**, see Punta Arenas Tour operators. 2½-hr crossing (can be rough and cold, watch for dolphins), US$11 pp, US$19 motorcycle, US$67 per vehicle. Boat disembarks at Bahía Chilota, 5 km from Porvenir, bus US$1.50; bus drops you where you want to go in town. Return from Porvenir varying times in afternoon between 1400 and 1900, daily except Mon. Timetable dependent on tides and subject to change; check in advance. Tabsa website gives monthly schedules. Reservations for cars essential, especially in summer. Tabsa have an office on Señoret, seafront in Porvenir, T258 0089, open Mon-Fri 0900-1200, 1400-1830.

Punta Delgada to Punta Espora (Bahía Azul) This crossing is via the Primera Angostura (First Narrows), 170 km northeast of Punta Arenas (Punta Espora is 80 km north of Porvenir) There are three boats working continuously. On board is a café, lounge, toilets and decks for getting splashed. Buses can wait up to 90 minutes to board. Boats run 0830-2400, 20 mins' crossing, US$21 per vehicle, US$7 motorcycle, foot passengers US$3, www tabsa.cl. The ferries takes about 4 trucks and 20 cars; before 1000 most space is taken by trucks. There is no bus service to or from this crossing. If hitching, this route is preferable as there is more traffic.

Porvenir *p819*

Air From Punta Arenas – weather and bookings permitting, **Aerovías DAP**, Señoret s/n, T258 0089, Porvenir, www.aeroviasdap.cl, details under Punta Arenas, Transport. Heavily booked so make sure you have your return reservation confirmed.

Bus The only public transport on Chilean Tierra del Fuego is Jorge Bastian's minibus Porvenir– Cerro Sombrero, T234 5406/8503-

3662, jorgebastian@hotmail.com, or the driver axelvig20@hotmail.com. Mon, Wed, Fri, leaves Sombrero 0830, 0700 on Mon, returns from Porvenir Municipalidad, 2 hrs, US$4.50.

Road All roads are good *ripio* except paved from Bahía Chilota to Porvenir and in Porvenir itself.

Puerto Williams *p820*

Air From Punta Arenas with DAP (details under Punta Arenas). Book well in advance; long waiting lists (be persistent). The flight is beautiful (sit on right from Punta Arenas) with superb views of Tierra del Fuego, the Cordillera Darwin, the Beagle Channel, and the islands stretching south to Cape Horn. Also army flights available (they are cheaper), but the ticket has to be bought through DAP. Also from the Aeroclub in Ushuaia (see Ushuaia, Transport). Airport is in town.

Boat Yaghan ferry of Broom, www.tabsa.cl, from **Punta Arenas** once a week, 24 passengers, US$165 for chair, US$230 for Pullman, 30-34-hr trip through beautiful channels. Will not take passengers if carrying petrol, so ask in advance. From **Ushuaia** with Ushuaia Boating, US$120 each way, which includes a 30-90 min crossing in a semi-rigid boat to Puerto Navarino, a jetty, the Alcaldía del Mar and 4 more houses, plus a few horses and cows. Despite Ushuaia Boating dealing with documents when you buy the ticket, there is a lot of hanging around at Puerto Navarino, but the setting is nice and they sometimes offer coffee and pastries for impatient passengers. Then it's a 1 hr ride in a combi on a lovely, *ripio* road past inlets and forests, river outflows, Bahía Mejillones and birdlife to Williams. For return make sure you are clear about transport arrangements. Also **Fernández Campbell** have a 1½-hr crossing from **Ushuaia**, Fri, Sat, Sun 1000, return 1500, US$125 for foreigners, tickets sold at **Naviera RFC** in Puerto Williams and **Zenit Explorer**, Juana Fadul 126, Ushuaia, T02901-433232.

Chilean Pacific Islands

Chile has two national parks in the Pacific: Juan Fernández Islands, a little easier to reach (and leave) now than in Robinson Crusoe's time, and the remarkable Easter Island.

Juan Fernández Islands → *Phone code: 032. Population: 500.*

This group of small volcanic islands is administered by CONAF and is situated 667 km west of Valparaíso. The **CONAF** office ⓘ *Vicente González 130, T268 0381, parque njfernandez@yahoo. com, Mon-Fri 0800-1250, 1400-1800,* can give information on flora, fauna and services. Park entry is US$5.50, children US$1.50. Declared a UN World Biosphere Reserve in 1977, the islands enjoy a mild climate and the vegetation is rich and varied. Fauna includes wild goats, hummingbirds and seals. The best time to visit is October-March; take insect repellent. The islands are named after Juan Fernández, the first European to visit in 1574. There are three islands, Robinson Crusoe, the largest, which was the home (1704-1709) of Alexander Selkirk (the original of Defoe's Robinson Crusoe), Alejandro Selkirk and Santa Clara, the smallest. Selkirk's cave on the beach of Robinson Crusoe, about 4 km northwest of the village, can be visited on a boat trip. The only settlement is San Juan Bautista on Robinson Crusoe Island, a fishing village of wooden frame houses, located on Bahía Cumberland on the north coast of the island: many facilities close to the shore were destroyed by the February 2010 tsunami. The islands are famous for langosta de Juan Fernández (a pincerless lobster) which is sent to the mainland.

Robinson Crusoe Island The remains of the **Fuerte Santa Bárbara**, the largest of the Spanish fortresses, overlook San Juan Bautista. The island has long been the target for treasure seekers who claim that looted gold from Inca times is buried there. Near Santa Bárbara are the **Cuevas de los Patriotas**, home to the Chilean independence leaders, deported by the Spanish after the Battle of Rancagua. South of the village is the **Mirador de Selkirk**, the hill where Selkirk lit his signal fires. A plaque was set in the rock at the look-out point by British naval officers from *HMS Topaze* in 1868; nearby is a more recent plaque placed by his descendants. (Selkirk, a Scot, was put ashore from *HMS Cinque Ports* and was taken off four years and four months later by a privateer, the *Duke*.) The Mirador is the only easy pass between the north and south sides of the island. Further south is the anvil-shaped **El Yunque**, 915 m, the highest peak on the island, where Hugo Weber, a survivor from the *Dresden*, lived as a hermit for 12 years. (The *Dresden* was a German cruiser, cornered by two British destroyers in Bahía Cumberland in 1915; the scuttled *Dresden* still lies on the seabed and a monument on the shore commemorates the event.) The only sandy beach on Robinson Crusoe is **Playa Arenal**, in the extreme southwest corner, two hours by boat from San Juan Bautista.

There are no exchange facilities. Only pesos and US dollars cash are accepted; no credit cards and no traveller's cheques.

ⓔ Juan Fernández Islands listings

For hotel and restaurant price codes, and other relevant information, see Essentials.

ⓔ Where to stay

Juan Fernández Islands *p824*
$$$$ Crusoe Island Lodge, T02-2946 1636, 9-9078 1301, www.crusoeislandlodge.com. An ecolodge which offers many packages and activities, as well as therapies in its spa. It also has a gourmet restaurant.
$$$$ Más a Tierra Ecolodge, Subida el Castillo 128, T09-5379 1915, www.masatierra ecolodge.com. Bed-and-breakfast or half-board available, 4 rooms with bath and terrace, price includes welcome drink, internet, use of kayaks, tours arranged.

See www.comunajuanfernandez.cl, www.
sernatur.cl and www.turismorobinsoncrusoe.
com for other accommodation options.

⊖ Transport

Juan Fernández Islands *p824*
Air Aerolíneas ATA, Av Diego Barros Ortiz
2012B, **Aeropuerto Arturo Merino Benítez**,
T2611 3670 (on Robinson Crusoe T9-7389

1826), www.aerolineasata.cl, and **LASSA**, Av
Larraín 7941, **Tobalaba**, T2734 3353, lassa@
tie.cl, fly the year round (subject to demand)
from **Santiago**, 2½ hrs (US$975 round trip).
Planes leave from Tobalaba Aerodrome in La
Reina (eastern outskirts of city) and land on an
airstrip in the west of the island; passengers
are taken by boat to San Juan Bautista (1½ hrs,
US$2 one way). For cargo by sea, see http://
navieraiorana.cl.

Rapa Nui/Easter Island → *Phone code: 032 and 039. Always 2 hrs behind the Chilean mainland.*

Known as the navel of the world by the original inhabitants, this is one of the remotest places on
earth. Isla de Pascua (Rapa Nui) is just south of the Tropic of Capricorn, 3790 km west of Chile and
4050 km from the Great Polynesian Archipelago (at Tahiti). Its nearest neighbour is Pitcairn
Island, some 2081 km away.

The cultural and archeological treasures of Easter Island were the first of any Pacific island
nation to be registered by UNESCO on its World Heritage list. From its past the most potent
symbols are the giant carved statues, *moai*, that appear trance-like in a stunning landscape, their
gaze fixed on a distant horizon on the Pacific. The tangible evidence of these statues, historic
dwellings and petroglyphs far exceeds that of any other in Polynesia, Melanesia and Micronesia.
Whereas other Pacific nations can claim an impressive intangible heritage (story telling,
music and dance), but little in terms of structures and artwork, Easter Island has both tangible
and intangible heritage of epic proportions. Here are some of the most impressive and
mysterious sites on earth. Climb Rano Raraku volcano, dotted with caves and moai, overlooking
the magnificent statues of Ahu Tongariki against the backdrop of waves crashing on the rocky
coast, or visit Rano Kau volcano with the ancient city of Orongo on its rim, overlooking both the
crater lake and the vast Pacific Ocean, and you cannot fail to be overawed.

Arriving at Easter Island
Information Isla de Pascua is officially part of V Región of Chile (Valparaíso). **Sernatur**
① *C Policarpo Toro s/n, T210 0255, lpascua@sernatur.cl, Mon-Fri 0900-1800, Sat 0900-1400*. Useful
websites include http://Islandheritage.org (**Easter Island Foundation**, in English), www.rapanui.
co.cl, the Easter Island Newspaper. The book, *A Companion to Easter Island*, by James Grant
Peterkin (the British Consul, c/o Easter Island Spirit, Tu'u Koihu s/n, T210 0024, james@
easterislandspirit.com), in English, is on sale on the island and in Santiago airport. Average
monthly temperatures vary between 15-17°C in August and 24° C in February, the hottest
month. Average annual rainfall is 1100 mm. There is some rain throughout the year, but the rainy
season is March to October (wettest in May). The tourist season is from September to April.
Anyone wishing to spend time exploring the island would be well-advised to speak to **CONAF**
first ① *Mataveri Otai s/n, T210 0236, hotu.pate@conaf.cl*; they also give good advice on special
interests (biology, archaeology, handicrafts, etc).

History of Easter Island
The island is triangular in shape, 24 km across, with an extinct volcano at each corner. It is now
generally accepted that the islanders are of Polynesian origin (see below for the historical and
cultural contexts). European contact with the island began in the 18th century, followed by
tragic Peruvian rule from 1862. The island was annexed by Chile in 1888.

The original islanders called the island *Te Pito o te Henua*, the navel of the world. The population
was stable at 4000 until the 1850s, when, for reasons described below, numbers were reduced.

The cultural development of Easter Island

Among the prominent theories concerning the colonization of Easter Island, those of the late Thor Heyerdahl, as expressed in *Aku-Aku, The Art of Easter Island* (1975), based on South American influence, became less widely accepted as the theory of Polynesian origin gained ascendency. It was believed that colonizers came from possibly the Marquesas Islands or Mangareva, between about AD 400-600 and by AD 1000 the island's society was established.

The very precise stone fitting of some of the *ahu*, and the tall gaunt *moai* with elongated faces and ears for which Easter Island is best known came quite late in the development of island culture. The *moai* were sculpted at the Rano Raraku quarry and transported on wooden rollers over more or less flat paths to their final locations; their red topknots were sculpted at and brought from the inland quarry of Puna Pau; and the rounded pebbles laid out checkerboard fashion at the *ahu* all came from the same beach at Vinapu.

The theory held that with the growth in sophistication of Easter Island society, almost all the island's trees were felled. The wood was used for building fishing vessels and most probably for transporting and supporting statues. Deforestation led to soil erosion, the extinction of up to half the native plants, loss of nesting sites for birds and no means of making fishing boats. Rapa Nui, according to Jared Diamond in *Collapse: How Societies Choose to Fail or Succeed* (2005), was "the clearest

example of a society that destroyed itself by overexploiting its own resources". What followed were brutal wars between the clans that erupted by the end of 17th century.

After the islanders had lost their clan territoriality and were concentrated at Hanga Roa, inter-clan rivalry was stimulated by the birdman cult at Orongo. The central feature was an annual ceremony in which the heads of the lineages, or their representatives, raced to the islets of Motu Nui, Motu Iti and Motu Kao to obtain the first egg of the sooty tern (known as the Manatara). The winning chief was named Bird Man, Tangata Manu, for the following year. It appears that the egg represented fertility to the cult, although it is less clear what the status of the Tangata Manu actually was.

The "ecocide" theory and almost everything to do with it was questioned by Carl Lipo and Terry Hunt (*The Statues that Walked* -2011). They claim that Polynesians arrived in about AD 1200, that the rats that arrived with them caused far greater destruction of the palm forests, by eating the tree roots, than the humans, that the statues were "walked", not rolled to their ceremonial sites (much as Heyerdahl demonstrated) and that the population, after rapid growth, was stable until the arrival of Europeans. The environment was damaged, but as other research has proposed, the people learnt how to prevent soil erosion by "sowing" stones on their fields and supplemented their diet with rat meat. Serious decline was precipitated by the arrival of European diseases, not before.

According to the 2012 census, it has about 5800 residents, of whom some 60% are descendants of the aboriginal Rapa Nui.Most live in the village of **Hanga Roa**. Rapa Nui and Spanish are the official languages. Some people speak English and/or French. Rapa Nui has its own script recorded on tablets. Although not widely used, it is being studied and may be implemented again. The islanders have preserved their indigenous songs and dances, and are extremely hospitable. About half the island, of low round hills with groves of eucalyptus, is used for horses and cattle, and over a third constitutes a **national park** (entry US$53, children US$9 – Chileans pay less, payable at the airport when flights arrive, or at the Conaf office, address above, 0900-1600).

The box, above, gives a very brief overview of theories of how *Easter Island* culture originated. Over 1000 years of isolation ended in 1722 with the visit of the Dutch admiral, Jacob Roggeven, on Easter Sunday 1722. A Spanish captain, Don Felipe González, arrived in 1770 and claimed the island for the King of Spain, but no Spanish ship came to make it official. British Captain James Cook stopped briefly in 1774, and a French admiral and explorer, le Comte de La Pérouse, spent 11 hours on the island in 1786. Early visitors spent very little time on the island because of the lack of wood and drinking water, but first encounters led to tragic consequences, first with the introduction of diseases, principally venereal, by whalers in the 1800s.

In 1862 eight Peruvian ships kidnapped one third of the population of the island, including the King. Most were sold to hard labour on plantations, others as domestic servants. Many died and international outcry forced Peru to repatriate the islanders. Even this task was handled with utmost neglect, so that, out of 1407 Rapa Nui originally taken, only 15 made it back to their homeland. Further indignities ensued, first in 1864, when the religious order, Société de Picpus, brought new diseases in its mission to christianize the eastern Pacific, followed by French sea captain Jean-Baptiste Onéxime Dutroux-Bornier, charged with transporting missionaries to the island, deciding to become its sole ruler. Dutroux-Bornier and the missionaries clashed as each shipped islanders out, the former to plantations in Tahiti, the latter to missions elsewhere. With only 175 islanders left, the Frenchman was murdered, but, historians believe, by that time, the culture and traditions of Rapa Nui had been irreversibly destroyed.

In 1888 Captain Policarpo Toro Hurtado took formal possession of the island and the chiefs ceded sovereignty to Chile 'for ever'. In fact, a single wool company became the new ruler and yet again treatment of the islanders was so appalling that in desperation, the Rapa Nui petitioned the Chilean government to allow them to emigrate en masse to Tahiti. A rebellion erupted in 1914 and the Chilean navy was sent to restore order. In 1953 the Chilean government took over the administration of the island, but it was not until 1967, the year of the first regular commercial flight, that relaxation of colonial rules took place and interests of the islanders were taken into consideration.

Modern Easter Island Although part of Chile, Easter Island is run (at least in theory) by an independent Council of Chiefs and elected local officials. Chile provides good education and health care for all and the local diet is much healthier than on many Pacific islands. The range of services includes a modern mobile phone network, reliable internet, a television station, stadium, gymnasiums, a modern bank and excellent running water and electricity. Foreigners and Chileans from the mainland cannot own land on Easter Island, even if they live and work there, or are married to a local. Nevertheless, islanders own very little land outside Hanga Roa; the national park covers more than a third of the island, but negotiations for land outside this being returned are in progress. Easter Islanders do not pay taxes and they refuse entry to insurance companies, junk food outlets, public buses and other concepts they find hostile to their traditional culture. In 2007, a constitutional reform gave Easter Island and Juan Fernández the status of special territories. Administratively, it belongs to the Valparaíso Region and is the only commune of the Provincia de Isla de Pascua. The flag of Easter Island is white charged with a red reimiro, a wooden pectoral ornament once worn by the women of the island. It was adopted on 9 May 2006.

Places on Easter Island

The unique features of the island are the 800 (or so) *moai*, huge stone figures up to 9 m tall and broad in proportion. One of them, on **Anakena** beach, was restored to its (probably) original state with a plaque commemorating Thor Heyerdahl's visit in 1955. Others have since been re-erected.

In theory, a tour of the main part of the island can be done on foot. This would need at least two days, returning to Hanga Roa and setting out again the next day as camping is not permitted in the park (see page 830). To see more, hire a bicycle, a horse or a vehicle. Even with a car you will need at least two nights as to see a minimum of sights requires one long day. Far better is to allow more time to explore. From Hanga Roa, take the road going southeast past the airport; at the oil tanks turn right to Vinapu, where there are two *ahu* and a wall whose stones are joined with Inca-like precision. Head back northeast along the south coast, past Vaihu (an *ahu* with eight broken *moai*; small harbour); Akahanga (ahu with toppled moai); Hanga Tetenga (one toppled moai, bones can be seen inside the *ahu*), Ahu Tongariki (once the largest platform, damaged by a tidal wave in 1960). Turn left to Rano Raraku (20 km), the volcano where the moai were carved. Many statues can be seen, some of them buried to the neck, a breathtaking sight. In the crater is a small lake surrounded by reeds (swimming possible beyond reeds). Good views and a good place to watch the sunrise.

The road heads north past 'the trench of the long-ears' and an excursion can be made to **Poike** to see the open-mouthed statue that is particularly popular with local carvers (ask farmer for permission to cross his land). On Poike the earth is red; at the northeast end is the cave where the virgin was kept before marriage to the victor of ceremonies during the birdman cult. The road along the north coast passes Ahu Te Pito Kura, a round stone called the navel of the world and one of the largest moai ever brought to a platform. It continues to Ovahe, where there is a very attractive beach with pink sand, some rather recently carved faces and a cave.

From Ovahe, one can return direct to Hanga Roa or continue to Anakena, site of **King Hotu Matua's village** and Thor Heyerdahl's landing place. From Anakena, a coastal path of variable quality passes interesting remains and beautiful cliff scenery. At Hanga o Teo there appears to be a large village complex, with several round houses, and further on there is a burial place, built like a long ramp with several ditches containing bones. From Hanga o Teo the path goes west then south, inland from the coast, to meet the road north of Hanga Roa.

The path around the north of the island skirts the island's highest point, the extinct volcano of Terevaka (507 m), to which you can trek for a view of the ocean on all sides.

A six-hour walk from Hanga Roa on the west coast passes **Ahu Tahai** (a moai with eyes and topknot, cave house, a 15-minute walk from town and in itself a great place for watching the sunset). Two caves are reached, one inland appears to be a ceremonial centre, the other (nearer the sea) has two 'windows' (take a strong flashlight and be careful near the 'windows'). Further north is Ahu Tepeu (broken *moai*, ruined houses). Beyond here you can join the path mentioned above, or turn right to Te Pahu cave and the seven moai at Akhivi, which look straight into the setting sun. Either return to Hanga Roa, or go to Puna Pau crater (two hours), where the topknots were carved (good views from the three crosses at the top).

Rano Kau, south of Hanga Roa, is another important site to visit; one finds the curious Orongo ruins here. The route south out of Hanga Roa passes the two caves of Ana Kai Tangata, one of which has paintings. If on foot you can take a path from the Orongo road, just past the CONAF sign, which is a much shorter route to Rano Kau crater. A lake with many reed islands lies 200 m below. On the seaward side is Orongo, where the birdman cult flourished, with many ruined buildings and petroglyphs. Out to sea are the 'bird islets', Motu Nui, Motu Iti and Motu Kao. It is very windy at the summit; good views at sunset, or under a full moon (it is easy to follow the road back to Hanga Roa in the dark).

In Hanga Roa is **Ahu Tautira**, in front of the football field and next to a swimming area marked out with concrete walls and a breakwater (cold water). Music at the 0900 Sunday Mass is 'enchanting', well worth going. **Museo Arqueológico Padre Sebastián Englert** ⓘ *2 km north of town, very near Ahu Tahai, T255 1020, www.museorapanui.cl, Tue-Fri 0930-1730, Sat, Sun, holidays 0930-1230, closed 25 Dec, 1 Jan, Good Friday and 1 May; open morning only 17 Sep, 24 and 31 Dec, US$2*, small but good collection of original items, history and maps; often arranges exhibitions, films and concerts. It has a good gift shop with books in Spanish and English, handicrafts and paintings and a great little café. In the same complex is the excellent **William Molloy Library** ⓘ *Tue-Fri 0930-1230, only locals are allowed to borrow books*. There is a cultural centre next to the football field, with an exhibition hall and souvenir stall.

⊚ Rapa Nui/Easter Island listings

*For hotel and restaurant price codes, and other
relevant information, see Essentials.*

⊜ Where to stay

Rapa Nui/Easter Island *p825*
Unless it is a particularly busy season, there is
no need to book in advance; mainland agencies
make exorbitant booking charges. The airport
information desk has an accommodation list.
Flights are met by large numbers of hotel and
residencial representatives with whom you can
negotiate. Alternatively, take a taxi to the centre
of Hanga Roa, drop your things in a café and
look around. Many places offer accommodation
and tours (rates ranging from US$25 to
US$150 pp, includes meals). Rates, especially in
residenciales, can be cheaper out of season and
if you do not take full board.
$$$$ Explora En Rapa Nui, reserve in Santiago
T02-2395 2800, in US T1-866 750 6699, or
through www.explora.com. All-inclusive hotel,
easily one of the poshest in the South Pacific.
Intentionally hard to find (take Cross Island
road, turn right about 6 km from town on the
wider unpaved road), transport provided for
guests, as are all food, drinks and tours. Views
of the ocean are tremendous and each room
has a jacuzzi.
$$$$ Gomero, Av Tu'u'Koihu, T210 0313, www.
hotelgomero.com. Comfortable place near the
beach, spotless, cosy rooms. Restaurant, pool.
$$$$ Hanga Roa, Av Pont, T02-2957 0300,
www.hotelhangaroa.cl. The largest hotel in
town, within walking distance of centre. Full
board, excellent ocean views, spa and pool.
$$$$ Iorana, Ana Magara s/n, outside Hanga
Roa, opposite airport, 30 mins' walk from town,
T210 0608 (Santiago T02-2695 2058), www.
ioranahotel.cl. 3-star, hot water morning and
evening, comfortable, small pool, good views.
$$$$ O'Tai, Te Pilo Te Henua s/n, T210 0250,
www.hotelotai.com. Great location, pool, lovely
gardens, restaurants, best rooms with terrace,
family-run.
$$$$ Taha Tai, Api Na Nui s/n, T255 1192,
www.hoteltahatai.cl. Well-kept bright
hotel with rooms or cabins, sea view, small
swimming pool, tours organized.

$$$$-$$$ Chez Cecilia, Policarpo Toro y
Atamu Tekema, near Tahai Moai, T210 0499,
www.rapanuichezcecilia.com. Packages with
tours offered, excellent food, Rooms, *cabañas*
or camping, quiet, free airport transfer.
$$$$-$$$ Taura'a, C Principal s/n, T210 0463,
www.tauraahotel.cl. Upmarket B&B, very comfy,
good beds, spacious bathrooms, nice garden,
good service. **Taura'a Tours** is also good.
$$$ Cabañas Mahevi, Kaituoe s/n, T8742
3987, maheva_hiturangi@hotmail.com.
Cabins for 3-4 people, furnished with
kitchen or microwave, breakfast available,
near airport, views of Ranu Kau volcano.
Packages up to 5 nights available, also
car hire, island tours.
$$$ Cabañas Sunset, near Ahu Tahai site and
old cemetery, T255 2171. Spotless *cabañas*
overlooking the sea, discounts for Handbook
users, ask for the owner, Ms 'China' Pakarati. She
also arranges full day tours for groups of 1-4.
$$$ HI Kona Tau, Avareipua, T210 0321,
HI hostel, **$** pp in dorms, all rooms with bath
$$$ Inaki Uhi, Atamu Tekena s/n, T255 1160,
www.inakiuhi.com. Clean hostel and a central,
good option. 15 rooms (triples available). Also
arranges a wide range of tours.
$$$ Mana Nui Inn, Tahai s/n, opp cemetery,
T210 0011, www.mananui.cl. Pleasant cabins
and rooms on north edge of town, airport
transfers, tours run.
$$$ Martín and Anita's hotel, Simón Paoa
s/n, opposite hospital in Hanga Roa, T210 0593,
www.hostal.co.cl. Full board and multi-day
packages available, good food. Can arrange car,
bike and horse hire, guides and tours.
$$$ Orongo, Atamu Tekena s/n, T210 0572,
www.hotelorongo.com. Half-board available
(excellent restaurant), good service, nice garden.
$$$ Res Tadeo y Lili, Apina Ichi s/n, T210 0422,
tadeolili@entelchile.net. Simple but clean,
French-Rapa Nui run, all rooms with sea view
and terrace, tours.
$$$-$$ Ana Rapu, Av Apina, T210 0540,
www.anarapu.cl. Camping US$15.
Legendary budget lodging with great
range of accommodation, rooms or cabins
sleep 1-4, all spotless. Bike and car hire, boat
trips, horse riding and other excursions.

$$ Mihinoa, Av Pont s/n, T255 1593, www.
camping-mihinoa.com. Campsite, which hires
out camping equipment, with a few rooms
and cabin. Huge kitchen for campers, airport
transfers, welcoming, exceptional value.
Camping Camping is not allowed anywhere
in the national park. Many people offer
campsites in their gardens, check availability of
water first. Some families can also provide food.

🍴 Restaurants

Rapa Nui/Easter Island *p825*
Some *residenciales* offer full board. Vegetarians
will have no problems on the island; locally
produced fruit and vegetables are plentiful
and cheaper than meat and other foodstuffs,
which are imported from mainland. Locally
caught fish is also good value. Wine and beer
are expensive by Chilean standards because of
freight charges.
$$$ La Kaleta,Hanga Roa, T255 2244. Superb
ocean views and great seafood. Try the tuna
steak or ceviche, arguably the best on the
island. Tucked away behind the diving schools.
$$$ Te Moana, Hanga Roa. Lovely outdoors
terrace with ocean views, good steaks, fresh
seafood, creative cuisine. Live music at weekends.
$$ Haka Honu, Av Policarpo Toro s/n. Popular
seafood restaurant, excellent tuna carpaccio,
great (and huge) salads. Also good for a cocktail
in the evening. Friendly staff, sea views.
$$ Tataku Vave, Caleta Hanga Piko s/n.
T255 1544. Worth the detour, this ocean front
restaurant offers great pastas and salads, as
well as seafood dishes. One-way taxi fare to the
restaurant included if you book in advance.
$ Mi Kafé Gelatería, Caleta Hanga Roa near
Mike Rapu Diving Center. For real coffee and
good ice cream.
$ Toromiro Café, Av Atamu Tekena s/n,
Excellent Jamaican coffee and great value for
money breakfast and lunch.

For inexpensive local and Chilean food head
to **Ariki o Te Pana** (also known as **Tia Berta**),
Av Atamu Tekena s/n, T 210 0171. Mon-Sat
lunch and dinner. Aunt Berta makes delicioos
empanadas, filled with tuna and cheese, meat,
cheese, veggies etc. Great value at US$6 per
huge empanada. Another local favourite,
Los Carritos, a group of a few cheap eateries
near the football field. Try tuna *empanadas*
and delicious fruit juices at **Carrito Hitu**, Tuu
Maheke s/n (near corner of Apina), which also
has a good *menú del día*.

On Av Te Pito o te Henua near Av Atamu
Tekena is **Donde el Gordo**, the best place for
completo (besides wraps, huge empanadas,
fruit juices etc, at very affordable prices).

🍸 Bars and clubs

Rapa Nui/Easter Island *p825*
Action begins after 0100. Drinks are expensive.
Piriti, near airport. Thu-Sat. **Toroko**, Caleta
Hanga Roa, near harbour. Daily. Slightly
"rougher" ambience. **Topa Tangi**, Atamu
Tekena. Thu and Sat 2300-0300. Popular pub.
On Thu has free shows with dancers.
Traditional music and entertainment
Several in town; one of the best is **Kari Kari** at
Hotel Hanga Roa, T210 0595. 3 times a week,
US$20, very elaborate show.

🎉 Festivals

Rapa Nui/Easter Island *p825*
Tapati, or Semana Rapa Nui, **end-Jan/
beginning-Feb**, lasts about 10 days. Dancing
competitions, singing, sports (horse racing,
swimming, modified decathlon), body-painting,
typical foods (lots of small booths by the
football field), necklace-making, etc. Everyone
gets involved, many tourists too. Only essential
activities continue outside the festival.

🛍 Shopping

Rapa Nui/Easter Island *p825*
All shops and rental offices close 1400-1700.
On Av Atamu Tekena, the main street, there
are lots of small shops and market stalls
(which may close during rain) and a couple of
supermarkets, cheapest **Kai Nene** or **Tumukai**
(good *panadería* inside).
Handicrafts Wood carvings, stone moais, are
available throughout Hanga Roa. The expensive
Mercado Artesanal, left of church, will give you
a good view of what is available – authentic,
no compunction to buy. Good pieces cost
from US$50 to US$200. Souvenirs at dozens of
decent places on Atamu Tekena.

● What to do

Rapa Nui/Easter Island *p825*
Diving Mike Rapu, Caleta Hanga Roa Otai s/n, T255 1055, www.mike rapu.cl. Diving courses, expeditions, fishing trips and kayaks. Orca, Caleta Hanga Roa, T255 0877, www. seemorca.cl, run by Michel and Henri García, very experienced (Henri is a member of the Cousteau Society), PADI courses, with dive shop and surf equipment rental. Both have similar prices: introductory dive US$70; single dive for experienced diver US$53-62; also night dives and boat trips with snorkeling (from US$26). Both at the harbour, all equipment provided.
Hiking To walk around the island in 1 or 2 days you would need to be in great shape. It is more pleasant to take it easy, but once you leave Hanga Roa services (including lodging and food) are scarce. So take plenty of food and water and inform your hotel or park rangers of your exact route. Sample trekking (and cycling) distances and times: Hanga Roa to Anakena Beach, 17 km, 4½ hrs (1¾ hrs by bike); Hanga Roa to Jau-Orongo, 4 km, 1 hr (30 mins); Hanga Roa to Rano Raraku, 25 km, 6½ hrs (3 hrs).
Horse riding The best way to see the island, provided you are fit, is on horseback: horses, US$65 for a day, including guide. Cabañas Pikera Uri, T210 0577, www.pantupikerauri.cl, offers several riding tours, as well as *cabañas* for overnight stays.

Tour operators
Many agencies, residenciales and locals arrange excursions around the island. The English of other tour guides is improving. Good free bilingual tourist maps at Sernatur information office, hotels and tour agencies. More detailed maps (recommended for driving or bicycling) are sold on Av Policarpo Toro for US$15-18, or at the ranger station at Orongo for US$10. Half-and full-day tours of the island by minibus cost US$60-100 pp, including guide, without lunch. For the best light go early or late in the day.
Aku-Aku Tours, Tu'u Koihu s/n, T210 0770, www.akuakuturismo.cl. Wide range of tours.
Hanga Roa Travel, T210 0158, hfritsch@ entelchile.net. English, German, Italian and Spanish spoken, offers good-value all-inclusive tours.

Haumaka Archeological Guide Services, Av Atamu Tekena y Hotu Matua, T210 0274. English spoken.
Rapa Nui Travel, Tu'u Koihu s/n, T210 0548, www.rapanuitravel.com. Recommended agency with years of experience. Ask for Terangi Pakarati, a well-informed and super friendly local guide, who speaks English, Spanish and Rapa Nui.

● Transport

Rapa Nui/Easter Island *p825*
Air The airport runway has been improved to provide emergency landing for US space shuttles! Airport terminal is tiny but it has several reasonably priced souvenir shops and a café. No internet, but good mobile phone signal. For those in transit, in the garden at the departure lounge stands one lonely *moai*. Taxi to town centre US$4. LAN fly daily in high season, less in low season, 5-5½ hrs going east, 3½-4 hrs going west. Most flights continue to **Papeete, Tahiti**. LAN office on Av Atamu Tekena s/n, near Av Pont, Mon-Fri 0900-1630, Sat 0900-1230, T210 0279/210 0920. For details of LAN's special sector fare to Easter Island and which must be purchased outside Chile, see page 651. The cheapest return fare from **Santiago**, booked well in advance, is about US$550, with occasional special deals available through travel agents. Under 24s and over 65s are often eligible for a 28% discount on some fares. If you fly between Papeete and Santiago or vice versa, you will be considered in transit and will not be allowed to exit the airport. So, if flying to or from Tahiti, check if you can stay over till another flight.
Car hire If you are hiring a car, do the sites from south to north since travel agencies tend to start their tours in the north. Many vehicle hire agencies on the main street. US$ 80-100 per day for a small 4WD with manual transmission (usually). In theory, a Chilean or international driving licence is necessary, but your national licence will usually do. If a rental company makes a fuss, go next door. **Moira Souvenir Rent a Car**, Te Pito o te Henua s/n, T210 0718. About US$60 a day for small, beat-up but functional 4WD, no papers asked for, just a reasonable deposit.

There is no insurance available, drive at your own risk; be careful at night; since deep potholes and wild horses are not uncommon. Speeding, drunk driving and poor driving skills are also a problem on the island. If you are hit, demand that the person who dented your car and the rental car agency settles the bill. If you hit something or someone, you will be expected to pay, cash only. The speed limit in Hanga Roa is under 30 kph. Check oil and water before setting out. There is only one petrol station, near the airport. A basic loop around the island is 50 to 80 km, depending whether you go off road or not. Motorbike hire: about US$60 a day including gasoline (Suzuki or Honda 250 recommended because of rough roads). You can also rent scooters (US$50 for 24 hrs), bicycles (from US$12 from your *residencial*) and quadbikes.

Taxi Taxis cost a flat US$4 within Hanga Roa. Longer trips can be negotiated, with the cost depending mainly on the time. For example, a round-trip to the beach at Anakena costs US$30 (per taxi); be sure to arrange for the taxi driver to pick you up at a predetermined time. **Radiotaxi Vai Reva**, Sergio Cortés, Petero Atamu s/n, T210 0399, 24 hrs, reliable. For touring the island, it is cheaper to hire a car or take a tour if there are more than 3 people sharing.

❶ Directory

Rapa Nui/Easter Island *p825*
Banks US dollars may be accepted, at poor rates. **Banco del Estado**, Av Pont, T210 0221. Mon-Fri 0800-1300, with an ATM. Accepts MasterCard and Cirrus, cash advances on Visa, reasonable rates for dollars or euros. **Banco Santander**, on Policarpo Toro on the waterfront, T251 8007, has an ATM that accepts Visa and MasterCard, Mon-Fri 0800-1300. It also has an ATM at the airport (departure area). There is another reliable ATM at the gas station shop on Av Hotu Matua. ATMs can dispense 10,000 pesos per transaction. Cash can be exchanged in shops, hotels, etc, at about 5% less than Santiago. Credit cards are widely accepted for purchases, but some places add a surcharge.
Internet and telephones Omotohi Cybercafé, Av Te Pito o te Henua, offers fast and reliable internet at US$3 per hr. Daily 0900-2200. Phone calls are expensive. The cheapest way to call home or mainland Chile is by internet from one of the Internet cafés.
Medical facilities Small but well-equipped Hospital Hanga Roa, Av Simón Paoa, near the church, T210 0215. **Pharmacy Cruz Verde**, Av Atamu Tekena. T255 1540. Large, modern.
Post office Half a long block up from Caleta Hanga Roa on Av Te Pito o te Henua, sells Easter Island stamps, post cards and will put a souvenir stamp in your passport on request. Mon-Fri 0900-1300, 1430-1800, Sat. 0900-1200.

Contents

Footprint features

Colombia

At a glance

⏰ **Time required** 2-3 weeks.

☀ **Best time** Dec-Feb generally driest months. Fiestas in many southern towns in Jan and carnival in Barranquilla in Feb/Mar.

✖ **When not to go** Christmas and Easter are the busiest holiday seasons. Apr/May and Oct/Nov are the wettest months.

Caribbean Sea

Península de la Guajira

Manaure

Riohacha

PN Tayrona

Santa Marta

Maicao

Barranquilla

4

Fonseca

Cartagena

3

Aracataca

Valledupar

To San Andrés & Providencia

Turbaco

Bosconia

Malagana

San Jacinto

Lago de Maracaibo

Tolú

Mompós

El Banco

PANAMA

Montería

Sincelejo

VENEZUELA

Capurganá

Caucasia

Turbo

Cúcuta

PNN Paramillo

Chigorodó

Barranca

Pamplona

Santa Fé de Antioquia

Puerto Berrío

Bucaramanga

Arauca

Puerto Carreño

Bahía Solano

San Gil

PNN El Cocuy

Tame

Medellín

El Valle

Chiquinquirá

Sogamoso

Trinidad

PNN El Tuparro

PNN Ensenada de Utría

Manizales

Nuquí

Quibdó

5

2

Tunja

Yopal

Istmina

Pereira

PNN Los Nevados

Zipaquirá

Pacific Ocean

Armenia

1

BOGOTÁ

RNN Puinawai

Juanchaco

Buga

Villavicencio

Pto Gaitán

Buenaventura

Palmira

Villavieja

Gorgona Island

Cali

Silvia

Santander

Neiva

PNN Serranía de la Macarena

Popayán

Tierradentro

PNN Tinigua

San José del Guaviare

Guapí

6

PN Puracé

La Macarena

Calamar

Tumaco

San Agustín

El Doncello

PNN Nukak

Junín

Belén

Florencia

PNN Chiribiquete

Ipiales

Pasto

Mocoa

ECUADOR

Pto Asís

PNN La Paya

BRAZIL

San Miguel

PNN Cahuinarí

Putumayo

PNN Amacayacu

Pto Nariño

PERU

Leticia

N

100 km

100 miles

★ **Don't miss ...**

1 Museo del Oro, page 852.
2 Zipaquirá, page 863.
3 Cartagena, page 880.
4 Ciudad Perdida, page 904.
5 La Zona Cafetera, page 931.
6 San Agustín and Tierradentro, page 946.

The adventurous will love this land of sun and emeralds, with its excellent opportunities for climbing, trekking and diving. The gold museum in Bogotá, the Lost City of the Tayrona and San Agustín have superb examples of cultures long gone. Among several fine colonial cities, the jewel is Cartagena, whose history of slavery and pirates can be seen in the massive fortifications. Today, pelicans share the beach with holidaymakers. Colombia's Caribbean, from Venezuela to the Panamanian isthmus, is the inspiration for Gabriel García Márquez's world of magical realism and is the land of accordion-led *vallenato* music. Of the country's many snow-capped mountain ranges, the Sierra Nevada de Santa Marta, with its secretive indígenas, is the most remarkable, rising straight out of the Caribbean. Also not to be missed is the cathedral inside a salt mine at Zipaquirá. There are mud volcanoes to bathe in, acres of flowers, coffee farms to visit and a CD library's worth of music festivals. In fact, dancing is practically a national pastime and having a good time is taken very seriously: as García Márquez once said, "five Colombians in a room invariably turns into a party." Despite the drug trade and the guerrilla violence which has scarred the minds and landscape of this beautiful country, Colombia is fast rebuilding its position on the tourist circuit.

Planning your trip

Where to go in Colombia

Bogotá, the capital, stands on a plateau in the eastern cordillera of the Andes. It epitomizes the juxtaposition of the historical and the modern, with many important colonial buildings and museums. Among its attractions are La Candelaria, the old centre of the city, and the magnificent Gold Museum, which houses a remarkable collection of prehispanic artefacts, one of the 'musts' of South America. Places to visit around Bogotá include the salt cathedral at Zipaquirá and the Chicaque Parque Natural, a fine preserved area of cloud forest.

Northeast from Bogotá, to Cúcuta on the Venezuelan border, the beautiful colonial town of **Villa de Leiva** is carefully preserved from the 18th century and well worth a visit. Further north, Santander department also has its attractions, including the most dramatic mountain scenery in Colombia in the **Parque Nacional Cocuy** and the **Chicamocha Canyon**. **Barichara** is one of the best kept colonial towns and nearby **San Gil** is an important adventure sports centre.

The obvious centre for exploring the north Caribbean coast and the tropical islands of San Andrés and Providencia is **Cartagena**. The city is a fashionable, modern beach resort and also the place where Colombia's colonial past can best be seen. Some of the greatest examples of Spanish architecture on the continent are to be found within the city's ramparts. **Santa Marta** to the northeast is a popular beach resort and the centre for the rocky coast to the east, including Taganga and **Parque Nacional Tayrona**. Treks to the **Ciudad Perdida** (Lost City), a major archaeological site, start in Santa Marta. Towards the Venezuelan border, **La Guajira**, a region of arid desert landscapes and home to the indigenous group, the Wayúu, is becoming increasingly popular and accessible to visit. Northeast from Cartagena is the northern port of **Barranquilla**, where Carnival rivals some of those in Brazil. Inland from here, up the Río Magdalena, is the fascinating colonial town of **Mompós**.

In northwest Colombia, **Medellín** is a modern, vibrant city with many fine new buildings, old restored architecture and friendly, outgoing people. There are many fascinating places to visit in the surrounding department of Antioquia, including the colonial towns of **Rionegro** and **Santa Fé de Antioquia**. Further west is **Chocó**, one of the world's wettest and most biodiverse regions. Here, the Pacific coast is almost undeveloped for tourism, with pristine forests descending the mountain slopes to the ocean, but destinations such as Bahía Solano and Nuquí on the Pacific, and Capurganá on the Caribbean coast, are beginning to open up. South of Medellín is the **Zona Cafetera**, with modern and colonial cities such as Manizales and Pereira, where coffee farms, in delightful countryside, welcome visitors.

Further south, in the Cauca Valley, is **Cali**, with its passion for salsa. Like Medellín it is shrugging off its notorious reputation from recent years. Off the Pacific coast, **Isla Gorgona**, is an unspoilt, idyllic island offering excellent diving. From **Popayán**, a city with a strong colonial feel, are the difficult routes to the important archaeological sites of **Tierradentro** and **San Agustín**. South of Popayán lie Pasto, a pleasant town in an attractive setting, and Ipiales for the border with Ecuador.

In Colombia's far southeastern corner, towards the border with Brazil, lies **Leticia** from where jungle treks start.

Best time to visit Colombia

The best time to visit is December-February. These are generally the driest months, but many local people are on holiday. It gets busy and very crowded during Christmas, early to mid-January and Easter, when many hotels put up their rates and transport can be overloaded. Climate is a matter of altitude: there are no real seasons, though some periods are wetter than others. Height in metres is given for all major towns. Generally, around 2000 m is 'temperate';

Driving in Colombia

Road Signposting is poor and roads may be in poor condition. There are toll stations every 60-100 km on major roads: toll is about US$3.50. Motorcycles don't have to pay.

Safety Lorry and bus drivers tend to be reckless, and stray animals are often encountered. Always check safety information for your route before setting out. Police and military checks are frequent in troubled areas, keep your documents handy. In town, only leave your car in an attended car park (*parqueadero*). Only park in the street if there is someone on guard, tip US$0.50.

Documents International driving licences are advised, especially if you have your own car. To be accepted, a national driving licence must be accompanied by an official translation if the original is in a language other than Spanish. To bring a car into Colombia, you must also have documents proving ownership of the vehicle, and a tourist card/transit visa. These are normally valid for 90 days and must be applied for at the Colombian consulate in the country which you will be leaving for Colombia. A *carnet de passages* is recommended when entering with a European registered vehicle. Only third-party insurance issued by a Colombian company is valid; there are agencies in all ports. You will frequently be asked for this document while driving. Carry driving documents with you at all times.

Car hire In addition to passport and driver's licence, a credit card may be asked for as additional proof of identity and to secure a returnable deposit to cover any liability not covered by the insurance. If renting a Colombian car, note that major cities have the *pico y placa* system which means cars are not allowed entry in the city during morning and afternoon rush hour depending on the day and car number plate (does not apply during the weekends and public holidays); see www.picoyplaca.info for information.

Fuel 'Corriente' 84 octane, US$5 per gallon. More expensive 'Premium 95' octane is only available in large cities. Diesel US$4.55.

anywhere higher will require warm clothing in the early mornings and evenings. There is heavy rain in many places in April-May and October-November though intermittent heavy rain can fall at any time almost anywhere.

Transport in Colombia

Air Avianca, www.avianca.com, is the national carrier. Other airlines are LAN Colombia, www.lan.com, Copa Airlines Colombia, www.copaair.com, Satena (government-owned, but linked with Avianca on some flights), www.satena.com, Easyfly, www.easyfly.com.co (a budget airline serving Bogotá, Medellín, Cartagena, Cúcuta, Bucaramanga and other smaller cities), Viva Colombia, www.vivacolombia.co (a budget airline serving Barranquilla, Bogotá, Bucaramanga, Cartagena, Medellín, Montería, Pereira, Neiva, Valledupar and other towns) and Aerolínea de Antioquia, ADA, www.ada-aero.com (based in Medellín, 19- to 32-seater planes serving most of the country). You cannot buy tickets with an international credit card online, but you can pay over the phone. Domestic airports vary in the services they offer and tourist facilities tend to close early on weekdays, and all Sunday. Local airport taxes are included in the price. Security checks can be thorough, watch your luggage. ▶▶ *For further information on airport taxes, see page 844.*

Always allow plenty of time if making international connections. The low-cost carriers are not always on time and bad weather can affect any domestic flight. Bus transport can also be delayed for a variety of reasons.

Bus Travel in Colombia is exciting. The scenery is generally worth seeing so travel by day: it is also safer and you can keep a better eye on your valuables. Almost all the main routes are paved, but the state of the roads, usually single-lane, varies considerably between departments. On main routes you usually have choice of company and type of bus. The cheapest (*corriente*) are basically local buses, stopping frequently, uncomfortable and slow, but offering plenty of local colour. Try to keep your luggage with you. *Pullman* (each company has a different name for the service) are long distance buses usually with a/c, toilets, hostess service, DVDs. Sit near the back with your iPod to avoid the movie and the need to keep the blinds down. Luggage is normally carried in a locked compartment against receipt. See these following bus company websites: **Berlinas del Fonce**, www.berlinasdelfonce.com, **Bolivariano**, www.bolivariano.com.co, **Copetran**, www.copetran.com.co, **Expreso Brasilia**, www.expreso brasilia.com, **Flota Magdalena**, www.flotamagdalena.com, **Expreso Palmira**, www.expreso palmira.com.co. *Velotax* and other *busetas* are slightly quicker and more expensive than ordinary buses to long-distance destinations. They may be called *colectivos*, or *vans* and are usually 12-20 seat vehicles, sometimes seven-seater cars or pick-up trucks. It is also possible to order a *puerta-a-puerta* (door-to-door) service at a reasonable price. When taxis provide this service they are *por puestos* (pay by seat) and do not leave till full. Fares shown in the text are middle of the range where there is a choice but are no more than a guide. Note that meal stops can be few and far between, and short; take your own food. Be prepared for climatic changes on longer routes and for the vagaries of a/c on buses, sometimes fierce, sometimes none. **If you entrust your luggage to the bus companies' luggage rooms, remember to load it on to the bus yourself; it will not be done automatically.** There are few interdepartmental bus services on holidays. During holidays and high season, arrive at the bus terminal at least an hour before the departure time to guarantee a seat, even if you have bought a ticket in advance. If you are joining a bus at popular or holiday times, not at the starting point, you may be left behind even though you have a ticket and reservation. Always take your passport (or photocopy) with you: identity and luggage checks on buses are frequent and on rare occasions you may be body-searched at army roadblocks.

Cycling Cycling is a popular sport. There are good shops for spares in all big cities. Around Calle13 with Cra 20 in front of La Sabana train station in Bogotá are a few repair and accessory shops.

Hitchhiking Hitchhiking (*autostop*) is unadvisable and not common. In safe areas, try enlisting the co-operation of the highway police checkpoints outside each town and toll booths. Truck drivers are often very friendly, but be careful of private cars with more than one person inside. Travelling on your own is not recommended.

Taxi Whenever possible, take an official taxi with a meter and ensure that it is switched on. If there is no meter, fix a price at the start of the journey. Official taxis should display the driver's ID with photo and additional legal tariffs that may be charged after 2000, on Sunday and fiestas. In some cities, fares are registered in units on the meter, which the driver converts to pesos with a fare table. This should be shown to the passenger. It is safest to call a radio taxi, particularly at night, rather than hailing one on the street. Bars, hotels and restaurants will order taxis for customers. The dispatcher will give you the cab's number which should be noted in case of irregularities. The last two digits of the number from where the call was made is *el clave*, the security code. Remember it as taxi drivers will ask for the code before setting off. Never get into a taxi if there are already passengers in it. If the taxi 'breaks down', take your luggage and find another taxi immediately. Taxis in some cities, such as Cali, have helpful Spanish phrases with English translation on display.

Where to stay in Colombia → *See Essentials for our hotel price guide.*
Hotels The more expensive hotels charge 16% VAT (IVA). Some hotels add a small insurance charge. From 15 December to mid-January, Easter and 15 June to 31 August and bank holidays

(*puentes*), hotels in holiday centres may increase prices by at least 20-30%. Prices are normally displayed at reception, but in quiet periods it is always worth negotiating. See **www.posadas turisticasdecolombia.gov.co** for a government-sponsored network of simple places to stay, mostly without modern luxuries.

Camping Sites are given in the text but also check locally very carefully before deciding to camp. Local tourist offices have lists of official sites, but they are seldom signposted on main roads. Permission to camp with tent, camper van or car is usually granted by landowners in less populated areas. Many haciendas have armed guards protecting their property: this can add to your safety. Vehicles may camp at truck drivers' restaurants, *balnearios campestres* with armed guards, or ask if you may overnight beside police or army posts.

Youth hostels Federación Colombiana de Albergues Juveniles ① *Cra 15, No 124-17 Torre B, Bogotá, T612 6422, hostels@fcaj.org.co*. The FCAJ is affiliated to Hostelling International, www.hi hostels.com. **Colombian Hostels**, www.colombianhostels.com.co, has a good network of 41 members around the country.

Food and drink in Colombia → *See Essentials for our restaurant price guide.*
Restaurants Colombia's food is regionally varied, most major cities have restaurants with non-local Colombian food. Small towns do not often cater for vegetarians, but this is changing. Restaurants in smaller towns often close on Sunday, and early on weekday evenings, but you will probably find something to eat near the bus station. The filling three-course *menú del día*, also known as *menú ejecutivo* (daily set lunch), is excellent value.

Food Some of the standard items on the menu are: *sancocho*, a meat stock (may be fish on the coast) with potato, corn (on the cob), yucca, sweet potato and plantain. *Arroz con pollo* (chicken and rice), a common Latin American dish, is excellent in Colombia. *Carne asada* (grilled beefsteak), usually an inexpensive cut, is served with *papas fritas* (chips) or rice and you can ask for a vegetable of the day. *Sobrebarriga* (belly of beef) is served with varieties of potato in a tomato and onion sauce. *Huevos pericos,* eggs scrambled with onions and tomatoes, are a popular, cheap and nourishing snack available almost anywhere, especially for breakfast. *Tamales* are meat pies made by folding a maize dough round chopped pork mixed with potato, rice, peas, onions and eggs wrapped in banana leaves (which you don't eat) and steamed. Other ingredients may be added such as olives, garlic, cloves and paprika. Colombians eat *tamales* for breakfast with hot chocolate. *Empanadas* are another popular snack; these are made with chicken or other meats, or vegetarian filling, inside a maize dough and deep-fried in oil. *Patacones* are cakes of mashed and baked *plátano* (large green banana). *Arepas* are standard Colombian fare; these are flat maize griddle cakes served instead of bread or as an alternative. *Pan de bono* is cheese flavoured bread, best enjoyed hot. *Almojábanas*, a kind of sour milk/cheese bread roll, great for breakfast when freshly made. *Buñuelos* are 4-6 cm balls of wheat flour and eggs mixed and deep-fried, also best when still warm. *Arequipe* is a sugar-based caramel syrup used with desserts and in confectionery, universally savoured by Colombians.

Regional specialities Bogotá and Cundinamarca: *Ajiaco de pollo* is a delicious chicken stew with maize, manioc (yuca), three types of potato, herbs and sometimes other vegetables, served with cream and capers, and pieces of avocado. *Chunchullo* (tripe), and *morcilla* (blood sausage) are popular dishes. *Cuajada con melado* (or *melao*) is a dessert of fresh cheese served with cane syrup, or *natas* (based on the skin of boiled milk). **Boyacá:** *Mazamorra* is a meat and vegetable soup with broad and black beans, peas, varieties of potato and cornflour. *Care* is a milk and maize drink, known as *mazamorro* in Antioquia and elsewhere and *peto* in Cundinamarca. *Puchero* is a stew based on chicken with potatoes, yuca, cabbage, turnips, corn (on the cob) and herbs. *Cuchuco*, another soup with pork and sweet potato. *Masato* is a slightly fermented rice beverage. *Longaniza* (long pork sausage) is also very popular. **Santander and Norte de Santander:** *Mute* is a soup of various cereals including corn. *Hormigas culonas* (large-bottomed black ants) is the most famous culinary delight of this area, served toasted, and particularly popular in Bucaramanga at Easter time. *Bocadillo veleño* is similar to quince jelly but made from guava. *Hallacas* are cornmeal turnovers with different meats, and whatever else is to hand, inside. *Carne oreada* is salted dried meat marinated in a *panela* (unrefined sugarcane) and pineapple sauce with the consistency of beef jerky.

    Cartagena and the north coast: Fish is naturally a speciality the coastal regions. In *Arroz con coco*, rice here is often prepared with coconut. *Cazuela de mariscos*, a soup/stew of shellfish and white fish, maybe including octopus and squid, is especially good. *Sancocho de pescado* is a fish stew with vegetables, usually simpler and cheaper than *cazuela*. *Chipichipi*, a small clam found along the coast in Barranquilla and Santa Marta, is a standard local dish served with rice. *Empanada* (or *arepa*) *de huevo* is deep fried with eggs in the middle. *Canasta de coco* is a pastry containing coconut custard flavoured with wine and topped by meringue. **Tolima:** *Lechona*, suckling pig with herbs is a speciality of Ibagué. **Antioquia:** *Bandeja paisa* consists of various types of grilled meats, usually pork, *chorizo* (sausage), *chicharrón* (pork crackling), sometimes an egg, served with rice, beans, potato, manioc and a green salad; this has now been adopted in other parts of the country. *Natilla*, a sponge cake made from cornflour and *salpicón*, a tropical fruit salad. **Cali and south Colombia:** the emphasis here is on corn, plantain, rice and avocado with the usual pork and chicken dishes. *Manjar blanco*, made from milk and sugar or molasses, served with biscuit is a favourite dessert. *Cuy, curí* or *conejillo de Indias* (guinea pig), is typical of the southern department of Nariño. *Mazorcas* (baked corn-on-the-cob) are typical of roadside stalls in the south.

Drink *Tinto*, the national small cup of black coffee, is taken at all hours and is usually sweetened. Colombian coffee is always mild. Coffee with milk is called *café perico*; *café con leche* is a mug of milk with coffee added. To make sure you get cold milk with your coffee, ask for it separately at an additional cost. *Agua de panela* is a common beverage (hot water with unrefined sugar), also made with limes, served with cheese. Many decent brands of beer are brewed, including *Costeña*, *Aguila*, *Club Colombia* and *Poker*. The local rum is good and cheap; ask for *ron* eg Ron Viejo de Caldas. *Aguardiente* is a 'rougher' cane-based spirit distilled with or without aniseed (*aguardiente anisado*). Try *canelazo*, cold or hot *aguardiente* with water, sugar, lime and cinnamon, common in Bogotá. Local table wines include Isabella; none is very good. Wine is very expensive, US$15 in restaurants for an average Chilean or Argentine wine, more for European and other wines.

Fruit and juices As well as fruits familiar in northern and Mediterranean climates, Colombia has a huge variety of local fruits: *chirimoyas* (a green fruit, white inside with pips); *curuba* (banana passion fruit); *feijoa* (a green fruit with white flesh, high in vitamin C); *guayaba* (guava); *guanábana* (soursop); *lulo* (a small orange fruit); *maracuyá* (passion fruit); *mora* (literally 'black berry' but dark red more like a loganberry); *papaya*; the delicious *pitahaya* (taken either as an appetizer or dessert); *sandía* (watermelon); *tomate de árbol* (tree tomato, several varieties normally used as a fruit); and many more. All can be served as juices, either with milk or water. Fruit yoghurts are nourishing and cheap; **Alpina** brand is good, *crema* style is best. Also, **Kumis** is a type of liquid yoghurt. Another drink you must try is *champús*, a corn base, with fruit and lemon.

Essentials A-Z

Accident and emergency
General line for all emergencies: T123; **Fire**: T119; **Red Cross emergency**: T132; **CAI Police**: T156. If you have problems with theft or other forms of crime, contact a *Centro de Atención Inmediata* (CAI) office for assistance (Al offices in Bogotá: downtown, Cra 24, No 82-77, T315 344 6195.

Electricity
110 Volts AC, alternating at 60 cycles per second. Most sockets accept both continental European (round) and North American (flat) 2-pin plugs.

Embassies and consulates
For all Colombian embassies and consulates abroad and for all foreign embassies and consulates in Colombia, see http://embassy.goabroad.com.

Festivals in Colombia
Public holidays: there are some 18 public holidays. The most important are:
1 Jan: New Year's Day; 6 Jan: Epiphany*;
19 Mar: St Joseph*; Maundy Thu; Good Fri;
1 May: Labour Day; Ascension Day*; Corpus
Christi*; 15 Jun: Sacred Heart*; 29 Jun: SS Peter and Paul*; 20 Jul: Independence Day; 7 Aug: Battle of Boyacá; 15 Aug: Assumption*; 12 Oct: Columbus' arrival in America* (Día de la Raza); 1 Nov: All Saints' day*; 11 Nov: Independence of Cartagena*; 8 Dec: Immaculate Conception; 25 Dec: Christmas Day.

When those marked with an asterisk (*) do not fall on a Mon, they will be moved to the following Mon. Public holidays are known as *puentes* (bridges).

Maps
Maps of Colombia are sold at the Instituto Geográfico Agustín Codazzi, Carrera 30, No 48-51, Bogotá, T369 4000, www.igac.gov.co, or from their offices in other large cities; see the website. They have a wide range of official, country-wide and departmental maps and atlases, but many are a few years old. In Bogotá, they are open Mon-Fri 0730-1545, maps are US$2.65-4.65 and you pay at the bank next door. There is a library and refreshments are available at lunchtime. A guide with detailed road maps is the annual *Guía de Rutas de Colombia* available at toll booths and some bookshops. Town maps are usually available

from local tourist offices. A good travel map, 1:1,500,000, is published by **Mapas NaTurismo**, www.mapas-naturismo.com, US$9.

Money → *US$1 = 1922 pesos, €1 = 2630 pesos (May 2014).*

The currency is the peso. New coins of 50, 100, 200, 500 and 1000 were introduced in 2012 (old and new coins were valid at the time of writing); there are notes of 1000, 2000, 5000, 10,000, 20,000 and 50,000 pesos (the last can be difficult to change). Change is in short supply, especially in small towns, and in the morning. Watch out for forged notes. The 50,000-peso note should smudge colour if it is real, if not, refuse to accept it. There is a limit of US$10,000 on the import of foreign exchange in cash, with export limited to the equivalent of the amount brought in.

Plastic/TCs/banks

Cash and TCs can in theory be exchanged in any bank, except the **Banco de la República**; go early to banks in smaller places to change these. In most sizeable towns there are *casas de cambio* (exchange shops), which are quicker to use than banks but sometimes charge higher commission. It's best to use euros and, even better, dollars. It can sometimes be difficult to buy and sell large amounts of sterling, even in Bogotá. Hotels may give very poor rates of exchange. Hotels are not allowed to accept dollars as payment by law. Some may open a credit card account and give you cash on that. It is dangerous to change money on the streets and you may well be given counterfeit pesos, or robbed. Also in circulation are counterfeit US$ bills. You must present your original passport when changing money (it will be photocopied and you may be fingerprinted, too). Take US$ cash with you for emergencies.

Credit cards

As it is unwise to carry large quantities of cash, credit cards are widely used, especially MasterCard and Visa; Diners Club is also accepted. American Express is only accepted in expensive places in Bogotá. Many banks accept Visa (Visaplus and ATH logos) and Cirrus/MasterCard (Maestro and Multicolor logos) to advance pesos against the card, or through

ATMs. There are ATMs for Visa and MasterCard everywhere but you may have to try several machines. All Exito supermarkets have ATMs. Credit card loss or theft: Visa call collect to T01-800-912 5713, MasterCard T01-800-912 1303.

ATMs do not retain cards – follow the instructions on screen. If your card is not given back immediately, do not proceed with the transaction and do not type in your pin number. There are reports of money being stolen from accounts when cards have been retained. ATMs dispense a frustratingly small amount of cash at a time. The maximum withdrawal is often 300,000 pesos (about US$150), which can accrue heavy bank charges over a period of time. For larger amounts try: **Davivienda** (500,000 per visit) and **Bancolombia** (400,000 per visit).

Note Only use ATMs in supermarkets, malls or where a security guard is present. Don't ask a taxi driver to wait while you use an ATM. Be particularly vigilant around Christmas time when thieves may be on the prowl. For information on **traveller's cheques** see Essentials at the front of the book.

Cost of travelling

Prices are a little lower than Europe and North America for services and locally produced items, but more expensive for imported and luxury goods. Modest, basic accommodation will cost about US$12-20 pp per night in Bogotá, Cartagena, Santa Marta and colonial cities like Villa de Leiva, Popayán or Santa Fé de Antioquia, but a few dollars less elsewhere. A *menú ejecutivo* (set lunch) costs about US$3.50-5.50 and breakfast US$2-3. A la carte meals are usually good value and fierce competition for transport keeps prices low. The typical cost of internet is US$1-4 per hr.

Opening hours

Business hours depend a lot on where you are, so enquire locally. Generally offices are open Mon-Fri 0800-1700, but in hotter zones may close for lunch, 1200-1400, closing 1830 or 1900. **Banks**: Mon-Thu 0900-1500, 1530 on Fri. **Shops**: open 0700 or 0800 till 2000 and on Sat, but may close for lunch; supermarkets have longer hours and are open on Sat and Sun, usually 0900-1900. Most businesses such as banks and airline offices close for official holidays while supermarkets and street markets may stay open.

Postal services

The name of the Colombian postal service is 4-72, www.4-72.com.co. It offers a range of services from normal and express post to electronic mail, but its reputation for reliability and value is poor. Private couriers, such as **Servientrega** (www.servientrega.com), **Deprisa** (www.deprisa.com – a branch of Avianca, related to UPS) and international brands, are commonly used to send letters and packages, but they are not cheap either.

Safety

Travellers confirm that the vast majority of Colombians are polite, honest and will go out of their way to help visitors and make them feel welcome. In general, anti-gringo sentiments are rare. However, in addition to the general advice given in Essentials, the following local conditions should be noted. Colombia is part of a major drug-smuggling route. Police and customs activities have greatly intensified and smugglers increasingly try to use innocent carriers. Do not carry packages for other people. Be very polite if approached by policemen in uniform, or if your hotel room is raided by police looking for drugs. Colombians who offer you drugs could be setting you up for the police, who are very active in Cali, on the north coast, San Andrés island and other tourist resorts.

There have been reports of travellers and Colombians being victims of *burundanga* (scopolamine), a drug obtained from a white flower, native to Colombia. At present, the use of this drug appears to be confined to major cities. It is very nasty, almost impossible to see or smell. It leaves the victim helpless and at the will of the culprit. Usually, the victim is taken to ATMs to draw out money. Be wary of accepting cigarettes, food and drink from strangers at sports events and in buses. In bars watch your drinks very carefully.

The internal armed conflict in Colombia is almost impossible to predict and the security situation changes from day to day. For this reason, it is essential to consult regularly with locals for up-to-date information. Taxi and bus drivers, local journalists, soldiers at checkpoints, hotel owners and Colombians who actually travel around their country are usually good sources of reliable information. Travelling overland between towns, especially during the holiday season and bank holiday weekends, has in general become much safer due to increased military and police presence along main roads. However, in some areas fighting between the armed forces and guerrilla groups continues even though, at the time of writing, peace talks between FARC and government are taking place. The following areas are known as *zonas calientes* (hot zones) where there is significant unrest: the rural areas down the eastern part of the country from **Arauca** and **Casanare** to **Meta**; **Caquetá** and some parts of **Putumayo**; the **Magdalena Medio** and **Norte de Santander**; from **Urabá** near the border with **Panamá** into northwestern **Antioquia** and parts of **Chocó**, the ports of **Buenaventura** and **Tumaco** on the north coast. Travellers wishing to go into rural areas in **Huila**, **Cauca** and **Nariño** departments should also seek advice. As a loose rule, the conflict is often most intense in coca growing areas, oil-producing regions and along Colombia's borders. Guerrilla activity usually increases in the run up to local and national elections. Incidents in cities, including **Bogotá**, may also occur. Apart from between major cities such as Cartagena, Bogotá, Bucaramanga and Medellín, do not travel between towns by road at night. If venturing into rural areas and hot zones ask first at your embassy. It is essential to follow this up with detailed enquiries at your chosen destination. If arriving overland, go to the nearest hotel favoured by travellers (given in the text) and make enquiries. **Note** that rural hot zones are often littered with land mines.

Amazonas and, to a lesser extent, **Los Llanos**, have always been difficult to visit because of their remoteness, the lack of facilities and the huge distances involved. Our text is limited to **Villavicencio**, **Florencia** and the **Leticia** region all of which are comparatively safe. They should only be visited by air, except Leticia where river routes are safe. Remoteness is also a factor in visiting **La Guajira** in the north, but many tours go there.

Taxes

Airport taxes

The airport departure tax is about US$36, payable in dollars or pesos; see www.elnuevodorado.com/tramites.html. It may be included in the ticket price. Travellers changing planes in Colombia and leaving the same day are exempt from this tax. When you arrive, ensure that all necessary documentation bears a stamp for your date of arrival. There is also an airport tax on internal flights, US$6 (varies according to airport), usually included in the ticket price.

VAT

16%. You can ask for an official receipt. Some hotels and restaurants add IVA (VAT) onto bills, but foreigners do not officially have to pay.

Telephone → *Country code T+57.*

Ringing: equal tones with long pauses. Engaged: short tones with short pauses. National and international calls can be made from public phone offices in all major cities and rural towns. You are assigned a cabin, place your calls, and pay on the way out. You can also make calls from street vendors who hire out mobile phones (usually signposted '*minutos*'). For call boxes, phone cards are the best option. It is relatively inexpensive to buy a pay-as-you go SIM card for your mobile phone. Mobile phone numbers start with a 3-digit prefix beginning with 3.

Time

Official time is 5 hrs behind GMT.

Tipping

In restaurants a 10% service charge is added to the bill, but the waiter/waitress will ask you if you wish to include it; the bill will state the tipping policy. Porters, cloakroom attendants and hairdressers US$0.05-0.25. It is not customary to tip taxi drivers, but it is appreciated.

Tourist information

National tourism is part of the Ministry of Commerce, Industry and Tourism, Calle 28, No 13A-15, Bogotá, www.mincit.gov.co, with its portal, **Proexport**, at the same address,

p 36, www.colombia.travel. See **Posadas Turísticas de Colombia** under Where to stay in Colombia, above. Departmental and city entities have their own offices responsible for tourist information: see the text for local details. These offices should be visited as early as possible for information on accommodation and transport, but also for details on areas that are dangerous to visit. Regional tourist offices are better sources of information on safety than the Bogotá offices; otherwise contact Colombia's representation overseas. See also Useful websites, below.

The **National Parks** service is at the Ministerio del Medio Ambiente, Vivienda y Desarrollo Territorial (Ministry of the Environment, www.minambiente.gov.co), Ecotourism office, Carrera 10, No 20-30, p 1, Bogotá, T01-353 2400, www.parques nacionales.gov.co, Mon-Fri 0800-1700 (which has a list of regional offices). Staff can provide information about facilities and accommodation, and have maps. If you intend to visit the parks, this is a good place to start and ask for up-to-date details and to obtain a permit. There is a library and research unit (*Centro de Documentación*) for more information. Some parks and protected areas require permits to visit; enquire here where these must be obtained before going to the park. Do not go directly to the parks themselves. Some prices vary according to high and low seasons. High season includes: weekends, Jun-Jul, Dec-Jan, public holidays and Semana Santa. **Aviatur** travel agency, Av 19, No 4-62, Bogotá, T587 5181, www.concesionesparquesnaturales.com, has the concession for accommodation in 3 parks: Tayrona Isla Gorgona and Los Nevados (addresses given in text, not always efficient). Foreigners over 18 can participate on the voluntary park ranger programme. Details from the Ecotourism office in Bogotá. You will have to provide photocopies of ID documents and Colombian entry stamp in your passport. A good level of Spanish is required.

The **Asociación Red Colombiana de Reservas Naturales de la Sociedad Civil**, Cra 71C, No 122-72, Bogotá, T313-357 4406, www.resnatur.org.co, is a network of privately owned nature reserves that works with local people to build a sustainable model of environmentally friendly tourism.

Other conservation websites

www.colparques.net Organización para la Promoción de los Parques Naturales de Colombia.
www.humboldt.org.co Site of Institute Von Humboldt, probably the most important environment research organization in Colombia. An excellent site describing different ecosystems and projects with ethnic communities (in Spanish).
www.natura.org.co Fundación Natura, excellent conservation information.
www.proaves.org Fundación ProAves, an NGO for the study and conservation of birds and their habitats; publishes a good *Field Guide to the Birds of Colombia*.

Useful websites

www.experienciacolombia.com A good tourism website.
www.ideam.gov.co Weather forecasts and climate information, in Spanish and English.
wsp.presidencia.gov.co The government website. You can also access:

Visas and immigration

Tourists are allowed to stay a maximum of 180 days in a calendar year. Make sure that, on entry, you are granted enough days for your visit. On entry you are given 90 days. If you wish to extend your permission to stay in Colombia, for a further 90 days, apply 2-3 days before your permit expires at a **Centro Facilitador de Servicios Migratorios** (**CFSM**) of Migración Colombia (www.migracioncolombia.gov. co gives a full list); it costs about US$40. Take 2 copies of your passport details, the original entry stamp, 2 passport photos and a copy of your ticket out of Colombia. This does not apply to visas. If you overstay an entry permit or visa, a *salvoconducto* can be applied for at a CFSM. The *salvoconducto* is only issued once for a period of 30 days and is usually processed within 24 hrs; it costs about US$24. Take 2 recent photos and copies of your passport. The **Migración Colombia** head office in Bogotá is, C 100, No 11B-27, T511 1150, www. migracioncolombia.gov.co (see the Directory

in Bogotá and other cities). Arrive early in the morning, expect long queues and a painfully slow bureaucratic process. **Note** Migración Colombia does not accept cash payments; these are made at the branches of Banco de Occidente with special payments slips (in Maicao, Leticia and Arauca, use Banco de Bogotá). An onward ticket may be asked for at land borders or Bogotá international airport. You may be asked to prove that you have sufficient funds for your stay.

To visit Colombia as a tourist, nationals of countries of the Middle East (except Israel and UAE), Asian countries (except Japan, South Korea, Phillipines, Indonesia and Singapore), Haiti, Nicaragua, and all African countries (except South Africa) need a **visa**. Always check for changes in regulations before leaving your home country. Visas are issued only by Colombian consulates. When a visa is required you must present a valid passport, 3 photos on a white background, the application form (in duplicate), US$80, onward tickets, and a photocopy of all the documents (allow 2 weeks maximum). A non-refundable charge of US$50 is made for any study made by the Colombian authorities prior to a visa being issued.

If you are going to take a Spanish course, you must have a student visa (US$50, plus US$15 charge), valid for one year. You may not study on a tourist visa. A **student visa** can be obtained while in Colombia on a tourist visa. Proof of sufficient funds is necessary. You must be first enrolled in a course from a bona fide university to apply for a student visa. Various business and other temporary visas are needed for foreigners who have to reside in Colombia for a length of time. The **Ministerio de Relaciones Exteriores**, C 10, No 5-51, T381 4000, www.cancilleria.gov. co, Mon-Fri 0800-1700, processes student and some work visas. In general, Colombian work visas can only be obtained outside Colombia at the appropriate consulate or and embassy. You must register work and student visas at a DAS office within 15 days of obtaining them, otherwise you will be liable to pay a hefty fine. Visas must be used within 3 months. Supporting documentary requirements for visas change frequently. Check with the appropriate consulate in good time before your trip.

When entering the country, you will be given the copy of your DIAN (Customs) luggage declaration. Keep it; you may be asked for it when you leave. If you receive an entry card when flying in and lose it while in Colombia, apply to any Migración Colombia office who should issue one and restamp your passport for free. Normally passports are scanned by a computer and no landing card is issued, but passports still must be stamped on entry. Note that to leave Colombia you must get an exit stamp from the Migración Colombia. They often do not have offices at the small border towns, so try to get your stamp in a main city.

Note It is highly recommended that you photocopy your passport details, including entry stamps which, for added insurance, you can have witnessed by a notary. Always carry a photocopy of your passport with you, as you may be asked for identification. This is a valid substitute for most purposes though not, for example, for cashing TCs or drawing cash across a bank counter. Generally acceptable for identification (eg to enter government buildings) is a driving licence, provided it is plastic, of credit card size and has a photograph. For more information, check with your consulate.

Weights and measures
Generally metric, but US gallons for petrol.

Bogotá

Bogotá, the fifth-largest city in Latin America, is a vast sprawling metropolis where, despite its modernity, it is not uncommon to see the horse and cart still in use on the streets. It is the cultural centre of the country with cosmopolitan restaurants and a vibrant night life. Predictably, there are staggering extremes of wealth and poverty, with the city segregated between the rich north and the poorer south. The capital has advanced in leaps and bounds since the mid-1990s, winning awards for its environmental efforts, libraries and transport systems, as well as improving quality of life. On Sundays, 0700-1400, the city's main streets are closed to traffic for the benefit of cyclists, joggers and rollerbladers. Emerald sellers do deals on street corners, but for a safer view of all that glitters, visit the Gold Museum, one of the most stunning collections of pre-Columbian treasures in the Americas. The old centre, La Candelaria, has countless well-preserved colonial buildings and important museums along cobbled, hilly streets. As Bogotá is Latin America's third highest city, it gets chilly at night. Warm clothes are needed.

Arriving in Bogotá → *Phone code: 1. Population: 9,600,000 million. Colour map 1, B3. Altitude: 2625 m. Mean temperature: 14°C.*

Orientation El Dorado **airport** is 15 km west of the centre. The long-distance **bus terminal**, Terminal de Transportes, is in the same direction as the airport, but not as far out. Some buses leave passengers at termini in the north and south of the city. Several types of **bus** cover urban routes. All stop when flagged down. There are also **TransMilenio** buses on dedicated lanes. **Taxis** are relatively cheap and easy to come by. ▶ *See Transport, page 860, for full details.*

The following **address system** is used throughout Colombia. The Calles (abbreviated 'C', or 'Cll') run at right angles across the Carreras ('Cra' or 'K'). The address Calle 10, No 12-45 would be the building on Calle 10 between Carreras 12 and 13 at 45 paces from Carrera 12; however transversals (Tra) and diagonals (Diag) can complicate the system. The Avenidas (Av), broad and important streets, may be either Calles (like 26) or Carreras (like 14). Avenida Jiménez de Quesada, one of Bogotá's most well-known streets, owes its lack of straightness to having been built over a river bed (a water feature now runs along it and it's called Eje Ambiental). Some streets in La Candelaria were renumbered in 2011 and the old names of blocks in this area are being reintroduced. The Calles in the south of the city are marked 'Sur' or 'S'; this is an integral part of the address and must be quoted.

To the east of the city are the mountains of the eastern cordillera, a useful landmark for getting your bearings. Most of the interesting parts of the city follow the foot of the cordillera in a south-north line. **La Candelaria**, full of character, occupies the area bounded by Avenida Jiménez de Quesada, C 6, Cra 3 and Cra 10. There is some modern infill but many of the houses are well preserved in colonial style, one or two storeys high with tiled roofs, projecting eaves, wrought ironwork and carved balconies. The main colonial churches, palaces and museums are concentrated around and above the Plaza Bolívar. Some hotels are found in this part, more along the margins. Cra 7 is pedestrians-only from C 11 (Plaza Bolívar) to C 24, 0800-1800. **Downtown Bogotá** runs in a band northeast along Cra 7 from Av Jiménez de Quesada to C 26. It is a thorough mix of styles including modern towers and run-down colonial and later buildings, together with a few notable exceptions. From C 50 to C 68 is **El Chapinero**, once the outskirts of the city and now a commercial district with a sprinkling of old, large mansions. Also known as 'Chapigay', it doubles up as the epicentre of Bogotá's gay scene, with many bars and clubs. Next to the National Park, along La Séptima (Cra 7) is **La Merced**, a cluster of English country-style houses. A few blocks further south, along Cra 4 between C 25 and C 27, is the Bohemian area of **La Macarena**, which was formerly inhabited by struggling artists, now fashionable with many good restaurants and bars. Beyond C 60, the main city continues to **North Bogotá**, which is split into various points of interest. Most of the best hotels, restaurants and embassies are in this area.

Because of the **altitude**, go easy and be careful with food and alcoholic drinks for the first day or so. Even though pavements can be congested, walking in the downtown area and in La Candelaria by day is recommended as distances are short and traffic is heavy on those streets that are not pedestrianized. North Bogotá is more spacious and buses and taxis are more convenient. Between the two and elsewhere, transport is necessary. Taxis, preferably radio taxis, are especially recommended at night; keep the doors locked. La Candelaria is relatively safe by day, but there continue to be reports of muggings and robberies by night. Anyone approaching you with questions, offering to sell something or making demands, may well be a thief or a con-artist. They may be well-dressed and plausible, may pose as plain-clothes officials, and often work in pairs. They are frequently active in and near the Plaza de Bolívar.

Tourist offices Instituto Distrital de Turismo, Cra 24, No 40-66, La Soledad, T217 0711, www. bogotaturismo.gov.co (in Spanish and English). There are 10 tourist-information kiosks dotted around the city, as well as some mobile units. They have 12 detailed tourist routes. La Candelaria ① *Cra 8, No 9-83, T283 7115, Mon-Sat 0700-1800, Sun and holidays 0900-1600,* two-hour tourist walks leave from here daily 1000 and 1400 (Tuesday and Thursday in English). El Dorado airport ① *at international and national arrivals, daily 0700-2200, and in Puente Aéreo, same hours.* **Bus station** ① *Módulo 5, local 127, T295 4460, Mon-Sat 0700-1900, Sun and holidays 0900-1600 and at the southern bus terminal, T775 3897, Mon-Sat 0700-1900.* **Parque de la Independencia (Quiosco de la Luz)** ① *Cra 7, C 26, T284 2664, Mon-Sat 0900-1700.* **Unicentro shopping centre** ① *Entrada Principal, T637 4482, Mon-Sat 1100-1900, Sun 1000-1800.* **Centro Internacional** ① *Cra 13, No26-62, T286 2248, Mon-Sat 0900-1800.* Also at the **Hacienda Santa Bárbara** shopping centre. **Cundinamarca tourist office** ① *C 26, No 51-53, T749 0000, www. cundinamarca.gov.co.* The following have listings on events, restaurants and clubs in Spanish: *Guía del Ocio* (known as GO, www.goguiadelocio.com.co, also for Cartagena), *Plan B* (www. planb.com.co, also in Medellín and Cali) and *Vive.in* (www.vive.in). **Note** Very little is open on Mondays. Most museums and tourist attractions are open Tuesday to Sunday, 0900-1700, but may be closed for a period in the middle of the day. Times change often. The best time to visit the churches is before or after Mass (not during). Mass times are 0700, 1200 and 1800.

Places in Bogotá

La Candelaria

When the *conquistadores* first arrived in the 16th century, the area was inhabited by the Chibcha people. The district, named after Nuestra Señora de la Candelaria, is where the conquistador Gonzalo Jiménez de Quesada founded Santafé (later renamed Bogotá) in 1538. Events in 1810 made La Candelaria synonymous with the Independence movement (see below), while the Franciscans and Jesuits founded schools and monasteries giving La Candelaria a reputation as a centre of learning. Among the oldest educational establishments is the **Colegio Nacional de San Bartolomé** ① *C 10, No 6-57*, founded 1573, now a prestigious school. The heart of the city and government is **Plaza Bolívar**, a good starting point for exploring the

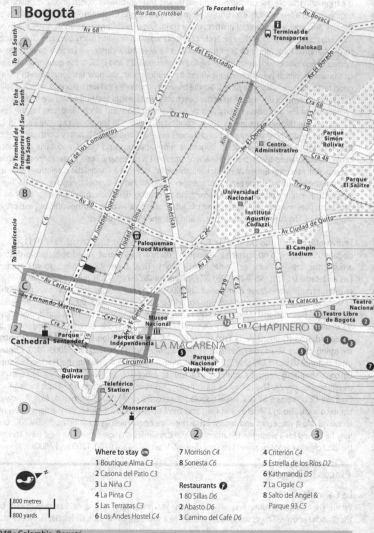

Bogotá

Where to stay 🛏
1 Boutique Alma *C3*
2 Casona del Patio *C3*
3 La Niña *C3*
4 La Pinta *C3*
5 Las Terrazas *C3*
6 Los Andes Hostel *C4*
7 Morrison *C4*
8 Sonesta *C6*

Restaurants 🍴
1 80 Sillas *D6*
2 Abasto *D6*
3 Camino del Café *D6*
4 Criterión *C4*
5 Estrella de los Ríos *D2*
6 Kathmandu *D5*
7 La Cigale *C3*
8 Salto del Angel & Parque 93 *C5*

800 metres
800 yards

colonial district. It is claimed that the first ever statue of South America's liberator, Simón Bolívar, stands here. Around the Plaza are the narrow cobbled streets and mansions of the Barrio La Candelaria. On the northern side of the Plaza is the **Corte Suprema de Justicia** (the supreme court of justice) destroyed by fire in 1985 after the now defunct M-19 guerrilla group stormed in. The court was wrecked and the present building was completed in 1999. On the west side of the plaza is the **Alcaldía Mayor de Bogotá** (the office of Bogotá's influential mayor and City Hall). On

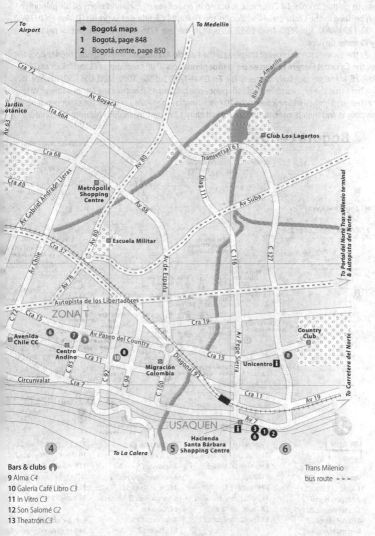

➡ **Bogotá maps**
1 Bogotá, page 848
2 Bogotá centre, page 850

Bars & clubs 🎵
9 Alma C4
10 Galería Café Libro C3
11 In Vitro C3
12 Son Salomé C2
13 Theatrón C3

Trans Milenio
bus route - - -

the south side is the **Capitolio Nacional** (congress), an imposing classical style structure with fine colonnades (1847-1925).

East of Plaza Bolívar The **Catedral** was rebuilt 1807-1823 in classical style. It has a notable choir loft of carved walnut and wrought silver on the altar of the Chapel of El Topo. The banner brought by Jiménez de Quesada to Bogotá is now in the sacristy and there is a monument to Jiménez inside the Cathedral. Gregorio Vásquez de Arce y Ceballos (1638-1711), the most famous painter in colonial Colombia, is buried in one of the chapels and many of his paintings can be seen in the Cathedral. Next door is the beautiful **Capilla del Sagrario** ① *Mon-Fri 0730-1200, 1300-1800, Sun 1500-1800, US$2.20*, built in the late 17th century, with several paintings by Vásquez de Arce.

At the southeastern corner of the plaza is the **Palacio Arzobispal**, with splendid bronze doors. See the **Casa del Florero** or **Museo de la Independencia** ① *on the corner of Plaza Bolívar at C 11, No 7-28, www.quintadebolivar.gov.co, Tue-Fri, 0900-1700, Sat-Sun 1000-1600, US$1.50, Sun free*. It was here that the first rumblings of independence began and it houses the famous flower vase that featured in the 1810 revolution. Its 10 rooms display the history of Colombia's independence campaigns and their heroes. It still has original early 17th-century Spanish-Moorish balconies.

② Bogotá centre

Bogotá maps
1 Bogotá, page 848
2 Bogotá centre, page 850

200 metres
200 yards

Where to stay ⊟
1 Abadia Colonial C3
2 Alegría's Hostel C2
3 Casa Platypus C4
4 Hostal Fátima C3
5 Hostal Martinik C3
6 Hostal Sue C4
7 Hostal Sue Candelaria C3
8 Hotel de la Opera B2
9 Masaya C3
10 Platypus C3
11 Swiss Hostal Martinik C3
12 Tequendama B5
13 The Cranky Croc C3

Restaurants ⑦
1 Al Wadi C6
2 Artesano C6
3 Asadero Capachos B4
4 Bulevar Sésamo C3
5 Construimos El Futuro C3
6 Enobra B6
7 La Cicuta C2
8 La Paella B2
9 La Totuma & Rosita C3
10 Moros y Cristianos C2
11 Panadería Pastelería La Vieja Suiza C3
12 Tábula C6
13 Yumi Yumi C4

Bars & clubs ⑦
14 Bogotá Beer Company C3

In the block behind it is the colonial **Plazuela de Rufino Cuervo**. Located here is the house of Manuela Sáenz, who was the mistress of Simon Bolívar. Inside is the **Museo de Trajes Regionales** ⓘ *C 10, No 6-18, www.museodetrajesregionales.com, Mon-Fri 0900-1600, Sat 0900-1400, US$1.50*, a small collection of traditional costumes from indigenous groups of Colombia. Beside it is the house in which Antonio Nariño printed in 1794 his translation of Thomas Paine's 'The Rights of Man' which had a profound influence on the movement for independence. You can read an extract of the text in Spanish on the wall of the building. Across from Plazuela de Rufino Cuervo is **San Ignacio**, a Jesuit church built in 1605. Emeralds from the Muzo mines in Boyacá were used in the monstrance and it has more paintings by Gregorio Vásquez de Arce. The **Museo de Arte Colonial** ⓘ *Cra 6, No 9-77, www.museocolonial.gov.co, closed for restoration early 2014*, is a fine colonial brick building. It belonged originally to the Society of Jesus, and was once the seat of the oldest University in Colombia and of the National Library. It has a splendid collection of colonial art and paintings by Gregorio Vásquez de Arce, all kinds of utensils, and two charming patios. Across Cra 6 is the **Palacio de San Carlos** ⓘ *C 10, No 5-51, T381 4000 (restricted access, book appointment)*, where Bolívar lived, which now houses the Foreign Ministry. Bolívar is said to have planted the huge walnut tree in the courtyard. On 25 September 1828, there was an attempt on his life. His mistress, Manuela, thrust him out of the window and he hid for two hours under the stone arches of the bridge across the Río San Agustín (now Calle 7). Santander, suspected of complicity, was arrested and banished.

Almost opposite the Palacio de San Carlos is the **Teatro Colón** ⓘ *C 10, No 5-32, T284 7420 (due to reopen in mid-2014)*. It is considered Colombia's most prestigious theatre. Its opulent style is typical of late 19th-century Italian architecture. South of the Palacio de San Carlos is the **Iglesia de María del Carmen** ⓘ *Cra 5, No 8-36*, the most striking church building in Bogotá, in neo-Gothic style, with excellent stained glass and walls in bands of red and white.

One block northeast of here is the **Casa de la Moneda** (Mint) ⓘ *C 11, No 4-21, www.banrep cultural.org, Mon-Sat 0900-1900, Sun and holidays, 1000-1700, closed Tue, free*. The building dates back to 1620 when Felipe III of Spain ordered its construction, making this the first mint in South America to produce gold coins. It houses Colombian and European art and sculptures and the machines used to produce gold and silver coins. The courtyard is worth seeing. In the same block is the **Museo Botero** ⓘ *same entrance, website and hours*. A well-displayed, excellent collection of Botero's own sculptures and paintings, this includes his fine modern and impressionist art including Picasso, Miró, Dalí and Monet. Well worth a visit. Also in this block is the Botero shop, the **Colección de Arte del Banco de la República**

15 Quiebra Canto *B4*

Churches ⛪
1 Catedral *B2*
2 Capilla del Sagrario & Palacio Arzobispal *B2*
3 La Tercera Orden *B4*
4 La Veracruz *B3*
5 Mária del Carmen *C2*

6 San Agustín *B2*
7 San Diego *B5*
8 San Francisco *B3*
9 San Ignacio *B2*
10 Santa Clara *B2*

Trans Milenio
bus route – – – – – –

and **La Manzana Café**. In the same street is the Banco de la República's modern **Biblioteca Luis Angel Arango** ① *No 4-14, hours as above, free*, one of the best endowed and arranged in South America, with three heavily used reading rooms, research rooms, art galleries, a splendid concert hall and a musical instrument collection.

A few blocks north of here is **Casa de Poesía Silva** ① *C 12C, No 3-41, T286 5710, http://casadepoesiasilva.com, Mon-Fri 0900-1300, 1400-1800, free*, house of the poet José Asunción Silva until his death in 1895. The restored colonial house, with a peaceful patio, has a museum, bookshop and a fine audio and book library with taped readings of almost every Spanish-speaking author. CDs are sold in the bookshop. There are also lectures and poetry readings.

Up from the Casa de Poesía to Calle 12C/ Carrera 2, turn right up a delightful narrow alleyway (Callejón del Embudo) to the **Plaza del Chorro de Quevedo** ① *C 12B y Cra 2*, which is believed to be the centre of the Muisca village of Teusaquillo and was certainly where Jiménez de Quesada took possession of the territory in the name of King Charles of Spain to form the kingdom of New Granada on 6 August 1538. The name dates from around 1800 when Father Francisco Quevedo provided a *chorro* (well) for the local people. Students take a break from their studies in the bars and cafés here, adding to the activity (and safety) of the area until about 2000.

The **Palacio de Nariño** (1906), the presidential palace and offices, occupies a large space due south of Plaza Bolívar. It has a spectacular interior and a fine collection of modern Colombian paintings. It is occasionally open to the public. The guard ceremonially changes Monday, Wednesday, Friday and Sunday, normally at 1730. To the south is the elaborately ornate Church of **San Agustín** (1637). It, too, has fine paintings by Vásquez Arce and the Image of Jesus, which was proclaimed Generalísimo of the army in 1812.

Up Calle 7 from the Palacio Nariño is the **Museo Arqueológico** ① *Cra 6, No 7-43, T243 0465, www.musarq.org.co, Tue-Fri 0830-1700, Sat 0900-1600, US$1.50, ISIC discount*, a fine and extensive collection of Latin American, pre-Columbian pottery, in the restored mansion of the Marqués de San Jorge. The house itself is a beautiful example of 17th-century Spanish colonial architecture. Below the Palacio Nariño is the **Museo del Siglo XIX** ① *Cra 8, No 7-93, Mon-Fri 0830-1730, Sat 0900-1300, US$1*, which has a fine collection of 19th-century items within a restored mansion. Nearby, the colonial **Santa Clara church and museum** ① *Cra 8, No 8-91, www.museoiglesia santaclara.gov.co, Tue-Fri 0900-1700, Sat-Sun 1000-1600, US$1.50*, has a fine interior. It is now a religious museum and concert hall. A block north of Santa Clara is the **Escuela de Artes y Oficios Santo Domingo** ① *C 10, No 8-73, T282 0534, www.eaosd.org, Mon-Fri 1000-1200, 1300-1500, Sat 0800-1200*, a school for traditional teaching trades and arts in a beautiful colonial building. Expensive craft items and furniture are sold.

Downtown Bogotá

At the junction of Cra 7 and Avenida Jiménez de Quesada, which marks the La Candelaria and Downtown boundary, is the **Plazoleta del Rosario** with, on its southern side, the **Colegio Mayo de Nuestra Señora del Rosario** (1651), a beautiful colonial building, now a university. Across the Avenida Jiménez de Quesada is the **Banco de la República**, the other side of which is **Parque Santander**, with a bronze statue of Santander, who helped Bolívar to free Colombia and was later its President. There is a handicraft market most days.

Also on Parque Santander is the wonderful **Museo del Oro** (Gold Museum) ① *C 16, No 5-41, T343 2222, www.banrepcultural.org/museo-del-oro, Tue-Sat 0900-1800 (leave by 1900), Sun and holidays 1000-1600 (leave by 1700), closed every Mon, 1 Jan, Good Friday, 1 May, 24, 25, 31 Dec, US$1.50, free on Sun, audioguides in Spanish, English and French, also guided tours in Spanish and English*. This unique collection is a must and a poignant reminder of why the *conquistadores* found Colombia and the rest of the continent so appealing. There are more than 35,000 pieces of pre-Columbian gold work in the total collection, most of which is held here. The rest are in other Museos de Oro sponsored by the Banco de la República throughout Colombia. The ancient gold objects discovered in Colombia were not made by primitive hammering alone, but show the use of virtually every technique known to modern goldsmiths. A tasteful light show in the Salón Dorado (Gold Room) highlights some 8000 pieces and should not be missed. Opposite the Gold Museum is **Galería Artesanal de Colombia** ① *C 16, block 5, Mon-Sun 0900-1900*, an arts and crafts market.

Also around Parque Santander: **San Francisco** church (mid-16th century) ① *www.templode sanfrancisco.com, 7 Masses a day, 9 on Sun*, with paintings of famous Franciscans, choir stalls, a famous ornate gold high altar (1622), and a fine Lady Chapel with blue and gold ornamentation. The remarkable ceiling is in Spanish-Moorish (*mudéjar*) style. Try to see this church when it is fully illuminated. The church of **La Veracruz**, first built five years after the founding of Bogotá, rebuilt in 1631, and again after the 1827 earthquake. José de Caldas, the famous scientist, was buried along with many other victims of the 'Reign of Terror' under the church. It has a bright white and red interior and a fine ceiling. **La Tercera Orden** is a colonial church famous for its carved woodwork along the nave and a high balcony, massive wooden altar reredos, and confessionals, built by the Third Franciscan Order in the 17th century.

Continuing north along Carrera 7, at Calle 26 you reach **Parque de la Independencia**, adorned with wax palms. In the park is the **Planetarium/Museo del Espacio** ① *T281 4150, www.idartes. gov.co, Tue-Sun 1000-1700, US$5.25 including dome and museum, reductions for students, children and seniors.* Behind is the impressive Moorish-style brick bullring, **La Santamaria**, Cra 6, No 26-50, see under What to do. Also at this junction (Carrera 7 and Calle 26) are the church and monastery of **San Diego**, a picturesque, restored old building. The Franciscan monastery with fine mudéjar ceiling was built in 1560 and the church in 1607 as its chapel. Local craft items are sold in one part of the old monastery. Across the street is the **Tequendama Hotel**, one of the city's finest. Near the park is the **Biblioteca Nacional** (www.bibliotecanacional.gov.co), with its entrance at Calle 24, No 5-60. On the corner is the **Museo de Arte Moderno** (Mambo) ① *C 24, No 6-00, www.mambogota.com, Tue-Sat 1000-1800, Sun-holidays 1200-1630, US$2, students and seniors half price*, with a well-displayed collection of Colombia's modern artists and foreign artists including Picasso, Dalí and Ernst. There is also a good shop. **Edificio Colpatria** ① *Cra 7, No 24-89, US$1.70*, the tallest building in this area and illuminated at night, is open Friday 1800-2100, Saturday 1100-2000, Sunday and holidays 1100-1500 for good views of the city from the 48th floor.

Museo Nacional ① *Cra 7, No 28-66, T381 6470, www.museonacional.gov.co, Tue-Sat 1000-1800, Sun 1000-1700, permanent collections free, various tours available*, is an old prison converted into a museum, founded by Santander in 1823. There is an excellent archaeological collection. Its top floor houses a fine art section, comprising national paintings and sculptures. Allow at least two hours to look round. There is a café.

In the link between Central and North Bogotá is Colombia's main state university, **Universidad Nacional**, housed in the Ciudad Universitaria. Be aware that the university's main entrance on Cra 30 is periodically the focal point of protests (sometimes violent) between students and riot police. Avoid the area during these times. There is an interesting, peaceful and well-organized **Jardín Botánico José Celestino Mutis** ① *Av 63, No 68-95, T437 7060, www.jbb.gov.co, Tue-Fri 0800-1700, Sat-Sun and holidays 0900-1700, US$1.35, children US$0.70, guided tours at weekends*. It has a large collection of orchids, plus roses, gladioli and trees from all over the country.

Maloka ① *Cra 68D, No 24A-51, near the bus terminal, www.maloka.org, daily 1000-1900, US$12 including everything*, is a complex of science and technology exhibits, screen cinema, ice rink, all under a dome. Entry is cheaper without cinema ticket.

Monserrate

① *T284 5700 (answer service in English too), www.cerromonserrate.com. The path is open Mon-Fri 0500-1800 for sports; 0800-1200 for the public with tour operators; 1200-1600 general public; weekends 0600-1600. The return fare is US$8 Mon-Sat 0700-1730, US$8.75, Mon-Sat 1730-2300; US$4.60 on Sun, on either the funicular (Mon-Sat 0700-1145; Sun 0530-1700, holidays 0600-1700), or the cable car (Mon-Sat 1200-2300, Sun 0900-1730). Both every 15 mins. Times change frequently.*

There is a very good view of the city from the top of **Monserrate** (3152 m), the lower of the two peaks rising sharply to the east. It is reached by a funicular railway, a cable car and a path. The new convent at the top is a popular shrine and pilgrimage site. At the summit, near the church, a platform gives a bird's-eye view of the city's tiled roofs, modern suburbs and of the plains beyond stretching to the rim of the Sabana. Sunrise and sunset can be spectacular. There are two upmarket touristy restaurants at the top, **Casa Santa Clara**, which also has a café, and **Casa San Isidro** (closed Sunday). Many people walk or run up Monserrate first thing in the morning. The path is dressed stone and comfortably graded all the way up with refreshment stalls half-way and frequent police presence. It is closed after dark. It takes about 1¼ hours up (if you don't stop – the record is reportedly 18 minutes). There is a health centre at the top if you need it. The bottom station and path entrance are not far from the top end of Avenida Jiménez de Quesada and Las Aguas terminus of the **TransMilenio**; you can walk there in daylight with the same precautions you would take anywhere else in the city. If you prefer you can take a taxi to or from the entrance. The walk up to **Guadalupe**, the higher peak opposite Monserrate, is not recommended.

At the foot of Monserrate is the **Quinta de Bolívar** ①*C 20, No 2-91 Este, T336 6419, www.quintadebolivar.gov.co, Tue-Sat 0900-1700, Sat-Sun 1000-1600, US$1.50, reductions for students and children, guided tours, in English on Wed 1100.* This is a fine colonial mansion, with splendid gardens and lawns. There are several cannons captured at the battle of Boyacá. The elegant house, once Bolívar's home, is now a museum showing some of his personal possessions and paintings of events in his career. Opposite the Quinta is the attractive campus of the prestigious private university, Los Andes.

North Bogotá

North of Calle 68 are expanding wealthy suburbs, shopping malls and classy restaurants, an area regarded as having the best hotels. Between Cra 4 and Cra 5 and Calle 68 and Calle 71 is the **Zona G** (for 'gourmet'), home to some of Bogotá's best (and most expensive) restaurants. The T-shaped pedestrianized area made up by Calle 83 and Cra 13 is Bogotá's **Zona Rosa** (also known as the Zona T) with many fashionable bars, clubs and restaurants. Further north the streets around Parque 93 have more expensive bars and restaurants, while at the very limits of the city, off Cra 7 between Calle 117 and Calle 119, is **Usaquén**, formerly a satellite town with a pleasant plaza, a popular evening and weekend excursion for *bogotanos* wishing to escape the metropolis.

North Bogotá is also noted for its huge, lavish shopping malls, which are worth a visit even if the prices don't grab you. The **Hacienda Santa Bárbara** has been constructed within a large country mansion, and parts of the colonial architecture, even some of the old gardens have been retained.

⦿ Bogotá listings

For hotel and restaurant price codes, and other relevant information, see Essentials.

⦿ Where to stay

IVA tax of 16% is charged by middle and more expensive hotels. It is additional to the bill but included in our price classification.
Note Always insist that taxi drivers at the airport or bus station take you to the address we quote. There are many small, cheap, unregistered hotels and *hostales* in parts of the

city which may be unsafe for tourists and are far from the sights.

La Candelaria *p847, map p850*
Several hostels and hotels are members of the Asociación de Alojamiento de la Candelaria (ASACAN), T311-530 2677, asacan@googlegroups.com.
$$$$ Hotel de la Opera, C 10, No 5-72, T336 2066, www.hotelopera.com.co. Once the residence of Simón Bolívar's personal guard. Opulent, exquisite rooms in colonial, republican

and deco style, 2 rooftop restaurants with superb views, spa facilities.

$$$ Abadia Colonial, C 11, No 2-32, T341 1884, www.abadiacolonial.com. Fine colonial building in the heart of this area. Comfortable rooms if a bit small, ask for a street-facing room, safe, Italian restaurant. Recommended.

$$$ Casa Platypus, Cra 3, No 12F-28, T281 1801, http://casaplatypus.wix.com/hotel#!. From the owner of the Platypus Hostel, this hotel is aimed at 'the parents of backpackers' or anyone with a larger budget. Beautiful colonial building overlooking the Parque de los Periodistas, excellent rooms with extra large beds and duvets, also has dorms (US$21), kitchen, dining room, roof terrace with views of Monserrate. Very helpful. Highly recommended.

$$$ Platypus, C 12F, No 2-43, T341 3104, http://platypushotel.wix.com/hostalplaty. As the first backpackers' hostel to open in Colombia, the Platypus has all the facilities you would expect and remains popular. Owner Germán Escobar's knowledge of Colombia is encyclopaedic. Has 12 private rooms with bath and several dorms with bunks (US$20). Recommended.

$$-$ Alegría's Hostel, Cra 2, No 9-46, T286 8047, www.alegriashostel.com. In the heart of La Candelaria, set around a pleasant patio. Private room and 4- to 10-bed dorms (US$10-13) available.

$$-$ The Cranky Croc, C 12D, No 3-46, T342 2438, www.crankycroc.com. Aussie-run hostel in a beautiful 300-year-old building, carefully restored to retain many of the original features. Excellent facilities, lounge with a fireplace. Has several private rooms with and without bath and dorms with bunks, US$12-14 pp.

$$-$ Hostal Fátima, C 12C, No 2-24, T281 6389, www.hostalfatima.com. A maze of brightly coloured rooms and sunny patios with lots of stained-glass windows and potted plants. Sauna, jacuzzi, weekly programme of events. Has several private rooms with and without bath as well as dorms with bunks (US$10). Long stays available. Also has a branch in Capurganá.

$$-$ Hostal Sue, C 12F, No 2-55 and **Hostal Sue Candelaria**, Cra 3, No 12C-18, T334 8894 and T341 2647, www.suecandelaria.com. Both have excellent facilities, including hot water and places to relax in hammocks. The first attracts those seeking a quieter atmosphere while the latter has a bar and has a younger crowd, keener on partying. Dorms with bunks (US$11).

$$-$ Swiss Hostal Martinik, Cra 4, No 11-88, T283 3180, www.hostalmartinik.com. New Canadian management, good location, US$11 pp in dorm, also private rooms, a bit dark but good facilities.

$ Masaya, Cra 2, No 12-48, T/47 1848, www masaya-experience.com. French-owned hostel with dorms for 5 to 10 (also private rooms with breakfast), tapas bar, games, excursions and cultural events. Has another branch in Santa Marta (**$$$-$**).

Downtown and El Chapinero *p852, maps p848 and p850*

$$$$ Tequendama, Cra 10, No 26-21, T382 0300, www.sht.com.co. One of Bogotá's traditional grand hotels, witness to some of Colombia's most important political events since its inauguration in 1953, now run by

Crowne Plaza. With 4 restaurants, a spa, pool and large rooms it is well equipped for the conferences it hosts.

$$$ Boutique Alma, Cra 5, No 57-79, Chapinero Alto, T704 2454, reservas@ hotelboutiquealma.com. In an 'English-style' house, quiet, well appointed, good reports, in a group with properties in Cali, San Andrés and elsewhere.

$$ Las Terrazas, C 54A, No 3-12, T255 5400, hotellasterrazas@yahoo.com. Well placed in a quiet area of Chapinero Alto, popular with foreigners. Each room has a large balcony with excellent views of the city. First 2 floors are student residences.

$$-$ La Pinta, C 65, No 5-67, T211 9526, www.lapinta.com.co, and **La Niña**, C 66, No 4a-07, T704 4323, www.lanina.com.co. 2 popular, welcoming hostels with private rooms, with and without bath, and dorms (US$11), Colombian-run, with gardens, tours and Spanish classes offered, lots of activities.

North Bogotá *p854, map p848*
Many hotel chains are well represented here, such as **Charleston**, www.hotelescharleston. com, **Estelar**, www.hotelesestelar.com, **Royal**, www.hotelesroyal.com, and **Sonesta**, www.sonesta.com (opposite Unicentro).

$$$$ Morrison, C 84 Bis, No 13-54, T622 3111, www.morrisonhotel.com. Handily located near the Zona T, contemporary British design, large rooms with thermo-acoustic windows. It looks out onto the beautiful Parque León de Greiff.

$$$ Casona del Patio, Cra 8, No 69-24, T212 8805, www.lacasonadelpatio.net. With 24 immaculate rooms set around a sunny patio and well situated near the Zona G, this is one of the best mid-range options. Recommended.

$$$-$ Los Andes Hostel, Cra 13A, No 79-07, El Lago, T530 4035, www.losandeshostel. com. 1 block from Zona T and its nightlife, with and without bath, safe, quiet, laundry facilities, airport pick-up, Spanish and salsa classes arranged.

❷ Restaurants

The more exotic and fashionable places to eat are in North Bogotá, but Candelaria has its bistros and good value, typical Colombian food. Take local advice if you want to eat really cheaply in markets or from street stalls.

Throughout the city there are a number of chains with several outlets. Don't miss **Crepes & Waffles**, www.crepesywaffles.com (see website for branches in Colombia and elsewhere), serving very good salads, pittas, crêpes, soups, vegetarian choices, plus lots of desserts, and **Crepes & Waffles**, www.wok. com.co, for Asian cuisine. Also **El Corral**, for hamburgers, pizzas, etc, with regular and **Gourmet** branches; **La Hamburguesería**, www.lahamburgueseria.com, for more than just burgers. Also the popular coffee shop chains **Juan Váldez** and **Oma**.

La Candelaria *p847, map p850*
$$$ La Cicuta, C 9, No 1-95, T283 0229. Mon-Fri 1200-1600, Sat-Sun 1200-1700, phone ahead. French cuisine in a lovely restaurant, overlooking a beautiful garden. Good vegetarian options.

$$ La Paella, C 11, No 5-13. Close to the Centro Cultural García Márquez, serves Spanish food and specializes in paellas.

$$ Moros y Cristianos, C 7, No 5-30. New location for this Cuban restaurant. Mon-Thu 1200-1600, Fri-Sat 1200-2400, Sun 1200-1800, live music Fri-Sat nights and Sun.

$$ Rosita, C 12B, No 1A-36. On Plazoleta Chorro de Quevedo, this is an excellent little breakfast and lunchtime spot.

$$-$ La Totuma, Cra 2, No 12B-58. On Callejón del Embudo, economic sushi other Japanese dishes. Colourful surroundings.

$ Bulevar Sésamo, Av Jiménez de Quesada 4-64. Busy vegetarian lunch spot; pay first and find a table; give ticket to waitress.

$ Construimos El Futuro, C 12D bis, No 2-19. Good breakfasts and *menú del día* served by a neighbourhood cooperative. Also has a supermarket, the **Hostal Casu**, www.caciquesuga muxi.com, restaurant and cultural centre **Hibiscus**.

$ Panadería Pastelería La Vieja Suiza, Cra 3 at C 12C. Closed Sun. Tiny place selling coffee, *pasteles*, vegetables, breads and cakes. Has hotel above.

$ Yumi Yumi, Cra 3, No 12F-40. Tiny hole-in-the-wall café-bar serving sandwiches, crêpes and juices. Thai curries on Tue night and 2 for

1 cocktails every night. 2 larger branches in North Bogotá.

Downtown Bogotá *p852, maps p848 and p850*

Many restaurants and cafes along Carrera 4A in Barrio La Macarena (behind the Bull Ring), as well as Zona G nearby.

$$$ Criterión, C 69A, No 5-75, T310 2810. Minimalist decor, expensive French-influenced menu, with shellfish and steak, large wine list.

$$$ Estrella de los Ríos, C 26D, No 4-50, La Macarena, T334 0502, www.estrelladelosrios. com. Estrella, the author of several cookbooks, calls her small place an 'anti-restaurant'. Her idea is that you should feel much like you are dining at home. Her food is Colombian and Caribbean. You must book 8 days in advance for a 7-course meal costing US$55, excluding alcohol. Highly recommended.

$$$-$$ Artesano, Cra 4A, No 27-12, www. artesanogourmet.com. Specializes in 'woodfire cooking': fish and meat dishes, as well as pizzas, plus pastas, sandwiches, etc. Also *pastelería*.

$$$-$$ Asadero Capachos, C 18, No 4-68, T243 4607, www.asaderocapachos.com. Closed Mon. Not for vegetarians, meat from the Llanos, simple menu, good food, live music Fri-Sun, busy.

$$$-$$ Enobra, Cra 4A, No 26A-37. Fashionable, chic restaurant with sparse decor serving tapas and various cuts of steak.

$$$-$$ La Cigale, C 69A, No 4-93, T249 6839, www.lacigale.com.co. French restaurant with a variety of Gallic specialities.

$$$-$$ Tábula, C 29 bis, No 5-90, www. elorigendelacomida.co/tabula. Tue-Sun 1200-1600, also Thu-Sat 1900-2300. Gourmet international menu in stylish surroundings a couple of blocks from La Macarena.

$$ Al Wadi, C 27, No 4A-14, www.restaurante alwadi.com. Healthy Lebanese food, including kebabs, falafel and rice dishes.

North Bogotá *p854, map p848*

North of C 76 there are 3 popular areas for eating and drinking: Zona T, also known as the Zona Rosa, C 83 and Cra 13; further north is Parque 93, surrounded by eating places, most of which have queues at lunchtime; and C 117 with Cra 6A and Cra 7 in Usaquén.

$$$ Abasto, Cra 6, No 119b-52, Usaquén, T215 1286. Decribed as "honest" food with the best organic ingredients, breakfast and market, gourmet coffees and teas.Many good reports.

$$$ Kathmandu, Cra 6, No 117-26, T213 3276, www.kathmandusite.com. Excellent Asian restaurant in Usaquén, with cocktails, events and a shop.

$$$ Salto del Angel, Cra 13, No 93A-45, T654 5454, www.saltodelangel.com.co. This huge restaurant on Parque 93 has a large, varied menu including steaks, ceviches and international options including fish and chips. On Sat-Sun, after dinner, the tables are cleared and it becomes a popular upmarket disco.

$$$-$$ 80 Sillas, C 118, No 6A-05, Usaquén, T744 9097. All kinds of ceviches and other seafood served in wooden elevated patios with encroaching ferns.

$$ Camino del Café, Cra 6A, No 117-26, Usaquén. Pleasant café with outdoor terrace and Wi-Fi. Good coffees, sandwiches, ice creams and cocktails.

🔊 Bars and clubs

La Candelaria *p847, map p850*

There are any number of bars and cafés around Plaza Chorro de Quevedo and along Cra 3 which come alive in the early evening.
Bogotá Beer Company, C 12D, No 4-02, www.bogotabeercompany.com, is the La Candelaria branch of this expanding chain of good pubs belonging to a microbrewery with 8 types of beer.
Quiebra Canto, Cra 5, No 17-76. In colonial house, world music, funk and salsa, best nights Wed, Thu, friendly crowd.

Downtown to North Bogotá *p854, map p848*

Most bars and clubs are concentrated in the Cra 11-13, C 80-86 region, known as the Zona Rosa. Some of these have live entertainment. Further south along Cra 7, from C 32 up to C 59 draws an edgier crowd of filmmakers, artists and students.
Alma Bar, C 85, No 12-51, T622 8289. Wed-Sat 1900-0300, entry US$11-17. Bar/club playing crossover Colombian/Western music.

Galería Café Libro, Cra 11A, No 93-42, T218 3435, www.galeriacafelibro.com.co. Tue-Sat. Restaurant, bar and dancing, with 2 other branches.

In Vitro, C 59, No 6-38, T666 9129. Tue 2000-0245, Fri-Sat 2100-0245. What started as a weekly meeting of friends to show their short films and documentaries has developed into one of Bogotá's hippest clubs. Has an eclectic mix of salsa, rock'n'roll and indie music.

Son Salomé, Cra 7, No 40-31, 2nd floor, T285 0547. Thu-Sat 1800-0300. Good local salsa bar, intimate, cosy atmosphere.

Theatrón, C 58, No 10-18, www.theatronde pelicula.com. Fri-Sat 2100-0300. In old large theatre, gay and mixed crowd, attracts international DJs, good atmosphere with 10 different zones. Be careful leaving the club at night, use a taxi.

⊕ Entertainment

Bogotá *p847, maps p848 and p850*

Cinema Consult *El Espectador*, www.vive.in, or www.planb.com.co for programmes. There are cinema complexes in the principal shopping centres; see for instance *CineColombia*, www.cinecolombia.com. Foreign films, old and new, are shown on weekend mornings in some commercial cinemas and there are many small screening rooms running features. **Cine Paraíso**, Cra 6, No 119B-56, Usaquén, T215 5316, foreign art films. **Cinemanía**, Cra 14, No 93A-85, mainstream and foreign art films. **Museo de Arte Moderno** shows Colombian and foreign films daily, all day. Admission, US$6-11.

There's an international film festival in Oct (Festival de Cine de Bogotá, www.bogocine. com) and a European film festival (Eurocine, www.festivaleurocine.com) in Apr/May.

Dance classes Punta y Taco, Salón de Baile, C 85, No 19A-25, T300-218 7199, www.puntay taco.com. Tango and salsa classes Mon-Fri 0800-2100, Sat 0800-1830, flexible class times, professional.

Theatre Many of the theatres are in the Candelaria area. For **Teatro Colón**, see details on page 851. Bogotá hosts the biennial **Ibero American Theatre Festival** (Apr, next 2016), www.festivaldeteatro.com.co. The **Temporada de Opera y Zarzuela** is held annually, starting in Apr, with international artists. In the city centre, **Centro Cultural Gabriel García Márquez**, C 11, entre Cras 5 y 6, has activities, concerts, dance classes and exhibitions; it also has a large **FCE** bookshop, **El Corral Gourmet** restaurant and **Banco de Bogotá**.

⊛ Festivals

Bogotá *p847, maps p848 and p850*

There are many local religious festivals and parades at Easter and Christmas. One of the best is the **Jan Fiesta de Reyes Magos** (Three Kings) in the suburb of Egipto (up the hill to the east of Candelaria) with traditional processions.

In **Apr/May** Feria Internacional del Libro (book fair) is held in **Corferias** (see below), www.feriadellibro.com. In **Jun-Jul** there is Rock al Parque, the biggest annual rock festival in Latin America (http://rockalparque.com.co). In **Sep**, Festival Internacional de Jazz. In **Dec** at Corferias is the **Expoartesanía** fair, www. expoartesanias.com, an excellent selection of arts and crafts and regional food from across Colombia. Highly recommended. There are events throughout the year at **Corferias**, Cra 37, No 24-67, www.corferias.com.

○ Shopping

Bogotá *p847, maps p848 and p850*

Heavy duty plastic for covering rucksacks etc, is available at several shops around C 16 and Av Caracas; some have heat sealing machines to make bags to size. In Barrio Gaitán, Cra 30 y C 65, are rows of leather shops. This is an excellent area to buy made-to-measure leather jackets, good value; not safe at night, go during the day.

Camping equipment Monodedo, Cra 16, No 82-22, T616 3467, www.monodedo. com. Good selection of camping and climbing equipment. Enquire here for information about climbing in Colombia. **Tatoo**, C 122, No 18-30, T629 9949. Complete outdoor gear suppliers.

Handicrafts Artesanías de Colombia, Claustro de Las Aguas, next to the Iglesia de las Aguas, Cra 3, No 18A-60; Cra 11 No 84-12 by CC Andino; and in **Plaza de los Artesanos**, Tr 48, No 63A-52. Beautiful but expensive designer crafts. **Centro Colombiano de Artesanos**, Cra 7, No 22-66, and **Colombia Linda**, Cra 7, No23-49, are 2 central craft galleries. **Tienda Fibrarte**, Cra 3, No 11-24. *Artesanías* from around Colombia and Latin America. Good fique products, coca tea. Credit cards accepted. **Galería Cano**, Ed Bavaria, Cra 13, No 27-98 (Torre B, Int 119), also at Unicentro, Airport and elsewhere, www.galeriacano.com.co. Sell textiles, pottery, and gold and gold-plated replicas of some of the jewellery on display in the Gold Museum. **Mercado de Pulgas** (fleamarket) on Cra 7/C 24, on Sun morning and holidays. A better fleamarket can be found at the Usaquén market around the plaza, Cra 7 y C 119B, on Sun, also a good arts and crafts market at the top of the hill in Usaquén. **Pasaje Rivas**, C10 y Cra 10. Persian-style bazaar. Hammocks, basketware, ceramics, cheap.

Jewellery The pavements and cafés along Av Jiménez, below Cra 7, and on Plazoleta del Rosario are used on weekdays (especially Fri) by emerald dealers. Rows of jewellers and emerald shops also along C 12 with Cra 6. Great expertise is needed in buying: bargains, but synthetics and forgeries abound. **Emerald Trade Centre**, Av Jiménez, No 5-43, p 1. Has a collection of outlets in one place. **GMC Galería Minas de Colombia**, Diag 20A, No 0-12, T281 6523, www.galeriaminasdecolombia.com, at foot of Monserrate diagonal from Quinta de Bolívar. Great choice of gold and emerald jewellery at good prices.

Markets Paloquemao food market, Cra 27 y C19. Bogotá's huge central market, good to visit just to see the sheer abundance of Colombia's tropical fruits and flowers. Cheap stalls serving

comida corriente. Safe. **San Andresito**, Cra 38 y C12. Popular contraband market, cheap alcohol, designer sports labels, electrical goods, football shirts. Relatively safe.

◑ What to do

Bogotá *p847, maps p848 and p850*
Bullfighting On Sun during the season (Jan-Feb), and occasionally for the rest of the year, at the municipally owned **Plaza de Toros de Santamaría**, Cra 6, No 26-50, T334 1482, near Parque Independencia. (Local bullfight museum at bullring, door No 6.)
Cycling The *Ciclovía* is a set of streets leading from Cra 7 to the west, closed to motor traffic every Sun and bank holidays, 0700-1400 for cyclists, joggers, rollerskaters etc. There are also the extensive *Cicloruta* paths. Recommended are **Bogotá Bike Tours**, Cra 3, No 12-72, La Candelaria, T281 9924, T312-502 0554, www.bogotabiketours.com. Bike tours (US$19 pp) at 1030, 1330, rentals (US$9.50 half-day), walking tours, cooking classes and more besides. Also **Bogotravel Tours**, C 12F, No 2-52, T282 6313, T313-368 0441, www.bogotraveltours.com. Bike tours (US$20) and rentals, emeralds tours, walking tours, party bus tour, Zipaquirá and Guatavita, Spanish classes, enthusiastic, local guides.
Football Tickets for matches at El Campín stadium can be bought in advance at **Federación Colombiana de Futbol**, Av 32, No 16-22, http://fcf.com.co. It is not normally necessary to book in advance, except for the local Santa Fe-Millionarios derby, and internationals. Take a cushion, matches Sun

at 1545, Wed at 2000. Big matches can be rowdy and sometimes violent.

Horse riding Cabalgatas Carpasos, Km 7 Vía La Calera, T368 7242. Horse riding at night too. **Cabalgatas San Francisco**, 47 km from the city near La Vega, T310-265 2706, http://cabalgatassanfrancis.wix.com/enovoa#!. Daily rides around coffee farms, in the mountains, by rivers and lakes, from US$25 per hr.

Rafting and kayaking Boga Travel, T313-832 9169, info@bogatravel.com. Expeditions throughout Colombia, many on the Río Magdalena, mostly by kayak, but also rafting, hiking, 4WD, camping and cultural trips.

Rock climbing La Gran Pared, Cra 7, No 50-02, T285 0903, www.granpared.com. Artificial rock-climbing wall in the centre of Bogotá. All levels of experience catered for, day rates available.

Trekking Sal Si Puedes, hiking group arranges walks every weekend and sometimes midweek on trails in Cundinamarca, and further afield at national holiday periods; very friendly, welcomes visitors. Hikes are graded for every ability, from 6 km to 4-day excursions of 70 km or more, camping overnight. Groups are often big (30-60), but it's possible to stray from the main group. Reservations should be made and paid for a week or so in advance at Cra 7, No 17-01, of 640, T283 3765, open Mon-Thu 0900-1700, Fri 0900-1400, www.salsipuedes.org. **Corporación Clorofila Urbana**, Cra 49B, No 91-41, T616 8711, www.clorofilaurbana.org, offers similar walking opportunities with an emphasis on environmental awareness. **Caminantes del Retorno**, T315-249 0090, www.caminantesdelretorno.com, is a group of guides with 25 years' experience of treks in out-of-the-way places in the country. A recommended operator is **Camina por Colombia**, Cra 7, No 22-31, of 226 B, T286 7487, https://sites.google.com/site/caminaporcolombia/, walks in different parts of Colombia. There are several other groups and operators.

Tour operators

Colombia Oculta, Cra 29, No 74-19 (by appointment only), T301 0213, www.colombiaoculta.org. Adventure tours throughout Colombia, ecotourism, programmed or personalized tours.

De Una Colombia Tours, Cra 24 (Parkway), No 39b-25, of 501, La Soledad, T368 1915, www.deunacolombia.com. Dutch-run tour agency with tailor-made trips throughout Colombia and an emphasis on introducing tourists to the country's people as well as its landscapes.

Eco-Guías, Cra 7, No 57-39, of 501, T347 5736 or T212 1423, www.ecoguias.com. Colombian/English team specializes in tailor-made trips, ecotourism, adventure sports, trekking, riding and tourism on coffee *fincas*, efficient, knowledgeable and well organized. Highly recommended.

Mantaraya Travel, Cra 11B, No 98-08, of 501, T691 0684, www.mantarayatravel.com. Offers tailor-made tours throughout Colombia (and South America), experienced, lots of activities and itineraries available.

More Local, C 120A, No 5-02, T215 5949, www.morelocal.co. Concentrates on authentic cultural and responsible travel in Amazonas, coffee region and around Bogotá, community visits include hikes and activities to suit all levels of experience, several European languages spoken, has associated reforestation projects.

Somos Aventureros, Cra 15, No 79-70, of 403, T467 3837, www.somosaventureros.com. Mon-Fri 0830-1800, Sat 0900-1300. Arranges a variety of tours and adventure sports throughout the country.

Universal Tourism, T300-485 6632, www.universaltourismcolombia.com. Individual and small-group tours with bilingual guides (several languages), focus on Colombia from a local's perspective.

🚌 Transport

Bogotá *p847, maps p848 and p850*
Air
El Dorado airport, on Av El Dorado, has 3 terminals: Terminal 1 for all domestic flights except **Avianca**, whose domestic flights use Puente Aéreo (Terminal 3). The new Terminal 2 is for all international flights (T266 2000 for the airport call centre, or visit www.elnuevodorado.com, Spanish only). Allow at least 2 hrs for checking in and security for all

flights. The terminals have ATMs which accept international credit cards. Use only uniformed porters. There is a baggage deposit in national arrivals, US$4 for 12 hrs. There are tourist offices in international arrivals and in domestic arrivals, see Arriving in Bogotá.

The taxi fare from airport to city is roughly US$15, more at night and early morning. Only take a yellow, registered taxi by getting a ticket from the official booth. There are *colectivos* (US$1.25 plus luggage pp) from airport to centre. A *bus satélite* connects the 3 terminals and the bus stop for the city. The TransMilenio extends to the airport on a route starting at C 100 on Cra 7, then taking 'Calle 26. It is usually too crowded for luggage.

For internal flights, which serve all parts of the country, see page 837. Reconfirmation is not necessary if booking online. Otherwise reconfirm all flights 48 hrs before departure.

Bus
Local Fares start at US$0.75, depending on length of route and time of day. Most buses have day/night tariff advertised in the window. Busetas (green) charge a little more and can be dirty. There are some *ejecutivo* routes (red and white) with plush seats, US$0.80, and *colectivos* (small vans), cramped but fast, charge US$0.80. Fares are also higher on holidays. The TransMilenio (www.transmilenio.gov.co), an articulated bus system running on dedicated lanes connects North, Central and South Bogotá. Corriente services stop at all principal road intersections, *expresos* limited stops only (*expresos* do not run on Sun). Journeys cost US$0.70, US$0.85 in rush hours; charge cards area available for frequent use. Using the TransMilenio is a good way of getting around, but it can be crowded and confusing. Make sure you know which bus stops at your destination. Taking luggage onto the TransMilenio is usually very difficult.

Long distance If going to towns in Boyacá or Cundinamarca for a long weekend, leave Bogotá before Fri 1200 as it can take 1½ hrs to get from Terminal to outskirts. Try to arrive back before 1300, or ask to be set down in North Bogota and take a TransMilenio bus to centre (see above regarding luggage).

The main **Terminal de Transportes** is at C 23, No 69-59, near Av Boyacá (Cra 72) between El Dorado (Av 26) and Av Centenario (C 13), sometimes referred to as Terminal El Salitre, T423 3600, www.terminalde transporte.gov. co. There is also access from Cra 68. It is divided into 5 modules; modules 1-3 have several bus companies serving similar destinations. Module 4 has a health centre and module 5 is for arrivals If possible, buy tickets at the ticket office before travelling to avoid overcharging and to guarantee a seat, especially during bank holidays. Fares and journey times are given under destinations below. If you are travelling to or from the north or northwest, you can significantly cut down on the journey time by taking the TransMilenio to Portal del Norte, or Portal de la 80 on C 80, thus avoiding an arduous journey through Bogotá's traffic. If you are travelling to or from the south, many buses use the **Terminal de Transportes del Sur**, C 57 Q Sur, No 65F-68 Autopista Sur, near the Portal del Sur TransMilenio terminus. This is as convenient for the centre of the city as the main terminal if you don't have large bags. To get to the main terminal take a bus marked 'Terminal terrestre' from the centre or a *buseta* on Cra 10. A taxi costs around US$6-8 from or to the centre, with a surcharge at night. Give your desired address at the kiosk in module 5, which will print out a slip with the address and price. At airport and bus terminals, unofficial taxis are dangerous and should be avoided. To get into town from the terminal take buses marked 'La Candelaria', 'Centro' or 'Germania'; ask the driver where to get off (the 'Germania' bus goes up to the centre and La Candelaria). Note there are two areas called La Candelaria, one in the north of the city and one in the south. Be sure to ask for La Candelaria in 'el centro histórico'.To get to North Bogotá from the terminal, take a bus heading in that direction on Cra 68.

International bus Ormeño, bus terminal modelo 2, T410 7522, has a service Lima-Caracas 3 days a week via Cúcuta; there is also a Bogotá-Lima service weekly. International tickets with Ormeño can only be bought at the bus terminal. Much better (and cheaper) is to do the trip in stages and enjoy the countries you are travelling through.

Taxi

See Taxis, page 838. Taxis are relatively cheap, with fares priced in units, starting at 25. The minimum fare is US$2.20. Average fare from North Bogotá to the centre US$6. Check for additional charges above what the meter states eg: night charge and rides to the airport. At busy times, empty taxis flagged down on the street may refuse to take you to less popular places. If you are going to an address out of the city centre, it is helpful to know the neighbourhood (barrio) you are going to as well as the street address, eg Chicó, Chapinero (ask at your hotel). Radio taxis are recommended for safety and reliability; when you call, the dispatcher gives you a cab number, confirm this when it arrives. Try these numbers and websites: T400 1111, www.autotaxiejecutivo.com; T481 1111, www.taxmilenio.com; T611 1111, www.coopteletaxi.com; or T210 0000, http://rtaxi.com.co.

❶ Directory

Bogotá *p847, maps p848 and p850*
Banks Some head offices are grouped around the Avianca building and the San Francisco church, others are in North Bogotá on or near C 72. The best way to obtain pesos in Bogotá is to use ATMs. Any other method will require your passport and, often, queues. Since it will probably require at least 2 or 3 attempts, either go downtown or in the north, where there are many banks. Unfortunately, there are no rules; there are countless ATMs accepting MasterCard, Visa and other cards; but machines may be down or out of cash, or just don't accept the cards stated. Several *cambios* on Av Jiménez de Quesada, between Cras 6 and 11, and in the north of the city. On Sun exchange is virtually impossible except at the airport. CC Hacienda Santa Bárbara has several *cambios*. **Orotur**, in the Hotel Tequendama building, is quick and efficient, cash only, including sterling. **Cambios New York Money**, in CC Unicentro, Av 15, No 123-30, loc 1-118, accepts sterling, efficient. **Car hire** Car hire is expensive in Colombia. There are lots of agencies at the airport. **Colombiana Rent a Car**, Av Boyacá, No 63-12, T473 8694, www.colombianarentacar.com. **Embassies and consulates** For all foreign embassies and consulates in Bogotá, see http://embassy.goabroad.com. **Immigration** Migración Colombia: Bogotá office (for extending entry permits), C 100, No 11B-27, T511 1150, www.migracioncolombia.gov.co. Mon-Fri 0800-1600. Migración will not authorize photocopies of passports; look in Yellow Pages for notaries.
Language courses Some of the best Spanish courses are in the Universidad Nacional (see map, page 848), T316 5000, www.unal.edu.co, or Universidad de los Andes, T339 4949, www.uniandes.edu.co, and Pontificia Universidad Javeriana, T320 8320, www.javeriana.edu.co. Good value Spanish courses at the Universidad Pedagógica, C 72, No 11-86, T610 8080. Good reports. Spanish World Institute, Cra 4A, No 56-56, T248 3399, www.spanishworldinstitute.com. Personalized courses from beginner to advanced, activities and events organized, 30 hrs US$270. Enquire at Platypus hostel for more information. Carmen Trujillo, T315-874 1325, carmen.trujillo@colombia quest.com, is recommended. English, French and Italian spoken. **Medical services** 24-hr emergency health service, T123. Cruz Roja Nacional, Av 68, No 66-31, T746 0909, www.cruzrojabogota.org.co. Has 11 vaccination centres in the city as well as emergency (T132) and other services. Santa Fe de Bogotá, C ra 7, No 117-15, T603 0303, www.fsfb.org.co, and El Bosque, C 134, No 7B-41, T649 9300, www.clinicaelbosque.com.co, are both modern, private hospitals, with good service.

Around Bogotá

The basin on which Bogotá stands, with high ranges of the Cordillera to the east, is known as La Sabana de Bogotá and is the centre of Colombia's important cut-flower industry. Around La Sabana are many places of interest in nearby towns for weekend excursions out of the city.

Zipaquirá → Phone code: 1. Colour map 1, B3. Population: 91,000. Altitude: 2650 m.

Twenty kilometres beyond Chía, on La Sabana with its flower greenhouses and dairy farms, is the famous rock salt mine, still producing salt after centuries. Within the mines, the **Salt Cathedral** ① www.catedraldesal.gov.co, 0900-1730, Sun Mass at 1200, various ticket combinations available starting at US$11.50; discounts for children and seniors, is one of the major attractions of Colombia. The entrance is in hills about 20 minutes' walk west of the town from Parque Villaveces. At the site, there is an information centre and the **Museo de la Salmuera** ① US$1.75, which explains how salt is produced. The original underground cathedral was dedicated in 1954 to Nuestra Señora del Rosario (patron saint of miners). Continuing deterioration made the whole cave unsafe and it was closed. A remarkable, new salt cathedral, minimalist in style, was opened on 16 December 1995. Inside, near the entrance, are the 14 Stations of the Cross, each sculpted by a different artist. Other sections of the cathedral follow to the Nave, 180 m below the surface, with huge pillars 'growing' out of the salt. All is discreetly illuminated and gives an austere impression.

Zipaquirá has a pleasant colonial plaza, which is dominated by a brick cathedral (see www.zipaquira-cundinamarca.gov.co). Tuesday is market day. In the town is the **Museo Quevedo Zornoza** ① Calle 3, No 7-69, Tue-Fri 0930-1200, 1400-1600, Sut-Sun 0900-1700, US$1, which displays musical instruments and paraphernalia including the piano of General Santander. The **Museo Arqueológico** ① C 1, No 6-21, T852 3499, next to the Parque Villaveces entrance, daily 1000-1800, US$2.25, houses more than 1500 pieces of pre-Columbian pottery.

Around Zipaquirá

Nemocón, 15 km northeast of Zipaquirá, has **salt mines** ① open daily 0900-1800, US$5.65, children and students half price and a church with original 17th-century frescos. There is a small but interesting **Museo de Sal** ① on the plaza, Tue-Sun 0900-1700, closed Tue after bank holiday, US$1, which includes history of the salt industry in the time of the Chibcha. ATM on main plaza. A side road connects with the Bogotá-Cúcuta highway. Some 8 km beyond Nemocón, with its own access to the main Tunja road, is **Suesca**, a centre of rock climbing on sandstone cliffs overlooking the Río Bogotá. ▶▶ See Transport, page 866.

Southwest of Bogotá

The picturesque Simón Bolívar Highway runs 132 km from Bogotá to **Girardot**, the former main river port for Bogotá. About 20 km along this road from the centre of Bogotá is Soacha, the end of the built-up area. A right fork here leads to the **Chicaque Parque Natural** ① www.chicaque.com, daily 0800-1700, US$6.75, with separate prices for lodging, guides, riding, a privately owned 300 ha park, principally cloud forest between 2100 m and 2700 m on the edge of the Sabana de Bogotá. It is a popular spot for walkers and riders at weekends with good facilities for day visitors and a Swiss-style refugio, cabins, camping and restaurant, about 45 minutes down the trail from the entrance (full board price US$103 double, camping US$31).

Northwest of Bogotá

The Sabana de Bogotá is dotted with farms and groves of eucalyptus. Two routes go to Honda (see Transport, below). The older road passes through the small towns of Fontibón, Madrid and **Facatativá**, 40 km from Bogotá. Some 3 km from Facatativá, on the road to the west, is the park of Piedras de Tunja, a natural rock amphitheatre with enormous stones, numerous indigenous pictographs and an artificial lake. The roads meet at **Villeta**, 71 km from Facatativá, a popular weekend resort. The road continues to Honda, half way to which is the interesting historical town of **Guaduas** (*Population: 33,000*; *Altitude: 1000 m*; *Phone code: 1*). In the main plaza is a statue of the heroine of independence, Policarpa Salavarrieta, the cathedral and one of several museums in the town. Sunday market. Nearby La Piedra Capira offers great views of Río Magdalena. Bus to Honda, US$4, one hour.

Honda On the west bank of the Río Magdalena, Honda was founded in 1539. Until the rise of first rail, then road transport, it was a major port for cargo and passengers from the centre of the country to the Caribbean. It is well known for its many bridges spanning the Ríos Magdalena and Guali, at whose junction the town lies. The historic centre has narrow, picturesque streets and the lively indoor market in a grand, early 20th-century building. There are two museums: **Museo del Río Magdalena** ① *at end of Calle del Retiro, irregular opening hours*, and **Casa Museo Alfonso López Pumarejo** ① *C13, No 11-75, Plaza América, Mon-Sat 0800-1200, 1400-1800, Sun 0900-1300, free*, dedicated to the ex-president (1934-38, 1942-45). El Salto de Honda (the rapids which separate the Lower from the Upper Magdalena) is just below the town. In February the Magdalena rises and fishing is unusually good. People come from all over the country for the fishing and the festival of the Subienda, the fishing season.

Beyond Honda the road passes cattle *fincas* and eroded outcrops on its way to La Dorada and, across the river, Puerto Salgar with a huge military base. The highway north towards Santa Marta and Medellín is being dualled. The road to Medellín leaves the south-north highway just before Puerto Triunfo. The other main road from Honda heads west to Manizales (see page 931).

Gateway to the Llanos

Through Colombia's longest tunnel, the impressive Buenavista, and along an 85-km road running southeast from Bogotá lies **Villavicencio** (*Phone code: 8; Population: 384,000; Altitude: 467 m*), capital of Meta Department. **Instituto de Turismo de Villavicencio** ① *C 37, No 29-57, p 6, Centro, T670 3975, www.turismovillavicencio.gov.co, Mon-Fri 0730-1530, see also Instituto de Turismo del Meta, Km 3, Vía Camino Ganadero, Parque Las Malocas, T661 4444, www. turismometa.gov.co*. Villavicencio, a modern town, is a good base for visiting Los Llanos (the plains), at the foot of the eastern slopes of the Eastern Cordillera stretching more than 800 km east as far as Puerto Carreño, on the Orinoco in Venezuela. Los Llanos is cowboy country and the never ending expanse of fertile plains makes it ideal for cattle raising, the area's main industry. The area is also rich in oil and the flames from distant oil refineries can be seen flickering on the horizon.

From Villavicencio, three roads run into the Llanos. To the north is a popular route known as the Ruta del Piedemonte Llanero. The road east from Villavicencio, known as the Amanecer Llanero, passes through the Apiay oil field before reaching **Puerto López** on the Río Meta, while the road south, the Ruta del Embrujo Llanero, leads to the **Parque Nacional Natural Sumapaz** ① *entry US$9, páramo at 3000-3600 m*, and where adventure sports such as whitewater rafting, paragliding and abseiling can be practised, and the Parque Nacional Natural Serranía de la Macarena. Tours to isolated parts of Los Llanos are just beginning to open up. One such is to **Caño Cristales**, a river in which plants, Macarenia clavigera, bloom deep red for a brief period and, together with other natural colours, make an amazing spectacle. The river, in the south of the Serranía de la Macarena, is reached from the town of La Macarena, to which there are weekly flights from Bogotá and local flights from Villavicencio. You must check in advance when the phenomenon is occurring as it can happen anytime between June and November. The area is protected and policed, but you cannot camp there. Agencies such as **Caminantes del Retorno** (see page 860) run tours.

For hotel and restaurant price codes, and other relevant information, see Essentials.

◉ Where to stay

Zipaquirá *p863*

$$ Cacique Real, Cra 6, No 2-36, T851 0209, www.hotelcaciquereal.com. Recently declared a Patrimonio Cultural, fine little hotel, lovely courtyard with hanging baskets, good rooms, car park.

$$-$ Casa Virrey, C 3, No 6-21, T852 3720, casavirreyorani@hotmail.com. Housed in a new building with comfortable rooms.

$ Torre Real, C 8, No 5-92, T851 1901, hoteltorrereal@yahoo.es. Light and airy rooms with large beds.

Around Zipaquirá: Suesca *p863*

$$$ La Esperanza, Cra 7 IC, No 98A-44, Km 1 along railway from Suesca, T226 7513, www.hotellaesperanza.com.co. With restaurant, conference centre, sauna, camping at Campamento Zhay, US$4pp, or rent a house or room sleeping 3-5, good for groups.

$$ Caminos de Suesca, Vereda Cacicazgo, Entrada a las Rocas, T310-341 9841. Hotel, restaurant and climbing centre offering packages that include adventure sports or just B&B, very helpful. Felipe Cadavid runs Vertical Extremo, www.verticalextremo.com Recommended.

Honda *p864*

$$$ Posada Las Trampas, Cra 10A, No 11-05, T310-343 5151, www.posadalastrampas.com. Boutique hotel in a converted mansion on Calle Las Trampas, suites and standard rooms, pool on the terrace, bar and business centre.

$$$-$$ Casa Belle Epoque, C 12, No 12A-21, Cuesta de San Francisco, T251 1176/310-481 4090, www.casabelleepoque.com. A lovely old house overlooking the market, with spacious, high-ceilinged rooms, all with fan or a/c, one small dorm (**$** pp), beautiful roof terrace with jacuzzi, pool, lots of antique, period touches. British-Colombian run, very helpful, advance booking preferred. Arranges horse riding, boat and fishing trips. Recommended.

$$-$ Riviera Plaza, C 14, No 12-19, T251 2125, T312-745 1446, hotelrivieraplaza@hotmail. com. Cheaper with fan, rooms around a large pool, which is open till 2200. End rooms have views over the Río Gualí and the colonial part of town. All meals extra, US$3.50, in restaurant 0700-2100.

$ Calle Real, Cra 11, No 14-40, T320-212 2931, opposite Teatro Honda. Central, safe, cheaper with fan, parking, restaurant, small rooftop pool.

$ Tolima Plaza, Cra 11, No 15-75, T310-298 6418, www.hoteltolimaplaza.com.co. Large, rambling hotel, pool, large car park. Rooms are a bit spartan but OK, with fan, US$12.50 pp in shared room. Helpful management.

Gateway to the Llanos: Villavicencio *p864*

$$$ Hotel del Llano, Cra 30, No 49-77, T671 7000, www.hoteldelllano.com. Tucked under the forested hills of the Cordillera Oriental, a smart option with good rooms, spa, sauna, pool, restaurant, tour agency.

$$$ María Gloria, Cra 38, No 20-26, T672 0197, www.hotelmariagloria.com. In an ugly building, with a good pool area with sauna and Turkish bath.

$$ Savoy, C 41, No 31-02, T662 6009. Simple rooms with a/c. Vegetarian restaurant downstairs.

$ Mochilero's Hostel, C 18, No 39-08-10, Barrio Balatá, T667 6723/310-297 8831, www.mochileroshostel.com. Hostel also offers salsa and yoga classes, adventure tours.

◉ Restaurants

Zipaquirá *p863*

There are several eating places near the plaza and there is a Plazoleta de Comidas in town.

Chía

$$$ Andrés Carne de Res, C 3, No 11-56, T863 7880, www.andrescarnederes.com. Thu-Sun. This arty, rustic restaurant and bar has become a tourist institution with typical food, highly original decor, 'performers' to liven things up and free arts and crafts workshops for children. Now also has a branch in North Bogotá, but this is the original.

Honda p864

Calle Centenario is the Zona Rosa, with restaurants, burger bars, discos, supermarkets, etc. It is buzzing at weekends. **Alejo Parrilla**, C Centenario, only Fri-Sun evenings, is best for meat. **Arepas La 21**, street stall at corner of Cra 21 y C Centenario, opposite restaurant **Sazón y Son**, sells *pinchos* (kebabs), *empanadas* and *torta de chócolo* (maize).

There are 2 economical fish restaurants by Río Magdalena a short walk from town, serving fresh catch of the day: **KZ (Donde Marta)**, and **El Mello**, both at Av Pacho María, Bahía 3.

⊛ Festivals

Honda p864

Semana Santa celebrations are good. See above for the festival of the Subienda.

Gateway to the Llanos: Villavicencio p864

Jun-Jul Torneo Internacional del Joropo, involving parades, singers and over 3000 couples dancing the *joropo* in the street. **Encuentro Mundial de Coleo** festival in **mid-Oct**. Colourful event, similar to rodeo in which cowboys tumble young calves by grabbing their tails and twisting them until they lose their balance.

◑ What to do

Around Zipaquirá: Suesca p863

Rock climbing For information call Monodedo climbing centre, T310-216 8119, www.monodedo.com (shop open at weekends). In Suesca turn right at the entrance to Las Rocas, past Rica Pizza restaurant. **Ricardo Cortés**, the owner of Rica Pizza, also arranges climbing trips and local accommodation. See also **Caminos de Suesca**, Where to stay.

⊖ Transport

Zipaquirá p863

Bus The Zipaquirá bus station is 15 mins' walk from the mines and cathedral. Many buses from **Bogotá**: from the Terminal de Transporte, take a bus from Módulo 3, otherwise from the Intermunicipio terminal at the Portal del Norte terminus of the **TransMilenio** in North Bogotá, US$2.20 each way on either route, 1½ hrs from Terminal de Transport, 45 mins from Portal

Norte. Zipaquirá can also be reached from Tunja (see page 867), by taking a Bogotá-bound bus and getting off at La Caro for connection to Zipaquirá, US$3.50. Note when arriving to C174 terminus from Zipaquirá you need to buy a **TransMilenio** bus ticket to leave the station. To avoid this, ask the driver to drop you off before the bus station.

Train La Sabana station at C 13, No 18-24, Bogotá. A slow tourist steam train runs on Sat, Sun and holidays at 0830 calling at Usaquén in the north of Bogotá, going north to Zipaquirá (1130) and Cajicá, back in Bogotá, La Sabana at 1740. Cost: adult US$24, child up to 12, US$14.75. Tickets should be bought in advance at La Sabana station, T375 0557, or Usaquén station, Trv 10, No 100-08, or from travel agents.

Southwest of Bogotá: Chicaque Parque Natural p863

Take a bus from Bogotá to Soacha and ask for continuing transport to the park, T368 3114/244 1230. If driving, there is a better route via Mosquera on the Honda road, left towards La Mesa and in 11 km left again on the road to Soacha, the park sign is 6 km along this road.

Honda p864

New bus terminal is on the outskirts, where Diagonal 17 meets the main road heading north to La Dorada. Buses to **Bogotá** take 2 routes, via Facatativá ('Faca') which is slower but has cheaper tolls and is used by most companies, and via La Vega and Calle 80 to the north. The roads diverge at Villeta. Several companies go to Bogotá, eg **Bolivariano, Copetran, Omega**, via Faca, US$8.30-13.25, 4-5 hrs; **Cundinamarca** go via La Vega, 3 a day, US$11 (also to **Zipaquirá**, US$12.70), also **Tax La Feria** *camioneta*, 8 a day, 3½ hrs, US$14 (for Cundinamarca and La Feria, T251 5300, 320-271 7039). **Omega** to **Bucaramanga**, US$36, 7 hrs, at 1830. To **Manizales**, US$15. Several daily buses to **Medellín**, Bolivariano, Flota Magdalena, US$18-19, 6 hrs.

Gateway to the Llanos: Villavicencio p864

Air LAN and Satena to **Bogotá** daily. Satena flies to Puerto Carreño and to destinations in the Llanos. **Bus** Station outside town, taxi US$1.50. To/from **Bogotá**, Bolivariano mini vans and others leave frequently, US$12, 1½ hrs.

Bogotá to the Venezuelan border

The main road route from Bogotá to Venezuela has some beautiful stretches and passes through, or near, several colonial towns. In Cundinamarca and Boyacá it gives access to the Laguna de Guatavita, perhaps the nearest place the Spaniards came to finding their El Dorado, historical battle sites and the Sierra Nevada del Cocuy, excellent climbing and hiking country. The principal towns, both with a strong colonial heritage, are Tunja and charming Villa de Leiva.

The highway crosses Santander and Norte de Santander Departments on its way to Cúcuta. That this was an important route for the Spaniards can be seen in the colonial villages, like Barichara, and the more important centres like Bucaramanga and Pamplona. There is also some grand scenery in the Chicamocha canyon and the eastern cordillera, with possibilities for adventure sports.

Bogotá to Villa de Leiva

Guatavita → *Phone code: 1. Colour map 1, B4. Population: 6700. Altitude: 2650 m.*
The modern town of Guatavita Nueva, 75 km from Bogotá, is a popular haunt for Bogotanos. It was rebuilt in replica colonial style when the old town of Guatavita was submerged by the reservoir. There is a small bullring, cathedral and two small museums, one devoted to the Muisca people and the other to relics of the old Guatavita church. There many artisan shops, which sell *ruanas*. Market day is Sunday. The tourist information booth can find accommodation.

Laguna de Guatavita, a sacred lake of the Muisca, is where the legend of El Dorado (see box, page 868) originated. Access to the Laguna del Cacique Guatavita y Cuchilla de Peñas Blancas park is only allowed with a permit from the **Corporación Autónoma Regional de Cundinamarca** (CAR) ① *Cra 7, No 36-45, Bogotá, T320 9000, www.car.gov.co, lake open Tue-Sun 0900-1600 but you can stay in the park till 1800, US$7.75, children and locals pay less.* The lake is a quiet, beautiful place; you can walk right round it, 1½ hours, or climb to the rim of the crater. From the park entrance there are guided walks and interpreted trails; guides speak English and Spanish. Opinions differ on whether the crater is volcanic or a meteorite impact, but from the rim at 3100 m there are extensive views over the countryside.

Tunja → *Phone code: 8. Colour map 1, B4. Population: 160,000. Altitude: 2800 m.*
Tunja, capital of Boyacá Department and 137 km from Bogotá, has some of the finest, well-preserved colonial churches of Colombia. When the Spaniards arrived in what is now Boyacá, Tunja was already an indigenous city, the seat of the Zipa, one of the two Chibcha kings. It was refounded as a Spanish city by Gonzalo Suárez Rendón in 1539. The **Cathedral** and five other churches are all worth visiting, particularly for their colonial woodwork and lavish decoration.

The **Casa del Fundador Suárez Rendón** ① *Plaza de Bolívar (Cra 9 19-56, next door to the cathedral), daily 0830-1230, 1400-1800, US$1,* is one of Colombia's few mansions of a Spanish conquistador (1539-1543) and has a peaceful courtyard with fine views of the valley; see the unique series of plateresque paintings on the ceilings. The **regional tourist office** is at ① *Cra 10, No 19-17, T742 6547, cultura.turismo@boyaca.gov.co.*

The market, near Plaza de Toros on the outskirts of town, is open every day (good for *ruanas* and blankets). Friday is main market day. During the week before Christmas (16-22 December), there is a lively festival with local music, traditional dancing and fireworks.

The battle of Boyacá was fought about 16 km south of Tunja, on the road to Bogotá. Overlooking the bridge at Boyacá is a large **monument to Bolívar** ① *daily 0800-1800, US$1.50 per car.* There are several other monuments, an exhibition hall and restaurant at the site. Bus from Tunja, US$1, ask for 'El Puente'. Bolívar took Tunja on 6 August 1819, and next day his troops, fortified by a British Legion, the only professional soldiers among them, fought the Spaniards on the banks of the swollen Río Boyacá. With the loss of only 13 killed and 53 wounded they

The Gilded Man

The basis of the El Dorado (Gilded Man) story is established fact. It was the custom of the Chibcha king to be coated annually with resin, on which gold dust was stuck, and then to be taken out on the lake on a ceremonial raft. He then plunged into the lake and emerged with the resin and gold dust washed off. The lake was also the repository of precious objects thrown in as offerings; there have been several attempts to drain it (the first, by the Spaniards in colonial times, was the origin of the sharp cut in the crater rim) and many items have been recovered over the years. The factual basis of the El Dorado story was confirmed by the discovery of a miniature raft with ceremonial figures on it, made from gold wire, which is now one of the most prized treasures of the Museo del Oro in Bogotá. Part of the raft is missing; the story is that the gold from it ended up in one of the finder's teeth! (Read John Hemming's *The Search for El Dorado* on the subject.)

captured 1600 men and 39 officers. Only 50 men escaped, and when these told their tale in Bogotá the Viceroy Samao fled in such haste that he left half a million pesos of the royal funds.

Villa de Leiva → *Phone code: 8. Colour map 1, B4. Population: 6800. Altitude: 2144 m.*

About 40 km west is the beautiful and unmissable colonial town of **Villa de Leiva** (also spelt Leyva) which has one of the largest plazas in the Americas. It is surrounded by cobbled streets, a charming, peaceful place. The town dates back to the early days of Spanish rule (1572), but unlike Tunja, it has been declared a national monument so will not be modernized. The first president of Nueva Granada, Andrés Días Venero de Leiva, lived in the town. Many of the **colonial houses** are now hotels, others are museums, such as the restored birthplace of the independence hero, **Casa de Antonio Ricaurte** ① *Cra 8 y C 15, T439 7800 ext 2066, Tue-Sun 0900-1200, 1400-1700, free.* Ricaurte was born in Villa de Leiva and died in 1814 at San Mateo, Venezuela, fighting with Bolívar's army. The house has a nice courtyard and garden. **Casa de Nariño** ① *Cra 9, No 10-25, Mon-Sat 0900-1230, 1400-1800, Sun 0830-1230, 1430-1700, free,* displays documents from the Independence period. The **Casa del Primer Congreso** ① *C 13 y Cra 9, on the corner of the plaza, free, Tue-Fri 0900-1200, 1400-1700, Sat 0900-1200,* in which the first Convention of the United Provinces of New Granada was held, is worth a visit if the local authority is not in session. On the Plaza Mayor the **Casa-Museo Luis Alberto Acuña** ① *US$1.10, daily 0900-1800,* houses fascinating examples of Acuña's work.

A **palaeontological museum** ① *15 mins' walk north of the town, Cra 9, No 11-42, T732 0466, www.ciencias.unal.edu.com (in Spanish only; click Museos), US$2, Tue-Sat 0900-1200, 1400-1700, Sun and holidays 0900-1500,* has well-displayed exhibits. The **Monasterio de las Carmelitas Descalzas** ① *Calle 14 y Cra 10, Sat, Sun and holidays 1000-1200, 1400-1700, US$2,* has one of the best museums of religious art in Colombia. Part of the monastery is the **Iglesia del Carmen** and the **Convento**, all worth a visit. The shops in the plaza and adjoining streets have a great selection of Colombian handicrafts.

Some colonial houses close Monday to Friday out of season, but the trip is worthwhile for the views and for long, peaceful walks in the hills. Many places, particularly restaurants, are closed Monday and Tuesday. Market day is Saturday, held in the Plaza de Mercado 0400-1300. During weekends and public holidays, the town is very crowded with Bogotanos. The helpful **tourist office** ① *Cra 9, No 13-04 just off the plaza, T732 0232, daily 0800-1800,* has local maps, gives advice on cheaper accommodation and bus schedules. Useful websites include www.villaleyvanos.com and www.villadeleyva.us. There is an ATM on the Plaza Mayor.

The wide valley to the west of Villa de Leiva abounds in fossils. Some 5 km along the road to Santa Sofía is the fossil of a dinosaur (possibly a Kronosaurus) found in 1977, now with a museum built around it. A second fossil found in 2000 nearby has been put alongside. Look for road signs to **El Fósil** ① *www.museoelfosil.com, daily 0800-1800, US$3*. About 2 km from El Fósil along this road is the turning for (1 km) the archaeological site of **Parque Arqueológico de Monquirá** or **El Infiernito** ① *Tue-Sun 0900-1200, 1400-1700, US$2.30 with guide*, where there are several carved stones believed to be giant phalli and a solar calendar. About 1 km beyond El Infiernito is the **Fibas Jardín del Desierto** ① *T311-222 2399, www.fibas.org, US$1, Wed-Sun 0830-1730, Mon and Tue with forewarning*, which sells cactus and desert plants. It features two mazes, based on indigenous designs, in which meditation exercises are held.

Some 6 km after the Infiernito turning is the **Monastery of Ecce-Homo** (founded 1620) ① *Tue-Sun 0900-1700, just knock on the door*; note the fossils on the floor at the entrance. It was built by the Dominicans between 1650 and 1695. It was reclaimed from the military in 1920, since when it has been repeatedly robbed; some of the religious art is now in the Chiquinquirá museum. What can be seen of the monastery is impressive, but the fabric and roof are in a poor state. There are buses from Villa de Leiva (0800-1615) to Santa Sofía, US$1.20; it is 30 minutes to the crossing, then a 2-km walk to the monastery. A tour of most of these attractions leaves the plaza at 0930, Saturday/Sunday, US$5.

About 12 km north of Villa de Leiva is a right turn for the **Santuario de Fauna y Flora de Iguaque** ① *www.parquesnacionales.gov.co, US$19 for foreigners, contact Organización*

Villa de Leiva

To ③ ② & Museo Paleontológico

200 metres
200 yards

To ③ ② & Museo Paleontológico

Monasterio de las Carmelitas Descalzas

Plazuela de San Agustín

Casa de Antonio Ricaurte

Museo Luis Alberto Acuña

Alcaldía

Casa del Primer Congreso

Plaza Mayor

Iglesia Parroquial

Parque Nariño

Plaza de Mercado

Casa de Antonio Nariño

San Francisco

To Santa Sofía, Ecce-Homo & El Fósil

To Bogotá, via Tunja or Chiquinquirá

Where to stay
1 Candelaria
2 Casa Vienna
3 Colombian Highlands & Hostal Renacer
5 El Marqués de San Jorge
6 El Molino la Mesopotamia
7 Hostal Sinduly
8 Plaza Mayor
9 Posada de los Angeles
10 Posada Don Blas

Restaurants
1 Casa Blanca
2 Casa Quintero (La Cocina de la Gata, Savia, Zarina)
3 Don Quijote
4 Olivas & Especias and Carnes & Olivas

Comunitaria Naturar Iguaque, T312-585 9892, naturariguaque@yahoo.es. The 6750-ha park is mainly high cloudforest of oak, fig and other temperate trees, many covered with epiphytes, lichens and bromeliads. There is also *páramo* (moorland) and a series of lakes at over 3400 m, and the mountains rise to 3800 m. At the visitor centre, Furachiogua, there is accommodation; camping with showers, toilets and cooking facilities. **Colombian Highlands** (see Where to stay, below) in Villa de Leiva are recommended for organized tours.

Ráquira → *Market day Sun.*

In the Chibcha language, **Ráquira** means 'city of pots' and with over 100 *artesanía* shops selling earthenware pottery in a village of just a dozen blocks, it is rightly considered the capital of Colombian handicrafts. In recent years there has been an influx of cheap products from Ecuador, somewhat diluting its appeal. The village itself, 25 km from Villa de Leiva, has been painted in an array of primary colours and has a picturesque plaza embellished with terracotta statues. Accommodation (**$$-$**) and places to eat on or near the plaza.

About 7 km along a very rough road, which winds up above Ráquira affording spectacular views, is the beautiful 16th-century **Monasterio Desierto de La Candelaria** ① *daily 0900-1700, US$1.50 plus US$0.55 to Hermit's Cave.* On the altar of the fine church is the painting of the Virgen de La Candelaria, dating from 1597, by Francisco del Pozo of Tunja. The painting's anniversary is celebrated each 1 February, in addition to 28 August, the saint's day of San Agustín. The convent has two beautiful cloisters, one featuring a 170-year-old dwarf orange tree, the other virtually untouched since the 17th century. They are lined with anonymous 17th-century paintings of the life of San Agustín.

Chiquinquirá → *Phone code: 8. Colour map 1, B3. Population: 45,000. Altitude: 2580 m.*

On the west side of the valley of the Río Suárez, 134 km from Bogotá and 80 km from Tunja, this is a busy market town for this large coffee and cattle region. In December thousands of pilgrims honour a painting of the Virgin whose fading colours were restored by the prayers of a woman, María Ramos. The picture is housed in the imposing **Basílica**, but the miracle took place in what is now the **Iglesia de la Renovación** ① *Parque Julio Flores.* In 1816, when the town had enjoyed six years of independence and was besieged by the Royalists, this painting was carried through the streets by Dominican priests from the famous monastery, to rally the people. The town fell, all the same. There are special celebrations at Easter and on 26 December, the anniversary of the miracle. The town is known for making toys and musical instruments.

⦿ Bogotá to Villa de Leiva listings

For hotel and restaurant price codes, and other relevant information, see Essentials.

⦿ Where to stay

Tunja *p867*
$$$ Hunza, C 21A, No 10-66, T742 4111, www. hotelhunza.com. One of several smart hotels in the **$$$-$$** ranges.
$$ Alicante, Cra 8, No 19-15, T744 9967, http:// www.hotelcasarealtunja.com/hotel-alicante. html. Minimalist design, sunny patio fringed by varieties of cactus, bright rooms, great value.
$$ Casa Real, C 19, No 7-65, T743 1764, www. hotelcasarealtunja.com. Sister hotel to **Alicante**.

A real bargain, comfortable rooms in a lovely colonial building with varnished wooden floorboards. Highly recommended.
$$ Posada San Agustín, C 23, No 8-63, T742 2986, www.posadadesanagustin.co. Beautiful colonial building on the Parque Pinzón, balustraded courtyard, antiques and old photos of Tunja, comfortable rooms, "a bit of a gem".
$ Conquistador de América, C 20, No 8-92, T742 3534. Lovely foyer with a bright skylight, rooms are small but comfortable.

Villa de Leiva *p868, map p869*
The town tends to be full of visitors at weekends and holidays when booking is

advisable. Book in advance for the Festival of Light.

$$$$-$$$ El Molino la Mesopotamia, Cra 8, 15A-265, T732 0235, www.lamesopotamia.com. A beautifully restored colonial mill filled with antiques, excellent home cooking, beautiful gardens, freshwater pool (US$2.50 for non-guests), memorable. Recommended.

$$$$-$$$ Plaza Mayor, Cra 10, No 12-31, T732 0425, www.hotelplazamayor.com.co. On the plaza, delightful octagonal courtyard with lemon trees, comfortable rooms and a good restaurant.

$$$ Candelaria, C del Silencio (Cra 18), No 8-12, T732 0534, www.hotelcandelaria. villadeleyva.com.co. Refurbished colonial building with 9 rooms of "monastic simplicity", in delightful location.

$$$ El Marqués de San Jorge, C 14, No 9-20, T732 0480, www.hospederiaelmarquesde sanjorge.com. Simple little place with rooms around a courtyard, cheaper Mon-Thu.

$$ Posada de los Angeles, Cra 10, No 13-94, T732 0562. Basic, clean rooms in a fine building 2 blocks from the plaza, restaurant, ask for a room overlooking the Iglesia del Carmen.

$$ Posada Don Blas, C 12, No 10-61, T732 0406. Sweet, simple little place 1 block from the plaza.

$$ Colombian Highlands and Hostal Renacer, Cra 9, No 11-02, T732 1201, T311-308 3739, www.colombianhighlands.com. 15-min walk from town, this hostel, belonging to English-speaking biologist Oscar Gilède, has some of the most comfortable rooms, private and shared, you are likely to find in a Colombian hostel. Extensive gardens, wood-fired pizza oven, hammocks, bike hire. Tour agency offering a variety of trips including adventure sports and scientific tours, excellent local information. Camping US$9.20-12, also tent rental.

$ Casa Vienna, Cra 10, No 19-114, T732 0711, www.casaviena.com. Austrian/Colombian-run, 10 mins from plaza, small, comfortable hostel with 3 rooms, dorm (US$9.50 pp), kitchen and communal area. Also runs Austrian bakery nearby and serves Indian food and pizza cooked in a wood-fired oven.

$ Hostal Sinduly, Cra 11, No 11-77, T320-429 4050, www.hosteltrail.com/hostalsinduly. Run by Austrian Manfred, 2 private rooms and a dorm in a colonial house 1 block from the plaza. English and German spoken.

Chiquinquirá *p870*

$$ El Gran, C 16 No 7A-55, T726 3700, www. elgranhotel.amawebs.com. Central, secure, comfortable, good restaurant.

$$ Sarabita, C 16, 8-12, T726 2079, hotelsarabita@yahoo.es. In a national monument, with pool and restaurant.

❼ Restaurants

Tunja *p867*

$ El Maizal, Cra 9, No 20-30, T742 5876. Good varied menu of local specialities.

$ La Cascada, Pasaje Vargas (C 19A), No 10-82. Popular at lunchtime, good value for lunches and breakfasts. There are other places on this street.

$ Pizza Nostra, C 19, No 10-36, T740 2040. Pizzas and lasagnes on a pedestrianized street.

Villa de Leiva *p868, map p869*

Villa de Leiva has dozens of good restaurants with varied international and local menus. Most, but not all, are concentrated in the town's upmarket food courts, Casa Quintero (on the plaza) and La Guaca (on C Caliente). Some are closed Mon-Wed.

$$ Don Quijote, La Guaca, C Caliente (Cra 9), Local 12. Award-winning Spanish restaurant with a 400-year-old kitchen.

$$ La Cocina de la Gata, Casa Quintero. Pleasantly decorated fondue restaurant, which also serves chicken and steak.

$$ Olivas & Especias, Cra 10, No 11-99. On the corner of the plaza, pizzas and pastas in homely surroundings. Next door's Carnes & Olivas (**$$$**) is also worth a try.

$$ Savia, Cra 9, No 11-75 (Casa Quintero). Great range of organic starters and interesting mains.

$$ Zarina, Cra 9, No 11-75 (Casa Quintero). Good Arabic and Oriental dishes as well as the usual chicken and steak.

$ Casa Blanca, C 13, No 7-06. Popular for regional specialities.

✿ Festivals

Villa de Leiva *p868, map p869*
Jan-Feb Astronomical festival, telescopes are set up in the Plaza for public use. **Virgen del Carmen, 13-17 Jul** annually. In **Aug** an international kite festival is held in the Plaza Major. **Nov** Festival de Gastronomía for the best individual dish cooked by the town's restaurants. **Festival of Light** is held every year from **7 Dec**.

⊖ Transport

Guatavita: Laguna de Guatavita *p867*
Bus Bogotá–Guatavita Nueva vía Autopista del Norte and Sesquilé, from Portal del Norte on the TransMilenio, US$4.50, 2-3 hrs, several departures morning; last return bus at 1730. A second route goes via La Calera, Tres Esquinas, Guasca and Guatavita Nueva. Also **Flota Valley de Tenza**, US$4, 3 a day. The routes meet at the entrance to the park but from Guatavita Nueva it's a 1½-hr walk to the park entrance, or you can share vehicle, about US$5 pp.

Tunja *p867*
Bus Bus station is 400 m steeply down from city centre. From **Bogotá** several

companies, 3-3½ hrs, 4½-5 hrs weekends and holidays, US$12. To **Villa de Leyva**, colectivos every 15 mins 0600-1830, US$4, 45-60 mins. To **Bucaramanga**, frequent services, 7 hrs, US$20-29.

Villa de Leiva *p868, map p869*
Bus The bus station is on Cra 9 between C 11 and C 12. Advisable to book the return journey on arrival at weekends. Buses to/from **Tunja**, 45-60 mins, US$4, every 15 mins from 0600 to 1800. To **Bogotá**, either go via Tunja, or 2 direct buses a day, 3½-4 hrs with Libertadores, US$7.50. To/from **Chiquinquirá**, 1½ hrs, US$4, 6 a day. To **Ráquira** see below. To **Iguaque National Park entrance**, 50 mins, US$2, at 0700 and 1000.

Ráquira *p870*
Buses from **Villa de Leiva** 4 a day, 30 mins, US$3.35. For the return, check if you have to change at Ramera. There are also buses to **Tunja** (3 a day) and **Bogotá**.

Chiquinquirá *p870*
Bus To **Tunja**, 3 hrs, US$8.50. To **Zipaquirá**, US$8.50. To **Bogotá**, 2½ hrs, US$7-8.50.

Sierra Nevada del Cocuy

A road runs northeast of Tunja to **Paipa** (41 km), noted for the **Aguas Termales** complex ⓘ *3 km to the southeast, T321-209 5655, www.termalespaipa.co, daily 0600-2200, water park/hydrotherapy US$6.70/21, children US$4.60/14.40*, and on 15 km to Duitama. From here it is 85 km to Soatá, one of the junctions for the **Parque Nacional Natural El Cocuy** ⓘ *entrance fee, US$25.20 for foreigners, payable at the park offices (C 5, No 4-22, T098-789 7280, El Cocuy, another office in Güicán), where you can also obtain a walking map. Guiding association Aseguicoc, T311-236 4275, aseguicoc@gmail.com. See also www.elcocuyboyaca.com and www. parquesnacionales.gov.co.* From either Soatá or, 20 km further north, by the bridge over the Río Chicamocha at **Capitanejo** are turnings to the attractive **Sierra Nevada del Cocuy** in the Eastern Cordillera, the best range in Colombia for mountaineering and rock climbing. The Sierra consists of two parallel north–south ranges about 30 km long, offering peaks of rare beauty (more than 22 are snow covered), lakes and waterfalls. The flora is particularly interesting, notably the thousands of *frailejones*.

   The park is accessible from the small towns of **El Cocuy** or, further north, **Güicán**. Either town is a perfect start or end point for hiking or climbing in the park. On the central plaza of El Cocuy is a model of the mountain area. One of the most spectacular hikes is from south to north (or vice versa), during which you will see a great part of what the park has to offer. It might appear an easy marked trail, but it is highly recommended to go with a guide as sudden changes in weather can cause visibility to drop to less than 10 m. You need to know where to camp and to get drinking water.

There is no accommodation on the longer treks in the park, so you must take all equipment. Basic food supplies can be bought in El Cocuy or Güicán, otherwise you should buy your food in Bogotá. There is no need to take ice axe or crampons, unless you are climbing Pan de Azúcar. Temperatures can drop below 0°C at night as most campsites are around 4000 m. The peak holiday periods (the last week in December, the first two weeks of January and Easter week) can get very busy. The best season for trekking is December to March but even in those months it can rain or be very foggy.

La Laguna de La Plaza is probably the most beautiful lake in the Sierra Nevada del Cocuy, surrounded by the snow tops of **Pan de Azúcar** and **Toti** in the west and Picos **Negro** and **Blanco** to the east. Just below Pan de Azúcar is **Cerro El Diamante**. At sunrise, this rock can change from grey to yellow, gold, red and orange if you are lucky with the weather. **Laguna Grande de la Sierra** is surrounded by Pan de Azúcar, Toti, Portales, Concavo and Concavito and is a perfect base camp for climbing one of these. **El Púlpito de Diablo** is an enormous, altar-shaped rock at 5000 m. From El Púlpito you can continue to climb up to the top of **Pan de Azúcar** (5100 m) overlooking Laguna de la Plaza on one side and Laguna Grande de la Sierra on the other. **Valle de los Cojines** is an enormous valley surrounded by snow peaks, filled with *cojines* (pillow plants). **Ritacuba Blanco** is the highest mountain of all (5322 m) and is not too difficult to climb. The views at the top over the Valle de Cojines and many other parts of the park are stunning.

◉ Sierra Nevada del Cocuy listings

For hotel and restaurant price codes, and other relevant information, see Essentials.

◉ Where to stay

Sierra Nevada del Cocuy p872

There are places to stay in El Cocuy and Güicán and *cabañas* on some of the trails into the park, eg Cabaña Guaicany, at the entrance to Valle de Lagunillas, T310-566-7554, guaicany@ hotmail.com, shared bath, great views of Ritacuba Blanco and other peaks, also possible to camp and to hire horses and/or guide. Cabañas Kanwara, at the foot of Ritacuba Blanca, T311-231 6004, the perfect starting point to climb the mountain or to walk to Laguna Grande de los Verdes, shared bath. Hacienda La Esperanza, T310-209 9812, www. cocuynevadohle.com, convenient for the walk to Laguna Grande de la Sierra, simple rooms with shared bath, good, horse riding.
$$ Casa Muñoz, Cra 5, No 7-28, El Cocuy, on the main plaza, T098-789 0028, T313-829 1073, www.hotelcasamunoz.com. With private and shared rooms, comedor.

$$ La Posada del Molino, Cra 3, No 7 51, El Cocuy, T8-789 0377, 312-352 9121, http:// elcocuycasamuseo.blogspot.co.uk. In a historic building, with private rooms, restaurant and information on tours to the national park.
$ pp **Hotel Villa Real**, El Cocuy, T311-475-6495, hotelvillareal@hotmail.com. Shared bath.

⊖ Transport

Sierra Nevada del Cocuy p872

Bus El Cocuy and Güicán can be reached by direct bus (early morning or late evening) from **Bogotá**, 10-12 hrs, US$25; buses also from **Tunja** US$14. Coming from Bucaramanga, change buses in Capitanejo. Around 0600 a milk truck leave the main plaza of El Cocuy, taking you to **Cabañas Guaicany** (the southern park entrance), **Finca la Esperanza** (for Laguna Grande de la Sierra) or to **Hacienda Ritacuba**, from where it's a 1-hr walk to **Cabañas Kanwarra**. Or take an *expreso* (private transport), US$45, from El Cocuy main plaza.

To Bucaramanga and Cúcuta

Socorro → *Phone code: 7. Colour map 1, B4. Population: 23,020. Altitude: 1230 m.*
The main road goes northeast for 84 km to Socorro, with steep streets and single storey houses set among graceful palms. It has a singularly large stone cathedral. The **Casa de Cultura** museum (opening hours vary) covers the local history and the interesting part played by Socorro in the fight for Independence. It is well worth a visit. There is a daily market.

San Gil → *Phone code: 7. Colour map 1, B4. Population: 33,000. Altitude: 1140 m.*
About 21 km beyond Socorro, northeast on the main road to Bucaramanga, is San Gil, an attractive colonial town with a good climate. It's a friendly, relaxed place and its main square is lively at night. San Gil is a centre for adventure sports (rafting, kayaking, parapenting, paragliding and caving) and is also a good place for biking, horse riding and walking. See What to do, page 879. Tourist office: **Instituto Municipal de Turismo y Cultura** ⓘ *C 12, No 10-24, T724 4617.* **Parque Gallineral** ⓘ *www.gallineral.sangil.com.co, daily 0800-1700, US$3, guides, some English speaking, tip them as they are not paid,* a delightful riverside park, covers 4 ha where the Quebrada Curití runs through a delta to the Río Fonce. It has a superb freshwater swimming pool and beautiful trees covered with moss-like tillandsia. Good view from **La Gruta**, the shrine overlooking the town (look for the cross). Visit **Juan Curi** waterfalls for abseiling or hiking (take a bus, US$3.50 return, towards Charalá and ask to be dropped off. There are two approaches, passing through private fincas. You may have to pay a small fee for access, about US$2. A return taxi fare is US$25).

Barichara → *Phone code: 7. Colour map 1, B4. Population: 10,000. Altitude: 1300 m.*
From San Gil a paved road leads 22 km to Barichara, a beautiful, quiet colonial town founded in 1741 and designated as a national monument. Among Barichara's places of historical interest are the Cathedral and three churches, the cemetery and the house of the former president Aquileo Parra Gómez (the woman next door has the key). There is a superb wide-ranging view from the *mirador* at the top of Carrera 10 across the Río Suárez to the Cordillera de los Cobardes, the last section of the Cordillera Oriental before the valley of the Magdalena.

An interesting excursion is to **Guane**, 9 km away by road, or two hours' delightful walk by *camino real* (historic trail), where there are many colonial houses and an archaeological museum in the **Parroquia San Isidro** ⓘ *daily 0800-1200, 1400-1800 (but times can be erratic), US$1.20.* It has an enormous collection of fossils found in the local area (which is constantly being added to), as well as Guane textiles and a mummified woman. Three good restaurants on the plaza serve regional food. From San Gil there is a three-day walk to the villages of Barichara, Guane, Villanueva, Los Santos, and the ghost town of Jordán, involving a spectacular descent of the Chicamocha canyon. Speak to Shaun at the **Macondo Hostal** in San Gil for more details of hostales and eating places on the way.

Between San Gil and Bucaramanga is the spectacular **Río Chicamocha canyon**, with the best views to the right of the road. There is a Parque Nacional visitor centre with panoramic views, activities, parking, snack bars and toilets and a 6.3-km **cable car** across the canyon ⓘ *www.parquenacionaldelchicamocha.com, Mon-Thu 0830-1830, Fri-Sun 0830-1900, but hours may change, US$21.60, including cable car and park entrance, children US$13.*

Bucaramanga → *Phone code: 7. Colour map 1, B4. Population: 539,000. Altitude: 960 m.*
The capital of Santander, 420 km from Bogotá, was founded in 1622 but was little more than a village until the latter half of the 19th century. The city's great problem is space for expansion. Erosion in the lower, western side topples buildings over the edge after heavy rain. The fingers of erosion, deeply ravined between, are spectacular. The metropolitan area of this modern, commercial city, has grown rapidly because of the success of coffee, tobacco and staple crops.

It is known as the 'city of parks' for its fine green spaces, eg Mejoras Públicas, de los Niños, San Pío and Las Palmas, but some areas, particularly Parque Centenario, are not very safe even in daylight.

The **Parque Santander** is the heart of the modern city, while the **Parque García Rovira** is the centre of the colonial area. On it stands the city's oldest church, **Capilla de Los Dolores** ① *C 35/ Cra 10*, a national monument. Just off Parque García Rovira is the **Casa de Cultura** ① *C 37, No 12-46, T642 0163, Mon-Sat 0900-1800, US$1*, in a fine colonial building with exhibitions, films and an *artesanía* display. The **Casa de Bolívar** ① *C 37, No 12-15, Tue-Sat 0900-1200, 1400-1800, US$1*, where Bolívar stayed in 1828. It is interesting for its connections with Bolívar's campaign in 1813. The **tourist office** ① *Instituto Municipal de Cultura, C 30, No 26-117, T634 1132, Mon-Fri 0800-1200, 1400-1830*, is friendly and knowledgeable. The departmental **Cultura y Turismo, Secretaría de Desarrollo** is at ① *C 37, No 10-30, T633 9666*. The **National Parks office** is at ① *Av Quebrada Seca No 30-44, T634 9418*.

Around Bucaramanga

In **Floridablanca**, 8 km southwest, is the **Jardín Botánico Eloy Valenzuela** ① *Tue-Sun 0800-1100, 1400-1630, US$2.60, children US$1.50*, take a Florida Villabel *bus from Cra 33, US$0.80*, or Florida Autopista *to the plaza and walk 1 km; taxi from centre, US$3*, belonging to the national tobacco agency. **Girón** a tobacco centre 9 km southwest of Bucaramanga on the Río de Oro, is a quiet and attractive colonial town. Its white buildings, beautiful church, bridges and cobbled streets are well preserved and the historic part of town unspoilt by modernization. Girón can be easily reached from Bucaramanga and makes a good day trip. By the river are *tejo* courts and open-air restaurants with *cumbia* and *salsa* bands. Bus from Cra 15 or 22 In Bucaramanga, US$1, taxi US$7. **Piedecuesta** is 18 km southeast of Bucaramanga. Here you can see cigars being handmade, furniture carving and jute weaving. Cheap, hand-decorated *fique* rugs can be bought. There are frequent buses to all the surrounding towns; taxi costs US$9. Corpus Christi processions in these towns in June are interesting. Bus from Cra 22, 45 minutes.

Bucaramanga to Pamplona

The road (paved but narrow) runs east to Berlín, and then northeast (a very scenic run over the Eastern Cordillera) to Pamplona, about 130 km from Bucaramanga. **Berlín** is an ideal place to appreciate the grandeur of the Eastern Cordillera and the hardiness of the people who live on the *páramo*. The village lies in a valley at 3100 m, the peaks surrounding it rise to 4350 m and the temperature is constantly around 10°C, although on the infrequent sunny days it may seem much warmer. There Is a tourist complex with cabins and there are several basic eating places.

Pamplona → *Phone code: 7. Colour map 1, B4. Population: 68,000. Altitude: 2200 m.*

Founded in the mountains in 1548, it became important as a mining town but is now better known for its university. It is renowned for its Easter celebrations. The climate is chilly. Pamplona is a good place to buy *ruanas* and has a good indoor market. The **Cathedral** in the spacious central plaza is the most attractive feature of this otherwise unprepossessing city. The **Iglesia del Humilladero**, adjoining the cemetery, is very picturesque and allows a fine view of the city. Museums include the **Casa Colonial** ① *C 6, No 2-56, Mon-Fri 0800-1200, 1400-1800; Sat 0800-1200, US$0.50*, archaeological museum, a little gem, and the **Museo de Arte Moderno** ① *C 5, No 5-75, Tue-Sun 0900-1200, 1400-1800*.**Tourist office** ① *C 5, No 6-45, T568 2880*, next to *alcaldía*, off Plaza Central. Very helpful, organizes tours and guides.

Cúcuta → *Phone code: 7. Colour map 1, B4. Population: 918,000. Altitude: 325 m.*

Some 72 km from Pamplona is the city of Cúcuta, capital of the Department of Norte de Santander, 16 km from the Venezuelan border. Founded in 1733, destroyed by earthquake 1875, and then rebuilt, its tree-lined streets offer welcome respite from the searing heat, as does the **cathedral**, on Avenida 5 between Calles 10 and 11. The **Casa de Cultura** (also known as Torre de

Reloj) ① *C13, No 3-67*, houses art exhibitions and the **Museo de la Ciudad** which covers the city's history and its part in the Independence Movement. For a border town, it is a surprisingly pleasant place to visit, with plenty of green spaces and a busy but non-threatening centre, but see Warning, page 880. **Corporación Mixta de Promoción de Santander** ① *C 10, No 0-30, T571 8981*, helpful. Tourist police at the bus station and airport. The international bridge between Colombia and Venezuela is southeast of the city.

Border with Venezuela → *Phone code: 7.*

Venezuela is 30 minutes ahead of Colombia. If you do not obtain an exit stamp, you will be turned back by Venezuelan officials and the next time you enter Colombia, you will be fined.

Colombian immigration ① *Migración Colombia (CFSM), Av 1, No 28-57, T583 5912, Mon-Fri 0730-1600*. Take a bus from the city centre to Barrio San Rafael, south towards the road to Pamplona. Shared taxi from border is US$9, then US$1.50 to bus station. Exit and entry formalities are also handled at the Migración Colombia office the white building on the lefthand side of road just before the international border bridge (Puesto Terrestre CENAF Villa del Rosario, Puente Internacional Simón Bolívar). See Venezuela chapter for Venezuelan immigration. There is no authorized charge at the border. For exchange, see Banks, page 880.

Venezuelan consulate ① *Av Aeropuerto Camilo Daza y C 17, Zona Industrial, T579 1954, http://cucuta.consulado.gob.ve, near airport, Mon-Thu 0800-1000, 1400-1500, Fri 0800-1000*. Nationals not requiring a visa are issued an automatic free tourist card by the Venezuelan immigration officers at the border. Overland visitors requiring a visa to Venezuela can get one here, or at the Venezuelan Embassy in Bogotá, although they may send you to Cúcuta. As requirements change frequently, it is recommended that all overland visitors check with a Venezuelan consulate in advance. Apply for visa at 0800 to get it by 1400. If you know when you will arrive at the border, get your visa in your home country.

Leaving and entering Colombia by private vehicle Passports must be stamped with an exit stamp at the white Migración Colombia building before the crossing. If not you will have to return later. Expect very long queues. Car papers must be stamped at the SENIAT office in Venezuela, see Venezuela chapter. With all the right papers, the border crossing is easy and traffic flows smoothly.

⊙ To Bucaramanga and Cúcuta listings

For hotel and restaurant price codes, and other relevant information, see Essentials.

● Where to stay

San Gil *p874*
$$ Macondo Hostel, Cra 8, No 10-35, T724 8001, www.macondohostel.com. Australian Shaun Clohesy has created more of a home-from-home than a hostel. Social area decked out with hammocks, garden, board games, free coffee and Wi-Fi, regular BBQs and other events, comfortable dorms (US$10-13), and a wealth of information on local activities. Recommended.

$$ Mansión del Sam, C 12, No 8-71, T724 6044, www.hotelmansionsangil.com. Colonial building on the corner of the Parque, most picturesque, large rooms (ask for a balcony) and pub/restaurant.
$$ La Posada Familiar, Cra 10, No 8-55, T724 8136. Small, 6 rooms set around a sunny courtyard. Recommended.
$$-$ Abril, C 8, No 9-63, T724 8795, hotelabrilsangilss@yahoo.es. Strangely laid out, but rooms have comfortable antique beds, fan.
$ Sam's VIP Hostel, Cr 10, No 12-33, p 2, main plaza, T724 2746, www.samshostel.com. Good reports on value and services, dorms and private rooms (**$$-$**) rooftop pool, adventure

activities, bar, sauna, English spoken, sister to Mansión del Sam.

$ Santander Alemán, C 10, No 15-07, T724 0329, www.hostelsantanderalemantv.com. Private and shared rooms, nice common areas including a roof terrace, hammocks, book exchange and adventure sports arranged.

Baricphara *p874*
$$$ Hostal Misión Santa Bárbara, C 5, No 9-12, T726 7163, www.hostalmisionsanta barbara.info. The place to stay if looking for some luxury. Each room is individually decorated with great taste and all open onto a delightful plant-filled courtyard. Good restaurant, spa, gym and pool.
$$ Coratá, Cra 7, No 4-08, T726 7110, hotelcorata@hotmail.com. Delightful colonial building with a fine courtyard, no fan or a/c but high ceilings keep you cool.
$$ La Mansión de Virginia, C 8, No 7-26, T726 7170, www.lamansiondevirginia.com. Impeccable colonial house with rooms around a lovely courtyard, comfortable beds, hot water. Recommended.
$$ La Posada de Pablo 2, C 3, No 7-30, T726 7719. One of several places belonging to Pablo. This one is next to the Iglesia de Jesús Resucitado and a gorgeous park. Good beds, rooms 10 and 11 have fine views.
$ Tinto, C 6, No 2-61, bloque E, casa 1, T310-280 0218, http://hosteltintobarichara.com. A short walk from the centre, private rooms and small dorms, good budget accommodation.
Camping Just outside Barichara on the road to San Gil is **La Chorrera**, a natural swimming pool, T726 7422, US$0.30 to bathe, US$1.60 to camp, meals by arrangement, clean, attractive.

Guane
$ Posada Mi Tierra Guane, Parque Principal, opposite museum, T310-488 4378, hildaui@ hotmail.com. Comfortable and charming small hostel with a pleasant courtyard. Some rooms have bunk beds. Recommended.

Bucaramanga *p874*
Due to being a centre for national conventions, it's sometimes hard to find a room.
$$$$-$$$ Dann Carlton, C 47, No 28-83, T697 3266, www.hotelesdann.com. Part

of the **Dann** hotel chain, top of the range, business class.
$$$ El Pilar, C 34, No 24-09, T634 7207, www. hotelpilar.com. Good rooms and lots of extras, parking, restaurant and accident insurance.
$$$ Guane, C 34, No 22-72, T634 7014, www. hotelguane.com. Smart hotel with large rooms, pool, gym and spa.
$$$-$$ Colonial Plaza, C 33, No 20-46, T645 4125, www.hotelcolonialplaza.inf.travel. It's not colonial but rooms are good, cheaper with fan. Restaurant.
$$ Kasa Guane, C 49, No 28-21, T657 6960, www.kasaguane.com. The best budget option in town. Owned by paragliding instructor Richi Mantilla of Colombia Paragliding, it's decorated with Guane culture artefacts, has private rooms and dorms (US$12-14), pool table, kitchen, dance classes and good local information.

Around Bucaramanga: Girón *p875*
$$$ Girón Chill Out, Cra 25, No 32-06, T315-475 3001, www.gironchillout.com. Suites and studios in a colonial house, boutique style, with restaurant.
$$ Las Nieves, C 30, No 25-71, T681 2951, www.hotellasnievesgiron.com. Characterful colonial building on the main plaza, large rooms. Street-facing rooms have balconies, good value restaurant. Much cheaper with fan.

Pamplona *p875*
$$$ El Solar, C 5, No 8-10, T568 2010, www. elsolarhotel.com. Beautifully restored colonial building. Rooms upstairs are enormous and have kitchen and balconies. Rooms downstairs, without kitchen, are cheaper. Also has by far the best restaurant in town.
$$-$ 1549 Hostal, C 8B, No 5-84, T568 0451, http://1549hostal.com. Another lovingly restored colonial building. Rooms are light and airy and decorated with great taste by owners Ricardo and Kokis. Coffee bar and *panadería* in a large courtyard. Highly recommended.

Cúcuta *p875*
$$$ Arizona Suites, Av 0, No 7-62, T573 1884, www.hotelarizonasuites.com. Central, all mod cons including safety boxes, Italian restaurant.
$$$ Casa Blanca, Av 6, No 14-55, T582 1600, www.hotelcasablanca.com.co.

Large pool, restaurant serving regional and international food.
$$ Acora, C 10, No 2-75, T573 1846, hotelacora@hotmail.com. Cosy, with fridge (cheaper without), good restaurant (closed Sat), good view for 7th floor, laundry service.
$$ Zaraya, C 11, No 2-46, T571 9436, www.hotelzaraya.com. Central, with restaurant, pool and sauna.
$ Hotel de la Paz, C 6, No 3-48, T571 8002. Basic rooms, but has a pool. 10% discount for stays longer than 5 days.
$ Lady Di, Av 7, No 13-76, T583 1922. A huge photo of Princess Di above the doorway and more photos throughout. Rooms are clean but basic.

🍴 Restaurants

San Gil *p874*
Few places open in the evening. The market, Cra 11 entre C13/14, is good for breakfast, fruit salads and juices.
$$-$ Gringo Mike's Sandwiches, C 12, No 8-35, T724 1695, www.colombianbike monkeys.com/gringo-mikes.html. Open 0800-1200, 1500-2200. US/British-run restaurant, with some lovely Mexican influences. Also runs bike tours (see Tours, below). Friendly staff, good nosh and cocktails. Recommended.
$ Donde Betty, Cra 9 y C 12, Parque Principal. Good for breakfast, *arepas*, scrambled eggs, fruit juices and people watching.
$ El Maná, C 10, No 9-49. Tue-Sun lunchtime and evenings. Set menus under US$5.
$ Pizzeria Pierrot, Cra 9, No 9-98. Open evenings. Best pizzas in town, home delivery.
$ Rogelia, Cra 10, No 8-09. Good for lunch, local specialities.

Barichara *p874*
$$ Color de Hormiga, C 8, No 8-44. Specializes in the *hormiga culona* (see below), here used in inventive ways. On a terrace with a pretty garden and views to the town below.
$ El Compá, C 5, No 4-48. Family-run restaurant serving regional food.

Bucaramanga *p874*
Try the *hormigas culonas* (a large, winged ant often eaten as a deep-friend, crunchy snack), a local delicacy available Mar-May (mostly sold in shops, not restaurants).
$$$ La Carreta, Cra 27, No 42-27, T643 6680, www.lacarreta.com.co. Established by football legend Roberto Pablo Janiot, tastefully restored, swish colonial building, *parrillas* and seafood.
$$$ Mercagán, C 33, No 42-12, T632 4949, www.mercaganparrilla.com. Steaks and hamburgers in a fine setting opposite the beautiful Parque San Pío.
$$ Di Marco, C 28, No 54-21. Tue-Sat lunch and dinner, Sun-Mon 1100-1600. Excellent meat
$$ El Viejo Chiflas, Cra 33 y C 34. Well-established, good, typical food from the region, generous portions. Recommended.
$$ La 22, Cra 22, No 45-18. This local canteen is so popular that at weekends you will struggle to be seated.
$$ Los Tejaditos, C 34, No 27-82. Popular for its varied menu of meat, seafood, pastas and salads.
$$ Tony, Cra 33A, No 33-67. Typical food, popular. Good *tamales* and *arepas*. Recommended.

Pamplona *p875*
Pamplona is famous for its bread. Particularly well known *panaderías* are **Chávez**, Cra 6, No 7-30 and **Araque**, Cra 5, No 8B-15. Try *pastel de horno, queso de hoja, pan de agua* or *cuca*, a kind of black ginger biscuit often topped with cheese. Pamplona even has a *cuca* festival in Sep/Oct of each year.
$$ La Casona, C 6, No 7-58, T568 3555. Local favourite serving meats and seafood.
$$-$ Delicias del Mar, C 6, No 7-60, T568 4558. Popular lunchtime venue specializing in fish.

Cúcuta *p875*
$$ Rodizio, Av Libertadores, No 10-121, Malecón II Etapa. Elegant, good service, big choice of meat dishes, seafood, salad bar.
$ Venezia, C 13, No 6AE-46, Condominio La Riviera, loc 5, T575 0006. Oven-fired pizzas. Lots of fast food outlets on the 3rd level of Centro Comercial Ventura Plaza, C 10 y 11 Diagonal Santander, also cinema and shops.

⊛ Festivals

Bucaramanga *p874*
Mar, or Apr Feria de artesanías (Handicraft
Fair) at the Centro de Exposiciones y Ferias
(CENFER). The annual **international piano
festival** is held here in **Aug-Sep** in the Auditorio
Luis A Calvo at the Universidad Industrial de
Santander, one of Colombia's finest concert
halls. The university is worth a visit for beautiful
grounds and a lake full of exotic plants.

⊙ What to do

San Gil *p874*
There are many adventure companies in
San Gil, some better equipped than others.
Main activities:
Abseiling (rappel) At Juan Curi waterfall, US$15.
Kayaking 3-day beginner's course US$196
on Río Fonce.
Parapenting Chicamocha canyon US$100
for 30-60 mins; Curiti, 20-30 mins US$40.
Rafting Río Fonce, best for beginners, US$17;
Ríos Chicamocha and Suárez, more advanced,
from US$70. Also offers caving, cycling, hiking,
horse riding and swimming.
Colombia Rafting Expeditions, Cra 10, No 7-83,
T311-283 8647, www.colombiarafting.com.
The best for rafting, with International Rafting
Federation-qualified guides. Also hydrospeed.
Colombian Bike Junkies, see **Gringo Mike's**
under Restaurants, above, www.colombian
bikejunkies.com. Downhill mountain biking
tours in the San Gil area, including visit to goat
farm or the Chicamocha canyon, and multi-
activity packages.
Exploracion Colombia Guides, Cra 11,
No 9-08, p 1, T724 9927, http://exploracol.jimdo.
com/exploracion-colombia-guides. Caving,
canyoning, paragliding and whitewater rafting.
Páramo Santander Extremo, Parque Principal,
Cra 4, No 4-57, Páramo, T725 8944, www.
paramosantanderextremo.com. Basedin nearby
Páramo, this company is best for abseiling and
canyoning. But it also has caving, rafting and
horse riding.

Bucaramanga *p874*
Parapenting At Mesa del Ruitoque
and Cañón de Chicamocha. Good

schools are **Las Aguilas**, Km 2 vía Mesa de
Ruitoque, Floridablanca, T678 6257, www.
voladerolasaguilas.com.co, and **Colombia
Paragliding**, T312-432 6266, www.colombia
paragliding.com, which also has a hostel for
those taking lessons.

⊝ Transport

San Gil *p874*
Bus Station 5 mins out of town by taxi on
road to Tunja. To **Bogotá**, US$19-32, 7-8 hrs;
Bucaramanga, US$11.25-14, 2½ hrs, sit on
right for lovely views of the Chicamocha
Canyon; **Barichara** from C 12, US$2.50,
45 mins, every 30 mins.

Bucaramanga *p874*
Air Palonegro, on 3 flattened hilltops south
of city. Taxi US$15, colectivo US$1, traffic
very slow to and from airport. Spectacular
views on take-off and landing. Daily flights
to **Bogotá**, **Cúcuta**, **Medellín**, **Cartagena**
and **Barranquilla**.
Bus Local buses cost US$1. The long distance
terminal is on the Girón road, T637 1000,
http://terminalbucaramanga.com, with
cafés, shops and showers. Taxi to centre,
US$5; bus US$1. To **Bogotá**, 8½ hrs, US$35
with **Berlinas del Fonce** (C 53, No 20-40, T630
4468, www.berlinasdelfonce.com, or at bus
terminal), and Copetran, 9½-10½ hrs, US$30.
To **Cartagena**, Copetran, US$45, 12-14 hrs.
Barranquilla, 13 hrs, US$62, Berlinas; US$40,
Copetran. **Santa Marta**, Copetran, 11-13 hrs,
US$40. To **Valledupar**, 9 hrs, US$35 with
Copetran. To/from **Pamplona**, US$18, 4-5 hrs.
To/from **Cúcuta**, 6-8 hrs, US$22. The trip to
Cúcuta is spectacular and passes through
cloud forests and *páramos*. Best to start the
journey early morning as thick fog usually
covers the mountains by afternoon. To
Medellín, US$40, 8 hrs. **Barrancabermeja**,
2½ hrs, US$11, paved road, scenic journey.
To **El Banco** on the Río Magdalena, US$34,
9 hrs, several companies, direct or change at
Aguachica. Hourly buses to **San Gil**, see above.
Other companies with local services to nearby
villages on back roads, eg the folk-art buses of
Flota Cáchira (C 32, Cra 33-34).
Taxi Most have meters, minimum fare US$2.50.

Pamplona *p875*

Bus To **Bogotá**, Berlinas del Fonce, US$43, 13 hrs. To **Cúcuta**, US$10, 2½ hrs. Colectivos or shared taxis to **Bucaramanga** and **Cúcuta** cost a few dollars more and usually cut the journey by 1 hr, with door-to-door pick-up and delivery. To **Berlín**, US$8. Buses leave from Cra 5 y C 4, minibuses to Cúcuta from Cra 5 y C 5.

Cúcuta *p875*

Air The airport is 5 km north of the town centre, T587 9797, 15 mins by taxi in normal traffic from the town and border, US$5, US$12 at night, US$12 to border. Daily flights to **Bogotá**, **Bucaramanga** and **Medellín**. It's cheaper to buy tickets in Colombia for these than in advance in Venezuela.

Bus Bus station: Av 7, No 1-50 (a really rough area). Taxi from bus station to town centre, US$2.50. **Copetran**'s private terminal is at Av 7, No 16N-33, Zona Industrial, T312-570 6380 (also at municipal terminal); taxi to town centre, US$3.50. The **Berlinas de Fonce** terminal is at Av 7, No 0-05, opposite the airport, T587 5105 (also at the main terminal). To **Bogotá**, 14½ hrs, US$45, frequent with **Berlinas del Fonce** and **Copetran**. To **Cartagena**, 18 hrs, **Copetran** 17 hrs, US$60, **Berlinas del Fonce** 19½ hrs, US$75. Reliable taxis service at the bus terminal, Cotranol, T572 6139, 314-413 2316 (Sr Orlando).

Warning To avoid scams and theft at Cúcuta bus terminal, go straight to the **Berlinas del Fonce** and **Copetran** terminals. Otherwise, on the 1st floor of the main terminal there is a tourist office for help and information and a café/snack bar where you can wait in comparative safety. Do not allow anyone to divert you from the service you want and don't let your belongings out of your sight. Report any theft to Migración Colombia, who may be able to help.

Border with Venezuela *p876*

Bus San Cristóbal, US$2 (Bolivariano), colectivo US$3.50; **San Antonio**, taxi US$10, bus and colectivo from C 7, Av 4/5, US$0.50 to Migración Colombia, then US$0.50 to SAIME in San Antonio. From Cúcuta to **Mérida** or beyond, go to San Antonio or (better) San Cristóbal and change. On any form of transport which is crossing the border, make sure that the driver knows that you need to stop to obtain exit/entry stamps etc. You will have to alight and flag down a later colectivo.

Directory

Bucaramanga *p874*
Banks Many banks in the city, lots with ATMs.

Cúcuta *p875*
Banks For the best exchange rates, it is recommended to change pesos to bolívares in Cúcuta and not in Venezuela. Exchange rates fluctuate throughout the day. There is an ATM tucked away on the left side of the international bridge in Venezuela. Good rates of exchange at the airport, or on the border. It is difficult to change pesos beyond San Antonio in Venezuela. Money changers on the street all around the main plaza and many shops advertise bolívares exchange. There are also plenty of *casas de cambio*.

Cartagena and the north coast

Caribbean Colombia is very different in spirit from the highlands: the coast stretches from the Darién Gap, through banana and palm plantations and swamps to the arid Guajira.

Cartagena → *Phone code: 5. Colour map 1, A2. Population: 1,200,000.*

Cartagena should not be missed. Besides being Colombia's top tourist destination and a World Heritage Site, it is one of the most vibrant and beautiful cities in South America. It's an eclectic mix of Caribbean, African and Spanish tastes and sounds. The colonial heart of Cartagena lies within 12 km of ramparts. Within the walled city, El Centro, is a labyrinth of colourful squares, churches, mansions of former nobles and pastel-coloured houses along narrow cobbled streets. Most of the upmarket hotels and restaurants are found here.

The sacking of Cartagena

Despite its daunting outer forts and encircling walls, Cartagena was challenged repeatedly by enemies. Sir Francis Drake, with 1300 men, broke in successfully in 1586, leading to the major reconstruction of the ramparts we see today. Nevertheless the Frenchmen Baron de Pointis and Ducasse, with 10,000 men, beat down the defences and sacked the city in 1697. But the strongest attack of all, by Sir Edward Vernon with 27,000 men and 3000 pieces of artillery, failed in 1741 after besieging the city for 56 days; it was defended by the one-eyed, one-armed and one-legged hero Blas de Lezo, whose statue is at the entrance to the San Felipe fortress.

The San Diego quarter, once home to the middle classes, and Plaza Santo Domingo perhaps best capture the lure of Cartagena. Less touristy and developed is the poorer Getsemaní neighbourhood, where colonial buildings of former artisans are being rapidly restored. Here are most of the budget hotels. Immediately adjoining Getsemaní is the downtown sector known as La Matuna, where vendors and fruit juice sellers crowd the pavements and alleys between the modern commercial buildings and banks. Cartagena is also a popular beach resort and along Bocagrande and El Laguito are modern high rise hotels on the seafront. During the high season the walled city becomes a playground for the rich and famous, while cruise liners dock at its port. Don't miss a drink at night in the cafés next to the city's oldest church, Santo Domingo, and in Plaza San Diego. Beyond Crespo on the road to Barranquilla is a fast-growing beach resort lined with luxury apartments. Trade winds during December-February provide relief from the heat.

Arriving in Cartagena

Orientation Rafael Núñez **airport** is 1.5 km east of the city in the Crespo district and the **bus terminal** is at least 35 minutes from town on the road to Barranquilla. The colonial centre should be explored on foot, but public transport is needed for the beach areas. ▶▶ *See Transport, page 890.*

Tourist information Turismo Cartagena de Indias ⓘ *Casa del Marqués del Premio Real, Plaza de la Aduana, T660 1583, Mon, Wed, Thu, Sat 0800-1900, Tue 0800-1200, 1400-1800, Sun 0900-1700 (very helpful and knowledgeable staff), and there are kiosks in Plaza de los Coches and Plaza de San Pedro Claver (Mon-Sat 0900-1300, 1500-1900, latter also Sun 0900-1700).* Corporación de Turismo Cartagena de Indias ⓘ *Av Blas de Lezo, Muelle Turístico, La Bodeguita, p 2, T655 0277, www. cartagenadeindias.travel (by appointment only).* The Instituto de Patrimonio y Cultura de Cartagena ⓘ *C del Tablón No 7-28, Edif Gonzales Porto, T664 5361, www.ipcc.gov.co,* may provide information. See also www.cartagenacaribe.com. For maps, Instituto Agustín Codazzi ⓘ *C 34, No 3A-31, Edif Inurbe, www.igac.gov.co, Mon-Fri 0800-1630.* This Is Cartagena is an independent collective offering lots of practical information, entertainment listings, details of volunteering projects and more, www.ticartagena.com.

Background

Cartagena de Indias was founded by Pedro de Heredia on 1 June 1533 and grew to be the most important port in the 'New World'. The core of the city was built on an island separated from the mainland by marshes and lagoons close to a prominent hill – the perfect place for a defensive port. There were then two approaches to it, Bocagrande, at the northern end of Tierrabomba island – the direct entry from the Caribbean – and Bocachica, a narrow channel at the south leading to the great bay of Cartagena, 15 km long and 5 km wide. (Bocagrande was blocked after Admiral Vernon's attack in 1741; see box, above.) The old walled city lies at the north end of the Bahía de Cartagena, with the Caribbean Sea to the west.

Cartagena historic centre

To Airport & Playa Marbella

Baluarte de Santa Catalina
Museo Fortificaci
Plaza de las Bóvedas

Caribbean Sea

SAN DIEGO

Old Plaza de Toros

Casa de Gabriel García Márquez

Campo

La Merced
Santo Toribio
Parque Fernández de Mora

Siete Infantes

Casa del Marqués de Valdehoyos

CENTRO

San Agustín
Soledad

Éxito Super-market

Santo Domingo
Plaza de Santo Domingo

Casa de los Condes de Pestagua

Cathedral
Palacio de la Inquisición
Plaza de Bolívar
Museo del Oro Zenú

LA MATUNA

Naval Museum

Plaza de los Coches
Torre del Reloj

Parque del Centenario

Plaza de la Aduana

San Pedro Claver

Museo de Arte Moderno

Plaza de la Independencia

Corporación de Turismo Cartagena de Indias

Tércera Orden
San Francisco

GETSEMANI

Playa de Barahona

Centro Internacional de Convenciones

Santísima Trinidad

Bahía de las Ánimas

To Bocagrande

100 metres
100 yards

Cartagena was one of the storage points for merchandise sent out from Spain and for treasure collected from the Americas to be sent back to Spain. A series of forts protected the approaches from the sea, and the formidable walls around the city made it almost impregnable.

Entering Bocachica by sea, the island of Tierrabomba is to the left. At the tip of a spit of land is the fortress of **San Fernando**. Opposite, right on the tip of Barú island, is the **Fuerte San José**. The two forts were once linked by heavy chains to prevent surprise attacks by pirates. Close to the head of the bay is Manga island, now a leafy residential suburb. At its northern end a bridge, **Puente Román**, connects it with the old city. This approach was defended by three forts: **San Sebastián del Pastelillo** built between 1558 and 1567 (the Club de Pesca has it now) at the north western tip of Manga Island; the fortress of **San Lorenzo** near the city itself; and the very powerful **Castillo San Felipe de Barajas** ① *daily 0800-1800, US$7.50, guides are available*, the largest Spanish fort built in the Americas. Built on San Lázaro hill, 41 m above sea level, to the east of the city, initial construction began in 1656 and was finished by 1741. Under the huge structure are tunnels lined with living rooms and offices. Some are open and lit; visitors pass through these and on to the top of the fortress. Good footwear is advisable for the damp sloping tunnels. Baron de Pointis, the French pirate, stormed and took it, but Admiral Vernon failed to reach it.

Yet another fort, **La Tenaza**, protected the walled city from a direct attack from the open sea. The huge encircling walls were started early in the 17th century and finished by 1798. They were on average 12 m high and 17 m thick, with six gates and even contained a water reservoir.

In order to link Cartagena with the Río Magdalena, the most important route to the interior of the continent, the Spaniards built a 114-km canal from the Bahía de Cartagena to Calamar on the river. Called the Canal del Dique, it is still in use.

Independence Cartagena was the first Colombian city to declare independence from Spain, in 1811. A year later Bolívar used the city as a jumping-off point for his Magdalena campaign. After heroic resistance, Cartagena was retaken by the royalists under Pablo Morillo in 1815. The patriots finally freed it in 1821.

Historic centre

The **Puente Román** leads from the island of Manga into Getsemaní. North of the bridge, in an interesting plaza, is the church of **Santísima Trinidad**, built 1643 but not consecrated until 1839. North of the church, at Calle Guerrero 10 lived Pedro Romero, who set the revolution of 1811 going with his cry of "Long Live Liberty". The chapel of **San Roque** (early 17th century), near the hospital of Espíritu Santo, is by the junction of Calles Media Luna and Espíritu Santo.

If you take Calle Larga from Puente Román, you come to the two churches and monastery of **San Francisco**. The oldest church (now a cinema) was built in 1590 after the pirate Martin Côte had destroyed an earlier church built in 1559. The first Inquisitors lodged at the monastery. From its courtyard a crowd surged into the streets claiming independence from Spain on 11 November 1811. The monastery is now used by the Corporación Universitaria Rafael Núñez. Originally part of the Franciscan complex, the **Iglesia de la Tercera Orden** on the corner of Calle Larga is worth a visit.

Past the San Francisco complex is **Plaza de la Independencia**, with the landscaped **Parque del Centenario** beyond. Alongside the Plaza, by the water, runs the **Paseo de los Mártires**, flanked by the busts of nine patriots executed in the square on 24 February 1816 by the royalist Morillo when he retook the city. At its western end, the **Torre del Reloj** (clock tower) is one of Cartagena's most prominent landmarks. Through its arches (the main entrance to the inner walled city), slaves from Africa were brought to the **Plaza de los Coches**, which served as a slave market. Around almost all the plazas of Cartagena arcades offer refuge from the tropical sun. On the west side of this plaza is the **Portal de los Dulces**, a favourite meeting place, where sweets are still sold. At night, the area becomes a popular place for an evening drink.

The **Plaza de la Aduana**, which has a statue of Columbus, is flanked by the **Palacio Municipal** and the old Customs House. The **Museo de Arte Moderno** ① *Mon-Sat 0900-1200, 1500-1800, US$3.50*, exhibits modern Colombian artists and has a shop. The **Art Gallery and Museum** ① *Banco Ganadero, Plaza de la Aduana*, has contemporary Latin American paintings. Continue southwest to the **Church of San Pedro Claver and Monastery** ① *Mon-Fri 0800-1730, Sat 0800-1600, US$4.25*. Built by Jesuits in 1603, it was later dedicated to San Pedro Claver, a monk in the monastery, who was canonized 235 years after his death in 1654. Known as the Slave of the Slaves (El Apóstol de los Negros), he used to beg from door to door for money to give to the black slaves brought to the city. His body is in a glass coffin on the high altar and his cell and the balcony from which he sighted slave ships are shown to visitors. The monastery has a pleasant courtyard filled with flowers and trees in which Pedro Claver baptised slaves.

The church and convent of **Santa Teresa** on the corner of C Ricaurte, was founded in 1609. It is now a hotel, renamed the **Charleston Santa Teresa** (Cra 3, No 31-23, www.hotelcharleston santateresa.com). Opposite is the **Museo Naval del Caribe** ① *C San Juan de Dios No3-62, T5-664 2440, www.museonavaldelcaribe.com, daily 1000-1730, US$3*, displaying the detailed naval history of Cartagena and the Caribbean.

The **Plaza de Bolívar** (the old Plaza Inquisición) has a statue of Bolívar. On its west side is the **Palacio de la Inquisición** ① *Mon-Sat 0900-1900, Sun 1000-1600, US$6.75*. It was first established in 1610 and the present building dates from 1706. The stone entrance with its coats of arms and ornate wooden door is well preserved. The whole building, with its balconies, cloisters and patios, is a fine example of colonial baroque. It has been restored with air-conditioned rooms. The small museum contains photographs of Cartagena from the 20th century, paintings of historical figures, models of colonial houses and a torture chamber (with reproductions of actual instruments). On the opposite side of the Plaza de Bolívar is the **Museo del Oro Zenú** ① *www.banrepcultural.org/Cartagena, Tue-Sat 0900-1700, Sun 1000-1500, free*. It has well displayed pre-Columbian gold and pottery.

The **Cathedral**, in the northeast corner of Plaza de Bolívar, was begun in 1575 and partially destroyed by Francis Drake. Reconstruction was finished by 1610. Great alterations were made between 1912 and 1923. It has a severe exterior, with a fine doorway and a simply decorated interior. See the gilded 18th-century altar, the Carrara marble pulpit, and the elegant arcades which sustain the central nave.

The church and monastery of **Santo Domingo**, Santo Domingo y Estribos, was built 1570 to 1579 and is now a seminary. Inside, a miracle-making image of Christ, carved towards the end of the 16th century, is set on a baroque 19th-century altar. There is also a statue of the Virgin with a crown of gold and emeralds. Opposite the church is a fine bronze sculpture by Fernando Botero, the *Gertrudis*, presenting an interesting juxtaposition between the colonial and the modern.

Plaza Santo Domingo and Calle Santo Domingo have lots of pavement cafés, restaurants and wandering musicians, an excellent place to go in the evening. In Calle Santo Domingo, No 33-29, is one of the great patrician houses of Cartagena, the **Casa de los Condes de Pestagua** (now restored by architect Alvaro Barrera Herrera with great care as a hotel, www.casapestagua.com). North of Santo Domingo is the magnificent **Casa del Marqués de Valdehoyos** ① *C de la Factoria 36-57*, home of some of the best woodcarving in Cartagena and used for cultural events and conferences.

The monastery of **San Agustín** (1580) is now the Universidad de Cartagena (at Universidad y La Soledad). From its chapel the pirate Baron de Pointis stole a 500-pound silver sepulchre. It was returned by the King of France, but the citizens melted it down to pay their troops during the siege by Morillo in 1815. (The luxury hotel **Casa San Agustín** is at Calle de la Universidad No 36-44, www.hotelcasasanagustin.com.) The church and convent of **La Merced**, Merced y Chichería, was founded 1618. The convent was a prison during Morillos reign of terror and its church is now the Teatro Heredia, beautifully restored. Building of the church of **Santo Toribio** ① *Badillo y Sargento*, began in 1729. In 1741, during Admiral Vernon's siege, a cannon ball fell into the church during Mass and lodged in one of the central columns; the ball is now in a recess in the west wall. The font of Carrara marble in the Sacristy is a masterpiece. There is a beautiful carved ceiling (mudéjar style) above the main altar. Opens for Mass at Mon-Fri 0630, 1200 and 1815, Sat 0630, 1200 and 1800, Sun 0800, 1000, 1800 and 1900, closed at other times. The church and monastery of **Santa Clara de Assisi**, built 1617-1621, have been converted into a fine hotel (Santa Clara, Calle del Torno, No 39-29, www. sofitel.com). Near the hotel is the orange **Casa de Gabriel García Márquez**, the most famous living Colombian author, on the corner of Calle del Curato.

North of Santa Clara is the **Plaza de las Bóvedas**. The walls of Las Bóvedas, built 1799, are some 12 m high and 15 to 18 m thick. From the rampart there is a grand view. At the base of the wall are 23 dungeons, now containing tourist shops. Both a lighted underground passage and a drawbridge lead from Las Bóvedas to the fortress of La Tenaza at the water's edge (see above). In the neighbouring Baluarte de Santa Catalina is the **Museo Fortificación de Santa Catalina** ① *www.fortificacionesdecartagena.com, daily 0800-1800, US$3.60, children US$2*, inside the city walls.

Casa de Núñez ① *just outside the walls of La Tenaza in El Cabrero district opposite the Ermita de El Cabrero, C del Coliseo, Tue-Sat 0900-1730, Sun 1300-1600, US$2*, was the home of Rafael Núñez, president (four times) and poet (he wrote Colombia's national anthem). His grandiose marble tomb is in the adjoining church.

Four of the sights of Cartagena are off our map. Two of them, the Fortress of San Fernando and the Castillo San Felipe de Barajas, across the Puente Heredia, have been described above. At **Convento La Popa** on La Popa hill (named after an imagined likeness to a ship's poop) ① *daily 0845-1730, US$3.50, children and students US$2*, nearly 150 m high, is the church and monastery of **Santa Cruz** and restored ruins of the convent dating from 1608. The only reason to visit is for good views of the harbour and the city. In the church is the beautiful little image of the Virgin of La Candelaria, reputed a deliverer from plague and a protector against pirates. Every year, in her honour, nine days before 2 February thousands of pilgrims go up the hill and on the day itself carry lighted candles. It can be unsafe to walk up on your own; seek local advice first. There are guided tours, or take a public bus to Teatro Miramar at the foot of the hill (US$0.50), then bargain for a taxi up, about US$11. If driving, take Cra 21 off Avenida Pedro de Heredia and follow the winding road to the top.

Beaches

Take a bus south from the Torre del Reloj (10 minutes), taxi US$2.50, or walk to **Bocagrande**, a spit of land crowded with hotels and apartment blocks. Sand and sea can be dirty and you will be hassled by vendors. But do not ignore the *palenqueras*, the black women who majestically carry bowls of fruits on their heads, serving excellent fruit salads on the beach. The **Hilton** hotel beach (www.cartagena.hilton.com, excellent hotel), at the end of the peninsula, is cleaner and has fewer vendors.

Northeast of the city is **Marbella**, just north of Las Bóvedas. The city continues beyond Marbella, with beaches along a spit of land between the sea and the Ciénaga de la Virgen. During the week, they are quiet and are decent for swimming, though sometimes there are dangerous currents. The promontory beyond the airport is built up with high rises, including many well-known hotels which have their own access to the beach. City buses run to Los Morros and Las Américas conference centre, carrying on towards La Boquilla.

The **Bocachica** beach, on Tierrabomba island, is also none too clean. Boats leave from Muelle Turístico. The round trip can take up to two hours each way and costs about US$2.50 with regular services. *Ferry Dancing*, about half the price of the faster, luxury boats, carries dancing passengers. Boats taking in Bocachica and the San Fernando fortress include *Alcatraz*, which runs a daily trip from the Muelle Turístico. Recommended.

Boats to the Islas del Rosario (see below) may stop at the San Fernando fortress and **Playa Blanca** on the Isla Barú for 2-2½ hours. Many consider this to be the best beach in the region, with stretches of white sand and shady palm groves. Take food and water since these are expensive on the island. Playa Blanca is crowded in the morning, with armies of hawkers, but the tour boats leave at 1400. If snorkelling, beware drunken jetski drivers. There are several fish restaurants on the beach, a growing number of upmarket places to stay and a few hammock and camping places (take repellent against sandflies if sleeping in a tent or *cabaña*). When taking boat trips be certain that you and the operator understand what you are paying for. You can arrange to be left and collected later, or you can try to catch an earlier boat on to Islas del Rosario or back to Cartagena with a boat that has dropped off people at the beach.

Islas del Rosario

The **Parque Nacional Corales del Rosario** embraces the Rosario archipelago (a group of 30 low-lying, densely vegetated coral islets 45 km southwest of the Bay of Cartagena, with narrow strips of fine sand beaches and mangroves) and the Islas de San Bernardo, a further 50 km south (see page 893). **Isla Grande** and some of the smaller islets are easily accessible by day trippers. Permits from National Parks office in Bogotá are needed for the rest, US$6 entrance fee; in Cartagena, C 4, No 3-20, Bocagrande, T665 6698. See also www.ecohotellacocotera.com. **Rosario** (the best conserved) and **Tesoro** both have small lakes, some of which connect to the sea. There is an incredible profusion of aquatic and birdlife. The **San Martín de Pajarales Aquarium** ① *US$11, not included in boat fares (check that it's open before setting out)* is an open sea aquarium; there are guides, but also shark and dolphin shows (Footprint does not endorse dolphins in captivity, see www.wdcs.org/captivity). Many of the smaller islets are privately owned. Apart from fish and coconuts, everything is imported from the mainland, fresh water included. **Hotel Caribe** in Bocagrande has scuba lessons in its pool and diving at its resort on Isla Grande, US$230 and up. Enquire in Bocagrande for other places to stay on the islands. Diving permits are organized by diving companies and are included in the tour price.

North of Cartagena

A good road continues beyond La Boquilla. On the coast, 50 km northeast, is **Galerazamba**, no accommodation but good local food. Nearby are the clay baths of **Volcán del Totumo** ① *US$2.50 adults, US$1.75 children, a bathe will cost you US$2, masseurs available for a small extra fee*, in beautiful surroundings. The crater is about 20 m high and the mud lake, at a comfortable temperature, 10 m across, is reputed to be over 500 m deep.

⊚ Cartagena listings

For hotel and restaurant price codes, and other relevant information, see Essentials.

⊜ Where to stay

Cartagena: Historic centre *p884, map p882*

Hotel prices rise substantially, up to 50%, during high season: Jun-Jul and 1 Nov-31 Mar, especially 15 Dec-31 Jan (dates are not fixed and vary at each hotel). Bargain in low season. There are a growing number of attractive boutique hotels in Cartagena. Most budget hostels are in Getsemaní. This area is very popular with travellers and has been smartened up, with many places to stay, eat and drink (lots of happy hour offers). Do not, however, walk alone late at night.

See the description of the **Historic centre**, above, for websites of colonial buildings converted to luxury hotels: Casa de Pestagua, Charleston Santa Teresa, San Agustín and Santa Clara. All are special places.

$$$$ Agua, C de Ayos, No 4-29, T664 9479, www.hotelagua.com.co. Exclusive, pricey, small boutique hotel, colonial, quiet, pleasant patio.

$$$$ Cartagena de Indias, C Vélez Daníes 33, No 4-39, T660 0133, www.movichhotels.com. Small hotel in a colonial building, comfortable, luxury accommodation with pool and terrace with great view of the city.

$$$$ El Marqués, C Nuestra Señora del Carmen, No 33-41, T664 7800, www. elmarqueshotelboutique.com. A house belonging to the Pestagua family, famous in the 1970s for its celebrity guests. The central courtyard has giant birdcages, hanging bells and large palm trees. The rooms are crisp and white. Peruvian restaurant, wine cellar and a spa. Exquisite.

$$$$ La Passion, C Estanco del Tabaco, No 35-81, T664 8605, www.lapassionhotel.com.

Moroccan-style chic, elegant and discreet comfort, helpful staff, breakfast served by the roof top pool, very pleasant. Some rooms have balconies. Massage treatments and boat trips to Islas del Rosario organized. Highly recommended.

$$$$-$$$ Casa La Fe, Parque Fernández de Madrid, C 2a de Badillo, No 36-125, T664 0306, www.casalafe. com. Discreet sign (pink building), run by British/Colombian team. Very pleasant converted colonial house, quiet, jacuzzi on roof, free bicycle use. Recommended.

$$$ Hostal San Diego, C de las Bóvedas 39-120, T660 1433, www.hostalsandiego.com. Near the delightful Plaza San Diego, this colonial building has modern rooms opening onto a tiled courtyard.

$$$ Las Tres Banderas, C Cochera de Hobo 38-66, T660 0160, www.hotel3banderas.com. Off Plaza San Diego, popular, helpful owner, very pleasant, safe, quiet, good beds, spacious rooms, massage treatments, small patio. Price depends on standard of room and season. Free ferry transport to sister hotel on Isla de la Bomba, has another hotel in Manzanillo.

$$$ Monterrey, Paseo de los Mártires Cra 8B, No 25-103, T650 3030, www.hotelmonterrey. com.co. Colonial style, nice terrace with jacuzzi, pool, business centre, comfortable rooms.

$$$-$$ Hostal Casa Baluarte, C Media Luna No 10-81, Getsemaní, T664 2208, www.hotelcasabaluarte.com. Small rooms in colonial house, family run, fan, laundry service. Offers massage and can arrange tours to the Islas del Rosario.

$$ El Viajero, C del Porvenir, No 35-68, p 2, T664 3289, www.hotelelviajero.com. Ideally located, more practical than attractive. Organizes tours.

$$ Hostal Santo Domingo, C Santo Domingo 33-46, T664 2268, hsantodomingopiret@yahoo. es. Prime location, rooms are simple and open onto a sunny patio. Gate is usually locked, so security is good.

$$ Marlin, C de la Media Luna, No 10-35, T664 3507, www.hotelmarlincartagena.com. Aquatic-themed hostel run by a friendly Colombian. Has a fine balcony overlooking the busy C de la Media Luna, free coffee, laundry service, lockers, tours and bus tickets organized. Recommended.

$$-$ Casa Viena, C San Andrés 30-53 Getsemaní, T668 5048, T320 538 3619, www.casaviena.com. Popular traveller hostel with very helpful staff who provide lots of information and sell tours and Brasilia bus tickets. Washing machine, TV room, book exchange, range of rooms from dorms to a few with private bath (**$$**), good value, security conscious. Enquire here for information about boats to Panama.

$$-$ Hostal La Casona, C Tripita y Media, Cra 10, No 31-32, T664 1301, http://hostallacasonacartagena.com. Has a breezy central courtyard and rooms for 1-6, some with private bath, with a/c or fan. Laundry service.

$$-$ Mamallena, C de la Media Luna, No 10-47, www.hostelmamallenacartagena.com. Rooms and dorms (some a/c), in same group as Mamallena hostels in Panama, www.mamallena.com. Thorough info on boat travel to Panama and on local activities, day tours. There's a small kitchen, café, breakfast, tea and coffee included.

$$-$ Villa Colonial, C de las Maravillas 30-60, Getsemaní, T664 4996, www.hotelvillacolonial.com. Safe, well-kept hostel run by friendly family, English spoken, cheaper with fan, tours to Islas del Rosario. Its sister hotel, **Casa Villa Colonial**, C de la Media Luna No 10-89, T664 5421, www.casavillacolonial.net, is more upmarket (**$$$**) and is also recommended.

$ El Viajero Hostel Cartagena (don't confuse with hotel of same name, above), C Siete Infantes No 9-45, T660 2598, www.hostelcartagena.com. Member of the Uruguayan chain of hostels, with a/c in rooms and dorms (average dorm bed price US$12 pp), busy and popular. Free internet and Wi-Fi.

$ Familiar, C El Guerrero No 29-66, Getsemaní, T664 2464. Fresh and bright, family-run hotel with rooms set around a colonnaded patio. Has a good noticeboard full of information. Recommended.

Beaches p886
Bocagrande

$$$$ Hotel Caribe, Cra 1, No 2-87, T665 0155, www.hotelcaribe.com. The first hotel to be built in Cartagena, retaining some splendour of bygone years. Beautiful grounds, large pool, beach bar, pricey restaurant. It has tour agencies and a dive shop.

$$$$ Playa Club, Av San Martín, No 4-87, T665 0552, www.hotelplayaclubcartagena.com. Some rooms are painted in lurid colours but are otherwise fine, inviting pool and direct access to the beach.

$$$$-$$$ Cartagena Millenium, Av San Martín No 7-135, T665 8711, www.hotelcartagenamillennium.com. Range of different suites and spacious rooms at various prices. Chic and trendy, minimalist decor, small pool, restaurant, good service.

$$$ Charlotte, Av San Martín 7-126, T665 9298, www.hotelescharlotte.com. Mediterranean-style decor, comfortable rooms, small pool, Italian restaurant, good.

Playa Blanca

$$$ Baruchica, Km 16, Vía Playa Blanca, on private beach on Isla Barú, T317-657 1315, http//baruchica.com. Ecolodge, B&B, owned and run by Olga Paulhiac, organic food, yoga available, evening cocktails, attentive service, delightful.
$ Hugo's Place, T310-716 1021. Hammocks with mosquito nets, fish meals served, camping.
Another place is **Mama Ruth** (recommended).

Islas del Rosario p886

$$$$ Isla del Pirata, book through **Excursiones Roberto Lemaitre**, T665 2952, www.hotelislapirata.com. Simple, comfortable *cabañas*, activities include diving, snorkelling, canoeing and petanque, good Caribbean restaurant. Prices include transport to the island, food and non-guided activities. Highly recommended.

Restaurants

There is a wide range of excellent, upmarket restaurants. **Crepes y Waffles** (6), **Jeno's Pizza** (4) and **Juan Valdez** (9) have outlets in the centre, Bocagrande and elsewhere. All restaurants are busy in high season, reservations recommended.

Cartagena: Historic centre *p884, map p882*

$$$-$$ Donde Olano, C Santo Domingo, No 33-08, e Inquisición, T664 7099. Tucked away, Art Deco style, intimate atmosphere, great seafood with French and Creole influences.

$$ Balkoon, C de Tumbamuertos, No 38-85, p 2 (above Zebra). Small restaurant with a nice balcony overlooking the Plaza de San Diego. Good atmosphere and good views.

$$ Bistro, C de los Ayos, No 4-46. Closed Sun. German-run restaurant with a relaxed atmosphere. Sofas, music, Colombian and European menu at reasonable prices, German bakery. Recommended.

$$ Juan del Mar, Plaza San Diego, No 8-18. Two restaurants in one: inside for expensive seafood, outside for fine, thin-crust pizzas, though you are likely to be harassed by street hawkers, as with any place on the street here.

$$ Lunarossa, C Media Luna y San Andrés. Italian place, with pastas, thin-crust pizzas and other dishes, also has a bar.

$$ Oh! La La, C de los Ayos. No 4-50. Café/restaurant serving good French and Colombian food. Next door are Jugoso juice bar and El Gallinero for ice creams, yoghurts and snacks.

$$ Perú Fusión, C de los Ayos, No 4-42. Good value Peruvian-style food, including ceviches.

$$ Teppanyaki, Plaza San Diego, No 8-28. Serves sushi and Thai food in smart surroundings.

$$ Zebra, Plaza San Diego, No 8-34. Café with wide selection of coffees, hot sandwiches and African dishes.

$$-$ Casa Suiza, C de la Soledad No 5-38. For breakfast, lunch such as lasagne, salads, cheeses dishes, also does take-away, Wi-Fi.

$$-$ La Casa de Socorro, C Larga, No 8B-112, Getsemaní, T664 4658, www.restaurantelacasa desocorro.com. Busy at lunchtime, excellent restaurant serving seafood and Caribbean dishes. There are 2 restaurants of the same name on the street and this is the original. Recommended.

$$-$ La Cocina de Pepina, Callejón Vargas, No 9A-6, T664 2944. Open daily 1200-1600. Serving Colombian-Caribbean fare, run by established chef and cookbook author María Josefina Yances Guerra.

$ El Coroncoro, C Tripita y Media, No 31-28. Typical restaurant, popular at lunchtime, main dishes from US$5.50. breakfasts US$3.75.

$ Este es el punto, C San Andrés No 30-35. Another popular restaurant, *comida corriente* at lunchtime, US$3.50, also serves breakfast.

$ La Esquina del Pan de Bono, San Agustín Chiquito No 35-78, opposite Plazoleta San Agustín. Breads, *empanadas*, *pasteles* and juices, popular for a quick snack.

$ La Mulata, C Quero, No 9-58. A popular lunchtime venue with locals, you get a selection of set menu dishes. Try the excellent seafood casserole and coconut lemonade. Wi-Fi.

$ Pizza en el Parque, C 2a de Badillo, No 36-153. This small restaurant serves delicious pizzas with some interesting flavours (pear and apple) which you can enjoy in the delightful atmosphere of Parque Fernández de Madrid.

Outside the centre

$$$ Club de Pesca, San Sebastian de Pastelillo fort, Manga island, T660 4594. Wonderful setting, excellent fish and seafood. Recommended.

Beaches: Bocagrande *p886*

$$$ Ranchería's, Av 1A, No 8-86. Mainly meats at this *parrilla* in thatched huts just off the beach.

$$$-$$ Arabe, Cra 3A, No 8-83, T665 4365. Upmarket Arab restaurant serving tagines, etc. A/c, indoor seating or pleasant outdoor garden.

$$$-$$ Carbón de Palo, Av San Martín, No 6-40. Steak heaven (and other dishes), cooked on an outdoor *parrilla*.

$ La Fonda Antioqueña, Cra 2, No 6-164. Traditional Colombian food served in an inviting atmosphere.

Bars and clubs

Cartagena *p880, map p882*
Most night life is found in the historic district. Many of the hotels have evening entertainment and can arrange *chiva* tours, usually with free drinks and live music on the bus.

Most places don't get going until after 2400, though the Cuban bars Donde Fidel, Portal de los Dulces, and Café Havana (see below) start a bit earlier and are recommended for Cuban salsa. The former is open daytime, with good atmosphere. Many clubs are on C del Arsenal. Most bars play crossover music.

Café del Mar, Baluarte de Santo Domingo, El Centro. The place to go for a drink at sundown.
Café Havana, C de la Media Luna y C del Guerrero, T310-610 2324, www.cafehavana cartagena.com. Thu-Sat 2030-0400. A fantastic Cuban bar/restaurant, which feels like it has been transported from Havana brick by brick. The walls are festooned with black-and-white portraits of Cuban salsa stars and live bands play most nights. No credit cards. Highly recommended.
Quiebra Canto, C Media Luna at Parque Centenario, next to **Hotel Monterrey** and above **Café Bar Caponero**, Getsemaní. Good for salsa, nice atmosphere, free admission.
Studio 54, C Larga, No 8B-24, Getsemaní. A popular gay bar.
Tu Candela, Portal de los Dulces. Where you can dance to 'crossover' in the vaults.

⊛ Festivals

Cartagena *p880, map p882*
Mid-Jan Festival Internacional de Música, www.cartagenamusicfestival.com, classical music festival with associated education programme for young musicians. **End-Jan** Hay Festival Cartagena, www.hayfestival.com. Franchise of the famous UK literary festival, with internationally renowned writers. Also **Cartagena de Indias Jazz Fest**, www. cartagenadeindiasjazz fest.com. **Jan-Feb** La Candelaria, religious processions and horse parades (see La Popa). There is an international film festival **2nd week of Mar**, www.ficcifestival.com. Independence celebrations, **2nd week of Nov**: masked people in fancy dress dance to the sound of *maracas* and drums. There are beauty contests, battles of flowers and general mayhem.

O Shopping

Cartagena *p880, map p882*
Handicrafts and jewellery Shopping is better in Bogotá. Good handicraft and emerald shops around Plaza de Bolivar and Plaza de las Bóvedas have the best selection in Cartagena. The Pierino Gallo building in Bocagrande has reputable jewellers. **El Centavo Menos**, C Román, No 5-08, Plaza de la Proclamación. Good Colombian handicrafts. **Santo Domingo,**

C Santo Domingo, No 3-34. Recommended for jewellery. **Upalema**, C San Juan de Dios, No 3-99, www.upalema.com. Good for handicrafts.

◐ What to do

Cartagena *p880, map p882*
City tours Many agencies, hotels and hostels offer them, US$22. There is also a hop-on, hop-off city sightseeing bus tour. A party tour on a chiva bus costs US$19.50. You can also rent bicycles for riding the city streets, eg **Bike Flag**, Av 1 No 02-38, Barrio el Laguito, T665 4462, bikeflag@hotmail. com or see Facebook, US$2.50 per hr.
Diving Discounts are sometimes available if you book via the hotels, enquire. Recompression chamber at the naval hospital, Bocagrande.
Cultura del Mar, C del Pozo, No 25-95, Getsemaní, T664 9312. Run by team of young, well-informed Colombians, diving, snorkelling and tours to Islas del Rosario, English spoken, environmentally responsible.
Diving Planet, C Estanco del Aguardiente, No 5-94, T664 2171, www.divingplanet.org. PADI open certificate course, PADI e-learning, snorkelling trips, English spoken. Associated hotel in Cartagena, **Puertas de Cartagena**, www.hotelpuertasdecartagena.com.
La Tortuga Dive Shop, Edif Marina del Rey, C 1, No 2-23, loc 4, Av del Retorno, El Laguito, Bocagrande, T665 6994/5, www.tortugadive. com. Fast boat, which allows trips to Isla Barú as well as Los Rosarios.

Tour operators
Aventure Colombia, C del Santísimo, No 8-55, T664 8500, T314-588 2378, www.aventure colombia.com. The only tour organizer of its kind in Cartagena, French/Colombian run, alternative tours across Colombia, local and national activities and expeditions, working (wherever possible) with local and indigenous groups. Focus on ecotourism and trekking, also organizes boat trips. Highly recommended.

⊖ Transport

Cartagena *p880, map p882*
Air
Rafael Núñez airport (www.sacsa.co) is 1.5 km from the city in Crespo district, reached by local

buses from Blas de Lezo, southwest corner of inner wall. Bus from one block from airport to Plaza San Francisco US$1. Taxi to Bocagrande US$8.50, to San Diego or the centre US$5. Casa de cambio (T656 4943, open Mon-Fri 0830-2030, Sat 0830-1700, Sun 0830-2100), better rates in town. Travel agents have offices on the upper level. Daily flights to all main cities, **San Andrés** and some international destinations, such as Fort Lauderdale and Panama. Flights can be overbooked Dec-Mar, so best to turn up at the airport early.

Bus

Local Within the city large buses (with no glass in windows) cost US$0.75 (a/c buses US$1, green and white **Metrocar** to all points recommended). From bus terminal to centre, 35 mins or more depending on traffic with Metrocar, US$1.
Long distance Bus terminal (www. terminal decartagena.com) is 30 mins from town on the road to Barranquilla, taxi US$9, or take city buses 'Terminal de Transportes', US$1. Several bus companies to **Barranquilla**, every 15 mins, 2-3 hrs, US$7-8; **Berlinastur** minibus service from Av 1, No 65-129, Crespo, T318-724 2424. Colectivos for **Barranquilla** leave from C 70, Barrio Crespo, every 2 hrs, US$14, centre to centre service. To **Santa Marta**, hourly, US$18, 4 hrs. Few buses go direct to Santa Marta from Cartagena, most stop in Barranquilla. To **Medellín** 665 km, US$48-53, more or less hourly from 0530, 13-16 hrs. Book early (2 days in advance at holiday times). The road is paved throughout, but in poor condition. To/from **Bogotá** via Barranquilla

and Bucaramanga, 16 a day, 21-28 hrs (depending on number of check-points), US$72-75, several companies. To **Magangué** on the Magdalena US$20, 4 hrs with Brasilia; to **Mompós**, see page 897. To **Riohacha**, US$24. Bus to **Maicao** on Venezuelan border, every hour 0500-1200, 2 in the evening, 12 hrs, US$30, with Brasilia.

Sea

Boats go every day or two from Cartagena to the San Blas Islands (**Panama**); the journey takes 5 days in all, 2 sailing to the archipelago and 3 touring the **San Blas islands**. The fare, about US$550 in 2014, includes food, water and snorkeling gear. Choose a boat carefully. Trips usually end at Porvenir and you can continue to Panama City for US$40 for a short speedboat trip and a 3-hr jeep ride to your chosen hotel/hostel. There are also public boats and buses. Officially, tourists entering Panama by boat have to pay an Immigration fee of US$105, but this does not seem to be consistently applied. You are advised to visit the Panamanian Consulate (address below) to check the facts (www.migracion.gob.pa may help). Many notices in hostels in Getsemaní advertise this trip; for example, **Casa Viena** and **Mamallena**. Also **Blue Sailing**, C San Andres 30-47, Getsemani, T310-704 0425, www.bluesailing.net (who offer day trips and charters as well), and **Sailing Koala**, T300-805 1816, www.sailingkoala.com, both of whom have trips to San Blas and Panama.

A new roll-on/roll-off ferry service was due to start in 2014, departing every Thu from

Cartagena to Cartí, Panama, 24 hrs, US$249 one way per passenger, www.sanblasferry.com.

Taxi
There are no meters; journeys are calculated by zones, each zone costing about US$1.50, though the minimum fare is US$4. Thus Bocagrande to Centro, 2 zones, is US$4. It is quite common to ask other people waiting if they would like to share, but, in any case, always agree the fare with the driver before getting in. Fares go up at night. A horse-drawn carriage can be hired for US$20, opposite Hotel El Dorado, Av San Martín, in Bocagrande, to ride into town at night (short ride). Also, a trip around the walled city, up to 4 people, US$20, from Torre del Reloj.

Beaches: Playa Blanca p886
There are three ways of getting to Playa Blanca. The most common is to take a bus from the centre to **Pasacaballo**, US$1. From there take a 5-min ferry over the Río Magdalena, US$0.55. Then take a motortaxi to Playa Blanca via **Santa Ana** (45 mins), US$4.50-5.50. Do not give money or gifts to children dancing on the roadway. Alternatively, fast boats to Playa Blanca leave **Bazurto** market, near La Popa, from 0700-0930 daily, US$13.75 one way. Public boats cost US$5.50-8.50. Neither the area nor the boats are particularly safe and boatmen can be persistent. Be sure to pay the captain and not his 'helpers' and arrange a return pick-up time. There are also touristy, expensive boats from the tourist dock (*Muelle Turístico*) at 0830 which stop at Playa Blanca as part of a tour, US$33.

Islas del Rosario p886
Travel agencies and hotels offer launch excursions from the Muelle Turístico, leaving hotels at 0700-0900 and returning 1530-1730, costing US$20-25, lunch included. The boats stop at San Martín de Pajarales (El Acuario, 1 hr) and Playa Blanca (2-2½ hrs). The boat trip is free if staying in one of the hotels. See Where to stay, above. Also, the Santa Clara Hotel has San Pedro de Majagua on Isla Grande, and Cultura de Mar (see Diving, above) has an ecohotel. There is an additional 'port tax' of US$6.60 payable at the entrance to the *Muelle* or on the

boat. Book in advance. For 5 or more, try hiring your own boat.

North of Cartagena: Volcán del Totumo
p887
Bus from **Cartagena** bus terminal to Galerazamba in the morning, US$2.25, 2 hrs, ask to be dropped off at Lomito Arena and walk 2 km along the main road to a right turn signposted 'Volcán del Totumo', 1.5 km along a poor road. Hitching possible. Taking a tour from Cartagena will cost more but will save a lot of time. A tour to the volcano including lunch is US$22 (US$16.50 without lunch).

① Directory

Cartagena *p880, map p882*
Banks There are many ATMs, the most convenient are in the Plaza de la Aduana, the banks in La Matuna (across from Parque del Centenario) and the **Exito** supermarket, Escallón y Boquete. In Bocagrande a number of banks can be found around Av San Martín y C 8. Never change money on the street under any circumstances. There are *cambios* in the arcade at Torre Reloj and adjoining streets (Carretas, Manuel Román y Pico, Colegio).
Consulates Panama, Cra 1, No 10-10, Bocagrande, T655 1055, consuladocartagena1@ hotmail.com. **Venezuela**, Cra 3, Edif Centro Ejecutivo, Bocagrande, p 14, T665 0382, http://cartagena.consulado.gob.ve/. Possible to get a visa the same day with all the required documents (see web page).
Language classes Amaury Martelo, amartesi@yahoo.com. Good, professional teacher. **Security** Carry your passport, or a photocopy, at all times. Failure to present it on police request can result in imprisonment and fines. There is a police station in Matuna (Central Comercial La Plazoleta), another in Barrio Manga. In Bocagrande there is a police station on Parque Flanaga. **Useful addresses** Migración Colombia: Cra 20B, No 29-18, T666 3092, open 0800-1200, 1400-1700. **Volunteering** If you are interested in working with local foundations/NGOs, contact **Cartagenitos**, www.volunteercolombia.org, who will find places for volunteers. See also www.ticartagena.com.

To Panama

Apart from the towns inland on the road to Medellín and the beaches around Tolú and Coveñas, this section is concerned with the furthest tip of Colombia on the Panama border at Darién. There are flights from Medellín and some Cartagena–Panama boat trips stop at the beautiful beaches here, but if going by road, check the latest information on security.

South from Cartagena

The highway south towards Medellín goes through **Turbaco**, 24 km (**Botanical Garden**, 1.5 km before village on the left, Tuesday-Sunday 0900-1600), **Malagana**, 60 km, **San Jacinto**, known for its cumbia music using gaitas and local craft work (handwoven hammocks) and **El Carmen de Bolívar**, 125 km.

Mompós

A road runs east from the highway at El Bongo to **Magangué** (*Phone code: 5; Population: 65,000; Altitude: 30 m*), on the western loop of the Río Magdalena. It is the port for the savannas of Bolívar. From here boats go to La Bodega where you pick up the road again for the small town of **Mompós**, also spelt Mompox (*Phone code: 5; Colour map 1, A3; Population: 41,585*), a UNESCO World Heritage Site on the eastern arm of the river. Alfonso de Heredia (brother of the founder of Cartagena) founded the town in 1540, but due to the silting up of the Río Magdalena here, little has changed in this sweltering, humid town since the early 20th century. Simón Bolívar stayed here frequently and wrote, "If I owe my life to Caracas, I owe my glory to Mompós" (a monument outside the Alcaldía proclaims this). Today, Mompós is one of Colombia's most beautiful colonial towns. Facing the river, on the Albarrada, is the old customs house and the mansions of Spanish merchants for whom this was an important stopping-off point on the Cartagena trade route. Rows of well-preserved buildings, some with balconies, have served as a backdrop in many Colombian films. Of its six churches, **Santa Bárbara**, **La Concepción** and **San Francisco** stand out. In the **Claustro de San Agustín** is a workshop where youngsters are taught local skills. The cemetery is of considerable historical interest. Mompós is packed during Easter week when visitors flock to see its ornate traditional processions. It is also known for its handworked silver jewellery and its wicker rocking chairs. The town is safe and peaceful. Guided tours of the city on foot or motortaxi cost US$6 per hour (guides approach you on the street). Boat trips can be taken along the Río Magdalena and into the surrounding wetlands, which provide excellent opportunities for birdwatching: three to four hours, US$14-17. In the early morning or at dusk, you can walk along the river back to look for birds, or in the afternoon, cross the river on the small ferry from beyond the Parque Santander, US$0.50, for a stroll on the opposite bank where birds can also be seen. Ferocious mosquitoes and the odd bat are a nuisance after dusk; take insect repellent and wear long sleeves.

Tolú to Turbo

On the coast, 35 km northwest of Sincelejo (the capital of Sucre Department) is **Tolú**, a fast developing holiday town popular for its mud volcanoes, offshore islands and diving. Along the *malecón* (promenade), there are plenty of bars and restaurants. Bicycle rickshaws armed with loud sound systems blast out vallenato, salsa and reggaeton. From Cartagena, the best approach is south from Malagana through San Onofre. This is also an easier and safer way for cyclists. There are two mud volcanoes to visit. The nearer is in San Antero, 30 minutes' drive from Tolú, and farther is in San Bernando del Viento, 1¼ hours (turn off the main road at Lorica). Both make good day trips; a six-hour trip to San Antero, including lunch and visits to other sights, costs US$55. From Tolú, another good trip is by boat three hours to Isla Múcura or Titipán in the **Islas de San Bernardo**. With all tour boats converging on the island at the same time, it gets very crowded, attracting plenty of beach vendors. There is a charge for everything, including sitting at a table. To enjoy the islands at your leisure, it is better to stay overnight. If camping, take your own supplies. Trips to the mangrove lagoons also recommended.

There are good beaches at **Coveñas**, 20 km further southwest (several *cabañas* on the beach and hotels). This is the terminal of the oil pipeline from the oilfields in the Venezuelan border area. Buses and *colectivos* from Tolú.

The main road south from Tolú passes **Montería**, the capital of Córdoba Department, on the east bank of the Río Sinú. It can be reached from Cartagena by air, by boat, or from the main highway to Medellín (US$48, nine hours).

Arboletes

Southwest of Tolú is the unremarkable town of Arboletes, near which is the largest mud volcano in the area. Dipping into this swimming pool-sized mud bath is a surreal experience – like bathing in treacle. It´s also very good for your skin. You can wash the mud off with a dip in the sea by walking down to the beach 100 m below. Arboletes is also a convenient stopover on the way to Turbo and the Darién coast. The **Volcán de Lodo** is a 15-minute walk from town on the road to Montería or a two-minute taxi ride (US$7 return – the driver will wait for you while you bathe). A mototaxi costs US$1.50. There is a small restaurant and changing rooms (US$0.50), plus a locker room (US$1 per bag) and showers (US$0.50).

To Capurganá

On the Gulf of Urabá is the port of **Turbo** (*Phone code: 4; Colour map 1, A2; Population: 127,000*), an important centre of banana cultivation. It is a rough community so it's best to move on quickly. There are various routes involving sea and land crossings around or through the **Darién Gap**, which still lacks a road connection linking the Panamanian Isthmus and South America.

The trek across the Darién is held in high regard by adventurers but we strongly advise against it, not simply because it is easy and fatal to get lost, but also because it has a heavy guerrilla and drug-trafficking presence, it is virtually deserted by police and the military and indigenous communities do not welcome tourists. The Caribbean coastline, however, heavily patrolled by Colombian and Panamanian forces, is safe.

Acandí

Acandí is a small fishing village on the Caribbean side of the Darién (populaton about 7000). It has a spectacular, forest-fringed bay with turquoise waters. To the south are other bays and villages, such as **San Francisco**. In March-June, thousands of leatherback turtles come here to lay their eggs. There are several *residencias* in Acandí.

Capurganá → *Colour map 1, A2. Phone code: 4.*

For many years, Capurganá and neighbouring Sapzurro have been one of the best kept secrets in Colombia: a glistening, untouched shore of crystal waters, coral reefs and quiet villages. Capurganá has developed into a resort popular with Colombians, increasingly visited by foreigners. There are no banks, ATMs or cars. Taxi rides are provided by horse and cart. The village has two beaches, La Caleta at the northern end, with golden sand, and Playa de los Pescadores, south of the village, fringed by palm and almond trees but with grey sand and pebbles. Ask the fishermen about fishing trips from here.

Several half- and full-day trips can be made by launch to neighbouring beaches, for example Aguacate, near which is a natural jacuzzi known as '*La Piscina*', and Playa Soledad, perhaps the most attractive beach in the area. You can also walk to Aguacate, 1½ hours along the coast, though not to Playa Soledad. Note that it can be difficult to obtain a return by launch if you walk.

A delightful half-day excursion is to **El Cielo**, a small waterfall in the jungle (open 0600-1700, entry US$1.75; 40-minute walk, take flip flops or waterproof boots for crossing a stream several times). Take the path to the left of the airport and keep asking for directions. Just before the waterfall a small restaurant serves *patacones* and drinks. Alternatively, you can hire horses to take you there. Another horse-ride is to El Valle de Los Ríos. The primary forest in this area is rich in wildlife, but you should take a guide. The trip includes lunch at a *ranchería*.

Another trip is to **Sapzurro**, a few kilometres north and the last outpost before Panama and Central America. The houses of this tiny village are linked by intersecting paths bursting with tropical flowers. It is set in a shallow horseshoe bay dotted with coral reefs, excellent for snorkelling, with a couple of underwater caves to explore. A day's walking trip (there are no cars here) is to the village of **La Miel**, on a gorgeous white-sand beach in Panama. This could qualify as the most relaxed border crossing in the world. The Colombian and Panamanian immigration officers share a hut and copy each other's notes. Be sure to take your passport; if only going to La Miel they won't stamp it but they will take your details. There are breathtaking views of Panama and back into Sapzurro at the frontier on the brow of the hill. You can arrange for a launch to pick you up and take you back to Sapzurro or Capurganá.

Colombian immigration Ask Migración Colombia in Cartagena, Medellín or Montería (C 28, No 2-27, T4-781 0841, cf.monteria@migracioncolombia.gov.co, Monday-Friday 0800-1200, 1400-1700) whether the immigration office in Capurganá is open.

Entering Panama Panamanian immigration at Puerto Obaldía will check all baggage for drugs. Requirements for entry are proof of US$600 in the bank and a yellow fever certificate. There is a **Panamanian consul** in Capurganá opposite the main square: T310-303 5285, nayi051991@hotmail.com. Check with the consul in Cartagena, Medellín, or the embassy in Bogotá (C 92, No 7A-40, T01-257 5067, www.panamaenelexterior.gob.pa/bogota) before setting out. **Note** Colombian pesos are impossible to change at fair rates in Panama.

◉ To Panama listings

For hotel and restaurant price codes, and other relevant information, see Essentials.

◉ Where to stay

Mompós *p893*
It is essential to book in advance for Semana Santa and other festival periods, when prices go up.
$$$ Bioma, C Real del Medio (Cra 2), No 18-59, T685 6733, www.bioma.co. Boutique style, cool and fresh, courtyard garden with running water, jacuzzi on roof terrace and a small pool. Rooms are large, mostly white, family rooms have 2 floors, restaurant (reserve in advance).
$$$ Hostal Doña Manuela, C Real del Medio (Cra 2), No 17-41, T685 5621/5142, hostalmompox@turiscolombia.com. A converted colonial merchant's house, an enormous, lovely building with a huge tree in the first courtyard which is home to many bats. Quiet and peaceful, good restaurant, pool open to the public for US$2 a day. Good service, knowledgeable managers.

Art gallery and jewellery shop. Check in advance if it's own.
$$$ Portal de la Marquesa, on the Albarrada, T685 6221, www.hotelportaldelamarquesa. com. New hotel in a converted colonial mansion, fronting the river, with gardens and patios, suites and standard rooms with modern facilities, cn arrange local guides an boat trips.
$$$-$$ La Casa Amarilla, Cra 1, No 13-59, T685 6326, www.lacasaamarillamompos.com. 1 block up from the Iglesia Santa Bárbara near the riverfront, 3 standards of room, master suites and suites, cheaper 'colonial' rooms, and a small dorm (US$9 pp), beautifully decorated. All rooms open onto a cloister-style colonial garden. English owner Richard McColl is an excellent source of information on Colombia. Laundry, book exchange, use of kitchen, roof terrace, bicycle hire, tours arranged to silver filigree workshops and to wetlands for birdwatching and swimming (US$10 pp). Recommended.
$$ Casa de España, C Real del Medio (Cra 2), No 17A-52, T313-513 6946, http://www.hotel

casaespanamompox.com. White rooms with a/c or fan, some for families.

$ Casa Hotel La Casona, Cra 2, No 18-58, T685 5307, www.hotelmompos.com. Fine colonial building with delightful courtyards and plants.

$ Casa Hotel Villa de Mompox, Cra 2, No 14-108, 500 m east of Parque Bolívar, T685 5208, http://hotelvillademompox.blogspot.co.uk. Charming, family run, decorated with antique bric-a-brac. Also arranges rooms for families during festivals.

$ San Andrés, C Rreal del Medio (Cra 2), No 18-23, T685 5886, http://hotelsanandresmompox.com. Another fine, restored colonial building, with nice sitting room and garden. Rooms for 1-5, cheaper with fan, on a corridor off the garden, spacious, use of kitchen, meals extra. Same owner as Islandés restaurant and tour company (river tours).

Tolú to Turbo *p893*
Tolú

$$ Alcira, Av La Playa, No 21-151, T288 5016, www.hotelalcira.amawebs.com. Modern, on the promenade, with restaurant and parking.

$$ pp Estado Natural Ecolodge, 7 km from San Bernardo del Viento, T320-573 4121, www.estado-natural.com. Rustic cabins on a beach, composting toilets and other sustainable practices, meals not included, cabins have kitchen, activities include birdwatching, windsurfing, trips to Isla Fuerte, riding and guided tours.

$$ Villa Babilla, C 20, No 3-40, Barrio el Cangrejo, T312-677 1325, www.villababilla hostel.com. Hostel run by Colombian/German team. 3 blocks from beach, well organized, dorms and private rooms, good restaurant, horse riding, bike hire, good information on diving and island tours. Recommended.

$$-$ Mar Adentro, Av La Playa 11-36, T286 0079, www.clubnauticomaradentro.com. Belonging to the good tour agency of same name. Nice rooms, cheaper with fan.

$ El Turista, Av La Playa, No 11-20, T288 5145. The cheapest option in town and good value for money. Next to all the tour agencies.

Islas de San Bernardo

$$$$ Punta Faro, Isla Múcura, T318-216 5521, www.puntafaro.com. Low-key luxury resort with 45 rooms in gorgeous setting by the sea, inside Corales del Rosario national park. Price includes all meals, buffet-style and return boat transfer from Cartagena (boats leave once a day in high season and Mon and Fri only in low season). Massage treatments, hammocks on the beach, eco walks around the island and a good sustainability policy. Highly recommended.

To Capurganá: Turbo *p894*

$$ Simona del Mar, Km 13 Vía Turbo, T842 3729, www.simonadelmar.com. A few kilometres outside town, so a good, safe option. *Cabañas* in a tranquil setting near the beach, good restaurant. A taxi to Turbo US$11. You can also ask colectivos to drop you there.

Capurganá *p894*

Accommodation and food are generally more expensive than in other parts of Colombia. Upmarket options include Tacarcuna Lodge (www.hotelesdecostaacosta.com/capurgana) and Bahía Lodge (www.bahia-lodge.com).

$$ Marlin Hostal, Playa de los Pescadores, T310-593 6409, http://hostalmarlin.com. The best mid-range option in town, good rooms, also bunks (**$**), good restaurant serving excellent fish.

$$ Cabaña Darius, T314-622 5638, www.dariuscapurgana.es.tl. In the grounds of Playa de Capurganá, excellent value, simple, comfortable rooms in tropical gardens, fan, breakfast included.

$ Hostal Capurganá, C del Comercio, T314-778 5738, http://hostalcapurgana.net. Comfortable, pleasant patio, well situated. Recommended.

$ Luna Verde Hostel, T313-812 7172, fabio@capurgana-sanblas.com. With double rooms, dorms (US$6) and hammocks, offers diving, snorkelling, treks and other activities, plus trips to San Blas and Panama.

$ Posada del Gecko, T314-525 6037, www.posadadelgecko.com. Small place with 5 rooms with bath and 3 cabins, gardens, popular café/bar that serves good Italian food.

Sapzurro

$ Paraíso Sapzurro, T824 4115, T313-685 9862. *Cabañas* on the beach at the southern end of the village, Chilean-run (ask for El Chileno),

higher price includes half board. Also has space for camping (US$3 or US$4 with tent hire).
$ Zingara Hospedaje, Camino La Miel, T313-673 3291, www.hospedajesapzurrozingara.com. Almost the last building in Colombia, 2 lovely *cabañas* overlooking the bay. The owners have a herb and vegetable garden and sell home-made chutneys. This also doubles up as the village pharmacy.

🍴 Restaurants

Mompós *p893*
$$$-$$ El Fuerte, on Parque Santander, T685 6762/314-564 0566, www.elfuertemompox.com. Art gallery of Walter Maria Gurth in a restored colonial building, displaying his wooden furniture, sometimes serves gourmet pizza. Book in advance.
$ Comedor Costeño, on the river front between Cs 18 and 19. Good local food, popular for lunch.
$ Islandés, on the river front between C 18 and 19. In same vein as **Comedor Costeño** and almost next door, same owner as **San Andrés** (see Where to stay).
$ Plaza Santo Domingo, outside the church of same name. Freshly cooked food is sold every night, also fresh juices, most activity Wed-Sun.

Capurganá *p894*
$$ Donde Josefina, Playa La Caleta, T316-779 7760. Exquisite seafood, served under a shady tree on the beach.
Many other places serving local food.

🎯 What to do

Capurganá *p894*
Dive and Green, near the jetty, T682 8825, www.diveandgreen.com. Dive centre offering PADI and NAUI, lots of courses and snorkelling. Excursions to San Blas. English spoken. Has rooms to let.

🚌 Transport

Mompós *p893*
Air The nearest airport is **Corozal**, which is near Sincelejo and to which there are regular flights from **Medellín** (US$95) and **Bogotá**.

It's 1 hr by colectivo from Corozal airport to Magangué, or 15 mins from Corozal to Sincelejo, then take a colectivo to Magangué, as below.
Bus and ferry There is no road from Magangué to Mompós. You have to take a fast *chalupa* (motorized canoe, 20 mins, life jacket provided), or the vehicle ferry (1 hr, food and drink on board) to La Bodega, then continue by road. Passengers can also take the vehicle ferry Magangué–La Bodega, free if you arrive as the ferry is leaving. In Maguangué it leaves from Yati, about 2 km outside town. The first vehicle ferry leaves La Bodega at 0600.

From **Cartagena**: direct bus with **Unitransco**, or **Brasilia** at 0630, US$23, 8 hrs, bus returns at 0430 from outside Iglesia Santa Bárbara (same fare Barranquilla–Mompós, 8½ hrs). **Toto Express**, T310-707 0838, runs a door-to-door colectivo service between Mompós and **Cartagena**, US$40, 6-7 hrs. Or take a **Cootransabanas Express** colectivo Trans 54, No 94-06, Via Estrella, from petrol station outside Cartagena bus terminal to Magangué, 0600-1700, 4 hrs, US$22, then *chalupa* to La Bodega, US$4, and finally colectivo to Mompós, US$6, 1¼ hrs. **Asotranstax** runs a door-to-door colectivo service between Mompós and **Santa Marta**, US$40, leaves Santa Marta 0300 and 1100, 6 hrs. To **Medellín**, colectivo to La Bodega, then *chalupa* to Magangué and finally bus with Brasilia, 12 hrs, US$47-52, or from Magangué take a colectivo to **Sincelejo**, US$9, 1½ hrs, then a **Brasilia** or **Rápido Ochoa** bus to Medellín, 8-10 hrs, US$38-42. For **Valledupar**–Mompós, see under Valledupar.

From **Bogotá**, Copetran and Omega have services to **El Banco** at 1700, 14 hrs, US$55, then take a 4WD to Mompós, US$16.50 (US$19.50 a/c), 1 hr. From **Bucaramanga**, Cotransmagdalena direct early morning bus, or this company, Copetran or Cotaxi bus to El Banco, several daily, US$33, then 4WD to Mompós, 9 hrs in all. **Note**: prices for transport rises Dec-Jan and at Easter.

Tolú to Turbo *p893*
Tolú
Brasilia hourly to **Cartagena** between 0715 and 1730, US$20. 12 a day to **Medellín** with Brasilia and **Rápido Ochoa**, US$38-43, via Montería except at night.

To Capurganá: Turbo p894

Buses From **Medellín**, buses every 1½ hrs to Turbo, 10-12 hrs, US$34. To **Montería**, US$18, 4-5 hrs. Fewer from **Cartagena**. Check safety carefully before travelling by road to/from Turbo.

Ferries Launches for **Capurganá** leave daily at 0700-0900, US$30, 2¾ hrs, T312-701 9839. Turbo's port is known as El Waffe. It's a spectacular journey that hugs the Caribbean shoreline of Darién. Rush for a seat at the back as the journey is bumpy and can be painful in seats at the front. **Note** Make sure that all your belongings, especially valuables, are in watertight bags and be prepared to get wet. There is a 10 kg limit on baggage, excess is US$0.30 per kg. From mid-Dec to end Feb the sea is very choppy and dangerous. We advise you not to make the journey at this time.

Capurganá p894

Air 1 flight daily to/from **Medellín** to Acandí with Aerolíneas de Antioquia (ADA), from US$110 one way. Twin Otter biplanes with 16 passenger capacity. Be sure to book ahead. Baggage limit of 10 kg. Excess is US$2 per kg.

Ferries Daily launch to **Turbo**, 0800, US$30. Launch Capurganá-**Sapzurro** US$7 (5 people minimum), 30 mins. Launch Capurganá-**Acandí** US$9. There are daily launches to **Puerto Obaldía** in Panama, US$20. From here it is possible to fly to **Panama City**, www.flyairpanama.com. It is also possible to catch a further launch from Puerto Obaldía to **Mulatuto**, US$20, and from there on to **Colón**, US$66.

ⓘ Directory

Mompós p893

Banks There are ATMs on C 18 by the junction with C del Medio.

Tolú to Turbo: Tolú p893

Banks There are several banks with ATMs on the Parque Principal.

Barranquilla → Phone code: 5. Colour map 1, A3. Population: 1,148,000.

Barranquilla lies on the western bank of the Río Magdalena, about 18 km from its mouth, which, through deepening and the clearing of silted sandbars, makes it a seaport as well as a river port. During recent years, the city's commercial and industrial importance and its port have declined. Few colonial buildings remain, but its historic centre is being revived. In the northwest of the city are pleasant leafy residential areas and parks. **Tourist information** can be found at the **Secretaría de Cultura, Patrimonio y Turismo** ⓘ *C 34, No 43-31, p 4, T339 9450, www.barranquilla.gov.co/cultura.*

Many people stay a night in Barranquilla because they can find better flight deals than to Cartagena or Santa Marta. It is worth a short stay as it is growing as a cultural centre, safety has improved, there are several things to do and see and handicrafts, the same as can be found elsewhere, are cheaper. The main reason people visit the city, however, is for its famous annual **Carnival**, held 40 days before Easter week, end-February/beginning of March. It's one of the oldest in Latin America and less commercial and touristy than the Rio Carnival. It is a UNESCO "masterpiece of the oral and intangible heritage of humanity". Pre-carnival parades and dances last through January until an edict that everyone **must** party is read out. Carnival itself lasts from Saturday, with the Batalla de las Flores, through the Gran Parada on Sunday, to the funeral of Joselito Carnaval on Tuesday. The same families going back generations participate, keeping the traditions of the costumes and dances intact. Prepare for three days of intense revelry and dancing with friendly and enthusiastic crowds, spectacular float processions, parades and beauty queens. Tickets for the spectator stands are sold in major restaurants and bars. **La Casa de Carnaval** ⓘ *Cra 54, No 49B-39, T319 7616, www.carnavaldebarranquilla.org*, is the official office and the best place for information.

The new **Catedral Metropolitana** ⓘ *Cra 45, No 53-120, opposite Plaza de la Paz*, has an impressive statue of Christ inside by the Colombian sculptor, Arenas Betancur. The church of **San Nicolás**, formerly the Cathedral, stands on Plaza San Nicolás, the central square, and before it is a small statue of Columbus. The commercial and shopping districts are round Paseo Bolívar, the main boulevard, a few blocks north of the old Cathedral, and in Avenida Murillo (C 45). A cultural centre, **Parque Cultural del Caribe**, is on the Paseo Bolívar end of Avenida Olaya Herrera (Carretera 46). It contains the **Museo del Caribe** ① *C36, No 46-66, T372 0581, www. culturacaribe.org, Tue-Fri 0800-1700, Sat-Sun 0900-1800, ticket office closes 1600 (1700 weekends), US$6*, an excellent introduction to the region, in Spanish only, but guided tours in English are available. Visits start on the top floor, at the Sala García Márquez, which has audiovisual displays and a library, then work your way down through floors dedicated to nature, indigenous people and cultures, languages, to a video musical presentation at the end. Outside is a large open space for theatre and children's games, and the **Cocina del Museo** restaurant. Not far away is the restored **Antiguo Edificio de la Aduana**, customs house (1919) ① *Vía 40 y C 36*, which has historical archives. The **Museo Romántico** ① *Cra 54, No 59-199, Mon-Fri 0900-1200, 1430-800, US$2.75*, covers the city's history with an interesting section on Carnival.

Barranquilla also attracts visitors because the most important national and international football matches are held here in Colombia's largest stadium, **Estadio Metropolitano** ① *Av Murillo, south of the city*. The atmosphere is considered the best in the country. South along the Magdalena, 5 km from the city, is **Soledad** (*Population: 16,000*); around the cathedral are narrow, colonial streets. Regular buses run from Paseo Bolívar and the church at Calle 33 y Carrera 41 to the attractive bathing resort of **Puerto Colombia**, 20 minutes, www.puerto colombia-atlantico.gov.co. The **Hotel Pradomar** ① *C 2, No 22-61, T309 6011, www.hotelpradomar. com* (**$$$** good beach bar, **Climandario Sunset Lounge**, and a restaurant), offers surfing lessons, as does surf school **Olas Puerto Colombia** ① *1313-817/ 0111, www.olascolombia.com*. February to May is the best time for taking classes; the biggest waves are seen from November to January. **Vía Parque Isla de Salamanca** ⓘ *www.parqueisladesalamanca.org, US$19.25*, is a national park, across the Río Magdalena from the city, comprising the Magdalena delta and the narrow area of beaches, mangroves and woods that separate the Ciénaga Grande de Santa Marta (see page 903) from the Caribbean. Its purpose is to restore the mangroves and other habitats lost when the highway to Santa Marta blocked off the channels that connect the fresh and salt water systems. There is lots of wildlife, but it is not yet geared up for tourism.

⓭ Barranquilla listings

For hotel and restaurant price codes, and other relevant information, see Essentials.

● Where to stay

Barranquilla *p898*
Prices rise significantly during Carnival, book well in advance. Most stay in the north zone, beyond the Catedral Metropolitano, C 50; there are a few hotels in the business zone, Cra 43-45, C 42-45.

$$$ Barranquilla Plaza, Cra 51B, No 79-246, T361 0333, www.hbp.com.co. Popular business hotel, 360° views from the 26th floor restaurant. All amenities including gym, spa, sauna.
$$$ El Prado, Cra 54, No 70-10, T369 7777, www.hotelelpradosa.com. A landmark in Barranquilla, 1930s building, traditional

service. Fantastic pool shaded by palm trees, various restaurants, tennis courts and a gym.
$$$ Majestic, Cra 53, No 54-41, T349 1010, www.hotelmajesticbarranquilla.com. An oasis of calm, fine pool, large, fresh rooms, restaurant.
$$$ Sonesta, C 106, No 50-11, T385 6060, www. sonesta.com. Overlooking the Caribbean, first class business and fitness facilities, restaurant. Shopping centre and nightclub nearby.
$ Meeting Point, Cra 61, No 68-100, El Prado, T318 5299, themeetingpoint.hostel.com). Italian/Colombian owned, the best choice for budget travellers. Dorms US$13-16, cheaper with fan and shared bath, also has private rooms, very helpful and congenial, eating places and cultural centres nearby. Recommended.

Hotels in the business district include:
$$ Girasol, C 44, No 44-103, T379 3191, www.el hotelgirasol.com. Safe, helpful manager, restaurant.
$$ San Francisco, C 43, No 43-128, T351 5532, www.sfcol.com/barranquilla.html. Bright rooms, courtyard full of songbirds, a good safe bet, restaurant.

🍴 Restaurants

Barranquilla *p898*
Many places, for all tastes and budgets, in El Prado. Many upmarket restaurants along Carreras 52-54 from Calle 70 to 93. There are numerous good Arab restaurants, especially Lebanese, in Barranquilla due to waves of Arab immigration in the 20th century.
$$$-$$ Arabe Gourmet, Cra 49C, No 76-181, www.arabegourmetrestaurante.com. Middle Eastern fare, more formal and expensive than other eateries in town.
$$$-$$ La Cueva, Cra 43 No 59-03, T379 0342, www.fundacionlacueva.org. Formerly a high-class brothel and a favourite haunt of Gabriel García Márquez and his literati friends during the 1950s. Its bohemian charm may have gone, but it's a Museo Centro Cultural, with a bar/restaurant and recommended for a visit. Good typical food, live music and other events.
$$$-$$ La Parrilla Libanesa, Cra 61, No 68-02, T360 6664, near **Meeting Point**. Well-regarded Lebanese place, colourful, outdoor terrace.
$$ Arabe Internacional, C 93, No 47-73, T378 2803. Good Arab cuisine in informal setting.
$$ Firenze Pizza, C 68, No 62-12, El Prado, T344 1067, near **Meeting Point**. Eat in or take-away.
$$-$ Los Helechos de Carlos, Cra 52, No 70, T356 7493. Offers *comida antioqueña* in a good atmosphere.

🍸 Bars and clubs

Barranquilla *p898*
Bar La 8, Cra 8, No 35-04. In an excellent area which is popular for nightlife. Take a taxi there and back.
Froggs Leggs, C 93, No 43-122, T359 0709, www.frogg.co. Popular bar, good atmosphere.
Henry's Café, C 80, No 53-18, CC Washington, T345 6431, http://henryscafe.co. Daily from

1600. Popular US-style bar and restaurant.
La Troja, C 74, No 44 esquina. Popular for salsa, not far from the old stadium.

🛍 Shopping

Barranquilla *p898*
There is a good value handicrafts market near the old stadium, which is at Cra 46 y C 74 (at the end of Transmetro).

🚌 Transport

Barranquilla *p898*
Air Ernesto Cortissoz airport is 10 km from the city. Daily flights to **Bogotá**, and **Medellín**, also to **Bucaramanga**, **Montería**, **San Andrés** and other Colombian destinations. International flights to **Miami** and **Panama City**. City bus from airport to town, US$0.90 (more on Sun). To town, take only buses marked 'centro' from 200 m to right when leaving airport; the bus to the airport (marked Malambo) leaves from Cra 44 up C 32 to Cra 38, then up C 30 to airport. Taxi to town: go to the central taxi kiosk, tell them your destination and you will be given a ticket with the price to pay the driver at end of ride. To centre: US$12.35, about 30 mins. See ticket for phone number for 20% discount on return. There is an ATM outside terminal entrance, a casa de cambio in the hall, closed after 1900. Also a tourist information desk.
Bus City buses cost US$0.90, a little more on Sun. The Transmetro is a dedicated bus service with two routes, Troncal Murillo and Troncal Olaya Herrera. It takes prepaid cards; single journey US$0.90 (US$0.95 on Sun and holidays).

The main bus terminal, Km 1.5 Prol Murillo, www.ttbaq.com.co, is south of the city near the Circunvalación. Take the Transmetro to Terminal de Transporte. To **Santa Marta**, US$7, **Expreso Brasilia**, 2 hrs. To **Valledupar**, same company, 5-6 hrs, US$15.50. To **Bucaramanga**, same company and **Berlinas del Fonce** US$45-62, 9-11 hrs. To **Bogotá**, 19 hrs, frequent, US$60 direct. To **Maicao**, US$27, 6 hrs (with Brasilia, frequent). To **Cartagena**, 2½-3 hrs, US$7-8, several companies. Brasilia Van Tours (Cra 35, No 44-63, T371 5226, as well as the bus terminal), and Berlinastur (Cra 43, No 71-43, T318-354 5454, Cra 46, No 95-27 and other offices), have mini-bus services to Cartagena and Santa Marta (US$8.25).

Taxi Taxis within the town cost about US$4 (eg downtown to northern suburbs).

⊙ Directory

Barranquilla *p898*
Banks Many ATMs. *Casa de cambio* El Cairo, C 76, No 48-30, T360 6433. TCs, euros, dollars, Mon-Fri and Sat 0900-1200. **Consulates** Panama, Cra 57, No 72-25, Edif Fincar p 2, T360 1870, www.panamaenelexterior.gob.pa/barranquilla. **Venezuela**, Edif Concasa, Cra 52, No 69-96, p 3, T368 2207, http://barranquilla.consulado.gob.ve, 0800-1500, visa issued same day, but you must be there by 0915 with all documents and US$30 cash; onward ticket may be requested. **Useful addresses** Migración Colombia: Cra 42, No 54-77, T351 3401.

Santa Marta, Tayrona and Ciudad Perdida

Santa Marta is a port with strong historical associations and popular beaches. Nearby are the Tayrona national park with pre-Columbian remains and the unspoilt Sierra Nevada de Santa Marta coastal range.

Santa Marta → *Phone code: 5. Colour map 1, A3. Population: 454,860.*

Santa Marta is Colombia's third largest Caribbean port and capital of Magdalena Department. It lies on a deep bay with high shelving cliffs to the north and south, at the mouth of the Río Manzanares. The snow-clad peaks of the Sierra Nevada, less than 50 km east, are occasionally visible. The main promenade (Carrera 1) along the sea front is lined with hotels, restaurants and bars and a beach reaching the port. Much more attractive beaches are to be found around Taganga and Parque Nacional Tayrona. Santa Marta is the base for treks to La Ciudad Perdida. The tourist office is on the **Plaza de la Catedral** ⓘ *C 16, No 4-15, T438 2587*. The staff are helpful, but do not have much information to hand. The **national parks office** ⓘ *C 17, No 4-06, Plaza de la Catedral, www.parquesnacionales.gov.co,* has an office for each of the four local parks.

Santa Marta was the first town founded by the *conquistadores* in Colombia, in 1525 by Rodrigo de Bastidas. Most of the famous sea-dogs – the brothers Côte, Drake and Hawkins – sacked the city despite the forts on the mainland. It was here that Simón Bolívar, his dream of Gran Colombia shattered, came to die. Almost penniless, he stayed at San Pedro Alejandrino *hacienda, see below*. He died, aged 47, on 17 December 1830, apparently from tuberculosis, and was buried in the Cathedral, but his body was taken to the Pantheon at Caracas 12 years later.

In the city centre, well-preserved colonial buildings and early churches still remain and more are currently being restored. There has been much investment in new business, such as bars and restaurants on Carrera 3, the hub of nightlife in the centre. Much of Carrera 3 and Calle 19 are pedestrianized and Carrera 5 has many kerbside stalls. On **Plaza de la Catedral** is the impressive white **cathedral** ⓘ *Cra 4, C 16/17, open for Mass daily at 0600 and 1800 (more frequently on Sun), possibly also at 1000,* on the site of what is claimed to be Colombia's oldest church and one of the oldest in Latin America. **Casa de la Aduana/Museo del Oro Tairona** ⓘ *C 14, No 2-07 on Parque Bolívar, Mon-Fri 0830-1800, Sat 0900-1300, free,* has an excellent archaeological collection, Tayrona culture exhibits and precolombian gold artefacts; visit recommended before going to Ciudad Perdida. At the time of writing the Casa de la Aduana was being restored; the Museo del Oro was in the Biblioteca Banco de la República next door, 2nd floor. **Museo Etnográfico de la Universidad del Magdalena** ⓘ *Cra 1, C 22, p 2, T431 7513, Mon-Sat 0800-1900, US$3,* traces the history of Santa Marta, its port and the Tayrona culture, well-displayed.

Quinta de San Pedro Alejandrino ⓘ *daily 0930-1700 (high season 0900-1730), US$6.60, discounts for students and children; take a bus or colectivo from the waterfront, Cra 1 C, in Santa Marta to Mamatoca and ask for the Quinta, US$0.50,* a 17th-century villa surrounded by gardens 5 km southeast of the city. Here is the simple room in which Simón Bolívar died, with a few of his belongings. Other paintings and memorabilia of the period are on display. This is an elegant memorial to Colombia's most revered man.

Sandy beaches and headlands stretch all along this coast, surrounded by hills, green meadows and shady trees. The largest sandy bay is that of Santa Marta, with Punta Betín, a rocky promontory protecting the harbour to the north and a headland to the south. The rugged Isla El Morro lies 3 km off Santa Marta, topped by a lighthouse. **Playa El Rodadero** is a

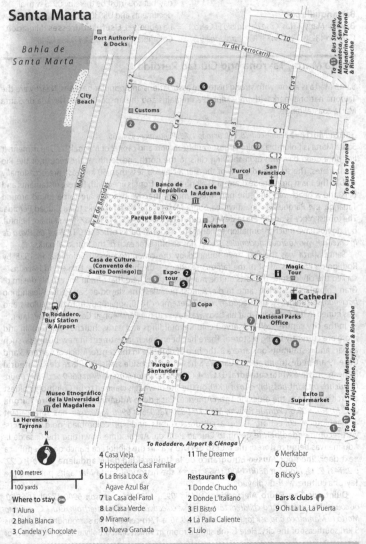

Santa Marta

Bahía de Santa Marta

Port Authority & Docks

City Beach

Av del Ferrocarril

To Bus Station, Mamatoco, San Pedro Alejandrino, Tayrona & Riohacha

Customs

To Bus to Tayrona & Palomino

Turcol
San Francisco

Banco de la República
Casa de la Aduana

Parque Bolívar

Avianca

Casa de Cultura (Convento de Santo Domingo)
Expo-tour

Magic Tour

Copa

Cathedral

National Parks Office

To Rodadero, Bus Station & Airport

Parque Santander

Museo Etnográfico de la Universidad del Magdalena

Exito Supermerkat

La Herencia Tayrona

To Bus Station, Mamatoco, San Pedro Alejandrino, Tayrona & Riohacha

N

100 metres
100 yards

To Rodadero, Airport & Ciénaga

Where to stay
1 Aluna
2 Bahía Blanca
3 Candela y Chocolate

4 Casa Vieja
5 Hospedería Casa Familiar
6 La Brisa Loca & Agave Azul Bar
7 La Casa del Farol
8 La Casa Verde
9 Miramar
10 Nueva Granada

11 The Dreamer

Restaurants
1 Donde Chucho
2 Donde L'Italiano
3 El Bistró
4 La Paila Caliente
5 Lulo

6 Merkabar
7 Ouzo
8 Ricky's

Bars & clubs
9 Oh La La, La Puerta

crowded, somewhat tacky beach resort, 4 km south of the city (local bus service, taxi, US$4.50-5.50). Many of the buses coming from Barranquilla and Cartagena stop at Rodadero on the way to Santa Marta.

Around Santa Marta

The paved coast road to Santa Marta from Barranquilla passes salt pans and skirts the **Ciénaga Grande de Santa Marta** ① *free*. There is a wildlife sanctuary, recognised by UNESCO and RAMSAR, which is not open to visitors, but on the large lake and its margins all types of water birds, plants and animals may be seen. Cutting off the egress from the lake to the sea to build the coast road killed large areas of mangrove and caused an ecological disaster, but a National Environment Programme is working to reopen the channels and restore the area. There are two villages built on stilts in the lake, Nueva Venecia and Buenavista. Ask at the Santuario de Flora y Fauna Ciénaga Grande de Santa Marta desk in national parks office in Santa Marta (T423 0752, see above) about guides and boatmen who take visitors to the lake from the community of Tasajera. On the east shore of the lagoon is **Ciénaga** (*Population: 100,000*), famous for its *cumbia* music.

Taganga

Close to Santa Marta is the popular former fishing village, turned beach resort of Taganga, set in a little bay with good views. It laid back and welcoming, but beaches east of Tayrona national park are becoming more favoured as 'in' places on the backpacker circuit. Swimming is good, especially on Playa Grande, 25 minutes' walk round coast or US$3 by boat. Taganga is quieter midweek, but busy at weekends. Good fresh fish is served at places along the beach. Taganga is a popular place for diving and several well-established dive shops offer good value PADI courses. There is a good book exchange shop but no ATMs.

Parque Nacional Tayrona

① www.parquesnacionales.gov.co, 0800-1700, US$20 foreigners, US$7 Colombians, US$3.80 children, parking extra. During high season, the park is very crowded. Sometimes it closes temporarily for a variety of reasons, but never for long. It's best to arrive early. For the address of the national parks office in Santa Marta, see page 901.

Stretching north of Taganga for some 85 km is the beautiful and mostly unspoilt coastline of Tayrona National Park, where the densely forested northern slopes of the Sierra Nevada fall into the Caribbean. Small, secluded bays with beaches of golden sand are guarded by giant boulders and islets. In the lush jungle vegetation and in the mangroves, you can see monkeys, iguanas, birds and maybe snakes. Of its 15,000 ha, 3000 are marine. There is accommodation at the eastern end, where the beaches and the accessible remnants of the Tayrona culture can only be reached on foot or horseback.

The park has four entrances: Bahía Concha, the closest to Santa Marta (entry US$3.85); Palangana for Neguanje and Playa Cristal; Calabazo for Pueblito and Cabo San Juan de Guía; El Zaino, at the east end of the park, 35 km from Santa Marta, for Cañaveral and Arrecifes, the most commonly used. At the El Zaino entrance you sign in and buy a ticket. From the gate colectivos make a 10-minute ride to **Cañaveral**, US$1.10, where there is a gift shop, a car park, a museum (closed) and the trail of Nueve Piedras, to a mirador (about 30 minutes there and back). A few metres from the car park is a juice bar, campsite, the road to the Ecohabs (see Where to stay) and horse hire at the start of the trail to Arrecifes (US$9 to ride to Arrecifes, US$13 to La Piscina, US$17.50 to Cabo San Juan, one way). See Transport, below, for how to get to El Zaino.

It is a one-hour walk through the forest from Cañaveral to **Arrecifes**. The trail is mostly level, apart from a couple of short, steep sections. At Arrecifes, beyond the cabins, campsites and eating places is a long beach backed by mangroves. On no account be tempted to swim here as the tides and surf are treacherous. Every year, people drown because they do not heed the warnings.

Walk on from Arrecifes to **La Piscina**, 40 minutes further. You pass a little beach, La Arenilla, two-thirds of the way along, with a *cevichería* and juice stall. La Piscina also has a couple of places selling drinks, one of which also sells food. The beach is narrow, but the swimming after the walk is divine; excellent snorkelling, too. From La Piscina you can walk on to **Cabo San Juan de Guía**, 45 minutes, which also has excellent bathing, places to eat and a popular campsite/hammock place. From Cabo San Juan you can return the way you came, take the boat to Taganga (see Transport, below), or walk 1½ hours on a clear path up to the archaeological site of **Pueblito**. A guided tour around the site is free, every Saturday or as arranged with a park guard. Other Tayrona relics abound. At Pueblito there are indigenous people; do not photograph them. From Pueblito you can continue for a pleasant two-hour walk up to Calabazo on the Santa Marta-Riohacha road. A circuit Santa Marta, Cañaveral, Arrecifes, Pueblito, Calabazo, Santa Marta in one day needs a 0700 start at least. It is easier (more downhill) to do the circuit in reverse, ask to be dropped at Calabazo. Tours can be arranged at several hotels and agencies in Santa Marta.

The beaches of Bahía Concha, Neguanje and Playa Cristal (a 10-minute boat ride from Neguanje) can be reached from Santa Marta by tours (eg from hostels), or in the case of Neguanje by colectivos from the market at 0700, return 1600.

It is advisable to inform park guards when walking in the park. Wear hiking boots and beware of bloodsucking insects. Take food, water and only necessary valuables. If you are staying overnight in one of the campsites or hammock places, remember to take all supplies with you as there is only a small store in the park.

Beyond Cañaveral on the Santa Marta–Riohacha road, is **Los Angeles**, with access to fine empty beaches, excellent for surfing. Here are the **Cabañas Los Angeles ($$$**, www.cabana santamartalosangeles.com, owner is Nohemi Ramos, also offers tours). Ten minutes west of Los Angeles is the mouth of the Río Piedras, the border of Tayrona Park, where you can bathe and enjoy sights to rival those in the park. At **Quebrada Valencia** ① *US$1.20*, several natural swimming pools amid waterfalls, with good views. From the marked roadside entrance, it is a pleasant 20 minutes' walk along a clear path, or horse ride, to the waterfalls. It can get overcrowded during high season. Drinks and snacks available along the way. The paved coastal road continues from Tayrona and crosses into Guajira Department at **Palomino**, 80 km from Santa Marta, which has a fine beach, a river running into the sea and fine views of the Sierra Nevada, including snow-capped Pico Bolívar. There are hotels, hostels and *cabañas*, with more under construction.

Ciudad Perdida → *Colour map 1, A3.*

Ciudad Perdida was called Teyuna by the Tayrona, meaning Mother Nature. The city covers 400 ha and was built around AD 700. It was the political and trading centre of the Tayrona. The circular and oval stone terraces were once the living quarters for some 1400-3000 people. The city was also an important religious and burial site. The Tayrona built sophisticated irrigation systems and walls to prevent erosion. By around 1600, the Tayrona were almost wiped out by the conquistadores and the few who survived were forced to flee. For the next four centuries, the city disappeared under the forest growth. In 1973, tomb looters searching for gold known to exist in burial urns and graves, rediscovered the city by chance. By 1975, the city was officially re-found, attracting local and international anthropologists and archeologists who started to excavate, leading to the first tourist groups in 1984. Today the area is a protected indigenous reserve, where three main indigenous groups, the Koguis, Arhuacos and Arsarios (Wiwa), continue to live.

The 20-km trek to the Lost City is, at times, gruelling and challenging. It is not a leisurely walk, but is well worth the effort for a rewarding and memorable experience. The trek is perhaps more spectacular than the archeological site itself. Depending on the length of tour, it starts and ends at Machete Pelao or El Mamey. Along with lush tropical humid and dry forests, abundant flora and fauna, there are crystal clear rivers, waterfalls and natural swimming pools. There are some

1200 steep slippery steps to climb to the summit of the city; the nearest campsite to the city is below these steps. Watch out for snakes. Along the way, you will pass friendly Kogui villages. Don't forget that Ciudad Perdida is in a national park: it is strictly forbidden to damage trees and collect flowers or insects. Only four agencies are licensed to take tours to Ciudad Perdida; see What to do, below. The price covers park permits. For archaeological information, see **ICANH** ① *C 12, No 2-41, Bogotá, T444 0544, www.icanh.gov.co.*

Parque Nacional Natural Sierra Nevada de Santa Marta
① *Entry US$11. For the latest information check with national parks offices in Santa Marta and Bogotá and the Fundación Pro Sierra Nevada, C 17, No 3-83, Santa Marta, T431 0551, www.prosierra.org.*
The Sierra Nevada, covering a triangular area of 16,000 sq km, rises abruptly from the Caribbean to 5800 m snow peaks in about 45 km, a gradient comparable with the south face of the Himalaya, and unequalled along the world's coasts. Pico Colón is the highest point in the country. Here can be found the most spectacular scenery and most interesting of Colombia's indigenous communities. The area has been a drugs-growing, processing and transporting region. For this reason, plus the presence of guerrilla and paramilitary groups, some local *indígenas* have been reluctant to welcome visitors. But the situation is improving and limited activities are now possible, such as the trek to Ciudad Perdida. From Valledupar, it is also possible to enter the Sierra, with permission from community leaders.

In the foothills, there are places to visit: **Minca**, 20 km from Santa Marta, is a village surrounded by coffee *fincas* and begonia plantations, with several charming places to stay. Horse riding, birdwatching and tours further into the Sierra Nevada can be arranged from here. About 45 minutes' walk beyond the village is **El Pozo Azul**, a local swimming spot under a waterfall, which is popular at weekends but almost always empty during the week. Beyond Minca, the partly paved road rises steeply to San Lorenzo which is surrounded by a forest of palm trees. On the way to San Lorenzo is **La Victoria**, a large coffee *finca* which offers tours to demonstrate the coffee-making process. You can stay in *cabañas* run by the park authorities near San Lorenzo.

Inland from Santa Marta
Aracataca, 60 km south of Ciénaga (see above) and 7 km before Fundación, is the birthplace of **Gabriel García Márquez**, fictionalized as Macondo in some of his stories (notably *100 Years of Solitude*). His home is now a **Casa Museo** ① *take Cra 5 away from plaza at corner with Panadería Delipán, museum is next to La Hojarasca café, open 0800-1700, with a break for lunch*. Different rooms have objects and quotations from his work in Spanish and English to provide an overview of his family life. You can also visit the **Casa del Telegrafista**, which houses a few dusty items. **Finca Macondo** (named after a type of tree) is 30 minutes from town. You can visit it in an afternoon; take a mototaxi, US$16.50 with wait. Other sites related to the stories are the river, where you can swim, and the railway station, through which coal trains pass.

Valledupar (*Phone code: 5. Colour map 1, A3. Population: 354,000. Altitude: 180 m*). South of Aracataca and Fundación is the important road junction of **Bosconia** (80 km). The main road continues to Bucaramanga while a road east goes towards Maicao and the Venezuelan border and a road west heads to the Río Magdalena (a side road at La Gloria on this road goes towards Mompós – see Transport, below). The easterly route goes 89 km to **Valledupar**, capital of César Department, on the plain between the Sierra Nevada de Santa Marta and the Sierra de Perijá. Continuing on this road takes you **Cuestecitas**, where you can turn north to Riohacha, or carry on to Maicao. Valledupar is the home of *vallenato* music and culture. On the main Plaza Alfonso López Pumarejo, with a dramatic statue of La Revolución en Marcha, is the cultural centre **Fundación Festival de la Leyenda Vallenata: Compai Chipuco** ① *C 16, No 6-05, T580 8710, tiendacompaichipuco@festivalvallenato.com*, a good place for information. It sells handicrafts, books and music and has a bar, restaurant and photographic exhibition of La Cacica, Consuelo

Araujonoguera, one of the founders of *El Festival de la Leyenda Vallenata*, which draws thousands of visitorseach April (26-30, www.festivalvallenato.com). Also of interest are **Escuela Vallenato Rafael Escalona** ① *C 15, No 6-95*, with photos of famous artists and personalities, and **Sayco** ① *Cra 5, No 13C-40*, a good private collection. There are other cultural events throughout September. At the **Centro Artesanal Calle Grande** ① *C 16, block 7*, lots of stalls sell hats, bags, jewellery, hammocks and some musical instruments. Opposite is **Artesanías El Cacique** ① *C 16, No 7-23*.

The Río Guatapurí runs cold and clear from the Sierra Nevada past the city. The **Balneario Hurtado** is a popular bathing spot, especially at weekends, with food, drink and music (the water is muddy after heavy rain). It is by the bridge just past the Parque de la Leyenda, the headquarters of the Vallenato Festival. From the centre take Carrera 9, the main commercial avenue, or, if cycling, the quieter Carrera 4. Across the bridge is **Ecoparque Los Besotes** (9 km), a dry forest wildlife reserve, good for birdwatching. A full-day tour from the city is to **La Mina** (20 km), a natural swimming pool by magnificent rocks, also popular at weekends. Another good excursion is to the Arhuaco community of **Nabusímake** ① *from Cra 7A, where it splits from Cra 7 (beyond 5 Esquinas), take a bus 1 hr to Pueblo Bello at 0600, then a jeep to Nabusímake, 1 a day, 2-2½ hrs, 15 km,* one of the most important centres of indigenous culture in the Sierra Nevada de Santa Marta. You have to stay the night as the jeep comes straight back. In Valledupar the **Casa Indígena** (Av Simon Bolivar, just past the accordion statue at end of Cra 9), is where the Indians from the Sierra gather. Go here if you need permission to go to remote places.

⊛ Santa Marta, Tayrona and Ciudad Perdida listings

For hotel and restaurant price codes, and other relevant information, see Essentials.

⊜ Where to stay

Santa Marta *p901, map p902*
In town
Do not stay at the north end of town near the port and beyond the old railway station, nor south of Rodadero beach. It's essential to book ahead during high season, particularly weekends, when some hotels increase their prices by 50%.
$$$$ La Casa del Farol, C 18, No 3-115, T423 1572, http://lacasadelfarol.com. A luxury boutique hotel with 6 rooms, all with its own style, roof terrace with pool, price includes breakfast, all modern conveniences, laundry service, beauty salon with massages.
$$$ Casa Vieja, C 12, No 1C-58, T431 1606, www.hotelcasavieja.com. Cheaper with fan, welcoming and has a good popular restaurant.
$$$ La Casa Verde, C 18, No 4-70, T431 4122, www.casaverdesantamarta.com. Only 5 suites, 'boutique' style, safe, small jacuzzi pool and juice bar.

$$$-$$ Nueva Granada, C 12, No 3-17, T421 1337, www.hotelnuevagranada.com. Colonial building with rooms round a pleasant courtyard, quiet, cheaper with fan, **$** in shared rooms, safe in rooms, small pool with jacuzzi, bike hire, includes breakfast, coffee and welcome drink. Reductions in low season. Recommended.
$$ Aluna, C 21, No 5-72, T432 4916, www. alunahotel.com. Irish-run, pleasant, large hostel in a converted 1920s villa with private rooms and dorms (US$17.60 pp), cheaper with fan, with roof terrace. Breakfast extra, café and a good noticeboard. Recommended. Under same ownership is **Finca Entre Ríos**, http://fincaentrerios.com/, 1 hr from Santa Marta, a working farm with rooms, full board **$$** pp, dorm **$** pp.
$$ Bahía Blanca, Cra 1, No 11-13, T422 7090, www.hotelbahiablanca.com. Rooms around pleasant courtyard, helpful staff, cheaper with fan and in low season. Good.
$$-$ La Brisa Loca, C 14, No 3-58, T431 6121, www.labrisaloca.com. Dorms from US$11 pp, US$26 with a/c, private rooms **$$**. US-owned, lively hostel, shared bath, meals extra, bar, pool and billiard room.

$$-$ The Dreamer Hostel, Cra 51, No 26D-161 Diagonal, Los Trupillos, Mamatoco, T433 3264, T300-251 6534, www.thedreamerhostel.com. Travellers' hostel in a residential district 15 mins from the centre on the way to Tayrona, 5 mins by taxi from the bus station. All rooms around a sunny garden and pool, dorms for 4-10 (US$7.50-10.50) and private rooms with and without bath, fan or a/c, bar, Italian restaurant, tour information and activities, good atmosphere. All services close by, including huge shopping mall, San Pedro Alejandrino, bus stop for Tayrona. Recommended.

$ Candela y Chocolate, C 12, No 3-01, T421 0977, www.candelaychocolate.com. Small B&B with dorm rooms only, for 5, 6 or 8 beds (US$9-10 pp, the smallest room has shared bath), all with fan, lockers.

$ Hospedería Casa Familiar, C 10C, No 2-14, T421 1697, www.hospederiacasafamiliar.freeservers.com. Run by an extremely helpful family, rooms with fan, roof terrace where you can cook your own food, bicycles for hire. Has its own dive shop and organizes trips to Tayrona and Ciudad Perdida. Recommended.

$ Miramar, C 10C, No 1C-59, T423 3276, www.hotelmiramar.com.co, 2 blocks from Malecón. Very knowledgeable and helpful staff at this backpacker favourite. Can be crowded, simple dorms and some better, pricier private rooms (US$16.50), motorbike parking, cheap restaurant. Often full. Online reservations are held until 1500 on the day of arrival. Tours to Ciudad Perdida, Tayrona, Guajira and local sites are available at the in-house tour operator. Airline tickets also sold here.

Taganga p903

$$$ Bahía Taganga, C 8, No 1B-35, T421 0653, www.bahiataganga.com. Unmissable sign on the cliff face. Overlooking bay, breakfast served on lovely terrace, hospitable, a/c, more expensive in new building, tastefully decorated.

$$$ La Ballena Azul, Cra 1, No 18-01, T421 9009, www.hotelballenaazul.com. Attractive hotel with French riviera touch, comfortable, spacious rooms with sea views, also run boat

tours to secluded beaches, horses for hire. Good restaurant on the beach, terrace bar.

$$ Casa Blanca, Cra 1, No 18-161, T421 9232, at the southern end of the beach, www. casablancahosteltaganga.com. Characterful, each room has its own balcony with hammock, US$19 in dorm. Good roof terrace, tour desk.

$$ Techos Azules, Sector Dunkarinca, Cabaña 1-100, T421 9141, www.techosazules.com. Off the road leading into town, *cabañas* with good views over the bay, private rooms and dorm US$12.50 pp (low season prices), free coffee, laundry service.

$$-$ La Casa de Felipe, Cra 5A, No 19-13, 500 m from beach behind football field, T421 9101, www.lacasadefelipe.com. Cosy traveller place run by knowledgeable French team of Jean-Phillipe and Sandra Gibelin. Good kitchen facilities, excellent restaurant, hospitable, relaxing hammock and spacious garden area with sea views, studio apartments (**$$$-$$**), dorms (US$9-14) and rooms. Good information on trips to Tayrona (maps provided), English spoken. Highly recommended.

$ Bayview, Cra 4, No 17B-57, T421 9560, www.hosteltrail.com/bayview. With a technicolour façade, pleasant rooms, dorms (US$11 pp), kitchen, BBQ area, Wi-Fi, lounges with DVD player.

$ pp Divanga B&B, C 12, No 4-07, T421 9092, also Casa Divanga, C 11, No 3-05, T421 9217, www.divanga.com. French-owned hostel, doubles with private bath or 3-person dorm, includes great breakfast, comfortable, 5 mins' walk from beach, nice views, attentive service, lovely atmosphere, good pool, HI affiliated. Recommended.

$ Pelikan Hostal, Cra 2, No 17-04, T421 9057, www.hosteltrail.com/hostels/hostalpelikan. Rooms with fan for 2-7 people, apartments, kitchen, laundry service, restaurant.

Parque Nacional Tayrona *p903*
Comfortable up-market cabins with thatched roofs (*ecohabs*) for 1-4 people cost from US$118 pp (half board, 4 people sharing, US$151 full board) at Cañaveral, cabins for 1-5 people at **Arrecifes** cost from US$78 pp (half board, US$121 full board; other packages available), bookable through **Aviatur** (Av 19, No 4-62, Bogotá, T1-607 1500,

www.concesionesparques naturales.com). They offer privacy, great views over sea and jungle; both have decent restaurants. Both have campsites US$7 pp in 5-person tent; hammocks US$14. Take insect repellent and beware falling coconuts and omnivorous donkeys.

Also at **Arrecifes** are various places to stay with double tents with mattress, US$22, hammocks, US$6.55 (US$8.20 with breakfast), US$4.50 to camp with own tent, toilets, meals. These include **Bukaru**, T310-691 3626; **El Paraíso**, T317-676 1614; **Los Bermúdez**, guide Luis Eduardo Muñoz, speaks English, viajesvara@ hotmail.com, T310-741 4672, 300-499 0943, also run tours, eg to Sierra Nevada and Guajira; **Yuluca** (there is also an ecohostel called **Yuluka** about 1 km from El Zaino entrance on the main road, http://eco-hostal-yuluka.com, **$$**, dorm US$26). At **Cabo de San Juan de Guía** there is a small restaurant and hammocks for hire (US$13 in high season, US$10 in low season); there are 2 *cabañas* on the rock that divides the 2 bays (US$50 high season, US$43 low); pitching your own tent costs US$7, tent hire for 2 costs US$19.

Beyond Cañaveral: Palomino
$$ Finca Escondida, Palomino, T315-627 5773, www.chillandsurfcolombia.com. Double rooms, dorms at US$17.60 pp, also camping and hammock space, direct access to beach which has good surf, surfing lessons, board rental, beach sports or just lazing, bar-restaurant, prices rise in high season.

$ pp The Dreamer on the Beach, Playa Donaire, Palomino, T300-609 7229, www. onthebeach.thedreamerhostel.com. Sister hostel to **The Dreamer** in Santa Marta, dorms and private suites (**$$$**), gardens, pool, restaurant, mini-market and access to activities.

Sierra Nevada de Santa Marta *p905*
$$$ Minca, on the hill to the right as you enter Minca, T421 9958, T317-437 3078, www.hotelminca.com. Converted convent with views of the valley below, formerly called La Casona, fully remodelled, with breakfast, bath, fan, hot water, restaurant and bar, various activities including birdwatching.

$$ Sans Souci, Minca, T421 9968, sanssouci minca @yahoo.com. Rambling house in beautiful garden, German owned, rooms in the house or separate apartments, pool, kitchen, discount in exchange for gardening. Stunning views.

$$ Sierra's Sound, C Principal, Minca, T321-522 1292, www.mincahotelsierrasound.com. Italian owned, overlooking a rocky river, hot water, home-made pasta, organized tours into the Sierra Nevada.

There are many more places to stay in town.

Inland from Santa Marta *p905*
Valledupar
$$$ Sonesta, Diag 10, No 6N-15, T574 8686, www.sonesta.com. Business class, next to CC Guatapurí Plaza, all amenities including pool and restaurant.

$$$-$$ Vajamar, Cra 7, No 16A-30, T573 2010, www.hotelvajamar.com. Smart city centre hotel, cheaper at weekends, pool, expensive food.

$$ Hostal Provincia, C 16A, No 5-25, T580 0558, www.provinciavalledupar.com. Private rooms and dorms for 6, US$12.50 pp, cheaper with fan. A very good choice, with a nice atmosphere, free use of bicycles, lots of information, helpful staff. Recommended.

$$ La Casa de Siempre, Cra 7, No 15-53, T584 5254, hotellacasadesiempre@hotmail.com. Colonial building in centre, lots of beds in rooms, no breakfast.

🍴 Restaurants

Santa Marta *p901, map p902*
In town
$$$-$$ El Bistró, C 19, No 3-68, T421 8080. Daily 1100-2300, happy hour 1700-1900. Meat dishes, pastas, salads, burgers, sandwiches and set lunches, neither a big place nor an extensive menu, wine list, Argentine influence throughout.

$$ Donde Chucho, C 19, No 2-07. A little expensive but well situated in the corner of Parque Santander. Serves mostly seafood.

$$ Donde L'Italiano, Cra 3, No 16-26. Mon-Sat 1130-1430, 1800-2230. Tasty Italian fare at reasonable prices, generous portions.

$$ Ouzo, Cra 3, No 19-29. Mediterranean, Italian, Greek, seating on the street, popular restaurant and bar.

$$ La Paila Caliente, C 18, No 4-60. Delightful restaurant with good Colombian/Caribbean food, à la carte at night, excellent value lunch middle day, US$3.85.

$$ Ricky's, Cra 1a, No 17-05. Beachside restaurant serving international food, including Chinese. Reasonably priced.

$$-$ Lulo, Cra 3, No 16-34, www.lulocafebar. com. Café and bar serving arepas, wraps, paninis, fresh juices, coffee and cocktails.

$ Merkabar, C 10C, No 2-11. Opens early for breakfast. Pastas, great pancakes, good juices and seafood. Family-run, good value and provides tourist information. Recommended.

Taganga *p903*
$$ Bitácora, Cra 1, No17-13. Seafood, pastas, burgers, steaks and salads, has a good reputation.

$ Yiu Nu Sagu, C 12, No 1-08. Beachside pizzería, large helpings.

Inland from Santa Marta: Aracataca *p905*
$ Gabo, Cra 4. Good breakfast, lunch and dinner.
$ La Hojarasca, next to the Casa Museo. Juices, snacks and drinks, clean and pleasant.

Valledupar *p905*
There are some cafés on the Plaza Alfonso López, but all types of restaurant on Cra 9 from C 15 down, heading towards Plaza del Acordeón.

Café de Las Madres, Plaza de las Madres, Cra 9, No 15-19. A nice shady place, with a limited selection: coffee, beer, ices.

🍸 Bars and clubs

Santa Marta *p901, map p902*
Santa Marta is a party town with many new clubs, discos and bars opening every week. In the evening wander along Cra 3 and C 17 and 18 either side of C 17 to see what's going on.

Agave Azul, C 14, No 3-58. In the same building as **La Brisa Loca**, Mexican happy hour 1700-2000.

Oh La La, La Puerta, C 17, No 2-29. Excellent bar and atmosphere in colonial house. Recommended.

Taganga *p903*
El Garaje, C 8, No, 2-127, T421 9003. Plays hip hop and other forms of electronic music. Starts late, finishes late.
Mojito Net, C 14, No 1B-61. Open 0800-0200, happy hour 1400-2100. Live music, open mic sessions, wine, cocktails, food and internet.

⚫ What to do

Santa Marta *p901, map p902*
New Frontiers Adventures, C 27, No 1C-74, close to Playa Los Cocos, T318-736 1565/317-648 6786, http://colombia. newfrontiersadventures.com. Trekking, birdwatching, diving and other adventures and ecotours, with English-speaking guides to Ciudad Perdida. Also in Venezuela.
Turcol, C 13, No 3-13, CC San Francisco Plaza loc 115, T421 2256, www.buritaca2000.com. Arranges trips to Ciudad Perdida, Tayrona, Pueblito, Guajira and provides a guide service.

Taganga *p903*
Adventure tours
Elemento, C 18. No 3-31, T421 0870, www. elementooutdoor.com. Mountain biking, hiking and other tours in the Sierra Nevada, Minca and Tayrona.

Diving
Oceano Scuba, Cra 2, No 17-46, T421 9004, www.oceanoscuba.com.co. PADI, NAUI, TDI and other courses, 2, 3 and 4 days.
Poseidon Dive Center, C 18, No 1-69, T421 9224, www.poseidondivecenter.com. PADI courses at all levels and the only place on the Colombian Caribbean coast to offer an instructor course. German owner, several European languages spoken. Own pool for beginners, also has rooms to rent (**$** pp), Wi-Fi.

Ciudad Perdida *p904*
Tours
Trips of 4-5 days are organized by 4 authorized agencies in Santa Marta: **Turcol** (see above), **Magic Tour** (C 16, No 4-41, Santa Marta, T421 5820, and C 14, No 1b-50, T421 9429, Taganga, www.magictourtaganga.com), **Expotour** (C 17, No 2-59, T421 9577, www.expotur-eco.com)

and **Wiwa Tour** (Cra 3, No 18-49, T420 3413). Other tour operators and hotels in Santa Marta or Taganga can make arrangements. The cost is US$330 pp. Under no circumstances should you deal with unauthorized guides, check with the tourist office if in doubt.

All tours include transport to the start of the trail and back, sleeping in hammocks with mosquito nets, food, insurance, guides and entrance fees. The companies list the clothes and equipment you should take, such as sleeping bag, insect repellent, water bottle, etc. Accommodation is in organized camping or cabin sites. Tours run all year; be prepared for heavy rain. Leave no rubbish behind and encourage the guides to ensure no one else does. Going on your own is not allowed.

Sierra Nevada de Santa Marta *p905*
Semilla Tours, Minca, T313-872 2434, http:// semillatours.com. Community tourism company offering tours in the region and elsewhere in Colombia. Also has volunteering opportunities and its own guesthouse, **Finca La Semilla**, www.fincalasemilla.blogspot.co.uk.

⚫ Transport

Santa Marta *p901, map p902*
Air Simón Bolívar, 20 km south of city; bus, US$1, taxi to Santa Marta, US$10-15, less to Rodadero. Daily flights to **Bogotá**, **Bucaramanga**, **Cali** and **Medellín**; connections to other cities. During the tourist season, get to the airport early and book well ahead (the same goes for bus reservations).
Bus Terminal southeast of the city, towards Rodadero, minibus US$0.70; taxi US$3 to centre, US$6 to Rodadero. To **Bogotá**, 7 daily, 16 hrs, US$61, **Brasilia** or Berlinas del Fonce. To **Medellín**, 6 daily, 15 hrs, US$48-53, BrasiliaorCopetran. Berlinas and Brasilia to **Bucaramanga** about 9 hrs, from US$40, frequent departures 0700-2200. Buses to **Barranquilla**, 7 daily, 2 hrs, US$7; Berlinastur minibus, Cra 3, No 8-69, Rodadero, and terminal, T318-743 4343, US$8.25. To **Cartagena**, 5 hrs US$18, Brasilia. To **Riohacha** US$11, 3 hrs. Frequent buses to **Maicao**, US$14 a/c, also cheaper non a/c, 4-5 hrs.

Taganga *p903*
Minibus from **Santa Marta** US$1 (frequent, 0600-2130).
Taxi US$5.50, 15-20 mins.

Parque Nacional Tayrona *p903*
Bus To get to the park entrance in El Zaino, take a **Cootrans Oriente 'La Guajira'** bus from the market in Santa Marta, Cra 11 y C11 outside the general store, or from in front of the **Buenavista** shopping centre in Mamatoca, near San Pedro Alejandrino and **The Dreamer**, US$3.30, every 15 mins from 0700, 1 hr, last back 1800-1830 (check on the day with the bus driver). Unless going to Pueblito and Calabazo, or taking the Taganga boat (see below), walk from Arrecifes to the car park and take the colectivo to the man road. At the car park there may be taxis waiting: US$33 per car, US$27 for one person to Santa Marta, or you may get lucky and find a cheaper ride back to Santa Marta. Hotels and hostels arrange tours, but there is no need to take guides (who charge US$25 or more pp for a day trip). There is a **boat** service from Taganga at 1000-1100 to Cabo San Juan, 1 hr journey, US$25 pp one way (and you have to pay park entry); returns to Taganga 1500-1600.

Beyond Cañaveral: Palomino
Take a Tayrona/Palomino bus from Santa Marta, as above.

Inland from Santa Marta: Aracataca *p905*
Bus Santa Marta—Aracataca, US$6.60 with Berlinas; **Barranquilla**, US$8.25, goes via Ciénaga (US$6.60). To/from **Valledupar**, US$7,

Valledupar *p905*
Air Flights from Barranquilla and Bogotá.
Bus The bus and air terminals are 3 km southeast of the town, close to each other, taxi, US$4.50. **Santa Marta**, 4 hrs, US$12, **Barranquilla**, 5-6 hrs, US$20, **Cartagena**, US$22, To **Mompós**, *puerta a puerta* with Lalo Castro, T312-673 5226, US$28.50; if he isn't going, **Veloz** or **Cootracegua** bus at 0400, 0800, or minibus from outside bus terminal to Santa Ana on the Río Magdalena, US$40, take a ferry across then motorbike taxi to Mompós, US$5-8. To **Bucaramanga**, 8 hrs, US$35.

Santa Marta *p901, map p902*
Banks Banks with ATMs in Plaza Bolívar and Plaza San Francisco. *Casas de cambio* on C 13 entre Cras 5 y 6, and C14 entre Cras 4 y 5.**Exito** supermarket, in the block bounded by C 19 y 20, Cra 5 y 6, has an ATM and a *cambio* which opens 1000-1300, 1400-1900, Sat 1000-1400. **Immigration** Migración Colombia, Cra 8, No 27-15, T421 7794. Mon-Fri 0800-1200, 1400-1700.

Taganga *p903*
Banks ATM, all major credit cards, next to police station ½ block up from **Poseidon Dive Center**.

Valledupar *p905*
Banks Exito supermarket, Cras 6 y 7, C 16 y 17, has ATMs.

To Venezuela

Roads head for the insalubrious border town of Maicao, but on the way is plenty of interest: lagoons where flamingos feed and the arid, empty Guajira Peninsula with its wildlife and special Wayúu culture.

Riohacha and around → *Phone code: 5. Colour map 1, A4. Population: 231,650.*
The port of Riohacha, 160 km east of Santa Marta and capital of La Guajira Department, comes alive at the weekend, when it fills with party-goers and music (almost always vallenato) springs up all over the place. It was founded in 1545 by Nicolás Federmann, and in early years its pearling industry was large enough to tempt Drake to sack it (1596). Pearling almost ceased during the 18th century and the town was all but abandoned. Today, there is a pleasant stretch of beach with shady palms and a long wooden pier in the centre. A promenade along the beachfront (Calle 1) is lined with banks, hotels, restaurants and tour

agencies. It is common to see Wayúus selling their wares and beautiful handmade *mochilas* (bags) along the seafront. Riohacha is a useful base for exploring the semi-desert landscape of La Guajira. Tourist office: **Dirección de Turismo de la Guajira** ⓘ *C 1, Av de La Marina No 4-42, T727 1015*, little information, better to ask tour operators. Ask for the University of the Guajira, which has an excellent resource centre related to the region and the Wayuú culture (ID is necessary to get in). See also www.riohacha-laguajira.gov.co.

Santuario Los Flamencos

ⓘ *At the time of writing the Parques Nacionales Naturales de Colombia was not listing an entry fee for this park. 95 km east of Santa Marta and 25 km short of Riohacha.*

There are several small and two large saline lagoons (Laguna Grande and Laguna de Navío Quebrado), separated from the Caribbean by sand bars. The latter is near Camarones (colectivo from Riohacha, roundabout between water tower and bus station, US$3) which is just off the main road. About 3 km beyond Camarones is 'La Playa', a popular beach to which some colectivos continue at weekends. Flamingos normally visit the large lagoons between October and December, during the wet season, though some birds are there all year. They are believed to migrate to and from the Dutch Antilles, Venezuela and Florida. Across Laguna de Navío Quebrado is community-run visitor centre called **Los Mangles**, with accommodation in cabañas, in hammocks (**$**), or camping. Meals are also available and the centre arranges birdwatching trips on foot or by boat (US$5 per person). A two day/one night package costs US$73 double; longer packages available. See http://ecoturismosantuario.weebly.com and www.parquesnacionales. gov.co. There are several bars and two stores on the beach.

Guajira Peninsula

Beyond Riohacha to the east is the arid and sparsely inhabited Guajira Peninsula. The *indígenas* here collect dividivi (the curved pods of trees used in tanning and dyeing), tend goats, and fish. They are Wayúu (or Guajiros), and of special interest are the coloured robes worn by the women. Their language is Wayuunaiki; beyond Cabo de Vela little Spanish is spoken. You'll see fields of cactii and fine views of flamingos and other brightly coloured birds. The sunsets and barren landscapes of the Guajira are magnificent.

Note The Guajira peninsula is not a place to travel alone; if not taking an organized tour, parties of three or more are recommended. If going in your own transport, check on safety before setting out. Also remember it is hot, easy to get lost, and there is little cover and very little water. Locals, including police, are very helpful in giving lifts. Stock up with provisions and water in Riohacha or Maicao. Elsewhere, what little there is, is expensive.

Manaure is known for its salt flats southwest of the town. If you walk along the beach past the salt works, there are several lagoons where flamingos congregate the year round (take binoculars). Local children hire out bicycles to travel to the lagoons and salt flats. Take plenty of sunblock and water and a torch/flashlight for returning in the evening. Around 14 km from Manaure in this direction is **Musichi**, an important haunt of the flamingos, sometimes out of the wet season, with the **Area Natural Protegida de los Flamencos Rosados**. From Manaure there are *busetas* to **Uribia** (US$3, 30 minutes), which has a Wayúu festival in June (www. festivalwayuu.com, no other reason to stop here), and thence to Maicao. You can get *busetas* from Uribia to Puerto Bolívar (from where coal from El Cerrejón mine is exported) and from there transport to **Cabo de Vela**, where the lagoons seasonally shelter vast flocks of flamingos, herons and sandpipers. It costs about US$8 from Uribia to Cabo de Vela, busetas run until 1400, few on Sunday, all transport leaves from the market and the journey is slow. There are fine beaches, but very strong currents offshore. Good walks through desert scrubland, eg to Pan de Azúcar hill (one hour from beach) and El Faro, with superb views of the coastline and desert. To enjoy deserted beaches, avoid Christmas and Easter when the *cabañas* and beaches are crowded and full of cars.

Parque Nacional Macuira

① *For information, T5-728 2636 in Riohacha. US$18, children US$4, registration and 30-min compulsory induction at Nazareth park office, guides US$20.*

Towards the northeast tip of the Guajira peninsula is the Serranía de Macuira, a range of hills over 500 m which creates an oasis of tropical forest in the semi-desert. Moisture comes mainly from clouds that form in the evening and disperse in the early morning. Its remoteness gives it interesting flora and fauna and indigenous settlements little affected by outsiders. To reach the area, travel northeast from Uribia either round the coast past Bahía Portete, or direct across the semi-desert, to the Wayúu village of **Nazareth** on the east side of the park. Someone may let you stay the night in a hammock in Nazareth. Otherwise, there is camping beside the park office. Macuira can be seen on two-day trips from Nazareth. Beyond Cabo de la Vela take a tour, as there is no public transport.

Another worthwhile, but arduous trip is the journey to **Punta Gallinas**, the northernmost tip of the South American continent. It takes up to eight hours on unpaved roads, followed by a boat journey (three hours, shorter in dry season) that's not for the fainthearted, but the magic of the place makes it all worth it. Few people make it this far north, adding to the isolated feel and special atmosphere. The nearby sand dunes of Taroa are also spectacular.

Maicao → *Phone code: 5. Colour map 1, A4. Population: 250,757. Altitude: 50 m.*

The paved highway runs from Riohacha to Maicao, 12 km from the Venezuelan border. It is hot, dusty and has a strong Arab presence, with several mosques and restaurants selling Arabic food. Clothing and white goods make up much of the business, but the city has a reputation for many black-market activities. Most commercial premises close early and after dark the streets are unsafe.

Border with Venezuela

Colombian immigration is at the border. **Migración Colombia** ① *C 16, No 3-28, Maicao, open 0800-1200, 1400-1700.* With all the right papers, the border crossing is easy and there are few traffic delays. Make sure your bus or *por puesto* driver stops for you to get exit and entry stamps at both country's immigration posts. There are plenty of money changers hanging around at the border crossing.

There is no Venezuelan consul in Maicao. If you need a visa, get it in Barranquilla, Cartagena or Riohacha. Entering Venezuela, a transit visa will only do if you have a confirmed ticket to a third country within three days. See 'Entering Venezuela', Venezuela chapter.

⊙ To Venezuela listings

For hotel and restaurant price codes, and other relevant information, see Essentials.

⊜ Where to stay

Riohacha *p911*
$$$ Arimaca, C 1, No 8-75, T727 3481. Impressive high tower with light, spacious rooms, some with reception room, all with balconies and magnificent sea views, pool on 2nd floor.
$$ Castillo del Mar, C 9, No 15-352, T727 5043. Reasonably priced, near the sea, a bit rough around the edges, but very pleasant

and helpful. Also has a travel agency. Recommended.
$ Internacional, Cra 7, No 13-37, T727 3483. Down an alleyway off the old market. Small, basic rooms with fan. Pleasant restaurant on the patio, a good option.
$ Yalconia del Mar, Cra 7, No 11-26, T727 3487. Cheaper with fan, small rooms, safe, helpful, half way between beach and bus station.

Guajira Peninsula *p912*
Manaure
$$ Palaaima, Cr 6, No 7-25, T717 8455, T314-581 6789. The best in town. Comfortable, cool

rooms, helpful. There are always Wayúu locals hanging around the hotel who are eager to talk about their culture and traditions.

Uribia
Basic *hostels* (**$**, no running water); most transport stops in Uribia.
$$ Juyasirain, Diag 2A, No 2B-04, T717 7284. The only more upmarket accommodation in town. Large, light and airy, with a pleasant patio restaurant.

Cabo de Vela
This area becomes very crowded during high season, but there are 60 hostels to choose from, mostly basic with hammocks, but some have TV, a/c. There is a telecom centre. Most places have hammock space on the beach, US$7. Fish meals cost US$4-6, including a large breakfast.

Maicao p913
$$$-$$ Hotel Maicao Internacional, C 12, No 10-90, T726 7184. Good rooms with a/c, rooftop pool and bar. A good option in Maicao, attentive staff.
$$ Los Médanos, Cra 10, No 11-25, T726 8822. Large rooms, a bit dark, minibar, restaurant and disco.
$$ Maicao Plaza, C 10, No 10-28, T726 0310. Modern, central, with spacious rooms.

⑦ Restaurants

Riohacha p911
Many ice cream and juice bars, and small *asados*, serving large, cheap selections of barbecued meat at the western end of the seafront. Western end also has a lovely row of brightlypainted huts selling fresh seafood and ceviche.
$$ La Tinaja, C 1, No 4-59. Lovely seafood in light, breezy setting. Recommended.
$$ Malecón, C 1A, No 3-43. Good selection of seafood and meat served in a palm-thatched barn looking out to sea, music and dancing in the evening.

⚙ Shopping

Riohacha p911
Market 2 km from town on Valledupar road; hammocks and bags woven by the Wayúu of the Guajira are sold.

⚙ What to do

Guajira Peninsula p912
Trips to the Guajira Peninsula are best arranged in Riohachawhere there are several operators, but can also be taken with national operators and others in Cartagena and Santa Marta. Tours to Cabo de la Vela, 1-2 days usually include Manaure (salt mines), Uribia, Pilón de Azucar and El Faro. All organize tours to Wayúu *rancherías* in the afternoon (includes typical goat lunch).

Uribia
Kaí Eco Travel, Diagonal 1B, No 8-68, T311-436 2830, also at Hotel Castillo del Mar in Riohacha and in Hotel Juyasirain, www.kaiecotravel.com. Run by a network of Wayúu families, organizes tours to Cabo de la Vela, Punta Gallinas and kitesurfing courses, prices include transport, accommodation and food. Highly recommended.
Kaishi, Plaza Principal, T717 7306 or 311-429 6315, T717 7306 or T311-429 6315, www.kaishitravel.com. Organizes jeep tours around La Guajira, with lodging.

⊖ Transport

Riohacha p911
Air Daily flight to **Bogotá**, 1 hr 35 mins.
Bus Main terminal is on C 15 (El Progreso). Coopcaribe Taxis travel throughout the region and can be picked up almost anywhere in town, especially close to the old market area near the Hotel Internacional: daily to **Uribia**, US$9, 1½ hrs, **Manaure** US$10, 1¾ hrs. Leave when full (4 people), be prepared to pay slightly more if there are no travellers. Early morning best for travel, transport is scarce in the afternoon. No buses leave from Riohacha direct to Cabo de la Vela: travel to Uribia and wait for a jeep (leaves when full, irregular service) to Cabo de La Vela, long and uncomfortable, unpaved

road. Take plenty of water with you. It is much easier and recommended to take a tour from Riohacha to Cabo de La Vela.

Maicao *p913*
Bus Buses to/from **Riohacha**, US$5.75, frequent, 1-1½ hr. **Santa Marta** 3 hrs, US$20. **Barranquilla**, US$34. **Cartagena**, US$34. Trucks leave regularly for **Cabo de Vela**, 2½-3 hrs, US$10 (can be uncomfortably crowded). Take water. **Fleta** is the local name for the faster taxis. Colectivos (*por puestos* in Venezuela), Maicao-**Maracaibo**, US$18.50, or microbus, US$15, very few buses to Venezuela after midday. Buses leave from the bus terminal where you can change money. Taxis from Maicao to Maracaibo

stop at both immigration posts and take you to your hotel.

O Directory

Riohacha *p911*
Banks Many are on or near Parque Almirante. **Consulates** Venezuela, Cra 7, No 3-08, p 2, T727 4076, riohacha.consulado.gob. ve (Mon-Thu 0800-1200, 1400-1700, Fri 0800-1300). If you need a visa, you should check all requirements for your nationality before arriving at this consulate. It is easier to get a Venezuelan visa in Barranquilla. **Immigration** Migración Colombia, C 5, No 4-48, 0800-1200, 1400-1700.

San Andrés and Providencia

Colombia's Caribbean islands of the San Andrés and Providencia archipelago are 480 km north of the South American coast, 400 km southwest of Jamaica, and 180 km east of Nicaragua. This proximity has led Nicaragua to claim them from Colombia in the past. In 2000, the Archipelago of San Andrés, Old Providence and Santa Catalina was declared a World Natural Heritage Site called the Seaflower Biosphere Reserve. San Andrés is larger and more developed than Providencia and has lost much of its colonial Caribbean feel. Both are very expensive by South American standards. Nevertheless, their surrounding islets and cays, good diving, white sand beaches and spectacular turquoise waters make them popular holiday resorts with Colombians and North Americans looking for winter sun. San Andrés is very crowded with Colombian shoppers looking for foreign-made, duty-free bargains, but international shoppers will find few bargains, and essentials and eating out are expensive. The original inhabitants, mostly descendants of Jamaican slaves, speak English, but the population has swollen with unrestricted immigration from Colombia. There are also Chinese and Middle Eastern communities.

Arriving in San Andrés and Providencia
Getting there A cheap way to visit San Andrés is by taking a charter flight from Bogotá or other major cities, accommodation and food included. See supplements in the local Colombian press. The airport at San Andrés is 15 minutes' walk to town centre; buses to centre and San Luis from across the road from the airport. » *See also Transport, page 919.*

Tourist information **San Andrés Tourist office** ① *Av Newball, opposite Restaurante La Regatta, T512 5058, securismosai@yahoo.com, Mon-Fri 0800-1200, 1400-1800, and kiosk at the end of Av 20 de Julio, across from the sea,* helpful, English spoken, maps and hotel lists. On arrival in San Andrés, you must buy a tourist card, US$27. It is also valid for Providencia. Do not lose it. You must also have an onward or return ticket. On Providencia is the **Centro Administrativo Aury** ① *T514 8054, securismoprovidencia@hotmail.com.*

San Andrés → *Phone code: 8. Population: 77,000.*
The 11-km-long San Andrés island is made of coral and rises at its highest to 104 m. The town, commercial centre, resort hotel sector and airport are at the northern end. A picturesque road circles the island. Places to see, besides the beautiful cays and beaches on the less developed southern side, include the Hoyo Soplador (South End), a geyser-like hole through which the

sea spouts into the air when the wind is in the right direction. The west side is less spoilt, but there are no beaches. Instead there is **The Cove**, the islands deepest anchorage, and **Morgan's Cave** (Cueva de Morgan, reputed hiding place for the pirate's treasure) which is penetrated by the sea through an underwater passage. Next to Cueva de Morgan is a **museum** ① *US$5*, with exhibitions telling the history of the coconut, paraphernalia from wrecks around the island and a replica pirate ship.

About 1 km south from Cueva de Morgan is **West View** ① *daily 0900-1700, small restaurant opposite entrance*, an excellent place to see marine life as the sea is very clear. At The Cove, a road crosses up to the centre of the island and back to town over La Loma, on which is a Baptist Church, built in 1847.

San Andrés is famous in Colombia for its different styles of music, including the local form of calypso, soca, reggae and church music. Concerts are held at the **Old Coliseum** (every Saturday at 2100 in the high season).

Boats leave from San Andrés in the morning for El Acuario (Rose Cay) and Haynes Cay, and continue to Johnny Cay in the afternoon (entry US$2.25), which has a white beach and parties all day Sunday (US$17 return). **El Acuario** has crystalline water and is a good place to snorkel. You can wade across to **Haynes Cay** where there is good food and a reggae bar at **Bibi's Place** (they organize full moon parties and civil and rasta weddings). If you want to avoid the crowds, hire a private boat and do the tour in reverse. Boats for the cays leave from Tonino's Marina between 0930 and 1030, returning at 1530, or from Muelle Casa de la Cultura on Avenida Newell. On San Andrés the beaches are in town and on the east coast. Best are at San Luis and Bahía Sonora/Sound Bay.

Providencia → *Phone code: 8. Population: 5500. 80 km north-northeast of San Andrés.*

Commonly called Old Providence, Providencia is mountainous, of volcanic origin. The barrier reef that surrounds it, the third largest in the world, is called Old Providence McBean Lagoon; it is easily visited (entry US$11). Providencia and its sister island **Santa Catalina** (an old pirate lair separated from Providencia by a channel cut to improve their defence) have an approximate surface of 22 sq km. The official languages of its 5500 inhabitants are Spanish and Caribbean English. Musical influences are the mento from the Antilles, calypso from Trinidad and reggae from Jamaica. The average temperature is 27°C; the rainiest months are October and November, while the driest are January to April. There are no high-rises, apartment blocks or shopping malls and its quieter atmosphere than San Andrés attracts more European visitors.

Superb views can be had by climbing from Casabaja/Bottom House or Aguamansa/Smooth Water to the peak (about one hour, US$15 with a guide). There are relics of the fortifications built on the island during its disputed ownership. Horse riding is available, and boat trips can be made to Santa Catalina and, to the northeast, Cayo Cangrejo/Crab Cay (entrance US$1.50, good snorkelling – see Tours, below). Santa Catalina is joined to the main island by the wooden Lover's Bridge (Malecón de los Enamorados). Go left after crossing this bridge (right is a dead end) and walk for about 500 m. Climb stairs to the Virgin statue for excellent views of Providencia. If you continue past the Virgin and go down the flight of stairs you will arrive at a very small beach (nice snorkelling). On the west side is a rock formation called Morgan's Head; from the side it looks like a profile.

Of the three main beaches, Manzanillo is the best preserved and wildest. Not much space for lying out, but pleasant for walking. **Roland's Roots Bar** has excellent live, traditional island music on weekends. South West Bay/Suroeste has stunning beaches and is the best for hanging out. There is access at each end. Agua Dulce is where most hotels and restaurants are. Between April-May, the island is awash with migrating black crabs.

⊙ San Andrés and Providencia listings

For hotel and restaurant price codes, and other relevant information, see Essentials.

⊕ Where to stay

San Andrés *p915*
Hotels quote rates pp, but we list prices for double rooms. Prices include half board, but most can be booked without meals. Most raise prices by 20-30% on 15 Dec. All this also applies to Providencia. The Decameron group has 5 hotels on San Andrés, www.decameron.com.

$$$$ Casa Harb, C 11, No 10-83, T512 6348, www.casaharb.com. Just outside town, this boutique hotel takes its inspiration from the Far East and is the most stylish on the island. Each room is individually decorated with antique furniture, enormous granite baths, infinity pool and home-cooked meals.

$$$$ Portobelo, Av Colombia, No 5A-69, T512 7008, www.portobelohotel.com. In a couple of buildings at the western end of the *malecón*, large beds.

$$$$ Sunset Hotel, Carretera Circunvalar Km 13, T513 0433, http://sunsethotelspa.com. On the western side of the island, ideal for diving or for getting away from the crowds. Bright, fresh rooms set around a salt-water swimming pool. Restaurant with international and regional food in a typical clapboard house, dive shop next door.

$$ Hernando Henry, Av Las Américas, No 4-84, T512 3416, www.hotelhernandohenry.com. At the back of town, shoddy but passable rooms, cheaper with fan, laundry service.

$$ La Posada de Lulú, Av Antioquia, No 2-28, T512 2919. Brightly coloured hostel, comfortable rooms and 2 apartments to rent for longer stays, excellent restaurant. Recommended.

$$ Posada Doña Rosa, Av Las Américas con Aeropuerto, T512 3649, http://posadarosa.blogspot.co.uk. A 2-min walk from the airport, this is a reasonable an economical option, use of kitchen, TV room, a short walk from the beach. Also has 2 apartments to rent.

$ pp El Viajero San Andrés, Av 20 de Julio 3A-122, T512 7497, www.sanandreshostel.com. Member of the Uruguayan hostel chain. Private en suite rooms and dorms (US$17-

26 per bed) with a/c. Rooms also have TV. Breakfast, internet and Wi-Fi included. Roof-terrace bar overlooking the sea. Cycle hire and money exchange.

Providencia *p916*
Rooms can be rented at affordable prices in local houses or *posadas nativas*.

Hotels in Agua Dulce are 10 mins by motor taxi (US$1) from centre or 1-hr walk. Suroeste is a 20-min walk from Agua Dulce. The Decameron group, www.decameron.com, represents 5 properties on the island, including **Cabañas Miss Elma**, T514 8229, and **Cabañas Miss Mary**, T514 8454, at Aguadulce.

$$$ Posada del Mar, Aguadulce, T514 8168, www.posadadelmarprovidencia. com. Pink and purple clapboard house with comfortable rooms, each with a terrace and hammock, hot water.

$$$ Sirius, Suroeste, T514 8213, www.sirius hotel.net. Large, colourful house set back from the beach. Large, light rooms, some with balconies, on the beach. Also dive centre, kayaks, wakeboarding, horse riding, massage. The owner speaks German, Italian and English. Half-board and diving packages available.

$$$ Sol Caribe Providencia, Agua Dulce, T514 8230, www.solarhoteles.com. Chain hotel with 2-5 night deals, pool, sea views, a/c, TV, fridge, bright.

$$ Old Providence, diagonal Alcaldía Municipal, Santa Isabel (centre), T514 8691. Above supermarket **Erika**, rooms are basic but clean.

❼ Restaurants

San Andrés *p915*
Good fish and seafood meals at San Luis beach.
$$$-$$ La Regatta, Av Newball, next to Club Naútico, T512 0437. Seafood restaurant on a pier, fine reputation.
$$$-$$ Margherita e Carbonara, Av Colombia, No 1-93. Good Italian, pizzas and coffee.
$$ Niko's, Av Colombia, No 1-93. Bills itself as a seafood restaurant though its steaks are actually better. Lovely setting by the water.

Providencia p916

Typical dish is *rondón*, a mix of fish, conch, yucca and dumplings, cooked in coconut milk. Fish and crab are most common. Corn ice cream is also popular – it tastes a little like vanilla but a little sweeter.

As well as hotels, good places include:
Arturo, on Suroeste beach, next to Miss Mary. **Café Studio**, between Agua Dulce and Suroeste. Great pies and spaghetti.
$$ Caribbean Place (Donde Martín), Aguadulce. *Bogoteño* chef Martín Quintero uses local ingredients.
$$ Roland's Roots bar, Playa Manzanillo, T514 8417, rolandsbeach@hotmail.com. Parties at Roland's bar-restaurant are legendary. The menu is mainly seafood. He also hires tents (**$**).

⊛ Festivals

San Andrés p915

Jun Jardín del Caribe. A folkloric festival.
20 Jul independence celebrations on San Andrés with various events.
Dec Rainbow Festival. Reggae and calypso music.

Providencia p916
The island holds its **carnival** in **Jun**.

O Shopping

Providencia p916
Arts and Crafts Café, Agua Dulce, T514 8297. French owners sell local crafts and delicious homemade cookies and ice cream.

⓸ What to do

San Andrés p915
Canopying Canopy La Loma, Vía La Loma-Barrack, T314-447 9868. Site at the top of the hill in San Andrés. 3 'flights' over the trees at 450 m, 300 m and 200 m all with spectacular views out to sea, US$17. Safety precautions and equipment are good.
Diving Diving off San Andrés is good; depth varies from 3 to 30 m, visibility from 10 to 30 m. There are 3 types of site: walls of seaweed and minor coral reefs, different types

of coral, and underwater plateaux with much marine life. It is possible to dive in 70% of the insular platform. Diving trips to the reef:
Banda Dive Shop, Hotel Lord Pierre, Local 102, T315-303 5428, www.bandadiveshop.com. PADI qualified, various courses. Fast boat and good equipment.
Sharky Dive Shop, Carretera Circunvalar Km 13, T512 0651, www.sharkydiveshop.com. Good equipment and excellent, English-speaking guides. PADI qualifications and a beginner's course held in the Sunset Hotel's saltwater pool.
Watersports and boat trips Cooperativa Lancheros, on the beach in San Andrés town. Can arrange fishing trips, wind-surfing, jet skiing and kite surfing. Snorkelling equipment can be hired for US$10.
Galeon Morgan, Centro Comercial New Point Plaza, T512 8787. Boat tours to El Acuario.

Providencia p916
Diving Recommended diving spots on the Old McBean Lagoon reef are Manta's Place, a good place to see manta rays; Felipe's Place where there is a submerged figure of Christ; and Stairway to Heaven, which has a large wall of coral and big fish.
Felipe Diving, South West Bay, T851 8775, www.felipediving.com. Mini and full courses, also rents snorkel equipment, can arrange lodging. Owner Felipe Cabeza even has a diving spot on the reef named after him. Warmly recommended. See also **Hotel Sirius**, above. PADI qualifications, mini courses.
Snorkelling and boat trips
Recommended snorkelling sites include the waters around Santa Catalina, where there are many caves to explore as well as Morgan's Head and lots of starfish; Hippie's Place, which has a little bit of everything; and El Faro (The Lighthouse), the end of the reef before it drops into deep sea.
Valentina Tours, T514 8548. Lemus Walter, aka Captain 'Hippie', T514 8548, T311-485 4805, organizes snorkelling, boat trips to the outlying cays and reefs, also boat hire, home-cooking and lodging in his house.
Tour operators Body Contact, Aguadulce, T514 8283. Owner Jennifer Archbold organizes excursions, fishing and hiking trips, currency exchange, accommodation, and more.

Walking A good 1.5-km walk over Manchineel Hill, between Bottom House (Casa Baja) and South West Bay, through tropical forest, fine views, many types of bird, iguanas and blue lizards. Guided tours depart twice a day at 0900 and 1500 from Bottom House. Enquire at **Body Contact**, see above, or Coralina, T514 9003.

⊝ Transport

San Andrés *p915*
Air Regular flights from **Bogotá**, **Cartagena**, **Cali** and **Medellín**. Copa once daily to **Panama City**. Sun flights are always heavily booked, similarly Jul-Aug, Dec-Jan.
Bus Buses run every 15 mins on the eastern side of the island, US$0.50, and more often at night and during the holidays.
Taxis around the island cost US$20, but in town fares double after 2200. To airport US$8.50.
Vehicle and bicycle hire Motorbikes are easy to hire, as are golf buggies, US$35. Cars can also be hired for 2 hrs or for a day. Passport may be required as deposit. Bikes are easy to hire, but they may be in poor condition.

Providencia *p916*
Air Satena and Searca fly from San Andrés twice a day. Bookable only in San Andrés. Essential to confirm flights to guarantee a seat.

Schedules change frequently. Taxi from airport to centre, US$10 (fixed).
Boat Catamaran *Sensation*, www.catamaranelsensation.com, sails Mon, Wed, Fri, Sun 0730, returns from Providencia 1530, US$32.50 one way, 3¼ hrs. Cargo boat trips leave from San Andrés, taking 7-8 uncomfortable hrs, 3 times a week, US$22. They usually leave at 2200, arriving in the early morning. *Miss Isabel*, *Doña Olga* and *Raziman* make the trip regularly. Speak directly to the captain at the port in San Andrés, or enquire at the Port Authority (Capitanía del Puerto) in San Luis.
Motoped hire US$35 per day from many hotels. No licence or deposit needed. Golf buggies are also available for US$83 per day.

⊙ Directory

San Andrés *p915*
Banks Banks close 1200-1400. ATMs available in town and at the airport. *Casa de cambio*, some shops and most hotels will change US$ cash **Immigration** Migración Colombia, Cra 7, No 2-70, T512 1818.

Providencia *p916*
Banks An ATM is tucked away just before the Lover's Bridge, on the road to Santa Catalina.
Useful numbers Police: T2. Medical: T11. Ambulance: T514 8016 at hospital.

Medellín and Chocó

Antioquia is the largest of the western departments, full of diversity and an important agricultural and commercial region. With its roots in the Cordilleras, it still has 100 km of Caribbean coastline. The people of Antioquia are called 'paisas'.

Stretching between the Cordillera Occidental and the Pacific Coast, from Panamá to Valle del Cauca, Chocó is one of Colombia's least developed and most beautiful departments.

Medellín → *Phone code: 4. Colour map 1, B2. Population: 2,636,000. Altitude: 1495 m.*

Medellín, capital of Antioquia, is considered by many to be the engine of Colombia and *paisas* are known for their canny business sense as well as their hospitality. Previously the home and headquarters of notorious narco-trafficker Pablo Escobar, Medellín has, since his death, shaken off its association with drugs and violence in what is one of the most remarkable turnarounds in Latin America. It is now a fresh, vibrant, prosperous city known for its progressive social politics and culture. In the centre, few colonial buildings remain, but large new buildings must, by law, incorporate modern works of art. Music, arts and gastronomy festivals attract many visitors and the flower festival, the **Desfile de Silleteros**, in August, is the most spectacular parade in

Colombia. Known as 'The City of Eternal Spring', Medellín has a pleasant, temperate climate year-round; warm during the day and cool in the evening.

Arriving in Medellín

Orientation The **International airport** (José María Córdova, also called Rionegro) is 28 km from Medellín and 9 km from the town of Rionegro. The **city airport**, Enrique Olaya Herrera, has regional flights to some destinations in Colombia.

The terminal for long-distance buses going north and east is **Terminal del Norte**, about 3 km north of the centre. For buses going south, **Terminal del Sur** is alongside the Olaya Herrera airport. The city's overground Metro is the best way to get around. The Terminal del Norte is close to Caribe station, but Terminal del Sur is 1.5-km taxi ride from Poblado station. ▶▶ *See also Transport, page 925.*

The city is based around the old and the new cathedrals, the former on Parque Berrío and the latter overlooking Parque de Bolívar. The main commercial area is three blocks away on Carrera 46. In the centre, Pasaje Junín (Cra 49) is closed to traffic from Parque de Bolívar to Parque San Antonio (C 46), as is the central part of Cra 52. In the south, El Poblado is an upmarket commercial and residential area. This is where many hotels, hostels and restaurants can be found. The area around Parque Lleras, known as the Zona Rosa, is where most of the bars and nightclubs are situated. West of the centre between Cerro El Volador and the Universidad Pontificia Bolivariana, Cra 70 and C 44 are busy commercial and entertainment sectors with many hotels, shopping centres and the huge **Atanasio Girardot** sports stadium nearby. Many central streets are named as well as numbered. Particularly important are: Cra 46, part of the inner ring road, which has several names but is known popularly as 'Av Oriental'; Cra 80/Cra 81/Diagonal 79, the outer ring road to the west, which is called 'La Ochenta' throughout; C 51/52, east of the centre is 'La Playa'; and C 33, which crosses the Río Medellín to become Calle 37, is called 'La Treinta y Tres'.

For your first view of the city, take the Metro, which connects with three cable cars which give great views over the city, especially at dusk. ▶▶ *See Transport, page 925.*

1 El Poblado

Medellín maps
1 El Poblado, page 920
2 Medellín centre, page 921
3 Medellín metro, page 922

Where to stay 😴
1 Acqua Hotel Express
2 Art
3 Black Sheep Hostel
4 Casa Blanca
5 Casa Kiwi
6 Diez
7 GEO Hostel
8 Park 10
9 Pitstop Hostel
10 Tiger Paw

Restaurants 🍴
1 Basílica
2 Eco Bar
3 Le Bon
4 Thaico
5 Triada
6 Verdeo

Tourist information Oficina de Turismo de Medellín ① *C 41, No 55-80, of 306, T261 6060, http://medellin.travel.* For information on the city, helpful staff, English spoken, has kiosks (PITs) at both airports, both bus terminals, at the Pueblito Paisa at the top of Cerro Nutibara, open daily, and in the Caja de Madera, Plaza Mayor (first floor, less regular hours). **Comfenalco** Medellín information service ① *C 50, No 53-43, T444 7110, www.comfenalco antioquia.com,* has booths in Plaza Botero

① *Cra 51, No 52A-48, T511 1211, Mon-Fri 0900-1900, Sat 0900-1800, Sun 1000-1300, 1400-1700,* has information in English, French and Spanish, very helpful staff, and several libraries throughout the city. See also www.medellintraveler.com and www.guia turisticademedellin.com. **National parks office** ① *C 49, No 78A-67, T422 0883.*

Centre

Plaza Botero (or de las Esculturas) ① *C 52 y Cra 52,* is dotted with 23 bronze sculptures by **Fernando Botero**, who is Colombia's leading contemporary artist, born in Medellín in 1932. One side of the plaza has **El Palacio de la Cultura Rafael Uribe**, formerly the governor's office, which is now a cultural centre and art gallery (free entry). Across, is the **Museo de Antioquia** ① *Cra 52, No 52-53, T251 3636, www.museodeantioquia.org.co, Mon-Sat 1000-1730, Sun and holidays, 1000-1630, US$5, metro stop: Parque Berrío,* well-displayed works of contemporary Colombian artists, including a large collection by Botero. More works by Botero can be seen in **Parque San Antonio** ① *between C 44/46 and Cra 46.* It includes the 'Torso Masculino' (which complements the female version in Parque Berrío), and the 'Bird of Peace' which was severely damaged by a guerrilla bomb in 1996. At Botero's request, it has been left unrepaired as a symbol of the futility of violence and a new one has been placed alongside to make the point yet more dramatically. **Parque de Bolívar**, with its flowering trees and a fountain display, is dominated by the **Catedral Metropolitana**, built between 1875 and 1931, claimed to be the third largest brick building in the world. Of the colonial churches near the centre, white **La Veracruz** ① *C 51, No 52-58, T512 5095, Mon-Sat 0700-1800, Sun Mass 0830-1000, 1200-1600,* is a national historical monument.

Outside the centre

To the north are **Joaquín Antonio Uribe botanical gardens** ① *Cra 52, No 73-298, T444 5500 ext 120, www.botanicomedellin.org, daily 0900-1700, free, metro Universidad,* are near the University

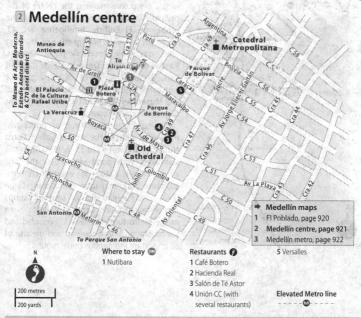

② **Medellín centre**

Museo de Antioquia
Catedral Metropolitana
Av de Greif
To Airport
Parque de Bolívar
El Palacio de la Cultura Rafael Uribe
Plaza Botero
La Veracruz
Parque de Berrío
Boyacá
Av 1 de Mayo
Old Cathedral
Ayacucho
Colombia
Pichincha
Av La Playa
San Antonio
Maturín
Av Oriental
To Parque San Antonio
To Museo de Arte Moderna, Estadio Anatasio Girardot & C70 hotel district

➡ Medellín maps
1 El Poblado, page 920
2 Medellín centre, page 921
3 Medellín metro, page 922

Where to stay 🛏
1 Nutibara

Restaurants 🍴
1 Café Botero
2 Hacienda Real
3 Salón de Té Astor
4 Unión CC (with several restaurants)
5 Versalles

Elevated Metro line
- - - - -Ⓜ- - - - -

N
200 metres
200 yards

of Antioquia campus, with 5500 species of plants, orchids and trees. There are two restaurants, one more economical than the other. Opposite the botanical gardens is the **Parque Explora** ① *Cra 52, No 73-75, T516 8300, www.parque explora.org, Tue-Sun 1000-1830 (ticket office closes 1700), US$10 for full tour, approximately 6-8 hrs*, a science and technology museum plus associated aquarium, planetarium (entry US$6) and other spaces. With more than 300 interactive scientific puzzles and games, this is fun for adults and heaven for kids.

③ Medellín Metro

> **Medellín maps**
> 1 El Poblado, page 920
> 2 Medellín centre, page 921
> 3 Medellín metro, page 922

Niquía
Bello
Madera
Santo Domingo
Andalucía
Acevedo
Popular
Arví
Tricentenario
Terminal del Norte
Caribe
Universidad
La Aurora
(Service Link)
Hospital
Vallejuelos
Juan XXIII
Prado
Santa Lucía
Estadio
Parque Berrío (see map detail)
San Javier
Floresta
Suramericana
Cisneros
San Antonio
Alpujarra
Exposiciones
Industriales
Olaya Herrera Airport
Terminal del Sur
Poblado (see map detail)
Aguacatala
Ayurá
Linea A
Linea B
Linea J
Envigado
Linea K
N
Linea L
Not to scale
Itagüí

West of the centre **Museo de Arte Moderno** ① *Cra 44, No 19A-100, T444 2622, www. elmamm.org, Mon-Fri 0900-1730, Sat 1000-1730, Sun 1000-1700, US$4, children, students with card and seniors free*, has a small collection, shows foreign films, has a variety of special visits and holds many events at other locations. **Biblioteca Pública Piloto para América Latina** ① *Cra 64, No 50-32, T460 0590, www. bibliotecapiloto.gov.co, Mon-Fri 0830-1900, Sat 0900-1800* is one of the best public libraries in the country, with art and photo exhibitions, readings and films. **Puntocero** ① *at the C 67 river bridge*, is an elegant steel double arch with a pendulum marking the centre of the city. In Alpujarra district, southwest of the centre are **El Edificio Inteligente** ① *C 43, No 58-01*, a highly energy-efficient building used jointly by Medellín's public services, **Parque de Los Pies Descalzos** (The Barefoot Park) ① *Cra 57, No 42-139*, a relaxing space with cafés, sand pits, Zen garden and fountains, and **Museo del Agua EPM** ① *T380 6954, www. museodelaguaepm.com.co*.

As you ride the metro you will notice two prominent hills in the Aburrá valley: **Cerro Nutibara** ① *C 30A y Cra 55, T235 8370*, in the southwest with good views over the city, where there is a stage for open air concerts, sculpture park, miniature Antioquian village (known as Pueblito Paisa), souvenir shops and restaurants; and **Cerro El Volador** (seen as the Metro turns between Universidad and Caribe stations), tree-covered and the site of an important indigenous burial ground.

⊙ Medellín listings

For hotel and restaurant price codes, and other relevant information, see Essentials.

● Where to stay

Medellín: centre *p921, map p921*
Most of the city's better accommodation are around Cra 70 and in El Poblado. There are hotels in the centre, some new, others old and faded, including the famous art deco **Nutibara Conference Plaza**, C 52A, No 50-46, T511 5111, http://hotelnutibara.com, fully remodelled and associated with **Nutibara Express**, C 52, No 50-19, and **Nutibara Poblado Suites**, Cra 31, No 16-221.

Medellín: outside the centre *p919, map p920*
Cra 70 (metro Estadio), is full of hotels in roughly the same price range. Although standards can vary they are good value. There are plenty of eateries, bars and discos as well.
$$$ Florida, Cra 70, No 44B-38, T260 4900, www.hotelfloridamedellin.com. A bit more upmarket than others, car park and restaurant.
$$$-$$ Lukas, Cra 70, No 44A-28, T260 1761, mercadeo@lukashotel.com, or see Facebook. Crisp rooms with safe and all facilities.
$$ Parque 70, C 46B, No 69A-11, T260 3339, www.hotelparque70.com. Good little hotel in a quiet cul-de-sac off Cra 70, cheper without a/c.
$$ Villa Real, Cra 70, No 45E-153, T414 4905, www.hotelvillarealmedellin.co. Comfortable, modern hotel, cheaper without street view or a/c, parking.
$ Hostal Medellín, Cra 69, No 46B-17, T260 2972, www.hostalmedellin.com. Spacious hostel, private rooms and dorms (US$11), German/Colombian run, popular with bikers. Garden with a hammock, pool table, organizes tours, close to Estadio Metro. Recommended.
$ Palm Tree Hostal, Cra 67, No 48D-63, T444 7256, www.palmtreemedellin.com (Metro Suramericana, behind Exito supermarket on C 50). Good backpackers' hostel, bike hire, book exchange and hammocks. Private rooms and dorms (US$15), free BBQ on Fri, dance classes on Mon.

El Poblado and around
There are many luxury and business class hotels in El Poblado, for instance **Diez**, C 10A, No 34-11, www.diezhotel.com, and **Medellín Royal**, Cra 42, No 5 Sur-130, T448 5700, www.hoteles royal.com, and the boutique-style **Art**, Cra 41, No 9-31, T369 7900, www.arthotel.com.co. Also many more hostels than we can list here. See also Arriving in Medellín, page 920.
$$$$ Park 10, Cra 36B No 11-12, T310 6060, www.hotelpark10.com.co. Quiet location, smart, all rooms have a reception area. Buffet breakfast, sauna, gym, business centre and spa, among other facilities.
$$$ Acqua Hotel Express, Cra 35, No 7-47, T448 0482, www.hotelacqua.com. A mid-range option close to Parque Lleras.
$$ GEO Hostel, Cra 35, No 8A-58, T311 7150, www.geohostel.com. Smart, modern mid-range option, close to the Zona Rosa, private rooms and dorms (US$13 pp).
$$-$ Black Sheep Hostel, Transversal 5A, No 45-133 (tell taxi drivers it's in Patio Bonito), T311 1589, T317-518 1369, www.blacksheep medellin.com (informative website about travelling in Colombia). Run by welcoming Kiwi, Kelvin, homely feel, well-organized, private rooms and dorms (US$11.50-12.50 pp), TV areas, popular weekly BBQ, washing machine, excellent service, Spanish lessons arranged. Information on paragliding. Recommended.
$$-$ Casa Blanca, Transversal 5A, No 45-256 (Patio Bonito), T586 5149, www.casablanca medellin.com. Large hostel with dorms (US$12.50) and private rooms, quiet location, parking for cars or motorbikes, pool table, table tennis.
$$-$ Casa Kiwi, Cra 36, No 7-10, T268 2668, www.casakiwihostel.com. Private rooms, semi-dorms and dorms, US$12 pp. Good travellers' hostel, hammock terrace, roof-top pool, bar and TV room with theatre seating. Near Parque Lleras, welcoming, paragliding arranged. Recommended.
$$-$ Pitstop Hostel, Cra 43E, No5-110, T352 1176, www.pitstophostel.com. A big hostel with party atmosphere, swimming pool, Irish bar, steam room, gym, pool table and a huge outdoor area. Dorms US$10.50-13 pp,

private rooms with and without bath for up to 4 people. Tours and events organized.
$$-$ Tiger Paw, Cra 36, No 10-49, T311 6079, www.tigerpawhostel.com. A variety of rooms, dorms US$10-11, US-owned, tourist packages, sports bar with micro brews and lots of activities.

❼ Restaurants

Medellín: centre *p921, map p921*
$$ Café Botero, Cra 52, No 52-43.
Excellent lunchtime venue in the Museo de Antioquia building. Fish, fine steaks and delicious puddings.
$$ Hacienda Real, Cra 49, No 52-98 (next door to Salón de Té Astor).
Pleasant restaurant with balcony seating, overlooking Pasaje Junín/Cra 49.
$$ Versalles, Pasaje Junín, No 53-59. Famous Argentine-run *pastelería* and restaurant, *parrillas* and empanadas, good-value set lunches. Lovely coffees and breakfasts too. Highly recommended.
$$-$ CC Unión CC, Cra 49 (Junín), No 52-107. Many eateries on the Balcón de Comidas of this commercial centre, including **San Miguel Cazuelas**, for typical dishes; **Malibú Gourmet Parrilla**, crêpes, pastas, salads; **Latin Coffee**, combos, crêpes, sandwiches; all do breakfasts.
$$-$ Salón de Té Astor, Cra 49, No 52-84. Delightful traditional tea and pastry house, famous for its chocolate delicacies.

Medellín: outside the centre *p919, map p920*
Several eateries on Cra 70, No 45E block, all serving *bandeja paisa* (**$$$**) and other cheaper lunches.
$$ La Margarita No 2, Cra 70, No 45E-11. Antioquian dishes in a nice, friendly atmosphere.
$$-$ Pomo d'Oro, C 42, No 71-24. Wide variety of pastas and sauces at reasonable prices.
$ Opera Pizza, C 42, No 70-22. *Paisas* swear these are the best pizzas in town.
$ ¡Orale!, C 41, No 70-138. Excellent little Mexican cantina with tables on the street. Another branch at Cra 43B, 10A-49, El Poblado, does Mexican and pizza. Recommended.

El Poblado and around
In Parque Lleras/Zona Rosa, there are so many places that it is impossible to mention them all. Those we do list have been found to be good, but recommendations change as places become fashionable. Just wander around and see what takes your fancy, but at weekends especially, don't leave it too late as places get very busy, with queues for tables.
$$$ Basílica, Cra 38, No 9-42. Steaks, sushi and Peruvian specialities on an open terrace on Parque Lleras.
$$$ Triada, Cra 38, No 8 (Vía Primavera)-08. Enormous restaurant/bar/club in the heart of the Zona Rosa, steaks, sushi, salads and Tex Mex, good atmosphere. Packed at weekends.
$$$-$$ Thaico, C 9A, No 37A-40. Good Thai food, popular spot for watching televised sports.
$$$-$$ Verdeo, Parque Explora, Cra 35, No 8A-3, www.ricoverdeo.com. Excellent vegetarian on a pedestrian alley.
$$ Le Bon, C 9, No 39-09. French café with lovely atmosphere. Often has jazz in the evening.

❼ Bars and clubs

Medellín *p919, maps p920 and p921*
In El Poblado, the best bars and clubs are in the Zona Rosa, around Parque Lleras; there are plenty of them. If the prices of the Zona Rosa get too much, an alternative after-hours location is Sabaneta, 11 km from the centre, with an attractive plaza. It's popular with young and old alike. There are several excellent bars and restaurants with lots of local history. Take a taxi from El Poblado, US$5.50. Also check out Medellín's local brewery, **Tres Cordilleras**, www.3cordilleras.com.
Canalón, Cra 40, No 75S-25, Sabaneta. Fri and Sat. A popular club in this area.
Eco Bar, Cra 8a, No 36-30, El Poblado. On an alley close to Parque Lleras, open-air seating on tree stumps.
El Viejo John, Cra 45, No 70 Sur-42, Sabaneta. A popular local spot with strings of chorizo hanging from the ceiling. Also serves typical dishes.
Fonda Sitio Viejo, C 70 Sur, No 44-25, Sabaneta. Another bar full of character. This one has photographs of every church in Medellín.

La Herrería, Cra 45, No 70 Sur-24, Sabaneta. Packed to the ceiling with pictures of local characters, Mexican sombreros, saddles and bananas.

Entertainment

Medellín *p919, maps p920 and p921*
Cinema Check the press and www.planb. com.co/medellin for movies, music, theatre and other cultural events. **Centro Colombo Americano**, Cra 45, No 53-24, T513 4444, www.colomboworld.com. Shows foreign art films, also holds cultural events, has a café and bookshop. The main malls have multiplexes.
Tango There are popular tango bars in El Envigado, a **Museo Casa Gardeliana**, Cra 45, No 76-50, T212 0968, info@casagardeliana.com, commemorating Carlos Gardel who died in a plane crash in Medellín in 1935, and an annual **Festival Internacional de Tango** in Jun. Salón Malaga, Cra 51, No 45-80, T231 2658, is one of Medellín's oldest tango bars.
Theatre Teatro Metropolitano, C 41, No 57-30, T232 2858, www.teatrometropolitano.com, major artistic presentations.

Festivals

Medellín *p919, maps p920 and p921*
Easter Semana Santa (Holy Week) has special Easter religious parades. **Jul** International Poetry Festival, see www.festivaldepoesiade medellin. org. Flower fair (Feria de las Flores/Desfile de Silleteros) is held annually in the **1st week of Aug** with spectacular parades and music, one of the finest shows in Colombia. **International Jazz and World Music Festival** in **Sep**, www. festivalmedejazz.com. There are many other music and cultural festivals throughout the year.

Shopping

Medellín *p919, maps p920 and p921*
Handicrafts There are *artesanía* shops on the top of Cerro Nutibara. Mercado Sanalejo, Parque Bolívar, open on the first Sat of every month except Jan, and before Christmas on Sat and Sun (handicrafts on sale at good prices). Every Nov the Feria Nacional de Artesanías is held in the Plaza Mayor exhibition centre.

What to do

Medellín *p919, maps p920 and p921*
Bullfights At the bullring of La Macarena, C 44 and Cra 63, in Jan and Feb.
Dance classes Academia Dance, Cra 46, No 7-9, T266 1522. Salsa classes, good reports.
Pablo Escobar tours A number of operators offer tours of the most significant places from the life and times of this notorious leader of the Medellín drugs cartel. Contact **Paisa Road**, T317-489 2629, www.paisaroad. com, or via hostels.
Sports complex Estadio Atanasio Girardot, Cra 74, C 50, football, baseball, velodrome, swimming, next to the *Estadio* Metro station. Just outside the station is EnCicla bicycle hire.
Tour operators Destino Colombia, C 50, No 65-42, CC Contemporáneo, loc 225, T260 6868, www.destinocolombia.com. Tours to nearby attractions in Antioquia and nationwide. Very well-informed English speaking guides. Can also arrange flights. Recommended. Real City Tours, T311-328 9905, www.real citytours.com. Pablo Alvarez-Correa leads tours from Poblado metro station 3 days a week (check in advance), about 4 hrs, in English, excellent, enthusiastic, pay by tip. Also has an Exotic Fruit Tour.

Transport

Medellín *p919, maps p920 and p921*
Air José María Córdova international airport (T562 2828, also called Rionegro) is 28 km, 40 mins, from Medellín by road and 9 km from the town of Rionegro. Taxi to town US$34 (US$28 city to airport). *Buseta* to centre, US$5, frequent service from 0400-2100, taking about 1 hr to the San Diego terminal on the small road (Cra 50A/C 53) behind Hotel Nutibara. To Rionegro from the airport US$0.25 bus, US$10 taxi. The airport has good shops and services, but no left luggage. Frequent services to **Bogotá, Cartagena**, and all major Colombian cities. Municipal airport: **Enrique Olaya Herrera**, airport information T365 6100, 10 mins by taxi from the centre, national flights only including to **Quibdó** (change here for **Nuquí**), **Acandí, Capurganá** and major cities. Taxi to centre or El Poblado, US$4.55.

Bus The terminal for long-distance buses going north and east is **Terminal del Norte** at Cra 64 (Autopista del Norte) y Transversal 78 (Cra 64C, No 78-58), T444 8020 or 267 7075, about 3 km north of the centre, with shops, cafés, left luggage, ATMs and other facilities. It is well policed. Walkway from Metro stop Caribe. Taxi to/from the centre US$3-US$6.25. From **Terminal del Norte**: To/from **Bogotá**, 9-12 hrs, US$28-31, several daily with 4 companies. To **Cartagena**, 15 hrs, US$48-53 (take food with you; the stops tend to be at expensive restaurants). Same fare to **Barranquilla**, 18 hrs, and to **Santa Marta**. To **Turbo**, US$34 with Gómez Hernández (the best), 10 hrs. To **Magangué** (for Mompós), US$47-52, with Rápido Ochoa.

For buses going south, **Terminal del Sur**, Cra 65, No 8B-91, T444 80 20, or T361 1499, alongside the Olaya Herrera airport. Similar services to Terminal del Norte plus a shopping centre. Take No 143 bus marked 'Terminal del Sur' from C 51 (in front of the Banco Popular) along Cra 46, or metro to Poblado, then a taxi for the remaining 1.5 km to the bus station, US$4.55. From **Terminal del Sur**: to **Quibdó**, 8-9 hrs, US$28, Flota Occidental, T444 5328. Frequent buses to **Manizales**, 6 hrs US$18, by Empresa Arauca. To **Pereira**, 6-8 hrs, US$17. Frequent buses for **Cali**, Flota Magdalena among others, US$30, 10-12 hrs. To **Popayán**, US$34, 12 hrs, Flota Magadalena. To **Ipiales**, US$53, 22 hrs.

Metro There are 2 lines: A from Niquía in the east to La Estrella in the south, B from San Javier to San Antonio, where they intersect, and three connecting cable cars, known as Metro

Cable: J from San Javier to La Aurora, K, serving the areas on the mountain slopes up to Santo Domingo Savio, and L from Santo Domingo, further up the mountains to Arví. Change at Acevedo on line A for this cable car, www. metrode medellin.gov.co. 0430-2300 weekdays, 0500-2215 Sun and holidays. 1 journey (anywhere on the system) US$1.

Taxi Meters are used; minimum charge US$3.50. **Radio taxis**: Cootransmede, T265 6565, Fem Taxi, T444 6340 (women only), Tax Andaluz, T444 5555, http://taxandaluz.co. Many others. For airport service, **Iván Agudelo Gómez**, T313-744 0667, T315-509 9035, up to 8 people.

⚙ Directory

Medellín p919, maps p920 and p921
Banks Most banks in the business zones have ATMs accepting international cards. Most *casas de cambio* are found in the shopping malls. **Immigration** Migración Colombia, C 19, No 80A-40 in Belén La Gloria section, T345 5500. **Language classes** Eafit University, Cra 49, No 7 Sur 50, Av Las Vegas, T261 9500, www.eafit.edu.co. Popular, well-organized Spanish courses. **Medical services** Hospital San Vicente de Paul, C 64/ Cra 51D, T444 1333, http://hospitaluniversitario. sanvicentefundacion.com, one of the best. Clínica Soma, C 51, No 45-93, T576 8400, www.soma.com.co, good doctor and general services. There is an emergency health clinic the Rionegro airport building. **Useful addresses** Tourist Police T265 5907. All emergencies T123.

Around Medellín

Medellín southeast to Bogotá

Five kilometres from Medellín airport is **Rionegro** (*Phone code: 4*) in a delightful valley of gardens and orchards. The **Casa de Convención** and the **cathedral** are worth a visit. There are colourful processions in Easter Week. There are various hotels and many places to eat in and near the plaza.

On the Medellín-Bogotá highway is **Marinilla**, 46 km from Medellín. A road north goes 25 km to **El Peñol** ① *US$5.75, car parking extra*, a precipitous, bullet-shaped rock which towers above the surrounding hills and the Embalse del Peñol reservoir. It has been eroded smooth, but a spiral staircase has been built into a crack from the base to the summit (649 steps). The views from the top are spectacular. At the entrance and summit are snack bars. The rock and the nearby town of **Guatapé** (*Phone code: 4; Population: 5000; Altitude: 1900 m*) are a popular excursion, especially at weekends. Ask the bus driver to drop you off at the small road leading to El Peñol, from where it's a 10-minute walk uphill to the entrance. Guatapé is 3 km further along the main road. All the houses are cheerfully painted, each with a distinctive frieze. The malecón is lined with restaurants and pleasure boats offering tours (US$20-50). There is also a zipline.

Another popular trip from Medellín is to **Reserva Natural Cañón del Río Claro** ① *www. rioclaroelrefugio.com, free,* clearly signed on the Medellín-Bogotá highway, three hours from either Medellín or Honda. The crystal-clean Claro river is lined with limestone cliffs and is a beautiful, tranquil place to relax and take leisurely walks along its banks. The reserve is noted for its incredible biodiversity with over 50 new species of plants discovered and more than 370 different species of bird identified since its foundation. Oilbirds live in the caves. Take an early bus, spend a day and a night at the reserve and continue to Honda the next day (or vice versa).

Santa Fé de Antioquia → *Phone code: 4. Colour map 1, B2. Population: 23,000. Altitude: 530m.*

Santa Fé de Antioquia (usually called Santa Fé), is 78 km from Medellín, just west of the Río Cauca, surrounded by mountainous green countryside. It is a safe, peaceful, well-preserved colonial town from where it is best to explore on horseback or bicycle. It is a popular weekend haunt with Antioquians. Santa Fé was founded as a gold mining town by the Spaniards in 1541 and became famous for its gold jewellery. Today, most of the gold mines have been abandoned but there is still some gold mining in the Río Cauca. In 1813, Santa Fé was declared the capital of the short-lived independent state of Antioquia, but in 1826, its status had collapsed and political control was lost to Medellín. The lively main plaza is dominated by a fine old Cathedral. There are several other churches worth seeing, notably Santa Bárbara. Next door is a **Museo de Arte Religioso/Museo Juan del Corral** ① *C 11, open weekends and holidays, 1000-1700,* which has a collection of items from colonial and more recent times. Opposite the Plaza Santa Bárbara is the site of a former slave market. Major local festivals at Easter, Christmas and New Year.

South from Medellín

Santa Bárbara (*Altitude: 1857 m*), 57 km south of Medellín on the main road via the town of Caldas, with stunning views in every direction of coffee, banana and sugar plantations, orange-tiled roofs and folds of hills. A further 26 km is **La Pintada**. Here the main road crosses the Río Cauca and continues via Marmato to Manizales. A left turn after La Pintada takes the particularly attractive road through Aguadas, Pácora and Salamina, all perched on mountain ridges, to Manizales. A turn right here, northwest, goes to some beautiful country on the west side of the Río Cauca.

This region can also be reached shortly after Caldas, by a road to the west which descends through Amagá to cross the Cauca at Bolombolo. From here, several attractive towns can be visited. **Jericó**, is an interesting Antioquian town with a large cathedral, several other churches, two museums and a good view from **Morro El Salvador**. **Andes** is a busy coffee-buying centre, several places to stay and to eat. **Jardín** is 16 km southeast of Andes. This pretty Antioquian village is surrounded by cultivated hills, passionfruit farms, trout farms and good horse riding. The plaza is full of flowering shrubs and trees. There is a delightful festival (*Fiesta de las Rosas*) in January. The **Templo Parroquial de la Inmaculada Concepción** is a National Monument and the small museum in the Casa Cultura has paintings and local artifacts.

⊙ Around Medellín listings

For hotel and restaurant price codes, and other relevant information, see Essentials.

⊕ Where to stay

Medellín southeast to Bogotá *p926*
$$$-$$ Refugio Río Claro, reservations in Medellín, T268 8855, T311-354 0119, www.rioclaroelrefugio.com. Tranquil spot, good value, delightful wooden lodges with great views of river (hotel, hostel and cabin accommodation). Includes 3 meals, restaurant service. Book ahead. Rafting trips, zip-lines over canyon and hiking trips are extra.
$$-$ El Encuentro, Vereda Quebrada Arriba, Guatapé, about 15 mins' walk from town, T861 1374, www.hostelelencuentro.com. Great views, nice rooms, good meals extra, plenty of activities can be arranged. A nice place for a short break from the city.
$$-$ Lake View Hostel, over the bridge at the end of the Malecón, Guatapé, T861 0097, or T311-329 9474, www.lakeviewhostel.com. Private rooms and dorms. Activities include boat tours, kayaking, mountain biking, hikes, riding, Spanish classes and fishing.

Santa Fé de Antioquia *p927*
It's best to book in advance at weekends and public holidays. Rates can be 40% more in high season and bank holiday weekends. Most hotels organize horse rides and town tours and offer weekend packages.
$$$ Hostal Tenerife, Cra 8, No 9-50, T853 2261, www.hotelcasatenerife.com.co. Beautifully decorated colonial house. Free use of house bikes, pool. Recommended.
$$$ Mariscal Robledo, Cra 10, No 9-70, T853 1111, www.hotelmariscalrobledo.com. Stylish colonial hotel. Nice pool area with palms. Good weekend lunch buffet. Recommended.
$$$-$$ Caserón Plaza, C 9, No 9-41, T853 2040, www.hotelcaseronplaza.com.co. Large colonial building, comfortable rooms, some with balconies looking onto pool. Sun deck has fantastic views, bike hire, cheaper Mon-Fri.
$$ Las Carnes del Tío, C 10, No 7-22, T853 3385, lascarnesdeltio@gmail.com. A restaurant

that also offers good rooms with huge bathrooms. Also dorms with shared bath.
$$-$ Hostal Plaza Mayor, Cra 9, No 9-59, Parque Principal, T853 3448. Popular with backpackers. There are hammocks, a small pool and a small *cabaña* with bunk beds.
$ Alejo, C 9, No 10-56, T853 1091. 1 block from the Parque Principal, small, basic rooms, restaurant serves cheap food.

South from Medellín: Jardín *p927*
Several *residencias* and restaurants by the plaza.
$$$ Hacienda Balandú, Vía Jardín Río Sucio, 800 m from town, T4-444 7110, www.comfenalcoantioquia.com. Comfortable rooms, pool, gardens, lake, spa, sports, used by birdwatching groups, good restaurant.

❼ Restaurants

Santa Fé de Antioquia *p927*
$ La Comedia, C 11, No 8-03, T853 1243. Café/bar/restaurant with music and art exhibitions. Colombian and international art house films.

⊖ Transport

Medellín southeast to Bogotá *p926*
Bus From Terminal del Norte in Medellín, desk 14, many buses to **El Peñol** and **Guatapé**, US$6 (US$9 shared taxi). To **El Peñol** from Rionegro, take a colectivo to Marinilla from near market, US$1. To **Río Claro**, take a Bogotá-bound bus and tell the driver you want to get off at Río Claro, 3 hrs.

Santa Fé de Antioquia *p927*
Bus The station is on the road to Turbo at the north end of Cras 9 and 10 (5 mins' walk to main plaza). To **Medellín** US$4 (numerous companies), 1 hr. To **Turbo**, US$25, 8-9 hrs, every 2 hrs or so.

South from Medellín *p927*
Bus Medellín-Andes, US$8. From Medellín (Terminal Sur), **Trans Suroeste Antioqueño** to **Jardín**, T444 4872, US$9.50, 6 a day, 3-4 hrs.

Department of Chocó

Chocó is one of the most biodiverse regions in the world and is all in the heavy rainbelt along Colombia's northwest coast, densely forested and sparsely inhabited. It is one of the rainiest regions on earth ('dry' season: December to March). In the northern part of the department, the mountain ranges rise directly from the ocean to reach a height of about 500 m. Transport is limited to water routes along the Pacific coast from Buenaventura in the south and up the rivers. Road access across the Cordillera Occidental from Medellín is via Bolívar.

Chocó is home to a number of indigenous groups, including the Embera, whose communities are based on hunting, fishing, and subsistence farming. The coastline is also dotted with poor black fishing communities. The main small tourist resorts on the Pacific coast are concentrated in Nuquí and Bahía Solano. The best time to go to Chocó is when humpback whales visit the area (beginning of July-October). Hotels usually offer all-inclusive packages for a three-night stay and arrange boat transport to and from the airport. Precautions against malaria, yellow fever, and dengue are recommended.

Quibdó → *Phone code: 4. Colour map 1, B2. Population: 162,000. Altitude: 50 m.*

Quibdó is on the eastern bank of the Río Atrato. Apart from the unstoppable partying during the city's fiestas, there is little to detain the visitor here. The San Pacho festival (20 September-5 October, www.sanpacho.com), for instance, has parades and a San Francisco de Asís procession. There is an interesting mural in the cathedral. Hordes of birds fly in to roost at dusk and there are magnificent sunsets, which locals watch from the waterfront promenade, El Malecón.

The road from Medellín to Quibdó is poor but OK.

Pacific coast

On the Gulf of Tribugá, surrounded by estuaries, mangroves and virgin beaches, the Afro-Colombian town of **Nuquí** gives access to the beaches and ecolodges up and down the Pacific coast. Visitors have to pay a US$4 tourism tax. The town holds a **Festival de la Migración Pacífica**, 24-29 August, to celebrate the migratory birds, turtles and whales which visit the region from April to October. To the south lies the wide curve of Playa Olímpica. To the north is another splendid beach. Various communities, Jobí, Coquí, Termales, Jurubidá, welcome visitors; the best place for information is the **NGO Mano Cambiada** ① *office opposite Nuquí airport, T310-348 6055 or T313-758 7653, corporacionmanocamhiada@yahoo.es, or on Facebook.* About 50 km north of Nuquí along the coast, **El Valle** has the best bathing and surfing beaches in the area. Between Nuquí and El Valle is **Parque Nacional Ensenada de Utría** ① *entry US$20.50, see Where to stay, below,* home to many aquatic species and birds. The surrounding hillsides are covered with pristine rainforest and there are mangroves and several magnificent beaches. Activities include diving over the coral reefs, swimming, trekking (national park guides obligatory, US$14 per day) and whale watching in season. Most hotels organize day trips to the Park, or you can hire a boat with a group from El Valle, takes 1 hour, or from Nuquí, minimum 1½ hours. Isla Playa Blanca is recommended as part of the trip. Boat prices start at US$150 and vary considerably, depending on time and number of passengers. Ask at hotels and Mano Cambiada for information. Insist on a life jacket and, on all boat trips, be prepared to get soaked – keep all valuables in watertight bags.

Bahía Solano → *Phone code: 816.*

The town lies on a large bay set against jungle covered hills. As a resort, it gets busy during holiday periods (the whale season and the fishing season, March to Easter), otherwise it's a functional fishing town. Good bathing beaches may be reached by launch or by walking about 1½ hours at low tide (for example Playa Mecana. Be sure to return before the tide rises or you will be stranded). Tourist information from the **Alcaldía** ① *T682 7418, www.bahia solano-choco.gov. co.* There are no ATMs in the town.

⊙ Department of Chocó listings

For hotel and restaurant price codes, and other relevant information, see Essentials.

⊖ Where to stay

Quibdó *p929*

There are few decent places to stay, but centrally located and safe is the **Malecón**, Cra 1, No 26A-60, p 2, T4-671 2725.

Pacific coast: Nuquí *p929*

Along the beach at the north end of town, there are several tourist hotels usually fully booked during the holiday period, best to make arrangements through travel agents in Medellín or Bogotá. It is possible to stay in Nuquí and Bahía Solano cheaply if you rent a basic room in a family house. Ask locals or look for rent signs on windows. Negotiate prices during low season.

The following are environmentally aware, award-winning and design-oriented locations:
Cabañas Pijiba, T4-474 5221, http://pijiba.wix.com/pijibalodge#!info/c17vo. Award-winning ecotourism development with full board. Comfortable wooden lodges with thatched roofs. Arranges guided trips, diving, forest walks, airport pick-up (45-min boat ride to hotel), from US$515 pp double for 2 nights, longer packages available.
El Cantil, T4-448 0767, www.elcantil.com. 35 mins south of Nuquí, several packages from about US$315 pp double for a 2-night package, full board, transfers and a trail walk included. Wooden cabins with sea view, bath, mosquito nets. Also surfing courses, hot springs trips, diving, whale watching in season.
Ensenada de Utria, lodge run by Mano Cambiada (address above) on a beautiful inlet in the national park. Comfortable cabins with bath, cold water, mosquito nets, no electricity (but solar power in the main building), good simple fresh food, wonderful staff. Guiding is included in packages, about US$400 pp for 3 nights.
Lodge Piedra Piedra, 45 mins south of Nuquí, T4-302 3438, 315-510 8216, www.piedrapiedra.com. Prices from US$820 double for 3-night package, full board.

Also all-inclusive, whale-watching and fishing packages, 3-7 days. Organizes local tours, wood and thatched lodges, camping, use of kitchen and kayak rental.

Pacific coast: El Valle *p929*

Cabañas El Almejal, T4-412 5050, www.almejal.com.co. Cabins with private bath, full board, price depends on the package. In private reserve, turtle conservation programme, educational programmes, lots of wildlife-watching opportunities.
$$-$ The Humpback Turtle Lodge/La Tortuga Jorobada, Playa Almejal, T312-756 3439, www.humpbackturtle.com. Surfing, surf kayaking, camping, dorms and private rooms, restaurant and bar, use of kitchen.

Bahía Solano *p929*

Mapara Crab, T2-331 9464. Run by Nancy and Enrique Ramírez, small, comfortable cabins on a private beach, 30 mins by boat from Bahía Solano. Enrique is a master sports fisherman and diving enthusiast.

There are hotels in Bahía Solano itself, see www.bahiasolano-choco.gov.co.

⊖ Transport

Quibdó *p929*

Air Flights daily to **Medellín**, **Bogotá** and nearby towns with **Satena**, **ADA** and **EasyFly**.
Bus Flota Occidental (T361 1312, or T671 1865 in Quibdó) from **Medellín**, daily at 1930, 8-9 hrs, US$28.

Pacific coast: Nuquí *p929*

Air Satena and ADA fly to Nuquí from **Medellín**, **Bogotá** and **Quibdó** (daily, from US$65-86; Medellín-Nuquí from US$100, from Bogotá from US$112).

Bahía Solano *p929*

Air There are flights from Medellín (from US$92), Bogotá, Cali and Quidbó to Bahía Solano with **Satena** and **ADA**.
Pickups run to **El Valle** throughout the day, 18 km (6 paved).

Quibdó *p929*
Banks Several ATMs. It is best to buy pesos before arriving.

La Zona Cafetera

Modern and colonial cities line the fertile western slopes of the Cordillera Central which is the centre of Colombia's coffee production. The three departments of Caldas, Quindío and Risaralda are generally known as the 'Zona Cafetera'. Much of the land here is between the critical altitudes for coffee of 800-1800 m, and has the right balance of rain and sunshine. The area has beautiful rolling countryside of coffee plantations, interspersed with bamboo, plantain and banana trees. The best way to enjoy the Zona Cafetera is to stay on a coffee farm, where you can tour the plantations and see how coffee is produced at harvest time. And of course, there is excellent, fresh, coffee all year round. In recent years, the Zona Cafetera has been building a reputation as an adventure sports destination, including rafting, kayaking and canopying (whizzing across ravines on steel cables).

Manizales and around

Rich in coffee and flowers, Manizales is one of the principal starting points for excursions to the Parque Nacional Los Nevados, which, as its name suggests, is dominated by snow-capped peaks. Earthquakes and volcanoes remain a feature of this volatile region.

Manizales → *Phone code: 6. Colour map 1, B2. Population: 414,000. Altitude: 2153 m.*
Manizales, 309 km from Bogotá, is dominated by its enormous concrete Cathedral and the Nevado del Ruiz volcano, which erupted catastrophically in November 1985. It sits on a mountain saddle, which falls away sharply from the centre into the adjacent valleys. The climate is humid (average temperature is 17°C, annual rainfall is 3560 mm), encouraging prodigious growth in the flowers that line the highways to the suburbs north and south. Frequently the city is covered in cloud. The best months of the year are from mid-December to early March. The area known as El Cable, east of the centre, is the Zona Rosa, with good restaurants and bars. The city looks down on the small town of Villa María, "the village of flowers", now almost a suburb.

Several earthquakes and fires have destroyed parts of the city over the years, so the architecture is predominantly modern with high-rise office and apartment blocks. Traditional styles are still seen in the suburbs and the older sections of the city. The departmental **Gobernación** building, opposite the Cathedral in the Parque de Bolívar, is an imposing example of neocolonial architecture and a national monument. Inside are a **tourist office** ① *C 22 y Cra 21, T884 2400 ext 351, 352,* and a local arts and crafts shop. The **bullring** ① *Av Centenario, T883 7629, www.cormanizales. com,* is an impressive copy of the traditional Moorish style. Along Avenida 12 de Octubre to the suburb of Chipre is a park, providing a great view to the west and paragliding opportunities (well visited on Sunday); El Tanque, on the Avenida, is a popular landmark and viewpoint.

Banco de la República ① *Cra 23, No 23-06 (behind the cathedral), Mon-Fri 0900-1000, 1100-1130, 1430-1830, free,* has a gold and anthropology museum, which at the time of writing was closed for renovation. The **Centro de Museos** ① *part of Caldas University, Cra 23, No 58-65, T886 2720, www.ucaldas.edu.co/museos, Mon-Fri 0830-1200, 1415-1800, take a 'Fátima' bus to the University,* has an art gallery, natural history museum and exhibitions on geology and archaeology.

About 8 km from Manizales is the **Parque Ecológico Río Blanco**, a 4343-ha protected cloudforest, considered by the World Wildlife Fund the best place for birdwatching in Colombia. To date, 348 species of bird have been identified, including 33 species of hummingbird. There are also 40 types of orchid, 350 species of butterfly and 50 species of mammal, including spectacled bear, ocelot and the white-tailed deer. There are several hikes of between 20 minutes and eight hours as well as a rangers' hut where 22 species of hummingbird come to feed. The park is managed by the **Fundación Ecológica Gabriel Arango Restrepo** ① *T310-422 1883, you must contact Sergio Ocampo before visiting, sergiofundegar@gmail.com, www.fundegar.com*.

Parque Nacional Los Nevados

The park has all the wild beauty of the high Cordillera, towering mountains (snowcapped above 4850 m), dormant volcanoes, hot springs and recent memories of tragic eruptions. The park comprises 58,000 ha and straddles the departments of Caldas, Quindío, Risaralda, and Tolima. Visitors should come prepared for cold, damp weather, and remember to give themselves time to acclimatize to the altitude. See under Ibagué, page 936, for Nevado del Tolima.

Tourist information **Oficina del Parque de Los Nevados** ① *Cra 23, No 70A-44, Manizales, T887 1611, Mon-Fri 0800-1730*, for information and entrance fees, US$17 for non-Colombians, including compulsory guide. In 2013, the Parque de los Nevados reopened after six months' closure owing to volcanic activity on **Nevado del Ruiz** (5400 m). While the southern section was open (0730 or 0900-1600, access from Salento, Pereira and Ibagué), the northern section (access from Manizales and Brisas and Murillo in Tolima department) was open only as far as Valle de las Tumbas, from 0800 to 1400. If you wish to enter the northern part of the park or intend to do some serious mountain climbing or mountain biking, apply to the above office in advance. The tourist office in Manizales can give advice on which parts of the park are open and can put you in touch with agencies who organize day trips to Nevado del Ruiz. Hotels and hostels offer trips to the park. Guides can be arranged and trips extended to the Parque Nacional de los Nevados and Nevado del Tolima. **Mountain Hostels**, see below, has information on trips and provides maps, which are also available at the **Instituto Geográfico** ① *C 21, No 23-22, p 7-8 Edif Atlas, Manizales, T884 5864, Mon-Fri 0745-1200, 1400-1745*.

The main road from Manizales to Bogotá goes east to Honda (see page 864). It passes through **Mariquita**, capital of a fruit-growing region (21 km before Honda). From Mariquita a road turns south to (32 km) **Armero**, which was devastated by the eruption of the Nevado del Ruiz volcano in November 1985. Over 25,000 people were killed as 10% of the ice core melted, causing landslides and mudflows. (Armero can be reached by colectivo from Honda and the road heads south to Ibagué via **Lérida**, 12 km south.)

⊙ Manizales and around listings

For hotel and restaurant price codes, and other relevant information, see Essentials.

⊕ Where to stay

Manizales *p931*
When planning a trip here, take into account price rises during the popular Feria de Manizales in Jan.

$$$$ Escorial, C 21, No 21-11, T884 7696, www.hotelesmanizales.com. Nicely decorated, central, parking, restaurant.
$$$ Regine's, C 65A, No 23B-113, T887 5360, www.regineshotel.com. In a quiet suburban street behind El Cable, good rooms. Breakfast

can be served in a small garden where there are smaller, cheaper rooms. Recommended.
$$$ Varuna, C 62, No 23C-18, T881 1122, www.varunahotel.com. Slick, minimal look, good restaurant. Rooms are large and comfortable, hydro massage showers. Recommended.
$$$-$ pp Hacienda Venecia, 3.5 km off the Chinchiná autopista, T320-636 5719, www.haciendavenecia.com. Delightful 4th generation coffee *finca* with 2 different types of accommodation: guesthouse with private or shared rooms (**$$-$**), or staying in the main *finca* itself (**$$$**), both have pools. Beautiful location and surroundings, attentive, English-speaking hosts, lunch and

dinners can be arranged, as well as a number of tours. A tour of the plantation itself is well worth it. Highly recommended.

$$-$ Mountain Hostels Manizales, C 66, No 23B-91, Barrio Palermo, T887 4736/887 0871, www.manizaleshostel.com (or mountainhostels on Facebook). Popular travellers' hostel, has all the expected facilities, hammocks, TV room, book exchange, bike rental, hot showers, free coffee, restaurant. Dorms and rooms with bath. Excellent information about trips to Los Nevados and coffee farms. Recommended.

$$-$ The Secret Garden, Km 3 Vía a Llanitos, Vereda La Floresta, sector La Alqueria, Villa María, T321-770 3020, http://thesecretgardenmanizales.com. Hostel and bistro with 3 rooms (1 shared) 30 mins from central Manizales, all meals extra, local produce and coffee, airport and bus terminal transfer, rural setting.

$ Basecamp, Cra 23, No 32-20, T882 1699. Perfectly situated hostel, 2 mins' walk from cable car station connecting the bus terminal with El Cable, American-Colombian run. Excellent facilities include a rooftop terrace and bar with extensive views, private rooms and dorms. American owner has years of experience organizing volcano tours in Guatemala and runs unusual tours to Los Nevados nearby.

🍴 Restaurants

Manizales *p931*
Apart from the hotels, the best restaurants are on or near Cra 23 in El Cable (La Zona Rosa) and Barrio Milán, a taxi ride from Cable Plaza, in the east of the city.

$$$-$$ Bologninis, C 77, No 21-116. Italo-Argentine restaurant with good pasta, steak and wines.

$ Don Juaco, C 65A, No 23A-44. Sandwiches, burgers and typical dishes.

$ Il Forno, Cra 23, No 73-86. Italian, pleasant, pastas, pizzas and salads. Good vegetarian dishes.

$ Pollos Asados Mario, C 23 esq Cra 22. Traditional Colombian *asadero* with the best rotisserie chicken in downtown. Also burgers and steaks.

⭐ Entertainment

Manizales *p931*
Cinema and theatre Centro Cultural y Convenciones los Fundadores, Cra 22 y C 33, www.ccclosfundadores.com, has interesting wood-carved mural by Guillermo Botero, who also has murals in the *Club Manizales* and *Hotel Las Colinas*. Many events held here.

🎉 Festivals

Manizales *p931*
The **Feria de Manizales** held in early **Jan** includes a coffee festival, bullfights, beauty parades and folk dancing as well as general partying. **Sep**, Festival Internacional de Teatro, www.festivaldemanizales.com.

🎯 What to do

Manizales *p931*
Colombia57, T886 8050, www.colombia57.com. Ex-pats Simon Locke, Russell Coleman, Brendan Rayment and team organize tailor-made trips for individuals or groups around the coffee zone and the rest of Colombia. Well organized, thoroughly researched with a commitment to sustainability and quality. Highly recommended.

🚌 Transport

Manizales *p931*
Air Airport 7 km east; flights are often delayed by fog. Buses to the centre US$1, taxi US$6. There are frequent flights to **Bogotá** and Medellín.
Bus Terminal at Cra 43, No 65-100, T878 7858, with a direct cable car system from the station up to the area of El Cable (US$0.75 per journey). To **Medellín**, many daily, 6 hrs, US$18 with **Arauca**; by **Flotaospina** mini van, 4½ hrs, US$18.50 (they also run to Cali and Pereira, 1½ hrs). Many buses to **Bogotá**, Bolivariano, US$17-33, 9 hrs. To **Honda**, US$15. **Cali**, hourly, 6 hrs, US$19, 4½ hrs, **Expreso Palmira**. **Pereira**, every 30 mins, 2 hrs, excellent road, beautiful scenery, US$6.25. **Armenia**, 3 hrs, US$10 with **Expreso Palmira**, hourly 0600-1800.

Parque Nacional Los Nevados *p936*
See above for sources of information on the
northern sector of the park. See under Pereira
for access from there.

❶ Directory

Manizales *p931*
Banks Banks are along Cra 23. **Immigration**
Migración Colombia: Cra 53, No 25A-35, T887
9600, Mon-Fri, 0080-1200, 1400-1700.

Pereira to Ibagué

Still in the shadow of the Nevados, this is a region of modern cities (in several cases rebuilt after earthquakes), delightful scenery and botanical parks and gardens. Coffee is still by far the most important agricultural product of the area, but many *fincas* have diversified into other crops and opened up to tourism, from day visits to overnight stays. No two *fincas* are the same; they range from beautiful historic country mansions to more modest accommodation options.

Pereira → *Phone code: 6. Colour map 1, B3. Population: 576,000. Altitude: 1411 m.*
Capital of Risaralda Department and 56 km southwest of Manizales, Pereira stands within sight of the *Nevados* of the Cordillera Central. Pereira is a pleasant modern city, founded in 1863, its past chequered by earthquake damage. The central **Plaza de Bolívar**, is noted for the striking sculpture of a nude Bolívar on horseback, by Rodrigo Arenas Betancur. There are other fine works of his in the city. The **Área Cultural Banco de la República** ① *C 18 bis 9-37, Mon-Fri 0830-1800, free*, features a library, art exhibitions and an auditorium with a programme of classical music. The **botanical garden** ① *on the campus of Universidad Tecnológica de Pereria, T321 2523, www. utp.edu.co/jardin, US$2.50, Mon-Fri, 0800-1500, Sat 0800-1300, book visits in advance and use a guide*, is good for bird watching and has bamboo forests and two-hour nature walks.

Tourist information: **Cámara de Turismo** for Risaralda ① *C 19, No 5-48, of 901, T325 4157.* **Corporación Autónomo Regional de Risaralda** (Carder) ① *Av de las Américas and C 46, No 46-40, T311 6511, www.carder.gov.co*, also has information. **Turiscafé** ① *T325 4157, www.turiscafe.net*, for good information on coffee farms in Risaralda in Spanish.

Fifteen kilometres from Pereira is **Santa Rosa de Cabal**, from where several thermal pools can be reached, including **Termales de Santa Rosa/Los Arbeláez** ① *T364 5500, http://termales.com. co, 0800-2000, US$10-11 (US$16 in high season)*. A 9-km unpaved road from Santa Rosa leads to the hot baths (early morning *chiva* or taxi, US$10 to entrance). The Termales de Santa Rosa are surrounded by forests, with waterfalls and nature walks. It's packed at the weekend, quiet during the week. **Hotel Termales de Santa Rosa de Cabal** (attached to the hot baths, **$$$**), comfortable, chalet style, with restaurant. Further along this road, midway between Pereira and Manizales, is **Chinchiná**, in the heart of the coffee zone. A coffee hacienda which takes day and overnight visitors (**$$$**) is **Finca Guayabal** ① *T314-772 4856, www.haciendaguayabal.com*, with a nature trail, full explanations of the coffee-growing process and lunch.

Northwest of Pereira, 30 km towards the Río Cauca, is **Marsella**, and the **Alexander von Humboldt Gardens** ① *T368 5258, www.jardinbotanicomarsella.com*, a carefully maintained botanical display with cobbled paths and bamboo bridges. Just outside the town is the **Ecohotel Los Lagos** ① *T368 5298, www.ecohotelloslagos.com.co*, previously a gold mine, then a coffee hacienda, and now restored as a hotel (**$$$**) and nature park with lakes.

Cartago (*Population: 135,000. Altitude: 920 m*), 25 km southwest of Pereira, is at the northern end of the rich Cauca Valley, stretching south for 240 km but no more than 30 km wide. Founded in 1540 and noted for its embroidered textiles, Cartago has some colonial buildings, like the fine **Casa del Virrey**, Calle 13, No 4-29, and the **cathedral**. From here, the Panamericana goes south along this valley to Cali and Popayán.

Parque Ucumari

From Pereira it is possible to visit the beautiful **Parque Ucumari** ① *park office, T325 4781, open daily for information, if visiting for the day and not staying overnight, entrance is free,* one of the few places where the Andean spectacled bear survives. From Pereira, a *chiva* leaves daily (0700, 0900, 1500, more frequently during high season) with **Transporte Florida** (T334-2721) from C12, No 9-40, to the village of El Cedral. From El Cedral it is a two- to 2½-hour walk to **La Pastora**, the park visitors' centre and refuge. There is excellent camping, or lodging at a refuge (**$**), meals extra. From La Pastora it is a steep, rocky one- to two-day hike to Laguna de Otún through beautiful scenery of changing vegetation (according to the national parks office, this sector was open in 2014 but check locally for the current situation, www.parquesnacionales.gov.co). The **Otún Quimbaya flora and fauna sanctuary** ① *T314-674 9248, www.parquesnacionales.gov.co, US$2.50, transport with La Florida, C 12, N 9-40, T334 2721, 3 a day, 4 on Sat-Sun,* forms a biological corridor between Ucumari and Los Nevados; it protects the last remaining area of Andean tropical forest in Risaralda. There are marked paths as well as *cabañas* (**$$**), camping (**$**) and meals available.

Pereira to Armenia

A 44 km road runs through the heart of the *Zona Cafetera*. A turn off at the *Posada Alemana* goes east for 9 km to **Salento** (*Phone code: 6; Population: 9400; Altitude: 1985 m*), well into the foothills of the Cordillera. This small town is brightly painted with an attractive plaza surrounded by traditional houses. Up Carrera 6 (continuation of the north side of the plaza), now lined with attractive craft shops and restaurants, is a 250-step climb. The 14 stations of the cross measure your progress to an outstanding viewpoint, overlooking the upper reaches of the Quindío and Cárdenas rivers known as the Cocora valley, possibly one of the finest views in Colombia. It is a popular weekend resort for Colombians for walking, riding and trekking but is quieter during the week. More places to eat and to stay are opening up constantly, but try to make arrangements early in the day, particularly at the weekend. Fiesta is in the first week of January and every Sunday night after mass the plaza is taken over by food, drink and craft stalls, with a lively atmosphere. **Tourist information** Alcaldía de Salento ① *Parque Principal, T759 3105, http://salento-quindio.gov.co.*

Valle de Cocora

The centre of the Cocora valley is 12 km up from Salento along a rough track, a picturesque two-hour walk, or by jeep, 35 minutes (US$1.50, Monday-Friday six departures from 0610 to last return at 1700; Saturday and Sunday 10 departures, last return 1800). Some 5 km beyond Cocora at 2770 m is the **Acaime Natural Reserve** with visitor centre, ponies for hire, beds for 20 and a small restaurant. There are humming birds, cloud forest and the most important area of wax palm (the national tree and one of the tallest trees of the world). In January is the Wax Palm Festival. Above Acaime there are many trails into the high mountains.

Armenia → *Phone code: 6. Colour map 1, B2. Population: 324,500. Altitude: 1838 m.*

The capital of Quindío Department was founded in 1889. In January 1999, an earthquake flattened much of the city. Impressive reconstruction continues and Armenia is as busy as ever. The fine example of Rodrigo Arenas Betancur's work, the **Monumento al Esfuerzo**, in the Plaza de Bolívar poignantly portrays the spirit of the local people. The **Museo del Oro Quimbaya** is at ① *Av Bolívar, C 40 norte-80, Tue-Sun 0900-1700.* **Parque de la Vida**, north of the city, has bamboo structures, waterfalls and a lakeside theatre.

Near Calarca, 6 km from Armenia, is **Jardín Botánico y Mariposario del Quindío** ① *T742 7254, www.jardinbotanicoquindio.org, daily 0900-1600, US$8.65,* featuring a huge covered butterfly house, with some 50 species of butterflies. There is also an insect zoo and forest walks. Twenty minutes south of Calarcá or Armenia is **Recuca** ① *daily 0900-1500, US$9 for day visit, US$16 with* lunch, reserve in advance, T310-830 3780, www.recuca.com, take bus Armenia-Barcelona, a coffee farm with tours experiencing all aspects of coffee-growing, also tastings. **Tourist information:** **Fondo Mixto de Promoción del Quindío** ⓘ *C 20, No 13-22, T741 7700, www.turismo cafeyquindio. com*, and **Corporación de Cultura y Turismo** ⓘ *Centro Administrativo Municipal CAM, p 4, T741 2991, www.armeniaculturayturismo.gov.co*.

Parque Nacional del Café

Some 12 km northwest of Armenia is **Montenegro**, near Pueblo Tapao (4 km) and the **Parque Nacional del Café** ⓘ *T741 7417, www.parquenacionaldelcafe.com, in high season, daily 0930-1800, low season, Wed-Sun and public holidays, 0930-1800, general entrance, US$11.70, or US$19.80-28.50 for additional activities and rides, parking US$1; take a bus or colectivo (US$0.50) from Armenia to Montenegro and then a jeep marked 'Parque' (US$0.25) or taxi (US$3) to the entrance*. There are restaurants, a coffee shop, a botanical garden, ecological walks, a Quimbaya cemetery, a tower with a fine view and an interesting museum which covers all aspects of coffee. A cableway links to a children's theme park (roller coasters, water rides etc). Beyond Montenegro is **Quimbaya**, known for its **Fiesta de Velas y Faroles** in December each year. About 7 km away is the **Parque Nacional de la Cultura Agropecuaria** (Panaca) ⓘ *T01-800 012 3999, www.panaca. com.co, Tue-Sun 0900-1800, US$17-26.50*, an educational theme park with many varieties of horses (and a very good show/display), cattle and other animals. A good family outing.

Ibagué and around → *Phone code: 8. Colour map 1, B2. Population: 421,000.*

Quindío Pass, 3350 m, is on the Armenia to Ibagué road (105 km), across the Cordillera Central. On the east side of the Pass is **Cajamarca**, in a beautiful setting at 1900 m with an interesting market on Sunday.

Ibagué (*Altitude: 1248 m*), capital of Tolima Department, lies at the foot of the Quindío mountains. See the Colegio de San Simón and the market (good tamales). The Parque Centenario is pleasant and there is a famous music conservatory. Try the local alcoholic drink called *mistela*. **Tourist office** ⓘ *Cra 3 entre C 10 y 11, p 2, T261 1111, www.tolimaturismo.gov.co*.

Just outside, on the Armenia road, a dirt road leads up the Río Combeima to El Silencio and the slopes of **Nevado del Tolima**, the southernmost *nevado* in the **Parque Nacional Los Nevados**. The climb to the summit (5221 m) takes two to three days, camping at least one night over 4000 m, ice equipment necessary. For safety reasons, visit Nevado del Tolima from Ibagué and not Manizales. A milk truck (*lechero*) leaves Ibagué marketplace for El Silencio between 0630 and 0730, US$2.50, two hours.

⦿ Pereira to Ibagué listings

For hotel and restaurant price codes, and other relevant information, see Essentials.

⬢ Where to stay

Pereira *p934*
$$$$ Hacienda San José, Entrada 16 cadena El Tigre, Km 4 Vía Pereira–Cerritos, T313 2612, www.haciendahotelsanjose.com. One of the oldest houses in the region, almost all of the features have been preserved. Breakfast included. Activities include horse riding and visits to one of the largest bamboo reserves in the region.

$$$ San Simón, C 19, No 7-41, T333 4595, www.hotelsansimon.com. One of the most central hotels available, with a cool, suave and trendy look. Healthy food served in sleek restaurant.
$$$ Soratama, Cra 7, No 19-20, T335 8650, www.hotelsoratama.com. Helpful staff, new 11th-floor Sky Lounge restaurant and bar with panoramic views. Discounts available Sat-Sun.
$$ Cataluña, C 19, No 8-61, T335 4527, www. hotelcatalunapereira.com. 2 floors up, airy rooms, popular restaurant, good value.
$ Sweet Home, Cra 11, No 44-30, T345 4453, www.sweethomehostel.com. Pereira's only

backpackers. Slightly out of town, but worth the trek. 3 dorms, 1 private room, all-day breakfast. Handy for the airport.

Coffee farms

There are far too many coffee farms in the Pereira/Armenia region to list here. They range from huge traditional haciendas to smaller, more modern farms. See www.clubhaciendas delcafe.com for a good selection.

$$ pp Finca Villa María, 12 km from Pereira, via Marsella, follow the signs, turning before La Bodega, unpaved 3-km road, T312-722 3006, fincavillamaria@hotmail.com. 25 mins by taxi from Pereria, US$9. Charming typical coffee hacienda set in beautiful countryside. Large rooms, peaceful, full board. Coffee plantations tours. Recommended.

$$ pp Villa Martha, from Pereria, via Marsella Km 9, Corregimiento Combia, via La Convención, T322 9994, T310-421 5920, villamarthacafeblogspot.co.uk. Modern *finca* with bamboo decor, pool and lovely gardens. Comfortable rooms, excellent service, includes breakfast and dinner (vegetarians catered for). Free pick-ups from airport/bus terminal in Pereria. Serves probably the best coffee in La Zona Cafetera.

Pereira to Armenia: Salento *p935*

$$ Hostal Ciudad de Segorbe, C 5, No 4-06, T759 3794, www.hostalciudaddesegorbe.com. Splendid old house around a courtyard, with music, TV and reading room, very pleasant, helpful Spanish owners. One room with disability access.

$$ La Posada del Café, Cra 6, No 3-08, T759 3012, www.laposadadelcafe.webs.com. Traditional house with rooms set around a garden, helpful, English-speaking owner.

$$-$ Tralala Hostel, Cra 7, No 6-45, T314-850 5543, www.hosteltralalasalento.com. Dutch-run hostel with dorms, and 3 private rooms (one with bathroom), cosy DVD/reading room, great views, Wellington boot hire. Recommended.

$ Camping Monteroca, Km 4 Vía Pereira–Salento, T315-413 6862, www.campingmonteroca.com. Beside the Río Quindío. Owner Jorge knows the area, its history and wildlife well. Well-maintained

campsite with clean showers, communal cooking area, TV lounge. Fantastic themed cabins, from tree house to "Hippie Hilton", all with hot showers, one has a jacuzzi. Museum of fossils and meteorites, a room dedicated to Simón Bolívar and a serpentarium.

$ pp La Casona de Lili, C 6, No 3-45, T625 1151, www.lacasadelilihostal.com. Good beds, tasteful decor, excellent breakfast, Lili is an enthusiastic hostess.

$ Las Palmas, C 6, No 3-02, T311-540 3828, LasPalmassalento@hotmail.com. Small, traditional hostel, comfortable rooms, good value.

$ Plantation House, Alto de Coronel, C 7, No 1-04, T316-285 2603, www.theplantation housesalento.com. Popular backpackers' hostel, with private rooms and dorms (US$10-11), outdoor seating area. Gorgeous views, bike hire. English/Colombian owned, the best local information, also offer tours of their coffee *finca* nearby. It's possible to stay the night on the top floor of the *finca* (**$**, US$8 dorm). Highly recommended.

Valle de Cocora *p935*

$$ Las Palmas de Cocora, Km 10 Valle de Cocora, T310-423 9080, http://laspalmas decocora.com. Comfortable rooms with beds and bunks. Restaurant serving trout (**$$**). Horses for hire (guide available at extra cost).

$$-$ Bosques de Cocora, Km 11 Vía Cocora, T312-288 6549, www.bosquesdecocora.com. Restaurant, with *finca* accommodation or tent hire with mattresses and bedding. Shower facilities and free coffee and hot chocolate.

Armenia *p935*

$$$ Centenario, C 21, No 18-20, T744 3143, www.hotelcentenario.com. Bright rooms, attentive staff, gym, sauna, parking.

$$ Café Plaza, Cra 18, No 18-09, T741 1500, hotelcafeplaza@hotmail.com. Near the Plaza Bolívar, a little noisy but simple, clean rooms with bath and TV, breakfast included.

$$ Zuldemayda, C 20, No 15-38, T741 0580, http://hotelzuldemayda.net. A popular central hotel in minimalist style.

$ Alferez, Cra 17, No 17-47, T744 2879. Very basic but safe, laundry service.

Parque Nacional del Café: Montenegro
p936
See also Coffee farms, above.
$$$ El Delirio, Km 1 vía Montenegro-Parque del Café, T745 0405, casadelirio@hotmail.com. Beautiful, traditional *finca* restored with immaculate taste, a "perfect place to unwind", pool, large gardens, delicious food.
$$ El Carriel, Km 1 vía Quimbaya-Filandia, T746 3612, elcarriel@hotmail.com. An excellent option if you are looking for an economic stay on a working coffee *finca*. Simple but comfortable rooms, hot water, restaurant. The coffee tour takes you through the whole coffee-making process.

Ibagué *p936*
$$$ Ambalá, C 11, No 2-60, T261 4444, www.hotelambala.com. Breakfast, TV, pool, sauna, parking, restaurant.
$$-$ Center, Cra 4, No 12-52, T263 7311, www.hotelcenteribague.com. Convenient location, helpful.

● Restaurants

Pereira *p934*
$$ Mediterráneo, Av Circunvalar, No 4-47. Steaks, seafood, fondus and crêpes in a relaxed atmosphere.
$$-$ Pasaje de la Alcaldía is a narrow alleyway next to the Alcaldía with a number of cheap eating options including French, Italian, Colombian and a few cafés.

Pereira to Armenia: Salento *p935*
$$-$ Balcones del Ayer, C 6, No.5-40, www.balconesdelayer.com. Serving trout, the local speciality, as well as good quality meat dishes. Efficient and recommended. Also has rooms to let (**$**).
$ Café Jesús Martín, Cra 6, No 6-14. Excellent little café with its own coffee from Señor Bedoya's father's *finca*. (see also What to do, below); has 2 coffee shops in Salento and 1 in Armenia.
$ El Rincón de Lucy, Cra 6, No 4-02. Excellent breakfasts, lunches and dinners, limited menu, but great value, tasty local food. Recommended.

Galería Café-Libro Salento, C 3, No 3-25 (Salida a Cocora). Art gallery and bookshop with vegetarian food and coffee, family run.

Armenia *p935*
$$ Café Quindío, Cra 19, No 33N-41. Gourmet coffee shop and restaurant next to Parque de la Vida, serving recipes such as chicken or steak in coffee sauce as well as international dishes. Also sells coffee products from its own farm.
$$ Keizaki, Cra 13, No 8N-39. Sushi and other Asian dishes. There are several other good restaurants on the same block.
$$ La Fogata, Cra 13, No 14N-39. One of Armenia's most popular restaurants, serving steaks, pork chops and typical dishes.
$$-$ Anis, C 10N, No 13-94. Excellent restaurant with a varied menu: steaks, pasta, salads, sandwiches, crêpes and other brunch options.
$ Natural Food Plaza, Cra 14, No 4-43. Vegetarian, varied menu and fruit juices. Also has a wholefood shop.

● Festivals

Ibagué *p936*
National Folklore Festival, in **Jun**. Tolima and Huila commemorate San Juan (**24 Jun**) and SS Pedro y Pablo (**29 Jun**) with fireworks, and music.

● What to do

Pereira *p934*
Colombia Eco Travel, Mz 10 Cs 28 Et 3, Bosque de la Acuarela, Dosquebradas, T311-319 3195, www.colombiaecotravel.com. Aims to provide responsible tours throughout Colombia, from day trips to longer tours.

Pereira to Armenia: Salento *p935*
Aldea del Artesano, book through Alejandro, T320-782 9128, aldeadelartesano@gmail.com. Craftworkers community project with handicraft courses and a shop.
Café Jesús Martín, Cra 6, No 6-14 (coffee shop), T316-620 7760, www.cafejesusmartin.com. 1-hr tours of local coffee roasting factory, Mon-Wed 0800-1000, but tours can also be arranged at other times, fun and informative. Also 4- to 5-hr tours visiting a coffee *finca* in

Quimbaya, plantation tour with explanation of coffee making and coffee and a brownie in the Salento coffee shop, minimum 3 participants. Recommended.

Armenia *p935*
Balsaje Los Remansos, C 16, No 6-12, Quimbaya, T314-775 4231, adal161@hotmail. com. *Balsaje* excursions (punting on bamboo rafts) on the Río La Vieja.

⊖ Transport

Pereira *p934*
Air Matecaña airport is 5 km to the south, bus, US$0.40. Daily flights to **Miami**, **Bogotá**, **Cali** and **Ibagué**; less frequent to other cities.
Bus Terminal is at C 17, No 23-157, 1.5 km south of city centre, T315-2323, www.terminal pereira.com. Bus to **Armenia**, 1 hr, US$4, a beautiful trip. To **Cartago**, US$1.50, 45 mins, Arauca *buseta* every 10 mins. To **Cali**, US$10-14, 4½-5 hrs, colectivo by day, bus by night. To **Medellín**, 6-8 hrs, US$17. To/from **Bogotá**, US$15-27, 7 hrs (route is via Girardot, Ibagué – both cities bypassed – and Armenia).

Pereira to Armenia: Salento *p935*
Bus To **Armenia** every 20 mins, US$2, 1 hr. To **Pereira**, hourly, US$3.50, 1 hr.

Armenia *p935*
Air El Edén, 13 km from city. Daily to **Bogotá** and **Medellín**. Fog can delay flights.
Bus Terminal at C 35, No 20-68, www. terminalarmenia.com. To **Ibagué**, US$9-11, 3 hrs. **Bogotá**, hourly, 7-9 hrs, US$15-24. **Cali**, US$10-15, 3 hrs, frequent.

Ibagué *p936*
Air Daily flights to **Bogotá**, **Cali** and **Medellín**, also to **Pereira**.
Bus Terminal is between Cras 1-2 and C 19-20, www.terminalibague.com. Tourist police at terminal helpful. Frequent services to **Bogotá**, US$1, 4 hrs. To **Cali** US$25; **Neiva**, US$15, 3½ hrs, and many other places.

ⓘ Directory

Pereira *p934*
Banks Banks around Plaza de Bolívar. Most have ATMs that take foreign cards. *Casas de cambio*: several around Cra 9/C 18.

Pereira to Armenia: Salento *p935*
Banks There are ATMs in the main plaza.
Language classes Marcia Pozos, T311-241 0727, marciapozos@yahoo.com, is a qualified Universidad Nacional Spanish tutor.

Cali and the Cauca Valley

The narrow Cauca valley has as its focus Cali, the country's southern industrial centre but at the same time one of Colombia's party hotspots. Cali calls itself the salsa capital of the world, and few would dispute that claim. The region is served by the Pacific port of Buenaventura. Some 56 km off the coast is the high-security prison turned national park of Gorgona Island.

Cali → *Phone code: 2. Colour map 1, B2. Population: 2,732,000. Altitude: 1030 m.*

Cali, Colombia's third city and capital of the Valle del Cauca Department, is the country's self-declared salsa capital. So if you're looking for *la rumba* and wanting to join swinging salsa couples on the dance floor, Cali should not to be missed. Sensuous, tropical rhythms are ubiquitous, seeming to seep from every part of the city's being. The region is set in a rich agricultural area producing sugar, cotton, rice, coffee and cattle. Cali was founded in 1536 and, until 1900, it was a leisurely colonial town. Then the railway came and Cali is now a rapidly expanding industrial complex serving the whole of southern Colombia.

Arriving in Cali

Orientation Alfonso Bonilla Aragón (Palmaseca) **airport** is 20 km from city. The **bus terminal** is at C 30N, No 2AN-29, 25 minutes' walk from the centre. For getting around the city there is the **MIO** metro system, with north-south and west-east trunk routes and some pre-trunk routes. Although the atmosphere in Cali is quite relaxed, carry your passport (or photocopy) at all times. Cali has some rough parts, particularly east or south of Cra 10 and C 15, and caution is needed when walking around the city, especially at night. Do not change money on the street under any circumstances and avoid all people who approach, offering to sell. ▶▶ *See also Transport, page 943.*

Tourist offices Secretaría de Cultura y Turismo ① *Cra 5, No 6-05, sala 102, T885 8855, www.cali. gov.co,* in the large red-brick Centro Cultural de Cali. The centre also has free exhibitions in the hallways and is one of the main entertainment venues in the city. **Puntos de Información Turística** ① *Cra 4 esq C 6, Mon-Fri 0730-1730, Sat 0800-1300,* good information. Also in the bus terminal (same hours as above) and a third, roving Punto de Información moves around the city. See http://cali.vive.in for cultural and entertainment news. **National parks office** ① *C 29N, No 6N-43, Santa Mónica, T667 6041,* (see also **Aviatur,** under Tour operators).

Cali

Where to stay 🛏
1 Apartahotel Colombia
2 Aparta Hotel Del Río
3 Casa Republicana
4 Colombian Hostel
5 El Viajero Hostel
6 Hostal Santa Rita
7 Hotel Boutique San Antonio
8 Iguana
9 Intercontinental & La Terraza Restaurant
11 La Casa Café
12 La Pinta Boogaloo
13 Pelican Larry
14 Posada de San Antonio
15 Tostaky

Restaurants 🍴
1 Carambolo
2 D'Toluca
3 El Solar
4 La Tartine
5 Ojo de Perro Azul
6 Pampero
7 Tortelli

Bars & clubs 🍸
8 Tin Tin Deo
9 Zaperoco

Places in Cali

The city's centre is the **Plaza de Caicedo**, with a statue of one of the independence leaders, Joaquín Caicedo y Cuero. Facing the plaza is the elegant **Palacio Nacional** and the **Cathedral**, seat of the influential Archbishop of Cali. Nearby is the renovated church and 18th-century monastery of **San Francisco** ① *Cra 6, C 9/10* with a splendidly proportioned domed belltower. Cali's oldest church, **La Merced** ① *C 7, between Cras 3 and 4*, has been restored by the Banco Popular. The adjoining convent houses two museums: **Museo de Arte Colonial** (which includes the church), a collection of 16th- and 17th-century paintings, and the **Museo Arqueológico** ① *Cra 4, No 6-59, T881 3229, Mon-Sat 0900-1245, 1345-1800, US$2.50*, with pre-Columbian pottery. **Museo del Oro** (also called Museo Calima) ① *C 7, No 4-69, www.banrepcultural.org/museodeloro, Tue-Fri 0900-1700, Sat 1000-1700, free*, has pre-Columbian gold work and pottery.

The **Museo La Tertulia** ① *Av Colombia, No 5-105 Oeste, T893-2939, www.museolatertulia.com, Tue-Sat 1000-1800, Sun 1400-1800, US$2.50*, exhibits South American, including local, modern art and shows unusual films. The neighbourhood of **San Antonio** (behind the **Intercontinental Hotel**) is the city's oldest area, where Cali's colonial past can still be felt. The area has a relaxed, bohemian atmosphere, especially at weekends when it's livelier. There are good views of the city from the 18th-century church of San Antonio.

◉ Cali listings

For hotel and restaurant price codes, and other relevant information, see Essentials.

● Where to stay

Cali *p939, map p940*

$$$$-$$$ Intercontinental, Av Colombia, No 2-72, T882 3225, www.intercontinental.com. On the edge of San Antonio, the most expensive hotel in town. Spa, outdoor pool and elegant restaurant, La Terraza, along with 4 others. Cheaper Sat-Sun.

$$$ Aparta Hotel Del Río, Av 2N, No 21N-05, T653 4224, www.apartahoteldelrio.com. Comfortable suites and rooms with good facilities (gym, sauna, pool, laundry), safe, good restaurant, parking.

$$$ Hostal Santa Rita, Av 3 Oeste, No 7-131, 1892 0021, www.hostalsantarita.com. Refurbished old house, west of the centre, pleasant area, good rooms, parking. Cheaper Sat-Sun.

$$$ Hotel Boutique San Antonio, Cra 6, No 2-51, T524 6364, www.hotelboutique sanantonio.com. Charming hotel with 10 sound-proofed rooms, own security system, cheaper at weekends.

$$$-$$ Posada de San Antonio, Cra 5, No 3-37, T893 7413, www.posadadesan antonio.com. Rooms set around a couple of patios, decorated with Calima artefacts, good value. 10% discount for Footprint readers.

$$ Apartahotel Colombia, C 31 Norte, No 2 Bis-48, T660 8001, www.facebook.com/pages/hotel-colombia-cali/7211013476. One block from bus terminal and close to Barrio Granada, steam room, restaurant, secure, English spoken.

$$ Casa Republicana, C 7, No 6-74, T896 0949, www.hotelcasarepublicana.com. Lovely plant-filled courtyard, good rooms (cheaper with fan) and a fine restaurant, welcoming. Recommended.

$$-$ La Pinta Booqaloo, Cra 3 Oeste, No 11-49, Bellavista, T892 2448, www.lapinta.com co. In a mansion in a quiet neighbourhood, private rooms (cheaper with shared bath) and dorms (US$8-18), restaurant, bar, pool, garden, cinema room, kitchen available, salsa classes arranged.

$$-$ Pelican Larry, C 20 Norte, No 6AN-44, Barrio Granada, T420 3955, www.hostel pelicanlarry.com. Rooms with and without bath, also has dorms. Close to Zona Rosa restaurants and bars, 15 mins' walk from bus terminal, hot water, laundry and internet extra, Sun night BBQ, Spanish lessons arranged, TV room, helpful staff.

$ Colombian Hostel, C 3bis, No 35A-70, San Fernando Viejo, T315-705 2343, www.colombianhostel.blogspot.co.uk. Colombian-owned hostel, dorms with and without bath and a private room (**$$**), cold water, welcoming and helpful.

$ El Viajero Hostel Cali & Salsa School, Cra 5 No 4-56, San Antonio, T893 8342, www.elviajerohostels.com/hostel-cali. Doubles (cheaper with shared bath) with TV, dorms (US$11 pp), salsa school, pool, open-air bar, cinema room and a stage for shows. Breakfast, internet and Wi-Fi included.
$ Iguana, Av 9 Norte, No 22N-46, T313-768 6024, www.iguana.com.co. In 2 suburban houses on the edge of fashionable Barrio Granada, dorm US$10 pp, popular backpackers' hostel so there can be a lot of *movimiento*. Private rooms, some with bath, garden, TV room with DVDs, Spanish and free salsa classes and good local information.
$ La Casa Café, Cra 6, No 2-13, T893 7011, www.lacasacafecali.blogspot.com. Nice backpackers' hostel and café. Simple rooms with high ceilings and wooden floorboards, dorm US$7.50; café hosts cultural and music evenings.
$ Tostaky, Cra 10, No 1-76, T893 0651, www.tostakycali.com. At the bottom of San Antonio park, good backpackers' hostel, French/Colombian-run, airy rooms and dorms (US$9) above a café open only to guests, hot water, shared bath, breakfast extra. Recommended.

🍴 Restaurants

Cali *p939, map p940*
In the centre, Parque de Peñón, just north of San Antonio, has an excellent selection of restaurants serving all types of international food, while San Antonio itself has many good restaurants and cafés. In the north, Barrio Granada has an enormous number of eating places to choose from.
$$$ Carambolo, C 14, No 9N-18/28, T667 5656, www.carambolo.com.co. Excellent themed restaurant with Latin and Mediterranean dishes. Friendly and recommended.
$$$ El Solar, C 15 Norte, No 9N-62, Barrio Granada, T653 4628, www.faroelsolar.co. Great atmosphere and a varied international menu, popular.
$$$ La Tartine, C 3 Oeste, No 1-74, T893 6617. Classic French-owned restaurant in an eccentric setting.
$$$ Tortelli, C 3 Oeste, No 3-15, T893 3227, www.restaurantetortelli.com. Little Italian restaurant serving great home-made pasta.

$$$-$$ Pampero, C 21N, No 9-17, Barrio Granada, T661 3117, www.pamperoparrilla argentina.com. Argentine steaks on pleasant terrace with good service. Recommended.
$$ D'Toluca, C 17N, No 8N-46, Barrio Granada, T668 9372, www.dtoluca.com. Open from 1200 Mon-Fri and from 1730 Sat-Sun until late. Good little Mexican restaurant serving fajitas, tacos and burritos at reasonable prices.
$$ Ojo de Perro Azul, Cra 9, No 1-27. Wed-Sun 1600-0100. Bright bohemian hangout with games, mixed drinks, *picadas*, *tostadas* and traditional Colombian dishes.

🍸 Bars and clubs

Cali *p939, map p940*
Cali's nightlife is legendary, especially the *salsatecas* – salsa-playing discos. The most popular with *caleños* can be found on Av 6 Norte where there are dozens to choose from, although salsa purists would direct you to **Zaperoco**, Av 5N, No 16-46, www.zaperocobar.com. An alternative is **Tin Tin Deo**, C 5, No 38-71, T514 1537, www.tintindeo.com, which attracts students and teachers and is more forgiving of salsa beginners. But it's not just salsa, there are bars playing rock, jazz, blues and electronic music as well.
Blues Brothers, Av 6AN, No 21-40, www.caliblues.net. Jazz and live rock bands.
Talberts Pub and **Bourbon St**, www.bourbon streetcali.com, C 17N, 8N, Barrio Granada. English and American themed bars, with same owner, English music generally, good live bands on Fri and good atmosphere in general.
   Barrio Juanchito has a range of salsa bars and discos, from thatched roofs to huge, hi-tech *salsatecas*. It is worth visiting just to watch couples dancing salsa and to join in, if you dare! Go with locals and couples; groups of foreign male tourists might have a hard time getting in. Most advisable to take a registered radio taxi there and back; 15-min ride out of Cali, across the bridge over the Río Cauca.

🎭 Entertainment

Cali *p939, map p940*
Cinema Alianza Colombo-Francesa, Av 6 N, No 21-34, T661 3431, http://cali.alianzafrancesa.org.co. Shows films.

Theatre Teatro Experimental, C 7, No 8-63, T884 3820. **Teatro Municipal**, Cra 5, No 6-64, T881 3131, www.teatromunicipal.gov.co. Major cultural activities, including opera and concerts. **Teatro La Máscara**, Cra 10, No 3-40, San Antonio, T893 6640, see Facebook. Women's theatre group.

⊛ Festivals

Cali *p939, map p940*
Feria de Cali (www.feriadecali.com) from **25 Dec to end of Dec or early Jan**, biggest Salsa festival in Latin America, bullfights at the Canaveralejo bullring, carnival in streets, horse parades, masquerade balls, sporting contests and general merry partying. **Aug/Sep** Festival Petronio Alvarez, www.festivalpetronioalvarez. com,celebrating Afro-Latino and Pacific music. **Sep** AjazzGo festival, www.ajazzgofestival. com, with international artists.

O Shopping

Cali *p939, map p940*
Best shopping districts are: Av 6N, from Río Cali to C 30 Norte and on Cra 5 in the south with several new shopping malls including: Chipichape, at the end of Av 6N. Vast, cinemas, **Librería Nacional** bookstore, good choice of restaurants and shops, supermarket.
Handicrafts Artesanías Pacandé, Av 6N, No 17A-53. Typical regional handicrafts.
La Caleñita, Cr 24, No 8-53. Good selection of typical handicrafts. **Parque Artesenal Loma de la Cruz**, C 5, Cras 15/16. Permanent handicraft market, nice setting and pleasant neighbourhood, safe, cafés around the park. Open 1130-2030. **Platería Ramírez**, C 1A, No 4B-44 Oeste, San Antonio. Good selection of jewellery, lessons offered in jewellery making.

⊕ What to do

Cali *p939, map p940*
Ciclovía On Sun, 0700-1400, C 9 is closed from north to south to allow people to cycle, run and exercise on the roadway.

Tours
Aviatur, T382 1616, www.aviatur.com; and at airport. For tours to Isla Gorgona, and other services.

⊖ Transport

Cali *p939, map p940*
Air Alfonso Bonilla Aragón (Palmaseca) airport, 20 km from city. Minibus from airport, from far end of pick-up road outside arrivals, to bus terminal (2nd floor), every 10 mins from 0500 up to 2100, approximately 30 mins, US$2.50. Taxi to city US$25, 30 mins. Frequent services to **Bogotá**, **Medellín**, **Cartagena**, **Ipiales** and other Colombian cities. International flights to Miami, New York, and Panama.
Bus Urban: MIO metro buses US$2 a ride, single tickets sold at the stations; for multiple journeys and to use pre-trunk routes you need a smart card, US$1.70, which you pre-charge, www.metrocali.gov.co. **Long-distance** Terminal is at C 30N, No 2AN-29, T668 3655, www.terminalcali.com, 25 mins' walk from the centre (leave terminal by the taxi stands, take first right, go under railway and follow river to centre, or go through tunnel, marked *túnel*, from the terminal itself. Left luggage, ATMs, showers and good food outlets. Buses between the bus station and the centre, US$0.50. Taxi from centre to bus station, US$4. To **Popayán**, many buses, US$7.50-12, 2½-3 hrs, also busetas and colectivos, US$12.50-25.50. To **Pasto**, US$23-34, 8-9 hrs. To **Ipiales** (direct), US$24-37, 10-11 hrs; to **San Agustín**, 9 hrs, US$23 with (Cootrans La Boyana buseta. To **Cartago**, US$10, 5 hrs. To **Armenia**, US$10-15. To **Manizales**, US$19, 7 hrs. To **Medellín**, US$30, 8-10 hrs. To **Bogotá**, 9-10 hrs, 4 companies, US$28-45. Busetas charge more than buses but save time; taxi-colectivos charge even more and are even quicker.
Taxi Ensure that taxi meters are used. Prices, posted in the window, minimum fare US$2.50. Extra charge on holidays, Sun and at night.

⊕ Directory

Cali *p939, map p940*
Banks Many banks and *casas de cambio* in the main commercial areas.
Immigration Migración Colombia: Av 3 norte, No 50N-20, T397 3510, Mon-Fri 0800-1200, 1400-1700.

Cauca and the coast

To reach the Pacific you have to cross the western arm of the Andes, with a number of parks and recreational areas. There are plenty of beaches to the northwest of the port of Buenaventura while away to the south are the isolated national park islands of Gorgona and Mapelo.

From Buga to the coast

From the colonial city of **Buga**, 74 km north of Cali on the Panamericana (1¼ hours by bus, US$4-5), the main road to Buenaventura passes the **Laguna de Sonso** reserve, good for birdwatching, before crossing the Río Cauca. Beyond the river, near the crest of the Cordillera, is another park, **Reserva Natural Bosque de Yotoco**, noted for orchids. The road continues to the man-made **Lago Calima**. Many treasures of the Calima culture are said to have been flooded by the lake, when the dam was built. This is an important centre for watersports, riding and other activities. The northern route round the lake goes through **Darién** at 1500 m with an **archaeological museum** ① *Tue-Fri 0800-1200, 1300-1700, Sat-Sun 1000-1800*, with good displays of Calima and other cultures. There are hotels in the village, and cabins at a Centro Náutico on the lakeside. Camping is possible near the village. Direct buses to Darién from Cali US$7, 2½ hours.

A popular excursion from Cali is to **San Cipriano**, 30 km on the road to Buenaventura. Get off the bus at Córdoba, from where rail cars, man-powered or motorbike-powered (US$2.50, only pay for the return leg when returning), go to the village in beautiful scenery. There are crystal-clear rivers and waterfalls and inner tubes can be rented for US$3 per day for floating downstream. The village and its surroundings are a national reserve of 8564 ha, entry US$1, www.reservasancipriano.tripod.com. Take insect repellent.

Buenaventura → *Phone code: 2. Colour map 1, B2. Population: 324,000. 145 km from Cali.*

Through a pass in the Western Cordillera is Buenaventura, Colombia's most important port handling some 80% of total exports, including coffee, sugar and frozen shrimp. It was founded in 1540, but not on its present site. It now stands on the island of Cascajal, on the Bay of Buenaventura, 20 km from the open Pacific. The commercial centre has some impressive buildings, but the rest of the town has steep unpaved streets lined with shacks on stilts. There is a festive atmosphere every night and the **Festival Folclórico del Litoral** is held in August. **Warning** This town is one of Colombia's main drug- and people-trafficking centres and has severe poverty; this has led to high levels of violent crime. Do not walk about at night and stick within a couple of blocks of the seafront.

Beaches around Buenaventura

Beaches are plentiful northwest of Buenaventura along the coast of the **Bahía de Málaga**. There is stunning scenery with virgin jungle, waterfalls and empty, black sand beaches. About 40 km from Buenaventura is **Juanchaco**, a small fishing village, the location of spectacular **dolphin** and **humpback whale** sightings between July and early October. By frequent launch from Buenaventura (*mueleturístico*), one hour. Beyond Juanchaco is **Ladrilleros**, a 30-minute walk, or take a mototaxi or jeep (5 minutes), one of the best and longest beaches. Simple accommodation in Juanchaco ($) but better in Ladrilleros: **$$$ Reserva Aguamarina**, T246 0285, www.reservaaguamarina. com, which also organizes whale watching, boat trips, fishing and birdwatching; **$$$ Palma Real**, T683 0049, www.hotelpalmarealcolombia.com, with a pool, good. Smaller places include **$$-$ Doña Francia**, T246 0373. Several small restaurants (good fish) and snack bars at the town end of the beach. Trips can be taken to other beaches, sea canals and mangrove forests.

Gorgona Island → *Colour map 1, B1. 150 km down the coast from Buenaventura.*

① *Visits to the island are managed and run by Aviatur, T587 5181, www.aviaturecoturismo.com. Accommodation is available in various houses and Aviatur offers 3-night packages from Bogotá, Medellín and Cali, from around US$400 pp (excluding flights). All visitors must have a permit before* *arriving at the island, from Aviatur. It is recommended to book accommodation and boat tickets well in advance during high season. Entrance fee US$18.90 for foreigners.*

Until 1984 the island of **Gorgona** was Colombia's high security prison (a sort of Alcatraz). The prison is derelict but some parts can still be clearly seen. Convicts were dissuaded from escaping by the poisonous snakes on the island and the sharks patrolling the 30 km to the mainland (both snakes and sharks are still there). The national park boasts many unspoilt, deserted sandy beaches. From the paths you can see monkeys, iguanas, and a wealth of flora and fauna. (Rubber boots are provided and recommended.) There is an abundance of birds (pelicans, cormorants, geese, herons) that use the island as a migration stop-over. Snorkelling and diving are rewarding, equipment can be hired (but take your own if possible), exotic fish and turtles to be seen. Killer whales visit the area from July-September.

Isla Malpelo

Declared a UNESCO site in 2006, Isla Malpelo is located 506 km from Buenaventura in the Pacific and is an acclaimed birdwatching haven with great diving opportunities. The island is considered to be one of the world's best places to observe hammerhead sharks in great numbers. Boats leave from Buenaventura, a 36-hour bumpy voyage. There are no places to stay on the island and camping is not allowed. Contact national parks office in Bogotá, T353 2400, www.parquesnacionales.gov.co. **Embarcaciones Asturias** in Buenaventura (T240 4048, barcoasturias@yahoo.com, see Facebook) offer an eight-day tour, with transport and accommodation. National park embarkation tax US$27; diving fee US$48 (90 for foreign vessels) per day.

ⓒ Cauca and the coast listings

For hotel and restaurant price codes, and other relevant information, see Essentials.

beds with crisp, white sheets, safe. 6th-floor restaurant for *almuerzos* and à la carte, a good option.

⬤ Where to stay

Buga *p944*
$ Buga Hostel and Holy Water Ale Café, Cra 13 4-83, T236 7752, http://bugahostel.com. A German/Colombian-run hostel with rooms, dorm (US$8) and its own micro brewery; the rooftop terrace has lovely views. They bake their own pizza and bread and also organize local tours.

Buenaventura *p944*
$$$$-$$$ Cosmos Pacífico, Cra 1a, No 3A-57, T01-644 4000, www.hotelescosmos.com.
$$$$-$$$ Estación, C 2, No 1A-08, T241 9512, www.sht.com.co. Grand old white building on seafront, good restaurant, pool. A Tequendama hotel.
$$ Los Delfines, C 1, No 5A-03, T241 5450, hotellosdelfines@mibuenaventura.com. 4 blocks up the hill from the *muelle*, good value, has a breezy terrace.
$$ Titanic, C 1, No 2A-55, T241 2046, www.hoteltitanicbuenaventura.com. About a block from the *muelle turístico*, good rooms and

ⓞ Transport

Buenaventura *p944*
Air Flights to **Cali** and **Bogotá**.
Road There are plenty of buses to **Cali**, US$10-12.75, 3 hrs. Colectivos and taxis run at ½-hourly intervals to Cali. The toll road to Cali is fully paved.

Gorgona Island *p944*
It is recommended to book tours through **Aviatur**, they arrange permits, transport and accommodation; their packages include a fast launch service to the island from the seaside town of **Guapi**, 1½ hrs one way, and transfer from airport to dock. **Satena** flies from Cali to Guapi. **Embarcaciones Asturias** (address under Isla Malpelo, above) offer a weekend package leaving Buenaventura on Fri 1900, returning Mon, including accommodation on boat, food, permit and snorkelling equipment. Alternatively, launches can be contracted in Buenaventura, 4 hrs to Gorgona.

Popayán, Tierradentro and San Agustín

The Pan-American Highway climbs out of the valley to Popayán, a historic city which gives access to the páramo of Puracé in the Cordillera Central and serves as a good base from which to visit some of Colombia's most exciting sights, including the burial caves of Tierradentro and, to the south, the remarkable archaeological site of San Agustín. The Cauca valley has strong indigenous cultures, notably the Páez people.

Popayán and Tierradentro

Popayán has retained its colonial character, even though it had to be fully restored after the March 1983 earthquake. The streets of two-storey buildings are in rococo Andalucian style, with beautiful old monasteries and cloisters of pure Spanish classic architecture. In contrast, the tombs of Tierradentro reveal much of the northern Andean world before the Spaniards arrived.

Popayán → *Phone code: 2. Colour map 1, C2. Population: 258,000. Altitude: 1760 m.*

Founded by Sebastián de Belalcázar, Francisco Pizarro's lieutenant, in 1536, Popayán became the regional seat of government, until 1717, to the Audiencia of Quito, and later to the Audiencia of Bogotá. It is now the capital of the Department of Cauca. The city lies in the Pubenza valley, a peaceful landscape of palm, bamboo, and the sharp-leaved agave. The early settlers, after setting up their sugar estates in the hot, damp Cauca valley, retreated to Popayán to live, for the city is high enough to give it a delightful climate. To the north, south, and east the broken green plain is bounded by mountains. The cone of the volcano Puracé (4646 m) rises to the southeast.

Places in Popayán The Cathedral ① *C 5, Cra 6*, beautifully restored, has a fine marble Madonna sculpture behind the altar by Buenaventura Malagón and the unusual statue of Christ kneeling on the globe. Among the other churches are **San Agustín** ① *C 7, Cra 6*, note the gilt altar piece; **Santo Domingo** ① *C 4, Cra 5*, used by the Universidad del Cauca; and **La Encarnación** ① *C 5, Cra 5*, also used for religious music festivals. Walk to **Belén** chapel ① *C 4 y Cra 0*, seeing the statues en route, and then continue to **El Cerro de las Tres Cruces** if you have the energy, and on to the equestrian statue of Belalcázar on the **Morrode Tulcán** which overlooks the city; this hill is the site of a pre-Columbian pyramid. A fine arcaded bridge, **Puente del Humilladero**, crosses the Río Molino at Cra 6. Public concerts and events are given in the gardens below. **Museo Negret y Museo Iberoamericano de Arte** (MIAMP) ① *C 5, No 10-23, http://museonegret.wordpress.com, Mon, Wed-Fri 0800-1200, 1400-1800, Sat-Sun 0900-1200, 1400-1700, free*, has works, photographs and furniture of Negret and exhibitions of contemporary art. **Casa Mosquera** ① *C 3, No 5-14, Tue-Sun 0900-1200, 1400-1800, US$1*, has collections of colonial religious art and historical objects in the house of four-times president Tomás Cipriano de Mosquera. **Museo de Historia Natural** ① *Cra 2, No 1A-25, daily 0900-1200, 1400-1700, US$1*, has good displays of archaeological and geological items with sections on insects (particularly good on butterflies), reptiles, mammals and birds.

During the week, the open markets are interesting – **Mercado Bolívar** ① *C 1N, Cra 5*, is best in the early morning – local foods such as *pipián*, *tamales* and *empanadas*. Another, better market, is **Mercado Esmeralda** on Calle 5 and Autopista.

The **tourist office** ① *Cra 5, No 4-68, T824 2251*, has a good selection of maps and brochures. **Cámara de Comercio de Cauca, Cultura y Turismo** ① *Cra 7, No 4-36, T824 3625, www.cccauca. org.co*. **National parks office** ① *Cra 9, No 25N-06, T823 1279*.

Silvia → *Phone code: 2. Colour map 1, C2. Population: 5000. Altitude: 2520 m.*

Silvia, in a high valley 59 km northeast of Popayán, is best known for its Tuesday market when the friendly local Guambianos come to town in their distinctive blue and fuchsia clothes. The market (also full of Otavalo from Ecuador) is at its best between 0600 and 0830 and is very colourful. Tourist information at the **Municipio** ① *C 9, No 2-49, on the plaza, T825 1011, http://silvia-cauca.gov.co, 0800-1200, 1400-1800.* For horse riding enquire at the tourist office or hotels.

Tierradentro → *Colour map 1, C2*

East of Popayán is **Inzá** which is 67 km beyond **Totoró**. There are several stone statues in the new plaza. Some 9 km beyond Inzá is the Cruce de Pisimbalá (or Cruce de San Andrés or just El Cruce), where a road turns off to **San Andrés de Pisimbalá** (4 km). The village, at the far end of the Tierradentro Park, has a unique and beautiful colonial church with a thatched roof; for the key ask behind the church. About 2 km or so before Pisimbalá is the **Tierradentro Museum** ① *0800-1600, may close for lunch,* with exhibits on indigenous culture. It has very good local information. The second floor is dedicated to the work of the Páez, not to be missed. The Páez people in the Tierradentro region can be seen on market days at Inzá (Saturday), and Belalcázar (Saturday); both start at 0600. The setting is spectacular, with small indigenous mountain villages (get exact directions before leaving).

Popayán To Bus Station, Airport & Pasto To ① & Cali

Where to stay 🛌
1 Auberge Camponhello *A2*
2 Caracol *B3*
3 Casa Familiar Turística *B2*
4 Dann Monasterio *B1*
5 HostelTrail Guesthouse *B1*
6 La Plazuela *B2*
7 Los Balcones *B2*
10 Pass Home *B1*

Restaurants 🍴
1 Capriccio *B2*
2 El Muro *B2*
3 Italiano *B2*
4 Jengibre Espacios Sabores *B2*
7 Lonchería La Viña *B2*
8 Madeira Café *B3*
9 Tequila's *B1*
10 Verde y Mostaza *B2*
11 Wipala *B3*

Bars & clubs 🍸
12 El Sotareño *B2*
13 Iguana Afro Video Bar *B1*

200 metres
200 yards

N

Parque Arqueológico Tierradentro ⓘ *Park and museum open 0800-1600, US$11.50, under-7s, over-60s free, students half price. See http://tierradentro.xtrweb.com. Walking between the sites, take a hat and plenty of water. It gets crowded at Easter.* At the archway opposite the museum or at Pisimbalá village you can hire horses or you can walk to the **Tierradentro** man-made burial caves painted with geometric patterns, a World Heritage Site. There are four cave sites: Segovia, El Duende, Alto de San Andrés and El Aguacate. The main caves are lit, but a torch is advisable. At **Segovia** (15 minutes' walk up behind the museum across the river), the guards are very informative (Spanish only) and turn lights on in the main tombs. Segovia has about 30 tombs, five of which can be lit. Fifteen minutes up the hill beyond Segovia is **El Duende** (two of four tombs are very good, faint paintings can be seen but take torch/flashlight). From El Duende continue directly up to a rough road descending to **Pisimbalá** (40 minutes). **El Tablón**, with eight stone statues, is just off the road 20-30 minutes' walk down. **El Alto de San Andrés** is 20 minutes from Pisimbalá. From the back of El Alto it is 1½ hours up and down hill, with a long climb to **El Aguacate** (superb views). Only one tomb is maintained although there may be 30 more. Guides are available. The area is good for birdwatching.

⦿ Popayán and Tierradentro listings

For hotel and restaurant price codes, and other relevant information, see Essentials.

⦿ Where to stay

Popayán *p946, map p947*
Prices can rise by 100% for Holy Week and festivals, eg 5-6 Jan, when it's essential to book in advance. It is not safe walking alone at night outside the central area.
$$$$ Dann Monasterio, C 4, No 10-14, T824 2191, www.hotelesdann.com. In what was the monastery of San Francisco, lovely grounds, pool, spa, gym, very good.
$$$-$$ La Plazuela, C 5, No 8-13, T824 1084, www.hotellaplazuela.com.co. Opposite Iglesia San José, beautiful colonial building, good-sized rooms with antique furniture set around a courtyard.
$$$-$$ Los Balcones, Cra 7, No 2-75, T824 2030, www.hotellosbalconespopayan.com. Huge and small rooms, antique furniture but up-to-date services.
$$ Auberge Campobello, C 33AN, No 14A-14, T823 5545, www.hostalcampobello.com. Off the Pan-American Highway, 300 m down road opposite **Torremolino** restaurant. Swiss/Colombian owners speak French, English, Spanish and Italian, safe, family atmosphere, nicely decorated, terrace, laundry service. Near bus station. Recommended.
$$-$ Pass Home, C 5, No 10-114, T316-448 9513, hotelpasshome@gmail.com. Relaxing

atmosphere, welcoming, free laundry service if staying 3 days. Recommended.
$ Caracol, C 4, No 2-21, T820 7335/311-626 8840, www.hostelcaracol.com. Private rooms and a dorm (US$10 pp), shared bath, café, book exchange, laundry service, kitchen, bike hire and tours.
$ Casa Familiar Turística, Cra 5, No 2-07, T824 4853. Popular, simple rooms with high ceilings, good notice boards for information and messages from other travellers.
$ Hostel Trail Guesthouse, Cra 11, No 4-16, T314-696 0805, www.hosteltrailpopayan.com. This excellent, efficient backpackers' hostel is run by Scottish couple Tony and Kim. The rooms are comfortable (cheaper with shared bath), cheaper dorms (US$9 pp), good communal areas, DVD room, bike hire, book shop and lockers. Extensive knowledge of the local area. Bike tours to nearby thermal springs. Recommended.

Tierradentro *p947*
Near the museum
$ Hospedaje Luzerna, next to the museum. Run by a lovely couple, this little place has clean, basic rooms and good showers (with 30 mins' notice).
$ Hospedaje Ricabet, near the museum, T312-795 4636. Flower-filled courtyard, clean rooms with bath and hot water. Rooms with a shared bath are a little cheaper.

$ La Portada, T311-601 7884. Bamboo building at jeep/bus stop in village; rooms with bath and hot water. Kind owners. Restaurant with excellent *menú del día*, fresh soups.
$ Residencias Pisimbalá, near the museum, T311-612 4645. Rooms with bath and hot water, cheaper with shared bath with cold water, good restaurant. Camping costs US$1.20 pp.

In the village
$ El Cauchito, T314-869 2936. Family-run, with 3 basic rooms, attentive service, shared bath, no hot water.
$ El Viajero, T317-746 5991. Another family home, basic but clean rooms, unheated shower. Food available.

🍴 Restaurants

Popayán *p946, map p947*
$$-$ Italiano, C 4, No 8-83, T824 0607. Swiss-run, excellent selection of pastas, pizzas, crêpes and fondues. Recommended.
$$-$ Tequila's, C 5, No 9-25. Mexican-run cantina with great Mexican food, reasonably priced. Also good cocktails. Recommended.
$ El Muro, Cra 8, No 4-11, T824 0539. Serves vegetarian *almuerzos* with daily menus. At night it converts into a dimly lit bar.
$ Jengibre Especias Sabores, Cra 7, No 2-38, T820 5456. Good for breakfast venue, *almuerzos* as well as á la carte options.
$ Lonchería La Viña, C 4, No 7-07, T824 0602. Open 24 hrs, *parrillada*, huge selection of steaks and salads.
$ Verde y Mostaza, Cra 4 y C 4. Popular with students for cheap fast food such as crêpes, pizzas and burgers.

Cafés
Popayán has a thriving café culture, with many in colonial buildings.
Capriccio, C 5, No 5-63. Popular with the locals, excellent frappes, brownies and ice creams.
Madeira Café, C 3 y Cra 5. Good selection of coffee, milkshakes, brownies, juices and cheesecakes.
Wipala, Cra 2, No 2-38. Art and café in lovely surroundings.

Autopista Norte
There is a good selection of typical food from the Cauca region in Popayán. For good food at reasonable prices, take a short taxi ride to the road to Cali to: **$$ Rancho Grande**, Autopista Norte 32N-50, T823 5788. 2 thatched restaurants, delicious *chuzos* (barbecued beef), credit cards accepted, open Sun.

🍷 Bars and clubs

Popayán *p946, map p947*
El Sotareño, C 6, No 8-05. This eccentric bar plays old tango LPs from the 1940s and 50s as well as *bolero* and *ranchero* music. The owner has a huge collection of vinyl records.
Iguana Afro Video Bar, C 4, No 9-67. Good music, jazz, salsa, friendly owner.

⚛ Festivals

Popayán *p946*
Easter processions, every night of **Holy Week** until Good Friday, are spectacular; at the same time there is an **International Religious Music Festival** and local handicraft fairs. The city is very crowded in Semana Santa. The children's processions in the following week are easier to see. As at Pasto (but less violent), there are the **Día de los Negros** on **5 Jan** and **Día de los Blancos** on **6 Jan**; drenching with water is not very common. These are part of the **Fiestas de Pubenza**, with plenty of local music.

🌀 What to do

Popayán *p946, map p947*
Tour operators
Alas y Raíces, T320-742 3470, www.alasyraices. org. Swiss-Colombian run, tour of coffee *finca* US$25 pp for 2 people, price includes transportation from Popayán (leaves 0930) to *finca*, plantation tour and traditional lunch. Also possible to visit waterfalls nearby and see the coffee toasting and grinding process. The *finca* has limited accommodation (**$$**, price includes breakfast and dinner). Recommended.

Tierradentro *p947*
Cayo Oidos Galindo, T310-229 2971, based in La Plata, spent 15 years working with

archaeologists from Banco de la República. Organizes tours of Tierradentro and surrounding villages with accommodation and food provided. Can arrange English-speaking guides. Recommended.

● Transport

Popayán *p946, map p947*
Air The airport is 20 mins' walk from the centre. Service twice-daily to **Bogotá**. All passengers need a Migración Colombia stamp on their boarding pass from the Migración Colombia office (see below), a quick formality.
Bus The bus terminal is opposite the airport, 15 mins' walk from the centre (Ruta 2-Centro bus, terminal to centre, US$0.50, or taxi, US$2), www.terminalpopayan.com. Luggage can be stored safely (receipt given). From the bus station, walk up Cra 11 and take a left at Calle 4 to reach the centre. Take care if you cross any of the bridges over the river going north, especially at night. To **Bogotá**, Expreso **Bolivariano**, US$39-44, 12-16 hrs. To **Cali**, US$7.50-12, 2½-3 hrs, or **Velotax** microbus, colectivos leave from the main plaza. To **Pasto**, US$18, 4-6 hrs, spectacular scenery (sit on right – night buses are not safe). To **Ipiales**, Expreso Bolivariano, US$19, 6-7 hrs, runs every hour but many buses arrive full from Cali, book in advance. To **San Agustín**: several companies go to **Pitalito**, US$16, 7 hrs (eg **Cootranshuila**) from where you can catch a taxi colectivo, US$3. Via Isnos **Cootranshuila**, US$15.50, or **Estelar**, several a day mainly mid morning to afternoon, US$17.50, 5-7 hrs. Sit on the left for the best views. To **Puracé**, **Cootranshuila** US$3, 2 hrs.
Taxi No meters; normal price within city is US$2.

Silvia *p946*
Bus From **Popayán**, daily **Coomotorista** and Belalcázar, several *busetas* in the morning, US$5.

Tierradentro *p947*
Bus The road from Popayán to **Tierradentro** is difficult and narrow, but with beautiful scenery. There are 4 daily buses from Pisimbalá to **Popayán**, but services are erratic. Otherwise, you must go to El Cruce. From Popayán daily 1030, US$15, 4-6 hrs to **Cruce Pisimbalá**. Best to take early buses, as afternoon buses will leave you at the Cruce in the dark. Walk uphill (about 2 km, 30 mins) to the museum and on, 20 mins, to the village. If you want to go to **Silvia**, take this bus route and change to a colectivo (US$2.50) at Totoró. Buses and *camionetas* from the Cruce to **La Plata** (en route to San Agustín, see below) US$8, 4-5 hrs or more frequent colectivo jeeps, US$10. If you cannot get a direct Cruce–La Plata bus, take one going to Páez (Belalcázar) (US$3.25), alight at Guadualejo, 17 km east of Inzá, from where there is a more frequent service to La Plata. The roads from Totoró and La Plata to Inzá are being paved.

● Directory

Popayán *p946, map p947*
Banks Several ATMs on main plaza. Best exchange rates offered at Titan, Cra 7, No 6-40, T824 4659, inside CC Luis Martínez, Mon-Fri 0800-1200, 1400-1700, Sat 0830-1200. **Immigration** Migración Colombia, C 4N, No 10B-66, T839 1051, Mon-Fri 0700-1200, 1400-1800, opposite bus terminal next to fire station, go early to extend visas. **Safety** Ask the Tourist Police about which areas of the city are unsafe.

Popayán to San Agustín

The two routes from Popayán to San Agustín go through the highlands of the Puracé National Park, with its volcanoes, hot springs and the sources of four great rivers. The goal of the journey is one of South America's great, but mysterious archaeological sites, which is also one of Colombia's main tourist destinations.

Puracé and Parque Nacional Puracé

ⓘ *The park is open all week, 0800-1700, US$11. For information contact Parque Nacional Puracé office in Popayán, Cra 9, No 25N-06, T521 2578, purace@parquesnacionales.gov.co, Mon-Fri*

0800-1745. It is recommended to book for the park here in advance, especially at Easter. At the time of writing the park was temporarily closed because of tensions between the park and its indigenous population.

Some 30 km from Popayán is the small town of Puracé, at Km 12, which has several old buildings. Behind the school a 500-m-long path leads to Chorrera de las Monjas waterfalls on the Río Vinagre, which is notable for the milky white water due to concentrations of sulphur and other minerals.

At Km 22, look for the spectacular San Francisco waterfall on the opposite side of the valley. At Km 23 is the turning right to Puracé sulphur mines (6 km) which can be visited by applying to **Industrias Puracé SA** ① *C 4, No 7-32, Popayán*, best through the Popayán tourist office. About 1 km along this road is a turning left leading in 1.5 km to **Pilimbalá** in the **Parque Nacional Puracé** at 3350 m. Here there is a park office, and seven sulphur baths (cold, no bathing). At Pilimbalá, near the park entrance, there is a restaurant and lodging (see below). The national park contains Volcán Puracé (4640 m), Pan de Azúcar (4670 m) with its permanent snow summit, and the line of nine craters known as the Volcanes los Coconucos. The park also encompasses the sources of four of Colombia's greatest rivers: the Magdalena, Cauca, Caquetá and Patía. Virtually all the park is over 3000 m. The Andean condor is being reintroduced to the wild here from Californian zoos. There are many other birds to be seen and fauna includes the spectacled bear and mountain tapir. Pilimbalá is a good base from which to explore the northern end of the park.

Before climbing or hiking in the national park get advice on which areas are safe and, preferably, hire a guide. The terrain can be difficult, or dangerous from volcanic fumes. Although the best weather is reported to be December-March and July-August, this massif makes its own climate, and high winds, rain and sub-zero temperatures can come in quickly at any time. Some military areas are mined.

Around Puracé

Continuing on the main road from Volcán Puracé to **La Plata** (whose central plaza has an enormous ceiba, planted in 1901), at Km 31 there is a viewpoint for Laguna Rafael, at Km 35 the **Cascada de Bedón** (also chemically charged water) and at Km 37 the entrance to the most northerly part of the Parque Nacional Puracé. Here there's a visitor centre, a **geology/ ethnology museum** ① *US$1*, and the very interesting **Termales de San Juan** ① *700 m from the road, US$0.50*, where 112 hot sulphur springs combine with icy mountain creeks to produce spectacular arrays of multi-coloured mosses, algae and lichens, a must if you are in the area (no bathing; accommodation available).

From La Plata one road goes 41 km east to the main Bogotá-Neiva-Pitalito highway, some 60 km south of Neiva, while a southerly road through Pital joins the same highway some 42 km before Pitalito.

Pitalito (*Phone code: 8; Population: 63,000; Altitude: 1231 m*) has little to offer the tourist, save convenient access to the **Parque Nacional Cueva de los Guácharos** ① *www.parquesnacionales. gov.co, US$19, cafetería, accommodation and camping available, equipment for hire*, which lies to the south. Between December and June swarms of oilbirds (*guácharos*) may be seen; they are nocturnal, with a unique radar-location system. The reserve also contains many of the unusual and spectacular cocks-of-the-rock and the limestone caves are among the most interesting in Colombia. The rangers are particularly friendly, providing tours and basic accommodation; permission to visit the park must be obtained from the national parks offices in Popayán or Bogotá. Check with them if the park is open.

Popayán to San Agustín direct

South of Puracé towards San Agustín is **Coconuco** (*Altitude: 2460 m*). Coconuco's baths, **Agua Hirviendo** ① *1.5 km beyond the Hotel de Turismo (see Where to stay), on a paved road (mostly), US$1.50*, have one major and many individual pools with an initial temperature of at least 80°C.

There is one pool where you can boil an egg in five minutes. A track from town is quicker than the road. It gets crowded at weekends, but during the week it is a fine area for walking and relaxing in the waters. About 6 km beyond Coconuco, near the road, are **Aguas Tibias** ① *T310-543 7172, www.termalesaguatibias.com, US$5*, warm rather than hot, with similar facilities for visitors. South of Coconuco by 24 km is **Paletará** with high grassland on a grand scale with the Puracé/Pan de Azúcar volcanoes in the background. Below the village (roadside restaurant and national park post) flows the infant Río Cauca. 10 km south of Paletará, the road enters the Parque Nacional Puracé and there is a track northeast to Laguna del Buey. The road then enters a long stretch of virgin cloud forest. This section links Paletará with Isnos and San Agustín. Heavy rain has weakened this stretch, 25 km of which are impassable to light vehicles and very tedious for buses and trucks. No efforts are being made currently to improve this road. Some 62 km from Paletará at the end of the cloud forest is Isnos (see page 953) followed by a steep drop to a dramatic bridge over the Río Magdalena and shortly to the main road between Pitalito and San Agustín. **Warning** Avoid travelling by night between Popayán and San Agustín, the roads are dangerous. Cyclists should avoid taking the direct route. Reports of theft on the buses between these towns; do not trust 'helpfuls' and do not put bags on the luggage rack.

San Agustín → *Phone code: 8. Colour map 1, C2. Population: 30,000. Altitude: 1700 m.*

The little town of San Agustín, near the source of the Río Magdalena, is a peaceful place with a few colonial houses and cobbled streets still intact. It is on every travellers' itinerary because of its proximity to the 'Valley of the Statues', where hundreds of large rough-hewn stone figures of men, animals and gods, dating from roughly 3300 BC to just before the Spanish conquest. Little is known of the culture which produced them or what exactly the stone sculptures represent. One theory suggests that this culture came from the Amazon region. The sculptures also display indigenous and Asian influences. No evidence of writing has been discovered, but traces of small circular bamboo straw-thatched houses have been found. The sites were burial and ceremonial sites where it is thought sacrifices, including of children, were made to the gods. Some sites were also residential areas. Various sculptures found here are exhibited in the National Museum at Bogotá. Only about 30% of the burial mounds in the area have been excavated and many of those that have been opened were previously ransacked by grave diggers, who had looted their precious statues. There are about 20 well-kept sites. The area offers excellent opportunities for hiking, although some trails to remote sites are not well marked, and other adventure sports. The rainy season is April-June/July, but it rains almost all year, hence the beautiful green landscape; the driest months are November-March.

For impartial advice visit the **Oficina Municipal de Turismo** ① *Plaza Cívica, C 3 y Cra 12, T837 3062 ext 15, www.sanagustin-huila.gov.co*, or the tourist police at **Oficina de Policía de Turismo** ① *C 3, No 11-86*. For cultural information there is a **Casa de Cultura** ① *Cra 11, No 3-61*. There are also four tour agencies calling themselves 'tourist offices'. They give out useful advice, but they also hold contracts with hotels and other operators.

Warning Enquire about safety before walking to the more distant monuments. Beware of 'guides' and touts who approach you in the street. Have nothing to do with anyone offering drugs, pre-Columbian objects, gold, emeralds or other precious minerals for sale.

Places near San Agustín The whole area leaves an unforgettable impression, from the strength and strangeness of the statues, and the great beauty of the rolling green landscape. The nearest archaeological sites are in the **Parque Arqueológico** ① *0800-1600, US$11.30 including museum, Parque Arqueológico and Fuente de Lavapatas, students half price, under 7s and over 60s free; if, at the end of the day, you wish to visit the following day for free, enquire first at the ticket office, it is recommended to hire a guide to gain a better understanding of the statues and what they represent. Guidebook in Spanish/English US$3.75.* The park is 3 km from San Agustín. The 130 statues and graves in the Parque are *in situ*, though those in the Bosque (a little wood) have been moved and rearranged, and linked by gravel footpaths. Originally, the statues were found lying down and covered in the graves. Those excavated have been placed upright next to the graves and fenced in. Beyond the central area are the carved rocks in and around the stream at the **Fuente de Lavapatas** in the park, where the water runs through carved channels. The **Alto de Lavapatas** ⓘ *closes at 1600*, above the Fuente, has an extensive view. You can get a good idea of the Parque, the Bosque and the museum in the course of three hours' walking, or add in El Tablón and La Chaquira (see below) for a full day. The **Museo Arqueológico** ⓘ *park entrance, 0800-1700*, displays pottery and information about San Agustín culture (Spanish only).

Around San Agustín

El Tablón is reached up Carrera 14, over the brow of the hill and 250 m to a marked track to the right. El Tablón (five sculptures brought together under a bamboo roof) is shortly down to the left. Continue down the path, muddy in wet weather, ford a stream and follow signs to the Río Magdalena canyon. **La Chaquira** (figures carved on rocks) is dramatically set half way down to the river. To walk to and from San Agustín is two hours.

At **La Pelota**, two painted statues were found in 1984 (three-hour return trip, six hours if you include El Tablón and La Chaquira, 15 km in all). Discoveries from 1984/1986 include some unique polychromed sculptures at **El Purutal** near La Pelota and a series of at least 30 stones carved with animals and other designs in high relief. These are known as **Los Petroglifos** and can be found on the right bank of the Río Magdalena, near the **Estrecho** (narrows) to which jeeps run.

Alto de los Ídolos ⓘ *0800-1600, US$3*, is about 10 km by horse or on foot, a lovely (if strenuous) walk, steep in places, via **Puente de la Chaquira**. Here on a levelled hill overlooking San Agustín are 13 uncovered tombs and statues dating from 100 BC-AD 600. These statues, known as *vigilantes*, each guard a burial mound. One is an unusual rat totem; stone crocodiles are believed by some to have strong links with the Amazon region. The few excavated have disclosed large stone sarcophagi. It is not certain whether the vigilantes bear a sculpted resemblance of the inmate.

Alto de los Ídolos can also be reached from **San José de Isnos** (5 km northeast) 27 km by road from San Agustín. The road passes the **Salto del Mortiño**, a 170 m fall 7 km before Isnos, 500 m off the road. The main plaza in **Isnos** has restaurants and cafés and a **Cootranshuila** bus office. Isnos' market day is Saturday (bus 0500, US$1.50, return 1100, 1300, otherwise bus from Cruce on Pitalito road, or hitch).

About 6 km north of Isnos is **Alto de las Piedras** ⓘ *0800-1700*, which has seven interesting tombs and monoliths, including the famous 'Doble Yo' and the tombs of two children. There are still over 90 tombs to be excavated. Only less remarkable than the statues are the orchids growing nearby. Some 8 km further is Bordones; turn left at end of the village and there is (500 m) parking for the **Salto de Bordones** falls ⓘ *US$0.50*, which is good for birdwatching.

Bogotá to San Agustín

ⓘ *Before travelling by road south to Neiva, check on safety.*

A lot of people travelling from Bogotá to San Agustín will pass through **Neiva**. The capital of Huila Department. Neiva is a modern city on the east bank of the Río Magdalena, surrounded by rich coffee plantations. There is a large and colourful market every day. South of Girardot, about 50 km before Neiva, is a small area (300 sq km) of scrub and arid eroded red soil known as the **Tatacoa** desert, with large cacti, isolated mesas and unusual wildlife. Four- or five-hour guided walks through the desert cost US$12 per person per day. From Villavieja hire a taxi to Tatacoa desert, US$25 return. There is also a museum next to Santa Bárbara church showing prehistoric finds in the area, entry US$1.25, 0730-1300, 1400-1700, weekends 0700-1730. On top of a small incline some 15 minutes' drive from Villavieja is the **Observatorio Astronómico de la Tatacoa** ⓘ *T879 7584, www.tatacoa-astronomia.com*, run by Javier Fernando Rua who gives an excellent talk every evening at 1830, US$3 per person (camping permitted, US$5.50 to hire tent).

Accommodation available in Villavieja (**$**, or several *posadas nativas*, run by local families, enquire at the **Asociación de Operadores Turísticos** on the Parque Principal, T314-315-2067; see www.villavieja-huila.gov.co). Daily bus from Neiva to Villavieja (Flotahuila and Coomotor from Neiva bus terminal) one hour, US$5. You can cross the Magdalena by motorized canoe near Villavieja for US$1.25, then 1.5 km to Aipe for buses on the Neiva-Bogotá road.

◉ Popayán to San Agustín listings

For hotel and restaurant price codes, and other relevant information, see Essentials.

● Where to stay

Puracé *p950*
$ Residencias Cubina, safe, cold showers, secure parking.

Parque Nacional Puracé: Pilimbalá *p951*
Saloon cars will struggle up the last stretch to the centre, but it's an easy 2.5 km walk from Km 23. Picnic shelters, restaurant and lodging in room with bath, **$** pp; also camping (tents and sleeping bags can be hired). Firewood is provided. Sleeping bags or warm clothing recommended to supplement bedding.

Around Puracé *p951*
La Plata
$ Cambis, C 4, No 4-28, T837 1891. Helpful, near bus station. Recommended.
   Other basic places to stay are **Berlín**, C 4, No 4-76 on the Plaza, T837 0229, and **El Portal de Valencia**, C 6, No 3-58, T837 6304.

Pitalito
$$ Hotel Calamó Plaza, Cra 5, No 5-45, T836 0603, www.hotelcalamoplaza.com. Hot water, pool, cafetería, parking.
$$-$ Hotel Yorytania Boutique, C 7, No 3-31, T836 6368, www.hotelyorytaniaboutique.com. Helpful, laundry service, café.

Popayán to San Agustín: Coconuco *p951*
$$ Hotel de Turismo, 500 m out of town, 10 mins' drive to the baths. The best, comfortable, hot water, price is full board, colonial-style hotel, restful atmosphere. There are several other modest hotels and restaurants in town.

At **Agua Hirviendo**, T827 7013/14/15, are 3 cabins that will hold up to 6, **$** pp.

San Agustín *p952*
Some hotels increase prices during Easter and Christmas by around 10-20%.
$$ Casa de Nelly, Km 2 Vía Parque Archeológico, T310-215 9067, www.hotelcasadenelly.co. On top of the hill on the road to the archeological park, colourful rooms and *cabañas* set in a gorgeous garden, home-cooked pastas and pizzas, hammocks.
$$ Yalconia, Vía al Parque Arqueológico, T837 3013, www.inturcol.com. By municipal pool, the only mid-range hotel in town, modern building, pool.
$ El Jardín, Cra 11, No 4-10, T837 3455, www.hosteltrail.com/hostels/eljardin. In town, colonial house with a colourful patio, simple rooms, dorms, restaurant with fixed-menu lunches.
$ La Casa de François, T837 3847, T314-358 2930, 200 m via El Tablón, www.lacasadefrancois.com. Just outside town, French-run, private rooms, dorms (US$11) and camping set in 2 ha of gardens, good breakfast, meals, crêpes and home-baked bread available, bike and horse hire.
$ Posada Campesina, Cra 14, Camino al Estrecho (on the route to El Tablón), 1 km from town, T837 3956, www.posadasturisticasde colombia.gov.co. A recommended farmhouse, owned by Doña Silvina Patiño, who makes good pizza and cheese bread, meals with family, simple working farm, shared bath, use of kitchen, camping possible, good walks nearby.
Camping Camping San Agustín, 1 km from town towards Parque Arqueológico, opposite clean public swimming pool, Las Moyas, T837 3804. US$7, plus charge pp with own tent, US$6 pp to hire tent, clean, pleasant, safe (guards), showers, toilets, lights, laundry service, horse hire.

Just outside San Agustín

$$ Hacienda Anacaona, Vía al Estrecho del Magdalena, 2 km from town, T311-231 7128, www.anacaona-colombia.com. Elegant traditional *finca*, attractive, beautiful views and garden, hammocks, restaurant, quiet. Camping allowed on grounds. Good.

$ pp Finca El Maco, 1 km from town, 400 m past Piscina Las Moyas, T837 3437, www. elmaco.ch. Swiss owned, working organic farm with colourful gardens, rustic, peaceful, cosy cabins for 1-6 (US$9-25 pp), also teepee, welcoming, laundry service, very good restaurant (reserve ahead), great local information; see Chaska Tours below.

$ pp Finca El Cielo, 3 km from San Agustín, Vía El Estrecho/Obando, T837 9398, www. fincaelcielo.com. Guesthouse and organic farm, overlookig Río Magdalena, restaurant, camping, swimming pool, tours organized in the area and beyond, also live music, dance and riding classes.

Bogotá to San Agustín: Neiva *p953*
$$$ Neiva Plaza, C 7, No 4-62, T871 0800, www.hotelneivaplaza.com. Neiva's traditional smart hotel for more than 50 years, good, comfortable rooms, restaurant, gym and pool.
$ Andino, C 9, No 5-82, T871 0184. Central, rooms are a little small and dark but clean.

🍴 Restaurants

San Agustín *p952*
Tap water in San Agustín is not safe to drink.
$$ Donde Richard, C 5, No 23-45. On the outskirts of town. Good steaks, chicken and fish, soups and salads, agreeable surroundings. Recommended.
$$-$ Surabhi, C 5, No 14-09. Tasty regional specialities and set lunches.
$ Brahama, C 5, No 15-11. This small restaurant serves Colombian fare and some good vegetarian options.
$ El Fogón, C 5, No 14-30, T837 3431. Family run, good *comida* and juices, fresh salads. Recommended.

⏱ Festivals

San Agustín *p952*
Santa María del Carmen in **mid-Jul** (date varies) in San Agustín. 2 festivals in **Jun** are San Juan (24th) with horse races and dances, and **San Pedro** (29th) with horse races, dances, fancy dress, and more. In the **1st week of Oct**, the Casa de Cultura celebrates **La Semana Cultural Integrada**, with folklore events from all parts of the country.

Bogotá to San Agustín: Neiva *p953*
Late Jun/early Jul Festival Nacional del Reinado del Bambuco, incorporating San Juan and San Pedro: dancing competitions, parades on the river and through the streets.

⚙ What to do

San Agustín *p952*
Guides There are countless guides in town offering tours of the various sites. Some give a better service than others. Enquire at your hotel or at the tourist office for advice. Some recommended names are **Marino Bravo**, T311-835 6736, takes walking, riding and minibus tours, authorized, professional, speaks English, French and Italian; **Gloria Amparo Palacios**, T311-459 5753, and **Carlos Bolaños**, T311-459 5753; **Fabio Burbano**, T837 3592, 311-867 5665, professional, reliable and knowledgeable, **Luis Alfredo Salazar**, T837 3426, speaks English, French, Italian. They charge US$15 for a half day, US$30 for a full day.
Chaska Tours, T837 3437, 311-271 4802, www.chaskatours.net. Run by Swiss René Suter (who also owns **Finca El Maco**), organizes tours around San Agustín and to Tierradentro, Puracé and the Tatacoa desert. English and German spoken. Recommended.
Horse riding You are strongly advised to hire horses for trips around San Agustín through hotels. The centre for horses, **Asociación de Acompañantes y Alquiladores de Caballos**, along C 5 on the road to the park, costs about US$12 per hr, per rider. If you require a guide, you must add the hire cost of his horse. Pacho, T311-827 7972, pachitocampesinito@ yahoo.es (also does tours to Lago Magdalena, the source of the Río Magdalena, US$27 for

guidance plus US$20 pp), and **Abuy**, T311-453 3959, are recommended and are contactable through **El Maco** or **La Casa de Nelly**. There are fixed tariffs for 20 standard trips.

Rafting Magdelana Rafting, C 5, No 16-04, T311-271 5333, www.magdalenarafting.com. Run by experienced Frenchman Amid Bouselahane, offers various rafting, kayaking and caving tours.

Vehicle tours Jeeps may be hired for 4-5 people. Prices vary according to the number of sites to be visited.

⊝ Transport

Parque Nacional Puracé *p951*
Bus Several daily to Puracé from **Popayán**, last returning 1700. Bus stops 3.5 km from Pilimbalá. All the places beyond Puracé village can be reached by bus from **Popayán** to La Plata. The bus service can be erratic so check time of last daylight bus to Popayán and be prepared to spend a cold night at 3000 m. The rangers will allow you to stay in the centre.

Around Puracé *p951*
La Plata
Bus To **Bogotá**, via Neiva, Coomotor, 9 hrs, in the evening, Cootranshuila, 5 a day, US$30. To **Popayán** 0500 and others, US$14, 5½ hrs. To **San Agustín**, direct US$15 or take a colectivo to Pitalito and change. For **Tierradentro** take a bus towards Popayán (leaves 0600-0630) and alight at the Cruce US$6. Private jeep hire La Plata–Tierradentro US$50, cheaper if you pick up other passengers. To **Pitalito**, 3½ hrs, US$12.

Pitalito
Bus At all bus stations in this region, both off and on buses, theft is common.

Plenty of buses and colectivos to **San Agustín**, US$3. Bus to **La Plata**, 3½ hrs, US$12. Bus to Bogotá, US$28-32. Bus to **Mocoa** (in the Putumayo), US$9-12, 7-8 hrs. To **Parque Nacional Cueva de los Guácharos** take a bus/*chiva* to Palestina, US$2.50, 1 hr, then a 40-min *chiva* to Mensura. From there, 8-km walk or horse ride to visitor centre.

San Agustín *p952*
Bus To **Bogotá** by colectivo (Taxis Verdes, C 3, No 10-27, T837 3068) 3 daily, direct or change at Neiva, go early US$29, 9-11 hrs, or by bus (**Coomotor**, C 3, No 10-71), 4 a day, US$28-32, 10-12 hrs. From **Bogotá**, Taxis Verdes will pick up at hotels (extra charge), T01-355 5555, www.taxisverdes.net. Alternatively, there are frequent services from Bogotá to **Neiva** as well as some to Pitalito. Most services going to Bogotá will stop at Neiva. To **Tierradentro**, check first if any of the tourist offices is running a jeep, otherwise, Taxis Verdes or colectivos leave frequently to **Pitalito** (30 mins), then a colectivo jeep from Pitalito to La Plata, US$12, 3½ hrs. Usually you can get a chiva, bus or colectivo, 2-3 hrs to Tierradentro (San Andrés de Pisimbalá) the same day. Do not take a night bus to Tierradentro. There are several daily buses from San Agustín to **Popayán** via Isnos with **Cootranshuila** (office on C 3, No 10-81) and Estelar, slow, bad unpaved road, 6-8 hrs, US$17.50; some Popayán-San Agustín buses drop passengers outside San Agustín. Do not travel between San Agustín and Popayán at night. The road is isolated and dangerous. It's best to book seats the day before.

Bogotá to San Agustin: Neiva *p953*
Air La Marguita, 1.5 km from city. Daily flights to/from **Bogotá** and principal cities. Taxi to bus terminal US$4.
Bus Station out of town, www.eltermina lneiva.com; bus from the centre leaves from the old terminal (Cra 2, Cs 5 y 6). To **Bogotá**, 6 hrs, US$16.60-29. Coomotor to **San Agustín**, US$15, 6 hrs. To **Pitalito**, US$12.50-14, 3 hrs. To **La Plata**, for Tierradentro, US$10-13, 2 hrs, frequent services (especially early morning, 0400, 0500). To **Popayán**, US$25, 8-11 hrs, poor road in parts.

ⓘ Directory

San Agustín *p952*
Banks Two banks with ATMs, but don't arrive short of cash.

Southern Colombia

This region includes the routes from Popayán to the border with Ecuador, Colombia's furthest stretch of Pacific coast and its toehold on the Amazon river. Pasto is the commercial outlet for the agricultural produce of the southern highlands and its history is tied up with the struggle for independence from Spain and the subsequent wrangling over Simón Bolívar's dream of Gran Colombia. The country's Amazonian port is Leticia, gateway to the jungle, Brazil and Peru.

South to Ecuador

From Popayán to Ecuador is scenic highland country, much of it open **páramo** intersected here and there by spectacular deep ravines. To the west is the long slope down to the Pacific including the mangrove swamps of much of the coast and the small port of Tumaco. To the east is the continental divide of the Cordillera Oriental and the beginning of the great Amazonian basin.

Pasto → *Phone code: 2. Population: 399,000. Altitude: 2534 m.*
From Popayán to Pasto is 285 km (five hours driving). The road drops to 700 m in the valley of the Río Patía before climbing to Pasto with big temperature changes.

Pasto, 88 km from Ecuador, is overlooked from the west by Volcán Galeras and to the east by green hills not yet suburbanized by the city, and is in a very attractive setting. It was founded in the early days of the conquest and retains some of its colonial character. During the wars of Independence, it was a stronghold of the Royalists and the last town to fall into the hands of the patriots after a bitter struggle. Then the people of Nariño Department, of which Pasto is capital, wanted to join Ecuador when that country split off from Gran Colombia in 1830, but were prevented by Colombian troops.

There are several churches worth visiting: ornate **San Juan Bautista** and **La Merced** ① *C 18A, No 25-11*, **Cristo Rey** ① *C 20, No 24-64* and **Santiago** ① *Cra 23 y C 13*, which has good views over the city to the mountains.

The **Museo de Oro del Banco de la República** ① *C 19, No 21-27, 1721 5777, www.banrepcultural.org/pasto, Tue-Fri 1000-1700, Sat 0900-1700, free,* has a small well-displayed collection of pre-Columbian pieces from the cultures of southern Colombia. **Museo Zambrano** ① *C 20, No 29-78, Mon-Sat 0800-1200, 1400-1600, free,* houses indigenous and colonial period arts, especially *quiteño* (from Quito). Every Sunday paddle ball is played on the edge of the town (bus marked 'San Lorenzo'), similar to the game played in Ibarra, Ecuador. The **tourist office** ① *just off the main plaza, C 18, No 25-25, p 2, T723 4962, www.turismonarino.gov.co, Mon-Fri 0800-1200, 1400-1800,* is friendly and helpful.

Volcán Galeras and around
The volcano, Galeras (4276 m), has been erupting frequently since 1989. Check at the tourist office whether it is safe to climb on the mountain and whether you need a permit (entry US$1). A road climbs up the mountain to a ranger station and police post at 3700 m, beyond which you are not permitted.

On the north side of the volcano lies the village of **Sandoná** ① *frequent buses and colectivos daily, US$3, 1½ hrs from Pasto,* where panama hats are made; they can be seen lying in the streets in the process of being finished. Sandoná market day is Saturday.

The Putumayo
About 25 km east of Pasto, on the road to Mocoa is **Laguna La Cocha**, the largest lake in south Colombia (sometimes called Lago Guamuez). In the lake is the **Isla de La Corota** nature reserve with interesting trees (entry US$0.50, 10 minutes by boat from the **Hotel Sindanamoy**, camping

possible, information T732-0493, corota@parquesnacionales.gov.co, or from the national parks office in Popayán or Bogotá).

A steep climb over the Sierra leads to a large statue of the Virgin marking the entry into the Putumayo. The road then descends steeply to Sibundoy and Mocoa, in the transitional zone between Andes and Amazon. There are hotels on the plaza in **Mocoa** and the Belgian-owned **$ Hostal Casa del Río** ① *Vereda Caliyaco, T08-420 4004, T314-304 5050, www.casadelriomocoa. com.* Beyond are the lowlands and the river towns of Puerto Asís and San Miguel (a crossing to Lago Agrio in Ecuador). For many years this was guerrilla territory, but it is opening up for ecotourism with lots of potential for visiting rivers and waterfalls and nature-watching. Seek local advice before heading to Ecuador this way.

Ipiales → *Phone code: 2. Colour map 1, C2. Population: 72,000. Altitude: 2898 m.*

Passing through deep valleys and a spectacular gorge, buses on the paved Pan-American Highway cover the 84 km from Pasto to Ipiales in 1½-2 hours. The road crosses the spectacular gorge of the Río Guáitara at 1750 m, near El Pedregal, where *choclo* (corn) is cooked in many forms by the roadside. **Ipiales**, "the city of the three volcanoes", is famous for its colourful Friday morning indigenous market. The main attraction is the Sanctuary of the Virgin of **Las Lajas** (US$0.55), about 7 km east of Ipiales. Seen from the approach road, looking down into the canyon, the Sanctuary is a magnificent architectural conception, set on a bridge over the Río Guáitara: close up, it is very heavily ornamented in the gothic style. The altar is set into the rock face of the canyon, which forms one end of the sanctuary with the façade facing a wide plaza that completes the bridge over the canyon. There are walks to nearby shrines in dramatic scenery. It is 10-15 minutes' walk down to the sanctuary from the village. There are great pilgrimages to it from Colombia and Ecuador (very crowded at Easter) and the Sanctuary must be second only to Lourdes in the number of miracles claimed for it. Colectivo taxis from Ipiales bus terminal go direct to Las Lajas (10 minutes), US$1 one way or US$3.50 by taxi. Several basic hotels and a small number of restaurants at Las Lajas.

Border with Ecuador

Ipiales is 2 km from the Rumichaca bridge across the Río Carchi into Ecuador. The border post stands on a concrete bridge, beside a natural bridge, where customs and passport examinations take place 24 hours. All Colombian offices are in one complex, Puesto Terrestre CENAF Rumichaca, Puente Internacional Rumichaca: **Migración Colombia** (immigration, exit stamp given here), customs, **INTRA** (Dept of Transportation, car papers stamped here; if leaving Colombia you must show your vehicle entry permit) and **ICA** (Department of Agriculture for plant and animal quarantine). There is also a restaurant, Telecom, clean bathrooms (US$0.10) and ample parking. See Ecuador chapter for the Ecuadorean side. The **Ecuadorean consulate** ① *Cra 7, No 14-10, p2, T773 2292, weekdays 0900-1230, 1430-1700,* is in the Migración Colombia complex. There are many money changers near the bridge on both sides. There are better rates on the Colombian side but check all calculations.

⊙ South to Ecuador listings

For hotel and restaurant price codes, and other relevant information, see Essentials.

⊙ Where to stay

Pasto *p957*
$$$ Galerías, Cra 26, No 18-71, p 3, T723 7390, www.hotel-galerias.com. In the town's main

shopping centre, good-sized rooms, parking, with a good restaurant.
$$$ Loft Hotel, C 18, No 22-33, T722 6733, www.lofthotelpasto.com. Comfortable, with minimalist decor, spa, gym. 20% discount if you show a copy of *Footprint*.
$$ Fernando Plaza, C 20, No 21B-16, T729 1432, www.hotelfernandoplaza.com. Smart,

lots of good details such as orthopaedic mattresses, restaurant.

$ Koala Inn, C 18, No 22-37, T722 1101, www.hosteltrail.com/hostels/koalainn. The best backpackers' option in town. Large, antiquated rooms, some with bath, laundry, cable TV,good local information. There is a small café serving decent breakfasts for US$3.50.

Ipiales *p958*
$$-$ Santa Isabel 2, Cra 7, No 14-27, T773 4172, www.hotelsantaisabel2.com. Smart, central, good services, parking, restaurant.
$ Belmonte, Cra 4, No 12-11, T773 2771. Basic but clean, shared bath.
$ Emperador, Cra 5, No 14-43, T725 2413. Central, best budget option, good rooms, hot water, parking.

🍴 Restaurants

Pasto *p957*
$ Inca Cuy, C 29, No 13-65, T723 8050. Down a narrow corridor behind the Plaza de Bombona, specializes in fried guinea pig (*cuy*); book ahead as it takes an hour to prepare.
$ Picantería Ipiales, C 19, No 23-37, T723 0393. Typical food from Nariño, specifically pork-based dishes, and *almuerzos*.

🎉 Festivals

Pasto *p957*
During the new year's fiesta there is a Día de los Negros on 5 Jan and a Día de los Blancos next day. On 'black day' people smear each others' faces in black grease. On 'white day' they throw talc or flour at each other. Local people wear their oldest clothes. On 28 Dec and 5 Feb, there is also a Fiesta de las Aguas when anything that moves gets drenched with water from balconies and even from fire engines' hoses. All towns in the region are involved in this legalized water war! In Pasto and Ipiales (see page 958), on 31 Dec, is the Concurso de Años Viejos, when huge dolls are burnt; they represent the old year and sometimes lampoon local people.

🛍 Shopping

Pasto *p957*
Handicrafts Pasto varnish (*barniz*) is mixed locally, to embellish the colourful local wooden bowls. Leather goods shops are on C 17 and C 18. Try the municipal market for handicrafts.

🚌 Transport

Pasto *p957*
Air Daily flights to **Bogotá and Cali**, 3 a week to **Puerto Asís**. The airport is at Cano, 40 km from Pasto; by colectivo (beautiful drive), 45 mins, US$2.50 or US$15 by taxi.
Bus Bus terminal at Cra 6, C 16, 4 km from centre, taxi, US$1. **Bogotá**, 18-23 hrs, US$49-58 (Bolivariano Pullman most direct, recommended). **Ipiales**, 2 hrs, US$3.50, sit on the left for the views. **Popayán**, ordinary buses take 10-12 hrs, US$11; expresses take 5-8 hrs, cost US$18. **Cali**, US$23-34, expresses, 8½-10 hrs.

The Putumayo: Laguna La Cocha *p957*
To La Cocha take a taxi from Pasto, a colectivo from C 20 y Cra 20, or a **bus** to El Encano and walk 20 mins from bus stop direct to lake shore.

Ipiales *p958*
Air San Luis airport is 6.5 km out of town. Flights to **Cali** and **Puerto Asís**. Taxi to Ipiales centre, US$5.
Bus Bus companies have individual departure points: *busetas/colectivos* mostly leave from main plaza. To **Popayán**, Expreso Bolivariano, US$19, 7½-8 hrs, hourly 0800-2000; also colectivo taxis, US$25. Expreso Bolivariano to **Cali**, US$24-37, 10-12 hrs. To **Pasto** US$3.50, 2-3 hrs. Frequent buses to **Bogotá** every 2 hrs, 20-24 hrs, US$54-60 (check if you have to change buses in Cali).

Border with Ecuador: Ipiales *p958*
Bus From Ipiales to **Tulcán**: *colectivo* from C 14 y Cra 11, US$1.05 to the border (buses to Ipiales arrive at the main plaza – they may take you closer to the colectivo point if you ask). Colectivo from border to **Tulcán** and to Tulcán bus station, US$1. Easiest to take a taxi from Ipiales to the border, US$4.15.

Car If entering Colombia by car, the vehicle should be fumigated against diseases that affect coffee trees, at the ICA office. The certificate must be presented in El Pedregal, 40 km beyond Ipiales on the road to Pasto. (This fumigation process is not always carried out.) You can buy insurance for your car in Colombia at Banco Agrario, in the plaza.

ⓘ Directory

Pasto *p957*
Banks *Casas de cambio*, Titan, Cra 26, No 18-71, at Cra 25, No 18-97, and C 19, No 24-86, by the main plaza. **Immigration** Migración Colombia: C 17, No 29-70, T731 1500, will give exit stamps if you are going on to Ecuador.

Ipiales *p958*
Banks It is not possible to cash TCs. *Casa de cambio* on the plaza. Money changers on street, in plaza and at border, but they may take advantage if the banks are closed.

Leticia and the Amazon

The extensive cattle lands from the Cordillera Central to the Orinoco are a good place to get away from it all in the dry season. Leticia, Colombia's port on the Amazon, is on the southern tip of a spur of territory which gives Colombia access to the great river, 3200 km upstream from the Atlantic. At the east edge of town is the land border with Brazil. The Brazilian port of **Tabatinga** starts directly at the border and the two cities function as one unit, but Leticia is safer and more expensive than Tabatinga. Across the river and downstream is a more relaxed and pleasant Brazilian town, **Benjamin Constant**, at the confluence of the Amazon and the Rio Javari (see Brazil chapter). On an island across from Leticia and Tabatinga is the small Peruvian town of **Santa Rosa**, which is prone to severe flooding in the rainy season.

Leticia → *Phone code: 8. Colour map 3, A5. Population: 35,000. Altitude: 82 m.*

Capital of Amazonas Department, the city is clean and modern. Changes in the height of the river sometimes mean that the water is quite a distance from town and port facilities. Parque Santander y Orellana is pleasant and is a popular meeting place. There is a well-equipped hospital. The best time to visit the area is in July or August, the early months of the dry season. Leticia is a good place to buy typical products of Amazon *indígenas* (for example, at *Museo Artesanal Uirapurú*, C 8, 10-35), and tourist services are better than in Tabatinga or Benjamin Constant. Housed in the beautiful Biblioteca del Banco de la República is the **Museo Etnográfico** ⓘ *Cra 11 9-43, www.banrepcultural.org/leticia, Mon-Fri 0830-1800, Sat 0900-1230, free*, which has displays on local ethnography and archaeology. For the border with Brazil, Colombia and Peru see the Brazil chapter, where Colombian, Brazilian and Peruvian procedures are detailed in one section. The **tourist office** is at ⓘ *C 8, entre Cra 9 y 10, T592 7567, Mon-Fri 0700-1200, 1400-1700, see www.amazonas.gov.co.* **Note** There is an obligatory US$10 environment tax payable upon arrival by plane in Leticia. You may also be asked for a yellow fever inoculation certificate on arrival; if you do not have this, an inoculation will be administered on the spot (not recommended).

Jungle trips from Leticia

Colombian operators run tours to several jungle reserves and lodges in Colombian, Brazilian and Peruvian territory. See What to do, below. **Reserva Natural Isla de los Micos** ⓘ *entry US$10.90; Decameron has the concession for the restaurant here*: there are few monkeys on the island now, those left are semi-tame. Native communities can be visited in the area, Huacarí of the Yagua people, opposite the island; Santa Sofía, upriver from the island, and Nazareth downriver, the latter two of the Ticuna people.

Parque Nacional Amacayacu ① *closed in 2013 due to flooding, the Leticia national parks office has the latest information and how to get there, C 10, No 15-60, T592 4872, www.parquesnacionales. gov.co* , 60 km upstream, at the mouth of the Matamata Creek, two hours from Leticia. There is a jungle walk to a lookout and a rope bridge over the forest canopy, with wonderful views over the surrounding jungle. There are various other guided day treks through the jungle.

Puerto Nariño A small, attractive settlement on the Río Loretoyacu, a tributary of the Amazon, beyond the Parque Nacional Amacayacu, 75 km from Leticia. Where the two rivers meet is a popular place to watch dolphins. Tours include Lago de Tarapoto to see pink and grey river dolphin – the latter when the water level is high (US$27-44 per person by motorized canoe) and walks to indigenous communities. **Fundación Natütama** ① *www.natutama.org, Mon and Wed-Fri 0800-1230, 1400-1700, US$5.50* works to preserve the marine life of this part of the Amazon by organizing educational programmes with local communities. They have an informative visitor centre with an elaborate display of underwater life.

⦿ Leticia and the Amazon listings

For hotel and restaurant price codes, and other relevant information, see Essentials.

French and Portuguese and organizes alternative tours of the Amazon.

⦿ Where to stay

Leticia *p960*

$$$ Malokamazonas, C 8, No 5-49, T592 6642, www.hotelmalokamazonas.es.tl. Family run, close to the border, a variety of rooms in thatched cabins, welcome drink, meals apart from breakfast extra, jacuzzi, laundry, cable TV, garden.

$$$ Yurupary, C 8, No 7-26, T592 4743, www.hotelyurupary.com. Good, large rooms, pool fringed with tropical plants. Also arranges tours into the Amazon through Yurupary Amazonas Tours and runs Aldea Yurupary in Puerto Nariño.

$$ Divino Niño, Cra 6, No 7-23, T592 5594, www.hoteldivinonino.com. Not central but good value, simple, cheaper with fan, welcoming, dorm US$10 pp.

$$ Fernando Real, Cra 9, No 8-80, T592 7362. Intimate atmosphere, **$** with fan, rooms open onto a flower-filled patio, minibar, good value.

$$ -$ Mahatu Hostel, Cra 7, No 1-40, T311-539 1265, www.mahatu.org. Far from the centre, a couple of private rooms with bath and dorms with fan (US$12.50 pp), kitchen, bar, nice ample grounds with ponds, small pool, hammocks, quiet location. Owner speaks English, Flemish,

Puerto Nariño *p961*

Increasingly travellers are choosing to stay in Puerto Nariño. Several options are available.

$$$ Casa Selva, Cra 6, No 6-78, T311-201 2153, www.casaselvahotel.com. Comfortable, airy, spotless rooms, with breakfast. Tours to Lago de Tarapoto and other destinations through their operator AT Amazonas Turismo Ecológico.

$$-$ Maloca Napu, C 4, No 5-72, 2 blocks from river, T315-607 4044, www.malocanapu.com. Simple private wooden rooms, dorms (US$10), quiet and relaxing. Breakfast provided.

$ Hospedaje Manguaré, C 4, No 5-52, T311-276 4873. Comfortable cabin-style rooms with fans and bath. Bunks in dorms are US$11 pp. It also doubles up as the town chemist.

⦿ Restaurants

Leticia *p960*

Several popular sidewalk restaurants near the corner of Cra 9 and C 8 serve good value set lunches (*comida corriente*) and à la carte in the evening; eg **$$-$ La Cava Amazónica**, Cra 9, also has an a/c dining room.

$ El Maná, Cra 8 No 10-24, open 0700-1900, closed Fri evening and Sat. Good vegetarian set lunches, fruit juices, fruit salad, breakfast.

⚙ What to do

Leticia *p960*
Tour operators
Full-day trips (eg to Puerto Nariño and Lago de Tarapoto) cost about US$75 pp.
Isaac Rodríguez, Cra 6N, No 7-91 apto 117, T312-314 0311, isaacdrc@gmail.com. Ministry of Tourism-registered guide.
Reserva Natural Palmarí, Cra 10 No 93-72, Bogotá, T01-610 3514, www.palmari.org. They operate a reserve on the Río Javarí (see Manaus to Colombia *Where to stay*, in the Brazil chapter).
SelvAventura, Cra 9, No6-85, T592 3977, 311-287 1307, www.selvaventuramazonas. com. Jungle tours and expeditions to natural reserves and indigenous territories, activities such as kayaking, trekking and canopying. English and several other languages spoken. Also run **Casa del Kurupira** hostel.
Turismo Verde, no storefront, Leticia, T311-508 5666, www.amazonheliconia. com. Run **Kurupira** floating hotel on the Colombian Amazon and **Heliconia Lodge** on the Río Javarí (see Brazil chapter).

Puerto Nariño *p961*
Tour guides
Ever Sinarahua (a boatman), **Clarindo López** and **Milciades Peña** are recommended for their local knowledge of flora and fauna and indigenous customs; they work with tour operators. Also, **Pedro Nel Cuello**, enquire through **Fundación Natutama** (see above), also recommended.

⚙ Transport

Leticia *p960*
Air Airport is 1 km north of the city; small terminal, few facilities. Expect to be searched before leaving Leticia airport, and on arrival in Bogotá from Leticia. Daily flights from Bogotá. **Satena** (Cra 11, No 9-42 loc 1, T312-457 6291) has flights to local Amazonas destinations.
Boat Different docks are used at different times depending on water levels, ask around. Motorboat to **Santa Rosa**, Peru, 0700-1800, US$1.65 pp; to cross at night arrange

ahead with a boatman, US$5.50 pp, beware overcharging and negotiate. If crossing to Santa Rosa in the early morning to catch the *rápido* to Iquitos, better to take a taxi to Tabatinga docks (it is not safe to walk) where a motorboat shuttles passengers starting 0230 (Colombia/Peru time), US$3 pp.
Taxi Airport to the centre US$4; Leticia (including airport) to Tabatinga (including Brazilian immigration and ports) US$11 during the day, US$16 at night, mototaxi US$2.70; mototaxi (one passenger only) within Leticia US$1.

Jungle trips from Leticia *p961*
Parque Nacional Amacayacu
Boat Speedboats to Puerto Nariño (see below) take passengers to the park, US$13.60 one way. Let them know when you wish to return; 2 companies on alternate days, make sure that your operator travels the day you want to return.

Puerto Nariño *p961*
Boat From **Leticia**, daily at 0800, 1100 and 1500, return 0730, 1100 and 1600 (check times as they often change), 2 hrs, US$16.

⚙ Directory

Leticia *p960*
Banks There are several banks with ATMs. Leticia is the best place to change money in the border area; cash only, no TCs. Good rates for US$ and reais, poor rates for soles. Reais and pesos colombianos are accepted in all three towns, soles are seldom used. Many street changers and cambios on C 8, near the market and port, beware of tricks; **Cambios El Opita**, C 8 No 10-105 is reliable.
Immigration Migración Colombia, C 9, No 9-62, T592 4877, Mon-Fri 0800-1200, 1400-1700. For entry and exit stamps go to Leticia airport, T592 4535, Mon-Fri 0800-1700, Sat-Sun 0800-1500, taxi from the centre US$4, mototaxi US$2.50.

Puerto Nariño *p961*
Internet and international calls (expensive) next to the school.

Contents

Ecuador

At a glance

⊙ **Time required** 2-5 weeks.

☼ **Best time** Jun-Aug, Christmas and New Year are good for fiestas.

✕ **When not to go** Jun-Sep and Dec-Jan are the busiest times. All year is good from a climatic point of view. In the highlands, the wettest months are Oct-Nov and Feb-May; Jan-May are hottest and rainiest on Pacific coast. In the jungle, wet months are Mar-Sep.

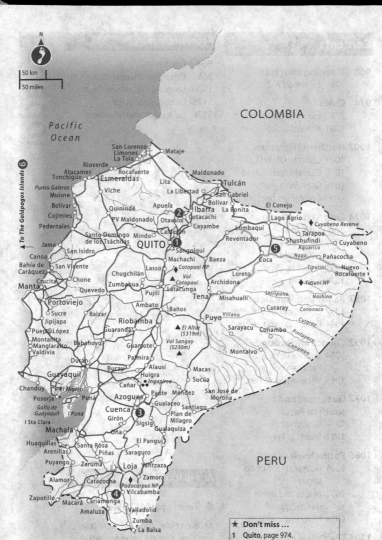

COLOMBIA

Pacific
Ocean

San Lorenzo
Limones
La Tola
Mataje

Rioverde
Atacames
Tonchigüe
Esmeraldas
Lita
Maldonado
Tulcán

Punta Galeras
Muisne
Viche
La Libertad
San Gabriel

Bolívar
Quinindé
Apuela
Ibarra
La Bonita
El Conejo

Cojímies
PV Maldonado
Otavalo
Cotacachi
Lago Agrio
Cuyabeno Reserve

Pedernales
Santo Domingo
de los Tsáchilas
Mindo
Cayambe
Lumbaquí
Tarapoa
Shushufindi
Cuyabeno

Jama
Calderón
Reventador
Aguarico

Canoa
San Isidro
QUITO
Sangolquí
Coca
Napo
Pañacocha

Bahía de
Caráquez
San Vicente
Machachi
Baeza
Tiputini
Nuevo
Rocafuerte

Manta
Chone
Chugchilán
Lasso
Cotopaxi NP
Vol
Cotopaxi
Loreto
Archidona
Yasuní NP
Nashino

Crucita
Quevedo
Zumbahua
Pujilí
Latacunga
Tena
Misahuallí
Shiripuno
Cononaco

Portoviejo
Ambato
Baños
Puyo
Villano
Curaray
Curaray
Conambo
Pintuyacu

Sucre
Jipijapa
Balzar
Riobamba
El Altar
(5319m)
Sarayacu
Conambo

Puerto López
Guaranda
Guamote
Vol Sangay
(5230m)
Montalvo

Montañita
Manglaralto
Valdivia
Babahoyo
Palmira
Alausí
Macas

Durán
Bucay
Huigra
Ingapirca
Cañar
Sucúa

Guayaquil
El Morro
Puná
Paute
Méndez
San José de
Morona

Chanduy
Posorja
Azogues
Gualaceo
Santiago

Golfo de
Guayaquil
I Puná
Cuenca
Girón
Sígsig
Plan de
Milagro
Gualaquiza

I Sta Clara
Machala
Oña
El Pangui

Huaquillas
Santa Rosa
Piñas
Saraguro

Arenillas
Puyango
Zaruma
Yantzaza

Alamor
Catacocha
Loja
Zamora

Zapotillo
Macará
Cariamanga
Podocarpus NP
Vilcabamba

Amaluza
Valladolid

Zumba

La Balsa

PERU

To The Galápagos Islands ⑥

N
50 km
50 miles

Tucked in between Peru and Colombia, this country is small enough for you to have breakfast with scarlet macaws in the jungle, lunch in the lee of a snow-capped peak and, at tea time, be eyeballed by an iguana whose patch of Pacific beach you have just borrowed.

A multitude of national parks and conservation areas emphasise the incredible variety of Ecuador. They include mangroves; an avenue of volcanoes – many of them active – striding across the Equator; forests growing on the dry Pacific coast, in the clouds and under the Amazonian rains; not forgetting all the animals and birds which flourish in these habitats. In fact, as Ecuador is one of the richest places in the world for birds, with some of the planet's most beautiful species, the country is a prime birdwatching destination.

The capital, Quito, and the southern highland city of Cuenca, are two of the gringo centres of South America, bursting at the seams with language schools, tour operators and restaurants. The smaller towns and villages of Ecuador offer the most authentic experience. Indulge your senses at one of their many markets, with dizzying arrays of textiles, ceramics, carvings and other crafts, not to mention the cornucopia of fresh produce.

The exotic wildlife of the Galápagos Islands will also keep you enthralled, whether it's watching an albatross take off on its flight path, swimming with marine iguanas, sea lions and penguins, or admiring the sexual paraphernalia of the Magnificent Frigatebird. If the Galápagos are beyond your budget, then Isla de la Plata, in Parque Nacional Machalilla, is a more accessible alternative for seeing marine life.

Planning your trip

Where to go in Ecuador

The capital, **Quito**, boasts some of the best-preserved colonial architecture in South America in its 'colonial city', while the 'modern Quito' is where you'll find most accommodation, restaurants, tour operators and language schools. From the capital many of the country's attractions are accessible by road in only a few hours. Day trips include nature reserves, hot springs, and, of course, the Equator. There is also good mountaineering and white-water rafting nearby. North of Quito is **Otavalo** with its outstanding handicrafts market, a regular one-day tour, but equally popular as a base for exploring nearby villages, more nature reserves and hiking or cycling routes. Carrying on towards the Colombian border is **Ibarra**, another good centre for visiting the north.

In the Central Sierra, south of Quito, is the national park surrounding **Cotopaxi**, one of Ecuador's most frequently climbed volcanoes. Further south is the **Quilotoa circuit**, a 200-km loop through small villages and beautiful landscapes, with lots of possibilities for trekking, cycling and riding. The starting point is Latacunga on the Pan-American Highway. On one of the main routes from the Sierra to the eastern jungle is **Baños**, a popular spa town with hiking, biking, adrenaline sports, horse riding and volcano watching opportunities close at hand. The heart of the central highlands is **Riobamba**, beneath Chimborazo volcano. This is another good base for climbing, biking and trekking, as well as the starting point for the famous railway ride over La Nariz del Diablo (The Devil's Nose). The archaeological site of **Ingapirca** is between Riobamba and **Cuenca**, a lovely colonial city in the Southern Sierra. Nearby is Cajas National Park. En route from Cuenca towards Peru are the provincial capital of **Loja**, close to Podocarpus National Park, and **Vilcabamba**, with a delightful climate and a favourite with travellers and expats alike. Several border crossings with Peru are accessible from Loja.

Ecuador's Pacific capital is **Guayaquil**, 45 minutes by air from Quito (eight hours by bus) and only four hours by bus south to the Peruvian border via Machala. Key areas of the city have been renewed, such as its historic riverfront. To the north stretch the **Pacific Lowlands** with beaches, pre-Columbian archaeological sites and small seaside resorts like Puerto López, Montañita, Canoa and Mompiche, as well as a few more developed ones like Salinas, Bahía de Caráquez and Atacames. Near Puerto López, **Parque Nacional Machalilla** contains dry tropical forest, offshore islands and marine ecosystems. It is a good place for riding, diving, whale watching, birdwatching and relaxing on the beautiful Los Frailes beach.

The **Oriente** (eastern lowlands) offers good opportunities for nature tourism, with a number of specially designed jungle lodges, mainly in the north. A stay in one of these places is best booked in Quito or from home, but you can head for jungle towns like Coca, Tena, Puyo or Misahuallí to arrange a tour with a local agency. The southern Oriente is less developed for tourism, but interest is growing, with Macas or Zamora as the places to aim for.

Ecuador is famous for its **hot springs** and, on either side of the Andes, there is great **birdwatching** in a wide variety of protected areas (see www.avesecuador.com). Other special interest activities include **diving**, **whitewater rafting** and various **volunteer programmes**. The nature destination par excellence, though, is the **Galápagos Islands**, 970 km west of the mainland. Tours, which are usually arranged in advance from Quito, Guayaquil or from home, traditionally involve cruising from island to island to see new species with each landfall, although land-based options are also available.

National parks Ecuador has an outstanding array of protected natural areas including a system of 43 national parks and reserves administered by the **Ministerio del Ambiente** ⓘ *Madrid E12-*

102 y Andalucía, T398 7600, ext 1420, www.ambiente.gob.ec/areas-protegidas-3/. Entry to national protected areas is free except for Parque Nacional Galápagos. Some parks can only be visited with authorized guides. For information on specific protected areas, contact park offices in the cities nearest the parks, they have more information than the ministry.

Best time to visit Ecuador

Ecuador is a year-round destination. The climate is unpredictable. As a general rule, however, in the **Sierra**, there is little variation by day or by season in the temperature: this depends on altitude. The range of shade temperature is from 6°C to 10°C in the morning, to 19°C to 23°C in the afternoon, though it can get considerably hotter in the lower basins. Rainfall patterns depend on whether a particular area is closer to the eastern or western slopes of the Andes. To the west, June to September are dry and October to May are wet (but there is a short dry spell in December or January). To the east, October to February are dry and March to September are wet. There is also variation in annual rainfall from north to south, with the southern highlands being drier. **Quito** is within 25 km of the Equator, but it stands high enough to make its climate much like that of spring in England, the days pleasantly warm and the nights cool. Rainy season is October to May with the heaviest rainfall in April. Rain usually falls in the afternoon. The day length (sunrise to sunset) is almost constant throughout the year.

Along the **Pacific coast**, rainfall also decreases from north to south, so that it can rain throughout the year in northern Esmeraldas and seldom at all near the Peruvian border. The coast, however, can be enjoyed year-round, although it may be a bit cool from June to November, when mornings are often grey with the *garúa* mists. January to May is the hottest and rainiest time of the year. Like the coast the **Galápagos** may receive *garúa* from May to December; from January to April the islands are hottest and brief but heavy showers can fall. In the **Oriente**, heavy rain can fall at any time, but it is usually wettest from March to September.

Ecuador's **high season** is from June to early September, which is also the best time for climbing and trekking. There is also a short tourist season in December and January. In resort areas at major fiestas, such as **Carnival**, **Semana Santa** (Easter), **Finados** (2 Nov) and over New Year, accommodation can be hard to find. Hotels will be full in individual towns during their particular festivals, but Ecuador as a whole is not overcrowded at any time of the year.

Transport in Ecuador

Air Airlines operating within Ecuador include: **Aerogal** ① *T1-800-237642 or T02-294 3100, www.aerogal.com.ec*, serving Quito, Guayaquil, Cuenca, Coca, Manta and Galápagos and international routes, code sharing with Avianca, to Bogotá, Cali, Medellín and Lima; **LAN** ① *T1-800-842526, www.lan.com*, Quito, Guayaquil, Cuenca, Manta and Galápagos and international routes to Miami, New York, Madrid, Cali, Medellín, Lima, Santiago and Buenos Aires; **TAME** ① *T1-700-500800 or T02-397 7100, www.tame.com.ec*, Quito, Guayaquil, Cuenca, Tulcán, Latacunga, Loja, Coca, Lago Agrio, Tena, Macas, Esmeraldas, Manta, Santa Rosa (Machala) and Galápagos and international flights to Bogotá, Cali, Caracas, Panamá, Habana, New York, Lima, São Paulo and Buenos Aires.

Bus Bus travel is generally more convenient and regular than in other Andean countries. Several companies use comfortable air-conditioned buses on their longer routes; some companies have their own stations, away from the main bus terminals, exclusively for these better buses. Bus company information and itineraries are found in www.ecuadorbuses.com, where tickets for some major routes can also be purchased online for US$3. **Note** Throughout Ecuador, travel by bus is safest during the daytime.

Driving in Ecuador

Roads A very good network of paved roads runs throughout most of the country. Maintenance of major highways is franchised to private firms, who charge tolls of US$1. Roads are subject to damage during heavy rainy seasons. Always check road conditions before setting out.

Safety Unexpected potholes and other obstructions, the lack of road signs, and local drivers' tendency to use the middle of the road make driving 'an experience'. Beware the bus drivers, who often drive very fast and rather recklessly. Driving at night is not recommended.

Documents To bring a foreign vehicle or motorcycle into the country, its original registration document (title) in the name of the driver is required. If the driver is not the owner, a notarized letter of authorization is required. All documents must be accompanied by a Spanish translation. A 90-day permit is granted on arrival, extensions are only granted if the vehicle is in the garage for repairs. No security deposit is required and you can enter and leave at different land borders. Procedures are generally straightforward but it can be a matter of luck. Shipping a vehicle requires more paperwork and hiring a customs broker. The port of Guayaquil is prone to theft and particularly officious. Manta and Esmeraldas are smaller and more relaxed,

but receive fewer ships. A valid driver's licence from your home country is generally sufficient to drive in Ecuador and rent a car, but an international licence is helpful.

Car hire To rent a car you must be 21 and have an international credit card. Surcharges may apply to clients aged 21-25. You may pay cash, which is cheaper and may allow you to bargain, but they want a credit card for security. You may be asked to sign two blank credit card vouchers, one for the rental fee itself and the other as a security deposit, and authorization for a charge of as much as US$8000 may be requested against your credit card account if you do not purchase the local insurance. The uncashed vouchers will be returned to you when you return the vehicle. Make sure the car is parked securely at night. A small car suitable for city driving costs around US$570 per week including unlimited mileage, tax and full insurance. A 4WD or pickup truck (recommended for unpaved roads) costs about US$1240 a week. Drop-off charges are about US$112.

Fuel There are two grades of petrol, 'Extra' (82 octane, US$1.48 per US gallon) and 'Super' (92 Octane, US$1.98-2.30). Both are unleaded. Extra is available everywhere, while Super may not be available in more remote areas. Diesel fuel (US$1.03) is notoriously dirty and available everywhere.

Vans and shared taxis These operate between major cities and offer a faster, more comfortable and more expensive alternative to buses. Some provide pickup and drop-off at your hotel.

Hitchhiking Public transport in Ecuador is so abundant that there is seldom any need to hitchhike along the major highways. On small out-of-the-way country roads however, the situation can be quite the opposite, and giving passers-by a ride is common practice and safe, especially in the back of a pick-up or truck. A small fee is usually charged, check in advance.

Train Empresa de Ferrocarriles Ecuatorianos ① *T1-800-873637, www.ecuadorbytrain.com*. A series of tourist rides have replaced regular passenger service along the spectacular Ecuadorean railway system, mostly restored in 2013. There are two classes of service, standard and plus; carriages are fancier in the latter and a snack is included. On some routes, an autoferro, a motorized railcar runs instead of the train. The following routes are on offer: **Quito to Machachi, El Boliche** (Cotopaxi) and **Latacunga; Alausí to Sibambe** via the Devil's Nose;

Ambato to Urbina; **Riobamba to Urbina** and **Colta**; **Ibarra to Salinas**; **El Tambo to Baños del Inca** near Ingapirca; **Durán** (outside Guayaquil) to Yaguachi and Bucay; and the Tren Crucero, an upmarket all inclusive tour of up to four days along the entire line from Quito to Durán. Details are given under What to do, in the corresponding cities.

Taxi In cities, all taxis must use meters.

Maps and guide books Instituto Geográfico Militar (IGM) ① *Senierges y Telmo Paz y Miño, east of Parque El Ejido, Quito, T02-397 5100, ext 2502, www.geoportaligm.gob.ec, Mon-Thu 0730-1600, Fri 0700-1430, take ID.* They sell country and topographic maps in a variety of paper and digital formats. Prices range from US$3 to US$7. Maps of border and sensitive areas are 'reservado' (classified) and not available for sale without a permit. Buy your maps here, they are rarely available outside Quito.

Where to stay in Ecuador → *See Essentials for our hotel price guide.*
Hotels Higher-class hotels are found mainly in provincial capitals and resorts, where self-styled boutique hotels are springing up. The larger cities also have an array of international hotels. In the countryside, a number of *haciendas* have opened their doors to paying guests. A few are in the **Exclusive Hotels & Haciendas of Ecuador** group, www.ehhec.com, and there are many other independent haciendas of good quality. Some are mentioned in the text. Larger towns and tourist centres have many more hotels than we can list. The hotels that are included are among the best in each category, selected to provide a variety of locations and styles. Additional hotels are found in www.hotelesecuador.com, www.ecuadorboutiquehotels.com, www.infohotel.ec and www.gulahotelesecuador.com. Many hotels do not include breakfast. Service of 10% and tax of 12% are added to better hotel bills. Some cheaper hotels apply only the 12% tax, but check if it is included. Some hotel rooms have very low wattage bulbs, keen readers are advised to take a head torch. All but the most basic establishments have Wi-Fi in their rooms or common areas.

Camping Camping in protected natural areas can be one of the most satisfying experiences during a visit to Ecuador. Organized campsites, car or trailer camping on the other hand are very uncommon. Because of the abundance of cheap hotels you should never *have to* camp in Ecuador, except for cyclists who may be stuck between towns. In this case the best strategy is to ask permission to camp on someone's private land, preferably within sight of their home for safety. It is not safe to pitch your tent at random near villages and even less so on beaches. *Camping gas* canisters are easily obtainable, but white gas, like US Coleman fuel, is not. Unleaded petrol (gasoline) is available everywhere and may be an alternative for some stoves.

Food and drink in Ecuador → *See Essentials for our restaurant price guide.*
Eating out The large cities have a wide selection of restaurants with Ecuadorean, international and fashionable fusion cuisine. Upmarket restaurants add 22% to the bill, 12% tax plus 10% service. All other places add the 12% tax, which is also charged on non-essential items in food shops. The cuisine varies with region, you can learn about it in www.ecuador.travel. The following are some typical dishes.

In the highlands *Locro de papas* (potato and cheese soup), *mote* (corn burst with alkali, a staple in the region around Cuenca, but used in a variety of dishes in the Sierra), *caldo de patas* (cowheel soup with *mote*), *llapingachos* (fried potato and cheese patties), *empanadas de morocho* (a fried ground corn shell filled with meat), *sancocho de yuca* (vegetable soup with manioc root), roast *cuy* (guinea pig), *fritada* (fried pork), *hornado* (roast pork), *humitas* (tender ground corn steamed in corn leaves), and *quimbolitos* (similar to *humitas* but prepared with wheat flour and steamed in *achira* lily leaves). *Humitas* and *quimbolitos* come in both sweet and savoury varieties.

On the coast *Empanadas de verde* (fried snacks: a ground plantain shell filled with cheese, meat or shrimp), *sopa de bola de verde* (plantain dumpling soup), *ceviche* (marinaded fish or seafood, popular everywhere, see below), *encocados* (dishes prepared with coconut milk, may be shrimp, fish, etc, very popular in the province of Esmeraldas), *cocadas* (sweets made with coconut), *viche* (fish or seafood soup made with ground peanuts), and *patacones* (thick fried plantain chips served as a side dish).

In Oriente Dishes prepared with yuca (manioc or cassava root) and river fish. *Maitos* (in northern Oriente) and *ayampacos* (in the south) are spiced meat, chicken or palm hearts wrapped in leaves and roasted over the coals.

Throughout the country If economizing ask for the set meal in restaurants: *almuerzo* at lunch time, *merienda* in the evening – cheap and wholesome; it costs US$2-4. *Fanesca*, a traditional Easter dish, is a filling fish soup with beans, many grains, ground peanuts and more; it is so popular that in Quito and main tourist spots it is sold throughout Lent, between Carnival and Easter. *Ceviche*, marinated fish or seafood which is usually served with popcorn and roasted maize (*tostado*), is very popular throughout Ecuador. Only *ceviche de pescado* (fish) and *ceviche de concha* (clams) which are marinated raw, potentially pose a health hazard. The other varieties of *ceviche* such as *camarón* (shrimp/prawn) and *langostino* (jumbo shrimp/king prawn) all of which are cooked before being marinated, are generally safe. The vegetarian variety, *ceviche de chochos*, prepared with lupin beans, is excellent and cheap. *Langosta* (lobster) is an increasingly endangered species but continues to be illegally fished; please be conscientious. *Menestra* is a bean or lentil stew, served with rice and grilled meat, chicken or fish. Ecuadorean food is not particularly spicy. However, in most homes and restaurants, the meal is accompanied by a small bowl of *ají* (hot pepper sauce) which may vary in potency. In addition to the prepared foods mentioned above, Ecuador offers a large variety of delicious fruits, some of which are unique to South America.

Drink The best fruit drinks are *naranjilla* (a tomato relative), *maracuyá* (passion fruit), *tomate de árbol* (tree tomato), *babaco* (related to papaya), *guanábana* (soursop), *piña* (pineapple), *taxo* (banana passion fruit) and *mora* (blackberry), but note that fruit juices are sometimes made with unboiled water. Main beers available are *Pilsener* and *Club*. Argentine and Chilean wines are available in cities. *Aguardiente* (unmatured rum, many brands) is popular, also known as *puntas*, *trago de caña*, or just *trago*. The usual soft drinks, known as *colas*, are widely available. In tourist centres and many upscale hotels and restaurants, good cappuccino and espresso can be found.

Essentials A-Z

Accident and emergency
For emergencies nationwide, T911.
For police, T101.

Disabled travellers
Ecuador for All (see page 994) is a tour operator catering to travellers with special needs.

Electricity
AC throughout, 110 volts, 60 cycles. Sockets are for twin flat blades, sometimes with a round earth pin.

Embassies and consulates
For all Ecuadorean embassies and consulates abroad and for all foreign

embassies and consulates in Ecuador,
see http://embassy.goabroad.com.

Festivals

1 Jan: New Year's Day; **6 Jan**: Reyes Magos
y Día de los Inocentes, a time for pranks,
which closes the Christmas-New Year holiday
season. **Carnival**: Mon and Tue before Lent,
celebrated everywhere in the country (except
Ambato) by throwing water at passers-by:
be prepared to participate. **Easter**: Holy
Thu, Good Fri, Holy Sat. **1 May**: Labour Day;
24 May: Battle of Pichincha, Independence.
Early Jun: Corpus Christi. **10 Aug**: first
attempt to gain the Independence of Quito.
9 Oct: Independence of Guayaquil. **2 Nov**:
All Souls' Day. **3 Nov**: Independence of
Cuenca. **6 Dec**: Foundation of Quito. **25 Dec**:
Christmas Day.

Internet

Cyber cafés are universal in all cities and towns
of Ecuador. Consequently we do not list them
in the text below. Wi-Fi is available in most
hotels and many cafés.

Money

The **US dollar** (US$) is the official currency of
Ecuador. Only US$ bills circulate. US coins are
used alongside the equivalent size and value
Ecuadorean coins. Ecuadorean coins have no
value outside the country. Many establishments
are reluctant to accept bills larger than US$20
because of counterfeit notes or lack of change.
There is no substitute for cash-in-hand when
travelling in Ecuador; US$ cash in small
denominations is by far the simplest and
the only universally accepted option. Other
currencies are difficult to exchange outside
large cities and fetch a poor rate.

Plastic/traveller's cheques/banks/ATMs

The most commonly accepted **credit cards**
are Visa, MasterCard, Diners and, to a lesser
extent, American Express. Cash advances on
credit cards can be obtained through many
ATMs (only Banco de Guayaquil for Amex),
but daily limits apply. Larger advances on
Visa and MasterCard are available from the
main branches of the following banks: **Banco
Bolivariano**, **Banco de Guayaquil** (Visa only),
Banco del Austro and **Banco del Pacífico**.
Paying by credit card may incur a surcharge
(at least 10%). TCs are not accepted by most
merchants, hotels or tour agencies in Ecuador.
They can be exchanged for cash at **Banco del
Pacífico** (main branches; US$5 commission,
maximum US$200 a day) and some **casas de
cambio** including Vaz Corp (in Quito, Otavalo,
Cuenca, Loja and Machala; 1.8% commission).
A passport is always required to exchange TCs.
American Express is the most widely accepted
brand, but they are no longer replaced in
Ecuador; if they are lost or stolen, you must file
a claim from home. A police report is required
if TCs are stolen. Internationally linked **ATMs**
are common, although they cannot be relied
on. Credit cards are easier to use in ATMs than
debit cards. ATMs are a focus for scams and
robberies, use them judiciously. Funds may be
rapidly wired to Ecuador by **Western Union** or
MoneyGram, high fees and taxes apply.

Cost of living/travelling

Despite dollarization, prices remain modest
by international standards and Ecuador is
still affordable for even the budget traveller.
A very basic daily travel budget in 2014
was about US$25 pp based on 2 travelling
together, but allow for higher costs in main
cities and resorts. For US$60 a day you can
enjoy a good deal of comfort. Internet use
is about US$0.60-1 per hr, US$2 in the
Galápagos. Bus travel is cheap, about US$1
per hr, flights cost almost 10 times as much
for the same route. An **International Student
Identity Card** (**ISIC**) may help you obtain
discounts when travelling. ISIC cards are
sold in Quito by Grupo Idiomas ① *Roca 130
y 12 de Octubre, p 2, T02-250 0264*. They need
proof of full-time enrolment in Ecuador or
abroad (minimum 20 hrs per week), 2 photos,
passport, US$20 and the application form
found in www.isic.com.ec.

Opening hours

Banks: open Mon-Fri 0830-1700. **Government offices**: variable hours Mon-Fri, most close for lunch. **Other offices**: 0900-1230, 1430-1800. **Shops**: 0900-1900; close at midday in smaller towns, open till 2100 on the coast.

Residence and retirement

Since 2005 a growing number of foreigners, many of them retirees, have settled in Ecuador. Expatriate colonies have sprung up in Cotacachi, Jama, Cuenca and Vilcabamba, among other locations. Real estate prices have soared in these areas and this, alongside cultural insensitivity on the part of some newcomers, has led to local resentment. If considering a move to Ecuador, you are strongly advised to come for an extended visit first, to get to know the country, blemishes and all. Note the public safety situation (see below), and remember that you are undertaking a major life-change, not merely looking for a place with lower prices and a better climate than your current home. Learning Spanish before you arrive is a prerequisite for a successful transition. Be cautious with the many real-estate agents, attorneys, middle-men and facilitators, be they foreign or Ecuadorean, who have made a growth industry of catering to expatriates.

Safety

Public safety is an important concern throughout mainland Ecuador; Galápagos is generally safe. Armed robbery, bag snatching and slashing, and holdups along the country's highways are among the most significant hazards. 'Express kidnapping', whereby victims are taken from ATM to ATM and forced to withdraw money, is a threat in major cities, and fake taxis (sometimes yellow official-looking ones, sometimes unmarked *taxis ejecutivos*) are often involved. Radio taxis are usually safer.

Secure your belongings at all times, be wary of con tricks, avoid crowds and congested urban transport, and travel only during the daytime. It is the larger cities, especially Guayaquil, Quito, Cuenca, Manta, Machala, Esmeraldas, Santo Domingo, and Lago Agrio which call for the greatest care. Small towns and the countryside in the highlands are generally safer than on the coast or in the jungle. The entire border with Colombia calls for precautions; enquire locally before travelling there.

Although much less frequent than in the past, sporadic social unrest remains part of life in Ecuador and you should not overreact. Strikes and protests are usually announced days or weeks in advance, and their most significant impact on tourists is the restriction of overland travel. It is usually best to wait it out rather than insisting on keeping to your original itinerary.

In Ecuador, drug sale, purchase, use or growing is punishable by up to 16 years' imprisonment.

Ecuador's active volcanoes are spectacular, but have occasionally threatened nearby communities. The **National Geophysics Institute** provides daily updates at www.igepn.edu.ec.

Tax

VAT/IVA 12%, may be reclaimed on departure if you show official invoices with your name and passport number; don't bother with bills under US$50. High surtaxes apply to imported luxury items

Airport taxes Departure tax is included in the ticket price: Quito, US$17 for domestic flights, US$60 for international; Guayaquil, US$5 for domestic, US$30 for international; Baltra (Galápagos), US$30.

Telephone

International phone code: +593. Calling within Ecuador dial the area code (02-07) + 7 digits for land lines, 09 +8 digits for cell phones. For local calls from a land line leave out the area code. Calling from abroad, leave out the 0 from the area code. Phone offices are called *cabinas*. **Note** Roaming may not work with foreign cell phones, for local use it is best to buy an Ecuadorean chip (US$6-7), but it must be registered using a local ID (*cédula*) number.

Time
Official time is GMT -5 (Galápagos, -6).

Tipping
In restaurants 10% may be included in the bill. In cheaper restaurants, tipping is uncommon but welcome. It is not expected in taxis. Airport porters, US$1-2, depending on the number of cases.

Tourist information
Ministerio de Turismo ① *El Telégrafo E7-58 y Los Shyris, Quito, T1-800-887476 or T02-399-9333, www.ecuador.travel*. Local offices are given in the text. The ministry has a Public Prosecutors Office, where serious complaints should be reported. Outside Ecuador, tourist information can be obtained from Ecuadorean Embassies. For information on parks and reserves, see National parks, page 966.

Useful websites
www.ecuador.travel A good introduction. www.ecuador.com; www.quitoadventure. com; www.paisturistico.com and www. explored.com.ec General guides with information about activities and national parks. www.ecuadorexplorer.com; www.ecuador-travel-guide.org; www.ecuaworld.com and www.thebestofecuador.com Are all travel guides; the latter includes volunteering options. www.saexplorers.org South American Explorers, has information about volunteering. www.trekkinginecuador.com and www. thefreeair.com For hiking information. www.paginasamarillas.info.ec, www.edina. com.ec and www.guiatelefonica.com.ec Telephone directories.

Visas and immigration
All visitors to Ecuador must have a passport valid for at least 6 months and an onward or return ticket, but the latter is seldom asked for. Citizens of some Middle Eastern, Asian and African countries require a visa to visit Ecuador, other tourists do not require a visa unless they wish to stay more than 90 days. Upon entry all visitors must complete an international embarkation/disembarkation card. Keep your copy, you will be asked for it when you leave.

Note You are required by Ecuadorean law to carry your passport at all times. Whether or not a photocopy is an acceptable substitute is at the discretion of the individual police officer, having it notarized can help. Tourists are not permitted to work under any circumstances.

Length of stay Tourists are granted 90 days upon arrival and there are no extensions except for citizens of the Andean Community of Nations. Visitors are not allowed back in the country if they have already stayed 90 days during the past 12 months. If you want to spend more time studying, volunteering etc, you can get a purpose specific visa (category '12-IX', about US$200 and paperwork) at the end of your 90 days as a tourist. There is no fine at present (subject to change) for overstaying but you will have difficulties on departure and may be barred from returning to Ecuador. Dirección Nacional de Migración (immigration) has offices in all provincial capitals; Visas for longer stays are issued by the Ministerio de Relaciones Exteriores (Foreign Office), through their diplomatic representatives abroad and administered in Quito by the Dirección General de Asuntos Migratorios and the Dirección Nacional de Extranjería. Visa information is found in http://cancilleria.gob.ec.

Weights and measures
Metric, US gallons for petrol, some English measures for hardware and weights and some Spanish measures for produce.

Quito

Few cities have a setting to match that of Quito, the second highest capital in Latin America after La Paz. The city is set in a hollow at the foot of the volcano Pichincha (4794 m). The city's charm lies in its colonial centre – the Centro Histórico as it's known – a UNESCO World Heritage Site, where cobbled streets are steep and narrow, dipping to deep ravines. From the top of Cerro Panecillo, 183 m above the city level, there is a fine view of the city below and the encircling cones of volcanoes and other mountains.

North of the colonial centre is modern Quito with broad avenues lined with contemporary office buildings, fine private residences, parks, embassies and villas. Here you'll find Quito's main tourist area in the district known as La Mariscal, bordered by Avenidas Amazonas, Patria, 12 de Octubre and Orellana.

Arriving in Quito → Phone code: 02. Colour map 11, A4. Population: 1,670,000. Altitude: 2850 m.

Orientation Mariscal Sucre airport is about 30 km northeast of the city. Long-distance bus services leave from terminals at the extreme edges of the city, **Quitumbe** in the south and **Carcelén** in the north. Some bus services also run to their own offices in modern Quito. There are four parallel public transit lines running north to south on exclusive lanes: the *Trole*, *Ecovía*, *Metrobus* and *Universidades*, as well as city buses.

Both colonial Quito and La Mariscal in modern Quito can be explored on foot, but getting between the two requires some form of public transport, using taxis is the best option. Quito is a long city stretching from north to south, with Pichincha rising to the west. Its main arteries run the length of the city and traffic congestion along them is a serious problem. Avenida Occidental or Mariscal Sucre is a somewhat more expedite road to the west of the city. The Corredor Periférico Oriental or Simón Bolívar is a bypass to the east of the city running 44 km between Santa Rosa in the south and Calderón in the north. Roads through the eastern suburbs in the Valle de los Chillos and Tumbaco can be taken to avoid the city proper. **Note** There are vehicular restrictions on weekdays 0700-0930 and 1600-1930, based on the last digit of the license plate, seniors are exempt. Colonial Quito is closed to vehicles Sunday 0900-1600 and main avenues across the city close Sunday 0800-1400 for the *ciclopaseo* (page 992).

Most places of historical interest are in colonial Quito, while the majority of the hotels, restaurants, tour operators and facilities for visitors are in the modern city to the north. The street numbering system is based on N (Norte), E (Este), S (Sur), Oe (Oeste), plus a number for each street and a number for each building, however, an older system of street numbers is also still in use. Note that, because of Quito's altitude and notorious air pollution, some visitors may feel some discomfort: slow your pace for the first 48 hours. ▶▶ *See also Transport, page 997.*

Tourist information Empresa Metropolitana Quito Turismo/Quito Visitor's Bureau ① *T299 3300, www.quito.com.ec*, has information offices with English-speaking personnel, brochures and maps, and an excellent website. They also run walking tours of the colonial city, see Paseos Culturales, page 991. **Airport** ① *in Arrivals area, T281 8363, open 24 hrs*. **Bus station** ① *Terminal Quitumbe, T382 4815, daily 0900-1730*. **Train station** ① *T261 7661, Mon-Fri 0800-1630*. **Colonial Quito** ① *Plaza de la Independencia, El Quinde craft shop at Palacio Municipal, Venezuela y Espejo, T257 2445, Mon-Fri 0900-1800, Sat 0900-2000, Sun 0900-1700*. **La Mariscal** ① *República del Cacao, Reina Victoria 258 y Pinto, near Plaza Foch, kiosk in the patio of the chocolate shop/café, T255 1566, Mon-Fri 0900-1800, Sat 0900-1400*; also sell tickets for the double decker bus tours, see page 992. General information about Quito is found in www.in-quito.com and photos in www.quitoenfotos.com.

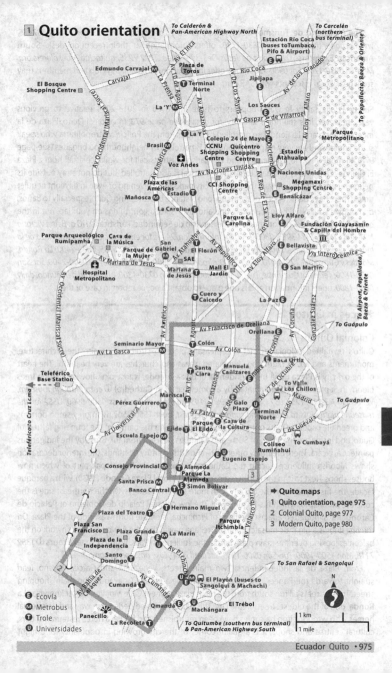

1 Quito orientation

To Calderón & Pan-American Highway North

To Carcelén (northern bus terminal)

To Papallacta, Baeza & Oriente

Estación Río Coca (buses to Tumbaco, Pifo & Airport)

Edmundo Carvajal

El Bosque Shopping Centre

Plaza de Toros

Río Coca

Jipijapa

Terminal Norte

Los Sauces

La 'Y'

La 'Y'

Brasil

Colegio 24 de Mayo

Voz Andes

CCNU Shopping Centre

Quicentro Shopping Centre

Estadio Atahualpa

Naciones Unidas

Plaza de las Américas

Estadio

CCI Shopping Centre

Megamaxi Shopping Centre

Mañosca

La Carolina

Benalcázar

Parque La Carolina

Eloy Alfaro

Parque Arqueológico Rumipamba

Casa de la Música

San Gabriel

Fundación Guayasamín & Capilla del Hombre

Parque de la Mujer

El Florón

SAE

Bellavista

Hospital Metropolitano

Mariana de Jesús

Mall El Jardín

San Martín

Cuero y Caicedo

La Paz

To Airport, Papallacta, Baeza & Oriente

Teleférico Base Station

Av Francisco de Orellana

Orellana

To Guápulo

Seminario Mayor

Colón

Av Colón

Baca Ortiz

Santa Clara

Manuela Cañizares

Mariscal

Pérez Guerrero

Galo Plaza

To Valle de Los Chillos

To Guápulo

Ejido

Av Patria

Casa de la Cultura

Terminal Norte

Parque El Ejido

Escuela Espejo

Coliseo Rumiñahui

To Cumbayá

Consejo Provincial

Eugenio Espejo

Santa Prisca

Alameda

Parque La Alameda

Banco Central

Simón Bolívar

3

Plaza del Teatro

Hermano Miguel

Parque Itchimbía

Plaza San Francisco

Plaza Grande

La Marín

Plaza de la Independencia

Santo Domingo

To San Rafael & Sangolquí

Cumandá

El Playón (buses to Sangolquí & Machachi)

Qmandá

El Trébol

Panecillo

Machángara

La Recoleta

To Quitumbe (southern bus terminal) & Pan-American Highway South

Quito maps
1 Quito orientation, page 975
2 Colonial Quito, page 977
3 Modern Quito, page 980

E Ecovía
M Metrobus
T Trole
U Universidades

N

1 km
1 mile

The **Ministerio de Turismo** ① *El Telégrafo E7-58 y Los Shyris, T399 9333 or T1-800-887476, www.ecuador.travel, Mon-Fri 0830-1730*, offers information at their reception desk. **South American Explorers** ① *Mariana de Jesús Oe3-32 y Ulloa, T222 7235, quitoclub@saexplorers.org, Mon-Fri 0930-1700, Sat 0900-1200*. They offer information, have a hiking club and members may store gear. Local discounts with SAE card.

Safety Public safety in Quito appears to have improved in 2013-2014 relative to previous years, however, it is still not a safe city, for details see page 972. In colonial Quito, Plaza de la Independencia and La Ronda are patrolled by officers from the **Policía Metropolitana** who speak some English and are very helpful. El Panecillo is patrolled by neighbourhood brigades (see page 978). In modern Quito, La Carolina and La Mariscal districts call for vigilance at all hours. Plaza El Quinde (Calle Foch y Reina Victoria) in La Mariscal is also patrolled, but do not stray outside its perimeter at night. Do not walk through any city parks in the evening or even in daylight at quiet times. There have been reports of scams on long distance buses leaving Quito, especially to Baños; do not give your hand luggage to anyone and always keep your things on your lap, not in the overhead storage rack nor on the floor. The **Servicio de Seguridad Turística** ① *HQ at Reina Victoria N21-208 y Roca, T254 3983, 0800-1800 for information, 24 hrs for emergencies; offices at: Plaza de la Independencia, Pasaje Arzobispal, Chile Oe4-66 y García Moreno, T295 5785, 0800-2400; La Ronda, Morales y Guayaquil, T295 6010, 0800-2400; airport, T394 5000, ext 3023, Mon-Fri 0600-2400, Sat-Sun 0600-1800; Terminal Quitumbe, Tue-Fri 0800-0000, Sat-Mon 0730-1800; and Mitad del Mundo, daily 0800-1800*, offers information and is one place to obtain a police report in case of theft.

Places in Quito

Colonial Quito
Quito's revitalized colonial district is a pleasant place to stroll and admire the architecture, monuments and art. At night, the illuminated plazas and churches are very beautiful. The heart of the old city is **Plaza de la Independencia** or **Plaza Grande**, whose pink-flowered arupo trees bloom in September. It is dominated by a somewhat grim **Cathedral** ① *entry through museum, Venezuela N3-117, T257 0371, Tue-Sat, 0900-1745, no visits during Mass 0600-0900, US$2 for the museum, night visits to church and cupolas on request*, built 1550-1562, with grey stone porticos and green tile cupolas. On its outer walls are plaques listing the names of the founding fathers of Quito, and inside are the tomb of Sucre and a famous Descent from the Cross by the indigenous painter Caspicara. There are many other 17th- and 18th-century paintings; the interior decoration shows Moorish influence. Facing the Cathedral is the **Palacio Arzobispal**, part of which now houses shops. Next to it, in the northwest corner, is the **Hotel Plaza Grande** (1930), with a baroque façade, the first building in the old city with more than two storeys. On the northeast side is the concrete **Municipio**, which fits in quite well. The low colonial Palacio de Gobierno or **Palacio de Carondelet**, silhouetted against the flank of Pichincha, is on the northwest side of the Plaza. On the first floor is a gigantic mosaic mural of Orellana navigating the Amazon. The ironwork on the balconies looking over the main plaza is from the Tuilleries in Paris. Visitors can take **tours** ① *T382 7118, Mon 1500-1900, Tue-Sun 0900-1900, Sat until 2200, take passport or copy*.

From Plaza de la Independencia two main streets, Venezuela and García Moreno, lead straight towards the Panecillo. Parallel with Venezuela is Calle Guayaquil, the main shopping street. These streets all run south from the main plaza to meet Calle Morales, better known as **La Ronda**, one of the oldest streets in the city. This narrow cobbled pedestrian way and its colonial homes with wrought iron balconies have been refurbished and house a hotel, restaurants, bars, cultural centres and shops. It is a quaint corner of the city growing in popularity for a night

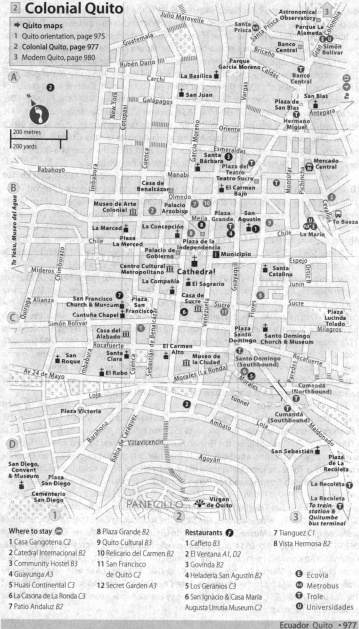

2 Colonial Quito

➡ Quito maps
1 Quito orientation, page 975
2 Colonial Quito, page 977
3 Modern Quito, page 980

200 metres
200 yards

Where to stay
1 Casa Gangotena C2
2 Catedral Internacional B2
3 Community Hostel B3
4 Guayunga A3
5 Huasi Continental C3
6 La Casona de La Ronda C3
7 Patio Andaluz B2
8 Plaza Grande B2
9 Quito Cultural B3
10 Relicario del Carmen B2
11 San Francisco de Quito C2
12 Secret Garden A3

Restaurants
1 Caffeto B3
2 El Ventana A1, D2
3 Govinda B2
4 Heladería San Agustín B2
5 Los Geranios C3
6 San Ignacio & Casa María Augusta Urrutia Museum C2
7 Tianguez C1
8 Vista Hermosa B2

Ⓔ Ecovía
Ⓜ Metrobus
Ⓣ Trole
Ⓤ Universidades

out or an afternoon stroll. On García Moreno N3-94 is the beautiful **El Sagrario** ⓘ *Mon-Fri, 0800-1800, Sat-Sun 1000-1400, no entry during Mass, free,* church with a gilded door. The **Centro Cultural Metropolitano** is at the corner of Espejo, housing the municipal library, a museum for the visually impaired, temporary art exhibits and the **Museo Alberto Mena Caamaño** ⓘ *entry on C Espejo, T395 2300, ext 155, www.centrocultural-quito.com, Tue-Sun 0900-1730, US$1.50.* This wax museum depicts scenes of Ecuadorean colonial history. The scene of the execution of the revolutionaries of 1809 in the original cell is particularly vivid. The fine Jesuit church of **La Compañía** ⓘ *García Moreno N3-117 y Sucre, T258 1895, Mon-Thu 0930-1830, Fri 0930-1730, Sat and holidays 0930-1600, Sun 1230-1600, US$4, students US$2,* has the most ornate and richly sculptured façade and interior. Many of its most valuable treasures are in vaults at the Banco Central. Diagonally opposite is the **Casa Museo María Augusta Urrutia** ⓘ *García Moreno N2-60 y Sucre, T258 0103, Tue-Fri 1000-1800, Sat-Sun 0930-1730, US$2,* the home of a Quiteña who devoted her life to charity, showing the lifestyle of 20th-century aristocracy.

Housed in the fine restored, 16th century Hospital San Juan de Dios, is the **Museo de la Ciudad** ⓘ *García Moreno 572 y Rocafuerte, T228 3879, www.museociudadquito.gob.ec, Tue-Sun 0930-1730, US$3, free entry on the last Sat of each month, foreign language guide service US$6 per group (request ahead).* A very good museum which takes you through Quito's history from prehispanic times to the 19th century, with imaginative displays; café by the entrance overlooking La Ronda. Almost opposite on García Moreno are the convent and museum of **El Carmen Alto** ⓘ *T228 1513, Wed-Sun 0930-1600, US$3, request ahead for guiding in English.* In 2013, this beautifully refurbished cloister opened its doors to the public for the first time since 1652.

On **Cerro Panecillo** ⓘ *Mon-Thu 0900-1700, Fri-Sun 0900-2100, US$1 per vehicle or US$0.25 per person if walking, for the neighbourhood brigade; entry to the interior of the monument US$2,* there is a statue of the Virgen de Quito and a good view from the observation platform. Although the neighbourhood patrols the area, it is safer to take a taxi (US$6 return from the colonial city, US$10 from La Mariscal, with a short wait). In the museum of the monastery of **San Diego** ⓘ *Calicuchima 117 y Farfán, entrance to the right of the church, T317 3185, Tue-Sat 1000-1300, 1400-1700, Sun 1000-1400, US$2,* (by the cemetery of the same name, just west of Panecillo). Guided tours (Spanish only) take you around four colonial patios where sculpture and painting are shown. Of special interest are the gilded pulpit by Juan Bautista Menacho and the Last Supper painting in the refectory, in which a *cuy* and *humitas* have taken the place of the paschal lamb.

Plaza de San Francisco (or Bolívar) is west of Plaza de la Independencia; here are the great church and monastery of the patron saint of Quito, **San Francisco** ⓘ *daily 0800-1200, 1500-1800.* The church was constructed by the Spanish in 1553 and is rich in art treasures. A modest statue of the founder, Fray Jodoco Ricke, the Flemish Franciscan who sowed the first wheat in Ecuador, stands nearby. See the fine wood-carvings in the choir, a high altar of gold and an exquisite carved ceiling. There are some paintings in the aisles by Miguel de Santiago, the colonial *mestizo* painter. The **Museo Franciscano Fray Pedro Gocial** ⓘ *in the church cloisters to the right of the main entrance, T295 2911, Mon-Sat 0900-1730, Sun 0900-1300, US$2,* has a collection of religious art. Also adjoining San Francisco is the **Cantuña Chapel** ⓘ *Cuenca y Bolívar, T295 2911, 0800-1200, 1500-1800, free,* with sculptures. Not far to the south along Calle Cuenca is the excellent archaeological museum **Museo Casa del Alabado** ⓘ *Cuenca 335 y Rocafuerte, T228 0940, Tue-Sat 0930-1730, Sun 1000-1600, US$4, guides extra, excellent art shop.* An impressive display of pre-Columbian art from all regions of Ecuador, amongst the best in the city. North of San Francisco is the church of **La Merced** ⓘ *Chile y Cuenca, 0630-1200, 1300-1800, free,* with many splendidly elaborate styles. Nearby is the **Museo de Arte Colonial** ⓘ *Cuenca N6-15 y Mejía, T228 2297, Tue-Sat 0900-1630, US$2,* housed in a 17th-century mansion, it features a collection of colonial sculpture and painting.

At **Plaza de Santo Domingo** (or Sucre), southeast of Plaza de la Independencia, is the church and monastery of **Santo Domingo** ① *daily 0630-1230, 1700-1830*, with its rich wood-carvings and a remarkable Chapel of the Rosary to the right of the main altar. In the monastery is the **Museo Dominicano Fray Pedro Bedón** ① *T228 0518, Mon-Sat 0915-1400, 1500-1630, US$2*, another fine collection of religious art. In the centre of the plaza is a statue of Sucre, facing the slopes of Pichincha where he won his battle against the Royalists. Just south of Santo Domingo, in the old bus station, is **Parque Qmanadá** ① *Tue-Sun 0900-1300, 1500-1800, busy on weekends*, with swimming pool, sport fields, gym and activities. **Museo Monacal Santa Catalina** ① *Espejo 779 y Flores, T228 4000, Mon-Fri 0900-1700, Sat 0900-1200, US$2.50*, said to have been built on the ruins of the Inca House of the Virgins, depicts the history of cloistered life. Many of the heroes of Ecuador's struggle for independence are buried in the monastery of **San Agustín** ① *Chile y Guayaquil, Mon-Sat 0715-1200, 1430-1715, Sun 0715-1315*, which has beautiful cloisters on three sides where the first act of independence from Spain was signed on 10 August 1809. Here is the **Museo Miguel de Santiago** ① *Chile 924 y Guayaquil, T295 1001, www.migueldesantiago.com, Mon-Fri 0900-1230, 1400-1700, Sat 0900-1230, US$2*, with religious art.

The **Basílica** ① *on Parque García Moreno, Carchi 122 y Venezuela, northeast of Plaza de la Independencia, T228 9428, 0900-1700 daily, US$2*, is very large, has many gargoyles (some in the shape of Ecuadorean fauna), stained glass windows and fine, bas relief bronze doors (begun in 1926; some final details remain unfinished due to lack of funding). Climb above the coffee shop to the top of the clock tower for stunning views. The **Centro de Arte Contemporáneo** ① *Luis Dávila y Venezuela, San Juan, T398 8800, Tue-Sun 0900-1700, free*, in the beautifully restored Antiguo Hospital Militar, built in the early 1900s, has rotating art exhibits. To the west of the city, the **Yaku Museo del Agua** ① *El Placer Oe11-271, T251 1100, www.yakumuseoagua.gob. ec, Tue-Sun 0900-1700, US$3, take a taxi*, has great views. Its main themes are water and nature, society and heritage, also a self-guided *eco-ruta*; great for children. Another must for children, south of the colonial city, is the **Museo Interactivo de Ciencia** ① *Tababela Oe1-60 Y Latorre, Chimbacalle, T251 1100*. East of the colonial city is **Parque Itchimbía** ① *T228 2017, park open daily 0600-1800, exhibits 0900-1630*; a natural look-out over the city with walking and cycle trails and a cultural centre housed in a 19th-century "crystal palace" which came from Europe, once housed the Santa Clara market.

Modern Quito

Parque La Alameda has the oldest **astronomical observatory** ① *T257 0765, ext 101, http://oaq. epn.edu.ec, museum Tue-Sat 1000-1700, US$2, observations on clear nights, call ahead for schedule*, in South America dating to 1873 (native people had observatories long before the arrival of the Europeans). There is also a splendid monument to Simón Bolívar, lakes, and in the northwest corner a spiral lookout tower with a good view. On Fridays and Saturdays from 1900 to 2100, there are very nice sound and light shows.

A short distance north of Parque La Alameda, opposite Parque El Ejido and bound by 6 de Diciembre, Patria, 12 de Octubre and Parque El Arbolito, is the **Casa de la Cultura**, a large cultural and museum complex. If you have time to visit only one museum in Quito, it should be the **Museo Nacional** ① *entrance on Patria, T222 3258, Tue-Fri 0900-1700, Sat-Sun 1000-1600, free, guided tours in English by appointment*, housed in the north side of the Casa de la Cultura. The **Sala de Arqueología** is particularly impressive with beautiful pre-Columbian ceramics, the **Sala de Oro** has a nice collection of prehispanic gold objects, and the **Sala de Arte Colonial** with religious art from the Quito School. On the east side of the complex are the museums administered by the **Casa de la Cultura** ① *enter from Patria and go left around the building, T290 2272, ext 420, Tue-Sat 0900-1300, 1400-1645, US$2*: **Museo de Arte Moderno**, paintings and sculpture since

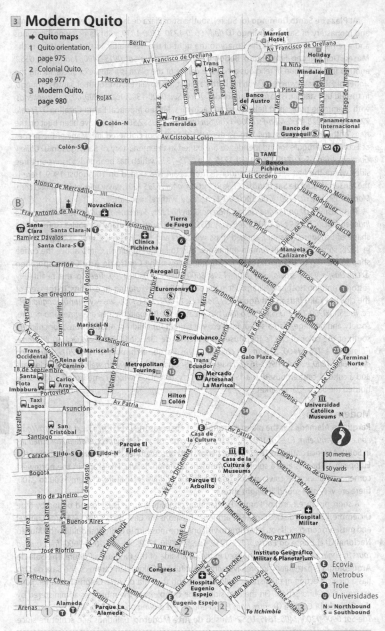

3 Modern Quito

➡ Quito maps
1 Quito orientation, page 975
2 Colonial Quito, page 977
3 Modern Quito, page 980

Marriott Hotel
Holiday Inn
Mindalae
Berlin
Av Francisco de Orellana
La Niña
La Pinta
Reina Victoria
Diego de Almagro
J Ascázubi
Rojas
Trans Loja
Veintimilla
F Pizarro
A Jervés
de Triana
R de Villalengua
E Gangotena
Santa María
Banco del Austro
La Bâbita
Trans Esmeraldas
Colón-N
Banco de Guayaquil
Panamericana internacional
Av Cristóbal Colón
Colón-S
TAME
Banco Pichincha
Luis Cordero
Alonso de Mercadillo
Baquerizo Moreno
Juan Rodríguez
Fray Antonio de Marchena
Novaclínica
Veintimilla
Tierra de Fuego
Lizardo García
Joaquín Pinto
Calama
Santa Clara
Santa Clara-N
Ramírez Dávalos
Santa Clara-S
Clínica Pichincha
Diego de Almagro
Manuela Cañizares
Mariscal Foch
Carrión
Aerogal
Amazonas
Gral Baquedano
Wilson
San Gregorio
Euromoney
Jerónimo Carrión
Vazcorp
Mariscal-N
Washington
Produbanco
Bolivia
Mariscal-S
Reina Victoria
Galo Plaza
Roca
Tamayo
Terminal Norte
Trans Occidental
Reina del Camino
Metropolitan Touring
Trans Ecuador
Robles
18 de Septiembre
Carlos Arroy
Portoviejo
Mercado Artesanal La Mariscal
Universidad Católica Museums
Taxi Lagos
Asunción
Hilton Colón
Av Patria
San Cristóbal
Santiago
Casa de la Cultura
Av Patria
Diego Ladrón de Guevara
Caracas
Ejido-S
Ejido-N
Parque El Ejido
Casa de la Cultura & Museums
Bogotá
Queseras del Medio
Río de Janeiro
Parque El Arbolito
Andrade C
Buenos Aires
Hospital Militar
José Riofrío
Juan Montalvo
Instituto Geográfico Militar & Planetarium
Feliciano Checa
Congress
Hospital Eugenio Espejo
Alameda
Parque La Alameda
Eugenio Espejo
To Itchimbía

E Ecovía
M Metrobus
T Trole
U Universidades
N = Northbound
S = Southbound

50 metres / 50 yards

980 · Ecuador Quito

1830 also rotating exhibits and **Museo de Instrumentos Musicales**, an impressive collection of musical instruments, said to be the second in importance in the world. Also on the east side are an art gallery for temporary exhibits and the **Agora**, a large open space used for concerts. On the west side are halls for temporary art exhibits, in the original old building, and the entrance to the **Teatro Nacional**, with free evening performances. On the south side are the **Teatro Demetrio Aguilera Malta** and other areas devoted to dance and theatre. Near the Casa de la Cultura, in the Catholic University's **cultural centre** ⓘ *12 de Octubre y Roca, T299 1700, ext 1710, Mon-Fri 0900-1900, Sat1000-1700*, are the **Museo Jijón y Caamaño**, with a private collection of archaeological objects, historical documents and art, very well displayed (closed for relocation in 2014); the **Museo Weilbauer**, with archaeological and photo collections; and temporary exhibits.

A focal point in La Mariscal, north of Parque El Ejido, is **Plaza del Quinde**, also called **Plaza Foch** (Reina Victoria y Foch), a popular meeting place surrounded by cafés and restaurants. At the corner of Reina Victoria and La Niña, known as **Plaza Yuyu**, is the excellent **Museo Mindalae** ⓘ *T223 0609, daily 0900-1800, US$3, 1st Sun of each month free*, which exhibits Ecuadorean crafts and places them in their historical and cultural context, as well as temporary exhibits, a good fair-trade, non-profit shop and restaurant. (For another handicrafts museum and shop, see **Folklore**, page 991.)

La Mariscal detail

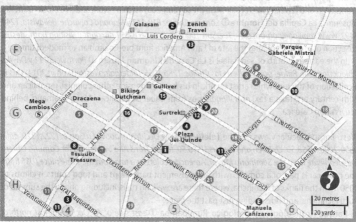

Where to stay 🛌
1 Anahi *C3*
2 Backpackers Inn *G6*
3 Café Cultura *C2*
4 Casa Helbling *C3*
5 Casa Joaquín *G4*
6 Cayman *F6*
7 City Art Hotel Silberstein *G4*
8 El Arupo *F6*
9 El Cafecito *F6*
10 Fuente de Piedra I *C3*
11 Fuente de Piedra II *H4*
12 Hostal de la Rábida *A3*
13 Hothello *C2*
14 La Cartuja *D3*
15 La Casa Sol *H6*
16 L'Auberge Inn *E2*
17 Nü House *G5*
18 Posada del Maple *G6*
19 Queen's Hostel *H5*
20 Sierra Madre *C3*
21 Travellers Inn *A3*

Restaurants 🍴
1 Baalbek *C3*
2 Chandani Tandoori *F5*
3 Chez Alain *H4*
4 Coffee Bar *G5*
5 Coffee Tree *C2*
6 El Hornero *B2*
7 Ethnic Coffee *C2*
8 Kallari *G4*
9 La Boca del Lobo *G5*
10 La Petite Mariscal *G6*
11 Las Menestras de la Almagro *H4, H5*
12 Mama Clorinda *G5*
13 Paléo *F5*
14 Sakti *C2*
15 Sushi/Siam *G5*
16 The Magic Bean *G5*
17 Yu Su *B3*

Bars & clubs 🍸
18 Bungalow Six *G5*
19 Cherusker *H5*
20 El Aguijón *G5*
21 Finn McCool's *H5*
22 No Bar *F5*
23 Seseribó *C3*
24 Turtle's Head *A3*
25 Varadero *A3*

North of La Mariscal is the large **Parque La Carolina**, a favourite recreational spot at weekends. Around it is the banking district, several shopping malls, hotels and restaurants. In the park is the **Jardín Botánico** ① *T333 2516, www.jardinbotanicoquito.com, Mon-Fri 1000-1700, Sat-Sun 0900-1700, US$3.50*, which has a good cross section of Andean flora. Also the **Vivarium** ① *T227 1820, daily 0930-1300, 1330-1730, US$3*, dedicated to protect endangered snakes, reptiles and amphibians, and the **Museo de Ciencias Naturales** ① *T244 9824, Mon-Fri 0800-1300,1345-1645, US$2*. Beyond La Carolina, on the grounds of Quito's former airport, is **Parque Bicentenario**, with sports fields and a great cycling track, right on the old tarmac.

Quito suburbs

East Built by Indian slaves in 1693, the **Santuario de Guápulo** ① *Mass Mon-Fri 1900, Sat 0700, Sun 0700-1200, 1600-1700*, perched on the edge of a ravine east of the city, is well worth seeing for its many paintings, gilded altars, stone carvings and the marvellously carved pulpit. The **Museo Fray Antonio Rodríguez** ① *Plaza de Guápulo N27-138, T256 5652, Mon-Fri 0900-1700, US$1.50*, has religious art and furniture, from the 16th to the 20th centuries. Guided tours (Spanish only) include a visit to the beautiful Santuario.

Museo Fundación Guayasamín ① *Bosmediano E15-68, Bellavista, northeast of La Mariscal, T244 6455, www.guayasamin.org, Tue-Sun 1000-1700, US$6, take a taxi*, is highly recommended. As well as the eponymous artist's works there are pre-Columbian, colonial and contemporary collections. Works of art and jewelery are for sale. Also presenting Guayasamín's work and five blocks from the museum is **La Capilla del Hombre** ① *Lorenzo Chávez E18-143 y Mariano Calvache, Bellavista, T244 8492, www.capilladelhombre.com, Tue-Sun 1000-1700, US$6 (US$1 discount if visiting both sites)*, a collection of murals depicting the fate of Latin America from pre-Columbian to modern times.

In the eastern suburb of San Rafael is **La Casa de Kingman Museo** ① *Portoviejo 111 y Dávila, 1 block from San Rafael park, Valle de los Chillos, T286 1065, undergoing restoration in 2014*. This is a collection of the renowned artist's work, in his home, alongside other colonial, republican and 20th-century art. Take a taxi or a *Vingala* bus from Isabel La Católica y Mena Caamaño, behind Universidad Católica.

West For spectacular views ride the **Teleférico** ① *Av Occidental above La Gasca, T222 1320, daily 0800-2000, US$8.50, children and seniors US$6.50, take a Trans Alfa bus bound for Comuna Obrero Independiente from the Seminario Mayor, América y Colón, or a taxi from the same place (US$1.50)*. The cable car is part of a complex with an amusement park, shops and food courts. It climbs to 4050 m on the flanks of Pichincha, where there are walking trails, including one to the summit of Rucu Pichincha, and horse riding just past the fence.

Parque Arqueológico y Ecológico Rumipamba ① *east side of Av Occidental just north of Mariana de Jesús, Wed-Sun 0830-1600, free, some English speaking guides*, is a 32-ha park on the slopes of Pichincha, where vestiges of human occupation of several pre-Inca periods, dating from 1500 BC to AD 1500, have been found. There are walking trails in some pockets of native vegetation. Northwest of Rumipamba, in the neighbourhood of San Vicente de la Florida is **Museo de Sitio La Florida** ① *C Antonio Costas y Villacrés, T380 3043, Wed-Sun 0800-1600, free, some English speaking guides, at north end of Marín-San Vicente bus line*. At this necropolis of the Quitus people, 10 17-m deep burial chambers, dating to AD 220-640, have been excavated. The elaborate dress and jewelry found in the tombs suggests most were prominent citizens.

Mitad del Mundo and around

The location of the equatorial line here (23 km north of central Quito) was determined by Charles-Marie de la Condamine and his French expedition in 1736, and agrees to within 150 m with modern GPS measurements. The monument forms the focal point of a leisure park built as a typical colonial town, with restaurants, gift shops, post office, travel agency, and has a very interesting **ethnographic museum** ① *T239 4806, 0900-1700 daily (very crowded on Sun), entry to complex US$3, children US$1.50, includes entrance to the pavilions; entry to the ethnographic museum US$3 (includes guided tour in Spanish or English)*, depicting indigenous cultures. There is also an interesting **model of old Quito**, about 10 m sq, with artificial day and night and an **insectarium**. The Museo Inti-Ñan ① *200 m north of the monument, T239 5122, www.museointinan.com.ec, 0930-1700 daily, US$4*, is eclectic, very interesting, has lots of fun activities and gives Equator certificates for visitors. Research about the equator and its importance to prehistoric cultures is carried out near Cayambe, by an organization called **Quitsa-to** ① *www.quitsato.org, daily 0800-1700, US$2*.

⊙ Quito listings

For hotel and restaurant price codes, and other relevant information, see Essentials.

● Where to stay

For websites with extensive lists of hotels see Where to stay, page 969. For lodgings near the airport, see Quito suburbs below. Near the Quitumbe bus terminal are a few simple establisments catering to short stay customers and there is one simple hostal (**$ Madrid**) opposite the Carcelén bus terminal, along busy Avenida Eloy Alfaro. Large international chain hotels are represented in the city and meet their international standards. For more information see: www.sheraton.com, www.radisson.com, www.swissotel.com, www.hilton.com, www.hojo.com (**Howard Johnson**), www.hiexpress.com (**Holiday Inn**), www.danncarltonquito.com, www.marriott.com, www.mercure.com, www.bestwestern.com, www.hotelquito.com (**Compass**).

Colonial Quito *p976, map p977*
$$$$ Casa Gangotena, Bolívar y Cuenca, T400 8000, www.casagangotena.com. Superb location by Plaza San Francisco, luxury accommodation in beautifully refurbished classic family home with rooms and suites, fine restaurant.
$$$$ Patio Andaluz, García Moreno N6-52 y Olmedo, T228 0830, www.hotelpatioandaluz.com. Beautifully reconstructed 16th-century mansion with large arches, balconies and patios, exclusive restaurant with Ecuadorean and Spanish cuisine, library, gift shop.

$$$$ Plaza Grande, García Moreno N5-16, Plaza de la Independencia, T251 0777, www.plazagrandequito.com. Exclusive top-of-the-line hotel with an exceptional location, 15 suites including a presidential suite for US$2000, jacuzzi in all rooms, climate control, 3 restaurants including La Belle Epoque, gourmet French cuisine and a wine cellar, mini-spa, 110/220V outlets
$$$ Catedral Internacional, Mejía Oe6-36 y Cuenca, T295 5438. Nicely restored colonial house with 15 carpeted rooms, heaters, small patio, popular restaurant, spa.
$$$ La Casona de La Ronda, Morales Oe1-160 y Guayaquil, T228 7538, www.lacasona delaronda.com. Tastefully refurbished colonial house in the heart of La Ronda, comfortable rooms and suite, restaurant.
$$$ Relicario del Carmen, Venezuela 1041 y Olmedo, 1228 9120, www.hotelrelicariodel carmen.com. Beautifully refurbished colonial house, good restaurant, cafeteria, good rooms and service, no smoking.
$$ Quito Cultural, Flores N4-160 y Chile, T228 8084, www.hostalquitocultural.com. Nicely refurbished colonial house, bright, rooftop terrace with nice views, patio with plants, a bit pricey.
$$ San Francisco de Quito, Sucre Oe3-17 y Guayaquil, T295 1241. Converted colonial building, breakfast served in attractive patio or underground cloisters, restaurant, suites are particularly good value, well run by owners, rooms to the street can be noisy.

$$ -$ Community Hostel, Cevallos N6-78 y Olmedo, T228 5108, communityhostel@gmail.com. Popular hostel with two double rooms and dorms for 4-6 (cheaper) comfy beds, shared bath (may have to wait for toilet in the morning), good showers, very clean and efficient, nice sitting area, breakfast available, kitchen facilities, helpful staff.

$ Huasi Continental, Flores N3-08 y Sucre, T295 7327. Colonial house, restaurant, private or shared bath, parking, good value.

In between the colonial and modern cities

$$$$ Mansión del Angel, Los Ríos N13-134 y Pasaje Gándara, T254 0293, www.mansiondelangel.com.ec. Luxurious hotel decorated with antiques in a beautifully renovated mansion, 15 ample rooms and a palacial suite, dinner available, nice gardens, lovely atmosphere.

$$-$ L'Auberge Inn, Colombia N15-200 y Yaguachi, T255 2912, www.auberge-inn-hostal.com. Nice spacious rooms, duvets, private or shared bath, excellent hot water, restaurant, spa, cooking facilities, parking, lovely garden, terrace and communal area, tour operator, helpful, good atmosphere. Highly recommended.

$$-$ Secret Garden, Antepara E4-60 y Los Ríos, T295 6704, www.secretgardenquito.com. Restored house, some rooms small and dark, lovely roof-top terrace restaurant, private or shared bath, cheaper in dorm, popular meeting and party place, can be noisy. Ecuadorean-Australian owned, also run a rustic lodge between Pasochoa and Cotopaxi, www.secretgardencotopaxi.com.

$ Chicago, Los Ríos N17-30 y Briceño, T228 1695. Popular family-run hostel, small rooms, cheaper in dorm, laundry and cooking facilities, a good economy option.

$ Guayunga, Antepara E4-27 y León, T228 3127, www.guayunga.com. Nice hostel with a few double rooms with and without bath and dorms for 3-9 (cheaper), interior patio, nice rooftop terrace with great views, parking.

Modern Quito *p979, map p980*

$$$$ Le Parc, República de El Salvador N34-349 e Irlanda, T227 6800, www.leparc.com.ec. Modern hotel with 30 executive suites, full luxury facilities and service, restaurant, spa, gym.

$$$$ Nü House, Foch E6-12 y Reina Victoria, T255 7845, www.nuhousehotels.com. Modern luxury hotel with minimalist decor, restaurant, some suites with jacuzzi, all furnishings and works of art are for sale.

$$$ Anahi, Tamayo N23-95 y Wilson, T250 8403, www.anahihotelquito.com. Very nice tastefully decorated suites, each one is different, ample bathrooms, buffet breakfast, safety box, fridge, terrace with nice views, good value.

$$$ Café Cultura, Robles E6-62, T250 4078, www.cafecultura.com. A well-established hotel with ample suites, social areas including wood-paneled library with fireplace, restaurant, attentive service. Planning to relocate.

$$$ Casa Joaquín, Pinto E4-376 y JL Mera, T222 4791, www.hotelcasajoaquin.com. Nicely refurbished hotel in the heart of La Mariscal, covered patio makes it warm, good service, a bit pricey, Belgian-run, new in 2013.

$$$ Cayman, Rodríguez E7-29 y Reina Victoria, T256 7616, www.hotelcaymanquito.com. Pleasant hotel, lovely diningroom, cafeteria, rooms a bit small, sitting room with fireplace, parking, garden, very good.

$$$ City Art Hotel Silberstein, Wilson E5-29 y JL Mera, T603 2213, www.cityartsilberstein.com. 10 comfortable rooms and suites in an attractively refurbished building, includes buffet breakfast.

$$$ Hostal de la Rábida, La Rábida 227 y Santa María, T222 2169, www.hostalrabida.com. Lovely converted home, bright comfortable rooms, good restaurant, parking, British-Italian run. Recommended.

$$$ Finlandia, Finlandia N32-129 y Suecia, T224 4288, www.hotelfinlandia.com.ec. Pleasant small hostel in residential area, buffet breakfast, restaurant, spacious rooms, sitting room with fireplace, small garden, parking, airport pick-up extra, helpful staff.

$$$ **Fuente de Piedra I & II**, Wilson E9-80 y Tamayo, T255 9775 and JL Mera N23-21 y Baquedano, T290 1332, www.ecuahotel.com. Nicely decorated modern hotels, comfortable, some rooms are small, nice sitting areas, pleasant.

$$$ **La Cartuja**, Plaza 170 y 18 de Septiembre, T252 3577, www.hotelacartuja.com. In the former British Embassy, beautifully decorated, spacious comfortable rooms, cafeteria, parking, lovely garden, very helpful and hospitable. Highly recommended.

$$$ **La Casa Sol**, Calama 127 y 6 de Diciembre, T223 0798, www.lacasasol.com. Nice small hotel with courtyard, 24-hr cafeteria, very helpful, English and French spoken, also run Casa Sol in Otavalo. Recommended.

$$$ **Sierra Madre**, Veintimilla E9-33 y Tamayo, T250 5687, www.hotelsierramadre.com. Fully renovated villa, comfortable, restaurant, nice sun roof, parking, English spoken.

$$$ **Villa Nancy**, Muros N27-94 y 12 de Octubre, T256 2483, www.hotelvillanancy.com. Quaint hotel in quiet residential area, buffet breakfast, parking, homey and comfortable, helpful multilingual staff. Recommended.

$$ **El Arupo**, Rodríguez E7-22 y Reina Victoria, T255 7543, www.hostalelarupo.com. Good hotel, cooking facilities, English and French spoken. Recommended.

$$ **Hothello**, Amazonas N20-20 y 18 de Septiembre, T256 5835. Small bright hotel, tastefully decorated rooms, heating, helpful multilingual staff.

$$ **Queen's Hostel/Hostal de la Reina**, Reina Victoria N23-70 y Wilson, T255 1844. Nice small hotel, popular among travellers and Ecuadoreans, cafeteria, cooking facilities, sitting room with fireplace.

$$-$ **Casa Helbling**, Veintimilla E8-152 y 6 de Diciembre, T222 6013, www.casahelbling.de. Very good, popular hostel, spotless, breakfast available, private or shared bath, laundry and cooking facilities, English, French and German spoken, pleasant atmosphere, good information, tours arranged, luggage storage, parking. Highly recommended.

$$-$ **Casona de Mario**, Andalucía 213 y Galicia (La Floresta), T254 4036, www.casonademario. com. Popular hostel, private or shared bath, hot water, laundry facilities, well equipped kitchen, parking, sitting room, nice garden, book exchange, long stay discounts, Argentine owner. Repeatedly recommended.

$$-$ **Posada del Maple**, Rodríguez E8-49 y 6 de Diciembre, T254 4507, www. posadadelmaple.com. Popular hostel, private or shared bath, also dorms, cooking facilities, warm atmosphere, free tea and coffee.

$$-$ **Travellers Inn**, La Pinta E4-435 y Amazonas, T255 6985, www.travellersecuador. com. In a nicely converted home, includes good breakfast, private or shared bath, parking, nice common area, bike rentals. Recommended.

$ **Backpackers Inn**, Rodríguez E7-48 y Reina Victoria, T250 9669, www.backpackersinn.net. Popular hostel, breakfast available, private or

shared bath, also dorms, laundry and cooking facilities, adequate dorms.

$ El Cafecito, Cordero E6-43 y Reina Victoria, T223 4862, www.cafecito.net. Popular with backpackers, good café including vegetarian, cheaper in dorm (US$8), 1 room with bath, relaxed atmosphere but can get noisy at night, Canadian owned.

Quito suburbs *p982*

$$$$ Hacienda Rumiloma, Obispo Díaz de La Madrid, T254 8206, www.haciendarumiloma. com. Luxurious hotel in a 40-ha hacienda on the slopes of Pichincha. Sumptuous suites with lots of attention to detail, lounges with antiques, good pricey restaurant, bar with fireplace, nice views, personalized attention from owners, ideal for someone looking for a luxurious escape not far from the city.

$$$ Hostería San Jorge, Km 4 via antigua Quito-Nono, to the west of Av Mariscal Sucre, T339 0403, www.eco-lodgesanjorge.com. Converted 18th-century hacienda on a 80-ha private reserve on the slopes of Pichincha, full board available, good pricey restaurant, heating, pool, sauna and jacuzzi, horse riding and birdwatching. Operates several nature reserves.

Quito airport

A hotel by the airport is under construction in 2014. Towns near the airport with accommodation include: Tababela, off highway E-35, 10 mins from the airport towards Quito (airport taxi US$10). Nearby, by the junction of E-35 and the Vía Interoceánica, is Pifo, also about 10 mins from the airport (taxi US$10). From Pifo you can go northwest to Quito, southwest to Sangolquí and points south or east to Papallacta and Oriente. Puembo, past Pifo on the Vía Interoceánica, is 20 mins from the airport (taxi US$15-20) and closer to Quito. Checa, north of the airport on the E-35, is about 15 mins away (taxi US$12-15). Further north on the E-35 is El Quinche, about 20 mins from the airport (taxi US$15-20). The latter 2 are convenient if going to Otavalo and points north, without going to Quito.

$$$ Garden Hotel San José, Manuel Burbano s/n, Barrio San José, Puembo, T239 0276, T1-800-180180, www.hosteriasanjose.com. 18th-century hacienda with 4 ha grounds, modern rooms, restaurant, pool, spa, airport transfers US$10 pp.

$$$ Hostal Su Merced, Julio Tobar Donoso, Puembo, T239 0251, www.sumerced.com. Nicely refurbished 18th-century hacienda house, well-appointed rooms with bathtubs, includes traditional breakfast, restaurant, sauna, gardens, airport transfers US$15 per vehicle.

$$ Hostal El Parque, 29 de Abril y 24 de Septiembre, opposite the main park in Tababela, T259 9008, patriciogarzon70@hotmail.com. Private or shared bath, gardens, meals available, airport transfers US$5 per vehicle.

$$ Hostal MarShyl, E-35 y Cuenca, El Quinche, T238 8327, www.marshyl.com. Functional rooms in 4-storey hotel, package rate including breakfast and airport transfers.

$$ Hostería San Carlos, Justo Cuello y Maldonado, Tababela, T359 9057, www. hosteriasancarlostababela.com. Hacienda style inn with ample grounds, restaurant, pool, jacuzzi, rooms with bath and dorms (US$18 pp), airport transfers US$5 per person.

$ Nevada, E-35 Km 26, outside Pifo, near the turnoff for Sangolquí, T238 0074. Simple economical rooms, noisy.

⑦ Restaurants

Eating out in Quito is excellent, varied, upmarket and increasingly cosmopolitan. There are many elegant restaurants offering Ecuadorean and international food, as well as small simple places serving set meals for US$2-50, the latter close by early evening and on Sun.

Colonial Quito *p976, map p977*

$$$ El Ventanal, Carchi y Nicaragua, west of the Basílica, in Parque San Juan, take a taxi to the parking area and a staff member will accompany you along a footpath to the restaurant, T257 2232, www.elventanal.ec, Tue-Sat 1100-1500, 1800-2200, Sun 1200-1600. International nouvelle cuisine with a varied menu including a number of seafood dishes, fantastic views over the city. 2nd branch with traditional Ecuadorean menu at Loja Oe4-09 y Venezuela, T228 5103.

$$$ Theatrum, Plaza del Teatro, 2nd floor of Teatro Sucre, T228 9669, www.theatrum.com. ec. Mon-Fri 1230-1600, 1930-2330, Sat-Sun 1900-2300. Excellent creative gourmet cuisine in the city's most important theatre, wide selection of fruit desserts which come with an explanatory card.

$$$-$$ Los Geranios, Morales Oe1-134, T295 6035. Mon-Fri 0900-0000, Sat 0900-0200, Sun 0900-1200. Upscale *comida típica*, in a nicely restored La Ronda house.

$$ Hasta la Vuelta Señor, Pasaje Arzobispal, 3rd floor. Mon-Sat 1100-2300, Sun 1100-2100. A *fonda quiteña* perched on an indoor balcony with *comida típica* and snacks, try *empanadas* (pasties) or a *seco de chivo* (goat stew).

$$ Tianguez, Plaza de San Francisco under the portico of the church. Mon-Tue 0930-1830, Wed-Sun 0930-2400. International and local dishes, good coffee, snacks, sandwiches, popular, also craft shop (closes 1830), run by Fundación Sinchi Sacha.

$$ Vista Hermosa, Mejía 453 y García Moreno. Mon-Sat 1400-2400, Sun 1200-2100. Good meals, drinks, pizza, live music on weekends, lovely terrace-top views of the colonial centre.

$ $-$ San Ignacio, García Moreno N2-60, at Museo María Agusta Urrutia, Mon-Thu 0800-1930, Fri-Sat 0800-2100, Sun 0800-1530. Good popular set lunch (US$4-4.50) with a choice of dishes and buffet salad bar; à la carte in the evening.

$ Govinda, Esmeraldas Oe3-115 y Venezuela. Mon-Sat 0800-1600. Vegetarian dishes, good value economical set meals and à la carte, also breakfast.

Cafés

Caffeto, Chile 930 y Flores. Mon-Sat 0800-1930. Variety of coffees, snacks, sandwiches, sweets.

Heladería San Agustín, Guayaquil N5-59 y Chile. Mon-Fri 1000-1630, Sat-Sun 1030-1530. Coffee, traditional homemade cakes, ices and lunch, a Quito tradition since 1858.

Modern Quito *p979, map p980*

There are many restaurants serving good economical set lunches along both Pinto and Foch, between Amazonas and Cordero.

$$$ Carmine, Catalina Aldaz N34-208 y Portugal, T333 2829, www.carmineristorante. com. Mon-Sat 1200-1530, 1900-2230, Sun 1200-1800. Creative international and Italian cuisine.

$$$ Chez Jérôme, Whymper N30-96 y Coruña, T223 4067. Mon-Fri 1230-1530, 1930-2330, Sat 1930-2330. Excellent French cuisine, traditional and modern dishes with a touch of local ingredients, good ambiance and service.

$$$ La Boca del Lobo, Calama 284 y Reina Victoria, T223 4083. Sun-Wed 1700-2330, Thu-Sat 1700-0100. Stylish bar-restaurant with eclectic food, drink, decor, and atmosphere, good food and cocktails, popular, good meeting place.

$$$ La Choza, 12 de Octubre N24-551 y Cordero, T223 0839. Mon-Fri 1200-1600, 1800-2200, Sat-Sun 1200-1700. Traditional Ecuadorean cuisine, good music and decor.

$$$ La Gloria, Valladolid N24-519 y Salazar, La Floresta, T252 7855. Daily 1200-1530, 1900-2200. Very innovative Peruvian and international cuisine, excellent food and service, same ownership as Theatrum.

$$$ La Petite Mariscal, Almagro N24 304 y Rodríguez, T09-8772 8010. Upmarket European cuisine with an Ecuadorean touch.

$$$ Sake, Paul Rivet N30-166 y Whymper, T252 4818. Mon-Sat 1230-1530, 1830-2300, Sun 12305-1600, 1830-2200. Sushi bar and other Japanese dishes, very trendy, great food and decor.

$$$ San Telmo, Portugal 440 y Casanova, T225 6946. Mon-Sat 1200-2300, Sun until 2200. Good Argentine grill, seafood, pasta, pleasant atmosphere, great service.

$$$ Zazu, Mariano Aguilera 331 y La Pradera, T254 3559, www.zazuquito.com. Mon-Fri 1230-1500, 1900-2230, Sat 1900-2230. Very elegant and exclusive dinning. International and Peruvian specialties, extensive wine list, attentive service, reservations required.

$$$-$$ La Briciola, Toledo 1255 y Salazar, T254 7138, www.labriciola.com.ec. Daily 1200-

2400. Extensive Italian menu, excellent food, homey atmosphere, very good personal service.

$$ Chez Alain, Baquedano E5-26 y JL Mera. Mon-Fri 1200-1530. Choice of good 4-course set lunches, pleasant relaxed atmosphere. Recommended.

$$ Il Risotto, Eloy Alfaro N34-447 y Portugal. Sun-Fri 1200-1500, 1800-2300. Very popular and very good italian cooking, live music Thu and Fri. A Quito tradition.

$$ Mama Clorinda, Reina Victoria N24-150 y Calama. Daily 1100-2300. Ecuadorean cuisine à la carte and set meals, filling, good value.

$$ Paléo, Cordero E5-36 y JL Mera. Mon-Sat 1200-1500 1830-2200. Authentic Swiss specialties such as rösti and raclette. Also good economical set lunch, pleasant ambiance. Recommended.

$$ Pekín, Whymper N26-42 y Orellana. Mon-Sat 1200-1500, 1900-2230, Sun 1200-2030. Excellent Chinese food, very nice atmosphere.

$$ Sushi/Siam, Calama E5-104 y JL Mera. Mon-Sat 1200-2300, Sun 1200-1600. Sushi bar, small portions, pleasant atmosphere with nice balcony, good-value happy hour 1700-1900.

$$ The Magic Bean, Foch E5-08 y JL Mera and Portugal y Los Shyris. Daily 0700-2200. Fine coffees and natural food, more than 20 varieties of pancakes, good salads, large portions, outdoor seating (also popular lodging, **$**).

$$-$ Baalbek, 6 de Diciembre N23-123 y Wilson. Daily 1200-1800. Authentic Lebanese cuisine, great food and atmosphere, friendly service.

$$-$ El Hornero, Veintimilla y Amazonas, República de El Salvador N36-149 y Naciones Unidas and on González Suárez. Daily 1200-2300. Very good wood oven pizzas, try one with choclo (fresh corn). Recommended.

$$-$ Las Palmeras, Japón N36-87 y Naciones Unidas, opposite Parque la Carolina. Daily 0800-1700. Very good *comida Esmeraldeña*, try their hearty viche soup, outdoor tables, popular, good value. Recommended.

$ Chandani Tandoori, JL Mera 1312 y Cordero. Mon-Sat 1100-2200. Good authentic Indian cuisine, economical set meals, popular, good value. Recommended.

$ Las Menestras de la Almagro, Almagro y Foch and Veintimilla y JL Mera. Mon-Sat 1200-0000, Sun 1230-2100. Breakfast, economical set lunches and a choice of *menestras* (grilled meat or chicken with stewed beans or lentils) and other local fare; large portions.

$ Sakti, Carrión E4-144 y Amazonas. Mon-Fri 0830-1800. Good quality and value vegetarian food, breakfast, set lunches and à la carte, fruit juices, great desserts (also a few rooms, **$$-$**).

$ Yu Su, Almagro y Colón, edif Torres de Almagro. Mon-Fri 1230-1600, 1800-2000, Sat 1230-1600. Very good sushi bar, pleasant, Korean run, takeaway service.

Cafés

Coffee Bar, Reina Victoria y Foch, open 24 hrs. Popular café serving a variety of snacks, pasta, burguers, coffee, Wi-Fi. Very similar are **Coffee Tree**, Amazonas y Washington, and **Coffee O**, next to Museo Mindalae, La Niña y Reina Victoria.

Ethnic Coffee, Amazonas y Roca, Edif Hotel Mercure Alameda. Mon-Fri 0930-2100. Nice café with gourmet coffee as well as a wide range of desserts, meals and drinks.

Kallari, Wilson y JL Mera, www.kallari.com. Mon-Fri 0800-1830, Sat 0900-1830. Fair trade café, breakfast, snacks, salad and sandwich set lunches, organic coffee and chocolate, crafts, run by an association of farmers and artisans from the Province of Napo working on rainforest and cultural conservation.

🎵 Bars and clubs

Note that a law forbids the sale and consumption of alcohol on Sun. In Colonial Quito, nightlife is concentrated along La Ronda.

Modern Quito *p979, map p980*
Bungalow Six, Almagro N24-139 y Calama. Tue-Sat 1900-0200, Sun 1200-1900. US-style sports bar and club. Popular place to hang out and watch a game or a film, dancing later on, varied music, cover US$5 (Thu free), ladies' night on Wed, happy hour 2000-2200.

Cherusker, Pinto y Diego de Almagro esquina. Mon-Fri 1500-2330, Fri-Sat 1500-0130. Various micro-brews and German food.

El Aguijón, Calama E7-35 y Reina Victoria. Tue-Sat 2100-0300. Bohemian bar/club, varied music, nice atmosphere, after 2200 entry US$6 with 1 free drink. Also concerts, theatre, art.

El Pobre Diablo, Isabel La Católica y Galicia E12-06, La Floresta. Mon-Sat 1230-0200. Relaxed atmosphere, friendly, jazz, sandwiches, snacks and nice meals, live music Wed, Thu and Sat, a popular place to hang out and chill.

Finn McCool's, Almagro N24-64 y Pinto. Daily 1100-0200. Irish-run pub, Irish and international food, darts, pool, table football, sports on TV, Wi-Fi, popular meeting place.

Flash Back, González Suárez N27-205 y Muros. Club, mostly English music, rock and 1980s music, older crowd, cover US$12.

La Juliana, 12 de Octubre N24-722 y Coruña. Thu-Sat 2130-0300. Popular club, live 1990s Latin music, cover US$12.

No Bar, Calama E5 01 y JL Mera. Mon-Sat 1900-0300. Good mix of Latin and Euro dance music, busy at weekends. Free drinks for women until 2200, Thu-Sat after 2200 entry US$5 with 1 free drink.

Ramón Antiguo, Mena Caamaño E12-86 e Isabel la Católica. 2100-0200. Live music Fri-Sat, cover US$5-10 depending on band. Great for salsa and other hip tropical music, popular with locals.

Seseribó, Veintimilla 325 y 12 de Octubre, T256 3598. Thu-Sat 2100-0100. Caribbean music and salsa, a must for salseros, very popular, especially Thu and Fri, cover US$8. Recommended.

Turtle's Head, La Niña 626 y JL Mera, T256 5544. Mon-Tue 1700-0300, Wed-Sat 1230-0300. Microbrews, fish and chips, curry, pool table, darts, fun atmosphere.

Varadero, Reina Victoria N26-99 y La Pinta. Mon-Thu1200-2400, Fri-Sat 1800-0300. Bar-restaurant, live Cuban music Wed-Sat, meals, snacks, good cocktails, older crowd.

✦ Entertainment

Quito *p974, maps p975, p977 and p980*
There are always many cultural events taking place in Quito, usually free of charge. **Culturas** monthly agenda is available at the tourist office and museums. Films are listed daily in El Comercio, www.elcomercio.com.

Cinema

Casa de la Cultura, Patria y 6 de Diciembre, T290 2272. Shows foreign films, often has documentaries, film festivals.

Ocho y Medio, Valladolid N24-353 y Guipuzcoa, La Floresta, T290 4720. Cinema and café, good for art films, programme available at *Libri Mundi* and elsewhere. There are several multiplexes, eg **Cinemark**, www.cinemark.com. ec and **Multicines**, www.multicines.com.ec

Dance schools

One-to-one or group lessons are offered for US$4-6 per hr.

Ritmo Tropical, Amazonas N24-155 y Calama, T255 7094, www.ritmotropicalsalsa.com, salsa, capoeira, merengue, tango and more.

Salsa y Merengue School, Foch E4-256 y Amazonas, T222 0427, also cumbia.

Music

Classical The **Orquesta Sinfónica Nacional**, T250 2815, performs at Teatro Sucre, Casa de la Música, Teatro Escuela Politécnica Nacional, in the colonial churches and regionally. **Casa de la Música**, Valderrama s/n y Mariana de Jesús, T226 7093, www.casadelamusica.ec, concerts by the Orquesta Sinfónica Nacional, Orquesta Filarmónica del Ecuador, Orquesta de Instrumentos Andinos and invited performers, Excellent acoustics.

Folk Folk shows at Palacio Arzobispal (entrance on C Venezuela, minimum donation US$1): Fri and Sat at 1930, Sun at 1200. Folk music is popular in *peñas* which come alive after 2230:

Noches de Quito, Washington E5-29 y JL Mera, T223 4855. Thu-Sat 2000-0300, show starts 2130. Varied music, entry US$6.

Ñucanchi, Av Universitaria Oe5-188 y Armero, T254 0967. Thu-Sat 2000-0300, show starts at 2130. Ecuadorean and other music, including Latin dance later in the night, entry US$8-10. **Ecuadorean folk ballet: Ballet Andino Humanizarte**, at Casa 707, Morales 707, La Ronda, T257 3486. Thu 2100, Fri-Sat 2130, US$5; plays and comedies are also often in their repertoire, restaurant on the premises. **Jacchigua**, at Teatro Demetrio Aguilera Malta, Casa de la Cultura, 6 de Diciembre y Patria, T295 2025, www.jacchiguaesecuador.com. Wed at 1930. Entertaining, colourful and touristy, reserve ahead, US$30. **Saruymanda**, at Palacio Arzobispal, Venezuela y Chile, Fri at 1930, minimum donation US$1, see above.

Theatre

Agora, open-air theatre of Casa de la Cultura, 12 de Octubre y Patria. Stages plays, concerts.
Teatro Bolívar, Espejo 847 y Guayaquil, T258 2486, www.teatrobolivar.org. Despite restoration work there are tours, presentations and festivals.
Teatro Sucre, Plaza del Teatro, Manabí N8-131 y Guayaquil, T295 1661. Beautifully restored 19th-century building, the city's main theatre.

✹ Festivals

Quito *p974, maps p975, p977 and p980*
New Year, Años Viejos: life-size puppets satirize politicians and others. At midnight on 31 Dec a will is read, the legacy of the outgoing year, and the puppets are burnt; good at Parque Bicentenario, where a competition is held, very entertaining and good humoured. On New Year's day everything is shut. **6 Jan** (may be moved to the weekend), colourful **Inocentes** procesion from Plaza de Santo Domingo at 1700. **Palm Sunday**, colourful procession from the Basílica, 0800-1000. The solemn **Good Friday** processions are most impressive. **24 May** is Independence, commemorating the Battle of Pichincha in 1822 with early morning cannon-fire and parades, everything closes. **Aug: Agosto Arte y Cultura**, organized by the municipality, cultural events, dance and music in different places throughout the city. The city's main festival, **Día de Quito**, celebrated **1-6 Dec**, commemorates the foundation of the city with elaborate parades, bullfights, performances and music in the streets, very lively. Hotels charge extra, everything except a few restaurants shuts on 6 Dec. Foremost among **Christmas** celebrations is the **Misa del Gallo**, midnight Mass. Nativity scenes can be admired in many public places. Over Christmas, Quito is crowded, hotels are full and the streets are packed with vendors and shoppers.

✪ Shopping

Quito *p974, maps p975, p977 and p980*
Shops open generally 0900-1900 on weekdays, some close at midday and most shut Sat afternoon and Sun. Shopping centres are open at weekends. In modern Quito much of the shopping is done in malls. For purchasing maps see Planning your trip, page 969.

Camping

Camping gas is available in many of the shops listed below, white gas is not.
Aventura Sport, Quicentro Shopping, 2nd level. Tents, good selection of glacier sunglasses, upmarket.
Camping Sports, Colón E6-39 y Reina Victoria. Sales only, well stocked.
Equipos Cotopaxi, 6 de Diciembre N20-36 y Patria. Ecuadorean and imported gear for sale.
Explora, Plaza Foch and several other locations in the city. Clothing and equipment for adventure sports. Also have public bulletin boards for travellers.
The Explorer, Reina Victoria N24-43 y Pinto, Plaza Foch. Sales and rentals, very helpful, will buy US or European equipment, also run tours.
Los Alpes, Reina Victoria N23-45 y Baquedano. Sales and good rental prices.
Mono Dedo, Rafael León Larrea N24-36 y Coruña, La Floresta, www.monodedo.com. Climbing equipment, part of a rock climbing club, lessons.
Tatoo, JL Mera N23-54 y Wilson and CC La Esquina in Cumbayá, www.ec.tatoo.ws. Quality backpacks and outdoor clothing.

Chocolate

Ecuador has exported its fine cacao to the most prestigious chocolatiers around the world for over 100 years. Today, quality chocolate is on offer in specialized shops and food stores.
Galería Ecuador, Reina Victoria N24-263 y García. Shop and café featuring Ecuadorean gourmet organic coffee and chocolate as well as some crafts.
República del Cacao, Reina Victoria y Pinto, Plaza Foch; Morales Oe1-166, La Ronda and at the airport. Chocolate boutique and café.

Handicrafts

Note that there are controls on export of arts and crafts. Unless they are obviously new handicrafts, you may have to get a permit from the **Instituto Nacional de Patrimonio Cultural** (Colón Oe1 93 y 10 de Agosto, T254 3527, offices also in other cities), before you can mail or take things home. Permits cost US$5 and take time.

A wide selection can be found at the following craft markets: **Mercado Artesanal La Mariscal**, Jorge Washington, between Reina Victoria and JL Mera, daily 1000-1800, interesting and worthwhile; **El Indio**, Roca E4-35 y Amazonas, daily 0900-1900; and **Centro de Artesanías CEFA**, 12 de Octubre1 738 y Madrid, Mon-Sat 0930-1830.

On weekends, crafts are sold in stalls at **Parque El Ejido** and along the Av Patria side of this park, artists sell their paintings. There are crafts and art shops along La Ronda and souvenir shops on García Moreno in front of the Palacio Presidencial

Recommended shops with an ample selection are:
Camari, Marchena 260 y Versalles. Fair Trade shop run by an artisan organization.
The Ethnic Collection, Amazonas y Roca, Edif Hotel Mercure Alameda, www.ethniccollection. com. Wide variety of clothing, leather, bags, jewellery and ceramic items. Also café next door.
Folklore, Colón E10-53 y Caamaño, also at Hotel Hilton Colón and Hotel Patio Andaluz. The store of the late Olga Fisch, who for decades encouraged craftspeople to excel.

Attractive selection of top quality, pricey handicrafts and rugs. Small museum upstairs.
Galería Latina, JL Mera 823 y Veintimilla. Fine selection of alpaca and other handicrafts from Ecuador, Peru and Bolivia, visiting artists sometimes demonstrate their work.
Hilana, 6 de Diciembre N23-10 y Veintimilla, www.hilana.com.ec. Beautiful unique 100% wool blankets, ponchos and clothing with Ecuadorean motifs, excellent quality, purchase by metre possible, reasonable prices.
Kallari, Crafts from Oriente at café, page 988.
La Bodega, JL Mera 614 y Carrión. Recommended for antiques and handicrafts.
Marcel Creations, Roca 766, entre Amazonas y 9 de Octubre. Panama hats.
Mindalae. Nice crafts at museum, page 981.
Productos Andinos, Urbina 111 y Cordero. Artisan's co-op, good selection, unusual items.
Saucisa, Amazonas N22-18 y Veintimilla, and a couple other locations in La Mariscal. Very good place to buy Andean music and instruments.

Jewellery

Argentum, JL Mera 614. Excellent selection, reasonably priced.
Ari Gallery, Bolívar Oe6-23, Plaza de San Francisco. Fine silver with ancestral motifs.
Taller Guayasamín, at the museum, see page 982. Jewellery with native designs.

⚙ What to do

Quito *p974, maps p975, p977 and p980*
Birdwatching and nature
The following are specialized operators:
Andean Birding, www.andeanbirding.com; BirdEcuador, www.birdecuador.com; **Neblina Forest**, www.neblinaforest.com; **Pluma Verde**, www.plumaverdetours.com.

City tours
Paseos Culturales. Walking tours of the colonial city led by English- or French-speaking officers of the Policía Metropolitana start at the Plaza de la Independencia tourist information office, Venezuela y Espejo, T257 2445. Departures with minimum 2 passengers at

0900, 1000, 1100, 1130 and 1400. Two choices: **Vida Cotidiana**, includes visits to museums, Tue-Sun, 2½ hrs, US$15, children and seniors US$7.70, includes museum entrance fees; and **Fachadas**, a daily historic buildings walking tour, 2 hrs, US$4. Arrange ahead for evening tours, US$5.

Quito Tour Bus, T245 8010, www.quitotourbus. com. Tours on double-decker bus, stops at 12 places of interest, it starts and ends at Naciones Unidas, south side. You can alight at a site and continue later on another bus. Hourly, 0900-1600, 3-hr ride, US$12, children and seniors US$6, ticket valid all day. Night tour US$10.

Climbing, trekking and walking

The following Quito operators specialize in this area, many also offer conventional tours and sell Galápagos and jungle tours. Note that independent guides are refused entry to national parks.

Andes Explorer, T247 2306, www.andes-explorer.com. Good-value budget mountain and jungle trips.

Campo Base, T259 9737, campobase_ec@ yahoo.com. Climbing, trekking, horse riding and cycling tours, run by Diego Jácome, very experienced climbing guide. Also operate a mountain lodge 15 km south of Sangolquí, good for acclimatization at 3050 m.

Campus Trekking, T234 0601, www. campustrekking.com.ec. Good-value trekking, climbing and cultural tours, 8- to 15-day biking trips, taylor made itineraries. Also run **Hostería Pantaví** near Ibarra, 8 languages spoken.

Climbing Tours, Amazonas N21-221 y Roca, T254 4358, www.climbingtour.com. Climbing, trekking and other adventure sports. Tours to regional attractions, also sell Galápagos and jungle tours. Well-established operator.

Compañía de Guías, Valladolid N24-70 y Madrid, T290 1551, www.companiadeguias. com. Climbing and trekking specialists. Speak English, German, French and Italian.

Cotopaxi Cara Sur, contact Eduardo Agama, T09-9800 2681, www.cotopaxicarasur.com. Offers climbing and trekking tours, runs Albergue Cara Sur on Cotopaxi.

Latitud 0°, Mallorca N24-500 y Coruña, La Floresta, T254 7921, www.latitud0.com. Climbing specialists, French spoken.

Original Ecuador, T323 7512, www. originalecuador.com. Runs 4- and 7-day highland tours which involve walking several hours daily, also custom made itineraries.

Sierra Nevada, Pinto E4-152 y Cordero, T255 3658, www.sierranevada.ec. Adventure expeditions: climbing, trekking, rafting and jungle, experienced multi-lingual guides. Also run a good hotel: www.hotelsierranevada.com.

TribuTrek, T09-9282 5404, www.tributrek.com. Hiking and trekking, cultural and budget tours.

Cycling and mountain biking

Quito has many bike paths and bike lanes on city streets, but mind the traffic and aggressive drivers. The city organizes a **ciclopaseo**, a cycle day, every Sun 0800-1400. Key avenues are closed to vehicular traffic and thousands of cyclists cross the city

in 29 km from north to south. This and other cycle events are run by **Fundación Ciclópolis**, Equinoccio N17-171 y Queseras del Medio, T322 6502, www.ciclopolis.ec; they also hire bikes, US$5.60 per *ciclopaseo* (must book Mon-Fri), US$11.20 per day on other days. Rentals also from **La Casa del Ciclista**, Eloy Alfaro 1138 y República, near the ciclopaseo route, T254 0339, US$3 per hr, US$12 per day. If staying a long time in the city, sign up with **BiciQ**, to use their bikes stationed throughout town. **Biciacción**, www.biciaccion.org, has information about routes in the city and organizes trips outside Quito.

Mountain bike tours Many operators offer bike tours, the following are specialists:
Aries, T09-9981 6603, www.ariesbikecompany. com. 1- to 3-day tours, all equipment provided.
Biking Dutchman, Foch E4-283 y Amazonas, T256 8323, after hours T09-9420 5349, www. biking-dutchman.com. 1- and several-day tours, great fun, good food, very well organized, English, German and Dutch spoken, pioneers in mountain biking in Ecuador.

Horse riding
Horse riding tours are offered on Pichincha above the gate of the *teleférico* (see page 982).
Green Horse Ranch, see page 1006.
Ride Andes, T09-9973 8221, www.rideandes. com. Private and set date tours in the highlands including stays in haciendas, also in other South American countries.

Motorbiking
Freedom Bike Rental, JL Mera N22-37 y Veintimilla, T250 4339, www.freedombikerental. com. Motorcycle rentals US$75-200 per day, scooter US$25, good equipment including mountain bikes, route planning, also tours.

Paragliding
Escuela Pichincha de Vuelo Libre, Carlos Endara Oe3-60 y Amazonas, T225 6592 (office hours), T09-9993 1206, parapent@uio.satnet. net. Offers complete courses for US$450 and tandem flights for US$65-US$105 (Pichincha).

Tour operators
Most operators also sell Galapagos cruises and jungle tours.
Advantage Travel, Gaspar de Villarroel 1100 y 6 de Diciembre, T336 0887, www. advantagecuador.com. Tours on the Manatee floating hotel on Río Napo and to Machalilla.
Andando Tours – Angermeyer Cruises, Moreno Bellido F6-167 y Amazonas, T323 8631, www.andandotours.com. Operate the Mary *Anne* sailing vessel and *Anahi* catamaran, as well as land-based highland tours, see www. humboltexpeditions.com.
Andean Travel Company, Amazonas N24-03 y Wilson, p 3, T222 8385, www.andeantc.com. Dutch-Ecuadorean-owned operator, wide range of tours including trekking and cruises on the *Galapagos Voyager*, *Galapagos Odyssey* and *Galapagos Grand Odyssey* vessels.

Creter Tours, Pinto E5-29 y JL Mera, T254 5491, www.cretertours.com.ec. Operate the *Treasure of Galapagos* catamaran and sell island-hopping tours.

Dracaena, Pinto E4-375 y Amazonas, T290 6644, www.amazondracaena.com. Runs good budget jungle tours to Cuyabeno and climbing and trekking trips, popular.

EcoAndes, Baquedano E5-27 y JL Mera, T222 0892, www.ecoandestravel.com. Classic and adventure tours, volunteer opportunities Also operate hotels in Quito.

Ecoventura, La Niña E8-52 y Almagro, T323 7393, www.ecoventura.com. Operate first-class Galápagos cruises and sell mainland tours.

Ecuador for All, T237 7430, www.ecuadorforall.com. Specialized tours to all regions of Ecuador for the mobility and hearing impaired traveller.

Ecuador Galapagos Travels (EGT), Veintimilla E10-78 y 12 de Octubre, Edif El Girón, Torre E, of 104, T254 7286, www.galapagos-cruises.ec, www.ecuadortravels.ec. Wide range of traditional and adventure tours throughout Ecuador; tailor made itineraries.

Ecuador Journeys, Manabi S1-146, Cumbaya, T603 5548, www.ecuadorianjourney.com. Adventure tours to off-the-beaten-path destinations, day tours, treks to volcanos, jungle trips, run **Emerald Forest Lodge** in Pañacocha, tours to expat hotspots.

Ecuador Treasure, Wilson E4266 y JL Mera, T09-9546 5822/09-8938 6999, www.ecuador treasure.com. Climbing, horse riding, cycling and trekking tours. Run **Chuquirahua Lodge**, near Reserva Los Ilinizas.

Enchanted Expeditions, de las Alondras N45-102 y de los Lirios, T334 0525, www.enchantedexpeditions.com. Operate the *Cachalote* and *Beluga* Galápagos vessels, sell jungle trips to Cuyabeno and highland tours. Very experienced.

Equateur Voyages Passion, in L'Auberge Inn, Gran Colombia N15-200 y Yaguachi, T322 7605, www.magical-ecuador.com. Full range

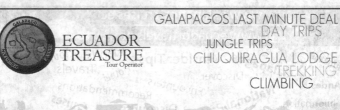

of adventure tours, run in highlands, coast and jungle. Also custom-made itineraries.

Galacruises Expeditions, 9 de Octubre N22-118 y Veintimilla, pb, T252 3324, www.islasgalapagos.travel. Galápagos cruises on the *Sea Man II* catamaran and other vessels. Also island hopping and land tours on Isabela, where they operate Casa Isabela on the Beach.

Galasam, Amazonas N24-214 y Cordero, T290 3909, www.galasam.net. Has a fleet of boats in different categories for Galápagos cruises. City tours, full range of highland tours and jungle trips to Siona Lodge in Cuyabeno.

Galextur, Portugal E10-271 y 6 de Diciembre, 1226 9626, www.galextur.com. Run land-based Galápagos tours with daily sailings. Operate **Hotel Silberstein** in Puerto Ayora and **City Art Hotel Silberstein** in Quito. Good service.

Geo Reisen, Shyris N36-46 y Suecia, T243 6081. Specializing in cultural, adventure and nature tours adapted for individuals, groups or families.

Gulliver, JL Mera N24-156 y Calama, T290 5036, www.gulliver.com.ec. Wide range of economical adventure and traditional tours. Operate **Hostería Papagayo** south of Quito.

Happy Gringo, Catalina Aldaz N34-155 y Portugal, Edif Catalina Plaza, of 207, T512 3486, www.happygringo.com. Tailor-made tours throughout Ecuador, Quito city tours, Otavalo, sell Galápagos, jungle and other destinations, good service. Recommended.

Klein Tours, Eloy Alfaro N34-151 y Catalina Aldaz, also Shyris N34-280 y Holanda, T226 7000, www.kleintours.com. Operate the *Galapagos Legend* and *Coral I* and *II* cruise ships.

Also run community based tours in Imbabura and highland tours with tailor-made itineraries, English, French and German spoken.

Latin Trails, T286 7832, www.latintrails.com, www.galapagoscatamarans.com, www.galapagosodyssey.com. Run cruises in various Galápagos vessels and offer a variety of land trips in several countries.

Metropolitan Touring, Av Las Palmeras N45-74 y Las Orquídeas, Amazonas N20-39 y 18 de Septiembre, Amazonas N40-80 y Naciones Unidas and at shopping centres, T1800-115115, T298 8200, www.metropolitantouring.com. A large organization operating in Ecuador, Peru, Chile and Argentina. Run several luxury Galápagos vessels, the **Finch Bay Hotel** in Puerto Ayora, Casa Gangotena in Quito and Mashpi Lodge west of Quito. Also adventure, cultural and gastronomy tours.

Positiv Turismo, Jorge Juan N33-38 y Atahualpa, T600 9401, www.positivturismo.com. Cultural trips, Cuyabeno, trekking and special interest tours, Swiss-run.

Pure! Ecuador, Muros N27-94 y González Suárez, T512 3358, www.pure-ecuador.com. A Dutch-local operator offering tours throughout Ecuador and the Galápagos, trips to Cotococha Amazon Lodge, and tailor-made tours.

Quasar Náutica, T244 6996, T1-800 247 2925 (USA), www.quasarnautica.com. Offer 7- to 10-day naturalist and diving Galápagos cruises on 8- to 16-berth yachts.

Rolf Wittmer Turismo/Tip Top Travel, Foch E7-81 y Almagro, T252 6938, www.rwittmer.com.

Run first class yachts: *Tip Top II, III* and *IV*.
Also tailor-made tours throughout Ecuador.
Safari Tours, Reina Victoria N25-33 y Colón,
Edif Banco de Guayaquil, p11, T255 2505, www.
safari.com.ec. Daily 0930-1830. Adventure travel,
personalized itineraries, mountain climbing,
cycling, rafting, trekking and cultural tours.
Also book Galápagos tours. Recommended.
Surtrek, Reina Victoria N24-151 y Calama, T250
0660, www.surtrek.com. Wide range of tours
in all regions, helicopter and ballon flights,
birdwatching, rafting, horse riding, mountain
biking and jungle tours, also sell domestic
flights and run **Las Cascadas Lodge**.
Tierra de Fuego, Amazonas N23-23 y
Veintimilla, T250 1418, www.ecuador
tierradefuego.com. Provide transport
and tours throughout the country,
domestic flight tickets, Galápagos bookings
and operate the *Guantanamera* yacht.

Tropic Journeys in Nature, Pasaje Sánchez
Melo Oe1-37 y Av Galo Plaza, T240 8741, www.
destinationecuador.com. Environmental and
cultural jungle tours to the **Huaorani Ecolodge**,
see page 1110; also day trips, Quito city, coast,
highlands, lodge-to-lodge mountain treks,
Amazon lodges and Galápagos land-based and
multisport tours. Community-based tourism
working with and donating a percentage of all
profits to **Conservation in Action**. Winner of
awards for responsible tourism.
Yacu Amu Experiences, Checoslovaquia
E10-137 y 6 de Diciembre, T246 1511, www.
yacuamu.com. Tailor-made adventure, nature
and cultural trips for active couples, families
and small groups.
Zenith Travel, JL Mera N24-234 y Cordero, T252
9993, www.zenithecuador.com. Good-value
Galápagos cruises as well as various land tours
in Ecuador and Peru. All gay Galápagos cruises
available. Multilingual service, knowledgeable
helpful staff, good value.

Train rides

The lovely refurbished train station, **Estación
Eloy Alfaro (Chimbacalle)**, with a railway
museum and working concert hall, is 2 km
south of the colonial city at Maldonado y
Sincholagua, T1-800-873637, T265 6142, www.
trenecuador.com, Mon-Fri 0800-1630. *Tren
Crucero*, a luxury tourist train, runs about twice
per month (but not every month) in either
direction between Quito and Durán, outside
Guayaquil, part of the route is run with a
historic steam locomotive. The complete route
takes 4 days and costs US$1270 one way, you
can also take it for segments from 1 to 3 days.
The tour includes visits to places of interest
and accommodation in luxury inns. See www.
trenecuador.com/crucero for details. Tourist
trains run Thu-Sun and holidays from Quito
to **Machachi** (at 0815, US$15-20), **El Boliche**
(0815, US$20-25) and **Latacunga** (motorized
rail car at 0800, transport only US$12 return,
you cannot purchase tickets to board at
Latacunga.). If you go only to Machachi, you will
have a long wait for the returning train, so it is a
better option to go to El Boliche. At the station

in the latter is **Restaurante Nuna**, and nearby, **Area Nacional de Recreación El Boliche**, a protected area abutting on Parque Nacional Cotopaxi. There are lovely views of Cotopaxi and Los Ilinizas. Purchase tickets in advance by phone, or at the station or **El Quinde craft shop**, Palacio Municipal, Venezuela y Espejo. You need each passenger's passport number and age to purchase tickets. Tours start with a visit to the railway museum.

Whitewater rafting
Río Blanco/Toachi tours cost US$87.
Ríos Ecuador (see Tena operators), T260 5828, www.riosecuador.com. Very professional, rafting and kayaking trips of 1-6 days, also kayak courses. Highly recommended.
Sierra Nevada (see page 992), excellent trips from 1 to 3 days, minimum 5 passengers, chief guide Edison Ramírez (fluent English/French) is certified by French Association des Rivieres des Eaux Rapides.

Mitad del Mundo *p982*
Calimatours, 30 m east of monument, Mitad del Mundo, T239 4796, www.mitaddelmundo tour.com. Tours to Pululahua and other sites in the vicinity.

⊖ Transport

Quito *p974, maps p975, p977 and p980*
Air
Details of internal air service are given under the respective destinations. Quito's new **Mariscal Sucre Airport** opened in 2013, T395 4200, www.quitoairport.aero (has information about current arrival and departures, airport services and airlines). It is in Tababela, off Highway E-35, about 30 km northeast of the city, at 2134 m above sea level. The tourist information office (arrivals level, T281 8363, open 24 hrs), will assist with hotel bookings. Set taxi rates to different zones of the city are posted by arrivals (US$24.50 to La Mariscal, US$26 to colonial Quito, US$33 to Quitumbe bus station, US$26.50 to Carcelén station); taxi rates from the city to the airport are about 12%

cheaper. Aero Servicios express bus, T604 3500, T1-800-237673, runs 24 hrs per day, between the new airport and the old airport in northern Quito (Parque Bicentenario), US$8, US$4 seniors and children. From Tababela, departures are hourly from 0000 to 0600 and every 30 mins during the day, taking a taxi from the old airport to your hotel is recommended; from Quito, departures are hourly from 1800 to 0300 and every 30 mins the rest of the day. HATS, T323 0113 or T09-8336 1610, shuttle bus to/ from hotels in La Mariscal, US$16 pp, minimum 4 passengers. Regional buses with limited stops, run every 15 mins, 0600-2145, between the airport and Terminal Quitumbe in the south and Terminal Río Coca in the north, US$2. Van services are good value for groups (US$35-40, minimum 3 passengers, US$5 per additional person), but require advanced arrangements: **Trans-Rabbit**, T290 2690, www.transrabbit. com.ec, or **Achupallas Tour**, T255 1614.

Note There is only one access road from the city to the airport and traffic is congested. It may take as much as 2 hrs to reach the airport, allow enough time. Additional access roads are under construction in 2014, one from Calderón in the north of Quito is due to be completed by the end of the year. If going to the airport from other cities, take a bus that bypasses Quito along highway E-35 (available from Baños, Ambato and Ibarra), get off at the airport roundabout and take the regional bus 4½ km from there. If coming from the east (Papallacta, Baeza or Oriente), go as far as Pifo and transfer to the regional bus there.

Bus
Local Quito has 4 parallel mass transit lines running from north to south on exclusive lanes, covering almost the length of the city. There are several transfer stations where you can switch from one line to another without cost. Feeder bus lines (*alimentadores*) go from the terminals to outer suburbs. Within the city the fare is US$0.25; the combined fare to some suburbs is US$0.40. Public transit is not designed for carrying heavy luggage and is often crowded.
Trole (T266 5016, Mon-Fri 0500-2345,

weekends and holidays 0600-2145, plus hourly overnight service with limited stops) is a system of trolley buses which runs along Av 10 de Agosto in the north of the city, C Guayaquil (southbound) and C Flores (northbound) in colonial Quito, and mainly along Av Maldonado and Av Teniente Ortiz in the south. The northern terminus is north of 'La Y', the junction of 10 de Agosto, Av América and Av de la Prensa; south of the colonial city are important transfer stations at El Recreo, known as Terminal Sur, and Morán Valverde; the southern terminus is at the Quitumbe bus station. Trolleys do not necessarily run the full length of the line, the destination is marked in front of the vehicle. Trolleys have a special entrance for wheelchairs. **Ecovía** (T243 0726, Mon-Sat 0500-2200, Sun and holidays 0600-2200), articulated buses, runs along Av 6 de Diciembre from Estación Río Coca, at C Río Coca east of 6 de Diciembre, in the north, to La Marín transfer station and on to Cumandá, east of colonial Quito. **Metrobus** (T346 5149, Mon-Fri 0530-2230, weekends and holidays 0600-2100) also runs articulated buses along Av de la Prensa and Av América from Terminal La Ofelia in the north to La Marín in the south. **Universidades** articulated buses run from 12 de Octubre y Veintimilla to Quitumbe bus terminal. There are also 2 types of **city buses**: *Selectivos* are red, and *Bus Tipo* are royal blue, both cost US$0.25. Along Av Universitaria and at the El Tejar and San Roque tunnels on Av Mariscal Sucre (Occidental) are interchanges where you can change buses without paying a second fare. Many bus lines go through La Marín and El Playón Ecovía/ Metrobus stations. Extra caution is advised here: pickpockets abound and it is best avoided at night. For **Quito Tour Bus**, see page 992.

Short distance Outer suburbs are served by green *Interparroquial* buses. Those running east to the valleys of Cumbayá, Tumbaco and the airport leave from the Estación Río Coca (see Ecovía above). Buses southeast to Valle de los Chillos leave from El Playón Ecovía/Metrobus station and from Isabel la Católica y Mena Caamaño, behind Universidad Católica. Buses going north (ie Calderón, Mitad del Mundo)

leave from La Ofelia Metrobus station. Regional destinations to the north (ie Cayambe) and northwest (ie Mindo) leave from a regional station adjacent to La Ofelía Metrobus station. Buses west to Nono from the Plaza de Cotocollao, to Lloa from C Angamarca in Mena 2 neighbourhood. Buses south to Machachi from El Playón, La Villaflora and Quitumbe. Buses to Baeza and El Chaco leave from Don Bosco E1-136 y Av Pichincha in La Marín.

Long distance Quito has 2 main bus terminals: **Terminal Quitumbe** in the southwest of the city, T398 8200, serves destinations south, the coast via Santo Domingo, Oriente and Tulcán (in the north). It is served by the Trole (line 4: El Ejido-Quitumbe, best taken at El Ejido) and the Universidades articulated buses, however it is advisable to take a taxi, about US$6, 30-45 mins to the colonial city, US$8-10, 45 mins-1 hr to La Mariscal. Arrivals and tourist information are on the ground floor. Ticket counters (destinations grouped and colour coded by region), and departures in the upper level. Left luggage (US$0.90 per day) and food stalls are at the adjoining shopping area. The terminal is large, allow extra time to reach your bus. Terminal use fee US$0.20. Watch your belongings at all times. On holiday weekends it is advisable to reserve the day before. The smaller **Terminal Carcelén**, Av Eloy Alfaro, where it meets the Panamericana Norte, T396 1600, serves destinations to the north (including Otavalo) and the coast via the Calacalí–La Independencia road. It is served by feeder bus lines from the northern terminals of the Trole, Ecovía and Metrobus; a taxi costs about US$5, 30-45 mins to La Mariscal, US$7, 45 mins-1 hr to colonial Quito. Ticket counters are organized by destination. See under destinations for fares and schedules; these are also listed in www.ecuadorbuses.com, where for US$3 you can also purchase tickets online for buses departing Quito. A convenient way to travel between Quitumbe and Carcelén is to take a bus bound for Tulcán, **Trans Vencedores** or **Unión del Carchi** (Booth 12), every 30 mins during the day, hourly at night, US$1, 1 hr; from Carcelén to Quitumbe, wait for a through bus arriving from the north; taxi between terminals, US$15.

Several companies run better quality coaches on the longer routes and some have terminals in modern Quito (departures at night), these include: **Flota Imbabura**, Larrea 1211 y Portoviejo, T223 6940, for **Cuenca** and **Guayaquil**; Transportes Ecuador, JL Mera N21-44 y Washington, T250 3842, hourly to **Guayaquil**; Transportes Esmeraldas, Santa María 870 y Amazonas, T250 9517, for **Esmeraldas**, **Atacames**, **Coca**, **Lago Agrio**, **Manta** and **Huaquillas**. Reina del Camino, Larrea y 18 de Septiembre, T321 6633, for **Bahía**, **Puerto López** and **Manta**; Carlos Aray Larrea y Portoviejo, T256 4406, for **Manta** and **Puerto López**; Transportes Occidentales, 18 de Septiembre y Versalles, for **Esmeraldas**, **Atacames**, **Salinas** and **Lago Agrio**; Transportes Loja, Orellana y Jerves, T222 4306, for **Loja** and **Lago Agrio**; San Cristóbal, Larrea y Asunción, T290 0457, for **Tulcán** and **Guayaquil**; in the same office is Transportes Chimborazo, for Riobamba. Transportes Baños, for **Baños** and Oriente destinations, has a ticket counter at Santa María y JL Mera, but buses leave from Quitumbe Panamericana Internacional, Colón E7-31 y Reina Victoria, T255 7133, ext 126 for national routes, ext 125 for international, for **Huaquillas**, **Machala**, **Cuenca**, **Loja**, **Manta**, **Guayaquil** and **Esmeraldas**. Also run international service to **Lima**, daily, changing buses in Aguas Verdes and Túmbes, US$85, 38 hrs. Ormeño Internacional, from Perú, Shyris N35-52 y Portugal, of 3B, T245 6632, Tue and Thu to **Lima**, US$90, Sat to **Bogotá**, US$90, Tue to **Caracas**, US$130. Rutas de América, Selva Alegre Oe1-72 y 10 de Agosto, T250 3611, www.rutasenbus.com, to **Lima**, 1 weekly, US$65; to **Caracas**, 2 weekly, US$135, 2½ days, does not go into Colombian cities, but will let passengers off by the roadside (eg Popayán, Palmira for Cali or Ibagué for Bogotá, all US$55). The route to **Peru** via Loja and Macará takes much longer than the Huaquillas route, but is more relaxed. Don't buy Peruvian (or any other country's) bus tickets here, they're much cheaper outside Ecuador.

Shared taxis and vans offer door-to-door service and avoid the hassle of reaching Quito's bus terminals. Reserve at least 2 days ahead. Taxis Lagos to **Otavalo** and **Ibarra**, see page 1015. Servicio Express, T03-242 6828 (Ambato) or T09-9924 2795, to **Ambato** (US$12) or **Latacunga** (US$10), 9 daily (fewer on Sun). Montecarlo Trans Vip, T03-294 3054 (Riobamba) or T09-8411 4114, to **Riobamba**, US$15. Autovip, T600 2582, to **Puyo**, US$30; to **Baños**, US$20. Río Arriba/Atenas Washington y Páez, T252 1336, to **Cuenca**, daily at 2300, US$25, 6 hrs. Sudamericana Taxis, to **Santo Domingo**, see page 1098. Esmetur Express T06-271 5498 (Esmeraldas) or T09-9226 0857, to **Esmeraldas**, US$25.

Taxi

Taxis are a cheap (from US$1) and efficient way to get around the city. Authorized taxis display a unit number on the windshield, the driver's photograph and have a working meter. They are safer and cheaper than unauthorized taxis. Expect to pay US$1-2 more at night when meter may not be used. At night it is safer to use a radio taxi, these have black markings in front, ie: Taxi Americano, T222 2333; Taxi Amigo, T222 2222; City Taxi, T263 3333. Make sure they give you the taxi number so that you get the correct vehicle, some radio taxis are unmarked. Taxis from the near suburbs have a red markings and those from the outer suburbs green. Note the registration and the licence plate numbers if you feel you have been seriously overcharged or mistreated. You may then complain to the transit police or tourist office. To hire a taxi by the hour costs from US$8 in the city, more out of town. For trips outside Quito, agree the fare beforehand: US$70-85 a day. Outside luxury hotels cooperative taxi drivers have a list of agreed excursion prices and most drivers are knowledgeable.

Train

There is no regular passenger service. For tourist rides, see Train rides, page 996.

Language schools in Quito

Quito is one of the most important centres for Spanish language study in Latin America with over 80 schools operating. There is a great variety to choose from. Identify your budget and goals for the course: rigorous grammatical and technical training, fluent conversation skills, getting to know Ecuadoreans or just enough basic Spanish to get you through your trip.

Visit a few places to get a feel for what they charge and offer. Prices vary greatly, from US$5 to US$22 per hour. There is also tremendous variation in teacher qualifications, infrastructure and resource materials. Schools usually offer courses of four or seven hours tuition per day. Many readers suggest that four is enough. Some schools offer packages which combine teaching in the morning and touring in the afternoon, others combine teaching with travel to various attractions throughout the country. A great deal of emphasis has traditionally been placed on one-to-one teaching, but remember that a well-structured small classroom setting is also recommended.

The quality of homestays likewise varies, the cost including half board runs from US$16 to US$20 per day (more for full board). Try to book just one week at first to see how a place suits you. For language courses as well as homestays, deal directly with the people who will provide services to you, avoid intermediaries and always get a detailed receipt.

If you are short on time then it can be a good idea to make your arrangements from home, either directly with one of the schools or through an agency, who can offer you a wide variety of options. If you have more time and less money, then it may be more economical to organize your own studies after you arrive. **South American Explorers** provides a list (free to members) of recommended schools and these may give club members discounts.

We list schools for which we have received positive recommendations each year. This does not imply that schools not mentioned are not recommended.

Mitad del Mundo and around *p982*
Bus From Quito take a 'Mitad del Mundo' feeder bus from La Ofelia station on the Metrobus (transfer ticket US$0.15), or from the corner of Bolivia y Av América (US$0.40). Some buses continue to the turnoff for Pululahua or Calacalí beyond. An excursion by **taxi** to Mitad del Mundo (with 1 hr wait) is US$25, or US$30 to include Pululahua. Just a ride from La Mariscal costs about US$15.

❶ Directory

Quito *p974, maps p975, p977 and p980*
Banks The highest concentration of banks and ATMs is in modern Quito. Many are along Av Amazonas, both in La Mariscal and La Carolina, and along Naciones Unidas between Amazonas and Los Shyris. In colonial Quito there are banks near the main plazas. To change TCs, **Banco del Pacífico**, Naciones Unidas E7-95 y Shyris and Amazonas y Veintimilla and **Casas de cambio**: All open Mon-Fri 0900-1730, Sat 0900-1245. **Euromoney**, Amazonas N21-229 y Roca, T252 6907. Change 10 currencies, 2% commission for Amex US$ TCs; **Mega Cambios**, Amazonas N24-01 y Wilson, T255 5849. 3% commission for US$ TCs, change cash euros, sterling, Canadian dollars; **Vazcorp**, Amazonas N21-169 y Roca, T252 9212. Change 11 currencies, 1.8% comission for US$ TCs, good rates, recommended. **Car hire** All the main international car rental companies are at the airport. For rental procedures see Driving in Ecuador, page 968. A local company is: **Simon Car Rental**, Los Shyris 2930 e Isla Floreana, T243 1019, www.simoncarrental.com, good rates and service. **Achupallas Tours**, T255 1614, and **Trans-Rabbit**, T290 2690, www.transrabbit.com.

ec, rent vans for 8-14 passengers, with driver, for trips in Quito and out of town. **Embassies and consulates** For all foreign embassies and consulates in Ecuador, see http://embassy. goabroad.com. **Immigration** Dirección Nacional de Migración, Amazonas 171 y República, T227 2835, Mon-Fri 0800-1200 and 1500-1800. **Language schools** Many schools offer study-travel programs. The following have received favourable reports: Academia de Español Quito, T255 3647. Amazonas, www.eduamazonas.com. Andean Global Studies, www.andeanglobalstudies. org. Beraca, www.beraca.net. Bipo & Toni's, www.bipo.net. Cristóbal Colón, www. colonspanishschool.com. Equinox, www. ecuadorspanish.com. Instituto Superior, www.instituto-superior.net. La Lengua, www. la-lengua.com. Mitad del Mundo, www.

mitadmundo.com.ec. Sintaxis, www.sintaxis. net. South American, www.southamerican.edu. ec. Universidad Católica, T299 1700 ext 1388, mejaramillo@puce.edu.ec. Vida Verde, www. vidaverde.com. **Medical services** For all emergencies T911.**Hospitals:** Metropolitano, Mariana de Jesús y Occidental, T226 1520, ambulance T226 5020. Very professional and recommended, but expensive. Clínica Pichincha, Veintimilla E3-30 y Páez, T256 2296, ambulance T250 1565. Also very good, and expensive. Voz Andes, Villalengua Oe 2-37 y Av 10 de Agosto, T226 2142, quick and efficient, fee based on ability to pay, a good place to get vaccines. **Police** 1101. Servicio de Seguridad Turística, Reina Victoria y Roca, T254 3983. Report robberies here or at Fiscalía de Turismo (Public Prosecutors Office), at Ministerio de Turismo, see Tourist information, page 973.

Around Quito

Papallacta → *Phone code: 06. Colour map 11, A4. Population: 950. Altitude: 3200 m.*
At the **Termas de Papallacta** ① *64 km east from Quito, 2 km from the town of Papallacta, 0600-2100, T02-250 4787 (Quito), www.papallacta.com.ec,* the best developed hot springs in the country, are 10 thermal pools, three large enough for swimming, and four cold plunge pools. There are two public complexes of springs: the regular **pools** ① *US$8,* and the **spa centre** ① *US$21 (massage and other special treatments extra).* There are additional pools at the Termas' hotel and cabins (see Where to stay, page 1004) for the exclusive use of their guests. The complex is tastefully done and recommended. In addition to the Termas there are nice municipal pools in the village of Papallacta (US$3) and several more economical places to stay (some with pools) on the road to the Termas and in the village. The view, on a clear day, of Antisana while enjoying the thermal waters is superb. Along the highway to Quito, are several additional thermal pools. Note that Quito airport is between Quito and Papallacta.

There are several walking paths in the **Rancho del Cañón private reserve** ① *behind the Termas, US$2 for use of a short trail, to go on longer walks you are required to take a guide for US$8-15 pp.* To the north of this private reserve is **Reserva Cayambe-Coca** ① *T02-211 0370.* A scenic road starts by the Termas information centre, crosses both reserves and leads in 45 km to Oyacachi. A permit from Cayambe-Coca headquartes is required to travel this road even on foot. It is a lovely 2-day walk, there is a ranger's station and camping area 1½ hours from Papallacta. Reserva Cayambe-Coca is also accessed from La Virgen, the pass on the road to Quito, where there is a ranger's station. **Ríos Ecuador,** see Tena operators, offer guiding service here.

Refugio de Vida Silvestre Pasochoa
① *45 mins southeast of Quito by car, very busy at weekends; park office at El Ejido de Amaguaña, T09-9894 5704, Quito office T256 3429, ext 21302.*
This natural park is set in humid Andean forest between 2700 m and 4200 m. The reserve has more than 120 species of birds (unfortunately some of the fauna has been frightened away by

the noise of the visitors) and 50 species of trees. There are walks of 30 minutes to eight hours. There are picnic and camping areas. Take a good sleeping bag, food and water.

Western slopes of Pichincha → *Phone code: 02. Altitude: 1200-2800 m.*

Despite their proximity to the capital (two hours from Quito), the western slopes of **Pichincha** and its surroundings are surprisingly wild, with fine opportunities for walking and birdwatching. This scenic area has lovely cloud forests and many nature reserves. The main tourist town in this area is Mindo. To the west of Mindo is a warm subtropical area of clear rivers and waterfalls, with a number of reserves, resorts and lodges.

Paseo del Quinde Two roads go from Quito over the western Cordillera before dropping into the northwestern lowlands. The old route via Nono (the only town of any size along this route) and Tandayapa, is dubbed the Paseo del Quinde (Route of the Hummingbird) or **Ecoruta**, see www. ecorutadelquinde.org. It begins towards the northern end of Avenida Mariscal Sucre (Occidental), Quito's western ring road, at the intersection with Calle Machala. With increased awareness of the need to conserve the cloud forests of the northwest slopes of Pichincha and of their potential for tourism, the number of reserves here is steadily growing. Keen birdwatchers are no longer the only visitors, and the region has much to offer all nature lovers. Infrastructure at reserves varies considerably. Some have comfortable upmarket lodges offering accommodation, meals, guides and transport. Others may require taking your own camping gear, food, and obtaining a permit. There are too many reserves and lodges to mention here; see *Footprint Ecuador* for more details.

At Km 62 on the Paseo del Quinde road is **Bellavista Cloud Forest Reserve**, a 700-ha private reserve with excellent birdwatching and botany in the cloud forest, There are 20 km of trails ranging from wheelchair access to the slippery/suicidal. See **Hostería Bellavista** below.

The new route From the Mitad del Mundo monument the road goes past **Calacalí**, whose plaza has an older monument to the Mitad del Mundo. Beyond Calacalí is a toll (US$0.80 for cars) where a road turns south to Nono and north to Yunguilla. Another road at Km 52 goes to Tandayapa and Bellavista. The main paved road, with heavy traffic at weekends, continues to Nanegalito (Km 56), Miraflores (Km 62), the turn-offs to the old road and to Mindo (Km 79), San Miguel de los Bancos, Pedro Vicente Maldonado and Puerto Quito, before joining the Santo Domingo-Esmeraldas road at La Independencia.

Pululahua ① *park office by the rim lookout, T239 6543, 0800-1700*, is a geobotanical reserve in an inhabited, farmed volcanic caldera. A few kilometres beyond the Mitad del Mundo, off the road to Calacalí, Mirador Ventanillas, a lookout on the rim gives a great view, but go in the morning, as the cloud usually descends around 1300. You can go down to the reserve and experience the rich vegetation and warm micro-climate inside. From the mirador: walk down 30 minutes to the agricultural zone then turn left. There are picnic and camping areas. A longer road allows you to drive into the crater via Moraspungo. To walk out this way, starting at the mirador, continue past the village in the crater, turn left and follow the unimproved road up to the rim and back to the main road, a 15-20 km round trip.

In **Nanegalito**, the transport hub for this area, is a **tourist information office** ① *T02-211 6222, Mon-Sun 0900-1700*. Just past the centre is the turn-off to Nanegal and the cloud forest in the 18,500-ha **Maquipucuna Biological Reserve** ① *www.maqui.org, knowledgeable guides: US$25 (Spanish), US$100 (English) per day for a group of 9*, which contains a tremendous diversity of flora and fauna, including Spectacled Bear, which can be seen when the aguacatillo trees are in fruit (around January) and about 350 species of birds. The reserve has 40 km of trails (US$10 per person) and a lodge (see below).

Next to Maquipucuna is **Santa Lucía** ⓘ *T02-215 7242, www.santaluciaecuador.com*. Access to this reserve is 30 minutes by car from Nanegal and a walk from there. Day tours combining Pululahua, Yunguilla (a community project near Calacalí) and Santa Lucía are available. Bosque Nublado Santa Lucía is a community-based conservation and eco-tourism project protecting a beautiful 650-ha tract of cloud forest. The area is very rich in birds (there is a Cock-of-the-rock lek) and other wildlife. There are waterfalls and walking trails and a lodge (see below).

At Armenia (Km 60), a few km beyond Nanegalito, a road heads northwest through Santa Clara, with a handicrafts market on Sunday, to the village and archaeological site of **Tulipe** (14 km; 1450 m). The site consists of several man-made "pools" linked by water channels. A path leads beside the Río Tulipe in about 15 minutes to a circular pool amid trees. The site **museum** ⓘ *T02-285 0635, www.museodesitiotulipe.com, US$3, Wed-Sun 0900-1600, guided tours (arrange ahead for English)*, has exhibits in Spanish on the Yumbos culture and the colonos (contemporary settlers). There is also an orchid garden. For reserves and tours in the area, see www.tulipecloudforest.org and www.cloudforestecuador.com.

The Yumbos were traders who linked the Quitus with coastal and jungle peoples between AD 800-1600. Their trails are called *culuncos*, 1 m wide and 3 m deep, covered in vegetation for coolness. Several treks in the area follow them. Also to be seen are *tolas*, raised earth platforms; there are some 1500 around Tulipe. **Turismo Comunitario Las Tolas** ⓘ *6 km from Tulipe, T02-286 9488*, offers lodging, food, craft workshops and guides to *tolas* and *culuncos*.

To the northwest of Tulipe are **Gualea** and **Pacto**, beyond which is **$$$$ Mashpi Lodge** and **Reserve**, www.mashpilodge.com. Back along the main road, by Miraflores, is **Tucanopy** (turn north at Km 63.5, closed Wednesday), www.tucanopy.com, a reserve with lodging, trails, canopy zip lines and conservation volunteer opportunities. At Km 79 is the turnoff for Mindo.

Mindo → *Phone code: 02. Colour map 11, A3. Population: 4300. Altitude: 1250 m.*

Mindo, a small town surrounded by dairy farms and lush cloud forest climbing the western slopes of Pichincha, is the main access for the 19,500-ha Bosque Protector Mindo-Nambillo. The town gets very crowded with Quiteños at weekends and holidays. The reserve, which ranges in altitude from 1400 m to 4780 m, features beautiful flora (many orchids and bromeliads), fauna (butterflies, birds including the Cock-of-the-rock, Golden-headed Quetzal and Toucan-barbet) and spectacular cloud forest and waterfalls. The region's rich diversity is threatened by proposed mining in the area. **Amigos de la Naturaleza de Mindo** ⓘ *1½ blocks from the Parque Central, T217 0115, US$4 for guided walk along a trail with bird feeders, guides for groups also available*, runs the **Centro de Educación Ambiental (CEA)**, 4 km from town, within the 17 ha buffer zone, capacity for 25-30 people. Lodging: **$** per person; full board including excursion: **$$** per person; use of kitchen: US$1.50. Arrangements have to be made in advance. During the rainy season, access to the reserve can be rough. Mindo also has orchid gardens and butterfly farms. Activities include visits to waterfalls, with rappelling in the La Isla waterfalls, 'canopy' zip lines, and 'tubing' regattas in the rivers. **Note** There is only one ATM, take cash.

West of Mindo → *Phone code: 02. Colour map 11, A3.*

The road continues west beyond the turn-off to Mindo, descending to the subtropical zone north of Santo Domingo de los Tsáchilas. It goes via San Miguel de los Bancos, Pedro Vicente (PV) Maldonado and Puerto Quito (on the lovely Río Caoni) to La Independencia on the Santo Domingo-Esmeraldas road. From San Miguel de Los Bancos a paved side-road also goes to Santo Domingo. The entire area is good for birdwatching, swimming in rivers and natural pools, walking, kayaking, or simply relaxing in pleasant natural surroundings. There are many reserves, resorts, lodgings and places to visit along the route, of particular interest to birdwatchers. There are tours from Quito. See Where to stay, below, for resorts.

For hotel and restaurant price codes, and other relevant information, see Essentials.

● Where to stay

Papallacta *p1001*

$$$$-$$$ Hotel Termas Papallacta, at the Termas complex, T289 5060. Comfortable heated rooms and suites, good expensive restaurant, thermal pools set in a lovely garden, nice lounge with fireplace, some rooms with private jacuzzi, also cabins for up to 6, transport from Quito extra. Guests have acces to all areas in the complex and get discounts at the spa. For weekends and holidays book 1 month in advance. Recommended.

$$ Antizana, on road to the Termas, a short walk from the complex, T289 5016. Simple rooms, private or shared bath, restaurant, pools, a good option.

$$ Coturpa, next to the Municipal baths in Papallacta town, T289 5040. Small fuctional rooms, breakfast available.

$$ La Choza de Don Wilson, at intersection of old unpaved road and road to Termas, T289 5027. Rooms with nice views of the valley, heaters, good popular restaurant, pools, massage, spa, attentive.

East of Papallacta

$$$$ Guango Lodge, near Cuyuja, 9 km east of Papallacta, T02-289 1880 (Quito),

www.guangolodge.com. In a 350 ha temperate forest reserve along the Río Papallacta. Includes 3 good meals, nice facilities, excellent birdwatching. Day visits US$5. Reserve ahead.

Western slopes of Pichincha *p1002*
Paseo del Quinde

$$$$ Tandayapa Bird Lodge, T244 7520 (Quito), www.tandayapa.com. Designed and owned by birders. Full board, comfortable rooms, some have a canopy platform for observation, large common area; packages including guide and transport from Quito.

$$$$-$$$ Bellavista Cloud Forest, T211 6232 (Bellavista), in Quito at Jorge Washington E7-25 y 6 de Diciembre, T290 1536, www.bellavistacloudforest.com. A dramatic lodge perched in beautiful cloud forest, with unique geodesic dome, bamboo house and half-timbered house, suites. Cheaper in dorm with shared bath. Full board, hot showers, birdwatching, botany and waterfalls. Camping US$7 pp. Package tours with guide and transport arranged from Quito. Best booked in advance. Recommended.

$$$ San Jorge, T339 0403, www.eco-lodge sanjorge.com. A series of reserves with lodges in bird-rich areas. One is 4 km from Quito (see Hostería San Jorge, page 986), one in Tandayapa at 1500 m and another in Milpe, off the paved road, at 900 m.

The new route

$$$$ Santa Lucía, T02-215 7242, www.santaluciaecuador.com. The lodge with panoramic views is a 1½-hr walk from the access to the reserve. Price includes full board with good food and guiding. There are cabins with private bath, rooms with shared composting toilets and hot showers and dorms ($ pp including food but not guiding).

$$$$-$$$ Maquipucuna Lodge, T02-250 7200, 09-9237 1945, www.maqui.org. Comfortable rustic lodge, includes full board with good meals using ingredients from own organic garden (vegetarian and vegan available). Rooms range from shared to rooms with bath, hot water, electricity. Campsite is 20 mins' walk from main lodge, under US$6 pp (food extra), cooking lessons, chocolate massages.

$$$ Hostería Sumak Pakari, Tulipe, 200 m from the village, T286 4716, www.hosteria sumakpakari.com. Cabins with suites with jacuzzi and rooms set in gardens, includes breakfast and museum fee, terraces with hammocks, pools, restaurant, sports fields.

$ Posada del Yumbo, Tulipe, T286 0121. Up a side street off the main road. Cabins in large property with river view, also simple rooms, electric shower, pool, horse riding. Also run Restaurant **La Aldea**, by the archaeologic site.

Mindo *p1003*

$$$$ Casa Divina, 1.2 km on the road to Cascada de Nambillo, T09-9172 5874, www.mindocasadivina.com. Comfortable 2-storey cabins, lovely location surrounded by 2.7 forested ha, includes breakfast and dinner, bathtubs, guiding extra, US-Ecuadorean run.

$$$$ El Monte, 2 km form town on road to CEA, then opposite Mariposas de Mindo, cross river on tarabita (rustic cable car), T217 0102, T09-9308 4675, www.ecuadorcloudforest. com. Beautifully-constructed lodge in 44-ha property, newer cabins are spacious and very comfortable, includes 3 meals, some (but not all) excursions with a *guía nativo* and tubing, other adventure sports and horse riding are extra, no electricity, reserve in advance. Recommended.

$$$ Séptimo Paraíso, 2 km from Calacalí-La Independencia road along Mindo access road, then 500 m right on a small side road, well signed, T09-9368 4417, www.septimoparaiso. com. All wood lodge in a 420-ha reserve, comfortable, expensive restaurant, pool and jaccuzi, parking, lovely grounds, great birdwatching, walking trails open to non-guests for US$10. Recommended.

$$ Caskaffesu, Sixto Durán Ballén (the street leading to the stadium) y Av Quito, T217 0100, caskaffesu@yahoo.com. Pleasant hostal with nice courtyard, restaurant serves international food, US-Ecuadorean run.

$$ El Descanso, 300 m from main street, take 1st right after bridge, T217 0213. Nice house with comfortable rooms, cheaper in loft with shared bath, ample parking. Recommended.

$$ Hacienda San Vicente (Yellow House), 500 m south of the plaza, T217 0124, Quito T02-223 6275. Family-run lodge set in 200 ha of very rich forest, includes excellent breakfast, nice rooms, good walking trails open to non-guests for US$5, reservations required, good value. Highly recommended for nature lovers.

$$-$ Jardín de los Pájaros, 2 blocks from the main street, 1st right after bridge, T217 0159. Family-run hostel, includes good breakfast, small pool, parking, large covered terrace, good value. Recommended.

$ Rubby, by the stadium, T09-9193 1853, rubbyhostal@yahoo.com. Well maintained hostal with homey feel, includes breakfast, other meals on request, private or shared bath, electric shower, nice balcony with hammocks, good value. English spoken, owner Marcelo Arias is a birding guide.

$ Sandy, 1 block from the main street, 1st right after bridge. Family run hostel in a wooden house, hot water, nice, good value.

West of Mindo *p1003*

$$$$ Arashá, 4 km west of PV Maldonado, Km 121, T02-390 0007, Quito T02-244 9881 for reservations, www.arasharesort.com. Well-run resort and spa with pools, waterfalls (artificial and natural) and hiking trails. Comfortable thatched cabins, price includes all meals (world class chef), use of the facilities (spa extra) and tours, can arrange transport from Quito, attentive staff, popular with families, elegant and very upmarket.

$$ Mirador Río Blanco, San Miguel de los Bancos, main road, at the east end of town, T02-277 0307. Popular hotel/restaurant serving tropical dishes, small rooms, parking, terrace with bird feeders (many hummingbirds and tanagers) and magnificent views of the river.

$$ Selva Virgen, at Km 132, east of Puerto Quito, T02-390 1317, www.selvavirgen.com. ec. Nice *hostería* in a 100-ha property owned by the Universidad Técnica Equinoccial (UTE). Staffed by students. Restaurant, spacious comfortable cabins with a/c, fridge, jacuzzi, and nice porch, cheaper in rooms with ceiling fan, pool, lovely grounds, part of the property is forested and has trails, facilities also open to restaurant patrons.

⑦ Restaurants

Western slopes of Pichincha *p1002*
Pululahua
$$$ El Cráter, on the rim of the crater, access along road to the Mirador, T239 6399, www. elcrater.com. Open 1200-1600. Popular upscale restaurant with excellent views. Fancy hotel.

④ What to do

Western slopes of Pichincha *p1002*
Pululahua
The Green Horse Ranch, Astrid Muller, T09-8612 5433, www.horseranch.de.
1- to 9-day rides, among the options is a 3-day ride to Bellavista.

Mindo
Mindo Extreme Bird, Sector Saguambi, just out of town on the road to CEA, T217 0188, www.mindobird.com, birdwatching, regattas, cycling, hiking, waterfalls, English spoken, very helpful.
Vinicio Pérez, T09-947 6867, www.bird watchershouse.com, is a recommended birding guide, he speaks some English.

⑧ Transport

Papallacta *p1001*
Bus From **Quito**, buses bound for Tena or Lago Agrio from Terminal Quitumbe, or buses to Baeza from La Marín (see page 1111), 2 hrs, US$2. The bus stop is east of (below) the village, at the junction of the main highway and the old road through town. A taxi to Termas costs US$1pp shared or US$3 private. The access to the Termas is uphill from the village, off the old road. The complex is a 40-min walk from town. To return to Quito, most buses pass in the afternoon, travelling back at night is not recommended. The Termas also offer van service from Quito, US$110-180.

Refugio de Vida Silvestre Pasochoa *p1001*
Bus From Quito buses run from El Playón to Amaguaña US$0.50 (ask the driver to let you off at the 'Ejido de Amaguaña'); from there follow the signs. It's about 8-km walk, with not much traffic except at weekends, or book a pick-up from Amaguaña, **Cooperativa Pacheco Jr**, T02-287 7047, about US$6.

Western slopes of Pichincha *p1002*
Pululahua
Bus Take a 'Mitad del Mundo' bus from La Ofelia Metrobus terminal. When boarding, ask if it goes as far as the Pululahua turnoff (some end their route at Mitad del Mundo, others at the Pululahua Mirador turnoff, others continue to Calacalí). It is a 30-min walk from the turn to the rim.

Tulipe
Bus From **Quito**, Estación La Ofelia, from 0615, US$1.50, 1¾ hrs: **Transportes Otavalo**, 6 daily, continue to Pacto (US$2, 2 hrs) and **Transportes Minas** 4 daily, continue to Chontal (US$2.50, 3 hrs). To **Las Tolas**, **Transportes Minas**, daily at 1730, US$2, 2½ hrs or take pick-up from Tulipe, US$5.

Mindo *p1003*
Bus From **Quito**, Estación La Ofelia, **Coop Flor del Valle**, T236 4393, Mon-Fri 0800, 0900,

1100, 1300, 1600, Sat and Sun 0740, 0820, 0920, 11, 1300, 1400, 1600 (last one on Sun at 1700 instead of 1600); Mindo-Quito: Mon-Fri 0630, 1100, 1345, 1500, Sat and Sun 0630, 1100 and hourly 1300-1700; US$2.50, 2 hrs; weekend buses fill quickly, buy ahead. You can also take any bus bound for Esmeraldas or San Miguel de los Bancos (see below) and get off at the turnoff for Mindo from where there are taxis until1930, US$0.50 pp or US$3 without sharing. **Cooperativa Kennedy** to/from **Santo Domingo** 6 daily, US$4, 3½ hrs, 0400 service from Mindo continues to **Guayaquil**, US$9, 9 hrs.

West of Mindo *p1003*
From **Quito**, Terminal Carcelén, departures every 30 min (**Coop Kennedy** and associates) to Santo Domingo via: **Nanegalito** (US$1.50, 1½ hrs), **San Miguel de los Bancos** (US$2.50, 2½ hrs), **Pedro Vicente Maldonado** (US$3, 3 hrs) and **Puerto Quito** (US$3.75, 3½ hrs). **Trans Esmeraldas** frequent departures from Terminal Carcelén and from their own station in La Mariscal, Santa María 870, also serve these destinations along the Quito-Esmeraldas route.

Northern Highlands

The area north of Quito to the Colombian border is outstandingly beautiful. The landscape is mountainous, with views of the Cotacachi, Imbabura, and Chiles volcanoes, as well as the glacier-covered Cayambe, interspersed with lakes. The region is also renowned for its artesanía.

Quito to Otavalo

On the way from the capital to the main tourist centre in northern Ecuador, the landscape is dominated by the Cayambe volcano.

Quito to Cayambe
At **Calderón**, 32 km north of the centre of Quito, you can see the famous bread figurines being made. Prices are lower than in Quito. On 1-2 November, the graves in the cemetery are decorated with flowers, drinks and food for the dead. The Corpus Christi processions are very colourful. Take a bus at La Ofelia Metrobus terminal.

The Pan-American Highway goes to **Guayllabamba**, home of the Quito zoo (www.quitozoo.org), where it branches, one road going through Cayambe and the second through Tabacundo before rejoining at Cajas. At 10 km past Guayllabamba on the road to Tabacundo, just north of the toll booth, a cobbled road to the left (signed Pirámides de Cochasquí) leads to Tocachi and further on to the **Parque Arqueológico Cochasquí** ① *T09-9822 0686, Quito T399 4405, http://parquecochasqui.blogspot.com, 0900-1600, US$3, entry only with a 1½-hr guided tour.* The protected area contains 15 truncated clay pyramids (tolas), nine with long ramps, built between AD 950 and 1550 by the Cara or Cayambi-Caranqui people. Festivals with dancing at the equinoxes and solstices. There is a site museum and views from the pyramids, south to Quito, are marvellous. From Terminal Carcelén, be sure to take a bus that goes on the Tabacundo road and ask to be let off at the turnoff. From there It's a pleasant 8-km walk. A taxi from Tabacundo costs US$12 or US$20 round trip with 1½-hour wait, from Cayambe US$15, US$25 round trip.

On the other road, 8 km before Cayambe, a globe carved out of rock by the Pan-American Highway is at the spot where the French expedition marked the Equator (small shop sells drinks and snacks). A few metres north is **Quitsato** ① *T02-236 3042, www.quitsato.org, US$1,* where studies about the equator and its importance to ancient cultures are carried out. There is a sun dial, 54 m in diameter, and **a solar culture exhibit,** with information about indigenous cultures

Northern Ecuador

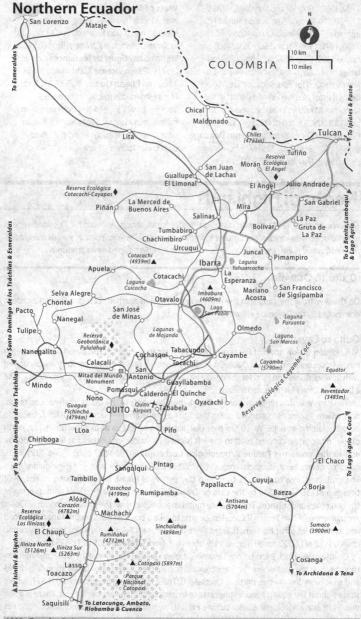

and archaeological sites along the equator; here too there are special events for the solstices and equinoxes.

Cayambe → *Phone code: 02. Colour map 11, A4. Population: 53,700.*

Cayambe, on the eastern (righthand) branch of the highway, 25 km northeast of Guayllabamba, is overshadowed by the snow-capped volcano of the same name. The surrounding countryside consists of a few dairy farms and many flower plantations. The area is noted for its *bizcochos* (biscuits) served with *queso de hoja* (string cheese). At the Centro Cultural Espinoza-Jarrín, is the **Museo de la Ciudad** ① *Rocafuerte y Bolívar, Wed-Sun 0800-1700, free*, with displays about the Cayambi culture and ceramics found at **Puntiachil**, an important but poorly preserved archaeologic site at the edge of town. There is a *fiesta* in March for the equinox with plenty of local music; also Inti Raymi solstice and San Pedro celebrations in June. Market day is Sunday.

Volcán Cayambe → *Altitude: 5790 m.*

Cayambe, Ecuador's third highest peak, lies within the **Reserva Ecológica Cayambe-Coca** ① *102-211 0370*. It is the highest point in the world to lie so close to the Equator (3.75 km north). The equator goes over the mountain's flanks. About 1 km south of Cayambe is an unmarked cobbled road heading east via Juan Montalvo, leading in 26 km to the Ruales-Oleas-Berge refuge at 4600 m. The *refugio* was being rebuilt in 2014 and was expected to reopen later that year. The standard climbing route, from the west, uses the refuge as a base. There is a crevasse near the summit which can be very difficult to cross if there isn't enough snow, ask the refuge keeper about conditions. There are nice acclimatization hikes around the refuge. Otavalo and Quito operators offer tours here.

⊙ Quito to Otavalo listings

For hotel and restaurant price codes, and other relevant information, see Essentials.

⊙ Where to stay

Cayambe *p1009*
$$$ Hacienda Guachaiá, south of Cayambe on the road to Cangahua, T236 3042, www.guachala.com. A nicely restored colonial hacienda, the chapel (1580) is built on top of an Inca structure. Simple but comfortable rooms in older section and fancier ones in newer area, fireplaces, delicious meals, covered swimming pool, parking, attentive service, good walking, horses for rent, excursions to nearby pre-Inca ruins, small museum.
$$$-$$ Jatun Huasi, Panamericana Norte Km 1½, T236 3777. US motel style, cabins and rooms with fireplace and frigo-bar, restaurant, indoor pool, spa, parking.
$$ Shungu Huasi, Camino a Granobles, 1 km northwest of town, T236 1847, www.shunguhuasi.com. Comfortable cabins in a

6.5-ha ranch, excellent Italian restaurant, heaters on request, nice setting, attentive service, offers horse riding and vehicle excursions. Recommended.
$ La Gran Colombia, Panamericana y Calderón, T236 1238. Modern multi-storey building, restaurant, parking, traffic noise. in front rooms.

⑦ Restaurants

Cayambe *p1009*
$$$ Casa de Fernando, Panamericana Norte Km 1.5. Varied menu, good international food.
$ Aroma, Bolívar 404 y Ascázubi. Large choice of set lunches and à la carte, variety of desserts, very good, closed Wed.

⊙ Transport

Cayambe *p1009*
Bus Flor del Valle, from La Ofelia, **Quito**, every 10 mins 0530-2100, US$1.25, 1½ hrs. Their Cayambe station is at Montalvo y Junín.

To **Otavalo**, from traffic circle at Bolívar y Av N Jarrín, every 15 mins, US$0.75, 45 mins.

Volcán Cayambe *p1009*
Road Most vehicles can go as far as the **Hacienda Piemonte El Hato** (at about 3500 m) from where it is a 3- to 4-hr walk, longer if heavily laden or if it is windy, but it is a beautiful walk. Regular pick-ups can often make it to 'la Z', a sharp curve on the road 30-mins' walk to the refugio. 4WDs can often make it to the refugio. Pick-ups can be hired by the market in Cayambe, Junín y Ascázubi, US$35, 1½-2 hrs. Arrange ahead for return transport. A milk truck runs from Cayambe's hospital to the hacienda at 0600, returning between 1700-1900.

Otavalo and around → *Phone code: 06. Colour map 11, A4. Population: 55,000. Altitude: 2530 m.*

Otavalo, only a short distance from the capital, is a must on any tourist itinerary in Ecuador. The Tabacundo and Cayambe roads join at Cajas, then cross the *páramo* and suddenly descend into the land of the *Otavaleños*, a thriving, prosperous group, famous for their prodigious production of woollens. The town itself, consisting of rather functional modern buildings, is one of South America's most important centres of ethno-tourism and its enormous Saturday market, featuring a dazzling array of textiles and crafts, is second to none and not to be missed. Men here wear their hair long and plaited under a broad-brimmed hat; they wear white, calf-length trousers and blue ponchos. The women's colourful costumes consist of embroidered blouses, shoulder wraps and many coloured beads. Indigenous families speak Quichua at home, although it is losing some ground to Spanish with the younger generation. Otavalo is set in beautiful countryside, with mountains, lakes and small villages nearby. The area is worth exploring for three or four days.

Arriving in Otavalo
Tourist offices Contact iTur ⓘ *corner of Plaza de Ponchos, Jaramillo y Quiroga, T292 1994, Mon-Fri 0800-1800, Sat 0800-1600,* for local and regional information.

Otavalo
The **Saturday market** comprises four different markets in various parts of the town with the central streets filled with vendors. The *artesanías* market is held 0700-1800, based around the Plaza de Ponchos (Plaza Centenario). The livestock section begins at 0500 until 0900, outside the centre, west of the Panamericana; go west on Calderón from the town centre. The produce market lasts from 0700 till 1400, in Plaza 24 de Mayo; it is scheduled to move to the old stadium, west of the centre in late 2014. The *artesanías* industry is so big that the Plaza de Ponchos is filled with vendors every day of the week. The selection is better on Saturday but prices are a little higher than other days when the atmosphere is more relaxed. Wednesday is also an important market day with more movement than other weekdays. Polite bargaining is appropriate in the market and shops. Otavaleños not only sell goods they weave and sew themselves, but they bring crafts from throughout Ecuador and from Peru and Bolivia. Indigenous people in the market respond better to photography if you buy something first, then ask politely. The **Museo Etnográfico Otavalango** ⓘ *Vía a Selva Alegre Km1, antigua Fábrica San Pedro, T09-8726 9827, Mon-Sat 0900-1700, call ahead, US$5,* displays on all cultural aspects of Otavaleño life; live presentations of local traditions for groups. The **Museo de Tejidos El Obraje** ⓘ *Sucre 6-08 y Olmedo, T292 0261, call ahead, US$2,* shows the process of traditional Otavalo weaving from shearing to final products. There are good views of town from **Centro de Exposiciones El Colibrí** ⓘ *C Morales past the railway line.*

Around Otavalo

Otavalo weavers come from dozens of communities. Many families weave and visitors should shop around as the less known weavers often have better prices and some of the most famous ones only sell from their homes, especially in Agato and Peguche. The easiest villages to visit are Ilumán (there are also many felt hatmakers in town and *yachacs*, or shamen, mostly north of the plaza – look for signs); Agato; Carabuela (many homes sell crafts including wool sweaters); Peguche. These villages are only 15-30 minutes away and have good bus service; buses leave from the Terminal and stop at Plaza Copacabana (Atahualpa y Montalvo). You can also take a taxi.

To reach the lovely **Cascada de Peguche**, from Peguche's plaza, facing the church, head right and continue straight until the road forks. Take the lower fork to the right, but not the road that

Otavalo

Where to stay 🛏
1 Acoma
2 Doña Esther
3 El Geranio
4 El Indio
5 El Indio Inn
6 María
7 Posada del Quinde
8 Rincón del Viajero
9 Riviera Sucre
10 Valle del Amanecer

Restaurants 🍴
1 Aly Allpa & Buena Vista
2 Deli
3 Fontana di Trevi
4 La Casa de Intag
5 Mi Otavalito
6 Oraibi
7 Quino
8 Salinerito
9 Shanandoa Pie Shop

Bars & clubs 🍸
10 Bohemios
11 Peña Amauta

heads downhill. From the top of the falls (left side, excellent views) you can continue the walk to Lago San Pablo. The *Pawkar Raimi* festival is held in Peguche before carnival. At the falls there is a small information centre (contributions are appreciated).

The **Ciclovía** is a bicycle path which runs along the old rail line 21 km between Eugenio Espejo de Cajas and Otavalo. Because of the slope, starting in Cajas is recommended. You can take a tour or hire a bike and take a bus bound for Quito to the bike path.

Lago San Pablo

There is a network of old roads and trails between Otavalo and Lago San Pablo, none of which takes more than two hours to explore. It is worth walking either to or back from the lake for the views. Going in a group is recommended for safety. A nice half-day excursion is via Cascada de Peguche, **Parque Cóndor** ① *on a hill called Curiloma, near the community of Pucará Alto, T304 9399, www.parquecondor.org, Wed-Sun 0930-1700, raptor flight demonstrations at 1130 and 1530, US$4.50, crowded on weekends*, a reserve and birds of prey rehabilitation centre, and back via **El Lechero**, a lookout by a tree considered sacred among indigenous people. From **San Pablo del Lago** it is possible to climb **Imbabura** volcano (4630 m, a serious climb and frequently under cloud), allow at least six hours to reach the summit and four hours for the descent. An alternative access is from La Esperanza or San Clemente (see page 1017). Easier, and no less impressive, is the nearby Cerro Huarmi Imbabura, 3845 m, it is not signed but several paths lead there. Take a good map, food and warm clothing.

ⓔ Otavalo and around listings

For hotel and restaurant price codes, and other relevant information, see Essentials.

● Where to stay

Otavalo *p1010, map p1011*
In town
Hotels may be full on Fri night before market.
$$$ Posada del Quinde, Quito y Miguel Egas, T292 0750, www.posadaquinde.com. Nicely decorated, all rooms around a lovely garden, also 2 suites, good restaurant, parking, US run.
$$$-$$ El Indio Inn, Bolívar 9-04 y Calderón, T292 2922, www.hotelelindioinn.com. Modern hotel, carpeted rooms and simple suites, restaurant, parking, spa.
$$ Acoma, Salinas 07-57 y 31 de Octubre, T292 6570, www.acomahotel.com. Lovely re-built home in colonial style, parking, nice comfortable rooms, some with balcony, 1 room with bathtub, 2 suites with kitchenette.
$$ Doña Esther, Montalvo 4-44 y Bolívar, T292 0739, www.otavalohotel.com. Nicely restored colonial house, a hotel for over 100 years, very good restaurant, rooms with nice wooden

floors, colourful decor, pleasant atmosphere, transfers to Quito or airport.
$$-$ El Indio, Sucre 12-14 y Salinas, near Plaza de Ponchos, T292 0060, www.hostalel indio.com. In multi-storey building, ask for a room with balcony, simple restaurant, parking, helpful service.
$$-$ Rincón del Viajero, Roca 11-07 y Quiroga, T292 1741, www.hostalrincondelviajero.com. Very pleasant hostel and meeting place. Simple but nicely decorated rooms, includes a choice of good breakfasts, private or shared bath, small parking, rooftop hammocks, sitting room with fireplace, camping, US-Ecuadorean run, good value. Recommended.
$$-$ Riviera Sucre, García Moreno 380 y Roca, T292 0241, www.rivierasucre.com. Older hotel with ample renovated rooms, good breakfast available, cafeteria, 1 room with shared bath, kitchen facilities, book exchange, bookshop with good selection of English and German titles, nice common areas, garden and courtyard, good meeting place. Recommended.
$$-$ Valle del Amanecer, Roca y Quiroga, T292 0990. Small rooms, nice courtyard

with hammocks, private or shared bath, bike hire, popular.

$ El Geranio, Ricaurte y Morales, T292 0185, hgeranio@hotmail.com. Breakfast available cheaper with electric shower, laundry and cooking facilities, quiet, family run, popular, runs trips. Good value, recommended.

$ María, Jaramillo y Colón, T292 0672. Bright rooms in multi-storey building, parking for small car. Good value.

$ Santa Fé, Roca 7-34 y García moreno, T292 3640, www.hotelsantafeotavalo.com. Modern, nice pine decoration, restaurant, run by indigenous Otavaleños, good value.

Camping, in Punyaro, Km 2 vía a Mojanda. US$5 pp, Camping area in a rural property, hot shower and Wi-Fi, arrange through **Rincón del Viajero**, above.

Out of town

$$$$ Ali Shungu Mountaintop Lodge, 5 km west of Otavalo by the village of Yambiro, T09-8950 9945, www.alishungumountaintoplodge. com. Country inn on a 16 ha private reserve. 4 comfortable nicely decorated guest houses for 6, each with living room, woodstove and kitchenette. Includes breakfast and dinner (vegetarian available), horseback riding, US run.

$$$$ Casa Mojanda, Vía a Mojanda Km 3.5, T09-9972 0890, www.casamojanda.com. Comfortable cabins set in a beautiful hillside. Breakfast and tasty dinner prepared with ingredients from own organic garden and short guided hike to waterfall; each room is decorated with its own elegant touch, outdoor hot tub with great views, quiet, good library, horse riding. Recommended.

$$$ Hacienda Pinsaquí, Panamericana Norte Km 5, 300 m north of the turn-off for Cotacachi, T294 6116, www.haciendapinsaqui. com. Converted hacienda with 30 suites, one with jacuzzi, restaurant with lovely dining room, lounge with fireplace, beautiful antiques, colonial ambience, gardens, horse riding, biking.

$$$ Las Palmeras de Quichinche, outside Quichinche, 15 mins by bus from Otavalo, T292 2607, www.laspalmerasinn.com. Cabins with terrace and fireplace in a rural setting,

restaurant, parking, nice grounds and views, pool table and ping-pong, British owned.

$$ La Casa de Hacienda, Entrance at Panamericana Norte Km 3, then 300 m east, T269 0245, www.hosteriacasadehacienda.com. Tasteful cabins with fireplace, restaurant, parking, advance reservations required for horse riding.

$$ La Luna de Mojanda, On a side-road going south off the Mojanda road at Km 4, T09-9315 6082, www.lalunaecuador.com. Pleasant hostel in nice surroundings, some rooms with fireplace, heater and private bath, others with shared bath, US$12 pp in dorm, camping US$8 pp, terrace with hammocks, pleasant dining room-lounge, transport information on hostel's web site, excursions arranged, popular. Recommended.

$$ Rose Cottage, Vía a Mojanda Km 3, T09-9772 8115, www.rosecottageecuador.com. Various rooms and prices in 7 separate houses, some with private bath, US$10 pp in dorm, camping US$4 pp, restaurant, hammocks, nice views.

Around Otavalo: Peguche *p1011*

$$$ La Casa Sol, near the Cascada de Peguche, T269 0500. Comfortable rustic construction set on a hillside. Rooms and suites with balcony, some with fireplace, lovely attention to detail, restaurant.

$$ Aya Huma, on the railway line in Peguche, T269 0164, www.ayahuma.com. In a country setting between the unused rail tracks and the river. Quiet, pleasant atmosphere, Dutch-Ecuadorean run, popular. Recommended.

Lago San Pablo *p1012*

$$$ Hacienda Cusín, by the village of San Pablo del Lago to the southeast of the lake, T291 8013, www.haciendacusin.com. A converted 17th-century hacienda with lovely courtyard and garden, fine expensive restaurant, rooms with fireplace, sports facilities (pool, horses, bikes, squash court, games room), library, book in advance, British run. Recommended.

$$$ Puerto Lago, 6 km from Otavalo, just off the Panamericana on the west side of the lake,

T292 0920, www.puertolago.com. Modern hostería in a lovely setting on the lakeshore, good expensive restaurant overlooking the lake, rooms and suites with fireplace, very hospitable, a good place to watch the sunset, includes the use of row-boats, pedalos and kayaks, other water sports extra.

$$ Green House, C 24 de Junio, Comunidad Araque, by the east shore of the lake, northwest of San Pablo del Lago, T291 9298, www.araquebyb.hostel.com. Family-run *hostal*, some rooms with bath, others with detached bath, dinner on request, sitting room with fireplace, rooftop terrace with views, transport.

⑦ Restaurants

Otavalo *p1010, map p1011*

$$ Quino, Roca 7-40 y Juan Montalvo. Tue-Sun 1030-2300, Mon1730-2300. Traditional coastal cooking and some meat dishes, pleasant seating around patio.

$$-$ Buena Vista, Salinas entre Sucre y Jaramillo, p2, www.buenavistaotavalo.com. 1200-2200, Sat from 0900, closed Tue. Bistro with balcony overlooking Plaza de Ponchos. Good international food, sandwiches, salads, vegetarian options, trout, good coffee, Wi-Fi.

$$-$ Deli, Quiroga 12-18 y Bolívar. Mon-Fri 1000-2100, Sat 0800-2200. Good Mexican and international food, also pizza, nice desserts, pleasant atmosphere, family run, good value.

$$-$ Fontana di Trevi, Sucre 12-05 y Salinas, 2nd floor. Daily 1300-2100. Overlooking Calle Sucre, good pizza and pasta, nice juices, friendly service.

$$-$ Mi Otavalito, Sucre y Morales. Good for set lunch and international food à la carte.

$$-$ Oraibi, Sucre y Colón. Wed-Sat 0800-2000. Vegetarian food in nice patio setting, pizza, salads, pasta, Mexican, breakfast, Swiss owned.

$ Aly Allpa, Salinas 509 at Plaza de Ponchos. Daily 0730-2030. Good-value set meals, breakfast and à la carte including trout, vegetarian, meat. Recommended.

Cafés

La Casa de Intag, Colón 465 y Sucre. Mon-Sat 0800-1800. Fair trade cafeteria/shop run by Intag coffee growers and artisans associations. Good organic coffee, breakfast, pancakes, sandwiches, sisal crafts, fruit pulp and more.

Salinerito, Bolívar 10-08 y Morales. Mon-Sat 0800-2200. Café/deli run by the Salinas de Guaranda coop. Good sandwiches, breakfast, coffee and juices. A good place to buy supplies such as cheese, coldcuts and chocolate.

Shanandoa Pie Shop, Salinas y Jaramillo. 1100-2100, Sat from 0900. Good fruit pies, milk shakes and ice-cream, popular meeting place, an Otavalo tradition.

⑦ Bars and clubs

Otavalo *p1010, map p1011*

Otavalo is generally safe but avoid deserted areas at night. Nightlife is concentrated at Morales y Jaramillo and C 31 de Octubre. Peñas are open Fri-Sat from 1930, entrance US$3.

Bohemios, Colón entre Bolívar y Sucre. Live folk music, also Latin music.

Peña Amauta, Morales 5-11 y Jaramillo. Good local bands, welcoming, mainly foreigners.

✳ Festivals

Otavalo *p1010, map p1011*

The **end of Jun** combines the Inti Raymi celebrations of the summer solstice (**21 Jun**), with the **Fiesta de San Juan** (**24 Jun**) and the **Fiesta de San Pedro y San Pablo** (**29 Jun**). These combined festivities are known as **Los San Juanes** and participants are mostly indigenous. Most of the action takes place in the smaller communities surrounding Otavalo, each one celebrates separately on different dates, some of them for a full week. The celebration begins with a ritual bath, the Peguche waterfall is used by Otavalo residents (a personal spiritual activity, best carried out without visitors and certainly without cameras). In Otavalo, indigenous families have costume parties, which at times spill over onto the streets. In the San Juan neighbourhood, near the Yanayacu baths, there is a week-long celebration with food, drink and music. **Fiesta del Yamor** and **Colla Raimi 1st 2 weeks of Sep**, feature local dishes, amusement parks, bands in the plaza and sporting events. **Oct**, Mes de la cultura, cultural events throughout the month. **Last Oct weekend**, Mojanda Arriba is an annual full day hike from Malchinguí over Mojanda to reach Otavalo for the foundation celebrations.

⏱ What to do

Otavalo *p1010, map p1011*
Horse riding Several operators offer riding tours. Half-day trips to nearby attractions cost US$25-35. Full-day trips such as Cuicocha or Mojanda run US$40-50.
Mountain bikes Several tour operators rent bikes and offer cycling tours for US$35-60 a day trip. See also Ciclovía, page 1012. Rentals cost US$10-12 per day **Hostal Valle del Amanecer** (see Where to stay), good bikes. **La Tierra** craft shop, Salinas 503 y Sucre, Plaza de Ponchos, good equipment. **Taller Ciclo Primaxi**, Ricaurte y Morales and in Peguche.

Tour operators
Most common tours are to indigenous communities, Cuicocha and Mojanda, US$20-30 pp. Independent travel to the Lagunas de Mojanda is not recommended because of public safety problems. Best go with a tour.
All about EQ, Los Corazas 433 y Albarracín, at the north end of town, T292 3633, www. all-about-ecuador.com. Interesting itineraries, trekking and horse riding tours, climbing, cycling, trips to Intag, Piñán, Cayambe, Oyacachi, volunteering on organic farms. English and French spoken. Recommended.
Ecomontes, Sucre y Morales, T292 6244, www. ecomontestour.com. A branch of a Quito operator, trekking, climbing, rafting, also sell tours to Cuyabeno and Galápagos.
Runa Tupari, Sucre y Quito, T292 2320, www.runatupari.com. Arranges indigenous homestays in the Cotacachi area, also the usual tours, trekking, horse riding and cycling trips; also transport.

Train rides
The track from Otavalo to Ibarra is being restored and a tourist ride is expected to operate by late 2014. Train station at Guayaquil y J Montalvo.

⊖ Transport

Otavalo *p1010, map p1011*
Note Never leave anything in your car or taxi in the street. There are public car parks at Juan Montalvo y Sucre, by Parque Bolívar, and on Quito between 31 de Octubre and Jaramillo.
Bus Terminal at Atahualpa y Ordóñez (no departures after 1830). To **Quito** 2 hrs, US$2, every 10 mins; all depart from the Terminal Carcelén in Quito, **Coop Otavalo** and **Coop Los Lagos** go into Otavalo, buses bound for Ibarra or Tulcán drop you off at the highway, this is inconvenient and not safe at night. From **Quito** or airport by taxi takes 1½ hrs. US$50 one way, US$80 return with 3 hrs wait; shared taxis with **Taxis Lagos** (in Quito, Asunción Oe2-146 y Versalles, T256 5992; in Otavalo, Av Los Sarances y Panamericana, T292 3203), who run a hotel to hotel service (to/from modern Quito only) and will divert to resorts just off the highway, Mon-Sat hourly, 5 departures on Sun, 1½ hrs, US$9.50 pp, buy ticket at least 1 day before, they also go from Quito to Ibarra. Tour operators also offer tranfers. Bus to **Ibarra**, every 4 mins, US$0.45, 40 mins. To **Peguche**, city bus on Av Atahualpa, every 10 mins, bus stops in front of the terminal and at Plaza Copacabana, US$0.20. To the **Intag region**, 5 daily.

Lago San Pablo *p1012*
Bus From **Otavalo** to San Pablo del Lago every 25 mins, more often on Sat, US$0.25, 30 mins; taxi US$4.

ⓘ Directory

Otavalo *p1010, map p1011*
Banks Banco del Austro, Sucre y Quiroga. Banco del Pacífico, Bolívar 614 y García Moreno. **Fax Cambios**, Salinas y Sucre, T292 0501, Mon-Sat 0745-1900, poor rates for cash

(7 currencies), 3% commission on TCs. **Vaz Corp**, Sucre 11-13 y Morales, T292 3500, Tue-Sat 0830-1700, exchange 8 currencies, 1.8% comission on TCs (minimum US$2). **Language schools** Instituto Superior de Español, Jaramillo 6-23 y Morales, T292 7354. **Mundo Andino Internacional**, Salinas 404 y Bolívar, T292 1864, www.mandinospanishschool.com. Salsa and cooking classes included. **Otavalo Spanish Institute**, 31 de Octubre 47-64 y Salinas, p 3, T292 1404, www.otavalospanish.com, also offers Quichua lessons.

Otavalo to the Colombian border

Northwest of Otavalo is Cotacachi from where a road goes west to the Cotacachi-Cayapas reserve and the subtropical Intag region. The main highway goes north to the city of Ibarra and beyond into the hot Chota Valley from where a branch road goes west to the subtropical valley of the Río Mira and the coastal town of San Lorenzo. The Panamericana reaches the border at the busy town of Tulcán, with its fantastic cemetery topiary.

Cotacachi → *Phone code: 06. Colour map 11, A4. Population: 17,700. Altitude: 2440 m.*
West of the road between Otavalo and Ibarra is Cotacachi, home to a growing expatriate community. Leather goods are made and sold here. There is also access along a secondary road from Otavalo through Quiroga. The **Casa de las Culturas** ① *Bolívar 1334 y 9 de Octubre*, a beautifully refurbished 19th-century building is a monument to peace. It houses a library, café and temporary exhibits. The **Museo de las Culturas** ① *García Moreno 13-41y Bolívar, Mon-Fri 0800-1200, 1400-1700, Sat-Sun 0800-1300, donations appreciated*, renovated in 2013, has good displays of early Ecuadorean history and regional crafts and traditions. For information, **Empresa Pública de Turismo** ① *at Hostería Cuicocha, by the lake (see below), T301 7218*. Additional tourist information and a city map are found in www.cotacachi.gob.ec. Local festivals include **Inti Raymi/San Juan** in June and **Jora** during the September equinox.

Laguna Cuicocha → *Altitude: 3070 m.*
① *15 km from Cotacachi, visitor centre has good natural history and cultural displays, daily 0800-1700.*
This crater lake is part of the **Reserva Ecológica Cotacachi-Cayapas**, which extends from Cotacachi volcano to the tropical lowlands on the Río Cayapas in Esmeraldas. It is a crater lake with two islands, which are closed to the public to protect the native species. There is a well-marked, 8-km path around the lake, which takes four to five hours and provides spectacular views of the Cotacachi, Imbabura and, occasionally, Cayambe peaks. The best views are in the morning, when condors can sometimes be seen. There is a lookout at 3 km, two hours from the start. Take water and a waterproof jacket. There is a shorter trail which takes 40 minutes. Motor boat rides around the islands, US$3.25 per person for minimum six persons.

    Warnings Enquire locally about safety before heading out and don't take valuables. Do not eat the berries which grow near the lake, as some are poisonous. The path around the lake is not for vertigo sufferers.

    To the northwest of Otavalo lies the lush subtropical region of **Intag**, reached along a road (being paved in 2014) that follows the southern edge of Cuicocha and continues to the town of **Apuela**. The region's primary cloudforest is threatened by a proposed large-scale copper mine, vigorously opposed by local communities. See **Defensa y Conservación Ecológica de Intag**, *www.decoin.org*, for local conservation and community development projects. The area's rivers will also be affected by an irrigation and hydroelectric scheme in the Piñan area, see Northwest of Ibarra, below. The **Asociación Agroartesanal de Café Río Intag (AACRI)** ① *on the main street opposite the health centre, T06-264 8489, www.aacri.com*, a fair trade organic coffee grower's association, offers tours of coffee, sisal and sugar cane plantations and processing plants, also lodging and volunteer opportunities. Beyond, are pleasant thermal baths at **Nangulví**. The area is rich in cloud forest and has several nature reserves. On the southwest boundary of the Cotacachi-Cayapas reserve is **Los Cedros Research Station** ① *T09-8460 0274, www. reservaloscedros.org*, 6400 ha of pristine cloud forest, with abundant orchids and bird life. Full board in **$$$** range.

Ibarra and around → *Phone code: 06. Colour map 11, A4. Pop: 137,000. Altitude: 2225 m.*

Ibarra the provincial capital is the main commercial centre and transport hub of the northern highlands. The city has an interesting ethnic mix, with blacks from the Chota valley and Esmeraldas alongside Otavaleños and other highland *indígenas*, mestizos and Colombian immigrants. For information: **Dirección de Turismo de Imbabura** ① *Bolívar y Oviedo, T295 5832, www.imbaburaturismo.gob.ec, Mon-Fri 0800-1300, 1500-1800*, and the municipal tourist office, **i-Tur** ① *Sucre y Oviedo, T260 8489, www.touribarra.gob.ec, free Wi-Fi, Mon-Fri 0800-1230, 1400-1730.*

On **Parque Pedro Moncayo** stand the Cathedral, the Municipio and Gobernación. One block away, at Flores y Olmedo, is the smaller Parque 9 de Octubre or **Parque de la Merced** after its church. Beyond the railway station, to the south and west of the centre, is a busy commercial area with several markets beyond which is the bus terminal. The **Museo Regional Sierra Norte** ① *Sucre 7-21 y Oviedo, T260 2093, Mon-Fri, 0830-1700, Sat 1000-1300, 1400-1600*, has interesting displays about cultures from northern Ecuador. **Bosque Protector Guayabillas** ① *Urbanización La Victoria, on the eastern outskirts of town, www.guayabillas.com, daily 0900-1730*, is a 54-ha park on a hill overlooking the city. There are trails, animals, volunteer opportunities, and accommodation. **Virgen del Carmen** festival is on 16 July and **Fiesta de los Lagos** is in the last weekend of September.

Off the main road between Otavalo and Ibarra is **San Antonio de Ibarra**, well known for its wood carvings. It is worth seeing the range of styles and techniques and shopping around in the galleries and workshops. About 8 km from Ibarra on the road to Olmedo is **La Esperanza**, a pretty village in beautiful surroundings. Some 15 km further along, by Angochagua is the community of **Zuleta**. The region is known for its fine embroidery. West of La Esperanza, along a road that starts at Avenida Atahualpa, and also 8 km from Ibarra, is the community of **San Clemente**, which has a very good grassroots tourism project, **Pukyu Pamba**, see Where to stay below. From either La Esperanza or San Clemente you can climb **Cubilche** volcano and **Imbabura**, more easily than from San Pablo del Lago. From the top you can walk down to Lago San Pablo (see page 1012). *Guías nativos* are available for these climbs.

Ibarra to the coast The spectacular train ride from Ibarra to San Lorenzo on the Pacific coast no longer operates. A tourist train runs on a small section of this route, see page 1023.

Some 24 km north of Ibarra is the turn-off west for **Salinas**, a mainly Afro-Ecuadorean village with a Museo de la Sal, and the very scenic road beside the Río Mira down to San Lorenzo. At 41 km from the turn-off are the villages of **Guallupe**, **El Limonal** (see Where to stay, below), and **San Juan de Lachas**, in a lush subtropical area. Ceramic masks and figurines are produced at the latter. In **Lita**, 33 km from Guallupe, there is nice swimming in the river. Beyond is the Río Chuchubi with waterfalls and swimming holes; here is **Las Siete Cascadas resort** ① *entry US$10, guide US$10 per group*, (see Where to stay below). It is 66 km from Lita to **Calderón**, where this road meets the coastal highway coming from Esmeraldas. Two kilometres before the junction, on the Río Tululbí, is **Hostería Tunda Loma** (see Where to stay, page 1103). About 7 km beyond is San Lorenzo (see page 1101).

Northwest of Ibarra Along a secondary road to the northwest of Ibarra is the town of **Urcuquí** with Yachay, a university and national research and technology centre, opened in 2014 in a beautiful historic hacienda, and a basic hotel. From just south of Urcuquí, a road leads via Irunguicho towards the **Piñán lakes**, a beautiful, remote, high *páramo* region, part of the Reserva Ecológica Cotacachi-Cayapas. The local community of Piñán (3112 m) has a tourism programme (www.pinantrek.com), with a well equipped refuge (US$12 per person, meals available), *guías nativos* (US$15 per day) and muleteers (US$12 per day, per horse). Another access to the hamlet of Piñán is via La Merced de Buenos Aires, a village reached form either Tumbabiro (see below) or Guallupe (on the road to the coast). Along the Tumabiro access is the community of Sachapamba, which offers meals and muleteers. The nicest lakes, Donoso and Caricocha, are one-hour walk from the community. They can also be reached walking from either Chachimbiro (see below), Irubí or Cuellaje in the Intag area. Otavalo agencies and hotels in Chachimbiro and Tumababiro also offer trekking tours to Piñán. Note that an irrigation and hydroelectric scheme, proposed in 2014, will affect this beautiful area. Beyond Urcuquí is the friendly town of **Tumbabiro**, with a mild climate, a good base from which to explore this region (several lodgings, see Where to stay page 1021); it can also be reached from Salinas on the road to the coast. Some 8 km from Tumbabiro along a side road, set on the slopes of an extinct volcano, is **Chachimbiro**, a good area for walking and horseback riding, with several resorts with thermal baths (see Where to stay, page 1021). The largest one, run by the provincial government, is **Santa Agua Chachimbiro** ⓘ *T264 8308, http://imbabura.gob.ec/chachimbiro, 0700-2000, entry to recreational pools US$5, to medicinal pools and spa US$10*, with several hot mineral pools, lodging, restaurants, zip line and horses for riding; weekends can be crowded.

North to Colombia

From Ibarra the Pan-American highway goes past Laguna Yahuarcocha (with a few hotels, a campground, see Where to stay, Ibarra, and many food stalls, busy on weekends) and then descends to the hot dry Chota valley, a centre of Afro-Ecuadorean culture. Beyond the turn-off for Salinas and San Lorenzo, 30 km from Ibarra, the highway divides. One branch follows an older route through Mira and El Angel to Tulcán on the Colombian border. At **Mascarilla**, 1 km along this road, ceramic masks are made (hostal run by the women's craft group, **El Patio de mi Casa**, T09-9449 4029, **$$** full-board). This road is paved and in good condition as far as **El Angel** (3000 m), but deteriorates thereafter. It is passable with 4WD and is a great mountain bike route.

El Angel's main plaza retains a few trees sculpted by José Franco (see Tulcán Cemetery, page 1019); market day Monday. The **Reserva Ecológica El Angel** ⓘ *T297 7597, office in El Angel near the Municipio; best time to visit May to Aug*, nearby protects 15,715 ha of *páramo* ranging in altitude from 3400 m to 4768 m. The reserve contains large stands of the velvet-leaved *frailejón* plant, also found in the Andes of Colombia and Venezuela. Also of interest are the spiny *achupallas, bromeliads* with giant compound flowers. The fauna includes *curiquingues* (caracara), deer, foxes, and a few condors. From El Angel follow the poor road north towards Tulcán for 16 km to **El Voladero** ranger station/shelter, where a self-guided trail climbs over a low ridge (30 minutes' walk) to two crystal-clear lakes. Pickups or taxis from the main plaza of El Angel charge US$25 return with one-hour wait for a day trip to El Voladero. A longer route to another area follows an equally poor road to Cerro Socabones, beginning at **La Libertad**, 3.5 km north of El Angel (transport El Angel-Cerro Socabones, US$30 return). It climbs gradually to reach the high *páramo* at the centre of the reserve and, in 40 minutes, the **El Salado** ranger station. From Socabones the road descends to the village of **Morán** (lodging and guides, transport with Sr Calderón, T09-9128 4022), the start of a nice three-day walk to Las Juntas, a warm area, off the Ibarra-San Lorenzo road.

Eastern route to the border

The second branch (the modern Pan-American Highway), in good repair but with many heavy lorries, runs east through the warm Chota valley to El Juncal, before turning north to reach Tulcán via Bolívar and San Gabriel. A good paved road runs between Bolívar and El Angel, connecting the two branches.

Bolívar is a neat little town where the houses and the interior of its church are painted in lively pastel colours. At the **Museo Paleontológico** ① by the north entrance to town, US$2, remains of a mammoth, found nearby, can be seen. There is a Friday market.

Some 16 km north of Bolívar is **San Gabriel**, an important commercial centre. The 60-m-high **Paluz** waterfall is 4 km north of town, beyond a smaller waterfall. To the southeast, 11 km from town on the road to Piartal is **Bosque de Arrayanes**, a 16-ha mature forest with a predominance of myrtle trees, some reaching 20 m, taxi US$5.

East of San Gabriel by 20 km is the tiny community of **Mariscal Sucre** also known as Colonia Huaqueña, the gateway to the **Guandera Reserve and Biological Station** ① *the reserve is part of Fundación Jatun Sacha. Reservations should be made at the Quito office, T02-331 7163, www. jatunsacha.org.* You can see bromeliads, orchids, toucans and other wildlife in temperate forest and *frailejón páramo*. From San Gabriel, take a taxi to Mariscal Sucre, one hour, then walk 30 minutes to the reserve, or make arrangements with Jatun Sacha.

Between San Gabriel and Tulcán is the little town of Julio Andrade, with **Hotel Naderic** and a Saturday market (good for horses and other large animals) and, afterwards, paddleball games. This is the beginning of the road to La Bonita, Lumbaqui and Lago Agrio. The road follows the frontier for much of the route. Make enquiries about safety before taking this beautiful route.

Tulcán → *Phone code: 06. Colour map 11, A4. Population: 61,900. Altitude: 2960 m.*

The chilly city of Tulcán is the busy capital of the province of Carchi. There is a great deal of informal trade here with Colombia, a textile and dry goods fair takes place on Thursday and Sunday. The two branches of the Panamericana join at Las Juntas, 2 km south of the city. In the **cemetery** ① *daily 0800-1800*, two blocks from Parque Ayora, the art of topiary is taken to beautiful extremes. Cypress bushes are trimmed into archways, fantastic figures and geometric shapes in *haut* and *bas* relief. To see the stages of this art form, go to the back of the cemetery where young bushes are being pruned. The artistry, started in 1936, is that of the late Sr José Franco, born in El Angel (see above), now buried among the splendour he created. The tradition is carried on by his sons. Around the cemetery is a promenade with fountains, souvenir and flower stalls and the **tourist office**, Unidad de Turismo ① *entrance to the cemetery, T298 5760, daily 0800-1800, turismo@gmtulcan.gob.ec, helpful.* Write in advance to request a guided tour of the cemetery. Two blocks south is the **Museo de la Casa de la Cultura** ① *Mon-Fri 0730-1300, 1500-1800*, with a collection of pre-Inca ceramics.

Safety Don't wander about at night. The area around the bus terminal is unsafe. Do not travel outside town (except along the Panamericana) without advance local enquiry.

Border with Colombia: Tulcán-Ipiales

The border is at **Rumichaca** (stone bridge), 5 km from Tulcán. Border posts with immigration, customs and agriculture control are on either side of a concrete bridge over the Río Carchi, opened in 2013, to the east of the natural stone bridge. This well organized border is open 24 hours. On the Ecuadorean side, next to immigration (T298 6169), is a tourist information office. There are money changers on both sides of the bridge, check all calculations. Ipiales, with all services, is 2 km from the border.

Otavalo to the Colombian border listings

For hotel and restaurant price codes, and other
relevant information, see Essentials.

Where to stay

Cotacachi p1016

$$$$ La Mirage, 500 m west of town, T291
5237, www.mirage.com.ec. Luxurious converted
hacienda with elegant suites and common
areas, includes breakfast and dinner, excellent
restaurant, pool, gym and spa (treatments extra),
beautiful gardens, tours arranged.

$$ Land of Sun, García Moreno 1376 y Sucre,
T291 6009. Refurbished colonial house in the
heart of town, restaurant in lovely patio, sauna,
parking. Recommended.

$$ Runa Tupari, a system of homestays in
nearby villages. Visitors experience life with
a indigenous family by taking part in daily
activities. The comfortable rooms have space
for 3, fireplace, bathroom and hot shower,
and cost US$30 pp including breakfast,
dinner and transport from Otavalo. Arrange
with Runa Tupari, www.runatupari.com, or
other Otavalo tour operators.

$$-$ La Cuadra, Peñaherrera 11-46 y González
Suárez, T291 6015, www.lacuadra-hostal.com.
Modern comfortable rooms, good matresses,
private or shared bath, kitchen facilities.

$ Bachita, Sucre 16-82 y Peñaherrera, T291
5063. Simple place, private or shared bath, quiet.

$ Munaylla, 10 de Agosto y Sucre, T291 6169.
Centrally located multi-storey building, rooms
a bit small, good value.

Laguna Cuicocha p1016

$$$ Hostería Cuicocha, Laguna Cuicocha, by
the pier, T264 8040, www.cuicocha.org. Modern
comfortable rooms overlooking the lake,
includes breakfast and dinner, restaurant.

$ Cabañas Mirador, on a lookout above the
pier, follow the trail or by car follow the road to
the left of the park entrance, T09-8682 1699,
miradordecuicocha@yahoo.com. Rustic cabins
with fireplace and modern rooms overlooking

the lake, good economical restaurant, trout is the
specialty, parking, transport provided to Quiroga
(US$4), Cotacachi (US$5), or Otavalo (US$10);
owner Ernesto Cevillano is knowledgeable about
the area and arranges trips.

Ibarra p1017

$$$$ Hacienda Pimán, 9 km northeast of
town, Quito T02-256 6090, www.hacienda
piman.com. Luxuriuosly restored 18th-century
hacienda. All inclusive 2- and 3-day packages
with a train ride and visit to El Angel Reserve.

$$$ Hacienda Chorlaví, Panamericana Sur
Km 4, T293 2222, www.haciendachorlavi.com.
In an old hacienda, comfortable rooms, very
good expensive restaurant, excellent parrillada,
pool and spa, busy on weekends, folk music
and crafts on Sat.

$$$ La Estelita, Km 5 Vía a Yuracrucito, T09-
9811 6058, www.laestelita.com.ec. Modern
hotel 5 km from the city on a hill overlooking
town and Laguna Yahuarcocha. Rooms and
suites with lovely views, good restaurant, pool,
spa, paragliding.

$$ Montecarlo, Av Jaime Rivadeneira 5-61
y Oviedo, near the obelisk, T295 8266, www.
hotelmontecarloibarra.ec. Nice comfortable
rooms, buffet breakfast, restaurant, heated pool
open on weekends, parking.

$$ Royal Ruiz, Olmedo 9-40 y P Moncayo,
T264 4653. Modern, comfortable carpeted
rooms, restaurant, solar heated water,
parking, long-stay discounts.

$ Fran's Hostal, Gral Julio Andrade 1-58 y
Rafael Larrea, near bus terminal, T260 9995.
Multi-storey hotel, bright functional rooms.

$ Finca Sommerwind, Autopista Yahuarcocha
Km 8, T09-3937 1177, www.finca-sommerwind.
com. Campground in a 12-ha ranch by
Laguna Yahuarcocha, US$3 pp in tent,
US$5 pp for camper vans, electricity, hot
shower, laundry facilities.

$ Las Garzas, Flores 3-13 y Salinas, T295 0985.
Simple comfortable rooms, sitting room doubles
as café-bar with a pleasant atmosphere.

Around Ibarra

$$$$ Hacienda Zuleta, by Angochahua, along the Ibarra-Cayambe road, T266 2032, Quito T02-603 6874, www.haciendazuleta.com. A 2000-ha working historic hacienda, among the nicest in the country. Superb accommodation and food, 15 rooms with fireplace, price includes all meals (prepared with organic vegetables, trout and dairy produced on the farm) and excursions, advance reservations required.

$$$-$$ Pukyu Pamba, In San Clemente, T266 0045, www.sclemente.com (in French). Part of a community-run program. Nicely built cottages with hot water on family properties, cheaper in more humble family homes, price includes 3 tasty meals and a guided tour, you are expected to participate in the family's activities. Horses and *guías nativos* available for more extended treks and visits to other communities.

$$ Casa Aída, in La Esperanza village, T266 0221. Simple rooms with good beds, includes dinner and breakfast, restaurant, shared bath, hot water, some English spoken, meeting place for climbing Imbabura.

Ibarra to the coast

$$$ Las Siete Cascadas, Km 111, 15 km past Lita, T09-9430 7434, lily_tarupi@hotmail.com. A-frame cabins with balconies in a 204-ha reserve, price includes full board and excursions to waterfalls and the forest, reserve well ahead.

$$-$ Parque Bambú, in El Limonal, about 600 m uphill from the main square, T301 6606, www.bospas.org. Small family-run reserve rich in bird life, private rooms with terrace, cheaper in dorm, splendid views of the valley, good breakfast, tasty meals available, camping, treks and horse-riding trips, can arrange excursions to mangroves, volunteer opportunities, Belgian run. Knowledgeable and recommended.

Northwest of Ibarra

$$$ Aguasavia, in Chachimbiro,15-min walk from Santa Agua complex, T06-264 8064, www.termasaguasavia.com. Community run modern hotel in a beautiful setting in the crater of La Viuda Volcano, includes 3 meals, rooms on groud floor with jacuzzi, thermal pools, trips.

$$$ Hacienda San Francisco, in the community of San Francisco, 5 km past Tumbabiro on the road to Chachimbiro, T293 4161, www.hosteriasanfrancisco.com. Intimate family run inn in tastefully converted hacienda stables, includes breakfast, expensive restaurant, full board packages available, small thermal pool, nice grounds, good walking, horse riding, tennis court, excursions to Piñán, best Thu to Sun when owners are in.

$$$ Santa Agua Chachimbiro, part of the recreational complex, T264 8063, in Ibarra T261 0250. Rooms and cabins (some with jacuzzi), includes 3 meals and access to spa and pools, restaurant, busy on weekends, reserve ahead.

$$$-$$ Hostería Spa Pantaví, 7 km from Salinas, at the entrance to Tumbabiro, T293 4185, Quito reservations T02-234 7476, www.hosteriaspapantavi.com. Stylish inn in a tastefully restored hacienda. Very comfortable rooms, decorated with the owner's original works of art, includes nice breakfast, good restaurant, pool, spa, nice gardens, attentive service, hikes and horses for rent, tours. Recommended.

$ Tío Lauro, 1 block from plaza, Tumbabiro, T293 4148. Nice *residencial*, simple rooms, meals on request, parking, friendly owner.

North to Colombia p1018
El Angel

$$$ Polylepis Lodge, T09-9403 1467, abutting the reserve, 14 km from El Angel along the road to Socabones. Rustic cabins with fireplace by a lovely 12-ha forest, includes 3 meals (vegetarian on request) and 3 guided walks, jacuzzi.

$$ Las Orquídeas, in the village of Morán, T09-8641 6936, castro503@yahoo.com. Mountain cabin with bunk beds, shared bath, includes 3 meals, horse riding and guide, run by Carlos Castro, a local guide and conservation pioneer.

$ Paisajes Andinos, Riofrío y 2a Transversal, T297 7577. Adequate, private or shared bath.

Eastern Route to the border p1019
San Gabriel

$ Gabrielita, Mejía y Los Andes, above the agricultural supply shop, T229 1832. Modern hostel, includes breakfast, best in town.

Tulcán p1019

$$ Grand Hotel Comfort, Colón y Chimborazo, T298 1452, www.grandhotelcomfort.com. Modern highrise hotel with rooms and suites with jacuzzi, fridge, safety box, restaurant with set lunch and à la carte, parking, new in 2013.

$$ Machado, Bolívar 403 y Ayacucho, T298 4221. Includes breakfast, comfy, parking.

$$ Sara Espíndola, Sucre y Ayacucho, on plaza, T298 6209. Comfortable rooms, with breakfast, spa, helpful.

$ Los Alpes, JR Arellano next to bus station, T298 2235. Restaurant, OK, good value.

$ Sáenz Internacional, Sucre y Rocafuerte, T298 1916. Very nice, modern, hot water, good value.

$ Torres de Oro, Sucre y Rocafuerte, T298 0296. Modern, nice, restaurant, parking.

🍴 Restaurants

Cotacachi p1016

A local specialty is *carne colorada* (spiced pork).
$$ D'Anita, 10 de Agosto, y Moncayo. Daily 0800-2100. Good set meal of the day, local and international dishes à la carte, popular, English spoken, good value.

$$-$ La Marqueza, 10 de Agosto y Bolívar. Daily 0730-2130. Set lunches and à la carte.

Espresso Río Intag, Imbabura y Rocafuerte. Mon-Fri 0800-2000, Sat 1000-2200, Sun 1030-1500. The best coffee, snacks, meeting place.

Ibarra p1017

$$ El Argentino, Sucre y P Moncayo, at Plazoleta Francisco Calderón. Tue-Sun. Good mixed grill and salads, small, pleasant, outdoor seating.

$$ Flor de Café, Av Teodoro Gómez 6-49 y Atahualpa. Daily. Crêpes, fondue, good breakfasts, bread, yoghurt, cold cuts, coffee.

$$ Pizza El Horno, Rocafuerte 6-38 y Flores. Closed Mon. Italian dishes, live music Sat night.

$$-$ La Cassona, Bolívar 6-47 y Oviedo. Daily. In a nice colonial patio, international, seafood and local dishes, also set lunch.

$ Casa Blanca, Bolívar 7-83. Closed Sun. Family run, in colonial house with patio, good set lunches and snacks. Recommended.

$ Inti Raymi, Av Pérez Guerrero 6-39 y Bolívar. Good simple vegetarian lunches.

Cafés and heladerías

Café Arte, Salinas 5-43 y Oviedo. Daily from1700. Café-bar with character, drinks, Mexican snacks, sandwiches, live music Fri-Sat night.

Heladería Rosalía Suárez, Oviedo y Olmedo. Excellent homemade *helados de paila* (fruit sherbets made in large copper basins), an Ibarra tradition since 1896. Highly recommended.

Olor a Café, Flores y Bolívar. Café/bar/cultural centre in an historic home, music, library.

Tulcán p1019

$ Café Tulcán, Sucre 52-029 y Ayacucho. Café, snacks, desserts, juices, set lunches.

$ Dubai, Chimborazo. Set lunch, à la carte and *comida típica*, popular.

$ Mama Rosita, Sucre entre Boyacá y Atahualpa. Typical Ecuadorean dishes, set lunch.

$ Tequila, Sucre entre Junín y Boyacá. Varied à la carte menu.

🍸 Bars and clubs

Ibarra p1017

Plazoleta Francisco Calderón on Sucre y Pedro Moncayo, has several café-bars with outdoor seating and a pleasant atmosphere.

Rincón de Myer, Olmedo 9-59. A bar with lots of character, attractively restored.

Sambucos and **Dream Cocktails**, Flores y Sucre. Bars/clubs, the in-places among Ibarreño youth.

⚙ What to do

Ibarra p1017

A unique form of paddle ball, **pelota nacional**, is played in the afternoon at Yacucalle, south of the bus station. Players have huge studded paddles for striking the 1-kg ball.

Cycling
Cycling Zone, Flores y Borja. Well-stocked shop, repairs, rentals, route information.

Paragliding

Fly Ecuador, Oviedo 9-13 y Sánchez Cifuentes, T295 3297, www.flyecuador.com.ec. Tandem flight US$67-90, course US$448, arrange ahead. Also at La Estelita, see Where to stay above.

Tour operators

EcuaHorizons, Bolívar 4-67 y García Moreno, T295 9904. Bilingual guides for regional tours. **Intipungo**, Rocafuerte 6-08 y Flores, T295 7766. Regional tours.

Train rides

A tourist train runs from Ibarra to **Salinas**, 29 km away, Wed-Sun and holidays at 1030, returning 1630, US$15-20 one way, US$20-25 return. When there is high demand, there is also ferrochiva (open sided motorized railcar) service at 0800 and 1230, US$15 one way, US$20 return. Purchase tickets in advance at any train station. In Ibarra, at Espejo y Colón, T295 5050, daily 0800-1630 or through T1-800-873637; you need each passenger's passport number and date of birth to purchase tickets. The ride takes 2 hrs with stops. Salinas is a mainly Afro-Ecuadorean town, here are the **Museo de la Sal**, an ethnographic cultural centre and eateries offering local cuisine. You can continue by bus from Salinas to **San Lorenzo**, see page 1101.

⊖ Transport

Cotacachi *p1016*

Bus Terminal at 10 de Agosto y Salinas by the market. Every 10 mins to/from Otavalo terminal, US$0.25, 25 mins; service alternates between the Panamericana and the Quiroga roads. To **Ibarra**, every 15 mins, US$0.45, 40 mins.

Laguna Cuicocha *p1016*

Pick-ups From Otavalo US$10. From **Cotacachi**, US$5 one way, US$10 return with short wait. From **Quiroga** US$5. Return service from the lake available from **Cabañas El Mirador**, same rates.

Los Cedros Research Station

Bus From Estación La Ofelia in Quito, **Trans Minas**, daily at 0615, 1000, 1530, 1800 to **Chontal**, US$2.50, 3 hrs; then a 5-hr **walk**; ask in Chontal for mules to carry luggage up. If the road is passable, 1 daily bus from Otavalo to Chontal.

Ibarra *p1017*

Bus Terminal is at Av Teodoro Gómez y Av Eugenio Espejo, southwest of the centre, T264 4676. Most inter-city transport runs from here. There are no ticket counters for regional destinations, such as Otavalo, proceed directly to the platforms. City buses go from the terminal to the centre or you can walk in 15 mins. To/from **Quito**, Terminal Carcelén, every 10 mins, US$2.50, 2½ hrs. Shared taxis with **Taxis Lagos** (Quito address under Otavalo Transport, in Ibarra at Flores 924 y Sánchez y Cifuentes, near Parque La Merced, T295 5150), buy ticket at least 1 day ahead, US$9.50 pp, 2½ hrs. To **Tulcán**, with **Expreso Turismo**, 9 daily, US$2.50, 2½ hrs. To **Otavalo**, platform 12, every 4 mins, US$0.45, 40 mins. To **Cotacachi**, platform 15, every 15 mins, US$0.45, 40 mins, some continue to **Quiroga**. To the coast, several companies, some go all the way to **San Lorenzo** US$4, 4 hrs, others only as far as **Lita**, US$3.50, 2 hrs. To **Ambato**, CITA goes via El Quinche and the Quito airport and bypasses Quito, 10 daily, US$5, 5 hrs. To **Baños**, Expreso Baños, also by the airport and bypasses Quito, at 0500 and 1430, US$6, 6 hrs. To **Lago Agrio**, Valle de Chota, at 0915, US$9, via La Bonita. To **Tumbabiro** via Urcuquí, Coop Urcuquí, hourly, US$0.75, 1 hr. To **Chachimbiro**, Coop Urcuquí, at 0700, 0730 and 1200, returning Mon-Fri at 1215 (Sat-Sun at 1300), 1530 and 1630, US$1.25, 1½ hrs, taxi US$40 return. Buses to La Esperanza, Zuleta and San Clemete leave from **Parque Germán Grijalva** (east of the Terminal Terrestre, follow C Sánchez y Cifuentes, south from the centre). To **La Esperanza**, every 20 mins, US$0.25, 30 mins. To **Zuleta**, hourly, US$0.52, 1 hr. To **San Clemente**, frequent, weekdays 0650-1840, Sat-Sun 0720-1500, US$0.25, 30 mins.

North to Colombia p1018
El Angel
Bus from **Ibarra** Terminal Terrestre to **Mira**, every 30 mins, US$0.90, 1 hr; to **El Angel**, hourly, US$1.30, 1½ hrs. El Angel to **Mira**, every 30 mins, US$.50, 20 mins. El Angel to **Tulcán**, US$1.30, 1½ hrs. El Angel to **Quito**, US$4, 4 hrs.

Eastern route to the border p1019
San Gabriel
Bus From **San Gabriel** to **Tulcán**, vans and jeeps US$0.70, shared taxis US$0.95, 30 mins, all from the main plaza. From San Gabriel to **Ibarra**, buses, US$1.65, 2 hrs. From San Gabriel to **Quito**, buses, US$3.50, 3½ hrs.

Tulcán p1019
Air TAME (T224 2101) to **Quito** Tue and Thu.
Bus The bus terminal is 1.5 km uphill from centre; best to take a taxi, US$1. To **Quito**, US$4, 5 hrs, every 15 mins, service to Terminal Carcelén, some continue to **Quitumbe**; from Quito, service from both terminals. To **Ibarra**, 2½ hrs, US$2.50. **Otavalo**, US$3, 3 hrs (they don't go in to the Otavalo Terminal, alight at the highway turnoff where taxis are available or transfer in Ibarra). To **Guayaquil**, 20 a day, 13 hrs, US$13. To **Lago Agrio**, 2 a day with **Putumayo**, US$7, 7 hrs, spectacular.

Border with Colombia p1019
Bus Minivans and shared taxis (US$1 pp) leave when full from Parque Ayora (near the cemetery); private taxi US$3.50. **Note** These vehicles cross the international bridge and drop you off on the Colombian side, where onward transport waits. Remember to cross back over the bridge for Ecuadorean immigration. Shared taxi border-Tulcán bus terminal, US$1 pp. Colectivo border-Ipiales, US$1.05, taxi US$4.15.

ⓘ Directory

Ibarra p1017
Banks Banco del Pacífico, Olmedo 715 y Moncayo. **Banco Pichincha**, Sucre 581 y Flores; **Cambio**, Sánchez y Cifuentes 10-70 y Velasco, several currencies and TCs.
Medical services Instituto Médico de Especialidades, Egas 1-83 y Av Teodoro Gómez de La Torre, T295 5612.

Tulcán p1019
Banks Banco del Austro, Ayacucho y Bolívar. Banco Pichincha, 10 de Agosto y Sucre. Few places accept credit cards. Nowhere in Tulcán to change TCs. Pesos Colombianos can easily be changed on Parque La Independencia, the bus terminal and the border. **Consulates** Colombia: Bolívar entre Ayacucho y Junín, T298 7302, Mon-Fri 0800-1300, 1430-1530, visas require 3days.

Cotopaxi, Latacunga and Quilotoa

An impressive roll call of towering peaks lines the route south of Quito, appropriately called the Avenue of the Volcanoes. This area obviously attracts its fair share of trekkers and climbers, while the less active tourist can browse through the many colourful indigenous markets and colonial towns that nestle among the high volcanic cones. The Panamericana heads south from Quito towards the central highlands' hub of Ambato. The perfect cone of Cotopaxi volcano is ever-present and is one of the country's main tourist attractions. Machachi and Latacunga are good bases from which to explore the region and provide access to the beautiful Quilotoa circuit of small villages and vast expanses of open countryside.

Cotopaxi and Latacunga

Machachi → *Phone code: 02. Colour map 11, A3. Population: 29,000. Altitude: 2900 m.*
In a valley between the summits of Pasochoa, Rumiñahui and Corazón, lies the town of **Machachi**, famous for its horsemen (*chagras*), horse riding trips, mineral water springs and crystal clear swimming pools. The water, 'Agua Güitig' or 'Tesalia', is bottled in a plant 4 km from the town, where there is also a sports/recreation complex with one warm and two cold pools, entry US$5. Annual highland 'rodeo', El Chagra, third week in July; tourist information office on the plaza. Just north of Machachi is Alóag, where an important road goes west to Santo Domingo and the coast.

Reserva Ecológica Los Ilinizas → *Phone code: 02. Colour map 11, A3-B3.*
Machachi is a good starting point for a visit to the northern section of the **Reserva Ecológica Los Ilinizas**. Below the saddle between the two peaks, at 4740 m, is the **refugio** ① *T8133 3483, office and café in El Chaupi, T367 4125, www.ilinizas-refuge.webs.com, US$15 per night, US$30 with dinner and breakfast, reserve ahead, take sleeping bag,* a shelter with capacity for 25. **Iliniza Norte** (5105 m) although not a technical climb, should not be underestimated, a few exposed, rocky sections require utmost caution. Some climbers suggest using a rope and a helmet is recommended if other parties are there because of falling rock; allow two to four hours for the ascent from the refuge. Take a compass, it's easy to mistake the descent. **Iliniza Sur** (5245 m) involves ice climbing despite the deglaciation: full climbing gear and experience are absolutely necessary. Access to the reserve is through a turnoff west of the Panamericana 6 km south of Machachi, then it's 7 km to the village of El Chaupi, which is a good base for day-walks and climbing **Corazón** (4782 m, not trivial). A dirt road continues from El Chaupi 9 km to 'La Virgen' (statue), pickup US$15. Nearby are woods where you can camp. El Chaupi hotels arrange for horses with muleteer (US$20-25 per animal).

Parque Nacional Cotopaxi → *Phone code: 03. Colour map 11, B4.*
① *Visitors to the park must register at the entrance. Park gates are open 0700-1500, although you can stay until 1800. Visitors arriving with guides not authorized by the park are turned back at the gate. The park administration, a small museum (0800-1200, 1300-1700) and the Paja Blanca restaurant and shelter, are 10 km from the park gates, just before Limpio Pungo. (See also Transport section below.) The museum has a 3D model of the park, information about the volcano and stuffed animals.*
Cotopaxi volcano (5897 m) is at the heart of a much-visited national park. This scenic snow-covered perfect cone is the second highest peak in Ecuador and a very popular climbing destination. Cotopaxi is an active volcano, one of the highest in the world, and its most recent eruption took place in 1904. Volcanic material from former eruptions can be seen strewn about the *páramo* surrounding Cotopaxi. The northwest flank is most often visited. Here is a high plateau with a small lake (Laguna Limpio Pungo), a lovely area for walking and admiring the delicate flora, and fauna including wild horses and native bird species such as the Andean Lapwing and the Chimborazo Hillstar hummingbird. The lower slopes are clad in planted pine forests, where llamas may be seen. The southwest flank, or Cara Sur, has not received as much impact as the west side. Here too, there is good walking, and you can climb Morurco (4881 m) as an acclimatization hike; condors may sometimes be seen. Just north of Cotopaxi are the peaks of Rumiñahui (4722 m), Sincholagua (4873 m) and Pasochoa (4225 m). To the southeast, beyond the park boundary, are Quilindaña (4890 m) and an area of rugged páramos and mountains dropping down to the jungle. The area has several large haciendas which form the Fundación Páramo (www.fundacionparamo.org), a private reserve with restricted access.

The **main entrance** to Parque Nacional Cotopaxi is approached from Chasqui, 25 km south of Machachi, 6 km north of Lasso. Once through the national park gates, go past Laguna Limpio Pungo to a fork, where the right branch climbs steeply to a parking lot (4600 m). From here it's a 30-minute to one-hour walk to the José Ribas refuge, at 4800 m; beware of altitude sickness. Walking from the highway to the refuge takes an entire day or more. The **El Pedregal entrance**, from the northwest, is accessed from Machachi via Santa Ana del Pedregal (21 km from the Panamericana), or from Sangolquí via Rumipamba and the Río Pita Valley. From Pedregal to the refuge car park is 14 km. There are infrequent buses to Pedregal (two a day) then the hike in is shorter but still a couple of hours. The **Ticatilín access** leads to the southwest flank. Just north of Lasso, a road goes east to the village of San Ramón and on to Ticatilín (a contribution of US$2 per vehicle may be requested at the barrier here, be sure to close all gates) and Rancho María. From the south, San Ramón is accessed from Mulaló. Beyond Rancho María is the private Albergue Cotopaxi Cara Sur (4000 m, see Where to stay below). Walking four hours from here you reach Campo Alto (4760 m), a climbers' tent camp.

Climbing Cotopaxi The ascent from the Ribas refuge takes five to eight hours, start climbing at 0100 as the snow deteriorates in the sun. A full moon is both practical and a magical experience. Check out snow conditions with the guardian of the refuge before climbing. The route changes from year to year due to deglaciation. Because of the altitude and weather conditions, Cotopaxi is a serious climb, equipment and experience are required. To maximize your chances of reaching the summit, make sure to be well acclimatized beforehand. Glimbing with a guide is compulsory. Agencies in Quito and throughout the Central Highlands offer Cotopaxi climbing trips. Note that some guides encourage tourists to turn back at the first sign of tiredness, don't be pressured, insist on going at your own pace. There is no specific best season to climb Cotopaxi, weather conditions are largely a matter of luck year-round. You can also climb on the southwest flank, where the route

Where to stay
1 Central
2 Rodelú
3 Rosim

4 Tiana & Tovar Expediciones

Restaurants
1 Café Abuela
2 Chifa China
3 Dragon Rojo

4 El Templario
5 Guadalajara Grill
6 Parilladas La Española
7 Pizzería Buon Giorno

is reported easier and safer than on the northwest face, but a little longer. To reach the summit in one day, you have to stay at Campo Alto (see above, and Where to stay below), from where it is 6 hours to the summit. The last hour goes around the rim of the crater with impressive views.

Lasso → *Phone code: 03. Colour map 11, B3. Altitude: 3000 m.*

Some 30 km south of Machachi is the small town of Lasso, on the railway line and off the Panamericana. In the surrounding countryside are several *hosterías*, converted country estates, offering accommodation and meals. Intercity buses bypass Lasso.

Latacunga → *Phone code: 03. Colour map 11, B3. Population: 103,000. Altitude: 2800 m.*

The capital of Cotopaxi Province is a place where the abundance of light grey pumice has been artfully employed. Volcán Cotopaxi is much in evidence, though it is 29 km away. Provided they are not hidden by clouds, which unfortunately is all too often, as many as nine volcanic cones can be seen from Latacunga; try early in the morning. The colonial character of the town has been well preserved. The central plaza, **Parque Vicente León**, is a beautifully maintained garden (locked at night). There are several other gardens in the town including **Parque San Francisco** and **Lago Flores** (better known as 'La Laguna'). **Casa de los Marqueses de Miraflores** ⓘ *Sánchez de Orellana y Abel Echeverría, T280 1382, Mon-Fri 0800-1200, 1400-1800, Sat 0900-1300, free,* in a restored colonial mansion has a modest museum, with exhibits on Mama Negra (see Festivals, page 1030), colonial art, archaeology, numismatics, a library and the Jefatura de Turismo, see below.

Casa de la Cultura ⓘ *Antonia Vela 3-49 y Padre Salcedo T281 3247, Tue-Fri 0800-1200, 1400-1800, Sat 0800-1500, US$1,* built around the remains of a Jesuit Monastery and the old Monserrat watermill, houses a nice museum with pre-Columbian ceramics, weavings, costumes and models of festival masks; also art gallery, library and theatre. It has week-long festivals with exhibits and concerts for all the local festivities. There is a Saturday **market** on the Plaza de San Sebastián (at Juan Abel Echeverría). Goods for sale include *shigras* (fine stitched, colourful straw bags) and homespun wool and cotton yarn. The produce market, Plaza El Salto has daily trading and larger fairs on Tuesday, Friday and Saturday. A tourist **train** runs from Quito to Latacunga, see page 996.

Tourist offices: **Cámara de Turismo de Cotopaxi** ⓘ *Quito 14-38 y General Maldonado, T280 1112, www.capturcotopaxi.com/fest.htm, Mon-Fri 0900-1300, 1400-1700,* local and regional information, Spanish only. **Jefatura de Turismo** ⓘ *Casa de los Marqueses, T280 8494, Mon-Fri 0800-1700,* local and regional information and maps.

ⓒ Cotopaxi and Latacunga listings

For hotel and restaurant price codes, and other relevant information, see Essentials.

● Where to stay

Machachi *p1025*

$$$ Papagayo, in Hacienda Bulívia, west of the Panamericana, take a taxi fom Machachi, T231 0002, www.hosteria-papagayo.com. Nicely refurbished hacienda, pleasant communal areas with fireplace and library, restaurant, jacuzzi, parking, central heating, homey atmosphere, horse riding, biking, tours, popular.

$$ La Estación y Granja, 3 km west of the Panamericana, by railway station outside the village of Aloasí, T230 9246, Quito T02-241 3784. Rooms in a lovely old home and newer section, also cabins, fireplaces, meals available (produce from own garden), parking, family run, hiking access to Volcán Corazón, reserve ahead.

$$ Sierra Loma, near Aloasí, 700 m south of Machachi train station, T09-9593 8256, www. sierraloma.com. Cabins in the forest for 4, with fireplace, includes breakfast, other meals on request, camping (**$**), package with meals, activities and transport from Quito available.

$ Chiguac, Los Caras y Colón, 4 blocks east of the main park, T231 0396, amsincholagua@gmail.com. Nice family-run hostel, comfortable rooms, good breakfast, other meals available, shared bath. Recommended.

Reserva Ecológica Los Ilinizas *p1025*

$$$$ Hacienda Umbria, off the road to El Chaupi, T09-8923 0143, http://haciendaumbria.com. Very exclusive accommodation in a 330-ha working hacienda on the slopes of El Corazón. Rooms with fireplace, gourmet meals with farm produce, open kitchen, outdoor and farm activities.

$$$-$$ Chuquiragua Lodge, 500 m before El Chaupi, then 200 m on a cobbled road, T367 4046, in Quito: T603 5590, www.ecuadortreasure.com. Inn with lovely views, a variety of rooms and prices, restaurant with roaring fireplace, spa. US$18 pp in dorm, camping US$5 pp with hot shower, horse riding, trekking, climbing, bike tours, and transport from Quito.

$$ La Llovizna, 100 m behind the church, on the way to the mountain, T367 4076. Pleasant hostel, sitting room with fireplace, includes breakfast and dinner, private or shared bath, ping pong, horse, bike and gear rentals, guiding, book in advance.

$$-$ Nina Rumy, near the bus stop in El Chaupi, T367 4088. Includes breakfast and supper, simple rooms with shared bath, electric shower, family run and very friendly.

Parque Nacional Cotopaxi *p1025*

All these inns are good for acclimatization at altitudes between 3100 m and 3800 m. Just below Limpio Pungo is the **Paja Blanca** shelter (**$** pp with breakfast, hot water) with 2 very basic huts and a couple of campsites (US$2 per tent, no facilities). The **José Ribas** refuge was being rebuilt in 2014 and was expected to reopen later that year. It will have capacity for 100 visitors and a restaurant, no public kitchen, bring a warm sleeping bag.

$$$-$$ Tambopaxi, 3 km south of the El Pedregal access (1 hr drive from Machachi) or 4 km north of the turn-off for the climbing

shelter, T02-222 0242 (Quito), www.tambopaxi.com. Comfortable straw-bale mountain shelter at 3750 m. 3 double rooms and several dorms (US$20 pp), duvets, includes breakfast, other meals available, camping US$7.50 pp, horse riding with advance notice.

$$ Albergue Cotopaxi Cara Sur, at the southwestern end of the park, at the end of the Ticatilín road, T09-8461 9264, www.cotopaxicarasur.com (see page 992). Very nice mountain shelter at 4000 m, day use US$1. Includes breakfast and dinner, use of kitchen, some cabins with private bath, hot shower, transport from Quito and climbing tours available, equipment rental. **Campo Alto** is a very basic tent camp (4780 m, US$8 pp), 4 hrs walk from the shelter, horse to take gear to Campo Alto US$15, muleteer US$15.

Outside the park

$$$$ Hacienda San Agustín de Callo, 2 access roads from the Panamericana, one just north of the main park access (6.2 km); the second, just north of Lasso (4.3 km), T03-271 9160, Quito T02-290 6157, www.incahacienda.com. Exclusive hacienda, the only place in Ecuador where you can sleep and dine in an Inca building, the northernmost imperial-style Inca structure still standing. Rooms and suites with fireplace and bathtub, includes breakfast and dinner, horse rides, treks, bicycles and fishing. Restaurant (**$$$**) and buildings open to non-guests (US$5-10).

$$$$ Hacienda Santa Ana, 10 mins from north entrance to Cotopaxi National Park, T02-222 4950, www.santaanacotopaxi.com. 17th-century former-Jesuit hacienda in beautiful surroundings. 7 comfortable rooms with fireplaces, central heating, great views, horse riding, hiking, trekking, climbing. Also run **Hotel Sierra Madre** in Quito.

$$$$ Hacienda Yanahurco, on access road to Quilindaña, 2 hrs from Machachi, T09-9612 7759, Quito T02-244 5248, www.haciendayanahurco.com. Large hacienda in wild area, rooms with fireplace or heater, includes meals, 2-4 day programs, all-inclusive.

$$$-$$ Chilcabamba, Loreto del Pedregal, by the northern access to the National Park,

T09-9946 0406, T02-237 7098, www.chilca bamba.com. Cabins and rooms, US$30.50 pp in dorm, magnificent views.

$$$-$$ Cuello de Luna, 2 km northwest of the park's main access on a dirt road, T09-9970 0330, www.cuellodeluna.com. Comfortable rooms with fireplace, includes breakfast, other meals available, US$22 pp in dorm (a very low loft). Can arrange tours to Cotopaxi, horse riding and biking.

$$$-$$ Tierra del Volcán, T09-9498 0121, Quito T02-600 9533, www.tierradelvolcan.com. 3 haciendas: Hacienda El Porvenir, a working ranch by Rumiñahui, between El Pedregal and the northern access to the park, 3 types of rooms, includes breakfast, set meals available, horses and mountain bikes for hire, camping, zip line; Hacienda Santa Rita, by the Río Pita, on the Sangolquí-El Pedregal road, with zip-lines, entry US$6, camping US$5 pp; and the more remote, rustic Hacienda El Tambo by Quilindaña, southeast of the park. Also offers many adventure activities in the park.

$$ Huagra Corral, 200 m east of Panamericana along the park's main access road, T03-271 9729, Quito T02-380 8427, www.huagracorral. com. Nicely decorated, restaurant, private or shared bath, heaters, convenient location, helpful, reserve ahead.

Lasso *p1027*

$$$$ Hacienda Hato Verde, Panamericana Sur Km 55, by entry to Mulaló, southeast of Lasso, T271 9348, www.haciendahatoverde. com. Lovely old hacienda and working dairy farm near the south flank of Cotopaxi, tastefully restored. 10 rooms with wood-burning stoves, includes breakfast, other meals available; horse riding (for experienced riders), trekking, trip up Cotopaxi Cara Sur, charming hosts.

$$$ Hostería La Ciénega, 2 km south of Lasso, T271 9052. An historic hacienda with nice gardens, rooms with heater or fireplace, good expensive restaurant.

$ Cabañas Los Volcanes, at the south end of Lasso, T271 9524, maexpediciones@yahoo.com. Small hostel, nice rooms, private or shared bath, discounts for HI members. Tours to Cotopaxi.

Latacunga *p1027, map p1026*

$$ Rodelú, Quito 16-31, T280 0956, www. rodelu.com.ec. Comfortable popular hotel, restaurant, nice suites and rooms except for a few which are very small, breakfast included starting the 2nd day.

$$ $ Rosim, Quito 16-49 y Padre Salcedo, T280 2172, www.hotelrosim.com. Centrally located, breakfast available, carpeted rooms, quiet and comfortable. Discounts in low season.

$$-$ Tiana, Luis F. Vivero N1-31 y Sánchez de Orellana, T281 0147, www.hostaltiana.com. Includes breakfast, drinks and snacks available, private or shared bath, US$10 pp in dorm, nice patio, kitchen facilities, luggage store, popular meeting place, good source of information for Quilotoa Loop.

$ Central, Sánchez de Orellana y Padre Salcedo, T280 2912. A multi-storey hotel in the centre of town, breakfast available, a bit faded but very helpful.

🍴 Restaurants

Machachi *p1025*
Not much to choose from in town.
$$$-$$ Café de la Vaca, 4 km south of town on the Panamericana. Daily 0800-1730. Very good meals using produce from their own farm, popular.
$$-$ Pizzeria Di Ragazzo, Av Pablo Guarderas N7-107, north of centre. Is reported good.

Latacunga *p1027, map p1026*
Few places are open on Sun. Many places along the Panamericana specialize in *chugchucaras*, a traditional pork dish. *Allullas* biscuits and string cheese are sold by the roadside.
$$ Parilladas La Española, 2 de Mayo 7-175. Mon-Sat 1230-2100. Good grill, popular with locals.
$$-$ Chifa China, Antonia Vela 6-85 y 5 de Junio. Daily 1030-2200. Good Chinese food, large portions.
$$-$ Guadalajara Grill, Quijano y Ordóñez y Vivero. Closed Sun. Good Mexican food.
$$-$ Pizzería Buon Giorno, Maldonado y Sánchez de Orellana. Mon-Sat 1300-2200. Great pizzas and lasagne, large selection. Popular and recommended.
$ Dragon Rojo, Amazonas y Pastaza. Open late. Chinese food, large portions, popular.
Café Abuela, Guayaquil 6-07 y Quito, by Santo Domingo church. Pleasant cosy café/bar, nicely decorated, drinks, sweets and sandwiches, popular with university students.
El Templario, Luis F Vivero y Sánchez de Orellana. Café/bar, microbrews, tapas, good atmosphere.

🎉 Festivals

Latacunga *p1027, map p1026*
The La Mama Negra is held **23-24 Sep**, in homage to the Virgen de las Mercedes. There are 5 main characters in the parade and hundreds of dancers, some representing the black slaves, others the whites. Mama Negra herself (portrayed by a man) is a slave who dared to ask for freedom in colonial times. The colourful costumes are called the Santísima Trajería. The civic festival of Mama Negra, with similar parade, is on the **1st or 2nd Sat in Nov** (but not 2 Nov, Día de los Muertos). It is part of the Fiestas de Latacunga, **11 Nov**.

🛍 Shopping

Latacunga *p1027, map p1026*
Artesanía Otavalo, Guayaquil 5-50 y Quito. A variety of souvenirs from Otavalo.

🎯 What to do

Latacunga *p1027, map p1026*
All operators offer day trips to Cotopaxi and Quilotoa (US$40 pp, includes lunch and a visit to a market town if on Thu or Sat, minimum 2 people). Climbing trips to Cotopaxi are around US$170 pp for 2 days (plus *refugio*), minimum 2 people. Trekking trips US$70-80 pp per day. **Note** Many agencies require passport as deposit when renting gear.
Greivag, Guayaquil y Sánchez de Orellana, Plaza Santo Domingo, L5, T281 0510, www.greivagturismo.com. Day trips.
Metropolitan Touring, Calle Guayaquil y Sánchez de Orellana, Plaza Santo Domingo, L6, T280 2985. See Quito operators. Airline tickets.
Neiges, Guayaquil 6-25, Plaza Santo Domingo, T281 1199, neigestours@hotmail.com. Day trips and climbing.
Tovar Expediciones, at Hostal Tiana, T281 1333. Climbing and trekking.

⛔ Transport

Machachi *p1025*
Bus To **Quito**, from El Playón behind the stadium, every 15 mins to Terminal Quitumbe, every 30 mins to Villa Flora and El Trebol, all US$0.75, 1½ hrs. To **Latacunga**, from the monument to El Chagra at the Panamericana, US$0.55, 1 hr.

Reserva Ecológica Los Ilinizas *p1025*
Bus From El Playón in Machachi, where buses from Quito arrive (see above), to **El Chaupi**

(every 20 mins, US$0.36, ½ hr), from where you can walk to the *refugio* in 7-8 hrs. A pick-up from El Chaupi to 'La Virgen' costs US$10, from Machachi US$25. It takes 3 hrs to walk with a full pack from 'La Virgen' to the *refugio*. Horses can be hired at any of the lodgings in El Chaupi.

Parque Nacional Cotopaxi *p1025*
Main park entrance and Refugio Ribas, take a Latacunga bus from Quito and get off at the main access point. Do not take an express bus as you can't get off before Latacunga. At the turnoff to the park there are usually vehicles from a local operator which go to the park. US$40 to the parking lot before the refuge for up to 3 passengers. From **Machachi**, pick-ups go via the cobbled road to El Pedregal on to Limpio Pungo and the refugio parking lot, US$40. From **Lasso**, full day trip to the park, US$70 return, contact **Cabañas los Volcanes**. From **Latacunga**, arrange with tour operators.

To **Cara Sur** from Quito, **Cotopaxi Cara Sur** offer transport to the **Albergue Cara Sur**, US$60 per vehicle up to 5 passengers. Alternatively take a Latacunga bound bus and get off at **Pastocalle**, and take a pick-up from there, US$15 per vehicle for up to 5 passengers.

Latacunga *p1027, map p1026*
Air The airport is north of the centre.1 daily flight to **Guayaquil** and **Coca** with TAME.
Bus Buses leave from the terminal on the

Panamericana just south of 5 de Junio, except **Transportes Santa**, which has its own terminal, 2 blocks away at Eloy Alfaro y Vargas Torres, T281 1659, serving **Cuenca** and **Loja** (4 daily), **Machala** and **Guayaquil** (3 daily). To **Quito**, every 15 mins, 2 hrs, US$2. To **Ambato**, 1 hr, US$1. To **Guayaquil**, US$7, 7 hrs. To **Saquisilí**, every 20 mins (see below). Through buses, which are more frequent, do not stop at Latacunga Terminal. During the day (0600-1700), they go along a bypass road 4 blocks west of the Terminal, and have small stations at Puente de San Felipe. At night they stop at the corner of Panamericana and Av 5 de Junio. To **Otavalo**, **Ibarra** and **Tulcán**, bypassing Quito, **Cita Express**, 12 daily from Puente de San Felipe; also with **Expreso Baños**. To **Baños**, every 20 mins from Puente de San Felipe. Buses on the Zumbahua, Quilotoa, Chugchilán, Sigchos circuit are given below. **Note** On Thu most buses to nearby communities leave from Saquisilí market instead of Latacunga.

⊙ Directory

Latacunga *p1027, map p1026*
Banks Banco de Guayaquil, Maldonado y Sánchez de Orellana. Banco Pichincha, C Quito, Parque Vicente León. **Medical services** Clínica Latacunga, Sánchez de Orellana 11-79 y Marqués de Maenza, T281 0260. Private, 24 hrs.

Quilotoa Circuit

The popular and recommended 200-km round trip from Latacunga to Pujilí, Zumbahua, Quilotoa crater, Chugchilán, Sigchos, Isinliví, Toacazo, Saquisilí, and back to Latacunga, can be done in two to three days by bus. It is also a great route for biking and only a few sections of the loop are cobbled or rough. Access is from either Pastocalle, north of Lasso or Latacunga. Hiking from one town to another can be challenging, especially when the fog rolls in. For these longer walks hiring a guide might not be unreasonable if you don't have a proper map or enough experience.

Latacunga to Zumbahua

A fine paved road leads west to **Pujilí** ⓘ *15 km, bus US$0.25*, which has a beautiful church. Good market on Sunday, and a smaller one on Wednesday. Colourful Corpus Christi celebrations. Beyond Pujilí, many interesting crafts are practised by the *indígenas* in the **Tigua valley**: paintings on leather, hand-carved wooden masks and baskets. **Chimbacucho**, also known as Tigua, is home to the Toaquiza family, most famous of the Tigua artists. The road goes on to

Zumbahua, then over the Western Cordillera to La Maná and Quevedo. This is a great paved downhill bike route. It carries very little traffic and is extremely twisty in parts but is one of the most beautiful routes connecting the highlands with the coast. Beyond Zumbahua are the pretty towns of **Piló** (two restaurants, small hostal and petrol pumps), **Esperanza de El Tingo** (two restaurants and lodging at **Carmita's**, T03-281 4657) and **La Maná** (two hotels).

Zumbahua → *Phone code: 03. Colour map 11, B3.*

Zumbahua lies 800 m from the main road, 62 km from Pujilí. It has an interesting Saturday market (starts at 0600) for local produce, and some tourist items. Just below the plaza is a shop selling dairy products and cold drinks. Friday nights involve dancing and drinking. Take a fleece, as it can be windy, cold and dusty. There is a good hospital in town, Italian-funded and run. The Saturday trip to Zumbahua market and the Quilotoa crater is one of the best excursions in Ecuador.

Quilotoa → *Phone code: 03. Colour map 11, B3.*

Zumbahua is the point to turn off for a visit to Quilotoa, a volcanic crater filled by a beautiful emerald lake. From the rim of the crater, 3850 m, several snowcapped volcanoes can be seen in the distance. The crater is reached by a paved road which runs north from Zumbahua (about 12 km, three- to five-hours' walk). There's a 300-m drop down from the crater rim to the water. The hike down takes about 30 minutes (an hour or more to climb back up). The trail starts at the village of Quilotoa, up the slope from the parking area, then, down a steepcanyon-like cut. You can hire a mule to ride up from the bottom of the crater (US$8), best arrange before heading down. There is a basic hostel by the lake and kayaks for rent. Everyone at the crater tries to sell the famous naïve Tigua pictures and carved wooden masks, so expect to be besieged (also by begging children). To the southeast of the crater is the village of Macapungo, which runs the Complejo Turístico Shalalá, see Where to stay, below. The Mirador Shalalá platform on offers great views of the lake. To hike around the crater rim takes 4½ to six hours in clear weather. Be prepared for sudden changes in the weather, it gets very cold at night and can be foggy. Always stay on the trail as trekkers have got lost and hurt themselves. For a shorter loop (three to four hours), start on the regular circuit going left when you reach the rim by Quilotoa village and follow it to Mirador Shalalá, a great place for a picnic; then backtrack for about five minutes and take the path down to the lake. To return, follow a path near the lake until you reach the large trail which takes you back up to Quilotoa village. If you are tired, right there you can hire a horse to take you up.

Chugchilán, Sigchos and Isinliví → *Phone code: 03. Colour map 11, B3.*

Chugchilán, a village in one of the most scenic areas of Ecuador, is 16 km by paved road from Quilotoa. An alternative to the road is a five- to six-hour walk around part of the Quilotoa crater rim, then down to Guayama, and across the canyon (Río Sigüí) to Chugchilán, 11 km. Outside town is a cheese factory and nearby, at Chinaló, a woodcarving shop. The area has good walking.

Continuing from Chugchilán the road, unpaved, runs to **Sigchos**, the starting point for the Toachi Valley walk, via Asache to San Francisco de las Pampas (0900 bus daily to Latacunga). There is also a highland road to Las Pampas, with two buses from Sigchos. Southeast of Sigchos is **Isinliví**, on the old route to Toacazo and Latacunga. It has a fine woodcarving shop and a pre-Inca pucará. Trek to the village of Guantualó, which has a fascinating market on Monday. You can hike to or from Chugchilán (five hours), or from Quilotoa to Isinliví in seven to nine hours.

From Sigchos, a paved road leads to **Toacazo** (**$$ La Quinta Colorada**, T271 6122, www.quintacolorada.com, price includes breakfast and dinner) and on to Saquisilí.

Saquisilí → *Phone code: 03. Colour map 11, B3.*

Some 16 km southwest of Lasso, and 6 km west of the Panamericana is the small but very important market town of Saquisilí. Its Thursday market (0500-1400) is famous throughout Ecuador for the way in which its seven plazas and some of its streets become jam-packed with people, the great majority of them local *indígenas* with red ponchos and narrow-brimmed felt hats. The best time to visit the market is 0900-1200 (before 0800 for the animal market). Be sure to bargain, as there is a lot of competition. This area has colourful Corpus Christi processions.

⦿ Quilotoa Circuit listings

For hotel and restaurant price codes, and other relevant information, see Essentials.

⬛ Where to stay

Latacunga to Zumbahua *p1031*
Tigua-Chimbacucho

$$ La Posada de Tigua, 3 km east of Tigua-Chimbacucho, 400 m north of the road, T305 6103, posadadetigua@yahoo.com. Refurbished hacienda, part of a working dairy ranch, 6 rooms, wood-burning stove, includes tasty home-cooked breakfast and dinner, pleasant family atmosphere, horses for riding, trails, nice views.

Zumbahua *p1032*

There are only a few phone lines in town, which are shared among several people. Expect delays when calling to book a room.
$ Cóndor Matzi, overlooking the market area, T09-8906 1572 or T03-281 2953 to leave message. Basic but best in town, shared bath, hot water, dinning room with wood stove, kitchen facilities, try to reserve ahead, if closed when you arrive ask at **Restaurante Zumbahua** on the corner of the plaza.
$ Richard, opposite the market on the road in to town, T09-9015 5996. Basic shared rooms and one shower with hot water, cooking facilities, parking.

Quilotoa *p1032*

$$ Quilotoa Crater Lake Lodge, on the main road facing the access to Quilotoa, T305 5816. Somewhat faded hacienda-style lodge, includes breakfast and dinner, dining room with fireplace, views.

Humberto Latacunga, a good painter who also organizes treks, runs 3 good hostels, T09-9212 5962, all include breakfast and dinner:
$$ Hostería Alpaca, www.alpacaquilotoa. com, the most upmarket, rooms with wood stoves; **$$-$ Cabañas Quilotoa**, on the access road to the crater, www.cabanasquilotoa.com, private or shared bath, wood stoves; **$ Hostal Pachamama**, at the top of the hill by the rim of the crater, private bath.
$ Complejo Shalalá, in Macapungo, T09-9312 2983, http://shalala.uphero.com. Community run lodge in a lovely 35-ha cloudforest reserve. Nice cabins, one with wheelchair access, includes breakfast and dinner, restaurant, trails.

Chugchilán *p1032*

$$$$-$$$ Black Sheep Inn, below the village on the way to Sigchos, T270-8077, www. blacksheepinn.com. A lovely eco-friendly resort which has received several awards. Includes 3 excellent vegetarian meals, private and shared bath, **$$** pp in dorms, spa, water slide, zip line, arrange excursions. Highly recommended.
$$ Hostal Mama Hilda, on the road in to town, T270 8015. Pleasant family-run hostel, warm atmosphere, large rooms some with wood stoves, includes good dinner and breakfast, private or shared bath, camping, parking, arrange trips. Highly recommended.
$$-$ Hostal Cloud Forest, at the entrance to town, T270 8016, www.cloudforesthostal.com. Simple popular family-run hostel, sitting room with wood stove, includes dinner and great breakfast, restaurant open to public for lunch, private or shared bath, also dorm, parking, very helpful.

Sigchos *p1032*

$ Jardín de los Andes, Ilinizas y Tungurahua, T271 2114. Basic but quite clean and friendly.

Isinliví *p1032*

$$$-$$ Llullu Llama, T09-9258 0562, www.llullullama.com. Farmhouse with cosy sitting room with wood stove, nicely refurbished in 2013, tastefully decorated rooms, shared ecological bath. Also rustic adobe cabins for four, with bath, stove and small terrace, new in 2014. All include good hearty dinner and breakfast. Warm and relaxing atmosphere, a lovely spot. Recommended.

Saquisilí *p1033*

$$ Gilocarmelo, by the cemetery, 800 m from town on the road north to Guaytacama, T09-9966 9734, T02-340 0924. Restored hacienda house in a 4 ha property. Plain rooms with fireplace, restaurant, pool, sauna, jacuzzi, nice garden.

$ San Carlos, Bolívar opposite the Parque Central. A multi-storey building, electric shower, parking, good value, but watch your valuables. Will hold luggage for US$1 while you visit the market.

⊙ Transport

Zumbahua *p1032*

Bus Many daily on the Latacunga-Quevedo road (0500-1900, US$1.25, 1½ hrs). Buses on Sat are packed full, get your ticket the day before. A pick-up truck can be hired from Zumbahua to **Quilotoa** for US$5-10 depending on number of passengers; also to **Chugchilán** for around US$30. On Sat mornings there are many trucks leaving the Zumbahua market for Chugchilán which pass Quilotoa. Pick-up Quilotoa–Chugchilán US$25.

Taxi Day-trip by taxi to Zumbahua, Quilotoa, and return to **Latacunga** is about US$60.

Quilotoa *p1032*

Bus From the terminal terrestre in Latacunga Trans Vivero daily at 1000, 1130, 1230 and 1330, US$2, 2 hrs. Note that this leaves from

Latacunga, not Saquisilí market, even on Thu. Return bus direct to Latacunga at 1300. Buses returning at 1400 and 1500 go only as far as Zumbahua, from where you can catch a Latacunga bound bus at the highway. Also, buses going through Zumbahua bound for Chugchilán will drop you at the turnoff, 5 mins from the crater, where you can also pick them up on their way to Zumbahua and Latacunga.Taxi from Latacunga, US$40 one way. For **Shalalá**, Trans Ilinizas from Latacunga to **Macapungo** at 1300, US$1.50, or go to Zumbahua and take a pick-up from there, US$5. From Macapungo it is a 30-min walk to the cabins.

Chugchilán *p1032*

Bus From **Latacunga**, daily at 1130 (except Thu) via Sigchos, at 1200 via Zumbahua; on Thu from **Saquisilí market** via Sigchos around 1130, US$2.25, 3 hrs. Buses return to Latacunga daily at 0300 via Sigchos, at 0400 via Zumbahua. On Sun there are 2 extra buses to Latacunga leaving 0900-1000. There are extra buses going as far as Zumbahua Wed 0500, Fri 0600 and Sun between 0900-1000; these continue towards the coast. Milk truck to Sigchos around 0800. On Sat also pick-ups going to/from market in Zumbahua and Latacunga. From **Sigchos**, through buses as indicated above, US$0.60, 1 hr. Pick-up hire to Sigchos US$25, up to 5 people, US$5 additional person. Pick-up to **Quilotoa** US$25, up to 5 people, US$5 additional person. Taxi from Latacunga US$60, from Quito US$100.

Sigchos *p1032*

Bus From **Latacunga** almost every hour, 0930-1600; returning to Latacunga most buses leave Sigchos before 0700, then at 1430 (more service on weekends); US$1.50, 2 hrs. From **Quito** direct service Mon-Sat at 1400 (more frequent Sun) with Reina de Sigchos; **also Fri 1700 with Ilinizas**; US$3, 3 hrs. To **La Maná** on the road to Quevedo, via Chugchilán, Quilotoa and Zumbahua, Fri at 0500 and Sun at 0830, US$3.50, 6 hrs (returns Sat at 0730 and Sun at 1530). To **Las Pampas**, at 0330 and 1400,

US$2.50, 3 hrs. From Las Pampas to **Santo Domingo**, at 0300 and 0600, US$2.50, 3 hrs.

Isinliví *p1032*
From **Latacunga** daily (except Thu), via Sigchos at 1215 (**14 de Octubre**) and direct at 1300 (**Trans Vivero**), on Thu both leave from Saquisilí market around 1100, on Sat the direct bus leaves at 1100 instead of 1300, US$1.80, 2½ hrs. Both buses return to Latacunga 0300-0330, except Wed at 0700 direct, Sun 1245 direct and Mon 1500 via Sigchos. buses fill quickly, be there early.

Connections to Chugchilán, Quilotoa and Zumbahua can be made in Sigchos. Bus schedules are posted on www.llullullama.com.

Saquisilí *p1033*
Bus Frequent service between **Latacunga** and Saquisilí, US$0.30, 20 mins; many buses daily to/from **Quito** (Quitumbe), 0530-1300, US$2, 2 hrs. Buses and trucks to many outlying villages leave from 1000 onwards. Bus tours from Quito cost US$45 pp, taxis charge US$80, with 2 hrs wait at market.

Ambato → *Phone code: 03. Colour map 11, B3. Population: 182,000. Altitude: 2700 m.*

Almost completely destroyed in the great 1949 earthquake, Ambato lacks the colonial charm of other Andean cities, though its location in the heart of fertile orchard-country has earned it the nickname of 'the city of fruits and flowers' (see Festival, page 1037). It is also a transport hub and the principal supply town of the central highlands, with a large Monday market and smaller ones Wednesday and Friday. **Tourist office: Ministerio de Turismo** ① *Guayaquil y Rocafuerte, T282 1800, Mon-Fri 0800-1700*, helpful.

The modern cathedral faces **Parque Montalvo**, where there is a statue of the writer Juan Montalvo (1832-1889), whose **house** ① *Bolívar y Montalvo, T282 4248, US$1*, can be visited. The **Museo de la Provincia** in the Casa del Portal (built 1900), facing Parque Montalvo, has a photo collection.

Northeast of Ambato is the colonial town of **Píllaro**, gateway to **Parque Nacional Los Llanganates**, a beautiful rugged area (for tours see **Sachayacu Explorer**, page 1044) The town is known for its colourful festivals: a *diablada* (devils parade) 1-6 January and Corpus Christi.

Ambato to Baños
To the east of Ambato, an important road leads to **Salasaca**, where the *indígenas* sell their weavings; they wear distinctive black ponchos with white trousers and broad white hats. Further east, 5 km, is **Pelileo**, the blue jean manufacturing capital of Ecuador with good views of Tungurahua. There are opportunities for cultural tourism, walking and paragliding in the area (contact **Blue I and Adventures** ① *T03-283 0236, bluelandsalasaca@yahoo.com.ar*). From Pelileo, the road descends to Las Juntas, where the Patate and Chambo rivers meet to form the Río Pastaza. About 1 km east of Las Juntas bridge, the junction with the road to Riobamba is marked by a large sculpture of a macaw and a toucan (locally known as Los Pájaros – the lower bird was destroyed by the volcano). It is a favourite volcano watching site. The road to Baños then continues along the lower slopes of the volcano.

Eight kilometres northeast of Pelileo on a paved side-road is **Patate**, centre of the warm, fruit growing Patate valley. There are excellent views of Volcán Tungurahua from town. The fiesta of **Nuestro Señor del Terremoto** is held on the weekend leading up to 4 February, featuring a parade with floats made with fruit and flowers.

Ambato to Riobamba and Guaranda
After Ambato, the Pan-American Highway runs south to Riobamba (see page 1044). About half way is **Mocha**, where guinea pigs (*cuy*) are bred for the table. You can sample roast *cuy* and other

typical dishes at stalls and restaurants by the roadside, **Mariadiocelina** is recommended. The highway climbs steeply south of Mocha and at the pass at **Urbina** there are fine views in the dry season of Chimborazo and Carihuayrazo.

To the west of Ambato, a paved road climbs through tilled fields, past the páramos of Carihuayrazo and Chimborazo to the great Arenal (a high desert at the base of the mountain), and down through the Chimbo valley to Guaranda (see page 1045). This spectacular journey reaches a height of 4380 m and vicuñas can be seen.

◉ Ambato listings

For hotel and restaurant price codes, and other relevant information, see Essentials.

● Where to stay

Ambato *p1035*
$$$ Ambato, Guayaquil 01-08 y Rocafuerte, T242 1791, www.hotelambato.com. A modern hotel near the heart of the city, good restaurant, 1 suite (**$$$$**), squash court, weekend discounts.
$$$ Florida, Av Miraflores 1131, T242 2007, www.hotelflorida.com.ec. Pleasant hotel in a nice setting, restaurant with good set meals, spa, weekend discounts.
$$$ Roka Plaza, Bolívar 20-62 y Guayaquil, T242 3845. Small stylish hotel in a refurbished colonial house in the heart of the city, sushi restaurant.
$$-$ Colony, 12 de Noviembre 124 y Av El Rey, near the bus terminal, T282 5789. A modern hotel with large rooms, parking, spotless.
$ $-$ Pirámide Inn, Cevallos y Mariano Egüez, T242 1920. Comfortable hotel, cafeteria, English spoken.

Ambato to Baños *p1035*
Salasaca and Pelileo
$ Hostal Pelileo, Eloy Alfaro 641, T287 1390. Shared bath, hot water, simple.
$ Runa Huasi, in Salasaca, 1 km north off main highway, T09-9984 0125, www.hostalrunahuasi. com. Simple hostel, includes breakfast and fruit, other meals on request, cooking facilities, nice views, guided walks.

Patate
$$$$ Hacienda Leito, on the road to El Triunfo, T285 9329, www.haciendaleito.com. Classy hacienda, spacious rooms, includes breakfast and dinner, great views of Tungurahua.
$$$$ Hacienda Manteles, in the Leito valley on the road to El Triunfo, T09-9871 5632, Quito T02-223 3484, www.haciendamanteles.com. Nice converted hacienda with wonderful views of Tungurahua and Chimborazo, includes breakfast, dinner, snacks, walk to waterfalls, hiking and horse riding. Reserve ahead.
$$$ Hostería Viña del Río, 3 km from town on the old road to Baños, T287 0314, www. hosteriavinadelrio.com. Cabins on a 22 ha ranch, restaurant, pool, spa and mini golf, US$6.72 for day use of facilities.

● Restaurants

Ambato *p1035*
$$ El Alamo Chalet, Cevallos 1719 y Montalvo. Open 0800-2300 (2200 Sun). Ecuadorean and international food. Set meals and à la carte, Swiss-owned, good quality.
$$ La Buena Mesa, Quito 924 y Bolívar. Mon-Sat 0900-2200. Good French cuisine, also set lunches. Recommended.
$$ La Fornace, Cevallos 1728 y Montalvo. Wood oven pizza. Opposite is **Heladería La Fornace**, Cevallos y Castillo. Snacks, sandwiches, ice-cream, very popular.
$ Govinda's, Cuenca y Quito. Mon-Sat 0800-2030, Sun 0800-1600. Vegetarian set meals and à la carte, also a meditation centre (T282 3182).

Cafés
Crème Brulée, Juan B Vela 08-38 y Montalvo. Daily 0900-2100. Very good coffee and pastries.
Pasterlería Quito, JL Mera y Cevallos. Daily 0700-2100. Coffee, pastries, good for breakfast.

✿ Festivals

Ambato p1035
Ambato has a famous festival in **Feb** or **Mar**, the **Fiesta de frutas y flores**, during carnival when there are 4 days of festivities and parades (best Sun morning and Mon night). Must book ahead to get a hotel room.

○ Shopping

Ambato p1035
Leather Ambato is a centre for leather: stores for shoes on Bolívar; jackets, bags, belts on Vela between Lalama and Montalvo. Take a local bus up to the leather town of Quisapincha for the best deals, everyday, but big market on Sat.

◐ What to do

Ambato p1035
Train rides An autoferro runs from Ambato to **Urbina** and back via **Cevallos**, Fri-Sun at 0800, US$15. The train station is at Av Gran Colombia y Chile, near the Terminal Terrestre, T252 2623; open Wed-Sun 0800-1630.

⊖ Transport

Ambato p1035
Bus The main bus station is on Av Colombia y Paraguay, 2 km north of the centre. City buses go there from Plaza Cevallos in the centre, US$0.25. To **Quito**, 3 hrs, US$2.50; also door to door shared taxis with **Servicio Express**, T242 6828 or T09-9924 2795, 9 daily departures (fewer on Sun), US$12. To **Cuenca**, US$8, 6½ hrs. To **Guayaquil**, 6 hrs, US$6. To **Riobamba**, US$1.25, 1 hr. To **Guaranda**, US$2, 3 hrs. To **Ibarra**, via the Quito airport and bypassing Quito, **CITA**, 8 daily, 5 hrs, US$5. To **Santo Domingo de los Tsáchilas**, 4 hrs, US$4. To **Tena**, US$5, 4½ hrs. To **Puyo**, US$3, 2½ hrs. To **Macas**, US$7, 5½ hrs. To **Esmeraldas**, US$8, 8 hrs. **Note** Buses to **Baños** leave from the Mercado Mayorista and then stop at the edge of town, 1 hr, US$1. Through buses do not go into the terminal, they take the Paso Lateral bypass road.

ⓘ Directory

Ambato p1035
Banks Banco de Guayaquil, JL Mera 514 y Sucre; Banco del Pacífico, Cevallos y Lalama, and Cevallos y Unidad Nacional.

Baños and Riobamba

Baños and Riobamba are both good bases for exploring the Sierra and their close proximity to high peaks gives great opportunities for climbing, cycling and trekking (but check for volcanic activity before you set out). The thermal springs at Baños are an added lure and the road east is one of the best ways to get to the jungle lowlands. On the other hand, anyone with the faintest interest in railways stops in Riobamba to ride the train on the famous section of the line from the Andes to Guayaquil, around the Devil's Nose.

Baños and around → *Phone code: 03. Colour map 11, B4. Population: 15,400. Altitude: 1800 m.*

Baños is nestled between the Río Pastaza and the Tungurahua volcano, only 8 km from its crater. Baños bursts at the seams with hotels, *residenciales*, restaurants and tour agencies. Ecuadoreans flock here on weekends and holidays for the hot springs, to visit the Basílica and enjoy the local *melcochas* (toffees), while escaping the Andean chill in a sub-tropical climate (wettest in July and August). Foreign visitors are also frequent; using Baños as a base for trekking, organizing a visit to the jungle, making local day trips on horseback or by mountain bike, or just plain hanging out.

Arriving in Baños

Tourist offices iTur ① *Oficina Municipal de Turismo, at the Municipio, Halflants y Rocafuerte, opposite Parque Central, Mon-Fri 0800-1230, 1400-1730, Sat-Sun 0800-1600*. Helpful, have colourful maps of the area, some English spoken. There are several private 'tourist information offices' run by travel agencies near the bus station; high-pressure tour sales, maps and pamphlets available. Local artist, J Urquizo, produces an accurate pictorial map of Baños, 12 de Noviembre y Ambato, also sold in many shops. There have been reports of thefts targeting tourists on Quito-Baños buses, take extra care of your hand-luggage.

In 1999, after over 80 years of dormancy, Tungurahua became active again and has remained so until the close of this edition. The level of activity is variable, the volcano can be quiet for weeks or months. Baños continues to be a safe and popular destination and will likely remain so unless the level of volcanic activity greatly increases. **Tungurahua is closed to climbers** and the direct road to Riobamba is often closed, but all else is normal. Since the level of volcanic activity can change, you should enquire locally before visiting Baños. The National Geophysical Institute posts reports on the web at www.igepn.edu.ec.

Places in Baños

The **Manto de la Virgen** waterfall at the southeast end of town is a symbol of Baños. The **Basílica** attracts many pilgrims. The paintings of miracles performed by Nuestra Señora del Agua Santa are worth seeing. There are various thermal baths in town, all charge US$2 unless otherwise noted. The **Baños de la Virgen** ① *0430-1700*, are by the waterfall. They get busy so best visit very early morning. Two small hot pools open evenings only (1800-2200, US$3). The **Piscinas Modernas** ① *Fri-Sun and holidays 0900-1700*, with a water slide, are next door. **El Salado baths** ① *0500-1700, US$3*, several hot pools, plus icy cold river water, repeatedly destroyed by volcanic debris (not safe when activity is high), 1.5 km out of town off the Ambato road. The **Santa Ana baths** ① *Fri-Sun and holidays 0900-1700*, have hot and cold pools in a pleasant setting, just east of town on the road to Puyo. All the baths can be very crowded at weekends and holidays; the brown colour of the water is due to its high mineral content.

As well as the medicinal baths, there is a growing number of spas, in hotels, as independent centres and massage therapists. These offer a combination of sauna, steam bath (Turkish or box), jacuzzi, clay and other types of baths, a variety of massage techniques (Shiatsu, Reiki, Scandinavian) and more.

Around Baños

There are many interesting **walks** in the Baños area. The **San Martín shrine** is a 45-minute easy walk from town and overlooks a deep rocky canyon with the Río Pastaza thundering below. Beyond the shrine, crossing to the north side of the Pastaza, is the **Ecozoológico San Martín** ① *T274 0552, 0800-1700, US$2.50*, with the **Serpentario San Martín** ① *daily 0900-1800, US$2*, opposite. 50 m beyond is a path to the **Inés María waterfall**, cascading down, but polluted. Further, a tarabita (cable-car) and ziplines span the entrance to the canyon. You can also cross the Pastaza by the **Puente San Francisco** road bridge, behind the kiosks across the main road from the bus station. From here a series of trails fans out into the hills, offering excellent views of Tungurahua from the ridge-tops in clear weather. A total of six bridges span the Pastaza near Baños, so you can make a round trip.

On the hillside behind Baños, it is a 45-minute hike to the **statue of the Virgin** (good views). Go to the south end of Calle JL Mera, before the street ends, take the last street to the right, at the end of which are stairs leading to the trail. A steep path continues along the ridge, past the statue. Another trail begins at the south end of JL Mera and leads to the **Hotel Luna Runtún**, continuing on to the village of Runtún (five- to six-hour round-trip). Yet another steep trail starts at the south end of Calle Maldonado and leads in 45 minutes to the **Bellavista cross**, with a lookout and a café (open 0900-2400). You can continue from the cross to Runtún.

The scenic road to Puyo (58 km) has many waterfalls tumbling down into the Pastaza. Many *tarabitas* (cable cars) and ziplines span the canyon offering good views. By the Agoyán dam and bridge, 5 km from town, is **Parque de la Familia** ① *daily 0900-1700, free*, with orchards, gardens, paths and domestic animals. Beyond, the paved road goes through seven tunnels between Agoyán and Río Negro. The older gravel road runs parallel to the new road, directly above the Río Pastaza, and is the preferred route for cyclists who, coming from Baños, should only go through one tunnel at Agoyán and then stay to the right avoiding the other tunnels. Between tunnels there is only the paved road, cyclists must be very careful as there are many buses and lorries. The area has excellent opportunities for walking and nature observation.

At the junction of the Verde and Pastaza rivers, 17 km from Baños is the town of **Río Verde** with snack bars, restaurants and a few places to stay. The Río Verde has crystalline green water

Where to stay 🛏
1 Alisamay *B1*
2 Apart-Hotel Napolitano *A4*
3 El Belén *B2*
4 El Oro *B1*
5 Finca Chamanapamba *A4*
6 Isla de Baños *C2*
7 La Casa Verde *A4*
8 La Chimenea *C4*
9 La Floresta *C2*
10 La Petite Auberge *C3*
11 Llanovientos *C1*
12 Los Pinos *B4*
13 Luna Runtún *A3*
14 Plantas y Blanco *C3*
15 Posada del Arte *C4*
16 Princesa María *B1*
17 Puerta del Sol *B4*
18 Samari *A4*
19 Sangay *C4*
20 Santa Cruz *C3*
21 Transilvania *B3*
22 Villa Santa Clara *C4*
23 Volcano *C4*

Restaurants 🍴
1 Ali Cumba *C3*
2 Café Blah Blah *B2*
3 Café Hood *B2*
4 Casa Hood *C3*
5 El Castillo *C4*
6 La Tasca *C4*
7 Mariane *C2*
8 Pancho's *C2*
9 Rico Pan *B2*
10 Swiss Bistro *C3*

Bars & clubs 🍸
11 Buena Vista *B3*
12 Ferchos *B3*
13 Jack Rock *B3*
14 Leprechaun *B3*
15 Peña Ananitay *B3*

and is nice for bathing. The paved highway runs to the north of town, between it and the old road, the river has been dammed forming a small lake where rubber rafts are rented for paddling. Near the paved road is **Orquideario** ① *open 0900-1700, closed Wed, US$1.50*, with nice regional orchids. Before joining the Pastaza the Río Verde tumbles down several falls, the most spectacular of which is **El Pailón del Diablo** (the Devil's Cauldron). Cross the Río Verde on the old road and take the path to the right after the church, then follow the trail down towards the suspension bridge over the Pastaza, for about 20 minutes. Just before the bridge take a side trail to the right (signposted) which leads you to **Paradero del Pailón**, a nice restaurant, and viewing platforms above the falls (US$1.50). The **San Miguel Falls**, smaller but also nice, are some five minutes' walk from the town along a different trail. Cross the old bridge and take the first path to the right, here is **Falls Garden** (US$1.50), with lookout platforms over both sets of falls. Cyclists can leave the bikes at one of the snack bars while visiting the falls and return to Baños by bus.

◉ Baños and around listings

For hotel and restaurant price codes, and other relevant information, see Essentials.

● Where to stay

Baños *p1037, map p1039*
Baños has plenty of accommodation but can fill during holiday weekends.
$$$$ Luna Runtún, Caserío Runtún Km 6, T274 0882, www.lunaruntun.com. A classy hotel in a beautiful setting overlooking Baños. Includes dinner, breakfast and use of pools (spa extra), very comfortable rooms with balconies and superb views, lovely gardens. Good service, English, French and German spoken, tours, nanny service.
$$$$ Samari, Vía a Puyo Km 1, T274 1855, www.samarispa.com. Upmarket resort opposite the Santa Ana baths, nice grounds, tastefully decorated hacienda-style rooms and suites, pool and spa, restaurant.
$$$ Finca Chamanapamba, on the east shore of the Río Ulba, a short ride from the road to Puyo, T274 2671, www.chamanapamba.com. 2 nicely finished wooden cabins in a spectacular location overlooking the Río Ulba and just next to the Chamanapamba waterfalls, very good café-restaurant serves German food.
$$$ Posada del Arte, Pasaje Velasco Ibarra y Montalvo, T274 0083, www.posadadelarte. com. Nice cosy inn, restaurant with vegetarian options, pleasant sitting room, some rooms have fireplace, terrace, US run.

$$$ Sangay, Plazoleta Isidro Ayora 100, next to waterfall and thermal baths, T274 0490, www. sangayspahotel.com. A traditional Baños hotel and spa with 3 types of rooms, buffet breakfast, good restaurant specializes in Ecuadorean food, pool and spa open to non-residents 1600-2000 (US$10), parking, tennis and squash courts, games room, car hire, disco, attentive service, mid-week discounts, British-Ecuadorean run. Recommended.
$$$ Volcano, Rafael Vieira y Montalvo, T274 2140, www.volcano.com.ec. Nice spacious modern hotel, large rooms with fridge, some with views of the waterfall, buffet breakfast, restaurant, heated pool, massage, nice garden.
$$ Alisamay, Espejo y JL Mera, T2741391, www.hotelalisamay.com. Rustic hotel, nice cosy rooms with balconies, includes breakfast and use of spa, gardens with pools.
$$ Apart-Hotel Napolitano, C Oriente 470 y Suárez, T274 2464, napolitano-apart-hotel@ hotmail.com. Large comfortable apartments with kitchen, fireplace, pool and spa, garden, parking. A bit pricey, daily rentals or US$600 per month.
$$ Isla de Baños, Halflants 1-31 y Montalvo, T274 0609, www.isladebanios.com. Nicely decorated comfortable hotel, includes European breakfast and steam bath, spa operates when there are enough people, pleasant garden.
$$ La Casa Verde, in Santa Ana, 1.5 km from town on Camino Real, a road parallell and north

of the road to Puyo, T09-8659 4189, www.
lacasaverde.com.ec. Very nice spacious hotel
decorated in pine, the largest rooms in Baños,
laundry and cooking facilities, very quiet, New
Zealand-run.

$$ La Floresta, Halflants y Montalvo, T274
1824, www.laflorestahotel.com. Nice hotel
with large comfortable rooms set around
a lovely garden, excellent buffet breakfast,
wheelchair accessible, parking, attentive
service. Warmly recommended.

$$ La Petite Auberge, 16 de Diciembre y
Montalvo, T274 0936, www.lepetit.banios.com.
Rooms around a patio, some with fireplace, good
upmarket French restaurant, parking, quiet.

$$-$ Los Pinos, Ricardo Zurita y C Ambato,
T274 1825. Large hostel with double rooms and
dorms (US$8-10 pp), spa, kitchen and laundry
facilities, pool table Argentine run, good value.

$$-$ Puerta del Sol, Ambato y Arrayanes (east
end of C Ambato), T274 2265. Modern hotel,
nicer than it looks on the outside, large well-
appointed rooms, pleasant dining area, laundry
facilities, parking.

$ El Belén, Reyes y Ambato, T274 1024, www.
hotelelbelen.com. Nice hostel, cooking facilities,
spa, parking, helpful staff.

$ El Oro, Ambato y JL Mera, T274 0736. With
bath, US$7 pp in dorm, laundry and cooking
facilities, good value, popular. Recommended.

$ La Chimenea, Martínez y Rafael Vieira, T274
2725, www.hostalchimenea.com. Nice hostel
with terrace café, breakfast available, private
or shared bath, US$7.50 pp in dorm, small
pool, jacuzzi extra, parking for small cars, quiet,
helpful and good value. Recommended.

$ Llanovientos, Martínez 1126 y Sebastián
Baño, T274 0682, www.llanovientos.banios.
com. Modern breezy hostel with wonderful
views, comfortable rooms, cafeteria, cooking
facilities, parking, nice garden. Recommended.

$ Plantas y Blanco, 12 de Noviembre y
Martínez, T274 0044, www.plantasyblanco.com.
Pleasant popular hostel decorated with plants,
private or shared bath, US$6-8 pp in dorm,
excellent breakfast available, rooftop cafeteria,
steam bath, classic films, bakery, French owned,
good value. Repeatedly recommended.

$ Princesa María, Rocafuerte y Mera, T274
1035. Spacious rooms, US$7 pp in dorm,
laundry and cooking facilities, parking, popular
budget travellers' meeting place, helpful and
good value.

$ Santa Cruz, 16 de Diciembre y Martínez,
T274 3527, www.santacruzbackpackers.com.
Large rooms, US$8 pp in dorm, fireplace in
lounge, small garden with hammocks, kitchen
facilities, mini pool on roof. New management
in 2013.

$ Transilvania, 16 de Diciembre y Oriente,
T274 2281, www.hostal-transilvania.com.
Multi-storey building with simple rooms,
includes breakfast, US$7.90 in dorm, Middle
Eastern restaurant, nice views from balconies,
large TV and movies in sitting room, pool table,
popular meeting place.

$ Villa Santa Clara, 12 de Noviembre y
Velasco Ibarra, T274 0349, www.hotelvilla
santaclara.com. Nice cabins in a quiet
location, laundry facilities, wheelchair
accessible, garden, spa, parking.

Around Baños p1038

$$$ Miramelindo, Río Verde, just north of
the paved road, T249 3004, www.miramelindo.
banios.com. Lovely hotel and spa, nicely
decorated rooms, good restaurant, pleasant
gardens include an orchid collection with over
1000 plants.

$$ Hostería Río Verde, between the paved
road and town, T288 4207 (Ambato), www.
hosteriarioverde.com. Simple cabins in a rural
setting, includes breakfast and use of spa, large
pool, restaurant specializes in trout and tilapia.

🍴 Restaurants

Baños p1037, map p1039

$$$ Swiss Bistro, Martínez y Alfaro. Tue-Sat
1200-2300, Sun 1200-1700, Mon 1800-2300.
International dishes and Swiss specialties,
Swiss run.

$$$-$$ La Tasca, 12 de Noviembre y Martínez.
Wed-Sun 1830-2230, Sat-Sun also 1230-1600.
Spanish cuisine, tapas, Spanish owned.

$$ Mariane, on a small lane by Montalvo y Halflants. Mon-Sat 1300-2200. Excellent authentic Provençal cuisine, large portions, lovely setting, pleasant atmosphere, popular, slow service. Highly recommended. **Hotel Mariane ($$)** at the same location, very clean and pleasant.

$$-$ Café Hood, Maldonado y Ambato, at Parque Central. Open 1000-2200, closed Wed. Mainly vegetarian but also some meat dishes, excellent food, English spoken, always busy. Also rents rooms.

$$-$ Casa Hood, Martínez between Halflants and Alfaro. Open 1200-2200. Largely vegetarian, but also serve some meat dishes, juices, milkshakes, varied menu including Indonesian and Thai dishes, good set lunch and desserts. Travel books and maps sold, book exchange, repertory cinema, occasional cultural events, nice atmosphere. Popular and recommended.

$ El Castillo, Martínez y Rafael Vieira, in hostel. Open 0800-1000, 1200-1330. Breakfast and good set lunch.

Cafés

Ali Cumba, 12 de Noviembre y Martínez. Daily 0700-1900. Excellent breakfasts, salads, good coffee (filtered, espresso), muffins, cakes, homemade bread, large sandwiches, book exchange. Danish-Ecuadorean run.

Café Blah Blah, Halflants y Matrínez. Daily 0800-2000. Cosy café serving very good breakfasts, coffee, cakes, snacks and juices, a popular meeting place.

Pancho's, Rocafuerte y Maldonado at Parque Central. Daily 1500-2200. Hamburgers, snacks, sandwiches, coffee,

Rico Pan, Ambato y Maldonado at Parque Central. Mon-Sat 0700-2000, Sun 0700-1300. Good breakfasts, hot bread (including whole wheat), fruit salads and pizzas, also meals.

🍸 Bars and clubs

Baños *p1037, map p1039*

Eloy Alfaro, between Ambato and Oriente has many bars including:

Buena Vista, Alfaro y Oriente. A good place for salsa and other Latin music.

Ferchos, Alfaro y Oriente. Tue-Sun 1600-2400. Café-bar, modern decor, snacks, cakes, good varied music, German-run.

Jack Rock, Alfaro y Ambato. A favourite traveller hangout.

Leprechaun, Alfaro y Oriente. Popular for dancing, bonfire on weekends, occasional live music.

🎭 Entertainment

Baños *p1037, map p1039*

Chivas, open-sided buses, cruise town playing music, they take you to different night spots and to a volcano lookout when Tungurahua is active.

Peña Ananitay, 16 de Diciembre y Espejo. Bar, good live music and dancing on weekends, US$2 cover.

🎉 Festivals

Baños *p1037, map p1039*

During Carnival and Holy Week hotels are full and prices rise.

Oct: Nuestra Señora de Agua Santa with daily processions, bands, fireworks, sporting events and partying through the month. Week-long celebrations ending **16 Dec**: the town's anniversary, parades, fairs, sports, cultural events. The night of **15 Dec** are the Verbenas, when each *barrio* hires a band and parties.

🛍 Shopping

Baños *p1037, map p1039*

Look out for jaw-aching toffee (*melcocha*) made in ropes in shop doorways, or the less sticky *alfeñique*.

Handicrafts Crafts stalls at Pasaje Ermita de la Vírgen, off C Ambato, by the market. Tagua (vegetable ivory made from palm nuts) crafts on Maldonado y Martínez. Leather shops on Rocafuerte between Halflants and 16 de Diciembre.

Las Orquídeas, Ambato y Maldonado by Parque Central and at **Hostal La Floresta**. Excellent selection of crafts, some guidebooks and coffee-table books.

Latino Shop, Ambato y Alfaro and 4 other locations. For T-shirts.

⏱ What to do

Baños *p1037, map p1039*
Potentially hazardous activities are popular in Baños, including mountaineering, white water rafting, canyoning, canopying and bridge jumps. Safety standards vary greatly. There is seldom any recourse in the event of a mishap so these activities are entirely at your own risk.
Bus tours The *chivas* (see entertainment, above) and a **double-decker bus** (C Ambato y Halflants, T274 0596, US$6) visit waterfalls and other attractions. Check about their destination if you have a specific interest such as El Pailón falls.
Canopying or zip line Involves hanging from a harness and sliding on a steel cable. Prices vary according to length, about US$10-20. Cable car, about US$1.50.
Canyoning Many agencies offer this sport, rates US$30 half day, US$50 full day.
Climbing and trekking There are countless possibilities for walking and nature observation near Baños and to the east. Tungurahua has been officially closed to climbers since 1999. There is nobody to stop you from entering the area, but the dangers of being hit by flying volcanic bombs are very real. Operators offer trekking and climbing tours to Cotopaxi and Chimborazo.
Cycling Many places rent bikes, quality varies, US$5-10 per day; check brakes and tyres, find out who has to pay for repairs, and insist on a helmet, puncture repair kit and pump. The following have good equipment:
Carrillo Hermanos, 16 de Diciembre y Martínez. Rents mountain bikes and motorcycles (reliable machines with helmets, US10 per hr).
Hotel Isla de Baños, cycling tours US$15-20.
Horse riding There are several places, but check their horses as not all are well cared for. Rates around US$6-8 per hr, US$40 per day. The following have been recommended:
Angel Aldaz, Montalvo y JL Mera (on the road to the statue of the Virgin).

Hotel Isla de Baños, see above. Horses for rent; 3½ hrs with a guide and jeep transport costs US$35 pp, English and German spoken.
José & Two Dogs, Maldonado y Martínez, T274 0746. Flexible hours.
Ringo Horses, 12 de Noviembre y Martínez (**Apart-hotel El Napolitano**). Nice horses, offers rides outside Baños.
Paragliding See www.aeropasion.net; US$60 per day.
Puenting Many operators offer this bungee-jumping-like activity from the bridges around Baños, US$10-15 per jump, heights and styles vary.
Whitewater rafting Fatal accidents have occurred, but not with the agencies listed here. Rates US$30 for half-day, US$60-70 for full-day. The Chambo, Patate and Pastaza rivers are all polluted. **Geotours** and **Wonderful Ecuador** are good (see below).

Tour operators
There are many tour agencies in town, some with several offices, as well as 'independent' guides who seek out tourists on the street (the latter are generally not recommended). Quality varies considerably; to obtain a qualified guide and avoid unscrupulous operators, it is best to seek advice from other travellers who have recently returned from a tour. We have received some critical reports of tours out of Baños, but there are also highly respected and qualified operators here. In all cases, insist on a written contract. Most agencies and guides offer trips to the jungle (US$50-70 per day pp). There are also volcano-watching, trekking and horse tours, in addition to the day-trips and sports mentioned above. Several companies run tours aboard a *chiva* (open-sided bus). The following agencies and guides have received positive recommendations but the list is not exhaustive and there are certainly others.
Expediciones Amazónicas, Oriente 11-68 y Halflants, T274 0506.
Explorsierra, Oriente y Halflants, T274 0514. Also rent equipment.
Geotours, Ambato y Halflants, next to Banco Pichincha, T274 1344, www.geotoursbanos. com. Also offer paragliding for US$60.

Imagine Ecuador, 16 de Diciembre y Montalvo, T274 3472, www.imagineecuador.com.
Sachayacu Explorer, Bolívar 229 y Urbina, in Píllaro, T287 5316 or T09-8740 3376, www.parquellanganates.com. Trekking in the Llanganates, jungle tours in Huaorani territory, Yasuní and as far as Peru, English spoken.
Wonderful Ecuador, Maldonado y Oriente, T274 1580, www.wonderfulecuador.org.

⊖ Transport

Baños *p1037, map p1039*
Bus City buses run from Alfaro y Martínez east to Agoyán and from Rocafuerte by the market, west to El Salado and the zoo. The long distance bus station is on the Ambato-Puyo road (Av Amazonas). To **Río Verde** take any Puyo bound bus, through buses don't go in the station, 20 mins, US$0.50. To **Quito**, US$3.50, 3 hrs, frequent service; going to Quito sit on the right for views of Cotopaxi, buy tickets early for weekends and holidays. For shared taxis from Quito, see *Autovip*, page 999. Note that buses from Quito to Baños are the target of thieves, take a shared taxi or bus to Ambato and transfer there. To **Ambato**, 1 hr, US$0.80. To **Riobamba**, the direct Baños-Riobamba road is sometimes closed due to Tungurahua's volcanic activity (also dangerous after rain), most buses go via Mocha, 1½ hrs, US$2. To **Latacunga**, 2 hrs, US$2. To **Otavalo** and **Ibarra** direct, bypassing Quito, Expreso Baños, at 0400 and 1440, US$6, 5½ hrs. To **Guayaquil**, 1 bus per day and one overnight, 6-7 hrs; or change in Riobamba. To **Puyo**, 1½ hrs, US$2. Sit on the right. You can cycle to Puyo and take the bus back (passport check on the way). To **Tena**, 3½ hrs, US$4. To **Misahuallí**, change at Tena. To **Macas**, 4½ hrs, US$6 (sit on the right).

ⓘ Directory

Baños *p1037, map p1039*
Banks Banco del Austro, Halflants y Rocafuerte, ATM. Banco del Pacífico, Halflants y Rocafuerte, Parque Central, ATM. Don Pedro, Halflants y Martínez, hardware store, open weekends, 3% commission on TCs. Also exchanges Euros and other currencies.
Language schools Spanish schools charge US$5.50-8 per hr, many also offer homestays. Baños Spanish Center, www.spanishcenterschool.com. Home Stay Baños, T274 0453. Mayra's, www.mayraspanishschool.com. Raíces, www.spanishlessons.org.

Riobamba and around

Guaranda and Riobamba are good bases for exploring the Sierra. Riobamba is the bigger of the two and is on the famous railway line from Quito to Guayaquil. Many indigenous people from the surrounding countryside can be seen in both cities on market days. Because of their central location Riobamba and the surrounding province are known as 'Corazón de la Patria' – the heartland of Ecuador – and the city boasts the nickname 'La Sultana de Los Andes' in honour of lofty Mount Chimborazo.

Riobamba → *Phone code: 03. Colour map 11, B3. Population: 162,000. Altitude: 2754 m. See map, page 1046.*

The capital of Chimborazo Province has broad streets and many ageing but impressive buildings. **Tourist office**: iTur ⓘ *Av Daniel León Borja y Brasil, T296 3159, Mon-Fri 0800-1230, 1430-1800*, municipal information office. The **Ministerio de Turismo** ⓘ *3 doors from iTur, in the Centro de Arte y Cultura, T294 1213, Mon-Fri 0830-1730*, is very helpful and knowledgeable.

The main square is **Parque Maldonado** around which are the **Cathedral**, the **Municipality** and several colonial buildings with arcades. The Cathedral has a beautiful colonial stone façade and an incongruously modern interior. Four blocks northeast of the railway station is the **Parque 21 de Abril**, named after the Batalla de Tapi, 21 April 1822, the city's independence from Spain.

The park, better known as **La Loma de Quito**, affords an unobstructed view of Riobamba and Chimborazo, Carihuairazo, Tungurahua, El Altar and occasionally Sangay. It also has a colourful tile tableau of the history of Ecuador; ask about safety before visiting. The **Convento de la Concepción** ① *Orozco y España, entrance at Argentinos y J Larrea, T296 5212, Tue-Sat, 0900-1230, 1500-1730, US$3*, has a religious art museum. **Museo del Ministerio de Cultura** ① *Veloz y Montalvo, T296 5501, Mon-Fri 0900-1700, free; temporarily closed in 2014*, has well-displayed exhibits of archaeology and colonial art. **Museo de la Ciudad** ① *Primera Constituyente y Espejo, at Parque Maldonado, T294 4420, Mon-Fri 0800-1230, 1430-1800, free*, in a beautifully restored colonial building, has an interesting historical photograph exhibit and temporary displays.

Riobamba is an important **market** centre where people from many communities congregate. Saturday is the main day when the city fills with colourfully dressed *indígenas* from all over Chimborazo, each wearing their distinctive costume; trading overflows the markets and buying and selling go on all over town. Wednesday is a smaller market day. The 'tourist' market is in the small **Plaza de la Concepción or Plaza Roja** ① *Orozco y Colón, Sat and Wed only, 0800-1500*, is a good place to buy local handicrafts and authentic Indian clothing. The main produce market is **San Alfonso**, Argentinos y 5 de Junio, which on Saturday spills over into the nearby streets and also sells clothing, ceramics, baskets and hats. Other markets in the colonial centre are **La Condamine** ① *Carabobo y Colombia, daily*, largest market on Fridays, **San Francisco** and **La Merced**, near the churches of the same name.

Guano is a carpet-weaving, sisal and leather working town 8 km north of Riobamba. Many shops sell rugs and you can arrange to have these woven to your own design. Buses leave from the Mercado Dávalos, García Moreno y New York, every 15 minutes, US$0.25, last bus back at 1900, taxi US$4.

Guaranda → *Phone code: 03. Colour map 11, B3. Population: 57,500. Altitude: 2650 m.*

This quaint town, capital of Bolívar Province, proudly calls itself 'the Rome of Ecuador' because it is built on seven hills. There are fine views of the mountains all around and a colourful market. Locals traditionally take an evening stroll in the palm-fringed main plaza, **Parque Libertador Simón Bolívar**, around which are the Municipal buildings and a large stone **Cathedral**. Towering over the city, on one of the hills, is an impressive statue of **El Indio Guaranga**; museum (free) and art gallery. Although not on the tourist trail, there are many sights worth visiting in the province, for which Guaranda is the ideal base. Of particular interest is the highland town of **Salinas**, with its community development projects (accommodations and tours available, see Where to stay), as well as the *subtrópico* region, the lowlands stretching west towards the coast.

Market days are Friday (till 1200) and Saturday (larger), when many indigenous people in typical dress trade at the market complex at the east end of Calle Azuay, by Plaza 15 de Mayo (9 de Abril y Maldonado), and at Plaza Roja (Avenida Gen Enríquez). Carnival in Guaranda is among the best known in the country. **Tourist office: Oficina Municipal de Turismo** ① *García Moreno entre 7 de Mayo y Convención de 1884, T298 5877, www.guaranda.gob.ec (in Spanish), Mon-Fri 0800-1200, 1400-1800*. Provides Information in Spanish and maps. www.gobiernodebolivar.gob. ec has information in Spanish about regional attractions.

Reserva Faunística Chimborazo → *See also Riobamba Tour operators.*

① *Information from Ministerio del Ambiente, Avenida 9 de Octubre y Duchicela, Quinta Macají, Riobamba, T261 0029, ext107, Mon-Fri 0800-1300, 1400-1700.* Visitors arriving without a guide or with guides not authorized by the ministry are turned back at the gate; exceptions are made for members of alpine clubs, apply for an entry permit at the Ministerio del Ambiente in Riobamba. The most outstanding features of this reserve, created to protect the camelids (vicuñas, alpacas and llamas) which were re-introduced here, are the beautiful snow-capped volcanos of **Chimborazo** and its neighbour **Carihuayrazo**. Chimborazo, inactive, is the highest peak in Ecuador (6310 m), while Carihuayrazo, 5020 m, is dwarfed by its neighbour. Day visitors can enjoy lovely views, a glimpse of the handsome vicuñas and the rarefied air above 4800 m. There are great opportunities for trekking on the eastern slopes, accessed from **Urbina**, west of the Ambato-Riobamba road, and of course climbing Ecuador's highest peak. Horse riding and trekking tours are offered along the Mocha Valley between the two peaks and downhill cycling from Chimborazo is popular.

To the west of the reserve runs the Vía del Arenal which joins San Juan, along the Riobamba–Guaranda road, with Cruce del Arenal on the Ambato-Guaranda road. A turn-off from this road leads to the main park entrance and beyond to the **Refugio Hermanos Carrel**, a shelter at 4800 m, from where it is a 45-minute walk to **Refugio Whymper** at 5000 m. The shelters were closed for reconstruction in early 2014 and expected to reopen later that year. The access from Riobamba (51 km, paved to the park entrance) is very beautiful. Along the Vía del Arenal past San Juan are a couple of small indigenous communities which grow a few crops and raise llamas and alpacas. They offer lodging and *guías nativos*, the area is good for acclimatization The *arenal* is a large sandy plateau at about 4400 m, to the west of Chimborazo, just below the main park entrance. It can be a harsh, windy place, but it is also very beautiful; take the time to admire the tiny flowers which grow here. This is the best place to see vicuñas, which hang around either in family groups, one male and its harem, or lone males which have been expelled from the group.

Climbing Chimborazo At 6310 m, this is a difficult climb owing to the altitude. Climbers must go with a certified guide working for an operator who has a special permit (*patente*). Rope, ice-axe, helmet and crampons must be used. It is essential to have at least one week's acclimatization above 3500 m. The best seasons are December and June-September. Deglaciation is making the climb more difficult and ice pinnacles, *penitentes*, sometimes prevent climbers reaching the main, Whymper summit.

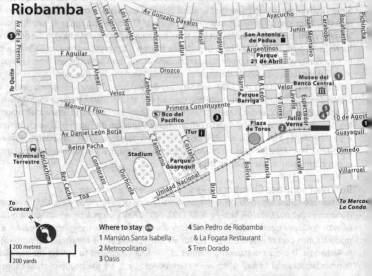

Riobamba

Where to stay
1 Mansión Santa Isabella
2 Metropolitano
3 Oasis
4 San Pedro de Riobamba
& La Fogata Restaurant
5 Tren Dorado

200 metres
200 yards

The Devil's Nose Train

This spectacular ride is popular with Ecuadorean and foreign tourists alike. In 2014, tourist trains ran from Alausí to Sibambe, the most scenic part of the trip including the **Devil's Nose**, and from Riobamba north to Urbina and south to Colta. The route Riobamba-Alausí-Sibambe is scheduled to operate in 2015. For details see What to do, page 1051.

Alausí → *Phone code: 03. Colour map 11, B3. Population: 10,500. Altitude: 2350 m.*

This picturesque town perched on a hillside is where many passengers join the train for the amazing descent over *La Nariz de Diablo* to Sibambe. There is good walking, a Sunday market and a **Fiesta de San Pedro** on 29 June.

Parque Nacional Sangay

Riobamba provides access to the central highland region of **Sangay National Park** ⓘ *information from Ministerio del Ambiente, see Reserva Chimborazo above*, a beautiful wilderness area with excellent opportunities for trekking and climbing. A spectacular but controversial road, good for downhill biking, runs from Riobamba to Macas in the Oriente, cutting through the park. Near Cebadas (with a good cheese factory) a branch road joins from **Guamote**, a quiet, mainly indigenous town on the Pan-American highway, which comes to life during its colourful Thursday market. At **Atillo**, south of Cebadas, an area of lovely páramo dotted with lakes, there is lodging (US$7 per person) and restaurant at Cabaña Saskines (T03-230 3290, atillosaskines@hotmail.com). **Sangay** (5230 m) is an active volcano, access to the mountain takes at least three days and is only for those who can endure long, hard days of walking and severe weather. Climbing Sangay can be dangerous even on a quiet day and a helmet to protect against falling stones is vital, November to January is a good time to climb it. Agencies in Quito and Riobamba offer tours or you can organize an expedition independently. A guide is essential, porters can be hired in the access towns of **Alao** and **Guargualla**. The latter has a **community tourism project** ⓘ *T03-302 6688, accommodation in Guargualla Chico US$12 pp, US$21 pp with dinner and breakfast, kitchen facilities. Guías nativos, US$30 per day, porters and horses US$15 per day. Also in Sangay National Park is the beautiful El Altar volcano (5315 m), whose crater is surrounded by nine summits. The most popular climbing and trekking routes begin beyond Candelaria at* **Hacienda Releche** *(see Where to stay).*

ⓦ Riobamba and around listings

For hotel and restaurant price codes, and other relevant information, see Essentials.

ⓦ Where to stay

Riobamba *p1044, map p1046*
$$$ Abraspungo, Km 3 on the road to Guano, T236 4275, www.haciendaabraspungo.com. Nice hotel in a country setting, comfortable rooms, includes buffet breakfast, excellent

Restaurants ⓕ
1 Bom Café
2 Helados de Paila
3 Jamones La Andaluza & Naranjo's
4 Lulu's
5 Mónaco Pizzería

restaurant, parking, attentive service. Recommended.

$$$ La Andaluza, 16 km north of Riobamba along the Panamericana, T294 9371, www. hosteriaandaluza.com. An old hacienda, rooms with heaters and roaring fireplaces, good restaurant, lovely views, good walking.

$$$ Mansión Santa Isabella, Veloz 28-48 y Carabobo, T296 2947, www.mansionsanta isabella.com. Lovely restored house with pleasant patio, comfortable rooms most with bathtub, duvets, restaurant serves set lunches and à la carte, bar in stone basement, parking, attentive service, British-Ecuadorean run. Recommended.

$$$ San Pedro de Riobamba, Daniel L Borja 29-50 y Montalvo, opposite the train station, T294 0586, www.hotelsanpedroderiobamba. com. Elegant hotel in a beautifully restored house in the centre of town, ample comfortable rooms, bathtubs, cafeteria, parking, covered patio, reservations required. Recommended.

$$ Rincón Alemán, Remigio Romero y Alfredo Pareja, Ciudadela Arupos del Norte, T260 3540, www.hostalrinconaleman.com. Family-run hotel in a quiet residential area north of the centre, nice ample rooms, laundry and cooking facilities, parking, fireplace, sauna, gym, garden, terrace, nice views, German spoken.

$$-$ Tren Dorado, Carabobo 22-35 y 10 de Agosto, near the train station, T296 4890, www. hoteltrendorado.com. Modern hotel with nice large rooms, buffet breakfast available (starting 0730, open to non-guests), restaurant, reliable hot water, good value. Recommended.

$ Metropolitano, Daniel L Borja y Lavalle, near the train station, T296 1714. One of the oldest hotels in Riobamba, built in 1912 and nicely restored. Ample rooms, breakfast available.

$ Oasis, Veloz 15-32 y Almagro, T296 1210, www.oasishostelriobamba.com. Small, pleasant, family-run hostel in a quiet location, laundry facilities, some rooms with kitchen and fridge, shared kitchen for the others, parking, nice garden, Wi-Fi US$1 per day, popular with backpackers. Recommended.

Guaranda p1045

$$$ La Colina, Av Guayaquil 117, on the road to Ambato, T298 0666, www.complejolacolina. com. Nicely situated on a quiet hillside overlooking the city. Bright spacious rooms, nice views, small covered swimming pool (not always open) and sauna (weekends only), gardens, parking, tours available.

$$ Bolívar, Sucre 704 y Rocafuerte, T298 0547, http://hotelbolivar.wordpress.com. Pleasant hotel with courtyard, small modern rooms, best quality in the centre of town. Restaurant next door open Mon-Fri for economical breakfasts and lunches.

$$ Mansión del Parque, 10 de Agosto y Sucre, T298 4468. Nicely restored colonial house, spacious rooms, some with balcony, cafeteria, good value.

$ El Marquez, 10 de Agosto y Eloy Alfaro, T298 1053. Pleasant hotel with family atmosphere, newer rooms with private bath are clean and modern, older ones with shared bath are cheaper, parking.

Salinas

$ Hotel Refugio Salinas, 45 min from Guaranda, T221 0044, www.salinerito.com. Pleasant community-run hotel, economical meals on request, private or shared bath, dining/sitting area with fireplace, visits to community projects, walking and horse riding tours, packages available, advance booking advised.

$ La Minga, by the main plaza, T221 0108, www.laminga.ec. Simple rooms with bath and dorms, meals on request, fullboard packages including tour available.

Reserva Faunística Chimborazo p1045

The following are all good for acclimatization; those in Urbina can be reached by autoferro from either Riobamba or Ambato.

$$ Refugio del Tren, at the Urbina railway station 2 km west of the highway, at 3619 m, T09-981 76400. Converted train station, shared bath, price includes dinner and breakfast, fireplace in common areas and one room, heaters.

$ Casa Cóndor, in Pulinguí San Pablo, Vía del Arenal, T03-235 4034, T09-8650 8152. Basic community-run hostel, dinner and breakfast available, use of cooking facilities extra, tours in the area.

$ Portal Andino, at 4200 m, 4- to 5-hr walk from Urbina, T09-9165 0788. Simple hostel with bunk-beds, shared bath, hot water, use of cooking facilities extra.

$ Posada de la Estación, opposite the Urbina railway station,T09-9969 4867, www.altamontana.net. Comfortable rooms with heaters, shared bath, meals available, wood stoves, magnificent views, trips and equipment arranged, tagua workshop, helpful. Also run **$ Urcu Huasi**, cabins at 4150 m, 10 km (2½ hrs walking) from Urbina, in an area being reforested with polylepis.

Alausí p1047

$$$$ Posada de las Nubes, on the north side of the Río Chanchán, 7 or 11 km from Alausí depending on the route, best with 4WD, pick-up from Alausí US$7, T293 0535 or T09-9315 0847, www.posadadelasnubes.com. Rustic hacienda house in cloud forest at 2600 m. Rooms are simple to basic for the price, some with bath, full board, hiking and horse riding, advance booking required.

$$$ La Quinta, Eloy Alfaro 121 y M Muñoz, T293 0247, www.hosteria-la-quinta.com. Nicely restored old house along the rail line to Riobamba. Pleasant atmosphere, some rooms are ample, restaurant, gardens, excellent views, not always open, reserve ahead.

$$ Gampala, 5 de Junio 122 y Loza, T293 0138, www.hotelgampala.com. Nicely refurbished modern rooms and 1 suite with jacuzzi (**$$$**), restaurant and bar with pool table.

$$-$ La Posada del Tren, 5 de Junio y Orozco, T293 1293. Nice, modern, parking.

$$-$ San Pedro, 5 de Junio y 9 de Octubre, T293 0089, hostalsanpedro@hotmail.com. Simple comfortable rooms, a few cheaper rooms in older section, restaurant downstairs, parking, nice owner.

Parque Nacional Sangay p1047
$ Hostal Capac Urcu, at Hacienda Releche, near the village of Candelaria, T301 4067. Basic rooms in small working hacienda. Use of kitchen (US$6) or meals prepared on request, rents horses for the trek to Collanes, US$11 per horse each way, plus US$12.50 per muleteer each way. Also runs the *refugio* at Collanes (same price), by the crater of El Altar: thatched-roof rustic shelters with solar hot water. The *refugio* is cold, take a warm sleeping bag.

Guamote

$$ Inti Sisa, Vargas Torres y García Moreno, T291 6529, www.intisisa.org. Basic but nice guesthouse, part of a community development project, most rooms with bath, US$18.75 pp in dorm, includes breakfast, other meals available, dining room and communal area with fireplace, horse riding and cycling tours to highland villages, reservations necessary.

🍴 Restaurants

Riobamba p1044, map p1046
Most places closed after 2100 and on Sun.
$$ Lulu's, Veloz 10-41 y Puruha. Tue-Sun 1230-1500, 1800-2200. Bar/restaurant with excellent set lunch and à la carte Ecuadorean and American food, no vegetarian options, nice ambiance.

$$ Mónaco Pizzería, Av de la Prensa y Francisco Aguilar. Mon-Fri 1500-2200, Sat-Sun 1200-2200. Delicious pizza and pasta, nice salads, good food, service and value. Recommended.

$ La Fogata, Av Daniel L Borja y Carabobo, opposite the train station. Daily 0700-2200. Simple but good local food, economical set meals and breakfast.

$ Naranjo's, Daniel L Borja 36-20 y Uruguay. Tue-Sun 1200-1500. Excellent set lunch, friendly service, popular with locals.

Cafés and bakeries

Bom Café, Pichincha 21-37 y 10 de Agosto. Mon-Sat 1000-1300, 1600-2200. Very nice European-style coffee shop, with a good choice of coffee and sandwiches.

Helados de Paila, Espejo y 10 de Agosto. Daily 0900-1900. Excellent homemade ice cream, coffee, sweets, popular.

Jamones La Andaluza, Daniel L Borja y Uruguay. Open 0900–2300. Indoor and outdoor seating, good coffee, sandwiches, salads, variety of cold-cuts and cheeses, tapas.

La Abuela Rosa, Brasil y Esmeraldas. Mon-Sat 1600-2100. Cafetería in grandmother's house serving typical Ecuadorean snacks. Nice atmosphere and good service.

Guaranda *p1045*

See also Where to stay. Most places close on Sun.

$$ Pizza Buon Giorno, Sucre at Parque Bolívar. Tue-Sun 1200-2200. Pizza and salads.

$$-$ La Bohemia, Convención de 1884 y 10 de Agosto. Mon-Sat 0800-2100. Very good economical set meals and pricier international dishes à la carte, nice decor and ambiance, very popular. Recommended.

$$-$ La Estancia, García Moreno y Sucre. Mon 1200-1500, Tue-Sat 1200-2100. Excellent buffet lunch for quality, variety and value, à la carte in the evening, nicely decorated, pleasant atmosphere, popular.

Cafés

Cafetería 7 Santos, Convención de 1884 y Olmedo. Mon-Sat 1000-2200. Pleasant café and bar with open courtyard. Good coffee and snacks, fireplace, live music Fri and Sat, popular.

El Taquito, 10 de Agosto y 9 de Abril. Daily 0700-2200. Small bar with Mexican snacks and meals.

Juad's, Convención de 1884 y Azuay. Mon-Sat 0900-1300, 1500-1900. Very good, popular, cappuccino, hot chocolate, sandwiches, fruit salad, pastries, go early. Recommended.

Salinerito, Plaza Roja. Daily 0800-1300, 1430-1900. Salinas cheese shop also serves coffee, sandwiches and pizza.

Alausí *p1047*

$$ El Mesón del Tren, Ricaurte y Eloy Alfaro. Tue-Sun 0700-0930, 1200-1430. Good restaurant, popular with tour groups, breakfast, set lunch and à la carte.

$$ Bukardia, Guatemala 107. 1300-2200, closed Wed. Meat specialties, snacks and drinks.

$ Flamingo, Antonio Mora y 9 de Octubre. 0700-2000, closed Sat. Good economical set meals. Also run **$$-$ Ventura Hostal**, simple.

🍸 Bars and clubs

Riobamba *p1044, map p1046*

Restobar La Rayuela, Daniel L Borja 36-30 y Uruguay. Mon-Sat 1200-2200, Sun 1200-1800. Trendy bar/restaurant, live music on Fri, sandwiches, coffee, salads, pasta.

San Valentín, Daniel L Borja y Vargas Torres. Mon-Sat 1800-0200. Very popular bar, good pizzas and Mexican dishes.

🎭 Entertainment

Riobamba *p1044, map p1046*

Casa de la Cultura, 10 de Agosto y Rocafuerte, T296 0219. Cultural events, cinema on Tue.

Super Cines, at El Paseo Shopping, Vía a Guano, 12 modern cinema halls, some films in 3-D.

🎉 Festivals

Riobamba *p1044, map p1046*

Fiesta del Niño Rey de Reyes, street parades, music and dancing, starts in **Dec** and culminates on **6 Jan**. Around **21 Apr** there are independence celebrations lasting several days, hotel prices rise. **29 Jun Fiestas Patronales** in honour of San Pedro. **11 Nov** is the festival to celebrate the 1st attempt at independence from Spain.

🛍 Shopping

Riobamba *p1044, map p1046*

Camping gear Some of the tour operators hire camping and climbing gear. **Marathon Explorer**, at Multiplaza mall, Av Lizarzaburu near the airport. High-end outdoor equipment and clothing. **Protección Industrial**, Rocafuerte 24-51 y Orozco, T296 3017. Outdoor equipment, rope, fishing supplies, rain ponchos.

Handicrafts Crafts sold at Plaza Roja on Wed and Sat. **Almacén Cacha**, Colón y Orozco, next to the Plaza Roja. A cooperative of indigenous people from the Cacha area, sells woven bags, wool sweaters, and other crafts, good value (closed Sun-Mon).

● What to do

Riobamba and around *p1044, map p1046*
Mountain biking Guided tours with support vehicle average US$50-60 pp per day. **Pro Bici**, Primera Constituyente 23-51 y Larrea, T295 1759, www.probici.com. Tours and rentals. **Julio Verne** (see Tour operators), very good tours, equipment and routes.

Tour operators
Most companies offer climbing trips (US$200 pp for 2 days to Chimborazo or Carihuayrazo) and trekking (US$85-100 pp per day).
Andes Trek, Esmeraldas 21-45 y Espejo, T2951275, www.goandestrek.com. Climbing and trekking, transport, equipment rental.
Expediciones Andinas, Vía a Guano, Km 3, across from **Hotel Abraspungo**, T236 4278, www.expediciones-andinas.com. Climbing expeditions run by Marco Cruz, a guide certified by the **German Alpine Club**, operate **$$$ Estrella del Chimborazo** lodge on south flank of mountain. Recommended.
Incañán, Brasil 20-28 y Luis A Falconí, T294 0508, www.incanian.com.ec. Trekking, cycling and cultural tours.
Julio Verne, El Espectador 22-25 y Daniel L Borja, 2 blocks from the train station, T296 3436, www.julioverne-travel.com. Climbing, trekking, cycling, jungle and Galápagos trips, transport, equipment rental, English spoken, Ecuadorean-Dutch-run, very conscientious and reliable. Uses official guides. Highly recommended.
Veloz Coronado, Chile 33-21 y Francia, T296 0916 (after 1900). Climbing and trekking.

The Devil's Nose Train *p1047*
In early 2014 the Devil's Nose Train departed from and returned to Alausí, Tue-Sun at 0800, 1100 and 1500 (the latter only if there are enough passengers), 2½ hrs return, US$25-35, includes a snack and folklore dance performance. From Riobamba, an autoferro (motorized rail car) ran from Riobamba to Urbina (Thu–Sun at 0800, US$11) and from Riobamba to Colta (Thu-Sun at 1200, US$15), dress warmly. Purchase tickets well in advance for weekends and holidays at any train station (Riobamba, T296 1038, Mon-Fri 0800-1630, Sat-Sun 0700-1500; Alausí, T293 0126, Tue-Sun 0700-1530), through the call centre (T1800-873637) or by email (reservasriobamba@ferrocarrilesdelecuador. gob.ec, then you have to make a bank deposit). Procedures change frequently, so enquire locally and check www.trenecuador.com.

● Transport

Riobamba *p1044, map p1046*
Bus **Terminal Terrestre** on Epiclachima y Av Daniel L Borja for most long distance buses including to Quito, Guayaquil and Cuenca. **Terminal Oriental**, Espejo y Cordovez, for Baños and the Oriente. **Terminal Intercantonal**, Av Canónigo Ramos about 2.5 km northwest of the Terminal Terrestre, for Guamote, San Juan and Cajabamba (Colta). Taxi from Terminal Terrestre to Oriental, US$1.50, from Terminal Intercantonal to the other terminals US$2. To **Quito**, US$3.85, 4 hrs, about every 30 mins; also door to door shared taxis with: **Montecarlo Trans Vip**, T301 5946 or T09-8411 4114, 6 daily, US$18 (US$5 extra for large luggage). To **Guaranda**, US$2, 2 hrs (sit on the right). To **Ambato**, US$1.25, 1 hr. To **Alausí**, see below. To **Cuenca**, 8 a day via Alausí, 5½ hrs, US$6. To **Guayaquil** via Pallatanga, frequent service, US$4.75, 5 hrs, spectacular for the first 2 hrs. The following from Terminal Oriental: to **Baños**, 2 hrs, US$2; to **Puyo** US$4, 4 hrs, to **Macas** via Sangay, 8 daily, 4 hrs, US$5 (sit on the left), also Unidos from the Terminal Terrestre at 0900.

Guaranda *p1045*
Bus Terminal at Eliza Mariño Carvajal, on road to Riobamba and Babahoyo; if you are staying in town get off closer to the centre. Many daily buses to: **Ambato**, US$2, 2 hrs. **Riobamba**, see

above. **Babahoyo**, US$3, 3 hrs; beautiful ride. **Guayaquil**, US$4, 5 hrs. **Quito**, US$5, 5 hrs.

Reserva Faunística Chimborazo p1045
There are no buses that will take you to the shelters. You can take a tour or arrange transport with a tour operator from Riobamba (US$35 one way, US$45 return with wait). You can also take a Riobamba-Guaranda bus, alight at the turn-off for the refuges and walk the remaining steep 8 km (5 km taking short-cuts) to the first shelter. For the eastern slopes, take a trekking tour, arrange transport from an agency or take a bus between Riobamba and Ambato, get off at the turnoff for **Posada La Estación** and Urbina and walk from there.

Alausí p1047
Bus To **Riobamba**, 1½ hrs, US$1.90, 84 km. To **Quito**, from 0600 onwards, 8 a day, 6 hrs, US$6; often have to change in Riobamba. To **Cuenca**, 4 hrs, US$5. To **Ambato** hourly, 3 hrs, US$3. To **Guayaquil**, 4 a day, 4 hrs, US$5. Coop Patria. Colombia y Orozco, 3 blocks up from the main street; Trans Alausí, 5 de Junio y Loza. Many through buses don't go into town, but have to be caught on the highway, taxi from town US$1.

Parque Nacional Sangay p1047
To **Atillo** from Parque La Dolorosa, Puruhá y Primera Constituyente, at 0545, 1200, 1500, 1800, US$2, 2 hrs Also Riobamba-**Macas** service goes through Atillo, see above. To **Alao**, from Parque La Dolorosa, 0555, 0630, 0730, 0845 and hourly 1145-1800, US$1.25, 1½ hrs. To **Guarguallá Grande** and **Chico** from Parque La Dolorosa daily at 1345 (return to Riobamba at 0545), US$ 1.75 (Grande), US$2 (Chico), 2 hrs. To **Candelaria**, fromTerminal Oriental, Mon-Fri 0630, 1015, 1215, 1515 and 1700, Sat-Sun 0630, 1215 and 1700 US$1.25, 1½ hrs. Alternatively, take a bus from the same terminal to Penipe, every ½ hr, US$0.40, 40 mins, and hire a pickup truck from there to Candelaria, US$15, 40 mins.

⊕ Directory

Riobamba p1044, map p1046
Banks Several banks with ATMs at Primera Costituyente y García Moreno. **Banco del Pacífico**, Daniel L Borja y Zambrano.

Guaranda p1045
Banks Banco Pichincha, Azuay y 7 de Mayo, ATM.

Cuenca and around

Founded in 1557 on the site of the Inca settlement of Tomebamba, much of Cuenca's colonial air has been preserved, with many of its old buildings renovated. Its cobblestone streets, flowering plazas and whitewashed buildings with old wooden doors and ironwork balconies make it a pleasure to explore. The climate is spring-like, but the nights are chilly. In 1999 Cuenca was designated a UNESCO World Heritage Site. It is home to a growing expat retiree community. The area is know for its crafts.

Arriving in Cuenca → *Phone code: 07. Colour map 11, C3. Population: 346,000. Altitude: 2530 m.*
Orientation The **Terminal Terrestre** is on Avenida España, 15 minutes' ride northeast of the centre, T284 2811. The **airport** is five minutes' beyond the Terminal Terrestre, T282 4811. Both can be reached by city bus, but best take a taxi at all hours (US$1.50-2.50 to the centre). The **Terminal Sur** for regional buses within the province is by the Feria Libre El Arenal on Avenida Las Américas. Many city buses pass here.

The city is bounded by the Río Machángara to the north and the Ríos Yanuncay and Tarqui to the south. The Río Tomebamba separates the colonial heart from the newer districts to the south. Avenida Las Américas is a ring road around the north and west of the city and the *autopista*, a multi-lane highway bypasses the city to the south. **➤➤** *See Transport, page 1062, for details.*

Tourist offices Ministerio de Turismo ① *Sucre y Benigno Malo, on Parque Calderón next to the Municipio, T282 1035, Mon-Fri, 0800-2000, Sat 0830-1730, Sun 0830-1330, helpful.* **Cámara de Turismo** ①*Terminal Terrestre, T284 5657, Mon-Sat 0830-1200, 1230-1800,* information about the city, including city and long distance bus routes; also at the airport. General information from **www.cuenca.com.ec.** To locate an establishment see **www.ubicacuenca.com.**

Safety Though safer than Quito or Guayaquil, routine precautions are advised. Outside the busy nightlife area around Calle Larga, the city centre is deserted and unsafe after 2300, taking a taxi is recommended. The river banks, the Cruz del Vado area (south end of Juan Montalvo), the Terminal Terrestre and all market areas, are not safe after dark.

Places in Cuenca

On the main plaza, **Parque Abdón Calderón**, are the Old Cathedral, **El Sagrario** ① *Mon-Fri 0900-1730, Sat-Sun 0900-1300, US$2,* begun in 1557, and the immense 'New' **Catedral de la Inmaculada**, started in 1885. The latter contains a famous crowned image of the Virgin, a beautiful altar and an exceptional play of light and shade through modern stained glass. Other churches which deserve a visit are **San Blas**, **San Francisco** and **Santo Domingo**. Many churches are open at irregular hours only and for services. The church of **El Carmen de la Asunción**, close to the southwest corner of La Inmaculada, has a flower market in the tiny **Plazoleta El Carmen** in front. There is a colourful daily market in **Plaza Rotary** where pottery, clothes, guinea pigs and local produce, especially baskets, are sold. Thursday is the busiest.

Museo del Monasterio de las Conceptas ① *Hermano Miguel 6-33 entre Pdte Córdova y Juan Jaramillo, T283 0625, www.museodelasconceptas.org.ec. Mon-Fri 0900-1830, Sat and holidays 1000-1300, US$2.50,* in a cloistered convent founded in 1599, houses a well displayed collection of religious and folk art, in addition to an extensive collection of lithographs by Guayasamín.

Pumapungo ① *C Larga y Huayna Capac, T283 1521, Mon-Fri 0900-1700, Sat 0900-1300,* is a mueum complex on the edge of the colonial city, at the actual site of Tomebamba excavations. Part of the area explored is seen at **Parque Arqueológico Pumapungo**. The **Sala Arqueológica** section contains all the Cañari and Inca remains and artifacts found at this site. Other halls in the premises house the **Sala Etnográfica**, with information on different Ecuadorean cultures, including a special collection of *tsantsas* (shrunken heads from Oriente), the **Sala de Arte Religioso**, the **Sala Numismática** and temporary exhibits. There are also book and music libraries, free cultural videos and music events. Three blocks west of Pumapungo, **Museo Manuel Agustín Landívar** ① *C Larga 2-23 y Manuel Vega, T282 1177, Mon-Fri 0800-1700, Sat 0900-1300, US$1,* is at the site of the small Todos los Santos ruins, with Cañari, Inca and colonial remains; ceramics and artifacts found at the site are also displayed.

Museo de las Culturas Aborígenes ① *C Larga 5-24 y Hermano Miguel, T283 9181, Mon-Fri 0830-1800, Sat 0900-1400, US$2; guided tours in English, Spanish and French, craft shop,* the private collection of Dr J Cordero Íñiguez, has a impressive selection of pre-Columbian archaeology. **Museo Remigio Crespo Toral** ① *C Larga 7-25 y Borreo. T282 1177, Mon-Fri 0900-1300, 1500-1800, Sat 0900-1300, free, temporarily closed in 2014,* in a beautiful colonial house refurbished in 2013, has important history, archaeology and art collections. **Museo del Sombrero** ①*C Larga 10-41 y Gral Torres, T283 1569, Mon-Fri 0900-1800, Sat 0900-1700, Sun 0930-1330,* shop with all the old factory machines for hat finishing.

On Plaza San Sebastián is **Museo Municipal de Arte Moderno** ① *Sucre 1527 y Talbot, T282 0838, Mon-Fri 0900-1700, Sat-Sun 0900-1300, free,* has a permanent contemporary art collection and art library. It holds a biennial international painting competition and other cultural activities. Across the river from the Museo Pumapungo, the **Museo de Artes de Fuego** ① *Las Herrerías y 10* *de Agosto, T409 6510, Mon-Fri 0800-1330, 1500-1730, free except for special events*, has a display of wrought iron work and pottery. It is housed in the beautifully restored Casa de Chaguarchimbana. Also south of city, accessed via Avenida Fray Vicente Solano, beyond the football stadium, is Turi church, orphanage and mirador; a tiled panorama explains the magnificent views.

Cuenca

Where to stay
1 Carvallo *B3*
2 Casa del Barranco *D3*
3 Casa del Río *C2*
4 Casa Ordóñez *B3*
5 Colonial *B3*
6 El Conquistador *B3*
7 El Príncipe *C3*
8 Hogar Cuencano *D3*
9 Inca Real *B2*
10 La Casona *E3*
11 La Cigale *C3*
12 La Orquídea *B3*
13 La Posada Cuencana *B2*
14 Macondo *A2*
15 Mansión Alcázar *B2*
16 Mercure El Dorado *B3*
17 Milán *C2*
18 Posada del Angel & Mangiare Restaurant *B1*
19 Posada Todos Santos *D4*
20 Santa Lucía *C3*
21 Turista del Mundo *D3*
22 Victoria *D3*
23 Yakumama *C3*

Restaurants
1 Balcón Quiteño *B4*
2 Bananas Café *C2*
3 Café Eucalyptus & Grecia *B3*
4 Coffee Tree *D3*
5 Di Bacco *B2*
6 El Carbón *B3*
7 El Maíz *E5*
8 Mixx Gourmet *C5*

There are sulphur baths at **Baños**, with a domed, blue church in a delightful landscape, 5 km southwest of Cuenca. These are the hottest commercial baths in Ecuador. Above **Hostería Durán** (see Where to stay) are four separate complexes of warm baths, **Merchán**, **Rodas** (www.hosteriarodas.com), **Durán** (www.novaqua.com.ec) and **Piedra de Agua** ① *www.piedradeagua.com.ec, entry US$2-10*. The latter two are better maintained, more exclusive and in addition to having several hot pools, offer a variety of treatments in their spas.

Ingapirca → *Phone code: 07. Colour map 1a, B3. Altitude: 3160 m.*

① *Daily 0800-1800, closed public holidays, US$6, including museum and tour in Spanish; bags can be stored. Small café.*

Ecuador's most important Inca ruin, at 3160 m, lies 8.5 km east of the colonial town of **Cañar** (hostales in **$** range). Access is from Cañar or **El Tambo**. The Inca Huayna Capac took over the site from the conquered Cañaris when his empire expanded north into Ecuador in the third quarter of the 15th century. Ingapirca was strategically placed on the Royal Highway that ran from Cuzco to Quito and soldiers may have been stationed there. The site shows typical imperial Cuzco-style architecture, such as tightly fitting stonework and trapezoidal doorways. The central structure may have been a solar observatory. Nearby is a throne cut into the rock, the **Sillón del Inca** (Inca's Chair) and the **Ingachugana**, a large rock with carved channels. A 10-minute walk away from the site is the **Cara del Inca**, or 'face of the Inca', an immense natural formation in the rock looking over the landscape. On Friday there is an interesting indigenous market at Ingapirca village.

A tourist autoferro runs from El Tambo 7 km to the small Cañari-Inca archaeological site of **Baños del Inca** or **Coyoctor** ① *site open daily 0800-1700, US$1; 2 departures Wed-Fri, US$7, includes entry to El Tambo museum and Coyoctor site, 5 departures Sat-Sun and holidays, US$5*, a massive rock outcrop carved to form baths, showers, water channels and seats overlooking a small amphitheatre. There is an interpretation centre with information about the site, a hall with displays about regional fiestas and an audiovisual room with tourist information about all of Ecuador.

9 Moliendo Café *D3*
10 Néctar *B3*
11 Raymipampa *B3*
12 San Sebas *B1*
13 Tiestos *C3*
14 Tutto Freddo *B3*
15 Viejo Rincón *C3*
16 Villa Rosa *B2*

Bars & clubs ⑤
17 La Mesa Salsoteca *B4*
18 MalAmado *C1*
19 Rue *D3*
20 Wunderbar *D3*

Inca Trail to Ingapirca

The three-day hike to Ingapirca starts at **Achupallas** (lively Saturday market, one hostel), 25 km from Alausí. The walk is covered by three 1:50,000 *IGM* sheets, Alausí, Juncal and Cañar. The Juncal sheet is most important, the name Ingapirca does not appear on the latter, you may have to ask directions near the end. Also take a compass and GPS. Good camping equipment is essential. Take all food and drink with you as there is nothing along the way. A shop in Achupallas sells basic foodstuffs. There are persistent beggars the length of the hike, especially children. Tour operators in Riobamba and Cuenca offer this trek for about US$250-320 per person, three days, everything included.

East of Cuenca

Northeast of Cuenca, on the paved road to Méndez in the Oriente, is **Paute**, with a pleasant park and modern church. South of Paute, **Gualaceo** is a rapidly expanding, modern town set in beautiful landscape, with a charming plaza and Sunday market. The **iTur** ① *at the Municipio, Gran Colombia y 3 de Noviembre, Parque Central, T225 5131, Mon-Fri 0800-1300, 1400-1700*, is very helpful, Spanish only. **CIDAP** ① *Loja y Sucre, Wed-Sun 0900-1300, free*, is a small crafts museum. A scenic road goes from Gualaceo to Limón in Oriente (closed for paving in 2014). Many of Ecuador's 4000 species of orchids can be seen at **Ecuagénera** ① *Km 2 on the road to Cuenca, T225 5237, www.ecuagenera.com, Mon-Sat 0730-1630, Sun 0930-1630, US$5 (US$3 pp for groups of 3 or more)*.

South of Gualaceo is **Chordeleg**, a touristy village famous for its crafts in wood, silver and gold filigree, pottery and panama hats. At the Municipio is the **Centro de Interpretación** ① *C 23 de Enero, Mon-Fri 0800-1300, 1400-1700*, an exhibition hall with fascinating local textiles, ceramics and straw work, some of which are on sale at reasonable prices. It's a good uphill walk from Gualaceo to Chordeleg, and a pleasant hour downhill in the other direction. South of Gualaceo, 83 km from Cuenca, **Sígsig**, an authentic highland town where women can be seen weaving hats 'on the move'. It has a Sunday market, two *residenciales* and an archaeology museum. A poor but scenic road goes from Sígsig to Gualaquiza in Oriente.

Parque Nacional Cajas

① *The park office is at Presidente Córdova 7-56 y Luis Cordero, Edif Morejón, p 2, T282 9853, www.etapa.net.ec/PNC, Mon-Fri 0800-1300 and 1500-1800. Entry free, overnight stay US$4 per night. Hiking information for Cajas and other areas around Cuenca in www.thefreeair.com.*

Northwest of Cuenca, Cajas is a 29,000-ha national park with over 230 lakes. The *páramo* vegetation, such as chuquiragua and lupin, is beautiful and the wildlife interesting. Cajas is very rich in birdlife; 125 species have been identified, including the condor and many varieties of hummingbird (the Violet-tailed Metaltail is endemic to this area). On the lakes are Andean gulls, Speckled Teal and Yellow-billed Pintails. On a clear morning the views are superb, even to Chimborazo, some 300 km away.

There are two access roads. The paved road from Cuenca to Guayaquil via Molleturo goes through the northern section and is the main route for Laguna Toreadora, the visitors' centre and Laguna Llaviuco. Skirting the southern edge of the park is a gravel secondary road, which goes from Cuenca via San Joaquín to the Soldados entrance and the community of Angas beyond. (See Transport, page 1062.) There is nowhere to stay after the *refugio* at Laguna Toreadora (see Where to stay, below) until you reach the lowlands between Naranjal and La Troncal.

The park offers ideal but strenuous walking, at 3150-4450 m altitude, and the climate is rough. There have been deaths from exposure. The best time to visit is August-January, when you may expect clear days, strong winds, night-time temperatures to -8°C and occasional mist. From February-July temperatures are higher but there is much more fog, rain and snow. It is best to arrive in the early morning since it can get very cloudy, wet and cool after about 1300. Cuenca tourist office has a good, one-page map of Cajas, but other local maps are not always exact. It is best to get the *IGM* maps in Quito (Chaucha, Cuenca, San Felipe de Molleturo, and Chiquintad 1:50,000) and take a compass and GPS. It is easy to get lost.

● Cuenca and around listings

For hotel and restaurant price codes, and other relevant information, see Essentials.

● Where to stay

Cuenca and around *p1052, map p1054*

$$$$ Carvallo, Gran Colombia 9-52, entre Padre Aguirre y Benigno Malo, T283 2063, www.hotelcarvallo.com.ec. Combination of an elegant colonial-style hotel and art/antique gallery. Very nice comfortable rooms all have bath tubs, restaurant, boutique with exclusive crafts and clothing.

$$$$ Mansión Alcázar, Bolívar 12-55 y Tarqui, T282 3918, www.mansionalcazar.com. Beautifully restored house, a mansion indeed, central, very nice rooms, restaurant serves gourmet international food, lovely gardens, quiet relaxed atmosphere.

$$$$ Oro Verde, Av Ordóñez Lazo, northwest of the centre towards Cajas, T409 0000, www.oroverdehotels.com. Elegant hotel, buffet breakfast, excellent international restaurant offers buffet lunch and à la carte dinner, small pool, parking.

$$$$ Santa Lucía, Borrero 8-44 y Sucre, T282 8000, www.santaluciahotel.com. An elegantly renovated colonial house, very nice comfortable rooms, buffet breakfast, excellent Italian restaurant, safe deposit box.

$$$ Casa Ordóñez, Lamar 8-59 y Benigno Malo, T282 3297, www.casa-ordonez.com. Nicely renovated colonial house with wood floors and 3 inner patios, nicely decorated rooms and common areas, down comforters, no smoking.

$$$ Inca Real, Gral Torres 8-40 entre Sucre y Bolívar, T282 3636, www.hotelincareal.com.ec. Refurbished colonial house with comfortable rooms around patios, good Spanish restaurant, parking.

$$$ La Casona, Miguel Cordero 2-124, near the stadium, T410 3501, www.lacasonahotel.com.ec. Very nice refurbished family home in a residential area, comfortable carpeted rooms, buffet breakfast, restaurant, parking.

$$$ La Posada Cuencana, Tarqui 9-46 y Bolívar, T282 6831. Small family run hotel, beautiful colonial style rooms, personalized service by owners

$$$ Mercure El Dorado, Gran Colombia 787 y Luis Cordero, T283 1390, www.eldoradohotel.com.ec. Elegant modern hotel, rooms have safe and mini-bar, buffet breakfast, cafeteria, spa, gym, business centre, parking.

$$$ Posada del Angel, Bolívar 14-11 y Estévez de Toral, T284 0695, www.hostalposadadelangel.com. A nicely restored colonial house, comfortable rooms, good Italian restaurant, parking, patio with plants, some noise from restaurant, English spoken, helpful staff. Recommended.

$$$-$$ Victoria, C Larga 6-93 y Borrero, T283 1120, www.grupo-santaana.net. Elegant refurbished hotel overlooking the river, comfortable modern rooms, excellent expensive restaurant, nice views.

$$ Casa del Barranco, Calle Larga 8-41 y Luis Cordero, T283 9763, www.casadelbarranco.com. Nicely restored colonial house, some rooms with lovely views over the river, cafeteria overlooking the river.

$$ Colonial, Gran Colombia 10-13 y Padre Aguirre, T284 1644, www.hostalcolonial.com. Refurbished colonial house with beautiful patio, carpeted rooms.

$$ El Príncipe, J Jaramillo 7-82 y Luis Cordero, T284 7287, www.hotelprincipe.com.ec. A refurbished 3-storey colonial house, comfortable rooms around a nice patio with plants, restaurant, parking.

$$ La Orquídea, Borrero 9-31 y Bolívar, T282 4511. Nicely refurbished colonial house, bright rooms, fridge, low season and long term discounts, good value.

$$ Macondo, Tarqui 11-64 y Lamar, T284 0697, www.hostalmacondo.com. Nice restored colonial house, large rooms, buffet breakfast, cooking facilities, pleasant patio with plants, garden, very popular, US run. Highly recommended.

$$ Milán, Pres Córdova 989 y Padre Aguirre, T283 1104, www.hotelmilan.com.ec. Multi-storey hotel with views over market, restaurant, popular.

$$ Posada Todos Santos, C Larga 3-42 y Tomás Ordóñez, near the Todos Santos Church, T282 4247, posadatodossantoscue@latinmail. com. Nice tranquil hostel decorated with murals, very good, attentive service, English spoken, group discounts.

$$-$ Casa del Río, Bajada del Padrón 4-07 y C Larga, T282 9659, hostalcasadelrio@hotmail. com. Pleasant quiet hostal on El Barranco overlooking the river, private or shared bath, breakfast available, nice views, attentive service.

$$-$ Turista del Mundo, C Larga 5-79 y Hermano Miguel, T282 9125, esperanzab65@ gmail.com. Popular hostel with comfortable rooms, private or shared bath, cooking facilities, nice terrace, very helpful.

$ Hogar Cuencano, Hermano Miguel 436 y C Larga, T283 4941, celso3515@yahoo.com. Nicely furnished family run hostal in the heart of the action, private or shared bath, 10 pp in dorm, cafeteria, cooking facilities (0700-1900), clean.

$ La Cigale, Honorato Vasquez 7-80 y Cordero, T283 5308, lacigalecuencana@yahoo.fr. Very popular hostel with private rooms and dorms for 4 (US$10 pp) to 6 (US$7 pp), excellent restaurant (**$**), can be very noisy.

$ Yakumama, Cordero 5-66 y Honorato Vásquez, T283 4353, www.hostalyakumama. com. Popular hostel, 2 private rooms and dorms with 2-6 beds US$7-9 pp, restaurant with Ecuadorean and Swiss dishes, bar, patio with plants and lounging area, terrace with hammocks, can get noisy.

Baños

$$$ Caballo Campana, Vía Misicata-Baños Km 4, on an alternative road from Cuenca to Baños (2 km from Baños, no public transport, taxi US$5 from the centre of Cuenca), T289 2360, www.caballocampana.com. Nicely rebuilt colonial hacienda house in 28 has with gardens and forest, heated rooms, suites and cabins, includes buffet breakfast, Ecuadorean and international cuisine, horse riding and lessons, sports fields, discounts for longer stays.

$$$ Hostería Durán, Km 8 Vía Baños, T289 2485, www.hosteriaduran.com. Includes buffet breakfast, restaurant, parking, has well-maintained, very clean pools (US$6.20 for non-residents), gym, steam bath, transport from Cuenca, camping. There are also a couple of cheap *residenciales*.

Ingapirca *p1055*

$$$ Posada Ingapirca, 500 m uphill from ruins, T221 7116, for reservations T283 0064 (Cuenca), www.grupo-santaana.net. Converted hacienda, comfortable rooms, heating, includes typical breakfast, excellent pricey restaurant, good service, great views.

$ El Castillo, opposite the ruins, T09-9998 3650, cab.castillo@hotmail.com. 3 simple cabins, restaurant with fireplace.

There are a couple of simple places in the village. Also good economical meals at **Intimikuna**, at the entrance to the archaeological site.

El Tambo

This is the nearest town to Ingapirca.

$ Chasky Wasy, Montenegro next to Banco del Austro, 1 block from the park, T09-9883 0013, tenezaca@hotmail.com. Nice hostel with ample rooms, parking nearby.

$ Sunshine, Panamericana y Ramón Borrero, at north end of town, T223 3394. Simple, family run, not always staffed, private or shared bath, restaurant nearby, traffic noise.

Inca Trail to Ingapirca *p1056*

$ Ingañán, Achupallas, T293 0663. Basic, with bath, hot water, meals on request, camping.

East of Cuenca *p1056*
Paute
$$$ Hostería Uzhupud, Km 32 Vía a Paute, T225 0329, www.uzhupud.com. Set in the beautiful Paute valley 10 km from town, deluxe, relaxing, rooms at the back have best views, swimming pools and sauna (US$15 for non-residents), sports fields, horse riding, gardens, lots of orchids. Recommended.
$ Cutilcay, Abdón Calderón, by the river, T225 0133. Older basic hostel, private or shared bath.

Gualaceo
$$-$ Peñón de Cuzay, Sector Bullcay El Carmen on the main road to Cuenca, T217 1515. In one of the weaving communities, spa and pool. Fills on weekends, book ahead.
$ Residencial Gualaceo, Gran Colombia 302 y FA Piedra, T225 5006. Older hotel, clean basic rooms, private or shared bath, parking.

Parque Nacional Cajas *p1056*
There is a *refugio* at Laguna Toreadora, cold, cooking facilities, and camping at Laguna Llaviuco. Other shelters in the park are primitive.
$$ Hostería Dos Chorreras, Km 21 Vía al Cajas, sector Sayausí, T245 4301, www.hosteriados chorreras.com. Hacienda-style inn outside the park. Heating, restaurant serves excellent fresh trout, reservations recommended, horse rentals with advanced notice.

❼ Restaurants

Cuenca *p1052, map p1054*
There is a wide selection and fast turnover of restaurants. Most places are closed on Sun evening. There are cheap *comedores* at the Mercados 9 de Octubre and 10 de Agosto.
$$$ El Carbón, Borrero 10-69 y Lamar, T283 3711. Mon-Wed 0700-1600, 1800-2200, Thu-Sat until 2400. Excellent charcoal-grilled meat served with a choice of fresh salads, seafood, wide choice of dishes and breakfasts, large portions enough for 2.
$$$ Villa Rosa, Gran Colombia 12-22 y Tarqui, T283 7944. Mon-Fri 1200-1430, 1900-2230. Very elegant restaurant in the centre of town,

excellent international and Ecuadorean food and service. A meeting place for business people.
$$$-$$ Balcón Quiteño, Sangurima 6-49 y Borrero, and Av Ordóñez Lazo 311 y los Pinos, T283 1928. Daily 0900-0100. Good Ecuadorean and international food and service, 1960s decor. Popular with locals after a night's partying.
$$$-$$ Tiestos, J Jaramillo 4-89 y M Cueva, T283 5310. Tue-Sat 1230-1500, 1830-2200, Sun 1230-1500. Superb international cuisine prepared on *tiestos*, shallow clay pans, comfortable feel-at-home atmosphere, very popular, reserve ahead.
$$ Café Eucalyptus, Gran Colombia 9-41 y Benigno Malo. Mon-Fri 1700-2300 or later, Sat 1900-0200. A pleasant restaurant, café and bar in an elegantly decorated house. Large menu with dishes from all over the world. British run, popular. Recommended.
$$ Di Bacco, Tarqui 9-61 y Bolívar, T283 2301, www.cuencadibaccorestaurant.com. Tue-Sun 1200-1500, 1700-2200. Excellent lasagna and other Italian dishes, very good set lunch, live music, theatre and other events (see web page), popular with expats.
$$ El Maíz, C Larga 1-279 y C de los Molinos, T284 0224. Mon-Sat 1200-2100 (variable, call ahead). Good traditional Ecuadorean dishes with some innovations, salads.
$$ Manglare, Estévez de Toral 8-91 y Bolívar, at Posada del Angel, T282 1360. Mon-Sat 1200-1500, 1730-2230, Sun 1200-1500. Excellent Italian food, home-made pasta, good value, very popular with locals.
$$ Raymipampa, Benigno Malo 8-59, at Parque Calderón. Mon-Fri 0830-2300, Sat-Sun 0930-2230. Good typical and international food in a nice central location, economical set lunch on weekdays, fast service, very popular, at times it is hard to get a table.
$$-$ Néctar, Benigno Malo 10-42 y Gran Colombia, p2, T284 4118. Mon-Sat 1200-1500, Fri 1800-2100. Good economical vegetarian set lunch and à la carte, vegan and raw options.
$$-$ Viejo Rincón, Pres Córdova 7-46 y Borrero. Mon-Fri 0900-2100, Sat 0900-1500. Tasty Ecuadorean food, very good set lunch and à la carte, popular.

$ Good Affinity, Capulíes 1-89 y Gran Colombia. Mon-Sat 0930-1530. Very good vegetarian food, vegan options, economical set lunch, nice garden seating.
$ Grecia, Gran Colombia y Padre Aguirre. Mon-Sat 1200-1500. Good quality and value set lunch.
$ Moliendo Café, Honorato Vásquez y Hermano Miguel. Mon-Sat 1100-2100. Tasty Colombian food including set lunch, friendly service.

Cafés

Bananas Café, C Larga 9-40 y Benigno Malo. Thu-Sun 0800-1600. Breakfast, snacks, light lunches, fruit juices, hot drinks, desserts, attentive service.
Coffee Tree, C Larga y Borrero, Plaza de la Merced. Mon-Thu 0800-2200, Fri-Sat 0800-2400, Sun 0800-2200. Very popular café/restaurant with a varied menu; one of the few places in Cuenca with outdoor seating and open Sun evening. Note that there are plans to remodel and change the name in mid 2014.
Mixx Gourmet, Parque San Blas 2-73 y Tomás Ordóñez. A variety of fruit and liquor flavoured ice cream, popular. Several others nearby.
Monte Bianco, Bolívar 2-80 y Ordóñez and a couple of other locations. Good ice-cream and cream cakes, good value.
San Sebas, San Sebastián 1-94 y Sucre, Parque San Sebastián. Tue-Sun 0830-1500. Outdoor café, popular for breakfast, good selection of giant sandwiches and salads.
Tutto Freddo, Bolívar 8-09 y Benigno Malo and several other locations. Daily 0900-2200. Good ice-cream, crêpes, pizza, sandwiches and sweets, reasonable prices, popular.

🌙 Bars and clubs

Cuenca *p1052, map p1054*
Calle Larga is a major destination for night life, with lots of bars with snacks and some restaurants. Av 12 de Abril, along the river near Parque de la Madre, and to the west of the centre, Plaza del Arte, Gaspar de Sangurima y Abraham Sarmiento, opposite Plazoleta El Otorongo, are also popular. Most bars open Wed-Thu until 2300, Fri-Sat until 0200.

La Mesa Salsoteca, Gran Colombia 3-36 entre Vargas Machuca y Tomás Ordóñez (no sign). Latin music, salsa, popular among travellers and locals, young crowd.
MalAmado, C San Roque y Av 12 de Abril. Pleasant atmosphere, good music, food, a good place for dancing, US$10-15.
Rue, at Parque de la Madre, Av 12 de Abril. Nice bar/restaurant with outdoor seating, no cover charge.
Wunderbar, entrance from stairs on Hermano Miguel y C Larga. Mon-Fri 1100-0200, Sat 1500-0200. A café-bar-restaurant, drinks, good coffee and food including some vegetarian. Nice atmosphere, book exchange, German-run.

🎭 Entertainment

Cuenca *p1052, map p1054*
Cinemas Multicines, Av José Peralta, complex of 5 theatres and food court, also at Mall del Río.
Dance Classes Cachumbambe, Remigio Crespo 7-79 y Guayas, p2, T288 2023. Salsa, merengue and a variety of other rhythms, group and individual classes.

🎉 Festivals

Cuenca *p1052, map p1054*
On **24 Dec** there is an outstanding parade: **Pase del Niño Viajero**, probably the largest and finest Christmas parade in all Ecuador. Children and adults from all the *barrios* and surrounding villages decorate donkeys, horses, cars and trucks with symbols of abundance. Little children in colourful indigenous costumes or dressed up as Biblical figures ride through the streets accompanied by musicians. The parade starts at about 1000 at San Sebastián, proceeds along C Bolívar and ends at San Blas about 5 hrs later. In the days up to, and just after Christmas, there are many smaller parades. **12 Apr** is the Foundation of Cuenca. On **Good Friday** there is a fine procession through the town to the Mirador Turi. **May-Jun** Septenario, the religious festival of Corpus Christi, lasts a week. On **3 Nov** is Independence of Cuenca, with street theatre, art exhibitions and night-

time dances all over the city. Cuenca hosts the **Bienal de Cuenca**, an internationally famous art competition The next one is due in 2015. Information from Bolivar 13-89, T283 1778, www.bienaldecuenca.org.

O Shopping

Cuenca *p1052, map p1054*

Camping equipment Bermeo Hnos, Borrero 8-35 y Sucre, T283 1522. **Explorador Andino**, Borrero 7-39 y Sucre. **Tatoo/Cikla**, Av Remigio Tamariz 2-52 y Federico Proaño, T288 4809, www.ec.tatoo.ws. Good camping, hiking, climbing and biking gear. Also rent bikes.Several other shops near the university, on or near Av Remigio Crespo. Equipment rental from **Apullacta**, see Tour operators.

Handicrafts There are many craftware shops along Gran Colombia, Benigno Malo and Juan Jaramillo alongside Las Conceptas. There are several good leather shops in the arcade off Bolívar between Benigno Malo and Luis Cordero. *Polleras*, traditional skirts worn by indigenous women are found along Gral Torres, between Sucre and Pres Córdova, and on Tarqui, between Pres Córdova and C Larga. For basketwork, take a 15 min bus ride from the Feria Libre (see Markets below) to the village of San Joaquín.

Arte, Artesanías y Antigüedades, Borrero y Córdova. Textiles, jewellery and antiques. **Artesa**, L Cordero 10-31 y Gran Colombia, several branches. Modern ceramic tableware. **Centro Artesanal Municipal 'Casa de la Mujer'**, Gral Torres 7-33. Crafts market with a great variety of handicrafts. **Colecciones Jorge Moscoso**, J Jaramillo 6-80 y Borrero. Weaving exhibitions, ethnographic museum, antiques and crafts. **El Barranco**, Hermano Miguel 3-23 y Av 3 de Noviembre. Artisans' cooperative selling a wide variety of crafts. **El Otorongo**, 3 de Noviembre by Plaza Otorongo, exclusive designs sold at this art gallery/café. **El Tucán**, Borrero 7-35. Good selection. Recommended. **Galápagos**, Borrero 6-75. Excellent selection. **La Esquina de las Artes**, 12 de Abril y Agustín Cueva, shops with exclusive crafts including textiles; also cultural events.

Jewellery Galería Claudio Maldonado, Bolívar 7-75, has unique pre-Columbian designs in silver and precious stones. **Unicornio**, Gran Colombia y Luis Cordero. Good jewellery, ceramics and candelabras. **Panama hats** Manufacturers have displays showing the complete hat making process, see also Museo del Sombrero, page 1053. **K Dorfzaun**, Gil Ramírez Dávalos 4-34, near bus station, T286 1707, www.kdorfzaun.com. Good quality and selection of hats and straw crafts, nice styles, good prices. English-speaking guides. **Homero Ortega P e Hijos**, Av Gil Ramírez Dávalos 3-86, T280 1288, www.homeroortega.com. Good quality.

Markets Feria Libre, Av Las Américas y Av Remigio Crespo, west of the centre. The largest market, also has dry goods and clothing, busiest Wed and Sat. **Mercado 9 de Octubre**, Sangurima y Mariano Cueva, busiest on Thu. Nearby at **Plaza Rotary**, Sangurima y Vargas Machuca, crafts are sold, best selection on Thu. Note this area is not safe. **Mercado 10 de Agosto**, C Larga y Gral Torres. Daily market with a prepared foods and drinks section on the 2nd floor.

O What to do

Cuenca *p1052, map p1054*

Day tours to Ingapirca or Cajas run about US$45-50 pp. Trekking in Cajas about US$60-100 pp per day, depending on group size. **Apullacta**, Gran Colombia 11-02 y Gral Torres, p 2, T283 7815, www.apullacta.com. Run city and regional tours (Cajas, Ingapirca, Saraguro), also adventure tours (cycling, horse riding, canopy, canyoning), sell jungle, highland and Galápagos trips; also hire camping equipment. **Metropolitan Touring**, Sucre 6-62 y Borreo, T284 3223, www.metropolitan-touring.com. A branch of the Quito operator, also sells airline tickets. **Pazhuca Tours**, T282 3231, info@pazhucatours. com.ec. Run regional tours and offer transport through **Van Service**, T281 6409, www.van service.com.ec, which also run city tours on a double-decker bus. The 1¾-hrs tour includes the main attractions in the colonial city and El Turi lookout. US$5, hourly departures 0900-1900 from the Old Cathedral.

Terra Diversa, C Larga 8-41 y Luis Cordero, T282 3782, www.terradiversa.com. Lots of useful information, helpful staff. Ingapirca, Cajas, community tourism in Saraguro, jungle trips, horse riding, mountain biking and other options. The more common destinations have fixed departures. Also sell Galápagos tours and flights. Recommended.

⊖ Transport

Cuenca *p1052, map p1054*

Air Airport is about a 20-min ride northeast of the centre. To **Quito** and **Guayaquil** with Aerogal (Aguilar 159 y Solano and Av España, T286 1041), **LAN** (Bolívar 9-18, T283 8078) and TAME (Florencia Astudillo 2-22, T288 9581).

Bus **Terminal Sur** for local services is at the Feria Libre on Av Las Américas. Many city buses pass here, not a safe area. City buses US$0.25. For the local **Baños**, city buses every 5-10 mins, 0600-2230, buses pass the front of the Terminal Terrestre, cross the city on Vega Muñoz and Cueva, then down Todos los Santos to the river, along 12 de Abril and onto Av Loja.

The long distance **Terminal Terrestre** is on Av España, 15 mins by taxi northeast of centre. Take daytime buses to enjoy scenic routes. To **Riobamba**, 5½ hrs, US$6. To **Baños** (Tungurahua), take a bus to Riobamba and a taxi to the Terminal Oriental. To **Ambato**, 6½ hrs, US$8. To **Quito**, US$10-12, 9 hrs, all buses arrive at Terminal Quitumbe in Quito; **Flota Imbabura** has several nighttime departures which continue to their own terminal in central Quito; van service with **Río Arriba/Atenas** (see To Guayaquil, below), daily at 2300, US$25, 6 hrs. To **Alausí**, 4 hrs, US$5; all Riobamba- and Quito-bound buses pass by, but few enter town. To **Loja**, 4 hrs, US$7.50, see www.viajerosinternacional.com; hourly van service with **Elite Tours**, Remigio Crespo 14-08 y Santa Cruz, T420 3088, also **Faisatur**, Remigio Crespo y Brazil, T404 4771, US$12, 3 hrs; taxi US$60. To **Vilcabamba**, van service daily at 1430 from

Hostal La Cigale, Honorato Vásquez y Luis Cordero, US$15, 4½ hrs. To **Saraguro**, US$5, 2½ hrs. To **Machala**, 4 hrs, US$5.50, sit on the left, wonderful scenery. To **Huaquillas**, 5 hrs, US$7 To **Guayaquil**, via Cajas and Molleturo, 4 hrs, or via Zhud, 5 hrs, both US$8; also hourly van service, 0500-2100, with **Río Arriba/Atenas**, Av Remigio Crespo 13-26 y Santa Cruz, near the Feria Libre, T420 3064, US$12, 3 hrs, reserve ahead; several others nearby. To **Macas** via Guarumales or Limón (closed in 2014), 7 hrs, US$8; spectacular scenery but prone to landslides, check in advance if roads are open. To **Gualaquiza**, in the southern Oriente, there are 2 routes, via Gualaceo and Plan de Milagro, US$5 (closed for paving in 2014) and via Sígsig, 6 hrs, US$6.25. To **Chiclayo** (Peru) via Tumbes, **Máncora** and **Piura**, with **Super Semería**, at 2200, US$18, 11 hrs (US$14 as far as Piura or Máncora).To Piura, also **Pullman Sucre**, connecting with CIFA in Huaquillas; direct service to Piura via Macará is available from Loja, 8 hrs.

Taxi US$1.50 for short journey; US$1.50 to the bus station; US$2 to airport; US$5 to Baños.

Ingapirca *p1055*

Bus Direct buses **Cuenca** to Ingapirca with Transportes Cañar Mon-Fri at 0900 and 1220, Sat-Sun at 0900, returning 1300 and 1545, US$2.50, 2 hrs. Buses run from Cuenca to Cañar (US$1.50) and El Tambo (US$2) every 15 mins. From **Cañar**, corner of 24 de Mayo and Borrero, local buses leave every 15 mins for Ingapirca, 0600-1800, US$0.50, 30 mins; last bus returns at 1700. The same buses from Cañar go through **El Tambo**, US$0.50, 20 mins. If coming from the north, transfer in El Tambo. Pick-up taxi from Cañar US$8, from El Tambo US$5.

Inca Trail to Ingapirca

From **Alausí to Achupallas**, small buses and pickups leave as they fill between 1100 and 1600, US$1, 1hr. Alternatively, take any bus along the Panamericana to **La Moya**, south of Alausí, at the turn-off for Achupallas, and a shared pick-up from there (best on Thu and Sun), US$0.50. To hire a pick-up from Alausí costs US$12-15, from La Moya US$10.

East of Cuenca *p1056*

Bus From Terminal Terrestre in Cuenca: to **Paute**, every 15 mins, US$0.75, 1 hr; to **Gualaceo**, every 15 mins, US$0.60, 50 mins; to **Chordeleg**: every 15 mins from Gualaceo, US$0.25; 15 mins or direct bus from Cuenca, US$0.70, 1 hr; to **Sigsig**, every 30 mins via Gualaceo, US$1.25, 1½ hrs.

Parque Nacional Cajas *p1056*

Bus From Cuenca's Terminal Terrestre take any **Guayaquil** bus that goes via Molleturo (not Zhud), US$2, 30 mins to turn-off for Llaviuco, 45 mins to Toreadora. **Coop Occidental** to Molleturo, 8 a day from the Terminal Sur/Feria Libre, this is a slower bus and may wait to fill up. For the Soldados entrance, catch a bus from Puente del Vado in Cuenca, daily at 0600,

US$1.25, 1½ hrs; the return bus passes the Soldados gate at about 1600.

Directory

Cuenca *p1052, map p1054*

Banks Banco del Pacífico, Gran Colombia 23-120 y Av Las Américas and Pres Córdova y Benigno Malo, ATM and TCs. Many banks with ATMs around Sucre y Borrero. **Vazcorp**, Gran Colombia 7-98 y Cordero, T283 3434, Mon-Fri 0830-1730, Sat 0900-1245, change 11 currencies, good rates, 1.8% comission for US$ AMEX TCs. **Car rental** Bombuscaro, España y Elia Liut, opposite the airport, T286 6541. Also international companies. **Immigration** E Muñoz 1-42 y Gran Colombia, T282 1112. **Language courses** Rates US$6-10 per hr.

Centro de Estudios Interamericanos (CEDEI), Gran Colombia 11-02 y General Torres, T283 9003, www.cedei.org. Spanish and Quichua lessons, immersion/volunteering programmes, also run the attached Hostal Macondo. Recommended. **Estudio Internacional Sampere**, Hermano Miguel 3-43 y C Larga, T284 2659, www.sampere.es. At the high end of the price range. **Sí Centro de Español e Inglés**, Bolívar 12-54 y Tarqui, T282 0429, www.sicentrospanishschool.com. Good teachers, competitive prices, homestays, volunteer opportunities, helpful and enthusiastic, tourist information available. Recommended. **Medical services** Emergencies T911. **Hospital Monte Sinaí**, Miguel Cordero 6-111 y Av Solano, near the stadium, T288 5595, several English-speaking physicians. **Hospital Santa Inés**, Av Toral 2-113, T281 7888; Dr Jaime Moreno Aguilar speaks English.

Cuenca to the Peruvian border

From Cuenca various routes go to the Peruvian border, fanning out from the pleasant city of Loja, due south of which is Vilcabamba, famous for its invigorating climate and lovely countryside.

South to Loja

The Pan-American Highway divides about 20 km south of Cuenca. One branch runs south to Loja, the other heads southwest through Girón, the Yunguilla valley (with a small bird reserve, see www.fjocotoco.org) and Santa Isabel (several hotels with pools and spas; cloud forest and waterfalls). The last stretch through sugar cane fields leads to Pasaje and Machala. The scenic road between Cuenca and Loja undulates between high, cold páramo passes and deep desert-like canyons.

Saraguro → *Phone code: 07. Colour map 11, C3. Population: 9500. Altitude: 2500 m.*

On the road to Loja is this old town, where the local people, the most southerly indigenous Andean group in Ecuador, dress all in black. The men are notable for their black shorts and the women for their pleated black skirts, necklaces of coloured beads and silver *topos*, ornate pins fastening their shawls. The town has a picturesque Sunday market and interesting Mass and Easter celebrations. Traditional festivities are held during solstices and equinoxes in surrounding communities. Necklaces and other crafts are sold around the plaza. Saraguro has a community tourism programme with tours and home-stay opportunities with indigenous families. Contact **Fundación Kawsay** ① *18 de Noviembre y Av Loja, T220 0331*, or the **Oficina Municipal de Turismo** ① *C José María Vivar on the main plaza, T220 0100 ext 18, Mon-Fri 0800-1200, 1400-1800. See also www.saraguro.org.* **Bosque Washapampa**, 6 km south has good birdwatching.

Loja → *Phone code: 07. Colour map 11, C3. Population: 191,000. Altitude: 2060 m.*

This friendly, pleasant highland city, encircled by hills, is a traditional gateway between the highlands and southern Amazonia. Loja has won international awards for its parks and its recycling programme. **Tourist offices**: iTur ① *José Antonio Eguiguren y Bolívar, Parque Central, T258 1251, Mon-Fri 0800-1300, 1500-1800, Sat 0900-1300.* Local and regional information and map, helpful, some English spoken. **Ministerio de Turismo** ① *Bolívar 12-39 y Lourdes, p 3, Parque San Sebastián, T257 2964, Mon-Fri 0830-1330, 1430-1700.* Regional information.

Housed in a beautifully restored house on the main park is the **Centro Cultural Loja** home of the **Museo de la Cultura Lojana** ① *10 de Agosto 13-30 y Bolívar, T257 3004, Mon-Fri 0830-1700, Sat-Sun 1000-1600, free,* with well-displayed archaeology, ethnography, art, and history halls. **Parque San Sebastián** at Bolívar y Mercadillo and the adjoining Calle Lourdes preserve the flavour of old Loja and are worth visiting. Loja is famed for its musicians and has two symphony orchestras. Musical evenings and concerts are often held around the town. The **Museo de Música** ① *Valdivieso 09-42 y Rocafuerte, T256 1342. Mon-Fri 0900-1300, 1500-1900, free,* honours 10 Lojano composers.

Parque Universitario Francisco Vivar Castro (Parque La Argelia) ① *on the road south to Vilcabamba, Tue-Sun 0800-1700, US$1, city bus marked 'Capulí-Dos Puentes' to the park or 'Argelia' to the Universidad Nacional and walk from there,* has trails through the forest to the *páramo.* Across the road is the **Jardín Botánico Reynaldo Espinosa** ① *Mon-Fri 0800-1600, Sat-Sun 0900-1730, US$1,* which is nicely laid out.

Parque Nacional Podocarpus

① *Headquarters at Cajanuma entrance, T302 4862. Limited information from Ministerio del Ambiente in Loja, Sucre 04-55 y Quito, T257 9595, parquepodocarpus@gmail.com, Mon-Fri 0800-1700. In Zamora at Sevilla de Oro y Orellana, T260 6606. Their general map of the park is not adequate for navigation, buy topographic maps in Quito.*

Podocarpus (950 m to 3700 m) is one of the most diverse protected areas in the world. It is particularly rich in birdlife, including many rarities, and includes one of the last major habitats for the Spectacled Bear. The park protects stands of *romerillo* or podocarpus, a native, slow-growing conifer. UNESCO has declared Podocarpus-El Cóndor (Cordillera del Cóndor) as a biosphere reserve. It includes a large area (1.14 million has) in the provinces of Loja and Zamora Chinchipe. The park itself is divided into two areas, an upper premontane section with spectacular walking country, lush cloud forest and excellent birdwatching; and a lower subtropical section, with remote areas of virgin rainforest and unmatched quantities of flora and fauna. Both zones are wet (rubber boots recommended) but there may be periods of dry weather October to January. The upper section is also cold, so warm clothing and waterproofs are indispensable year-round.

Entrances to the upper section: at Cajanuma, 8 km south of Loja on the Vilcabamba road, from the turn-off it is a further 8 km uphill to the guard station; and at San Francisco, 24 km from Loja along the road to Zamora. Entrances to the lower section: Bombuscaro is 6 km from Zamora, the visitor's centre is a 30-minute walk from the car park. **Cajanuma** is the trailhead for the demanding eight-hour hike to **Lagunas del Compadre**, a series of beautiful lakes set amid rock cliffs, camping is possible there (no services). Another trail from Cajanuma leads in one hour to a lookout with views over Loja. At **San Francisco**, the *guardianía* (ranger's station) operated by Fundación Arcoiris, offers nice accommodation (see below). This section of the park is a transition cloud forest at around 2200 m, very rich in birdlife. This is the best place to see podocarpus trees: a trail (four hours return) goes from the shelter to the trees. The **Bombuscaro** lowland section, also very rich in birdlife, has several trails leading to lovely swimming holes on the Bombuscaro River and waterfalls; Cascada La Poderosa is particularly nice.

Conservation groups working in and around the park include: **Arcoiris** ① *Ciprés 12-202 y Acacias, La Pradera, T257 2926, www.arcoiris.org.ec;* **Naturaleza y Cultura Internacional** ① *Av Pío Jaramillo y Venezuela, T257 3691, www.natureandculture.org.*

Loja to the Peruvian border

Of all the crossings from Ecuador to Peru, by far the most efficient and relaxed is the scenic route from Loja to Piura via Macará (see below). Other routes are from Vilcabamba to La Balsa (see page 1070), Huaquillas (page 1082) and along the Río Napo in the Oriente (page 1108). There are smaller border crossings without immigration facilities (passports cannot be stamped) at Jimbura, southeast of Macará; and Lalamor, west of Macará.

Leaving Loja on the main paved highway going west, the airport at **La Toma** (1200 m) is reached after 35 km. La Toma is also called **Catamayo**, where there is lodging. At Catamayo, where you can catch the Loja-Macará-Piura bus, the Pan-American Highway divides: one branch runs west, the other south.

On the western road, at San Pedro de La Bendita, a road climbs to the much-venerated pilgrimage site of **El Cisne**, dominated by its large incongruous French-style Gothic church. Vendors and beggars fill the town and await visitors (see Festivals, page 1067). Continuing on the western route, **Catacocha** is spectacularly placed on a hilltop. Visit the Shiriculapo rock for the views. There are pre-Inca ruins around the town; small archaeological **Museo Hermano Joaquín Liebana** ⓘ *T268 3201, 0800-1200, 1400-1800*. From Catacocha, the road runs south to the border at Macará.

Another route south from Catamayo to Macará is via **Gonzanamá**, a sleepy little town (basic *hostales*), famed for the weaving of beautiful *alforjas* (multi-purpose saddlebags), and **Cariamanga**, a regional centre (various hotels, banks). From here the road twists along a ridge westwards to **Colaisaca**, before descending steeply through forests to **Utuana** with a nature reserve (www.fjocotoco.org) and **Sozoranga** (one hotel), then down to the rice paddies of **Macará**, on the border. There is a choice of accommodation here and good road connections to Sullana and Piura in Peru.

Border with Peru: Macará-La Tina The border is at the Río Macará, 2.5 km from Macará, where a new international bridge was opened in 2013. There are plans to build a border complex, in the meantime, immigration, customs and other services are housed in temporary quarters nearby. The border is open 24 hours. Formalities are straightforward, it is a much easier crossing than at Huaquillas. In Macará, at the park where taxis leave for the border, there are money changers dealing in soles. Shared taxi Macará-border, US$0.30, private US$1. On the Peruvian side, minivans and cars run to Sullana; avoid arriving in Sullana after dark.

⊚ Cuenca to the Peruvian border listings

For hotel and restaurant price codes, and other relevant information, see Essentials.

⊜ Where to stay

Saraguro *p1064*
$ Achik Huasi, on a hillside above town, T220 0058, or through **Fundación Kawsay**, T220 0331. Community-run hostería in a nice setting, private bath, hot water, parking, views, tours, taxi to centre US$1.
$ Saraguro, Loja 03-2 y A Castro, T220 0286. Private or shared bath, nice courtyard, electric shower, family-run, basic, good value.

Loja *p1064*
$$$$-$$$ Grand Victoria, B Valdivieso 06-50 y Eguiguren, ½ a block from the Parque Central, T258 3500, www.grandvictoriabh. com. Rebuilt early-20th century home with 2 patios, comfortable modern rooms and suites, includes buffet breakfast, restaurant, small pool,

spa, gym, business centre, frigobar, safety box, parking, weekend discounts.
$$$-$$ Libertador, Colón 14-30 y Bolívar, T256 0779, www.hotellibertador.com.ec. A very good hotel in the centre of town, comfortable rooms and suites, includes buffet breakfast, good restaurant, indoor pool (US$6 for non-guests), spa, parking.
$$ Bombuscaro, 10 de Agosto y Av Universitaria, T257 7021, www. bombuscaro.com.ec. Comfortable rooms and suites, includes buffet breakfast and airport transfers, restaurant, car rental, good service. Recommended.
$ Londres, Sucre 07-51 y 10 de Agosto, T256 1936. Economical hostel in a well-maintained old house, shared bath, hot water, basic, clean, good value.
$ Vinarós, Sucre 11-30 y Azuay, T258 4015, hostalvinaros@hotmail.com. Pleasant hostel with simple rooms, eletric shower, parking, good value.

Parque Nacional Podocarpus *p1065*

At **Cajanuma**, there are cabins with beds, bring warm sleeping bag, stove and food. At San Francisco, the *guardianía* (ranger's station), operated by **Fundación Arcoiris** offers rooms with shared bath, hot water and kitchen facilities, US$8 pp if you bring a sleeping bag, US$10 if they provide sheets. Ask to be let off at Arcoiris or you will be taken to Estación San Francisco, 8 km further east. At **Bombuscaro** there are cabins with beds and an area for camping.

Loja to the Peruvian border *p1065*
Catamayo

$$ MarcJohn's, Isidro Ayora y 24 de Mayo, at the main park, T267 7631, granhotelmarcjohns@hotmail.com. Modern multi-storey hotel, suites with jacuzzi and fridge, fan, restaurant, includes airport transfers.

$$ Rosal del Sol, a short walk from the city on the main road west of town, T267 6517. Ranch-style building, comfortable rooms with fan, restaurant not always open, small pool, parking, includes airport transfer, welcoming owner.

$ Reina del Cisne, Isidro Ayora at the park, T267 7414. Simple adequate rooms, hot water, cheaper with cold water, fan, small pool, gym, parking, good value.

Macará

$ Bekalus, Valdivieso y 10 de Agosto, T269 4043. Simple adequate hostel, a/c, cheaper with fan, cold water.

$ El Conquistador, Bolívar y Abdón Calderón, T269 4057. Comfortable hotel, some rooms are dark, request one with balcony, includes simple breakfast, electric shower, a/c or fan, parking.

❼ Restaurants

Saraguro *p1061*
Several restaurants around the main plaza serve economical meals.

$$-$ Turu Manka, 100 m uphill from Hostal Achik Huasi. Wide selection. The food is average, but it is still one of the better choices in town.

Loja *p1064*

$$ Lecka, 24 de Mayo 10-51 y Riofío, T256 3878. Tue-Fri 1630-2200, Sat 1800-2200. Small quaint restaurant serving German specialties, very good food, friendly owners.

$$-$ Casa Sol, 24 de Mayo 07-04 y José Antonio Eguiguren. Daily 0830-2330. Small place serving breakfast, economical set lunches and regional dishes in the evening. Pleasant seating on balcony.

$$-$ Pizzería Forno di Fango, 24 de Mayo y Azuay, T258 2905. Tue-Sun 1200-2230. Excellent wood-oven pizza, salads and lasagne. Large portions, home delivery, good service and value.

$ Alivinatu, 10 de Agosto 12-53 y Bernardo Valdivieso, in the health food shop. Mon-Sat 0830-1400, 1500-1900. Very good fresh fruit or vegetable juices prepared on the spot. Also snacks and set lunches with vegetarian options.

$ Angelo's, José Félix de Valdivieso 16-36 y Av Universitaria. Mon-Sat 0800-1600. A choice of good quality set lunches, friendly service.

Cafés

Café Ruskina, Sucre 07-48 y 10 de Agosto. Mon-Sat 0900-1300, 1500-2000. Coffee, cream cakes, other sweets and regional snacks such as humitas.

El Sendero, Bolívar 13-13 y Mercadillo, upstairs Tue-Sat 1530-2200. Fruit juices, coffee and snacks, nice balcony overlooking Parque San Sebastián, ping pong and other games, library.

Molino Café, José A Eguiguren y Sucre. Mon-Sat 0800-2000. Small place, breakfast, choice of coffees, snacks, sandwiches, economical set lunches.

❁ Festivals

Loja *p1064*
Aug-Sep Fiesta de la Virgen del Cisne, hundreds of faithful accompany the statue of the Virgin in a 3-day 74 km pilgrimage from El Cisne to Loja cathedral, beginning **16 Aug**. The image remains in Loja until **1 Nov** when the return pilgrimage starts. Town is crowded Aug-Sep.

⛔ What to do

Loja p1064

Aratinga Aventuras, Lourdes 14-80 y Sucre, T258 2434, T08-515 2239, www.exploraves.com. Specializes in birdwatching tours, overnight trips to different types of forest. Pablo Andrade is a knowledgeable guide.

🚍 Transport

Saraguro p1064

Bus To **Cuenca** US$5, 2½ hrs. To **Loja**, US$1.75, 1½ hrs. Check if your bus leaves from the plaza or the Panamericana.

Loja p1064

Air The airport is at La Toma (Catamayo), 35 km west (see Loja to the Peruvian border, p1065): taxi from airport to Catamayo town US$2, to Loja shared taxi US$5 pp, to hire US$20 (cheaper from Loja) eg with Jaime González, T256 3714 or Paul Izquierdo, T256 3973; to Vilcabamba, US$40. There are 1-2 daily flights to Quito and 1 daily to **Guayaquil** with TAME (24 de Mayo y E Ortega, T257 0248).

Bus All buses leave from the Terminal Terrestre at Av Gran Colombia e Isidro Ayora, at the north of town, 10 mins by city bus from the centre; left luggage; US$0.10 terminal tax. Taxi from centre, US$1. To **Cuenca**, almost every hour (www.viajerosinternacional.com), 4 hrs, US$7.50. Van service with **Elite Tours**, 18 de Noviembre 01-13, near Puerta de la Ciudad, T256 0731 and **Faisatur**, 18 de Noviembre y Av Universitaria, T258 5299, US$12, 3 hrs; taxi US$60. **Machala**, 10 a day, 5-6 hrs, US$6 (3 routes, all scenic: via Piñas, for **Zaruma**, partly unpaved and rough; via Balsas, paved; and via Alamor, for **Puyango petrified forest**). **Quito**, regular US$12-14; Transportes Loja semi-cama US$17 to Quitumbe, US$20 to La Mariscal, cama US$40 to La Mariscal, 12 hrs. **Guayaquil**, US$10 regular, US$12 semi-cama, 8 hrs. To **Huaquillas**, 6 hrs direct. To **Zumba** (for Peru), 10 daily including Sur Oriente at 0500 to make connections to Peru the same day and Cariamanga at 0900, US$7.50, 7 hrs but delays possible, road construction in

2014; **Nambija** at 2400 direct to the border at La Balsa (only in the dry season), U$10, 8 hrs. To **Catamayo** (for airport) every 15 mins 0630-1900, US$1, 1hr. To **Macará**, see below. To **Piura (Peru)**, Loja Internacional, via Macará, at 0700, 1300 and 2300 daily, US$12, 8-9 hrs including border formalities. Also **Unión Cariamanga** at 0600 and 2400.

Parque Nacional Podocarpus p1065

For **Cajanuma**, take a Vilcabamba bound bus, get off at the turnoff, US$1, it is a pretty 8-km walk from there. Direct transport by taxi to Cajanuma, about US$10 (may not be feasible in the rainy season) or with a tour from Loja. You can arrange a pick up later from the guard station. Pickup from Vilcabamba, US$20. To the **San Francisco section**, take any bus between Loja and Zamora, make sure you alight by the Arcoiris *guardianía* and not at Estación Científica San Francisco which is 8 km east. To the **lower section: Bombuscaro** is 6 km from Zamora, take a taxi US$6 to the entrance, then walk 1 km to the visitor's centre.

Loja to the Peruvian border p1065
Macará

Bus Transportes Loja and Cariamanga have frequent buses, daily from Macará to **Loja**; 6 hrs, US$6. Direct Loja-**Piura** buses can also be boarded in Macará, US$4 to Piura, 3 hrs. Transportes Loja also has service to **Quito**, US$15, 15 hrs, and **Guayaquil**, US$11, 8 hrs.

ⓘ Directory

Loja p1064

Banks Several banks with ATMs around the Parque Central. Vazcorp, B Valdivieso y 10 de Agosto, change euros, Peruvian soles and other South American currencies, also TCs, 1.8% commission. A couple of shops along José Antonio Eguiguren change cash euros and soles. **Embassies and consulates** Peru, Zoilo Rodríguez 03-05, T258 7330, Mon-Fri 0900-1300, 1500-1700. **Medical services** Clínica San Agustín, 18 de Noviembre 10-72 y Azuay, T257 3002.

Vilcabamba to Peru

Vilcabamba → *Phone code: 07. Colour map 11, C3. Population: 4900. Altitude: 1520 m.*
Once an isolated village, Vilcabamba is today home to a thriving and colourful expatriate community. It is popular with travellers and a good place to stop on route between Ecuador and Peru. The whole area is beautiful and tranquil, with an agreeable climate. There are many places to stay and good restaurants. The area offers many great day-walks and longer treks, as well as ample opportunities for horse riding and cycling. A number of lovely private nature reserves are situated east of Vilcabamba, towards Parque Nacional Podocarpus. Trekkers can continue on foot through orchid-clad cloud forests to the high *páramos* of Podocarpus. Artisans sell their crafts in front of the school on weekends. Tourist office: **iTur** ① *Diego Vaca de Vega y Bolívar, on the corner of the main plaza, T264 0090, daily 0800-1300, 1500-1800*, has various pamphlets, helpful.

Rumi Wilco ① *10-min walk northeast of town, take C Agua de Hierro towards C La Paz and turn left, follow signs, US$2 valid for the duration of your stay in Vilcabamba.* This 40-ha private nature reserve has several signed trails. Many of the trees and shrubs are labelled with their scientific

Vilcabamba

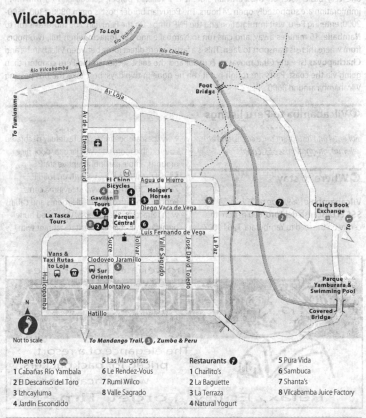

Not to scale

To Mandango Trail, ③ *, Zumba & Peru*

Where to stay 🛏
1 Cabañas Río Yambala
2 El Descanso del Toro
3 Izhcayluma
4 Jardín Escondido
5 Las Margaritas
6 Le Rendez-Vous
7 Rumi Wilco
8 Valle Sagrado

Restaurants 🍴
1 Charlito's
2 La Baguette
3 La Terraza
4 Natural Yogurt
5 Pura Vida
6 Sambuca
7 Shanta's
8 Vilcabamba Juice Factory

and common names. There are great views of town from the higher trails, and it is a very good place to go for a walk. Over 100 species of birds have been identified here. Volunteers are welcome. Climbing **Mandango**, 'the sleeping woman' mountain is a scenic half-day walk. The signed access is along the highway, 250 m south of the bus terminal. Be careful on the higher sections when it is windy and always enquire beforehand about public safety, armed robberies have taken place and tourists have been hurt. South of Vilcabamba, 45 km on the road to Zumba is the 3500 ha bird and orchid rich **Reserva Tapichalaca** ① *T250 5212, www.fjocotoco.org, entry US$15, lodge ($$$)*.

Border with Peru: La Balsa

Many daily buses run on the scenic road from Loja via Vilcabamba to **Zumba** (see Loja, Transport, page 1068), 112 km south of Vilcabamba. It is a 1½-hour rough ride by *ranchera* (open-sided bus) from Zumba to the border at La Balsa, there is a control on the way, keep your passport to hand. La Balsa is just a few houses on either side of the international bridge over the Río Canchis; there are simple eateries, shops, money changers (no banks here or in Zumba), and one very basic hotel on the Peruvian side. It is a relaxed border, Ecuadorean customs and immigration are supposedly open 24 hours. The Peruvian border post is open 0800-1300, 1500-2000; entering Peru, visit immigration and the PNP office. On the Peruvian side mototaxis run to **Namballe**, 15 minutes away, and cars run to Namballe and **San Ignacio** when full, two hours, from where there is transport to **Jaén**. This is a faster, more direct route between Vilcabamba and **Chachapoyas** (see the Chacapoyas to Ecuador and the coast section in the Peru chapter) than going via the coast. Parts are rough but it can be done in two days; best take the bus passing Vilcabamba around 0600.

◉ Vilcabamba to Peru listings

For hotel and restaurant price codes, and other relevant information, see Essentials.

◉ Where to stay

Vilcabamba *p1069, map p1069*
$$$ El Descanso del Toro, 800 m from the centre on the road to Yamburara, T264 0007, www.descansodeltoro.com. Tastefully decorated comfortable rooms, all with jacuzzi, pool, nice grounds, ample parking, attentive staff.
$$-$ Izhcayluma, 2 km south on road to Zumba, T302 5162, www.izhcayluma.com. Popular inn with comfortable rooms and cabins with terrace and hammocks. Very good buffet breakfast available, excellent restaurant with

wonderful views, private or shared bath, also dorm US$8.50 pp, very nice grounds, pool, massage centre, yoga centre and lessons, lively bar, billiards, ping-pong, parking, bird observation platform, walking map and route descriptions, English and German spoken, helpful. Highly recommended.

$$-$ Jardín Escondido, Sucre y Diego Vaca de Vega, T264 0281. Nicely refurbished old house around a lovely patio, bright comfortable rooms, restaurant, cheaper in dorm, small pool, English spoken.

$$-$ Las Margaritas, Sucre y Clodoveo Jaramillo, T264 0051. Small family-run hotel with comfortable nicely-furnished rooms, includes good breakfast, intermittent solar-heated water, parking, garden.

$$-$ Le Rendez-Vous, Diego Vaca de Vega 06-43 y La Paz, T09-9219 1180, www.rendezvousecuador.com. Very comfortable rooms with terrace and hammocks around a lovely garden. Private or shared bath, pleasant atmosphere, attentive service, French and English spoken. Recommended.

$ Cabañas Río Yambala, Yamburara Alto, 4 km east of town (taxi US$3), T09-9106 2762, www.vilcabamba-hotel.com. Cabins with cooking facilities in a beautiful tranquil setting on the shores of the Río Yambala, hot water, sauna, monthly rates available. No shops or restaurants nearby, bring food. Tours to Las Palmas private nature reserve. English spoken.

$ Rumi Wilco, 10-min walk northeast of town, take C Agua de Hierro towards C La Paz and turn left, follow the signs from there, www.rumiwilco.com. Cabins in the Rumi Wilco reserve. Lovely setting on the shores of the river, very tranquil, private or shared bath, laundry facilities, fully furnished kitchens, discounts for long stays and volunteers, camping US$3.50 pp, friendly Argentine owners, English spoken. Recommended.

$ Valle Sagrado, Av de la Eterna Juventud y Luis Fernando de Vega, T09-9936 1699. Basic rooms around nice ample grounds, cheaper in dorm, electric shower, laundry and cooking facilities, parking, trekking tours.

Vilcabamba to Peru: Zumba *p1070*

$$-$ Emperador, Colón y Orellana, T230 8063. Adequate rooms, private bath.

$ San Luis, 12 de Febrero y Brasil, T230 8017. Rooms on top floor are nice, private or shared bath, attentive service, refurbished in 2013.

❼ Restaurants

Vilcabamba *p1069, map p1069*
Around the Parque Central are many café/bar/restaurants with pleasant sidewalk seating; too many to list, see map, page 1069.

$$ Shanta's, 800 m from the centre on the road to Yamburara. Tue-Sun 1300-2100. Specialties are pizza (excellent), trout, frogs legs, filet mignon and *cuy* (with advance notice). Also vegetarian options, good fruit juices and drinks. Nicely decorated rustic setting, pleasant atmosphere and attentive service. Recommended.

$$-$ Natural Yogurt, Bolívar y Diego Vaca de Vega. Daily 0800-2200. Breakfast, home-made yoghurt, a variety of savoury and sweet crêpes, some pasta dishes.

$ Charlito's, Diego Vaca de Vega y Sucre. Tue-Sun 1000-2200. Salads, pasta, pizza, soup, sandwiches with tasty homemade wholemeal bread.

$ Vilcabamba Juice Factory, Sucre y Luis Fernando de Vega, on the Parque Central. Healthy juices, vegan food available, run by a naturopath, popular with expats.

La Baguette, Luis Fernando de Vega y Sucre, small French bakery, great bread and pastries.

❹ What to do

Vilcabamba *p1069, map p1069*
See Where to stay, above, for more options.
Cycling El Chino, Sucre y Diego Vaca de Vega, T09-8187 6347, chinobike@gmail.com. Mountain bike tours (US$25-35), rentals (US$2 per hr, US$10 per day) and repairs. Also see La Tasca Tours, below.
Horse riding half day US$30, full day with lunch US$40, overnight trips US$60 per day full board.

Gavilán Tours, Sucre y Diego Vaca de Vega, T264 0209, gavilanhorse@yahoo.com. Run by a group of experienced horsemen.

Holger's Horses, Diego Vaca de Vega y Valle Sagrado, T09-8296 1238. Holger Granda, good horses and saddles, German spoken.

La Tasca Tours, Sucre at the plaza, T09-8556 1188. Horse and bike tours with experienced guides, René and Jaime León.

Massage Beauty Care, Diego Vaca de Vega y Valle Sagrado, T09-8122 3456, daily 1000-1800, Karina Zumba, facials, waxing, Reiki, 1 hr US$15; **Shanta's** (see Restaurants, above), T09-8538 5710, Lola Encalada, very good 1½-hr therapeutic massage US$30, also does waxing. Recommended.

⊖ Transport

Vilcabamba *p1069, map p1069*
Loja to Vilcabamba, a nice 1-hr bus ride; from Loja's Terminal Terrestre, **Vilcabambaturis** mini-buses, every 15-30 mins, 0545-2115, US$1.30, 1 hr; or *taxirutas* (shared taxis) from José María Peña y Venezuela, 0600-2000, US$1.75, 45 mins; taxi, US$15. To **Loja**, vans and shared taxis leave from the small terminal behind the market. For **Parque Nacional Podocarpus**, taxis charge US$20 each way, taking you right to the trailhead at Cajanuma. To **Cuenca** vans at 0800 from **Hostería Izhcayluma**, then pick-up passengers at **Hostal Jardín Escondido**,

US$15, 4-4½ hrs, Cuenca stop at Hostal La Cigale. To **Zumba** buses originating in Loja pass Vilcabamba about 1 hr after departure and stop along the highway in front of the market (1st around 0600, next 1000), US$6.50, 5-6 hrs, expect delays due to road construction in 2014. To **Quito** (Quitumbe) Transportes Loja (tickets sold for this and other routes at Movistar office, Av de la Eterna Juventud y Clodoveo Jaramillo) at 1900, with a stop in Loja, US$18, 13-14 hrs.

Vilcabamba to Peru: Zumba *p1070*
Terminal Terrestre in Zumba, 1 km south of the centre. From Zumba to **La Balsa**, *rancheras* at 0800, 1430 and 1730, US$1.75, 1-1½ hrs. From La Balsa to Zumba at 1200, 1730 and 1930. Taxi Zumba-La Balsa, US$30. To **Loja**, see above. In Zumba, petrol is sold 0700-1700.

❶ Directory

Vilcabamba *p1069, map p1069*
Airline offices TAME agent, Bolívar y Montalvo, T264 0437. **Banks** No banks, several standalone ATMs, next to iTur and by the church, but not all cards accepted. **Book exchange** Craig's, in Yamburara, 1 km east of town, follow Diego Vaca de Vega, 2500 books in 12 languages, and art gallery. **Language courses** Spanish classes with Catalina Carrasco, T09-8267 8960, catycarrasco@yahoo. com; Marta Villacrés, T09-9751 3311.

Guayaquil and south to Peru

Guayaquil is hotter, faster and louder than the capital. It is Ecuador's largest city, the country's chief seaport and main commercial centre, some 56 km from the Río Guayas' outflow into the Gulf of Guayaquil. Industrial expansion continually fuels the city's growth. Founded in 1535 by Sebastián de Benalcázar, then again in 1537 by Francisco Orellana, the city has always been an intense political rival to Quito. Guayaquileños are certainly more lively, colourful and open than their Quito counterparts. Since 2000, Guayaquil has cleaned-up and 'renewed' some of its most frequented downtown areas, it boasts modern airport and bus terminals, and the Metrovía transit system.

Thriving banana plantations and other agro-industry are the economic mainstay of the coastal area bordering the east flank of the Gulf of Guayaquil. The Guayas lowlands are subject to flooding, humidity is high and biting insects are fierce. Mangroves characterize the coast leading south to Huaquillas, the main coastal border crossing to Peru.

Arriving in Guayaquil → *Phone code: 04. Colour map 11, B2. Population: 2,370,000. Altitude: 4 m.*
Orientation **José Joaquín de Olmedo** international airport is 15 minutes north of the city centre by car. Not far from the airport is the **Terminal Terrestre** long distance bus station. Opposite this terminal is the northern terminus of the **Metrovía** rapid transit system. ▶▶ *See also Transport, page 1080.*

A number of hotels are centrally located in the downtown core, along the west bank of the Río Guayas, where you can get around on foot. The city's suburbs sprawl to the north and south of the centre, with middle-class neighbourhoods and some very upscale areas in the north, where some elegant hotels and restaurants are located, and poorer working-class neighbourhoods and slums to the south. Road tunnels under Cerro Santa Ana link the northern suburbs to downtown. Outside downtown, addresses are hard to find; ask for a nearby landmark to help orient your driver. From May-December the climate is dry with often overcast days but pleasantly cool nights, whereas the hot rainy season from January-April can be oppressively humid.

Tourist offices **Centro de Información Turística del Municipio** ① *Clemente Ballén y Pichincha, at Museo Nahim Isaías, T232 4182, Tue-Fri 0830-1600,* has pamphlets and city maps. There are also information booths at the Malecón 2000 by the clock tower, and at the Terminal Terrestre. **Ministerio de Turismo, Subsecretaría del Litoral** ① *Av Francisco de Orellana, Edif Gobierno del*

1 Guayaquil orientation

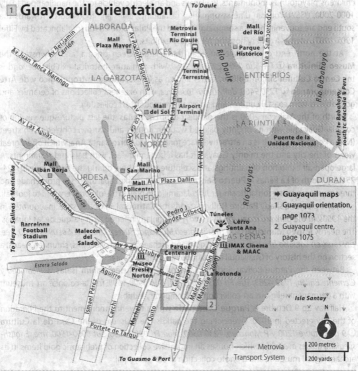

⮕ **Guayaquil maps**
1 Guayaquil orientation, page 1073
2 Guayaquil centre, page 1075

━━━ Metrovía
Transport System

200 metres
200 yards

Litoral, p 8 and counter on the ground floor, Ciudadela Kennedy, T268 4274, www.ecuador.travel, Mon-Fri 0900-1700. Information about the coastal provinces of Ecuador and whale watching regulations.

Safety The Malecón 2000, parts of Avenida 9 de Octubre, Las Peñas and Malecón del Estero Salado are heavily patrolled and reported safe. The rest of the city requires precautions. Do not go anywhere with valuables, for details see page 972. Parque Centenario is also patrolled, but the area around it requires caution. 'Express kidnappings' are of particular concern in Guayaquil; do not take a taxi outside the north end of the Malecón 2000 near the MAAC museum, walk south along the Malecón as far as the Hotel Ramada, where there is a taxi stand; whenever possible, call for a radio taxi.

Guayaquil

Places in Guayaquil

A wide, tree-lined waterfront avenue, the Malecón Simón Bolívar runs alongside the Río Guayas from the **Palacio de Cristal**, past **Plaza Olmedo**, the Moorish clock tower, by the imposing **Palacio Municipal** and **Gobernación** and the old Yacht Club to Las Peñas. The riverfront along this avenue is an attractive promenade, known as **Malecón 2000** ① *daily 0700-2400*, where visitors and locals can enjoy the fresh river breeze and take in the views. There are gardens, fountains, childrens' playgrounds, monuments, walkways and an electric vehicle for the handicapped (daily 1000-2000, US$2). You can dine at upmarket restaurants, cafés and food courts. Towards the south end are souvenir shops, a shopping mall and the **Palacio de Cristal** (prefabricated by Eiffel 1905-1907), used as a gallery housing temporary exhibits.

At the north end of the Malecón is an **IMAX** large-screen cinema, and downstairs the **Museo Miniatura** ① *Tue-Sun 0900-2000, US$1.50*, with miniature historical exhibits. Beyond is the **Centro Cultural Simón Bolívar**, better known as MAAC, **Museo Antropológico y de Arte Contemporaneo** ① *T230 9400, daily 0900-1630, free*, with excellent collections of ceramics and gold objects from coastal cultures and an extensive modern art collection.

North of the Malecón 2000 is the old district of **Las Peñas**, the last picturesque vestige of colonial Guayaquil with its brightly painted wooden houses and narrow, cobbled main street (Numa Pompilio Llona). It is an attractive place for a walk to **Cerro Santa Ana**, which offers great views of the city and the mighty Guayas. It has a bohemian feel, with bars and restaurants. A large open-air exhibition of paintings and sculpture is held here during the *fiestas julianas* (24-25 July). North of La Peñas is **Puerto Santa Ana**, with upmarket apartments, a promenade and three museums: to the romantic singer Julio Jaramillo, to beer in the old brewery, and to football.

By the pleasant, shady **Parque Bolívar** stands the **Cathedral**, in Gothic style, inaugurated in the 1950s. In the park are many iguanas and it is popularly referred to as Parque de las Iguanas. The nearby **Museo Municipal** ① *in the Biblioteca Municipal, Sucre y Chile, Tue-Sat 0900-1700, free, city tours on Sat, also free* has paintings, gold and archaeological collections, shrunken heads, a section on the history of Guayaquil and a good newspaper library.

Between the Parque Bolívar and the Malecón is the **Museo Nahim Isaías** ① *Pichincha y Clemente Ballén, T232 4283, Tue-Fri 0830-1630, Sat-Sun 0900-1600, free*, a colonial art museum with a permanent religious art collection and temporary exhibits.

Halfway up 9 Octubre is **Parque Centenario** with a towering monument to the liberation of the city erected in 1920. Overlooking the park is the museum of the **Casa de la Cultura** ① *9 de Octubre 1200 y P Moncayo, T230 0500, Mon-Fri 0900-1800, Sat 0900-1500, free, English-speaking guides available*, which houses an impressive collection of prehistoric gold items in its archaeological museum; and a photo collection of old Guayaquil.

West of Parque Centenario, the **Museo Presley Norton** ① *Av 9 de Octubre y Carchi, T229 3423, Tue-Sat 0900-1700, free,* has a nice collection of coastal archeology in a beautifully restored house. At the west end of 9 de Octubre are **Plaza Baquerizo Moreno** and the **Malecón del Estero Salado**, another pleasant waterfront promenade along a brackish estuary. It has various monuments, eateries specializing in seafood, and rowing boats and pedal-boats for hire.

2 Guayaquil centre

➔ Guayaquil maps
1 Guayaquil orientation, page 1073
2 Guayaquil centre, page 1075

N

100 metres
100 yards

Ⓜ Metrovía

Where to stay 🛏
1 Continental
2 Elite Internacional
3 Grand Hotel Guayaquil
4 Hampton Inn
5 Las Peñas & California Café
6 La Torre
7 Manso
8 Nueve de Octubre
9 Oro Verde
10 Palace
11 Ramada
12 Savoy II
13 Unipark

Restaurants 🍴
1 Asia
2 Fruta Bar
3 La Parrilla del Ñato
4 Las Tres Canastas
5 La Tasca Vasca
6 Ollantay
7 Resaca

Places outside the city

Parque Histórico Guayaquil ① *Vía Samborondón, near Entrerías, T283 2958, Wed-Sun 0900-1630, free; CISA buses to Samborondón leave from the Terminal Terrestre every 20 mins, US$0.25.* The park recreates Guayaquil and its rural surroundings at the end of the 19th century. There is a natural area with native flora and fauna, a traditions section where you can learn about rural life, an urban section with old wooden architecture, and eateries. A pleasant place for a family outing. The **Botanical Gardens** ① *Av Francisco de Orellana, in Ciudadela Las Orquídeas (bus line 63), T289 9689, daily 0800-1600, US$3, guiding service for up to 5 visitors US$7 (Spanish), US$10 (English),* are northwest. There are over 3000 plants, including 150 species of Ecuadorean and foreign orchids (most flower August to December). One area emulates the Amazon rainforest and has monkeys and other animals.

Bosque Protector Cerro Blanco ① *Vía a la Costa, Km 16, T09-8622 5077 (Spanish), fundacionprobosque@ymail.com, US$4, additional guiding fee US$10-15 depending on trails visited, camping US$20 for group of 8, lodge available.* The reserve, run by **Fundación Pro-Bosque**, is set in tropical dry forest with an impressive variety of birds (over 200 species), many reptiles and with sightings of monkeys and other mammals. Unfortunately it is getting harder to see the animals due to human encroachment in the area. Reservations required during weekdays, for groups larger than eight at weekends, and for birders wishing to arrive before or stay after normal opening hours (0800-1600). Take a **CLP** bus from the Terminal Terrestre, a **Cooperativa Chongón** bus from Antepara y 10 de Agosto (hourly) or a taxi (US$8-10). On the other side of the road, at Km 18 is **Puerto Hondo**, where *rowboat trips* ① *through the mangroves are offered, T09-9140 0186, US$15 for a group of 7, 1hr, reserve ahead.*

Heading east then south from Guayaquil, 22 km beyond the main crossroads at Km 50 on the road to Machala, lies the **Reserva Ecológica Manglares Churute** ① *free entry, camping and use of basic cabins; boat tour US$20-40, depending on group size (2-4 hrs recommended to appreciate the area), arrange several days ahead through the Dirección Regional, Ministerio del Ambiente in Guayaquil, 9 de Octubre y Panamá, Edif Banco Pichincha, p 9, T232 0383, ext 102.* Buses (CIFA, Ecuatoriano Pullman, 16 de Junio) leave the Terminal Terrestre every 30 mins, going to Naranjal or Machala; ask to be let off at the Churute information centre. The reserve can also be reached by river. It is a rich natural area with five different ecosystems created to preserve mangroves in the Gulf of Guayaquil and forests of the Cordillera Churute. Many waterbirds, monkeys, dolphins and other wildlife can be seen. There is a trail through the dry tropical forest (1½ hours' walk) and you can also walk (one hour) to Laguna Canclón or Churute, a large lake where ducks nest. Near the park is **Monoloco Lodge ($)**, www.monoloco.ec, tours available.

⊙ Guayaquil listings

For hotel and restaurant price codes, and other relevant information, see Essentials.

⊙ Where to stay

Guayaquil *p1074, maps p1073 and p1075*
Guayaquil has some of the best top-class accommodation in Ecuador. For major chain hotels see: www.hilton.com (**Hilton Colón** and **Hampton Inn**, both excellent), www. oroverdehotels.com (**Oro Verde** and **Unipark**),

www.hotelcontinental.com.ec, www.hojo. com (**Howard Johnson**), www.hdoral.com (**Best Western**), www.sheraton.com and www.sonesta.com/guayaquil . There are several refurbished mid-range (**$$**) hotels on Junín between Gen Córdova and Escobedo but decent economy places are few and far between; the latter are concentrated around Parque Centenario, not a safe area.

$$$$ Mansión del Río, Numa Pompilio Llona 120, Las Peñas, T256 6044, www.mansiondelríoec.com. Elegant boutique hotel in a 1926 mansion, period European style, river view, buffet breakfast, airport transfers, 10 mins from city centre.

$$$ Castell, Av Miguel H Alcivar y Ulloa, by the Parque Japonés, Kennedy Norte, T268 0190, www.hotelcastell.com. Modern comfortable hotel in a quiet location in the north of the city, includes buffet breakfast, restaurant, a/c, convenient for the airport.

$$$ Grand Hotel Guayaquil, Boyacá 1600 y 10 de Agosto, T232 9690, www.grandhotel guayaquil.com. A traditional Guayaquil hotel, central, includes buffet breakfast, good restaurants, pool, gym and sauna.

$$$ Nazú B&B, Ciudadela La Cogra, Manzana 1, Villa 2, off Av Carlos Julio Arosemena Km 3½ (taxi from bus terminal or airport US$6-8, Metrovía '28 de Mayo' stop, best without luggage), T220 1143. Lovely suburban guesthouse with a variety of rooms and suites with a/c, includes dinner and breakfast, pool, parking, terrace with views of the city, English and German spoken, refurbished and under new management in 2014.

$$$ Palace, Chile 214 y Luque, T232 1080, www.hotelpalaceguayaquil.com.cc. Modern hotel, includes buffet breakfast, restaurant, 24-hr cafetería, traffic noise on Av Chile side, good value for business travellers.

$$$ Ramada, Malecón 606 e Imbabura, T256 5555, www.hotelramada.com. Excellent location right on the Malecón, rooms facing the river are more expensive, includes buffet breakfast, restaurant, a/c, pool, spa.

$$$-$$ Casa Alianza, Av Segunda 318 y Calle 12, Los Ceibos (taxi from bus terminal US$6 7, 15 min walk from 'Te de Guayas' Metrovía stop, only without luggage), T200 3041. Good hostel, far from the centre, a variety of rooms and prices, cafetería, a/c, private or shared bath, group rooms, run by a Norwegian NGO, Spanish classes available.

$$ La Torre, Chile 303 y Luque, p 13-15, T253 1316. Popular hotel in a downtown office tower, long flight of stairs to get into the building, comfortable rooms, cafetería, a/c, nice views, reasonably quiet for where it is, popular, advance booking advised, good value.

$$ Las Peñas, Escobedo 1215 y Vélez, T232 3355. Nice hotel in a refurbished part of downtown, ample modern rooms, cafetería, a/c, quiet despite being in the centre of town, good value. Recommended.

$$ Manso, Malecón 1406 y Aguirre, upstairs, T252 6644, www.manso.ec. Nicely refurbished hostel in a great location opposite the Malecón. Rooms vary from fancy with a/c, private bath and river view, to simpler with shared bath and fan, and a 4-bed dorm (US$15 pp), English spoken.

$$ Savoy II, Junín 627 y Boyacá, T231 0206. Central location, simple rooms with private bath, hot water, a/c.

$$ Tangara Guest House, Manuela Sáenz y O'Leary, Manzana F, Villa 1, Ciudadela Bolivariana, T228 4445, www.tangara-ecuador. com. Comfortable hotel in a nice area by the university and near the Estero Salado, a/c, fridge, convenient for airport and bus terminal but also along the flight path, so it is noisy.

$$-$ Elite Internacional, Baquerizo Moreno 902 y Junín, T256 5385. Completely refurbished old downtown hotel, better rooms have a/c, private bath, hot water; **$** with fan, shared bath and cold water.

$ Nueve de Octubre, 9 de Octubre 736 y García Avilés, T256 4222. Busy 8-storey hotel in a central location. Simple functional rooms, those facing the street are larger but noisy, restaurant, private bath, cold water, a/c, cheaper with fan, parking extra. Fills early and does not accept reservations. Good value.

🍴 Restaurants

Guayaquil *p1074, maps p1073 and p1075*
Main areas for restaurants are the centre with many in the larger hotels, around Urdesa and the residential and commercial neighbourhoods to the north.

$$$ Lo Nuestro, VE Estrada 903 e Higueras, Urdesa, T238 6398. Daily 1200-2300. Luxury restaurant with typical coastal cooking, good seafood platters and stuffed crabs, colonial decor.

$$$ Manny's, Av Miraflores 112 y C Primera, Miraflores, T220 2754; also in Urdesa and

Kennedy. Daily 1000-2400. Well known crab house with specialties such as *cangrejo al ajillo* (crab in garlic butter), good quality and value.

$$$-$$ Cangrejo Criollo, Av Rolando Pareja, Villa 9, La Garzota, T262 6708. Mon-Sat 0900-0100, Sun 0900-2300. Excellent, varied seafood menu.

$$$-$$ La Parrilla del Ñato, VE Estrada 1219 y Laureles in Urdesa; Av Francisco de Orellana opposite the Hilton Colón; Luque y Pichincha downtown; and several other locations, T268 2338. Daily 1200-2300. Large variety of dishes, salad bar, also pizza by the metre, good quality, generous portions. Try the *parrillada de mariscos*, available only at the Urdesa and Kennedy locations. Recommended.

$$$-$$ La Trattoria da Enrico, Bálsamos 504 y las Monjas, Urdesa, T238 7079. Mon-Sat 1230-2330, Sun 1230-2200. Very exclusive Italian restaurant since 1980, the best in food and surroundings, good antipasto.

$$$-$$ Riviera, VE Estrada 707y Ficus, Urdesa, and Mall del Sol, T288 3790. Daily 1230-2330. Extensive Italian menu, good pasta, antipasto, salads, bright surroundings, good service.

$$$-$$ Sion Lung, VE Estrada 621 y Ficus, Urdesa, also Av Principal, Entre Ríos, T288 8213. Daily 1200-2230. Chinese food, a variety of rice (*chaulafán*) and noodle (*tallarín*) dishes.

$$ La Canoa, at Hotel Continental. Open 24 hrs. Regional dishes rarely found these days, with different specials during the week, a Guayaquil tradition.

$$ La Tasca Vasca, Clemente Ballén 422 y Chimborazo, downtown. Mon-Sat 1200-1600, 1900-2300. Spanish cuisine, specialties include *paella* and *pulpo a la gallega* (octopus).

$$-$ Asia, Sucre 321 y Chile, downtown, also VE Estrada 508 y Las Monjas, Urdesa and in shopping centres in the north. Daily 1100-2130. Chinese food, large portions, popular.

$ Manso, Malecón 1406 y Aguirre, downtown at the hotel. Small dining area serving innovative set lunches and snacks. Tables overlooking the river are nice.

$ Ollantay, Tungurahua 508 y 9 de Octubre, west of downtown. Good vegetarian food.

Cafés and snacks

Aroma Café, Malecón 2000 by Tomás Martínez. Daily 1200-2300. Café, also serves regional food, nice garden setting.

California, Escobedo 1215 y Vélez, below Hotel Las Peñas. Mon-Sat 0700-2000, Sun 0800-1500. Good and popular for breakfast, snacks, drinks, sweets and à la carte meals.

Fruta Bar, Malecón e Imbabura, VE Estrada 608 y Monjas, Urdesa. Excellent fruit juices and snacks, unusual African decor, good music.

Las Tres Canastas, Vélez y García Avilés and several other locations. Breakfast, snacks, safe fruit juices and smoothies.

⊙ Bars and clubs

Guayaquil *p1074, maps p1073 and p1075*
Guayaquil nightlife is not cheap. Most discos charge a cover of around US$5-10 on weekdays, US$10-15 at weekends, and drinks are expensive. There are clubs and bars in most of the major hotels, as well as in the northern suburbs, especially at the Kennedy Mall. Also in vogue are the Las Peñas area, and the Zona Rosa, bounded by the Malecón Simón Bolívar and Rocafuerte, C Loja and C Roca. Both these areas are considered reasonably safe but take a radio taxi back to your hotel. Yellow street cabs have been involved in holdups here.

La Paleta, Escalón 176, Las Peñas. Tue-Sat from 2000. Good music, great drinks and snacks. US$10-15 cover Fri and Sat, popular, reserve.

Praga, Rocafuerte 636 y Mendiburo. Tue-Sat from 1830. US$10-16 cover, live music Fri-Sat. Pleasant atmosphere, several halls, varied music.

Resaca, Malecón 2000, at the level of Junín. Daily 1130-2400. Lovely setting, live tropical music Fri-Sat night. Also serves set lunches on weekdays, regional dishes and pricey drinks.

Vulcano, Rocafuerte 419 y Padre Aguirre. Fri-Sat from 2230. Cover US$7-8. Popular gay bar which attracts a mixed crowd, varied modern music.

⊕ Entertainment

Guayaquil *p1074, maps p1073 and p1075*
Party boats See What to do, below.
Cinemas are at the main shopping centres and cost US$3-4. The IMAX Cinema, Malecón 2000, projects impressive films on its oversize screen.
Theatre **Centro Cívico**, Quito y Venezuela, excellent theatre/concert facility, home to the Guayaquil Symphony which gives free concerts.

⊛ Festivals

Guayaquil *p1074, maps p1073 and p1075*
The foundation of Guayaquil is celebrated on **24-25 Jul**, and the **city's independence** on **9-12 Oct** Both holidays are lively and there are many public events; cultural happenings are prolonged throughout Oct.

⊙ Shopping

Guayaquil *p1074, maps p1073 and p1075*
There are many shopping malls, noisy but air conditioned for cooling off on hot days.
Camping equipment Casa Maspons, Ballén 517 y Boyacá. For camping gas.
Handicrafts Mercado Artesanal del Malecón 2000, at the south end of the Malecón, has many kiosks selling varied crafts. **Mercado Artesanal**, Baquerizo Moreno between Loja and J Montalvo. Greatest variety, almost a whole block of stalls with good prices. In Albán Borja Mall are: **El Telar** with a good variety of *artesanías* and **Ramayana**, with nice ceramics.
Malls Centro Comercial Malecón 2000 is at the south end of the Malecón. **Centro Comercial San Marino**, Av Francisco de Orellana y L Plaza Dañín. Huge, one of the largest in South America. **Mall del Sol** is near the airport on Av Constitución y Juan Tanca Marengo. It has craft shops.

⊙ What to do

Guayaquil *p1074, maps p1073 and p1075*
Boat tours The gulf islands and mangroves can be visited on tours from Guayaquil, Puerto

Hondo or Puerto El Morro. **Isla Santay**, a Ramsar site wetland with walking trails has a community tourism programme, as does **Puná**, the largest of the islands. **Capitan Morgan**, Muelle Malecón y Sucre, 1-hr tours on the river with nice city views, Tue-Fri at 1600, 1800 and 1930, Sat and Sun at 1230, 1400, 1600, 1800 and 1930, Fri and Sat also at 2130; US$7. Also 2-hr party cruises, Thu 2130-2330, Fri-Sat from 2330-0200, US$15, with live music, open bar and dancing. **Cruceros Discovery**, Muelle Malecón y Tomás Martínez, 1-hr river cruises, US$7, Tue-Fri from 1600, Sat-Sun from 1300, and party trips.
Tour operators A 3-hr city tour costs about US$14 pp in a group. See Guayaquil Vision for bus tours of the city. Tours to coastal haciendas, offer a glimpse of rural life.
Centro Viajero, Baquerizo Moreno 1119 y 9 de Octubre, of 805, T230 1283, T09-9235 7745 24-hr service, www.centroviajero.com. Custom-designed tours to all regions, travel information and bookings, flight tickets, car and driver service, well informed about options for Galápagos, helpful, English, French and Italian spoken. Recommended.
Galasam, Edif Gran Pasaje, 9 Octubre 424, ground floor, T230 4488, www.galapagos-islands.com. Galápagos cruises, city tours, tours to reserves near Guayaquil, diving trips, also run highland and jungle tours and sell flight tickets.
Guayaquil Visión, ticket booth at Olmedo y Malecón, T292 5332, www.guayaquilvision.com. City tours on a double-decker bus, US$6-17 depending on route, departs from Plaza Olmedo and the Rotonda, Malecón at the bottom of 9 de Octubre. Also tours to attractions outside the city and night-time party tours.
La Moneda, Av de las Américas 406, Centro de Convenciones Simón Bolívar, of 2, T269 0900, ecuador@lamoneda.com.ec. City and coastal tours; whale watching, also other regions.
Metropolitan Touring, Francisco De Orellana, Edif. World Trade Center, CC Millenium Galery, PB, T263 0900, www.metropolitan-touring.com. High-end land tours and Galápagos cruises.
Train rides The train station is in Durán, across the river from Guayaquil, T215 4254,

reservations T1800-873637, www.trenecuador.com, Mon-Fri 0800-1630, Sat-Sun 0730-1530. For information on the luxury *Tren Crucero* from Durán to Quito, see page 996. An *autoferro* runs through rice paddies from Durán to Yaguachi and back Thu-Sun and holidays at 0900 and 1315, US$12, 4 hrs return. A second route is from Durán to Bucay, Sat-Sun and holidays at 0800 returning by bus at 1800, US$20. Tickets are also sold at the railcar in Malecón 2000, Malecón y Aguirre, Wed-Fri 1000-1600, Sat-Sun 1000-1530.

☺ Transport

Guayaquil *p1074, maps p1073 and p1075*
Air
José Joaquín de Olmedo is a modern airport with all services including banks (change only cash euros at poor rates) and luggage storage. The information booth outside international arrivals (T216 9000, open 24 hrs) has flight, hotel and transport information. It is 15 mins to the city centre by taxi, US$5, and 5-10 mins to the bus terminal, US$3. Fares from the airport to other areas are posted at exit doors and on www.taxiecuadorairport.com. Official airport taxis are more expensive but safer than those out on the street. It is along line 2 of the Metrovía, but neither the Metrovía nor buses to the centre (eg Línea 130 'Full 2') are safe or practical with luggage. For groups, there are van services such as **M&M**, T216 9294, US$15 to centre.

Many flights daily to **Quito** (sit on the right for the best views) and **Galápagos**, see page 1122, with **Aerogal** (Junín 440 y Córdova, T231 1028, T1-800-237642), **LAN** (Gen Córdova 1042 y 9 de Octubre, and in Mall del Sol, T1-800-101075) and **TAME** (9 de Octubre 424 y Chile, T268 9127 and Galerías Hilton Colón, T268 9135 or T1-700-500800). **TAME** also flies to **Esmeraldas**, **Latacunga**, **Loja** and **Coca**.
Bus Metrovía (T213 0402, www.metrovia-gye.com.ec, US$0.25) is an integrated transport system of articulated buses running on exclusive lanes and *alimentadores* (feeder buses) serving suburbs from the terminuses. One line runs from the Terminal Río Daule, opposite the

Terminal Terrestre, in the north, to the Terminal El Guasmo in the south. In the city centre it runs along Boyacá southbound and Pedro Carbo northbound. A second line goes from the Terminal Río Daule along Avenida de las Américas then past the centre to Terminal 25 de Julio in the southern suburbs. A third line goes from the centre (transfer points at Biblioteca Municipal and IESS) along C Sucre to the northwest as far as Bastión Popular and provides access to neighbourhoods such as Urdesa, Miraflores, and Los Ceibos. The Metrovía is a good way of getting around without luggage or valuables. It is very crowded at peak hours.

City buses (US$0.25) are only permitted on a few streets in the centre; northbound buses go along Rumichaca or the *Malecón*, southbound along Lorenzo de Garaicoa or García Avilés. They get very crowded at rush hour.
Taxis Using a radio taxi, such as **Samboroncar**, T284 3883, or **Vipcar**, T239 3000, is recommended. Short trips costs US$2,50, fares from the centre to Urdesa, Policentro or Alborada are around US$4-5. Taxis are supposed to use a meter, but in mid-2014, not all drivers where using them.

Long distance The Terminal Terrestre, just north of the airport, is off the road to the Guayas bridge. The Metrovía, opposite the bus station, and many city buses (eg Línea 84 to Parque Centenario) go from to the city centre but these are not safe with luggage; take a taxi (US$3-4). The bus station doubles as a shopping centre with supermarket, shops, banks, post office, calling centres, internet, food courts, etc. Incoming buses arrive on the ground floor, where the ticket offices are also located. Regional buses depart from the second level and long distance (interprovincial) buses depart from the 3rd level. The terminal is very large, so you need to allow extra time to get to your bus. Check the board at the entrance for the location of the ticket counters for your destination, they are colour-coded by region.

Several companies to **Quito**, 8 hrs, US$10, US$12 for express buses which go at night; also non-stop, a/c services, eg **Transportes Ecuador**, Av de las Américas y Hermano Miguel, opposite the airport terminal, T228 9509. To **Cuenca**, 4 hrs via Molleturo/Cajas, 5 hrs via Zhud, both US$8, both scenic; also hourly van service, 0500-2100, with **Río Arriba/Atenas**, Centro de Negocios El Terminal, Bloque C, of 38, Av de las Américas y entrada a Bahía Norte, T09 8488 9269, US$12, 3 hrs, reserve ahead; several others at the same address, departures every 30-40 min. **Riobamba**, 5 hrs, US$5. To **Santo Domingo de los Tsáchilas**, 5 hrs, US$5. **Manta**, 4 hrs, US$4. **Esmeraldas**, 8 hrs, US$8. To **Bahía de Caráquez**, 6 hrs, US$5. To **Ambato**, 6 hrs, US$6. Frequent buses to **Playas**, 2 hrs, US$2.60; and to **Salinas**, 2½ hrs, US$3.70. To **Santa Elena**, 2hrs, US$2.50, change here for **Puerto López**. To **Montañita** and **Olón**, CLP, at 0520, 0620, 0900, 1300, 1500 and 1640, 3¼hrs, US$5.70. For the **Peruvian border**, to **Huaquillas** direct, 4½-5 hrs, US$6-7; van service with **Transfrosur**, Chile 616 y Sucre, T232 6387, hourly 0500-2000, Sun 0700-2000, 4 4½ hrs, US$13.50; to **Machala**, 3 hrs, US$4-5, also hourly vans with **Oro Guayas**, Clemente Ballén y Chile, T232 0934, US$12, 3 hrs. To **Zaruma**, 8 buses daily, US$6.50, 6 hrs; also vans, **Rutas Zarumeñas**, T213 0389, US$12, 5 hrs. To **Loja**, with Trans Loja, 8 daily, US$10, 9-10 hrs. Direct bus to **Tumbes** (Peru) 10 daily, 5½ hrs, US$6; to **Piura** (Peru) via **Máncora**, with CIFA, T213 0379, www.cifainternacional.com, regular service at 0720, 1820 and 2100, 10-11 hrs, US$13; and double-decker bus-cama at 1950 and 2330, US$17; also with Ecuatoriano Pullman, and CIVA, daily at 2130, semi-cama US$17, cama

US$20. To **Chiclayo** (Peru) with **Super Semería**, at 2200 daily, US$25, 12 hrs. To **Lima** with Cruz del Sur, T213 0179, www.cruzdelsur.com.pe, Tue, Fri, Sun at 1400, US$75 (including meals), 27 hrs. With **Ormeño**, Centro Comercial El Terminal (near Terminal Terrestre), Of C34, T213 0847, 4 weekly to **Lima**, US$80; Sat to **Bogotá**, US$100; Tue and Sun to **Caracas**, US$150.

ⓓ Directory

Guayaquil p1074, maps p1073 and p1075
Banks Most banks have their main branches (with many ATMs) downtown and others in the shopping malls. The airport and Terminal Terrestre both have ATMs. **Banco del Pacífico**, P Ycaza 200 y Panamá for TCs and cash advances. No casas de cambio in centre, only a few street changers along 9 de Octubre dealing in cash euros; be careful. **Car hire** All the main car rental agents are at the airport. **Immigration** Av Río Daule, near the bus terminal, T214 0002. **Medical services** Emergencies T911. Hospitals: a reliable hospital is Clínica Kennedy, Av San Jorge y la 9na, T228 9666. Also has branches in Ciudadela La Alborada XIII, Mz-1227 and Entre Ríos. It has many specialists (Dr Roberto Morla speaks German) and a very competent emergency department. Also reliable are: Clínica Alcívar, Coronel 2301 y Azuay, T258 0030; Clínica Guayaquil, Padre Aguirre 401 y General Córdova, T256 3555 (Dr Roberto Gilbert speaks English and German)

South to Peru

Machala → Phone code: 07. Colour map 11, C2. Population: 249,000. Altitude: 4 m.
The capital of the province of El Oro is a booming agricultural town in a major banana producing and exporting region. It is unsafe, somewhat dirty and oppressively hot. For the tourist, the only reasons for stopping here are to go to the beautiful tranquil uplands of El Oro, and to catch a through CIFA bus to Peru (also runs from Guayaquil) for the beaches around Máncora. **Tourist office** ⓘ 25 de Junio y 9 de Mayo, Municipio, iturmachala@hotmail.com, Mon-Fri 0800-1230, 1500-1800, Spanish only. Some 30 km south along the road to Peru is **Santa Rosa** with the regional airport.

Puerto Bolívar, on the Estero Jambelí among mangroves, is a major export outlet for over two million tonnes of bananas annually. From the old pier canoes cross to the beaches of **Jambelí** (hourly 0730-1500, US$2.40 return) on the far side of the mangrove islands which shelter Puerto Bolívar from the Pacific. The beaches are crowded at weekends, deserted during the week and not very clean. Boats can be rented for excursions to the **Archipiélago de Jambelí**, a maze of islands and channels just offshore, stretching south between Puerto Bolívar and the Peruvian border. These mangrove islands are rich in birdlife (and insects for them to feed on, take repellent), the water is very clear and you may also see fish and reefs.

Zaruma → *Phone code: 07. Colour map 11, C3. Population: 10,800. Altitude: 1300 m.*

Southeast from Machala is the lovely old gold-mining town of Zaruma (118 km). It is reached from Machala by paved road via Piñas, by a scenic dirt road off the main Loja-Machala road, or via Pasaje and Paccha on another scenic dirt road off the Machala-Cuenca road.

Founded in 1549, Zaruma is a delightful town perched on a hilltop, with steep, twisting streets and painted wooden buildings. The **Tourist office** ⓘ *in the Municipio, at the plaza, T297 3533, Mon-Fri 0800-1200, 1400-1800, Sat 0900-1600, Sun 0900-1300,* is very friendly and helpful. They can arrange for guides and accommodation with local families. Next door is the small **Museo Municipal** ⓘ *free, ask for the key at the tourist office if closed.* It has a collection of local historical artefacts. The Zaruma area has a number of prehispanic archaeological sites and petroglyphs are also found in the region. Tours with **Oroadventure** ⓘ *at the Parque Central, T297 2761,* or with English speaking guide **Ramiro Rodríguez** ⓘ *T297 2523.* Zaruma is also known for its excellent Arabica coffee freshly roasted in the agricultural store basement, the proud owner will show you around if the store isn't busy. On top of the small hill beyond the market is a public swimming pool (US$1), from where there are amazing views over the hot, dry valleys. For even grander views, walk up **Cerro del Calvario** (follow Calle San Francisco); go early in the morning as it gets very hot. At **Portovelo**, south of Zaruma, is the largest mine in the area. Its history is told inside a mine shaft at the **Museo Magner Turner** ⓘ *T294 9345, daily 0900-1100, 1400-1700, US$1.* The area has virtually no tourists and is well worth a visit.

Piñas, 19 km west of Zaruma, along the road to Machala is a pleasant town which conserves just a few of its older wooden buildings. Northwest of Piñas, 20 minutes along the road to Saracay and Machala, is **Buenaventura**, to the north of which lies an important area for bird conservation, with over 310 bird species recorded, including many rare ones. **The Jocotoco Foundation** (www.fjocotoco.org) protects a 1500-ha forest in this region, with 13 km of trails, entry US$15, **$$$$** category lodge, advance booking required.

Bosque Petrificado Puyango → *Altitude: 360 m.*

ⓘ *110 km south of Machala, west of the Arenillas-Alamor road, T293 2106 (Machala), bosquepuyango@hotmail.com, 0800-1530, free.* At Puyango, a dry-forest reserve, a great number of petrified trees, ferns, fruits and molluscs, 65 to 120 million years old, have been found. Over 120 species of birds can be seen. There is a camping area, no accommodation in the village, but ask around for floor space or try at the on-site information centre. If not, basic accommodation is available in **Las Lajas**, 20 minutes north (one residencial) and **Alamor**, 20 km south (several hotels, eg **$ Rey Plaza**, T07-268 0256).

Huaquillas → *Phone code: 07. Colour map 11, C2. Population: 50,400. Altitude: 12 m.*

The stiflingly hot Ecuadorean border town of Huaquillas is something of a shopping arcade for Peruvians. The border runs along the Canal de Zarumilla and is crossed by two international bridges, one at the western end of Avenida La República in Huaquillas and a second newer one further south.

Border with Peru: Huaquillas-Tumbes

The best way to cross this border is on one of the international buses that run between Ecuador and Peru. Border formalities are only carried out at the new bridge, far outside the towns of Huaquillas

(Ecuador) and Aguas Verdes (Peru). There are two border complexes called CEBAF *(Centro Binacional de Atención Fronteriza)*, open 24 hours, on either side of the bridge; they are about 4 km apart. Both complexes have Ecuadorean and Peruvian customs and immigration officers so you get your exit and entry stamps in the same place. If crossing with your own vehicle however, you have to stop at both border complexes for customs and, on the Ecuadorean side, you also have to stop at the customs *(aduana)* post at Chacras, 7 km from the Ecuadorean CEBAF, on the road to Machala. If you do not take one of the international buses, the crossing is inconvenient. See details in the Peru chapter. A taxi from Huaquillas to the Ecuadorean CEBAF costs US$2.50, to the Peruvian CEBAF US$5. See Peru chapter for transport to Tumbes and beyond. Those seeking a more relaxed crossing to or from Peru should consider Macará (see page 1066) or La Balsa (see page 1070).

◉ South to Peru listings

For hotel and restaurant price codes, and other relevant information, see Essentials.

● Where to stay

Machala *p1081*
$$$$ Oro Verde, Circunvalación Norte in Urbanización Unioro, T298 5444, www.oroverde hotels.com. Includes buffet breakfast, 2 restaurants, nice pool (US$6 for non-guests), beautiful gardens, tennis courts, full luxury. Best in town.
$$ Oro Hotel, Sucre y Juan Montalvo, T293 0032, www.orohotel.com. Includes breakfast, pricey restaurant and cheaper café downstairs, a/c, fridge, parking, nice comfortable rooms but those to the street are noisy, helpful staff. Recommended.
$ San Miguel, 9 de Mayo y Sucre, T292 0474. Good quality and value, some rooms without windows, hot water, a/c, cheaper with fan, fridge, helpful staff.

Zaruma *p1082*
$$ Hostería El Jardín, Barrio Limoncito, 10-min walk from centre (taxi US$1.50), T297 2706. Lovely palm garden and terrace with views, internet, parking, comfortable rooms, small zoo, family-run. Recommended.
$$-$ Roland, at entrance to town on road from Portovelo, T297 2800. Comfortable rooms (some are dark) and nicer more expensive cabins, restaurant with lovely views, pool, parking.
$ Blacio, C Sucre, T297 2045. Hot water, modern, ask for rooms with balcony.
$ Romería, on the plaza facing the church, T297 2173. Old wooden house with balcony, a treat.

Huaquillas *p1082*
$$-$ Hernancor, 1 de Mayo y 10 de Agostso, T299 5467, grandhotelhernancor@gmail.com. Cafeteria, nice rooms with a/c.
$$-$ Sol del Sur, Av La República y Chiriboga, T251 0898, www.soldelsurhotel.amawebs.com. Nice rooms, a/c, small bathrooms, parking.
$ Vanessa, 1 de Mayo y Hualtaco, T299 6263, www.hotelvanessa-ec.com. A/c, internet, fridge, parking, pleasant.

🍴 Restaurants

Machala *p1081*
The best food is found in the better hotels.
$$ Mesón Hispano, Av Las Palmeras y Sucre. Very good grill, attentive service, outstanding for Machala.
$ Chifa Gran Oriental, 25 de Junio entre Guayas y Ayacucho. Good food and service, clean place. Recommended.

Zaruma *p1082*
$$ Giuseppe, C Pichincha s/n. Mon-Sat 1100-2100. Good pizzas.
$$-$ 200 Millas, Av Honorato Márquez, uphill from bus station. Good seafood.
$ Cafetería Uno, C Sucre. Good for breakfast and Zaruma specialties, best *tigrillo* in town.

◉ Transport

There may be military checkpoints on the roads in this border area, keep your passport to hand.

Machala p1081

Air The regional airport is at Santa Rosa, 32 km from Machala; taxi US$12. To **Quito**, TAME (J Montalvo y Pichincha, T293 0139); 4 daily flights Mon-Fri, 2 on Sat-Sun.

Bus There is no Terminal Terrestre. Do not take night buses into or out of Machala as they are prone to hold-ups. To **Quito**, with **Occidental** (Buenavista entre Sucre y Olmedo), 10 hrs, US$10, 8 daily, with **Panamericana** (Colón y Bolívar), 7 daily. To **Guayaquil**, 3 hrs, US$5, hourly with **Ecuatoriano Pullman** (Colón y Rocafuerte), **CIFA** (Bolívar y Guayas) and **Rutas Orenses** (Tarqui y Rocafuerte), half-hourly, US$5, 3 hrs; also hourly vans with **Oro Guayas**, Guayas y Pichincha, T293 4382, US$12, 3 hrs. There are 3 different scenic routes to **Loja**, each with bus service. They are, from north to south: via **Piñas** and **Zaruma**, partly paved and rough, via **Balsas**, fully paved; and via **Arenillas** and **Alamor**, for **Puyango** petrified forest. Fare to **Loja**, 6 hrs, US$6, several daily with **Trans Loja** (Tarqui y Bolívar). To **Zaruma**, for bus service see below; also vans, **Oro y Plata**, Rocafuerte y Tarqui, US$5, 2 hrs. To **Cuenca**, half-hourly with **Trans Azuay** (Sucre y Junín), 4 hrs, US$5. To **Huaquillas, with** CIFA and Ecuatoriano Pullman, direct, 1½ hr, US$2.30, every 20 mins. To **Piura**, in Peru, with **CIFA**, 4 a day, US$8-10, 6 hrs; also to **Máncora**, 5 daily, US$6, 5hrs and **Tumbes**, 7 daily, US$3, 3 hrs.

Zaruma p1082

Bus To/from **Machala** with Trans Piñas or TAC, half-hourly, US$3.50, 3 hrs; also vans, **Oro y Plata**, 10 de Agosto by market, US$5, 2 hrs; and shared taxis (near the terminal), US$7. To **Piñas**, take a Machala bound bus, US$1, 1 hr. To **Guayaquil**, 8 buses daily US$6.50, 6 hrs; also vans, **Rutas Zarumeñas**, T297 3098, US$12, 5 hrs. To **Quito**, 5 daily, US$11, 12 hrs, note that TAC has a terminal in Quito at Almagro y La Niña; to **Cuenca**, 3 daily (Trans Azuay at 0730, US$7, 6 hrs and **Loja**, 4 daily, US$5, 5 hrs (may have to change at Portovelo).

Puyango p1082

Puyango is west of the highway: alight from bus at turn-off at the bridge over the Río Puyango. Bus from **Machala**, Trans Loja 0930, 1300 and 2200, **CIFA** at 0600 and 1500, US$3.50, 2½ hrs. From **Loja**, Trans Loja 0900, 1430 and 1930, US$5, 5 hrs. From **Huaquillas**, Trans Loja at 0730 and **Unión Cariamanga** at 1130, US$2, 1½ hrs. You might be able to hire a pick-up from the main road to the park, US$3. Pick-up from Alamor to Puyango US$25 return, including wait.

Huaquillas p1082

Bus There is no Terminal Terrestre, each bus company has its own office, many on Teniente Cordovez. If you are in a hurry, it can be quicker to change buses in Machala or Guayaquil. To **Machala**, with **CIFA** (Santa Rosa y Machala) and **Ecuatoriano Pullman**, direct, 1½ hrs, US$2.30, every hour between 0800 and 2000; via Arenillas and Santa Rosa, 2 hrs, every 20 mins. To **Quito**, with **Occidental**, every 2 hrs, 12 hrs, US$10; with **Panamericana**, 11½ hrs, 3 daily via Santo Domingo; 2 daily via **Riobamba** and **Ambato**, 12 hrs. To **Guayaquil**, frequent service with CIFA and Ecuatoriano Pullman, 4½-5 hrs, US$6-7, take a direct bus; van service to downtown Guayaquil with **Transfrosur**, C Santa Rosa y Av La República, T299 5288, hourly 0500-2000, Sun 0700-2000, 4-4½ hrs, US$13.50. To **Cuenca**, 8 daily, 5 hrs, US$6. To **Loja**, 6 daily, 6 hrs, US$6.

⊙ Directory

Machala p1081

Banks Banco del Pacifico, Rocafuerte y Junín, ATM and TCs. For ATM: Banco de Guayaquil and Banco Pichincha, both at Rocafuerte y Guayas. **Embassies and consulates** Peruvian Consulate, Urb Unioro, Mz 14, V 11, near Hotel Oro Verde, T293 0680, Mon-Fri 0900-1800.

Huaquillas p1082

Banks Banks do not change money here. Many street changers deal in soles and US$ cash. Do not change more US$ than you need to get to Tumbes, where there are reliable cambios, but get rid of all your soles here as they are difficult to exchange further inside Ecuador. Only clean, crisp US$ bills are accepted in Peru.

Pacific lowlands

This vast tract of Ecuador covers everything west of the Andes and north of the Guayas delta. Though popular with Quiteños and Guayaquileños, who come here for weekends and holidays, the Pacific Lowlands receive relatively few foreign visitors, which is surprising given the natural beauty, diversity and rich cultural heritage of the coast. Here you can surf, watch whales, visit archaeological sites, or just relax and enjoy some of the best food this country has to offer. Parque Nacional Machalilla protects an important area of primary tropical dry forest, pre-Columbian ruins, coral reef and a wide variety of wildlife. Further north, in the province of Esmeraldas, there are not only well-known party beaches, but also opportunities to visit the remaining mangroves and experience two unique lifestyles: Afro-Ecuadorean on the coast and indigenous Cayapa further inland. Coastal resorts are busy and more expensive from December to April, the temporada de playa.

Guayaquil to Puerto López

Southwest of Guayaquil is the beach resort of Playas and, west of it, the Santa Elena Peninsula, with Salinas at its tip. From the town of Santa Elena, capital of the province of the same name, the coastal road stretches north for 737 km to Mataje on the Colombian border; along the way are countless beaches and fishing villages, and a few cities. Puerto López is the perfect base for whale watching and from which to explore the beautiful Parque Nacional Machalilla.

Playas and Salinas → *Phone code: 04. Colour map 11, B1. Population: 45,600 and 36,300 respectively.*
The beach resorts of Playas and Salinas remain as popular as ever with vacationing Guayaquileños. The paved toll highway from Guayaquil divides after 63 km at El Progreso (Gómez Rendón). One branch leads to **Playas** (General Villamil), the nearest seaside resort to Guayaquil. Bottle-shaped ceibo (kapok) trees characterise the landscape as it turns into dry, tropical thorn scrub. In Playas a few single-sailed balsa rafts, very simple but highly ingenious, can still be seen among the motor launches returning laden with fish. In high season (*temporada* – December to April), and at weekends, Playas is prone to severe crowding, although the authorities are trying to keep the packed beaches clean and safe (thieving is rampant during busy times). Out of season or midweek, the beaches are almost empty especially north towards Punta Pelado (5 km). Playas has six good surf breaks. There are showers, toilets and changing rooms along the beach, with fresh water, for a fee. Many hotels in our **$$-$** ranges. Excellent seafood and typical dishes from over 50 beach cafés (all numbered and named). Many close out of season. **Tourist office** ① *on the Malecón, Tue-Fri 0800-1200, 1400-1800, Sat-Sun 0900-1600.*

Salinas, surrounded by miles of salt flats, is Ecuador's answer to Miami Beach. **Turismo Municipal** ① *Eloy Alfaro y Mercedes de Jesús Molina, Chipipe, T277 3931, Tue-Fri 0800-1700, Sat 0800-1400.* There is safe swimming in the bay and high-rise blocks of holiday flats and hotels line the seafront. More appealing is the (still urban) beach of Chipipe, west of the exclusive Salinas Yacht Club. In December-April it is overcrowded, its services stretched to the limit. Even in the off season it is not that quiet. On the south shore of the Santa Elena peninsula, 8 km south of La Libertad, built on high cliffs is **Punta Carnero**, with hotels in the **$$$-$$** range. To the south is a magnificent 15-km beach with wild surf and heavy undertow, there is whale watching in season.

North to Puerto López
The '**Ruta del Spondylus**' north to Puerto López in the province of Manabí parallels the coastline and crosses the Chongón-Colonche coastal range. Most of the numerous small fishing villages

along the way have good beaches and are slowly being developed for tourism. Beware of rip currents and undertow.

Valdivia → *Phone code: 04. Colour map 11, B2.*

San Pedro and Valdivia are two unattractive villages which merge together. There are many fish stalls. This is the site of the 5000-year-old Valdivia culture. Many houses offer 'genuine' artefacts (it is illegal to export pre-Columbian artefacts from Ecuador). Juan Orrala, who makes excellent copies, lives up the hill from the **Ecomuseo Valdivia** ① *T08-9011 9856, daily, US$1.50*, which has displays of original artefacts from Valdivia and other coastal cultures. There is also a handicraft section, where artisans may be seen at work, and lots of local information. At the museum is a restaurant and five rooms with bath to let. Most of the genuine artefacts discovered at the site are in museums in Quito and Guayaquil.

Manglaralto → *Phone code: 04. Colour map 11, B2. Population: 30,800*

Located 180 km northwest of Guayaquil, this is the main centre of the region north of Santa Elena. There is a tagua nursery; ask to see examples of worked 'vegetable ivory' nuts. It is a nice place, with a quiet beach, good surf but little shade. **Pro-pueblo** is an organization working with local communities to foster family run orchards and cottage craft industry, using tagua nuts, *paja toquilla* (the fibre Panama hats are made from), and other local products. They have a craft shop in town (opposite the park), an office in San Antonio south of Manglaralto, T278 0230, and headquarters in Guayaquil, T268 3569, www.propueblo.com. **Proyecto de Desarrollo Ecoturístico Comunitario** ① *contact Paquita Jara T09-9174 0143*, has a network of simple lodgings with local families (US$9 per person), many interesting routes into the Cordillera Chongón Colonche and whale watching and island tours.

Montañita and Olón → *Phone code: 04. Colour map 11, B2.*

About 3 km north of Manglaralto, **Montañita** has mushroomed into a major surf resort, packed with hotels, restaurants, surf-board rentals, tattoo parlours and craft/jewellery vendors. There are periodic police drug raids in Montañita and several foreigners are serving long sentences in jail. At the north end of the bay, 1 km away, is another hotel area with more elbow-room, Baja Montañita (or Montañita Punta, Surf Point). Between the two is a lovely beach where you'll find some of the best surfing in Ecuador. Various competitions are held during the year. At weekends in season, the town is full of Guayaquileños. Beyond an impressive headland and a few minutes north of Montañita is **Olón**, with a spectacular long beach, still tranquil but starting to get some of the overflow from Montañita. Nearby is **El Cangrejal**, a 7-ha dry tropical forest with mangroves.

Ayampe to Salango → *Phone code: 04. Colour map 11, B2.*

North of Montañita, by **La Entrada**, the road winds up and inland through lush forest before continuing to the small, tranquil village of **Ayampe** (tourism is growing here, with many popular places to stay at south end of the beach). North of Ayampe are the villages of **Las Tunas**, **Puerto Rico** and **Río Chico**. There are places to stay all along this stretch of coast. Just north of Río Chico is **Salango**, with an ill-smelling fish processing plant, but worth visiting for the excellent **Salango archaeological museum** ① *at the north end of town, daily 0900-1200, 1300-1700, US$1*, housing artefacts from excavations right in town. It also has a craft shop and, at the back, nice rooms with bath in the $ range. There is a place for snorkelling offshore, by Isla Salango.

Puerto López → *Phone code: 05. Colour map 11, B2. Population: 11,600.*

This pleasant fishing town is beautifully set in a horseshoe bay. The beach is best for swimming at the far north and south ends, away from the fleet of small fishing boats moored offshore. The town is popular with tourists for watching Humpback Whales from approximately mid-June to September, and for visiting Parque Nacional Machalilla and Isla de la Plata.

Parque Nacional Machalilla

① *Park office in Puerto Lópe, C Eloy Alfaro y García Moreno, daily 0800-1200, 1400-1600.*

The Park extends over 55,000 ha, including Isla de la Plata, Isla Salango, and the magnificent beach of **Los Frailes** and preserves marine ecosystems as well as the dry tropical forest and archaeological sites on shore. At the north end of Los Frailes beach is a trail through the forest leading to a lookout with great views and on to the town of Machalilla (don't take valuables). The land-based part of the park is divided into three sections which are separated by private land, including the town of Machalilla. The park is recommended for birdwatching, especially in the cloud forest of Cerro San Sebastián (see below); there are also howler monkeys, several other species of mammals and reptiles.

Puerto López

To Machalilla & Manta

To ③ ⑦ & Fish Market

Río Pital

Abdón Calderón

González Suárez

Lascano

Montalvo

Machalilla

To ②

Atahualpa

Machalilla Nat Park Office

Eloy Alfaro

General Córdova

García Moreno

Ⓢ Banco Pichincha

Mariscal Sucre

To Montañita & Guayaquil

N

Not to scale

Where to stay 🛏
1 Itapoa
2 La Terraza
3 Mandála
4 Máxima
5 Ruta del Sol
6 Sol Inn
7 Victor Hugo
8 Villa Colombia

Restaurants 🍴
1 Bellitalia
2 Carmita
3 Patacón Pisao
4 Whale Café

About 5 km north of Puerto López, at Buena Vista, a dirt road to the east leads to **Agua Blanca** (park kiosk at entry). Here, 5 km from the main road, in the national park, amid hot, arid scrub, is a small village and a fine, small **archaeological museum** ① *0800-1800, US$5 for a 2-hr guided tour of the museum, ruins (a 45-min walk), funerary urns and sulphur lake, horses can be hired for the visit, camping is possible and there's a cabin and 1 very basic room for rent above the museum for US$5 per person; pick-up from Puerto López US$8,* containing some fascinating ceramics from the Manteño civilization. **San Sebastián**, 9 km from Agua Blanca, is in tropical moist forest at 800 m; orchids and birds can be seen and possibly Howler Monkeys. Although part of the national park, this area is administered by the Comuna de Agua Blanca, which charges an entry fee; you cannot go independently. It's five hours on foot or by horse. A tour to the forest costs US$40 per day including guide, horses and camping (minimum two people), otherwise lodging is with a family at extra cost.

About 24 km offshore is **Isla de la Plata**. Trips are popular because of the similarities with the Galápagos. Wildlife includes nesting colonies of Waved Albatross (April to November), frigates and three different booby species. Whales can be seen from June to

September, as well as sea lions. It is also a pre-Columbian site with substantial pottery finds, and there is good diving and snorkelling, as well as walks. Take a change of clothes, water, precautions against sun and seasickness (most agencies provide snorkelling equipment). You can only visit with a tour and staying overnight is not permitted.

Puerto López to Manta

North of Machalilla, the road forks at **Puerto Cayo**, where whale-watching tours may be organized July-August. One road follows the coast, partly through forested hills, passing Cabo San Lorenzo with its lighthouse. The other route heads inland through the trading centre of **Jipijapa** to **Montecristi**, below an imposing hill, 16 km before Manta. The town is renowned as the centre of the panama hat industry. Also produced are varied straw- and basketware, and wooden barrels which are strapped to donkeys for carrying water. Ask for José Chávez Franco, Rocafuerte 203, where you can see panama hats being made. Some 23 km east of Montecristi is **Portoviejo**, capital of Manabí province, a sweltering unsafe commercial city.

◉ Guayaquil to Puerto López listings

For hotel and restaurant price codes, and other relevant information, see Essentials.

● Where to stay

Salinas *p1085*

$$$-$$ El Carruaje, Malecón 517, T277 4282. Comfortable rooms, some with ocean view, all facilities, good restaurant, electric shower, a/c, fridge, parking.

$$ Francisco I and II, Enríquez Gallo y Rumiñahui, T277 4106; Malecón y Las Palmeras, T277 3751. Both are very nice, comfortable rooms, restaurant, a/c, fridge pool.

$$ Travel Suites, Av 5 Y C 13, T277 2856, maguerra@telconet.net. Modern, a/c, kitchenette with fridge, very good value in low season.

$ Las Olas, C 17 y Av Quinta, T277 2526, pachecobolivar@hotmail.com. Hot water, a/c, spotless, good value.

$ Porto Rapallo, Av Edmundo Azpiazu y 24 de Mayo, T277 1822. Modern place in a quiet area, hot water, a/c, cheaper with fan, good value.

Valdivia *p1086*

$$ Valdivia Ecolodge, at Km 40, just south of San Pedro, T291 6128. Screened cabins without walls in a nice location above the ocean, fresh and interesting.Restaurant, pool and access to nice bathing beach.

Manglaralto *p1086*

See also **Proyecto de Desarollo Ecoturístico Comunitario**, page 1086.

$$-$ Manglaralto Sunset, 1 block from the Plaza, T09-9440 9687, manglaralto_beach@ yahoo.com. Nice modern place, comfortable rooms with a/c, hammocks, cafeteria bar, electric shower, parking.

Montañita *p1086*

There are many places to stay in town; the quieter ones are at Montañita Punta. Prices are negotiable in low season.

$$$-$$ Balsa Surf Camp, 50 m from the beach in Montanita Punta, T206 0075, www.balsasurfcamp.com. Very nice spacious cabins with terrace, hammocks in garden, fan, parking, surf classes and rentals, French-Ecuadorean run. Recommended.

$$ La Casa del Sol, in Montañita Punta, T09-6863 4956, www.casadelsolmontanita.com. A/c, some rooms are dark, fan, restaurant/bar, surf classes and rentals, yoga drop-in (US$8).

$$ Pakaloro, in town at the end of C Guido Chiriboga, T206 0092. Modern 4-storey building with lots of wood, ample rooms with balcony and hammock, fan, shared kitchen, nice setting by the river, good value.

$$ Rosa Mística, Montañita Punta, T09-9798 8383, www.hostalrosamistica.net. Tranquil place, small rooms, cheaper ones away from beach, a/c, garden.

$$-$ La Casa Blanca, C Guido Chiriboga, T09-9918 2501. Wooden house, rooms with bath, mosquito nets, hammocks, good restaurant and bar.

$$-$ Las Palmeras, Malecón at south end of town, T09-8541 9938. Quiet, fan, laundry, English spoken.

$$-$ Sole Mare, on the beach at the north end of Montañita Punta, T206 0119. In a lovely setting on the beach, fan, garden, parking, English spoken, good value. Recommended.

Olón

$$$ Samai, 10 mins from town by taxi (US$5), T09-462 1316, www.samailodge. com. Rustic cabins in a natural setting, great views, restaurant/bar, pool, jacuzzi, advance booking required.

$$ Isramar, Av Sta. Lucia, ½ block from the beach, T278 8096. Rooms with bath and fan, small garden, restaurant/bar, friendly owner Doris Cevallos.

$$-$ La Mariposa, a block from the beach, near church, T09 8017 8357, www.la mariposahostal.com. 3-storey building, nice ocean views from top floor, Italian run, English and French also spoken, good value, opened in 2013.

Ayampe to Salango *p1086*
Ayampe

$$ Finca Punta Ayampe, south of other Ayampe hotels, Quito T09-9189 0982, www. fincapuntaayampe.com. Bamboo structure high on a hill with great ocean views, restaurant, hot water, mosquito nets, helpful staff.

$$-$ Cabañas de la Iguana, Ayampe, T08-9016 3825, www.hotelayampe.com. Cabins for 4, mosquito nets, cooking facilities, quiet, relaxed family atmosphere, knowledgeable and helpful, organizes excursions, good choice.

Las Tunas-Puerto Rico

$$$-$$ La Barquita, by Las Tunas, 4 km north of Ayampe, T05-234 7051, www.hosteriala barquita.com. Restaurant and bar are in a boat

on the beach with good ocean views, rooms with fan and mosquito nets, pool, nice garden, games, tours, Swiss-run.

Salango *p1086*

$$ Islamar, on a hilltop south of Salango, T09-9385 7580, Guayaquil T04-228 7001, www. hosteria-islamar.com.ec. Ample comfortable cabins, restaurant, lovely views of Isla Salango, camping in your own tent **$** pp, parking for motor-homes. Offers paragliding and diving, Swiss-Ecuadorean run, advance booking advised.

Puerto López *p1087, map p1087*

$$$ Victor Hugo, north along the beach, T230 0054, www.victorhugohotel.com.ec. Ample rooms with bamboo decor, balconies, pool.

$$ La Terraza, on hill overlooking town (moto-taxi US$0.50), T09-8855 4887, www.laterraza. de. Spacious cabins, great views over the bay, gardens, restaurant (only for guests), crystal-clear pool and jacuzzi, parking, German run.

$$ Mandála, Malecón at north end of the beach, T230 0181, www.hosteriamandala.info. Nice cabins decorated with art, fully wheelchair accessible, gorgeous tropical garden, good restaurant only for guests, fan, mosquito nets, games, music room, Swiss-Italian run, English spoken, knowledgeable owners. Highly recommended.

$$ Ruta del Sol, Malecón y Mariscal Sucre, T230 0236. Nice modern hotel near the pier, a/c, hot water, restaurant.

$$-$ Itapoa, on a lane off Abdón Calderón, between the Malecón and Montalvo, T09-9314 5894. Thatched cabins around large garden, hot water, cheaper in dorm, family run, English spoken.

$ Máxima, González Suárez y Machalilla, T230 0310, www.hotelmaxima.org. Cheaper with shared bath, mosquito nets, laundry and cooking facilities, parking, modern, English spoken, good value.

$ Sol Inn, Montalvo entre Eloy Alfaro y Lascano, T230 0248, hostal_solinn@hotmail. com. Bamboo and wood construction, private or shared bath, hot water, fan, laundry and cooking facilities, garden, pool table, popular, relaxed atmosphere.

$ Villa Colombia, García Moreno behind market, T230 0189, www.hostalvillacolombia.com. Rooms with hot water, fan, cooking facilities, mosquito nets, garden with hammocks, small parking area.

Puerto López to Manta p1088

There are other places to stay but many close out of season.

$ Luz de Luna, 5 km north of Puerto Cayo on the coastal road, T261 6031, Quito T02-240 0562, www.hosterialuzdeluna.com. On a clean beach, comfortable spacious rooms with balcony, full board **$$**, restaurant, cold water in cabins, shared hot showers available, fan and mosquito net, pool, disco, quieter in low season when discounts are available.

$ Puerto Cayo, south end of beach, Puerto Cayo, T261 6019, T09-9752 1538. Good restaurant, fan, comfortable rooms with hammocks and terrace overlooking the sea.

❼ Restaurants

Salinas p1085

A couple of blocks inland from the Malecón are food stalls serving good *ceviches* and freshly cooked seafood.

$$$ La Bella Italia, Malecón y C 17, near Hotel El Carruaje. Good pizza and international food.

$$$-$$ Amazon, Malecón near Banco de Guayaquil, T277 3671. Elegant upmarket eatery, grill and seafood specialties, good wine list.

$$ Oyster Catcher, Enríquez Gallo entre C 47 y C 50. Oct-May. Restaurant and bar, friendly place, safe oysters, enquire here about birdwatching tours with local expert Ben Haase.

$ El Mayquito, Av 2 y C 12. Simple place with very good food and friendly service.

Montañita p1086

$$$-$$ Tikilimbo, opposite Hotel Casa Blanca. Good quality, vegetarian dishes available.

$$ Hola Ola, in the center of town. Good international food and bar with some live music and dancing, popular.

$$ Marea Pizzeria Bar, 10 de Agosto y Av 2. Open evenings only. Real wood-oven pizza, very tasty. Recommended.

$$ Rocío, 10 de Agosto y Av 2, inside eponymous hotel. Good Mediterranean food.

Salango p1086

$$ El Delfín Mágico. Excellent, order meal before visiting museum because all food is cooked from scratch, very fresh and safe.

Puerto López p1087, map p1087

$$$ Bellitalia, north toward the river, T09-9617 5183. Mon-Sat 1800-2100. Excellent authentic Italian food, homemade pasta, attentive owners Vittorio and Elena. Reservations required. Highly recommended.

$$ Carmita, Malecón y General Córdova. Tasty fish and seafood, a Puerto López tradition. Try the *camarones en salsa de maní* (prawns in peanut sauce).

$$ Patacón Pisao, Gen Córdova, half a block from the malecón. Colombian food, giant *patacones* and *arepas*.

$$ Whale Café, towards the south end of the Malecón. Good pizza, stir-fried Asian dishes, Thai specialties, sandwiches, vegetarian salads, cakes and pies. Nice breakfast, famous for pancakes. US-run, open irregular hours, evenings only.

⓸ What to do

Salinas p1085

Ben Haase, at Museo de Ballenas, Av Enríquez Gallo 1109 entre C47 y C50, T277 7335, T09-9961 9257. Expert English speaking naturalist guide runs birdwatching tours to the Ecuasal salt ponds, US$50 for a small group. Also whale watching and trips to a sea lion colony.

Fernando Félix, T238 4560, T09-9827 4475. English-speaking marine biologist, can guide for whale watching and other nature trips, arrange in advance.

Montañita p1086

Surfboard rentals all over town from US$4 per hr, US$15 per day.

Ayampe to Salango p1086
Ayampe
Otra Ola, beside Cabañas de la Iguana, www. otraola.com. Surf lessons and board rental, Yoga and Spanish classes. Very nice enthusiastic owners, Vanessa and Ryan from Canada.

Puerto López p1087, map p1087
Whale watching Puerto López is a major centre for trips from Jun to Sep, with many more agencies than we can list; avoid touts on the street. Whales can also be seen elsewhere, but most reliably in Puerto López. There is a good fleet of small boats (16-20 passengers) running excursions, all have life jackets and a toilet, those with 2 engines are safer. All agencies offer the same tours for the same price. Beware touts offering cheap tours to "La Isla", they take you to Isla Salango not Isla de la Plata. In high season: US$40 pp for whale watching, Isla de la Plata and snorkelling, with a snack and drinks, US$25 for whale watching only (available Jun and Sep). Outside whale season, tours to Isla de la Plata and snorkelling cost US$35. Trips depart from the pier around 0800 and return around 1700. Agencies also offer tours to the mainland sites of the national park. A day tour combining Agua Blanca and Los Frailes costs US$25 pp plus US$5 entry fee. There are also hiking, birdwatching, kayaking, diving (be sure to use a reputable agency, there have been accidents) and other trips.
Aventuras La Plata, on malecón, T230 0189, www.aventuraslaplata.com. Whale watching tours.
Cercapez, at the Centro Comercial on the highway, T230 0173. All-inclusive trips to San Sebastián, with camping, local guide and food run US$40 pp per day.
Exploramar Diving, Malecón y Gral Córdova, T230 0123, www.exploradiving.com. Quito based, T02-256 3905. Have 2 boats for 8-16 people and their own compressor to fill dive tanks. PADI divemaster accompanies qualified divers to various sites, but advance notice is required, US$120 pp for all-inclusive diving day tour (2 tanks). Also offer diving lessons. Recommended.

Palo Santo, Malecón y Abdón Calderón, T230 0312, palosanto22@gmail.com. Whale watching tours.

⊖ Transport

Playas p1085
Bus Trans Posorja and Trans Villamil to **Guayaquil**, frequent, 2 hrs, US$2.60; taxi US$25.

Salinas p1085
Bus To **Guayaquil**, Coop Libertad Peninsular (CLP), María González y León Avilés, every 5 mins, US$3.70, 2½ hrs. For **Montañita**, **Puerto López** and points north, transfer at La Libertad (not safe, take a taxi between terminals) or Santa Elena. From La Libertad, every 30 mins to Puerto López, US$4, 2½ hrs; or catch a Guayaquil-Olón bus in Santa Elena.

Manglaralto p1086
Bus To **Santa Elena** and **La Libertad**, US$1.25, 1 hr. Transfer in Santa Elena for Guayaquil. To **Guayaquil** direct, see Olón schedule below. To **Puerto López**, 1 hr, US$1.50.

Montañita and Olón p1086
Bus Montañita is just a few mins south of Olón, from where CLP has direct buses to **Guayaquil** at 0445, 0545, 1000, 1300, 1500, 1700 (same schedule from Guayaquil), US$5.50, 3 hrs; or transfer in Santa Elena, US$1.50, 1½ hrs. To **Puerto López**, every 30 mins, US$2, 45 mins.

Puerto López p1087, map p1087
Mototaxis all over town, US$0.50.
Bus To **Santa Elena** or **La Libertad**, every 30 mins, US$4, 2½ hrs. To **Montañita** and **Manglaralto**, US$2.50, 1 hr. To **Guayaquil**, direct with Cooperativa Jipijapa via Jipijapa, 10 daily, US$4.50, 4 hrs; or transfer in Olón or Santa Elena. Pick-ups for hire to nearby sites are by the market, east of the highway. To/from **Manta**, direct, hourly, US$3, 2½ hrs; or transfer in Jipijapa. To **Quito** with Reina del Camino, office in front of market, daily 0800 and 2000; and **CA Aray**, 5 daily, 9 hrs, US$13; some buses go to Quitumbe others to their private stations.

Parque Nacional Machalilla *p1087*
Bus To Los Fraîles: take a bus towards Jipijapa (US$0.50), mototaxi (US$5), or a pick-up (US$8), and alight at the turn-off just south of the town of Machalilla, then walk for 30 mins. No transport back to Puerto López after 2000 (but check in advance). To Agua Blanca: take tour, a pick-up (US$7), mototaxi (US$10 return with 2 hrs wait) or a bus bound for Jipijapa (US$0.50); it is a hot walk of more than 1 hr from the turning to the village. To Isla de la Plata: the island can only be visited on a day trip. Many agencies offer tours, see Puerto López above.

Puerto López to Manta *p1088*
Bus From Jipijapa (terminal on the outskirts) to **Manglaralto** (2 hrs, US$2), to **Puerto López** (1 hr, US, 1, these go by Puerto Cayo), to **Manta** (1 hr, US$1), to **Quito** (10 hrs, US$9).

Montañita *p1086*
Banks Banco Bolivariano, and one other ATM (not always working, bring some cash). **Language courses** Montañita Spanish School, on the main road 50 m uphill outside the village, T206 0116, www.montanitaspanishschool.com.

Puerto López *p1087, map p1087*
Banks Banco Pichincha, large building at south end of Malecón, for ATM; only one in town, best bring some cash.
Language courses La Lengua, Abdón Calderón y García Moreno, east of the highway, T09-233 9316 or Quito T02-250 1271, www.la-lengua.com.

Manta and Bahía de Caráquez

Two quite different seaside places: Manta a rapidly growing port city, prospering on fishing and trade; Bahía de Caráquez a relaxed resort town and a pleasant place to spend a few days. It is proud of its 'eco' credentials. Just beyond Bahía, on the other side of the Río Chone estuary, is the village of Canoa, boasting some of the finest beaches in Ecuador.

Manta and around → *Phone code: 05. Colour map 11, B2. Population: 230,000.*

Ecuador's second port after Guayaquil is a busy town that sweeps round a bay filled with all sorts of boats. A constant sea breeze tempers the intense sun and makes the city's *malecones* pleasant places to stroll. At the gentrified west end of town is Playa Murciélago, a popular beach with wild surf (flags indicate whether it is safe to bathe), with good surfing from December to April. Here, the Malecón Escénico has a cluster of bars and seafood restaurants. It is a lively place especially at weekends, when there is good music, free beach aerobics and lots of action. Beyond El Murciélago, along the coastal road are San Mateo, Santa Marianita, San Lorenzo and Puerto Cayo, before reaching Machalilla and Puerto López. The **Museo Centro Cultural Manta** ① *Malecón y C 19, T262 6998, Mon-Fri 0900-1630, Sat-Sun 1000-1500, free*, has a small but excellent collection of archaeological pieces from seven different civilizations which flourished on the coast of Manabí between 3500 BC and AD 1530. Three bridges join the main town with its seedy neighbour, **Tarqui. Tourist offices**: Ministerio de Turismo ① *Paseo José María Egas 1034 (Av 3) y C 11, T262 2944, Mon-Fri 0900-1230, 1400-1700*; Dirección Municipal de Turismo ① *C9 y Av 4, T261 0171, Mon-Fri 0800-1700*; and Oficina de Información ULEAM ① *Malecón Escénico, T262 4099, daily 0900-1700*; all helpful and speak some English. Manta has public safety problems, enquire locally about the current situation.

Crucita → *Phone code: 05. Colour map 11, B2. Population: 14,900.*

A rapidly growing resort, 45 minutes by road from either Manta or Portoviejo, Crucita is busy at weekends and holidays when people flock here to enjoy ideal conditions for paragliding, hang-gliding and kite-surfing. The best season for flights is July to December. There is also an abundance of sea birds in the area. There are many restaurants serving fish and seafood along the seafront. A good one is **Motumbo**, try their *viche*, they also offer interesting tours and rent bikes.

North to Bahía

About 60 km northeast of Manta (30 km south of Bahía de Caráquez) are **San Clemente** and, 3 km south, **San Jacinto**. The ocean is magnificent but be wary of the strong undertow. Both get crowded during the holiday season and have a selection of *cabañas* and hotels. Some 3 km north of San Clemente is **Punta Charapotó**, a high promontory clad in dry tropical forest, above a lovely beach. Here are some nice out-of-the-way accommodations and an out-of-place upmarket property development.

Bahía de Caráquez and around → *Phone code: 05. Colour map 11, B2. Population: 26,400.*

Set on the southern shore at the seaward end of the Chone estuary, Bahía has an attractive riverfront laid out with parks along the Malecón which goes right around the point to the ocean side. The beaches in town are nothing special, but there are excellent beaches nearby between San Vicente and Canoa and at Punta Bellaca (the town is busiest July-August). Bahía has declared itself an 'eco-city', with recycling projects, organic gardens and ecoclubs. Tricycle rickshaws called 'eco-taxis' are a popular form of local transport. Information about the eco-city concept can be obtained from **Río Muchacho Organic Farm** in Canoa (page 1097) or the **Planet Drum Foundation**, www.planetdrum.org. **Tourist offices**: Ministerio de Turismo, T269 1124, and **Dirección Municipal**, T269 1044, www.bahiadecaraquez.com, both at Bolívar y Padre Laennen, Mon-Fri 0830-1300, 1430-1730, Sat 0000-1300. The **Museo Bahía de Caráquez** ① *Malecón Alberto Santos y Aguilera, T269 2285, Tue-Sat 0830-1630, free*, has an interesting collection of archaeological artefacts from prehispanic coastal cultures, a life-size balsa raft and modern sculpture. Bahía is a port for international yachts, with good service at **Puerto Amistad** ① *T269 3112.*

The Río Chone estuary has several islands with mangrove forest. The area is rich in birdlife, and dolphins may also be seen. **Isla Corazón** has a boardwalk through an area of protected mangrove forest and there are bird colonies at the end of the island which can only be accessed by boat. The village of **Puerto Portovelo** is involved in mangrove reforestation and runs an eco-tourism project (tour with *guía nativo* US$6 per person). You can visit independently, taking a Chone-bound bus from San Vicente or with an agency. Visits here are tide-sensitive, so even if you go independently, it is best to check with the agencies about the best time to visit. Inland near Chone is **La Segua** wetland, very rich in birds; Bahía agencies offer tours here. **Saiananda** ① *5 km from Bahía along the bay, T239 8331, owner Alfredo Harmsen, biologist, reached by taxi or any bus heading out of town, US$2*, is a private park with extensive areas of reforestation and a large collection of animals, a cactus garden and spiritual centre. Also offer first-class accommodation (**$$** including breakfast) and vegetarian meals served in an exquisite dining area over the water.

San Vicente and Canoa → *Phone code: 05. Colour map 11, B2.*

On the north side of the Río Chone, **San Vicente** is reached from Bahía de Caráquez by the longest bridge in Ecuador. Some 17 km beyond, **Canoa**, once a quiet fishing village with a splendid 200-m-wide beach, has grown rapidly and is increasingly popular with Ecuadorean and foreign tourists. It has lost some of its charm along the way, but it is still pleasant on weekdays, crowded, noisy and dirty on weekends and especially holidays. The choice of accommodation and restaurants is very good. The beautiful beach between San Vicente and Canoa is a good walk, horse or bike ride. Horses and bicycles can be hired through several hotels. Surfing is good, particularly during the wet season, December to April. In the dry season there is good wind for windsurfing. Canoa is also a good place for hang-gliding and paragliding. Tents for shade and chairs are rented at the beach for US$3 a day. About 10 km north of Canoa, the **Río Muchacho organic farm** (www.riomuchacho.com, see What to do, page 1097) accepts visitors and volunteers, it's an eye-opener to rural coastal (*montubio*) culture and to organic farming.

North to Pedernales → *Phone code: 05. Colour map 11, A2. Population: 35,600.*

The coastal road cuts across Cabo Pasado to **Jama** (1½ hours; cabins and several *hostales*), then runs parallel to the beach past coconut groves and shrimp hatcheries, inland across some low hills and across the Equator to **Pedernales**, a market town and crossroads with nice undeveloped beaches to the north. In town, where beaches are less attractive, they cater to the *quiteño* holiday market. A poor unpaved road goes north along the shore to Cojimíes. The main coastal road, fully paved, goes north to Chamanga, El Salto and Esmeraldas. Another important road goes inland to El Carmen, where it divides: one branch to Santo Domingo de los Tsáchilas, another to La Concordia. The latter is the most direct route to Quito.

Santo Domingo de los Tsáchilas → *Phone code: 02. Colour map 11, A3. Population: 319,000.*

In the hills above the western lowlands, Santo Domingo, 129 km from Quito, is an important commercial centre and transport hub. It is capital of the eponymous province. The city is noisy and dangerous, caution is recommended at all times in the market areas, including the pedestrian walkway along 3 de Julio and in peripheral neighbourhoods. Sunday is market day, shops and banks close Monday instead. It was known as 'Santo Domingo de los Colorados', a reference to the traditional red hair dye, made with *achiote* (annatto), worn by the indigenous Tsáchila men. Today the Tsáchila only wear their indigenous dress on special occasions. There are less than 2000 Tsáchilas left, living in eight communities off the roads leading from Santo Domingo towards the coast. Their lands make up a reserve of some 8000 ha. Visitors interested in their culture are welcome at the **Complejo Turístico Huapilú**, in the Comunidad Chigüilpe, where there is a small but interesting museum (contributions expected). Access is via the turn-off east at Km 7 on the road to Quevedo, from where it is 4 km. Tours are run by travel agencies in town. The Santo Domingo area also offers opportunities for nature trips and sports activities, such as rafting. **Cámara de Turismo** ⓘ *Río Mulaute y Av Quito, T275 2146, Mon-Fri 0830-1300, 1430-1800, English spoken.*

◉ Manta and Bahía de Caráquez listings

For hotel and restaurant price codes, and other relevant information, see Essentials.

● Where to stay

Manta and around *p1092*
All streets have numbers; those above 100 are in Tarqui (those above C110 are not safe).
$$$$ Oro Verde, Malecón y C 23, T262 9200, www.oroverdehotels.com. Includes buffet breakfast, restaurant, pool, all luxuries.
$$$ Vistalmar, C M1 y Av 24B, at Playa Murciélago, T262 1671. Exclusive hotel over-looking the ocean. Ample cabins and suites

tastefully decorated with art, a/c, pool, cabins have kitchenettes, gardens by the sea. A place for a honeymoon.
$$ Manakin, C 20 y Av 12, T262 0413. A/c, comfortable rooms, small patio, nice common areas.
$$ YorMar, Av 14 entre C 19 y C 20, T262 4375. Nice rooms with small kitchenette and patio, electric shower, a/c, parking.
$$-$ Donkey Den, in Santa Marianita, 20 mins south of Manta, T09-9723 2026, www.donkeydenguesthouse.com. Nice rooms right on the beach where kite-surfing is popular, private or shared bath, dorm for 5 US$15 pp,

cooking facilities, breakfast available, popular with US expats, taxi from Manta US$10.
$ Centenario, C 11 #602 y Av 5, enquire at nearby Lavamatic Laundry, T262 9245, josesanmartin@hotmail.com. Pleasant hostel in a nicely refurbished old home in the centre of town. Shared bath, hot water, fan, cooking facilities, nice views, quiet location, good value.

Tarqui
$$-$ Chávez Inn, Av 106 y C 106, T262 1019. Modern hotel, a/c, fridge, small bright rooms.

Crucita *p1092*
$ Cruzita, towards the south end of beach, T234 0068. Very nice hostel right on the beach with great views, meals on request, cold water, fan, small pool, use of kitchen in the evening, parking, good value. Owner Raul Tobar offers paragliding flights and lessons. Recommended.
$ Hostal Voladores, at south end of beach, T234 0200, www.parapentecrucita.com. Simple but nice, restaurant, private or shared bath, hot water, small pool, sea kayaks available. Owner Luis Tobar offers paragliding flights and lessons.
$ Italia, C 9 y 25 de Mayo, at the south end of town, T234 0291. Pleasant place, restaurant serves pizza, electric shower, small pool, parking, nice patio.

North to Bahía *p1093*
$$ Peñón del Sol, on the hillside near Punta Charapotó, T09-9941 4149, penondelsol@hotmail.com. Located on a 250 ha dry tropical forest reserve, meals on request, shared bath, cold water, great views, camping possible.
$$-$ Hotel San Jacinto, on the beach between San Jacinto and San Clemente, T261 5516, www.hotelsanjacinto.com. Pleasant location right by the ocean, restaurant, hot water, fan, older place gradually being refurbished and looking good.
$ Sabor de Bamboo, on the ocean side of the road to Punta Charapotó, T09-8024 3562. Nice simple wooden cabins with sea breeze, cold water, restaurant and bar, music on weekends, wonderfully relaxed place, friendly owner Meier, German and English spoken.

Bahía de Caráquez *p1093*
$$$ La Piedra, Circunvalación near Bolívar, T269 0154, www.hotellapiedra.com. Modern hotel with access to the beach and lovely views, good expensive restaurant, a/c, pool (US$2 for non-guests, only in low season), good service, bicycle rentals for guests.
$$-$ La Herradura, Bolívar e Hidalgo, T269 0446, www.laherradurahotel.com. Older well-maintained hotel, restaurant, a/c, cheaper with fan and cold water, nice common areas, cheaper rooms are good value.
$ Bahía Hotel, Malecón y Vinueza. A variety of different rooms, those at the back are nicer, fan, parking.
$ Coco Bongo, Cecilio Intriago y Arenas, T09-8544 0978. Nice hostel with a pleasant atmosphere, private bath, cheaper in dorm, breakfast available, electric shower, ceiling fan, mosquito nets, cooking facilities, popular.

Canoa *p1093*
There are over 60 hotels in Canoa.
$$$ Hostería Canoa, 1 km south of town, T261 6380, www.hosteriacanoa.com. Comfortable cabins and rooms, good restaurant and bar, a/c, pool, sauna, whirlpool.
$$ La Vista, on the beach towards the south end of town, T09-9228 8995. All rooms have balconies to the sea, palm garden with hammocks, good value. Recommended.
$ Baloo, on the beach at south end of the village, T261 6355, www.baloo-canoa.com. Wood and bamboo cabins, restaurant, private or shared bath, hot water, British run.
$ Bambú, on the beach just north of C Principal, T09-8926 5225, www.hotelbambuecuador.com. Pleasant location and atmosphere. A variety of rooms and prices, good restaurant including vegetarian options, private or shared bath, also dorm, camping possible (US$3.50 pp with your own tent), hot water, fan, surfing classes and board rentals. Dutch-Ecuadorean owned, very popular and recommended.
$ Coco Loco, on the beach toward the south end of town, T09-8764 6459, www.hostalcocoloco.weebly.com. Pleasant breezy hotel with nice views, café serves breakfast and snacks,

bar, private or shared bath, also dorm, hot showers, cooking facilities, surfboard rentals, excellent horse riding, English spoken, popular.

North to Pedernales *p1094*
Jama
$$$ Samvara, 300 m from the highway, turnoff 13 km north of Jama, T09-9128 2278, www. samvara-ecolodge.com. Thatched cabins on 6 ha of land, includes breakfast and dinner, beach and pool, lovely secluded setting, camping possible (US$15 pp in on-site tents, US$8 pp in your own tent), Swiss-Ecuadorean run.

$$$-$$ Punta Prieta Guest House, by Punta Prieta, T09-9225 9146, Quito T02-286 2986, www.puntaprieta.com. Gorgeous setting on a headland high above the ocean with access to pristine beaches. Meals available, comfortable cabins with fridge, suites and rooms with shared bath, balcony with hammocks, nice grounds.

$ Palo Santo, C Melchor Cevallos, by the river in Jama town, T241 0441, luchincevallos@hotmail. com. Thatched cabins on pleasant grounds, cold water, ceiling fan.

Pedernales
There are many other hotels in all price ranges.
$$ Agua Marina, Jaime Roldós 413 y Velasco Ibarra, T268 0491. Modern hotel, cafeteria, a/c, pool, parking.

$$ Cocosolo, on a secluded beach 20 km north of Pedernales (pickups from main park US$1, 30 mins), T09-9921 5078. A lovely hideaway set among palms. Cabins and rooms, camping possible, restaurant, horses for hire, French and English spoken.

$ Mr John, Plaza Acosta y Malecón, 1 block from the beach, T268 0235. Modern hotel, cold water, fan, parking, rooms facing the beach can be noisy at weekends. Good value.

Santo Domingo de los Tsáchilas *p1094*
$$$ Tinalandia, 16 km from Santo Domingo, on the road to Quito, poorly signposted, look for a large rock painted white; T09-9946 7741, in Quito T244 9028, www.tinalandia.com. Includes full board, nice chalets in cloud forest

reserve, great food, spring-fed pool, good birdwatching, entry US$10 for non-guests.
$$$ Zaracay, Av Quito 1639, 1.5 km from the centre, T275 0316, www.hotelzaracay.com. Restaurant, gardens and swimming pool, parking, good rooms and service. Advance booking advised, especially on weekends.

$$-$ Royal Class, Cadmo Zambrano y César López, near the bus station, T274 3348. Multi-storey modern hotel, a/c, cheaper with fan, parking, the best choice near the bus station, reasonably quiet location, good value.

$ Safiro Internacional, 29 de Mayo 800 y Loja, T276 0706. Comfortable modern hotel, cafeteria, hot water, a/c, good value.

Restaurants

Manta and around *p1092*
Restaurants on Malecón Escénico serve local seafood.
$$ Club Ejecutivo, Av 2 y C 12, top of Banco Pichincha building. First class food and service, great view.

$$ El Marino, Malecón y C 110, Tarqui. Open for lunch only. Classic fish and seafood restaurant, for *ceviches*, *sopa marinera* and other delicacies.

$ Café Trovador, Av 3 y C 11, Paseo José María Egas. Closes 2100. Very good coffee, snacks, sandwiches and economical set lunches.

$ Peberes, Av 1 entre C 13 y C 14. Good quality and set lunch, popular with locals.

Bahía de Caráquez *p1093*
$$ Puerto Amistad, on the pier at Malecón y Vinueza. Mon-Sat 1200-2400. Nice setting over the water, international food and atmosphere, popular with yachties.

$$-$ Arena-Bar Pizzería, Riofrío entre Bolívar y Montúfar, T269 2024. Daily 1700-2400. Restaurant/bar serving good pizza, salads and other dishes, nice atmosphere, also take-away and delivery service. Recommended.

$$-$ Muelle Uno, by the pier where canoes leave for San Vicente. Daily 1000-2400. Good grill and seafood, lovely setting over the water.

$ Doña Luca, Cecilio Intriago y Sergio Plaza, towards the tip of the peninsula. Daily 0800-

1800. Simple little place serving excellent local fare, *ceviches*, *desayuno manabita* (a wholesome breakfast), and set lunches. Friendly service, recommended.

Canoa *p1093*
$$ Amalur, behind the soccer field. Daily 1200-2100. Fresh seafood and authentic Basque specialties, try the *lomo de chancho adobado*, attentive service, modest portions.
$$-$ Surf Shak, at the beach. Daily 0800-2400. Good for pizza, burgers and breakfast, best coffee in town, Wi-Fi US$1 per hr, popular hangout for surfers, English spoken.
$ Oasis, C Principal, 2 blocks from the beach. Good set meals, tasty and abundant.

Santo Domingo de los Tsáchilas *p1094*
$$$ Parrilladas Che Luis, on the road to Quito. Tue-Sun 1200-2300. One of the best grills in town.
$$-$ La Cocina de Consuelo, Av Quito y Chimbo. 0700-2230, Sun and Mon to 1700. Very good à la carte dishes and 4-course set meals.

What to do

Manta and around *p1092*
Delgado Travel, Av 6 y C 13, T262 2813, vtdelgad@hotmail.com. City and regional tours, whale watching trips, Parque Nacional Machalilla, run *Hostería San Antonio* at El Aromo, 15 km south of Manta.

Canoa *p1093*
Canoa Thrills, at the beach next to Surf Shak. Surfing tours and lessons, sea kayaking. Also rent boards and bikes. English spoken.
Río Muchacho Organic Farm, J Santos y Av 3 de Noviembre, T258 8184, www.riomuchacho. com. Bookings for the organic farm and eco-city tours. Hikes from Canoa to Río Muchacho and around Río Muchacho. Knowledgeable and helpful with local information. Recommended.
Wings and Waves, T09-8519 8507 or ask around for Greg. Paragliding flights and lessons.

Santo Domingo de los Tsáchilas *p1094*
Turismo Zaracay, 29 de Mayo y Cocaniguas, T275 0546, zaratur@andinanet.net. Tours to Tsáchila commune, minimum 5 persons; rafting, fishing trips, bird/butterfly watching tours, English spoken.

Transport

Manta and around *p1092*
Air Eloy Alfaro airport. TAME (T390 5052), Aerogal (T262 8899) and LAN to **Quito** several daily.
Bus Most buses leave from the terminal on C 7 y Av 8 in the centre. A couple of companies have their own private terminals nearby. To **Quito**, 9 hrs, US$7-8, some go to Quitumbe, others continue to private terminals further north. **Guayaquil**, 4 hrs, US$4, hourly. **Esmeraldas**, 3 daily, 10 hrs, US$8. **Santo Domingo**, 7 hrs, US$6. **Portoviejo**, 45 mins, US$0.75, every 10 mins. **Jipijapa**, 1 hr, US$1, every 20 mins. **Bahía de Caráquez**, 3 hrs, US$3, hourly.

Crucita *p1092*
Bus Run along the Malecón. There is frequent service to **Portoviejo**, US$1, 1 hr and **Manta**, US$1.20, 1½ hrs.

North to Bahía *p1093*
Bus From San Clemente to **Portoviejo**, every 15 mins, US$1.25, 1¼ hrs. To **Bahía de Caráquez**, US$0.50, 30 mins, a few start in San Clemente in the morning or wait for a through bus at the highway. Mototaxis from San Clemente to Punta Charapotó, US$0.50.

Bahía de Caráquez *p1093*
Boat Motorized canoes (*lanchas* or *pangas*) cross the estuary to **San Vicente**, from the dock opposite C Ante, US$0.30.
Bus The Terminal Terrestre is at the entrance to town. To **Quito**, Reina del Camino, regular service to Quitumbe at 0620 and 2145 (from Quitumbe 1030, 2300), 8 hrs, US$7.50, Ejecutivo to their own station (18 de Septiembre y Larrea) at 0800 and 2215 (from Quito 1200, 2330), US$10. To **Santo Domingo**, 5 hrs,

US$5-7.50. To **Guayaquil**, every 30 mins, 6 hrs, US$6-7. To **Portoviejo**, 2 hrs, US$2. To **Manta**, 3 hrs. US$3. To **Puerto López**, change in Manta, Portoviejo or Jipijapa.

San Vicente and Canoa *p1093*
San Vicente
Bus The terminal is by the market on the San Isidro road, take an eco-taxi tricycle to get there. To **Portoviejo**, US$2.50, 2½ hrs. To **Guayaquil**, US$6, 6½ hrs. To **Quito** (Quitumbe), with **Reina del Camino** at 1000 and 2100 (from Quitimbe 0830 and 2100), US$7.50, 7½ hrs, more services from Bahía, or take a bus to **Pedernales** US$3, 2½ hrs and change. For **Esmeraldas** and northern beaches, take a bus to **Chamanga**, at 0810, 1430 or 1700, US$4.50, 3¼ hrs, and transfer there.

Canoa
Bus To/from **San Vicente**, every 30 mins, 0600-1900, 30 mins, US$0.50; taxi US$5. Taxi to/from Bahía de Caráquez, US$7. To **Pedernales**, hourly 0600-1800, 2 hrs, US$2.50. To **Quevedo**, 4 daily, where you can get a bus to **Quilotoa** and **Latacunga**. To **Quito**, direct bus nightly or transfer in Pedernales or San Vicente.

Pedernales *p1094*
Bus To **Santo Domingo**, every 15 mins, 3½ hrs, US$4, transfer to Quito. To **Quito** (Quitumbe) direct **Trans Vencedores**, 7 daily via Santo Domingo, US$6.25, 5 hrs; also starting in Jama at 0815 and 2300. To **Chamanga**, hourly 0600-1700, 1½ hrs, US$2, change there for **Esmeraldas**, 3½ hrs, US$3.50. To **Bahía de Caráquez**, shared vans from Plaza Acosta 121 y Robles, T268 1019, 7 daily,US$4.50.

Santo Domingo de los Tsáchilas *p1094*
Bus The bus terminal is on Av Abraham Calazacón, at the north end of town, along the city's bypass. Long distance buses do not enter the city. Taxi downtown, US$1, bus US$0.25. As it is a very important transportation centre, you can get buses going everywhere in the country. To **Quito** via Alóag US$3, 3 hrs; via San Miguel de los Bancos, 5 hrs; also **Sudamericana Taxis**, Cocaniguas y 29 de Mayo, p 2, T275 2567, door to door shared taxi service, 6 daily 0500-1700, US$13, 3 hrs. To **Ambato** US$4, 4 hrs. To **Loja** US$13, 11 hrs. To **Guayaquil** US$5, 5 hrs. To **Huaquillas** US$10, 10 hrs, via Guayaquil. To **Esmeraldas** US$3, 3 hrs. To **Atacames**, US$4, 4hrs. To **Manta** US$6, 7 hrs. To **Bahía de Caráquez** US$5, 6 hrs. To **Pedernales** US$4, 3½ hrs.

Directory

Manta and around *p1092*
Banks Many banks with ATMs in the centre. **Language courses** Academia Sur Pacífico, Av 24 y C 15, Edif Barre, p3, T261 0838, www.surpacifico.k12.ec.

Bahía de Caráquez *p1093*
Banks Banco de Guayaquil, Av Bolívar y Riofrío. ATM.

San Vicente and Canoa *p1093*
Banks Banco Pichincha in San Vicente for ATM. No ATMs in Canoa. **Language courses** Sundown, at Sundown Inn, in Canoa, on the beach, 3 km toward San Vicente, contact Juan Carlos, T09-9143 6343, www.ecuadorbeach.com, US$7 per hr.

Northern lowlands

A mixture of palm lined beaches, mangroves (where not destroyed for shrimp production), tropical rainforests, Afro-Ecuadorean and Cayapa Indian communities characterize this part of Ecuador's Pacific lowlands as they stretch north to the Colombian border.

North to Atacames
North of Pedernales the coastal highway veers northeast, going slightly inland, then crosses into the province of Esmeraldas near **Chamanga** (*San José de Chamanga, Population: 4400*),

a village with houses built on stilts on the freshwater estuary. This is a good spot from which to explore the nearby mangroves, there is one basic *residencial* and frequent buses north and south. Town is 1 km from the highway. Inland, and spanning the provincial border is the **Reserva Ecológica Mache-Chindul**, a dry forest reserve. North of Chamanga by 31 km and 7 km from the main road along a poor side road is **Mompiche** with a lovely beach and one of Ecuador's best surfing spots. The town and surroundings have been affected by the opening of an international resort complex and holiday real-estate development 2 km south at Punta Portete. The main road continues through El Salto (reported unsafe), the crossroads for **Muisne**, a town on an island with a beach (strong underow), a selection of hostels and a mangrove protection group which offers tours.

The fishing village of **Tonchigüe** is 25 km north of El Salto. South of it, a paved road goes west and follows the shore to **Punta Galera**, along the way is the secluded beach of **Playa Escondida** (see Where to stay below). Northeast of Tonchigüe by 3 km is Playa de **Same**, with a beautiful, long, clean, grey sandy beach, safe for swimming. The accommodation here is mostly upmarket, intended for wealthy Quiteños, but it is wonderfully quiet in the low season. There is good birdwatching in the lagoon behind the beach and some of the hotels offer whale watching tours in season. Ten kilometres east of Same and 4 km west of Atacames, is **Súa**, a friendly little beach resort, set in a beautiful bay. It gets noisy on weekends and the July to September high season, but is otherwise tranquil.

Atacames → *Phone code: 06. Colour map 11, A2. Population: 18,700.*

One of the main resorts on the Ecuadorean coast, Atacames, 30 km southwest of Esmeraldas, is a real 24-hour party town during the high season (July-September), at weekends and national holidays. Head instead for Súa or Playa Escondida (see above) if you want peace and quiet. Most hotels are on a peninsula between the Río Atacames and the ocean. The main park, most services and the bus stops are south of the river. Information from **Oficina Municipal de Turismo** ① *on the road into town from Esmeraldas, T273 1912, Mon-Fri 0800-1230, 1330-1600.*

Camping on the beach is unsafe. Do not walk along the beach from Atacames to Súa, as there is a risk of mugging. Also the sea can be very dangerous, there is a powerful undertow and people have drowned.

Esmeraldas → *Phone code: 06. Colour map 11, A2. Population: 186,000.*

Capital of the eponymous province, Esmeraldas is a place to learn about Afro-Ecuadorean culture and some visitors enjoy its very relaxed swinging atmosphere. Marimba groups can be seen practising in town, enquire about schedules at the tourist office. Ceramics from La Tolita culture (see below) are found at the **Museo y Centro Cultural Esmeraldas** ① *Bolívar y Piedrahita, US$1, English explanations*. At the **Centro Cultural Afro** ① *Malecón y J Montalvo, T272 7076, Tue-Sun 0900-1630, free, English explanations*, you can see 'La Ruta del Esclavo', an exhibit showing the harsh history of Afro-Ecuadoreans brought as slaves to Ecuador (some English explanations). Despite its wealth in natural resources, Esmeraldas is among the poorest provinces in the country. Shrimp farming has destroyed much mangrove, and timber exports are decimating Ecuador's last Pacific rainforest. **Tourist office: Ministerio de Turismo** ① *Bolívar y Ricaurte, Edif Cámara de Turismo, p3, T271 1370, Mon-Fri 0900-1200, 1500-1700.* Mosquitoes and malaria are a serious problem throughout Esmeraldas province, especially in the rainy season (January to May). Most *residenciales* provide mosquito nets (*toldos* or *mosquiteros*), or buy one in the market near the bus station. Town suffers from water shortages and is not safe.

North of Esmeraldas

From Esmeraldas, the coastal road goes northeast to Camarones and Río Verde, with a nice beach, from where it goes east to **Las Peñas**, once a sleepy seaside village with a nice wide beach, now a holiday resort. With a paved highway from Ibarra, Las Peñas is the closest beach to any highland capital, only four hours by bus. Ibarreños pack the place on weekends and holidays. From Las Peñas, a secondary road follows the shore north to **La Tola** (122 km from Esmeraldas) where you can catch a launch to Limones. Here the shoreline changes from sandy beaches to mangrove swamp; the wildlife is varied and spectacular, especially the birds. The tallest mangrove trees in the world (63.7 m) are found by **Majagual** to the south. In the village of **Olmedo**, just northwest of La Tola, the Unión de Mujeres runs an ecotourism project; they have accommodation, cheap meals and tours in the area. La Tola itself is not a pleasant place to stay, women especially may be harassed; Olmedo is a better option, see Where to stay below. To the northeast of La Tola and on an island on the northern shore of the Río Cayapas is **La Tolita**, a small, poor village, where the culture of the same name thrived between 300 BC and AD 700. Many remains have been found here, several burial mounds remain to be explored and looters continue to take out artefacts to sell.

Limones (also known as Valdez) is the focus of traffic downriver from much of northern Esmeraldas Province, where bananas from the Río Santiago are sent to Esmeraldas for export. The Cayapa Indians live up the Río Cayapas and can sometimes be seen in Limones, especially during the crowded weekend market, but they are more frequently seen at Borbón (see below). Two shops in Limones sell the very attractive Cayapa basketry. There has been a great deal of migration from neighbouring Colombia to the Limones, Borbón and San Lorenzo areas. Smuggling, including drugs, is big business and there are occasional searches by the authorities. Mosquito-borne diseases are another hazard, always take a net. Accommodation is basic.

Borbón → *Phone code: 06. Colour map 11, A2. Population: 8100.*

From Las Peñas, the coastal highway runs inland to **Borbón**, upriver from La Tola, at the confluence of the Cayapas and Santiago rivers, a lively, dirty, busy and somewhat dangerous place, with a high rate of malaria. It is a centre of the timber industry that is destroying the last rainforests of the Ecuadorean coast. Ask for Papá Roncón, the King of Marimba, who, for a beer or two, will put on a one-man show. Cayapa handicrafts are sold in town and at the road junction outside town, Afro musical instruments are found at **Artesanía** on 5 de Agosto y Valdez. The local fiestas with marimba music and other Afro-Ecuadorean traditions are held the first week of September. The bakery across from the church is good for breakfast. Sra Marcia, one block from the Malecón serves good regional food.

Upriver from Borbón are Cayapa or Chachi Indian villages and Afro-Ecuadorean communities, you will see the Chachis passing in their canoes and in their open long-houses on the shore. To visit these villages, arrangements can be made through **Hostal Brisas del Río**. Alternatively, around 0700, canoes arrive at the malecón in Borbón and return to their homes around 1000. You can arrange to go with them. For any independent travel in this area take a mosquito net, food and a means of water purification. Upriver along the Río Cayapas, above its confluence with the Río Onzole, are the villages of **Pichiyacu** and **Santa María** (two hours). Beyond is **Zapallo Grande**, a friendly place with many gardens (3½ hours) and **San Miguel**, beautifully situated on a hill at the confluence of the San Miguel and Cayapas rivers (four hours). Along this river are a couple of lodges, the ride is not comfortable but it is an interesting trip. San Miguel is the access to the lowland section of **Reserva Ecológica Cotacachi-Cayapas**, about 30 minutes upriver. The community also runs its own 1200 ha forest reserve, abutting on the national reserve, and has an ecotourism project with accommodation and guiding service.

From Borbón, the costal road goes northeast towards **Calderón** where it meets the Ibarra-San Lorenzo road. Along the way, by the Río Santiago, are the nature reserves of **Humedales de Yalare**, accessed from **Maldonado**, and **Playa de Oro** (see below). From Calderón, the two roads run together for a few kilometres before the costal road turns north and ends at **Mataje** on the border with Colombia. The road from Ibarra continues to San Lorenzo.

San Lorenzo → *Phone code: 06. Colour map 1a, A3. Population: 28,500.*

The hot, humid town of San Lorenzo stands on the Bahía del Pailón, which is characterized by a maze of canals. It is a good place to experience the Afro-Ecuadorean culture including marimba music and dances. There is a local festival 6-10 August and groups practise throughout the year; ask around. At the seaward end of the bay are several beaches without facilities, including San Pedro (one hour away) and Palma Real (1¾ hours). On weekends canoes go to the beaches around 0700-0800 and 1400-1500, US$3. Note that this area is close to the Colombian border and it may not be safe, enquire with the Navy (Marina). From San Lorenzo you can visit several natural areas; launches can be hired for excursions (see Transport, page 1104) and trips are organized by **Bosque de Paz** (page 1021). There are mangroves at **Reserva Ecológica Cayapas-Mataje**, which protects islands in the estuary northwest of town. **Reserva Playa de Oro** ⓘ *www.touchthejungle. org, see Where to stay, page 1103*, has 10,406 ha of Chocó rainforest, rich in wildlife, along the Río Santiago. Access is from **Selva Alegre** (a couple of basic *residenciales*), off the road to Borbón.

Border with Colombia: San Lorenzo-Tumaco

The Río Mataje is the border with Colombia. From San Lorenzo, the port of Tumaco in Colombia can be reached by a combination of boat and land transport. Because this is a most unsafe region, travellers are advised not to enter Colombia at this border. Go to Tulcán and Ipiales instead.

ⓦ Northern lowlands listings

For hotel and restaurant price codes, and other relevant information, see Essentials.

ⓦ Where to stay

North to Atacames *p1098*
Mompiche
There are several economical places in the town. Camping on the beach is not safe.
$$-$ Iruña, east along the beach, vehicle access only at low tide, T09-9497 5846, teremompiche@yahoo.com. A lovely secluded hideaway with cabins of different sizes and prices. Large terraces and hammocks, meals on request, fan, nice gardens.
$ Gabeal, 300 m east of town, T09-9969 6543. Lovely quiet place with ample grounds and beachfront. Bamboo construction with ocean views, balconies, small rooms and cabins, restaurant serves breakfast and lunch in season, discounts in low season.

Tonchigüe to Punta Galera
$$ Playa Escondida, 10 km west of Tonchigüe and 6 km east of Punta Galera, T273 3106, www.playaescondida.com.ec. A charming beach hideaway set in 100 ha with 500 m beachfront stretching back to dry tropical forest. Run by Canadian Judith Barett on an ecologically sound basis. Nice rustic cabins overlooking a lovely little bay, excellent restaurant (**$$$** with full board), private showers, shared composting toilets, camping US$5 pp, good birdwatching, swimming and walking along the beach at low tide. Also offers volunteer opportunities.

Same
$$$-$$ Cabañas Isla del Sol, at south end of beach, T273 3470, www.cabanasisladelsol.com. Comfortable cabins, meals available in high season, electric shower, a/c, cheaper with fan, pool, boat tours and whale watching in season.

$$Casa de Amigos, by the entrance to the beach, T247 0102. Restaurant, electric shower, a/c, nice rooms with balconies, use of kayaks and surfboards included, English and German spoken.
$La Terraza, on the beach, T247 0320, pepo@hotmail.es. Nice rooms and cabins for 3-4 with balconies, hammocks and large terrace, spacious, hot water, a/c, fan, mosquito net, some rooms have fridge, good restaurant open in season, Spanish run.

Súa
$Buganvillas, on the beach, T273 1008. Nice, room 10 has the best views, pool, helpful owners.
$Chagra Ramos, on the beach, T273 1006. Ageing hotel with balconies overlooking the beach, restaurant, cold water, fan, parking, good service.
$Sol de Súa, across from beach toward west end of town, T273 1021. Cold water, ceiling fan, mosquito net, simple cabins on ample grounds with palm trees, camping possible.

Atacames *p1099*
Prices rise on holiday weekends, discounts may be available in low season. There are many more hotels than we can list.
$$$Juan Sebastián, towards the east end of the beach, T273 1049. Large upmarket hotel with cabins and suites, restaurant, a/c, 3 pools and small spa (US$10 for non-guests), fridge, parking, popular with Quiteños.
$$Carluz, behind the stadium, T273 1456. Nice hotel in a good, quiet location. Comfortable suites for 4 and apartments for 6, good restaurant, a/c, fan, pool, fridge, parking.
$$Cielo Azul, towards the west end of the beach, near the stadium, T273 1813, www.hotelcieloazul.com. Restaurant, fan, pool, fridge, rooms with balconies and hammocks, comfortable and very good.
$$-$Tahiti, toward east end of beach, T276 0085, lucybritogarcia@yahoo.com.ar. Good restaurant, cheaper with cold water, pool, parking, ample grounds.

$Chill Inn, Los Ostiones y Malecón, T276 0477, www.chillinnecuador.com. Small backpacker's hostel with bar, good beds, fan, parking, balcony with hammocks, good breakfast available, Swiss run, helpful.
$Jarfi, Los Ostiones, 1 block from the beach by the footbridge, T273 1089. Hot water, pool, simple bungalows, good value.

Esmeraldas *p1099*
Hotels in the centre are poor; better to stay in the outskirts.
$$Apart Hotel Esmeraldas, Libertad 407 y Ramón Tello, T272 8700. Good restaurant, a/c, fridge, parking, excellent quality.
$Andrés, Sucre 812 y Piedrahita, T272 5883. Simple hostel in a multi-storey building, cold water, fan.
$Galeón, Piedrahita 330 y Olmedo, T272 3820. Cold water, a/c, cheaper with fan, good.
$Zulema 2, Malecón y Rocafuerte. Modern concrete hostel with large rooms, cold water, fan, parking.

North of Esmeraldas *p1100*
Las Peñas
$Mikey, by the beach, T278 6031. Cabins with kitchenettes, private bath, hot water, pool.

Olmedo
$Casa del Manglar, a 20-min walk or short boat ride from La Tola, T278 6126 (Catalina Montes or her son Edwin). A wood cabin with porch by the shore. Dormitory for 15 people, meals available, shared bath, mosquito nets, quiet and pleasant. Take drinking water or means of purification. Organizes tours to mangroves, La Tolita and other sights.

Limones
$Colón, next to the church at the main park, T278 9311. A good hostel for where it is, with bath, cold water, fan.

Borbón *p1100*
$Brisas del Río Santiago, Malecón y 23 de Noviembre, T278 6211. Basic concrete hostel

with good air circulation, private bath, cold water, fan, mosquito net, meeting point for travellers going upriver. Owner Sr Betancourt can arrange canoes for excursions.

San Miguel

In villages like **Pichiyacu** (ethnic Chachi) and Santa María (Afro-Ecuadorean), local families can provide accommodation.

$$$ Eco-Lodge San Miguel, above the village of San Miguel, contact Fundación Verde Milenio, Quito, T02-290 6192, www.verde milenio.org. Community-run lodge with lovely views, 7 bedrooms, shared bath. Price includes transport from Borbón, 3 meals and excursion to the forest. Advance booking advised.

San Lorenzo *p1101*

Expect to be mobbed by children wanting a tip to show you to a hotel or restaurant. Also take insect repellent.

$$$ Playa de Oro, on the Río Santiago, upriver from Borbón, contact Ramiro Buitrón at Hotel Valle del Amanecer in Otavalo, T06-292 0990, www.touchthejungle.org. Basic cabins with shared bath, includes 3 meals and guided excursion.

$$ Tunda Loma, Km 17 on the road to Ibarra (taxi from San Lorenzo US$5), T278 0367. Beautifully located on a hill overlooking the Río Tululbí. Wood cabins, includes breakfast, restaurant, warm water, fan, organizes tubing trips on the river and hikes in the forest.

$ Pampa de Oro, C 26 de Agosto y Tácito Ortiz, T278 0214. Adequate family run hotel, with bath, cold water, fan, mosquito net.

$ San Carlos, C Imbabura near the train station, T278 0284. Simple concrete hotel, private or shared bath, cold water, fan, mosquito nets.

🍴 Restaurants

North to Atacames *p1098*
Mompiche

$$-$ Pizza Luz, on the beach between town and Hotel Gabeal. Opens around 1830. Excellent pizza, bar-stool seating, popular.

$ Comedor Margarita, on main street, 2 blocks from the beach. Daily from 0730. Basic *comedor* serving tasty local fare, mostly fish and seafood.

Same

$$$ Seaflower, by the beach at the entrance road. Excellent international food.

Súa

$ Churuco's, diagonally across from the park, 100 m from the beach. Wed-Sun 0900-2100. Simple *comedor* serving good set meals and local snacks, generous portions, good value.

Atacames *p1099*

The beach is packed with bars and restaurants offering seafood, too many to list.

$$ Da Giulio, Malecón y Cedros. Weekdays 1700-2300, weekends from 1100. Spanish and Italian cuisine, good pasta.

$$-$ El Tiburón, Malecón y Súa. Good seafood.

$$-$ Le Cocotier, Malecón y Camarones. Very good pizza.

Esmeraldas *p1099*

There are restaurants and bars by Las Palmas beach offering regional specialties.

$$ Chifa Asiático, Cañizares y Bolívar. Chinese and seafood, a/c, excellent.

$$-$ El Manglar, Quito y Olmedo. Good *comida esmeraldeña*.

$ Tapao.con, 6 de Diciembre 1717 y Piedrahita. A popular place for typical dishes such as *tapado*, *encocado* and *ceviche*.

San Lorenzo *p1101*

$ El Chocó, C Imbabura. Good fish and local specialties. Also economical set lunches and the best *batido de borojó* (milkshake) in town.

🚌 Transport

North to Atacames *p1098*

Bus Hourly from **Chamanga** to **Esmeraldas**, US$3.50, 3½ hrs, and to **Pedernales**, US$2, 1½ hrs. **Mompiche** to/from **Esmeraldas**, 5 a day, US$3, 3½ hrs, the last one from Esmeraldas about 1630. To **Playa Escondida**: take a ranchera or bus from Esmeraldas or Atacames for Punta Galera or Cabo San Francisco, 5 a day, US$2, 2 hrs. A taxi from Atacames costs US$12 and a pick-up from Tonchigüe US$5. To **Súa** and **Same**: Buses every 30 mins to and from **Atacames**, 15 mins, US$0.35. Make sure it drops you at Same and not at Club Casablanca.

Atacames p1099
Bus To **Esmeraldas**, every 15 mins, US$0.80, 1 hr. To **Guayaquil**, US$9, 8 hrs, Trans Esmeraldas at 0830 and 2245. To **Quito**, various companies, about 10 daily, US$8, 7 hrs, Trans Esmeraldas has service from its own terminal in La Mariscal. To **Pedernales**, Coop G Zambrano, 4 daily, US$4, 4 hrs or change in Chamanga.

Esmeraldas p1099
Air Gen Rivadeneira Airport is along the coastal road heading north. A taxi to the city centre (30 km) costs US$6, buses to the Terminal Terrestre from the road outside the airport pass about every 30 mins. If headed north towards San Lorenzo, you can catch a bus outside the airport. TAME (Bolívar y 9 de Octubre, T272 6863), 1-2 daily flights to **Quito**, continuing to **Cali** (Colombia) Mon, Wed, Fri; to **Guayaquil**, 1 daily Mon, Wed, Fri.
Bus Trans-Esmeraldas (10 de Agosto at Parque Central, recommended) and Panamericana (Colón y Salinas) have *servicio directo* or *ejecutivo* to Quito and Guayaquil, a better choice as they are faster buses and don't stop for passengers; they also run to their own terminals in La Mariscal in Quito. Frequent service to **Quito** via Santo Domingo or via Calacalí, US$7, 6 hrs; ask which terminal they go to before purchasing ticket. To **Ibarra**, 9 hrs, US$10, via Borbón. To **Santo Domingo**, US$3, 3 hrs. To **Ambato**, 6 a day, US$8, 8 hrs. To **Guayaquil**, hourly, US$8, *directo*, 8 hrs. To **Bahía de Caráquez**, via Santo Domingo, US$8, 9 hrs. To **Manta**, US$8, 10 hrs. La Costeñita and El Pacífico, both on Malecón, to/ from **La Tola**, 8 daily, US$3.75, 3 hrs. To **Borbón**, frequent service, US$3.50, 3 hrs. To **San Lorenzo**, 8 daily, US$4.50, 4 hrs. To **Súa**, **Same** and **Atacames**,

every 15 mins from 0630-2030, to Atacames US$0.80, 1 hr. To **Chamanga**, hourly 0500-1900, US$3.50, 3½ hrs, change here for points south.

North of Esmeraldas p1100
Ferry There are launches between **La Tola** and **Limones** which connect with the buses arriving from Esmeraldas, US$3, 1 hr, and 3 daily Limones-**San Lorenzo**, 2 hrs US$3. You can also hire a launch to **Borbón**, a fascinating trip through mangrove islands, passing hunting pelicans, approximately US$10 per hr.

Borbón p1100
Bus To **Esmeraldas**, US$3.50, 3 hrs. To **San Lorenzo**, US$1.60, 1 hr.
Ferry 4 launches a day run to communities upriver, 1030-1100. Check how far each one is going as only one goes as far as **San Miguel**, US$8, 4 hrs.

San Lorenzo p1101
Bus Buses leave from the train station or environs. To **Ibarra**, 10 daily, 4 hrs, US$4. To **Esmeraldas**, via Borbón, 8 daily, US$4.50, 4 hrs.
Ferry Launch service with Coopseturi, T278 0161; and Costeñita, both near the pier. All services are subject to change and cancellation. To **Limones**, 4 daily, US$3, 2 hrs. To **La Tola**, US$6, 4 hrs. To **Palma Real**, for beaches, 2 daily, US$3, 2 hrs. To hire a boat for 5 passengers costs US$20 per hr.

● Directory

Atacames *p1099*
Banks Banco Pichincha, Espejo y Calderón by the plaza, for ATM. There are a few other stand-alone ATMs in town and along the beach.

Esmeraldas *p1099*
Banks For ATMs, several banks on C Bolívar in the centre.

San Lorenzo *p1101*
Banks Banco Pichincha, C Ponce y Garcés, has the only ATM in town; bring some cash.

The Oriente

East of the Andes the hills fall away to tropical lowlands. Some of this beautiful wilderness remains unspoiled and sparsely populated, with indigenous settlements along the tributaries of the Amazon. Large tracts of jungle are under threat, however: colonists are clearing many areas for agriculture, while others are laid waste by petroleum development. The Ecuadorean jungle, especially the Northern Oriente, has the advantage of being relatively accessible and tourist infrastructure here is well developed. The eastern foothills of the Andes, where the jungle begins, offer the easiest access and a good introduction to the rainforest for those with limited time or money. Further east lie the few remaining large tracts of primary rainforest, teeming with life, which can be visited from several excellent (and generally expensive) jungle lodges. Southern Oriente is as yet less developed for tourism, it offers good opportunities off the beaten path but is threatened by large mining projects.

Arriving in the Oriente

Getting there There are commercial flights from Quito to Lago Agrio, Coca and Macas; and from Guayaquil to Coca via Latucunga. From Quito, Macas and Shell, light aircraft can be chartered to any jungle village with a landing strip. Western Oriente is also accessible by scenic roads which wind their way down from the highlands. Quito, via Baeza, to Lago Agrio and Coca, Baños to Puyo, and Loja to Zamora are fully paved, as is almost all of the lowland road from Lago Agrio south to Zamora. Other access roads to Oriente are: Tulcán to Lago Agrio via Lumbaqui, Riobamba to Macas, and three diffrent roads from Cuenca. These go to Méndez via Guarumales, Plan de Milagro via Paute (closed for paving in 2014), and Gualaquiza via Sígsig. Some roads are narrow and tortuous and subject to landslides in the rainy season, but all have regular bus service and all can be attempted in a jeep or in an ordinary car with good ground clearance. Deeper into the rainforest, motorized canoes provide the only alternative to air travel.

Jungle tours These fall into four basic types: lodges, guided tours, indigenous ecotourism and river cruises. When staying at a jungle lodge, you will need to take a torch (flashlight), insect repellent, protection against the sun and a rain poncho that will keep you dry when walking and when sitting in a canoe. See also Lodges on the Lower Napo (page 1109) and the Upper Napo (page 1116). All jungle lodges must be booked in advance. **Guided tours** of varying length are offered by tour operators and independent guides. These should, in principle, be licensed by the Ecuadorean **Ministerio de Turismo**. Tour operators and guides are mainly concentrated in Quito, Baños, Puyo, Tena, Misahuallí, Coca, and, to a lesser extent, Macas and Zamora.

A number of indigenous communities and families offer **ecotourism** programmes in their territories. These are either community-controlled and operated, or organized as joint ventures between the indigenous community or family and a non-indigenous partner. These programmes usually involve guides who are licensed as *guías nativos* with the right to guide within their communities. You should be prepared to be more self-sufficient on such a trip than on a visit to a jungle lodge or a tour with a high-end operator. Take a light sleeping bag, rain jacket, trousers (not only shorts), long-sleeve shirt for mosquitoes, binoculars, torch, insect repellent, sunscreen and hat, water-purifying tablets, and a first aid kit. Wrap everything in several plastic bags to keep it dry. Most lodges provide rubber boots, indepedent guides may not.

River cruises offer a better appreciation of the grandeur of Amazonia, but less intimate contact with life in the rainforest. Passengers sleep and take their meals onboard comfortable river boats, stopping on route to visit local communities and make excursions into the jungle.

Jungle travel without a guide is not recommended. Some indigenous groups prohibit the entry of outsiders to their territory, navigation in the jungle is difficult, and there is a variety of dangerous animals. For your own safety as well as to be a responsible tourist, the jungle is not a place to wander off on your own.

Health and safety A yellow fever vaccination is required. Anti-malarial tablets are recommended, as is an effective insect repellent. There may be police and military checkpoints in the Oriente, so always have your passport handy. Caution is advised in the province of Sucumbíos, enquire about public safety before visiting sites near the Colombian border.

Northern Oriente

Much of the Northern Oriente is taken up by the Parque Nacional Yasuní, the Cuyabeno Wildlife Reserve and most of the Cayambe-Coca Ecological Reserve. The main towns for access are Baeza, Lago Agrio and Coca.

Quito to the Oriente

From Quito to Baeza, a paved road goes via the **Guamaní pass** (4064 m). It crosses the Eastern Cordillera just north of **Volcán Antisana** (5705 m), and then descends via the small village of **Papallacta** (hot springs, see page 1001) to the old mission settlement of Baeza. The trip between the pass and Baeza has beautiful views of Antisana (clouds permitting), high waterfalls, *páramo*, cloud forest and a lake contained by an old lava flow.

Baeza → *Phone code: 06. Colour map 11, A4. Population: 2000. Altitude 1900 m.*

The mountainous landscape and high rainfall have created spectacular waterfalls and dense vegetation. Orchids and bromeliads abound. Baeza, in the beautiful Quijos valley, is about 1 km from the main junction of roads from Lago Agrio and Tena. The town itself is divided in two parts: a faded but pleasant **Baeza Colonial** (Old Baeza) and **Baeza Nueva** (New Baeza), where most shops and services are located. There are hiking trails and rafting possibilities in the area.

Beyond Baeza

From Baeza a road heads south to Tena, with a branch going east via Loreto to Coca, all paved. Another paved road goes northeast from Baeza to Lago Agrio, following the Río Quijos past the villages of **Borja** (8 km from Baeza, very good *comedor* **Doña Cleo** along the highway, closed Sun) and **El Chaco** (12 km further, simple accommodation and kayaking at **$ La Guarida del Coyote**) to the slopes of the active volcano **Reventador**, 3560 m. Check www.igepn.edu.ec and enquire locally about volcanic activity before trekking here; simple **$ Hostería El Reventador** at the bridge over the Río Reventador; **Ecuador Journeys** offers tours, see page 994. Half a kilometre south of the bridge is signed access to the impressive 145-m **San Rafael Falls** (part of **Reserva Ecológica Cayambe-Coca**), believed to be the highest in Ecuador. It is a pleasant 45-minute hike through cloud forest to a *mirador* with stunning views of the thundering cascade. Many birds can be spotted along the trail, including Cock-of-the-rock, also monkeys and coatimundis. In 2014 the falls could still be visited but the former ranger station had been converted to headquarters of a hydro-electric project (www.ccs.gob.ec) which will use up to 70% of the water in the Río Quijos, leaving only 30% to go over the falls – the death knell for Ecuador's most beautiful cascade.

Lago Agrio → *Phone code: 06. Colour map 11, A5. Population: 63,500. Altitude 300 m.*

The capital of Sucumbíos province is an old oil town with close ties to neighbouring Colombia, and among the places in Ecuador which has been most affected by conflict there. The name comes from Sour Lake, the US headquarters of Texaco, the first oil company to exploit the Ecuadorean Amazon in the 1970s. It is also called Nueva Loja or just 'Lago'. If taking a Cuyabeno tour from Lago Agrio, it is worth leaving Quito a day or two early, stopping en route at Papallacta, Baeza or San Rafael falls. Lago Agrio is not a safe place, return to your hotel by 2000. Alternatively you can overnight at more tranquil **Cascales** (**$ Paraíso Dorado**, small, pleasant), 35 minutes before Lago Agrio, and still meet your tour party in Lago the following morning. There is a border crossing to Colombia north of Lago Agrio but it is also unsafe. Seek local advice from the **Ministerio de Turismo** ① *Narváez y Añazco, upstairs, T283 2488, Mon-Fri 0830-1300, 1400-1800.*

Cuyabeno Wildlife Reserve

This large tract of rainforest, covering 602,000 ha, is located about 100 km east of Lago Agrio along the Río Cuyabeno, which eventually drains into the Aguarico. In the reserve are many lagoons and a great variety of wildlife, including river dolphins, tapirs, capybaras, five species of caiman, ocelots, 15 species of monkey and over 500 species of birds. This is among the best places in Ecuador to see jungle animals. The reserve is very popular with visitors but there have been occasional armed hold-ups of tour groups here, best enquire before booking a tour. Access is either by road from Lago Agrio, or by river along the Río Aguarico. Within the reserve, transport is mainly by canoe. In order to see as many animals as possible and minimally impact their habitat, seek out a small tour group which scrupulously adheres to responsible tourism practices. Most Cuyabeno tours are booked through agencies in Quito.

Coca → *Phone code: 06. Colour map 11, A5. Population: 52,400. Altitude 250 m.*

Officially named **Puerto Francisco de Orellana**, Coca is a hot, noisy, bustling oil town at the junction of the Ríos Payamino and Napo. It is the capital of the province of Orellana and is a launch pad from where to visit more remote jungle parts. The view over the water is nice, and the riverfront **Malecón** can be a pleasant place to spend time around sunset; various indigenous groups have craft shops here. Hotel and restaurant provision is adequate, but electricity, water and, ironically for an oil-producing centre, petrol supplies are erratic. Information from **iTur** ① *Chimborazo y Amazonas, by the Malecón, 1288 0532, Mon-Sat 0800-1200, 1400-1800, www.orellanaturistica.gob.ec* and the **Ministerio de Turismo** ① *Cuenca y Quito, upstairs, T288 1583, Mon-Fri 0830-1700.*

Jungle tours from Coca Coca provides access to **Parque Nacional Yasuní** and the **Reserva Huaorani**. Tours to the park and reserve really need a minimum of five days but shorter visits of 3-4 days are worthwhile along the Río Napo, where the lodges are concentrated. Wildlife in this area is under threat: insist that guides and fellow tourists take all litter back and ban all hunting and shooting; it really makes a difference. The majority of tours out of Coca are booked through agencies in Quito but there are a few local operators. Quality varies so try to get a personal recommendation, prices are around US$70-80 per person per day. **Note** If a guide offers a tour to visit the Huaorani, ask to see his/her permission to do so, which should be issued by the Huaorani organization **NAWE**.

The paved road to Coca via Loreto passes through **Wawa Sumaco**, where a rough road heads north to **Sumaco National Park**; 7 km along it is **$$$$-$$$ Wildsumaco** ① *T06-301 8343, www.wildsumaco.com*, a comfortable birdwatching lodge with full board, excellent trails and many rare species. Just beyond is the village of Pacto Sumaco from where a trail runs through the park to the *páramo*-clad summit of **Volcan Sumaco** (3732 m), six to seven days round-trip. Local guides may be hired, there are 3 nice shelters along the route and a basic community-run hostel in the village (www.sumacobirdwatching.com, try T06-301 8324 but not always staffed).

Coca to Nuevo Rocafuerte and Iquitos (Peru)

Pañacocha is halfway between Coca and Nuevo Rocafuerte, near a magnificent lagoon. Here are a couple of **lodges** (see Lodges on the Lower Napo) and Coca agencies and guides also run tours to the area (see Tour operators). Entry to Pañacocha reserve US$10. There are basic places to stay and eat in Pañacocha village.

Following the Río Napo to Peru is rough, adventurous and requires plenty of time and patience. There are two options: by far the least expensive is to take a motorized canoe from Coca to **Nuevo Rocafuerte** on the border. This tranquil riverside town has simple hotels, eateries, a phone office and basic shops. It can be a base for exploring the endangered southeastern section of **Parque Nacional Yasuní** (see www.yasuni-itt.gob.ec); local guides are available. Ecuadorean immigration for exit stamps is next to the navy dock; if the officer is not in, enquire in town. Peruvian entry stamps are given in **Pantoja**, where there is a decent municipal *hospedaje*, **$ Napuruna**. Shopkeepers in Nuevo Rocafuerte and Pantoja change money at poor rates. In addition to immigration, you may have to register with the navy on either side of the border so have your passport at hand. See Transport, page 1112, for boat services Coca-Nuevo Rocafuerte and onward to Pantoja and Iquitos. See also the Peru chapter, under Iquitos Transport.

The second option for river travel to Iquitos is to take a tour with a Coca agency, taking in various attractions on route, and continuing to Iquitos or closer Peruvian ports from which you can catch onward public river transport. Ask carefully about these tours as they may involve many hours sitting in small, cramped craft; confirm all details in advance.

⦿ Northern Oriente listings

For hotel and restaurant price codes, and other relevant information, see Essentials.

⦿ Where to stay

Baeza *p1106*
$ Gina, Jumandy y Batallón Chimborazo, just off the highway in the old town, T232 0471. Hot water, parking, pleasant, good value.
$ La Casa de Rodrigo, in the old town, T232 0467, rodrigobaeza@andinanet.net. Modern and comfortable, hot water, friendly owner offers rafting trips, kayak rentals and birdwatching.
$ Samay, Av de los Quijos, in the new town, T232 0170. Private or shared bath, electric shower, older place but friendly and adequate, simple rooms, good value.

Around Baeza
$$$$ Cabañas San Isidro, near Cosanga, 19 km south of Baeza, T02-289 1880 (Quito), www.cabanasanisidro.com. A 1200-ha private nature reserve with rich bird life, comfortable accommodation and warm hospitality. Includes 3 excellent meals, reservations required.
$ Hostería El Reventador, on main highway next to bridge over the Río Reventador, turismovolcanreventador@yahoo.com. Meals on request, hot water, pool, simple rooms, busy at weekends, mediocre service but well located for San Rafael Falls and Volcán Reventador.

Lago Agrio *p1107*
Virtually everything can be found on the main street, Av Quito.
$$$ Gran Hotel de Lago, Km 1½ Vía Quito, T283 2415, granhoteldelago@grupodelago. com. Restaurant, a/c, pool, parking, cabins with nice gardens, quiet. Recommended.
$$ Arazá, Quito 536 y Narváez, T283 1287, www.hotel-araza.com. Quiet location away from centre, buffet breakfast, restaurant, a/c, pool (US$5 for non-residents), fridge, parking, comfortable, nice. Recommended.

$$ El Cofán, 12 de Febrero 3915 y Quito, T283 0526, elcofanhotel@yahoo.es. Restaurant, a/c, fridge, parking, older place but well maintained.
$$-$ Lago Imperial, Colombia y Quito, T283 0453, hotellagoimperial@hotmail.com. A/c, cheaper with fan and cold water, central location, good value.
$ Casa Blanca, Quito 228 y Colombia, T283 0181. Electric shower, fan, nice bright rooms.
$ Gran Colombia, Quito y Pasaje Gonzanamá, T283 1032. Good restaurant, hot water, a/c, cheaper with fan and cold water, more expensive rooms also have fridge, parking, centrally located, modern and good value.

Cascales
$ Paraíso Dorado, on the highway at the east end of town, T280 0421. A small place, meals on request, cold water, mosquito nets, very helpful.

Coca *p1107*
$$ El Auca, Napo y García Moreno, T288 0600, www.hotelelauca.com. Restaurant, disco on weekends, a/c, cheaper with fan, parking, a variety of different rooms and mini-suites. Comfortable, nice garden with hammocks, English spoken. Popular and centrally located but can get noisy.
$$ Heliconias, Cuenca y Amazonas, T288 2010, heliconiaslady@yahoo.com.Upmarket restaurant, pool (US$5 for non-guests), spotless. Recommended.
$$ La Misión, by riverfront 100 m downriver from the bridge, T288 0260, www.hotelamision. com. A larger hotel, restaurant and disco, a/c and fridge, pool (US$2 for non-guests), parking, a bit faded but still adequate.
$$-$ Amazonas, 12 de Febrero y Espejo, T288 0444, hosteriacoca@hotmail.com. Nice quiet setting by the river, away from centre, restaurant, electric shower, a/c, parking.
$$-$ Río Napo, Bolívar entre Napo y Quito, T288 0872. A/c, cheaper with fan, small modern rooms.
$ Omaguas, Cuenca y Quito, T288 2436, h_omaguas@hotmail.com. Restaurant, hot water, a/c, parking, small modern rooms.
$ San Fermín, Bolívar y Quito, T288 0802. Hot water, a/c (cheaper with fan, shared bath and

cold water), ample parking, variety of different rooms, nicely furnished, popular and busy, good value, owner organizes tours. Recommended.

Jungle tours from Coca *p1107*
Lodges on the Lower Napo
All Napo lodges count travel days as part of their package, which means that a '3-day tour' spends only 1 day actually in the forest. Most lodges have fixed departure days from Coca (eg Mon and Fri) and it is very expensive to get a special departure on another day. For lodges in Cuyabeno, see page 1111; for lodges on the Upper Napo, see page 1116, for southern Oriente lodges see page 1117.
Amazon Dolphin Lodge, Quito office: Amazonas N24-236 y Colón, T02-250 4037, www.amazondolphinlodge.com. On Laguna de Pañacocha, 4½ hrs downriver from Coca. Special wildlife here includes Amazon river dolphins and giant river otters as well as over 500 species of birds. Cabins with private bath, US$600-700 for 4 days.
Napo Wildlife Center, Quito office: Pje Yaupi N31-90 y Mariana de Jesús, T02-600-5893, USA T1-866-750-0830, UK T0-800-032-5771, www. ecoecuador.org. Operated by and for the local Añangu community, 2½ hrs downstream from Coca. This area of hilly forest is rather different from the low flat forest of some other lodges, and the diversity is slightly higher. There are big caimans and good mammals, including giant otters, and the birdwatching is excellent with 2 parrot clay-licks and a 35-m canopy tower. US$820 for 4 days. Recommended.
La Selva, Quito office: Mariana de Jesús E7-211 y La Pradera, T02-255 0995, www. laselvajunglelodge.com. An upmarket lodge, 2½ hrs downstream from Coca on a picturesque lake. Surrounded by excellent forest, especially on the far side of Mandicocha. Bird and animal life is exceptionally diverse. Many species of monkey are seen regularly. A total of 580 bird species have been found, one of the highest totals in the world for a single elevation. Comfortable cabins and excellent meals. High standards, most guides are biologists. 45-m canopy tower. US$765-1100 for 4 days.

Pañacocha Emerald Forest Lodge, Quito office: Ecuador Journeys (see Quito operators), T02-603 5548, www.ecuadorianjourney.com. Located 5 hrs from Coca, on the Río Pañayacu and surrounded by primary forest. Run by the Quito operator and Luis García, a legendary jungle guide. 6 comfortable cabins with solar power, private bath, shower, large deck, common areas, canopy tower, US$440 for 4 days.

Sacha, Quito office: Julio Zaldumbide y Valladolid, T02-256 6090, www.sachalodge.còm. An upmarket lodge 2½ hrs downstream from Coca. Very comfortable cabins, excellent meals. The bird list is outstanding; the local bird expert, Oscar Tapuy (Coca T06-2881486), can be requested in advance. Canopy tower and 275-m canopy walkway. Several species of monkey are commonly seen. Nearby river islands provide access to a distinct habitat. US$790 for 4 days.

Sani, Quito office: Washington E4-71 y Amazonas, T02-222 8802, www.sanilodge.com. All proceeds go to the Sani Isla community, who run the lodge with the help of outside experts. It is located on a remote lagoon which has 4- to 5-m-long black caiman. This area is rich in wildlife and birds, including many species such as the Scarlet Macaw which have disappeared from most other Napo area lodges. There is good accommodation and a 35-m canopy tower. An effort has been made to make the lodge accessible to people who have difficulty walking; the lodge can be reached by canoe (total 3½ hrs from Coca) without a walk. US$715 for 4 days. Good value, recommended.

Lodges in the Reserva Huaorani

Huaorani Ecolodge, operated by Tropic Journeys in Nature in Quito (see page 996), a joint venture with several Huaorani communities who staff the lodge; winner of sustainable tourism awards. Small (10 guests), wooden cabins, solar lighting, upgraded in 2013, a spontaneous, rewarding and at times challenging experience. Includes much community involvement, rainforest hikes, conservation area, kayaking (US$40 per day), dug out canoe trips. Tours arrive by small plane from Shell and leave on the Vía Auca to Coca.

River journeys are non-motorized except the last stretch from Nenquepare Camp (cabins, refurbished kitchen and bathrooms) where the last night is spent, to the road. From US$730 for 4 days. Prices do not include land and air transport from Quito to the Lodge, or return from Coca to Quito.

Otobo's Amazon Safari, www.rainforest camping.com. 8 day/7 night camping expeditions in Huaorani territory, access by flight from Shell to Bameno (US$1540 pp), or by road from Coca then 2-day motorized canoe journey on the Ríos Shiripuno and Cononaco (US$1,050 pp) All meals and guiding included.

Shiripuno, Quito T02-227 1094, www. shiripunolodge.com. A lodge with capacity for 20 people, very good location on the Río Shiripuno, a 4-hr canoe ride downriver from the Vía Auca. Cabins have private bath. The surrounding area has seen relatively little human impact to date. US$360 for 4 days, plus US$20 entry to Huaorani territory.

Coca to Nuevo Rocafuerte and Iquitos
p1108

$ Casa Blanca, Malecón y Nicolás Torres, T238 2184. Rooms with a/c or fan, nice, simple, welcoming. There are a couple of other basic places to stay in town.

🍴 Restaurants

Baeza *p1106*
$ El Viejo, east end of Av de los Quijos, the road to Tena in the new town. Daily 0700-2100. Good set meals and à la carte.
$ Gina, Batallón Chimborazo, just off the highway in the old town. Daily 0730-2200. Trout is the speciality, good and popular.

Lago Agrio *p1107*
There are good restaurants at the larger hotels (see above); also many cheap *comedores*.

Coca *p1107*
$$ Denny's, Alejandro Labaka by the airport. Mon-Sat 0800-2000, Sun 1200-1400. Steaks, ribs and other US-style meals and drinks, friendly.

\$\$-\$ Pizza Choza, Rocafuerte entre Napo y Quito. Daily 1800-2200. Good pizza, friendly owner, English spoken.

\$ La Casa del Maito, Espejo entre Quito y Napo. Daily 0700-1700. *Maitos* and other local specialties.

\$ Ocaso, Eloy Alfaro entre Napo y Amazonas. Mon-Sat 0600-2100, Sun 0600-1400. Set meals and à la carte, popular with locals.

◑ What to do

Cuyabeno Wildlife Reserve *p1107*
Prices do not include transport to Lago Agrio.
Magic River Tours, Lago Agrio (no storefront), T09-9736 0670, www.magicrivertours.com. Good quality and value 5- to 8-day canoe tours, half-day paddling, half-day motorized, camping and accommodation in rustic cabins, US\$330-800, book well in advance.

The following agencies are all in Quito:
Dracaena, page 994. US\$260 for 4 days.
Ecuador Verde País, Calama E6-19 y Reina Victoria, T02 222 0614, www.cabanasjamu.com. Run **Jamu Lodge**, good service, US\$230-265 for 4 days.
Galasam, page 1079. Operates *Siona Lodge*, www.sionalodge.com, US\$360 for 4 days.
Neotropic Turis, Pinto E4-360, Quito, T02-252 1212, www.neotropicturis.com. Operate the Cuyabeno Lodge by the Laguna Grande, English speaking guides, US\$220-350 for 4 nights.

Coca *p1107*
Jungle tours from Coca
See also page 1107.
Ecu-Astonishing, near Hotel La Missión, T288 0251, jjarrin1@msn.com. Julio Jarrín offers tours to his own cabins near Pañacocha.
Luis Duarte, at Casa del Maito (see Restaurants above), T288 2285, cocaselva@hotmail.com. Regional and trips to Iquitos.
Sachayacu Explorer, in Píllaro near Baños (see page 1035), T03-287 5316, info@parquelanganates.com. Although not based in Coca, experienced jungle guide Juan Medina offers recommended jungle tours and trips to Iquitos. Advance arrangements required.

Wildlife Amazon, Robert Vaca at Hotel San Fermín (see Where to stay above), T288 0802. Jungle tours and trips to Iquitos.

River cruises on the lower Río Napo
Manatee, Quito office: Advantage Travel, Gaspar de Villarroel N 40-143 y 6 de Diciembre, T02-336 0887, www.manateeamazonexplorer.com. This 30-passenger vessel sails between Coca and Pañacocha. US\$795 for 4 days. First-class guides, excellent food, en suite cabins. They also operate the new **Anakonda**, www.anakondaamazoncruises.com, a luxury cruise vessel on the Napo.

Coca to Nuevo Rocafuerte and Iquitos
p1108
Juan Carlos Cuenca, Nuevo Rocafuerte, T06-238 2257, is a *guía nativo* who offers tours to Parque Nacional Yasuní, about US\$60 per day.

● Transport

Baeza *p1106*
Bus Buses to and from **Tena** pass right through town. If arriving on a **Lago Agrio** bus, get off at the crossroads (la "Y") and walk or take a pick-up for US\$0.25. From **Quito**, 5 daily (3 on Sun), with **Trans Quijos**, T02-295 0842, from Don Bosco E1-136 y Av Pichincha (beside the overpass at La Marín, an unsafe area), US\$3, 2½ hrs. These continue to Borja and El Chaco.

Lago Agrio *p1107*
Air Airport is 5 km southeast of the centre. TAME (Orellana y 9 de Octubre, T283 0113) and Aerogal (at the airport, T283 0333) daily to **Quito**. Book several days in advance. If there is no space available to **Lago Agrio** then you can fly to **Coca** instead, from where it is only 2 hrs by bus on a good road.
Bus Terminal terrestre is north of town, but buses for Coca leave from the market area on Orellana, 3 blocks south of Av Quito. To **Quito** (2 routes: through Cascales, and, slightly longer via Coca and Loreto), US\$8, 7-8 hrs. **Baeza** 5 hrs. **Coca**, US\$3, 2 hrs. **Tena**, US\$7, 7 hrs.

Coca *p1107*

Air Flights to **Quito**, **Latacunga** and **Guayaquil** with TAME (C Quito y Enrique Castillo, T288 0768) and **Aerogal** (at the airport T288 1742), several daily (fewer on weekends), reserve as far in advance as possible.

Bus Long distance buses depart from company offices in town; local destinations, including **Lago Agrio**, are served from the terminal on 9 de Octubre north of the centre. To **Quito**, 10 hrs, US$10, several daily 1030-2200. To **Tena**, 5 hrs, US$7. To **Baeza**, US$7.50, 8 hrs. To **Baños**, US$11, 8½ hrs.

River Down the Río Napo to **Nuevo Rocafuerte** on the Peruvian border, 50-passenger motorized canoes leave Coca daily except Sat, 0730, 10-12 hrs; returning at 0500, 12-14 hrs; US$15. Details change often, enquire locally, buy tickets at the dock a day in advance and arrive early for boarding.

From Nuevo Rocafuerte boats can be hired for the 30 km trip down river to the Peruvian border town of **Pantoja**, US$60 per boat, try to share the ride. Departure dates of riverboats from **Pantoja to Iquitos** are irregular, about once a month, be prepared for a long wait. Try to call Iquitos or Pantoja from Coca to enquire about the next sailing; full details are given in the Peru chapter under Iquitos, Transport. For the journey, take a hammock, cup, bowl, cutlery, extra food and snacks, drinking water or purification, insect repellent, toilet paper, soap, towel, cash dollars and soles in small notes; soles cannot be purchased in Coca.

⊕ Directory

Lago Agrio *p1107*
Banks For ATMs: Banco de Guayaquil, Quito y 12 de Febrero; Banco Pichincha, 12 de Febrero y Añasco. Several **Casas de Cambio** on Quito between Colombia and Pasaje Gonzanamá, change euros and Colombian pesos.

Coca *p1107*
Banks For ATMs: Banco Pichincha, Quito y Bolívar; Banco Internacional, 9 de Octubre y Cuenca.

Central and southern Oriente

Quito, Baños, Puyo, Tena and Puerto Misahuallí are all starting points for cental Oriente. Further south, Macas, Gualaquiza and Zamora are the main gateways. All have good road connections.

Archidona → *Phone code: 06. Colour map 11, B4. Population: 12,700. Altitude: 550 m.*

Archidona, 65 km south of Baeza and 10 km north of Tena, has a striking, small painted church and not much else but there are some interesting reserves in the surrounding area. The road leaving Archidona's plaza to the east goes to the village of **San Pablo**, and beyond to the Río Hollín. Along this road, 15 km from Archidona, is **Reserva El Para** ⊕ *owned by Orchid Paradise (see Where to stay, page 1115); guided tours US$5 pp plus US$20 for transport.* This 500-ha forest reserve has many rare birds and a nice waterfall. Tours can also be arranged to the **Izu Mangallpa Urcu (IMU) Foundation** ⊕ *contact Elias Mamallacta in Archidona, T288 9383 or T08-9045 6942, US$50 per day for accommodation (private rooms, mosquito nets) and guiding, minimum 2 people.* This reserve was set up by the Mamallacta family to protect territory on Galeras mountain. There is easy walking as well as a tougher trek, the forest is wonderful.

Tena and around → *Phone code: 06. Colour map 11, B4. Population: 37,500. Altitude: 500 m.*

Relaxed and friendly, Tena is the capital of Napo Province. It occupies a hill above the confluence of the Ríos Tena and Pano, there are nice views of the Andean foothills often shrouded in mist. Tena is Ecuador's most important centre for whitewater rafting and also offers ethno-tourism. It makes a good stop en route from Quito to points deeper in Oriente. The road from the north passes the old airstrip and market and heads through the town centre as Avenida 15 de

Noviembre on its way to the bus station, nearly 1 km south of the river. Tena is quite spread out. A pedestrian bridge and a vehicle bridge link the two halves of town. **iTur and Ministerio de Turismo** ① *Malecón, sector El Balnerio, Mon-Fri 0730-1230, 1400-1700*, several information offices under one roof. See also map, below.

Misahuallí → *Phone code: 06. Colour map 11, B4. Population: 5300. Altitude: 400 m.*

This small port, at the junction of the Napo and Misahuallí rivers, is perhaps the best place in Ecuador from which to visit the 'near Oriente', but your expectations should be realistic. The area has been colonized for many years and there is no extensive virgin forest nearby (except at **Jatun Sacha** and **Liana Lodge**, see Lodges on the Upper Río Napo, page 1116). Access is very easy however, prices are reasonable, and while you will not encounter large animals in the wild, you can still see birds, butterflies and exuberant vegetation – enough to get a taste for the jungle. Beware the troop of urban monkeys by the plaza, who snatch food, sunglasses, cameras, etc. There is a fine, sandy beach on the Río Misahuallí, but don't camp on it as the river can rise unexpectedly. A narrow suspension bridge crosses the Río Napo at Misahuallí and joins

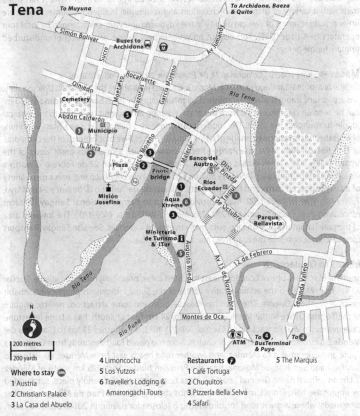

Tena

To Muyuna
To Archidona, Baeza & Quito

C Simón Bolívar
Buses to Archidona
Sucre
Olmedo
Montalvo
Rocafuerte
Amazonas
García Moreno
Río Tena
Av Jumandy
Cemetery
Abdón Calderón
Municipio
JL Mera
García Moreno
Plaza
Foot bridge
Banco del Austro
Díaz Pineda
Ríos Ecuador
Malecón
Misión Josefina
Aqua Xtreme
9 de Octubre
Tandalia
Parque Bellavista
Ministerio de Turismo & ITur
Augusto Rueda
Av 15 de Noviembre
12 de Febrero
Segunda Vallejo
Río Tena
Río Pano
Montes de Oca
To ④, BusTerminal & Puyo
ATM
To ④

N
200 metres
200 yards

Where to stay 🛏
1 Austria
2 Christian's Palace
3 La Casa del Abuelo
4 Limoncocha
5 Los Yutzos
6 Traveller's Lodging & Amarongachi Tours

Restaurants 🍴
1 Café Tortuga
2 Chuquitos
3 Pizzería Bella Selva
4 Safari
5 The Marquis

the road along the south shore. There is an interesting **Mariposario** (butterfly farm) ① *US$2.50*, where several colourful species can be observed and photographed close up, also an orchid garden and an entomologic display. Make arrangements through **Ecoselva** (See What to do, page 1119). At Chichicorumi, outside Misahuallí, is **Kamak Maki** ① *US$2.50, T09-9982 7618, www.museokamakmaki.com*, an ethno-cultural museum run by the local Kichwa community.

Puyo → *Phone code: 03. Colour map 11, B4. Population: 40,000. Altitude: 950 m.*

The capital of the province of Pastaza feels more like a lowland city anywhere in Ecuador rather than a typical jungle town. Visits can nonetheless be made to nearby forest reserves and tours deeper into the jungle can also be arranged from Puyo. It is the junction for road travel into the northern and southern Oriente (80 km south of Tena, 130 km north of Macas), and for traffic heading to or from Ambato via Baños; all on paved roads. The Sangay and Altar volcanoes can occasionally be seen from town. **Tourist offices**: iTur ① *Francisco de Orellana y 9 de Octubre, T288 5122, daily 0800-1600; also at Treminal Terrestre, Wed-Sun 0900-1600.*

Omaere ① *T288 3174, Tue-Sun 0900-1700, US$3, access by footbridge off the Paseo Turístico, Barrio Obrero,* is a 15.6-ha ethnobotanical reserve located in the north of Puyo. It has three trails with a variety of plants, an orchidarium and traditional indigenous homes. There are other private reserves of varying quality in the Puyo area and visits are arranged by local tour operators (see page 1119). You cannot however expect to see large tracts of undisturbed primary jungle here.

Macas → *Phone code: 07. Colour map 11, B4. Population: 20,700. Altitude: 1050 m.*

Capital of Morona-Santiago province, Macas is situated high above the broad Río Upano valley. It is a pleasant tranquil place, established by missionaries in 1563. **Sangay volcano** (5230 m) can be seen on clear mornings from the plaza, creating an amazing backdrop to the tropical jungle surrounding the town. The modern cathedral, with beautiful stained-glass windows, houses the much-venerated image of La Purísima de Macas. Five blocks north of the cathedral, at Don Bosco y Riobamba, the **Parque Recreacional,** which also affords great views of the Upano Valley, has a small orchid collection. The Sunday market on 27 de Febrero is worth a visit. **Fundación Chankuap** ① *Soasti y Bolívar, T270 1176, www.chankuap.org,* sells a nice variety of locally produced crafts and food products. **Ministerio de Turismo** ① *Bolívar y 24 de Mayo, T270 1480, Mon-Fri 0800-1700.* Macas provides access to **Parque Nacional Sangay** ① *Macas office, Juan de la Cruz y Guamote, T270 2368, Mon-Fri 0800-1300, 1400-1700.* The lowland area of the park has interesting walking with many rivers and waterfalls. See also Sangay Transport (page 1052) for notes on the road from Macas to Riobamba.

Macas to Gualaquiza

South of Macas lies one of Ecuador's least touristed areas, promising much to explore. **Sucúa**, 23 km from Macas, is the administrative centre of the Shuar indigenous people who inhabit much of southern Oriente. The town has most services and some attractions nearby; enquire at the **Tourist Office** in the Municipio. **Logroño**, 24 km further south, has a large limestone cave nearby; to visit contact Mario Crespo, T07-391 1013. It is another 31 km to (Santiago de) **Méndez**, a crossroads with a modern church. A mostly paved road descends from Cuenca via Paute and Guarumales to Méndez, and another road heads east from Méndez via Patuca to Santiago and San José de Morona, near the Peruvian border. Some 26 km south of Méndez is **Limón** (official name General Leónidas Plaza Gutiérrez), a busy, friendly place, surrounded by impressive hills. From Limón the road climbs steeply 10 km to **Plan de Milagro**, another crossroads, where a great road for birdwatching (closed for paving in 2014), descends from

Cuenca via Gualaceo. Next are **Indanza**, 5 km south, then **San Juan Bosco**, 16 km further, with striking views of Cerro Pan de Azucar (2958 m) rising abruptly out of the jungle, before the road reaches Gualaquiza, 55 km ahead.

Gualaquiza → *Phone code 07. Colour map 11, C3. Population 9500. Altitude 850 m.*

A pleasant town with an imposing church on a hilltop, Gualaquiza's pioneer-settlement charm is threatened by large mining projects in the area. Fortunately, tourism offers an alternative as there are also lovely waterfalls, good rivers for tubing, caves, and undeveloped archaeological sites nearby. Information and tours from the **Oficina Municipal de Turismo** ⓘ *García Moreno y Gonzalo Pesántez, T278 0783, Mon-Fri 0730-1230, 1330-1630*, and from Leonardo Matoche at **Canela y Café**.

At Gualaquiza a very rough and narrow road forks northwest to climb steeply to Cuenca via **Sígsig**. The paved road south from Gualaquiza passes El Pangui and Yantzaza (55 km), 8 km south of which is **Zumbi**, with basic hotels on the plaza. At Zumbi, a bridge crosses the Río Zamora and a side road goes southeast to Guayzimi and the beautiful **Alto Nangartiza** region, with **Reserva El Zarza**. The upper Río Nangaritza flows through Shuar territory and a magnificent jungle-covered gorge with 200-m-high walls. There are also oilbird caves and other natural attractions. There is bus service to the area from Zamora, and tours are available form **Cabañas Yankuam** (see Where to stay, page 1118) and Zamora tour operators. South of Zumbi, the broad valley of the Río Zamora becomes progressively narrower, with forested mountains and lovely views. It is 35 km to Zamora.

Zamora → *Phone code 07. Colour map 11, C3. Population: 14,000. Altitude. 950 m.*

The colonial mission settlement of Zamora, at the confluence of the Ríos Zamora and Bombuscaro, has an increasingly boom-town feeling due to large mining projects in the area. It is reached by road from Gualaquiza (see above) or Loja, 64 km away. The road from Loja is beautiful as it wanders from *páramo* down to high jungle, crossing mountain ranges of cloud forest, weaving high above narrow gorges as it runs alongside the Río Zamora. The town itself is hilly, with a pleasant climate. It gives access to the **Alto Nangaritza** (see above) and is the gateway to the lowland portion of **Parque Nacional Podocarpus** (see page 1065). Between town and the park is **Copalinga**, a bird-rich private reserve (see Where to stay, page 1118). There are two *orquidearios*, **Tzanka** ⓘ *José Luis Tamayo y Jorge Mosquera, T260 5692, US$2* and **Pafinia** ⓘ *Av del Ejército Km 2, T260 5911*. For information about the town: **Unidad de Turismo** ⓘ *Municipio, Diego de Vaca y 24 de Mayo, by the plaza, T260 5316, ext 110, Mon-Fri 0800-1230, 1400-1730*.

◎ Central and southern Oriente listings

For hotel and restaurant price codes, and other relevant information, see Essentials.

◐ Where to stay

Archidona *p1112*

$$$$-$$$ Hakuna Matata, Vía Shungu Km 3.9, off the road between Tena and Archidona, T288 9617, www.hakunamat.com. Comfortable cabins in a lovely setting by the Río Inchillaqui. Includes 3 meals, walks,

river bathing and horse riding. Excellent food, Belgian hosts, pleasant atmosphere. Warmly recommended.

$$$ Huasquila, Vía Huasquila, Km 3.5, Cotundo, T237 6158, www.huasquila.com. Wheel chair accessible bungalows and Kichwa style cabins, includes breakfast and dinner, jungle walks, caving, rock art.

$$$ Orchid Paradise, 2 km north of town, T288 9232. Cabins in nice secondary forest with lots of birds. Full board or cheaper with only breakfast, owner organizes tours in the area.

$ Regina, Rocafuerte 446, 1 block north of the plaza, T288 9144. Private or shared bath, cold water, ample parking, pleasant, family-run.

Tena *p1112, map p1113*

$$ Christian's Palace, JL Mera y Sucre, T288 6047. Restaurant, a/c, cheaper with fan, pool, modern and comfortable.

$$ La Casa del Abuelo, JL Mera 628, T09-9900 0914, www.tomas-lodge.com. Nice quiet place, comfortable rooms, small garden, hot water, ceiling fan, parking, tours. Recommended.

$$ Los Yutzos, Augusto Rueda 190 y 15 de Noviembre, T09-9567 0160, www.uchutican. com/yutzos. Comfortable rooms and beautiful grounds overlooking the Río Pano, quiet and family-run. A/c, cheaper with fan, parking.

$ Austria, Tarqui y Díaz de Pineda, T288 7205. Spacious rooms, with a/c, cheaper with fan, ample parking, quiet, good value.

$ Limoncocha, Sangay 533, Sector Corazón de Jesús, on a hillside 4 blocks from the bus station, ask for directions, T284 6303, http:// limoncocha.tripod.com. Concrete house with terrace and hammocks, some rooms with a/c, private or shared bath, hot water, fan, laundry and cooking facilities, breakfast available, parking, German-Ecuadorean run, enthusiastic owners organize tours. Out of the way in a humble neighbourhood, nice views, pleasant atmosphere, good value.

$ Traveler's Lodging, 15 de Noviembre 438 y 9 de Octubre, T288 6372, www.amarongachi. com. Many different rooms and prices, front ones noisy, best to look around and choose for yourself, some rooms with a/c, cheaper with fan, Amarongachi Tours on the premises.

Misahuallí *p1113*

$$$$ El Jardin Aleman, jungle lodge on shores of Río Mishualli, 3 km from town, T289 0122, www.eljardinaleman.com. Comfortable rooms with bath, hot water. Price includes 3 meals and river tour, set in protected rainforest.

$$$$ Hamadryade, behind the Mariposario, 4 km from town, T09-8590 9992, www. hamadryade-lodge.com. Luxury lodge in a 64-ha forest reserve, 5 designer wood cabins, packages include breakfast, dinner and excursions, French chef, pool, lovely views down to the river.

$$$ Hostería Misahuallí, across the river from town, T289 0063, www.hosteriamisahualli. com. Cabins for up to 6 in a nice setting, includes breakfast, other meals on request, electric shower, fan, pool and tennis court, lovely sunsets.

$$-$ Banana Lodge, 500 m from town on road to Pununo, T289 0190, www. bananalodge.com. Nicely decorated hostel, ample rooms, cheaper in dorm, huge garden with hammocks, breakfast available, cooking facilities, parking, US$4 pp for campervans, opened in 2013, Russian-Ecuadorean run.

$$-$ Cabañas Río Napo, cross the suspension bridge, then 100 m on the left-hand side, T09-9990 4352. Nice rustic cabins with thatch roof, private bath, hot water, ample grounds along the river, run by a local Kichwa family, enthusiastic and friendly.

$$-$ El Paisano, Rivadeneyra y Tandalia, T289 0027, www.hostalelpaisano.com. Restaurant, hot water, mosquito nets, small pool, helpful.

$ Shaw, Santander on the Plaza, T289 0163, hostalshaw@hotmail.com. Good restaurant, hot water, fan, simple rooms, annexe with kitchen facilities and small pool, operate their own tours, English spoken, very knowledgeable. Good value. Recommended.

Lodges on the Upper Río Napo

Casa del Suizo, Quito office: Julio Zaldumbide y Valladolid, T02-256 6090, www.casadel suizo.com. On north shore at Ahuano, resort with capacity for 200, comfortable rooms, well-tended grounds, pool, gift shop, great river views. Swiss-Ecuadorean owned. US$99 per night.

Cotococha, Quito office: Muros N27-94 y González Suárez, T512 3358, www.cotococha. com, along the road east of Puerto Napo. Comfortable well-screened cabins. Jungle walks, tubing, waterfalls and community visits. US$320 for 4 days.

Jatun Sacha Biological Station, east of Ahuano and easily accessible by bus, Quito T02-331 7163, www.jatunsacha.org. A 2500-ha reserve for education, research and tourism. 507 birds, 2500 plants and 765 butterfly species have been identified. Basic cabins with shared bath, cold water, good self-guided trails, canopy tower. US$30 per night, day visit US$6, guiding US$20 per group. Good value.

Liana Lodge, on Río Arajuno near its confluence with the Napo, Tena T06 301 7702, www.amazoonico.org. Comfortable cabins with terraces and river views on a 1700-ha reserve. *Centro de rescate* has animals on site. US$250 for 4 days. Recommended. Also arranges stays at **Runa Wasi**, next door; basic cabins run by the local Kichwa community, US$25 per night with 3 meals, guiding extra.

Yachana, Quito office: Reina Victoria N24-217 y Roca, T02-252 3777, www.yachana. com. Located in the village of Mondaña, 2 hrs downstream from Misahuallí or 2½ hrs upstream from Coca. Proceeds go toward supporting community development projects. For 4 days: US$510-760. Recommended.

Puyo *p1114*

$$$$ Altos del Pastaza Lodge, access from Km 16 of Puyo-Macas road, Quito office: Leonardo Murialdo E11-04 y los Nardos, T09-9767 4686, www.altosdelpastazalodge.com. Attractive lodge in 65-ha reserve overlooking the Río Pastaza, pool. Don't expect much wildlife, but a nice place to relax, 1- to 4-day packages include meals and walking tours.

$$$$ Las Cascadas Lodge, Quito office: Amazonas N23-87 y Wilson, T02-250 0530, www.surtrek.com. First-class lodge 40 km east of Puyo, 8 rooms with terraces, includes full board, activities and transport from/to Quito, waterfalls; 3- and 4-day packages available.

$$$ El Jardín, Paseo Turístico, Barrio Obrero, T288 6101, www.eljardinrelax.com.ec. Nice rooms and garden, good upmarket restaurant.

$$ Delfín Rosado, Ceslao Marín y Atahualpa, T288 8757. Pool, modern rooms with a/c.

$$ Las Palmas, 20 de Julio y 4 de Enero, 5 blocks from centre, T288 4832, hostal_laspalmas_puyo@yahoo.com. Comfortable new rooms with a/c and fridge, older ones with fan are cheaper (best upstairs), private bath, hot water.

$$ San Luís-Memon's, one block from bus terminal, T288 4064. Nice modern rooms, rooftop terrace with restaurant, good choice for late arrivals or early departures.

$ Colibrí, Av Manabí entre Bolívar y Galápagos, T288 3054. Hot water, private bath, parking, away from centre, simple but nice, good value, offers tours. Recommended.

Southern Oriente jungle lodges

Kapawi, Quito office: Foch E7-38 y Reina Victoria, T02-600 9333, www.kapawi.com. A top-of-the-line lodge located on the Río Capahuari near its confluence with the Pastaza, not far from the Peruvian border. Run by the local Achuar community and accessible only by small aircraft and motor canoe. The biodiversity is good, but more emphasis is placed on ethno-tourism here than at other upmarket jungle lodges. US$1265 for 4 days includes land and air transport from Quito.

Macas *p1114*

$$$$ Arrayán y Piedra, Km 7 Vía a Puno, T304 6448. Large resort style lodging, nice rooms, pool, ample grounds, restaurant with very good food, but variable service.

$$$ Casa Upano, Av La Ciudad, Barrio La Barranca, 1 km from centre, T270 2674, www.realnaturetravel.com. A family-run B&B in a private home, other meals available with advance notice, excellent food, parking, ample comfortable rooms, huge garden with many birds, day-visit US$5 with advance notice. Very helpful, English spoken, organize birdwatching tours. Warmly recommended.

$ Casa Blanca, Soasti 14-29 y Sucre, T270 0195. Hot water, small pool, modern and comfortable, very helpful, good value, often full, book in advance.

$ Nivel 5, Juan de la Cruz y Amazonas, T270 1240. Nice modern multi-storey hotel, hot water, fan, pool, parking.

Macas to Gualaquiza p1114

Sucúa

$$$ Lucelinda, 1 km vía a Cuenca, T274 2118. Comfortable rooms with fans, large clean pool, good restaurant.

$$ Arutam, Vía a Macas Km 1, north of town, T274 0851. Restaurant, pool and sauna, parking, modern comfortable rooms, nice grounds, sports fields, well suited to families.

Several other hotels (**$**) in town.

Méndez

$ Interoceánico, C Quito on the plaza, T276 0245. Hot water, parking, smart and modern, good value.

Limón

$ Dream House, Quito y Bolívar, T277 0166. With restaurant, shared bath, hot water, adequate.

San Juan Bosco

$ Antares, on the plaza, T304 2128. Restaurant, hot water, indoor pool, simple functional rooms, helpful owner.

Gualaquiza p1115

$ Gran Hotel, Orellana y Gran Pasaje, T278 0722. Modern concrete building, hot water, fan, parking, small rooms, some without windows.

$ Wakis, Orellana 08-52 y Domingo Comín, T278 0138. Older simple place with small rooms, private or shared bath, cold water, enthusiastic owner speaks English.

Alto Nangaritza

$$ Cabañas Yankuam, 3 km south of Las Orquideas, T260 5739 (Zamora), www.lindoecuadortours.com. Rustic cabins, includes breakfast, other tasty meals on request, private or shared bath, good walking in surrounding jungle-clad hills, organizes trips up the Río Nangaritza. Family-run. Reservations required, 1 week advance notice preferred.

Zamora p1115

With the ongoing mining boom, many new hotels have opened since 2012.

$$$-$$ Copalinga, Km 3 on the road to the Bombuscaro entrance of Parque Nacional Podocarpus, T09-9347 7013, www.copalinga.com. Nice comfortable cabins with balcony in a lovely setting, includes very good breakfast, other delicious meals available if arranged in advance, more rustic cabins with shared bath are cheaper, excellent birdwatching, walking trails. Belgian run, English, French and Dutch spoken, attentive, reserve ahead. Highly recommended.

$$ Samuria, 24 de Mayo y Diego de Vaca, T260 7801, hotelsamuria@hotmail.com. Modern bright hotel, comfortable well furnished rooms, restaurant, parking.

$ Betania, Francisco de Orellana entre Diego de Vaca y Amazonas, T260 7030, hotel-betania@hotmail.com. Modern, functional, breakfast available, hot water.

$ Wampushkar, Diego de Vaca y Pasaje Vicente Aldeán, T260 7800. Nice modern hotel, ample rooms, hot water, parking, good value.

🍴 Restaurants

Tena p1112, map p1113

$$$ The Marquis, Amazonas entre Calderón y Olmedo, daily 1200-1600, 1800-2200. Upmarket restaurant serving good steaks.

$$ Chuquitos, García Moreno by the plaza. Mon-Sat 0800-2100, Sun 1100-2100. Good food, à la carte only, seating on a balcony overlooking the river. Pleasant atmosphere, attentive service and nice views. Popular and recommended. *Araña Bar* downstairs.

$$ Pizzería Bella Selva, Malecón south of the footbridge; second location on east side. Daily 1100-2300. Pizza and pasta.

$ Safari, Av 15 de Noviembre y F Monteros, Mon-Sat 0700-2300, Sun 0700-1600. Set meals, good quality and value.

Café Tortuga, Malecón south of the footbridge, Mon-Sat 0700-1930, Sun 0700-1300. Juices, snacks and sweets, nice location, spotless, friendly Swiss owner. Recommended.

Misahuallí *p1113*

$$$ El Jardín, 300 m past bridge to Ahuano. Daily 1200-1600, 1800-2200. Variety of dishes, beautiful garden setting.

$$-$ Doña Gloria, Arteaga y Rivadeneyra by corner of plaza. Daily 0730-2030. Good set meals.

Puyo *p1114*

$$$-$$ Tapas y Topes, opposite Parque Acuático near bus terminal. Daily 1100-1500, 1700-2400. Wide variety of tasty dishes.

$$ Pizzería Buon Giorno, Orellana entre Villamil y 27 de Febrero. Mon-Sat 1200-2300, Sun 1400-2300. Good pizza, lasagne and salads, pleasant atmosphere, very popular. Recommended.

El Fariseo Café, Atahualpa entre 27 de Febrero y General Villamil. Open 0700-2200. Good cakes and the best coffee in town.

Escobar Café, Atahualpa y Orellana. Daily 0630-2400. Good for early breakfast, sandwiches, bar at night, attractive bamboo decor.

Macas *p1114*

$$ Junglab, Bolívar entre Guamote y Amazonas, T270 2448. Tue-Sun 1200-2230. Delicious creative meals using local produce.

$$-$ La Italiana, Soasti y Sucre. Mon-Sat 1200-2300. Great pizzas, pasta and salads.

$ La Choza de Mama Sara, 10 de Agosto y 9 de Octubre. Mon-Sat 0830-2100. Traditional Macabeo cuisine such as ayampacos and yuca and palm tamales, served for breakfast. Also a choice of set lunches, good value.

$ Rincón Manabita, Amazonas y 29 de Mayo. Mon-Fri 0700-2200, Sat-Sun 0700-1600. Good breakfasts and a choice of set meals which are delicious and filling. Also à la carte.

Zamora *p1115*

$ Agate, near main plaza. Mon-Fri midday only. Good set lunch and à la carte.

$ King Ice, Diego de Vaca y José Luis Tamayo, by the plaza. Daily 0900-2400. Snacks and a few à la carte dishes.

Spiga Pan, 24 de Mayo, ½ block downhill from the plaza. Great bakery with a variety of hot bread, cream cakes and fresh fruit yoghurt. A very good option in this otherwise un-gastronomic town.

⏱ What to do

Tena *p1112, map p1113*

Rafting tours cost US$50-70 per day, safety standards vary between operators. Avoid touts selling tours on the street.

Amarongachi Tours at Hostal Traveler's Lodging (see Where to stay above), jungle tours.

AquaXtreme, Malecón Francisco de Orellana 248, T288 8746, www.axtours.com. Offers rafting, kayaking, canyoning and horse riding.

Limoncocha, at Hostal Limoncocha (see Where to stay above), rafting, kayaking and jungle, English and German spoken.

Ríos Ecuador, Tarqui 230 y Díaz de Pineda, T288 6727, www.riosecuador.com. Highly recommended whitewater rafting and kayak trips, and a 4-day kayaking school (US$320).

Misahuallí *p1113*

Jungle tours (US$45-80 pp per day) can be arranged by most hotels as well as the following:

Ecoselva, Santander on the plaza, T289 0019, ecoselva@yahoo.es. Recommended guide Pepe Tapia speaks English and has a biology background. Well organized and reliable.

Runawa Tours, in La Posada hotel, on the plaza, T09-9818 1961, www.misahualliamazon. com. Owner Carlos Santander, tubing, kayak and jungle tours.

Teorumi, on the plaza, T289 0203, www.teorumi.com. Offers tours to the Shiripuno Kichwa community.

Puyo *p1114*

All of the following offer jungle tours of varying lengths, US$25-50 pp per day.

Coka Tours, 27 de Febrero y Ceslao Marín, T288 6108, denisecoka@gmail.com.

Naveda Santos, at the Terminal Terrestre, upstairs, T288 3974. Owner, Marco Naveda.
Selvavida Travel, Ceslao Marín y Atahualpa, T288 9729, www.selvavidatravel.com. Specializes in rafting and Parque Nacional Yasuní.

Macas *p1114*

Tours to indigenous communities and lowland portions of Parque Nacional Sangay, cost about US$50 per day.
Insondu, Bolívar y Soasti, T270 2533.
Planeta Tours, Domingo Comín 7-35 y Soasti, T270 1328.
Real Nature Travel Company, at Casa Upano, see Where to stay, above. Run by RhoAnn Wallace and professional birdwatching guide Galo Real, English spoken.

Zamora *p1115*

BioAventura, at Orquideario Tzanka (see page 1115), T09-9381 4472. Fernado Ortega offers downhill bike rides along the old road Loja-Zamora.
Cabañas Yankuam, see page 1118. Offer tours to the Alto Nangaritza.
Wellington Valdiviezo, T09-9380 2211, lindozamoraturistico@yahoo.es. Tours to the Alto Nangaritza, Shuar communities, adventure sports, visits to shamans. Contact in advance.

⊖ Transport

Tena *p1112, map p1113*
Air Airport at Ahuano. TAME to **Quito** on Mon, Wed and Fri.
Bus Run-down Terminal Terrestre on 15 de Noviembre, 1 km from the centre (taxi US$1). To **Quito**, US$6, 5 hrs. To **Ambato**, via Baños, US$5, 4½ hrs. To **Baños**, US$4, 3½ hrs. To **Riobamba**, via Ambato, US$6, 5½ hrs. To **Puyo**, US$3, 2 hrs. To **Coca and Lago Agrio**, fares given above. To **Misahuallí**, see below. To **Archidona**, from Amazonas y Bolívar by market, every 20 mins, US$0.25, 15 mins.

Misahuallí *p1113*
Bus Local buses run from the plaza. To **Tena**, hourly 0600-1900, US$1, 45 mins. Make long-distance connections in Tena. To **Quito**, 1 direct bus a day at 0830, US$7, 5 hrs.
River No scheduled passenger service, but motorized canoes for 8-10 passengers can be chartered for touring.

Puyo *p1114*
Air The nearest airport to Puyo is at Shell, 13 km. Military flights to jungle villages are not open to foreigners, but light aircraft can be chartered starting around US$300 per hr.
Bus Terminal Terrestre on the outskirts of town, a 10- to 15-min walk from the centre; taxi US$1. To **Baños**, US$2, 1½ hrs. To **Ambato**, US$3, 2½ hrs. To **Quito**, US$5, 5 hrs via Ambato. To **Riobamba**, US$4, 3½ hrs. To **Tena**, see above. To **Macas**, US$5, 2½ hrs.

Macas *p1114*
Air Small modern airport within walking distance at Cuenca y Amazonas. To **Quito**, Thu and Sun with TAME (office at airport T270 4940) Sit on left for best views of Volcán Sangay. Air taxis available to jungle villages, US$600 per hr for 9 passengers.
Bus Terminal Terrestre by the market. To **Puyo**, see above. To **Baños**, US$6, 4½ hrs. To **Quito**, via Puyo, Baños and Ambato, US$8, 8 hrs. To **Riobamba** through Parque Nacional Sangay, a beautiful ride, 6 daily, US$5, 4 hrs. To **Cuenca**, US$8, 8 hrs, via Méndez and Guarumales (mostly paved) or via Plan de Milagro and Gualaceo (closed 2014). To **Gualaquiza**, US$8, 8 hrs, where you can get a bus to Zamora and Loja (see below). To **Sucúa**, hourly, US$0.90, 30 min. To **9 de Octubre**, for **PN Sangay**, US$1.50, 45 mins.

Gualaquiza *p1115*
Bus To **Macas**, see above. To **Cuenca**; via Sígsig, 4 daily, US$6.25, 6 hrs; or via Plan de Milagro and Gualaceo (closed 2014). To **Zamora**, US$3.50, 3½ hrs. To **Loja**, US$6, 5½ hrs.

Alto Nangaritza

To **Las Orquídeas**, with Trans Zamora, from Zamora at 0400, 0645, 1115 and 1230, US$3.80, 3½ hrs; from Yantzaza at 0440, 0740, 1150 and 1310, US$2.50, 3½ hrs; with **Unión Yantzaza**, from Yantzaza at 0430, 0930, 1130, 1430 and 1630; from Loja at 1415, 1510, US$6.20, 5½ hrs.

Zamora *p1115*

Bus Leave from Terminal Terrestre. To **Loja**, frequent, 1½-2 hrs, US$2.40; to **Gualaquiza**, US$3.50, 3½ hrs, where you transfer for Macas.

⊕ Directory

Tena *p1112, map p1113*
Banks For ATMs: Banco del Austro, 15 de Noviembre y Díaz de Pineda;

Banco Pichincha, 15 de Noviembre y Tena, on the way to bus terminal.

Puyo *p1114*
Banks For ATM: Banco del Austro, Atahualpa entre 27 de Febrero y 9 de Octubre; Banco de Guayaquil, Ceslao Marín y 20 de Julio; Banco Pichincha, 10 de Agosto y Orellana.

Macas *p1114*
Banks For ATMs: Banco del Austro, Soasti y Domingo Comín; Banco Pichincha, Soasti y 10 de Agosto.

Zamora *p1115*
Banks For ATMs: Banco del Austro, Jorge Mosquera by the Plaza; also Banco Pichincha.

Galápagos Islands

A trip to the Galápagos Islands is an unforgettable experience. The islands are world-renowned for their fearless wildlife but no amount of hype can prepare the visitor for such a close encounter with nature. Here you can snorkel with penguins, sea lions and the odd hammerhead shark, watch giant 200-kg tortoises lumbering through cactus forest and enjoy the courtship display of the blue-footed booby and magnificent frigatebird, all in startling close-up.

Lying on the Equator, 970 km west of the Ecuadorean coast, the Galápagos consist of six main islands, 12 smaller islands and over 40 islets. The islands have an estimated population of 27,000, but this does not include many temporary inhabitants. Santa Cruz has 16,600 inhabitants, with Puerto Ayora the main city and tourist centre. San Cristóbal has a population of 7900 with the capital of the archipelago, Puerto Baquerizo Moreno. The largest island, Isabela, is 120 km long and forms over half the total land area of the archipelago, some 2500 people live there, mostly in and around Puerto Villamil on the south coast. Floreana, the first island to be settled, has about 160 residents.

Background

The Galápagos have never been connected with the continent. Gradually, over many hundreds of thousands of years, animals and plants from over the sea somehow migrated there and as time went by they adapted themselves to Galápagos conditions and came to differ more and more from their continental ancestors. Unique marine and terrestrial environments, due to the continuing volcanic formation of the islands in the west of the archipelago and its location at the nexus of several major marine currents, have created laboratory-type conditions where only certain species have been allowed access. The formidable barriers which prevent many species from travelling between the islands, has led to a very high level of endemism. A quarter of the species of shore fish, half of the plants and almost all the reptiles are found nowhere else. In many cases different forms have evolved on the different islands. Charles

Darwin recognized this speciation within the archipelago when he visited the Galápagos on the *Beagle* in 1835 and his observations played a substantial part in his formulation of the theory of evolution.

This natural experiment has been under threat ever since the arrival of the first whaling ships and even more so since the first permanent human settlement. New species were introduced and spread very rapidly, placing the endemic species at risk. Quarantine programmes have since been implemented in an attempt to prevent the introduction and spread of even more species, but the rules are not easy to enforce. There have also been campaigns to eradicate some of the introduced species on some islands, but this is inevitably a very slow, expensive and difficult process.

One striking feature of the islands is the tameness of the animals. The islands were uninhabited when they were discovered in 1535 and the animals still have little instinctive fear of man.

Plant and animal species are grouped into three categories. **Endemic species** are those which occur only in the Galápagos and nowhere else on the planet. Examples of Galápagos endemics are the Galápagos marine and Galápagos land iguana, Galápagos fur sea lion, flightless cormorant and the 'daisy tree' (*scalesia pedunculata*). **Native species** make their homes in the Galápagos as well as other parts of the world. Examples include all three species of boobies, frigate birds and the various types of mangroves. Although not unique to the islands, these native species have been an integral part of the Galápagos ecosystems for a very long time. **Introduced species** on the other hand are very recent arrivals, brought by man, and inevitably the cause of much damage. They include cattle, goats, donkeys, pigs, dogs, cats, rats and over 500 species of plants such as elephant grass (for grazing cattle), and fruit trees. The unchecked expansion of these introduced species has upset the natural balance of the archipelago. The number of tourists also has grown steadily: from 11,800 in 1979, to 68,900 in 2000, to 204,400 in 2013. From 2007 to 2010, Galápagos was on the UNESCO list of endangered World Heritage Sites. Although it is now off the list, promoting environmental conservation and sustainable development in the face of growing tourism and population remains a substantial challenge.

Arriving in the Galápagos Islands → *Phone code: 05. Colour map 10.*

Getting there

Airports at **Baltra**, across a narrow strait from Santa Cruz, and **Puerto Baquerizo Moreno**, on San Cristóbal, receive flights from mainland Ecuador. The two islands are 96 km apart and on most days there are local flights in light aircraft between them, as well as to **Puerto Villamil** on Isabela. There is also speedboat service between Puerto Ayora (Santa Cruz) and the other populated islands. There are no international flights to Galápagos.

AeroGal, **LAN** and **TAME** all fly from Quito and Guayaquil to Baltra or San Cristóbal. Baltra receives more flights but there is at least one daily to each destination. You can arrive at one and return from the other. You can also depart from Quito and return to Guayaquil or vice versa, but you may not buy a one-way ticket. The return airfare varies considerably, starting at about US$500 from Quito, US$400 from Guayaquil (2014 prices). See also Fees and inspections, below.

Airport transfers Two buses meet flights from the mainland at Baltra: one runs to the port or *muelle* (10 minutes, no charge) where the cruise boats wait; the other goes to Canal de Itabaca, the narrow channel which separates Baltra from Santa Cruz. It is 15 minutes to the

Canal, free, then you cross on a small ferry, US$0.80. On the other side, buses (US$1.80, may involve a long wait while they fill) and pickup truck taxis (US$18 for up to four passengers) run to Puerto Ayora, 45 minutes. For the return trip to the airport, buses leave the *Terminal Terrestre* on Avenida Baltra in Puerto Ayora (2 km from the pier, taxi US$1) at 0700, 0730 and 0830 daily.
➤ *See also Transport, page 1136.*

Getting around

Emetebe Avionetas ① *Guayaquil at Hotel City Plaza, T04-230 9209, see Directory for local offices,* offers inter-island flights in light aircraft. Two daily flights except Sun between **Puerto Baquerizo Moreno** (San Cristóbal), **Baltra** and **Puerto Villamil** (Isabela). Fares US$155-170 one way; baggage allowance 25 lbs.

Fibras (fibreglass speedboats for about 20 passengers) operate daily between Puerto Ayora and each of Puerto Baquerizo Moreno, Puerto Villamil, and Puerto Velasco Ibarra (Floreana); US$30-35 one way, two hours or more depending on the weather and sea. Tickets are sold by several agencies in Puerto Baquerizo Moreno, Puerto Ayora, and Puerto Villamil. This can be a wild ride in rough seas, life vests should be provided, take drinking water.

Information and advice

A recommended bilingual web site is www.galapagospark.org. It describes each visitor site and gives details of guides and tourist vessels operating in the islands.

Tourist offices Puerto Ayora: iTur ① *Av Charles Darwin y 12 de Febrero, T252 6614 ext 22, www.santacruz.gob.ec, Mon-Fri 0730-1230, 1400-1930, Sat-Sun 1600-1930,* has information about Puerto Ayora and Santa Cruz Island; **Ministerio de Turismo** ① *Charles Binford y 12 de*
Febrero, T252 6174, Mon-Fri 0830-1300, 1430-1700, is mostly an administrative office but also receives complaints about agencies and vessels. **Puerto Baquerizo Moreno: Municipal tourist office** ① *Malecón Charles Darwin y 12 de Febrero, T252 0119 ext 120, Mon-Fri 0730-1230, 1400-1800,* is downstairs at the Municipio **Ministerio de Turismo** ① *12 de Febrero e Ignacio Hernández, T252 0704, Mon-Fri 0830-1230, 1400-1730,* operates as in Santa Cruz, above. **Puerto Villamil: Municipal tourist office** ① *by the park, T252 9002, ext 113, Mon-Fri 0730-1230, 1400-1700,* has local information.

Fees and inspections A US$10 fee is collected at Quito or Guayaquil airport, where a registration form must be completed. You can also pre-register on line at www.gobiernogalapagos.gob.ec, or ask your tour operator to do so for you. Bags are checked prior to flights to Galápagos, no live animals, meat, dairy products, fresh fruit or vegetables may be taken to the islands. On arrival, every

foreign visitor must pay a US$100 National Park fee. All fees are cash only. Be sure to have your passport to hand at the airport and keep all fee receipts throughout your stay in the islands. Bags are checked again on departure, as nothing may be taken off the islands. Puerto Villamil charges a US$5 port fee on arrival in Isabela.

Basic rules Do not touch any of the animals, birds or plants. Do not transfer sand, seeds or soil from one island to another. Do not leave litter anywhere; nor take food on to the uninhabited islands, which are also no-smoking zones. There is increasingly close contact between people and sea lions throughout Galápagos. Never touch them however, and keep your distance from the male 'beach-masters', they have been known to bite. Always take food, plenty of water and a compass or GPS if hiking on your own. There are many crisscrossing animal trails and it is easy to get lost. Also watch out for the large-spined opuntia cactus; and the poisonwood tree (*manzanillo*) found near beaches, contact with its leaves or bark can cause severe skin reactions.

What to take A remedy for seasickness is recommended. A good supply of sun block and skin cream to prevent windburn and chapped lips is essential, as are a hat and sunglasses. You should be prepared for dry and wet landings, the latter involving wading ashore; keep photo equipment and other delicate items in plastic bags. The animals are so tame that you will take far more photos than you expected; if you run out of memory cards they can be bought in Puerto Ayora, but best to take your own. Snorkelling equipment is particularly useful as much of the sea-life is only visible under water. The cheaper boats may not provide equipment or it may be of poor quality. If in doubt, bring your own. Good sturdy footwear is important, boots and shoes soon wear out on the abrasive lava terrain. Always bring some US$ cash to Galápagos, there are only a few ATMs and they may be out of order.

Tipping A ship's crew and guides are usually tipped separately. Amounts are often suggested onboard or in agencies' brochures, but these should be considered in light of the quality of service received and your own resources.

If you have problems Raise any issues first with your guide or ship's captain. Serious complaints are rare but may filed with **iTur** or **Ministerio de Turismo** offices in Puerto Ayora or Puerto Baquerizo Moreno, see Tourist offices above.

Best time to visit The Galápagos climate can be divided into a hot season (December-May), when there is a possibility of heavy showers, and the cool or *garúa* (mist) season (June to November), when the days generally are more cloudy and there is often rain or drizzle. July and August can be windy, force four or five. Daytime clothing should be lightweight. (Clothing generally, even on 'luxury cruises', should be casual and comfortable.) At night, however, particularly at sea and at higher altitudes, temperatures fall below 15°C and warm clothing is required. The sea is cold July-October; underwater visibility is best January to March. Ocean temperatures are usually higher to the east and lower at the western end of the archipelago. Despite all these climatic variations, conditions are generally favourable for visiting Galápagos throughout the year.

High season for tourism is June to August and December to January, when last-minute arrangements are generally not possible. Some boats may be heavily booked throughout the year and you should plan well in advance if you want to travel on a specific vessel at a specific time.

Overseas agencies

Galápagos Classic Cruises, 6 Keyes Rd, London NW2 3XA, T020-8933 0613, www.galapagoscruises.co.uk. Specialists in cruises and diving holidays to the islands including tailor-made land tours in Ecuador and additions to Peru and Bolivia on request.
Galápagos Holidays, 14 Prince Arthur Av, Suite 311, Toronto, Ontario M5R 1A9, T416-413 9090, T1-800-661 2512 (toll free), www.galapagosholidays.com.
Galápagos Network, 5805 Blue Lagoon Dr, Suite 160, Miami, FL 33126, T305-2626264, www.ecoventura.com.
INCA, 1311 63rd St, Emeryville, CA 94608, T510-420 1550, www.inca1.com.

International Expeditions, 1 Environs Park, Helena, Alabama, 35080, T205-428 1700, T1-855-232 7134, www.ietravel.com.
Select Latin America, 3.51 Canterbury Court, 1-3 Brixton Road, Kennington Park Business Centre, London SW9 6DE, T020-7407 1478, www.selectlatinamerica.com. Tailor-made holidays and small group tours.
Sol International, PO Box 1738, Kodak, TN 37764, T931-536 4893, T1-800-765 5657, www.solintl.com.
Wilderness Travel, 1102 Ninth St, Berkeley, CA 94710, T510 558 2488, T1-800-368 2794, www.wildernesstravel.com.

Choosing a tour

There are a growing number of options for visiting Galápagos but the best remains the traditional **live-aboard cruise** (*tour navegable*), where you travel and sleep on a yacht, tour boat or cruise ship. These vessels travel at night, arriving at a new landing site each day. Cruises range from three to 14 nights, seven is recommended. Itineraries are controlled by the National Park to distribute cruise boats evenly throughout the islands. All cruises begin with a morning flight from the mainland on the first day and end on the last day with a midday flight back to the mainland. The less expensive boats are normally smaller and less powerful so you see less and spend more time travelling; also the guiding may be mostly in Spanish. The more expensive boats have air conditioning, hot water and private baths. All boats have to conform to certain minimum safety standards; more expensive boats are better equipped. Boats with over 20 passengers take quite a time to disembark and re-embark people, while the smaller boats have a more lively motion, which is important if you are prone to seasickness. Note also that there may be limitations for vegetarians on the cheaper boats. The least expensive boats (economy class) cost about US$200 per person per day and a few of these vessels are dodgy. For around US$250-350 per day (tourist and tourist superior class) you will be on a better, faster boat which can travel more quickly between visitor sites, leaving more time to spend ashore. Over US$400 per day are the first-class and luxury brackets, with far more comfortable and spacious cabins, as well as a superior level of service and cuisine. No boat may sail without a park-trained guide.

The table on page 1126 lists live-aboard tour vessels; for dive boats see page 1134. The sailing vessels listed also have motors, and many frequently operate under engine power. All details are subject to change. Captains, crews and guides regularly change on all boats. These factors, as well as the sea, weather and your fellow passengers will all influence the quality of your experience.

Island-hopping is another option for visiting Galápagos, whereby you spend a night or two at hotels on some of the four populated islands, travelling between them in speedboats. You cover less ground than on a cruise, see fewer wildlife sites, and cannot visit the more distant islands. Island-hopping is sold in organized packages but visitors in no rush can also travel between and explore the populated islands independently and at their leisure.

Galápagos tourist vessels

Name	Description	Capacity	Website
Silversea	cruise ship	100	silversea.com
Galápagos Legend	cruise ship	100	kleintours.com
Xpedition	cruise ship	100	galapagosxpedition.co.uk
Santa Cruz	cruise ship	90	galapagosvoyage.com
Nat Geo Edeavour	cruise ship	80	expeditions.com
Eclipse	cruise ship	48	galapagos-eclipse.com
Nat Geo Islander	cruise ship	48	expeditions.com
Isabela II	cruise ship	40	galapagosvoyage.com
Millenium	cruise ship	40	galasam.net
Coral I	motor yacht	36	kleintours.com
Evolution	cruise ship	32	galapagosexpeditions.com
La Pinta	cruise ship	32	lapintagalapagoscruise.com
Coral II	motor yacht	20	kleintours.com
Eric	motor yacht	20	ecoventura.com
Flamingo I	motor yacht	20	ecoventura.com
Galápagos Adventure	motor yacht	20	various
Letty	motor yacht	20	ecoventura.com
Aída María	motor yacht	16	various
Amigo I	motor vessel	16	various
Anahi	motor catamaran	16	andandotours.com
Angelito I	motor yacht	16	angelitogalapagos.com
Archipel II	motor yacht	16	various
Athala II	motor catamaran	16	various
Beluga	motor yacht	16	enchantedexpeditions.com
Cachalote	2-mast schooner	16	enchantedexpeditions.com
Carina	motor yacht	16	various
Cormorant Evolution	motor catamaran	16	cormorantgalapagos.com
Darwin	motor vessel	16	various
Edén	motor yacht	16	various
Estrella del Mar I	motor yacht	16	galasam.net
Floreana	motor yacht	16	yatefloreana.com
Fragata	motor yacht	16	various
Galap Adventure II	motor yacht	16	various
Galap Journey I	motor catamarans	16	galapagosjourneycruises.com
Galapagos Odyssey	motor yatch	16	galapagosodyssey.com

Name	Description	Capacity	Website
Galapagos Vision I	1-mast catamaran	16	various
Galapagos Voyager	motor yatch	16	galapagos-voyager.com
Galaxy	motor yacht	16	various
Golondrina I	motor vessel	16	various
Grace	motor yatch	16	galapagosexpeditions.com
Gran Monserrat	motor yacht	16	various
Guantanamera	motor yacht	16	various
Integrity	motor yacht	16	various
Liberty	motor yacht	16	various
Majestic	motor vessel	16	www.galasam.com.ec
Mary Anne	3-mast barquentine	16	andandotours.com
Monserrat	motor vessel	16	various
Monserrat II	motor vessel	16	various
Ocean Spray	motor catamaran	16	galapagosoceanspray.com
Pelíkano	motor vessel	16	various
Queen Beatriz	motor catamaran	16	various
Queen of Galap	motor catamaran	16	galasam.net
Reina Silvia	motor yacht	16	reinasilvia.com
Samba	motor yacht	16	various
San José	motor yacht	16	various
San Juan II	motor vessel	16	various
Sea Man II	motor catamaran	16	various
Tip Top II	motor vessel	16	rwittmer.com
Tip Top III	motor yacht	16	rwittmer.com
Tip Top IV	motor yacht	16	rwittmer.com
Treasure of Galap	motor catamaran	16	treasureofgalapagos.com
Xavier III	motor vessel	16	various
Yolita II	motor yacht	16	various
Albatros	motor yacht	14	various
Beagle	2-mast schooner	13	angermeyercruises.com
Amazonía	1-mast catamaran	12	various
Encantada	2-mast schooner	12	scubagalapagos.com
New Flamingo	motor vessel	12	various
Merak	1 mast sailer	8	various

Day tours (*tour diario*) are yet another alternative, based mostly out of Puerto Ayora. Some take you for day-visits to National Park landing sites on nearby unpopulated islands, such as Bartolomé, Seymour, Plazas and Santa Fe (US$140-240), and can be quite good. Others go for the day to the populated islands of Isabela or Floreana, with no stops permitted along the way. The latter require at least four hours of speedboat travel and generally leave insufficient time to enjoy visitor sites; they are not recommended.

None of the above options is cheap, with the flight from the mainland and entry fees alone amounting to about US$600. Galápagos is such a special destination for nature-lovers however, that most agree it is worth saving for and spending on a quality tour. If nature is not your great passion and you are looking mainly for an exotic cruise or beach holiday, then your money will go further and you will likely have a better experience elsewhere.

Booking a tour in advance You can book a Galápagos cruise in several different ways: 1) over the internet; 2) from either a travel agency or directly though a Galápagos wholesaler in your home country; 3) from one of the very many agencies found throughout Ecuador, especially in Quito (see page 993) but also in other tourist centres and Guayaquil (page 1079); or 4) from local agencies, mostly in Puerto Ayora but also in Puerto Baquerizo Moreno. The trade-off is always between time and money: booking from home is most efficient and expensive, last-minute arrangements in Galápagos are cheapest and most time-consuming, while Quito and Guayaquil are intermediate. It is not possible to obtain discounts or make last-minute arrangements in high season (see Best time to visit, above). Surcharges may apply when using a credit card to purchase tours on the islands, there are limits to ATM withdrawals and no cash advances on weekends, so bring cash if looking for a last-minute cruise. Also, if looking for a last-minute sailing, it is best to pay your hotel one night at a time since hoteliers may not refund advance payments. Especially on cheaper boats, check carefully about what is and is not included (eg drinking water, snorkelling equipment, etc).

The islands

Santa Cruz: Puerto Ayora → *Phone code: 05. Population: 12,600.*
Santa Cruz is the most central of the Galápagos islands and the main town is Puerto Ayora. About 1.5 km from the pier is the **Charles Darwin Research Station** ① *at Academy Bay, www. darwinfoundation.org, office Mon-Fri 0700-1600, visitor areas 0600-1800 daily, free.* A visit to the station is a good introduction to the islands. Collections of several of the rare sub-species of giant tortoise are maintained on the station as breeding nuclei, together with tortoise-rearing pens for the young. The **Centro Comunitario de Educación Ambiental** ① *east end of Charles Binford, Mon-Fri 0730-1200, 1400-1700, Sat morning only, free,* has an aquarium and exhibits about the Galápagos Marine Reserve.

There is a beautiful beach at **Tortuga Bay**, 45 minutes' easy walk (2.5 km each way) west from Puerto Ayora on an excellent cobbled path through cactus forest. Start at the west end of Calle Charles Binford; further on there is a gate where you must register, open 0600-1800 daily, free. Make sure you take sun screen, drinking water, and beware of the very strong undertow. Do not walk on the dunes above the beach, which are a marine tortoise nesting area. At the west end of Tortuga Bay is a trail to a lovely mangrove-fringed lagoon, with calmer warmer water, shade, and sometimes a kayak for rent.

Las Grietas is a lovely gorge with a natural pool at the bottom which is popular and splendid for bathing. Take a water taxi from the port to the dock at Punta Estrada (five minutes, US$0.50). It is a five-minute walk from here to the **Finch Bay hotel** and 15 minutes further

Puerto Ayora

Where to stay
1 España
2 Estrella de Mar
3 Lobo de Mar
4 Los Amigos
5 Peregrina
6 Silberstein
7 Sol y Mar

Restaurants
1 El Descanso del Guía
2 Il Giardino
3 Isla Grill
4 La Dolce Italia
5 La Garrapata
6 Rincón del Alma

over rough lava boulders to Las Grietas – well worth the trip.

The Puerto Ayora-Baltra road goes through the agricultural zone in the highlands. The community of **Bellavista** is 7 km from the port, and **Santa Rosa** is 15 km beyond. The area has National Park visitor sites, walking possibilities and upmarket lodgings. **Los Gemelos** are a pair of large sinkholes, formed by collapse of the ground above empty magma chambers. They straddle the road to Baltra, beyond Santa Rosa. You can take a taxi or airport bus all the way; otherwise take a bus to Santa Rosa, then walk one hour uphill. There are several **lava tubes** (natural tunnels) on the island. Some are at **El Mirador**, 3 km from Puerto Ayora on the road to Bellavista. Two more lava tubes are 1 km from Bellavista. They are on private land, it costs US$1.50 to enter the tunnels (bring a torch) and it takes about 30 minutes to walk through them. Tours to the lava tubes can be arranged in Puerto Ayora.

The highest point on Santa Cruz Island is **Cerro Crocker** at 864 m. You can hike here and to two other nearby 'peaks' called **Media Luna** and **Puntudo**. The trail starts at Bellavista where a rough trail map is painted as a mural on the wall of the school. The round trip from Bellavista takes six to eight hours. A permit and guide are not required, but a guide may be helpful. Always take food, water and a compass or GPS.

Another worthwhile trip is to the **El Chato Tortoise Reserve**, where giant tortoises can be seen in the wild during the dry season (June to February). In the wet season the tortoises are breeding down in the arid zone. Follow the road that goes past the Santa Rosa school to 'La Reserva'. At the end of the road (about 3 km) you reach a faded wooden memorial to an Israeli tourist who got lost here. Take the trail to the right (west) for about 45 minutes. There are many confusing trails in the reserve itself; take food, water and a compass or GPS. If you have no hiking experience, horses can sometimes be hired at Santa Rosa or arrange a tour from Puerto Ayora.

Tortoises can also be seen at **Cerro Mesa** and at several private ranches, some of which have camping facilities; eg **Butterfly Ranch** ① *Hacienda Mariposa, entry US$3, camping US$25 pp including breakfast, access at Km 16, just before Santa Rosa, walk 1 km from here, make previous arrangements at Moonrise Travel.*

San Cristóbal: Puerto Baquerizo Moreno → *Phone code: 05. Population: 7200.*

Puerto Baquerizo Moreno, on San Cristóbal island, is the capital of the archipelago. Electrical energy here is provided by wind generators in the highlands, see www.eolicsa.com.ec. The town's attractive *malecón* has many shaded seats shared by tourists, residents and sea lions. The **cathedral** ① *on Av Northía y Cobos, 0900-1200, 1600-1800,* has interesting artwork combining religious and Galápagos motifs.

To the north of town, opposite **Playa Mann** (suitable for swimming), is the Galápagos National Park visitor centre or **Centro de Interpretación** ① *T252 0138, ext 123, daily 0700-1700, free.* It has excellent displays of the natural and human history of the islands including contemporary issues, recommended. A good trail goes from the Centro de Interpretación to the northeast through scrub forest to **Cerro Tijeretas**, a hill overlooking town and the ocean, 30 minutes away. From here a rougher trail continues 45 minutes to **Playa Baquerizo**. Frigatebirds nest in this area and can be observed gliding overhead; there are sea lions on the beaches below. To go back from Cerro Tijeretas, if you take the trail which follows the coast, you will end up at **Playa Punta Carola**, a popular surfing beach, too rough for swimming. To the south of Puerto Baquerizo Moreno, 30 minutes' walk past the stadium and high school (ask for directions), is **La Lobería**, a rocky shore with sea lions, Marine Iguanas, and a rough trail leading to beautiful cliffs with many birds, overlooking the sea.

Five buses a day run the 6 km inland from Puerto Baquerizo Moreno to **El Progreso**, US$0.20, 15 minutes, then it's a 2½-hour walk to **El Junco lake**, the largest body of fresh water in Galápagos. Pick-up trucks to El Progreso charge US$2, or you can hire them for touring: US$20 to El Junco (return with wait), US$40 continuing to the beaches at **Puerto Chino** on the other side of the island, past a man-made tortoise reserve. Camping is possible at Puerto Chino with a permit from the National Park, take food and drinking water. At El Junco there is a path to walk around the lake in 20 minutes. The views are lovely in clear weather but it is cool and wet in the *garúa* season, so take adequate clothing. Various small roads fan out from El Progreso and make for pleasant walking. **Jatun Sacha** (www.jatunsacha.org) has a volunteer centre on an old hacienda in the highlands beyond El Progreso, working on eradication of invasive species and a native plant nursery; US$15 taxi ride from town, take repellent.

Boats go to **Punta Pitt** in the far north of San Cristóbal where you can see all three species of booby (US$65 for a tour). Off the northwest coast is **Kicker Rock** (León Dormido), the basalt remains of a crater; many seabirds, including nazca and blue-footed boobies, can be seen around its cliffs (fivehour trip, including snorkelling, recommended, US$40).

Isabela: Puerto Villamil → *Phone code: 05. Population 2300.*

This is the largest island in the archipelago, formed by the coalesced lava flows of six volcanoes. Five are active and each has (or had) its own separate sub-species of giant tortoise. Isabela is also the island which is changing most rapidly, driven by growing land-based tourism. It remains a charming place but is at risk from uncontrolled development. Most residents live in Puerto Villamil. In the highlands, there is a cluster of farms at Santo Tomás. There are several lovely beaches right by town, but mind the strong undertow and ask locally about the best spots for swimming.

It is 8 km west to **Muro de las Lágrimas**, built by convict labour under hideous conditions. It makes a great day-hike or hire a bicycle (always take water). Short side-trails branch off the road to various attractions along the way, and a trail continues from the Muro to nearby hills with lovely views. Along the same road, 30 minutes from town, is the **Centro de Crianza**, a breeding centre for giant tortoises surrounded by lagoons with flamingos and other birds. In the opposite direction, 30 minutes east toward the *embarcadero* (pier) is **Concha de Perla Lagoon**, with a nice access trail through mangroves and a small dock from which you can go swimming with sea lions and other creatures. Tours go to **Las Tintoreras**, a set of small islets in the harbour where white-tipped reef sharks and penguins may be seen in the still crystalline water (US$25 per person). There are also boat tours to **Los Túneles** at Cabo Rosa (US$65 per person, a tricky entrance from the open sea), where fish, rays and turtles can be seen in submerged lava tunnels.

Sierra Negra Volcano has the second-largest basaltic caldera in the world, 9 km by 10 km. It is 19 km (30 minutes) by pickup truck to the park entrance (take passport and National Park entry receipt), where you start the 1½ hour hike to the crater rim at 1000 m. It is a further 1½ hours walk along bare brittle lava rock to **Volcán Chico**, with several fumaroles and more stunning views. You can camp on the crater rim but must take all supplies, including water, and obtain a permit the day before from the National Park office in Puerto Villamil. A tour including transport and lunch costs about US$50 per person. Highland tours are also available to **La Cueva de Sucre**, a large lava tube with many chambers; be sure to take a torch if visiting on your own. A bus to the highlands leaves the market in Puerto Villamil at 0700 daily, US$0.50, ask the driver for directions to the cave and return times.

Floreana: Puerto Velasco Ibarra → *Phone code: 05. Population: 160.*

Floreana is the island with the richest human history and the fewest inhabitants, most living in Puerto Velasco Ibarra. You can easily reach the island with a day tour boat from Puerto Ayora, but these do not leave enough time to enjoy the visit. A couple of days stay is recommended, however note that there may not always be space on boats returning to Puerto Ayora, so you must be flexible. Services are limited, one shop has basic supplies and there are a handful of places to eat and sleep, none is cheap (see Where to stay, page 1133). Margaret Wittmer, one of the first settlers on Floreana, died in 2000, but you can meet her daughter and granddaughter.

La Lobería is a beautiful little peninsula (which becomes an island at high tide), 15 minutes walk from town, where sea lions, sea turtles, marine iguanas and various birds can be seen. The climate in the highlands is fresh and comfortable, good for walking and birdwatching. A *ranchera* runs up to **Asilo de La Paz**, with a natural spring and tortoise area, Monday to Saturday 0600 and 1500, returning 0700 and 1600; Sun 0700 returning 1000. Or you can walk down in three to four hours, detouring to climb **Cerro Allieri** along the way.

Post Office Bay, on the north side of Floreana, is visited by tour boats. There is a custom (since 1792) for visitors here to place unstamped letters and cards in a barrel, and deliver, free of charge, any addressed to their own destinations.

◉ Galápagos Islands listings

For hotel and restaurant price codes, and other relevant information, see Essentials.

● Where to stay

Santa Cruz *p1128, map p1129*
Puerto Ayora
Reservations are advised in high season.

$$$$ Angemeyer Waterfront Inn, by the dock at Punta Estrada, T252 6561, www. angermeyer-waterfront-inn.com. Gorgeous location overlooking the bay. Includes buffet breakfast, restaurant, very comfortable modern rooms and apartments, some with kitchenettes, a/c, attentive service.

$$$$ Silberstein, Darwin y Piqueros, T252 6277, Quito T02-225 0553, www.hotel silberstein.com. Modern and comfortable with lovely grounds, pool in tropical garden, a/c, buffet breakfast, restaurant, bar, spacious rooms and common areas, very nice.

$$$$ Sol y Mar, Darwin y Binford, T252 6281, www.hotelsolymar.com.ec. Right in town but with a priviledged location overlooking the bay. Inculdes buffet breakfast, restaurant, bar, pool, jacuzzi.

$$$ Estrella de Mar, by the water on a lane off 12 de Febrero, T252 6427. Nice quiet location with views over the bay. A/c, fan, fridge, spacious rooms, sitting area.

$$$ Jean's Home, Punta Estrada, T252 6446. Comfortably refurbished home in a lovely out-of-the-way location, a/c, family run, English and German spoken.

$$$ Lobo de Mar, 12 de Febrero y Darwin, T252 6188, Quito T02-250 2089, www. lobodemar.com.ec. Modern building with balconies and rooftop terrace, great views over the harbour.A/c, small pool, fridge, modern and comfortable, attentive service.

$$$ Santa Fe Suites, Charles Binford entre Juan Montalvo y Las Ninfas, T252 6419, www. santafegalapagos.com.ec. Spacious modern rooms with kitchenettes (older rooms are smaller and cheaper), a/c, pool.

$$ España, Berlanga y 12 de Febrero, T252 6108, www.hotelespanagalapagos.com. Pleasant and quiet, spacious rooms, a/c ($ with fan), small courtyard with hammocks, good value.

$$ Peregrina, Darwin e Indefatigable, T252 6323, peregrinagalapagos@yahoo.com. Away from the centre of town, a/c, nice rooms and common areas, small garden, family run, homey atmosphere.

$ Los Amigos, Darwin y 12 de Febrero, T252 6265. Small place, basic rooms with shared bath, cold water, laundry facilities, use of kitchen for breakfast only, good value.

Highlands of Santa Cruz

$$$$ Galápagos Safari Camp, T09-9179 4259, www.galapagossafaricamp.com. Luxury resort

with a central lodge and accommodation in comfortable, en-suite tents. Includes breakfast and dinner, swimming pool, organizes tours and activities.

$$$$ Semilla Verde, T301-3079, www.gps.ec. Located on a 5 ha property being reforested with native plants, comfortable rooms and common areas, includes breakfast, other meals available or use of kitchen facilities, British-Ecuadorean run, family atmosphere.

San Cristóbal *p1130*
Puerto Baquerizo Moreno

$$$$ Miconia, Darwin e Isabela, T252 0608. Restaurant, a/c, small pool, large well-equipped gym, modern if somewhat small rooms, some with fridge.

$$$ Blue Marlin, Española y Northia, T252 0253, info@bluemaringalapagos.ec. Ample modern rooms are mostly wheelchair accessible, bathtubs, a/c, pool, fridge.

$$$ Casablanca, Mellville y Darwin, T252 0392, www.casablancagalapagos.com. Large white house with lovely terrace and views of harbour.Each room is individually decorated by the owner who has an art gallery on the premises.

$$ Bellavista, Darwin y Melville, T252 0352, agat74@yahoo.com. Ample modern rooms with a/c and fridge.

$$ Casa de Nelly, Northía y Roldós, T252 0112. 3-storey building in a quiet location, bright comfortable rooms, a/c, kitchen facilities, family run.

$$ Mar Azul, Northía y Esmeraldas, T252 0139. Nice comfortable lodgings, electric shower, a/c (cheaper with fan), fridge, kitchen facilities, pleasant. Same family runs 2 more expensive hotels nearby.

$ San Francisco, Darwin y Villamil, T252 0304. Simple rooms with private bath, cold water, fan, kitchen facilities, good value.

El Progreso

$$ Casa del Ceibo, T301 0160, Pto Baquerizo Moreno T252 0248. 2 unique rooms, one up in the branches of a huge kapok tree, the other under its roots. Private bath, hot water, ingenious design, US$1 to visit, advance booking required.

Isabela p1130
Puerto Villamil
Many hotels have opened in recent years, more than we can list below.
$$$$ La Casa de Marita, at east end of beach, T252 9238, www.galapagosisabela.com. Tastefully chic, includes breakfast, other meals on request, a/c and fridge, very comfortable, each room is slightly different, some have balconies; **$$$** across the road away from the sea. A little gem and recommended.
$$$$-$$$ Albemarle, on the beachfront in town, T252 9489, www.hotelalbemarle.com. Attractive Mediterranean-style construction, restaurant, bright comfortable rooms with wonderful ocean views, a/c, small pool, British-Ecuadorean run, attentive owner.
$$$ La Laguna, Los Flamencos y Los Petreles, T349 7940. Pleasant rooms with a/c, attractive balconies and common areas, jacuzzi.
$$$-$$ Caleta Iguana, Antonio Gil at west end of the beach, T301 6612, www. caletaiguana.com. Comfortable rooms with fridge and fan, terrace overlooking the ocean, nice views, popular with upmarket surfers.
$$ Casa Isabela on the Beach, on the beachfront in town, T252 9103, casitadelaplaya@hotmail.com, Quito office: Galacruises, www.islasgalapagos.travel. Pleasant house on the beach, rooms with a/c, some have balconies, nice ocean views.
$$ The Jungle, off Antonio Gil at the west edge of town, T301 6690. Nice rooms with a/c, beach views, meals on request, secluded location away from the centre.
$$ San Vicente, Cormoranes y Pinzón Artesano, T252 9140. Very popular and well organized hotel which also offers tours and kayak rentals, includes breakfast, other meals on request or use of cooking facilities, a/c, jacuzzi, rooms a bit small but nice, family run.
$ Hostal Villamil, 10 de Marzo y Antonio Gil, T252 9180. A/c, kitchen and laundry facilities, small patio with hammocks, family run and very friendly, good value. Recommended.

Highlands of Isabela
$$ Campo Duro, T09-8545 3045, refugiodetortugasgigantes@hotmail.com. Camping (tents provided), includes breakfast and dinner, nice ample grounds, giant tortoises may be seen (US$2 to visit), friendly owner.

Floreana: Puerto Velasco Ibarra p1131
$$$$ Lava Lodge, book through **Tropic Journeys in Nature**, www.destinationecuador. com. Wooden cabins on the beach a short distance outside town, family-owned, full board, kayak, snorkel and SUP equipment, guided tours to wildlife and historic sites, popular with groups.
$$$ Hostal Santa María, opposite the school, T252 4904. Nice modern rooms with private bath, hot water, fan, fridge, screened windows, friendly owner Sr Claudio Cruz.
$$$ Hotel Wittmer, right on Black Beach, T252 4873. Lovely location with beautiful sunsets, simple comfortable rooms, electric shower, fan, very good meals available, family run, German spoken, reservations required.
$$ Sra Lelia Cruz, opposite the school, T252 4901. 2 rooms for rent in a private home, shared bath, hot water, kitchen, meals also available, good value (for Floreana).

❼ Restaurants

Puerto Ayora p1128, map p1129
$$$ Angermeyer Point, at Punta Estrada across the bay, take a water-taxi, T252 7007. Daily 1800-2230. Former home of Galápagos pioneer and artist Carl Angermeyer, with his works on display. Gorgeous setting over the water (take insect repellent). Excellent, innovative and varied menu, attentive service. Reservations advised. Highly recommended.
$$$ Il Giardino, Charles Darwin y Charles Binford, T252 6627. Open 0800-2230, closed Tue. Very good international food, service and atmosphere, excellent ice-cream, very popular.
$$$ Isla Grill, Charles Darwin y Tomás de Berlanga, T252 4461. Tue-Sun 1200-2200. Upmarket grill, seafood and pizza.
$$$ La Dolce Italia, Charles Darwin y 12 de Febrero. Daily 1100-1500, 1800-2200.

Italian and seafood, wine list, a/c, pleasant atmosphere, attentive owner.

$$$-$$ La Garrapata, Charles Darwin between 12 de Febrero and Tomás de Berlanga. Mon-Sat 0900-2200. Good food, attractive setting and nice music.

$$ Kiosks, along Charles Binford between Padre Herrera and Rodríguez Lara. Many kiosks serving local fare, including a variety of seafood, outdoor seating, lively informal atmosphere, busy at night.

$$ Rincón del Alma, Charles Darwin e Islas Plaza, across from navy base. Mon-Sat 0830-2100. Traditional old place serving *ceviche* and seafood, also economical set lunch.

$ El Descanso del Guía, Charles Darwin y Los Colonos. Daily 0645-1945. Good set meals, very popular with locals.

Puerto Baquerizo Moreno *p1130*
$$$ Miramar, upstairs at Malecón y Cobos. Daily 1800-2300. Seafood and international dishes, cocktails, lovely ocean views, great sunsets, slow service.

$$$-$$ La Playa, Av de la Armada Nacional, by the navy base. Daily 0930-2330. Varied menu, fish and seafood.

$$$-$$ Rosita, Ignacio de Hernández y General Villamil. Daily 0930-1430, 1700-2230. Old-time yachtie hangout, good food, large portions, nice atmosphere, à la carte and economical set meals. Recommended.

$$$-$$ Sheanovi, Ignacio de Hernández y General Villamil. Daily 1700-2300. Small place with varied menu, nice views from 2nd floor terrace.

$$ Descanso del Marinero, Northia y Española. Open 0800-2100, closed Tue. *Ceviches* and seafood, pleasant outdoor seating.

$ Several simple places serving economical set meals on Northia between Española and 12 de Febrero.

Mockingbird Café, Española y Hernández. Mon-Sat 0730-2330, Sun from 0930. Fruit juices, brownies, snacks, internet.

Isabela *p1130*
Puerto Villamil
$$$-$$ There are various outdoor restaurants around the plaza, all with similar menus featuring seafood, **Cesar's** and **Los Delfines** are reported good.

$ Tropical, Las Fragatas ½ block from Plaza. Daily 1200-1400, 1800-1930. Simple set lunch, grill at night, popular with locals.

Floreana: Puerto Velasco Ibarra *p1131*
Meals available at hotels or from a couple of restaurants catering to tour groups, **$$$-$$**, all require advance notice.

$ The Devil's Crown, 100 m from the dock on the road to the highlands. Set lunch and dinner on most days, ask in advance.

O Shopping

Most items can be purchased on the islands but cost more than in mainland Ecuador. Do not buy anything made of black coral as it is an endangered species.

Puerto Ayora *p1128, map p1129*
There is an attractive little **Mercado Artesanal** (craft market) at Charles Darwin y Tomás de Berlanga. **Proinsular**, opposite the pier, is the largest and best stocked supermarket.

Puerto Baquerizo Moreno *p1130*
Galamarket, Isabela y Juan José Flores, is a modern well-stocked supermarket.

O What to do

Puerto Ayora *p1128, map p1129*
Cycling Mountain bikes can be hired from travel agencies in town. Prices and quality vary.
Diving Only specialized diving boats are allowed to do diving tours. It is not possible to dive as part of a standard live-aboard cruise nor are dive boats allowed to call at the usual land visitor sites. The following vessels offer live-aboard diving tours: *Darwin Buddy* and *Wolf Buddy*, www.buddydive-galapagos.com;

Deep Blue, www.deepbluegalapagosdiving.com; *Galápagos Agressor I and II*, www.aggressor.com; *Galápagos Sky*, www.ecoventura.com; *Humboldt Explorer*, www.galasam.com. Cruises cost US$4000-5000 for 7 days. National Park rules prohibit collecting samples or souvenirs, spear-fishing, touching animals, or other environmental disruptions. Experienced dive guides can help visitors have the most spectacular opportunities to enjoy the wildlife. There are several diving agencies in Puerto Ayora, Baquerizo Moreno and Villamil (see Tour operators, below) offering courses, equipment rental, and dives; prices and quality vary. On offer in Puerto Ayora are diving day trips (2 dives, US$175-250) and daily tours for up to 1 week in the central islands. There is a hyperbaric chamber in Puerto Ayora at **Centro Médico Integral**, Marchena y Hanny, T252 4576, www.sssnetwork.com. Check if your dive operator is affiliated with this facility or arrange your own insurance from home. To avoid the risk of decompression sickness, divers are advised to stay an extra day on the islands after their last dive before flying to the mainland, especially to Quito at 2840 m above sea level.
Dive Center Silberstein, opposite Hotel Silberstein, T252 6028, www.divingalapagos.com. Nice comfortable boat for up to 8 guests, English-speaking guides, good service, dive courses and trips for all levels of experience.
Galápagos Sub-Aqua, Av Charles Darwin e Isla Floreana, T252 6350, Guayaquil T04-230 5514, www.galapagos-sub-aqua.com. Instructor Fernando Zambrano offers full certificate courses up to PADI divemaster level. Repeatedly recommended.
Nautidiving, Av Charles Darwin, T252 7004, www.nautidiving.com. Offers day-trips to central islands as well as longer trips.
Scuba Iguana, Charles Darwin near the research station, T252 6497, www.scuba iguana.com. Matías Espinoza runs this long-time reliable and recommended dive operator. Courses up to PADI divemaster.
Horse riding For riding at ranches in the highlands, enquire at **Moonrise Travel**.

Snorkelling Masks, snorkels and fins can be rented from travel agencies and dive shops, US$5 a day, deposit required. Closest place to snorkel is by the beach near the Darwin Station.
Surfing There is surfing at Tortuga Bay and at other more distant beaches accessed by boat. There is better surfing near Puerto Baquerizo Moreno on San Cristóbal. The **Lonesome George** agency rents surfboards, see below.

Tour operators
Avoid touts offering cheap tours at the airport or in the street. Also be wary of agencies who specialize in cut-rate cruises.
Galacruises Expeditions, see page 995.
Galasam, see pages 995, 1079 and 1111.
Happy Gringo, see page 995.
Lonesome George, Av Baltra y Enrique Fuentes, T252 6245, lonesomegrg@yahoo.com. Run by Victor Vaca. Sells tours and rents: bicycles (US$3 per hr), surf-boards (US$30 per day) snorkelling equipment and motorcycles.
Moonrise Travel, Av Charles Darwin y Charles Binford, T252 6348, www.galapagosmoonrise.com. Last-minute cruise bookings, day-tours to different islands, bay tours, airline reservations, run guesthouse in Punta Estrada. Owner Jenny Devine is knowledgeable.
Zenith Travel, see page 953.

Puerto Baquerizo Moreno *p1130*
Cycling Hire bikes from travel agencies, US$20 per day.
Diving There are several dive sites around San Cristóbal, most popular being Kicker Rock, Roca Ballena and Punta Pitt, full day about US$200, see Tour operators below.
Kayaking Rentals US$10 per hr; from Islander's Store, Av J Roldós, above cargo pier, T252 0348; and **Galápagos Eco Expedition**, Av de la Armada, next to La Playa restaurant.
Surfing There is good surfing in San Cristóbal, the best season is Dec-Mar. Punta Carola near town is the closest surfing beach; other spots are Canon and Tongo Reef, past the navy base. There is a championship during the local *fiesta*, the 2nd week of Feb.

Tour operators

Chalo Tours, Darwin y Villamil, T252 0953, chalotours@hotmail.com. Specializes in diving and snorkelling.

Sharksky, Darwin y Española, T252 1188, www.sharksky.com. Highlands, snorkelling, island-hopping, last-minute cruise bookings and gear rental. Also has an office on Isabela. Swiss-Ecuadorean run, English, German and French spoken, helpful.

Wreck Bay Dive Center, Darwin y Wolf, T252 1663, www.wreckbay.com. Reported friendly and respectful of the environment.

Puerto Villamil *p1130*

Hotels also arrange tours. Kayak rentals at Hotel San Vicente.

Carapachudo Tours, Escalecias y Tero Real, T252 9451. Mountain biking downhill from Sierra Negra, full day including lunch, US$42. Also rentals: good bikes US$3 per hr, US$20 per day; snorkelling gear US$5 per day; surf boards US$4 per hr.

Galápagos Dive Center, 16 de Marzo y Tero Real, T301 6570. Dive trips, diving gear sale and rental.

Isabela Dive Center, Escalecias y Alberto Gil, T252 9418, www.isabeladivecenter.com.ec. Diving, land and boat tours.

⊝ Transport

Puerto Ayora *p1128, map p1129*

Sea *Fibras* (fibreglass speedboats) depart daily from the pier near the Proinsular supermarket for the following islands: **San Cristóbal** at 1400; **Isabela** at 0730 and 1400; **Floreana** at 0700; all fares US$30-35.

Pick-up truck taxis These may be hired for transport throughout town, US$1. A *ranchera* runs up to the highlands from the **Tropidurus** store, Av Baltra y Jaime Roldóss, 2 blocks past the market: to **Bellavista** US$0.25, 10 mins; **Santa Rosa** US$1, 20 mins. For airport transfers, see page 1122.

Water taxis (*taxis acuáticos*) From the pier to Punta Estrada or anchored boats, US$0.60 during the day, US$1 at night.

ⓘ Directory

Puerto Ayora *p1128, map p1129*

Airline offices Aerogal, Rodríguez Lara y San Cristóbal, T252 6798. Emetebe, at the airport, T252 4755. **LAN**, Av Charles Darwin e Islas Plaza, T1-800-101075. **TAME**, Av Charles Darwin y 12 de Febrero, T252 6527. **Banks** Banco del Pacífico, Av Charles Darwin y Charles Binford, T252 6282; also Av Baltra y 10 de Marzo; Mon-Fri 0800-1530, Sat 0930-1230. ATM, cash advances (Mon-Fri) and TCs (US$5 commission per transaction, up to US$200 a day). Also ATMs next to Proinsular supermarket; at Banco Pichincha, Av Baltra on the way to Highlands and several others. **Medical services** Hospitals: there is a hospital on Av Baltra for first aid and basic care. For anything serious, locals usually fly to the mainland. **Yacht agents** Galápagos Ocean Services (Peter Schiess), Charles Darwin next to Garrapata restaurant, T09-9477 0804, www.gos.ec. Naugala Yacht Services (Jhonny Romero), T252 7403, www.naugala.com.

Puerto Baquerizo Moreno *p1130*

Airline offices Aerogal, at the airport, T252 1118. **Emetebe**, at the airport, T252 0615. **TAME**, Charles Darwin y Manuel J Cobos, T252 1351. **Banks** Banco del Pacífico, Melville y Hernández, same hours and services as in Puerto Ayora. COOPCCP, Wolf y Charles Darwin, for ATM. **Medical services** There is a hospital providing only basic medical care.

Puerto Villamil *p1130*

Airline offices Emetebe, Antonio Gil y Las Fragatas, T252 9155. **Banks** There are no banks or ATMs, bring US$ cash. MoneyGram, in La Isla supermarket, Tero Real y Escalecias, for international funds transfer.

Contents

Paraguay

At a glance

⏱ **Time required** 1-3 weeks.

☂ **Best time** Sep/Oct and Mar-May
are not too hot or wet.

✖ **When not to go** Heaviest
rains Nov-Mar; Dec-Feb can be
excessively hot.

★ Don't miss ...
1 Plaza de los Héroes, Asunción, page 1147.
2 Itaipú, page 1165.
3 Jesuit missions, page 1170.
4 The Chaco, page 1180.

BOLIVIA

Mayor Pablo Lagerenza

PN Defensores del Chaco

Bahía Negra

Gral Eugenio A Garay

FN Madrejón

PN Tte Agripino Enciso

Fuerte Olimpo

BRAZIL

Fortín Infante Rivarola

Vallemí

PN Serranías San Luís

Bella Vista

Mariscal Estigarriba

Filadelfia

Loma Plata

PN del Cerro Corá

Pedro Juan Caballero

Neuland

4

Chaco

Río Verde

Yby Yaú

Capitán Badó

Pozo Colorado

Concepción

Horqueta

Pirahú

Puerto Antequera

Santa Rosa

Salto del Guairá

San Pedro

Nuevo Germania

Mbaracayú Forest Reserve

Rosario

Tacuara

Curuguaty

ARGENTINA

Benjamin Aceval
Villa Hayes

25 de Diciembre

San Estanislao

Limoy

Represa de Itaipú

ASUNCION

San Lorenzo

Caraguatuy

Mbutuy

1

Paraguarí

Coronel Oviedo

2

Colonia Independencia

Ciudad del Este

Carapeguá

Sapucai

Ybicuí NP

Villarrica

Ybicuí

Caazapá

Caacupé

Villa Florida

San Rafael NP

Pilar

San Juan Bautista

Santa Rosa

Obligado

Bella Vista

San Ignacio Guazú

Coronel Bogado

Jesús

Hohenau

Trinidad

Paso de Patria

Ayolas

Cosme y Damián

San Encarnación

3

BRAZIL

ASUNCIÓN

Luque

Altos

Tobatí

Areguá

San Bernardino

San Lorenzo

Lago Ypacaraí

Capiatá

Ñemby

Itauguá

Ypacaraí

Caacupé

San Antonio

Río Paraguay

Ypane

Guarambaré

Itá

Pirayú

Piribebuy

Villeta

Nueva Italia

Yaguarón

Paraguarí

Chololó

Puerto Paraíso

N

100 km
100 miles

An air of mystery hangs over this under-explored pocket of South America, a country of farmland, nature and folklore. From the hot, wild and impenetrable Chaco in the northwest to the lush forests of the southeast, there is abundant birdlife, a number of rivers to navigate and fantastic opportunities to experience rural tourism. Although dwarfed by its giant neighbours Brazil and Argentina, Paraguay covers some 407,000 sq km, roughly the same size as California. It is at the confluence of six eco-regions, Paraná-Paraíba interior forest, cerrado, humid chaco, dry chaco pantanal and *pastizales* (grasslands) of Mesoptamia, resulting in a variety of landscapes and panoramas as well as rich flora and fauna.

Land-locked Paraguay has had a strange history of charismatic leaders, steadfastness and isolation. Paraguayans are proud of their Guaraní culture and heritage, evident in the widespread use of it as the officially recognized indigenous language, which is still taught in schools. Although difficult to pronounce for many outsiders, the Guaraní language cannot mask the warmth of Paraguayan hospitality. Music, too, marks Paraguay apart from its neighbours: emotive songs and European dances accompanied by virtuoso harp players and guitarists.

Yet in other ways, Paraguay is not so separate. It shares with Argentina and Brazil remains of the mission settlements (*reducciones*) built by Jesuits near the banks of the Río Paraná, testimony to one of the major social experiments on the continent. Paraguayans are renowned for their passion for football and a dedication to a daily consumption of yerba mate (*Ilex paraguariensis*); either with ice-cold water (*tereré*) on hot days, or hot water (*mate*) on cold days. Today the country is part of the Latin American and Caribbean Economic System, with trade routes to Argentina and Brazil well established and the road to Bolivia finally completed: Paraguay's infamous Ruta 9, the Trans-Chaco Highway, remains one of the great road adventures in South America.

Planning your trip

Where to go in Paraguay

Paraguay is divided into two main regions separated by the Río Paraguay. The capital, **Asunción**, sits between the two; to the east of the river lies the Región Oriental (approximately 40%) and to the west the Región Occidental (approximately 60%), better known simply as the Chaco. Unless coming from Buenos Aires or Santa Cruz, it is best to plan your travels to either of these regions from Asunción.

The capital, Paraguay's largest city, sits on a bay of the Río Paraguay. The expansion of the city's metropolitan area means it now rubs shoulders with a dozen neighbouring cities to form Gran Asunción. Asunción is the political and commercial heart of the country and much of its architecture dates from the early 1800s.

Región Oriental makes up most of the fertile agricultural part of the country. The towns and villages are quiet and traditional; many have unique crafts associated with them. There are also many signs of Jesuit heritage, best exemplified at the ruins of the former mission settlements at Santísima Trinidad de Paraná and Jesús de Tavarangüé, declared World Heritage Sites by UNESCO in 1993 (along with a third, Santos Cosme y Damián), close to the city of Encarnación. From here you can cross the Río Paraná to the Argentine city of Posadas. Paraguay's eastern border with Brazil has several frontier posts, but the main one is Ciudad del Este, a duty-free shopper's paradise (or hell, depending on your point of view), where you can visit Itaipú, until recently the largest hydroelectric dam in the world. Across the Friendship Bridge from Ciudad del Este is Foz do Iguaçu in Brazil and the magnificent Iguaçu Falls.

North of Asunción there is one main town, Concepción, and the most interesting route there, if you have the time, is by river boat from the capital. The boat ride takes at least a day, so quicker ways are via the Chaco, along part of the Trans-Chaco Highway or across the Cordillera and San Pedro Departments along Ruta 3. Beyond Concepción, the Río Paraguay leads to the Brazilian and Bolivian Pantanal, which can also be reached by road.

Región Occidental, or Chaco, makes up the western half of the country. Divided into three departments, Presidente Hayes (also known as Bajo Chaco), Boquerón and Alto Paraguay (or Alto Chaco), the Chaco begins as a marshy palm savanna, but becomes an increasingly impenetrable and dry scrub forest as it approaches the border with Bolivia. The Trans-Chaco Highway crosses the Chaco but apart from scattered military outposts, there are few urbanized areas for 400 km until you reach the Mennonite colonies of Filadelfia, Loma Plata and Neuland which make up the Chaco Central region. A relatively short distance further northwest is the former military base of Mariscal Estigarribia. This is not a region in which to venture off the beaten track alone and unprepared.

National parks and nature tourism Paraguay is a confluence of globally important eco-regions and is rich in biodiversity. This abundance of wildlife, particularly birds, is most visible in the Chaco, especially in its remote national parks, along the Río Pilcomayo, and the frontier with Bolivia. It is been estimated that the Pantanal has the highest concentration of fauna in the New World. Current estimates include between 10,000-13,000 plant species, 100,000 invertebrates (including 765 of butterfly), 300 species of fish, 120 reptiles, 100 amphibians, 687 birds and 171 mammals. For more details, visit **Fauna Paraguay** (www.faunaparaguay.com). Paraguay has an extensive network of state-protected areas, 83 in all, covering – on paper at least – almost 7% of the country's territory. Exactly what constitutes a protected area is confusing at best and the criteria can change from year to year. To complicate matters further, of this number, 27 are private reserves which are maintained by outside entities (in some cases, the Itaipú and Yacyretá dam authorities) but which are in one way or another supervised by Paraguay's **Secretaría Nacional de Turismo (SENATUR**, www.senatur.gov.py) or **Secretaría del Ambiente (SEAM**, www.seam.gov.py). As of January 2014, there are 21 national parks (including one under water), plus eight monuments, six biological reserves or refuges, four protected landscapes, three wilderness areas, two wildlife refuges and a welter of other reserves, as well as six international protected areas. An additional 10 reserves of varying types are planned for creation between 2014 and 2015. Unfortunately many of these protected areas exist solely on paper, and the whole system is under-funded. As beautiful and unique as these areas are, infrastructure is in most cases rudimentary at best (if it exists at all), and visiting them is not always easy. Always contact the relevant institutions and authorities first, and never venture in without prior permission (and a good all-terrain vehicle). Due to overlapping jurisdictions and differing criteria, there is as yet no official list of all of Paraguay's 83 protected areas (public and private) from either SENATUR or SEAM. The most reliable online source is the National Parks of Paraguay blog (http://nationalparksofparaguay.blogspot.com). However, SEAM's **Sistema Nacional de Áreas Protegidas del Paraguay (SINASIP**, www.seam.gov.py/areas-protegidas.html) offers some useful information on state-protected areas, as well as a 2007-edition map. For the reserves managed by the Itaipú and Yacyretá authorities, contact the relevant environmental departments. For private reserves contact the following conservation NGOs: **Guyra Paraguay** ① *Gaetano Martino 215 y Ite Ross, Asunción, 1021-229097, www.guyra.org.py*, which has a wealth of information for birdwatchers, naturalists and biologists as well as the capacity, infrastructure and expertise to organize tailor-made ecotours to all parts of the country, including some of the more remote locations not provided by other tour operators (highly recommended); **Fundación Moisés Bertoni para la Conservación de la Naturaleza** ① *Prócer Carlos Argüello 208, Asunción, T021-608740, www.mbertoni.org.py*, which manages the Mbaracayú Reserve, one of two remaining pristine Atlantic Forest reserves in the region, as well as the lesser-known Tapyta Reserve; **Pro Cosara** ① *Hohenau II, Itapúa, T0768-295046, www.procosara.org*, which works for the protection of the San Rafael Nature Reserve in eastern Paraguay and which welcomes volunteers at the ecological station (www.faunaparaguay.com/ecosaravolunteers.html); **Para la Tierra** ① *San Pedro del Ycuamandiyú, T0985-260074, www.paralatierra.org*, which works for the protection of the Laguna Blanca Reserve and also welcomes volunteers. **Desarrollo Turístico Paraguayo (DTP**, offices in Asunción, Encarnación and Ciudad del Este, www.dtp.com.py), the country's largest and best-known tourism agency, can organize adventure tours to different parts of the country.

Best time to visit Paraguay

The climate is sub-tropical, with a marked difference between summer and winter and often from one day to the next. December to February (summer) can be very hot and humid, with temperatures from 25°C to 40°C, and even higher in the Chaco. From March to May (autumn) and September to November (spring) the heat is less oppressive, a good time for travelling. During winter (June-August) the temperature can range from 0°C at night to 28°C in the day. Temperatures below freezing are very rare. Some rain falls each month, but the heaviest rains tend to occur from October to April.

Transport in Paraguay

Air There are scheduled services to most of the main parts of the country from Silvio Pettirossi airport. Domestic fares are subject to US$4 tax, payable in guaraníes or dollars.

Driving in Paraguay

Road Around 10% of roads are paved. Roads serving the main centres are in good condition and are continually being upgraded. A highway links Asunción with Iguazú Falls (six hours). Potholes are a hazard, especially in Asunción. Unsurfaced roads may not be passable in bad weather, especially November-April. There are regular police checks; it's advisable to lock doors.

Safety Beware of stray cattle on the road at night. Driving at night is not advisable.

Documents Neither a *carnet de passages* nor *libreta de pasos por aduana* is required for a car or motorcycle, but the carnet may make entry easier. Temporary admission for a private vehicle is usually 30 days.

Organizations Touring y Automóvil Club Paraguayo (TACP), 25 de Mayo y Brasíl, p 2, Asunción, T021-210550, www.tacpy. com.py, produces a road map and provides information about weather and roads. Information also from the office of the traffic police in Asunción, T021-493390.

Car hire Weekly and free-km rates available. Rates from US$45 per day to US$150 for 4WD.

Fuel Unleaded only (some has sugar-cane alcohol added). Most vehicles are diesel-powered. 95 octane US$0.74 per litre; 97 octane US$0.86 per litre; diesel US$0.70 per litre. Motor fuel and oil are sold by the litre. There are few service stations in the Chaco.

Bus Along most main roads, buses will stop at almost any junction to collect or drop off passengers, so all timetables are approximate.

Train Most of the 441-km rail network closed in early 2001, with the last stretch sealed off in 2012. Neither freight trains to Encarnación, nor the tourist steam train service (*Tren del Lago*) from Asunción's Botánico station, to Sapucai via Areguá is now run. After a large number of components of the historic railway system were dismantled and sold for scrap, plans to recommence tourist trains were tabled in 2012 in favour of using the rail bed as a commuter road from Asunción to Ypacaraí, to be completed in 2014. It should be noted, however, that tourist train service between Luque and Aregua is being prepared, with possible extensions to Ypacaraí and Sapucai, where the railroad's old workshops function as a museum. Thanks to intense lobbying by Ferrocarriles del Paraguay (FEPASA), it is entirely possible that another tourist train will at some point run again from Asunción to at least Aregua, paralleling the new motorway.

Maps A general map of the country can be purchased at most bookstores in Asunción and at bus terminals. The **Touring y Automóvil Club Paraguayo (TACPy**, www.tacpy.com.py), publishes an annual guide (latest edition 2010) in Spanish and English, with maps, US$25 for non-members (also online price), US$22 for members (in person), but more detailed maps are available from **Instituto Geográfico Militar** ① *Av Artigas casi Av Perú, T021-206344*; take your passport.

Where to stay in Paraguay → *See Essentials for our hotel price guide.*

Many hotels are in our **$$-$** ranges, often good ones with private shower and toilet, but there are very few hostels with dormitory accommodation (US$10-15 per person). Most hotels have two rates – one for a room with a/c, the other without. Almost all include breakfast.

Food and drink in Paraguay → *See Essentials for our restaurant price guide.*

Eating out Lunch is usually served between 1130-1300 in most restaurants and bars. Evening meals are hard to find in small towns, but options exist in larger cities.

Food Typical local foods include *chipa*, a cheese bread that comes in a number of varieties: *almidón*, made with yuca flour; *barrero*, made with corn flour; *manduví*, made with peanuts (better warm than cold). *Chipa so'o* is maize bread with minced meat filling; *chipa guazú* is made with fresh corn; *sopa paraguaya* is a kind of sponge of ground maize and cheese. These make a great side dish, or can be enjoyed on their own. *Soyo* is a soup of different meats and vegetables; *albóndiga* a soup of meat balls; *bori bori* another type of soup with diced meat, vegetables, and small balls of maize mixed with cheese. The beef is excellent in the better restaurants (best cuts are *lomo* and *lomito*) and can be enjoyed with *chorizo* (sausage), *morcilla*, *chipa guazú*, *sopa paraguaya* and a variety of salads. *Parrillada completa* is recommended and there are many *churrascarías* (barbecues) serving huge quantities of meat, with salad, vegetables and pasta. River fish include *surubí* and *dorado*, which are prepared in many different ways. Although vegetarian restaurants are scarce, there are lots of fruits, salads and vegetables, as well as the non-meat varieties of *empanada*, such as *choclo*, *palmito* or *cuatro quesos*.

Drink The most popular drink among Paraguayans is *tereré* (cold mate with digestive herbs) for warm days and hot mate to warm you up on cold days. *Cocido* is a type of tea made by burning (traditionally with a red ember) the yerba with some sugar; this can be served with or without milk. Paraguayan beers are very good, the better brands being *Baviera*, *Pilsen* and *Munich*. These are lager-types, but you can sometimes find darker beers in the winter. The better brands of the national sugarcane-based spirit, *cana*, include *Aristocrata* (known as 'Arl'), *Fortín* and *Tres Leones*. You can find most global brand soft drinks, including *Guaraná* (originally from Brazil). *Mosto* is a very sweet but refreshing juice from sugarcane. And there is a wonderful variety of fresh fruit juices.

Essentials A-Z

Accident and emergency
Ambulance and police emergency T911.

Electricity
220 volts AC, 50 cycles, but power surges and voltage drops are frequent. European 2 round pin plugs are used. Visitors from North America should bring an inexpensive adaptor, as few hotels outside Asunción offer 110-volt service.

Embassies and consulates
For Paraguayan embassies and consulates abroad and for all foreign embassies and consulates in Paraguay, see http://embassy.goabroad.com.

Festivals
Public holidays
1 Jan; **1-3 Feb** (San Blas, patron of Paraguay, but as of 2014 re-named Day of Paraguayan

Democracy to commemorate the departure of the dictator Alfredo Stroessner in 1989); **1 Mar** (National Heroes' Day, on the anniversary of the death of former president Francisco Solano López); **Wed of Holy Week**; **Maundy Thu**; **Good Fri**; **1 May** (Labour Day); **14 May** (Independence); **12 Jun** (Paz del Chaco); **24 Jun** (San Juan); **15 Aug** (founding of Asunción); **16 Aug** (Children's Day, in honour of the boys who died at the Battle of Acosta Nu, see page 1147); **29 Sep** (victory of Boquerón, decisive battle in the Chaco War); **8 Dec** (Virgen de Caacupé/Inmaculada Concepción); **25 Dec**.

Internet
Average cost in towns is US$0.75-1.25 per hr.

Money → US$1=₲4425, €1=₲6030
(May 2014).
The guaraní (plural guaraníes) is the unit of currency, symbolized by ₲ (the letter G

crossed). There are bank notes for 2000, 5000, 10,000, 20,000, 50,000 and 100,000 guaraníes and coins for 50, 100, 500 and 1000 guaraníes. Get rid of all your guaraníes before leaving Paraguay; there is no market for them elsewhere.

Plastic/TCs/banks Asunción is a good place for obtaining US$ cash on MasterCard or Visa especially if heading for Brazil. ATMs for Visa and MasterCard are common in Asunción and offer good rates of exchange. They accept credit and debit cards and give dollars and guaraníes. Many banks in Asunción (eg HSBC, Citibank, ABN AMRO, Interbanco) give US$ cash, but charge up to 5.5% commission. Rates for most other foreign currencies are reasonable. *Casas de cambio* and banks may want to see customers' records of purchase before accepting TCs, if they will accept them at all. Try Banco Continental, which charges 7% commission on TCs. Visa and MasterCard cash advances are possible in Asunción, Ciudad del Este and Encarnación, but only for credit (not debit) cards. Street dealers operate from early morning until late at night, even on public holidays, but double check that they are giving you the right exchange (have your own calculator handy) and the right amount of cash. **Cost of travelling** Allow US$50-60 per person per day to cover main expenses, unless staying in the cheapest hotels and not moving around much.

Opening hours
Banks: Mon-Fri 0845-1500. **Commercial office hours**: 0730-1100 or 1300, and 1430 or 1500-1800 or 1900. **Government offices**: 0700-1130 in summer, 0730-1200 in winter, open Sat. **Museums**: usually Mon-Fri 0800-1200, and 1330-1700. As a rule, Paraguay does not follow the regional norm of closing its museums on Mon. **Shops, offices and businesses**: open around 0700; some may close 1200-1500 for lunch and siesta.

Safety
Paraguay is generally safe and visitors are treated courteously. At election times there

may be demonstrations in the capital, but the country as a whole is very calm. Beware police seeking bribes, especially at Asunción bus station and at border crossings. See www.mspbs.gov.py for current health issues in Paraguay.

Tax
Airport tax US$31, payable on departure in US$ or guaraníes (cheaper).
VAT/IVA 10% (5% for some purchases).

Telephone→ *Country code +595.*
Ringing: equal long tones with long pauses. Engaged: equal short tones with equal pauses. Directory enquiries and information: T112. To make calls between provinces, an access code ("0") followed by a 2-, 3- or, rarely, 4-digit city code are required, then the 6- or 7-digit number (a few cities, such as Ciudad del Este and Villarrica have 7-digit, as well as 6-digit numbers). Mobile phone numbers have the 3-digit prefix of the carrier, of which there are four. These always start with 9. This is followed by 6 digits. You can use a prepaid SIM card, with prior registration at one of the official carrier's offices.

Time
Standard time GMT -4 hrs begins early Apr. Summer time GMT -3 hrs begins early Oct (dates change yearly).

Tipping
Restaurants, 10%. Taxis, 10%. In supermarkets, tip the check-out boys who pack bags; they are not paid.

Tourist information
Secretaría Nacional de Turismo Palma 468 y 14 de Mayo, Asunción, T021-494110/441530, www.senatur.gov.py or www.paraguay.travel.

Useful websites
http://www.paraguaytierradelagua.com Tri-lingual tourism information on the country.
http://discoveringparaguay.com/home A blog about living and travelling in Paraguay.

www.cabildoccr.gov.py Centro Cultural de la República El Cabildo, the government's official cultural website (in Spanish).
www.portalguarani.com Portal to the arts and letters of Paraguay, also includes information on coin and stamp collecting, museums and music.
www.presidencia.gov.py The government's official website (in Spanish).
http://lanic.utexas.edu/la/sa/paraguay Enormous bi-lingual portal for information on all things Paraguay; maintained by University of Texas' Latin American Network Information Center.

See Asunción, Entertainment (page 1154) for online newspapers.

Visas and immigration

A passport valid for 6 months after the intended length of stay is required to enter Paraguay and tourist visas are issued at the point of entry for a stay of up to 90 days. Visas are extendible for an additional 180 days for US$40 for each 90-day period. Visitors are registered on arrival by the immigration authorities and proof of onward travel is required (although not always asked for). Citizens of the following countries do not require visas in advance: EU member states, Israel, Japan, Norway, South Africa, Switzerland, countries of South and Central America.

Citizens of the following countries require visas either in advance or upon arrival (Visa en Arribo) only at Silvio Pettirossi International Airport: Valid for 90 days only, the costs are as follows: Australia (US$135), Canada (US$150), New Zealand (US$140), Russia (US$160), Taiwan (US$100) and the United States (US$160). Fees are payable in these countries' respective national currencies or guaraníes only; credit cards not accepted. Only citizens of the countries listed above can obtain a visa upon arrival. Citizens of all others countries other than the two groups above must apply previously at a Paraguayan embassy or consulate in person (not by mail) for a fee of US$160. Present a valid passport, a passport photo, a covering letter and proof of onward travel and economic solvency. At the time of going to press, new regulations were being drawn up regarding the issue of visas, so you must double-check at a consulate or www.mre.gov.py before arrival which nationalities need a visa, how much they cost and which Paraguayan consulates issue them. Make sure you're stamped in and out of Paraguay to avoid future problems. If you do not get an entrance stamp in your passport you can be turned back at the border, or have to pay a fine of US$45 or the equivalent in guaraníes when leaving Paraguay.

Weights and measures

Metric.

Asunción

Asunción was founded in 1537 on the eastern bank of a calm bay in the Río Paraguay. It is the longest continually inhabited area in the River Plate Basin and in colonial times was referred to as the "Mother of Cities" because it was from here that missionaries and military expeditions alike set off to establish other cities. The centre is a testament to 19th-century ideals, with names reflecting its heroes and battles. Tree-lined avenues, parks and squares break up the rigid grid system. In July and August the city is drenched in colour with the prolific pink bloom of lapacho trees, which grow everywhere.

Arriving in Asunción → *Phone code: 021. Colour map 6, C6. Population: 515,587 (city); 2,164,316 (urban area).*

Getting there Silvio Pettirossi International **airport** is in Luque, 16 km northeast of the city centre, from which taxis, buses and an airport-to-hotel minibus service run. It takes about 45 minutes to go from the airport to town. The **bus terminal**, Terminal de Omnibus Asunción, T551740, www.mca.gov.py/toa.htm, is south of the centre at the intersection of Avenidas Fernando de la Mora y República Argentina, 30-45 minutes away by taxi or bus. **▶▶** *See Transport, page 1157, for details.*

Orientation Asunción's historic centre (along with other sites throughout the city) has recently undergone a renaissance in terms of popularity and government support and there are now a number of tours that take in many of its best-known buildings and spaces. The restoration of several historically significant buildings in the centre (eg Palacio de Gobierno) and outside (eg Casa de las Artes Escénicas Edda de los Ríos) was supposed to coincide with Paraguay's independence bicentennial (2011), but work continues. As a result, opening hours may change without notice.

Most of the historical sights of interest are in a relatively small area by the river, so walking between them is not a problem. Likewise, many central hotels and restaurants are within walking distance of these sights. Places outside the city´s centre, for example Villa Morra (see below), are easily reached by taxi or bus. If going by taxi, give driver the specific street address but also the name of the nearest intersection. The often-used "casi" (near) and "esquina" (corner) both mean "at the corner of". Almost all locations in Asunción are referred to in this manner (in this chapter "y" is used). The bus system is extensive and runs 0600-2200 (2400 on a few routes); buses stop at signs before every street corner. Asunción is very spread out and transport so slow that you need to allow 60-90 minutes to get beyond its limits.

Tourist offices **Secretaría Nacional de Turismo** ① *Palma 468, T494110/441530, www.senatur. gov.py or www.paraguay.travel, daily 0700-1900.* Helpful, with a good free map, information on all parts of Paraguay and bookstore. Both the airport and bus terminal have tourist information desks. Check for special tours being run from the tourist office, sometimes run by Senatur, sometimes in conjunction with agencies. The city of Asunción's municipal website **www.mca. gov.py** also has up-to-date information in Spanish, as does the Cabildo (see below), which intermittently publishes an official bulletin of cultural events and news.

Places in Asunción

Historic centre

At the bottom of Avenida Colón, just before it joins El Paraguayo Independiente, are the colonial façades of **La Recova**, shops selling local arts and crafts (see Shopping, below). The main river port and **Aduana** (Customs) are at this same junction. Every Saturday afternoon from 1500 there are cultural activities at the port (Puerto Abierto). Continue along El Paraguayo Independiente to a small plaza on your left with a statue of the former dictator, Alfredo Stroessner. After his deposition, the statue was crushed and placed inside a block of concrete, only his hands and face protruding. Next to this is the **Palacio de Gobierno** (1857), undergoing restoration in 2014, built in the style of Versailles by Alan Taylor as a palace for Francisco Solano López (1860-1869). In later years Taylor was forced to use child labour as all adult men were enlisted to fight in the Triple Alliance War. It now houses government departments. Down the side of the palace towards the river is a platform for viewing the back of the building. Directly opposite the Palace is the **Manzana de la Rivera** ① *Ayolas 129 y El Paraguayo Independiente, T445085, Mon-Sat 0700-2000, museum and cultural centre Mon-Fri 0800-2100, Sat 1000-2000, Sun 1000-1900, library Mon-Fri 0700-1900, Sat 0800-1200*, 10 buildings and a patio area, of which nine buildings are restored, dating from 1700s. They include **Casa Viola** with Museo Memoria de la Ciudad with historical photos and city information, **Casa Clari**, with exhibition halls and a bar, the Miguel Acevedo cultural centre, the Ruy Díaz de Guzmán auditorium, and **Casa Vertúa**, the municipal library. These collectively represent the most complete set of colonial era buildings in the city.

A block away from the Palace is the **Congreso Nacional**, built in steel and glass representing a huge ship moored on the river bank and incorporating part of the old congress building. On **Plaza de la Independencia** (often referred to as Plaza Constitución or Plaza Juan de Salazar) there is a small memorial to those who died in the struggle for democracy (also look out for statues of the frog and the dog). On the Plaza are the **Antiguo Colegio Militar** (1588) originally a Jesuit College, now home to government ministries, the **Cabildo** (1844-1854) ① *Mon-Fri 0900-1900, Sat 0800-1200, free*, since 2003 the **Centro Cultural de la República** ① *T443094, http://cabildoccr.gov.py*, with temporary exhibitions, indigenous and religious art, museum of music, film and video on the top floor, and the **Catedral Metropolitana** (mid-17th century, rebuilt 1842-1849) ① *T449512, seldom open, but hours posted in front, possible to view the interior before, after or during Sunday Mass*. The altar, decorated with Jesuit and Franciscan silver, is very beautiful. From the Plaza turn right onto Alberdi and to your right is the **Correos** (old post office), the Palacio Patri in colonial times, with a lovely planted courtyard and a small museum. At Alberdi and Presidente Franco is the **Teatro Municipal Ignacio Pane** ① *T445169, www.teatromunicipal.com.py, for information on events*, fully restored to its former belle époque glory. The **Estación Central del Ferrocarril Carlos Antonio López** ① *Eligio Ayala y México, just below Plaza Uruguaya, T447848*, was built 1861-1864 with British and European help. Paraguay had the first passenger carrying railway in South America. No trains now run from the station, but it has a small **museum** ① *Mon-Fri, 0800-1600, US$2.25*, featuring the old ticket office, machinery from Wolverhampton and Battersea and the first steam engine in Paraguay, the **Sapucai** (1861). **Plaza Uruguaya**, at the nexus of calles México, Eligio Ayala, 25 de Mayo and Antequera, with its shady trees and fountain is another spot to stop and rest in the daytime. From here take Mariscal Estigarribia towards Plaza de Los Héroes.

Mariscal Estigarribia becomes Palma at its intersection with Independencia Nacional (the names of all streets running east to west change at this point). On **Plaza de los Héroes** is the **Panteón Nacional de los Héroes** ① *Palma y Chile, open daily*, which is based on Les Invalides in Paris, begun during the Triple Alliance War and finished in 1937. It contains the tombs of Carlos Antonio López, Mariscal Francisco Solano López, Mariscal Estigarribia, the victor of the Chaco War, an unknown child-soldier, and other national heroes. The child-soldiers honoured in the Panteón were boys aged 12-16 who fought at the battle of Acosta Ñu in the War of the Triple Alliance, 15 August 1869. Most of the boys died and somewhere between 60%-70% of adult

Paraguayan men were killed during the war. Plaza de los Héroes is made up of four separate squares with different names. These include Plaza Libertad and Plaza de la Democracia.

On weekdays in the Plaza at Chile y Oliva (Plaza Libertad) there are **covered market stalls** selling traditional Paraguayan arts and crafts in wood, cotton and leather. Along Palma indigenous women sell colourful woven bags, beads and baskets. You may be approached by indigenous men selling bags, whistles, bows and arrows or feather headdresses. A few blocks further along Palma near its intersection with Alberti is the tourist information office (address above); it has craft stalls for those not wishing to buy on the street. On Saturday morning, till 1200, Palma becomes a pedestrian area, with stalls selling arts, crafts, clothes and during the summer there is entertainment outside the tourist office. On Sunday there are stalls selling second-hand or antique items around Plaza de los Héroes. (If looking for more handicraft and traditional items, visit also the nearby Plaza de la Democracia bordering Olivia and NS de la Asunción.) From Palma turn right at 14 de Mayo to the **Casa de la Independencia** (1772) ⓘ *14 de Mayo y Pdte Franco, www.casadelaindependencia.org.py, Mon-Fri 0800-1800, Sat 0800-1300, free, has toilets*, with a historical collection; the 1811 anti-colonial revolution was plotted here. The **Iglesia de Encarnación** ⓘ *14 de Mayo y Víctor Haedo, T490860*, partially restored after

Asunción

Where to stay
1 Amalfi C4
3 Aspen Apart Hotel C1
4 Asunción Palace B1
5 Bavaria A6
6 Black Cat Hostel A3
8 Cecilia B6
9 Chaco B4
10 City C3

11 Crowne Plaza B6
12 El Lapacho A6
13 El Viajero Hostel C3
14 Granados Park B2
16 La Española C4
17 Las Margaritas B2
18 Maison Suisse A6
19 Palmas del Sol A6
20 Paramanta A6

21 Portal del Sol A6
22 Res Itapúa C6
23 Sabe Center B4
24 Sheraton A6
25 Westfalenhaus A6

Restaurants
1 Bar Leo B1
2 Bellini B2

1148 · Paraguay Asunción

a fire in 1889 by an Italian immigrant who offered his services gratis on condition that he be free to select the best materials. Thanks to a 2013 publicity campaign, the Ministry of Public Works has committed to a complete restoration of the church. In spite of the ongoing work, it is, when open, a tranquil place to end your tour.

Heading out of the centre along Avenida Mariscal López

The **Museo Nacional de Bellas Artes** ⓘ *E Ayala 1345 y Curupayty, T211578, www.cultura.gov.py, Tue-Fri 0700-1800, Sat 0800-1400, free, guided tour*, shows the development of Paraguayan art and its European precursors, largely the collection of Juan Silvano Godoy. The **Museo Histórico Militar** ⓘ *in the Ministry of National Defence, Mcal López y 22 de Septiembre (surrender passport on entry), T223965, Mon-Fri 0700-1300, free*, has articles from both the Triple Alliance and the Chaco Wars. These include blood-stained flags from the Triple Alliance as well as clothes and personal possessions of Franciso Solano López and his Irish mistress, Eliza Lynch. The national cemetery, **Cementerio Recoleta** ⓘ *Av Mcal López y Chóferes del Chaco*, resembles a miniature city with tombs in various architectural styles. It contains the tomb of Madame Lynch (ask guide to show you the location), and, separately, the tomb of her baby daughter Corrine (Entrada 3 opposite Gran Unión supermarket). Beyond Chóferes del Chaco, between Avenida Mcal López and Avenida España, is **Villa Morra**, a smart residential and commercial zone with bars, restaurants and shopping centres. On the southeast outskirts of Asunción, at Km 12, is the fast-growing city of **San Lorenzo** (*population 320,878*). Reached via Ruta 2 (Mariscal Estigarribia Highway) or take buses 12, 18, 56, 26 and get off at central plaza with blue, 18th-century neo-Gothic cathedral. The **Museo Arqueológico y Etnográfico Guido Boggiani** ⓘ *Bogado 888 y Saturio Ríos, 1584717, 1½ blocks from plaza, Tue-Fri 1500-1800, Sat 0900-1200, 1500-1800, ring the bell if door is shut*, is staffed by a very helpful lady who explains the exhibits, which include rare Chamacoco feather art, and a well-displayed collection of tribal items from the northern Chaco from the turn of the 20th century. The shop across the road sells crafts at good prices. There's also a daily market.

Heading out of the centre along Avenida España

Museo Etnográfico Dr Andrés Barbero ⓘ *España 217 y Mompox, T441696, www.museobarbero.org.py, Tue-Fri 0700-1100, 1500-1700, free*, houses a good collection of tools and weapons of the various Guaraní cultures. The **Centro de Artes Visuales** ⓘ *Grabadores del Cabichuí entre Cañada y Emeterio Miranda,*

3 Bolsi *B3*
4 Café Literario *B4*
5 El Bar de la Preferida *B6*
6 El Molino *A6*
7 La Flor de la Canela *A5*
8 La Vienesa *B3*
11 Lido Bar *B3*
12 Munich *A4*
13 Paseo Carmelitas *A6*

14 San Roque *B5*
15 Taberna Española *C1*

Bars & clubs ⚫
16 Britannia Pub *B5*
17 Rivera *B2*

T607996, exhibitions open Thu-Sat 1530-2000, shop and café Wed-Sat 1530-2000, take bus 30 or 44A from the centre past Shopping del Sol, ask driver for Cañada, includes contemporary art in **Museo del Barro** ⓘ *T607996, www.museodelbarro.org, Tue 1530-2000, Wed-Sat 0900-1200, 1530-2000, free, guided tours US$3.25,* the most popular museum in the country by far, and the **Museo de Arte Indígena** ⓘ *www.museodelbarro.org/exhibicion/museo-de-arte-indigena,* which contains indigenous art and outstanding displays of rarely seen colonial art. Highly recommended.

Luque (*population 361,662, take bus 30*), founded 1636, has an attractive central plaza with some well-preserved colonial buildings and a pedestrianized area with outdoor cafés. It is famous for the making of Paraguayan harps and guitars and for fine filigree jewellery in silver and gold at very good prices, many shops on the main street. Luque is aware of its colonial heritage: the partial demolition in 2012 of two colonial-era houses in its centre was halted by the government. There is tourist information at Plaza General Aquino, which also holds the mausoleum of José Elizardo Aquino, a hero of the disastrous War of the Triple Alliance. There are some fine musical instrument shops on the road to Luque along Avenida Aviadores del Chaco. **Guitarras Sanabria** ⓘ *Av Aviadores del Chaco 2574 casi San Blas, T614974, www. arpasgsanabria.com.py,* is one of the best-known firms.

Other places in Asunción

Six kilometres east, the 245-ha **Jardín Botánico y Zoológico** ⓘ *Av Artigas y Primer Presidente, T663311, www.mca.gov.py/zoo.htm, daily 0700-1700, US$1.10,* lies along the Río Paraguay, on the former estate of the López family. The gardens are well-maintained, with signed walks and a rose garden, and are bordered by the 18-hole Asunción Golf Club. In addition to claiming almost 340 species of flora and fauna, this is a good place to buy local crafts including jewellery and cloth bags, but you'll need insect repellent if taking any of the side trails. In the gardens are the former residences of Carlos Antonio López, a two-storey typical Paraguayan country house with verandas, now housing a **Museo de Historia Natural** and a library, and that of Solano López, a two-storey European-inspired mansion which is now the **Museo de Historia Natural e Indigenista y Herbario** ⓘ *both museums are free, Mon-Sat 0730-1130, 1300-1730, Sun 0900-1300. Getting there: by bus Nos 2, 6, 23, and 40, US$0.60, 35 mins from Luis A Herrera, or Nos 24, 35 or 44B from Oliva or Cerro Corá.* Neither museum is in good condition.

Around Asunción

Many villages close to Asunción can be visited on a day trip: eg Areguá and San Bernardino on Lago Ypacaraí (see page 1160), Altos, great views over the lake, Itauguá (traditional ñandutí "spider web" lace and handicrafts centre).

Alternatively take a tour from any travel agent (see What to do, page 1155) of the **Circuito de Oro** or Camino Franciscano. Destinations for both tours vary from operator to operator, but those of the Circuito de Oro tend to include (by distance from Asunción), Fernando de la Mora, San Lorenzo, Julián Augusto Saldivar, Itá, Yaguarón, Paraguarí, Piribebuy, Caacupé, Ypacaraí, Itauguá and Capiatá, 160 km on paved roads on Rutas 1 and 2, seven hours. The route goes through the rolling hills of the Cordillera, no more than 650 m high, which are beautiful, with hidden waterfalls and a number of spas: Chololó, Piraretá (near Piribebuy) and Pinamar (between Piribebuy and Paraguarí) are the most developed.

The **Camino Franciscano** is similar, but longer and some towns from the Circuito de Oro overlap, but usually includes some combination of the historical towns of Capiatá, Ypané, Itá, Yaguarón, Villarrica, Valenzuela, Piribebuy, Caacupé, Caazapá, Tobatí, Atyrá, and Altos.

◉ Asunción listings

For hotel and restaurant price codes, and other relevant information, see Essentials.

● Where to stay

Hotel bills do not usually include service charge. Look out for special offers. For Asunción's Sheraton (**$$$$**), see www. sheraton-asuncion.com.py; or **Crowne Plaza** (**$$$$**); see www.crowneasuncion.com.py. Near the bus terminal, there are several hotels on Av F de la Mora and quieter places on C Cedro, adjoining Mora, all quite similar; turn left from front of terminal, 2 mins' walk.

Asunción *p1146, map p1148*
$$$$ Granados Park, Estrella y 15 de Agosto, T497921, www.granadospark.com.py. Luxury, top-quality hotel, range of suites with all facilities, good restaurant *Il Mondo*.
$$$$ Resort Yacht y Golf Club Paraguayo, 14 km from town, at Lambaré, on own beach on the Río Paraguay, T906121, www.resortyacht. com.py. 7 restaurants and cafés, super luxury, with pool, gym, spa, golf, tennis, airport transfers, many extras free, special deals.
$$$$-$$$ Hotel Westfalenhaus, Sqto 1° M Benítez 1577 con Santísima Trinidad, T292374, www.westfalenhaus.com.py. Comfortable, German-run, half board, weekly rates and self-catering apartments, pool, safe deposit box, international restaurant, *Piroschka*, gym, massage and spa, English, German and Spanish spoken.
$$$$-$$$ Sabe Center, 25 de Mayo y México, T450093, www.sabecenterhotel. com.py. Luxury hotel in modern tower, with all facilities, discounts available. English and Spanish spoken.
$$$ Aspen Apart Hotel, Ayolas 581 y Gral Díaz, T496066, www.aspen.com.py. Modern, lots of marble, 50 suites and apartments, pool, sauna, gym, cheaper longer stays.
$$$ Cecilia, Estados Unidos 341 y Estigarribia, T210365, www.hotelcecilia.com.py. Comfortable suites, weekend specials,

pool with a view, sauna, gym, airport transfers, parking, medical service.
$$$ Chaco, Caballero 285 y Estigarribia, T492066, www.hotelchaco.com.py. Central 1970s hotel, parking nearby, rooftop swimming pool, bar, good restaurant (**$$$**).
$$$ Las Margaritas, Estrella y 15 de Agosto, T448765, www.lasmargaritas.com.py. Modern, central business hotel, safe in room, restaurant, terrace grill, gym, sauna, pool. English, German, Portuguese spoken.
$$$ Maison Suisse, Malutín 482, Villa Morra, T600003, www.maisonsuisse.info. Convenient for shops, restaurants and bars, rooms with disabled access, pool, garden, gym, buffet breakfast in "Suizoguayo" style.
$$$ Paramanta, Av Aviadores del Chaco 3198, T607053, www.paramantahotel.com.py. Mid-way between airport and centre, buses stop outside, bar, restaurant, pool, gym, gardens, and many other services. English, German, Portuguese spoken.
$$$-$$ Bavaria, Chóferes del Chaco 1010, T600966, www.hotel-bavaria-py.com. Comfortable, colonial style, beautiful garden, pool, good value rooms and suites with kitchens, fridge, English, German spoken, very helpful staff.
$$ Amalfi, Caballero 877 y Fulgencio R Moreno y Manuel Domínguez, T494154. Modern, comfortable, spacious rooms, frigobar, safe downstairs, small bar and comedor. Recommended.
$$ Asunción Palace, Colón 415 y Estrella, T492153, www.asuncionhotel palace.com. Historic building dating from 1858. 24 rooms, fridge, very helpful, elegant, laundry. English spoken.
$$ City, NS de la Asunción con Humaitá, T491497, www.cityhotel.com.py. Good, all meals available in restaurant.
$$ El Lapacho, República Dominicana 543 casi Av España, T210662, www.lapacho. com.py. Family-run, welcoming, comfortable, cheaper rooms available. Favourite with backpackers and students. Convenient for

local services, 10 mins from centre by bus, pool, parking.

$$ La Española, Herrera 142 y F Yegros, T449280, www.hotellaespanola.galeon.com. Central, poor breakfast, credit cards accepted, airport pick-up, laundry, luggage storage, restaurant, parking.

$$ Palmas del Sol, España 202, T449485, www.hotelpalmasdelsol.com. Linked to Portal del Sol, very helpful, good buffet-style breakfast, a/c and fan, small pool, English, German spoken.

$$ Portal del Sol, Av Denis Roa 1455 y Santa Teresa, T609395, www.hotelportaldelsol.com. Comfortable hotel, some rooms sleep 4, free airport pick-up, pool.

$ Black Cat Hostel, Eligio Ayala 129 casi Independencia Nacional, T449827, www. hostelblackcat.com. Central backpacker hostel in a historic building, dorms for 8 and 16, private rooms for 1-2 (**$$**), shared bath, helpful with travel advice, breakfast included, English spoken. Recommended.

$ El Viajero Asunción, Alberdi 734, T444563, www.elviajerohostels.com/fr/hostel-asuncion. Private and shared dorms all en suite with a/c. Breakfast included. Cable TV and DVDs. Wide common areas, swimming pool.

$ Residencial Itapúa, Fulgencio R Moreno 943, T445121. Breakfast available, cheaper with fan, kitchen for snacks, no cooking, quiet, comfortable.

Out of the city: San Lorenzo

$$$ Estancia Oñondivemi, tourism farm, Km 27.5 on Ruta 1 just past the turn off to Ruta 2, Juan Augusto Saldivar, 30 mins from Asunción, T029-5 20344 or T981-441460, www.onondivemi.com.py. A pleasant escape from the city. Serves all meals, food organically grown on site. Horse riding, fishing, swimming, nature walks (they have a nearby property with a waterfall, lovely for swimming), attractive accommodation with a/c, cheaper with fan. Groups welcome.

Camping If camping, take plenty of insect repellent. The pleasant site at the Jardín Botánico, tents and vehicles permitted,

cold showers and 220v electricity, busy at weekends. Lock everything in vehicle.

⑦ Restaurants

Asunción *p1146, map p1148*
Many restaurants are outside the scope of the map. A few restaurants close at weekends, but may open at night. A good meal in the food halls at the shopping malls, which you pay for by weight, as you do in some of the city centre restaurants, is about US$2.30-4. Average price of a good meal in quality restaurants: US$20-25. The following are open most days of the week, day and night. For Spanish-language reviews see asunciongourmet.blogspot.com.

$$$ Acuarela, Mcal López casi San Martín, T601750, www.acuarela.com.py. Very good *churrascaría* and other Brazilian dishes.

$$$ Bolsi, Estrella 399 y Alberdi, T491841, www. bolsi.com.py. One of Asunción's longest-operating eateries. Enormously popular. Wide choice of wines, good for breakfast, excellent food (Sun 1200-1430) in large servings. Has great diner next door, lower prices, also popular.

$$$ Ciervo Blanco, José A Flores 3870 casi Radiooperadores del Chaco, T212918, ciervoblanco@yahoo.com. For meat dishes and parrillada and Paraguayan music shows.

$$$ Fabio Rolandi's, Mcal López y Infante Rivarola, T610447, www.restauranterolandi.com. Delicious pasta, steak and fish. Recommended.

$$$ La Pergola Jardín, Perú 240 y José Bergés, T214014, www.lapergola.com.py. Under the same ownership as **Bolsi**, excellent.

$$$ Mburicao, González Rioobó 737 y Chaco Real, T660048, www.mburicao.com. Mediterranean food. Highly recommended.

$$$ Paulista Grill, San Martín casi Mcal López, T608624, www.paulistagrill.com.py. A good *churrascaría*, good value, cheaper in the week, popular with groups.

$$$ Shangrila, Aviadores del Chaco y San Martín, T661618, www.shangri-la.com.py. Very good food at upmarket Chinese.

$$$ Sukiyaki, Hotel Uchiyamada, Constitución 763 y Luis A de Herrera, T222038. Good Japanese.

$$$ Taberna Española, Ayolas 631 y General Díaz, T441743. Spanish food, very good.

$$$-$$ El Chef Peruano, General Garay 431 y Del Maestro, T605756. Good-quality Peruvian food, popular with groups.

$$$-$$ Tierra Colorada Gastro, Santísima Trinidad 784 y Tte Fernández, T663335, http://tierracoloradagastro.com. Out of the centre in Barrio Mburucuya, toward Parque Ñu Guasu in Luque. Paraguayan-fusion dishes, deliberately healthy, many using indigenous recipes and produce from farms in the area; good reputation.

$$ Bellini, Palma 459 y 14 de Mayo. 3-course pasta buffet or à la carte, good value and popular.

$$ Lido Bar, Plaza de los Héroes, Palma y Chile, T446171. Daily 0700-2300. An institution in Asunción, great location across from Panteón, loads of character. Good for breakfast, empanadas and watching the world go by. Good quality and variety, famous for fish soup, delicious, very popular. Recommended.

$$ Munich, Eligio Ayala 163, T447604. Pleasant, old-fashioned, with a shady patio, popular with business people.

$$ San Roque, Eligio Ayala y Tacuary, T446015. Traditional, "an institution" and one of the oldest restaurants in town, relatively inexpensive. Recommended.

$ La Vienesa, Alberdi y Oliva, T612793, www.lavienesa.com.py. Wide menu, meat dishes, fish, pasta, pizza, Mexican, lots of breads and sweets, coffee. Also does by weight and take away. Popular at lunchtime. Also at Av España y Dominicana, Villa Morra.

$ Tapei, Tte Fariña 1049 y Brasil y Estados Unidos, T201756. Serves stylish Chinese and vegetarian by weight. Recommended.

Cafés and snacks

Most cheap lunch places close around 1600.
Bar Leo, Colón 462 y Olivia, T490333. Small, clean place for lunch buffet, takeaway and empanadas and tortas.

Café Literario, Mcal Estigarribia 456, T491640. Mon-Fri 1600-2200. Cosy café/bar, books and good atmosphere. Occasional cultural events with Alianza Francesa.

El Bar de la Preferida, Estados Unidos 341 y 25 de Mayo, T202222, www.hotelcecilia.com.py/index-3.html. Bar with meals served by kilo, Mon-Sat from 1200, different availability each day. Part of **Hotel Cecilia** and not to be confused with restaurant by the same name.

El Café de Acá, Tte Vera 390 casi Dr Mora, T623583, www.elcafedeaca.com. Serving coffee as in the old days.

El Molino, España 382 y Brasil, T225351. Good value, downstairs for sandwiches and homemade pastries, upstairs for full meals in a nice setting, good service and food (particularly steaks) but pricey. Bakery as well. Recommended.

Heladería París, 6 locations: Brasilia y Abelardo Brugada, Roca Argentina 982, Quesada y San Roque González, Felix Bogado y 18 Julio, Julio Correa y Molas López 143, and NS de Asunción y Quinta Avenida, www.hparis.com.py. Café/bar/ice cream parlour. Popular.

La Flor de la Canela, Tacuary 167 y Eligio Ayala, T498928, www.laflordelacanela.com.py. Cheap Peruvian lunches.

Michael Bock, Pres Franco 828, T495847. Excellent bread and sweet shop, specializing in German pastries.

Quattro D (4D), San Martín y Dr Andrade, T615168. Ice cream parlour offering great range of flavours, also weekday lunches from about US$1 and up.

🍸 Bars and clubs

Asunción p1146, map p1148
Bars
The best up-to-date online source for bars and clubs in Asunción, Ciudad del Este and anywhere else in Paraguay is www.asunfarra.com.py. *Asunción Viva* is a weekly listing of what's going on in the city; its monthly version costs US$1.65 (free at tourist office).

Paseo Carmelitas, Av España y Malutín, Villa Morra, small but upscale mall has several popular bars, such as El Bar, Kamastro, Kilkenney Irish Pub, Liquid and the very chic Sky Resto & Lounge (T600940, www.sky lounge.com.py) as well as restaurants and shops. To get there, take bus 30 from Oliva, which goes along Mcal López, but returns on España, or bus 31 to Mcal López.

Britannia Pub, Cerro Corá 851, T443990, www.britannia-pub.com. Evenings only, closed Mon. Good variety of drinks, German spoken, popular expat hangout, book exchange.

Café Bohemia, Senador Long 848 casi España, T662191. Original decor and atmosphere, Mon and Tue live blues/jazz, alternative at weekends.

Déjà Vu, Galería Colonial, Av España casi San Rafael, T615098. Popular, open every day from 0800.

Rivera, Estrella con 14 de Mayo y Alberdi. Central bar on second floor, balcony, good for drinks and music.

Clubs

Av Brasilia has a collection of clubs such as **Ristretto Café & Bar** (No 671 y Siria, T224614, http://ristrettocafebar.jimdo.com) and **Mouse Cantina** (No 803 y Patria, T228794).

Café Proa, Padre Juan Pucheú 549 casi España at same corner as French Embassy, T222456. Tango classes every night, light snacks and drinks, very pleasant.

Coyote, Sucre 1655 casi San Martín, T662114, www.coyote.com.py. Several dance floors and bars, affluent crowd, see website for other events in different locations including Ciudad del Este and San Bernardino. Recommended.

Face's, Av Mcal López 2585 (technically in Fernando de la Mora), T671421/672768, www.faces.com.py. Also in Ciudad del Este. Largest club in Paraguay, shows nightly.

Glam, Av San Martin 1155 y Agustín Barrios, T331905, www.glam.com.py. Along with Coyote and Face's (see above), one of Asunción's most popular clubs. Thu, Fri and Sat.

Trauma, 25 de Mayo 760 y Antequera y Tacuary, T981-204020. Gay/transvestite/mixed, Fri, Sat, 2300.

⊕ Entertainment

Asunción *p1146, map p1148*
Cinema and theatre See newspapers for films, performances of concerts, plays and ballets. For online listings, check *ABC Digital* (www.abc.com.py), *Última Hora* (www.ultimahora.com) and *La Nación* (www.lanacion.com.py). See also *Asunción Viva*, above, and the monthly *Asunción Quick Guide* (www.quickguide.com.py). Cinema admission US$5 (Wed and matinées half price). Most shopping malls have modern cinemas; see Shopping centres, below. For the **Teatro Municipal**, see above. Various cultural centres also put on films, theatrical productions and events: **Alianza Francesa**, Mcal Estigarribia 1039 y Estados Unidos, T210503, http://alianzafrancesapy.blogspot.com. **Centro Cultural Paraguayo Americano**, España 352 entre Brasil y Estados Unidos, T224831, www.ccpa.edu.py. **Centro Paraguayo-Japonés**, Av Julio Corea y Domingo Portillo, T607277, www.centroparaguayojapones. blogspot.com. **Goethe-Zentrum Asunción**, Juan de Salazar 310 y Artigas, T226242, www.goethe.de/ins/pa/asu.

⊛ Festivals

Asunción *p1146, map p1148*
Two weeks in **Jul**, **Expo**, an annual trade show at Mariano Roque Alonso, Km 14.5 on the Trans-Chaco Highway, www.expo.com.py. The biggest fair in the country with local and international exhibitors. Packed at weekends. Bus from centre takes 30 mins.

⊙ Shopping

Asunción *p1146, map p1148*
Bookshops English-language books are expensive throughout Paraguay. Better prices and selections are had in Argentina and Brazil. 'Books', at Shopping del Sol, T611730, and Mcal López 3971, also opposite Villa Morra shopping centre, T603722, www.libreriabooks.com. Very good for English books, new titles and classics. **El Lector** at San Martín y Austria, T610639 (has café and internet connection), www.ellector.com.py. Has a selection of foreign material and a range of its own titles on Paraguay.

Crafts Check the quality of all handicrafts carefully; in the city, lower prices usually mean lower quality. Many leading tourist shops offer up to 15% discount for cash; many others will not accept credit cards, so ask even if there are signs in window saying they do. For leather goods there are several places on Colón and on Montevideo including: **Boutique Irene**, No 463; **Boutique del Cuero**, No 329; and **Galería Colón 185** (recommended). Also **La Casa del Portafolio**, Av Palma 302, T492431. **Artes de Madera** at Ayolas 222. Wooden articles and carvings. **Casa Overall 1**, Mcal Estigarribia y Caballero, T448657, good selection. Also **No 2** at 25 de Mayo y Caballero, T447891. **Casa Vera**, Estigarribia 470, T445868, www.casavera.com.py, for Paraguayan leatherwork, cheap and very good. **Doña Miky**, O'Leary 215 y Pres Franco, recommended. **Folklore**, Mcal Estigarribia e Iturbe, T494360, good for music, woodcarvings and other items. **Victoria, Arte Artesanía**, Iturbe y Ayala, T450148, interesting selection of wood carvings, ceramics etc. Recommended. **La Recova**, near the waterfront, long Asunción's general-purpose market, has served as an open-air and covered emporium for all manner of handicrafts and traditional goods (including better-grade hammocks, leather and silver products) for more than 150 years. It takes some searching to find the best deals, but the markets here are endlessly colourful and vibrant, with wares usually cheaper than what are being sold in Plaza Libertad or along Av Palma.

Note that Paraguay's famous ñanduti lace can be purchased in several Asunción shops, but as with musical instruments and hammocks, often these products are less expensive and better grade when purchased in the countryside.

Markets Mercado Cuatro in the blocks bounded by Pettirossi, Perú and Av Dr Francia, is a huge daily market selling food, clothing, electrical items, DVDs, CDs, jewellery, toys, is a great place to visit. Good, cheap Chinese restaurants nearby. **Shopping Mariscal López** (see below) has a fruit and vegetable market, Tue, in the car park, and a small plant/flower market, including orchids, Wed, at the entrance.

Shopping centres Asunción has a number of modern Shopping Malls with shops, ATMs, cafés, supermarkets, cinemas and food halls all under one a/c roof. Most also offer Wi-Fi coverage. In the centre is **Mall Excelsior** (Chile y Manduvirá, T443015, www.mallexcelsior. com). **Shopping Villa Morra** (Av Mcal López y San Roque González, T603050, www.svm.com. py). **Shopping Mariscal López** (Quesada 5050 y Charles de Gaulle, behind Shopping Villa Morra, T611272, www.mariscallopez.com.py). **Shopping del Sol** (Av Aviadores de Chaco y D F de González, T611780, www.delsol.com.py).

⏻ What to do

Asunción *p1146, map p1148*

Football Asunción (technically next-door Luque) is the permanent home of the South American Football Confederation, CONMEBOL (www.conmebol.com), on the autopista heading towards the airport, opposite Ñu Guazú Park. This imposing building with its striking 'football' fountain houses offices, a hall of fame, extensive football library and a new museum with interactive exhibits, T494628 in advance for visits. See also **Asociación Paraguaya de Futbol**, www.apf.org.py. **Estadio Defensores del Chaco**, Mayor Martínez 1393 y Alejo García, T480120, is the national stadium, hosting international, cup and major club matches.

Horse riding Club Hípico Paraguayo, Av Eusebio Ayala y Benjamín Aceval, Barrio San Jorge Mariano Roque Alonso, T756148. Actually 9 different athletic clubs in one; scene of many Asunción society events. Members club (US$55 per month but daily rates available) open to the public. Friendly and helpful.

Nature tourism See page 1140.

Rural tourism *Turismo rural* is an enjoyable way to visit the country and get a feel for a Paraguayan way of life that revolves around agriculture and ranching. It is not as advanced as rural tourism in Argentina, Chile or Uruguay, amenities are modest and there is little concerted promotion of estancias, but the sector is slowly growing in Paraguay, particularly in the southeast (in Paraguarí, Caaguazú, Guairá and Caazapá departments) and to the east and northeast of Asunción (in Cordillera and San Pedro departments). The **Touring y Automóvil Club Paraguayo (TACPy**, 25 de Mayo y Brasíl, p 2, T210550, www.tacpy.com.py) is a potential source of information on rural tourism, although it now focuses primarily upon three regions: mission tours (to Villa Florida, San Ignacio Guazú, Santa María de Fé and Santiago Apóstol); the Alto Paraná (including Itaipú, the Salto de Monday falls and Ciudad del Este); and Guairá (essentially the city of Villarrica). Thanks to increased government support for its mission, however, the **Paraguayan Rural Tourism Association** (APATUR), Don Bosco 881, T497028, turismo@tacpy.com.py, is expected to take over this role. With advance notice, it can help organize visits to ranches and farms throughout the country's more accessible regions and is also attempting to showcase Paraguay's rural folk art and music. One-day tour prices are about US$60-95 pp including accommodation, food and drink (not alcohol). All the ranches promoted by APATUR supposedly have good facilities, although what constitutes "good" is still a subjective matter as there is as yet no accepted standardization. Transport to and from these ranches from Asunción is sometimes included in the package. Visitors experience living on a ranch, can participate in a variety of activities, and enjoy typical food, horse riding, photo safaris and nature watching. See the **Ministry of Tourism** (SENATUR) website, www.senatur.gov.py, Turismo rural page, under ¿Qué hacer?, for a list of several ranches that welcome tourists. All visits should be arranged at least one week in advance and confirmed prior to leaving Asunción.

Tours

Many agencies offer day tours of the **Circuito de Oro** or **Camino Franciscano** (from US$50), with the possibility of different stops for each agency, so ask in advance which locations are included on the itinerary. Trips to local *estancias*, Encarnación and the former Jesuit Missions, Itaipú and Iguazú or the Chaco region are all offered as 1-, 2- or 4-day tours. Most agencies will also provide personalized itineraries on request. Many more city tours, especially those focusing on architecture and culture, are also now available and, in the wake of Paraguay's 2010 bicentennial, often take in several recently restored historic buildings. For more information contact **SENATUR** or the **Paraguayan Association of Travel Agencies and Tourism (ASATUR)**, Juan O'Leary 650, p 1, T494728, www.asatur.org.py. Also, Paraguay's official national cultural organ, the Cabildo (address above), offers several options for itineraries throughout the country and capital. **Canadá Viajes**, Rep de Colombia 1061, T211192, www.canadaviajes.com.py. Good Asunción and Chaco tours.

Crucero Paraguay, Av Costanera y Montevideo, T447710/440669, crucero@cruceroparaguay.info. The Chaco Programme, a slow-speed cruiser, leaves Asunción Bay on weekends starting Fri at 0700 to Sun at 1700. Cuñataí, at Sporting Club de Puerto Sajonia, T420375. Boat tours of Asunción and Río Paraguay, departures Sun, 1700, 140-people capacity.

Inter Tours, Perú 436 y España, T211747, www.intertours.com.py. One of Paraguay's biggest full-service tour agencies. Tours to Chaco, Iguazú and Jesuit missions. Highly recommended.

Crucero Paraguay

Menno Travel, Rep de Colombia 1042 entre Brasil y EEUU, T493504, mennotra@tigo.com.py. German spoken.

Time Tours, Asunción Super Centro, loc 197, T449737, info@timetours.com.py. Fluent English, runs Camino Franciscano tours. Recommended.

Vips Tour, México 782 entre Fulgencio R Moreno y Herrera, T441199, also at Senador Long 790 y Tte Vera, T615920, www.vipstour.com. Asunción, estancia and Chaco tours.

Guides

Oscar Daniel González, T981-21 7082, osgonzaga1@hotmail.com. Private tours of the Circuito de Oro, US$70 pp per day, in Spanish.

⊖ Transport

Asunción *p1146, map p1148*

Air Silvio Pettirossi Airport, T645600. Several agencies have desks where you can book a taxi to your hotel, up to US$30. Bus 30 goes every 15 mins between the red bus stop outside the airport and Plaza de los Héroes, US$1, difficult with luggage. Minibus service from your hotel to airport run by **Tropical**, T424486, book in advance, US$2.70 (minimum 2 passengers, or pay for 2). The terminal has a tourist office (free city map and hotel information), bank (turn right as you leave customs – better rates in town), post office (0800-1800), handicraft shop (good quality, expensive), restaurant and several travel agencies who arrange hotel bookings and change money (very poor rates). Left luggage US$5 per day per item.

Bus City buses: Journeys within greater Asunción US$0.75. Buses can be busy at rush hours. Turnstiles are awkward for large backpacks. Keep your ticket for inspection until you leave bus.

Long-distance: The Terminal de Omnibus, TOA, is south of the centre at República Argentina y Fernando de la Mora, T551740, www.mca.gov.py/toa.htm. Local bus No 8 is the only direct one from Oliva, which goes via Cerro Corá and Av Brasil from the centre, and stops on the opposite side of Av F de la Mora to the terminal, US$0.75. From the terminal to the centre it goes via Brasil, FR Moreno, Antequera, Plaza Uruguaya and E Ayala. Get out between Chile and Alberdi for Plaza de los Héroes. Other buses, eg No 31, follow more circuitous routes. Taxi to/from centre, recommended if you have luggage, US$8-10, journey time depends on the amount of traffic, about 45 mins. The terminal has a bus information desk, free city/country map, restaurant (quite good), café, *casas de cambio* (poor rates), ATM, post office, phone booths and shops. There are many touts for bus companies at the terminal. Allow yourself time to choose the company you want and don't be tricked into buying the wrong ticket. Better companies include **Nuestra Señora de la Asunción**, T289 1000, www.nsa.com.py, has booking office at main terminal and at Mcal Estigarribia y Antequera, off Plaza Uruguaya (mainly for its tours), and at Benjamin Constant 984, opposite Aduanas. Some of its buses are direct, ie they don't stop everywhere and anywhere. RYSA, T557201/551726, www.rysa.com.py, has a booking office at Ayala y Antequera by Plaza Uruguaya. Also recommended are **Crucero del Norte** (T224555), **La Ovetense** (T551585), **Nasa-Golondrina** (T558451) for domestic destinations. Bus company offices are on the top floor of the terminal. Local departures, including for Yaguarón and Paraguarí, are boarded from the basement. Bus fares within Paraguay are given under destinations, also available on TOA's website. Note that all journey times are approximate.

To Argentina There is a road north from Asunción (passing the Jardín Botánico on Primer Presidente) to a concrete arch span bridge (Puente Remanso – US$1.25 toll, pedestrian walkway on upstream side, 20 mins to cross) which leads to the border at Puerto Falcón (about 40 km) and then to **Clorinda** in Argentina. The border is open 24 hrs; local services are run by **Empresa Falcón** to **Puerto Falcón**: US$1.50, every hr, last bus from Falcón to the centre of Asunción 1830; from Falcón to **Clorinda** costs US$0.75, but direct from Asunción to Clorinda is US$1.20. **Note** Buses don't wait for you to go through formalities: if you cannot process in time, wait for the same company's next bus and present ticket, or buy a new ticket.

Buses to **Buenos Aires** (18 hrs) daily, many companies, via Rosario and Santa Fe (fares range from US$35-75). To **Resistencia** and **Corrientes**, many daily, US$9.75 to Resistencia, US$13 to Corrientes; many drug searches on this road. To **Salta**, take a bus to **Resistencia**, then change to **Flecha** or **La Veloz del Norte**, or take a bus on the route through the Chaco, as below.

To Brazil Many Paraguayan buses advertise that they go to destinations in Brazil, when, in fact you have to change buses and book again at the border. Services to **Campo Grande** and **Corumbá** via Pedro Juan Caballero and Ponta Porã do not stop for immigration formalities. Check all details carefully. **Nuestra Señora de la Asunción** and others, and the Brazilian company **Pluma** (T551725, www.pluma.com. br) have direct services via Ciudad del Este to **Foz do Iguaçu** (Brazil), US$30-35, 5-6 hrs. To **Curitiba**, with **Pluma** and others, daily, 15½ hrs, US$55. To **Florianópolis**, Pluma and **Catarinense**, US$72 (T551738, www. catarinense.net), you may have to change in Cascavel. To **Porto Alegre**, Uneleste (T442679), Tue, Thu, US$66. To **São Paulo**, Pluma, Sol and Brújula, 20 hrs, US$55-86. Pluma to **Rio de Janeiro**, US$98 (not daily); Transcontinental (T557369) to **Brasília** 3 a week, US$105.

To Bolivia Via the Chaco, to Santa Cruz, Yacyretá, T551725, Mon, Wed, Fri, and Sat at 2030, US$44.50. Also **Pycazú**, T555235, Thu, Sat 2100, **Palma Loma**, T558196, **Río Paraguay**, T555958, both daily, and **Stel Turismo**, T551647. All fares US$52-64. All buses normally travel via Mariscal Estigarribia, for Paraguayan immigration where foreigners must get an exit stamp; La Patria; Infante Rivarola at the border (no stamps are given here); Ibibobo, for Bolivian immigration; and Villamontes. From here buses go either to Yacuiba for Argentina (Pocitos and on to Salta on Ruta 54), or direct to Santa Cruz. Advertised as 21 hrs, the trip can take 2 days to Santa Cruz if the bus breaks down. Some food provided on both Salta and Santa Cruz routes, but take your own, plus extra water just in case; also take toilet paper. The buses can be very crowded. In summer the route can be very hot and dusty, but in winter, it can be cold at night.

Unless specifically advertised (eg Nasa-Golodrina), buses to Bolivia do not go through Filadelfia or the other Mennonite colonies, so take a local service from Asunción (see page 1186). After visiting the Chaco, you can usually get on a Bolivia-bound bus in Mariscal Estigarribia, where the bus companies have agents (see page 1184), but enquire in advance with their offices in Asunción.

River boat To escape the city take a short trip across the river to the **Mbiguá Club** (rather run down), fare US$4.50. Ask at Aduanas for information. A small launch leaves every 20 mins from the pier at the bottom of Montevideo to **Chaco-i**, a strip of land between the Ríos Paraguay and Pilcomayo, US$0.75 each way. The Argentine town of Clorinda is just the other side of the Pilcomayo, but there are no ferries or immigration for crossing here.

For boat travel to **Concepción**, see under Concepción, Transport, page 1179. If you want more luxury take a cruise on the **Crucero Paraguayo**, see Tours, above. Reservations also available through larger tour operators.

Taxi Taxi meters start at US$1.15 and rise in US$0.10 increments. There is a late night surcharge after 2200 to 0500. There are many taxi ranks throughout the city. Taxis can either be hailed or call **Radiotaxi** (recommended), T550116/311080.

Train At the time of writing, no tourist steam trains were running from Asunción.

⊙ Directory

Asunción *p1146, map p1148*
Banks See Money section in Planning your trip. Lots of ATMs, accepting credit and debit cards, give dollars and guaraníes. Many *casas de cambio* on Palma, Estrella and nearby streets (Mon-Fri 0730-1200, 1500-1830, Sat 0730-1200). All rates are better than at frontiers. They change dollars, euros, Brazilian reais, Argentine pesos and a few will accept sterling notes or Bolivianos. **Car hire** Fast Rent a Car, Prof

Chávez 1276 y Santa Rosa, T605462, www.
fastrentacar.com.py. Good, helpful. Also
other companies at the airport. Note that
all Paraguayan car hire agencies require
payment in US dollars as well as a deposit
secured by a credit card of between US$500-
1000. **Embassies and consulates** For
all Paraguayan embassies and consulates
abroad and for all foreign embassies and
consulates in Paraguay, see http://embassy.
goabroad.com. **Immigration** Caballero
y Eligio Ayala, T446066, www.migraciones.
gov.py. **Language schools** Idipar
(Idiomas en Paraguay), Manduvirá 963,
T447896, www.idipar.net. Offers courses in
Spanish or Guaraní. Private or group lessons
available, also offers accommodation with
local families and volunteer opportunities.
Good standard. IPEE, Lugano 790 y Ayolas,
T447482. Spanish or Guaraní, in individual
or group classes. Recommended. One2One,
Cecilio da Silva 980, T613507, www.one2one.
com.py. Good for immersion or business
Spanish (as well as other languages).
Medical services Private hospitals: Centro

Médico Bautista, Av Argentina y Cervera,
T688900, www.cmb.org.py. Sanatorio San
Roque, Eligio Ayala y Pa'í Pérez, T228600,
www.sanroque.com.py, 24 hrs. Public
hospital: Centro de Emergencias Médicas, Av
Gral Santos y Teodoro S Mongelos, T284900.
Post offices The historic post office at
Alberdi, between Benjamín Constant y El
Paraguayo Independiente, does not have
postal services. The main office is at 25 de
Mayo 340 y Yegros, T498112, Mon-Fri 0700-
2000, Sat 0700-1200. Poste Restante (ask at
the Casillas section) charges about US$0.50
per item, but you may have to insist they
double-check if you are expecting letters.
Packages under 2 kg should be handed in at
the small packages window, up to 20 kg at
the 'Encomiendas' office. A faster and more
reliable way to send parcels is by EMS, the
post office courier service from the same
office. Customs inspection of open parcel
required. Register all important mail. There
are sub-offices at Shopping del Sol, Mall
Excelsior and in certain suburbs, but mail
takes longer to arrive from these offices.

Región Oriental: East of Asunción

To the east of the Río Paraguay lie the most fertile lands and the most populated region of the country. Of the vast rainforests that once covered it, only a few isolated patches have not been converted to farmland. Rutas 2, 3 and 7 (a continuation of 2) all head east towards the border with Brazil, taking the traveller near tranquil villages known for their arts and crafts, German colonies, the occasional Franciscan mission, and small towns associated with the country's bloody past. In contrast to the quiet of the countryside, Rutas 1 and 8 run south and east, and lead to the southern Paraneña (the country's breadbasket and home to its gauchos), the former Jesuit missions and then merge at Coronel Bogado before reaching the Río Paraguay in Encarnación. Ciudad del Este, a straight shot across Rutas 2 and 7, is a crossroads for all manner of merchandise, much of it illegal, and the world's largest stolen car market, while the giant Itaipú dam has irreversibly changed the landscape. Along the border (and shared with Brazil and Argentina) are the Iguazú Falls, still the top draw for most visitors to Paraguay.

Itauguá → *Phone code: 0294. Population: 148,721.*

At Km 30 on Ruta 2, founded in 1728, Itauguá, now Paraguay's fastest-growing city, is where
the famous *ñandutí*, or spiderweb lace, is made. There are some 320 different designs. Prices
are lower than in Asunción and the quality is better; there are many makers. Almost all of the
best *talleres* are located directly off the highway and can be accessed by bus. To watch the lace

being made, ask around. The old town lies two blocks from the main highway. Worth seeing are the **market** ① *0800-1130, 1500-1800, closed Sun*, the church of Virgen del Rosario and the **Museo de Historia Indígena** ① *Km 25, daily 0800-1130, 1500-1800, US$0.60*, a beautiful collection of carvings of Guaraní mythological creatures, and the **Museo Parroquial San Rafael** ① *daily 0800-1130, 1500-1800*, free, with a display of indigenous art and Franciscan artefacts. There is a four-day **Festival de Ñandutí** in early July, including processions and the crowning of Señorita Ñandutí. Many of Paraguay's best traditional musicians perform during the festival. There are also musical evenings on **Viernes Culturales** (Cultural Fridays) in January and February. Itauguá is also the birthplace of Juan Crisóstomo Centurión, the only Paraguayan military leader to win a battle in the War of the Triple Alliance and an architect of the country's rebirth. The best guide for information about town is online: www.itaugua.com.py.

Areguá → *Phone code: 0291. Population: 15,814.*

At **Capiatá** (Ruta 2, Km 20, fine colonial church), a left turn goes to **Areguá**, Paraguay's strawberry capital and a centre of better-grade crafts (lots of artesanías). Founded in 1541 this is a pretty colonial village, 30 km east of Asunción and also easily reached from Luque's main road. It sits on the slopes above **Lago Ypacaraí**. Formerly the summer capital of the country's elite, from its attractive church at the highest point in town there is one of the best views of the lake, its two nearby cerros (Kõi and Ita'o) and surroundings. It has an interesting ceramics cooperative, a museum, arts and crafts exhibition and on its outskirts a remarkable Dominican convent, originally a castle built for Francisco Solano López and his mistress Eliza Lynch and later purchased by one of Paraguay's grandes dames, **Carlota Palmerola** ① *open daily 0800-1700, US$2.15*. Guided tours of the convent and other sites in town leave Sun 0900, return 1500, from SENATUR's office in Asunción, T433500, US$6.50. There is also a memorial in the centre to its most famous son, Gabriel Casaccia Bibolini, who many consider the founder of modern Paraguayan literature. There is a good German-run restaurant in the centre of the village. From here boat trips run across the lake at weekends to San Bernadino.

San Bernardino and Lago Ypacaraí → *Phone code: 0512. Population, 7220.*

At Km 48 on Ruta 2 a branch road, 8 km long, leads off to **San Bernardino**, originally a Swiss German colony settled by the eminent botanist Emilio Hassler and known locally as 'Samber', on the east bank of **Lago Ypacaraí**. In the past few decades it has replaced Areguá as the country's summer resort for the rich. The lake, 24 km by 5 km, has facilities for swimming and watersports and sandy beaches (ask locally about pollution levels in the water). There are frequent cruises from the pier during the tourist season. As well as for Paraguay's elite, it is now the main vacation spot for all of Asunción from December to February, which means that it is lively and crowded at weekends in the summer, with concerts, pubs and nightclubs, but as a result it is commercialized. During the week and off season it is a tranquil resort town, with lakeside tourism clearly the main draw. In town itself, visit **Casa Büttner** ① *Colonos Alemanes, T0984-933158, free*, an estate built by the German immigrant Julio Büttner in 1882. It saw Paraguay's first automobile and bus and also was the site of the country's first formal carpentry and ice-making factories. The house is still owned by Büttner's descendants and part of it serves as the town's library, a tea house and a crafts centre. It also has a wealth of information for travellers. Boats can be hired on the lake and there is good walking in the neighbourhood, for example from San Bernardino to **Altos**, which has one of the most spectacular views of the lake, wooded hills and valleys (round trip three hours). Shortly after the turn off from the main road towards San Bernardino is a sign to **La Gruta**; turn right here to a secluded park (Ypacaraí). There are grottos with still water and overhanging cliffs. No buses run after 2000 and taxis are expensive. The town is one of the few in Paraguay to have an official tourist guide agency (**SanBer Tour** ① *T0981-607829, sanber_tour_py@hotmail.com*), which offers five different tours. Tourist information is in **Casa Hassler** ① *between General Morinigo and Emilio Hassler, T0512-232974, http://sanbernardino.gov.py/casa-hassler*, which is also the town's cultural centre.

Caacupé → *Phone code: 0511. Colour map 6, C6. Population: 30,738.*

At Km 54 on Ruta 2, this is a popular resort and religious centre on the Azcurra escarpment. The centre is dominated by the modern Basilica of Our Lady of the Miracles, with a copper roof, stained glass and polychrome stone esplanade, consecrated by Pope John Paul II in 1988 (small fee to climb the tower). There is an ATM on the plaza between the supermarket and **Hotel El Mirador**.

Thousands of people from Paraguay, Brazil and Argentina flock to the shrine, especially for the **Fiesta de la Inmaculada Concepción** on 8 December, known locally as the Fiesta de la Virgen de Caacupé, or 'the black virgin'. Besides fireworks and candlelit processions, pilgrims watch the agile gyrations of Paraguayan bottle-dancers; they weave in intricate measures whilst balancing bottles pyramided on their heads. The top bottle carries a spray of flowers and the more expert dancers never let drop a single petal. The bottles contained blessed water, which is believed to come from the nearby spring of Tupasy Ykuá, which the Virgin revealed to early settlers. Caacupé is also well known for its Carnaval celebrations.

Tobatí, a town 15 km north of Caacupé along a marked branch road, specializes in woodwork. The town's highly regarded **Villa Artesenal** is 1 km walk from the bus stop outside the house of the late **Zenon Páez**, a world famous sculptor. It produces wonderful masks (some reputedly of pre-Columbian ancestry), coca-fibre hammocks and furniture. The Villa also has a small permanent exhibition and annual traditional handicrafts fair. There are some amazing rock formations on the way to Tobatí. To get there, take a bus from the corner below the park on the main Asunción road in Caacupé.

Piribebuy → *Phone code: 0515. Population: 13,106.*

Beyond Caacupé, at Km 71 on Ruta 2, a paved road runs 13 km due south to the town of Piribebuy, founded in 1636 and noted for its strong local drink, *caña*. In the central plaza is the church (1640), with fine sculptures, high altar and pulpit. The town is officially one of Paraguay's 'heroic cities' in recognition of its staunch defence during a major battle in the War of the Triple Alliance (1869), commemorated by the **Museo Histórico Pedro Pablo Caballero** ① *Mariscal Estigarribia y Yegros, free*, which also contains pristine artefacts from the Chaco War. Buses from Asunción by Transportes Piribebuy. Near the town are the attractive falls of Piraretá and more than 15 hot springs (popular on weekends). The branch road continues via Chololó, 13 km south, and reaches Ruta 1 at Paraguarí, 28 km from Piribebuy (see page 1169). Between Piribebuy and Paraguarí is an outdoor and adventure centre, **Eco-reserva Mbatoví** ① *T021-444844, or T0971-659820, for reservations and information visit www.mbatovi.com.py, entry US$35*, with a visitor centre. It includes an outdoor pursuits course and a three-hour guided walk, taking in early settlements, local folklore and beautiful scenery.

Caraguatay → *Phone code: 0517. Population: 1776.*
A turn-off from Eusebio Ayala (Km 73) on Ruta 2 goes 20 km northeast to Caraguatay, a singular town with a unique history. Founded by the Spanish in 1770, it later served as the summer

residence of Francisco Solano López and his Irish mistress Eliza Lynch. The town's centre boasts several beautiful colonial-era buildings and on the 24 of September, it celebrates the feast day of its patron saint, the Virgen de las Mercedes, with traditional dances and music that are no longer seen elsewhere in the country. Remarkably for a town of less than 5000 inhabitants, it has given the country three presidents. Caraguatay is also the centre of an interesting economic experiment: it sends more workers abroad than any other municipality in Paraguay and the remittances returned have gone into making it one of the country's more upscale communities, with amenities and public services not easily found elsewhere. For more information, see http://caraguatay-ciudad.blogspot.com.

Vapor Cué National Park

Some 5 km from Caraguatay is the Vapor Cué National Park, where boats from the War of the Triple Alliance are preserved. Although officially a national park, it is more of an open-air museum. Next to the (indoor) museum is a hotel with pool, **Hotel Nacional de Vapor Cué ($$**, T0517-222395). Frequent buses run from Asunción to Caraguatay.

Coronel Oviedo and around → *Phone code 0521. Colour map 6, C6. Population: 64,485.*
Coronel Oviedo, at the junction of west-east highway Ruta 2 and the major north-south Ruta 8, is an important route centre, although hardly worth a stop. Buses drop passengers for connections at the junction (El Cruce). Ruta 8 runs north to Santa Rosa del **Mbutuy**, continuing as Ruta 3 to Yby Yaú, where it meets Ruta 5 (westward to Concepción and eastward to Pedro Juan Caballero). At Mbutuy (Km 56, parador, restaurant, petrol station) Ruta 10 branches off northeast to the Brazilian frontier on the Río Paraná at **Saltos de Guaíra** (*Phone code: 046*), named after the waterfalls now under the Itaipú lake. There is a 900-ha wildlife reserve, **Refugio Biológico Mbaracayú**, administered by the Itaipú dam company, www.itaipubinacional.gov.py. Saltos de Guaíra, a free port, can also be reached by a paved highway (the Supercarretera Itaipú) which runs north from Hernandarias, via Colonia Limoy to meet Ruta 10 at Cruce Carolina Andrea.

Mbaracayú Forest Nature Reserve ① *To visit, first contact the Moisés Bertoni Foundation in Asunción for details (see National parks, page 1140 for address); entry US$7.50. 2 bus companies from Asunción to Curuguaty, daily, 6 hrs, US$20. From Curuguaty to Ygatimi local buses take 1 hr, not all paved. From Villa Ygatimi it is 25 km to the park on a dirt road, T034-720147 for the park staff to arrange transport; US$15, 3-5 hrs Ygatimi to the park.* Not to be confused with the nearby Refugio Biológico Mbaracayú mentioned above, this federally protected reserve covers 64,406 ha of Paraguay's rapidly disappearing Interior Atlantic forest. It is the largest area representative of this ecosystem in good conservation status in Paraguay. It contains 53% of all mammal species (nearly 100) and 58% of all bird species (411) found in eastern Paraguay. There are trails (US$2 with guide, US$5 to hire bike, guide US$6 extra), canoes (US$8, guide US$8), waterfalls (US$20) and spectacular view points. There are also two indigenous communities, the Aché and Guaraní. There is a visitor centre, 3-km walk from the entrance, and small museum at Villa Ygatimi, also lodging (13 rooms, each with Wi-Fi and a/c, with or without bath, and meals are available). Packages of seven, 15 and 30 days can be booked.

Villarrica → *Phone code: 0541. Colour map 6, C6. Population: 56,385.*

Villarrica, 42 km south of Coronel Oviedo on Ruta 8, is delightfully set on a hill rich with orange trees. Founded in 1570 and moved seven times before settling in its current location in 1682, it is a very pleasant, friendly place, with a fine cathedral, built in traditional style with veranda, and various pleasant parks. The **Museo Municipal Maestro Fermín López** (closed weekends) behind the church in a wonderfully restored building dating from the War of the Triple Alliance has a foreign coin collection; please contribute. Products of the region are tobacco, cotton, sugar, yerba mate, hides, meat and wine produced by German settlers. There is a large student population and the town is the cultural hub of the region. Its Carnaval Guaireño is one of the most spectacular events the nation and attracts large crowds every year. For more information, see www.villarrica.gov.py, www.villarricache ciudad.com or www.villarrica-online.com.

There are several German colonies near Villarrica. Some 7 km north is an unsigned turn off to the east, then 20 km to tiny **Colonia Independencia**, which has some beautiful beaches on the river (popular in summer). German-speaking travellers can also visit the German cooperative farms (these are not Mennonite communities, but rather German settlements established in the early 20th century). A great mate and wine producing area and, at harvest time, there is a wine festival. They also have a good beer festival in October.

Ciudad del Este

Where to stay
1 Austria
2 California
3 El Caribeño
4 Convair
5 Mi Abuela
6 Munich

Restaurants
1 Cantina Napoli, Patussi Grill, Pizza Hut, Rélax Heladería y Café
2 Gouranga
3 Yrupé

East from Coronel Oviedo

The paved Ruta 7 runs 195 km through farmed areas and woods and across the Caaguazú hills. From here it continues to the spectacular 500-m singlespan 'Friendship Bridge' across the Paraná (to Brazil) at Ciudad del Este.

Ciudad del Este → *Phone code: 061.*
Colour map 7, C1. Population: 396,091.

Originally founded as Ciudad Presidente Stroessner in 1957 and 327 km from Asunción at the eastern terminus of Ruta 7, this was the fastest growing city in the country until the completion of the Itaipú hydroelectric project, for which it is the centre of operations. Ciudad del Este, the country's second-largest city, has been described as the biggest shopping centre in Latin America, attracting Brazilian and Argentine visitors who find bargain prices for electrical goods, watches and perfumes. However, it is a counterfeiter's paradise and can be quite dangerous. Check everything properly before making a purchase and ensure that shops pack what you actually bought. The main shopping street is Avenida San Blas, lined with shopping malls and market stalls, selling a huge variety of goods. Almost any vehicle advertised for sale, should you be tempted, was stolen in Brazil or Bolivia. Many jewels and stones are also counterfeit; be especially careful with touts advertising amethysts or emeralds. Watch the exchange rates if you're a short-term visitor. Parts of the city are dirty and frantic during business hours, but away from the Avenidas San Blas and Adrián Jara the pace of life is more relaxed and the streets and parks are green and quiet. **Tourist office** ① *Adrián Jara y Mcal Estigarribia, by the urban bus terminal, T511626, open 0700-1900, helpful.*

Around Ciudad del Este The **Monday Falls** (Salto del Monday) ① *0730-1800, US$1.20, taxi US$25 return*, where the Río Monday drops into the Paraná gorge, are worth seeing. They were proclaimed a protected area by the government in 2012. Camping and meals available. North of the city is the popular beach resort and biological refuge called **Tatí Yupí** ① *www.itaipu. gov.py/es/turismo/refugio-tati-yupi.*

Border with Brazil

The border crossing over the Friendship Bridge to Foz do Iguaçu is very informal, but is jammed with vehicles and pedestrians all day long. No passport stamps are required to visit Ciudad del Este for the day if coming from Brazil. Motorcycle taxis (helmet provided, hang on tight) are a good option if you have no luggage. There are lots of minibuses, too. On international buses, eg from Florianópolis to Ciudad del Este and Asunción, or from Foz to Asunción, the procedure is: non-Brazilians get out at immigration for an exit stamp, then take the bus across the bridge to Paraguayan immigration where everyone gets out for an entry stamp. On buses from Asunción to Foz and beyond, non-Paraguayans get out at Paraguayan immigration for an exit stamp, then the bus takes all passengers across the river to Brazilian immigration for the entry stamp. Make sure you get all entry and exit stamps.

If going to Foz for the day, note that buses marked "Foz do Iguaçu" do not – in spite of both the law and what you may be told – always stop at Paraguayan immigration before crossing into Brazil. This is unlikely to cause problems with Brazilian authorities, but make absolutely certain to pick up a Paraguayan exit stamp and a Brazilian entry stamp to re-enter Paraguay later. On return to Paraguay you do not need a Brazilian exit stamp or Paraguayan entry stamp because your original entry stamp covers you till you finally leave the country. Without the stamps you may have some explaining to do upon returning to Ciudad del Este, but the problem is common. You shouldn't face difficulties as long as your paperwork is in order. For local bus services, see Transport, below.

Although Ciudad del Este is a tax-free shopping destination for Brazilians, the same is not true in reverse. Technically there is a Paraguayan import tax of up to 60% on anything purchased in Brazil costing more than US$300. This applies to Paraguayan citizens only (and even then is not usually enforced), but keep all receipts for any items purchased in Brazil and make sure the price is denominated in reais.

There is a friendly tourist office in the customs building on the Paraguayan side, open 24 hours. You can get out of the bus here, rather than going to the bus terminal. Taxis wait just beyond immigration, US$4.50-5.50 to most places in Ciudad del Este, but settle price before getting in as there are reports of exorbitant fares. Remember to adjust your watch to local time (Brazil is one hour ahead). Although Paraguay observes daylight saving throughout the country, only some states in Brazil (including Paraná) do so (see Brazil chapter for details). **Brazilian consulate** ① *Ciudad del Este, Pampliega 205 y Pa'í Pérez, T061-500985, consulado. deleste@itamaraty.gov.br, Mon-Fri 0800-1400*, issues visas. **Argentine consulate** ① *Av Boquerón y Adrián Jara, Edificio China p 7, T061-500945, www.embajada-argentina.org.py/V2/consulados/ consulado-gral-en-cde, Mon-Fri 0800-1300.*

Itaipú and around

① T061-599 8040, www.itaipu.gov.py, daily 0800-1800. Bus tours of the external facilities daily, free, with film show (several languages). Take passport. Buses going to Hernandarias will drop you at the Centro de Recepción de Visitas.

The Itaipú project, a huge hydroelectric scheme covering an area of 1350 sq km and still subject to controversy among environmental groups, is close to Ciudad del Este (peaceful protests continue on an almost daily basis in Ciudad del Este as well as near the plant itself). It is currently the world's largest generator of renewable clean energy and well worth a visit. Tours of the plant offer panoramic views of the power plant featuring dam and spillway, run for 90 minutes and start hourly between 0800-1600, US$10. There is an interesting biological sanctuary, **Bella Vista**, that has successfully re-settled flora and fauna dislodged during the construction of the dam and offers 2½-hour guided tours Wednesday-Monday 0830, 1000, 1430, 1530, US$8.25. There is a light show every Friday and Saturday, 1830-2100, book in advance (phone as above, or call Brazilian side, +55-45-3520 6676, www.turismoitaipu.com.br).

On the way to Itaipú is **Zoológico Regional y Vivero Forestal** *① on the Supercarretera Itaipú, 11.5 km from Ciudad del Este, www.itaipu.gov.py/en/tourism/local-zoo, Tue-Sat 0800-1130, 1430-1700, Sun 0800-1130, free*, a zoo and nursery containing native animals and plants. The nursery has more than 500 species and annually plants some 200,000 ornamental, forest and fruit trees. Nearby is the **Museo de la Tierra Guaraní** *① T061-599 8632, www itaipu.gov.py/en/tourism/museum-guarani-land*, which offers a view of the science and culture of the Guaraníes via natural history displays and interactive screens.

Hernandarias (*population 86,213*), just north of Ciudad del Este grew rapidly with the building of Itaipú. The Supercarretera Itaipu runs north to Cruce Carolina Andrea, where it meets Ruta 10 for Saltos de Guaíra (see above, page 1162). This road gives access to two biological reserves on the Itaipú lake, **Itabó** (80 km) and, a further 80 km north, **Limoy**. For information on both, see www.itaipu.gov.br/en/the-environment/reserves-and-sanctuaries.

⊚ East of Asunción listings

For hotel and restaurant price codes, and other relevant information, see Essentials.

⚫ Where to stay

San Bernardino *p1160*
Other than those listed, there are plenty of hotels, many with good restaurants, from the super luxury Sol de San Ber down. Book hotels in advance during fiestas.
$$$ Del Lago, Tte Weiler 401 y Mcal López, near lake in town, T232201, www.hoteldellago.org. With breakfast, attractive 1888 building renovated as a museum, upgraded, safe, regional decor, restaurant, bar and grill, pool, lovely gardens.
$$$ Pueblo Hotel San Bernardino, C 8 entre C 5 y Mbocayá, T232195, pueblohotel@ gmail.com. Swimming pool, a/c, by the lake. Weekend packages also available.
$$ Los Alpes, Ruta General Morínigo Km 46.5, 3 km from town, T232083, www.hotellosalpes.com.py. Lovely gardens, 2 swimming pools, excellent self-service restaurant, children's playground, beach 1 km away, frequent buses to centre.
Camping Brisas del Mediterráneo, Ruta Kennedy a 2000 m from Copaco, T232459, www.paraguay-hostel.com. With campsite (US$9, Oct-Apr), rooms (**$$-$**), meals, beach and games.

Caacupé *p1161*
Cheaper than Lago Ypacaraí. Prices increase during the Fiesta de la Inmaculada Concepción.

\$ El Mirador, T242652, on plaza. With bath.
\$ Katy María, Eligio Ayala y Dr Pino, T242860, beside Basílica, www.katymaria.com. Well-kept, welcoming, Wi-Fi.
\$ Virgen Serrana, plaza, T242366. A/c, cheaper with fan.

Tourism farm
\$\$\$\$ Estancia Aventura, Km 61.5, Ruta 2, T981-441804, www.estancia-aventura.com. 91 ha of countryside, 7-day packages. Owner speaks German, English, Spanish. Good, horse riding, tennis, swimming, tours, can arrange airport pick-up from Asunción. Expensive but worth it.

Piribebuy *p1161*
\$\$\$ La Quinta, 10 km from Piribebuy, 19 km from Paraguarí, 82.5 km from Asunción along Ruta 1 and then branch road from Piribebuy (take bus to Piribebuy then bus to Chololó, bus passes in front of hotel), T971-11 7444, www.laquinta.com.py. Price based on 4 sharing in cabins, also suites, also open for day visits, own stream and is close to falls at Piraretá and Chololó.
\$ Viejo Rincón, Maestro Fermín López y Tte Horacio Gini, T0515-212251. Reasonable.

Coronel Oviedo and around *p1162*
\$\$-\$ Quincho Porá, Aquidaban 235, Coronel Oviedo, T521-202963/9-7286 4236, www.2cv-tours.de/hostel.htm. Owned by Walter Schäffer who runs Citröen 2CV and Land Rover tours in Paraguay and South America. Good hostel, German/Paraguayan, lots of information, hammock space, bar.

Villarrica *p1162*
There are more hotels than can be listed here. Book rooms in advance during fiestas.
\$\$\$ Villarrica Palace Hotel, Ruta 8 Blas Garay, turn right on road entering Villarrica, T42832, www.sosahoteles.com/villaricapalace. Large modern hotel, restaurant, parking, pool, sauna.
\$\$ Ybytyruzú, C A López y Dr Bottrell, T42390, www.hotelybytyruzu.com. Best in town, breakfast, more with a/c, restaurant.

\$ Guairá, Mcal López y Talavera, T42369. With bath and a/c, cheaper with fan, welcoming.

Colonia Independencia
\$\$ Hotel Tilinski, out of town, T0548-265240. Peaceful, German spoken, swimming pool (filled with river water), meals for residents.

Ciudad del Este *p1163, map p1163*
\$\$\$ California, C A López 180, T501838, www.hotelcalifornia.com.py. Several blocks from commercial area, large, modern with swimming pool, lit clay tennis court, attractive gardens, good restaurant.
\$\$ Austria, E R Fernández 165, T504213, www.hotelaustriarestaurante.com. Above good restaurant, good breakfast, Austrian family, good views from upper floors, popular with shopping trips and groups. Warmly recommended.
\$\$ Convair, Adrián Jara y Pioneros del Este, T508555, www.hotelconvair.com. In shopping district, comfortable, restaurant good, pasta festival on Thu, pool.
\$\$ El Caribeño, Fernández 136, T512460, http://hotelcaribeno.com.py. On 3 floors around central car parking area, plain rooms but spotless, helpful. Recommended.
\$\$ Mi Abuela, Adrián Jara y Pioneros del Este, T500333, www.miabuelahotel.com. Small, off a central patio, restaurant, opposite Convair.
\$\$ Munich, Fernández 71 y Miranda, T500347. A/c, frigobar, parking. Recommended.

❼ Restaurants

Villarrica *p1162*
Many eating places on CA López and General Díaz. At night on the plaza with the Munici-palidad stands sell tasty, cheap steaks.

Ciudad del Este *p1163, map p1163*
\$\$ Patussi Grill, Monseñor Francisco Cedzchiz casi Av Alejo García, T502293, www.patussigrill.com. Tue-Sat 1100-1500, 1800-2300, Sun 1100-1600. Good churrasquería, Wi-Fi. At the same junction, T513204, is **\$\$ Cantina Napoli**, pizzas and

pastas. Also **Pizza Hut, Relax Heladería y Café**, T501671, Mon-Fri 1600-2400, Sat 1630-0100 (closed Sun) and **Librería El Foro**.
$ Gouranga, Pampliega y Eusebio Ayala, T510362. Vegetarian restaurant with a menu that changes daily, also juices, desserts, sandwiches, burgers, etc.
$ Yrupé, Curupayty y A Jara (part of **Executive Hotel**, T512215, www.executivehotel.com.py/restaurant.html), T509946. Good buffet lunch for US$5.50 including ice cream. Also desserts, coffee and Wi-Fi.
Supermarkets Area Iris, A Jara y Av Pioneros del Este. Open 0700-1930, Sun 0800-1300. Serves good value meals. **Shopping del Este**, by Puente de Amistad, has good restaurants. Another good collection of restaurants is at **Centro Gastronómico Epoca**, on Rogelio Benítez, some distance southeast of centre, near Lago de la República. Other shopping centres, eg **Corazón**, have a Patio de Comidas.

⏻ What to do

San Bernardino *p1160*
Aventura Xtrema, NS de la Asunción y Hassler, T981-682243, San Bernardino, www.aventuraxtrema.com.py. Offers backpacker tours and a variety of adventure tours: horse riding, caving, canoes, hiking, cycling and more.

⊖ Transport

Itauguá *p1159*
Bus Frequent from **Asunción**, 1 hr, US$0.75.

Areguá *p1160*
Bus From **Asunción**, bus from Shopping del Sol, Nos 11 or 111, may take scenic route through villages, 45-60 mins; alternatively take local bus to Capiatá and change.

San Bernardino *p1160*
Bus From **Asunción**, 3 companies: Altos, Loma Grande and Ciudad de San Bernadino, every 10 mins, 45 km, 1-2 hrs, US$1.25.

Caacupé *p1161*
Bus From **Asunción**, US$1.25, get off at Basilica (closer to centre) rather than Caacupé station.

Coronel Oviedo and around:
Salto del Guaíra *p1162*
Bus **Asunción** to **Coronel Oviedo**, US$4.50. From Asunción to **Saltos del Guaíra**, US$13.50-15, 4 companies, several daily; to **Ciudad del Este**, US$12. **To Brazil** Regular launches cross the lake to Guaíra, 20 mins. Also hourly bus service, 30 mins, US$1.75. Buses run north of the lake to Mondo Novo, where they connect with Brazilian services. Brazilian consulate is at Canindeyú 980, casi Pasajae Morán, T24-2305.

Villarrica *p1162*
Bus To **Coronel Oviedo**, US$2.50. To **Asunción**, frequent, US$5-6.50, 3½ hrs (La Guaireña). Also direct service to **Ciudad del Este**, see below.

Colonia Independencia
Bus Direct to **Asunción**, 3 daily (US$5, 4 hrs), as well as to **Villarrica**.

Ciudad del Este *p1163, map p1163*
Air International airport, Aeropuerto Guaraní; departure tax US$16. To **Asunción**, TAM daily en route from **São Paulo**. TAM, Av San Blas con Patricio Colman, Km 2, Shopping Zuni, T506030-35.

Bus Terminal is south of the centre, T510421 (No 4 bus from centre, US$0.70, taxi US$5, recommended). Many buses to and from **Asunción**, US$16.50-20 rápido, 4½ hrs, at night only; US$11 *común*, 5 hrs minimum. **Nuestra Señora** recommended (they also have an office in Shopping Mirage, Pampliega y Adrián Jara), Rysa (T510396) and others. To **Villarrica**, many daily with La Guaireña and La Carapagueña, US$8, 4 hrs. To **Pedro Juan Caballero**, 7 hrs, overnight US$18, García and others. To **Concepción**, García, 11 hrs, 2 per day. To **Encarnación** (for Posadas and Argentina), paved road, frequent, 4-5 hrs, US$12 (this is cheaper than via Foz do Iguaçu). There are international services to Argentina and Brazil.

Border with Brazil *p1164*
Bus Two bus companies cross the international bridge between Ciudad del Este and Foz's bus terminals: **Pluma**, T061-510434, www.pluma. com.br, daily 0700-1830 each way every 10 mins, 30-40 mins, US$2, and **Rafagnin**, T +55-45-3523 1986 (Brazil; no office in Paraguay) 0800-1900, US$3; speak to the driver about waiting at the immigration posts at either end of the bridge. Most buses will not wait at immigration, so disembark to get your exit stamp, walk across the bridge (10 mins) and obtain your entry stamp; keep your ticket and continue to Foz on the next bus free. Paraguayan taxis cross freely to Brazil (US$30), but it is cheaper and easier to walk across the bridge and then take a taxi, bargain hard. You can pay in either currency (and often in Argentine pesos). Obtain all necessary exit and entry stamps.
To Argentina Direct buses to **Puerto Iguazú**, leave frequently from outside

the terminal, US$2.50. If continuing into Argentina, you need to get Argentine and Paraguayan stamps (not Brazilian), but bus usually does not stop, so ask driver if he will. Also check what stamps you need, if any, if making a day visit to Puerto Iguazú.

Itaipu and around: Hernandarias *p1165*
Bus Frequent from **Ciudad del Este**, US$1.

❶ Directory

Villarrica *p1162*
Bus ATM at gas station at northern end of town.

Ciudad del Este *p1163, map p1163*
Banks Local banks (open Mon-Fri 0730-1100). Many *casas de cambio* on Adrián Jara y Curupayty. There is a *casa de cambio* 20m beyond the entry post; rates are no different from in town and much safer than using the street changers, of which there are plenty. Money changers (not recommended) operate at the bus terminal but not at the Brazilian end of the Friendship Bridge.

Región Oriental: South of Asunción

Ruta 1 runs south from Asunción to Encarnación and the Argentine border. This is an attractive area of fertile landscapes, sleepy towns and the historically important Jesuits settlements, the ruins of some of which have been restored and now have interpretive and even multimedia exhibits.

Itá → *Phone code 024. Population 17,469.*
Itá (Km 37 on Ruta 1) Paraguay's second-oldest town, settled as a Franciscan mission in 1539, is famous for rustic pottery, but also sells wood, leather and textile items including hammocks and exquisite cloth dolls. There is a **Centro de Artesanía** in the centre. At the town's entrance you can visit the workshop of **Rosa Brítez**, a local ceramics artist and Paraguay's most famous artisan, recognized by UNESCO. Its Franciscan church, San Blas, also in the centre, was built in 1698 and has an interesting museum (free) featuring traditional crafts. The town has a lagoon which is reputed never to dry up. For information on the maestra Rosa Britez's taller, see www.portalguarani.com/724_rosa_britez.html.

Yaguarón → *Phone code 0533. Population, 8926.*

Also founded in 1539, Yaguarón (Km 48), was a key centre of the Franciscan missions in colonial times. At the centre of the town, marooned on an island of green, mown grass, stands the church of **San Buenaventura** ⓘ *daily 0700-1100, 1330-1630, on Sun morning only,* with its external bell-tower. The simplicity and symmetry of the exterior is matched by the ornate carvings and paintings of the interior. The tints, made by the *indígenas* from local plants, are still bright on the woodcarvings and the angels have Guaraní faces. Built in Hispano-Guaraní baroque style by the Franciscans between 1640 and 1775, it was reconstructed in 1885 and renovated in the late 20th century. Stations of the Cross behind the village lead to a good view of the surroundings.

Museo Dr José Gaspar Rodríguez de Francia ⓘ *leaving the church, 500 m down the road to your left at Pirayú 325, T177797 Tue-Sun 0930-1430, free guided tour in Spanish,* has artefacts from the life of Paraguay's first dictator, 'El Supremo', plus paintings and artefacts from the 18th century. The 18th-century single-storey adobe building with bamboo ceilings and tiled roof belonged to Francia's father. The fiesta patronal, **San Buenaventura**, is in mid-July. At the festivals for **San Roque** (16 August, first Sunday in September) music is provided by the Banda Peteke Peteke, a unique group that plays the mimby flute and two small drums. There are a few basic hotels (**$**).

Paraguarí and around → *Colour map 6, C6. Phone code: 531. Population: 12,661.*

Founded 1775 and located at Km 63 along Ruta 1, this is the north entrance to the mission area, at the foot of a range of hills. Its restored church has two bell towers, separate from the main structure. Buses between Asunción and Encarnación stop here. One km from the centre is an interesting military museum, the **Museo Histórico de la Artillería** ⓘ www.portalguarani. com/detalles_museos_exposiciones.php?id=4&id_exposicion=59, *inside the nearby military base with cannons and artefacts from the Chaco War. Free, but prior permission to visit is required as it is still military property.* Its chapel holds a remarkable statue of Santa Bárbara, which is brought out on her feast day (4 December). You can stroll to the top of Cerro Perö for views from the cross on top. More challenging is a one-hour climb through dense forest to the summit of Cerro Jhu, ask for directions in Barrio San Miguel behind the abandoned train station. Paraguarí retains many customs from its Spanish founders and is seen as Paraguay's capital of bullfighting.

Sapucai (*phone code 0539; population 2354*), 25 km east of Paraguarí, recently the terminus of the tourist train from Asunción, is the location of the **workshops** ⓘ *Mon-Fri, take a bus from Asunción at 0700, 1200, 88 km, 3 hrs, being restored,* where you can see old and abandoned wood-burning steam locomotives. There is also a small museum attached, T263218. Tour operators like to point out that as such, it is the world's last steam locomotive repair shop (although travellers not fascinated by steam locomotives may want to give it a miss). Close by is Paraguay's first viaduct, constructed by English engineers in 1897. The neighbourhood in which they lived is still known as Villa Inglesa and has several original houses constructed in late Victorian style. There are also some *hospedajes* (**$**). For information on Sapucai, see www.sapucai.net.

Northeast from Paraguarí 15 km is **Chololó** ⓘ *bus US$1,* with a small but attractive series of waterfalls and rapids with bathing facilities and walkways, mainly visited in the summer

que Nacional Ybycuí

0800-1700, www.salvemoslos.com.py/pny.htm. For camping get a permit from the Secretaría el Ambiente, Madame Lynch 3500, in Asunción (see National parks, page 1140).

At **Carapeguá** (phone code 0532; population 6825), Km 84 on Ruta 1 (hospedaje on main street, basic, friendly; blankets and hammocks to rent along the main road, or buy your own, made locally and cheaper than elsewhere), a road turns off to Acahay, Ybycuí and the Parque Nacional Ybycuí, 67 km southeast. This is one of the most accessible national parks, if you have a car, and is one of the few remaining stands of Atlantic forest in eastern Paraguay. It contains 5000 ha of virgin forest and was founded in 1973. Good walks, a beautiful campsite and lots of waterfalls. At the entrance is a well set out park and museum, plus the reconstructed remains of the country's first iron foundry (La Rosada). Crowded on Sunday but deserted the rest of the week; guides available. The only shops (apart from a small one at the entrance selling drinks, eggs, etc, and a good T-shirt stall which helps support the park) are at **Ybycuí**, 30 km northwest.

Ruta 1 continues through **Villa Florida**, 162 km from Asunción, on the banks of the Río Tebicuary. It's a popular spot in January-February for its sandy beaches and the fishing is first-rate. The **Hotel Nacional de Villa Florida** ($$, T083-240207) and the Touring y Automóvil Club's **Hotel-Parador Villa Florida** (Km 156, T083-240205, www.tacpy.com.py) would make a convenient places to stop when travelling on this route.

The Jesuit missions

In 1578 Jesuit missionaries came to what is now the border region of Brazil, Argentina and Paraguay to convert the Guaraníes to Christianity. The first mission in Paraguay was established in 1610 at San Ignacio Guazú. Together these two groups developed a pioneering economic and social system that emphasized collaboration and; to some extent, integration between the two societies. In 1767, by decree of Charles III of Spain, the Jesuits were expelled and local wealthy landowners took the Guaraníes as slave workers. More than thirty missions, or reducciones, were built. Eight of these remain in Paraguay in varying states of repair and three have been inscribed as UNESCO World Heritage Sites. Numerous Asunción-based tour operators offer tours of these missions. For local tours, **Emitur** ① T0782-20286, emitur. misiones@gmail.com, offers area tours and visits to local ranches. Also see **Cámara Paraguaya de Turismo de las Misiones Jesuíticas** ① Mcal Estigarribia 1031 y Curupayty, Encarnación T071-205021, rutajesuiticapy@hotmail.com, for information. For information on the UNESCO inscribed missions, see http://whc.unesco.org/en/list/648.

San Ignacio Guazú and around → Phone code 0782. Population, 17,422.

At Km 226 at the intersection of Rutas 1 and 4, this is a delightful town on the site of a former Jesuit reducción (guazú means big in Guaraní). Several typical Hispano-Guaraní buildings survive. Each Sunday night at 2000 a folklore festival is held in the central plaza, free, very local, "fabulous". The **Museo Jesuítico** ① T0782-232223, www.portalguarani.com/museos.php? pormustytr=MzU=, daily 0800-1130, 1400-1730, US$1, housed in the former Jesuit art workshop, reputedly the oldest surviving civil building in Paraguay, contains a major collection of Guaraní art and sculpture from the missionary period. The attendant is very knowledgeable, but photos are not allowed. Nearby is the **Museo Histórico Sembranza de Héroes** ① T975-631352, www.portalguarani.com/1565javier_yubi/20665_museo_historico_semblanza_de_ ...es 76__por_javier_yubi.html, Mon-Fri 0700-1200, 1300-1700, free, with displays on the

Santa María de Fé is 12 km northeast along a cobbled road. The **Museo Jesuítico** ① T0781-283332, www.portalguarani.com/detalles_museos_exposiciones.php?id=4&id_exposicion=11 Tue-Sun 0830-1130, 1300-1700, US$1 (photos allowed), in restored mission buildings contains 60 Guaraní sculptures among the exhibits. It is considered one of the country's finest museums for mission art. The modern church has a lovely altarpiece of the Virgin and Child (the key is kept at a house on the opposite side of the plaza). There is also the **Santa María Cooperative and Educational Fund**, begun by English journalist Margaret Hebblethwaite, which sponsors education and craftwork (notably appliqué) and organizes local activities for visitors. Santa María de Fé was between 1960-76 the home of the radically utopian **Ligas Agrarias Cristianas** (Christian Agrarian League) until forcibly suppressed by Stroessner. There is a hotel on the plaza, see www.santamaria hotel.org (see below) and www.santamariadefe.org.

At **Santa Rosa** (Km 248; phone code 0858; population 8902), founded 1698, only the Nuestra Señora de Loreto chapel of the original Jesuit church survived a fire. The current building dates from 1884. The chapel houses the **Museo Jesuítico de Santa Rosa** ① by appointment only, 0730-1130, 1430-1600 (ask at parroquia), T858-285221, www.portalguarani.com/detalles_museos_exposiciones.php?id=4&id_exposicion=18, free, on the walls are frescoes in poor condition; exhibits include a sculpture of the Annunciation considered to be one of the great works of the Hispanic American Baroque. Daily buses from San Ignacio Guazú.

Southwest to Pilar Ruta 4 (paved) from San Ignacio (see above) goes southwest to **Pilar** (phone code: 086; population 31,612), on the banks of the Río Paraguay. Capital of Ñeembucú district, the town is known for its fishing (one of the largest fishing festivals in South America is held here during Holy Week), manufacturing and historical Cabildo (now a museum). This area saw many bloody battles during the War of the Triple Alliance and you can visit **Humaitá**, with the Basílica de Nuestra Señora de Pilar, the old church of San Carlos, **Paso de Patria**, **Curupayty** and other historic battle sites. In early January the town's **Fiesta Hawaiana** attracts tens of thousands of visitors. Pilar is unique in the country for having a successful youth tourism initiative. There are hotels in the **$$-$** range.

Ayolas, Santiago and San Cosme

At Km 262 on Ruta 1 a road leads to the former reducción at Santiago and the town of **Ayolas** (phone code 072; population 15,386) founded 1840, although not by Jesuits, standing on the banks of the Aña Cuá river. **Santiago** is an important former Jesuit centre (founded 1651) with a modern church containing a fine wooden carving of Santiago slaying the Saracens. More wooden statuary in the **Museo Tesoros Jesuíticos** ① T0975-762008, Mon-Sat 0800-1100, 1400-1700, Sun 0900-1100, free (guided tour US$2.15), next door (ask around the village for the key-holder). There is an annual **Fiesta de la Tradición Misionera**, in January or February, with music, dance, horsemanship and other events. Beyond is Ayolas, the area has been influenced by the construction of the Yacyretá dam and is good for fishing. There is the Museo Regional Yacyretá and, 12 km from Ayolas, the **Refugio Faunístico de Atinguy** ① Mon-Sat 0830-1130, 1330-1630, Sun and holidays 0830-1130, www.portalguarani.com/detalles_museos_otras_detalles.php?id=99&id_otras=367, free, run as a research and educational facility by the **Entidad Binacional Yacyretá (EBY)** to study the fauna affected by the dam. EBY also has a reserve on the **island of Yacyretá** ① for visits to the project, T072-222141, or T021-445055, www.eby.gov.py. Cross the river to Ituzaingó, Argentina (linked via road to Corrientes and Posadas). Follow the new paved road from Ayolas to the **San Cosme y Damián** former reducción or leave Ruta 1 at Km 333. This is the only ex-Jesuit mission in the country still used for religious services. When the Jesuits were expelled from Spanish colonies in 1767, the **church and ancillary buildings** ① 0700-1130, 1300-1700 US$5.50 (T0985-732956 for tickets), also valid for Trinidad and Jesús, see below, were unfinished.

A huge project has followed the original plans. Some of the *casas de indios* are in private use for other purposes, such as the cultural centre and parts of the **Centro de Interpretación Astronómica Buenaventura Suárez** ① *daily 0700-2000, www.astropar.org/html/sancosmey damian.html.* For the tourist committee T0985-110047; guide Rolando Barboza T0985-732956.

Encarnación → *Phone code: 071. Colour map 6, C6. Population: 94,572.*

A bridge connects this busy port, the largest town in the region (founded 1614, known as La Perla del Sur), with the Argentine town of Posadas across the Alto Paraná. The old town was badly neglected at one time as it was due to be flooded when the Yacyretá-Apipé dam was completed. Since the flooding, however, what is not under water has been restored and a modern town has been built higher up with a pronounced emphasis on catering to tourism. The town exports the products of a rich area: timber, soya, mate, tobacco, cotton, and hides. It is fast losing its traditional, rural appearance, but its pre-Lenten Carnival is the best known in the country. The town is a good base for visiting nearby Jesuit mission sites, the inland playa San José and the newly constructed malecón along the Río Paraná. Bizarrely, Encarnación, in the extreme south, holds the distinction of being the only place in Paraguay outside of the Chaco ever to receive snowfall. A tourist office was due to open in 2014. Till then the **Gobernación** ① *Av Irrazábal y Pedro Juan Caballero, T204568, www.itapua.gov.py*, and the **Municipalidad** ① *Kreuser y Estigarribia, www.encarnacion. gov.py*, have some information. Otherwise contact the numbers given for the individual Jesuit *reducciones*.

Encarnación

To Ruta 6 to Ciudad del Este & Jesuit Missions
To Ruta 1 to Asunción
Avda Gral B Caballero
Constitución
25 de Mayo
Villarrica
Arq TR Pereira
Plaza Central
14 de Mayo
Cerro Corá
Wiessen
Curupayty
Kreuser
Cabañas
Municipalidad
Memmel
To Gobernación & Bridge to Argentina
Sgto Reverhon
Bruguez
PJ Caballero
Gral Escobar
Pre Gonzalez
P. Winquel
Carlos Antonio López
Lomas Valentinas
Independencia
Tte González
Av Irrazábal
Dr JL Mallorquín
Mcal LR Estigarribia
To Ferry to Posadas (2 Blocks)
To 3 (3 blocks)
N
200 metres
200 yards

Where to stay
1 Casa de la Y
2 Central
3 Cristal
4 De La Costa
5 De La Trinidad
6 Germano
7 Paraná
8 Viena

Restaurants
1 American Grill
2 Hiroshima

Border with Argentina
The San Roque road bridge connects Encarnación with **Posadas**. Formalities are conducted at respective ends of the bridge. Argentine side has different offices for locals and foreigners; Paraguay has one for both. **Note** Paraguay is one hour behind Argentina, except during Paraguayan summer time (October-April).

Santísima Trinidad del Paraná and Jesús de Tavarangüé

Northeast from Encarnación along Ruta 6 towards Ciudad del Este are the two best-preserved Jesuit former *reducciones*. These are both recognized as UNESCO World Cultural Heritage Sites. The hilltop site of **Trinidad** ① *US$5.50, joint ticket with Jesús and San Cosme y Damián, T0985-810053 (parroquia), Oct-May 0700-1900, Apr-Sep 0700-1730, light and sound show Thu-Sun 2000, summer, 1900, winter,* built 1706-1760, has undergone significant restoration. Note the partially restored church, the carved stone pulpit, the font and other masonry and relief sculpture. Also partially rebuilt is the bell-tower near the original church (great views from the top). You can also see another church, a college, workshops and indigenous living quarters. It was founded in 1706 by Padre Juan de Anaya; the architect was Juan Bautista Prímoli. For information or tours (in Spanish and German), ask at the visitor centre; guide T0985-772803 or T0985-753997, www.turismojesusytrinidad.com.py. There are three *artesanías* nearby and craft demonstrations in the afternoon. The **Jesuito Snack Bar** at the turnoff from the main road has decent food. One kilometre from Trinidad is Parque Ecológico **Ita Cajón** ① *T0985-726971, US$4.35,* an enormous clearing where the stone was quarried for the former *reducción*. Frequent folklore events are held here. The municipal office of Trinidad (T071-270165, Mon-Fri 0700-1300) in the centre of town also has information and a brochure.

About 12 km northwest of Trinidad, along a rough road (which turns off 300 m north from Trinidad entrance) is **Jesús de Tavarangüé**, now a small town where another group of Jesuits settled in 1763. In the less than four years before they were expelled they embarked on a huge construction programme that included the church, sacristy, residencia and baptistry, on one side of which is a **square tower** ① *T09-8573 4340, www.turismojesusytrinidad.com.py, Oct-May 0700-1900, Apr-Sep 0700-1730, US$5.50 as above, guide.* There is a fine front façade with three great arched portals in a Moorish style. The ruins have been restored. There are beautiful views from the main tower. The municipal office of Jesús (T071-270150, Mon-Fri 0700-1300) in the centre of town also has information and a brochure.

German colonies on the road to Ciudad del Este

From Trinidad the road goes through or near a number of German colonies including **Hohenau** (Km 36) and **Parque Manantial** ① *Km 35, 500 m from main road, T0775-232250, manantial@tigo.com.py, open 0830-2200.* The park is in a beautiful location and has three pools, a good restaurant, bar, lovely camping ground and complete facilities, horse riding, tour of the countryside by jeep and cross country tours to the nearby Jesuit ruins. It's a good place to stop off on the way to Ciudad del Este. Major credit cards accepted and national phone calls can be made at no extra charge.

The next colony is **Obligado**, 35 km from Encarnación; it has an ATM in the centre of town. About 5 km further north is **Bella Vista** (Km 42, also has ATM), the yerba mate capital of Paraguay. The plantations, **Pajarito** ① *T0767-240240, www.pajarito.com.py,* and **Selecta** ① *T0767-240247, www.selecta.com.py, accept visitors.* From the port you can cross the Río Paraná to Corpus in Argentina by ferry (for cars weekdays only; foot passengers US$2.50), making a good circuit between the Paraguayan and Argentine Jesuit missions. There are immigration and customs facilities.

ⓘ South of Asunción listings

For hotel and restaurant price codes, and other relevant information, see Essentials.

ⓘ Where to stay

Parque Nacional Ybycuí *p1170*
$$$ Estancia Santa Clara, Km 141, Ruta 1, Caapucú, T021-605729, www.estancia santaclara.com.py. Tourism farm offering rural activites in a beautiful setting between Paraguarí and San Ignacio Guazú, full board or visit for the day (mini-zoo). Reserve in advance.
$$ Hotel Pytu'u Renda, Av General Caballero 509 y Quyquyho, Ybycuí, T0534-226364. Good food, cooking facilities.

San Ignacio Guazú and around *p1170*
$$ Hotel Rural San Ignacio Country Club, Ruta 1, Km 230, T0782-232895, gusjhave@ hotmail.com. With full board and Wi-Fi in cabins. Also has shaded camping, US$6 pp, without tent or meals, but other services included, hot water, electricity, tennis, swimming pool, ping pong table, pool, impressive place and very helpful owner, Gustavo Jhave.
$$ Parador Altamirano, Ruta 1, Km 224, T0782-232334. Modern, on outskirts, with a/c ($ pp without), recommended, 24-hr restaurant.
$$ Santa María Hotel, Santa María de Fé, T0781-283311/0981-861553, www. santamariahotel.org. With breakfast, other meals extra. Activities offered include day tours of Santa María and 2-week tours to other Jesuit towns and the region.
$$-$ La Casa de Loly, Mcal López 1595, San Ignacio, T0782-232362, http://lacasadeloli. com.py, on outskirts. Nice atmosphere, cabañas and rooms, pool, a/c, with breakfast, other meals on request.

Ayolas, Santiago and San Cosme *p1171*
$$ Hotel Nacional de Turismo Ayolas, Av Costanera, Villa Permanente, T072-222273, infohotelturismoayolaspy@gmail.com. Over-looking the river, popular with fishing groups.

Encarnación *p1172, map p1172*
$$$-$$ De La Costa, Av Rodríguez de Francia 1240 con Cerro Corá, T205694, www.delacostahotel.com.py. Smart hotel on the new Costanera, with pool, garden, parking and restaurant.
$$$-$$ De La Trinidad, Mcal Estigarribia y Memmel, T208099, www.hoteldelatrinidad. com.py. New tower-block hotel of a good standard, close to bus station, 6 categories of room with all modern facilities, with spa, restaurant, pool, parking.
$$ Cristal, Mcal Estigarribia 1157 y Cerro Corá, T202371, www.hotelcristal.com.py. With pool and restaurant, helpful staff.
$ pp Casa de la Y, Carmen de Lara Castro 422, entre Yegros y Molas, Barrio San Roque, T985-77 8198, casadelay@gmail.com (Casa Delay on Facebook). Quiet location a short distance from most attractions and facilities (bus terminal transfer US$5), shared rooms with bath, garden, breakfast included, other meals available, Wi-Fi, welcoming and attractive.
$ Central, Mcal López 542 y C A López, Zona Baja, T203454, soyparte@encarnacion.com.py. With breakfast, nice patio, German spoken.
$ Germano, General Cabañas y C A López, opposite bus terminal, T203346. Cheaper without bath or a/c, German and Japanese spoken, small, very accommodating. Highly recommended.
$ Paraná, Estigarribia 1414 y Tomas R Pereira y Villarrica, T204440. Good breakfast, helpful. Recommended.
$ Viena, PJ Caballero 568, T205981. With breakfast, German-run, good food, garage.

German colonies on the road to Ciudad del Este *p1173*
$$$-$$ Papillón, Ruta 6, Km 45, Bella Vista, T0767-240235, www.papillon.com.py. A/c, pool, gardens, very pleasant, German, French, English, Flemish spoken, excellent and popular restaurant, full and half-board available. Highly recommended. Organizes excursions in the area.

Restaurants

Paraguarí and around p1169
La Frutería, Ruta 1, Km 61, T531-432406, about 2.5 km before the town. Wide selection of fruit, outdoor seating and a restaurant serving *empanadas*, hamburgers, beer, fruit salad. Highly recommended.

Encarnación p1172, map p1172
$$ American Grill, Ruta Internacional y Av San Blas, T71-204829. Good *churrasquería*.
$$ Hiroshima, 25 de Mayo y L Valentinas (no sign), T206288. Tue-Sun 1130-1400, 1900-2330. Excellent Japanese, wide variety, fresh sushi.

Transport

Yaguarón p1169
Bus Every 15 mins from **Asunción**, US$1.25.

Paraguarí and around p1169
Bus City buses leave from lower level of the Asunción terminal every 15 mins throughout the day, but much faster to take an Encarnación-bound bus from the upper level, same fare US$1.75.

Parque Nacional Ybycuí p1170
Bus There are 2 per day, 1000 and 1600 from **Ybycuí**, US$1.25, take bus going to the Mbocaya Pucú colony that stops in front of the park entrance. From Asunción take a bus to Acahay, **Transportes Emilio Cabrera**, 8 daily and change, or bus to Ybycuí, 0630, US$2.25.

San Ignacio Guazú p1170
Bus Regular services to/from **Asunción**, US$6.50 *común*, up to 4½ hrs; to **Encarnación**, frequent, US$8 *común*.

Santa María
Bus From **San Ignacio** from the Esso station, 6 a day from 0500, 45 mins.

San Cosme y Damián
Bus From **Encarnación**, La Cosmeña and Perla del Sur, US$4, 2½ hrs.

Encarnación p1172, map p1172
Bus The bus terminal is at Mcal Estigarribia y Memmel. Good cheap snacks. To/from **Asunción**, 8 companies including **La Encarnacena** (recommended, T203448, www.laencarnacena.com.py), **Rysa** (T203311), at least 4 a day each, 6 hrs, US$13-15.50. Stopping (*común*) buses are much slower (6-7 hrs). To **Ciudad del Este**, US$13, several daily, 4 hrs.

Border with Argentina p1172
Bus Take any 'Posadas/Argentina' bus from opposite bus terminal over the bridge, US$1.25, 30 mins. Keep all luggage with you and retain bus ticket; buses do not wait. After formalities (queues common), use ticket on next bus. **Cycles** are not allowed to use the bridge, but officials may give cyclists a lift. **Ferry** costs US$2. Immigration formalities must be undertaken at the main offices. **Taxi** costs US$12.50 (at least).

Santísima Trinidad del Paraná and Jesús de Tavarangüé p1173
Bus Many go from **Encarnación** to and through Trinidad, take any bus from the terminal marked Hohenau or Ciudad del Este, US$2.50 (beware overcharging). A **taxi** tour from Encarnación costs about US$40. Bus direct **Encarnación-Jesús** 0800; buses run **Jesús-Trinidad** every hr (30 mins, US$1), from where it is easy to get back to Encarnación, so do Jesús first. Last bus Jesús-Trinidad 1700; also collective taxis, return Trinidad-Jesús US$6. No buses on Sun. Enquire locally as taxis may overcharge.

Directory

Encarnación p1172, map p1172
Banks Banco Continental, Mcal Estigarribia 1418, Visa accepted. Banco Itapúa, 14 de Mayo (next to church). Sudameris Bank, Carlos Antonio López y 14 de Mayo. *Casas de cambio* for cash on Mcal Estagarribia. Moneychangers at the Paraguayan side of the bridge but best to change money in town.
Consulates Argentine Vice Consulate, Artigas 960, T201066, cenca@mrecic.gov.ar, Mon-Fri 0800-1300. Brazil Vice Consulate, Memmel 452, T203950, epgbrvc@itacom.com.py.

hero
Chac

North of Asunción

The winding Río Paraguay is 400 m wide and is still the main trade route for the products of northern Paraguay, in spite of a paved highway built to Concepción. With the start of the rainy season, most farms and rural communities lose their overland connection to the outside world. Boats carry cattle, hides, yerba mate, tobacco and timber.

Asunción to Concepción

Travelling north from Asunción by river (nowadays mostly done by aquidaban, a more upscale version of a cargo boat, usually with a few sleeping cabins), you first come across Puente Remanso in Mariano Roque Alonso, the bridge that marks the beginning of the Trans-Chaco Highway. Just further upstream is Villa Hayes, 31 km above Asunción, founded in 1786 but renamed in 1879 after the US president who arbitrated the territorial dispute with Argentina in Paraguay's favour. Further upstream at 198 km is Puerto Antequera and 100 km beyond that is Concepción. By road there are two alternative routes. One is via the Trans-Chaco Highway (Ruta 9) and Pozo Colorado (five to seven hours). The Pozo Colorado-Concepción road, 146 km, is completely paved and offers spectacular views of birdlife. The other route, also fully paved, is Ruta 3 to to Yby Yaú and then west along Ruta 5 (seven to nine hours).

At Santa Rosa del Aguaray, 108 km north of San Estanislao, there is petrol, *pensión* and restaurants. A paved road (Ruta 11) runs southwest for 27 km to **Nueva Germania** founded in 1866 by Bernhard Förster and Elisabeth Nietzsche (the philosopher's sister) to establish a pure Aryan colony (follow signs to **Hotel Germania**, $ with a/c, very clean). From Nueva Alemania, this road goes on to San Pedro del Ycuamandiyú (48 km), and Puerto Antequera on the Río Paraguay (another 14 km). East of Santa Rosa, 23 km, is $ Rancho Laguna Blanca ① *T021-424760 or T0981-558671, www.lagunablanca.com.py, day visits US$4.50, camping US$6.70, dormitory US$18 (US$21.65 for 2)*, a nature reserve, family farm and rural tourism centre offering lots of activities including riding, trekking, kayaking and birdwatching (one of the few in this area open year-round). A further 23 km north of Santa Rosa, a dirt road runs northeast through jungle for 105 km to the interesting town of **Capitán Badó**, which forms the frontier with Brazil. About 50 km north of the turn off to Capitán Badó is Yby Yaú, see page 1177. From Capitán Badó a road follows the frontier north to Pedro Juan Caballero (another 119 km).

Concepción → *Phone code: 0331. Colour map 6, B6. Population: 60,346.*

Concepción, 422 km north of Asunción Via Ruta 9 and 5 (or 439 via Ruta 3), stands on the east bank of the Río Paraguay. It is known as La Perla del Norte for its climate and setting. To appreciate the colonial aspect of the city, walk away from the main commercial streets. At Plaza La Libertad are the Catedral and Municipalidad. Sunsets from the port are beautiful. The town is the trade centre of the north, doing a considerable business with Brazil. The **Brazilian Vice Consulate** ① *Pdte Franco 972, T242655, Mon-Fri 0800-1400, brvcconcep@tigo.com.py*, issues visas, but go early to ensure same-day processing. The market, a good place to try local food, is east of the main street, Agustín Pinedo (which is a kind of open-air museum). From here Avenida Presidente Franco runs west to the port. Along Avenida Agustín Pineda is a large statue of María Auxiliadora with the Christ Child. There are stairs to balconies at the base of the monument which offer good views of the city. The **Museo Municipal Ex-Cuartal Militar** ① *Mcal López, in the Teatro Municipal building, diagonally opposite the Municipality, Mon-Sat 0700-1200, www. portalguarani.com/detalles_museos_exposiciones.php?id=4&id_exposicion=6, free*, contains a dusty collection of local items and faded photographs. You must ask for it to be opened and it's worth a look. The city historian, Sr Medina, offers good sightseeing tours; ask for him. Plaza Agustín Fernando de Pinedo has a permanent craft market. About 9 km south is a bridge across the Río Paraguay, which makes for an interesting walk across the shallows and islands to the west bank and the Chaco, about an hour return trip, taxi US$10. At weekends, the top of the bridge becomes a party venue for the city's youth. The island in the Río Paraguay facing Concepción is Isla Chaco'i, a planned free trade zone and tourism complex, but at present largely uninhabited, where you can stroll through the fields. Row boats take passengers to the island from the shore next to the port, US$0.50 per person. For more information visit the town's website, www.concepcion-py.com.

East of Concepción

There is a 215-km road (Ruta 5 – fully paved) from Concepción, eastwards to the Brazilian border. This road goes through Horqueta, Km 50, a cattle and lumber town of 12,948 people. Further on the road is very scenic. From **Yby Yaú** (junction with Ruta 8 south to Coronel Oviedo) the road continues to Pedro Juan Caballero.

Ten kilometres east of Yby Yaú Ruta 5 continues through the pleasant **Parque Nacional Cerro Corá** (12,038 ha, www.salvemoslos.com.py/pncc.htm), the site of Mariscal Francisco Solano López' death and the final defeat of Paraguay in the War of the Triple Alliance. To reach the park from the main entrance, however, take the left turn, a signed branch road, some 6 km out of Yby Yaú. Not far from the park's entrance is a monument to Solano López and other national heroes; the site is constantly guarded. It has hills and cliffs (some with pre-Columbian caves and petroglyphs), camping facilities, swimming and hiking trails. The rocky outcrops are spectacular and the warden is helpful and provides free guides. When you have walked up the road and seen the line of leaders' heads, turn right and go up the track passing a dirty-looking shack (straight on leads to a military base). The park's administration office (not a recommended entry point) is 5 km east of the main entrance at Km 180 back on Ruta 5.

Pedro Juan Caballero → *Phone code: 0336. Colour map 7, B1. Population: 81,650.*

This border town is separated from the Brazilian town of Ponta Porã by a road (Dr Francia on the Paraguayan side, on the Brazilian side either Rua Marechal Floreano or Avenida Internacional), which anyone can cross (see below for immigration formalities). Ponta Porã is the more modern and prosperous of the two towns; everything costs less on the Paraguayan side. **Shopping China** is a vast emporium on the eastern suburbs of town, reputed to have the best shopping in the Americas (has to be seen to be believed). **Maxi** is a large well-stocked supermarket with **Mr Grill** restaurant in the centre. You can pay in guaraníes, reais or US$, at good exchange rates. **Arte Paraguaya**, Mcal López y Alberdi, has a selection of crafts from all over the country. In recent years the town has attracted a prominent criminal element (based not so much on smuggling as drugs) and care should be taken at all times.

Border with Brazil

This is a more relaxed crossing than Ciudad del Este and generally much faster. For day crossings you do not need a stamp, but passports must be stamped if travelling beyond the border towns (ask if unsure whether your destination is considered beyond). If you fail to get a stamp when entering Paraguay, you will be fined US$45 when you try to leave. **Paraguayan immigration** ① *T0336-272195, Mon-Fri 0700-2100, Sat 0800-2100, Sun 1900-2100, take bus line 2 on the Paraguayan side, or any Brazilian city bus that goes to the Rodoviária, taxi US$7.50, is in the* customs building on the eastern outskirts of town near *Shopping China*. Then cross bridge and report to Brazilian federal police in Ponta Porã (closed Sat-Sun). The **Brazilian** vice consulate ⓘ *Mcal Estigarribia 250, T0336-273562, administracion.pjcaballero@itamaraty.gov.br, Mon-Fri 0800-1300*, issues visas, fees payable only in guaraníes, take passport and a photo, go early to get visa the same day. There is another crossing to Brazil at Bella Vista on the Río Apá, northwest of PJ Caballero; buses run from the Brazilian border town of Bela Vista to Jardim and on to Campo Grande. There is a Paraguayan immigration office at Bella Vista, but no Brazilian Policia Federal in Bela Vista. To cross here, get Paraguayan exit stamp then report to the local Brazilian police who may give a temporary stamp, but you must later go to the Policia Federal in either Ponta Porã or Corumbá. Do not fail to get the proper stamp later or you will be detained upon re-entering Paraguay.

North of Concepción

Aquidabán cargo boats (expensive) go north of Concepción to Vallemí, Fuerte Olimpo, **Bahía Negra**, and intermediate points along the upper Río Paraguay, through the Pantanal de Nebileque (see Transport, below). This is a route to Bolivia, but because of the time involved, it is important to get a pre-dated exit stamp in Concepción (address below) if you wish to leave Paraguay this way. Near Bahía Negra on the banks of the Río Negro is **Los Tres Gigantes biological station** ⓘ *contact Guyra Paraguay, T021-223567, www.guyra.org.py/areas-de-conservacion/pantanal-paraguayo, in advance for details*. It can only be reached by boat (ask for Don Aliche) and is a wonderful place to see Pantanal wildlife, including (with luck) jaguar and giant anteater. There is accommodation and full board can be arranged for roughly US$110.

ⓞ North of Asunción listings

For hotel and restaurant price codes, and other relevant information, see Essentials.

● Where to stay

Asunción to Concepción *p1176*
$$$ Estancia Jejui, set on the Río Jejui, 65 km north of Tacuara on Ruta 3, address in Asunción, Telmo Aquino 4068, T021-600227, http://jejui.coinco.com.py. All rooms with a/c, bathroom and hot water, full board, fishing, horse riding, tennis, boat rides extra.

Concepción *p1176*
$$$ Concepción Palace, Mcal López 399 y E A Garay, T241858, www.concepcionpalace. com.py. By far the nicest hotel in town. With all mod cons, pool, restaurant, Wi-Fi throughout, large rooms.
$$-$ Francés, Franco y C A López, T242383, www.hotelfrancesconcepcion.com. With a/c, cheaper with fan, breakfast, nice

grounds with pool (small charge for non-guests), restaurant, parking.
$$-$ pp Granja El Roble, in Dieciseis (16 km from Concepción on road to Belén), T09-8589 8446, www.paraguay.ch. Working farm and nature reserve with various sleeping options, full board with homegrown food, camping US$10, lots of activities including boat trips, tubing on Río Ypané, tours to the Chaco, aquarium, very good bird and wildlife-watching (special trips arranged, including for scientists), local information including on routes to Bolivia, internet, Wi-Fi. Excellent value, prices are not negotiable. Phone in advance to arrange transport if required.
$ Center, Presidente Franco e Yegros, T242360. More basic and cheaper than others, popular.
$ Concepción, Don Bosco y Cabral near market, T242506. With simple breakfast, a/c, cheaper with fan, family run, good value.
$ Victoria, Franco y PJ Caballero 693, T242256, hotelvictoria@hotmail.es. Pleasant rooms, a/c, fridge, cheaper with fan, restaurant, parking.

Pedro Juan Caballero *p1177*

$$$-$$ Eiruzú, Mcal López y Mcal Estigarribia, T272435, http://hoteleiruzu.blogspot.com. A/c, fridge and pool, starting to show its age but still good.

$$$-$$ Porã Palace, Alberdi 30 y Dr Francia, T273021, www.porapalacehotel.com. A/c, fridge, balcony, restaurant, pool, OK, rooms in upper floor have been refurbished and are nicer.

$ Victoria, Teniente Herrero y Alberdi, near bus staton, T272733. Electric shower and a/c, cheaper with fan, family run, simple. Cheapest decent lodgings in town. Cash only.

🍴 Restaurants

Concepción *p1176*

$ Hotel Francés, good value buffet lunch, à la carte in the evening.

$ Hotel Victoria, set lunches and à la carte, grill in *quincho* across the street.

$ Palo Santo, Franco y PJ Caballero, T241454. Good Brazilian food and value.

$ Ysapy, Yegros y Mcal Estigarribia at Plaza Pineda. Daily 1630-0200. Pizza and ice-cream, terrace or sidewalk seating, very popular.

⊖ Transport

Concepción *p1176*

Bus The terminal is on the outskirts, 8 blocks north along General Garay, but buses also stop in the centre, Av Pinedo, look for signs Parada Omnibus. A shuttle bus (Línea 1) runs between the terminal and the port. Taxi from terminal or port to centre, US$4.75; terminal to port US$6. To **Asunción**, many daily with Nasa-Golondrina (T242744, Asunción 940332), 3 with La Santaniana, plus other companies, US$13-16, 5½ hrs via Pozo Colorado, 9 hrs via Coronel Oviedo. To **Pedro Juan Caballero**, frequent service, several companies, US$12.50, 4-5 hrs. To **Horqueta**, 1 hr, US$2.50. To **Filadelfia**, Nasa-Golondrina direct at 0730 Mon, Sat, US$15, 5 hrs, otherwise change at Pozo Colorado. To **Ciudad del Este**, García direct at 1230 daily, US$25, 9 hrs, or change at Coronel Oviedo.

Boat To/from **Asunción**, the only boat taking passengers is the *Guaraní*, which has a 2-week sailing cycle on the Asunción-Fuerte Olimpo route and is very slow, but nice and welcomes tourists. To make arrangements for the boat, speak to the owner and captain, Julio Desvares, T982-873436, or Don Coelo, T972-678695. To **Bahía Negra** and intermediate points along the upper Río Paraguay, the **Aquidabán** sails Tue 1100, arriving Bahía Negra on Fri morning and returns the same day to Concepción, arriving on Sun, US$21.70 to Bahía Negra, US$39 for a berth (book by the Fri of the week before, at least). Meals are sold on board (US$2.20), but take food and water. Tickets sold in office just outside the port, T242435, Mon-Sat 0700-1200. From Bahía Negra to **Puerto Suárez** (Bolivia) you must hire a boat to Puerto Busch, about US$85-95, then catch a bus. There are sporadic ferries from Concepción to Isla Margarita, across from Porto Murtinho, Brazil. Ask for prices and times at dock and note that service does not include anything other than standing room. A regular ferry, for 1 vehicle and a few passengers, US$44 per vehicle, goes between Capitán Carmelo Peralta (customs and immigration service at west end of town) and Porto Murtinho (no immigration, head for Ponta Porã, Corumbá or Campo Grande; obtain visa in advance). **Note** If planning to go to Bolivia or Brazil by this route, you must enquire before arriving at the border, even in Asunción, about exit and entry formalities. Visas for either country must be obtained in advance. There is an immigration office in Concepción (see below), but not further towards Brazil.

Pedro Juan Caballero *p1177*

Bus To **Concepción**, as above. To **Asunción**, quickest route is via Yby Yaú, Santa Rosa and 25 de Diciembre, about 6 hrs. La Santaniana has nicest buses, *bus cama* US$22; *semicama* US$15.50; *común* US$13.25. Also Amambay and Nasa-Golondrina 2 a day on the quick route. To **Bella Vista**, Perpetuo Socorro 3 a day, US$8, 4 hrs. To **Campo Grande** Amambay 3 a day, US$21, 5 hrs, they stop at Policia Federal in Ponta Porã for entry stamp.

Concepción *p1176*

Banks TCs cannot be changed. Several ATMs in town. **Norte Cambios**, Pdte Franco y 14 de Mayo, www.nortecambios.com.py, Mon-Fri 0830-1700, Sat 0830-1100, fair rates for US$ and euros, cash only. **Financiera Familiar**, Pdte Franco y General Garay, US$ cash only. **Immigration** Registro Civil, Pdte Franco y Caballero, T972-193143. **Internet, post office and telephones** All on Pdte Franco.

Pedro Juan Caballero *p1177*

Banks Many *cambios* on the Paraguayan side, especially on Curupayty between Dr Francia and Mcal López. Good rates for buying guaraníes or reais with US$ or euros cash, better than inside Brazil, but TCs are usually impossible to change and there is only one ATM. Banks on Brazilian side do not change cash or TCs but have a variety of ATMs. **BBVA**, Dr Francia y Mcal Estigarribia, Mon-Fri 0845-1300, changes US$ cash to guaraníes only, and has Cirrus ATM. **Norte Cambios**, Curupayty y Mcal López, Mon-Fri 0830-1630, Sat 0830-1100, fair rates for cash, 5% commission for TCs.

The Chaco

West of the Río Paraguay is the Chaco, a wild expanse of palm savanna and marshes (known as Humid, or Bajo Chaco, closest to the Río Paraguay) and dry scrub forest and farmland (known as Dry, or Alto Chaco, further northwest from the river). The Chaco is one of the last homelands of Paraguay's indigenous peoples, now numbering some 27,000 inhabitants. Birdlife is spectacular and abundant. Large cattle estancias dot the whole region and, until recently, agriculture was developed mainly by German-speaking Mennonites from Russia in the Chaco Central. Increasingly, though, large-scale deforestation to make way for cattle has been taking place. Through this vast area the Trans-Chaco Highway (Ruta 9) runs to Bolivia. Much of the region is perfect for those who want to escape into wilderness with minimal human contact and experience nature at its finest and who know the risks involved in traversing the terrain. Although the government has made much of its interest in promoting tourism in the Chaco, it is also considerably lacking in infrastructure, so travellers should prepare accordingly.

Visiting the Chaco

Getting there The Paraguayan Chaco covers more than 24 million ha, but once away from the vicinity of Asunción, the average density is far less than one person to the sq km. A single major highway, the Ruta Trans-Chaco, runs in an almost straight line northwest towards the Bolivian border, ostensibly forming part of the *corredor bi-oceánico*, connecting ports on the Pacific and Atlantic oceans, although it has yet to live up to its expectations. The elevation rises very gradually from 50 m opposite Asunción to 450 m on the Bolivian border. Paving of the Trans-Chaco to the Bolivian border (the military outpost of Fortín Sargento Rodríguez) was completed in 2007, but in spite of being graded twice a year, several paved sections are showing signs of wear and tear, with repairs to potholes few and far between. Sand berms also form at will in some sections and must be avoided. Most travellers cross to Bolivia not through Sargento Rodríguez, but through another military base to the southwest, Infante Rivarola, which is gained by turning left from the Ruta Trans-Chaco in Estancia La Patria onto a hard-packed road. ▶▶ *See also Transport, page 1186.*

Getting around Most bus companies have some a/c buses on their Chaco routes (a great asset December-March), enquire in advance. There is very little local public transport between the main Mennonite towns, you must use the buses heading to/from Asunción to travel between them as well as Mariscal Estigarribia. Bus passengers and motorists should always carry extra food and especially water; climatic conditions are harsh and there is little traffic in case of a breakdown. No private expedition should leave the Trans-Chaco without plentiful supplies of water, food and fuel. No one should venture onto the dirt roads alone and since this is a major smuggling route from Bolivia, it is unwise to stop for anyone at night. There are service stations at regular intervals along the highway in the Bajo and Chaco Central, but beyond Mariscal Estigarribia there is one stop for diesel only and no regular petrol at all until Villamontes in Bolivia, a long drive. Winter temperatures are warm by day, cooler by night, but summer heat and mosquitoes can make it very unpleasant (pyrethrum coils, *espirales*, are sold everywhere). Any unusual insect bites should be examined immediately upon arrival, as Chagas disease is endemic in the Chaco.

Information Consejo Regional de Turismo Chaco Central (**CONRETUR**) coordinates tourism development of the three cooperatives and the private sector. Contact **Hans Fast** ① *T0492-52422, Loma Plata, fast@telesurf.com.py*. The **Fundación para el Desarrollo Sustentable del Chaco** ① *Deportivo 935 y Algarrobo, Loma Plata, T0492-252235, www.desdelchaco.org.py*, operates conservation projects in the area and has useful information but does not offer tours. Always examine in detail a tour operator's claims to expertise in the Chaco. ➤➤ *For Tour operators, see page 1186. See also under individual towns for local tourist offices.*

Background

The **Bajo Chaco** begins on the riverbank just west of Asunción across the Río Paraguay. It is a picturesque landscape of palm savanna, much of which is seasonally inundated because of the impenetrable clay beneath the surface, although there are 'islands' of higher ground with forest vegetation. Cattle ranching on huge, isolated estancias is the prevailing economic activity. Except in an emergency, it is not advisable to enter an estancia unless you have prior permission from the owner.

In the **Chaco Central**, the natural vegetation is dry scrub forest, with a mixture of hardwoods and cactus. The *palo borracho* (bottle tree) with its pear-shaped, water-conserving trunk, the *palo santo*, with its green wood and beautiful scent, and the tannin-rich *quebracho* (literally meaning axe-breaker) are the most noteworthy native species. This is the best area in Paraguay to see large mammals, especially once away from the central Chaco Mennonite colonies.

The **Alto Chaco** is characterized by low dense thorn and scrub forest which has created an impenetrable barricade of spikes and spiny branches resistant to heat and drought and very tough on tyres. Towards Bolivia cacti become more prevalent as rainfall decreases. There are a few estancias in the southern part, but beyond Mariscal Estigarribia there are only occasional military checkpoints. Summer temperatures often exceed 45°C.

Reserva de la Biosfera del Chaco

This is the crown jewel of Paraguay's national park system, albeit one without infrastructure and nearly impossible to visit. **Guyra Paraguay**, which currently co-manages the national parks in this region, is possibly the best option for arranging a tour (see page 1141 and What to do, below). Note that any expedition to the Reserve will be a very costly undertaking and must be cleared with government authorities well ahead of time. The 4.7-million-ha biosphere reserve in the Chaco and Pantanal ecosystems is a UNESCO Man and Biosphere Reserve and includes: **Parque Nacional Defensores del Chaco** (www.salvemoslos.com.py/pdchaco.htm), considered a pristine environment and the gateway to the seventh-largest ecosystem in Latin America. It is some 220 km from Filadelfia, but has only one staffed ranger station at Madrejón in the southeastern corner with very limited facilities: some water, restricted electricity and a small shop for truckers. There were no other ranger stations in operation at the time of writing. **Parque Nacional Teniente Agripino Enciso** (www.salvemoslos.com.py/pntae.htm) is 20 km from La Patria. Nasa minibuses run from Filadelfia to Teniente Enciso via Mariscal Estigarribia and La Patria. The Reserve also contains Médanos del Chaco (www.salvemoslos.com.py/pnmc. htm) and Río Negro (www.salvemoslos.com.py/pnrn.htm) national parks; the Cerro Chovoreca monument; and the Cerro Cabrera-Timané reserve. All are north of the Trans-Chaco, mostly along the Bolivian border, and all face the threat of deforestation. Most of Paraguay's few remaining jaguars are found here. Puma, tapir and peccary also inhabit the area, as well as taguá (an endemic peccary) and a short-haired guanaco. **Cerro León** (highest peak 600 m), one of the only hilly areas of the Chaco, is located within this reserve.

The Trans-Chaco Highway

To reach the Ruta Trans-Chaco, leave Asunción behind and cross the Río Paraguay to Villa Hayes. Birdlife is immediately more abundant and easily visible in the palm savanna, but other wildlife is usually only seen at night, and otherwise occurs mostly as road kills. The first service station after Asunción is at Km 130. **Pirahú**, Km 252, has a service station and is a good place to stop for a meal; it has a/c, delicious empanadas and fruit salad. The owner of the **Ka-Í** parador owns an old-fashioned carbon manufacturing site 2 km before Pirahú. Ask for him if you are interested in visiting the site. At Km 271 is **Pozo Colorado** and the turning for Concepción (see page 1176). There are two restaurants, a basic hotel (**$** with fan, cheaper without), supermarket, hospital, a service station and a military post. The **Touring y Automóvil Club Paraguayo** provides a breakdown and recovery service from Pozo Colorado (T0981-939611, www.tacpy. com.py). At this point, the tidy Mennonite homesteads, with flower gardens and citrus orchards, begin to appear. At Km 282, 14 km northwest of Pozo Colorado, is **Rancho Buffalo Bill**, T021-298381, one of the most pleasant places to stop off or eat, beside a small lake. The estancia has limited but good accommodation (**$$-$**), ask at restaurant. Horse riding, nature walks and camping are good options here. At Km 320 is **Río Verde**, with fuel, police station and restaurant. The next good place to stay or eat along the Trans-Chaco is **Cruce de los Pioneros**, at Km 415, where accommodation (**$$-$ Los Pioneros**, T0491-432170, hot shower, a/c), limited supermarket, vehicle repair shop, and fuel are available. A paved road runs from Cruce Boquerón, just northwest of Cruce de los Pioneros, to Loma Plata.

Mennonite communities

The Chaco Central has been settled by Mennonites, Anabaptists of German extraction who began arriving in the late 1920s. There are three administratively distinct but adjacent colonies: Menno (from Russia via Canada); Fernheim (directly from Russia) and Neuland (the last group to arrive, also from Russia, after the Second World War). Among themselves, the Mennonites speak 'plattdeutsch' ('Low German'), but they readily speak and understand 'hochdeutsch' ('High German'), which is the language of instruction in their schools. Increasingly, younger Mennonites speak Spanish and some English. The people are friendly and willing to talk about their history and culture. Altogether there are about 80 villages with a population of about 18,000 Mennonites and 20,000 *indígenas* from eight distinct groups (they occupy the lowest rung on the socioeconomic ladder).

The Mennonites have created a remarkable oasis of regimented prosperity in this harsh hinterland. Their hotels and restaurants are impeccably clean, services are very efficient, large modern supermarkets are well stocked with excellent dairy products and all other goods, local and imported. Each colony has its own interesting museum. All services, except for hotels, a few restaurants and one gas station in Filadelfia, close on Saturday afternoon and Sunday. The main towns are all very spread out and have no public transport except for a few expensive taxis in Filadelfia. Walking around in the dust and extreme heat can be tiring. Transport between the three main towns is also limited, see Transport, page 1186.

Filadelfia → *Phone code: 0491. Colour map 6, B5. Population: 11,742.*

Also known as Fernheim Colony, Filadelfia, 466 km from Asunción, is the largest town of the region. The **Jacob Unger Museum** ① *C Hindenburg y Unruh, T32151, US$1 including video*, provides a glimpse of pioneer life in the Chaco, as well as exhibiting artefacts of the indigenous peoples of the region. The manager of the Hotel Florida will open the museum upon request, mornings only. Next to the museum is **Plaza de los Recuerdos**, a good place to see the *samu'u* or *palo borracho* (bottle tree). A bookstore-cum-craft shop, **Librería El Mensajero**, next to Hotel Florida, is run by Sra Penner, very helpful and informative.

Apart from the website, www.filadelfiaparaguay.com, there is no tourist infrastructure in Filadelfia. General information may be obtained from the co-op office.

Loma Plata → *Phone code: 0492. Population: 4118.*

The centre of Menno Colony, Loma Plata is 15 km east of Filadelfia. Although smaller than Filadelfia, it has more to offer the visitor, but few transport services. It has a good museum **Museo de la Colonia Menno** ① *Mon-Fri 0700-1130, 1400-1800, Sat 0700-1300, US$1.85.* **Balneario Oasis swimming complex** ① *Nord Grenze, 700 m past airport north of Loma Plata, T52704, US$2, Sep-Apr 1500-2100, except Sun and holidays, 1100-2100*, has three pools with slides and snack bar, a welcome break from the summer heat. **Tourist office** (contact Walter Ratzlaff) ① *next to the Chortitzer Komitee Co-op, T492-52301, turismo@chortitzer.com.py, Mon-Fri 0700-1130, 1400-1800, Sat 0700-1300*, very helpful.

Wetlands around Loma Plata To the southeast of Loma Plata is the Riacho Yacaré Sur watershed, with many salt water lagoons, generally referred to as Laguna Salada. This is a wonderful place to see waterbirds such as Chilean flamingos, swans, spoonbills and migratory shorebirds from the Arctic. There are extensive walks though the eerily beautiful landscape. **Laguna Capitán**, a 22-ha recreation reserve, 30 km from town, has several small lagoons, a swimming lake, basic bunk bed accommodation (**$**, shared bath), kitchen facilities, meals on request, camping. Reserve directly at T0983-344463, English and German spoken, also helpful for tour organizing, or through the Cooperative information office in Loma Plata. There is no public transport. Taxi US$30 one way; full-day tour combining Laguna Capitán with visit to the Cooperative's installations and museum, US$85 per group plus transport. Guides are required for visits. **Laguna Chaco Lodge** ① *70 km from town, T252235*, a 2500-ha private reserve, is a Ramsar wetland site (no accommodation). The lovely Laguna Flamenco is the main body of water surrounded by dry forest. Large numbers of Chilean flamingos and other water birds may be seen here. **Campo María**, a 4500-ha reserve owned by the Chortitzer Komitee (www.choritzer.com.py), but 90 km from town, also has a large lake and can be visited on a tour.

The **Indigenous Foundation for Agricultural and Livestock Development (FIDA)** ① *30 km from Neuland, Filadelfia and Loma Plata, T0491-432321, www.ascim.org*, located within Yalve Sanga, is a collective of 1762 indigenous inhabitants organized into 11 agricultural villages. The community has its own legal capacity and is the legal owner of 6000 ha of property. Yalve Sanga is the first indigenous version of the Mennonite cooperative colonies and provides an interesting insight into the lives of the communities. Limited handicrafts are sold in the Yalve Sanga supermarket (better selection in Neuland).

Neuland → *Phone code: 0493. Population: 4217.*

Neuland, also known as Neu-Halbstadt, is 381 km northwest of Asunción. To the extent that the High Chaco has a tourism infrastructure at all, it is located squarely in Neuland, a well organized town. There is a small **Museo Histórico** with objects brought by the first Mennonies from Russia, set in the building of the first primary school of the area. **Neuland Beach Park** ⓘ *US$1.75, pool, snack bar with a/c.* **Parque la Amistad**, 500 m past pool, is 35 ha of natural vegetation where paths have been cleared for nature walks. Most spectacular are the wild orchids (September-October), cacti and birdlife. **Enrique (Heinz) Weibe** ⓘ *T971-701634, hwiebe@neuland.com.py* is the official guide of the Neuland colony; also ask for **Harry Epp** ⓘ *contact through Neuland Co-op office, T0493-240201, www.neuland.com.py, Mon-Fri 0700-1130, 1400-1800, Sat 0700-1130,* who is very knowledgeable about the flora and fauna and is an informative and entertaining guide. He also gives tours of Neuland in a horse drawn carriage. Phone booths and post office are in centre of town next to the supermarket.

Fortín Boquerón, 27 km from Neuland, was the site of the decisive battle of Chaco War (September 1932) and includes a memorial, a small, well-presented museum and walks around the remainder of the trenches. **Campamento Aurora Chaqueña** is a park 15 km from town on the way to Fortín Boquerón, there is simple accommodation with fan (**$**, take your own food and water). **Parque Valle Natural**, 10 km from Neuland on the way to Filadelfia, is an *espartillar*, a dry riverbed with natural brush around it and a few larger trees. Camping is possible although there is only a small covered area. All three sites are easily reached from Neuland as part of a package tour.

Mariscal Estigarribia and on to Bolivia → *Colour map 6, B5. Population: 14,035.*

At 525 Km from Asunción, Mariscal Estigarribia's few services are spread out over four km along the highway: three gas stations, a couple of small supermarkets (**La Llave del Chaco** is recommended), two mediocre hotels, and one remarkably excellent restaurant. The immigration office (supposedly 24 hours, but often closed in the small hours) is at the southeast end of town near the Shell station. All buses stop at the terminal (**Parador Arami**), at the northwest end of town, where travellers entering from Bolivia are subject to thorough searches for drugs. The people are friendly and helpful.

There are no reliable services of any kind beyond Mariscal Estigarribia. At **La Patria**, 125 km northwest, the road divides: 128 km west to Infante Rivarola (no immigration post – use Mariscal Estigarribia) continuing to Villamontes, Bolivia, with Bolivian immigration at Ibibobo; 128 km northwest to Sargento Rodríguez continuing to Boyuibe, Bolivia (not used by public transport). There are customs posts at either side of the actual border in addition to the main customs offices in Mariscal Estigarribia and Villamontes.

On the Bolivian side, from the border to Villamontes (Ruta 11), the road is gravel and in good condition even after rain, and a 4WD is no longer indispensable. From Villamontes, a paved road runs north to Santa Cruz and south to Yacuiba on the Argentine border. Take small denomination dollar notes as it is impossible to buy bolivianos before reaching Bolivia (if entering from Bolivia only *casas de cambio* in Santa Cruz or Puerto Suárez have guaraníes).

The Chaco listings

For hotel and restaurant price codes, and other relevant information, see Essentials.

Where to stay

The Trans-Chaco Highway *p1182*

$$$ pp Estancia Golondrina, José Domingo Ocampo, Km 235, San Luis, T026-262893, or Asunción office, Pastor Ibáñez 2275 casi Av Artigas, T021-293540 (weekdays only), www. estanciagolondrina.com. Take the unpaved road to the right, 15 km to the ranch. A good place for combining rural and ecotourism. The ranch has extensive agricultural land as well as 12,000 ha of protected virgin forest (Reserva Ypetí) and abundant wildlife. There are trails for walking or horse riding, boat trips on the river, picturesque accommodation (a/c, private bathroom, very comfortable) overlooking the river. Price includes all meals, activities and transportation from the main road.

Filadelfia *p1183*

$$-$ Golondrina-Avenida, Av Hindenburg 635-S at entrance to town, T433111, www. hotelgolondrina.com/?Avenida. Modern, 4 types of room with breakfast, a/c, fridge in the best (cheapest with fan, shared bath, no breakfast), restaurant.
$$-$ Golondrina-Centro, Industrial 194-E, T432218, www.hotelgolondrina.com/?Centro. Modern, spacious common areas with game room. Spanish and German spoken.
$ Florida, Av Hindenburg 165-S opposite park, T432152/4, http://hotelfloridachaco. com. Fridge, a/c, breakfast, cheaper in basic annex with shared bath, fan and without breakfast. Pool (US$1.50 per hr for non-guests), restaurant ($) for buffet and à la carte.
There is a Touring y Automóvil Club Paraguayo hotel at Transchaco Km 443, www.tacpy.com.py.

Loma Plata *p1183*

$$-$ Loma Plata Inn, Eligio Ayala y Manuel Gondra, T252166/253235, www.lomaplata

innhotel.com. Near southern roundabout and Nasa bus office, with restaurant.
$$-$ Mora, Sandstrasse 803, T252255. With breakfast, a/c, Wi-Fi, new wing has spacious rooms with fridge, nice grounds, family run, good value, good breakfast, basic meals on request. Recommended.
$$-$ Pensión Loma Plata, J B Reimer 1805, T252829. A/c, breakfast, comfortable rooms, homely atmosphere, very helpful, good value. Includes breakfast, other meals on request.

Neuland *p1184*

$$-$ Hotel Boquerón, Av 1 de Febrero opposite the Cooperative, T0493-240306, www.neuland.com.py/en/services/hotel-restaurant-boqueron. With breakfast, a/c, cheaper in older wing without TV, restaurant.
$ Parador, Av 1 de Febrero y C Talleros, T0493-24056/. With breakfast, a/c, cheaper with fan and shared bath, restaurant.

Mariscal Estigarribia *p1184*

$ Parador Arami, northwest end of town and far from everything, also known as *la terminal*, T0494-247277. Functional rooms, a/c, meals on request, agents for Stel Turismo and Nasa buses.

Restaurants

Filadelfia *p1183*

$$ El Girasol, Unruh 126-E y Hindenburg, T320780. Mon-Sat 1100-1400, 1800-2300, Sun 1100-1400. Good buffet and *rodizio*, cheaper without the meat.

Loma Plata *p1183*

$$ Chaco's Grill, Av Dr Manuel Gondra, T252166. Buffet, *rodizio*, very good, patio, live music.
$ Norteño, 3 Palmas 990, T252447. Good, simple, lunch till 1400 then open for dinner.
$ Pizzería San Marino, Av Central y Dr Gondra. Daily 1800-2300. Pizza and German dishes.
$ Unión, Av Central, north of roundabout, halfway to airport. Daily 0800-1300, 1700-2200. Good standard food.

Mariscal Estigarribia p1184

$$ Italiano, southwest end of town behind Shell station, T0494-247231. Excellent, top quality meat, large portions, an unexpected treat. Italian owner is friendly and helpful, open for lunch and dinner.

<a> What to do

Many agencies in Asunción offer Chaco tours. Note that some are just a visit to Rancho Buffalo Bill and do not provide a good overview of attractions. Hans Fast and Harry Epp also run tours to national parks. In Loma Plata ask around for bicycle hire to explore nearby villages. For more complete tailor-made tours, contact **Guyra Paraguay** (www.guyra.org.py). This birding organization does not offer tours of the Chaco, but can make excellent referrals to those operators that meet its high standards.

<a> Transport

Filadelfia p1183
Bus From **Asunción**, Nasa-Golondrina, 3 daily except Sat, US$15.50; also Stel Turismo, 1 overnight; 6 hrs. To **Loma Plata**, Nasa-Golondrina 0800 going to Asunción, 0600 and 1900 coming from Asunción, 1 hr, US$3.50. To **Neuland**, local service Mon-Fri 1130 and 1800, 1 hr, US$3.50. Also Stel Turismo at 1900 and Nasa-Golondrina at 2130, both coming from Asunción. To **Mariscal Estigarribia**, Nasa at 0500 Mon and Fri, continuing to La Patria and Parque Nacional Teniente Enciso (see page 1182), 5-6 hrs, US$12.50, returns around 1300 same day (confirm all details in advance).

Loma Plata p1183
Bus Asunción, Nasa-Golondrina, daily 0600, 7-8 hrs, US$15.50. To **Filadelfia**, Mon-Fri 1300, Sat 1100, Sun 1200, daily 2130, all continuing to Asunción.

Neuland p1184
Bus To **Asunción**, Stel Turismo at 1900 (1230 on Sat), via Filadelfia, 7-8 hrs, US$15.50. Local service to **Filadelfia**, Mon-Fri 0500, 1230.

Mariscal Estigarribia p1184
Bus From **Filadelfia**, Nasa-Golondrina 1100 daily; **Asunción**, Nasa-Golondrina, daily 1430, and Pycasu 3 daily, US$15.50; Stel, 2 a day, US$17.75, 7-8 hrs. Buses from Asunción pass through town around 0300-0400 en route to Bolivia: Yaciretá on Tue, Thu, Sat, Sun (agent at Barcos y Rodados petrol station, T0494-247320); Stel Turismo daily (agent at Parador Arami, T0494-247230). You can book and purchase seats in advance but beware overcharging, the fare from Mariscal Estigarribia should be about US$10 less than from Asunción.

<a> Directory

Filadelfia p1183
Banks Banco Itaú ATM, Av Hindenburg 775 y Caraya. Fernheim Cooperative Bank, Hindenburg opposite the Cooperative building, changes US$ and euro cash, no commission for US$ TCs (although must be from major issuer). **Internet** At Shopping Portal del Chaco and opposite Radio ZP30. **Telephone** Copaco on Hindenburg, opposite supermarket, Mon-Sat 0700-2100, Sun 0700-1200, 1500-2000.

Loma Plata p1183
Banks Chortitzer Komitee Co-op, Av Central, Mon-Fri 0700-1730, Sat 0700-1100, good rates for US$ and euros, US$1.25 commission per TC, Banco Itaú ATM outside. ATMs also at bank at southern roundabout and by the Nasa bus office. **Internet** Microtec, Fred Engen 1207, Mon-Sat 0800-1130, 1400-2200, US$1 per hr. **Telephone** Copaco, Av Central near supermarket, Mon-Sat 0700-2000, Sun 0700-1200, 1500-2000.

Neuland p1184
Banks Neuland Cooperative changes US$ cash and TCs, Mon-Fri 0700-1130, 1400-1800, Sat 0700-1130.

Mariscal Estigarribia p1184
Banks No banks. Shell station best for US$, cash only. **Telephone** Copaco, 1 street back from highway, ask for directions.

Contents

Peru

At a glance

⏱ **Time required** 2-6 weeks.

🌤 **Best time** Dec-Apr on the coast; Oct-Apr in the sierra; Apr-Oct driest in the jungles. Jun for fiestas, especially in Cuzco; carnival is celebrated everywhere.

✖ **When not to go** 28-29 Jul is a major holiday; transport and hotels are booked up. Roads in sierras and jungle can be impassable Nov-Apr. Coast is dull and damp May-Nov.

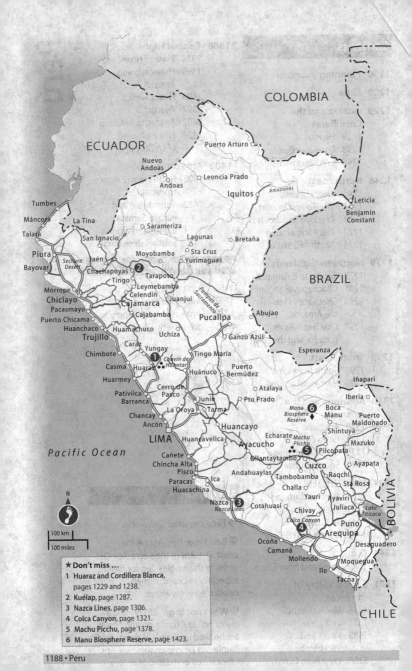

COLOMBIA

ECUADOR

Tumbes
Máncora
La Tina
Talara
Piura
Bayovar

Nuevo
Andoas
Andoas
Puerto Arturo
Leoncia Prado

Iquitos
Amazonas

Leticia
Benjamín
Constant

Sarameriza
San Ignacio
Jaén
Chachapoyas
Mórrope
Chiclayo
Pacasmayo
Puerto Chicama
Huamachuco
Trujillo
Caraz Yungay
Chimbote
Casma Huaraz
Huarmey
Patívilca
Barranca
Chancay
Ancón

Sechura Desert
Moyobamba
Sta Cruz
Yurimaguas
Lagunas
Bretaña

Tarapoto
Tingo
Leymebamba
Celendín
Juanjuí
Cajamarca
Cajabamba
Uchiza
Ganzo Azúl
Abujao
Pucallpa

Pampas de Sacramento

BRAZIL

Chavín de
Huántar
Tingo María
Puerto
Bermúdez
Huánuco
Atalaya
Cerro de
Pasco
Junín Pto Prado
La Oroya Tarma

Esperanza

Iñapari
Iberia

Pacific Ocean

LIMA

Huancavelica

Huancayo

Cañete
Chincha Alta
Pisco
Paracas
Huacachina

Ica

Nazca
Nazca Lines

Andahuaylas

Ayacucho
Echarate
Ollantaytambo
Machu
Picchu
Cuzco
Tambobamba
Challa
Yauri
Cotahuasí
Chivay
Colca Canyon

Ocoña
Camaná
Mollendo
Ilo

Manu
Biosphere
Reserve
Boca
Manu
Shintuyá
Pilcopata

Puerto
Maldonado
Mazuko

Ayapata
Raqchi
Sta Rosa
Ayaviri
Juliaca
Puno
Arequipa

Lake
Titicaca

BOLIVIA

Desaguadero
Moquegua
Tacna

CHILE

N

100 km
100 miles

Cuzco, capital of the Inca world, is now one of South America's premier tourist destinations, with its access to Machu Picchu and the Inca Trail, the Sacred Urubamba Valley and a buzzing nightlife. On the border with Bolivia is Lake Titicaca, blessed with a magical light and fascinating islands. But in Peru, the Egypt of the Americas, this is just the tip of the pyramid.

The coastal desert may sound uninhabitable, yet pre-Inca cultures thrived there. They left their monuments in sculptures etched into the surface of the desert, most famously at Nazca. Civilization builders welcomed gods from the sea and irrigated the soil to feed great cities of adobe bricks. After the Incas came the Spanish *conquistadores*, who left some of their own finest monuments. You can trek forever amid high peaks and blue lakes, cycle down remote mountainsides, look into canyons deeper than any others on earth, or surf the Pacific rollers. There are enough festivals to brighten almost every day of the year, while the spiritual explorer can be led down mystical paths by a shaman.

East of the Andes the jungles stretch towards the heart of the continent with some of the richest biodiversity on earth. And, should you tire of nature, there is always Lima: loud, brash, covered in fog for half the year, but with some of the best museums, most innovative restaurants and liveliest nightlife in the country.

Planning your trip

Where to go in Peru

Lima, the sprawling capital, is daunting at first sight, but worth investigating for its museums, colonial architecture and nightlife. Routes radiate in every direction and great steps have been taken to improve major roads linking the Pacific with the highlands. Travelling overland does, however, take time, so if on a short visit, try to stick to one area.

North of Lima it is only seven hours to Huaraz, in the Cordillera Blanca, the country's climbing and trekking centre. Mountaineering and hiking can be easily linked with the archaeological site at Chavín, east of Huaraz, or with the pre-Inca cities Sechín, Chan Chán and the Huaca de la Luna, the last two close to the colonial city of Trujillo. Heading up the coast, there is plenty of evidence of pre-Columbian culture, particularly around Chiclayo, beaches for surfing (eg Chicama) or watching traditional fishing techniques, and wildlife parks in the far north near Tumbes. (Tumbes, and the nearby Piura-Sullana route are the gateways to Ecuador.) In the northern highlands, Cajamarca is a pleasant base for exploring archaeological sites, thermal baths and beautiful countryside. From here, or by a route from Chiclayo, there is access to the Chachapoyas region where a bewildering number of prehispanic cities and cultures are being opened up to visitors. Going east from here is one of the less-travelled, but nonetheless beautiful roads into the jungle lowlands.

South of Lima are Peru's most deservedly famous tourist destinations. The chief focus is Cuzco, where Spanish colonial and Inca architecture are united, and the Sacred Valley of the Incas, with the mountain-top city of Machu Picchu as the highlight of a historical and cultural treasure trove. Regular trips from Cuzco extend to Puno on the shores of Lake Titicaca (on the overland route to Bolivia), in which islands are frequently visited to see a unique way of life. Arequipa, a fine city at the foot of El Misti volcano, gives access to the canyons of Colca and, for those with more time, the even deeper Cotahuasi. A much-travelled railway links Cuzco, and Puno, but the Cuzco–Puno road has now been paved, offering new opportunities for exploring these high-altitude regions. On the southern coastal route is the Paracas Peninsula (near Pisco), reputed to be home to the largest sea-lion colony on earth, and offshore Ballestas Islands, one of the best places to see marine birdlife in the world. The mysterious Nazca Lines, whose meanings still stir debate, etched in the stony desert, should not be missed if you are on the Lima–Arequipa road, or taking the Pan-American Highway south to Tacna and Chile.

The **Central Highlands** are reached by road from Lima, Pisco and Nazca, the main centres being Huancayo, Huancavelica and Ayacucho. There is much of historical interest here and the Mantaro Valley and Ayacucho are good areas for buying handicrafts. From Ayacucho you can continue to Cuzco by bus, over the altiplano to Abancay, then into and out of the Apurímac river canyon.

Another route into the **Peruvian jungle** runs from the Central Highlands to Pucallpa, but the most popular journeys are by air to the Amazon city of Iquitos, from where boats can be taken to Brazil, or from Cuzco to the spectacular Manu Biosphere Reserve and the Tambopata area (reached from Puerto Maldonado). This has some of the highest levels of biodiversity in the world, providing wonderful opportunities for animal and plant lovers.

Best time to visit Peru

Each of Peru's geographical zones has its own climate. The **coast**: summer (December-April); temperatures 25-35°C; hot and dry; these are the best months for swimming. Winter (May-November); temperature drops and it is cloudy. On the coast, climate is determined by cold sea-water adjoining deserts: prevailing inshore winds pick up so little moisture over the cold Peruvian current that only May-November does it condense. The resultant blanket of cloud and sea mist extends from the south to about 200 km north of Lima. This *garúa* dampens isolated coastal zones of vegetation (called *lomas*) and they are grazed by livestock driven down from the mountains. During the *garúa* season, only the northern beaches near Tumbes are warm enough for swimming.

The **sierra**: April-October is the dry season, hot and dry during the day, around 20-25°C, cold and dry at night, often below freezing. November-April is the wet season, dry and clear most mornings, some rainfall in the afternoon, with average temperatures of 18°C (15°C at night).

Peru's high season is June-September, which is the best time for hiking the Inca trails or trekking and climbing elsewhere in the country. At this time the days are generally clear and sunny, though nights can be very cold at high altitude. The highlands can be visited at other times of the year, though during the wettest months of November-April some roads become impassable and hiking trails can be very muddy.

The **jungle**: April-October, dry season, temperatures up to 35°C. This is the best time to visit the jungle. In the south, a cold front can pass through at night. November April, wet season, heavy rainfall at any time, humid and hot. During the wet season, it only rains for a few hours at a time, which is not enough to spoil your trip, but enough to make some roads virtually impassable.

National parks in Peru

Peru has 68 national parks and protected areas. For information see **El Servicio Nacional de Áreas Naturales Protegidas por el Estado** (Sernanp), Calle Diecisiete 355, Urb El Palomar, San Isidro, Lima, T01-717 7500, www.sernanp.gob.pe

Transport in Peru

Air Carriers serving the major cities are **Star Peru**, T01-705 9000, www.starperu.com, **LAN**, T01-213 8200, www.lan.com, **Avianca/TACA**, T01-511 8222, www.avianca.com, and **Peruvian Airlines**, T01-716 6000, www.peruvianairlines.pe. For destinations such as Andahuaylas, Ayacucho, Cajamarca, Jauja, Huánuco, Huaraz and Pisco flights are offered by **LC Peru** T01-204 1313, www. lcperu.pe. Flights start at about US$100 one-way anywhere in the country from Lima, but prices vary greatly between airlines, with LAN being the most expensive for non-Peruvians. Prices often increase at holiday times (Semana Santa, May Day, Inti Raymi, 28-29 July, Christmas and New Year), and for elections. During these times and the northern hemisphere summer, seats can be hard to come by, so book early. Flight schedules and departure times often change and delays are common. In the rainy season cancellations occur. Flights into the mountains may well be put forward one hour if there are reports of bad weather. Flights to jungle regions are also unreliable. Always allow an extra day between national and international flights, especially in the rainy season. Internal flight prices are fixed in US dollars (but can be paid in soles) and have 18% tax added. Flights must be reconfirmed at least 24 hours in advance. You can do this online or in the town you will be leaving from. Be at the airport well ahead of your flight.

Bus Services along the coast to the north and south as well as inland to Huancayo, Ayacucho and Huaraz are generally good, but on long-distance journeys it is advisable to pay a bit extra and travel with a reliable company. Whatever the standard of service, accidents and hold-ups on buses do occur, especially at night; seek local advice before travelling on a night bus. All major bus companies operate modern buses with two decks on interdepartmental routes. The first deck is called *bus cama*, the second *semi cama*. Both have seats that recline, *bus cama* further than *semi cama*. These buses usually run late at night and are more expensive than ordinary buses which tend to run earlier in the day. Many buses have toilets and show movies. Each company has a different name for its regular and *cama* or *ejecutivo* services. **Cruz del Sur** and **Ormeño** are bus lines covering most of the country. **Cruz del Sur**, generally regarded as a class above the others, accepts Visa cards and gives 10% discount to ISIC and Under26 cardholders (you may have to insist). There are many smaller but still excellent bus lines that run only to

Driving in Peru

Road According to the Ministry of Transport and Communications, 48% of Peru's roads are paved, including the Pan-American Highway which runs north-south through the coastal desert. The aim is for 85% to be paved by 2016. Tolls, US$1.35-2.60, are charged on most major paved roads. Mountain roads that are unpaved can be good, but some are very bad. Each year they are affected by heavy rain and mud slides, especially on the east slopes of the mountains. Some of these roads can be dangerous or impassable in the rainy season. Check with locals (not with bus companies, who only want to sell tickets) as accidents are common at these times.

Documents You must have an international driving licence and be over 21 to drive in Peru. If bringing in your own vehicle you must provide proof of ownership; a *libreta de pasos por aduana* or *carnet de passages* is accepted and recommended, although not officially required. You cannot officially enter Peru with a vehicle registered in someone else's name. On leaving Peru there is no check on the import of a vehicle. All vehicles are required to carry Peruvian insurance (SOAT, Seguro Obligatorio para Accidentes de Tránsito) and spot checks are frequent, especially in border areas. SOAT can be purchased for as little as one month (US$10) at larger border crossings, but only during office hours (Monday-Friday 0800-1800).

Organizations The Touring y Automóvil Club del Perú, Avenida Trinidad Morán 698, Lince, Lima, T611 9999, www.touring peru.com.pe, with offices in several provincial cities, offers help to tourists and particularly to members of the leading motoring associations.

Car hire The minimum age for renting a car is 25. If renting a car, your home driving licence will be accepted for up to six months. Car hire companies are given in the text. Always check that the vehicle you rent has a spare wheel, toolkit and functioning lights etc.

Fuel From 84 octane to 97 octane petrol/gasoline is sold, ranging from US$4.70 to US$6.45. Diesel costs about US$5. Unleaded fuel (90, 95 and 97 octane) is available in large cities and along the Panamericana, but rarely in the highlands.

specific areas. An increasing number accept internet bookings and you may find good deals on the websites. For bus lines, see page 1225 For a centralized information and booking site, visit https://busportal.pe. Some bus terminals charge a usage fee of about US$0.50 which you pay at a kiosk before boarding. Many also charge for the toilet, about US$0.35 with paper and US$0.25 without. Take a blanket or warm jacket when travelling in the mountains. Where buses stop it is possible to buy food on the roadside. With the better companies you will get a receipt for your luggage, which will be locked under the bus. On local buses watch your luggage and never leave valuables on the luggage rack or floor, even when on the move. If your bus breaks down and you are transferred to another line and have to pay extra, keep your original ticket for refund from the first company.

Combis operate between most small towns on one- to three-hour journeys. This makes it possible, in many cases, just to turn up and travel within an hour or two. Combis can be minibuses of varying age and comfort, or slightly more expensive, faster but often overfilled car colectivos, called *autos*, or *cars*. These usually charge twice the bus fare. They leave only when full. They go almost anywhere in Peru; most firms have offices. Book one day in advance and they pick you up at your hotel or in the main plaza.

Note Prices of bus tickets are raised by 60-100%, two or three days before Semana Santa, 28 July (Independence Day – Fiestas Patrias), Christmas and special local events. Tickets are sold out two or three days in advance at this time and transport is hard to come by.

Hitchhiking Hitchhiking is difficult. Freight traffic has to stop at the police *garitas* outside each town and these are the best places to try (also toll points, but these are further from towns). Drivers usually ask for money but don't always expect to get it. In mountain and jungle areas you usually have to pay drivers of lorries, vans and even private cars; ask the driver first how much he is going to charge, and then recheck with the locals.

Taxi Taxi prices are fixed in the mountain towns, about US$1-1.50 in the urban area. Fares are not fixed in Lima although some drivers work for companies that do have standard fares. Ask locals what the price should be and always set the price beforehand; expect to pay US$3-5 in the capital. The main cities have taxis which can be hired by phone, which charge a little more, but are reliable and safe. Many taxi drivers work for commission from hotels. Choose your own hotel and get a driver who is willing to take you. Taxis at airports are more expensive; seek advice about the price in advance. In some places it is cheaper to walk out of the airport to the main road and flag down a cab. Another common form of public transport is the mototaxi, a three-wheel motorcycle with an awning covering the double-seat behind the driver. Fares are about US$1.

Train The main railways are Puno–Juliaca–Cuzco, Cuzco–Machu Picchu and Lima–Huancayo, with a continuation to Huancavelica in the Central Highlands. Details are given in the text below.

Maps The **Instituto Geográfico Nacional** in Lima sells a selection of maps, see page 1222. Another official site is **Ministerio de Transporte** ① *Jr Zorritos 1203, Lima centre, T01-615 7800, www.mtc.gob.pe.* Lima 2000's *Mapa Vial del Perú* (1:2,200,000) is probably the most correct road map available. Maps can also be obtained from the **South American Explorers** (see page 1199).

A good tourist map of the Callejón de Huaylas and Cordillera Huayhuash, by Felipe Díaz, is available in many shops in Huaraz, including Casa de Guías. **Alpenvereinskarte Cordillera Blanca Nord 0/3a** and **Alpenvereinskarte Cordillera Blanca Süd 0/3b** at 1:100,000 are the best maps of that region, US$24, available in Huaraz and Lima, but best bought outside Peru. **Cordillera Huayhuash map**, 1:50,000 (The Alpine Mapping Guild, 2nd ed, 2004) is recommended, available in Huaraz at Café Andino, US$15.

Where to stay in Peru → *See Essentials for our hotel price guide.*

Hotels All deluxe and first class hotels charge 18% in state sales tax (IGV) and 10% service charges. Foreigners should not have to pay the sales tax on hotel rooms. Neither is given in the accommodation listings, unless specified. Places that offer accommodation have a plaque outside bearing the letters H (Hotel), Hs (Hostal), HR (Hotel Residencial) or P (Pensión) according to type. A hotel has 51 rooms or more, a hostal 50 or fewer; the categories do not describe quality or facilities. Many hotels have safe parking for motor cycles. All hotels seem to be crowded during Christmas and Easter holidays, Carnival and at the end of July; Cuzco in June is also very busy. **iPeru** advises that all accommodations registered with them are now listed on their website: www.peru.travel.

Camping Camping is easy in Peru, especially along the coast. There can be problems with robbery when camping near a small village. Avoid such a location, or ask permission to camp in a backyard or *chacra* (farmland). Most Peruvians are used to campers, but in some remote places, people have never seen a tent. Be casual about it, do not unpack all your gear, leave it inside your tent (especially at night) and never leave a tent unattended. Camping gas in little blue bottles is available in the main cities. Those with stoves designed for lead-free gasoline should use *ron de quemar*, available from hardware shops (*ferreterías*). White gas is called *bencina*, also available from hardware stores.

Youth hostels Contact **Asociación Peruana de Albergues Turísticos Juveniles** ① *Av Casimiro Ulloa 328, Miraflores, Lima, T446 5488, www.limahostell.com.pe or www.hostellingperu.com.pe.*

Food and drink in Peru → *See Essentials for our restaurant price guide.*

Restaurants in Peru A normal lunch or dinner costs US$5-8, but can go up to about US$80 in a first-class restaurant, with drinks and wine. (See under Lima Restaurants for information on high-end dining.) Middle- and high-class restaurants may add 10% service, but not include the 18% sales tax in the bill (which foreigners do have to pay); this is not shown on the price list or menu, check in advance. Lower-class restaurants charge only tax, while cheap, local restaurants charge no taxes. Lunch is the main meal and most restaurants serve one or two set lunch menus, called *menú ejecutivo* or *menú económico* (US$2-3). The set menu has the advantage of being served almost immediately and it is usually cheap. The *menú ejecutivo* costs US$2.50-4 or more for a three-course meal with a soft drink and it offers greater choice and more interesting dishes. Chinese restaurants (*chifas*) serve good food at reasonable prices.

Peruvian cuisine The best **coastal** dishes are seafood based, the most popular being *ceviche*. This is a dish of raw white fish marinated in lemon juice, onion and hot peppers. Traditionally, *ceviche* is served with corn-on-the-cob, *cancha* (toasted corn), yucca and sweet potatoes. *Tiradito* is *ceviche* without onions made with plaice. Another mouth-watering fish dish is *escabeche* – fish with onions, hot green pepper, red peppers, prawns (*langostinos*), cumin, hard-boiled eggs, olives, and sprinkled with cheese (it can also be made with chicken). For fish on its own, don't miss the excellent *corvina*, or white sea bass. You should also try *chupe de camarones*, which is a shrimp stew made with varying ingredients. Other fish dishes include *parihuela*, a popular bouillabaisse which includes *yuyo de mar*, a tangy seaweed, and *aguadito*, a thick rice and fish soup said to have rejuvenating powers. A favourite northern coastal dish is *seco de cabrito*, roasted kid (baby goat) served with the ubiquitous beans and rice, or *seco de cordero* which uses lamb instead. Also good is *ají de gallina*, a rich and spicy creamed chicken, and duck is excellent. *Humitas* are small, stuffed dumplings made with maize. The *criollo* cooking of the coast has a strong tradition and can be found throughout the country. A dish almost guaranteed to appear on every restaurant menu is *lomo saltado*, a kind of stir-fried beef with onions, vinegar, ginger, chilli, tomatoes and fried potatoes, served with rice. Other popular examples are *cau cau*, made with tripe, potatoes, peppers, and parsley and served with rice, and *anticuchos*, which are shish kebabs of beef heart with garlic, peppers, cumin seeds and vinegar. *Rocoto relleno* is spicy bell pepper stuffed with beef and vegetables, *palta rellena* is avocado filled with chicken or Russian salad, *estofado de carne* is a stew that often contains wine and *carne en adobo* is a cut and seasoned steak. Two good dishes that use potatoes are *causa* and *carapulca*. On coastal menus *causa* is made with mashed potato wrapped around a filling, which often contains crabmeat. On other occasions, *causa* has yellow potatoes, lemons, pepper, hard-boiled eggs, olives, lettuce, sweet cooked corn, sweet cooked potato, fresh cheese, and served with onion sauce.

The staples of **highland** cooking, corn and potatoes, come in a variety of shapes, sizes and colours. A popular potato dish is *papa a la huancaína*, which is topped with a spicy sauce made with milk and cheese. The most commonly eaten corn dishes are *choclo con queso*, corn on the cob with cheese, and *tamales*, boiled corn dumplings filled with meat and wrapped in a banana leaf. Most typical of highland food is *pachamanca*, a combination of meats (beef, lamb, pork, chicken), potatoes, sweet potatoes, corn, beans, cheese and corn humitas, all slow-cooked in the ground, dating back to Inca times.

The main ingredient in jungle cuisine is fish, especially the succulent, dolphin-sized *paiche*, which comes with the delicious *palmito*, or palm-hearts, and yucca and fried bananas. *Tocacho* is green banana, cooked and ground to a chunky paste, usually served with pork (*cecina*) and sausage (*chorizo*). *Juanes* are a jungle version of tamales, stuffed with chicken and rice.

Meat dishes are many and varied. *Ollucos con charqui* is a kind of potato with dried meat, *sancochado* is meat and all kinds of vegetables stewed together and seasoned with ground garlic and *lomo a la huancaína* is beef with egg and cheese sauce. Others include *fritos*, fried pork, usually eaten in the morning, *chicharrones*, deep fried chunks of pork ribs and chicken or fish, and *lechón*, suckling pig. A delicacy in the highlands is *cuy*, guinea pig. Very filling and good value are the many soups on offer, such as *caldos* (broths): eg *de carnero, verde,* or *de cabeza,* which includes a sheep's head cooked with corn and tripe. Also *yacu-chupe,* a green soup made from potato, with cheese, garlic, coriander, parsley, peppers, eggs, onions, and mint, *and sopa a la criolla* containing thin noodles, beef heart, egg, vegetables and pleasantly spiced.

Peruvian fruits are of good quality: they include bananas, the citrus fruits, pineapples, dates, avocados (*paltas*), eggfruit (*lúcuma*), custard apple (*chirimoya*) which can be as big as your head, quince, papaya, mango, guava, the passion-fruit (*maracuyá*) and the soursop (*guanábana*).

Drink The most famous local drink is *pisco,* a clear brandy which, with egg whites and lime juice, makes the famous pisco sour. The most renowned brands come from the Ica valley. The best wines are also from Ica, *Tabernero, Tacama* (especially its Selección Especial and Terroix labels), *Ocucaje* and *Santiago Queirolo* (in particular its Intipalka label). Beer is of the lager type, the best known brands being *Cusqueña* and *Arequipeña* brands (lager) and *Trujillo Malta* (porter). In Lima only *Cristal* and *Pilsen* are readily available. Other brands, including some Brazilian beers, are coming onto the market, but there is little difference between any of them, Seek out the microbreweries which are springing up, eg in Huaraz. *Chicha de jora* is a maize beer, usually home-made and not easy to come by, refreshing but strong, and *chicha morada* is a soft drink made with purple maize. The local rival to Coca Cola, the fluorescent yellow *Inca Cola,* is made from lemongrass. Peruvian coffee is good, but the best is exported and many cafés only serve coffee in liquid form or Nescafé. There are many different kinds of herb tea: the commonest are *manzanilla* (camomile) and *hierbaluisa* (lemon grass). *Mate de coca* is frequently served in the highlands to stave off the discomforts of altitude sickness.

Essentials A-Z

Accident and emergency
Emergency medical attention (Cruz Roja) T115. Fire T116. Police T105, www.pnp.gob.pe (Policía Nacional del Perú), for police emergencies nationwide. Tourist Police, Jr Moore 268, Magdalena, 38th block of Av Brasil, Lima, T01-460 1060/0844, daily 24 hrs They are friendly, helpful and speak English and some German.

Electricity
220 volts AC, 60 cycles throughout the country, except Arequipa (50 cycles). Most 4- and 5-star hotels have 110 volts AC. Plugs are American flat-pin or twin flat and round pin combined.

Embassies and consulates
For all Peru embassies and consulates abroad and for all foreign embassies and consulates in Peru, see http://embassy.goabroad.com.

Festivals
Two of the major festival dates are **Carnaval**, which is held over the weekend before Ash Wed, and **Semana Santa** (Holy Week), which ends on Easter Sun. Carnival is celebrated in most of the Andes and Semana Santa throughout Peru. Another important festival is **Fiesta de la Cruz**, held on 1 May in much of the central and southern highlands and on the coast. In Cuzco, the entire month of Jun is one huge *fiesta*, culminating in Inti Raymi, on 24 Jun, one of Peru's prime tourist attractions. 1 Aug is the National Day of the Alpaca, with events in major alpaca-rearing centres across the country. Another national festival is **Todos los Santos** (All Saints) on 1 Nov, and on 8 Dec is Festividad de la Inmaculada Concepción. A full list of local festivals is listed under each town. Apart from those listed above, the main holidays are: 1 Jan, New Year; 6 Jan, **Bajada de Reyes**; 1 May, Labour Day; 28-29 Jul, Independence (Fiestas Patrias); 7 Oct, Battle of Angamos; 24-25 Dec, Christmas. **Note** Most businesses close for the official holidays but supermarkets and street markets may be open. Sometimes holidays that fall mid-week will be moved to the following Mon. The high season for foreign tourism in Peru is Jun-Sep while national tourism peaks at Christmas, Semana Santa and Fiestas Patrias.

Prices rise and rooms and bus tickets are harder to come by.

Money → *US$1 = S/2.79; €1 = S/3.77 (Jun 2014).*

Currency The new sol (s/) is divided into 100 céntimos. Notes in circulation are: S/200, S/100, S/50, S/20 and S/10. Coins: S/5, S/2, S/1, S/0.50, S/0.20, S/0.10 and S/0.05 (being phased out). Some prices are quoted in dollars (US$) in more expensive establishments, to avoid changes in the value of the sol. You can pay in soles, however.

Warning Forged US$ notes and forged soles notes and coins are in circulation. Always check your money when you change it, even in a bank (including ATMs). Hold sol notes up to the light to inspect the watermark and that the colours change according to the light. The line down the side of the bill spelling out the bill's amount should appear green, blue and pink. Fake bills are only pink and have no hologram properties. There should also be tiny pieces of thread in the paper (not glued on). In parts of the country, forged 1-, 2- and 5-sol coins are in circulation. The fakes are slightly off-colour, the surface copper can be scratched off and they tend to bear a recent date. Posters in public places explain what to look for in forged soles. See also www.bcrp.gob.pe, under **Billetes y Monedas**. Try to break down large notes whenever you can as there is a shortage of change in museums, post offices, even shops. Taxi drivers are notorious in this regard – one is simply told 'no change'. Do not accept this excuse.

Credit cards, ATMs and banks Visa (by far the most widely accepted card in Peru), MasterCard, American Express and Diners Club are all valid. There is often an 8-12% commission for all credit card charges. Bank exchange policies vary from town to town, but as a general rule the following applies (but don't be surprised if a branch has different rules): BCP (Mon-Fri 0900-1800, Sat 0900-1300) changes US$ cash to soles; cash advances on Visa in soles only; VíaBCP ATM with US$2 surcharge for Visa/Plus, MasterCard/Cirrus, Amex. **BBVA Continental** changes US$ cash to soles, some branches change TCs at US$12 commission; B24 ATM for Visa/Plus has US$5 charge. **Interbank** (Mon-Fri 0900-1815, Sat 0900-1230) changes US$ cash and TCs to soles,

TCs to US$ cash for US$5 per transaction up to US$500; branches have **Global Net** ATMs (see below). **Scotiabank** (Mon-Fri 0915-1800, Sat 0915-1230) changes US$ cash to soles, cash advances on MasterCard; ATM for Visa, MasterCard, Maestro and Cirrus; charges US$3.50 per cheque to change TCs. There are also **Global Net** and **Red Unicard** ATMs that accept Visa, Plus and MasterCard, Maestro and Cirrus (the former makes a charge per transaction). ATMs usually have a maximum withdrawal limit of between US$140 and US$200. It is safest to use ATMs during banking hours. At night and on Sun there is more chance of the transaction going wrong, or false money being in the machine. ATMs usually give US$ if you don't request soles and their use is widespread. Availability decreases outside large towns. In smaller towns, take some cash. Businesses displaying credit card symbols, on the other hand, are less likely to take foreign cards.

All banks' exchange rates are considerably less favourable than *casas de cambio* (exchange houses). Long queues and paperwork may be involved. US$ and euros are the only currencies which should be brought into Peru from abroad (take some small bills). There are no restrictions on foreign exchange. Few banks change euros. Some banks demand to see 2 documents with your signature for changing cash. Always count your money in the presence of the cashier. A repeatedly recommended *casa de cambio* is LAC Dolar, Jr Camaná 779, 1 block from Plaza San Martín, p 2, T428 8127, also at Av La Paz 211, Miraflores, T242 4069. Open Mon-Sat 1000-1800, good rates, very helpful, safe, fast, reliable, 2% commission on cash and TCs, will come to your hotel if you're in a group. Another recommended *casa de cambio* is **Virgen P Socorro**, Jr Ocoña 184, T428 7748. Open daily 0830-2000, safe, reliable and friendly. In Lima, there are many *casas de cambio* on and around Jr Ocoña off the Plaza San Martín. In 2014 there was no real advantage in changing money on the street, but should you choose to do so, it does avoid paperwork and queuing. Use only official street changers, such as those around Parque Kennedy and down Av Larco in Miraflores (Lima). They carry ID cards and wear a green vest. Check your soles before handing over your US$ or euros, check their calculators, etc, and don't change money in crowded areas. If using their services think about taking a taxi after changing, to avoid being followed. **Moneygram**, Ocharan 260, Miraflores, T447 4044. Safe and reliable agency for sending and receiving money. Locations throughout Lima and the provinces. Exchanges most world currencies and TCs. Soles can be exchanged into US$ at the exchange desks at Lima airport, and you can change soles for US$ at any border. US$ can also be bought at the various borders.

Note No one, not even banks, will accept US$ bills that look 'old', damaged or torn.

Cost of travelling The average budget is US$45-60 pp a day for living fairly comfortably, including transport. Your budget will be higher the longer you stay in Lima and Cuzco and depending on how many internal flights you take. Rooms range from US$7-11 pp for the most basic *alojamiento* to US$20-40 for mid-range places, to over US$90 for more upmarket hotels (more in Lima or Cuzco). Living costs in the provinces are 20-50% below those in Lima and Cuzco. The cost of using the internet is generally US$0.60-1 per hr, but where competition is not fierce, rates vary from US$1.50 to US$4.

Students can obtain very few reductions in Peru with an international students' card, except in and around Cuzco. To be any use in Peru, it must bear the owner's photograph. An ISIC card can be obtained in Lima from **Intej**, Av San Martín 240, Barranco, T01-247 3230; also Portal de Panes 123, of 303, Cuzco, T084-256367; Mercaderes 329, p 2, of 34, Arequipa, T054-284756; Av Mariscal Castilla 3909-4089, El Tambo, 7o piso del Edificio de Administración y Gobierno de la UNCP, anexo 6060, Huancayo, T064-481081; www.intej.org.

Opening hours

Banks: see under Money, above. Outside Lima and Cuzco banks may close 1200-1500 for lunch. **Government offices**: Jan-Mar Mon-Fri 0830-1130; Apr-Dec Mon-Fri 0900-1230, 1500-1700, but these hours change frequently. **Offices**: 0900-1700; most close on Sat. **Shops**: 0900 or 1000-1230 and 1500 or 1600-2000. In the main cities, supermarkets do not close for lunch and Lima has some that are open 24 hrs. Some are closed on Sat and most are closed on Sun.

Postal services

The central Lima post office is on Jr Camaná 195 near the Plaza de Armas. Mon-Fri 0730-1900, Sat 0730-1600. Poste Restante is in the same building but is considered unreliable. In Miraflores the main post office is on Av Petit Thouars 5201 (same hours). There are many small branches around Lima and in the rest of the country, but they are less reliable. For express service: **EMS**, next to central post office in downtown Lima, T533 2020.

Safety

The following notes on personal safety should not hide the fact that most Peruvians are hospitable and helpful. For general hints on avoiding crime, see Security, in Essentials. All the suggestions given there are valid for Peru. The police presence in Lima and Cuzco, and to a lesser extent Arequipa and Puno, has been greatly stepped up. Nevertheless, be aware that assaults may occur in Lima and centres along the Gringo Trail. Also watch for scammers who ask you, "as a favour", to change dollars into (fake) soles and for strangers who shake your hand, leaving a chemical which will knock you out when you next put your hand to your nose.

Outside the Jul-Aug peak holiday period, there is less tension, less risk of crime, and more friendliness.

Although certain illegal drugs are readily available, anyone carrying any is almost automatically assumed to be a drug trafficker. If arrested on any charge the wait for trial in prison can take a year and is particularly unpleasant. If you are asked by the narcotics police to go to the toilets to have your bags searched, insist on taking a witness. **Drug use or purchase is punishable by up to 15 years' imprisonment. There are a number of foreigners in Peruvian prisons on drug charges.**

Many places in the Amazon and in Cuzco offer experiences with Ayahuasca or San Pedro, often in ceremonies with a shaman. These are legal, but always choose a reputable tour operator or shaman. Do not go with the first person who offers you a trip. Single women should not take part. There are plenty of websites for starting your research. See also under Iquitos, page 1419. Tricks employed to get foreigners into trouble over drugs include slipping a packet of cocaine into the money you are exchanging, being invited to a party or somewhere involving a taxi ride, or simply being asked on the street if you want to buy cocaine. In all cases, a plain clothes 'policeman' will discover the planted cocaine, in your money, at your feet in the taxi, and will ask to see your passport and money. He will then return them, minus a large part of your cash. Do not get into a taxi, do not show your money, and try not to be intimidated. Being in pairs is no guarantee of security, and single women may be particularly vulnerable. Beware also thieves dressed as policemen asking for your passport and wanting to search for drugs; **searching is only permitted if prior paperwork is done**.

In Cuzco many clubs and bars offer coupons for free entry and a free drink. The drinks are made with the cheapest, least healthy alcohol; always watch your drink being made and never leave it unattended. Sadly, the free entry-and-drink system doesn't appear to apply to Peruvians who are invariably asked to pay for entry to a disco, even if their tourist companions get in for nothing. We have also received reports of nightclubs and bars in Lima and Cuzco denying entrance to people solely on the basis of skin colour, assumed economic status or sexual orientation. This discrimination should be discouraged.

Insurgency Indications are that Sendero Luminoso and MRTA remain active in scattered parts of the country and to a limited degree. In the first half of 2014 there were no reports of threats to those parts of Peru of tourist interest, but it is important to be aware of the latest situation.

For up-to-date information contact the **Tourist Police** (see Accident & emergency), your embassy or consulate, fellow travellers, or **South American Explorers** (Lima T444 2150, Cuzco T245484, or in Quito). You can also contact the **Tourist Protection Bureau** (Indecopi). As well as handling complaints, they will help if you have lost, or had stolen, documents.

Tax
Airport taxes US$31 on international flight departures; US$9.40 on internal flights (when making a domestic connection in Lima, you don't have to pay airport tax; contact airline

personnel at baggage claim to be escorted you to your departure gate). Regional airports have lower departure taxes. Both international and domestic airport taxes should be included in the price of flight tickets, not paid at the airport. 18% state tax is charged on air tickets; it is included in the price of the ticket.
VAT/IGV/IVA 18%.

Telephone → *Country code+51.*
Easiest to use are the independent phone offices, *locutorios*, all over Lima and other cities. They take phone cards, which can be bought in *locutorios*, or in the street nearby. There are payphones throughout the country. Some accept coins, some only phone cards and some take both.

The numbering system for digital phones is as follows: for Lima mobiles, add 9 before the number, for the departments of La Libertad 94, Arequipa 95, Piura 96, Lambayeque 97; for other departments, add 9 – if not already in the number – and the city code (for example, Cuzco numbers start 984). Note also that some towns are dominated by Claró, others by Movistar (the 2 main mobile companies). As it is expensive to call between the two you should check, if spending some time in one city and using a mobile, which is the best account to have.

Red Privada Movistar (RPM) and **Red Privada Claró (RPC)** are operated by the respective mobile phone companies. Mobile phone users who subscribe to these services obtain a 6-digit number in addition their 9-digit mobile phone number. Both the 6- and 9-digit numbers ring on the same physical phone. The RPM and RPC numbers can be called from anywhere in Peru without using an area code, you just dial the 6 digits, and the cost is about 20% of calling the 9-digit number. This 80% discount usually also applies when calling from *locutorios*. Many establishments including hotels, tour operators and transport companies have both RPM and RPC numbers.

Time
GMT -5.

Tipping
Restaurants: service is included in the bill, but tips can be given directly to the waiter for

exceptional service. **Taxi drivers**: none (bargain the price down, then pay extra for good service). **Cloakroom attendants and hairdressers** (very high class only): US$0.50-1. **Porters**: US$0.50. **Car wash boys**: US$0.30. **Car 'watch' boys**: US$0.20. If going on a trek or tour, it is customary to tip the guide as well as the cook and porters.

Tourist information

Tourism promotion and information is handled by **PromPerú**, Edif Mincetur, C Uno Oeste 50, p 13 y 14, urb Córpac, San Isidro, T01-616 7300, or Av República de Panamá 3647, San Isidro, T616 7400, www.promperu.gob.pe. See also www. peru.travel. PromPerú runs an information and assistance service, **i perú**, T01-574 8000 (24 hrs). Main office: Jorge Basadre 610, San Isidro, Lima, T616 7300 or 7400, iperulima@promperu.gob.pe, Mon-Fri 0830-1830. Also a 24-hr office at Jorge Chávez airport; and throughout the country.

There are tourist offices in most towns, either run by the municipality, or independently. Outside Peru, information can be obtained from Peruvian embassies/consulates. **Indecopi** T224 7777 (in Lima), T0800-44040 (in the Provinces), www.indecopi.gob.pe, is the government-run consumer protection and tourist complaint bureau. They are friendly, professional and helpful. An excellent source of information is **South American Explorers**, in Lima (see page 1201) and Cuzco. See also Essentials. They have information on travellers held in prison, some for up to 1 year without sentencing, and details on visiting regulations. A visit will be really appreciated!

Useful websites

www.caretas.com.pe The most widely read weekly magazine, *Caretas*.
www.leaplocal.org Recommends good quality guides, helping communities benefit from socially responsible tourism.
www.minam.gob.pe Ministerio del Ambiente (Spanish).
www.peruthisweek.com Informative guide and news service in English for people living in Peru.
www.peruviantimes.com The *Andean Air Mail & Peruvian Times* internet news magazine.
www.terra.com.pe TV, entertainment and news (in Spanish).

Visas and immigration

Tourist cards No visa is necessary for citizens of EU countries, most Asian countries, North and South America, and the Caribbean, or for citizens of Andorra, Belarus, Finland, Iceland, Israel, Liechteinstein, Macedonia, Moldova, Norway, Russian Federation, Serbia and Montenegro, Switzerland, Ukraine, Australia, New Zealand and South Africa. A Tourist Card (TAM – Tarjeta Andina de Migración) is free on flights arriving in Peru, or at border crossings for visits up to 183 days. The form is in duplicate, the original given up on arrival and the copy on departure. A new tourist card must be obtained for each re-entry. If your tourist card is stolen or lost, get a new one from **Migraciones**, Digemin, Av España 730, Breña, Lima, T200 1081, www. migraciones.gob.pe, Mon-Fri 0830-1300.
Tourist visas For citizens of countries not listed above (including Turkey), visas cost US$37.75 or equivalent, for which you require a valid passport, a departure ticket from Peru (or a letter of guarantee from a travel agency), 2 colour passport photos, 1 application form and proof of economic solvency. Tourist visas are valid for 183 days. In the first instance, visit the Migraciones website (as above) for visa forms.

Keep ID, preferably a passport, on you at all times. You must present your passport when reserving travel tickets. To avoid having to show your passport, photocopy the important pages of your passport – including the immigration stamp, and have it legalized by a 'Notario público'. We have received no reports of travellers being asked for onward tickets at the borders at Tacna, Aguas Verdes, La Tina, Yunguyo or Desaguadero. Travellers are not asked to show an onward flight ticket at Lima airport, but you will not be able to board a plane in your home country without one.

Under Decree 1043 of Jun 2008, once in Peru tourists may not extend their tourist card or visa. It's therefore important to insist on getting the full number of days to cover your visit on arrival (it's at the discretion of the border official). If you exceed your limit, you'll pay a US$1-per-day fine.
Business visas If receiving money from Peruvian sources, visitors must have a business visa: requirements are a valid passport, 2 colour passport photos, return ticket and a letter

from an employer or Chamber of Commerce stating the nature of business, length of stay and guarantee that any Peruvian taxes will be paid. The visa allows the holder to stay 183 days in the country. On arrival business visitors must register with the Dirección General de Contribuciones for tax purposes.

Student visas These must be requested from Migraciones (address above) once you are in Peru. In addition to completing the general visa form you must have proof of adequate funds, affiliation to a Peruvian body, a letter of consent from parents or tutors if you are a minor. Full details are on the Migraciones website (in Spanish).

If you wish to change a tourist visa into another type of visa (business, student, resident, etc), you may do so without leaving Peru. Visit Migraciones and obtain the relevant forms.

Weights and measures
Metric.

Lima

Lima's colonial centre and suburbs, shrouded in fog which lasts eight months of the year, are fringed by the pueblos jóvenes *which sprawl over the dusty hills overlooking the city. It has a great many historic buildings, some of the finest museums in the country and its food, drink and nightlife are second to none. Although not the most relaxing of South America's capitals, it is a good place to start before exploring the rest of the country.*

Arriving in Lima → *Phone code: 01. Colour map 3, C2. Population: 8.6 million (metropolitan area).*
Orientation All international flights land at Jorge Chávez **airport**, 16 km northwest of the Plaza de Armas. Transport into town by taxi or bus is easy. If arriving in the city by **bus**, most of the recommended companies have their terminals just south of the centre, many on Avenida Carlos Zavala. This is not a safe area and you should take a taxi to and from there.

Downtown Lima can be explored on foot by day; at night a taxi is safest. Miraflores is 15 km south of the centre. Many of the better hotels and restaurants are here and in neighbouring San Isidro. Three types of bus provide an extensive public transport system; all vehicles stop when flagged down. Termini of public transport vehicles are posted above the windscreens, with the route written on the side. However good the public transport system or smart your taxi, one thing is unavoidable, Lima's roads are congested almost throughout the whole day. Allow plenty of time to get from A to B and be patient.➤➤ *For detailed information, see Transport, page 1225.*

Addresses Several blocks, with their own names, make up a long street, a jirón (often abbreviated to Jr). Street corner signs bear both names, of the jirón and of the block. In the historic centre blocks also have their colonial names.

Climate Only 12° south of the equator, one would expect a tropical climate, but Lima has two distinct seasons. The winter is May-November, when a garúa (mist) hangs over the city, making everything look grey. It is damp and cold, 8-15°C. The sun breaks through around November and temperatures rise to 30°C or more. Note that the temperature in the coastal suburbs is lower than the centre because of the sea's influence. Protect against the sun's rays when visiting the beaches around Lima, or elsewhere in Peru.

Tourist information i perú has offices at Jorge Chávez **international airport**① T574 8000, open 24 hrs; **Casa Basadre** ① Av Jorge Basadre 610, San Isidro, T616 7300 or 7400, Mon-Fri 0900-1800; and **Larcomar shopping centre** ① Módulo 10, Plaza Principal, Miraflores, T445 9400, Mon-Fri 1100-1300, 1400-2000. There is a **Municipal tourist kiosk** on Pasaje Escribanos, behind the Municipalidad, near the Plaza de Armas, T632 1542, www.munlima.gob.pe. Ask about guided walks in the city centre. There are eight **Miraflores kiosks**: Parque Central; Parque Salazar; Parque del Amor; González Prada y Avenida Petit Thouars; Avenida R Palma y Avenida Petit Thouars; Avenida Larco y Avenida Benavides; Huaca Pucllana (closed Saturday afternoon); and Ovalo Gutiérrez. **South American Explorers** ① *Enrique Palacios 956, Miraflores, T445 3306/447 7731 (dial 011-51-1 from USA), www.saexplorers.org.* See also Essentials, at the front of the book. For an English website, see www.limaeasy.com and for an upmarket city guide see www.limainside.net.

Background

Lima, capital of Peru, is built on both sides of the Río Rímac, at the foot of Cerro San Cristóbal. It was originally named *La Ciudad de Los Reyes*, in honour of the Magi, at its founding by conquistador Francisco Pizarro in 1535. From then until the independence of the South American republics in the early 19th century, it was the chief city of Spanish South America. The name Lima, a corruption of the Quechua name *Rimac* (speaker), was not adopted until the end of the 16th century.

The Universidad de San Marcos was founded in 1551, and a printing press in 1595, both among the earliest of their kind in South America. Lima's first theatre opened in 1563, and the Inquisition was introduced in 1569 (it was not abolished until 1820). For some time the Viceroyalty of Peru embraced Colombia, Ecuador, Bolivia, Chile and Argentina. There were few cities in the Old World that could rival Lima's power, wealth and luxury, which was at its height during the 17th and early 18th centuries. The city's wealth attracted many freebooters and in 1670 a protecting wall 11 km long was built round it, then destroyed in 1869. The earthquake of 1/46 destroyed all but 20 houses, killed 4000 inhabitants and ended its pre-eminence. It was only comparatively recently, with the coming of industry, that Lima began to change into what it is today.

Modern Lima is seriously affected by smog for much of the year, and is surrounded by 'Pueblos Jóvenes', or settlements of squatters who have migrated from the Sierra. Villa El Salvador, a few kilometres southeast of Lima, may be the world's biggest 'squatters' camp' with 350,000 people building up an award winning self-governing community since 1971.

Over the years the city has changed out of recognition. Many of the hotels and larger business houses have relocated to the fashionable suburbs of Miraflores and San Isidro, thus moving the commercial heart of the city away from the Plaza de Armas.

Half of the town-dwellers of Peru now live in Lima. The metropolitan area contains 8.6 million people, nearly one-third of the country's total population, and two-thirds of its industries. Callao, Peru's major port, runs into Lima; it is a city in its own right, with over one million inhabitants. Within its boundaries is the Jorge Chávez airport. The docks handle 75% of the nation's imports and some 25% of its exports. Callao has a serious theft problem, avoid being there in the evening.

Places in Lima

The traditional heart of the city, at least in plan, is still what it was in colonial days. An increasing number of buildings in the centre are being restored and the whole area is being given a new lease of life as the architectural beauty and importance of the Cercado (as it is known) is recognized. Most of the tourist attractions are in this area. Some museums are only open 0900-1300 from January-March, and some are closed in January.

Plaza de Armas (Plaza Mayor)

One block south of the Río Rímac lies the Plaza de Armas, or Plaza Mayor, which has been declared a World Heritage Site by UNESCO. Running along two sides are arcades with shops: Portal de Escribanos and Portal de Botoneros. In the centre of the plaza is a bronze fountain dating from 1650. The **Palacio de Gobierno**, on the north side of the Plaza, stands on the site of the original palace built by Pizarro. The changing of the guard is at 1145-1200. To take a tour register two days in advance at the Oficina de Turismo (ask guard for directions); the free, 45-minute tours are in Spanish and English Monday-Friday, 0830-1300, 1400-1730. The **Cathedral** ① *T427 9647, Mon-Fri 0900-1700, Sat 1000-1300; entry to cathedral US$3.65, ticket also* including *Museo Arzobispado US$11*, was reduced to rubble in the earthquake of 1746. The reconstruction, on the lines of the original, was completed 1755. Note the splendidly carved stalls (mid-17th century), the silver-covered altars surrounded by fine woodwork, mosaic-covered walls bearing the coats of arms of Lima and Pizarro and an allegory of Pizarro's commanders, the 'Thirteen Men of Isla del Gallo'. The remains of Francisco Pizarro, found in the crypt, lie in a small chapel, the first on the right of the entrance. The **Museo de Arte Religioso** in the cathedral, has sacred paintings, portraits, altar pieces and other items, as well as a café and toilets. Next to the cathedral is the **Archbishop's Palace and museum** ① *T01-427 5790, www. palacioarzobispaldelima.com, Mon-Sat 0900-1700*, rebuilt in 1924, with a superb wooden balcony. Permanent and temporary exhibitions are open to the public.

Around the Plaza de Armas

Just behind the Municipalidad de Lima is **Pasaje Ribera el Viejo**, which has been restored and is now a pleasant place, with several good cafés with outdoor seating. Nearby is the **Casa Solariega de Aliaga** ① *Unión 224, T427 7736, Mon-Fri 0930-1300, 1430-1745, US$11, knock on the door and wait to see if anyone will let you in, or contact in advance for tour operators who offer guided visits.* It is still occupied by the Aliaga family and is open to the public and for functions. The house

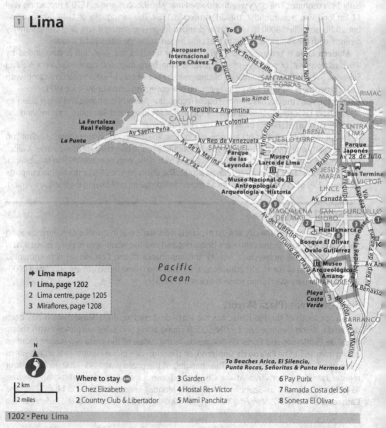

■ Lima

➡ Lima maps
1 Lima, page 1202
2 Lima centre, page 1205
3 Miraflores, page 1208

Pacific Ocean

To Beaches Arica, El Silencio, Punta Rocas, Señoritas & Punta Hermosa

Where to stay 🛏		
1 Chez Elizabeth	3 Garden	6 Pay Purix
2 Country Club & Libertador	4 Hostal Res Víctor	7 Ramada Costa del Sol
	5 Mami Panchita	8 Sonesta El Olivar

contains what is said to be the oldest ceiling in Lima and is furnished entirely in the colonial style. The **Casa de la Gastronomía Nacional Peruana** ① *Conde de Superunda 170, T426 7264, www.limacultura.pe, guided tours US$.5.25, behind the Correo Central,* has an extensive permanent collection of objects and displays on Peruvian food, historic and regional. It also has temporary exhibitions on the same theme. All signs are in Spanish.

The area from the east side of the Palacio de Gobierno (Calle Carabaya) along the second block of Ancash has been designated the tourist circuit of the Calles El Rastro y Pescadería, with the **Museo de Sitio Bodega y Quadra** ① *Ancash 213, Tue-Sun 0900-1700, free.* It stretches from the railway station to San Francisco, including the Casa de la Literatura and several historic houses. The area is to be pedestrianized.

The baroque church of **San Francisco** ① *on the 1st block of Jr Lampa, corner of Ancash, a few blocks from the Plaza de Armas, T426 7377 ext 111, www.museocatacumbas.com, daily 0930-1645, guided tours only, US$2.75, students half price, US$0.40 children,* was finished in 1674 and withstood the 1746 earthquake. The nave and aisles are lavishly decorated in Mudéjar style. The monastery is famous for the Sevillian tilework and panelled ceiling in the cloisters (1620). The Catacombs under the church and part of the monastery are well worth seeing. The late 16th-century **Casa de Jarava** or **Pilatos** ① *Jr Ancash 390,* is opposite San Francisco church. Close by, **Casa de las Trece Monedas** ① *Jr Ancash 536,* still has the original doors and window grills. **Parque de la Muralla** ① *open 0900-2000,* on the south bank of the Rímac, incorporates a section of the old city wall, fountains, stalls and street performers. There is a cycle track, toilets and places to eat both inside and near the entrance on Calle de la Soledad.

The **Palacio Torre Tagle** (1735) ① *Jr Ucayali 363, Mon-Fri during working hours,* is the city's best surviving example of secular colonial architecture. Today, it is used by the Foreign Ministry, but visitors are allowed to enter courtyards to inspect the fine, Moorish-influenced wood-carving in balconies and wrought iron work. At Ucayali 391 and also part of the Foreign Ministry is the Centro Cultural Inca Garcilaso, which holds cultural events. **Casa de la Rada,** or **Goyeneche** ① *Jr Ucayali 358,* opposite, is a fine mid-18th-century French-style town house which now belongs to a bank. The patio and first reception room are open occasionally to the public. **Museo Banco Central de Reserva** ① *Jr Ucayali at Jr Lampa, T01-613 2000 ext 2655, Tue-Fri 1000-1630, Wed 1000-1900, Sat-Sun 1000 1300, free, photography prohibited.* This is a large collection of pottery from the Vicus or Piura culture (AD 500-600) and gold objects from Lambayeque, as well as 19th- and 20th-century paintings: both sections highly recommended. **San Pedro** ① *3rd block of Jirón Ucayali, Mon-Sat 0930-1145, 1700-1800,* finished by Jesuits in 1638, has marvellous

SAN JUAN DE LURIGANCHO

Cerro San ▲ Cristóbal

Av Independencia

SANTA ANITA

Cerro El Agustino ▲

Av N Ayllón

Av Nicolás Arriola

Av Metropolitana

Av de Evitamiento

ATE

To Puruchuco

LA MOLINA

SAN BORJA

■ Museo de la Nación & Ⅲ Gran Teatro Nacional

Av Javier Prado Este

Hipódromo de Monterrico

MONTERRICO

Av Panamericana Sur

Av Primavera

Av Aviación

Av Alonso de Molina

■ Museo de Oro del Perú

Av Tomás Marsano

El Tren Eléctrico ———

Metropolitano bus line ▪▪▪▪

To Chorrillos

9 Tambopacaya

altars with Moorish-style balconies, rich gilded wood carvings in choir and vestry, and tiled throughout. Several Viceroys are buried here; the bell called La Abuelita, first rung in 1590, sounded the Declaration of Independence in 1821.

Between Avenida Abancay and Jr Ayacucho is **Plaza Bolívar**, where General José de San Martín proclaimed Peru's independence. The plaza is dominated by the equestrian statue of the Liberator. Behind lies the Congress building which occupies the former site of the Universidad de San Marcos. Behind the Congress is the Mercado Municipal (or Central) and the Barrio Chino, with many *chifas* and small shops selling oriental items. Block 700 of Ucayali is pedestrianized, in 'Chinese' style. The whole area is jam-packed with people. **Museo del Congreso y de la Inquisición** ① *Plaza Bolívar, C Junín 548, near the corner of Av Abancay, T311 7777, ext 5160, www.congreso.gob.pe/museo.htm, daily 0900-1700, free, students offer to show you round for a tip; good explanations in English.* The main hall, with a splendidly carved mahogany ceiling, remains untouched. The Court of Inquisition was held here from 1584; 1829-1938 it was used by the Senate. In the basement there is a recreation *in situ* of the gruesome tortures. A description in English is available at the desk.

The 16th-century **Santo Domingo church and monastery** ① *T427 6793, monastery and tombs open Mon-Sat 0900-1230, 1500-1800; Sun and holidays morning only, US$1.65,* is on the first block of Jr Camaná. The Cloister, one of the most attractive, dates from 1603. The second Cloister is less elaborate. Beneath the sacristy are the tombs of San Martín de Porres, one of Peru's most revered saints, and Santa Rosa de Lima (see below). In 1669, Pope Clement presented the alabaster statue of Santa Rosa in front of the altar. Behind Santo Domingo is **Alameda Chabuca Granda**, named after one of Peru's greatest singers. In the evening there are free art and music shows and you can sample foods from all over Peru. A couple of blocks beyond Santo Domingo is **Casa de Osambela** or **Oquendo** ① *Conde de Superunda 298, T01-427 7987 (ask Lizardo Retes Bustamante if you can visit).* It is said that José de San Martín stayed here after proclaiming independence from Spain. The house is typical of Lima secular architecture with two patios, a broad staircase leading from the lower to the upper floor, fine balconies and an observation tower. It is now the Centro Cultural Inca Garcilaso de la Vega and headquarters of various academies. A few blocks west is **Santuario de Santa Rosa** ① *Av Tacna, 1st block, T425 1279, daily 0930-1300, 1500-1800, free to the grounds,* a small but graceful church. A pilgrimage centre; here are preserved the hermitage built by Santa Rosa herself, the house in which she was born, a section of the house in which she attended to the sick, her well, and other relics.

San Agustín ① *Jr Ica 251, T427 7548, daily 0830-1130, 1630-1900, ring for entry,* is west of the Plaza de Armas: its façade (1720) is a splendid example of churrigueresque architecture. There are carved choir stalls and effigies, and a sculpture of Death, said to have frightened its maker into an early grave. The church has been restored after the last earthquake, but the sculpture of Death is in storage. **Las Nazarenas church** ① *Av Tacna, 4th block, T423 5718, daily 0700-1200, 1600-2000,* is built around an image of Christ Crucified painted by a liberated slave in 1655. This, the most venerated image in Lima, and an oil copy of El Señor de los Milagros (Lord of Miracles), encased in a gold frame, are carried on a silver litter the whole weighing nearly a ton through the streets on 18, 19, and 28 October and again on 1 November (All Saints' Day). *El Comercio* newspaper and local pamphlets give details of times and routes.

Northeast of Plaza de Armas

From the Plaza, passing the Palacio de Gobierno on the left, straight ahead is the **Desamparados** railway station, which now houses fascinating exhibitions on Peruvian themes. **The Puente de Piedra**, behind the Palacio de Gobierno, is a Roman-style stone bridge built in 1610, crossing the Río Rímac to the district of that name. On Jr Hualgayoc is the bullring in the **Plaza de Acho**, inaugurated on 20 January 1766, with the **Museo Taurino** ① *Hualgayoc 332, T482 3360, Mon-Sat 0800-1600, US$1, students US$0.50, photography US$2.* Apart from matador's relics, the museum contains good collections of paintings and engravings, some of the latter by Goya. There are two

Lima centre

To Panamericana Norte

RIMAC

Convento & Alameda de los Descalzos
Paseo de Aguas

To Cerro San Cristóbal

Madera
Purus
Yutay

Jr Cajamarca

Museo Taurino
Plaza de Acho

Ramón Espinoza
Hector

Alameda Chabuca Granda
Jr Conde de Superunda

Santo Domingo

Hurtado
Chiclayo
Ayacucho de Mendoza
Marañón
Palma

Jr Tayacaja
Jr Angares
Santuario de Santa Rosa
Jr Cañete
Jr Chancay
Jr Huancavelica

Río Rímac
Puente de Piedra
Julian Piñeyro

Museo de Sitio Bodega y Quadra

Las Nazarenas
Av Tacna
Ica
Jr Callao
Casa Oquendo
Casa de la Gastronomía
Casa de Aliaga
Palacio de Gobierno

Parque de la Muralla

Teatro Municipal
Tacna
Jr Cailloma
Municipalidad
Plaza de Armas
Fertur
San Francisco

pte Ricardo

San Marcelo
San Agustín
Jr Camaná
Cathedral
Casa Iarava

Casa de Las Trece Monedas
Plaza Italia

Jr Rufino Torico
Jr Ica
Jr de la Unión
Teatro Segura
La Merced
Museo Banco Central
Palacio Torre Tagle
Plaza Bolívar

Jr Ancash
Av Ayacucho

Jr Nicolás de Piérola
Jr Ocoña
Jr Moquegua
Casa de la Rada
Ucayali
San Pedro
Museo del Congreso y de la Inquisición
Congress

Jesús María
Augusto N Wiese
Jr Lampa
Jr Miró Quesada
Mercado Municipal

Gran Hotel Bolívar
Plaza San Martín
Teatro Segura
Jr Puno
Jr Abancay
Jr Andahuaylas
Jr Huallaga
Jr Junín

Info Perú
Belén
Contumazá
Colmena
Parque Universitario
BARRIO CHINO
Jr Miró Quesada
Huanta

Plaza Francia
Av Uruguay
Jr Pamilea
Jr Azángaro
Jr Cusco

Av Roosevelt

To Cruz del Sur Terminal (150m)
To Plaza 2 de Mayo
To Plaza 2 de Mayo (Wilson)

Estación Central
Av España
Miguel
Jr Sandia
Jr Leticia
Av Nicolás de Piérola
Leticia
Jr Puno

Museo de Arte Italiano
M Cuadros
Ormeño
Jr Montevideo

Paseo Colón
Plaza Grau
Cavassa
Carlos Zavala
Av Grau

Museo de Arte de Lima
Parque de la Exposición
Polvos Azules
Raimondi
G Naranjo

Museo Metropolitano
Av 28 De Julio
Flores
Cromotex
León de Huánuco

Plaza Bolognesi (200m)
To Breña & Immigration
Av Petit Touars
Parque Hernán Velarde
Estadio Nacional
Movil
Julio César
Humboldt
Bauzate y Mesa
Ittsa

Metropolitano

To Parque de la Reserva, Miraflores & San Isidro
To Perúbus/Soyuz (6 blocks), Línea buses (1 1/2 blocks), Horna buses (2 1/2 blocks) San Isidro (Corpac), Miraflores & Barranco

➜ Lima maps
1 Lima, page 1202
2 Lima centre, page 1205
3 Miraflores, page 1208

N

200 metres
200 yards

Where to stay
1 Hostal España
2 Hostal Iquique
3 Hostal Roma
4 Hostal San Francisco
5 La Posada del Parque
6 Lima Sheraton
7 Maury
8 Pensión Ibarra
9 The Clifford Hotel

Restaurants
1 Acllahuasy
2 Azato
3 Bar Cordano
4 Chifa San Joy Lao
5 De César
6 Estadio Futbol Sports Bar
7 La Catedral del Pisco
8 La Choza Náutica
9 L'Eau Vive
10 Rovegno
11 Salon Capon
12 Wa Lok

Bars & clubs
13 El Rincón Cervecero
14 Piano Bar Munich

bullfight seasons: October to first week in December and during July. The **Convento de Los Descalzos** ① *on the Alameda de Los Descalzos in Rímac, T481 0441, daily 1000-1300, 1500-1800, except Tue, US$1, guided tour only, 45 mins in Spanish (worth it)*, was founded in 1592. It contains over 300 paintings of the Cuzco, Quito and Lima schools which line the four main cloisters and two ornate chapels. The chapel of El Carmen was constructed in 1730 and is notable for its baroque gold leaf altar. The museum shows the life of the Franciscan friars during colonial and early republican periods. The cellar, infirmary, pharmacy and a typical cell have been restored.

Cerro San Cristóbal ① *visited on a 1-hr minibus tour, departing from in front of Santo Domingo, Camaná y Conde Superunda, daily 1000-2100; departures every 15 mins, US$3*, dominates downtown Lima. It includes a look at the run-down Rímac district, passes the Convento de los Descalzos (see above), ascends the hill through one of the city's oldest shanties with its brightly painted houses and spends about 20 minutes at the summit, where there is a small museum and café. Excellent views on a clear day. The second half of the trip is a historical tour. **Urbanito** buses ① *T01-424 3650, www.urbanito.com.pe, 3 hours, weekends and holidays*, also run from the Plaza de Armas on a tour of central Lima, which includes Cerro San Cristóbal.

South of Plaza de Armas

The Jr de La Unión, the main shopping street, runs to the Plaza de Armas. It has been converted into a pedestrian precinct which teems with life in the evening. In the two blocks south of Jr Unión, known as Calle Belén, several shops sell souvenirs and curios. **La Merced** ① *Unión y Miró Quesada, T427 8199, 0800-1245, 1600-2000 (Sun 0700-1300, 1600-2000); monastery daily 0800-1200 and 1500-1730*, is in Plazuela de la Merced. The first Mass in Lima was said here on the site of the first church to be built. The restored façade is a fine example of colonial Baroque. Inside are some magnificent altars and the tilework on some of the walls is noteworthy. A door from the right of the nave leads into the Monastery. The cloister dates from 1546. Jr de la Unión leads to **Plaza San Martín**, which has a statue of San Martín in the centre. The plaza has been restored with colourful flower beds and is now a nice place to sit and relax. On its west side is the refurbished **Gran Hotel Bolívar** ① *Jr de la Unión 958, T619 7171, www.granhotelbolivar.com.pe*, which has a huge stained-glass dome over the entrance lobby. Its **El Bolivarcito** bar calls itself 'La Catedral del Pisco Sour'.

Museo de Arte Italiano ① *Paseo de la República 250, T423 9932, Tue-Fri 0900-1900, Sat-Sun 1100-1700, US$1*, is in a wonderful neoclassical building, given by the Italian colony to Peru on the centenary of its independence. Note the remarkable mosaic murals on the outside. It consists of a large collection of Italian and other European works of art and houses the **Instituto de Arte Contemporáneo**, which has many exhibitions.

Museo de Arte de Lima ① *Paseo Colón 125, T204 0000, www.mali.pe, Tue-Sun 1000-2000, Sat 1000-1700, US$2.15 minimum, US$4.30 suggested, children, students and over-65s US$1.40, guides US$1, bilingual guides available 1030-1600, signs in English*, is in the Palacio de la Exposición, built in 1868 in Parque de la Exposición (designed by Gustave Eiffel). There are more than 7000 exhibits, giving a chronological history of Peruvian cultures and art from the Paracas civilization up to today. It includes excellent examples of 17th- and 18th-century Cuzco paintings, a beautiful display of carved furniture, heavy silver and jewelled stirrups and also pre-Columbian pottery. The Filmoteca (movie club) is on the premises and shows films just about every night. See the local paper for details, or look in the museum itself. The **Gran Parque Cultural de Lima** ① *0800-2030*, is in the grounds. Inaugurated in January 2000, this large park has an amphitheatre, Japanese garden, food court and children's activities. Relaxing strolls through this green, peaceful and safe oasis in the centre of Lima are recommended. **Museo Metropolitano** ① *Av 28 de Julio, T433 7122, www.limacultura.pe, Tue-Sun 0900-1700, US$1.40*, has audiovisual displays and temporary exhibitions about the history of Lima, also lectures and a library

In **Parque de la Reserva** is the **Circuito Mágico del Agua** ① *block 8 of Av Arequipa and going up towards the centre, Santa Beatriz, Wed-Sun and holidays 1600-2200, US$1.50*, a display of

13 fountains, the highest reaching 80 m, enhanced by impressive light and music shows four times a night, great fun and very popular.

San Borja and Surco

Museo de la Nación ① *Javier Prado Este 2465, T476 9878, www.mcultura.gob.pe/museo-de-la-nacion-exposiciones, Tue-Sun 0900-1700, closed major public holidays, US$2.50. 50% discount with ISIC card,* in the huge **Banco de la Nación** building, is the museum for the exhibition and study of the art and history of the aboriginal races of Peru. There are good explanations in Spanish and English on Peruvian history, with ceramics, textiles and displays of many ruins in Peru. It is arranged so that you can follow the development of Peruvian precolonial history through to the time of the Incas. A visit is recommended before you go to see the archaeological sites themselves. There are displays of the tomb of the Señor de Sipán, artefacts from Batán Grande near Chiclayo (Sicán culture), reconstructions of the friezes found at Huaca La Luna and Huaca El Brujo, near Trujillo, and of Sechín and other sites. A photographic record of the events of 1980-2000, **Yuyanapaq,** is also on display. Temporary exhibitions are held in the basement, where there is also a Ministerio de Cultura bookshop. The museum has a cafetería. To get there, take a taxi from downtown Lima or Miraflores US$3.20. From Avenida Garcilaso de la Vega in downtown Lima take a combi with a "Javier Prado/Aviación" window sticker. Get off at the 21st block of Javier Prado at Avenida Aviación. From Miraflores take a bus down Avenida Arequipa to Avenida Javier Prado (27th block), then take a bus with a "Todo Javier Prado" or "Aviación" window sticker.

The **Museo de Oro del Perú** ① *Alonso de Molina 1100, Monterrico, Surco (between blocks 18 and 19 of Av Primavera), Lima 33, T345 1292, www.museoroperu.com.pe, daily 1030-1800, closed 1 Jan, 1 May, 28 Jul, 25 Dec, US$11.55, children under 11 US$5.60, multilingual audioguides,* houses an enormous collection of Peruvian gold, silver and bronze objects, together with an impressive International array of arms and military uniforms from Spanish colonial times to the present day and textiles from Peru and elsewhere. Allow plenty of time to appreciate all that is on view. It is directed by the **Fundación Miguel Mujica Gallo**. 167 of its pieces can be seen in the **Sala Museo Oro del Perú**, in Larcomar (see below).

Pueblo Libre

The original museum of anthropology and archaeology is **Museo Nacional de Antropología, Arqueología e Historia** ① *Plaza Bolívar in Pueblo Libre, not to be confused with Plaza Bolívar in the centre, T463 5070, Tue-Sat 0900-1700, Sun and holidays 0900-1600, US$4, students US$1.20, guides available for groups.* On display are ceramics of the Chimú, Nazca, Mochica and Pachacámac cultures, a new display on the Paracas culture (2013), various Inca curiosities and works of art, and interesting textiles. **Museo Nacional de Historia** ① *T463 2009, Tue-Sat 0900-1700, Sun and holidays 0900-1600, US$3.65,* in a mansion occupied by San Martín (1821-1822) and Bolívar (1823-1826) is next door. It exhibits colonial and early republican paintings, manuscripts and uniforms. Take any public transport on Avenida Brasil with a window sticker saying "Todo Brasil." Get off at the 21st block called Avenida Vivanco. Walk about five blocks down Vivanco. The museum will be on your left. From Miraflores take bus SM 18 Carabayllo-Chorrillos, marked "Bolívar, Arequipa, Larcomar", get out at block 8 of Bolívar by the Hospital Santa Rosa, and walk down Avenida San Martín five blocks until you see the 'blue line'; turn left. The 'blue line' marked on the pavement, very faded, links the Museo Nacional de Antropología, Arqueología e I Iistoria to the Museo Larco (see below), 15 minutes' walk. Taxi from downtown US$3; from Miraflores US$4.

Museo Larco de Lima ① *Av Bolívar 1515, T461 1312, www.museolarco.org, 0900-2200, 0900-1800 24 Dec-1 Jan; texts in Spanish, English and French, US$10.55 (half price for students, seniors US$8.75), disabled access, photography not permitted.* Located in an 18th-century mansion, itself built on a seventh-century pre-Columbian pyramid, this museum has a collection which gives an excellent overview on the development of Peruvian cultures through their pottery. It has the world's largest collection of Moche, Sicán and Chimú pieces. There is a Gold and Silver of

Ancient Peru exhibition, a magnificent textile collection and a fascinating erotica section. Don't miss the storeroom with its vast array of pottery, unlike anything you'll see elsewhere. There is a library and computer room for your own research and a good café open during museum hours, see below. It is surrounded by beautiful gardens, has a new entrance and park outside. Take any bus to the 15th block of Avenida Brasil. Then take a bus down Avendia Bolívar. From Miraflores, take the SM 18 Carabayllo-Chorrillos, see above, to block 15 of Bolívar. Taxi from downtown, Miraflores or San Isidro, 15 minutes, US$4. Follow the 'blue line' marked on the pavement to the Museo Nacional de Antropología, Arqueología e Historia (see above), 15 minutes' walk.

San Isidro

To the east of Avenida La República, down Calle Pancho Fierro, is **El Olivar**, an olive grove planted by the first Spaniards which has been turned into a park. Some 32 species of birds have been recorded there. Between San Isidro and Miraflores, is **Huallamarca** ① *C Nicolás de Rivera 201 and Av Rosario, T222 4124, 0900-1700, closed Mon, US$1.75. Take bus 1 from Av Tacna, or*

minibus 13 or 73 to Choquechaca, then walk. An adobe pyramid of the Maranga (Lima) culture, it dates from about AD 100-500, but has later Wari and Inca remains. There is a small site museum. There are many good hotels and restaurants in San Isidro; see Where to stay, page 1212 and Restaurants, page 1217.

Miraflores

Avenida Arequipa continues to the coast, to the most important suburb of Lima (see Where to stay and Youth hostels, page 1213; and Restaurants, page 1217). Together with San Isidro and Barranco this is the social centre of Lima.

Parque Kennedy, the Parque Central de Miraflores is located between Avenida Larco and Avenida Mcal Oscar Benavides (locally known as Avenida Diagonal). This extremely well-kept park has a small open-air theatre with performances Thursday-Sunday and an arts and crafts market most evenings of the week. The house of the author **Ricardo Palma** ⓘ *Gral Suárez 189, T445 5836, http://ricardopalma.miraflores.gob.pe, Mon-Fri 0915-1245, 1430-1700, US$2.20,*

100 metres

100 yards

Where to stay 🛏
1 Albergue Turístico Juvenil Internacional *D3*
2 Albergue Verde *D2*
3 Alemán *A3*
4 Antigua Miraflores *B1*
5 Belmond Miraflores Park *D1*
6 Blue House *C1*
7 Casa Andina *D2*
8 Casa Andina Private Collection *C3*
9 Casa Andina Select *C2*
10 Casa de Baraybar *A1*
11 Casa del Mochilero *A2*
12 Casa Rodas *B3*
13 Condor's House *A1*
14 El Carmelo *B1*
15 Explorer's House *A1*
16 Flying Dog *B2 , C2*
17 Friend's House *C1*
18 Hitchhikers B&B Backpackers *B1*
19 Hostal El Patio *C2*
20 HosteLima *A3*
21 Inka Frog *A2*
22 José Antonio *C1*
23 JW Marriott *D1*
24 La Casa Nostra *D2*
25 La Castellana *C2*
26 Loki Backpackers *A1*
27 Pariwana *B3*
28 Pirwa *B3*
29 Pirwa B&B *A3*
30 San Antonio Abad *D3*
31 Señorial *D1*
32 Sipán *D2*
33 Sonesta Posadas del Inca & Café La Máquina *C2*
34 The Lighthouse *A2*

Restaurants 🍴
1 Ache & Amaz *D2*
2 Alfresco *B1*
3 AlmaZen *B2*
4 Café Café *B2*
5 Café de la Paz *D2, C2*
6 Café Tarata *C2*
7 Central *D1*
8 C'est si bon *A2*
9 Chef's Café *C2*
10 Chifa Internacional *D2*
11 El Huarike *B3*
12 El Kapallaq *B3*
13 El Parquetito *B2*
14 El Rincón Gaucho *D1*
15 Fiesta Gourmet *D2*
16 Govinda *D2*
17 Haiti *B3*
18 IK *A2*
19 La Gloria *B3*
20 La Lucha *B2*
21 La Preferida *D3*
22 Las Brujas de Cachiche *B1*
23 Las Tejas *C2*
24 La Tiendecita Blanca *B3*
25 La Trattoria *C3*
26 Lobo del Mar – Octavio Otani *C1*
27 Madre Natura *A3*
28 Mama Olla *C2*
29 Manifiesto *B2*
30 Panchita *B3*
31 Pizza Street *B2*
32 Punto Azul *C2*
33 Rafael *C1*
34 San Antonio *A3, D2*
35 Saqra *C2*
36 Sí Señor *B1*

Bars & clubs 🍸
37 Media Naranja *B2*
38 Murphy's *C3*
39 The Old Pub *B2*
40 Treff Pub Alemán *C2*

🚇 Metropolitano

➡ **Lima maps**
1 Lima, page 1202
2 Lima centre, page 1205
3 **Miraflores, page 1208**

includes video and guided tour, is now a museum explaining the author's life and work. At the end of Avenida Larco and running along the Malecón de la Reserva is the renovated **Parque Salazar** and the modern shopping centre called **Centro Comercial Larcomar**. Here you will find expensive shops, hip cafés and discos and a wide range of restaurants, all with a beautiful ocean view. The 12-screen cinema is one of the best in Lima and even has a 'cine-bar' in the 12th theatre. Don't forget to check out the Cosmic Bowling Alley with its black lights and fluorescent balls. A few hundred metres to the north is the famous **Parque del Amor** where on just about any night you'll see at least one wedding party taking photos of the newly weds.

Museo Arqueológico Amano ① *Retiro 160, 11th block of Av Angamos Oeste, Miraflores), T441 2909, www.fundacionmuseoamano.org.pe, open by appointment only Mon-Fri 1500-1630, donations (photography prohibited).* The collection is of artefacts from the Chancay, Chimú and Nazca periods, owned by the late Mr Yoshitaro Amano. It has one of the most complete exhibits of Chancay weaving, and is particularly interesting for pottery and pre-Columbian textiles, all superbly displayed and lit. Take a bus or colectivo to the corner of Avenida Arequipa y Avenida Angamos and another one to the 11th block of Avenida Angamos Oeste. Taxi from downtown US$3.20; from Parque Kennedy US$2.25.

Poli Museum ① *Almte Cochrane 466, T422 2437, tours cost US$15 per person irrespective of the size of the group, allow 2 hrs, call in advance to arrange tours.* This is one of the best private collections of colonial and pre-Columbian artefacts in Peru, including material from Sipán. At General Borgoño, eighth block s/n, turn off Avenida Arequipa at 45th block, is **Huaca Pucllana** ① *T01-445 8695, www.miraflodesperu.com/huacapucllana/, US$4.25, students US$2, includes 45-min tour in Spanish or English, 0900-1600, closed Tue,* a pre-Inca site which is under excavation. Originally a Lima culture temple to the goddesses of sea and moon (AD 200-700), it became a Wari burial site (AD 700-900) before being abandoned. Later Ychsma occupation (AD 1000-1470) and subsequent looting followed. It has a small site museum with some objects from the site itself, a garden of traditional plants and animals and a souvenir shop (see Restaurants, below).

Barranco

This suburb further south was already a seaside resort by the end of the 17th century. The attractive public library, formerly the town hall, stands on the plaza. It contains the helpful **municipal tourist office** ① *T719 2046.* Nearby is the interesting *bajada,* a steep path leading down to the beach. The **Puente de los Suspiros** (Bridge of Sighs) crosses the *bajada* to the earthquake-damaged La Ermita church (only the façade has been restored) and leads towards the Malecón, with fine views of the bay. Barranco is quiet by day but comes alive at night (see Restaurants and Bars sections). The 45-minute walk from Miraflores to Barranco along the Malecón is nice in summer. There are many old mansions in the district, in a variety of styles. Several are being renovated, particularly on Calle Cajamarca and around San Francisco church. The main artistic focus is contemporary; a number of artists have their workshops here and there are several chic galleries (see also **Hotel B**, below). **Museo de Arte Contemporáneo de Lima (MAC Lima)** ① *Av Miguel Grau beside the municipal stadium, near Miraflores, T652 5100, www.mac-lima.org.pe, US$2.25, Tue-Sun 1000-1700, with guided tour,* has permanent Latin American and European collections and holds temporary exhibitions. **MATE (Asociación Mario Testino)** ① *Av Pedro de Osma 409, T251 7755, www.mate.pe, US$5.55, Tue-Sat 1100-2000, Sun 1100-1800, with audio tour (no other explanations),* is the world-renowned fashion photographer's vision of modern art, with a shop and excellent café/restaurant. Next door, by contrast, and equally important is the **Museo de Arte Colonial Pedro de Osma** ① *Av Pedro de Osma 423, T467 0141, www.museopedrodeosma.org, Tue-Sun 1000-1800, US$6.75, students half price, guided tours in English or Spanish.* A private collection of colonial art of the Cuzco, Ayacucho and Arequipa schools.

Lima beaches

In summer (December-April) the city's beaches get very crowded at weekends and lots of activities are organized. Even though the water of the whole bay has been declared unsuitable for swimming, Limeños see the beach more as part of their culture than as a health risk. Do not camp on the beaches as robbery is a serious threat and, for the same reason, take care on the walkways down. Don't take any belongings with you to the beach, only what is really necessary.

The *Circuito de Playas*, which begins with Playa Arica (30 km from Lima) and ends with San Bartolo (45 km from Lima), has many great beaches for all tastes. The beaches of **Miraflores**, **Barranco** and **Chorrillos** are very popular and sand and sea get dirty. It's much better to take a safe taxi 40 km south to **Punta Rocas**, **Señoritas** or **Silencio**. **Punta Hermosa** has frequent surfing and volleyball tournaments. If you really want the height of fashion head to **Asia**, Km 92-104, some 20 beaches with boutiques, hotels, restaurants and condos.

Pachacámac

① *T430 0168, http://pachacamac.cultura.pe, Tue-Sat 0900-1700, Sun 0900-1600; closed public holidays except by appointment. US$3.50, includes the museum, students US$1.75, guide US$7.*
When the Spaniards arrived, Pachacámac in the Lurín valley was the largest city and ceremonial centre on the coast. A wooden statue of the creator-god, after whom the site is named, is in the site museum. Hernando Pizarro was sent here by his brother in 1533 in search of gold for Inca emperor Atahualpa's ransom. In their fruitless quest, the Spaniards destroyed images and killed the priests. The ruins encircle the top of a low hill, whose crest was crowned with a **Temple of the Sun**, now partially restored. Slightly apart is the reconstructed **House of the Mamaconas**, where the 'chosen women' spun fine cloth for the Inca and his court. An impression of the scale of the site can be gained from the top of the Temple of the Sun, or from walking or driving the 3 km circuit, which is covered by an unmade road for cars and tour buses. The site is large and it is expected that tourists will be visiting by vehicle. There are six parking areas.

ⓔ Lima listings

For hotel and restaurant price codes, and other relevant information, see Essentials.

● Where to stay

Central Lima is not as safe at night as the more upmarket areas of Miraflores, San Isidro and Barranco. If you are only staying a short time and want to see the main sites, it is convenient, but do take care. San Isidro is the poshest district while Miraflores has a good mix of places to stay, great ocean views, bookstores, restaurants and cinemas. From here you can then commute to the centre by bus (45 mins minimum) or by taxi (30 mins minimum). Barranco is a little further out. All hotels in the upper price brackets charge 18% state tax and service on top of prices. In hotels foreigners pay no tax and the amount of service charge is up to the hotel. Neither is included in the prices below, unless otherwise stated. All those listed below have received good recommendations.

Lima has several international, high-class chain hotels: JW Marriott, www.marriott.com; Lima Sheraton, www.sheraton.com.pe; Sofitel Royal Park, www.sofitel.com; Swissôtel Lima, www.lima.swissotel.com; Westin, www.starwoodhotels.com. All are recommended.

There are dozens of hostels offering dormitory accommodation and charging US$10-17 pp, usually including a simple breakfast, hot water in shared bathrooms, kitchen facilities, bar and living room. Double rooms with private bathrooms are also offered, which aren't much more expensive, starting at about US$30. Some hostels are linked to travel agents or adventure tour companies.

Lima *p1201, maps p1202 and p1205*
Near the airport
$$$$ Ramada Costa del Sol, Av Elmer Faucett s/n, T711 2000, www.ramada.com. Within the airport perimeter. Offers day rates as well as overnights if you can't get into the city. Good

service, buffet breakfast, but high-priced because of lack of competition and expensive extras.

$$ Hostal Residencial Víctor, Manuel Mattos 325, Urb San Amadeo de Garagay, Lima 31, T01-569 4662, www.hostalvictor.com. 5 mins from the airport by taxi, or phone or email in advance for free pick-up, large comfortable rooms, hot water, 10% discount for Footprint book owners, American breakfast (or packed breakfast for early departure), evening meals can be ordered locally, 2 malls with restaurants, shops, cinemas, etc nearby, very helpful.

$$-$ Pay Purix, Av Japón (formerly Bertello Bolatti), Mz F, Lote 5, Urb Los Jazmines, 1a Etapa, Callao, T484 9118, www.paypurix.com. 3 mins from airport, can arrange pick-up (taxi US$6, US$2 from outside airport). Hostel with doubles and dorms, convenient, washing machine, English spoken, CDs, DVDs, games and use of kitchen.

Central Lima

$$$ The Clifford Hotel, Parque Hernán Velarde 27, near 1st block of Av Petit Thouars, Sta Beatriz, T433 4249, www.thecliffordhotel.com. pe. Nicely converted, republican town house in a quiet and leafy park. Rooms and suites, has a bar, café and conference room.

$$$ Maury, Jr Ucayali 201, T428 8188, hotmaury@rcp.net.pe. The most luxurious hotel in the historical centre, secure. The bar is reputed to be the home of the first-ever pisco sour (this is, of course, disputed!).

$$ La Posada del Parque, Parque Hernán Velarde 60, near 1st block of Av Petit Thouars, Santa Beatriz, between centre and San Isidro, T433 2412, www.incacountry.com. A charmingly refurbished old house with a collection of fine handicrafts, in a safe area, comfortable rooms, breakfast 0800-0930, airport transfer 24 hrs for US$18 for 1-3 passengers (US$8 pp for larger groups), no credit cards, cash only. Always check the website for special offers and gifts. The owners speak good English. Excellent value. Gay friendly. Has an agreement with the nearby Lawn Tennis Club (Arenales 200 block) for guests to eat at the good-value **Set Point** restaurant and use the gym.

$$-$ Hostal España, Jr Azángaro 105, T427 9196, www.hotelespanaperu.com. A long-standing travellers' haunt, rooms or dormitories,

fine old building, motorcycle parking, laundry service, roof garden, good café, can be very busy.

$$-$ Hostal Iquique, Jr Iquique 758, Breña (discount for SAE members), T433 4724, www.hostal-iquique-lima.com. Rooms on top floor at the back are best, from singles with shared bath to triples with private bath, well-kept if a bit noisy and draughty, use of kitchen, warm water, safe, airport pick up.

$ Hostal Roma, Jr Ica 326, T427 7576, www.hostalroma.8m.com. Over 35 years in the business, rooms sleep 1-4, private or shared bath, hot water, often full, luggage deposit and safe box, motorcycle parking, airport transfers (Roma Tours arranges city tours – but shop around if you want to, flight reservations). Next door is **Café Carrara**.

$ Hostal San Francisco, Jr Azángaro 127, T426 2735. Dormitories with and without bathrooms, safe, Italian/Peruvian owners, good service, café.

$ Pensión Ibarra, Av Tacna 359, 1402 y 1502, (elevator to 14th/15th floors doesn't run all hours), no sign, T427 8603/1035, pensionibarra@gmail.com. Breakfast US$4, discount for longer stay, basic, noisy, use of kitchen, balcony with views of the city, helpful owners (2 sisters), hot water, full board available (good small café almost next door). Reserve in advance; taxis can't stop outside so book airport pick-up (US$18.50) for safe arrival.

San Isidro *p1208, map p1202*

$$$$ Country Club, Los Eucaliptos 590, T611 9000, www.hotelcountry.com. Excellent, fine service, luxurious rooms, good bar and restaurant, classically stylish with a fine art collection.

$$$$ Libertador Hotels Peru, Los Eucaliptos 550, T518 6300, www.libertador.com.pe. Overlooking the golf course, full facilities for the business traveller, large comfortable rooms in this relatively small hotel, fine service, good restaurant.

$$$$ Sonesta El Olivar, Pancho Fierro 194, T712 6000, www.sonesta.com/Lima. Excellent, one of the top 5-star hotels in Lima overlooking El Olivar park, modern, good restaurant and bar, terrace, gym, swimming pool, quiet, very attentive, popular.

$$$ Garden, Rivera Navarrete 450, T200 9800, www.gardenhotel.com.pe. Good beds, small restaurant, ideal for business visitors, convenient, good value.

$$ Chez Elizabeth, Av del Parque Norte 265, San Isidro, T9980 07557, http://chezelizabeth. typepad.fr. Family house in residential area 7 mins' walk from Cruz del Sur bus station. Shared or private bathrooms, TV room, laundry, airport transfers.

$ Albergue Juvenil Malka, Los Lirios 165 (near 4th block of Av Javier Prado Este), San Isidro, T442 0162, www.youthhostelperu.com. Dormitory style, 4-8 beds per room, also private doubles (**$$**), English spoken, laundry, climbing wall, nice café, airport transfer.

San Miguel and Magdalena del Mar
South of San Isidro, on the seaward side of Pueblo Libre.

$$ Mami Panchita, Av Federico Gallessi 198 (ex-Av San Miguel), San Miguel, T263 7203, www.mamipanchita.com. Dutch-Peruvian owned, English, Dutch and Spanish spoken, includes breakfast and welcome drink, comfortable rooms with bath, hot water, living room and bar, patio, email service, book exchange, airport transfers, 15 mins from airport, 15 mins from Miraflores, 20 mins from historical centre. Frequently recommended.

$ Tambopacaya, Jr Manco Capac 212 (block 31 of Av Brasil), Magdalena del Mar, T261 6122, www.tambopacaya.com. All rooms and dorms have private bath, hot water, use of kitchen, laundry, guided tours, airport transfers, convenient for airport and centre.

Miraflores p1209, map p1208
$$$$ Casa Andina Private Collection, Av La Paz 463, T213 4300, www.casa-andina.com. Top of the range hotel in this recommended Peruvian chain (see below), modern, well-appointed large rooms with safe, cable TV, Wi-Fi, good bathrooms. Fine food in **Alma** restaurant and good value café, **Sama**, first class service, bar, pool and gym.

$$$$ Belmond Miraflores Park, Av Malecón de la Reserva 1035, T610 4000, www.miraflores park.com. An Orient Express hotel, excellent service and facilities, beautiful views over the ocean, top class. Rooftop, open-air, heated pool and spa which looks out over the ocean, open to the public when you buy a spa treatment.

$$$$ Sonesta Posadas del Inca, Alcanfores 329, T241 7688, www.sonesta.com/Miraflores/. Part of renowned chain of hotels, convenient location, cable TV, a/c, restaurant.

$ $$ Alemán, Arequipa 4704, T445 6999, www.hotelaleman.com.pe. No sign, comfortable, quiet, garden, excellent breakfast, smiling staff.

$$$ Antigua Miraflores, Av Grau 350 at C Francia, T201 2060, www.antiguamiraflores. com. A small, elegant hotel in a quiet but central location, excellent service, tastefully furnished and decorated, gym, good restaurant. Recommended.

$$$ Casa Andina, Av 28 de Julio 1088, T241 4050, www.casa-andina.com. Also at Av Petit Thouars 5444, T447 0263, in Miraflores. These Classic hotels in this chain have similar facilities and decor. Very neat, with many useful touches, comfortable beds, fridge, safe, laundry service, buffet breakfast, other meals available. Check website for discounts and for the more upmarket **Casa Andina Select** at Schell 452, T416 7500 (**$$$$-$$$**), with disabled facilities.

$$$ Casa de Baraybar, Toribio Pacheco 216, T652 2262, www.casadebaraybar.com. 1 block from the ocean, extra long beds, a/c or fan, colourful decor, high ceilings, 24-hr room service, laundry, airport transfers free for stays of 3 nights. Bilingual staff. Recommended.

$$$ La Castellana, Grimaldo del Solar 222, T444 4662, www.castellanahotel.com. Pleasant, good value, nice garden, safe, expensive restaurant, laundry, English spoken.

$$$ José Antonio, 28 de Julio 398 y C Colón, T445 7743, www.hotelesjoseantonio.com. Good in all respects, including the restaurant, large modern rooms, jacuzzis, swimming pool, business facilities, helpful staff speak some English.

$$$ San Antonio Abad, Ramón Ribeyro 301, T447 6766, www.hotelsanantonioabad.com. Secure, quiet, helpful, tasty breakfasts, 1 free airport transfer with reservation, justifiably popular, good value.

$$$ Señorial, José González 567, T445 0139, www.senorial.com. 100 rooms, with restaurant, room service, comfortable, nice garden, parking, good services.

$$$-$$ Hostal El Patio, Diez Canseco 341, T444 2107, www.hostalelpatio.net. Very nice suites and rooms, comfortable, English and

French spoken, convenient, *comedor*, gay friendly. Very popular, reservations are essential. **$$$-$$ Inka Frog**, Gral Iglesias 271, T445 8979, www.inkafrog.com. Self-styled "Exclusive B&B", comfortable, nice decor, lounge with huge TV, rooftop terrace, good value.

$$ Casa Rodas, Av Petit Thouars 4712, T447 5761, and Tarapacá 250, T242 4872, www.casarodas.com. Both houses have rooms for 2, 3 or 4, good beds (**$$$** with private bath), hot water, helpful staff.

$$ El Carmelo, Bolognesi 749, T446 0575, www.hostalelcarmelo.com.pe. Great location a couple of blocks from the Parque del Amor, small restaurant downstairs serving *criolla* food and *ceviche*, good value, comfortable, breakfast extra.

$$ La Casa Nostra, Av Grimaldo del Solar 265, T241 1718. Variety of rooms (from singles to quad), all with private bath, good service, convenient, safe, money exchange, laundry, tourist information. Popular.

$$ Sipán, Paseo de la República 6171, T241 3758, www.hotelsipan.com. Very pleasant, on the edge of a residential area next to the Vía Expresa (which can be heard from front rooms). Economical meals available in restaurant, 24-hr room service, security box, secure parking. Airport transfers available.

$$-$ Albergue Turístico Juvenil Internacional, Av Casimiro Ulloa 328, San Antonio, T446 5488, www.limahostell.com.pe. Dormitory accommodation or a double private room, basic cafeteria, travel information, laundry facilities, swimming pool often empty, extra charge for breakfast, safe, situated in a nice villa; 20 mins' walk from the beach. Bus No 2 or colectivos pass Av Benavides to the centre.

$$-$ Condor's House, Martín Napanga 137, T446 7267, www.condorshouse.com. Award-winning, quiet hostel, two categories of dorm rooms with lockers, good bathrooms, also doubles, good meeting place, TV room with films, book exchange, *parrillada* prepared once a week, bar. Helpful staff.

$$-$ Explorer's House, Av Alfredo León 158, by 10th block of Av José Pardo, T241 5002, http://explorershouselima.com. No sign, but plenty of indications of the house number, dorm with shared bath, or double rooms with

bath, hot water, laundry service, Spanish classes, English spoken, very welcoming.

$$-$ Flying Dog, Diez Canseco 117, T212 7145, www.flyingdogperu.com. Also at Lima 457 and Olaya 280, all with dorms, doubles, triples, quads. All on or near Parque Kennedy, with kitchen, lockers, but all with different features. They have others in Cuzco, Iquitos and Arequipa.

$$-$ HosteLima, Cnel Inclán 399, T242 7034, www.hostelima.com. Private double rooms and brightly-painted dorms, close to Parque Kennedy, helpful staff, safe, bar/restaurant and snack shop, movie room, Play Station 3, travel information.

$$-$ The Lighthouse, Cesareo Chacaltana 162, T446 8397, www.thelighthouseperu.com. Near Plaza Morales Barros, British/Peruvian run, relaxed, small dorm or private rooms with private or shared bath. Good services, small indoor patio.

$$-$ Loki Backpackers, José Galvez 576, T651 2966, www.lokihostel.com. In a quiet area, the capital's sister to the party hostel of the same name in Cuzco, doubles or dorms, good showers, cooked breakfast extra, Fri barbecues, lockers, airport transfers.

$$-$ Pariwana, Av Larco 189, T242 4350, www.pariwana-hostel.com. Party hostel with doubles and dorms in the heart of Miraflores, individual lockers with power outlets so you can leave your gadgets charging in a safe place. Always lots going on here.

$$-$ Pirwa, González Prada 179, T444 1266 and Coronel Inclán 494 (B&B), T242 4059, www.pirwahostelsperu.com. Members of a chain of hostels in Peru (Cuzco, Arequipa, Puno, Nazca); González Prada is a bit cheaper but both have choice of dorms and double rooms, lockers, transfers arranged, bike rental.

$ Albergue Verde, Grimaldo del Solar 459, T445 3816, www.albergueverde.com. Nice small hostal, comfortable beds, friendly owner, Arturo Palmer, airport and bus terminal pick up.

$ Blue House, José González 475, T445 0476, www.bluehouse.com.pe. A true backpacker hostel, most rooms with bath including a double, basic but good value for the location, terraza with parrilla, films to watch.

$ Casa del Mochilero, Cesareo Chacaltana 130A, T444 9089, pilaryv@hotmail.com (casa-del-mochilero on Facebook). Ask for Pilar or Juan, dorms or double room on terrace, all with shared bath, breakfast and internet extra, hot water, lots of information.

$ Friend's House, José González 427, T446 3521, FriendsHouseLimaPeru on Facebook. Very popular, reserve in advance. Near Larcomar shopping centre, plenty of good information and help, family atmosphere. Highly recommended. They have another branch at Jr Manco Cápac 368, T446 6248, with dormitory accommodation with shared bath and hot water. Neither branch is signed, except on the bell at No 427.

$ Hitchhikers B&B Backpackers, Bolognesi 400, T242 3008, www.hhikersperu.com. Located close to the ocean, mixture of dorms (1 girl-only) and private rooms with shared or private bath (**$$**), nice patio, plenty of parking, airport transfers.

Barranco *p1210*

$$$$ B, San Martín 301, T700 5106, www.hotelb.pe. Boutique hotel in an early 20th-century mansion. Beautifully redesigned as a luxury hotel in theoriginal building and a contemporary wing, eclectic design features and a large collection of mostly modern art, next to Lucía de la Puente gallery and convenient for others, blog and Facebook give cultural recommendations, highly regarded Mediterranean/Peruvian restaurant, cocktail bar, plunge pool, excellent service. In Relais y Châteaux group.

$$-$ Barranco's Backpackers Inn, Mcal Castilla 260, T247 1326, www.barranco backpackersperu.com. Ocean view, colourful rooms, all en suite, shared and private rooms, tourist information.

$$-$ Domeyer, C Domeyer 296, T247 1413, www.domeyerhostel.net. Private or shared rooms sleeping 1-3 people in a historic house. Hot water 24 hrs, laundry service, secure, gay friendly.

$$-$ Safe in Lima, Alfredo Silva 150, T252 7330, www.safeinlima.com. Quiet, Belgian-run hostal with family atmosphere, single, double and triple rooms, very helpful, airport pick-up US$28, good value, reserve in advance, lots of information for travellers.

$ The Point, Malecón Junín 300, T247 7997, www.thepointhostels.com. Rooms range from doubles to large dormitories, all with shared

bath, very popular with backpackers (book in advance at weekends), laundry, gay friendly, restaurant, bar, party atmosphere most of the time, but also space for relaxing, weekly barbecues, travel centre.

⑦ Restaurants

18% state tax and 10% service will be added to your bill in middle- and upper-class restaurants. Chinese is often the cheapest at around US$5 including a drink.

Lima *p1201, map p1205*
Central Lima

$$$ Wa Lok, Jr Paruro 864 and 878, Barrio Chino, T427 2656. Good dim sum, cakes and fortune cookies (when you pay the bill). English spoken, very friendly. Also at Av Angamos Oeste 700, Miraflores, T447 1329.

$$ Chifa San Joy Lao, Ucayali 779. A *chifa* with a good reputation, one of several on the pedestrianized part of the Barrio Chino.

$$ L'Eau Vive, Ucayali 370, also opposite the Torre Tagle Palace, T427 5612. Mon-Sat, 1230-1500 and 1930-2130. Run by nuns, fixed-price lunch menu, Peruvian-style in interior dining room, or à la carte in either of dining rooms that open on to patio, excellent, profits go to the poor, Ave María is sung nightly at 2100.

$$ Salon Capon, Jr Paruro 819. Good dim sum, at this recommended *chifa*. Also has a branch at Larcomar shopping centre, which is **$$**, elegant and equally recommended.

$$-$ Bar Cordano, Ancash 202 y Carabaya (in Calles El Rastro y Pescadería zone). Historic tavern serving Peruvian food and drinks, great atmosphere, favoured by politicians.

$$-$ De César, Ancash 300, T428 8740. Open 0700-2300. Old-fashioned atmosphere, apart from the 3 TVs, breakfasts, snacks, seafood, meat dishes, pastas, pizza, juices, coffees and teas. Good food.

$$-$ Roveqno, Arenales 456 (near block 3 of Arequipa), T424 8465. Italian and Peruvian dishes, home-made pasta, also serves snacks and sandwiches and has a bakery. Good value.

Acllahuasy, Jr Ancash 400. Around the corner from Hostal España. Daily 0700-2300. Good Peruvian dishes.

Lima's new gastronomy

Lima attracts terms such "gastronomic capital of South America", which is reflected in the fact that the **Mistura** festival in September 2013 attracted 500,000 visitors. There are several restaurants that are championed as the height of culinary excellence. They are often priced beyond the average traveller's budget, but a meal at one of these could be the ideal way to celebrate a special occasion. Most serve à la carte and a tasting menu. At the heart of much of today's Peruvian gastronomy are traditional ingredients, from the coast, the Andes and the jungle. The star chefs all recognize the debt they owe to the cooks of the different regions. Their skill is in combining the local heritage with the flavours and techniques that they have learnt elsewhere, without overwhelming what is truly Peruvian.

Gastón Acurio is usually credited with being the forerunner of the evolution of Peruvian cuisine. He is also recognized for his community work. With **Astrid y Gastón Casa Moreyra** (Av Paz Soldán 290, San Isidro, www.astridygaston.com), Acurio and his wife Astrid have moved their flagship restaurant from Miraflores to this historic house in San Isidro. It has been completely remodelled and opened in 2014. Other ventures include *ceviche* at **La Mar** (Av Lar 770, Miraflores, T421 3365, www.lamarcebicheria.com), *anticuchos* at **Panchita** (Av 2 de Mayo 298, Miraflores, T242 5957, see Facebook page) and his chain of **T'anta** cafés, eg behind the Municipalidad in the city centre, at Pancho Fierro 115 in San Isidro and in Larcomar.

Central (Santa Isabel 376, Miraflores, T446 9301, www.centralrestaurante.com.pe) presents Virgilio Martínez' award-winning, sophisticated recipes fusing Peruvian ingredients and molecular cuisine.

Manifiesto (Independencia 130, Miraflores, T249 5533, www.manifiesto. pe) is billed as "Tacna meets Italy", bringing together the birthplace and family roots of chef Giacomo Bocchio.

Rafael Osterling has two restaurants in the city: **Rafael** (San Martín 300, Miraflores, T242 4149, www.rafaelosterling.com), celebrated for its classic Peruvian dishes incorporating flavours from around the globe, especially the Mediterranean, and **El Mercado** (H Unanue 203, Miraflores, T221 1322), which concentrates on seafood, reflecting all the influences on Peruvian cooking.

At **IK** (Elias Aguirre 179, Miraflores, T652 1692, reservas@ivankisic.pe, see Facebook page), molecular gastronomy meets Peruvian ingredients at the late Ivan Kisic's restaurant.

Lima 27 (Santa Lucía 295 – no sign, T221 5822, www.lima27.com) is a modern restaurant behind whose black exterior you will find contemporary Peruvian cuisine. It's in the same group as **Alfresco** (Malecón Balta 790, T242 8960, www.restaurantealfresco.com), **Cala on Costa Verde** (http://calarestaurante.com), and a new sandwich bar, **Manduca**, in Jockey Plaza.

Pedro Miguel Schiaffino's **Malabar** (Camino Real 101, San Isidro, T440 5200, http://malabar.com.pe) takes the Amazon and its produce as the starting point for its dishes, as does Schiaffino's **Amaz** (Av La Paz 1079, Miraflores, T221 9393). This eatery is in a group of four places under the Hilton Hotel. Also here is **Ache** (Av La Paz 1055, T221 9315, achecocinanikkei on Facebook) which specializes in Japanese fusion cuisine.

La Picantería (Moreno 388 y González Prada, Surquillo, T241 6676, www.picanteria sdelperu.com) serves excellent seafood, first-class ceviche, has a fish-of-the-day lunch menu and a good bar.

At **AlmaZen** (Federico Recavarrén 298 y Galvez, T243 0474) you will find one of the best organic slow-food restaurants in Latin America.

Beyond Lima there are many innovative restaurants in Cuzco and Arequipa and don't forget that the regional cooking that provided inspiration for Peru's growing international fame is still very much alive and well, often in much more modest surroundings than the fine dining settings of the capital. One such place that has moved to the capital is **Fiesta Gourmet** (Av Reducto 1278, T242 9009, www.restaurantfiestagourmet.com), which specializes in food from Chiclayo and the north coast: superb food in fancy surroundings.

La Catedral del Pisco, Jr de la Unión 1100 esq Av Uruguay 114, T330 0079, lacatedraldelpisco@hotmail.com. Open 0800-2200. *Comida criolla*, drinks, free Peruvian coffee (excellent) or pisco sour for Footprint owners, live music at night, Wi-Fi.

Breña
$$ La Choza Náutica, Jr Breña 204 and 211 behind Plaza Bolognesi, T423 8087, www.chozanautica.com. Good *ceviche* and friendly service; has 3 other branches.
$ Azato, Av Arica 298, 3 blocks from Plaza Bolognesi, T423 0278. Excellent and cheap Peruvian dishes.

Pueblo Libre *p1207*
$$$-$$ Café del Museo, at the Museo Larco, Av Bolívar 1515, T462 4757. Daily 0900-2200, seating inside and on the terrace. Specially designed interior, selection of salads, fine Peruvian dishes, pastas and seafood, a tapas bar of traditional Peruvian foods, as well as snacks, desserts and cocktails. Highly regarded.
$$ $ Antigua Taberna Queirolo, Av San Martín 1090, 1 block from Plaza Bolívar, T460 0441, http://antiguatabernaqueirolo.com. Atmospheric old bar with glass-fronted shelves of bottles, marble bar and old photos, owns bodega next door. Serves simple lunches, sandwiches and snacks, good for wine, does not serve dinner.

San Isidro *p1208*
$$$ Antica Pizzería, Av Dos de Mayo 732, T222 8437. Very popular, great ambience, excellent food, Italian owner. Also in Barranco at Alfonso Ugarte 242, www.anticapizzeria.com.pe.
$$$ Chifa Titi, Av Javier Prado Este 1212, Corpac, 1224 8189, www.chifatiti.com. Regarded by many as the best Chinese restaurant in Lima with over 60 years in operation.
$$$-$$ Segundo Muelle, Av Conquistadores 490, T717 9998, www.segundomuelle.com. *Ceviches* and other very good seafood dishes, including Japanese, popular.
$$ Chez Philippe, Av 2 de Mayo 748, T222 4953, www.chez-philippe.net. Pizza, pasta and crêpes, wood oven, rustic decor (same owners as Pizza B&B in Huaraz) and a huge choice of beers.

$$ Como Agua para Chocolate, Pancho Fierro 108, T222 0297. Dutch-Mexican owned restaurant, specializing in Mexican food as the name suggests, also has a very amusing Dutch night once a month. SAE members get a discount.
Havanna, Miguel Dasso 165, www.havanna.pe. Branch of the Argentine coffee and *alfajores* chain, others in the city include **Larcomar**.
News Café, Av Santa Luisa 110. Mon-Fri 1000-2300, Sat 1200-2300, Sun 1200-1700. Great salads and desserts, popular and expensive. With another branch at Av Larco 657, Miraflores.

Miraflores *p1209, map p1208*
Calle San Ramón, known as 'Pizza Street' (across from Parque Kennedy), is a pedestrian walkway lined with outdoor restaurants/bars/discos open until the wee small hours. It's very popular, with good-natured touts trying to entice diners and drinkers with free offers.
$$$ El Kapallaq, Av Petit Thouars 4844, T444 4149. Mon-Fri 1200-1700 only. Prize-winning Peruvian restaurant specializing in seafood and fish, excellent *ceviches*.
$$$ El Rincón Gaucho, Av Armendáriz 580, T447 4778. Good grill, renowned for its steaks.
$$$ Huaca Pucllana, Gral Borgoño cuadra 8 s/n, alt cuadra 45 Av Arequipa, T445 4042, www.resthuacapucllana.com. Facing the archaeological site of the same name, contemporary Peruvian fusion cooking, very good food in an unusual setting, popular with groups.
$$$ La Gloria, Atahualpa 201, T445 5705, www.lagloriarestaurant.com. Mon-Sat from 1300 and again from 2000. Popular upmarket restaurant serving Peruvian food, classic and contemporary styles, good service.
$$$ La Preferida, Arias Araguez 698, T445 5180, http://restaurantelapreferida.com. Daily 0800-1700. Seafood restaurant and tapas bar, with delicious *ceviches*, also has a branch in Monterrico.
$$$ La Trattoria, Manuel Bonilla 106, T446 7002, www.latrattoriadimambrino.com, 1 block from Parque Kennedy. Italian cuisine, popular, good desserts. Has another branch, **La Bodega**, opposite entrance to Huaca Pucllana.

$$$ Las Brujas de Cachiche, Av Bolognesi 472, T447 1883, www.brujasdecachiche.com.pe. Mon-Sat 1200-2400, Sun 1230-1630. An old mansion converted into bars and dining rooms, fine traditional food (menu in Spanish and English), live *criollo* music.

$$$ Rosa Náutica, T445 0149, www.larosanautica.com. Daily 1230-0200. Built on old British-style pier (Espigón No 4), in Lima Bay. Delightful opulence, fine fish cuisine, experience the atmosphere by buying a beer in the bar at sunset.

$$$ Saqra, Av La Paz 646, T650 88 84, www.saqra.pe. Mon-Thu 1200-2400, Fri-Sat 1200-0100. Colourful and casual, indoor or outdoor seating, interesting use of ingredients from all over Peru, classic flavours with a fun, innovative twist, inspired by street food and humble dishes, vegetarian options, many organic products. Also good cocktail bar. Go with a group to sample as many dishes as possible.

$$$ Sí Señor, Jr Bolognesi 706, T445 3789. Mexican food, cheerful, interesting decor, huge portions.

$$$-$$ Chifa Internacional, Av República de Panamá 5915, T445 3997, www.chifainternacional.com. Open 1230-1530 (1600 on Sat), then from 1900, Sun 1200-2315. Great *chifa* in San Antonio district of Miraflores.

$$$-$$ Las Tejas, Diez Canseco 340, T444 4360. Daily 1100-2300. Good, typical Peruvian food, especially *ceviche*.

$$$-$$ Punto Azul, San Martín 595, Benavides 2711, with other branches in San Isidro, Surco and San Borja, http://puntoazulrestaurante.com. Tue-Sun 1100-1600 (San Martín 595 also open Mon-Sat 1900-2400). Popular, well-regarded chain of seafood and *ceviche* restaurants.

$$ Café Tarata, Pasaje Tarata 260, T446 6330. Good atmosphere, family-run, good varied menu.

$$ El Huarike, Enrique Palacios 140, T241 6086. Fashionable, interesting combinations of *ceviche* and sushi, also cooked seafood dishes.

$$ El Parquetito, Lima 373 y Diez Canseco, T444 0490. Peruvian food from all regions, good menu, serves breakfast, eat inside or out.

$$ Lobo del Mar – Octavio Otani, Colón 587, T242 1871. Basic exterior hides one of the oldest *cevicherías* in Miraflores, excellent, a good selection of other seafood dishes.

$$ Mama Olla, Pasaje Tarata 248. Charming café on a pedestrian walkway, huge menu, big portions.

$ Govinda, Schell 630. Vegetarian, from Hare Krishna foundation, lunch *menú* US$3.

$ Madre Natura, Chiclayo 815, T445 2522, www.madrenaturaperu.com. Mon-Sat 0800-2100. Natural foods shop and eating place, very good.

Café Café, Martin Olaya 250, at the corner of Av Diagonal. Very popular, good atmosphere, over 100 different blends of coffee, good salads and sandwiches, very popular with 'well-to-do' Limeños. Also in Larcomar.

Café de la Paz, Lima 351, middle of Parque Kennedy. Good outdoor café right on the park, expensive, great cocktails, with another branch on Pasaje Tarata.

Café La Máquina, Alcanfores 323. Friendly small café and bar with good cocktails, interesting sandwiches and great cakes.

C'est si bon, Av Cdte Espinar 663. Excellent cakes by the slice or whole, best in Lima.

Chef's Café, Av Larco 375 and 763. Nice places for a sandwich or coffee.

Haiti, Av Diagonal 160, Parque Kennedy. Open almost round the clock daily. Great for people watching, good ice cream.

La Lucha, Av Benavides y Olaya (under Flying Dog), on Parque Kennedy, with a small branch nearby between Olaya and Benavides and another on Ovalo Gutiérrez. Excellent hot sandwiches, limited range, choice of sauces, great juices, *chicha morada* and *café pasado*. Good for a wholesome snack.

La Tiendecita Blanca, Av Larco 111 on Parque Kennedy. One of Miraflores' oldest, expensive, good people-watching, very good cakes, European-style food and delicatessen.

Pan de la Chola, Av La Mar 918, El-Pan-de-la-Chola on Facebook. Café and bakery specializing in sourdough bread, teas, juices and sweets.

San Antonio, Av 28 de Julio y Reducto (many other eating places at this junction), Av Angamos Oeste 1494, Rocca de Vergallo 201, Magdalena del Mar and Av Primavera 373, San Borja. Fashionable *pastelería* chain with hot and cold lunch dishes, good salads, inexpensive, busy.

Barranco *p1210*

$$$ Canta Rana, Génova 101, T247 7274. Sun-Mon 1200-1800, Tue-Sat 1200-2300. Good *ceviche*, expensive, small portions, but the most popular local place on Sun.

$$$ La 73, Av Sol Oeste 176, casi San Martín, at the edge of Barranco. Mostly meat dishes, has a lunch menu, look for the Chinese lanterns outside, good reputation.

$$$ La Costa Verde, on Barranquito beach, T247 1244, www.restaurantecostaverde.com. Daily 1200-2400, Sun buffet. Excellent fish and wine, expensive but considered one of the best.

$$$ La Pescadería, Grau 689, T477 0966, www. lapescaderia.pe. A recommended *cevichería*.

$$$-$$ Tío Mario, Jr Zepita 214, on the steps to the Puente de Suspiros. Excellent *anticuchería*, serving delicious Peruvian kebabs, always busy, fantastic service, varied menu and good prices.

$$ Las Mesitas, Av Grau 341, T477 4199. Open 1200-0200. Traditional tea rooms-cum-restaurant, serving Creole food and traditional desserts which you won't find anywhere else, lunch *menú* served till 1400 US$3.

$$-$ Sóngoro Cosongo, Ayacucho 281, T247 4730, at the top of the steps down to Puente de Suspiros, www.songorocosongo.com. Good-value *comida criolla*, "un poco de todo".

La Boteca, Grau 310-312. Smart-looking café bar.

Expreso Virgen de Guadalupe, San Martín y Ayacucho. Café and vegetarian buffet in an old tram, also seating in the garden, more expensive at weekends.

Tostería Bisetti, Pedro de Osma 116, www.cafe bisetti.com. Coffee, cakes and a small selection of lunchtime dishes, service a bit slow but a nice place.

🔊 Bars and clubs

Lima *p1201, map p1205*

Central Lima

The centre of town, specifically Jr de la Unión, has many discos. It's best to avoid the nightspots around the intersection of Av Tacna, Av Piérola and Av de la Vega. These places are rough and foreigners will receive much unwanted attention.

For latest recommendations for gay and lesbian places, check www.gayperu.com.

El Rincón Cervecero, Jr de la Unión (Belén) 1045, www.rinconcervecero.com.pe. German-style pub, fun.

Estadio Futbol Sports Bar, Av Nicolás de Piérola 926 on the Plaza San Martín, T428 8866. Mon-Wed 1215-2300, Thu 1215-2400, Fri-Sat 1215-0300, Sun 1215-1800. Beautiful bar with a disco, international football theme, good international and creole food.

Piano Bar Munich, Jr de la Unión 1044 (basement). Small and fun.

Miraflores *p1209, map p1208*

La Tasca, Av Diez Canseco 117, very near Parque Kennedy, part of the *Flying Dog* group and under one of the hostels (see Where to stay, above). Spanish-style bar with cheap beer (for Miraflores). An eclectic crowd including ex-pats, travellers and locals. Gay-friendly. Small and crowded.

Media Naranja, Schell 130, at bottom of Parque Kennedy. Brazilian bar with drinks and food.

Murphy's, Schell 619, T01-447 1082. Mon-Sat from 1600. Happy hours every day with different offers, lots of entertainment, very popular.

The Old Pub, San Ramón 295 (Pizza St), www. oldpub.com.pe. Cosy, with live music most days.

Treff Pub Alemán, Av Benavides 571-104, T444 0148, www.treff-pub-aleman.com (hidden from the main road behind a cluster of tiny houses signed "Los Duendes"). A wide range of German beers, plus cocktails, good atmosphere, darts and other games.

Barranco *p1210*

Barranco is the capital of Lima nightlife. The following is a short list of some of the better bars and clubs. Pasaje Sánchez Carrión, right off the main plaza, used to be the heart of it all. Watering holes and discos line both sides of this pedestrian walkway. Av Grau, just across the street from the plaza, is also lined with bars, eg **The Lion's Head Pub**, Av Grau 268 p 2, **Déjà Vu**, No 294. Many of the bars in this area turn into discos later on.

Ayahuasca, San Martín 130. In the stunning Berninzon House from the Republican era, chilled out lounge bar with several areas for eating, drinking and dancing. Food is expensive and portions are small, but go for the atmosphere.

Barranco Beer Company, Grau 308, T247 6211, www.barrancobeer.com. Closed Mon, open from 1900 on Tue, 1200 on Wed-Sun, closes 1700 on Sun. New artisanal brewhouse.

El Dragón, N de Piérola 168, T715 5043, www.eldragon.com.pe. Popular bar and venue for music, theatre and painting.

Juanitos, Av Grau, opposite the park. Open from 1600-0400. Barranco's oldest bar, where writers and artists congregate, a perfect spot to start the evening.

La Noche, Bolognesi 307, at Pasaje Sánchez Carrión, www.lanoche.com.pe. A Lima institution with high standard, live music, Mon is jazz night, all kicks off at around 2200.

La Posada del Angel, 3 branches, Pedro de Osma 164 and 214, T247 0341, see Facebook. These are popular bars serving snacks and meals.

La Posada del Mirador, Ermita 104, near the Puente de los Suspiros (Bridge of Sighs), see Facebook. Beautiful view of the ocean, but you pay for the privilege.

Santos Café & Espirituosos, Jr Zepita 203, just above the Puente de Suspiros, T247 4609, also on Facebook. Mon-Sat 1700-0100. Favourite spot for trendy young professionals who want to drop a few hundred soles, relaxed, informal but pricey.

Sargento Pimienta, Bolognesi 757, www. sargentopimienta.com.pe. Tue-Sat from 2200. Live music, always a favourite with Limeños.

Victoria, Av Pedro de Osma 135. New upmarket pub in the beautiful Casa Cillóniz, a selection of beers, cocktails, snacks and live music.

⊕ Entertainment

Lima p1201, maps p1202, p1205 and p1208
Cinemas
The newspaper *El Comercio* lists cinema information in the section called *Luces*. Mon-Wed reduced price at most cinemas. Most films are in English with subtitles and cost from US$7-8.75 in Miraflores and malls, US$3-4 in the centre. The best cinema chains in the city are **Cinemark**, **Cineplanet** and **UVK Multicines**. **Filmoteca de Lima**, at **Centro Cultural PUCP** (cultural centre of the Universidad Católica), Camino Real 1075, San Isidro, T616 1616, http://cultural.pucp.edu.pe. **Cinematógrafo de Barranco**, Pérez Roca 196, Barranco, T264 4374.

Small independent cinema showing a good choice of classic and new international films.

Peñas
De Rompe y Raja, Manuel Segura 127, T636 1518, www.derompeyraja.pe. Thu, Fri, Sat. Popular for music, dancing and *criolla* food.

Del Carajo, Catalino Miranda 158, Barranco, T247 7977, www.delcarajo.com.pe. All types of traditional music.

La Candelaria, Av Bolognesi 292, Barranco, T247 1314, www.lacandelariaperu.com. Fri-Sat 2130 onwards. A good Barranco *peña*.

La Estación de Barranco, Pedro de Osma 112, T477 5030, www.laestaciondebarranco.com. Good, family atmosphere, varied shows.

Las Brisas de Titicaca, Héroes de Tarapacá 168, at 1st block of Av Brasil near Plaza Bolognesi, T715 6960, www.brisasdeltiticaca. com. A Lima institution.

Sachun, Av del Ejército 657, Miraflores, T441 0123, www.sachunperu.com. Great shows on weekdays as well.

Theatre
El Gran Teatro Nacional, at the corner of Avs Javier Prado and Aviación, San Borja. Capable of seating 1500 people, it holds concerts, opera, ballet and other dance as well as other events. Most professional plays are staged at **Teatro Segura**, Jr Huancavelica 265, T427 9491. **Teatro Municipal**, Jr Ica 377, T315 1300 ext 1767, see Facebook. Completely restored after a fire, with full programmes and with a theatre museum on Huancavelica. There are many other theatres in the city, some of which are related to cultural centres, eg CCPUCP (see Cinemas, above). **Instituto Cultural Peruano-Norteamericano**, Jr Cusco 446, Lima Centre, T706 7000, central office at Av Angamos Oeste 160, Miraflores, www.icpna.edu.pe. **Centro Cultural Peruano Japonés**, Av Gregorio Escobedo 803, Jesús María, T518 7450, www. apj.org.pe. All have various cultural activities. The press gives details of performances. Theatre and concert tickets booked through Teleticket, T01-613 8888, Mon-Fri 0900-1900, www.teleticket.com.pe. For cultural events, see **Lima Cultural**, www.limacultura.pe, the city's monthly arts programme.

☸ Festivals

Lima *p1201, maps p1202, p1205 and p1208*
18 Jan Founding of Lima. Semana Santa, or Holy Week, is a colourful spectacle with processions. **28-29 Jul** Independence, with music and fireworks in the Plaza de Armas on the evening before. **30 Aug** Santa Rosa de Lima. **Mid-Sep** Mistura, www.mistura.pe, a huge gastronomy fair in Parque Exposición, with Peruvian foods, celebrity chefs, workshops and more. **Oct** The month of Our Lord of the Miracles; see Las Nazarenas church, page 1204.

○ Shopping

Lima *p1201, maps p1202, p1205 and p1208*
Bookshops
Crisol, Ovalo Gutiérrez, Av Santa Cruz 816, San Isidro, T221 1010, below Cine Planet. Large bookshop with café, titles in English, French and Spanish. Also in Jockey Plaza Shopping Center, Av Javier Prado Este 4200, Surco, T436 0004, and other branches, www.crisol.com.pe.
Epoca, Av Cdte Espinar 864, Miraflores, T241 2951. Great selection of books, mostly in Spanish.
Ibero Librerías, Av Diagonal 500, T242 2798, Larco 199, T445 5520, in Larcomar, Miraflores, and other branches, www.iberolibros.com. Stocks Footprint Handbooks as well as a wide range of other titles.

Camping equipment
It's better to bring all camping and hiking gear from home. Camping gas (the most popular brand is Doite, which comes in small blue bottles) is available from any large hardware store or bigger supermarket.
Alpamayo, Av Larco 345, Miraflores at Parque Kennedy, T445 1671. Mon-Fri 1000-1330, 1430-2000, Sat 1000-1400. Sleeping mats, boots, rock shoes, climbing gear, water filters, tents, backpacks etc, very expensive but top quality equipment. Owner speaks fluent English and offers good information.
Altamira, Arica 880, Parque Damert, behind Wong on Ovalo Gutiérrez, Miraflores, T445 1286. Sleeping bags, climbing gear, hiking gear and tents.
Camping Center, Av Benavides 1620, Miraflores, T445 5981, www.campingperu.com. Mon-Fri

1000-2000, Sat 1000-1400. Selection of tents, backpacks, stoves, camping and climbing gear.
El Mundo de las Maletas, Preciados 308, Higuereta-Surco, T449 7850. Daily 0900-2200. For suitcase repairs.
Tatoo, CC Larcomar, locs 123-125B, T242 1938, www.tatoo.ws. For top-quality imported ranges and own brands of equipment.
Todo Camping, Av Angamos Oeste 350, Miraflores, near Av Arequipa, T2421318. Sells 100% deet, blue gas canisters, lots of accessories, tents, crampons and backpacks.

Handicrafts
Miraflores is a good place for high quality, expensive handicrafts; there are many shops on and around the top end of Av La Paz (starting at Av Ricardo Palma).
Agua y Tierra, Diez Canseco 298 y Alcanfores, Miraflores, T444 6980. Fine crafts and indigenous art.
Arte XXI, Av La Paz 678, Miraflores, T01-447 9777, www.artemania-21.com. Gallery and store for contemporary and colonial Peruvian paintings
Artesanía Santo Domingo, Plazuela Santo Domingo, by the church of that name, in Lima centre, T428 9860. Good Peruvian crafts.
Centro Comercial El Alamo, corner of La Paz y Diez Canseco, Miraflores. *Artesanía* shops with good choice.
Dédalo, Paseo Sáenz Peña 295, Barranco, T477 0562. A labyrinthine shop selling furniture, jewellery and other items, as good as a gallery. It also has a nice coffee shop and has cinema shows. Has other branches on Parque Kennedy and at Larcomar.
Kuntur Wasi, Ocharán 182, Miraflores, opposite Sol de Oro hotel, look for the sign above the wall, T01-447 7173, kunturh@speedy. com.pe. English-speaking owners are very knowledgeable about Peruvian textiles; often have exhibitions of fine folk art and crafts.
La Casa de la Mujer Artesana, Juan Pablo Ferandini 1550 (Av Brasil cuadra 15), Pueblo Libre, T423 8840, www.casadelamujerartesana.com. Mon-Fri 0900-1300, 1400-1700. A cooperative run by the Movimiento Manuela Ramos, excellent quality work mostly from *pueblos jóvenes*.
Las Pallas, Cajamarca 212, Barranco, T477 4629. Mon-Sat 0900-1900. Very high quality handicrafts, English, French and German spoken.

Luz Hecho a Mano, Berlín 399, Miraflores, T446 7098, www.luzhechoamano.com. Lovely handmade handbags, wallets and other leather goods including clothing which last for years and can be custom made.

Museo de la Nación, address above, often hosts specialist handicrafts markets presenting ore individual work from across Peru during national festivals.

There are bargains in high-quality Pima cotton. Shops selling **alpaca** items include:
Alpaca 859, Av Larco 859, Miraflores. Good quality alpaca and baby alpaca products.
Kuna by Alpaca 111, Av Larco 671, Miraflores, T447 1623, www.kuna.com.pe. High quality alpaca, baby alpaca and vicuña items. Also in Larcomar, loc 1-07, Museo Larco, the airport, Jockey Plaza, at hotels and in San Isidro.

Jewellery
On Cs La Esperanza and La Paz, Miraflores, dozens of shops offer gold and silverware at reasonable prices.
Ilaria, Av 2 de Mayo 308, San Isidro, T512 3530, www.ilariainternational.com. Jewellery and silverware with interesting designs. There are other branches in Lima, Cuzco, Arequipa and Trujillo.

Maps
Instituto Geográfico Nacional, Av Aramburú 1190, Surquillo, T475 9960, www.ign.gob.pe. Mon-Fri 0830-1645. It has topographical maps of the whole country, mostly at 1:100,000, political and physical maps of all departments and satellite and aerial photographs. You may be asked to show your passport when buying these maps.
Lima 2000, Av Arequipa 2625 (near the intersection with Av Javier Prado), T440 3486, www.lima2000.com.pe. Mon-Fri 0900-1300, 1400-1800. Has excellent street maps of Lima, from tourist maps, US$5.55, to comprehensive books US$18. Also has country maps (US$5.55-9.25), maps of Cuzco, Arequipa, Trujillo and Chiclayo and tourist maps of the Inca Trail, Colca, and Cordillera Blanca. **South American Explorers** (see page 1201) also stocks these and IGN maps.

Markets
All are open 7 days a week until late(ish).

Av Petit Thouars, in Miraflores. At blocks 51-54 (near Parque Kennedy, parallel to Av Arequipa). An unnamed crafts market area, usually called **Mercado Inca**, with a large courtyard and lots of small flags. This is the largest crafts arcade in Miraflores. From here to C Ricardo Palma the street is lined with crafts markets.
Feria Nacional de Artesanía de los Deseos y Misterios, Av 28 de Julio 747, near junction with Av Arequipa and Museo Metropolitano. Small market specializing in charms, remedies, fortune-telling and trinkets from Peru and Bolivia.
Mercado 1, Surquillo, cross Paseo de le República from Ricardo Palma, Miraflores and go north 1 block. Food market with a huge variety of local produce. C Narciso de la Colina outside has various places to eat, including Heladería La Fiorentina, No 580, for excellent ice creams.
Parque Kennedy, the main park of Miraflores, hosts a daily crafts market from 1700-2300.
Polvos Azules, on García Naranjo, La Victoria, just off Av Grau in the centre of town. The 'official' black market, sells just about anything; it is generally cheap and very interesting; beware pickpockets.

⏻ What to do

Lima p1201, maps p1202, p1205 and p1208
Cycling
Bike Tours of Lima, Bolívar 150, Miraflores, T445 3172, www.biketoursoflima.com. Offer a variety of day tours through the city of Lima by bike, also bicycle rentals.
BikeMavil, Av Aviación 4023, Surco, T449 8435, see Facebook page. Mon-Sat 1030-2000. Rental service, repairs, tours, selection of mountain and racing bikes.
Buenas Biclas, Domingo Elías 164, Miraflores, T241 9712, www.buenasbiclas.com. Mon-Fri 1000-2000, Sat 1000-1400. Mountain bike specialists, knowledgeable staff, good selection of bikes, repairs and accessories.
Casa Okuyama, Manco Cápac 590, La Victoria, T330 9131. Mon-Fri 0900-1300, 1415-1800, Sat 0900-1300. Repairs, parts, try here for 28-in tyres, excellent service.
Cycloturismo Peru, T99-9012 8105, www.cicloturismoperu.com. Offers goodvalue cycling trips around Lima and beyond, as well as bike rental. The owner, Aníbal Paredes, speaks good

English, is very knowledgeable and is the owner of **Mont Blanc Gran Hotel**.
Mirabici, Parque Salazar, T673 3903. Daily 0800-1900. Bicycle hire, US$7.50 per hr (tandems available); they also run bike tours 1000-1500, in English, Spanish and Portuguese. Bikes to ride up and down Av Arequipa can be rented on Sun 0800-1300, US$3 per hr, leave passport as deposit, www.jafibike.com.
Perú Bike, T260 8225, www.perubike.com. Experienced agency leading tours, professional guiding, mountain bike school and workshop.

Diving
Peru Divers, Av Defensores del Morro 175, Chorrillos, T251 6231, www.perudivers.com. Owner Lucho Rodríguez is a certified PADI instructor who offers certification courses, tours and a wealth of good information.

Hiking
Trekking and Backpacking Club, Jr Huáscar 1152, Jesús María, Lima 11, T423 2515, T94-3866 794, www.angelfire.com/mi2/tobac. Sr Miguel Chiri Valle, treks arranged, including in the Cordillera Blanca.

Paragliding
Aeroxtreme, Trípoli 345, dpto 503, T242 5125, www.aeroxtreme.com. One of several outfits offering parapenting in Lima, 20 years' experience.
Andean Trail Perú, T99-836 3436, www.andeantrailperu.com. For parapenting tandem flights, US$53, and courses, US$600 for 10 days. They also have a funday for US$120 to learn the basics. Trekking, kayaking and other adventure sports arranged.

Textiles/cultural tours
Puchka Perú, www.puchkaperu.com. Web-based operator specializing in textiles, folk art and markets. Fixed-date tours involve meeting artisans, workshops, visit to markets and more. In association with Maestro Máximo Laura, world-famous weaver, http://maximolauratapestries.com, whose studio in Urb Brisas de Santa Rosa III Etapa, Lima can be visited by appointment, T577 0952, karinaguilar@maximolaura.com. See also Museo Máximo Laura in Cuzco.

Tour operators
Do not conduct business anywhere other than in the agency's office and insist on a written contract.
The Andean Experience Co., Sáenz Peña 214, Barranco, T700 5100, www.andean-experience.com. Offers tailor-made itineraries designed to match each traveller's personal interests, style and preferences to create ideal Peru trips.
Aracari Travel Consulting, Schell 237, of 602, Miraflores, T651 2424, www.aracari.com. Regional tours throughout Peru, also 'themed' and activity tours, has a very good reputation.
Coltur, Av Reducto 1255, Miraflores, T615 5555, www.coltur.com. Very helpful, experienced and well-organized tours throughout Peru.
Condor Travel, Armando Blondet 249, San Isidro, T615 3000, www.condortravel.com. Highly regarded operator with tailor-made programmes, special interest tours, luxury journeys, adventure travel and conventional tourism. One-stop shopping with own regional network.
Dasatariq, Av Reducto 1255, Miraflores, T447 2741, www.dasatariq.com. Also in Cuzco. Well-organized, helpful, with a good reputation.
Domiruth Travel Service S.A.C, Jr Rio de Janeiro 216-218, Miraflores, T610 6000, www.domiruth.com. Tours throughout Peru, from the mystical to adventure travel. See also **Peru 4x4 Adventures**, part of Domiruth, www.peru4x4adventures.com, for exclusive 4WD tours with German, English, Spanish, Italian and Portuguese-speaking drivers.
Ecocruceros, Av Arequipa 4964, of 202, Miraflores, T226 8530, www.islaspalomino.com. Daily departures from Plaza Grau in Callao to see the sea lions at Islas Palomino, 4 hrs with 30-40 mins wetsuit swimming with guide, snack lunch, US$48 (take ID), reserve a day in advance.
Excursiones MYG, T241 8091, www.excursionesmyg.com. Offers a variety of tours in Lima and surroundings, including historic centre, nighttime, culinary tours, Caral, and further afield.
Explorandes, C San Fernando 287, Miraflores, T2006100, www.explorandes.com. Award-winning company. Offers a wide range of adventure and cultural tours throughout the country. Also offices in Huaraz and Cuzco (see pages 1235 and 1363).

Fertur Peru Travel, C Schell 485, Miraflores, T242 1900; and Jr Junín 211, Plaza de Armas, T427 2626; also in Cuzco at San Augustin 317, T084-221304; (USA/Canada T(1) 877-247 0055 toll free, UK T020-3002 3811), www.fertur-travel.com. Mon-Fri 0900-1900, Sat 0900-1600. Siduith Ferrer de Vecchio, CEO of this agency, is highly recommended; she offers tour packages and up-to-date, correct tourist information on a national level, and also great prices on national and international flights, discounts for those with ISIC and youth cards and **South American Explorers** members. Other services include flight reconfirmations, hotel reservations and transfers to and from the airport or bus or train stations.

Il Tucano Peru, Elías Aguirre 633, Miraflores, T444 9361, 24-hr number T01-975 05375, www.iltucanoperu.com. Personalized tours for groups or individuals throughout Peru, also 4WD overland trips, first-class drivers and guides, outstanding service and reliability.

Info Perú, Jr de la Unión (Belén) 1066, of 102, T425 0414, www.infoperu.com.pe. Mon-Fri 0900-1800, Sat 0930-1400. Run by a group of women, ask for Laura Gómez, offering personalized programmes, hotel bookings, transport, free tourist information, sale of maps, books and souvenirs, English and French spoken.

InkaNatura Travel, Manuel Bañon 461, San Isidro, T440 2022, www.inkanatura.com. Also in Cuzco and Chiclayo, experienced company with special emphasis on both sustainable tourism and conservation, especially in Manu and Tambopata, also birdwatching, and on the archaeology of all of Peru.

Lima Mentor, T624 9360, www.limamentor.com. Contact through web, phone or through hotels. An agency offering cultural tours of Lima using freelance guides in specialist areas (eg gastronomy, art, archaeology, Lima at night), entertaining, finding different angles from regular tours. Half-day or full day tours.

Lima Tours, N de Piérola 589 p 18, T619 6900, www.limatours.com.pe. Very good for tours in the capital and around the country; programmes include health and wellness tours.

Peru For Less, ASTA Travel Agent, Luis García Rojas 240, Urb Humboldt, US office: T1-877-269 0309; UK office: T+44-203-002 0571; Peru (Lima) office: T273 2486, Cuzco T084-254800, www.peruforless.com. Will meet or beat any published rates on the internet from outside Peru. Good reports.

Peru Rooms, Av Dos de Mayo 1545 of 205, San Isidro, T422 3434, www.perurooms.com. Internet-based travel service offering 3- to 5-star packages throughout Peru, cultural, adventure and nature tourism.

Rutas del Peru SAC, Av Enrique Palacios 1110, Miraflores, T445 7249, www.rutasdelperu.com. Bespoke trips and overland expeditions in trucks.

Viajes Pacífico (Gray Line), Av Paseo de la República 6010, p 7, T610 1911, www.graylineperu.com. Tours throughout Peru and within South America.

Viracocha, Av Vasco Núñez de Balboa 191, Miraflores, T445 3986, peruviantours@viracocha.com.pe. Very helpful, especially with flights, adventure, cultural, mystical and birdwatching tours.

Open-top bus tours Mirabús, T242 6699, www.mirabusperu.com. Goes from Parque Kennedy Tue-Sun at 1000 to Pachacámac and back with a stop at Pántanos de Villa wildlife sanctuary, US$30. **Mirabús** runs other tours of the city and Callao (from US$3.75 to US$28) – eg Lima half day by day, Lima by night, Costa Verde, Callao, Gold Museum, Miraflores. Similar services are offered by **Turibus**, from Larcomar, T230 0909, www.turibusperu.com.

Private guides The MITINCI (Ministry of Industry Tourism, Integration and International Business) certifies guides and can provide a list. Most are members of **AGOTUR** (Asociación de Guías Oficiales de Turismo), Av La Paz 678, Miraflores (for correspondence only), www.agotur.com. Book in advance. Most guides speak a foreign language.

⊖ Transport

Lima *p1201, maps p1202, p1205 and p1208*
Air
Arrivals or departures flight information T511 6055, www.lap.com.pe. **Jorge Chávez Airport**, 16 km from the centre of Lima.

Information desks can be found in the national and international foyers. There is also a helpful desk in the international Arrivals hall, which can make hotel and transport reservations. There are many smart shops, places to eat and drink and, in international Arrivals, mobile phone rentals.

Global Net ATM, *Casas de cambio* (money changing kiosks) and a bank can be found in many parts of Arrivals and Departures. Exchange rates are marginally poorer than outside. There are public telephones around the airport and a **Telefónica** *locutorio*, daily 0700-2300. Internet facilities are more expensive than in the city. Most of the terminal has free Wi-Fi. There are postal services.

Transport from the airport *Remise* taxis from desks outside International Arrivals and National Arrivals: **Taxi Green**, T484 4001, www.taxigreen.com.pe; **Mitsu**, T261 7788, www.mitsoo.net; and **CMV**, T219 0266, http://cmvtaxi.pe. As a rough guide, these companies charge US$20-30 to the centre, US$22-32 to Miraflores and San Isidro, a bit more to Barranco. In the same place is the desk of

Peruvian Shuttle, T373 5049, www.peruvian-shuttle.com, which runs private, shared and group transfers to the city; fares US$7-18 shared, depending on number of passengers, US$22-40 private. There are many taxi drivers offering their services outside Arrivals with similar or higher prices (more at night). To get to Miraflores by combi, take the "Callao-Ate" with a big red "S" ("La S"), the only direct link from the airport to Miraflores. Catch it outside of the airport, on Av Faucett, US$0. 55. From downtown Lima go to the junction of Alfonso Ugarte and Av Venezuela where many combis take the route "Todo aeropuerto – Avenida Faucett", US$0.50. At anytime other than very late at night or early in the morning luggage won't be allowed on public buses.

Note Do not take the cheapest, stopping buses to the centre along Av Faucett. They are frequently robbed. Pay more for a non-stop bus, or better still take one of the options above. Nor go to the car park exit and find a taxi without an airport permit outside the perimeter. Although much cheaper than those inside, they are not safe.

Bus
Local The bus routes are shared by buses, combis (mid-size) and colectivos (mini-vans or cars); the latter run from 0600-0100, and less frequently through the night, they are quicker and stop wherever requested. Buses and combis charge about US$0.40-0.45, colectivos a little more. On public holidays, Sun and from 2400 to 0500 every night, a small charge is added to the fare. None is particulary safe; it is better to take a taxi (see below for recommendations).

Lima centre–Miraflores: Av Arequipa runs 52 blocks between downtown Lima and Parque Kennedy in Miraflores. There is no shortage of public transport on this avenue; they have 'Todo Arequipa' on the windscreen. When heading towards downtown from Miraflores the window sticker should say 'Wilson/Tacna'. To get to Parque Kennedy from downtown look on the windshield for 'Larco/Schell/Miraflores', 'Chorrillos/Huaylas' or 'Barranco/Ayacucho'.

Lima centre–Barranco: Lima's only urban freeway, Vía Expresa, runs from Plaza Grau in the centre of town, to the northern tip of

Barranco. This 6-lane thoroughfare, locally known as *El Zanjón* (the Ditch), with the **Metropolitano** bus lane in the middle, is the fastest way to cross the city. Buses downtown for the Vía Expresa can be caught on Av Tacna, Av Wilson (also called Garcilaso de la Vega), Av Bolivia and Av Alfonso Ugarte.

The **Metropolitano** is a system of articulated buses running on dedicated lanes of the Vía Expresa/Paseo de la República (T01-203 9000, www.metropolitano.com.pe). The Estación Central is in front of the **Sheraton** hotel. The southern section runs to Matellini in Chorrillos (estimated journey time 32 mins). For Miraflores take stations between Angamos and 28 de Julio; for Barranco, Bulevar is 170 m from the Plaza. The northern branch runs to Naranjal in Comas, a 34-min journey. Stations Estación Central to Ramón Castilla serve the city centre. Tickets are prepaid and recharge able, from S/.5-100, each journey is S/.2 (US$0.70). Buses run from 0500-2300 daily with shorter hours on Sun and on some sections. From 0600-0900, 1635-2115 Mon-Fri express services run between certain stations. Buses are packed in rush hour.

Long distance There are many different bus companies, but the larger ones are better organized, leave on time and do not wait until the bus is full. For approximate prices, frequency and duration of trip, see destinations. Leaving or arriving in Lima by bus in the rush hour can add an extra hour to the journey.

Note In the weeks either side of 28/29 Jul (Independence), and of the Christmas/New Year holiday, it is practically impossible to get bus tickets out of Lima, unless you book in advance. Bus prices double at these times.

Cruz del Sur, T311 5050 (telephone sales), www.cruzdelsur.com.pe. The main terminal is at Av Javier Prado 1109, La Victoria, with *Cruzero* and *Cruzero Suite* services (luxury buses) and *Imperial* service (quite comfortable buses and periodic stops for food and bathroom breaks, a cheap option with a quality company) to most parts of Peru. Another terminal is at Jr Quilca 531, Lima centre, for *Imperial* services to Arequipa, Ayacucho, Chiclayo, Cuzco, Huancayo, Huaraz, and Trujillo. There are sales offices throughout the city.

Ormeño and its affiliated bus companies depart from and arrive at Av Carlos Zavala 177, Lima centre, T427 5679; also Av Javier Prado Este 1057, Santa Catalina, T472 1710, www.grupo-ormeno.com.pe. **Ormeño** offers *Royal Class* and *Business Class* service to certain destinations. These buses are very comfortable with bathrooms, hostess, etc. They arrive and depart from the Javier Prado terminal, but the Carlos Zavala terminal is the best place to get information and buy any Ormeño ticket. **Cial**, República de Panamá 2460, T207 6900 ext 119, and Paseo de la República 646, T207 6900 ext 170, www.expresocial.com, has national coverage. **Flores**, with terminals at Av Paseo de le República 683, Av Paseo de le República 627 and Jr Montevideo 523, T332 1212, www. floreshnos.net, has departures to many parts of the country, especially the south. Some of its services are good quality.

Other companies include: **Oltursa**, Aramburú 1160, San Isidro, T708 5000, www.oltursa.pe. A reputable company offering top end services to **Nazca**, **Arequipa** and destinations in **northern Peru**, mainly at night. Tepsa, Javier Prado Este 1091, La Victoria, T617 9000, www.tepsa.com.pe, also at Av Gerardo Unger 6917, Terminal Plaza Norte, T533 1524 (not far from the airport, good for those short of time for a bus connection after landing in Lima). Services to the north as far as **Tumbes** and the south to **Tacna**.

Transportes Chanchamayo, Av Nicolás Arriola 535, La Victoria, T265 6850, www. transporteschanchamayo.com. To **Tarma**, **San Ramón** and **La Merced**. Ittsa, Paseo de la República 809, T423 5232, www.ittsabus.com. Good service to the north, **Chiclayo**, **Piura**, **Tumbes**. Transportes León de Huánuco, Av 28 de Julio 1520, La Victoria, T424 3893. Daily to **Huánuco**, **Tingo María**, **La Merced** and **Pucallpa**. Línea, Paseo de la República 941-959, Lima Centre, T424 0836, www.transporteslinea. com.pe, also has a terminal at Terminal Plaza Norte (see above under Tepsa), T533 0739. Among the best services to destinations in the **north**. Móvil, Av Paseo de La República 749, Lima Centre near the national stadium, T716 8000 (also Av Alfredo Mendiola 3883, Los Olivos), www.moviltours.com.pe, to **Huaraz** and **Chiclayo** by *bus cama*, and **Chachapoyas**. Soyuz, Av México 333, T205 2370, www.soyuz. com.pe. To **Ica** every 7 mins, well organized. As **PerúBus**, www.perubus.com.pe, the same company runs north to **Huacho** and **Barranca**. Cavassa, Raimondi 129, Lima Centre, T431 3200, also at Terminal Plaza Norte, www. turismocavassa.com.pe. To **Huaraz**. Also Julio César, José Gálvez 562, La Victoria, T424 8060, www.transportesjuliocesar.com.pe (also at Plaza Norte). Recommended to arrive in Huaraz and then use local transport to points beyond. Good. To **Cuzco**: Cromotex, Av Nicolás Arriola 898, Santa Catalina, Av Paseo de La República 659, T424 7575, www.cromotex.com.pe, also to **Arequipa**.

Bus or colectivo to Pachacámac from Lima From the Pan-American Highway (southbound) take a combi with a sticker in the window reading "Pachacámac/Lurín" (US$0.85). Let the driver know you want to get off at the ruins. A taxi will cost approximately US$5.50, but if you don't ask the driver to wait for you (an extra cost), finding another to take you back to Lima may be a bit tricky. For organized tours contact one of the tour agencies listed above.
International buses Ormeño, address above. To: **Guayaquil** (29 hrs with a change of bus at the border, US$56), **Quito** (38 hrs, US$75), **Cali** (56 hrs, US$131), **Bogotá** (70 hrs, US$141), **Caracas** (100 hrs, US$150), **Santiago** (54 hrs, US$102), **Mendoza** (78 hrs, US$159), **Buenos Aires** (90 hrs, US$148), **São Paulo** (90 hrs). A maximum of 20 kg is allowed pp. Cruz del Sur also has services to **Guayaquil**, 3 a week, US$85, **Buenos Aires**, US$250, and **Santiago**, US$155. El Rápido, Av Rivera Navarrete 2650, Lince, T441 6651, www. elrapidoint.com.ar. Service to Argentina and Uruguay only. Note that international buses are more expensive than travelling from one border to another on national buses.
Warning The area around the bus terminals is very unsafe; thefts and assaults are more common in this neighbourhood than elsewhere in the city. You are strongly advised either to take a bus from a company which has a terminal away from the Carlos Zavala area (eg Cruz del Sur, Oltursa, Ormeño), or to take a taxi to and from your bus. Make sure your luggage is well guarded and put on the right bus. It is also important not to assume that buses leave from the place where you bought the tickets.

Taxi

Taxis do not use meters although some have rate sheets (eg Satelital, T355 5555, www.3555555satelital.com). Agree the price of the journey beforehand and insist on being taken to the destination of your choice. At night, on Sunday and holidays expect a surcharge of 35-50% is made. The following are taxi fares for some of the more common routes, give or take a sol. From downtown Lima to: Parque Kennedy (Miraflores), US$4. Museo de la Nación, US$3.75. San Isidro, US$3.75. Barranco US$4.75. From Miraflores (Parque Kennedy) to: Museo de la Nación, US$2.75. Archaeology Museum, US$3.75. Barranco, US$4.80. By law, all taxis must have the vehicle's registration number painted on the side. They are often white or yellow, but can come in any colour, size or make. Licensed and phone taxis are safest, but if hailing a taxi on the street, local advice is to look for an older driver rather than a youngster. There are several reliable phone taxi companies, which can be called for immediate service, or booked in advance; prices are 2-3 times more than ordinary taxis; eg to the airport US$15, to suburbs US$10. Some are, Moli Taxi, T479 0030; Taxi Real, T215 1414, www.taxireal.com; Taxi Seguro, T241 9292; Taxi Tata, T274 5151; TCAM, run by Carlos Astacio, T99-983 9305, safe, reliable. If hiring a taxi by the hour, agree on price beforehand, US$7-9. Recommended, knowledgeable drivers: César A Canales N, T436 6184, T99-687 3310, only speaks Spanish, reliable. Hugo Casanova Morella, T485 7708 (he lives in La Victoria), for city tours, travel to airport, etc. Mario Salas Pantoja, T99-908 1888. Very reliable and helpful, airport transfers for US$12 or hourly rate for city tours/museum visits etc. Speaks basic English. Mónica Velásquez Carlich, T425 5087, T99-943 0796, vc_monica@hotmail. com. For airport pick-ups, tours, speaks English, most helpful, frequently recommended. **Note** Drivers don't expect tips; give them small change from the fare.

Train

Details of the service on the Central Railway to Huancayo are given under Huancayo, page 1394. The first route of the Tren Eléctrico (Metro) runs from Av Grau in the centre of Lima south to Villa El Salvador, 0600-2230. Each journey costs S/.1.50 (US$0.55); pay by swipe card S/.5 (US$1.75). To connect with the Tren Eléctrico from the Metropolitano, take a bus from Estación Central to Grau or Gamarra. Construction work has started on the next section.

● Directory

Lima *p1201, maps p1202, p1205 and p1208*
Car hire Most companies have an office at the airport, where you can arrange everything and pick up and leave the car. It is recommended to test drive before signing the contract as quality varies. It can be much cheaper to rent a car in a town in the Sierra for a few days than to drive from Lima; also companies don't have a collection service. Cars can be hired from: **Paz Rent A Car**, Av Diez Canseco 319, of 15, Miraflores, T446 4395, T99-939 9853, www.perupazconsortium.com.pe. **Budget**, T204 4400, www.budgetperu.com. Prices range from US$35 to US$85 depending on type of car. Make sure that your car is in a locked garage at night. **Embassies and consulates** For foreign embassies and consulates in Lima, see http://embassy.goabroad.com. **Language schools** Hispana, San Martín 377, Miraflores, T446 3045, www.hispanaidiomas.com. 20- to 60-hr travellers' programmes and other courses, also salsa, surf and gastronomy. **Instituto de Idiomas** (Pontífica Universidad Católica del Perú), Av Camino Real 1037, San Isidro, T626 6500, http://idiomas.pucp.edu.pe. Spanish for foreigners courses. **El Sol School of Languages**, Grimaldo del Solar 469, Miraflores, T242 7763, http://elsol.idiomasperu.com. Private tuition, also small groups. Family homestays and volunteer programmes available. **Independent teachers** (enquire about rates): **AC Spanish Classes (Luis Villanueva)**, Diez Canseco 497, Miraflores, T247 7054, www.acspanishclasses.com. Flexible, reliable, helpful. **Srta Susy Arteaga**, T534 9289, T99-989 7271, susyarteaga@hotmail.com, or susyarteaga@yahoo.com. **Srta Patty Félix**, T521 2559, patty_fel24@yahoo.com. **Medical**

services (Also worth contacting consulate for recommendations.) **Hospitals: Clínica Anglo Americano**, Alfredo Salazar 350, San Isidro, a few blocks from Ovalo Gutiérrez, T616 8900, www.angloamericana.com.pe. Stocks Yellow Fever and Tetanus. **Clínica Internacional**, Jr Washington 1471 y Paseo Colón (9 de Diciembre), downtown Lima, T619 6161, www.clinicainternacional.com.pe. Good, clean and professional, consultations up to US$35, no inoculations. **Instituto de Medicina Tropical**, Av Honorio Delgado 430 near the Pan American Highway in the Cayetano Heredia Hospital, San Martín de Porres, T482 3903, www.upch.edu.pe/tropicales/. Good for check-ups after jungle travel. **Clínica del Niño**, Av Brasil 600 at 1st block of Av 28 de Julio, Breña, T330 0066, www.isn.gob.pe. **Centro Anti-Rabia de Lima**, Jr Austria 1300, Breña, T425 6313. Open Mon-Sat 0830-1830. **Clínica Padre Luis Tezza**, Av El Polo 570, Monterrico, T610 5050, www.clinicatezza.com.pe. Clinic specializing in a wide variety of illnesses/disorders, etc, expensive; for stomach or intestinal problems. **Clínica Ricardo Palma**, Av Javier Prado Este 1066, San Isidro, T224 2224, www.crp.com.pe. For general medical consultations, English spoken. **Clínica Good Hope**, Malecón Balta 956, Miraflores, T610 7300, www.goodhope.org.pe. Has been recommended, will make visitsto hotels; prices similar to US. **International Health Department**, at Jorge Chávez airport, T517 1845. Open 24 hrs a day for vaccinations. **Useful addresses** Tourist Police, Jr Moore 268, Magdalena at the 38th block of Av Brasil, T460 1060, open daily 24 hrs. For enquiries, Av España y Av Alfonso Ugarte, Lima; and Colón 246, Miraflores, T243 2190. They are friendly and very helpful, English spoken. It is recommended to visit when you have had property stolen. **Immigration**: Av España 730, Breña, Mon-Fri 0830-1300. Provides new entry stamps if passport is lost or stolen. **Intej**, Av San Martín 240, Barranco, T247 3230. They can extend student cards, change flight itineraries bought with student cards.

Huaraz and the Cordilleras

The spectacular Cordillera Blanca is an area of jewelled lakes and snowy mountain peaks attracting mountaineers and hikers in their thousands. Huaraz is the natural place to head for. It has the best infrastructure and the mountains, lakes and trails are within easy reach. This region, though, also has some sites of great archaeological significance, the most notable of which must be Chavín de Huantar, one of Peru's most important pre-Inca sites. Large multinational mining projects have brought new prosperity as well as social change and ecological damage to the area.

Arriving in Huaraz and the Cordilleras

North from Lima the Pan-American Highway parallels the coast. A series of roads climb up to Huaraz, in the Callejón de Huaylas, gateway to Parque Nacional Huascarán. Probably the easiest route to Huaraz is the paved road which branches east off the Pan-American Highway north of Pativilca, 203 km from Lima. The road climbs increasingly steeply to the chilly pass at 4080 m (Km 120). Shortly after, Laguna **Conococha** comes into view, where the Río Santa rises. A road branches off from Conococha to **Chiquián** (see page 1247) and the **Cordilleras Huayhuash** and **Raura** to the southeast. After crossing a high plateau the main road descends gradually for 47 km until **Catac**, where another road branches east to Chavín and on to the **Callejón de Conchucos** (eastern side of the Cordillera Blanca). Huaraz is 36 km further on and the road then continues north between the towering Cordillera Negra, snowless and rising to 4600 m, and the snow-covered Cordillera Blanca. The alternative routes to the Callejón de Huaylas are via the Callán pass from Casma to Huaraz (see page 1250), and from Chimbote to Caraz via the Cañón del Pato (page 1249).

Huaraz → *Phone code: 043. Colour map 3, B2. Population: 115,000. Altitude: 3091 m.*

The main town in the Cordillera Blanca, 420 km from Lima, Huaraz is expanding rapidly as a major tourist centre, but it is also a busy commercial hub, especially on market days. It is a prime destination for hikers and a Mecca for international climbers.

Arriving in Huaraz

Tourist offices iPerú ① *Pasaje Atuspuria, of 1, Plaza de Armas, T428812, iperuhuaraz@ promperu. gob.pe, Mon-Sat 0800-1830, Sun 0830-1400. Also at Jr San Martín cuadra 6 s/n, open daily 0800-1100, and at Anta airport when flights arrive.* **Policía de Turismo** ① *Av Luzuriaga on Plaza de Armas, around the corner from iPerú, T421351, divtueco_huaraz@yahoo.com, Mon-Sat 0730-2100,* is the place to report crimes and resolve issues with tour operators, hotels, etc. All female officers, limited English spoken. **Indecopi** ① *Av Gamarra 671, T423899, www.indecopi.gob.pe,* government consumer protection office, very effective but not always quick. Spanish only. Huaraz has its share of crime, especially since the arrival of mining and during the high tourist season. Women should not go to surrounding districts and sites alone. Muggings have taken place on the trails to Rataquena lookout, just above the city, and between the Monterrey thermal baths and Wilcawain ruins. See also www.andeanexplorer.com.

Places around Huaraz

Huaraz, capital of Ancash department, was almost completely destroyed in the earthquake of May 1970. The Plaza de Armas has been rebuilt. A new **Cathedral** is still being built. The setting, at the foot of the Cordillera Blanca, is spectacular. The main thoroughfare, Avenida Luzuriaga, is bursting at the seams with travel agencies, climbing equipment hire shops, restaurants, cafés and bars. A good district for those seeking peace and quiet is La Soledad, six blocks uphill from the Plaza de Armas on Avenida Sucre. Here, along Sucre as well as Jr Amadeo Figueroa, are many hotels and rooms for rent in private homes. **Museo Arqueológico de Ancash** ① *Ministerio de Cultura, Plaza de Armas, Mon-Sat 0900-1700, Sun 0900-1400,* contains stone monoliths and *huacos* from the Recuay culture, well labelled. The **Sala de Cultura SUNARP** ① *Av Centenario 530, Independencia, T421301, Mon-Fri 1700-2000, Sat 0900-1300, free,* often has interesting art and photography exhibitions by local artists.

About 8 km to the northeast is **Willkawain** ① *Tue-Fri 0830-1600, Sat-Sun 0900-1330, US$1.75, take a combi from 13 de Diciembre and Jr Cajamarca, US$0.50, 20 min, direct to Willkawain.* The ruins (AD 700-1100, Huari Empire) consist of one large three-storey structure with intact stone roof slabs and several small structures. About 500 m past Willkawain is Ichicwillkawain with

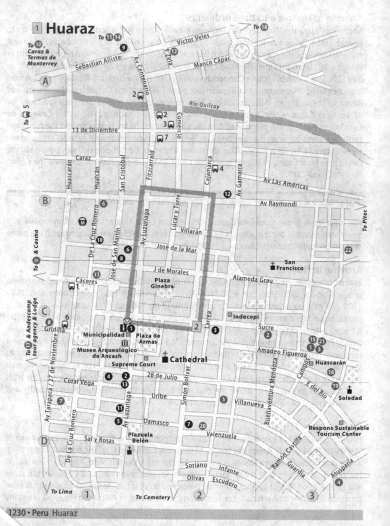

several similar but smaller structures. A well-signed trail climbs from Wilkawain to Laguna Ahuac (Aguak Cocha, 4580 m), 12 km return, a demanding acclimatization hike, no services along the way. North of Huaraz, 6 km along the road to Caraz, are the thermal baths at **Monterrey** (at 2780 m) ① *the lower pool is US$0.85; the upper pool, which is nicer (closed Mon for cleaning), US$1.35; also individual and family tubs US$1.35 per person for 20 mins; crowded at weekends and holidays.* There are restaurants and hotels. City buses along Avenida Luzuriaga go as far as Monterrey (US$0.22), until 1900; taxi US$2-3. **Note** that it is not safe to walk between Monterrey to Willkawain.

200 metres

200 yards

Where to stay 😊
1 Albergue Churup C3
2 Alojamiento El Jacal C3
3 Alojamiento Soledad C3
4 Andino Club D3
5 Angeles Inn D2
6 Backpackers B1
7 Benkawasi D1
8 Casa Jaimes C1
9 Edward's Inn B1
10 El Patio A1
11 Hatun Wasi A1
12 Hostal Colomba A2
13 Hostal Quintana C1
14 Jo's Place A2
15 La Cabaña C3
16 La Casa de Zarela C3
17 Lodging Caroline C1
18 Lodging House Ezama A3
19 Olaza's B&B D3
20 Res NG D2
21 Res Sucre C3
22 San Sebastián B3

Restaurants 🍴
1 Bistro de los Andes C2
2 Café El Centro C1
3 Cafetería y Juguería C2
4 California Café C1
5 Chifa Jim Hua D1
6 Fuente de Salud B1
7 Huaraz Querido D2
8 Las Puyas B1
9 Mi Comedia A1
10 Panadería La Alameda B1
11 Panadería Montserrat D1
12 Papa Loca B2
13 Pizza Bruno D1

Transport 🚌
1 Sandoval/Chavín Express C1
2 Combis to Caraz A1, A2
3 Combis to Wilcawain A2
4 Julio César B2
5 Móvil Tours A1
6 Terminal de Transportistas Zona Sur C1
7 Trans Huandoy A2

➡ **Huaraz maps**
1 Huaraz, page 1230
2 Huaraz centre, page 1232

⊙ Huaraz listings

For hotel and restaurant price codes, and other relevant information, see Essentials.

🛏 Where to stay

Huaraz *p1229, maps p1230 and p1232*
Hotels fill up rapidly in high season (May-Sep), especially during public holidays and special events when prices rise (beware overcharging). Touts meet buses and aggressively "suggest" places to stay. Do not be put off your choice of lodging; phone ahead to confirm.
$$$$-$$$ Andino Club, Pedro Cochachín 357, some way southeast of the centre (take a taxi after dark), T421662, www.hotelandino. com. Swiss-run hotel with very high standards, excellent restaurant, variety of rooms including panoramic views, balcony, fireplace, jacuzzi and sauna.
$$$ El Patio, Av Monterrey, 250 m downhill from the Monterrey baths, T424965, www. elpatio.com.pe. Very colonial-style with lovely gardens, comfortable rooms, singles, doubles and triples, some with balconies, also 4 lodges with fireplaces. Meals on request, bar.
$$$ Hostal Colomba, Francisco de Zela 210, just off Centenario across the river, T421501, www.huarazhotel.com. Lovely old hacienda, family-run, garden with playground and sports, safe parking, gym and well-equipped rooms sleeping 1-6, comfortable beds, restaurant.
$$$ The Lazy Dog Inn, 30 mins' drive from Huaraz (US$10 by taxi), close to the boundary of Huascarán National Park, 3.1 km past the town of Marian, close to the Quebrada Cojup, T943 789330, www.thelazydoginn. com. Eco-tourism lodge actively involved in community projects, water recycling systems and composting toilets. Beautifully designed

in warm colours, great location gives access to several mountain valleys. Organizes horse riding and hiking trips. Excellent home-cooked breakfast and dinner included. Canadian owned, English spoken. Recommended.

② Huaraz centre

Where to stay
1 Oscar's Hostal

Restaurants
1 Café Andino &
    Familia Meza Lodging
2 Chilli Heaven
3 Créperie Patrick
4 El Horno Pizzería Grill
5 Encuentro
6 Maialino
7 Pizza B&B
8 Pizzería Landauro
9 Rinconcito Minero
10 Rossanero
11 Sabor Salud
12 Trivio

Bars & clubs
13 '13 Buhos'
14 Amadeus
15 Extreme &
    Monttrek Agency
16 Taberna Tambo

50 metres
50 yards

$$$-$$ San Sebastián, Jr Italia 1124, T426960, www.sansebastianhuaraz.com. Elegant, modern hotel, comfortable beds with duvets, parking available, helpful, good views.

$$-$ Albergue Churup, Jr Amadeo Figueroa 1257, T424200, www.churup.com. 13 rooms with private bath or 2 dorms with shared bath, hot water, fire in sitting room on 4th floor, cafeteria, use of kitchen 1800-2200, lots of information, laundry, book exchange, English spoken, Spanish classes, adventure travel tours, extremely helpful. Airport transfers and free pick-up from bus.

$$-$ Edward's Inn, Bolognesi 121, T422692, www.huaraz.com/edwards. With or without bath, nice garden, laundry, breakfast extra, insist on proper rates in low season, popular. Edward speaks English and has 30 years' experience trekking, climbing and guiding in the area. He also rents gear.

$$-$ Hatun Wasi, Jr Daniel Villayzán 268, T425055. Family-run hotel next to Jo's place. Spacious rooms, with hot water, pleasant roof terrace, ideal for breakfasts, with great views of the Cordillera.

$$-$ La Casa de Zarela, J Arguedas 1263, T421694, www.lacasadezarela.hostel.com. Hot water, use of kitchen, laundry facilities, popular with climbers and trekkers, owner Zarela who speaks English organizes groups and is very knowledgeable.

$$-$ Residencial NG, Pasaje Valenzuela 837, T421831, www.residencialng.com. Breakfast, hot water, good value, helpful, has restaurant.

$ Alojamiento El Jacal, Jr Sucre 1044, T424612, reservaseljacal@yahoo.es. With or without shower, hot water, helpful family, garden, laundry facilities.

$ Alojamiento Soledad, Jr Amadeo Figueroa 1267, T421196, www.lodgingsoledad.com. Simple breakfast, private and shared bath, abundant hot water, use of kitchen, family home and atmosphere, secure, trekking information and tours. Warmly recommended.

$ Andescamp Hostel, Jr Huáscar 615, T423842, www.andescamphostel.com. See Trekking and climbing, below.

$ Angeles Inn, Av Gamarra 815, T422205, solandperu@yahoo.com. No sign, look for **Sol Andino** travel agency in same building (www.solandino.com), laundry facilities, garden,

➜ **Huaraz maps**
1 Huaraz, page 1230
2 Huaraz centre, page 1232

hot water, owners Max and Saul Angeles are official guides, helpful with trekking and climbing, rent equipment.

$ Backpackers, Av Raimondi 510, T421773, www.huaraz.com/backpackers. Breakfast not included. Dorms or private room with bathroom. Spacious, hot showers, good views, energetic staff, a real bargain, but heavy traffic outside.

$ Benkawasi, Parque Santa Rosa 928, 10 mins from centre, T423150, http://huarazbenkawasi. com. Doubles, also rooms for 3, 4 and dorm, hot water, breakfast US$5, laundry, games room, pick-up from bus station. Owner Benjamín Morales also has **Xtreme Bar**, **Infinite Tours** for mountain bike hire and tours of the National Park and a lodge at Playa Tortugas, near Casma (arranges downhill biking from Huaraz).

$ Casa Jaimes, Alberto Gridilla 267, T422281, 2 blocks from the main plaza, www.casajaimes. com. Dormitory with hot showers, laundry facilities, has maps and books of the region. Noisy but otherwise good.

$ Familia Meza, Lúcar y Torre 538, behind Café Andino (enquire here), T421203. Shared bath, hot water, laundry facilities, popular with trekkers, mountaineers and bikers.

$ Hostal Quintana, Mcal Cáceres 411, T426060, www.hostal-quintana.com. English, French, Italian and Spanish spoken, mountain gear rental, 2 of the owner's sons are certified guides and can arrange itineraries, laundry facilities, café popular with trekkers.

$ Jo's Place, Jr Daniel Villayzan 276, T425505, www.huaraz.com/josplace. Safe, hot water at night, nice mountain views, garden, terrace, English owner, warm atmosphere, popular.

$ La Cabaña, Jr Sucre 1224, T423428. Shared and double rooms, hot showers, laundry, popular, safe for parking, bikes and luggage, English and French spoken, good value.

$ Lodging Caroline, Urb Avitentel Mz D-Lt 1, T422588, http://carolinelodging.com. Colourful dorms in main building or private rooms in newer annex. Gay friendly. 10-min walk from centre, free pickup from bus station (phone ahead), hot water, tourist information, laundry, helpful. Compare tours offered here with those of established operators.

$ Lodging House Ezama, Mariano Melgar 623, Independencia, T423490, 15 mins' walk from Plaza de Armas (US$0.50 by taxi), www.huaraz.

com/ezama. Light, spacious rooms, hot water, safe, helpful.

$ Oscar's Hostal, La Mar 624, T422720, cvmonical@hotmail.com. Hot water, cheap breakfast next door, good beds, cheaper in low season, helpful.

$ Residencial Sucre, Sucre 1240, T422264, filibertor@terra.com.pe. Private house, kitchen, laundry facilities, hot water, English, German and French spoken, mountaineering guide, Filiberto Rurush, can be contacted here.

⑦ Restaurants

Huaraz p1229, maps p1230 and p1232
$$$ Créperie Patrick, Luzuriaga 422. Excellent crepes, fish, quiche, spaghetti and good wine.
$$$ Pizza Bruno, Luzuriaga 834. Open from 1600-2300. Best pizza, excellent crêpes and pastries, good service, French owner Bruno Reviron also has a 4WD with driver for hire.
$$$-$$ Mi Comedia, Av Centenario 351, T587954. Open 1700-2300. Wood-oven pizzas, rustic European style, very good service.
$$$-$$ Trivio, Parque del Periodista. Open for lunch and dinner. Creative food, good coffee, nice view.
$$ Bistro de los Andes, Plaza de Armas 2nd floor, T426249. Great food, owner speaks English, French and German. Plaza branch has a nice view of the plaza. Wide range of dishes including breakfasts.
$$ Chilli Heaven, Parque Ginebra, T396085. Run by a British biker, specializing in spicy food (Mexican, Indian, Thai), book exchange.
$$ El Horno Pizzería Grill, Parque del Periodista, T043-424617. Good atmosphere, fine grilled meats and nice location.
$$ Fuente de Salud, J de la Mar 562. Vegetarian, also meat and pasta dishes, serves good soups and breakfast.
$$ Huaraz Querido, Bolívar 981. Open for lunch only. Very popular place for great ceviche and other fish dishes.
$$ Maialino, Parque Ginebra, T940-241660. Popular for Italian and local dishes, cosy, welcoming, set meal for lunch and dinner costs US$2.50.
$$ Papa Loca, Av Raimondi 903, T978-495271, papalocarestaurant on Facebook. Tue-Sun 1700-2300. Varied menu from

Peruvian to British and Irish, good quality and value. Recommended.

$$ Pizza B&B, La Mar 674, beside laundry of same name. Excellent traditional sauces for pizza and pasta, and desserts.

$$ Pizzería Landauro, Sucre, on corner of Plaza de Armas. Closed 1200-1800 and Sun. Very good for pizzas, Italian dishes, sandwiches, breakfasts, nice atmosphere.

$$ Rinconcito Minero, J de Morales 757. Breakfast, lunch, vegetarian options, coffee and snacks

$$ Sabor Salud, Luzuriaga 672, upstairs. Pizzeria with vegetarian and Italian food.

$$-$ Chifa Jim Hua, Luzuriaga y Damasco. Large, tasty portions, economical *menú*. Mon-Sat 0900-1500, 1800-2400, Sun 1800-2200.

$$-$ Encuentro, Parque del Periodista and Julian de Morales 650, www.restaurant encuentro.com. Opens 0700. Breakfast, lunch and dinners, very busy, good.

$ Las Puyas, Morales 535. Popular with gringos, good *sopa criolla* and trout, also serves breakfast.

Cafés

Café Andino, Lúcar y Torre 538, 3rd floor, T421203, www.cafeandino.com. Peruvian/American-owned café-restaurant-bar with book exchange and extensive lending library in many languages. A great place to relax and meet other travellers, nice atmosphere, warmly recommended. Owner Chris Benway also runs **La Cima Logistics**, www.lacimalogistics.com, for custom outfitting in Cordilleras Blanca and Huayhuash.

Café El Centro, 28 de Julio 592. Good breakfast for US$1.30-2, great chocolate cake and apple pie.

Cafetería y Juguería, Sucre 806. Cheap café just above the Plaza. Serves excellent yogurt and honey drinks, among other treats.

California Café, 28 de Julio 562, T428354, http://huaylas.com/californiacafe/california.htm. Excellent breakfast, great coffee and chocolate cake, book exchange. Californian owner is a good source of information on trekking in the Cordillera Huayhuash and security issues.

Panadería La Alameda, Juan de La Cruz Romero 523 near market. Excellent bread and sweets.

Panadería Montserrat, Av Luzuriaga 928. Good bakery and café, cheap, pleasant atmosphere, good for a snack.

Rossanero, Luzuriaga entre Sucre y J de Morales, 2nd floor. 'Sofa-cafe' with extensive menu, ice cream, reasonable prices.

🎵 Bars and clubs

Huaraz *p1229, maps p1230 and p1232*
13 Buhos Bar, José de la Mar 2nd floor, above Makondo's. Afternoon, evening, and nightspot, very popular, owner makes his own craft beer. Good music, games, nice ambience.

Amadeus, Parque Ginebra. Bar-disco.

Taberna Tambo, José de la Mar 776. Open 1000-1600, 2000-early hours. Folk music daily, disco, full on, non-stop dance mecca. Very popular with both locals and gringos.

Vagamundo, J de Morales 753. Popular bar with snacks and football tables.

Xtreme, Luzuriaga 646. Open 1900-0200. Very popular with *gringos*, soft music.

✿ Festivals

Huaraz *p1229, maps p1230 and p1232*
Patron saints' day, **El Señor de la Soledad**, week starting **3 May**. **Semana del Andinismo**, in **Jun**, international climbing week. **San Juan** and **San Pedro** throughout the region during the last week of **Jun**. **Aug**, Inkafest mountain film festival, dates change each year.

O Shopping

Huaraz *p1229, maps p1230 and p1232*
Clothing For local sweaters, hats, gloves and wall hangings at good value, **Pasaje Mcal Cáceres**, off Luzuriaga, in the stalls off Luzuriaga between Morales and Sucre, Bolívar cuadra 6, and elsewhere. **Last Minute Gifts**, Lúcar Y Torre 530, 2nd floor, and **Peru Magico**, Sucre ½ block from Plaza, both sell hats, clothing, souvenirs and jewelry.
Markets The central market offers various canned and dry goods, as well as fresh fruit and vegetables. Beware pickpockets in this area. There are also several supermarkets in town (see Huaraz centre map), do not leave valuables in bags you check while shopping.

⏰ What to do

Huaraz *p1229, maps p1230 and p1232*
Try to get a recommendation from someone who has recently returned from a tour or trek, or see **South American Explorers'** recommendations in the Lima office. All agencies run conventional tours to Llanganuco (US$12 per person, very long day) and Chavín (8-10 hrs, US$14 per person), entry tickets not included. Many hire equipment.

Horse riding
Posada de Yungar, at Yungar (about 20 km on the Carhuaz road), T421267, 967 9836. Swiss run. Ask for José Flores or Gustavo Soto. US$4.50 per hr on nice horses; good 4-hr trip in the Cordillera Negra.
Sr Robinson Ayala Gride, T423813. Contact him well in advance for half-day trips (enquire at **El Cortijo** restaurant, on Huaraz-Caraz road, Km 6.5). He is a master paso rider.

Mountain biking
Mountain Bike Adventures, Lúcar y Torre 530, T424259, www.chakinaniperu.com. Contact Julio Olaza. US$60 pp for day trip, all included, various routes, excellent standard of equipment. Julio speaks excellent English and also runs a book exchange, sells topo maps and climbing books.

Trekking and climbing
Trekking tours cost US$50-70 pp per day, climbing US$100-140 pp per day. Many companies close in low season.
Active Peru, Gamarra 699 y Sucre, T423339, www.activeperu.com. Offers classic treks, climbing, plus standard tours to Chavín and Llanganuco, among others, good in all respects, Belgian owner speaks Dutch, German and English.
Alpa-K, Parque Ginebra 30-B, above Montañero, www.alpa-k.org. Owner Bertrand offers tours throughout Peru and has a B&B (**$**) on the premises. French, Spanish and some English spoken.
Andean Footsteps, Carretera Huaraz-Caraz Km 14, Paltay, and Jr José Olaya 103, Huaraz, T943-318820, www.andeanfootsteps.com. British/Peruvian operation (Yvonne Danson and David Maguiña), specializing in treks, climbs and tours with a commitment to using local personnel and resources. Local projects are sponsored.
Andean Kingdom, Parque Ginebra next to Casa de Guías, T425555, www.andeankingdom.com. Free information, maps, climbing wall, rock and ice climbing, including multi-day courses, treks, equipment rental, English and some Hebrew spoken, can be very busy. The company has a Refugio de Montaña, **Hatun Machay** (**$**), near the excellent rock-climbing site of Hatun Machay in the Cordillera Negra, with kitchen facilities and heating, transport arranged.
Andescamp, Jr Huáscar 625, T423842, or 1943-563424, www.andescamphostel.com. Popular agency and hostel, especially with budget travellers. Only qualified guides used for climbing trips. Variety of treks, mountaineering expeditions and courses, rafting, paragliding and other adventure sports. Hostel has dorms and private rooms, some with bath, and snack bar.

Cordillera Blanca Adventures, run by the Mejía Romero family, Los Nogales 108, T421934, www.cordillerablanca.org. Experienced, quality climbing/trekking trips, good guides/equipment.
Explorandes, Gamarra 835, T421960, www.explorandes.com.
Galaxia Expeditions, Parque del Periodista, T425355, www.galaxia-expeditions.com. Usual range of tours, climbing, hiking, biking, equipment hire, etc. Go to the office to buy tours direct, do not buy from unscrupulous sub-contractors.
Huascarán, Jr Pedro Campos 711, Soledad, T424504, www.huascaran-peru.com. Contact Pablo Tinoco Depaz, one of the brothers who run the company. Good 4-day Santa Cruz trip. Good food and equipment, professional service, free loan of waterproofs and pisco sour on last evening.
Kallpa, José de la Mar y Luzuriaga, p 2, T427868. Organizes treks, rents gear, arranges arrieros and mules, very helpful.
Montañero, Parque Ginebra 30-B, T426386, www.trekkingperu.com. Run by veteran mountain guide Selio Villón, German, French and English spoken.
Monttrek, Luzuriaga 646, upstairs, T421124, monttrek@terra.com.pe. Good trekking/climbing information, advice and maps, ice and rock climbing courses (at Monterrey), tours to Laguna Churup and the 'spectacular' Luna Llena tour; also hire mountain bikes, run ski instruction and trips, and river rafting. Helpful, conscientious guides. Next door in the Pizzería is a climbing wall, good maps, videos and slide shows. For new routes/maps contact Porfirio Cacha Macedo, 'Pocho', at Monttrek or at Jr Corongo 307, T423930.
Peruvian Andes Adventures, José Olaya 532, T421864, www.peruvianandes.com, www.perutrekkingclimbing.com. Run by Hisao and Eli Morales, professional, registered mountain and trekking guides. All equipment and services for treks of 3-15 days, climbing technical and non-technical peaks, or just day walks. Vegetarians catered for.
Quechua Explorer, Sucre 705 of 4, T422886, www.quechuaexplorer.com. Hiking, mountaineering, rock and ice climbing, rafting, biking, cultural and ecological tourism, experienced and friendly guides.

Quechuandes, Av Luzuriaga 522, T943-562339, www.quechuandes.com. Trekking, mountaineering, rock climbing, ice climbing, skiing, mountain biking and other adventure sports, guides speak Spanish, Quechua, English and/or French. Animal welfare taken seriously with weight limits of 40kg per donkey.
Respons Sustainable Tourism Center, Jr Eulogio del Rio 1364, Soledad, T956-125568, www.respons.org. Sustainable tourism initiatives, community based, with trekking, homestays, tours, volunteering and other responsible travel ideas.

Guides

Aritza Monasterio, through *Casa de Guías*. Speaks English, Spanish and Euskerra.
Augusto Ortega, Jr San Martín 1004, T424888, is the only Peruvian to have climbed Everest.
Casa de Guías, Plaza Ginebra 28-g in Huaraz, T421811. Mon-Sat 0900-1300, 1600-1800. This is the climbers' and hikers' meeting place. Has a full list of all members of the Asociación de Guías de Montaña del Perú (AGMP) throughout the country. It is useful with information, books, maps, arrangements for guides, *arrieros*, mules, etc. It operates as an agency and sells tours. Notice board, postcards and posters for sale and has a good restaurant (open 0700-1100, 1700-2300).
Christopher Benway, La Cima Logistics, cafeandino@hotmail.com. Makes custom arrangements for climbing and trekking trips.
Filiberto Rurush Paucar, Sucre 1240, T422264 (**Lodging Casa Sucre**), speaks English, Spanish and Quechua.
Genaro Yanac Olivera, T422825, speaks good English and some German, also a climbing guide.
Hugo Sifuentes Maguiña, Siex (Sifuentes Expeditions), Jr Huaylas 139, T426529, www.siexperu.com. Trekking, rock climbing and less adventurous tours.
Koky Castañeda, T427213, or through **Skyline Adventures**, or **Café Andino**. Speaks English and French, UIAGM Alpine certified.
Max, Misael and Saul Angeles, T456891 or 422205 (**Sol Andino** agency), speak some English, know Huayhuash well.
Máximo Henostrosa, T426040. Trekking guide with knowledge of the entire region.

Ted Alexander, Skyline Adventures, Pasaje Industrial 137, Cascapampa, Huaraz, T427097, www.skyline-adventures.com. US outward bound instructor, very knowledgeable.
Tjen Verheye, Jr Carlos Valenzuela 911, T422 569, is Belgian and speaks Dutch, French, German, and reasonable English, runs trekking and conventional tours and is knowledgeable about the Chavín culture.

Prices The Dirección de Turismo issues qualified guides and *arrieros* (muleteers) with a photo ID. Note down the name and card number in case you should have any complaints. Prices are currently set at: *arriero*, US$18 per day; donkey or mule, US$8 per day; trekking guides US$40-70 per day (more for foreign guides); climbing guides US$90-200 per day (more for foreign guides), depending on the difficulty of the peak; cooks US$30-40 per day; all subject to change. You are required to provide or pay for food and shelter for all *arrieros*, porters, cooks and guides. Associations of *arrieros*: Humacchuco-Llanganuco (for porters and cooks), T943-786497, victorcautivo@ hotmail.com. **Pashpa Arrieros**, T830540/83319. **Musho Arrieros**, T230003/814416. **Collon Arrieros** (for llama trekking), T833417/824146.

Camping gear The following agencies are recommended for hiring gear: Andean Kingdom, Galaxia Expeditions, Monttrek, Kallpa and Montañero. Also Skyline, Andean Sport Tours, Luzuriaga 571, T043-421612, and MountClimb, Jr Mcal Cáceres 421, T426060, mountclimb@yahoo.com. Casa de Guías rents equipment and sells dried food. Check all camping and climbing equipment very carefully before taking it. Quality varies and some items may not be available, so it's best to bring your own. All prices are standard, but not cheap, throughout town. All require payment in advance, passport or air ticket as deposit and rarely give any money back if you return gear early. Many trekking agencies sell screw-on camping gas cartridges. White gas (*bencina*) is available from *ferreterías* on Raymondi below Luzuriaga and by Parque Ginebra. Along the most popular routes, campers have complained that campsites are dirty, toilet pits foul and that rubbish is not taken away by groups. Do your share to make things better.

Tour operators

Chavín Tours, José de la Mar, T421578, www.chavintours.com.pe. All local tours, long-standing agency based in Lima.
Pablo Tours, Luzuriaga 501, T421145, www.pablotours.com. For all local tours, also with many years of operation.

⊖ Transport

Huaraz *p1229, maps p1230 and p1232*
Air LC Peru flies twice daily to/from **Lima**, 1 hr.
Bus To/from **Lima**: 7-8 hrs, US$17-30 (Móvil prices). Large selection of ordinary service and luxury coaches throughout the day. Many of the companies have their offices along Av Raymondi and on Jr Lúcar y Torre. Some recommended companies are: **Cavassa**, Jr Lúcar y Torre 446, T425767; **Rodríguez**, J de Morales 650, T429253; **Cruz del Sur**, Bolívar Mz C Lote 12, T728726; **Empresa 14**, Fitzcarrald 216, T421282, terminal at Bolívar 407; **Julio César**, Prol Cajamarca s/n, cuadra 1, T396443; **Móvil**, Av Confraternidad Internacional Oeste 451, T422555; **Oltursa**, Av Raymondi 825, T423717; **Z-Buss**, Av Raymondi, T428327.

Other long-distance buses To **Casma** via the Callán pass and Pariacoto (150 km) 7 hrs, US$12, the lower section of the road is very poor, landslides and closures are common (sit on the left for best views): **Transportes Huandoy**, Fitzcarrald 261, T427507 (terminal at Caraz 820), daily at 0800, 1000 and 1300. **Yungay Express**, Raymondi 930, T424377, 3 a day. They continue to Chimbote, 185 km. To Chimbote via Caraz and the Cañon del Pato (sit on the right for the most exciting views) *Yungay Express*, daily, US$14, 10 hrs. Other companies go to **Chimbote** via Pativilca, 7 hrs (to **Pativilca**, 160 km, 4 hrs). Most continue to **Trujillo**, all buses go at night, 8-9 hrs, US$17-30: **Línea** (Simón Bolívar 450, T726666), **Móvil** and **Empresa 14**, addresses above.

Within the Cordillera Blanca Several buses and frequent minivans run daily, 0500-2000, between Huaraz and **Caraz**, 1¼ hrs, US$2, from the parking area by the bridge on Fitzcarrald, no luggage racks, you might have to pay an extra seat for your bag. To **Chavín**, 110 km, 2 hrs (sit on left side for best views), US$6: Sandoval/Chavín Express, Mcal

Cáceres 338, 3 a day. Also Trans Río Mosna, Mcal Cáceres 265, T426632, 3 a day; buses go on to Huari, 4 hrs, US$7.50.

To **Chacas**, US$7, and **San Luis**, an unforgettable ride via the 4700-m-high Punta Olímpica tunnel, US$8, at 0700 with **Virgen de Guadalupe**, Caraz 607. **Renzo**, Raymondi 821, T425371, runs to Chacas daily (0615, 1400), **Piscobamba** and **Pomabamba** (0630, best, and 1900). **Los Andes**, same office as Yungay Express, T427362, daily 0630 to Yungay, US$1, Lagunas de Llanganuco, US$7, Yanama, US$7, Piscobamba, US$8 and Pomabamba, US$9, 8 hrs. This route is also served by **La Perla de Alta Mayo**, daily 0630, 8 hrs to Pomabamba, US$9. To **Sihuas**, also Sandoval/Chavín Express, Tue/Fri 0800; **Perú Andino**, 1 a week, 8 hrs, US$11.

Colectivos to **Recuay**, US$0.75, and **Catac**, US$0.85, daily at 0500-2100, from Gridilla, just off Tarapacá (Terminal de Transportistas Zona Sur). To **Chiquián** for the Cordillera Huayhuash (see below). To **Huallanca** (Huánuco), the route now taken is the paved road through Conococha, Chiquián, Aquia to Huansala, then by good dirt road to Laguna Pachacoto and Huallanca to La Unión (paving under way). Departs Huaraz twice a day, first at 1300, with **Trans El Rápido**, Bolognesi 216, T422887, US$8. Frequent daily service from Huallanca to Huánuco.

Taxi Standard fare in town is about US$1, more at night; radio taxis T421482 or 422512.

Cordillera Blanca

Apart from the range of Andes running along the Chile-Argentina border, the highest mountains in South America lie along the Cordillera Blanca and are perfectly visible from many spots. From Huaraz alone, you can see more than 23 peaks of over 5000 m, of which the most notable is Huascarán (6768 m), the highest mountain in Peru. Although the snowline is receding, the Cordillera Blanca still contains the largest concentration of glaciers found in the world's tropical zone and the turquoise-coloured lakes, which form in the terminal moraines, are the jewels of the Andes. Here also is one of Peru's most important pre-Inca sites, at Chavín de Huantar.

Parque Nacional Huascarán

Established in July 1975, the park includes the entire Cordillera Blanca above 4000 m, with an area of 3400 sq km. It is a UNESCO World Biosphere Reserve and part of the World Heritage Trust. The park's objectives are to protect the flora, fauna, geology, archaeological sites and scenic beauty of the Cordillera. Take all your rubbish away with you when camping. The park charges visitors US$8 for three daytime visits; no camping, no overnight stays. For visits of up to 21-30 days (ie for trekking and climbing trips) a permit costing US$25 (70 soles) must be bought. Fees for visiting the national park are collected in the park office in Huaraz (see below) and at rangers posts at Llanganuco and Huascarán (for the Llanganuco to Santa Cruz trek), at Collón on the way up the Quebrada Ishinca. The **park office** ① *Jr Federico Sal y Rosas 555, by Plazuela Belén, T422086, pnhuascaran@sernanp.gob.pe; Mon-Fri 0830-1300, 1430-1700*, is principally administrative, with no information for visitors.

Regulations state that local guides are mandatory everywhere in the park except designated 'Recreation Zones' (areas accessible by car). Tourists must hire a licensed tour operator for all activities and those operators may only employ licensed guides, cooks, arrieros and porters. Fees, regulations and their implementation change frequently, always confirm details in Huaraz.

Trekking and climbing in the Cordillera Blanca

The Cordillera Blanca offers popular backpacking and trekking, with a network of trails used by the local people and some less well-defined mountaineers' routes. Most circuits can be hiked in five days. Although the trails are easily followed, they are rugged with high passes, between 4000 and 5000 m, so backpackers should be fit and acclimatized to the altitude, and carry all equipment. Essential items are a tent, warm sleeping bag, stove, and protection against wind and rain (the weather is unreliable and you cannot rule out rain and hail storms even in the dry season). Less stamina is required if you hire mules to carry equipment. The season is from May to September, although conditions vary from year to year. The rainy season in Huaraz is December-March.

Advice to climbers The height of the Cordillera Blanca and the Callejón de Huaylas ranges and their location in the tropics create conditions different from the Alps or even the Himalayas. Fierce sun makes the mountain snow porous and glaciers move more rapidly. Deglaciation is rapidly changing the face of the Cordillera. Older maps do not provide a reliable indication of the extent of glaciers and snow fields (according to some studies 15% of the range's glaciers have disappeared since the 1970s), so local experience is important. If the rules prohibiting independent treks or climbs have not been implemented (see above), move in groups of four or more, reporting to the Casa de Guías (see page 1236) or the office of the guide before departing, giving the date at which a search should begin, and leaving your embassy's telephone number, with money for the call. International recommendations are for a 300 m per day maximum altitude gain. Be wary of agencies wanting to sell you trips with very fast ascents (but ask around if this is what you want).

It is imperative that all climbers carry adequate insurance (it cannot be purchased locally). Be well prepared before setting out on a climb. Wait or cancel your trip when the weather is bad. Every year climbers are killed through failing to take weather conditions seriously. Climb only when and where you have sufficient experience. Rescue services, while better than in the past, may not be up to international standards. In the event of an emergency try calling the **Casa de Guías**, T427545 or T421811; Edson Ramírez at the national park office, T944 627946 or T943-626627; or the Police, T105. Satellite phones can be rented through the Casa de Guías and there is cell-phone coverage in some (but not all) parts of the Cordillera Blanca.

Note Before heading out on any route, always enquire locally about public safety. The Cordillera Blanca is generally safe, but muggings have taken place on the way to Laguna Churup and to the Mirador Rataquenua above Huaraz; see also above concerning Monterrey. On all treks in this area, respect the locals' property, leave no rubbish behind, do not give sweets or money to children who beg and remember your cooking utensils and tent would be very expensive for a *campesino*, so be sensitive and responsible.

Huaraz to Chavín → *For guides and prices, see Huaraz listings, page 1236.*
South of Huaraz is **Olleros** (*Altitude: 3450 m*). The spectacular and relatively easy three- to four-day hike to Chavín, along a pre-Columbian trail, starts from Olleros. Some basic meals and food supplies available. At 38 km via the main road from Huaraz is **Catac** (two basic hotels and a restaurant), where a paved road branches east for Chavín.

A good place to see the impressive Puya Raimondi plants is the Pumapampa valley. A 14-km gravel road from Pachacoto goes to the park entrance (4200 m), where there is a park office. You can spend the night here. Walking up the road from this point, you will see the gigantic plants, whose flower spike, which can reach 12 m in height, takes 100 years to develop. The final flowering (usually in May) is a spectacular sight. Another good spot, and less visited, is the **Queshque Gorge**. Follow the Río Queshque from Catac (see above); it's easy to find.

From Catac to Chavín is a magnificent journey. The road passes Lago Querococha, has good views of the Yanamarey peaks and, at the top of the route, is cut through a huge rock face, entering the Cahuish tunnel at 4516 m. (The tunnel has no light and is single lane; a small stream runs inside. Cyclists must have a strong light so that trucks and buses can see them.) On the other side it descends the Tambillo valley, then the Río Mosna gorge before Chavín.

Chavín de Huantar
① *Tue-Sun 0900-1600, US$3.50, students half price, Spanish-speaking guides will take groups at an extra charge.*

Chavín de Huantar, a fortress temple, was built about 800 BC. It is the only large structure remaining of the Chavín culture which, in its heyday, is thought to have held influence in a region between Cajamarca and Chiclayo in the north to Ayacucho and Ica in the south. In December 1985, UNESCO designated Chavín a World Heritage Trust Site. The site is in good condition despite the effects of time and nature. The main attractions are the marvellous carved stone heads (*cabezas clavas*) and designs in relief of symbolic figures and the many tunnels and culverts which form an extensive labyrinth throughout the interior of the pyramidal structure. The carvings are in excellent condition, and the best are now in the Museo Nacional Chavín. The famous Lanzón dagger-shaped stone monolith of 800 BC is found inside one of the temple tunnels. In order to protect the site some areas are closed to visitors. All the galleries open to the public have electric lights. The guard is also a guide and gives excellent explanations of the ruins. The **Museo Nacional Chavín** ① *1 km north of town and 1.6 km from the site, Tue-Sun, 0900-1700, US$3.50* has a comprehensive collection of items, gathered from several deposits and museums, including the Tello obelisk dating from the earliest period of occupation of Chavín (c 100BC) and many impressive *cabezas clavas*.

In high season, the site is busy with tourists all day through. You will receive an information leaflet in Spanish at the entrance.

The town of Chavín → *Altitude: 3140 m.*
Just north of the ruins, Chavín, painted colonial yellow and white, has a pleasant plaza with palm and pine trees. There are a couple of good, simple hotels and restaurants; local *fiesta* July 13-20.

Chavín to Pomabamba → *225 km in total, gravel road, parts rough.*
From Chavín one circuit by road back to Huaraz is via Huari, San Luis, Yanama and Yungay (see page 1242) but the bus service is infrequent. The road north from Chavín descends into the Mosna river canyon. The scenery is quite different from the other side of the Cordillera Blanca, very dry and hot. After 8 km it reaches **San Marcos**, the town that has been most heavily impacted by the huge **Antamina** gold mine. Hotels may be full with mine workers and public safety is a concern. After 32 km is **Huari**, perched on a hillside at 3150 m, with various simple hotels (**$** Huagancu 2, Jr Sucre 335, T630434, clean and good value) and restaurants. **Fiesta of Nuestra Señora del Rosario** first two weeks of October, main day 7th.

There is a spectacular **two- to three-day walk** from Huari to Chacas via Laguna Purhuay. Alberto Cafferata of Caraz writes: "The Purhuay area is beautiful. It has splendid campsites, trout, exotic birds and, at its north end, a 'quenual' forest with orchids. This is a microclimate at 3500 m, where the animals, insects and flowers are more like a tropical jungle, fantastic for ecologists and photographers." A day walk to Laguna Purhuay, starting at the village of Acopalca (taxi from Huari to Acopalca US$3.50, to Puruhuay US$14) is a nice alternative for those who don't want to do the longer walk to Chacas. The lake is inside Parque Nacional Huascarán. There is a visitors' centre, food kiosk and boat rides.

In **Chacas**, 10 km south of San Luis on a paved road, is a fine church. The local *fiesta* (**Virgen de la Asunción**) is on 15 August, with bullfights, a famous *carrera de cintas* and fireworks. There are hostels (**$**), shops, restaurants and a small market. A spectacular paved road and 4700-m-high tunnel through Punta Olímpica, opened in 2013, connects Chacas with Carhuaz in the Callejón de Huaylas.

It is a **three-day hike** from Chacas to Marcará via the Quebradas Juytush and Honda (lots of condors to be seen). The Quebrada Honda is known as the Paraíso de las Cascadas because it contains at least seven waterfalls. From Huari the road climbs to the Huachacocha pass at 4350 m and descends to **San Luis** at 3130 m, 60 km from Huari (**$** Hostal Puñuri, Ramón Castilla 151, T043-830408, with bath and hot water, a few basic restaurants, shops and a market).

Some 20 km north of San Luis, a road branches left to **Yanama**, 45 km from San Luis, at 3400 m. It has a good comfortable hotel, **Andes Lodge Peru**, T043-943 847423, www.andeslodgeperu.com

($$, full board available, excellent food and services, fabulous views). The village retains many traditional features and is beautifully surrounded by snow-capped peaks. A day's hike to the ruins above the town affords superb views.

A longer circuit to Huaraz can be made by continuing from San Luis 62 km to **Piscobamba**. There are a couple of basic hotels, also a few shops and small restaurants. Beyond Piscobamba by 22 km, is **Pomabamba**, worth a visit for some very hot natural springs (the furthest are the hottest). There are various hotels ($) near the plaza and restaurants.

From Pomabamba a dusty road runs up the wooded valley crossing the puna at Palo Seco, 23 km. The road then descends steeply into the desert-like Sihuas valley, passing through the village of Sicsibamba. The valley is crossed half an hour below the small town of **Sihuas**, a major connection point between the Callejón de Conchucos, Callejón de Huaylas, the upper Marañón and the coast. It has a few $ hotels and places to eat. From Sihuas it is possible to travel, via Huancaspata, Tayabamba, Retamas and Chahual to Huamachuco along a road which is very poor in places and involves crossing the Río Marañón twice. Using this route, it is possible to travel from Cuzco to Quito through the Andes entirely by public transport. This journey is best undertaken in this direction though the road can take over two days (if it's not impassable) in the wet season.

Caraz → Altitude: 2290 m. Colour map 3, B2.

This pleasant town is a good centre for walking, parasailing and the access point for many excellent treks and climbs. Tourist facilities are expanding as a more tranquil alternative to Huaraz, and there are great views of Huandoy, Huascarán and surrounding summits in July and August. In other months, the mountains are often shrouded in cloud. Caraz has a milder climate than Huaraz and is more suited to day trips. The ruins of **Tumshukaiko** are 1½ km from the Plaza de Armas in the suburb of Cruz Viva, to the north before the turn-off for Parón. There are seven platforms from the Huaraz culture, dating from around 2000-1800 BC, but the site is in poor shape. The **Museo Arqueológico Municipal** is on San Martín, half a block up from the plaza. The **tourist office**, at Plaza de Armas, next to the municipality, T391029 ext 143, has limited information. There are three ATMs in the centre. On 20 January is the fiesta **Virgen de Chiquinquirá**. In the last week of July is **Semana Turística**.

Treks from Caraz

A good day walk goes from Caraz by the lakes of Miramar and Pampacocha to Huaripampa, where you can get a pickup back to Caraz. A longer full-day walk with excellent views of Huandoy and Huascarán follows the foothills of the Cordillera Blanca east of the main Río Santa valley, from Caraz south through the villages of Chosica and Ticrapa. It ends at Puente Ancash on the Caraz–Yungay road, from where frequent transport goes back to Caraz.

A large stand of **Puya Raimondi** can be seen in the Cordillera Negra southwest of Caraz. Beyond Pueblo Libre is a paved road which heads west via Pamparomás and Moro to join the Panamerican highway south of Chimbote. After 45 km (1½ hours) are the Puya Raymondi plants at a place called **Winchos**, with views of 145 km of the Cordillera Blanca and to the Pacific. The plants are usually in flower May or October. Take warm clothing, food and water. You can also camp near the puyas and return the following day. The most popular way to get there is to rent a bike (US$18 per day), go up by public transport (see below), and ride back down in four or five hours. Or form a group (eg via the bulletin board at **Pony's Expeditions**, Caraz) and hire a car which will wait for you (US$60 for five). From Caraz, a minibus for Pamparomás leaves from Ramón Castilla y Jorge Chávez around 0830, two hours, US$3 (get there at about 0800 as they often leave early). From the pass (El Paso) or El Cruce it is a short walk to the plants. Return transport leaves between 1230 and 1300. If you miss the bus, you can walk back to Pueblo Libre in four hours, to Caraz in six to eight hours, but it is easy to get lost and there are not many people to ask directions along the way.

Laguna Parón From Caraz a narrow, rough road goes east 32 km to beautiful Laguna Parón ① *US$3.50*, in a cirque surrounded by several, massive snow-capped peaks, including Huandoy, Pirámide Garcilazo and Caraz. The gorge leading to it is spectacular. It is a long day's trek for acclimatized hikers (25 km) up to the lake at 4150 m, or a four- to five-hour walk from the village of Parón, which can be reached by combi (U$2.50). Camping is possible. There is no trail around the lake and you should not attempt it as it is slippery and dangerous, particularly on the southern shore; tourists have been killed here.

Santa Cruz Valley One of the best known treks in the area is the beautiful three- to five-day route from Vaquería, over the 4750 m Punta Unión pass, to Quebrada Santa Cruz and the village of Cashapampa. It can be hiked in either direction. Starting in Cashpampa, you climb more gradually to the pass, then down to Vaquería or the Llanganuco lakes beyond. Along this 'clockwise' route the climb is gentler, giving more time to acclimatize, and the pass is easier to find, although on the other hand, if you start in Vaquería and finish in Cashapampa you ascend for one day rather than three in the other direction. You can hire an *arriero* and mule in Cashapampa, prices given in Listings, What to do, see page 1245. Campsites are at Llamacorral and Taullipampa before Punta Unión, and Quenoapampa (or Huaripampa) after the pass. You can end the hike at Vaquería on the Yanama-Yungay road and take a minibus or, better, an open truck from there (a beautiful run). Or end the walk a day later with a night at the Yuraccorral campsite, at the Llanganuco lakes, from where cars go back to Yungay. This trek is very popular and offered by all tour agencies in Huaraz and Caraz.

Yungay → *Colour map 3, B2.*

The main road goes on 12 km south of Caraz to Yungay which was completely buried during the 1970 earthquake by a massive mudslide; a hideous tragedy in which 20,000 people lost their lives. The earthquake and its aftermath are remembered by many older residents of the Callejón de Huaylas. The original site of Yungay, known as Yungay Viejo, desolate and haunting, has been consecrated as a *camposanto* (cemetery). The new settlement is on a hillside just north of the old town. It has a pleasant plaza and a concrete market, good on Wednesday and Sunday. October 17 is the **Virgen del Rosario** fiesta and October 28 is the anniversary of the founding of the town. The tourist office is on the corner of the Plaza de Armas.

Lagunas de Llanganuco

The Lagunas de Llanganuco are two lakes nestling 1000 m below the snowline beneath Huascarán and Huandoy. The first you come to is Laguna Chinancocha (3850 m), the second Laguna Orconcocha (3863 m). The park office is situated below the lakes at 3200 m, 19 km from Yungay. Accommodation is provided for trekkers who want to start the Llanganuco-Santa Cruz trek from here. From the park office to the lakes takes about five hours (a steep climb). For the last 1½ hours, a nature trail, Sendero María Josefa (sign on the road), takes 1½ hours to walk to the western end of Chinancocha where there is a control post, descriptive trail and boat trips on the lake. Walk along the road beside the lake to its far end for peace and quiet among the quenual trees, which provide shelter for 75% of the birdlife found in the park.

Carhuaz → *Colour map 3, B2.*

After Yungay, the main road goes to **Mancos** (8 km south, 30 minutes) at the foot of Huascarán. There is a dormitory at **La Casita de mi Abuela**, some basic shops and restaurants. From Mancos it is 14 km to Carhuaz, a friendly, quiet mountain town with a pleasant plaza. There is very good walking in the neighbourhood (eg to thermal baths; up the Ulta valley). Market days are Wednesday and Sunday (the latter is much larger). The local fiesta of **Virgen de las Mercedes**, 14-24 September, is rated as among the best in the region.

⊙ Cordillera Blanca listings

For hotel and restaurant price codes, and other relevant information, see Essentials.

⊖ Where to stay

Chavín *p1240*

$$-$ La Casona, Wiracocha 130, Plaza de Armas, T454116, www.lacasonachavin.com.pe. In a renovated house with attractive courtyard, single, double and triple rooms, some with balcony overlooking Plaza or courtyard, nice breakfast, laundry, parking.

$$-$ R'ikay, on 17 de Enero 172N, T454068. Set around 2 patios, modern, best in town, variety of room sizes, hot water, restaurant does Italian food in the evening. Recommended.

$ Hostal Chavín, Jr San Martín 141-151, half a block from the plaza, T454055. Pleasant courtyard, hot water, will provide breakfast for groups, best of the more basic hotels but beds are poor.

$ Inca, Wiracocha 170, T754021, www.huaraz.com/hotelinca. Rooms are cheaper without bath, good beds, hot water on request, nice garden.

Caraz *p1241*

$$$-$$ Los Pinos Lodge, Parque San Martín 103 (also known as Plazuela de la Merced), T391130, www.lospinoslodge.pe. Nice comfortable rooms, patio, gardens, parking, cosy bar, tourist information. Recommended. Also have a nearby annex nearby called **Caraz Backpacker ($)**.

$$$-$$ O'Pal Inn, Km 265.5, 5 min south of Caraz, T391015, www.opalsierraresort.com. Scenic, family bungalows, suites and rooms, swimming pool, includes breakfast, restaurant, games room.

$$-$ La Alameda, Av Noé Bazán Peralta 262, T391177, www.hotellaalameda.com. Comfortable rooms, hot water, ample parking, pleasant gardens.

$ Caraz Dulzura, Sáenz Peña 212, about 12 blocks from the city centre, T392090, www.hostalcarazdulzura.com. Modern building in an old street, hot water, comfortable, airy rooms, restaurant and bar.

$ Chavín, San Martín 1135 just off the plaza, T391171. Get a room overlooking the street,

many others have no window. Warm water, breakfast extra, guiding service, tourist info.

$ Hostal La Casona, Raymondi 319, 1 block east from the plaza, T391334. With or without bath, hot water, lovely little patio, noisy at night.

$ La Perla de los Andes, Daniel Villar 179, Plaza de Armas, next to the cathedral, T392007, http://huaraz.com/perladelos andes. Comfortable rooms, hot water, helpful, average restaurant.

$ San Marco, San Martín 1133, T391558. Comfortable rooms with private or shared bath, hot water, patio.

Yungay *p1242*

$ Complejo Turístico Yungay (COMTURY), Prolongación 2 de Mayo 1012, 2.5 km south of the new town, 700 m east of main road in Aura, the only neighbourhood of old Yungay that survived, T788656. Nice bungalows, pleasant country setting, hot water, fireplace, restaurant with regional specialities, camping possible.

$ Hostal Gledel, Av Arias Graziani, north past plaza, T793048, www.huaraz.com/gledel. Owned by Sra Gamboa, who is hospitable and a good cook, shared bath, hottish water, no towels or soap, cheap meals prepared on request, nice courtyard.

$ Hostal Sol de Oro, Santo Domingo 7, T493116, www.huaraz.com/soldeoro. Most rooms with bath, hot water, comfortable, breakfast and dinner on request, good value, best in town.

Lagunas de Llanganuco *p1242*

$$$$-$ Llanganuco Mountain Lodge, Lago Keushu, Llanganuco Valley, close to Huascarán park entrance (booking office in Huaraz: Gamarra 699), T943 669580, www.llanganucomountainlodge.com. 2 luxury rooms, 2 standard rooms and 10-bed dormitory. Room rate is seasonal and full board with a packed lunch, dorm beds can be with or without meals, modern, camping area, excellent food in restaurant, helpful staff, fine views and limitless possibilities for trekking (equipment rental and logistics), British-owned.

Carhuaz *p1242*

$$ pp **Casa de Pocha**, 1.5 km out of town towards Hualcán, at foot of Nevado Hualcán, ask directions in town, T943-613058 (mob 1800-2000), www.socialwellbeing.org/lacasadepocha.htm. Including breakfast and dinner, country setting, entirely solar and wind energy powered, hot water, sauna and pool, home-produced food (vegetarian available), horses for hire, camping possible, many languages spoken. Book in advance.

$$ El Abuelo, Jr 9 de Diciembre 257, T394456, www.elabuelohostal.com. Modern, comfortable 3-star, laundry, restaurant, large garden with organic fruit and veg, parking, credit cards accepted. Knowledgeable owner is map-maker, Felipe Díaz.

$ Hostal Señor de Luren, Buin 549, 30 m from Plaza de Armas, T668806. Hot water, safe motorcycle parking, very hospitable.

$ 4 family-run *hospedajes* operate as part of a community development project. All have private bath and hot water. The better 2 are: **Hospedaje Robri**, Jr Comercio 935, T394505. Modern. **Alojamiento Las Torresitas**, Jr Amazonas 603, T394213.

🍴 Restaurants

Chavín *p1240*

$$-$ Chavín Turístico, middle of 17 de Enero. The best in town, good *menú* and à la carte, delicious apple pie, nice courtyard, popular. Also run a hostal nearby.

$$-$ La Portada, towards south end of 17 de Enero. In an old house with tables set around a pleasant garden.

$ La Ramada, towards north end of main street, 17 de Enero. Regional dishes, also trout and set lunch.

Caraz *p1241*

$$ Venezia, Av Noé Bazán Peralta 231, T784813. Good homemade pasta, Italian owner.

$$-$ Entre Panes, Daniel Villar 211, half a block from the plaza. Closed Tue. Variety of excellent sandwiches, also meals. Good food, service and atmosphere.

$$-$ La Punta Grande, D Villar 595, 10 mins' walk from centre. Closes 1700. Best place for local dishes.

$$-$ La Terraza, Jr Sucre 1107, T301226. Good *menú* as well as pizza, pasta, juices, home made ice cream, sandwiches, sweets, coffee and drinks.

$ Jeny, Daniel Villar on the plaza next to the Cathedral. Local fare at reasonable prices, ample variety.

Cafés

Café de Rat, Sucre 1266, above *Pony's Expeditions*. Breakfast, vegetarian dishes, good pizzas, drinks and snacks, darts, travel books, nice atmosphere.

El Turista, San Martín 1117. Open in morning and evening only. Small, popular for breakfast, ham omelettes and ham sandwiches are specialities.

Heladería Caraz Dulzura, D Villar on the plaza. Homemade ice cream.

Panificadora La Alameda, D Villar y San Martín. Good bread and pastries, ice cream, popular with locals. The excellent *manjar blanco* for which the town earned it's nickname 'Caraz dulzura' is sold here and at several other shops on the same street.

Yungay *p1242*

$$ Alpamayo, Av Arias Graziani s/n. At north entrance to town, good for local dishes, lunchtime only.

$ Café Pilar, on the main plaza. Good for juices, cakes and snacks.

Carhuaz *p1242*

$$ La Bicharra, just north of Carhuaz on main road, T943-780893 (mob). Innovative North African/Peruvian cooking, lunch only, busy at weekends, call ahead to check if they are open on weekdays.

🍸 Bars and clubs

Caraz *p1241*

Airu Resto Bar, at Los Pinos Lodge, Parque San Martín. Open 1800-2200. Serves wines and piscos.

🛍 Shopping

Caraz *p1241*

Camping supplies Fresh food in the market. Some dried camping food is available from

Pony's Expeditions, who also sell camping gaz canisters and white gas.

O What to do

Caraz *p1241*

Agencies in Caraz arrange treks in the Cordillera Huayhuash, as well as more local destinations.
Apu-Aventura, Parque San Martín 103, 5 blocks west of plaza, T391130, www.apu aventura.pe. Range of adventure sports and equipment rental.
Pony's Expeditions, Sucre 1266, near the Plaza de Armas, T391642, www.ponyexpeditions. com. Mon-Sat 0800-2200. English, French, Italian and Quechua spoken. Owners Alberto and Aidé Cafferata are knowledgeable about treks and climbs. They arrange local tours, offer accommodation at **Pony's Lodge ($$)** and **Backpacker Los Ponys ($)**, trekking, transport for day excursions, and rental of a 4WD vehicle with driver (US$125 per day plus fuel). Also maps and books for sale, equipment hire and mountain bike rental (US$18 for a full day). Well organized and reliable. Highly recommended.

O Transport

Chavín *p1240*

Bus It is much easier to get to Chavín (even walking!) than to leave the place by bus. All buses to **Huaraz** originate in Huari or beyond. They pass through Chavín at irregular hours and may not have seats available. Buying a ticket at an agency in Chavín does not guarantee you will get a seat or even a bus. For buses from **Huaraz**, see under Huaraz. Sandoval/Chavín Express goes through around 1200, 1600 and 1700 daily, **Río Mosna** at 0430 and then 4 between 1600-2200. Bus to Huaraz takes 2 hrs. To **Lima**, 438 km, 12 hrs, US$14, with Trans El Solitario and Perú Andino daily. Locals prefer to travel to Huaraz and then take one of the better companies from there.

To other destinations in the Callejón de Conchucos, either use buses coming from Huaraz or Lima, or hop on and off combis which run between each town. To **San Marcos**, 8 km, and **Huari**, 38 km, take one of the cars or combis which leave regularly from the main plaza in Chavín, every 20 mins and 30 mins

respectively. There are buses during the day from Lima and Huaraz which go on to **Huari**, with some going on to **San Luis**, a further 61 km, 3 hrs; **Piscobamba**, a further 62 km, 3 hrs; and **Pomabamba**, a further 22 km, 1 hr; such as El Solitario which passes through Chavín at 1800.

Chavín to Pomabamba *p1240*
Huari

Bus Terminal Terrestre at Av Circunvalación Baja. To **Huaraz**, 4 hrs, US$5.50, Sandoval/ Chavín Express 3 a day. Also runs to **San Luis** and **Lima**.

Yanama

Bus Daily between **Yungay** and Yanama over the 4767-m Portachuelo de Llanganuco (3 hrs, US$7.50), continuing to Pomabamba.

Pomabamba

To **Piscobamba**, combis depart hourly, 1 hr, US$1.50. There are no combis from Piscobamba to San Luis. To **Lima**, 18 hrs, US$15, via San Luis (4 hrs, US$5), Huari (6 hrs, US$7.50) and Chavín (9 hrs, US$9) with El Solitario Sun, Mon and Thu at 0800; via **Yungay** and **Huaraz** with La Perla del Alto Mayo, Wed, Thu, Sat, Sun, 16 hrs.

Sihuas

Bus To **Pomabamba**, combi from Av 28 de Julio near the market at 1100, 4 hrs, US$7 (returns 0200). To **Huaraz**, via Huallanca, with Cielo Azul, daily at 0830, 10 hrs, US$11. To **Tayabamba**, for the Marañón route north to Huamachuco and Cajamarca: **Andía** passes through from Lima on Sat and Sun at 0100, La Perla del Alta Mayo passes through Tue, Thu 0000-0200; also **Garrincha** Wed, Sun around 0800; all 8 hrs, US$11, the beginning of a long wild ride. To **Huacrachuco**, Andía, passes through Wed, Sat 0100. To **Chimbote**, Corvival on Wed, Thu and Sun morning, 9 hrs, US$9; La Perla del Alta Mayo Tue, Thu, Sun. To **Lima** (19 hrs, US$20) via Chimbote, **Andía** Tue, Sun 0200, Wed, Sat 1600; and 3 other companies once or twice a week each.

Caraz *p1241*

Bus From Caraz to **Lima**, 470 km, 9 companies, daily, US$11-30 (El Huaralino,

T996-896607, **Huaraz Buss**, T943-469736, Zbuss, T391050, **Cooperativa Ancash**, T391126, all on Jr Cordova; **Rochaz**, Pasaje Olaya, T794375, **Cavassa**, Carretera Central, T392042, Yungay Express, Av Luzuriaga, T391492, **Móviltours**, east end of town, www.moviltours. com.pe, **Rodríguez**, Daniel Villar, T635631), 10-11 hrs. All go via Huaraz and Pativilca. To **Chimbote**, Yungay Express, via Huallanca, Casma and Cañon del Pato, 3 daily, US$9, 7 hrs. Sit on right for best views. To **Trujillo**, via Casma with **Móviltours**. To **Huaraz**, combis leave 0400-2000, 1¼ hrs, US$2, no luggage racks, you might have to pay an extra seat for your bag. They leave from a terminal on the way out of town, where the south end of C Sucre meets the highway. To **Yungay**, 12 km, 15 mins, US$0.70. To **Huallanca** and **Yuramarca** (for the Cañon del Pato), combis and cars leave from Córdova y La Mar, 0700-1600, US$2.50.

Treks from Caraz *p1242*
Laguna Parón
To the village of **Parón**, *colectivos* from Ramón Castilla y Jorge Chávez, close to the market, 1 hr, US$1.50. Taxi from Caraz to the lake, US$40-45 for 4 passengers. **Pony's Expeditions** have a pool of well-trained drivers who make daily departures to Laguna Parón at 0800, US$60 for 4, including 1-hr visit to the lake and 1-hr walk. Also, you can hire a bike (US$18 per day), take a car up and ride back down.

Santa Cruz Valley
To **Cashapampa** (Quebrada Santa Cruz) colectivo/minbus from Ramón Castilla y Jorge Chávez, Caraz, leave when full from 0600 to 1530, 1½ hrs, US$2. Yanama to Yungay combis

can be caught at Vaquería between 0800-1400, US$4, 2 hrs.

Yungay *p1242*
Buses and colectivos run all day to **Caraz**, 12 km, US$0.50, and **Huaraz**, 54 km, 1½ hrs, US$1. To lakes **Llanganuco**, combis leave when full, especially 0700-0900, from Av 28 de Julio 1 block from the plaza, 1 hr, US$2.50. To **Yanama**, via the Portachuelo de Llanganuco Pass, 4767m, 58 km, 3½ hrs, US$5; stopping at María Huayta (for the Llanganuco–Santa Cruz trek), after 2 hrs, US$3. To **Pomabamba**, via Piscobamba, **Trans Los Andes**, daily at 0700-0730, the only company with a ticket office in Yungay; **Transvir** and **La Perla de Alta Mayo** buses coming from Huaraz, 0730, stop if they have room, 6-7 hrs, US$6. After passing the Llanganuco lakes and crossing the Portachuelo the buses descend to Puente Llacma; where it is possible to pick up buses and combis heading south to San Luis, Chacas and Huari.

Carhuaz *p1242*
All transport leaves from the main plaza. To **Huaraz**, colectivos and buses leave 0500-2000, US$1, 40 mins. To **Caraz**, 0500-2000, US$1, 1 hr. Buses from Huaraz to **Chacas** in the Cordillera Blanca, 87 km, 4 hrs, US$5.75, pass through Carhuaz about 40 mins after leaving Huaraz. The road works its way up the Ulta valley to the pass at Punta Olímpica from where there are excellent views. The dirt road is not in good condition due to landslides (can be closed in the wet season). **Renzo** daily buses pass through en route to **San Luis** (see page 1240), a further 10 km, 1½ hrs.

Cordillera Huayhuash

The Cordillera Huayhuash, lying south of the Cordillera Blanca, has azure trout-filled lakes interwoven with deep *quebradas* and high pastures around the hem of the range and is perhaps the most spectacular cordillera for its massive ice faces that seem to rise sheer out of the Puna's contrasting green. You may see tropical parakeets in the bottom of the gorges and condors circling the peaks. The complete circuit is very tough; allow 10-12 days. Fees are charged by every community along the way, adding up to about US$80 for the entire circuit. Take soles in small denominations and insist on getting a receipt every time. The trail head is at **Cuartel Huain**, between Matacancha and the **Punta Cacanan** pass (the continental divide at 4700 m). There are up to eight passes over 4600 m, depending on the route. A half-circuit is also possible, but there are many other options. Both ranges are approached from Chiquián in the north,

Oyón, with links to Cerro de Pasco to the southeast, **Churín** in the south or Cajatambo to the southwest. The area offers fantastic scenery and insights into rural life.

Chiquián is a town of narrow streets and overhanging eaves. **Semana Turística**: first week of July. Buy all your food and supplies in Huaraz as there are only basic supplies in Chiquián and almost nothing in the hamlets along the route. **Mule hire** It may take a day to bring the mules to your starting point from Llamac or Pocpa where they are kept. (Very basic supplies only can be bought in either village.) Ask for mules (US$6 per day) or horses (US$7 per day) at the hotels or restaurants in Chiquián. A guide for the Huayhuash is **Sr Delao Callupe**, ask for him in Chiquián.

Cajatambo is the southern approach to the Cordillera Huayhuash, a small market town with a beautiful 18th-century church and a lovely plaza. There are various hotels (**$**) and some good restaurants around the plaza. Note that the road out of Cajatambo is not for the fainthearted. For the first three to four hours it is no more than a bus-width, clinging to the cliff edge.

⊙ Cordillera Huayhuash listings

For hotel and restaurant price codes, and other relevant information, see Essentials.

● Where to stay

Cordillera Huayhuash *p1246*
$ Hostal San Miguel, Jr Comercio 233, Chiquián, T447001. Nice courtyard and garden, clean, many rooms, popular.
$ Hotel Huayhuash, 28 de Julio 400, Chiquián, T447049. Private bathroom, hot water, restaurant, laundry, parking, modern, great views, information and tours.
$ Los Nogales de Chiquián, Jr Comercio 1301, T447121, http://hotelnogaleschiquian. blogspot.com. Traditional design, with private or shared bath, hot water, cafeteria, parking. Recommended.

● Restaurants

Cordillera Huayhuash *p1246*
$ El Refugio de Bolognesi and **Yerupajá**, on Tarapacá, both offer basic set meals.
$ Panificadora Santa Rosa, Comercio 900, on the plaza, Chiquián, for good bread and sweets, has coin-operated phones and fax.

● Transport

Cordillera Huayhuash *p1246*
Coming from Huaraz, the road is now paved beyond Chiquián to Huansala, on the road to Huallanca (Húanuco). 2 bus companies run from **Huaraz to Chiquián**, 120 km, 3½ hrs: **El Rápido**, at Bolognesi 216, T422887, at 1345, and **Chiquián Tours**, on Tarapacá behind the market. From Chiquián to Huaraz: buses leave the plaza at 0500 daily, US$1.75, except El Rápido, Jr Figueredo 216, T447049, at 0500 and 1330, US$3.65. Also colectivo Chiquián-Huaraz 1500, 3 hrs, US$2.45 pp. There is also a connection from **Chiquián to Huallanca** (Húanuco) with buses from Lima in the early morning and combis during the day, which leave when full, 3 hrs, US$2.50. From Huallanca there are regular combis on to La Unión, 1 hr, US$0.75, and from there transport to Huánuco. From Cajatambo buses depart for **Lima** at 0600, US$9, daily with **Empresa Andina** (office on plaza next to Hostal Cajatambo), **Tour Bello**, 1 block off the Plaza, and **Turismo Cajatambo**, Jr Grau 120 (in Lima, Av Carlos Zavala 124 corner of Miguel Aljovín 449, T426 7238).

North coast

The north of Peru has been described as the Egypt of South America, as it is home to many ruined pre-Inca treasures. Many tourists pass through without stopping on their way to or from Ecuador, missing out on one of the most fascinating parts of the country. Along a seemingly endless stretch of desert coast lie many of the country's most important pre-Inca sites: Chan-Chán, the Moche pyramids, Túcume, Sipán, Batán Grande and El Brujo. The main city is Trujillo, while Chiclayo is more down to earth, with one of the country's largest witchdoctors' market. The coast is also famous for its deep-sea fishing, surfing, and the unique reed fishing boats at Huanchaco and Pimentel. Inland lies colonial Cajamarca, scene of Atahualpa's last stand. Further east, where the Andes meet the jungle, countless unexplored ancient ruins await the more adventurous traveller.

North of Lima

The Pan-American Highway is four-lane (several tolls, about US$2.65) to Km 101, by **Huacho**, which is by-passed, 19 km east of **Puerto Huacho** (several hotels in Huacho, and good restaurants, eg **Cevichería El Clásico**, Calle Inca s/n, open 1000-1800; **La Estrella**, Avenida 28 de Julio 561). The beaches south of the town are clean and deserted.

Caral and Paramonga → *Phone code: 01.*
A few kilometres before Barranca (by-passed by the Highway) a turning to the right (east) at Km 184 leads to **Caral** ① *0900-1700; entry US$4, all visitors must be accompanied by an official guide, US$7 per group, in the car park is the ticket office, toilets, handicrafts stalls; for details, Proyecto Especial Caral, Av Las Lomas de la Molina 327, Urb Las Lomas, Lima 12, T205 2500, www.caralperu.gob.pe, UNESCO World Heritage Site*. This ancient city, 26 km from the coast, dates from about 2600 BC. Many of the accepted theories of Peruvian archaeology have been overturned by Caral's age and monumental construction. It appears to be easily the oldest city in South America. The dry, desert site lies on the southern fringes of the Supe valley, along whose flanks there are more ruins, 19 out of 32 of which have been explored. Caral covers 66 ha and contains eight significant pyramidal structures. To date seven have been excavated by archaeologists from the University of San Marcos, Lima. They are undertaking careful restoration on the existing foundations to re-establish the pyramidal tiers. It is possible to walk around the pyramids. A viewpoint provides a panorama across the whole site. The site is well organized, criss-crossed by marked paths which must be adhered to. Allow at least two hours for your visit. You can stay or camp at the **Casa del Arqueólogo**.

Some 4 km beyond the turn-off to Huaraz at Pativilca, beside the Panamericana, are the well preserved ruins of the **Chimú temple of Paramonga** ① *US$1.80; caretaker may act as guide*. Set on high ground with a view of the ocean, the fortress-like mound is reinforced by eight quadrangular walls rising in tiers to the top of the hill. Between Pativilca and Chimbote the mountains come down to the sea. The road passes by a few very small protected harbours in tiny rock-encircled bays, such as **Huarmey**, with a fine beach and (**$**) **Jaime Crazy** ① *Manuel Scorza 371 y 373, Sector B-8, Huarmey, T043-400104, www.jaimecrazyperu.com*, a hostel offering trips to beaches, archaeological sites, farming communities, volunteering and all sorts of activities.

Casma and Sechín → *Phone code: 043. Colour map 3, B2. Population: 22,600.*
Casma has a pleasant Plaza de Armas, several parks and two markets including a good food market. It is a base from where to explore **Sechín** ① *daily 0800-1800, photography best around midday, US$1.80 (children and students half price); ticket also valid for the Max Uhle Museum by the ruins and Pañamarca*, an archaeological site in the Nepeña Valley, north of Casma. Frequent colectivos leave from in front of the market in Casma, US$0.50 pp, or motorcycle taxi US$1, one

of the most important ruins 5 km away on the Peruvian coast. It consists of a large square temple completely faced with about 500 carved stone monoliths narrating, it is thought, a gruesome battle in graphic detail. The style is unique in Peru for its naturalistic vigour. The complex as a whole is associated with the pre-Chavín Sechín culture, dating from about 1600 BC. Three sides of the large stone temple have been excavated and restored, but you cannot see the earlier adobe buildings inside the stone walls because they were covered up and used as a base for a second storey, which has been completely destroyed.

Chimbote → *Phone code: 043. Colour map 3, B2. Population: 296,600.*

The port of Chimbote serves the national fishing industry and the smell of the fishmeal plants is overpowering. As well as being unpleasant it is also unsafe. Take extensive precautions, always use taxis from the bus station to your hotel and don't venture far. **Note** The main street, Avenida Víctor Raul Haya de la Torre, is also known by its old name, José Pardo. At weekends boat trips go around the bay to visit the cliffs and islands to see the birdlife and rock formations.

Chimbote to Callejón de Huaylas

Just north of Chimbote, a road branches northeast off the Pan American Highway and goes up the Santa valley following the route of the old Santa Corporation Railway which used to run as far as **Huallanca** (Ancash – not to be confused with the town southeast of Huaraz), 140 km up the valley. At Chuquicara, three hours from Chimbote (paved – very rough thereafter), is Restaurante Rosales, a good place to stop for a meal (you can sleep here, too, but it's very basic). At Huallanca there are also places to stay and eat. Fuel is available. At the top of the valley by the hydroelectric centre, the road goes through the very narrow and spectacular **Cañón del Pato**. You pass under tremendous walls of bare rock and through almost 40 tunnels, but the flow of the river has been greatly reduced by the hydroelectric scheme. After this point the road is paved to the Callejón de Huaylas and south to Caraz and Huaraz.

An alternative road for cyclists (and vehicles with a permit) is the 50-km private road known as the 'Brasileños', used by the Brazilian company Odebrecht which has built a water channel for the Chavimochic irrigation scheme from the Río Santa to the coast. The turn-off is 35 km north of the Santa turning, 15 km south of the bridge in Chao, on the Pan American Highway at Km 482. It is a good all-weather road via Tanguche. Permits are obtainable from the Chavimochic HQ at San José de Virú, US$7.50, or from the guard at the gate on Sunday.

⚫ North of Lima listings

For hotel and restaurant price codes, and other relevant information, see Essentials.

⚫ Where to stay

Casma and Sechín *p1248*
$$ El Dorado Inn, Av Garcilazo de la VegaMz J, Lt 37, T411795. 1 block from the Panamericana. With fan, pool, restaurant and tourist information.
$$ Hostal El Farol, Túpac Amaru 450, T411064, www.elfarolinn.com. Very nice, rooms and suites, hot water, swimming pool, pleasant garden, good restaurant, parking, information.
$ Gregori, Luis Ormeño 530, T711073. Rooms with or without bath, café downstairs.

$ Las Dunas, Luis Ormeño 505, T711057. An upgraded and enlarged family home, welcoming.

Chimbote *p1249*
Plenty of hotels, so try to negotiate a lower rate.
$$ Cantón, Bolognesi 498, T344388. Modern, higher quality than others, has a good but pricey chifa restaurant.
$$ Ivansino Inn, Av José Pardo 738, T321811, www.ivansinoinn.com. Includes breakfast, comfortable, modern.
$ Hostal El Ensueño, Sáenz Peña 268, 2 blocks from Plaza Central, T328662. Cheaper rooms without bath, very good, safe, welcoming.
$ Hostal Karol Inn, Manuel Ruiz 277, T321216. Hot water, good, family run, laundry, cafetería.

$ Residencial El Parque, E Palacios 309, on plaza, T345572. Converted old home, hot water, nice, secure.

🍴 Restaurants

Casma and Sechín *p1248*
Cheap restaurants on Huarmey. The local ice-cream, *Caribe*, is available at Ormeño 545.
$ Tío Sam, Huarmey 138. Specializes in fresh fish, wins awards for its ceviche. Recommended.
$ Venecia, Huarmey 204. Local dishes; popular.

⏰ What to do

Casma and Sechín *p1248*
Sechín Tours, in Hostal Monte Carlo, Casma, T411421. Organizes tours in the local area. The guide, Renato, only speaks Spanish but has knowledge of local ruins and can be contacted at renatotours@yahoo.com.

🚌 Transport

North of Lima *p1248*
Bus AméricaMóvil (Av Luna Pizarro 251, La Victoria, T01-423 6338; in Huacho T01-232 7631) and Zeta (Av Abancay 900, T01-426 8087; in Huacho T01-239 6176) run every 20-30 mins **Lima–Huacho**, from 0600 to 2000, 2½ hrs, US$6 (more expensive at weekends).

Caral and Paramonga *p1248*
Bus To **Barranca** stops opposite the service station (*el grifo*) at the end of town. From **Lima** to Barranca, 3½ hrs, US$7.50. As bus companies have their offices in Barranca, buses will stop there rather than at Pativilca or Paramonga. Bus from Barranca to **Casma** 155 km, several daily, 2½ hrs, US$6. From Barranca to **Huaraz**, take a minibus from C Lima to the gas station in Pativilca where you can catch a bus, colectivo or truck on the good, paved road to Huaraz.

To **Caral**, Empresa Valle Sagrado Caral leave from terminal at Berenice Dávila, cuadra 2, Barranca, US$2.75 shared, or US$35 private service with 1½ hrs at the site. Taxi to the ruins US$10 one way. The ruins are 25 km along a road which runs up the Supe valley from Km 184 of the Panamericana (signed). Between Kms 18 and 19 of this road a track leads across the valley to the ruins, though the river may be impassable Dec-Mar, 30 mins. Tours from Lima usually allow 1½ hrs at Caral, with a 3-hr journey each way, stopping for morning coffee and for lunch in Huacho on the return.

Buses run only to Paramonga port (3 km off the Highway, 4 km from the Paramonga ruins, about 15 mins from Barranca).
Taxi From Paramonga to the ruins and return after waiting, US$9, otherwise take a Barranca-Paramonga port bus, then a 3 km walk.

Casma and Sechín *p1248*
Bus Half hourly from **Lima** to **Chimbote** which can drop you off in Casma, 370 km, 6 hrs, US$18. If going to **Lima** many of the buses from Trujillo and Chimbote stop briefly opposite the petrol station, block 1 of Ormeño or, if they have small offices, along blocks 1-5 of Av Ormeño. To **Chimbote**, 55 km, it is easiest to take a **Los Casmeños** colectivo, which depart when full from in front of the petrol station, block 1 of Ormeño, or from Plaza Poncianos, 45 mins, US$.50. To **Trujillo** it is best to go first to Chimbote bus station and then take an **América Express** bus. To **Huaraz** (150 km), via Pariacoto, buses come from Chimbote, 6-7 hrs, US$12. **Transportes Huandoy**, Ormeño 166, T712336, departs at 0700, 1100 and 1400, while **Yungay Express**, Ormeño 158, departs at 0600, 0800 and 1400. This difficult but beautiful trip is worth taking in daylight. From Casma the first 50 km are paved, a good dirt road follows for 20 km to **Pariacoto** (basic lodging). From here to the **Callán pass** (4224 m) the road is rough (landslides in rainy season), but once the Cordillera Negra has been crossed, the gravel road is better with lovely views of the Cordillera Blanca (150 km to Huaraz). Most Huaraz buses go via Pativilca, which is further but the road is much better, 6 hrs, **Móvil Tours** and **Trans Chinchaysuyo**, all run at night.

Chimbote *p1249*
Warning Under no circumstances should you walk to the centre: minibus costs US$0.50, taxi US$1.50. There are no hotels near the terminal; some companies have ticket offices in the centre.
Bus The station is 4 km south on Av Meiggs. From **Lima**, to Chimbote, 420 km, 5½ hrs,

US$15-20. Frequent service with many companies. To **Trujillo**, 130 km, 2 hrs, US$6, América Express buses every 20 mins till 2100. To **Huaraz** most companies, with the best buses, go the 'long way round', ie down the Pan-americana to Pativilca, then up the paved highway, 7 hrs, US$14. The main companies start in Trujillo and continue to **Caraz**. To Huaraz via Pariacoto, 7 hrs, US$14, **Trans Huandoy** (Etseturh), T354024, at 0600, 1000 and 1300, 7 hrs, and **Yungay Express** at 0500, 0700 and 1300. To **Caraz** via Cañón del Pato, 7-8 hrs,

US$12, **Yungay Express** at 0830 (for a description of this route see above). Sit on the left-hand-side for the best views. If arriving from Caraz via the Cañón del Pato there is usually time to make a connection to Casma or Trujillo/Huanchaco and avoid overnighting in Chimbote. If travelling to Caraz, take **Línea** 0600 or earlier from Trujillo to make the 0830 bus up the Cañón del Pato. If overnighting is unavoidable, Casma is near enough to stay in but you will need to buy your Caraz ticket the day before; the bus station is on the Casma side of Chimbote.

Trujillo and around → Phone code: 044. Colour map 3, B2. Population: 1,539,774.

The capital of La Libertad Department, 548 km from Lima, disputes the title of second city of Peru with Arequipa. The compact colonial centre, though, has a small-town feel. The greenness surrounding the city is a delight against the backcloth of brown Andean foothills and peaks. Founded by Diego de Almagro in 1534 as an express assignment ordered by Francisco Pizarro, it was named after the latter's native town in Spain. Nearby are some of Peru's most important Moche and Chimú archaeological sites and a stretch of the country's best surfing beaches.

Arriving in Trujillo

Orientation The **airport** is west of the city, the entry to town is along Avenida Mansiche. There is no central bus terminal. **Bus stations** are spread out on four sides of the city beyond the inner ring road, Avenida España. There are few hotels around them, but plenty of taxis. Insist on being taken to your hotel of choice. A new Terminal Terrestre is being built. ▸▸ *See also Transport, page 1261.*

Trujillo is best explored on foot. The major sites outside the city, Chan Chán, the Moche pyramids and Huanchaco beach are easily reached by public transport, but take care when walking around. A number of recommended guides run tours to these and other places. **Note** The city is generally safe, but take care beyond the inner ring road, Avenida España, as well as obvious places around bus stops and terminals, and at ATMs and internet cafés.

Tourist offices i perú ① *Diego de Almagro 420, Plaza de Armas, T294561, iperutrujillo@prom peru. gob.pe, Mon-Sat 0900-1800, Sun 1000-1400*. Also useful: **Municipalidad de Trujillo, Sub-Gerencia de Turismo** ① *Av España 742, T044-244212, anexo 119, sgturismo@munitrujillo.gob.pe*. The **Tourist Police** ① *Independencia 572, in the Ministerio de Cultura building, policia_turismo_tru @ hotmail.com, open Mon-Sat 0800-2000*, provide useful information and can help with reports of theft, some speak English. **Indecopi** ① *Santo Toribio de Mogrovejo 518, Urb San Andrés II etapa, T295733, sobregon@indecopi.gob.pe*, for tourist complaints. **Gobierno Regional de la Libertad** ① *Dirección de Turismo, Av España 1800, T296221*, for information on regional tourism. Useful websites include www.xanga.com/TrujilloPeru and www.laindustria.com.

Places in Trujillo

The focal point is the pleasant and spacious **Plaza de Armas**. The prominent sculpture represents agriculture, commerce, education, art, slavery, action and liberation, crowned by a young man holding a torch depicting liberty. Fronting it is the **Cathedral** ① *0700-1230, 1700-2000*, dating from 1666, with its museum of religious paintings and sculptures next door (Monday-Friday 0900-1300, 1600-1900, Saturday 0900-1300, US$1.45). Also on the Plaza are the **Hotel Libertador**, the colonial style Sociedad de Beneficencia Pública de Trujillo and the Municipalidad. The

Universidad de La Libertad, second only to that of San Marcos at Lima, was founded in 1824. Two beautiful colonial mansions on the plaza have been taken over. The Banco Central de Reserva is in the Colonial-style **Casa Urquiaga (or Calonge)** ① *Pizarro 446, Mon-Fri 0930-1500, Sat-Sun 1000-1330, free 30-min guided tour, take passport,* which contains valuable pre-Columbian ceramics. The other is **Casa Bracamonte (or Lizarzaburu)** ① *Independencia 441,*

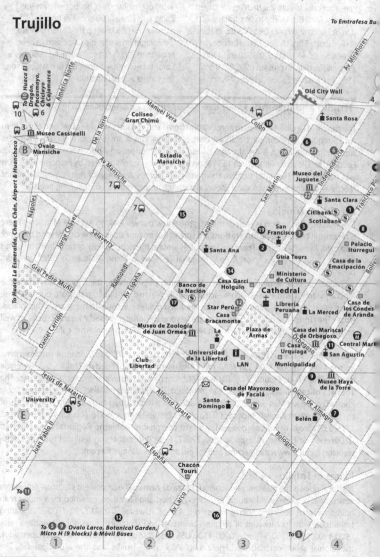

Trujillo

To Emtrafesa Bu

To Huaca El Dragón
To Pacasmayo, Chiclayo & Cajamarca

A
10
6
3

Museo Cassinelli

América Norte

Manuel Vera

Colón

Old City Wall

4

Santa Rosa

Ovalo Mansiche

B

De la Torre

Coliseo Gran Chimú

Estadio Mansiche

Av Mansiche

Napoles

Jorge Chavez

Salaverry

7

7

Zepita

San Martín

10

18

21

20

23

6

6

Museo del Juguete

22

Santa Clara

Citibank
Scotiabank

1

Independencia

Francisco Pi

To Huaca La Esmeralda, Chan Chán, Airport & Huanchaco

15

19

San Francisco

3

2

Palacio Iturregui

C

Raimondi

Santa Ana

Guía Tours

Ministerio de Cultura

Casa de la Emacipación

Casa Garci Holguín

14

Casa de los Condes de Aranda

Bolív

Gral Pedro Muñiz

Banco de la Nación

17

Star Perú

Casa Bracamonte

La

12

Cathedral

Librería Peruana

La Merced

Casa del Mariscal O de Orbegoso

Casa Urquiaga

D

Daniel Carrión

Museo de Zoología de Juan Ormea

Club Libertad

Universidad de la Libertad

Plaza de Armas

LAN

San Agustín

Central Mark

Municipalidad

Museo Haya de la Torre

9

7

Jesús de Nazareth

Alfonso Ugarte

Casa del Mayorazgo de Facalá

Santo Domingo

Diego de Almagro

Belén

E

University

13

5

Juan Pablo II

Av España

2

Bolognesi

F

To 11

Av Larco

Chacón Tours

To 5 5 Ovalo Larco, Botanical Garden, Micro H (9 blocks) & Móvil Buses

12

13

1

2

16

3

To 5

4

which houses the Seguro Social de Salud del Perú and has occasional exhibitions. Opposite the Cathedral on Independencia, is the **Casa Garci Olguín** (Caja Nuestra Gente), recently restored but boasting the oldest façade in the city and Moorish-style murals. The buildings that surround the Plaza, and many others in the vicinity, are painted in bright pastel colours. Near the Plaza de Armas is the spacious 18th-century **Palacio Iturregui**, now occupied by the **Club Central**

N

200 metres
200 yards

Where to stay
1 Casa de Clara *F6*
2 Chan Chán Inn *A5*
3 Colonial *C4*
4 Continental *D4*
5 El Gran Marqués *F2*
6 El Mochilero *B4*
7 Gran Bolívar *B5*
8 Hostal El Centurión *F4*
9 Hostal Malibú *F2*
10 Hostería El Sol *A1*
11 Kallpa *F1*
12 Libertador *D3*
13 Res Vanini *F2*
14 Turismo *D5*

Restaurants
1 Asturias, Café Oviedo,
   Demarco & Romano *C4*
2 Café Amaretto *C3*
3 Casona Deza *C4*
4 Cevichería Puerto Morí *B4*
5 Chelsea *B5*
6 Dulcería Doña Carmen *B4*
7 El Chileno *E4*
8 El Kluv *C4*
9 El Mochica *E4*
10 El Sol *B3*
11 Juguería San Agustín *D4*
12 Le Nature *F2*
13 Pizzería Pizzanino *E1*
14 Rincón de Vallejo *C3*
15 Rincón de Vallejo 2 *C2*
16 Romano-Rincón Criollo *F3*
17 Sabor Supremo *D2*
18 Sal y Pimienta *B3*
19 Trujillo Señorial *C3*

Bars & clubs
20 Canana *B3*
21 El Estribo *B4*
22 Juguete *C4*
23 Stradivarius *B4*

Transport
1 Buses to Huaca del Sol y
   de la Luna *D6*
2 Combi A to Chan Chán &
   Huanchaco *E2, E5*
3 Combis A & B; & Micros B, H
   & H-Corazón to Chan Chán
   & Huanchaco *B1*
4 Combi B & Micro B: to
   Chan Chán &
   Huanchaco *A4, B3*
5 Micro H to Chan Chán &
   Huanchaco *E1*
6 El Dorado *B1*
7 Ittsa *B2, C2*
8 Oltursa & Flores *A5*
9 Ormeño *A5*
10 Turismo Díaz, Horna &
    Tarapoto Tours *B1*

① *Jr Pizarro 688, restricted entry to patio, US$1.85 to see the ceramics, 0830-1000.* An exclusive and social centre of Trujillo, it houses a private collection of ceramics. **Casa Ganoza Chopitea** ① *Independencia 630 (see Casona Deza under Restaurants, below),* is considered architecturally the most representative of the viceroyalty in the city. It combines baroque and rococo styles and is also known for the pair of lions that adorn its portico.

Other mansions, still in private hands, include **Casa del Mayorazgo de Facalá** ① *Pizarro 314, another entrance on Bolognesi, Mon-Fri 0915-1230,* now Scotiabank. **Casa de la Emancipación** ① *Jr Pizarro 610 (Banco Continental), Mon-Sat, 0900-1300, 1600-2000,* is a museum in the building where independence from Spain was planned and was the first seat of government and congress in Peru. The **Casa del Mariscal de Orbegoso** ① *Orbegoso 553, open 0930-2000,* is the **Museo de la República** owned by the BCP bank. It also holds temporary exhibitions. **Museo Haya de la Torre (Casa del Pueblo)** ① *Orbegoso 664, Mon-Sat 0900-1300, 1600-2000, free,* is a small, well-presented museum about the life of the founder of the APRA party and one of the leading twentieth-century socialists in the Americas, in the house in which he was born. It holds a cinema club once a week.

One of the best of the many churches is the 17th-century **La Merced** ① *at Pizarro 550, 0800-1200, 1600-2000, free,* with picturesque moulded figures below the dome. **El Carmen** ① *at Colón y Bolívar, open for Mass Sun 0700-0730,* church and monastery, has been described as the 'most valuable jewel of colonial art in Trujillo' but it is rarely open. Likewise **La Compañía** ① *near Plaza de Armas,* now an auditorium for cultural events.

Museo de Arqueología ① *Junín 682 y Ayacucho, Casa Risco, T249322, Mon-Fri 0830-1430, US$1.85,* houses a large and interesting collection of thematic exhibits. The **Museo del Juguete** ① *Independencia 705 y Junín, Mon-Sat 1000-1800, Sun 1000-1300, US$1.85, children US$0.70, café open 0900-2300,* is a toy museum containing examples from prehistoric times to 1950, collected by painter Gerardo Chávez. Downstairs is the Espacio Cultural Angelmira with a café bar; in a restored *casona*, worth a visit. Gerardo Chávez has opened the **Museo de Arte Moderno** ① *Av Industrial, 3.5 km from centre, T215668, 0930-1700, Sun 0930-1400, US$3.50, students half price,* which has some fine exhibits, a peaceful garden and friendly staff. The basement of the **Cassinelli garage** ① *Av N de Piérola 607, T231801, behind a petrol station, 1000-1300, 1430-1800, US$2.45,* contains a private collection of Mochica and Chimú pottery which is recommended. **Museo de Zoología de Juan Ormea** ① *Jr San Martín 368, Mon-Fri 0700-1850, US$0.70,* has interesting displays of Peruvian animals. There is also a **botanical garden** ① *Mon-Sat 0800-1700, free,* about half a block beyond the Ovalo Larco, southwest of the city centre.

Huacas del Sol and de la Luna

① *0900-1600 (last entry, but site open till sunset), US$4 (students US$2, children US$0.40), booklet in English or Spanish US$2.85. All tickets are sold at the Museo Huacas de Moche – see below. You have to go with a guide on a 1-hr tour in English, French or Spanish. Groups can be up to 25 people and quite rushed. See Proyecto Huaca de la Luna, Jr San Martín 380, Trujillo, T221269, www.huacas.com. The visitors' centre (T834901) has a café showing videos and a souvenir shop and good toilets. In an outside patio craftsmen reproduce ceramics in designs from northern Peru.*

A few kilometres south of Trujillo are the huge and fascinating Mochè pyramids, the Huaca del Sol and the Huaca de la Luna. Until the Spaniards destroyed a third of it in a vain search for treasure, Huaca del Sol was the largest man-made structure in the western hemisphere, at 45 m high. It consisted of seven levels, with 11 or 12 phases of construction over the first six centuries AD. Today, about two thirds of the pyramid have been lost and it is closed to the public. Huaca de la Luna, 500 m away, received scant attention until extensive polychrome moulded decorations were uncovered since 1990. The colours on these remarkable geometric patterns and deities have faded little and it is now possible to view impressive friezes of the upper four levels on the northern exterior wall of the *huaca*. The highest mural is a 'serpent' which runs the length of the wall, beneath it there are repeated motifs of 'felines' holding decapitated heads of warriors, then repeated motifs of 'fishermen' holding fish against a bright blue background and, next, huge 'spider/crab' motifs. The bottom two levels show dancers or officials grimly holding hands and, below them, victorious warriors following naked prisoners past scenes of combat and two complex scenes, similar to those at Huaca Cao Viejo at El Brujo (see below). Combined with intricate, brightly painted two-dimensional motifs in the sacrificial area atop the huaca, and with new discoveries in almost every excavation, Huaca de la Luna is now a truly significant site well worth visiting.

The **Templo Nuevo**, or Plataforma III, represents the period 600 to 900 AD and has friezes in the upper level showing the so-called Rebellion of the Artefacts, in which weapons take on human characteristics and attack their owners. Also new was the **Museo Huacas de Moche** ① *5 mins' walk from Huaca de la Luna, www.huacasdemoche.pe, daily 0900-1600, US$1, students US$0.75, children US$0.40,* the site museum. Three halls display objects found in the huacas, including beautiful ceramics, arranged thematically around the Moche themselves, the cermonial complex, daily life, the deities of power and of the mountains and priests who worshipped them. Food is available on Sunday at the nearby town of Moche.

Chan Chán
① *5 km from Trujillo. 0900-1600, arrive well before that. Site may be covered up if rain is expected. Tickets cost US$3.80 (US$2 with ISIC card, children US$0.35), include entrance fees for Chan Chán, Huaca El Dragón and Huaca La Esmeralda (for 2 days). Official guides, US$10, wait by the souvenir shops, toilets here too. See note about safety, page 1262.*

These vast, unusually decorated crumbling ruins of the imperial city of the Chimú domains are the largest adobe city in the world. The ruins consist of 10 great compounds built by Chimú kings. The 11- to 12-m high perimeter walls surrounded sacred enclosures with usually only one narrow entrance. Inside, rows of storerooms contained the agricultural wealth of the kingdom, which stretched 1000 km along the coast from near Guayaquil to the Carabayllo Valley, north of Lima.

Most of the compounds contain a huge walk-in well which tapped the ground water, raised to a high level by irrigation further up the valley. Each compound also included a platform mound which was the burial place of the king, with his women and his treasure, presumably maintained as a memorial. The Incas almost certainly copied this system and transported it to Cuzco where the last Incas continued building huge enclosures. The Chimú surrendered to the Incas around 1471 after 11 years of siege and cutting off the irrigation canals.

The dilapidated city walls enclose an area of 28 sq km containing the remains of palaces, temples, workshops, streets, houses, gardens and a canal. What is left of the adobe walls bears either well-restored, or modern fibreglass fabrications of moulded decorations showing small figures of fish, birds, fishing nets and various geometric motifs. Painted designs have been found on pottery unearthed from the debris of a city ravaged by floods, earthquakes, and *huaqueros* (grave looters). The **Ciudadela de Nik-An** (formerly called Tschudi) is the part that visitors see.

The **site museum** ① *US$1, 0830-1630,* on the main road, 100 m before the turn-off, has objects found in the area, displays and signs in Spanish and English.

The partly restored temple, **Huaca El Dragón** ① *0930-1630 (in theory), on the west side of the Pan-American Highway in the district of La Esperanza; combis from Huayna Cápac y Los Incas, or Av España y Manuel Vera marked 'Arco Iris/La Esperanza', taxi costs US$2,* dating from Huari to Chimú times (AD 1000-1470), is also known as **Huaca Arco Iris** (rainbow), after the shape of friezes which decorate it. The poorly preserved **Huaca La Esmeralda** is at Mansiche, between Trujillo and Chan Chán, behind the church and near the Mall Aventura shopping centre. Buses to Chan Chán and Huanchaco pass the church at Mansiche.

El Brujo
① *Daily 0900-1600, US$4 (US$2 with ISIC card, children US$0.35). Shops and toilets at the entrance. See www.fundacionwiese.com.*

A complex collectively known as El Brujo, 60 km north of Trujillo, is considered one of the most important archaeological sites on the north coast. Covering 2 sq km, it was a ceremonial centre for up to 10 cultures, including the Moche. Huaca Cortada (or El Brujo) has a wall decorated with high relief stylized figures. Huaca Prieta is, in effect, a giant rubbish tip dating back 5000 years, which once housed the very first settlers. It was first investigated by the US archaeologist Junius Bird in the late 1940s leading him to establish the chronology of prehistoric Peru that prevails today, cementing the place of this unremarkable *huaca* in Peruvian history. Huaca Cao Viejo has extensive friezes, polychrome reliefs up to 90 m long, 4 m high and on five different levels. The mummy of a tattooed, pregnant woman, La Señora de Cao, dating from AD 450, has also been found. Her mausoleum, with grave goods, can be visited in an excellent, purpose-built museum. In front of Cao Viejo are the remains of one of the oldest Spanish churches in the region. It was common practice for the Spaniards to build their churches near these ancient sites in order to counteract their religious importance. Excavations will continue for many years. Trujillo travel agencies run tours and there is a trail system for exploring the site.

Huanchaco and around

An alternative to Trujillo is this fishing and surfing village, full of hotels, guest houses and restaurants. It is famous for its narrow pointed fishing rafts, known as *caballitos* (little horses) *de totora*, made of totora reeds and depicted on Mochica, Chimú and other cultures' pottery. Unlike those used on Lake Titicaca, they are flat, not hollow, and ride the breakers rather like surfboards (fishermen offer trips on their *caballitos* for US$1.75, be prepared to get wet; groups should contact Luis Gordillo, El Mambo, T461092). You can see fishermen returning in their reed rafts at about 0800 and 1400 when they stack the boats upright to dry in the fierce sun. Overlooking Huanchaco is a huge church (1535-1540) from the belfry of which are extensive views. Post office at Grau y Manco Capac, open Monday-Saturday 1300-1800.

Puerto Chicama (**Malabrigo**), is claimed by surfers as the best surf beach in Peru, with the longest left-hand point-break in the world. The best waves are March-October (high point May-June) and the sand is clean. It is 70 km north of Trujillo, turn off Panamericana at Paiján. There is a 1-km-long fishing pier, huge, abandoned warehouses and the remains of the railway to Casa Grande cooperative from the town's sugar-exporting days. There are a few *hospedajes* and simple places to eat in town (shop early by the market for fresh seafood) and a string of small places line the clifftop south of town, Distrito El Hombre. The best places to eat are here (eg **Chicama**, Arica 625); avoid the shacks that line the beach.

⊚ Trujillo and around listings

For hotel and restaurant price codes, and other relevant information, see Essentials.

⊜ Where to stay

Trujillo *p1251, map p1252*
$$$$ El Gran Marqués, Díaz de Cienfuegos 145-147, Urb La Merced, T481710, www.elgran marques.com. Price includes breakfast, modern, minibar, pool, sauna, jacuzzi, restaurant.
$$$$ Libertador, Independencia 485, Plaza de Armas, T232741, www.libertador.com. pe. Modern hotel in historic building, lovely place to stay. Comfortable rooms, excellent service, swimming pool in a flower-filled patio,

sauna, cafetería and restaurant, breakfast extra, excellent buffet lunch on Sun.
$$$ Gran Bolívar, Bolívar 957, T222090, www.granbolivarhotel.net. In converted 18th-century house, restaurant and room service, café, bar, laundry, gym, parking.
$$$-$$ Kallpa, Díaz de las Heras s/n, Urb Vista Hermosa, T281266, www.kallpahotel.pe. A smart new boutique hotel, welcoming, English spoken, well below usual boutique hotel prices.
$$ Colonial, Independencia 618, T258261, www.hostalcolonial.com.pe. Attractive but small rooms, hot showers, basic breakfast, good restaurant, especially for set lunch. Recommended.

$$ Continental, Gamarra 663, T241607, www.
perunorte.com/hcontinental. Modern but old-
fashioned hotel opposite the market, with hot
water, good breakfast, helpful, safe.
$$ Hostal El Centurión, Paraguay 304, Urb El
Recreo, T201526, www.hostalelcenturion.com.
About 20 mins' walk from the Plaza, modern,
good rooms, well kept, safe but no a/c, simple
restaurant, good service.
$$ Hostal Malibú, Av Larco 1471, Urb La
Merced, T284811, www.hostalmalibu.com.
Variety of rooms, restaurant, room service,
mini-bar, laundry, massage, currency exchange.
Also sister hotel of same name at Av Larco
1000, Huanchaco.
$ Casa de Clara, Cahuide 495, T243347, http://
trujilloperu.xanga.com. Backpackers' hostal, hot
water, good food, helpful, information, lodging
packages with meals and tours, laundry service,
use of kitchen with permission and charge for
gas, meeting place and lots going on, many
languages spoken (see Clara Bravo and Michael
White, What to do, below). Restaurants nearby.
$ Chan Chán Inn, Av Ejército 307, T298583,
chanchaninn@hotmail.com. Close to several
bus terminals so noisy, with or without
breakfast, popular with backpackers, café,
laundry, money exchange, information.
$ El Mochilero, Independencia 887, T297842,
Elmochilerotrujilloperuoficial on Facebook.
A variety of dorms and rooms, only one with
bath, electric showers, breakfast US$1.75, fridge
for guests' use. Tours arranged, information.
$ Hostería El Sol, Brillantes 224, Urb Santa Inés,
T231933, hosteriaelsol@gmail.com, near bus
terminals on Av Nicolás de Piérola. With hot
shower, restaurant, all meals available.
$ Residencia Vanini, Av Larco 237, outside
Av España, T200878, enriqueva@hotmail.com.
Youth hostel in a converted private house,
a good option but not in the centre, some
rooms with bath, others with shared shower.
$ Turismo, Gamarra 747, T244181. Central, good
services, restaurant, parking, travel agency

El Brujo *p1256*
$ Hospedaje Jubalu, Libertad 105, Magdalena
de Cao, T995 670600. With hot water.
No internet in town and limited shopping.

Huanchaco *p1256*
$$$-$$ Bracamonte, Los Olivos 160, T461162,
www.hotelbracamonte.com.pe. Comfortable,
modern, contemporary decor, good, pool,
secure, good restaurant offers lunch *menú* and
some vegetarian dishes, English spoken, laundry
service, games room. Highly recommended.
$$$-$$ Hostal Huankarute, La Rivera 312,
T461705, www.hostalhuankarute.com.
On the sea-front, with small pool, bar, sun
terrace, bicycle rental; some rooms larger,
more luxurious and more pricey, all with
ocean view. Recommended.
$$$-$$ Las Palmeras, Av Larco 1150, sector
Los Tumbos, T461199, www.laspalmerasde
huanchaco.com. One of the best, rooms with
terrace, hot water, dining room, pool and
gardens. Rooms on top floor with sea view cost
more than ground floor rooms with pool view.
$$ El Malecón, Av La Rivera 322, T461275,
www.hostalelmalecon.com. Overlooking the
sea, some rooms with terrace, hot water, café,
helpful staff.
$$ Hostal Huanchaco, Larco 185 on Plaza,
T461272, www.huanchacohostal.com.
With hot water, pool, good but pricey
cafetería, video, pool table.
$$ Hostal Los Esteros, Av Larco 618, T461300,
www.losesteroshuanchaco.com. Rooms with
sea view for 1-4 people, hot water, laundry,
restaurant, safe parking, bicycle hire, can
arrange surfing and *caballitos de totora* trips.
$$ Residencial Sol y Mar, La Rivera 400,
T461120, ctsolymar1@hotmail.com. Breakfast
extra, with pool, restaurant and garden.
$$-$ Hostal Cocos Beach, Av Larco 1500,
Los Tumbos, T461023, www.hostelcocosbeach.
com. Opposite the beach, rooms with beds
and bunks, hot water, restaurant, surfing
lessons, car rental, tours arranged.
$$-$ Huanchaco Inn, Los Pinos 528, T461158.
Rooms with and without bath, hot water, use
of kitchen, laundry service, small pool.
$ Cherry's, Los Pinos 448, T462066. Owner Juan
Carlos speaks English, rooms with private or
shared bath, hot water, kitchen, shop, bar, roof
terrace, laundry, even a small swimming pool.
$ Hospedaje My Friend, Los Pinos 533,
T461080. Dorm rooms with shared bath
upstairs, with hot water, TV room, information.
Tours arranged, but service is erratic. Popular

place with surfers, good for meeting others and for a meal in the restaurant on ground floor (open 0800-1800).

$ La Casa Suiza, Los Pinos 308, T461285, www.lacasasuiza.com. This Huanchaco institution has a variety of rooms with/without bath, breakfast US$3, BBQ on the roof, book exchange.

$ Las Brisas, Raymondi 146, T461186, http://facebook.com/lasbrisashuanchaco. Hot water, café, comfortable.

$ McCallum Lodging, Los Ficus 460, T462350, http://mccallumlodginghouse.wordpress.com/the-hostel/. Private rooms and dorms, hot water, hammocks, home-cooked meals available and recipes shared, laundry, baggage and surfboard storage, family atmosphere, highly considered by locals and tourists.

$ Ñaylamp, Av Víctor Larco 123, northern end of seafront in El Boquerón, T461022, www.hostalnaylamp.com. Rooms set around a courtyard with patios and garden, others have sea view, dorms, hammocks, good beds, hot water, camping, tents available to hire, laundry, safe, Italian food, good breakfasts.

Puerto Chicama
At Distrito El Hombre (several close out of season):
$$$ Chicama Beach, T576130, www.chicamabeach.com. 3-star, hot water, swimming pool for kids and adults, restaurant, bar, laundry, parking, open all year.

$$$ Chicama Surf Resort, T576206, www.chicamasurf.com. Exclusive, with surfing classes, boats to the waves, spa, restaurant, infinity pool, open all year.

$ El Hombre is the backpacker place, OK, very friendly.

$ Hostal Los Delfines, T943 296662. Owner Tito Venegas, guests can use well-equipped kitchen, rooms with balcony, hot water, spacious.

$ Sueños de Chicama, is the furthest from town and the cheapest.

In town there are several cheaper places; Hostal El Naipe, Tacna 395, is arguably the best.

❼ Restaurants

Trujillo *p1251, map p1252*
A speciality is *shambar*, a thick minestrone made with pork, served on Mon. All along Pizarro are restaurants to suit all tastes and budgets. On the west side of the central market at Grau y Ayacucho are several small, cheap restaurants. On sale everywhere is *turrón*, a nougat-type sweet.

$$$ Romano-Rincón Criollo, Estados Unidos 162, Urb El Recreo, 10-min walk from centre, T244207. Northern Peruvian cuisine, *menú* for US$5.60, smart.

$$$-$$ El Mochica, Bolívar 462. Good typical food with live music on special occasions.

$$ Casona Deza, Independencia 630, T434866, CasonaDezaCafe on Facebook. Open 0800-2200, from 0900 on Sun. An atmospheric pizzeria in a restored colonial house with period furniture and a patio surrounded by frescoes.

$$ Chelsea, Estete 675, T257032. Open 1145-1645, 1700-0100, on Sun. Restaurant/bar. Buffet Criollo US$8.70, special shows on Fri (live music, fee US$3.50) and Sat (Marinera dance show, US$5.25). Recommended.

$$ Demarco, Pizarro 725. Popular at midday for lunchtime menus and for its cakes and desserts, good service.

$$ Le Nature, Marcelo Corne 338, in a residential district off Av Larco, T209674. Mon-Thu 1000-2200, Fri, Sun 1000-1600, Sat 1900-2200. Probably the best vegetarian food in town.

$$ Pizzería Pizzanino, Av Juan Pablo II 183, Urb San Andrés, opposite University. Good for pizzas, pastas, meats, desserts, evening only.

$$ Romano, Pizarro 747. International food, good *menú*, breakfasts, coffee, excellent milkshakes, cakes.

$$-$ Cevichería Puerto Mori, Estete 482, T346752. Very popular, they serve only good seafood. At the same location are 2 more fish restaurants, but not of the same quality.

$ Asturias, Pizarro 741. Nice café with a reasonable *menú*, good pastas, cakes and sandwiches.

$ Café Oviedo, Pizarro 737. With soups, vegetarian options, good salads and cakes, helpful.

$ El Sol, Zepita 203, T345105. Mon-Sat 0800-2200, Sun 0800-1600. Vegetarian, lunch *menú* and à la carte.

$ Juguería San Agustín, Bolívar 526. Good juices, good *menú*, sandwiches, ice creams, popular, excellent value. Also at Av Larco Herrera y Husares de Junín.

$ Rincón de Vallejo, Orbegoso 303. Good *menú*, typical dishes, very crowded at peak times. Second branch at Av España 736.

$ Sabor Supremo, Diego de Almagro 210, T220437. Menú US$1.75, also à la carte, vegetarian food, vegan on special request.
$ Sal y Pimienta, Colón 201. Very popular for lunch, US$1 and US$1.85, close to buses for Huanchaco and Chan Chán.
$ Trujillo Señorial, Gamarra 353, T204873. Mon-Sat 1300-1530. Restaurant and hotel school, good *menú* US$2.60-3, food nicely presented, good value.

Cafés
Café Amaretto, Gamarra 368. Smart, good selection of real coffees, "brilliant" cakes, sweets, snacks and drinks.
Casona Deza, Independencia 630. Comfortable café/bar selling home-made pasta and pizza and good coffee in an old mansion.
Dulcería Doña Carmen, San Martín 814. Serves local specialities such as *alfajores*, *budin*, *king kong*, etc.
El Chileno, Ayacucho 408. Café and ice cream parlour, popular.
El Kluv, Junín 527 (next to Metro Market). Italian owned, fresh, tasty pizzas at noon and in the late afternoon.
Fitopán, Bolívar 406. Good selection of breads, also serves lunches.

Huanchaco *p1256*
There are about 30 restaurants on the beachfront, recommended on Av Larco are
$$ Estrella Marina, No 740, Los Herrajes, No 1020, **Lucho del Mar**, No 750. Many close in the low season and at night.
$$$ Big Ben, Av Larco 1182, near A Sánchez, T461869. Open 1130-1730. Seafood and international, very good.
$$$ Club Colonial, La Rivera 514, on the beachfront, T461015. Open 1100-2300. A smart restaurant and bar, French-speaking Belgian owner.
$$$ El Mochica, Av Larco 700, T461963. Same owners and quality as this restaurant in Trujillo, due to reopen after rebuilding in 2014.
$$$ Huanchaco Beach, Av Larco 602, T461484. One of the best for quality in town, popular with tours.
$$$-$$ El Kero, Av La Ribera 612, T461184. Open 0800-midnight. Very popular meeting place and good restaurant.

$$$-$$ El Sombrero, Av Larco 800. Smart new restaurant serving good ceviche and seafood, most tables have great sea view.
$$ Casa Tere, Plaza de Armas, T461197. For best pizzas in town, also pastas, burgers and breakfasts.
$$ La Barca, Raimondi 117, T461855. Very good seafood, well-run, popular.
$$ Sabes?, Av Larco 920, T461555. Opens at 2000. Pub with food, internet café, popular, British-owned.
$$-$ Menuland, Los Pinos 250, T773579. Managed by a German/Peruvian couple, English, German, Italian spoken. Peruvian and international dishes, breakfast, lunch *menú* for US$1.75. Also has 2 double rooms (**$**), book exchange.
$ La Charapita, Huáscar 162. Modest but popular restaurant serving large portions.

Cafés
Argolini, Av Rivera 400. Convenient for people staying in the Los Pinos/Los Ficus area for fresh bread, cakes, ice cream, coffee and juices.
Chocolate, Av Rivera 772. Open 0730-1900. Dutch/Peruvian management, serves breakfast, also some vegetarian food, coffee and cakes. Also offers B&B.

🍸 Bars and clubs

Trujillo *p1251, map p1252*
Bar/Café Juguete, Junín y Independencia. Open to midnight. An old style café serving good coffee. Has a good pasta restaurant attached.
Bar/Café Stradivarius, Colón 327. Open in the evenings only. An attractive café with sofas,
Canana, San Martín 788, T232503. Bars and restaurant, disco, live music at weekends (US$1.50-3), video screens (also has travel agency). Recommended, but take care on leaving.
El Estribo, San Martín 809, T204053. A club playing a wide genre of sounds and attracting a mixed crowd.

🎉 Festivals

Trujillo *p1251, map p1252*
The 2 most important festivals are the National Marinera Contest (end of **Jan**) and the Festival Internacional de La Primavera (last week of

Sep), with cultural events, parades, beauty pageants and Trujillo's famous **Caballos de Paso**.

Huanchaco *p1256*
In the 1st week of **May** is the **Festival del Mar**, a celebration of the disembarkation of Taycanamo, the leader of the Chimú period. A procession is made in Totora boats. **29 Jun**, **San Pedro**, patron saint of fishermen: his statue is taken out to sea on a huge totora-reed boat. There are also surf competitions. Carnival and New Year are also popular celebrations.

O Shopping

Trujillo *p1251, map p1252*
Bookshops Librería Peruana, Pizarro 505, just off the Plaza. Best selection in town, also postcards, ask for Sra Inés Guerra de Guijón. SBS, Jr Bolívar 714 and in Mall Aventura, Av Mansiche block 20, also in Plaza Real Mall, Prol Av César Vallejo (behind UPAO University), California (take taxi or green California micro A). **Handicrafts** 120 Artesanía por Descubrir, Las Magnolias 403, California, www.tienda120. blogspot.com. Art gallery designs and handmade crafts, near Real Plaza. **APIAT**, craft market, Av España and Zela. The largest craft market in the city, good for ceramics, totora boats, woodwork and leather, competitive prices. **Artesanía del Norte**, at Dulcería La Libertad, Jr Pizarro 758, and at the Huacas del Sol y de la Luna, www.artesaniadelnorte.com. Sells items mostly to the owner, Mary Cortijo's, design using traditional techniques. **Trama Perú**, Pizarro 754, T243948, www.tramaperu. com. Daily 1000-2200. High-quality, hand-made art objects, authorized Moche art replicas. **Markets** Mercado Central, on Gamarra, Ayacucho and Pasaje San Agustín. **Mercado Unión**, between Av Santa and Av Perú. A little safer than others, also has repairs on shoes, clothes and bags.

Huanchaco *p1256*
El Quibishi, entrance to Huanchaco at south end of beach. Main *artesanía* market; also has a food section.

☉ What to do

Trujillo *p1251, map p1252*
Tour operators
Prices vary and competition is fierce so shop around for the best deal. Few agencies run tours on Sun and often only at fixed times on other days. Their groups are usually large. To Chan Chán, El Dragón and Huanchaco, 4-4½ hrs for US$8-9 pp. To Huacas del Sol and de la Luna, 2½-3 hrs for US$8-9 pp. To El Brujo, US$27-34 pp, 4-5 hrs. City tours cost US$3.50 pp, 2-2½ hrs. Prices do not include entrance fees.
Chacón Tours, Av España 106-112, T255212. Sat afternoon and Sun morning. Recommended for flights etc, not local tours.
Guía Tours, Independencia 580, T234856. Also Western Union agent.

Guides
Many hotels work on a commission basis with taxi drivers and travel agencies. If you decide on a guide, make your own direct approach and always agree what is included in the price. The Tourist Police (see Directory) has a list of guides; average cost US$7 per hr. Beware of cowboy outfits herding up tourists around the plazas and bus terminals for rapid, poorly translated tours. Also beware scammers offering surfing or salsa lessons and party invitations. **Clara Bravo**, Cahuide 495, T243347, http://trujilloperu.xanga.com. An experienced tourist guide who speaks Spanish, English, German and understands Italian; archaeological tour US$20 for 6 hrs, city tour US$7 pp, US$53 per car to El Brujo, with extension to Sipán, Brüning Museum and Túcume possible (tours in Lambayeque involve public transport, not included in cost). Clara works with English chartered accountant **Michael White** (same address, microbewhite@yahoo.com, also speaks German, French and Italian), who provides transport. He is very knowledgeable about tourist sites. They run tours any day of the week; 24-hr attention, accommodate small groups. **Luis Ocas Saldaña**, Jr José Martí 2019, T949-339593, guianorteperu@hotmail. com. Very knowledgeable, helpful, covers all of northern Peru. **Gustavo Prada Marga**, at Chan Chán, an experienced guide. **Alfredo Ríos Mercedes**, riosmercedes@hotmail.com, T949-

657978. Speaks English. **Jannet Rojas Sánchez**, Alto Mochica Mz Q 19, Trujillo, T949-344844. Speaks English, enthusiastic, works also for **Guía Tours**. **José Soto Ríos**, Atahualpa 514, dpto 3, T949-251489. He speaks English and French.

Huanchaco *p1256*
Surfing
There are plenty of surf schools. Equipment rental US$8.75/day, one lesson US$14-15.50. See also Casa Amelia, Av Larco 1150, T461351; http://casaamelia.net.
Indigan, Deán Saavedra 582 (next to soccer field), T462591. Jhon and Giancarlos Urcía for lessons, surf trips and rentals. Also offer lodging at their home.
Muchik, Av Larco 650, T462535, www.escueladetablamuchik.com. Instructors Chico and Omar Huamanchumo are former surf champions, also repairs. Arrange trips to other surf sites.
Olas Norte, Los Ficus 450, see Facebook. Individual and group lessons, prices include full equipment.
Onechako, Av La Ribera Norte, escuelasurfone chako@hotmail.com. Owner Tito Lescano. *Caballito de totora* riding lessons. Surf trips to other surf beaches in the North. Restaurant/bar.
Yenth Ccora, Av Larco 500, T949 403871, http://yenthccora.blogspot.co.uk. Surfing equipment manufacture, repair, rental and surfing school.

⊖ Transport

Trujillo *p1251, map p1252*
Air To **Lima**, 1 hr, daily flights with **LAN**, **Star Perú** and **Avianca/TACA**. Taxi to airport, US$6-8 depending on length of journey. The military **Grupo Aéreo 42** (J Alfonso Ugarte 642, Centro Cívico, T995-566264), has passenger flights on 2 routes in the north: Trujillo, Chiclayo, Chachapoyas, Tarapoto, Chiclayo, Trujillo (twice a week) and Trujillo, Chiclayo, Cajamarca, Mendoza, Juanjui, Tarapoto, Yurimaguas, Iquitos (out Wed, return Thu, plus Iquitos, Yurimaguas, Tarapoto, Chiclayo, Trujillo on Sun).
Bus Micros (small buses with 25 or more seats) and combis (up to 15 passengers), on all routes, cost US$0.50-0.60; colectivos (cars carrying 6 passengers), US$0.50, tend to run on

main avenues starting from Av España. None is allowed inside an area bounded by Av Los Incas in the east to Ovalo Mansiche in the west and the north and south perimeters of Av España.

A large new bus terminal for southbound buses has been built between Ovalos Grau and La Marina. Over time all bus companies will relocate here, but at the time of writing many maintain their own terminals. **Note** On Fri-Sun nights year round the better bus services must be pre-booked 2-3 days in advance. To and from **Lima**, 561 km, 9-10 hrs in the better class buses, average fare US$22-32, 10 hrs or more in the cheaper buses, US$11-16. There are many bus companies doing this route, among those recommended are: **Cruz del Sur**, Amazonas 437 near Av Ejército, T261801, the only one with a morning service to Trujillo at 0800; **Turismo Díaz**, Nicolás de Piérola 1079 on Panamericana Norte, T201237; **Línea**, Av América Sur 2857, T297000, 3 levels of service, also to **Chimbote** hourly, **Huaraz**, 9 hrs, **Cajamarca** 5 a day, **Chiclayo**, hourly (from Carrión by Av Mansiche, T235847, on the hour), and **Piura**, 2300. Also **Flores** (Av Ejército 346, T208250), **Ittsa** (Av Juan Pablo 1110, T284644, for southern destinations, Av Mansiche 145, T222541, for northern destinations – good service), **Móvil**, Av América Sur 3959, T286538. **Oltursa**, Av Ejército 342, T263055, 3 *bus cama* services to Lima.

Small **Pakatnamú** buses leave when full, 0400-2100, from Av N de Piérola 1092, T206594, to **Pacasmayo**, 102 km, 1¼ hrs, US$5.50. To **Chiclayo**, 4 hrs from Trujillo, from US$5.50, several companies. Among the best are Emtrafesa, Av Túpac Amaru 185, T471521, on the half-hour every hour; also to **Jaén**, 9 hrs; **Piura**, 6 hrs, US$15 (Ittsa's 1330, or Línea's 1415 buses are good choices); Ittsa also goes to **Talara**, 2200, 9 hrs, US$16.

Direct buses to **Huaraz**, 319 km, via Chimbote and Casma (169 km), with **Línea** and **Móvil**, 8 hrs, US$17-30. There are several buses and colectivos to **Chimbote**, with **América Express** from Av La Marina 315, 135 km, 2 hrs, US$6, departures every 30 mins from 0530 (ticket sales from 0500); then change at Chimbote (see above – leave Trujillo before 0600 to make a connection from 0800). Ask Clara Bravo and Michael White (see Guides, above) about transport to Caraz avoiding

Chimbote (a worthwhile trip via the Brasileños road and Cañon del Pato).

To **Cajamarca**, 300 km, 7-8 hrs, US$10-27: with **Línea**, and **Emtrafesa**, see above, at 2145. To **Huamachuco**, 170 km, 5-6 hrs, see page 1285.

Taxi Taxis in town charge US$1 within Av España and US$1.20 within Av América; always use official taxis, which are mainly yellow, or cooperative taxis, which have the company logo on the side. Beware of overcharging, check fares with locals. Taxi from in front of Hotel Libertador, US$12 per hr, about the same as a tour with an independent guide or travel agent for 1-2 people.

Huacas del Sol and de la Luna *p1254*
Combis every 15 mins from Ovalo Grau and, less safe, Galvez y Los Incas. They leave you a long walk from the site. On the return go to Ovalo Grau for onward connections. US$0.40. Taxis about US$5; few at site for return, unless you ask driver to wiat.

Chan Chán *p1255*
Take any transport between Trujillo and Huanchaco (see below) and ask to get out at the turn-off to Chan Chán, US$0.50. A taxi is US$5 from Trujillo to the ruins, US$1 from museum to ruins, US$3 to Huanchaco. **Note** There are police at the entrance to the site, but it is a 25-min walk to the ticket office. Take care if not taking a car on this track. On no account walk the 4 km from Chan Chán or on to Buenos Aires beach, as there is serious danger of robbery and of being attacked by dogs.

El Brujo *p1256*
The complex can be reached by taking one of the regular buses from Trujillo to Chocope, US$1.25, every 10 mins, 1 hr, and then a colectivo to Magdalena de Cao, US$0.75 (leave when full), 15 mins, then a mototaxi taking up to 3 people to the site, US$7.50 including 1½ hr wait.

Huanchaco *p1256*
2 combi routes run between Trujillo and Huanchaco, A and B, **Caballitos de Totora** company (white and black). 4 micros run between Trujillo and Huanchaco: A, B (also

known as Mercado Mayorista), H (UPAO) and H-Corazón (with red heart, Mercado Hermelinda), **Transportes Huanchaco**, red, yellow and white. They run 0500-2030, every 5-10 mins. Fare is US$0.75 for the journey (25 mins by combi, 45-60 mins by microbus). The easiest place to pick up any of these combis or micros is Ovalo Mansiche, 3 blocks northwest of Av España in front of the Cassinelli museum. In Trujillo, combi A takes a route on the south side of Av España, before heading up Av Los Incas. Combi B takes the northerly side of Av España. Micro A from Huanchaco goes to the 28 de Julio/Costa Rica junction where it turns west along Prolongación César Vallejo, passing the UPAO university and Plaza Real shopping centre, continuing to the Av El Golf (the terminus for return to Huanchaco on almost the same route). From Huanchaco to the city centre on other routes, ask the cobrador to let you off near C Pizarro on Av España. For the **Línea, Móvil Tours** and southern bus terminals, take micro H. It also goes to Ovalo Grau where you can catch buses to the Huacas del Sol and de la Luna. For **Cruz del Sur, Ormeño, Flores,** etc, take combi or micro B from Huanchaco. For **Oltursa** take micro H, Taxis US$4-5.

Puerto Chicama
Combis from Trujillo (Santa Cruz terminal, Av Santa Cruz, 1 block from Av America Sur), US$2, 1½ hrs. Also **Dorado** buses, Av N de Piérola 1062, T291778, US$2 (via Chocope, US$0.75, and Paiján, US$0.60 to Chicama). Buses stop just off Plaza Central, opposite Comisaria.

🛈 Directory

Trujillo *p1251, map p1252*
Medical services Hospital Belén, Bolívar 350, T245281. Clínica Peruano Americana, Av Mansiche 810, T231261, English spoken, good. **Useful addresses** Immigration: Av Larco 1220, Urb Los Pinos, T282217. Open Mon-Fri 0815-1230, 1500-1630.

Huanchaco *p1256*
Medical services Centro de Salud, Jr Atahualpa 128, T461547.

Chiclayo and around

Lambayeque department, sandwiched between the Pacific and the Andes, is a major agricultural zone, especially for rice and sugar cane. It boasts a distinctive cuisine and musical tradition, and an unparalleled ethnographic and archaeological heritage. Chiclayo's witchcraft market is famous and excavations at nearby adobe pyramid cities are uncovering fabulous treasures.

Chiclayo → *Phone code: 074. Colour map 3, B1. Population: 750,000.*

Since its inception in the 16th century, Chiclayo has grown to become a major commercial hub, but it is best known for the spectacular cache of prehispanic archaeological treasures that lie at its doorstep. **Tourist offices**: i perú ① *Sáenz Peña 838, T205703, iperuchiclayo@promperu.gob.pe, 0900-1900, Sun 0900-1300*; also at the airport (daily). For complaints and tourist protection, **Indecopi** ① *Los Tumbos 245, Santa Victoria, T206223, aleyva@indecopi.gob.pe, Mon-Fri 0800-1300, 1630-1930*. The **tourist police** ① *Av Sáenz Peña 830, T236700, ext 311, 24 hrs a day*, are very helpful and may store luggage and take you to the sites themselves. There are tourist kiosks on the Plaza and on Balta.

In the city itself, on the Plaza de Armas, is the 19th-century neoclassical **Cathedral**, designed by the English architect Andrew Townsend. The private **Club de la Unión** is on the Plaza at the corner of Calle San José. The new Palacio Municipal contains a Centro Documental de la Memoria Histórica de Chiclayo. Continue five blocks north on Balta, the busiest commercial street, to the **Mercado Modelo**, one of northern Peru's liveliest and largest daily markets. Don't miss the handicrafts stalls (see **Monsefú**) and the well organized section (off Calle Arica on the south side) of ritual paraphernalia used by traditional curers and diviners (*curanderos*): herbal medicines, folk charms, curing potions, and exotic objects including dried llama foetuses to cure all manner of real and imagined illnesses. At **Paseo de Artesanías**, 18 de Abril near Balta south of the Plaza, stalls sell handicrafts in a quiet, custom-built open-air arcade. Another relaxing spot here is the **Paseo de las Musas**, with its gardens and imitation Greek statues.

Monsefú and the coast

The traditional town of **Monsefú**, southwest, is known for its music and handicrafts; there's a good market, four blocks from the plaza. Handicraft stalls open when potential customers arrive (see Festivals, page 1269). Beyond Monsefú are three ports serving the Chiclayo area. **Pimentel**, 8 km from Chiclayo, is a beach resort which gets very crowded on Sundays and during the summer (US$4 to rent a chair and sunshade). Most of the seafront has been bought up by developers, but the main plaza is an oasis of green. There are several seafood restaurants (**El Muelle de Pimentel**, Rivera del Mar cuadra 1, T453142, is recommended). You can walk along the restored pier for US$0.25. Sea-going reed boats (*caballitos de totora*) are used by fishermen and may be seen from the pier returning mid-morning or late morning or late afternoon on the beach. The surfing between Pimentel and the Bayovar Peninsula is excellent, reached from Chiclayo (14.5 km) by road branching off from the Pan-American Highway. Nearby **Santa Rosa** has little to recommend it other than to see the realities of the fisherfolks' life and it is not safe to walk there from Pimentel. The most southerly is **Puerto Eten**, a quaint port with some nice wooden buildings on the plaza, 24 km by road from Chiclayo. Its old railway station has been declared a national heritage. In the adjacent roadstead, Villa de Eten, panama hats are the local industry, but it is not as picturesque. The ruined Spanish town of **Zaña**, 51 km south of Chiclayo, was destroyed by floods in 1726, and sacked by English pirates on more than one occasion. There are ruins of five colonial churches and the convents of San Agustín, La Merced and San Francisco.

Lambayeque

About 12 km northwest from Chiclayo is Lambayeque, a good base from which to explore the Chiclayo area. Its narrow streets are lined by colonial and republican houses, many retaining their distinctive wooden balconies and wrought-iron grill-work over the windows, but many in very bad shape. On Calle 2 de Mayo see especially **Casa de la Logia o Montjoy**, whose 64-m-long balcony is said to be the longest in the colonial Americas. It has been restored and can be visited (free). At 8 de Octubre 345 is **Casona Descalzi** ① *T283433, 1100-1700 daily*, which is well preserved as a good restaurant. It has 120 carved iguana heads on the ceiling. **Casona Iturregui Aguilarte**, at No 410, is, by contrast, seriously neglected. Also of interest is the 16th-century **Complejo Religioso Monumental de San Francisco de Asís** and the baroque church of the same name which stands on Plaza de Armas 27 de Diciembre.

Chiclayo

Where to stay 🛌
1 Casa de la Luna *B1*
2 Costa del Sol *C3*
3 Embajador *A3*
4 Garza *C3*
5 Gran Hotel Chiclayo *B1*
6 Hosp Concordia *C3*
7 Hosp San Eduardo *C3*
8 Inti *B2*
9 Muchik Hostel *B3*
10 Pirámide Real *C3*
11 Santa Rosa *B2*
12 Sicán *C2*
13 Sol Radiante *C2*
14 Sunec *C2*

Restaurants 🍴
1 Balta 512 *C3*
2 Boulevar *B2*
3 Café 900 *C3*
4 Café Astoria *C2*
5 D'Onofrio *C3*
6 El Huaralino *C1*
7 Fiesta *B1*
8 Hebrón *C3*
9 Kaprichos *A3*
10 La Panadería *B2*
11 La Parra *C3*
12 La Plazuela *B1*
13 Las Américas *B3*
14 Roma *C3*
15 Tradiciones *C2*

Transport 🚌
1 Brüning Express to
  Lambayeque *B1*
2 Cial *C1*
3 Civa *C3*
4 Colectivos to
  Lambayeque *A2*
5 Colectivos to
  Puerto Etén *A3*
6 Cruz del Sur *C3*
7 Emtrafesa *C3*
8 Línea *C2*
9 Móvil *C2*
10 Oltursa *B1*
11 Tepsa *C2*
12 Transportes Chiclayo *B1*

The reason most people visit is to see the town's two museums. The older of the two is the **Brüning Archaeological Museum** ① *0900-1700, US$2.75, a guided tour costs an extra US$2.75*, in a modern building, specializing in Mochica, Lambayeque/Sicán and Chimú cultures. Three blocks east is the more recent **Museo de las Tumbas Reales de Sipán** ① *Av Juan Pablo Vizcardo y Guzmán 895, T283977, www.museotumbasrealessipan.pe, 0900-1700, closed Mon, US$3.55, moto taxi from plaza US$0.60*, shaped like a pyramid. The magnificent treasure from the tomb of 'The Old Lord of Sipán' (see below), and a replica of the Lord of Sipán's tomb are displayed here. A ramp from the main entrance takes visitors to the third floor, from where you descend, mirroring the sequence of the archaeologists' discoveries. There are handicrafts outside and in the museum shop and a **tourist office** ① *Tue-Sun 1030-1400, 1500-1730*.

On the plaza in **Mórrope**, on the Pan-American Highway 20 km north of Lambayeque, is one of the earliest churches in northern Peru, **San Pedro de Mórrope** (1545), an adobe and *algarrobo* structure beautifully renovated and painted. It contains the tomb of the cacique Santiago Cazusol. Next to it is the more modern parish church.

Sipán
① *Daily 0900-1700, entrance for tombs and museum is US$2.85; guide at site US$8 (may not speak English). To visit the site takes about 3-4 hrs. There are comedores outside the site.*
At this imposing complex a short distance east of Chiclayo (turn-off well signed in the centre of Pomalca), excavations since 1987 in one of three crumbling pyramids have brought to light a cache of funerary objects considered to rank among the finest examples of pre-Columbian art. Peruvian archaeologist Walter Alva, former leader of the dig, continues to probe the immense mound that has revealed no less than 12 royal tombs filled with 1800-year-old offerings worked in precious metals, stone, pottery and textiles of the Moche culture (circa AD 1-750). In the most extravagant Moche tomb discovered, El Señor de Sipán, a priest was found clad in gold (ear ornaments, breast plate, etc), with turquoise and other valuables.

In another tomb were found the remnants of what is thought to have been a priest, sacrificed llama and a dog, together with copper decorations. In 1989 another richly appointed, unlooted tomb contained even older metal and ceramic artefacts along with what was probably a high-ranking shaman or spiritual leader, called 'The Old Lord of Sipán'. Three tombs are on display, containing replicas of the original finds. **Museo de Sitio Huaca Rajada** ① *daily 0900-1700, US$2.85*, concentrates on the finds at the site, especially Tomb 14 (the 'Sacerdote-Guerrero', or Priest-Warrior), the decorative techniques of the Moche and the roles that archaeologists and local communities play in protecting these precious discoveries. You can wander around the previously excavated areas of the Huaca Rajada to get an idea of the construction of the burial mound and adjacent pyramids. For a good view, climb the large pyramid across from the excavated Huaca Rajada.

A 4000-year-old temple, **Ventarrón**, was uncovered about 20 km from Sipán in 2007 by Walter Alva; his son, Ignacio, is now in charge of the dig. It predates Sipán by some 2000 years and shows three phases of development. Its murals, which appear to depict a deer trapped in a net, are claimed to be the oldest in the Americas and there is evidence of cultural exchange with as far away as the Amazon. A project to build a site museum and improved access will take until 2015, until then entry, with guide, is US$2.

East from Pomalca is Chongoyape, just before which is the turning to the **Chaparrí** private ecological reserve, 34,000 ha, set up and run by the Comunidad Muchik Santa Catalina de Chongoyape, 75 km from Chiclayo. Visitors can go for the day or stay at the **Chaparrí EcoLodge** ① *US$10.50 for entry to the reserve, www.chaparri.org, for day visits T978-896377, see Where to stay, below*. All staff and guides are locals; for every 10 people you have to have a local guide (this provides work and helps to prevent rubbish). There are no dogs or goats in the area so the forest is recuperating; it contains many bird and mammal species of the dry forest, including white-winged guan and spectacled bear. There is a Spectacled Bear Rescue Centre where bears rescued from captivity live in semi-wild enclosures. The Tinajones reservoir is good for birdwatching.

Túcume

ⓘ T835026, www.museodesitiotucume.com, open 0800-1700, US$4.50, students US$1, children US$0.30, guide US$7.

About 35 km north of Chiclayo, not far from the Panamericana and Túcume Nuevo, lie the ruins of this vast city built over 1000 years ago. A short climb to the two *miradores* on **Cerro La Raya** (or **El Purgatorio**) offers the visitor an unparalleled panoramic vista of 26 major pyramids, platform mounds, walled citadels and residential compounds flanking a ceremonial centre and ancient cemeteries. One of the pyramids, Huaca Larga, where excavations are still being undertaken, is the longest adobe structure in the world, measuring 700 m long, 280 m wide and over 30 m high. There is no evidence of occupation of Túcume previous to the Sicán, or Lambayeque people who developed the site AD 1000-1375 until the Chimú conquered the region, establishing a short reign until the arrival of the Incas around 1470. The Incas built on top of the existing structure of **Huaca Larga** using stone from Cerro La Raya. Among the other pyramids which make up this huge complex are: **Huaca El Mirador** (90 m by 65 m, 30 m high), **Huaca Las Estacas**, **Huaca Pintada** and **Huaca de las Balsas**, which is thought to have housed people of elevated status such as priests. A walkway leads around the covered pyramid and you can see many mud reliefs including fishermen on rafts.

Not much of the site is open to view, only the miradores mentioned above and the walk through the site there, as lots of study is going on. There is a pleasant dry forest walk to Huaca I, with shade, bird- and lizard-watching. A new site museum is due to open in late 2014.

The town of **Túcume Viejo** is a 20-minute walk beyond the site. Look for the side road heading towards a new park, opposite which is the ruin of a huge colonial church made of adobe and some brick. The surrounding countryside is pleasant for walks through mango trees and fields of maize. **Fiesta de la Purísima Concepción**, the festival of the town's patron saint, is eight days prior to Carnival in February, and also in September.

Ferreñafe and Sicán

The colonial town of **Ferreñafe**, 20 km northeast of Chiclayo, is worth a visit, especially for the **Museo Nacional Sicán** ⓘ T286469, Museo-Nacional-Sican on Facebook, Tue-Sun 0900-1700, US$4, students half price, good explanations in Spanish, café and gift shop. This excellent new museum on the outskirts of town houses objects of the Sicán (Lambayeque) culture from near Batán Grande. **Tourist office**: the Mincetur ⓘ on the Plaza de Armas, T282843, citesipan@mincetur.gob.pe, is helpful.

The entrance to **El Santuario Histórico Bosque de Pómac** ⓘ visitors' centre, dalemandelama@gmail.com, 0900-1700, free, a guide (Spanish only) can be hired with transport, US$3.45, horses for hire US$6, which includes the ruins of **Sicán**, lies 20 km beyond Ferreñafe along the road to Batán Grande (from the Panamericana another entrance is near Túcume). Visiting is not easy because of the arid conditions and distances involved: it is 10 km to the nearest *huaca* (pyramid). At the visitors' centre food and drinks are available and camping is permitted. The guide covers a two-hour tour of the area which includes at least two *huacas*, some of the most ancient carob trees and a mirador (viewpoint), which affords a beautiful view across the emerald green tops of the forest with the enormous pyramids dramatically breaking through. Sicán has revealed several sumptuous tombs dating to AD 900-1100. The ruins comprise some 12 large adobe pyramids, arranged around a huge plaza, measuring 500 m by 250 m, with 40 archaeological sites in total. The city, of the Sicán (or Lambayeque culture), was probably moved to Túcume (see above), 6 km west, following 30 years of severe drought and then a devastating El Niño related flood in AD 1050-1100. These events appear to have provoked a rebellion in which many of the remaining temples on top of the pyramids were burnt and destroyed. The forest itself has good birdwatching possibilities.

North of Chiclayo

On the old Pan-American Highway 885 km from Lima, **Olmos** is a tranquil place (several hotels and **Festival de Limón** last week in June). A paved road runs east from Olmos over the Porculla Pass, branching north to Jaén and east to Bagua Grande (see page 1297).

Olmos is the best base for observing the critically endangered white-winged guan, a bird thought extinct for 100 years until its rediscovery in 1977. On the outskirts is the white-winged guan captive breeding centre, **Zoocriadero Bárbara d'Achille** ① *Km 103, Olmos*, which also has an aviary of rescued birds, and the **Asociación Cracidae Perú** (director Fernando Angulo Pratolongo) ① *Torres Paz 708, Chiclayo, T074-238748*. Captive breeding started in 1979 and the first reintroduction into the wild was made in 2001 at Chaparrí (see page 1265). One place where the guans can be seen in the wild is Quebrada Limón (or Frejolillo), where guides from the local community check on the guans' whereabouts in order to take visitors to see them in the early morning. Ask at the breeding centre for how to get there.

The old Pan-American Highway continues from Olmos to Cruz de Caña and Piura. At Lambayeque the new Pan American Highway branches off the old road for 190 km straight across the **Sechura Desert**, a large area of shifting sands separating the oases of Chiclayo and Piura. **Note** Solo cyclists should not cross the desert as muggings have occurred. Take the safer, inland route. In the desert, there is no water, fuel or accommodation. Do not attempt this alone.

⊙ Chiclayo and around listings

For hotel and restaurant price codes, and other relevant information, see Essentials.

⊜ Where to stay

Chiclayo *p1263, map p1264*

$$$ Costa del Sol, Balta 399, T227272, www.costadelsolperu.com. Non-smoking 'rooms, smart, small pool, sauna, jacuzzi, Wi-Fi, ATM. **Páprika** restaurant, good value Sun buffets, vegetarian options.

$$$ Gran Hotel Chiclayo (Casa Andina Select), Villareal 115, T511-2139739, www.casa-andina.com. Large, modern hotel for corporate and leisure guests, pool, safe car park, changes dollars, jacuzzi, entertainments, restaurant. Now operated by **Casa Andina**.

$$$ Inti, Luis Gonzales 622, T235931, www.intihotel.com.pe. More expensive rooms with jacuzzi, family rooms available, welcome cocktail, airport transfer included, parking, safe and fridge in room, restaurant, helpful staff.

$$$ Sunec, Izaga 472, T205110, www.sunechotel.com.pe. Modern hotel in a central location, parking and small pool, opened in 2013.

$$ Embajador, 7 de Enero 1388, 1½ blocks from Mercado Modelo, T204729, http://hotelembajadorchiclayo.com. Modern, bright, good facilities, 20 mins' walk from centre, small comfortable rooms, small restaurant,

excellent service, free pick-up from bus office, tours arranged.

$ Hospedaje Concordia, 7 de Enero Sur 235, Urb San Eduardo, T209423. Rooms on 2nd floor bigger than 3rd, modern, pleasant, no meals, laundry service, view of Parque San Eduardo.

$ Hospedaje San Eduardo, 7 de Enero Sur 267, Urb San Eduardo, T208668. No meals, colourful decor, modern bathrooms, fan, Wi-Fi, public phone, quiet, hot water.

$ Muchik Hostel, Vicente de la Vega 1127. Singles, doubles and dorm, with fan, pleasant common area, safe.

$ Pirámide Real, MM Izaga 726, T224036. Compact and spotless, good value, no meals, safe in room, fan, very central.

$ Santa Rosa, L González 927, T224411. Rooms with windows are bright and spacious, best at rear. Hot water, fan, laundry, good value.

$ Sicán, MM Izaga 356, T208741, hsican@hotmail.com. With breakfast, hot water, fan, comfortable, restaurant and bar, laundry, parking, welcoming and trustworthy.

$ Sol Radiante, Izaga 392, T237858. Hot water, comfortable, pleasant, family-run, laundry, tourist information. Pay in advance.

Lambayeque *p1263*

$$$ Hostería San Roque, 2 de Mayo 437, T282860, www.hosteriasanroque.com. In a fine, extensive colonial house, beautifully refurbished, helpful staff, bar, swimming pool, lunch on request. Single, double, triple, quad rooms and dorm for groups of 6, **$**.

$ Hostal Libertad, Bolívar 570, T283561, www.hostallibertad.com. 1½ blocks from plaza, big rooms, fridge, secure.

$ Hostal Real Sipán, Huamachuco 664, opposite Brüning Museum. Modern, an option if arriving late at night.

Mórrope

$$-$ La Casa del Papelillo, San Pedro 357, T955-624734, http://lacasadelpapelillo. blogspot.com/. 3 rooms in a remodeled 19th-century home, one with private bath, includes breakfast, communal areas, cultural events, discounts for community volunteer work. Owner Cecilia is knowledgeable and helpful.

Sipán: Chaparrí p1265

$$$$ EcoLodge Chaparrí, T984-676249 or in Chiclayo T452299, www.chaparrilodge.com. A delightful oasis in the dry forest, 6 beautifully decorated cabins (more being built) and 5 double rooms with shared bath, built of stone and mud, nice and cool, solar power. Price is for 3 meals and a local guide for one day, first-class food. Sechuran foxes in the gardens; hummingbirds bathe at the pool about 0600 every day. Recommended.

Túcume p1266

$$ pp Los Horcones, T951-831705, www. loshorconesdetucume.com. Rustic luxury in the shadow of the pyramids, with adobe and algarrobo rooms set in lovely garden with lots of birdlife. Good food, pizza oven, breakfast included. Note that if rice is being grown nearby in Jan-May there can be a serious mosquito problem.

North of Chiclayo: Olmos p1267

$$$ Los Faiques, Humedades Alto, Salas, T979-299932, www.losfaiques-salas.com. Very pretty place in a quiet forest setting, buffet breakfast, excellent restaurant.

$ El Remanso, San Francisco 100, T427158, elremansolmos@yahoo.com. Like an hacienda with courtyards, small pool, whitewashed rooms, colourful bedding, flowers and bottled water in room, hot water (supposedly). Price is full board, good restaurant. Charming owner. Several other places to stay.

Restaurants

Chiclayo p1263, map p1264

For delicious, cheap *ceviche*, go to the **Nativo** stall in the Mercado Central, a local favourite.

$$$ El Huaralino, La Libertad 155, Santa Victoria. Wide variety, international and creole, but mixed reports of late.

$$$ Fiesta, Av Salaverry 1820 in 3 de Octubre suburb, T201970, www.restaurantfiesta gourmet.com. Gourmet local dishes, excellent food and service, beautifully presented, daily and seasonal specials, fabulous juices, popular business lunch place.

$$$ Sabores Peruanos, Los Incas 136. Tue-Sun 1200-1700. Great Peruvian seafood and meat dishes.

$$ Balta 512, Balta 512, T223598. First-class local food, usually good breakfast, popular with locals.

$$ Boulevar, Colón entre Izaga y Aguirre. Good, friendly, *menú* and à la carte.

$$ Hebrón, Balta 605. For more upmarket than average chicken, but also local food and *parrilla*, good salads. Also does an excellent breakfast and a good buffet at weekends.

$$ Kaprichos, Pedro Ruíz 1059, T232721. Chinese, delicious, huge portions.

$$ Las Américas, Aguirre 824. Open 0700-0200. Good service.

$$ Roma, Izaga 706. Open all day. Wide choice, breakfasts, snacks and meals.

$$ Tradiciones, 7 de Enero Sur 105, T221192. Daily 0900-1700. Good variety of local dishes, including ceviche, and drinks, nice atmosphere and garden, good service.

$ Café Astoria, Bolognesi 627. Open 0800-1200, 1530-2100. Breakfast, good-value *menú*.

$ La Parra, Izaga 746. Chinese and creole, *parrillada*, very good, large portions, cheerful.

$ La Plazuela, San José 299, Plaza Elías Aguirre. Good food, seats outside.

Café 900, MM Izaga 900, www.cafe900.com. Nice atmosphere in a remodeled old house, good food, popular with locals, sometimes has live music.

D'Onofrio, Balta y Torres Paz. Good ice cream.

La Panadería, Lapoint 847. Good choice of breads, including *integral*, snacks and soft drinks.

Lambayeque *p1203*
A Lambayeque specialty is the 'King Kong', a giant *alfajor* biscuit filled with manjar blanco and other sweets. San Roque brand (www.sanroque.com.pe), sold throught Peru, is especially good.
$$ Casona Descalzi, address above. Open for lunch only. Good menu, including traditional northern dishes.
$$ El Cántaro, 2 de Mayo 180, http://restaurant elcantaro.com. Lunch only. For traditional local dishes, à la carte and a good *menú*.
$$ El Pacífico, Huamachuco 970, T283135. Open for lunch only. Renowned for its enormous plates of *arroz con pato* and *causa norteña*.
$$ El Rincón del Pato, A Leguía 270. Lunch only. Offers 40 different duck dishes.
$$-$ Sabor Norteño, Bolívar 440. One of the few restaurants open in the early evening.
$ Café Cultural La Cucarda, 2 de Mayo 263, T284155. Open evening only. Small alternative café, decorated with rescued antiques, delicious pastries, pies and cakes. Recommended.

⊕ Festivals

Chiclayo *p1263, map p1264*
6 Jan Reyes Magos in Mórrope, Illimo and other towns, a recreation of a medieval pageant in which pre-Columbian deities become the Wise Men. On **4 Feb** Túcume devil dances (see below). **14 Mar** El Señor Nazareno Cautivo, in Lambayeque and Monsefú, whose main celebration of this festival is **14 Sep**. Holy Week, traditional Easter celebrations and processions in many villages. **2-7 Jun** Divine Child of the Miracle, Villa de Eten. **27-31 Jul** Fexticum in Monsefú, traditional foods, drink, handicrafts, music and dance. **5 Aug** Pilgrimage from the mountain shrine of Chalpón to Motupe, 90 km north of Chiclayo; the cross is brought down from a cave and carried in procession through the village. At Christmas and New Year, processions and children dancers (*pastorcitos* and *seranitas*) can be seen in many villages, eg Ferreñafe, Mochumi, Mórrope.

⊙ What to do

Chiclayo *p1263, map p1264*
Lambayeque's museums, Sipán and Túcume (see Around Chiclayo) can easily be visited by public transport. Local operators run 3-hr tours to Sipán; Túcume and Lambayeque (5 hrs); Sicán is a full-day tour including Ferreñafe and Pómac; also to Zaña and coastal towns.
InkaNatura, Manuel María Izaga 730, of 203, T979-995024, www.inkanatura.net. Mon-Fri 0915-1315, 1515-1915, Sat 0915-1315. Run historical and nature tours throughout northern Peru. Good service.

Horse riding
Rancho Santana, in Pacora, T979-712145, www.cabalgatasperu.com. Relaxing tours on horseback, half-day (US$15.50), 1-day (US$22.50) or 3-day tours, including to Santuario Bosque de Pómac, Sicán ruins and Túcume, Swiss-run (Andrea Martin), good horses. Also **$** a bungalow, a double room and camping (tents for hire) at the ranch with safe parking for campervans. Frequently recommended.

⊖ Transport

Chiclayo *p1263, map p1264*
Air José Abelardo Quiñones González airport 1 km from town, T233192; taxi from centre US$4. Arrive 2 hrs before flight; be prepared for manual search of hand luggage; no restaurant or bar in departure lounge.
    Daily flights to/from **Lima** and **Piura** with LAN (MM Izaga 770) and StarPerú (MM Izaga 459, T225204), direct or via **Trujillo**. The military **Grupo Aéreo 42** (Av Balta 901, T979-975537) has passenger flights to Chiclayo originating in Trujillo or Iquitos; see page 1261 for routes and schedules.
Bus No terminal terrestre; most buses stop outside their offices on Bolognesi. To **Lima**, 770 km, US$25-36: **Civa**, Av Bolognesi 714, T223434; **Cruz del Sur**, Bolognesi 888, T225508; **Ormeno**, Haya de la Torre 242, 2 blocks south of Bolognesi, T234206; **Ittsa**, Av Bolognesi 155, T233612; **Línea**, Bolognesi 638, T222221, *especial* and *bus cama* service; **Móvil**, Av Bolognesi 195, T271940 (goes as far as Tarapoto); **Oltursa**, ticket office at Balta e Izaga, T237789, terminal at Vicente de la Vega 101, T225611; **Tepsa**, Bolognesi 504-36 y Colón,

T236981; **Transportes Chiclayo**, Av L Ortiz 010, T223632. Most companies leave from 1900 onwards. To **Trujillo**, 209 km, with **Emtrafesa**, Av Balta 110, T600660, every 15 mins, 4 hrs, US$5.50, and **Línea**, as above. To **Piura**, 4 hrs, US$5.50, **Transportes Chiclayo** leave 15 mins throughout the day; also **Línea** and **Emtrafesa** and buses from the **Cial/Flores** terminal, Bolognesi 751, T239579. To **Sullana**, US$8.50. To **Tumbes**, US$9, 9-10 hrs; with **Cial**, **Cruz del Sur** or **El Dorado**. Some companies on the route northwards arrive full from Lima. Many buses go on to the **Ecuadorean border** at **Aguas Verdes**. Go to the *Salida* on Elías Aguirre, mototaxi drivers know where it is, be there by 1900. All buses stop here after leaving their terminals to try and fill empty seats, so discounts may be possible. To **Cajamarca**, 260 km, US$9-20, eg **Línea**, 4 a day; others from Tepsa terminal, Bolognesi y Colón, eg **Días**, T224448. To **Chachapoyas**, US$13.50-25: **Civa** 1730 daily, 10-11 hrs; **Transervis Kuelap**, in Tepsa station, 1830 daily, **Móvil**, at 2000. To **Jaén**, US$7.75-9.60, many companies, but **Móvil** US$11.55-15.50. To **Tarapoto**, 18 hrs, US$25-29, with **Móvil**, also **Tarapoto Tours**, Bolognesi 751, T636231. **Civarun** to **Guayaquil** at 1825, *semi-cama* US$34.75, *cama* US$42.50, also **Super Semería**, US$25, 12 hrs, via Piura, Máncora, Tumbes; they also go to Cuenca.
Taxi Mototaxis are a cheap way to get around; US$1 anywhere in city.

Monsefú and the coast *p1263*
Combis to **Monsefú** cost US$0.75 from Balta y Pedro Ruiz, or Terminal Epsel, Av Castañeda Iparraguirre s/n. The **ports** may be visited on a half-day trip. Combis leave from Av L Ortiz y San José, Chiclayo, to Pimentel, US$1.10. Taxi Chiclayo-Pimentel US$6, 20 mins. Colectivos to Eten leave from 7 de Enero y Arica.

Lambayeque *p1263*
Colectivos from **Chiclayo** US$0.75, 25 mins, from Pedro Ruíz at the junction with Av Ugarte. Also **Brüning Express** combis from Vicente de la Vega entre Angamos y Av L Ortiz, every 15 mins, US$0.50. **Trans Lambayeque** colectivo from Plaza Elias Aguirre, US$0.90, Some major bus lines have offices in Lambayeque and can drop you off there.

Sipán *p1265*
Combis to Sipán leave from Plaza Elías Aguirre and from terminal Epsel, US$1, 1 hr.

Chaparrí
Take a public bus from Leoncio Prado y Sáenz Peña, Chiclayo, to **Chongoyape** (1¼ hrs, US$1.50), then a mototaxi to **Chaparrí**, US$10.

Túcume *p1266*
Combis from **Chiclayo**, Av Leguía, 15 m from Angamos, US$1, 45 mins; mototaxi from highway/new town to ruins US$0. 75. Combi Túcume-**Lambayeque**, US$0.75, 25 mins.

Ferreñafe and Sicán *p1266*
Colectivos from Terminal Epsel, Chiclayo, to the centre of Ferreñafe leave every few mins, or from 8 de Octubre y Sáenz Peña, 40 mins, U$1, take a mototaxi to the museum, 5 mins, US$1.75. Alternatively, combis for Batán Grande depart from Av N de Piérola, Chiclayo, and pass the museum every 15-20 mins, 40 mins, US$1.

❶ Directory

Chiclayo *p1263, map p1264*
Medical services Ambulance: Max Salud, 7 de Enero 185, T234032.

Piura and around → *Phone code: 073. Colour map 3, A1. Population: 377,500.*

A proud and historic city, Piura was founded in 1532, three years before Lima, by the conquistadores left behind by Pizarro. The city has two well-kept parks, Cortés and Pizarro (with a statue of the *conquistador*, also called Plaza de las Tres Culturas), and public gardens. Old buildings are kept in repair and new buildings blend with the Spanish style of the old city. Three bridges cross the Río Piura to Castilla, the oldest from Calle Huancavelica, for pedestrians (Puente San Miguel), another from Calle Sánchez Cerro, and the newest from Avenida Panamericana Norte, at west end of town. The winter climate, May-September, is very pleasant although nights can be cold and the wind piercing; December to March is very hot.

Tourist offices Information at the **tourist office** ⓘ *Ayacucho 377, T320249, iperupiura@ prom peru.gob.pe, Mon-Sat 0830-1900, Sun 0830-1400. Also at the airport.* **Dirección Regional de Turismo** ⓘ *Av Fortunato Chirichigno, Urb San Eduardo, T308229, at the north end of town, helpful when there are problems, open 0900-1300, 1600-1800.* **Indecopi** ⓘ *Av Los Cocos 268, Urb Club Grau, T308549, dnavarro@indecopi.gob.pe.*

Piura

Where to stay 🛏
1 California
2 El Almirante
3 El Sol
4 Esmeralda
5 Hosp Aruba
6 Hostal Los Jardines
7 Hostal Moon Night
8 LP Los Portales
9 San Miguel

Restaurants 🍴
1 Alex Chopp's
2 Brosti Chopp
3 Carburmer &
Picantería Los Santitos
4 Chalán de la Avenida
5 Chalán del Norte
6 D'Pauli
7 El Otro Romano &
Piura Tours

8 Ganímedes
9 Italia
10 La Pera Madura
11 Romano

Places in Piura

Standing on the **Plaza de Armas** is the **cathedral**, with gold covered altar and paintings by Ignacio Merino. A few blocks away is **San Francisco**, where the city's independence from Spain was declared on 4 January 1821, nearly eight months before Lima. The birthplace of Admiral Miguel Grau, hero of the War of the Pacific with Chile, is **Casa Museo Grau** ① *Jr Tacna 662, opposite the Centro Cívico, 0800-1300, 1600-1900, free*. It is a museum and contains a model of the *Huáscar*, the largest Peruvian warship in the War of the Pacific, which was built in Britain. It also contains interesting old photographs. Local craftwork is sold at the **Mercado Modelo**. The small **Museo Municipal Vicús** ① *Sullana, near Huánuco, Mon-Sat 0800-2200, Sun 0800-1200*, includes 60 gold artefacts from the local Vicús culture. It also has an art section.

Catacaos 12 km to the southwest of Piura, is famous for its *chicha, picanterías* (local restaurants, some with music), tooled leather, gold and silver filigree jewellery, wooden articles, straw hats (expensive) and splendid celebrations in Holy Week. About 2 km south of Catacaos is the **Narihualá** archaeological site.

The port for the area, 50 km from Piura, **Paita** is flanked on three sides by a towering, sandy bluff. It is a major fishing port with a long history. Several colonial buildings survive. Bolívar's mistress, Manuela Sáenz, lived the last 24 years of her life in Paita, after being exiled from Quito. She supported herself until her death in 1856 by weaving, embroidering and making candy, after refusing the fortune left her by her husband. On a bluff looming over Paita is a small colonial fortress built to repel pirates, who attacked it frequently. Nearby beaches include **Colán**, to the north, with various hotels, restaurants and a long sandy beach (beware the stingrays); and less developed **Yasila**, a fishing village to the south.

⊛ Piura and around listings

For hotel and restaurant price codes, and other relevant information, see Essentials.

⊜ Where to stay

Piura and around *p1270, map p1271*
To be sure of a room in Piura, book the hotel of your choice in advance.
$$$$ LP Los Portales, Libertad 875, Plaza de Armas, T321161, www.losportaleshoteles.com.pe. Includes welcome cocktail, attractively refurbished, the city's social centre, elegant, hot water, pleasant terrace, nice pool.
$$$ Esmeralda, Loreto 235, T331205, www.hotelesmeralda.com.pe. Variety of room sizes, hot water, frigobar, comfortable, good, restaurant.
$$ El Almirante, Ica 860, T335239. With fan, modern, laundry, meals, parking, owner is knowledgeable about the Ayabaca area.
$$ El Sol, Sánchez Cerro 411, T324461. Hot water, frigobar, small pool, snack bar, parking, payment in advance, some rooms can be noisy.
$$ San Miguel, Lima 1007, Plaza Pizarro, T305122, www.sanmigueldepiura.com. Modern, comfortable, café.

$$-$ Hostal Los Jardines, Av Los Cocos 136, T326590, www.hotellosjardines.com. Hot water, laundry, parking, good value.
$ California, Jr Junín 835, upstairs, T328789. Shared or private bath, own water-tank, some hot water, mosquito netting on windows, roof terrace, brightly decorated. The best of the hostels in this area.
$ Hospedaje Aruba, Junín 851, T303067. Small rooms, no windows, but comfortable, shared bath, fan on request.
$ Hostal Moon Night, Junín 899, T336174. Comfortable, modern, spacious, with or without bath, cold water.

❼ Restaurants

Piura and around *p1270, map p1271*
$$$ Carburmer, Libertad 1014, T332380. Very good lunches and dinners, also serves pizza.
$$$ Picantería Los Santitos, in the same precinct is Carburmer. Lunch only, wide range of traditional dishes in a renovated colonial house.

$$ Alex Chopp's, Huancavelica 538, T322568. A la carte dishes, seafood, fish, chicken and meats, beer, popular at lunchtime.
$$ Brosti Chopp, Arequipa 780, T303753. Similar, but with lunch *menú* for US$1.45.
$$ Romano, Ayacucho 580. Mon-Sat 0700-2300. Popular with locals, extensive menu, excellent set meal for US$1.55. Recommended. Also has **$$ El Otro Romano**, Ayacucho 579, Tue-Sun 0900-1700, offering the same fare.
$ Ganímedes, Lima 440, T329176. A good vegetarian restaurant, very popular set lunch, à la carte is slow but well worth it.
$ Italia, Grau 172. For breakfasts, snacks, desserts and juices.

Cafés
Chalán del Norte several branches for sandwiches, sweets, and very good ice cream, Tacna 520 on Plaza de Armas, Grau 173 and 450 (**Chalán de la Avenida**).
D'Pauli, Lima 541. Sweets, cakes and ice-cream.
La Pera Madura, Arequipa 168, next to Cine Municipal. Daily 1700-2300. For local specialities, plus tamales and other snacks.

⚙ What to do

Piura and around *p1270, map p1271*
Piura Tours, C Ayacucho 585, T326778, piuratours@speedy.com.pe. The manager Mario speaks good English.

⊖ Transport

Piura and around *p1270, map p1271*
Air Capitán Guillermo Concha airport is in Castilla, 10 mins from the centre by taxi (US$1.85). It has gift shops and 2 car rental agencies (see below). Daily flights with **LAN** (Av Grau 140) to **Lima** via **Chiclayo**. Flights with **Saereo** Mon, Wed, Fri, 1325, to **Machala** (Santa Rosa) US$87, **Guayaquil** US$120 and **Quito** US$185, one way.
Bus Most companies are on Av Sánchez Cerro, blocks 11, 12 and 13. To **Lima**, 1038 km, 14-15½ hrs, US$30-45. Most buses stop at the major cities on route; **Ittsa**, Sánchez Cerro 1142, T308645; **Línea**, Sánchez Cerro 1215, T327 821; **Tepsa**, Loreto 1195, T306345. To **Chiclayo** and **Lambayeque**, 190 km, 4 hrs, from US$5.50, **Trans Chiclayo**, Sánchez Cerro 1121, T308455;

several others. Also several daily buses to **Trujillo**, 7 hrs, 487 km, US$15, to travel by day change in Chiclayo. To **Tumbes**, 282 km, 4½ hrs, US$8.50, several buses daily, eg **Cruz del Sur** (Av Circunvalación 160, T337094, also to Lima), **Cial** (Bolognesi 817, T304250) and **Emtrafesa** (Los Naranjos 255, T337093, also to Chiclayo and Trujillo); also colectivos, US$12. To **Paita**, Trans Dora, Sánchez Cerro 1391, every 20 mins, 1 hr, US$1.50; also from Paita terminal on Av Gullman, just off Sánchez Cerro. To **Máncora**, US$5.50, 3 hrs, with **Eppo**, T304543, www.eppo.com.pe.

To Ecuador To **Machala** and **Guayaquil**, the fastest route if you are heading directly to Quito, **CIFA**, Los Naranjos y Sánchez Cerro (cuadra 11-12) opposite Emtrafesa, T305925, 5 a day, Machala US$7, 6 hrs, Guayaquil US$13-17, 9 hrs. **Ecuatoriana Pullman**, on Av Loreto, 0830, 2030 to **Guayaquil** via Sullana, Tumbes and Machala, US$17-20, 10 hrs. Otherwise, go to Tumbes and travel on from there for the Aguas Verdes crossing. To **Loja**, the best option if you want to visit the southern or central highlands of Ecuador. **Transportes Loja**, Sánchez Cerro 1480, T305446, at 0930, 1300, 1900, US$12, 8-9 hrs, to **Macará** US$5. Or **Unión Cariamanga**, Sánchez Cerro (cuadra 18) y Av Vice, Urb Santa Ana, T969-900135, at 1330 and 2000. Alternatively take a bus to **Sullana**, 38 km, 30 mins (US$0.50), **Eppo**, **Sullana Express** and **Turismo del Norte**, all on 1100 block of Sánchez Cerro; also colectivos (US$1). To **La Tina** on the Ecuadorean frontier, is a further 128 km, 1¾ hrs, US$3.50. It's best to take an early bus to Sullana (start at 0430, leave when full), then a colectivo (see under Sullana).

Catacaos *p1272*
Combis From **Piura** to Catacaos leave when full from bus terminal at block 12 of Av Sánchez Cerro, US$0.50, 20 mins.

ⓘ Directory

Piura and around *p1270, map p1271*
Car hire Ramos, T348668, www.ramos rentacars.com. At airport, and others.
Consulates Ecuadorean consulate, Av Chirichigño 505 y F Elguero, Urb El Chipe, T308027. Mon-Fri 0800-1400. **Immigration** Av Integración Urbana y Av Sullana, T335536.

North to Ecuador

Sullana, built on a bluff over the fertile Chira valley, is a busy, modern place 38 km north of Piura. Here the Pan-American Highway forks. To the east it crosses the Peru-Ecuador border at La Tina and continues via Macará to Loja and Cuenca. The excellent paved road is very scenic. The more frequently used route to the border is the coastal road which goes from Sullana northwest towards the Talara oilfields, and then follows the coastline to Máncora and Tumbes.

Border at La Tina-Macará The border crossing is problem-free and both sides are open 24 hours. A new international bridge was opened in 2013 and there are plans to build a border complex. In the meantime immigration, customs and other services are housed in temporary quarters nearby; officials are generally helpful. There are no money changers right at the bridge, only at the park in Macará where vehicles leave for the border. On the Peruvian side, there is one *hospedaje* and several eating places on the road down to the bridge. On the Ecuadorean side, Macará is a small city with all services, 2.5 km past the bridge.

Máncora and Punta Sal

Máncora, a resort stretching along the Panamerican Highway, is popular with young Limeños, Chileans and Argentines and as a stop-off for travellers, especially surfers, on the Peru-Ecuador route. Development here has been rapid and haphazard. The area is crowded and noisy during the December-February high season, beaches can get dirty, drugs and scams (many involving mototaxis) abound and public safety is an important concern. Enquire locally about which sections are currently safe. More tranquil beaches such as Las Pocitas and Vichayito are being developed to the south. Surfing on this coast is best November-March and boards and suits can be hired from several places on Avenida Piura, US$10 per day. **Tourist office: iPerú** ① *Av Piura 250, Thu-Sun 1000-1700*. See www.vivamancora.com.

At 22 km north of Máncora, Km 1187, is the turn-off for **Punta Sal**, marked by a large white arch (El Arco) over the track leading into Punta Sal (2 km). Punta Sal boasts a 3-km-long white sandy beach and a more upmarket clientèle than Máncora, with accommodation (and prices) to match. There is no town centre nor services such as banks, ATMs or restaurants independent of hotels; it is very quiet in the low season. There is one bank and various ATMs in Máncora. Taking a taxi from Máncora to Punta Sal is safest, 20 minutes, US$14; mototaxi 40 minutes, US$10. **Zorritos**, 27 km south of Tumbes, is an important fishing centre with a good beach. At **Caleta La Cruz** is the only part of the Peruvian coast where the sea is warm all year, 16 km southwest of Tumbes. It was here that Pizarro landed in 1532. Regular colectivos, US$0.30 each way.

Tumbes and around → *Phone code: 072. Colour map 3, A1. Population: 94,750.*

The most northerly of Peruvian towns (265 km north of Piura), Tumbes is a garrison town. Most tourists stop only briefly to get transport connections to the beaches to the south, or to Ecuador to the north. The most striking thing is the bright and cheery modern public buildings. The **Malecón Benavides**, a long promenade beside the Tumbes river, has rainbow-coloured archways and a monstrous statue called El Beso (the Kiss). The Plaza de Armas sports a large structure of many colours and even the **cathedral** ① *entry during morning and evening Mass*, (1903, restored in 1985) has green and pink stripes. Calles Bolívar and San Martín (Paseo de la Concordia) make for a pleasant wander and there is a small artesans' market at the top end of San Martín (approaching Plaza Bolognesi). On Calle Grau, there are the tumble-down colonial houses, many of which are no longer in use. **Tourist office** is in the **Centro Cívico** ① *Bolognesi 194, 2nd level, on the plaza, T524940, dirceturtumbes@gmail.com, Mon-Fri 0730-1300, 1400-1630*. **Pronaturaleza** ① *Bq 0B-14, 4 Etapa, Urb Casas Fonavi, T993-583445, comunicaciones@ pronaturaleza.org*, has specialized information about national parks in the area, of which there are three important ones: The **Santuario Nacional los Manglares de Tumbes** protects 3000 ha of Peru's remaining 4750 ha of mangrove forest.

The **Parque Nacional Cerros de Amotape** protects 90,700 ha of varied habitat, but principally the best preserved area of dry forest on the west coast of South America. The **Zona Reservada de Tumbes** (75,000 ha) lies northeast of Tumbes between the Ecuadorean border and Cerros de Amotape. It protects dry equatorial forest and tropical rainforest. The Río Tumbes crocodile, which is a UN Red-data species, is found at the river's mouth, where there is a small breeding programme, and in its upper reaches.

Border with Ecuador The best way to cross this border is on one of the international buses that run between Peru (Piura, Máncora or Tumbes) and Ecuador (Huaquillas, Machala, Guayaquil or Cuenca). If travelling from further south in Peru, do not take a bus all the way to the border; change to an Ecuador-bound bus in Piura, Máncora or Tumbes. Formalities are only carried out at the new bridge, far outside the border towns of **Aguas Verdes** (Peru) and **Huaquillas** (Ecuador). There are two border complexes called **CEBAF** *(Centro Binacional de Atención Fronteriza)*, open 24 hours on either side of the bridge. Both complexes have Peruvian and Ecuadorean immigration officers so you get your exit and entry stamps in the same place. If crossing with your own vehicle however, you may have to stop at both border complexes for customs.

If you do not take one of the international buses then the crossing is hot, harrowing and transport between the two sides via the new bridge and border complex is inconvenient and expensive (see Transport, below). Travellers often fall victim to thefts, muggings, shakedowns by minor officials and countless scams on both sides. Never leave your baggage unattended and do your own arithmetic when changing money. Those seeking a more relaxed crossing to or from Ecuador should consider La Tina-Macará or Namballe-La Balsa.

⦿ North to Ecuador listings

For hotel and restaurant price codes, and other relevant information, see Essentials.

⦿ Where to stay

North to Ecuador: Sullana *p1274*
Take care by the market. Do not arrive at night.
$$ Hostal La Siesta, Av Panamericana 400, T502264, www.lasiestasullana.com. At entrance to town, hot water, fan, pool, restaurant, laundry.
$ Hospedaje San Miguel, C J Farfán 204, T502789. Private/shared bath, good showers, basic, helpful, rooms sprayed against mosquitoes, café.
$ Hostal Lion's Palace, Grau 1030, T502587. With fan, patio, pleasant, quiet, no breakfast.

Máncora and Punta Sal *p1274*
Máncora town
There are at least 50 hotels in and around Máncora, heavily booked in high season. The main strip of the Panamericana is known as Av Piura from the bridge for the first couple of blocks, then Av Grau to the end of town. The better hotels are at the southern end of town, with a small concentration of mid-range

hotels just over the bridge. Hotels to the left look onto the beach directly in front of the best surf and often have beach entrances as well as road entrances. As the most popular with tourists, they are all noisy at night from nearby discos, which go until around 0200 week nights and 0600 at weekends. Prices can increase by 100% or more in high season (Dec-Mar). Many hotels have even higher rates for Christmas, New Year, Easter and Independence Day holidays when the resort is full to bursting. When checking into any hotel, expect to pay up front and make sure you get a receipt as you will most likely be asked to pay again the next time the receptionist sees you. Take every precaution with your valuables, theft is common. Mosquitoes are bad at certain times of the year, so take plenty of bug spray.
$$$ Don Giovanni, Pje 8 de Noviembre s/n, T258525, www.dongiovannimancora.com. 3-storey Indonesian-style beachfront hotel, includes breakfast, restaurant and ice-cream parlour, kitesurfing classes available.
$$ Del Wawa, beachfront, T258427, www.delwawa.com. This relaxed and spacious Spanish-owned hotel is popular with serious

surfers and kitesurfers. Hotel service poor, rooms noisy, food average, but great location and nice restaurants round the corner.

$$ Kon Tiki, Los Incas 200, T258138, www.kontikimancora.net. On hill with lighhouse, great views, cabins with thatched roofs, hammocks, kitchen facilities, bar. Transport to/from bus station provided. Advance booking required.

$$ Las Olas, beachfront, T258099, www.lasolasmancora.com. Smart, cabin-style rooms, top floor rooms have best view of ocean, hammocks and gardens, includes breakfast.

$$ Punta Ballenas Inn, Km 1164, south of Cabo Blanco bridge at the south entrance to town, T630844, www.puntaballenas.com. Lovely setting on beach, garden with small pool, expensive restaurant.

$$-$ Kokopelli Beachpackers, Av Piura 209, T258091, www.hostelkokopelli.com. Popular hostel 3 mins' walk from beach, with pool, bar, good food, good meeting place, lots of facilities. Rooms for 2, 4 or 8, mixed or female only, all with bath, hot water.

$$-$ Laguna Surf Camp, T01-99 401 5628, www.vivamancora.com/lagunacamp. 50 m from the sea, thatched roofs, cabins sleeping up to 6 people (US$11 pp), also cabins around small communal area with hammocks, pool and restaurant. Good surf lessons, helpful staff.

$$-$ Loki del Mar, Av Piura 262, T258484, www.lokihostel.com. In the Loki group of hostels, seafront, bright white and modern muti-storey building, doubles with private bath or dorms with 4-6 beds and lockable closets, bar, restaurant, pool, lots of activities. Be ready for loud music and parties. Advance booking required.

$ Casa del Turista, Av Piura 224, T258126. Family-run, TV, roof terraces giving sea views, good value and location. Recommended.

Quebrada Cabo Blanco

Crossing the bridge into Máncora, a dirt track leads downhill to the right, to the Quebrada Cabo Blanco, signed to La Posada Youth Hostel. The many hotels at the end of the track require better lighting for guests returning at night (robberies have occurred), but the hotels are relatively quiet and relaxing.

$$ Kimbas Bungalows, T258373, www.kimbasbungalowsmancora.com. Relaxed spot with charming thatched bungalows, Balinese

influences, nice garden with hammocks, pool, some rooms have hot water, good value. Recommended.

$$ La Posada, T258328, hlaposada@hotmail.com. IYHF affiliated hostel, dorms (US$20 pp), camping (US$12 pp) and rooms with private bath, fan, garden with hammocks, pool, cooking facilities, parking,

Las Pocitas and Vichayito

South of Máncora, a stretch of beautiful beach with rocks on the shore, behind which little pools (or *pocitas*) form at low tide. Vichayito, a separate beach around a headland from Las Pocitas, is better reached from Los Organos than Máncora. There are over 40 hotels in this area.

$$$$ Arennas, Antigua Panamericana Norte Km 1213, T258240, www.lasarenasdemancora.com. Smart, luxury pool or beachfront suites, all modern facilities, with central bar and restaurant serving imaginative dishes, beautiful pool, palm-lined beach frontage, very romantic.

$$$ Las Pocitas, Antigua Panamericana Norte Km 1215, T258432, www.laspocitasmancora.com. Great location, rooms with ocean views, lovely palm-lined beach, terrace, pool, restaurant and bar.

$$$ Máncora Beach Bungalows, Antigua Panamericana Norte Km 1215, Lima T01-201 2060, www.mancora-beach.com. Comfortable rooms with ceiling fan, terrace and hammocks, good restaurant, good value for this price range.

$$$ Puerto Palos, along the old Pan-American Highway 2 km south of Máncora (10 mins by mototaxi, US$2), T258199, www.puertopalos.com. Variety of rooms, fan, suites have a/c. Excellent, nice pool overlooking ocean, hammocks, sunbeds, umbrellas, good restaurant. Friendly and hospitable.

$$ Marcilia Beach Bungalows, Antigua Panamericana Norte Km 1212, T09-9468 5209, www.marciliadevichayito.com. Nice rustic bamboo cabins with ocean views, includes breakfast, family run.

Punta Sal

There is a huge new resort of the Colombian Royal Decameron group here, www.decameron.com.

$$$$ Punta Sal, Panamericana Norte Km 1192, Punta Sal Chica, T596700/540088, www.puntasal.com.pe. A beautiful complex of bungalows along a fine sandy beach, with pool, bar decorated with photos of big game fishing, fine restaurant. Most deals are all-inclusive, but massages and whale-watching trips are extra. Good food and service.

$$$-$ Waltako Beach Town, Panamericana 1199, Canoas de Punta Sal, T998-141976, www.waltakoperu.com. Thatched cabins for 2, 4 or 6 people, with kitchenette, porch and hammock. Camping on the beach if you bring your own tent. Restaurant and bar, bicycles, quad bikes and horses for hire. Volunteers welcomed for conservation and reforestation work.

$$ Hospedaje El Bucanero, at the entrance to Playa Punta Sal, set back from the beach, T540118, www.elbucaneropuntasal.com. The most happening place in Punta Sal, popular with travellers, rates rise in high season, a variety of rooms, pool, restaurant, bar and gardens.

$$ Huá, on the beach at the entrance to Playa Punta Sal, T540023, www.hua-puntasal.com. A rustic old wooden building, pleasant terrace overlooking ocean, hammocks, quiet, restful, good food, friendly service.

$$-$ Las Terrazas, opposite Sunset Punta Sal, T507701. One of the more basic and cheaper hotels in Punta Sal in operation since 1989, restaurant has sea view, some rooms better than others, those with own bath and sea view twice the price. Helpful owners.

$ Hospedaje Orillas del Mar, San Martín 496, Cancas. The best of the basic *hostales* lining the beach and Panamericana; a short walk from Punta Sal Chica beaches.

Zorritos

$ Hostal Grillo Tres Puntas, Panamericano Norte Km 1235, T794830, www.casagrillo.net. On the beach, rustic bamboo cabins, quiet and peaceful. Great food prepared by Spanish chef-owner, Leon, who breeds Peruvian hairless dogs. Lukewarm showers, Wi-Fi in dining area, camping possible on the beach.

Tumbes and around *p1274*

Av Tumbes is still sometimes referred to by its old name of Teniente Vásquez. At holiday times it can be very difficult to find a room.

$$$ Costa del Sol, San Martín 275, Plazuela Bolognesi, T523991, www.costadelsolperu.com.

The only high class hotel in town, hot water, minibars, a/c, good restaurant, garden, pool, excellent service. Parking for an extra fee. Rooms which look onto the Plaza Bolognesi are noisy.

$$ Lourdes, Mayor Bodero 118, 3 blocks from main plaza, T522966. Welcoming place. Narrow corridor leading to cell-like rooms which are plushly decorated with a mixture of antique and modern furniture. Good bathrooms, fans in each room.

$$-$ Asturias, Av Mcal Castilla 307, T522569. Comfortable, hot water, a/c or fan, restaurant, bar and laundry. Accepts credit cards.

$ Hostal Tumbes, Filipinas s/n, off Grau, T522203, or T972 852954. Small, dark, basic but cleanish rooms with fans and bath. Good cheap option.

🍴 Restaurants

Máncora and Punta Sal *p1274*

Máncora

Máncora is packed with restaurants. Plenty of sushi, pizza and grills; most are pricey, the cheaper places are north along Av Piura. At a small open-air commercial centre called **The Birdhouse** are: **Green Eggs and Ham**, open 0730-1300 for great breakfasts at US$3.35, 8 options including waffles, pancakes or eggs and bacon, plus optional extra portions, juice or coffee included. Papa Mo's milk bar, directly underneath Green Eggs and Ham, with comfy seats which are practically on the beach and a selection of drinks.

Along the main strip of the Panamericana:

$$$ Pizzería Mamíferos, Av Piura 346. Tue-Sun 1800-2300. Wood-oven pizzas and lasagna.

$$$-$$ Josil, near The Birdhouse. Closed Sun. Very good Sushi bar.

$$$-$$ Tao, Av Piura. Closed Wed. Good Asian food and curries.

$$ Angela's Place/Cafetería de Angela, Av Piura 396, www.vivamancora.com/deangela. Daily 0800-2300. A great option for a healthy breakfast or lunch and heaven for vegetarians and whole-food lovers, home-made bread, yogurts, fresh fruit etc.

$$ Don César, hard to find, ask around or take a mototaxi. Closed Sun. Good fresh sea food, very popular with locals.

$ Café La Bajadita, Av Piura, has an impressive selection of delicious home-made desserts and cakes.

Tumbes and around *p1274*
Cheap restaurants on the Plaza de Armas, Paseo de la Concordia and near the markets.
$$-$ Budabar, Grau 309, on Plaza de Armas, T525493. One of a kind chill out lounge offering traditional food and comfy seating with outdoor tables and cheap beer, popular in the evenings.
$$-$ Chifa Wakay, Huáscar 413. Open evenings only. A large, well-ventilated smart restaurant offering the usual Chifa favourites.
$$-$ Classic, Tumbes 185. Look for it almost under the bridge over the river, heading south. Popular for local food.
$$-$ Los Gustitos, Bolívar 148. Excellent menús and à la carte. Popular, good atmosphere at lunchtime.
$ Sí Señor, Bolívar 119 on the plaza. Good for snacks, cheap lunch menus.
Cherry, San Martín 116. Open 0800-1400, 1700-2300. Tiny café offering an amazing selection of cakes and desserts, also fresh juices, shakes, sandwiches, hot and cold drinks and traditional *cremoladas* (fruit juice with crushed ice).

⚙ What to do

Máncora and Punta Sal *p1274*
Many agencies on Av Piura offer day-trips to Manglares de Tumbes and Isla del Amor for snorkelling, as well as private transport in cars and vans.
Iguanas Trips, Av Piura 306, T632762, www.iguanastrips.com. Run by Ursula Behr, offers a variety of adventure tourism trips, horseriding and camping in the nearby national parks and reserve zones.
Samana Chakra, in the eponymous hotel, T258604, www.samanachakra.com. Yoga classes, US$5 per hr.
Surf Point Máncora, on the beach next to Hostal del Wawa. Surf classes US$17.50 per hr, kitesurfing (season Mar-Sep) US$50 per hr. Surfboard, body-board and paddle-board rentals.

⊖ Transport

North to Ecuador: Sullana *p1274*
Bus Several bus companies including **Ormeño** share a Terminal Terrestre outside the centre. To **Tumbes**, 244 km, 4-5 hrs, US$8, several buses daily. To **Chiclayo** and **Trujillo** see under Piura. To **Lima**, 1076 km, 14-16 hrs, several buses daily, most coming from Tumbes, luxury overnight via Trujillo with **Ittsa** (T503705), also with **Ormeño** and **Tepsa** (José de Lama 236, T502120). To **Máncora**, Eppo, frequent, 2½ hrs, US$4.50.

Border with Ecuador: La Tina-Macará *p1274*
Bus Buses leave frequently from Ecuadorean side for Loja, so even if you are not taking the through bus (see under Piura), you can still go from Sullana to Loja in a day. From the border to Sullana, cars may leave before they are full, but won't charge extra.
Shared taxis Station wagons leave from Sullana to the international bridge from Terminal Terrestre La Capullana, off Av Buenos Aires, several blocks beyond the canal. They leave when full, US$8 per person, 1¾ hrs. It's best to take a taxi or mototaxi to and from the terminal. From the border to Macará is 2.5 km; pick-ups charge US$0.50 pp, or US$1.50 for whole vehicle.

Máncora and Punta Sal *p1274*
Bus To **Sullana** with Eppo, every 30 mins, 0400-1830, US$4.50, 3½ hrs; to **Piura**, US$5.50, 4 hrs;, also colectivos, 2 hrs, US$9; to **Tumbes** (and points in between), minibuses leave when full, US$5.50, 1½ hrs. Several companies to **Lima**, US$28-70, 18 hrs; to **Chiclayo**, Tran Chiclayo, US$17.50, 6h; **Trujillo** US$25, 9 hrs. To **Ecuador: Machala** (US$14, 5 hrs) and **Guayaquil** (US$17.50, 8 hrs), CIFA and Super Semería, at 0800, 1100 and 1300; Guayaquil direct at 2300 and 2330; **Cuenca**, Super Semería at 2300 and 2400, US$20.

Tumbes and around *p1274*
Air Daily flights to and from **Lima** (LAN, Bolognesi 250).
Bus Daily to and from **Lima**, 1320 km, 18-20 hrs, depending on stopovers, US$34-45 regular fare), US$60 (Cruz del Sur VIP, Tumbes Norte

319, T896163). **Civa**, Av Tumbes 518, T525120. Several buses daily. Cheaper buses usually leave 1600-2100, more expensive ones 1200-1400. Except for luxury service, most buses to Lima stop at major cities en route. Tickets to anywhere between Tumbes and Lima sell quickly, so if arriving from Ecuador you may have to stay overnight. Piura is a good place for connections in the daytime. To **Sullana**, 244 km, 3-4 hrs, US$8, several buses daily. To **Piura**, 4-5 hrs, 282 km, US$8.50 with **Trans Chiclayo** (Tumbes 466, T525260), **Cruz del Sur**, **El Dorado** (Piura 459, T523480) 6 a day; **Comité Tumbes/Piura** (Tumbes N 308, T525 977), US$12 pp, fast cars, leave when full, 3½ hrs. To **Chiclayo**, 552 km, 7-8 hrs, US$9, several each day with **Cruz del Sur**, **El Dorado**, and others. To **Trujillo**, 769 km, 10-11 hrs, from US$15, **Ormeño** (Av Tumbes s/n, T522228), **Cruz del Sur**, **El Dorado**, **Emtrafesa**, Tumbes Norte 596, T522894. Transport to the border with Ecuador, see below.

To Ecuador **CIFA**, Av Tumbes 958, to **Machala**, US$4, and **Guayaquil**, 5 a day, luxury bus at 1000, US$8.50, 5 hrs to Guayaquil.

Border with Ecuador *p1275*
Between Tumbes and the border If you cannot cross on an international bus (the preferred option), then take a taxi from Tumbes to the new bridge, 17 km, US$12; bridge to **Huaquillas**, US$2.50-5. **Entering Peru** From the new bridge to: **Tumbes,** city or airport, US$17; **Punta Sal**, US$50; **Máncora**, US$60.

ⓘ Directory

Máncora and Punta Sal *p1274*
Medical services Clínica Medical Center, Av Panamericana s/n, T258601.

Tumbes and around *p1274*
Consulates Ecuadorean Consulate, Bolívar 129, p 3, Plaza de Armas, T525949, consultum@ speedy.com.pe. Mon-Fri 0800-1400. **Medical services** 24 Hour Emergency Clinic, Av Mariscal Castilla 305, T525341. Consultancy hours Mon to Fri 0800 1400.

Northern Highlands

Leaving the Pacific coast behind, you climb in a relatively short time up to the Sierra. It was here, at Cajamarca, that the defeat of the Incas by the Spaniards began, bringing about cataclysmic change to this part of the world. But, unlike this well-documented event, the history of the Incas' contemporaries and predecessors has to be teased out of the stones of their temples and fortresses, which are shrouded in cloud in the 'Eyebrow of the Jungle'.

Trujillo to Cajamarca

To the northeast of Trujillo is Cajamarca, an attractive colonial town surrounded by lovely countryside and the commercial centre of the northern mountain area. It can be reached by the old road (now paved) via Huamachuco and Cajabamba, or via Ciudad de Dios. The former road takes two hours from Huamachuco to Cajabamba and three hours from Cajabamba via San Marcos to Cajamarca (as opposed to nine hours via Ciudad de Dios, see below). It is also more interesting, passing over the bare *puna* before dropping to the Huamachuco valley.

Huamachuco → *Colour map 3, B2. Altitude: 3180 m. www.munihuamachuco.gob.pe.*
This colonial town formerly on the royal Inca Road, 181 km from Trujillo, has the largest main plaza in Peru, with fine topiary, and a controversial modern **cathedral**. There is a colourful **Sunday market**, with dancing in the plaza, and the Founding of Huamachuco festival, second week in August, with spectacular fireworks and the amazing, aggressive male dancers, called *turcos*. **Museo Municipal Wamachuko** ⓘ *Sucre 195, Mon-Sat 0900-1300, 1500-1900, Sun 0900-1200, free,* displays artefacts found at nearby **Cerro Amaru** (a hill-top system of wells and water worship) and **Marca Huamachuco** ⓘ *daily 0900-1700, allow 2 hrs, 4 hrs to explore fully.* Access is

via a poor vehicle road or a mule track (preferable for walking), off the road to Sanagorán, there is an archway at the turn-off, 5 km from Huamachuco, mototaxi to turnoff US$2; combis to Sanagorán in the morning. These hilltop pre-Inca fortifications rank in the top 10 archaeological sites in Peru. They are 3 km long, dating back to at least 300 BC though many structures were added later. Its most impressive features are: El Castillo, a remarkable circular structure with walls up to 8 m high located at the highest point of the site, and El Convento complex, five circular structures of varying sizes towards the northern end of the hill. The largest one has been partially reconstructed. The extensive Huari ruins of **Wiracochapampa** are 3 km north of town, 45 minutes' walk, but much of the site is overgrown.

Cajabamba is a small market town and a useful stop-over point between Cajamarca and Huamachuco. A new thermal bath complex, **La Grama**, is 30 minutes by combi (US$1) from Cajabamba, with a pool, very hot individual baths and an adjoining small *hostal*.

Pacasmayo → *Colour map 3, A2. Population: 12,300.*
Pacasmayo, 102 km north of Trujillo, is the port for the next oasis north. It has a nice beach front with an old Customs House and a very long pier. Resort El Faro is 1 km away, with surfing at the point and kite- and windsurfing closer to town. There are maritime festivals at New Year and Semana Santa. Away from the front it is a busy commercial centre.

Some 20 km further north on the Panamericana is the main road connection from the coast to Cajamarca at a junction called **Ciudad de Dios**. The paved 175 km road branches off the Pan-American Highway soon after it crosses the Río Jequetepeque. The river valley has terraced rice fields and mimosas may often be seen in bloom, brightening the otherwise dusty landscape.

Cajamarca → *Phone code: 076. Colour map 3, B2. Population: 201,000. Altitude: 2750 m.*
At Cajamarca Pizarro ambushed and captured Atahualpa, the Inca emperor. This was the first showdown between the Spanish and the Incas and, despite their huge numerical inferiority, the Spanish emerged victorious, executing Atahualpa in the process. The nearby **Yanacocha gold mine** ⓘ *www.yanacocha.com.pe*, has brought new wealth to the town (and major ecological concerns and social problems) and Cajamarca is the hub of tourism development for the whole of the northwest via the *Circuito Turístico Nororiental* (Chiclayo-Cajamarca-Chachapoyas). **Tourist offices**: **Dirección Regional de Turismo** and **Ministerio de Cultura** ⓘ *in the Conjunto Monumental de Belén, Belén 631, T362601, cajamarca@mcultura.gob.pe, Mon-Fri 0900-1300, 1500-1730.* **Sub-Gerencia de Turismo of the Cajamarca Municipality** ⓘ *Av Alameda de los Incas, Complejo Qhapac Ñan, T363626, www.municaj.gob.pe*, opposite UNC university on the road to Baños del Inca. The **University tourist school** ⓘ *Del Batán 289, T361546, Mon-Fri 0830-1300, 1500-2200*, offers free advice and leaflets. **Indecopi** ⓘ *Apurímac 601, T363315, mcastillo@indecopi.gob.pe.*

Complejo Belén ⓘ *Tue-Sat 0900-1300, 1500-1800, Sun 0900-1300, US$1.55, valid for more than 1 day, a ticket is also valid for the Cuarto de Rescate, a guide for all the sites costs US$2.85 (US$5.75-8.50 for guides in other languages).* The complex comprises the tourist office and Institute of Culture, a beautifully ornate church, considered the city's finest. See the inside of the dome, where eight giant cherubs support an intricate flowering centrepiece. In the same courtyard is the **Museo Médico Belén**, which has a collection of medical instruments. Across the street is a maternity hospital from the colonial era, now the **Archaeological and Ethnological Museum**, Junín y Belén. It has a range of ceramics from all regions and civilizations of Peru. The **Cuarto de Rescate** ⓘ *entrance at Amalia Puga 750, Tue-Sat 0900-1800, Sun 0900-1300*, is not the actual ransom chamber but in fact the room where Atahualpa was held prisoner. A red line on the wall is said to indicate where Atahualpa reached up and drew a mark, agreeing to have his subjects fill the room to the line with treasure. A new roof protects the building from the weather and pollution.

You can also visit the plaza where Atahualpa was ambushed and the stone altar set high on **Santa Apolonia hill** ⓘ *US$0.60, take bus marked Santa Apolonia/Fonavi, or micro A*, where he is said to have reviewed his subjects. There is a road to the top, or you can walk up from Calle 2 de Mayo, using the steep stairway. The view is worth the effort, especially at sunrise (but go in a group).

The **Plaza de Armas**, where Atahualpa was executed, has a 350-year-old fountain, topiary and gardens. The **Cathedral** ⓘ *0800-1000, 1600-1800*, opened in 1776, is still missing its belfry, but the façade has beautiful baroque carving in stone. On the opposite side of the plaza is the 17th-century **San Francisco Church** ⓘ *Mon-Fri 0900-1200, 1600-1800*, older than the Cathedral and with more interior stone carving and elaborate altars. The attached **Museo de Arte Colonial** ⓘ *Mon-Sat 1430-1800, US$1, entrance is behind the church on Amalia Puga y Belén*, is filled with colonial paintings and icons. The guided tour of the museum includes entry to the church's spooky catacombs.

The city has many old colonial houses with garden patios, and 104 elaborately carved doorways: see the **Bishop's Palace**, across the street from the Cathedral; the **palace of the Condes de Uceda**, at Jr Apurímac 719 (now occupied by BCP bank); and the **Casa Silva Santiesteban** (Junín y 2 de Mayo).

Museo Arqueológico Horacio H Urteaga ⓘ *Del Batán 289, Mon-Fri 0700-1445, free, donations accepted*, of the Universidad Nacional de Cajamarca, has objects of the pre-Inca Cajamarca and other cultures. The university maintains an experimental arboretum and agricultural station, the **Museo Silvo-agropecuario** ⓘ *Km 2.5 on the road to Baños del Inca*, with a lovely mural at the entrance.

Cajamarca

Where to stay 🛏
1 Cajamarca
2 Costa del Sol
3 El Cabildo
4 El Cumbe Inn
5 El Ingenio
6 El Portal del Marqués
7 Hosp Los Jazmines
8 Hostal Becerra
9 Hostal Perú
10 La Casona del Inca
11 Los Balcones de La Recoleta

Restaurants 🍴
1 Bella's Café Lounge
2 Casa Club
3 Cascanuez
4 De Buena Laya
5 Don Paco
6 El Pez Loco
7 El Zarco
8 Heladería Holanda
9 Om-Gri
10 Pascana
11 Pizzería El Marengo
12 Pizzería Vaca Loca
13 Querubino
14 Salas
15 Sanguchón.com

Excursions About 6 km away are the sulphurous thermal springs of **Los Baños del Inca** ① *0500-2000, T348385, www.ctbinca.com.pe, US$0.70, combis marked Baños del Inca cost US$0.20, 15 mins, taxis US$2.30.* The water temperature is at least 72° C. Atahualpa tried the effect of these waters on a festering war wound and his bath is still there. The complex is renewed regularly, with gardens and various levels of accommodation (see Where to stay, below). The main baths are divided into five categories, with prices ranging from US$1.75-2.10, all with private tubs and no pool. Sauna US$3.50, massage US$7 (take your own towel; soaps are sold outside). Only spend 20 minutes maximum in the water; obey instructions; many of the facilities allow bathers in shifts, divided by time and/or sex.

Other excursions include **Llacanora**, a typical Andean village in beautiful scenery (13 km southeast; nice walk downhill from Baños del Inca, two hours). **Ventanillas de Otusco** ① *8 km, 0800-1800, US$1.10, combi US$0.20,* part of an old pre-Inca cemetery, has a gallery of secondary burial niches. There are good day walks in this area; local sketch maps available.

A road goes to **Ventanillas de Combayo** ① *occasional combis on weekdays; more transport on Sun when a market is held nearby, 1 hr, some 20 km past the burial niches of Otusco.* These are more numerous and spectacular, being located in an isolated, mountainous area, and distributed over the face of a steep 200-m-high hillside.

Cumbe Mayo, a *pampa* on a mountain range, is 20 km southwest of Cajamarca. It is famous for its extraordinary, well-engineered pre-Inca channels, running for 9 km across the mountain tops. It is said to be the oldest man-made construction in South America. The sheer scale of the scene is impressive and the huge rock formations of Los Frailones ('big monks') and others with fanciful names are strange indeed. On the way to Cumbe Mayo is the Layzón ceremonial centre. There is no bus service; guided tours run from 0900-1300 (recommended in order to see all the pre-Inca sites); taxi US$15. To walk up takes three to four hours (take a guide, or a tour, best weather May-September). The trail starts from the hill of Santa Apolonia (Silla del Inca), and goes to Cumbe Mayo straight through the village and up the hill; at the top of the mountain, leave the trail and take the road to the right to the canal. The walk is not difficult and you do not need hiking boots. Take a good torch. The locals use the trail to bring their goods to market.

The **Porcón** rural cooperative, with its evangelical faith expressed on billboards, is a popular excursion, 30 km northwest of Cajamarca. It is tightly organized, with carpentry, bakery, cheese and yoghurt-making, zoo and vicuñas. A good guide helps to explain everything. If not taking a tour, contact **Cooperativa Agraria Atahualpa Jerusalén** ① *Chanchamayo 1355, Fonavi 1, T825631.*

Some 93 km west of Cajamarca is the mining town of Chilete, 21 km north of which on the road to San Pablo is **Kuntur Wasi**. The site was devoted to a feline cult and consists of a pyramid and stone monoliths. Extensive excavations are under way and significant new discoveries are being made (excellent site museum). There are two basic *hostales* in Chilete; very limited facilities.

◉ Trujillo to Catamarca listings

For hotel and restaurant price codes, and other relevant information, see Essentials.

◉ Where to stay

Huamachuco *p1279*

$$ Real, Bolívar 250, T441402, www.hotelreal huamachuco.com. Modern, sauna, majority of fittings are wood, pleasant with good service.

$$ Santa María, Grau 224, T348334. An enormous new, sparsely furnished edifice offering the best-quality rooms in town, with restaurant.

$$-$ Hostal Santa Fe, San Martín 297, T441019, www.actiweb.es/luisnv83/. Good value, hot water, parking, restaurant.

$ Hostal Huamachuco, Castilla 354, on the plaza, T440599. With private or shared hot showers, small rooms but large common areas, good value, has parking.

Cajabamba

$ Hostal Flores, Leoncio Prado 137, on the Plaza de Armas, T551086. With electric shower, cheaper without bath, clean but rooms are gloomy, nice patio; no breakfast.

Pacasmayo p1280
$$ La Estación, Malecón Grau 69, T521515, www.hotellaestacion.com.pe. Restaurant on ground floor, all meals extra, some rooms with terrace overlook sea, others face street, fan, good beds.

$$ Libertad, Leoncio Pardo 1-D, T521937, www.hotellibertad.com. 2 km from beach by petrol station, safe, restaurant/bar, parking, efficient and nice.

$$ Pakatnamú, Malecón Grau 103, T522368, www.actiweb.es/hotelpakatnamu. Historic building on seafront with verandahs and balconies, rooms and suite have seaview.

$ Duke Kahanamoku, Ayacucho 44, T521889, www.eldukepacasmayo.com. Surfing place, with classes and board rental, breakfast extra, hot water.

Cajamarca p1280, map p1281
$$$$ Costa del Sol, Cruz de Piedra 707, T362472, www.costadelsolperu.com. On the Plaza de Armas, part of a Peruvian chain, with airport transfer, welcome drink; restaurant, café and bars, pool, spa, casino, business centre.

$$$ El Ingenio, Av Vía de Evitamiento 1611-1709, T368733, www.elingenio.com. Colonial style buildings 1½ blocks from new El Quinde shopping mall. With solar-powered hot water, spacious, very relaxed.

$$ Cajamarca, Dos de Mayo 311, T362532, hotelcajamarca@gmail.com. 3-star in beautiful colonial mansion, sizeable rooms, hot water, food excellent in Los Faroles restaurant.

$$ El Cabildo, Junín 1062, T367025. Includes breakfast, in historic monument with patio and modern fountain, full of character, elegant local decorations, comfortable, breakfast served.

$$ El Cumbe Inn, Pasaje Atahualpa 345, T366858, www.elcumbeinn.com. Includes breakfast and tax, comfortable, variety of rooms, hot water, evening meals on request, small gym, will arrange taxis, very helpful.

$$ El Portal del Marqués, Del Comercio 644, T368464, www.portaldelmarques.com. Attractive converted colonial house, laundry,

safe, parking, leased restaurant El Mesón del Marqués has good lunch *menú*. Casino with slot machines.

$$ La Casona del Inca, 2 de Mayo 458-460, Plaza de Armas, T367524, www.casonadel incaperu.com. Upstairs, old building, traditional style, some rooms overlooking plaza, some with interior windows, good beds, breakfast in café on top floor, tours, laundry.

$$ Los Balcones de la Recoleta, Amalia Puga 1050, T363302, hslosbalcones@speedy.com.pe. Beautifully restored 19th-century house, central courtyard full of flowers, some rooms with period furniture, internet.

$ Hospedaje Los Jazmines, Amazonas 775, T361812. In a converted colonial house with courtyard and café, 14 rooms with hot water, all profits go to disabled children, guests can visit the project's school and help.

$ Hostal Becerra, Del Batán 195, T367867. With hot water, modern, pleasant, will store luggage until late buses depart.

$ Hostal Perú, Amalia Puga 605, on Plaza, T365568. With hot water, functional rooms in old building around central patio used by El Zarco restaurant, wooden floors, credit cards taken.

Los Baños del Inca
$$$$-$$$ Laguna Seca, Av Manco Cápac 1098, T584300, www.lagunaseca.com.pe. In pleasant surroundings with thermal streams, private hot thermal baths in rooms, swimming pool with thermal water, restaurant, bar, health spa with a variety of treatments, disco, horses for hire.

$$$ Hostal Fundo Campero San Antonio, 2 km off the Baños road (turn off at Km 5), T368237. An old *hacienda*, wonderfully restored, with open fireplaces and gardens, 15 mins walk along the river to Baños del Inca, riding on *caballos de paso*, own dairy produce, fruit and vegetables, catch your own trout for supper; try the *licor de sauco*.

$$-$ Los Baños del Inca, see above, 1348385. Various accommodation: bungalows for 2 to 4 with thermal water, fridge; Albergue Juvenil, not IYFH, hostel rooms with bunk beds or double rooms, private bath, caters to groups, basic. Camping possible. Restaurant offers full board.

🍴 Restaurants

Huamachuco *p1279*

$$-$ Bull Grill, R Castilla 364. Smart new place specializing in meat dishes, with a cool bar at the back.

$ Café Somos, Bolognesi 665. Good coffee, large turkey/ham sandwiches and excellent cakes.

$ Doña Emilia, Balta 384, on Plaza de Armas. Good for breakfast and snacks.

$ El Viejo Molino, R Castilla 160. Specializes in local cuisine, such as cuy.

Cajabamba

$ Cafetería La Otuscana, Grau 929. Daily 0730-2200. Good bakery, sweets and sandwiches.

$ Don Lucho, Jr Leoncio Prado 227. Good local trout and other à la carte dishes.

Cajamarca *p1280, map p1281*

$$$ Pascana, Av Atahualpa 947. Well-known and recommended as the best in town, near the new Qhapac Ñan Municipality. Their **Taberna del Diablo** is the top disco in town.

$$$ Querubino, Amalia Puga 589, T340900. Mediterranean-style decoration, a bit of everything on the menu, including pastas, daily specials, breakfasts, cocktails, coffees, expensive wines otherwise reasonable, popular.

$$ Casa Club, Amalia Puga 458-A, T340198. Open 0800-2300. Menú, including vegetarian, and extensive selection à la carte, family atmosphere, slow but attentive service.

$$ Don Paco, Amalia Puga 390, T362655. Opposite San Francisco. Typical, including novo andino, and international dishes, tasty food, desserts, drinks.

$$ El Pez Loco, San Martín 333. Recommended for fish dishes.

$$ Om-Gri, San Martín 360, near the Plaza de Armas. Opens 1300 (1830 Sun). Good Italian dishes, small, informal, French spoken.

$$ Pizzería El Marengo, Junín 1201. Good pizzas and warm atmosphere, T368045 for delivery.

$$ Salas, Amalia Puga 637, on the main plaza, T362867. Open 0700-2200. A Cajamarca tradition, fast service, excellent local food (try their *cuy frito*), best *tamales* in town.

$$-$ De Buena Laya, 2 de Mayo 343. With a rustic interior, popular with hostales, offers Novo Cajamarquino cuisine; lunchtime menú US$3.50.

$$-$ El Zarco, Jr Del Batán 170, T363421. Sun-Fri 0700-2300. Very popular, also has short *chifa* menu, good vegetarian dishes, excellent fish, popular for breakfast.

$ Pizzería Vaca Loca, San Martín 330. Popular, best pizzas in town.

Cafés

Bella's Café Lounge, Junín 1184, T345794. For breakfasts, sandwiches, great desserts and coffee from Chanchamayo, Wi-Fi, a place to linger, check emails and relax, owner Raul speaks English. Popular with visitors to the city.

Cascanuez, Amalia Puga 554. Great cakes, extensive menu including *humitas*, breakfasts, ice creams and coffees, highly regarded.

Heladería Holanda, Amalia Puga 657 on the Plaza de Armas, T340113. Dutch-owned, easily the best ice-creams in Cajamarca, 50 flavours (but not all on at the same time), try *poro poro*, *lúcuma* or *sauco*, also serves coffee. Four branches, including at Baños del Inca. Ask if it is possible to visit their factory. They assist deaf people and single mothers.

Sanguchón.com, Junín 1137. Best burgers in town, sandwiches, also popular bar.

🎉 Festivals

Cajamarca *p1280, map p1281*

The pre-Lent **Carnival** is very spectacular and regarded as one of the best in the country; it is also one of the most raucous. In Porcón, 16 km to the northwest, **Palm Sunday** processions are worth seeing. **24 Jun** San Juan in Cajamarca, Chota, Llacanora, San Juan and Cutervo. An agricultural fair is held in **Jul** at Baños del Inca; on the first Sun in **Oct** is the **Festival Folklórico** in Cajamarca.

🛍 Shopping

Cajamarca *p1280, map p1281*
Handicrafts Specialities including gilded mirrors and cotton and wool saddlebags (*alforjas*). Items can be made to order. The market on Amazonas is good for *artesanía*. There are stalls near the Belén complex (Belén and/or 2 de Mayo) and along the steps up to Santa Apolonia hill. At Jr El Comercio 1045, next to the Police office, is a **Feria Artesenal**, as

well as **El Molino** at 2 de Mayo. All offer a good range of local crafts.

⚙ What to do

Cajamarca *p1280, map p1281*
Agencies around the Plaza de Armas offer trips to local sites and further (eg Kuntur Wasi, Kuélap), trekking on Inca trails, riding *caballos de paso* and handicraft tours. Cumbe Mayo, US$6.50-8.50, 4-5 hrs at 0930. Porcón, US$6.50-8.50, 4-5 hrs at 0930. Otusco, US$4.50-7, 3-3½ hrs at 1530. City tour, US$7, 3 hrs at 0930 or 1530. Kuntur Wasi is a full day. There are also 2 day/3 night tours to Kuélap and Cutervo National Park.
Cumbemayo Tours, Amalia Puga 635 on the plaza, T362938. Guides in English and French, standard tours.
Mega Tours, Amalia Puga 691 on the plaza, T341876, www.megatours.org. Conventional tours, full day and further afield, ecotourism and adventures.

⊖ Transport

Huamachuco *p1279*
Bus To/from **Trujillo**, 170 km, 5-6 hrs, US$9-15 (see page 1262): the best service is **Fuentes** (J Balta 1090, Huamachuco, T41090 and Av R Palma 767, Trujillo, T204581); **Tunesa** (Suárez 721, T441157). To **Cajabamba**, Trans Los Andes, Pje Hospital 109, 3 combis a day, 2 hrs, US$7.50.

Cajabamba
Bus To/from **Cajamarca**, 127 km, US$7.50, 3 hrs, several companies. Combis, 3 hrs, US$8.

Cajamarca *p1280, map p1281*
Air To/from **Lima**: LC Peru (Comercio 1024, T361098), daily except Sat, LAN (Cruz de Piedra 657) and Star Perú (Junín 1300, T367243). The military **Grupo Aéreo 42** (Amalia Pugla 605, T970-029134) has passenger flights to Cajamarca originating in Trujillo or Iquitos; see page 1261 for routes and schedules. Airport 5 km from town; taxi US$8.
Bus Buses in town charge US$0.35. To **Lima**, 870 km, 12-14 hrs, US$27-53, including several luxury services, many buses daily. To **Trujillo**, 295 km, 7 hrs, US$10-27, regular buses daily 0900-2230 most continue to Lima. To **Chiclayo**, 265 km, 6 hrs, US$9-20, several buses daily; you have to change buses to go on to Piura and Tumbes. To **Celendín**, 107 km, 3½ hrs, US$6, usually 2 a day with CABA, Royal Palace's and Rojas. To **Chachapoyas**, 336 km, 11-12 hrs, US$18, **Virgen del Carmen**, Atahualpa 333A, T983-915869, at 0500, to **Leymebamba**, US$11.55, 9-10 hrs. The route follows a paved road through beautiful countryside. Among the bus companies are: CABA, Atahualpa 299, T366665 (Celendín); Civa, Ayacucho 753, T361460 (Lima); Cruz del Sur, Atahualpa 606, T361737 (Lima). Emtrafesa, Atahualpa 315, T369663 (to Trujillo). Línea, Atahualpa 318, T363956 (Lima, Trujillo, Chiclayo). Móvil, Atahualpa 405, T340873 (Lima). Rojas, Atahualpa 309, T340548 (to Cajabamba; Celendín); Royal Palace's, Reina Forje 130, T343063 (Lima, Trujillo, Celendín); Tepsa, Sucre y Reina Forje, T363306 (Lima); Turismo Días, Av Evitamiento s/n, T344322 (to Lima, Chimbote, Trujillo, Chiclayo).
Taxi US$2 within city limits. Mototaxis US$0.75. Radio taxi: El Sol, T368897, 24 hrs. Taxi Super Seguro, T507090.

Chachapoyas region

Cajamarca is a convenient starting point for the trip east to the department of Amazonas, which contains the archaeological riches of the Chachapoyans, also known as Sachupoyans. Here lie the great pre-Inca cities of Vilaya (not yet developed for tourism) and the immense fortress of Kuélap, among many others. It is also an area of great natural beauty with waterfalls, notably Gocta, cliffs and caves. The road is paved but prone to landslides in the rainy season. It follows a winding course through the mountains, crossing the wide and deep canyon of the Río Marañón at Balsas. The road climbs steeply with superb views of the mountains and the valleys below. The fauna and flora are spectacular as the journey alternates between high mountains and low forest.

Celendín → *Phone code: 076. Colour map 3, B2.*

East from Cajamarca, this is the first town of note, with a pleasant plaza and cathedral, predominantly blue. Festival 16 July to 3 August (**Virgen del Carmen**). There is also a fascinating local market on Sunday which is held in three distinct areas. At 0630 the **hat market** is held by the Alameda, between Ayacucho and 2 de Mayo at Jorge Chávez. You can see hats at every stage of production, but it is over within an hour or so. Then at 0930 the **potato market** takes place at 2 de Mayo y Sucre and, at the other end of town, the **livestock market** on Túpac Amaru. The most popular local excursion is to the hot springs and mud baths at **Llanguat**, 20 km, US$2.75 by limited public transport. **Multired** ATM beside **Banco de la Nación** on 2 de Mayo may not accept all foreign cards; take cash.

Leymebamba and around → *Phone code: 041. Colour map 3, B2. Altitude: 2250 m.*

There are plenty of ruins – many of them covered in vegetation – and good walking possibilities around this pleasant town at the source of the Utcubamba River. The main attraction in the area is its spectacular museum, see below.

La Congona, a Chachapoyan site, is well worth the effort, with stupendous views. It consists of three hills: on the vegetation-covered conical hill in the middle, the ruins are clustered in a small area, impossible to see until you are right there. The other hills have been levelled. La Congona is the best preserved of three sites in this area, with 30 round stone houses (some with evidence of three storeys) and a watch tower. The two other sites, **El Molinete** and **Cataneo**, are nearby. All three sites can be visited in a day but a guide is advisable. It is a brisk three hours' walk from Leymebamba, first along the rough road to Fila San Cristóbal, then a large trail. The road starts at the bottom of Jr 16 de Julio.

At **Laguna de los Cóndores**, in 1996, a spectacular site consisting of six burial *chullpas*, containing 219 mummies and vast quantities of ceramics, textiles, woodwork, *quipus* and everyday utensils from the late Inca period, was discovered near a beautiful lake in a lush cloudforest setting. The trip to Laguna de los Cóndores takes 10-12 hours on foot and horseback from Leymebamba. An all-inclusive tour for the three-day muddy trek can be arranged at Leymebamba hotels (ask for Sinecio or Javier Farge) or with Chachapoyas operators, US$70 per person. The artefacts were moved to the excellent **Museo Leymebamba** ⓘ *outside San Miguel, on the road to Celendín, T041-816803, www.museoleymebamba.org, Tue-Sun about 0930-1630, entry US$5.75. Taxi from Leymebamba US$2.75, mototaxi US$2.* From Leymebamba, walk to the village of 2 de Mayo, ask for the trail to San Miguel, then take the footpath uphill, the road is much longer. It is beautifully laid-out and very informative. Across the road is **Kentitambo** (T971-118273, **$$$$-$$$** in two comfortable cabins, restaurant, lovely grounds with hummingbirds), **Kentikafe**, offering snacks, and **Mishqui**, offering meals on request.

The road to Chachapoyas follows the Utcubamba River north. In the mountains rising from the river, are a number of archaeological sites. Before **Yerbabuena** (important Sunday market, basic *hospedaje*), a road heads east to **Montevideo** (basic *hospedaje*) and beyond to the small village of San Pedro de Utac, where you can hike up to the impressive but overgrown ruins of Cerro Olán.

The burial *chullpas* of **Revash**, of the Revash culture (AD 1250), are reached from either **San Bartolo** (30-45 minutes' walk) or a trail starting past **Puente Santo Tomás** (1½ to two hours' walk). Both access points are along roads going west from Yerbabuena. The town of **Jalca Grande** (or La Jalca), at 2800 m, is reached along a road going east at **Ubilón**, north of Yerbabuena. Jalca Grande has the remains of a Chachapoyan roundhouse, a stone church tower, a small **museum** ⓘ *US$1.80*, with ceramics and textiles, and one very basic *hospedaje*.

Tingo → *Phone code: 041. Colour map 3, B2. Altitude: 1800 m.*

Situated at the junction of the Tingo and Utcubamba rivers, 40 km north of Leymebamba and 37 km south of Chachapoyas, Tingo is the access for Kuélap. A road climbs steeply from Tingo to Choctámal, where it divides. The left branch climbs east to Lónguita, María, Quizango and Kuélap.

Kuélap → *Altitude: 3000 m.*

① *0800-1700, US$4.30, guides available for US$7 per group (Rigoberto Vargas Silva has been recommended). The ticket office at the car park has a small but informative Sala de Interpretacion.*
Kuélap is a spectacular pre-Inca walled city which was re-discovered in 1843. It was built continuously from AD 500 up to Inca times and is said to contain three times more stone than the Great Pyramid at Giza in Egypt. The site lies along the summit of a mountain crest, more than 1 km in length. The massive stone walls, 585 m long by 110 m wide at their widest, are as formidable as those of any pre-Columbian city. Some reconstruction has taken place, mostly of small houses and walls, but the majority of the main walls on all levels are original, as is the inverted, cone-shaped main temple. The structures have been left in their cloud forest setting, the trees covered in bromeliads and moss, the flowers visited by hummingbirds.

Chachapoyas → *Phone code: 041. Colour map 3, B2. Population: 30,000. Altitude: 2350 m.*
The capital of the Department of Amazonas, founded in 1538 retains its colonial character. The city's importance as a crossroads between the coast and jungle began to decline in the late

Chachapoyas

Where to stay 🛏
1 Aventura Backpackers Lodge *A1*
2 Belén *A1*
3 Casa Vieja *A1*
4 Casona Monsante *B2*
5 Chachapoyas Backpackers *B2*
6 El Dorado *A1*
7 Las Orquídeas *A1*
8 Posada del Arriero *B1*
9 Puma Urco *B2*
10 Quiocta *B2*
11 Revash *B2*
12 Rumi Huasi *A2*
13 Vilaya *B2*
14 Vista Hermosa *A1*

Restaurants 🍴
1 Batán del Tayta *B2*
2 Dulcería Santa Elena *B2*
3 El Edén *A2*
4 El Tejado *A1*
5 Fusiones *A1*
6 Heladería San Antonio *B2*
7 La Tushpa *B1*
8 Matalaché *B3*
9 Panadería Café San José *B2*
10 Paraíso de las Pizzas *A1*
11 Romana *B1*

Transport 🚌
1 Cars to Huancas & Mendoza *A2*
2 Cars to Lamud & Luya *A1*
3 Combis to Bagua Grande & Moyobamba *A1*
4 Cars to Huancas & Mendoza *A2*
5 Combis to Pedro Ruiz *A1*
6 Trans Rollers to Kuelab & Pizuquia *A2*
7 Cars to Pedro Ruíz & Bagua Grande *A2*
8 Civa *A2*
9 Virgen del Carmen to Celendín & Cajamarca *A2*
10 Karlita to Leymebamba *A2*
12 Móvil Tours *B3*
13 El Expreso & Transervis Kuelab *B3*
14 GH Bus *A3*

1940s, however archaeological and ecological tourism have grown gradually since the 1990s and have brought increasing economic benefits to the region. The cathedral, with a lovely modern interior, stands on the spacious Plaza de Armas. **Ministerio de Cultura Museum** ① *Ayacucho 904, T477045, amazonas@mcultura.gob.pe, Mon-Fri 0800-1300, 1500-1700, free*, contains a small collection of artefacts and mummies, with explanations in Spanish. The **Museo Santa Ana** ① *Jr Santa Ana 1054, T790988, Sun-Fri 0900-1300, 1500-1800, US$2*, has colonial religious art and pre-Hispanic ceramics and textiles. Jr Amazonas, pedestrianized from the Plaza de Armas uphill to Plaza Burgos, makes a pleasant stroll. **Tourist offices**: iPerú ① *on the Plaza de Armas, T477292, iperuchachapoyas@promperu.gob.pe, Mon-Sat 0900-1800, Sun 0900-1300.* **Huancas** ① *autos leave from Jr Ortiz Arrieta 370, 0600-1800, 20 min, US$1.15 or 2-hr walk*, is a small village to the north of Chacha where rustic pottery is produced. Walk uphill from town to the **Mirador** ① *1 km from the plaza, US$0.70, viewing tower, crafts on sale*, for magnificent views into the deep canyon of the Río Sonche, with tumbling waterfalls. At **Huanca Urco**, 5 km from Huancas, past the large prison complex, are ruins, remains of an Inca road and another *mirador* with fine views including Gocta Waterfall in the distance.

Levanto, due south of Chachapoyas, was built by the Spaniards in 1538, directly on top of the previous Chachapoyan structures, as their first capital of the area. Nowadays Levanto is an unspoilt colonial village overlooking the massive canyon of the Utcubamba River. Kuélap can, on a clear day, be seen on the other side of the rift. A 30-minute walk from Levanto towards Chachapoyas are the overgrown ruins of **Yalape**, which seems to have been a massive residential complex, extending over many hectares. Local people can guide you to the ruins.

East of Chachapoyas
In the district of Soloco, south of the Chachapoyas-Mendoza road is **Parjugsha**, Peru's largest cave complex, about 300 m deep and with some 20 km of galeries (10 km have been explored and connected). Spelunking experience is essential.

The road east from Chachapoyas continues on to **Mendoza** (2½ hours), centre of the coffee producing region of Rodríguez de Mendoza. It is the starting point of an ethnologically interesting area in the Guayabamba Valley, where there is an unusually high incidence of fair-skinned people. Close by are the caves at Omia, Tocuya thermal baths, Mirador Wimba and Santa Natalia waterfall. For information ask for Michel Ricardo Feijoó Aguilor in the municipal office, mifeijoo@gmail.com; he can help tourists arrange a guide, accommodation, etc. A recommended guide is Alfonso Saldana Pelaez, fotoguiaalsape@gmail.com.

Northwest of Chachapoyas
On a turn-off on the Chachapoyas-Pedro Ruiz road, at Km 37, is the village of **Luya**. Here the road divides, one branch goes north to **Lamud**, a convenient base for several interesting sites, such as San Antonio and Pueblo de los Muertos, and the **Quiocta cave** ① *entry US$2, tours from Chachapoyas, or arranged at the Lamud Oficina de Turismo; it's 30 mins by car from Lamud, then a 10-min walk*. The cave is 560 m long, 23 m deep, has four chambers with stalactites and stalagmites and a stream running through it. There are petroglyphs at the mouth, a man-made wall, human skulls set in depressions and other, partly buried human remains

The second road goes south and west to Cruzpata, the access for **Karajía** ① *US$2, take binoculars*, where remarkable, 2.5-m-high sarcophagi set into an impressive cliff face overlook the valley. The viewpoint is 2½ hours' walk from Luya or 30 minutes from Cruzpata (*autos from Luya to Cruzpata, 0600-1700, US$3, one hour*). **Chipuric** is another site 1½ hours' walk from Luya. In a lush canyon, 1½ hours' walk from the road to Luya is **Wanglic**, a funeral site with large circular structures built under a ledge. Nearby is a beautiful waterfall, a worthwhile excursion. Ask for directions in Luya. Best to take a local guide (US$7 a day). The road to Luya and Lamud is unpaved, see Chachapoyas Transport for how to get there.

Chachapoyas region listings

For hotel and restaurant price codes, and other relevant information, see Essentials.

Where to stay

Celendín *p1286*

$$-$ Hostal Celendín, Unión 305, Plaza de Armas, T555041, hcgustavosd1@hotmail.com. Some rooms with plaza view, central patio and wooden stairs, hot water, pleasant, has 2 restaurants: Rinconcito Shilico, 2 de Mayo 816, and Pollos a la brasa Gusys.

$ Hostal Imperial, Jr Dos de Mayo 568, 2 blocks from the plaza, T555492. Large rooms, good mattresses, hot water, Wi-Fi, parking, decent choice.

$ Loyer's, José Gálvez 410, T555210. Patio with wooden balcony all round, nice, singles, doubles and family rooms.

$ Maxmar, Dos de Mayo 349, T555330. Cheaper without bath, hot shower extra, basic, parking, good value, owners Francisco and Luis are very helpful.

$ Mi Posada, Pardo 300, next to Atahualpa bus, T074-979-758674. Includes breakfast, small cheerful rooms, family atmosphere.

$ Orange B&B, Jr Unión 333, T770590, www.celendinperu.com. One bedroom in family of the owners of the original *hostal*, which is being built in a new location on the edge of town. See the website for developments. In the meanwhile you can ask for advice on the area by emailing Susan van der Wielen in advance. Tours offered. This is also the HQ for Proyecto Yannick, a charity for children and the families of children with Down's Syndrome, www.proyectoyannick.org. See the website or contact Orange if you would like to help.

$ Raymi Wasi, Jr José Gálvez 420, T976-551133. With electric shower, cheaper without, large rooms, has patio, quiet, parking, good value, restaurant and karaoke.

Leymebamba *p1286*

$$ La Casona, Jr Amazonas 223, T630301, www.casonadeleymebamba.com. Nicely refurbished old house with balcony, attractive common area, restaurant upstairs with good view over roof tops, simple rooms with solar hot water, arrange tours and horses.

$ Laguna de los Cóndores, Jr Amazonas 320, ½ a block from the plaza, T797908. Nice courtyard, breakfast available, electric shower, also runs the shelter at Laguna de los Cóndores and offers tours of 1-8 days.

$ La Petaca, Jr Amazonas 426, on the plaza, T999-020599. Good rooms with hot water, breakfast available, café, helpful.

Tingo *p1286*

$$ Estancia Chillo, 5 km south of Tingo towards Leymebamba, T630510/979-340444. On a 9-ha farm, dinner and breakfast included, with bath, hot water transport, horse riding. Friendly family, a lovely country retreat. The walk from Chillo to Kuélap, is shorter than from Tingo.

$ Albergue León, along the south bank of the Río Tingo, just upriver from the highway, T941 715685, hildegardlen@yahoo.es. Basic, private or shared bath, electric shower, guiding, arrange horses, run by Lucho León who is knowledgeable.

$ Albergue Tingo, on the main highway, just north of the Río Tingo, T941-732251. Adequate rooms with electric shower, restaurant.

Kuélap *p1287*

Walking up from Tingo, the last house to the right of the track (**El Bebedero**) offers very basic rooms with bed, breakfast and dinner, helpful. It may be fully booked by archaeologists, but **Gabriel Portocarrero**, the caretaker, runs a hostel just below the ruins, basic, friendly. **Sra Juanita**, T989-783432, the home of archaeologist Arturo Ruiz Estrada, basic rooms with shared bath, cold water, includes breakfast, good.

María, 2½ hrs from Kuélap on the vehicle road to Choctámal has 10 *hospedajes*, some with bath and hot water; meals available. All these places are in the **$** range.

Choctámal

$$ Choctámal Marvelous Spatuletail Lodge, 3 km from village towards Kuélap at Km 20, T041-941-963327, www.marvelousspatuletail.com. Book in advance. Heated rooms, hot showers, hot tub, telescope for star-gazing. Meals US$8-10. Offers horse riding and a chance to see the endangered Marvellous spatuletail hummingbird.

Chachapoyas *p1287, map p1287*

$$$ Casa Andina Classic, Km 39 Carretera Pedro Ruiz (13 km from Chacha), T969-335840, www.casa-andina.com. Colonial-style hacienda some way outside Chachapoyas, some rooms in modern annex, with safe, pool, gardens, restaurant, Wi-Fi in public areas.

$$$ Casa Vieja, Chincha Alta 569, T477353, www.casaviejaperu.com. Converted old house with lovely courtyard, very nicely decorated, all rooms different, comfy beds, family atmosphere, good service, living room and *comedor* with open fire, includes breakfast, good café, Wi-Fi and library. Repeatedly recommended.

$$ Casona Monsante, Amazonas 746, T477702, www.lacasonamonsante.com. Converted colonial house with patio, orchid garden, comfortable rooms decorated with antiques.

$$ Las Orquídeas, Ayacucho 1231, T478271, www.hostallasorquideas.com. Converted home, nicely decorated rooms, hot water, large garden.

$$ Posada del Arriero, Grau 636, T478945, www.posadadelarriero.net. Old house nicely refurbished in modern style, rooms are a bit plain, courtyard, helpful staff.

$$ Puma Urco, Amazonas 833, T477871, www.hotelpumaurco.com. Comfortable rooms, includes breakfast, TV, frigobar, Wi-Fi, Café Café next door, hotel and café receive good reports, run tours with Turismo Explorer.

$$ Vilaya, Ayacucho 734, T477664. Ample carpeted rooms, parking.

$$-$ Quiocta, Amazonas 721, T477698. Brightly painted rooms, hot water, family run.

$$-$ Revash, Grau 517, Plaza de Armas, T477391, revash9@hotmail.com. Traditional house with patio, stylish decor, steaming hot showers, breakfast available, helpful owners, good local information, popular. Operate tours and sell local crafts.

$ Aventura Backpackers Lodge, Jr Amazonas 1416, www.chachapoyashostal.com. Dorms with bunk beds, use of kitchen, good value.

$ Belén, Jr Ortiz Arrieta 540, Plaza de Armas, T477830, www.hostalbelen.com. With hot water, nicely furnished, pleasant sitting room overlooking the Plaza, good value.

$ Chachapoyas Backpackers, Jr Dos de Mayo 639, T478879, www.chachapoyasbackpackers.com. Simple 2- and 3-bed dorms with shared bath, electric shower, a good budget option,

same owners as Turismo Explorer tour operator. Lovely family run place. Recommended.

$ El Dorado, Ayacucho 1062, T477047, ivvanovt@hotmail.com. With bathroom, electric shower, helpful staff, a good economical option.

$ Rumi Huasi, Ortiz Arrieta 365, T791100. With and without bath, electric shower, small rooms, simple and good.

$ Vista Hermosa, Puno 285, T477526. Nice ample rooms, some have balconies, electric shower, good value.

Levanto

$ Levanto Marvelous Spatuletail Lodge, behind the church, T478838, www.marvellousspatuletail.net. 2 circular buildings with tall thatched roofs, 4 bedrooms with 2 external bathrooms, can accommodate 12 people, hot shower, lounge with fireplace and kitchen, meals US$8-10, must book ahead.

Northwest of Chachapoyas *p1288*

$ Hostal Kuélap, Garcilaso de la Vega 452, on the plaza, Lamud. With or without bath or hot water, basic.

Restaurants

Celendín *p1286*

$$-$ La Reserve, José Gálvez 313. Good quality and value, extensive menu, from Italian to *chifa*.

$ Carbón y Leña, 2 de Mayo 410. For chicken, *parrillas* and pizzas.

$ Juguería Carolin, Bolognesi 384. Daily 0700-2200. One of the few places open early, for juices, breakfasts and caldos.

Chachapoyas *p1287, map p1287*

$$$ Batán del Tayta, La Merced 604. Closed Sun. Excellent innovative local cuisine, generous portions. Recommended.

$$ El Tejado, Santo Domingo 424. Daily for lunch only, but hours vary. Excellent upscale *comida criolla*. Large portions, attentive service, nice atmosphere and setting. Good-value *menú ejecutivo* on weekdays.

$$ La Tushpa, Jr Ortiz Arrieta 753. Mon-Sat 1300-2300. Good grilled meat and *platos criollos*, wine list, very clean kitchen, attentive service.

$$ Paraíso de las Pizzas, Chincha Alta 355. Open to 2200. Good pizzas and pastas, family run.

$$-$ Romana, Amazonas 1091. Daily 0700-2300. Choice of set meals and à la carte, good service.

$ El Edén, Grau by the market. Sun-Thu 0700-2100, Fri 0700-1800. Simple vegetarian, a variety of dishes à la carte and economical set meals.

$ Matalaché, Ayacucho 616. Daily 0730-1530, 1800-2230. Famous for their huge *milanesa* (breaded beef); also serves *menú*.

Dulcería Santa Elena, Amazonas 800. Open 0900-2230. Old-fashioned home-made desserts.

Fusiones, Chincha Alta 445. Mon-Sat 0730-1130, 1600-2100. Breakfast, fair-trade coffee, juices, snacks, Wi-Fi, book exchange, volunteer opportunities.

Heladería San Antonio, 2 de Mayo 521 and Amazonas 856. Good home-made ice-cream, try the *lúcuma* and *guanábana* flavours.

Panadería Café San José, Ayacucho 816. Mon-Sat 0630-2200. Bakery and café, good breakfasts, sweets and snacks.

⏱ What to do

Chachapoyas *p1287, map p1287*
The cost of full-day trips depends on season (higher Jul-Sep), distance to a site, number of passengers and whether meals are included. Several operators have daily departures to Kuélap, US$15-19, Gocta, US$13.50-15, Quiocta and Karajía, US$19-27, and Museo de Leymebamba and Revash, US$31-39. All inclusive trekking tours to Gran Vilaya cost about US$46-50 pp per day.

Amazon Exepdition, Jr Ortiz Arrieta 508, Plaza de Armas, T798718, http://amazonexpedition.com.pe. Day tours and multi-day treks.

Andes Tours, at Hostal Revash. Daily trips to Kuélap and Gocta, other tours to ruins, caves and trekking. Also less-visited destinations, combining travel by car, on horseback and walking.

Cloudforest Expeditions, Jr Puno 368, T477610, www.kuelapnordperu.com. English and German spoken.

Nuevos Caminos, at Café Fusiones, T479170, www.nuevoscaminostravel.com. Alternative community tourism throughout northern Peru, volunteer opportunities.

Turismo Explorer, Jr Grau 509, T478162. Daily tours to Kuélap, Gocta and other destinations, trekking tours including Laguna de los Cóndores and other archaeological sites, transport service.

Vilaya Tours, T+51(0)41 477506, www.vilayatours.com. All-inclusive treks to off-the-beaten-path destinations throughout northern Peru. Run by Robert Dover, a very experienced and knowledgeable British guide, book ahead.

Guides Martín Chumbe, T941-994650, martin.chumbe@yahoo.es, or through **Restaurante Las Rocas**, Jr Ayacucho, at the Plaza. Specializes in longer trips.

⊖ Transport

Celendín *p1286*
Bus To **Cajamarca**, 107 km, 3½ hrs; with Royal Palace's, Jr Unión y José Gálvez, by Plaza de Armas, at 1400 daily; also **CABA** 2 a day, and Rojas 3 a day. Cars to Cajamarca leave when full from Ovalo Agusto Gil, Cáceres y Amazonas, 2½ hrs, US$9 pp. From the same place they go to **Chachapoyas**, 6 hrs, US$18 pp. **Virgen del**

Carmen, Cáceres 112 by Ovalo A Gil, T792918, to Chachapoyas, daily at 0900, US$11.55, 6 hrs to **Leymebamba**, US$7.75.

Leymebamba and around p1286
To **Chachapoyas**, 2½ hrs (fills quickly, book ahead), cars US$7.75; *combis* US$4, eg **Transportes Karlita**, Jr Amazonas corner 16 de Julio on the plaza, 0400 and 0500, **Mi Cautivo**, Jr San Agustín ½ block from the plaza, Mon-Sat 0500 and 0700, Sun 1100 and 1700, **Hidalgo Tours**, Jr Bolívar 608, 0500. **Virgen del Carmen**, Jr 16 de Julio at Plaza, buses from Cajamarca pass Leymebamba at about 1400 en route to Chacha; from Chacha they pass at 0800 for Celendín US$7.75, and Cajamarca US$11:55, 8 hrs.

Kuélap p1287
There are 4 options: **1**) Take a tour from Chachapoyas (3 hrs each way in vehicle, including lunch stop on return, 3 hrs at the site). **2**) Hire a vehicle with driver in Chachapoyas, US$45 per vehicle, or US$54 with wait. **3**) Take Trans Rollers combi from Chachapoyas to the end of the road, near the ruins. It returns right away, so you will have to spend the night at Kuélap, María (2-2½ hrs walk), Choctámal (4-5 hrs walk) or Tingo (see option 4). From Tingo you may get transport back to Chachapoyas later in the day. **4**) Take a combi from Chachapoyas to Tingo, spend the night, then take the 5 hrs' strenuous walk uphill from Tingo; take waterproofs, food and drink, and start early as it gets very hot. Only the fit should try to ascend and descend in one day on foot. In the rainy season it is advisable to wear boots; at other times it is hot and dry (take all your water with you as there is nothing on the way up).

Chachapoyas p1287, map p1287
Air   The military **Grupo Aéreo 42** (Grau 505, T947-490770) has passenger flights to Chachapoyas originating in **Trujillo** or **Iquitos**; see page 1261 for routes and schedules.
Bus   To **Chiclayo** (9 hrs, US$15-25), **Trujillo** (12 hrs, US$23-29) and **Lima** (20-22 hrs, US$44-52), best is **Móvil**, Libertad 464, T478545; to Lima daily at 1300; to Trujillo and Chiclayo at 1930. **Civa**, Salamanca y Ortiz Arrieta, T478048 (to Chiclayo also at 1815). **Transervis Kuelap**,

Jr Union 330, T478128, to Chiclayo Tue and Sat at 1900, other days at 2000. **GH Bus**, station at C Evitamiento (take a taxi), tickets can be bought on Jr Grau entre Trujillo y Amazonas, T479200, to Lima at 1030, to Chiclayo at 2000, to Trujillo 1930. **El Expreso**, Jr Unión 330, to Chiclayo 1930 daily. To **Celendín** (8-9 hrs) and **Cajamarca** (11-12 hrs): Virgen del Carmen, Salamanca 956, 0500 daily, US$11.55 to Celendín, US$18 to Cajamarca, 11 hrs. To **Pedro Ruiz** (1 hr), for connections to Chiclayo, Jaén, or Tarapoto, cars leave from Grau 310 y Salamanca, 0600-1800 (1800-2200 they depart from Grau in front of the market), US$3.85; combis every 2 hrs 0600-1800, from Ortiz Arrieta 370, US$2, also **Diplomáticos** vans, as they fill 0500-1900, from Libertad cuadra 10. To **Bagua Grande** for connections to Jaén, cars from Grau between Libertad and Salamanca 0600-1800 and Grau by the market 1800-0600, US$8.50, 2 hrs, also combis/vans with **Evangelio Poder de Dios**, Jr Libertad 1048, US$6. This company also goes to **Moyobamba** (connections to Tarapoto), 0700, US$9.75, 5 hrs.
Regional   To **Kuélap** US$6, 3 hrs (will only go to Kuélap if they have enough passengers); **María** US$6, 2½ hrs; **Lónguita** US$4.60, 2 hrs; **Choctámal** US$3.85, 1½ hrs; **Tingo** US$3.10, 1 hr: with **Roller's**, Grau y Salamanca, combi or car, at 0400 (return from Kuélap around 0700); with **Sr José Cruz**, Grau 331, combi or car at 0530 (returns from María at 0800); with **Trans Shubet**, Pasaje Reyes off Grau, cars to Lónguita around 1400-1500. To **Tingo**, also with **Brisas del Utcubamba**, Grau 332, cars bound for Magdalena, 0500-1800 or transport going to Yerbabuena or Leymebamba. Vehicles going to Chachapoyas pass Tingo from 0500. To **Leymebamba**, 83 km, 3 hrs, US$4, reserve ahead: **Transportes Karlita**, Salamanca cuadra 9, 1300, 1600; **Mi Cautivo**, Pasaje David Reina y Grau, vans at 1200 and 1600; **Hidalgo Tours**, Jr Grau corner Pasaje David Reina, at 1300. For **Revash**, Comité Santo Tomás, to **Santo Tomás**, at 1000, 1300, 1500 (return at 0300, 0400, 0500), US$4.30, 3 hrs; get off at **Cruce de Revash** (near Puente Santo Tomás), US$4.30, 2½ hrs; or with the same company to **San Bartolo** at 1400 (return 0600), US$4.30, 3 hrs. To **Jalca Grande**, from Jr Hermosura y Salamanca, 2 combis depart Mon-Fri from 1330 onwards, US$4.30,

3 hrs (return 0300-0400). To **Levanto**, cars from Av Cuarto Centenario y Sociego southeast end of town, daily 1200-1300, US$2.90. To **Mendoza** (86 km), Guayabamba, Ortiz Arrieta 372,

US$7.75, 2½ hrs, combis from same address US$6. To **Luya** and **Lamud**, from Libertad y Chincha Alta, cars 0400-1800, US$2.85, 1 hr to Lamud, same price to Luya.

Chachapoyas to the Amazon

From Chachapoyas the road heads north through the beautiful Utcubamba canyon for one hour to a crossroads, **Pedro Ruíz** (two hotels and other lodgings; basic restaurants), where you can return to the coast, head to Jaén for Ecuador, or continue east to Tarapoto and Yurimaguas, making the spectacular descent on a paved road from high Andes to jungle. In the rainy season, the road may be subject to landslides. On route to Tarapoto are **Rioja** (198 km, with several hotels), Nueva Cajamarca (reported unsafe) and Moyobamba.

Gocta
South of Pedro Ruíz is the spectacular **Gocta Waterfall** (771 m, the upper waterfall is 231 m, the lower waterfall is 540 m), one of the highest in the world. From Pedro Ruíz, take the Chachapoyas road for 18 km to Cocahuayco where there are two roads up to Gocta, along either bank of the Cocahuayco River. The first turn-off leads up to the village of **San Pablo de Valera** (1934 m, 6 km from main road, 20 minutes by car) from which it is a one- to 1½-hour walk to a mirador, and then 30-60 minutes to the base of the upper waterfall, 6.3 km in all. The second turn-off, 100 m further on the main road, leads up to the village of **Cocachimba** (1796 m, 5.3 km, 20 minutes), from which it is a 1½- to 2½-hour, 5.5-km walk to the base of the lower waterfall, of which there is an impressive view. Both routes go through about 2 km of lovely forest; the San Pablo trail is somewhat flatter. A trail connecting both banks starts on the San Pablo side at the mirador. It is a much smaller trail than the others, quite steep and not signposted past the mirador. There is a suspension foot-bridge over the main river. It joins the Cocachimba trail about three quarters of the way to the base of the lower falls. If you start the hike at San Pablo and finish at Cocachimba you can arrange transport to return to San Pablo at the end of the day. Or you can take transport to San Pablo to begin the hike if lodged in Cocachimba. The ride is about 30 minutes. To see both sides in one day you need to start very early, but this is a great way to get the full experience. Each community offer similar services: entry fee is US$4, guides (compulsory) cost US$11, horses can be hired for US$11 (they can only go part of the way), rubber boots and rain ponchos are available for hire, US$1.20 (it is always wet by the falls). The best time to visit is May-September, the dry season. In the wet season the falls are more spectacular, but it is cold, rainy and the trails may be slippery. Both towns have a **community tourist information office** ① *San Pablo, T041-631163, daily 0800-1730; and Cocachimba, T041-630569, daily 0800-1730.* Several more waterfalls in this area are now becoming accessible, including **Yumbilla**, 895 m (124 m higher than Gocta), although in eight tiers. For more information about expeditions to Yumbilla, other falls and related projects, see the Florida-based NGO, **Amazon Waterfalls Association**, www.amazonwaterfalls.org.

Moyobamba → *Phone code: 042. Colour map 3, B2. Population: 14,000. Altitude: 900 m.*
Moyobamba, capital of San Martín department, is a pleasant town, in the attractive Río Mayo valley. The area is renowned for its orchids and there is a Festival de la Orquídea over three days around 1 November. Among several places to see orchids is **Orquideario Waqanki** ① *www.waqanki.com, 0700-1800, US$0.55,* where the plants have been placed in trees. Just beyond are **Baños Termales San Mateo** ① *5 km southeast, 0600-2200, US$0.55,* which are worth a visit. **Puerto Tahuishco** is the town's harbour, a pleasant walk north of the centre, where boat trips can be taken. **Morro de Calzada** ① *Rioja combi to the Calzada turnoff, US$0.55, mototaxi to the start of the trail US$2.50,* is an isolated outcrop in white sand forest, good for birdwatching. A path through forest leads to the top and a lookout (1½ hours), but enquire about public safety beforehand. The main road that

goes to Pomacochas and Pedro Ruiz climbs through the **Bosque de Protección Alto Mayo**, with the Long-whiskered Owlet reserve and the Abra Patricia pass (Rioja T558467).

Tourist offices: Oficina Municipal de Información ① *Jr Pedro Canga 262, at Plaza, T562191 ext 541, Mon-Fri 0800-1300, 1430-1715, no English spoken*. **Dircetur** ① *Jr San Martín 301, T562043, Mon-Fri 0800-1300, 1430-1730*, has leaflets and map, English spoken. Also see www.moyobamba.net.

Tarapoto → *Phone code: 042. Colour map 3, B2. Altitude: 350 m. Population: 120,000*

Tarapoto, the largest commercial centre in the region, is a very friendly place. Information from: **Oficina Municipal de Información** ① *Jr Ramírez Hurtado, at plaza, T526188, Mon-Sat 0800-1300, 1500-2000, Sun 0900-1300*, and **Dircetur** ① *Jr Angel Delgado Morey, cuadra 1, T522567*. **Lamas** 22 km from Tarapoto, off the road to Moyobamba, has a native community, descendants of the Chancas people, who live in the Wayku neighbourhood below the centre. There is a small **Museo Los Chankas** ① *Jr San Martín 1157, daily 0830-1300, 1430-1800, US$1.15*, with ethnological and historical exhibits. In upper part of town is a *mirador*, opposite is **$ Hosp Girasoles** (T042-543439, stegmaiert@yahoo.de, breakfast available, nice views, pizzeria and friendly knowledgeable owners). Cars from Tarapoto: Avenida Alfonso Ugarte, cuadra 11, US$1.45, 30 minutes.

Tarapoto stands at the foot of the forested hills of the **Area de Conservación Regional Cordillera Escalera** (149,870 ha), good for birdwatching and walking. By the conservation area and within easy reach of town are the 9-ha **El Amo del Bosque Sector** ① *Urawasha 5 km walk (9 km by car) from town, T524675 (after 1900)*, knowledgeable owner Sr José Macedo, offers guided tours; and 20-ha **Wayrasacha** ① *6-km walk (10 km by car) from the city, T522261, www.wayrasacha.com.pe*, run by Peruvian-Swiss couple, César Ramírez and Stephanie Gallusser, who offer day trips, overnight stays in a basic shelter and volunteer opportunities, English and French spoken. Within the conservation area, about 15 km from Tarapoto on the spectacular road to Yurimaguas are the 50-m falls of **Ahuashiyacu** ① *US$1.15, tours available or transport from La Banda de Shilcayo*. This is a popular place with locals. There are many other waterfalls in the area. Past Ahuashiyacu, the road climbs to a tunnel (stop at the police control for birdwatching, mototaxi US$6), after which you descend through beautiful forest perched on rocky cliffs to Pongo de Caynarachi (several basic *comedores*), where the flats start.

⊚ Chachapoyas to the Amazon listings

For hotel and restaurant price codes, and other relevant information, see Essentials.

⊛ Where to stay

Gocta *p1293*
San Pablo
$ Hospedaje Las Gardenias, T941-718660, Basic rooms with shared bath, cold water, economical meals available.
Gocta, just outside town on the way to the falls, T984-007033. A comfortable hotel with camping facilities, under construction in 2014.

Cocachimba
$$$ Gocta Andes Lodge, Cocachimba, T041-630552 (Tarapoto T042-522225), www.goctalodge.com. Beautifully located lodge overlooking the waterfall, ample rooms with

balconies, lovely terrace with pool, restaurant. Packages available with other hotels in the group.
$ Hospedaje Gallito de la Roca, T630048. Small simple rooms with shared bath, cold water, economical meals available.
$ Hospedaje Las Orquídeas, T631265. Simple rooms in a family home, shared bath, cold water, restaurant.

Moyobamba *p1293*
$$$ Puerto Mirador, Jr Sucre, 1 km from centre, T562050, www.hotelpuertomirador. com. Buffet breakfast, lovely grounds, views overlooking river valley, pool, good restaurant, credit cards accepted.
$$ Orquídea del Mayo, Jr San Martín 432, T561049, orquideadelmayohostal@hotmail. com. Modern comfortable rooms with bath, hot water.

$$ Río Mayo, Jr Pedro Canga 415, T564193. Central, modern comfortable rooms, frigobar, small indoor pool, parking.

$$-$ El Portón, Jr San Martín 449, T866121, casahospedajeelporton@hotmail.com. Pleasant modern rooms with fan, hot water, nice grounds with hammocks, kitchen facilities.

$ Atlanta, Alonso de Alvarado 865, T562063, atlantainn@hotmail.com. Hot water, parking, fan, good value but front rooms noisy.

$ Cobos, Jr Pedro Canga 404, T562153. Private bath, cold water, simple but good.

$ La Cueva de Juan, Jr Alonso de Alvarado 870, T562488, lacueva870@hotmail.com. Small courtyard, private bath, hot water, central but reasonably quiet, good value.

Tarapoto p1294

Several **$** *alojamientos* on Alegría Arias de Morey, cuadra 2, and cheap basic hotels by the bus terminals.

$$$ Puerto Palmeras, Carr Belaúnde Terry Km 614, T524100. Large, modern complex, popular with families, lots of activities and entertainment. Nice rooms, helpful staff, good restaurant, pleasant grounds with pool, mountain bikes, horses and small zoo, airport transfers. Private reserve outside town.

$$$ Puma Rinri Lodge, Carretera Shapaja Chasuta Km 16, T526694, www.pumarinri.com. Lodge/resort hotel on the shores of the Río Huallaga, 30 km east of Tarapoto. Offers a variety of all-inclusive packages.

$$ Huingos Lodge, Prolongación Alerta cuadra 6, Sector Takiwasi, T524171, www.huingoslodge.com. Nice cabins in lovely grounds by the Río Shilcayo, fan, electric shower, frigobar, kitchen facilities, hammocks, HI afiliated, mototaxi from bus stations US$1.55-2.

$$ La Patarashca, Jr San Pablo de la Cruz 362, T528810, www.lapatarashca.com. Very nice hotel with large rooms, cheaper without a/c, rustic, restaurant, electric shower, large garden with hammocks, tours arranged.

$$ Luna Azul, Jr Manco Capac 276, T525787, www.lunaazulhotel.com. Modern, central, includes breakfast and airport transfers, with bath, hot water, a/c or fan, frigobar.

$$-$ El Mirador, Jr San Pablo de la Cruz 517, 5 blocks uphill from the plaza T522177, www.elmiradortarapoto.blogspot.com. With bath, electric shower, fan, Wi-Fi, laundry facilities, breakfast available, hammocks on rooftop terrace with nice views, tours arranged. Family-run and very welcoming.

$$-$ La Posada Inn, San Martín 146, T522234, laposada_inn@yahoo.es. Convenient but ageing town centre hotel, a/c or fan, electric shower, fridge, nice atmosphere. **El Merendero** restaurant on ground floor.

$ San Antonio, Jr Jiménez Pimentel 126, T525563. Rooms with private bath, hot water and fan, good value.

Restaurants

Moyobamba p1293

$$-$ Kikeku, Jr Pedro Canga 450, next to casino. Open 24 hrs. Good *chifa*, also *comida criolla*, large portions, noisy.

$$-$ La Olla de Barro, Pedro Canga 398. Daily 0800-2200. Tourist place serving regional food and other Peruvian dishes.

$ El Avispa Juane, Jr Callao 583. Mon-Sat 0730-1600, Sun 0800-1500. Regional specialities menu Mon-Sat and snacks, popular.

$ La Buena Salud, 25 de Mayo 227, by market. Sun-Fri 0800-1500. Vegetarian set meals, breakfast and fruit juices.

Helados La Muyuna, Jr Pedro Canga 529. Good natural jungle fruit ice cream.

Tarapoto p1294

Several restaurants and bars around Jr San Pablo de la Cruz corner Lamas – a lively area at night.

$$$-$$ Chalet Venezia, Jr Alegría Arias de Morey 298, www.restaurantcafechaletvenezia.com. Tue-Sun 1200-2300. Upmarket Italian-Amazonian fusion cuisine, wine list, elegant decor, interior or terrace seating.

$$$-$$ Real Grill, Jr Moyobamba on the plaza. Daily 0830-2400. Regional and international food. One of the best in town.

$$-$ Chifa Cantón, Jr Ramón Castilla 140. Mon-Fri 1200-1600, Sat-Sun 1200-2400. Chinese, very popular and clean.

$ El Manguaré, Jr Moyobamba corner Manco Cápac. Mon-Sat 1200-1530. Choice of set meals and à la carte, good food and service.

Café Plaza, Jr Maynas corner Martínez, at the plaza. Open 0730-2300. Breakfast, coffee, snacks, juices, Wi-Fi, popular.

Helados La Muyuna, Jr Ramón Castilla 271. Open 0800-2400 except closed Fri from 1700 until Sat at 1830. Good natural ice cream and drinks made with jungle fruits, fruit salads,

⊖ Transport

Chachapoyas to the Amazon *p1293*
Pedro Ruíz Many buses on the **Chiclayo-Tarapoto** and Chiclayo-**Chachapoyas** routes pass through town. Bus fare to Chiclayo US$11.50-19; to Tarapoto US$11.50-15.50. Cars or combis are more convenient for Chacha or Bagua. To **Chachapoyas**, cars US$4, combis US$2, 1 hr. To **Bagua Grande**, cars US$4.75, combis US$4, 1hr. To **Jaén**, Trans Fernández bus from Tarapoto passes Pedro Ruiz about 1400-1500 or take a car to Bagua Grande and transfer there. To **Moyobamba**, cars US$10.70, 4 hrs. To **Nueva Cajamarca**, cars US$9.75, combis US$7.75, 3-3½ hrs, then a further 20 mins to **Rioja**, car US$1.15, combi US$0.75. From Rioja to **Moyobamba**, 21 km, 20 mins, car US$1.15, combi, US$0.75.

Gocta *p1293*
The easiest way to get to Gocta is with a tour from Chachapoyas; in high season there are also tours from Pedro Ruiz. Cocahuayco, near the turn-offs for San Pablo and Cocachimba is 16 km from Pedro Ruiz and about 35 km from Chachapoyas. A taxi from Pedro Ruiz to San Pablo or Cocachimba costs US$2 pp (there are seldom other passengers to share) or US$10 for the vehicle. Sr Fabier, T962-922798, offers transport service to San Pablo, call ahead to find out when he will be in Pedro Ruiz. A moto-taxi from Pedro Ruiz costs US$6, beware of overcharging and dress warmly, it is windy and cold. Cars and mototaxis wait at 5 Esquinas, along the road to Chachapoyas, 4 blocks from the highway. A taxi from Chachapoyas costs US$30, or US$38 with 5-6 hrs wait. Arrange return transport ahead or at the tourist offices in San Pablo or Cocachimba. It is difficult to get transport from Cocahuayco to either Chachapoyas or Pedro Ruiz, passing vans are generally full.

Moyobamba *p1293*
Long distance The bus terminal is 12 blocks from the centre on Av Grau (mototaxi US$0.55).

No service originating in Moyobamba, all buses are on-route to/from Tarapoto. Several companies heading west to **Pedro Ruiz** (US$9, 4 hrs), **Jaén** (US$9, 7 hrs), **Chiclayo** (US$15-US$23, 12 hrs). To book on long-haul buses, you may have to pay the fare to the final destination even if you get off sooner.
Regional Empresa San Martín, Benavides 276, and ETRISA, Benavides 244: cars to **Tarapoto**, US$7.75, vans US$4, 2 hrs; to **Rioja** US$1.15, 20 mins, vans US$0.75; to **Nueva Cajamarca**, US$2, vans US$1.55, 40 mins. Combis cost about 50% less on all routes. To **Chachapoyas**, Evangelio Poder de Dios, Grau 640, at 1500, US$9.75, 5 hrs.

Tarapoto *p1294*
Air US$3 per taxi airport to town, mototaxi US$1.15. To **Lima**, with LAN (Ramírez Hurtado 183, on the plaza, T529318), Avianca/TACA and Star Perú (San Pablo de la Cruz 100, T528765) daily. Star Perú to **Iquitos** daily (Mon, Wed, Fri via Pucallpa), LAN to Iquitos Mon, Thu. The military Grupo Aéreo 42 (J Martínez de Compagñon 688, T972-990630) has passenger flights to Tarapoto originating in **Trujillo** or **Iquitos**; see page 1261 for routes and schedules.
Buses From Av Salaverry, blocks 8-9, in Morales; mototaxi from centre, US$1.15, 20 mins. To **Moyobamba**, 116 km, US$3.85, 2 hrs; to **Pedro Ruiz**, US$11.50-15.50 (companies going to Jaén or Chiclayo), 6 hrs; **Chiclayo**, 690 km, 15-16 hrs, US$25-29; and **Lima**, US$46-52, *cama* US$64, 30 hrs. To **Jaén**, US$13.50-15.50, 9-10 hrs, Fernández 4 a day. For **Chachapoyas**, go to Moyobamba and take a van from there. To **Piura** US$23, 16 hrs, with Sol Peruano, at 1200. To **Tingo María**, US$27, and **Pucallpa**, US$35, Mon, Wed, Fri 0500, Tue, Thu, Sat 0830, Transamazónica and Transmar alternate days; there have been armed holdups on this route.
Regional To **Moyobamba**, cars with Empresa San Martín, Av Alfonso Ugarte 1456, T526327 and ETRISA, Av Alfonso Ugarte 1096, T521944, both will pick you up from your hotel, US$7.70, 2 hrs; combis with Turismo Selva, Av Alfonso Ugarte, cuadra 11, US$4, 2½ hrs. To **Yurimaguas**, Gilmer Tours, Av Alfonso Ugarte 1480, frequent minibuses, US$5.75, 2½ hrs; cars with **Empresa San Martín**, see above, US$7.75, 2 hrs; **Turismo Selva** vans US$4, 8 daily.

Chachapoyas to Ecuador and the coast

The road from Pedro Ruíz (see page 1293) goes west to Bagua Grande and then follows the Río Chamaya. It climbs to the Abra de Porculla (2150 m) before descending to join the old Pan-American Highway at Olmos (see page 1267). From Olmos you can go southwest to Chiclayo, or northwest to Piura. **Bagua Grande** is the first town of note heading west. It has several hotels (eg **$$-$ Río Hotel**, Jr Capac Malku 115, www.riohotelbaguagrande.blogspot.com, good) but is hot, dusty and unsafe. Pedro Ruiz or Jaén are more pleasant places to spend the night.

To Ecuador

Some 50 km west of Bagua Grande, a road branches northwest at Chamaya to **Jaén** (*Phone code: 076; Colour map 3, B2; Population: about 100,000*), a convenient stopover en route to the jungle or Ecuador. It is a modern city surrounded by rice fields. A **Museo Hermógenes Mejía Solf** ① *2 km south of centre, T976-719590, Mon-Fri 0800-1400, mototaxi US$0.60,* displays pre-Columbian artefacts from a variety of cultures and newly-discovered temples close to Jaén, at Monte Grande and San Isidro, are revealing more finds, dating back possibly to 3500 BC. Festival, **Nuestro Señor de Huamantanga**, 14 September.

A road runs north to **San Ignacio** (109 km, first 55 km are paved), near the border with Ecuador. San Ignacio (*fiesta* 30 July) is a pleasant town with steep streets in the centre of a coffee growing area. The nearby hills offer excursions to waterfalls, lakes, petroglyphs and ancient ruins. West of San Ignacio is the **Santuario Tabaconas-Namballe** ① *Sernanp, Huancabamba s/n, Sector Santiago, downhill from the centre in San Ignacio, T960-218439,* a 32,125-ha reserve, at 1700-3800 m protecting the spectacled bear, mountain tapir and several ecosystems including the southernmost Andean *páramo*. From San Ignacio the unpaved road, being widened, runs 45 km through green hills to **Namballe**. The border is 15 minutes from town at **La Balsa**, with a simple lodging and a simple *comedor*, a few small shops and money changers, but no lodgings. To leave Perú head directly to immigration (0830-1300, 1500-2000, otherwise find the officer at his house), when entering see immigration first, then the PNP and return to immigration. From the frontier transport goes to Zumba and then to Vilcabamba and Loja. ▶▶ *See Transport, page 1298.*

⊛ Chachapoyas to Ecuador and the coast listings

For hotel and restaurant price codes, and other relevant information, see Essentials.

⊜ Where to stay

To Ecuador *p1297*
Jaén
$$ Casa del Sol, Mcal Castilla 140, near Plaza de Armas, T434478, hotelcasadelsol@hotmail. com. Modern confortable rooms with frigobar, parking, suites with Jacuzzi.
$$ El Bosque, Mesones Muro 632, T431184, hoteleraelbosque@speedy.com.pe. On main road by bus terminals. Quiet rooms at the back, gardens, frigobar, solar hot water, pool, good restaurant.
$$ Hostal Valle Verde, Mcal Castilla 203, Plaza de Armas, T432201. Modern, large comfortable rooms and beds, a/c or fan, hot water, frigobar, parking.

$$ Prim's, Diego Palomino 1341, T431039, www.primshotel.com. Includes breakfast, good service, comfortable, hot water, a/c or fan, frigobar, Wi-Fi, friendly, small pool.
$ Cancún, Diego Palomino 1413, T433511. Good rooms with hot water, fan, good value.
$ Danubio, V Pinillos 429, T433110. Older place, nicely refurbished, many different rooms and prices, some cheaper rooms have cold water only, fan, good.

North of Jaén

$ Gran Hotel San Ignacio, Jr José Olaya 680 at the bottom of the hill, T076-356544, granhotel-sanignacio@hotmail.com. Restaurant for breakfast and good lunch *menú*, modern comfortable rooms, upmarket for San Ignacio.

$ **Hostal Maldonado**, near the plaza, Namballe, T076-830011 (community phone). Private bath (cheaper without), cold water, basic.

$ **La Posada**, Jr Porvenir 218, San Ignacio, T076-356180. Simple rooms which are cheaper without bath or hot water, restaurant.

$ **Sol de la Frontera**, 1 km north of Namballe, 4 km from La Balsa, T976 116781, T01-247 8881 in Lima, www.hotelsoldelafrontera. com. British-run by Isabel Wood. Comfortable rooms in bungalows, bathtubs, gas water heaters, continental breakfast, set in 2.5 ha of countryside. A good option if you have your own vehicle or bring some food. Meals only available for groups with advance booking. Camping and campervans.

❶ Restaurants

To Ecuador *p1297*
Jaén
$$-$ **La Cabaña**, Bolívar 1332 at Plaza de Armas. Daily 0700-0000. Daily specials at noon, à la carte in the evening, popular.

$$-$ **Lactobac**, Bolívar 1378 at Plaza de Armas. Daily 0730-0000. Variety of à la carte dishes, snacks, desserts, good *pollo a la brasa*. Very popular.

$ **Ebenezer**, Mcal Ureta 1360. Sun-Thu 0700-2130, Fri 0700-1600. Simple vegetarian restaurant serves economical midday *menú* and à la carte.

$ **Gatizza**, Diego Palomino 1503. Mon-Sat 0830-1800. Tasty and varied *menú*.

Cenfrocafé, San Martín 1528. Mon-Sat 0730-1330, 1600-2300. Serve a variety of coffees, sandwiches, *humitas* and desserts, Wi-Fi. Cenfrocafé, www.cenfrocafe.com.pe, is a Jaén-based coffee farmers organization.

❷ Transport

Chachapoyas to Ecuador and the coast
p1297
Many buses pass through **Bagua Grande** en route from Chiclayo to Tarapoto or Chachapoyas and vice versa. Cars to **Jaén** from Mcal Castilla y Angamos at the west end of town, US$4, combis US$2.50, 1 hr. From R Palma 308 at the east end of town, cars leave to **Pedro Ruiz**, US$4.60, combis US$4, 1 hr; to **Chachapoyas**, US$9.75, combis US$5.75, 2½ hrs.

To Ecuador *p1297*
Jaén
Bus Terminals are strung along Mesones Muro, blocks 4-7, south of centre; many ticket offices, always enquire where the bus actually leaves from. Some companies also have offices in the centre: eg Civa, Mcal Ureta 1300 y V Pinillos (terminal at Bolívar 935). To **Chiclayo**: US$7.75-15.50, 6 hrs, many companies, **Móvil** more expensive than others. Cars to Chiclayo from terminal at Mesones Muro cuadra 4, US$27, 5 hrs. To **Lima**: Móvil at 1500, 16 hrs, *bus cama* US$46, *semi-cama* US$38.50. Civa, 1700, US$35-42. Service to Lima also goes through **Trujillo**. To **Piura** via Olmos: Sol Peruano, at 2200, US$15.50, 8 hrs. To **Tarapoto**, 490 km, US$13.50-15.50, 9-10 hrs; Fernández, 4 a day. To **Moyobamba**, US$11.50-13.50, 7 hrs, same service as Tarapoto, likewise to **Pedro Ruiz**: US$6-7.75, 3½ hrs. To **Bagua Grande**, cars from Mesones Muro cuadra 6, 0400-2000, US$4, 1hr; combis from cuadra 9, US$2.50. To **Chamaya**: cars from Mesones Muro cuadra 4, 0500-2000, US$1, 15 min. To **San Ignacio** (for Ecuador), cars from Av Pacamuros, cuadra 19, 0400-1800, US$7.75, 2 hrs; combis from cuadra 17, US$4.60, 3 hrs.

North of Jaén
Bus From San Ignacio to **Chiclayo**, with Civa, Av San Ignacio 386, daily at 1830, US$11.55, 10-11 hrs; with Trans Chiclayo, Av San Ignacio 406, 1945 daily. To **Jaén**, from *óvalo* at south end of Av Mariano Melgar: prices above.

To **Namballe** and **La Balsa** (border with Ecuador), cars leave from Sector Alto Loyola at north end of town, way above the centre, US$6 to Namballe, US$6.55 to La Balsa, 1½ hrs. Taxi or moto-taxi Namballe-La Balsa, US$1.15. In Ecuador, *rancheras* (open-sided buses) run from La Balsa to Zumba at 1200, 1700 and 1915, US$1.75, 1¾ hrs; Zumba to La Balsa 0800, 1430 and 1700. There are Ecuadorean military controls before and after Zumba; keep your passport to hand.

South coast

The Pan-American Highway runs all the way south from Lima to the Chilean border. This part of Peru's desert coast has its own distinctive attractions. The most famous, and perhaps the strangest, are the mysterious Nazca Lines, whose origin and function continue to puzzle scientists the world over. But Nazca is not the sole archaeological resource here: remains of other pre-Columbian civilizations include outposts of the Inca empire itself. Pisco and Ica are the main centres before Nazca. The former, which is near the famous Paracas marine reserve, is named after the latter's main product, the pisco grape brandy and a number of places are well known for their bodegas.

South from Lima

Beyond the beaches which are popular with Limeños the road passes near several towns: eg Chincha with its Afro-Peruvian culture. The Paracas peninsula, near Pisco, is one of the world's great marine bird reserves and was home to one of Peru's most important ancient civilizations. Further south, the Ica valley, with its wonderful climate, is home to that equally wonderful grape brandy, pisco. Most beaches have very strong currents and can be dangerous for swimming; if unsure, ask locals.

Cañete Valley

A paved road runs inland from Cañete, mostly beside the Río Cañete, to **Lunahuaná** (40 km). It is 8 km beyond the Inca ruins of **Incawasi**, which dominated the valley. In the week it's very quiet, but on Sunday the town is full of life with pisco tastings from the valley's *bodegas*, food and handicrafts for sale in the Plaza and lots of outdoor activities. Several places offer rafting and kayaking: from November-April rafting is at levels IV-V. May-October is low water, levels I-II only. A festival of adventure sports is held every February. **Fiesta de la Vendimia**, grape harvest, first weekend in March. At the end of September/beginning October is the **Fiesta del Níspero** (medlar festival). There are several hotels, ranging from **$$** to **$**, and *restaurantes campestres* in the area. **Tourist office** in the Municipalidad (T284 1006), opposite the church, open daily.

Beyond Lunahuaná the road ascending the Cañete Valley leaves the narrow flood-plain and runs 41 km, paved, through a series of gorges to the San Jerónimo bridge. A side road heads to Huangáscar and the village of Viñac, where **Mountain Lodges of Peru** has its **Viñak-Reichraming Lodge** (**$$$** pp full board, T01-421 6952, www.refugiosdelperu.com, see page 1385), a wonderful place to relax or go horse riding or walking (superb views, excellent food). The main road carries on to market town of **Yauyos** (basic accommodation, 5 km off the road). After the attractive village of **Huancaya** (several *hospedajes*, T01-810 6086/7, municipal phone, and ask for details) the valley is transformed into one of the most beautiful upper valleys in all Peru, on a par with Colca. Above Huancaya the high Andean terrain lies within the **Reserva Paisajística Nor Yauyos-Cochas** (**Sernanp** contact Juan Carlos Pilco, pilco_traveler@hotmail.com; regional office RPNYC, Avenida Francisco Solano 107, San Carlos, Huancayo T064-213064) and the river descends through a series of absolutely clear, turquoise pools and lakes, interrupted by cascades and white water rapids. The valley has perhaps the best pre-Columbian terracing anywhere in Peru. Further upstream **Llapay** is a good base because it is in the middle of the valley (**$** Hostal Llapay, basic but very friendly, will open at any hour, restaurant). Beyond Llapay, the Cañete valley narrows to an exceptionally tight canyon, with a road squeezed between nothing but rock and rushing water for the steep climb to the 4600-m pass. Beyond, the road drops to Huancayo (see page 1390).

Pisco and around → *Phone code: 056. Colour map 3, C3. Population: 82,250.*

The largest port between Callao and Matarani is a short distance to the west of the Pan-American Highway and 237 km south of Lima. In August 2007, an earthquake of 7.9 on the Richter scale struck the coast of Peru south of Lima killing 519 people, with 1366 injured and 58,500 homes destroyed. Hardest hit was the province of Ica; in the city of Pisco almost half of all buildings were destroyed. Also affected was **Chincha Alta**, 35 km north of Pisco, where the negro/criollo culture thrives. The famous festival, **Verano Negro**, is at the end of February while, in November, the **Festival de las Danzas Negras** is held in El Carmen, 10 km south. In October 2011, another earthquake, this time of 6.9 on the Richter scale, occurred off the coast of Ica, leaving one dead, 1705 homeless and 515 damaged or destroyed houses.

A 317-km paved road goes to Ayacucho in the sierra, with a branch to Huancavelica. At Castrovirreyna it reaches 4600 m. The scenery on this journey is superb. **Tambo Colorado**, one of the best-preserved Inca ruins in coastal Peru, is 38 km from the San Clemente junction, up the Pisco valley. It includes buildings where the Inca and his retinue would have stayed. Many of the walls retain their original colours. On the other side of the road is the public plaza and the garrison and messengers' quarters. The caretaker will act as a guide, he has a small collection of items found on the site. See https://www.facebook.com/TamboColorado for details of a French research project here.

Paracas National Reserve

ⓘ *US$1.75 pp; agency tours cost US$9 in a bus with 20 people, 1100-1500.*

Down the coast 15 km from Pisco Puerto is the bay of **Paracas**, sheltered by the Paracas peninsula. The name means 'sandstorm' (these can last for three days, especially in August; the wind gets up every afternoon, peaking at around 1500). Paracas can be reached by the coast road from San Andrés, passing the fishing port and a large proportion of Peru's fishmeal industry. Alternatively, go down the Pan-American Highway to 14.5 km past the Pisco turning and take the road to Paracas across the desert. In town is the **Museo Histórico de Paracas** ⓘ *Av Los Libertadores Mz Jl Lote 10, T955-929514, www.museohistoricoparacas.com*, with exhibits from the pre-Columbian cultures of the region.

The peninsula, a large area of coast to the south and the Ballestas Islands is a national reserve (Peru's most visited in 2013), and one of the best marine reserves, with the highest concentration of marine birds in the world. It's advisable to see the peninsula as part of a tour: it is not safe to walk alone and it is easy to get lost. The **Julio C Tello** site museum was being rebuilt in 2014 after the 2007 earthquake. Tours follow a route through the reserve, including to a *mirador* of **La Catedral** rock formation, which collapsed in 2007. Longer tours venture into the deserts to the south. About 14 km from the museum is the pre-Columbian Candelabra (**Candelabro** in Spanish) traced in the hillside, at least 50 m long, best seen from the sea (sit on left side of boat). The tiny fishing village of **Lagunilla** is 5 km from the museum across the neck of the peninsula. Eating places there are poor value (watch out for prices in dollars), but almost all tours stop for lunch here.

Ballestas Islands

Trips to the **Islas Ballestas** leave from the jetties in Paracas town. The islands are spectacular, eroded into numerous arches and caves (*ballesta* means bow, as in archery), which provide shelter for thousands of seabirds, some of which are very rare, and hundreds of sea lions. The book *Las Aves del Departamento de Lima* by Maria Koepcke is useful (see also www.avesdelima. com/playas.htm). You will see, close up, thousands of inquisitive sea lions, guano birds, pelicans, penguins and, if you're lucky, dolphins swimming in the bay. Most boats are speedboats with life jackets, some are very crowded; wear warm clothing and protect against the sun. The boats pass Puerto San Martín and the Candelabra en route to the islands.

Ica and Huacachina → *Phone code: 056. Colour map 3, C3. Population: 161,410.*

Ica, 70 km southeast of Pisco, is Peru's chief wine centre and is famous for its *tejas*, a local sweet of *manjarblanco*. It suffered less damage than Pisco, but one side of the Plaza de Armas collapsed in the earthquake. The **Museo Regional** ⓘ *Av Ayabaca, block 8, T234383, Mon-Wed 0800-1900,*

Thu-Sun 0900-1800, US$4, students US$2.15, tip guides US$4-5, take bus 17 from the Plaza de Armas (US$0.50), has mummies, ceramics, textiles and trepanned skulls from the Paracas, Nazca and Inca cultures; a good, well-displayed collection of Inca *quipus* and clothes made of feathers. Behind the building is a scale model of the Nazca lines with an observation tower; a useful orientation before visiting the lines. The kiosk outside sells copies of motifs from the ceramics and textiles. **Dircetur** ① *Av Grau 148, T238710, ica@mincetur.gob.pe*. Some tourist information is available at travel agencies.

Wine *bodegas* that you can visit are: **La Caravedo**, Panamericana Sur 298, T01-9833 4729, with organic production and sophisticated presentation; **El Carmen**, on the right-hand side when arriving from Lima (has an ancient grape press made from a huge tree trunk); **El Catador** ① *Fondo Tres Esquinas 102, T962629, elcatadorcristel@yahoo.es, 1000-1800, US$1.50, 10 km outside Ica, in the district of Subtanjalla, combi from the 2nd block of Moquegua, every 20 mins, US$0.75, taxi takes 10 mins, good tours in Spanish*. The shop sells home-made wines, pisco and crafts associated with winemaking. In the evening it is a restaurant-bar with dancing and music, best visited during harvest, late February to early April. Near El Catador is **Bodega Alvarez**, whose owner, Umberto Alvarez, is very hospitable. The town of Ocucaje is a popular excursion from Ica for tours of the **Ocucaje winery** ① *Ctra Panamericana Sur, Km 335.5, T01-251 4570, www.ocucaje. com*, which makes wines and *pisco*.

About 5 km from Ica, round a palm-fringed lake and amid amazing sand dunes, is the oasis and summer resort of **Huacachina** ① *take a taxi from Ica for US$1.75, or colectivo from Bolívar black 2 in Ica, return from behind Hotel Mossone, US$0.75*, a popular hang-out for people seeking a change from the archaeology and chill of the Andes. Plenty of cheap hostels and bars have opened, playing pop and grunge as opposed to pan-pipe music. Paddleboats can be rented and sandboarding on the dunes has become a major pastime. For the inexperienced, note that sandboarding can be dangerous. Dune buggies also do white-knuckle, rollercoaster tours for US$20 (plus a municipal small fee), most start between 1600 and 1700 for sunsets, some at 1000, 2½ hours.

◉ South from Lima listings

For hotel and restaurant price codes, and other relevant information, see Essentials.

● Where to stay

Pisco and around *p1299*
$$ Posada Hispana Hostal, Bolognesi 222, T536363, www.posadahispana.com. Some rooms with loft and bath, also rooms with shared bath, hot water, can accommodate groups, comfortable, breakfast extra, has **Café de la Posada**, information service, English, French, Italian and Catalan spoken.
$$-$ El Candelabro, Callao y Pedemonte, T532620, www.hoteleselcandelabro.com. Modern, pleasant, all rooms with bath, fridge, restaurant.
$$-$ Hostal San Isidro, San Clemente 103, T536471, http://sanisidrohostal.com. With or without bath, hot water, safe, welcoming, nice pool and cafetería, pizzería, free laundry facilities, games room, English spoken, parking.

Breakfast not included, free coffee in mornings, use of kitchen. Arranges dune buggy tours and other excursions.
$$-$ San Jorge Residencial, Jr Barrio Nuevo 133, T532885, www.hotelsanjorgeresidencial. com. Smart and modern. Hot water, secure parking, breakfast is served in the restaurant, also lunch and dinner, swanky and spacious, café/bar in garden.
$ Hostal Los Inkas Inn, Prol Barrio Nuevo Mz M, Lte 14, Urb San Isidro, T536634. Affordable, rooms and dorms have private bath, fan, safes, rooftop games area, small pool.
$ Hostal Tambo Colorado, Av Bolognesi 159, T531379, www.hostaltambocolorado.com. Welcoming, helpful owners are knowledgeable about the area, hot water, small café/bar, use of kitchen.

Paracas *p1300*
$$$$ Hotel Paracas Luxury Collection Resort, Av Paracas 173, T581333, www.libertador.com.

pe. The reincarnation of the famous Hotel Paracas, as a resort with spa, pools, excellent rooms in cottages around the grounds, access to beach, choice of restaurants, bar.

$$$$ La Hacienda Bahía Paracas, Lote 25, Urb Santo Domingo, T01-213 1000, www.hoteles lahacienda.com. Next to **Doubletree** but not connected, rooms and suites, some with access straight to pool, spa, choice of restaurants, bar.

$$$$-$$$ Doubletree Guest Suites Paracas, Lote 30-34, Urb Santo Domingo on the outskirts, T01-617 1000, www.doubletree.com. Low rise, clean lines and a comfortable size, built around a lovely pool, on beach, water sports, spa, all mod cons and popular with families.

$$$ El Mirador, at the turn-off to El Chaco, T545086, www.elmiradorhotel.com. Hot water, good service, boat trips arranged, meals available, large pool, tranquil gardens, relaxing.

$$$ Gran Palma, Av Principal Mz D lote 03, half block from plaza, T01-665 5932, www. hotelgranpalma.com. Central, convenient for boats, best rooms have sea view, buffet breakfast on the terrace.

$$ Brisas de la Bahía, Av Principal, T531132, www.brisasdelabahia.com. Good, family-run hostal, convenient position for waterfront and bus stops, ask for a back room, good breakfast.

$$ Los Frayles, Av Paracas Mz D lote 5, T545141, www.hostallosfrayles.com. Variety of simple, well-kept rooms, ocean view, breakfast extra, roof terrace, tourist information, transfers to/from bus arranged.

$$ Mar Azul, Alan García Mz B lote 20, T534542, www.hostalmarazul.com. Family run overlooking the sea although most rooms face away from ocean, comfortable, hot water, breezy roof terrace with sea view for breakfast (included), helpful owner Yudy Patiño. Also **Ballestas Expeditions** for local tours.

$$ Santa María, Av Paracas s/n, T545045, www.hostalsantamariaparacas.com. Smart rooms, hot water, no view. El Chorito restaurant, mainly fish and seafood. Also has **Santa María 2**, round the corner in lovely converted house (same contact numbers), not all rooms have view but has rooftop terrace. **Santa María 3**, under construction on the approach road, will have more facilities and pool.

$ Backpackers House, Av Los Libertadores, beside museum, T635623, www.paracas backpackershouse.com.pe. Rooms with and without bath, private and dorms, at high season prices rise to **$$-$**. Good value, comfortable, tourist information.

$ Hostal El Amigo, El Chaco, T545042, hostalelamigo@hotmail.com. Simple, hot water, no food, no internet but very helpful staff.

Ica and Huacachina p1300

Ica

Hotels are fully booked during the harvest festival and prices rise. Many hotels are in out of town residential neighbourhoods, insist taxis go to the hotel of your choice.

$$$$-$$$ Las Dunas, Av La Angostura 400, T256224, www.lasdunashotel.com. Lima office: Av Vasco Núñez de Balboa 259, Lima, T213 5000. Variety of rooms and suites. Prices are reduced on weekdays. Packages available. Complete resort with restaurant, swimming pool, many sporting activities and full-day programmes.

$$$ Villa Jazmín, Los Girasoles Mz C-1, Lote 7, Res La Angostura, T258179, www.villajazmin. net. Modern hotel in a residential area near the sand dunes, 8 mins from the city centre, solar heated water, restaurant, buffet breakfast, pool, tours arranged, airport and bus transfers, helpful staff, tranquil and very good.

$$ Princess, Santa Magdalena D-103, Urb Santa María, T215421, www.hotelprincess.com. pe. Taxi ride from the main plaza, small rooms, hot water, frigobar, pool, tourist information, helpful, peaceful, very good.

$ Arameli, Tacna 239, T239107. 1 block from the Plaza de Armas, is a nice place to stay, good value, café on 3rd floor.

Huacachina

$$$ Mossone, east end of the lake, T213630, www.dmhoteles.pe. Faded elegance, hacienda-style with a view of the lagoon, full board available, good buffet breakfast, large rooms, bilingual staff, lovely courtyard, bicycles and sandboards, large, clean swimming pool.

$$ Hostal Huacachinero, Av Perotti, opposite Hostal Salvatierra, T217435, http:// elhuacachinero.com. Spacious rooms, sparsely furnished but comfortable beds, nice atmosphere, pool, outside bar and restaurant, parking, offers tours and buggy rides.

$$ Hostería Suiza, Malecón 264, T238762, hostesuiza@terra.com.pe. Overlooking lake, lovely grounds, quiet, safe parking.

$ Carola del Sur (also known as **Casa de Arena II**), Av Perotti s/n, T237398. Basic rooms, popular, small pool, restaurant/bar, hammocks, access to Casa de Arena's bigger pool, noisy at night, pressure to buy tours.

$ Casa de Arena, Av Perotti s/n, T215274. Basic rooms and dorms, thin walls, bar, small pool, laundry facilities, board hire, popular with backpackers but grubby, check your bill and change carefully, don't leave valuables unattended, disco next door.

$ Hostal Rocha, T222256, kikerocha@hotmail. com. Hot water, with or without bath, family run, kitchen and laundry facilities, board hire, small pool, popular with backpackers, but a bit run-down.

$ Hostal Salvatierra, T232352, http:// salvaturgroup.galeon.com. An old building, with or without bath, not on waterfront, charming, pool, relaxing courtyard, rents sandboards, good value.

See also **Desert Adventures**, under What to do, below.

🍴 Restaurants

Pisco and around *p1299*
$$ $ As de Oro, San Martín 472, T532010. Closed Mon. Good food, not cheap but always full at lunchtime, swimming pool.
$ Café Pirata, Callao 104, T534343. Open 0630-1500, 1800-2200, closed Sun. Desserts, pizzas, sandwiches, coffee and lunch menu.
$ Chifa Lisen, Av San Martín 325, T535527. Open 1230-1530, 1800-2200. Chinese food and delivery.

Paracas *p1300*
Several eating places on the Malecón by Playa El Chaco, all with similar menus and prices (in our **$$** range) and open for breakfast, eg **Bahía**; **Brisa Marina**, varied menu, mainly seafood; **Johnny y Jennifer**. All have vegetarian options. Better value *menús* are available at lunchtime on the main road, eg Lobo Fino. Higher quality food within walking distance of the centre is at the **Hotel Paracas' restaurant and Trattoria**, **$$$**, both open to the public.

Ica and Huacachina *p1300*
$$-$ Anita, Libertad 133, Plaza de Armas. Local dishes, breakfast, à la carte a bit expensive for what's offered, but set menus at US$4.50 are good value.
$ Carne y pescao, Av Juan José Elías 417, T228157. Seafood and, at night, grilled chicken and *parrilladas*.
$ Plaza 125, C Lima 125, T211816. On the plaza, regional and international food as well as breakfast, good-value set lunches.
D'lizia, Lima 155, Plaza de Armas, T237733, www.delizia.com.pe. Also in the Patio de comidas at Plaza Vea mall and in Urb Moderna. Modern and bright, for breakfasts, lunches, sandwiches, snacks, ice cream, cakes and sweets, juices and drinks.
Tejas Helena, Cajamarca 137. The best *tejas* and locally made chocolates are sold here.

Huacachina
$ La Casa de Bamboo, Av Perotti s/n, next to Hostería Suiza, T776649. Café-bar, English breakfast, marmite, Thai curry, falafel, vegetarian and vegan options, book exchange, games.
$ Moroni, T238471. Open 0800 till late. Only restaurant right on the lake shore, serving a variety of Peruvian and international foods.

🎉 Festivals

Ica and Huacachina *p1300*
Festival Internacional de la Vendimia wine harvest in early **Mar**. The image of El Señor de Luren, in a fine church in Parque Luren, draws pilgrims from all Peru in **Oct** (3rd Mon), when there are all-night processions; celebrations start the week before.

⚙ What to do

Paracas *p1300*
There are agencies all over town offering trips to the Islas Ballestas, the Paracas reserve, Ica, Nazca and Tambo Colorado. A 2-hr boat tour to the islands costs US$13-15 pp, including park entrance fee and tax, departure 0800. Usually, agencies will pool clients together in 1 boat, 40 people per boat. Do not book tours on the street. An agency that does not pool clients is **Huacachina**,

based in Ica, with an office in Paracas, T056-215582, www.huacachinatours.com.

Zarcillo Connections, Independencia A-20, Paracas, T536636, www.zarcilloconnections. com. With long experience for trips to the Paracas National Reserve, Tambo Colorado, trekking and tours to Ica, Chincha and the Nazca Lines and surrounding sites. Agent for **Cruz del Sur** buses. Also has its own hotel, Zarcillo Paradise, in Paracas.

Ica and Huacachina *p1300*

In Ica, agencies offer city tours, Nazca Lines, Paracas, Islas Ballestas, buggies and sandboarding: **AV Dolphin Travel**, C Municipalidad 132, of 4, T256234, www.av-dolphintravelperu.com; **Desert Travel**, Lima 171, inside Tejas Don Juan on Plaza, T227215, desert_travel@hotmail.com.

Desert Adventures, Huacachina, T228458, www.desertadventure.net. Frequently recommended for sandboarding and camping trips into the desert by 4WD and buggies, French, English and Spanish spoken. Also to beaches, Islas Ballestas and Nazca Lines flights. Has an associated hostel, **Desert Nights**, which has a good reputation, English spoken, food available.

Ica Desert Trip, Bolívar 178, T237373, www.ica deserttrip.com. Roberto Penny Cabrera (speaks Spanish and English) offers 1-, 2- and 3-day trips off-road into the desert, archaeology, geology, etc. 4 people maximum, contact by email in advance. Take toilet paper, something warm for the evening, a long-sleeved loose cotton shirt for daytime and long trousers. Recommended, but "not for the faint-hearted".

⊖ Transport

Cañete Valley *p1299*

Soyuz bus Lima-**Cañete** every 7 mins, US$5; combi Cañete-**Lunahuaná**, US$2.75. Cars run from the Yauyos area to **Huancayo**, US$7.50. Ask locally where and when they leave. Public transport between villages is scarce and usually goes in the morning. When you get to a village you may have to wait till the early evening for places to open up.

Pisco and around *p1299*

Air Capitán RE Olivera airport is being redeveloped from a military base into an alternative airport for Lima. By 2017 it expected to be a major international hub. **LCPerú's** Lima-Pisco-Cuzco flights offer views of the Nazca Lines. They also have Nazca overflights from Pisco in large-windowed Twin Otter Vistaliners (www.lcperu.pe), as does **Aerodiana** (Av Casimiro Ulloa 227, San Antonio, Lima, T447 6824, www.aerodiana.com.pe).

Bus Buses drop passengers at San Clemente on Panamericana Sur (**El Cruce**); many bus companies and tour agencies have their offices here. It's a 10-km taxi ride from the centre, US$8, US$10 to Paracas. Colectivos leave from outside Banco Continental (plaza) for El Cruce when full, US$2. To **Lima**, 242 km, 4 hrs, US$7.50. The best company is **Soyuz**, every 7 mins. **Ormeño** has an office in Pisco plaza and will take you to El Cruce to meet their 1600 bus. **Flores** is the only company that goes into Pisco town, from Lima and Ica, but buses are poor and services erratic. To **Ica**, US$1.25 by bus, 45 mins, 70 km, with **Ormeño**, also colectivos. To **Nazca**, 210 km, take a bus to Ica and then change to a colectivo. To **Ayacucho**, 317 km, 8-10 hrs, US$12-20, several buses daily, leave from El Cruce, book in advance and take warm clothing as it gets cold at night. To **Huancavelica**, 269 km, 12-14 hrs, US$12, with **Oropesa**, coming from Ica. To Arequipa, US$17, 10-12 hrs, 2 daily. To **Tambo Colorado** from near the plaza in Pisco, 0800, US$2.50, 3 hrs; also colectivos, US$2 pp. Alight 20 mins after the stop at Humay; the road passes right through the site. Return by bus to Pisco in the afternoon. For transport back to Pisco wait at the caretaker's house. Taxi from Pisco US$30. Tours from Pisco agencies US$15 with guide, minimum 2 people.

Paracas *p1300*

Cruz del Sur has 2 direct buses a day to its Paracas terminal, regular bus from US$9, luxury services US$30-35 from **Lima**, US$15 to **Nazca**. Agencies in Paracas sell direct transfers between Paracas and Huacachina, **Pelican Perú**, 1100 daily, US$7, comfortable and secure.

Taxi From **Pisco** to Paracas about US$3; combis when full, US$1.75, 25 mins.

Ica and Huacachina *p1300*

Bus All bus offices are on Lambayeque blocks 1 and 2 and Salaverry block 3. To **Pisco**, 70 km, as above; to Paracas junction US$1.15. To **Lima**, 302 km, 4 hrs, US$21-34, on upmarket buses, several daily including **Soyuz** (Av Manzanilla 130, every 7 mins 0600-2200) and **Ormeño** (at Lamba yeque 180). To **Nazca**, 140 km, 2 hrs, several buses (US$3.50) and colectivos (US$5) daily, including **Ormeño**, **Flores**, 4 daily, and **Cueva** (José Elias y Huánuco), hourly on the hour 0600-2200. To **Arequipa** the route goes via Nazca (see Nazca).

Nazca and around

Set in a green valley amid a perimeter of mountains, Nazca's altitude puts it just above any fog which may drift in from the sea. The sun blazes the year round by day and the nights are crisp. Nearby are the mysterious, world-famous Nazca Lines. Overlooking the town is Cerro Blanco (2078 m), the highest sand dune in the world, popular for sandboarding and parapenting.

Nazca Town → *Phone code: 056. Colour map 3, C3. Population: over 50,000. Altitude: 598 m.*
In the town of Nazca (140 km south of Ica via Pan-American Highway, 444 km from Lima) there are two important museums. **Museo Antonini** ① *Av de la Cultura 600, eastern end of Jr Lima, 1523444, cahuachi@terra.com.pe or CISRAP@numerica.it, 0900-1900, ring the bell, US$6, including guide. 10-min walk from the plaza, or short taxi ride.* This museum houses the discoveries of Professor Orefici and his team from the huge pre-Inca city at Cahuachi (see below), which, Orefici believes, holds the key to the Nazca Lines. Many tombs survived the huaqueros and there are displays of mummies, ceramics, textiles, amazing *antaras* (panpipes) and photos of the excavations. In the garden is a prehispanic aqueduct. Recommended. The **Maria Reiche**

Nazca

Where to stay 🛏
1 Alegría
2 Casa Andina Classic
3 Hostal Alegría
4 Maison Suisse
5 Majoro
6 Nasca
7 Nazca Lines
8 Paredones Inn
9 Posada de Don Hono
10 Posada Guadalupe
11 Sol de Nasca

Restaurants 🍴
1 Chifa Guang Zhou
2 Coffee Break
3 El Huarango & Travel Service
4 Fuente de Soda Jumbory
5 Kañada
6 La Choza
7 La Taberna
8 Los Angeles
9 Mamashana & Vía La Encantada
10 Panadería
11 Rico Pollo

Planetarium ① *Hotel Nazca Lines, T522293, shows usually at 1900 and 2115 in English, 2000 in Spanish; US$7 (students half price)*, offer introductory lectures every night about the Nazca Lines, based on Reiche's theories, which cover archaeology and astronomy. The show lasts about 45 minutes, after which visitors are able to look at the moon, planets and stars through telescopes. There is a small market at Lima y Grau, the Mercado Central at Arica y Tacna and a supermarket, Raulito, at Grau 245. The **Virgen de la Guadalupe** festival takes place 29 August-10 September. **Tourist police** ① *Av Los Incas cuadra 1, T522105*.

Nazca Lines

Cut into the stony desert about 22 km north of Nazca, above the Ingenio valley on the Pampa de San José, along the Pan-American Highway, are the famous Nazca Lines. Large numbers of lines, not only parallels and geometrical figures, but also designs such as a dog, an enormous monkey, birds (one with a wing span of over 100 m), a spider and a tree. The lines, best seen from the air, are thought to have been etched on the Pampa Colorada sands by three different groups – the Paracas people 900-200 BC, the Nazcas 200 BC-AD 600 and the Huari settlers from Ayacucho at about AD 630.

The Nazcas had a highly developed civilization which reached its peak about AD 600. Their polychrome ceramics, wood carvings and adornments of gold are on display in many of Lima's museums. The Paracas was an early phase of the Nazca culture, renowned for the superb technical quality and stylistic variety in its weaving and pottery. The Huari empire, in conjunction with the Tiahuanaco culture, dominated much of Peru from AD 600-1000.

Origins of the lines The German expert, Dr Maria Reiche, who studied the lines for over 40 years, mostly from a step ladder, died in 1998, aged 95. She maintained that they represent some sort of vast astronomical pre-Inca calendar. In 1976 Maria Reiche paid for a platform, the mirador, from which three of the huge designs can be seen – the Hands, the Lizard and the Tree. Her book, *Mystery on the Desert*, is on sale for US$10 (proceeds to conservation work) in Nazca. In January 1994 Maria Reiche opened a small **museum** ① *US$1. At the Km 421 marker, 5 km from town, take micro from in front of Ormeño terminal, US$0.75, frequent*. Viktoria Nikitzhi, a colleague of Maria Reiche, gives one-hour lectures about the Nazca Lines at **Dr Maria Reiche Center** ① *US$5, Av de los Espinales 300, 1 block from Ormeño bus stop, T969 9419, viktorianikitzki@hotmail.com*. She also organizes tours in Jun and Dec (phone in advance to confirm times; also ask about volunteer work). See the Planetarium, above. Another good book is *Pathways to the Gods: the mystery of the Nazca Lines*, by Tony Morrison (Michael Russell, 1978).

Other theories abound: claims that the lines are the tracks of running contests (Georg A von Breunig, 1980, and English astronomer Alan Sawyer); that they represent weaving patterns and yarns (Henri Stirlin) and that the plain is a map demonstrating the Tiahuanaco Empire (Zsoltan Zelko). Johan Reinhard proposes that the Lines conform to fertility practices throughout the Andes, in common with the current use of straight lines in Chile and Bolivia.

Another theory is that the ancient Nazcas flew in hot-air balloons, based on the idea that the lines are best seen from the air (Jim Woodman, 1977 and, in part, the BBC series *Ancient Voices*). A related idea is that the lines were not designed to be seen physically from above, but from the mind's eye of the flying shaman. Both theories are supported by pottery and textile evidence which shows balloonists and a flying creature emitting discharge from its nose and mouth. There are also local legends of flying men. Thhe depiction in the desert of creatures such as a monkey or killer whale also indicates the qualities needed by the shaman in his spirit journeys.

After six years' work at La Muña and Los Molinos, Palpa (43 km north of Nazca), and using photogrammetry, Peruvian archaeologist Johny Isla and Markus Reindel of the Swiss-Liechtenstein Foundation deduced that the lines on both the Palpa and Nazca plains are offerings dedicated to the worship of water and fertility, two elements which also dominate on ceramics and on the engraved stones of the Paracas culture. Isla and Reindel believe that the

Palpa lines predate those at Nazca and that the lines and drawings themselves are scaled up versions of the Paracas drawings. This research proposes that the Nazca culture succumbed not to drought, but to heavy rainfall, probably during an El Niño event.

Other excursions

The Nazca area is dotted with over 100 cemeteries and the dry, humidity-free climate has perfectly preserved invaluable tapestries, cloth and mummies. At **Chauchilla** ① *30 km south of Nazca, last 12 km a sandy track, US$3*, grave robbing *huaqueros* ransacked the tombs and left bones, skulls, mummies and pottery shards littering the desert. A tour takes about two hours. Gold mining is one of the main local industries and a tour usually includes a visit to a small family processing shop where the techniques used are still very old-fashioned.

To the **Paredones ruins and aqueduct** ① *US$3.55 entry also includes 4 other archeological sites: El Telar Geoglyphs, Acueductos de Cantayoc, Las Agujas Geoglyphs and Acueductos de Ocongalla*. The ruins, also called Cacsamarca, are Inca on a pre-Inca base; they are not well preserved. The underground aqueducts, built 300 BC-AD 700, are still in working order and worth seeing. Cantayoc Aqueducts, Las Agujas and El Telar Geoglyphs are a 30 minutes to one-hour walk through Buena Fe (or organize a taxi from your hotel), to see markings in the valley floor and ancient aqueducts which descend in spirals into the ground. The markings consist of a triangle pointing to a hill and a telar (cloth) with a spiral depicting the threads. Climb the mountain to see better examples.

Cahuachi ① *US$3.50 entry, US$17 pp on a tour, US$12-15 in private taxi, minimum 2 people; see also the Museo Antonini, above*, one hour to the west of the Nazca Lines along a rough dirt track, comprises some 30 pyramids. Only 5% of the site has been excavated so far, some of which has been reconstructed. It could be larger than Chan Chán, making it the largest adobe city in the world. Some 4 km beyond Cahuachi is a site called **El Estaquería**, thought to have been a series of astronomical sighting posts, but more recent research suggests the wooden pillars were used to dry dead bodies and therefore it may have been a place of mummification.

Reserva Nacional De San Fernando is a gathering place for birds, continental and oceanic mammals. It was established in 2011 as a national reserve to protect migratory and local wild life such as the Humboldt penguin, sea lions, the Andean fox, condor, guanaco, dolphins and whales. San Fernando is located in the highest part of the Peruvian coastal desert, in the same place as Cerro Blanco, the highest dune in the world. Here is where the Nazca Plate lifts the continental plate, generating moist accumulation in the ground with resulting seasonal winter flora and a continental wildlife corridor between the high coastal mountains and the sea. Full-day and two-day/one-night tours are offered by some agencies in town.

Road from Nazca towards Cuzco

Two hours out of Nazca on the newly paved road to Abancay and Cuzco is the **Reserva Nacional Pampas Galeras** at 4100 m, which has a vicuña reserve. There is an interesting Museo del Sitio, also a military base and park guard here. Entry is free. At Km 155 is **Puquio**, then it's another 185 km to **Chalhuanca**. Fuel is available in both towns. There are wonderful views on this stretch, with lots of small villages, valleys and alpacas.

South of Nazca

Ten kilometres north of the fishing village of **Chala** (*Phone code: 054, 173 km from Nazca, many restaurants*) are the large pre-Columbian ruins of **Puerto Inca** on the coast. This was the port for Cuzco. The site is in excellent condition: the drying and store houses can be seen as holes in the ground (be careful where you walk). On the right side of the bay is a cemetery, on the hill a temple of reincarnation, and the Inca road from the coast to Cuzco is clearly visible. The road was 240 km long, with a staging post every 7 km so that, with a change of runner at every post, messages could be sent in 24 hours. The site is best appreciated when the sun is shining.

◉ Nazca and around listings

For hotel and restaurant price codes, and other relevant information, see Essentials.

◉ Where to stay

Nazca *p1305, map p1305*

If arriving by bus beware of touts who tell you that the hotel of your choice is closed, or full. If you phone or email the hotel they will pick you up at the bus station free of charge day or night.

$$$ Casa Andina Classic, Jr Bolognesi 367, T01-213 9739, www.casa-andina.com. This recommended chain of hotels' Nazca property, offering standardized services in distinctive style. Bright, modern decor, central patio with palm trees, pool, restaurant.

$$$ Maison Suisse, opposite airport, T522 434, www.nazcagroup.com. Comfortable, safe car park, expensive restaurant, pool, suites with jacuzzi, good giftshop, shows video of Nazca Lines. Also has camping facilities. Its packages include flights over Nazca Lines.

$$$ Majoro, Panamericana Sur Km 452, T522490, www.hotelmajoro.com. A charming old hacienda about 5 km from town past the airstrip so quite remote, beautiful gardens, pool, slow and expensive restaurant, quiet and welcoming, good arrangements for flights and tours.

$$$ Nazca Lines, Jr Bolognesi 147, T522293. With a/c, rather dated rooms with private patio, hot water, peaceful, restaurant, safe car park, pool (US$9-10.50 pp includes sandwich and drink), they can arrange package tours which include 2-3 nights at the hotel plus a flight over the lines and a desert trip.

$$$-$$ Oro Viejo, Callao 483, T521112, www.hoteloroviejo.net. Has a suite with jacuzzi and comfortable standard rooms, nice garden, swimming pool, restaurant and bar. Recommended.

$$ Alegría, Jr Lima 166, T522497, www.hotel alegria.net. Small breakfast, bus terminal transfers. Rooms with hot water, cafeteria, pool, garden, English, Hebrew, Italian and German spoken, laundry facilities, book exchange, restaurant, ATM, parking, OK but can be noisy from disco and traffic. Also has a tour agency and guests are encouraged to buy tours (see What to do), flights and bus tickets arranged.

$$ La Encantada, Callao 592, T522930, www. hotellaencantada.com.pe. Pleasant modern hotel with restaurant, laundry and parking.

$$ Paredones Inn, Jr Lima 600, T522181. 1 block from the Plaza de Armas, modern, colourful rooms, great views from roof terrace, laundry service, bar, suites with minibar, microwave, jacuzzi, helpful staff.

$$ Posada de Don Hono, Av María Reiche 112, T506822, laposadadedonhono1@hotmail. com. Small rooms and nice bungalows, good café, parking.

$ Hostal Alegría, Av Los Incas 117, opposite Ormeño bus terminal, T522497. Basic, hot water, hammocks, nice garden, camping, restaurant.

$ Nasca, C Lima 438, T522085, marionasca13@ hotmail.com. Hot water, with or without bath, laundry facilities, new annexe at the back, nice garden, safe motorcycle parking.

$ Posada Guadalupe, San Martín 225, T522249. Family run, lovely courtyard and garden, hot water, with or without bath, good breakfast, relaxing. (Touts selling tours are nothing to do with hotel.)

$ Sol de Nasca, Callao 586, T522730. Rooms with and without hot showers, restaurant, pleasant, don't leave valuables in luggage store.

South of Nazca *p1307*

$$$-$$ Puerto Inka, 2 km along a side road from Km 610 Panamericana Sur (reservations T054-778458), www.puertoinka.com.pe. Bungalows on the beautiful beach, hammocks outside, indoor games room, disco, breakfast extra, great place to relax, kayaks, boat hire, diving equipment rental, pleasant camping US$5, low season discounts, used by tour groups, busy in summer.

❼ Restaurants

Nazca *p1305, map p1305*

$$$-$$ Vía La Encantada, Bolognesi 282 (website as hotel above). Modern, stylish with great food, fish, meat or vegetarian, good value lunches.

$$-$ Mamashana, Bolognesi 270. Rustic style with a lively atmosphere, for breakfast, grills, pastas and pizzas.

$$-$ La Choza, Bolognesi 290. Nice decor with woven chairs and thatched roof, all types of food, live music at night. Single women may be put off by the crowds of young men hanging around the doors handing out flyers.

$$-$ La Taberna, Jr Lima 321, T521411. Excellent food, live music, popular with gringos, it's worth a look just for the graffiti on the walls.

$ Chifa Guang Zhou, Bolognesi 297, T522036. Very good.

$ El Huarango, Arica 602. National and international cuisine. Relaxed family atmosphere and deliciously breezy terrace.

$ Kañada, Lima 160, nazcanada@yahoo.com. Cheap, good *menú*, excellent pisco sours, nice wines, popular, display of local artists' work, email service, English spoken, helpful.

$ Los Angeles, Bolognesi 266. Good, cheap, try *sopa criolla*, and chocolate cake.

$ Rico Pollo, Lima 190. Good local restaurant with great chicken dishes.

Coffee Break, Bolognesi 219. Open 0700-2300 except Sat. For real coffee and good pizzas.

Fuente de Soda Jumbory, near the cinema. Good *almuerzo*.

Panadería, Bolognesi 387.

☺ What to do

Nazca *p1305, map p1305*
All guides must be approved by the Ministry of Tourism and should have an official identity card. Touts (*jaladores*) operate at popular hotels and the bus terminals using false ID cards and fake hotel and tour brochures. They are rip-off merchants who overcharge and mislead those who arrive by bus. Only conduct business with agencies at their office, or phone or email the company you want to deal with in advance. Some hotels are not above pressurising guests to purchase tours at inflated prices. Taxi drivers usually act as guides, but most speak only Spanish. Do not take just any taxi on the plaza for a tour, always ask your hotel for a reputable driver.

Air Nasca Travel, Jr Lima 185, T521027, guide Susi recommended. Very helpful and competitive prices. Can do all types of tours around Nazca, Ica, Paracas and Pisco.

Algería Tours, Lima 186, T523431, http://alegriatoursperu.com. Offers inclusive tours, guides with radio contact and maps can be provided for hikes to nearby sites. Guides speak English, German, French and Italian. They also offer adventure tours, such as mountain biking from 4000 m in the Andes down to the plain, sandboarding, and more.

Félix Quispe Sarmiento, 'El Nativo de Nazca'. He has his own museum, Hantun Nazca, at Panamericana Sur 447 and works with the Ministerio de Cultura, tours off the beaten track, can arrange flights, knowledgeable, ask for him at Kañada restaurant.

Fernández family, who run the **Hotel Nasca**, also run local tours. Ask for the hotel owners and speak to them direct.

Huarango Travel Service, Arica 602, T522141, huarangotravel@yahoo.es. Tours around Ica, Paracas, Huacachina, Nazca and Palpa.

Mystery Peru, Simón Bolívar 221, T01-435 0051, T956-691155, www.mysteryperu.com. Owned by Enrique Levano Alarcón, based in Nazca with many local tours, also packages throughout Peru.

Nazca Perú 4x4, Bolognesi 367 (in Casa Andina), T522928, or 1975-017029. Tubular 4WD tours to San Fernando National Reserve and other off-the-beaten-track locations.

Tours of the Nazca Lines
On land Taxi-guides to the mirador, 0800-1200, cost US$5-8 pp, or you can hitch, but there is not always much traffic. Travellers suggest the view from the hill 500 m back to Nazca is better. Go early as the site gets very hot. Or take a taxi and arrive at 0745 before the buses.

By air Small planes take 3-5 passengers to see the Nazca Lines. Flights last 30-35 mins and are controlled by air traffic personnel at the airport to avoid congestion. The price for a flight is around US$130 pp. You also have to pay US$10 airport tax. It is best to organize a flight with the airlines themselves at the airport. They will weigh you and select a group of passengers based on weight, so you may have to wait a while for your turn. Flights are bumpy with many tight turns – many people get airsick so it's wise not to eat or drink just before a flight. Best times to fly are 0800-1000 and 1500-1630 when there is less turbulence and better light (assuming there is no fog). Make sure you clarify everything before getting on the plane and ask for a receipt. Also let them know in

advance if you have any special requests. Taxi to airport, US$5, bus, US$0.25 (most tours include transport). **Note** Be aware that fatal crashes by planes flying over the lines do occur. Some foreign governments advise tourists not to take these flights and some companies will not provide insurance for passengers until safety and maintenance standards are improved.
Aero Diana, see above under Pisco, Air, and **Aero Paracas**, T01-641 7000, www.aeroparacas. com, offer daily flights over the Lines.
Alas Peruanas, T522444, http://alasperuanas. com. Flights can also be booked at **Hotel Alegría**. Experienced pilots. They also offer 1-hr flights over the Palpa and Llipata areas, where you can see more designs and other rare patterns (US$130 pp, minimum 3) and Nazca and Palpa combined (US$250). See the website for promotional offers. All **Alas Peruanas** flights include the BBC film of Nazca.

⊖ Transport

Nazca *p1305, map p1305*
Bus It is worth paying the extra for a good bus – reports of robbery on the cheaper services. Over-booking is common.
    To **Lima**, 446 km, 7 hrs, several buses and colectivos daily, US$23-26. **Ormeño**, T522058, *Royal Class* at 0530 and 1330 from Hotel Nazca Lines, normal service from Av Los Incas, 6 a day; **Civa**, Av Guardia Civil, T523019, normal

service at 2300; **Cruz del Sur**, Lima y San Martín, T523713, via Ica and Paracas, luxury service, US$39-55. **Ormeño** to **Ica**, 2 hrs, US$3.50, 4 a day. For **Pisco** (210 km), 3 hrs, buses stop 5 km outside town (see under Pisco, Transport), so change in Ica for direct transport into Pisco. To **Arequipa**, 565 km, 9 hrs, US$19-22.50, or US$28-52 *bus cama* services: **Ormeño**, from Av Los Incas, Royal Class at 2130, 8 hrs, also **Cruz del Sur** and **Oltursa**, Av los Incas 103, T522265, reliable, comfortable and secure on this route. Delays are possible out of Nazca because of drifting sand across the road or because of mudslides in the rainy season. Travel in daylight if possible. Book your ticket on previous day.
    Buses to Cuzco, 659 km, via **Chalhuanca** and **Abancay** (13 hrs). The highway from Nazca to Cuzco is paved and is safe for bus travellers, drivers of private vehicles and motorcyclists. To **Cuzco** with **Ormeño**, US$50, and **Cruz del Sur**, 2015, 2100, US$50-70.

South of Nazca: Puerto Inca *p1307*
Taxi from **Chala** US$8, or take a colectivo to Nazca as far as the turnoff for Puerto Inca, Km 610, if it has space, about US$6, beware overcharging.

ⓘ Directory

Nazca *p1305, map p1305*
Useful addresses Police: at Av Los Incas, T522105, or T105 for emergencies.

Arequipa and the far south

The colonial city of Arequipa, with its guardian volcano, El Misti, is the ideal place to start exploring southern Peru. It is the gateway to two of the world's deepest canyons, Colca and Cotahuasi, whose villages and terraces hold onto a traditional way of life and whose skies are home to the magnificent condor. From Arequipa there are routes to Lake Titicaca and to the border with Chile.

Arequipa → *Phone code: 054. Colour map 6, A1. Population: 1 million. Altitude: 2380 m.*

The city of Arequipa, 1011 km from Lima, stands in a beautiful valley at the foot of El Misti volcano, a snow-capped, perfect cone, 5822 m high, guarded on either side by the mountains Chachani (6057 m), and Pichu-Pichu (5669 m). The city has fine Spanish buildings and many old and interesting churches built of sillar, a pearly white volcanic material almost exclusively used in the construction of Arequipa. The city was re-founded on 15 August 1540 by an emissary of Pizarro, but it had previously been occupied by Aymara Indians and the Incas. It is the main commercial centre for the south and is a busy place. Its people resent the general tendency to believe that everything is run from Lima. It has been declared a World Cultural Heritage site by UNESCO.

Arriving in Arequipa

Orientation The **airport** is 7 km west. It takes about half an hour to town. The main **bus terminal** is south of the centre, 15 minutes from the centre by colectivo, 10 minutes by taxi.
▶ *See also Transport, page 1330.*

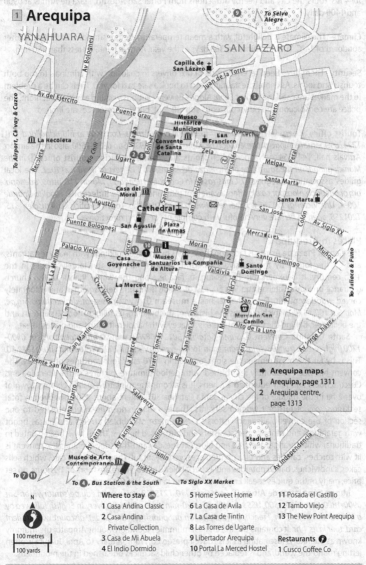

Arequipa

Where to stay 🛏
1 Casa Andina Classic
2 Casa Andina Private Collection
3 Casa de Mi Abuela
4 El Indio Dormido
5 Home Sweet Home
6 La Casa de Avila
7 La Casa de Tintin
8 Las Torres de Ugarte
9 Libertador Arequipa
10 Portal La Merced Hostel
11 Posada el Castillo
12 Tambo Viejo
13 The New Point Arequipa

Restaurants 🍴
1 Cusco Coffee Co

➡ **Arequipa maps**
1 Arequipa, page 1311
2 Arequipa centre, page 1313

The main places of interest and the hotels are within walking distance of the Plaza de Armas. If you are going to the suburbs, take a bus or taxi. A cheap tour of the city can be made in a *Vallecito* bus, 1½ hours for US$0.50. It is a circular tour which goes down Calle Jerusalén and Calle San Juan de Dios. Alternatively an **open-top bus** ① *T203434, www.bustour.com.pe, US$17 for 4 hrs*, tours the city and nearby attractions from Portal San Agustín, Plaza de Armas at 0900 and 1400 daily.

Climate The climate is delightful, with a mean temperature before sundown of 23°C, and after sundown of 14°C. The sun shines on 360 days of the year. Annual rainfall is less than 150 mm.

Security There have been recent reports of taxi drivers in collusion with criminals to rob both tourists and locals. Ask hotels, restaurants, etc, to book a safe taxi for you. Theft can be a problem in the market area and the park at Selva Alegre. Be very cautious walking anywhere at night. The police are conspicuous, friendly, courteous and efficient, but their resources are limited.

Tourist office i perú ① *central office is in the Plaza de Armas, Portal de la Municipalidad 110, T223265, iperuarequipa@promperu.gob.pe, Mon-Sat 0830-1930, Sun 0830-1600,* also in the airport Arrivals hall, T444564, only open when flights are arriving. **Municipal tourist office** ① *in the Municipalidad, on the south side of the Plaza de Armas, No 112 next to iPerú, T211021.* The local guides' association, **Adegopa** ① *Claustros de la Compañía, tienda 11, Morán 118, http://adegopa. org or adegopa.blogspot.co.uk,* offers a variety of tours and activities. **Indecopi** ① *Hipólito Unanue 100-A, Urb Victoria, T212054, mlcornejo@indecopi.gob.pe.* The **Tourist Police** ① *Jerusalén 315, T201258, open 24 hrs,* are very helpful with complaints or giving directions.

Places in Arequipa

The elegant **Plaza de Armas** is faced on three sides by arcaded buildings with many restaurants, and on the fourth by the massive **Cathedral**, founded in 1612 and largely rebuilt in the 19th century. It is remarkable for having its façade along the whole length of the church (entrance on Santa Catalina and San Francisco). Inside is the fine Belgian organ and elaborately carved wooden pulpit. The Cathedral has a **museum** ① *www.museocatedralarequipa.org.pe, Mon-Sat 1000-1700,* which outlines the history of the building, its religious objects and art and the belltower. Behind the Cathedral there is an alley with handicraft shops and places to eat.

Santa Catalina Convent ① *Santa Catalina 301, T608282, www.santacatalina.org.pe, 0900-1700 (high season from 0800, last admission 1600), evening visits till 2000 on Tue and Thu, US$12.50.* This is by far the most remarkable sight, opened in 1970 after four centuries of mystery. The convent has been beautifully refurbished, with period furniture, pictures of the Arequipa and Cuzco schools and fully equipped kitchens. It is a complete miniature walled colonial town of over 2 ha in the middle of the city at Santa Catalina 301, where about 450 nuns lived in total seclusion, except for their women servants. The few remaining nuns have retreated to one section of the convent, allowing visitors to see a maze of cobbled streets and plazas bright with geraniums and other flowers, cloisters and buttressed houses. These have been painted in traditional white, orange, deep red and blue. On Tuesday and Thursday evenings the convent is lit with torches, candles and blazing fireplaces, very beautiful. There is a good café, which sells cakes, sandwiches, baked potatoes and a special blend of tea. There are tours of 1½ hours, no set price, many of the guides speak English or German (a tip of US$6 is expected).

Museo Santuarios de Altura ① *La Merced 110, T215013, www.ucsm.edu.pe/santury, Mon-Sat 0900-1800, Sun 0900-1500, US$5.25 includes a 20-min video of the discovery in English followed by a guided tour in English, French, German, Italian or Spanish (tip the guide), discount with student card, tour lasts 1 hr.* It contains the frozen Inca mummies found on Mount Ampato; the mummy known as 'Juanita' is fascinating as it is so well preserved. From January to April, Juanita is often jetting round the world, and is replaced by other child sacrifices unearthed in the mountains.

② Arequipa centre

➡ **Arequipa maps**
1 Arequipa, page 1311
2 Arequipa centre, page 1313

| 50 metres |
| 50 yards |

Where to stay 🛏
1 Casablanca Hostal B1
2 Casa de Melgar A2
3 Hostal Regis A1
4 Hostal Santa Catalina A1
5 Hostal Solar A2
6 La Casa de Margott A2
7 La Fiorentina A2
8 La Posada del Cacique A2
9 La Posada del Virrey A2
10 Los Andes B&B B1
11 Sonesta Posadas
   del Inca B1

Restaurants 🍴
1 Antojitos de Arequipa B2
2 Ary Quepay A2
3 Bóveda San Agustín B1
4 Bruno Pizzería A1
5 Café Capriccio B2
6 Café Manolo B2
7 Café Valenzuela B2

8 Chicha B1
9 Crepísimo A1
10 El Asador A1
11 El Turko B2
12 Fez B1
13 La Alemana B1
14 La Canasta B2
15 Lakshmivan A2
16 La Trattoria del
   Monasterio A1
17 Mandala A2
18 Paladar 1900 B1
19 Qochamama A1
20 Ras El Hanout y
   los 40 Sabores A1
21 Sonccollay B1
22 Suri B2
23 Wayrana B1
24 Zig Zag A1

Bars & clubs 🍸
25 Casona Forum &
   Déjà Vu A1
26 Farren's B1

Arequipa is said to have the best preserved colonial architecture in Peru, apart from Cuzco. As well as the many fine churches, there are several fine seignorial houses with large carved tympanums over the entrances. Built as single-storey structures, they have mostly withstood earthquakes. They have small patios with no galleries, flat roofs and small windows, disguised by superimposed lintels or heavy grilles. Good examples are the 18th-century **Casa Tristán del Pozo**, or **Gibbs-Ricketts house** ① *San Francisco 108, Mon-Sat 0915-1245, 1600-1800*, with its fine portal and puma-head waterspouts (now a bank). **Casa del Moral** ① *Moral 318 y Bolívar, Mon-Sat 0900-1700, Sun 0900-1300, US$1.80, US$1 for students*, also known as Williams house. It is now a bank and has a museum. **Casa Goyeneche** ① *La Merced 201 y Palacio Viejo*, also a bank office, ask the guards to let you view the courtyard and fine period rooms. The oldest district is **San Lázaro**, a collection of tiny climbing streets and houses quite close to the **Hotel Libertador**, where you can find the ancient **Capilla de San Lázaro**.

Among the many fine churches is **La Compañía** ① *General Morán y Alvarez Thomas*, the main façade (1698) and side portal (1654) are striking examples of the florid Andean *mestizo* style. To the left of the sanctuary is the **Capilla Real** (Royal Chapel) ① *Mon-Fri 0900-1230, 1500-1930, Sat 1130-1230, 1500-1800, Sun 0900-1230, 1700-1800, with mass every day at 1200, free but donations box by the main altar*. Its San Ignacio chapel has a beautiful polychrome cupola. Also well worth seeing is the church of **San Francisco** ① *Zela 103, US$1.65*, opposite which is the interesting **Museo Histórico Municipal** ① *Plaza San Francisco 407, Mon-Fri 0900-1700, US$0.70*, with much war memorabilia and some impressive photos of the city in the aftermath of several notable earthquakes. **La Recoleta** ① *Jr Recoleta 117, T270966, Mon-Sat 0900-1200, 1500-1700, US$1.50*, a Franciscan monastery built in 1647, stands on the other side of the river, on Recoleta. A seldom-visited gem it contains a variety of exhibits. As well as several cloisters and a religious art museum, the pre-Columbian art museum contains ceramics and textiles produced by cultures of the Arequipa area. Most impressive however is the museum of Amazon exploration featuring many artifacts as well as photos of early Franciscan missionaries in the Amazon. The library, containing many antique books, is available for supervised visits at 45 minutes past the hour for 15 minutes when the museum is open.

The central **San Camilo market**, between Perú, San Camilo, Piérola and Alto de la Luna, is worth visiting, as is the **Siglo XX market**, to the east of the rail station. **Museo de Arte Contemporáneo** ① *Tacna y Arica 201, T221068, Tue-Fri 1000-1700, Sat-Sun 1000-1400, US$1*, in the old railway station, is dedicated to painting and photography from 1900 onwards. The building is surrounded by gardens and has a Sunday market. Universidad de San Agustín's **Archaeological Museum** ① *Alvarez Thomas y Palacio Viejo, T288881, Mon-Fri 0815-1700*, has an interesting collection of ceramics and mummies, tracing the region's history from pre-Columbian times to the Republican era.

Excursions near Arequipa

At **Yanahuara**, 2 km northwest, is a 1750 *mestizo*-style church, with a magnificent churrigueresque façade, all in sillar (opens 1500). On the same plaza is a *mirador*, through whose arches there is a fine view of El Misti with the city at its feet, a popular spot in the late afternoon. The **Museo Pre Inca de Chiribaya** ① *Miguel Grau 402, www.museochiribaya.org, Mon-Sat 0830-1900, Sun 0900-1500*, has a good collection of vessels and well-preserved textiles from a culture that had a high importance in the area before the arrival of the Incas. To get to Yanahuara, cross the Puente Grau, turn right up Avenida Bolognesi.

Some 3 km past **Tingo**, beside the Río Sabandía on the Huasacanche road, is **La Mansión del Fundador** ① *0900-1700, US$4.50*. Originally owned by the founder of Arequipa, Don Garcí Manuel de Carbajal, it has been restored as a museum with original furnishings and paintings; also has cafetería and bar.

About 8 km southeast of Arequipa is the **Molino de Sabandía** ① *US$3.75, ring bell for admission; round trip by taxi US$6*. This is the first stone mill in the area, built in 1621. It has been fully restored and the guardian diverts water to run the grinding stones when visitors arrive. Adjoining Sabandía is **Yumina** ① *tourist fee of US$6 payable, which may be asked for on the bus to Chivay*, with many Inca terraces which are still in use.

Climbing El Misti and Chachani At 5822 m, El Misti volcano offers a relatively straightforward opportunity to scale a high peak. There are three routes for climbing the volcano; all take two days. The northeast route starts from the Aguada Blanca reservoir, reached by 4WD, from where a four-hour hike takes you to the Monte Blanco camp at 4800 m. Then it's a five- to six-hour ascent to the top. Two hours takes you back down to the trail. The southwest route involves taking a 4WD vehicle to the trailhead at Pastores (3400 m), followed by a hike of five or six hours to a camp at 4700 m. A five-hour climb takes you to the summit, before a three-hour descent to the trail. A southern route (Grau) also starts at 3400 m, with a camp at 4610 m, followed by a five-hour hike to the summit and a two-hour descent. Be prepared for early starts and take plenty of water, food and protection against the weather. Favoured months are May to September.

Climbing Chachani (6057 m), northwest of El Misti, is also popular. This peak retains its icy covering longer than El Misti, though this is fast disappearing. Remember that both summits are at a very high altitude and that this, combined with climbing on scree, makes it hard going for the untrained. Always contact an experienced guiding agency or professional guide in Arequipa as you should never climb alone (see What to do, page 1319).

⊙ Arequipa listings

For hotel and restaurant price codes, and other relevant information, see Essentials.

⊕ Where to stay

Arequipa *p1310, maps p1311 and p1313*
When arriving by bus, do not believe taxi drivers who say the hotel of your choice is closed or full. This applies to many of the popular hotels, drivers will try to take you to another hotel which pays them a high commission. Phone in advance, or ring the door bell and check for yourself.

$$$$ Casa Andina Private Collection, Ugarte 403, T226907, www.casa-andina.com. Luxury hotel in a restored 18th-century mansion, former Casa de la Moneda. 5 large suites in colonial building, 36 rooms in modern extension off 2nd courtyard. Gourmet restaurant, room service, business centre, roof terrace with views.

$$$$ Libertador Arequipa, Plaza Simón Bolívar, Selva Alegre, T215110, www.libertador.com. pe. Safe, large comfortable rooms, good service, swimming pool (cold), gardens, good meals, pub-style bar, cocktail lounge, squash court.

$$$$ Sonesta Posadas del Inca, Portal de Flores 116, T215530, www.sonesta.com/ arequipa. On Plaza de Armas, all the services associated with this chain, comfortable modern rooms, Inkafé restaurant and bar overlooking plaza, good food, tiny outdoor pool, business centre with internet.

$$$ Casa Andina Classic, C Jerusalén 603, T202070, www.casa-andina.com. Part of the attractive Casa Andina chain, with breakfast, comfortable and colourful, central, modern, good restaurant, safe, parking.

$$$-$$ La Casa de Margott, Jerusalén 304, T229517, www.lacasademargott.com. Family-run, bright with a massive palm tree in patio, spacious, convenient, small bar/café, security box.

$$ Casablanca Hostal, Puente Bolognesi 104, a few metres from the Plaza de Armas, T221327, www.casablancahostal.com. Super stylish *hostal*, lovely minimalist rooms in a colonial building. Ambient lighting, rooms with exposed stone walls, hot water, most with balcony.

$$ Casa de Mi Abuela, Jerusalén 606, T241206, www.lacasademiabuela.com. Safe, hot water, laundry, swimming pool, rooms at the back are quieter and overlook the garden, English spoken, parking, restaurant and piano bar, breakfast or evening snacks on patio or in beautiful garden.

$$ Hostal Solar, Ayacucho 108, T241793, www.hostalsolar.com. Colonial building, hot water, good breakfast served in nice patio, sun lounge on roof, very secure, multilingual staff.

$$ La Casa de Avila, San Martín 116, Vallecito, T213177, www.casadeavila.com. Rooms with hot water on 2 floors around spacious, sunny garden, computers for guests' use, can arrange airport/bus station pick-up, recommended Spanish courses held in the garden and other activities.

$$ La Casa de Tintin, Urbanización San Isidro F1, Vallecito, T284700, www.hoteltintin.com. 15 mins' walk, 5 mins by taxi from the Plaza de Armas, Belgian/Peruvian-owned, hot water, garden, terrace, sauna, massage, laundry service, restaurant, café and bar, mountain bike rental, very pleasant and comfortable.

$$ Posada el Castillo, Pasaje Campos 105, Vallecito, T201828, www.posadaelcastillo.com. Dutch/Peruvian-owned, in an old house decorated with utensils found in the renovation, 20 mins by taxi from city centre. Variety of rooms and suites, some with balcony and view of El Misti, wonderful breakfast in new annexe, pool, lovely gardens, a good choice.

$$-$ Portal La Merced Hostel, La Merced 131, T330481, PortalLaMercedHostel on Facebook. Quiet, central, private rooms and dorms, beds only so-so, good breakfast, good service, laundry, travel agency.

$ Casa de Melgar, Melgar 108, T222459, www.lacasademelgar.com. 18th-century building, excellent rooms with bath, hot water (solar), safe, courtyard, good breakfast buffet. Good taxi driver (Angel).

$ El Indio Dormido, Av Andrés Avelino Cáceres B-9, T427401, http://members.tripod. com/h_indio_dormido/. Close to bus terminal, free transport to centre, rooms with bath, kitchen, cafeteria, parking, laundry, TV room, very helpful, family-run.

$ Home Sweet Home, Rivero 509A, T405982, www.homesweethome-peru.com. Run by María and daughter Cathy, who runs a travel agency and speaks Spanish, English, Italian, French, very helpful, warm and inviting atmosphere, substantial fresh breakfast included. Private or shared bath, hot water all day, simple rooms.

$ Hostal Regis, Ugarte 202, T226111, hostalregis@hotmail.com. Colonial house, French-style interior, hot water all day, use of fridge and laundry facilities, sun terrace with good views, street-facing rooms with sound-proofed windows, safe deposit, video rental and guide books and English language magazines for reference, tours arranged, but poor breakfast.

$ Hostal Santa Catalina, Santa Catalina 500, T243705, www.hostalsantacatalinaperu.com. On busy corner, rooms arranged around a courtyard, roof terrace with great views, helpful staff. Simple rooms with fridge, private or shared bath, hot water, laundry, security box. Can arrange trips and accommodation in other cities.

$ La Fiorentina, Puente Grau 110, T202571. With or without bath, hot water, comfortable, family atmosphere, tours arranged, laundry facilities, café bar and TV room.

$ La Posada del Cacique, Puente Grau 219 and at Jerusalén 404, T202170, posadadelcacique@yahoo.es. At Puente Grau is an old house with tall ceilings, teeny patio, sun terrace, hot water, English spoken, family atmosphere, private or shared bath, also dorm accommodation, breakfast available, laundry service, will pick up from terminal. Jerusalén branch is good value and helpful, with roof terrace, bar, café/restaurant.

$ La Posada del Virrey, Puente Grau 103, T224050. Spacious rooms with and without bath, dorms, hot water, kitchen and laundry facilities, helpful, café bar, small patio.

$ Las Torres de Ugarte, Ugarte 401, T283532, www.hotelista.com. Round the corner from Santa Catalina convent, hot water, laundry service, reflexology, roof terrace, parking, safe, luggage store. Some rooms are bungalow style in colonial part at the back.

$ Los Andes Bed & Breakfast, La Merced 123, T330015, www.losandesarequipa.com. Good value, kitchen use, hot water, large rooms with waxed wood floors and minimalist decor, TV rooms, pleasant roof terrace.

$ Lula's B&B, in Cayma, T272517, 959 992995, www.bbaqpe.com. Same owners as **Ari Quipay** language school, Lula (Peruvian) and her husband (Swiss) speak Spanish, English, German and French, with airport/bus terminal pick-up, modern, charming, quiet, meals available.

$ The New Point Arequipa, Palacio Viejo 325, T286920, www.thepointhostels.com. Very central, small, medium and large dorms, great place to meet other travellers, information on nightlife, lots of services (laundry, DVDs etc), games room and travel centre.

$ Tambo Viejo, Av Malecón Socabaya 107, IV Centenario, T288195, www.tamboviejo.com. 5 blocks south of the plaza near the rail station. 15 rooms ranging from double with bath to dormitory, quiet, English and Dutch spoken, walled garden, hot water, choice of 8 fresh breakfasts (extra), vegetarian restaurant, laundry service, safe deposit, coffee shop, bar, book exchange (2 for 1), money changed, tourist information for guests, bike rental, luggage store extra, tours and volcano climbs arranged. For a small fee, you can use the facilities if passing through. Free pick-up from bus terminal 0700-2300 (call when arriving), US$10 for airport pick-up.

❼ Restaurants

Arequipa *p1310, maps p1311 and p1313*

$$$ Chicha, Santa Catalina 210, int 105, T287360. The menu of mostly local and fusion dishes is created by Gastón Acurio, fine dining in a historic building opposite Santa Catalina.

$$$ Paladar 1900, San Francisco 227. In the same group as **El Turko**, stylish, contemporary design, Peruvian cuisine with a modern twist.

$$$ Wayrana, Santa Catalina 200, T285641. Traditional Arequipa dishes with a modern twist, specializing in sea food, *cuy*, and alpaca. Beautiful colonial building with stylish interior design.

$$$ Zig Zag, Zela 210, T206020. In a colonial house, European (including Swiss) and local dishes, meats include ostrich and alpaca, delicious. Book in advance.

$$$-$$ El Cebillano, C Misti 110, Yanahuara, T484866. Excellent cevichería in Yanahuara suburb, with good seafood, attentive service and long queues at weekends.

$$$-$$ La Trattoria del Monasterio, Santa Catalina 309, T204062, www.latrattoriadel monasterio.com. A fusion of Italian and Arequipeño styles and ingredients, in a cloister in the Convento,

$$ Ary Quepay, Jerusalén 502. Open 1000-2400. Excellent local meat and vegetarian dishes, very touristy but fun.

$$ Café-Restaurante Bóveda San Agustín, Portal San Agustín 127-129, T243596. Opens at 0700. Attractive, downstairs bar type atmosphere, upstairs balcony overlooking the Plaza de Armas, good value breakfasts and lunches, evening specials.

$$ Crepisimo at Santa Catalina 208, T206620. Great coffee and a huge variety of sweet and savoury crepes, magazines and board games.

$$ Sonccollay, Portal de San Agustin 149, www.sonccollay.com. Open 0800-2200. Serving 'Inca and Pre-Inca' dishes, stone-cooked alpaca steaks and meats are a speciality (you can view the kitchen), entertaining owner, copious *chicha* and generous pisco sours. It has a seafood branch, **Qochamama**, Ugarte 300 p 2, T231407, which is more of a bar in the evening.

$$-$ El Asador, Zela 201, T223414. Good value for alpaca steaks, *parrillada*, pleasant atmosphere, good music.

$ Bruno Pizzería, Jerusalén y Santa Marta. Pizzas and pastas with good lunch and dinner menus.

$ El Turko, San Francisco 223-25. Open 0700-2200. Bright café/bar selling kebabs, coffee, breakfasts recommended, good sandwiches. Has a branch at the airport.

$ Fez, San Francisco 229 and **Istanbul**, San Francisco 231-A. More up-market restaurants run by same company as **El Turko**. Delicious falafel and Middle Eastern fast food, including vegetarian. Good coffee, pleasant courtyard.

$ Lakshmivan, Jerusalén 408, T228768. Vegetarian whole food restaurant, set breakfast, lunch and dinner options for under US$2.50, pleasant courtyard, good value and healthy, but slow service.

$ Mandala, Jerusalén 207, T229974. Good-value vegetarian, breakfast, 3 set menus for lunch, buffet, dinner, friendly staff.

$ Ras El Hanout y los 40 Sabores, Santa Catalina 300 B-1, T212424, www.raselhanout40. com. Moroccan 'resto-lounge', breakfast, tagines, keftas, salads, juices and world music.

Cafés

Antojitos de Arequipa, Morán 125-A. An Arequipeñan institution, sells traditional sweets.

Café Capriccio, Mercaderes 121. Not that cheap, but excellent coffee, cakes, etc. Very popular with local business people. Also has **Capriccio Gourmet** on Santa Catalina, which is also good.

Café Manolo, Mercaderes 107 and 113. Great cakes and coffee, also cheap lunches.

Café Valenzuela, Morán 114. Fantastic coffee (also sells beans and ground coffee), locals' favourite.

La Canasta, Jerusalén 115. Excellent baguettes twice daily, also serves breakfast and delicious apple and brazil nut pastries, courtyard seating.

Cusco Coffee Co, La Merced 135, T281152. Good variety of coffees, cakes, average sandwiches, comfy sofas, Wi-Fi.

La Alemana, San Francisco 137. Wide choice of sausages, plus very good *empanadas* and sandwiches. Good value and popular.

Suri, Portal de Flores 128, T237202. The best chicken pie in Arequipa and more, great for a cheap quick snack while you look out on the Plaza.

Typical Arequipeño food is available at the San Camilo market. *Picanterías*, also called *restaurantes típicos*, are also places to find highly spiced dishes. The local chocolate is excellent: **La Ibérica**, in Patio del Ekeko, Mercaderes 141 (see Shopping); also at Morán 160, is top quality, but expensive. There are mini *chocolaterías* everywhere.

🌙 Bars and clubs

Arequipa *p1310, maps p1311 and p1313*

Casona Forum, San Francisco 317. Opens 1800 every day. Huge complex which hosts the Retro Bar, Zero pool bar, Forum Rock Café, Terrasse lounge and Chill Out Sofa Bar. With live music, underground club with huge imitation waterfall and top floor classy restaurant with great views of the city.

Déjà Vu, San Francisco 319-B. Open 2000-2400. Café/restaurant and bar, good food, DJ evenings, shows movies, has rooftop bar and often live music, weekend drinks specials, popular. **Farren's**, Pasaje Catedral. Good meeting place, pool table, great music.

⊛ Festivals

Arequipa *p1310, maps p1311 and p1313*
A full list of the department's many festivals is available locally from iPerú.
10 Jan Sor Ana de Los Angeles y Monteagudo, festival for the patron saint of Santa Catalina monastery. **Mar-Apr** Semana Santa celebrations involve huge processions every night, culminating in the burning of an effigy of Judas on Easter Sunday in the main plazas of Cayma and Yanahuara, and the reading of his will, containing criticisms of the city authorities. **27 Apr** The celebration of the apostle Santiago. **May** is known as the Mes de Las Cruces, with ceremonies on hilltops throughout the city. **3 Aug** A procession through the city bearing the images of Santo Domingo and San Francisco. **6-31 Aug** Fiesta Artesanal del Fundo El Fierro is a sale and exhibition of *artesanía* from all parts of Peru, taking place near Plaza San Francisco. **6-17 Aug** Celebration of the city's anniversary (the 15th, many events including a mass ascent of El Misti). **2 Nov** Day of the Dead celebrations in cemeteries.

O Shopping

Arequipa *p1310, maps p1311 and p1313*
Alpaca goods, textiles and clothing
Alpaca 21, Jerusalén 115, of 125, T213425. Recommended.
Kuna by Alpaca 111, in the Patio del Ekeko (see below), Casona Santa Catalina, Santa Catalina 210, Local 1-2, T282485, in the **Hotel Libertador**, T223303, www.kuna.com.pe. High-quality alpaca and wool products. See also www.incalpaca.com.
Las Clausulas de La Compañía, Morán 140. Handicrafts shopping centre in a colonial setting, containing many alpaca knitwear outlets including a factory outlet in the second patio.
Michell y Cia, Juan de la Torre 101, T202525, www.michell.com.pe. Factory outlet, excellent place for alpaca yarn in huge variety of colours, also a clearance room for baby and adult alpaca yarn is sold. They also sell other types of wool. Alpaca garments also for sale. 1920s machinery on display. Michell has opened an outlet, **Sol Alpaca**, Santa Catalina 210 (inside La Casona Santa Catalina), T221454, with branches in Lima and Cuzco, for their latest lines in alpaca and pima cotton clothing.
Millma's Baby Alpaca, Pasaje Catedral 117, T205134, millmas@hotmail.com. 100% baby alpaca goods, run by Peruvian family, high quality, beautiful designs, good prices.

Bookshops
Librería El Lector, San Francisco 213. Wide selection, including of Peruvian authors, book exchange in various languages (2 for 1), stocks *Footprint*.
Librerías San Francisco has branches at Portal de Flores 138, San Francisco 102-106 and 133-135. Books on Arequipa and Peru, some in English.
SBS Book Service, San Francisco 125, T205317. Has a good selection of travel books etc.

Markets
The covered market opposite the Teatro Municipal in C Mercaderes is recommended for knitted goods, bags, etc.
Note that in both Arequipa and Cuzco it is becoming common to find painted and unpainted souvenir condor feathers in the markets. Condors are being killed for this trade. It is illegal in Peru to sell or purchase condor feathers and the crime carries a sentence of 4 years in prison.
Fundo del Fierro, the large handicraft market behind the old prison on Plaza San Francisco, is also worth a visit.

Shopping centres
Patio del Ekeko, Mercaderes 141. A commercial centre with upmarket handicrafts, **Kuna by Alpaca 111** (see above), **Ilaria** for fine jewellery, **La Ibérica** chocolate shop (also at Morán 160), café, internet, cinema and **Museo de Arte Textil** upstairs (Mon-Sat 1000-2030, Sun 1000-1530).

◐ What to do

Arequipa *p1310, maps p1311 and p1313*
Climbing, cycling, rafting and trekking
International recommendations are for a
300 m per day maximum altitude gain.
Be wary of agencies wanting to sell you
trips with very fast ascents.
Julver Castro, who has an agency called
Mountrekk, T601833, julver_mountrekk@
hotmail.com. A climbing guide recommended
as experienced and "full of energy".
Colca Trek, Jerusalén 401 B, T206217, www.
colcatrek.com.pe. Knowledgeable and English-
speaking Vlado Soto is one of the best guides
for the Cotahuasi Canyon and is recommended
for climbing, trekking and mountain biking in
the Colca Canyon. He also rents equipment and
has topographical maps.
Cusipata, Jerusalén 402-A, T203966, www.
cusipata.com (shared office with **Andina
Travel**). Recommended as the best local
rafting operator, very popular half-day trips,
run 6-day trips on the Río Colca. May-Dec,
Río Chili 1 day kayak courses, also trekking
and mountain bike tours.
Naturaleza Activa, Santa Catalina 211,
T204182, naturactiva@yahoo.com. Experienced
guides, knowledgeable, climbing and trekking.
Sacred Road Tours, Jerusalén 400, T212332,
www.sacredroad.com. Arranges hiking and
rock climbing in Colca Canyon and elsewhere,
experienced guides led by Arcadio Mamani,
equipment available.
Selern Services, Urb Puerta Verde F13,
José LB y Rivero, Arequipa, T348685,
see Facebook. Trekking, adventure tourism,
mountain climbing.
Volcanyon Travel, C Villalba 414, T205078,
mario-ortiz@terra.com.pe. Trekking and some
mountain bike tours in the Colca Canyon, also
volcano climbing.
Carlos Zárate Aventuras, Santa Catalina 204,
of 3, T202461. Run by Carlos Zárate of the
Mountaineering Club of Peru. Good family
run business that always works with qualified
mountain guides. A specialist in mountaineering
and exploring, with a great deal of information
and advice and some equipment rental. Carlos
also runs trips to one of the supposed sources of
the Amazon, Nevado Mismi, as well as trekking

in the Cotahuasi canyon and climbing tougher
peaks such as Coropuna.

Tour operators
Many agencies on Jerusalén, Santa Catalina
and around Plaza de Armas sell air, train and
bus tickets and offer tours of Colca, Cotahuasi,
Toro Muerto and city. Prices vary greatly so
shop around; check carefully what is included
in the cheapest of tours and that there are
enough people for the tour to run. Travel
agents frequently work together to fill buses
and there are lots of touts. Many tourists prefer
to contract tours through their hotel. If a travel
agency puts you in touch with a guide, make
sure he/she is official. The following have been
recommended as helpful and reliable.
Al Travel Tours, Santa Catalina 203, of 7, ask for
Miguel Fernández T959-391436/971-858704
(mob), www.aitraveltours.com. Peruvian/Dutch
tour operator offering cultural and adventure
tours for groups or individuals, volunteer work
and Spanish courses, large book exchange.
Andina Travel Service, Jerusalén 309-402A,
T225082, www.andinatravelaqp.com. Good
tours of Colca Canyon, guide Gelmond Ynca
Aparicio is very enthusiastic.
Colca Explorer, Mariscal Benavides 201 Selva
Alegre, T202587, www.colca-explorer.com.
Agency associated with **Amazonas Explorer**
in Cuzco, with many options in Colca and
southern Peru: from classic local tours to
horse riding, mountain biking, fishing in
remote lakes, climbing, treks and visiting
alpaca farms on the altiplano.
Colca Journeys, C Rodríguez Ballón 533,
Miraflores, T973-901010, www.colcajourneys.
com. Specializes in and operates tours to the
Colca Valley and Cotahuasi Valley.
Giardino Tours, at **Casa de Mi Abuela** (see
above), T221345, www.giardinotours.com.
Professional company offering tours and
transport, has own properties in Arequipa
and Colca (eg delightful **La Casa de
Mamayacchi** in Coporaque), community
tourism options, good information.
Land Adventure, Residencial La Peña A-20,
Sachaca (outside city), T959-941570, www.
landadventures.net. 'Sustainable' tour operator
with good guides for communities in Colca,
trekking, climbing, downhill biking.

Pablo Tour, Jerusalén 400-AB-1, T203737, www.pablotour.com. Family-run agency, owns several hostals in Cabanaconde and knows area well, 3-day mixed tours in the Colca Canyon with mountain biking, trekking and rafting, free tourist information, maps for sale, bus and hotel reservation service. Son Edwin Junco Cabrera can sometimes be found in the office, he speaks fluent French and English.

Vita Tours, Jerusalén 302, T284211, www.vitatours.com.pe. Tours in the Arequipa area, including to the coast, and in the Colca Canyon where they have a hotel, **La Casa de Lucila**.

⊖ Transport

Arequipa *p1310, maps p1311 and p1313*
Air
Rodríguez Ballón airport is 7 km from town, T443464. Two desks offer hotel reservations and free transport to town; also car rentals. To and from **Lima**, 1 hr 10 mins, several daily with **LAN**, **Peruvian Airlines** (also to **Tacna**) and **Star Perú**. LAN and Star Perú also serve **Juliaca**, 30 mins, LAN continuing to **Cuzco**, 1 hr 10 mins from Arequipa. Local buses and combis go to about 500 m from the airport, look for ones marked 'Río Seco', 'Cono-Norte' or 'Zamacola'. Best to use a radio taxi company listed below.

Bus
A new urban rapid transit system, **Arequipa Bus** is being introduced, with dedicated bus lanes and less polluting vehicles.

There are 2 terminals at Av Andrés A Cáceres s/n, Parque Industrial, south of the centre, 15 mins by colectivo US$0.50, or taxi US$2.50. The older **Terminal Terrestre** has a tourist office, shops and places to eat. The newer **Terrapuerto**, across the car park, has a tourist office (which makes hotel reservations) and its own *hostal* (**$** without breakfast), T421375. Terminal tax US$0.50. Buses may not depart from the terminal where you bought your ticket. All the bus companies have offices in Terminal Terrestre and several also have offices in Terrapuerto.

Note Theft is a serious problem in the bus station area. Take a taxi to and from the bus station and do not wander around with your belongings. No one is allowed to enter the terminal 2100-0500, so new arrivals cannot be met by hoteliers between those hours; best not to arrive at night.

To **Lima**, 1011 km, 16-18 hrs, services from US$22 to US$56. **Cruz del Sur** (T427375), **Enlaces** (T430333), **Tepsa** (T054-608079), **Ormeño** (T424187) are recommended. The road is paved but drifting sand and breakdowns may prolong the trip.

To **Nazca**, 566 km, 9 hrs, US$19-22.50 (US$30-52 on luxury services), several buses daily, mostly at night; most buses continue to Ica (US$30-42) and Lima. Also US$12 to **Chala**, 8 hrs. To **Moquegua**, 213 km, 3 hrs, US$7.50-12, several buses and colectivos daily. To **Tacna**, 320 km, 6-7 hrs, from US$18, 17 buses daily with **Flores**.

To **Cuzco**, all buses go via Juliaca or Puno, US$14-47, 10 hrs. Most companies go overnight, eg **Enlaces, Cial, Ziva** and **Ormeño**, but a few in daytime. There is a quick paved road to **Juliaca**, US$11-27, 4-5 hrs (Cruz del Sur; also **Trans Julsa**, T430843, hourly buses, reliable), and **Puno**, 5 hrs, US$11-27 **Cruz del Sur**. Most buses and colectivos continue to Puno.

Taxi
US$8 airport to city (can be shared). From US$1 around town. **Alo 45**, T454545; **Taxitel**, T452020; **Taxi 21**, T212121; **Turismo Arequipa**, T458888.

ⓘ Directory

Arequipa *p1310, maps p1311 and p1313*
Language courses Centro de Intercambio Cultural Arequipa (CEICA), Urb Universitaria G-9, T250722, www.ceica-peru.com. Individual classes US$145 for 20 hrs' tuition, US$109 for groups of 3 or more, rooms with families (US$90 per week for a single room with breakfast, US$107 half board, US$119 full board), also dance lessons, history and cultural classes, excursions. **Escuela de Español Ari Quipay** (EDEAQ), T272517, T959 992995 (mob), www.edeaq.com. Peruvian/Swiss-run, experienced, multilingual staff, recognized by Peruvian Ministry of Education, in a colonial house near the Plaza de Armas, one-to-one and group classes, home stay available (see **Lula's B&B** under Where to stay). Instituto Cultural Peruano Alemán, Ugarte 207, T228130, www.icpa.org.pe. Good language classes. **Llama Education**, Casabella, lote A6, Cerro Colorado, T274069,

www.arequipaspanish.com/index.html.
Professional, with personal attention, owner
María Huaman is very helpful. Individual
and small group tuition, home stays
and cultural exchanges. **Spanish School
Arequipa**, Av San Martín 116, T213177, www.
spanishschoolarequipa.com. Standard Spanish
lessons or courses tailored for travellers or
volunteers, accommodation with families or
on site at Casa de Avila, see above. **Silvana
Cornejo**, 7 de Junio 118, Cerrito Los Alvarez,
Cerro Colorado, T254985, silvanacor@yahoo.
com. Negotiable rates for group, she speaks
German fluently. Her sister Roxanna also is
a teacher. **Cecilia Pinto Oppe**, Puente Grau
108 (in Hostal La Reyna), T959-961638, www.
cepesmaidiomasceci.com. Good-value lessons,
held in a café which helps orphaned children.
Carlos Rojas Núñez, Filtro 405, T285061,

carlrojas@mixmail.com. Private or group lessons
to students of all levels, encourages conversation,
knowledgeable on culture and politics. **Medical
services** Hospitals: Regional Honorio
Delgado, Av A Carrión s/n, T238465/231818
(inoculations). **Central del Sur**, Filtro y Peral s/n,
T214430 in emergency. Clinics: **Clinic Arequipa
SA**, Puente Grau y Av Bolognesi, T599000,
www.clinicarequipa.com.pe, fast and efficient
with English-speaking doctors and all hospital
facilities. **Paz Holandesa**, Villa Continental,
C 4, No 101, Paucarpata, T432281, www.
pazholandesa.com. Dutch foundation dedicated
to helping the impoverished, which also has
a travel clinic for tourists. Dutch and English
spoken, 24-hr service. Highly recommended
(see their website if you are interested in
volunteering). **Emergencies**: Ambulance
T289800; also **San Miguel**, T283330 (24 hrs).

Colca Canyon → *You must buy a tourist ticket for US$26.50 (valid 10 days), at a checkpoint on the road to Chivay when entering the canyon.*

The Colca Canyon is deep: twice as deep as the Grand Canyon. The Río Colca descends from 3500 m
above sea level at Chivay to 2200 m at Cabanaconde. In the background looms the grey, smoking
mass of Sabancaya, one of the most active volcanoes in the Americas, and its more docile neighbour,
Ampato (6288 m). Unspoiled Andean villages lie on both sides of the canyon, inhabited by the
Cabana and Collagua peoples, and some of the extensive pre-Columbian terraced fields are still in
use. High on anyone's list for visiting the canyon is an early-morning trip to the Cruz del Cóndor, to
see these majestic birds at close quarters. From January to April is the rainy season, but this makes
the area green, with lots of flowers. This is not the best time to see condors. May to December is the
dry, cold season when there is more chance of seeing the birds. Conditions vary annually, though.

From Arequipa there are two routes to **Chivay**, the first village on the edge of the Canyon:
the old route, via Cayma, and the new paved route, through Yura, following the railway, longer
but quicker. The two routes join at Cañahuas where you can change buses to/from Juliaca or
Chivay without going to Arequipa. The road from Cañahuas to Puno via Patahuasi, Imata and
Juliaca has been improved with a daily tourist transport service (see Transport, below). It can be
cold in the morning, reaching 4825 m in the Pata Pampa pass, but the views are worth it. Cyclists
should use the Yura road; better condition and less of a climb at the start. The old dirt route runs
north from Arequipa, over the altiplano. About an hour out of Arequipa is the **Aguada Blanca
National Vicuña Reserve**. If you're lucky, you can see herds of these rare animals near the road.
This route affords fine views of the volcanoes Misti, Chachani, Ampato and Sabancaya. Chivay
is the chief linking point between the two sides of the canyon; there is a road bridge over the
river here (others at Yanque and Larl). The road continues northeast to **Tuti** (small handicrafts
shop), and **Sibayo** (*pensión* and grocery store). A long circuit back to Arequipa heads south from
Sibayo, passing through **Puente Callalli**, **Chullo** and **Sumbay**. This is a little-travelled road, but
the views, with vicuña, llamas, alpacas and Andean duck are superb. Crossing the river at Chivay
going west to follow the canyon on the far side, you pass the villages of **Coporaque**, **Ichupampa**
(a footbridge crosses the river between the two villages and foot and road bridges connect the
road between Coporaque and Ichupampa with Yanque), **Lari**, **Madrigal** (footbridge to Maca)
and **Tapay** (connected to Cabanaconde by a footbridge).

Chivay to Cabanaconde

Chivay (3600 m) is the gateway to the canyon. The **Maria Reiche Planetarium and Observatory** ① *in the grounds of the Casa Andina hotel, 6 blocks west of the Plaza between Huayna Capac and Garcilazo (www.casa-andina.com), US$6, discounts for students,* makes the most of the Colca's clear Southern Hemisphere skies with a powerful telescope and two 55-minute presentations per day at 1830 (Spanish) and 1930 (English). There is a very helpful **tourist office** in the Municipalidad on the west side of the plaza (closed at weekends). The tourist police, also on the plaza, can give advice about locally trained guides. **Traveller's Medical Center (TMC)** ① *Ramón Castilla 232, T531037.* There is a Globalnet ATM close to the plaza.

The hot springs of **La Calera** ① *US$5.25 to bathe, half price just to go in, regular colectivos (US$0.25), taxi (US$1.50) or a 1-hr walk from town,* are 4 km away and are highly recommended after a hard day's trekking.

From Chivay, the main road goes west along the Colca Canyon. The first village encountered is **Yanque** (8 km, excellent views), with an interesting church containing superbly renovated altar pieces and paintings, a museum on the opposite side of the plaza, and a bridge to the villages on the other side of the canyon. A large thermal swimming pool is 20 minutes walk from the plaza, beside the renovated colonial bridge on the Yanque-Ichupampa road, US$0.75. The road continues paved to **Achoma** (**Hospedaje Cruz del Cóndor** on the plaza and a campsite) and **Maca**, which barely survived an earthquake in November 1991. Then comes the tiny village of **Pinchollo**, with **Hospedaje Refugio del Geyser** (Calle Melgar s/n, behind municipality, T054-959-007441/958-032090, basic with good local information). From here it is a 30-minute walk on a dirt track to the geyser **Hatun Infiernillo**. The Mirador, or **Cruz del Cóndor** ① *where you may be asked to show your tourist ticket,* is at the deepest point of the canyon. The view is wonderful and condors can be seen rising on the morning thermals (0900, arrive by 0800 to get a good spot) and sometimes in the late afternoon (1600-1800). Camping here is officially forbidden, but if you ask the tourist police in Chivay they may help. **Milagros'** 0630 bus from Chivay stop here very briefly at around 0800 (ask the driver to stop), or try hitching with a tour bus at around 0600. Buses from Cabanaconde stop at about 0700 (**Andalucía**) or 0830 (**Reyna**), which leave Cabanaconde's plaza 30 minutes earlier.

From the Mirador it is a 20-minute ride in tourist transport, 40 minutes by local bus on a paved road to **Cabanaconde** (3287 m). You can also walk, three hours by the road, or two hours by a short cut following the canyon. It is the last village in the Colca Canyon, friendly, typical, but basic (it does have 24-hour electricity). The views are superb and condors can be seen from the hill just west of the village, a 15-minute walk from the plaza, which also gives views of the agrcultural terraces, arguably the most attractive in the valley, to the south of the village. Cabanaconde is an excellent base for visiting the region, with interesting trekking, climbing, biking and horse riding. Many are keen to encourage respectful tourism in the area and several locally owned tourism businesses have opened in the village.

There's a friendly tourist information office, T280212, willing to give plenty of advice, if not maps. It's a good place to find trekking guides and muleteers (US$30 a day mule and guide).

Two hours below Cabanaconde is **Sangalle**, an 'oasis' of palm trees and swimming areas and three campsites with basic bungalows and toilets (three to 4½ hours back up, ask for the best route in both directions, horses can be hired to carry your bag up, US$5.85), a beautiful spot, recommended. A popular hike involves walking east on the Chivay road to the Mirador de Tapay (before Cruz del Cóndor), then descending to the river on a steep track (four hours, take care). Cross the bridge to the north bank. At the village of San Juan de Chuccho you can stay and eat at a basic family hostel, of which there are several. **Hostal Roy** and **Casa de Rebelino** ($) are both good. US$2 will buy you a good meal. From here pass **Tapay** (also possible to camp here) and the small villages of Malata and Cosnirhua, all the time heading west along the north side of the Río Colca (take a guide or ask local directions). After about three hours walking, cross another bridge to the south bank of the Río Colca, follow signs to Sangalle, spend the night and return to Cabanconde on the third day. This route is offered by many Arequipa and local agencies.

⊙ Colca Canyon listings

For hotel and restaurant price codes, and other relevant information, see Essentials.

⊙ Where to stay

Chivay to Cabanconde *p1322*
Chivay
$$$ Casa Andina, Huayna Cápac s/n, T531020, www.casa-andina.com. Attractive cabins with hot showers and a cosy bar/dining area, a member of the recommended hotel chain, heating, parking.
$$$ Estancio Pozo del Cielo, C Huáscar B-3, Sacsayhuaman-Chivay over the Puente Inca from Chivay amid pre Inca terraces, T531041 (Alvarez Thomas 309, Arequipa, T205838), www.pozodelcielo.com.pe. Very comfortable, warm rooms, good views, good service and restaurant.
$$ Colca Inn, Salaverry 307, T531088, www.hotelcolcainn.com. Good mid-range option, modern, hot water, decent restaurant, basic breakfast.
$$ Cóndor Wasi, Av Polonia s/n, on the road to La Calera hot springs, 1 km from Chivay, T799032, T959-444956, condorwasi@ hotmail.com. Rustic rooms with bath, hot water, very tranquil.
$$ Posada del Colca, Salaverry 325, T959-784940, laposadadelcolca@hotmail.com, also on Facebook. Central, good rooms, hot water.
$ Hospedaje Restaurant Los Portales, Arequipa 603, T531164, www.losportales dechivay.com. Good value, though beds have rather 'floppy' mattresses. Restaurant downstairs.
$ La Casa de Lucila, M Grau 131, T531109, http://vitatours.com.pe. Comfortable, hot water, coffee, guides available.
$ La Pascana, Puente Inca y C Siglo XX 106, T531001, hrlapascana@hotmail.com. Northwest corner of the Plaza. Excellent value with spacious en suite rooms, hot water, most rooms overlook a pleasant garden. Parking and a good restaurant.
$ Rumi Wasi, Sucre 714, 6 blocks from plaza (3 mins' walk), T531146. Good rooms, hot water, helpful, mountain bike rental (in poor condition).

Yanque
$$$$ Colca Lodge, across the river from Yanque, T531191, office at Mariscal Benavides 201, Selva Alegre, Arequipa, T202587, www. colca-lodge.com. Very relaxing, with beautiful hot springs beside the river, spend at least a day to make the most of the activities on offer. Day passes available. Rooms heated with geothermal energy, solar heated water.
$$$$ Las Casitas del Colca, Av Fundo La Curiña s/n, Yanque, T959-672688, www. lascasitasdelcolca.com. Under new management of the GHL group, with luxury cottages made of local materials with underfloor heating and plunge pools. Has a gourmet restaurant, bar, vegetable garden and farm, offers cookery and painting courses, the spa offers a variety of treatments, swimming pool.
$$$ Collahua, Av Collahua cuadra 7, Yanque, or in Arequipa at Mercaderes 212, Galerías Gamesa, T226098, www.hotelcollahua.com. Modern bungalows just outside Yanque, with heating, solar-powered 24-hr hot water and plush rooms, pool, restaurant.
$$$ Eco Inn, Lima 513, Yanque, T 837112, www.ecoinnhotels.com. Perched high on a bluff with incredible views over the valley and newly-restored Ullo Ullo ruins. Large, comfortable rooms in cabins, restaurant open from 0530 for buffet breakfast, WI-FI In lobby and restaurant.
$$ Tradición Colca, on main road. In Arequipa C Argentina 108, Urb Fecia JL Bustamante y Rivero, T424926, www.tradicioncolca.com. Adobe construction, rooms with private bathroom, gas stove. Spa treatment room in the garden, massages, sauna, jacuzzi (1800-2045). Restaurant, bar, games room, observatory and planetarium (30 min session at 1900, free for guests), horse riding from 2 hrs to 2 days, guided hiking tour to Ullu Ullu, also has a travel agency in Arequipa.
$ Casa Bella Flor Sumaq Wayta Wasi, Cuzco 303, T253586, www.casabellaflor.com. Charming small lodge run by Sra Hilde Checca, flower-filled garden, tasteful rooms, good meals (also open to non-residents), Hilde's uncle, Gregorio, guides visitors to pre-Columbian sites.

$ Rijchariy Colca Lodge, on the track leading down to the footbridge over the river, T764610. Great views, garden, comfortable rooms, restaurant.

Cabanaconde

$$ Kuntur Wassi, C Cruz Blanca s/n, on the hill above the plaza, T233120, www.arequipacolca.com. Excellent, 3-star, fine traditional meals on request. Creative design with rooms spaced between rock gardens and waterfalls. Viewing 'tower' and conference centre above. Owners Walter and María very welcoming and knowledgeable about treks.

$$ Posada del Conde, C San Pedro, T441030. Smart hotel and a lodge. Cheaper in low season, with hot shower, comfortable beds, good food. Local guides and horses for hire.

$ Hostal Valle del Fuego, 1 and 2 blocks from the plaza on C Grau y Bolívar, T959-611241, www.hvalledelfuego.com. Rooms with comfortable beds, all with hot water, laundry facilities, restaurant. The Junco family have plenty of information, with a small family 'empire', including the Arequipa agency **Pablo Tour**, the **Oasis Paradise** in Sangalle (discounts for clients of Valle del Fuego) and a bar, the **Casa de Pablo Club** at the end of the street. They usually meet the incoming buses. Popular.

$ Majestic Colca, Miguel Grau s/n near C San Pedro, T958-060433. Modern, hot water, rooftop terrace and restaurant.

$ Pachamama Home, San Pedro 209, T767277, T959-316322, www.pachamamahome.com. Backpacker hostel, with and without bath, family atmosphere, hot water, lots of information, good bar/pizzería **Pachamama** next door, try the Colca Sour, made from a local cactus. You can help with teaching and activities for village children.

$ Virgen del Carmen, Av Arequipa s/n, T832159, 5 blocks up from the plaza. Hot showers, may even offer you a welcoming glass of *chicha*.

🍴 Restaurants

Chivay *p1322*
Several restaurants serve buffet lunches for tour groups, US$5 pp, also open to the general public. Of the few that open in the evening, most have folklore shows and are packed with tour groups. When walking in the valley meals and drinks can be taken in any of the larger lodges. For local cheeses and dairy products, visit **Productos del Colca**, Av 22 de Agosto in the central market.

$$ El Balcón de Don Zacarías, Av 22 de Agosto 102 on plaza, T531108. Breakfast, the best lunch buffet in town, à la carte menu, novo andean and international cuisine.

$$-$ Lobos Pizzería, José Gálvez 101, T531081. Has good pizzas and pastas, fast service and good bar, popular. Has mountain biking information and **Isuiza Turismo y Aventura** agency, T959-860870.

$$-$ McElroys's Irish Pub, on the plaza. Bar run by a Peruvian and an Irishman, warm, good selection of drinks (sometimes including expensive Guinness), sandwiches, pizza, pasta and music. Mountain bikes for hire. Accepts Visa.

$$-$ Yaraví, Plaza de Armas 604, T489109. Arequipeña food, vegetarian options and the most impressive coffee machine in town.

$ Innkas Café-Bar, main plaza No 706, T531209. Coffee, sandwiches, *menú*, pizzas, pool table, nice atmosphere.

$ Ruadhri Irish Pub, Av Salaverry 202. Nothing Irish about it, but still a popular hang-out offering pizzas, pastas and sandwiches, has happy hour and a pool table.

Cabanaconde *p1322*
$$-$ Casa de Pablo Club, C Grau. Excellent fresh juices and pisco sour, cable TV (football!), small book exchange and some equipment hire.

$ Las Brisas del Colca, main plaza, T631593. Pleasant, serves breakfast, tourist menu, à la carte dishes, juices and sandwiches.

$ Don Piero, signposted just off main plaza. Excellent choice and good information.

$ Pizzería Bar Bon Appetit, Jorge Chávez s/n, main plaza, T630171. Pizzas, pastas, breakfast, and vegetarian.

$ Rancho del Colca, on plaza. Mainly vegetarian.

✪ Festivals

Colca Canyon *p1321*
Many in the Colca region: **2-3 Feb** Virgen de la Candelaria, Chivay, Cabanaconde, Maca, Tapay. **Feb**: Carnaval, Chivay. **3 May** Cruz de la Piedra, Tuti. **13 Jun** San Antonio, Yanque, Maca. **14 Jun** San Juan, Sibayo, Ichupampa. **21 Jun** Anniversary of Chivay. **29 Jun** San Pedro y

San Pablo, Sibayo. **14-17 Jul** La Virgen del Carmen, Cabanaconde. **25 Jul** Santiago Apóstol, Coporaque. **26 Jul-2 Aug** Virgen Santa Ana, Maca. **15 Aug** Virgen de la Asunta, Chivay. **8 Dec** Immaculada Concepción, Yanque, Chivay. **25 Dec** Sagrada Familia, Yanque. Many of these festivals last several days and involve traditional dances and customs.

⊙ What to do

Colca Canyon *p1321*
Tours
It is not always possible to join a tour in Chivay; it is best to organize it in Arequipa and travel with a group. From Arequipa a '1-day' tour to the Mirador at Cruz del Cóndor costs US$25-30, depart Arequipa at 0400, arrive at the Cruz del Cóndor at 0800-0900, expensive lunch stop at Chivay and back to Arequipa by 2100. For many, especially for those with altitude problems, this is too much to fit into one day (the only advantage is that you don't have to sleep at high altitude). 2-day tours are about US$30-40 pp with an overnight stop in Chivay or Yanque; more expensive tours range from US$45 to US$90. Most agencies will have a base price for the tour and then different prices depending on which hotel you pick. Allow at least 2-3 days to appreciate the Colca Canyon fully, more if planning on trekking.

Trekking
There are many hiking possibilities in the area, with *hostales* or camping for longer treks. Make sure to take enough water, or purification, as it gets very hot and there is not a lot of water available. Moreover, sun protection is a must. Some treks are impossible if it rains heavily in the wet season, but this is very rare. Ask locals for directions as there are hundreds of confusing paths going into the canyon. In Cabanaconde trekking and adventure sports can be organized quite easily

at short notice. Buy food for longer hikes in Arequipa. Topographical maps are available at the *Instituto Geográfico Nacional* in Lima, and at Colca Trek or Pablo Tour in Arequipa. See above for some of the the main treks.

Chivay *p1322*
Ampato Adventure Sports, Plaza de Armas (close to **Lobos Pizzería**), Chivay, T531073, www.ampatocolca.com. Offer information and rent good mountain bikes, but rarely open.
Colca-Turismo, Av Salaverry 321, Chivay, T503368, guide Zacarías Ocsa Osca, zacariasocsa@hotmail. com, seems to offer a professional service.

Cabanaconde *p1322*
Chiqui Travel & Expeditions, San Pedro s/n, T958-063602. Small, but professional and reliable, organizes trekking, biking and horse riding.
Guías Locales Aproset, T958-099332. Association of local guides, can organize *arrieros* and mules for independent treks.

⊙ Transport

Colca Canyon *p1321*
Bus La Reyna (T430612), **Trans Milagros**, T531115, and **Andalucía**, T694060, have almost hourly departures daily from Arequipa to **Chivay**, US$4.50, 6 hrs, some continuing to **Cabanaconde**, US$6, a further 75 km, 2 hrs. Buses return to Arequipa from bus station in Chivay, 3 blocks from the main plaza, next to the stadium. None offers a secure service; it may be better to take tourist transport, even if staying a few days, then join another group for the return. Combis and colectivos leave from the terminal to any village in the area. Ask the drivers.
Chivay-Cabanaconde Bus at 0500. Buses run infrequently in each direction, fewer on Sun. Buses leave Cabanaconde for Arequipa from 0730 to 1500 from the Plaza de Armas. To **Cuzco** from Chivay take a bus to Cañahuas and change there for a bus to Juliaca, then carry on to Cuzco.

Cotahuasi Canyon

Toro Muerto
ⓘ *US$2; entrance 2 km from the road, site 2 km from the entrance.*
West of Arequipa, a dirt road branches off the Pan-American to Corire, Aplao (small museum containing Wari cultural objects from the surrounding area) and the Río Majes valley. The

world's largest field of petroglyphs, covering 5 sq km, at Toro Muerto is near Corire, where there are several hotels and restaurants near the plaza and excellent shrimp restaurants by the river. For Toro Muerto, turn off on the right heading back out of Corire; one-hour walk; ask directions. The higher you go, the more interesting the petroglyphs, though some have been ruined by graffiti. The designs range from simple llamas to elaborate human figures and animals and are thought to be Wari (AD 700-1100) in origin. The sheer scale of the site, some 6000 sculpted rocks, is awe-inspiring and the view is wonderful (UNESCO World Heritage Site). Take plenty of water, sunglasses and sun cream. At least an hour is needed to visit the site.

Cotahuasi Canyon

Beyond Aplao the road heads north through **Chuquibamba**, where the paving ends (festivals 20 January; 2-3 February; 15 May), traversing the western slopes of Nevado Coropuna (6425 m), before winding down into **Cotahuasi** *(Phone code: 054; Population: 3200; Altitude: 2680 m).* The peaceful colonial town nestles in a sheltered hanging valley beneath Cerro Huinao. Its streets are narrow, the houses whitewashed. There is a small museum with **tourist information** ① *Centenario 208, Mon-Fri 0800-1300, 1400-1700, helpful,* Local festival is 4 May.

Several kilometres away a canyon has been cut by the Río Cotahuasi, which flows into the Pacific as the Río Ocuña. At its deepest, at Ninochaca (just below the village of Quechualla), the canyon is 3354 m deep, 163 m deeper than the Colca Canyon and the deepest in the world. From this point the only way down the canyon is by kayak and it is through kayakers' reports since 1994 that the area has come to the notice of tourists (it was declared a Zona de Reserva Turística in 1988). There is little agriculture apart from some citrus groves, but in Inca times the road linking Puerto Inca and Cuzco ran along much of the canyon's course. Note that the area is not on the tourist route and information is hard to come by.

Following the Río Cotahuasi to the northeast up the valley, you come to **Tomepampa** (10 km), a neat hamlet at 2700 m, with painted houses and a chapel. The hotsprings of **Luicho** (33° to 38°C) ① *18 km from Cotahuasi, 24 hrs, US0.50-1.75,* are a short walk from the road, across a bridge. Beyond is **Alca** (20 km, at 2750 m, one *hostal*), above which are the small ruins of Kallak, Tiknay and a "stone library" of rock formations. All these places are connected by buses and combis from Cotahuasi. Buses leave Alca for Arequipa around 1400, combis hourly from 0600-1800. **Puica** ① *connected to Alca by combi (2 hrs, US$1.50,* is the last village of any significance in the valley, hanging on a hillside at nearly 3700 m. Nearby attractions include: Churca and a vast prairie of Puya Raimondi cacti; the Ocoruro geysers; and the ruins of Maucallacta. Horses can be hired for US$5 a day, and locals can act as guides.

One of the main treks in the region follows the Inca trade road from Cotahuasi to Quechualla. From the football pitch the path goes through Piro, the gateway to the canyon, and Sipia (three hours, two suspension bridges to cross), near which are the powerful, 150-m-high Cataratas de Sipia (take care near the falls if it is windy). Combis from Cotahuasi to Velinga go to within an hour's walk of the Cataratas; they leave 0630 and 1200, passing the Sipia drop off one hour later; return four hours later. It's best to visit at midday. A road is being built from this point to the falls, and may be complete by the time you read this. The next three-hour stretch to Chaupo is not for vertigo sufferers as the road (track) is barely etched into the canyon wall, 400 m above the river in places. At Chaupo ask permission to camp; water is available. Next is Velinga (currently the end of the road), from where you can reach the dilapidated but extensive ruin of Huña, and the charming village of **Quechualla** at 1980 m. The deepest part of the canyon is below Quechualla. Ask Sr Carmelo Velásquez Gálvez for permission to sleep in the schoolhouse.

Several tour operators in Arequipa run four-day trips to Cotahuasi, taking in the Sipia falls and the Puya Raimondi cacti. They can also organize adventure activities. **Cotahuasi Trek** (www.cotahuasitrek.com) is a specialist adventure company based in Cotahuasi, owned by Marcio Ruiz, locally renowned guide.

⚫ Cotahuasi Canyon listings

For hotel and restaurant price codes, and other relevant information, see Essentials.

⚫ Where to stay

Cotahuasi *p1326*

$$ Valle Hermoso, Tacna 108-110, T581057, www.hotelvallehermoso.com. Nice and cosy, includes breakfast, beautiful views of the canyon, comfortable rooms, large garden, restaurant uses home-grown fruit and veg.

$ Casa Primavera, in Tomepampa, T212982. Family-run hostel, some rooms with private bath, kitchen facilities, courtyard and common areas, meals on request.

$ Cotahuasi, Arequipa 515, T581029/959-397163, hotel_cotahuasi@hotmail.com. New, with TV, hot water, clean.

$ Hostal Alcalá II, Arequipa 116, T581090. Very good, hot showers, excellent beds, doubles and triples. Run by same family as **$ Hostal Alcalá**, main plaza, Alca, T452258. One of the best hostales in the valley, 2 rooms with shower, others shared, hot water, restaurant, good food. Prices vary according to season and demand.

$ Hostal Fany Luz, Independencia 117, T581002. Basic but amenable, shared hot showers, double room with cold water only.

⚫ Restaurants

Cotahuasi *p1326*

3 small restaurants/bars on Jr Arequipa offer basic fare, best is BuenSabor, opposite Hostal Alcalá II. There are many well-stocked tiendas, particularly with fruit, vegetables and local wine.

$ El Pionero, Jr Centenario. Clean, good *menú*.

$ R y M, on main square, prepares typical soups.

⚫ Transport

Toro Muerto *p1325*

Empresa Del Carpio buses to **Corire** leave from **Arequipa** main terminal hourly from 0500, 3-4 hrs, US$5. Ask to be let out at the beginning of the track to Toro Muerto, or from the plaza in Corire take a taxi, US$10 including 2-hr wait.

Cotahuasi *p1326*

There is a modern bus station 10 mins' walk from the Plaza. Buses daily from **Arequipa** bus terminal, 10-11 hrs, US$11: **Cromotex** at 1700 and 1800; **Reyna** at 1630; all return from Cotahuasi at the same times. They stop for refreshments in Chuquibamba, about halfway. Both companies continue to **Tomepampa** and **Alca**.

⚫ Directory

Cotahuasi *p1326*

Useful services PNP, on plaza; advisable to register with them on arrival and before leaving. Maps: some survey maps in Municipalidad and PNP; they may let you make photocopies (shop on the corner of the plaza and Arequipa). Sr Chávez has photocopies of the sheets covering Cotahuasi and surroundings. The *Lima 2000* 1:225,000 map of the Colca and Cotahuasi canyons has information about the small villages throughout the canyon as well as about interesting places to visit.

South to Chile

Moquegua → *Phone code: 053. Colour map 6, A1. Population: 110,000. Altitude: 1412 m.*

This town 213 km from Arequipa in the narrow valley of the Moquegua River enjoys a sub-tropical climate. The old centre, a few blocks above the Pan-American Highway, has winding, cobbled streets and 19th-century buildings. The Plaza de Armas, with its mix of ruined and well-maintained churches, colonial and republican façades and fine trees, is one of the most interesting small-town plazas in the country. **Museo Contisuyo** ① *on the Plaza de Armas, within the ruins of Iglesia Matriz, T461844, www.museocontisuyo.com, daily 0800-1300, 1430-1730, Tue 0800-1200, 1600-2000, US$0.50,* covers the cultures which thrived in the Moquegua and Ilo valleys, including the Huari, Tiahuanaco, Chiribaya and Estuquiña, who were conquered by the Incas. Artefacts are well displayed and explained in Spanish and English. **Día de Santa Catalina**,

25 November, is the anniversary of the founding of the colonial city. **Dircetur regional tourist office** ① *Ayacucho 1060, T462236, moquegua@mincetur.gob.pe, Mon-Fri 0800-1630.*

A highly recommended excursion is to **Cerro Baúl** (2590 m) ① *30 mins by colectivo, US$2,* a tabletop mountain with marvellous views and many legends, which can be combined with the pleasant town of Torata, 24 km northeast.

The Carretera Binacional, from the port of Ilo to La Paz, has a breathtaking stretch from Moquegua to Desaguadero at the southeastern end of Lake Titicaca. It skirts Cerro Baúl and climbs through zones of ancient terraces to its highest point at 4755 m. On the altiplano there are herds of llamas and alpacas, lakes with waterfowl, strange mountain formations and snow-covered peaks. At Mazo Cruz there is a PNP checkpoint where all documents and bags are checked. Approaching Desaguadero the Cordillera Real of Bolivia comes into view. The road is fully paved and should be taken in daylight.

Tacna → *Phone code: 052. Colour map 6, A1. Population: 174,366. Altitude: 550 m.*

Only 36 km from the Chilean border and 56 km from the international port of Arica, Tacna has free-trade status. It is an important commercial centre and Chileans come for cheap medical and dental treatment. Around the city the desert is gradually being irrigated. The local economy includes olive groves, vineyards and fishing. Tacna was in Chilean hands from 1880 to 1929,

Tacna

Where to stay
1 Copacabana
2 Dorado
3 El Mesón
4 Gran Hotel Tacna
5 Hostal Anturio
6 Hostal Bon Ami
7 La Posada del Cacique
8 Roble 18 Residencial

Restaurants
1 Café Zeit
2 Cusqueñita
3 Da Vinci
4 Fu-Lin
5 Il Pomodoro
6 Koyuki
7 Un Limón
8 Verdi

400 metres
400 yards

when its people voted by plebiscite to return to Peru. Above the city (8 km away, just off the Panamericana Norte), on the heights, is the **Campo de la Alianza**, scene of a battle between Peru and Chile in 1880. The cathedral, designed by Eiffel, faces the Plaza de Armas, which contains huge bronze statues of Admiral Grau and Colonel Bolognesi. They stand at either end of the Arca de los Héroes, the triumphal arch which is the symbol of the city. The bronze fountain in the Plaza is said to be a duplicate of the one in the Place de la Concorde (Paris) and was also designed by Eiffel. The **Parque de la Locomotora** ① *daily 0700-1700, US$0.30; knock at the gate under the clock tower on Jr 2 de Mayo for entry*, near the city centre, has a British-built locomotive, which was used in the War of the Pacific. There is a very good railway museum at the station.

Tourist offices i perú ① *San Martín 491 (Plaza de Armas), T425514, Mon-Sat 0830-1930, Sun 0830-1400*. Also at the airport in the Arrivals hall which is usually manned when flights are scheduled to arrive, and **Terminal Terrestre Internacional** ① *Mon-Sat 0830-1500*. There is another office at the **border** ① *Thu-Sat 0830-1730*. A city map and regional information is available from **Dircetur** ① *Blondell 50, p 3, T422784, Mon-Fri 0730-1530*. See also www.turismotacna.com. **Tourist police** ① *Pasaje Calderón de la Barca 353, inside the main police station, T414141 ext 245*.

Border with Chile

There is a checkpoint before the border, which is open 0800-2300 (24 hours Friday and Saturday). You need to obtain a Peruvian exit stamp and a Chilean entrance stamp; formalities are straightforward (see below). If you need a Chilean visa, you have to get it in Tacna (address below). Peruvian time is one hour earlier than Chilean time March October; two hours earlier September/October to February/March (varies annually). No fruit or vegetables are allowed into Chile or Tacna.

Crossing by private vehicle For those leaving Peru by car buy *relaciones de pasajeros* (official forms, US$0.45) from the kiosk at the border or from a bookshop; you will need four copies. Next, return your tourist card, visit the PNP office, return the vehicle permit and finally depart through the checkpoints.

Exchange Money-changers can be found at counters in the international bus terminal; rates are much the same as in town.

◉ South to Chile listings

For hotel and restaurant price codes, and other relevant information, see Essentials.

◉ Where to stay

Moquegua *p1327*
Most hotels do not serve breakfast.
$ Alameda, Junín 322, T463971. Includes breakfast, large comfortable rooms, welcoming.
$ Hostal Adrianella, Miguel Grau 239, T463469. Hot water, safe, helpful, tourist information, close to market and buses, bit faded.
$ Hostal Carrera, Jr Lima 320-A (no sign), T462113. With or without bath, solar-powered hot water (best in afternoon), laundry facilities on roof, good value.

$ Hostal Plaza, Ayacucho 675, T461612. Modern and comfortable, good value.

Tacna *p1328, map p1328*
$$$ Gran Hotel Tacna, Av Bolognesi 300, T424193, www.granhoteltacna.com. Includes breakfast, internet, pool open to non-guests with purchases in restaurant or bar, disco, gardens, safe car park, English spoken.
$$ Copacabana, Arias Aragüez 370, T421721, www.copahotel.com. With breakfast, good rooms, restaurant, pizzería.
$$ Dorado, Arias Aragüez 145, T415741, www.doradohoteltacna.com. Modern and comfortable, good service, restaurant.

$$ El Mesón, H Unanue 175, T425841, www.mesonhotel.com. Central, modern, comfortable, safe.

$ Hostal Anturio, 28 de Julio 194 y Zela, T244258. Cafeteria downstairs, breakfast extra, good value.

$ Hostal Bon Ami, 2 de Mayo 445, T244847. With or without bath, hot water best in afternoon, simple, secure.

$ La Posada del Cacique, Arias Aragüez 300-4, T247424, laposada_hostal@hotmail. com. Antique style in an amazing building built around a huge spiral staircase.

$ Roble 18 Residencial, H Unanue 245, T241414, roble18@gmail.com. One block from Plaza de Armas. Hot water, English, Italian, German spoken.

🍴 Restaurants

Moquegua p1327

$ Moraly, Lima y Libertad. Mon-Sat 1000-2200, Sun 1000-1600. The best place for meals. Breakfast, good lunches, *menú* US$1.75.

Tacna p1328, map p1328

$$ DaVinci, San Martín 596 y Arias Araguez, T744648. Mon-Sat 1100-2300, bar Tue-Sat 2000-0200. Pizza and other dishes, nice atmosphere.

$$ Il Pomodoro, Bolívar 524 y Apurimac. Closed Sun evening and Mon 1200. Upscale Italian serving set lunch on weekdays, pricey à la carte in the evening, attentive service.

$ Cusqueñita, Zela 747. Open 1100-1600. Excellent 4-course lunch, large portions, good value, variety of choices. Recommended.

$ Fu-Lin, Arias Araguez 396 y 2 de Mayo. Mon-Sat 0930-1600. Vegetarian Chinese.

$ Koyuki, Bolívar 718. Closed Sun evening. Generous set lunch daily, seafood and à la carte in the evening. Several other popular lunch places on the same block.

$ Un Limón, Av San Martín 843, T425182. *Ceviches* and variety of seafood dishes.

Café Zeit, Deústua 150, CafeZeit on Facebook. German-owned coffee shop, cultural events and live music as well as quality coffee and cakes.

Verdi, Pasaje Vigil 57. Café serving excellent *empanadas* and sweets, also set lunch.

🚌 Transport

Moquegua p1327

Bus All bus companies are on Av Ejército, 2 blocks north of the market at Jr Grau, except **Ormeño**, Av La Paz casi Balta. From **Lima**, US$30-42, 15 hrs, many companies with executive and regular services. To **Tacna**, 159 km, 2 hrs, US$6, hourly buses with **Flores**, Av del Ejército y Andrés Aurelio Cáceres. To **Arequipa**, 3½ hrs, US$7.50-12, several buses daily. Colectivos for these 2 destinations leave when full from Av del Ejercito y Andrés Aurelio Cáceres, almost double the bus fare – negotiate. To **Desaguadero** and **Puno**, San Martín-Nobleza, 4 a day, 6 hrs, US$12. Mily Tours, Av del Ejército 32-B, T464000, colectivos to Desaguadero, 4 hrs, US$20.

Tacna p1328, map p1328

Air The airport (T314503) is at Km 5 on the Panamericana Sur, on the way to the border. To go from the airport directly to Arica, call the bus terminal (T427007) and ask a colectivo to pick you up on its way to the border, US$7.50. Taxi from airport to Tacna centre US$5-6. To **Lima**, 1½ hrs; daily flights with **LAN** (Av San Martín 259, T428346) and **Peruvian Airlines** (Av San Martín 670 p2, T412699, also to **Arequipa**).

Bus Two bus stations on Hipólito Unánue, T427007, 1 km from the plaza (colectivo US$0.35, taxi US$1 minimum). One terminal is for international services (ie Arica), the other for domestic, both are well organized, local tax US$0.50, baggage store, easy to make connections to the border, Arequipa or Lima. To **Moquegua** and **Arequipa**, 6 hrs (prices above) frequent buses with **Flores** (Av Saucini behind the Terminal Nacional, T426691). Also **Trans Moquegua Turismo** and **Cruz del Sur**. To **Nazca**, 793 km, 12 hrs, several buses daily, en route for Lima (fares US$3 less than to Lima). Several companies daily to **Lima**, 1239 km, 21-26 hrs, US$26-62 *bus-cama*, eg **Oltursa** or Civa. **Cruz del Sur** (T425729), charges US$43. Buses to **Desaguadero**, **Puno** and **Cuzco** leave from Terminal Collasuyo (T312538), Av Internacional in Barrio Altos de la Alianza neighbourhood; taxi to centre US$1. **San Martín-Nobleza** in early morning and at night to **Desaguadero**, US$22, and **Puno**, US$18, 8-10 hrs.

At **Tomasiri**, 35 km north of Tacna, passengers' luggage is checked. Do not carry anything on the bus for anyone else. Passports may be checked at Camiara, a police checkpoint some 60 km from Tacna. **Sernanp** also has a post where any fruit will be confiscated in an attempt to keep fruit fly out of Peru.

To **La Paz**, Bolivia, the quickest and cheapest route is via Moquegua and Desaguadero; it also involves one less border crossing than via Arica and Tambo Colorado.

Border with Chile: Tacna *p1329*
Road 56 km, 1-2 hrs, depending on waiting time at the border. Buses to Arica charge US$2.50 and colectivo taxis US$7.50 pp. All leave from the international terminal in Tacna throughout the day. Colectivos which carry 5 passengers only leave when full. As you approach the terminal you will be grabbed by a driver or his agent and told that the car is "just about to leave". This is hard to verify as you may not see the colectivo until you have filled in the paperwork. Once you have chosen a driver/agent, you will be rushed to his company's office where your passport will be taken from you and the details filled out on a Chilean entry form. You can change your remaining soles at the bus terminal. It is 30 mins to the Peruvian border post at Santa Rosa, where all exit formalities are carried out. The driver will hustle you through all the procedures. A short distance beyond is the Chilean post at Chacalluta, where again the driver will show you what to do. All formalities take about 30 mins. It's a further 15 mins to Arica's bus terminal. A Chilean driver is more likely to take you to any address in Arica.
Train Station is at Av Albaracín y 2 de Mayo. In 2014 no trains were running on the cross-border line to **Arica**.

ⓘ Directory

Tacna *p1328, map p1328*
Consulates Bolivia, Av Bolognesi 175, Urb Pescaserolli, T245121, Mon-Fri 0830-1630. **Chile**, Presbítero Andía block 1, T423063. Open Mon-Fri 0800-1300. **Useful addresses** Immigration, Av Circunvalación s/n, Urb El Triángulo, T243231.

Lake Titicaca

Straddling Peru's southern border with Bolivia are the sapphire-blue waters of mystical Lake Titicaca, a huge inland sea which is the highest navigable lake in the world. Its shores and islands are home to the Aymara and Quechua, who are among Peru's oldest peoples. Here you can wander through traditional villages where Spanish is a second language and where ancient myths and beliefs still hold true. Newly paved roads climb from the coastal deserts and oases to the high plateau in which sits Lake Titicaca (Arequipa-Yura-Santa Lucía-Juliaca-Puno; Moquegua-Desaguadero-Puno). The steep ascents lead to wide open views of pampas with agricultural communities, desolate mountains, small lakes and salt flats. It is a rapid change of altitude, so be prepared for some discomfort and breathlessness.

Puno and around → *Phone code: 051. Colour map 6, A2. Population: 100,170. Altitude: 3855 m.*

On the northwest shore of Lake Titicaca, Puno is capital of its department and Peru's folklore centre with a vast array of handicrafts, festivals and costumes and a rich tradition of music and dance. Puno gets bitterly cold at night: from June to August the temperature at night can fall to -25°C, but generally not below -5°C.

Arriving in Puno
Tourist offices i perú ⓘ *Jr Lima y Deústua, near Plaza de Armas, T365088, iperupuno@ promperu. gob.pe, daily 0830-1930.* Helpful English-speaking staff, good information and maps. Municipal website: www.munipuno.gob.pe. Dircetur ⓘ *Ayacucho 684, T364976, puno@mincetur.gob.pe,*

with a desk at the Terminal Terrestre. **Indecopi** ⓘ *Jr Deústua 644, T363667, jpilco@indecopi. gob.pe*, is the consumer protection bureau. **Tourist police** ⓘ *Jr Deústua 558, T354764, daily 0600-2200*. Report any scams, such as unscrupulous price changes, and beware touts (see page 1337).

Places around Puno

The **Cathedral** ⓘ *Mon-Fri 0800-1200, 1500-1800, Sat-Sun until 1900*, completed in 1657, has an impressive baroque exterior, but an austere interior. Across the street from the Cathedral is the **Balcony of the Conde de Lemos** ⓘ *Deústua y Conde de Lemos, art gallery open Mon-Fri 0800-1600* where Peru's Viceroy stayed when he first arrived in the city. The **Museo Municipal Dreyer** ⓘ *Conde de Lemos 289, Mon-Sat 1030-2200, Sun 1600-2200, US$5 includes 45-min guided tour*, has been combined with the private collection of Sr Carlos Dreyer. A short walk up Independencia leads to the **Arco Deústua**, a monument honouring those killed in the battles of Junín and Ayacucho. Nearby, is a mirador giving fine views over the town, the port and the lake beyond. The walk from Jr Cornejo following the Stations of the Cross up a nearby hill, with fine views of

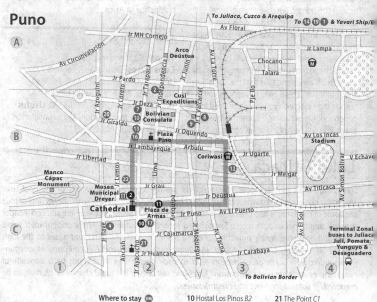

Puno

To Juliaca, Cuzco & Arequipa
To ⑭ ⑲ ① & Yavari Ship/B

Lake Titicaca, has been recommended, but be careful and don't go alone (the same applies to any of the hills around Puno, eg Huajsapata).

Avenida Titicaca leads to the port from where boats go to the islands. From its intersection with Avenida Costanera towards the pier, one side of the road is lined with the kiosks of the **Artesanos Unificados de Puno**, selling crafts. Closer to the port are food kiosks. On the opposite side of the road is a shallow lake where you can hire **pedal boats** ① *US$0.70 pp for 20 mins*. At the pier are the ticket counters for transport to the islands. The **Malecón Bahía de los Incas**, a lovely promenade along the waterfront, extends to the north and south; it is a pleasant place for a stroll and for birdwatching. The **Yavari** ① *0815-1715, free but donations of US$6 welcome to help with maintenance costs*, the oldest ship on Lake Titicaca, is berthed near the entrance to the **Sonesta Posada del Inca** hotel and is you have to go through the hotel to get to it. Alternatively, a boat from the port costs US$2 return, with wait. The ship was built in England in 1862 and was shipped in kit form to Arica, then by rail to Tacna and by mule to Lake Titicaca. The journey took six years. The *Yavari* was launched on Christmas Day 1870. Project addresses: England: 12 Back Lane, Great Bedwyn, Wiltshire SN8 3NX, yavarilarken@gmail.com. In Puno: T051-369329, yavariguldentops@hotmail.com.

Puno centre

Visit www.yavari.org. Another old ship is the **MN Coya** ① *moored in Barrio Guaje, beyond the Hotel Sonesta Posada del Inka, T368156, has a restaurant on board*, built in Scotland and launched on the lake in 1892. Berthed next to Coya is Hull (UK)-built *MS Ollanta*, which sailed the lake from 1926 to the 1970s.

Around Puno

Anybody interested in religious architecture should visit the villages along the western shore of Lake Titicaca. An Inca sundial can be seen near the village of **Chucuito** (19 km), which has an interesting church, La Asunción, and houses with carved stone doorways.

Juli, 80 km, has some fine examples of religious architecture. **San Pedro** on the plaza, is the only functioning **church** ① *open 0630-1130, 1400-1600, except Tue when only for mass at 0700 and Sun for Mass at 0730, 1100 and 1800, free, but donations appreciated*. It contains a series of paintings of saints, with the Via Crucis scenes in the same frame, and gilt side altars above which some of the arches have baroque designs. **San Juan Letrán** ① *daily 0800-1600, US$1.50*, has two sets of 17th-century paintings of the lives of St John the Baptist and of St Teresa, contained in sumptuous gilded frames. San Juan is a museum. It also has intricate *mestizo* carving in pink stone. **La Asunción** ① *daily 0800-1630, US$1.20*, is also a museum. The nave is empty, but its walls are lined with colonial paintings with no labels. The original painting on the walls of the transept can be seen. Its fine bell tower was damaged by earthquake or lightning. Outside is an archway and atrium which date from the early 17th century. Needlework, other weavings, handicrafts and antiques are offered for sale in town. Colectivo Puno-Juli US$1.50; return from Juli outside market at Ilave 349.

A further 20 km along the lake is **Pomata** (bus from Juli US$0.75, US$2 from Puno), whose red sandstone church of **Santiago Apóstol** ① *daily 0700-1200, 1330-1600, US$1, but if guardian is not there, leave money on table,* has a striking exterior and beautiful interior, with superb carving and paintings. At **Zepita**, near Desaguadero, the 18th-century Dominican church is also worth a visit.

Near Puno are the *chullpas* (pre-Columbian funeral towers) of **Sillustani** ① *32 km from Puno on a good road, US$2, take an organized tour; about 3-4 hrs, leave 1430, US$15-18, tours usually stop at a Colla house on the way, to see local products,* in a beautiful setting on a peninsula in Lake Umayo. John Hemming writes: "Most of the towers date from the period of Inca occupation in the 15th century, but they are burial towers of the Aymara-speaking Colla tribe. The engineering involved in their construction is more complex than anything the Incas built – it is defeating archaeologists' attempts to rebuild the tallest 'lizard' *chullpa*." There is a museum and handicraft sellers wait at the exit. Photography is best in the afternoon light, though this is when the wind is strongest. The scenery is barren, but impressive. There is a small community at the foot of the promontory.

Llachón → *Population: 1300.*
At the eastern end of the Península de Capachica, which encloses the northern side of the Bahía de Puno, the pretty farming villages of Llachón, Santa María and Ccotos have become a focus of community-based tourism. On Capachica there are currently six organizations, each with a dozen or more families and links to different tour operators in Puno, Cuzco or abroad. The scenery is very pretty, with sandy beaches, pre-Inca terracing, trees and flowers. The view of the sunset from the Auki Carus hill is reckoned to be better even than from Taquile. Visitors share in local activities and 70% of all produce served is from the residents' farms. Throughout the peninsula the dress of the local women is very colourful, with four-cornered hats called *monteros*, matching vests and colourful *polleras*. The peninsula is good for hiking, mountain biking and sailing; boats can be hired. Off the east coast of the peninsula is the island of Ticonata, whose community tourism association offers accommodation in round houses and various activities (www.ticonatatours. com). It's a short boat ride from Ccotos, or from Amantaní. Motor boats from Puno take 3½ hours.

⊚ Puno and around listings

For hotel and restaurant price codes, and other relevant information, see Essentials.

⊜ Where to stay

Puno *p1331, map p1332*
A number of luxury hotels are opening in and around the city. Prices vary according to season. Many touts try to persuade tourists to go to a hotel not of their own choosing. Be firm.
$$$$ Casa Andina Private Collection Puno, Av Sesquicentenario 1970, T363992. This recommended chain's lakeshore luxury property. The group also has **$$ Casa Andina Tikarani**, Independencia 185, T367803, heating, non-smoking rooms, safe, central, business centre. Visit www.casa-andina.com.

$$$$ Libertador Lago Titicaca, on Isla Esteves linked by a causeway 5 km northeast of Puno (taxi US$3), T367780, www.libertador.com.pe. Modern hotel with every facility, built on a Tiahuanaco-period site, spacious, good views, phone, bar, good restaurant, disco, good service, parking.
$$$$ Sonesta Posadas del Inca, Av Sesquicentenario 610, Huaje, 5 km from Puno on the lakeshore, T364111, www. sonesta.com/laketiticaca/. 62 rooms with heating, facilities for the disabled, local textile decorations, good views, **Inkafé** restaurant has an Andean menu, folklore shows.
$$$ Hacienda Puno, Jr Deústua 297, T356109, www.lahaciendapuno.com. Refurbished colonial house, with buffet breakfast, rooms and suites with good bathrooms, restaurant with local specialities, comfortable.

$$$ Intiqa, Jr Tarapacá 272, T366900, www.intiqahotel.com. Built around a sunny courtyard with good restaurant. Stylish, rooms have heaters, professional staff. Associated with **La Casa de Wiracocha**, at No 260, for select Peruvian handicrafts.

$$$ Plaza Mayor, Deústua 342, T366089, www.plazamayorhostal.com. Comfortable, well-appointed, good big beds, buffet breakfast, hot water, laundry, restaurant.

$$$ Puno Plaza, Jr Puno 425, T351424, http://tierravivahoteles.com. Tastefully decorated modern hotel overlooking the Plaza de Armas, includes buffet breakfast, very comfortable rooms, all with bathtub or jacuzzi, heater, safety box, good restaurant.

$$$-$$ Tierra Viva Plaza, Jr Grau 270, 1 block from plaza, T367520, www.tierravivahoteles.com. Heating, non-smoking rooms, safe, central, business centre, parking.

$$ Casona Colón Inn, Tacna 290, T351432, www.coloninn.com. Colonial style, good rooms with hot shower, good service, safe, restaurant **Sol Naciente** and pizzería **Europa**, the Belgian manager Christian Nonis is well known, especially for his work on behalf of the people on Taquile island.

$$ Conde de Lemos, Jr Puno 681, T369898, www.condelemosinn.com. Convenient, comfy, plush modern hotel, heating, washing machine, elevator, wheel chair friendly, restaurant.

$$ El Buho, Lambayeque 142, T366122, www.hotelbuho.com. Hot water, nice rooms with heaters, restaurant, safe, discount for Footprint book owners, travel agency for trips and flights.

$$ Hostal Imperial, Teodoro Valcarcel 145, T352386, www.hostalimperial.com. Basic but big rooms, good hot showers, safe, helpful, stores luggage, comfortable.

$$ Hostal Italia, Teodoro Valcarcel 122, T367706, www.hotelitaliaperu.com. 2 blocks from the station. With breakfast, cheaper in low season, good, safe, hot water, good food, small rooms, staff helpful.

$$ Hostal Pukara, Jr Libertad 328, T368448, pukara@terra.com.pe. Excellent, English spoken, helpful service, central, quiet, free coca to drink in evening, American breakfast included, dining room on top floor, lots of stairs.

$$ Posada Don Giorgio, Tarapacá 238, T363648, www.posadadongiorgio.com.

Comfortable, hot water, large rooms, nicely decorated, traditional architecture.

$$ Sillustani, Tarapacá 305 y Lambayeque, T351881, www.sillustani.com. Hot water, safety deposit, heaters, well-established, popular, reservations advised.

$$ Tambo Real, Jr Santiago Giraldo 362, T366060, www.tamborealtitikaka.com. Good value, bright rooms, good bathrooms, family-owned, helpful, tea and coffee in the lobby all day.

$$ pp MN Yavari, Muelle del Hotel Sonesta Posadas del Inca, T369329 (in Lima T01-255 7268), reservasyavari@gmail.com. B&B is available on board, 3 twin bunk rooms with shared bath. Dinner served on request downstairs in the Victorian saloon.

$ Hospedaje Residencial Margarita, Jr Tarapacá 130, T352820, www.hostal margaritapuno.com. Large building, family atmosphere, cold rooms, heaters on request, hot water, tours can be arranged.

$ Hostal Los Pinos, Tarapacá 182, T367398, hostalpinos@hotmail.com. Family run, helpful, small breakfast, cold rooms, heater on request, hot showers, safe, laundry facilities, tours organized.

$ Inka's Rest, Pasaje San Carlos 158, T368720, http://inkasresthostel.com. Several sitting areas hot water, heating, double or twin rooms with private or shared bath and a dorm, cooking and laundry facilities, a place to meet other travellers, reserve ahead.

$ Los Uros, Teodoro Valcarcel 135, T352141, www.losuros.com. Private or shared bath, hot water, breakfast available, quiet at back, small charge to leave luggage, laundry, heating costs extra.

$ The Point, Av Ayacucho 515-517, T351427, www.thepointhostels.com. Quieter than some of the other Point hostels, 1 block from main plaza, with dorms for 1-4 people, each with bath, hot water, bar, restaurant, travel centre, hammocks.

Around Puno: Chucuito p1333

$$$$ Titilaka Lodge, Comunidad de Huencalla s/n, on a private peninsula near Chucuito, T01-700 5111 (Lima), www.titilaka.com. Luxury boutique hotel offering all-inclusive packages in an exclusive environment on the edge of the lake. Plenty of activities available.

$$ Las Cabañas, Jr Tarapacá 538, T369494, T951-751196, www.chucuito.com. Rooms and cottages, lakeside, breakfast included, other meals available, events and conferences held here, will collect you from Puno if you phone in advance.

$ Sra Nely Durán Saraza, Chucuíto Occopampa, T951 586240 (mob). 2 nice rooms, one with lake view, shared bath, hot water, breakfast and dinner available, very welcoming and interesting.

Llachón p1334
Families offer accommodation on a rotational basis and, as the community presidents change each year, the standard of facilities changes from year-to-year and family-to family. All hosts can arrange boat transport to Amantaní. Among those who offer lodging ($ per bed, meals extra) are: Tomás Cahui Coila, **Centro Turístico Santa María Llachón**, T951 923595, www.exploretiticaca.com; **Primo Flores**, Santa María, T951-821392/951-680040/951-410901, primopuno@hotmail.com; **Valentín Quispe**, T051-951-821392 (mob), llachon@yahoo.com. But do recognize that there are other families who accept guests.

❼ Restaurants

Puno p1331, map p1332
$$ IncAbar, Lima 348, T368031. Open for breakfast, lunch and dinner, interesting dishes in creative sauces, fish, pastas, curries, café and couch bar, nice decor.
$$ Internacional, Moquegua 201, T352502. Very popular, excellent trout, good pizzas, service variable.
$$ La Hostería, Lima 501, T365406. Good set meal and à la carte dishes including local fare like alpaca and *cuy*, pizza, also breakfast, music in the evening.
$$ La Plaza, Puno 425, Plaza de Armas. Good food, international dishes and *comida nueva andina*, good service.
$$ Mojsa, Lima 635 p 2, Plaza de Armas. Good international and *novo andino* dishes, also has an arts and crafts shop.
$$ Tradiciones del Lago, Lima 418, T368140, www.tradicionesdelago.com. Buffet, à la carte and a big selection of Peruvian food.

$$ Tulipans, Lima 394, T351796. Sandwiches, juices and a lunchtime menu are its staples. One of the few places in Puno with outdoor seating in a pleasant colonial courtyard, a good option for lunch.
$$-$ Don Piero, Lima 360. Huge meals, live music, try their '*pollo coca-cola*' (chicken in a sweet and sour sauce), slow service, popular, tax extra.
$$-$ Pizzería/Trattoria El Buho, Lima 349 and at Jr Libertad 386, T356223. Open 1800 onwards. Excellent pizza, lively atmosphere, pizzas US$2.35-3.
$ Casa Grilll La Estancia, Libertad 137, T51-365469. Salad bar, huge steaks, grilled meat and peruvian food. Very popular with locals for huge lunches and a few beers.
$ Chifa Nan Hua, Arequipa 378. Tasty Chinese, big portions.
$ Govinda, Deústua 312. Closes at 2000. Cheap vegetarian lunch menus.
$ Ukukus, Libertad 216 and Pje Grau 172, T367373, 369504. Good combination of Andean and novo andino cuisine as well as pizzas and some Chinese *chifa* style.
$ Vida Natural, Tacna 141. Breakfast, salads, fruits, also vegetarian meals midday and evening.

Cafés
Cafetería Mercedes, Jr Arequipa 144. Good menú US$1.50, bread, cakes, snacks, juices.
Casa del Corregidor, Deústua 576, aptdo 2, T365603. In restored 17th-century building, sandwiches, good snacks, coffee, good music, great atmosphere, nice surroundings with patio. Also has a Fair Trade store offering products directly from the producers.
Ricos Pan, Jr Lima 424. Mon-Sat 0600-2300. Café and bakery, great cakes, excellent coffees, juices and pastries, breakfasts and other dishes. Branches at Arequipa cuadra 3 and Moquegua 330.

❼ Bars and clubs

Puno p1331, map p1332
Dómino, Libertad 443. Happy hour 2000-2130 Mon-Thu. "Megadisco", good.
Positive, Jr Lima 382. Drinks, large-screen TV, modern music, occasional heavy metal groups.
Pub Ekeko's, Lima 355. Happy hour 2000-2200. Live music every night.

⊛ Festivals

Puno *p1331, map p1332*
Feb At the **Fiesta de la Virgen de la Candelaria**, 1st 2 weeks in **Feb**, bands and dancers from all the local towns compete in a *Diablada*, or Devil Dance. The festivities are better at night on the streets than the official functions in the stadium. Check the dates in advance as Candelaria may be moved if pre-Lentern carnival coincides with it. A candlelight procession through darkened streets takes place on **Good Friday**. **3 May Festividad de las Cruces**, celebrated with masses, a procession and the Alasita festival of miniatures. **29 Jun** Colourful festival of **San Pedro**, with a procession at Zepita (see page 1334). **4-5 Nov** Pageant dedicated to the founding of Puno and the emergence of Manco Cápac and Mama Ocllo from the waters of Lake Titicaca.

⊙ Shopping

Puno *p1331, map p1332*
Markets Puno is the best place in Peru to buy alpaca wool articles, bargaining is appropriate. Along the avenue leading to the port is the large **Mercado Artesanal Asociación de Artesanos Unificados**, daily 0900-1800. Closer to the centre are **Mercado Coriwasi**, Ugarte 150, daily 0800-2100 and **Central Integral de Artesanos del Perú** (CIAP), Jr Deústua 576, Mon-Sat 1000-1800. The **Mercado Central**, in the blocks bound by Arbulú, Arequipa, Oquendo and Tacna has all kinds of food, including good cheeses as well as a few crafts. Beware pickpockets in the market. You will be hassled on the street and outside restaurants to buy woollen goods, so take care.

⊙ What to do

Puno *p1331, map p1332*
Watch out for unofficial tour sellers, *jalagringos*, who offer hotels and tours at varying rates, depending on how wealthy you look. They are everywhere: train station, bus offices, airport and hotels. Ask to see their guide's ID card. Only use agencies with named premises, compare prices and only hand over money at the office, never on the street or in a hotel.

Agencies organize trips to the Uros floating islands (see page 1339) and the islands of Taquile and Amantaní, as well as to Sillustani, and other places. The standard tour is two days, one night, visiting the Uros, staying in either Taquile or Amantaní and then visiting the other island the next day (from US$26.50 pp). Choose an agency that allows you to pay direct for your lodging so you know that the family is benefiting. Make sure that you settle all details before embarking on the tour. We have received good reports on the following:
All Ways Travel, Casa del Corregidor, Deústua 576, p 2, T353979, and at Tacna 281, p 2, T355552, www.titicacaperu.com. Very helpful, kind and reliable, speak German, French, English and Italian. They offer a unique cultural tour to the islands of Anapia and Yuspique in Lake Wiñaymarka, beyond the straits of Tiquina, "The Treasure of Wiñaymarka", departures Thu and Sun.
CEDESOS, Centro para el Desarrollo Sostenible (Centre for Sustainable Development), Jr Moquegua 348 Int p 3, T367915, www.cedesos.org. A non-profit NGO which offers interesting tours of Capachica peninsula with overnight stops in family homes, going to the less visited islands where there are few tourists.
Cusi Expeditions, Jr T Varcarcel 164, T369072, reservascusi@terra.com.pe. They own most of the boats which operate the standard tours of the Islands. You will very likely end up on a Cusi tour so it's best to buy from them directly to get the best price and the most accurate information.
Edgar Adventures, Jr Lima 328, T353444, www.edgaradventures.com. English, German and French spoken, very helpful and knowledgeable. Constantly exploring new areas, lots of off-the-beaten-track tours, eg kayaking tour of Llachón. Community-minded, promote responsible tourism. Consistently recommended.
Kontiki Tours, Jr Melgar 188, T353473, www.kontikiperu.com. Receptive tour agency specializing in special interest excursions.
Nayra Travel, Jr Lima 419, of 105, T337934, www.nayratravel.com. Small agency run by Lilian Cotrado and her helpful staff, traditional local tours and a variety of options in Llachón. Can organize off-the-beaten track excursions for a minimum of 2 people. Recommended.
Peru Up to Date, Arequipa 340, T950-857371, www.peruuptodate.com. New, offers tours in the Puno and Titicaca area.

Pirámide Tours, Jr Rosendo Huirse 130, T366107, www.titikakalake.com. Out of the ordinary and classic tours, flexible, personalized service, modern fast launches, very helpful, works only via internet, overseas clients.
Titikaka Explorers, Jr Puno 633 of 207, T368903, www.titikaka-explorer.com. Good service, helpful.

⊖ Transport

Puno *p1331, map p1332*
Bus All long-distance buses, except some Cuzco services and buses to La Paz (see below), leave from the Terminal Terrestre, which is at 1 de Mayo 703 y Victoria, by the lake, T364733. It has a tourist office, snack bars and toilets. Platform tax US$0. 50. Small buses and colectivos for Juliaca, llave and towns on the lake shore between Puno and Desaguadero, including Yunguyo, leave from the Terminal Zonal, Av Bolívar between Jrs Carabaya and Palma. To **Juliaca**, 44 km, 1 hr, bus US$1, minibus US$2. Daily buses to **Arequipa**, 5 hrs via Juliaca, 297 km, most buses take this route, US$15 (**Destinos, Julsa, Señor de Milagros**, or **Sur Oriente**, most have a morning and evening bus – better quality buses go at night); **Cruz del Sur**, T368524, US$19-25. To **Moquegua**, US$7.50-9, and **Tacna**, US$18. To **Lima**, 1011 km, 21 hrs, all buses go through **Arequipa**, sometimes with a change of bus. See Arequipa, page 1330. For services to La Paz or Copacabana (Bolivia), see page 1344.

To **Cuzco**, 388 km, 5-7 hrs. There are 3 levels of service: regular via Juliaca, US$12, 7 hrs; direct, without stopping in Juliaca, with **Tour Perú**, Jr Tacna, T365517; www.tourperu.com.pe, at 0800, US$15 and 2130 (*bus cama* US$18), 6 hrs; tourist service with 5 stops (Pukará, Sicuani for lunch, La Raya, Raqchi and Andahuayllillas), leave at 0730, US$60, includes lunch, 10 hrs, with **Inka Express**, Jr Tacna 346 and at the Terminal Terrestre, T365654, www.inkaexpress.com.pe (leaves from the Terminal and may pick up from hotel on request), **First Class**, Tacna 280-300, T364640, or **Turismo Mer**, Jr Tacna 336, T367223, www.turismomer.com. In high season, reserve 2 days ahead. **Note** It is advisable to travel by day, for safety as well as for the views. If you wish to travel by bus and cannot go direct, it is no problem to take separate buses to Juliaca, then to Sicuani, then to Cuzco.

To **Puerto Maldonado**, several daily along Route 4 of the Interoceanic Highway, a dramatic road via Juliaca, the San Gabán gorge and **Mazuko**, where the branches of the new road from Cuzco, Puerto Maldonado and Juliaca converge, **Transporte Santa Cruz**, US$27, 10-12 hrs. Other services start from Juliaca or from Arequipa via Juliaca.
Boats on Lake Titicaca Boats to the islands leave from the terminal in the harbour (see map); *trici-taxi* from centre, US$1.
Taxi 3-wheel 'Trici-Taxis', cost about US$0.25 per km and are the best way to get around.
Trains The railway runs from Puno to Juliaca (44 km), where it divides, to Cuzco (381 km) and Arequipa (279 km; no passenger service). To **Cuzco**, *Andean Explorer*, US$156, Cuzco to Puno US$268, Mon, Wed, Fri (Apr-Oct) and Sat at 0800, arriving in Cuzco at about 1800; try to sit on the right hand side for the views. The train stops at La Raya. The ticket office is open 0700-1700 Mon-Fri, 0700-1200 Sat, Sun and holidays; in high season buy several days in advance, passport required. The station is well guarded by police and sealed off to those without tickets.

Llachón *p1334*
Boats Only 1 weekly public boat from Llachón to **Puno**, Fri 0900, returning to Llachón Sat 1000, US$1.50, 3½ hrs. The daily 0800 boat to Amantaní may drop you off at Colata (at the tip of the peninsula), a 1-hr walk from Llachón, confirm details in advance. Returning to Puno, you can try to flag down the boat from Amantaní which passes Colata between 0830 and 0930. In Santa María (Llachón), boats can be hired for trips to **Amantaní** (40 mins) and **Taquile** (50 mins), US$30 return, minimum 10 passengers. **Combis** run daily from Bellavista market (known as El Contrabando) in Puno to **Capachica**, from 0700 to 1600, 1½ hrs, US$1.35, where you get another combi or bus to **Llachón**, leave when full, 30 mins, US$1.

⊙ Directory

Puno *p1331, map p1332*
Consulates Bolivia, Jr Arequipa 136, T351251, consular visas take about 48 hrs, Mon-Fri 0800-1400. **Useful addresses** Immigration: Ayacucho 280, T357103, Mon-Fri 0800-1300, 1500-1700.

The islands

The Uros
① US$2 entry.
The people of Uros or the 'floating islands' in Puno Bay fish, hunt birds and live off the lake plants, most important of which are the reeds they use for their boats, houses and the very foundations of their islands. Visitors to the floating islands encounter more women than men. These women wait every day for the tour boats to sell their handicrafts. The few men one does see might be building or repairing boats or fixing their nets. The rest are out on the lake, hunting and fishing. The Uros cannot live from tourism alone and it is better to buy handicrafts or pay for services than just to tip. They glean extra income from tourists offering overnight accommodation in reed houses, selling meals and providing Uro guides for two-hour tours. Organized tour parties are usually given a boat building demonstration and the chance to take a short trip in a reed boat. Some islanders will also greet boat loads of tourists with a song and will pose for photos. The islanders, who are very friendly, appreciate gifts of pens, paper, etc for their two schools. This form of tourism on the Uros Islands is now well-established and, whether it has done irreparable harm or will ultimately prove beneficial, it takes place in superb surroundings. Take drinking water as there is none on the islands.

Taquile
① US$3 to land. Contact Munay Taquile, the island's community-based travel agency, Titicaca 508, Puno, T351448, www.taquile.net
Isla Taquile, 45 km from Puno, on which there are numerous pre-Inca and Inca ruins, and Inca terracing, is only about 1 km wide, but 6-7 km long. Ask for the (unmarked) **museum of traditional costumes**, which is on the plaza. There is a co-operative shop on the plaza that sells exceptional woollen goods, which are not cheap, but of very fine quality. Each week different families sell their products. Shops on the plaza sell postcards, water and dry goods. The principal festivals are from 2-7 June, and the **Fiesta de Santiago** from 25 July to 2 August, with many dances in between. Native guides in Taquile, some speaking English and/or German, charge US$5 for two-hour tours. If you are staying over, you are advised to take some food, particularly fruit, bread and vegetables, water, plenty of small-value notes, candles and a torch, toilet paper and a sleeping bag. Take precautions against sunburn and take warm clothes for the cold nights. It is worth spending a night on Taquile to observe the daily flurry of activity around the boatloads of tourists: demonstrations of traditional dress and weaving techniques, the preparation of trout to feed the hordes. When the boats leave, the island breathes a gentle sigh and people slowly return to their more traditional activities.

Amantaní
① US$3 to land.
Another island worth visiting, is Amantaní, very beautiful and peaceful. There are six villages and ruins on both of the island's peaks, **Pacha Tata** and **Pacha Mama**, from which there are excellent views. There are also temples and on the shore there is a throne carved out of stone, the **Inkatiana**. On both hills, a fiesta is celebrated on 15-20 January, **Pago a la Tierra or San Sebastián**. The festivities are very colourful, musical and hard-drinking. There is also a festival on 9 April, **Aniversario del Consejo** (of the local council), and a **Feria de Artesanías**, 8-16 August. The residents make beautiful textiles and sell them quite cheaply at the Artesanía Cooperativa. They also make basketwork and stonework. The people are Quechua speakers, but understand Spanish. Islanders arrange dances for tour groups (independent travellers can join in), visitors dress up in local clothes and join the dances. Small shops sell water and snacks.

Anapia and Yuspique
In the Peruvian part of the Lago Menor are the islands of **Anapia**, a friendly, Aymara-speaking community, and **Yuspique**, on which are ruins and vicuñas. The community has organized

committees for tourism, motor boats, sailing boats and accommodation with families (**All Ways Travel**, see page 1337, arranges tours). To visit Anapia independently, take a colectivo from Yunguyo to Tinicachi and alight at Punta Hermosa, just after Unacachi. Boats to Anapia leave Punta Hermosa on Sunday and Thursday at 1300 (they leave Anapia for Yunguyo market on the same days at 0630); bus from Puno Sunday, Tuesday, Thursday, US$6. It's two hours each way by boat. On the island ask for José Flores, who is very knowledgeable about Anapia's history, flora and fauna. He sometimes acts as a guide.

◉ The islands listings

For hotel and restaurant price codes, and other relevant information, see Essentials.

⊕ Where to stay

The Uros *p1339*
Oscar Coyla, T051-951-824378 is the representative for the Uros community. Accommodation costs US$5 pp, simple meals are extra or US$10 pp full board including tour. **René Coyla Coila**, T051-951-743533 is an official tour guide who can advise on lodging and **Armando Suaña**, T051-951-341374 is another native guide offering accommodation in Kantati.

Taquile *p1339*
The Community Tourism Agency **Munay Taquile** (see above) can arrange accommodation in a **Casa Rural**, **Albergue Rural**, or **Hotel Rural**. Someone will approach you when you get off the boat if you don't have anything booked in advance. Lodging rates US$15-25 pp full board. Most Taquileños have a room in which they can accommodate visitors (*Casa Rural*). Since some families have become the favourites of tour groups they have been able to build bigger and better facilities (eg with showers and loos) (*Albergue* or *Hotel Rural*) and those which are in need of the income are often shunned as their facilities may be more basic. Instead of staying in the busy part around the main square, the Huayllano community is hosting visitors. This is on the south side of the island. Contact **Alipio Huatta Cruz**, T051-951 668551 or T951-615239 or you can arrange a visit with **All Ways Travel**, see page 1337.

Amantaní *p1339*
The **Presidente del Comité Turístico de Amantaní** is Senón Tipo Huatta, T051-951 832 308. Rate is up to US$25 pp full board. If you are willing to walk to a more distant communities, you might get a better price and you are helping to share the income. Some families that one can contact are: **$$ Kantuta Lodge**, T051-630238, 951 636172, www.kantutalodge.com, run by Richard Cari and family, full board; **Hospedaje Jorge Cari**, basic, but nice family, great view of lake from room, or **Ambrosio Mamani**; or **Familia Victoriano Calsin Quispe**, Casilla 312, Isla Amantaní, T051-360220/363320.

❼ Restaurants

Taquile *p1339*
There are many small restaurants around the plaza and on the track to the Puerto Principal (eg Gerardo Huatta's **La Flor de Cantuta**, on the steps; **El Inca** on the main plaza). Meals are generally fish, rice and chips, omelette and *fiambre*, a local stew. Meat is rarely available and drinks often run out. Breakfast consists of pancakes and bread.

Amantaní *p1339*
There is 1 restaurant, **Samariy**. The artificially low price of tours allows families little scope for providing anything other than basic meals, so take your own supplies if you so wish.

⊖ Transport

The Uros *p1339*
Boat Asociación de Transporte los Uros, at the port, T368024, aeuttal@hotmail.com, 0800-1600. Motorboat US$5, 0600-1600 or whenever there are 10 people. Agencies charge US$12-15.

Taquile *p1339*
Boats Centro de Operadores de Transporte Taquile, at the port, T205477, 0600-1100, 1400-1800. In high season, boats go at 0730

and 0800, stopping at the **Uros** on the way, returning at 1400 and 1430, in low season only one boat travels, US$7.50 one way. Organized tours cost US$18-25.

Amantaní p1339
Boats Transportes Unificados Amantaní, at the port, T369714, 0800-1100. 2 daily boats at 0815, one direct, the 2nd one stops at Uros, they return at 0800 the next day, one directo **Puno**, the 2nd one stops at **Taquile**. US$7.50 one way direct, US$18 return with stops at **Uros** and Taquile. Amantaní-Taquile costs US$3. If you stop in Taquile on the way back, you can continue to Puno at 1200 with the Amantaní boat or take a Taquile boat at 1400 (also 1430 in high season). Purchasing one-way tickets gives you more flexibility if you wish to stay longer on the islands.

To Cuzco

Juliaca → *Phone code: 051. Colour map 6, A2. Population: 134,700. Altitude: 3825 m.*

Freezing cold at night, hygienically challenged and less than safe, Juliaca, 289 km northeast of Arequipa, is not particularly attractive. As the commercial focus of an area bounded by Puno, Arequipa and the jungle, it has grown very fast into a noisy chaotic place with a large impermanent population, lots of contraband and more *tricitaxis* than cars. Monday, market day, is the most disorganized of all. A Sunday woollens market, **La Dominical**, is held near the exit to Cuzco. The handicrafts gallery, **Las Calceteras**, is on Plaza Bolognesi. Túpac Amaru market, on Moquegua seven blocks east of railway line, is a cheap market. **Tourist office**, Dircetur ① *Jr Noriega 191, p 3, T321839, Mon-Fri 0730-1530.*

The unspoiled little colonial town of **Lampa**, 31 km northwest of Juliaca is known as the 'Pink City'. It has a splendid church, La Inmaculada, containing a copy of Michelangelo's 'Pietà' cast in aluminium (guided tours of the church, crypt and mausoleum, US$3.50), many Cuzqueña school paintings and a carved wooden pulpit. To see a plaster copy of the 'Pietà' in the Municipalidad, a donation is requested. **Kampac Museo** ① *Jr Ayacucho y Alfonso Ugarte, T951-820085, owner Profesor Jesús Vargas can be found at the shop opposite, no charge for admission and tour but contributions appreciated*, small private museum featuring an eclectic collection of sculptures and ceramics from a number of Peruvian cultures. Lampa has a small Sunday market and celebrates a fiesta of **Santiago Apóstol** on 6-15 December. There is a fine colonial bridge just south of the town.

At **Pucará**, 63 km west of Juliaca on the road to Cuzco, Route 4, a fully paved branch of the Interoceanic Highway, heads north across the vast alpaca-grazed altiplano to Macusani (4400 m, always cold, basic hotels). The dramatic road then descends past the mining supply towns of Olachea and San Gabán, to Puente Iñambari, Mazuko and Puerto Maldonado. This off-the-beaten-path route through the Cordillera Carabaya connects Lake Titicaca and the southern jungle (see Transport below). Along the way are rock formations, petroglyphs and the glaciated summits of Allin Cápost surrounded by lakes and valleys ideal for trekking.

Puno to Cuzco

The road Puno-Juliaca-Cuzco is fully paved and in good condition. Bus services are an acceptable alternative to the train, at an average altitude of 3500 m. There is much to see on the way, but neither the daytime buses nor the trains make frequent stops. You would have to be using your own transport, or taking buses from town to town to sample what the places en route have to offer, eg pottery bulls at Pucará (rooms available at the station); knitted alpaca ponchos and pullovers and miniature llamas at Santa Rosa (rooms available). There are also hotels in **Ayaviri**, whose speciality is a mild, creamy cheese (US$4 per kg).

The road and railway crosses the altiplano, climbing to **La Raya**, the highest pass on the line; 210 km from Puno, at 4321 m (local market; toilets US$0.20). Up on the heights breathing may be a little difficult, but the descent along the Río Vilcanota is rapid. To the right of **Aguas Calientes**, the next station, 10 km from La Raya, are steaming pools of hot water in the middle of the green grass; a startling sight (US$0.15). The temperature of the springs is 40°C, and they show beautiful deposits of red ferro-oxide. Communal bathing pools and a block of changing rooms have been opened. At **Maranganí**, the river is wider and the fields greener, with groves of eucalyptus trees.

At 38 km beyond La Raya pass is **Sicuani** (*Phone code: 084; Altitude: 3690 m*), an important agricultural centre. Excellent items of llama and alpaca wool and skins are sold on the railway station and at the Sunday morning market. Around Plaza Libertad there are several hat shops. The bus terminal is in the newer part of town, which is separated from the older part and the Plaza by a pedestrian walkway and bridge. Several hotels (**$**) lie on the west side of the pedestrian bridge. (For more information about places between Sicuani and Cuzco, see page 1370.)

⦿ To Cuzco listings

For hotel and restaurant price codes, and other relevant information, see Essentials.

⦿ Where to stay

Juliaca *p1341*
The town has water problems in dry season.
$$$ Hotel Don Carlos, Jr 9 de Diciembre 114, Plaza Bolognesi, T323600, www.hoteles doncarlos.com. Comfortable, modern facilities, hot water, heater, good service, breakfast, restaurant and room service. Also has **Suites Don Carlos**, Jr M Prado 335, T321571.
$$ Royal Inn, San Román 158, T321561, www.royalinnhoteles.com. Rooms and suites with heaters, includes breakfast, good restaurant (**$$-$**).
$$ Sakura, San Román 133, T322072, hotelsakura@hotmail.com. Quiet, hot water, basic rooms in older section with shared bath.
$$-$ Hostal Luquini, Jr Brasesco 409, Plaza Bolognesi, T321510. Comfortable, patio, helpful staff, reliable hot water in morning only, motorcycle parking.

Lampa
$ Hospedaje Estrella, Jr Municipal 540. Simple rooms, with or without private bath, hot water, very friendly, breakfast included, a good alternative to staying in Juliaca.

⦿ Restaurants

Juliaca *p1341*
$ Dory's, Jr San Martín 347. Sun-Thu 0800-2000, Fri 0800-1400. Simple vegetarian.
$ El Asador, Unión 119. Open 1800-2400. Chicken, grill and pizza, good food and service, pleasant atmosphere.
Ricos Pan, Jr San Román y Jorge Chávez. Good bakery with café, popular.

⦿ Transport

Juliaca *p1341*
Air Manco Cápac airport is small but well organized. To/from **Lima**, 2¼ hrs, 3 a day with LAN (T322228 or airport T324448) via **Arequipa** (30 mins), **Cuzco** and direct, StarPerú (T326570) once a day via Arequipa, and **Avianca/TACA**, Beware over-charging for ground transportation. If you have little luggage, regular taxis and combis stop just outside the airport parking area. Taxi from Plaza Bolognesi, US$2.75; taxi from airport US$3.50, or less from outside airport gates. Airport transfers from **Puno** US$5.50 pp with **Camtur**, Jr Tacna 336, of 104, T951 967652 and **Rossy Tours**, Jr Tacna 308, T366709. Many Puno hotels offer an airport transfer. Taxi between Puno and the airport, about US$30. If taking regular public transport to Juliaca and a taxi to the airport from there, allow extra time as the minibuses might drive around looking for passengers before leaving Puno.
Bus To **Puno**, minibuses from Jr Brasesco near Plaza Bolognesi, leave when full throughout the day, US$2, 1 hr. To **Capachica** for Llachón, from Cerro Colorado market, leave when full 0500-1700, US$2, 1½ hrs. To **Lampa**, cars (US$1) and combis (US$0.75) leave when full from Av Circunvalación, block 6 west, 30 mins.

Long distance The terminal terrestre is at the east end of San Martín (cuadra 9, past the Circunvalación). Most bus companies have their offices nearby on San Martín. To **Lima**, US$38 normal, US$70 'Imperial', 20 hrs; with Ormeño 1630, 2000. To **Cuzco**, US$8-17, 5-6 hrs; Power (T321952) hourly, several others. To **Arequipa**, US$15, 4-5 hrs, Julsa (T331952) hourly, several others. To **Puerto Maldonado** via **Mazuko**, where the branches of the Interoceanic Highway from Cuzco, Puerto Maldonado and Juliaca converge, US$27, 12 hrs; several companies leave from M Nuñez cuadra 11, "El Triángulo" by the exit to Cuzco, 1300-1500. To **Macusani**, Alianza (Av Ferrocarril y Cahuide) 1300, 1700, 1815, US$3.50, 3 hrs; Jean (M Núñez y Pje San José), 0845, 1330, 1800; also minibuses from Pje San José, leave when full, US$4.25. See below for how to get to the Bolivian border and page 1344 for transport.

Puno to Cuzco: Sicuani p1342
Bus To Pucará, Ayaviri and Azángaro, from Las Mercedes terminal. To **Cuzco**, 137 km, US$1.50.

Border with Bolivia → *Peruvian time is 1 hr behind Bolivian time.*

There are three different routes across the border:

Puno-La Paz via Yunguyo and Copacabana **Peruvian immigration** is five minutes' drive from **Yunguyo** and 500 m from the Bolivian post; open 0700-2000 (Peruvian time), Bolivian immigration is open 0730-1930 (Bolivian time). Be aware of corruption here and look out for official or unofficial people trying to charge you a fee, on either side of the border (say that you know it is illegal and ask why only gringos are approached to pay the 'embarkation tax').

Bolivian consulate is at Jr Grau 339, T856032, near the main plaza in Yunguyo, open Monday-Friday 0830-1500. US citizens need a visa for Bolivia, it can be obtained in advance or right at the border (see Bolivia chapter for details). There are a couple of *casas de cambio* on the Peruvian side of the border offering slightly lower rates than in Yunguyo, but better rates than the shops on the Bolivian side. US dollars cash and soles can also be exchanged at *cambios* in Copacabana. In Yunguyo best rates for US dollars cash and Bolivianos at **Farmacia Loza**, Jr Bolognesi 567, Plaza 2 de Mayo. Also *cambios* on Plaza de Armas, and street changers who deal in dollars, bolivianos and euros.

Puno-Desaguadero **Desaguadero** is a bleak unsavoury place, with poor restaurants and dubious accommodation. Friday is the main market day, when the town is packed. There is a smaller market on Tuesday and at other times Desaguadero is deserted. There is no need to stop here as all roads to it are paved and if you leave La Paz, Moquegua or Puno early enough you should be at your destination before nightfall. Minibuses Puno-Desaguadero hourly 0600-1900, 2½ hours, US$2. Taxi US$33. **Peruvian border office** is open 0700-2000, Bolivian 0830-2030 (both local time). It is easy to change money on the Peruvian side. This particular border crossing allows you to stop at Tiahuanaco en route.

Along the east side of Lake Titicaca This is the most remote route, via **Huancané**, **Moho** (several basic *hostales*), **Cambria** (access to Isla Suasi), **Conima** and **Tilali**. Some walking may be involved between Tilali and **Puerto Acosta** (Bolivia, 13 km). Make sure you get an exit stamp in Puno, post-dated by a couple of days. From Juliaca there are minibuses to Huancané, Moho and Tilali, the last village in Peru with very basic lodgings (see Transport, below). The road is all paved. From Tilali it is 3-km walk to the international frontier. Puerto Acosta in Bolivia is a further 10 km. You must get a preliminary entry stamp at the police station on the plaza, then the definitive entry stamp at Migración in La Paz.

⊙ Border with Bolivia listings

For hotel and restaurant price codes, and other relevant information, see Essentials.

⊙ Where to stay

Border with Bolivia: Yunguyo p1343
$ Hostal Isabel, San Francisco 110, near Plaza de Armas, T951 794228. With or without bath, nice rooms and courtyard, electric shower, parking, friendly. A few other cheap places to stay.

North shore of Lake Titicaca
$$$$ Hotel Isla Suasi, T01-213 9739, a Casa Andina Private Collection hotel, www.casa-andina.com. The hotel is the only house on this tiny, tranquil, private island. There are beautiful

terraced gardens, best Jan-Mar. The non-native eucalyptus trees are being replaced by native varieties. You can take a canoe around the island to see birds and the island has vicuñas, a small herd of alpacas and vizcachas. The sunsets from the highest point are beautiful. Facilities are spacious, comfortable and solar-powered, rooms with bath, hot water, hot water bottles. Price includes full board, national drinks, entrance to island, all transport (suite boat from Puno 2¼ hrs direct), services and taxes. Massage room and sauna, internet extra.

US$0.50, taxi US$3, 8 km, 15 mins. **Note** Don't take a taxi Yunguyo-Puno without checking its reliability first, driver may pick up an accomplice to rob passengers.

To La Paz by hydrofoil or catamaran
There are luxury services combining bus and boat travel from Puno to La Paz by Crillon Tours hydrofoil, www.titicaca.com, with connections to tours, from La Paz, to Cuzco and Machu Picchu. Similar services, by catamaran, are run by Transturin, www.transturin.com (Jr Puno 633, of 3, Puno).

⊖ Transport

Border with Bolivia: Yunguyo *p1343*
Bus The road is paved from Puno to Yunguyo and the lakeside scenery is interesting. From Puno to **Copacabana**, US$8, 3 hrs, and **La Paz**, US$18, the best direct services are with **Tour Peru**, Jr Tacna, www.tourperu.com.pe, direct service to Copacabana leave Puno daily at 0730, and to La Paz at 0700. **Panamericano**, Jr Tacna 245, T369010, and **Litoral** (at Terminal Terrestre, cheaper, but thefts reported on night buses).

To **Yunguyo**, from the Terminal Regional in Puno, minibuses hourly 0600-1900, 2½ hrs, US$2.70 (return from Jr Cusco esq Arica, 1 block from Plaza 2 de Mayo). From Yunguyo to the border (Kasani), from Jr Titicaca y San Francisco, 1 block from Plaza de Armas, shared taxis US$0.30 pp, taxi US$2.50, 5 mins. From Kasani to Copacabana, minibuses

Along the east side of Lake Titicaca *p1343*
From Juliaca, minibuses for **Moho** via **Huancané** depart when full throughout the day from Jr Moquegua y Av El Maestro, north of Mercado Tupac Amaru, US$2.20, 1½ hrs. Minibuses for **Tilali** depart when full from Jr Lambayeque y Av Circunvalación Este, also near the market, US$3.60, 3 hrs. On market days trucks may go to Puerto Acosta and La Paz. Try hitching to catch bus from **Puerto Acosta** to **La Paz** (daily) about 1400 (note Bolivian time is 1 hr ahead of Peru), more frequent service on Sun, 5 hrs, US$6. If you are in a hurry and miss the bus, ask the truck to drop you off 25 km further in Escoma, from where there are frequent minivans to La Paz. Buses leave La Paz for Puerto Acosta at 0600 daily. Transport from Puerto Acosta to border only operates on market days, mostly cargo trucks.

Cuzco

The ancient Inca capital is said to have been founded around AD 1100, and since then has developed into a major commercial and tourism centre of 428,000 inhabitants, most of whom are Quechua. Today, colonial churches, monasteries and convents and extensive pre-Columbian ruins are interspersed with countless hotels, bars and restaurants that cater to the over one million tourists who visit every year. Almost every central street has remains of Inca walls, arches and doorways; the perfect Inca stonework now serves as the foundations for more modern dwellings. This stonework is tapered upwards (battered); every wall has a perfect line of inclination towards the centre, from bottom to top. The curved stonework of the Temple of the Sun, for example, is probably unequalled in the world.

Arriving in Cuzco → *Phone code: 084. Colour map 3, C4. Altitude: 3310 m.*
Orientation The **airport** is to the southeast of the city and the road into the centre goes close to Wanchac station, at which **trains** from Puno arrive. The **bus terminal** is near the Pachacútec statue in Ttio district. Transport to your hotel is not a problem from any of these places by taxi or in transport arranged by hotel representatives.

Inca society

Cuzco was the capital of the Inca empire – one of the greatest planned societies the world has known – from its rise during the 11th century to its death in the early 16th century. (See John Hemming's *Conquest of the Incas* and B C Brundage's *Lords of Cuzco* and *Empire of the Inca*.) It was solidly based on other Peruvian civilizations which had attained great skill in textiles, building, ceramics and working in metal. Immemorially, the political structure of the Andean *indígena* had been the *ayllu*, the village community; it had its divine ancestor, worshipped household gods, was closely knit by ties of blood to the family and by economic necessity to the land, which was held in common. Submission to the *ayllu* was absolute, because it was only by such discipline that food could be obtained in an unsympathetic environment. All the domestic animals, the llama and alpaca and the dog, had long been tamed, and the great staple crops, maize and potatoes, established. What the Incas did – and it was a magnificent feat – was to conquer enormous territories and impose upon the variety of *ayllus*, through an unchallengeable central government, a willing spiritual and economic submission to the State. The common religion, already developed by the classical Tiwanaku culture, was worship of the Sun, whose vice-regent on earth was the absolute Sapa Inca. Around him, in the capital, was a religious and secular elite which never froze into a caste because it was open to talent. The elite was often recruited from chieftains defeated by the Incas; an effective way of reconciling local opposition. The mass of the people were subjected to rigorous planning. They were allotted land to work, for their group and for the State; set various tasks (the making of textiles, pottery, weapons, ropes, etc) from primary materials supplied by the functionaries, or used in enlarging the area of cultivation by building terraces on the hill-sides. Their political organization was simple but effective. The family, and not the individual, was the unit. Families were grouped in units of 10, 100, 500, 1000, 10,000 and 40,000, each group with a leader responsible to the next largest group. The Sapa Inca crowned the political edifice; his four immediate counsellors were those to whom he allotted responsibility for the northern, southern, eastern and western regions (suyos) of the empire.

Equilibrium between production and consumption, in the absence of a free price mechanism and good transport facilities, must depend heavily upon statistical information. This the Incas raised to a high degree of efficiency by means of their *quipus*: a decimal system of recording numbers by knots in cords. Seasonal variations were guarded against by creating a system of state barns in which provender could be stored during years of plenty, to be used in years of scarcity. Statistical efficiency alone required that no one should be permitted to leave his home or his work. The loss of personal liberty was the price paid by the masses for economic security. In order to obtain information and to transmit orders quickly, the Incas built fine paved pathways along which couriers sped on foot. The whole system of rigorous control was completed by the greatest of all their monarchs, Pachacuti, who also imposed a common language, Quechua, as a further cementing force.

The centre of Cuzco is quite small and possible to explore on foot. Taxis in Cuzco are cheap and recommended when arriving by air, train or bus and especially when returning to your hotel at night. On arrival in Cuzco, respect the altitude: two or three hours rest after arriving makes a great difference; avoid meat and smoking, eat lots of carbohydrates and drink plenty of clear, non-alcoholic liquid; remember to walk slowly. To see Cuzco and the surrounding area properly (including Pisac, Ollantaytambo, Chinchero and Machu Picchu) you need five days to a week, allowing for slowing down because of the altitude. ▶▶ See Transport, page 1366.

Tourist information Official tourist information ① *Portal Mantas 117-A, next to La Merced church, T222032, open Mon-Sat 0800-2000, Sun 0800-1300.* There is also an **i perú** tourist information desk at the **airport** ① *T237364, daily 0800-1600*, and another at ① *Av El Sol 103, of 102, Galerías Turísticas, T252974, iperucusco@ promperu.gob.pe, daily 0830-1930.* **Dircetur** ① *Plaza Túpac Amaru Mz 1 Lte 2, Wanchac, T223761, Mon-Fri 0800-1300*, gives out good map. Other information sources include **South American Explorers** ① *Atocsaycuchi 670, T245484, www. saexplorers.org, Mon-Fri 0930-1700, Sat 0930-1300*. It's worth making the climb up the steps to the large new clubhouse which has a garden. Sells good city map, members get many local discounts, has comprehensive recycling centre. As with SAE's other clubhouses, this is the place

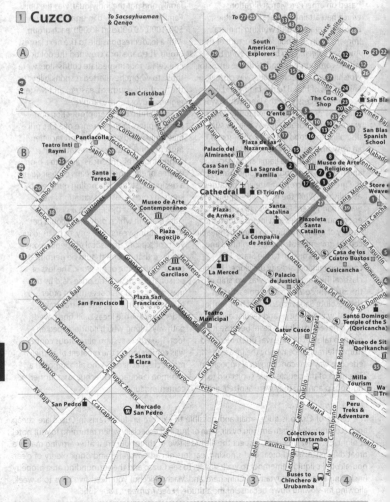

Cuzco

to go for specialized information, member-written trip reports and maps. Also has rooms for rent. For full details on **South American Explorers**, see Essentials. Many churches close to visitors on Sunday. See also www.aboutcusco.com and www.cuscoonline.com.

Visitors' tickets A combined entry ticket, called *Boleto Turístico de Cusco (BTC)*, is available to most of the sites of main historical and cultural interest in and around the city, and costs as follows: 130 soles (US$46/35) for all the sites and valid for 10 days; or 70 soles (US$25/19) for either the museums in the city, or Sacsayhuaman, Qenqo, Puka Pukara and Tambo Machay, or Pisac, Ollantaytambo, Chinchero and Moray; the 70 soles ticket is valid for one day. The BTC can

➡ Cuzco maps
1 Cuzco, page 1346
2 Around Plaza de Armas, page 1348

Where to stay 🛏
1 Albergue Casa Campesina *C4*
2 Albergue Municipal *B2*
3 Andenes al Cielo *B4*
4 Cahuide *A1*
5 Casa Andina Koricancha *C4*
6 Casa Andina Private Collection Cusco *C5*
7 Casa Andina San Blas *B5*
8 Casa Cartagena *A3*
9 Casa de la Gringa *A4*
10 Casa Elena *B4*
11 Casa San Blas & Tika Bistro *B4*
12 Casona Les Pleiades *A4*
13 El Arqueólogo & Divina Comedia Restaurant *A3*
14 El Balcón Colonial *A3*
15 El Grial *A3*
16 El Mercado *C1*
17 El Monasterio *B3*
18 Estrellita *C5*
19 Flying Dog Hostel *A3*
20 Hitchhikers B&B Backpackers Hostel *B2*
21 Hosp El Artesano de San Blas *A4*
22 Hosp Inka *A4*
23 Hostal Amaru *B4*
24 Hostal Casa de Campo *A3*
25 Hostal El Balcón *B1*
26 Hostal Killipata *B1*
27 Hostal Kuntur Wasi *A3*
28 Hostal Loki *B1*
29 Hostal María Esther *A3*
30 Hostal Pakcha Real *A4*
31 Hostal Qorichaska *C1*
32 Hostal Tikawasi *A3*
33 La Encantada *A3*
34 Los Apus Hotel & Mirador *A3*
35 Maison de la Jeunesse *D4*
36 Mamá Simona Hostel *C1*
37 Marani *A4*
38 Niños/Hotel Meloc *C1*
39 Novotel *C4*
40 Palacio del Inka Luxury Collection *C4*
42 Palacio Nazarenas *B3*
43 Pensión Alemana *A3*
44 Piccola Locanda & L'Osteria Restaurant *B2*
45 Quinua Villa Boutique *A3*
46 Rumi Punku *A3*
47 Sonesta Hotel Cusco *E6*
48 The Blue House *A4*
49 The Walk on Inn *B2*

Restaurants 🍴
1 Aldea Yanapay *B4*
2 A Mi Manera *B3*
3 Baco *B4*
4 Café El Ayllu *D3*
5 Café Punchay *A3*
6 Chocolate *B4*
7 Cositas Café y Arte *B4*
8 El Encuentro *B4*
9 El Paisa *E5*
10 Granja Heidi *B4*
11 Inkanato *C4*
12 Inka Panaka *A4*
13 Jack's Café *B4*
14 Juanito's Sandwich Café *A4*
15 Justina *B3*
16 Kuska...fé *B4*
17 La Bodega 138 *B4*
18 Le Soleil *C4*
19 Los Toldos *D3*
20 Macondo *A4*
21 Manu Café *E6*
22 Pachapapa *B4*
23 Panadería El Buen Pastor *A4*
24 Venezia *A4*

Bars & clubs 🍸
25 Bar 7 *A3*
26 Km 0 (Arte y Tapas) *A4*
27 Museo del Pisco *B4*

N

100 metres
100 yards

be bought at the offices of **Cosituc** ⓘ *Av El Sol 103, of 102, Galerías Turísticas, T261465, Mon-Sat 0800-1800, Sun 0800-1300, or Yuracpunku 79-A (east of centre, go along Recoleta), www.cosituc. gob.pe or www.boletoturisticocusco.net*, or at any of the sites included in the ticket. For students with an ISIC card the BTC costs 70 soles (US$25), which is only available at the Cosituc office upon presentation of the ISIC card. Take your ISIC card when visiting the sites, as some may ask to see it. Photography is not allowed in the churches, nor in museums.

Entrance tickets for the Santo Domingo/Qoricancha, the Inka Museum (El Palacio del Almirante) and La Merced are sold separately, while the Cathedral (including El Triunfo and La Sagrada Familia), La Compañía, San Blas and the Museo de Arte Religioso del Arzobispado are included on a religious buildings ticket which costs 50 soles (US$17.50) and is valid for 10 days. Each of these sites may be visited individually. Machu Picchu ruins and Inca trail entrance tickets are sold electronically at www.machupicchu.gob.pe, at the **Dirección Regional de Cultura Cusco** ⓘ *Av de la Cultura 238, Condominio Huáscar, T236061, www.drc-cusco.gob.pe, Mon-Fri 0715-1600, and other outlets listed on the machupicchu.gob.pe website.*

Security Police patrol the streets and stations, but still be vigilant. On no account walk back to your hotel after dark from a bar or club, strangle muggings and rape do occur. Pay for a taxi called by the club's doorman and make sure the taxi is licensed. Other areas in which to take care include San Pedro market (otherwise recommended), the San Cristóbal area, and at out-of-the-

② Around Plaza de Armas

way ruins. Also take special care during Inti Raymi. **Tourist Police** ① *Plaza Túpac Amaru, Wanchac, T512351 or T235123, polturcusco_74@hotmail.com*. If you need a *denuncia* (report for insurance purposes), which is available from the Banco de la Nación, they will type it out. Always go to the police when robbed, even though it will cost you some time. **Indecopi** ① *Av Manco Inca 209, Wanchac, T252987, mmarroquin@indecopi.gob.pe; toll free T0800-44040 (24-hr hotline, not available from payphones,* is the consumer protection bureau.

Places in Cuzco

The heart of the city in Inca days was *Huacaypata* (the place of tears) and *Cusipata* (the place of happiness), divided by a channel of the Saphi River. Today, Cusipata is Plaza Regocijo and Huacaypata is the Plaza de Armas, around which are colonial arcades and four churches. To the northeast is the early 17th-century baroque **Cathedral** ① *US$9, daily 1000-1800*. It is built on the site of the Palace of Inca Wiracocha (*Kiswarcancha*). The high altar is solid silver and the original altar *retablo* behind it is a masterpiece of Andean wood carving. The earliest surviving painting of the city can be seen, depicting Cuzco during the 1650 earthquake. In the far right hand end of the church is an interesting local painting of the Last Supper replete with *cuy, chicha*, etc. In the sacristy are paintings of all the bishops of Cuzco. The choir stalls, by a 17th-century Spanish priest, are a magnificent example of colonial baroque art. The elaborate pulpit and the sacristy are also notable. Much venerated is the crucifix of El Señor de los Temblores, the object of many

Plateros detail

50 metres
50 yards

Where to stay N
1 Andean Wings *A1*
2 Casa Andina Catedral *C3*
3 Casa Andina Classic - Cusco Plaza *C2*
4 EcoPackers *A1*
5 El Procurador del Cusco *A2*
6 Hostal Resbalosa *A3*
7 Hostal Royal Frankenstein *B1*
8 La Casona Inkaterra *B3*
9 Loreto Boutique Hotel *C2*
10 Marqueses *B1*
11 Pariwana *C1*
12 Pirwa *B3*
13 Sonesta Posadas del Inca *B2*
14 The Point *C1*
15 Tierra Viva Cusco Plaza *A3*

Restaurants N
1 Amaru *Plateros detail*
2 Café El Ayllu *B3*
3 Café Halliy *Plateros*
4 Café Perla *C3*
5 Chicha, El Truco & Taberna del Truco *B1*
6 Cicciolina *C3*
7 Dolce Vita *C3*
8 Dos por Tres *C1*
9 El Encuentro *A2, C3*
10 El Fogón *Plateros*
11 Fallen Angel restaurant & Guesthouse *B3*
12 Fusiones & Night Sky Disco *C2*
13 In canto & Greens Organic *C3*
14 Inka Grill *B2*
15 Kusikuy *B3*
16 La Bondiet *C1*
17 La China *A1*
18 La Retama *B2*
19 La Tertulia *B2*
20 Limo *D3*
21 MAP Café *B3*
22 Pachacútec Grill & Bar *B2*
23 Pucará *Plateros*
24 Sara *C3*
25 The Muse *C3*
26 Tunupa *B2*
27 Tupananchis *C1*
28 Víctor Victoria *A2*
29 Yahuu! Juice Bar *B2, C1*
30 Yaku Mama *A2*

Bars & clubs N
31 Cross Keys Pub *A2*
32 El Garabato Video Music Club *B2*
33 Extreme *B3*
34 Indigo *A2*
35 Kamikaze *B2*
36 Los Perros Bar *A2*
37 Mama África *B2*
38 Mythology *B3*
39 Norton Rat's Tavern & Hostal Goçta Cusco *C3*
40 Paddy's Pub *C3*
41 Rosie O'Grady's *C3*
42 Ukuku's *Plateros detail*

➡ **Cuzco maps**
1 Cuzco, page 1346
2 Around Plaza de Armas, page 1348

pilgrimages and viewed all over Peru as a guardian against earthquakes. The tourist entrance to the Cathedral is through the church of **La Sagrada Familia** (1733), which stands to its left as you face it. Its gilt main altar has been renovated. **El Triunfo** (1536), on the right of the Cathedral, is the first Christian church in Cuzco, built on the site of the Inca Roundhouse (the *Suntur Huasi*). It has a statue of the Virgin of the Descent, reputed to have helped the Spaniards repel Manco Inca when he besieged the city in 1536.

On the southeast side of the plaza is the beautiful **La Compañía de Jesús** ① *US$3.55, or by religious buildings ticket, daily 0900-1750*, built on the site of the Palace of the Serpents (*Amarucancha*, residence of Inca Huayna Capac) in the late 17th century. Its twin-towered exterior is extremely graceful, and the interior rich in fine murals, paintings and carved altars. Nearby is the **Santa Catalina church** ① *Arequipa at Santa Catalina Angosta, daily 0900-1200, 1300-1700, except Fri 0900-1200, 1300-1600, joint ticket with Santo Domingo US$5.25*, convent and museum, built upon the foundations of the *Acllahuasi* (House of the Chosen Women). There are guided tours by English-speaking students; tip expected. **Museo Machupicchu** (Casa Concha) ① *Santa Catalina Ancha 320, T255535, Mon-Sat 0900-1700, US$7*, is a new museum which features objects found by Hiram Bingham during his initial excavations of Machu Picchu in 1912, returned by Yale University to the Peruvian government in 2010

If you continue down Arequipa from Santa Catalina you come to Calle Maruri. Between this street at Santo Domingo is **Cusicancha** ① *US$1.75, Mon-Fri 0730-1600, sometimes open at weekends*, an open space showing the layout of the buildings as they would have been in Inca times.

La Merced ① *on Plazoleta Espinar, Calle Márquez, church Mon-Fri 0800-1700, Sat 0900-1600; monastery and museum 1430-1700, except Sun, US$1*. The church was first built 1534 and rebuilt in the late 17th century. Attached is a very fine monastery with an exquisite cloister. Inside the church are buried Gonzalo Pizarro, half-brother of Francisco, and the two Almagros, father and son. The church is most famous for its jewelled monstrance, which is on view in the monastery's museum during visiting hours.

Much **Inca stonework** can be seen in the streets and most particularly in the Callejón Loreto, running southeast past La Compañía de Jesús from the main plaza. The walls of the Acllahuasi (House of the Chosen Women) are on one side, and of the **Amarucancha** on the other. There are also Inca remains in Calle San Agustín, to the east of the plaza. The stone of 12 angles is in Calle Hatun Rumiyoc halfway along its second block, on the right-hand side going away from the Plaza. The **Palacio Arzobispal** stands on Hatun Rumiyoc y Herrajes, two blocks northeast of Plaza de Armas. It was built on the site of the palace occupied in 1400. It contains the **Museo de Arte Religioso** ① *0800-1800, included on the religious buildings ticket, or US$5.35*, a collection of colonial paintings and furniture. The collection includes the paintings by the indigenous master, Diego Quispe Tito, of a 17th-century Corpus Christi procession that used to hang in the church of Santa Ana.

The **Palacio del Almirante**, just north of the Plaza de Armas, is impressive. It houses the **Museo Inka** ① *Cuesta del Almirante 103, T237380, Mon-Fri 0800-1900, Sat 0900-1600, US$4*, which is run by the Universidad San Antonio de Abad, the museum exhibits the development of culture in the region from pre-Inca, through Inca times to the present day: textiles, ceramics, metalwork, jewellery, architecture, technology. See the collection of miniature turquoise figures and other offerings to the gods. Weaving demonstrations are given in the courtyard. On the northwest side of the Plaza de las Nazarenas, No 231, is **Museo de Arte Precolombino** ① *www.map.org.pe, 0900-2200, US$7, US$3.50 with student card; under same auspices as the Larco Museum in Lima, MAP Café (see Restaurants, below)*, housed in the **Casa Cabrera**. This beautiful museum is set around a spacious courtyard and contains many superb examples of pottery, metalwork (largely in gold and silver), wood carvings and shells from the Moche, Chimú, Paracas, Nazca and Inca cultures. There are some vividly rendered animistic designs, giving an insight into the way Peru's ancient people's viewed their world and the creatures that inhabited it. Every exhibit carries explanations in English and Spanish. Highly recommended. The **Convento de las Nazarenas**, also on Plaza de las Nazarenas, is now a hotel. You can see the Inca-colonial doorway with a mermaid motif, but ask permission to view the lovely 18th-century frescos inside. In the San Blas district, now firmly on the tourist map, the small church of **San Blas** ① *Plazoleta San Blas, Carmen Bajo, 0800-1800, on the religious buildings ticket, or US$5.35* has a beautiful carved *mestizo* cedar pulpit, which is well worth seeing. **Museo Máximo Laura** ① *Carmen Alto 133, T227383, http://museomaximolaura. com, daily 1000-2000*, displays 24 prize-winning exhibits by this celebrated textile artist (see page 1223), with workshop, gallery and shop. See also Shopping, Local crafts, below.

Santo Domingo, southeast of the main Plaza, was built in the 17th century on the walls of the **Qoricancha, Temple of the Sun** ① *Mon-Sat 0830-1730, Sun 1400-1700 (closed holidays), US$2, or joint ticket with Santa Catalina US$5.25, English-speaking guides, tip of US$2-3 expected*, and from its stones. Excavation has revealed more of the five chambers of the Temple of the Sun, which shows the best Inca stonework to be seen in Cuzco. The Temple of the Sun was awarded to Juan Pizarro, the younger brother of Francisco, who willed it to the Dominicans after he had been fatally wounded in the Sacsayhuaman siege. The baroque cloister has been gutted to reveal four of the original chambers of the great Inca temple – two on the west have been partly reconstructed in a good imitation of Inca masonry. The finest stonework is in the celebrated curved wall beneath the west end of Santo Domingo. This was rebuilt after the 1950 earthquake, at which time a niche that once contained a shrine was found at the inner top of the wall. Below the curved wall was a garden of gold and silver replicas of animals, maize and other plants. Excavations have revealed Inca baths below here, and more Inca retaining walls. The other superb stretch of late Inca stonework is in C Ahuacpinta outside the temple, to the east or left as you enter.

Museo de Sitio Qorikancha (formerly Museo Arqueológico) ① *Av El Sol, Mon-Sat 0900-1200, 1300-1700, Sun 0800-1400, entrance by BTC*, is under the garden below Santo Domingo. It contains a limited collection of pre-Columbian items, Spanish paintings of imitation Inca royalty dating from the 18th century, and photos of the excavation of Qoricancha. The palace called **Casa de los Cuatro Bustos**, whose colonial doorway is at San Agustín 400, is now the **Hotel Libertador**. The general public can enter the hotel from Plazoleta Santo Domingo, opposite the Temple of the Sun/Qoricancha.

Museo de Historia Regional ① *in the Casa Garcilaso, C Garcilaso y Heladeros, 0730-1700, entrance by BTC*, tries to show the evolution of the Cuzqueño school of painting. It also contains Inca agricultural implements, colonial furniture and paintings. **San Francisco** ① *on Plaza San Francisco, 3 blocks southwest of the Plaza de Armas, 0600-0800, 1800-2000*, is an austere church reflecting many indigenous influences. Its monastery is being rebuilt and may be closed. **San Pedro** ① *in front of the San Pedro market, Mon-Sat 1000-1200, 1400-1700*, was built in 1688. Its two towers were made from stones brought from an Inca ruin.

Museo de Plantas Sagradas, Mágicas y Medicinales ① *Santa Teresa 351, T222214, www. museoplantascusco.org, Mon-Sat 0800-2100, Sun 0800-1800, US$5.50*, has nine exhibition rooms detailing the history and uses of plants such as coca, Ayahuasca and San Pedro.

Above Cuzco, on the road up to Sacsayhuamán, is **San Cristóbal**, built to his patron saint by Cristóbal Paullu Inca. The church's atrium has been restored and there is a sidewalk access to the Sacsayhuamán Archaeological Park. North of San Cristóbal, you can see the 11 doorway-sized niches of the great Inca wall of the **Palacio de Colcampata**, which was the residence of Manco Inca before he rebelled against the Spanish and fled to Vilcabamba.

Sacsayhuaman

① *Daily 0700-1730; free student guides, give them a tip.*

There are some magnificent Inca walls in this ruined ceremonial centre, on a hill in the northern outskirts. The Incaic stones are hugely impressive. The massive rocks weighing up to 130 tons are fitted together with absolute perfection. Three walls run parallel for over 360 m and there are 21 bastions. Sacsayhuaman was thought for centuries to be a fortress, but the layout and architecture suggest a great sanctuary and temple to the Sun, which rises exactly opposite the place previously believed to be the Inca's throne – which was probably an altar, carved out of the solid rock. Broad steps lead to the altar from either side. The hieratic, rather than the military, hypothesis was supported by the discovery in 1982 of the graves of priests, who would have been unlikely to be buried in a fortress. The precise functions of the site, however, will probably continue to be a matter of dispute as very few clues remain, owing to its steady destruction. The site is about a 30-minute walk up Pumacurco from Plaza de las Nazarenas. A new Gran Museo del Tawantinsuyo was under construction here in 2014.

Along the road from Sacsayhuaman to Pisac, past a radio station, is the temple and amphitheatre of **Qenqo** with some of the finest examples of Inca stone carving *in situ*, especially inside the large hollowed-out stone that houses an altar. On the same road are **Puka Pukara** (Red Fort, but more likely to have been a *tambo*, or post-house), wonderful views; and the spring shrine of **Tambo Machay**, which is in excellent condition. Water still flows by a hidden channel out of the masonry wall, straight into a little rock pool traditionally known as the Inca's bath. Take a guide to the sites and visit in the morning for the best photographs. Carry your multi-site ticket, there are roving ticket inspectors. You can visit the sites on foot, a pleasant walk of at least half a day through the countryside; take water, sun protection, and watch out for dogs. Alternatively, take the Pisac bus or the Señor del Huerto combi up to Tambo Machay (US$0.70) and walk back.

⏹ Cuzco listings

For hotel and restaurant price codes, and other relevant information, see Essentials.

⏹ Where to stay

Cuzco *p1344, maps p1346 and p1348*
Book more expensive hotels several months in advance, particularly for the week or so around Inti Raymi, when prices are greatly increased. Prices given are for the high season in Jun-Aug. When there are fewer tourists hotels may drop their prices by as much as half. Always check for discounts. Be wary of unlicensed hotel agents for medium-priced hotels who are often misleading about details; their local nickname is *jalagringos* (gringo pullers), or *piratas*. Taxis and tourist minibuses meet new arrivals and (should) take you to the hotel of your choice, but be insistent. Since it is cold here and many hotels have no heating, ask for an *estufa*, a heater which some places will provide for an extra charge. Many places will store your luggage when you go trekking, but always check valuables and possessions before and after depositing them with hotel/hostel staff.

International chain hotels in Cuzco include JW Marriott (www.marriott.com), Novotel (www.novotel.com) and Sonesta (www.sonesta.com).

Around the Plaza de Armas
$$$$ Andean Wings, Siete Cuartones 225, T243166, www.andeanwingshotel.com. In a restored 17th-century house, in the same group as Casa de la Gringa and Another Planet, 5-star, intimate, suites, some with jacuzzi, are individually designed (one is accessible for the disabled), spa, restaurant and bar.

$$$$ The Fallen Angel Guest House, Plaza Nazarenas 221, T258184, www.fallenangel incusco.com. A 4-room luxury hotel above the restaurant of the same name. Each suite is decorated in its own lavish style (with living room, dining room, bathroom, feather duvets, heating), very comfortable and a far cry from the usual adaptation of colonial buildings elsewhere in the city. With all amenities, excellent service.

$$$$ La Casona Inkaterra, Plazoleta Las Nazarenas 113, T223010, www.inkaterra.com. A private, colonial-style boutique hotel in a converted 16th-century mansion, built on the site of Manco Cápac's palace. 11 exclusive suites, all facilities, concierge service with activities and excursions, highly-regarded and the height of luxury.

$$$ Casa Andina Classic – Cusco Plaza, Portal Espinar 142, T231733, www.casa-andina. com. 40-room hotel near plaza, ATM and safe deposit box. Equally recommendable are Casa Andina Koricancha, San Agustín 371, T252633,

Casa Andina Catedral, Santa Catalina Angosta 149, T233661, and the Casa Andina San Blas, Chihuampata 278, San Blas, T263964, all of which are in the same vein.

$$$ Loreto Boutique Hotel, Pasaje Loreto 115, T226352, www.loretoboutiquehotel.com. Great location; 12 spacious rooms with original Inca walls, upgraded to "boutique" status. Laundry service, will help organize travel services including guides and taxis, free airport pick-up.

$$$ Marqueses, Garcilaso 256, T264249, www.hotelmarqueses.com. Spanish colonial style, with 16/17th-century style religious paintings and 2 lovely courtyards. Rooms have heavy curtains and some are a little dark; luxury rooms have bath and shower. Buffet breakfast.

$$$ Sonesta Posadas del Inca, Portal Espinar 108, T712 6060, www.sonesta.com. Includes buffet breakfast, warmly decorated rooms with heating, safe, some rooms on 3rd floor have view of Plaza, very helpful, English spoken, restaurant with Andean food, excellent service.

$$$ Tierra Viva Cusco Plaza, Suecia 345, T245858, www.tierravivahoteles.com. Boutique hotel in the former residence of Gonzalo Pizarro. Rooms and suites have comfortable beds, heating, minibar, safe, with excellent breakfast. Exemplary service, airport transfers.

$$-$ EcoPackers Hostel, Santa Teresa 375, T231800, www.ecopackersperu.com. Ecologically friendly, well-regarded hostal in a colonial casona, double rooms with en suite or dorms for 4-18 people, communal kitchen, games room, bar, large-screen TV room, Wi-Fi, garage for bicycles or motorcycles.

$ Hostal Resbalosa, Resbalosa 494, T224839, www.hostalresbalosa.com. Private or shared bath, hot water in the mornings and evenings, ask for a room with a view, dorm beds, laundry facilities, full breakfast extra.

$ Hostal Royal Frankenstein, San Juan de Dios 260, 2 blocks from the Plaza de Armas, T236999, www.hostal-frankenstein.net. Eccentric place but a frequent favourite, with private or shared bath, hot water, safe, kitchen, small charge for computer, heater and laundry, German-owned, German and English spoken.

$ Pariwana, Mesón de la Estrella 136, T233751, www.pariwana-hostel.com. Variety of rooms in a converted colonial mansion with courtyard, from doubles with bath to dorms sleeping 10, also girls only dorm, restaurant, bar/lounge, English spoken, lots of activities.

$ Pirwa Hostels, T244315, www.pirwahostels cusco.com. This chain of hostels offers a range of rooms from private doubles with bath to dorms, in colonial buildings, lockers, 24-hr reception: Pirwa Suecia, Suecia 300, the B&B branch; Pirwa Posada del Corregidor, Portal de Panes 151 (Plaza de Armas); Pirwa Backpackers San Blas, Carmen Alto 283, and Pirwa Backpackers Colonial, Plaza San Francisco 360.

$ The Point, Mesón de la Estrella 172, T252266, www.thepointhostels.com. Dormitory accommodation, also has doubles and singles, hot showers, good party atmosphere.

Beyond the Plaza, including San Blas
$$$$ Casa Andina Private Collection Cusco, Plazoleta de Limacpampa Chico 473, T232610, www.casa-andina.com. The most upmarket and comfortable in this group, in a 16th-century mansion with 4 courtyards, enriched oxygen available in the rooms, plus a gourmet

restaurant serving local cuisine and a bar with an extensive pisco collection.

$$$$ Casa Cartagena, Pumacurco 336, T261171, www.casacartagena.com. In a converted monastery and national heritage building, super-deluxe facilities with Italian design and colonial features, 4 levels of suite, La Chola restaurant, extensive complimentary Qoya spa, enriched oxygen system, and all services to be expected in a Luxury Properties group hotel.

$$$$ El Mercado, C Siete Cuartones 306, T582640, www.elmercadotunqui.com. On the site of a former market close to the Plaza de Armas, owned by Mountain Lodges of Peru, superior rooms and suites, restaurant, bar, helpful staff.

$$$$ El Monasterio (Belmond), C Palacios 136, Plazoleta Nazarenas, T604000, www.monasteriohotel.com. 5-star, beautifully restored Seminary of San Antonio Abad (a Peruvian National Historical Landmark), including the Baroque chapel, spacious comfortable rooms with all facilities (some rooms offer an oxygen-enriched atmosphere to help clients acclimatize), very helpful staff (buffet breakfast open to non-residents, will fill you up for the rest of the day), good restaurants, lunch and dinner à la carte, business centre with internet for guests.

$$$$ Palacio del Inka Luxury Collection, Plazoleta Santo Domingo 259, T231961, www.libertador.com.pe. 5-star, good, especially the service, warm and bright, Inti Raymi restaurant, excellent, live music in the evening.

$$$$ Palacio Nazarenas (Belmond), Plazoleta Nazarenas 144, T582222, www.palacio nazarenas.com. Housed in a beautifully restored building, outdoor swimming pool, spa, history booklet and cooking classes. Opened in 2013.

$$$$-$$$ Casa San Blas, Tocuyeros 566, just off Cuesta San Blas, T237900, www.casasanblas.com. An international-standard boutique hotel with bright, airy rooms decorated with traditional textiles. Breakfast, served in the Tika Bistro downstairs. Pleasant balcony with good views, attentive service.

$$$ El Arqueólogo, Pumacurco 408, T232522, www.hotelarqueologo.com. Includes breakfast, hot water, heating extra, helpful, French and English spoken, will store luggage, garden, cafeteria and kitchen. Same group as Vida Tours, Ladrillo 425, T227750, www.vidatours.com. Traditional and adventure tourism.

$$$ Los Apus Hotel & Mirador, Atocsaycuchi 515 y Choquechaca, San Blas, T264243, www.losapushotel.com. Includes breakfast and airport transfer, full of character, very clean and smart, central heating, disabled facilities.

$$$ Rumi Punku, Choquechaca 339, T221102, www.rumipunku.com. An Inca doorway leading to a sunny courtyard, comfortable rooms, helpful staff, safe, sauna, jacuzzi, gym.

$$$-$$ Andenes al Cielo, Choquechaca 176, T222237, www.andenesalcielo.com. At the foot of the San Blas district, 15 rooms in renovated historic home, most expensive rooms have fireplaces, all with either balconies or patios, heating. Buffet breakfast, free airport pick up, gym.

$$$-$$ Cahuide, Saphi 845, T222771, www.hotelcahuide-cusco.com. Hot water, good rooms and suites, quiet, good laundry service, helpful, good value breakfasts.

$$$-$$ Hostal Casa de Campo, Tandapata 298 (at the end of the street), T244404,

www.hotelcasadecampo.com. Some of the top rooms have a *lot* of steps up to them, hot water, includes bus/airport/rail transfer with reservations, 10% discount for Footprint book owners, safe deposit box, sun terrace, quiet, relaxing, all rooms have great views, Dutch and English spoken, take a taxi after dark.

$$$-$$ Hostal El Balcón, Tambo de Montero 222, T236738, www.balconcusco.com. Warm atmosphere, very welcoming, quiet, laundry, sauna, bar, meals on request, English spoken, wonderful views, beautiful garden.

$$$-$$ Hostal Tikawasi, Tandapata 491, T231609, www.tikawasi.com. Includes heating, family-run, lovely garden overlooking the city. Stylish, modern rooms with good views, comfortable beds.

$$$-$$ La Encantada, Tandapata 354, T242206, www.encantadaperu.com. Good beds, rooftop spa, fabulous views of the city. Swiss-Peruvian owned.

$$$-$$ Piccola Locanda, Resbalosa 520, T252551, www.piccolalocanda.com. Steep walk up from the Plaza de Armas, colourful Peruvian/Italian-run B&B. Rooftop terrace with 360º views, excellent restaurant L'Osteria, a TV room, pleasant courtyard. Private or shared bath. Associated with Perú Etico tour company and 2 children's projects.

$$$-$$ Quinua Villa Boutique, Pasaje Santa Rosa A-8, T242646, www.quinua.com.pe. A beautifully built living museum, 5 different apartments, each with a different theme and kitchen.

$$$-$ Hostal Amaru, Cuesta San Blas 541, T225933, www.amaruhostal.com. Private or shared bath. Price includes airport/train/bus pick-up. Oxygen, kitchen for use in the evenings, laundry, book exchange. Rooms around a pretty colonial courtyard, some with no windows, good beds, pleasant, relaxing, some Inca walls. Also has **$$ Hostal Amaru II**, Chihuampata 642, San Blas, T223521, www.amaruhostal2.com, and **$$-$ Hosteria de Anita**, Alabado 525-5, T225933, www.amaruhostal.com/hosteria_de_anita, with rooms or dorm beds, safe, quiet, good breakfast.

$$ Casa Elena, Choquechaca 162, T241202, www.casaelenacusco.com. French/Peruvian hostel, very comfortable, helpful staff, good choice.

$$ Casona Les Pleiades, Tandapata 116, T506430, www.casona-pleiades.com. Small guesthouse in renovated colonial house, cosy and warm, generous hosts, hot water, video lounge and book exchange, café, free airport pickup with reservation, lots of info, being expanded in 2014.

$$ El Grial, Carmen Alto 112, T223012, www.hotelelgrial.com. Family-run, 2 star hostel, in a 17th-century building, coffee shop, laundry service.

$$ Hostal Kuntur Wasi, Tandapata 352-A, San Blas, T227570, www.hospedajekunturwasi.com. Great views, cheaper without bath, use of kitchen and laundry (both extra), owner speaks a bit of English and is very helpful and welcoming, a pleasant place to stay.

$$ Hostal María Esther, Pumacurco 516, T224382, http://hostalmariaesther.free.fr/. Very comfortable, helpful, garden.

$$ Marani, Carmen Alto 194, San Blas, T249462, www.hostalmarani.com. Full of character, set around a courtyard, breakfast available, Dutch-owned hostel associated with Hope Foundation (www.stichtinghope.org), which builds schools, helps teachers and hospitals, good value.

$$ Niños/Hotel Meloc, Meloc 442, T231424, www.ninoshotel.com. Modern decor in colonial building. Hot water, excellent breakfast extra, restaurant, laundry service, luggage store, English spoken, run as part of the Dutch foundation Niños Unidos Peruanos and all profits are invested in projects to help street children. Also has **Niños 2/Hotel Fierro**, on C Fierro 476, T254611, with all the same features.

$$ Pensión Alemana, Tandapata 260, San Blas, T226861, www.cuzco.com.pe. Colonial-style modern building. Swiss owned, welcoming, comfortable, discount in low season.

$$-$ Flying Dog Hostel, Choquechaca 469, T253997, www.flyingdogperu.com. Shared and private rooms and family suites, bar, living room with TV and DVD, buffet breakfast.

$$-$ Hitchhikers B&B Backpackers Hostel, Saphi 440, T260079, www.hhikersperu.com. Located close to the plaza, mixture of dorms and 1- to 3-bed private rooms with private or shared bath, laundry service.

$$-$ Hostal Loki, Cuesta Santa Ana 601, T243705, www.lokihostel.com/en/cusco. Huge hostel in a restored viceroy's residence on the steep Cuesta Santa Ana, dorms and rooms set around a beautiful courtyard, comfortable beds, hot water, free internet. A great meeting place.

$$-$ Mamá Simona Hostel, Ceniza 364, San Pedro, near the market, T260408, www.mamasimona.com. Traditional old house with rooms around a courtyard, doubles (with heating) and dorms, duvets, shared bathrooms, hot water, towel rental, full breakfast available, laundry service, helpful.

$$-$ Hostal Qorichaska, Nueva Alta 458, some distance from centre, T228974, www.qorichaskaperu.com. Rooms are clean and sunny, the older ones have traditional balconies. Also has dorms, mixed and men or women only. Laundry service. A good choice.

$ Albergue Casa Campesina, Av Tullumayo 274, T233466. Shared bath, lovely place, funds support the Casa Campesina organization (www.cbc.org.pe), which is linked to local *campesina* communities (see also Store of the Weavers under Shopping, below).

$ The Blue House, Kiskapata 291 (parallel and above Tandapata), T242407, www.thebluehouse.info. Cosy family hostal, good value. Reductions for longer stays, meals (except breakfast) US$3, hot shower, DVDs, great views.

$ Casa de La Gringa, Tandapata y Pasñapacana 148, T241168, www.casadelagringa.com. Each room individually decorated, lots of art and colour, 24-hr hot water, DVD, CD player in the common areas, heaters in the main lounges. See also Another Planet (Tour operators), below.

$ El Balcón Colonial, Choquechaca 350, T238129, balconcolonial@hotmail.com. Family house, fairly basic rooms, hot showers, good home cooking, use of family kitchen, laundry facilities extra, comfortable, safe, generous hosts.

$ Estrellita, Av Tullumayo 445, parte Alta, T234134. Most rooms with shared bath, 2 with private bath, basic but excellent value, safe parking available for bikes.

$ Hospedaje El Artesano de San Blas, Suytucato 790, San Blas, T263968, manosandinas@yahoo.com. Many bright and airy rooms overlooking courtyard, quiet, taxis leave you at Plaza San Blas, then it's a steep walk uphill for 5-10 mins.

$ Hospedaje Inka, Suytucato 848, T231995, http://hospedajeinka.weebly.com. Taxis leave you at Plaza San Blas, walk steeply uphill for

5-10 mins, or phone the hostal. Private or shared bath. Wonderful views, spacious rooms, very helpful owner, Américo.

$ Hostal Killipata, Killichapata 238, just off Tambo de Montero, T236668, www.hospedaje killipatacusco.com. Family-run lodging with variety of room sizes, private or shared bath, good showers, hot water and fully equipped kitchen. Breakfast is extra.

$ Hostal Pakcha Real, Tandapata 300, San Blas, T237484, www.hostalpakchareal.com. Family run, hot water, relaxed, with or without bath. Breakfast, cooking and laundry facilities extra. Airport/train/bus pick-up, but call ahead if arriving late.

$ The Walk on Inn, Suecia 504, T235065, www.walkoninn.com.pe. 2 blocks from the Plaza, private or shared bathrooms, breakfast extra, laundry service, free airport/bus station pick-up.

Youth hostels

$ Albergue Municipal, Quiscapata 240, San Cristóbal, T252506, albergue@municusco.gob.pe. Dormitories and double rooms, great views, bar, cafeteria, laundry, discount for members, luggage store.

$ El Procurador del Cusco, Coricalle 440, Prolongación Procuradores, T243559, http://hostelprocuradordelcusco.blogspot.com. Price includes use of the basic kitchen (no fridge) and laundry area, with or without bath, basic rooms, but upstairs is better, helpful, good value.

$ Maison de la Jeunesse (affiliated to HI, www.hihostels.com), Av El Sol, Cuadra 5, Pasaje Grace, Edif San Jorge (down a small side street opposite Qoricancha) T235617, hostelling cusco@hotmail.com. Double rooms with bath or a bed in a dorm with shared bath; HI discount. TV and video room, lockers, cooking facilities and hot water.

⊘ Restaurants

Cuzco *p1344, maps p1346 and p1348*
Around the Plaza de Armas
There are many good cheap restaurants on Procuradores, Plateros and Tecseccocha.

$$$ Chicha, Plaza Regocijo 261, p 2 (above El Truco), T240520. Daily 1200-2400. Specializes in regional dishes created by restaurateur Gastón Acurio (see under Lima, Restaurants), Peruvian cuisine of the highest standards in a renovated colonial house, at one time the royal mint, tastefully decorated, open-to-view kitchen, bar with a variety of pisco sours, good service.

$$$ Cicciolina, Triunfo 393, 2nd floor, T239510. Sophisticated cooking focusing largely on Italian/Mediterranean cuisine, impressive wine list. Good atmosphere, great for a special occasion.

$$$ El Truco, Plaza Regocijo 261. Open 0900-0100. Excellent local and international dishes, buffet lunch 1200-1500, nightly folk music at 2045, next door is **Taberna del Truco**.

$$$ Fallen Angel, Plazoleta Nazarenas 320, T258184. Sun from 1500. International and *Novo Andino* gourmet cuisine, great steaks, genuinely innovative interior design, worth checking out their events.

$$$ Fusiones, Av El Sol 106, T233341. Open 1100-2300. In the La Merced commercial centre, 2nd floor. *Novo Andino* and international cuisine in a chic contemporary setting, fine wines.

$$$ Incanto, Santa Catalina Angosta 135, T254753. Daily 1100-2400. Under same ownership as **Inka Grill** and with the same standards, restaurant has Inca stone work and serves Italian dishes (pastas, grilled meats, pizzas), and desserts, accompanied by an extensive wine list. Also Peruvian delicatessen.

$$$ Inka Grill, Portal de Panes 115, Plaza de Armas, T262992. Specializing in *Novo Andino* cuisine, also home-made pastas, wide vegetarian selection, live music, excellent coffee and home-made pastries 'to go'.

$$$ Kusikuy, Suecia 339, T292870. Mon-Sat 0800-2300. Local, national and international dishes, good service, set lunch unbeatable value at only US$2.

$$$ La China, Santa Teresa 364, 2nd floor, T506462. Reportedly one of the best *chifas* in Cuzco.

$$$ La Retama, Portal de Panes 123, 2nd floor, T226372. Good food (also *Novo Andino*) and service, live music and dance, art exhibitions.

$$$ Limo, Portal de Carnes 236, T240668. On 2nd floor of a colonial mansion overlooking the Plaza de Armas, Peruvian cuisine of the highest standard, with strong emphasis on fish and seafood, fine pisco bar, good service and atmosphere.

$$$ MAP Café, in Museo de Arte Precolombino, Plaza de las Nazarenas 231. Café by day (1000-1830), from 1830 to 2200 serves superb international and Peruvian-Andean cuisine, innovative children's menu, minimalist design and top-class service.

$$$ Pachacútec Grill and Bar, Portal de Panes 105, Plaza de Armas. International cuisine, seafood and Italian specialities, folk music nightly.

$$$ Tunupa, Portal Confiturias 233, p 2, Plaza de Armas. Large restaurant, small balcony overlooking Plaza, international, Peruvian and *Novo Andino* cuisine, good buffet US$15, nicely decorated, cocktail lounge, live music and dance at 2030.

$$$ Tupananchis, Portal Mantas 180, T245159. Tasty *Novo Andino* and fusion cuisine in a sophisticated atmosphere.

$$ Greens Organic, Santa Catalina Angosta 135, upstairs, T243379. Exclusively organic, but not wholly vegetarian, ingredients in fusion cuisine and a fresh daily buffet, very good.

$$ Pucará, Plateros 309. Mon-Sat 1230-2200. Peruvian and international food (no language skills required as a sample plate of their daily menu is placed in the window at lunchtime), nice atmosphere.

$$ Sara, Santa Catalina Ancha 370, T261691. Vegetarian-friendly organic café bistro, stylish and modern setting, menu includes both traditional Peruvian dishes as well as pasta and other international dishes.

$ El Encuentro, Santa Catalina Ancha 384, Choquechaca 136 and Tigre 130. One of the best value eateries In Cuzco, 3 courses of good healthy vegan food and a drink for US$2, very busy at lunchtime.

$ El Fogón, Plateros 365. Huge local *menú del día*, good solid food at reasonable prices. Very popular.

$ Víctor Victoria, Tecseccocha 466, T252854. Israeli and local dishes, first-class breakfasts, good value.

Cafés

Amaru, Plateros 325, p 2. Limitless coffee and tea, great bread and juices, even on 'non-buffet' breakfasts, colonial balcony. Also has bar.

Café El Ayllu, Almagro 133, T232357, and Marqués 263, T255078. Classical/folk music, good atmosphere, superb range of milk products, wonderful apple pastries, good selection for breakfast, great juices, quick service. A Cuzco institution.

Café Halliy, Plateros 363. Popular meeting place, especially for breakfast, good for comments on guides, has good snacks and 'copa Halliy' (fruit, muesli, yoghurt, honey and chocolate cake), also good vegetarian *menú* and set lunch.

Café Perla, Santa Catalina Ancha 304, on the plazoleta, T774130. Extensive menu of light meals, sandwiches, desserts and coffee, including beans for sale roasted on the premises. Popular.

Dolce Vita, Santa Catalina Ancha 366. Open 1000-2100. Delicious Italian ice cream.

Dos por Tres, Marquez 271. Popular for over 20 years, great coffee and cakes.

La Bondiet, Plaza Espinar y Plateros 363. Clean, simple café with a huge selection of sweet and savoury pastries, *empanadas*, good sandwiches, juices and coffee. A local favourite.

La Tertulia, Procuradores 44, p 2. Open until 2300. Breakfast served 0630-1300, includes muesli, bread, yoghurt, eggs, juice and coffee, all you can eat for US$3, superb value, vegetarian buffet daily 1800-2200, set dinner and salad bar for US$3.50, also fondue and gourmet meals, book exchange, newspapers, classical music.

Yahuu! Juice Bar, Portal Confitería 249 and Marqués 200. Fresh inexpensive juices and smoothies as well as sandwiches (at Portal Confitería).

Yaku Mama, Procuradores 397. Good for breakfast, unlimited fruit and coffee.

Beyond the Plaza, including San Blas

$$$ A Mi Manera, Triunfo 393, T222219. Imaginative *Novo Andino* cuisine with open kitchen. Great hospitality and atmosphere.

$$$ Baco, Ruinas 465, T242808. Wine bar and bistro-style restaurant, same owner as Cicciolina. Specializes in BBQ and grilled meats, also veggie dishes, pizzas and good wines. Unpretentious and comfy, groups welcome.

$$$ Pachapapa, Plazoleta San Blas 120, opposite church of San Blas, T241318. A beautiful patio restaurant in a colonial house, good Cusqueña and other dishes, at night diners can sit in their own, private colonial dining room, attentive staff.

$$$-$$ Divina Comedia, Pumacurco 406, T437640. Daily 1230-1500, 1830-2300. An elegant restaurant just 1 block from the Monasterio hotel, diners are entertained by classical piano and singing. Friendly

atmosphere with comfortable seating, perfect for a special night out, reasonable prices.

$$ El Paisa, Av El Sol 819, T501717. Open 0900-1700. Typical northern Peruvian dishes including *ceviche* and goat.

$$ Granja Heidi, Cuesta San Blas 525, T238383. Delicious yoghurt, granola, ricotta cheese and honey and other great breakfast options. Also vegetarian dishes, a very good midday *menú* and steak at night. Highly recommended.

$$ Inkanato, San Agustín 280, T222926. Good food, staff dressed in Inca outfits and dishes made only with ingredients known in Inca times, calls itself a "living museum".

$$ Inka Panaka, Tandapata 140, T235034. Artistic flair, gallery of local artists' work. *Novo Andino* cuisine, and tasty innovative treats. Several vegetarian options, also breakfast.

$$ Jack's Café, Choquechaca y San Blas, T806960. Excellent varied menu, generous portions, relaxed atmosphere, can get very busy at lunchtime, expect a queue in high season.

$$ Justina, Palacios 110. Mon-Sat from 1800. Good value, good quality pizzería, with wine bar. It's at the back of a patio.

$$ La Bodega 138, Herrajes 138, T260272. Excellent pizza, good salads and pasta. Warm and welcoming.

$$ Le Soleil, C San Agustin 275, in *La Lune* hotel, T240543, www.restaurantelesoleilcusco.com. Closed Wed. Excellent restaurant using local products to make classic French cuisine.

$$ Los Toldos, Almagro 171 and San Andrés 219. Grilled chicken, fries and salad bar, also *trattoria* with home-made pasta and pizza, delivery T229829.

$$ Macondo, Cuesta San Blas 571, T229415. Interesting restaurant with an imaginative menu, good food, well-furnished, gay friendly.

$$ The Muse, C Triunfo 338, 2nd floor, T242030. Restaurant lounge serving an international menu, lots of veggie options, live music every night, balcony seating, Wi-Fi. British owner Claire is a great source of information.

$$-$ Aldea Yanapay, Ruinas 415, p 2. Good café serving breakfast, lunch and dinner. Run by a charity which supports children's homes (www.aldeayanapay.org).

$ Café Punchay, Choquechaca 229, T261504. German-owned vegetarian restaurant, with a variety of pasta and potato dishes, good range of wines and spirits, large screen for international sports and you can bring a DVD for your own private movie showing.

$ Kushka...fé, Choquechaca 131-A and Espaderos 142, T258073. Great food and value in a nice setting, English spoken.

$ Venezia, Carmen Alto 154, San Blas. Only 4 tables, "exquisite gourmet" food at ridiculously low prices, opened in 2013.

Cafés

Chocolate, Choquechaca 162. Good for coffee and cakes, but don't miss the gourmet chocolates.

Cositas Café y Arte, Pasaje Inca Roca 108 and 110, T236410. Inventive local cuisine in a small, art-filled café. Profits support local social projects such as arts and crafts which are on sale in the café.

Juanito's Sandwich Café, Qanchipata 596. Great grilled veggie and meaty burgers and sandwiches, coffee, tea and hot chocolate. Juanito himself is a great character and the café stays open late.

Manu Café, Av Pardo 1046. Good coffee and good food too.

Panadería El Buen Pastor, Cuesta San Blas 579. Very good bread, *empanadas* and pastries, proceeds go to a charity for orphans and street children.

✿ Bars and clubs

Cuzco *p1344, maps p1346 and p1348*
Bars
Bar 7, Tandapata 690, San Blas, T506472. Good food and drinks in a trendy bar which specializes in local ingredients.

Cross Keys Pub, Triunfo 350 (upstairs), T229227, www.cross-keys-pub-cusco-peru.com. Open 1100-0130. Run by Barry Walker of **Manu Expeditions**, a Mancunian and ornithologist, cosy, darts, cable sports, pool, bar meals, plus daily half price specials Sun-Wed, great pisco sours, very popular, great atmosphere, free Wi-Fi.

Indigo, Tecseccocha 2, p 2, T260271. Shows 3 films a day. Also has a lounge and cocktail bar and serves Asian and local food. A log fire keeps out the night-time cold.

Km 0 (Arte y Tapas), Tandapata 100, San Blas. Mediterranean themed bar tucked in behind San Blas, good snacks and tapas, with live music every night (around 2200).

Los Perros Bar, Tecseccocha 436. Open 1100-0100. Great place to chill out on comfy couches, excellent music, welcoming, good coffee, tasty meals available (including vegetarian), book exchange, English and other magazines, board games. Has a take-away only branch at Suecia 368, open 2400 to 0600 for good quality, post-club food.

Museo del Pisco, Santa Catalina Ancha 398, T262709, museo-del-pisco on Facebook. A bar where you can sample many kinds of pisco; tapas-style food served.

Norton Rat's Tavern, Santa Catalina Angosta 116. Open 0700-0230. On the corner of the Plaza de Armas, fine balcony, also serves meals, cable TV, popular, English spoken, pool, darts, motorcycle theme. Also runs **Hostal Gocta Cusco**.

Paddy's Pub, Triunfo 124 on the corner of the plaza. Open 1300-0100. Irish theme pub, deservedly popular, good grub.

Rosie O'Grady's, Santa Catalina Ancha 360, T247935. Open 1100 till late (food served till 2400). Good music, tasty food, good value.

Clubs

El Garabato Video Music Club, Espaderos 132, p 3. Daily 1600-0300. Dance area, lounge for chilling, bar, live shows 2300-0030 (all sorts of styles) and large screen showing music videos.

Extreme, C Suecia. Movies in the late afternoon and early evening, but after midnight this place really gets going with an eclectic range of music, from 60's and 70's rock and pop to techno and trance.

Kamikaze, Plaza Regocijo 274, T233865. *Peña* at 2200, good old traditional rock music, candle-lit cavern atmosphere, entry US$2.50.

Mama Africa, Portal de Panes 109. Cool music and clubber's spot, good food with varied menu, happy hour till 2300, good value.

Mythology, Portal de Carnes 298, p 2. Mostly an early 80's and 90's combination of cheese, punk and classic, popular. Food in served in the jungle-themed **Lek Café**. They also show movies in the afternoons.

Ukuku's, Plateros 316. US$1.35 entry, very popular, good atmosphere, good mix of music including live shows nightly. Also has a **restaurant** at Carmen Alto 133, good value and fabulous views.

ⓔ Entertainment

Cuzco *p1344, maps p1346 and p1348*
Folklore Regular nightly folklore show at
Centro Qosqo de Arte Nativo, Av El Sol 604,
T227901. Show from 1900 to 2030, entrance
on BTC ticket. **Teatro Inti Raymi**, Saphi 605,
nightly at 1845, US$4.50, well worth it.
Teatro Municipal, C Mesón de la Estrella 149
(T227321 for information 0900-1300 and
1500-1900). Refurbished in 2013. Plays,
dancing and shows, mostly Thu-Sun.
They also run classes in music and dancing
from Jan to Mar which are great value.

ⓕ Festivals

Cuzco *p1344, maps p1346 and p1348*
Carnival in Cuzco is a messy affair with flour,
water, cacti, bad fruit and animal manure being
thrown about in the streets. **Easter Monday**:
procession of El Señor de los Temblores (Lord
of the Earthquakes), starting at 1600 outside
the Cathedral. A large crucifix is paraded
through the streets, returning to the Plaza
de Armas around 2000 to bless the tens of
thousands of people who have assembled
there. **2-3 May** Vigil of the Cross takes place
at all mountaintops with crosses on them, a
boisterous affair. **Jun** Q'Olloriti, the Snow Star
Festival, is held at a 4700 m glacier north of
Ocongate (Ausangate) 150 km southeast of
Cuzco. Several agencies offer tours. (The date is
moveable.) On **Corpus Christi** day, the Thu after
Trinity Sunday, all the statues of the Virgin and
of saints from Cuzco's churches are paraded
through the streets to the Cathedral. The Plaza
de Armas is surrounded by tables with women
selling *cuy* (guinea pig) and a mixed grill called
chiriuchu (*cuy*, chicken, tortillas, fish eggs,
water-weeds, maize, cheese and sausage) and
lots of Cusqueña beer. **24 Jun** The pageant
of **Inti Raymi**, the Inca festival of the winter
solstice, is enacted in Quechua at 1000 at the
Qoricancha, moving on to Sacsayhuaman at
1300. Tickets for the stands can be bought a
week in advance from the Emufec office, Santa
Catalina Ancha 325, US$80, less if bought
Mar-May. Travel agents can arrange the whole
day for you, with meeting points, transport,
reserved seats and packed lunch. Those who

try to persuade you to buy a ticket for the right
to film or take photos are being dishonest. On
the night before Inti Raymi, the Plaza de Armas
is crowded with processions and food stalls.
Try to arrive in Cuzco 15 days before Inti Raymi.
28 Jul Peruvian Independence Day. Prices
shoot up during these celebrations. **Aug**
On the last Sun is the **Huarachicoy** festival at
Sacsayhuaman, a spectacular re-enactment of
the Inca manhood rite, performed in dazzling
costumes by boys of a local school. **8 Sep
Day of the Virgin** is a colourful procession of
masked dancers from the church of Almudena,
at the southwest edge of Cuzco, near Belén,
to the Plaza de San Francisco. There is also
a splendid fair at Almudena, and a free bull
fight on the following day. **1 Nov** All Saints'
Day, celebrated everywhere with bread dolls
and traditional cooking. **8 Dec** Cuzco day,
when churches and museums close at 1200.
24 Dec Santuranticuy, 'the buying of saints',
with a big crafts market in the plaza, very noisy
until early hours of the 25th. This is one of the
best festivals with people from the mountains
coming to celebrate Christmas in Cusco.

ⓞ Shopping

Cuzco *p1344, maps p1346 and p1348*
Arts and crafts
In the Plaza San Blas and the surrounding area,
authentic Cuzco crafts still survive. A market is
held on Sat. Many leading artisans welcome
visitors. Among fine objects made are Biblical
figures from plaster, wheatflour and potatoes,
reproductions of pre-Columbian ceramics and
colonial sculptures, pious paintings, earthenware
figurines, festive dolls and wood carvings.
    Cuzco is the weaving centre of Peru and
excellent textiles can be found at good value.
Be very careful of buying gold and silver objects
and jewellery in and around Cuzco. Do not buy
condor feathers, painted or unpainted, as it is
illegal to sell or purchase them. Condors are
being killed for this trade. The prison sentence
is 4 years.
Agua y Tierra, Plazoleta Nazarenas 167, and
Cuesta San Blas 595, T226951. Excellent quality
crafts from rainforest communities.
Apacheta, San Juan de Dios 250, T238210, www.
apachetaperu.com. Replicas of Pre-Inca and Inca

textiles, ceramics, alpaca goods, contemporary art gallery, books on Andean culture.

Inkantations, Choquechaca 200. Radical baskets made from natural materials in all sorts of weird and wonderful shapes. Also ceramics and Andean weavings. Interesting and original.

Mercado Artesanal, Av El Sol, block 4, is good for cheap crafts.

Pedazo de Arte, Plateros 334B. A tasteful collection of Andean handicrafts, many designed by Japanese owner Miki Suzuki.

La Pérez, Urb Mateo Pumacahua 598, Huanchac, T232186. A big co-operative with a good selection; they will arrange a free pick-up from your hotel.

Seminario, Portal de Carnes 244, Plaza de Armas, sells the ceramics of Seminario-Behar (see under Urubamba, page 1372), plus cotton, basketry, jewellery, etc.

Bookshops

Centro de Estudios Regionales Andinos Bartolomé de las Casas, Av Tullumayo 465, T233472, www.cbc.org.pe. Mon-Sat 1100-1400, 1600-1900. Good books on Peruvian history, archaeology, etc.

Jerusalem, Heladeros 143, T235408. English books, guidebooks, postcards, book exchange (3 for 1).

Camping equipment

For renting equipment, there are several places around the Plaza area. Check the equipment carefully as it is common for parts to be missing. A deposit of US$100 is asked, plus credit card, passport or plane ticket. White gas (bencina), US$1.50 per litre, can be bought at hardware stores, but check the purity. Stove spirit (alcoól para quemar) is available at pharmacies; blue gas canisters, costing US$5, can be found at hardware stores and camping shops. You can also rent equipment through travel agencies.

Edson Zuñiga Huillca, Mercado Rosaspata, Jr Abel Landeo P-1, T802831, 993 7243 (mob). 3 mins from Plaza de Armas, for repair of camping equipment and footwear, also equipment rental, open 24 hrs a day, 7 days a week, English and Italian spoken.

Tatoo, Plazoleta Espinar, T254211, www.tatoo. ws. High-quality hiking, climbing and camping gear, not cheap, but Western brand names and their own lines.

Fabrics and alpaca clothing

Alpaca Golden, Portal de Panes 151, T251724, alpaca.golden@terra.com.pe. Also at Plazoleta Nazarenas 175. Designer, producer and retailer of fine alpaca clothing.

The Center for Traditional Textiles of Cuzco, Av El Sol 603, T228117, www.textilescusco.org. A non-profit organization that seeks to promote, refine and rediscover the weaving traditions of the Cuzco area. Tours of workshops, weaving classes, you can watch weavers at work. Also run 3-day weaving courses. Over 50% of the price goes direct to the weaver. Recommended.

Hilo, Carmen Alto 260, T254536. Fashionable Items designed individually and handmade on-site. Run by Eibhlin Cassidy, she can adjust and tailor designs.

Josefina Olivera, Portal Comercio 173, Plaza de Armas. Daily 1100-2100. Sells old textiles and weavings, expensive but worth it to save pieces being cut up to make other item.

Kuna by Alpaca 111, Plaza Regocijo 202, T243233, www.kuna.com.pe. High-quality alpaca clothing with outlets also in hotels El Monasterio, Libertador and Machu Picchu Sanctuary Lodge.

Store of Weavers (Asociación Central de Artesanos y Artesanas del Sur Andino Inkakunaq Ruwaynin), Av Tullumayo 274, T233466. Store run by 6 local weaving communities, some of whose residents you can see working on site. All profits go to the weavers themselves.

Food and natural products

Choco Museo, Garcilaso 210, 2nd floor, also in Ollantaytambo, T 244765, www.chocomuseo. com. Offers chocolate making classes and runs trips to their cocoa plantation.

The Coca Shop, Carmen Alto 115, San Blas, T260774. Tiny shop selling an interesting selection of sweets and chocolates made using coca leaf flour. There is also plenty of information about the nutritional values of coca leaves.

La Cholita, Av El Sol and at airport. Special chocolates made with local ingredients.

Jewellery

Calas, Siete Angelitos 619-B, San Blas. Handmade silver jewellery in interesting designs and alpaca goods from the community of Pitumarca.

Ilaria, Portal Carrizos 258, T246253. Branches in hotels **Monasterio**, **Libertador** and at the airport. For recommended jewellery and silver.

Inka Treasure, Triunfo 375, T227470. With branches at Av Pardo 1080, Plazoleta Nazarenas 159 and Portal de Panes 163. Also at the airport and the airport in Juliaca. Fine jewellery including goldwork, mostly with pre-Columbian designs, and silver with the owner's designs. Tours of workshops at Av Circunvalación, near Cristo Blanco. The stores also incorporte the work of famed jeweller Carlos Chakiras.

Mullu, Triunfo 120, T229831. Mon-Sat 1000-2100. Contemporary silver jewellery with semi-precious stones and cotton clothing with interesting designs.

Spondylus, Cuesta San Blas 505, T226929. A good selection of interesting gold and silver jewellery and fashion tops with Inca and pre-Inca designs.

Markets

Wanchac, Av Garcilaso (southeast of centre) and **San Pedro Market**, opposite Estación San Pedro, sell a variety of goods. **El Molino**, beyond the Terminal Terrestre, sells everything under the sun at knock-down prices, but quality not guaranteed and nothing touristy, fascinating, crowded, don't take valuables and go there by colectivo or taxi. **Confraternidad**, beside the Wanchaq train station, is similar to El Molino and closer to town.

Music

Taki Museo de Música de los Andes, Hatunrumiyoc 487-5. Shop and workshop selling and displaying musical instruments, owner is an ethno-musicologist. Recommended for anyone interested in Andean music.

⚙ What to do

Cuzco *p1344, maps p1346 and p1348*
For a list of recommended Tour operators for Manu, see page 1429. There are many travel agencies in Cuzco. The sheer number and variety of tours on offer is bewildering and prices for the same tour can vary dramatically. Always remember that you get what you pay for and that, in a crowded market, organization can sometimes be a weak point. In general you should only deal directly with the agencies themselves. You can do this when in town, or you can raise whatever questions you may have in advance (or even in Cuzco), and get replies in writing, by email. Other sources of advice are visitors returning from trips, who can give the latest information, and the trip reports for members of the South America Explorers. Students will normally receive a discount on production of an ISIC card. Do not deal with guides who claim to be employed by agencies listed below without verifying their credentials. City tours cost about US$10-15 for 4 hrs; check what sites are included and that the guide is experienced.

Only a restricted number of agencies are licensed to operate **Inca Trail** trips. Sernanp, Av José Gabriel Cosio 308, Urb Magisterial, 1 etapa, T229297, www.sernanp.gob.pe, verifies operating permits (see Visitors' tickets, above, for Dirección de Cultura office). Unlicensed agencies will sell Inca Trail trips, but pass clients on to the operating agency. This can cause confusion and booking problems at busy times. Current advice is to book your preferred dates as early as possible, between 2 months and a year in advance, depending on the season when you want to go, then confirm nearer the time. There have been many instances of disappointed trekkers whose bookings did not materialize. Don't wait to the last minute and check your operator's cancellation fees. **Note** See page 1383, under Inca Trails, for regulations governing the trail. Note also that many companies offer treks as alternatives to the Inca Trail and its variations to Machu Picchu. Unlike the Inca Trail, these treks are unregulated. Ensure that the trekking company does not employ the sort of practices (such as mistreating porters, not clearing up rubbish) which are now outlawed on the trails to Machu Picchu.

The Cuzco soccer stadium was renovated in 2014 and, If you are a fan, it is worth going to see a game.

Inca Trail and general tours

Amazon Trails Peru, Tandapata 660, T437374, or T984-714148, www.amazontrailsperu.com. Trekking tours around the area, including the Inca Trail, Salkantay and Choquequirao. Also well-equipped and well-guided trips to Manu.

Alpaca Expeditions, Heladeros 157, T254278. Offers responsible treks focusing on the Inca Trail.

Andean Treks, Av Pardo 705, T225701, www.andeantreks.com. Manager Tom Hendrickson uses high-quality equipment and satellite phones. This company organizes itineraries, from 2 to 15 days with a wide variety of activities in this area and further afield.

Andina Travel, Plazoleta Santa Catalina 219, T251892, www.andinatravel.com. Specializes in trekking and biking, notably the Lares Valley, working with traditional weaving communities.

Big Foot, Triunfo 392 (oficina 213), T233836, www.bigfootcusco.com. Tailor-made hiking trips, especially in the remote corners of the Vilcabamba and Vilcanota mountains; also the Inca Trail.

Ch'aska, Garcilaso 265 p 2, of 6, T240424, https://chaskatours.com. Dutch-Peruvian company offering cultural, adventure, nature and esoteric tours. They specialize in the Inca Trail, but also llama treks to Lares, treks to Choquequirao.

Culturas Peru, Tandapata 354A, T243679, www.culturasperu.com. Swiss-Peruvian company offering adventure, cultural, ecological and spiritual tours. Also specialize in alternative Inca trails.

Destinos Turísticos, Portal de Panes 123, oficina 101-102, Plaza de Armas, T228168, www.destinosturisticosperu.com. The owner speaks Spanish, English, Dutch and Portuguese and specializes in package tours from economic to 5-star budgets. Advice on booking jungle trips and renting mountain bikes. Very helpful.

EcoAmerica Peru, T999-705538, www.eco americaperu.com. Associated with America Tours (La Paz, Bolivia). Owned by 3 experienced consultants in responsible travel, conservation and cultural heritage. Specializes in culture, history, nature, trekking, biking and birding tours. Knowledgeable guides, excellent customer service for independent travellers, groups or families. Also sell tours and flights to Bolivia.

Enigma Adventure, Jirón Clorinda Matto de Turner 100, Urb Magisterial 1a Etapa, T222155, www.enigmaperu.com. Run by Spaniard Silvia Rico Coll. Well-organized, innovative trekking expeditions including a luxury service, Inca Trail and a variety of challenging alternatives. Also cultural tours to weaving communities, Ayahuasca therapy, climbing and biking.

Explorandes, Paseo Zarzuela Q-2, Huancaro, T238380, www.explorandes.com. Experienced high-end adventure company. Arrange a wide variety of mountain treks; trips available in Peru and Ecuador, book through website also arranges tours across Peru for lovers of orchids, ceramics or textiles. Award-winning environmental practices.

Fertur, C San Agustín 317, T221304, www.fertur-travel.com. Mon-Fri 0900-1900, Sat 0900-

1200. Cuzco branch of the Lima tour operator, see page 1224.

Gatur Cusco, Puluchapata 140 (a small street off Av El Sol 3rd block), T223496, www.gaturcusco.com. Esoteric, ecotourism, and general tours. Owner Dr José (Pepe) Altamirano is knowledgeable in Andean folk traditions. Excellent conventional tours, bilingual guides and transportation. Guides speak English, French, Spanish and German. They can also book internal flights.

Habitats Peru, Condominio La Alborada B-507, T246271, www.habitatsperu.com. Bird watching and mountain biking trips offered by Doris and Carlos. They also run a volunteer project near Quillabamba.

Hiking Peru, Portal de Panes 109, of 6, T247942, T984-651414, www.hikingperu.com. 8-day treks to Espíritu Pampa; 7 days/6 nights around Ausangate; 4-day/3-night Lares Valley Trek.

Inca Explorers, C Peru W-18, T241070, www.incaexplorers.com. Specialist trekking agency for small group expeditions in socially and environmentally responsible manner. Also 2-week hike in the Cordillera Vilcanota (passing Nevado Ausangate), and Choquequirao to Espíritu Pampa.

InkaNatura Travel, Ricardo Palma J1, T255255, www.inkanatura.com. Offers tours with special emphasis on sustainable tourism and conservation. Knowledgeable guides.

Llama Path, San Juan de Dios 250, T240822, www.llamapath.com. A wide variety of local tours, specializing in Inca Trail and alternative treks, in environmental campaigns and porter welfare. Many good reports.

Machete Tours, Triunfo 392, T224829, T440 351 (Lima office), www.machetetours.com. Peruvian and Danish owners. Tours cover all Peru and also Bolivia and Chile. All guides speak good English. Adventure tours arranged using local accommodation or family camping areas. Tours are eco-friendly and benefit the local community.

Peru Treks, Av Pardo 540, T222722, www.perutreks.com. Trekking agency set up by Englishman Mike Weston and his wife Koqui González. They pride themselves on good treatment of porters and support staff and have been consistently recommended for professionalism and customer care, a portion of

profits go to community projects. The company specializes in trekking and cultural tours in the Cuzco region. Treks offered include Salkantay, the Lares Valley and Vilcabamba Vieja.

Q'ente, Choquechaca 229, p 2, T222535, www.qente.com. Their Inca Trail service is recommended. Also private treks to Salkantay, Ausangate, Choquequirao, Vilcabamba and Q'eros. Horse riding to local ruins costs US$35 for 4-5 hrs. Very good, especially with children.

Sky Travel, Santa Catalina Ancha 366, interior 3-C (down alleyway near Rosie O'Grady's pub), T261818, www.skyperu.com. English spoken. General tours around city and Sacred Valley. Inca Trail with good-sized double tents and a dinner tent (the group is asked what it would like on the menu 2 days before departure). Other trips include Vilcabamba and Ausangate (trekking).

Southamerica Planet, Garcilaso 210, of 201 (2nd floor, T251145, www.southamericaplanet.com. Peruvian/Belgian-owned agency offering the Inca Trail, other treks around Cuzco and packages within Peru, as well as Bolivia and Patagonia.

Tambo Tours, 4405 Spring Cypress Rd, Suite 210, Spring, TX 77388, USA, T1-888-2-GO-PERU (246-7378), T001-281 528 9448, www.2GO PERU.com. Long established adventure and tour specialist with offices in Peru and the US. Customized trips to the Amazon and archaeological sites of Peru, Bolivia and Ecuador.

Tanager Tours, T01-669 0825, T984-742711, T984-761790 (mob), www.tanagertours.com. Specializes in birdwatching tours throughout Peru but all will also arrange other tours. Owners live in Cuzco but currently no office. Most of their tours are arranged via the internet and they contact clients at their accommodation.

T'ika Trek, no storefront, UK T07768-948366, www.tikatrek.com. Run by Fiona Cameron, a long-term resident of Peru and keen hiker and biker. With over 10 years in the Cuzco tourism business Fiona provides high-quality personalized tours all over Peru as well as to the Galápagos Islands (Ecuador). Focus is on small groups and families.

Trekperu, Av República de Chile B-15, Parque Industrial, Wanchac, T261501, www.trekperu.com. Experienced trek operator as well as other adventure sports and mountain biking. Offers 'culturally sensitive' tours. Cusco Biking Adventure includes support vehicle and good camping gear (but providing your own sleeping bag).

United Mice, Av Pachacútec 454 A-5, T221139, www.unitedmice.com. Inca Trail and alternative trail via Salkantay and Santa Teresa, well-established and reputable. Good guides who speak languages other than Spanish. Discount with student card, good food and equipment. City and Sacred Valley tours and treks to Choquequirao.

Wayki Trek, Av Pardo 506, T224092, www.waykitrek.net. Budget travel agency with a hostel attached, recommended for their Inca Trail service. Owner Leo knows the area very well. Treks to several almost unknown Inca sites and interesting variations on the 'classic' Inca Trail with visits to porters' communities. Also treks to Ausangate, Salkantay and Choquequirao.

Rafting, mountain biking and trekking

When looking for an operator please consider more than just the price of your tour. Competition between companies in Cuzco is intense and price wars can lead to compromises in safety. Consider the quality of safety equipment (lifejackets, etc) and the number and experience of rescue kayakers and support staff. On a large and potentially dangerous rivers like the Apurímac and Urubamba (where fatalities have occurred), this can make all the difference.

Amazonas Explorers, Av Collasuyo 910, Miravalle, PO Box 722, www.amazonas-explorer.com. Experts in rafting, inflatable canoeing, mountain biking, horse riding and hiking. English owner Paul Cripps has great experience. Most bookings from overseas (in UK, T01874-658125, Jan-Mar; T01437-891743, Apr-Dec), but they may be able to arrange a trip for travellers in Cuzco with advance notice. Rafting and inflatable canoeing includes Río Urubamba, Río Apurímac, Río Tambopata (including Lake Titicaca). Also 5-day/4-night Inca Trail, alternatives to the Inca Trail and Choquequirao to Machu Picchu, an excellent variation of the Ausangate Circuit and a trek to Espíritu Pampa. Multi-activity and family trips are a speciality. Mountain biking trips all use state-of-the-art equipment, expert guides and support vehicles where appropriate. All options are at the higher end of the market and are highly recommended. Amazonas Explorer are members of www.onepercentfortheplanet.org, donating 1% of their turnover to a tree-planting project in the Lares watershed.

Apumayo, Jr Ricardo Palma N-5, Santa Mónica, Wanchaq, T246018, www.apumayo.com. Mon-Sat 0900-1300, 1600-2000. Urubamba rafting (from 0800-1530 every day); 3- to 4-day Apurímac trips. Also mountain biking to Maras and Moray in Sacred Valley, or from Cuzco to the jungle town of Quillabamba. This company also offers tours for disabled people, including rafting.

Apus Perú, Cuichipunco 366, T232691, www.apus-peru.com. Conducts most business by internet, specializes in alternatives to the Inca Trail, strong commitment to sustainability, well-organized. Associated with Threads of Peru NGO which helps weavers.

Eric Adventures, Urb Santa María A1-6, San Sebastián, T272862, www.ericadventures.com. Specialize in many adventure activities. They clearly explain what equipment is included in their prices and what you will need to bring. They also rent motorcross bikes for US$70-90 per day, mountain bikes and cars and 4WDs. Prices are more expensive if you book by email. A popular company.

Medina Brothers, contact Christian or Alain Medina on T225163 or T984-653485/ T984-691670. Family-run rafting company with good equipment and plenty of experience. They usually focus on day rafting trips in the Sacred Valley, but services are tailored to the needs of the client.

Pachatusan Trek, Villa Union Huancaro G-4, B 502, T231817, www.pachatusantrek.com. Offers a wide variety to treks, as alternatives to the Inca Trail, professional and caring staff, "simply fantastic".

River Explorers, Pasaje Los Zafiros B-15, T260926 or T958-320673, www.riverexplorers.com. An adventure company offering mountain biking, trekking and rafting trips (on the Apurímac, Urubamba and Tambopata). Experienced and qualified guides with environmental awareness.

Terra Explorer Peru, T237352, www.terraexplorerperu.com. Offers a wide range of trips from high-end rafting in the Sacred Valley and expeditions to the Colca and Cotahuasi canyons, trekking the Inca Trail and others, mountain biking, kayaking (including on Lake Titicaca) and jungle trips. All guides are bilingual.

Cultural tours

Milla Tourism, Av Pardo 800, T231710, www.millaturismo.com. Mon-Fri 0800-1300, 1500-1900, Sat 0800-1300. Mystical tours to Cuzco's Inca ceremonial sites such as Pumamarca and The Temple of the Moon. Guide speaks only basic English. They also arrange cultural and environmental lectures and courses.

Shamans and drug experiences

San Pedro and Ayahuasca have been used since before Inca times, mostly as a sacred healing experience. If you choose to experience these incredible healing/teaching plants, only do so under the guidance of a reputable agency or shaman and always have a friend with you who is not partaking. If the medicine is not prepared correctly, it can be highly toxic and, in rare cases, severely dangerous. Never buy from someone who is not recommended, never buy off the streets and never try to prepare the plants yourself.

Another Planet, Tandapata y Pasñapacana 148, San Blas, T241168, or T974-792316, www.anotherplanetperu.org. Run by Lesley Myburgh, who operates mystical and adventure tours in and around Cuzco, and is an expert in San Pedro cactus preparation. She arranges San Pedro sessions for healing in the garden of her house outside Cuzco. Tours meet at La Casa de la Gringa, see Where to stay, above.

Etnikas Travel & Shamanic Healing, Herrajes 148, T244516, www.etnikas.com. A shamanic centre now offering travel for mind, body and spirit and the sale of natural products from the Andes and the jungle. Expensive but serious in their work.

Sumac Coca Travel, San Agustín 245, T260311. Mystical tourism, offering Ayahuasca and San Pedro ceremonies, and also more conventional cultural tourism. Professional and caring.

Private guides

As most of the sights do not have any information or signs in English, a good guide can really improve your visit. Either arrange this before you set out or contract one at the sight you are visiting. A tip is expected at the end of the tour. Tours of the city or Sacred Valley cost US$50 for half-day, US$65 full day; a guide to Machu Picchu

charges US$80 per day. A list of official guides is held by **Agotur Cusco**, C HelaHeros 157, Of 34-F, p 3, T233457. **South American Explorers** has a list and contact details for recommended local guides. See also www.leaplocal.org.

⊖ Transport

Cuzco *p1344, maps p1346 and p1348*

Air

The airport is at Quispiquilla, near the bus terminal, 1.6 km from centre, airport information T222611/601. **Note** The airport can get very busy. Check in 2 hrs before your flight. Flights may be delayed or cancelled during the wet season, or may leave early if the weather is bad. To **Lima**, 55 mins, over 30 daily flights with **Avianca/TACA, Star Perú, LAN, Peruvian Airlines** and LC Perú (on its Lima, Pisco, Cuzco route). To **Arequipa**, 30 mins daily with LAN. To **Juliaca** (for Puno), 1 hr daily with LAN. To **Puerto Maldonado**, 30 mins, with LAN and Star Perú. To **La Paz**, Amazonas (www.amaszonas.com) 1 hr daily except Sat. Taxi to and from the airport costs US$3.50 (US$7.25 from the official taxi desk). Colectivos cost US$0.30 from Plaza San Francisco or outside the airport car park. Many representatives of hotels and travel agencies operate at the airport, with transport to the hotel with which they are associated. Take your time to choose your hotel, at the price you can afford. Also in baggage retrieval are mobile phone rentals, ATMs, LAC Dollar money exchange, an Oxyshot oxygen sales stand and an i perú office. There are phone booths, restaurant, cafeteria and a Tourist Protection Bureau desk.

Bus

Long distance Terminal on Av Vallejo Santoni, block 2 (Prolongación Pachacútec), colectivo from centre US$0.50, taxi US$2. Platform tax US$0.35. Buses to **Lima** (20-24 hrs) go via **Abancay**, 195 km, 5 hrs (longer in the rainy season), and **Nazca**, on the Panamerican Highway. This route is paved but floods in the wet season often damage large sections of the highway. If prone to travel sickness, be prepared on the road to Abancay, there are many, many curves, but the scenery is magnificent. At Abancay, the road forks, the other branch going to **Andahuaylas**, a further

138 km, 10-11 hrs from Cuzco, and **Ayacucho**, another 261 km, 20 hrs from Cuzco. On both routes at night, take a blanket or sleeping bag to ward off the cold. All buses leave daily from the Terminal Terrestre. **Molina**, who also have an office on Av Pachacútec, just past the railway station, have buses on both routes. They run 3 services a day to Lima via Abancay and Nazca, and one, at 1900, to Abancay and Andahuaylas. **Cruz del Sur**'s service to Lima via Abancay leaves at 0730 and 1400, while their more comfortable services depart at 1500 and 1600. **San Jerónimo** and **Los Chankas** have buses to Abancay, Andahuaylas and Ayacucho at 1830. **Turismo Ampay** and **Turismo Abancay** go 3 times a day to Abancay, and **Expreso Huamanga** once. **Bredde** has 5 buses a day to Abancay. Fares: Abancay US$18, Andahuaylas US$22, Nazca US$28, Lima also US$38-49; also US$50-70 (*Cruz del Sur Cruzero* and *VIP* classes). In Cuzco you may be told that there are no buses in the day from Abancay to Andahuaylas; this is not so as **Señor de Huanca** does so. If you leave Cuzco before 0800, with luck you'll make the connection at 1300 – worth it for the scenery. **Ormeño** has a service from Cuzco to Lima via Arequipa which takes longer (22 hrs), but is a more comfortable journey.

To Lake Titicaca and Bolivia To **Juliaca**, 344 km, 5-6 hrs, US$8-17. The road is fully paved, but after heavy rain buses may not run. To **Puno**, via Juliaca, US$8-17; direct, US$15 (*bus cama* US$18); 6 hrs. Tourist service with 5 stops, **First Class** and **Inka Express** (Av La Paz C-32, Urb El Ovalo, Wanchac, T24/887, www. inkaexpress.com), calling at Andahuaylillas church, Raqchi, La Raya, Sicuani and Pucará, US$60, lunch included. **Note** It is safest to travel by day on the Juliaca-Puno-Cuzco route.

To **Arequipa**, 521 km, US$14-47; **Cruz del Sur** use the direct paved route via Juliaca and have a *Cruzero* services at 2000 and 2030, 10 hrs, US$25-47. Other buses join the new Juliaca-Arequipa road at Imata, 10-12 hrs (eg **Carhuamayo**, 3 a day).

To **Puerto Maldonado**, **Móvil** (Terminal Terrestre, T238223), **Transportes Iguazú**, **Machupicchu**, **Palomino** and **Mendivil**, all from Terminal Terrestre, several daily, see page 1431.

To the **Sacred Valley**: To **Pisac**, 32 km, 1 hr, US$1.50, from C Puputi on the outskirts of the city, near the Clorindo Matto de Turner school

and Av de la Cultura. Colectivos, minibuses and buses leave whenever they are full, between 0600 and 1600. Buses returning from Pisac are often full. The last one back leaves around 2000. Taxis charge about US$20 for the round trip. To Pisac, **Calca** (18 km beyond Pisac) and **Urubamba** a further 22 km, buses leave from Av Tullumayo 800 block, Wanchac, US$1.50. Combis and colectivos leave from 300 block of Av Grau, 1 block before crossing the bridge, for **Chinchero**, 23 km, 45 mins, US$1.50; and for **Urubamba** a further 25 km, 45 mins, US$1.50 (or US$2.25 Cuzco-Urubamba direct, US$2.25 for a seat in a colectivo taxi). To **Ollantaytambo** from Av Grau, 0745, 1945, US$4, or catch a bus to Urubamba. Also Cruz del Sur, at Terminal Terrestre, 3 a day, 2 hrs, US$7. Direct taxi-colectivo service to Ollantaytambo from C Pavitos, leaves when full, US$5. Tours can be arranged to Chinchero, Urubamba and Ollantaytambo with a Cuzco travel agency. To Chinchero, US$9 pp; a taxi costs US$35 round-trip. Usually only day tours are organized for visits to the valley, US$25-30. Using public transport and staying overnight in Urubamba, Ollantaytambo or Pisac allows more time to see the ruins and markets.

Taxi
In Cuzco they are recommended when arriving by air, train or bus. They have fixed prices but you have to stay alert to overpricing: in the centre US$1.50 in town (50% more after 2100 or 2200). In town it is advisable to take municipality-authorized taxis that have a sticker with a number on the window and a chequerboard pattern on the side. Safer still are licensed taxis, which have a sign with the company's name on the roof, not just a sticker in the window. These taxis are summoned by phone (**llama taxi**) and are more expensive (**Aló Cusco** T222222, **Ocarina** T247080). Trips to **Sacsayhuaman**, US$10; ruins of **Tambo Machay** US$15-20 (3-4 people); day trip US$50-85.

Train
To Juliaca and Puno, **Perú Rail** trains leave from the Av El Sol station, Estación Wanchac, T238722. When arriving in Cuzco, a tourist bus meets the train to take visitors to hotels whose touts offer rooms. Machu Picchu trains leave from Estación San Pedro, opposite the San Pedro market.

The train to **Puno**, the *Andean Explorer* leaves at 0800, Mon, Wed, Fri (Apr-Oct) and Sat, arriving at Puno around 1800, sit on the left for views. The train makes a stop to view the scenery at La Raya. Always check whether the train is running, especially in the rainy season, when services may be cancelled. Cuzco to Puno costs US$268, Puno to Cuzco US$156. The ticket office at Wanchac station is open Mon-Fri 0700-1700, Sat, Sun and holidays 0700-1200. The Perú Rail office at Portal de Carnes 214 is open Mon-Fri 1000-2200, Sat, Sun and holidays 1400-2300 (take you passport or a copy when buying tickets). Buy tickets on www.perurail.com, or through a travel agent. Meals are served on the train. To **Ollantaytambo** and **Machu Picchu**, see page 1381.

● Directory

Cuzco *p1344, maps p1346 and p1348*
Banks Most banks are on Av El Sol and all have ATMs. There are also ATMs around the Plaza de Armas, in San Blas and on Av Cultura. Many travel agencies and casas de cambio change dollars. **LAC Dollar**, Av El Sol 150, T257762, Mon-Sat 0900-2000, has a delivery service to central hotels. Street changers hang around Av El Sol blocks 2-3. **Consulates** For foreign consulates in Cuzco, see http://embassy. goabroad.com. Bolivia, Av Osvaldo Baca 101, p 1, Urb Magisterio, T231845, Mon-Fri 0900-1200, 1500-1700. **Language schools** Academia Latinoamericana de Español, Plaza Limacpampa 565, T243364, www.latinoschools. com. The same company also has schools in Ecuador (Quito) and in Bolivia (Sucre). They can arrange courses that include any combination of these locations using identical teaching methods and materials. Professionally run with experienced staff. Many activities per week, including dance lessons and excursions to sites of historical and cultural interest. Good homestays. Private classes US$170 for 20 hrs, groups also available. **Acupari**, the German-Peruvian Cultural Association, San Agustín 307, T242970, www.acupari.com. Spanish classes are run here. **Amauta Spanish School**, Suecia 480, T262345, www.amautaspanish.com. Spanish classes, one-to-one or in small groups, also Quechua classes and workshops in Peruvian cuisine, dance and music, group tuition (2-6 people) US$140 for 20 hrs. They have pleasant accommodation on the same street, as well as a free internet café for students, and can arrange excursions and help find voluntary work. They also have a school in Urubamba and can arrange courses in Tambopata, Lima and Argentina. **Amigos Spanish School**, Zaguán del Cielo B-23, T242292, www.spanishcusco. com. Certified, experienced teachers, friendly atmosphere. All profits support a foundation for disadvantaged children. Private lessons or US$150 for 20 hrs of classes in a small group. Comfortable homestays and extra-curricular activities available, including a 'real city tour' through Cuzco's poor areas or cooking classes. **Excel**, Cruz Verde 336, T235298, www.excel-spanishlanguageprograms-peru.org. Very professional, US$7 per hr for one-to-one lessons. US$229 for 20 hrs with 2 people, or US$277 with homestay, one-on-one for 20 hrs. **Fairplay Spanish School**, Pasaje Zavaleta C-5, Wanchac, T984-789252, www.fairplay-peru.org. This relatively new NGO teaches Peruvians

who wouldn't normally have the opportunity (Peruvian single mothers, for example) to become Spanish teachers themselves over several months of training. The agency then acts as an agent, allowing these same teachers to find work with visiting students. Classes with these teachers cost US$4.50 or US$6 per hr, of which 33% is reinvested in the NGO, the rest going direct to the teachers. Can also arrange volunteer work and homestay programmes. **San Blas Spanish School**, Carmen Bajo 224, T247898, www.spanishschoolperu.com. Groups, with 4 clients maximum, US$110 for 20 hrs tuition (US$210 one-to-one). **Massage and therapies** Casa de la Serenidad, Santa María P-8, San Sebastián, T984671867, www.shamanspirit.net. A shamanic therapy centre run by a Swiss-American healer and Reiki Master who uses medicinal 'power' plants. It

also has bed and breakfast and has received very good reports. **Medical services** Clinics: Hospital Regional, Av de la Cultura, T227661, emergencies T223691. **Clínica Pardo**, Av de la Cultura 710, T240387. 24 hrs daily, trained bilingual personnel, complete medical assistance coverage with international insurance companies, highly regarded. **Clínica Paredes**, Calle Lechugal 405, T225265, www.sos-mg.com. 24 hrs daily, excellent service, emergency doctors speak good English. **Motorcycle hire** Perú Mototours, Saphi 578, T232742, www.perumototours.com. Helpful, good prices and machines. **Useful addresses** Migraciones, Av El Sol s/n, block 6 close to post office, T222741, Mon-Fri 0800-1300. ISIC-Intej office, Portal de Panes 123, of 107 (CC Los Ruiseñores), T256367, cusco@intej. org. Issues international student cards.

Southeast from Cuzco

There are many interesting villages and ruins on this road. **Tipón** ruins ① US$3.60, between the villages of Saylla and Oropesa, are extensive and include baths, terraces, irrigation systems, possibly an agricultural laboratory and a temple complex, accessible from a path leading from just above the last terrace (5-km climb from village; take a combi from Cuzco to Oropesa, then a taxi). **Oropesa**, whose church contains a fine ornately carved pulpit, is the national 'Capital of Bread'. Try the delicious sweet circular loaves known as *chutas*.

At **Huambutío**, north of the village of Huacarpay, the road divides; northwest to Pisac and north to **Paucartambo**, on the eastern slope of Andes. This remote town, 80 km east of Cuzco, has become a popular tourist destination. In the Centro Cultural is the Museo de los Pueblos, with exhibits on the history, culture, textiles and society of the region, including the **Fiesta de la Virgen del Carmen** (Mamacha Carmen). This is a major attraction, with masked dancers enacting rituals and folk tales: 15-17 July. (There is basic accommodation in town.) From Paucartambo, in the dry season, you can go 44 km to **Tres Cruces**, along the Pilcopata road, turning left after 25 km. Tres Cruces gives a wonderful view of the sunrise in June and July: peculiar climatic conditions make it appear that three suns are rising. Tour agencies in Cuzco can arrange transport and lodging.

Further on from Huacarpay are the Huari (pre-Inca) ruins of **Piquillacta** ① daily 0700-1730, US$3.60. Buses to Urcos from Avenida Huáscar in Cuzco will drop you at the entrance on the north side of the complex, though this is not the official entry. The Piquillacta Archaeological Park also contains the Laguna de Huacarpay (known as Muyna in ancient times) and the ruins that surround it: Kañarakay, Urpicancha and the huge gateway of Rumicolca. A guide will help to find the more interesting structures. It's good to hike or cycle and birdwatch around the lake.

Andahuaylillas is a village 32 km southeast from Cuzco, with a fine early 17th-century church (the 'Andean Sistine Chapel'), with frescoes, a splendid doorway and a gilded main altar. Taxi colectivos go there from block 17 of Av La Cultura (opposite university), as does the Oropesa bus (from Avenida Huáscar in Cuzco) via Tipón, Piquillacta and Rumicolca. The next village, **Huaro**, also has a church whose interior is entirely covered with colourful frescoes.

Beyond Andahuaylillas is **Urcos**, whose lake is a popular picnic spot (follow the clear path). There are three very basic hostales. A spectacular road from Urcos crosses the Eastern Cordillera to Puerto Maldonado in the jungle (see page 1423). Some 47 km after passing the snow line

Hualla-Hualla pass, at 4820 m, the super-hot thermal baths of **Marcapata** ⓘ *173 km from Urcos, US$0.20,* provide a relaxing break.

Some 82 km from Urcos, at the base of **Nevado Ausangate** (6384 m), is the town of **Ocongate**, which has two hotels on the Plaza de Armas and the **Parador de Ausangate** (T221601, www. paradordelausangate.com), which can arrange hiking, horse riding, fishing and biking. Beyond Ocongate is **Tinqui**, the starting point for hikes around Ausangate and in the Cordillera Vilcanota. On the flanks of the Nevado Ausangate is Q'Olloriti, where a church has been built close to a glacier and has become a place of pilgrimage (see Cuzco, Festivals, page 1360).

Hiking around Ausangate ⓘ *Entry US$7.50 at Tinqui.* The hike around the mountain of Ausangate takes five days: spectacular, but quite hard, with a pass over 5000 m and camping above 4000 m, so you need to be acclimatized. Temperatures in high season (April-October) can drop well below zero at night. It is recommended to take a guide and/or *arriero. Arrieros* and mules can be hired in Tinqui for US$12 per day for an *arriero,* US$10 for a mule, but more for a saddle horse. *Arrieros* also expect food. Make sure you sign a contract with full details. Buy all food supplies in Cuzco. Maps are available at the **IGN** in Lima or **South American Explorers**, who also have latest information.

From Urcos to Sicuani (see page 1342), the road passes **Cusipata** (with an Inca gate and wall), **Checacupe** (with a lovely church) and **Tinta**, 23 km from Sicuani (church with brilliant gilded interior and an interesting choir vault). There are frequent buses and trucks to Cuzco, or take the train from Cuzco. Continuing to Sicuani, **Raqchi** is the scene of the region's great folklore festival starting on 24 June, **Wiracocha**, when dancers come from all over Peru. Raqchi is also the site of the **Viracocha Temple** ⓘ *US$3, take a bus or truck from Cuzco towards Sicuani, US$2.50.* John Hemming wrote: "What remains is the central wall, which is adobe above and Inca masonry below. This was probably the largest roofed building ever built by the Incas. On either side of the high wall, great sloping roofs were supported by rows of unusual round pillars, also of masonry topped by adobe. Nearby is a complex of barracks-like buildings and round storehouses. This was the most holy shrine to the creator god Viracocha, being the site of a miracle in which he set fire to the land – hence the lava flow nearby. There are also small Inca baths in the corner of a field beyond the temple and a straight row of ruined houses by a square. The landscape is extraordinary, blighted by huge piles of black volcanic rocks." You can do a homestay here with pottery classes and a walk to the extinct volcano.

◉ Southeast from Cuzco listings

For hotel and restaurant price codes, and other relevant information, see Essentials.

◉ Where to stay

Ausangate *p1370*
$ Ausangate, Tinqui. Very basic, but warm, friendly atmosphere.
$ Hostal Tinqui Guide, on the right-hand side as you enter Tinqui. Meals available. Sr Crispin, the owner, is knowledgeable and can arrange guides, mules, etc. He and his brothers can be contacted in Cuzco on T227768. All have been recommended as reliable sources of trekking and climbing information, for arranging trips. Also recommended is Teofilo Viagara, who lives 30 mins above the village; ask around to contact him by radio.

◉ Transport

Southeast from Cuzco: Paucartambo
p1369
Bus A minibus leaves daily for Paucartambo from Av Huáscar in **Cuzco**, US$8, 3-4 hrs; alternate days Paucartambo-Cuzco. Trucks and a private bus leave from the Coliseo, behind Hospital del Seguro in Cuzco, 5 hrs, US$3. Agencies in Cuzco arrange round trips on 15-17 Jul.

Ausangate *p1370*
Bus From Cuzco, to **Tinqui** from Av Tomasatito Condemayta, corner of the Coliseo Cerrado in Cuzco, daily at 1600, 3-4 hrs, US$7. **Huayna Ausangate** is a recommended company, ticket office near the Coliseo Cerrado.

Sacred Valley of the Incas

The name conjures up images of ancient rulers and their god-like status, with the landscape itself as their temple. And so it was, but the Incas also built their own tribute to this dramatic land in monuments such as Machu Picchu, Ollantaytambo, Pisac and countless others. For the tourist, the famous sights are now within easy reach of Cuzco, but the demand for adventure, to see lost cities in a less 21st-century context, means that there is ample scope for exploring. But if archaeology is not your thing, there are markets to enjoy, birds to watch, trails for mountain-biking and a whole range of hotels to relax in. The best time to visit is April to May or October to November. The high season is June-September, but the rainy season, from December to March, is cheaper and pleasant enough.

Pisac → *Phone code: 084. Colour map 3, C4.*

Pisac, 30 km north of Cuzco, has a traditional Sunday morning **market**, at which local people sell their produce in exchange for essential goods. It is also a major draw for tourists who arrive after 0800 until 1700. Pisac has other, somewhat less crowded but more commercial markets every second day. Each Sunday at 1100 there is a Quechua Mass. On the plaza are the church and a small interesting **Museo Folklórico**. The **Museo Comunitario Pisac** ① *Av Amazonas y Retamayoc K'asa, museopisac@gmail.com, daily 1000-1700, free but donations welcome* has a display of village life, created by the people of Pisac. There are many souvenir shops on Bolognesi. Local fiesta: 15 July.

High above the town on the mountainside is a superb **Inca fortress** ① *0700-1730, guides charge about US$5, you must show your BTC multi-site ticket to enter.* The walk up to the ruins begins from the plaza (but see below), past the Centro de Salud and a control post. The path goes through working terraces, giving the ruins a context. The first group of buildings is Pisaqa, with a fine curving wall. Climb then to the central part of the ruins, the Intihuatana group of temples and rock outcrops in the most magnificent Inca masonry. Here are the Reloj Solar ('Hitching Post of the Sun') – now closed because thieves stole a piece from it, palaces of the moon and stars, solstice markers, baths and water channels. From Intihuatana, a path leads around the hillside through a tunnel to Q'Allaqasa, the military area. Across the valley at this point, a large area of Inca tombs in holes in the hillside can be seen. The end of the site is Kanchiracay, where the agricultural workers were housed. Road transport approaches from this end. The descent takes 30 minutes. At dusk you will hear, if not see, the *pisaca* (partridges), after which the place is named. Even if going by car, do not rush as there is a lot to see and a lot of walking to do. Road transport approaches from the Kanchiracay end. The drive up from town takes about 20 minutes. Walking up, although tiring, is recommended for the views and location. It's at least one hour uphill all the way. The descent takes 30 minutes on foot. Combis charge US$0.75 per person and taxis US$7 one way up to the ruins from near the bridge. Then you can walk back down (if you want the taxi to take you back down, usually from a lower level, it will be another US$7).

Pisac to Urubamba

Calca, 2900 m, is 18 km beyond Pisac. There are basic hotels and eating places and buses stop on the other side of the divided plaza. **Fiesta de la Vírgen Asunta** 15-16 August. The ruins of a small Inca town, **Huchuy Cuzco** ① *US$7.15 for trek and entry*, are dramatically located on a flat esplanade almost 600 m above Calca, from where a road has been built to the ruins. Alternatively, a steep trail goes to the site from behind the village of Lamay, across the river. A magnificent one- or two-day trek leads to Huchuy Cuzco from Tambo Machay, the route once taken by the Inca from his capital to his country estate.

The **Valle de Lares** is beautiful for walking and cycling, with its magnificent mountains, lakes and small villages. You start near an old hacienda in Huarán (2830 m), cross two passes over 4000 m and end at the hot springs near Lares. From this village, transport runs back to Calca. Alternatively, you can add an extra day and continue to Ollantaytambo. You can also start in Lares and end in Yanhuara. Several agencies in Cuzco offer trekking and biking tours to the region. Miguel Angel Delgado in Cuzco, T973-275881, mikyyuta@yahoo.com, has been recommended as a trekking guide for this area.

About 3 km east of Urubamba, **Yucay** has two grassy plazas divided by the restored colonial church of Santiago Apóstol, with its oil paintings and fine altars. On the opposite side from Plaza Manco II is the adobe palace built for Sayri Túpac (Manco's son) when he emerged from Vilcabamba in 1558. In Yucay monks sell milk, ham and eggs from their farm on the hillside.

Urubamba → *Phone code: 084. Altitude: 2863 m.*

Like many places along the valley, Urubamba is in a fine setting with snow-capped peaks in view. Calle Berriózabal, on the west edge of town, is lined with pisonay trees. The large market square is one block west of the main plaza. The main road skirts the town and the bridge for the road to Chinchero is just to the east of town. Visit **Seminario-Bejar Ceramic Studio** ① *Berriózabal 111, T201002, www.ceramicaseminario.com.* Pablo Seminario and his workshop have investigated and use pre-Columbian techniques and designs, highly recommended. For local festivals, May and June are the harvest months, with many processions following ancient schedules. Urubamba's main festival, **El Señor de Torrechayoc**, occupies the first week of June.

About 6 km west of Urubamba is **Tarabamba**, where a bridge crosses the Río Urubamba. Turn right after the bridge to **Pichingoto**, a tumbled-down village built under an overhanging cliff. Also, just over the bridge and before the town to the left of a small, walled cemetery is a salt stream. Follow the footpath beside the stream to Salineras, a small village below which are a mass of terraced Inca salt pans which are still in operation (entry US$2.50); there are over 5000. The walk to the salt pans takes about 30 minutes. Take water as this side of the valley can be very hot and dry.

The Sacred Valley

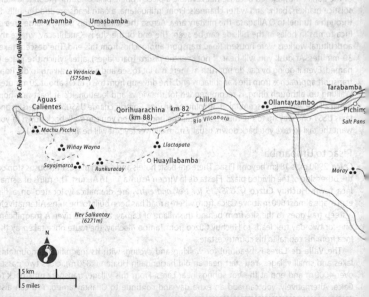

To Chaullay & Quillabamba

Amaybamba   Umasbamba

La Verónica ▲
(5750m)

Tarabamba

Aguas
Calientes   Chillca   Ollantaytambo   Pinching

Qorihuarachina   km 82
(km 88)   Río Vilcanota   Salt Pans

Machu Picchu

Wiñay Wayna   Llactapata

Sayajmarca   Runkuracay   Huayllabamba

Moray

Nev Salkantay
▲
(6271m)

N

5 km
5 miles

Chinchero and Moray

Chinchero (3762 m) ① *site 0700-1730, on the BTC combined entrance ticket (see page 1347)*, is just off a direct road to Urubamba. It has an attractive church built on an Inca temple. The church has been restored to reveal in all their glory the interior paintings. The ceiling, beams and walls are covered in beautiful floral and religious designs. The church is open on Sunday for Mass and at festivals; ask in the tourist office in Cuzco for other times. Recent excavations there have revealed many Inca walls and terraces. The food market and the handicraft market are separate. The former is held every day, on your left as you come into town. The latter, on Sunday only, is up by the church, small, but attractive. On any day but Sunday there are few tourists. Fiesta, day of the Virgin, on 8 September. Much of the area's character will change if a plan to build a new airport for Cuzco on nearby agricultural land goes ahead.

At Moray, there are three 'colosseums', used by the Incas, according to some theories, as a sort of open-air crop nursery, known locally as the laboratory of the Incas. The great depressions contain no ruined buildings, but are lined with fine terracing. Each level is said to have its own microclimate. It is a very atmospheric place which, many claim, has mystical power, and the scenery is absolutely stunning (entry US$3.50, or by BTC). The most interesting way to get to Moray is from Urubamba via the Pichingoto bridge over the Río Urubamba. The path passes by the spectacular **salt pans**, still in production after thousands of years, taking 1½ to two hours to the top. The village of Maras is about 45 minutes further on, then it's 9 km by road or 5 km through the fields to Moray. Tour companies in Cuzco offer cycle trips to Moray. There are no hotels at all in the area, so take care not to be stranded. (See Transport, for further details on how to get there.)

Ollantaytambo → *Colour map 3, C4. Phone code: 084. Altitude: 2800 m.*
① *Inca ruins open 0700 1730. If possible arrive very early, 0700, before the tourists. Admission is by BTC visitor's ticket, which can be bought at the site. Guides at the entrance.*

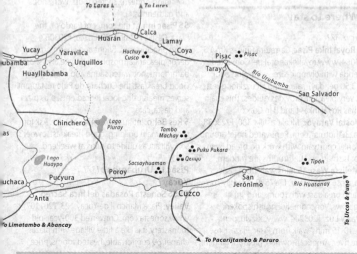

The Inca town, or *Llacta*, on which the present-day town is based is clearly seen in the fine example of Inca *canchas* (blocks), which are almost entirely intact and still occupied behind the main plaza. Entering Ollantaytambo from Pisac, the road is built along the long wall of 100 niches. Note the inclination of the wall: it leans towards the road. Since it was the Inca's practice to build with the walls leaning towards the interiors of the buildings, it has been deduced that the road, much narrower then, was built inside a succession of buildings. The road out of the plaza leads across a bridge, down to the colonial church with its enclosed *recinto*. Beyond is Plaza Araccama (and car park) with the entrance to the archaeological site.

The so-called **Baño de la Ñusta** (bath of the princess) is of grey granite, and is in a small area between the town and the temple fortress. Some 200 m behind the Baño de la Ñusta along the face of the mountain are some small ruins known as Inca Misanca, believed to have been a small temple or observatory. A series of steps, seats and niches have been carved out of the cliff. There is a complete irrigation system, including a canal at shoulder level, some 6 inches deep, cut out of the sheer rock face. The flights of terraces leading up above the town are superb, and so are the curving terraces following the contours of the rocks overlooking the Urubamba. These terraces were successfully defended by Manco Incas warriors against Hernando Pizarro in 1536. Manco Inca built the wall above the site and another wall closing the Yucay valley against attack from Cuzco. These are visible on either side of the valley.

The temple itself was started by Pachacútec, using Colla Indians from Lake Titicaca – hence the similarities of the monoliths facing the central platform with the Tiahuanaco remains. The massive, highly finished granite blocks at the top are worth the climb to see. The Colla are said to have deserted halfway through the work, which explains the many unfinished blocks lying about the site.

On the west side of the main ruins, a two-dimensional 'pyramid' has been identified in the layout of the fields and walls of the valley. A fine 750 m wall aligns with the rays of the winter solstice on 21 June. It can be appreciated from a high point about 3.5 km from Ollantaytambo.

◉ Sacred Valley of the Incas listings

For hotel and restaurant price codes, and other relevant information, see Essentials.

⬤ Where to stay

Pisac *p1371*
$$$ Royal Inka Pisac, Carretera Ruinas Km 1.5, T203064, www.royalinkahotel.pe. Converted hacienda with olympic-size swimming pool (US$3.50 per day), sauna and jacuzzi for guests only, very pleasant, provides guides. This chain also has Royal Inkas I and II in Cuzco.
$$ Hostal Varayoc, Mcal Castilla 380, T223638, luzpaz3@hotmail.com. Renovated hotel around a colonial courtyard with working bread oven. Decor is smart and bathrooms are modern.
$$ Melissa Wasi, 15 mins walk from Pisac Plaza, close to the river, T797589. A family-run bed and breakfast with rooms and small bungalows. Very homely, English spoken.
$$ Paz y Luz, T203204, www.pazyluzperu. com. 10-15 mins' walk from Pisac Plaza, close to the river. American-owned, pleasant garden,

nicely designed rooms, breakfast included. Diane Dunn offers healing from many traditions (including Andean), sacred tours, workshops and gatherings.
$$ Pisac Inn, at the corner of Pardo on the Plaza, Casilla Postal 1179, Cuzco, T203062, www.pisacinn.com. Bright and charming local decor, pleasant atmosphere, private and shared bathrooms, hot water, sauna and massage. Good breakfast, the **Cuchara de Palo** restaurant serves meals using local ingredients, plus pizza and pasta, café.
$ Res Beho, Intihuatana 642, T203001. Ask for room in main building, good breakfast, owner's son will act as guide to ruins at weekend.

Pisac to Urubamba *p1371*
Yucay
$$$$ Sonesta Posadas del Inca Sacred Valley, Plaza Manco II de Yucay 123, T201107, www.sonesta.com. Converted 300-year-old monastery, it is like a little village with plazas, chapel, 69 comfortable, heated rooms, price

includes buffet breakfast. Lots of activities can be arranged, canoeing, horse riding, mountain biking, etc. **Inkafe** restaurant is open to all, serving Peruvian, fusion and traditional cuisine with a US$15 buffet. Recommended.

$$$ La Casona de Yucay, Plaza Manco II 104, T201116, www.hotelcasonayucay.com. This colonial house was where Simón Bolívar stayed during his liberation campaign in 1824. With heating, 2 patios and gardens, **Don Manuel** restaurant and bar.

$$$ The Green House, Km 60.2 Huaran, T984 770130, www.thegreenhouseperu.com. A charming, Wi-Fi-free retreat, only 4 rooms, breakfast included, comfortable lounge, restaurant, small kitchen for guests, beautiful garden, restricted internet. No children under 10. Information on walks and day trips in the area. Activities include hiking, biking, horse riding and rafting. Intimate, beautiful and relaxing.

Urubamba *p1372*

$$$$ Casa Andina Private Collection Sacred Valley, paradero 5, Yanahuara, between Urubamba and Ollantaytambo, T984 765501, www.casa-andina.com. In its own 3-ha estate, with all the facilities associated with this chain, plus **Valle Sagrado Andean Cottage** for family and long-stay accommodation, 'Sacred Spa', gym, planetarium, good restaurant, adventure options.

$$$$ Río Sagrado (Belmond), Km 76 Carretera Cuzco–Ollantaytambo, T201631, www.rio sagrado.com. 4 km from Urubamba, set in beautiful gardens overlooking the river with fine views. Rooms and villas, **Mayu Wilka** spa, restaurant and bar, offers various packages.

$$$$ Sol y Luna, Fundo Huincho, west of town, T201620, www.hotelsolyluna.com. Award-winning bungalows and suites set off the main road in lovely gardens, pool, excellent gourmet restaurant, wine tastings, spa, handicrafts shop. Also has **Wayra** lounge bar and dining room, open to non-guests, for freshly cooked, informal lunches. Arranges adventure and cultural activities and traditional tours. Profits go to **Sol y Luna** educational association.

$$$$ Tambo del Inka, Av Ferrocarril s/n, T581777, www.luxurycollection.com/vallesagrado. A resort and spa on the edge of town, in gardens by the river. Completely remodelled with a variety of rooms and suites, fitness centre, swimming pools, **Hawa** restaurant, bar, business facilities and lots of activities arranged.

$$$ Casa Colibrí, Km 2.5 on road to Ollantaytamba, T205003, www.casacolibri ecolodge.com. Delightful, spacious rooms and casitas made of local stone, wood and adobe, set in beautiful gardens to attract bees, butterflies and hummingbirds. Very restful, hammocks, meditation room, excellent homegrown food, swings and table tennis, popular with couples, families and yoga groups.

$$ Las Chullpas, Querocancha s/n, 3 km from town, T201568, www.chullpas.pe. Very peaceful, excellent breakfast, vegetarian meals, English and German spoken, Spanish classes, natural medicine, treks, riding, mountain biking, camping US$3 with hot shower. Mototaxi from town US$2.50, taxi (ask for Querocancha) US$4.

$$ Posada Las Tres Marías, Zavala 307, T201006, www.posadatresmarias.com. A little way from the centre, quiet. Comfortable, hot water, no TV, lovely garden and shady terrace, can provide early breakfast.

$ Hospedaje Buganvilla, Jr Convención 280, T205102, 984 618900. Sizable rooms with hot water, breakfast on request, quiet, bright, good value, very pleasant.

$ Hospedaje Los Jardines, Jr Convención 459, T201331, www.hospedajelosjardines.blogspot.co.uk. Attractive guesthouse with comfortable rooms, hot water, non-smoking, delicious breakfast US$3.25 extra (vegans catered for), safe, lovely garden, laundry. **Sacred Valley Mountain Bike Tours** also based here.

Chinchero *p1373*

$$ La Casa de Barro, Miraflores 157, T306031 www.lacasadebarro.com. Modern hotel, with hot water, heating, bar, restaurant serving 'fusion' food using organic local produce, tours arranged.

Ollantaytambo *p1373*

$$$$ Pakaritampu, C Ferrocarril s/n, T204020, www.pakaritampu.com.Modern, well-appointed rooms, TV room, restaurant and bar, laundry, safe and room service. Adventure sports can be arranged. Lunch and dinner are extra. Excellent quality and service, but room 8 looks onto the railway station car park.

$$$ El Albergue Ollantaytambo, within the railway station gates, T204014, www.elalbergue. com. Owned by North American artist Wendy Weeks. Also has Café Mayu on the station and a good restaurant. Characterful rooms, rustic elegance, some larger than others, some with safe, lovely gardens, great showers and a eucalyptus steam sauna. Books for sale and exchange, also handicrafts. Private transport can be arranged to nearby attractions, also mountain-biking, rafting and taxi transfers to the airport.

$$$ Hostal Sauce, C Ventiderio 248, T204044, www.hostalsauce.com.pe. Smart, simple decor and views of the ruins from 3 of the 6 rooms as well as from the dining room, food from own farm.

$$ Apu Lodge, Calle Lari, T797162, www. apulodge.com. On the edge of town, great views of the ruins and surrounding mountains. Run by Scot Louise Norton and husband Arturo, good service, quiet, nice garden, good buffet breakfast, can help organize tours and treks. They work with Leap Local (www.leaplocal.org) guides project.

$$ Hostal Iskay II, Patacalle s/n, T204004, www.hostaliskay.com. In the Inca town. Great location but car access is difficult. Only 6 rooms, hot water, free tea and coffee, use of kitchen. Good reports.

$$ Hostal K'uychipunku, K'uychipunku 6, T204175. Close to Plaza Araccama, hot water, modern, some rooms with view, courtyard.

$$ Hotel Sol Ollantay, C Ventiderio s/n by the bridge between the 2 plazas, T204130, www. hotelsolperu.com. Tastefully renovated with good views from most rooms, hot water.

$$ KB Tambo, between the main plaza and the ruins, T204091, http://kbperu.com. Spacious, comfortable rooms, suites, garden view or standard, comfy mattresses, heaters on request, hot water, flower-filled garden, good restaurant (**$$**), breakfast extra. Reserve in advance. Also offers adventure tours.

$$ Las Orquídeas, near the start of the road to the station, T204032. Hot water, fairly small but nice rooms, flower-filled patio, discounts for 2 or more nights.

$$ Tika Wasi, C Convencion s/n, T204166, www.tikawasihotel.com. Great location close to the archaeological site, good service and comfortable rooms.

$ Hostal Chaska Wasi, Plaza de Armas, T204045. Private rooms and dorms, hammocks, hot showers, free hot drinks, laundry. Owner Katy is very friendly.

$ Hostal Plaza Ollantaytambo, beside the police station on the main plaza, T436741, hostalplazaollantaytambo@gmail.com. Basic rooms but with private bath, hot water and Wi-Fi. Opened in 2013.

$ Hostal Tambo, C Horno, north of the plaza, T773262 or T984-489094, paula1_79@hotmail. com. Cheaper for groups, breakfast extra. Once past the door you emerge into a garden full of fruit trees and flowers. Small, rooms for up to 3 people, basic, shared bath downstairs in the courtyard, hot water.

Camping

Restaurant Huatucay, at the edge of the Inca town, between Patacalle and the road to Patacancha, has camping for US$3.60 pp. There are toilets, a minimarket and the restaurant serves typical food.

❼ Restaurants

Pisac p1371

$$-$ Miski Mijuna Wasi, on the Plaza de Armas, T203266. Serves tasty local food, typical and Novo Andino, also international dishes. Has a *pastelería* also.

$$-$ Mullu, Plaza de Armas 352 and Mcal Castilla 375, T208182. Tue-Sun 0900-1900. Café/ restaurant related to the Mullu store in Cuzco, also has a gallery promoting local artists.

$ Doña Clorinda, on the plaza opposite the church. Tasty food, including vegetarian.

$ Valle Sagrado, Av Amazonas 116 (the main street where buses go towards Urubamba). Good quality, generous portions and a lunchtime buffet that includes vegetarian options. Go early before the tour groups arrive.

Bakery, Mcal Castilla 372. Good wholemeal bread, excellent cheese *empanadas*.

Blue Llama Café, corner of the plaza opposite Pisac Inn, T203135, www.bluellamacafe.com. Cute, colourful café with a huge range of teas, good coffee, breakfasts and daily menus.

Ulrike's Café, C Pardo 613, T203195. Has possibly the best apple crumble with ice cream, excellent coffee, smoothies and a wide range of international dishes. Good value 3-course daily *menú*. A good place to chill out.

Urubamba *p1372*

$$$ Tunupa, on road from Urumamba to Ollantaytambo, on riverbank. Buffet lunch 1200-1500, US$15, dinner 1800-2030. Same owners as Tunupa in Cuzco, colonial-style hacienda, excellent food and surroundings, pre-Columbian and colonial art exhibitions.

$$$-$$ El Huacatay, Arica 620, T201790, http://elhuacatay.com. Mon-Sat. A small restaurant with a reputation for fine, creative fusion cuisine (local, Mediterranean, Asian).

$$ Coffee Tree, Plaza de Armas, www.perucoffeetree.com. Daily 0700-2200, closed Feb. Has a proper coffee machine. Breakfast, lunch and dinner available.

$$ El Fogón, Parque Pintacha, T201534. Peruvian food.

$$ El Maizal, on the main road, before the bridge, T201454. Country-style restaurant, buffet service with a variety of Novo Andino and international choices, beautiful gardens, open daytime only.

$$ Tres Keros, Av Señor de Torrechayoc, T201701. Novo Andino cuisine, try the lamb chops.

$ La Chepita, Av 1 de Mayo, M6, in a small plaza. The place to go on Sun for regional food in the biggest portions you have ever seen. Get 1 plate between 2.

$ Pizza Wasi, Av Mcal Castilla 857, T434751 for delivery. Good pizzas and pastas. Mulled wine served in a small restaurant with nice decor, good value. Has another branch on Plaza Araccama in Ollantaytambo.

Ollantaytambo *p1373*

There are restaurants all over town offering *menú turístico*, pizzas, pastas, juices and hot drinks.

$$ Papa's, C Horno at the plaza, T436700. Restaurant and lounge open 1000-2200. Serving Tex-Mex, local dishes, pizzas, soups, salads, and desserts.

$$ Heart's Café, Av Ventiderio s/n, T204013, www.heartscafe.org. Open 0700-2100. Mainly wholefood restaurant serving international and Peruvian dishes, including vegetarian, box lunch and takeaway available, good coffee. All profits to education and self-help projects in the Sacred Valley. Deservedly popular.

$$ Il Cappuccino and Kusicoyllor, Plaza Araccama. Good coffee and continental and American breakfasts. Also serves *menú turístico*, lunch and dinner, desserts, juices and light meals.

$$ Mayupata, Jr Convención s/n, across bridge on the way to the ruins, on the left, T204083. Opens 0600 for breakfast, and serves lunch and dinner. International choices and a selection of Peruvian dishes, desserts, sandwiches and coffee. Bar has fireplace; river view, relaxing atmosphere.

$$ Tawachaki, close to the Ollantaytambo ruin. Good alpaca steak and great views of the ruins.

$$-$ Alcázar Café, C del Medio, 50 m from Plaza, T204034. Vegetarian, but also offers meat and fish, and pasta. Arranges excursions to Andean communities.

$ La Ñusta, Plaza de Armas corner of Chaupi Calle, ask here about their *hospedaje*. Popular, good food, snacks, soups, salads and juices.

Calicanto, on the righthand side just before the bridge leading to Plaza Araccama. For coffees and light meals, etc, overlooking the river that divides the town.

⊛ Festivals

Ollantaytambo *p1373*

On the Sun following Inti Raymi, there is a colourful festival, the **Ollanta-Raymi**. **6 Jan** The Bajada de Reyes Magos (the Magi), with dancing, a bull fight, local food and a fair. **End-May/early-Jun** 50 days after Easter, Fiesta del Señor de Choquekillca, patron saint of Ollantaytambo, with several days of dancing, weddings, processions, masses, feasting and drinking. **29 Oct** The town's anniversary, with lots of dancing in traditional costume and many local delicacies for sale.

◑ What to do

Urubamba *p1372*

Horse riding Perol Chico, 5 km from Urubamba at Km 77, T084-974-798 890/974-780020, www.perolchico.com. Dutch/Peruvian owned and operated, 1- to 14-day trips, good horses, riding is Peruvian Paso style.

Trekking Haku Trek, contact Javier Saldívar, T984 613001, www.hakutrek.com. Cooperative tourism project in the Chicón valley (the mountain valley above Urubamba), run by residents of the community, 1- and 2-day hiking trips based at a simple eco-lodge; profits are used to fund reforestation of the area.

● Transport

Urubamba *p1372*
Bus Terminal, west of town on the main road, about 3 km from centre. From Urubamba to **Calca**, **Pisac** (US$2, 1 hr) and **Cuzco**, about 2 hrs, US$2.25; also buses to Cuzco via Chinchero, same fare. Combis run to **Ollantaytambo**, 45 mins, US$0.75.

Chinchero and Moray *p1373*
Road There is a paved road from the main road between Chinchero and Urubamba to the village of Maras and from there an unmade road in good condition leads to Moray, 9 km. Ask in Maras for the best route to walk, other than on the main road. Any bus between Urubamba and Cuzco via Chinchero passes the clearly marked turning to Maras. From the junction taxi colectivos charge US$2.50 pp to Maras, or you can walk (30 mins). There is public transport from Chinchero to Maras; it stops running

between 1700 and 1800. Taxi to Moray, 1-hr wait then take you to the salt pans, from where you can walk back to the Urubamba-Ollantaytambo road, US$25.

Ollantaytambo *p1373*
Bus Colectivos leave all day for Urubamba and Cuzco from 1 block east of the main plaza. Direct bus Ollantaytambo to **Cuzco** at 0715 and 1945, US$4; also Cruz del Sur, 3 a day, US$7. Direct taxi colectivo service from C Pavitos, Cuzco, leaves when full US$3.60 to Ollantaytambo. Minibuses and taxis leave the small Terminal de Transportes just up from Ollantaytambo station (10-15 mins' walk from the plaza) at train times for Urubamba and Cuzco, US$6 shared to either place, but they may try to charge much more as a private service only. Say you'll go to the colectivo terminal and they may reduce the price. Transfers and tours with **Aló K'antuyoc**, at the hostel of that name on Av Ferrocarril, T204147. See also under trains to and from Machu Picchu, page 1381. There are colectivos and mototaxis at the Plaza for the station when trains are due. You won't be allowed in the station unless you have previously bought a ticket (and it is best to buy tickets in Cuzco).

Machu Picchu → *Colour map 3, C4.*

There is a tremendous feeling of awe on first witnessing Machu Picchu. The ancient citadel (42 km from Ollantaytambo by rail) straddles the saddle of a high mountain (2380 m) with steep terraced slopes falling away to the fast-flowing Urubamba river snaking its hairpin course far below in the valley floor. Towering overhead is Huayna Picchu, and green jungle peaks provide the backdrop for the whole majestic scene. Machu Picchu is a complete Inca city. For centuries it was buried in jungle, until Hiram Bingham stumbled upon it in 1911. It was then explored by an archaeological expedition sent by Yale University. The ruins – staircases, terraces, temples, palaces, towers, fountains and the famous Intihuatana (the so-called 'Hitching Post of the Sun') – require at least a day. Take time to appreciate not only the masonry, but also the selection of large rocks for foundations, the use of water in the channels below the Temple of the Sun and the surrounding mountains.

Arriving at Machu Picchu
Entrance to Machu Picchu The site is open from 0600 to 1730. Only 2500 visitors are allowed entry each day. Entrance fee to Machu Picchu only is 128 soles (US$45.50), 65 for Peruvians, 63 with ISIC card (US$23 and US$22.40 approximately). To climb Huayna Picchu you have to buy a ticket for site entry and the climb and specify whether you are going to go 0700-0800 or 1000-1100 (only 400 people are allowed up at one time), 152 soles (US$54). There is also a combined Machu Picchu and Museum ticket, 150 soles (US$53.30). There is a fourth Machu Picchu and Montaña ticket for 142 soles (US$50.50). Because of the limit on numbers it is wise to reserve

your ticket online in advance at www.machupicchu.gob.pe. You can pay online with Visa or at a number of outlets given on the website. These include branches of Banco de la Nación, **Centro Cultural de Machu Picchu** ① *Av Pachacútec cuadra 1, Aguas Calientes, 0500-2200 (also i perú here, of 4, T211104, iperumachupicchu@promperu.gob.pe, daily 0900-1300, 1400-2000)*, **Dirección Regional de Cultura** in Cuzco (see page 1348), **AATC** ① *C Nueva Baja 424, Cuzco*, offices of **PerúRail** and **Inca Rail** in Cuzco, **Hotel Monasterio**. Other websites offer tickets for sale, at an inflated price. Do not buy (fake) tickets on the street in Cuzco. You can deposit your luggage at the entrance for a small fee, but small bags may be taken into the ruins. Guides are available at the site, they are often very knowledgeable and worthwhile. The official price for a guide is US$80 for a full tour for one to 10 people. Site wardens are also informative, in Spanish only. A guarded gate by the river in Aguas Calientes opens only at 0530, so it is not possible to walk up to the ruins to be there before the first buses. After 1100 the ruins fill rapidly with visitors who have arrived by train. It is best to arrive before then. The **Sanctuary Lodge** is located next to the entrance, with a self-service restaurant. Take your own food and drink if you don't want to pay hotel prices, and take plenty of drinking water. Note that food is not officially allowed into the site and drink can only be carried in canteens/water bottles. There are toilets at the entrance. Sandflies are a problem, especially in the dry season, so take insect repellent and wear long clothes. Also take protection against the sun and rain showers.

New regulations were announced in early 2014 but had not yet come into effect at the close of this edition. They would require that all visitors be accompanied by a guide, that they follow one of the three established routes without turning back and that they limit stops at certain places to there to five minutes; all in the interest of mitigating crowding and maintaining an orderly flow of tourists through the site. Be aware also that entry may be limited to morning-, or afternoon-only tickets.

Around the site

Huayna Picchu, the mountain overlooking the site (on which there are also ruins), has steps to the top for a superlative view of the whole site, but it is not for those who are afraid of heights and you shouldn't leave the path. The climb takes up to 90 minutes but the steps are dangerous after bad weather. Visitors are given access to the main path at 0700 and 1000 daily, latest return time 1500 (maximum 200 people per departure). Check with the Ministerio de Cultura in Aguas Calientes or Cuzco for current departure times and to sign up for a place. Another trail to Huayna Picchu, down near the Urubamba, is via the Temple of the Moon, in two caves, one above the other, with superb Inca niches inside. For the trail to the Temple of the Moon: from the path to Huayna Picchu, take the marked trail to the left. It is in good shape, although it descends further than you think it should and there are very steep steps on the way. After the Temple you may proceed to Huayna Picchu, but this path is overgrown, slippery in the wet and has a crooked ladder on an exposed part about 10 minutes before reaching the top (not for the faint-hearted). It is safer to return to the main trail to Huayna Picchu, although this adds about 30 minutes to the climb. The round trip takes about four hours. Before doing any trekking around Machu Picchu, check with an official which paths may be used, or which are one-way.

The famous Inca bridge is about 45 minutes along a well-marked trail south of the Royal Sector. The bridge (on which you cannot walk) is spectacularly sited, carved into a vertiginous cliff-face. East of the Royal Sector is the path leading up to **Intipunku** on the Inca Trail (60 minutes, fine views). Climbing Machu Picchu mountain is another excellent option which gives a completely different view of the site and surrounding valleys. The route is steep and takes up to three hours.

Aguas Calientes

Those with more time should spend the night at Aguas Calientes (also known as Machu Picchu Pueblo) and visit the ruins early in the morning, when fewer people are around. Most hotels and restaurants are near the railway station, on the plaza, or on Avenida Pachacútec, which leads from the plaza to the **thermal baths** ① *0500-2030, US$3.15, 10 mins walk from the town*, (a communal pool, smelling of sulphur, best early in the morning) good bar for cocktails in the pool. You can rent towels and bathing costumes (US$3) at several places on the road to the baths; basic toilets and changing facilities and showers for washing *before* entering the baths; take soap and shampoo, and keep an eye on valuables. The **Museo Manuel Chávez Ballón** ① *Carretera Hiram Bingham, Wed-Sun 0900-1600, see above for tickets*, displays objects found at Machu Picchu.

⊙ Machu Picchu listings

For hotel and restaurant price codes, and other relevant information, see Essentials.

⊙ Where to stay

Machu Picchu *p1378*
$$$$ Machu Picchu Sanctuary Lodge, reservations as for the **Hotel Monasterio** in Cuzco, which is under the same management (Belmond), T084-984-816956, www.sanctuary lodge.net. Comfortable, good service, helpful staff, food well-cooked and presented. Electricity and water 24 hrs a day, prices are all-inclusive, restaurant for residents only in the evening, but the buffet lunch is open to all. Usually fully booked well in advance, try Sun night as other tourists find Pisac market a greater attraction.

Aguas Calientes *p1379*
$$$$ Casa del Sol, Av Imperio de los Incas 608, on the railroad, T211118, www.hoteles casadelsol.com. 5-storey hotel with lift/elevator, different room categories with river or mountain views, nice restaurant, beautiful spa. Shower service and changing room available after check out.
$$$$ Inkaterra Machu Picchu Pueblo, Km 104, 5 mins walk along the railway from town, T211122. Reservations: C Andalucía 174, Miraflores, Lima, T01-610 0400; in Cuzco at Plaza las Nazarenas 113 p2, T234010, www.inkaterra.com. Beautiful colonial-style bungalows in village compound surrounded by cloud forest, lovely gardens with a lot of steps between the public areas and rooms, pool, excellent restaurant, offer tours to Machu Picchu, several guided walks on and off the property, buffet breakfasts included in price. Good baggage service to coordinate with train arrivals and departures. Also has the Café Inkaterra by the railway line.
$$$$ Sumaq Machu Picchu, Av Hermanos Ayar Mz 1, Lote 3, T211059, www.sumaqhotel

peru.com. Award-winning 5-star hotel on the edge of town, between railway and road to Machu Picchu. Suites and luxury rooms with heating, restaurant and bar, spa.
$$$ Gringo Bill's (Hostal Q'oñi Unu), Colla Raymi 104, T211046, www.gringobills.com (in Cuzco Av El Sol 520, T223663). With hot water, laundry, money exchange, pretty rooms, good beds, balconies, lot of coming and going, good restaurant, breakfast from 0500, packed lunch available. Views of the plaza are now obscured by the monstrous new municipal building.
$$$ La Cabaña, Av Pachacútec Mz 20, Lote 3, T211048, www.lacabanamachupicchu.com. With hot water, café, laundry service, helpful, popular with groups.
$$$ Presidente, Av Imperio de los Incas, at the old station, T211034, www.hostalpresidente. com. Adjoining **Hostal Machu Picchu**, see below, more upmarket but little difference, rooms without river view cheaper.
$$$-$$ Hostal Wiracocha Inn, C Wiracocha, T211088, www.wiracochainn.com. Hot water, small garden, helpful, popular with groups, also has higher-priced suites.
$$$-$$ Rupa Wasi, Huanacaure 105, T211101, www.rupawasi.net. Charming 'eco-lodge' up a small alley off Collasuyo, laid back, comfortable, great views from the balconies, purified water available, organic garden, good breakfasts, half-board available, excellent restaurant, **The Tree House**, and cookery classes.
$$ Hospedaje Quilla, Av Pachacútec 23 between Wiracocha and Tupac Inka Yupanki, T211009. Hot water, rents bathing gear for the hot springs.
$$ Hostal Imperio de los Inkas, Av Pachacútec 602, at the old station, T211105, totemsito@gmail.com. Functional, quiet, family-owned *hostal*, group rates, good value.
$$ Hostal Machu Picchu, Av Imperio de los Incas 135, at the old station, T211065, sierrandina@gmail.com. Functional, quiet,

Wilber, the owner's son, has travel information, hot water, nice balcony over the Urubamba, grocery store.

$$ Hostal Místico, Av Pachacútec Mz 19 lote 12, T211051, http://elmisticohostal.com. Good breakfast, free Wi-Fi but pay for use of computer, quiet, new-wave-ish, comfortable, near thermal baths.

$$-$ Las Bromelias, Colla Raymi, T211145, just off Plaza before Gringo Bill's. Cheaper without bath, small, hot water.

$ Hostal Pirwa, C Túpac Inka Yupanki 103, T214315, www.pirwahostelscusco.com. In the same group as in Cuzco, Lima and elsewhere.

$ Terrazas del Inca, C Wiracocha M-18-4, T211114, www.terrazasdelinca.com. Safety deposit box, kitchen use, helpful staff.

Camping The only official campsite is in a field by the river, just below Puente Ruinas station, toilets, cold showers, US$6 per tent. Do not leave your tent and belongings unattended.

⑦ Restaurants

Aguas Calientes *p1379*
The old station and Av Pachútec are lined with eating places, many of them *pizzerías*. Tax is often added as an extra to the bill.

$$$ Café Inkaterra, on the railway, just below the Machu Picchu Pueblo Hotel. US$15 for a great lunch buffet with scenic views of the river.

$$ Indio Feliz, C Lloque Yupanqui, T211090. Great French cuisine, excellent value and service, set 3-course meal for US$20, good pisco sours in the new bar, great atmosphere.

$$ Inka Wasi, Av Pachacútec. Very good choice, has an open fire, full Peruvian and international menu available.

$$ Inka's Pizza Pub, on the plaza. Good pizzas, also changes money.

$$ Pueblo Viejo, Av Pachacútec (near plaza). Good food in a spacious but warm environment. Price includes use of the salad bar.

$$ Toto's House, Av Imperio de los Incas, on the railway line. Same owners as **Pueblo Viejo**. Good value and quality *menú*, buffet from 1130-1500.

$ Discovery, Plaza de Armas, T211355. The best coffee and internet connection in Aguas Calientes. Several computers and Wi-Fi.

$ Govinda, Av Pachacútec y Túpac Inka Yupanki. Vegetarian restaurant with a cheap set lunch.

La Boulangerie de Paris, Jr Sinchi Roca, www.laboulangeriedeparis.net. Coffee, sandwiches, quiche and great French bread.

ⓑ Bars and clubs

Aguas Calientes *p1379*
Wasicha Pub, C Lloque Yupanqui. Good music and atmosphere, the place to party after the Trail.

ⓔ Transport

Machu Picchu *p1378*
Bus Buses leave **Aguas Calientes** for Machu Picchu as they fill from 0530 until 1500, 25 mins US$19 return, US$10 single, children US$10, valid 48 hrs. The bus stop in Aguas Calientes is 50 m from the railway station, with the ticket office opposite. Tickets can also be bought in advance at **Consettur** in Cuzco, Av Infancia 433, Wanchaq, T222125, www.consettur.com, which saves queuing when you arrive in Aguas Calientes. Buses return from the ruins to Aguas 0700-1730. The walk up from Aguas Calientes follows a poor path and crosses the motor road (take care). The road is also in poor condition and landslides can cause disruptions.

Train Two companies operate: PerúRail (Av Pachacútec, Wanchac Station, T581414, www.perurail.com) to Machu Picchu from Poroy, near Cuzco, from Urubamba and from Ollantaytambo. Inca Rail, joint operation with Andean Railways (Portal de Panes 105, Plaza de Armas, Cuzco, T233030, or Lima T613 5288, www.incarail.com) from Ollantaytambo to Machu Picchu. They go to Aguas Calientes (the official name of this station is 'Machu Picchu'). The station for the tourist trains at Aguas Calientes is on the outskirts of town, 200 m from the **Pueblo Hotel** and 50 m from where buses leave for Machu Picchu ruins. There is a paved road between Aguas Calientes and the start of the road up to the ruins. **Note** Services may be disrupted in the rainy season, especially Jan-Feb.

There are 4 classes of PerúRail tourist train: **Vistadome** (recommended, US$87 one-way from Poroy, US$60-84 from Ollantaytambo); **Expedition** (US$77 Poroy-Machu Picchu one-way, US$56-65 from Ollantaytambo); **Auto Vagón** (from the Hotel Tambo del Inka in

Urubamba, US$80); and the luxurious **Belmond Hiram Bingham** service with meals, drinks and entertainment (US$356 one way from Poroy). Services from Poroy and Urubamba run once a day; those from Ollantaytambo 5 times a day each. Seats can be reserved even if you're not returning the same day. These trains have toilets, video, snacks and drinks for sale. You must have your original passport to travel on the trains to Machu Picchu. Tickets for all trains may be bought at Wanchac station and Portal de Carnes 214, Plaza de Armas, in Cuzco, at travel agencies, or via PerúRail's website, www.perurail.com.

Inca Rail has 4 trains a day Ollantaytambo-Machu Picchu, 0640, 0720, 1115 and 1636, returning 0830, 1430, 1612 and 1900), US$47-67 one way tourist class, US$135 one way executive class. Carriages have a/c and heating, snacks and drinks served.

Tourists may not travel on the local train to Machu Picchu, but there are ways to avoid the train. Take a bus from Cuzco towards Quillabamba at 0800, 0900 or 1900, US$9. It is best not to travel overnight; confirm all bus and train times locally, especially in the rainy season.

Get out at **Santa María** (about 7 hrs) where minibuses wait to go to **Santa Teresa**, 2 hrs, US$7. From Santa Teresa you have to cross the bridge over the Río Urubamba and walk 6 km to the Central Hidroeléctrica, a nice, flat road, or take a combi, US$4. From the Hidroeléctrica train station it's 40 mins on the local train to Aguas Calientes (US$20 for tourists, about 3 a day in high season) or you can walk along the railway in 2-3 hrs (at Km 114.5 is **$** pp Hospedaje Mandor, about 2 km from bridge to Machu Picchu). To return, walk or take the local train from Aguas Calientes to Santa Teresa to catch a bus to Santa María, then take a bus back to Cuzco. If using this route, don't forget you can pre-book your ticket for Machu Picchu online or in Cuzco, if you don't want to buy it in Aguas Calientes.

Another option is to take a **Machu Picchu By Car** tour, which agencies in Cuzco run over 1 or 2 nights. Passengers are taken to the Hidroeléctrica station via Ollantaytambo and Abra Málaga, with an overnight stay in Aguas Calientes, or Santa Teresa. The tour includes transport, lodging, Machu Picchu entry, some meals and guide, US$115-160 pp.

Inca trails

The most impressive way to reach Machu Picchu is via the centuries-old Inca Trail that winds its way from the Sacred Valley near Ollantaytambo, taking three to five days. The spectacular hike runs from Km 88, Qorihuayrachina (2299 m), a point immediately after the first tunnel 22 km beyond Ollantaytambo station. A sturdy suspension bridge has now been built over the Río Urubamba. Guided tours generally start at Km 82, Piscacucho, reached by road. Rules for hiking the trail are detailed below. What makes this hike so special is the stunning combination of Inca ruins, unforgettable views, magnificent mountains, exotic vegetation and extraordinary ecological variety.

Arriving at the Inca Trail

Equipment The Inca Trail is rugged and steep, but the magnificent views compensate for any weariness which may be felt. It is cold at night, however, and weather conditions change rapidly, so it is important to take not only strong footwear, rain gear and warm clothing but also food, water, water purification for when you fill bottles from streams, insect repellent, a supply of plastic bags, coverings, a good sleeping bag, a torch/flashlight and a stove for preparing hot food and drink to ward off the cold at night. A stove using white gas (*bencina*, available from hardware stores in Cuzco) is preferable. A tent is essential, but if you're hiring one in Cuzco, check carefully for leaks. Walkers who have not taken adequate equipment have died of exposure.

All the necessary equipment can be rented; see page 1361 under Camping equipment and What to do. Good maps of the Trail and area can be bought from **South American Explorers** in Lima or Cuzco. If you have any doubts about carrying your own pack, reasonably priced porters/guides are available. Carry a day-pack for your water, snacks, etc, in case you walk faster than the porters and you have to wait for them to catch you up.

The above applies only to those who trek with a licensed guide (see below). Most people sign on with an agency, which should provide all gear. Independent trekking is not permitted.

Tours Travel Agencies in Cuzco arrange transport to the start, equipment, food, etc, for an all-in price for all treks that lead to the Machu Picchu Historical Sanctuary. Prices start at about US$540-620 per person for a four-day/three-night trek on the Classic Inca Trail and rise according to the level of service given. If the price is significantly lower, you should be concerned as the company will be cutting corners and may not be paying the environment the respect the regulations were designed to instil. All are subject to strict rules and must be licensed. Tour operators taking clients on any of the Inca Trails leading to the Machu Picchu Historical Sanctuary have to pass an annual test. Groups of up to seven independent travellers who do not wish to use a tour operator are allowed to hike the trails if they contract an independent, licensed guide to accompany them, as long as they do not contact any other persons such as porters or cooks. There is a maximum of 500 persons per day, including guides and porters, allowed on the Classic Inca Trail. Operators pay US$15 for each porter and other trail staff; porters are not permitted to carry more than 20 kg. Littering is banned, as is carrying plastic water bottles (canteens only may be carried). Pets and pack animals are prohibited. Groups have to use approved campsites only.

Trail tickets On all hiking trails (Km 82 or Km 88 to Machu Picchu, Salkantay to Machu Picchu, and Km 82 or Km 88 to Machu Picchu via Km 104) adults must pay US$95, students and children under 15 US$47. On the Camino Real de los Inkas from Km 104 to Wiñay-Wayna and Machu Picchu the fee is US$55 per adult, US$31 for students and children and Salkantay to Huayllabamba and Km 88, US$95. All tickets must be bought at the Dirección de Cultura office in Cuzco; tickets are only sold on presentation of a letter from a licensed tour operator on behalf of the visitor, including full passport details. Tickets are non-refundable and cannot be changed so make sure you provide accurate passport details to your tour operator. None is sold at the entrance to any of the routes. See page 1362 on the need to reserve your place on the Trail in advance. You can save a bit of money by arranging your own transport back to Ollantaytambo in advance, either for the last day of your tour, or by staying an extra night in Aguas Calientes and taking the early morning train, then take a bus back to Cuzco. Make sure your return train ticket to Cuzco has your name on it (spelt absolutely correctly) for the tourist train, otherwise you have to pay for any changes.

Advice Four days would make a comfortable trip (though much depends on the weather). Allow a further day to see Machu Picchu when you have recovered from the hike. You cannot take backpacks into Machu Picchu; leave them at ticket office. The first two days of the Trail involve the stiffest climbing, so do not attempt it if you're feeling unwell. Leave all your valuables in Cuzco and keep everything inside your tent, even your shoes. Security has, however, improved

in recent years. Always take sufficient cash to tip porters and guides at the end (S/.50-100 each, but at your discretion). Avoid the July-August high season and check conditions in the rainy season from November to April (note that this can vary). In the wet it is cloudy and the paths are very slippery and difficult. **The Trail is closed each February for cleaning and repair.**

The Trail

The trek to the sacred site begins either at Km 82, **Piscacucho**, or at Km 88, **Qorihuayrachina**, at 2600 m. In order to reach Km 82 hikers are transported by their tour operator in a minibus on the road that goes to Quillabamba. From Piri onward the road follows the riverbank and ends at Km 82, where there is a bridge. The Inca Trail equipment, food, fuel and field personnel reach Km 82 (depending on the tour operator's logistics) for the Sernanp staff to weigh each bundle before the group arrives. When several groups are leaving on the same day, it is more convenient to arrive early. Km 88 can only be reached by train, subject to schedule and baggage limitations. The train goes slower than a bus, but you start your walk nearer to Llaqtapata and Huayllabamba. (See below for details of variations in starting points for the Inca Trail.)

The walk to **Huayllabamba**, following the Cusichaca River, needs about three hours and isn't too arduous. Beyond Huayllabamba, a popular camping spot for tour groups, there is a camping place about an hour ahead, at **Llulluchayoc** (3200 m). A punishing 1½-hour climb further is **Llulluchapampa**, an ideal meadow for camping. If you have the energy to reach this point, it will make the second day easier because the next stage, the ascent to the first pass, **Warmiwañuska** (Dead Woman's Pass) at 4200 m, is tough; 2½ hours.

Afterwards take the steep path downhill to the Pacaymayo ravine. Beware of slipping on the Inca steps after rain. Tour groups usually camp by a stream at the bottom (1½ hours from the first pass). It is no longer permitted to camp at **Runkuracay**, on the way up to the second pass (a much easier climb, 3900 m). Magnificent views near the summit in clear weather. A good overnight place is about 30 minutes past the Inca ruins at **Sayacmarca** (3500 m), about an hour on after the top of the second pass.

A gentle two-hour climb on a fine stone highway leads through an Inca tunnel to the third pass. Near the top there's a spectacular view of the entire Vilcabamba range. You descend to Inca ruins at **Phuyupatamarca** (3650 m), well worth a long visit, even camping overnight.

From there steps go downhill to the magnificent ruins of **Wiñay-Wayna** (2700 m, entry US$5.75), with impressive views of the cleared terraces of Intipata. Access is possible, but the trail is not easily visible. There is a campsite which gets crowded and dirty. After Wiñay-Wayna there is no water and no camping till the official site below Puente Ruinas. The path from this point goes more or less level through jungle until the steep staircase up to the **Intipunku** (two hours), where there's a fine view of Machu Picchu, especially at dawn, with the sun alternately in and out, clouds sometimes obscuring the ruins, sometimes leaving them clear.

Get to Machu Picchu as early as possible, preferably before 0830 for best views but in any case before the tourist trains in high season.

Alternative Inca trails

The **Camino Real de los Inkas** starts at Km 104, where a footbridge gives access to the ruins of Chachabamba and the trail which ascends, passing above the ruins of Choquesuysuy to connect with the main trail at Wiñay-Wayna. This first part is a steady, continuous ascent of three hours (take water) and the trail is narrow and exposed in parts. Many people recommend this short Inca Trail. Good hiking trails from Aguas Calientes (see page 1379) have been opened along the left bank of the Urubamba, for day hikes crossing the bridge of the hydroelectric plant to Choquesuysuy. A three-night trek goes from Km 82 to Km 88, then along the Río Urubamba to Pacaymayo Bajo and Km 104, from where you take the Camino Real de los Inkas.

Two treks involve routes from **Salkantay**: one, known as the **High Inca Trail** joins the classic Trail at Huayllabamba, then proceeds as before on the main Trail through Wiñay Wayna to

Machu Picchu. To get to Salkantay, you have to start the trek in Mollepata, northwest of Cuzco in the Apurímac valley. **Ampay** buses run from Arcopata on the Chinchero road, or you can take private transport to Mollepata (three hours from Cuzco). Salkantay to Machu Picchu this way takes three nights. The second Salkantay route, known as the **Santa Teresa Trek**, takes four days and crosses the 4500-m Huamantay Pass to reach the Santa Teresa valley, which you follow to its confluence with the Urubamba. The goal is the town of Santa Teresa from where you can go to La Hidroeléctrica station for the local train to Aguas Calientes (see page 1382). On this trek, **Machu Picchu Lodge to Lodge** ① *Mountain Lodges of Peru, T084-243636 (in Lima T01-421 6952, in North America T1-510-525 8846, in Europe T43-664-434 3340), www.mountainlodgesofperu.com*, a series of lodges have been set up. Fully guided tours take seven days, going from lodge to lodge, which are at Soraypampa (**Salkantay Lodge and Adventure Resort**), Huayraccmachay (**Wayra Lodge**), Collpapampa (**Colpa Lodge**) and Lucmabamba (**Lucma Lodge**). Contact **Mountain Lodges of Peru** for rates, departure dates and all other details, also for their new five- or seven-day, Lodge-to-Lodge route from Lamay to Ollantaytambo (http://laresadventure.com).

Inca Jungle Trail This is offered by several tour operators in Cuzco: on the first day you cycle downhill from Abra Málaga to Santa María (see Train, page 1381), 2000 m, three to four hours of riding on the main Quillabamba–Cuzco highway with speeding vehicles inattentive to cyclists on the road. It's best to pay for good bikes and back-up on this section. Some agencies also offer white-water rafting in the afternoon. The second day is a hard 11-km trek from Santa María to Santa Teresa. It involves crossing three adventurous bridges and bathing in the hot springs at Santa Teresa (US$1.65 entry). The third day is a six-hour trek from Santa Teresa to Aguas Calientes. Some agencies offer ziplining as an alternative. The final day is a guided tour of Machu Picchu.

Vitcos and Vilcabamba

The Incas' last stronghold is reached from **Chaullay**, a village on the road between Ollantaytambo and Quillabamba. The road passes through Peña, a beautiful place with snowy peaks on either side of the valley, then the climb to the pass begins in earnest — on the right is a huge glacier. Soon on the left, Verónica begins to appear in all its huge and snowy majesty. After endless zig-zags and breathtaking views, you reach the Abra Málaga pass (road is paved to here). The descent to the valley shows hillsides covered in lichen and Spanish moss. At Chaullay, the road crosses the river on the historic Choquechaca bridge.

From Chaullay you can drive, or take a daily bus or truck (four to seven hours) to the village of **Huancacalle**, the best base for exploring the nearby Inca ruins of **Vitcos**, with the palace of the last four Inca rulers from 1536 to 1572, and **Yurac Rumi** (or **Chuquipalta**), the impressive sacred white rock of the Incas. There are a few restaurants, shops and basic places to stay at Huancacalle. There are two hostals: **$ El Ultimo Refugio de Manco Inca**, T846010, clean hostal run by the Quispicusi family that also run the INC office, excellent information; and **$ Sixpac Manco**, managed by the Cobos family. Alternatively villagers will let you stay on their floor, or you can camp near the river below the cemetery. Allow time for hiking to, and visiting Vitcos. It takes one hour to walk from Huancacalle to Vitcos, 45 minutes Vitcos–Chuquipalta, 45 minutes Chuquipalta-Huancacalle. Horses can be hired.

The road from Chaullay continues to **Vilcabamba La Nueva**. You can also hike from Huancacalle; a three-hour walk through beautiful countryside with Inca ruins dotted around. There is a missionary building run by Italians, with electricity and running water, where you may be able to spend the night.

Vilcabamba Vieja

Travellers with ample time can hike from Huancacalle to **Espíritu Pampa**, the site of the **Vilcabamba Vieja** ruins (entry US$11), a vast pre-Inca ruin with a neo-Inca overlay set in deep jungle at 1000 m. The site is reached on foot or horseback from Pampaconas. From Chaullay, take a truck to Yupanca, Lucma or Pucyura: there rent horses or mules and travel through breathtaking countryside to Espíritu Pampa. From Huancacalle a trip will take three or four days on foot, with a further day to get to Chihuanquiri and transport back to Quillabamba. The Ministerio de Cultura charge for this trek is US$38, students US$19. It is advisable to take local guides and mules. Ask around in Huancacalle for guides. The **Sixpac Manco** hostal has various guides and other people in the village will offer their services. Distances are considerable and the going is difficult. *Sixpac Manco*, by Vincent R Lee (available in Cuzco), has accurate maps of all archaeological sites in this area, and describes two expeditions into the region by the author and his party, following in the footsteps of Gene Savoy, who first identified the site in the 1960s. His book, *Antisuyo*, is also recommended reading. The best time of year is May to November, possibly December. Outside this period it is very dangerous as the trails are very narrow and can be thick with mud and very slippery. Insect repellent is essential, also painkillers and other basic medicines. Make enquiries about safety in Cuzco before setting out on treks in this area.

◉ Vitcos and Vilcabamba listings

For hotel and restaurant price codes, and other relevant information, see Essentials.

◉ Transport

Huancacalle *p1385*
Bus Four companies leave Cuzco's bus terminal for **Quillabamba**, taking 6-8 hrs

for the 233 km, depending on season, US$9 (**Ampay** is best company). Then take a **combi** from Quillabamba, 0900 and 1200, US$3.30 to Huancacalle, 3-4 hrs. On Fri they go all the way to Vilcabamba. You can also take a taxi.

West from Cuzco

Beyond Anta on the Abancay road, 2 km before Limatambo at the ruins of **Tarahuasi** (US$6), a few hundred metres from the road, is a very well-preserved **Inca temple platform**, with 28 tall niches, and a long stretch of fine polygonal masonry. The ruins are impressive, enhanced by the orange lichen which give the walls a honey colour.

Along the Abancay road 100 km from Cuzco, is the exciting descent into the Apurímac canyon, near the former Inca suspension bridge that inspired Thornton Wilder's *The Bridge of San Luis Rey*.

Choquequirao
ⓘ *Entry US$13.50, students US$6.75.*

Choquequirao is another 'lost city of the Incas', built on a ridge spur almost 1600 m above the Apurímac. It is reckoned to be a larger site than Machu Picchu, but with fewer buildings. The main features of Choquequirao are the **Lower Plaza**, considered by most experts to be the focal point of the city. The **Upper Plaza**, reached by a huge set of steps or terraces, has what are possibly ritual baths. A beautiful set of slightly curved agricultural terraces run for over 300 m east-northeast of the Lower Plaza.

The **Usnu** is on a levelled hilltop, ringed with stones and giving awesome 360° views. The **Ridge Group**, still shrouded in vegetation, is a large collection of unrestored buildings some 50-100 m below the Usnu. The **Outlier Building**, isolated and surrounded on three sides by sheer drops of over 1.5 km into the Apurímac Canyon, possesses some of the finest stonework within Choquequirao. **Capuliyoc**, nearly 500 m below the Lower Plaza, is a great set of agricultural terraces, visible on the approach from the far side of the valley. One section of terraces is decorated with llamas in white stone.

There are three ways in to Choquequirao. None is a gentle stroll. The shortest way is from **Cachora**, a village on the south side of the Apurímac, reached by a side road from the Cuzco-Abancay highway, shortly after Saywite. It is four hours by bus from Cuzco to the turn-off, then a two-hour descent from the road to Cachora (from 3695 m to 2875 m). Guides (Celestino Peña is the official guide) and mules are available in Cachora. From the village you need a day to descend to the Río Apurímac then seven hours to climb up to Choquequirao. Allow one or two days at the site then return the way you came. This route is well signed and in good condition, with excellent campsites and showers en route. Horses can be hired to carry your bags. The second and third routes take a minimum of eight days and require thorough preparation. You can start either at Huancacalle, or at Santa Teresa, between Machu Picchu and Chaullay. Both routes involve an incredible number of strenuous ascents and descents. You should be acclimatised for altitudes ranging from 2400 m to between 4600 and 5000 m and be prepared for extremes of temperature. In each case you end the trail at Cachora. It is possible to start either of these long hikes at Cachora, continuing even from Choquequirao to Espíritu Pampa. Note, the government approved the construction of an aerial cableway to Choquequirao in 2013, due for completion in late 2015.

Saywite → *3 km from the main road at Km 49 from Abancay, 153 km from Cuzco, US$4, students US$2. Altitude: 3500 m.*

Beyond the town of Curahuasi, 126 km from Cuzco, is the large carved rock of Saywite. It is a UNESCO World Heritage Site. The principal monolith is said to represent the three regions of jungle, sierra and coast, with the associated animals and Inca sites of each. It is fenced in, but ask the guardian for a closer look. It was defaced, allegedly, when a cast was taken of it, breaking off many of the animals' heads. Six further archaeological areas fall away from the stone and its neighbouring group of buildings. The site is more easily reached from Abancay than Cuzco.

⦿ West from Cuzco listings

For hotel and restaurant price codes, and other relevant information, see Essentials.

⦿ Where to stay

Choquequirao *p1386*

$$ pp Casa de Salcantay, Prolongación Salcantay s/n, Cachora, T984 281171, www. salcantay.com. Price includes breakfast, dinner available if booked in advance. Dutch-run hostel with links to community projects, comfortable, small, Dutch, English, German spoken, can help with arranging independent treks, or organize treks with tour operator.

$$ pp Los Tres Balcones, Jr Abancay s/n, Cachora, www.choquequirau.com. Hostel designed as start and end-point for the trek to Choquequirao. Breakfast included, comfortable, hot showers, restaurant and pizza oven, camping. Shares information with internet café. They run a 5-day trek to Choquequirao,

US$500-650 (depending on numbers), with camping gear (but not sleeping bag), all meals and lunch at the *hostel* afterwards, entrance to the ruins, horses to carry luggage, transport from Cuzco and bilingual tour guide.

$ La Casona de Ocampo, San Martín 122, Cachora, T237514. Rooms with hot shower all day, free camping, owner Carlos Robles is knowledgeable.

⦿ Transport

Choquequirao *p1386*

From Cuzco take the first Abancay bus of the morning with **Bredde** at 0600, buy your ticket the night before to get a seat. Buses run from Abancay (Jr Prado Alto entre Huancavelica y Núñez) to **Cachora** at 0500 and 1400, return 0630 and 1100, 2 hrs, US$2.50. Cars run from the Curahuasi terminal on Av Arenas, Abancay, US$10 for whole vehicle.

Central Highlands

The Central Andes have many remote mountain areas with small typical villages, while larger cities of the region include Ayacucho and Huancayo. The vegetation is low, but most valleys are cultivated. Secondary roads are often in poor condition, sometimes impassable in the rainy season; the countryside is beautiful with spectacular views and the people are friendly. Three paved roads, from Lima, Pisco and Nazca, connect the Central Highlands to the coast. Huancayo lies in a valley which produces many crafts; the festivals are very popular and not to be missed.

Lima to Huancayo

The Central Highway more or less parallels the course of the railway between Lima and Huancayo (335 km). With the paving of roads from Pisco to Ayacucho and Nazca to Abancay, there are now more options for getting to the Sierra and the views on whichever ascent you choose are beyond compare. You can also reach the Central Highlands from Cuzco (via Abancay and Andahuaylas) and from Huaraz (via La Unión and Huánuco), so Lima is not the sole point of access overland.

Chosica and Marcahuasi
Chosica (860 m) is the real starting place for the mountains, 40 km from Lima. It's warm and friendly and a great place to escape the big city. Beyond the town looms a precipitous range of hills almost overhanging the streets. There are some basic *hostales* and, outside town, weekend resorts (see www.chosica.com). Up the Santa Eulalia valley 40 km beyond Chosica, is **Marcahuasi**, a table mountain (US$4) about 3 km by 1 km at 4000 m, near the village of **San Pedro de Casta**. There are three lakes, a 40-m-high 'monumento a la humanidad', and other mysterious lines, gigantic figures, sculptures, astrological signs and megaliths, which the late Daniel Ruzo describes in his book, *La Culture Masma*, Extrait de l'Ethnographie, Paris, 1956. A more widely accepted theory is that the formations are the result of wind erosion. The trail starts south of the village of San Pedro, and climbs southeast to the *meseta*; it's three hours' walk to the *meseta*; guides are advisable in misty weather. Donkeys for carrying bags cost US$8 to hire, horses US$10. Tourist information is available at the municipality on the plaza. At shops in San Pedro you can buy everything for the trip, including bottled water. Tours can be arranged with travel agencies in Lima.

Chosica to Huancayo
For a while, beyond Chosica, each successive valley looks greener and lusher, with a greater variety of trees and flowers. Between Río Blanco and **Chicla** (Km 127, 3733 m), Inca contour-terraces can be seen quite clearly. After climbing up from **Casapalca** (Km 139, 4154 m), there are glorious views of the highest peaks, and mines, from the foot of a deep gorge. The road ascends to the Ticlio Pass, before the descent to **Morococha** and **La Oroya**. A large metal flag of Peru can be seen at the top of Mount Meiggs, not by any means the highest in the area, but through it runs Galera Tunnel, 1175 m long, in which the Central Railway reaches its greatest altitude, 4782 m. The railway itself is a magnificent feat of engineering, with 58 bridges, 69 tunnels and six zigzags, passing beautiful landscapes. It is definitely worth the ride on the new tourist service (see Transport, below). **La Oroya** (3755 m) is the main smelting centre for the region's mining industry. It stands at the fork of the Yauli and Mantaro rivers. Any traveller, but asthmatics in particular, beware, the pollution from the heavy industry causes severe irritation. (For places to the east and north of La Oroya, see page 1404.)

Jauja The old town of **Jauja** (*Phone code: 064; Population: 16,000; Altitude: 3400 m, www.jaujaperu. info*), 80 km southeast of La Oroya, was Pizarro's provisional capital until the founding of Lima. It has a colourful Wednesday and Sunday market. The **Museo Arqueológico Julio Espejo Núñez**

① *Jr Cusco 537, T361163, Mon and Wed 1500-1900, Sun 0900-1200, 1400-1700, donations welcome, knock on door of La Casa del Caminante opposite where the creator and curator lives*, is a quaint but endearing mix of relics from various Peruvian cultures, including two mummies, one still wrapped in the original shroud. The **Cristo Pobre** church is supposedly modelled after Notre Dame and is something of a curiosity. Department of Junín **tourist office** ① *Jr Grau 528, T362897, junin@ mincetur.gob.pe*. On a hill above Jauja there is a fine line of Inca storehouses, and on hills nearby the ruins of Huajlaasmarca, with hundreds of circular stone buildings from the Huanca culture (John Hemming). There are also ruins near the **Paca lake**, 3.5 km away. The western shore is lined with restaurants; many offer weekend boat trips, US$1 (combi from Avenida Pizarro US$0.50).

On the road to Huancayo 18 km to the south, is **Concepción** (*Altitude: 3251 m*), with a market on Sunday. From Concepción a branch road (6 km) leads to the **Convent of Santa Rosa de Ocopa** ① *0900-1200 and 1500-1800, closed Tue, 45-min tours start on the hour, US$1.25, colectivos from the market in Concepción, 15 mins, US$0.50*, a Franciscan monastery set in beautiful surroundings. It was established in 1725 for training missionaries for the jungle. It contains a fine library with over 25,000 volumes, a biological museum and a large collection of paintings.

⦿ Lima to Huancayo listings

For hotel and restaurant price codes, and other relevant information, see Essentials.

manjar, recommended as the best in and around town, buses on the Lima route stop here.

⊜ Where to stay

Chosica and Marcahuasi: San Pedro de Casta *p1388*
Locals in town will put you up, **$**; ask at tourist information at the municipality. Take all necessary camping equipment for Marcahuasi trek.
$ Marcahuasi, just off the plaza. Private or shared bath, the best hotel in San Pedro; it also has a restaurant. There are 2 other restaurants.

Chosica to Huancayo: La Oroya *p1388*
$ Hostal Chavín, Tarma 281; and **$ Hostal Inti**, Arequipa 117, T391098. Both basic.

Jauja *p1388*
$ Hostal Manco Cápac, Jr Manco Cápac 575, T361620, T99-974 9119. Central, good rooms, private or shared rooms, garden, good breakfast and coffee.
$ Hostal María Nieves, Jr Gálvez 491, 1 block from the Plaza de Armas, T362543. Safe, helpful, large breakfast, hot water all day, parking. Good.

⊘ Restaurants

Chosica to Huancayo: La Oroya *p1388*
$$ El Tambo, 2 km outside town on the road to Lima. Good trout and frogs, sells local cheese and

Jauja *p1388*
$ Centro Naturista, Huarancayo 138 (no sign). Fruit salad, yoghurt, granola, etc, basic place.
$ D'Chechis, Jr Bolívar 1166, T368530. Lunch only, excellent.
$ Ganso de Oro, R Palma 249, T362166. Good restaurant in hotel of same name (which is not recommendable), varied prices, unpretentious.
$ La Rotonda, Tarapacá 415, T368412. Good lunch menú and pizzas in the evening.

⊖ Transport

Chosica *p1388*
Colectivos for Chosica leave from Av Grau, **Lima**, when full, between 0600 and 2100, US$1. Most **buses** on the Lima-La Oroya route are full; colectivo taxi to La Oroya US$7.50, 3 hrs, very scenic, passing the 2nd highest railway in the world.

San Pedro de Casta/Marcahuasi
Bus To San Pedro de Casta minibuses leave **Chosica** from Parque Echenique, opposite market, 0900 and 1500, 4 hrs, US$3.50; return 0700 and 1400.

Chosica to Huancayo: La Oroya *p1388*
Bus To Lima, 4½ hrs, US$8. To **Jauja**, 80 km, 1½ hrs, US$2. To **Tarma**, 1½ hrs, US$2.50.

To **Cerro de Pasco**, 131 km, 3 hrs, US$3. To **Huánuco**, 236 km, 6 hr, US$7.50. Buses leave from Zeballos, adjacent to the train station. Colectivos also run on all routes.

Jauja *p1388*
Air LC Peru has 2 daily flights from **Lima** to Francisco Carle airport, just outside Jauja, 45 mins, price includes transfer to Huancayo (marketed 'Lima-Huancayo').
Bus To **Lima**: US$15; with Cruz del Sur, Pizarro 220, direct, 6 hrs, US$22-29 *bus cama*. Most

companies have their offices on the Plaza de Armas, but their buses leave from Av Pizarro. To **Huancayo**, 44 km, takes 1 hr and costs US$2.25. Combis to Huancayo from 25 de Abril y Ricardo Palma, 01¼ hrs, US$2.50. To **Cerro de Pasco**, Turismo Central from 25 de Abril 144, 5 hrs, US$6. Turismo Central also goes to **Huánuco**, 8 hrs, US$15. To **Tarma**, US$3, hourly with **Trans Los Canarios** and Angelitos/San Juan from Jr Tarma; the latter continues to **Chanchamayo**, US$8. Colectivos to Tarma leave from Junín y Tarma when full.

Huancayo and around → *Phone code: 064. Colour map 3, C3. Population: over 500,000. Altitude: 3271 m.*

The city is in the Mantaro Valley. It is the capital of Junín Department and the main commercial centre for inland Peru. All the villages in the valley produce their own original crafts and celebrate festivals all year round. At the important festivals in Huancayo, people flock in from far and wide with an incredible range of food, crafts, dancing and music. The Sunday market gives a little taste of this every week (it gets going after 0900), but it is better to go to the villages for local handicrafts. Jr Huancavelica, 3 km long and four stalls wide, still sells clothes, fruit, vegetables, hardware, handicrafts and traditional medicines and goods for witchcraft. There is also an impressive daily market behind the railway station and a large handicrafts market between Ancash and Real, block 7, offering a wide selection.

Tourist offices The regional office is in Jauja; see above. Small **tourist information booth** ① *Plaza Huamanmarca, Real 481, T238480/233251*. **Indecopi** ① *Moquegua 730, El Tambo, T245180, abarrientos@indecopi.gob.pe*, is the consumer protection office.

The **museum** ① *at the Salesian school, north of the river on Pasaje Santa Rosa, Mon-Fri 0900-1800, Sun 1000-1200, US$1.75*, is a fascinating cabinet of curiosities with everything ranging from two-headed beasts to a collection of all the coins of the United States of America. The **Parque de Identidad Wanka** ① *on Jr San Jorge in the Barrio San Carlos northeast of the city, entry free, but contributions are appreciated*, is a mixture of surrealistic construction interwoven with native plants and trees and the cultural history of the Mantaro Valley.

Mantaro Valley
The whole Mantaro valley is rich in culture. On the outskirts of town is **Torre-Torre**, impressive, eroded sandstone towers on the hillside. Take a bus to Cerrito de la Libertad and walk up. The ruins of **Warivilca** (15 km) ① *1000-1200, 1500-1700 (museum mornings only), US$0.15, take a micro for Chilca from C Real*, are near **Huari**, with the remains of a pre-Inca temple of the Huanca tribe. Museum in the plaza, with deformed skulls, and modelled and painted pottery of successive Huanca and Inca occupations of the shrine.

East of the Mantaro River The villages of **Cochas Chico** and **Cochas Grande**, 11 km away, are where the famous *mate burilado*, or gourd carving, is done. You can buy them cheaply direct from the manufacturers, but ask around. Beautiful views of the Valle de Mantaro and Huancayo. *Micros* leave from the corner of Amazonas and Giráldez, US$0.25.

Hualahoyo (11 km) has a little chapel with 21 colonial canvases. **San Agustín de Cajas** (8 km) makes fine hats, and **San Pedro** (10 km) makes wooden chairs; **Hualhuas** (12 km) fine alpaca weavings which you can watch being made. The weavers take special orders; small items can be finished in a day. Negotiate a price.

The town of **San Jerónimo** is renowned for the making of silver filigree jewellery; Wednesday market. Fiesta on the third Saturday in August. There are ruins two to three hours' walk above San Jerónimo, but seek advice before hiking to them.

Between Huancayo and Huancavelica, **Izcuchaca** is the site of a colonial bridge over the Río Mantaro. On the edge of town is a fascinating pottery workshop whose machinery is driven by a water turbine (plus a small shop). A nice hike is to the chapel on a hill overlooking the valley; about one to 1½ hours each way.

Huancayo

Museo, Colegio Salesiano

To Jauja, La Oroya, Tarma & Lima

To Bus Terminal

Río Shullcas

To Parque de Identidad Wanka &

Sto Domingo

San Antonio

Ayacucho

Centenario

Cusco

2 de Mayo

Puno

Municipalidad

Cathedral

Casa de Artesano

Paseo La Breña

Plaza de la Constitución

Av Giráldez

Río Florido

Cars to Tarma

Lima

Transportes Angelitos/San Juan & Combis & Colectivos to Jauja, San Jerónimo & La Concepción

Plaza Amazonas

Trains to Lima

Loreto

Callixio

Colectivos to Jauja Huamanmarca

Ica

Buses to Huailhuas, Cajas & Huamancaca

Plaza Huamanmar

La Inmaculada

Ica

Wholesale

Piura

Mercado Artesanal

Coliseo Municipal

Sunday Market

Cajamarca

Huánuco

Tarapacá

Empresa Molina

Trans Yuri

Angaraes

To Train Station (2 blocks)

To Train Station (6 blocks)

To Train Station

200 metres
200 yards

Where to stay
1 Casa Alojamiento de Aldo y Soledad Bonilla *C2*
2 El Marquez *A2*

3 Hosp Familiar Tachi *B2*
4 Hosp Piccolo *B2*
5 Kiya *B2*
6 La Casa de La Abuela *A3*
7 Los Balcones *A2*
8 Peru Andino *A3*
9 Presidente *C2*
10 Retama Inn *C2*
11 Turismo *B2*

Restaurants
1 A La Leña *B2*
2 Café El Parque *B2*
3 Chifa El Centro *B2*
4 Chifa Xu *B2*
5 Detrás de la Catedral *B2*
6 Donatelo's *B2*
7 El Inka *A2*
8 El Olímpico *B2*

9 El Paraíso *C2*
10 ImaginArte *A2*
11 La Cabaña *B3*
12 La Pérgola *A2*
13 Panadería Koky *B2*
14 Pizzería Antojitos *B2*

For hotel and restaurant price codes, and other relevant information, see Essentials.

◐ Where to stay

Huancayo *p1390, map p1391*
Prices may be raised in Holy Week. **Note** The Plaza de Armas is called Plaza Constitución.
$$$ Presidente, C Real 1138, T231275, http://huancayo.hotelpresidente.com.pe. Helpful, classy, safe, serves breakfast, restaurant, convention centre.
$$$ Turismo, Ancash 729, T235611, http://turistases.hotelpresidente.com.pe/. Restored colonial building, same owner as Presidente, with more atmosphere, elegant, rooms quite small, Wi-Fi extra, quiet. Restaurant (**$$-$**) serves good meals, fine service.
$$$-$$ El Marquez, Puno 294, T219202, www.elmarquezhuancayo.com. Good value, efficient, popular with local business travellers, safe parking.
$$ Kiya, Giráldez 107, T214955, www.hotelkiya.com. Comfortable although ageing, hot water, helpful staff. Spectacular view of Plaza.
$ Casa Alojamiento de Aldo y Soledad Bonilla, Huánuco 332, ½ block from Mcal Cáceres bus station, T232103. Cheaper without full board, colonial house, owners speak English, laundry, secure, relaxing, nice courtyard, tours arranged, best to book ahead.
$ Hospedaje Familiar Tachi, Huamanmarca 125, T219980, saenz_nildy@hotmail.com. Central but not the safest area, small, comfortable, hot water, private or shared showers, family run, nice atmosphere and views from terrace.
$ Hospedaje Piccolo, Puno 239. With hot water, good beds, well-kept.
$ La Casa de la Abuela, Prolongación Cusco 794 y Gálvez, T234383, www.incasdelperu.org/casa-de-la-abuela. Doubles with or without private bath and dorms, 15 mins out of town. Hot shower, light breakfast, laundry facilities, meals available, sociable staff, owner speaks English, good meeting place, free pickup from bus station if requested in advance. Discount for Footprint Handbook readers.
$ Los Balcones, Jr Puno 282, T214881. Comfortable rooms, hot water, helpful staff,

elevator (practically disabled-accessible). View of the back of the Cathedral.
$ Peru Andino, Pasaje San Antonio 113-115, one block Parque Túpac Amaru, in 1st block of Francisco Solano (left side of Defensoría del Pueblo), 10-15 mins' walk from the centre (if taking a taxi, stress that it's *Pasaje* San Antonio), T223956. Hot showers, several rooms with bath, laundry and kitchen facilities, breakfast and other meals on request, safe area, cosy atmosphere, run by Sra Juana and Luis, who speak some English, organize trekking and mountain bike tours, bike hire, Spanish classes. Can pick up guests at Lima airport with transfer to bus station.
$ Retama Inn, Ancash 1079, T219193, http://hotelretamainnhuancayo.blogspot.co.uk/. All amenities, comfortable beds, hot water, TV, café/bar, helpful, breakfast extra.

Mantaro Valley *p1390*
In Izcuchaca, ask in stores off the plaza. Many locals are enthusiastic about renting a room to a gringo traveller for a night. You may well make a friend for life.

❼ Restaurants

Huancayo *p1390, map p1391*
Breakfast is served in Mercado Modelo from 0700. Better class, more expensive restaurants, serving typical dishes for about US$5, plus 18% tax, drinks can be expensive. Lots of cheap restaurants along Av Giráldez.
$$ Detrás de la Catedral, Jr Ancash 335 (behind Cathedral as name suggests), T212969. Pleasant atmosphere, excellent dishes. Charcoal grill in the corner keeps the place warm on cold nights. Considered by many to be the best in town.
$$ El Olímpico, Giráldez 199. Long-established, one of the more upscale establishments offering Andean and Creole dishes; the real reason to go is the owner's model car collection displayed in glass cabinets.
$$ La Cabaña, Av Giráldez 652. Pizzas, ice cream, *calentitos*, and other dishes, excellent atmosphere, live folk music Thu-Sun.
$$ Pizzería Antojitos, Puno 599. Attractive, atmospheric pizzería with live music some nights.

$$-$ Chifa Xu, Giráldez 208. Good food at reasonable prices, always-bustling atmosphere.
$ A La Leña, Paseo la Breña 144 and on Ancash. Good rotisserie chicken and salads, popular.
$ Chifa El Centro, Giráldez 238, T217575. Another branch at Av Leandra Torres 240. Chinese food, good service and atmosphere.
$ Donatelo's, Puno 287. Excellent pizza and chicken place, with nice atmosphere, popular.
$ La Pérgola, Puno 444. Pleasant atmosphere, overlooking the plaza, 4-course *menú*.

Cafés
Café El Parque, Giráldez y Ancash, on the main plaza. Popular place for juices, coffee and cakes.
El Inka, Puno 530. Popular *fuente de soda*, with coffee, Peruvian food, desserts, milkshakes.
El Paraíso, Arequipa 428, and another opposite at No 429. Both vegetarian places, OK.
ImaginArte, Jr Ancash 260. Open from 1800. Principally an art gallery, often displaying work based on ethnic Peruvian culture. Good coffee and cakes.
Panadería Koky, Ancash y Puno, serves Hotel Marquez. Open 0700-2300, lunch 1230-1530. Good for breakfasts, lunches, sandwiches, capuccino and pastries, fancy atmosphere, free Wi-Fi.

🍸 Bars and clubs

Huancayo *p1390, map p1391*
Peñas All the *peñas* have folklore shows with dancing, open normally Fri, Sat and Sun from 1300 to 2200. Entrance fee is about US$3 pp. Eg **Ollantaytambo**, Puno, block 2, and **Taki Wasi**, Huancavelica y 13 de Noviembre.

⚙ Festivals

Huancayo *p1390, map p1391*
There are so many festivals in the Mantaro Valley that it is impossible to list them all. Nearly every day of the year there is some sort of celebration in one of the villages.
Jan 1-6, New Year celebrations; 20, **San Sebastián y San Fabián** (recommended in Jauja). **Feb** There are carnival celebrations for the whole month, with highlights on 2, **Virgen de la Candelaria**, and 17-19 **Concurso de Carnaval**. **Mar-Apr** Semana Santa, with

impressive Good Friday processions. **May Fiesta de las Cruces** throughout the whole month.
Jun 15 **Virgen de las Mercedes**; 24, **San Juan Bautista**; 29, **Fiesta Patronal. Jul** 16, **Virgen del Carmen**; 24-25, **Santiago. Aug** 4, **San Juan de Dios**; 16, **San Roque**; 30, **Santa Rosa de Lima. Sep** 8, **Virgen de Cocharcas**; 15, **Virgen de la Natividad**; 23-24, **Virgen de las Mercedes**; 29, **San Miguel Arcángel. Oct** 4, **San Francisco de Asís**; 18, **San Lucas**; 28-30 culmination of month-long celebrations for **El Señor de los Milagros. Nov** 1, **Día de Todos los Santos. Dec** 3-13, **Virgen de Guadalupe**; 8, **Inmaculada Concepción**; 25, **Navidad** (Christmas).

🛍 Shopping

Huancayo *p1390, map p1391*
Thieves in the market hand out rolled up paper and pick your pocket while you unravel them.
Crafts All crafts are made outside Huancayo in the many villages of the Mantaro Valley, or in Huancavelica. The villages are worth a visit to learn how the items are made.
Casa de Artesano, on the corner of Real and Paseo La Breña, at Plaza Constitución. Has a wide selection of good quality crafts.

⌚ What to do

Huancayo *p1390, map p1391*
Tour operators
American Travel & Service, Plaza Constitución 122, of 2 (next to the Cathedral), T211181, T964-830220. Wide range of classical and more adventurous tours in the Mantaro Valley and in the Central Jungle. Transport and equipment rental possible. Most group-based day tours start at US$8-10 pp.
Incas del Perú, Av Giráldez 652, T223303, www.incasdelperu.org. Associated with the **La Cabaña** restaurant and **La Casa de la Abuela**. Run jungle, biking and riding trips throughout the region, as well as language and volunteer programs. Very popular with travellers in the region.
Peruvian Tours, Plaza Constitución 122, p 2, of 1, T213069. Next to the Cathedral and **American Travel & Service**. Classic tours of the Mantaro valley, plus day trips up to the Huaytapallana Nevados above Huancayo, plus long, 16-hr excursions to Cerro de Pasco and Tarma.

Guides

Marco Jurado Ames, T201260 or T964-227050 (mob), andinismo_peru@yahoo.es. Rock climbing and mountaineering, organizes long-distance treks on the 'hidden paths of Peru'. Many of these include Huancayo, such as a trek to Machu Picchu from the Amazon lowlands via Choquequirao and Inca Trail to Pariaccacca in the central Andes. Can start in Huancayo or Lima.

⊝ Transport

Huancayo *p1390, map p1391*

Bus The new bus terminal for buses to many destinations is 3 km north of the centre in the Parque Industrial. Some companies retain their own terminal in the centre, eg **Cruz del Sur**, Av Ferrocarril N 151, T223367. There are regular buses to **Lima**, 6-7 hrs on a good paved road, US$11-28 (**Oltursa** fares). For other fares and daytime buses take a bus from/to Yerbateros terminal in Lima (San Luis district, taxi there US$4.50), US$12. Travelling by day is recommended for the fantastic views and for safety; most major companies go by night (take warm clothing). Recommended companies:, **Turismo Central** and **Transportes Rogger**, Lima 561, T233488.

To **Ayacucho**, 319 km, 9-10 hrs, US$15-17 with **Molina**, C Angaráes 334, T224501, a day, recommended; 1 a day with **Turismo Central** US$13. The road is paved for the first 70 km, then in poor condition and is very difficult in the wet. Take warm clothing. (**Note** If driving to Ayacucho and beyond, roads are "amazingly rough". Don't go alone. Count kilometres diligently to keep a record of where you are: road signs are poor.) After Izcuchaca, on the railway to Huancavelica, there is a good road to the Quichuas hydroelectric scheme, but after that it is narrow with hair-raising bends and spectacular bridges. The scenery is staggering.

To **Huancavelica**, 147 km, 5 hrs, US$4. Many buses daily, including **Transportes Yuri**, Ancash 1220, 3 a day. The road has been paved and is a delightful ride, much more comfortable than the train (if you can find a driver who will not scare you to death). A private car from Huancayo costs US$18-23 pp depending on your negotiating skills.

To **Cerro de Pasco**, 255 km, 5 hrs, US$7.50. Several departures. Alternatively, take a bus to La Oroya, about every 20 mins, from Av Real about 10 blocks north of the main plaza. From La Oroya there are regular buses and colectivos to Cerro. The road to La Oroya and on to Cerro is in good condition. To **Huánuco**, 7 hrs, **Turismo Central** at 2115, US$9, good service.

To **Chanchamayo** Angelitos/San Juan, Ferrocarril 161 and Plaza Amazonas, every 1½ hrs, and **Tans Los Canarios** hourly service via Jauja to Tarma, 3 hrs, US$6, some of which continue on to La Merced, 5 hrs, US$7.50.

To **Yauyos**, cars at 0500 from Plaza de los Sombreros, El Tambo, US$7.50. It is a poor road with beautiful mountain landscapes before dropping to the valley of Cañete; cars go very fast.

To **Jauja**, 44 km, 1 hr. Colectivos and combis leave every few mins from Huamanmarca y Amazonas, and Plaza Amazonas, US$2.50. Ones via San Jerónimo and Concepción have 'Izquierda' on the front. Taxi to Jauja US$15, 45 mins. Most buses to the Mantaro Valley leave from several places around the market area. Buses to **Hualhuas** and **Cajas** leave from block 3 of Pachitea. Buses to **Cochas** leave from Amazonas y Giráldez.

Train There are 2 unconnected railway stations. The Central station serves **Lima**, via La Oroya: there is irregular service, about once a month, operated by **Ferrocarril Centro Andino**, Av José Gálvez Barrenechea 566, p 5, San Isidro, Lima, T01-226 6363, see www.ferrocarrilcentral.com.pe for next departure date. There are *turístico* and *clásico* fares, US$125 and US$70 return, respectively. The train leaves Lima at 0700, 11 hrs, returning at 0700, 3 or 4 days later. Coaches have reclining seats, heating, restaurant, tourist information, toilets, and nurse with first aid and oxygen. Tickets are sold online and by Lima agencies.

From the small station in Chilca suburb (15 mins by taxi, US$2), trains run to **Huancavelica**, on a narrow gauge (3 ft), Mon-Sat 0630, 1230, Sun 1400. There are 38 tunnels and the line reaches 3676 m. This "classic" Andean train journey on the *Tren Macho* takes 7 hrs and has fine views, passing through typical mountain villages where vendors sell food and crafts. In some places, the train has to reverse and change tracks.

Huancayo *p1390, map p1391*
Language classes Incas del Perú
(see What to do, above) organizes Spanish
courses for beginners for US$100 per week,
including accommodation at Hostal La Casa

de La Abuela, see above, and all meals, also
home-stays and weaving, playing traditional
music, Peruvian cooking and lots of other
things. Katia Cerna is a recommended teacher,
T225332, katiacerna@hotmail.com. She
can arrange home stays; her sister works
in adventure tourism.

Huancavelica → *Phone code: 064. Colour map 3, C3. Population: 37,500. Altitude: 3660 m.*

Huancavelica is a friendly and attractive town, surrounded by huge, rocky mountains. It was
founded in the 16th century by the Spanish to exploit rich deposits of mercury and silver. It
is predominantly an indigenous town, and people still wear traditional costume. There are
beautiful mountain walks in the neighbourhood. The Cathedral, located on the Plaza de Armas,
has an altar considered to be one of the finest examples of colonial art in Perú. Also very
impressive are the five other churches in town. The church of San Francisco, for example, has no
less than 11 altars. Sadly, though, most of the churches are closed to visitors. **Tourist office:**
Dircetur ① *Jr Victoria Garma 444, T452938.* Very helpful.
   Bisecting the town is the Río Huancavelica. South of the river is the main commercial centre.
North of the river, on the hillside, are the **thermal baths** ① *0600-1500, US$0.15 for private rooms,
water not very hot, US$0.10 for the hot public pool, also hot showers, take a lock for the doors.* The
handicraft sellers congregate in front of the Municipalidad on M Muñoz and the Biblioteca on
the Plaza de Armas (V Toledo). Most handicrafts are transported directly to Lima, but you can still
visit craftsmen in neighbouring villages. The Potaqchiz hill, just outside the town, gives a fine
view, about one hour walk up from San Cristóbal. **Ministerio de Cultura** ① *Plazoleta San Juan de
Dios, T453420,* is a good source of information on festivals, archaeological sites, history, etc. Gives
courses on music and dancing, and lectures some evenings. There is also an interesting but small
Museo Regional ① *Arica y Raimondi, Mon-Sat 1000-1300, 1500-1900.*

Huancavelica to Ayacucho

The direct route from Huancavelica to Ayacucho (247 km) goes via **Santa Inés** (4650 m), 78 km.
Out of Huancavelica the road climbs steeply with switchbacks between herds of llamas and
alpacas grazing on rocky perches. Around Pucapampa (Km 43) is one of the highest habitable
altiplanos (4500 m), where the rare and highly prized ash-grey alpaca can be seen. Snow-covered
mountains are passed as the road climbs to 4853 m at the Abra Chonta pass, 23 km before Santa
Inés. By taking the turnoff to Huachocolpa at Abra Chonta and continuing for 3 km you'll reach
one of the highest drivable passes in the world, at 5059 m. Nearby are two lakes (Laguna
Choclacocha) which can be visited in 2½ hours. 52 km beyond Santa Inés at the Abra de
Apacheta (4750 m), 98 km from Ayacucho, the rocks are all the colours of the rainbow, and
running through this fabulous scenery is a violet river. See Transport, below, for road services and
lodging options on this route.
   There is another route to Ayacucho from Huancayo, little used by buses, but which involves
not so much climbing for cyclists. Cross the pass into the Mantaro valley on the road to **Quichuas**.
Then to **Anco** and **Mayocc** (lodging). From here the road crosses a bridge after 10 km and in
another 20 km reaches **Huanta** in the picturesque valley of the same name. It celebrates the
Fiesta de las Cruces during the first week of May. Its Sunday market is large and interesting. Then
it's a paved road 48 km to Ayacucho. On the road from Huanta, 24 km from Ayacucho, is the site
of perhaps the oldest known human settlement in South America, 20,000 years old, evidence of
which was found in the cave of **Pikimachay**. The remains are now in Lima's museums.

⊚ Huancavelica listings

For hotel and restaurant price codes, and other relevant information, see Essentials.

⊜ Where to stay

Huancavelica *p1395*

$$$ Presidente, Plaza de Armas, T452760, http://huancavelica.hotelpresidente.com. pe/. Lovely colonial building, higher-priced suites available, heating, parking, safe, laundry, restaurant and café.

$ Ascención, Jr Manco Capac 481 (Plaza de Armas), T453103. A hidden treasure, no sign, use wooden door next to the Comisaría and follow the sign that says "Hotel". Very comfortable, wooden floors, with or without bath, hot water.

$ Camacho, Jr Carabaya 481, T453298. Shared showers, hot water morning only, secure, old-fashioned, good value.

$ La Portada, Virrey Toledo 252, T453603. Large rooms with private bath or small, basic rooms with shared bath with extra charge for TV. Lots of blankets, unlimited coca tea, helpful staff, good value, secure metal doors. Women may be put off by the public urinal in the shared shower area, but there is a better bathroom by the cafeteria.

$ San José, Jr Huancayo 299, T452958. Solar hot water in daytime, cheaper without bath or TV, secure, nice beds, helpful but basic.

Huancavelica to Ayacucho *p1395*

$ Alojamiento Andino, in Santa Inés, and a very friendly restaurant, **El Favorito**, where you can sleep. Several others.

$ Hostal Recreo Sol y Sombra, in Quichuas. Charming, small courtyard, helpful, basic.

⊘ Restaurants

Huancavelica *p1395*

$$-$ Mochica Sachún, Av Virrey Toledo 303. Great *menú* US$1.50, full meals available, sandwiches, friendly.

$$-$ Roma II, Manco Capac 580, T452608. Open 1800-2300. Pizzas, smells delicious, friendly staff, delivery available.

$ Chifa El Mesón, Manchego Muñoz 153, T453570. Very popular, standard *chifa* fare. Delivery available.

$ Joy, Virrey Toledo 230. Creole and regional dishes, sandwiches, long-established, award-winning, bright. Also **Joy Campestre**, Av de los Incas 870. Serves typical Peruvian regional dishes in leisurely country environment.

⊛ Festivals

Huancavelica *p1395*

The whole area is rich in culture. **Fiesta de los Reyes Magos y los Pastores**, **4-8 Jan**. Fiesta **del Niño Perdido** is held on **2nd Sun in Jan**. **Pukllaylay Carnavales**, celebration of the first fruits from the ground (harvest), **20 Jan-mid Mar**. Semana Santa, Holy Week. **Toro Pukllay** festival **last week of May, 1st week of Jun**. Fiesta de Santiago is held in **May and Aug** in all communities. **Los Laijas** or **Galas** (scissors dance), **22-28 Dec**.

⊝ Transport

Huancavelica *p1395*

Bus All bus companies have their offices on, and leave from the east end of town, around Parque M Castilla, on Muñoz, Iquitos, Tumbes and O'Donovan. To **Huancayo**, 147 km, 5 hrs, US$4, paved road, **Transportes Yuri** and **Transportes Ticllas** (O'Donovan 500). To **Lima** via Huancayo, 445 km, 13 hrs minimum, US$14. Most buses to Huancayo go on to Lima, there are several a day. The other route is to **Pisco**, 269 km, 12 hrs, US$12 and **Ica**, US$13, 1730 daily, with Oropesa, O'Donovon 599. Buy your ticket 1 day in advance. The road is poor until it joins the Ayacucho-Pisco road, where it improves. Most of the journey is done at night. Be prepared for sub-zero temperatures in the early morning as the bus passes snowfields, then for temperatures of 25-30°C as the bus descends to the coast. **Train** See under Huancayo; trains leave for Huancayo Mon-Sat 0630, 1230, Sun 0630.

Huancavelica to Ayacucho *p1395*

There is no direct transport from Huancavelica to Ayacucho, other than 0430 on Sat with **San**

Juan Bautista (Plazoleta Túpac Amaru 107, T803062), US$8. Otherwise you have to go to Rumichaca just beyond Santa Inés on the paved Pisco-Ayacucho road, also with San Juan Bautista, 0430, 4 hrs, then wait for a passing bus to Ayacucho at 1500, US$3, or try to catch a truck. Rumichaca has only a couple of foodstalls and some filthy toilets. This route is one of the highest continuous roads in the world. The journey is a cold one but spectacular as the road rarely drops below 4000 m for 150 km. The best alternative is to take a colectivo Huancavelica-Lircay, a small village with $ unnamed *hostal*

at Sucre y La Unión, with bath and hot water, much better than Hostal El Paraíso, opposite, also with bath, cheaper without (Transportes 5 de Mayo, Av Sebastián Barranca y Cercado, US$7.55, 2½ hrs, leave when full). The same company runs from Lircay Terminal Terrestre hourly from 0430 to Julcamarca (colonial church, Hostal Villa Julcamarca, near plaza, no tap water, really basic), 2½ hrs, US$6, then take a minibus from Julcamarca plaza to Ayacucho, US$4, 2 hrs; beautiful scenery all the way. Another option is to take the train to Izcuchaca, stay the night and take the colectivo (see above).

Ayacucho → *Phone code: 066. Colour map 3, C3. Population: 170,000. Altitude: 2748 m.*

A week can easily be spent enjoying Ayacucho and its hinterland. The climate is lovely, with warm, sunny days and pleasant balmy evenings, and the people are very hospitable. Semana Santa celebrations are famous throughout South America. Ayacucho was founded on 25 April 1540. On the Pampa de Quinua, on 9 December 1824, the decisive Battle of Ayacucho was fought, bringing Spanish rule in Peru to an end. In the middle of the festivities, the Liberator Simón Bolívar decreed that the city be named Ayacucho, 'Place of the Dead', instead of its original name, Huamanga.

The city is built round the Plaza Mayor, the main plaza, with the Cathedral, Municipalidad, Universidad Nacional de San Cristóbal de Huamanga (UNSCH) and various colonial mansions facing on to it. It is famous for its Semana Santa celebrations, its splendid market and its 33 churches. **Tourist offices:** iPerú ① *Portal Municipal 45, on the Plaza, T318305, iperuayacucho@promperu.gob.pe, daily 0830-1930, Sun 0830-1430.* Very helpful. Also has an office at the airport. **Dirección Regional de Industria y Turismo** (Dircetur) ① *Asamblea 481, T312548. Mon-Fri 0800-1700,* friendly and helpful. **Tourist Police** ① *Arequipa cuadra 1, T312055.*

Places in Ayacucho

The **Cathedral** ① *daily 1700-1900, Sun 0900-1700,* built in 1612, has superb gold leaf altars. It is beautifully lit at night. On the north side of the Plaza Mayor, at Portal de la Unión 37, are the **Casona de los Marqueses de Mozobamba del Pozo,** also called Velarde-Alvarez. Recently restored as the **Centro Cultural de la UNSCH,** frequent artistic and cultural exhibitions are held here; see the monthly Agenda Cultural. The **Casona Chacón** ① *Portal de la Unión 28, in the BCP building,* displays temporary exhibitions. North of the Plaza is **Santo Domingo** (1548) ① *9 de Diciembre, block 2, Mass daily 0700-0800.* Its fine façade has triple Roman arches and Byzantine towers.

Jr 28 de Julio is pedestrianized for two blocks. A stroll down here leads to the prominent **Arco del Triunfo** (1910), which commemorates victory over the Spaniards. Through the arch is the church of **San Francisco de Asís** (1552) ① *28 de Julio, block 3, daily for morning Mass and 1730-1830.* It has an elaborate gilt main altar and several others. Across 28 de Julio from San Fancisco is the **Mercado de Abastos Carlos F Vivanco,** the packed central market. As well as all the household items and local produce, look for the cheese sellers, the breads and the section dedicated to fruit juices.

Santa Clara de Asís ① *Jr Grau, block 3, open for Mass,* is renowned for its beautifully delicate coffered ceiling. It is open for the sale of sweets and cakes made by the nuns (go to the door at Nazareno 184, it's usually open). On the 5th block of 28 de Julio is the late 16th-century **Casona Vivanco,** which houses the **Museo Andrés A Cáceres** ① *Jr 28 de Julio 508, T066-812360, Mon-Sat 0900-1300, 1400-1800. US$1.25.* The museum has baroque painting, colonial furniture, republican

Ayacucho

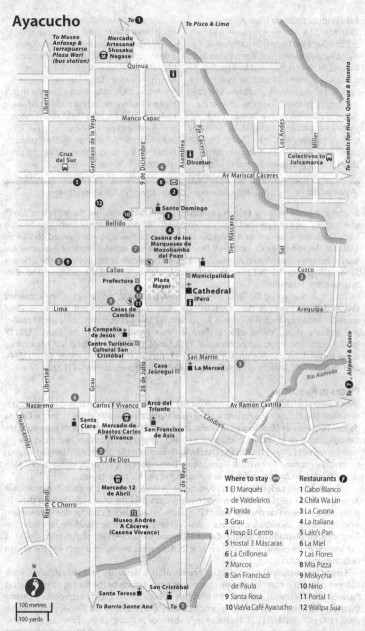

To Museo Anfasep & terrapuerto Plaza Wari (bus station)

Mercado Artesanal Shosaku Nagase

Quinua

To Pisco & Lima

To Huari, Quinua & Huanta

Libertad

Manco Capac

Garcilaso de la Vega

9 de Diciembre

Asamblea

Pje Cáceres

Los Andes

Miller

Cruz del Sur

Dircetur

Av Mariscal Cáceres

Colectivos to Julcamarca

Santo Domingo

Bellido

Casona de los Marqueses de Mozobamba del Pozo

Tres Máscaras

Sol

Cuzco

Callao

Prefectura

Plaza Mayor

Municipalidad

Cathedral

iPerú

Casas de Cambio

Arequipa

Lima

La Compañía de Jesús

Centro Turístico Cultural San Cristóbal

San Martín

La Merced

Río Alameda

To Airport & Cuzco

Casa Jáuregui

Libertad

Grau

28 de Julio

Nazareno

Carlos F Vivanco

Arco del Triunfo

Av Ramón Castilla

Huancasolar

Santa Clara

Mercado de Abastos Carlos F Vivanco

San Francisco de Asís

Londres

S J de Dios

2 de Mayo

Raymondi

C Chorro

Mercado 12 de Abril

Museo Andrés A Cáceres (Casona Vivanco)

N

100 metres
100 yards

Santa Teresa

San Cristóbal

To Barrio Santa Ana

To

Where to stay	Restaurants
1 El Marqués de Valdelirios	1 Cabo Blanco
2 Florida	2 Chifa Wa Lin
3 Grau	3 La Casona
4 Hosp El Centro	4 La Italiana
5 Hostal 3 Máscaras	5 Lalo's Pan
6 La Crillonesa	6 La Miel
7 Marcos	7 Las Flores
8 San Francisco de Paula	8 Mía Pizza
9 Santa Rosa	9 Miskycha
10 ViaVia Café Ayacucho	10 Nino
	11 Portal 1
	12 Wallpa Sua

and contemporary art, and exhibits on Mariscal Cáceres' battles in the War of the Pacific. Further south still, on a pretty plazuela, is **Santa Teresa** (1683) ① *28 de Julio, block 6, daily Mass, usually 1600*, with its monastery. The nuns here sell sweets and crystallized fruits and a *mermelada de ají*, made to recipe given to them by God; apparently it is not picante. **San Cristóbal** ① *Jr 28 de Julio, block 6, rarely open*, was the first church to be founded in the city (1540), and is one of the oldest in South America. With its single tower, it is tiny compared with Santa Teresa, which is opposite.

The 16th-century church of **La Merced** ① *2 de Mayo, open for Mass*, is the second oldest in the city. The high choir is a good example of the simplicity of the churches of the early period of the Viceroyalty. **Casa Jáuregui**, opposite, is also called **Ruiz de Ochoa** after its original owner. Its outstanding feature is its doorway, which has a blue balcony supported by two fierce beasts with erect penises.

Museo de Anfasep (Asociación Nacional de Familiares de Secuestrados Detenidos y Desaparecidos del Perú) ① *Prol Libertad 1226, 15 mins' walk from Mercado Artesanal Shosaku Nagase, or mototaxi, entry free but give a donation*, provides an insight into the recent history of this region during the violence surrounding the Sendero Luminoso campaign and the government's attempts to counter it.

For a fascinating insight into Inca and pre-Inca art and culture, a visit to **Barrio Santa Ana** is a must. The district is full of *artesanía* shops, galleries and workshops (eg **Wari Art Gallery** ① *Jr Mcal Cáceres 302, T312529, acwari@hotmail.com*, for textiles, and **Julio Gálvez** ① *Plazoleta Santa Ana 12, T314278*, for remarkable sculptures in alabaster – *piedra de huamanga*). Galleries are closed on Sunday.

Excursions

The Inca ruins of **Vilcashuamán** are 120 km the south, beyond Cangallo. Vilcashuamán was an important provincial capital, the crossroads where the road from Cuzco to the Pacific met the empire's north-south highway. Tours can be arranged with travel agencies in Ayacucho, US$13 per person, only with eight passengers, full day tour (0500-1800), including **Intihuatana** (Inca baths about one hour uphill from the village of Vischongo, one hour from Vilcashuamán, also Puya Raimondi plants at Titankayuq national sanctuary, one hour walk from Vischongo); alternatively stay overnight (three hotels, $, basic but clean). Market day is Wednesday. Buses and colectivos run from Avenida Cuzco 350, daily 0400-1500, four hours, US$7.50

A good road going north from Ayacucho leads to **Huari** ① *22 km from Ayacucho, 0800-1700, US$1*, dating from the 'Middle Horizon' (AD 600-1000), when the Huari culture spread across most of Peru. This was the first urban walled centre in the Andes. The huge irregular stone walls are up to 3-4 m high and rectangular houses and streets can be made out. The most important activity here was artistic: ceramics, gold, silver, metal and alloys such as bronze, which was used for weapons and for decorative objects. The ruins now lie in an extensive *tuna* cactus forest (don't pick the fruit). There is a museum at the site.

Quinua village, 37 km northeast of Ayacucho, has a charming cobbled main plaza and many of the buildings have been restored. There is a small market on Sunday. Nearby, on the Pampa de Quinua, a 44-m-high obelisk commemorates the battle of Ayacucho. A reenactment of the battle is held on 9 December, with college students playing the roles of Royalist and South American soldiers. The village's handicrafts are recommended, especially ceramics. Most of the houses have miniature ceramic churches on the roof. San Pedro Ceramics, at the foot of the hill leading to the monument, and Mamerto Sánchez, Jr Sucre, should be visited, but there are many others. **Fiesta de la Virgen de Cocharcas**, around 8 September. Trips can be arranged to Huari, La Quinua village and the battlefield; US$12 per person, minimum four people. Combis leave from Paradero a Huari Quinua, corner of Jr Ciro Alegría and Jr Salvador Cavero, when full from 0700; 40 minutes to Huari, US$1, then on to Quinua, 25 minutes, US$0.75 (US$1.50 from Ayacucho – ask the driver to go all the way to the Obelisco for an extra US$0.75).

⊙ Ayacucho listings

For hotel and restaurant price codes, and other relevant information, see Essentials.

⊜ Where to stay

Ayacucho *p1397, map p1398*

$$ San Francisco de Paula, Jr Callao 290, T312353, www.hotelsanfranciscodepaula.com. A bit like a museum with a nice patio, popular choice. Comfortable rooms and some suites with hot water. Will book El Encanto de Oro in Andahuaylas.

$$ Santa Rosa, Jr Lima 166, T314614, www.hotelsantarosa.com.pe. Lovely colonial courtyard in building with historical associations, roof terrace, warm rooms, hot water, attentive staff, car park, good restaurant with good value *menú*.

$$ ViaVia Café Ayacucho, Portal Constitución 4, Plaza de Armas, T312834, www.viaviacafe.com. Single, double and triple rooms with private bath, solar hot water 24 hrs, TV room, Spanish, Dutch and English spoken. The attached ViaVia restaurant and travellers' café overlooks the Plaza, offering international and Peruvian food, a lunch menú, lounge and live music on Sat, cultural events and tourist information.

$ El Marqués de Valdelirios, Alameda Valdelirios 720, T317040. Lovely colonial-style mansion, beautifully furnished, pick-up from the airport, hot water, bar, reserve at least 24 hrs in advance.

$ Florida, Jr Cuzco 310, T312565. Small, pleasant, quiet, patio with flowers, hot water from electric showers.

$ Grau, Jr San Juan de Dios 192, T312695, hotelgrau192@hotmail.com. Rooms on 3rd floor by the markets, with or without bath, hot water, laundry facilities, good value, safe but noisy, breakfast extra.

$ Hospedaje El Centro, Av Cáceres 1048, T313556. Rooms without bath and TV are cheaper than with, large rooms, hot water, good value, on a busy avenue.

$ Hostal 3 Máscaras, Jr 3 Máscaras 194, T312921, www.hoteltresmascaras.galeon.com. New rooms with bath better, but with less character, than the old ones without, nice colonial building with patio, hot water, breakfast extra, car park.

$ La Crillonesa, El Nazareno 165, T312350, www.hotelcrillonesa.com. Good value, hot water, laundry facilities, great views from roof terrace, loads of information, very helpful, Carlos will act as a local tour guide and knows everyone.

$ Marcos, 9 de Diciembre 143, T316867. Comfortable, modern, in a cul-de-sac half a block from the Plaza, quiet, hot water, price includes breakfast in the cafetería.

⊘ Restaurants

Ayacucho *p1397, map p1398*

Those wishing to try *cuy* should do so in Ayacucho as it's a lot cheaper than Cuzco. For a cheap, healthy breakfast, try *maca*, a drink of maca tuber, apple and quinoa, sold outside the market opposite Santa Clara, 0600-0800.

$$ Las Flores, Jr José Olaya 106, Plaza Conchopata, east of city. Daily 0900-1900. Specializes in *cuy*. Taxi US$1 from centre.

$$ Miskycha, Jr Callao 274. In a colonial mansion with regional decoration, good typical food and pleasant, helpful staff.

$$-$ La Casona, Jr Bellido 463. Open 1200-2200. Dining under the arches and in dining room, regional specialities, try their *puca picante*, *mondongo* and *cuy*, and a wide menu.

$$-$ Los Manglares de Tumbes, Av 26 de Enero 415, T315900. The best-established *cevichería* of several on this avenue, also does home delivery.

$$-$ Nino, Jr 9 de Diciembre 205, on small plaza opposite Santo Domingo church, T814537. Daily. Pleasant decor, terrace and garden (look for the owls in the trees); chicken, *parrillas*, pastas, pizzas, including take-away.

$ Cabo Blanco, Av Maravillas 198, T818740, close to Shosaku Nagase market (see Shopping). Open 0800-1800. *Ceviches*, seafood and fish dishes, small place with personal service. Also serves, beers, wines and cocktails.

$ Chifa Wa Lin, Asamblea 257. Very popular Chinese, said to be the best in town.

$ La Italiana, Jr Bellido 486, T317574. Open 1700-2300. Pizzería with a huge wood-burning oven for all to see.

$ Mía Pizza-Pizzería Karaoke, Av Mcal Cáceres 1045, T313273. Open 1800-0200. Pizzas *a la leña*, pastas and karaoke (also has a bar to get you in the mood for singing).

$ Wallpa Sua, Jr Garcilazo de la Vega 240.
A good chicken place, also with *parrillas*.
There are other chicken places in town,
eg **Tutos**, Jr Bellido 366, T312154 for delivery.

Cafés

Centro Turístico Cultural San Cristóbal, 28 de
Julio 178, some expensive cafés (eg **Lalo's**, No
115, open 0900-2100, café, pizza delivery and
bar) as well as other restaurants; all have tables
in the pleasant courtyard.
La Miel, Portal Constitución 11-12, on the Plaza,
T317183, 2 locations. Good coffee, hot drinks,
juices, shakes, cakes and snacks, also ice creams.
Lalo's Pan, Mcal Cáceres 1243. For breakfasts,
burgers and pies.
Portal 1, Portal Constitución 1. A good café
on the corner of the plaza serving snacks, light
meals and ice cream.

✷ Festivals

Ayacucho *p1397, map p1398*
The area is well-known for its festivals throughout
the year. Almost every day there is a celebration
in one of the surrounding villages. Check with the
tourist office. **Carnival in Feb** is reported as a wild
affair. **Semana Santa** begins on the Fri before
Holy Week. There follows one of the world's finest
Holy Week celebrations, with candle-lit nightly
processions, floral 'paintings' on the streets,
daily fairs (the biggest on Easter Saturday), horse
races and contests among peoples from all
central Peru. All accommodation is fully booked
for months in advance. Many people offer
beds in their homes during the week. Look out
for notices on the doors and in windows of
transport companies. **25 Apr** Anniversary of
the founding of Huamanga province. **1-2 Nov**
Todos Los Santos and Día de los Muertos.

O Shopping

Ayacucho *p1397, map p1398*
Handicrafts Ayacucho is a good place to buy
local crafts including filigree silver, which often
uses *mudéjar* patterns. Also look out for little
painted altars which show the manger scene,
carvings in local alabaster, harps, or the pre-Inca
tradition of carving dried gourds. The most
famous goods are carpets and *retablos*. In both

weaving and *retablos*, scenes of recent political
strife have been added to more traditional
motifs. For carpets, go to Barrio Santa Ana, see
under Places above. **Familia Pizarro**, Jr UNSCH
278, Barrio Belén, T313294. Works in textiles and
piedra huamanga (local alabaster) and Carnival
masks, good quality and all pieces individually
made. They also have rooms for visitors to stay
and take classes. **Mercado 12 de Abril**, Chorro
y San Juan de Dios. For fruit and vegetables.
Shosaku Nagase, on Jr Quinua y Av Maravillas,
opposite Plazoleta de María Parado de Bellido.
A large handicraft market.

☾ What to do

Ayacucho *p1397, map p1398*
A&R Tours, Jr 9 de Diciembre 130, T311300,
www.viajesartours.com. Open daily 0800-2000,
offers tours in and around the city. **Morochucos
Rep's**, Jr 9 de Diciembre 136, T317844, www.
morochucos.com. Dynamic company with
tours locally and to other parts of Peru,
flight and bus tickets. **Urpillay Tours**, Portal
Constitución 4, T315074, urpillaytours@ terra.
com. All local tours and flight tickets. **Wari
Tours**, Lima 138, T311415. Local tours. **Willy
Tours**, Jr 9 de Diciembre 107, T314075. Personal
guides, also handles flight and bus tickets.

⊖ Transport

Ayacucho *p1397, map p1398*
Air From/to **Lima**, 55 mins, with LC Peru (Jr 9
de Diciembre 160, T316 012) daily. **StarPerú**,
Portal Constitución 17, T316660. Taxi airport-
city centre US$3.
Bus Bus terminal **Terrapuerto Plaza Wari** at
final Av Javier Pérez de Cuéllar s/n, T311710,
northwest of centre, 10 mins. All bus companies
are installed here, but some may retain sales
counters in the centre (eg **Cruz del Sur**, Av Mcal
Cáceres 1264, T312813). To **Lima**, 8 hrs on a
good paved road, vía Ica, several companies
US$14-22 (**Molina** has the most services), plus
Cruz del Sur US$26 *regular*, US$37 *suite* and *VIP*
services, Tepsa US$37 presidencial;; and Civa,
US$26-41. For **Pisco**, 332 km, take a Ica/Lima
bus and get out at San Clemente, 5 hrs, 10 mins
from Pisco, and take a bus or combi (same fare
to San Clemente as for Ica).

To **Huancayo**, 319 km, 9-10 hrs, US$15-18, 3 daily with **Molina**, also **Turismo Central**, Manco Cápac 499, T317873, US$13 at 2030. The road is paved but poor as far as Huanta, thereafter it is rough, especially in the wet season, except for the last 70 km (paved). The views are stunning.

For **Huancavelica**, take a Libertadores 0730, or **Molina** 0800 bus as far as **Rumichaca**, US$3, where combis wait at 1030 for Huancavelica, 4 hrs. Otherwise take a Huancayo bus as far as **Izcuchaca**, then take another bus, a longer route.

Ayacucho to Cuzco

Beyond Ayacucho are two highland towns, Andahuaylas and Abancay, which are possible stopping, or bus-changing places on the road to Cuzco. The road towards Cuzco climbs out of Ayacucho and crosses a wide stretch of high, treeless páramo before descending through Ocros to the Río Pampas (six hours from Ayacucho). It then climbs up to **Chincheros**, 158 km from Ayacucho, and Uripa (good Sunday market).

Andahuaylas

Andahuaylas is about 80 km further on, in a fertile valley. It offers few exotic crafts, but beautiful scenery, great hospitality and a good market on Sunday. On the north side is the Municipalidad, with a small **Museo Arqueológico**, which has a good collection of pre-Columbian objects, including mummies. A good nearby excursion is to the **Laguna de Pacucha** ⓘ *colectivo from Av Los Chankas y Av Andahuaylas, at the back of the market, US$1, 40 mins*. On the shore is the town of Pacucha with a family-run hostal ($ on road from plaza to lake) and various places to eat. A road follows the north shore of the lake and a turn-off climbs to **Sóndor** ⓘ *US$0.65*, an Inca archaeological site at 3300 m. Various buildings and small plazas lead up to a conical hill with concentric stone terracing and, at the summit, a large rock or *intihuatana*. Each 18-19 June Sóndor Raymi is celebrated. Taxi from Andahuaylas, US$10; walk from Pachuca 8-10 km, or take a colectivo to Argama (also behind Andahuaylas market), which passes the entrance. With any form of public transport you will have to walk back to Pacucha, unless very lucky. **Tourist office: Dircetur** ⓘ *Av Túpac Amaru 374, T421627*.

Abancay → *Phone code: 084; Altitude: 2378 m*

Nestled between mountains in the upper reaches of a glacial valley, the friendly town of Abancay is first glimpsed when you are many kilometres away. The town is growing in importance now that the paved Lima-Nazca-Cuzco road passes through. **Tourist office** ⓘ *Lima 206, 0800-1430*, or Dircetur, *Av Arenas 121, p 1, T321664, apurimac@mincetur.gob.pe*. **Santuario Nacional de Ampay** ⓘ *US$1.50*, north of town, has lagoons called Angasccocha (3200 m) and Uspaccocha (3820 m), a glacier on Ampay mountain at 5235 m and flora and fauna typical of these altitudes. By public transport, take a colectivo to Tamburco and ask the driver where to get off. To get to the glacier you need two days' trekking, with overnight camping. See page 1386 for sites of interest between Abancay and Cuzco.

ⓔ Ayacucho to Cuzco listings

For hotel and restaurant price codes, and other relevant information, see Essentials.

ⓔ Where to stay

Andahuaylas *p1402*
$El Encanto de Apurímac, Jr Ramos 401 (near Los Chankas and other buses), T723527. With hot water, very helpful.
$El Encanto de Oro, Av Pedro Casafranca 424,

T723066, www.encantodeoro.4t.com. Modern, comfy, hot water, laundry service, restaurant, organizes trips on request. Reserve in advance.
$Las Américas, Jr Ramos 410, T721646. Near buses, bit gloomy in public areas, rooms are fine if basic, cheaper without bath, hot water, helpful.
$Sol de Oro, Jr Juan A Trelles 164, T721152. Good value, good condition, hot water, laundry service, garage, tourist information, restaurant alongside, near buses.

Abancay *p1402*

$$-$ Turistas, Av Díaz Barcenas 500, T321017, www.turismoapurimac.com. The original building is in colonial style, rooms a bit gloomy, breakfast not included. Newer rooms on top floor (best) and in new block are more expensive, including breakfast. Good restaurant (**$$**), wood panelled bar, parking.

$ Apurímac Tours, Jr Cuzco 421, T321446. Modern building, rooms with bath have tiny bathrooms, hot water, good value, helpful.

$ Hostal Arenas, Av Arenas 192, T322107. Well-appointed rooms, good beds, hot showers, helpful service, restaurant.

$ Imperial, Díaz Barcenas 517, T321538. Great beds, hot water, spotless, very helpful, parking, good value, cheaper without bath or breakfast.

🍴 Restaurants

Andahuaylas *p1402*

$ El Dragón, Jr Juan A Trellas 279. A recommended chifa serving huge portions, excellent value (same owner as Hotel El Encanto de Apurímac).

$ Il Gatto, Jr G Cáceres 334. A warm pizzería, with wooden furniture, pizzas cooked in a wood-burning oven.

$ Nuevo Horizonte, Jr Constitución 426. Vegetarian and health food restaurant, open for breakfast.

Abancay *p1402*

$ Focarela Pizzería, Díaz Bárcenas 521, T083-322036. Simple but pleasant décor, pizza from a wood-burning oven, fresh, generous toppings, popular (ask for *vino de la casa*!).

$ Pizzería Napolitana, Díaz Barcenas 208. Wood-fired clay oven, wide choice of toppings.

⏰ What to do

Abancay *p1402*

Apurimak Tours, at Hotel Turistas, see Where to stay. Run local tours and 1- and 2-day trips to Santuario Nacional de Ampay: 1-day, 7 hrs, US$40 per person for 1-2 people (cheaper for more people). Also a 3-day trip to Choquequirao including transport, guide, horses, tents and food, just bring your sleeping-bag, US$60 pp. **Carlos Valer**, guide in Abancay – ask for him at Hotel Turistas, very knowledgeable and kind.

🚌 Transport

Ayacucho to Cuzco *p1402*

Ayacucho to Andahuaylas, 261 km, takes 10-11 hrs (more in the rainy season), the road is being paved. It's in good condition when dry, but landslides occur in the wet. The scenery is stunning. Daytime buses stop for lunch at Chumbes (4½ hrs), which has a few restaurants, a shop selling fruit, bread and refrescos, and some grim toilets. **Los Chankas**, Pasaje Cáceres 150, T312391, at 0630 (without toilet) and 1900 (with toilet), US$15. **Celtur**, Pasaje Cáceres 174, T313194, 1830, US$15. Los Chankas' 1900 and Celtur are direct to **Cuzco**, but you still have to change buses in Andahuaylas. There are no other direct buses to Abancay or Cuzco.

Andahuaylas to Ayacucho Los Chankas, Av José María Arguedas y Jr Trelles, T722441, 0600 and 1800 or 1840, one coming from Cuzco. To **Abancay**, Señor de Huanca, Av Martinelli 170, T721218, 3 a day, 5 hrs, US$6; Los Chankas at 0630, US$7.50. To **Cuzco**, San Jerónimo, Av José María Arguedas 425, T801767, via Abancay, 1800 or 1830, also 1900 Sun, US$22, and Los Chankas. To **Lima**, buses go via Ayacucho or Pampachiri and Puquio: US$20. On all night buses, take a blanket.

In **Abancay**, 138 km from Andahuaylas, 5 hrs, the new Terminal Terrestre is on Av Pachacútec, on the west side of town. Taxi to centre US$1, otherwise it's a steep walk up to the centre. Several companies have offices on or near the El Olivo roundabout at Av Díaz Bárcenas y Gamarra, others on Av Arenas. Buses go to **Cuzco**, **Andahuaylas**, and **Nazca** (464 km, via Chalhuanca and Puquio), continuing to **Lima**. To **Cuzco**, 195 km, takes 4½ hrs, US$14-18. To Lima, Oltursa, US$66, Tepsa US$71. The scenery en route is dramatic, especially as it descends into the Apurímac valley and climbs out again.

Bus companies, all leave from Terminal Terrestre; office addresses are given: **Bredde**, Gamarra 423, T321643, 5 a day to Cuzco. **Los Chankas**, Díaz Bárcenas 1011, El Olivo, T321485. **Molina**, Gamarra 422, T322646. 3 a day to Cuzco, to Andahuaylas at 2330. **San Jerónimo**, to Cuzco at 2130 and Andahuaylas at 2130. **Señor de Huanca**, Av Arenas 198, T322377, 3 a day to Andahuaylas. Several others to Lima and Cuzco.

East and north of La Oroya

A paved road heads north from La Oroya towards Cerro de Pasco and Huánuco. Just 25 km north of La Oroya a branch turns east towards Tarma, then descends to the little-visited jungles of the Selva Central. This is a really beautiful run. North of La Oroya the road crosses the great heights of the Junín pampa and the mining zone of Cerro de Pasco, before losing altitude on its way to the Huallaga Valley. On this route you can connect by road to the Cordillera Blanca via La Unión.

Tarma and around → *Phone code: 064. Colour map 3, C3. Population: 55,000. Altitude: 3050 m.*
Founded in 1534, Tarma, 60 km from La Oroya, is a growing city but still has a lot of charm. The **Semana Santa celebrations** are spectacular, with a very colourful Easter Sunday morning procession in the main plaza. Accommodation is hard to find at this time, but you can apply to the Municipalidad for rooms with local families. The town is also notable for its locally made fine flower-carpets. Good, friendly market around Calle Amazonas and Ucayali. The surrounding countryside is beautiful. **Tourist office** ① *2 de Mayo 775 on the Plaza, T321010, ext 107, turismo@ munitarma.gob.pe, Mon-Fri 0800-1300, 1500-1800, very helpful; see www.tarma.info.* Around 8 km from Tarma, the small town of **Acobamba** has *tapices* made in San Pedro de Cajas which depict the Crucifixion. There are festivities during May. About 2 km up beyond the town is the **Santuario de Muruhuay**, with a venerated picture painted on the rock behind the altar.

Beyond Tarma the road is steep and crooked but there are few places where cars cannot pass one another. In the 80 km between Tarma and La Merced the road, passing by great overhanging cliffs, drops 2450 m and the vegetation changes dramatically from temperate to tropical. The towns of San Ramón and La Merced are in the province of **Chanchamayo**. **San Ramón** (*population 25,000*) is 11 km before La Merced and has several hotels (**$$$-$**) and restaurants. There are regular combis and colectivos between the two towns. **La Merced** (*population 20,000*) lies in the fertile Chanchamayo valley. Asháninka Indians can usually be found around the central plaza selling bows, arrows, necklaces and trinkets. There is a festival in the last week of September. There are several hotels (**$$-$**) and restaurants. For information, visit **Dircetur** ① *Pardo 110, San Ramón, T064-331265.*

About 25 km from La Merced along the road to Oxapampa, a road turns northeast to **Villa Rica**, centre of an important coffee growing area (hotels and restaurants). A very poor dirt road continues north to Puerto Bermúdez and beyond to join the Tingo María-Pucallpa road at Von Humboldt, 86 km from Pucallpa. **Puerto Bermúdez** is a great base for exploring further into the San Matías/San Carlos national reserve in the Selva Central Peruana, with trips upriver to the Asháninka communities. Tours are arranged by **Albergue Humboldt** (see Where to stay, below). To go further downriver to Pucallpa, there is road transport via Ciudad Constitución, about US$20 over two stages.

North of La Oroya
A paved road runs 130 km north from La Oroya to Cerro de Pasco. It runs up the Mantaro valley through canyons to the wet and mournful Junín pampa at over 4250 m, one of the world's largest high-altitude plains. An obelisk marks the battlefield where the Peruvians under Bolívar defeated the Spaniards in 1824. Blue peaks line the pampa in a distant wall. This windswept sheet of yellow grass is bitterly cold and the only signs of life are the youthful herders with their sheep and llamas. The road follows the east shores of the Lago Junín. The town of **Junín** lies some distance south of the lake and has the somewhat desolate feel of a high *puna* town, bisected by the railway (two hotels, **$, Leo** is very dirty).

The **Junín National Reserve** ① *US$5, ticket from Sernanp in Junín, Jr San Martín 138, T064-344146,* protects one of the best birdwatching sites in the central Andes where the giant coot and even flamingos may be spotted. It is easiest to visit from the village of Huayre, 5 km south of Carhuamayo, from which it is a 20-minute walk down to the lake. Fishermen are usually around to take visitors out on the lake. Carhuamayo is the best place to stay: **Gianmarco**, Maravillas 454, and **Patricia**, Tarapacá 862, are the best of several basic *hostales*. There are numerous restaurants along the main road.

Cerro de Pasco → *Phone code: 063. Population: 70,000. Altitude: 4330 m.*

This long-established mining centre, 130 km from La Oroya, is not attractive, but is nevertheless very friendly. Copper, zinc, lead, gold and silver are mined here, and coal comes from the deep canyon of Goyllarisquisga, the 'place where a star fell', the highest coal mine in the world, 42 km north of Cerro de Pasco. The town is sited between Lago Patarcocha and the huge abyss of the mine above which its buildings and streets cling precariously. Nights are bitterly cold.

Southwest of Cerro de Pasco by 40 km is **Huayllay**, near which is the **Santuario Huayllay (Bosque de Piedras)** ① *US$1, camping is permitted within the Sanctuary; Sernanp in Junín administers the site and there is a Comité del Santuario Nacional de Huayllay.* These unique weathered limestone formations are in the shape of a tortoise, elephant, alpaca, etc. At the Sanctuary (4100-4600 m), 11 tourist circuits through the spectacular rock formations have been laid out. The village of Huallay is 6 km southwest the sanctuary; it has a municipal hostel and other hotels. A festival of sports and music is held here 6-8 September. The Central Highway from Cerro de Pasco continues northeast another 528 km to Pucallpa, the limit of navigation for large Amazon river boats. The western part of this road (Cerro de Pasco-Huánuco) has been rebuilt into an all-weather highway. The sharp descent along the nascent **Río Huallaga** is a tonic to travellers suffering from *soroche*. The road drops 2436 m in the 100 km from Cerro de Pasco to Huánuco, and most of it is in the first 32 km. From the bleak high ranges the road plunges below the tree line offering great views. The only town of any size before Huánuco is **Ambo**.

Huánuco → *Phone code: 062. Colour map 3, B3. Population: 118,814. Altitude: 1894 m.*

This is an attractive Andean town on the Upper Huallaga with an interesting market. **Tourist office** ① *Gen Prado 716, on the Plaza de Armas, T512980.* A website giving local information is www.webhuanuco.com. About 5 km away on the road west to La Unión is **Kótosh** (*Altitude: 1912 m*) ① *US$0.75, including a guide around a marked circuit which also passes through a small botanical garden of desert plants, taxi US$5 from the centre, with 30 mins' wait.* At this archaeological site, the Temple of Crossed Hands, the earliest evidence of a complex society and of pottery in Peru, dates from 2000 BC. From Huánuco, a spectacular but very poor dirt road leads to **La Unión**, capital of Dos de Mayo district. It's a fast developing town with a couple of hotels ($) and restaurants, but electricity can be a problem and it gets very cold at night. On the pampa above La Unión is the large archaeological site of **Huánucopampa** or **Huánuco Viejo** ① *US$1.50, allow 2 hrs,* a 2½-hour walk from the town, an important Inca administrative centre with residential quarters (taxi US$6.50-9.50 with wait). It has impressive stonework and a fine section of Inca road running north and south. The route to the Callejón de Huaylas goes through **Huallanca**, an attractive town, with mining projects nearby. See Transport, below.

⊚ East and north of La Oroya listings

For hotel and restaurant price codes, and other relevant information, see Essentials.

⊜ Where to stay

Tarma and around *p1404*
$$$ Hacienda Santa María, 2 km out of town at Vista Alegre 1249, Sacsamarca, T321232, www.haciendasantamaria.com. A beautiful

(non-working) 17th-century hacienda, beautiful gardens and antique furniture. Includes breakfast. Excellent guides for local day trips.
$$$ Los Portales, Av Castilla 512, T321411, www.losportaleshoteles.com.pe. On the edge of town, hot water, heating, 1950s building with old furnishings, includes breakfast, good restaurant.
$$$-$$ Hacienda La Florida, 6 km from Tarma, T341041, www.haciendalaflorida.com.

18th-century working hacienda owned by German-Peruvian couple Inge and Pepe, who also arrange excursions. Variety of rooms sleeping 1-4, adjoining family rooms, dorm for groups and an independent house; all with hot water, meals available, lots of home-grown organic produce. Also camping for US$5.

$$ Normandie, beside the Santuario de Muruhuay, Acobamba, T064-341028, Lima T01-365 9795, www.hotelnormandie.com.pe. Rooms with hot water, bar, restaurant, tours offered.

$ El Caporal, Lima 616, T323636, hostalelcaporal@yahoo.es. Includes breakfast, good location, comfortable, hot water.

$ Hospedaje Residencial El Dorado, Huánuco 488, T321914, www.hospedajeeldoradotarma. com. Hot water, rooms set round a patio, 1st floor better, safe, welcoming, secure parking.

$ Hostal Aruba, Jr Moquegua 452 near the market, T322057. Hot water, nice rooms with tile floors, good value.

$ Hostal Central, Huánuco 614, T322625. Cheaper without bath, hot water, laundry facilities, bit rundown but popular, has observatory (opens Fri 2000, US$1 for non-guests).

$ La Colmena, Jauja 618, T321157. Well-maintained old building, convenient for Huancayo buses.

Puerto Bermúdez

$ Albergue Cultural Humboldt, by the river port (La Rampa), T063-963-722363, http:// alberguehumboldt.free.fr. The owner, Basque writer Jesús, has created a real haven for backpackers, with maps, library and book exchange. Rooms sleep 1-3, or there are hammocks and tents. Meals available, Spanish and Peruvian food. Jesús arranges tours, from day trips to camping and trekking in primary forest. Recommended.

Cerro de Pasco *p1405*

$ Hostal Arenales, Jr Arenales 162, near the bus station, T723088. Modern, TV, hot water in the morning.

$ Señorial, Jr San Martín 1, in the district of San Juan, 5 mins north of Cerro by taxi, T422802, hotelsenorial@hotmail.com. The most comfortable in town, hot water, fine view across the mine pit.

$ Welcome, Av La Plata 125, opposite the entrance to the bus station, T721883. Some rooms without window, hot water 24 hrs.

Huánuco *p1405*

$$$ Grand Hotel Huánuco (Inka Comfort), Jr D Beraún 775, T514222, www.grandhotel huanuco.com. With restaurant, pool, sauna, gym and parking.

$ El Roble, Constitución 629, T512515. Without bath, cheap and good value.

$ Hostal Miraflores, Valdizán 560, T512848, www.granhostalmiraflores.com. Hot water, private bathroom, quiet, safe, laundry service.

$ Imperial, Huánuco 581, T518737. With hot showers, quiet and helpful. Recommended.

$ Las Vegas, 28 de Julio 940, on Plaza de Armas, T512315. Small rooms, hot water, restaurant next door. Good.

Huallanca

$ Hostal Yesica, L Prado 507. Hot water, shared bathroom, the best of the basic ones.

$ Hotel Milán, 28 de Julio 107. Modern, hot water, best in town, good restaurant.

🍴 Restaurants

Tarma and around *p1404*

$ Chavín, Jr Lima 270 at Plaza de Armas. Daily 0730-2230. Very good quality and variety in set meals (weekdays only), also à la carte.

$ Chifa Roberto Siu, Jr Lima 569 upstairs. A good option for Chinese food, popular with locals.

$ Comedor Vegetariano, Arequipa 695. Open 0700-2100, but closed Fri after lunch and Sat. Vegetarian, small and cheap, sells great bread.

$ Señorial/Pollería El Braserito, Huánuco 138. Señorial is open daily 0800-1530, El Braserito, daily 1800-2300. Good *menú*, extensive choice of à la carte dishes.

Cerro de Pasco *p1405*

$ Los Angeles, Jr Libertad, near the market. Excellent *menú* for US$1.50. Recommended.

$ San Fernando, bakery in the plaza. Opens at 0700. Great hot chocolate, bread and pastries.

Huánuco *p1405*

$ Chifa Men Ji, 28 de Julio, block 8. Good prices, nice Chinese food.

$ Govinda, Prado 608. Reckoned to be the best vegetarian restaurant.

$ La Olla de Barro, Gral Prado 852, close to main plaza. Serves typical food, good value.

$ Pizzería Don Sancho, Prado 645. Best pizzas in town.

⊛ Festivals

Huánuco *p1405*
20-25 Feb Carnaval Huanuqueño. **3 May** La Cruz de Mayo. **16 Jul** Fiesta de la Virgen del Carmen. **12-18 Aug** Tourist Week in Huánuco. **28-29 Oct** Fiesta del Señor de Burgos, the patron of Huánuco. **25 Dec** Fiesta de los Negritos.

⊖ Transport

Tarma and around *p1404*
Bus To **Lima**, 231 km (paved), 6 hrs, US$15. Transportes Junín, Amazonas 667, 7 a day, with *bus cama* night bus (in Lima: Av Nicolás Arriola 198, T01-224 9220). Trans La Merced, Vienrich 420, 3 a day. Trans Los Canarios, Jr Amazonas 694 (2 daily) start in Tarma. Transportes Chanchamayo, Callao 1002, T321882, 2 a day, en route from Chanchamayo. To **Jauja**, US$2, and **Huancayo**, US$3, Transportes Angelitos/San Juan, from the stadium, 0800-1800, every 1¼ hrs; Trans Los Canarios about 1 per hr, 0500-1800; Trans Junín at 1200 and 2400. Colectivos depart when full from Callao y Jauja, 2 hrs, US$4, and 3 hrs, US$6, respectively. To **Cerro de Pasco**, Empresa Junín, Amazonas 450, 4 a day, 3 hrs, US$2.50. Also colectivos when full, 2 hrs, US$4. Buses to **La Oroya** leave from opposite the petrol station on Av Castilla block 5, 1 hr, US$1.50, while colectivos leave from the petrol station itself, 45 mins, US$2. To **Chanchamayo**, Transportes Angelitos/San Juan, 13 daily, 0600-2100, to La Merced US$1.75; Trans Junín, 4 a day, to San Ramón US$1.75, 1½ hrs, La Merced US$2.75, 2 hrs. Combis, US$1.75, and colectivos, US$4, from the stadium to La Merced.

Colectivos and Canary Tours **combis** to **Acobamba** and up to **Muruhuay**, 15 mins, US$0.30 and 0.45 respectively.

Note The local names for colectivos are 'carros' and 'stations'.

San Ramón
Air Flights leave from San Ramón. There is a small airstrip where **Aero Montaña**, T064-331074, rfmamsa@hotmail.com, has air taxis that can be chartered (*viaje especial*) to the jungle towns, with a maximum of 3 people, but you have to pay for the pilot's return to base. Flights cost US$250 per hr. **Puerto Bermúdez** takes 33 mins. You can also just go to the air base, across the river, on the east side of town.

La Merced
Bus Many buses go here from **Lima**: Expreso Satipo, Junín, La Merced and Chanchamayo each have several buses during the day, US$8 *regular*, US$11 *cama* upper level, US$12.50 *cama* lower level, 7-8 hrs. To **Tarma** Transportes Angelitos/San Juan, hourly, 2½ hrs, US$1.75, or colectivos, just over 1 hr, US$4. To **Puerto Bermúdez**, Empresa Transdife and **Villa Rica** have 4WD pick-ups between 0400 and 0600 and may pick up passengers at their hotels. You must purchase tickets in advance, the vehicles get very full. US$14 in front, US$8 in the back (worth spending the extra money), 8-10 hrs or more.

Cerro de Pasco *p1405*
Bus There is a large bus station. To **Lima** several companies including Carhuamayo and Transportes Apóstol San Pedro, hourly 0800-1200, plus 4 departures 2030-2130, 8 hrs, US$8. If there are no convenient daytime buses, you could change buses in La Oroya. To **Carhuamayo, Junín** and **La Oroya**: buses leave when full, about every 20-30 mins, to Carhuamayo 1 hr, US$1; to Junín 1½ hrs, US$1; to La Oroya, 2½ hrs, US$2. Colectivos also depart with a similar frequency, 1½ hrs, US$2.50, to La Oroya. To **Tarma**, Empresa Junín, 0600, 1500, 3 hrs, $2.50. Colectivos also depart hourly, 1½ hrs, US$4. To **Huancayo**, various companies leave throughout the day, 5 hrs, US$4. To **Huánuco**, buses and cars leave when full, about half hourly, 2½ hrs and 1½ hrs, US$2 and US$4 respectively.

Huayllay
Minibuses to Huallay from Cerro de Pasco's terminal leave throughout the day, about 1 hr, US$1. They return until 1800-1900.

Huánuco *p1405*

Air Airport T513066. From **Lima**, StarPerú and **LCPeru** (2 de Mayo 1355, T518113), daily, 55 mins.

Bus To **Lima**, US$18-25, 8 hrs. León de Huánuco, Malecón Alomía Robles 821, 3 a day. Also **Bahía Continental**, Valdizán 718, recommended, **Transportes El Rey**, 28 de Julio 1215 (28 de Julio 1192, La Victoria, Lima). The majority of buses of all companies leave 2030-2200, most also offer a bus at 0900-1000. A colectivo to Lima, costing US$23, leaves at 0400, arriving at 1400; book the night before at Gen Prado 607, 1 block from the plaza. Recommended. To **Cerro de Pasco**, 3 hrs, US$2, colectivos under 2 hrs, US$4. All leave when full from the Ovalo Carhuayna on the north side of the city, 3 km from the centre. To **Huancayo**, 7 hrs, US$6: **Turismo Central**, Tarapacá 530, at 2100. Colectivos run to **Tingo María**, from block 1 of Prado close to Puente Calicanto, 2½ hrs, US$5. Also **Etnasa**, 3-4 hrs, US2. For **Pucallpa**, take a colectivo to Tingo María, then a bus from

there. This route has many checkpoints and robberies can occur. Travel by day and check on the current situation regarding safety. To **La Unión**, Turismo Unión, daily 0730, 7 hrs, US$5; also Turismo Marañón daily 0700. This is a rough road operated also by El Niño colectivos, Aguilar 530, leave when full, US$7.15.

La Unión

Bus To **Huánuco**: Turismo Unión, Jr Comercio 1224 daily at 0600, US$8, 7 hrs. Also **Turismo Marañón**, Jr Comercio 1309, daily at 0700 (no afternoon/evening departures). *El Niño* colectivos, Jr Comercio 12, T062-515952, 5 hrs. To **Huallanca (Huánuco)**, combis leave from the market, about hourly, when full and follow the attractive Vizcarra valley, 1 hr, US$2. *El Rápido* runs to **Huaraz** 0400, 4½ hrs, US$8, or change in Huallanca. Combis leave when full about half hourly, from the corner of Comercio y 28 de Julio in Huallanca for La Unión. They also go to Laguna Pacahacoto from where another combi can be taken to Huaraz.

Amazon Basin

Cooled by winds sweeping down from the Andes but warmed by its jungle blanket, this region contains important tropical flora and fauna. In the north of the region, Iquitos, on the Amazon itself, is the centre of jungle exploration. It is a very varied landscape, with grasslands and tablelands of scrub-like vegetation, inaccessible swamps, and forests up to 2000 m above sea level. The principal means of communication in the jungle is by its many rivers, the most important being the Amazon, which rises high up in the Andes as the Marañón, then joins the Ucayali to become the longest river in the world. The northern tourist area is based on the River Amazon itself with, at its centre, a sizeable city, Iquitos. Although it has lost its rubber-boom dynamism, Iquitos is still at the heart of life on the river. There are jungle lodges upstream and down, each with its own speciality and level of comfort, but none more than half a day away by fast boat. To get right into the wilds, head for Peru's largest national reserve, Pacaya-Samiria, accessed by boat from Iquitos or the little town of Lagunas.

North from Huánuco to Pucallpa

Huánuco to Tingo María

The journey to Tingo María from Huánuco, 135 km, is very dusty but gives a good view of the jungle. Some 25 km beyond Huánuco the road begins a sharp climb to the heights of Carpish (3023 m). A descent of 58 km brings it to the Huallaga River again; it then continues along the river to Tingo María. The road is paved from Huánuco to Tingo María, including a tunnel through the Carpish hills. Landslides along this section are frequent and construction work causes delays. Although this route is reported to be relatively free from terrorism, robberies do occur and it is advisable to travel only by day.

Situated on the middle Huallaga, in the Ceja de Montaña, on the edge (literally 'eyebrow') of the mountains, **Tingo María** (*Phone code: 062; Population: 20,560; Altitude: 655 m; Annual* *rainfall: 2642 mm*) is isolated for days in the rainy season. The altitude prevents the climate from being oppressive. The Cordillera Azul, the front range of the Andes, covered with jungle-like vegetation to its top, separates it from the jungle lowlands to the east. The mountain which can be seen from all over the town is called La Bella Durmiente (the Sleeping Beauty). The meeting here of highlands and jungle makes the landscape extremely striking. Bananas, sugar cane, cocoa, rubber, tea and coffee are grown. The main crop of the area, though, is coca, grown on the *chacras* (smallholdings) in the countryside, and sold legitimately and otherwise in Tingo María. A small university outside the town, beyond the **Hotel Madera Verde**, has a little **museum-cum-zoo** ⓘ *free but a small tip would help to keep things in order*; it also maintains botanical gardens in the town. About 6.5 km from Tingo, on a rough road, is a fascinating cave, the **Cueva de las Lechuzas** ⓘ *US$1 for the cave, take a torch, and do not wear open shoes, getting there: take a motorcycle-taxi from town, US$1.75; cross the Río Monzón by new bridge.* There are many oilbirds in the cave and many small parakeets near the entrance. **Tourist office** ⓘ *Av Ericson 158, T562310, perucatapress@gmail.com.* Note that Tingo María is a main narco-trafficking centre and although the town is generally safe, it is not safe to leave it at night. Always keep to the main routes.

Tingo María to Pucallpa

From Tingo María to the end of the road at Pucallpa is 255 km, with a climb over the watershed – the Cordillera Azul – between the Huallaga and Ucayali rivers. The road is in poor shape for most of the journey, but some paving is in progress. Travel by day: it is safer the views are tremendous as you go from the high jungle to the Amazon Basin. Sit on the righthand side of the bus. When the road was being surveyed it was thought that the lowest pass over the Cordillera Azul was over 3650 m high, but an old document stating that a Father Abad had found a pass through these mountains in 1757 was rediscovered, and the road now goes through the pass of Father Abad, a gigantic gap 4 km long and 2000 m deep. At the top of the pass is a Peruvian Customs house; the jungle land to the east is a free zone. Coming down from the pass the road bed is along the floor of a magnificent canyon, the Boquerón Abad. It is a beautiful trip through luxuriant jungle, ferns and sheer walls of bare rock, punctuated by occasional waterfalls plunging into the roaring torrent below. East of the foot of the pass the all-weather road goes over the flat pampa, with few bends, to the village of **Aguaytía** (narcotics police outpost, gasoline, accommodation and restaurants). From Aguaytía the road continues for 160 km to Pucallpa – five hours by bus. There is a service station three hours before Pucallpa.

Pucallpa → *Phone code: 061. Colour map 3, B3. Population: 400, 000.*

Pucallpa is a rapidly expanding jungle town on the Río Ucayali, navigable by vessels of 3000 tons from Iquitos, 533 nautical miles away. Different 'ports' are used depending on the level of the river, they are all just mud banks without any facilities (see Transport, below).The economy of the area includes sawmills, plywood factories, oil refinery, fishing and boat building. Large discoveries of oil and gas are being explored. Local festivals are **Carnival** in February, **San Juan** on 24 June, and the Ucayali regional fair in October. The town is hot and dusty between June and November and muddy from December to May. **Note** There is narcotics activity in the area. The city itself is safe enough to visit, but don't travel at night. **Museo Regional** ⓘ *Carretera Federico Basadre Km 4.2, park entry US$1.10, Mon-Fri 0800-1630, Sat and Sun 0900-1730,* has some good examples of Shipibo ceramics, as well as some delightful pickled snakes and other reptiles. **Tourist office** Dircetur ⓘ *Jr 2 de Mayo 111, T578400, ucayali@mincetur.gob.pe, Mon-Fri 0730-1300, 1330-1515.* Information also at **Gobierno Regional de Ucayali (GOREU)** ⓘ *Raimondi block 220, T575018, www.regionucayali.gob.pe.*

Around Pucallpa The main attraction is **Lago Yarinacocha** ⓘ *to the northeast of Pucallpa, 20 mins by colectivo or bus along Jr Ucayali, US$0.50, or 15 mins by taxi,* an oxbow lake linked to the Río Ucayali by a canal at the northern tip of its west arm. River dolphins can be seen here. Puerto

Callao, also known as Yarinacocha or Yarina, is the main town, at the southern tip, reached by road from Pucallpa. There are a number of restaurants and bars here and it is popular at weekends. From Yarina, a road continues along the western arm to **San José**, **San Francisco** and **Santa Clara** (bus US$0.75). The area is populated by the Shipibo people, who make ceramic and textile crafts. The area between the eastern arm of the lake and the Río Ucayali has been designated as a reserve. Here, towards the northwestern shore of the east arm is the beautifully located **Jardín Botánico Chullachaqui** ① *free*, which can be reached by boat from Puerto Callao to Pueblo Nueva Luz de Fátima, 45 minutes, then one hour's walk to the garden (ask at Moroti-Shobo on the Plaza de Armas in Puerto Callao).

◉ North from Huánuco to Pucallpa listings

For hotel and restaurant price codes, and other relevant information, see Essentials.

● Where to stay

Tingo María *p1408*

$$$-$$ Madera Verde, Av Universitaria s/n, out of town on the road to Huánuco, near the University, T561800. Wooden chalets, cabins and rooms in beautiful surroundings, breakfast included, restaurant, 2 swimming pools, butterfly farm, free entry to wildlife rescue centre.

$$ Albergue Ecológico Villa Jennifer, Km 3.4 Carretera a Castillo Grande, 10 mins from Tingo María, T962-603509, www.villajennifer.net. Danish-Peruvian owned, includes breakfast, 2- to 4-night packages, US$50-90, and tours to local sites, pool, mini-zoo, birdwatching, restaurant, laundry service, phone ahead to arrange bus station pick-up. Rooms are surrounded by local flora, with lots of birdlife.

$$ Nueva York, Av Alameda Perú 553, T562406, joferjus@hotmail.com. Central and noisy, cheaper without bath and TV, laundry, good value, restaurant.

$ Hostal Marco Antonio, Jr Monzón 364, T562201. Quiet, restaurant of the same name next door.

Pucallpa *p1409*

$$$ Sol del Oriente, Av San Martín 552, T575154, www.soldelorientehoteles.com. Price includes breakfast and airport transfer, a/c, pool, mini-zoo, good restaurant, bilingual guides.

$$$-$$ Grand Hotel Mercedes, Raimondi 610, T575120, www.granhotelmercedes.com. Pucallpa's first hotel, still family-run, with some refurbished rooms, modern facilities with

old-fashioned ambiance, includes breakfast, hot water, a/c, fridge, pool, restaurant.

$$-$ Antonio's, Jr Progreso 545, T573721, antonios_hs@hotmail.com. A variety of rooms and prices, cheaper in older rooms or with fan, breakfast extra, cable TV, garden, pool, jacuzzi, parking, airport pick-up.

$$-$ Arequipa, Jr Progreso 573, T571348, www.hostal-arequipa.com. Good, a/c or fan, breakfast, comfortable, safe, restaurant, pool.

$ Barbtur, Raimondi 670, T572532. Cheaper without bath, central, good beds, cold water, friendly but noisy.

$ Komby, Ucayali 360, T571562. Cold water, fan, ample rooms, pool, very noisy street but back rooms are quiet, good value.

$ La Suite de Petita's Inn, Jr Fitzcarraldo 171, T572831. Includes simple breakfast, cold water, fan, fridge, parking.

Around Pucallpa: Yarinacocha *p1409*

$$$ Jana Shobo Amazonian Lodge, Lake Yarinacocha, T596943, www.otaku.ch/cyberboogie/JanaShoboweb/index_EN.htm. Small lodge is set in 10 ha of forest on the lakeshore. Bunk beds or camping. Price includes meals and airport transfer, packages and tours available. Living room, reading room and kitchen.

$$$ pp Pandisho Amazon Ecolodge, north of the village of 11 de Agosto, towards the northern tip of the eastern shore of the west arm, T061-799214, www.amazon-ecolodge. com (in Pucallpa, Pasaje Bolívar 261, T961-994227). Full board, good resort with cabins by the lakeshore, includes packages of varying length and rainforest expeditions. Also has lodges in Pacaya-Samiria, near Pucallpa at Honoria and near Iquitos.

$ **Los Delfines**, opposite Electroucayali in Puerto Callao. With bath, fan, fridge, some with TV.

🍴 Restaurants

Tingo María p1408
$ **El Antojito 2**, Jr Chiclayo 458. Local food.
$ **Girasol**, Av Raimondi 253, T562065. Chicken, burgers, cakes and fruit juices.

Pucallpa p1409
$$-$ **C'est si bon**, Jr Independencia 560 y Pasaje Zegarra, Plaza de Armas. Daily 0800-2400. Chicken, snacks, drinks, sweets, ice cream.
$$-$ **Chifa Xin Xin**, Jr Tarapacá 515 and Av Raimondi 603. Daily 1200-1600 and 1830-2300. Authentic Chinese cooking, set meals and à la carte.
$$-$ **El Viajero**, Jr Libertad 374. Sun-Fri 0800-1630. Choice of good set meals, also à la carte, very popular.
$$-$ **La Favorita**, Jr Adolfo Morey e Inmaculada. Daily 0800-1600. Regional and home cooking, good set meals Mon-Sat and *parrilladas* on Sun, popular.
$ **Tropitop Heladería**, Jr Sucre y Tarapacá 401 (Plaza de Armas). Good, cheap, typical breakfasts.

🛍 Shopping

Pucallpa p1409
Many Shibipo women carry and sell their products around Pucallpa and Yarinacocha.
Agustín Rivas, at Jr Tarapacá 861, above a small restaurant whose entrance is at No 863 (ask for it). For local wood carvings visit the workshop of this sculptor, whose work is made from huge tree roots.
Artesanías La Anaconda, Pasaje Cohen by Plaza de Armas, good selection of indigenous crafts.

🚌 Transport

Tingo María p1408
Bus To **Huánuco**, 119 km, 3-4 hrs, US$2 with Etnasa (not recommended – theft and drug-trafficking); take a micro, US$2, or colectivo, US$5, 2 hrs, several daily. Direct buses continue to Lima, 10 hrs, with Trans Rey, US$22 *bus cama*, León de Huánuco and

Bahía Continental (recommended, T01-424 1539), US$15. To **Pucallpa**, 5 hrs, US$15. Ucayali Express colectivos leave from Raimondi y Callao and Selva Express, Av Tito Jaime 218, T562380. Buses take 7-8 hrs, US$8.50, eg Etposa.

Pucallpa p1409
Air To **Lima** and **Iquitos**, daily 1 hr, flights with LAN (Jr Tarapacá 805 y San Martín, T579840) and Star Perú (7 de Junio 865, T590585). Airport taxis charge US$6 to town, outside taxis charge US$3.
Bus There are regular bus services to **Lima**, several companies, 18-20 hrs (longer in the rainy season, Nov-Mar), US$11-12.50 *regular*. Transmar, Av Raimondi 770, T579778 (in Lima Av Nicolás de Pierrola 197, T01-265 0190), US$17.50 *regular*, US$28 *bus cama* with a/c, US$25 *bus cama* without a/c. To **Tingo María**, bus US$8.50, 7-8 hrs, bound for Lima, also Etposa, 7 de Junio 843, at 1700. Or 5 hrs, US$15 by combi, leave from early morning, Turismo Ucayali, 7 de Junio 799, T593002, and Selva Express, Jr 7 de Junio 811, T579098. Take blankets as the crossing of the Cordillera at night is bitterly cold.
Ferry Boats to all destinations dock around Puerto Inmaculada, 2 blocks downriver from the Malecón Grau, at the bottom of Jr Inmaculada, unless the water level is very high, in which case they dock at Puerto Manantay, 4 km south of town. To **Iquitos** down the Ucayali and Amazon rivers, 3-4 days, longer if the water level is low and larger boats must travel only by day, hammock US$40, berth US$140 double. Henry is a large company with departures Mon, Wed, Fri and Sat from Puerto Henry at the bottom of Jr Manco Capac, by Jr Arica; their newer boats, *Henry 6* and *7*, have some cabins with private bath. Another good boat is *Pedro Martín 2* sailing from Puerto Inmaculada.
    You must ask around for the large boats to Iquitos. A mototaxi to any of the ports costs US$0.75 from the Plaza de Armas, taxis charge US$3. Departure times are marked on chalk boards on the deck. Schedules seem to change almost hourly. Do not pay for your trip before you board the vessel, and only pay the captain. Some boat captains may allow you to live on board a couple of days before sailing. Bottled

drinking water can be bought in Pucallpa, but not cheaply. See General hints for river travel, page 1420.

❶ Directory

Pucallpa *p1409*
Cultural centres Art school: Usko Ayar Amazonian School of Painting, in the house of artist Pablo Amaringo (died 2009), a former *vegetalista* (healer), Jr LM Sánchez, Cerro 465-467, see Facebook page. The school provides art classes for local people, and is dependent upon selling their art. The internationally renowned school welcomes overseas visitors for short or long stays to study painting and learn Spanish and/or teach English with Peruvian students. **Police** Policia Nacional, Jr Independencia 3rd block, T575211.

Yurimaguas and Pacaya-Samiria

Yurimaguas
The Río Huallaga winds northwards for 930 km. The Upper Huallaga is a torrent, dropping 15.8 m per kilometre between its source and Tingo María. The Lower Huallaga moves through an enervation of flatness, with its main port, Yurimaguas, below the last rapids and only 150 m above the Atlantic Ocean, yet distant from that ocean by over a month's voyage. Between the Upper and Lower lies the Middle Huallaga: the third of the river which is downstream from Tingo María and upstream from Yurimaguas.

Downriver of Tingo María, beyond Bellavista, the orientation is towards **Yurimaguas** (*Phone code: 065; Population: 25,700*), which is connected by road with the Pacific coast, via Tarapoto (120 km) and Moyobamba (see page 1294). It's a very relaxed jungle town and, as the roadhead on the lower Río Huallaga, is an ideal starting point for river travel in the Peruvian Amazon. A colourful Mercado Central is open from 0500-1200, full of fruit and animals, many, sadly, for the pot. Excursions in the area include the gorge of Shanusi and the lakes of Mushuyacu and Sanango. **Concejo Regional tourist office** ❶ *Mariscal Castilla 118, of 2, Mon-Fri 0745-1545, www.yurimaguas.net.*

Pacaya-Samiria
All river traffic to Iquitos stops at **Lagunas**, 12 hours from Yurimaguas, one of the entry points to the Pacaya-Samiria Reserve. The **reserve office** ❶ *Iquitos, SERNANP, Jorge Chávez 930/942, T223555, www.pacayasamiria.org, Mon-Fri 0700-1300, 1500-1700*, has general information and an updated list of tour operators authorized to enter the reserve. Entry costs US$2 for a day visit, US$23 for three days, US$46 for seven days, payable at the ranger stations. Pacaya-Samiria Reserve, at 2,080,000 ha, is the country's second largest protected area. It is bounded by the rivers Marañón and Ucuyali, narrowing to their confluence near the town of Nauta. The reserve's waterways and wetlands provide habitat for several cats including puma and jaguar, manatee, tapir, river dolphins, giant otters, black cayman, boas, 269 species of fish and 449 bird species. Many of the animals found here are in danger of extinction. There are 208 population centres in the area of the reserve, 92 within the park, the others in the buffer zone. Five native groups plus *colonos* live in the region.

The reserve can only be visited with an authorized guide arranged through a tour operator or a local community tourism association. Native guides generally speak only Spanish and native tongues. A list of authorized community associations is found in the reserve's web page and iPerú in Iquitos has a list of authorized operators. Most of the reserve is off-limits to tourists, but eight areas have been set up for visitors, these have shelters or camping areas, conditions are generally simple and may require sleeping in hammocks. Trips are mostly on the river and often include fishing. Four circuits are most commonly offered. All are rich in wildlife. 1) The basin of the Yanayacu and Pucate rivers is the most frequently visited; Laguna El Dorado is an important attraction in this area. It is accessed from **Nauta** on the Marañón, two hours by paved road from

Iquitos and three hours by *peque peque* or 1½ hours by *deslizador* from there to the reserve. Note that Nauta has pirate guides; best arrange a tour with an operator. 2) The middle and lower Samiria, accessed from Leoncio Prado (with a couple of *hospedajes*), 24 hours by *lancha* from Iquitos along the Marañón. Several lakes are found in this area. 3) The lower Pacaya, mostly flooded forest, accessed from Bretaña, on the Canal de Puinahua, a shortcut on the Ucayali, 24 hours by *lancha* from Iquitos. This area is less frequently visited than others. 4) The Tibilo-Pastococha area in the western side of the park, also in the Samiria basin, accessed from Lagunas on the Río Huallaga, 10-12 hours by *lancha* or three hours by *deslizador* from Yurimaguas and 48 hours by *lancha* from Iquitos. Another way of visiting the reserve is on a cruise, sailing along the main rivers on the periphery of the park. These tours are offered by some Iquitos operators.

◉ Yurimaguas and Pacaya-Samiria listings

For hotel and restaurant price codes, and other relevant information, see Essentials.

◔ Where to stay

Yurimaguas *p1412*
$$$-$$ Río Huallaga, Arica 111, T768329, www.riohuallagahotel.com. Nice modern hotel overlooking the river, safety box, pool, bar, rooftop restaurant with lovely views.
$$-$ Luis Antonio, Av Jaúregui 407, T352061, hostal_luis_antonio@hotmail.com. Cold water, small pool, a/c at extra cost, breakfast, very helpful.
$$-$ Posada Cumpanama, Progreso 403, T352905, http://posadacumpanama.blogspot.com. Rooms cheaper with shared bath, breakfast extra, tastefully decorated, pool, very pleasant.
$ Hostal Akemi, Jr Angamos 414, T352237, www.hostalakemi.com. Decent rooms with hot water, cheaper without a/c, some with frigobar, restaurant, pool, helpful owner, good value.
$ Hostal El Caballito, Av Jaúregui 403, T352864. Cold water, small bathroom, fan, pleasant, good value.
$ Hostal El Naranjo, Arica 318, T352650, www.hostalelnaranjo.com.pe. A/c or fan, hot water, frigobar, small pool, with restaurant.

Pacaya-Samiria: Lagunas *p1412*
Basic places in town include: all **$ Eco**, Jr Padre Lucero, near cemetery, T503703; **Hostal Miraflores**, Miraflores 1 block from plaza; **Samiria**, Jr José Cárdenas, near the market.

Pacaya-Samiria: Nauta
Basic places in town include: all **$ La Granja Azul**, near entrance to town; **Nauta Inn**, Manuel Pacaya by Laguna Sapi Sapi, T411025.

Pacaya-Samiria Reserve *p1412*
$$$$ Pacaya Samiria Amazon Lodge, www.pacayasamiria.com.pe. In Iquitos T065-225769. Beautifully designed lodge on a hill overlooking the Marañón, just inside the reserve but close to road and town. All buildings in indigenous style, with balconies and en-suite bathrooms, restaurant, bar. Community visits and specialist birdwatching trips included in the price, but boat trips (also included) can be long. Camping trips can be arranged deeper inside the reserve.

◑ What to do

Yurimaguas *p1412*
Samiria Expeditions, Río Huallaga Hotel, www.peruselva.com. Tours to lakes, day and multi-day trips to Pacaya-Samiria, work with Hauyruro Tours in Lagunas.

Pacaya-Samiria *p1412*
Community associations in many of the villages around the reserve run tours. **Consorcio Rumbo al Dorado**, www.yacutayta.org, groups 3 communities in the Yanayacu-Pucate region. In the community of San Martín de Tipishca in the Samiria Basin are **Asiendes** (Asociación Indígena en Defensa de la Ecología Samiria), T965-861748, asiendesperu@hotmail.com and **Casa Lupuna**. 5 associations operate in Lagunas; a tour operator is **Huayruro Tours**, T065-401203, www.peruselva.com. In Bretaña the **Gallán** family offer tours. Community tours cost US$46-

70 pp per day, agency tours arranged in Iquitos start at US$80. Make sure you know exactly what is included: park fees, lodging, food, transport, guide. Also what the trip involves: most of the day in a canoe, walking, hunting, fishing, type of accommodation.

⊖ Transport

Yurimaguas p1412

Air The military Grupo Aéreo 42 (Bolívar 128, T981-664986) has passenger flights to Yurimaguas originating in Trujillo or Iquitos; see page 1261 for routes and schedules.
Bus The road to Tarapoto is paved. Paredes Estrella, Mariscal Cáceres 220, 0830 daily to **Lima** (32-34 hrs, US$38.50) via **Tarapoto** (US$4), **Moyobamba** (US$7.75, 5-6 hrs), **Pedro Ruiz** (US$17.50), **Chiclayo** (US$27) and **Trujillo**

(US$33). Also **Ejetur**, 0500 to Lima. Faster than the bus to Tarapoto are: **Gilmer Tours**, C Victor Sifuentes 580, frequent mini-buses, US$5.75, 2½ hrs; cars (eg **San Martín**) US$7.75; and combis (Turismo Selva, Mcal Cáceres 3rd block) US$4.
Ferry There are 6 docks in all. To **Iquitos** from Embarcadero La Boca, 3 days/2 nights, Eduardo/Gilmer company is best, Elena Pardo 114, T352552 (see under Iquitos, Tansport). To **Lagunas** for Pacaya Samiria Reserve, from Embarcadero Abel Guerra at 0900, US$11.55, 10 hrs.

⊙ Directory

Yurimaguas p1412
Banks Several banks with ATMs. Casa de cambio Progreso, Progreso 117, changes US$ cash.

Iquitos and around → Phone code: 065. Colour map 3, A4. Population: 600,000.

Iquitos stands on the west bank of the Amazon and is a chief town of Peru's jungle region. Some 800 km downstream from Pucallpa and 3646 km from the mouth of the Amazon, the city is completely isolated except by air and river. Its first wealth came from the rubber boom (late 19th century to second decade of 20th century). The main economic activities are logging, commerce and petroleum and it is the main starting point for tourists wishing to explore Peru's northern jungle. It is hot, dirty and noisy from the tens-of-thousands of mototaxis and motorcycles that fill the streets.

The incongruous **Iron House/Casa de Fierro** stands on the Plaza de Armas, designed by Eiffel for the Paris exhibition of 1889. It is said that the house was transported from Paris by a local rubber baron and is constructed entirely of iron trusses and sheets, bolted together and painted silver. It now houses a pharmacy. Of special interest are the older buildings, faced with *azulejos* (glazed tiles). They date from the rubber boom of 1890 to 1912, when the rubber barons imported the tiles from Portugal and Italy and ironwork from England to embellish their homes. The **Casa de Barro** on the Plaza (house of the controversial rubber baron Fitzcarrald), is now a bank. **Museo Amazónico** ① *Malecón Tarapacá 386, T234221, Mon-Sat 0800-1300, 1430-1730, Sun 0800-1230, free, some guides speak English, tip expected*, in the Prefectura, has displays of native art and sculptures by Lima artist Letterstein. **Museo de Culturas Indígenas Amazónicas** ① *Malecón Tarapacá 332, T235809, 0800-1930, US$5.25*, the private museum of Dr Richard Bodmer, who owns the **Casa Morey** hotel (see below), celebrating cultures from the entire Amazon region. Ask here about historic Amazonian boats (www.amazoneco.com). The waterfront by Malecón Maldonado, known as 'Boulevard', is a pleasant place for a stroll and gets busy on Friday and Saturday evenings.

Belén, the picturesque, lively waterfront district, is worth visiting, but is not safe at night. Most of its huts are built on rafts to cope with the river's 10 m change of level during floods (January-July); now they're built on stilts. On Pasaje Paquito are bars serving local sugar cane rum. The main plaza has a bandstand made by Eiffel. In the high season canoes can be hired on the waterfront for a tour of Belén, US$3 per hour. The market at the end of the Malecón is well worth visiting, though you should get there before 0900 to see it in full swing.

Tourist offices: i perú ① *Jr Napo 161, of 4, T236144, iperuiquitos@promperu.gob.pe, Mon-Sat 0900-1800, Sun 0900-1300,* also at the airport, at flight times. Both offices are helpful. If arriving by air, go first to this desk. They will give you a list of hotels, a map, tell you about the touts outside the airport etc. Both www.iquitosnews.com and www.iquitostimes.com have articles, maps and information. See also www.jungle-love.org. **Indecopi** ① *Putumayo 464, T243490, jreategui@ indecopi.gob.pe, Mon-Fri 0830-1630.*

Iquitos

Where to stay 🛏
1 Casa Morey
2 El Dorado Isabel
3 El Dorado Plaza
4 El Sitio
5 Flying Dog Hostel
6 Green Track Hostel
7 Hostal El Colibrí
8 La Casa Fitzcarraldo
9 La Casona
10 Las Amazonas Inn
11 Marañón
12 Royal Inn
13 Samiria Jungle
14 Sol del Oriente
15 Victoria Regia

Restaurants 🍴
1 Amazon Bistro
2 Antica Pizzería
3 Ari's Burger
4 Chez Maggy Pizzería
5 El Carbón
6 El Sitio
7 Fitzcarraldo
8 Helados La Muyuna
9 Huasaí
10 La Gran Maloca
11 María's Café
12 Panadería Tívoli
13 Yellow Rose of Texas

Bars & clubs 🍸
14 Arandú
15 Camiri
16 La Parranda
17 Noa Noa

Excursions

There are pleasant beaches at **Tipishca** on the Río Nanay, reached in 20 minutes by boat from Puerto de Santa Clara near the airport, it gets quite busy at weekends, and, quieter, **Santa Rita**, reached from Puerto de Pampa Chica, on a turnoff, off the road to the airport. Beaches appear when the river is low, July-September. **Pilpintuhuasi Butterfly Farm** ① *near the village of Padre Cocha, T232665, www.amazonanimalorphanage.org, US$7.75, students US$4, includes guided tour, Tue-Sun 0900-1600, guided tours at 0930, 1100, 1330 and 1500*, as well as butterflies, has a small well-kept zoo, Austrian-Peruvian run. Colectivo from Bellavista to Padre Cocha takes 20 minutes, walk from there. If the river is high, boats can reach Pilpintuhuasi directly (no need to walk), a speedboat charges US$25 return including waiting time (pay at the end).

Along the road to Nauta, which is 100 km from Iquitos, are several attractiosn and balnearios. At Km 4.5 on the road to Nauta is **Centro de Rescate Amazónico** ① *http://gonzalomatosuria. blogspot.com/p/fundacion-iquitos-centro-de-rescate_20.html, daily 0900-1500, free, must show ID*, where orphaned manatees are nursed until they can be released. A good place to see this endangered species. The beautiful **Lake Quistococha** in lush jungle is at Km 6.5, with a fish hatchery at the lakeside. There's a two-hour walk through the surrounding jungle on a clearly marked trail, bars and restaurants on the lakeside and a small beach. Boats are for hire on the lake and swimming is safe but take insect repellent against sandflies.

Allpahuayo-Mishana Reserve ① *SERNANP, Jorge Chávez 930/942, T223555, Mon-Fri 0700-1300, 1500-1700, reserve fees: US$8.50, students US$6.25*. On the Río Nanay, some 25 km south of Iquitos by the Nauta road or two hours by boat from Bellavista, this reserve protects the largest concentration of white sand jungle (*varillales*) in Peru. Part of the Napo ecoregion, biodiversity here is among the highest in the Amazon basin. It has several endangered species including two primates, several endemic species; the area is rich in birds (475 species have been recorded). Within the reserve are **Zoocriadero BIOAM**, Km 25, a good birdwatching circuit in land belonging to the Instituto Nacional de Innovación Agraria (INIA); **Jardín de Plantas Medicinales y Frutales** ① *at Km 26.8, 0800-1600, guiding 0800-1000*; and at Km 28, **El Irapay** interpretation centre ① *Mon-Sat 0830-1430*, with a trail to Mishana village by the river.

Border with Brazil

Details on exit and entry formalities seem to change frequently, so when leaving Peru, check in Iquitos first at Immigration or with the Capitanía at the port. Boats stop in Santa Rosa for Peruvian exit formalities. Santa Rosa has five simple hotels, **Diana** and **Las Hamacas** are reported better than the others, price around US$15 for a double. All other details are given in the Brazil chapter.

ⓔ Iquitos and around listings

For hotel and restaurant price codes, and other relevant information, see Essentials.

⊖ Where to stay

Iquitos *p1414, map p1415*
Around Peruvian Independence Day (27 and 28 Jul) and Easter, Iquitos can get crowded and prices rise at this time.

$$$$ El Dorado Plaza, Napo 258 on main plaza, T222555, www.grupo-dorado.com. Good accommodation and restaurant, bar, business-type hotel, pool, prices include service, small breakfast, welcome drink and transfer to/from airport. Also owns **$$$ El Dorado Isabel**, Napo 362, T232574.

$$$$ Samiria Jungle, Ricardo Palma 159, T223232, www.samiriajunglehotel.com. Modern upmarket hotel, includes airport transfers, large suites and rooms, frigobar, bathtub, restaurant, bar, pool, meeting rooms.

$$$ Casa Morey, Raymondi y Loreto, Plaza Ramón Castilla, T231913, www.casamorey.com. Boutique hotel in a beautifully restored historic rubber-boom period mansion. Great attention to detail, includes airport transfers, ample comfortable rooms, pool, good library.

$$$ Sol del Oriente, Av Quiñónez Km 2.5

on the way to the airport, T260317, www.
soldelorientehoteles.com. Airport transfers, pool,
internet in hall, nice gardens, deco a bit kitsch.
$$$ Victoria Regia, Ricardo Palma 252,
T231983, www.victoriaregiahotel.com. Free
map of city, safe deposit boxes in rooms, good
restaurant, indoor pool.
$$$-$$ La Casa Fitzcarraldo, Av La Marina
2153, T601138, http://casafitzcarraldo.com/.
Prices vary according to room. Includes
breakfast and airport transfer, with Wi-Fi,
satellite TV, minibar, 1st-class restaurant,
treehouse, pool in lovely gardens, captive
animals. The house was the home of Walter
Saxer, the executive-producer of Werner
Herzog's famous film, lots of movie and
celebrity memorabilia.
$$$-$$ Marañón, Fitzcarrald y Nauta 289,
T242673, http://hotelmaranon.com. Multi-
storey hotel, spotless comfortable rooms, a/c,
convenient location, small pool.
$$ Royal Inn & Casino, Aguirre 793, T224244,
www.royalinncasinohotel.com. Modern,
comfortable, frigobar and, bidet, airport
transfer, good.
$$-$ Flying Dog Hostel, Malecón Tarapacá
592, T223755, www.flyingdogperu.com. Nice
old house, pleasant 4 bed dorms and private
rooms with bath and a/c or fan, clean kitchen,
lockers, arrange tours.
$$-$ Hostal Colibrí, Raymondi 200, T241737,
hostalelcolibri@hotmail.com. 1 block from Plaza
and 50 m from the river so can be noisy, nicely
refurbished house, a/c or fan, hot water, secure,
good value, breakfast extra, helpful staff.
$$-$ La Casona, Fitzcarald 147, T234 394,
www.hotellacasonaiquitos.com.pe. In building
dating from 1901, now modernized, hot water,
fan or a/c, kitchen facilities, small patio, pool,
popular with travellers. Opposite, at Fitzcarald
152, is Hostal La Casona Río Grande, with
smaller rooms, fan. Transport to either from
the airport with advance reservation.
$ Green Track Hostel, Ricardo Palma 540,
T997 829118, www.greentrack-travel.com.
Nice hostel, dorms with a/c or fan, 1 private
room with bath, free pick up with advanced
booking, English spoken, helpful owners,
tours arranged to Tapiche Ohara's Reserve.
$ El Sitio, Ricardo Palma 541, T234932.
Fan, private bath, cold water, good value.

$ Las Amazonas Inn, Ricardo Palma 460,
T225367, las_amazonas_inn_iquitos@yahoo.es.
Simple rooms with electric shower, a/c, kitchen
facilities, breakfast available, pleasant owner.

🍴 Restaurants

Iquitos *p1414, map p1415*
Local specialities Try palm heart salad
(*chonta*), or *a la Loretana* dish on menus; also
try *inchicapi* (chicken, corn and peanut soup),
cecina (fried dried pork), *tacacho* (fried green
banana and pork, mashed into balls and eaten
for breakfast or tea), *juanes* (chicken, rice, olive
and egg, seasoned and wrapped in bijao leaves
and sold in restaurants) and the *camu-camu*, an
acquired taste, said to have one of the highest
vitamin C concentrations in the world. For a
good local breakfast, go to the Mercado Central,
C Sargento Lores, where there are several
kioskos outside, popular and cheap. Avoid
eating endangered species such as paiche,
caiman or turtle, which are sometimes on
menus. Try the local drink *chuchuhuasi*, made
from the bark of a tree, which is supposed to
have aphrodisiac properties (for sale at Arica
1046), and *jugo de cocona*, and the alcoholic
cola de mono and *siete raices* (aguardiente
mixed with the bark of 7 trees and wild honey),
sold at Musmuqui, Raymondi 382, Mon-Sat
from 1900.
$$$ Al Frío y al Fuego, on the water, go to
Embarcadero Turístico and their boat will pick
you up, T224862. Mon 1830-2300, Tue-Sat
1130-1600 and 1830-2300, Sun 1130-1600.
Good upscale floating restaurant with regional
dishes, seafood specialties.
$$$ Fitzcarraldo, Malecón Maldonado 103 y
Napo. Smart, pizza, also good pastas and salads.
$$$ La Gran Maloca, Sargento Lores 170,
opposite Banco Continental. Closes 2000 on Sun,
other days 2300. A/c, high class regional food.
$$ Ari's Burger, Plaza de Armas, Próspero 127.
Medium-priced fast food, breakfasts, popular
with tourists but hygiene questionable.
$$ Yellow Rose of Texas, Putumayo 180.
Open 24 hrs so you can wait here if arriving
late at night. Varied food including local dishes,
Texan atmosphere, good breakfasts, lots of
information, also has a bar, Sky TV and Texan
saddle seats.

$$-$ Antica Pizzería, Napo 159. Sun-Thu 0700-2400, Fri-Sat 0700-0100. Very nice pizza and Italian dishes, pleasant ambiance especially on the upper level, also serves breakfast, try the *desayuno Loretano*.

$$-$ Arapaíma Gigas, Carr a Zungarococha Km 1. Open for lunch. Just outside the city, a restaurant with its own fish farm in a lake. They catch whatever you request and cook it immediately; ceviche de paiche on Sun.

$$-$ Chez Maggy Pizzería, Raymondi 177. Daily 1800-0100. Wood oven pizza and homemade pasta.

$ El Carbón, La Condamine 115. Open 1900-2300 only. Grilled meats, salads, regional side-dishes such as tacacho and patacones.

$ El Sitio, Sargento Lores 404. Mon-Sat 1930-2230. A simple place for *anticuchos* for all tastes including vegetarian, popular.

$ Huasaí, Fitzcarrald 131. Open 0715-1615, closed Mon. Varied and innovative menu, popular, good food and value, go early.

Cafés

Amazon Bistro, Malecón Tarapacá 268. Upscale French bistro/bar on the waterfront, drinks, snacks, breakfasts and meal of the day. Trendy and popular.

Helados La Muyuna, Jr Próspero 621. Good natural jungle fruit ice cream. Second location on Napo near Malecón.

María's Café, Nauta 292. Opens 0800, closed Mon and 1230-1600. Breakfasts, sandwiches, burgers, coffee and cakes, with desserts of the day.

Panadería Tívoli, Ricardo Palma, block 3, a variety of good bread and sweets.

🍸 Bars and clubs

Iquitos *p1414, map p1415*
Arandú, Malecón Maldonado. Good views of the river.

Camiri, Pevas at the shore. Floating bar, pleasant atmosphere.

La Parranda, Pevas, cuadra 1. Drinks, live music, dancing, Latin music, 80s rock.

Noa Noa, Pevas y Fitzcarrald. Popular disco with cumbia and Latin music.

⊛ Festivals

Iquitos *p1414, map p1415*
5 Jan Founding of Iquitos. **Feb-Mar** Carnival. **3rd week in Jun** Tourist week. **24 Jun** San Juan. **28-30 Aug** Santa Rosa de Lima. **8 Dec** Immaculate Conception, celebrated in Punchana, near the docks.

○ Shopping

Iquitos *p1414, map p1415*
Hammocks in Iquitos cost about US$12.
Amazon Arts & Crafts: Mercado Artesanal Anaconda, by the waterfront at Napo. Asociación de Artesanos El Manguaré, kiosks on Jr Nauta, block 1. **Comisesa**, Arica 471, sells rubber boots, torches (flashlights), rain ponchos and other gear. **Mad Mick's Trading Post**, Putumayo 163, top floor, next to the Iron House, hires out rubber boots for those going to the jungle. **Mercado Artesanal de Productores**, 4 km from the centre in the San Juan district, on the road to the airport, take a colectivo. Cheapest in town with more choice than elsewhere.

◑ What to do

Iquitos *p1414, map p1415*
Jungle tours from Iquitos Agencies arrange 1-day or longer trips to places of interest with guides speaking some English. Package tours booked in your home country, over the internet or in Lima are much more expensive than those booked locally. Take your time before making a decision and don't be bullied by the hustlers at the airport (they get paid a hefty commission). You must make sure your tour operator or guide has a proper licence (check with i perú). Do not go with a company which does not have legal authorization; there are many unscrupulous people about. Find out all the details of the trip and food arrangements before paying (a minimum of US$50 per day). Speed boats for river trips can be hired by the hour or day at the Embarcadero Turístico, at the intersection of Av de la Marina and Samánez Ocampo in Punchana. Prices vary greatly, usually US$15-20 per hr, US$80 for speedboat, and are

negotiable. In fact, all prices are negotiable, except **Muyuna**, **Heliconia Lodge** and **Explorama**, who do not take commissions.

There are several agencies that arrange river cruises in well-appointed boats. Most go to the Pacaya-Samiria region, very few towards Brazil. In addition to the vessels of Aqua and Delfín (see below), other options include La Amatista of the Dorado hotel group, the Aquamarina, Arapaima and Queen Violeta group and Estrella Amazónica. Contact a company like Rainforest Cruises, www.rainforestcruises.com, for options.

General information and advice Take a long-sleeved shirt, waterproof coat and shoes or light boots on jungle trips and binoculars and a good torch, as well as espirales to ward off the mosquitoes at night – they can be bought from pharmacies in Iquitos. Premier is the most effective local insect repellent. The dry season is from Jul-Sep (Sep is the best month to see flowers and butterflies).

This is an important place for ayahuasca tourism. There are legitimate shamans as well as charlatans. **Karma Café**, Napo 138, is the centre of the scene in town. See also the work of Alan Shoemaker, who holds an International Amazonian Shamanism Conference every year, Soga del Alma, Rómulo Espinar 170, Iquitos 65, alanshoemaker@hotmail.com. Before taking ayahuasca in a ceremony with a shaman, read the note on page 1197.

Amazon Yarapa River Lodge, Av La Marina 124, www.yarapa.com. On the Río Yarapa, in a pristine location, award-winning in its use of ecofriendly resources and work with local villages, flexible and responsible, its field laboratory is associated with Cornell University. Arranges trips to Pacaya-Samiria.

Aqua Expeditions, Iquitos 1167, T601053, www.aquaexpeditions.com. Luxury river cruises of 3, 4, or 7 nights on the *M/V Aria* (from US$2835 pp) and the *M/V Aqua* (from US$2685 pp), both designed by architect Jordi Puig to look like floating town houses rather than boats, with massive picture windows in each a/c suite. Amazing food with local delicacies on the gourmet tasting menu, good shore excursions with knowledgeable local guides.
Blue Morpho Tours, Av Guardia Civil 515, T263454, www.bluemorphotours.com. A rustic

camp on Carretera Nauta, Km 52.5. Centre for shamanic studies and workshops, 9-day shamanic trips, all inclusive except for bar and snacks.
Chullachaqui Eco Lodge, Raymondi 138, Iquitos, T965-705919, http://amazoniantrips. com/chullachaqui-eco-lodge/. 2 hrs by speed boat up the Amazon on the Río Tapira. Thatched timber cabins, basic accommodation, private bath, communal dining room, hammock room, insect screens, tours with naturalist guides to see river dolphins and other wildlife.
Cumaceba Amazonia Tours, Putumayo 184 in the Iron House, T232229, www.cumaceba.com. Overnight visits to Cumaceba Lodge, 35 km from Iquitos, and tours of 1-4 nights to the Botanical Lodge on the Amazon, 80 km from Iquitos, birdwatching tours, ayahuasca ceremonies.
Dawn on the Amazon, Malecón Maldonado 185 y Nauta, T223730, www.dawnonthe amazon.com. Offer a variety of day tours around Iquitos on the luxurious 20 passenger *Dawn on the Amazon III* (US$199 pp). Also offer custom-made cruises for several days. Their wooden vessels are decorated with carvings of jungle themes. Also has a bar/restaurant in town.
Delfín, Av Abelardo Quiñones Km 5, San Juan Bautista, T262721, www.delfinamazoncruises. com. Luxury cruises in the Delfín I and Delfín II (the cheaper of the 2), 3- and 4-night expeditions to Pacaya-Samiria, with daily activities including kayaking, bird and wildlife watching, fresh organic food, from US$2400 pp.
Explorama Tours, by the riverside docks on Av La Marina 340, T252530, www.explorama.com, are highly recommended, with over 40 years in existence, certainly the biggest and most established. Their sites are: **Ceiba Tops**, 40 km (1½ hrs) from Iquitos, is a comfortable resort, 75 a/c rooms with electricity, hot showers, pool with hydromassage and beautiful gardens. The food is good and, as in all Explorama's properties, is served communally. There are attractive walks and other excursions, a recommended jungle experience for those who want their creature comforts, US$340 pp for 1 night/2 days. **Explorama Lodge** at Yanamono, 80 km from Iquitos, 2½ hrs from Iquitos, has palm-thatched accommodation with separate bathroom and shower facilities connected by covered walkways, cold water, no

electricity, good food and service. US$455 for 3 days/2 nights. **Explornapo Lodge** at Llachapa on the Sucusai creek (a tributary of the Napo), is in the same style as Explorama Lodge, but is further away from Iquitos, 160 km (4 hrs), and is set in 105,000 ha of primary rainforest, so is better for seeing wildlife, US$1,120 for 5 days/4 nights (all 2014 basic prices). Nearby is the impressive canopy walkway 35 m above the forest floor and 500 m long, 'a magnificent experience and not to be missed'. It is associated with the Amazon Center for Tropical Studies (ACTS), a scientific station, only 10 mins from the canopy walkway. **Explor Tambos**, 2 hrs from Explornapo, offer more primitive accommodation, 8 shelters for 16 campers, bathing in the river, offers the best chance to see fauna. Close to Explornapo is the ReNuPeRu medicinal plant garden, run by a curandero.

Gerson Pizango, T965-013225. Local, English-speaking and award-winning guide who will take you to his village 2½ hrs by boat, from where you can trek and camp or stay and experience village life. Expert at spotting wildlife, knowledgeable about medicinal plants, interesting and varied expeditions benefitting the community. In the village, accommodation is in a hut by the riverside where there are pink and grey dolphins, private room with mosquito net. US$50-70 pp per day depending on length of trip and size of party, includes food, water, camping gear, boots, raincoats, torches, binoculars, fishing rods, machetes.

Heliconia Lodge, Ricardo Palma 259, T231959 (Lima T01-421 9195), www.heliconialodge. com.pe. On the Río Amazonas, 80 km from Iquitos. Surrounded by rainforest, islands and lagoons full of wildlife, this is a beautiful place for resting, birdwatching, looking for pink dolphins, jungle hikes. Organized packages from 1 to 4 nights, all-inclusive. Good guides, food and flexible excursions according to guest's request. The lodge has a traditional, rustic yet comfortable design, swimming pool, hot water and electricity at certain times of day and 1700 to 2200.

Muyuna Amazon Lodge, Putumayo 163, ground floor, T242858, www.muyuna.com. 140 km from Iquitos, also on the Yanayacu, before San Juan village. 1- to 5-night packages available. Everything is included in the price.

Good guides, accommodation, food and service; very well organized and professional, flexible, radio contact, will collect passengers from airport if requested in advance. Amenities are constantly updated with new ecological considerations. It is easy to see animals here and you can even find rareties such as the piuri (wattled curaçao, *Crax globulosa*). They offer birdwatching trips. Because of the isolated location they guarantee that visitors will see animals. Also visits to the Butterfly Farm and manatee rescue centre and city tours. Highly recommended.

Paseos Amazónicos Ambassador, Pevas 246, T231618, www.paseosamazonicos.com, operates the **Amazonas Sinchicuy Lodge**. The lodge is 1½ hrs from Iquitos on the Sinchicuy river, 25 mins by boat from the Amazon river. The lodge consists of several wooden buildings with thatched roofs on stilts, cabins with bathroom, no electricity but paraffin lamps are provided, good food, and plenty activities, including visits to local villages. Recommended. They also have Tambo Yanayacu and Tambo Amazónico lodges, organize visits to Pacaya Samiria and local tours.

Tapiche Ohara's Reserve, contact through Green Track Hostel, www.greentrack-jungle. com. On the Río Tapiche, a tributary of the Ucayali, 11 hrs up river from Iquitos. Fully screened wood cabins with thatched roofs, custom designed trips according to the visitor's interests, 4 nights/5 days US$840 pp.

🚌 Transport

Iquitos p1414, map p1415

Air Francisco Secada Vigneta airport, T260147. Taxi to the airport costs US$6; *mototaxi* (motorcycle with 2 seats), US$3.10. A bus from the airport, US$0.75, goes from the main road; most go through the centre of town. To **Lima**, daily; LAN (direct or via Tarapoto), **Peruvian Airlines** and **Star Perú** (direct or via Tarapoto, also daily to Pucallpa). The military **Grupo Aéreo 42** has passenger flights to Iquitos originating in Trujillo; see page 1261 for routes and schedules.

Ferry General hints for river travel: large passenger and cargo vessels are called *lanchas*, smaller faster craft are called *rápidos* or *deslizadores* (speedboats). *Yates* are small to medium wooden colectivos, usually slow, and *chalupas* are small motor launches used to ferry passengers from the lanchas to shore. For information about boats, go to the corresponding ports of departure for each destination, except for speed boats to the Brazil/Colombian border which have their offices clustered on Raymondi block 3. When river levels are very high departures may be from alternative places.

Lanchas leave from Puerto Henry and Masusa, 2 km north of the centre, a dangerous area at night. The first night's meal is not included. Always deal directly with boat owners or managers, avoid touts and middle-men. All fares are negotiable. You can buy either a ticket to sling your hammock on deck, or for a berth in a cabin sleeping 2 to 4 people.

A hammock is essential. A double, of material (not string), provides one person with a blanket. Board the boat many hours in advance to guarantee hammock space. If going on the top deck, try to be first down the front; take rope for hanging your hammock, plus string and sarongs for privacy. On all boats, hang your hammock away from lightbulbs (they aren't switched off at night and attract all sorts of strange insects) and away from the engines, which usually emit noxious fumes. Guard your belongings from the moment you board. It's safer to club together and pay for a cabin in which to lock your belongings, even if you sleep outside in a hammock. There is very little privacy; women travellers can expect a lot of attention. There are adequate washing and toilet facilities, but the food is rice, chicken and beans (and whatever can be picked up en route) cooked in river water. Stock up on drinking water, fruit and tinned food. Vegetarians must take their own supplies. There is usually a bar on board. Take plenty of prophylactic enteritis tablets; many contract dysentery on the trip. Also take insect repellent and a mosquito net. If arriving in Iquitos on a regular, slow boat, take extreme care when disembarking. Things get very chaotic at this time and theft and pickpocketing is rife. Some of the newer boats have CCTV to deter theft.

To **Pucallpa**, 4-5 days up river along the Amazon and Ucayali (can be longer if the water level is low), larger boats must travel only by day, hammock US$40, berth US$140 double. **Henry** (T263948) is a large company with 4 departures per week from Puerto Henry; *Henry 5, 6* and *7* have some cabins with bath. Another good boat is *Pedro Martín 2* from Puerto Masusa. To **Yurimaguas**, 3-4 days up river along the Amazon, Marañón and Huallaga, hammock space US$40, berth US$119-134 double. The **Eduardo/Gilmer** company, T960404, with 8 boats is recommended, they sail from Puerto Masusa several per week, but not Sun; *Eduardo I* and *Gilmer IV* have berths with bath for US$192.

The most convenient way to travel to the border with Brazil and Colombia is on a *rápido* to **Santa Rosa**, 8-10 hrs downriver, US$75, Tue-Sun, from the Embarcadero Turístico at 0600; be at the port 0445 for customs check, board 0500-0530. Motorized canoes cross from Santa Rosa to **Tabatinga** (Brazil) US$1.75 pp and **Leticia** (Colombia), US$1.65 pp. From Santa Rosa to Iquitos, Tue-Sun at 0400, board 0300, 10-12 hrs upstream, get immigration entry stamp the day before. *Rápidos* carry life jackets and have bathrooms, a simple breakfast and lunch are included in the price. Luggage limit is 15 kg. Purchase tickets in advance from company offices, open Mon-Sat. In Iquitos: **Golfinho**, Raymondi 378, T225118, www.transportegolfinho.com; **Transtur**, Raymondi 384, T221356. In Tabatinga: **Golfinho**, Marechal Mallet 306, T3412 3186; **Transtur**, Marechal Mallet 290, T8113 5239. Tickets are also on sale in Leticia, but the price is higher. *Lanchas* to Santa Rosa, which may continue Islandia, leave from the Puerto Pesquero or Masusa (enquire at T250440), Mon-Sat at 1800 (depart Santa Rosa at 1200), 2-3 days downriver, US$31 in hammock, US$50 in cabin. For additional details, see Brazil and Colombia chapters.

To **Pantoja** (for Ecuador), 5-7 days up river on the Napo, a route requiring plenty of time, stamina and patience. There are irregular departures once or twice a month; ask in Iquitos about sailings, eg **Radio Moderna** (Iquitos T250440), or T830055 – a private phone in Pantoja village. Fare is about US$38, US$3 per day extra for berth if you can get one. The vessels are usually cargo boats which carry live animals, some of which are slaughtered en route.

Crowding and poor sanitation are problems on some of the boats. Take a hammock, cup, bowl, cutlery, extra food and snacks, drinking water or purification, insect repellent, toilet paper, soap, towel, cash dollars and soles in small notes. To shorten the voyage, or visit towns along the way, you can go to **Indiana**, daily departures from **Muelle de Productores** in Iquitos, US$5, 45 mins, then take a mototaxi to **Mazán** on the Río Napo. From Mazán, there are *rápidos* to **Santa Clotilde** on Mon, Tue, Thu, Fri and Sat at 0600 (Santa Clotilde to Mazán Tue, Wed, Fri, Sat and Sun), US$31 includes a snack, 4-5 hrs, information from **Familia Ruiz**, Iquitos T251410. You can board boats in Mazan or Santa Clotilde. There is no public transport from Pantoja to **Nuevo Rocafuerte** (Ecuador), you must hire a private boat, US$60 per boat. For details of boats beyond Nuevo Rocafuerte, see Ecuador chapter, Coca, Transport, River.

Excursions: To **Nauta**, Trans del Sur buses from Libertad y Próspero, 0530-1900, US$3.10,

2 hrs; vans from Av Aguirre cuadra 14 by Centro Comercial Sachachorro, leave when full, US$4, 1½ hrs.

To **Lake Quistococha**, **combis** leave every hour until 1500 from Moore y Bermúdez, Iquitos, US$1; the last one back leaves at 1700. City bus from Tacna y Mcal Cáceres, US$0.40.

❶ Directory

Iquitos *p1414, map p1415*
Consulates Brazil, Sargento Lores 363, T235153, www.abe.mre.gov.br. Mon-Fri 0800-1400, visas issued in 2 days. **Colombia**, Calvo de Araujo 431, T231461, Mon-Fri 0800-1100. **Note** There is no Ecuadorean consulate. If you need a visa, you must get it in Lima or in your home country. **Medical services** Clínica Ana Stahl, Av la Marina 285, T252535. **Useful addresses** Immigration: Mcal Cáceres 18th block, T235371, Mon-Fri 0800-1615. **Tourist police**: Sargento Lores 834, T242081.

Southeastern jungle

The southern *selva* is in Madre de Dios department, which contains the Manu National Park (2.04 million ha), the Tambopata National Reserve (254,358 ha) and the Bahauja-Sonene National Park (1.1 million ha). The forest of this lowland region (*Altitude: 260 m*) is technically called Sub-tropical Moist Forest, which means that it receives less rainfall than tropical forest and is dominated by the floodplains of its meandering rivers. The most striking features are the former river channels that have become isolated as ox-bow lakes. These are home to black caiman and giant otter. Other rare species living in the forest are jaguar, puma, ocelot and tapir. There are also howler monkeys, macaws, guans, currasows and the giant harpy eagle. As well as containing some of the most important flora and fauna on Earth, the region also harbours gold-diggers, loggers, hunters, drug smugglers and oil-men, whose activities have endangered the unique rainforest. Moreover, the construction of the *Interoceánica*, a road linking the Atlantic and Pacific oceans via Puerto Maldonado and Brazil, will certainly bring more uncontrolled colonization in the area, as seen so many times in the Brazilian Amazon.

Arriving in Manu

Access to Manu The multiple use zone of Manu Biosphere Reserve is accessible to anyone and several lodges exist in the area (see Lodges in Manu below). The reserved zone is accessible by permit only. Entry is strictly controlled and visitors must visit the area under the auspices of an authorized operator with an authorized guide. Permits are limited and reservations should be made well in advance. In the reserved zone the only accommodation is in the comfortable **Manu Lodge** or in the comfortable but rustic **Casa Machiguenga** in the Cocha Salvador area. Several companies have tented safari camp infrastructures, some with shower and dining facilities, but all visitors sleep in tents. The entrance fee to the Reserved Zone is 150 soles pp (about US$55) and is included in package tour prices.

Useful addresses **In Lima** Asociación Peruana para la Conservación de la Naturaleza (APECO) ① *Parque José Acosta 187, p 2, Magdalena del Mar, T01-264 0094, comunicapeco@apeco. org.pe.* **Pronaturaleza** ① *Doña Juana 137, Urb Los Rosales, Santiago de Surco, T01-271 2662, and in Puerto Maldonado, Jr Cajamarca cuadra 1 s/n, T082-571585, comunicaciones@pronaturaleza. org.* **In Cuzco Perú Verde** ① *Ricardo Palma J-1, Santa Mónica, Cuzco, T084-226392, www. peruverde.org.* This is a local NGO that can help with information and has free video shows about Manu National Park and Tambopata National Reserve. Friendly and helpful and with information on research in the jungle area of Madre de Dios. The **Amazon Conservation Association** (ACCA) ① *Av Oswaldo Baca 402, Urb Magisterio, Cuzco, T084-222329, www.amazon conservation.org, Jr Cusco 499, T082-573237, Puerto Maldonado* is another NGO whose mission is to protect biodiversity by studying ecosystems and developing conservation tools to protect land while suporting local communities. Further information can be obtained from the **Manu National Park Office** ① *Av Micaela Bastidas 310, Cuzco, T084-240898, open 0800-1400.* They issue the permit for the Reserved Zone.

Climate The climate is warm and humid, with a rainy season from November to March and a dry season from April to October. Cold fronts from the South Atlantic, called *friajes*, are characteristic of the dry season, when temperatures drop to 15-16° C during the day, and 13° C at night. Always bring a sweater at this time. The best time to visit is during the dry season when there are fewer mosquitoes and the rivers are low, exposing the beaches. This is also a good time to see nesting and to view animals at close range, as they stay close to the rivers and are easily seen. Note that this is also the hottest time. A pair of binoculars is essential and insect repellent is a must.

Manu Biosphere Reserve

No other reserve can compare with Manu for the diversity of life forms; it holds over 1000 species of birds and covers an altitudinal range from 200 m to 4100 m above sea-level. Giant otters, jaguars, ocelots and 13 species of primates abound in this pristine tropical wilderness, and uncontacted indigenous tribes are present in the more remote areas, as are indigenous groups with limited access.

The reserve is one of the largest conservation units on Earth, encompassing the complete drainage of the Manu River. It is divided into the **Manu National Park** (1,692,137 ha), where only government sponsored biologists and anthropologists may visit with permits from the Ministry of Agriculture in Lima; the **Reserved Zone** (257,000 ha) within the Manu National Park, set aside for applied scientific research and ecotourism, and the **Cultural Zone** (92,000 ha), which contains acculturated native groups and colonists, where the locals still employ their traditional way of life. Among the ethnic groups in the Cultural Zone are the Harakmbut, Machiguenga and Yine in the Amarakaeri Reserved Zone, on the east bank of the Alto Madre de Dios. They have set up their own ecotourism activities. Associated with Manu are other areas protected by conservation groups, or local people (for example the Blanquillo reserved zone) and some cloud forest parcels along the road. The **Nahua-Kugapakori Reserved Zone**, set aside for these two nomadic native groups, is the area between the headwaters of the Río Manu and headwaters of the Río Urubamba, to the north of the alto Madre de Dios.

Cuzco to Puerto Maldonado via Mazuko

This route is Cuzco-Urcos-Quincemil-Mazuko-Puerto Maldonado. Bus details are given under Transport, below. The road from Cuzco to Puerto Maldonado has been upgraded as part of the Interoceánica highway and the road's susceptibility to bad weather has declined. **Quincemil**, 240 km from Urcos on the road to Mazuko, is a centre for alluvial gold-mining with many banks. Hunt Oil is building a huge oil and gas facility here; its exploration lot controversially overlaps the Amarakaeri Communal Reserve. Accommodation is available in **$ Hotel Toni**, friendly, clean, cold shower, good meals. The changing scenery is magnificent. Puente Iñambari is the junction of three sections of the Interoceanic Highway, from Cuzco, Puerto Maldonado and Juliaca. However, this is only a small settlement and transport stops 5km further north at Mazuko. In the evenings, Mazuko is a hive of activity as temperatures drop and the buses arrive. There is regular traffic to Puerto Maldonado, including colectivos, three hours, US$11. **$ Hostal Valle Sagrado** is the best of many places to stay. The Highway beyond Mazuko cuts across lowland rainforest, large areas of which have been cleared by migrants engaged in small-scale gold mining. Their encampments of plastic shelters, shops and prostibars now line the Highway for several kilometres. A worthwhile stop on the route is the **Parador Turístico Familia Méndez**, Km 419, 45 minutes from Puerto Maldonado, www.paradormendez.com, which prepares local dishes from home-grown ingredients and has a trail network on the surrounding forest.

Cuzco to Puerto Maldonado via Pilcopata and Itahuania

The arduous 255 km trip over the Andes from Cuzco to Pilcopata takes about eight to 12 hours by bus or truck (10 hours to two days in the wet season). On this route, too, the scenery is magnificent. From Cuzco you climb up to the pass before Paucartambo (very cold at night), before dropping down to this mountain village at the border between the departments of Cuzco and Madre de Dios. The road then ascends to the second pass (also cold at night), after which it goes down to the cloud forest and then the rainforest, reaching **Pilcopata** at 650 m (eight hours).

Pilcopata to Itahuania After Pilcopata, the route is hair-raising and breathtaking, passing through **Atalaya**, the first village on the Alto Madre de Dios River and tourist port for hiring boats to Boca Manu (basic accommodation). The route continues to Salvación, where a Park Office and Park Entrance are situated. There are basic hostals and restaurants. Basic restaurants can be found in Pilcopata and Atalaya.

The road, which bypasses the previous port of **Shintuya**, continues to **Itahuania**, the starting point for river transport. Rain often disrupts wheeled transport, though. The road is scheduled to continue to Nuevo Edén, 11 km away, and Diamante, so the location of the port will be determined by progress on the road. Eventually, the road will go to Boca Colorado. **Note** It is not possible to arrange trips to the Reserved Zone of the National Park from Itahuania, owing to park regulations. All arrangements, including permits, must be made in Cuzco.

Itahuania to Puerto Maldonado Cargo boats leave for the gold mining centre of Boca Colorado on the Río Madre de Dios, via Boca Manu, but only when the boat is fully laden (see Transport below). Very basic accommodation can be found here, but it is not recommended for lone women travellers. From Colorado you can take a colectivo taxi to Puerto Carlos, cross the river, then take another colectivo to Puerto Maldonado; 4½ hours in all.

Boca Manu is the connecting point between the rivers Alto Madre de Dios, Manu and Madre de Dios. It has a few houses, an air strip and some food supplies. It is also the entrance to the Manu Reserve and to go further you must be part of an organized group. The park ranger station is located in Limonal. You need to show your permit here. Camping is allowed if you have a permit. There are no regular flights from Cuzco to Boca Manu. These are arranged the day before, if there are enough passengers. Check at Cuzco airport; or with the tour operators in Cuzco.

To the Reserved Zone Upstream on the Río Manu you pass the **Manu Lodge** (see Where to stay, below), on the Cocha Juárez, three or four hours by boat. You can continue to Cocha Otorongo, 2½ hours and Cocha Salvador, 30 minutes, the biggest lake with plenty of wildlife. From here it is two to three hours to Pakitza, the entrance to the National Park Zone. This is only for biologists with a special permit.

Between Boca Manu and Colorado is **Blanquillo**, a private reserve (10,000 ha). Bring a good tent with you and all food if you want to camp and do it yourself, or alternatively accommodation is available at the **Tambo Blanquillo** (full board or accommodation only). Wildlife is abundant, especially macaws and parrots at the macaw lick near **Manu Wildlife Centre**. There are occasional boats to Blanquillo from Shintuya; six to eight hours.

Puerto Maldonado → *Phone code: 082. Colour map 3, C5. Pop: 45,000. Altitude: 250 m.*

Puerto Maldonado is an important starting point for visiting the south eastern jungles of the Tambopata Reserve or departing for Bolivia or Brazil. It overlooks the confluence of the rivers Tambopata and Madre de Dios and, because of the gold mining and timber industries, the immediate surrounding jungle is now cultivated. A bridge, as part of the Interoceánica highway, has been built across the Río Madre de Dios. Even before its completion business activity in the town was growing fast. There are tourist offices at the airport and at **Dircetur** ① *Urb Fonavi, take a moto-taxi to the Posta Médica which is next door.*

The beautiful and tranquil **Lago Sandoval** is a one-hour boat ride along the Río Madre de Dios, and then a 5-km walk into the jungle (parts of the first 3 km are a raised wooden walkway; boots are advisable). Entry to the lake costs US$9.50. You must go with a guide; this can be arranged by the boat driver. Boats can be hired at the Madre de Dios port for about US$25 a day, minimum two people (plus petrol) to go to Lago Sandoval (don't pay the full cost in advance).

Jungle tours from Puerto Maldonado

Trips can be made to **Lago Valencia**, 60 km away near the Bolivian border, four hours there, eight hours back. It is an ox-bow lake with lots of wildlife. Many excellent beaches and islands are located within an hour's boat ride. Mosquitoes are voracious. If camping, take food and water.

It is quite easy to arrange a boat and guide from Puerto Maldonado (see Tour operators below) to the **Tambopata National Reserve** (TNR) ① *Sernanp, Av 28 de Julio 482, Puerto Maldonado, T573278*, between the rivers Madre de Dios, Tambopata and Heath. Some superb ox-bow lakes can be visited and the birdwatching is wonderful.

The **Bahuaja-Sonene National Park**, declared in 1996, stretches from the Heath River across the Tambopata, incorporating the Río Heath National Sanctuary. It is closed to visitors.

Río Las Piedras

Lying to the northeast of, and running roughly parallel to the Río Manu, this drainage runs some 700 km from rainforest headwaters in the Alto Purús region. The lower, more easily accessible section of the river, closer to Puerto Maldonado and outside state protection, runs through rich tropical forests, very similar to those in the Manu and Tambopata areas. Close to 600 species of birds, at least eight primate species and some of the Amazon's larger mammals, giant otter, jaguar, puma, tapir and giant anteater, are all present. Hunting pressure has resulted in wildlife being shier than in Manu or Tambopata, but this remains an excellent wildlife destination. See www.arbioperu.org and www.relevantfilms.co.uk/propied/las-piedras/.

To Iberia and Iñapari

Daily public transport runs to **Iberia** and **Iñapari** on the border with Brazil. This section of the Interoceánica road takes a lot of traffic and can be dangerous for motorcyclists as a result. No primary forest remains along the road, only secondary growth and small *chacras* (farms). There are picturesque *caseríos* (settlements) that serve as processing centres for the brazil nut. Some 70% of the inhabitants in the Madre de Dios are involved in the collection of this prized nut.

Iberia, Km 168, has three hotels, the best is **$ Hostal Aquino**, basic, cold shower. It's a small frontier town, much quieter and more laid back than Iñapari on the border. The old Fundo María Cristina rubber plantation, now a research centre, can be visited to see the whole rubber production process. Allow one hour; five minutes south of town, US$0.50 by mototaxi.

Iñapari, at the end of the road, Km 235, has a growing problem with Haitian refugees trying to enter Brazil by the back door. Hundreds are stuck in transit. The town has a basic hotel and a restaurant, but **Assis Brasil** across the border is much more attractive and has three hotels, two restaurants and shops. A suspension bridge now links the two countries.

There is a road from Assis Brasil into Brazil and connections to Cobija in Bolivia from Brasiléia. There are no exchange facilities en route and poor exchange rates for Brazilian currency at Iñapari. Crossing between Peru and Bolivia on this route is not easy.

Crossing to Brazil
Public transport stops near **immigration in Iñapari**. Exit stamps can be obtained at immigration, open 0930-1300, 1500-1930 daily (Brazilian side 0830-1200, 1400-1830). In Assis Brasil, there is no Policía Federal office. You have to travel on to Brasiléia to obtain your Brazil entry stamp at Policía Federal in the Rodoviária (bus station). You must have a yellow fever certificate to enter Brazil.

● Southeastern jungle listings

For hotel and restaurant price codes, and other relevant information, see Essentials.

● Where to stay

Manu Biosphere Reserve *p1423*
Lodges in Manu
Most jungle lodges are booked as package deals for 3 days, 2 nights, or longer, with meals, transport and guides, see websites below for offers.
Amazon Yanayacu Lodge, Cahuide 824, Punchana, T065-250822, www.amazon yanayaculodge.com. About 1 hr by boat above Diamante village on the southern bank of the Madre de Dios, close to a small parrot *collpa* (mineral lick). Using local river transport to arrive at the lodge rates are very reasonable, prices depend on length of stay. The lodge also offers several different itineraries in Manu.
Amazonia Lodge, on the Río Alto Madre de Dios just across the river from Atalaya, T084-816131, www.amazonialodge.com; in Cuzco at Matará 334, p 3, T084-231370. An old tea hacienda run by the Yabar Calderón family, famous for its bird diversity and fine hospitality, a great place to relax, meals included, birding or natural history tours available, contact Santiago in advance and he'll arrange a pick-up.
Casa Machiguenga, near Cocha Salvador, upriver from Manu Lodge. Contact **Manu Expeditions** or **Apeco** NGO, T084-225595. Machiguenga-style cabins run by local communities with NGO help.
Cock of the Rock Lodge, on the road from Paucartambo to Atalaya at 1600 m, www.

tropicalnaturetravel.com. Next to a Cock of the Rock *lek*, 10 private cabins with en-suite bath.
Erika Lodge, on the Alto Madre de Dios, 25 mins from Atalaya, offers basic accommodation and is cheaper than the other, more luxurious lodges. Contact Manu Ecological Adventures (see below).
Manu Cloud Forest Lodge, at Unión, at 1800 m on the road from Paucartambo to Atalaya, owned by **Manu Nature Tours**, 6 rooms with 16-20 beds.
Manu Learning Centre, Fundo Mascoitania, a 600-ha reserve within the cultural zone, T84-262433, www.crees-expeditions.com. 45 mins from Atalaya by boat, a conservation and volunteer programme run by the crees foundation, now welcoming tourists here and at their new, luxury lodge, **Romero Rainforest Lodge**, a day away by boat.
Manu Lodge, on the Manu river, 3 hrs upriver from Boca Manu towards Cocha Salvador, run by **Manu Nature Tours** and only bookable as part of a full package deal with transport.
Manu Wildlife Center, 2 hrs down the Río Madre de Dios from Boca Manu, near the Blanquillo macaw lick. Book through **Manu Expeditions**, which runs it in conjunction with the conservation group **Peru Verde**, www. manuwildlifecenter.com. 22 double cabins, with private bathroom and hot water. Also canopy towers for birdwatching and a tapir lick.
Pantiacolla Lodge, 30 mins downriver from Shintuya. Owned by the Moscoso family. Book through **Pantiacolla Tours** (see page 1431).

Cuzco to Puerto Maldonado via Pilcopata and Itahuania *p1424*
Turismo Indígena Wanamei, Av El Sol 814 p 2, of 212, Cuzco, T234608, T984-754708, or Av 26 de Diciembre 276, Puerto Maldonado, T082-572 539, www.ecoturismowanamei.com. An initiative by the people of the Amarakaeri Communal Reserve, located between Manu and Tambopata. They offer 4- to 9-day trips starting and ending in Cuzco. Accommodation includes lodges, communities and camping. The trips aim not only to offer excellent wildlife viewing opportunities but also an insight in to the daily life of indigenous peoples. It's advised that you speak Spanish
$ Hospedaje Manu, Boca Colorado, on street beside football field. Cell-like rooms, open windows and ceilings but comfy mattresses and mosquito netting.
$ Sra Rubella in Pilcopata. Very basic but friendly.
$ Yine Lodge, next to Boca Manu airport. A cooperative project run between **Pantiacolla Tours** and the Yine community of Diamante, who operate their own tours into their community and surroundings. Also **$ Hostal** in Boca Manu run by the community. Basic accommodation.

Puerto Maldonado *p1425*
New hotels catering for business travellers are springing up.
$$$ Don Carlos, Av León Velarde 1271, T571029, www.hotelesdoncarlos.com. Nice view over the Río Tambopata, a/c, restaurant, airport transfers, good.
$$$ Wasaí Lodge & Expeditions, Plaza Grau 1, T572290, www.wasai.com. In a beautiful location overlooking the Madre de Dios River, with forest surrounding cabin-style rooms, shower, small pool with waterfall, good restaurant (local fish a speciality). They can organize local tours and also has a lodge on the Río Tambopata (see page 1429).
$$$-$$ Cabañaquinta, Cuzco 535, T571045, www.hotelcabanaquinta.com. A/c or fan, frigobar, laundry, free drinking water, good restaurant, lovely garden, very comfortable, airport transfer. Request a room away from the Interoceanic Highway.
$$ Anaconda Lodge, 600 m from airport, T982 611039 (mob), www.anacondajunglelodge.com. With private or shared bath, Swiss/Thai-owned

bungalows, hot showers, swimming pool, Thai restaurant or Peruvian food and pizza if you prefer, tours arranged, has space for camping, very pleasant, family atmosphere.
$$ Paititi Hostal, G Prada 290 y Av León Velarde, T574667, see Facebook page. All mod-cons, executive and standard rooms. Reserve in advance.
$$ Perú Amazónico, Jr Ica 269, T571799, peruamazonico@hotmail.com. Modern, comfortable and good.
$ Amarumayo, Libertad 433, 10 mins from the centre, T573860. Comfortable, with pool and garden, good restaurant.
$ Hospedaje El Bambú, Jr Puno 837, T793880. Basic and small but well kept rooms with fan, family atmosphere, breakfast and juices not included in price but served in dining room. A good budget option.
$ Hospedaje Español, González Prada 670, T572381. Comfortable, set back from the road, In a quiet part of town.
$ Hospedaje La Bahía, 2 de Mayo 710, T572127. Cheaper without bath or TV, large rooms, a good choice.
$ Tambopata Hostel, Av 26 de Diciembre 234, www.tambopatahostel.com. The only real backpacker hostel in town, dorm beds, hammocks or camping. Nice atmosphere, they also organize local tours.

Jungle tours from Puerto Maldonado: Tambopata *p1425*
Some of the lodges along the Tambopata river offer guiding and research placements to biology and environmental science graduates. For more details send an SAE to **TReeS**: UK – J Forrest, PO Box 33153, London, NW3 4DR, www.tambopata.org.uk.

Lodges on the Río Madre de Dios
Most jungle lodges are booked as package deals for 3 days, 2 nights, or longer, with meals, transport and guides, see websites below for offers.
$$ Casa de Hospedaje Mejía, to book T571428, visit **Ceiba Tours**, L Velarde 420, T573567, turismomejia@hotmail.com. Attractive but basic rustic lodge close to Lago Sandoval, full board can be arranged, canoes are available.

Eco Amazonia Lodge, on the Madre de Dios, 1 hr down-river from Puerto Maldonado (office Jr Lambayeque 774, T573491). In Lima: Enrique Palacios 292, Miraflores, T01-242 2708, in Cuzco Garcilazo 210, of 206, T084-236159, www.ecoamazonia.com.pe. Basic bungalows and dormitories, good for birdwatching, has its own Monkey Island with animals taken from the forest.

El Corto Maltés, Billinghurst 229, Puerto Maldonado, T573831, www.cortomaltes-amazonia.com. On the Madre de Dios, halfway to Sandoval which is the focus of most visits. Hot water, huge dining room, well run.

Estancia Bello Horizonte, 20 km northeast of Puerto Maldonado, Loreto 252, Puerto Maldonado, T572748, www.estanciabellohorizonte.com. In a nice stretch of forest overlooking the old course of the Madre de Dios, now a huge aguajal populated with macaws. A small lodge with bungalows for 30 people, with private bath, hot water, pool, butterfly house. Transport, all meals and guide (several languages offered) included, US$220 for 3 days/2 nights. The lodge belongs to APRONIA, an organization that trains and provides employment for orphaned children. Suitable for those wanting to avoid a river trip.

Inkaterra Reserva Amazónica Lodge, 45 mins by boat down the Madre de Dios. To book: Inkaterra, Andalucía 174, Miraflores L18, Lima, T01-610 0400; Plaza Nazarenas 167 p 2, Cuzco T084-245314, and Cuzco 436, Puerto Maldonado, www.inkaterra.com. Tastefully redecorated hotel in the jungle with suites and bungalows, solar power, good food in huge dining room supported by a big tree. Jungle tours in its own 10,000 ha plus their new canopy walk; also tours to Lago Sandoval.

Sandoval Lake Lodge, 1 km beyond Mejía on Lago Sandoval, book through InkaNatura, address under Manu, Tour operators. Usual access is by canoe after a 3-km walk or rickshaw ride, huge bar and dining area, electricity, hot water.

Lodges on the Tambopata

Lodges on the Tambopata are reached by vehicle to Bahuaja port, 15 km up river from Puerto Maldonado by the community of Infierno, then by boat. Under a new scheme, a central booking office is being set up to offer the services of over 15 small lodges and *casas de hospedaje* along the Tambopata river under the names: **Tambopata Ecotourism Corridor** and **Tambopata Homestays** (www.tambopataecotours.com). Further details on the website of location, style of accommodation, facilities, cost, etc. See lodge websites for prices of packages offered.

Explorers Inn, book through **Peruvian Safaris**, Alcanfores 459, Miraflores, Lima, T01-447 8888, www.peruviansafaris.com. Just before the La Torre control post, adjoining the TNR, in the part where most research work has been done, 58 km from Puerto Maldonado. 2½ hrs up the Río Tambopata (1½ hrs return), one of the best places in Peru for seeing jungle birds (580 plus species have been recorded), butterflies (1230 plus species), also giant river otters, but you probably need more than a 2-day tour to benefit fully from the location. Offers tours through the adjoining community of La Torre. The guides are biologists and naturalists undertaking research in the reserve. They provide interesting wildlife-treks, including to the macaw lick (*collpa*).

Posada Amazonas Lodge, on the Tambopata river, 1½ hrs by vehicle and boat upriver from Puerto Maldonado. Book through **Rainforest Expeditions**, San Francisco de Paula Ugariza 813, Of 201, San Antonio-Miraflores, Lima, T01-241 4880, reservations at T01-997 903650, www.perunature.com. A collaboration between the tour agency and the local native community of Infierno. Attractive rooms with cold showers, visits to Lake Tres Chimbadas, with good birdwatching including the Tambopata Collpa. Offers trips to a nearby indigenous primary health care project where a native healer gives guided tours of the medicinal plant garden. Service and guiding is very good. The **Tambopata Research Centre**, the company's more intimate, but comfortable lodge, about 6 hrs further upriver. Rooms are smaller than Posada Amazonas, shared showers, cold water. The lodge is next to the famous Tambopata macaw clay lick. 2 hrs from Posada Amazonas, Rainforest Expeditions also has the **Refugio Amazonas**, close to Lago Condenados. It is the usual stopover for those visiting the collpa. 3 bungalows accommodate

70 people in en suite rooms, large, kerosene lit, open bedrooms with mosquito nets, well-designed and run, atmospheric. There are many packages at the different lodges and lots of add-ons.

Tambopata Eco Lodge, on the Río Tambopata, to make reservations Nueva Baja 432, Cuzco, T084-245695, operations office Jr Gonzales Prada 269, Puerto Maldonado, T571726, www.tambopatalodge.com. Rooms with solar-heated water, good guides, excellent food. Trips go to Lake Condenado, some to Lake Sachavacayoc, and to the Collpa de Chuncho, guiding mainly in English and Spanish, naturalists programme provided.

Wasaí Lodge and Expeditions, Río Tambopata, 120 km (3 hrs by speedboat) upriver from Puerto Maldonado, contact Las Higueras 257, Residencial Monterrico, La Molina, Lima 12, T01-436 8792, or Plaza Grau 1, Puerto Maldonado, T082-572290, www.wasai.com. Kayaking, zip line, fishing, photography tours, mystic tours, wildlife observation, volunteering, etc. Also tours to the Chuncho Clay Lick and Sandoval Lake. Guides in English and Spanish.

Río Las Piedras

Amazon Rainforest Conservation Centre, contact Pepe Moscoso, Jr Los Cedros B-17, Los Castaños, Puerto Maldonado, T082-573655, www.laspiedrasamazontour.com. Roughly 8 hrs up Río Las Piedras, overlooking a beautiful oxbow lake, Lago Soledad, which has a family of giant otters. Comfortable bungalows, with bath and hot water. Activities include a viewing platform 35 m up an ironwood tree, a hide overlooking a macaw lick, and walks on the extensive trail network. Most trips break the river journey half way at Tipishca Lodge, overlooking an oxbow lake with a family of otters (same website as above).

Las Piedras Biodiversity Station, T082-573922. A small lodge in a 4000-ha concession of 'primary' rainforest 90 km up the Río Las Piedras. Visitors camp en route to the lodge. 20 beds in 10 rooms, central dining-room, shared bath, no electricity, library, guiding in English/Spanish. Minimum package is for 4 days/3 nights. Birdwatching trips cost more.

🍴 Restaurants

Puerto Maldonado p1425
$$-$ Burgos's, León Velarde 129. Serves traditional dishes and has a good set lunch menu.
$$-$ Carne Brava, on the Plaza de Armas. One of the smart new joints for a steak and chips.
$$-$ El Hornito/Chez Maggy, on the plaza. Cosy, good pizzas, busy at weekends.
$$-$ Kuskalla, Av 26 de Diciembre 195. Peruvian/Brazilian fusion food with views of the Madre de Dios and Tambopata rivers.
$ D'Kaoba, Madre de Dios 439. Serves the most delicious *pollos a la brasa* in town.
$ La Casa Nostra, Velarde 515. Sells huge fruit juices for US$0.50, as well as *tamales, papas rellenas* and enormous fancy cakes, great coffee.
$ Namaste, Av León Velarde 469. Moroccan and Indian food, sandwiches, breakfasts and set lunches, in chilled out surroundings.
Gustitos del Cura, Loreto 258, Plaza de Armas. Open 0800-2300, closed Wed. Ice-cream and juice parlour run by the APRONIA project for homeless teenagers, offering unusual flavours.

🍸 Bars and clubs

Puerto Maldonado p1425
El Asadero, Arequipa 246, east side of Plaza. Popular *menú* at lunchtime, great sandwiches later in the day, cool bar in the evening.
El Witite, Av León Velarde 153. Fri and Sat. A popular, good disco, latin music.
Le Boulevard, behind El Hornito. Live music, popular.
T-Saica, Loreto 335. An atmospheric bar with live music at weekends.
Vikingo, León Velarde 158. A popular bar and open-air disco.

⚙ What to do

Manu Biosphere Reserve p1423
Warning Beware of pirate operators on the streets of Cuzco who offer trips to the Reserved Zone of Manu and end up halfway through the trip changing the route "due to emergencies", which, in reality means they have no permits to operate in the area. Some unscrupulous tour guides will offer trips to see the uncontacted tribes of Manu. On no account make any

attempt to view these very vulnerable people. The following companies organize trips into the Multiple Use and Reserved Zones. Contact them for more details.

Amazon Trails Peru, C Tandapata 660, San Blas, Cuzco, T084-437374, or T984-714148, www.amazontrailsperu.com. Offers tours to Manu National Park and Blanquillo clay lick; runs 2 lodges in Manu. Operated by ornithologist Abraham Huamán, who has many years' experience guiding in Manu, and his German wife Ulla Maennig. Well-organized tours with knowledgeable guides, good boatmen and cooks, small groups, guaranteed departure dates. Also trekking in Cuzco area. Run the **Amazon Hostel** next door to office in Cuzco (T236770).

Bonanza Tours, Suecia 343, T084-507871, www.bonanzatoursperu.com. 3- to 8-day tours to Manu with local guides, plenty of jungle walks, rafting, kayaking and camp-based excursions with good food. Tours are high quality and good value.

Expediciones Vilca, Plateros 359, Cuzco, T084-244751, www.manuvilcaperu.com. Offers tours at economical prices.

Greenland Peru, in Cuzco: Celasco Astete C-12, T246572, www.greenlandperu.com. Fredy Domínguez is an Amazonian and offers good-value trips to Manu with comfortable accommodation and transport and excellent food cooked by his mother. Experienced, knowledgeable and enthusiastic, he speaks English.

InkaNatura, in Cuzco: Ricardo Palma J1, T084-255255, in Lima: Manuel Bañón 461, San Isidro, T01-440 2022, www.inkanatura.com. Tours to Manu Wildlife Centre and Sandoval Lake Lodge (see above) with emphasis on sustainable tourism and conservation. Knowledgeable guides. They also run treks in Cuzco area.

Manu Adventures, Plateros 356, Cuzco, T084-261640, www.manuadventures.com. This company operates one of the most physically active Manu programmes, with options for a mountain biking descent through the cloudforest and 3 hrs of whitewater rafting on the way to **Erika Lodge** on the upper Río Madre de Dios. Also jungle specialists.

Manu Expeditions and Birding Tours, Jr Los Geranios 2-G, Urb Mariscal Gamarra, 1a Etapa, Cuzco, T084-225990, www.manuexpeditions.com. Owned by ornithologist Barry Walker, 3 trips available to the reserve and Manu Wildlife Center.

Manu Learning Centre, Fundo Mascoitania, a 600-ha private reserve near Salvación, operated by CREES, San Miguel 250, Cuzco, T084-262433 (in UK 5-6 Kendrick Mews, London, SW7 3HG, T020-7581 2932), www.crees-manu.org. A multi-use centre in the Cultural Zone for ectourism, research, volunteers and school groups for rainforest conservation and community development. They run expeditions, tours and field courses.

Manu Nature Tours, Av Pardo 1046, Cuzco, T084-252721, www.manuperu.com. Owned by Boris Gómez Luna, run lodge-based trips, owners of **Manu Lodge** and part owners of **Manu Cloudforest Lodge**; Manu is the only lodge in the Reserved Zone, open all year, situated on an oxbow lake, providing access to the forest, guides available; activities include river-rafting

and canopy-climbing. Highly recommended for experiencing the jungle in comfort.
Oropéndola, Av Circunvalación s/n, Urb Guadalupe Mz A Lte 3, Cuzco, T084-241428, www.oropendolaperu.org. Guide Walter Mancilla Huamán is an expert on flora and fauna. 5-, 7- and 9-day tours from US$800 pp plus park entrance. Good reports of attention to detail and to the needs of clients.
Pantiacolla Tours SRL, Garcilaso 265, interior, p 2, of 12, Cuzco, T084-238323, www.pantiacolla.com. Run by Marianne van Vlaardingen and Gustavo Moscoso. They have tours to the Pantiacolla Lodge (see Where to stay, page 1426) and also 8-day camping trips. Pantiacolla has started a community-based ecotourism project, called the Yine Project, with the people of Diamante in the Multiple Use Zone.

Puerto Maldonado *p1425*
Guides
All guides should have a carnet issued by the Ministry of Tourism (DIRCETUR), which also verifies them as suitable guides for trips to other places and confirms their identity. Check that the carnet has not expired. Reputable guides are Hernán Llave Cortez, Romel Nacimiento and the Mejía brothers, all of whom can be contacted on arrival at the airport, if available. Also recommended: Carlos Borja Gama, a local guide offering specialist birdwatching and photography trips as well as traditional jungle tours, speaks several languages. Contact him through Wasaí or see www.carlosexpeditions.com.
Víctor Yohamona, T082-982-686279 (mob), victorguideperu@hotmail.com. Speaks English, French and German. Boat hire can be arranged through the Capitanía del Puerto (Río Madre de Dios), T573003. **Perú Tours**, Loreto 176, T082-573 244. Organize local trips. See also Ceiba Tours, under Casa de hospedaje Mejía, above.

☺ Transport

Cuzco to Puerto Maldonado: via Urcos and Mazuko *p1423*
Bus The *Interoceánica* is paved all the way. There are many daily buses, US$19-30 (*económico* or *semi-cama*), 10-11 hrs, from the Terminal Terrestre in **Cuzco** with **Transportes Iguazú** (one of the cheapest, less reliable, no toilet), **Mendivil, Machupicchu, Palomino** and **Móvil Tours** (one of the better companies, at Tambopata 529, Puerto Maldonado, T082-795785). All are on Av Tambopata, blocks 3 and 5 in Puerto Maldonado. There are also daily buses from **Mazuko** to Puerto Maldonado with Transportes Bolpebra and Transportes Señor de la Cumbre, 4 hrs, US$6.

Juliaca to Puerto Maldonado: via Mazuko
Road The 4th stage of the Interoceanic Highway is now open and several buses run daily from Arequipa and Puno, stopping in Juliaca, crossing the altiplano and joining the Cuzco-Puerto Maldonado section of the Highway at Puente Iñambari, 5 km from the gold-mining town of Mazuko. **Trans Continental Sur, Aguilas** and **Santa Cruz** buses leave Juliaca 1300-1500, 12 hrs, US$27. **Trans Wayra** from Puno (US$27) and Arequipa; **Trans Mendivil** from Cuzco (US$30), Puno and Arequipa.

Cuzco to Puerto Maldonado: via Pilcopata and Itahuania *p1424*
Road From the Coliseo Cerrado in Cuzco 3 buses run to **Pilcopata** Mon, Wed, Fri, returning same night, US$10. They are fully booked even in low season. The best are Gallito de las Rocas; also Unancha from C Huáscar near the main plaza. Trucks to Pilcopata run on same days, returning Tue, Thu, Sat, 10 hrs in wet season, less in the dry. Only basic supplies are available after leaving Cuzco, so take all camping and food essentials, including insect repellent. Transport can be disrupted in the wet season because the road is in poor condition, although improvements are being made. *Camioneta* service runs between Pilcopata and **Salvación** to connect with the buses, Mon, Wed, Fri. The same *camionetas* run **Itahuania-Shintuya-Salvacion** regularly, when sufficient passengers, probably once a day, and 2 trucks a day. On Sun, there is no traffic. To **Boca Manu** you can hire a boat in Atalaya, several hundred dollars for a *peke peke*, more for a motor boat. It's cheaper to wait or hope for a boat going empty up to Boca Manu to pick up passengers, when the fare will be US$15 per passenger. •

Itahuania-Boca Manu in a shared boat is US$7.50. A private, chartered boat would be over US$100. From Itahuania, cargo boats leave for the gold mining centre of **Boca Colorado** on the Río Madre de Dios, via Boca Manu, but only when the boat is fully laden; about 6-8 a week, 9 hrs, US$20. From Boca Colorado colectivos leave from near football field for Puerto Carlos, 1 hr, US$5, ferry across river 10 mins, US$1.65; colectivo Puerto Carlos-Puerto Maldonado, 3 hrs, US$10, rough road, lots of stops (in Puerto Maldonado **Turismo Boca Colorado**, Tacna 342, T082-573435, leave when full). Tour companies usually use own vehicles for the overland trip from Cuzco to Manu.

Puerto Maldonado *p1425*
Air To **Lima**, daily with LAN and Star Perú via Cuzco. Moto-taxi from town to airport US$2.25, taxi US$3.50, 8 km. **Road and ferry** A standard journey by **moto-taxi** in town costs US$0.60, a ride on a **motorbike** US$0.30. For **Boca Manu** and **Itahuania** take a colectivo to **Boca Colorado** (see above) and then take a cargo boat (no fixed schedule).

From Itahuania there is transport to Pilcopata and Cuzco. To **Iberia** and **Iñapari** for Brazil, daily combis from Jr Ica y Jr Piura, recommended companies are **Turismo Imperial** and Turismo **Real Dorado**. To Iberia 2½ hrs, US$6.50; to Iñapari 3½ hrs, US$8.50. **Móvil** (see above) also have daily service to **Rio Branco** (Brazil), 1200, US$35. To **Juliaca**, several companies offer daily services via San Gabán, at 1900 and 1700 respectively, 18 hrs, US$17. For all routes, ask around the bus offices for colectivo minibuses.

Directory

Puerto Maldonado *p1425*
Consulates Bolivian Consulate, on the north side of the plaza. **Motorcycle hire** Scooters and mopeds can de hired from **San Francisco** and others, on the corner of Puno and G Prado for US$1.75 per hr, off-road motorbikes cost US$3.50 per hr. Passport and driver's licence must be shown. **Useful addresses** Peruvian immigration, 28 de Julio 465, get your exit stamp here.

Contents

Uruguay

At a glance

⏱ **Time required** 1-2 weeks.
☀ **Best time** Dec-Mar best. Carnival and Holy Week are the biggest festivals, particularly in Montevideo.
✖ **When not to go** Coastal resorts are packed out in Jan and can be all shut up in Jun-Sep.

ARGENTINA

BRAZIL

★ Don't miss ...
1 Mercado del Puerto, page 1448.
2 Estancia tourism, page 1451.
3 Colonia del Sacramento, page 1455.
4 Punta del Este, page 1470.

Bella Unión

Río Cuareim

Artigas

Termas del Arapey

Rivera

Salto

Termas de Daymán

Minas de Corrales

Aceguá

Termas de Guaviyú

Tacuarembó

Paysandú   Guichón

Tambores

Curtina

Ansina

Las Toscas

Melo

Río Uruguay

Tres Bocas

Paso de los Toros

Rincón del Bonete (Lago Artificial)

Río Negro

Fray Bentos

Mercedes

Carlos Reyes

Quebrada de los Cuervos

Soriano

Palmitas

Durazno

Cerro Chato

Sarandí del Yi

Treinta y Tres

José R Varela

Dolores

Trinidad

Sarandí Grande

Nueva Palmira

Cardona

Calera de las Huérfanas

Nueva Helvecia

Florida

Cerro Colorado

Pirajá

Lascano

Chuy

Carmelo

Rosario

San José de Mayo

Aiguá

Velásquez

Castillo

Conchillas

Colonia del Sacramento

Colonia Valdense

Canelones

Sta Rosa

Minas Solís

Libertad

Río de la Plata

Atlántida

San Carlos

La Paloma

MONTEVIDEO

Piriápolis

Punta del Este

Maldonado

Atlantic Ocean

N

20 km

20 miles

Uruguay is a land of rolling hills, best explored on horseback, or by staying at the many estancias that have opened their doors to visitors. It also has its feet in the Atlantic Ocean and one of the best ways to arrive is by ferry across the shipping lanes of the Río de la Plata. Montevideo, the capital and main port, is refurbishing its historical centre to match the smart seaside neighbourhoods, but its atmosphere is far removed from the cattle ranches of the interior.

West of Montevideo is Colonia del Sacramento, a former smuggling town turned gambling centre, and a little colonial treasure where race horses take their exercise in the waters of the Río de La Plata. Up the Río Uruguay there are pleasant towns, some with bridges to Argentina, some with hot springs. Also by the river is Fray Bentos, the town that lent its name to corned beef for generations, now home to an industrial museum.

Each summer, millions of holidaymakers flock to Punta del Este, one of the most famous resorts on the continent, but if crowds are not your cup of *mate* (the universal beverage), go out of season. Alternatively, venture up the Atlantic coast towards Brazil for emptier beaches and fishing villages, sea lions, penguins and the occasional old fortress. And anywhere you go, take your binoculars because the birdwatching is excellent.

Planning your trip

Where to go in Uruguay

Montevideo, the capital, is the business heart of the country and has an interesting Ciudad Vieja (old city). The highlights are Mercado del Puerto, the former dockside market, which has become an emporium for traditional food and drink, the magnificently restored Teatro Solís and the pedestrianized Calle Sarandí. Within the city limits are a number of beaches, which continue along the north shore of the Río de la Plata and on to the Atlantic seaboard. The most famous resort is **Punta del Este** which, in season (December to February), is packed with Argentines, Brazilians and locals taking their summer break. Beyond Punta del Este, particularly in the department of Rocha, there are quieter beaches with less infrastructure, but with sand dunes and other natural features. Along the coast, impressive villas and condominiums blend with their surroundings, a sort of museum of contemporary South American architecture under the open sky.

West of the capital is **Colonia del Sacramento**, a unique remnant of colonial building in this part of the continent. It is well preserved, standing on a small peninsula, and has one of the principal ferry ports for passenger traffic from Buenos Aires. Consequently it is a popular, if costly place, well worth a visit, as is the nearby historic town of Carmelo. Continuing west you come to the confluence of the Río Uruguay with the Plata estuary. Up river are the last vestiges of the meat canning industry at **Fray Bentos**, which has a museum commemorating what used to be one of Uruguay's main businesses. Further upstream are towns such as **Paysandú** and the historic **Salto**, from which you can cross to Argentina, and the hot springs which have been developed into resorts.

The centre of the country is mainly agricultural land, used for livestock and crops. Many *estancias* (farms/ranches) accept visitors. Daytrips out of Montevideo, Punta del Este, or Colonia to an *estancia*, usually involve a meal, handicraft shopping and an educational element. The ranches that offer lodging let you take part in the daily tasks, as these are working farms; you can do as much or as little as you like. Horse riding is the main activity and is suitable for all. Fishing, hunting and wine-tasting are also offered at some.

Best time to visit Uruguay

The climate is temperate, often windy, with summer heat tempered by Atlantic breezes. Winter (June to September) is damp; temperatures average 10-16°C, but can sometimes fall to freezing. Summer (December to March) temperatures average 21-27°C. There is always some wind and the nights are relatively cool. The rainfall, with prolonged wet periods in July/August, averages about 1200 mm at Montevideo and some 250 more in the north, but the amount varies yearly.

Most tourists visit during the summer, which is also high season, when prices rise and hotels and transport need advance bookings. In the low season on the coast many places close, although increasingly they're staying open longer to encourage international and local visitors.

Transport in Uruguay

Flight connections If flying from Uruguay to make an international connection in Buenos Aires, make sure your flight goes to Ezeiza International Airport (eg **American Airlines** or **Air Europa**), not Aeroparque (almost all **Aerolíneas Argentinas** flights). Luggage is not transferred automatically to Ezeiza and you will have to travel one hour between the airports by taxi or bus. If you need a visa to enter Argentina, you must get a transit visa (takes up to four weeks to process in Montevideo), just to transfer between airports. See also Tax for airport taxes, page 1440.

Driving in Uruguay

Road Driving is very expensive by South American standards: fuel costs are high and many roads have tolls (passenger vehicles US$2.50, payable in UR$, AR$, US$ or reais). Roads are generally good condition, with a significant proportion paved or all-weather. In rural areas, motorists should drive with their headlights on even in daylight, especially on major roads. Uruguayans are polite drivers: outside Montevideo, trucks will move to let you pass and motorists will alert you of speed traps.

Documents 90-day admission is usually given without any problems. Entry is easier and faster with a *carnet de passages*, but it is not essential. Without it you will be given a temporary import paper which must be surrendered on leaving the country. Insurance is required by law. For more information, see www.aduanas.gub.uy ('preguntas frecuentes').

Organizations **Automóvil Club del Uruguay**, Av del Libertador 1532, T1707, www.acu.com.uy. Reciprocity with foreign automobile clubs is available; members do not have to pay for affiliation.

Fuel All gasoline is unleaded: 97 octane, US$1.98 per litre, 95 octane, US$1.90, *especial* 87 octane, US$1.89 per litre; diesel, US$1.82 per litre. Filling stations may close weekends.

Bus and road All main cities and towns are served by good companies originating from the Tres Cruces Terminal in Montevideo (www.trescruces.com.uy, for schedules and fares, but purchase must be made in person and early if travelling to popular destinations at peak holiday time). There are good services to neighbouring countries. Details are given in the text. Driving your own or a rented vehicle (see page 1454) is a viable way to explore Uruguay, as it allows flexibility and access to further destinations. **Hitching** is not easy.

Train The passenger services are slow commuter services from Montevideo. See page 1454.

Maps Automóvil Club del Uruguay (www.acu.com.uy, see box, above), publishes road maps of the city and country, as do **Esso** and **Ancap**. **ITMB** of Vancouver also publish a country map (1.800,000). Official maps are issued by **Servicio Geográfico Militar** ① *Av 8 de Octubre 3255, T2487 1810, www.ejercito.mil.uy/cal/sgm.*

Where to stay in Uruguay → *See Essentials for our hotel price guide.*

There is an increasingly wide range of accommodation in all categories (slightly fewer mid-range hotels). Luxury accommodation and *estancias* are particularly good. See www.ahru.com.uy and text for further information.

Camping There are lots of sites. Most towns have municipal sites (quality varies). Many sites along the Ruta Interbalnearia, but most of these close off season. The Tourist Office in Montevideo issues a good guide to campsites and youth hostels; see references in main text. See also www.solocampings.com/uruguay.

Youth hostels Many good quality hostels can be found in Montevideo and other cities and towns (see recommendations in Where to stay sections). **Hostelling International** ① *Colonia 1086 p9 Of 903, Montevideo, www.hosteluruguay.org*, has 19 member hostels.

Food and drink in Uruguay → *See Essentials for our restaurant price guide.*

Restaurants Dinner hours are generally 2000-0100. Restaurants usually charge *cubierto* (bread and place setting), costing US$1-3, and more in Punta del Este. Lunch is generally served from 1230-1500, when service often stops until dinner. A *confitería* is an informal place which serves meals at any time, as opposed to a *restaurante*, which serves meals at set times. Uruguay does not as yet have a great selection of international restaurants, although this is slowly changing. Vegetarians may have to stick to salads or pasta, as even the "meatless dishes" may contain some meat. There are a few more vegetarian restaurants in Montevideo and, surprisingly, in some of the smaller beach resorts, attracting a more 'alternative' crowd.

Food In most places, you have two choices: meat or Italian food. Beef is eaten at almost all meals. Most restaurants are *parrilladas* (grills) where the main cuts are *asado* (ribs); *pulpa* (no bones), *lomo* (fillet steak) and entrecote. Steak prices normally indicate the quality of the cut. Also very popular are *chorizos* and *salchichas*, both types of sausage. More exotic Uruguayan favourites include *morcilla* (blood sausage, salty or sweet), *chinchulines* or *chotos* (small or large intestines), *riñones* (kidneys) and *molleja* (sweetbreads). *Cordero* (lamb) and *brochettes* (skewers/kebabs) are also common. Grilled *provolone*, *morrones* (red peppers), *boniatos* (sweet potatoes), and *chimichurri* sauce are also omnipresent. *Chivitos* (large, fully loaded steak sandwiches) and *milanesa* (fried breaded chicken or beef) are also popular; usually eaten with mixed salad (lettuce, tomato, onion), or chips. All Italian dishes are delicious, from bread to pastas to raviolis to desserts. Pizza is very common and good. Seafood includes squid, mussels, shrimp, salmon, and *lenguado* (sole). For snacks, *medialunas* (croissants) are often filled with ham and/or cheese, either hot or cold; toasted sandwiches and quiches/pies are readily available; *frankfurters,* known as *panchos* are hot dogs; *picada* (crackers or breads, cheese, olives, coldcuts) is a common afternoon favourite. Desserts, mostly of Italian origin, are excellent. *Dulce de leche* (similar to caramel) and *dulce de membrillo* (quince paste) are ubiquitous ingredients. As in Argentina, *alfajores* are a favourite sweet snack. Ice cream is excellent everywhere. High quality olive oil is produced near Punta del Este, see www.colinasdegarzon.com for tours and tastings. Punta del Este and surroundings also host a food and wine festival in October.

Drink The beers are good (**Patricia** has been recommended). Local wines vary, but tannat is the regional speciality (eg **Don Pascual, Pisano**) and several bodegas offer tours. See www.bodegasdeluruguay.com.uy and www.uruguaywinetours.com. Whisky is the favourite spirit in Uruguay, normally Johnny Walker. There is also a national brand, Dunbar whisky Uruguayo, a blended whisky that still has a little way to go before reaching international standards, but worth a sample. The local spirits include *uvita, caña* and *grappamiel* (honey liquor). In the Mercado del Puerto, Montevideo, a *medio medio* is half still white wine, half sparkling white (elsewhere a *medio medio* is half *caña* and half whisky). *Espillinar* is a type of Uruguayan rum. Try the *clericó*, a mixture of white wine and fruit juices. Very good fresh fruit juices and mineral water are common. *Mate* is the drink of choice between meal hours. Coffee is good, normally served espresso-style after a meal. Milk, sold in plastic containers, is excellent, skimmed to whole (*descremada* to *entera*)

Essentials A-Z

Accident and emergency
Emergency T911. Ambulance T105 or 911. Medical emergencies T1727.

Fire service T104. Road police T108. Road information: T1954. Tourist Police in Montevideo, at Colonia 1021, T0800-8226.

Electricity

220 volts 50 cycles AC. Various plugs used: round 2-pin or flat 2-pin (most common), oblique 2-pin with earth, 3 round pins in a line.

Embassies and consulates

For all Uruguayan embassies and consulates abroad and for all foreign embassies and consulates in Uruguay, see http://embassy.goabroad.com.

Festivals in Uruguay

Public holidays 1 Jan, 6 Jan; Carnival; Easter week (Tourism Week); 19 Apr; 1 and 18 May, 19 Jun; 18 Jul; 25 Aug (the night before is **Noche de la Nostalgia**, when people gather in *boliches* to dance to old songs); 12 Oct; 2 Nov; 25 Dec.

Carnival begins in late Jan/early Feb and lasts for some 40 days until Carnival week, officially Mon and Tue before Ash Wed (many firms close for the whole week). The most prominent elements in Carnival are Candombe, representing the rituals of the African slaves brought to Río de la Plata in colonial times, through drumming and dance. The complex polyrhythms produced by the mass of drummers advancing down the street in the 'Llamadas' parades are very impressive. The other main element is Murga, a form of street theatre with parody, satire, singing and dancing by elaborately made-up and costumed performers.

Business also comes to a standstill during Holy Week (or Tourism Week), which coincides with La Semana Criolla del Prado (horse-breaking, stunt riding by gauchos, dances and song) Department stores close only from Good Fri. Banks and offices close Thu-Sun. Easter Mon is not a holiday. Also in Mar/Apr Tacuarembó, in the north, hosts gaucho festival Patria Gaucha. A weekend of Oct is chosen annually for celebrating the Día del Patrimonio (Heritage Day) throughout the country: hundreds of buildings, both public or private, including embassies, are open to the public for that day only. Also special train services run.

Money → *US$1=23.05, €1=31.42 (Jun 2014)*. The currency is the *peso uruguayo*. Bank notes: 20, 50, 100, 200, 500, 1000 and 2000 pesos uruguayos. Coins: 1, 2, 5, 10 and 50 (the latter is rare) pesos. Any amount of currency can be taken in or out.

There's no restriction on foreign exchange transactions (so it is a good place to stock up with US$ bills, though AmEx and some banks refuse to do this for credit cards; most places charge 3% commission for such transactions).

Dollars cash can be purchased when leaving the country. Changing Argentine pesos into Uruguayan pesos is usually a marginally worse rate than for dollars. Brazilian *reais* get a much worse rate. US$, Argentina pesos or Brazilian reais notes are accepted for some services, including hotels and restaurants in the main tourist centres.

Cost of travelling Prices vary considerably between summer and winter in tourist destinations, Punta del Este being one of the most expensive summer resorts in Latin America. In Montevideo, allow US$70-80 daily for a cheap hotel, eating the *menú del día* and travelling by bus. Internet price varies, around US$1 per hr at Antel *telecentros*.

Credit cards In some places there is a 10% charge to use Visa and MasterCard. **Banred**, www.banred.com.uy, is the largest ATM network from where you can withdraw US$ or pesos with a Visa or MasterCard. **HSBC, Lloyds TSB, BBVA, Citibank** all have Banred ATMs. **Banco de la República** (BROU) branches have Banred, Link and Cirrus ATMs. ATMs can also be found in supermarkets. Most cheaper hotels outside major cities do not accept credit cards.

Postal services

The main post office in Montevideo is at Misiones 1328 y Buenos Aires; 0800-1800 Mon-Fri, 0800-1300 Sat and holidays. **Poste restante** at main post office will keep mail for 1 month. Other branches in the capital: on Av Libertador 1440, next to Montevideo Shopping Center, 0800-1300, and under the Intendencia at corner of Av 18 de Julio and Ejido, Mon-Fri 1000-2000, Sat 1700-2200.

Safety

Personal security offers few problems in most of Uruguay. Petty theft does occur in Montevideo, most likely in tourist areas or markets. Beggars are often seen trying to sell small items or simply asking for money. They are not dangerous. The Policía Turística patrols the streets of the capital. In December 2013, Uruguay became the first country in the world to legalize cannabis/marijuana, as a drug-fighting measure. At the time of writing, the measure did not appear to have any significant impact on visitors. Bear in mind that crossing borders while in possession of drugs is still a serious offence.

Tax

Airport tax US$19 on all air travellers leaving Uruguay for Buenos Aires, Aeroparque, but US$40 to Ezeiza and all other countries (payable in US$, or local currency), and a tax of 3% on all tickets issued and paid for in Uruguay. Domestic airport tax is US$2.

VAT/IVA 22%, 10% on certain basic items.

Telephone → Country code +598.
Ringing: long equal tones, long pauses. Engaged: short tones, short pauses.

In Uruguay, fixed line numbers are 8 digits long. There are no area codes. Mobile phone numbers are prefixed by 9 if calling from outside Uruguay and 09 if calling within the country. **Antel** *telecentros* in cities are good places to find phone, internet and other means of communication.

Time

GMT -3 (Oct-Mar -2).

Tipping

Restaurant and cafés usually include service, but an additional 10% is expected. Porters at the airport: US$1 per piece of luggage. Taxis: 5-10% of fare.

Tourist information

Ministry of Tourism Rambla 25 de Agosto de 1825 y Yacaré, T2188 5100, www.turismo.gub.uy. For birdwatching, contact: **Avesuruguay/Gupeca** Canelones 1198, Montevideo, T2902 8642, www.avesuruguay.org.uy, Mon-Fri 1600-2000. Uruguay is creating a system of national parks under the heading **Sistema Nacional de Areas Protegidas** (SNA), see www.snap.gub.uy (Spanish only).

Useful websites

www.welcomeuruguay.com Excellent bilingual regional guide to all tourist related businesses and events.
www.turismodeluruguay.com A tourism portal in English, Spanish and Portuguese.
www.brecha.com.uy *Brecha*, a progressive weekly listing films, theatres and concerts in Montevideo and provinces, US$2 (special editions sometimes free). Recommended.

Visas and immigration

A passport is necessary for entry except for nationals of most Latin American countries, who can get in with national identity documents for stays of up to 90 days. Nationals of the following countries need a visa for a tourist visit of less than 3 months: China, Egypt, Guyana, Morrocco and the majority of Caribbean, African, Middle Eastern, Central Asian and Asian states. Visas cost US$42, and you need a passport photo, hotel reservations or letter of invitation and a ticket out of Uruguay. Visa processing may take 2-4 weeks. Visas are valid for 90 days and usually multiple entry. Tourist cards (obligatory for all tourists, obtainable on entry) are valid for 3 months, extendable for a similar period at the **Migraciones office** C Misiones 1513, T2152 1800, www.dnm.minterior.gub.uy. If entering and leaving Uruguay overland (bus or ferry), you may on departure be asked to show the ticket with which you arrived in the country.

Weights and measures

Metric.

Working hours

Shops: Mon-Fri 1000-1900; Sat 1000-1300; **shopping malls**: daily 1000-2200. In small towns or non-tourist areas, there is a break for lunch and siesta, between 1300 and 1600. **Businesses**: 0830-1200, 1430-1830 or 1900. **Banks**: Mon-Fri 1300-1700 (some till 1800). **Government offices**: Mon-Fri 1200-1800 in summer; Mon-Fri 1000-1700 (rest of the year).

Montevideo

Montevideo, the capital, is a modern city that feels very much like a town. Barrios retain their personality while the city gels into one. The main areas, from west to east are: the shipping port, downtown, several riverside and central neighbourhoods (Palermo, Punta Carretas, Pocitos), the suburbs and Carrasco International airport, all connected by the Rambla. Everything blends together – architecture, markets, restaurants, stores, malls, stadiums, parks and beaches – and you can find what you need in a short walk.

Montevideo, officially declared a city in 1726, sits on a promontory between the Río de la Plata and an inner bay, though the early fortifications have been destroyed. Spanish and Italian architecture, French and Art Deco styles can be seen, especially in Ciudad Vieja. The city not only dominates the country's commerce and culture: it accounts for 70% of industrial production and handles almost 90% of imports and exports. In January and February many locals leave for the string of seaside resorts to the east. The first football World Cup was held in Centenario Stadium and won by Uruguay in 1930.

Arriving in Montevideo → *Colour map 8, B6. Population: 1,340,535 (2012).*

Orientation Carrasco International **airport** is east of the centre, with easy connections by bus or taxi (20-30 minutes to downtown). Many visitors arrive at the port by boat from Buenos Aires, or by boat to Colonia and then bus to the Tres Cruces bus terminal just north of downtown. Both port and terminal have good facilities and tourist information.

The Ciudad Vieja can be explored on foot. From Plaza de la Independencia buses are plentiful along Avenida 18 de Julio, connecting all parts of the city. Taxis are also plentiful, affordable and generally trustworthy, although compact. *Remises* (private driver and car) can be rented by the hour. **Note** Street names are located on buildings, not street signs. Some plazas and streets are known by two names: for instance, Plaza de la Constitución is also called Plaza Matriz. It's a good idea to point out to a driver the location you want on a map and follow your route as you go. Also, seemingly direct routes rarely exist owing to the many one-way streets and, outside the centre, non-grid layout. ▶▶ *See Transport, page 1452.*

Tourist offices Tourist information for the whole country is at the **Tres Cruces bus terminal** ① *T2409 7399, trescruces@mintur.gub.uy, Mon-Fri 0800-2200, Sat-Sun 0900-2200*; at the **Ministry of Tourism** ① *Rambla 25 de Agosto de 1825 y Yacaré (next to the port), T21885, ext111*; and at **Carrasco international airport** ① *T2604 0386, carrasco@mintur.gub.uy, 0800-2000*; which has good maps. For information on Montevideo, at **Mercado del Puerto** ① *Rambla 25 de Agosto de 1825 y Maciel, T2916 1513, also at Piedras and Pérez Castellano 1424, T2916 5287, Intendencia de Montevideo, Av 18 de Julio esq Ejido, at airport, port and Tres Cruces, all helpful. Pick up a copy of *Descubrí Montevideo*, useful city guide with an English version, downloadable from the municipal website or www.descubrimontevideo.uy. Check also at the municipal website for weekend tours, www.montevideo.gub.uy. For the **Tourist Police** ① *Colonia 1021, T0800 8226.* See also www.montevideo.com.uy and www.cartelera.com.uy.

Maps Best street maps of Montevideo are at the beginning of the *Guía Telefónica* (both white and yellow page volumes). Free maps in all tourist offices and some museums. Downloadable map at www.montevideo.gub.uy. Guía *Eureka de Montevideo* is recommended for streets, with index and bus routes (US$8.50-10 from bookshops and newspaper kiosks).

Places in Montevideo

City centre

In the **Ciudad Vieja** is the oldest square in Montevideo: the **Plaza de la Constitución** or **Matriz**. On one side is the **Catedral** (1790-1804), with the historic **Cabildo** (1804) ① *JC Gómez 1362, T2915 9685, Mon-Fri 1200-1745, Sat 1000-1600, free,* opposite. It contains the **Museo y Archivo Histórico Municipal**. The Cabildo has several exhibition halls. On the south side is the **Club Uruguay** (built in 1888), which is worth a look inside. See also the unusual fountain (1881), surrounded by art and antique vendors under the sycamore trees.

West along Calle Rincón is the small **Plaza Zabala**, with a monument to Bruno Mauricio de Zabala, founder of the city. North of this Plaza are: the **Banco de la República** ① *Cerrito y Zabala* and the **Aduana** ① *Rambla 25 de Agosto.* Several historic houses belong to the Museo Histórico Nacional (see www.mec.gub.uy, or www.museohistorico.gub.uy): **Museo Histórico Nacional (Casa de Rivera)** ① *Rincón 437, T2915 1051, Mon-Fri 1100-1700, free,* is an early 19th-century mansion of the first president of the republic. Its rooms are dedicated to various stages of Uruguayan history. **Palacio Taranco, Museo de Artes Decorativas** ① *25 de Mayo 376, T2915 6060, Mon-Fri 1230-1730,*

Montevideo Ciudad Vieja & Centre

Where to stay ⬤
1 Arapey *A4*
2 Balfer *B6*
3 El Viajero Downtown Hostel & Suites *B5*
4 Don *A1*
5 El Viajero Ciudad Vieja Hostel *A3*
6 Embajador *B6*
7 Europa *A6*
8 Four Points by Sheraton *B6*
9 Hispano *B4*
10 Iberia *B5*
11 Klee Internacional *B6*
13 London Palace *B5*
15 Montevideo Hostel *B4*
16 Nh Columbia *B3*
17 Oxford *B5*
18 Palacio *B3*
19 Palermo Art Hostel *C6*
20 Plaza Fuerte *B3*
21 Radisson Victoria Plaza *A4*
22 Red Hostel *C6*

free, whose garden overlooks Plaza Zabala, a palatial mansion in turn-of-the-20th-century French style, with sumptuously decorated rooms, and a museum of Islamic and Classical pottery and glass. It was first built as a theatre in 1793 and rebuilt in 1908 after it was bought by the Ortiz de Taranco family. Also in the Ciudad Vieja is the **MAPI, Museo de Arte Precolombino e Indígena** ① *25 de Mayo 279, T2916 9360, www.mapi.org.uy, Mon-Fri 1130-1730, Sat 1000-1600, US$3*, in a 19th-century mansion, bringing together public and private collections of local and non-Uruguayan artefacts.

The main port is near the Ciudad Vieja, with the docks three blocks north of Plaza Zabala. Three blocks south of the Plaza is the Río de la Plata. Cross the Rambla from the docks to visit the **Mercado del Puerto** (see Restaurants, page 1448) and the adjacent **Museo del Carnaval** ① *Rambla 25 de Agosto 1825, T2915 0807, www.museodelcarnaval.org, daily 1100-1700 (closed Tue, Apr-Dec), US$3*, a small exhibition with colourful pictures and costumes from the February celebrations. Proceed south one block to Cerrito, east two blocks to the **Banco de la República** and church of **San Francisco** (1864) ① *Solís 1469*, south across Plaza Zabala to Peatonal Sarandí (pedestrianized street) and east to Plaza de la Independencia (see next paragraph), stopping at the aforementioned historical sites as desired. Restoration efforts are slow but steady. Although safe by day, with many tourist police, common sense, even avoidance, is recommended at night.

Recently opened in a 19th-century building in the centre is **Museo Andes 1972** ① *Rincón 619, T2916 9461, www.mandes.uy, Mon-Sat 1000-1700*, a small museum commemorating the 1972 plane crash in which a Uruguayan rugby team survived 72 days in the Andean mountains. Not recommended for children under 12.

Between the Ciudad Vieja and the new city is the largest of Montevideo's squares, **Plaza de la Independencia**, a short distance east of Plaza de la Constitución. Numerous cafés, shops and boutiques line Peatonal Sarandí. Two small pedestrian zones full of cafés, live music (mostly after 2300) and restaurants, Peatonal Bacacay and Policia Vieja, lead off Sarandí. Below his statue (1923) in the middle of Plaza de la Independencia is the subterranean marble mausoleum of Artigas. Just west of the plaza is **Museo Torres García** ① *Sarandí 683, T2916 2663, www.torresgarcia.org.uy, Mon-Sat 1000-1800, US$3.10, free Wed, bookshop*. It has an exhibition of the paintings of Joaquín Torres García (1874-1949), one of Uruguay's foremost contributors to the modern art movements of the 20th century, and five floors dedicated to temporary exhibitions of contemporary Uruguayan and international artists. At the eastern end is the **Palacio Salvo** ① *Plaza Independencia 846-848*, built 1923-1928. The first skyscraper in Uruguay and the tallest South American structure of its time, opinions are divided on

23 Sur Hotel *C5*

Restaurants ❼
1 Bosque Bambú *B5*
2 Café Bacacay & Panini's Boutique *B3*
3 Corchos *A3*
4 El Fogón *B5*
5 Los Leños Uruguayos *B5*
6 Mercado del Puerto *A1*
8 Subte Pizzería *B6*
9 Tartar *B5*
10 Viejo Sancho *B6*

its architectural merit. Currently it houses a mixture of businesses and residences. The famous tango, *La Cumparsita*, was written in a former café at its base. On the southern side is the **Museo de la Casa de Gobierno** ① *Palacio Estévez, Plaza Independencia 776, Mon-Fri 1000-1700*, with an exhibition of Uruguay's presidential history. Just off the plaza to the west is the splendid **Teatro Solís** (1842-69) ① *Reconquista y Bartolomé Mitre, T2-1950 3323, www.teatrosolis.org.uy, guided visits on Tue-Sun 1100, 1200, 1600 (Sat also at 1300), Wed free, otherwise US$1 in Spanish (US$2.20 for tours in other languages)*. It has been entirely restored to perfection, with added elevators, access for disabled people, marble flooring and impressive attention to detail. Built as an opera house, Teatro Solís is now used for many cultural events, including ballet, classical music, even tango performances. Check press for listings. Tickets sold daily 1100-1900.

Avenida 18 de Julio runs east from Plaza de la Independencia. The **Museo de Arte Contemporaneo** ① *18 de Julio 965, 2nd floor, T2900 6662, Tue-Sat 1400-2000, free*, holds temporary exhibitions. In the **Museo del Gaucho y de la Moneda** ① *Av 18 de Julio 998, Palacio Heber Jackson, T2900 8764, Mon-Fri 1000-1700, free*, the Museo de la Moneda has a survey of Uruguayan currency and a collection of Roman coins. Museo del Gaucho is a fascinating history of the Uruguayan gaucho and is highly recommended. Between Julio Herrera and Río Negro is the **Plaza Fabini**, or **del Entrevero**, with a statue of *gauchos* engaged in battle, the last big piece of work by sculptor José Belloni. Beneath the plaza is the **Centro Municipal de Exposiciones – Subte** ① *www.subte.montevideo.gub.uy, Tue-Sun 1200-1900, free*, temporary exhibitions of contemporary art, photography, etc. In the **Plaza Cagancha** (or Plaza Libertad) is a statue of Peace. The restored **Mercado de la Abundancia** ① *San Jose 1312*, is an attractive old market with handicrafts, good local restaurants with lunch specials and tango dancing by Joventango three evenings a week. The **Palacio Municipal** (La Intendencia) is on the south side of Avenida 18 de Julio, just before it bends north, at the statue of **El Gaucho**. It often has interesting art and photo exhibitions and there is a huge satellite image of the city displayed on the main hall's floor. The road which forks south from the Gaucho is Constituyente, and leads to the beach at Pocitos. **Museo de Historia del Arte** ① *Ejido 1326, T1950 2191, Tue-Sun 1330-1900, free*, is also in the Palacio Municipal. **Centro de Fotografía** ① *Palacio Municipal (San José 1360, T1950 1219, www.montevideo.gub.uy/fotografia), Mon-Fri 1000-1900, Sat 0930-1430, free*, has photography exhibitions.

The immense **Palacio Legislativo** ① *from Plaza Fabini head along Av del Libertador Brig Gen Juan Lavalleja (known as Av Libertador), 5 blocks east of Plaza de la Independencia (buses 173, 175 from C Mercedes), guided visits hourly Mon-Fri 0900-1800 (3 a day in summer), US$3.10*, was built 1908-1925 from local marble: there are 52 colours of Uruguayan marble in the Salón de los Pasos Perdidos, 12 types of wood in the library. Other rooms are also beautiful. Not far, and dramatically changing the city skyline, is the 160-m-high **Antel building** ① *Paraguay y Guatemala, Aguada, T2928 8517, free guided visits Mon, Wed, Fri 1530-1700; Tue, Thu 1030-1200*, with a public terrace on the 26th floor for panoramic bay views.

Outside the centre

Centro Cultural y Museo de la Memoria ① *Av de las Instrucciones 1057, Prado, T2355 5891, http://museodelamemoria-montevideo.blogspot.co.uk/, Mon-Sat 1300-1900, free*, is a fascinating space commemorating the horrors of Uruguay's 1970s-80s dictatorship. **Museo Municipal de Bellas Artes Juan Manuel Blanes** ① *Millán 4015, Prado, T2336 2248, http://blanes.montevideo.gub.uy/, Tue-Sun 1215-1745, free, take buses 148 or 149 from Mercedes*, in the ex-Quinta Raffo (a late 19th-century mansion) is dedicated to the work of the artist Blanes (1830-1901). It also has a room of the works of Pedro Figari (1861-1938), a lawyer who painted strange, naive pictures of peasant life and ceremonies of the Afro-Uruguayans, also other Uruguayan artists' work. **Museo Zoológico** ① *Rambla República de Chile 4215, Buceo, T2622 0258, Tue-Sat 1015-1545, free, take bus 104 from 18 de Julio*, is well displayed and arranged, recommended, great for children. Closed for refurbishment at the time of writing, check with tourist board for reopening details.

In the **Puerto del Buceo**, following the coast eastwards away from the centre, the ship's bell of *HMS Ajax* and rangefinder of the German pocket-battleship, *Graf Spee*, can be seen at the **Naval Museum** ① *Rambla Charles de Gaulle y Luis A de Herrera, Buceo, T2622 1084, 0800-1200, 1400-1800, closed Thu, free*. Both ships were involved in the Battle of the River Plate (13 December 1939) after which *Graf Spee* was scuttled off Montevideo. The museum also has displays of documentation from this battle, naval history from the War of Independence onwards and on the sailing ship *Capitán Miranda*, which circumnavigated the globe in 1937-1938.

Parque Batlle y Ordóñez (reached eastwards of Avenida 18 de Julio), has numerous statues: the most interesting group is the well-known **La Carreta** monument, by José Belloni, showing three yoke of oxen drawing a wagon. In the grounds is the **Estadio Centenario**, the national 65,000-seater football stadium and a football museum, an athletics field and a bicycle race-track (bus 107). The **Planetarium** ① *next to the Jardín Zoológico, at Av Rivera 3275, T2622 9109, take bus 60 from Av 18 de Julio, or buses 141, 142 or 144 from San José*, gives good, 40-minute shows on Saturday and Sunday (also Tuesday-Friday on holidays), free.

From the Palacio Legislativo, Avenida Agraciada runs northwest to **Parque Prado**, the oldest of the city's many parks, about 5 km from Avenida 18 de Julio (bus 125 and others). Among fine lawns, trees and lakes is a rose garden planted with 850 varieties and the monument of **La Diligencia** (the stage coach). Part of the park is the adjacent **Jardín Botánico** ① *daily summer 0700-1800, winter 0700-1700, guided tours, T2336 4005. It is reached via Av 19 de Abril (bus 522 from Ejido next to Palacio Municipal), or via Av Dr LA de Herrera (bus 147 from Paysandú)*. The most popular park is **Parque Rodó**, on Rambla Presidente Wilson, with an open-air theatre, an amusement park, and a boating lake. At the eastern end is the **Museo Nacional de Artes Visuales** ① *Tomás Giribaldi 2283 esq Herrera y Reissig, T2711 6054, www.mnav.gub.uy, Tue-Sun 1400-1700, free*, a collection of contemporary plastic arts, plus a room devoted to Blanes. Recommended.

Within the city limits, the **Punta Carretas**, **Pocitos** and **Buceo** neighbourhoods are the nicest, with a mix of classical homes, tall condos, wonderful stores, services, restaurants, active beaches, parks, and two major malls: the **Montevideo Shopping Center**, on the east edge of Pocitos (Herrera 1290 y Laguna, 1 block south of Rivera, www.montevideoshopping.com.uy, and **Punta Carretas Shopping** (Ellauri 350, close to Playa Pocitos in the former prison, www.puntacarretasweb.com.uy). Outside the city along Rambla Sur, the affluent **Carrasco** suburb has large homes, quieter beaches, parks and services. **Parque Roosevelt**, a green belt stretching north, and the international airport are nearby. The express bus D1 (US$1.40) runs every 20 minutes Monday to Saturday (about every hour Sunday and holidays) along Avenida 18 de Julio and the Rambla and is about 30 minutes quicker, and more comfortable, to Carrasco.

At the western end of the bay is the **Cerro**, or hill ① *getting there: bus from centre to Cerro: 125 'Cerro' from Mercedes*, 139 m high (from which Montevideo gets its name), with the Fortaleza General Artigas, an old fort, at the top. It is now the **Museo Militar** ① *T2313 6716, Wed-Sun 1000-1700, free (fort visit US$0.90)*. It houses historical mementos, documentation of the War of Independence and has one of the only panoramic views of Montevideo. The Cerro is surmounted by the oldest lighthouse in the country (1804).

Bathing **beaches** stretch along Montevideo's water front, from Playa Ramírez in the west to Playa Carrasco in the east. The waterfront boulevard, Rambla Naciones Unidas, is named along its several stretches in honour of various nations. Bus 104 from Aduana, which goes along Avenida 18 de Julio, gives a pleasant ride (further inland in winter) past Pocitos, Punta Gorda and all the beaches to Playa Miramar, beyond Carrasco, total journey time from Pocitos to Carrasco, 35 minutes. The seawater, despite its muddy colour (sediment stirred up by the Río de la Plata), is safe to bathe in and the beaches are clean. Lifeguards are on duty during the summer months.

For hotel and restaurant price codes, and other relevant information, see Essentials.

⊜ Where to stay

Non-residents are exempt from paying 22% IVA tax, which is usually listed separately in upper category hotels, but may be included in cheaper and mid-range options; check when booking. High season is 15 Dec-15 Mar, book ahead; many beach hotels only offer full board during this time. After 1 Apr prices are reduced and some hotel dining rooms shut down. During Carnival, prices go up by 20%. The city is visited by Argentines at weekends: many hotels increase prices. Midweek prices may be lower than those posted.

The tourist office has information on the more expensive hotels. Holiday Inn, www.holidayinn.com.uy, Ibis, www.ibis.com, and others, are represented. For more information and reservations contact Asociación de Hoteles y Restaurantes del Uruguay, Gutiérrez Ruiz 1215, T2908 0141, www.ahru.com.uy. All those listed below have been recommended.

City centre *p1442, map p1442*
$$$$ Don, Piedras 234, T2915 9999, www.donhotel.com.uy. Boutique hotel in 1930s building opposite Mercado del Puerto. With breakfast, 3 standards of room, all modern services including safe in room, restaurant.
$$$$ Four Points by Sheraton, Ejido 1275, T2901 7000, www.fourpointsmontevideo.com. Stylish hotel in the heart of Montevideo with all the mod cons. Indoor pool on the 10th floor, overlooking the city, spa treatments, cosy bar and fine dining.
$$$$ Radisson Victoria Plaza, Plaza Independencia 759, T2902 0111, www.radisson.com/montevideouy. Excellent restaurant (rooftop, fine views, Mon-Fri, lunchtime only), less formal restaurant in lobby, luxurious casino in basement, with new 5-star wing, art and antiques gallery, business centre (for guests only), pool, spa.

$$$ Balfer, Z Michelini 1328, T2902 0073, www.hotelbalfer.com. Good, safe deposit, excellent breakfast.
$$$ Embajador, San José 1212, T2902 0012, www.hotelembajador.com. Sauna, swimming pool in the summer, parking, medical services, free computer use, excellent all round.
$$$ Europa, Colonia 1341, T2902 0045, www.hoteleuropa.com.uy. Comfortable, spacious rooms, good choice in this price range, buffet breakfast, restaurant, parking.
$$$ Hispano, Convención 1317, T2900 3816, www.hispanohotel.com. Comfortable with good services, laundry, parking.
$$$ Klee Internacional, San José 1303, T2902 0606, www.klee.com.uy. Very comfortable, good value in standard rooms, spacious, buffet breakfast, heater, minibar, good view.
$$$ London Palace, Río Negro 1278, T2902 0024, www.lphotel.com. Well-established, convenient, excellent breakfast, parking. Associated with restaurant El Fogón (see below).
$$$ NH Columbia, Rambla Gran Bretaña 473, T2916 0001, www.nh-hotels.com. 1st class, overlooking the river in Ciudad Vieja. Well-appointed rooms, restaurant, sauna, fitness room.
$$$ Oxford, Paraguay 1286, T2902 0046, www.hoteloxford.com.uy. Good buffet breakfast, safes, laundry service, parking.
$$$ Plaza Fuerte, Bartolomé Mitre 1361, T2915 6651, www.plazafuerte.com. Restored 1913 building, historical monument, safe, restaurant, pub.
$$$-$$ Iberia, Maldonado 1097, T2901 3633, www.internet.com.uy/hoiberia. Very helpful staff, bike rental, stereos, minibar. US$6 for breakfast. Modern and refurbished.
$$$-$$ Sur Hotel, Maldonado 1098, T2908 2025, www.surhotel.com. Colourful, refurbished, welcoming, some rooms with balconies. Good continental breakfast for US$5, 24-hr room service, jacuzzi in 2 rooms.
$$ Arapey, Av Uruguay 925, near Convención, T2900 7032, www.arapey.com.uy. Slightly run-

down old building, in central location. Variety of rooms with fan, heating, no breakfast.

$$ El Viajero Ciudad Vieja Hostel, Ituzaingó 1436, T2915 6192, www.ciudadviejahostel.com. HI affiliate, hostel with lots of services (Spanish and tango lessons, bike hire, city tours, laundry, theatre tickets, football), double rooms and shared bedrooms (**$**), safes, airport transport, helpful staff.

$$ Palacio, Bartolomé Mitre 1364, T2916 3612, www.hotelpalacio.com.uy. Old hotel, a bit run-down, superior rooms with balconies, laundry service, stores luggage, no breakfast, frequently booked, good value.

$$-$ El Viajero Downtown Hostel and Suites, Soriano 1073, T2908 2913, www.elviajero hostels.com. Private en suite with a/c and TV, dorms en suite (**$**), breakfast included, BBQ area, bar, outdoor terrace, free Wi-Fi, bike rental.

$$-$ Red Hostel, San José 1406, T2908 8514, www.redhostel.com. By the Intendencia, hostel with dorms and 1 double, all with shared bath, cheerful, computers, safe, breakfast, roof terrace and kitchen. Closed at the time of writing, but re-opening Dec 2014.

$ pp Montevideo Hostel, Canelones 935, T2908 1324, www.montevideohostel.com. uy. HI affiliate. Open all year, 24 hrs (seasonal variations), dormitory style, kitchen, breakfast included, can be noisy in street-facing rooms, bicycle hire US$6.60 all day. Family-run. Recommended.

Outside the centre p1444
Tres Cruces, Palermo

$$$ Days Inn, Acevedo Díaz 1821, T2400 4840, www.daysinn.com.uy. Buffet breakfast, safe, coffee shop and health club, look for promotional offers.

$$$ Tres Cruces, Miguelete 2356 esq Acevedo Díaz, T2402 3474, www.hoteltres cruces.com.uy. Safe, café, decent buffet breakfast. Disabled access.

$$$-$$ Palermo Art Hostel, Gaboto 1010, T2410 6519, www.palermoarthostel.com. Cosy and colourful, bar and live music, private and shared rooms (**$**), pool, terrace, bike rental, near beach and US Embassy, a good choice.

East of the centre (Punta Carretas, Pocitos)

$$$$-$$$ Ermitage, Juan Benito Blanco 783, T2710 4021, www.ermitagemontevideo.com. Near Pocitos beach, remodelled 1945 building, rooms, apartments and suites, some with great views, buffet breakfast.

$$$$-$$$ Pocitos Plaza, Juan Benito Blanco 640, Pocitos, T2712 3939, www. pocitosplazahotel.com.uy. Modern building in pleasant residential district, next to the river, with large functional rooms, buffet breakfast, gym and sauna.

$ pp Pocitos Hostel, Av Sarmiento 2641 y Aguilar, T2711 8780, www.pocitos hostel.com. Rooms for 2 to 6 (mixed and women only), use of kitchen, *parrilla*, towels extra (US$2), Spanish classes.

Carrasco
$$$$ Belmont House, Av Rivera 6512, T2600 0430, www.belmonthouse.com.uy. 5-star, 28 beautifully furnished rooms, top quality, excellent restaurant Allegro, pub/bar Memories, English tea room 1700-2000, pool, 3 blocks from beach.

$$$$ Cottage, Miraflores 1360, T2600 1111, www.hotelcottage.com.uy. In a prime location next to wide beaches and in quiet residential surroundings, very comfortable, simply furnished rooms with minibar, restaurant Rambla, bar 1940, pool in a lovely garden, excellent.

$$$$ Regency Suites, Gabriel Otero 6428, T2600 1383, www.regencysuites.com.uy. Good boutique-style hotel with all services, fitness centre, pool, restaurant Cava and pub/wine bar, a couple of blocks from the beach. In same group and price range is the contemporary Regency Rambla, Rep de México 6079, T2601 5555, www.regencyrambla.com.uy

$$$$ Sofitel Montevideo Casino Carrasco & Spa, Rambla México 6451, T2604 6060, www. sofitel.com. This 100-year-old hotel and casino has been beautifully restored over a period of three years and offers 93 rooms and 23 suites on the Carrasco waterfront. State-of-the-art relaxing So Spa, fantastic bar and excellent restaurant. Recommended.

🍴 Restaurants

There is a 22% tax on restaurant bills that is usually included, plus a charge for bread and service (*cubierto*) that varies between US$1-3 pp.

City centre *p1442, map p1442*

$$$ Café Bacacay, Bacacay 1306 y Buenos Aires, T2916 6074, www.bacacay.com.uy. Closed Sun. Good music and atmosphere, food served, try the specials.

$$$ Corchos, 25 de Mayo 651, T2917 2051, www.corchos.com.uy. Mon-Fri 1100-1700, also Fri night 2000-2400. Bistro, wine bar and wine shop, 3 different lunchtime set menus from US$10, specializes in Uruguayan wines and gourmet dishes to accompany them.

$$$ Crocus, San Salvador y Minas (Palermo), T2411 0039. Closed Sun. Excellent meals with French and Mediterranean touches.

$$$ El Fogón, San José 1080. Open 1200-0000. Good value typical food, always full, arrive by 2000.

$$$ El Mercado del Puerto, opposite the Aduana, Calle Piedras, between Maciel and Pérez Castellanos (take 'Aduana' bus), www.mercadodelpuerto.com.uy. Don't miss eating at this 19th-century market building. Choose from delicious grills cooked on huge charcoal grates or more international fare like Spanish tapas and pasta. Best to go at lunchtime, especially Sat; the atmosphere's great, open until 1800 (last orders 1700). Inside the Mercado del Puerto, those recommended are: **Roldós**, sandwiches, most people start with a *medio medio* (half still, half sparkling white wine). **El Palenque**, famed as the finest restaurant, try their excellent *clericó*. **La Estancia del Puerto**, **Cabaña Verónica**, **La Chacra del Puerto**. By far the busiest at lunchtime any day of the week is **Empanadas Carolina** with over 20 varieties to choose from.

$$$ Los Leños Uruguayos, San José 909, T2900 2285. www.parrilla.com.uy. Good and smart *parrilla*, with an extensive and varied menu, including rice and pasta dishes, fish and seafood.

$$$ Panini's Boutique, Bacacay 1341 (also at 26 de Marzo 3586, Pocitos). Deli and lunchtime café. Good salads and meal deals.

$$$ Viejo Sancho, San José 1229. Closed Sun. Excellent, popular, set menus for US$12.50 pp.

$$ Bosque Bambú, San José 1060. Asian, vegan and vegetarian buffet, eat-in or take-away. Also food shop.

$$ Subte Pizzería, Ejido 1327, T2902 3050. An institution, cheap and good.

$ Tartar, San José 1096, T2902 3154. Tiny café selling fresh fruit juices, *empanadas*, savoury pies and *chivitos*. Lunchtime specials US$4.50.

Outside the centre *p1444*
In and around Pocitos

$$$ Bar Tabaré, Zorrilla de San Martín 152/54, T2712 3242. Wonderful restaurant in a converted old *almacén* (grocery shop). Great wines and entrées.

$$$ Da Pentella, Luis de la Torre 598, esq Francisco Ros, T2712 0981. Amazing Italian and seafood, artistic ambience, great wines.

$$$ Francis, Luis de la Torre 502 esq JM Montero, Punta Carretas, T2711 8603, http://francis.com.uy. Wide-ranging menu, including *parrilla*, sushi, pastas and seafood, fashionable with prices to match. Has another branch in Carrasco.

$$$ La Otra, Tomás Diago 752 y Juan Pérez, T2711 3006. Specializes in meat, lively.

$$$ Pantagruel, Obligado 1199 esq Maldonado, T2709 1436. Closed Sun evening and Mon. Varied menu including *parrilla* and Mediterranean, good quality and value.

$$$ Spaghetteria 32, Franzini y Carlos Berg, T2710 9769. Closed Mon. Very good Italian choice, serving excellent home-made pasta.

$$$ El Viejo y el Mar, Rambla Gandhi 400 y Solano García, Punta Carretas, T2710 5704. Fishing community atmosphere with a great location by the river.

$$ Pizzería Trouville, 21 de Septiembre y Francisco Vidal (also at Pereira y 26 de Marzo). A traditional pizza place with tables outside, next to the beach.

$$ Tranquilo Bar, 21 de Septiembre 3104. Very popular restaurant/bar, great lunch menu.

Carrasco/Punta Gorda

Several restaurants on Av Arocena close to the beach, packed Sun midday.

$$$ Café Misterio, Costa Rica 1700, esq Av Rivera, T2601 8765. Lots of choice on menu, sushi, cocktails. Completely new decor and menu every 6 months.

$$$ García, Arocena 1587, T2600 2703. Spacious, indoor and outdoor seating, large wine selection, rack of lamb is a speciality.

$$$ Hemingway, Rambla Méjico 5535, on west side of Punta Gorda, T2600 0121. Decent food, worth going for amazing sunset views of river and city, great outdoor seating.

Confiterías Café Brasilero, Ituzaingó 1447, half a block from Plaza Matriz towards the port. Small entrance; easy to miss. A must, one of the oldest cafés in Montevideo and a permanent hangout of one of the greatest Latin American writers, Eduardo Galeano. Others include: **Amaretto**, 21 de Septiembre y Roque Graseras, Punta Carretas. Excellent Italian coffee and pastries. **Bar Iberia**, Uruguay esq Florida, Locals' bar. **Manchester Bar**, 18 de Julio 899. Good for breakfasts. **Oro del Rhin**, Convención 1403 (also at Pocitos riverfront, on Plaza Cagancha and at shopping malls). Mon-Fri 0830-2000 (Sat till 1400), open since 1927 it retains the feel of an elegant *confitería* serving good cakes and sandwiches or vegetable pies for lunch.

Options with multiple locations Several good restaurants and establishments have locations in many neighbourhoods and serve typical Uruguayan fare. Among these are family restaurants: **La Pasiva**, **Don Pepperone** and **Il Mondo della Pizza**. A popular bakery chain is **Medialunas Calentitas**, great for coffee and croissants. Two popular *heladerías* are **La Cigale** and **Las Delicias**.

🍸 Bars and clubs

Montevideo *p1441, map p1442*
Boliches

Head to Sarandí, Bacacay or Bartolomé Mitre in Ciudad Vieja, or to Pocitos and Punta Carretas. Discos charge US$5-10. Bars/discos/pubs offering typical local nightlife:

503 Bar, Aguilar 832, just north of Ellauri. Open all day 1930-0400. Pool tables, only steel tip dart bar in town, small wood frame entrance, no sign.

Baar Fun-Fun, Ciudadela 1229, Ciudad Vieja, T2915 8005, www.barfunfun.com. Hangout of local artists, founded in 1895, used to be frequented by Carlos Gardel, where *uvita*, the drink, was born. Great music Fri and Sat. Recommended.

El Lobizón, Zelmar Michelini 1264, www. ellobizon.com. Popular restaurant open till very late with rock and fusion live performances.

El Pony Pisador, Bartolomé Mitre 1326, Ciudad Vieja. Popular with the young crowd. Live music. Also at LA de Herrera e Iturriaga, Pocitos.

La Ronda, Ciudadela 1182 y Canelones. Closed Sun, Mon. Drinks, good food, interesting music and events, with **Cheesecake Records** next door (see Facebook).

The Shannon Irish pub, Bartolomé Mitre 1318, www.theshannon.com.uy. Pub with almost daily live shows and DJs on Thu.

Viejo Mitre, Bartolomé Mitre 1321, Ciudad Vieja. Open till late all week. Mixed music, outside tables.

Outside the centre *p1444*
At or near Parque Rodó

Living, Paullier y Hugo Prato (tullving on Facebook). Wed-Sun 2100-0500. Popular corner bar.

El Mingus, San Salvador 1952 esq Jackson, T2410 9342, www.elmingus.com. Jazz and blues, homemade food, drinks, great atmosphere.

'W' Lounge, Rambla Wilson y Requena García. Fri-Sat 2300. Live music on Sat, fashionable place for young people, rock, electronica, Latin.

🎭 Entertainment

Montevideo *p1441, map p1442*
Cinema See http://cultura.montevideo.gub. uy for listings. Blockbusters often appear soon after release in US, most others arrive weeks or months later. Most films are in English (except non-English and animated features). Modern malls (Montevideo Shopping, Punta

Carretas, Portones) house several cine-theatre companies each, including 3D halls. Independent art theatres: **Cine Universitario**, 2 halls: Lumière and Chaplin, Canelones 1280, also for classic and serious films. **Cinemateca** film club, www.cinemateca.org.uy, has 4 cinemas: Cinemateca 18, 18 de Julio 1280, T2900 9056; Sala **Cinemateca y Sala Dos**, Dr L. Carnelli 1311, T2419 5795; and Sala **Pocitos**, A Chucarro 1036, T2707 4718. The Cinemateca shows great films from all over the world and has an extended archive. It organizes film festivals. Tickets US$6; members US$1 or free.
Tanguerías El Milongón, Gaboto 1810, T2929 0594, www.elmilongon.com.uy. A show that may include dinner beforehand, Mon-Sat 2100. For tango, milonga, candombe and local folk music. Recommended. **Joventango**, at Mercado de la Abundancia, Aquiles Lanza y San José, T2901 5561, www.joventango.org. Cheap and atmospheric venue, Sun 1930, Mon, Fri and Sun 2130. **Tango a Cielo Abierto**, Tango Under the Open Sky, in front of **Bar Facal**, Paseo Yi and 18 de Julio, T2908 7741 for information. Free and very good Uruguayan tango shows every day at noon on a wooden stage. Highly recommended. **Sala Zitarrosa**, 18 de Julio 1012, T2901 7303, www.salazitarrosa.com.uy is a very popular music venue. **Museo del Vino**, Maldonado 1150, www.museodelvino.com.uy. Wine bar and tango show Sat 2200.
Theatres Montevideo has a vibrant theatre scene. Most performances are only on Fri, Sat and Sun, others also on Thu. Apart from **Teatro Solís** (see Places in Montevideo, above), recommended are **Teatro del Centro Carlos E Sheck**, Plaza Cagancha 1168, T2902 8915, and **Teatro Victoria**, Río Negro 1479 y Uruguay, T2901 9971. See listings in the daily press and *La Brecha*. Prices are around US$15; performances are almost exclusively in Spanish starting around 2100 or earlier on Sun. **Teatro Millington-Drake** at the **Instituto Cultural Anglo-Uruguayo** (known as the 'Anglo'), San José 1426, T2902 3773, www.anglo.edu.uy, puts on occasional productions, as do the theatres of the **Alianza Cultural Uruguay-Estados Unidos**, Paraguay 1217, T2902 5160, www.alianza.edu.uy

(good library), and the **Alliance Française**, Blvr Artigas 1271, T2400 0505, www.alianzafrancesa. edu.uy (concerts, library, excellent bookshop). Many theatres close Jan-Feb.

O Shopping

Montevideo *p1441, map p1442*
The main commercial street is Av 18 de Julio, although malls elsewhere have captivated most local shoppers. Many international newspapers can be bought on the east side of Plaza Independencia.
Bookshops The Sun market on Tristán Narvaja and nearby streets is good for secondhand books. Every December daily in the evening is **Feria IDEAS +**, a book, photography and crafts fair, at Plaza Florencio Sánchez (Parque Rodó), with readings and concerts (www.ideasmas.com). The selection of English and American books in Montevideo is poor. The following specialize in foreign publications: **Bookshop SRL**, JE Rodó 1671 (at Minas y Constituyente), T2401 1010, www. bookshop.com.uy, also has 12 other branches across Montevideo and in other parts of the country. **Ibana**, International Book and News Agency, Convención 1485 (also Benito Blanco 845). **El Libro Inglés**, Cerrito 483, Ciudad Vieja. **Librería Papacito**, 18 de Julio 1409 and 888, T2908 7250/2900 2872, www.libreriapapacito. com. Good selection of magazines and books, wide range of subjects from celebrity autobiographies to art. **Puro Verso**, Yi 1385, T2901 6429, www.libreriapuroverso.com. Very good selection in Spanish, small secondhand section in English, excellent café, chess tables. It has another branch on Sarandí 675, **Más Puro Verso**, with good restaurant on 2nd floor.
Galleries There are many good art galleries. **Galería Latina**, Juan C Gómez 1420, Paseo de la Matriz, T2916 3737, www.galerialatina.com.uy, is one of the best, with its own art publishing house. Several art galleries and shops lie along C Pérez Castellanos, near Mercado del Puerto.
Handicrafts Suede and leather are good buys. There are several shops and workshops around Plaza Independencia. Amethysts,

topazes, agate and quartz are mined and polished in Uruguay and are also good buys. For authentic, fairly-priced crafts there is **Mercado de los Artesanos**, www.mercadodelosartesanos. com.uy, on Plaza Cagancha (No 1365), at Espacio Cultural R Barradas, Pérez Castellano 1542, and at Mercado de la Abundancia, San José 1312, T2901 0550, all branches closed Sun. For leather goods, walk around C San José y W Ferreira Aldunate. **Montevideo Leather Factory**, Plaza Independencia 832, www. montevideoleatherfactory.com. Recommended. **Manos del Uruguay**, San José 1111, and at Shopping Centres, www.manos.com.uy. A non-profit organization that sells very good quality, handwoven woollen clothing and a great range of crafts, made by independent craftsmen and women from all over Uruguay.

Markets Calle Tristán Narvaja (and nearby streets), opposite Facultad de Derecho on 18 de Julio. On Sun, 0800-1400, there is a large, crowded street market here, good for silver and copper, and all sorts of collectibles. **Plaza de la Constitución**, a small Sat morning market and a Sun antique fair are held here. **Villa Biarritz**, on Vásquez Ledesma near Parque Rodó, Punta Carretas. A big market selling fruit, vegetables, clothes and shoes (Tue and Sat early – 1600, and Sun in Parque Rodó, 0800-1400).

⭘ What to do

Montevideo *p1441, map p1442*
Sports
Rugby (www.rugbynews.com.uy), volleyball, tennis, cycling, surfing (www.olasyvientos.com), windsurfing and kitesurfing; lawn bowling, running, and walking are popular.
Basketball is increasingly popular; games can be seen at any sports club (**Biguá** or **Trouville**, both in Punta Carretas/Pocitos neighbourhoods). See www.fubb.org.uy for schedules.
Football (soccer) is the most popular sport. Seeing a game in **Centenario Stadium** is a must, located in Parque Batlle. If possible, attend a game with Uruguay's most popular teams, **Nacional** or **Peñarol**, or an international match. General admission tickets (US$5-15) can be bought outside before kickoff for sections Amsterdam, América, Colombes, Tribuna Olímpica. Crowds in Uruguay are much safer than other countries, but it's best to avoid the *plateas*, the end zones where the rowdiest fans chant and cheer. Sit in Tribuna Olímpica under or opposite the tower, at midfield. **Parque Central**, just north of Tres Cruces, **Nacional's** home field, is the next best venue. Other stadiums are quieter, safer and also fun. For information try www.tenfieldigital.com.uy, but asking a local is also advisable.
Golf Uruguay has 11 golf courses in total, between Fray Bentos and Punta del Este. Apart from Jan-Feb, Jul-Aug, you should have no problem getting onto the course, see www.aug.com.uy.

Tours
The **Asociación de Guías de Turismo de Montevideo**, T2970 0416, www.uruguias.com, runs historical and architecture tours. Check times and availability in English. Tours of the city are organized by the **Municipalidad**, see www. montevideo.gub.uy (go to Paseos) for details.

For visiting the several wineries around Montevideo, see www.loscaminosdelvino. com.uy. Also **The Wine Experience**, T9967 5750, http://thewine-experience.com, offering a variety of tours in Montevideo, Colonia, Carmelo and Punta del Este.

Day tours of Punta del Este are run by many travel agents and hotels, US$50-100 with meals.

Information on *estancias* can be found at **Lares** (see below), which represents many *estancias* and *posadas*; at the tourist offices in Montevideo; or general travel agencies and those that specialize in this field:
Cecilia Regules Viajes, Bacacay 1334, Plaza Independencia, T2916 3012, www.cecilia regulesviajes.com. Very good, knowledgeable, specialist in *estancias*, variety of tours in Uruguay, and skiing in Argentina.
Estancias Gauchas, Cecilia Regules Viajes, agent for an organization of 280 estancias offering lunch and/or lodging, English, French and Portuguese spoken. Full list of estancias (Establecimientos Rurales) at www.turismo.

gub.uy. Ask at these organizations about horse riding, too.

Fanáticos Fútbol Tours, Pablo de María 1592 bis, T2986 2325, www.futboltours.com.uy. Tour operator dedicated to Uruguay's national sport. Bilingual tours of several football stadiums, organizes tickets to matches. Free walking tours.

Jetmar, Plaza de la Independencia 725, T2902 0793, www.jetmar.com.uy. A helpful tour operator. Many branches.

JP Santos, Colonia 951, T2902 0300, www.jpsantos.com.uy. Helpful agency.

Lares, Wilson Ferreira Aldunate 1322, T2901 9120, www.larestours.com. Specializes in nature and cultural tours, including birdwatching, wine and gastronomy, art, trekking, horse riding and estancia tourism. Very experienced. Recommended.

Odile Beer Viajes, Plaza Independencia 723 of 102, T2902 3736, www.odiletravel.com. ISO-certified agency offering personalized service in a variety of fields, including sports (marathons, too), city cycling tours, gourmet and wine, bird and whale watching.

Rumbos, WTC, L A de Herrera 1248 Of 330, T2628 5555, www.rumbosturismo.com. Caters specifically for independent travellers, very helpful.

TransHotel, Acevedo Díaz 1671, T2402 9935, www.transhotel.com.uy. Accommodation, eco-tourism, sightseeing and tailor-made itineraries.

Turisport Ltda, San José 930, T2902 0829, www.turisport.com.uy (also in Pocitos). American Express for travel and mail services, good; sells Amex dollar TCs on Amex card.

⊖ Transport

Montevideo *p1441, map p1442*
Air
The main airport is at Carrasco, 21 km outside the city, T2604 0329, www.aeropuertode carrasco.com.uy; 24-hr exchange facilities. If making a hotel reservation, ask them to send a taxi to meet you; it's cheaper than taking an airport taxi. To Montevideo 30 mins by taxi or *remise* (official fares US$42-60, depending on

destination in the city, by van US$13 (payable in Uruguayan or Argentine pesos, reais, US$ or euros), T2604 0323, www.taxisaeropuerto. com; about 50 mins by bus. Buses, Nos 700, 701, 704, 710 and 711, from Terminal Brum, Río Branco y Galicia, go to the airport US$1.30 (crowded before and after school hours); dark brown 'Copsa' bus terminates at the airport. COT buses connect city and airport, US$5.50, and Punta del Este, US$9.

Air services to **Argentina**: for the Puente Aéreo to Buenos Aires, check in at Montevideo airport, pay departure tax and go to immigration to fill in an Argentine entry form before going through Uruguayan immigration. Get your stamp out of Uruguay, surrender the tourist card you received on entry and get your stamp into Argentina. There are no immigration checks on arrival at Aeroparque, Buenos Aires.

Bus
Local City buses are comfortable and convenient, see **Sistema de Transporte Metropolitano (STM)** pages on www. montevideo.gub.uy and www.cutcsa.com.uy. A single fare, US$1, may be paid on the bus, otherwise you can buy a rechargeable smart card for multiple journeys at designated places throughout the city. Buses D1 (see Carrasco, page 1445), D2, D3, 5, 8, 9, 10 and 11 charge US$1.40. There are many buses to all parts from 18 de Julio; from other parts to the centre or old city, look for those marked 'Aduana'. For Punta Carretas from city centre take bus No 121 from Calle San José.

Remises Fares from US$32 from airport to city; **Remises Carrasco**, T2606 1412, www.remisescarrasco.com.uy; **Remises Urbana**, T2400 8665.

Long distance (within Uruguay) During summer holidays buses are often full; it is advisable to book in advance (also for Fri and weekend travel all year round). Excellent terminal, Tres Cruces, Bulevar Artigas 1825 y Av Italia, T2401 8998 (10-15 mins by bus from the centre, Nos CA1, 64, 180, 187, 188 – in Ciudad Vieja from in front of Teatro Solís); it has a shopping mall, tourist office, internet café, restaurants, left luggage (free for 2 hrs at a time, if you have a ticket for that day, then US$2 up to 4 hrs, 12-24 hrs US$5), post and phone offices, toilets, good medical centre, **Banco de Montevideo** and **Indumex** *cambio* (accepts MasterCard). Visit www.trescruces.com.uy for bus schedules. Fares and journey times from the capital are given under destinations.

Summerbus, T4277 5781, www.summerbus. com is a new hop-on hop-off, door-to-door backpackers' service, taking travellers from hostel to hostel, with stops in Montevideo and all along the coast up to **Punta del Diablo**. Tickets from US$12 can be bought online or at hostels.

To Argentina (ferries and buses) You need a passport when buying international tickets. Direct to **Buenos Aires**: Buquebus, at the docks, in old customs hall, Terminal Fluvio-Marítima; Terminal Tres Cruces, Local 28/29, Carrasco airport, Hotel Radisson, and Punta Carretas Shopping, local Miranda; in all cases T130, www.buquebus.com. 1-3 daily, 3 hrs, from US$105 tourist class, one way (cheaper if booked online; 3 classes of seat); departure tax included in the price of tickets. At Montevideo dock, go to Preembarque 30 mins before departure, present ticket, then go to Migración for Uruguayan exit and Argentine entry formalities. The terminal is like an airport and the seats on the ferries are airplane seats. On board there is duty-free shopping, video and poor value food and drinks. Services via Colonia: bus/ferry and catamaran services by Buquebus: from 5 crossings daily from 1 to 3 hrs from Colonia, depending on vessel, fares: US$53 tourist class one way on slower vessel, US$72 tourist class on faster vessel (very good last minute deals available online in low season). All have 2½-hr bus connection Montevideo-Colonia from Tres Cruces. There are also bus connections to **Punta del Este**, 2 hrs, and **La Paloma**, 5 hrs, to/from Montevideo. Cars and motorcycles are carried on either route. Schedules and fares can be checked on www.buquebus.com, who also have flights between Uruguay and Argentina.

Fares increase in high season, Dec-Jan, when there are more sailings. If you want to break your journey in Colonia, you will have to buy your own bus ticket on another company to complete the trip to/from Montevideo. **Colonia Express**, at Tres Cruces bus terminal local 31A, T2401 6666, and at the dock in Colonia, www. coloniaexpress.com, makes 2-3 crossings a day between Colonia and Buenos Aires in fast boats (no vehicles) with bus connections to/ from Montevideo, Punta del Este and other Uruguayan towns. Fares range from US$18 to US$35 one way, depending on type of service and where bought, or US$45 65 with bus connections to/from Montevideo. **Seacat**, www.seacatcolonia.com, 3 fast ferries to Colonia, 1 hr, US$33-42 one way, with bus to Montevideo US$40-52, and to Punta del Este US$58-66. Offices: Río Negro 1400, at Tres Cruces locales 28/29, T2915 0202, and in Colonia. **Bus de la Carrera** (T2402 1313, www. busdelacarrera.com.uy), **Belgrano** (T2402 8445, www.grabelgrano.com.ar), **El Cóndor** (T2401 4764) and **Cauvi** (T2401 9196) run road services to Buenos Aires for US$51-59, 7½-8½ hrs.

Services to **Carmelo** and **Tigre** (interesting trip): bus/motor launch service by **Cacciola**, 2 a day, www.cacciolaviajes.com, US$48. Advanced booking is advisable on all services at busy periods. On through buses to Brazil and Argentina, you can expect full luggage checks both by day and night.

To Paraguay, Brazil, Chile If intending to travel through Uruguay to Brazil, do not forget to have Uruguayan entry stamped into your passport when crossing from Argentina. Without it you will not be able to cross the Brazilian border. To **Asunción**, Paraguay, US$142, 22 hrs, Wed, Sat (also Mon in high season) at 1300 with EGA, T2402 5165, www. ega.com.uy (and Río Branco 1417, T2902 5335), recommended, meals served, and **Sol de Paraguay**, T2400 3939, Thu, Sun. The through bus route is via Paysandú, Salto, Posadas, Encarnación, to Asunción (there are passport checks at Salto, Posadas and Encarnación). There are very comfortable daily buses to **Porto**

Alegre with EGA and TTL (Tres Cruces local B 27, T2401 1410, www.ttl.com.br), US$87-111, 12 hrs, and **São Paulo** (US$235, 30 hrs, 1 a week each via Florianópolis, US$155, Camboriú, US$165, 20 hrs, and Curitiba, US$187, 23 hrs). Some private tour companies in Montevideo offer excellent deals on overland bus tours to places like Iguazú, Rio de Janeiro, Salvador, Bariloche and Santiago (eg **MTUR Viajes**, www.mturviajes.com.uy, recommended).

Taxi
The meter starts at about US$0.90 in *fichas*, which determine fares as shown on a table in taxi. Tipping is not expected but welcomed, usually by rounding up the fare. Do not expect change for large peso notes. Prices go up on Sat, Sun, holidays and late at night.

Train
Uruguayan railways, **AFE**, use outdated trains, but interesting rides for enthusiasts. The old train station has been abandoned, replaced by a nice new terminus next to the Antel skyscraper, known as **Nueva Estación Central** at Paraguay y Nicaragua (Aguada), T2924 8080, www.afe.com.uy. Passenger trains currently only run Mon-Sat along the 25 de Agosto line. Most commuter trains run north between Montevideo and Progreso (about 5-10 a day), passing some of the country's poorest areas. Fewer services go beyond Progreso. To Progreso (55 mins, US$1.40), to Canelones (1 hr 20 mins, US$2), to Santa Lucía (1 hr 40 mins, US$2.45), to 25 de Agosto (1 hr 45 mins, US$2.90. Occasionally, long distance services and a steam-engine run for special events, such as the 48-hr celebration of the Día del Patrimonio (Heritage Day) in Oct. More information, T2924 7328.

Directory

Montevideo *p1441, map p1442*
Banks Don't trust the few black market money changers offering temptingly good rates. Many are experienced confidence tricksters. *Casas de cambio* and banks only open 1300-1700 (some till 1800). Airport bank daily 0700-2200. Most banks are along 25 de Mayo, Cerrito or Zabala, and on Plaza Matriz, in Ciudad Vieja, and in the centre along Av 18 de Julio. Exchange houses along 18 de Julio, but shop around for best rates (rates for cash are better than for TCs, but both are often better than in banks, and quicker service). **Car hire** It is wise to hire a small car (1.3 litre engine) as Uruguay is relatively flat and gas prices are high. A small car can be negotiated for about US$90 per day, free mileage, including insurance and collision damage waiver, if you are hiring a car for at least 3 days (rates are lower out of season). Cheaper weekly rates available. Best to make reservations before arrival. Autocar, Mercedes 863, T2908 5153, www.autocar. com.uy. Economical, helpful. Punta Car, Cerro Largo 1383, T2900 2772, www.puntacar.com.uy, also at Aeropuerto Carrasco and other locations nationwide. Snappy, Andes 1363, T2900 7728, www.snappy.com.uy. Sudancar, Av Italia 2665, T2480 3855, www.sudancar.com.uy. See Essentials for international agencies. Most car companies don't allow their cars to be taken abroad. To travel to Argentina or Brazil, you can use Maxicar rentals in Salto, see page 1468. **Embassies and consulates** For all foreign embassies and consulates in Montevideo, see http://embassy.goabroad. com. **Internet and telephones** At Antel *telecentros*. **Language schools** Academia Uruguay, Juan Carlos Gómez 1408, T2915 2496, www.academiauruguay.com. **Medical services** Hospital Británico, Av Italia 2420, T2487 1020, www.hospitalbritanico.com.uy. Recommended.

Western Uruguay

West of Montevideo, Route 1, part of the Pan-American Highway, heads to the UNESCO World Heritage Site of Colonia del Sacramento and the tranquil town of Carmelo. Off the road are the old British mining town of Conchillas and the Jesuit mission at Calera de las Huérfanas. Other roads lead to the Río Uruguay, Route 2 from Rosario to Fray Bentos, and Route 3 via San José de Mayo and Trinidad to the historic towns of Paysandú and Salto. The latter passes farms, man-made lakes and the river itself. There are also many hot-spring resorts.

Colonias Valdense and Suiza

Route 1 to Colonia de Sacramento is a four-lane highway. At Km 121 from Montevideo the road passes Colonia Valdense, a colony of Waldensians who still cling to some of the old customs of the Piedmontese Alps. For tourist information, T4558 8412. A road branches off north here to Colonia Suiza, a Swiss settlement also known as **Nueva Helvecia** (*Population: 10,642*), with lovely parks, gardens and countryside. In the town is the Santuario de Nuestra Señora De Schönstatt, all walls are covered by plants, and the first steam mill in Uruguay (1875). The Swiss national day is celebrated with great enthusiasm.

The highway skirts Rosario (130 km from Montevideo, 50 km before Colonia del Sacramento), called 'the first Uruguayan Museum of Mural Art'. Dozens of impressive murals are dotted around the city, some with bullfights, some abstract designs.

Colonia del Sacramento → *Colour map 8, B5. Population: 26,231. See also map, page 1456.*
ⓘ *All museums Fri-Mon 1115-1630, closed either Tue, Wed or Thu, except Museo Archivo Regional (shut Sat-Sun) and Museo Naval (shut Mon-Wed), combined tickets US$2.25. See www.museos.gub.uy.*
Founded by Portuguese settlers from Brazil in 1680, Colonia del Sacramento was a centre for smuggling British goods across the Río de la Plata into the Spanish colonies during the 18th century. The small historic section juts into the Río de la Plata, while the modern town extends around a bay. It is a lively place with streets lined with plane trees, a pleasant Plaza 25 de Agosto and a grand Intendencia Municipal (Méndez y Avenida Gen Flores, the main street). The town is kept very trim. The best beach is Playa Ferrando, 1.5 km to the east, easily accessible by foot or hired vehicle. There are regular connections by boat with Buenos Aires and a free port.

The **Barrio Histórico**, with its narrow streets (see Calle de los Suspiros), colonial buildings and reconstructed city walls, is charming because there are few such examples in this part of the continent. It has been declared Patrimonio Cultural de la Humanidad by UNESCO. The old town can be easily seen on foot in a day (wear comfortable shoes on the uneven cobbles), but spend one night there to experience the illuminations by nostalgic replica street lamps. The **Plaza Mayor** is especially picturesque and has parakeets in the palm trees. Grouped around it are the **Museo Municipal**, in a late-18th-century residence, rebuilt in 1835 (with indigenous archaeology, historical items, natural history, palaeontology), the **Casa Nacarello** next door (18th century; depicting colonial life), the **Casa del Virrey** (in ruins), the **Museo Portugués** (1717) with, downstairs, an exhibition of beautiful old maps, the ruins of the Convento de San Francisco, to which is attached the **Faro** (lighthouse, entry US$0.90, daily 1300-sunset, from 1100 at weekends, on a clear day you can see Buenos Aires), and the **Museo Naval** ⓘ *Calle Enríquez de la Peña y San Francisco, T42622 1084*, opened in the historic Casa de Lavalleja in 2009. At the Plaza's eastern end is the **Portón del Campo**, the restored city gate and drawbridge. Just north of the Plaza Mayor is the **Museo Archivo Regional** (1750), collection of maps, police records 1876-1898 and 19th-century watercolours. The **Iglesia Matriz**, on Calle Vasconcellos (beside the

Plaza de Armas/Manuel Lobo), is the oldest church in Uruguay (late 17th century). Free concerts are held occasionally. At the end of Calle Misiones de los Tapes, the tiny **Museo del Azulejo** (1740-1760, rebuilt 1986), houses a collection of Portuguese, French and Catalan tiles, plus the first Uruguayan tile from 1840. At Calles de San José y España, the **Museo Español** (1720, rebuilt 1840), displays Spanish colonial items plus modern paintings by Uruguayan Jorge Páez Vilaró. At the north edge, the fortifications of the **Bastión del Carmen** can be seen; nearby is

Colonia del Sacramento

Where to stay	8 Hostel El Español	17 Radisson Hotel &
1 Don Antonio Posada	9 Italiano	Casino Colonia &
2 El Capullo Posada	10 Posada de la Flor	Restaurant Del Carmen
3 El Viajero B&B	11 Posada del Angel	18 Romi
4 El Viajero Hostel	12 Posada del Gobernador	
5 Esperanza & Artemisa Spa	13 Posada del Virrey	**Restaurants**
6 Hostal de los Poetas	14 Posada Manuel de Lobo	1 Arcoiris
7 Hostel Colonial	15 Posada Manuel de Lobo	2 Club Colonia
	16 Posada Plaza Mayor	

the Centro Cultural Bastión del Carmen, Rivadavia 223, in a 19th-century glue and soap factory, with frequent theatre productions. In the third week of January, festivities mark the founding of Colonia. The **Feria de la Ciudad** ⓘ *Campus Municipal, Fosalba y Suárez*, is a crafts fair worth a visit. Kids will love the **Acuario** ⓘ *Calle Virrey Cevallos 236, esq Rivadavia, www.acuario.com.uy, Wed-Mon 1400-1800, 1600-2000 in summer, US$1.75* in the Barrio Histórico.

Around the bay is **Real de San Carlos** ⓘ *5 km, take 'Cotuc' or 'ABC' buses from Av Gral Flores, leaving Barrio Histórico, US$0.80*, an unusual, once grand but now sad tourist complex, built by Nicolás Mihanovich 1903-1912. The elegant bull-ring, in use for just two years, is falling apart (closed to visitors, bullfighting is banned in Uruguay). The casino, the nearest to Buenos Aires then (where gambling was prohibited), failed when a tax was imposed on Mihanovich's excursions; also disused is the huge Frontón court. Only the racecourse (Hipódromo) is still operational (free, except three annual races) and you can see the horses exercising on the beach and in the water.

Tourist offices Information from the **Old Gate** ⓘ *Manuel Lobo e Ituzaingó, T4522 8506, www.coloniaturismo.com, daily 0800-2000 (0900-1900 in winter)*. Hotel reservations office at Flores y Rivera. Also an information desk at bus terminal, daily 0900-2000, year-round. **Centro BIT** ⓘ *Calle Odriozola 434 (next to the port), www.bitcolonia.com*, is a large building complex with an official **tourist information centre** ⓘ *daily 0900-2000, 0900-1800 low season*, restaurant, terrace, gift shop and a permanent exhibition on the country and region (show entry US$2.25). Visit www.guiacolonia.com.uy and www.colonianet.com.

Conchillas, 50 km from Colonia and 40 km from Carmelo, is a former British mining town from the late 19th century. It preserves dozens of buildings constructed by C H Walker and Co Ltd. Tourist information is available at the **Casa de la Cultura** ⓘ *daily 0800-1400*, on Calle David Evans. The police station is also a good source of information. Direct buses from Colonia; road well marked on Route 21.

Carmelo → *Population: 18,041.*

From Colonia, Route 21 heads northwest to Carmelo (77 km) on the banks of Arroyo Las Vacas. A fine avenue of trees leads to the river,

3 El Drugstore & Viejo Barrio
4 El Torreón
6 La Bodeguita
7 La Casa de Jorge Páez Vilaró
9 Mercosur
10 Mesón de la Plaza
11 Parrillada El Portón
12 Punta Piedra
13 Pulpería de los Faroles
14 Tasca del Sur

crossed by the first swing bridge built 1912. Across the bridge is the Rambla de los Constituyentes and the Fuente de las Tentaciones. The church, museum and archive of El Carmen is on Plaza Artigas (named after the city's founder). In the **Casa de la Cultura Ignacio Barrios (IMC)** ① *19 de Abril 246, T4542 3840*, is a tourist office and museum. Historically a mining centre, it is said that many luxurious buildings in Buenos Aires were made from the grey granite of Cerro Carmelo (mines flooded and used for watersports). It is one of the most important yachting centres on Río de la Plata and its microclimate produces much wine.

Calera de Las Huérfanas (Estancia Belén or de las Vacas) is the remains of one of the area's main Jesuit missions. Vines were introduced and lime was exported for the construction of Buenos Aires. After the expulsion of the Jesuits, its production sustained an orphanage in Buenos Aires. It's in relatively good state and is best reached by car (exit from Route 21 clearly marked, some 10 km before Carmelo, see www.caleradelashuerfanas.org).

Between Carmelo and Nueva Palmira, another river port, is the colonial monument, **Capilla de Narbona** (Route 21, Km 263), built in the early 18th century. At **Bodega y Granja Narbona** ① *Ruta 21, Km 268, T4540 4160, www.narbona.com.uy*, wine, cheese and other produce are available, as well as a fine restaurant and exclusive hotel rooms.

Mercedes → *Colour map 8, B5. Population: 44,826.*

This livestock centre is best reached by Route 2 from the main Colonia-Montevideo highway. Founded in 1788, it is pleasant town on the Río Negro, a yachting and fishing centre during the season. Its charm (it is known as 'the city of flowers') derives from its Spanish-colonial appearance, though it is not as old as the older parts of Colonia. There is an attractive *costanera* (riverside drive) and a jazz festival in January (www.jazzalacalle.com.uy).

West of town 5 km is the **Parque y Castillo Barón de Mauá** ① *T4532 2201*, dating from 1857. It has a mansion which contains the **Museum of Palaeontology** ① *T4532 2201, museoberro@gmail.com, daily 1100-1700, free, on the ground floor*. The building is worth wandering around to see the exterior, upper apartments and stable block. Cheese, wine and olive oil are produced. It takes 45 minutes to walk to the park, a pleasant route passing Calera Real on the riverbank, dating back to 1722, the oldest industrial ruins in the country (lime kilns hewn out of the sandstone). At the **tourist office** ① *Detomasi 415, T4532 2733, www.sorianoturismo.com*, maps and hotel lists are available.

Fray Bentos → *Colour map 8, B5. Population: 25,047.*

Route 2 continues westwards (34 km) to Fray Bentos, the main port on the east bank of Río Uruguay. Here in 1865 the Liebig company built its first factory producing meat extract. The original plant, much extended and known as **El Anglo**, has been restored as the **Museo de la Revolución Industrial** ① *T4562 2918/3690, daily 0930-1730, US$2.20 including a 1½-hr guided tour 1000 and 1500 in Spanish, leaflet in English, Tue free*. The office block in the factory has been preserved complete with its original fittings. Many machines can be seen. Within the complex is the Barrio Inglés, where workers were housed, and La Casa Grande, where the director lived (guided tours of Casa Grande Tuesday, Thursday, Sunday 1200). There are **beaches** to the northeast and southwest. **Tourist office** ① *25 de Mayo 3400, T4562 2233, turismo@rionegro.gub.uy, Mon-Fri 0900-1800, Sat 0900-1500*.

Crossing to Argentina

About 9 km upriver from Fray Bentos is the San Martín International Bridge (vehicles US$6; pedestrians and cyclists may cross only on vehicles, officials may arrange lifts).

Paysandú → *Colour map 8, A5. Population: 78,868.*

North of Fray Bentos, 110 km, is this undulating, historic city on the east bank of the Río Uruguay. Along Route 3, it's 380 km from Montevideo. Summer temperatures can be up to 42°C. There is a 19th-century **basilica** ① *daily 0700-1145, 1600-2100*. The **Museo Histórico Municipal** ① *Zorrilla de San Martín y Leandro Gómez, Tue-Sun 0900-1400*, has good collection of guns and furniture from the time of the Brazilian siege of 1864-1865. **Museo de la Tradición** ① *Av de los Iracundos, north of town at the Balneario Municipal, 0900-1400 daily, Sun also 1800-2100, reached by bus to Zona Industrial*, gaucho articles, is also worth a visit. **Tourist office** ① *Plaza Constitución, 18 de Julio 1226, T4722 6220, www.paysandu.gub.uy and www.turismopaysandu.com, Mon-Fri 0900-1900, Sat-Sun 0800-1800 (2000 in summer), and at Plan de la Costa, Balneario Municipal.*

Around Paysandú

The **Central Termal Guaviyú** ① *Ruta 3 Km 431.5, T4755 2049, guaviyu@paysandu.gub.uy, US$3.75-4.50, getting there: 50 mins by bus, US$3, 6 a day*, thermal springs 60 km north, with four pools, restaurant, three motels (**$$$-$$** for three to five people) and private hotel with own thermal pools (**$$$**, Villayío) and excellent cheap camping facilities. Along Route 90, 83 km east, is the **Centro Termal Almirón** ① *Ruta 90 Km 83, T4740 2873, www.almirontermal.comn@paysandu.gu*, with camping, apartments and motels. The **Meseta de Artigas** ① *110 km north of Paysandú, 15 km off the highway to Salto, no public transport, free*, is 45 m above the Río Uruguay, which here narrows and at low water forms whirlpools at the rapids of El Hervidero. It was used

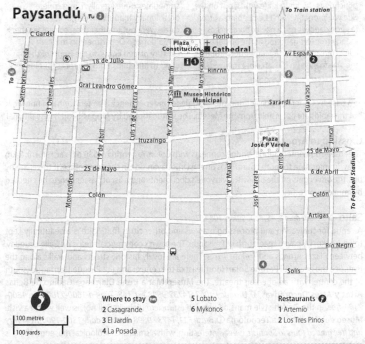

Paysandú

Where to stay
2 Casagrande
3 El Jardín
4 La Posada
5 Lobato
6 Mykonos

Restaurants
1 Artemio
2 Los Tres Pinos

Wreckers, revolutionaries and gauchos

Uruguay's passion for rural life began in 1603 with Hernando Arias and the first shipment of cattle and horses to the Banda Oriental.

Today, a typical day on an *estancia* begins at the hearth, perhaps with a warming *mate*, before a horseride. The fireplace may be decorated with signs of present and past ownership, each brand burnt into the fireplace representing a personal history, but one element unites them all: the myth of the gaucho.

You might be forgiven for imagining yourself a latter-day gaucho as you put your foot in the *copa* (a cupped stirrup) and mount a sturdy Uruguayan horse, perhaps of the same breed as the one that Napoleon had shipped back to carry him around a wintry Europe. However, your thick poncho might well be the only piece of gaucho gear that you are wearing. Gauchos sometimes used ponchos as shields in knife fights, but on the ride you probably won't be needing a *facón* (a large dagger), nor a pair of *bombachas* (baggy trousers gathered at the ankle) or *culero* (an apron of soft leather tied around the waist, open on the left side) to avoid lacerations from a lasso during branding and gelding. Horses on tourism estancias are used to novice riders, and *rebenques* (short whips) are best kept unused by your side. You'll find the Uruguayan horse a compliant platform for launching your *boleadoras* (three stones, covered with hide, on ropes tied at the middle, are used for entangling the legs of cattle). At this point you may learn whether your horse is a *pingo*, a gaucho's favourite horse, or *flete*, an ordinary cargo beast.

Riding along extensive *cuchillas* (ridges) and crossing rivers will bring to mind the nomadic gaucho lifestyle, and the revolutionary (largely gaucho) guerrilla bands. A *montonera* was a band of gauchos organized to drive the Brazilians and Argentinians out of Uruguay. Patriot leader Artigas was a *gaucho-caudillo* (boss).

Uruguayan life is built from livestock, sometimes quite literally. Houses were occasionally made from cattle hide. And cattle were put to other uses: coastal ranchers in Maldonado Department in the 19th century placed lights on the horns of their cows to lure ships onto the rocks for plunder.

as a base by General Artigas during the struggle for independence. The terrace has a fine view, but the rapids are not visible from the Meseta. The statue topped by Artigas' head is very original.

Crossing to Argentina

The José Artigas international bridge connects with Colón, Argentina (US$6 per car, return), 8 km away. Immigration for both countries is on the Uruguayan side in the same office. If travelling by bus, the driver gets off the bus with everyone's documents and a list of passengers to be checked by immigration officials.

Salto → *Colour map 8, A5. Population: 108,197.*

A centre for cultivating and processing oranges and other citrus fruit, Salto is a beautifully kept town 120 km by paved road north of Paysandú. The town's commercial area is on Calle Uruguay, between Plazas Artigas and Treinta y Tres. There are lovely historic streets and walks along the river. See the beautiful **Parque Solari** (northeast of the centre) and the **Parque Harriague** (south of the centre) with an open-air theatre. The **Museo María Irene Olarreaga Gallino de Bellas Artes y Artes Decorativas** ① *Uruguay 1067, T4732 9898 ext 148, Tue-Fri 1600-2100, Sun 1800-2100, free*, in the French-style mansion of a rich *estanciero* (Palacio Gallino), is well worth a visit. **Museo del Hombre y La Tecnología** ① *Brasil 511, T4732 9898, ext 151, daily 1300-1900, free entry and free guided tours in Spanish*, is very interesting, with a small archaeological museum. There is

National pride

The indigenous Charrúas were remarkably brave, but they were also inhospitable and rallied against European explorers. They killed Spaniard Juan Díaz de Solís, the navigator who first charted Montevideo in 1515. Between early explorer visits, they learned to ride captured horses, still slinging stones on suede straps in defiance of and indifference to the superior Spanish swords. Their aggression, despite the impossible odds, led to their eradication when the last remaining natives were massacred in 1831. Nevertheless, their legacy lives on. *Mate*, the native tea, is now the national beverage, proudly sipped and shared throughout Uruguay. And the national soccer team is nicknamed *Los Charrúas* because, after winning the first and fourth FIFA World Cups in 1930 and 1950, against powerhouses Argentina and Brazil, people recognized that 'fight to the finish' attitude in the players. In fact, in Uruguay, it is a great compliment to be described as having *garra Charrúa*, meaning strength, resourcefulness, bravery and determination.

a Shrove Tuesday carnival. **Tourist office** ⓘ *Uruguay 1052, T4733 4096, www.salto.gub.uy, Mon-Sat 0800-1900, free map; and at the international bridge, T4732 8933, salto@mintur.gub.uy.*

The most popular tourist site in the area is the large dam and hydroelectric plant **Represa de Salto Grande** ⓘ *taxi to dam US$20.50; guided tours 0700-1600 (museum 0700-1500) arranged by Relaciones Públicas office, T4732 6131/7777, rrppmi@saltogrande.org; visitors centre at the plant,* 14 km from Salto, built jointly by Argentina and Uruguay. A road runs along the top of the dam to Argentina. By launch to the **Salto Chico** beach, fishing, camping.

Near the dam (2 km north on ex-Route 3) is **Parque Acuático Termas de Salto Grande** ⓘ *open all year 1000-1800 (longer Jan and Feb), US$8.50, T4733 4411, www.hotelhoracioquiroga. com,* 4 ha, in a natural setting. There are several pools, slides, hydro massages, water jets and a man-made waterfall.

Crossing to Argentina

North of the town, at the Salto Grande dam, there is an international bridge to Concordia, Argentina, open 24 hours a day, all year. Passengers have to get off the bus to go through immigration procedures. Buses don't go on Sundays. Both Argentine and Uruguayan immigration offices are on the Argentine side.

Termas del Daymán and other springs

About 10 km south of Salto on Route 3, served by bus marked 'Termas' which leave from Calle Brasil every hour, are Termas del Daymán, a small town built around curative hot springs. It is a nice place to spend a night, though it is crowded in the daytime; few restaurants around the beautifully laid out pools. **Complejo Médico Hidrotermal Daymán** ⓘ *T4736 9090, www. viatermal.com/spatermaldayman, use of facilities US$4.50, multiple different treatments at additional cost,* has a spa and separate pools (external and internal), showers and jacuzzis. There is also Acuamania, a theme park, nearby.

The road to **Termas del Arapey** branches off Route 3 to Bella Unión, at 61 km north of Salto, and then runs 19 km east and then south. Pampa birds, rheas and metre-long lizards in evidence. Termas del Arapey is on the Arapey river south of Isla Cabellos (Baltasar Brum). The waters at these famous thermal baths contain bicarbonated salts, calcium and magnesium.

To the Brazilian border: Bella Unión → *Colour map 8, A5.*

Route 3 goes north to the small town of Bella Unión, from where an international bridge 5 km away crosses to the Brazilian town of Barra de Quaraí. This village lies next to a unspoilt area of densely wooded islands and beautiful sandbanks on the Río Uruguay, at the triple frontier point. About 80 km northwest is Uruguaiana which takes the main international bus traffic between Brazil and Argentina.

To the Brazilian border: Artigas → *Colour map 8, A6. Population: 44,905.*

From near Bella Unión Route 30 runs east to Artigas, a frontier town in a cattle raising and agricultural area (excellent swimming upstream from the bridge). The town is known for its good quality amethysts. There is a bridge across the Río Cuareim to the Brazilian town of Quaraí. The Brazilian consul is at Lecueder 432, T4772 5414, vcartigas@mre.gov.br.

⦿ Western Uruguay listings

For hotel and restaurant price codes, and other relevant information, see Essentials.

● Where to stay

Colonia Suiza (Nueva Helvecia) *p1455*
$$$$ Nirvana, Av Batlle y Ordóñez, T4554 4081, www.hotelnirvana.com. Restaurant (Swiss and traditional cuisine), half- and full-board available, see website for promotions, sports facilities, 25 ha of park and gardens, poolside bar. Recommended.
$$ Del Prado, Av G Imhoff, T4554 4169, www.hoteldelprado.info. Open all year, huge buffet breakfast, pool, hostel accommodation **$**.
Camping Several campsites south of Route 1 on Río de la Plata. A good one at Blancarena is **Camping Enrique Davyt** (access from La Paz village east of Colonia Valdense), T4587 2110, campinged@adinet.com.uy, US$3 pp (discount for longer stays).

Tourism farms
$$$$ pp Finca Piedra, Ruta 23, Km 125, Mal Abrigo, northwest of San José de Mayo (convenient for Montevideo or Colonia), T4340 3118, www.fincapiedra.com. Price is full board, various rooms in different parts of this 1930s estancia and vineyard, lots of outdoor activities including riding, tours of the vines, wine-tasting, pool, caters for children. Many activities free.
$$$$ La Vigna, T4558 9234, Km 120 Ruta 51 to Playa Fomento, www.lavigna.com.uy.

Wonderful boutique eco-hotel, solar-powered and recycled furniture. Offers horse riding and art lessons. Good food, all farm reared and organic. Owner is a cheese-maker, excellent produce. Highly recommended.
$$$ El Galope Farm & Hostel, Cno Concordia, Colonia Suiza, T9910 5985, www.elgalope.com. uy. Access on Route 1 Km 114.5. Discounts for HI members, limited to 10 guests, 6 km from Nueva Helvecia, **$** in bunk bed, use of kitchen, sauna US$10, 2½-hr riding US$35 (beginners US$25 with lesson), bicycles US$1 per hr, walking, English, French, German and Spanish spoken.
$$$ El Terruño, Paraje Minuano, Ruta 1, Km 140, 35 km before Colonia, T4550 6004, www.estanciaelterrunio.com. Price includes breakfast, horse-rides and activities.
$$$ pp Estancia Don Miguel, 6 km from Pueblo Cufré, access from Ruta 1 Km 121 y Ruta 52, T4550 2041, www.estanciadonmiguel. com. Rustic, working farm, full board, good activities including massage and reiki, Swedish and English spoken.

Colonia del Sacramento *p1455, map p1456*
Choice is good including several recently renovated 19th-century *posada* hotels.

Barrio Histórico
$$$$-$$$ El Capullo Posada, 18 de Julio 219, T4523 0135, www.elcapullo.com. Spacious living area, English and American owners, stylish boutique-style rooms, outdoor pool and *parrilla*.

$$$$-$$$ Posada Plaza Mayor, Del Comercio 111, T4522 3193, www.posadaplazamayor.com. In a 19th-century house, beautiful internal patio with lemon trees and Spanish fountain, lovely rooms with a/c or heating, English spoken.

Centre

$$$$ Radisson Hotel and Casino Colonia, Washington Barbot 283, T4523 0460, www.radissoncolonia.com. Great location overlooking the jetty, contemporary architecture, casino attached. 2 pools, jacuzzi, highly regarded restaurant **Del Carmen**, very good.

$$$$-$$$ Don Antonio Posada, Ituzaingó 232, T4522 5344, www.posadadonantonio.com. 1850 building, buffet breakfast, garden, pool, excellent.

$$$$-$$$ Hotel Esperanza & Artemisa Spa, Gral Flores 237, T4522 2922, www.hotelesperanzaspa.com. Charming, with buffet breakfast, sauna, heated pool and treatments.

$$$ Italiano, Intendente Suárez 103-105, 14522 7878, www.hotelitaliano.com.uy. Open since 1928, it has been renovated with comfortable rooms, cheaper rates Mon-Thu (low season). Large outdoor and indoor pools, gym, sauna, good restaurant. Recommended.

$$$ Posada del Angel, Washington Barbot 59, T4522 4602, www.posadadelangel.net. Early 20th-century house, pleasant, warm welcome, gym, sauna, pool.

$$$ Posada de la Flor, Ituzaingó 268, T4523 0794, www.posada-delaflor.com. Cheaper Mon-Thu. At the quiet end of C Ituzaingó, next to the river and to the Barrio Histórico, simply decorated rooms on a charming patio and roof terrace with river views.

$$$ Posada del Gobernador, 18 de Julio 205, T4522 2918, www.delgobernador.com. Cheaper Sun-Thu. Charming, with open air pool, garden.

$$$ Posada del Virrey, España 217, T4522 2223, www.posadadelvirrey.com. Large rooms, some with view over bay (cheaper with small bathroom and no balcony), with buffet breakfast. Recommended.

$$$ Posada Manuel de Lobo, Ituzaingó 160, T4522 2463, www.posadamanueldelobo.com. Built in 1850. Large rooms, huge baths, limited

parking, some smaller rooms, nice breakfast area inside and out.

$$$ El Viajero B&B, Odriozola 269, T4522 8645, www.elviajerobb.com. Very well located modern building with river views, bike rental, 13 private rooms with a/c and TV.

$$$-$$ Romi, Rivera 236, T4523 0456, www.hotelromicolonia.com. 19th-century *posada*-style downstairs, with lovely tiles at entrance. Airy modernist upstairs and simple rooms. Recommended.

$$ El Viajero Hostel Suites Colonia (HI affiliate), Washington Barbot 164, T4522 2683, www.elviajerohostels.com. Private en suite with a/c and TV, dorms en suite with a/c, fireplace for winter, terrace and BBQ area for the summer, breakfast included, free Wi-Fi. Quirky art on walls, recently renovated.

$$ Hostal de los Poetas, Mangarelli 677, T4523 1643, www.guiacolonia.com.uy. Some distance from the Barrio Histórico but one of the cheapest, a few simple bedrooms with a/c and TV and a lovely breakfast room, tiny exuberant garden.

$$ Hostel Colonial, Flores 440, T4523 0347, www.hostelcolonial.com.uy. HI affiliated. Pretty patio and quirky touches, such as barber's chair in reception. **$** in dorm. Kitchen, bar with set meals, free use of bikes (all ancient), run down and noisy, but popular.

$$ Hostel El Español, Manuel Lobo 377, T4523 0759, www.hostelelespaniol.com. Good value, **$** pp with shared bath in dorms, breakfast included, TV room. Part of the HoLa network of hostels. Recommended.

Carmelo *p1457*

$$ Timabe, 19 de Abril y Solís, T4542 5401, www.ciudad carmelo.com/timabe. Near the swing bridge, with a/c or fan, dining room, parking, good.

Camping At Playa Seré, hot showers.

Mercedes *p1458*

$$$ Rambla Hotel, Av Asencio 728, T4533 0696. Riverside 3-star hotel with quite good rooms.

$$ Ito, Eduardo V Haedo 184, T4532 4919. Basic though decent rooms in an old house.

Tourism Farm **$$$$** pp La Sirena Marinas del Río Negro, Ruta 14, Km 4, T9910 2130/4530 2271, www.lasirena.com.uy. *Estancia* dating from 1830, picturesque, on the river, birdwatching, fishing, waterskiing, accommodation, meals, full board (**$$$** double room with breakfast) friendly owners Rodney, Lucia and Patricia Bruce. Warmly recommended.

Fray Bentos *p1458*
$$ **Colonial**, 25 de Mayo 3293, T4562 2260, www.hotelcolonial.com.uy. Attractive old building with patio. A/c and breakfast extra, **$** without bath.
$$ **Plaza**, 18 de Julio y 25 de Mayo, T4562 2363, www.plazahotelfraybentos.com.uy. Comfortable, a/c, internet, with breakfast, on the Plaza Constitución.
Camping At the Club Remeros, on Rambla Costanera (opposite Parque Roosevelt), T4562 2236.

Paysandú *p1459, map p1459*
Book hotels in advance during Holy Week.
$$$ **Casagrande**, Florida 1221, Plaza Constitución, T4722 4994, www.hotel casagrande.com.uy. Welcoming, buffet breakfast, restaurant, parking, very good.
$$$ **El Jardín**, Montevideo 1085, T4722 3745, www.hoteljardin.com. Comfortable family-run residence with private parking, and a neat garden.
$$$ **Mykonos**, 18 de Julio 768, T4722 0255, www.hotelmykonos.com.uy. Buffet breakfast, mostly a business hotel with good services.
$$ **Lobato**, Leandro Gómez 1415, T4722 2241, hotellobato@adinet.com.uy. With buffet breakfast, modern, good.
$$ **La Posada**, José Pedro Varela 566, T4722 7879, www.hotellaposada.com.uy. Patio with BBQ, buffet breakfast, laundry service.
Camping Camping Club de Pescadores, Rambla Costanera Norte, T4722 2885, www.clubdepescadorespaysandu.com. US$3.50 pp per day plus US$6 per tent, electricity, hot showers after 1800.
Tourism farms **$$$$-$$$** Hostería y Estancia La Paz, Colonia La Paz, 15 km south

of Paysandú, T4720 2272, www.estancialapaz. com.uy. Excellent rustic rooms, pool, customized gaucho experiences, horse riding, birdwatching. Half- and full-board available. Highly recommended.
$$$ pp **Estancia Resort La Calera**, 60 km from Guichón, 150 km east of Paysandú, T2601 0340, www.lacalera.com. 44 rooms, 6 superior rooms and 24 studios, all with fireplace and kitchenette, 2 pools, horse riding and wagon rides, rodeo, sheep shearing, conference facilities. Self-catering. Highly recommended.

Salto *p1460*
$$$$ **Hotel Horacio Quiroga**, at Parque del Lago, T4733 4411, www.hotelhoracioquiroga. com. Best in town although some distance from centre, at the Termas complex, sports facilities, spa treatments, staffed by nearby catering school, special packages in season.
$$$ **Los Cedros**, Uruguay 657, T4733 3984, www.loscedros.com.uy. In centre, comfortable 3-star hotel, buffet breakfast, conference room.
$$ pp **Concordia**, Uruguay 749, T4733 2735. Oldest hotel in Uruguay, founded 1860, Carlos Gardel stayed here, fine courtyard, pleasant breakfast room.
$$ **Español**, Brasil 826, T4733 4048, www. hotelespanolsalto.com. Central, functional, with regular services, café and parking.

Termas del Daymán *p1461*
$$$ **Termas de San Nicanor**, 12 km from Termas de Daymán, Km 485, Route 3, T4730 2209, www.termassannicanor.com. Estancia and gaucho experience, excellent nature watching, private pool. Recommended. Also camping (US$10 pp), good facilities.
$$$-$$ **Del Pasaje**, near Ruta 3, T4736 9661, www.hoteldelpasaje.com. Hotel rooms, apartments for 2, 4, 6 or 7 people and cabañas. Situated in front of the Parque Acuático Acuamania.
$$ **Bungalows El Puente**, Calle 6 y Circunvalación, near the bridge over Río Dayman, T4736 9876, includes discount to thermal baths. 13 bungalows for 2 to 7 people, cheaper without a/c, kitchen.

\$\$ Estancia La Casona del Daymán, Ruta 3 Km 483, 3 km east of the bridge at Daymán, T4733 2735. Well-preserved farm, horse riding.

\$\$ Hostal Canela, Los Sauces entre Los Molles y Calle 1, T4736 9121, www.hostal canela.com.uy. HI affiliated. Good value, with kitchenette, pool, gardens.

\$\$ pp La Posta del Daymán, Ruta 3, Km 487, T4736 9801, www.lapostadeldayman.com. A/c, half- and full-board or breakfast only (cheaper, but still **\$\$**, in hostel), thermal water in more expensive rooms, thermal pool, good restaurant, long-stay discounts, camping. Recommended. Also hydrothermal complex.

Camping See Termas de San Nicanor, above.

Termas del Arapey

\$\$\$ Hotel Termas del Arapey, T4768 2441, www.hoteltermasdelarapey.com. Safe, indoor/outdoor pool, restaurant, spa, half-board available.

Camping US\$2.20 pp, good facilities.

Artigas *p1462*

There are a few hotels in town and the **Club Deportivo Artigas**, Pte Berreta and LA de Herrera, 4 km from city, T4772 2532, open all year, rooms (**\$**) and camping (US\$2.50 pp plus US\$1.50 per tent), restaurant, no cooking facilities.

Camping At Club Zorrilla, T4772 4341.

🍴 Restaurants

Colonia Suiza (Nueva Helvecia) *p1455*

\$\$\$-\$\$ Don Juan, main plaza. Snack bar/ restaurant excellent food, pastries and bread.

Colonia del Sacramento *p1455, map p1456*

\$\$\$ La Bodeguita, Del Comercio 167, T4522 5329. Daily 2030. Its terrace on the river is the main attraction of this lively pizza place that also serves good *chivitos* and pasta. Celebrating its 20th anniversary in 2014.

\$\$\$ La Casa de Jorge Páez Vilaró, Misiones de los Tapes 65, T4522 9211. Closed Wed. Attractively set at an artist's former residence, it offers a short though varied and fine menu, only 8 tables.

\$\$\$ El Drugstore, Vasconcellos 179, T4522 5241. Hip, fusion food: Latin American, European, Japanese, good, creative varied menu, good salads and fresh vegetables. Music and show.

\$\$\$ Mesón de la Plaza, Vasconcellos 153, T4522 4807. 140-year-old house with a leafy courtyard, elegant dining, good traditional food.

\$\$\$ Parrillada El Portón, Gral Flores 333, T4522 5318. Excellent *parrillada*. Small, relatively smart, good atmosphere. House speciality is offal and great sausages.

\$\$\$ Pulpería de los Faroles, Misiones de los Tapes 101, T4523 0271. Inviting tables (candlelit at night) on the cobbled plaza, for a varied menú that includes tasty salads, seafood and local wines.

\$\$\$ Punta Piedra, Ituzaingó y Gen Flores 248, T4522 2236. Daily 0900-0000. Set in a stone building, smart, great range of meat dishes, local wines, *parrilla*, *chivitos*, pastas.

\$\$\$ Viejo Barrio (VB), Vasconcellos 169, T4522 5399. Closed Wed. Very good for home-made pastas and fish, renowned live shows.

\$\$\$-\$\$ El Torreón, end of Av Gen Flores, T4523 1524. One of the best places to enjoy a sunset meal with views of the river. Set in an historic tower with in- and outdoor seating. Also serves toasties and cakes

\$\$\$-\$\$ Mercosur, Flores y Ituzaingó, T4522 4200. Popular, varied dishes. Also café serving homemade cakes. All you can eat buffet US\$18. Cash only, but accepts 5 currencies including euros.

\$\$ Club Colonia, Gen Flores 382, T4522 2189. Good value, frequented by locals, good sturdy grub, traditional Uruguayan fare.

\$\$ Tasca del Sur, Las Flores s/n. Daily from 1200 until late in high season. For a change from *parrilla* and pasta, this tiny place does excellent tacos, quesadillas and fajitas. The chef takes his time about things, but it's worth the wait. Recommended.

Arcoiris, Av Gral Flores at Plaza 25 de Agosto. Open till 0130. Very good ice cream.

Mercedes *p1458*

\$\$\$ Casa Bordó, Paysandú 654, T4532 9817. French-owned and an unmissable stopover on the routes of Uruguay.

\$\$\$-\$\$ Parador La Rambla, Rambla
Costanera y 18 de Julio, T4532 7337. For good
Spanish-influenced meals on the riverside.

Fray Bentos *p1458*
\$\$\$ Wolves, at Barrio Anglo, T4562 3604.
Good homemade pastas next to the museum.
\$\$\$-\$\$ Juventud Unida, 18 de Julio 1130,
T4562 3365. The restaurant of a local football
club is a popular place for varied meals.
Several other cafés and pizzerías on 18 de
Julio near Plaza Constitución.

Paysandú *p1459, map p1459*
\$\$\$ Artemio, 18 de Julio 1248. Simple,
reputation for serving "best food in town"
\$\$\$ Los Tres Pinos, Av España 1474, T4724
1211, www.lostrespinos.com.uy. *Parrillada*,
very good, as well as its pastas and fish. Wine
cellar, events.

Salto *p1460*
\$\$\$ La Caldera, Uruguay 221, T4732 4648.
Closed Mon lunchtime. Good *parrillada* and
local wines, also seafood.
\$\$\$ La Casa de Lamas, Chiazzaro 20, T4732
9376. Fish and homemade pasta.
\$\$\$ La Trattoria (at Club de Uruguay),
Uruguay 754, T4733 6660. Breakfast and good-
value meals, especially excellent pasta.

O Shopping

Colonia del Sacramento *p1455, map p1456*
There's a large artist community, Uruguayan
and international, with good galleries across
town. El Almacén, Real 150, creative gifts.
Paseo del Sol, Del Comercio 158, is a small
commercial centre selling local gifts. Oveja
Negra, De la Playa 114, recommended for
woollen clothes. Leather shops on C Santa Rita,
next to Yacht Club. At Arteco, Rambla de las
Américas y Av Mihanovich (Real de San Carlos)
and Gadec, on C San Miguel (opposite Puerta
de la Ciudadela) local artisans sell their produce.

O What to do

Colonia Suiza (Nueva Helvecia) *p1455*
Finca La Rosada, Federico Fisher s/n, Nueva
Helvecia, T4554 7026, www.larosada.com.uy.
A soft-fruit farm, famous for its blueberries,
pick-your-own in season, offers tours with
lunch or tea, plus local sites.

Colonia del Sacramento *p1455, map p1456*
City tours available with **Destino Viajes**, General
Flores 341, T4522 5343, destinoviajes@adinet.
com.uy. **Asociación Guías de Turismo de
Colonia**, T4522 2309, www.asociacionguias
colonia.blogspot.com, organizes walking tours
(1 hr, in Spanish, US\$6.50, other languages
US\$8.75, book in advance) in the Barrio
Histórico, daily 1100 and 1500 from tourist
office next to Old Gate.
    A new hop-on, hop-off city tour bus, run by
Buquebus, www.busturistico.com.uy, stops
at 10 different stops in and around Colonia,
US\$25 valid all day, 1st bus 1100, last 1900.

Paysandú *p1459, map p1459*
Bodega Leonardo Falcone, Av Wilson
Ferreira Aldunate y Young, T4722 7718, www.
bodegaleonardofalcone.com.uy. Winery tours
at one of Uruguay's finest wine makers.

O Transport

Colonia Suiza (Nueva Helvecia) *p1455*
Bus Montevideo-Colonia Suiza, frequent,
with **COT**, 2-2½ hrs, US\$8.15; **Turil**, goes to
Colonia Suiza and Valdense; to **Colonia del
Sacramento**, frequent, 1 hr, US\$4. Local
services between Colonia Valdense and
Nueva Helvecia connect with Montevideo/
Colonia del Sacramento buses.

Colonia del Sacramento *p1455, map p1456*
Road There are plenty of filling stations between
Colonia and the capital. If driving north to
Paysandú and Salto, especially on Route 3, fill up
with fuel and drinking water at every opportunity,
stations are few and far between. From Colonia to
Punta del Este by-passing Montevideo: take Ruta

11 at Ecilda Paullier, passing through San José de Mayo, Santa Lucía and Canelones, joining the Interbalnearia at Km 46.

Bus All leave from bus terminal on Av Buenos Aires y Manuel de Lobo, 7 blocks east of the Barrio Histórico, between the ferry port and the petrol station (free luggage lockers, tourist info desk, ATM, exchange, café and internet). To **Montevideo**, several services daily, 2¼-2¾ hrs, COT, T4522 3121, **Chadre**, T4522 4734, and **Turil**, T4522 5246, from US$11.30. **Turil** to **Col Valdense**, 1 hr, US$4. **Chadre** to **Conchillas**, US$2.50. To **Carmelo**, 1½ hrs, **Chadre** and **Berrutti**, T4522 5301, US$5. **Chadre** to **Mercedes**, 3½ hrs, US$12, **Fray Bentos**, 4 hrs, US$14.50, **Paysandú**, 6 hrs, US$21.50 and **Salto**, 8 hrs, US$29.40. **Nossar**, T4522 2934, to **Durazno**, 3 hrs, US$15.

Ferry Book in advance for all sailings in summer. Fares and schedules given under Montevideo, Transport. To **Buenos Aires**: from 5 crossings daily, with **Buquebus** (T130), cars carried. **Colonia Express**, office at the port, T4522 9676, www.coloniaexpress.com, makes 2-3 crossings a day between Colonia and **Buenos Aires** (50 min) in fast boats (no vehicles carried) with bus connections to/from **Montevideo, Punta del Este** and Uruguayan towns. **Seacat**, www.seacatcolonia.com, 3 fast ferries to Buenos Aires, 1 hr, office in Colonia T4522 2919. **Note** Passports must be stamped and Argentine departure tax paid even if only visiting Colonia for 1 day.

Taxi A Méndez y Gral Flores, T4522 2920. Taxi in the centre $3.50 flat fee.

Carmelo *p1457*

Bus To **Montevideo**, US$15.50-18, Intertur, Chadre and Sabelín. To **Fray Bentos** (US$9), **Salto** (US$23.50), with Chadre from main plaza 0655, 1540. To **Colonia**, see above. To **Buenos Aires**: via Tigre, across the Paraná delta, an interesting bus/boat ride past innumerable islands: **Cacciola** 2 a day; T2908 2244, www.cacciolaviajes.com, see Montevideo page 1453.

Mercedes *p1458*

Bus To **Paysandú**, with Sabelín, in bus terminal, 1½-2 hrs, US$8-9; also **Chadre** on the Montevideo-Bella Unión route. To **Montevideo**, US$18, 3½ hrs, CUT, **Agencia Central** and **Sabelín**. To **Gualeguaychú**, 2 hrs, US$10, ETA CUT, Ciudad de Gualeguay (not Sun).

Fray Bentos *p1458*

Bus Terminal at 18 de Julio y Blanes. To/from **Montevideo**, CUT, 4-5 hrs, US$20, also **Chadre** and **Agencia Central**. To **Mercedes**, ETA, US$2, 5 daily (not Sun).

Crossing to Argentina: Fray Bentos *p1458*

Bus To **Buenos Aires**, 4 hrs, US$38.50, CITA. To **Gualeguaychú**, 1½ hrs, US$7, ETA CUT (not Sun).

Paysandú *p1459, map p1459*

Bus Can be hard to get a seat on buses going north. Terminal at Zorrilla y Artigas, T4722 3225. To/from **Montevideo**, US$24 (Núñez/Viajes Cynsa, Copay, T4722 2094, 4 a day, US$22.50), 5-6 hrs, also **Chadre** and **Agencia Central**. To **Salto**, Agencia Central, Alonso, T4733 3969, 1½-2 hrs, 9 a day, US$8. To **Rivera**, US$21, Copay, 0400 Mon-Sat. To **Fray Bentos**, 2 a day, 2 hrs direct, US$8. To **Colonia** by Chadre, 0750, 1750, 6 hrs, US$20.

Crossing to Argentina: Paysandú *p1460*

Bus To **Colón**, Copay, Río Uruguay, 45 min-1 hr, US$5.

Salto *p1460*

Bus Terminal 15 blocks east of centre at Batlle y Blandengues, café, shopping centre, *casa de cambio*. Take taxi to centre. To/from **Montevideo**, 5½-7½ hrs, US$35-43 (Norteño, Núñez, Agencia Central and Chadre). Chadre, Cotabu and Hernández to **Termas del Arapey**, 1½ hrs, daily, US$5. Also **Agentur**, 1 to 2 a day, US$6, via C Treinta y Tres. To **Bella Unión**, 2 hrs, US$12, 2 a day. To **Colonia**, 0555, 1555, 8 hrs, US$29.40; to **Fray Bentos**, same times, US$17.

Crossing to Argentina: Salto *p1461*

Bus To **Concordia**, Chadre and Flecha Bus, 2 a day each Mon-Fri, 2 on Sat, no buses Sun,

US$5, 1¼-1½ hrs. To **Buenos Aires**, US$50, Flecha Bus.

Launch To **Concordia**, US$4, 15 mins, 4 a day (not Sun), depart port on C Brasil; immigration either side of river, quick and easy.

Artigas *p1462*
Bus To **Salto**, COA, T4772 2268, US$15. Turil and COT from **Montevideo** 7-7½ hrs, US$42 via Durazno, Paso de los Toros and Tacuarembó.

⊙ Directory

Colonia del Sacramento *p1455, map p1456*
Banks Banks open afternoon only. Most museums and restaurants accept Argentine pesos or US$, but rarely euros. HSBC, De Portugal 183 (Barrio Histórico), Mon-Fri 1300-1700. **Cambio Dromer**, Flores 350, T4522 2070, Mon-Fri 1000-1800, Sat 1000-1700 (branch at **Casino Radisson** daily 1400-0400). **Cambio Colonia** and **Western Union**, Av Flores y Lavalleja, T4522 5032. **Car hire** In bus terminal: **Avis** (main hall), T4522 9842, from

US$150 per day, **Hertz** (50 m from entrance), T4522 9851, from US$90 per day. **Thrifty** by port, also at Flores 172, T4522 2939, where there are bicycles too (US$3 per hr), scooters (US$7 per hr) and golf buggies (US$15 per hr) for hire, recommended as traffic is slow and easy to navigate. **Consulates** Argentine Consulate and Cultural Centre, Flores 209, T4522 2093, open weekdays 1300-1800.

Paysandú *p1459, map p1459*
Banks *Casas de cambio* on 18 de Julio: Cambio Fagalde, No 1004; **Cambio Bacacay**, No 1039; change TCs, Sat 0830-1230.
Consulates Argentina, Gómez 1034, T4722 2253, Mon-Fri 1300-1800.

Salto *p1460*
Banks *Casas de cambio* on Uruguay. **Car hire** Maxicar, Paraguay 764, T4733 5554, 9943 5454, www.maxicarsalto.com. 24 hrs, cars allowed to travel to Argentina and Brazil.
Consulates Argentina, Artigas 1162, T4733 2931, Mon-Fri 0900-1400.

Eastern Uruguay

Resorts line the coast from Montevideo to Punta del Este, the ultimate magnet for summer holidaymakers, especially from Argentina. Out of season, it is quieter and you can have the beaches to yourself, which is pretty much the case the closer you get to Brazil year round. Inland are cattle ranches, some of which welcome visitors, quiet lagoons and hills with expansive views.

East from Montevideo

This beautiful coast consists of an endless succession of small bays, beaches and promontories, set among hills and woodlands. The beach season runs from December to the end of February. An excellent four-lane highway leads to Punta del Este and Rocha, and a good two-lane highway to Chuy, near the Brazilian border. This route takes in the most important Uruguayan beach resorts, as well as Parque Nacional Santa Teresa and other natural attractions. If driving there are four tolls each way (about US$2.40 each), but this route is the easiest and the most comfortable in Uruguay with sufficient service stations along the way.

Piriápolis → *Colour map 8, B6. Population: 8830.*
This resort set among hills, 101 km from Montevideo, is laid out with an abundance of shady trees, and the district is rich in pine, eucalyptus and acacia woods. It has a good beach, a yacht harbour, a country club, a motor-racing track (street circuit) and is particularly popular with Argentines. It was, in fact, founded in the 1890s as a bathing resort for residents of Buenos Aires.

Next to the marina is a small cable car (with seats for two) to the top of **Cerro San Antonio** ⓘ *US$4, 10 mins ride, free car park and toilets at lower station (also reached by car, bus or on foot)*. Magnificent views of Piriápolis and beaches, several restaurants. Recommended, but be careful when disembarking. North of the centre, at **Punta de Playa Colorada**, is a marine rescue centre ⓘ *www.sosfaunamarina.com*, that looks after injured sea creatures before releasing them to the wild. **Tourist office**, Asociación de Turismo ⓘ *Paseo de la Pasiva, Rambla de los Argentinos, T4432 5055, www.destinopiriapolis.com, summer 0900-2400, winter 1000-1800*.

About 6 km north on the R37 is **Cerro Pan de Azúcar** (Sugar Loaf Hill) ⓘ *getting there: take bus 'Cerro Pan de Azúcar' and get off after 6 km*, crowned by a tall cross with a circular stairway inside, fine coastal views. There is only a steep path, marked by red arrows, up to the cross. Just north of Piriápolis R 37 passes the **La Cascada** municipal park (open all year, small waterfall, old woodlands, picnic area, toilets) which contains the house of Francisco Piria, the founder of the resort, **Museo Castillo de Piria** ⓘ *daily in summer, 1000-1730 (winter Tue-Sun 1000-1530)*. About 4 km beyond Cerro Pan de Azúcar is the village of Pan de Azúcar, which has a **Museo al Aire Libre de Pintura** where the walls of the buildings have been decorated by Uruguayan and Argentine painters, designers and writers with humorous and tango themes, known as the Mural Circuit (direct bus every hour from Piriápolis).

Portezuelo and Punta Ballena

R93 runs between the coast and the Laguna del Sauce to Portezuelo, which has good beaches. The **Arboreto Lussich** ⓘ *T4257 8077, 1000-1800, free*, on the west slope of the Sierra de la Ballena (north of R93) contains a unique set of native and exotic trees. There are footpaths, or you can drive through; two *miradores*; worth a visit. From Portezuelo drive north towards the R9 by way of the R12 which then continues, unpaved, to Minas. Just off R12 is **El Tambo Lapataia** ⓘ *1 km east from Solanas, then 4 km north, T4222 0303, www.lapataiapuntadeleste.com*, a dairy farm open to the public, selling cheese, ice cream, *dulce de leche*, home-made pizzas and pastas. Also farming activities and organic garden.

At Punta Ballena there is a wide crescent beach, calm water and very clean sand. The place is a residential resort but is still quiet. At the top of Punta Ballena there is a panoramic road 2.5 km long with remarkable views of the coast. **Casa Pueblo**, the house and gallery of Uruguayan artist Carlos Páez Vilaró who passed away in 2014, is built in a Spanish-Moroccan style on a cliff over the sea; the gallery can be visited (daily, 1000 sunset, US$6), there are paintings, collages and ceramics on display, and for sale; open all year. Walk downhill towards the sea for a good view of the house.

Maldonado → *Colour map 8, B6. Population: 65,865.*

The capital of Maldonado Department, 140 km east of Montevideo, is a peaceful town, sacked by the British in 1806. It has many colonial remains and the historic centre has been restored. It is also a dormitory suburb of Punta del Este. Worth seeing is the **El Vigía watch tower** ⓘ *Michelini y Pérez del Puerto*; the Cathedral (started 1801, completed 1895), on Plaza San Fernando; the windmill; the **Cuartel de Dragones exhibition centre** ⓘ *Pérez del Puerto y 18 de Julio, by Plaza San Fernando*, and the **Cachimba del Rey** ⓘ *on the continuation of 3 de Febrero, almost Artigas*, an old well – legend claims that those who drink from it will never leave Maldonado. **Museo Mazzoni** ⓘ *Ituzaingó 789, T4222 1107, summer 0800-2200, winter 1300-1800, free*, has regional items, indigenous, Spanish, Portuguese and English. **Museo de Arte Americano** ⓘ *Treinta y Tres 823 y Dodera, T4222 2276, http://maam-uruguay.blogspot.com, 1800-2200, Dec and Feb Fri-Sun only (closed winter)*, a private museum of national and international art, interesting. **Tourist office** ⓘ *Dirección General de Turismo, Edificio Municipal, T4222 3333, www.maldonado.gub.uy*.

Punta del Este → *Colour map 8, B6.*

About 7 km from Maldonado and 139 km from Montevideo (a little less by dual carriageway), facing the bay on one side and the open waters of the Atlantic on the other, lies the largest and best known of the resorts, **Punta del Este** (population 9200), part of the municipality of Maldonado, particularly popular among Argentines and Brazilians. The narrow peninsula of Punta del Este has been entirely built over. On the land side, the city is flanked by large planted forests of eucalyptus, pine and mimosa. Two blocks from the sea, at the tip of the peninsula, is the historic monument of El Faro (lighthouse); in this part of the city no building may exceed its height. On the ocean side of the peninsula, at the end of Calle 25 (Arrecifes), is a shrine to the first mass said by the Conquistadores on this coast, 2 February 1515. Three blocks from the shrine is Plaza General Artigas, which has a *feria artesanal* (handicraft market); along its side runs Avenida Gorlero, the main street. There are two casinos, a golf course, and many beautiful holiday houses. **Museo Ralli of Contemporary Latin American Art** ⓘ *Curupay y Los Arrayanes s/n, Barrio Beverly Hills, T4248 3476, www.museoralli. com.uy, Tue-Sun 1400-1800 closed Jun-Sep, free.* Worth a visit but a car (or bike – cycle path all the way from Punta del Este) is needed.

Punta del Este has excellent bathing **beaches**, the calm Playa Mansa on the bay side, the rough Playa Brava on the ocean side. There are some small beaches hemmed in by rocks on this side of the peninsula, but most people go to where the extensive Playa Brava starts. Papa Charlie beach on the Atlantic (Parada 13) is preferred by families with small children as it is safe. Quieter beaches are at La Barra and beyond.

There is an excellent yacht marina, yacht and fishing clubs. There is good fishing both at sea and in three nearby lakes and the Río Maldonado. **Tourist information** ⓘ *Liga de Fomento, Parada 1, T4244 6519, open summer 0800-1800, winter 1100-1700; in bus station T4249 4042; at Rambla Claudio Williman (Mansa side), T4223 0050; at Plaza Artigas, Av Gorlero, T4244 6510; and at airports.* See the websites www.puntaweb.com, www.puntadeleste.com and www.vivapunta.com.

Isla de Gorriti, visited by explorers including Solís, Magellan and Drake, was heavily fortified

Punta del Este

To ④
To ②   To ③

Rambla Costanera
Alsina
Villa Serrana
Francia

Playa Mansa

Playa Brava

Izaurraga (31)
Focas (30)
Gorlero (22)
Mesana (24)
Resalsero (26)

Gaviotas (29)
Meros (28)
Playa El Emir

Bauprés (18)
Remanso (20)
Muergos (27)
Shrine of First Mass

Río de la Plata

Arrecifes (25)
Plaza Gen Artigas
Corral (23)

Yacht Club
Galerna (21)
Comodoro Gorlero (19)

Yacht Marina
Estrecho (17)

Obenque (11)
Salina (9)

2 de Febrero (14)
Trinquete (13)
Virazón (10)
Faro (7)

Playa los Ingleses

Pampero (6)
Cnan Miranda (7)
Faro (5)

Rambla Gral Artigas
Faro
Puesta del Sol (4)
Isla de Lobos (2)

N

Sargos (2)

200 metres
200 yards

Where to stay 🛏
1 Agupy
2 Conrad
3 El Viajero Hostel
4 El Viajero Manantiales Hostel
5 Gaudi
6 Iberia
7 Punta del Este Hostel
8 Remanso
9 Tánger

Restaurants 🍴
3 Gure-etxe
4 Il Barreto
5 Isidora
7 Lo de Charlie
8 Lo de Tere
9 Los Caracoles
10 Viejo Marino
12 Yatch Club Uruguayo

by the Spanish in the 1760's to keep the Portuguese out. The island, densely wooded and with superb beaches, is an ideal spot for campers (0800-1830, 0900-1700 in winter, entry US$13.50; boats from 0930-1700, return 1015-1815, US$15, T4244 6166; **Don Quico Cruceros**, also does fishing trips, T4244 8945). On **Isla de Lobos**, which is a government reserve within sight of the town, there is a huge sea-lion colony; public boat US$20 per person (leaves 1200), tour US$30-50. Tickets should be booked in advance (T4244 1716, or **Dimartours** T4244 4750, www.dimartours.com.uy).

Beaches east of Punta del Este

Between the Peninsula and the mouth of the Río Maldonado, a road runs along the coast, passing luxurious houses, dunes and pines. Some of the most renowned architects of Uruguay and Argentina design houses here. Several of the beaches east of Punta del Este are excellent for surfing, more so the further east towards Brazil you travel. First in line after the main resort is **La Barra**, a fashionable, very hip and happening place, especially for summer nightlife. Punta del Este "downtown", on the peninsula, is increasingly turning into a service centre and many visitors are choosing to base their stay in other, less built-up beach resorts. La Barra has a good collection of beaches, art galleries, bars and restaurants (take a bus from Punta del Este terminal or taxi US$20). The **Museo del Mar Sirenamis** ⓘ *1 km off the coast road, watch for signs, T4277 1817, www.museodelmar.com.uy, summer daily 1030-2030 winter 1100-1700, US$7,* has an extensive collection on the subject of the sea, its life and history and on the first beach resorts. The coast road climbs a headland here before descending to the beaches further north, Montoya and **Manantiales** (reached by Condesa bus; taxi US$30). Some 30 km from Punta del Este is the former fishing village of **Faro José Ignacio**, now increasingly luxurious, alternative and arty. It has an old **lighthouse** ⓘ *summer daily 1100-2030, winter 1100-1330, 1430-1830, US$0.75,* a beach club and other new developments, now the road is paved. Coastal R10 continues east of José Ignacio to La Paloma and further north.

La Paloma and around → *Colour map 8, B6. Population: 3554.*

Protected by an island and a sandspit, this is a good port for yachts. The surrounding scenery is attractive, with extensive wetlands nearby. You can walk for miles along the beach. The pace is more relaxed than Punta del Este. **Tourist office** ⓘ *in La Paloma bus station, T9995 6662,* very helpful. **Department of Rocha office** ⓘ *Rutas 9 y 15, T4472 3100, www.turismorocha.gub.uy, daily 0800-2000.*

Coastal R10 runs to Aguas Dulces (regular bus services, **Rutas del Sol,** cover the whole coast). About 10 km from La Paloma is **La Pedrera**, a beautiful village with stunning views and sandy beaches. Beyond La Pedrera the road runs near pleasant fishing villages which are rapidly being developed with holiday homes, for example **Barra de Valizas**, a small, very laidback hide-away, 50 minutes north. At **Cabo Polonio** (permanent population 80), visits to the islands of Castillos and Wolf can be arranged to see sea lions and penguins. It has two great beaches: the north beach is more rugged, while the south is tamer by comparison. Both have lifeguards on duty (though their zone of protection only covers a tiny portion of the endless stretches of beach). The village is part of a nature reserve. This limits the number of people who are allowed to stay there since the number of lodgings is limited and camping is strictly forbidden (if you arrive with a tent, it may be confiscated). During January or February (and especially during Carnival), you **have** to reserve a room in one of the few posadas or hotels, or better yet, rent a house (see Where to stay, below). From Km 264 on the main road all-terrain vehicles run 8 km across the dunes to the village (several companies, around US$5; tourist office by the terminal, open 1000-1800, T9996 8747). Day visitors must leave just after sundown (see Transport, below). Ask locally in Valizas about walking there, three to four hours via the north beach (very interesting, but hot, unless you go early). There are also pine woods with paths leading to the beach or village.

The **Monte de Ombúes** ⓘ *open in summer months, from Jan, free, basic restaurant with honest prices* is a wood containing a few *ombú* trees (*Phytolacca dioica* – the national tree), *coronilla* (*Scutia buxifolia*) and *canelón* (*Rapanea laetevirens*). It has a small circuit to follow and a good hide for birdwatching. To reach the woods from Km 264, go 2 km north along R10 to the bridge. Here take a boat with guide, 30 minutes along the river (**Monte Grande** recommended as they visit both sides of the river, montegrande@adinet.com.uy). You can also walk from Km 264 across the fields, but it's a long way and the last 150 m are through thick brush. The bridge is 16 km from Castillos on R9 (see next paragraph): turn onto R16 towards Aguas Dulces, just before which you turn southwest onto R10.

From **Aguas Dulces** the road runs inland to the town of **Castillos** (ATM, shops, taxi rank and bus terminal on the main plaza, easy bus connections to Chuy), where it rejoins R9. A **tourist office** ⓘ *Aguas Dulces/Castillos crossroads on R9, T9981 7068, open 1000-1300, 1700-2200,* has details on hotels.

Punta del Diablo
At Km 298 there is a turn to a fishing village in dramatic surroundings, with three fine beaches, Playa de la Viuda to the south, Playa del Pescador in the centre and Playa del Rivero to the north. Punta del Diablo is very rustic, good for surfing and popular with young people in high season, but from April to November the solitude and the dramatically lower prices make it a wonderful getaway for couples or families. Increased popularity has brought more lodging and services year round, although off-season activity is still extremely low compared to summer. **Municipal tourist office** ⓘ *T4477 2412, daily 0800-2200.* See www.portaldeldiablo.com.

Parque Nacional Santa Teresa
ⓘ *100 km from Rocha, 308 km from Montevideo, open 0800-2000 to day visitors (open 24 hrs for campers), T4477 2101/03 ext 209.*
This park has curving, palm-lined avenues and plantations of many exotic trees. It also contains botanical gardens, fresh-water pools for bathing and beaches which stretch for many kilometres (the surf is too rough for swimming). It is the site of the impressive colonial fortress of Santa Teresa, begun by the Portuguese in 1762 and seized by the Spanish in 1793. The fortress houses a **museum** ⓘ *Wed-Sun 1300-1900 (winter Fri-Sun 1200-1800), US$1,* of artefacts from the wars of independence. Old cemetery nearby, several cafés and snack bars open high season. On the inland side of Route 9, the strange and gloomy Laguna Negra and the marshes of the Bañado de Santa Teresa support large numbers of wild birds. A road encircles the fortress; it's possible to drive or walk around even after closing. From there is a good view of Laguna Negra.

There are countless campsites (open all year), and a few cottages to let in the summer (usually snapped up quickly). At the *capatacia*, or administrative headquarters, campers pay US$4 pp per night. The park (entrance free) is well-kept and has numerous facilities attached to the different campsites, including cafés, supermarkets, telephones, post office, laundry services and several small restaurants. Beautiful isolated beaches also abound (six main beaches, several smaller ones). Practically every amenity is closed off-season. The bathing resort of **La Coronilla** is 10 km north of Santa Teresa, 20 south of Chuy; it has the **Karumbé** ⓘ *Ruta 9, Km 314, T09-991 7811, www.karumbe. org, Jan-Apr 1000-1900,* marine turtle center. There are several hotels and restaurants, most closed in winter (tourist information T9977 7129). Montevideo–Chuy buses stop at La Coronilla.

Chuy → *Colour map 7, inset. Population: 11,037. For details of Chuí in Brazil see the Brazil chapter.*
At Chuy, 340 km from Montevideo, the Brazilian frontier runs along the main street, Avenida Internacional, which is called Avenida Brasil in Uruguay and Avenida Uruguaí in Brasil. The Uruguayan

side has more services, including supermarkets, duty-free shops and a casino. **Tourist office** ① *on the plaza, T4474 3627, infochuy@turismorocha.gub.uy, 0900-2200*. See www.chuynet.com.

On the Uruguayan side, on a promontory overlooking Laguna Merín and the gaúcho landscape of southern Brazil, stands the restored fortress of **San Miguel** ① *Wed-Sun 1300-1900 (high season), Thu-Sun 1300-1900 (low season), US$0.90, bus from Chuy US$1.50, Rutas del Sol buses from Montevideo go here after passing through Chuy*, dating from 1734 and surrounded by a moat. It is set above a 1500-ha wetland park, which is good for birdwatching and is 10 km north of Chuy along Route 19 which is the border. There is a small museum of *criollo* and *indígena* culture (entrance included in the fortress ticket), displaying, among other artefacts, old carriages and presses. Not always open in low season. A fine walk from here is 2 km to the Cerro Picudo. The path starts behind the museum, very apparent. Tours (US$10 from Chuy) end for the season after 31 March.

Border with Brazil

Uruguayan passport control is 2.5 km before the border on Ruta 9 into Chuy, US$2 by taxi, 20 minutes walk, or take a town bus; officials friendly and cooperative. Ministry of Tourism kiosk here is helpful, especially for motorists, T4474 4599. Tourists may freely cross the border in either direction as long as they do not go beyond either country's border post. Taking a car into Brazil is no problem if the car is not registered in Brazil or Uruguay. (Uruguayan rental cars are not allowed out of the country. Although you can freely drive between Chuy and Chuí, if you break down/have an accident on the Brazilian side, car rental insurance will not cover it: park in Chuy, even if only one metre from Brazil, and walk.) From the border post, Ruta 9 bypasses the town, becoming BR-471 on the Brazilian side, leading to Brazilian immigration, also outside town. **Brazilian consulate** ① *Tito Fernández 147, T4474 2049, Chuy, open 0900-1300*. For buses to Brazilian destinations, go to the rodoviária in Chuí (details in the Brazil chapter). The bus companies that run from Chuy into Brazil ask for passports – make sure you get yours back before boarding the bus.

Entering Uruguay You need a Brazilian exit stamp and a Uruguayan entry stamp (unless visiting only Chuí), otherwise you'll be turned back at customs or other official posts. Those requiring a visa will be charged around US$80 depending on the country.

● East from Montevideo listings

For hotel and restaurant price codes, and other relevant information, see Essentials.

● Where to stay

Piriápolis *p1468*
Many hotels along the seafront, most close end-Feb to mid-Dec. Book in advance in high season. Many others than those listed here.
$$$ pp **Argentino Hotel**, Rambla de los Argentinos y Armenia, T4432 2791, www.argentinohotel.com.uy. A fine hotel and landmark designed by Piria with casino, 2 restaurants, medicinal springs, sauna and good facilities for children and teenagers.

$$$ Escorial, Rambla de los Argentinos 1290, T4432 2537, www.hotelescorial.com. With mini-bar, safe in room, pool, parking, children's playground, laundry service.
$$$-$$ Rivadavia, Rambla de los Argentinos y Trápani, T4432 2532, www.hotelrivadavia.com. Open all year (much cheaper in winter), restaurant, parking.
$ pp **Hostel Piriápolis**, Simón del Pino 1136 y Tucumán, T4432 0394, www.hostelpiriapolis.com.uy. Rooms for 2-4 (open all year), private rooms **$$**, 240 beds, non-HI members pay more, hot showers, cooking facilities, student cards accepted.
Camping El Toro, Av de Mayo y Fuente de Venus, T4432 3454, doubles in bungalows, and

tents. Also **Piriápolis Fútbol Club**, at Misiones y Niza, just behind bus station, T4432 3275, piriapolisfc@adinet.com.uy, US$5.75.

Portezuelo and Punta Ballena p1469
$$$$ Hotel-Art Las Cumbres, Ruta 12 Km 3.5, 4 km inland, T4257 8689, www.cumbres.com.uy. Themed as an artist's house-studio, on a wooded hill with great views over Laguna del Sauce and the coast, highly regarded, pool, restaurant and tea room (expensive but popular).
$$$$ Casa Pueblo, T4257 8611, www.club hotelcasapueblo.com. Highly recommended hotel and apartments, spa and, lower down the hill, **Restaurant Las Terrazas**.
Camping Punta Ballena, Km 120, Parada 45, T4257 8902, www.campingpuntaballena.com. US$11.50 pp per night (US$9 in low season), many facilities, very clean. Also has tents for hire, US$4.50 tent only, and cabins for 4-8 people (**$$$**).

Maldonado p1469
Hotel accommodation is scarce in summer; cheaper than Punta del Este, but you will have to commute to the beach. Basic 1-2 star places (**$$**), open all year, include: **Catedral**, Florida 830 casi 18 de Julio, T4224 2513, www.hotelcatedral.com.uy, central, and
$$$-$$ Colonial, 18 de Julio 841 y Florida, T4222 3346, www.colonialhotel.com.uy.
$$ Celta, Ituzaingó 839, T4223 0139. Helpful, Irish owner, No 7 bus stop outside.
$$ Isla de Gorriti, Michelini 884, T4224 5218. Nice courtyard. Recommended.
Camping El Edén, Balneario Las Flores, T4438 0565, www.eledencamping.com, US$9, also has *cabañas* for 2-6 people.

Punta del Este p1470, map p1470
Note Streets on the peninsula have names and numbers; lowest numbers at the tip. Hotels are plentiful but expensive: we list recommended ones only. Rates in the few hotels still open after the end of Mar are often halved. Visitors without a car have to take a hotel on the peninsula, unless they want to spend a fortune on taxis.

On the peninsula
$$$$ Conrad Hotel y Casino, Parada 4, Playa Mansa, T4249 1111, www.conrad. com.uy. Luxurious hotel with spa, concerts and events, wonderful views. Book in advance in high season.
$$$$ Remanso, C 20 y 28, T4244 7412, www. hotelremanso.com.uy. Some rooms **$$$** low season, comfortable, businesslike, pool, jacuzzi, safe, open all year (also 2 suites in **$$$$** range). 2-4-bed rooms. Recommended.
$$$ Iberia, C 24, No 685, T4244 0405, www.iberiahotel.com.uy. **$$$$** in high season, disabled access, garage opposite.
$$$ Tánger, C 31 entre 18 y 20, T4244 1333, www.hoteltanger.com. Closed May-Aug.
$$$$ in highest season, safe, disabled access, 2 pools.
$$$-$$ Gaudi, C Risso, parada 1, by bus terminal, T4249 4116, www.hotelgaudi.com.uy. Open all year. 2-star. Good, convenient, safe, fridge, bar.
$$-$ Agupy (formerly 1949 hostel), Esq 30 y 18, T4244 0719. Close to the bus terminal and beaches. New ownership. Rooms with sea view.
$$-$ pp **Punta del Este Hostel**, C 25 No 544 y 24, T4244 1632, www.puntadelestehostel.com. US$17-40 in dorm (price depends on season; no doubles), lockers, central, basic.
$ El Viajero Brava Beach Hostel and Suites, Av Francia y Charrua, T4248 0331, www.el viajerobravabeach.com. Private en suite with TV, dorms en suite (**$**) with a/c, breakfast included, cable TV and DVDs, bar, fireplace, free Wi-Fi, near bus station.

Beaches east of Punta del Este p1471
San Rafael (Parada 12)
$$$$ La Capilla, Viña del Mar y Valparaíso, behind San Marcos, T4248 4059, www.lacapilla. com.uy. Open all year. **$$$** in low season, kitchenette in some rooms, safes in rooms, gardens, pool, good.
$$$$-$$$ San Rafael, Lorenzo Batlle y Pacheco, Parada 11 Playa Brava, T4248 2161, www.hotelsanrafael.com.uy. Open all year. Large hotel, heating, safe, spa. Business and events facilities.

La Barra

$$$$ Hostal de la Barra, Ruta 10, Km 161.300, T4277 1521, www.hostaldelabarra.net. Open all year. In low season prices **$$$**. A small hotel, not a hostel, with sea view, forest view and loft rooms, neat, Christmas, Carnival and Semana Santa require 7 or 4-night minimum stays.

$$$$ Kalá, Pedregal s/n, Altos de Montoya, T4277 3500, www.kalahotel.com. A boutique hotel with 12 rooms, with breakfast, bars, pools and jacuzzi, bicycles.

$$$$ Mantra, Ruta 10, Parada 48, T4277 1000, www.mantraresort.com. Open all year. Very good and award-winning, but you will need a car to move around, great pool, spa, casino, restaurants, concerts, own cinema and wine bar.

$$$$ La Posta del Cangrejo, hotel/restaurant, Ruta 10 Km 160, T4277 0021, www.lapostadelcangrejo.com. Nice location, smart, prices reduced in low season. Recommended.

$$-$ pp Backpacker de La Barra, C 9, No 2306, 0.5 km off main road, T4277 2272, www.backpackerdelabarra.com. Youth hostel style, price depends on dates and class of room (**$$$$** in luxury double, high season), café, pool, gardens, laundry, bike hire, breakfast included.

Camping Camping San Rafael, Camino Aparicio Saravia, T4248 6715, www.campingsanrafael.com.uy. Good facilities, US$8.50-12.50 for 2, also has *cabañas*, Wi-Fi, bus 5 from Maldonado.

Manantiales

$$-$ pp El Viajero Manantiales Beach Hostel, Ruta 10, Km 164, T4277 4427, www.elviajerohostels.com. Private and shared dorms, swimming pool, open-air bar, BBQ area and terrace, breakfast included, free Wi-Fi.

Faro José Ignacio

$$$$ Estancia Vik, Camino Eugenio Saiz Martínez, Km 8, José Ignacio, T9460 5212, www.vikretreats.com. Also owned by the Vik family, this impeccable haven of laidback luxury offers one of the finest *estancia* stays in Uruguay. Excellent green credentials, extensive views across the José Ignacio Lagoon, exquisite asados, modern and traditional art in the rooms and suites. Horse riding and other activities offered.

$$$$ Posada del Faro, C de la Bahía y Timonel, T4486 2110, www.posadadelfaro.com. Exclusive hotel overlooking the sea, 12 rooms in 3 standards, pool, bar, restaurant.

$$$$ Playa Vik, C Los Cisnes, T4486 2611/19, www.vikretreats.com. Six luxurious beach houses, as well as accommodation in the main building, the Pavillion, all overlooking the sea and gardens. Fabulous modern art throughout the property, infinity pool, gym, spa and BBQ dining room. Also Bahía Vik (www.vikretreats.com) set to open autumn 2014.

La Paloma *p1471*

$$$$-$$$ Palma de Mallorca, on Playa La Aguada, In nearby La Aguada, I4479 6739, www.hotelpalmademallorca.com. Right on the ocean. Discounts for longer stays, heated pool, parking.

$$$ Bahía, Av del Navío s/n, entre Solari y Del Sol, T4479 6029, www.elbahia.com.uy. Breakfast, double or triple rooms, clean and simple, quite old fashioned, laundry, half-board available.

Youth hostels $ pp Altena 5000 at Parque Andresito, T4479 6396. 50 beds in 4 rooms, HI discounts, good meals, kitchen, open all year.

$ pp Ibirapitá, Av Paloma s/n, near bus station and beach, T4479 9303, www.hostelibirapita.com. Cheaper in mixed dorm and for HI members, doubles **$$**. Buffet breakfast, surf boards, bicycles.

Camping In Parque Andresito, Ruta 15, Km 1500, T4479 6081, complejoandresito@adinet.com.uy. Overpriced, thatched *cabañas* for rent, from US$52 per day with maid and kitchen facilities, sleep 4-6. Grill del Camping for *parrillas*.

Northeast of La Paloma

At Cabo Polonio you cannot camp. There are *posadas*, some listed below, or you can rent a house; see www.cabopolonio.com or www.portaldelcabo.com.uy for all options. Water is drawn from wells (*cachimbas*) and there is no electricity (some houses have generators, some gas lamps, otherwise buy candles). There are 4 shops for supplies, largest is El Templao. At La Pedrera, **Aguas Dulces** and **Barra de Valizas** there are various places to stay and lots of cheap cabins for rent.

$$$ La Perla, Cabo Polonio, T4470 5125, www.laperladelcabo.com. Open all year. Restaurant and snack bar, spa, visits to lighthouse.

$$$ Posada Mariemar, Cabo Polonio, T4470 5164, T987 5260, mariemar@cabopolonio.com. Nice owners, own electricity generator, hot water, with breakfast, restaurant, open all year.

$$$ Posada Valizas, C Tomás Cambre, 1 block from Plaza de los Barcos, Barra de Valizas, T4475 4067, www.posadavalizas.com. Tranquil and lovely, small-scale posada. Peaceful garden setting, attentive service. Highly recommended.

$$$-$$ La Pedrasanta, C Cabo Polonio (Cedron), La Pedrera, T4479 2179, www.posada lapedrasanta.com. Lovely, arty Italian/Argentine-run *posada* and restaurant. Pleasant garden, Tuscan cuisine, friendly owners. Recommended.

$$-$ pp Cabo Polonio Hostel, T9944 5943, www.cabopoloniohostel.com. Small wooden hostel, hot showers, shared rooms, doubles available outside high season, kitchenettes, solar power, bar, good fresh food, can arrange tours and riding.

$$-$ pp Reserva Ecológica La Laguna, 2 km north of Aguas Dulces, T4475 2118/9960 2410. Rustic cabins on the shore a lake, also hostel lodging, day rates for adults and children, full and half-board available, close to beach, horse riding, trekking, sailing, hydrobikes, meditation. Always phone in advance for directions and reservation.

Youth hostels $ pp El Viajero La Pedrera Hostel and Suites, Calle Ventevo s/n, La Pedrera, T4479 2252, www.elviajero hostels.com. Private en suite, dorms en suite, breakfast included, bar, wide common areas, gorgeous garden, free Wi-Fi.

Camping Camping PP, Ruta 10 Km 226.5, T4479 2069, La Pedrera, www.campingpp. com.uy. US$7.50-11.50 camping, also has cabins for 2 to 6 people.

Punta del Diablo *p1472*
In high season you should book in advance; www.portaldeldiablo.com gives a full list of choices.

$$$$ Aquarella, Av No 5, ½ block from beach, T4477 2400, www.hotelaquarella.com. Pool, jacuzzi, great views, gourmet restaurant.

$$$$-$$$ Terrazas de la Viuda, C del Indio, T9968 1138, www.terrazasdelaviuda.com. Pleasant hotel with spacious rooms and pool, overlooking the beach. Also nearby sister hotel **La Viuda del Diablo** (www.laviudadeldiablo.com), on the beach itself, with restaurant and beach bar open to the public, Good, fresh seafood.

$$$-$$ Hostería del Pescador, on road into village, Blv Santa Teresa, T4477 2017, www.portaldeldiablo.com. Rooms for 2-6, price vary for season and day of week, restaurant, pool.

$ pp El Diablo Tranquilo Hostel and Bar, Av Central, T4477 2647, www.eldiablotranquilo.com. Shared and private rooms, breakfast and cooking facilities, year round. Separate bar that is one of the nightlife hotspots. Highly recommended. Also **El Diablo Tranquilo Playa Suites** on the beach, run by the same team, double suites with fireplaces (**$$$-$$**).

$ pp Punta del Diablo Hostel, Km 298, Ruta 9 parada 2, T4477 2655, www.puntadeldiablo hostel.com. Mid-Dec to end-Feb. Discounts for HI members. With kitchen, camping (US$8-10 pp), bicycles.

$$-$ Unplugged Hostel, C 10, www.unpluggedhostel.com. Dorm-only hostel not far from the beach. sociable place, outdoor communal area for *asados* and pizzas, free computer, good place to meet other travellers.

Parque Nacional Santa Teresa: La Coronilla *p1472*

$$$$ Hotel Parque Oceánico, Ruta 9 km 312,5, T4476 2883, www.hotelparqueoceanico.com.uy. Open year-round. 4-star hotel in excellent location. 3 pools, 1 indoor, 2 outdoor, games room, full- and half-board options. Good restaurant also open to the public. Extensive grounds, short walk to endless beaches. Hiking, birdwatching, horse riding on the beach, forest walks. Highly recommended.

Chuy *p1472*
All hotels are open the year round.

$$$ Parador El Fortín de San Miguel, Paraje 18 de Julio, near San Miguel fortress, T4474

6607, www.elfortin.com. Excellent, full and half-board available, colonial-style hotel. Beautiful rooms, gym, 2 pools, restaurant. Recommended. You don't have to go through Uruguayan formalities to get there from Brazil.

$$$-$$ Nuevo Hotel Plaza, Av Artigas y C Arachanes, T4474 2309, www.hotelplaza. chuynet.com. On plaza, bath, good buffet breakfast, very helpful, good, restaurant El Mesón del Plaza.

$$ Alerces, Laguna de Castillos 578, T4474 2260, hotelalerceschuy@adinet.com.uy. 4 blocks from border. Bath, breakfast, heater, pool.

$$ Victoria, Numancia 143, T4474 3547. Price includes breakfast, simple and clean, parking.

Camping From Chuy buses run every 2 hrs to the Complejo Turístico Chuy campsite, Ruta 9 Km 331, turn right 13 km, T4474 9425, www. complejoturisticochuy.com. Good bathing, many birds. *Cabañas* and hostal accommodation for 2 people or more start at **$$$**, depending on amenities, camping from US$12.50 pp.

🍴 Restaurants

Portezuelo and Punta Ballena *p1469*
$$$ Medio y Medio, Cont Camino Lussich s/n, Punta Ballena, T4257 8791, www.medioymedio. com. Jazz club and restaurant, music nightly and good food.

$$$-$$ Las Vertientes, Camino de Los Ceibos, 2 km on the Route 9, T4266 9997, www.lasvertientes.com.uy. Country restaurant, fresh food which all comes from own farm, good salads and sweets.

Maldonado *p1469*
$$$-$$ Lo de Rubén, Santa Teresa 846 y Florida, T4222 3059, www.loderuben.com.uy. Open every day. *Parrillada*, best restaurant in town.

$$$-$$ Taberna Patxi, Dodera 944, T4223 8393. Very good Basque food with authentic recipes.

Punta del Este *p1470, map p1470*
Many enticing ice cream parlours on Gorlero. There are many more excellent restaurants beyond the peninsula.

$$$ Gure-etxe (also in La Coronilla), Calle 9 y 12, T4244 6858. Seafood and Basque cuisine.

$$$ Los Caracoles, Calle 20 y 28, T4244 0912. Excellent food (international, *parrilla*, seafood) at good prices.

$$$ Isidora, Rambla Artigas, esq 21, T4244 9646, www.isidora.com.uy. Smart, by the port, international cuisine beautifully presented.

$$$ Lo de Charlie, Calle 12 y 9, T4244 4183. Fish, including tuna and octopus, plus pasta and *parrilla* standards.

$$$ Lo de Tere, Rambla Artigas y 21, T4244 0492, www.lode tere.com. Good local food, open all year but closed Wed in winter, 20% discount if eating lunch before 1300 or dinner before 2100. Highly recommended.

$$$ Viejo Marino, Calle 11 entre 14 y 12, Las Palmeras, T4244 3565. Fish restaurant, busy, go early.

$$$ Yatch Club Uruguayo, Rambla Artigas y 8, T4244 1056, www.ycu.org.uy. Very good, fish, seafood, views over the port (not to be confused with the Yacht Club, C 10 y 13, with expensive restaurant).

$$ Il Barreto, C 9 y 10, T4244 5565. Daily year-round. Italian vegetarian, good value.

Beaches east of Punta del Este *p1471*
La Barra
$$$ Baby Gouda Deli Café, Ruta 10, Km 161, T4277 1874. Alternative food, yoga and Arab dances.

$$$-$$ Restaurant T, Ruta 10, Km 49.5, T4277 1356. Old-style, Italian and French as well as local dishes, good wine selection. Claims to be the only "real" bistro in Punta del Este.

Faro José Ignacio
$$$ La Huella, Los Cisnes on Playa Brava, T4486 2279, www.paradorlahuella.com. Excellent, award-winning seafood, on the beach, also has a bar.

$$$ La Susana, Ruta 10 Km 182.5, T4486 2823, www.lasusana.com. A new addition to José Ignacio's food scene, **La Susana** is a beach club, bar and eatery during the day and gourmet restaurant at night. Fabulous location right on the beach for sunset cocktails (excellent range).

Delicious, easy-going international cuisine. Recommended.

$$$ Marismo, Ruta 10 Km 185, T4486 2273. Romantic, outdoor tables around a fire, highly regarded.

$$$ Mostrador Santa Teresita, C Las Garzas y Los Tordos, T4486 2861. A long table with main courses on one side, desserts on the other, you can choose what size of plate you want, good food.

Manantiales

$$$ Cactus y Pescados, Primera Bajada a Playa Bikini y Ruta 10, T4277 4782. Very good seafood, international menu.

La Paloma *p1471*

$$$ La Marea, Av Solari y Av Paloma, near tourist office, T4479 7456. Very popular, has outstanding seafood.

$$ Arrecife, Av Solari y C de la Virgen, T4479 6837. First class, serving pizzas, *parrilla* and a good range of salads.

$$ Da Carlis, Av Solari, T4479 7873. Moderate prices, pizzas plus Uruguayan food.

Northeast of La Paloma

In **Cabo Polonio**, there are a few restaurants, some with vegetarian options, so you don't have to bring any food with you. Fish is on the menu when the sea is calm enough for the fishermen to go out. The most expensive and fashionable is **La Puesta**, on the south beach. At weekends during the summer there are DJs, dancing and live music. For self-catering, the stores sell fruit, vegetables, meat, etc. There are several restaurants in **Castillos** including **$$$ La Strada**, 19 de Abril, and several restaurants in **Punta del Diablo**, mostly colourful huts grouped around the sea front serving excellent fish. A couple of pizza places too.

$$ Chivito Veloz, Aguas Dulces. Good, large portions for US$5.

Parque Nacional Santa Teresa *p1472*

$$ La Ruta, L Fernández Tunón, La Coronilla, T4476 2788. This small round restaurant at the entrance to town may be your only option if you are driving in the evening and off season from Chuy to Punta or Montevideo. Good meat dishes. Off season, most restaurants in La Coronilla and around are closed.

Chuy *p1472*

$$-$ Fusion, Av Brasil 387 y Numancia. Good food, traditional Uruguayan fare and pizzas. Recommended

$$-$ Restaurant Jesús, Av Brasil 603 y L Olivera. Good value and quality.

🍸 Bars and clubs

Punta del Este *p1470, map p1470*
Hop, Rambla Artigas y C 12, T4244 6061. Bar and restaurant, popular drinking spot.
Moby Dick, Rambla Artigas 650, T4244 1240, www.mobydick.com.uy. Mock English-style pub by the port, open until the early hours, very popular.
Ocean Club, Parada 12 de la Playa Brava, T4248 4869. Very fashionable and smart club playing mostly pop and house. Dress up.

⊖ Transport

Piriápolis *p1468*
Road Piriápolis may be reached either by following the very beautiful R10 from the end of the Interbalnearia, or by taking the original access road (R37) from Pan de Azúcar, which crosses the R93. The shortest route from Piriápolis to Punta del Este is by the Camino de las Bases which runs parallel to the R37 and joins the R93 some 4 km east of the R37 junction.
Bus Terminal on Misiones, 2 blocks from Hotel Argentino, T4432 4141. To/from **Montevideo**, US$6.50, 1½ hrs. To **Punta del Este**, US$6, 50 mins. To **Maldonado**, US$5, 40 mins. For **Rocha**, **La Paloma** and **Chuy**, take bus to Pan de Azúcar and change.

Maldonado *p1469*
Bus Av Roosevelt y Sarandí, T4222 9300. To/from **Montevideo**, 2 hrs, US$9; to **Minas**, 2 hrs, 6 a day, US$6. To **San Carlos** take a local bus 3 blocks from the main bus station, US$2.50.

Punta del Este *p1470, map p1470*

Air Direct daily Boeing 737 flights from Buenos Aires to the new Punta del Este airport during the high season. **Capitán Curbelo** (formerly Laguna del Sauce, T4255 9777), handles flights to Buenos Aires, 40 mins. Airport tax US$31. Exchange facilities, tax-free shopping. Regular bus service to airport from Punta del Este (will deliver to and collect from private addresses and hotels), US$5, 90 mins before departure, also connects with arriving flights. Taxi US$30-40; *remise* around US$35 depending on destination (T4255 9100). El Jagüel airport is used by private planes.

Bus **Local** Traffic is directed by a one-way system, town bus services start from C 5 (El Faro), near the lighthouse.

Long distance Terminal at Av Gorlero, Blvd Artigas and C 32, T4248 6810 (served by local bus No 7); has toilets, newsagent, café, free luggage storage and Casa de Cambio. To/from **Montevideo** via Carrasco airport, COT (T4248 6810), US$9, just over 2 hrs, many in the summer; at least hourly in winter. To **Piriápolis**, US$6. To **San Carlos** (US$2.50) for connections to Porto Alegre, Rocha, La Paloma, Chuy. Direct to **Chuy**, 4 hrs, US$18. Local bus fare about US$1. For transport Montevideo-Buenos Aires, **Buquebus** T130, at bus terminal, loc 09, buses connect with ferries. Also **Colonia Express** and Seacat.

The hop on, hop-off **Summerbus** (www.summerbus.com, see Montevideo transport page 1453) also stops in Punta del Este and many other parts of the coast.

La Paloma *p1471*

Bus Frequent to and from **Rocha**, US$2.65, and to and from **Montevideo** (5 hrs, US$15.50). 4 buses daily to **Chuy**, US$12, 3½ hrs, 2 a day to **San Carlos**, **Pan de Azúcar** and **Aguas Dulces**, all with Rutas del Sol, www.rutasdelsol.com.uy. Northeast of La Paloma, some Montevideo-Chuy buses go into **Punta del Diablo**, 4 km from the main road (taxi to the centre US$5.50, 'golf cart taxi' much cheaper at US$1.10).

To **Cabo Polonio**, Rutas del Sol from Montevideo, US$20, 4-5 hrs, and any of the coastal towns to Km 264, where you catch the truck to the village (see above).

Chuy *p1472*

Bus To **Montevideo** (COT, Cynsa, Rutas del Sol) US$23-25, 4¾-6 hrs, may have to change buses in San Carlos; to **Maldonado** US$11. International buses passing through en route from Montevideo to Brazil either stop in Chuy or at the border. Make sure the driver knows you need to stop at Uruguayan immigration. Sometimes everybody must get off for customs check. If looking for onward transport, if there is a free seat, most companies will let you pay on board.

❶ Directory

Punta del Este *p1470, map p1470*

Banks Best rates of exchange from BROU, which opens earlier and closes later than the other banks and accepts MasterCard, but no TCs. Many ATMs at banks on the peninsula and at Punta Shopping (Roosevelt). Also *casas de cambio*, eg **Indumex**, Av Av Roosevelt parada 6, Brimar, C 31 No 610. **Car hire** Punta Car, Artigas 101 y Risso, T4248 2112, www.puntacar.com.uy. And others. **Scooter hire** US$51 per day, with drivers licence (US$50 fine if caught without it) and ID documents from **Filibusteros**, Av Artigas y Parada 5, T4248 4125. They also rent out bicycles (US$3.50 per hr, US$7.50 per half day, US$10 per day, includes padlocks).

La Paloma *p1471*

Useful services Bike rental from El Tobo, T4479 7881, US$3.50 a day. One bank which changes TCs; also internet, a supermarket and post office.

Chuy *p1472*

Banks Several *cambios* on Av Brasil, eg Gales, Artigas y Brasil, Mon-Fri 0830-1200, 1330-1800, Sat 0830-1200, and in World Trade Center, open 1000-2200; on either side of Gales are Aces and Val. All give similar rates, charging US$1 plus 1% commission on TCs, US$, pesos and reais. On Sun, try the casino, or look for someone on the street outside the *cambios*. No problem spending reais in Chuy or pesos in Chuí.

Two roads run towards Melo, heart of cattle-ranching country: Route 8 and Route 7, the latter running for most of its length through the Cuchilla Grande, a range of hills with fine views. Route 8 via Minas and Treinta y Tres is the more important of these two roads to the border and it is completely paved.

Minas and around → *Colour map 8, B6. Population: 39,909.*

This picturesque small town, 120 km north of Montevideo, is set in wooded hills. Juan Lavalleja, the leader of the Thirty-Three who brought independence to the country, was born here, and there is an equestrian statue to Artigas, said to be the largest such in the world, on the Cerro Artigas just out of town. The church's portico and towers, some caves in the neighbourhood and the countryside are worth seeing. Good confectionery is made in Minas; you can visit the largest firm, opposite Hotel Verdun. Banks are open 1300-1700 Monday to Friday. There is a tourist office at the bus station. See www.lavalleja.gub.uy and www.destinominas.com.uy.

The **Parque Salus**, on the slopes of Sierras de las Animas, is 8 km to the south and very attractive; take the town bus marked 'Cervecería Salus' from plaza to the Salus brewery, then walk 2 km to the mineral spring and bottling plant (**$$$ Parador Salus**, T4443 1652, www. paradorsalus.com.uy, good). It is a lovely three-hour walk back to Minas from the springs. The Cascada de Agua del Penitente waterfall, 11 km east off Route 8, is interesting and you may see wild rheas nearby. It's hard to get to off season. The Minas area is popular for mountain biking.

To the Brazilian border

Route 8 continues north via **Treinta y Tres** (*Population: 27,304*) to Melo (also reached by Route 7), near Aceguá close to the border. In **Melo** (*Population: 54,674*), there are places to stay and exchange rates are usually better than at the frontier. If crossing to Brazil here, Brazilian immigration is at Bagé, not at the border. At 12 km southeast of Melo is the Posta del Chuy (2 km off Route 26). This house, bridge and toll gate (built 1851) was once the only safe crossing place on the main road between Uruguay and Brazil. It displays gaucho paintings and historical artefacts.

Río Branco was founded in 1914, on the Río Yaguarón. The 1-km-long Mauá bridge across the river leads to Jaguarão in Brazil. The Brazilian vice-consulate in Río Branco is at 10 de Junio 379, T4675 2003, bravcrb@gmail.com, Monday-Friday 0800-1200 and 1400-1800. For road traffic, the frontier at Chuy is better than Río Branco or Aceguá. There is a toll 68 km north of Montevideo.

An alternative route to Brazil is via Route 5, the 509-km road from Montevideo to the border town of Rivera, which runs almost due north, bypassing Canelones and Florida before passing through Durazno. After crossing the Río Negro, it goes to Tacuarembó. South of the Río Negro is gently rolling cattle country, vineyards, orchards, orange, lemon and olive groves. North is hilly countryside with steep river valleys and cattle ranching. The road is dual carriageway as far as Canelones.

East of Florida, Route 56 traverses the countryside eastwards to **Cerro Colorado**, also known as Alejandro Gallinal, which has an unusual clock tower.

Durazno → *Colour map 8, B6. Population: 35,862.*

On the Río Yí 182 km from Montevideo, Durazno is a friendly provincial town with tree-lined avenues and an airport. There is a good view of the river from the western bridge. See http://durazno.gub.uy.

Dams on the Río Negro have created an extensive network of lakes near **Paso de los Toros** (*Population: 14,205; 66 km north of Durazno, bus from Montevideo, 3½ hrs, US$16.50*), with camping and sports facilities. Some 43 km north of Paso de los Toros a 55-km road turns east to **San Gregorio de Polanco**, at the eastern end of Lago Rincón del Bonete. The beach by the lake is excellent, with opportunities for boat trips, horse riding and other sports.

Tacuarembó → *Colour map 8, B6. Population: 54,994.*

This is an agro-industrial town and major route centre 390 km north of Montevideo. The nearby Valle Edén has good walking possibilities. Some 23 km west of Tacuarembó, along Route 26, is the **Carlos Gardel Museum** ① *daily 1000-1700, US$1*, a shrine to the great tango singer who was killed in an air crash in Medellín (Colombia). Uruguay, Argentina and France all claim him as a national son. The argument for his birth near here is convincing. Large-scale gaucho festival in March/April, www.patriagaucha.com.uy.

Brazilian border

Rivera (*Population: 71,222*) is divided by a street from the Brazilian town of Santana do Livramento. Points of interest are the park, the Plaza Internacional, and the dam of Cañapirú. Uruguayan immigration is at the end of Calle Sarandí y Presidente Viera, 14 blocks, 2 km, from the border (take bus along Agraciada or taxi from bus terminal for around US$2). There is also a tourist office here, T4623 1900. Luggage is inspected when boarding buses out of Rivera; there are also three checkpoints on the road out of town. The Brazilian consulate is at Ceballos 1159, T4622 3278, consbrasrivera@adinet.com.uy. Remember that you must have a Uruguayan exit stamp to enter Brazil and a Brazilian exit stamp to enter Uruguay.

⊕ Montevideo north to Brazil listings

For hotel and restaurant price codes, and other relevant information, see Essentials.

⊖ Where to stay

Minas *p1480*
$$ Posada Verdun, W Beltrán 715, T4422 4563, www.hotelposadaverdun.com. Good, à la carte restaurant with wood-fired oven on the premises.
Camping Arequita, Camino Valeriano Magri, T4440 2503. Beautiful surroundings, cabañas (for 2 people with shared bathroom US$22), camping US$4.50 each.

To the Brazilian border *p1480*
Treinta y Tres
$$-$ La Posada, Manuel Freire 1564, T4452 1107, www.hotellaposada33.com. With breakfast, Wi-Fi, good overnight stop.
$ pp Cañada del Brujo, Km 307.5, Ruta 8, Sierra del Yerbal, 34 km north of Treinta y Tres, T4452 2837, T9929 7448, www.pleka.com/

delbrujo. Isolated hostel, no electricity, basic but "fantastic", dorm, local food, meals extra, owner Pablo Rado drives you there (US$15), cycling, trekking on foot or horseback, trips to Quebrada de los Cuervos. Recommended.

Melo
$$ Virrey Pedro de Melo, J Muñiz 727, T4642 2673, www.hotelvirreypedrodemelo.com. Better rooms in new part, 3-star, minibar, Wi-Fi, café.

Cerro Colorado
$$$$ San Pedro de Timote, Km 142, R7, 14 km west of Cerro Colorado, T4310 8086, www.sanpedrodetimote.uy. A famous colonial-style *estancia*, working ranch, landscaped park, 3 pools, cinema, gym, horse riding, good restaurant.
$$$ Arteaga, 7 km off R7 north of Cerro Colorado, T2707 4766, arteaga@parada arteaga.com. Typical European *estancia*, famous, beautiful interior, pool.

Durazno *p1480*

There are a few hotels (**$$-$**).

Camping At 33 Orientales, in park of same name by river, T4362 2806. Nice beach, hot showers, toilets, laundry sinks.

Tourism Farm **Estancia Albergue El Silencio**, Ruta 14 Km 166, 10 km west of Durazno, T4362 2014 (or T4360 2270, HI member), www.estancia-el-silencio.com. About 15 mins' walk east of bridge over Río Yí where bus stops, clean rooms, riding, swimming, birdwatching. Recommended.

Paso de los Toros

$$-$ Sayonara, Sarandí 302 y Barreto, T4664 2535. 2 blocks from centre, renovated old residence, rooms with bath, a/c and cable TV. Breakfast extra.

San Gregorio de Polanco

$$ Posada Buena Vista, De Las Pitangueras 12, T4369 4841. Overlooking lake, breakfast extra, snack bar, good, prices rise Dec-Easter.

Tacuarembó *p1481*

$$$ Carlos Gardel, Ruta 5 Km 387,500, T4633 0306, www.hotelcarlosgardel.com.uy. Internet, pool, restaurant, meeting room.

$$$ Tacuarembó, 18 de Julio 133, T4632 2105, www.tacuarembohotel.com.uy. Breakfast, central, Wi-Fi, safe, restaurant, large pool, parking.

$$ Central, Gral Flores 300, T4632 2841. Ensuite bathrooms, rooms with or without a/c, laundry service.

$$ pp Panagea, 1 hr from Tacuarembó, T9983 6149, http://panagea-uruguay.blogspot.com. Estancia and backpackers' hostel, working cattle and sheep farm, home cooking, lots of riding, electricity till 2200 is only concession to modern amenities, many languages spoken.

Camping Campsites 1 km out of town in the Parque Laguna de las Lavanderas, T4632 4761, and 7 km north on R26 at Balneario Iporá.

Brazilian border: Rivera *p1481*

$$$ Uruguay Brasil, Sarandí 440, T4622 3068, www.hoteluruguaybrasil.com.uy.

Buffet breakfast, minibar, Wi-Fi area, laundry service, restaurant.

$$$-$$ Casablanca, Agraciada 479, T4622 3221, www.casablanca.com.uy. Comfortable and pleasant.

Camping Municipal site near AFE station, and in the Parque Gran Bretaña 7 km south along R27.

⑦ Restaurants

Minas *p1480*

Restaurants include **Complejo San Francisco de las Sierras**, Ruta 12 Km 347 (3 km from Minas); **Ki-Joia**, Diego Pérez in front of Plaza Libertad. **Irisarri**, C Treinta y Tres 618. Best pastry shop, *yemas* (egg candy) and *damasquitos* (apricot sweets).

⊖ Transport

Minas *p1480*

Bus To **Montevideo**, US$8, several companies, 2 hrs. To **Maldonado**, US$6, 7 a day, 1½-2 hrs (COOM).

To the Brazilian border: Melo *p1480*

Bus To **Montevideo** US$28, 5-7 hrs (Núñez, EGA). 3 buses daily to Río Branco.

Durazno *p1480*

Bus To **Montevideo** US$13, 2½ hrs.

Tacuarembó *p1481*

Bus From **Montevideo**, US$26, 4-5 hrs.

Brazilian border: Rivera *p1481*

Bus Terminal at Uruguay y Viera (1.5 km from the terminal in Santa Ana). To/from **Montevideo**, US$35, 5½-7 hrs (Agencia Central, Turil, Núñez). To **Paysandú**, Copay, T4622 3733, at 0400, 1600, US$21 To **Tacuarembó**, US$7 (Núñez, Turil), no connections for Paysandú. To **Salto**, Mon and Fri 1630, 6 hrs, US$27. For **Artigas**, take bus from Livramento to Quaraí, then cross bridge.

Contents

Footprint features

Venezuela

At a glance

⟳ **Time required** 2-3 weeks.

☁ **Best time** Highlands are
driest Oct-May, good for trekking.
Llanos best at start of the rainy
season Oct-Dec. Don't miss San Juan
Bautista celebrations on 24 Jun.

✖ **When not to go** Avoid
Maracaibo Jul-Sep. High seasons
at Carnival, Easter, mid-Jul to mid-
Sep and Christmas to New Year.

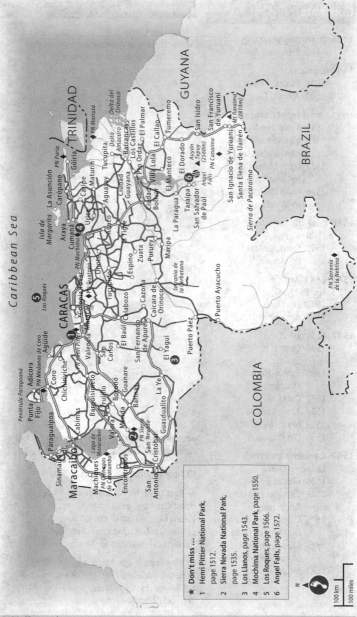

★ Don't miss ...
1 Henri Pittier National Park,
   page 1512.
2 Sierra Nevada National Park,
   page 1535.
3 Los Llanos, page 1543.
4 Mochima National Park, page 1550.
5 Los Roques, page 1566.
6 Angel Falls, page 1572.

Caribbean Sea

TRINIDAD

GUYANA

BRAZIL

COLOMBIA

CARACAS

Maracaibo

Peninsula Paraguaná
Punta Fijo   Adícora
Paraguaipoa   Coro   Chichiriviche
Sinamaica   Aguide
PN Ciénagas
Machiques de Catatumbo   Barquisimeto
Lago de   Cabimas
Maracaibo   Valera
Trujillo   Boconó
Encontrados   Bailadores   Barinas
PN Sierra   Guanare
La Ye
San Nevada
Cristóbal   Guasdualito
San
Antonio

Valencia Maracay
San   Calabozo
Carlos
El Baúl
San Fernando
de Apure
El Yagui
El Sombrero

Puerto Páez

Puerto Ayacucho

Serranía
de la Cerbatana

PN Serranía
de la Neblina

Los Roques
PN Morrocoy

Puruey
Zuata
Espino
Cazorla
Caicara de
Orinoco

Maripa

Isla de
Margarita
La Asunción
Cariaco Cumaná
Araya
Cumaná   PN Mochima
Ojedo
Barcelona
El Tigre

La Paragua

San Salvador
de Paúl
Tarapaí

Carúpano
PN Paria
Güiria
PN Mariusa
Delta del
Orinoco
Delta
Amacuro

Maturín
Aguay
Uverito
Ciudad
Guayana
Ciudad
Bolívar
El Manteco

El Dorado

San Isidro
San Francisco
de Yuruaní
Santa Elena de Uairén

Sierra de Pacaraima

Los Castillos
El Palmar
El Callao
Tumeremo

Vila Lola

Auyán
Tepuy
(2560m)
Angel
Falls
PN Canaima
San Ignacio de Yuruaní

Roraima
(2810m)

N
100 km
100 miles

Venezuela is where the Andes meet the Caribbean. The Orinoco river separates great plains from the table-top mountains of the Gran Sabana, where waterfalls tumble in sheer drops into the forest and lost worlds are easy to imagine. More recent innovations – cable cars up to the high peaks, hang gliders for jumping off them – are now part of the scene at Mérida, capital of Venezuela's Andes. Lying at the heart of the country – geographically and spiritually – are the *llanos* (plains), a vast area of flat savannah the size of Italy and home to an immense variety of birds, exotic mammals and reptiles, such as caiman (alligators), giant anacondas, anteaters, pumas, jaguars and giant otters, to name but a few.

These plains flood seasonally, but when the waters retreat, the birds and animals share their territory with cattle and the *llanero* cowboys, renowned for their hospitality towards visitors. A few *hatos* – cattle ranches – welcome tourists while another alternative is a budget tour from Mérida. If the sea is more to your taste, head for the country's seductive coastline – the longest in the Caribbean at over 2500 km. Venezuela's waters play host to some of the best (and least known) diving in the region with three marine national parks. Pick of the bunch are Islas Los Roques, an archipelago of emerald and turquoise lagoons and dazzling white beaches. At the other end of the country, the Amazon is home to humid rainforests and rare plants and animals as well as over 20 different ethnic groups. This part of Venezuela is very much frontier territory and remains wild and untamed, as it was when the country received its first foreign visitor back in 1498. So overwhelmed was Columbus by what he saw that he described it as 'Paradise on Earth'.

Planning your trip

Where to go in Venezuela

Caribbean coast Venezuela has the longest coastline in the Caribbean with numerous palm-fringed beaches of white sand. **Caracas**, at 1000 m, is hidden from the Caribbean by Monte Avila, one of Venezuela's national parks, but you don't have to go too far beyond the mountain to find good beaches. Some 320 km west of the capital is the Parque Nacional Morrocoy, with many islands close to the shore. North of Morrocoy is the historic town of Coro, surrounded by sand dunes, and the Paranaguá Peninsula. Parque Nacional Mochima, east of Caracas, has some excellent beaches and a multitude of islets to explore. Further east are unrivalled beaches on the Paria Peninsula, as well as Isla de Margarita, one of the country's principal tourist destinations. The Islas Los Roques, 166 km due north of the central coast, is a beautiful archipelago, still unspoilt despite the growth in tourist interest.

The Andes Venezuela's Andes have some gorgeous scenery, with snow-capped peaks and remote, historic villages. The main centre for adventure is Mérida, in the Sierra Nevada of the same name. It has abundant accommodation and eco-tour companies, which can arrange treks, climbing and other excursions. Two of its claims to fame are the highest cable car in the world, ascending the 4776-m Pico Espejo, and the shop selling the largest number of ice-cream flavours in the world.

The Llanos Life in the *llanos* revolves around the cycle of wet and dry seasons; the movement of cattle, the mainstay of the region's economy, depends on it. In the flat grasslands are slow running rivers which flood in the rainy season, creating a huge inland sea. When the rains cease, the whole area dries out completely. South of the cattle lands are forests and the tributaries of the Río Orinoco. Just after the May-November wet season, this is a paradise for nature lovers, with a spectacular variety of birds (323 species), monkeys, big cats, anaconda, river dolphins, caiman and capybara. Tours to the *llanos* are run from Mérida and there are ecotourism ranches which offer you the chance to get to know the lifestyle of the plains.

Guayana and the Orinoco Above the grasslands of the Gran Sabana rise mysterious *tepuis*, flat-topped mountains from which spring magnificent waterfalls and rivers. The Angel Falls, the highest in the world, are one such wonder, usually seen from a plane, but also reachable by a two- to three-day trip upriver. There are many other falls in the Gran Sabana and a few places to stay, the most popular being Canaima camp on a lagoon on the Río Carrao. Where Venezuela meets Brazil and Guyana is Mount Roraima; to reach its summit is one of the country's most adventurous excursions. The Orinoco delta is remote, but trips can be made from the small town of Tucupita. Amazonas is well off the beaten track, but accessible from Puerto Ayacucho. Much of the rainforest is protected and you need permission from the authorities to visit areas beyond the reach of a tour company.

Best time to visit Venezuela

The climate is tropical, with changes between the seasons being a matter of wet and dry, rather than hot and cold. Temperature is determined by altitude. The dry season in Caracas is December to April, with January and February the coolest months (there is a great difference between day and night temperatures at this time). The hottest months are July and August. The Caribbean coast is generally dry and rain is particularly infrequent in the states of Sucre, in the east, and Falcón, in the northwest. The lowlands of Maracaibo are very hot all year round; the least hot months are July to September. South of the Orinoco, in the Gran Sabana and Parque Nacional

Canaima, the dry season is November to May. The same months are dry in the *llanos*, but the best time to visit is just after the rains, when the rivers and channels are still full of water and the humidity is not too high. In the Andes, the dry season is October to May, the best time for climbing or hiking. The days are clear, but the nights are freezing cold. The rains usually begin in June, but in the mountains the weather can change daily. High season, when it is advisable to book in advance includes: Carnival, Easter, 15 July-15 September and Christmas to New Year.

National parks in Venezuela

Encompassing 16% of the national territory, Venezuela has 43 national parks, 30 national monuments and various other refuges and reserves, some of which are mentioned in the text. A full list is published by the **Instituto Nacional de Parques (Inparques)** ① *Salida del Distribuidor Santa Cecilia, Edif Sur del Museo de Transporte, Caracas, T273 2811 (Caracas), www.inparques. gob.ve (site not active in 2014)*. Each park has a regional director and its own guards (*guardaparques*). Permits are required to stay in the parks (up to five), although this is not usually necessary for those parks visited frequently. A few parks charge a fee on arrival, such as Los Roques and Canaima. For more details, visit the **Ministerio del Poder Popular para el Ambiente** ① *Centro Simón Bolívar, Torre Sul, Caracas, T408 1111, www.minamb.gob.ve.*

Transport in Venezuela → *See also box, page 1488.*

Air Venezuela's most important cities are served by domestic flights from Caracas. The most extensive coverage is offered by state-owned carrier **Conviasa**, www.conviasa.aero. Other lines include **Aeropostal**, www.aeropostal.com, **Aserca**, www.asercaairlines.com, **Avlor**, aviorair.com, **Rutaca**, www.rutaca.com.ve, **Laser**, www.laser.com.ve, and **Venezolana**, www.ravsa.com.ve. **LTA (Aereotuy)**, www.tuy.com connects Caracas with Porlamar, Los Roques and camps at Boral (Maturin) and Arekuna (Canaima). None of Venezuela's airlines is great. Lost luggage, delays and cancellations without compensation are common. Beware of overbooking during holidays, especially at Caracas airport; check in at least two hours before departure. If you book a ticket online with a credit card, you may be told at check-in that your tickets is 'reserved but not purchased'. Check with your card company that you have not been charged twice.It is essential to reconfirm all flights, international and domestic, 72 hours in advance. At the time of research (March 2014), many ticket agents were refusing to sell international flights to foreign tourists because of their exploitation of the parallel exchange rate.

Bus and taxi Buses on most long-distance routes come in four standards, *normal*, *semi-ejecutivo*, *ejecutivo* and *bus-cama*. Fares are set by the authorities and you should see them posted on bus office windows. There are numerous services between the major cities and many services bypass Caracas. Buses stop frequently, but there may not always be a toilet at the stop. For journeys in

Driving in Venezuela

Road The four-lane *autopistas* are quite good, but generally roads are in poor shape. Potholes are often marked by a pile of stones or sticks left by road-users to highlight the danger. Road congestion and lengthy delays are normal during holidays. Traffic jams are common in Caracas and car parks are usually crowded.

Safety As infrastructure is not improving and spare parts for cars are scarce and expensive, serious road accidents are common. The situation is not helped by reckless driving at extremely high speed. If you have an accident and someone is injured, you will be detained as a matter of routine, even if you are not at fault. Carry a spare tyre, wheel block, jack, water and the obligatory breakdown triangle. Use private car parks whenever possible. Car-jackings have soared in recent years, so be alert and try to drive in daylight and in populated areas.

Documents Minimum driving age is 18. A valid driving licence from your own country, or international driving licence (preferred) is required. Neither a *carnet de passages*, nor a *libreta de pasos por aduana* is officially required, but is recommended. You should also have copies of vehicle and insurance documents and passport with you at all times since stops at National Guard and local police checkpoints (*alcabalas*) are frequent. Drive slowly through these and stop to show your documents if instructed to do so. Before shipping your vehicle to Venezuela, go to a Venezuelan consul to obtain all necessary documentation. You must also go to a Venezuelan consul in the country in which you land your car if other than Venezuela.

Organizations Touring y Automóvil Club de Venezuela, Torre Phelps, p 15, of A y C, Plaza Venezuela, Caracas, T0212-781 9743, www.automovilclubvenezuela.com, issues *libreta de pasos por aduana* and a separate form for taking a car only to Colombia. See www.automovilclubvenezuela.com/documentos.php.

Car hire It is a good idea to hire a car; many of the best places are off the beaten track. You need a credit card to rent a vehicle. Rates for a car start at about US$50 per day, not including insurance, collision damage waiver, taxes or GPS if you book in advance. Prices are higher paying on the spot.

Fuel 91 and 95 octane, unleaded, cost US$0.01 a litre; diesel, US$0.01 a litre.

Warning There is a fine for running out of fuel.

a/c buses take a sleeping bag or similar because the temperature is set to freezing. This is most important on night journeys, which otherwise are fine. Also take earplugs and eyemask to protect against the loud stereo and violent Hollywood screenings. For journeys longer than six hours, it is essential to buy your ticket in advance, although they may not always be available until the day of departure. Sometimes hoteliers and tour operators have inside connections which can save a lot of hassle. The colectivo taxis and minibuses (jitneys), known as *por puesto*, seem to monopolize transport to and from smaller towns and villages. For longer journeys they are normally twice as expensive as buses, but faster, often breaking local speed limits. They are sometimes an unreliable and risky mode of transport, but great places to meet the locals, learn about the area and discuss politics. If first on board, wait for other passengers to arrive. Do not take a *por puesto* on your own unless you want to pay for the whole vehicle. Outside Caracas, town taxis are relatively cheap, and they are becoming popular for tourists and locals, for security reasons. Phone *Líneas de Taxi* and ask for interstate trip fares.

Hitchhiking Hitchhiking (*cola*) is not recommended as it is unsafe. It is illegal on toll roads and, theoretically, for non-family members in the back of pick up trucks. Avoid hitchhiking around Guardia Nacional posts (see also Safety, below).

Maps The best country map is **International Travel Maps'** *Venezuela Travel Reference Map*. They also publish *Caracas (Venezuela) ITM City Map* (Vancouver, Canada, www.itmb.ca); buy directly or at a good travel agency. Also see **Google Maps** and the recently updated Caracas Street Map by **www.dubbele.com**, pre-loaded on your phone before you leave home (download can take time).

Where to stay in Venezuela → *See Essentials for our hotel grade price guide.*

Using the new Sicad 2 exchange rate or the parallel market (see Money, below), value for money is quite high. For the ultra-thrifty, there are foreign-run, no-frills places catering for backpackers. The major cities, Isla Margarita, Los Roques, Guayana and Amazonas have higher room rates (eg US$20-60). Rooms are cheaper without a/c. In the Andean region prices are lower, starting at around US$5-10 per person. If comfort and cleanliness is what you are after, the price of a basic three-star (Venezuelan 'four star') hotel room with a/c, private bath and breakfast will be in our **$$-$** range, depending on location and whether it's a hotel or *posada*. A prior reservation will not guarantee you a room. If you can, insist on seeing the room before paying; if you don't, you will probably be given the worst possible room.

A group of 20 *posadas*, mostly in the west of the country, have joined together under the banner **El Circuito de la Excelencia**, www.circuitodelaexcelencia.com, to offer high quality, distinctive lodging, food and service. **Casa Tropical** (main office) ① *CC Paseo Las Mercedes, Sector La Cuadra, Local 26, Caracas, T212-993 2939, www.casa tropical.com.ve*, offers interesting accommodation in seven properties on the central coast, in Ciudad Bolívar, Canaima and Amazonas.

Elizabeth Kline's Guide to Camps, Posadas and Cabins in Venezuela 2013-14, published every two years or so (US$35, purchasing information from klineposada@yahoo.com) is incredibly detailed and doesn't pull its punches. *La Guía Valentina Quintero* also covers the whole country, suggesting routes, where to stay and eat, published biannually, www.valentinaquintero.com.ve.

Camping Camping in Venezuela is risky because of crime. Camping, with or without a vehicle, is not possible at the roadside. If camping on the beach, for the sake of security, pitch your tent close to others, even though they play their radios loud.

Food and drink in Venezuela → *See Essentials for our restaurant price guide.*

Restaurants in Venezuela As with lodging, eating out is cheap if you change dollars using Sicad 2. Midday used to be the best time to find a three-course *menú ejecutivo* or *cubierto*, but increasingly many places offer only à la carte, quoting scarcity of supplies. Minimum price for a basic meal is US$2, not including drinks. Hotel breakfasts are likely to be poor. It is better and cheaper in a *fuente de soda* and cheaper still in a *pastelería* or *arepería*.

Food There is excellent local fish (such as *pargo* or red snapper, *carite* or king fish), crayfish, small oysters and prawns. Although it is a protected species, turtle may appear on menus in the Península de Paraguaná as *ropa especial*. Of true Venezuelan food there is *sancocho* (vegetable stew with meat, chicken or fish); *arepas*, bland white maize bread; toasted *arepas* served with various fillings or the local salty white cheese, are cheap, filling and nutritious; *cachapas*, a maize pancake wrapped around white cheese; *pabellón*, of shredded meat, beans, rice and fried plantains; and *empanadas*, maize-flour pies of cheese, meat or fish. At Christmas there are *hallacas*, maize pancakes stuffed with chicken, pork, olives, boiled in a plantain leaf. A *muchacho* (boy) on the menu is a cut of beef. *Ganso* is not goose but beef. *Solomo* and *lomito* are other cuts of beef. *Hervido* is chicken or beef with vegetables. On the Península de Paraguaná roast kid (*asado de chivo*) and kid cooked in coconut are served. *Contorno* with a meat or fish dish is a choice of fried chips, boiled potatoes, rice or yuca. *Caraotas* are beans; *cachitos* are filled *croissants*. *Pasticho* is what Venezuelans call Italian lasagne. The main fruits are bananas, oranges, grapefruit, mangoes, pineapple and pawpaws. *Lechoza* is papaya, *patilla* water melon, *parchita* passion fruit, and *cambur* a small banana. Excellent strawberries are grown at Colonia Tovar, 90 minutes from Caracas, and in the Andes. Delicious sweets are *huevos chimbos*, egg yolk boiled and bottled in sugar syrup, and *quesillo*, made with milk, egg and caramel. **Note** Venezuelans dine late!

Drink Venezuelan rum is very good; recommended brands are *Cacique, Pampero* and *Santa Teresa*. There are four good beers: *Polar* (the most popular, sold as Polar, Ice, Solera and Solera Light), *Regional, Cardenal* and *Zulia* (a *lisa* is a glass of keg beer; for a bottle of beer ask for a *tercio*). Brazilian *Brahma* beer is brewed in Venezuela. There is a good local wine in Venezuela. The *Polar* brewery joined with Martell (France) to build a winery in Carora. **Bodegas Pomar** also sells a champagne- style sparkling wine. Look out for Pomar wine festivals in March and September. Liqueurs are cheap, try the local *ponche crema*. Coffee is very cheap (*café con leche* is milky, *café marrón* much less so, *café negro* is black); it often has sugar already added, ask for "sin azúcar". Try a *merengada*, a delicious drink made from fruit pulp, ice, milk and sugar; a *batido* is the same but with water and a little milk; *jugo* is the same but with water. A *plus-café* is an after-dinner liqueur. *Chicha de arroz* is a sweet drink made of milk, sugar and vanilla. Fruit juices are very good, ask for "jugo natural, preparado en el momento" for the freshest juice.

Essentials A-Z

Accident and emergency
Dial T171 for the integrated emergency system.
CICPC (**Cuerpo de Investigaciones Científicas, Penales y Criminalísticas**), Av Urdaneta entre Pelota y Punceres; Edif Icauca, mezzanina 2, Caracas, T0800-272 4224, www.cicpc.gob.ve. For registering crimes throughout the country.

Electricity
120 volts, 60 cycles. Plugs are US-style 'A' and 'B' types, 2-pin flat and 2-pin flat with optional D-shaped earth.

Embassies and consulates
The Ministry of Foreign Affairs website is www.mppre.gob.ve. For Venezuelan embassies and consulates abroad and for all foreign embassies and consulates in Venezuela, see http://embassy.goabroad.com.

Festivals in Venezuela
Public holidays
1 Jan; **Carnival** on the Mon-Tue before Ash Wed (everything shuts down Sat-Tue; book a place to stay in advance). Thu-Sat of Holy Week. **19 Apr** (Declaration of Independence). **1 May**. **Early Jun** at Corpus Christi (the eighth Thu after Thu of Semana Santa) in San Francisco de Yare, 90 km from Caracas, some 80 male 'Diablos' of all ages, dressed all in red and wearing horned masks, dance to the sound of their drums and rattles. **24 Jun**, Battle of Carabobo and

the feast day of San Juan Bautista, celebrated on the central coast where there were once large concentrations of plantation slaves who considered San Juan their special Saint; the best-known events are in villages such as Chuao, Cata and Ocumare de la Costa. **5 Jul** (Independence). **24 Jul** (Bolívar's birthday). **12 Oct**, Día de la Resistencia Indígena. **25 Dec**.

Other holidays
From 24 Dec-1 Jan, museums are closed, most restaurants close 24-25 Dec (except for fast-food outlets) and there is no long-distance public transport on 25 Dec, while other days are often booked solid. On New Year's Eve, everything closes and does not open for at least a day. Business travellers should not visit during Holy Week or Carnival. There are extra holidays only for banks which are set every year according to religious festivals, dates vary.

Money → *1 US$= BsF 6.30 (Cencoex); US$1= BsF 10.0 (Sicad); US$1= BsF 49.04 (Sicad 2) (Apr 2014).*
The unit of currency is the bolívar fuerte (BsF), introduced in 2008. There are coins for 1 bolívar fuerte, 50, 25, 12.5, 10, 5 and 1 céntimos, and notes for 2, 5, 10, 20, 50 and 100 bolívares fuertes. Have small coins and notes to hand, since in many shops and bars and on public transport large notes may be hard to change.

Official and unofficial currency exchange Venezuela has had an exchange control regime since 2003 to prevent capital flight. In Apr 2014, 3 official rates were in operation. Applicable to 'priority sectors' of food, medicine and staples, the official rate set by the Centro de Comercio Exterior (Cencoex) was US$1 = BsF 6.3. The next and most commonly used **exchange rate** was the Sistema Complimentario de Administración de Divisas (Sicad) set at US$1 = BsF 10.8. The third official exchange rate, Sicad 2, was a brand new forex system with government-controlled currency supplies and rates determined by market demand. It stood at US$1 = BsF 49.04. At the time of research, the Venezuelan government had indicated that it intended to make Sicad 2 available to tourists. All prices in this book have been calculated on its basis.

Prices at anything other than the Sicad 2 rate are extremely high for foreign visitors. Unfortunately, the practical details of how travellers will access the rate were not available at the time of research. Neither was it clear if Sicad 2 would be effective in eliminating the 'parallel' (ie black) market in foreign currencies. The unofficial exchange of dollars is illegal in Venezuela, but it has long been common practice among importers, exporters and travellers. The rate fluctuates depending on many factors, including government foreign currency reserves and the price of oil. In Apr 2014, it stood at around US$1 = BsF 68. If the Sicad 2 rate is unavailable and you do decide to change money on the black market, the process is relatively straight-forward. You should conduct the transaction with a trusted and senior member of staff at a hotel or tour operator, never with strangers on the street. The unofficial rate can be checked on the internet before you enter Venezuela, but once inside the country you will find those websites blocked (search twitter instead). You will probably not be offered the full parallel rate, but remember the exchange is illegal and involves risk to the changer. You will also be fined if caught in the act.

If the situation remains uncertain, you can investigate wiring money to a foreign-based account which will release cash in Venezuela, or, if you have friends living in Venezuela with an overseas bank account, sending money there.

Plastic, TCs, cash At the time of research, Sicad 2 had not been fully implemented and *Casas de cambio* were on the point of being given permission to use it. Previously they changed cash dollars and TCs at the poor Cencoex rate (US$1 = BsF 6.3); only Banco del Tesero at some international airports changed money at the slightly more favourable Sicad rate (US$1 = BsF 10.8). Most ATMs and credit card transactions also used Sicad, often with a high commission attached. ATMs are widespread but highly unreliable and not recommended. Some require a Venezuelan ID number and you should speak to your card issuer about this before leaving home. Despite the security risks, it is best to bring all the cash you need for your trip in US dollars and change small amounts at a time. For obvious reasons, only bolívares purchased officially can be converted back and you will need the original exchange receipt (currently up to 30% of original amount may be changed). If you run short of cash, your best bet is to cross the border to Colombia (San Antonio to Cúcuta is easiest), spend the night in Cúcuta and withdraw as much as possible in Colombian pesos from an ATM. Then return to Venezuela and buy bolívares. Some tour operators and foreign-owned hotels may also be able to provide you with cash or services in exchange for funds transferred via Paypal, but you must set up your account before arriving in Venezuela.

Cost of travelling If using the Sicad 2 rate, you will need a daily budget of around US$20-40 for 'mid-range' lodging and dining, depending on the region. On a very basic budget, you can get by on less than US$15 per day. First class travel can be had for US$50-70 daily, often for much less, and multi-day treks and all-inclusive packages to Angel Falls and Roraima are quite reasonable. Please bear in mind that Venezuela's economic situation is extremely unpredictable. The new Sicad 2 exchange mechanism signifies a massive devaluation of the BsF and is highly likely to accelerate inflation, rendering some prices in this book inaccurate. Exchange regulations are subject to change at any moment and you can check the three official rates at Cencoex, www.centrodecomercioexterior.com. Other measures introduced in 2014 were designed to bring some stability to consumer markets and to end shortages of basic shopping items. Before you travel, find out what the current situation is.

Opening hours
See also under Festivals, page 1490.
Banks: Mon-Fri 0830-1530 only. **Businesses**: 0800-1800 with a midday break. **Government offices**: 0800-1200 are usual hours, although they vary. Officials have fixed hours, usually 0900-1000 or 1500-1600, for receiving visitors. **Shops**: Mon-Sat 0900-1300, 1500-1900.

Generally speaking, Venezuelans start work early, and by 0700 everything is in full swing. Most firms and offices close on Sat.

Postal services
Post offices are run by Ipostel, whose main branch is at Urdaneta y Norte 4, near Plaza Bolívar, Caracas, see www.ipostel.gob.ve, for branches, Mon-Fri 0800-1630. It has an overseas package service; packages should be ready to send, also at airport. MRW, throughout the country, T0800-304 0000, see www.mrw.com.ve, for branches. 24-hr service, more reliable than Ipostel.

Safety
Venezuelans are generally honest, helpful, and hospitable people. The vast majority of visitors to the country do not encounter any problems, but you should be aware that street crime in big cities has soared in recent years. Most of the trouble occurs at night in poor barrios, but nonetheless caution is strongly advised when navigating the downtown and bus station districts of Caracas, Maracaibo and Valencia. Carry only as much money as you need, dress like the locals, don't wear jewellery or expensive sunglasses, don't take out smartphones in the street. During the day is mostly trouble-free, as long as you are aware of where you are going. Ask your hotel about any unsafe areas. It is not advisable to walk after dark: always take a taxi from a well-marked, recognizable company with a number, or get someone to recommend a driver. This applies even to tourist centres like Mérida and Ciudad Bolívar. You **must** speak at least basic Spanish to be able to get yourself around. Few people in the street will speak English, and even fewer in rural areas. Outside the big cities you will feel less unsafe, but still need to be careful in quieter rural areas.

Note The British Foreign and Commonwealth Office currently advises against all travel to within 80 km of the Colombian border due to the risk of kidnapping by drug traffickers and paramilitaries. The more popular destinations (such as beaches and national parks) are used to having travellers. You still need to watch out for scams, cons and petty thieving. If you are seeking an isolated beach, make enquiries about which are safe beforehand. Stay away from political rallies (unless you are there to join them) and protest marches, as they can turn violent. Foreigners may find themselves subject to harassment or abuse, or to thorough police identity and body searches. Carry a copy of your passport and, if searched, watch the police like a hawk, in case they try to plant drugs to your bags. Do not photograph people without permission. Carry a mobile, keep the number of a trusted Venezuelan contact handy, and be prepared to call him or her, or your embassy if a police search becomes threatening.

Tax
Airport tax International passengers do not pay airport tax at Maiquetía International Airport as it is included in the price of tickets. At all other airports, a maximum of US$2 is levied on domestic flights, US$9.75 on international flights, which must be paid after check-in and before proceeding to security. The rate changes annually, for the latest check www.aeropuerto-maiquetia.com.ve. Exit stamps are payable by overland travellers at some borders, US$2.50. Correct taxes are not advertised and you may be overcharged. Under 2s do not pay tax.
VAT/IVA 12%.

Telephone → *Country code +58.*
Ringing: long equal tones with equal long pauses. Engaged: short equal tones, with equal pauses. Mobile phone codes are generally 0412, 0414, 0416, or 0424. The national phone carrier is **CANTV**, which has offices country-wide, many of which also have internet. Everywhere there are independent phone offices, sometimes just tables, offering landline

and mobile calls. Phone cards for local calls are sold in multiples of BsF 5.

Time
4½ hrs behind GMT.

Tipping
Taxi drivers do not expect to be tipped. Hotel porters, US$1-2; airport porters US$4 per piece of baggage. Restaurants add 10% of bill for staff wages; tip a further 5-10%.

Tourist information
In charge of tourism is the **Ministerio del Poder Popular para el Turismo**, Av Francisco de Miranda con Av Principal de La Floresta, Lull Mintur (Frente al Colegio Universitario de Caracas), Chacao, Caracas, T0212-208 4651, www.venezuelaturismo.gob.ve and www.mintur.gob.ve. **Venetur**, Centro Empresarial Centro Plaza, Torre B, p 16, Los Palos Grandes, Caracas, T0500-TURISMO (887 4766), www.venetur.gob.ve, Mon-Fri 0900-1730, is the state-owned and operated travel agency, aimed at facilitating travel for nationals and foreigners, making reservations and arranging tours. In Caracas, go to **Corpoturismo**, Parque Central, Torre Oeste, p 35, 36 y 37, T507 8800.

Outside Venezuela, contact Venezuelan embassies and consulates. Read and heed the travel advice at websites below.

Useful websites
www.gobiernoenlinea.gob.ve Government site.
www.venezuelatuya.com Tourism, history, geography, cuisine, traditions and more.
www.turismo.net.ve Tourism portal and related blog at www.turismo.venezuela.net.ve.
www.audubonvenezuela.org Site of the not-for-profit conservation organization.

Visas and immigration
Entry is by passport, or by passport and visa. Immigration forms are issued by airlines to visitors from all EU and other Western European countries, Australia, Canada, New Zealand, South Africa, USA and most South and Central American and Caribbean countries. Forms are processed for an entrance stamp upon arrival. Valid for 90 days, entrance stamps cannot be extended. At some overland border crossings (including San Antonio) visitors are given only 30 days. Overstaying will lead to arrest and a fine when you try to depart. For citizens of some countries, tourist, transit, student, and business visas must be sought in advance. To check if you need a visa, see www.mppre.gob.ve. Requirements vary and include 2 passport photos, passport valid for 6 months, references from bank and employer, proof of foreign residence, demonstration of non-emigration to a consular official, proof of economic conditions, documentation of assets, and an onward or return ticket. The fee is US$30-43. For a 90-day extension go to the Servicio Administrativo de Identificación, Migración y Extranjería, **SAIME**, Av Baralt, Edif Mil, p 3, on Plaza Miranda in Caracas, T0800-SAIME00 or T0800-724 6300, www.saime.gob.ve (go to Extranjería, Prórroga de Visa); take passport, tourist visa, photographs and return ticket; passport with extension returned at end of day. SAIME offices in many cities do not offer extensions. If coming from Manaus or travelling onward to other countries in Latin America, you will need a yellow fever inoculation certificate. Carry your passport with you at all times as police do spot checks and anyone found without ID is immediately detained. You may also be asked to provide passport number in some restaurants and shops. Military checkpoints are common, especially in border zones, where all transport is stopped and you may be searched very thoroughly. Have documents ready and make sure you know what entry permits you need; soldiers may not know rules for foreigners. Business visitors on short visits are advised to enter as tourists, otherwise they'll have to obtain a tax clearance certificate (*solvencia*) before they can leave. Do not lose the carbon copy of your visa as this has to be surrendered when leaving.

Weights and measures
Metric.

Caracas

Founded in 1567, Caracas lies in a rift in thickly forested mountains which rise abruptly from a lush green coast to heights of 2000 m to 3000 m. The small basin in which the capital lies runs some 24 km east and west. For all its Caribbean appeal, it is not the gentlest of introductions to South America. Some enjoy its pleasant, year-round climate, its parks and cosmopolitan nightlife. Others are drawn to see firsthand the Bolivarian revolution in action. But others find it loud, congested and unsettling. By way of escape, there are several nearby excursions to mountain towns, the colonial district of El Hatillo, the Parque Nacional El Avila/Waraira Repano, beaches and Los Roques, a beautiful Caribbean atoll reached by a short flight.

Arriving in Caracas → *Phone code: 0212. Colour map 1, A6. Population: around 3 million (metropolitan region, 2011). Altitude: 960 m.*

Orientation The **airport** for international and domestic flights, Maiquetía, is 28 km from Caracas. There are three main **bus terminals** in different parts of the city; where you arrive depends upon where you travelled from. For getting around the city, there is a metro and various types of bus services, as well as taxis. ▶▶ *See also Transport, page 1506.*

In the centre, each street corner has a name: addresses are generally given as 'Santa Capilla and Mijares' (*Santa Capilla y* – sometimes *a* – *Mijares*), rather than the official 'Calle Norte 2, No 26'. In the east, 'y' or 'con' are used for street intersections. Modern multi-storeyed edifices

Caracas

Where to stay 🛏
1 Avila
2 Eurobuilding
3 Paseo Las Mercedes

Restaurants 🍴
2 La Castañuela
3 La Montanara
4 Mokambo

dominate and few colonial buildings remain intact. A 10-km strip from west to east, fragmented by traffic-laden arteries, contains several centres: Plaza Bolívar, Plaza Venezuela, Sabana Grande, Chacaíto, Altamira, La California and Petare. The Avila mountain is always north.

Tourist offices Corpoturismo ① *Parque Central, Torre Oeste, p 35, 36 y 37, T576 5696/507 8815*. Online local guides in Spanish include http://laguiadecaracas.net and www.guiacaracas. com. Information can also be found on the Alcaldía's website, www.caracas.gob.ve, and on www.ciudadccs.info.

Climate Maximum 32°C July-August, minimum 9°C January-February.

Security Safety in Caracas has deteriorated in recent years and crime rates and kidnappings have risen significantly. You should be on the lookout from when you arrive; there are many pirate taxis and rip-off merchants at the international airport. It is best not to arrive in Caracas at night. Avoid certain areas such as all western suburbs from the El Silencio monument to Propatria, the areas around the Nuevo Circo and La Bandera bus stations, the area around the *teleférico*, Chapellín near the Country Club, and Petare. It is not advisable to walk at night in the city, except in the municipality of Chacao (Altamira, Chacao and Los Palos Grandes) and in Las Mercedes. Street crime is common, even armed robbery in daylight. Carry handbags, cameras, etc, on the side away from the road as motorcycle bag-snatchers are notorious. Police checks are frequent, thorough and can include on-the-spot searches of valuables. Bribes are sometimes asked for. See also Safety, page 1492.

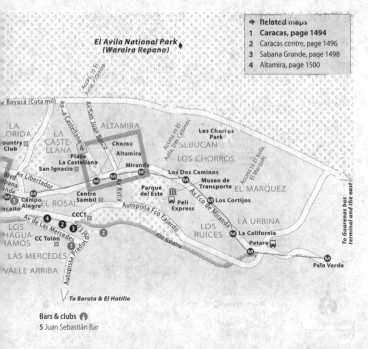

→ **Related maps**
1 **Caracas, page 1494**
2 Caracas centre, page 1496
3 Sabana Grande, page 1498
4 Altamira, page 1500

El Avila National Park
(Waraira Repano)

Bars & clubs 🍸
5 Juan Sebastián Bar

Places in Caracas

Centre

ⓘ Many museums close on Mon and at lunchtime.

The shady **Plaza Bolívar**, with its fine equestrian statue of the Liberator and pleasant colonial cathedral, is still the official centre of the city, though no longer geographically so. In the **Capitolio Nacional**, the National Assembly, which consists of two neoclassical-style buildings, the **Legislative Palace** and the **Federal Palace** *ⓘ Tue-Sun, 0900-1200, 1400-1700,* the Elliptical Salon has some impressive paintings and murals by the Venezuelan artist Martín Tovar y Tovar. The present **Cathedral** dating from 1674 has a beautiful façade, the Bolívar family chapel and paintings by Michelena, Murillo and an alleged Rubens 'Resurrection'. Bolívar was baptized in this Cathedral and the remains of his parents and wife are here. The **Museo Sacro** *ⓘ Plaza Bolívar, de la Torre a Gradillas, Tue-Sun 1000-1700,* has colonial religious paintings and images and has an art gallery, handicrafts, café and bookshop. Concerts and other cultural events are held at weekends.

The **Consejo Municipal** (City Hall) on Plaza Bolívar contains three **museums** *ⓘ all 3 open Tue-Fri 0930-1200, 1500-1800; Sat and Sun 0930-1800,* and feature a collection of the paintings of Emilio Boggio, a Venezuelan painter; the Raúl Santana Museum of the Creole Way of Life, a collection of miniature figures in costumes, all handmade by Raúl Santana; and the Sala de Arqueología Gaspar Marcano, exhibiting ceramics, mostly discovered on the coast.

Casa Natal del Libertador *ⓘ Sur 1 y Este 2, Jacinto a Traposos, opposite Plaza El Venezolano, T541 2563, Tue-Fri 0800-1600, Sun and holidays 1000-1600, free,* is a fascinating reconstruction of

2 Caracas centre

To Panteón Nacional (4 blocks)

N

200 metres
200 yards

Where to stay		4 El Conde	Restaurants	
1 Alex		5 Limón	1 Bar Basque	
2 Avila			2 Café Casa Veroes	
3 Dal Bo Hostel			4 La Cita	

the house where Bolívar was born (24 July 1783). Interesting pictures and furniture and murals tell Bolívar's life story. The first house, of adobe, was destroyed by an earthquake. The second was later pulled down. The **Museo Bolivariano** is next door and contains the Liberator's war relics.

San Francisco ① *Av Universidad y San Francisco (1 block southwest of Plaza Bolívar)*, the oldest church in Caracas, rebuilt 1641, should be seen for its colonial altars. **Santa Teresa** ① *between La Palma and Santa Teresa, just southeast of the Centro Simón Bolívar*, has good interior chapels and a supposedly miraculous portrait of Nazareno de San Pablo (popular devotions on Good Friday).

Panteón Nacional ① *Av Norte y Av Panteón, Tue-Sun 0900-1200, 1400-1630*. The remains of Simón Bolívar, the Liberator, lie here in the Plaza Panteón. The tomb of Francisco Miranda (the Precursor of Independence), who died in a Spanish prison, has been left open to await the return of his body, likewise the tomb of Antonio José de Sucre, who was assassinated in Colombia. Every 25 years the President opens Bolívar's casket to verify that the remains are still there.

Museo Histórico Fundación John Boulton ① *Final Av Panteón, Foro Libertador, Casa N 3, next to the Panteón Nacional, T861 4685, www.fundacionboulton.com, Tue-Sat 1000-1600*, contains good collections of 19th-century art and objects, furniture, maps, metals and coins and objects and documents relating to the life of Simon Bolívar.

Museo de Arte Colonial ① *Quinta Anauco, Av Panteón, San Bernardino, 1551 8190, www.quintadeanauco.org.ve, Tue-Fri 0900-1200 and 1400-1600, Sat-Sun and holidays 1000-1600, US$0.80*. This delightful house in the beautiful suburb of San Bernardino, was built in 1720 and was formerly the residence of the Marqués del Toro. Everything from the roof to the carpet has been preserved and the house contains a wealth of period furniture and sculpture and almost 100 paintings from the colonial era.

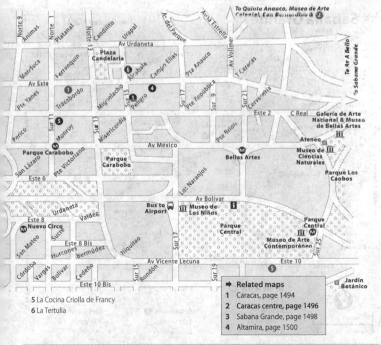

5 La Cocina Criolla de Francy
6 La Tertulia

➡ **Related maps**
1 Caracas, page 1494
2 Caracas centre, page 1496
3 Sabana Grande, page 1498
4 Altamira, page 1500

Parque Central to Sabana Grande

There are two good museums located at the **Parque Central**, a jungle of concrete edifices between Avenida Bolívar and Avenida Lecuna. The **Museo de Arte Contemporáneo** ⓘ *Parque Central, Cuadra Bolívar, T573 8289, www.fmn.gob.ve/fmn_mac.htm, Tue-Fri 0900-1700, Sat-Sun 1000-1700, free,* has some 3000 works on display, including modern sculptures and the works by, among others, Miró, Chagall, Matisse and Picasso, one of the finest collections of modern art in South America. The **Museo de los Niños** ⓘ *Parque Central, next to east Tower, Nivel Bolívar, T575 0695, www.maravillosarealidad.com, Mon-Fri 0900-1700, Sat-Sun and holidays 1000-1700, US$1.40, children US$1.20,* is an extremely popular and highly sophisticated interactive science museum.

Parque Los Caobos is a peaceful place to wander if you are visiting the **Plaza de los Museos** (see below). It also contains **Bosque de las Esculturas**, an open-air sculpture exhibition near the Plaza de los Museos entrance. By the entrance in Avenida México is the **Museo de Bellas Artes** ⓘ *www.fmn.gob.ve/fmn_mba.htm, free, Mon-Fri 0900-1600, Sat-Sun and holidays 1000-1700,* the oldest museum in Caracas, designed by Carlos Raúl Villanueva. It contains a permanent collection of contemporary and 19th-century works by mainly Venezuelan and South American artists and also has a good café surrounded by outdoor sculptures. Adjacent is the **Galería de Arte Nacional** ⓘ *T576 8707, www.fmn.gob.ve/fmn_gan.htm, Mon-Fri 0900-1700, Sat-Sun and holidays 1000-1700,* displays the history of Venezuelan art and also houses the **Cinemateca Nacional** ⓘ *www.cinemateca.gob.ve,* an arts and experimental cinema complex. **Museo de Ciencias Naturales** ⓘ *Plaza de los Museos, Los Caobos, T577 5103, www.fmn.gob.ve/fmn_mc.htm, Mon-Fri 0900-1700, Sat-Sun and holidays 1030-1800,* has archaeological, particularly pre-Columbian, zoological and botanical exhibits, interesting temporary shows.

③ Sabana Grande

➡ **Related maps**
1 Caracas, page 1494
2 Caracas centre, page 1496
3 **Sabana Grande, page 1498**
4 Altamira, page 1500

Where to stay 🛏
2 Crillón
3 Cristal
4 Gran Meliá
5 Nelson's Place
7 Plaza Palace

Restaurants 🍴
1 Da Guido
6 Jaime Vivas
7 La Huerta

Bars & clubs 🍸
9 El Maní Es Así

Universidad Central de Venezuela ① *Ciudad Universitaria, near Plaza Venezuela, www.ucv. ve*, is one of the most successful expressions of modern architecture in Latin America. Designed by Carlos Raúl Villanueva, it was declared a World Heritage Site by UNESCO in 2000. Among its important works of art are 'Floating Clouds' by Alexander Calder in the auditorium, murals by Victor Vasarely, Wilfredo Lam, Fernand Léger and sculptures by Jean Arp and Henri Laurens.

Jardín Botánico ① *near Plaza Venezuela, entrance by Ciudad Universitaria, Mon-Sun 0830-1630*, has collections of over 2000 species; 10,000 trees from 80 species grow in the arboretum alone. Here is the world's largest palm tree (*Corypha Sp*) and the elephant apple tree with its huge edible fruit.

East of Plaza Venezuela, the mid-town neighbourhood of Sabana Grande is bisected by the pedestrianised Boulevard Sabana Grande (actual name Avenida Abraham Lincoln), which connects with eastern Caracas. It has been cleaned up in recent years and is now a popular commercial district filled with shops, eateries and a book market – a great place to observe everyday Caraqueño life.

Eastern Caracas → *See map, page 1494.*
To the east of Sabana Grande is the safest and most fashionable area of the city, known as the golden belt of Caracas. It includes Country Club, Las Mercedes, Valle Arriba, Chacao, La Castellana, Altamira, Los Palos Grandes and Sebucán and has the best hotels and residential districts. In early 2014, eastern Caracas was the epicenter for anti-government protests.

Plaza Alfredo Sadel is an open space where public events take place all year round. It's on Avenida Principal of Las Mercedes, an old residential neighbourhood that has been transformed into an exclusive commercial zone.

Plaza Bolívar de Chacao ① *Av Mohedano, entre Ribas y Páez*, marks the spot where the town of Chacao was born, in the grounds of the Hacienda San Diego. Opposite is Iglesia San José, its patron saint. It's a popular meeting place and a stage for art exhibitions and folklore shows. **Plaza Francia** ① *Av Francisco de Miranda, entre Av Luis Roche y Av San Juan Bosco, Altamira*, commonly called Plaza Altamira, is a well-known landmark with an obelisk, a fountain and a Metro station. **La Estancia** ① *just along from the Altamira metro exit, www.pdvsalaestancia.com*, is a cultural centre with good exhibitions, regular activities and events including free yoga and music. It is set in a lovely park with beautiful trees and manicured lawns, the perfect place to escape from the hectic city. **Plaza Los Palos Grandes** ① *3a Av entre 2a y 3a Transversal, Los Palos Grandes*, at the heart of the fashionable neighbourhood of the same name, has a library, a coffee shop and mural. It is a good place to start a tour of the area and has an open market on Saturdays.

Parque Nacional del Este (officially Parque Gerneralísimo Francisco de Miranda) ① *closed Mon, opens 0530 for joggers, 0830 for others, till 1700, Miranda metro station*, is the largest park in Caracas and a popular place to relax, especially at weekends. It has a boating lake, cactus garden, tropical birds, some caged animals and reptiles as well as the **Humboldt Planetarium** ① *T234 9188, www.planetario humboldt.com*. **Museo de Transporte** ① *Parque Nacional del Este (to which it is connected by a pedestrian overpass), T234 2234, www.automotriz.net/museo-del-transporte, Sun 0900-1700*, has a large collection of locomotives and old cars.

Other parks and urban excursions
At the foot of the Avila mountain, the **Parque Los Chorros** ① *Tue-Fri 0830-1630, Sat-Sun 0830-1800, take bus from Los Dos Caminos station to Lomas de Los Chorros*, has impressive waterfalls and forest walks. **Paseo Los Próceres**, not far from the Escuela Militar, is a monument to the Venezuelan Independence heroes and is popular with walkers, runners and cyclists. It can be reached from Metro Los Símbolos. The refurbished **Parque Ezequiel Zamora/El Calvario**, west of El Silencio, with the Arch of Confederation at the entrance, has a good view of Centro Simón Bolívar. It has a small Museo Ornitológico, botanical gardens and a picturesque chapel. Near here is the Cuartel 4 de Febrero (4-F), the barracks in 23 de Enero district, also known as the Cuartel de

la Montaña and now home to the **Museo de la Revolución** ⓘ *T672-1719, www.milicia.mil.ve, Tue-Sun 1000-1600 (take a taxi, sketchy neighbourhood)*, the final resting place of the body of President Hugo Chávez, who died in March 2013. His body is entombed within a sombre, temperature-controlled marble sarcophagus. A 2-km Bulevar de la Dignidad will connect E Calvario with the site of the new museum via the Plaza 4 de Febrero. The densely wooded **Parque Caricuao** ⓘ *Tue-Sun 0900-1630: take metro to Caricuao Zoológico, then 5-min walk up Av Principal La Hacienda*, is at the southwest end of the Metro line, and part of Parque Nacional Macuro. A pleasant day out.

El Hatillo ⓘ *take a bus or taxi from central Caracas, about 20-30 mins' drive, depending on traffic*, once a separate village now subsumed by the city sprawl, is one of the few places in Caracas

4 Altamira

➡ Related maps
1 Caracas, page 1494
2 Caracas centre, page 1496
3 Sabana Grande, page 1498
4 Altamira, page 1500

100 metres
100 yards

Where to stay
3 Caracas Palace
4 Chacao & Suites
5 La Floresta
6 Pestana Caracas
7 Renaissance
8 Residencia Montserrat
9 The VIP

Restaurants
1 Amapola
2 Aprile
3 Arabica Coffee Bar
4 Arepa Factory Tradicional
5 Avila Burger
7 Catar
8 Chez Wong
9 Come a Casa
10 El Alazán

11 El Presidente
12 Miga's
14 St Honoré

Bars & clubs
15 360° Rooftop Bar

that has retained its colonial architecture. Built around a central plaza, its peaceful streets of multi-coloured houses offer a fine selection of cafés, restaurants, shops and small galleries. It is a wonderful spot to escape from the city and to shop for handicrafts, but it's busy at weekends. It holds an annual international music festival, usually in October, but dates vary.

⊚ Caracas listings

For hotel and restaurant price codes, and other relevant information, see Essentials.

⊜ Where to stay

The cheapest hotels are in the downtown area, but this is not a safe part of town at night, or even in the day with a backpack. Sabana Grande, which has a wide range of hotels, is not safe after 2000. If you don't want to stay in the suburbs or centre, spend a little more and go to the upmarket Chacao, Altamira, La Castellana districts (all easily reached by metro), where it is relatively safe to stroll around during the day. There are hotels on the coast, close to the airport, if you do not want to go into the city. If you book from abroad, make sure you receive written confirmation before beginning your journey.

Central area *p1496, map p1496*
The cheapest hotels are around the Nuevo Circo bus terminal (not a safe area). Plaza Bolívar and its surrounding streets are busy by the day, but by night are deserted and unsafe.
$$ Alex, Ferrenquín esq la Cruz, T578-0437, www.hotelalex.com.ve. A modern, new high-rise option boasting a bold contemporary lobby with tropical aquariums, 100 rooms on 14 floors with crisp furnishings and funky carpets, flat-screen TVs, Wi-Fi, gym, small pool, and restaurant.
$ Dal Bo, Av Sur 2 y Av Universidad, esq San Francisco, T0424-215 0799, www.dalbohostal. hostel.com. Cosy hostel with small dorms, 1½ blocks from Plaza Bolívar, on 1st floor of an old building. Wi-Fi, tourist info, console games and Blu-Ray DVDs. A sociable option. Prices are in US dollars, payment in dollars or euros only.
$ El Conde, Av Sur 4 esq El Conde, T862 2007, hotel_elconde@hotmail.com. Elegant old hotel, well located for those wanting to stay in the historic centre, but the rooms are very run-down. It's also hard to get a reservation. Own restaurant and bar.

$ Limón, Av Lecuna, Frente Parque Central, T571 6457, Bellas Artes metro. Recently remodeled red brick building with a restaurant attached. Safe, parking, well located for museums and galleries.

San Bernardino *map p1496*
Residential area 2 km north of Bellas Artes metro.
$$ Avila, Av Jorge Washington, T555 3000, www.hotelavila.com.ve. Founded by Nelson Rockerfeller in 1942, now a bit past its heyday but still a pleasant and tranquil retreat set in lush tropical gardens. Most staff speak English and German, there are fans, mosquito screens, pool, Metrobus nearby, a good restaurant and poolside bar, and travel agency. A 20-min drive from the centre.

Sabana Grande/Chacaíto *p1498, map p1498*
This is a busy area with restaurants and shops, but most close by early evening and it is unsafe to be out after 2000 when crowds and atmosphere change. The western fringes of Sabana Grande around Plaza Venezuela should be avoided entirely after sunset.
$$$$ Gran Meliá, Av Casanova y El Recreo, T762 8111, www.gran-melia.com/en. Beyond the ugly concrete 1970s exterior, the **Gran Melía** boasts a sumptuous marble lobby, James Bond staircases and glittering crystal chandeliers. However, it is past its heyday. Mixed rooms and good facilities including business centre, gourmet buffets, restaurants, fitness centre (at extra cost), spa, pool area, piano bar.
$$$-$$ Nelson's Place, C El Recreo, Edif 6, p 2, Apt 623, T231 9729, www.nelson.com.ve. By prior reservation only, Nelson Agelvis has 1 excellent fully furnished apartment (**$$$**) complete with Wi-Fi, cable TV, kitchen, and lounge, and 1 economical room (**$$**), both conveniently located in a residential block next to El Recreo shopping mall. Exceptional

hospitality, attention and travel information. A comfortable introduction to Caracas. Prices in dollars. Highly recommended.

$$ Plaza Palace, Av Los Mangos, Las Delicias, T762 4821, plaza_palace_hotel@hotmail.com. A secure building located on a quiet residential street. Amenities include parking and business facilities. Helpful, English spoken.

Chuao/Las Mercedes map p1494

An upmarket commercial district southeast of the centre and Sabana Grande, no metro station.

$$$ Eurobuilding Hotel & Suites, Calle La Guarita, Chuao, T902 1111, www.eurobuilding.com.ve. A modern 5-star hotel that's part of an international chain. It has a well-furnished all-suite wing, large pool, gym, spa, barber, restaurants, weekend rates.

$$ Hotel Paseo Las Mercedes, CC Paseo Las Mercedes, Las Mercedes, T993 1244, www.hotelpaseolasmercedes.com. Located in the shopping mall with fine restaurants and bars on the doorstep. Comfortable, spacious rooms with good service.

Chacao, Altamira, La Castellana
map p1500

These 3 districts, east of Gran Sabana and the centre, are adjacent to each other, and are a respectable commercial and residential zone.

$$$$ Pestana Caracas, 1 Av Urb Santa Eduvigis, T208 1900, www.pestana.com. Luxury hotel near Miranda metro station and Parque del Este, business-oriented with all facilities, fitness centre, pool, restaurant and penthouse bar.

$$$$ Renaissance, Av Eugenio Mendoza con C Urdaneta, La Castellana, T908 4222, www.marriott.com/ccsbr. A well-located hotel with bright contemporary decor, tasteful and well-equipped rooms, Asian restaurant, lounge bar, pool and gym. Good reports.

$$$ Caracas Palace, Av Luis Roche con Av Francisco Miranda, Altamira, T771 1000, www.caracaspalace.com. A popular luxury hotel well-located at the heart of Chacao on the Plaza Francia. It boasts a crisp white marble lobby and sweeping staircase, 2 restaurants, pool, spa, gym and business centre.

$$$ Hotel Chacao and Suites, Av Francisco de Miranda y Av José Félix Sosa, T956 6900,

www.hotelchacaonsuites.com. A smart new luxury option with modern, stylish, minimalist decor, spacious carpeted rooms and well-equipped suites to suit executive travellers. Amenities include Wi-Fi and restaurant.

$$$ The VIP, 3 Transversal con Av San Juan Bosco, Altamira, T349 4300, www.thevipcaracas.com. Young, stylish boutique hotel with good sized, crisply attired rooms, some with balconies, as well as a fine gourmet restaurant and slick lounge bar.

$ La Floresta, Av Avila Sur, T263 1955, www.hotelafloresta.com. Simple, reasonable, generic rooms with cable TV, hot water and Wi-Fi. A bit dated and the remodeled rooms are better; some have a nice view over the park. Good location near Altamira metro and Plaza Francia. Parking.

$ Residencia Montserrat, Av Avila Sur, T263 3533, www.hotelmontserrat.com.ve. A good 3-star option with a range of reasonable rooms and apartments, but ask to see before accepting. Near Plaza Francia and Altamira metro. Pleasant, well run, helpful, parking. Wi-Fi in lobby.

Near airport
See Litoral Central, page 1510.

🍴 Restaurants

Thanks to the creative input of generations of immigrants, Caracas' restaurant scene is extensive and diverse. There are more decent establishments than can be listed here, but an excellent online guide is www.miropopic.com.

Central area p1496, map p1496
There a lots of classic Spanish haunts in the downtown area, full of atmosphere and history. You should use taxis at night as it is unsafe. Call ahead for reservations.

$$ Bar Basque, Alcabala a Peligro, La Candelaria, T572 4857. Intimate and well-established, this is a renowned family-run Caracas favourite that has been serving fine home-cooked Basque cuisine for three generations. Just a handful of tables and an excellent menu of fresh seafood, poultry and meat dishes. One of the best.

$$ Café Casa Veroes, Veroes a Jesuítas, T564 7457. Mon-Fri 1100-1530. Sophisticated traditional Venezuelan food in a colonial house built in 1759 (www.casadelahistoriade venezuela.com). A bastion of elegance in an otherwise shabby neighbourhood. Great ambiance and a changing menu.

$$ La Cita, Esquina de Alcabala, La Candelaria, T573 8819. Serving traditional Spanish food for 56 years, including seafood, fish stews and paella. Bustling, festive and packed at lunchtime. Book ahead.

$$ La Cocina Criolla de Francy, Av Este 2 y Sur 11, La Candelaria, T576 9849. Open 0900-1800, closed Sun. Founded by Francy Moncada, his kitchen serves wholesome traditional Venezuelan cuisine, including rabbit, lamb, and arepitas. A good place to sample local flavours.

$$ La Tertulia, Alcabala a Urapal, La Candelaria, T574 1476. Family-run tapas restaurant with an extensive menu and daily specials. Famous for its lamb chops, octopus, tapas and Spanish-style fresh fish. Busy at noon.

Sabana Grande *p1498, map p1498*
This area has some cafés, bars (*tascas*) and restaurants. Places on the Sabana Grande Boulevard are good for people watching. There is also an array of fast food joints in CC El Recreo, most of them on the 6th floor.

$$ Da Guido, Av Fco Solano, T763 0937. A long running Italian restaurant and Sabana Grande institution, as reliable as it was 50 years ago. It has a small menu of hearty home-cooked fare, simple, fresh, and authentic, the way good Italian food should be. Has a 2nd branch at 6 Av con 5 Transversal, Altamira, T266 9927, equally popular.

$$ La Huerta, Av Fco Solano con 1ra Av de Las Delicias, www.lahuerta.com. Spanish *tasca* with a dash of Venezuelan, including tapas, seafood paella, rabbit, goat, and lamb. Popular with locals watching Spanish football. A good stock of wine.

$ Jaime Vivas, C San Antonio, T763 4761. The place for hearty local Caracas food, especially *pabellón*. Simple, no frills, and a bit dated, but maintains loyal clientele.

Chuao/Las Mercedes *map p1494*
The area has a good selection of upmarket restaurants and US-style steakhouses and chains.

$$$ Astrid y Gaston, Londres entre Av Caroní y Nueva York, T993 1119, Las Mercedes, www.astridygaston.com. High-end Peruvian restaurant, one of the finest in Caracas, serving traditionally flavoured seafood and specials like rabbit and kid.

$$ Coco Thai and Lounge, CC Tolón, piso 3, Las Mercedes. Excellent Thai, Vietnamese, and Japanese cuisine, including tasty chicken in coconut curry, duck spring rolls and sashimi. Excellent presentation and flavours, great ambience, open-air terrace and striking eastern decor.

$$ La Castañuela, C Trinidad con C París. Good paella and seafood in generous portions. Popular and festive at weekends with live music and dancing. Attentive service.

$$ La Montanara, C Caroní con Madrid, Las Mercedes, T991 2812. An authentic Italian trattoria (some say the best in the city) and one of the most popular restaurants in the district. Great atmosphere, often buzzing and full with diners, so be prepared to wait.

$$ Mokambo, C Madrid con Monterrey, Las Mercedes, T991 2577. A pleasant brunch, lunch and dinner spot frequented by well-to-do crowds. They serve creative Mediterranean cuisine.

Altamira, La Castellana *map p1500*
$$$ Aprile, 4 Av con 5 Transversal, Altamira, T264 5775. Upscale and fashionable Italian restaurant serving ceviche, pastas, steak and fries. Smart interior, cosmopolitan vibe. Reservations a must

$$ Chez Wong, Edif IASA, Plaza La Castellana, T266 5015, www.chezwong.com.ve. Creative and unconventional Chinese food, including good dimsum and Peking duck. Minimalist decor.

$$ El Alazán, Av Luis Roche, entre 5 y 6 Transversal, Altamira, T285 0208, www.elalazan. com. Carnivores should not miss this place, one of the best places in Caracas to enjoy a slab of prime beef. Big, noisy, popular and an institution for 3 decades. Good wines.

Los Palos Grandes *p1499*
$$ Amapola, 1 Av entre 1 y 2 Transversal, T283 3680. Creative Venezuelan dishes handed down by Grandmother and an imaginative use of local flavours. Bright, light decor and an outdoor terrace.

$$ Avila Burger, 6 Transversal entre 3 y 4, Cuadra Gastronómica, www.avilaburger.com. Buzzing gourmet burger joint with an enticing array of hearty options. Fun and casual.

$$ Catar, Cuadra Gastronómica, 6 Transversal, T285 0649. Relaxed, stylish café/restaurant with an eclectic menu. Closed Mon. Try the delicious thin crust pizzas and a melt-in-the-mouth chocolate pudding. Good selection for vegetarians. Several other good restaurants in this gastronomic block.

$$ Come a Casa, 1 Av con 1 Transversal, T283 1707. Low-key Sicilian-style trattoria serving wholesome home-cooked pasta. Cosy atmosphere and outdoor terrace.

$ Arepa Factory Tradicional, 2 Transversal entre Av Andrés Bello y 2 Av, T285 1125. Don't be put off by the name, this fast-food joint serves Venezuelan gourmet *arepas* with sophisticated fillings.

$ El Presidente, 3 Av entre 1 y 2 Transversal. An unpretentious local institution serving wholesome home-cooked fare. Ideal for a quick lunch.

Cafés and bakeries

Arabica Coffee Bar, Av Andrés Bello con 1 Transversal, T283 7024. Good Venezuelan coffee with great pastries, the best *empanadas* in the city. Small and cosy.

Miga's, Av Luis Roche con 1 Transversal, opposite Altamira Suites Hotel, www.migas. com.ve. Busy café/bakery/ deli chain with a dozen or so outlets selling fresh breads, cakes, salads, sandwiches and meat dishes, some vegetarian options, open late. OK, convenient, nothing special.

St Honoré, 1 Transversal con Av Andrés Bello, T286 7982. Popular café and bakery with covered terrace, good for lunch. Some of the best bread in town, often recommended, but also closed for renovation at the time of research (Mar 2014).

🎧 Bars and clubs

Caracas *p1494, maps p1494, p1496, p1498 and p1500*

Caracas has a vibrant nightlife. Clubs don't usually come to life until after 2300, and then go on to the early hours. Las Mercedes district is full of busy, trendy bars. Always take care when leaving in the small hours.

Bars

360° Rooftop Bar, 19th floor of **Altamira Suites Hotel**, 1 Av, Los Palos Grandes. Hip, sophisticated wine bar with panoramic views of the city, snack on pizza or sushi and sip delicious cocktails. A must just for the views.

Centro Comercial San Ignacio, see Shopping, has many fashionable, though pricey bars and the occasional nightclubs, popular with wealthy young Venzuelans. Try **Whisky Bar** (Nivel Blandín), usually packed, trendy and friendly crowd, long bar with terrace area, open daily. Or **Suka** (Nivel Blandín) with giant hammock and good cocktails.

La Suite bar, Centro Comercial Tolón Fashion Mall, PB, Las Mercedes, T300 8858. Another popular lounge bar, lavish decor, attracts wealthy 20-something crowd. Mix of music from house to 80s. Tango on Mon, boleros on Tue, jazz on Wed, varied music with invited DJ nights Thu-Sat.

Clubs

El Maní es Así, Av Fco Solano y C El Cristo, Sabana Grande, T763 6671, www.elmaniesasi. com. Tue-Sun till 0400/0500. Famous for its live salsa and dancing, casual.

Juan Sebastián Bar, Av Venezuela entre C Sorocaima y C Mohedano, El Rosal, T951 3750. Closed Sun. Caracas' temple of jazz, live music.

Moulin Rouge, Av Fco Solano, Sabana Grande. Club famous for its live rock music.

🎭 Entertainment

Caracas *p1494, maps p1494, p1496, p1498 and p1500*

For details of cinemas and other events, see the newspapers, *El Universal* (the cinema page on www.el-universal.com has full listings) and *El Nacional*.

Ateneo de Caracas, Av La Salle, Quinta La Colina, Colinas de Los Caobos. Concerts, ballet, theatre and film festivals. **Centro de Acción Social para la Música**, Boulevard Amador Bendayán de Quebrada Honda, Los Caobos (metro Colegio de Ingenieros), concert hall built for the Youth and Children's Orchestras of Venezuela. See the web page of *El Sistema* (FundaMusical Bolívar) for forthcoming concerts and events: www.fundamusical.org.ve.

Centro de Estudios Latinoamericanos Rómulo Gallegos (CELARG), Av Luis Roche con 3ra Transversal, Altamira, T285 2721, www.celarg.org.ve. Cultural centre with cinema showing alternative films, theatre, exhibitions, talks. Trasnocho Cultural, Urb Las Mercedes, Centro Comercial Paseo Las Mercedes, Nivel Trasnocho, T993 1910, www.trasnochocultural.com. Theatre, cinemas, exhibitions, lounge bar with live DJs Thu-Sat, bookshop, café and yoga centre.

⚄ Festivals

Caracas *p1494, maps p1494, p1496, p1498 and p1500*
3 May, Velorio de la Cruz de Mayo still celebrated with dances and parties in some areas.

◑ Shopping

Caracas *p1494, maps p1494, p1496, p1498 and p1500*
Most shopping takes place in Caracas' numerous malls, such as: **Centro Sambil**, Av Libertador, 1 block south of Chacao Metro, one of the largest in South America; **CC El Recreo**, Av Casanova y El Recreo, Sabana Grande; **CC Tolon** and **Paseo Las Mercedes**, both on Av Principal de Las Mercedes, and the exclusive **San Ignacio**, several blocks north of Chacao Metro.
Chocolate Blue Moon, C La Paz, Plaza de El Hatillo, T963 3023. Divine chocolatier with small café selling hot chocolate mixes. La Praline Chocolatier, Av Andrés Bello con 3ra Transversal, Los Palos Grandes, T284 7986, www.lapraline.com.ve. Ultimate heaven for chocaholics, delicious chocolates crafted from Venezuelan cacao. The packets of hot chocolate make great gifts.
Handicrafts Good-quality Sun craft market between Museo de Bellas Artes and Museo de Historia Natural (metro Bellas Artes). Hannsi, C Bolívar, El Hatillo, T963 5577, www.hannsi.com.ve. A superstore of

Venezuelan crafts and products made up of numerous small rooms.
Markets Mercado Quinta Crespo, off Av Baralt, El Silencio metro, daily, one of the largest central food markets, shabby but vibrant. Mercado de Chacao, Av Avila, 3 blocks north of Chacao metro, 0800-1200, daily except Sun. Good food, fruit and veg market. **Mercado Peruano**, Colegio de Ingenieros metro, Blvd Amador Bendayán, from 0900 on Sun, popular small Peruvian food market with ceviche stalls.

◑ What to do

Caracas *p1494, maps p1494, p1496, p1498 and p1500*
Baseball
The popular baseball season is from late Sep-Jan. The capital's local team, Los Leones del Caracas, plays at the Estadio Universitario, Los Chaguaramos. Tickets can be bought at the stadium's box office, www.leones.com.

Tours
Akanan, C Bolívar, Edf Grano de Oro, pb loc C, Chacao, T715 5433, www.akanan.com. Excellent and professionally managed eco-tour operator with an emphasis on nature and adventure with riding, cycling, climbing, rafting, hiking and other outdoor activities outside Caracas. Small groups, personalized service and years of experience working with documentary film crews. Recommended.
Alborada Venezuela, Plaza La Castellana, Torre IASA, oficina 101, T263 1820, www.alboradavenezuela.com. Tours focusing on nature conservation, also specialist interest, adventure trips and tours beyond Venezuela.
Alpiviajes, Av Sucre, Centro Parque Boyacá, Torre Centro, Los Dos Caminos, T285 0410, www.alpiviajes.com. Tours throughout Venezuela, including fishing trips and adventure sports, English spoken, good for flights and advice. Flying safari tours in private plane. Recommended.
Ascanio Birding Tours, Apartado Postal 78006, La Urbina 1074 Caracas, T242 4949, www.abtbirds.com. Specialists in birdwatching tours in Venezuela and neighbouring countries.
Candes Turismo, Av Francisco de Miranda, Edif Roraima, p 3, of 3C, T953 1632,

www.candesturismo.com. Well-established tour operator, range of destinations, helpful, efficient, English, Italian, German spoken.

Cóndor Verde, Av Caura, Torre Humboldt, M 3, Prados del Este, T655 0100, www.condor verdetravel.com. Operate throughout the country, well-established, German run.

Kayaman, T0414-124 2725, www.kayaman. com. Dedicated to kayaking, courses and construction. See related company, **Rafting Barinas**, page 1545.

Natoura Travel & Adventure Tours, C 31 entre Av Don Tulio y prol Av 6 No 5-27, Mérida 5101, T274-252 4216 (in US T303-800 4639), www. natoura.com. Tailor-made tours throughout Venezuela. Specialists in adventure tours and ecotourism. See also page 1534.

Osprey Travel, Av Casanova, Sabana Grande, 2 Av de Bello Monte, Edif La Paz, p 5, of 51, T0414-310 4491, www.ospreyexpeditions. com. Tours in Venezuela (also Colombia and Panama), diving, language courses, advice from English speaking staff. Office opens by appointment. Recommended.

Tucaya, Quinta Santa Marta, 1 Av Urbanización Campo Claro, Los Dos Caminos, T234 9401, www.tucaya.com. Small company with good reputation, popular with French speakers.

Venezuela X, T0414-255 1591, www.venezuela x.com. Adventure tours of all types, on land, water and in the air, for all levels. Have a base camp south of Barinas for rafting, trekking and mountain biking trips, T0273-400 3625.

⊖ Transport

Caracas *p1494, maps p1494, p1496, p1498 and p1500*

Air

The **airport** for international and domestic flights, Maiquetía, www.aeropuerto-maiquetia. com.ve, is 28 km from Caracas near the port of La Guaira, and has 2 terminals: Maiquetía (national) and Simón Bolívar (international), 5 mins apart via an a/c walkway from international to national, but an open-air sidewalk from national to international (less secure after dark). In both terminals, many people offer to change money on the black market. There is no way of knowing if they are trustworthy. Always allow plenty of time to get to the airport as the route can be very congested (minimum 30 mins, up to 2-3 hrs in heavy traffic). It is unsafe to travel between Maiquetía and the city in the hours of darkness. For evening or pre-dawn flights, it is recommended you stay in one of the hotels near the airport (see Litoral Central, Where to stay, below). International passengers must check in at least 3 hrs before departure or they may lose their seat. National flights need 2 hrs check in. It is best not to arrive at the airport without having arranged a pick up. There have been incidents of foreigners getting taken in what seem to be marked taxis, only to be driven off, robbed and left in the middle of nowhere. If the hotel does not have its own taxis, ask them to contact a driver. On no account go with one of the freelance or unlicensed drivers who crowd the terminal. Official taxis are all black with a yellow logo. You buy tickets from official counters and will be accompanied to the taxi by a member of staff. Double check the driver's ID. The fare varies depending on time of day and district, US$8-13. See also the private firm, **Taxi to Caracas**, www. taxitocaracas.com. Airport **shuttle buses** are run by **Sitssa**, T572 1609, from national terminal, level 2, to the Alba Caracas Hotel, 0600-1900, US$1.25. Also **UCAMC**, from the national terminal exit. To get to the airport, catch it under the flyover at Bolívar and Av Sur 17, Parque Central, 250 m from Bellas Artes metro (poorly lit at night, not safe to wait here in the dark), or at metro stations such as Parque Central and Gato Negro. The service runs 0500-2200, every 30 mins, 1-2 hrs, depending on traffic, US$3. If heading for a hotel in Chacao or Altamira on arrival, get off at Gato Negro metro station (same fare) and take metro from there (with luggage only at off-peak times). The shuttle bus or *por puesto* to airport can also be caught at Gato Negro metro station. Watch your belongings around Gato Negro. An alternative is to take a bus to Catia La Mar and get out at the airport. Taxis remain the best and safest option, however.

Bus

Local TransMetrópoli buses (www. transmetropoli.com.ve) run on 22 routes mostly from El Silencio or Chacaíto to the suburbs,

0500-2100; they have wheelchair access. Also being introduced is a mass transport system, **BusCaracas**, using magnetic cards, single journey BsF1.50. Regular buses are overcrowded in rush hour and charge extra after 2100. Bus tickets cost BsF1.50. Por puesto minibuses, known as *busetas, carmelitas* or *carritos* run on regular routes; fares depend on the distance travelled within the city.

Long distance The Terminal Oriente at Guarenas for **eastern destinations** is clean, modern and relatively safe. It can be reached by numerous buses from the city centre and Petare. Take a taxi at night.

The La Bandera terminal for all **western** destinations is a 500 m, unsafe walk from La Bandera metro station on Line 3. City buses that pass are prominently marked 'La Bandera'. Give yourself plenty of time to find the bus you need although there are bus agents who will assist in finding a ticket for your destination. Tickets are sold in advance except for nearby destinations such as **Maracay** and **Valencia**. Those first on get the best seats so it is advisable to arrive an hour before departure. There is a left luggage office, cash machines, restaurant and many food and drink kiosks.

The more upscale **Aeroexpresos Ejecutivos**, Av Principal De Bello Campo, Quinta Marluz, Bello Campo, Chacao, www.aeroexpresos.com. ve (timetables and prices available online), a private bus company, runs regular services to Barquisimeto, Ciudad Bolívar, El Tigre, Maracaibo, Maracay, Maturín, Puerto La Cruz, Puerto Ordaz, San Felix and Valencia. Prices are more expensive than others, but worth it for the more comfortable and modern buses and for the extra security. Other good companies are: **Peli Express**, Corredor Vial Parque del Este, Los Dos Caminos (to Puerto La Cruz, Barinas, El Vigia, Mérida, Coro, Punto Fijo and Maracaibo); and **Rodovías**, 150-m walk from metro station Colegio de Ingenieros, Galpon Terminal Rodovías, Local Pc 7-A, Urbanización Los Caobos, www.rodovias.com.ve (to the east, Valencia and Maracaibo).

Buses to places near Caracas leave from the old Nuevo Circo bus station (eg **Los Teques, Higuerote, Catia La Mar, La Guaira**).

Sat and Sun morning and public holidays are bad for travel into/out of Caracas. Always take identification when booking a long-distance journey. Times and fares of buses are given under destinations.

Car

Car hire Self-drive cars are available at both terminals of the airport (offices open 0700-2100) and in town. Some of have counters at domestic air terminals and hotels. See rates on page 1488.

Metro

The metro is a/c, clean, safe, comfortable and quick, although poorly signed and often packed, especially at rush hours. Operates 0530-2300, no smoking, no heavy luggage, www.metrodecaracas.com.ve. There lines are: **Line 1** (west-east) from Propatria to Palo Verde, **Line 2** (north-south), from El Silencio to Las Adjuntas, with connection to Caricuao Zoológico and a continuation from Las Adjuntas to Los Teques (Alí Primera); **Line 3**, south from Plaza Venezuela via El Valle to La Rinconada, **Line 4**, extending Line 2 west-east from Capuchinos to Plaza Venezuela/ Zona Rental, with a continuation through Las Mercedes and Chuao to Parque del Este being built. Lines 5 and 6 are planned. A single ticket costs BsF1.50, BsF3 return, whereas a 10-journey (*multi abono*) ticket is BsF13.50. Student discounts are available with ISIC card; apply at Parque del Este station. There are also *Metrotarjetas* (pre-paid cards) for 20, 30 and 40 trips. Metrobuses connect with the Metro system: get transfer tickets (*boleto integrado*, BsF1.50) for services to southern districts, route maps displayed at stations; retain ticket after exit turnstile. Metrobuses are modern, comfortable, recommended but infrequent. *Metrocable* systems opened 2010 from Parque Central (Line 4) to San Agustín barrio and from Palo Verde to Mariche. Good selection of maps at shops in Altamira and La California stations.

Motorcycle

Motorcycles may not be ridden in Caracas between 2300 and 0500.

Taxi

Even though they are a legal requirement, meters are never used. Negotiate fares in advance; always offer 10% less than the driver's first quote and bargain hard. Minimum fares in the city are about US$8-10 during the day, with longer trips up to US$17.50. Taxi drivers are authorized to charge an extra 20% on night trips after 1800, on Sun and all holidays, and extra for answering telephone calls. After 1800 drivers are selective about destinations. Beware of taxi drivers trying to renegotiate fixed rates because your destination is in 'a difficult area'. See warning above under Air about pirate taxis. See also under Air (or in Yellow Pages) for radio taxis. **Note** Never tell a driver it's your first visit to Caracas.

⊕ Directory

Caracas *p1494, maps p1494, p1496, p1498 and p1500*

Banks See also Money, page 1490. Plenty of ATMs around the city and most of the banks have branches in the major shopping centres

(Sambil, San Igancio, El Tolón). For money exchange and other services including travel, go to **Italcambio**, www.italcambio.com, the official government exchange office and take ID. Offices at Av Urdaneta, esq Animas a Platanal, Edif Camoruco, Nivel Pb, El Centro, T565 0219, CC Mercapo, El Cementerio, at CC El Recreo shopping centre, in Sabana Grande, and others in the capital and around the country. **Italcambio** also at national and international terminals at airport (open public holidays). **La Moneda**, Centro Financiero Latino, Av Fco Solano, Edif San Germán, Sabana Grande, open Mon-Fri only. **Viajes Febres Parra**, Av Libertador, Edif CC Libertador, PB, Loc 4 y 5, La Florida, and at airport. **Embassies and consulates** For all foreign embassies and consulates in Caracas, see http://embassy.goabroad.com. Many are open to the public only in the morning, some are closed on Fri. **Medical services** Clínica Avila, Av San Juan Bosco con 6ta Transversal, Altamira, T276 1111, www.clinicaelavila.com.

Around Caracas

Between the capital and the Caribbean coast is the national park of El Avila, not only a popular recreational area for caraqueños, but also a refuge for wildlife within earshot of the city and a good place for birdwatching and hiking. The coast itself is also a favourite weekend escape, although it can get busy. Nor, at weekends, can you expect to have Colonia Tovar to yourself, a German immigrant town to which city folk flock for the local produce and mild climate.

Wairara Repano/Monte Avila → *Colour map 1, A6.*

The 85,192-ha **Parque Nacional El Avila** (renamed **Waraira Repano** in 2008) forms the northern boundary of Caracas. The green slopes rise steeply from both the city and from the central Caribbean coast. Despite being so close to the capital, fauna includes red howler monkeys, jaguar and puma. There are also several species of poisonous snake. Access is from Caracas, with several marked entrances along the Cota Mil (Avenida Boyacá), designed for hikers. The park is closed Monday and Tuesday morning.

A **cable railway**, the **Teleférico Warairarepano** ⓘ *Final Av Principal de Maripérez (Simón Rodríguez), T901 5555 or 793 5960, www.ventel.gob.ve, Tue-Sun 0800-2000, closed Mon, US$2, students with card, children 4-12, over 60s and disabled US$0.80, taxi from Colegio de Ingenieros metro station, US$3,* runs up to Monte El Avila (2175 m). The 20-minute cable car ride offers fantastic views of Caracas on clear days and is highly recommended. Courting couples wander the restaurant, food stalls and skating rink at the summit, El Avila station. From here you can look down the other side of Monte Avila over the village of Galipán all the way to the Caribbean sea. The **Humboldt Hotel** on the summit has been refurbished and is open for guided tours but not yet for sleeping. From El Avila station you can take a 4WD *carrito* to the village of Galipán, www.galipan.net, founded by Spanish immigrants from the Canary Islands and today a popular weekend excursion with *caraqueños*. The village has plentiful good restaurants serving excellent pork sandwiches and rich hot chocolate, as well as stone-built cabins and stalls selling strawberries and cream, jams and flowers. There are *posadas* for overnight stays. Also worth visiting is the old coffee hacienda **Los Venados**, where there are picnic areas and a **zip wire** (known as 'canopy') ① *Senderos Aéreos, T0416-177 4017, www.senderosaereos.com, Tue-Sun 0900-1500, (Sat-Sun only in low season), US$4*. El Avila station can also be reached in 45 minutes by shared 4WD *carritos* that leave regularly from the entrance to the park at San Bernardino, US$0.50 (on the edge of sketchy *barrios*, take care). Alternatively, trucks leave from the **Avila** hotel, US$1 per person or US$12 for the whole vehicle. A recommended trip is to ride up in a vehicle and hike back down (note that it is cold at the summit, around 13°C, take a sweater).

Listed below are three good places to start a hike. **Advice** Hikers should go in groups of at least three, for mountain and personal safety. If you want to camp, inform any Puesto de Guardaparques of your route, where you intend to stay and get their permission; also leave a mobile phone number with them. Always take water and something for the cold at altitude. The unfit should not attempt any of the hikes. **Inparques'** Caracas office is at Avenida F de Miranda, Parque Generalísimo Francisco de Miranda, opposite Parking 2, T273 2807.

Pico Naiguatá (2765 m) This is a very strenuous hike. Take the metro to La California, then a bus going up Avenida Sanz, ask for the Centro Comercial El Marqués. From there walk up Avenida Sanz towards Cota Mil (Avenida Boyacá), about four blocks. At the end of Avenida Sanz, underneath the bridge, is the entrance to the Naiguatá trail. In about 40 minutes you reach La Julia *guardaparques* station.

Pico Oriental (2600 m) From the Altamira metro station take a bus to 'La entrada de Sabas Nieves', where the **Tarzilandia** restaurant is. From here a dirt road leads up to the **Sabas Nieves** *guardaparques* station, a steep 20- to 40-minute hike with good views of the city, popular with keep fit *caraqueños*. The path to Pico Oriental starts at the back of Sabas Nieves and is extremely easy to follow. **Note** Paths beyond Sabas Nieves are shut in dry season (roughly February-June depending on the year) to prevent forest fires.

Hotel Humboldt (2150 m) This is a relatively easy route of three hours. Take the Metro bus from Bellas Artes station to El Avila stop; opposite is a grocery. Turn the corner and walk two blocks up towards the mountain. At the top of the street turn left; almost immediately on your right is the park entrance. **Note** This area is not safe before 0800 or after dark. Plenty of people take this route, starting 0830-0900, giving enough time to get up and down safely and in comfort.

Litoral Central

The Litoral Central is the name given to the stretch of Caribbean Coast directly north of Caracas. A paved road runs east from Catia La Mar, past the airport and then through the towns of Maiquetía, **La Guaira**, Venezuela's main port, dating back to 1567, and Macuto. This became the state of Vargas in January 1999 and in December that year was the focus of Venezuela's worst natural disaster of the 20th century. Prolonged heavy rains on deforested hillsides caused flash floods and landslides, killing and causing to disappear an estimated 30,000 people and leaving 400,000 homeless. From La Guaira a panoramic road runs to the beaches at Chichiriviche de la Costa, Puerto Cruz (nice beach, no shade, bars) and Puerto Maya (very nice beach with shade and services).

Colonia Tovar → *Phone code: 0244. Municipal population: 16,500. Altitude: 1890 m.*
www.colonia-tovar.com

This picturesque mountain town was founded in 1843 by German immigrants from Kaiserstuhl in the Black Forest; a small **museum** ① *1000-1800, Sat-Sun and holidays*, tells the history of the founding pioneers. They retained their customs and isolation until a paved road reached the settlement in 1963. It is now very touristy, attracting hordes of weekend visitors, but the blond hair, blue eyes and Schwartzwald-accented German of the inhabitants remain, as do many traditions and dances. Local produce includes breads, blackberry jam, bratwurst and beer. Colonia Tovar offers delightful landscapes, a mild climate, old architecture and dignified hospitality in its many restaurants, cafés and hotels.

⊚ Around Caracas listings

For hotel and restaurant price codes, and other relevant information, see Essentials.

⊕ Where to stay

Litoral Central *p1509*
If you're arriving or leaving the airport at odd times, there are some good choices in Catia La Mar and Macuto as an alternative to Caracas. These places often provide free transfers, or a taxi costs about US$4, 5-20 mins depending on traffic.
$$$ Eurobuilding Express Maiquetía, Av La Armada, T700 0700, maiquetia@eurobuilding. com.ve. Useful business hotel with pool, tennis, airport transfer.
$$$ Olé Caribe, Final Av Intercomunal, El Playón, 1160, Macuto, T620 2000, www. hotelolecaribe.com. A good, if expensive bet near the airport, safe in room, breakfast, pool.
$$-$ Catimar, Urb Puerto Viejo Av Principal, Catia La Mar, T351 7906, www.hotelcatimar. com. Price includes transfers to and from airport (you may have to phone them from Asistencia al usuario desk), nice bar, restaurant, basic rooms, expensive for what's offered. Near small Puerto Viejo beach, said to be safe, with a few restaurants (**Brisas del Mar, Puerto Mar**), snack bar.
$$-$ Posada Doña Alcinda, Av Principal La Atlántida Calle 7, T619 1605, www.posada alcinda.com. Suites and standard rooms, bar, airport transfer, diving courses and other activities can be arranged.
$ Buena Vista Inn, Av el Hotel y C 4, Qta Buenavista Inn, Urb Playa Grande, Catia la Mar, T352 9163, http://buenavistainn.com.ve. Convenient for airport, pick-up extra.
$ Posada Il Prezzano, Av Principal de Playa Grande c/c 5, Catia La Mar, T351 2626, www.ilprezzano.com.ve. Italian-run, spotless, pleasant, good value, restaurant.

$ Santiago, Av La Playa, Urb Alamo, Macuto, T213 3500, www.hotelsantiago.com.ve. Comfortable, restaurant with live music, pool, secure parking, 15 mins' drive to airport.

⑦ Restaurants

Waraira Repano/Monte Avila *p1508*
$$$ Casa Pakea, Carretera San Antonio de Galipán, Sector Manzanares, a la derecha de la Rosa Mística, T415 5353. Special transport from Hotel Avila, San Bernardino, or from the cable car station in Galipán. Fabulous restaurant in a wonderful location at the top of Monte Avila, traditional Basque food.
$$$ La Galipanier, Galipán, T414-249 1978, www.legalipanier.com. Hot soups and Swiss-style fondues. A bit classy and a very romantic setting overlooking the valley.

⑩ What to do

Waraira Repano/Monte Avila *p1508*
Centro Excursionista Caracas, Av Santa Sofia Sur, Zona Polideportivo, Urb Santa Sofia. El Cafetal, Caracas, cecaracas@gmail.com.

⊝ Transport

Colonia Tovar *p1509*
The 1½ hrs' windy drive up from Caracas on Ruta 4, through La Yaguara, El Junquito and the Parque Nacional Macarao, is easy during the week, but murder (2½-4 hrs) at weekends: long traffic jams, few picnic spots or accommodation, definitely not recommended. It is generally easy to get a lift if there are no buses.
Bus Take the metro to La Yaguara and from there take a *por puesto* to El Junquito (1 hr if no traffic, US$0.50), then change for Colonia Tovar (1 hr, US$0.50). Last public transport to Caracas 1800, later at weekends.

West from Caracas

The Central Highlands run through this varied region. North of the highlands is the Caribbean, with secluded coves and popular resorts such as Puerto Colombia. Straddling the mountains is the birders' paradise of Parque Nacional Henri Pittier. Two coastal national parks, Morrocoy, which lies offshore, and Los Médanos, around the old city of Coro, are further highlights of this area. West of Coro is the city and lake of Maracaibo, for most Venezuelans, a region summed up in three letters – oil. For others, it can be summed up in four letters – heat. Both are certainly true. To the south, though, are the eastern extremities of the Andean mountain chain, with quaint villages, lakes and high passes on the way to the Sierra Nevada de Mérida.

Maracay and around

Maracay is a hot, thriving industrial city and is the gateway to Henri Pittier National Park. The city has some pleasant leafy residential neighbourhoods and is the centre of an important agricultural area. The great basin in which lies the Lago de Valencia and the industrial town of Valencia is 100 km west of Caracas. The basin, which is only 450 m above sea-level, receives plenty of rain and is one of the most important agricultural areas in the country.

Maracay → *Phone code: 0243. Colour map 1, A6. Population: 1.2 million. Altitude: 445 m.*

In its heyday Maracay was the favourite city of Gen Juan Vicente Gómez (dictator, 1909-1935) and some of his most fantastic whims are still there. **Jardín Las Delicias** (Avenida Las Delicias, en route to Choroni; take an Ocumare bus from terminal) with its beautiful zoological garden (closed Monday), park and fountain, built for his revels. The heart of the city is **Plaza Girardot**, on which stands the attractive, white **Cathedral**, dating back almost to the city's foundation in 1701. There is an interesting collection of prehispanic artefacts in the museum of the **Museo de Antropología e Historia** ⓘ *south side of the plaza, T247 2521, Tue-Sun 0800-1200, 1400-1800, free.* The opposite end of the same building has rooms dedicated to Gómez and Bolívar. **Plaza Bolívar**, said to be the largest such-named plaza in Latin America, is 500 m east. The **Museo Aeronáutico de las Fuerzas Aéreas Venezolanas** ⓘ *Av Las Delicias con Av 19 de Abril, 1 block from Plaza Bolívar, T233 3812, Sat-Sun 0900-1700,* has an interesting collection of aircraft and memorabilia. The **San José festival** is on 16-25 March. Tourist office for the state, **Iatur** ⓘ *Hotel Golf Maracay, Urb Las Delicias, Final Urb Canturrana, T242 2284; municipal website www.uragua.gob.ve.*

Parque Nacional Henri Pittier

Parque Nacional Henri Pittier

A land of steep, lush, rugged hills and tumbling mountain streams, the 107,800-ha park, rises from sea-level in the north to 2430 m at Pico Cenizo, descending to 450 m towards the Lago de Valencia. Named after Swiss conservationist and engineer Henri Pittier, the park was established in 1937 and is the oldest in the country. Estimates of bird species range from 20 to 50 (about 42% of all species in Venezuela), including seven different eagles and eight kites. The park extends from the north of Maracay to the Caribbean and south to the valleys of Aragua. The dry season is December-March and the rainy season (although still agreeable) is April-November. The variation in altitude gives a great range of vegetation, including impressive lower and upper cloud forests and bamboo.

Two paved roads cut through the Park. The Ocumare (western) road climbs to the 1128-m-high Portachuelo pass, guarded by twin peaks (38 km from Maracay). At the pass is Rancho Grande, the uncompleted palace/hotel Gómez was building when he died (in a state of disrepair). It is close to the bird migratory routes, September and October are the best months. There are many trails in the vicinity. Permits to visit the park, walk the trails near the **Estación Biológica Alberto F Yépez at Rancho Grande** ⓘ *bioestacion@gmail.com*, or stay at the station are available from the admin offices at the Facultad de Agronomía, Universidad Central de Venezuela, Maracay campus.

Aragua Coast

To Cata and Cuyagua The road to the coast from Rancho Grande goes through **Ocumare de la Costa** (*Population: 10,405, 48 km from Maracay*), to La Boca de Ocumare and **El Playón** (hotels and restaurants at both places). The road is very busy at weekends. Some 20 minutes west by boat is **La Ciénaga**, a pretty place, but little shade. A few kilometres east is **Bahía de Cata**, now overdeveloped, particularly at the west end, while the smaller beach at **Catita** is reached by fishing boat ferries (10 minutes, US$0.50), or a 20-minute walk, tricky over rocks at the start. In Cata town (5 km inland) is the small colonial church of San Francisco; devil dancers here fulfil an ancient vow by dancing non-stop through the morning of 27 July each year. Cuyagua beach, unspoilt, is 23 km further on at the end of the road. Good surfing, dangerous rips for swimmers. Devil dancers here too, on movable date in July/August.

To Choroní The second twisty and narrow (eastern) road through the Parque Nacional Henri Pittier is spectacular and goes over a more easterly pass (1830 m), to **Santa Clara de Choroní**, a small colonial town with attractive, pastel single-storey houses. The **Fiesta de San Juan** on 31 May is worth seeing. Choroní is a good base for walking. There are many opportunities for exploring the unmarked trails, some originating in picturesque spots such as the river pools, 'pozos', of El Lajao (beware of the dangerous whirlpool), and Los Colores, 6 km above Choroní. Other recommended 'pozos' are La Virgen, 10 km from Choroní, and La Nevera, 11 km away.

Puerto Colombia and around → *Phone code: 0243. Colour map 1, A6.*

Just beyond Choroní is the popular fishing village of **Puerto Colombia**, a laid-back place with several narrow streets lined with colonial buildings. During high season, its small main bay attracts arts and crafts sellers. It is a good place to stay and spend a couple of days beach hopping with boat rides to different bays. Five minutes' walk across the river lies Puerto Colombia's main attraction; the dazzling long stretch of white beach, Playa Grande, lined with palm trees beneath mountains. There is a row of good fish restaurants at the beach entrance. At weekends drummers drum and dancers gyrate and the beach gets crowded with campers and families. At other times it's more peaceful, with brightly painted fishing boats in the river and frigate birds wheeling overhead. If swimming, beware the strong undertow. There are public showers at the entrance. Many fishing boats are for hire in the harbour, US$15 for a day trip. A very bumpy, 30-minute ride east goes to **Cepe**, another beautiful long beach with good swimming, popular with campers. Boats charge US$4 per person return, usually take six to

10 people. From the beach, there is a delightful 25-minute walk to **Pueblo de Cepe** through the Henri Pittier park. Several places on the beach serve fish, salad and *tostones*. Most locals bring their own supplies in the obligatory beer cooler. From the beautiful unspoiled beach there are fishing and scuba diving trips. The latter, with guide and equipment, explore the only bit of coral on this stretch of the coast. At Cepe's west end, you can climb the hill and descend to **Playa Escondida**, a deserted but more rocky beach. Other beaches include: to the east, before Cepe, Valle Seco (some shade, natural pool protected by reef) and **Chuao** (boat US$10 per person return to each). To the west are: Diario (small, no shade), Aroa (lovely, with river and palms, rough sea but one safe bathing area, no services, take everything with you, three hours' hike from Choroní, go early) and Uricao (also isolated); boat to Uricao US$12 per person return.

◉ Maracay and around listings

For hotel and restaurant price codes, and other relevant information, see Essentials.

● Where to stay

Maracay p1511
Budget hotels are in streets around Plaza Girardot.
$$-$ Princesa Plaza, Av Miranda Este entre Fuerzas Aéreas y Av Bermúdez, T232 0177, www.hotelprincesaplaza.com.ve. Large commercial hotel, 1 block east of Plaza Bolívar, convenient, inexpensive restaurant.
$ Caroní, Ayacucho Norte 197, Bolívar, T554 4465. Hot showers, comfortable, cheap. Recommended.
$ Mar del Plata, Av Santos Michelena 23, T246 4313, mardelplatahotel@gmail.com. Central, with hot water, excellent.
$ Posada El Limón, C El Piñal 64, El Limón suburb, near Parque Nacional Henri Pittier, T283 4925, www.posadaellimon.com. Dutch owned, some way from centre, Caracas airport transfers in good car with English-speaking driver, relaxed and pleasant, family atmosphere, spacious rooms, dorm, laundry, pool, good restaurant, parking, trips to Parque with guide.

Aragua Coast p1512
Ocumare de la Costa
$$ De La Costa Eco-Lodge, California 23, T993 1986, www.ecovenezuela.com. Comfortable, upmarket lodge near beach, with outdoor bar serving food, restaurant, roof terraces with good sea views, pool, landscaped gardens, excursions, equipment hire, specialist bilingual guides. Includes breakfast.
Most *posadas* are in El Playón and websites like www.turismodeplaya.com give a selection.

Expect to pay **$$-$**. Recommendations change annually, but see **Posada Angel**, www.posadaangelencostadeoro.blogspot.com, or **Posada La Estancia**, www.posadalaestancia.com.

La Ciénaga
$$$ pp all-inclusive **Coral Lagoon Lodge**, La Ciénaga, T217 7966, www.ecovenezuela.com. A dive resort accessible only by boat. Beautiful location on waterfront with view of mountains. 6 rooms in 2 cabins sleeping 2-4 people, fans, solar power with back-up generator, rainwater and seawater used. Hammocks, deckchairs, kayaks and snorkelling. Diving with PADI and SSI instructors to underwater grottos, canyons, reefs and wrecks.

Choroní
See www.choroni.info for listings and locations of many hotels and *posadas*.
$$ Hacienda El Portete, C El Cementerio, T991 1255, www.elportechoroni.com. Restored cocoa plantation, colonial-style large grounds, pool, restaurant, many children's facilities, excursions.
$$ Hacienda La Aljorra, 1 km south in La Loma, T218 8841, laaljorra@hotmail.com. On roadside, out of town, **$$** on weekdays, breakfast included, hot water, 300-year old cacao hacienda in 62 ha of wooded hillside. Large rooms, relaxing and peaceful.
$ Posada Colonial El Picure, C Miranda No 34-A, T991 1296, www.hosteltrail.com/posadaelpicure. Colonial house in village centre, backs onto river. Popular with travellers, welcoming, 4 dorms and a private room, restaurant with vegetarian options.

Puerto Colombia and around *p1512*
There are dozens of *posadas* for all budgets in town, but most are fully booked during high season when prices rise by around 40%.

$$ Hostal Casa Grande 1, Morillo 33, T991 1251, www.hostalcasagrande.net. One of the best in town, attractive colonial decor, pool, gardens, parking, spa at weekends. Excellent. Also has newer **Casa Grande 2**, same street, with restaurant.

$ Casa Luna, next to Hostal Colonial, Morillo 35, no obvious sign, T951 5318, www.jungletrip. de. Colonial house, 4 basic rooms and 1 dorm, fan, shared bath, German and English spoken, tourist information. Ask here for **Casa Nova** and **Posada Alfonso**, both **$$-$**, most rooms with bath. Tours to Pittier park, diving trips and airport transfers.

$ Costa Brava, Murillo 9, near Malecón, T991 1057, suarezjf@cantv.net. Cheaper in low season. Basic, cheaper without bath, fans, laundry, good food, parking, English spoken, family run. Recommended.

$ Hostal Vista Mar, C Colón at western end, T991 1250, http://hostalvistamar.net. On seafront, pleasant, terraces with hammocks, some rooms with sea view, some with a/c, helpful, secure parking.

$ La Posada de Choroní, Calle Principal, 2 blocks from Malecón, T991 1191, www. laposadadechoroni.3a2.com. Rooms are cheaper without TV and in low season, hot water, colonial with rooms off central garden, parking.

$ Posada Alonso, near checkpoint, T0416-546 1412, alons0243@hotmail.com. Quiet, hammocks, laundry. Recommended.

$ Posada Doña Enriqueta, Color 3, T991 1158, just off the seafront, www.hosteltrail.com/posadadonaenriqueta. Basic rooms, books tours, helpful, 40% discount Mon-Thu.

$ Posada Pittier, on road to Choroní, 10-min walk from Puerto Colombia, T991 1028, www.posadapittier.com. Small, immaculate rooms, more expensive at weekends, cheaper without breakfast, good meals, helpful, garden. Recommended.

$ Posada Turpial, José Maitin 3, T991 1123, www.posadaturpial.com. Colonial house, well-organized, cosy, attractive, nice atmosphere, good restaurant, rooms around patio, safety deposit box, German and English spoken. Book

in advance. Owners run travel agency www. turpialtravel.com and organize local tours, dive trips. Recommended.

$ Hostal Colonial, on Morillo, opposite bus stop, T431 8757, http://choroni.net. Popular hostel, good value, with fan, laundry, German owner. Also good tours in the Pittier park.

Camping is possible on Playa Grande, no permission needed and showers on beach; beware of theft. Crowded during high season.

Cepe and Chuao
Several *posadas* in Chuao, but some distance from the beach (those listed are closer). Camping is permitted on Chuao and Cepe beaches.

$ El Gran Cacao, 200 m up the hill from the port at Chuao, T872 4680. Comfortable, with a/c or fan. Recommended.

$ La Luzonera, on the plaza, T242 1284, posadaluzonera@yahoo.com. The best of the cheaper options, with restaurant (**$$** half board), also has 2 houses for rent.

$ La Terraza del Morocho, Av Principal Las Tejerías 44, Chuao, T0414-450 3341. Helpful, ask about guides for excursions.

🍴 Restaurants

Maracay *p1511*
Many excellent restaurants in the Av Las Delicias area and a variety of cheap restaurants in streets around Plazas Girardot and Bolívar.

Puerto Colombia *p1512*
Several places in town serve fish and seafood.
$$-$ Mango, Trino Rangel. Informal setting in patio, delicious catch of the day, pastas, vege- tarian options, generous portions. Recommended.

$$-$ Willy, Vía Playa Grande 1, just after bridge along the river. Very popular, good seafood and meat dishes. In low season only opens Fri-Sun.

🎯 What to do

Puerto Colombia *p1512*
Jungle Trip Choroní, see Casa Luna, Where to stay, above. Good trips in the national park.
Posada Puerto Escondido, Cepe, T241 2114, www.puertoescondido.com.ve. Offers a variety of courses and trips to a variety of dive sites.

Transport

Maracay p1511

Bus The bus station is 2 km southeast of the centre, taxi US$1.50. It has two sections, Terminal Oriente for long distance and Terminal Nacional for regional buses. *Por puesto* marked 'Terminal' for the bus station and 'Centro' for the centre (Plaza Girardot). To **Maracaibo**, AeroExpresos, US$7. To **Valencia**, US$1.50, 1 hr, and **Caracas**, US$2-3 by *autobus*, 5 daily, US$4 by *microbus*, 1½-2 hrs. **Mérida** US$7, 12 hrs; Ciudad Bolívar, US$7, 10 hrs. To **Coro**, US$6, 7¾ hrs.

Parque Nacional Henri Pittier p1512, map 1511

Bus Depart from Maracay Terminal; pay full fare to **Ocumare** or hitch from the alcabala at El Limón.

Aragua Coast p1512
El Playón
Bus From **Maracay**, 2-2½ hrs, US$1.25. To **Cata** from El Playón US$0.50 from plaza, from Ocumare de la Costa US$1.

Choroní

Bus There is a single, new bus station between Choroní and Puerto Colombia, serving both. **Maracay-Choroní**, beautiful journey Henri Pittier park, every 2 hrs from 0630-1700, more at the weekend, US$1.25, 2½-3 hrs. Road congested at holidays and weekends.

Puerto Colombia p1512

Bus From **Maracay** terminal leave from platform 5. Buses to Maracay depart every hour from 0500 till 1700, US$4.50, 2-3 hrs. **Taxi** From **Maracay** US$5 pp, 1-1½ hrs.

Directory

Puerto Colombia p1512

Banks The nearest banks are in Maracay (also **Italcambio** (Amex), Av Aragua con C Bermúdez, C C Maracay Plaza, p 1, loc 110K, T234 9778, Mon-Fri 0800-1700, Sat 0900-1300). There are no ATMs in Choroní or Puerto Colombia and credit cards are accepted by very few places. Take enough cash.

Valencia and around

Founded in 1555, Valencia is the capital of Carabobo State and Venezuela's third largest city. It's the centre of its most developed agricultural region and the most industrialized. Near the city are several groups of petroglyphs while the coast has some very popular beach areas. Best known of these is the Morrocoy national park, but you have to seek out the quiet spots.

Valencia → *Phone code: 0241. Colour map 1, A5. Population: over 2 million. Altitude: 480 m.*
A road through low hills thickly planted with citrus, coffee and sugar runs 50 km west from Maracay to the valley in which Valencia lies. It is hot and humid with annual rainfall of 914 mm. Like its Spanish namesake, Valencia is famous for its oranges.

The **Cathedral**, first built in 1580, is on the east side of **Plaza Bolívar**. The statue of the Virgen del Socorro (1550) in the left transept is the most valued treasure; on the second Sunday in November (during the Valencia Fair) it is paraded with a richly jewelled crown. The city's handsome **Plaza de Toros** ① *south end of Av Constitución beyond the ring road* is the second largest in Latin America after Mexico City (it is also used for shows). The magnificent former **residence of General Páez** ① *Páez y Boyacá, open Tue-Sun at 0900, closed for lunch Tue-Fri and at 1400 Sat-Sun, free*, is now a museum. Páez was the hero of the **Carabobo** battle, the site of which is 30 km southwest of Valencia on the highway to San Carlos (bus from Avenida Bolívar Sur y Calle 75 or Avenida 5 de Julio). The monument surrounded by splendid gardens and the view over the field from the *mirador* where the Liberator directed the battle in 1814 is impressive. Other attractive buildings are the **Casa de los Celis** (1766) ① *Av Soublette y C Comercio, T617 6867, Tue-Sun 0900-1600*, a well-restored colonial house and National Monument which also houses the **Museo de Arte e Historia**, and the **Casa Estrella** (1766) ① *Av Soublette y C Colombia, Tue-Fri 0900-1700, Sat-Sun from 1000*, now a historical museum and cultural centre.

Around Valencia

Most important of the region's petroglyphs can be found at the **Parque Arqueológico Piedra Pintada** (part of Parque Nacional San Esteban), where lines of prehispanic stone slabs, many bearing swirling glyphs, march up the ridges of Cerro Pintado. At the foot of Cerro Las Rosas is the **Museo Parque Arqueológico Piedra Pintada** ① *Sector Tronconero, vía Vigirmia, Guacara, T041-571 596, Tue-Sun 0800-1700, free*, has 165 examples of rock art and menhirs (tours, parking, café).

Other extensive ancient petroglyphs have been discovered at **La Taimata** near Güigüe, 34 km east of Valencia on the lake's southern shore. There are more sites on rocks by the Río Chirgua, reached by a 10 km paved road from Highway 11, 50 km west of Valencia. About 5 km past Chirgua, at the **Hacienda Cariaprima**, is a remarkable 35-m-tall geoglyph, a humanoid figure carved into a steep mountain slope at the head of the valley.

Coast north of Valencia

Puerto Cabello (*Colour map 1, A5, Phone code: 0242, Population: 185,000*), 55 km from Valencia, was one of the most important ports in the colonial Americas, from which produce was transported to the Dutch possessions. Puerto Cabello has retained its maritime importance and is Venezuela's key port. Plaza Bolívar and the colonial part of town are by the waterfront promenade at Calle 24 de Julio.

To the east is **Bahía de Patanemo**, a beautiful, tranquil horseshoe-shaped beach shaded by palms. It has three main sectors, Santa Rita, Los Caneyes and Patanemo itself, with the village proper, further from the beach than the other two. All three have lodging, but it may be difficult to find meals midweek (try at *posadas*). Offshore is the lovely **Isla Larga** (no shade or facilities), best reached by boat from Quizandal, US$2, 15 minutes. There are several cafés along the beachfront. Nearby are two sunken wrecks that attract divers. From Puerto Cabello, take a *por puesto* from the terminal, 20 minutes, US$0.50, a taxi US$2.

Parque Nacional Morrocoy → *Colour map 1, A5.*

Palm-studded islets and larger islands (*cayos*) with secluded beaches make up Parque Nacional Morrocoy. The largest and most popular of the islands within the park is **Cayo Sombrero**, with two over-priced fish restaurants. No alcohol is sold on this or other islands; be aware of hidden extra costs and take your own supplies. It is very busy at weekends and during holidays and is generally dirty and noisy. But there are some deserted beaches, with trees on which to sling a hammock. For peace and quiet, take boats to the farthest cayos. **Playuela** is beautiful and is considered to have one of the nicest beaches of all. It has a small restaurant at weekends and there's a nice walk to Playuelita. **Boca Seca** is also pleasant, with shade and calm water suitable for children, but it can be windy. **Cayo Borracho**, one of the nicest islands, has become a turtle-nesting reserve, closed to visitors. **Playa Azul**, a nice small cayo, has shallow water. The water at **Pescadores** is very shallow. **Los Muertos** has two beaches with shade, mangroves and palms. **Mero**'s beach is beautiful, with palms, but is windy. With appropriate footwear it is possible to walk between some of the islands. Calm waters here are ideal for waterskiing while scuba diving is best suited to beginners. Only by diving to deeper waters will you see coral, although in all locations there are still fish to watch. Take insect repellent against *puri puri* (tiny, vicious mosquitoes) and flies.

Adjoining the park to the north is a vast nesting area for scarlet ibis, flamingos and herons, the **Cuare Wildlife Sanctuary**, a Ramsar site. Most of the flamingos are in and around the estuary next to Chichiriviche, which is too shallow for boats but you can walk there or take a taxi. Birds are best watched early morning or late afternoon.

Tucacas and Chichiriviche → *Phone code: 0259. Colour map 1, A5*

Tucacas is a hot, busy, dirty town, where bananas and other fruit are loaded for Curaçao and Aruba. Popular and expensive as a beach resort, it has garish high-rise blocks and casinos. A few kilometres beyond Tucacas, towards Coro, is **Chichiriviche** (*Population: 7000*), smaller, more relaxed, but lined with tacky shops, also dirty and not that attractive. Both provide access to Parque Nacional Morrocoy, each town serving separate *cayos*, but only as far as Cayo Sombrero. Apart from this and the diving options, few have a good word to say about Tucacas or Chichiriviche.

⊙ Valencia and around listings

For hotel and restaurant price codes, and other relevant information, see Essentials.

⊙ Where to stay

Valencia *p1515*
There are several business hotels, also ones for all budgets along the very long Av Bolívar
$$ Dinastía, Av Urdaneteo y Av Cedeño, T858 8139, www.dinastiahotel.com. Central, just off Av Bolívar, all services, restaurant.
$ Marconi, Av Bolívar 141-65, T823 4843. Small, modern hotel, simple rooms, helpful, safe, laundry, recommended, take bus or colectivo from bus station to stop after 'El Elevado' bridge.

Coast north of Valencia *p1516*
At **Patanemo** there are hotels and *posadas* in the village (eg **Chachita** C Bolívar 99, T302 3068, and María Lucía, T421 1191).
$$-$ Posada Edén, Final Av Principal Los Caneyes, T0416 442 4955. The best *posada* in the region, small, comfortable, hot water, restaurant and pool.
$$-$ Posada Santa Margarita, Bolívar 4-36, Puerto Cabello, T361 4112, www.posadasantamargarita.com.ve. Converted colonial house in historic district, 2 blocks from waterfront promenade, day trips, attractive rooms, cheaper with fan, roof terrace, restaurant, small pool. Book in advance.
$ Posada Natal Mar, at entrance to Caneyes sector, 100 m from turn-off to Bahía de Patanemo, T0412-536 7961. Small but clean rooms, but no windows, restaurant upstairs.

Parque Nacional Morrocoy *p1516*
Camping is allowed at **Cayo Paiclá** and **Cayo Sol** but not year round and you must first make a reservation with **Inparques** (National Parks), Av Libertador, Tucacas, T812 0053 (Falcón office: Intercomunal Coro-La Vela, sector Sabana Larga, Jardín Botánico Dr León Croizat, Coro, Estado Falcón, T0268-277 8582); reserve at least 8 working days in advance; US$2.35 per night, 7 nights max, pay in full in advance (very complicated procedure). Very few facilities and no fresh water at **Paiclá. Playa Azul** and **Paiclá** have ecological toilets. At weekends and holidays it is very crowded and litter-strewn (beware rats).
$$$-$$$ pp Villa Mangrovia on Lizardo Spit between Tucacas and Chichiriviche, T0259-889 1299, posadamangrovia@yahoo.es. One of few places in the park itself. 6 rooms, superb food and service, charming owner, good birdwatching. Book via **Last Frontiers**, in UK, T01296-653000.

Tucacas *p1516*
Chichiriviche has a wider choice of budget places. Most hotels and restaurants in Tucacas are on the long Av Libertador, the main street.
$$ Aparto Posada del Mar, Av Silva, T812 0524, www.apartoposadadelmar.com. Variety of rooms with a/c, pool, restaurant, Wi-Fi, private jetty and windsurfing centre.
$ Manaure, Av Silva (opposite Posada del Mar), T812 1011/818 6121, www.paradormanaure.com. Modern, low-rise hotel, a/c, hot water, pool, good.
$ Posada Amigos del Mar, C Nueva, near bus stop, beyond Hospital Viejo, T812 3962. Organizes trips to cayos and diving, use of kitchen, with fan.

Chichiriviche *p1516*
There are plenty of reasonably priced *posadas*, eg **Casa Manantial**, Playa Sur, 50 m from beach, T818 6248, www.posadacasamanantial.com.ve (**$**), **La Riviera**, Playa Norte, T815 0369, www.posadalariviera.com, and **Morokkue**, Playa Norte, T818 6492, www.morokkue.com.ve (**$**).
$ Morena's Place, Sector Playa Norte, 10 mins walk from bus stop, T815 0936, posadamorenas@hotmail.com. Beautifully decorated house, fan, hammocks, helpful hosts, English spoken.

$ Posada Alemania, Av Cuare, T881 1283, www.karibik-pur-venezuela.de. German-run, runs tours, rents snorkel gear, 200 m from Playa Sur, nice garden.

$ Posada El Profe, 2 Calle Playa Norte, T416 1166, www.posadaelprofe.com. Welcoming B&B, several languages spoken, tours and information, contact Aminta in advance for best deals.

$ Posada Sol, Mar y Arena, Mariño y Partida, T815 0306, solmaryarena@cantv.net. Small rooms, welcoming, upstairs terrace with a grill, 1 block from sea, tours and all-inclusive packages offered.

$ Posada Villa Gregoria, C Mariño y R Yáñez, 1 block north of bus stop behind the large water tank, T818 6359, www.villagregoriaresort.webs. com. Spanish-run, helpful, relaxing, good value, fan or a/c, laundry, small rooms, hammocks, garden, secure parking. Tours, English spoken.

⏻ What to do

Tucacas *p1516*
Diving
Frogman Dive Center, CC Bolívar, Plaza Bolívar, T0414-340 1824, www.frogmandive. com. Introductory, Open Water and Advanced courses, dive trips to Morrocoy, shop.
Submatur, C Ayacucho 6, near Plaza Bolívar, T812 0082, morrocoysubmatur1@cantv.net. Experienced owner, runs 4-day PADI courses and day trips with 2 dives; also rents rooms, **$**, fan and kitchen.

⊖ Transport

Valencia *p1515*
Air The airport is 6 km southeast of centre. Taxi airport-bus terminal US$5. Daily flights to **Maracaibo**, **Porlamar**, **Caracas**, **Puerto Ordaz** and other cities (often via Caracas). Dutch Antilles Express, www.flydae.com, flies to **Curaçao** 6 days a week.
Bus Terminal is 4 km east of centre, part of shopping mall **Big-Low** (24-hr restaurants). Entry to platforms by *ficha* (token), US$1. Left luggage. Minibus to centre, frequent and cheap, but slow and confusing route at peak times; taxi from bus station to centre, US$5 (official

drivers wear ID badges). To **Caracas**, frequent buses with **Aeroexpresos Ejecutivos** and others, 2½ hrs, US$3-4. Likewise to **Maracaibo**, US$5-7, 8 hrs. **Mérida**, 10-12 hrs, US$8. **Puerto Cabello**, US$0.80, 1 hr. To **Coro**, US$6, 4½ hrs. To **Ciudad Bolívar**, US$8, 10 hrs.

Around Valencia *p1516*
Parque Arqueológico Piedra Pintada
Bus To **Vigírima** 20 km northeast of Valencia at regular intervals (US$0.50), ask to get off at the 'Cerro Pintado' turn-off.

Parque Nacional Morrocoy *p1516*
Ferry From **Tucacas**: prices per boat from US$10 return to **Paiclá** to US$25 return to **Cayo Sombrero** (max 7 per boat). The ticket office is on the left of the car entrance to the Park. Boats to Boca Seca and Playuelita only leave from Tucacas. **From Chichiriviche**: tickets are per boat and vary according to distance, around US$10-25. Prices are set for each cayo and there are long and short trips. There are 2 ports: one in the centre, one at Playa Sur. Ask for the ticket system to fix the price and to ensure you're picked up on time for return trip.

Tucacas *p1516*
Bus Frequent *por puesto* from **Valencia**, US$2.30, bus US$1. To **Coro**, US$3, 3 hrs.

Chichiriviche *p1516*
Bus To **Coro**, take a bus from the station on Av Zamora to **Sanare**, US$0.50, every 20 mins, then another to Coro, US$2, 3 hrs. Direct buses from **Valencia**.

ⓘ Directory

Valencia *p1515*
Banks Italcambio, Av Bolívar Norte, Edif Talia, loc 2, T822 7777. Amex travel services, Visa TCs, a long way north of centre in Urbanización Los Sauces, get off bus at junction with C 132; also at airport, Mon-Fri 0800-1700, Sat morning only and CCs Metrópolis and Sambil Valencia.

Tucacas *p1516*
Banks Banesco offers a facility of cash advances on credit cards.

Coro and around

The relaxed colonial city of Coro, with its sand-dune surroundings, sits at the foot of the arid, windswept Paranaguá Peninsula. Inland from Coro, the Sierra de San Luis is good walking country in fresher surroundings.

Coro → Phone code: 0268. Colour map 1, A5. Population: 244,340. Mean temperature: 28°C.

Coro, the capital of the Falcón state and former capital of the country, is a UNESCO World Heritage Site. Founded in 1527, it became an important religious centre for Christians and Jews alike. The city, 177 km from Tucacas, is relatively clean and well-kept and its small colonial part has several shaded plazas and beautiful buildings, many of which date from the 18th century. Recently, efforts have been made to preserve and restore its colonial heritage. In the rainy season the centre may flood. **Corfaltur tourist office** ⓘ *Paseo Alameda entre Falcón y Palmasola, T253 0260, http://corfaltur.blogspot.co.uk*, English spoken, helpful. **State tourist office Fondo Mixto de Turismo** ⓘ *C Bolívar, CC Don Salim, of 3 y 4, T251 3698.*

The **Cathedral**, a National Monument, was begun in 1583. **San Clemente church** ⓘ *Mass Mon-Sat 1930*, has a wooden cross in the plaza in front, which is said to mark the site of the first Mass said in Venezuela; it is believed to be the country's oldest such monument. There are several interesting colonial houses, such as **Los Arcaya** ⓘ *Zamora y Federación*, one of the best examples of 18th-century architecture, with the **Museo de Cerámica**, small but interesting, with a beautiful garden. **Los Senior** ⓘ *Talavera y Hernández*, where Bolívar stayed in 1827, houses the **Museo de Arte de Coro** ⓘ *T251 5265, www.fmn.gob.ve/ fmn_coro.htm, Mon-Sat 0900-1900, Sun 0900-1700, free*, exhibiting some interesting modern artwork. Opposite is the **Museo Alberto Henríquez** ⓘ *T252 5299*, which has the oldest synagogue in Venezuela (1853), if not South America. Built 1764-1765, **Las Ventanas de Hierro** ⓘ *Zamora y Colón, Tue-Sat 0900-1200, 1500-1800, Sun 0900-1300, US$0.20*, is now the **Museo de Tradición Familiar**. Just beyond is the **Casa del Tesoro** (or del Obispo) ⓘ *C Zamora, T252 8701, free*, an art gallery showing local artists' work. There are other handicraft galleries in the centre, such as **Centro Artesanal Generalísimo Francisco de Miranda** ⓘ *C Zamora, near Plaza San Clemente*. The **Jewish cemetery** ⓘ *C 23 de*

Coro

Where to stay 🛏
1 El Gallo
2 Intercaribe
3 Miranda Cumberland
4 Posada Casa Tun Tun
5 Posada Don Antonio
6 Posada La Casa de los Pájaros
7 Villa Antigua

Restaurants 🍴
1 Barra del Jacal
4 Mersi
5 Panadería Costa Nova

Enero esq C Zamora, visit by prior arrangement only, enquire at the Museo Alberto Henríquez or your hotel, is the oldest on the continent, founded by Jews who arrived from Curaçao in the early 19th century. It has suffered rain damage and is being restored.

The **Museo de Coro 'Lucas Guillermo Castillo'** ① *C Zamora by San Francisco, T251 5645, Tue-Sat 0900-1230, 1500-1830, Sun 0900-1400, reopened after repair in late 2013*, is in an old monastery, and has a good collection of church relics.

Coro is surrounded by sand dunes, **Los Médanos de Coro**, which form an impressive **national park** ① *0800-1700, www.losmedanos.com; outside town on the main road to Punto Fijo: take bus marked 'Carabobo' from C35 Falcón y Av Miranda, or up Av Los Médanos and get off at the end, just after Plaza Concordia, from there walk 500 m to entrance, or take a taxi*. The place is guarded by police and is generally safe, but stay close to the entrance and on no account wander off across the dunes. Kiosk at entrance sells drinks and snacks.

The historic part of the town's port, **La Vela de Coro** (population: 40,000), is included in the UNESCO World Heritage Site, with some impressive colonial buildings, lovely sea front, wooden traditional fishing boats and historic church. It has an unmistakable Caribbean feel, but it is in urgent need of facelift (taxi from Coro US$4). On the road to La Vela, near the turning, is the interesting **Jardín Botánico Xerofito Dr León Croizat** ① *Sector Sabana Larga, T277 8451, drfalcon@inparques.gov.ve, Tue-Fri 0800-1200, 1300-1600, Sat and Sun 0900-1700, free, getting there: take Vela bus from corner of C Falcón, opposite Banco Coro, and ask to be let off at Pasarela del Jardín Botánico – the bridge over the road*. It is backed by UNESCO and has plants from Africa, Australia, etc. Tours in Spanish.

Paraguaná Peninsula → *Phone code: 0269. Colour map 1, A5. Population: 210,000.*

Punto Fijo and around This area is a must for windsurfers and is a great place for walking and flamingo spotting. The western side of the peninsula is industrialized, with oil refineries at Cardón and Amuay connected by pipeline to the Lago de Maracaibo oilfields. The main town is **Punto Fijo**, a busy, unappealing place, whose duty-free zone attracts shoppers with cheap electrical goods and alcohol. It has a range of hotels and *posadas*, but the residential area of **Judibana**, about 5 km away, is better, with shopping centre, cinema and restaurants.

Adícora A quiet if run-down little resort on the east side of the peninsula. The beaches are very windswept and not great but they are popular with wind- and kite-surfers. There are three windsurfing schools in town. Adícora is also a good base for exploring the beautiful, barren and wild peninsula where goats and wild donkeys roam.

Cerro Santa Ana (830 m) is the only hill on the peninsula and commands spectacular views. The entrance is at El Moruy; take bus to Pueblo Nuevo (0730-0800), then take one to Punto Fijo and ask to be dropped off at the entrance to Santa Ana. From the plaza walk back to the signpost for Pueblo Nuevo and take the dirt road going past a white building; 20 m to the left is **Restaurant La Hija**. Walk 1 km through scrubby vegetation (watch out for dogs) to the **Inparques** office (closed Monday to Friday but busy at weekends). Register here before attempting the steep three-hour climb. It's safer to go on Saturday or Sunday. Some *posadas* in Coro arrange trips to the Peninsula.

Laguna Boca de Caño (also called Laguna Tiraya) is a nature reserve north of Adícora, inland from Supi, along a dirt track that is usually fit for all vehicles. There is abundant bird life, particularly flamingos. It is the only mangrove zone on the east of the peninsula.

Sierra de San Luis

South of Coro, on the road to Barquisimeto, the Sierra, includes the **Parque Nacional Juan C Falcón**, with tropical forest, caves and waterfalls. Visit it from the picturesque village of **Curimagua**; jeeps leave from Coro terminal, US$2.25, one hour. The lovely colonial town of **Cabure** is the capital of the Sierra. Jeeps leave from Coro terminal, 58 km, 1¼ hours, US$2.25. As well as hotels, Cabure has restaurants, bars, a bakery, supermarket and pharmacy. A few kilometres up the road is a series of beautiful waterfalls, called the Cataratas de Hueque. **The Spanish Road** is a fantastic three-hour walk through orange groves and tropical forest from Curimagua to Cabure. You will see many butterflies along the way. The path is not well marked, so it is best to hire a guide. Take water. It's very muddy in rains; take insect repellent and good shoes and be prepared to get wet. Ask at any of the hotels listed below. To walk the Spanish Road from Coro in one day, take transport to Cabure, ask to be dropped at the turn-off for the **Posada El Duende** (see below) and walk uphill 1 km to the Posada, where you begin the trek. The path eventually comes out to the Curimagua-Coro paved road, where you can take transport back to Coro.

✪ Coro and around listings

For hotel and restaurant price codes, and other relevant information, see Essentials.

● Where to stay

Coro *p1519, map p1519*
Coro has several excellent *posadas* catering for travellers; book well in advance, especially in Dec.

$ El Gallo, Federación 26, T252 9481, www. hosteltrail.com/posadaelgallo. In colonial part, French/ Venezuelan owned, relaxed, spacious, shared baths, courtyard with hammocks, dorms and private rooms, some English spoken, sandboarding, see Eric for tours to Sierra San Luis, a 1-day tour includes lunch.

$ Intercaribe, Av Manaure entre Zamora y Urdaneta, T251 1811, http://hotelintercaribe. jimdo.com. Bland, modern, pool, a/c, small rooms.

$ Miranda Cumberland, Av Joseta Camejo, opposite old airport, T252 2111, www.hotel escumberland.com. Large modern hotel, good value, restaurant, good pool area, travel agency.

$ Posada Casa Tun Tun, Zamora 92, entre Toledo y Hernández, T404 4260, http://casa tuntun.vefblog.net. Run by knowledgeable and welcoming Belgian couple. Restored colonial house with 3 attractive patios, kitchen facilities, laundry, relaxing hammock areas and dipping pool, dorms and rooms with and without bath and lovely decor. Good value, nice atmosphere, free morning coffee, changes US$. Highly recommended.

$ Posada Don Antonio, Paseo Talavera 11, T253 9578. Central, small rooms, parking.

$ Posada La Casa de los Pájaros, Monzón 74 entre Ampies y Comercio, T252 8215. Colonial house 6 blocks from centre, restored by the owners with local art and antiques, rooms with and without bath, hammock space, meals available, use of kitchen for small fee, laundry service, trips to local sights. Recommended.

$ Villa Antigua, C 50 Comercio 46, 1252 7499/0414-682 2924. Colonial style, fountain in courtyard, restaurant.

Camping About 30 km east of Coro at La Cumara, nice, good beach and dunes.

Adícora *p1520*
$$$-$$ Archie's Surf Posada, Playa Sur, T988 8285, www.kitesurfing venezuela.com. At entrance to Adícora, 5 mins' walk to centre. German-run, well established, organizes wind and kite surfing lessons. Also trips, horse riding and airport pick-ups. Furnished bungalows for 4-12, apartments for 2-4, hammocks. Prices in Euros/dollars. Good reports.

$ Hacienda La Pancha, Vía Pueblo Nuevo, 5 km from Adícora in the hills, T0414-969 2649, www.haciendalapancha.tripod.com. Beautiful, old, colonial-style house set in countryside, nice owners, restaurant, pool, no children.

$ Posada La Casa Rosada, C Comercio de Adícora, on Malecón, T988 8004, www.posadala casarosada.com. Pleasant, cosy, rooms for 2-8 people, garden and hammocks, breakfast extra, good restaurant. Recommended.

Sierra de San Luis *p1520*
Curimagua
$ Finca El Monte, Vía La Soledad, 5 km from the village, T404 0564, www.hosteltrail.com/ fincaelmonte/. Run by a Swiss couple on an eco-friendly basis. Peaceful, beautiful views, colonial style, hot water, meals, hammocks. Tours round the park include birdwatching and cave tours. English, German and French spoken. Highly recommended.

Cabure

In town are several budget options.

$ Hotel El Duende, 20 mins uphill from village, T0416-225 6491. A beautiful 19th-century *posada* and garden, price depends on size of room, fan, cold water, good restaurant, horse riding, walking, peaceful. Recommended.

🍴 Restaurants

Coro *p1519, map p1519*

$ Barra del Jacal, Av Manaure y C 29 Unión. Outdoors, pizza and pasta.

$ Mersi, C 56 Toledo y Zamora. Good pizzas and *empanadas*.

Cafés

Panadería Costa Nova, Av Manaure, opposite Hotel Intercaribe. Good bread, sandwiches and pastries, open late.

🎉 Festivals

Coro *p1519, map p1519*

26 Jul, Coro Week. **Oct**, Cine en la Calle, programme of open-air films on Paseo Talavera. **Nov-Dec**, Tambor Coriano in many places. **28 Dec** Los Locos de La Vela (La Vela).

⚙ What to do

Coro *p1519, map p1519*

Contact *posadas* in town for tours, eg La Casa de los Párajos.

🚌 Transport

Coro *p1519, map p1519*

Air Airport open for domestic flights; see also Las Piedras, below, for flights.

Bus Terminal is on Av Los Médanos, entre Maparari y Libertad, buses go up C 35 Falcón, US$0.15, taxi US$1.20. To/from **Caracas** US$5, 6-8 hrs; **Maracaibo**, US$3.50, 4 hrs, *por puesto* US$5; **Tucacas**, every 20 mins, US$3, 3-4 hrs; **Punto Fijo**, *por puesto* US$1.50.

Punto Fijo *p1520*

Air Airport at **Las Piedras**: *por puestos* from C Garcés y Av Bolívar (don't believe taxis who say there are no *por puestos* from airport to town); taxi from Punto Fijo US$2, from bus terminal US$1.50. Daily flights to **Curaçao** with **Insel Air**, www.fly-inselair.com.

Bus Terminal is in Carirubana district; *por puestos* to **Pueblo Nuevo**, **Adícora**, **Coro**, **Valencia** and **Maracaibo**. To **Maracay**, **Barquisimeto**, **Maracaibo** (US$4) and **Caracas** (US$6). Expresos Occidente has a terminal on C Comercio entre Ecuador y Bolivia.

Adícora *p1520*

Bus Several daily to and from **Coro**, from 0630-1700, US$1, 1 hr; to and from **Pueblo Nuevo** and **Punto Fijo**, several daily from 0600-1730.

ⓘ Directory

Punto Fijo *p1520*

Banks Many banks on Av Bolívar y Comercio accept Visa and Mastercard. Italcambio at the airport.

From Maracaibo to Colombia

To the heart of Venezuela's oil business on the shores of Lake Maracaibo: not many tourists find their way here. Those that do are usually on their way to Colombia via the border crossing on the Guajira Peninsula to the north. If you've got the time to stop and can handle the heat, Maracaibo is the only town in Venezuela where occasionally you'll see indigenous people in traditional dress going about their business and nearby are reminders of prehispanic and oil-free customs.

Maracaibo → *Phone code: 0261. Colour map 1, A4. Population: 2.1 million.*

Maracaibo, capital of the State of Zulia, is Venezuela's second largest city and oil capital. The region is the economic powerhouse of the country with over 50% of the nation's oil production coming from the Lago de Maracaibo area and Zulia state. The lake is reputedly the largest fresh water reserve in South America. A long cement and steel bridge, Puente General Rafael Urdaneta, crosses

Lago de Maracaibo, connecting the city with the rest of the country. Maracaibo is a sprawling modern city with wide streets. Some parts are pleasant to walk around, apart from the intense heat (or when it is flooded in the rainy season), but as in the rest of the country, security is becoming an issue. The hottest months are July to September, but there is usually a sea breeze from 1500 until morning. The **tourist office** is **Corzutur** ① *Av 18, esq C 78 (Dr Portillo), Edif Lieja, p 4, T783 4928.*

Places in Maracaibo The traditional city centre is **Plaza Bolívar**, on which stand the **Cathedral** (at east end), the **Casa de Gobierno**, the **Asamblea Legislativa** and the **Casa de la Capitulación** (or Casa Morales) ① *Mon-Fri 0800-1600, free,* a colonial building and national monument. The Casa houses libraries, a gallery of work by the Venezuelan painter, Carmelo Fernández (1809-1887), several exhibition halls and a stunning interior patio dedicated to modern art. Next door is the 19th-century **Teatro Baralt**, hosting frequent subsidized concerts and performances.

Running west of Plaza Bolívar is the **Paseo de las Ciencias**, a 1970s development which levelled all the old buildings in the area. Only the **Iglesia de Santa Bárbara** stands in the Paseo. The Paseo de La Chinita continues west from Santa Bárbara to the Basílica de Nuestra Señora de Chiquinquirá. **Calle Carabobo** (one block north of the Paseo de las Ciencias) is a very good example of a colourful, colonial Maracaibo street. One block south of the Paseo is **Plaza Baralt** ① *Av 6*, stretching to Calle 100 and the old waterfront market (**Mercado de Pulgas**). The impressive **Centro de Arte de Maracaibo Lía Bermúdez** ① *Mon-Fri 0800-1200, 1400-1600, Sat-Sun 0930-1700*, in the 19th-century Mercado de Pulgas building, displays the work of national and international artists. It is a/c, a good place to escape the midday heat and for starting a walking tour of the city centre. Its walls are decorated with beautiful photographs of Maracaibo. The Centro holds frequent cultural events, including the **Feria Internacional de Arte y Antigüedades de Maracaibo (FIAAM)**. The new part of the city round **Bella Vista** and towards the university is in vivid contrast with the small **old town** near the docks. The latter, with narrow streets and brightly painted, colonial style adobe houses, has hardly changed from the 19th century, although many buildings are in an advanced state of decay. The buildings facing **Parque Urdaneta** (three blocks north of Paseo de las Ciencias) have been well-restored and are home to several artists. Also well preserved are the church of **Santa Lucía** and the streets around. This old residential area is a short ride (or long walk) north from the old centre. **Parque La Marina**, on the shores of the lake, contains sculptures by the Venezuelan artist, Jesús Soto (1923-2005).

Paseo de Maracaibo, or Vereda del Lago, 25 minutes' walk from Plaza Bolívar, is a lakeside park near the **Hotel del Lago**. It offers walks along the shores of the lake, stunning views of the Rafael Urdaneta bridge and of oil tankers sailing to the Caribbean. The park attracts a wide variety of birds. To get there take a 'Milagro' *por puesto* or a 'Norte' bus northbound and ask the driver to let you off at the entrance. Opposite is the **Mercado de los Indios Guajiros** (see Shopping).

Maracaibo to Colombia

About one hour north is the Río Limón. Take a bus (US$0.50, from terminal or Avenida 15 entre Calle 76 y 77) to **El Moján**, riding with the Guajira Indians as they return to their homes on the peninsula. From El Moján, *por puestos* go to **Sinamaica** (US$1; taxi US$2.50).

Sinamaica is the entry point to the territory of Añu people (also known as Paraujanos) who live in stilt houses on Sinamaica lagoon (these houses inspired the invading Spaniards to christen the place 'Little Venice'). Some 15,000 Añu live in the area, although official numbers say there are only 4000. Their language is practically extinct (UNICEF has supported a project to revive it). The Añu use fibres to make handicrafts. To get to the lagoon, take a truck (US$0.50) from Sinamaica's main plaza on the paved road to Puerto Cuervito (5 minutes), where the road ends at the lagoon. You can hitch a ride on a shared boat to one of the settlements for a few bolívares, or you can hire a boat by the hour (US$7 per hour, ask for Víctor Márquez, recommended). Main settlements on the lagoon are El Barro, La Bocita and Nuevo Mundo. **Parador Turístico de la Laguna de Sinamaica** has decent food, clean bathrooms and an excellent handicraft shop with local produce.

Beyond Sinamaica, the paved road past the Lagoon leads to the border with Colombia. Along the way you see Guajira people, the men with bare legs, on horseback; the women with long, black, tent-shaped dresses and painted faces, wearing the sandals with big wool pom-poms which they make and sell, more cheaply than in tourist shops. The men do nothing: women do all the work, tending animals, selling slippers and raising very little on the dry, hot, scrubby Guajira Peninsula.

Border with Colombia → *Colombia is 1 hr behind Venezuela.*

If you travel on the road between Maracaibo and the border, even if you are planning to visit just Sinamaica and its lagoon, carry your passport with you. Police and army checkpoints are numerous. They are friendly but can get tough if you don't have your documents, or don't cooperate. The border operates 24 hours. You need an exit card and stamp to leave Venezuela, payable in bolívares only. Ask for 90 days on entering Colombia and make sure you get an entry stamp from the Colombian authorities. From the frontier to Maicao, it's a 15-minute drive. Also see Colombia chapter.

⊙ From Maracaibo to Colombia listings

For hotel and restaurant price codes, and other relevant information, see Essentials.

⊙ Where to stay

Maracaibo *p1522*
It is best to reserve well in advance.
$$$ Kristoff, Av 8 Santa Rita con C 68 No 68-48, T796 1000, www.hotelkristoff.com. In the north of the city some distance from centre. Large hotel, with all services, fully refurbished, nice pool open to non-residents, disco, laundry service, restaurant.
$$ Hotel El Paseo, Av 1B y C 74, Sector Cotorrera, T792 4422, www.hotelelpaseo.com.ve. All rooms with breathtaking view of the lake, good, top of the range. **Girasol**, revolving restaurant on top floor with great view, international dishes.
$$ Venetur Maracaibo, Av 2 (El Milagro), near Club Náutico, T794 4222, www.venetur.gob.ve. With 360 rooms, some overlooking the lake. It was the Intercontinental, but is now part of Venetur.
$ Acuario, C 78 (also known as Dr Portillo) No 9-43, Bella Vista, T797 1123, www.hotel acuario.net. Safe, small rooms, safe parking.
$ Doral, C 75 y Av 14A, T797 8385, www.hotel doral.com. North of the city. Safe, decent rooms, helpful. Recommended.
$ Gran Hotel Delicias, Av 15 esq C 70, T797 0983, www.granhoteldelicias.com. North of the city. Old-style modern hotel, bland, restaurant, pool, disco, accepts credit cards.
$ Posada Oleary, Av Padilla, C 93 No 2A-12, Santa Lucía, T723 2390, www.posadaoleary.com.

Small *posada* across from Hospital Central, convenient location, bright, safe.
$ Trece 27, C 79 (Dr Quintero) entre Av 13 y Av 13A, T935 5544, www.hotelmaracaibo trece27.com. New hotel north of the centre with modern facilities, parking, near services on Av Delicias and 5 de Julio.

⊙ Restaurants

Maracaibo *p1522*
A range of US chains and Chinese restaurants (mostly on Av 8 Santa Rita) and pizzerías in the north of town. There are many good restaurants around the Plaza de la República, C77/5 de Julio and Av 31, in Bella Vista. Many places to eat and bars on Calle 72 and 5 de Julio. Most restaurants are closed on Sun. Many restaurants on *palafitos* (stilts) in Santa Rosa de Agua district, good for fish (*por puesto* US$0.25 to get there); best to go at lunchtime.
$$ El Zaguán, on C Carabobo (see above). Serves traditional regional cooking, friendly service, good menu and food, pleasant bar.
$$-$ Koto Sushi, Av 11 entre C 75 y 76, Tierra Negra, T798 8954. Japanese food.
$$-$ Mi Vaquita, Av 3H con C 76. Texan steak house, popular with wealthy locals, bar area for dancing, pricey drinks. No sandals allowed.
$$-$ Peruano Marisquería, Av 15 (Delicias) y C 69, T798 1513. Authentic Peruvian seafood dishes and international cuisine.
$ Bambi, Av 4, 78-70. Italian run with good cappuccino, pastries, recommended. Has other branches.

$ Pizzería Napolitana, C 77 near Av 4. Closed Tue. Excellent food but poor service.
$ Yal-la, Av 8 C 68, opposite **Hotel Kristoff**, T797 8863. Excellent, authentic Lebanese/Middle Eastern restaurant at very reasonable prices. Great vegetarian food.

⊛ Festivals

Maracaibo *p1522*
Virgen del Rosario, 5 Oct; 24 Oct; 18 Nov,
NS de Chiquimquira (La Chinita), processions, bullfights – the main regional religious festival.

O Shopping

Maracaibo *p1522*
There are several modern malls with all services and amenities, including multiplex cinemas. The most luxurious is **Centro Lago Mall**.
Handicrafts and markets El Mercado de los Indios Guajiros, open market at C 96 y Av 2 (El Milagro). A few crafts, some pottery, hammocks, etc. **Las Pulgas**, south side of C 100 entre Av 10 y 14. The outdoor market, enormous, mostly clothes, shoes, and household goods. Most of the shops on **C Carabobo** sell regional crafts, eg **La Salita. El Turista**, C 72 y Av 3H, in front of Centro Comercial Las Tinajitas, T792 3495.

⊖ Transport

Maracaibo *p1522*
Air La Chinita airport is 25 km southwest of city centre (taxis US$7; no *por puestos*). Good bookshop in arrivals sells city map; several good but overpriced eateries; **Italcambio** for exchange, daily 0600-1800, no commission; car hire outside. Frequent flights to **Caracas, Valencia, Barquisimeto, San Antonio,** and **Porlamar**. International flights to **Miami**.
Bus The bus station is 1 km south of the old town. It is old and chaotic, unsafe at night. Taxi to the city US$3-4. Ask for buses into town, local services are confusing. Several fast and comfortable buses daily to **Valencia**, US$6-7, 8 hrs. **San Cristóbal**, US$7, 6-8 hrs. **Barquisimeto**, 4 hrs, US$4. **Coro**, US$3.50, 4 hrs. **Caracas**, US$8-10, 10-13 hrs (Aeroexpresos Ejecutivos from Av 15 con C 90 – Distribuidor las Delicias, T783 0620). **Mérida**, from US$6, 5-7 hrs.

Local *Por puestos* go up and down Av 4 from the old centre to Bella Vista. Ruta 6 goes up and down C 67 (Cecilia Acosta). The San Jacinto bus goes along Av 15 (Las Delicias). Buses from Las Delicias also go to the centre and terminal. From C 76 to the centre *por puestos* marked 'Las Veritas' and buses marked 'Ziruma'. Look for the name of the route on the roof, or the windscreen, passenger's side. Downtown to Av 5 de Julio in a 'Bella Vista' *por puesto* costs US$0.55-0.90, depending on distance. Taxis minimum US$2.50; from north to centre US$3 (beware overcharging, meters are not used). Public transport is being completely overhauled, but it will take years to complete. New large and small red public buses (government-owned) connect the north, centre and other parts of the city at US$0.15. Old private buses charge US$0.20.
Metro An elegant light-rail system is being developed. 6 stations of the first line are in operation, from Altos de la Vanega, southwest of the centre, to Libertador, via Sabaneta and Urdaneta: Mon-Fri 0600-2000, Sat-Sun 0800-1800. Basic fare US$0.10. An extension to Línea 1 and Línea 2 are planned.

Border with Colombia *p1524*
Maracaibo-Maicao
Bus Busven direct at 0400. Other buses operate during the morning, US$5. Or take a *colectivo* from Maracaibo bus terminal (5 passengers), US$6.50 pp; shop around, plus US$1 road toll, 2-3 hrs. Some drivers are unwilling to stop for formalities; make sure the driver takes you all the way to Maicao and arrive before the last bus to Santa Marta or Cartagena (1630).

⊕ Directory

Maracaibo *p1522*
Banks All banks shut at 1530, exchange morning only. Best for dollars and TCs is **Casa de Cambio de Maracaibo**, C 78 con Av 9B. Italcambio, has branches at the airport, Lago Mall (by Hotel Venetur Maracaibo), Centro Sambil (Av Guajira, ZI Norte) and CC Aventura (Av 12 y 13 con C 74 y 75). *Cambio* at bus terminal will change Colombian pesos into bolívares at a poor rate. **Medical services** Hospital Coromoto, Av 3C, No 51, El Lago, T790 0017.

From the lowlands to Mérida

The arid, fruit-growing area around the city of **Barquisimeto** *(Phone code: 0251. Colour map 1, A5. Population: 900,000. Altitude: 565 m. Mean temperature: 25° C)* leads to the lush Andean foothills of Trujillo state. The heart of old Barquisimeto is **Plaza Bolívar**, with a statue of the Liberator, the white-painted **Iglesia Concepción** and the **Palacio Municipal** ① *Cra 17 y C 25*, an attractive modern building. It is now Venezuela's fourth largest city and capital of Lara state. For information contact: **Fondo Mixto de Turismo** ① *Cra 19 esq C 14, CC Santiago Plaza, T252 1125*. On 28 December (morning) is the fiesta of **La Zaragoza**, when colourfully clad people are accompanied by music and dancing in the street. Huge crowds watch **La Divina Pastora** procession in early January, when an image of the Virgin Mary is carried from the shrine at Santa Rosa village into the city.

There are good air and road connections: buses from Caracas take 5½ hours, from Coro seven hours and from Barinas in the *Llanos*, five hours. Buses to Mérida (eight hours) take the Panamericana, which runs at the foot of the Andes near the border with Zulia state, via Agua Viva and El Vigía. More scenic routes take roads which climb towards the mountains, passing colonial towns and entering an increasingly rugged landscape. One such passes is the busy agricultural centre of **Quíbor** *(Phone code: 0253, Population: 40,295)*, 24 km southwest of Barquisimeto. Festivals on 18 January (**NS de Altagracia**) and 12 June (**San Antonio de Padua**).

Boconó and Niquitao

Some 165 km southwest of Quíbor is **Boconó** (Population: 95,750), built on steep mountain sides and famed for its crafts. The **Centro de Acopio Artesanal Tiscachic** is highly recommended for *artesanía* (turn left just before bridge at entrance to town and walk 350 m). From Boconó there is a high, winding, spectacular paved road to Trujillo (see below).

Niquitao, a small town one hour southwest of Boconó, is still relatively unspoilt. Excursions can be made to the Teta de Niquitao (4007 m), two hours by jeep, the waterfalls and pools known as Las Pailas, and a nearby lake. Southwest of Niquitao, by partly paved road is **Las Mesitas**; continue up towards **Tuñame**, turn left on a good gravel road (no signs), cross pass and descend to **Pueblo Llano** (one basic hotel and restaurant), from where you can climb to the Parque Nacional Sierra Nevada at 3600 m, passing Santo Domingo (see also below). Good hiking in the area.

Valera → *Phone code: 0271. Colour map 1, A5. Population: 130,000.*

From the Panamericana in the lowlands, a road goes to the most important town in Trujillo state, Valera. Here, you can choose between two roads over the Sierra, either via Boconó and down to the Llanos at Guanare and Barinas, or via Timotes and Mucuchíes to Mérida. There are several upmarket business hotels, few decent budget ones, and lots of good Italian restaurants on the main street.

Trujillo → *Phone code: 0272. Colour map 1, A5. Population: 59,000. Altitude: 805 m.*

From Valera a road runs via the restored colonial village of **La Plazuela** to the state capital, Trujillo. This beautiful historic town consists of two streets running uphill from the Plaza Bolívar. It's a friendly place with a warm, subtropical climate. The **Centro de Historia de Trujillo**, on Avenida Independencia, is a restored colonial house, now a museum. Bolívar lived there and signed the 'proclamation of war to the death' in the house. A 47-m-high monument to the **Virgen de la Paz** ① *0900-1700, US$0.50*, with lift, was built in 1983; it stands at 1608 m, 2½ hours walk from town and gives good views to Lake Maracaibo but go early. Jeeps leave when full from opposite **Hotel Trujillo** (20 minutes, US$0.75 per person). For tourist information, visit the **Corporación Trujillana de Turismo** ① *Av Principal La Plazuela, Trujillito, T236 1455*.

Road to the high Andes

After **Timotes** the road climbs through increasingly wild, barren and rugged country and through the windy pass of **Pico El Aguila** (4118 m) in the Sierra de la Culata, best seen early morning, otherwise frequently in the clouds. This is the way Bolívar went when crossing the Andes to liberate Colombia, and on the peak is the statue of a condor. At the pass is the tourist restaurant **Páramo Aguila**, reasonably priced with open fire. People stop for a hot chocolate or a *calentado*, a herb liquor drunk hot. There are also food and souvenir stalls, and horses for hire (high season and weekends). Across from the monument is a small chapel with fine views. A paved road leads from here 2 km to a CANTV microwave tower (4318 m). Here are tall *frailejones* plants. Continuing north as a lonely track the road goes to the **Piñango lakes** (45 km) and the traditional village of **Piñango** (2480 m), 1½ hours. Great views for miles before the road reaches the Panamericana and Lago de Maracaibo.

Santo Domingo (*Phone code: 0274; Population: 6000; Altitude: 2178 m*), with good handicraft shops and fishing, is on the spectacular road up from Barinas to Mérida, before the Parque Nacional Sierra Nevada. Festival: 30 September, **San Gerónimo**. The tourist office is on the right leaving town, 10 minutes from the centre.

⊚ From the lowlands to Mérida listings

For hotel and restaurant price codes, and other relevant information, see Essentials.

⊜ Where to stay

Boconó *p1526*
$ Estancia de Mosquey, Mosquey, 10 km from Boconó towards Biscucuy, T0272-414 8322, 10414-723 4246, www.estancia-mosquey. com. Family run, great views, rooms and cabañas, good beds, good restaurant, pool, recommended. There are other hotels and *posadas* in town, some on or near Plaza Bolívar, one opposite the bus station.

Niquitao *p1526*
$ Posada Turística de Niquitao, T0414-727 8217/0416-771 7860, http://posada niquitao. com. Rooms around a patio in a restored old house, some with bunks, restaurant, tours arranged with guide, also has small museum.

Trujillo *p1526*
$ Los Gallegos, Av Independencia 5-65, T236 3193. With hot water, a/c or fan, with or without TV. As well as several other places.

Road to the high Andes *p1526*
Timotes
$ Caribay, Av Bolívar 41, T0271-828 9126. With bar and restaurant.
$ Las Truchas, north entrance to town, T0271-808 0500, www.andes.net/lastruchas. 44 cabins, with and without kitchen. Also has a Restaurant.

Santo Domingo
$$$-$$ La Trucha Azul, east end of town, 1898 8111, www.latruchaazul.com. Rooms with open fireplace, also suites and cabins.
$$-$ Los Frailes, between Santo Domingo and Laguna Mucubají at 3700 m. 10274-417 3440, or T0212-976 0530, reservacioneshlf@gmail.com, www.hotellosfrailes.blogspot.com. Cheaper in low season, includes breakfast. Beautiful former monastery, specializes in honeymoon packages, rooms are simple, international menu and wines.
$$-$ Moruco, T898 8155/8070, out of town. Good value, beautiful, also cabins, good food, bar.
$ Paso Real, on the other side of the river from Los Frailes, T0414-974 7486. A good place to stay, heating, restaurant.

⊖ Transport

Valera *p1526*
Bus The terminal is on the edge of town. To **Boconó**, US$2.50, 3 hrs; to **Trujillo**, *por puestos*, 30 mins, US$0.50; to **Caracas**, 9 hrs, US$7 (direct at 2230 with Expresos Mérida); to **Mérida**, 4 daily with Trans Barinas, US$3.25, 4½ hrs; *por puestos* to **Mérida**, 3 hrs, US$4, leave when full (travel by day for views and, especially in the rainy season, safety); to **Maracaibo**, *micros* every 30 mins till 1730, 4 hrs, US$3.

Road to the high Andes *p1526*
Santo Domingo
Bus Buses or *busetas* pass in both directions every 2 hrs all day. **Mérida** 2 hrs, US$1.50 *por puesto*; **Barinas** 1½ hrs, US$2.

Mérida and around

Venezuela's high Andes offer hiking and mountaineering, and fishing in lakes and rivers. The main tourist centre is Mérida (674 km from Caracas), but there are many interesting rural villages. The Transandean Highway runs through the Sierra to the border with Colombia, while the Pan-American Highway runs along the foot of the Andes through El Vigía and La Fría to join the Transandean at San Cristóbal.

The Sierra Nevada de Mérida, running from south of Maracaibo to the Colombian frontier, is the only range in Venezuela where snow lies permanently on the higher peaks. Several basins lying between the mountains are actively cultivated; the inhabitants are concentrated mainly in valleys and basins at between 800 m and 1300 m above sea level. The towns of Mérida and San Cristóbal are in this zone.

Mérida → *Phone code: 0274. Colour map 1, A4. Population: 237,725. Altitude: 1640 m.*

Mérida stands on an alluvial terrace – a kind of giant shelf – 15 km long, 2.5 km wide, within sight of Pico Bolívar, the highest in Venezuela. The mountain is part of the Five White Eagles group, visible from the city. The summits are at times covered in snow, but the glaciers and snow are retreating. Founded in 1558, the capital of Mérida State retains some colonial buildings but is mainly known for its 33 parks and many statues. For tourists, its claims to fame are the great opportunities for adventure sports and the buzz from a massive student population.

The heart of Venezuelan mountaineering and trekking is the Andes, with Mérida as the base, and there are several important peaks and some superb hikes. Bear in mind that high altitudes will be reached and acclimatization is essential. Suitable equipment is necessary and you may consider bringing your own. In the Sierra Nevada is mountain biking, whitewater rafting, parapenting and horse riding. See also the Tour operators listed in What to do, page 1533.

Arriving in Mérida

Orientation Mérida's **airport** is on the main highway, 5 km southwest of the centre. The **bus terminal** is 3 km from the centre of town on the west side of the valley, linked by a frequent minibus service to Calle 25 entre Avenidas 2 y 3, US$0.25. City bus fares rise at weekends. A trolley bus system from the southern suburb of Ejido to La Hechicera in the north has been opened as far as Calle 40 (currently free), but as yet does not connect the downtown area. Mérida may seem safe, but theft does occur. Avoid the Pueblo Nuevo area by the river at the stairs leading down from Avenida 2, as well as Avenida 2 itself. ▶▶ *See also Transport, page 1534.*

Tourist information Next to the airport is the **Corporación Merideña de Turismo**, on Avenida Urdaneta beside the airport, T262 2371, cormetur@merida.gob.ve. It's open Monday-Saturday low season 0800-1200 and 1400-1800, high season 0800-1800. They supply a useful map of the state and town. Also in the bus terminal, same hours, have a map of the city (free) and at the airport. At Parque Las Heroínas, at the zoo in Chorros de Milla park and at the Mercado Principal, low season 0800-1200, 1400-1800, high season 0830-1830. **Inparques** (National Parks) Sector Fondur, Parcelamiento Albarrega, Calle 02, paralela a Av Las Américas, T262 1529, www.inparques.gob.ve. Map of Parque Nacional Sierra Nevada (mediocre) US$1; also, and easier, at Teleférico for permits.

Places in Mérida

In the city centre is the attractive **Plaza Bolívar**, on which stands the **cathedral**, dark and heavy inside, with **Museo Arquidiocesano** beside it, and **Plaza de Milla**, or **Sucre** ① *C 14 entre Avs 2 y 3*, always a hive of activity. The **Parque de las Cinco Repúblicas** ① *C 13, entre Avs 4 y 5, beside the* *barracks*, is renowned for having the first monument in the world to Bolívar (1842, replaced in 1988) and contains soil from each of the five countries he liberated (photography strictly prohibited). Three of the peaks known as the Five White Eagles (Bolívar, 5007 m, La Silla del Toro, 4755 m, and León 4740 m) can be clearly seen from here.

Plaza Las Heroínas, by the lowest station of the *teleférico* (see below) is busy till 2300, a recently renovated outdoor party zone, with artists exhibiting their work. Many cheap hotels, restaurants and tour operators are also located here.

Less central parks include **Plaza Beethoven** ① *Santa María Norte*, a different melody from Beethoven's works chimes every hour, but the site is now neglected and run-down; *por puestos/ busetas*, run along Avenida 5, marked 'Santa María' or 'Chorro de Milla', US$0.45. The **Jardín Botánico** ① *located on the way to La Hechicera, www.ciens.ula.ve/jardinbotanico, open daily, 360 days a year, US$1.50*, has been recently remodeled and contains the largest collection of bromeliads in South America, sculptures, a canopy walkway, and botanical specimens from a range of eco-systems. The **Jardín Acuario** ① *beside the aquarium, high season daily 0800-1800, low season closed Mon, US$0.25; (busetas leave from Av 4 y C 25, US$0.25, passing airport)*, is an exhibition centre, mainly devoted to the way of life and the crafts of the Andean *campesinos*.

Mérida has several museums: the small **Museo Arqueológico** ① *Av 3, Edif del Rectorado de la Universidad de los Andes, just off Plaza Bolívar, T240 2344, http://vereda.ula.ve/museo_ arqueologico, Tue-Sat 0800-1200, 1400-1800, Sun 1400-1800, US$0.50*, with ethnographic and pre-Columbian exhibits from the Andes. **Museo de Arte Moderno** ① *Av 2 y C 21, T252 4380, Mon-Fri 0800-1600, Sat-Sun 0800-1300, free*, is in the Centro Cultural Don Tulio Febres Cordero, which is a run-down but still impressive concrete building with political murals in front of its main entrance, and has several galleries and theatres.

⚜ Mérida listings

For hotel and restaurant price codes, and other relevant information, see Essentials.

🛏 Where to stay

Mérida *p1528, map p1530*
Book ahead in school holidays and Feria del Sol. High season is mid Jul to mid-Jan.
$$-$ El Tisure, Av 4 entre C 17 y 18, T252 6061, www.venaventours.com/hoteltisure. A well-maintained colonial-style option, centrally located with 28 simple, calm, attractive rooms, including one enormous Presidential suite with a jacuzzi. Helpful and hospitable.
$$-$ Posada Casa Alemana-Suiza, El Encanto, Av 2 No 38-130, T263 6503, www.casa-alemana. com. Stylish guesthouse with a nice family atmosphere. Rooms are spacious, including a suite overlooking Pico Bolívar. Amenities include breakfast salon, kitchen, living room and bar, billiard room, chimney room, and roof top-terrace overlooking the Andes. Bus station pick-up available, parking, discount in low season and for long stays, laundry service, English and German spoken. Also runs good tours and activities.

$$-$ Posada Casa Sol, Av 4 entre C15 y C16, T252 4164, www.posadacasasol.com. Renovated colonial-era house with lovely rooms in distinctive, tasteful style, modern art on walls, hot water, Wi-Fi, beautiful garden, large breakfast included. Very helpful, English, German and Italian spoken. Limited parking. The best in town, highly recommended.
$ El Escalador, C 23 entre Avs 7 y 8, T252 2411, el_escalador_andino@hotmail.com. A very simple little guesthouse run by a kindly old lady. Doubles or rooms with bed and bunks, hot water, Wi-Fi, free coffee, tourist information.
$ La Montaña, C 24 No 6-47 entre Av 6 y 7, T252 5977, www.posadalamontana.com. A friendly little *posada* with 19 rooms set around a courtyard, all with hot water, safe, fan, fridge, and Wi-Fi. Very helpful, English spoken, excellent restaurant. Mountain views from the sun terrace. Recommended.
$ Los Bucares de Mérida, Av 4 No 15-5, T252 2841, www.losbucares.com. Colonial-style with tranquil inner courtyards, attractive wood beams and red tile roofs. Simple white-washed rooms with hot water, cheaper (and noisier) at

the front. Amenities include parking and *cafetín*.
$ Montecarlo, Av 7 entre C 24 y C 25, T252
5981, www.andes.net/hotelmontecarlo.
Simple rooms painted a calming sky blue.
Ask for back one with view of mountain,
safe, parking, hot water, restaurant.
$ Posada Alemania, Av 2 entre C 17 y 18, No

17-76, T252 4067, www.posadaalemania.com.
Relaxed family atmosphere, cosy rooms with
and without bath, leafy patio, laundry service,
kitchen, communal areas, book exchange, and a
good tourist information and eco-tourism office.
Popular with backpackers, discounts for long
stays, breakfast included. English and German

Mérida

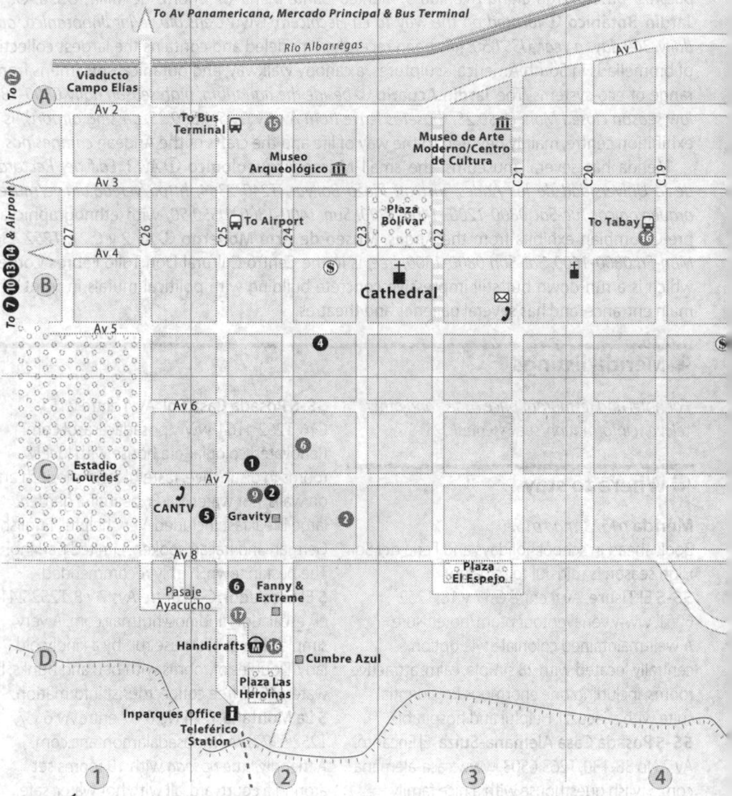

Where to stay
2 El Escalador *C2*
3 El Tisure *B5*
6 La Montaña &
   restaurant *C2*
7 Los Bucares de Mérida *B6*
9 Montecarlo *C2*
11 Posada Alemania *A5*
12 Posada Casa
   Alemana-Suiza *A1*
13 Posada Casa Sol *B5*
14 Posada Doña Pumpa *B6*

16 Posada Guamanchi &
   Guamanchi Tours *D2*
17 Posada Luz Caraballo *A6*
19 Posada Suiza
   & Colibrí Tours *B5*

Restaurants
1 Buona Pizza *C2*
2 Buona Pizza Express *C2*

3 Café Tekeños *A6*
4 Chipen *B2*
5 Delicias Mexicanas *C2*
6 El Atico del Cine *D2*
7 El Encuentro *B1*
8 El Sabor de los Quesos *A6*
9 El Vegetariano *B4*
10 Heladería La
   Coromoto *B1*

spoken, German owner. Recommended.

$ Posada Doña Pumpa, Av 5 y C 14, T252
7286, www.donapumpa.com. 16 simple,
spacious, well-maintained rooms with good
showers at this quiet guesthouse. English-
speaking owner, parking.

$ Posada Guamanchi, C 24, No 8-86, T252

2080, www.guamanchi.com. Owned by tour
operator of same name, if on a tour you are
will receive a discount. Rooms and dorms of
varying size, including 6 matrimonials with
private terrace and hammock and Wi-Fi.
Good communal areas, including terraces
overlooking the plaza, shared fridges, kitchens,
TV room. Recommended.

$ Posada Luz Caraballo, Av 2 No 13-80,
on Plaza de Milla, T252 5441. Colonial-style
building with antique typewriters in the lobby,
hot water, superb cheap restaurant, good bar,
parking, secure.

$ Posada Suiza, Av 3 entre C 17 y 18, No 17-
59, T252 4961, www.posada-suiza.net.
A 19th century colonial home converted
to a guesthouse. Private rooms for 2 to 6
people, Wi-Fi in communal areas, internal
patios. Adventure tours (trekking, rafting,
riding, expeditions) with **Colibrí Tours**,
same phone, www.colibri-tours.com.

🍴 Restaurants

Mérida *p1528, map p1530*
Good restaurants in Centro Comercial La
Hechicera, Av Alberto Carnevalli, northeast of
the centre: **La Chistorra**, T244 0021, a seafood
bar and restaurant, open 1200-2400, Spanish
food. Next door is **Sushi'tei**, with Japanese
chef, very friendly, wide range of dishes, sushi,
sashimi and traditional Japanese recipes.

$$ La Abadía, Av 3 entre C 17 y 18, T251 0933,
www.abadiacafe.com. Kitsch and atmospheric
old restaurant set in an early 20th-century
abbey and attended by waiters in habits.
Good varied menu of salads, soups, meat, pasta,
and chicken. Romantic and recommended.
Also here is **Abadía Tours** travel agency.

$$ El Chipen, Av 5, No 23-67, T252 5015.
Established 50 years ago, El Chipen is the oldest
restaurant in Mérida and often recommended
by locals. They serve Spanish and Venezuelan
food, excellent trout and cordon bleu. Lots of
character and old world style.

$$ El Encuentro, Av 4 y C 29, at Hotel Chama,
T935 2602, www.restaurantelencuentro.com.
Open 1200-2200 (till 2300 Fri-Sat, Sun till 1800).
Smart joint, moderately classy, serving gourmet
international and Venezuelan cuisine, including
seafood starters, fish, meat, chicken, pasta and

11 La Abadía *B5*
12 La Astilla *A6*
13 La Ciboulette *B1*
14 T-Café *B1*

Bars & clubs 🍸
15 Birosca Carioca *A2*
16 El Hoyo del Queque *B4*
17 La Botana *D2*

risotto, wines and cocktails. Good presentation, the place for an intimate evening meal.

$$-$ La Astilla, C 14, No 2-20, Plaza de Milla. Colourful pizzería filled with hanging plants and nostalgic music, varied menu, frequented by locals and groups. Good ambience, reasonable food, average service.

$$-$ La Ciboulette, Av 4 y C 29, T252-4851, next to **Hotel Chama**. Mon-Sat 1800-2300. Formerly Café Mogambo, a sophisticated European-style bistro with eclectic gastronomic offerings, including tapas and fine wine. Occasional live music.

$ Buona Pizza, Av 7 entre C 24 y 25, T252 7639. Daily 1200-2300. Thick-crust pizzas, popular with the locals and often buzzing in the evening. Express branch opposite and 2 other branches.

$ Café Tekeños, C 14 y Av 3, just of Plaza Milla. A casual, bohemian eatery in a lovely rustic colonial building, liberally adorned with interesting art and antiques. They serve hot chocolate, juices and *tequeños* – tasty fried dough sticks with a variety of fillings. Recommended.

$ Delicias Mexicanas, C 25, entre Av 7 y 8, next to **Hotel Altamira**. Closed Tue. Authentic Mexican joint with colourful furniture and art work by Diego Rivera. They serve old favourites from the homeland including *burritos*, fajitas, tacos, and *chilaquiles*. Not really gourmet, but servings are massive.

$ El Atico del Cine, C 25 near Plaza Las Heroínas. Movie-themed restaurant, bar, and café set in a cosy upstairs attic. They serve pizza and other international fare. Casual place, sociable vibe. Recommended.

$ El Sabor de los Quesos, on Plaza de Milla. Cheap and popular locals' pizzería, very busy, painted green and white with an inner patio.

$ El Vegetariano, Av 4 y C 18. Low-key little vegetarian café. Wholesome menu includes unpretentious pastas, paella, Carpaccio, good salads, pasties, cake and juices.

Ice cream parlours

Heladería La Coromoto, Av 3 y C 29, T523525. Tue-Sun 1415-2100. Proud Guinness record holder serving the most ice cream flavours in the world, over 800, at least 60 choices daily, eg trout, avocado.

🍸 Bars and clubs

Mérida *p1528, map p1530*
There is no cover charge for nightclubs but always take your passport or a copy. Use taxis to get back as the streets are deserted.

Birosca Carioca, Av 2 y C 24. Popular alternative hang-out, with live music, grunge, rock, metal, Indie music. Take care outside.

El Hoyo del Queque, Av 4 across the road from **Alfredo's**. Open 1200-2400, usually packed, good meeting place, youthful student crowd. The best local bands play here, some nights free. Recommended.

La Botana, Plaza las Heroínas. Raucous reggae bar that's packed with drinkers on a Fri and Sat night. Live music and DJs. They also serve pizza.

Los Cibeles, Av 3 y C 25. Mon-Sat 1200-0100. A popular salsa bar with an alternative vibe and a mixed crowd of young and old.

🎉 Festivals

Mérida *p1528, map p1530*
For 2 weeks leading up to Christmas there are daily song contests between local students on Plaza Bolívar, 1700-2200. **Feria del Sol**, held on the week preceding Ash Wednesday. This is also the peak bullfighting season.

1-2 Jan, Paradura del Niño; **15 May**, San Isidro Labrador, a popular festival nationwide, but especially in Mérida.

🛍 Shopping

Mérida *p1528, map p1530*
Camping shops 5007, Av 5 entre C 19 y 20, CC Mediterráneo, T252 6806. Recommended.
Eco Bike, Av 7 No 16-34, www.ecobike.com.ve. For mountain bikes and equipment. Many tour operators rent equipment.
Handicrafts Handicraft market on La Plaza de Las Heroínas, opposite *teleférico*. **Mercado Principal** on Av las Américas (buses for bus station pass by), has many small shops, top floor restaurant has regional *comida típica*, bargaining possible.

The Lighthouse of Maracaibo

In the south and southwest of the Lago de Maracaibo is the Catatumbo delta, a huge swamp with fast flowing, navigable rivers, luxurious vegetation and plentiful wildlife, one of the most fascinating trips in the whole country. Its nightly displays of lightning over the lake at the **Parque Nacional Ciénagas del Catatumbo**, best seen from May to November or December, have yet to be explained. Indigenous people thought that it was produced by millions of fireflies meeting to pay the homage to the creator gods. Early scientific thought was that the constant silent flashing at three to ten second intervals was caused by friction between hot air moving south from Zulia and Falcón and cold currents from Andes. Latest theories suggest it is the result of clashes between the methane particles from the marsh and the lake system between the Catatumbo and Bravo rivers. It has been proved that this phenomenon is a regenerator of the planet's ozone layer.

Whatever its origin, the spectacle is truly unique, best observed from Congo Mirador right after nightfall. Several operators run tours from Mérida, which may be the best way because they have bilingual nature guides, who have information about birds, butterflies and flora and boat transport (see below).

Going independently is a real tropical adventure and not fully safe because of illegal immigration and contraband coming from Colombia. To get to the Mirador takes three to four hours by motorboat from the port of Encontrados. Travel should be arranged in a group. Boatman will ask about US$30. If staying overnight on the boat, take plenty of water and food, mosquito repellant and antiseptics. Security can be hired at **Encontrados**, a small town with basic services. It is at the entrance to the **Parque Nacional Ciénagas de Juan Manuel de Aguas Blancas y Aguas Negras**, known for impressive vegetation and migrating birds. It is open from 0700-1600 and the Catatumbo lightning can be seen from some parts of the park, even from Encontrados. If not going on a tour, you must get a permit from Inparques to enter the park. In town hotels: $ Hostería Juancho, Calle Piar 74, T0275-615 0448, basic, and $ Hotel La Nona Magdalena, Avenida Principal, near Plaza Bolívar, T0275-414 2951, central, food. Restaurants close around 1600.

To get to Encontrados takes about four hours by car from Maracaibo, three to four hours from San Cristóbal. Drive south from Maracaibo on Machiques-Colón road then, at El Manguito, take a road to Encontrados, over 70 km from the intersection. Approximately 90 minutes by por puesto or two hours by bus from La Fría and Encontrados.

⏱ What to do

Mérida *p1528, map p1530*
Parapenting All agencies offer jumps. Conditions in Mérida are suitable for flying almost all year round. It takes on average 50 mins to get to a launch site and tandem jumps last 25-40 mins. There are 7 main sites. Price US$60. Can take own equipment and hire a guide.
Xtreme Adventours, Av 8, C24, Plaza Las Heroínas, T252 7241, xatours@hotmail.com. Specializes in parapenting (latest equipment, safety) and many other adventure options, plus tours in the region. Also offers tours from Mérida to Canaima, Margarita and Los Roques.

Tour operators
Arassari Trek, C 24 No 8-301 (beside the teleférico), T0414-746 3569, www.arassari.com. Run by Tom and Raquel Evenou (based in Switzerland), mostly for rafting tours, but also Roraima, Los Llanos, canyoning, and horse-trekking.
Catatumbo Tour, T0414-756 2575, www.catatumbotour.com. Alan Highton and his team specialize in 2-day trips to Catatumbo to see the lightning, visit the communities of the region and experience the variety of habitats between the Andes and the delta. They have a camp at Ologa lagoon. Naturalist tours to other parts of the country offered. Very experienced, several languages spoken.

Fanny Tours, C 24, No 8-31, T252 2952, T0414-747 1349, www.fanny-tours.com. Patrizia Rossi, José Albarrán for parapenting (the first to do it), reliable. Apart from parapenting, specializes in mountain biking, with and without jeep support, bike hire, rafting; Llanos, Catatumbo, canyoning, trekking to mountains and some climbing; also tours combining all types of sport. Recommended.

Gravity Tours, C 24 entre Av 7 y 8, 1 block from cable car, T251 1279, T0424-760 8327, www.gravity-tours.com. Bilingual guides, natural history and adventure tours, some extreme, including rock climbing, rafting, biking, Llanos trips and Gran Sabana.

Guamanchi Tours, C 24, No 8-86, T252 2080, www.guamanchi.com. Owned by John and Joëlle Peña. Specializes in mountaineering and safari tours to Los Llanos, with 22 years experience, including working with documentary crews. Good service, ethical ethos and constantly updated equipment. They also offer rafting and kayaking from beginner to extreme, biking, birdwatching, paragliding, pendulum jumping and tours of Amazonas. They have a *posada* in town (see above) and at Los Nevados (see below). German, French, Italian and English spoken. Recommended.

Natoura Travel and Adventure Tours, C 31 entre Av Don Tulio y prol Av 6 No 5-27 (Diagonal Bomberos ULA), Mérida 5101, T252 4216, in US T303-800 4639, in Germany T05906-303364, in France T0970-449206, www.natoura.com. Daily 0830-1800. Friendly, award-winning company organizing tours throughout Venezuela, run by José Luis Troconis and Renate Reiners, English, French, German and Italian spoken, climbing, trekking, rafting, horse riding, mountain biking, birdwatching and equipment hire. Their self-drive option allows you to rent a car and they will reserve accommodation for your route. Repeatedly recommended.

⊖ Transport

Mérida *p1528, map p1530*
Air Mérida receives several flights a week from **Caracas** with **Avior** (book direct with airline only). The airport has a tourist office, car hire and **Italcambio** offices. More frequent flights to/from Caracas connect airports at San Antonio (3-5 hrs by road), or **El Vigía** (1½-2½ hrs away, shared taxi US$8 per car, an official will direct you to a taxi and set the price); both are served by several airlines.

Bus The terminal has 2 levels, the upper one for small buses, minivans and cars to nearby places, the lower for interstate buses. Taxis line up outside the main entrance; you will be shown to a taxi. A small exit tax of US$0.35 is charged for journeys in the state, US$0.50 for long distance, payable at one of 2 kiosks leading to buses. Make sure you pay, officials check buses before departure. On interstate buses, it is essential to book in advance; for buses within the state you pay on board. The terminal has a tourist office, phones, toilets, luggage store and places to eat. Fares: **Caracas**, US$7-10; **Maracay**, US$7; **Valencia**, US$9; **Coro**, US$7; **Maracaibo**, US$6.

Transportes Barinas (T263 4651), to **Barinas** (US$2.50) via **Apartaderos** (US$1.45), to **Guanare** (US$3.50) and **Valera** (US$3.25). From upper level of terminal: **Táchira Mérida**, to **San Cristóbal** (US$3.25, 6 hrs) and **San Antonio**. Also to Jaji, Chiguará, Apartaderos, Barinas, El Vigía, Valera. **Líneas Unidas**, T263 8472, *por puesto* microbus with TV, and car, to **Maracaibo**, 1000, 2130; also **Fraternidad del Transporte**, T263 1187, 1000, 1400, 2145. If heading for **Ciudad Bolívar**, change buses in Valencia or Maracay.
Taxi In town US$1-2.

ⓘ Directory

Mérida *p1528, map p1530*
Banks Italcambio at airport; this is often the easiest place to change cash and TCs. **Consulates** Colombia, Final Av Universidad Quinta Noevia, Casa No 80, Sector Vuelta de Lola, T245 9724, www.cancilleria.gov.co.co, open 0730-1330.
Language schools Iowa Institute, Av 3 y C 18, T935-9775, iowalanguageinstitute@gmail.com. Competitive prices, fully qualified teachers, homestays arranged. Recommended. Latinoamericano de Idiomas, CC Mamayeya, p 4, of C-5-38, T244 7808. Contact Marinés Asprino, Conjunto Residencial Andrés Bello, Torre C, p 5, Apt 6-1, T271 1209 for private lessons and cheap accommodation. Recommended. Carolina Tenías, 17 years' experience in

private lessons for travellers, grammar and conversation, T252 4875, or T0416-971 1445. **Medical services** Doctors: Dr Aldo Olivieri, Av Principal La Llanita, La Otra Banda, Centro Profesional El Buho, 09, T244 0805, T0414-374 0356, aldrolia250@cantv.net, very good, gastroenterologist, speaks English and Italian. Dr Giotto Guillén Echeverria, Centro Médico La Trinidad, C 42 entre Avs Urdaneta y Gonzalo Picón, T263 9685, T0416-674 0707. Specialist in infections, speaks French. **Useful addresses** Immigration office: SAIME, Av 4 y C 16, quinta San Isidro N0 4-11, Parroquia Sagrario,

T251 8588, Mon-Sat 0800-1700. **Tourist police:** The CICPC will provide a *constancia* reporting the crime and listing the losses. Their office is on Av Las Américas, at Viaducto Miranda, T262 0343. Open daily but they won't issue a *constancia* on Sun. To get there, take any bus marked 'Terminal Sur' or 'Mercado' leaving from C 25. You can also get a *constancia* from the *Prefectura Civil del Municipio Libertador*, but it can take all day and is only valid for a limited period; at Av 4 No 21-69, just off Plaza Bolívar; opening hours variable. Tourist offices may be better than police if you need to register a theft for insurance purposes.

Sierra Nevada de Mérida

The Sierra is a mixture of the wild and isolated and the very touristy. In the latter group fall the cable car up Pico Espejo and villages designed to lure the shopper, but it is not difficult to escape the tour groups. There are routes from the mountains to the *llanos* and to Colombia.

Parque Nacional Sierra Nevada (South)

Close to Mérida is the popular hiking area around Los Nevados, with the added attraction of the highest cable car in the world (if it's running). The further you go from Mérida, the greater the off-the-beaten-track possibilities for hiking and exploration that arise.

Since this is a national park, you need a permit from the **Inparques** (National Parks) offices in Mérida (see Arriving in Mérida above) to hike and camp overnight. Permits are not given to single hikers (except to Los Nevados), a minimum of two people is needed. Have your passport ready. Return permit after your hike; park guards will radio the start of trek to say you've reached the end. If camping, remember that the area is 3500-4200 m so acclimatization is necessary. The night temperatures can fall below freezing so a -12°C sleeping bag is necessary, plus good waterproofs. Conditions are much more severe than you'd think after balmy Mérida. Don't leave litter. Some treks are very difficult so check with the tourist office before leaving. Water purification is also recommended. See Mérida Tour operators and Parque Nacional Sierra Nevada (North) below.

Pico Espejo The world's highest and longest aerial cableway (built by the French in 1957-1960) runs to Pico Espejo (4765 m) in four stages. The teleférico was closed in late 2008 and a new system was due to open, along with improved hiking trails, in 2015. When operating, its final station is at Pico Espejo, with a change of car at every station, all of which have cafés, toilets and advice. Beware altitude sickness: there is oxygen and a nursing station at higher points. Barinas is the ground level station, Plaza de las Heroínas; you can hire, or buy, hats, gloves and scarves here, the Venezuelans all do. La Montaña (2442 m) is the second station with a small Museo del Montañismo. You pass over various levels of forest. Next is La Aguada (3452 m), then Loma Redonda (4045 m). From here you can start the trek to Los Nevados (see below); you must inform Inparques if trekking to Los Nevados. Pause for 10 minutes at Loma Redonda before the last stage to Pico Espejo, where there is a statue of Nuestra Señora de las Nieves. Next door to Pico Espejo is Pico Bolívar (Mucumbari, where the sun sleeps) with Humboldt behind. It has remnants of a glacier. In the other direction, closest is La Silla del Toro and you can see a statue of Francisco Miranda with the Venezuelan flag on an outcrop. On a clear day you can see the blue haze of the Llanos to the east and, west, as far as Sierra de Cocuy and Guicán in Colombia. Across Río Chama you can see Sierra de la Culata. It is advisable to spend only 30 minutes at Pico Espejo. Apart from Los Nevados trek, the only safe part to walk down is Loma Redonda to La Aguada; a rough but clear trail, two hours; wear boots, not for children or the elderly, take water.

Los Nevados Los Nevados (*Altitude: 2711 m*) is a colonial town with cobbled streets, an ancient chapel and a famous fiesta on 2 May. From here, it is a very testing two-day trek to **Pico Espejo**, with a strong chance of altitude sickness as the ascent is more than 1600 m. It is best done November-June early in the morning (before 0830 ideally), before the clouds spoil the view. In summer the summit is clouded and covered with snow and there is no view. **Do not attempt Pico Espejo alone; go with a guide, it is easy to get lost.** Reputable trekking companies provide suitable clothing; temperatures can be 0° C. August is the coldest month.

From Los Nevados to **Loma Redonda** takes five to seven hours, four hours with mules (14 km). The hike is not too difficult; breathtaking views; be prepared for cold rain in the afternoon, start very early. The walk from Los Nevados to the village of **El Morro** (24 km) takes seven to nine hours (very steep in parts). (It's 47 km to Mérida; jeeps do the trip daily.) Sr Oviller Ruiz provides information on the history of the church of San Jacinto (the patron saint, whose fiesta is on 16 August) and the indigenous cemetery. The town, with its red tiled roofs, is an interesting blend of the colonial and the indigenous.

It is possible to hike from Pico Espejo to the cloud forest at La Mucuy (see below), two to three days walking at over 4000 m altitude, passing spectacular snow peaks and Lagos Verde and Coromoto. A tent and a warm sleeping bag are essential, as is a good map. If you start at Pico Espejo you will be at the highest point first, so although you will be descending, you may have altitude sickness from the word go.

Parque Nacional Sierra Nevada (North) and Sierra de La Culata

The Transandean highway snakes its way through the rugged mountain landscape, past neat, little towns of red-tiled roofs, steep fields and terraces of maize and potatoes. Just outside Mérida a side road goes to El Valle, known for *pasteles de trucha, vino de mora* and handicraft shops. The snow-tipped peaks of the high sierras watch over this bucolic scene, with Pico Bolívar lording it over them all. Throughout the park you will see a plant with felt-like leaves of pale grey-green, the *frailejón* (or great friar, *espeletia*), which blooms with yellow flowers from September to December. There are more than 130 species; tall ones grow at less than 1 cm a year.

Tabay At 12 km from Mérida, Tabay (*30 minutes; Altitude 1708 m; Population 17,000*) is named after an indigenous tribe. Its Plaza Bolívar has an attractive church, trees and plants. Around it are mini mercados, **Pizzería Valentina** (best in town), **Pastelitos** (at bus stop from Mérida, for empanadas in morning), and other transport stops. Jeeps run a regular service to **La Mucuy** cloud forest, 0600-2200, they are labelled (US$1 one way if five passengers). They drop you at the Guardaparques. There is nothing to pay for a day visit, but you pay per night if making the Travesía to Pico Espejo and the Teleférico (or alternative route) down to Mérida. When going back to Tabay, you may have to wait for a jeep; the driver will charge extra for backpacks. Jeeps also go to the **Aguas Termales** (from a different stop, just off Plaza Bolívar, US$0.80). It is possible to walk and there are signs. The man-made pool has 38°C water. The area is also good for walking and horse riding (see **Mano Poderosa**, Where to stay), all Mérida agencies go here.

Beyond Tabay the road goes through **Mucurubá** (2400 m) with a pleasant Plaza Bolívar and blue and white church, colonial buildings and handicrafts, and passes the **Monumento al Perro Nevado**. It depicts Simón Bolívar, the Indian boy, Tinjaca, the Mucuchíes dog, Snowy, and the father and son who gave Bolívar the dog in 1813. According to legend, both Tinjaca and Nevado were devoted to Bolívar until their death on the same day at the Battle of Carabobo, 1821. At **Mucuchíes** (*Phone code: 0274; Population: 9175; Altitude: 2983 m*) the statue of the Liberator on Plaza Bolívar also features Tinjaca and Snowy. Also on the Plaza is a wooden statue of San Isidro, patron saint of farmers; all rural communities honour him on 15 May. The patron saint of Mucuchíes is San Benito; this festival (and several others) on 27-30 December is celebrated by participants wearing flower-decorated hats and firing blunderbusses. **Tourist office** on Calle 9 as you enter from Mérida; internet at Calle 9 Independencia.

The road leads up from Mucuchíes to **San Rafael de Mucuchíes** (*Altitude: 3140 m; Fiesta 24 October*). You should visit the remarkable church, pieced together from thousands of stones, by the late Juan Félix Sánchez (born 1900), nationally renowned as a sculptor, philosopher and clown. The chapel is dedicated to the Virgen de Coromoto; it was blessed by Pope John Paul II. The tombs of Sánchez and his companion of 50 years, Epifania Gil, are inside. Next door is his house, now a museum with photos, weavings and sculptures. Opposite is the library given by him to the community. He built a similar chapel at El Tisure. The picturesque road continues to Apartaderos (two hours from Mérida). It follows the Río Chama valley in the heart of the cultivated highlands and the fields extend up to the edge of the *páramo*, clinging to the steep slopes. Main crops are potatoes (four harvests a year) onions, garlic and carrots. East of the Río Chama is the Sierra Nevada; to the west is the Sierra de La Culata. There are handicrafts, *posadas* and eateries.

Apartaderos (*Phone code: 0274; Altitude: 3342 m*) is at the junction of Route 7 and the road over the Sierra Nevada to Barinas. About 3 km above Apartaderos, a narrow paved road (signposted) turns west off the highway at Escuela Estatal 121 and winds its way to **Llano del Hato** (3510 m) and on to the **Centro de Investigaciones de Astronomía** (3600 m) ① *T0274-245 0106, www.cida.ve, the 4 telescopes and modern facilities are open Wed-Sat 1500-1900, Apr-Jan subject to weather conditions(check website for details), US$0.50 for adults, US$0.25 under-18s and students with card, seniors and under-8s free.* At least two view-points on the way in give great views of the Lake Mucubají plateau. A good paved road descends 7 km from Llano del Hato to the Mérida highway at La Toma, just above Mucuchíes. Many prehispanic terraces and irrigation systems, adobe houses and ox-ploughed fields (*poyos*) are visible from the road.

Three kilometres beyond the junction of the roads from Barinas and Valera is the entrance to the **Parque Nacional Sierra Nevada** (Línea Cultura bus from Mérida ends at the junction, two hours; taxis run from bus stop to park, US$2.35). At the turn-off to the park is a motel and restaurant. Near the entrance is **Laguna Mucubají**, at 3600 m, with free campsite; visitors' centre, bookshop, good maps, interesting museum. A two- to 2½-hour walk takes you to **Laguna Negra** and back (1½ hours on horseback, US$3-4 to hire a horse, guide US$1.50). A further 1½-hour walk from Laguna Negra is the beautiful **Laguna Los Patos**. There are many *frallejón* plants here. Guides (not always necessary) are at Laguna Mucubají or the hotels in Santo Domingo. *Páramo* tours to this area usually include Pico El Aguila (see Road to the high Andes, page 1526).

From Mérida to the Panamericana

There are three routes from Mérida to the Panamericana which runs at the foot of the Andes near the border with Zulia state. The most northerly of them is the most interesting. This beautiful journey, starting in the highlands from Mérida, heads west. It passes La Chorrera waterfall on the way to La Encrucijada (restaurant and service station), where a side road leads to **Jají** (*Phone code: 0274*), a pretty, restored colonial village with white-washed houses, cobbled streets, arches on the exits to the plaza and a white and blue church. Most houses are given over to handicrafts shops. There are a few hotels and others in the hills, where there is good walking. *Buseta* from Mérida bus terminal, hourly, 50 minutes, US$0.50. From La Encrujidada the road passes dairy farms before its descent through cloud forest. Towns passed on the way are San Eusebio and Mirabel. This is prime birdwatching territory as the road, paved but rough in parts, twists down through several habitats. **La Azulita**, 73 km, four hours from Mérida, is the base for birdwatching tours, with several lodges nearby. A modern cathedral stands on the Plaza. From La Azulita, the road meets the Panamericana at Caño Zancudo, passing en route the Cascada Palmita. Turn south for El Vigía, one of the hottest zones in South America, and routes to Lago de Maracaibo and Catatumbo.

El Vigía is where the second route from Mérida meets the Panamericana. Transandean Route 7 leaves Mérida and passes through El Ejido, originally known as Las Guayabas, or 'the city of honey and flowers'. El Ejido and surrounding villages in the sugar cane zone are known for handicrafts and ceramics. One such historic town is **Mesa de los Indios** (www.andes.net/mesadelosindios), where sugarcane is produced, 5 km from El Ejido towards Jaji, 1¼ hours from Mérida. It is famous for its musical traditions and for its artists. Every Saturday *La Retreta de Antonio Valero*, a youth group band, plays wind and percussion instruments in the plaza at 2000. Travellers may donate a wind instrument to the youngsters. Buses to La Mesa leave the plaza in El Ejido. The main road follows the Chama valley, to Lagunillas and Tovar.

Lagunillas was founded in the 16th century by Spaniard Juan Rodríguez Suárez on the site of a pre-hispanic ceremonial centre. Its elaborately choreographed dances honouring a beautiful indigenous princess can be seen at festivities taking place on 15 May. More can be learned at **Museo Arqueológico Julio César Salas** ⓘ *on Parque Sucre*. **San Juan de Lagunillas**, 2 km away, is where Mérida was originally supposed to be built. Locals (and allegedly doctors) say that the climate is one of the healthiest in the world. There are botanical gardens and a colourful fiesta on 24 June.

Near Estanques, a winding road leads towards **Chiguará**, one of the best-preserved coffee towns in Venezuela. Bizarrely, it contains a theme park: **La Montaña de los Sueños** ⓘ *www.montanadelossuenos.com, 1300-2100, daily, ticket office open 1300-1700, US$7, children and senior citizens US$5, food available*, devoted to the history of the Venezuelan film industry (1950s to 1970s), complete with sets, old aeroplanes, limousines, cameras and posters. There are also displays of local television, commercial music and theatre. Chiguará is 45 km from Mérida: take bus or por puesto towards El Vigía and ask to be dropped at junction for Chiguará, from where you have to hitch or wait for infrequent bus or por puesto.

Beyond Estanques the main highway for bus and heavy traffic turns off Route 7. Near the intersection on the right is 19th-century **Hacienda La Victoria** with an interesting coffee museum. The highway descends from the grey, scarred mountains before the thickly wooded tropical hillsides above the plains. Buses between Mérida and San Crístobal then belt along the Panamericana to La Fría from where a four-lane motorway goes to San Cristóbal. The third route leaves the Transandean road at **Tovar** (*Phone code: 0275, 96 km from Mérida*), passing through Zea, a pleasant town in the foothills.

From Mérida to Táchira

From Tovar the road continues to **Bailadores** (fiesta from Christmas to Candlemas, 2 February), and **La Grita**, a pleasant town in Táchira state (Sunday market, fiesta 6 August). Near Bailadores is the pleasant Parque La Cascada India Carú, named after a legendary princess whose tears at the death of her warrior lover created the waterfall. This route takes the wild and beautiful old mountain road over Páramo de La Negra to San Cristóbal. Mérida- San Cristóbal buses go via La Fría, not this road; by public transport change in Tovar and La Grita.

San Cristóbal → *Phone code: 0276. Colour map 1, B4. Population: 297,620. Altitude: 830 m.*

The capital of Táchira State was founded in 1561. Today it's a large, busy, but friendly place built over hills and ravines, although a few blocks in historic centre, around the cathedral, retain a colonial air. You need to know which district you are in for orientation, eg La Concordia for the bus station. The **Fiesta de San Sebastián** in second half of January is a major international event, with parades, trade shows, and much more; book ahead, prices rise. **Tourist office**: Cotatur ⓘ *Av España con Av Carabobo, T357 9655, www.cotatur.gob.ve; see also www.traveltachira.com*. Helpful. Inparques ⓘ *Parque Metropolitano, Av 19 de Abril, T346 6544*. **Note** San Cristóbal was a centre of major anti-government protest in 2014.

On Sunday, take a taxi to **Peribeca** (US$13.25 one way), a tiny colonial village with handicraft shops, restaurants and sellers of dairy products, fruit desserts and bewildering variety of liqueurs and infusions. The pretty handicraft alley is next to the modern church. There are four *posadas* and many restaurants open for Sunday lunch (the best is **El Solar de Juancho**). Alternatively, on Monday, go to the wholesale vegetable market of **Táriba**, just off highway going north. The town's huge white Basílica de la Virgen de la Consolación (1959) can be seen from the highway.

San Cristóbal to San Antonio → *Phone code: 0276. Colour map 1, B4. Population: 52,600.*

The border town of San Antonio is 55 km from San Cristóbal by a paved, congested road. At **Capacho** (25 km from San Antonio) is an interesting old Municipal Market building, with lions at the four corners.

San Antonio is connected by international bridge with Cúcuta on the Colombian side (16 km); continue by road or air to Bogotá. San Antonio has a colonial cathedral and some parks, but is not tourist-oriented. Avenida Venezuela leads to Venezuelan customs. You can catch most transport here, to Cúcuta, San Cristóbal, even to Caracas, but the bus terminal is off the road to the airport: at the roundabout at end of Avenida Venezuela, turn left (Calle 11), take a Circunvalación combi marked Terminal (US$0.30). Also buses to airport. There is a festival on 13-20 May.

Border with Colombia This is the main crossing point between the two countries and the border formalities are geared towards locals. Few foreigners travel overland here. Make sure you get a Venezuelan exit stamp at **SAIME** ① *Cra 9 entre 6 y 7, Antiguo Hospital San Vicente, T771 2282.* You will have to fill out a departure card and pay departure tax across the street. **Colombian consulate** ① *Av 1 de Mayo No 8-52, T771 5890, open 0800-1400*; better to get a visa in Mérida. The border is open 24 hours but **note** Venezuelan time is 30 minutes ahead of Colombian. Colombian formalities are taken care of right after the bridge: immigration procedures are straightforward with only a passport check and stamp. Colombian and Venezuelan citizens do not need any immigration formalities. Foreigners can arrange exit and entry stamps 0800-1800, often much later. If you only travel to Cúcuta (even to spend the night), no immigration formalities are needed. Just cross the bridge by bus, taxi or por puesto and return the same way. If you plan to travel further to Colombia, however, you will need both Venezuelan exit stamp and Colombian entry stamp.

Entering Venezuela, get your passport stamp at immigration and take bus, por puesto or taxi across the bridge. Ask the driver to take you to Venezuelan immigration, otherwise you will be taken to the centre of San Antonio and will have to backtrack. You can also cross the bridge on foot. Information centre is at the end of the bridge on Venezuelan side. Go to **SAIME** for entry formalities then look for a bus or por puesto to San Cristóbal on Av Venezuela, or go to the bus station (taxi from SAIME US$1.50). If Venezuelan customs is closed at weekends, it is not possible to cross from Cúcuta. There is a customs and Guardia Nacional post at Peracal outside San Antonio; be prepared for luggage and strip searches. There may be more searches en route.

If crossing by private vehicle, car documents must be stamped at the SENIAT office at the Puente Internacional, just before San Antonio. Two different stamps are needed at separate **SENIAT buildings** ① *Mon-Fri 0800-1200, 1330-1700, Sat 0800-1200, final Av Venezuela, Edif Nacional San Antonio de Táchira, T771 1620, www.seniat.gob.ve.* It's essential to have proof of car/motorbike ownership. You must check in advance if you need a visa and a *carnet de passages* (see box in Essentials chapter). See Cúcuta, Colombia chapter, for details on exit formalities. Once in Venezuela, you may find police are ignorant of requirements for foreign cars.

◉ Sierra Nevada de Mérida listings

For hotel and restaurant price codes, and other relevant information, see Essentials.

◉ Where to stay

Los Nevados *p1536*
$ pp El Buen Jesús, T252 5696. Hot water, meals available.

$ pp Posada Bella Vista, behind church. Hot water, hammocks, great views, restaurant.

$ pp Posada Guamanchi, T252 2080, www.guamanchi.com. Solar power, great views, with and without bath, 2 meals included. Recommended.

El Morro
$ Posada run by Doña Chepa, as you enter from Los Nevados, warm. Recommended.

$ pp Posada El Orégano, including meals, basic, good food. Recommended.

Tabay *p1536*

$$ Casa Vieja, Transandina via Páramo, San Rafael de Tabay, inside the Parador Turístico El Paramito, T0274-417 1489, www.casa-vieja-merida.com. Plant-filled colonial house, German and Peruvian owners, good doubles, hot water, breakfast and dinner available, good food, relaxing, very helpful, information on independent trips from Tabay and transport, English, French and German spoken. Travel agency, **Caiman Tours**, for Llanos, wildlife and adventure tours, see also www.birds-venezuela. de and www.nature-travel.net. From the bus terminal in Mérida take a bus via Mucuchíes or Apartaderos, 30 mins to Tabay, get off exactly 1.5 km after the gas station in Tabay village (just after you pass Plaza Bolívar); the bus stop is called El Paramito. There is a sign on the road pointing left. Free pick-up from the airport or terminal with reservation. They also have a second *posada* in the village of Altamira de Cáceres. Warmly recommended.

$ La Casona de Tabay, on the Mérida road 1.5 km from the plaza, T0274-283 0089, posadalacasona@cantv.net. A beautiful colonial-style hotel, surrounded by mountains, comfortable, home cooking, family-run. Take *por puesto*, 2 signposts.

$ pp Posada de la Mano Poderosa, beyond San Rafael de Tabay on road to Mucuchíes, T0414-742 2862. Dorms, lovely, quiet, hot showers, good food, great value, get off at La Plazuela then walk 15 mins towards Vivero Fruti Flor.

Mucuchíes

$$-$ Los Conquistadores, Av Carabobo 14, T872 0350, www.losconquistadoreshotelresort. com. Nice decor, modern, heating, lots of facilities like pool tables and other games, garden, parking, restaurant 0800-2200, tasca, and bike hire. Arranges transport for tours, ATM.

$ Posada Los Andes, Independencia 25, T872 0151, T0414-717 2313. Old house on street above plaza, run by Las Hermanas Pironi Belli, 5 cosy rooms, hot water, shared bathrooms, TV in living room, excellent restaurant (breakfast extra, criollo and Italian food, 0800-2030). Highly recommended.

San Rafael de Mucuchíes

$ Casa Sur, Independencia 72, T872 0342, T0416-275 1684, njespindola@yahoo.com. Hot water, heating, breakfast extra, other meals on request.

$ El Rosal, Bolívar 37, T872 0331, T0416-275 3254. Hot water, good, also cabins with kitchenette (**$$**), no breakfast, café nearby, restaurant for groups, tasca at weekends.

$ Posada San Rafael del Páramo, just outside San Rafael, 500 m from the Capilla de Piedra, on road to Apartaderos, T872 0938. Charming converted house with lots of interesting sculpture and paintings, hot water, heating, also cabin with kitchenette, walking and riding tours (guide extra). Recommended.

Apartaderos *p1537*

$$ Hotel Parque Turístico, main road, T888 0094. Cheaper in low season. Attractive modern chalet-style building, heating, very hot showers, helpful owner, expensive restaurant. Recommended.

$$-$ Hotel y Restaurante Mifafí, on main road, T888 0131, refugioturisticomifafi@hotmail. com. Cheaper without heating, pleasant rooms and cabins, hot water, good food. A welcoming, reliable choice.

$ Posada Viejo Apartaderos, outside town, coming from Mucuchíes, T888 0003, *posada* viejoapartaderos@cantv.net. Next to *bomba*, with La Matica de Rosa restaurant, T271 2209, Sra Marbeles. Open only in high season. Good value, good restaurant with reasonable prices.

From Mérida to the Panamericana *p1537*
Jají

$$ pp Estancia La Bravera, 18 km from Jají towards La Azulita, T0212-978 2627, 414-293 3306, www.estancialabravera.com. Cabins in beautiful flower gardens in the cloud forest, great for birdwatching and for relaxing, hot water, includes breakfast and dinner, lunch extra, uses home produce, holds an annual Estancia Musical (Aug). Recommended.

$$ Hacienda El Carmen, Aldea La Playa, 2 km from Jají (there is public transport), T414-639 2701, T0414-630 9562, www.haciendael carmen.com.ve. On a working dairy and coffee-processing farm, built 1863, fascinating buildings, lovely rooms, one with jacuzzi (**$$**), some simpler rooms, breakfast included, coffee tours, owner Andrés Monzón.

$$ Hacienda Santa Filomena, 5 mins from Jají, T 658 2943, T0412-247 9020, www.santafilomena.com.ve. Stay and dine on a 19th-century coffee farm. Used by birders.

$$-$ Posada Restaurant Aldea Vieja, C Principal, just off Plaza, T0426-926 0367, http://aldeavieja.com. Colonial-style main building, also cabins for 4-8, lovely views, simple rooms, hot water, meals extra, playground.

$ Posada Turística Jají, beside the Prefectura, on the plaza, T416 6333. 4 rooms with hot water, no TV, historic, 2 fountains, restaurant 0800-2100, breakfast included if staying a few days.

La Azulita

$ El Tao, on a side road beyond Remanso, 4-5 km, 6 mins in car from La Azulita, T0274-511 3088, T0416-175 0011, www.eltaomerida.com. Taoist owners and oriental-style spa with saunas, and natural therapies, many birds, favoured by birders and other groups, lovely gardens, very safe and peaceful, nice public areas. Cabins for 2-4, restaurant, boxed lunches and early breakfast for birding groups.

$ Posada Turística La Azulita, on Plaza Bolívar. Rooms around restaurant in courtyard, OK food. Some other lodgings in town.

$ Remanso del Quebradón, close to junction, T0416-775 7573, www.remanso.com.ve. 4 rooms, on a small coffee farm with fruit trees in the gardens, restaurant, popular with birdwatchers.

Mesa de los Indios

$$ Posada Papá Miguel, C Piñango 1, T0274-417 4315, T0414-747 9953, www.posada papamiguel.com. Rustic and characterful, a good place to stay if staying to hear the music on Sat night.

San Cristóbal *p1538*

Cheapest hotels around the bus station (eg **Río de Janeiro**, C 1, No 7-27, Urb Juan Maldonado, La Concordia, by bus station, T347 7666, and **Tropical**, Prol 5ta Av No 7472, opposite bus station, T347 2932), **$$** business hotels in the centre and more upmarket places in the northwestern suburbs.

$$ Del Rey, Av Ferrero Tamayo, Edif El Rey, T343 0561. Good showers, fridge, kitchenette, laundry, no breakfast but *panadería* in building, pizzas. Recommended.

$$ Lidotel, Sambil San Cristóbal Mall, Autopista Antonio José de Sucre, Las Lomas, T510 3333, www.lidotelhotelboutique.com. Attached to an enormous, posh shopping mall, with all the luxuries of 4-star hotel, pool, very well run. Recommended.

$ Posada Turística Don Manuel, Cra 10 No 1-104, just off Av 19 de Abril, Urb La Concordia, T347 8082. Rooms are across street; Sra Carmen will direct you. Hot water, family run, fridge, fan, limited kitchen facilities, no breakfast, parking. Sleeps 8, always book in advance, convenient.

$ Posada Rincón Tachirense, Av Ferrero Tamayo con C 3, N Ft-19, La Popita, T341 8573, www.posadarincontachirense.com. Not central, down hill from **Del Rey**, cheaper with shared bath, comfortable, breakfast and will ring out for pizza. Recommended.

San Cristóbal to San Antonio *p1539*
Capacho

$ La Molinera, 20 mins from San Cristóbal at Capacho, municipalidad de Independencia, T788 3117. Rooms and suites in a beautiful, traditional *posada* with swimming pool and handmade furniture. Good Tachirense food in its restaurant.

San Antonio

Many hotels near town centre.

$ Adriático, C6 y Cra 6, T771 5757. Not far from Av Venezuela, 3-star, functional.

$ Neveri, C 3, No 3-13, esq Carrera 3, T771 5702. Safe, parking nearby, 1 block from Customs, opposite Guardia Nacional barracks. No food, dated. Internet next dor.

Restaurants

San Cristóbal *p1538*

El Barrio Obrero has the main concentration of eateries, bars and discos. Try **Rocamar**, Cra 20 y C 14, for seafood. Also pizza places and *pastelerías*.

$$-$ La Olleta, Cra 21, no 10-171, just off plaza, Barrio Obrero, T356 6944. Smart, simple decor, Venezuelan and international with creative touches, well presented.

Around town there are many *panaderías* and *pastelerías* for snacks as well as bread and cakes, coffee and other drinks, eg **América**, Cra 8, Edif La Concordia, no 4-113, La Concordia (several on Cra 8 y C 4, La Concordia); also **Táchira** branches.

San Antonio *p1539*
$ Rosmar, Cra 6 y C 6, opposite Hotel Adriático. Very popular for lunch, several choices, OK food.

⊙ Transport

Los Nevados *p1536*
Jeep Los Nevados-**Mérida**, late afternoon (depart 0700 from Plaza Las Heroínas in Mérida), 5-6 hrs, US$4 pp, US$15 per jeep, very rough and narrow but spectacular.

Tabay *p1536*
Regular bus service from **Mérida** C 19 entre Avs 3 y 4, every 10 mins, US$0.50; taxi US$2-3 (more at night).

Apartaderos *p1537*
Bus To **Mérida** from turn-off to Barinas; bus to **Barinas** on the road over the Sierra Nevada is unreliable, best to catch it in Mérida.

San Cristóbal *p1538*
Air Airport at Santo Domingo, 40 km away. Helpful tourist kiosk with leaflets, map of San Cristóbal US$0.50. Taxi to San Cristóbal US$5, can take as little as 35 mins, but normally much more, lots of traffic, nice scenery (tourist office says no other option). Daily flights to/from **Caracas**. Alternatively fly to San Antonio (see below) for better public transport links.
Bus Local buses cost US$0.40. 'Intercomunal' goes from Av Ferrero Tamayo (northwest) to Bus Terminal. 'Tusca' from Av Ferrero Tamayo to centre. Taxis US$2.50 for a short run.

The bus station is in La Concordia, in the southeast. It is a bus terminal, shopping mall, market, phone exchange and food court all lumped together. Terminal tax US$0.10, paid on bus before departure. Company offices are grouped together, but **Expresos Occidente** have their own terminal nearby. To **Mérida**, US$3.25, 5 hrs, with **Táchira-Mérida** (buy ticket

on bus); also **Expreso Unido**. Buses to Mérida go via the Panamericana, not over the Páramo. National Guard Control at La Jabonesa, just before San Juan de Colón, be prepared for luggage search. To **Maracaibo**, 6-8 hrs, US$7. To **Caracas**, US$8-10, 15 hrs; **Valencia**, US$9. To **Barinas**, US$3.25. To **San Fernando de Apure** via **Guasdualito**, US$8. To **San Antonio**, 1¼ hrs (but San Cristóbal rush hour can add lots of time), US$0.80, **Línea San Antonio**, T347 0976 (San Antonio 771 2966) and **Unión de Conductores**, T346 0691 (San Antonio 771 1364). To **Cúcuta**, **Línea Venezuela**, T347 3086 (Cúcuta T0270-583 6413) and **Fronteras Unidas**, T347 7446 (Cúcuta T0270 583 5445), US$1.35, Mon-Fri 0800-1200, 1400-1800. Opposite terminal on Rugeles, **Coop de Conductores Fronterizos** cars, T611 2256, to **San Antonio**.

San Antonio *p1539*
Air The airport has exchange facilities (mainly for Colombian pesos). Taxis run to SAIME (immigration) in town, and on to Cúcuta airport. Flights to **Caracas**.
Bus From terminal several companies to **Caracas**, via the Llanos, Valencia and Maracay. All *bus-cama*: Caracas US$10. **Expresos San Cristóbal** have office on Av Venezuela, close to Customs, 1800 to Caracas, 13-14 hrs; **Expresos Mérida**, Av Venezuela, No 6-17, at 1900. **Táchira-Mérida** to **Mérida** and **Barquisimeto**; **Expresos Unidos** to Mérida. To **San Cristóbal**, catch a bus on Av Venezuela.

Border with Colombia *p1539*
Air It is cheaper, but slower, to fly Caracas–San Antonio, take a taxi to Cúcuta, then take an internal Colombian flight, than to fly direct Caracas-Colombia. The airport transfer at San Antonio is well organized and taxi drivers make the 25-min trip with all stops.
Bus On Av Venezuela *por puestos/colectivos* to **Cúcuta** charge US$0.50, and buses US$0.25 payable in bolívares or pesos, 30 mins. Some say to terminal, others to centre. Taxi to Cúcuta, US$4. On any transport that crosses the border, make sure the driver knows you need to stop to obtain stamps. *Por puesto* drivers may refuse to wait. Taxi drivers will stop at all the offices.

Los Llanos and Amazonas

A spectacular route descends from the Sierra Nevada to the flat llanos, one of the best places in the world to see birds and animals. This vast, sparsely populated wilderness of 300,000 sq km – one third of the country's area – lies between the Andes to the west and the Orinoco to the south and east. Southwest of the Guayana region, on the banks of the Orinoco, Puerto Ayacucho is the gateway to the jungles of Venezuela. Although it takes up about a fifth of the country, Amazonas and its tropical forests is for the most part unexplored and unspoilt.

Los Llanos

The *llanos* are veined by numerous slow-running rivers, forested along their banks. The flat plain is only varied here and there by *mesas*, or slight upthrusts of the land. About five million of the country's 6.4 million cattle are in the *llanos*, but only around 10% of the human population. When the whole plain is periodically under water, the *llaneros* drive their cattle into the hills or through the flood from one *mesa* to another. When the plain is parched by the sun and the savanna grasses become inedible they herd the cattle down to the damper region of the Apure and Orinoco. Finally they drive them into the valley of Valencia to be fattened.

In October and November, when the vast plains are still partially flooded, wildlife abounds. Animals include capybara, caiman, monkeys, anacondas, river dolphins, pumas and many bird species. Though you can explore independently, towns are few and distances are great. It's better to visit on a tour from Mérida (page 1533), or stay at one of the ecotourism *hatos* (see below).

Guanare → *Phone code: 0257. Colour map 1, B5. Population: 32,500.*
An excellent road goes to the western *llanos* of Barinas from Valencia. It goes through San Carlos, Acarigua (an agricultural centre and the largest city in Portuguesa state) and Guanare, a national place of pilgrimage with a cathedral containing the much venerated relic of the Virgin of Coromoto. The **Santuario Nacional Nuestra Señora de Coromoto** ① *25 km form Guanare on road to Barinas, open 0800-1700*, is on the spot where the Virgin appeared to Cacique Coromoto in 1652. An imposing modern basilica dedicated to the Virgin, it was inaugurated by Pope John Paul II in 1996. Buses run from Calle 20 y Carrera 9, Guanare, every 15 minutes (US$0.25). Pilgrimages to Coromoto are 2 January and 11 September and Candlemas is 2 February.

Barinas → *Phone code: 0273. Colour map 1, A5. Population: 345,000.*
The road continues to Barinas, the capital of the cattle-raising and oil-rich state of Barinas. A few colonial buildings remain on the plaza: the **Palacio del Marqués** and the **Casa de la Cultura**. Also here is the beautifully restored, 19th-century **Escuela de Música**; the cathedral is to the east. The shady Parque Universitario, just outside the city on Avenida 23 de Enero, has a botanical garden. **Tourist office** ① *C Arzobispo Méndez, edif Vifran, p 1, diagonal al Banco Exterior, T552 7091*. Helpful, maps, no English spoken; kiosks at airport and bus station.

San Fernando de Apure → *Phone code: 0247. Colour map 1, A6. Population: 171,660.*

At Lagua, 16 km east of Maracay, a good road leads south to San Fernando de Apure. It passes through San Juan de los Morros, with natural hot springs; Ortiz, near the crossroads with the San Carlos-El Tigre road; the Guárico lake and Calabozo. Some 132 km south of Calabozo, San Fernando is the hot and sticky capital of Apure state and a fast-growing trade and transport hub. From San Fernando travel east to Ciudad Bolívar (page 1568) or south to Puerto Ayacucho (see below).

San Fernando to Barinas

From San Fernando a road heads west to Barinas (468 km). It's a beautiful journey, but the road can be in terrible condition, eg between Mantecal, La Ye junction and Bruzual, a town just south of the Puente Nutrias on the Río Apure. In the early morning, many animals and birds can be seen, and in the wet season caiman (alligators) cross the road. **Mantecal** is a friendly cattle-ranching town with hotels and restaurants. **Fiesta**, 23-26 February.

⊙ Los Llanos listings

For hotel and restaurant price codes, and other relevant information, see Essentials.

⊙ Where to stay

Barinas *p1543*

$ El Palacio, Av Elías Cordero con C 5, T552 6947. Good value, parking, near bus terminal so front rooms are noisy.

$ Internacional, C Arzobispo Méndez on Plaza Zamora, T552 2343, hotelinternacional_3@ hotmail.com. Safe, good restaurant.

$ Varyná, Av 23 de Enero, near the airport, T533 2477. Hot water, restaurant, parking. Recommended.

Staying at a tourist ranch

An alternative to travelling independently or arranging a tour from Mérida is to stay at a tourist ranch. Most are in Apure state and can be reached from Barinas or San Fernando de Apure.

$$ Hato Chinea Arriba, the closest *hato* to Caracas, is a 5 mins' drive from Calabozo, T0414-322 0785, www.haciendachineaarriba. com. Prices all-inclusive. Owner Francisco Leitz speaks French, German and English.

$$ Hato El Cedral, about 30 mins by bus from Mantecal (see above). Address: Av La Salle, edif Pancho p 5, of 33, Los Caobos, Caracas, T0212-781 8995, www.elcedral.com. A 53,000-ha ranch, where hunting is banned. Fully inclusive price, tax extra (high season Nov-Apr), a/c, hot water, land and river safaris, guides, pool. The government has nationalized the ranch,

see www.venetur.gob.ve for this and other nationalized ranches.

$$ Hato La Fe, Km 51 between Calabozo and San Fernando de Apure at Corozopando in Guárico state, www.ecoposadalafe.com. All-inclusive tours include animal-watching trips and horse riding. 8 bedrooms in a colonial-style house, pool, camping available.

$$ pp Hato Piñero, a safari-type lodge at a working ranch near El Baúl (turn off Tinaco-El Sombrero road at El Cantón). 2-night, 3-day packages cost US$120 pp, including food, lodging, tours with local guides, but not return transport from Caracas. Bird- and animal-watching trips. The ranch has been bought by the government, but still accepts visitors and tour groups. Contact Ascanio Birding Tours in Caracas, www.abtbirds.com, well in advance to make a reservation. From Caracas, 6 hrs; from Ciudad Bolívar, 9 hrs.

$ pp Rancho Grande, close to Mantecal, T0416-873 1192. Run by very friendly and knowledgeable Ramón Guillermo González. All inclusive, good wildlife spotting and horse riding trips, 4-day packages.

San Fernando de Apure *p1544*

Most hotels are within 1 block of the intersection of Paseo Libertador and Av Miranda.

$ El Río, Av María Nieves, near the bus terminal, T341 1928. Good value.

$ Gran Hotel Plaza, C Bolívar, T342 1746, 2 blocks from the bus terminal, www.granhotel plaza.com. Good, safe hotel with parking.

$ La Torraca, Av Boulevard y Paseo Libertador by Plaza Bolívar, T342 2777. Rooms have balcony overlooking centre of town. Recommended.
$ Trinacria, Av Miranda, near bus terminal, T342 3578. Huge rooms, fridge.

⚙ What to do

Barinas *p1543*
Campamento Colibrí, Plaza Bolívar Caño Grande, La Acequia, T0273-514 3022, T0414-748 0064, www.campamentocolibri.com. Rafting trips in association with Colibrí Tours in Mérida.
Grados Alta Aventura, Altamira de Cáceres, T0416-877 4540, http://www.grados.com.ve/ 2011. For rafting trips, kayaking, birdwatching and other adventures, in a historic town.
Rafting Barinas, T0273-311 0388, www.rafting barinas.com. With Campamento Aguas Bravas, Carretera nacional vía San Cristóbal, La Acequia, Caño Grande, Km 4, for rafting excursions.

⊖ Transport

Barinas *p1543*
Air Aeropuerto Nacional, Av 23 de Enero. Flights to **Caracas**.
Bus To **Mérida**, 6 a day with Transportes Barinas, US$2.50, spectacular ride through the mountains, 5-7 hrs (sit on right for best views); also to **Valera** at 0730, 1130, US$3, 7 hrs. To **Caracas**, US$7, 8 hrs, a few companies go direct or via **Maracay** and **Valencia**. To **San Cristóbal**, several daily, US$3.50, 5 hrs; to **San Fernando de Apure**, US$4.50, 9 hrs with Expresos Los Llanos at 0900, 2300; the same company also goes to **Maracaibo** (at 2000 and 2200, US$7, 8 hrs).

From Barinas there is a beautifully scenic road to Apartaderos, in the Sierra Nevada de Mérida (see page 1537). Motorists travelling east to Ciudad Bolívar can either go across the *llanos* or via San Carlos, Tinaco, El Sombrero, Chaguaramas, Valle de la Pascua (see below) and El Tigre. The latter route requires no ferry crossings and has more places with accommodation.

San Fernando de Apure *p1544*
Air Aeropuerto Las Flecheras, Av 1 de Mayo, T341 0139. Flights to **Caracas**.
Bus Terminal is modern and clean, not far from centre; US$1.75 taxi. To **Caracas**, US$5, 7 hrs; to **Maracay**, US$7; to **Puerto Ayacucho**, US$7, 8 hrs; to **Calabozo**, 1½ hrs, US$2.

San Fernando to Barinas *p1544*
Bus San Fernando de Apure-Mantecal 3½ hrs, US$4, Mantecal-Barinas, 4 hrs, US$4.

Amazonas

Much of Amazonas is stunningly beautiful and untouched, but access is only by river. The more easily accessible places lie on the course of the Orinoco and its tributaries. The best time to visit is October to December after the rains, but at any season, this is a remote part of the country.

San Fernando to Puerto Ayacucho

Due south of San Fernando de Apure is **Puerto Páez** (*Phone code: 0247; Population: 4500*) at the confluence of the Meta and Orinoco rivers; here there is a crossing to El Burro west of the Caicara-Puerto Ayacucho road. On the opposite bank of the Meta from Puerto Páez is Puerto Carreño in Colombia. Route 2 runs south from San Fernando to Puerto Páez, crossing several major rivers. Between the Capanaparo and Cinaruco rivers is the **Parque Nacional Cinaruco-Capanaparo** (also called **Santos Luzardo**), reached only from this road. If this road is closed, to get to Puerto Ayacucho from San Fernando involves a minimum 15-hour detour via the Caicara ferry.

From Caicara a new paved road runs 370 km southwest to Puerto Ayacucho. The turn off to **El Burro**, where the boat crosses the Orinoco to Puerto Páez (ferry US$1), is 88 km north of Puerto Ayacucho (*taxi* El Burro-Puerto Ayacucho, two hours US$3).

Puerto Ayacucho → *Phone code: 0248. Colour map 1, B6. Population: 41,240.*
The capital of the State of Amazonas is 800 km via the Orinoco from Ciudad Bolívar, but no direct boats journey up river. At the end of the dry season (April), it is very hot and humid. It is deep in the

wild, across the Orinoco from Casuarito in Colombia. **Museo Etnológico Monseñor Enzo Ceccarelli** ① *Av Río Negro, Tue-Sat 0830-1200, 1430-1830, Sun 0900-1300, US$0.50,* has a library and collection of regional exhibits, recommended. In front of the museum is a market, Plaza de los Indios, open every day, where *indígenas* sell handicrafts. One block away is the cathedral. Prices in Puerto Ayacucho are generally higher than north of the Orinoco. **Tourist office** is in the Gobernación building, Avenida Río Negro, T521 0033. **Note** Malaria is prevalent in this area; so make sure you take precautions.

Excursions November to December is the best time, when rivers are high but the worst of the rains has passed. In the wettest season, May-June, it may be difficult to organize tours for only a few days. At any time of year, permission from the military may be required to travel independently on the rivers.

You can walk up **Cerro Perico** for good views of the town, or go to the Mirador, 1 km from centre, for good views of the Ature rapids. A recommended trip is to the village of Pintado (12 km south), where petroglyphs described by Humboldt can be seen on the huge rock **Cerro Pintado**. This is the most accessible petroglyph site of the many hundreds which are scattered throughout Amazonas.

Some 35 km south on the road to Samariapo is the **Parque Tobogán de la Selva**, a pleasant picnic area based around a steeply inclined, smooth rock over which the Río Maripures cascades. This waterslide is great fun in the wet season; crowded on Sunday, take swimsuit and food and drink. A small trail leads up from the slide to a natural jacuzzi after about 20 minutes. Enquire at agencies in town about tours.

The well-paved road from Puerto Ayacucho to Samariapo (63 km) was built to bypass the rapids which here interrupt the Orinoco, dividing it into 'Upper' and 'Lower'; the powerful Maripures Rapids are very impressive.

⊙ Amazonas listings

For hotel and restaurant price codes, and other relevant information, see Essentials.

● Where to stay

Puerto Ayacucho *p1545*
$$-$ Orinoquia Lodge, on the Río Orinoco, 20 mins from airport, book through Wao Turismo, T0212-214 1027, www.waoturismo. com, Cacao Travel, www.cacaotravel.com, or through, T0212-977 1234, www.casatropical. com.ve. Nice setting, comfortable lodgings in thatched huts, full board.
$$-$ Gran Hotel Amazonas, Av Evelio Roa y Amazonas, T521 5633, or T0212-635 2166, www.amazonas.travel. Refurbished, with a/c, fridge, pool, restaurant and bar.
$ Posada Manapiare, Urb Alto Parima, 2da entrada, casa 1, T521 3954. Pleasant, good services, lots of information, excellent choice, with restaurant, small pool, safe parking.
$ Res Internacional, Av Aguerrevere 18, T521 0242. A/c (cheaper without); comfortable, shower, locked parking, safe but basic, good

place to find tour information and meet other travellers, if no room available you can sling up your hammock, bus drivers stay here and will drive you to the terminal for early starts.

Río Manapiare area
$$$ Campamento Camani, in a forest clearing on the banks of the Río Alto Ventuari, 2 hrs by launch from San Juan de Manapiare, T521 4865, www.campamentocamani.com. From Puerto Ayacucho daily aerotaxi takes 50 mins. Maximum 26 at any one time, mosquito nets, all amenities, excursions available. Has 2-, 3- and 4-night packages including transport, full board and jungle excursions.

● What to do

Amazonas *p1545*
It is strongly recommended to go on tours organized by tour agents or guides registered in the Asocación de Guías, in the Cámara de Turismo de Puerto Ayacucho, Casa de la Piedra, on the Arteria Vial de la Av Orinoco with

Av Principal (the house on top of the large rock). Some independent guides may not have permission to visit Amazonas. Those listed below arrange permits and insurance but shop around. **Coyote Expediciones**, Av Aguirrevere 75, T521 4582, T0416-448 7125, coyotexpedition@ cantv.net. Helpful, professional, English spoken, organizes trips staying in indigenous villages. **Expediciones Aguas Bravas Venezuela**, Av Río Negro, No 32-2, in front of Plaza Rómulo Betancourt, T521 4458/0541, aguasbravas@ cantv.net. Whitewater rafting, 2 daily 0900-1200 and 1500-1800, 3-13 people per boat, reservations required at peak times, take insect repellent, sun protector, light shoes and swimsuit. See also Rafting Barinas, page 1545.

⊖ Transport

Puerto Ayacucho *p1545*
Air Airport 7 km southeast along Av Orinoco.
Bus Expresos del Valle to **Ciudad Bolívar** (US$25, 10 hrs; take something to eat, bus stops once for early lunch), **Caicara, Puerto Ordaz** and **San Félix**; Cooperativa Cacique to **San Fernando de Apure**, US$7, 8 hrs; both companies in bus terminal. Expresos La Prosperidad to **Caracas** and **Maracay** from Urb Alto Parima. Bus from **Caracas**, daily, US$10, 12 hrs (but much longer in wet season).
Ferry Ferry service across the Orinoco to Casuarito, US$0.60.

East coast

Beautiful sandy bays, islands, forested slopes and a strong colonial influence all contribute to make this one of the most visited parts of the country. The western part, which is relatively dry, has the two main cities, Puerto La Cruz and Cumaná, which is possibly the oldest Hispanic city on the South American mainland. As you go east, you find some splendid beaches.

Off shore are two of Venezuela's prime holiday attractions, Isla de Margarita, a mix of the overdeveloped and the quiet, and the island paradise of the Los Roques archipelago.

Caracas to Puerto La Cruz

Very much a holiday coastline, the first part takes its name from the sweeping Barlovento bay in Miranda state. Onshore trade winds give the seaboard a lusher aspect than the more arid landscape elsewhere.

It is some five hours from Caracas to Puerto La Cruz through Caucagua, from which there is a 58 km road northeast to **Higuerote** (*Phone code: 0234. Population: 25,000*); the best beaches are out of town. A coastal road from Los Caracas to Higuerote has many beaches and beautiful views.

Parque Nacional Laguna de Tacarigua
At 14 km before Higuerote on the road from Caucagua is Tacarigua de Mamporal, where you can turn off to the **Parque Nacional Laguna de Tacarigua**. The 39,100-ha national park is an important ecological reserve, with a lagoon separated from the sea by a landspit, mangroves, good fishing and many water birds, including flamingos (usually involving a day-long boat trip to see them, the best time to see them is 1700-1930; permit required from *Inparques* at the *muelle*, US$1, open 0500-1830). Around 20,700 ha of the park are offshore. Boats leave from the Inparques *muelle* and can be hired to anywhere in the park (about US$2.50 per person). The beaches beyond here are unspoilt and relaxing, but mosquitoes are a problem after sunset.

Puerto La Cruz and around → *Phone code: 0281. Colour map 2, A1.*
Originally a fishing village, Puerto La Cruz (*Population: 454,000*) is now a major oil refining town and busy, modern holiday resort. Tourist facilities are above average, if expensive, and the sea is polluted.

The seafront avenue, Paseo de La Cruz y El Mar (formerly Paseo Colón), extends to the eastern extremity of a broad bay. To the west the bay ends at the prominent El Morro headland. Most hotels, restaurants, bars and clubs are along Paseo de La Cruz y El Mar, with excellent views of Bahía de Pozuelas and the islands of the Parque Nacional Mochima (see below). Vendors of paintings, jewellery, leather and hammocks are on Paseo de La Cruz y El Mar in the evening.

The **Santa Cruz** festival is on 3 May, while 8 September is the **Virgen del Valle**, when boats cruise the harbour clad in palms and balloons; afternoon party at El Faro, Chimana, lots of salsa and beer.

The main attractions of Puerto La Cruz lie offshore on the many islands of the beautiful Parque Nacional Mochima and in the surrounding waters. For details of how to get there, see below. The tourist office is **Fondoturismo** ①*C Bolívar, Ed Araya, local 3 PB, T267 1632, Mon-Fri 0800-1300*, very helpful and friendly.

⊙ Caracas to Puerto La Cruz listings

For hotel and restaurant price codes, and other relevant information, see Essentials.

⊖ Where to stay

Puerto La Cruz *p1547, map p1549*
Newer, upmarket hotels are at Lechería and El Morro; cheaper hotels are concentrated in the centre, though it's not easy to find a cheap hotel.
$$$ Venetur Puerto La Cruz, Paseo de La Cruz y El Mar, east edge of the centre, T500 3611, www.venetur.gob.ve. 5-star hotel with all facilities, including gym, spa, marina and beach access.
$$-$ Rasil, Paseo de La Cruz y El Mar y Monagas 6, T262 3000, www.hotelrasil.com. ve. Rooms, suites and bungalows, 3 restaurants, bar, pool, tour office, gym, money exchange, car rental, convenient for ferries and buses.
$$-$ Riviera, Paseo de La Cruz y El Mar 33, T267 2111, www.hotelriviera.com.ve. Seafront hotel, some rooms have balcony, bar, watersports, very good location, restaurant, poor breakfast.
$ Caribbean Inn, Freites, T267 4292, hotelcaribbean@cantv.net. Big rooms, well kept small pool, very good service.
$ Gaeta, Paseo de La Cruz y El Mar y Maneiro, T265 0411, gaeta@telcel.net.ve. Modern, good location but very small rooms, restaurant.
$ Senador, Miranda y Bolívar, T267 3522, hotelsenadorplc@cantv.net. Back rooms quieter, restaurant with view, parking.

⊘ Restaurants

Puerto La Cruz *p1547, map p1549*
Many on Paseo de La Cruz y El Mar, eg **Tío Pepe**, delicious sea food. **O Sole Mio**, cheap, excellent, wide variety. **Trattoria Dalla Nonna**, Italian food.
$ El Guatacarauzo, de La Cruz y El Marnear Pizza Hut. Live music, salsa, good atmosphere and value.
$ La Colmena, next to **Hotel Riviera**. Vegetarian.
$ Salmorejo, Miranda y Honduras. For chicken and seafood, with a terrace.

Cafés
Heladería Tropic, Galería Colón on Paseo de La Cruz y El Mar. Good ice cream.

⊙ What to do

Puerto La Cruz *p1547, map p1549*
Diving Several companies, mostly on Paseo de La Cruz y El Mar, run diving courses. They're a bit more pricey than Santa Fe and Mochima. Hotels and travel agents also organize trips. The nearest recompression chamber is on Isla Margarita.
Kayaking Jakera, www.jakera.com. Sea kayaks for rent from their lodge at Playa Colorada (T0293-808 7057), trips to whole country arranged (lodge in Mérida too, office C 24, No 8-205, Plaza Las Heroínas, Mérida, T0274-252 9577, 0416-887 2239), also Spanish lessons and volunteering. Chris and Joanna are helpful, English spoken.

Puerto La Cruz *p1547, map p1549*
Bus Bus terminal to the east of town; *por
puesto* terminal at Av Juncal y Democracia,
many buses also stop here. **Aeroexpresos
Ejecutivos** to/from **Caracas** 5 a day, 5 hrs,
US$4.50 (T267 8855, next to ferry terminal),
highly recommended (also to **Maracay**,
US$6, **Valencia**, US$7, and **Barquisimeto**).
Other companies to **Caracas** charge US$4.
To **Ciudad Bolívar** US$3.75; to **Ciudad
Guayana** US$7.50. To **Cumaná**, bus US$1.50,
1½ hrs. To **Carúpano**, US$2.50, 5 hrs. *Por puesto*
to **Playa Colorado** US$1 and to **Santa Fe**
US$2. Along Av 5 de Julio runs a bus marked

'Intercomunal'. It links Puerto La Cruz with
the city of Barcelona (which has the nearest
airport) and intervening points. Another
Barcelona bus is marked 'Ruta Alternativa' and
uses the inland highway via the Puerto La Cruz
Golf and Country Club and Universidad de
Oriente, US$0.25.
Ferry For details of ferries to Isla de Margarita,
see page 1565.

❶ Directory

Puerto La Cruz *p1547, map p1549*
Banks Italcambio, Av Ppal de Lechería,
CC Galery Center, Loc 10, T287 2066 Oficambio,
Mancim y Honduras, open 0000-1045 Mon-Fri

Puerto La Cruz

To Cumaná & Parque Nacional Mochima

Caribbean Sea

Marina

Plaza Colón

Plaza Bolívar

Por Puesto Terminal

Por Puestos to Conferry Terminal

Anzoátegui

To Car Ferry Terminal

To Caracas & Barcelona

| 200 metres |
| 200 yards |

Where to stay 🛏
1 Caribbean Inn
4 Gaeta
6 Rasil
7 Riviera
8 Senador
9 Venetur Puerto La Cruz

Restaurants 🍴
1 El Guatacarauzo
2 Heladería Tropic & Galería Colón
3 La Colmena
4 O Sole Mio
5 Salmorejo
6 Tío Pepe
7 Trattoria Dalla Nonna

Parque Nacional Mochima

Beyond the cities of Barcelona and Puerto La Cruz, the main focus is the Mochima National Park, one of the country's most beautiful regions. Hundreds of tiny Caribbean islands, a seemingly endless series of beaches backed by some of Venezuela's most beautiful scenery and little coves tucked into bays, all offer excellent snorkelling, fishing and swimming.

Visiting Parque Nacional Mochima Tour companies offer trips to the islands from Puerto La Cruz, but you can also go independently with the cooperative boatmen, *peñeros*. One dock, **Transtupaco**, is next to *Venetur Puerto La Cruz*. The other *Embarcadero de Peñeros*, is on the point at the southwest end of Paseo de La Cruz y El Mar, by Calle Anzoátegui. Departures from 0900-1000, return at 1600-1630; US$2.50 per person. If beaches are full, the authorities will stop boats leaving. Tourist office in Puerto La Cruz provides tour operators for day trips to various islands for swimming or snorkelling; six-hour trip to four islands costs US$30 per person, including drinks. The islands to the east (Isla de Plata, Monos, Picuda Grande and Chica and the beaches of Ña Cleta, Conoma and Conomita) are best reached from the ports at **Guanta**, called Barinita and Valle Seco, US$5 (taxi from town, or *por puesto* from C Freites between Avenida 5 de Julio and C Democracia, and ask to be dropped off at the Urb Pamatacualito). **Note** Boat trips to the islands can also be taken from **Santa Fe** or **Mochima** (see below).

Note At Christmas, Carnival and Easter this part of the coast becomes extremely congested so patience is needed as long queues of traffic can develop. Accommodation is very hard to find and prices increase by 20-30%. To prevent littering and pollution, especially on the islands, carry out all your rubbish (no alcohol in glass bottles may be taken). Camping on the islands in Parque Nacional Mochima is possible, but not advisable. To stay overnight you need a permit from Inparques, Parque Andrés Eloy Blanco, US$1.50. Only camping gas cookers allowed. On day trips, take your own food as the island restaurants are expensive. When hiring a parasol for the day, make sure exactly what is included in the price and beware 'extra services'.

Around the park Starting east from Puerto La Cruz is the Costa Azul, with the islands of the Parque Nacional Mochima offshore. Highway 9 follows the shore for much of the 85 km to Cumaná, but a new highway is being built. The road is spectacular but if driving take great care between Playa Colorada and Cumaná. It passes the 'paradise-like' beaches of **Conoma** and **Conomita**. Further along is **Playa Arapito** (*posada, $*, restaurant, parking extra). Here boats can be hired to **La Piscina**, a beautiful coral reef near some small islands, for good snorkelling (with lots of dolphins); US$10 per boat.

    Playa Colorada is a popular beach (Km 32) with beautiful red sands and palm trees (take a *por puesto* from corner of terminal in Puerto La Cruz, US$0.80). Nearby are **Playa Vallecito** (camping free, security guard, bar with good food and bottled water on sale, plenty of palm trees for slinging a hammock) and **Playa Santa Cruz**. At **Playa Los Hicacos** is a lovely coral reef.

    In Sucre State 40 km from Puerto La Cruz is **Santa Fe** (*Phone code: 0293*), larger and noisier than Mochima, but a good place to relax. The attractive beach is cleaned daily. It has a market on Saturday. Jeep, boat or diving tours available. Fishermen offer boat trips, for around US$15 per person to Playas Colorada or Blanca; it's cheaper to hire your own boat, or hitch to Colorada.

    The little village of **Mochima** beyond Santa Fe, is 4 km off the main road (hitching difficult). It's busy at weekends but almost deserted through the week. Boats take tourists to nearby beaches, such as Playa Marita and Playa Blanca (excellent snorkelling, take own equipment). Both have restaurants, but take food and water to be safe. Boats to the nearby beaches cost US$8-10 (up to six people), depending on distance. Arrange with the boatman what time he will collect you. There are also five- to six-island trips, US$15-20. Canoeing trips are available and walks on local trails and to caves (ask for information, eg from Carlos Hernández, or Rodolfo Plaza, see Diving, below).

Parque Nacional Mochima listings

For hotel and restaurant price codes, and other relevant information, see Essentials.

Where to stay

Parque Nacional Mochima *p1550*
Playa Colorada
$$ Sunset Inn, Av Principal, T0416-887 8156. Clean, comfortable, pool, hot water.
$ Quinta Jaly, C Marchán, T808 3246/0416-681 8113. Hot water, very quiet, also 1 bungalow sleeps 6, family atmosphere, English and French spoken, use of kitchen, laundry facilities, good breakfast extra, multilingual library. Recommended.
$ Villa Nirvana, 6-min walk uphill from beach, opposite *Jaly*, run by Sra Rita who is Swiss, T808 7844. Rooms with fan or a/c, also mini- apartments with kitchen for 2-6 people, hot water, kitchen facilities, English, French and German spoken, book exchange, laundry, breakfast extra.

Santa Fe
$$$-$$ Playa Santa Fe Resort and Dive Center, T231 0051, www.santaferesort.com. Renovated *posada* with rooms and suites, laundry service, owner Howard Rankell speaks English, can arrange transport to beaches, kitchen.
$ Bahía del Mar, T231 0073/T0426-481 7242, www.posadabahiadelmar.com. Pleasant rooms with a/c or fan, upstairs rooms have a cool breeze, owners María and Juan speak French and some English.
$ Café del Mar, first hotel on beach, T231 0009, www.turismodeplaya.com/MOCHIMA/CafedelMar.htm. A/c or cheaper with fan, good restaurant. Rogelio Alcaraz speaks English and Italian, arranges tours to islands.
$ Cochaima, on beach, T642 07828. Run by Margot, noisy, popular, a/c or fan, safe. Recommended.
$ La Sierra Inn, near Café del Mar, T231 0042. Self-contained garden suite with fridge and cooker, run by Sr José Vivas, English spoken, helpful, tours to islands. Recommended.
$ Las Palmeras, T231 0008, www.laspalmerassantafe.blogspot.com. Behind **Cochaima**,

fan, room for 5 with fridge and cooker. Price negotiable, ask about light work in exchange for longer stays. English, German, Italian and Portuguese spoken
$ Petit Jardin, behind **Cochaima**, T231 0036/T0416-387 5093, www.lepetitjardin-mochima.com. A/c or fan, hot water, kitchen, pool, helpful.
$ Siete Delfines, on beach, T808 8064, T0416-317 9290, lossietedelfinessantafe@hotmail.com. Cheaper without breakfast, safe, fan, bar, good meals in restaurant, owner speaks English.

Mochima
Various apartments are available for larger groups, look for signs.
$ Posada Doña Cruz, T416 6114. A/c, cable TV. Run by José Cruz, family also rents rooms at **Posada Mama Cruz** on the plaza with a/c and living room.
$ Posada El Embajador, Av W Larrazabal, T416 3437, by the jetty. Good value, comfortable, breakfast, boat trips arranged.
$ Posada Gaby, at end of road with its own pier next to sea, T431 0842/0414-773 1104. A/c or fan, breakfast available, lovely place.
$ Posada Mochimero, on main street in front of Restaurant Mochimero, T0414 773 8782. A/c or fan, rooms with bath.
$ Villa Vicenta, Av Principal, T414 0868. Basic rooms with cold water and larger rooms with balcony, also cold water, dining room, owner Otilio is helpful.

Restaurants

Parque Nacional Mochima *p1550*
Santa Fe
$ Club Naútico, open for lunch and dinner. Fish and Venezuelan dishes.
$ Los Molinos (Julios), open from 0800. Beach bar serves sandwiches, hamburgers and cocktails.

Mochima
$ El Mochimero, on waterfront 5 mins from jetty. Highly recommended for lunch and dinner.
$ Il Forno de Mochima, main street. Run by Roberto Iorio, for those who would like a change from seafood, homemade pastas and pizza.

$ Puerto Viejo, on the plaza. Good food, if a bit pricey, good views.

⚙ What to do

Parque Nacional Mochima *p1550*
Mochima
Diving Francisco García, runs a diving school and shop (**Aquatics Diving Center**, T267 3963, or T0412-947 6375, www.scubavenezuela.com), C La Marina at Plaza Apolinar. Equipment hire, courses, trips.
Rodolfo Plaza runs a diving lodge and school (La Posada de los Buzos, T416 0856/T0414-980 6244, www.laposadadelosbuzos.com) and hires equipment, also walking, rafting (mochimarafting@hotmail.com), kayaking and canoeing trips.

⚙ Transport

Parque Nacional Mochima *p1550*
Santa Fe
Getting there from **Cumaná**, take *por puesto* 1 block down from the Redonda del Indio, along Av Perimetral, US$1.50. It may be difficult to get a bus from **Puerto La Cruz** to stop at Santa Fe, take a *por puesto* (depart from terminal, US$1.50, 1 hr), or taxi, US$5 including wait.

Mochima
Bus From **Cumaná** to Mochima take a bus from outside the terminal and ask to be let off at the street where the transport goes to Mochima, US$1; change here to crowded bus or jeep (US$0.25). No buses between Santa Fe and Mochima, take a *por puesto*, bargain hard on the price, US$7-10 is reasonable. Bus to Cumaná, 1400, US$1.

Cumaná → *Phone code: 0293. Colour map 2, A1. Population: 365,000.*

Cumaná was founded in 1521 to exploit the nearby pearl fisheries. It straddles both banks of the Río Manzanares. Because of a succession of devastating earthquakes (the last in 1997), only a few historic sites remain. Cumaná is a charming place with its mixture of old and new. Like any other city it is not safe at night, the port area (1.5 km from the centre) especially so. Main festivals are 22 January, Santa Inés, a pre-Lenten carnival throughout the state of Sucre and 2 November, the **Santos y Fideles Difuntos** festival at El Tacal.

A long public beach, **San Luis**, is a short bus ride from the centre of town; take the 'San Luis/ Los Chaimas' bus. The least spoilt part is the end by the *Hotel Los Bordones*.

The **Castillo de San Antonio de la Eminencia** (1686) has 16 mounted cannons, a draw- bridge and dungeons from which there are said to be underground tunnels leading to the Santa Inés church. Restored in 1975, it is flood-lit at night (but don't go there after dark, it's not safe). **Castillo de Santa María de la Cabeza** (1669) is a rectangular fortress with a panoramic view of San Antonio and the elegant homes below. **Convento de San Francisco**, the original Capuchin mission of 1514, was the first school on the continent; its remains are on the Plaza Badaracco Bermúdez facing the beach. The **Church of Santa Inés** (1637) was the base of the Franciscan missionaries; earthquakes have caused it to be rebuilt five times. A tiny 400-year-old statue of the Virgen de Candelaria is in the garden. The **home of Andrés Eloy Blanco** (1896- 1955) ① *0800-1200, 1430-1730, free,* one of Venezuela's greatest poets and politicians, on Plaza Bolívar, has been nicely restored to its turn-of-the-century elegance. On the opposite side of the plaza is **La Gobernación** around a courtyard lined by cannon from Santa María de la Cabeza; note the gargoyles and other colonial features. There are markets selling handicrafts and food on both sides of the river.

The **Museo Gran Mariscal de Ayacucho** ① *Consejo Municipal in Parque Ayacucho, Tue-Fri 0845-1130, 1545-1830; free tours,* commemorates the battle of Ayacucho: with portraits, relics and letters of Bolívar and José Antonio Sucre (Bolívar's first lieutenant). **Museo del Mar** ① *Av Universidad with Av Industrial, Tue-Sun 0830-1130, 1500-1800, US$1, getting there: take San Luis minibus from the cathedral,* has exhibits of tropical marine life, at the old airport.

For information contact **Corsotur** ① *C Sucre 49, T441 0136, open mornings only.* This office is very helpful, English spoken. See also www.sucreturistico.com and www.turismosucre.com.

Cumaná listings

For hotel and restaurant price codes, and other relevant information, see Essentials.

⊖ Where to stay

Cumaná *p1552, map p1553*

$$ Los Bordones, at end of Av Universidad on the beach, T400 0350, www.los bordones.com. Pool, restaurant, a hotel with all-inclusive options.

$$ Nueva Toledo Suites, end of Av Universidad, close to San Luis beach, T414 9311, www.nuevatoledo.com. Pool, beach bar, good value all-inclusive deals.

$ Bubulina's, Callejón Santa Inés, ½ a block west of Santa Inés church, T431 4025, bubulinas10@hotmail.com. In the historic centre, beautifully restored colonial building, hot water, good service, German spoken.

$ Posada San Francisco, C Sucre 16, near Santa Inés, T431 3926, posadafrancisco@cantv.net. Renovated colonial house, courtyard, spacious rooms, hot water, cheaper rooms with fan, very helpful, bar, restaurant. Recommended.

$ Posada Tempera, C Páez 7, behind the Cathedral, T431 2178, www.tempera-posada. com. Charming, comfortable small *posada* in historic centre, hot water, a/c, Wi-Fi, good

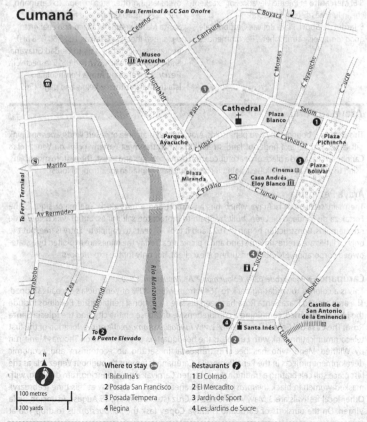

Cumaná

To Bus Terminal & CC San Onofre

Where to stay
1 Bubulina's
2 Posada San Francisco
3 Posada Tempera
4 Regina

Restaurants
1 El Colmao
2 El Mercadito
3 Jardín de Sport
4 Les Jardins de Sucre

100 metres
100 yards

breakfast extra, laundry service, parking outside or in nearby guarded parking lot. Also here is Topaz tour operator, www.topaz.com.fr.
$ Regina, Arismendi y Av Bermúdez, T431 1073. Hot water, restaurant, helpful.

❼ Restaurants

Cumaná p1552, map p1553
All central restaurants close Sun lunchtime. After dark take a taxi.
$$ Les Jardins de Sucre, Sucre 27, in front of the Santa Inés church. French food, good service, outdoor seating. Recommended.
$ El Colmao on Plaza Pichincha, C Sucre. Serves very good fish, with charming service, karaoke.
$ El Mercadito at Puente Elevado. For excellent cheap lunches, fish and seafood.
$ Jardín de Sport, Plaza Bolívar. Outdoor café, good food, noisy atmosphere. Recommended.

❹ What to do

Cumaná p1552, map p1553
Posadas San Francisco, Tempera and Bubulina's can help arrange local tours, as well as sailing and diving trips.

❺ Transport

Cumaná p1552, map p1553
Bus Terminal 3 km northwest of the centre on Av Las Palomas, just before the junction with the peripheral road. Local bus into centre US$0.25, taxi US$1-2. To **Puerto La Cruz**, US$1.50, 1½ hrs. To **Güiria**, US$4, Expresos Los Llanos once a day, por puesto US$5 (6-7 hrs), beware of overcharging, often stop in Irapa. To **Carúpano**, US$2, 2-3 hrs. To **Caripe**, you have to go to **Santa María**, south of Cariaco, and change to por puesto there. To **Caracas**, US$5.50 (7-8 hrs), frequent service; many daily to **Ciudad Guayana** and **Ciudad Bolívar**, US$7 and US$5 respectively.
Ferry For Ferries to **Araya Peninsula** and **Isla de Margarita**, see below and page 1565.

Araya to Paria

This section is bounded by two peninsulas, Araya, which is an area of desert landscapes and pink salt lakes, and Paria, a finger of land stretching out to the most easterly point on Venezuela's Caribbean coast and a place of peaceful, coastal towns, beaches and forest. The eastern mountains, rising to 2000 m at their highest point, receive abundant rainfall in their tropical forest.

Araya Peninsula

The main settlement is Araya which has an airport and a ferry dock. The major sight is the Fortaleza de Santiago de León, built by Spain to protect the salt mines, but of which very little now remains. Construction began in 1622 and it took 47 years to complete. Entry is free, but the only facilities are a refreshment stand and a picnic area. Today the mines are exploited by a state-owned corporation, ENSAL. Windsurfing is excellent, but only for the experienced.

Carúpano → Phone code: 0294. Colour map 2, A1. Population: 170,000.

This is a colonial town dating back to 1647, from which 70% of Venezuela's cocoa is shipped. The area around Plaza Santa Rosa has been declared a national heritage site. Buildings include the **Museo Histórico**, containing a comprehensive database on the city, and the **Iglesia Santa Rosa**. The **Casa del Cable** ① T331 3847, www.fundacionthomasmerle.org.ve, location of the first telecommunications link with Europe, is the headquarters of the Fundación Thomas Merle, run by Wilfried Merle, who has been instrumental in setting up ecotourism and economic development projects in the Paria Peninsula. Carúpano is famous throughout Venezuela as the last place still celebrating a traditional pre-Lenten Carnival: days of dancing, rum drinking, with masked women in black (negritas). Book well ahead for places to stay at this time (February). Other local festivals are 3 May, **Velorios de la Cruz** (street dances); 15 August, **Asunción de la Virgen**. On the outskirts of Carúpano is **Playa Copey** (ask the por puesto/bus to drop you at

Playa Copey if arriving from Cumaná or other westerly points, or take a taxi from town, US$8). See www.carupano.org.

Caripe → *Phone code: 0292. Population: 31,335.*

A paved road runs inland from Carúpano to Caripe via Cariaco and Santa María, two hours. Caripe is an attractive town set in gorgeous mountain scenery. There is a lively daily market. It is 12 km from the famous Cueva del Guácharo and a good place to escape from the beaches. It's especially good for walking and biking. At San Francisco, on the Maturín-Cumaná road (212 km, all paved but twisty; beautiful tropical mountain scenery), is a branch road running 22.5 km northeast to Caripe. **Feria de las Flores** is on 2-12 August and **NS del Pilar** is 10-12 October. See http://caripe.net. To get to Caripe from Caracas you must go to **Maturín** (*Phone code: 0291. Colour map 2, A1*), the capital of Monagas state, offering relatively expensive accommodation), then take a *por puesto*. Alternatively go to Cumaná and then to Santa María for *por puesto* services.

Cueva del Guácharo

① *0830-1600, US$2.50 with compulsory guide in Spanish, speak some English and German. Leave backpacks at the ticket office, photography is not allowed. To go further into the caves permits from Inparques in Caracas are needed.*

This remarkable cave was discovered by Humboldt and has since been penetrated 10.5 km along a small, crystal-clear stream. In the first caves live around 18,000 *guácharos* (oil birds) with an in-built radar system for sightless flight. Their presence supports a variety of wildlife in the cave: blind mice, fish and crabs in the stream, yellow green plants, crickets and ants. For two hours at dusk (about 1900) the birds pour out of the cave's mouth. Through a very narrow entrance is the **Cueva del Silencio** (Cave of Silence). About 2 km in is the **Pozo del Viento** (Well of the Wind).

Wear old clothes, stout shoes and be prepared to get wet. In the wet season it can be a bit slippery; tours in the cave may be closed in August-September because of rising water level. There is a caving museum with good cafeteria. Opposite the road is a paved path to **Salto Paila**, a 25-m waterfall, about 30 minutes' walk, guides available for US$3.65. A beautiful path, built by Inparques, starts at the caving museum, with some nice shelters for picnics. Camping is allowed by the cave for US$1.50, or you can sleep without a tent under the roof by the café for free.

Between Cariaco and Casanay, **Las Aguas de Moisés** ① *T0414-780 2013, www.lasaguas demoises.com, open 0800-1600, US$3, US$2 for seniors and children, ask to be let off from bus or por puesto on Cariaco-Carúpano route*, is a tourist park containing 11 large thermal pools. The waters are said to be curative and there are lots of sporting and other activities. Camping (**$**) is available, or **Hotel Faraón** (T555 1036).

Paria Peninsula

Río Caribe This lovely fishing village (*Phone code: 0294; Population: 51,100; 20 km east of Carúpano*) used to be a major cacao-exporting port. It is a good jumping-off point for the beautiful beaches of **Playa Medina** (in an old coconut plantation, 25 km east) and **Pui Puy**, both famous for their crystal-clear water and golden sands. Playa Medina is safe, has shade for rent and stalls selling food and drink; it is crowded at weekends and holidays. Cabins at the beach are very expensive (**$$$** per person). To get to Playa Medina, take a taxi, US$15 return trip per car, US$16 to Pui Puy, as *camionetas* do not go to the beaches, only to the entrance, from where it's two hours' walk or more (not safe). Surfing at Playas Pui Puy and Querepare; visit **Querepare** between May and August to watch sea turtles laying their eggs.

Further east is the delightful village of **San Juan de las Galdonas** and some great beaches. Near Chacaracual, 15 minutes' drive from Río Caribe is **Paria Shakti** ① *T611 8767/T0416-517 9676, paraishakti@gmail.com, see Facebook*, a 1.6-ha cacao plantation and holistic health centre that offers factory tours and massages. Next door, visit **Aguasana**, a *hacienda* with mineral-rich hot springs and mud pools (see Where to stay, below). Recommended guide: Eli Monroy (T0426-985

7670, or through **Posada Shalimar**). Near Bohordal is **Campamento Hato Rio de Agua**, a buffalo ranch available for day visits and milk factory tours; many species of birds can be seen (also see Where to stay). Day trips are also available to **Caño de Ajíes** with a visit to a waterfall and the estuary which flows into the Golfo de Paria; you can see crocodiles, birds and snakes. It is part of the Parque Nacional Turuépano. A trip by car and boat costs US$100.

Güiria At Bohordal, the paved road from Río Caribe across the mountains meets Route 9, which continues to the pleasant town of **Irapa** (*Population: 28,576; hotels, bus connections*). The paved highway continues 42 km to **Güiria** (*Phone code: 0294; Colour map 2, A2; Population: 36,860, www. guiria.com.ve*), a friendly, peaceful town and a badly littered beach. **Feria de la Pesca**, 14 July.

Macuro A quiet town on the tip of the Peninsula, Macuro (*Population: 2100*) is accessible by boat (two hours from Güiria) and by a new road from Güiria (20 km paved, the remainder passable by 4WD). It was around here that Columbus made the first recorded European landing on the continent on 5 August 1498. Locals like to believe the landing took place at Macuro, and the town's official new name is Puerto Colón. There is a small **Museo de Macuro** on Calle Bolívar, 1 block from Posada Beatriz; ask here about walking tours and boat trips. A big party is held here every year on 12 October to mark the official 'discovery' of America. Restaurants only open at weekends. There are also a few basic shops and a pharmacy. The boat to Güiria leaves at 0500, arrive early, US$2 per person.

The beach is unattractive but the coast on the north side of the peninsula is truly wonderful; crystal-clear water and dazzling sands backed by dense jungle. A highly recommended trip for the adventurous is the hike to **Uquire** and **Don Pedro** on the north coast; four to six hours' walk, places to hang a hammock or pitch a tent. **Note** This part of the peninsula is a national park; you need a permit from Inparques in Caracas.

⊙ Araya to Paria listings

For hotel and restaurant price codes, and other relevant information, see Essentials.

⊙ Where to stay

Araya *p1554*
$ Araya Mar, El Castillo, T437 1382/T0414-777 3682. Hot water, good restaurant, arranges car and boat tours to the Salinas and around Araya, parking. Good restaurant serves Venezuelan food. Recommended.
$ Araya's Wind, beside the Fortaleza in front of beach, T0414-189 0717. Some rooms with bath, cold water.
$ Lagunasal, C El Progreso, T437 1290/T0424-849 9730, see Facebook. Modern *posada*, 100 m from the dock, with good services.

Carúpano *p1554*
$$-$ Hotel Euro Caribe Internacional, Av Perimetral Rómulo Gallegos, T331 3911, www.eurocaribehotel.com. Well located, some rooms with sea view, attentive staff, parking, good Italian restaurant.

$$-$ La Colina, Av Rómulo Gallegos 33, behind **Hotel Victoria**, T332 2915. Restaurant on terrace, beautiful view, comfortable rooms. Recommended.
$ Lilma, Av Independencia, 3 blocks from Plaza Colón, T331 1361, hotellilma@hotmail. com. Hot water, restaurant, *tasca*, cinema.
$ Victoria, Av Perimetral Rómulo Gallegos, T331 2832, hotelvictoria@hotmail.com. Safe but basic, hot water.

Playa Copey
$$-$ Posada Nena, 1 block from the beach, T331 7297, www.venezuela-vacaciones.com. Hot water, games room, good restaurant, public phone, good service, German spoken, owner Volker Alsen offers day trips to Cueva del Guácharo, Mochima, Medina and other Venezuelan destinations. Recommended.
$ Posada Casa Blanca, Av Principal, 5 mins from **Posada Nena**, T331 6896, www.posada casablanca.com. Hot water, safe, good family atmosphere, private stretch of beach

illuminated at night, Spanish restaurant, German spoken, discounts for long stays.

Caripe *p1555*
$$-$ Finca Agroturística Campo Claro, at Teresén, T555 1013/0414 770 8043, www. haciendacampoclaro.com. Cabins for 4-15 people with cooking facilities and hot water, also rooms (**$**), restaurant for residents, horse riding.
$$-$ Samán, Enrique Chaumer 29, T545 1183, www.hotelsaman.com. Also has more expensive suites, comfortable, pool, parking, not so welcoming to backpackers.

Río Caribe *p1555*
As well as those listed, there are other *posadas* and private, unmarked pensions; ask around.
$$ Posada Caribana, Av Bermúdez 25, T263 3649, www.parquenivaldito.com. Beautifully restored colonial house, tastefully decorated, a/c or fan, restaurant, bar, excursions. Ask about *posada* at Playa Uva.
$ La Posada de Arlet, 24 de Julio 22, T646 1290. English and German spoken, bar, arranges day trips to local beaches. Recommended.
$ Pensión Papagayos, 14 de Febrero, 1 block from police station, opposite *liceo*, T646 1868. Charming house and garden, shared bath with hot water (single sex), use of kitchen, nice atmosphere, owner Cristina Castillo.
$ Posada Shalimar, Av Bermúdez 54, T646 1135, www.posada-shalimar.com. Francisco González speaks English, very helpful, can arrange tours to and provide information about local beaches and other areas. Beautiful rooms situated around pool have a/c. Recommended.
$ Posada Villa Antillana, Rivero 32, T646 1413, posadavillaantillana@hotmail.com. In the village, small, in a converted colonial house, with fan, English spoken.

San Juan de las Galdonas
$$$-$$ Playa Galdonas, T889 1892. 4-star, overlooking the main beach, hot water, bar/ restaurant, swimming pool, English and French spoken, arranges boat tours to Santa Isabel and beaches.
$ pp Habitat Paria, T511 9571, www.soaf.info/ hp/. With breakfast and supper, huge, splendid, zodiac theme, fan, bar/ restaurant, terraces, garden. The *posada* is right behind Barlovento

beach on the right hand side of San Juan. Can arrange boat tours. Recommended.
$ Posada Las Tres Carabelas, T0416-894 0914, lastrescarabelas3@gmail.com. Fans and mosquito nets, restaurant, wonderful view, owner Javier knowledgeable about local area.

Outside Río Caribe
$$ Hato Río de Agua, T332 0527. Rustic cabins with fans, private bathrooms, restaurant on a buffalo ranch (see above), price includes breakfast and tours of dairy factory.
$ pp Hacienda Posada Aguasana, T417 0648/ T0414-304 5687, www.posadaaguasana.com. Attractive rooms with fans near hot springs, price includes breakfast and dinner. 3-7 packages available, with and without transfers.

Güiria *p1556*
$ Plaza, esq Plaza Bolívar, T982 0022. Basic, restaurant, luggage store.
$ Timón de Máximo, C Bideau, 2 blocks from plaza, T982 1535. Hotel with good créole restaurant. Recommended.
$ Vista Mar, Valdez y Trincheras, T982 1055. Hot water, fridge, restaurant.

Macuro *p1556*
$ Posada Beatriz, C Mariño y Carabobo. Basic, clean, with bath, fan.

🍴 Restaurants

Araya *p1554*
Eat early as most places close before 2000. Hamburger stalls around the dock and 2 *panaderías*.
$ El Timonel de Fabi. *Tasca* across from dock, Venezuelan food, karaoke.
$ Eugenía, in front of **Posada Helen**. For good value meals.
$ Las Churuatas de Miguel, on the beach near dock. Fish and typical food.

Carúpano *p1554*
$$-$ El Fogón de La Petaca, Av Perimetral on the seafront. Traditional Venezuelan dishes, fish.
$$-$ La Madriguera, Av Perimetral Rómulo Gallegos, in **Hotel Eurocaribe**. Good Italian food, some vegetarian dishes, Italian and English spoken.

$ Bam Bam, kiosk at the end of Plaza Miranda, close to seafront. Tasty hotdogs and hamburgers.

$ El Oasis, Juncal in front of Plaza Bolívar. Open from 1700, best Arabic food in Carúpano.

$ La Flor de Oriente, Av Libertad y Victoria, 4 blocks from Plaza Colón. Open from 0800, arepas, fruit juice and main meals, good, large portions, good, food, reasonable prices, very busy at lunchtime.

Other options include the **food stalls** in the market, especially the one next to the car park, and the *empanadas* in the Plaza Santa Rosa.

Caripe *p1555*

$$ Tasca Mogambo, next to Hotel Saman. Good, local food.

$$ La Trattoria, C Cabello. Wide variety of good food, popular with locals and tourists.

Río Caribe *p1555*

$$ Mi Cocina, on the road parallel to Av Bermúdez, 3 mins' walk from Plaza Bolívar. Very good food, large portions.

Güiria *p1556*

Everywhere is closed Sun, except for kiosks on Plaza Bolívar.

$$ El Limón, C Trinchera near C Concepcion. Good value, outdoor seating.

$$ Rincón Güireño, corner of Plaza Sucre. Good for breakfast (also rents rooms, **$**).

⊖ Transport

Araya *p1554*

Ferry Cumaná-Araya ferry with **Naviarca** car ferry, T0293-432 2144, www.grancacique. com.ve, shuttles back and forth 24 hrs a day, US$0.10 pp, US$0.50-1 per car. At weekends it usually makes only 1 trip each way. To get to ferry terminal take taxi in Cumaná, US$1 (avoid walking; it can be dangerous), take a *tapadito* (passenger ferry in a converted fishing boat, leave when full, crowded, stuffy, US$0.10) to Manicuare and *camioneta* from there to Araya (15 mins). Return ferries from Araya depart from main wharf at end of Av Bermúdez. Ferries to **Isla de Margarita**, *tapaditos* depart from **Chacopata** (1 hr, US$2 one way). To get to Chacopata from Carúpano,

take a *por puesto* at the stop diagonal to the market entrance (where the fish is unloaded), US$1, 1½ hrs.

Carúpano *p1554*

Air The airport is 15 mins' walk from the centre, US$1 by taxi. Check with **Rutaca** (T0501-788 2221), which occasionally offers flights to Caracas through Porlamar.

Bus To **Caracas,** US$8, 9 hrs, to Terminal de Oriente. For other destinations such as **Cumaná,** US$2-3, 2 hrs, **Puerto La Cruz,** US$2.50, 4 hrs (Mochima/Santa Fé), **Güiria,** US$2.75, 3 hrs *por puestos* are a better option. They run more frequently and make fewer stops. Buses do not go from Carúpano to Caripe, you have to take a *por puesto* to **Cariaco,** US$0.75, then another to **Santa María,** US$1.50, then another to Caripe, US$1.

Caripe *p1555*

Bus Terminal 1 block south of main plaza. For **Carúpano,** take *por puestos* to Santa María and Cariaco (see above), similarly for **Río Caribe** and **Las Aguas de Moisés.** To get to **Cumaná,** go to Santa María and catch transport from there. Bus to **Maturín** several daily, 2½ hrs, US$2.50; Maturín-**Caracas** costs US$6, 7½ hrs. *Por puestos* run from Maturín to Ciudad Bolívar.

Cueva del Guácharo *p1555*

Bus Frequent from **Caripe** to the caves. If staying in Caripe, take a *por puesto* (a jeep marked Santa María-Muelle), at 0800, see the caves and waterfall and catch the Cumaná bus which goes past the caves between 1200 and 1230. Taxis from Caripe US$1.50, hitching possible. *Por puesto* from Cumaná US$4, 2 hrs. Private tours can be organized from Cumaná for about US$10 pp, with guide.

Río Caribe and San Juan de las Galdonas *p1555*

Bus Direct from **Caracas** (Terminal del Oriente) to Río Caribe , 10 hrs, and from **Maturín,** US$8. *Por puesto* Carúpano-Río Caribe, US$1, or taxi US$3. Buses depart Río Caribe from the other Plaza Bolívar, 7 blocks up from pier. Jeep Carúpano-San Juan de las Galdonas 1100, 1½ hrs; *camioneta* from Río Caribe from stop near petrol station, 0600 till 1300, US$1.50.

Güiria *p1556*
Bus Depart Plaza Sucre, at top end of
C Bolívar: to **Maturín** (0400, US$3, 6 hrs),
Caripito, **San Félix**, **Cumaná**, US$4,
Puerto La Cruz, US$5, and **Caracas**, US$8.
Ferry To **Macuro**: daily 1100-1200 from
the Playita, US$1-3, return 0500, 2 hrs.
To **Trinidad** A ferry leaves every Wed at
1530 for Chaguaramas, Trinidad (leaves
Trinidad at 0830, Wed), 3½ hrs, US$115 one
way (tax extra), operated by **Pier 1 Cruises**,
T2-949-821556 (Miguel Acosta), www.pier1tt.
com. There is a US$23 exit tax from Venezuela
(US$13 from Trinidad).

❶ Directory

Carúpano *p1554*
Banks It is not easy to change foreign
currency in Carúpano.

Güiria *p1556*
Useful services Immigration: visas can't
be arranged in Güiria, should you need one;
maximum length of stay 14 days (but check).
For more than 14 days, get visa in Caracas.
Remember to get exit stamp before leaving
Venezuela. Officially, to enter Trinidad and
Tobago you need a ticket to your home country,
but a return to Venezuela is usually enough.

Isla de Margarita → *Colour map 2, A1.*

Margarita is the country's main Caribbean holiday destination and is popular with both
Venezuelans and foreign tourists. The island's reputation for picture-postcard, white-sand
beaches is well-deserved. Some parts are crowded but there are undeveloped beaches and
colonial villages. Porlamar is the most built up and commercial part of the island while Juan
Griego and La Restinga are much quieter.

It is advisable to reserve ahead, especially in high season, to get the best value for
accommodation. Despite the property boom and the frenetic building on much of the coast and
in Porlamar, much of the island has been given over to natural parks. Of these the most striking
is the Laguna La Restinga.

The western part, the Peninsula de Macanao, is hotter and more barren, with scrub, sand
dunes and marshes. Wild deer, goats and hares roam the interior, but 4WDs are needed to
penetrate it. The entrance to the Peninsula de Macanao is a pair of hills known as **Las Tetas de
María Guevara**, a national monument covering 1670 ha. There are mangroves in the **Laguna de
las Marites** natural monument, west of Porlamar.

Other parks are **Cerro El Copey**, 7130 ha, and **Cerro Matasiete y Guayamurí**, 1672 ha (both
reached from La Asunción). The climate is exceptionally good and dry. Roads are good and a
bridge links the two parts. Nueva Esparta's population is over 437,000, of whom 185,000 live in
Porlamar. The capital is La Asunción.

Visiting Isla de Margarita

Getting there and around There are many national, international and charter flights to Isla de
Margarita. There also ferries from La Guaira (Caracas), Puerto La Cruz and Cumaná. Car hire is a
good way of getting around (see Directory, below). Women should avoid walking alone at night
on the island and no one should go to the beaches after dark, except El Yaque (see below).
▶ *See also Transport, page 1565.*

Tourist information Isla de Margarita: The private **Cámara de Turismo** ① *2da Entrada Urb
Jorge Coll, Av Virgen del Valle, Qta 6, Pampatar, T262 0683,* have free maps and are very helpful.
Corpotur, the state tourism department, can be contacted on T262 2322, Centro Artesanal
Gilberto Menchini, Los Robles, www.corpoturmargarita.gob.ve. Travel agencies can also provide
a tourist guide to Margarita. The best map is available from *Corpoven*. See also www.islamargarita.
com and http://margaritaislandnews.blogspot.co.uk. Many offices close for lunch.

Porlamar → *Phone code: 0295.*

Most of the island's high-rise hotels are at Porlamar which is 20 km from airport and 28 km from Punta de Piedra, where ferries dock. If you're seeking sun and sand, then head for the north coast towns where the beaches tend to be lined with low-rise hotels and thatched restaurants. Porlamar's beaches are nothing special, but it makes up for what it lacks in this department with its shops (see Shopping below). At Igualdad y Díaz is the **Museo de Arte Francisco Narváez**, which has some good displays of the work of this local sculptor and other Venezuelan artists. At night everything closes by 2300.

The **Bella Vista** beach is busy but clean and has lots of restaurants lining the seafront. **Playa Concorde** is small, sheltered and tucked by the marina. **Playa Morena** is a long, barren strip of sand for the Costa Azul hotel zone east of the city. **La Caracola** is a popular beach for a young crowd.

Boats go from Punta de Piedra, El Yaque and La Isleta to the **Isla de Coche** (11 by 6 km), which has 4500 inhabitants and one of the richest salt mines in the country (see Transport below). They also go, on hire only, to **Isla de Cubagua**, which is totally deserted, but you can visit the **ruins of Nueva Cádiz** (which have been excavated). Large private yachts and catamarans take tourists on day trips to Coche.

La Asunción → *Population: 27,500.*

The capital of La Asunción located a few kilometres inland from Porlamar. It has several **colonial buildings**, a **cathedral**, and the **fort of Santa Rosa** ⓘ *Mon 0800-1500, the rest of the week 0800-*

Isla de Margarita

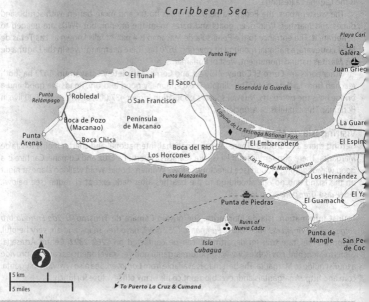

1800, which features a famous bottle dungeon. There is a **museum** in the Casa Capitular, and a good local **market**, worth browsing for handicrafts. Nearby is the **Cerro Matasiete** historical site, where the defeat of the Spanish on 31 July 1817 led to their evacuation of the island.

Pampatar → *Population: 25,000.*

For a more Venezuelan atmosphere go northeast to Pampatar, which is set around a bay favoured by yachtsmen as a summer anchorage. Pampatar has the island's largest fort, **San Carlos de Borromeo**, which was built in 1662 after the Dutch destroyed the original. Jet skis can be hired on the clean and pretty beach. A fishing boat can be hired for 2½ hours, four to six passengers; shop around for best price; it's good fun and makes for a worthwhile fishing trip.

Eastern and northern beaches

Playa Guacuco, reached from La Asunción by a road through the Guayamurí reserve, is a local beach with a lot of surf, fairly shallow, palm trees, restaurants and car park. Playa Parguito further up the east coast is best for surfing (strong waves; full public services).

Playa El Agua has 4 km of white sand with many kiosks and shady restaurants on the beach and on Calle Miragua. The sea is very rough in winter (dangerous for children), but fairly shallow; beware the strong cross current when you are about waist deep. This beach gets overcrowded at Venezuelan holiday times. The fashionable part is at the south end. The beach is 45 minutes by bus from Porlamar (US$1). See also www.playaelagua.info.

Manzanillo is a picturesque bay between the mountains on the northeast point of the island with apartments, beach houses and good places to eat (cheaper than Playa El Agua). Playa Escondida is at the far end. Puerto Fermín/El Tirano is where Lope de Aguirre, the infamous conquistador, landed in 1561 on his flight from Peru.

The coast road is interesting, with glimpses of the sea and beaches to one side. There are a number of clifftop look-out points. The road improves radically beyond Manzanillo, winding from one beach to the next. **Playa Puerto la Cruz** (wide and windy) adjoins **Pedro González**, with a broad sweeping beach, running from a promontory (easy to climb) to scrub and brush that reach down almost to the water's edge. **Playa Caribe** is a fantastic curve of white sand with moderate surf. Chairs and umbrellas can be hired from the many beach bars.

Juan Griego (*Population: 28,256*) is further west, a fast-expanding town whose pretty bay is full of fishing boats. The little fort of La Galera is on a promontory at the northern side, beyond which is a bay of the same name with a narrow strip of beach lined with many seafront restaurants.

Playa El Yaque

Playa El Yaque on the south coast, near the airport, is a Mecca for wind- and kitesurfers. The winds are perfect from mid-June to mid-October and the water is shallow enough to stand when you fall off (see What to do, below). After dark it becomes an open-air disco, the safest beach on the island at night. Most visitors come on package deals and therefore accommodation is expensive, but cheaper places to stay can be found. There is no public transport; a taxi from Porlamar costs US$8. **Cholymar** travel agency will change money and there is a *casa de cambio* in the Hotel California.

La Restinga and around

This is the 22-km sandbar of broken seashells that joins the eastern and western parts of Margarita. Behind the *restinga* is the eponymous **national park**, designated a wetland of international importance. More than 100 species of birds live here, including the blue-crowned parakeet, which is endemic to Margarita. There are also marine turtles and other reptiles, dolphins, deer, ocelots, seahorses and oysters. *Lanchas* can be taken into the fascinating lagoon and mangrove swamps to the beach from landing stages at the eastern end (US$2.50 for 30 minutes, US$15 for an hour trip in a boat taking five, plus US$2.50 entrance fee to park). Bus from Porlamar US$2. On La Restinga beach you can look for shellfish in the shallows (sun protection is essential) and delicious oysters can be bought here.

The **Peninsula de Macanao**, over the road bridge from La Restinga, is mountainous, arid, barely populated and a peaceful place to get away from the holidaymakers on the main part of Isla Margarita. It also has some good beaches that are often deserted and is a good place for horse riding. Punta Arenas is a very pleasant beach with calm water and is the most popular. It has some restaurants, chairs and sunshades. Further on is the wilder Playa Manzanillo. It's best visited in a hire car as public transport is scarce. **Boca del Río**, near the road bridge, has a **Museo Marino** ① *T291 3231, www.museomarino.com, daily 0900-1630, US$3, US$2 children and seniors*, which has interesting collections of marine life, organized by ecosystem, and also features a small aquarium.

◉ Isla de Margarita listings

For hotel and restaurant price codes, and other relevant information, see Essentials.

● Where to stay

Porlamar *p1560*
Many luxury hotels are grouped in the Costa Azul suburb east of Porlamar, but they now pepper most of the northeast coast of the island. Most hotels and tour operators work on a high season/low season price system. High season prices (Christmas, Easter and Jun-Aug) can be up to 35% higher. Flights and hotels are usually fully booked at this time. In low season, bargaining is possible.
$$$$ Bella Vista, Av Santiago Mariño, T261 7222, www.hbellavista.com. Large hotel with all services, pool with sea views, beach, car hire, travel agency, French restaurant, and restaurant serving *comida criolla*.

$$-$ Imperial, Av Raul Leoni, via El Morro, T261 6420, www.hotelimperial.com.ve. Modern, best rooms have sea view, parking, balcony, safe, restaurant, parking, English spoken.
$$-$ Margarita Princess, Av 4 de Mayo, T263 6777, www.hotelmargaritaprincess. com.ve. Large, comfortable rooms, balcony, restaurant, small pool.
$$-$ María Luisa, Av Raúl Leoni entre Campos y Fermín, T261 0564, www.hotelmarialuisa.com. ve. With a pool and some beach views.
$ For You, Av Santiago Mariño, T263 8635, foryouhotel@hotmail.com. Modern, bland rooms but good service, roof restaurant, bar.
$ Posada Casa Lutecia, Final C Campos Cedeño y Marcano, T263 8526, casalutecia@ mail.com. Lovely bright rooms with personal touch, French-owned, café with outdoor seating near beach.

La Asunción p1560
$$ Ciudad Colonial, C La Margarita, T416 7647, isbeeu@cantv.net. Upmarket apartments minimum 4 people, swimming pool, accepts credit cards, restaurant.
$ Posada Restaurant Ticino Da´Rocco, Crucero de Guacuco, vía Playa El Agua, C San Onofre, sector Camoruco, T242 2727, posadaticino@gmail.com. Pool, restaurant, accepts credit cards.

Playa Guacuco p1561
$$ Guacuco Resort, Vía Playa Guacuco, T242 3040, www.guacucoresort.com. Stylish, comfortable apartments for up to 4 people with balcony or terrace, 1 km from the beach and 300 m off the road, self-catering, tranquil, beautiful tropical gardens with birds, spa, pool and bar.

Playa El Agua p1561
Most *posadas* are on C Miragua, which is near the beach.
$$$-$$ Coco Paraíso, Av Principal, T249 0117/ 0414-092 2403, www.cocoparaiso.com.ve, Pleasant, large rooms, pool, 3 mins from beach, English and German spoken.
$$ Costa Linda, C Miragua, T249 1303, www.hotelcostalinda.com. Lovely rooms in colonial-style house, relaxing, safe, pool, restaurant and bar, accepts credit cards, English and German spoken.
$$ Costa Linda Beach, C Miragua. T415 9961, hotelcostalinda@cantv.net. Comfortable rooms, pool, bar and restaurant, gym
$$ Margarita Tropical Villa, C Díaz Ordaz, T249 0558, www.casatrudel.com. Canadian run, small place, patio with hammocks, 5 mins from beach, Wi-Fi, king-size beds, use of kitchen, hot water shower.
$$-$ Doña Romelia, Av 31 de Julio (1 km before Playa Manzanillo), 10-min walk to Playa El Agua, T249 0238, http://www. hotelposadadonaromelia.blogspot.com. Very attractive rustic-style hotel, bright rooms with balconies and hammocks, nice pool area and garden. Well-run, helpful staff. Recommended.
$ Chalets de Belén, Miragua 3, T249 1707, jesush30@yahoo.com. 2 chalets for 4 and 6, kitchen, good value, parking, no hot water, also 2 double rooms, **$** (with discounts in the low season).

$ Hostería El Agua, Av 31 de Julio vía Manzanillo, T249 1297, hosteriaelagua@ hotmail.com. Simple, hot water, safe, restaurant/bar, on roadside 4 mins' walk from beach, English spoken.

Juan Griego p1561
$$ The Sunset Posada Turística, T253 2168, losavila@verizon.net, on Facebook. Apartments sleep 4-8, good value, some with beachfront balconies.
$ Hostel El Caney, Giulliana Torrico 17, Rue Guevara, T253 5059, http://elcaney. free.fr. Shared kitchen, small pool, English and French spoken, weekly rentals.
$ Patrick's, El Fuerte, T253 6218, www.hotel patrick.com. Good travellers hostel, rooms with fine sunset views, excellent restaurant and bar, near beach. English spoken, will arrange salsa and Spanish lessons. Recommended.

Playa El Yaque p1562
$$ El Yaque Motion, T0426-288 07885 (English, German), T0416-596 5139 (Spanish), www.elyaquemotion.com. 400 m from beach. German run, popular with wind- and kitesurfers (lessons and equipment hire available), well-established, kitchen, laundry, roof terrace, cheaper with shared bath, rents 3 apartments for 4-8 people, English spoken, good.
$ Sail Fast Shop, T263 3449, herbert@ sail fast.com. Basic rooms 300 m from the beach, ask for Herbert Novak at the Sail Fast Shop opposite Hotel Yaque Paradise. Rooms with private bath, some with a/c, kitchen facilities.

La Restinga and around: Península de Macanao p1562
$$ Makatao, T0412-092 7187, www.makatao. com. Run by Dr Alexis Vásquez, price includes transfer, food, some therapies, natural drinks and lodging in the singular rooms. The doctor runs health, 'eco-relax' and therapy programs, and there are mud baths at the *campamento*.

🍴 Restaurants

Porlamar p1560
The upmarket dining is in Urb Costa Azul on Av Bolívar. There are plenty of eating places on Campos and 4 de Mayo.

$$ La Casa del Mero, Av Raúl Leoni. Good place for a cocktail on the water, serves seafood, steaks and chicken.
$$ La Pimienta, Cedeño entre Campos y Fermín. Good seafood.
$ Dragón Chino, Av Principal, 4 de Mayo. Great Chinese.
$ El Pollo de Carlitos, Marcano y Martínez. Pleasant location, good food.
$ El Punto Criollo, Igualdad near *Hotel Porlamar*. Excellent value *comida margariteña*.

🍸 Bars and clubs

Porlamar *p1560*
Several bars in the Centro Comercial Costal Azul.

Playa El Yaque *p1562*
Several beach bars; best bar is **Los Surf Piratas**, drinks and dancing from 2130.

🎉 Festivals

Isla de Margarita *p1559, map p1560*
Many religious festivals, including **19 Mar** at Paraguachí (**Feria de San José**, 10 days); **26 Jul** at Punta de Piedras; **31 Jul** (Batalla de Matasiete) and **15 Aug** (Asunción de la Virgen) at La Asunción; **1-8 Sep** at El Valle; **4-11 Nov** at Boca del Río, **4-30 Nov** at Boca del Pozo; **5-6 Dec** at Porlamar; **27 Dec-3 Jan** at Juan Griego. See map for locations.

🛍 Shopping

Porlamar *p1560*
Margarita's status as a duty-free zone attracts Venezuelan shoppers, who go in droves for clothing, electronic goods and other items. Street sellers lay out their handicrafts on Av Santiago Mariño in the afternoon. When buying jewellery, bargain, don't pay by credit card (surcharges are imposed) and get a detailed guarantee of the item. Av Santiago Mariño and surroundings are the place for designer labels, but decent copies can be found on Blvds Guevara and Gómez and around Plaza Bolívar in the centre. For bargains on denims, T-shirts, shorts, swimming gear and bikinis, take a bus to Conejeros market (from Fraternidad, Igualdad a Velásquez).

Pampatar *p1501*
Centro Comercial La Redoma, Av Jovito Villalba. A good small mall for food, clothing, medicines, and more. Also has a cyber café.

🎯 What to do

Porlamar *p1560*
Sailing The motor yacht **Viola Festival** can be hired for mini cruises to the island of Coche, contact **Festival Tours**, Calle Marcano, CC Paseo Terrazul, loc P1-8, Costa Azul, T264 9554, www.violafestival.com. There are other yachts offering island cruises, fishing trips, etc.

Playa El Agua *p1561*
Tour shops in Playa El Agua are the best places to book scuba diving and snorkelling trips: most go to Los Frailes, a small group of islands to the north of Playa Agua, and reputedly the best diving and snorkelling in Margarita, but it's also possible to dive at Parque Nacional La Restinga and Isla Cubagua. Prices from US$75 pp for an all-inclusive full day (2 dives). Snorkelling is about two-thirds the price of scuba diving.
Enomis Divers, Av 31 de Julio, CC Turístico, Playa El Agua, loc 2, sector La Mira, T249 0366, www.divemargarita.com. PADI school, diving trips, many programmes and certifications offered.

Playa El Yaque *p1562*
Sailboards, **kite surf** and **kayaks** can be hired on the beach from at least 5 well-equipped companies, who also offer lessons. An hour's lesson costs US$55. English, German, French and Portuguese spoken. Enquire at **El Yaque Motion** (see Where to stay, above) for more information about wind and kite surfing. See also www.velawindsurf.com. A 20-min boat ride to Isla Coche leaves from next door to **El Yaque Motion**, a recommended spot for advanced kiters. Rescue service available at the beach.

La Restinga and around: Peninsula de Macanao *p1562*
Horse riding You can ride on the peninsula at **Ranch Cabatucan**, 2 km from Guayacancito on the road to Punta Arenas, T416 3584, www.cabatucan.com.

⊕ Transport

Porlamar *p1560*

Air There are too many flight options to list here: check with local offices for details. Gen Santiago Mariño Airport, between Porlamar and Punta de Piedras, has the international and national terminals at either end, www.aeropuerto-margarita.gob.ve. Taxi from Porlamar US$5, 20-30 mins. All national airlines have routes to **Margarita**. Many daily flights to/from **Caracas**, 45-min flight; tickets are much cheaper if purchased in Venezuela. To **Canaima** and to **Los Roques** with LTA.

Bus Local Buses and *por puestos* serve most of the island, buses US$0.35-75, *por puestos* minimum fare US$1, few services at night when you should take a taxi anyway.

Long distance Several bus companies in Caracas sell through tickets from **Caracas** to Porlamar, arriving about midday, US$4. Buses return to Caracas from La Paralela bus station in Porlamar.

Ferry From **Puerto La Cruz** to Margarita (Punta de Piedras): **Conferry**, Los Cocos terminal, Puerto La Cruz, freefone T0501-2663 3779, www.conferry.com. Price varies according to class of seat, 2½-4½ hrs, 4-6 a day, night departures too (check times, extra ferries during high season). Fast ferry, passengers US$5 from mainland to island, US$10 return, over-60s and children under-13 about half price (proof of age required), cars US$37.

Conferry office in **Porlamar**, Av Terranova con Av Llano Adentro, Mon-Fri 0800-1730, Sat 0800-1200. **Gran Cacique**, 2-3 fast ferries a day Puerto la Cruz-Punta de Piedras, US$7-10 one way, also takes cars, US$10-12, and motorbikes, US$6-7, T0281-263 0935 (Puerto La Cruz ferry terminal), T0295-239 8339 (Punta de Piedras, or Av Santiago Mariño, Edif Blue Sky, loc 3, Porlamar, T0295-264 2945). It is most advisable to book in advance, especially if travelling with a car or motorbike during high season. To get to terminal in Puerto La Cruz, take 'Bello Monte' *por puesto* from Libertad y Anzoátegui, 2 blocks from Plaza Bolívar. From **Cumaná** ferry terminal, El Salado, **Gran Cacique**, T0293-432 0011, 2-3 a day, US$6-8 one way (children

3-7 and over-60s half price), and **Naviarca**, T0293-433 5577, continuous service, US$5 one way for passengers (children 3-7 and over-60s half price), motorcycles US$5-7, cars US$6-10. **Navibus**, T0295-500 6284, www.navibus.com.ve, a new service, has 2 sailings a day from Puerto la Cruz and Cumaná: US$4-5.50 and 3 respectively (children 2-7, over-60s and disabled half price), motorcycles US$6 and 4, cars US$10-12 and US$8-11. **Note** Ferries are very busy at Sat, Sun and Mon. Buying tickets can be a complex business with a lot of confusing queuing. Cars are checked by SENIAT for their legality and to prevent the smuggling of tax-free goods to the mainland.

Taxi Taxi for a day is US$5 per hr, minimum 3 hrs. Always fix fare in advance; 20% extra after 2100 and on Sun. Taxi from Porlamar to Playa El Agua, US$4.

⊕ Directory

Porlamar *p1560*

Banks Banks on Avs Santiago Mariño and 4 de Mayo, open 0830-1130, 1400-1630. **Casas de cambio**: Italcambio, CC Jumbo, Av 4 de Mayo, Nivel Ciudad, T265 3240, at airport and at CC Sambil Margarita. **Car hire** Several offices at the airport and at the entrance to Hotel Bella Vista, others on Av Santiago Mariño. Check the brakes, bodywork and terms and conditions of hire thoroughly. Scooters can also be hired. Motor bikes may not be ridden 2000-0500. **Note** Fill up before leaving Porlamar as service stations are scarce. Roads are generally good and most are paved. Signposts are often nonexistent. Free maps are confusing, but it's worth having one with you. Avoid driving outside Porlamar after dark. Beware of robbery; park in private car parks.

Pampatar *p1561*

Language schools Centro de Lingüística Aplicada, Corocoro Qta, Cela Urb, Playa El Angel between Porlamar and Pampatar, T262 8198, http://cela-ve.com (a useful website worth visiting is www.insel-margarita-venezuela.de).

Los Roques → *Colour map 1, A6. Phone code: 0237.*

ⓘ *National park entry BsF254 for 15 days (US$5.20 at the Sicad 2 exchange rate), children under 4 and seniors over 65 free.*

The turquoise and emerald lagoons and dazzling white sands of the Archipelago de Los Roques make up one of Venezuela's loveliest national parks. For lazing on an untouched beach, or for snorkelling and diving amid schools of fish and coral reefs, these islands cannot be beaten. Diving and snorkelling are best to the south of the archipelago. The islands tend to be very busy in July-August and at Christmas. See www.los-roques.com, www.losroques.org and www.consejocomunallosroques.org. Also look out for the excellent *Guía del Parque Nacional Archipiélago Los Roques* (Ecograph, 2004).

The islands of Los Roques, with long stretches of white beaches and over 20 km of coral reef in crystal-clear water, lie 166 km due north of La Guaira; the atoll, of about 340 islets and reefs, constitutes a national park of 225,153 ha. There are many bird nesting sites (eg the huge gull colonies on Francisqui and the pelicans, boobies and frigates on Selenqui); May is nesting time at the gull colonies. For more detailed information visit www.fundacionlosroques.org.

This is one of the least visited diving spots in the Caribbean; best visited midweek as Venezuelans swarm here on long weekends and at school holidays, after which there is litter on every island. (Low season is Easter to July.) There are at least seven main dive sites offering caves, cliffs, coral and, at Nordesqui, shipwrecks. There are many fish to be seen, including sharks at the caves of Olapa de Bavusqui. Prices are higher than the mainland and infrastructure is limited but the islands are beautiful and unspoiled. Camping is free, but campers need a permit from **Inparques** ⓘ *T0212-273 2811 in Caracas, or the office on Plaza Bolívar, Gran Roque, Mon-Fri 0830-1200 and 1400-1800, weekends and holidays 0830-1200 and 1430-1730; also the small office by the runway where you pay the entry fee.* Average temperature 29°C with coolish nights. You will need strong sunblock as there is no shade and an umbrella is recommended.

Gran Roque (*Population: 1200*) is the only permanently inhabited island. The airport is here, as is the national guard, a few grocery stores, public phones (offering expensive internet), a bank with an ATM, medical facilities, dive shops, a few restaurants and accommodation. There is nowhere to change traveller's cheques. Park Headquarters are in the scattered fishing village. Tourist information is available from the very helpful **Oscar Shop**, directly in front as you leave the airstrip. Boat trips to other islands can be arranged here or at *posadas* (round trip US$12.75-41, depending on distance), which are worthwhile as you cannot swim off Gran Roque.

You can negotiate with local fishermen for transport to other islands: you will need to take your own tent, food and (especially) water. You may also have to take your own snorkeling equipment, unless it is provided by your package tour operator. **Madrisqui** has a good shallow beach and joins Pirata Cay by a sandspit. **Francisqui** is three islands joined by sandspits, with calm lagoon waters to the south and rolling surf to the north. You can walk with care from one cay to the other, maybe swimming at times. There's some shade in the mangrove near the bar at La Cueva. **Crasqui** has a 3-km beach with beautiful water and white sand. **Cayo de Agua** (one hour by fast boat from Gran Roque) has an amazing sandspit joining its two parts and a nice walk to the lighthouse where you'll find two natural pools.

◉ Los Roques listings

For hotel and restaurant price codes, and other relevant information, see Essentials.

● Where to stay

In most places on Islas Los Roques, breakfast and dinner are included in the price.

Los Roques: Gran Roque *p1566*
There are over 60 *posadas* on Gran Roque.
$$$ pp **El Botuto**, on seafront near Supermercado W Salazar, T0416-621 0381, www.posadaelbotuto.com. Nice airy rooms with fan, good simple food, locally owned. Trips to other islands and watersports arranged.

$$$ pp **Piano y Papaya**, near Plaza Bolívar towards seafront, www.losroques.com. Very tasteful, run by Italian artist, with fan, $$ pp for bed and breakfast, credit cards and TCs accepted, Italian and English spoken, laundry service.

$$$ pp **Posada Acquamarina**, C 2 No 149, T0412-310 1962, www.posada-acquamarina.com. All-inclusive, rooms have a/c, private bathrooms with hot water, terrace. Owner Giorgio very helpful, speaks Italian and some French, can arrange flights from Caracas. Excursions to other islands.

$$$ pp **Posada Caracol**, on seafront near airstrip, T414 5566, www.caracolgroup.com. Delightful, full-board with excursions, credit cards and TCs accepted, Italian and English spoken, good boats.

$$$ pp **Posada Doña Magalis**, Plaza Bolívar 46, T0414-287 7554, www.magalis.com. Simple place, locally owned, with a/c, cheaper with shared bath, includes trips to other islands, soft drinks, breakfast and dinner, delicious food, mostly fish and rice.

$$ pp **Roquelusa**, C 3 No 214, behind supermarket, T0414-369 6401. A cheaper option, basic, with cold water, a/c.

○ What to do

Los Roques p1566
Many *posadas* arrange water sports such as windsurfing and kitesurfing (especially good at Francisqui), diving, sailing and fishing.
Diving For health reasons you must allow 12 hrs to elapse between diving and flying back to the mainland. Lots of courses and packages available. Cayo de Agua and Francisqui recommended for snorkelling. Boats and equipment rentals can be arranged. Ecobuzos, 3 blocks from the airstrip, T0295-262 9811/0416-696 5775, www.ecobuzos.com.

Very good, new equipment, modern boats, experienced dive masters. PADI courses (US$280) and beginner dives available.
Sailing Fully equipped yachts can be chartered for US$200-400 per night for 2 people, all inclusive, highly recommended as a worthwhile way of getting some shade on the treeless beaches. Ask at **Angel & Oscar Shop**, or **Posada Mediterraneo**, T0414-215 2292, www.posadamediterraneo.com, associated with **Pez Ratón** fishing lodge, www.pezraton.com.

⊖ Transport

Los Roques p1566
Air Flights from **Maiquetía** or **Porlamar**. LTA (www.tuy.com), **Chapi Air** (T0212-355 1349, reservacioneschapiair@gmail.com), **Blue Star** (T0412-310 1962, www.bluestar.us) and **Los Roques Airlines** (T0212-635 2155, www.losroques-airlines.com) all fly from Maiquetía (Aeropuerto Auxiliar) once a day, 40 mins, US$100-200 round trip, more expensive if booked outside of Venezuela. Tax of about US$10 is payable. Some carriers charge more at weekends. Remember that small planes usually restrict luggage to 10 kg. They offer full-day (return flight, meals and activities) and overnight packages. It's best to buy a return to the mainland as buying and confirming tickets and finding offices open on the islands is difficult.

⊙ Directory

Los Roques p1566
Banks ATM on Plaza Bolívar, but take cash from the mainland.

Canaima and the Orinoco Delta

In Parque Nacional Canaima, one of the largest national parks in the world, you'll find the spectacular Angel Falls, the highest in the world, and the mysterious "Lost World" of Roraima (described under South to Brazil). Canaima is the tourist centre for the park, but indigenous communities are now accepting tourists. The historic Ciudad Bolívar on the Río Orinoco is a good starting place for the superb landscapes further south. Further east, beyond the industrial city of Ciudad Guayana, the Orinoco Delta is developing as a tourist destination.

Guayana, south of the Orinoco River, constitutes half of Venezuela, comprising rounded forested hills and narrow valleys, rising to ancient flat-topped tablelands on the borders of Brazil. These savannahs interspersed with semi-deciduous forest are sparsely populated. So far, communications have been the main difficulty, but a road that leads to Manaus passes through Santa Elena de Uairén on the Brazilian frontier (see page 1579). The area is Venezuela's largest gold and diamond source, but its immense reserves of iron ore, manganese and bauxite are of far greater economic importance.

Ciudad Bolívar → *Phone code: 0285. Colour map 2, A1, Population: 371,000.*

Ciudad Bolívar is on the narrows of the Orinoco, some 300 m wide, which gave the town its old name of Angostura, 'The Narrows'. It is 400 km from the Orinoco delta. It was here that Bolívar came after defeat to reorganize his forces, and the British Legionnaires joined him. At Angostura he was declared President of the Gran Colombia he had yet to build and which was to fragment before his death. With its cobbled streets, pastel buildings and setting on the Orinoco, it is one of Venezuela's most beautiful colonial towns.

Places in Ciudad Bolívar

At the Congress of Angostura, 15 February 1819, the representatives of the present day Venezuela, Colombia, Panama and Ecuador met to proclaim Gran Colombia. The building, on **Plaza Bolívar**, built 1766-1776 by Manuel Centurión, the provincial governor, houses a museum, the **Casa del Congreso de Angostura**, with an ethnographic museum in the basement. Guides give tours in Spanish only. Also on this plaza is the **Cathedral** (which was completed in 1840), the

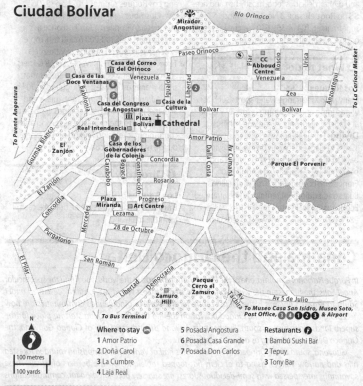

Ciudad Bolívar

Where to stay		Restaurants
1 Amor Patrio	5 Posada Angostura	1 Bambú Sushi Bar
2 Doña Carol	6 Posada Casa Grande	2 Tepuy
3 La Cumbre	7 Posada Don Carlos	3 Tony Bar
4 Laja Real		

Casa de Los Gobernadores de la Colonia (also built by Centurión in 1766), the Real Intendencia, and the Casa de la Cultura. Also here, at Bolívar 33, is the house where Gen Manuel Piar, the Liberator of Guayana from the Spanish, was held prisoner before being executed by Bolívar on 16 October 1817, for refusing to put himself under Bolívar's command. The restored Plaza Miranda, up Calle Carabobo, has an art centre. The present legislative assembly and Consejo Municipal are between Plaza Bolívar and Plaza Miranda. In 1824, when the town was still known as Angostura a Prussian physician to Bolívar's troops invented the bitters; the factory moved to Port of Spain in 1875.

Museum at Casa del Correo del Orinoco ① *Paseo Orinoco y Carabobo, Mon-Fri 0930-1200, 1430-1700*, houses modern art and history exhibits of the city. Museo Casa San Isidro ① *Av Táchira, Tue-Sun 0900-1700, free, knowledgeable guides*, is a colonial mansion where Simón Bolívar stayed for two weeks. It has antique furniture and an old garden. Museo de Arte Moderno Jesús Soto ① *Av Germania, 0930-1730, weekends and holidays 1000-1700, free, guide in Spanish only*, is located some distance from the centre in pleasant gardens. It has works by Venezuela's celebrated Jesús Rafael Soto and other modern artists from around the world. Recommended. The best views of the city are from Fortín El Zamuro ① *C 28 de Octubre y Av 5 de Julio, daily except Mon, free, guides available*, dating from 1902, strategically located at one of the tallest points of the city.

The Paseo Orinoco skirts the riverbank and heads west out of town; it is a relaxing place to stroll but unsafe after dark. Speedboats go across the river to the small, picturesque town of Soledad (US$0.25, one way, five minutes) on a journey that offers great views of colonial centre, the bridge and the river itself. Security can be an issue at either end; don't cross at night. There are no other passenger boat services. The Angostura Bridge can be seen from the waterfront paseo. This is the first bridge across the Orinoco, 1668 m long, opened in 1967, again with great views (cyclists and walkers are not allowed to cross, you must flag down a car or truck).

West of the centre is El Zanjón, an area of vegetation typical of the region. East is Parque El Porvenir, with botanical gardens (entrance on Calle Bolívar), but it is unsafe to wander unless accompanied by staff. Outside the airport is the *Río Caroní* aeroplane, which Jimmy Angel landed on top of Auyán Tepuy (see page 1573).

The tourist office Is Dirección de Turismo ① *Av Bolívar, Quinta Yeita 59, T632 2362, Mon-Fri 0800-1200, 1400-1730*. Helpful, English spoken. State website: www.e-bolivar.gov.ve, see also www.turismobolivar.gob.ve.

To Ciudad Bolívar from the coast and the llanos Ciudad Bolívar can be reached easily by roads south from Caracas and Puerto La Cruz. The Caracas route, via Valle de la Pascua, and the Puerto La Cruz route, via Anaco, meet at El Tigre (*Population: 198,770*), which has good hotels and services. From the *llanos*, from Chaguaramas turn south through Las Mercedes (hotel $) to Cabruta (*Population: 9000*), 179 km, road in very bad shape, daily bus to Caracas, US$3, basic hotel. Then take a ferry from opposite the airport to Caicara (car ferry 1½ hours, *lanchas* for pedestrians 25 minutes). An 11.2-km bridge across the Orinoco is being built between Cabruta and Caicara (due to open in 2015). Alternatively, from San Fernando de Apure take a bus to Calabozo (*Population: 152,000*) and *por puesto* to El Sombrero (*Population: 31,000; US$0.25*), where you can catch the Ciudad Bolívar bus.

Tours can be made into the area south of the Río Orinoco from Maripa (*Colour map 2, A1*), travelling on the Río Caura. These include visits to indigenous villages, river bathing, jungle treks to waterfalls with explanations of wildlife and vegetation, usually starting from Ciudad Bolívar (see What to do, below).

Ciudad Bolívar listings

For hotel and restaurant price codes, and other relevant information, see Essentials.

Where to stay

Ciudad Bolívar *p1568, map p1568*

$$ Posada Casa Grande, C Boyacá 8, T632 4639, www.cacaotravel.com (the HQ of Cacao Travel is here). A handsome colonial building converted to a tasteful 4-star hotel. Well-attired rooms overlook a central patio upstairs there's a rooftop terrace with a bar and small pool. Professional service, good meals by prior arrangement, breakfast included. Recommended.

$ Amor Patrio, Amor Patrio 30, T0414-854 4925, www.posadaamorpatrioaventura.com. A simple, friendly guesthouse with a tranquil little patio. 5 rooms have fan and shared bathroom, a/c is extra. No Wi-Fi but an internet terminal is available. Also laundry service and tours. Run by Gerd Altmann, German and English spoken. Recommended.

$ La Cumbre, Av 5 de Julio, T632 7709, www.holacumbre.com. Secluded hill-top retreat with commanding views. Rooms are large and simple, some overlook the town and Orinoco river below. Resort-style facilities include a great pool, restaurant, bar, and terraces, maybe noisy at weekends. Take a taxi, you can't walk.

$ Laja Real, Av Andrés Bello y Jesús Soto, opposite airport, T617 0100, www.hotellaja real.com. A reasonable 1980s hotel, but some of the rooms appear not to have been renovated for a while. Good for early morning flights, excellent pool (US$5 for non-residents), sauna, gym, parking, restaurant. Not bad.

$ Posada Angostura, same contact details as Posada Casa Grande above, also on C Boyacá. Handsome rooms in old colonial house, some rooms have river view, hot water, travel agency, unwelcoming service. Excellent food.

$ Posada Doña Carol, Libertad 28, T634 0989, jmaury2008@hotmail.com. Basic and hospitable guesthouse with a mixture of rooms, including one large quadruple with an outdoor patio-balcony. Very helpful, can prepare meals, organize bus tickets, tours. Communal fridges, refreshments and Wi-Fi.

$ Posada Don Carlos, C Boyacá 26 y Amor Patrio, just 30 m from Plaza Bolívar, T632 6017, www. posada-doncarlos.com. Stunning colonial house. 6 private double rooms with a/c, or 4 cheaper rooms with fan and shared facilities. Breakfast and dinner available, lovely patio, bar, tours. Good vibe, helpful, popular. Recommended.

Outside town

$ Posada La Casita, Av Ligia Pulido, Urb 24 de Julio, T617 0832, www.posada-la-casita.com. Beautiful leafy grounds at this secluded hotel, also home to a small private zoo. Lodging is in spacious and immaculately clean apartments or in tasteful garden *casitas*. Amenities include pool, laundry service, hammocks, food and drink at extra cost. Free pick up from airport or bus terminal (ring in advance), free shuttle service into town. The owner runs **Gekko Tours**. German and English spoken, helpful. Prices in Euros.

Restaurants

Ciudad Bolívar *p1568, map p1568*
Many restaurants close at 1700.

$$ Bambú Sushi Bar, Av 5 de Julio, inside Hotel La Cumbre, take a taxi. Authentic sushi rolls served up on a breezy hill overlooking the city. In the same hotel, **Restaurante El Mirador**, serving grilled fish and meat, isn't bad either.

$$ Tepuy, Av Andrés Bello y Jesús Soto, opposite airport and inside Hotel Laja Real. Slightly formal place with very attentive service. Good pasta with prawns, as well as meat, chicken and fish, wines and cocktails.

$$ Tony Bar, Av Táchira y Mario Briceño Iragory. Very good stone-baked Italian-style pizzas, pastas, chicken, and general *típico* fare. Service isn't stellar, but the food makes up for it. A few blocks from the airport, but easiest to jump in a taxi. Recommended.

$$-$ Mercado La Carioca, Octava Estrella y Paseo Orinoco, on the banks of the river. Daily from 0600-1500. The best place for eating tasty local food. Great view. Various stalls and excellent local food with a range of prices.

$ Mirador Angostura, Paseo Orinoco. Unpretentious *comida criolla* with views over the river.

Cafés and fast food

Several fast food restaurants around **Museo de Arte Moderno Jesús Soto**.
Café Estilo, Av Andrés Bello, opposite **Laja Real Hotel** and very near airport. Open 0900-1200, 1500-1900. Boutique and café with homemade sweets, comfortable, spotless. Run by very nice elderly couple. Recommended.

◑ What to do

Ciudad Bolívar *p1568, map p1568*
Competition is stiff in Ciudad Bolívar. Do not agree to, or pay for a tour in the bus station or on the street. Always ask to be taken to the office. Always ask for a receipt (and make sure that it comes on paper bearing the company logo) and only take a tour that starts in Ciudad Bolívar. If you fall prey to a con artist, make a *denuncio* at the police station and inform genuine travel agents.

Ciudad Bolívar is the best place to book a tour to Canaima, but you will pick up cheaper deals for trips to Roraima and the Gran Sabana from Santa Elena. Most agents in Ciudad Bolívar sell tours run by just a handful of operators, but sometimes add commission. Always ask who will be running the actual tour; it may be cheaper to book from them directly. Get independent recommendations on standards of guiding, food, time-keeping, etc. For 3 days/2 nights tours to Canaima including flights, you pay around US$260-400 pp depending on accommodation, or around US$110 for 1-day tour that includes flights to Canaima, flight near the Angel Falls, boat ride across Canaima lagoon (just a few mins) and food (see page 1575 for flights to Canaima).
Bernal Tours, T632 6890, T0414-854 8234 (mob in Spanish), T0414-899 7162 (in English), www.bernaltours.com. Agency is run by descendents of Peruvian adventurer Tomás Bernal from Arequipa (see page 1572). They use *indígena* guides and their own eco lodge at Canaima lagoon overlooking the falls.
Gekko Tours, run by Pieter Rothfuss at airport (also **Posada La Casita**), T632 3223, T0414-854 5146, www.gekkotours-venezuela.de. Established family business with 18 years of experience.

Soana Travel, run by Martin Haars at **Posada Don Carlos**, Boyacá 26, T632 6017, T0414-864 6616, www.posada-doncarlos.com. English and German spoken. Professional and reliable.
Tiuna Tours, at airport, T416-686 1192, tiunatoursca@gmail.com. Cheapest option for Canaima, have a camp that takes 180 people.

● Transport

Ciudad Bolívar *p1568, map p1568*
Air It's possible to fly to **Canaima** independently, but an organized tour is highly recommended. Several flights leave daily with **Transmandú** (T0285-632 1462, www.transmandu.com), **Sundance Air** (Gekko Tours, T0285-632 3223) and **La Montaña** (T0414-853 2624), less frequently, with other charter airlines. One-way tickets cost around US$100; try to book at least 24-48 hrs in advance. A 20-person charter to Santa Elena can be arranged with **Transmandú**, subject to weather conditions, US$1600 (US$80/pp). Flights to **Caracas**, 5 6 a week, 1 hr with Rutaca. **Note** Puerto Ordaz/Ciudad Guayana is a busier flight hub and some tours start from there. Taxi to Ciudad Guayana US$5-7; to historic centre US$1.50.
Bus Terminal at junction of Av República and Av Sucre. Left luggage. To get there take bus marked Terminal going west along Paseo Orinoco (US$0.15). Buy bus tickets in advance. Hourly to **Caracas** US$5, 8-9 hrs. 10 daily to **Puerto La Cruz**, US$3.25, 5 hrs. 1 daily to **Cumaná**, US$4, 7 hrs. Daily to **Valencia**, via Maracay, US$4.80, 8-9 hrs, with Aeroexpresos Ejecutivos. **El Dorado** US$3.20. To **Santa Elena de Uairén** with several companies, Occidente and Línea Los Llanos recommended for comfort, US$6.25, 12-13 hrs. To **Ciudad Guayana** hourly from 0700, US$1-2, 1½ hrs. 2 daily to **Caicara**, US$4 (including 2 ferry crossings), 7-8 hrs, with Coop Gran Mcal Sucre. 2 daily to **Puerto Ayacucho**, US$6.25, 10-12 hrs with Línea Amazonas or Coop Gran Mcal Sucre, take food.
Taxi US$1.50 to virtually anywhere in town. US$1.20 from bus station to town centre.

Canaima and Angel Falls → *Colour map 2, B1.*

① *Park entry US$24 pp (BsF150; Venezuelans pay BsF100) paid to Inparques on arrival in Canaima.* Canaima National Park, a UNESCO World Heritage Site since 1994, is one of the most unspoilt places on earth. At over 3 million ha, it is the second largest national park in Venezuela, the sixth largest on the planet. It is a world apart, with its fantastic table mountains, waterfalls which include the world's highest (Angel Falls), caves, deep forests and indigenous cultures.

At Canaima camp, the Río Carrao tumbles spectacularly over Ucaima, Golondrina and Hacha Falls into the lagoon, which has beautiful tannin-stained water with soft beige beaches. It's a lovely spot, but it also has the air strip and is the centre of operations for river trips to indigenous areas and to Angel Falls. The falls are named after Jimmie Angel, the US airman who first reported their existence in 1935. Two years later he returned and crash landed his plane, the *Río Caroní*, on top of Auyán Tepuy. The site is marked with a plaque. The sheer rock face was climbed in 1971 by three Americans and an Englishman, David Nott, who recounted the 10-day adventure in his book *Angels Four* (Prentice-Hall). Hugo Chávez said that the falls should be called by an indigenous name: Kerepakupai Merú. A second indigenous name is Parekupa Vena.

There is a famous 'tunnel' between Sapo and Sapito Falls (where Río Carrao passes behind Isla Anatoliy), where one can walk behind the huge waterfall – a must for any visitor. It is essential to be accompanied by guide. The easiest way to get there is from Tomás Bernal Camp on Isla Anatoliy (five minutes boat ride from Canaima Camp). It's a 25-minute walk from there. Plastic raincoats are usually provided by the guide, or wear a swim suit. Wrap your camera and other belongings in a plastic bag. No matter what, you will get completely soaked in the middle of the tunnel. The path behind the waterfall is extremely slippery and should be taken only by the reasonably fit. Wrap your hand in an extra plastic bag, so it's not cut by the rough rope. When taking photos from behind the wall of water, experiment with camera speeds for the best effects.

Warning There is one more, invisible, waterfall on Canaima Lagoon, at the opposite end from Canaima Camp. It is called Salto Ara. The lagoon is a terrace and at Salto Ara all the water goes down one step. It is invisible from the surface, the only indicator is foam rising as if from nowhere. This fall is extremely dangerous: do not swim or take a boat near it. This is where Tomás Bernal, the Peruvian discoverer of the above tunnel, lost his life in 1998 after the engine of his boat broke down. He is buried on Isla Anatoliy.

Canaima

There are several tourist lodges at Canaima and many package tours visit on two-day/one-night and three-day/two-night trips from Ciudad Bolívar or Ciudad Guayana. These offer a variety of activities and longer ones usually include a day-trip to the Angel Falls (a long, bottom-numbing day). There is also a great variety of prices, depending on the class of lodging chosen (US$260-400; more expensive from Ciudad Guayana, more still if you start in Caracas). Do not forget swimwear, insect repellent and sun cream; waterproof clothing may be advisable. Do not walk barefoot because there are chiggers, or *niguas*, in the lagoon's sand beaches.

Trips to the Angel Falls

The Angel Falls, the highest in the world (979 m – its longest single drop is 807 m), 70 km downriver from Canaima, are best reached by plane to Canaima from Ciudad Bolívar or Ciudad Guayana. Trips by boat upriver to the Angel Falls operate May-January, depending on the level of the water in the rivers. Boats literally fly up and down river over the boulders (not for faint-hearted), but even during the rainy season you may have to get out and push in places. Most trips starting from Canaima make an overnight stop on one of the islands, continuing to the Falls the next day. More relaxing, with more stops at beauty spots, are 44-hour, 'three-day' trips. **Inparques** ① *Av Guayana, Edif Centro Empresarial Alta Vista, p 8, Puerto Ordaz, Ciudad Guayana, T0286-966 2033.* Ask here if you need a *permiso de excursionistas* to go on one tour and come back with another, giving yourself more time at the Falls. You may have to pay extra to do this, up to US$10 (take all food and gear). Trips can be arranged with agencies in Ciudad Bolívar (see above) or at Canaima airport. All *curiaras* (dugouts) must carry first aid, life jackets, etc. Take wet weather gear, swimwear, mosquito net for hammock and insect repellent and a plastic bag to protect your camera/day bag. The light is best on the falls in the morning.

The cheapest way to fly over the falls is on scheduled flights from Ciudad Bolívar. From Canaima a 45-minute flight costs around US$100 per person and does some circuits over and alongside the falls; departures only if enough passengers.

Kamarata

The largest of the tepuis, **Auyán Tepuy** (700 sq km) is also one of the more accessible. **Kamarata** is a friendly indigenous settlement with a Capuchin mission on the plain at the east foot of the tepuy. It has a well-stocked shop but no real hotels; basic rooms can be found for under US$10 per person, camping also possible at the mission (mosquito nets necessary and anti-malarial pills advised). Take food, although there is one place to eat, and locals may sell you dinner. The whole area is within the Parque Nacional Canaima.

Pemón families in Kamarata have formed co-operatives and can arrange *curiaras*, tents and porters for various excursions: see What to do, below.

Kavác

About a two-hour walk northwest of Kamarata, this is an indigenous-run resort consisting of a dozen thatched huts (*churuatas*) for guests, a small shop, and an excitingly short airstrip serviced by Cessnas from Ciudad Bolívar, Santa Elena, and Isla Margarita; flights from the north provide excellent views of Angel Falls and Auyán Tepuy. There is a vehicle connection with Kamarata but it is expensive because all fuel has to be flown in.

The prime local excursion is to **Kavác Canyon** and its waterfall known as La Cueva, which can be reached by joining a group or by setting out early west up the Río Kavác. A natural jacuzzi is encountered after a 30 minute wade along the sparkling stream, after which the gorge narrows dramatically until the falls are reached. Go in the morning to avoid groups of day-trippers from Porlamar. The sun's rays illuminate the vertical walls of the canyon only for a short time around 1100. Be prepared to get wet; swimwear and shoes with good grip, plus a dry change of clothing are recommended; also insect repellent, as there is a mosquito and midge invasion around dusk. Late afternoon winds off the savannah can make conditions chilly. Most visitors to Kavác are on tours from Canaima, or elsewhere, so it may be difficult to book lodging at the camp (basic rooms or hammocks). If you go independently, take food with you. There is an entry charge for visitors.

Uruyén

South of Auyán Tepuy and west of Kamarata, **Uruyén** is similar to Kavác, only smaller and more intimate. It also has a beautiful canyon and is the starting point for treks up Auyán Tepuy. The camp is run by the Carvallo family. See also www.angelconservation.org/lodges.html.

⊚ Canaima and Angel Falls listings

For hotel and restaurant price codes, and other relevant information, see Essentials.

⊜ Where to stay

Canaima *p1572*
Most lodges and camps are booked up by package tour companies.

$$$$ Wakü Lodge (Canaima Tours), T0286-962 0559, www.wakulodge.com. The best option in Canaima, 4-star luxury, romantic, comfortable, a/c, good food, right on lagoon, free satellite/ Wi-Fi internet for guests. Specializes mainly in all-inclusive packages. Recommended.

$$ pp Campamiento Canaima, T0289-540-2747, www.venetur.gob.ve. Run by **Venetur**

as a luxury resort with 105 rooms, restaurant, meeting room. Superb views of the lagoon.

$$ pp Campamiento Ucaima Jungle Rudy, T0289-808 9241, T0286-952 1529 in Puerto Ordaz, www.junglerudy.com. Run by daughters of the late 'Jungle' Rudy Truffino, full board with a variety of tour packages, 1-hr walk from Canaima above Hacha Falls, bilingual guides.

$$ pp Parakaupa Lodge, 5 mins from airport, on southwestern side of lagoon, Caracas T0212-287 0517, parakaupa@etheron.net. Attractive rooms with bath, hammocks views over the lagoon and falls, restaurant, full board.

$$ pp Tapuy Lodge, 50 m from Canaima beach, T212-993 2939 (reservations), T0414-287 7554, www.casatropical.com.ve. Next to the beach with expansive views of the mountains. Rooms are pleasant and include bath and a/c. Facilities include restaurant and bar. Attentive service and good reputation. One of the best. Recommended.

$ Camp Wey Tepuy, in the village, T0414-989-6615, www.weytepuy.com.ve. Cheap and basic with some reported deficiencies. Fan, shower, bar, a range of tours available.

$ Kusary, close to Parakaupa Lodge, near airport, T0286-962 0443. Basic but clean, with bath, fan, food available, ask for Claudio at Tienda Canaima.

Camping and hammocks

Camp for free in Canaima, but only around the *fuente de soda*; fires are not permitted. No tents available for hire. Otherwise, best place to rent a hammock or camp is at **Campamento Tomás Bernal (Bernal Tours)** on Isla Anatoliy, T0414-854 8234 Spanish, T0414-899 7162 English, www.bernaltours.com. Camp has capacity for 60 hammocks. Also 4 beds in open for elderly travellers, 4 rooms with private bath. Clean bathrooms. Package (**$$$ pp**) includes flight, bilingual guide, hammock, mosquito repellent, all meals, boat trip across lagoon, raincoat. Bernal Tours also has a camp on Ratoncito Island by Angel Falls.

Campamento Tiuna (Tiuna Tours) has camping space and lodging (**$ pp**). Some families in the village rent hammocks (**$ pp**).

Restaurants

Canaima *p1572*
Food is expensive at the lodges. A cheaper option is **Simon's** restaurant in the village which is used by many agencies. It is advisable to take food, though there are various stores, both on the west side, **Tienda Canaima**, or in the indian village, selling mainly canned foods. A *fuente de soda* overlooks the lagoon. There is an expensive snack bar at the airport selling basic food, soft drinks and coffee; also souvenir shop.

What to do

Canaima *p1572*
You can do walking expeditions into the jungle to indigenous villages with a guide, but negotiate the price. Other excursions are to the Mayupa Falls, including a canoe ride on the Río Carrao (US$18, half day), to Yuri Falls by jeep and boat (US$15, half day); to Isla Orquídea (US$25, full day, good boat ride, beach barbecue); to Saltos de Sapo and Sapito (3 hrs, US$10).

Guides in Canaima Fierce competition at the airport but agencies pretty much offer the same thing at the same price. Some package tours to Canaima are listed under Caracas and Ciudad Bolívar Tour operators. Agents may tell you that guides speak English: some do, but many don't.
Bernal Tours (see above).
Excursiones Kavác, T424-950 1294, or T414-342 3088. Several local companies use or otherwise recommend Excursiones Kavác as a well-structured and economical option. In Canaima, they operate a basic lodge, Campamento Churúm, along with a rustic camp near the falls.
Kamaracoto Tours and **Tiuna Tours** for trips to Salto Sapo, Kavác, Salto Angel; they will also help with finding accommodation.

Kamarata *p1573*
Macunaima Tours (Tito Abati), **Excursiones Pemón** (Marino Sandoval), and **Jorge and Antonio Calcaño II** run local tours.

For details on climbing Auyán Tepuy and many other tours in the region, contact **Kamadac** in Santa Elena, run by Andreas Hauer (T0289-995 1408, T0414-886 6526, www.abenteuer-venezuela.de).

⊖ Transport

Canaima *p1572*

Air There are flights from **Caracas** to Canaima with **Conviasa**, but these require a change in Puerto Ordaz. Many travelers prefer to go independently to **Puerto Ordaz** or **Ciudad Bolívar** and have their chosen tour operator or lodging organize onward flights to Canaima. LTA runs day excursions out of **Isla Margarita**, to Canaima, with a possible overflight of Angel Falls if conditions permit, but this airline's reliability has come under scrutiny (T0212-212 3110, www.tuy.com).

The flight to Canaima from **Ciudad Bolívar** is spectacular and takes 1 hr each way, overflying mining towns of San Isidro and Los Barrancos, as well as the vast artificial lake at Guri and the Yuri Falls. For more information see page 1571.

Kamarata *p1573*

Air Transmandú from **Ciudad Bolívar** (2 hrs).

Kavác *p1573*

Air A day excursion by light plane to Kavác from **Canaima** (45 mins' flight) can be made with any of the tour operators at the airport, US$100. There are also flights from **Ciudad Bolívar** with **Transmandú**. Trips from Ciudad Bolívar can be arranged for 5 days/4 nights including Kavác and Angel Falls for US$300-500.

Ciudad Guayana and the Orinoco Delta

Ciudad Guayana → *Phone code: 0286. Colour map 2, A2. Population: 790,000 (2009).*

In an area rich in natural resources 105 km downriver from Ciudad Bolívar, Ciudad Guayana was founded in 1961 with the merger of two towns, San Félix and Puerto Ordaz, on either bank of the Río Caroní where it spills into the Orinoco. Today, they are technically a single city, but most locals to refer to them as if they were separate settlements. Ciudad Guayana is hot, humid, sprawling and futuristic. Its wide avenues, lack of sidewalks and public transport reflect the functional vision of the US-owned Orinoco Mining Company, which had its headquarters here and was nationalized in 1976. The city lacks any aesthetic charm and is unsuitable for casual strolling.

East of the Caroní is the commercial port of **San Félix** and the Palúa iron-ore terminal. It is a very dangerous part of the city and there is no reason for you to visit it. Across the Caroní by the 470 m concrete bridge is the wealthier settlement of **Puerto Ordaz** (airport), the iron-ore port connected by rail with the Cerro Bolívar open-cast iron mine. The second bridge across the Río Orinoco, Puente Orinoquia, 3156 m long, was opened in Ciudad Guayana in 2006.

Visitors should be particularly careful while exploring Ciudad Guyana: it is surrounded by some desperately poor neighbourhoods. Violent crime, including rape, is unfortunately very common. And so is police unwillingness to answer 171 calls, let alone to investigate.

Excursions Unlike elsewhere in Venezuela, there is little emphasis on arts and culture. However, beyond the urban functionality are some pleasant parks, all well kept and free to enter. Just up the Caroní at Macagua, some truly beautiful cataracts called Salto Llovizna are in the **Parque Nacional La Llovizna** ① *open from early morning till 1630, taxi, US$2.50*, which covers 26 islands separated by narrow waterways and connected by 36 footbridges. Also in the park are hydroelectric plants, but these do not spoil the views of the larger and smaller falls, diverse fauna, including monkeys, and magnificent plants growing from the falling water. There are several trails. A facility on the **hydroelectric dam** ① *Tue-Sun 0900-2100*, houses an ecological museum, art exhibitions and displays on the dam's construction, and a café. Near La Llovizna, the iron-tinted waterfall in the pretty **Parque Cachamay** (about 8 km from centre, near the **Guayana Hotel**; closes 1700) is worth a visit. A third park, adjoining Cachamay, is **Loefling Wildlife Park**, with tapirs, capybaras and capuchin monkeys.

Los Castillos, supposedly where Sir Walter Raleigh's son was killed in the search for El Dorado, are two old forts down the Orinoco from San Félix (one hour by *por puesto*, US$1, or take a tour).

Tucupita → *Phone code: 0287, Colour map 2, A2, Population: 73,000. Climate: very humid.*

A worthwhile side trip along asphalted roads can be made to Tucupita, on the Orinoco delta. Though capital of Delta Amacuro state and the main commercial centre of the delta, there's a one-horse feel about it. **Tourist office** ① *Parque Central de Tucupita Módulos II y III, Av Mons A García de Espinosa, by the Terminal de Pasajeros.* Tourists should go there first for tour information.

For a three- to four-day trip to see the delta, its fauna and the indigenous *Warao*, either arrange boats through the tourist office (see above). Boats are not easy to come by and are expensive except for large groups. Bargain hard and never pay up front.

Excursions often only travel on the main river, not in the *caños* where wildlife is most often seen. To avoid disappointment, be sure to determine where your guide intends to take you before you leave. If the river level rises after a downpour, arrangements may be cancelled. On all trips agree in advance exactly what is included, especially that there is enough food and water for you and your guide. Hammocks and mosquito repellents are essential.

Barrancas → *Colour map 2, A2. Population: 13,000.*

An interesting and friendly village, founded in 1530, Barrancas is one of the oldest villages in the Americas, but its precolonial past dates back to 1000 BC. Situated on the Orinoco, it can be reached by road from Tucupita (63 km), or from Maturín. It has two basic hotels ($). The village has a large community of Guyanese people who speak English. It is possible to take a boat to the *Warao* villages of **Curiapo** and **Amacuro** (near Guyana border), check at harbour.

◉ Ciudad Guayana and the Orinoco Delta listings

For hotel and restaurant price codes, and other relevant information, see Essentials.

● Where to stay

Ciudad Guayana: Puerto Ordaz *p1575*
$$$ Venetur Orinoco, Av Guayana, Parque Punta Visat, T713 1000, www.venetur.gob.ve. It overlooks La Llovizna in Parque Cachamay, far from centre, great location but poor value. Get one of the newer rooms with a good view.
$$ Doral Inn Hotel, C Neverí, opposite the airport, T952 6803, doralinn@bolivar.travel. A good option for early morning flights. Generic rooms are massive and spotless with white marble floors, a/c, cable TV, and Wi-Fi. Next door, Hotel Mara is good too, but twice the price.
$ Casa del Lobo, of Wolfgang Löffler of Lobo Tours, C Zambia 2, Africana Manzana 39, T961 6286, www.lobo-tours.de. Homely *posada* with room for 8 people, free transfer from airport. 'El Lobo' speaks English and German.
$ Posada Turística Alonga, Urb La Corniza, Av Canadá, manz 10, casa 14, T923 3154, posadaalonga@hotmail.com. Family-run *posada* in a quiet residential area, see Facebook.
$ Residencias Tore, C San Cristóbal y Cra Los Andes, T923 1389, www.residenciastore.com.ve.

Ecologically aware hotel with solar heated water, restaurant, laundry and Wi-Fi. Simple, pleasant, quiet rooms have flat screen TVs and sparkling bathrooms.

Tucupita *p1576*
$ Saxxi, on main road into Tucupita, 10 mins from centre, T721 2112, www.deltaorinocomis palafitos.com. Comfortable, hot water, a/c, bar/restaurant, disco Fri-Sat, pool. Also has camps Mis Palafitos and Orinoco Bujana Lodge, **$$**, T721 1733. All inclusive.
$ Pequeño, La Paz, T721 0523. Basic but clean, fan, good value, safe, stores luggage, orchid garden, popular, closes at 2200.

❼ Restaurants

Ciudad Guayana *p1575*
There are plenty of restaurants and cafés on Cras Tumeremo and Upata, off Av Las Américas. Fast food and upmarket eateries in Ciudad Comercial Altavista.
Mall Orinokia, on Av Guayana, Altavista, close to the bus terminal. Huge, super-modern shopping mall with restaurants, cafés and travel agencies. Multi-screen cinema.

El Arepazo Guayanés, C La Urbana, Puerto Ordaz, T922 4757. The oldest and best *arepería* in Ciudad Guyana, open 24 hrs.

Mi Rinconcito, across the street from Mall Orinokia (Altavista), T962 1554. Famous for its *cachapas* and live music at the end of the week.

⚙ What to do

Ciudad Guayana *p1575*

Lobo Tours, see Casa del Lobo, Where to stay. Wolfgang Löffler will tailor his tours to fit your demands. Trips organized to the Gran Sabana and Orinoco Delta, but will put together other excursions. Very helpful, all-inclusive, excellent cooking. English and German spoken.

Tucupita *p1576*

Some boat owners visit hotels in the evenings looking for clients and may negotiate a price. Ask Pieter Rothfuss at Gekko Tours/Posada La Casita in Ciudad Bolívar about a trip through the southern part of the delta and into the Sierra Imataca highlands. The following (and Mis Palafitos – see Hotel Saxxi) are registered with the tourist board and have insurance (this does not necessarily guarantee a good tour).

Aventura Turística, C Centurión 62, T0414-879 5821, and at bus station, a_t_d_1973@ hotmail.com, www.hosteltrail.com/atd. 2 camps in the northern part of the delta, all inclusive tours, English and French spoken.

Tucupita Expeditions, opposite hospital, T0295-249 1823, T0414-789 8343, www.orinocodelta.com. 2- to 5-night tours to lodges and camps in the delta.

⊖ Transport

Ciudad Guayana *p1575*

Air Daily flights from Puerto Ordaz to **Caracas**, **Maracaibo**, **Porlamar** and short-haul destinations. Walk 600 m to gas station on main road for buses to San Félix or Puerto Ordaz.
Bus Terminals at San Félix and close to Puerto Ordaz airport; long-distance buses at both. Public transport in Ciudad Guayana is very limited. Free local buses are infrequent. Minibuses are fast and cheap; San Félix-Puerto Ordaz, US$0.60; buses run until 2100. Several buses daily to **Santa Elena de Uairén** (via El Callao), US$6, 10 hrs, night buses with Los Llanos and Occidente recommended for comfort, but you'll miss the scenery. **El Callao** (US$2.50), **Tumeremo** (US$3), **El Dorado** (US$4) and Km 88 with Turgar. **Ciudad Bolívar** US$1-2, 1 hr. 8 daily to **Caracas**, US$6-9, 10 hrs. 8 daily to **Puerto La Cruz**, US$5, 6 hrs. 2 daily to **Cumaná**, US$5, 8 hrs. To **Tucupita**, US$3, 3 hrs, leaving from San Félix bus terminal with Expresos Guayanesa, booking office opens 1 hr before departure, be there early, passport check just before Tucupita. San Felix bus terminal is not a safe place, especially at night.
Taxi San Félix-Puerto Ordaz US$1.50 minimum, Puerto Ordaz-airport US$2, San Félix bus terminal-Puerto Ordaz bus terminal US$3, bus terminal-centre US$2, centre-San Félix bus terminal US$2.

Tucupita *p1576*

Bus *Por puesto* from **Maturín** US$4, 2-3 hrs; bus to Maturín, US$2, 3-4 hrs, Expresos Guayanesa, US$3.25 with Expresos Los Llanos recommended. 2 daily to **San Félix**, US$3, see above. 2 daily to **Caracas**, US$7, 12-13 hrs.

Barrancas *p1576*

Bus Tucupita-Barrancas, US$1, return at 0945 and 1700.

ⓘ Directory

Ciudad Guayana *p1575*

Banks Banks will not exchange Brazilian currency. **Car hire** Many agencies at airport. A car is very useful here, eg for local excursions, or taking a road trip through the Gran Sabana to Brazil. **Consulates** Brazil, Cra Tocoma, Edif Eli-Alti, of 4, Alta Vista, T961 2995, consbras@cantv.net, 0900-1200, 1400-1800. Helpful, visa issued promptly.

Ciudad Guayana to Santa Elena de Uairén

Travelling south from Ciudad Guayana to the Brazilian border is popular with Venezuelans, as well as for overland travellers heading in or out of Brazil via Boa Vista. The road to the border at Santa Elena de Uairén passes across the beautiful Gran Sabana and is paved, with all bridges in place.

Visiting Ciudad Guayana to Santa Elena de Uairén

Getting around A 4WD is only necessary off the main road, especially in the rainy season. You may need spare tanks of gasoline if spending a lot of time away from the main road (eg in Kavanayen and El Paují) and have a gas-guzzling vehicle. Carry extra water and plenty of food. Small eating places may close out of season. There are Guardia Nacional checks at the Río Cuyuní (Km 8), at Km 126, and at San Ignacio de Yuruaní (Km 259), and a military checkpoint at Luepa (Km 143); all driving permits, car registration papers, and ID must be shown. ➡ *See also Transport, page 1582.*

Advice In the towns as far as El Dorado, there are hotels, but many cater for local business, legitimate or otherwise, and for short-stay clients. Water is rationed in many places and hot water in hotels is rare south of Ciudad Guayana, except in the better hotels of Santa Elena. Towns usually have a bank, but don't rely on it for getting money. Camping is possible but a good waterproof tent is essential. A small fee is payable to the *indígenas* living around Kaui, Kama and similar villages (see also under Parque Nacional Canaima). Insect repellent and long- sleeved/ trousered clothes are needed against *puri-puri* (small, black, vicious biting insects) and mosquitoes (especially in El Dorado, at Km 88 and at Icabarú). See www.lagransabana.com.

To Tumeremo

South from Ciudad Guayana Highway 10 is a four-lane *autopista* as far as **Upata** (*Phone code: 0288; Population: 91,000*). Buy provisions opposite the petrol station. At 18 km beyond **Guasipati** is **El Callao** (*Population: 27,400*) on the south bank of the Río Yuruari, off the highway, a small, clean, bright town whose renowned pre-Lenten carnival has a touch of calypso from British Caribbean immigrants who came to mine gold in the late 19th century (all prices rise for carnival). The town has many jewellery shops and restaurants.

On another 41 km is **Tumeremo** (*Colour map 2, A2. Population: 24,300*), which is recommended as the best place to buy provisions and gasoline, all grades at a normal price (better than El Dorado).

El Dorado → *Phone code: 0288. Colour map 2, B2. Population: 9000.*

This hot, dirty and noisy town is 76 km from Tumeremo, 278 km from Ciudad Guayana, and 7 km off the road on the Río Cuyuní. On a river island is the prison made famous by Henri Charrière/ Papillon's stay there in 1945. El Dorado's economic mainstay is its gas station (daily 0800-1900).

El Dorado to Santa Elena de Uairén

The turn-off to El Dorado is marked Km 0; distances are measured from here by green signs 2 km apart. The wall of the Gran Sabana looms above **Km 88** (also called **San Isidro**), where gasoline and expensive supplies can be bought. The highway climbs steeply in sharp curves for 40 km before reaching the top. The road is in very good condition and presents no problem for conventional cars. 4WDs may be better in the wet season (May-October). At Km 100 the huge **Piedra de la Virgen** (sandy coloured with black streaks) is passed before the steepest climb (La Escalera) enters the beautiful **Parque Nacional Canaima** (see page 1572).

The landscape is essentially savannah, with clusters of trees, moriche palms and bromeliads. Typical of this area are the large abrupt *tepuis* (flat-topped mountains or mesas), hundreds of waterfalls, and the silence of one of the oldest plateaus on earth. At Km 119 (sign can only be seen going north) a short trail leads to the 40 m **Danto ('Tapir') Falls**, a powerful fall wreathed in mosses and mist. The falls are close to the road (about five minutes slippery walk down on the left-hand side), but not visible from it. The **Monumento al Soldado Pionero** (Km 137) commemorates the army engineers who built the road from the lowlands, finally opened in 1973; barbecues, toilets, shelters are now almost all in ruins. Some 4 km beyond is **Luepa**; everyone must stop at the military checkpoint a little way south. There is a popular camping place at Luepa, on the right going south. You may be able to rent a tent or you can hang a hammock in an open-sided shelter (very cold at night, no water or facilities, buy meals from a tour group, but pricey). The Inparques station at Luepa has guestrooms for visitors of Inparques, but they may let you stay for a small fee. You can camp at a site on Río Aponwao on the left hand side of the road going south.

Some 8 km beyond Luepa, a poor, graded gravel road leads 70 km west to **Kavanayén** (little traffic, best to have your own vehicle with high clearance, especially during the wet season, take snacks; the road can be cycled but is slow, lots of soft, sandy places). Accommodation is at the Capuchin mission, **$**, also in private homes. One of the two grocery stores will prepare food, or the restaurant opposite serves cheap breakfasts and dinners, order in advance.

The settlement is surrounded by *tepuis*. Off the road to Kavanayén are the falls of **Torón Merú** and **Chinak-Merú** (also called Aponwao), 105 m high and very impressive. Neither is a straightforward detour, so get full instructions before setting out. Chinak-Merú is reached via the Pemón village of **Iboribó**. A day's walk west of Kavanayén are the lovely falls on the **Río Karuay**.

For the remaining 180 km to Santa Elena de Uairén few people and only a few Pemón Indian villages are to be seen. San Juan and San Rafael de Kamoiran and **Rápidos de Kamoiran** are passed. The 5-m Kawí falls on the **Kaüi** River are at Km 195, while at Km 201.5 are the impressive 55 m high **Kama Merú** falls (US$1 to walk to bottom of falls). Also a small lake, handicrafts, a small shop, canoe trips. Cabins and *churuatas* can be rented, also camping. Buses can be flagged down going south or north three times a day; check times in advance.

At Km 237 the Río Arapán cascades over the charming **Quebrada Pacheco** (Arapán Merú); pools nearby where you can swim. Tour groups often stop here. A path up the opposite side of the main falls leads to an isolated natural pool 20 minutes walk away, in the middle of the savannah. **Warning** Do not go beyond the red line at Pacheco: there is a hidden fall which has claimed lives. There is a Campamento at Arapán. Next is **Balneario Saro Wapo** on the Río Soruapé (Km 244), a good place for swimming and picnics, natural whirlpool, restaurant. 10 minutes downriver is a natural waterslide. At Km 250 is the Pemón village of Kumarakapai, San Francisco de Yuruaní (see page 1583), whose falls (Arapena-merú) can be seen from the bridge, followed, 9 km of bends later, by the smaller **San Ignacio de Yuruaní** (strict military checkpoint; excellent regional food).

A trail at Km 275 leads to the **Quebrada de Jaspe** where a river cuts through striated cliffs and pieces of jasper glitter on the banks. Visit at midday when the sun shines best on the jasper, or at 1500 when the colour changes from red to orange, dazzlingly beautiful.

Santa Elena de Uairén → *Phone code: 0289. Colour map 2, B2. Municipal population: 33,500.*

This booming, pleasant frontier town was established by Capuchin Monks in 1931. The mid-20th-century **cathedral** ⓘ *daily 0530-1900, mass Mon-Sat 0630 and 1830, Sun 0630 and 2030*, built from local stone, is a famous landmark. Thanks to its relaxed atmosphere and many hotels, Santa Elena is an agreeable place in which to spend time. It has Arab and Chinese communities and you are as likely to hear Portugese spoken as you are Spanish.

Border with Brazil

The 16 km road to the border is paved. The entire road links Caracas with Manaus in four days with hard driving; see Northern Brazil, in Brazil chapter, for a description of the road from the border and Brazilian immigration formalities. Modern customs and immigration facilities are at the border and the crossing is straightforward on both sides (for more information, see Transport, page 1583). Staff at the Ministry of Justice and the Guardia Nacional headquarters (T960 3765/995 1189/995 1958) have been recommended as helpful with entry and exit problems. You can get a visa at the **Brazilian consulate** ⓘ *Edif Galeno, C Los Castaños, Urbanización Roraima del Casco Central, T995 1256, vcsantaelena@mre.gov.br; open 0800-1400.*

For entry to Venezuela, some nationalities who cross the border from Boa Vista, Brazil, need a visa. It is not required by western Europeans, whose passport must be valid for a year, but check with a consulate before leaving home. A yellow fever vaccination certificate is required. Ask well in advance for other health requirements (eg malaria test certificate). Entering by car, keep photocopies of your licence, the Brazilian permission to leave and Venezuelan entry stamp. Allow two hours for formalities when crossing by private vehicle and don't cross during the lunch hour. Fresh fruit and vegetables may not be brought into Venezuela. There are frequent road checks when heading north from Santa Elena. SENIAT (the customs authority) has its Aduana Principal Ecológica outside the town and there may be up to eight more thorough searches, mainly for drugs. Luggage will be sealed before loading into the bus hold in Santa Elena. These checks may mean you arrive in Ciudad Bolívar after dark. There is no public transport on the Venezuelan side, hitch or take a taxi from Brazil.

El Paují

A road leaves the highway 8 km south of Santa Elena and after passing through a tunnel of jungle vegetation emerges onto rolling savannah dotted with *tepuis*. The road has been considerably improved and has been paved for 20 km. The rest is graded, but deteriorating. It can take between two to four hours to reach El Paují. Take advice before setting out, as rain can rapidly degrade the road. At Km 58 is a Guardia Nacional checkpoint at Paraitepuí, waterfall nearby.

El Paují, 17 km further on, is an agricultural settlement with a growing foreign population. It is a lovely area, with good walking. Excellent sights: **Chirica Tepuy**, huge, beautiful, jet black, set in rolling savannah; **Río Surucún**, where Venezuela's largest diamond was found; **Salto Catedral** (61 km off the road), beautiful small hollow, lovely falls, excellent swimming (camping, shop); **Salto La Gruta**, impressive falls; and **Pozo Esmeralda**, 1.5 km outside El Paují towards Icabarú (400 m south of road), fine rapids, waterfall you can stand under and pools. At Los Saltos de Paují are many powerful falls; going from El Paují towards Santa Elena, before crossing the first bridge, take track on left for about 500 m. A good walk is to the small hill, 2 km from El Paují beyond the airfield; views from the crest over **El Abismo**, the plunging escarpment marking the end of Gran Sabana highlands and the start of the Amazon rainforest. It takes an hour to reach the top, and the walk is highly recommended. Guides, though not necessary, are in the village. A recommended guide is German-speaking Marco. Small campsite (lovely early morning or sunset).

Apiculture is the main activity of El Paují and there's an **International Honey Festival** every summer. The honey made in this area is delicious; buy it at the shop in El Paují or Salto Catedral.

◎ Ciudad Guayana to Santa Elena de Uairén listings

For hotel and restaurant price codes, and other relevant information, see Essentials.

● Where to stay

To Tumeremo: Upata *p1578*
$ Andrea, Plaza Miranda, T221 3656. Decent rooms, a/c, hot water, fridge in some rooms. Credit cards accepted, Chinese restaurant, safe parking, good.

El Dorado to Santa Elena de Uairén
p1578
$$ pp La Barquilla de Fresa, at Km 84.5. Book via Alba Betancourt in Caracas T0288-808 8710, T0426-991 9919, www.strawberrybirds.com. English and German spoken. Birdwatching tours; inventory of bird species here has

reached more than 300 species. Full board lodging, reservations and deposit required.

Rápidos de Kamoiran
$ Campamento Rápidos de Kamoiran, Km 172, T0289-540 0009, www.rapidosde kamoiran.blogspot.com. Clean, with fan, well-kept, cold water, also has camping, also restaurant, gasoline, and picnic spot by rapids.

Santa Elena de Uairén *p1579*
$$-$ Cabañas Friedenau, Av Ppal de Cielo Azul, off Av Perimetral, T995 1353, see Facebook. Self-contained chalets, nice grounds, vegetarian food, parking, transfer to Puerto Ordaz, bikes, horseriding, trips to Roraima (see below), English spoken. Recommended.

$$-$ **Gran Sabana**, Carretera Nacional Via Brasil, 10 km from border, T995 1810, www. hotelgransabana.com. Large resort-style hotel with 58 rooms, one of the most upscale in town but past its heyday. Pool, parking, café, tours.

$$-$ **Posada L'Auberge**, C Urdaneta, T995 1567, www.l-auberge.net. Brick-built guesthouse with good rooms and shared balcony, a/c, Wi-Fi, cable TV, hot water, parking, tourist information. Family-run. Recommended.

$$-$ **Villa Fairmont**, Urb Akurimá, T995 1022, at north edge of town, www.lagransabana. com/villafairmont. Large place up on a hill with pool, jacuzzi, restaurant, parking, bar. Reasonable rooms but check before accepting.

$ **Kiamantí**, outside town 1 km from bus terminal, T995 1952, http://kiamanti.blogspot. com/. Very simple little cabins, full board, fan, hot water, parking, pool.

$ **Lucrecia**, Av Perimetral, T995 1105, near old terminal, www.hotellucrecia.com.ve. Motel-style lodgings with a small pool, parking and restaurant. Rooms have a/c or fan, hot water, cable TV, Wi-Fi. Helpful.

$ **Michelle**, C Urdaneta, T416 1257, www.hostel trail.com/posadamichelle. Popular backpacker place, helpful. Basic rooms have fan, hot water, Wi-Fi. Shower and changing room available if you're waiting for a night bus.

$ **Posada Ana**, Sector Piedra Canaima, T414-385 2846, 15 mins from Santa Elena. Boasts a commanding position on a mountainside and expansive views of the landscape. They offer simple, brightly painted private rooms, dorms, shared kitchen, and campground.

$ **Villa Apolpó**, on the road to the airport, turn left at the **Hotel Gran Sabana**, T995 2018, www.posadaturisticavillapoipo.blogspot.com. Very nice rooms, hot water, fan. For groups but will take independent travellers if you ring ahead. Use of kitchen or full board. Bunk beds or hammocks available in large *churuata*.

$ **Ya-Koo Ecological Camp**, 2 km on unpaved road to Sampai Indian community, up mountain behind Santa Elena, T995 1742, www.ya-koo.com. *Cabañas* in beautiful 10-ha site, full board, spacious rooms, hot water, natural pool. Cheaper in low season. Recommended if you have a car.

El Paují *p1580*

$$-$ pp **Campamento Amaribá**, 3.5 km outside El Paují on road from Santa Elena, transport available from airstrip, T0416-533 4270, amaribapauji@yahoo.com. Comfortable cabins with mosquito nets, good facilities, full board, kitchen, tours arranged, very hospitable. Also dance, healing and therapy centre.

$ **Campamento El Paují**, 3.5 km outside El Paují on road from Santa Elena, transport available from airstrip, T995 1431, T0426-691 8966, dianalez@gmail.com, or contact through **Maripak**. Beautiful cabins with spectacular views over the Gran Sabana, food available, camping US$6 per tent. Recommended.

$ **Cantarana** tourist camp, 25 km from town, T0415 212 0662 (in Caracas T0212-234 0255), www.gran-sabana.info. Basic accommodation, breakfast and dinner included, owners, Alfonso and Barbara Borrero, speak German, English and Spanish, waterfall and lovely surroundings.

$ **Maripak**, near the airstrip and small store, T0414-772 3070, www.maripak.com.ve, or reserve in Caracas T0212-234 3631. Cabins for 2/3 with bath, meals extra, good food, tours, camping.

$ **Weimure**, 2 km out, outside El Paují on road from Santa Elena, pauji0@yahoo.com. Beautiful cabin close to river, dynamic architect owner.

🍴 Restaurants

Santa Elena de Uairén *p1579*
Several restaurants on Mcal Sucre. The local river fish, Lau Lau, is good. Avoid seafood.

$ **Alfredo's**, Av Perimetral, at the end of C Urdaneta. Tasty pizzas at good prices.

$ **Peixada e Restaurant Do Léo**, C Zea, between C Peña and C Icabarú. Unpretentious Brazilian barbeque with chicken, sausages and chorizos, pay by weight, also a good selection of salads for vegetarians. Recommended.

$ **Tumá Serö**, a cheap and bustling gastronomic market where you can pick up wholesome arepas, soup, pizzas, burgers.

$ **Venezuela Primero**, Av Perimetral. Dated interior but often recommended for its chicken, meat and fish.

Gran Sabana Deli, C Bolívar, T995 1158. A large café with pavement seating selling good hot coffee, imported ham, cheese, salami, fresh bread, olives, cakes, and pastries.

● What to do

Santa Elena de Uairén p1579

Santa Elena is the most economical place to book tours of the Gran Sabana, Roraima, and other tepuis. Many interesting attractions lie along the highway and can be covered in an undemanding day-trip. Trips to Roraima typically last 5-6 days, but it can be done in 4. An all-inclusive package (transport, guide, sleeping bag, mattress, map, food, tent, and porter) costs US$270. The same tour without a porter costs US$200; loads are typically 10 kg plus your own luggage. The cheapest option, including only transport and guide, costs US$130.

Alvarez Treks, office in the bus station, T414-385 2846, www.saltoangelrsta.com. An excellent range of Gran Sabana tours by Francisco Alvarez. The 'traditional' tour is physically undemanding, follows the highway, a good trip for families and seniors. The moderately demanding 'non-traditional' tour offers a more intimate experience of the landscape with hikes through rivers and rainforests. The combination tour offers a bit of both, while the Extreme Tour is a 6-hr day with stops at waterfalls and swimming holes; 4-people minimum. Also tours of Roraima, Angel Falls, Los Llanos, and the Orinoco Delta. Knowledgeable, helpful, recommended.

Backpacker Tours, C Urdaneta, T995 1430, T0414-886 7227, www.backpacker-tours.com. 1- to 5-day, all-inclusive jeep tours through the Gran Sabana, visiting little-known falls in the Kavanayen area. Trekking to nearby Chirikayen Tepuy, 3-4 days and to Roraima (minimum 4 persons), plus more. German and English spoken. Recommended. Also have own $ Posada **Kamadac**, C Urdaneta, T995 1408, T0414-886 6526, www.abenteuer-venezuela.de. Run by Andreas Hauer, tours of Gran Sabana, all-inclusive tour to Roraima, and also more adventurous tours to Auyán Tepuy from which Angel Falls cascades, difficult. Recommended.

Roberto's Mystic Tours, Urdaneta, casa 6, T416 0686, www.mystictours.com.ve. As the author of several books about Roraima and the Gran Sabana, Roberto is very knowledgeable about the local environment and culture. His tours include a complete briefing of the region's ecological,

botanical and energetic properties. Excellent tours, very helpful, highly recommended.

Ruta Salvaje, C Mcal Sucre, at the junction opposite the petrol station, T995 1134, www.rutasalvaje.com. Well-established adventure tour specialists offering white-water rafting, parapenting and paramotoring, traditional and non-traditional day tours of the Gran Sabana, treks to Roraima, and tours of Angel Falls.

● Transport

To Tumeremo: Upata p1578

Bus To **Ciudad Bolívar**, US$3.50. To **San Félix** (Ciudad Guayana), US$1.75. To **Santa Elena**, US$5.

Tumeremo p1578

Bus To **Caracas**, US$10. To **Ciudad Bolívar**, US$6, 6 a day, 6½ hrs. To **Santa Elena**, 8-10 hrs, with **Líneas Orinoco**, 2 blocks from plaza. **El Dorado**, US$1, 1½ hrs.

El Dorado p1578

Bus All buses stop on main plaza. From **Caracas**, Expresos del Oriente, at 1830 daily, US$12, 14½ hrs (925 km). The Orinoco bus links with **Ciudad Bolívar** (6 hrs, US$4) and **Santa Elena**, as does Transmundial (better, leaving 1100, US$4 to **Santa Elena**, US$4 to San Félix, 4 hrs).

El Dorado to Santa Elena de Uairén p1578

Km 88 (San Isidro)

Bus Frequent *por puestos* from **El Dorado** to Km 88, 1 hr, US$1. Most non-luxury buses stop at the petrol station to refuel. Or get a ride with jeeps and trucks (little passes after 1030).

Santa Elena de Uairén p1579

Air Airport, 8 km from the centre. Scheduled flights from Caracas with **Conviasa** only (unreliable); infrequent charters from **Ciudad Bolívar** subject to weather conditions.

Bus The bus terminal on road to Ciudad Bolívar is 2-km/30 mins' walk from town, taxi US$1.50. Get to terminal 30 mins in advance for SENIAT baggage check for contraband. From **Caracas** there are direct buses (eg **Expresos Los Llanos**), US$15, or you can go to Ciudad Bolívar or to Ciudad Guayana and then take a bus direct to Santa Elena. 10 buses daily from Santa Elena to **Ciudad Bolívar**, US$6, Expresos Los Llanos and Expresos Occidente recommended for comfort, 10-12 hrs. 10 daily to **Ciudad Guayana** and **San Félix**, US$5, 10-11 hrs.

To the border The best way to reach the border is with a *por puesto* taxi, US$1.50. They depart from the intersection of C Roscio and C Icabarú. Check that they drop you at the 2 immigration offices, 750 m apart, before going onward to the town of Pacaraima, where you can pick up connections to Boa Vista. Alternatively, from the bus station, there are 3 buses daily to **Boa Vista**, US$3, 4 hrs, Eucatur.

El Pauji *p1580*
Road From **Santa Elena** by jeep, US$3-5 if full, more if not, daily at around 0600-0700 and 1500-1600 from Plaza Bolívar. Also at **Panadería Gran Café**, C Icabarú. To get further than El Pauji, 4WD vehicle is necessary: **Cantarana**, US$7, and **Icabarú**, US$8.

ⓘ Directory

Santa Elena de Uairén *p1579*
Banks ATMs are unlikely to accept non-Venezuelan credit cards. Try shops in the centre, C Urdaneta, for dollars cash, or Brazilian reais. Try at border with Brazilians entering Venezuela. Ask the bus driver on the Santa Elena-Boa Vista bus the best place for favourable bolívares/reais rates: in Santa Elena at Sucre y Perimetral; in Brazil at the first stop after the border. Check with travellers going in opposite direction what rates should be.

Mount Roraima → *Altitude: 2810 m.*

An exciting trek is to the summit of Mount Roraima, at one time believed to be the '**Lost World**' made famous by Arthur Conan Doyle's novel. 'Roroima' is a word in the Pemón Indian language meaning 'The great blue-green'. Due to the tough terrain and extreme weather conditions, this hike is only suitable for the fit. Supplies for a week or more should be bought in Santa Elena. If a tour company is supplying the food, check what it is first; vegetarians may go hungry.

San Francisco de Yuruaní

The starting point is this Pemón village, 9 km north of the San Ignacio military checkpoint (where you must register). There are three small shops selling basic goods but not enough for Roraima hike. Meals are available and tents can be hired, about US$10 each per day, quality of tents and stoves is poor; better equipment is available in Santa Elena.

Paraitepui

The road to Paraitepui (which is signposted), the nearest village to the mountain, leaves the highway 1 km south of San Francisco. It is in good condition, with three bridges; the full 25 km can be walked in seven hours. You can sleep for free in the village if hiring a guide; camping is permitted. Few supplies are available; a small shop sells basics. The villagers speak Tauripán, the local dialect of the Pemón linguistic group, but now most of them also speak Spanish.

Climbing Roraima

The foot trail winds back and forth on a more direct line than the little-used jeep track; it is comparatively straightforward and adequately marked descending from the heights just past Paraitepui across rolling hills and numerous clear streams. The goal, Roraima, is the mountain on the right, the other massive outcrop on the left is Mata Hui (known as Kukenán after the river which rises within it). If leaving the village early in the day, you may reach the Río Cuquenán crossing by early afternoon (good camping here). Three hours' walk brings you to a lovely bird-filled meadow below the foothills of the massif, another perfect camping spot known as *campamento base* (10 hours to base camp from Paraitepui). The footpath now climbs steadily upwards through the cloud forest at the mountain's base and becomes an arduous scramble over tree trunks and damp rocks until the cliff is reached. From here it is possible to ascend to the plateau along the 'easy' rock ledge which is the only route to the top. Walkers in good health should take about four hours from the meadow to the top. The summit is an eerie world of stone and water, difficult to move around easily. There are not many good spots to camp; but there are various overhanging ledges which are colourfully known as 'hoteles' by the guides. Red painted arrows lead the way to the right after reaching the summit for the main group of these. A marked track leads to the survey pillar near the east cliff where Guyana, Brazil and Venezuela meet; allow a day as the track is very rough. Other sights include the Valley of the Crystals, La Laguna de Gladys and various sinkholes.

The whole trip can take anywhere between five days and two weeks. The dry season for trekking is November-May (with annual variations); June-August Roraima is usually enveloped in cloud. Do not remove crystals from the mountain; on-the-spot fines up to US$100 may be charged. Thorough searches are made on your return. Take your rubbish back down with you.

◉ Mount Roraima listings

For hotel and restaurant price codes, and other relevant information, see Essentials.

◍ Where to stay

San Francisco de Yuruaní *p1583*
$ Arapena Posada, T0414-095.7613.
Small and basic.
$ El Caney de Yuruaní, T0416-289 2413.
Clean, basic rooms, fan, restaurant.
$ Mínima T0414-886 6771.
Camping Permitted just about anywhere, free. Plenty of mosquitos at night.

Climbing Roraima *p1583*
Camping Full equipment including stove is essential (an igloo-type tent with a plastic sheet for the floor is best for the summit, where it can be wet), wear thick socks and boots to protect legs from snakes, warm clothes for the summit (much mist, rain squalls and lightning at night) and effective insect repellent – biting *plaga* (*blackflies*) infest the grasslands. The water on the summit and around the foot of Roraima is very pure, but as more do the trek, the waters are becoming dirtied. Bring bottled water or a purifier for the savannah. Fires must not be lit on top of Roraima, only gas or liquid fuel stoves. Litter is appearing along the trail; please take care of the environment.

◍ What to do

Climbing Roraima *p1583*
Guides and tours The National Guard requires all visitors to have a guide beyond Paraitepui; you will be fined. Go with a guide or tour operator from Santa Elena or from San Francisco; ask at **Arapena**, or **El Caney de Yuruaní**. Those hired on the street or in Paraitepui have no accident insurance cover. Guides can help for the hike's final stages (easy to get lost) and for finding best camping spots. Guides in San Francisco de Yuruaní cost US$15 a day, more if they carry your supplies. Check the camping gear for leaks, etc, and be clear about who is providing the guide's food.

Guides in Paraitepui cost US$10 a day, Spanish- speaking guides. The **Ayuso** brothers are the best-known guides. Ask for El Capitán, he is in charge of guides. Parking at Inparques US$2.

◍ Transport

San Francisco de Yuruaní *p1583*
Bus From **Santa Elena** bus will let you off here and pick up passengers en route northwards (no buses 1200-1900). Jeep to **Paraitepui** US$40. Cheapest is Oscar Mejías Hernández, ask in village.

Contents

At a glance

⌚ **Time required** 1-2 weeks each for Guyana and Suriname; Guyane 1 week, 2 if exploring beyond the coast.

☀ **Best time** Guyana: coolest months Aug-Oct; travel is good Aug-Apr. Suriname: year-end festival is Surifesta, mid-Dec to 1st week of Jan; Holi Phagwa (Hindu spring festival) in Mar. Guyane: Aug-Nov; Carnival Feb/Mar.

✘ **When not to go** Guyana: Georgetown is very crowded on Republic Day, 23 Feb; wettest months May-Jul, Dec and Jan. Suriname: Prices highest 15 Mar-15 May, Jul-Sep and during year-end Surifesta. Guyane: Wettest months May-Jul, but rains start Nov.

Guianas

★ Don't miss ...

Atlantic Ocean

VENEZUELA

Morawhanna
Mabaruma
Port Kaituma
Matthews Ridge
Towakaima
Shell Beach
Charity
Anna Regina
Adventure
Supenaam
Parika
Bartica
Rockstone
Kyk-over-al
Issano
GEORGETOWN
Wakenaam I
Leguan I
New Amsterdam
Rosignol
Linden
Corriverton/
Springlands
Ituni
Kwakwani
Nieuw Nickerie
Totness
Boskamp
Braamspunt
PARAMARIBO
Matapica
Galibi
Les Hattes
Awara
Mana
St-Laurent du Maroni
Albina
Moengo
Ndensavanne
Langa Tabiki
Stoelmanseiland
Cottica
Kourou
Iles du Salut
CAYENNE
Roura
Kaw
Regina
Cacao
St-Georges de l'Oyapock
R Oyapock

R Corentyne
R Berbice
R Demerara
R Essequibo
R Mazaruni
R Cuyuni
R Courono
R Maroni
R Mana
R Lawa
R Litani

Werushima Range
Kaieteur National Park
Imbaimadai
Mt Roraima
Pakaraima Mts
Orinduik
Kato
Kaieteur Falls
Mahdia
Mabura Hill
Kurupukari
Iwokrama
Rainforest
Programme
Iwokrama Canopy Walkway
Surama
Rock View
Annai
Karanambu
Apoteri
Yupukari
Maparri
Maco-Moco Falls
Lethem
Bonfim
Dadanawa
Aishalton
Rupununi Savanna
Kanuku Mountains
Dome Hill
Sipaliwini NR

GUYANA

BRAZIL

SURINAME

R Coppename
Washabo
Apoera
Blanche Marie Falls
Kabalebo
Lucie
Bakhuis Mountains
Raleigh Falls
Voltzberg NR
Raleighvallen
Tafelberg NR
Julianatop (1280m)
Frederik Willem de Vierdevallen
Eilerts de Haan NR
Central Suriname
Nature Reserve
Kasikasima
Pelelu Tepu
Drie Tabiki
Kumalu
Van Blomme-
steinmeer Lake
Afobaka
Brokopondo
Brownsberg NP
Brokopondo
Santigron
Nieuw
Nickerie

GUYANE

Mont St-Marcel
Maripasoula
Saül

N

50 km
50 miles

Guyana's coastal region is dominated by a mixture of Calypso music, Dutch drainage systems, Hindu temples, rice and Demerara sugar. Leaving the sea behind, travelling by river-boat or by plane, it is a land of rainforests, which gives way to wildlife-rich savannahs and isolated ranches. Waterfalls tumble over jasper rocks, or, at Kaieteur, into a chasm almost five times the height of Niagara. Suriname, too, has the intriguing combination of Dutch, Asian and African, which influences the culture, food and street life. And, like its neighbour, when you head inland, you enter a different world of bronze-tinted rivers, jungles and Amerindian villages.

Despite having geographical features shared by other South American countries, Suriname and Guyana are classed as Caribbean states. Guyane, on the other hand, is an overseas department of France. It has a famous penal colony – now closed – circled by sharks, a European space programme whose launches can be witnessed and jungle adventure in the undeveloped interior. All this within the context of a corner of South America where coffee and croissants are served and the prices are more than Parisian.

Guyana

Planning your trip

Where to go in Guyana

Despite being on the Atlantic, **Georgetown**, capital of Guyana, is known as the 'Garden City of the Caribbean'. This gives some idea of the country's orientation, in trade and cultural terms. The coast, where most of the population live, is a mix of coconut palms and calypso music, Dutch place names and techniques for draining the land, Hindu temples and Islamic mosques, all of which reflect the chequered history of the country. The thinly populated interior is different again, with life revolving around the rivers in the tropical forest, or, further south, the scattered ranches of the Rupununi Savannah. The improvement of the road from Georgetown to Lethem on the Brazilian border, with a minibus service, opens up the interior for easier exploration, but this area remains largely untouched, with many places reached by river boat or plane. Highlights include the Kaieteur Falls, among the highest in the world, the Orinduik Falls on the border with Brazil and the Iwokrama Rainforest Reserve, with the Iwokrama Canopy Walkway. Travelling on any of the rivers, many with excellent beaches, is the most interesting way to get around. On the coast there are no beaches for bathing, but in the far northwest is Shell Beach, a protected area for marine turtles and birdlife.

Best time to visit Guyana

Although hot, the climate is not unhealthy. Mean shade temperature throughout the year is 27°C; the mean maximum is about 31°C and the mean minimum 23°C. The heat is tempered by cooling breezes from the sea and is most appreciated in the warmest months, August to October. There are two wet seasons, from May to June, and from December to the end of January, although they may extend into the months either side. In the south and the Rupununi the wet season is May to July or August. Rainfall averages 2300 mm a year in Georgetown. Note that the Republic Day celebrations (23 February, float parade) last for one day, but there are other activities (Children's Costume Competition, etc) which take place during the preceding days. Also, in the two weeks prior to 23 February, many large companies hold Mashramani Camps at which public participation is encouraged. Hotels in Georgetown are very full, as they are also during international cricket. See also Festivals, below.

Transport in Guyana

Air Most flights to the interior leave from Ogle, some 15 minutes from Georgetown. For scheduled flights between Georgetown and Lethem see page 1609, and services to Kaieteur and Rupununi, see page 1608. Scheduled services to many parts of Guyana are offered by **Trans Guyana Airways** (TGA), Ogle, T222 2525, **Air Services Limited** (ASL), Ogle, T222 4357, and **Air Guyana – Wings**, Ogle, T222 6513. Scheduled flights to northwestern Guyana are operated by **Sky West Travel**, T225 4206, skywest@bbgy.com. Charter flights from Ogle are flown by **Roraima Airways**, RAL, Lot 8 Eping Avenue, Bel Air Park, Georgetown, T225 9648, www.roraimaairways.com, and **Air Services Ltd**, **ASL**, Ogle Aerodrome, T222 4357, asl@solutions2000.net. Domestic airlines are very strict on baggage allowance on internal flights: 20 lb pp.

Public road transport Minibuses and collective taxis, an H on their number plate, run between Georgetown and the entire coast from Charity to Corriverton; also to Linden. Minibuses run daily from Georgetown to Lethem. All taxis also have an H on the number plate and it is recommended only to use those painted yellow.

Driving in Guyana

Roads Most coastal towns are linked by a good 296-km road from Springlands in the east to Charity in the west; the Essequibo river is crossed by ferry, the Berbice by a toll bridge and the Demerara by a toll bridge, which, besides closing at high tide for ships to pass through (two to three hours) is subject to frequent closures (an alternative ferry operates only one trip daily: from Rosignol to New Amsterdam in the morning, return in the afternoon). Apart from a good road connecting Timehri and Linden, continuing as good dirt to Mabura Hill, and the new Georgetown-Lethem road, most other roads in the interior are very poor.

Safety Traffic drives on the left.

Documents No *carnet de passages* is required for driving a private vehicle.

Car hire Several companies in Georgetown (most are listed in the Yellow Pages of the phone directory).

Fuel Gasoline costs US$4.80 a gallon.

River There are over 960 km of navigable river, an important means of communication. Ferries and river boats are described here; also contact the Transport and Harbours Department, Water St, Georgetown. Six-seater river boats are called *ballahoos*, three- to four-seaters *corials*; they provide the transport in the forest. The ferry across the Corentyne to Suriname carries vehicles; it operates twice daily.

Maps Maps of country and Georgetown (US$6) from **Department of Lands and Surveys** ① *Homestreet Av, Durban Backland (take a taxi), T226 0524 in advance,* poor stock. Rivers and islands change frequently, so maps only give a general direction. A local guide can be more reliable. Free country and city maps are available from most tour operators and hotels. Georgetown and Guyana maps in **Explore Guyana**. *Guyana ITMB* map is recommended.

Where to stay in Guyana → *See Essentials for our hotel price guide.*
Almost all hotels in Georgetown have electricity generators, water pumps and overhead tanks to deal with any interruptions in supply. When booking an a/c room, ensure it also has natural ventilation.

Food and drink in Guyana → *See Essentials for our restaurant price guide*
Local food The blend of different influences – Indian, African, Chinese, Creole, English, Portuguese, Amerindian, North American – gives distinctive flavour to Guyanese cuisine. One well-known dish, traditional at Christmas, is pepper-pot: meat cooked in bitter cassava (casareep) juice with peppers and herbs. Some popular local dishes are cook-up-rice, curry (chicken, beef, mutton) with rice, dhal pouri or roti and metagee. All are available in Creole restaurants. Seafood is plentiful and varied, as are tropical fruits and vegetables. The staple food is rice. In the interior wild meat is often available, eg wild cow, or *labba* (a small rodent).

Drink Rum is the most popular drink. There is a wide variety of brands, all cheap, including the best which are very good and cost US$3.50 a bottle. Demerara Distillers Ltd produces two prize-winning brands, the 12-year-old **King of Diamonds** premium rum, and the 15-year-old **El Dorado** (voted the best rum in the world every year since 1999, US$45 in Georgetown, US$25 at airport duty free). Demerara Distillers, the makers of these rums, have a distillery tour and visit to their rum heritage, US$15. High wine is a strong local rum. There is also local brandy and whisky (**Diamond Club**), which are worth trying. **D'Aguiar's Cream Liqueur**, produced and bottled by Banks DIH Ltd, is excellent (and strong). The local beer, **Banks**, made partly from rice is good and cheap. There is a wide variety of fruit juices produced by Topco. Mauby, a local drink brewed from the bark of a tree, and natural cane juice are delightful thirst quenchers available from Creole restaurants and local vendors.

Essentials A-Z

Accident and emergency
Police T911; Fire T912; Ambulance T226 9449.

Electricity
110 volts in Georgetown; 220 volts elsewhere, including some Georgetown suburbs. Plugs as in US.

Embassies and consulates
For a full list of Guyanese overseas representatives and of foreign representation in Guyana, visit http://embassy.goabroad.com.

Festivals in Guyana
Public holidays 1 Jan, New Years' Day; 23 Feb, Republic Day and Mashramani festival; Good Fri, Easter Mon; Labour Day, 1 May; Arrival Day, 5 May; Independence Day, 26 May (instigated in 1996); Caricom Day, first Mon in Jul; Freedom Day, first Mon in Aug; Christmas Day, 25 Dec, and Boxing Day, 26 Dec. Hindu and Muslim festivals follow a lunar calendar, and dates should be checked as required: Phagwah, usually Mar; Eid ul-Adah, end of Ramadan; Eid el Azah; Youm un Nabi; Deepavali, usually Nov.

Around 21-28 Aug, Jam Zone Summer Break is held at the Guyana National Stadium and Splashmins Resort on the Linden Soesdyke Highway with concerts, pageants, fashion shows and sporting events.

Money → US$1 = G$200; €1 = G$272 (May 2014).
The unit is the Guyanese dollar. There are notes for 20, 100, 500 and 1000 dollars. Coins are for 1, 5 and 10 dollars. Official exchange rate is adjusted weekly in line with the rate offered by licensed exchange houses (*cambios*). There are ATMs in Georgetown. Also take cash dollars or euros. No *cambio* changes TCs. They only buy US or Canadian dollars, euros and pounds sterling. Most *cambios* accept drafts (subject to verification) and telegraphic transfers, but not credit cards. Rates vary slightly between *cambios* and from day to day and some *cambios* offer better rates for changing over US$100. Rates for changing TCs are good on the black market. Banks in Georgetown that accept TCs are Demerara Bank (South Rd and Camp St), **Guyana Bank of Trade and Industry** (GBTI, 47 Water St) and Republic

Bank (38-40 Water St). All charge commission. Republic Bank and *cambios* accept euros at best rates. Demerara Bank, Republic Bank and GBTI have opened branches at Diamond on the east bank of Demerara, open Mon-Fri (except Wed) 0800-1400, Sat 0800-1230. Note that to sell Guyanese dollars on leaving, you will need to produce your *cambio* receipt. The black market on America St ('Wall St') in Georgetown still operates, but rates offered are no better than the *cambio* rate. To avoid being robbed on the black market, or if you need to change money when *cambios* are closed, go by taxi and ask someone (preferably a friend) to negotiate for you. The black market also operates in Molson Creek/ Springlands, the entry point from Suriname, and where the bus stops for launches between Bonfim and Lethem at the Brazilian border.

Cost of travelling The devaluation means that, for foreigners, prices for food and drink are low at present. Even imported goods may be cheaper than elsewhere and locally produced goods such as fruit are very cheap. Hotels, tours and services in the interior are subject to energy and fuel surcharges, making them less cheap.

Opening hours
Banks: 0800-1400 Mon-Thu, Fri 0800-1430. **Markets**: 0800-1600, Mon-Sat, except Wed 0900-1200, Sun 0800-1000. **Shops**: 0830-1600, Mon-Thu, 0830-1700 Fri, 0830-1200 Sat.

Postal services
The main post office is on North Rd, Georgetown, opposite the National Museum. There is another on Regent St, opposite Bourda market. There are postal centres in Lethem and at Rock View, Annai.

Tax
Airport tax This is G$4000 (US$20, £12, €14), payable in Guyanese dollars or foreign currency equivalent at Cheddi Jagan International airport. For international departures from Ogle airport, tax is G$2500 (US$12.35, £8, €9.45). **VAT** 16%.

Telephone → Country code +592.
Ringing: a double ring, repeated regularly. Engaged: equal tones, separated by equal pauses.

Time
4 hrs behind GMT; 1 hr ahead of EST (but the same as EST during US daylight saving).

Tourist information
Ministry of Tourism, Industry and Commerce, 229 South Rd near Camp St, Georgetown, T226 2505, www.mintic.gov.gy, creates tourism policy. The Guyana Tourism Authority, National Exhibition Center, Sophia, Georgetown, T219 0094, www.guyana-tourism.com, promotes the development of the tourism industry. Tourism and Hospitality Association of Guyana (THAG), office and information desk at 157 Waterloo St, T225 0807, www.exploreguyana.com. Private organization covering all areas of tourism, with an 80-page, full-colour magazine called *Explore Guyana*, available from the Association at PO Box 101147, Georgetown, or phone above number. See also www.turq.com/guyana. For information and lots of useful links, visit www.guyana.org. The government agency's site is www.gina.gov. See also www.wwfguianas.org, of WWF Guianas Programme, 285 Irving St, Queenstown, Georgetown, T223 7802, the WWF conservation initiative covering the 3 Guianas. For birdwatching see www.guyanabirding.com and its associated newsletter, *Guyana Birding News*.

Visas and immigration
The following countries do not need a visa to visit Guyana: Australia, Canada, Japan, New Zealand, Norway, Switzerland, USA, EU countries (except Cyprus, Czech Republic, Estonia, Hungary, Latvia, Lithuania, Malta, Poland, Slovak Republic and Slovenia) and the Commonwealth countries. Visitors are advised to check with the nearest embassy, consulate or travel agent for changes to this list. All visitors require a passport with 6 months' validity and all nationalities, apart from those above, require visas. To obtain a visa, 3 photos, evidence of sufficient funds, a travel itinerary and, if coming from a country with yellow fever, a yellow fever certificate are required. If Guyana has no representation in your country, apply to the Guyana Embassy in Washington DC, or the Guyana Consulate General in New York. Tourist visas cost US$25 for a period of one month initially, then US$25 for each additional month. Employment and student visas cost US$140 for 3 years in the first instance and an additional US$140 for each 3-year renewal. Business visas cost US$140 for 5 years in the first instance and US$140 for each 5-year renewal. Visitors from those countries where they are required arriving without visas are refused entry, unless a tour operator has obtained permission for the visitor to get a visa on arrival. To fly in to Guyana, an exit ticket is required, at land borders an onward ticket is usually not asked for.

Weights and measures
Metric since 1982, but imperial is widely used.

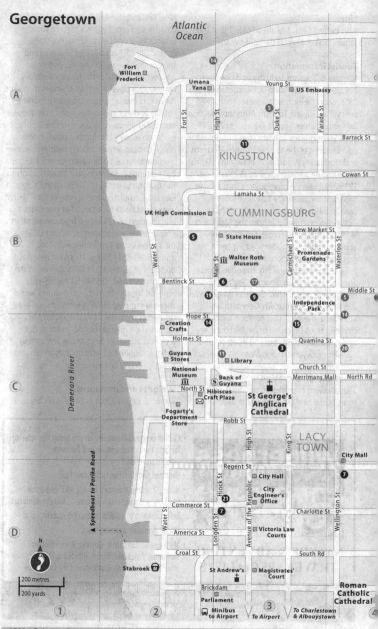

Georgetown

Atlantic Ocean

Fort William Frederick

Umana Yana

Young St

US Embassy

Fort St

High St

Duke St

Parade St

Barrack St

KINGSTON

Cowan St

Lamaha St

UK High Commission

CUMMINGSBURG

New Market St

State House

Carmichael St

Waterloo St

Water St

Main St

Walter Roth Museum

Promenade Gardens

Bentinck St

Middle St

Independence Park

Creation Crafts

Hope St

Quamina St

Holmes St

Guyana Stores

Church St

Library

North Rd

Demerara River

National Museum

Bank of Guyana

Merrimans Mall

North St

Hibiscus Craft Plaza

St George's Anglican Cathedral

Fogarty's Department Store

Robb St

LACY TOWN

City Mall

Regent St

Hinck St

City Hall

King St

Wellington St

Charlotte St

City Engineer's Office

Commerce St

Water St

Longden St

Avenue of the Republic

America St

Victoria Law Courts

Croal St

South Rd

N

200 metres
200 yards

Speedboat to Parika Road

Stabroek

St Andrew's

Magistrates' Court

Roman Catholic Cathedral

Brickdam

Parliament

Minibus to Airport

To Airport

To Charlestown & Albouystown

Where to stay 🏨

1 Ariantze *B4*
2 Atlantic Inn *A4*
3 Brandsville's Apartments *A4*
4 Cara Lodge &
   Bottle Bar & Restaurant *C4*
5 Cara Suites, Bistro 176 *B4*
6 Duke Lodge *A3*
7 El Dorado Inn *C4*
8 Grand Coastal Inn *B4*
9 Herdmanston Lodge *B4*
10 Hotel Glow *B2*
11 Hotel Tower &
   Flame restaurant *C3*
12 Melbourne Inn *B4*
13 Millenium Manor *D4*
14 New Tropicana *B4*
15 Ocean Spray International *A4*
16 Pegasus Guyana *A2*
17 Rima Guest House *B3*
18 Roraima Residence Inn *B4*
19 Sleepin Guesthouse *C4*
20 Waterchris *C4*
21 Windjammer International
   Cuisine & Comfort Inn *A4*

Restaurants 🍴

1 Brazil Churrascaria *D4*
2 Church's Chicken *B4*
3 Coalpot *C4*
4 Flava's Grill *B4*
5 German's *B2*
6 Golden Coast *B3*
7 Gravity Lounge
   & United Center Mall *D4*
8 Hacks Halaal *D3*
9 Hibiscus Restaurant
   and Lounge *B3*
10 Juice Power *B4*
11 Lily's *A3*
12 Maggie's Snackette *B4*
13 Mario's Pizza & Quizno's *B4*
14 New Thriving *B4*
15 Oasis Café *C3*
16 Popeye's *B4*
17 Shanta's *B4*
18 The Coffee Bean
   Café and Eatery *C4*
19 The New Palm Court *B2*
20 The Vintage Wine and Cheese
   Lounge *B4*
21 Upscale *D3*

Bars & clubs 🍸

22 704 Sports Bar *B4*
23 Club Ice *C4*

Georgetown → *Colour map 2, B3.*
Population: 200,000.

Guyana's capital, and chief town and port, is on the east bank of the mouth of the Demerara river. The climate is tropical, with a mean temperature of 27°C, but the trade winds provide welcome relief. The city is built on a grid plan, with wide tree-lined streets and drainage canals following the layout of the old sugar estates. Parts of the city are very attractive, with white-painted wooden 19th-century houses raised on stilts and a profusion of flowering trees. In the evening the sea wall is crowded with strollers and at Easter it is a mass of colourful kites.

Arriving in Georgetown

Orientation Cheddi Jagan International Airport is at Timehri, 40 km south of Georgetown, while Ogle International Airport is 8 km from the city. Taxis and minibuses run to Georgetown from both.

Minibuses run regularly to most parts of the city, mostly from Stabroek market or Avenue of the Republic. Collective taxis ply set routes at a fixed fare; they stop at any point on request. Taxis can be taken within and and outside the city limits. ▶▶ *See Transport, page 1607.*

Security This is a beautiful city, but check with your hotel, tour operator, the police or government authorities about unsafe areas. Don't walk the streets at night: always take a taxi, especially if going to Sheriff Street for the nightlife. At all times, avoid Albouystown (south of the centre) and the Tiger Bay area, just one block west of Main Street. Leave your valuables in your hotel. These problems are restricted to Georgetown and nearby villages; the interior remains as safe as ever.

Places in Georgetown

Although part of the old centre was destroyed by fire in 1945, there are some fine 19th-century buildings, particularly on or near High Street and the Avenue of the Republic. **St George's Anglican Cathedral**, which dates from 1889 is 44 m high and is said to be the world's tallest free-standing wooden building. It was designed by Sir Arthur Blomfield, who placed the supporting columns either side of the altar, leaving nothing but open space between ceiling and floor. Above the altar is a chandelier given by Queen Victoria. Other fine buildings on High St are the Gothic-style **City Hall** (1888), the City Engineer's Office, the Victoria Law Courts (1887) and the Magistrates' Court. The **Public Buildings**, on Brickdam, which house Parliament, are an impressive neo-classical structure built in 1839. Opposite is **St Andrew's Presbytery** (18th century). **State House** on Main St is the residence of the president. Much of the city centre is dominated by the imposing tower above **Stabroek market** (1881). At the head of Brickdam is an aluminium arch commemorating independence. Nearby is a monument to the 1763 slave rebellion, surmounted by an impressive statue of Cuffy, its best-known leader. Near the **Pegasus** hotel on Seawall Rd is the **Umana Yana**, a conical thatched structure built by a group of Wai Wai Amerindians using traditional techniques for the 1972 conference of the Non-Aligned Movement. The **National Museum** ① *opposite the post office, Mon-Fri 0900-1630, Sat 0900-1200, free*, has exhibits from Guyana and elsewhere, including a model of Georgetown before the fire and a good natural history section. The **Walter Roth Museum of Anthropology** ① *Main St, Mon-Fri 0800-1300, 1400-1640*, has artefacts from Guyana's nine Amerindian tribes and serves as a research centre for indigenous people.

The **Botanical Gardens** (20 minutes' walk from Anglican Cathedral, entry free), covering 50 ha, have Victorian bridges and pavilions, palms and lily ponds (undergoing continual improvements). The gardens are safe in daylight hours, but keep to the marked paths. Do not go to the gardens after dark. Near the southwest corner is the former residence of the president, Castellani House, which now houses the renovated **National Art Collection**, and there is also a large mausoleum containing the remains of the former president, Forbes Burnham, which is decorated with reliefs depicting scenes from his political career. Look out for the rare cannonball tree (*Couroupita Guianensis*), named after the appearance of its poisonous fruit. The Botanical Gardens offer great birdwatching. The city has 200 bird species from 39 families many of which can be seen in the gardens. Flycatchers, tanagers, hummingbirds and many migrating species such as peregrine falcons and warblers can be found around the capital, but the true stars are the blood-coloured woodpecker, which is endemic to the Guiana Shield, and festive parrot. Both are regularly spotted in the gardens. Tour operators offer birdwatching tours.

The **zoo** ① *0800-1800, US$1.50 for adults, half price for children; to use personal video US$11*, is being upgraded, together with the Botanical Gardens and National Park (2014). It carries the WWF logo and has educational programmes. It has a collection of local animals including manatees, which can be seen throughout the day. The zoo also boasts a breeding centre for endangered birds which are released into the wild. There are also beautiful tropical plants in the **Promenade Gardens** ① *Middle St, open 0830-1630*, and in the **National Park** on Carifesta Avenue, which has a good public running track. Near the southeast corner of the Botanic Gardens is the well-equipped Cliff Anderson Sports Hall. Nearby is the **National Cultural Centre**, an impressive air-conditioned theatre with a large stage. Performances are also given at the **Theatre Guild Playhouse** in Parade Street.

The **Georgetown Cricket Club** at Bourda was one of the finest cricket grounds in the tropics. For the ICC World Cup in 2007, a new stadium was built at **Providence** on the east bank of Demerara right next to **Ramada Georgetown Princess Hotel** (8 km from the city on the airport road, take bus 42 or a taxi). It has fine modern stands but not enough protection from sun and rain.

Outside Georgetown

The interior of Guyana is a land of great rivers, dramatic waterfalls, rainforests and savannahs. On the coast are turtle-nesting grounds and sea defences. You can stay at working ranches and secluded resorts. At all times, expect superb nature watching.

Southeast to Suriname

New Amsterdam (*Population: 25,000. 104 km southeast of Georgetown*) On the east bank of the Berbice River, near its mouth, is picturesque New Amsterdam. From Georgetown, take a minibus (44, or express No 50) or collective taxi to Rosignol on the west bank of the Berbice, US$6, then cross the river. A floating bridge goes from Cotton Tree to Palmyra Village (5 km from New Amsterdam); a toll is charged.

Corriverton (*Population: 31,000*) The road continues east from New Amsterdam (minibus No 50, US$3.50-4.25), to **Springlands** and **Skeldon** at the mouth of the Corentyne River. The towns are officially known as Corriverton (Corentyne River Town). Springlands is 2 km long, so you need to know where you want to get off the bus. There are the Republic Bank and Guyana National Commercial Bank. Suriname dollars can officially be changed into Guyanese dollars here. A ferry sails twice daily from Moleson, or Crabwood Creek, 13 km south of Springlands, to South Drain/Canawaima in Suriname, 40 km south of Nieuw-Nickerie (see Transport, below).

West from Georgetown

The road crosses the 2-km-long floating Demerara bridge (opens often for shipping, US$1 for cars, pedestrians free). Speedboats cross the Demerara from Stabroek market (US$1 every 30 minutes). The road continues 42 km, past rice paddies, *kokers* and through villages to **Parika**, a growing town on the east bank of the Essequibo River (minibus US$3). It has a Sunday market, 0600-1100, and three banks. Two ferries, the Kanawan and Sabanto, cross the river to **Supenaam** on the west bank at at high tide, mostly twice a day (schedules can be checked at the Transport and Harbours Department, T225 9355, or 225 9350); or speedboat US$8.50 (can be very wet). From Supenaam minibuses or taxis (US$7.50 per person) go to Charity through Adventure and Anna Regina. Nearby there is a resort at **Lake Mainstay**. You can visit a hot and cold lake, which varies in temperature, and the Wayaka Mainstay Amerindian Community, 13 km from Anna Regina. Mainstay is 2½ hours by road and ferry from Georgetown (depending on tides). The road goes on to **Charity**, a pleasant town with loud bars, various hotels and a lively market on Monday (quiet at other times).

Border with Venezuela Near the border with Venezuela are the small ports of **Morawhanna** (Morajuana to the Venezuelans) and **Mabaruma**. Mabaruma has replaced Morawhanna as capital of the region since it is less at risk from flooding. If arriving from Venezuela, make sure that the official who stamps your passport is not an imposter. You may only be given a five-day temporary visa, to be renewed on arrival in Georgetown.

Shell Beach Part of a protected area of Atlantic coastline, Shell Beach is some 145 km long, from the Pomeroon River to the Venezuelan border. It safeguards the nesting grounds of leatherback, green, hawksbill and olive Ridley turtles. Nesting activity begins in late March and continues, with hatching, until mid-August. Former turtle hunters have been retrained to patrol and identify nest sites, which are logged using global positioning satellite equipment. The project receives support from WWF. The coast consists of areas of mangrove swamps with beaches formed entirely of eroded shell particles. There are large flocks of scarlet ibis. Other birds include Amazon parrots, macaws, toucans, woodpeckers and crab hawks. Iguanas are usually seen in the mangroves, with sightings of rare river dolphin on the narrower stretches of river.

The camp consists of a thatched dining area and huts for the staff and igloo-type tents for guests, with fly-sheets and mosquito netting (vital in the rainy season, when there are 'blizzards' of mosquitos). Showers and toilets are basic. Food is very good. An Arawak family runs the camp and offers daily activities of fishing and birdwatching. They are excellent English-speaking guides. Turtle watching is available in season.

Fort Island and Bartica From Parika (see above) a vehicle ferry runs up the Essequibo River to Bartica on Tuesday, Thursday and Friday at 0550, returning the same day; Saturday at 0900, returning Sunday, US$2.50 one way. The 58-km journey takes six hours, stopping at **Fort Island**; boats come out from riverside settlements to load up with fruit. There are also flights from Ogle five days a week (see Transport, below). On Fort Island is a Dutch fort (built 1743, restored by Raleigh International in 1991) and the Dutch Court of Policy, built at the same time. There is also a small village; the rest of the island is dairy farms. River taxis run from Parika to Bartica all day, US$12.50 per person.

Bartica, at the junction of the Essequibo and Mazaruni rivers, is the 'take-off' town for the gold and diamond fields and the interior generally. Opposite Bartica, at the mouth of the Mazaruni, is Kaow Island, with a lumber mill. The *stelling* (wharf) and market in Bartica are very colourful. Bars flank the main street. Easter regatta, mostly power boats.

Southwest of Bartica The Essequibo is navigable to large boats for some miles upstream Bartica. The Cuyuni flows into the Mazaruni three miles above Bartica, and above this confluence the Mazaruni is impeded for 190 km by thousands of islands, rapids and waterfalls. To avoid this stretch of treacherous river a poor road runs from Bartica to Issano, where boats can be taken up the more tranquil upper Mazaruni. At the confluence of the Mazaruni and Cuyuni rivers are the ruins of the Dutch stronghold **Kyk-over-al**, once the seat of government for the Dutch county of Essequibo. Nearby are the **Marshall Falls** (30-60 minutes by boat from Bartica, US$250 per boat for a group of six to eight, US$200 per charter, return), which are beautiful, but too dangerous for swimming. You can swim in the nearby bay, part of the Rainbow River Marshall Falls property (day trippers may have to pay an entrance fee).

Kaieteur National Park ⓘ *Permission to enter park must be obtained from the National Parks Commission, Georgetown, T225 9142 (arranged by tour operators).* The **Kaieteur Falls**, on the Potaro River, nearly five times the height of Niagara, with a drop of 228 m, are almost 100 m wide. Ranking with the Niagara, Victoria and Iguazú Falls in majesty and beauty, they have the added attraction of being surrounded by unspoilt forest. Lying within a national park, there is also plenty of wildlife: tapirs, ocelots, monkeys, armadillos, anteaters and birds. At the falls themselves, one can see the magnificent silver fox, the Guianan cock-of-the-rock and the white-collared swift, also known as Makonaima bird, which lives behind the falls. At dusk the swifts swoop in and out of the gorge before passing through the deluge to roost behind the water. The golden rocket frog lives in the giant tank bromeliad and are endemic to this area. In the dry months, April and October, the flow of the falls is reduced; in January and June/July the flow is fullest. In the height of the wet season (June), the overland route is difficult and not recommended.

The **Pakaraima Mountains** stretch from Kaieteur westwards to include the highest peak in Guyana, **Mount Roraima**, once believed to be the inspiration for Conan Doyle's *Lost World*. Roraima is very difficult to climb from the Guyanese side, but **Wilderness Explorers** offer trips via Brazil and Venezuela.

Orinduik Falls Orinduik Falls are on the Ireng River, which forms the border with Brazil; the river pours over steps and terraces of jasper, with a backdrop of the Pakaraima Mountains. There is good swimming at the falls which are a 25-minute flight from Kaieteur.

South from Georgetown: to Brazil

Linden (*Population: 60,000. 112 km south of Georgetown*) The second-largest town in Guyana is a bauxite mining town on the banks of the Demerara River. The two towns are linked by a good road (slow for the first part to Timehri); police checks are to stop drug and gun running. Linden's opencast mine is 60-90 m deep and is said to have the world's longest boom walking dragline. The town is dominated by a disused alumina plant and scarred by old bauxite pits. In town is the lovely colonial guesthouse on the Demerara River, run by the mining company.

From Linden rough roads suitable for four-wheel drive vehicles run south to the bauxite mining towns of **Ituni** and **Kwakwani**. The road south to the logging centre at Mabura Hill is in excellent condition; from here a good road runs west to Mahdia, with a pontoon crossing of the Essequibo, and another road continues south from Mabura Hill to Kurupukari on the route to Lethem. A good road goes west from Linden to Rockstone ferry on Essequibo River. From Rockstone roads run north to Bartica and southwest to Issano.

Rupununi Savannah This is an extensive area of dry grassland in the far southwest of Guyana, with scattered trees, termite mounds and wooded hills. The rivers, creeks and ponds, lined with Ite palms and other trees, are good for seeing wildlife. Among a wide variety of birds, look out for macaws, toucan, parrots, parakeets, osprey, hawks and jabiru storks (take binoculars). Many of the animals are nocturnal and seldom seen. The region is scattered with Amerindian villages and a few large cattle ranches which date from the late 19th century: the descendants of some of the Scots settlers still live here. Links with Brazil are much closer than with the Guyanese coast; many people speak Portuguese and most trade is with Brazil. See http://rupununi.org.

In the wet season (May to July/August), much of the Savannah may flood and malaria mosquitoes and *kabura*/sandflies are widespread. The best time to visit is October to April. River bathing is good, but beware of dangerous stingrays and black caiman. Note that a permit from the Home Affairs Ministry is usually required to visit Rupununi, unless you go with a tour operator. Check in advance if your passport is sufficient. A separate permit to visit Amerindian villages is needed from the Minister of Amerindian Affairs, the President's office in Georgetown.

Lethem A small but scattered town on the Brazilian border (see below), this is the service centre for the Rupununi and for trade with Brazil. There are many small stores, a small hospital (T772 2006), a police station (T772 2011) and government offices. A big event at Easter is the rodeo, visited by cowboys from all over the Rupununi. Prices are about twice as high as in Georgetown. About 2.5 km south of town at St Ignatius there is a Jesuit mission dating from 1911 and a peanut processing plant which produces the purest form of peanut butter. In the nearby mountains there is good birdwatching and there are waterfalls to visit.

Border with Brazil The Takutu River separates Lethem from Bonfim in Brazil. The crossing is about 1.6 km north of Lethem and 2.5 km from Bonfim. A new bridge across the river has been built. Formalities are tight on both sides of the border and it is important to observe them as people not having the correct papers and stamps will have problems further into either country. Visas for Brazil have to be obtained in Georgetown at the Brazillian Embassy. You must have a yellow fever certificate. All procedures for exit and entry are carried out at the Guyanese immigration office at the border. Immigration is supposedly open 24 hours, but officers usually go home at 1800. If arriving from Brazil, buy some Guyanese dollars in Boa Vista, or use the black market at the river, although some hotels in Lethem change money as well as sell bus and plane tickets.

Annai This remote Amerindian village is located in the northern savannahs, south of the Iwokrama Rainforest Programme. It is possible to trek over the plains to the Rupununi River, or through dense jungle to the mountains. About one or two hours on foot are the villages of Kwatamang and Wowetta where Raleigh International built a health and community Centre in 1995. Some 25 km north of Annai is the Amerindian village of **Surama** which organizes its own ecotourism activities through the village council and can accommodate guests in the new **Ecotourism Lodge**, info@suramaecolodge.com, 3 km from the river bank near a manakin lek. A harpy eagle nest nearby has proven very reliable over the last four years, with good sightings. Comfortable chalets (**$**), guided walks and river tours. The forest is beautiful, with many animals especially at dawn on the dirt road between Surama and the Lethem-Georgetown road. Birdwatching (US$5 per person per day), night trekking (US$5) and boating (US$40-62 per boat) are arranged; every visitor pays a village fee of US$7.50. Bookings are made via **Wilderness Explorers** (www.wilderness-explorers.com) in Georgetown, who have formed a partnership with Surama community to develop tourism; through **The Rock View Lodge** (see Where to stay, below), or through Iwokrama. Transport to Surama can be arranged from Rock View, who can also organize transport from the Lethem-Guyana road. An airstrip opened in 2012.

Iwokrama Rainforest Programme ⓘ *For information and prices, which change frequently, contact the administrator, Iwokrama International Centre for Rainforest Conservation and Development, 77 High St, Kingston, Georgetown, PO Box 10630, T225 1504, www.iwokrama.org.* This is a 360,000-ha project, set up by Guyana and the Commonwealth to conserve habitats such as primarily tropical forest. As well as conservation, the Programme will involve studies on the sustainable use of the rainforest and ecotourism. It is hoped that the results will provide a database for application worldwide. The Field Station is at Kurukupari, near the Arawak village of Fairview (which has an airstrip), on the northern boundary of the reserve. You can meet research teams, take boat trips and stay at satellite camps deep in the forest (Clearwater on the Burro-burro, Kabocalli and Turtle Mountain on the Essequibo). Fishing is good, especially for peacock bass. Well-trained rangers, who speak their native language and English, escort visitors through the forest on many trails. One goes to Turtle Mountain (45 minutes by boat, then 1½ hours' walk), go early for great views of the forest canopy. Another trek is to the top of Mount Iwokrama, a difficult 20-km round trip; for the less fit there is a 10-km trail to the foot of the mountain to a pleasant stream and Amerindian petroglyphs. There are set rates for boat and Land Rover use and for field assistants to accompany you.

There is a 33-m-high **Iwokrama Canopy Walkway**, managed by **Wilderness Explorers**, Surama, Rock View Lodge and Iwokrama International Centre, under the name of Community And Tourism Services (CATS); for information contact **Wilderness Explorers** ⓘ *US$ 25 pp for a day visit including entry to the walkway and qualified guide with good birding knowledge, www. iwokramacanopywalkway.com (see Georgetown, Tour operators).* The walkway allows visitors to walk among the treetops and see the birds and monkeys of the upper canopy. Night excursions are available on the walkway. There is a library with birding books and a small arts and crafts shop. See Where to stay, page 1602, **Atta Rainforest Lodge**.

⊙ Guyana listings

For hotel and restaurant price codes, and other relevant information, see Essentials.

● Where to stay

Georgetown *p1593, map p1592*
It's best to book in advance. There isn't much choice in the lower price categories and many small hotels and guesthouses are full of long-stay residents, while some are rented by the hour. If in doubt, go to a larger hotel for first night and look around next day in daylight. There are several business hotels, hotels near the north shore (eg **$$$$-$$$ Ocean Spray International**, 46 Stanley Pl, Kitty, T227 3763/5, www.oceanspray.co.gy; **$$$ Atlantic Inn**, 56 Chirch Rd and First Ave, Soubryanville, T225 5826, www.atlaticinngy.com, and apartments

(eg **$$$$ Eddie Grant's Blue Wave**, 8-9 North Rd, Bourda, T227-8897, www.bluewave-gy.com; **$$$-$$ Brandsville's Apartments**, 88-90 Pike St, Campbellville, T227 0989, bransville@gol.net.gy).
$$$$ Pegasus Guyana, Seawall Rd, PO Box 101147, T225 2856, www.pegasushotelguyana. com. Very safe, a/c, comfortable, fridge, lovely swimming pool, gym, tennis, business centre, massage and yoga, restaurants (eg **Aromas**). 24-hr back-up electricity.
$$$$ Ramada Georgetown Princess, Providence, East Bank Demerara, next to Cricket World Cup stadium, 15-20 mins' drive out of the city, T265 7001, www.ramada.com (rebranding 2014). 250 rooms all with a/c, huge pool with 2 pool-side bars, restaurants, including **Providence** for international and local food, **Club Next** and casino.

$$$$-$$$ Cara Suites, 176 Middle St, T226 1612/5, www.carahotels.com. Luxurious, secure, self-contained rooms with kitchen, grocery, shoeshine, laundry, internet access, airport pick-up.

$$$$-$$$ Duke Lodge, Duke St, Kingston, T231 7220, www.rorairamaairways.com. Opposite US Embassy, beautiful antique-style guesthouse 5 mins from central Georgetown, with breakfast, Wi-Fi, swimming pool, fine restaurant.

$$$$-$$$ Roraima Residence Inn, R8 Eping Av, Bel Air Park, T225 9648, www.roraimaairways.com. A small hotel with good standards, a/c and pool.

$$$ Cara Lodge, 294 Quamina St, T225 5301, www.carahotels.com. A Heritage House hotel, 150-year-old converted mansion, 36 rooms, broadband (DSL) Internet in rooms, good service, superb, restaurant, bar, taxi service, laundry, business centre with internet, conference room.

$$$ El Dorado Inn, 295 Quamina and Thomas Sts, T225 3966, www.eldorado-inn.com. Good hotel with nicely appointed rooms in central location. Also has **$$$$** suites.

$$$ Millenium Manor, 43 Hadfield St, T223 0541, http://milleniummanor.com. 3 standards of room with all facilities, modern, comfortable, helpful staff.

$$$ Tropical View International, 33 Delph St, Campbellville, T227 2216/7, http://tropicalview internationalhotel.shutterfly.com. Smart, modern hotel in a residential area, rooms with windows, all mod cons, Wi-Fi, breakfast included.

$$$-$$ Ariantze, 176 Middle St, T227 0152, www.ariantzesidewalk.com. Fans, or a/c in deluxe rooms. Includes small breakfast, see Restaurants, below. Very good but can be noisy from music and nightclub next door.

$$$-$$ Grand Coastal Inn, 2 Area M Le Ressouvenir, 5 km out of city, T220 1091, www.grandcoastal.com. 3 standards of room, with breakfast and drinking water, dining room, laundry, business centre with internet, car rental, tours, good.

$$$-$$ Hotel Tower, 74-75 Main St, T227 2015, hoteltower@solutions2000.net. A/c, old-fashioned and overpriced, lively bar, **Main Street Café** and **Flame** restaurant, swimming pool (membership for non-residents), gym, Muneshwer's travel agency.

$$$-$$ Windjammer International Cuisine and Comfort Inn, 27 Queen St, Kitty, T227 7478, www.windjammergy.com. 30 very comfy, rooms, a/c, hot water, 2 bridal suites.

$$ City Holiday Inn, 314 Sheriff St, Campbellville, T225 4425. Various rooms, bath, fan, mosquito net, no restaurant but several nearby, breakfast available, laundry, 15-20 mins from centre. Recommended.

$$ Herdmanston Lodge, 65 Peter Rose and Anira Sts, Queenstown, T225 0808, www.herd manston lodge.com. In a lovely old house, pleasant district, with breakfast, restaurant, Wi-Fi throughout, very comfortable.

$$ Waterchris, 184 Waterloo St, T227 1980, waterchris@mail.com. A/c (suppose d), TV, hot water, phone (**$** with fan), simple and run-down wooden rooms, some with shared bath next to a noisy TV lounge, poor plumbing.

$$-$ Hotel Glow, 23 Queen St, Kitty, T227 0863. Clean, a/c or fan, some with TV, 24-hr restaurant, breakfast extra, taxi or minibus to centre.

$$-$ Melbourne Inn, 29 Sherrif St, Campbellville, T226 7050, www.melbourne inn.com. On this famous street, rooms with and without a/c, some with kitchen, all with bath, car hire.

$$-$ Sleepin Guesthouse, 151 Church St, Alberttown, T223 0991, www.sleepinguest house.com. A/c, cheaper with fan, some rooms with kitchenette, Wi-Fi, meals served, also has car hire. Also **Sleepin International**, 24 Brickdam, Stabroek, T 223-0991, www.sleep ininternationalhotel.com. Slightly better.

$ New Tropicana, 177 Waterloo St, T227 5701, www.newtropicanahotel.com. With fan, aimed at backpackers, Wi-Fi, café downstairs, central, can accommodate groups, Spanish and Portuguese spoken.

$ Rima Guest House, 92 Middle St, T225 7401, rima@networksgy.com. Good central area, well-run, modern, popular with backpackers, no a/c, hot, communal bath and toilets, good value, internet, safe, mosquito nets, restaurant (breakfast US$6, lunch/dinner US$8). Mrs Nellie Singh is very helpful. Highly recommended, book ahead.

Resorts near Georgetown

$$$ pp Timberhead, operated by **Tropical Adventures Ltd**, 10 Providence, East Bank Demerara, T223-5108, geb@solutions 2000.

net. In the Santa Amerindian Reserve (founded 1858), situated on a sandy hill overlooking Savannah and the Pokerero Creek, 3 beautiful native lodges with bath and kitchen facilities, well run, good food, lovely trip up the Kamuni River to get there, much wildlife to be seen, 212 species of bird have been recorded, activities include swimming, fishing, jungle trails, visit to Santa Mission Arawak village, volleyball, US$79 pp for a day trip (minimum 2 people), US$153 pp per night (including transport, meals, bar, guide, accommodation). Recommended.

Arrowpoint Nature Resort, contact at R8 Eping Av, Bel Air Park, Georgetown, T225 9648. In the heart of the Santa Mission Amerindian reservation, offers a "back to nature experience", excellent birdwatching, with numerous other activities such as mountain biking, canoeing.

Pandama Restreat and Winery, Plot 9 Madewini, Soesdyke/Linden Highway (just before Splashmin's Fun Park), T654 1865/627 7063, www.pandamanaretreat.com. Tucked away in sand forest along the Madewini Creek, good for relaxation, offers a wide range of programmes with a spiritual, educational and artistic focus, aimed at small groups. Produces quality wines from local fruit.

New Amsterdam *p1595*

$$ Church View Guest House, 3 Main and King Sts, T333 2880. Breakfast US$3-4.50, room rate includes 1 hr in gym, a/c, cheaper without, phone, TV, clean. Recommended.

$$ Little Rock Hotel, 65 Vrymans Erven, T333 3758. **$** without a/c, hot water, a/c, TV, phone, fridge, breakfast US$3-5, lunch/ dinner US$4-5. Also **$$$-$$ Little Rock Suites**, 10 Main and Church Sts, T333 2727, irtvs@guyana.net.gy.

$$ Parkway, 4 Main St, T333 6438. Clean, a/c, safe, with bath, breakfast US$2.55-4, lunch/ dinner US$4-5. Recommended.

$ Astor, 7 Strand. All rooms self-contained, breakfast US$2.45, charming owner.

Berbice resorts

$$$$ Cortours, Springlands, Berbice, T339 2430, cortoursinc@yahoo.com. Offers package tours to Orealla village, Cow Falls and Wanatoba Falls for overnight visits and Peacock bass fishing.

$$ pp Dubalay Ranch, a working ranch on the Berbice River, 147 km from the river mouth,

has forest, savannah and swamp habitats, with some 300 bird species, deer, large cats, water buffalo and Dutch colonial remains. Activities include boat trips (US$25 with guide), riding (US$15 for first hr, then US$10 per hr), birdwatching (US$15), jeep tours (US$30), night time wildlife trips (US$50), custom-made packages, or just relaxing. Cheaper rates for scientists or students, includes 3 meals and soft drinks/juices, but not transport to the ranch (US$230 return from/to Georgetown) or activities. Small parties preferred; advance booking essential. Contact **Wilderness Explorers**, see Tour operators, Georgetown.

Corriverton *p1595*

$$ Mahogany, in Skeldon. With bath, TV, fridge, hot water, clean, lunch/dinner US$2.60-3.25. Recommended.

$$ Par Park, in Skeldon. With bath and a/c, hot water, TV, no meals available.

$ pp Swiss Guest House, Springlands, T339 2329. Pakistani run, with bath and fan, no meals, helpful, simple accommodation.

Others include **$$ Riverton Suites**, Lot 78 Springlands, T335 3039, and **$ Paraton Inn**, K & L 78, Corriverton, T335 3025.

West from Georgetown: Lake Mainstay *p1595*

$$$ Lake Mainstay Resort, T226 2975. 40 cabins with a/c, cheaper without lake view, also single rooms, beachfront on the lake, restaurant, bars, swimming, boating, other sports, birdwatching and nature trails, entertainment. Breakfast US$7, lunch US$10.45 and dinner US$12.75. Day trips US$87 pp (8-10 passengers). This fee includes road and boat transport, snacks, activities and entry fees. With own transport entrance fee is US$2.90 without meals and drinks.

Adel's Eco Resort, Akawini Creek, Pomeroon River, T771 5391/617 0398/629 4198, www. adelresort.com. In a pristine location 3 hrs from Georgetown, ideal for relaxation and tours of the Pomeroon river and Akawini Creek, fishing, etc. All-inclusive accommodation.

In Charity are **Hotel Purple Heart**, Restaurant and Bar, T225 2535, hotelpurple@yahoo.com, and **Xenon**, 190 Charity, T771 4989/629 6231.

Border with Venezuela: Mabaruma p1595

There is a **Government Guest House**, 2 rooms with bath or shared bath, clean, book in advance.
$ Kumaka Tourist Resort, Maburama, contact **Somwaru Travel Agency**, Georgetown, T225 9276. Meals, bath, run down; offers trips to Hosororo Falls, Babarima Amerindian settlement, rainforest, early examples of Amerindian art.

Bartica p1596

$$$-$ Platinum Inn International, Lot 7, First Av, T455 3041, www.platinumparadise. bravehost.com. Range of rooms from suite with a/c, cable TV and fridge, to fan and TV, weekend packages available, internet, tours arranged, restaurant and bar.
$$ Marin Hotel, 19 Second Av, T455 2243.
$$$ with a/c, with bath, TV, phone, fridge, meals available (breakfast US$5, lunch and dinner US$12).
$$-$ The New Modern Hotel & Nightclub, 9 First Av, T455 2301, near ferry. 2 standards of room, with bath and fan. Recommended. Good food, best to book ahead.

Resorts near Bartica

$$$$-$$$ Baganara Island Resort, beautiful house on Baganara Island in Essequibo River a few miles south of Bartica, www.baganara.net. Price depends on season and standard of room, full board, private beach, watersports, airstrip; day trips US$85 pp (minimum 12), includes road and boat transport, snacks, lunch, local soft drinks, VAT, activities and guide. Transport to resort US$30 pp return.
$$$$-$$$ Hurakabra River Resort, on the West Bank of the Essequibo, about 2 hrs from Georgetown, booking office 168 Century Palm Gardens, Durban Backlands, Lodge T225 3557/226 0240, www.hurakabragy.com. This nature resort has a choice of 3 lodgings, the grand Mango Tree Villa, which can sleep up to 8, Bucksands Lodge, 3 mins away by boat, sleeps up to 10, or Bamboo Cottage, for 2-4 people, all are on the waterfront with tropical forest behind, bamboo groves, mango trees and abundant birdlife.
$$ pp WilAmo Family House, 6.5 km from Bartica, wilf@networksgy.com. A family house on the western bank of the Essequibo River. Maid service and cook available but bring own food.

Kaieteur National Park p1596

$ The rest house at the top of the Falls is open for guests, but is basic; enquire and pay first at the National Parks Commission, Georgetown, T225 9142 (if planning to stay overnight, you must be self-sufficient, whether the guesthouse is open or not; take your own food and a hammock, it can be cold and damp at night; the warden is not allowed to collect money).

Linden p1596

$$ Barrow's Dageraad Inn, 82 Manni St, Mackenzie, T444 6799, dunbarr@ networksgy. com. Breakfast, US$3.50, all double/twin, hot water, a/c, TV, fridge.
$$ Watooka Guesthouse, 130 Riverside Drive, Watooka, T444 2162/6194/2634, watookacomplex@yahoo.com. In a historic building, old British charm with a tropical flavour, comfortable a/c rooms on ground and 1st floors, swimming pool, restaurant and bar.
$$-$ Hotel Star Bonnett, 671 Industrial Area, 1.5 km out of town on Georgetown Rd, T444 6505. Various standards of room, all with a/c and TV, clean, breakfast US$4, good lunches (US$4-5).
$ Summit Hotel, 6 Industrial Area, McKenzie, T444 6500. Cheaper shared rooms available, breakfast extra.

Rupununi Savannah p1597

For the first 2 ranches and Maipaima Eco-Lodge below, contact **Wilderness Explorers**. All transport is arranged.
$$$$ pp Dadanawa Ranch, Duane and Sandy de Freitas, 96 km south of Lethem, one of the world's largest ranches, each bedroom has a verandah (being upgraded). Their tour operator, **Rupununi Trails**, T+44-796-152 1951, www. rupununitrails.com, can organize trekking, birding, horse riding and fishing trips, rainforest adventures and camping with *vaqueros*. Tours also to the **Upper Rewa River**, minimum 14 days in conjunction with **Wilderness Explorers**: one of the most spectacular wildlife destinations in South America. Very remote and expensive but a high chance of seeing big cats, other large mammals and Harpy Eagle.
$$$$ pp Karanambu Ranch, http://karanam bu.com. Dianne McTurk, 96 km northeast of Lethem, on the Rupununi River, unique old home, 5 cottages with bath (1 suitable for a

family), mosquito net, toiletries, good meals, Wi-Fi, fishing, excellent birdwatching and boat rides with guides, including to see Victoria Amazonica flowers which open at dusk. 24 km from Yupukari Amerindian village, trips possible. For many years Dianne McTurk reared and rehabilitated orphaned giant river otters, but has not had to do so for a while. She hopes that her education programme has stopped the killing of otters.

Caiman House Field Station, at Yupukari village, www.rupununilearners.org. A centre for black caiman research and projects with the community, such as public library, furniture making. There is a guest house, rooms with bath, and rooms in the field station, Wi-Fi. Guests can help with research, walk local trails, and go birdwatching.

Rewa Eco-Lodge, Rewa Village, North Rupununi, contact through **Wilderness Explorers**. This lodge is on the Rewa River, 2-3 hrs by boat from Kwatamang Landing, which is 5 km from Annai. 4 bedrooms in 2 benabs with shared bath and toilets; 3 cabins with ensuite facilities; one benab with dining room; hammocks, solar lighting. Packages include sport fishing in Bat Creek, Harpy eagle or wild cats viewing, Arapaima spotting; also excellent birdwatching. 2- and 3-night packages available.

Lethem *p1597*

$$$ Maipaima Eco-Lodge, 56 km from Lethem in Nappi village, Kanuku Mountains, T772 2085, www.fosterparrots.com/etguyana. html. Community-run lodge with plenty of wildlife-viewing opportunities, hikes in rainforest and to waterfalls. One of the best activities is the hike to Jordon Falls, 4-6 hrs through pristine forest to a waterfall that has had fewer than 100 visitors. Two cabins (with more being built) and a large *benab* (dining hall), each cabin sleeps 4, buildings are elevated and connected by walkways. Hammock accommodation **$**.

$$$ Manari Ranch, 20 mins' drive north of Lethem on Manari Creek, contact through **Wilderness Explorers**. Great atmosphere, comfortable rooms and good food, savannah treks, drifts down river and out into the Ireng River, bird and wildlife watching provided.

$$$ Ori Hotel and Restaurant, T772 2124, orihotel@yahoo.com, or contact through **Wilderness Explorers**. Self-contained cabins and rooms with Wi-Fi, fridge, bar, breakfast US$8, lunch or dinner US$12, excellent view of mountains from upper balcony, changes reais to Guyana dollars.

$ Cacique Guest House, T772 2083. With bath, fan, clean, breakfast extra, lunch/dinner US$8.50-10.50.

$ Savannah Inn, T772 2035 (Georgetown T227 4938), savannahinn@futurenetgy.com, or book through **Wilderness Explorers**. Including breakfast, a/c cabins with bath (cheaper with fan), phone, fridge, clean, bar, breakfast US$8, lunch or dinner US$12, changes reais into Guyanese dollars, tours arranged, will take you to airport.

$ Takutu, T772 2034. Simple a/c and fan-cooled rooms, also hammock space, fridge, clean, breakfast extra. Lunch/dinner US$8.50-10.50.

Annai *p1597*

$$$ The Rock View Lodge, Annai, T226 5412, www.rockviewlodge.com, to book, or through **Wilderness Explorers**. Colin Edwards and family, guesthouse with 8 self-contained rooms, hot water, fans, bars, Wi-Fi, natural rock swimming pool; in the Pakaraima foothills, where the savannah meets the Iwokrama Rainforest Programme (see below). Pony treks, nature tours for painting, photography and fishing, regional Amerindian and other local cooking, full board. Recommended.

$ The Oasis, Rock View's second facility on the Lethem-Georgetown road. With a bar, churrascaria restaurant, shop, accommodation in comfortable a/c rooms or hammock space. Onward air tickets and buses can be booked from here and tours from Rock View or for Surama/Iwokrama. Interesting nature trail in front of the Oasis up a forest-covered hill – sweeping views of the savannah – channel billed toucans very common.

Iwokrama *p1598*

$$$ pp Atta Rainforest Lodge. For visits to the Iwokrama Canopy Walkway, 8 rooms with bath, with a bar, dining area and Wi-Fi. Mosquito nets provided. Restaurant serves breakfast, lunch and dinner. The overnight trip rate includes entry to the Iwokrama Canopy Walkway, trained guide, 3 meals. Visitors can experience the dawn chorus and be on the walkway at dusk and into the night. Have new and extended trails. Birds include crimson fruitcrow, white-winged potoo and a family of black curassow that regularly feed in the lodge's gardens.

At **Iwokrama Field Station**, the River Lodge is one of the most comfortable in South America in a beautiful setting on the banks of the Essequibo, next to pristine forest, full of giant moura trees and kapoks. It has 2 types of accommodation, in free standing cabins or in a terrace of rooms. Tourists pay a fee for the bed and a user fee. The cabins are comfortable, with bath and veranda. Meals served in huge dining research area with a library and bar which offers alcoholic beverages at extra cost; breakfast US$8, lunch US$12, dinner US$15. Wi-Fi available. Reservations for all Iwokrama lodges and information from **Wilderness Explorers**, see Georgetown, Tour operators, or from **Rock View** (see above).

Camps

Maparri Wilderness Camp. Contact Wilderness Explorers for rates and bookings. It is on the Maparri River, in the Kanuku Mountains, recognized by Conservation International as one of the few remaining pristine Amazonian areas, rich in flora and fauna. It is easy to watch macaws, herons, toucans, kingfisher, maybe harpy eagles. With luck, you can see tayra, labba, ocelot, agouti, monkeys, tapir, even jaguar. Various treks are arranged. It can only be reached by air and river. **Maparri Camp** is built of wood, with open sides, and has hammocks with mosquito nets. The site overlooks a waterfall; the river water is crystal clear (unlike most rivers in Guyana) and the fall and surrounding pools are safe for swimming. The camp is merely a framework. Simple, nutritional meals, and fish from the river, are prepared over an open fire.

❼ Restaurants

Georgetown *p1593, map p1592*
A 10% service may be added to the bill. Many restaurants are closed on public holidays.

Restaurants are categorized according to their most expensive dishes. All have much cheaper options on menus.

$$$ Bistro 176, at Cara Suites, see above. Restaurant and bar offering local and international cuisine.

$$$ Bottle Bar and Restaurant at Cara Lodge. Very good, pleasant surroundings, must book, also open for breakfast.

$$$ Café Tepuy, R 8 Eping Av, Bel Air Park, T225 9648. Serves both international and local cuisine.

$$$ Flame, 74-75 Main St in **Hotel Tower**, T227 2011. Good but pricey local and international cuisine.

$$$ Flava's Grill, 300 Thomas St, South Cummingsburg, T227 7509. For local cuisine.

$$$ Gravity Lounge, United Center Mall, Camp and Regent Sts, T226 8858. Top-end restaurant and VIP lounge on the 6th floor, panoramic views.

$$$ Golden Coast, Main and Middle Sts. Chinese, good food, huge portions, classy.

$$$ The New Palm Court, 35 Main St. Bar and restaurant with international and vegetarian food as well as drinks.

$$$ Play Land, American Italiano Family Restaurant, Lot 70, Park St, Enterprise, East Coast Demerara, T229 7100, info@playland italiano.com. Out of town, but a good place to enjoy Italian food in a Guyanese setting.

$$$-$$ Lily's, 87C Barrack St, T231 9804, lilysfastfoodcafe@gmail.com. A whole range of different dishes, from breakfast to traditional, Cajun/Creole, Caribbean, Asian, burgers and sandwiches.

$$$-$$ Xie Xie, 159A West Barr and Alexander Sts. High-quality food with a great atmosphere.

$$$-$ Coalpot, Carmichael St, opposite Bishop's High School in New Town. Good lunches starting at US$1.80, up to US$13.15 (no shorts allowed, cheaper cafetería).

$$$-$ New Thriving, Main St, the building before Customs House, T225 0038. A/c, buffet restaurant with large, oily portions.

$$$-$ Poolside, at Pegasus hotel. BBQ, pizza, live bands.

$$ Brazil Churrascaria, 208 Alexander St, Lacytown. All you can eat for US$15. Great.

$$ Church's Chicken, Camp and Middle Sts. For chicken and fries.

$$ The Coffee Bean Café and Eatery, 133 Church St, South Cummingsburg, T223 2222. For coffees, teas, juices, pastries, breakfasts and lunches of wraps, sandwiches and pastas.

$$ Hibiscus Restaurant and Lounge, 91 Middle St, T231 3624, dburgess@network sgy.com. Typical sports bar, varied Western menu, outdoor area, popular hang out bar.

$$ JR Burgers, 3 Sandy Babb St, Kitty, T226 6614. Popular. Also in the City Mall. In the same building is Altitude Lounge and Bar, same phone, a cocktail bar serving local food. Also a drive-thru section next door.

$$ Kamboat, 51 Sheriff St, Campbellville, T225 8323 (delivery T225 8090). Recommended for Chinese.

$$ Mario's Pizza, Camp and Middle Sts, T231 2639. Oppsite Church's Chicken. Variety of pizza.

$$ Popeye's, 1e Vissengen Rd and Duncan St, T223 6226. Serves chicken.

$$ White Castle Fish Shop, 21 Hadfield and John St, Werk-en-rust, T223 0921. Casual open-air bar, for great fried fish and chips. Delivery available.

$$-$ German's, 8 New Market St, North Cummingsburg, T227 0079. Creole food with and emphasis on traditional soups, for which it is best known.

$$-$ Hacks Halaal, 5 Commerce St, T226 1844. Specializes in creole foods and snacks, local juices.

$$-$ Main Street Café, at Hotel Tower. Good breakfast and other meals.

$$-$ Shanta's, The Puri Shop, 225 Camp and New Market St, Cummingsburg, T226 4365. Local cuisine, a wide variety of Indian and African dishes, casual in-house dining or take-away.

$ Jerry's at New Tropicana, 177 Waterloo St, T225 2988. Open 24 hrs. Big portions, cheap beer, karaoke Wed, Fri, Sat. Slow service. Fresh daily baking.

$ Oasis Café, 125 Carmichael St, South Cummingsburg, T226 9916, www.oasiscafegy. com. Fashionable and safe, has Wi-Fi access. Serves creole food, mainly lunch. Probably the best cofee in Georgetown. Recommended. Also Oasis Lounge at the Cheddi Jagan International Airport. Creole food, snacks, etc.

$ Upscale, Commerce and Hinck Sts, T225 4721. Popular, poetry night Tue, comedy night Fri.

Sheriff St is some way from the centre but is 'the street that never sleeps' full of late night Chinese restaurants (eg Buddy's Mei Tung Restaurant, No 137, T231 4100, very good); and has some good bars including Burns Beat (US$5.50 for night club section), Club Monaco, Royal Castle (Sheriff and Garnett Sts) for chicken burgers. Also Antonio's Grill, 172 Sheriff and Fifth Streets, T225 7933, serves both international and local cuisine; Cambo, No 76 (also at 119 Regent St, Lacytown); Maharaja Palace, T219 4346, for Indian food, and VIP Kids Zone, No 279 with John Smith St.

Cafés

The Dutch Bottle Café, 10 North Rd, Bourda, T231 6560. Serves a mix of Guyanese and international food, has Wi-Fi access.

Juice Power, Middle St, past the hospital. Excellent fruit juices, also sells drinking water.

Maggie's Snackette, 224 New Market St, Cummingsburg, T226 2226. Authentic Guyanese food, cakes, pastries and fruit drinks, very popular.

Quizno's, Camp and Middle Sts, T225 1527. Lunches, sandwiches, salads, soups and subs.

Corriverton *p1595*

Mansoor, in Skeldon. Good Indian food. Several good Chinese restaurants within a few blocks of Springlands town centre.

Bartica *p1596*

Riverview Beach Bar, at Goshan near Bartica (Camp Silo bible study centre). Popular hotel and bar, disco, nice beach, safe swimming.

Lethem *p1597*

$$-$ Mann's Café, T686 0122. Excellent local cuisine with Brazilian flare, good service, a/c, buffet style.

The Airport Shop, good snacks, bar.

Foo Foods, T772 2010. Recommended for snacks.

⚙ Bars and clubs

Georgetown *p1593, map p1592*

Lively at night, mainly with gold miners, traders and overseas Guyanese. Most nightclubs sell imported, as well as local Banks beer; many sell drinks by the bottle rather than shot, this works out cheaper. Don't walk home at night; take a taxi. See above for Sheriff Street.

704 Sports Bar, Lamaha and Albert Sts, Queenstown. Sports, entertainment and food.
Club Ice, 71 5th St, Alberttown, T223 6266.
The Edge in Hotel Tower, 74-75 Main St.
El Club Latino, 57 Hadfield and Lime Sts, Werk-En-Rust, T227 4600.
The Loft Night Club and Bar, 3rd St, Alberttown.
Mojo's, 45 Main St, North Cummingsburg, T225 7775, albert16642004@yahoo.com.
The Vintage Wine and Cheese Lounge, 218 Lamaha and Camp St, T231 9631.

⊕ Entertainment

Georgetown p1593, map p1592
Cinema Avinash Theatre, Water St, South Cummingsburg, avinashtheaters@gmail.com. 2 a/c theatres. Two cinemas also at the Fun City Arcade at the Princess Hotel (see Ramada Gorgetown Princess, above), T265 7212, princessfuncity@yahoo.com. The Arcade has more than 80 games.
Theatre There are 2 theatres.

○ Shopping

Georgetown p1593, map p1592
The main shopping area is Regent St.
Crafts Items that are a good buy: Amerindian basketwork, hammocks, wood carvings, pottery, and small figures made out of Balata, a rubbery substance tapped from trees in the interior. Look for such items in the markets (also T-shirts), or craft shops. **Creations Craft**, Water St; **Amerindian Hostel**, Princess St, **Hibiscus Craft Plaza**, outside General Post Office. Others are advertised in the papers.

Department stores and other shops
Fogarty's and **Guyana Stores**, Church St, both of which stock a wide range of goods (good T-shirts at the latter). Footsteps Mega Store, 141 Camp and Regent St, in the United Center Mall, for a wide range of goods, from clothing to furniture and household items (also at Camp and Charlotte Sts and America and Longden Sts). The **City Mall**, Regent and Camp Sts, T225 6644, is a small mall with everything from food to jewellers. **Georgetown Reading and Research Centre**, Woolford Ave, in the Critchlow Labour College, offers a wide range of books, used and new, at really great prices.
Gold Sold widely, often at good prices but make sure you know what you are buying. Do not buy it on the street.
Markets Most Guyanese do their regular shopping at the 4 big markets: **Stabroek** (don't take valuables), **Bourda**, **La Penitence** and **Kitty**.

◑ What to do

Georgetown p1593, map p1592
The tourism sector is promoting ecotourism in the form of environmentally friendly resorts and camps on Guyana's rivers and in the rainforest (see below). There is much tropical wildlife to be seen. Tours to Amerindian villages close to Georgetown cost US$90-120.
Dagron Tours, 91 Middle St, T223 7921, www.dagron-tours.com. Adventure and eco-tours within Guyana and in neighbouring countries and the Caribbean.
Earth Tours Ltd, 106 Lamaha St, North Cummingsburg, T223 7847, navindranarine@ hotmail.com. Tours to Iwokrama, Kaieteur Falls

and fishing trips to the east coast, Demerara River, Canal no 1 and Canal no 2.

Evergreen Adventures, Ogle Aerodrome, Ogle, East Coast Demerara, T222 8053, reservations@ evergreenadventuresgy.com. Tours on the Essequibo River to Baganara Island.

Rainforest Tours, 5 Avenue of the Republic and Robb St, T227 2011 or T231 5661, www. rftours.com. Frank Singh, day and overland trips to Kaieteur, Santa Mission, Essequibo/Mazaruni; also Pakaraima Mountain hike, Kukubara to Orinduik, 5 days from one Amerindian village to another. Has a desk in Hotel Tower, 74-75 Main St, T231 5661.

Roraima Airways, R8 Eping Av, Bel Air Park, T225 9648. Day trips to Kaieteur and Orinduik Falls.

Splashmin's, 48 High St, Werk-en-rust, Georgetown, T223 7301, www.splashmins.com. A water fun park on the Linden highway, 1 hr from the city, entrance and transportation from Georgetown: adult US$6, child US$5, with own transport, entry adult US$3.55, children over 7 US$2.50, children 6 and under free. Also has a resort ($$$).

Torong Guyana, 56 Coralita Av, Bel Air Park, T225 0876/226 5298, toronggy@networksgy.com. Air, land and river advice and logistical support to all destinations in Guyana, bespoke tours country-wide and excellent trips to Kaieteur.

Wilderness Explorers, 141 Fourth St, Campbellville, T227 7698, www.wilderness-explorers.com. (In London: c/o Claire Antell, 46 Melbourne Rd, London SW19 3BA,

T020-8417 1585.) Offer ready-made or custom-designed itineraries. Tours to all of Guyana's interior resorts, day and overland tours to Kaieteur Falls, horse trekking, hiking and general tours in the Rupununi (agents for **Ranches of the Rupununi**) and rainforest (trips to Iwokrama Rain Forest Programme and joint managers of Iwokrama Canopy Walkway, see page 1598). Tours also in Suriname, Guyane, Brazil, Venezuela, Barbados, Dominica, St Lucia and Trinidad and Tobago. Specialists in nature, adventure and birdwatching tours. Free tourism information, booklet and advice available. General sales agents for Air Services Ltd and Trans Guyana Airways. Recently won Honourable Mention in Pioneers of Prosperity competition. Representatives: North America: T202-630 7689. Europe: Claudia Langer, claudia@ wilderness-explorers.com.

Wonderland Tours, 85 Quamina and Carmichael Sts, T225 3122, T225 9795. (24 hrs), day trips to Kaieteur and Orinduik Falls, Santa Mission, Essequibo and Mazaruni rivers, city tours; special arrangements for overnight stays available, recommended.

Travel agents
Connections Travel, 6 Av of the Republic.
Frandec, Carmichael and Quamaina Sts, opposite Beacon Snackette, T226 3076, www. frandec travel.com. Mr Mendoza. Repeatedly recommended (no tours to the interior).
H and R Ramdehol, 215 South Rd, Lacytown.

Jim Bacchus, 34-37 Water St,
WM Fogarty Building.
Muneshwers Ltd, 45-47 Water St.

Bartica *p1596*
B Balkarran, 2 Triangle St, T455 2544.
A good boatman and guide.
Essequibo Adventure Tours, 52 First Av,
Bartica, T455 2441, sbell@guyananet.gy.
Jet boat and tours on the Essequibo/
Mazaruni and Cuyuni Rivers.

⊖ Transport

Georgetown *p1593, map p1592*
Air Cheddi Jagan International Airport is
at Timehri, 40 km south of Georgetown (a
new terminal is to be built). From the airport,
take minibus No 42 to Georgetown US$1.70,
1-1½ hrs (from Georgetown leaves from next
to Parliament building); for a small charge they
will take you to your hotel (similarly for groups
going to the airport). A taxi costs US$20-25 (use
approved airport taxis). Check in 3 hrs before
most flights and contact the airline the day
before your flight to hear if it has been delayed,
or brought forward. There are 3 duty-free
shops. Some spirits are more expensive than
downtown. There is also an exchange house,
open usual banking hrs; if closed, plenty of
parallel traders outside (signboard in the
exchange house says what the rate is). It is
difficult to pay for flight tickets at the airport
with credit cards or TCs. The exchange desk
will change TCs for flight ticket purchases.

Ogle, for internal flights, LIAT international
flights and most flights to Suriname (**Suriname
Airways** also have a flight on Tue and Sat
from Cheddi Jagan), has an extended runway
and new immigration and customs facilities.
It is 15 mins from Georgetown; taxi US$7.50,
minibus from Market to Ogle US$1.

Flights are often booked up weeks in
advance (especially at Christmas and in Aug)
and are frequently overbooked, so it is essential
to reconfirm an outward flight within 72 hrs of
arrival, which can take some time, and difficult
to change your travel plans at the last minute. A
number of travel agents are now computerized,
making the process easier. Check for special
deals on flights to neighbouring countries.

Foreigners must pay for airline tickets in US$
(most airlines do not accept US$100 bills), or
other specified currencies. Luggage should
be securely locked as theft from checked-in
baggage is common.
Bus Within the city, minibuses run regularly
to most parts, mostly from Stabroek market
or Avenue of the Republic, standard fare G$80
(US$0.40) very crowded. It is difficult to get
a seat during rush hours. There are regular
services by minibuses and collective taxis to
most coastal towns from the Stabroek Market.
Minibuses leave early; arrive before 0700. To
Moleson Creek for the crossing to Suriname,
No 65 from opposite the City Hall, Av of the
Republic between Regent and Charlotte Sts,
leaves when full, US$35. This is not a safe area
early in the morning, if there are no other
passengers waiting take a taxi to Moleson Creek
from Georgetown, US$125. **Avenish**, T642 5161,
offers this service. Be sure he takes you to the
legal ferry, via immigration and not the illegal
crossing further north. If, by mistake, you get on
a bus going only as far as **Springlands**, US$10,
15 mins before Moleson Creek, 3-4 hrs, the
driver will probably take you for a little extra
money (check with the driver in Georgetown
where his bus is going); you can also break the
journey at New Amsterdam. To **Rossignol**, US$5;
to **Parika**, No 32, US$3.25; to **Linden**, No 43,
US$5.50. Ask other passengers what the fare is.
Note For visiting many parts of the interior,
particularly Amerindian districts, permits are
required in advance from the **Ministry of
Home Affairs** and the **Minister of Amerindian
Affairs**, 236 Thomas St, South Cummingsburg.
If venturing out of Georgetown on your own,
check beforehand whether you need a permit
for where you intend to visit. Permits can be
difficult to obtain and may require some time.
Apply before arrival in Guyana. **Wilderness
Explorers** offer a service for obtaining permits.
Taxi Taxis charge US$1.50 for short journeys,
US$3 for longer runs, with higher rates at night
(a safe option) and outside the city limits.
Collective taxis ply set routes at a fixed fare;
they stop at any point on request. Certain hand
signals are used on some routes to indicate
the final destination (ask). Special taxis at
hotels and airports, marked 'special' on the
windscreen, charge US$2 for short journeys

around town, US$4 for longer runs, stops and waiting time extra, or you can negotiate a 'by the hour' deal, usually US$7.50.

Southeast to Suriname *p1595*
Air TGA/GUM Air (code share) fly Georgetown–Paramaribo Mon-Sat (2 a day except Thu and Sat), US$180 one way (US$300 return). Surinam Airways fly Paramaribo–Georgetown–Miami, and return, Tue and Sat, US$100 (US$267 return).
Boat To Suriname: a ferry from Moleson, or Crabwood Creek, 13 km south of Springlands, to South Drain/Canawaima (40 km south of Nieuw-Nickerie, paved road) runs twice daily at 0900 and 1300, check-in 0630-0800 and 1030-1200, US$10 single (US$15 return for 21 days), bicycles free, motorbikes US$5, cars US$15, 30-min crossing. Immigration forms are handed out on board. At the ferry point is a hut/bar where you can buy Suriname dollars.
Bus Direct buses **Georgetown–Moleson Creek**, see above. Entering Guyana, you may be able to join a Paramaribo–Georgetown minibus at Immigration. Direct buses Georgetown–Paramaribo are operated by Dougla, T226 2843, US$60 including ferry ticket; they pick up and drop off at hotels. Minibuses to **Paramaribo** by Bobby's, T226 8668, Lambada, Bin Laden, T264 2993/624 2411, US$35; they pick up and drop off at hotels. Check visa requirements for Suriname before travelling.

Border with Venezuela: Mabaruma
p1595
Air TGA flies from **Georgetown** Mon, Wed, Fri, Sat US$80 one way, US$160 return.
Boat A ferry runs every other Tue from **Georgetown** at 1500 (US$8.35) to Mabaruma. The journey is surprisingly rough and 'you will have to fight for hammock space and watch your possessions like a hawk'. For assistance with transport contact Mr Prince through the Government Guest House. Boats also go from Charity (see page 1595) when there is demand. Ask for Peanut or Gavin. Boats go out to sea so you will get very wet, can be rough, 6 hrs, costs up to US$100 per boat.

Shell Beach *p1595*
Air/boat Fly **Georgetown-Mabaruma**, then take a motorized canoe to Shell Beach,

1 hr (good trip in the early morning for birdwatching); the last 20 mins is from the mouth of the Waini River along coast to Shell Beach camp, which can be a jolting ride. Or from Georgetown by canoe along some very interesting waterways. Allow 3-4 days. Contact **Wilderness Explorers**, see above.

Bartica *p1596*
Air Flight from **Ogle** to Bartica Mon, Wed, Fri 0700, 1630, Sat 0700, Sun 1630. The morning flight lands at **Baganara** only, with a boat connection to Bartica; the afternoon flight lands at Bartica only, with a boat to Baganara if there are passengers to or from Baganara.

Kaieteur and Orinduik Falls *p1596*
Organized tours A trip to the Kaieteur Falls costs US$280 with most operators, minimum 5 people. The trip includes 2 hrs at Kaieteur Falls, 2 hrs at Orinduik Falls, lunch, drinks, park entrance fee and guide; sit on left for best views, take swimming gear. Trips depend on the charter plane being filled; there is normally at least 1 flight per week. Cancellations only occur in bad weather or if there are insufficient passengers. Operators offering this service are **Wilderness Explorers** (guarantees flight to Kaieteur Falls for flights booked as part of a package), **Wonderland Tours**, **Torong Guyana**, **Rainforest Tours**, and **Nature Tours**. Another option is Kaieteur Falls with **Baganara Island Resort** for US$255 pp. To charter a plane privately costs US$1200 to Kaieteur and Orinduik. **Air Services Ltd** offer a Kaieteur only flight on Sat and Sun for US$220 (includes national park registration); flight must be full, last minute cancellations not uncommon. **Rainforest Tours** in Georgetown offer overland trips to Kaieteur for US$3000 for groups of 3 minimum; rate includes all transport, meals, camping gear, guides and flight back to Georgetown. Minibuses run daily from Georgetown as far as Mahdia, via Mabura Hill.

On the Rupununi *p1597*
Transport around the Rupununi is difficult; there are a few 4WD vehicles, but ox-carts and bicycles are more common on the rough roads. From Lethem transport can be hired for day-trips to the Moco-Moco Falls and the Kumu Falls

and to the Kanuku Mountains (4WD and driver to Moco-Moco US$72.50, long, rough ride and walk, but worth it). Trucks may also be hired to visit Annai, 130 km northeast (see below) along a poor road, 4 hrs' journey, US$200. All trucks leaving town must check with the police.

Lethem *p1597*
The **Airport Shop** can arrange horse hire for US$8 per hr, and Land Rovers and trucks at US$3 per mile. **Savannah Inn** has good 4WD vehicles for hire with driver. For birdwatching trips and transport contact Loris Franklin, T772 2105, or through the Airport Shop. Best time to ask about vehicle hire (with driver), or horse is when plane arrives. Car hire is expensive.
Ali TGA flies **Georgetown**–Lethem Georgetown daily at 0800, return 1000, plus Mon, Fri, Sat 1300, return 1500, US$142 one way, US$268 return. Stops are available at Annai and Karanambu Ranch. ASL have a scheduled service to Lethem daily at 1015 (extra charge to stop at Annai or Karanambu). **Wings Aviation** flies Georgetown–Lethem Georgetown Tue, Thu and Sat.
Road The road from Georgetown to Lethem via Mabura Hill and Kurupukari is now all-weather. It provides a through route from Georgetown to Boa Vista (Brazil). After Linden, it runs 100 km to Mabura Hill, then 50 km to Frenchman's Creek and on to the Essequibo. After the river and Iwokrama (see below) the road goes through jungle to Rock View (see above), the stop for Annai. Then the road crosses the Rupununi. Minibuses leave when full for Lethem, US$70 one way; most can be found on Church St between Cummings and Light Sts. **P and A** provides a reliable service. Most are Mon-Sat, but Guy Braz, 28 Sheriff St, Campbellville, T231 9752/3, guybraz_cindy@ yahoo.com, operate every day.

Border with Brazil *p1597*
From Lethem to immigration at the crossing (1.6 km), take a colectivo taxi, or pickup, US$3-5. There is no toll to cross the bridge. Taxi from Guyanese immigration to Brazil, US$5. Buses from **Bonfim** to Boa Vista (Brazil) 4-5 a day, 2½ hrs, US$8; colectivos charge US$12 pp, 1½ hrs.

Annai *p1597*
Road TGA agent in Annai is Colin Edwards and the Rock View Lodge is beside the airstrip. Rock View-Georgetown by scheduled bus (see under Lethem), or Land Rover US$70 return. From **Karanambu** to **Rock View** by boat and jeep costs US$380 for up to 4 people, fascinating trip.

Iwokrama *p1598*
Road 1¼ hrs by road from Annai or Surama. Coming from **Georgetown**, you have to cross the Essequibo at Kurupukari; ferry runs 0800-1700, hoot for service, US$35 for a car, pick-up or small minibus, US$55 for 15-seat minibus, US$125 truck.

⚙ Directory

Georgetown *p1593, map p1592*
Airline offices International: Caribbean Airlines, 63 Robb St, Robbstown, T1-800-744 2225, or 221 2202, www.caribbean-air lines.com (Caribbean, Miami, New York, Toronto, London – codeshare with BA). Surinam Airways, 110 Duke and Barrack St, Kingston, T225 4249, www.flyslm.com (flies Suriname-Guyana-Miami twice a week). For domestic flights see Getting around, page 1588. **Car hire** Available through numerous companies (the Guyana Telephone book lists some of them and the rest can be found in the *Yellow Pages*). Budget at Ocean View Hotel, US$105, plus US$250 deposit for minimum of 3 days. Shivraj, 98 Hadfield St, Werk-en-Rust, T226 0550/225 4785, carl@ solution.com. US$54.65 plus US$220 deposit. A permit is needed from local police; rental agencies can advise. **Embassies and consulates** Brazilian Embassy, 308 Church St, Queenstown, T225 7970, guibrem@solutions 2000.net. Visa issued next day, 90 days, 1 photo, US$12.75. Suriname Embassy, 171 Peter Rose and Crown St, Queenstown, T225 2846/2631, surnmemb@gol.net.gy. Consular section open Mon, Wed, Fri morning only, but visa application can be handed in at any time. Venezuelan Embassy, 296 Thomas St, South Cummingsburg, T226 6749, embveguy@gol.net.gy. **Exchange houses** *(cambios)* A good, safe *cambio* is Kayman Sankar, Lamaha St. There is a *cambio* next to Rima Guest House, Middle St. Roving

cambios at entrance to Stabroek Market, take care. To buy Suriname dollars, go to **Swiss House**, a *cambio* in the unsafe market area around Water St and America St, known locally as 'Wall St'. There are others that will change Suriname dollars. **Medical services** Well-equipped private hospitals include **St Joseph's**, Parade St, Kingston; **Prashad's**, Thomas St, doctor on call at weekends, 24-hr malaria clinic, T226 7214/9 (US$2 to US$8 per day; medical consultations US$8 to US$15); **Balwant Singh's**, 314 East St, South Cummingsburg, T225 4279/227 1087. If admitted to hospital you must bring sheets and food (St Joseph's provides these). The **Georgetown Hospital** is understaffed even though facilities have improved. Recommended doctor, **Dr Clarence Charles**, 254 Thomas St, surgery 1200-1400 hrs.

Suriname

Planning your trip

Where to go in Suriname

Like its neighbours, Suriname has been influenced by a variety of cultures, African, Asian, European and Amerindian. Markets, customs, festivals and food all reflect this. In Paramaribo, the capital, there is some fine wooden architecture, dating from the Dutch colonial period, and there are important Jewish monuments. Colonial buildings can be seen everywhere. Probably the main attraction is the tropical, Amazonian flora and fauna in this very sparsely populated country. Much of the interior is untouched and largely uninhabited. Infrastructure is limited, so tourist lodges, Amerindian and Maroon villages can only be reached by small boat or plane. The Maroons, descendants of escaped slaves, have maintained traditional African culture for centuries and, together with the Amerindians, have a special bond with the tropical rainforest and its biodiversity. Nature reserves, such as the Central Suriname Nature Reserve, formed by the Raleigh Falls, Eilerts de Haan mountain and Tafelberg reserves, Brownsberg, Wia-Wia and Galibi are given in the text below. Suriname is famous as nesting ground for marine turtles. There are no beaches to speak of; the sea and rivers around the coast are muddy, and mosquitoes can be a problem. Some recreational facilities have improvised beaches on the riverbanks (eg White Beach Resort, Overbridge, on the Suriname river).

Best time to visit Suriname

The climate is tropical and moist, but not very hot, since the northeast trade wind makes itself felt throughout the year. In the coastal area the temperature varies on an average from 23° to 31°C, during the day; the annual average is 27°C and on a monthly basis it ranges from 26° to 28°C. The average annual rainfall is about 2340 mm for Paramaribo and 1930 mm for the western division. The seasons are: small rainy season from November to February; small dry season from February to April; large rainy season from April to August; large dry season from August to November. Neither one of these seasons is, however, either very dry or very wet. The degree of cloudiness is fairly high and the average humidity is 82. The climate of the interior is similar but with higher rainfall. The high seasons, when everything is more expensive, are 15 March to 15 May, July to September and 15 December to 15 January.

Transport in Suriname

Air Internal services are run by **Gum Air** (Doekhieweg 3, Zorg en Hoop Airfield, T498760, www.gumair.com), a small air charter firms. **Hi Jet** is a helicopter charter company at Zorg en Hoop airport (T432577). There are no scheduled flights, only charters. The air companies fly to several Amerindian and Maroon villages. Most settlements have an airstrip, but internal air services are limited. These flights are on demand.

Driving in Suriname

Roads 26% of roads are paved. East-west roads: From Albina to Paramaribo to Nieuw-Nickerie is paved. North-south roads: the road Paramaribo-Paranam-Afobaka-Pokigron is open. The road to the western interior, Zanderij-Apura, crosses the Coppename River; thereafter small bridges are in poor shape (take planks to bridge gaps). On the unpaved Moengo-Blakawatra road (eastern Suriname), the bridge across the Commewijne River is closed to traffic.
Note The **Surinaamse Auto Rally Klub**, www.sarkonline.com, has information on rallying and other motoring events.
Road safety Driving is on the left, but many vehicles have left-hand drive. There is a 24 hour emergency service

for motorists: Wegenwacht, Sr Winston Churchillweg 123, T484691/487540.
Documents All driving licences accepted; you need a stamp from the local police and a deposit. To drive a foreign-registered vehicle requires no carnet or other papers. People wishing to travel from Suriname to either Guyana or Guiane by car need special vehicle insurance, available from **Assuria Insurance Company**, Grote Combeweg 37, Paramaribo, T473400, www.assuria.sr. Although an international driver's licence is accepted in Suriname and Guyana, a special permit is required to drive for longer than one month.
Fuel Gasoline is sold as diesel, 'regular', unleaded, or super unleaded (more expensive): US$1.57 per litre.

Road Details of buses and taxis are given in the text below. **Hitchhiking** is possible but neither common nor advisable.

Where to stay in Suriname → See Essentials for our hotel price guide.

Hotels (and restaurants) are rare outside Paramaribo, but accommodation in the interior is excellent if organized through a tour operator. Many have their own resorts. Going alone, you usually have to supply your own hammock and mosquito net, and food and drink. A tent is less useful in this climate. Do not travel independently without taking some local currency.

Food and drink in Suriname → See Essentials for our restaurant price guide.

Surinamese cuisine is as rich and varied as the country's ethnic makeup. High-quality rice is the main staple. Cassava, sweet potatoes, plantain, and hot red peppers are widely used. Pom is a puree of the tayer root (a relative of cassava) tastily spiced and served with chicken. Moksie Alesie is rice mixed with meat, smoked chicken and fish, white beans, tomatoes, peppers and spices. Pindasoep (peanut soup) with plantain dumplings or noodles) and okersoep met tayerblad (gumbo and cassava soup) are both worth a try. Petjil are cooked vegetables served with peanut sauce. Well-known Indonesian dishes include bami (fried noodles) and nasi goreng (fried rice), both spicy and slightly sweet. Among the Hindustani dishes are roti, somosa and phulawri (fried chickpea balls). Among Suriname's many tropical fruit, palm nuts such as the orange-coloured awarra and the cone-shaped brown maripa are most popular.

   Drink The local beer is called Parbo and the best-selling rums are Borgoe, Mariënburg and Black Cat, all distilled by **Suriname Alcoholic Beverages** (SAB, www.sabrum.com). There are many fruit juices to sample, as well as the various non-alcoholic drinks of the different ethnic communities.

Essentials A-Z

Accident and emergency
Police: Emergency T115; other police numbers T471111/7777/3101. **First Aid centre**: Academic Hospital, T442222. **Medical emergency**: T113. **Fire Brigade**: T110 or T473333/491111/451111.

Electricity
110/127 volts AC, 60 cycles. Plug fittings: usually 2-pin round (European continental type).

Embassies and consulates
For all Surinamese embassies and consulates abroad and for all foreign embassies and consulates in Suriname, see http://embassy.goabroad.com.

Festivals in Suriname
Avond Vierdaagse (Four-Day Walk) starting on the 1st Wed after Easter is a carnival parade of the young and old dressed in traditional costumes or just simple outfits; it is organized by Bedrijven Vereniging Sport en Spel (BVVS), Johannes Mungrastraat 48, Paramaribo, T461020. **Surifesta** is a year-end festival, from mid-Dec to the first week of Jan, with shows, street parties, flower markets, culminating in Het Vat on 31 Dec. At **The Suriname Jazz Festival**, www.jazzfestivalsuriname.com, local and international jazz musicians perform in Paramaribo; it is held annually in Oct. **Nationale Kunstbeurs/National Art Fair/National Art Exhibition**, in Vormingscentrum Ons Erf, Prins Hendrikstraat, Paramaribo (Oct/Nov).
Public holidays 1 Jan, New Year; Holi Phagwa (Hindu spring festival, date varies each year, generally in Mar, interesting but watch out for throwing of water, paint, talc and coloured powder); Good Fri; Easter (two days); 1 May (Labour Day); 1 Jul (Emancipation Day); 25 Nov (Independence Day); Christmas (2 days). Diwali, the Hindu Festival of Light (in Oct) is not a national holiday. For Muslim holidays see note under Guyana (Eid el Fitr is called Bodo by the Javanese Muslims and is a public holiday).

Money → *US$1 = SRD3.30, €1 = SRD4.49 (May 2014).*
As of 1 Jan 2004, the unit of currency is the Suriname dollar (SRD, replacing the Suriname guilder (SF) at the rate of 1000 to 1), divided into 100 cents. There are notes for 1, 2.50, 5, 10, 20, 50 and 100 dollars. Coins are for 1 and 2.50 dollars and 1, 5, 10 and 25 cents (the 25-cent coin is usually known as a *kwartje*, 10-cent *dubbeltje* and 5-cent *stuiver*). Euros are readily exchanged in banks and with licensed money changers (*cambios*). On arrival at the Johan Adolf Pengel airport, you can exchange a wide variety of currencies into Surinamese dollars, including reais, Trinidad and Tobago dollars and Barbados dollars. In Paramaribo *cambios* at various locations are open till late and on Sat, but only accept US dollars and euros. Officially visitors must declare foreign currency on arrival. When arriving by land, visitors' funds are rarely checked, but you should be prepared for it. To check daily exchange rates for US dollars, euros, pounds sterling and Netherlands Antilles guilders, visit the Central Bank site, www.cbvs.sr/english/publicaties-dagkoers.htm. Confusingly, prices in stores are quoted in 3 currencies: SRD for small items; US$ for small items, sometimes euros; euros for books, upmarket clothing and real estate, but sometimes also quoted in US$.

Opening hours
Banks: Mon-Fri 0900-1400 (airport bank is open when flights operate). **Government offices**: Mon-Thu 0700-1500, Fri 0700-1430. **Shops and businesses**: Mon-Fri 0900-1630, Sat 0900-1300.

Safety
Street crime in Paramaribo has been reduced through intensive police surveillance. Although beggars and/or drug addicts are a nuisance day or night, they are rarely dangerous. Paramaribo tends to be safer than Georgetown or Cayenne, but it's still wise to be cautious after dark and take care around the markets and docks. Do not photograph military installations. If in doubt, ask first. If travelling to the interior, enquire at your hotel, the tourist information centre or any other tourist authority about the safety situation in the areas you plan to visit. Malaria exists at some places in the interior.

Tax

Airport tax Departure tax is included in the air fare.

Telephone → *Country code +597*

Ringing: equal tones and long pauses. Engaged: equal tones with equal pauses. Telesur (TeleG) and Digicel. All **Telesur Dienstencentrum** offices offer email, fax, local and international phone and computer services. Phone cards for cheap international calls are available in newsagents, shops and hotels in Paramaribo, a better deal than Telesur card. **Telesur**, Heiligenweg 14, Paramaribo, T474242, www.sr.net, with branches nationwide. In Nieuw Nickerie the telephone office is with the post office on Oost-Kanaalstraat, between Gouverneurstraat and R P Bharosstraat. If phoning within the city, omit 0 from the prefix. Mobile services are provided by Telesur (TeleG) and Digicel.

Time

Official time GMT -3.

Tourist information

Suriname Tourism Foundation Dr J F Nassylaan 2, T424878, www.suriname-tourism.org (in English). Also try Stinasu or METS Travel and Tours, see Paramaribo Tour operators.

Useful websites

http://lanic.utexas.edu/la/sa/suriname. The University of Texas site, lots of links.
www.kabinet.sr.org Office of the President.
www.conservation.org/global/suriname
Conservation International site. Information on Suriname, including the Central Suriname Nature Reserve.
www.scf.sr.org The Suriname Conservation Foundation.
www.whsrn.org Western Hemisphere Shorebird Reserve Network, in which are the Bigi Pan, Wia Wia and Coppenamemonding reserves.
www.wwfguianas.org Set up in 1998, the WWF Guianas Programme (Henck Aaronstraat 63, Suite E, Paramaribo, T422357) is a conservation initiative covering the 3 Guianas.

Visas and immigration

Visitors must have a valid passport and a visa. Nationalities that do not need a visa include: Israel, Japan, some South American countries and Caricom member states. Nationals of the following countries, however, may apply for a tourist card: the majority of EU countries (not Bulgaria, Cyprus, Ireland, Poland, Romania), Bolivia, Canada, Norway, Panama, Paraguay, Peru, Uruguay, Switzerland, USA and foreigners of Surinamese origin. The card is valid for one entry by air of 90 days (but after 30 days you must apply to the Immigration Department, address below, for an extension) and costs €20/US$25. It can be obtained at a Surinamese Embassy or Consulate, the tourist card counter at Schiphol Airport, Amsterdam, T020-622 6717, or on arrival at Johan Adolf Pengel Airport. You need a passport valid for 6 months and a return flight ticket. For all other nationals, to obtain a visa in advance, you must apply to a Surinamese Embassy or Consulate up to 6 weeks before your scheduled departure to Suriname. You need to fill in an application form (which can be obtained online) and submit it with a copy of your passport photo page, stating the purpose of your trip and flight number. You will then be issued with a letter and another form to be completed with a passport photo and presented on arrival at Johan Pengel Airport where the visa fee must be paid. A 3-month tourist visa, single entry: €40; multiple entry. €40/US$45 for 2 months, €150 (US$210) for 12 months. A visa for US passport holders is US$100 for 5 years, multiple entry. A transit visa costs €10 (US$13). A business visa costs from €50 (US$60) (2 months) to €300 (US$360 – 2 years). See the websites of the Suriname consulate in The Netherlands, www.consulaatsuriname.nl, the embassy in the US, www.surinameembassy.org, or consulate in Miami, www.scgmia.com, for latest details (prices vary in some cases). If arriving by land or sea, you cannot use a Visa on Arrival document; you must obtain a visa sticker from a consulate. Procedures at consulates vary: in Cayenne visa applications normally take 1 day, 2 passport photos are required. In Georgetown visa applications can be submitted at any time, but only collected when the consular section is open on Mon, Wed and Fri morning. If applying when the consulate is open, visas are usually processed on the same day. Make sure your name on the visa matches exactly that on your passport. On entry into Suriname (by land or air) your passport will be stamped by the military police for 30 days. If you wish to stay in Suriname longer than three months, you must apply at least 3 months in advance for Authorization of Temporary Stay (*Machtiging Kort Verblijf*, MVK) which is subject to a E10 administration fee, a €40 or US$45 fee and a US$150 finalization charge. An exit stamp is given by the military police at the airport or land border. If you want a

multiple entry or have any other enquiries, go to the Immigration Department/Registration of Foreigners, Mr J Lachmonstraat 166-8, Paramaribo, T597-490666, Mon-Fri 0700-1430, or The Ministry of Foreign Affairs, consular section, Henck Arronstraat 23-25 (opposite Surinaamsche Bank), Paramaribo. **Note** If you arriving from Guyana, Guyane or Brazil in theory you need a certificate of vaccination against yellow fever to be allowed entry. It is not always asked for.

Weights and measures
Metric.

Paramaribo

Where to stay
1 Best Western Elegance
2 Courtyard Paramaribo (Marriott)
3 Eco-Resort Inn
4 Fanna
5 Guest House 24
6 Guest House Albergo Alberga
8 Guesthouse Centre
9 Guesthouse Sabana
10 Krasnapolsky
11 Queens Hotel & Casino
12 Residence Inn
13 Royal Torarica
14 Savoie
15 Spanhoek
16 Torarica
17 Zeelandia Suites
18 Zus & Co

Restaurants
1 Bali
2 Café de Punt, Mambo, 'T Lekkerbekje & Zanzibar
3 Chi Min
4 DOK 204
5 Dumpling #1
6 Garden of Eden

Paramaribo → Colour map 2, B5. Population: 242,946 (2009 estimate).

The capital and main port, lies on the Suriname River, 12 km from the sea. There are many attractive colonial buildings along the waterfront whose fusion of European architecture and South American craft led to the historic centre's UNESCO listing (http://whc.unesco.org/en/list/940). The **Governor's Mansion** (now the Presidential Palace) is on Onafhankelijkheidsplein (also called Eenheidsplein and, originally, Oranjeplein). Many beautiful 18th- and 19th-century buildings in Dutch (neo-Normanic) style are in the same area. A few have been restored.

Arriving in Paramaribo

Orientation The airport is 47 km south. There's no central bus station. ►► *See Transport, page 1623.*

Getting around There are very few regular **buses**; the few services that are left leave from Heiligenweg. There are privately run 'wild buses', also known as 'numbered buses' which run on fixed routes around the city; they are minivans and are severely overcrowded. **Taxis** generally have no meters, average price US$2.50. The price should be agreed upon beforehand to avoid trouble. Recommended is **Tourtonne's Taxi**, T475734/425380, tourtaxi87@yahoo.com, reliable and good value, will collect from airport with advance notice. If hiring a taxi for touring, beware of overcharging. If you're a hotel guest, let the hotel make arrangements.

Tourist information Suriname Tourist Foundation ⓘ *main office JF Nassylaan 2, T424878, www.suriname-tourism.org. Mon-Fri 0730-1500. Branch office at the Zeelandia Complex, T479200, Mon-Fri 0900-1530.* Or ask at operators like METS. A city tour costs about US$32-45.

Places in Paramaribo

Fort Zeelandia houses the **Suriname Museum** ⓘ *T425871, Tue-Fri 0900-1400, Sun 1000-1400, US$2*, restored to this purpose after being repossessed by the military. The whole complex has been opened to the public again and its historic buildings can be visited. The fort itself now belongs to the **Stichting (foundation) Surinaams Museum** ⓘ *www.surinaams museum.net*, and is generally in good condition. The old wooden officers' houses in the same complex have been restored with Dutch funding. Look for Mr F H R Lim A Postraat if you wish to see what Paramaribo looked like only a comparatively short time ago. The 19th-century **Roman Catholic St Peter and Paul Cathedral** (1885), built entirely of wood, is one of the largest wooden buildings in the Americas. This twin towered, neo-Gothic building with a rose

7 Pannekoek en
   Poffertjes Café
8 Power Smoothie
9 Roopram Rotishop
10 Roti Joose
11 Spice Quest
12 'T VAT'
13 Uncle Ray & Warungs

Bars & clubs 🍷
14 Broki
15 Touché

window is both impressive and beautiful, but has just been restored with funds from the European Union. Much of the old town, dating from the 19th century, and the churches have been restored. Other things to see are the colourful **market** and the waterfront, **Hindu temples** in Koningstraat and Wanicastraat (finally completed after years of construction), one of the Caribbean's largest **mosques** at Keizerstraat (take a magnificent photo at sunset). There are two **synagogues**: one next to the mosque at Keizerstraat 88, the other (1854) on the corner of Klipstenstraat and Heerenstraat (closed, now houses an internet café and IT business unit). The **Numismatisch Museum** ① *Mr FHR Lim A Postraat 7, T520016, www.cbvs.sr Mon-Fri 0800-1400*, displaying the history of Suriname's money, is operated by the Central Bank. A new harbour has been constructed about 1.5 km upstream. Two pleasant parks are the **Palmentuin**, with a stage for concerts, and the **Cultuurtuin**. The latter is a 20-minute walk from the centre. National dress is normally only worn by the Asians on national holidays and at wedding parties, but some Javanese women still go about in sarong and klambi. A university (Anton de Kom Universiteit van Suriname) was opened in 1968. There is one public swimming pool at Weidestraat. There is an exotic Asian-flavour market area on Jozef Israelstraat. There is a Sunday morning flea market on Tourtonnelaan.

An interesting custom throughout Suriname are birdsong competitions, held in parks and plazas on Sunday and holidays. People carrying their songbird (usually a small black twa-twa) in a cage are frequently seen; on their way to and from work or just taking their pet for a stroll.

Outside Paramaribo

Inland from Paramaribo
An interesting excursion for a half or full day is to take a minibus tour, or taxi, to **Leonsberg** on the Suriname River (**Stardust Hotel**, with mid-priced restaurant, café, pool, games; **Rust Pelikan** restaurant at the waterfront; at restaurants try *saoto* soup and other Javanese specialities, overlooking the river), then ferry to **Nieuw-Amsterdam**, the capital of the predominantly Javanese district of Commewijne. There's an **open-air museum**① *open mornings only except Fri 1700-1900, closed Mon*, inside the old fortress that guarded the confluence of the Suriname and Commewijne rivers. There are some interesting plantation mansions left in the Commewijne district (some can be visited on tours and you can stay at the **Hotel Frederiksdorp**① *T453083, www.frederiksdorp.com*, which dates from around 1760 and is a good base for turtle-watching; see Where to stay, below). Tours cost about US$90-95 with an operator, or about half that if arranged direct with a boat owner. From Leonsberg or Paramaribo, there are boat trips to the confluence of the Suriname and Commewijne rivers, calling at villages, Nieuw-Amsterdam and plantations. With luck river dolphins can be seen en route. **Braamspunt**, a peninsula with nice beaches at the mouth of the Suriname River, is 10 km from Paramaribo. The area is threatened by the invasion of the sea. Take a boat from the Leonsberg scaffold.

South of Paramaribo
You can drive to **Jodensavanne** (Jews' Savannah, established 1639), south of Paramaribo on the opposite bank of the Suriname River, where a cemetery and the foundations of one of the oldest synagogues in the Western Hemisphere are being restored. You can also visit the healing well. There is no public transport and taxis won't go because of the bad road. It is still only 1½ hours with a suitable vehicle. There's a bridge across the Suriname River to Jodensavanne. **Blakawatra** is one of the most beautiful spots in Suriname (shame about the amount of rubbish lying around). This was the scene of much fighting in the civil war. A full day trip to Jodensavanne and Blakawatra, returning to Paramaribo via Moengo, has been recommended if you can arrange the transport. Bus to Blakawatra at 0800, a three-hour trip. **Powaka**, about 90 minutes south of the capital, is a primitive village of thatched huts but with electric light and a small church. In the surrounding forest one can pick mangoes and other exotic fruit. About 5 km from the International Airport there is a resort called **Colakreek**① *US$3*, so named for the colour of the

water, but good for swimming (busy at weekends), lifeguards, water bicycles, children's village, restaurant, bar, tents or huts for overnight stay (plenty of package tours available starting at US$90 for a day visit). The village of **Bersaba**, 40 km from Paramaribo close to the road to the airport, is a popular area for the Coropinakreek. Many people go there at weekends and holidays, as well as to the neighbouring village of Republiek.

About 30 km southwest of Paramaribo, via **Lelydorp** (District Wanica; **Hotel De Lely**, Sastrodisomoweg 41; **The Lely Hills** casino), is the Bush Negro village of **Santigron**, on the east bank of the Saramacca River. Minibuses leave Paramaribo at 0530 and 1500, two hours. They return as soon as they have dropped off passengers in the village, so make sure you will have a bus to return on. There is no accommodation in Santigron. Nearby is the Amerindian village of **Pikin Poika**. These two villages make a good independent day trip. Tour agencies also visit the area about twice a month, including canoe rides on the Saramacca River and a Bush Negro dance performance (US$108 for one day).

By bus or car to **Afobakka**, where there is a large dam on the Suriname River. There is a government guest house (price includes three meals a day) in nearby **Brokopondo** village. Victoria is an oil-palm plantation in the same area.

On the way to Brokopondo Lake is the **Bergendal Eco & Cultural River Resort** ⓘ *Domineestraat 37-39, Paramaribo, T597-475050, www.bergendalresort.com; book online, or via the Hotel Krasnopolsky*, on the Suriname River, 85 km/1½ hours by road and river from the capital. Day visits (US$95) and overnight stays in three types of comfortable cabins are offered (from US$136). Activities include canopy tours, hiking, mountain bikes and kayaking.

An hour by car from Brokopondo, are the hills of **Brownsberg National Park** ⓘ *US$6*, which overlook the Professor Dr Ir van Blommensteinmeer reservoir. It features good walking, ample chances to see wildlife (it includes 400 species of birds) and three impressive waterfalls. **Stinasu** and other tour operators run all-inclusive tours from Paramaribo (two-day tours US$170-184, price includes transport, accommodation, food and guide; one-day tour US$82). Independent visits are possible. Minibuses for Brownsweg leave Saramaccastraat in Paramaribo daily when full, be there 0800-0900, two hours, US$15. Trucks converted into buses do the trip for less. Go to Stinasu at least 24 hours in advance and pay for accommodation in their guest houses (US$124 sleeping nine – there are larger houses, or US$20 to camp, US$15 to sling hammock) or to arrange for a vehicle to pick you up in Brownsweg. Take your own food. A one-day tour with an agency costs US$60-92.

Tukunari Island, in the van Blommesteinmeer, is about three hours' drive from Paramaribo to Brokopondo then a two-hour canoe ride. The island is near the village of Lebi Doti, where Aucaner Maroons live.

Several tour operators organize boat tours with stays in lodges on the Suriname River. See, for example, **Anaula Nature Resort** and **Danpaati Eco Lodges** in What to do, below.

Saramacca villages and **Awarradam**. There are many Saramacca villages along the Gran Rio and Pikin Rio, both Suriname River tributaries. These are fascinating places, set up in the 17th and 18th centuries by escaped slaves, originally from Ghana, who preserve a ceremonial language, spirituality and traditions. **METS** has a comfortable lodge on the Gran Rio at Awarradam, in front of a beautiful set of rapids in thick forest, and many other agencies, such as **Sun** and **Forest**, organize culturally sensitive tours to the villages. Independent visitors are also welcome. METS also combines tours to Awarradam with visits to **Kasikasima** and **Palumeu**. In the far south of Suriname are a series of dramatic granite mountains rising out of pristine forest. The highest is Mount Kasikasima, near the Trio and Wajana Amerindian village of Palumeu. METS has a comfortable river lodge here and visitors learn about the lifestyle of the villagers. They and other operators also organize expeditions up the mountain, which involve a strenuous climb, rewarded by incredible views over the rainforest. METS tours to Awarradam are four to five days, US$730; Awarradam and the Gran Rio River jungle camp, five days US$885; Palumeu, four to five days, US$730; Kasikasima, eight days, US$995. Combinations of Awarradam and Palumeu and Awarradam and Kasikasima are available.

Raleighvallen/Voltzberg Nature Reserve ① *US$15*, (78,170 ha) is a rainforest park, southwest of Paramaribo, on the Coppename River. It includes Foengoe Island in the river and Voltzberg peak; climbing the mountain at sunrise is an unforgettable experience. The reserve can be reached by air, or by road (180 km) followed by a three- to four-hour boat ride. This reserve has been joined with Tafelberg and Eilerts de Haan reserves to create the **Central Suriname Nature Reserve** (1.592 million ha – 9.7% of Suriname's total land area). The Reserve is now part of the UNESCO's World Heritage List. Tourist facilities have been opened, to which Stinasu and others do four-day tours, all-inclusive with transport, food and guides for US$410-490 (www.raleighvallen.com).

Stoelmanseiland, on the Lawa River in the interior, and the Maroon villages and rapids in the area can be visited on an organized tour. Price US$680 per person for five days (three, five and eight tours possible; check precisely what is included). They are, however, more easily reached by river from St-Laurent du Maroni and Maripasoula in Guyane.

West of Paramaribo

A narrow but paved road leads through the citrus and vegetable growing areas of **Wanica** and **Saramacca**, linked by a bridge over the Saramacca River. At **Boskamp** (90 km from Paramaribo) is the Coppename River. The Coppename bridge crosses to **Jenny** on the west bank. The Coppename Estuary is the **Coppenamemonding Nature Reserve**, protecting many shorebird colonies, mangrove and other swamps.

A further 50 km is **Totness**, where there was once a Scottish settlement. It is the largest village in the Coronie district, along the coast between Paramaribo and Nieuw-Nickerie on the Guyanese border. There is a good government guesthouse. The road (bad, liable to flooding) leads through an extensive forest of coconut palms. Bus to Paramaribo at 0600. 40 km further west, 5 km south of the main road is **Wageningen**, a modern little town, the centre of the Suriname rice-growing area. One of the largest fully mechanized rice farms in the world was established here (**Hotel de Wereld**, Molenweg, T233149). A little outside Wageningen is the **Guesthouse Hira** (T88-10992, or T453083), where you can stay and learn to cook with a Hindustani family. The **Bigi-Pan** area of mangroves is a birdwatchers' paradise; boats may be hired from local fishermen. **METS** includes Bigi Pan in its two-day tours to Nickerie, US$245.

Nieuw-Nickerie (*Population: 13,000, district 45,000, mostly East Indian*) on the south bank of the Nickerie River 5 km from its mouth, opposite Guyana, is the main town and port of the Nickerie district and is distinguished for its rice fields. It's a clean, ordered town with a lot of mosquitoes.

Border with Guyana

Ferry to Moleson Creek (for Springlands) From South Drain/Canawaima (Suriname, 40 km from Nieuw-Nickerie, excellent road) to Moleson/Crabwood Creek (Guyana), it's a 30-minute trip on the twice-daily ferry. Immigration forms are handed out on the boat. Queues can be long and slow to enter Suriname: run to get to the front. People over 60 may be given preference. Suriname is one hour ahead of Guyana. If entering Suriname from Guyana, you can change money at a hut at the ferry point, or failing that one of several banks in Nieuw-Nickerie. On departure, you can change Suriname dollars into Guyanese or US$ at Corriverton or in Georgetown.

Blanche Marie Falls, 320 km from Paramaribo on the road to Apoera on the Corantijn river, is a popular destination. **Washabo** near Apoera, which has an airstrip, is an Amerindian village. No public transport runs from Paramaribo to the Apoera-Bakhuis area, but Stinasu tours run to Blanche Marie and Apoera, US$375 per person, minimum five people, four days (www.blanche-marie.com) and there are charter flights to the Washabo airstrip. Irregular small boats sail from Apoera to Nieuw-Nickerie and to Springlands (Guyana).

East of Paramaribo to Guyane

Eastern Suriname was the area most severely damaged during the civil war. A paved road connects Meerzorg (bridge across the river) with Albina, passing through the districts of

Commewijne and Marowijne. There is little population or agriculture left here, although the road is being improved, cutting the journey time to 1½-two hours.

There are two **nature reserves** on the northeast coast of Suriname. Known primarily as a major nesting site for sea turtles (five species including the huge leatherback turtle come ashore to lay their eggs), **Wia-Wia Nature Reserve** (36,000 ha) also has nesting grounds for some magnificent birds. The nesting activity of sea turtles is best observed from April to July (July is a good month to visit as you can see adults coming ashore to lay eggs and hatchlings rushing to the sea at high tide). Since the beaches and turtles have shifted westwards out of the reserve, accommodation is now at **Matapica** beach, not in the reserve itself. Stinasu offers two-day tours which take a bus to Leonsberg, then a boat to Johannes Margareta (one hour), where you change to another boat for the one hour ride through the swamps to Matapica. Lodging is in Stinasu's lodge (two-day trip costs US$130 per person, departures Tuesday and Saturday, minimum five people), or you can also stay in hammocks. Suitable waterproof clothing should be worn. Book through **Stinasu** (T88-58495, www.matapica.com) or other agencies; keep your receipts or you will be refused entry. Early booking is essential.

There are more turtle-nesting places at the **Galibi Nature Reserve** (T US$5.1 day entry, near the mouth of the Marowijne River as well as several Carib Indian villages. From Albina it is a three-hour (including 30 minutes on the open sea) boat trip to Galibi. Here you can stay at the **Warana Lodge** (US$50 pp), which has cooking facilities, a refrigerator, rooms with shower and toilet, powered mostly by solar energy. Make arrangements through Stinasu who run all-inclusive, two-day tours, US$184 per person, minimum five (www.galibi-suriname.com), **METS**, US$238 for two days, US$286 for three days (see What to do, below), or **Myrysji Tours** (Grlegstraat 41, Paramaribo, T453151, http://galibi-tours.com), two- and three-day tours staying at their own lodge at Christiaankondre at the mouth of the Marowijne River.

East of Moengo, 160 km up the Cottica River from Paramaribo, the scars of war are most obvious. **Albina** is on the Marowijne River, the frontier with Guyane. Once a thriving, pleasant town and then a bombed-out wreck, it is now recovering with shops, a market and restaurants (it's still not very inviting, though). **The Creek Hotel** (with eight rooms) is on the northern outskirts of town; the owner speaks English.

Border with Guyane

Customs and immigration on both sides close at 1900, but in Albina staff usually leave by 1700. Be wary of local information on exchange rates and transport to Paramaribo. Changing money on the Suriname side of the border is illegal; the nearest bank, **de Surinaamsche Bank**, is in Moengo, otherwise **Hakrinbank** at Tamanredjo (Commewijne), or **Multitrack Money Exchange** not far from the Dr Jules Albert Wijdenbosch bridge in Meerzorg. Suriname dollars are not recognized in Guyane; when crossing to Suriname, pay for the boat in euros, or get the minivan driver to pay and he will stop at a cambio before reaching Paramaribo so you can change money and pay him. Immigration is at either end, next to the ferry terminal. Have your passport stamped before getting the boat.➤ *See Transport, page 1623.*

⦿ Suriname listings

For hotel and restaurant price codes, and other relevant information, see Essentials.

⦿ Where to stay

Paramaribo *p1615, map p1614*
Service charge at hotels is 5-10%. New, expensive hotels are opening, eg **$$$$** Courtyard

Paramaribo (Marriott), Anton Dragtenweg 52-54, T560000, www.marriott.com, and **$$$$-$$$** Best Western Elegance, Frederick Derbystraat 99-100, T420007, www.bestwestern suriname.com. The Suriname Museum in Zorg-en-Hoop now has a good guest house; book in advance. Beware: many cheap hotels not listed are 'hot pillow' establishments.

$$$$-$$$ Krasnapolsky, Domineestraat 39, T475050, www.krasnapolsky.sr. A/c, central, travel agency, shopping centre, exhibition hall in lobby, good breakfast and buffet, 5 eating options, poolside bar, business centre and conference facilities, swimming pool.

$$$$-$$$ Queen's Hotel and Casino, Kleine Waterstraat 15, T474969, www.queenshotel suriname.com. Including breakfast, service charge and tax. A/c, swimming pool, minibar, restaurant terrace, free entrance for hotel guests to Starzz disco.

$$$$-$$$ Spanhoek, Domineestraat 2-4, T477888, www.spanhoekhotel.com. Delightful boutique hotel, funky, trendy décor, lovely bathrooms, continental breakfast with Surinamese delicacies.

$$$$-$$$ Torarica, Mr Rietbergplein, T471500, www.torarica.com. One of the best in town, very pleasant, book ahead, swimming pool and other sports facilities, sauna, casino, tropical gardens, a/c, central, 3 expensive restaurants (Plantation Room, European; The Edge, with live entertainment; good poolside buffet on Fri evening), superb breakfast, business centre with internet and conference facilities. Its sister hotel, the **$$$ Royal Torarica**, Rietbergplein, T473500, www.royaltorarica. com. More for business than leisure, but comfortable rooms, river view, pool and other sports facilities, lobby restaurant. Has subsidiary **Tangelo Bar and Terrace**, at Mr Rietbergplein 1.

$$$ Eco-Resort Inn, Cornelis Jongbawstraat 16, T425522, www.ecoresortinn.com. Use of Torarica facilities, good atmosphere and value, restaurant (mid-range), bar, Ms Maureen Libanon is very helpful, business centre.

$$$ Guesthouse Amice, Gravenberchstraat 5 (10 mins from centre), T434289, www. guesthouse-amice.sr. Quiet area, room with balcony more expensive, a/c, comfortable, breakfast, airport transfer and tours available.

$$$ Residence Inn, Anton Dragtenweg 7, T521414, www.resinn.com. Minibar, laundry, including breakfast, credit cards accepted, in a residential area, pool, tennis court, a/c bar and Matutu restaurant, European and Surinamese food (mid-range), airport transfer.

$$$ Zeelandia Suites, Kleine Waterstraat 1a, T424631, www.zeelandiasuites.com. Smart, business-style suites with all mod cons next to a lively bar and restaurant area. At same address is Discover Suriname Tours, T421818, www.discoversurinametours.com.

$$$-$$ De Luifel, Gondastraat 13 (about 15 mins from centre), T439933, www.hotel deluifel.com. A/c, warm water, mid-priced European restaurant, special 'business-to-business' deal: 1 night with breakfast, laundry, airport transfer, car hire and taxes included.

$$ Guest House Albergo Alberga, Lim A Po Straat 13, T520050, www.guesthousealbergo alberga.com. Central, in a 19th-century house, very pleasant, terrace and TV area, spotless rooms, a/c or fan (cheaper), breakfast extra, pool, excellent value, book in advance. Recommended.

$$ Guesthouse Centre, Van Sommelsdijck-straat 4, T426310, www.guesthousecentre.com. A/c, new, good value, convenient, parking.

$$ Guesthouse Sabana, Kleine Waterstraat 7, T424158, opposite Torarica. A/c, safe, helpful.

$ Fanna, Prinsessestraat 31, T476789. From a/c with bath to basic, breakfast extra, safe, family run, English spoken.

$ Guest House 24, Jessurunstraat 24, T420751, http://twenty4suriname.com/twenty4.html. Simple but well-maintained rooms, bar, buffet breakfast, Wi-Fi, pleasant, "backpackers' paradise". In the same group is Zus & Zo Guesthouse, Grote Combeweg 13a, T520905, info@zusenzo suriname.com, with café and arts and crafts centre, and Fietsenin Suriname (see Cycling, below).

Inland from Paramaribo *p1616*

$$$$ De Plantage, Km 23.5 on the east-west trail at Tamanredjo, Commewijne, 40 mins from Paramaribo, T356567, www.deplantagecomme wijne.com. Price is for 2-night stay. Lovely chalets for 2-4 on an old cocoa plantation, restaurant, pool, jungle walks and observation tower, bicycles for rent.

$$$ Overbridge River Resort, 1 hr south of the capital, via Paranam (30 km), then 9.5 km to Powerline mast 20-21, then 7.5 km to resort, or 60 km by boat down Suriname River. Reservations, Oude Charlesburgweg 47, Paramaribo, T422565, www.overbridge.net. Cabins by the river, price includes breakfast, weekend and other packages available.

$$$-$$ Residence Inn, R P Bharosstraat 84, Nieuw Nickerie, PO Box 4330, T210950/1, www.resinn.com. Best in town, prices higher at weekend, central, a/c, bath, hot water, business centre (email etc extra), laundry, good restaurant (Matutu, $$), bar.

$$ pp **Hotel Frederiksdorp**, T453083, www.frederiksdorp.com. In an old coffee plantation, apartments, bar, restaurant, museum, conference facilities and email.

$ Ameerali, Maynardstraat 32-36, Nieuw Nickerie, T231212. A/c, good, restaurant (**$$**) and bar.

❼ Restaurants

Paramaribo *p1615, map p1614*
Meat and noodles from stalls in the market are very cheap. There are some good restaurants, mainly Indonesian and Chinese. Blauwgrond is the area for typical, cheap, Indonesian food, served in *warungs* (Indonesian for restaurants).

Indonesian
Try a *rijsttafel* in a restaurant such as **Sarinah** (open-air dining), Verlengde Gemenelandsweg 187. Javanese foodstalls on Waterkant are excellent and varied, lit at night by candles. Try *bami* (spicy noodles) and *petjil* (vegetables), recommended on Sun when the area is busiest. In restaurants a dish to try is *gadogado*, an Indonesian vegetable and peanut concoction.

$$ Bali, Ma Retraiteweg 3, T422325. Very good food, service and atmosphere, check bill.

$$ Jawa, Kasabaholoweg 7. Famous restaurant.

Chinese
$$ Chi Min, Cornelis Jongbawstraat 83. For well-prepared Chinese food. Recommended.

$$ Dumpling #1, Dr JF Nassylaan 12, T477904. Daily 1800-2300, Tue-Sat 0930-1500, Sun 0800-1300. Simple, well-prepared Chinese dumplings and other such dishes. Generous portions, popular with children.

Others
$$$ Spice Quest, Dr Nassylaan 107, T520747. Open 1100-1500, 1800-2300, closed Mon. Same management as **Dumpling #1**. Creative menu, open-air and indoor seating, Japanese style setting. Recommended.

$$ Café De Punt, Kleine Waterstraat 17. Café opposite **Torarica**.

$$ DOK 204, Anton Dragenweg 204, T311461. Surinamese dishes in an intimate restaurant decorated with a nautical theme.

$$ Garden of Eden, Virolastraat via Johannes Mungrastraat. Attractive garden area and lounge bar/restaurant serving Thai food.

$$ Mambo, opposite **Torarica**, next to Sabana Guesthouse. Local and international cuisine.

$$ Martin's House of Indian Food, Hajaraystraat 19, T473413. Good value and tasty Indian food with friendly service and covered outside dining.

$$ 'T Lekkerbekje, Sommelsdijckstraat (near Guesthouse Centre). Specializes in fish.

$$ 'T VAT', opposite **Torarica**, www.hetvat suriname.com. A smart little square with lots of little bars and restaurants, popular after work for early evening meeting and drinking.

$$ Zanzibar, Sommelsdijckstraat 1, near Hotel Torarica, T471848. Tue-Sun 2000 till late. Surinamese and international cuisine, entertainment.

$$-$ Roopram Rotishop, Zwartenhovenbrug- straat 23, T478816. Rotis and accompanied fillings in an a/c fast-food style dining room, generous portions, *roti aard* particularly good.

$ Mix Food, Zeelandiaweg 1. Good location, view of river and close to Fort Zeelandia. Surinamese main dishes and snacks and sandwiches.

$ Pannekoek en Poffertjes Café, Sommelsdijckstraat 11, T422914. Thu, Sun 1000-2300, Fri-Sat 1000-0100. Specializes in 200 different sorts of pancakes.

$ Power Smoothie, Zwartenhovenbrugstraat and Wilhelminastraat. Healthy fast food.

$ Roti Joose, Zwartenhovenbrugstraat 9. Well-known roti shop in centre of town.

$ Uncle Ray at Waterkant by the Javanese *warungs*, opposite Central Bank of Suriname. Local Creole food.

❶ Bars and clubs

Paramaribo *p1615, map p1614*
All are liveliest Thu-Sat.

Ballrom Energy, L'Hermitageweg 25, T497534. Younger crowd.

Broki, Waterkant next to the Ferry Docks. Hammock bar, good food and atmosphere.

Lindeboom, Wilhelminastraat 8 (near Torarica). Sun-Thu 1600-0100, Fri-Sat 1600-0300. Popular spot, live entertainment.

El Molina, J A Pengelstraat, T478485. Fri-Sat from 2300. Cosy disco, lots of soul music/ golden oldies.

The Jungle, Wilhelminastraat 60-62. For all ages.

Millennium, Petrus Dondersstraat 2, Rainville suburb. Popular with all ages but mostly the over-30s; Grill restaurant inside.

Rumors Grand Café, in the lobby of **Hotel Krasnapolsky**, T475050. Every Fri live entertainment (jamming) with "Time Out".

Starzz Disco, Kleine Waterstraat 5-7, T474993. Fri-Sat 2300.

Touché, Waaldijk/Dr Sophie Redmondstraat 60. Fri-Sat only 2300. Small restaurant, the best disco.

Uptown Café, upstairs at Spanhoek Passage, T406181. Special entertainment programme every Fri-Sat.

ⓔ Entertainment

Paramaribo *p1615, map p1614*
There are many casinos in the city, including at major hotels.

ⓞ Shopping

Paramaribo *p1615, map p1614*
Arts and crafts Amerindian and Maroon carvings are better value at workshops on Nieuwe Domineestraat and Neumanpad. Many jewellers in the centre sell at reasonable prices. Local ceramics are sold on the road between the airport and Paranam, but are rather brittle. Old Dutch bottles are sold. **Arts & Crafts**, Kersten Shopping Mall. Amerindian goods, batik prints, basketwork and drums. **Cultuurwinkel**, Anton de Komstraat. Bosneger carvings, also available at **Hotel Torarica**.

Bookshops Second-hand books, English and Dutch, are bought and sold in the market. The kiosk in Krasnapolsky Hotel sells books. **Boekhandel Univers NV**, Henck Aaronstraat 61. Recommended for nature, linguistic and scholarly books on Suriname. **Kersten**, Domineestraat. One of 2 main bookshops in the city, selling English-language books. **Vaco**, opposite Krasnapolsky. The other main bookshop, also selling English books; try here for maps.

Music The following sell international and local music on CD (the latter is heavily influenced by Caribbean styles): **Beat Street** in Steenbakkerijstraat, near Krasnapolsky Hotel. **Boom Box**, Domineestraat, opposite Krasnapolsky Hotel. **Disco Amigo**, Wagenwegstraat, opposite Theater Star.

Shopping centres Hermitage Shopping Mall, Vieruurbloem Straat, 5 mins in taxi south of centre. The only place open until 2100, with chemists, money exchange, top quality boutiques, coffee shops and music stores. Also **Maretraite Mall** on Topaas Straat, north of the city.

Supermarkets Many, well stocked. **Choi's**, Johannes Mungrastraat, some way from centre. Excellent selections of Dutch and other European goods, also Rossignol Deli in same complex. Another branch at the corner of Thurkowweg and Tweekinderenweg. **Tulip** supermarket on Tourtonnelaan sells many North American and European products.

ⓞ What to do

Paramaribo *p1615, map p1614*
If intending to take a tour to the jungle and either Amerindian or Maroon villages, check how much time is spent in the jungle itself and on the conditions in the villages.

Access Suriname Travel, Prinsessestraat 37, T424533, www.surinametravel.com. Sells all major tours in Suriname and can supply general travel information on the country, manager Syrano Zalman is helpful.

Anaula Nature Resort, Wagenwegstraat 55, Paramaribo, T410700, www.anaulanature resort.com. A comfortable resort near the Ferulassi Falls about an hour's boat trip from Atjonie village, 4½ hrs' drive from Paramaribo (or reached by air). It has lodges for 2-5 people, cold water, restaurant and bar, swimming pool; activities include forest and Maroon village excursions; 3- and 4-day packages from US$325-382 pp, all inclusive.

Captain Moen's Dolphin Tours, bookable through METS, see below. Cruises to see brackish water or Guiana dolphin, the profosu (*Sotalia Guianensis*), daytime on the Commewijne river and to the beach at Braamspunt, 0900-1300, and sunset from

Leonsberg to the Johannes Margareta plantation, 1615-1915, US$37.50. Both include refreshments and snacks, lifejackets on board.
Cardy Adventures and Bike Rental, Cornelis Jongbawstraat 31 (near Eco Resort), T422518, www.cardyadventures.com. Mon-Sat 0800-1900, Sun 0830-1830. Bike rental (bike rental@cardyadventures.com) and standard and adventure tours throughout the country, English spoken, very helpful, efficient, excellent food.
Danpaati Eco Lodges, Anniestraat 14, T471113, www.danpaati.net. Danpaati River Lodge in Upper Suriname (Boven Suriname) offers 3- and 4-day packages, or nightly rates of US$102 in cabins on Danpaati island, 345 km south of Paramaribo, excursions to the forest, on the river and to villages, has an associated health care project.
Ma-Ye-Du, Matoeliestraat 22, T410348, www.facebook.com/mayedu. Tours to Maroon villages in Marowijne River.
METS Travel and Tours (Movement for Eco-Tourism in Suriname), Dr JF Nassylaan 2, Paramaribo, T477088, www.surinamevacations.com. Mon-Fri 0800-1600. Runs a variety of tours and is involved with various community projects. Several of their trips to the interior are detailed in the above. They also offer city and gastronomy tours. Can be booked through any Surinam Airways outside Suriname.
Stinasu is the Foundation for Nature Preservation in Suriname, Cornelis Jongbawstraat 14, T476597, PO Box 12252, Paramaribo, www.stinasu.com (website not working at time of research – see destination websites above). Mon-Thu 0700-1500, Fri 0700-1430. It offers reasonably priced accommodation and provides tour guides on the extensive nature reserves throughout the country. One can see 'true wilderness and wildlife' with them.
Suriname Experience, Chopinstraat 27, Ma Retraite 3, Paramaribo North, T453083, www.surinameexperience.com. Very knowledgeable agency about Suriname.
Waldo's Travel Service, Kerkplein 10, T425428, www.waldostravel.sr. For all tours within Suriname.
Waterproof Tours, Lizelaan 4, T454434, www.waterproofsuriname.com. Tours of the waters in and around Suriname, dolphin and caiman watching, birdwatching, river trips.

Wilderness Explorers, see page 1606 (www.wilderness-explorers.com) offer a wide range of tours to Suriname, Guyana and French Guyana. They have a UK office T020-8417 1585 for advice and a list of UK operators who sell the 3 Guianas.

Cycling
Cardy Adventures and Bike Rental, see above.
Fietsen in Suriname, Grote Combeweg 13a, T520781, www.fietseninsuriname.com. Good quality bikes for rent. Tours with knowledgeable guides, good value, bike repair. Recommended.
Koen's Verhuur Bedrijf, Van Sommelsdijck-straat 6, T08-876106. Mon-Sat 1000-1700, also rents scooters.

West of Paramaribo: Nieuw Nickerie
p1618
Manoetje Tours, Crownstraat 11, NieuwNickerie, T231991 (Hans Overeem). Boat tours to, among other places, Apoera, Orealla, Corantijn.

⊖ Transport

Paramaribo *p1615, map p1614*
Air Johan Pengel International Airport is 47 km south of Paramaribo. Minibus to town costs US$20 pp (eg De Paarl, T403610, or Buscovery/Le Grand Baldew, who have a booth in the arrival hall, Tourtonnelaan 59, T474713, www.legrandbaldew.com/www.buscoverytours.com); bus costs US$15 with Ashruf taxi company, T454451 (it makes many stops), taxi proper costs about US$35, but negotiate. Hotels **Krasnapolsky**, **Torarica**, **Eco Resort Inn** and **Residence Inn** offer free transfers to and from the international airport for guests with room reservation. There is a guesthouse near the airport. Internal flights and flights to Georgetown leave from Zorg en Hoop airfield in a suburb of Paramaribo (minibus 8 or 9 from Steenbakkerijstraat). See below for airline offices.
Bus To **Nickerie** from Dr Sophie Redmondstraat, near **Hotel Ambassador**, minibuses leave when full between 0500 and 1000, US$6.50, 3 hrs. There are also buses after 1200, but the price then depends on the driver,

4-5 hrs, extra for large bag. (Taxis from the same area are slightly faster, US$15.) Verify fares in advance and beware overcharging.

Minibus taxis to Albina US$15, 2 hrs from Paramaribo cross the new bridge; there is also a bus from the station near the ferry services in Paramaribo at 0830, return 1300, US$3.50 (take an APB or PBA bus, which has a plainclothes policeman on board). A **shared taxi** costs US$27, while a private taxi will charge US$92 (drivers have a poor reputation for honesty). There are irregular bus services to other towns. For full details ask drivers or enquire at the tourist office. There is much jostling in the queues and pure mayhem when boarding vehicles. They are all minivans and have no luggage space. Try to put bags under your seat or you will have to hold it in your lap.

Direct **minibuses** to **Georgetown** via South Drain (fare does not include ferry crossing), US$35, pick up and drop off at hotels: Bobby's, T498583 (very cramped); Lambada Bus Service, Keizerstraat 162. T411 073, and Bin Laden, T0-210944/0-8809271. Buscovery/Le Grand Baldew (address above), organizes 3- and 4-day trips to Georgetown and Cayenne respectively, US$815 (they also do tours around the country).

West of Paramaribo: Nieuw Nickerie
p1618
Bus For services, see under Paramaribo. The bus station is next to the market on G G Maynardstraat.
Boat Ferry to **Moleson Creek** (for Springlands): from South Drain to Moleson/Crabwood Creek (Guyana), ferry twice a day, US$10, cars US$15, pick ups US$20. T472447 to check if ferry is running on holidays. Taxi bus from Nickerie market to **South Drain** at 0730, but can pick you up from your hotel. Bus Paramaribo-South Drain: US$7. See under Paramaribo, for companies.

Border with Guyane *p1619*
Boat Pirogues take people across the river to **St-Laurent du Maroni** for about US$6.75, check if cost is in Suriname dollars

or euros. Most leave from 200 m north of the immigration pier, at the same place that minibuses leave for **Paramaribo** (2-3 hrs). The car ferry charges US$5.75 for foot passengers, US$47 per car, US$21 motorbike, payable only in euros. If you don't want to take a shared minibus taxi or a private taxi from Paramaribo (see above), ask to join a Stinasu tour to Galibi to get to Albina. A bus leaves at 1300, US$3.50.

ⓘ Directory

Paramaribo *p1615, map p1614*
Airline offices Surinam Airways, Dr Sophie Redmondstraat 219, T432700, www.flyslm.com (to/from Amsterdam, joint operation with KLM, Hofstraat 1, T411811, Miami via Aruba and via Georgetown twice a week, and Caribbean). Caribbean Airlines, Wagenwegstraat 36, T520034 (to/from Port of Spain, www.caribbean-airlines.com). Gum Air, Doekhieweg 03, Zorg en Hoop Airport, T498760, www.gumair.com (Gum Air and Trans Guyana fly Paramaribo-Guyana daily, T433830). For Air France (flights between Cayenne and Europe), T473838.
Banks The main banks that offer exchange are: de Surinaamsche Bank (www.dsbbank.sr); Finabank (open on Sat); Hakrinbank (www.hakrinbank.com); RBC Royal Bank (www.rbcroyalbank.com). **Car hire** Avis, Kristalstraat 1, T551158, www.avis.com; Europcar, Kleine Waterstraat 1, T424631, www.europcar.com. Hertz at Real Car, Van 't Hogerhuysstraat 19, T402833, ckcmotor@sr.net; SPAC, Verl Gemenelandsweg 139A, T490877. From US$30 per day, hotel delivery, drivers available. U-Drive, T490803, Wheelz, HD Benjaminstraat 20, T442929, 887 9366 or 8802361 after 1600 and at weekends, killit@sr.net. Mastercard accepted, US$35-110 daily (tax not included).
Embassies and consulates Brazil, Maratakastraat 2, T400200, brasilemb. paramaribo@itamaraty.gov.br. Guyana, Gravenstraat 82, T477895, guyembassy@sr.net. Netherlands, van Roseveltkade 5, T477211, www.nederlandseambassade.sr.

Guyane

Planning your trip

Where to go in Guyane

Guyane is an Overseas Department of France, upon which it is heavily dependent. The capital, Cayenne, is on a peninsula at the mouth of the river of the same name. Like its neighbours, Guyane has a populated coastal strip and much of the country remains sparsely populated and underdeveloped despite French aid. The department is known internationally for its space station at Kourou, home to the European Ariane space programme, where economic activity and investment is concentrated. The site has been used to launch over half the world's commercial satellites and employs about 1500 personnel, with 7000 related jobs. Tourism is slowly being developed and is increasing, as in all the Guianas, with adventure trips into the forests making up for the lack of good beaches. The Parc Amazonien de Guyane (www.parcsnationaux.fr) covers 2 million ha of the interior and with neighbouring reserves in Brazil such as Tumucumaque, Maricuru and Grão-Pará forms the world's largest protected tropical forest. Almost all visitors are from France and Belgium. Over 10,000 tourists arrive annually, but their numbers are dwarfed by the 60,000 other visitors, businessmen and those who work in the space programme. An unusual attraction is the remains of the former penal colony, notably the Iles du Salut, made famous by Henri Charrière's book *Papillon*.

Best time to visit Guyane

The best months to visit are between August-November. The climate is tropical with heavy rainfall. Average temperature at sea level is fairly constant at 27°C. There is often a cool ocean breeze. Night and day temperatures vary more in the highlands. The rainy season is November-July, sometimes with a dry period in February and March. The great rains begin in May

Transport in Guyane

Air Internal air services are by **Air Guyane** (see Airline offices, Cayenne). These flights are always heavily booked, so be prepared to wait, or phone. There are scheduled flights to Maripasoula, Saül and St-Laurent. Baggage allowance 10 kg. There are also helicopter companies with domestic services.

Road There are no railways, and about 1000 km of road. It is now possible to travel overland to Cayenne from Suriname and onwards to Macapá in Brazil. The latter takes about 24 hours from Cayenne with half a day's waiting in St-Georges de l'Oyapock for the Brazilian bus to leave. The roads are much improved. Combis (minivans) ply the coastal roads between St-Laurent, Cayenne and St-Georges de l'Oyapock. Transport is expensive, around US$2 per 10 km. **Hitchhiking** is reported to be easy and widespread.

Boat One- to three-ton boats which can be hauled over the rapids are used by the gold-seekers, the forest workers, and the rosewood establishments. Ferries are free. Trips by motor-canoe (*pirogue*) up-river from Cayenne into the jungle can be arranged.

Where to stay in Guyane → *See Essentials for our hotel price guide.*

There are few hotels under our **$$$** bracket and almost no restaurants under the **$$$** bracket. Accommodation in Guyane is more expensive than Paris, but food is better value. The **Comité du Tourisme de la Guyane** (see Tourist information, below) has addresses of furnished apartments for rent (**Locations Clévacances**) and **Gîtes**, which are categorized as **Gîtes d'Amazonie**, with

Driving in Guyane

Roads The main road, narrow, but now paved, runs for 270 km from Pointe Macouris, on the roadstead of Cayenne, to Mana and St-Laurent. It also runs to Régina and St-Georges de l'Oyapock on the Brazilian border.

Documents There are no formalities for bringing a private car across the Guyane-Surinam border, but you must ensure that your insurance is valid.

Car hire A convenient way to get around. There are 14 agencies in Cayenne; those at the airport open only for flight arrivals. **Budget** (www.budget-guyane.com),

Europcar (loc@groupesgtm.com) and **Sixt** (sancarlocation@wanadoo.fr) have offices. A local agency is **Jasmin**, T308490, jrac@nplus.gf. All types of car available, from economy to luxury to pick-ups and jeeps. Cheapest rates are about €30/US$41 a day, km extra, €200/US$273 per week including km, insurance extra. Check insurance details carefully; the excess is very high. Motorcycle hire, also a good way to get around, at Avenida Pasteur and Dr Gippet, from US$30-US$35 per day.

Fuel Gasoline/petrol costs about €1.66/US$2.26 per litre, diesel €1.54/US$2.10.

accommodation in hammocks or *carbets* (imitation Amerindian huts), **Carbets d'Hôtes**, which include breakfast, and **Gîtes Panda Tropiques Label**, which are approved by the WWF.

Essentials A-Z

Electricity
220 volts. Plugs are the same as mainland Europe.

Embassies and consulates
A full list of France's overseas representation can be found at www.mfe.org or http://embassy.goabroad.com.

Festivals in Guyane
Public holidays These are the same as in Metropolitan France, with the addition of **Slavery Day**, 10 Jun. **Carnaval** (Feb or Mar). Guyane's Carnaval is joyous and interesting. It is principally a Créole event, but with some participation by all the different cultural groups in the department (best known are the contributions of the Brazilian and Haitian communities). Celebrations begin in Jan, with festivities every weekend, and culminate in colourful parades, music, and dance during the 4 days preceding Ash Wed. Each day has its own motif and the costumes are very elaborate. On Sat night, a dance called *Chez Nana – Au Soleil Levant* is held, for which the women disguise themselves beyond recognition as *Touloulous*, and ask the men to dance. They are not allowed to refuse. On Sun there are parades in downtown Cayenne. Lundi Gras (Fat

Mon) is the day to ridicule marriage, with mock wedding parties featuring men as brides and women as grooms. *Vaval*, the devil and soul of Carnaval, appears on Mardi Gras (Fat Tue) with dancers sporting red costumes, horns, tails, pitch-forks, etc. He is burnt that night (in the form of a straw doll) on a bonfire in the Place des Palmistes. Ash Wed is a time of sorrow, with participants dressed in black and white.

Money → *US$1 = €0.73 (May 2014)*.
The currency is the euro. Take euros with you; many banks do not offer exchange facilities, but ATMs are common. Good rates can be obtained by using Visa or MasterCard (less common) to withdraw cash from any bank in Cayenne, Kourou and St-Laurent du Maroni. It is possible to pay for most hotels and restaurants with a Visa or MasterCard. American Express, Eurocard and Carte Bleue cards are also accepted.

Banks Most banks have ATMs for cash withdrawals on Visa, sometimes MasterCard, never Amex. The Post Office exchanges cash and TCs at good rates, but complicated and time-consuming. Exchange facility at the airport. Central pharmacy may help when banks are closed. Almost impossible to change dollars outside Cayenne or Kourou.

Opening hours
They vary widely between different offices, shops and even between different branches of the same bank. There seem to be different business hours for every day, but they are usually posted. Most shops and offices close for a few hours around midday.

Postal services
The main post office is on Route de Baduel, 2 km from the centre of Cayenne (take a taxi or 20 mins on foot).

Telephone → *Country code +594.* Ringing: equal tones with long pauses. Engaged: equal tones with equal tones.

Time
GMT -3.

Tourist information
The French Government tourist offices can usually provide leaflets on Guyane; also **Comité du Tourisme de la Guyane** 1 rue Clapeyron, 75008 Paris, T33-1-4294 1516, guyanaparis@ tourisme-guyane.com. In Guyane: **Comité du Tourisme de la Guyane** 12 rue Lallouette, BP 801, 97300 Cayenne, T05-94-296500, www.tourisme-guyane.com. See also www.cr-

guyane.fr. **Note** The Amerindian villages in the Haut-Maroni and Haut-Oyapock areas may only be visited with permission from the Préfecture in Cayenne *before* arrival in Guyane.

Visas and immigration
Passports are not required by nationals of France and most French-speaking African countries carrying identity cards. For EU visitors, documents are the same as for Metropolitan France (that is no visa, no exit ticket required – check with a consulate in advance). EU passport must be stamped; be sure to visit immigration if arriving from Suriname or Brazil, it is easy to miss. No visa required for most nationalities (except for those of Guyana, Suriname, some Eastern European countries – not Croatia, and Asian – not Japan – and other African countries) for a stay of up to 3 months, but an exit ticket out of the country is essential (a ticket out of one of the other Gulanas is not sufficient); a deposit is required otherwise. If you stay more than 3 months, income tax clearance is required before leaving the country. A visa costs 60 euros, or equivalent (US$82).

Weights and measures
Metric.

Cayenne → *Population: 58,500-61,550 (est). Colour map 2, B6.*

The capital and the chief port of Guyane is on the island of Cayenne at the mouth of the Cayenne River. Founded by French traders in 16th-century, but taking its name from an Amerindian prince, Cayenne remained relatively isolated until after the Second World War when Guyane became part of metropolitan France and Rochambeau airport was constructed.

Arriving in Cayenne
Getting there Cayenne is 645 km from Georgetown (Guyana) and 420 km from Paramaribo (Suriname) by sea. ▶▶ *See also Transport, page 1634.*

Tourist offices Comité du Tourisme de la Guyane ① *12 rue Lallouette, BP 801, 97300 Cayenne, T296500, www.tourisme-guyane.com, Mon, Tue, Thu 0730-1300, 1430-1730, Wed, Fri 0730-1330,* is helpful and has lots of brochures, but very little in English. Cayenne also has a municipal tourist office at this address, T272940.

Places in Cayenne
There is an interesting museum, the **Musée Départemental Franconie** ① *1 rue de Rémire, near the Place de Palmistes, T295913, http://musee.cg973.fr/ws/collections/app/report/index.html different hours every day, closed Tue, Sun, Thu afternoon and Sat afternoon, US$4.* Its exhibits include pickled snakes and the trunk of the 'late beloved twin-trunked palm' of the Place de

Palmistes. There is a good entomological collection and excellent paintings of convict life. Next door is the municipal library. **L'Orstom** ① *Route de Montabo, Mon and Fri 0700-1330, 1500-1800, Tue-Thu 0700-1300*, a scientific research project with a research library and permanent exhibits on Guyane's ecosystems and archaeological finds. **Musée des Cultures Guyanaises** ① *78 rue Mme Payé, T314172, mcg87@wanadoo.fr, Mon, Tue 0800-1245, 1500-1745, Wed 0800-1245, Thu, Fri 0800-1215, 1500-1745, Sat 0800-1145, US$2.75, 18-25 year-olds US$1.35, children free*, has a small collection of crafts from tribal communities. Also worth a visit is **La Crique**, the colourful but dangerous area around the Canal Laussat (built by Malouet in 1777); the Jesuit-built residence (circa 1890) of the Prefect (**L'Hôtel-de-Ville**) in the Place de Grenoble; the **Place des Amandiers** (also known as the **Place Auguste-Horth**) by the sea; the Place des Palmistes, with assorted palms; a pool and five cinemas. The **market** on Monday, Wednesday, Friday and Saturday mornings has a great Caribbean flavour, but is expensive. There are bathing beaches (water rather muddy) around the island, the best is Montjoly, but watch out for sharks. Minibuses run from the terminal to Rémire-Montjoly for beaches, US$3. They leave when full; check when the last one returns (about 1830, earlier at weekends). There is a walking trail called **Rorota** which follows the coastline and can be reached from Montjoly or the Gosselin beaches. Another trail, **Habitation Vidal** in Rémire, passes through former sugar cane plantations and ends at the remains of 19th-century sugar mills.

Some 43 km southwest of Cayenne is **Montsinéry**, with a nearby **zoo** ① *Macouria, T317306, www.zoodeguyane.com, daily 0930-1730, US$22, children US$13*, featuring Amazonian flora and fauna, a walking trail, canopy walkway, zipline and other activities.

Cayenne

Where to stay
1 Best Western Amazonia
2 Central
3 Des Amandiers
4 Ker Alberte
5 Ket Tai
6 La Belle Etoile & Villa Soleil

Restaurants
1 Café de la Gare
3 La Petite Maison
4 La Sarrasine
5 Le Café Crème
6 Le Paris-Dakar
7 Le Patriarche
8 Le Sandouicherie
9 Paris-Cayenne

Bars & clubs
10 des Palmistes

Outside Cayenne

The European space centre at Kourou is one of the main attractions, especially when a rocket is being launched. In stark contrast are the abandoned penal settlements. Beyond is largely unexplored jungle. Also in this section are the routes to Suriname and Brazil.

West to Suriname

Kourou (*Population: 20,000, 56 km west of Cayenne*) This is where the main French space centre (Centre Spatial Guyanais), used for the European Space Agency's Ariane programme, is located. It is also used by the Russians to launch Soyuz and Vega (a joint mission with other European countries). It is referred to by the Guyanais as 'white city' because of the number of French families living there. Tourist attractions include bathing, fishing, sporting and a variety of organized excursions. **Tourist information** ① *T329833, Mon, Tue, Thu 0800-1330, 1500-1800, Wed, Fri 0800-1400.*

The **space centre** occupies an area of about 750 sq km along 50 km of coast, bisected by the Kourou River. **Public guided tours** are given Monday to Thursday at 0815 and 1315 (Friday 0815 only). Tours last 3½ hours, but are only in French; under eights are not admitted. Advance reservations can be made but are not necessary on a weekday, T326123, visites.csg@wanadoo.fr, Monday to Friday 0800-1200. No tours during a launch or on the days before or after. The **Musée de l'Espace** ① *T335384, Mon-Fri 0800-1800, Sat 1400-1800, US$9.55 (5.45 with reservation for a tour), no public transport, take a taxi or hitch*, can be visited without reservation. To watch a launch you must write to CNES at Centre Spatial Guyanais, Relations Publiques, BP 726, 9/387 Kourou Cedex, T334453, saying you want to attend; phone or fax to find out when launches take place, or www.cnes-csq.fr for the email address. Supply full names and ID; ask for your invitation from Centre d'acceuil du CSG. Invitations must be collected two to three days before the launch; if you hear nothing, it's probably full, but you can try wait-listing (arrive early). Alternatively, you can watch the launch for free, from 10 km, at Montagne Carapa at Pariacabo. Also see www.esa.int/Education and www.arianespace.com.

Iles du Salut The Iles du Salut (many visitors at weekends), opposite Kourou, include the Ile Royale, the **Ile Saint-Joseph**, and the **Ile du Diable**. They were the scene of the notorious convict settlement built in 1852; the last prisoners left in 1953. One of their most famous residents was Henri Charrière, who made a miraculous escape to Venezuela. He later recounted the horrors of the penal colony and his hair-raising escape attempts in his book *Papillon* (some say Charrière's book is a compilation of prisoners' stories). There is a museum in the Commander's House on Ile Royale; brochures for sale. The Ile du Diable (Devil's Island), a rocky islet almost inaccessible from the sea, was where political prisoners, including Alfred Dreyfus, were held (access to this island is strictly forbidden). You can see monkeys, agoutis, turtles, hummingbirds and macaws, and there are many coconut palms. Paintings of prison life, by François Lagrange (the inspiration for Dustin Hoffman's character in the film *Papillon*) are on show in the tiny church. Visit the children's graveyard, mental asylum and death cells. These are not always open, but the church is open daily. Conservation work is underway. Three guided tours in French are given weekly.

Sinnamary and St-Laurent du Maroni Between Kourou and Iracoubo, on the road west to St-Laurent, is **Sinnamary** (116 km from Cayenne, bus Line 4, US$27, no bus Sunday, US$13.50 from Kourou), a pleasant town where Galibi Indians at a mission make artificial flowers, for sale to tourists. Carvings and jewellery are on sale here. **Tourist information** ① *T346883, 0730-1230 (1500-1800 Mon, Wed).* There are three- to five-day excursions up the Sinnamary River. Scarlet ibis can be seen in numbers on the Sinnamary estuary at Iracoubo (tourist information T345938, ot.iracoubo@wanadoo.fr, Monday-Saturday 0900-1700).

St-Laurent du Maroni (*Population: 25,000*), formerly a penal transportation camp, is now a quiet colonial town 250 km from Cayenne on the river Maroni, bordering Suriname. Market days Wednesday and Saturday, 0700-1400 It can be visited as a day tour from Cayenne if you hire a car, but note that everything closes for a long siesta. The old **Camp de Transportation** (the original penal centre) can be wandered round at will, but a guide is needed to enter the cells (an absolute must if visiting the country). **Guided tours of Les Bagnes** (prison camps) July-August daily 0930, 1100, 1500, 1630, rest of year Monday 1500, 1630, Tuesday-Saturday as July-August, Sunday 0930, 1100, chilling, buy tickets from tourist office here, €5/US$6.80. See also www.bagne-st-jean.com on the **Camp de la Relégation** at St-Jean du Maroni, US$6.80. **Tourist office: Office du Tourisme** ① *1 esplanade Laurent Baudin, 97393 St-Laurent du Maroni, T342398, www.ot-saintlaurentdumaroni.fr, Mon-Fri 0730-1800, Sat 0730-1245, 1445-1745, Sun 0900-1300 (1500 Jul and 1630 Aug)*; has leaflet with self-guided walking tour.

Border with Suriname Make sure you obtain proper entry stamps from immigration, not the police, to avoid problems when leaving. Customs and immigration, 2 km south of the centre, close at 1900. There are aggressive touts on the St-Laurent and Albina piers. It is best to change money in the Village Chinois in St-Laurent (dangerous area); although rates are lower than in Paramaribo, it is illegal to change money in Albina. Beware theft at St-Laurent's black market. Surinamese consul is at 26A rue Justin Catayée, T344969, Monday-Friday 0900-1200, 1400-1600 (1530 Friday).

Around St-Laurent About 3 km from St-Laurent, along the Paul Isnard road, is Saint-Maurice, where the rum distillery of the same name can be visited, Monday to Friday 0730-1130. At Km 73 on the same dirt road is access to **Voltaire Falls**, 1½ hours' walk from the road. Some 7 km south of St-Laurent on the road to St-Jean du Maroni is the Amerindian village of **Terre Rouge**; canoes can be hired for day trips up the Maroni River (see Maripasoula below).

Some 40 km north of St-Laurent du Maroni is **Mana**, a delightful town with rustic architecture near the coast (tourist office, T278409, Mon-Sat 0800-1300, 1500-1800). 20 km west of Mana following the river along a single track access road is **Les Hattes**, or Yalimapo, an Amerindian village. About 4 km further on is Les Hattes beach where leatherback turtles lay their eggs at night; season April to August with May/June peak. No public transport to Les Hattes and its beach, but hitching possible at weekends; take food and water and mosquito repellent. The freshwater of the Maroni and Mana rivers makes sea bathing pleasant. It is very quiet during the week.

Aouara, or Awala, an Amerindian village with hammock places, is 16 km west of Les Hattes. It also has a beach where leatherback turtles lay their eggs; they take about three hours over it. Take mosquito nets, hammock and insect repellent.

There are daily flights from Cayenne to **Maripasoula**; details in Air transport, page 1625, local office T372141. It is up the Maroni from St-Laurent (two- to four-day journey up river in *pirogue*). There may be freight canoes that take passengers (€40/US$53) or private boats (€180/US$236), which leave from St-Laurent; four- to five-day tours with **JAL-Voyages** or other Cayenne operators cost €575/US$755.

South to Brazil

About 28 km southeast of Cayenne is the small town of **Roura**, which has an interesting church. An excursion may be made to the Fourgassier Falls several kilometres away (**L'Auberge des Cascades**, excellent restaurant). From Cayenne the road crosses a new bridge over the Comte River. Excursions can be arranged along the Comte River. Nearby is Dacca, a Laotian village. For information about the area contact the **Roura tourist office** ① *T270827, otroura@wanadoo.fr*.

From Roura a paved road, RD06, runs southeast towards the village of **Kaw**, on an island amid swamps which are home to much rare wildlife including caimans. The village is reached from where the Roura road ends at the river at Approuague. Basic rooms available; take insect repellent.

At Km 53 on another road southeast to Régina is the turn-off to **Cacao** (a further 13 km), a small, quiet village, where Hmong refugees from Laos are settled; they are farmers and produce fine traditional handicrafts. The Sunday morning market has local produce, Laotian food and embroidery. Canoe/kayak rental behind **Degrad Cacao** restaurant, T270830, US$3 per hour, good wildlife trips upriver. Ask the Comité du Tourisme de la Guyane for *gîtes* in the area.

Southwest of Kaw on the river Approuague is **Régina**, linked with Cayenne by a paved road. A good trip is on the river to Athanase with G Frétigne, T304551. A paved road runs from Régina to St-Georges de l'Oyapock (difficult in the rainy season).

Saül This remote gold-mining settlement in the 'massif central' is the geographical centre of Guyane. The main attractions are for the nature-loving tourist. Beautiful undisturbed tropical forests are accessible by a very well-maintained system of 90 km of marked trails, including several circular routes. There is running water and electricity; tourist office T374500, in the town hall. Another fascinating overland route goes from Roura (see above) up the Comte River to Belizon, followed by a 14- to 16-day trek through the jungle to Saül, visiting many villages en route, guide recommended. Meals from **Restaurant Pinot**. Two markets sell food.

Border with Brazil **St-Georges de l'Oyapock**, with its small detachment of the French Foreign Legion who parade on Bastille Day, is 15 minutes downriver from Oiapoque in Brazil, €5/US$6.55 per person by motorized canoe, bargain for a return fare. A bridge between the two countries has been built, but remains closed until the BR-156 to Macapá has been paved. The tourist office is in the library to the left of the town hall, T370401. There are bars, restaurants, supermarkets with French specialities, a post office and public telephones which take phonecards. Thierry Beltran, Rue Henri Sulny, T370259, offers guided river and forest tours. A pleasant day trip is to the **Saut Maripa** rapids (not very impressive with high water), located about 30 minutes upstream along the Oyapock River, past the Brazilian towns of Oiapoque and Clevelândia do Norte. Hire a motorized *pirogue* (canoe) to take you to a landing downstream from the rapids. Then walk along the trolley track (used to move heavy goods around the rapids) for 20 minutes to the rundown huts by the rapids (popular and noisy at weekends). There are more rapids further upstream on the way to Camopi.

Immigration, for entry/exit stamps: look for PAF (Police Federal), set away from the river about 10 minutes walk behind the Mairie; fork left at 'Farewell Greeting' sign from town (this may change when the border bridge is in service). Open daily 0700-1200, 1500-1800 (often not open after early morning on Sunday, so try police at the airport); French, Portuguese and English spoken. One of the Livre Service supermarkets and **Hotel Chez Modestine** will sometimes change dollars cash into euros at poor rates; if entering the country here, change money before arriving in St-Georges. Brazilian reais are accepted in shops at poor rates.

⊚ Guyane listings

For hotel and restaurant price codes, and other relevant information, see Essentials.

⊜ Where to stay

Cayenne *p1627, map p1628*
Most hotels are in the centre. A few of the better ones are in the suburb of Monjoly, next to a coarse sand beach and muddy sea, but the best district in Cayenne nonetheless. Hotels rarely add tax and service to their bill, but stick

to prices posted outside or at the desk. B&B accommodation (gîte) is available from €45/US$62 a night (breakfast included) – contact the tourist office for details.
$$$$ Ker Alberte, 4 rue de Docteur Sainte-Rose, T257570, www.hotelkeralberte.com. Central, in a converted old house, boutique hotel with good service, decorated with modern art, modern facilities, courtyard pool, restaurant.
$$$$-$$$ La Belle Etoile and Villa Soleil, 74 rue Lt Goinet, T257085, www.prestigelocations.fr.

The first is a brand new building with 6 deluxe suites on 3 floors, while the latter is the ground floor of a Creole villa, quaint, old style. All suites with kitchens, safe, a/c, washing machines. Very good.

$$$$-$$$ Novotel, Route de Montabo, Chemin St Hilaire, T303888, www.novotel.com. Beach-side hotel 3 km from the centre set in a tropical garden, 3 standards of room, gym, pool, 2 tennis courts and a respectable French and Creole restaurant, ultra-modern and business-friendly. Car hire available.

$$$ Best Western Amazonia, 28 Av general de Gaulle, T288300, www.bestwestern.com. A/c, pool, central location, good buffet breakfast extra.

$$$ Central Hotel, corner rue Molé and rue Becker, T256565, www.centralhotel-cayenne.fr. Good location, 100 m from the Place de Palmistes, a/c rooms. Special prices for groups and business travellers. Book in advance through the net.

$$$ Hotel des Amandiers, Place Auguste-Horth, T289728. Pleasant, tranquil and breezy location next to a park on a little peninsula at the north end of town, a/c rooms, popular restaurant with varied menu and good service.

$$ Ket-Tai, Av de la Liberté corner Blvd Jubelin, T289777, g.chang@wanadoo.fr. The best cheapie in town, top end of this range, simple a/c rooms, en suites, look at a few before deciding.

Around Rémire-Montjoly

$$$ Motel du Lac, Chemin Poupon, Route de Montjoly, T380800, moteldulac@orange.fr. In a protected area, very peaceful, garden, convenient for the airport, pool, bar, restaurant.

Near Matoury and the airport

$$ $ La Chaumiere, Chemin de la Chaumière (off the road to Kourou), 97351 Matoury, T255701, www.lachaumierecayenne.com. Set in gardens, thatched huts, restaurant, pool, at bottom end of this price band, good value, but cabs to town push up cost.

Apartment rentals

A good option, but what's on offer changes often. Best to reserve through the tourist office who publish a brochure, *Guides des hébergements*, with full details and pictures. Contact them in advance through the website.

Kourou *p1629*
Hotel rooms and rates are at a premium when there's an Ariane rocket launch (1 a month).

$$$$ Atlantis, near Lac Bois Diable, T321300, www.atlantiskoura.com. A/c, modern, pool, best value for business visitors.

$$$$ Hôtel des Roches, Pointe des Roches, T320066, www.hoteldesroches.com. Fair, a/c, includes breakfast, pool with bar, beach, Le Paradisier and Le Créolia restaurants, cybercafé and Wi-Fi.

$$$$ Mercure Ariatel, Av de St-Exupéry, Lac Bois Diable, T328900, www.mercure.com. Overlooking a lake, 9 hole golf course nearby and pool. See Restaurants, below.

$$$-$$ Le Ballahou, 1 et 3 rue Amet Martial, T220022, www.ballahou.com. Small apart-hotel, some rooms with cooking facilities, also studios, a/c, TV, modern. Book ahead, reception open 1200-1400, 1700-1900.

Iles du Salut *p1629*
$$$$ Auberge Iles du Salut, on Ile Royale (BP 324, 97378 Kourou, T321100, www.ilesdusalut. com). Full board. 60-bed hotel, hammock space (US$14); former guard's bungalow (**$$$**), main meals are excellent; pricey gift shop (especially when cruise ship is in), good English guidebook for sale.

Sinnamary *p1629*
$$$ Hôtel du Fleuve, 11 rue Léon Mine, T345400, infohoteldufleuve@orange.fr. Gardens, restaurant, internet access, pool, one of the grandest hotels west of Cayenne, breakfast extra.

St-Laurent du Maroni *p1630*
$$$$-$$$ Le Relais des 3 Lacs, 19-21 Domaine du Lac Bleu, T340505, www.relais des3lacs.com. A/c, cheaper with fan, shuttle to town centre, restaurant, gardens, pool.

$$$ La Tentiaire, 12 Av Franklin Roosevelt, T342600, tentiaire@wanadoo.fr. A/c, the best, breakfast extra, phone, pool, secure parking.

$$$ Star, 26 rue Thiers, T341084, hotelstar973@ yahoo.fr. A/c, pool.

$$ Chez Julienne, rue Gaston Monnerville, 200 m past Texaco station, T341153. A/c, TV, a/c, shower, good value.

Around St-Laurent p1630
Voltaire Falls
$$$$ Auberge des Chutes Voltaires, www.aubergechutes voltaire.com. Price is for half-board. Double rooms with shared bath, hammock space US$68 half-board, US$6.55 to hire hammock (more with mosquito net), other meals available.

Mana
Gîte Angoulême, PK 206/207 RN1 Saut Sabbat, T346490, aubergedangouleme973@gmail.com. Beside the river Mana, hammock in a *carbet* US$20, gîte from **$$$** without meal, all meals available, US$20.

Les Hattes
Gîtes, all at Commune Awala-Yalimapo: Ailumi Weyulu, T347245, ailumlweyulu@ mediaserv.net; **Chez Judith et Denis**, T342438; Pointe les Hattes, **Chez Rita**, T341809, gitechezrita@gmail.com.

South to Brazil p1630
Roura
$$ Auberge des Orpailleurs, 9 km after the Cacao turnoff on the road from Cayenne to Régina, on the banks of the Orapu River, T09710-447855 (net phone), www.aubergedes orpailleurs.com. 6 rooms and also hammock spaces, breakfast extra. Canoes, trails and butterfly and moth collecting. Restaurant.
$$ Auberge du Camp Caïman, RD06 29 km from Roura, T307277. Tourist camp (much less to hang hammock), tours arranged to watch caiman in the swamps.

Régina
$ Alberge de l'Approuague, Lieu-dit Corossony, 97390 Régina, T370802. Price is for hammock space, cheaper with own hammock, also rooms **$$**, meals expensive, great views of the forest.

Border with Brazil: St Georges de l'Oyapock p1631
Accommodation is cheaper on the Brazilian side.
$$$ Caz Cale, rue E Elfort, 1st back from riverfront, just east of the main square, T370054. A/c, a/c rooms with TV, cheaper with fan.

$$ Chez Modestine, on the main square, T370013, modestine@wanadoo.fr. A/c or fan, price for single room, restaurant.

Restaurants

Cayenne p1627, map p1628
There are very few decent French *patisseries* and *boulangeries*. Many restaurants close on Sun. There are many small Chinese restaurants serving the same fare: noodles, rice, soups etc.
$$$ Cric-Crac at Motel Beauregard, Rémire-Montjoly, T354100. Créole cooking, lovely atmosphere.
$$$ La Kaz Kréol, 35 Av D'Estrées, T390697. Créole cooking served by waitresses in costume, delights include stuffed cassava, agouti stew and sauerkraut of papaya.
$$$ La Marina, 24 bis rue Molé, T301930. For seafood, beef and chicken dishes.
$$$ La Petite Maison, 23 rue Féliz Eboué, T385839. In an old building, on 2 floors, with a good varied menu.
$$$ La Sarrasine, 55 rue Lt Goinet, T317238. Good fish, salads, crêpes and quiches in an intimate dining room. Good wine list and service. At the lower end of the price range.
$$$ Le Paris-Dakar, 103 rue Lt. Becker, T305517. Closed Sun, Mon lunch. African cooking from Zaire, Senegal, Benin and the Ivory Coast, like tropical fish on pureed aubergine, excellent vegetarian platter.
$$$ Le Patriarche, rues Voltaire at Samuel Lubin, T317644. Excellent classical French and Creole cooking, one of the best in Guyane and very good value for this country. Reserve in advance.
$$$ Paris-Cayenne, 59 rue de Lallouette, T317617. French cooking with tropical twist, nice decor.
$$$-$$ Café de la Gare, 42 rue Léopold Hélder, T284796. Great little restaurant with club playing classy live music every Thu and weekend. Good atmosphere, 20-40 something crowd.
$$$-$$ Le Café Crème, 42 rue Justin Catayée, T281256. Pastries, sandwiches, juices, breakfasts and coffee.
$$ Le Sandouicherie, rue Félix Eboué at Lt Goinet, T289170. French bread sandwiches, snacks, juices and breakfasts, a/c.

Snacks

Vans around Place des Palmistes in evenings sell cheap, filling sandwiches. Along the Canal Laussant there are Javanese snack bars: try *bami* (spicy noodles) or *saté* (barbecued meat in a spicy peanut sauce). Also along the canal are small, cheap Créole restaurants, not very clean.

Kourou *p1629*

$$$ Le Bistrot du Lac, Hotel Mercure Ariatel, T328900. Named chef, Dominique Pirou, has one of the best tables in Guyane, serving French Creole dishes like Grouper in wild mushroom sauce and Tiger prawns in citrus. The hotel's Le Ti-Gourmet (**$$$-$$**) serves upmarket snacks.
$$$-$$ Le P'tit Café, 11 Place Monnerville, T228168. A good value set lunch and a respectable à la carte menu.
$$ Le Karting, Zone Portuaire de Pariacabo (at the entrance to Kourou), T320539 (closed Sat-Sun). Excellent lunch set meal with a big choice of starters and mains. Evening BBQ Tue and Fri.
$ Cheap Chinese (also takeaway), eg: **Chinatown**, 66 rue Duchesne, T321769. Recommended.
    Many vans sell sandwiches filled with Créole food.
Le Glacier des 2 Lacs, 68 Ave des 2 Lacs, T321210. Ice cream, cakes, teas, very good.

St-Laurent du Maroni *p1630*

$$$ La Goelette, Balaté Plage, 2.5 km from St-Laurent, T342897. Closed Sun evening and Mon. In a converted fishing boat on the river, serving fish and game. Nice atmosphere in the evenings.
$$$ Tipic Kreol's, corner of rues Tourtet and Thiers (next to Star Hotel), T340983. Excellent restaurant/bar, créole menu, popular for lunch, good service.
$$ Le Mambari, 7 rue Rousseau, T343590. Pizzas and light French food served in a large, upmarket *palapa*. Open until late.
$ Many cheap Chinese restaurants.

Bars and clubs

Cayenne *p1627, map p1628*
Acropolys, Route de Cabassou, 3 km from town, T319781. Club music, Wed-Sat, huge dance floor.

Bar des Palmistes, Place des Palmistes. Good spot for cocktails and people-watching, opposite the Place des Palmistes.

Kourou *p1629*
Clibertown, rue Guynemer, L'Anse, T694-404042, see Facebook; at the entrance to Kourou overlooking the lake. The most popular in town by far.

Shopping

Cayenne *p1627, map p1628*
Bookshops Librairie Guyanaise Médiastore, 20-22 rue Louis Blanc, place Schoelcher.

What to do

Cayenne *p1627, map p1628*
Look under Rechercher les professionnels on www.tourisme-guyane.com for listings of local tour operators. Tours to the interior start at about US$200 pp per day. Pick-ups from the airport and accommodation in Cayenne for a night or 2 are usually part of the package. Full details on the company websites, some in English.
JAL-Voyages, 26 Av Gen de Gaulle, T316820, www.jal-voyages.com. Range of tours on the Mahury, Mana, Approuague rivers, on a houseboat on the Kaw marshes (US$94, very good accommodation, food and birdwatching) and Devil's Island, little English spoken. Recommended.
Takari Tour Amazonie, 21 Blvd Jubelin, T311960, www.takaritour.com. Long-established company, recommended for tours to the interior.
Thomas Cook, 2 Place du Marché, T255636, tcookguyane@orange.fr. Flights, changes Thomas Cook TCs, English spoken.

Kourou *p1629*
Guyanespace Voyages, A Hector Berlioz, T223101, guyanespace@wanadoo.fr.

Transport

Cayenne *p1627, map p1628*
Air Cayenne-Rochambeau Airport (T353882/89) 16 km from Cayenne, 20 mins by taxi, and 67 km from Kourou (US$60-80). *Cambio*

changes US$ and Brazilian reais, Cirrus and Visa Plus ATMs for withdrawing Euros. Only taxis (US$25 day, US$30 night, you can bargain or share). Cheapest route to town is taxi to Matoury US$10, then bus to centre US$2. Cheapest return to airport is by collective taxi from corner of Av de la Liberté and rue Malouet to Matoury (10 km) for US$2.40, then hitch or walk.

Bus Regular local services run by SMTC, Place du Marché, US$1.50 (ticket office 2682 route de la Madeleine, T302100, www.smtc-guyane.fr) Mon-Fri 0800-1200, 1500-1700). Interurban terminal at corner of rue Molé and Av de la Liberté. For bus schedules see www.cg973.fr/-Transport-interurbain-. To **St-Laurent du Maroni**, take a Line 6 bus direct, 3¼ hrs, US$41, or Line 8 via Kourou and **Iracoubo** US$ 34, 2 a day. **Roura**, US$6.55, and **Kaw**, US$15, Mon-Fri (Roura-Kaw US$8.55). **Régina** Line 9, 8 a day, 6 on Sun, US$27, 1½ hrs, to **St-Georges del' Oyapock** US$41 from Cayenne, US$13.75 from Régina. Take a cab to the bus stop. **Shared taxis** (collectifs) From the *gare routière* by the Canal Laussat early morning (Kourou US$20, St Laurent US$60). Other taxis at the stand on Place des Palmistes, corner of Av Gen de Gaulle and Molé.

Kourou *p1629*
Taxi US$10, Lopez T320560, Gilles 1320307, Kourou 1321444.
Bus To **Cayenne**, leaves place Monseigneur A Marie, Line 8 bus, US$11. Line 7 to St-Laurent du Maroni, 4 a day, 2 on Sun, US$34.
Shared taxis To Cayenne 0600, 0630, 0700, 1330, US$20. Taxi to Cayenne or airport, US$60 (US$85 at night). To St-Laurent du Maroni US$55 by *taxi collectif* (irregular) or minibus from Shell station.

Iles du Salut *p1629*
Boat Sailing boats and motorboats go from Kourou to the islands: **Iles du Salut** sailing catamaran, 98 passengers, from Ponton des Boulourous in Kourou, T320995, at 0830, return at 1630, US$57 return, 1 hr each way (book in advance). The 28-passenger *Royal Ti'Punch* (same price, same jetty, same phone) leaves at 0800, returns 1600. Motorboats are the 99-passenger *Ti Royal* (same price) and the *Angelina* (T320995 for reservations). The 12-seater *St Joseph* sails between Ile Royale

and Ile Saint-Joseph, weather permitting, for US$7. Tickets may be obtained direct or from agencies in Cayenne or Kourou. Some offer transport from Cayenne, US$20 extra. No sailings between Ile Royale and Ile du Diable. See www.ilesdusalut.com for all sailings.

St-Laurent du Maroni *p1630*
Air Service with Air Guyane from Cayenne, Mon, Wed, Fri, Sun, US$120.
Bus To **Cayenne** Lines 6 and 8 as above.
Minibuses meet the ferry from Suriname, leaving when full from rue du Port, 3 hrs (not until 1830/1900), US$50. Ask the minibus to pick up your luggage from your hotel. If none direct change in Iracoubo. To **Mana** 4 daily, 2 on Sun, US$11.
Shared taxis To Cayenne, 8 people, 3½ hrs, and to Kourou, US$55 (ask someone to call one for you).
Freight pirogues Sometimes take passengers inland along the Maroni River, but they can be dangerous as they tend to be overladen, often with dubious captains. Better to fly to **Maripasoula** (US$118) and return on a pirogue as they are empty going down river. Alternatively, groups can hire a *pirogue* for about US$200 a day.

Border with Suriname *p1630*
Boat Vehicle and passenger ferry to **Albina** 2-4 crossings a day, 30 mins. Passengers US$5.75 one way, car US$47, motorbike US$21 one way, payable only in euros. Speedboats US$6.75.
Minibuses and taxis Transport to/from Paramaribo meets the Albina ferry.

South to Brazil: Cacao *p1631*
Minibus From Cayenne, Mon-Fri 0725, 1600, return Mon-Fri 0600, 1725, US$20.

Saül *p1631*
Air Service with Air Guyane from Cayenne, daily except Sat, US$97. Try airport even if flight full. By *pirogue* from Mana up Mana River, 9-12 days, then 1 day's walk to Saül, or from St-Laurent via Maripa-soula along Moroni and Inini rivers, 15 days and 1 day's walk to Saül, expensive. Air Guyane also flies from Cayenne to **Maripasoula**, daily, US$163.

St-Georges de l'Oyapock *p1631*

Minibuses To **Cayenne**, price and schedule as above, or change in Régina. Taxi to Cayenne, US$72. Buses to **Macapá** leave late afternoon, 10 hrs; book when you arrive in Oiapoque (Brazilian side).

⊙ Directory

Cayenne *p1627, map p1628*

Airline offices Air Caraïbes, Rochambeau airport, T0820-835835, www.aircaraibes.com, flies to Paris, Pointe-à-Pitre, Fort-de-France, Port-au-Prince, Saint-Martin and Dominican Republic. **Air France**, T0820-820820, www.air france.com. **Air Guyane**, Rochambeau airport, T293630, www.airguyane.com. **Embassies and consulates** Brazilian, 444 chemin St Antoine, T296010, cg.caiena@ itamaraty.gov.br. Suriname, 3 Ave L Héder, T282160, cg.sme. cay@wanadoo.fr, Mon-Fri 0900-1200. English spoken, visa takes 2 hrs, proof of travel out of Venezuela or Guyana. For US and Canada, apply to embassies in Paramaribo.

Contents

Falkland Islands/Islas Malvinas

At a glance

⏱ **Time required** 1-2 weeks.
☀ **Best time** Oct-Apr.
✖ **When not to go** Outside wildlife breeding seasons.

Planning your trip

Where to go in the Falklands/Malvinas

These remote South Atlantic outposts, where there are more penguins than people, are the only part of South America where the British monarch's head appears on the stamps. Windswept they may be, but the islands are a haven for wildlife and a paradise for those who wish to see it: albatross nest in the tussac grass, sea lions breed on the beaches and dolphins cruise off the coast. About 640 km (400 miles) east of the South American mainland, the Falklands Islands/Islas Malvinas are made up of two large islands and over 748 smaller ones. The islands' remoteness adds to the charm of being able to see elephant seals, dolphins, whales, albatross, cormorants, geese and, above all, penguins at close range. Based on 2010 census figures from Falklands Conservation, there are about 400,000 breeding pairs of five species of penguin (king, magellanic, gentoo, rockhopper, macaroni) in the Islands. This compares with a human population of just 2931 (according to the 2012 census). The capital, Stanley, is a small, modern town, with reminders of its seafaring past in the hulks of sailing ships in the Harbour. To visit the camp, as the land outside Stanley is known, 4WD vehicles make tours and you can fly to farming and island outposts for warm hospitality, huge skies and unparalleled nature watching.

In accordance with the practice suggested by the UN, we are calling the islands by both their English and Spanish names.

Best time to visit the Falklands/Malvinas

Best months to visit are October to April; some places to stay are only open in these months. This is the best time for most wildlife watching, too; see below. The islands are in the same latitude south as London is north. The climate is cool and oceanic, dominated by persistent westerly winds which average 16 knots. Long periods of calm are rare except in winter. Though not always inclement, weather is very changeable but temperatures vary relatively little. At Stanley, the capital, the mean temperature in summer (January/February) is 15.4°C, but temperatures frequently exceed this on the islands. In winter (June/July/August) 4.9°C. Stanley's annual rainfall of about 600 mm is slightly higher than London's. In the drier camp, outside Stanley, summer drought sometimes threatens local water supplies. A dusting of snow may occur at any time of the year. Always wear water and windproof clothing; wear good boots and a peaked hat to protect the eyes from rain or hail. Sunblock is essential.

Best time for wildlife For wildlife enthusiasts, especially ornithologists, the islands are an exceptional destination. King and gentoo penguins are present the year round. Rockhoppers are on land October to May, magellanic penguins September to April. The black-browed albatross breeding season is September to May. Elephant seals are ashore September-December; adults haul out late January/early February to moult for 25 days. Sea lions can be seen December-March. Sei whales usually arrive in Falkland waters in January/February and remain till May/June. Other whale species may be seen in the same period, but not usually close to shore. Orcas are best seen on Sea Lion Island when sea lion pups are going to sea. Commerson's and Peale's dolphins are present the year round, but the former are less evident in winter. The most common birds are upland geese; other frequently seen geese are kelp and ruddy-headed. The flightless steamer duck (logger duck) can be seen in many places, as can Falkland skuas, southern giant petrels, Patagonian crested duck, speckled teal, grebes, shags, gulls and shorebirds such as magellanic and blackish oystercatchers. The rarest bird of prey in the world, the striated caracara (Johnny Rook) can easily be seen in several places (Sea Lion, Carcass, Weddell). Smaller birds that are easy to see include the striking long-tailed meadowlark, dark-faced ground tyrant, Falkland thrush and pipit. In islands unaffected by introduced predators you'll see the friendly tussacbird and the rarer Cobb's wren. There are many other common bird species (227 recorded in total) and, for botanists, plants of interest. For wildlife calendar, booklists, checklists and reports: **Falklands Conservation** ⓘ *Jubilee Villas, corner of Philomel St and Ross Rd (access from Philomel St), Stanley, T22247 (14 East Hatley, Sandy, Bedfordshire SG19 3JA, UK, T01767-650639), www.falklandsconservation.com, Mon-Fri 0800-1200, 1300-1630, also sells clothing, badges and books.*

Getting to the Falklands/Malvinas

Air Flights from Santiago to Mount Pleasant, via Punta Arenas with **LAN** ⓘ *www.lan.com*, leave every Saturday and, once a month, stop at Río Gallegos in Argentina on both the outward and return flight. April 2014 fares: return from Santiago £643, Punta Arenas £533. Fares include Chilean airport taxes, but exclude Falklands embarkation tax: see Tax, page 1642. See www.falklandislands.com, which is updated regularly with latest fare information. Passengers should confirm flights 24 hours before departure. For more information on LAN flights, see the website (tickets may be bought online), or contact **International Tours and Travel Ltd** ⓘ *1 Dean St, Stanley, FIQQ 1ZZ, T+500-22041, se.itt@horizon.co.fk or visit www.falklandislands.travel.*

The UK Ministry of Defence operates an airbridge to the Falkland Islands twice a week (at the time of writing). They depart from RAF Brize Norton, Oxfordshire, and take about 20 hours including a refuelling stop in Ascension Island at the half way point (passengers can stop over if they wish). Fares: £2,222 return, group rates £1,999 for six or more; premium economy return: £3,850. Falkland Islands residents and contract workers receive a discount. The £22 exit tax is included in MoD flights. Confirm luggage allowance in advance and confirm the flight itself

24 hours before departure. For the latest MoD schedules and prices, contact the **Falkland Islands Company Travel Department** ① *T27633, fic.travel@horizon.co.fk*, or the **Falkland Islands Government Office** ① *T020-7222 2542, travel@falklands.gov.fk*, in London.

Airport information Mount Pleasant airport (code MPN) is 35 miles from Stanley. **Falkland Islands Tours and Travel** ① *Lookout Industrial Estate, Stanley, T21775, fitt@horizon. co.fk*, book online at www.falklandtravel.com, and **Penguin Travel** (Falkland Islands Company) ① *Crozier Place, Stanley, T27630, www.the-falkland-islands-co.com*, transport passengers and luggage to and from the capital for £17.50 single. Departing passengers should make reservations. See also Taxis, page 1652.➤➤ *For airport departure tax, see Tax, page 1642.*

Boat Cruise ships en route to/from South America, South Georgia and the Antarctic are also a popular way to visit the Islands. Vessels typically visit between October and April each year. Passengers usually land for tours of Stanley and nearby sites, pub lunch, farmhouse tea, and call at outlying islands, such as Saunders, Carcass, West Point, New and Sea Lion Islands. Further details of companies that include the Falklands/Malvinas in their itineraries can be found on **www.falklandislands.com** and at **www.iaato.org**. Alternatively you can contact local port agents **Sulivan Shipping** ① *T22626, www.sulivanshipping.com*, and **Penguin Travel** (Falkland Islands Company) ① *T27630, www.penguintravel-falklands.com*.

Length of stay As flights from Chile only go once a week, stays in multiples of seven days are the only option. In one week you can see Stanley and a couple of nearby attractions, plus a bit of West Falkland or one or two islands, but the inter-island flight schedules will determine how much time you can stay on the outer islands. In two weeks you can see much more of East and West Falkland and several outer islands. The airbridge from the UK offers more flexibility. Cruise ship passengers do not disembark for more than a few hours.

Transport in the Falklands/Malvinas

The only paved roads are in Stanley. Outside Stanley, the major road to the airport at **Mount Pleasant** is part paved, but requires great care. Other roads are single track, of consolidated earth and stone. None should be driven at speed; look out for sheep or cattle, cattle grids and sudden hills, bends and junctions. On East and West Falkland, roads connect most of the settlements. Elsewhere, tracks require 4WD or quad bikes. Off-road driving in the boggy terrain is a skill not easily learned by short-term visitors and is not permitted by any car-hire company. Tour guides and drivers can be engaged to visit many places on the islands and taxis are readily available for journeys around Stanley. The Jetty Visitor Centre (see Tourist information below) and the Museum (see page 1643) stock a range of maps, 1:50,000 map (£4), A3 road maps (£3.50). ➤➤ *See also Transport, page 1651.*

Note Over 30,000 landmines were laid by Argentine forces during the 1982 Conflict, of which almost 20,000 are still on the ground. Of the 111 landmine fields across the Falklands, 75% are located around Stanley. The fields are fenced, mapped and clearly marked and no civilian injuries or casualties have ever occurred. Should you spot anything unusual, make a note of its location and contact the Bomb Disposal Unit, T53939, or the police (see below). Please note, it is illegal to enter any area designated as minefield, or to remove minefield signage.

Where to stay and eat in the Falklands/Malvinas ➜ *See Essentials for our hotel and restaurant price guide.*

Pre-booked accommodation is obligatory before being allowed entry. Advance reservation when travelling around is essential. Almost all places to stay in Stanley and on the islands have comfortable rooms, power showers, towels, heating, honesty bars (where they have a bar) and, when not self-catering, good local food. For self-catering you can get supplies, including ready-prepared meals, in Stanley. Stores in Port Howard and Fox Bay on West Falkland open only at specified times, usually three days a week. See www.falklandislands.com.

On the outer islands bear in mind that the wildlife you will see is inextricably linked with where you stay because there is no choice of lodging. Fortunately this is not a hardship.

Essentials A-Z

Accident and emergency
The emergency telephone number is T999. Stanley Police Station T28100. Hospital Reception T28000.

Activities in the Falklands/Malvinas
Fishing for trout and mullet (South Atlantic cod) is superb. The main rivers are the Chartres and Warrah on West Falkland, and the San Carlos on East Falkland. The season for trout is officially 1 Sep to 30 Apr, but 2 distinct runs: Sep to mid-Nov and Mar/Apr. A licence is not required for rod and line fishing; catch and release is encouraged. Mullet may be caught at any time. Falkland Islands zebra trout are protected and must never be caught. Most land is privately owned, including rivers and streams, always get permission from the owner, some of whom charge a fee. Ask travel agents about regulations for specific areas and changes to daily bag limits. **Golf**: Stanley's 18-hole course costs £5 a round; no club rental so you need to find clubs to borrow. **Hiking and touring**: See Stanley Tour operators.

See also 'Best time for wildlife' above for tips on watching birds and other animals.

Electricity
220/240 volts at 50 cycles. Rectangular, 3-blade plug as in the UK.

Festivals in the Falklands/Malvinas Public holidays
1 Jan (New Year's Day), **Good Friday** (Easter), 21 Apr (Queen's birthday), 14 Jun (Liberation Day), **1st Mon in Oct** (Peat Cutting Monday), 8 Dec (Battle Day). The main social event is the Christmas period, 24 Dec (Christmas Eve), 25 Dec (Christmas Day), 26 Dec (Boxing Day and start of Stanley sports meeting), to 2-4 Jan. Everything closes except places to stay and eat and food shops/supermarkets.

Internet
Public internet access is improving. Sure South Atlantic (Ross Rd), who has the monopoly, gives access, as does the **Jetty Visitor Centre** (Ross Rd) and many hotels and guest houses in Stanley. Internet costs £1 for 10 mins. Broadband access is now standard, island-wide and the number of Wi-Fi hotspots increasing. Purchase a card to use Wi-Fi (see Telephone, below).

Money → US$1 = £0.60; €1 = £0.81 (May 2014). The Falklands pound (£) is on a par with sterling. Local notes and coins. UK notes and coins are also legal tender. Falklands pounds cannot be used outside the islands. Currency from Ascension Island, where the airbridge stops, is not accepted. Foreign currency (including US dollars and euros) and traveller's cheques (TCs – US$ or £ only) can be changed at the **Standard Chartered Bank**, Ross Rd, Stanley, www.sc. com/fk/. All establishments accept pounds sterling, many also accept US dollars and some accept euros (check when booking). Credit cards and TCs are only accepted by a handful of operators. Visitors are advised to take cash where possible, or discuss alternative payment methods with operators prior to arrival. There are no ATMs on the Islands.

Opening hours
Banks: 0830-1500 (Wed 0900-1500). **Offices**, including government departments: Mon-Fri 0800-1200, 1300-1630 (the 1200-1300 lunch hour in Stanley is religiously observed).

Post

There is direct and dependable air mail service from the UK. Heavy parcels come by sea from the UK every month. A weekly DHL service is operated via **Falkland Islands Chamber of Commerce**, PO Box 378, Stanley, T22264, commerce@horizon. co.fk. Inter-island mail service is carried out by FIGAS, Falkland Island Government Air Service.

Tax

Airport tax Departing passengers by air on LAN pay an embarkation tax of £22, payable in Falklands pounds, sterling or dollars (there are no exchange facilities or ATM at Mt Pleasant).

Telephone → *International phone code = +500.*
Sure South Atlantic, Ross Rd, Stanley, www.sure.co.fk, Mon-Fri 0800-1630, is the telecommunications provider. The islands' telephone system has direct dialling worldwide. Sure has roaming agreements with a limited number of overseas networks. Check the Sure website for the latest information on mobile phone coverage and usage, Wi-Fi hotspots and weather forecasts. Those not covered can purchase a local SIM card from Sure or at the West Store Entertainment Centre for £30, including £10 credit, valid 60 days. Mobile phone coverage extends to most parts of East Falkland, some parts of West Falkland and may spread further. Handsets will generally need to be network unlocked to accept the local SIM card. Phones cannot be rented, but cheap Samsung and Nokias are on sale. Mobile help line T131. Phone cards for international calls and Wi-Fi access cost from £5-10 at Sure, Kelper Stores, the Jetty Centre; calls to UK £0.90 per min, to rest of world £1 (offpeak £0.60 and £0.80 respectively).

Time

GMT -4 in winter (May-Aug), -3 in summer. Some people use 'Camp time' (as opposed to 'Stanley time'), which does not use daylight saving.

Tourist information

The **Falkland Islands Tourist Board**, PO Box 618, Stanley, F1QQ 1ZZ, T22215, runs the **Jetty Visitor Centre**, at the head of the Public Jetty, Ross Rd,

Stanley, open daily during summer 1000-1700, from 0900 Sat, 1000-1600 Sun, winter Thu-Sun 1100-1430, www.falklandislands.com. This has information on accommodation, tours, transport and activities, and offers internet, postal service and public telephones and access cards. It has a free visitor guide in English, Spanish and German. It sells local books, DVDs, crafts, stamps, first day covers and postcards. The **Falkland Islands Government London Office** (FIGO), Falkland House, 14 Broadway, Westminster, London SW1H 0BH, T020-7222 2542, www. falklands.gov.fk, will answer enquiries.

Useful websites

www.falklandnews.com Falkland Islands News Network.
http://en.mercopress.com Merco Press, South Atlantic News Agency.
www.penguin-news.com *Penguin News* weekly newspaper.

Visas and immigration

All travellers must have full, current passports to visit the Islands. Citizens of Britain, North America, Mercosur, Chile, Japan, South Korea and most Commonwealth countries and the EU are permitted to visit the islands without a visa, as are holders of UN and International Committee of the Red Cross passports. Other nationals should apply for a visa from the Travel Coordinator at **Falkland House** in London (see above), the Immigration Department in Stanley (see Useful addresses, 1652 1735), or a British Embassy or Consulate. Visas cost £20. All visitors require a visitor permit, provided for the length of time you need on arrival. You must have a return ticket and sign a declaration that you have accommodation, sufficient funds to cover the cost of your stay and evidence of medical insurance (including cover for aero-medical evacuation). Work permits are not available. Do not stay beyond the valid period of your permit or visa without applying to the Immigration Office for an extension.

Weights and measures

Metric. On East Falkland miles are used; on West Falkland kilometres.

Stanley and around

The capital, Stanley, on East Falkland, is the major population centre. Its residents live mostly in houses painted white, many of which have brightly-coloured corrugated iron roofs. Surrounded by rolling moorland, Stanley fronts the enclosed Harbour. The outer harbour of Port William is larger but less protected.

Places in and around Stanley

The **Museum** ① *Britannia House, Ross Rd West, T27428, www.falklands-museum.com, Mon-Fri 0930-1200, 1330-1600 (in summer, no lunch break), Sat and Sun 1400-1600, £3 (under 16 free),* merits a visit. The manager is Mrs Leona Roberts. The ticket includes a visit to Cartmell Cottage (by prior appointment, £1 to visit separately), one of the original pioneer houses on Pioneer Row, whose interior reflects life in the late 19th century and the 1940s. Note, the Museum was due to move In 2014 to new premises in the Dockyard.

You can walk the length of the harbour front, from the wreck of the *Jhelum* (built in 1839 for the East India Company, now beginning to collapse) in the west, to the iron-built *Lady Elizabeth* at the far eastern end of the harbour (228 ft, with three masts still standing). A Maritime History Trail along the front has interpretive panels; a book describing the Stanley wrecks is sold at the museum. On the way you will pass Government House, the Anglican Cathedral (most southerly in the world, built in 1892) with a whalebone arch outside, several monuments commemorating the naval battle of 1914, the Royal Marines and the 1982 liberation. Among the latter are the Memorial Wood, off Ross Road East, where every tree is named for a British and Falkland casualty. Where Ross Road East turns inland, you can carry on east along the coastal path, past the FIPASS floating harbour and around the head of the bay to *Lady Elizabeth*. At low tide you can walk out to her. Follow the bay round and eventually you will come to **Gypsy Cove**, four miles, two hours walk each way from centre (10 minutes by car). It features a colony of magellanic penguins, black-crowned night herons and other shorebirds. Occasionally visitors can also spot orca, elephant seals, sea lions and variable hawks. Observe minefield fences which prevent close inspection of the penguins (Yorke Bay, where the Argentine forces landed In 1982, is off limits).

The **public library**, T27147, in the Community School, has a good selection of books on travel and flora/fauna. During the December holidays, the sports meeting at the race course attracts visitors from all over the Islands. The equally popular West and East Falkland sports, at the end of the shearing season in February/March rotate among the settlements.

Outside Stanley

Cape Pembroke lighthouse sits on the end of Cape Pembroke Peninsula and is open to the general public (an access key is available from the Museum for a £5 charge). The Cape itself offers great day walking, with plenty of wildlife watching: dolphins, whales and numerous bird species. There is also an impressive memorial to the crew of the *Atlantic Conveyor*, a supply ship sunk by Argentine forces during the 1982 Conflict.

Sparrow Cove, **Kidney Cove**, and adjacent areas, only a short distance from Stanley by boat, are good areas to see four species of penguin and other wildlife. Tours are the only way to get there.

East Falkland

On **Long Island**, 20 miles from Stanley, is a 22,000-acre sheep farm belonging to a sixth generation Falkland Island family, whose traditional way of life, with a dairy and using sheep dogs and island-bred horses to gather sheep, is popular with cruise passengers and day trippers.

Stanley

There are excellent hikes along the beach and shore of Berkeley Sound, with rockhopper, gentoo and magellanic penguins.

Volunteer Point, on the peninsula north of Berkeley Sound, is a **wildlife sanctuary** ① *1 Nov to Apr, £15, included in tour price, £7.50 for each extra day. Good toilets at the site.* In recent years the wardens have offered lodging at £55 pp per night and camping opportunities Nov-Apr (T32000, or ask the landowner, Jan Cheek, T21372, jancheek@horizon.co.fk). Check with the Falkland Islands Tourist Board, T22281, for up-to-date information. On cruise ship days many vehicles go in convoy to Volunteer Point. It contains the only substantial nesting colony of king penguins outside of South Georgia (the most accessible site in the world). Gentoo and magellanic penguins, geese and other birds can be photographed easily, but keep a respectful distance. Sea lions and dolphins may be seen from the beautiful beach. It is on a private farm approximately 2½ to three hours drive from Stanley: one hour to Johnson's Harbour on a good road (37 miles), then 1½ to two hours over the camp (12 miles, no permanent track). Visits are arranged with local guides who know the route and understand local conditions.

Bertha's Beach, a 10-minute drive from Mount Pleasant Military Complex, is popular for its beautiful white sand beach with abundant bird life. Dolphins often come close to shore as they hunt in the shallows. To get through the locked gate to the beach, ask for the key from the farm manager at Fitzroy (T33384).

Beyond Mount Pleasant, the road divides, one branch turning north to San Carlos (see below), the other going to **Darwin** (1½ hours from Stanley), a little community with the skeletal remains of the *Vicar of Bray* (last survivor of the California Gold Rush fleet). Another old iron ship, the *Garland*, can be seen up the bay. Just before Darwin is the Argentine cemetery for those killed in the 1982 conflict, and just beyond, the larger settlement of **Goose Green**. The **Galley Café** is usually open 0900-2100; contact Trudi Lee (T32228) about self-catering

Where to stay
1 Bennett House B&B
2 Kay's B&B
3 Lafone Guest
4 Lookout Lodge
5 Malvina House
6 Shorty's Motel & Diner
7 Susana Binnie's
8 The Paddock B&B
9 Waterfront Hotel
   & Kitchen.café

Restaurants
1 Bittersweet
2 Bread Shop
3 Deano's
4 Globe
5 Jacs
6 Lighthouse Seaman's
   Centre
7 Michelle's Café
8 Stanley Arms
9 Tasty Treat
10 The Narrows
11 Victory
12 Wirebird
13 Woodbine Takeaway

in a three-bedroom house, open all year. From Goose Green a road runs to the ferry dock for West Falkland at New Haven (35 minutes). Apart from a gentoo colony, there is nothing at the ramp. **North Arm** is one of four settlements in the flat expanses of Lafonia, a three-hour drive from Stanley. Bull Point is the most southerly point of East Falkland; its wildlife includes 32 species of birds. Also near North Arm are Tweeds Valley, 53 species of flora and fauna, and Fanny Cove, with some great rock formations. These locations can only be reached off-road so a tour guide is necessary.

The road to **San Carlos** is hilly, with lovely views of higher mountains inland and the bays and inlets of Falkland Sound to the west. San Carlos (two hours from Stanley) is a picturesque waterside settlement and an excellent base for exploring upper East Falkland. Here is the English cemetery from the 1982 conflict and a museum covering the conflict and the local way of life. See **Kingsford Valley Farm** below for lodging. Nearby is the ruin of the Ajax Bay Refrigeration plant, used as the British forces base in 1982. Tours from Kingsford Valley Farm, or contact the owners, Gerald and Doreen Dixon, Wreck Point, T31115. The new road network makes it possible to head north to Port San Carlos, Elephant Beach Farm (see Where to stay for both) and Cape Dolphin. At **Elephant Beach Farm**, a 1½-hour drive from Stanley, gentoo penguins and many other bird species, sea lions, Commerson's and Peale's dolphins can be seen. The private property offers fishing for Falkland mullet in the tidal lagoon, and fossicking among the whale skeletons on the coast. **Cape Dolphin**, at the northernmost tip of East Falkland, includes three species of penguin, storm petrels, sea lions, the occasional whale and large numbers of ducks and birds on Swan Pond. Allow a full day to make the most of the cape; camping is also possible by prior arrangement. You can return to Stanley on the North Camp road via Teal Inlet and Estancia.

Outer islands Bleaker Island, hardly bleak, has a wonderful coastline with white sandy beaches and sheltered coves. Bird species include rockhoppers, magellanic and gentoo penguins, waterfowl, ruddy-headed geese, Falkland skuas and an impressive imperial shag colony. The area north of the settlement was declared a National Nature Reserve in 1999. One of the key features of the island is Big Pond, where you can spot Chiloe wigeon, silvery and white tufted grebes, speckled and silver teal and occasionally the rare flying steamer duck. The Island is owned and run by Phyll and Mike Rendell (T32491, mrendell@horizon.co.fk; see www.bleakerisland.com); see Cobb's Cottage and Cassard House, below.

Sea Lion Island in the southeast, 35 minutes' flight from Stanley, is a wildlife sanctuary, a delightful place to explore and relax. The lodge (see Where to stay), open in the austral summer, is within easy reach of the wildlife. Many southern sea lions breed on the beaches; it is also the largest breeding ground for southern elephant seals in the islands. Up to three pods of orca whales are resident around the island and can be seen cruising the shore in search of elephant seal and sea lion pups risking their first swim (summer months). The island also has magnificent bird life: gentoo, magellanic and rockhopper penguins, giant petrels (known locally as stinkers), imperial shag, flightless steamer and other ducks, black-crowned night herons, tussacbird, oystercatcher (magellanic and blackish) and striated caracara. Also on the island is the *HMS Sheffield* memorial.

West Falkland

On West Falkland, there live fewer than 100 adults. **Port Howard** is one of the principle settlements, a neat, picturesque place, and the largest privately owned farm in the Islands with approximately 42,000 sheep and 1000 cattle running across 200,000 acres. The original settlement is 3.5 km south and Bold Cove is the site of the first British landing by Captain John Strong in 1690. It's an excellent base to explore West Falkland (see Port Howard Lodge, below). Activities include trout fishing; 4WD tours to wildlife and flora, 1982 war relics, fossil beds; hiking to Mount Maria.

About an hour west of Port Howard a road branches northwest to **Hill Cove** settlement, another 30 minutes drive. You can visit the largest forest in the Falklands (an experiment in shelter planting). Further west is **Crooked Inlet** farm at Roy Cove. Joy and Danny Donnelly run the sheep farm and still use horses for sheep work (see Where to stay). The settlement is very photogenic, particularly in late spring when the yellow gorse blooms; commanding views over King George Bay to Rabbit, Hammock and Middle Islands.

In the centre of West Falkland is **Little Chartres Farm** (see Where to stay, below), which is an ideal base for trips to all points and for trout fishing. West is a beautiful road to Dunnose Head, a centre for Falklands wool craft (ask if staying locally) and Shallow Harbour, passing the Narrows and Town Point nature reserves. To the south is Fox Bay, the largest settlement; half is government-owned, half, Fox Bay West, is private. The road passes Hawksnest Ponds, where swans may be seen, in a region of 2000 lakes and ponds. **Port Stephens** is a spectacular piece of country at the southwestern tip of West Falkland. Accessible by road and air, the area has rugged headlands, home to rockhopper and gentoo penguins, as well as many unusual geological formations at Indian Village and breathtaking coastal scenery. ►► *See Where to stay, below.*

Outer islands **Pebble Island** is the third largest offshore island and is thought to be named after the unusual pebbles found on its beaches. Pebble is home to more than 40 species including gentoo, rockhopper, macaroni and magellanic penguins, imperial shag, waterfowl, and black-necked swans. Sea lions can also be found on the coast. The eastern half of Pebble Island contains large ponds and wetlands with many waterfowl and wading birds. See Where to stay, below.

Saunders Island, besides a representative sample of wildlife, contains the ruins of the 18th-century British outpost at Port Egmont. There is a small group of king penguins at the Neck, a three-hour walk, 45 minutes by Land Rover from the settlement. Gentoo, magellanic, rockhoppers, imperial shag and black-browed albatross can also be seen here, as well as dolphins wave surfing and whales spouting. A further 1½ to two hours' walk goes to the point where elephant seals can be seen. At the Rookery, on the north coast, you can see rockhoppers, imperial shag and black-browed albatross. Another good place is the bay just north of the

Falkland Islands/Islas Malvinas

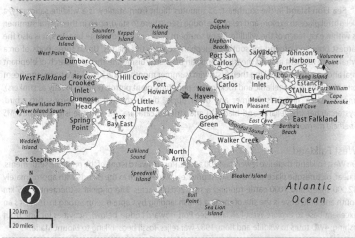

Settlement with many gentoo and magellanic penguins. There are many other wildlife sites on this large island.

Carcass Island, taking its name from *HMS Carcass* which visited in the late 18th century, is west of Saunders. One of the most spectacular and attractive islands for wildlife and scenery, species include striated caracara, gentoo and magellanic penguins, gulls, geese and elephant seals. The island also has great examples of tussac grass. The island is cat, rat and mice free, allowing small bird species such as Cobb's wren to flourish. A recommended trip from Carcass is on Michael Clark's boat, *Condor*, to West Point Island, to see a large colony of black-browed albatross and rockhoppers. Dolphins may be seen on the way. Crossing is about an hour each way, £231 for the boat.

Weddell Island, in the southwest, named after explorer James Weddell, is the third largest island of the archipelago, a little bigger than Malta but with only two residents (and then only October to March). It has self-catering accommodation, an interesting history and, despite what some books suggest, plenty of wildlife. This includes magellanic and gentoo rookeries, sea lions in the tussac grass, imperial shags, shore birds, geese and introduced species such as Patagonian grey fox and nine reindeer. In the surrounding waters are albatross, Peale's and Commerson's dolphins. Good hikes straight out of the settlement.

New Island, at the extreme west edge of the archipelago, is a nature reserve owned by the **New Island Conservation Trust** (www.falklandswildlife.com). The aim of the project, begun in 1973 by Ian Strange, is to ensure that the island operates as a reserve in perpetuity. There is a fully equipped field station in the settlement for scientific studies. The **Captain Charles Barnard Memorial Museum and Visitor Centre** is visited by passengers on cruise vessels. Contact can be made through the Trust's website.

◉ Stanley and around listings

For hotel and restaurant price codes, and other relevant information, see Essentials.

◐ Where to stay

Stanley *p1643, map p1644*

$$$$ Malvina House, 3 Ross Rd, T21355, www.malvinahousehotel.com. Very good, spacious executive and standard rooms, full board available, power showers, hot drinks, central heating, TV, nice restaurant (open to all daily except Sun evening – guests only), bar, sauna/jacuzzi, laundry, Wi-Fi broadband for guests.

$$$ pp Lafone House, T22891, arlette@horizon.co.fk. Owned and run by Arlette Betts, luxury B&B, good harbour views, evening meals on request, very good food.

$$$ The Paddock B&B, 38 Davis St, T21466, www.waterfronthotel.co.fk. Central B&B with spacious rooms, welcoming, internet hotspot, parking, money exchange, laundry, Spanish spoken.

$$$ Waterfront Hotel, 36 Ross Rd, T21462, www.waterfronthotel.co.fk. Comfortable rooms, most en suite, TV, modern facilities, welcoming, internet and Wi-Fi, exercise machine with great view, Waterfront kitchen café offers lunch and dinner, very helpful.

$$ pp Bennett House B&B, 14 Allardyce St, T21191, celiastewart@horizon.co.fk. Owned and run by Celia Stewart. Central, excellent home baking and breakfast, 3 rooms, 2 en suite, good views, welcoming. Camping £10 pp per night.

$$ pp Kay's B&B, 14 Drury St, T21071, kay@horizon.co.fk. Excellent value and rightly popular, shared bath, dinner, lunch and packed lunch available £8, good food. Camping £5 per tent per night, £4 for breakfast and shower in house for campers.

$$ pp Lookout Lodge, Keil Canal Rd, contact Caroline Cotter, T22834, lookoutlodge@cwimail.fk. Bunkhouse-style accommodation, single rooms, shared facilities. Price is bed only, meals extra, breakfast only or full board.

$$ pp **Shorty's Motel**, Snake Hill, T22861, www.shortys-diner.com. All rooms en suite, laundry, internet, next to **Shorty's Diner**.

$$ pp **Susana Binnie's**,3 Brandon Rd, T21051. Central B&B with 1 double room, shared bath, Spanish spoken.

East Falkland *p1643*

$$$$-$$$ pp **Sea Lion Lodge**, Sea Lion Island, T32004, sealion_lodge @horizon.co.fk or www.sealionisland.com. 1 Sep-31 Mar, high season prices Nov-end Feb, full board, some single rooms with shared bath, purpose-built, picture windows, comfortable, central heating, good bathrooms, good home cooking, packed lunches available for when you wish to go wildlife-watching, orientation tours, internet.

$$$ **Darwin Lodge**, Fiona and Graham Didlick, T31313, www.darwin-house.com. Comfortable accommodation in 6 en suite rooms, suitable for families, living room, conservatory, good walking in the area, tours can be arranged. Open daily for lunch and dinner on request.

$$$ pp **Race Point Farm**, Port San Carlos, John and Michelle Jones, T41012, jhjones@horizon. co.fk. Full board or B&B at the Big House, TV, DVD, laundry facilities, internet and telephone; also comfortable, child-friendly self-catering cottage, meals available on request. Gentoo rookeries, magellanic and rockhopper penguins at Fanning Head and Rookery Sands Beach. Good walks and excellent trout fishing on the San Carlos river. Guided 4WD tours available, also horse riding and quad biking.

$$ pp **Elephant Beach Farm**, contact John and Mandy MacLeod, T41030. Self-catering cottage sleeps up to 8, traditional Falkland Island meals by request. DVD, video, games etc, gas stove only for cooking. Tours of north coastline. Open all year.

$$ pp **Kingsford Valley Farm**, San Carlos settlement, East Falkland, T32233, kvf@horizon. co.fk. On a working farm owned and run by kind hosts Terence and Sheila McPhee. 2 comfortable self-catering cottages, one with 2-bedrooms, the other with 3, both include cots, children very welcome. Central heating, 24-hr power, TV, video, CD, enclosed gardens, meals on request,

close to trout fishing, San Carlos cemetery and museum. Terence McPhee offers wildlife and general tours on East Falkland.

Cobbs Cottage, Bleaker Island, T21084 (Stanley), T32491/32494 (Bleaker Island), mrendell@horizon.co.fk (Mike and Phyl Rendell). 30-min flight south from Stanley, finished to a high standard throughout. Good wildlife. Also on Bleaker Island is **Cassard House** (**$$$-$$**), 4 en suite bedrooms, well-equipped kitchen, local decorations, high standards.

North Arm: 4 houses have self-catering, fully equipped, sleeping 5-10 people. The farm has a small shop for everyday items and frozen food, but take your own supplies. En route to Bull Point are 4 houses for rent, basic self-catering with peat stove and diesel generator (they are off-road, so a guide is needed). Take sleeping bags/bedding, towels and food. A taste of old-style Falkland life. Contact Steven Dickson and Emma Reid, T32080.

West Falkland *p1645*

$$$ pp **Little Chartres Farm**, West Falkland, F1ZZ 1QQ, T42215, email through www. falklandislands.com. Operated by Lesley and Jim Woodward, who are very accommodating, 2 comfortable rooms with bath between, plus 1 smaller room, self-catering only. Excellent trout fishing, hiking, wildlife watching and tours available. They also have **Top Dip Shanty** (**$** pp) right on the Chartres estuary for more rustic lodging, self-catering, fuel and water provided.

$$$ **Pebble Island Lodge**, Pebble Island, T41093, www.pebblelodge.com. This well-appointed lodge is run by Jacqui Jennings and Allan White. En suite rooms, central heating, full board, lounge, TV and DVD, phone and internet and island tours.

$$$ **Port Howard Farm Cottages**, Myles and Critta Lee, T41096, phfarm@horizon.co.fk. 3 houses at Port Howard, good starting point for touring West Falkland, cosy, good views, price is for self-catering.

$$$ pp **Port Howard Lodge**, Port Howard, West Falkland, T42187, porthowardlodge@ horizon.co.fk. Sue Lowe and Wayne Brewer. Prices seasonal, full board, all rooms en suite, central heating, honesty bar, excellent food. Wayne takes Land Rover tours (£30 for general interest) and will drive to first class trout fishing spots, rod hire. Has a small war museum, and the chance to see the workings of a traditional large sheep station.

$$$-$$ pp Carcass Island, T41106, lorraine@horizon.co.fk. Owned and run by Rob and Lorraine McGill. Rooms are in the main farmhouse, full board, excellent food, honesty bar, lounge with TV and DVDs, gardens, open summer only. Tours to sites on the island, perfect combination of hospitality and wildlife.

$$$-$$ pp Saunders Island, Suzan and David Pole-Evans, T41298, saunders@cwimail.fk. At the settlement are 2 self-catering cottages, for 10 and 6, **$$** pp per night. Self-catering Portakabin sleeping 8 at the Neck, with 24-hr power, heating, cooker (**$$$** pp, transport £50). Self-catering **Rookery Inn**, within walking distance of the Rookery, is modern, sleeps 4, 24-hr power, kitchen/diner, shower room, heating (**$$$** pp, transport £20). Towels provided in all lodgings. A shop at the settlement sells supplies. Near the Rookery cottage is a backpackers Portakabin for 2, bunks, cooker, long-drop toilet. Camping £10 pp per night.

Crooked Inlet Farm, Roy Cove, Danny and Joy Donnelly, T41102, j.d.donnelly@horizon.co.fk. A comfortable self-catering property. Also trout fishing, riding Falklands' style or guided 4WD tours of the area.

Port Stephens, T42307, par@horizon.co.fk. Self-catering accommodation in 2-bedroom house, with kitchen/diner, central heating, DVDs, in the settlement, a great base to explore the region, very helpful hosts, Peter and Ann Robertson, who run the farm here.

Shallow Bay Self Catering, 25 mins from Hill Cove settlement, contact Paul and Davina Peck, T41007, psb@horizon.co.fk or daepeck@horizon. Accommodation in the original stone home. Meals available on request.

Weddell Island, T42398, m.j.beaton@horizon. co.fk. Martin and Jane Beaton, 3 self-catering cottages, sleeping 2, 4 and 8 people, £145-200 per night, well-equipped with kitchen and microwave, washing machine, central heating,

DVD, free wildlife tour if you stay 2 nights, lovely setting on an inlet. Open Oct-Mar.

🍴 Restaurants

Stanley *p1643, map p1644*
Most places are casual; for fine dining, **Malvina House**. At Sun lunchtime the pubs do food, but in the evening **The Narrows**, **Shorty's Diner** and **Stanley Arms** are open. Besides local lamb, beef and fish (kingclip, toothfish, squid), try diddle-dee berry jam and, in the autumn, tea-berry buns.

Bittersweet, 58 John St. Closed Sun. Offers speciality coffees and chocolates handmade in the Islands. Café or take-away a chocolate treat.

The Bread Shop, corner Dean St and Fitzroy Rd. Mon-Sat. Wide range of breads, sandwiches, snacks, all freshly baked.

Deano's Bar, 40 John St, T21296. Serving fresh local fish and chips and 100% home-made local beef burgers as part of their extensive menu; also popular are Saint Helenian curries and fishcakes. Beers and spirits from around the world, big screen satellite TV as well as pool and darts.

Jacs, John St, T21143, knipe@horizon.co.fk. Mon-Sat 0900-1600 except Wed 0900-1400. Small, pleasant café with home-made cakes and sandwiches, great value.

Lighthouse Seaman's Centre, over the bridge next to FIPASS ('The Seaman's Mission'). Open all day for seamen, 1000-1600 for general public, Sun 1200-1600. Tea/coffee, snacks. Internet and Wi-Fi hotspot.

Michelle's Café, Philomel St. Mon-Thu 0800-1600, Fri 0800-0030, Sat 1030-0030. Home baking a speciality, all food cooked to order, eat in, take-away or delivery.

The Narrows Bar, 39 Ross Rd East at Kelper Stores, T22272. Daily 1200-1330, 1800-2000, Sun carvery 1200-1330, book in advance. Daily specials, good pub food. Has Wi-Fi hotspot and internet centre, sells phone and Wi-Fi cards.

Shorty's, Snake Hill. Open 6 days (seasonal), Mon-Fri 0900-2030, Sat-Sun till 2000. Good fast food, lots of choice, eat in or take-away, good value.

Stanley Arms Bar, 1 John Biscoe Rd, T22259. Good pub food, daily specials.

Tasty Treat, Philomel St, T22500. Hot and cold food, including fish and chips, Chilean and Saint Helenian dishes, breads, pastries, eat in or take-away.

Victory Bar, 1A Philomel St, T21199. Daily for specials, lunch, evening meals Mon, Tue and Thu 1600-2030. Traditional English pub food, children welcome.

Waterfront Kitchen Café, 36 Ross Rd at Waterfront B&B. Open Tue-Sat for lunch with daily specials and dinner à la carte. Full bar and wine service.

West Store Café, FIC West Store, Ross Rd. Closed Sun. Choice of coffees and other hot drinks, freshly made sandwiches, panini, pastries and cakes.

Wirebird, 46 John St. Open daily for St Helenian and other dishes including a Sunday carvery.

Woodbine Takeaway, 29 Fitzroy Rd, T21102. Closed Sun and Mon. Fish and chips and pizza.

🍷 Bars and clubs

Stanley p1643, map p1644
The pubs include: **Beagle Bar**, at Malvina House Hotel, **Deano's Bar**, see above, **Narrows Bar**, see above, **Stanley Arms**, see above, **The Globe**, Philomel St, near the public jetty, open daily, bar menu, different entertainment every night; **The Trough**, Airport Rd, BYO, check Penguin News for opening dates (usually Sat night), live music and funky chill-out lounge, and **The Victory**, see above.

🛍 Shopping

Stanley p1643, map p1644
In Stanley there are a number of gift shops, **Capstan Gift Shop**, opposite West Store, wide selection, including books. **Harbour View**, Ross Rd. **The Pink Shop**, John St, for arts and crafts, books, pictures. **The Pod**, next to the Jetty Visitors Centre. **Studio 52**, Ross Rd, stocks a range of locally designed gifts including artwork and jewellery. The **Boathouse** sells great underwater photography. Good souvenirs from the **Falklands Conservation Shop**, Jubilee Villas, Philomel St.

For groceries: **FIC West Store** (Ross Rd), Mon-Fri 0830-2000, Sat 0900-1800, Sun 0900-1700, also has an entertainment centre, **Kelper Family Stores** (39 Ross Rd East, 3 other locations), Mon-Fri 0730-2100, Sat-Sun 0900-2100, **Stanley Growers Garden Centre** (Stanley Airport Rd), **Seafish Chandlery and Supermarket** (Stanley Airport Rd), **Stanley Services** (Stanley Airport Rd).

⚙ What to do

Stanley p1643, map p1644
Tour operators
See www.falklandislands.com for details of overseas operators.

Beauchene Fishing Company Ltd, T22260, http://beauchenefishing.com. Sightseeing tours, excursions, evening cruises and day charters out of Stanley on the *B-Mar* launch are all available.

Falkland Islands Company-Flights, T27633, fic.travel@horizon.co.fk. Local booking agent for the MoD charter flight via Brize Norton, UK.

Falkland Island Holidays (a division of Stanley Services Limited), PO Box 117 Stanley), T22622, www.falklandislandsholidays.com. Offer tailor-made itineraries for birding, wildlife, photography, battle, fishing and walking interests. Also organize internal flights, accommodation, tours/excursions and transfers.

Golden Fleece Expedition Cruises, contact: Jerome Poncet, T42316, www.goldenfleeceexp. co.fk. Specializes in film-work, scientific surveys or tourism around the Falklands, South Georgia or Antarctica.

International Tours and Travel Ltd, 1 Dean St, PO Box 408, T22041, www.falklandislands.travel. Handle inbound tourist bookings, book FIGAS flights, arrange tours, etc, and are the Falkland Island agents for **LAN**. Recommended.

Penguin Travel, Crozier Place, T27630, www. penguintravel-falklands.com. Wildlife tours on foot, or by 4WD, Stanley tours, battlesite tours.

South Atlantic Marine Services, Carol and Dave Eynon, PO Box 140, T21145, dceynon@ horizon.co.fk. Overland tours, boat trips, safaris and have a dive centre with deck recompression chamber (PADI courses).

Guided tours

Comprehensive list at www.falklandislands.com.
Adventure Falklands, PO Box 223, T21383, pwatts@horizon.co.fk. Patrick Watts offers tours of battlefield and other historical sights, ornithological trips and more. Recommended.
Charley's Tours, T51588, rowland@cwimail.fk. Charlene Rowland offers flexible, customized itineraries including wildlife, battlefields, fishing and general Falklands life. Trips to West Falkland and camping can also be arranged.
Cross Country Expeditions, T21494, scm@ horizon.co.fk. Wildlife and fishing tours, airport transfers and lodging with Sam Miller.
Discovery Falklands, T21027, T51027 (mob), discovery@horizon.co.fk. Tony Smith specializes in battlefield tours, wildlife, general interest, historical, also provides logistical support and guidance for visiting TV Crews and media personnel. Highly recommended.
France's Falkland Forays, 7 Snake Hill, T21624, france@cwimail.fk. Graham France's city, golf, penguin watching and historical tours.
Kidney Cove Safari Tours, T31001, allowe@ horizon.co.fk. Adrian and Lisa Lowe, offer overland 4WD tours to see 4 species of penguins at Kidney Cove, close to Stanley.
Top Town Tours, T21443 or 52834, jay.bee@ horizon.co.fk. John Birmingham offers Stanley tours, Goose Green, New Haven, Darwin, San Carlos, Port San Carlos; also bicycle hire.
Ubique Tours, T52285, frank.vera@horizon. co.fk. Frank Leyland takes wildlife, battlefield and historical interest tours around Stanley and East Falkland.

⊖ Transport

Falkland Islands/Islas Malvinas

Air The Falkland Islands Government Air Service (FIGAS, T27219, reservations@figas. gov.fk) flies to farm settlements and settled outer islands on a shuttle service that varies daily according to demand. To book a seat, contact FIGAS with as much notice as possible; daily schedules are announced the previous afternoon on local radio and by fax and telephone. One-way airfares in 2014 cost up to £150 one way, but fares depend on distance (Visa and MasterCard accepted); luggage limit 20 kg. Services daily Oct-end Mar, 6 days a week otherwise; no flights on 1 Jan, Good Friday, 21 Apr, 14 Jun, 25 Dec. Services and fares are continually under review. FIGAS tickets are also available from **Stanley Services Travel** and **International Tours and Travel Ltd**, see What to do, above. Flights leave from Stanley Airport, 3 miles east of town on the Cape Pembroke peninsula. 10-15 mins by car.

Car hire Falklands 4X4, Crozier Place, Stanley, T27663, www.falklands4x4.com. Rents Land Rover Defender, Discovery and Freelander. **Falklands Islands Tours and Travel**, Lookout Industrial Estate, Stanley, T21775, www. falklandtravel.com. **Stanley Services Ltd**, Travel Division, Airport Rd, Stanley, T22622, info@ falklandislandsholidays.com. Rents Mitsubishi Pajeros. Rented vehicles may not be taken off road and may not travel on the ferry between East and West Falkland. On West Falkland Port Howard Farm may rent a vehicle if one is spare.

Ferry A drive-on, drive-off ferry sails between New Haven (East) and Port Howard (West) on a variable schedule, usually twice a day. The same vessel, *MV Concordia Bay*, runs twice-monthly cargo services to the outer islands and when on this duty does not operate as a car ferry. For schedules T22300, www.workboat.co.fk; office is on Philomel St, behind the Globe Tavern. If the wind is wrong it will not sail. Cars £50 (must be booked in advance), foot passengers £20, child under 16 £10, under 5 £5.
Taxis Fares within Stanley, £3, to Stanley airport £6. **Town Taxis**, T52900. Other taxis operate at selected hours; ask in town for contact details.

❶ Directory

Stanley *p1643, map p1644*
Medical services Hospitals: Stanley has an excellent hospital, King Edward Memorial Hospital (KEMH), dental service included. T28000. **Post offices** On Ross Rd, open Mon-Fri 0800-1630. **Philatelic Bureau** (they sell stamps from South Georgia and the Antarctic Territories), T27159, www.falklandstamps.com. **Telephone** See Sure South Atlantic, page 1642. Directory enquiries T181. Operator Services T20800. **Useful addresses** Immigration: Customs and Immigration Department, 3 H Jones Rd, T27340, admin@customs.gov.fk.

Beyond the Falklands

South Georgia

South Georgia, in the Southern Ocean in latitudes 54° to 55° south and longitude 36° to 38° west, has an area of 3755 sq km, but no permanent residents. There are two British Antarctic Survey stations, King Edward Point and Bird Island, and a marine officer at the former is the government's representative who has responsibility for local administration (go@gov.gs). His duties include those of Harbour Master, Customs and Immigration Officer, Fisheries Officer and Postmaster. Visitors normally arrive by cruise ship from Ushuaia, Punta Arenas or Stanley. Some also come by chartered yachts. Intending visitors, who are not part of tour groups, must submit a request through the **Commissioner** ⓘ *Government House, Stanley, Falkland Islands, South Atlantic, T+500-28200, info@gov.gs*. There is a landing fee of £110 for up to three days. See also Information for Visitors on the **South Georgia website**: www.sgisland.gs.

South Georgia is a largely chain of high (almost 3000 m), snow-covered glaciated mountains. At King Edward Point, near sea level, snow falls on an average of nearly 200 days annually, but the coastal area is free from snow and partially covered by vegetation in summer. This is the port of entry and is 1 km from Grytviken. Wildlife consists of most of the same species found in the Falkland Islands/Islas Malvinas, but in much larger numbers, especially penguins, albatross, and seals. In 2011 a Habitat Restoration Programme to eliminate all non-native mammals began which was primarily to eradicate rodents. The first phase of eradicating reindeer, introduced in 1909, was completed in 2013. Points of interest are the abandoned whaling stations (although asbestos and other hazards restrict access to all except Grytviken), the little white whalers' church, and several shipwrecks. The explorer, Sir Ernest Shackleton lies in the whalers' cemetery at Grytviken. A **South Georgia Museum** (www.sght.org) has been established where the whaling station is now decontaminated and rearranged as a display featuring amazing steam industrial archaeology. Inside is a display of artefacts, photographs and other items about the old Antarctic whaling and sealing industries with descriptions of the history of the island, including the Argentine invasion in 1982, and much about the wildlife. The museum has a shop which sells a good selection of books and many other items. The island issues distinctive stamps which are sold by the Post Office and museum. There is a South Georgia Association.

The **South Sandwich Islands**, some 500 km southeast of South Georgia, are uninhabited but administered by the same government as South Georgia. Although very rarely visited they are a spectacular chain of 11 volcanoes, several of which are active.

The Antarctic

Antarctica, the fifth largest continent, is 99.8% covered with perpetual ice. Although access is difficult, the annual number of tourists now exceeds the number of personnel on government research programmes. It is well known for its extraordinary scenery, wildlife, scientific stations, and historic sites. The weather may be spectacularly severe, thus visits are confined to the brief summer. Presently 25 countries operate 60 scientific stations (45 remain open during winter). A wintering population of about 1200 lives in a continent larger than Europe. The **Antarctic Heritage Trust**, www.heritage-antarctica.org, with headquarters in New Zealand and Britain, and some other organizations maintain several historic huts where organized groups are admitted. Many current research stations allow visitors for a couple of hours during a conducted tour. Of the historic huts, the one at **Port Lockroy**, established in 1944 and now a museum, has become the most-visited site. The historic huts used by Scott, Shackleton, Mawson, and Borchgrevink during the 'heroic age' of exploration are on the Australian and New Zealand side of Antarctica thus very distant from South America.

Information There are many of specialist and general books about Antarctica, but the current best single source of information remains *Antarctica: Great Stories from the Frozen Continent* by Reader's Digest (first published Sydney 1985, with several later editions). General information may be found at the **Scott Polar Research Institute**, www.spri.cam.ac.uk, including links to other sites. Also useful is the website of **International Association of Antarctica Tour Operators**, **IAATO** (see below). Most national operators also have sites dedicated to their work but often with much more information. The **Council of Managers of National Antarctic Programmes**, in Christchurch, is the best source for these details: www.comnap.aq.

Governance of Antarctica is principally through the Antarctic Treaty (1959) signed by all countries operating there (50 countries were parties to the Treaty in 2014, these represent over 80% of the Earth's population). Most visitors will be affected by several provisions of the Treaty, in particular those of the Environmental Protocol of 1991. These are principally for protection of wildlife (prohibiting harmful interference with animals or plants, especially when breeding), respecting protected areas and scientific research, alerting visitors to the need to be safe and prepared for rapid deterioration of weather, and keeping the environment pristine. Details will be found on www.iaato.org/visitor-guidelines. Seven countries have territorial claims over parts of Antarctica and three of these overlap (Antártida Argentina, British Antarctic Territory, and Territorio Chileno Antártico); the Treaty has neutralized these with provision of free access to citizens of contracting states. Some display of sovereignty is legitimate and many stations operate a Post Office where philatelic items and various souvenirs are sold.

The region south of South America is the most accessible part of the Antarctic, therefore over half the scientific stations are there or on adjacent islands. Coincidentally it is one of the most spectacular areas with many mountains, glaciers and fjords closely approachable by sea. Four ports are used: Stanley, Punta Arenas, Ushuaia and Puerto Williams, the last two are major bases for yachts. The **South Shetland Islands** and **Antarctic Peninsula** are most frequently visited, but ships also reach the **South Orkney Islands** and many call at South Georgia at the beginning or end of a voyage. Most vessels are booked well in advance by luxury class passengers but sometimes late opportunistic vacancies may be secured by local agencies. Ships carrying 45-280 tourists land passengers at several sites during a couple of week's voyage. Some much larger vessels also visit; these generally do not land passengers but merely cruise around the coasts. During the 2013-2014 austral summer about 37,405 visitors reached Antarctica, of whom 25,526 landed on the continent.

Voyages from South America and the Falkland Islands/Islas Malvinas involve at least two days each way crossing the Drake Passage where sea conditions may be very uncomfortable. No guarantee of landings, views or wildlife is possible and delays due to storms are not exceptional. Conversely, on a brilliant day, some of the most spectacular sights and wildlife anywhere may be seen. Visitors should be well prepared for adverse conditions with warm clothing, windproof and waterproof clothing, and good boots for wet landings. Weather and state of the sea can change quickly without warning.

In 1991 the **International Association of Antarctica Tour Operators** was formed ⓘ *320 Thames St, suite 264, Newport, Rhode Island, 02840, USA, T+1-401-841 9700, www. iaato.org.* It represents the majority of companies and can provide details of most offering Antarctic voyages. Many vessels have a principal contractor and a number of other companies bring smaller groups, thus it is advantageous to contact the principal. **Antarctic Logistics and Expeditions (ALE)/Adventure Network International (ANI)** ⓘ *3478 South Main St, Salt Lake City, Utah 84115, USA, T+1-801-266 4876, info@antarctic-logistics.com,* provides flights to Antarctica from Punta Arenas where there is a **local office** ⓘ *RAAL, B O'Higgins 568, Punta Arenas, Chile, Oct-Jan.* Wheeled aircraft fly as far as an inland summer camp at Union Glacier (79·75°S, 83·50°W), the only land-based tourist facility, whence ski-aircraft proceed to the South Pole, vicinity of Mount Vinson (4892 m, Antarctica's highest peak), and elsewhere. Other flights go from Punta Arenas and Cape Town. 'Flightseeing' is made by Qantas from Australia aboard aircraft which do not land but spend about four hours over the continent (and about the same getting there and back).

Some private yachts carry passengers; enquire at Ushuaia or Puerto Williams, or the other ports listed. Travelling with the Argentine, Chilean, French or Russian supply ships may sometimes be arranged at departure ports. These are much cheaper than cruise ships but have limited itineraries as their principal object is to supply stations.

Index → Entries in bold refer to maps

Advertisers' index

Acknowledgements

The *South American Handbook* moves into its 10th decade with assistance, once again, from many people. Those who have helped with the individual chapters are acknowledged below, but Ben Box is also grateful to the following for their invaluable support during the preparation of this edition: above all, the team at Footprint who put the book together: Patrick, Felicity, Nicola, Emma, Kevin, Angus, Liz and Kirsty; also Sarah Cameron, Liz Harper, William H Coleman Inc and, last but not least, Chris Pickard, Claire Antell and the Latin American Travel Association committee who so kindly recognized the *Handbook*'s coverage of Latin America in their 2014 awards.

For specific chapter information, our warmest thanks go to the following contributors:

In Argentina, Nicolás Kugler, who updated the Buenos Aires and the Cuyo sections; Chris Wallace, who updated Córdoba and Northwest Argentina; Anna Maria Espsäter, who updated Patagonia. Anna Maria would like to thank Nicolás Kugler in Buenos Aires; **Turismo Ushuaia**: Alejandro and Frances from **Galeazzi-Basily B&B**, Ushuaia; Daniel from Tzion B&B, Ushuaia.

In Bolivia: Robert and Daisy Kunstaetter, authors of *Footprint Bolivia*, who would like to thank: Saúl Arias, Jill Benton, Carlos Fiorillo, Petra Huber, Alistair Matthew, Beatriz Michel, Fabiola Mitru, Bastian Müller, Derren Paterson, Tandil Rivera, Mariana Sánchez, Martin Stratker and Remy van den Berg.

For Brazil we are most grateful to Alex and Gardênia Robinson, authors of *Footprint Brazil*.

For the Chile chapter, Anna Maria Espsäter updated Patagonia. Anna Maria would like to thank **Australis Expedition Cruises**, with special thanks to Leandro S Bruno and Marcelo Gallo; Gareth Lyons and Simon Heyes of **Senderos**; the staff at **Tierra Patagonia**. Chris Wallace updated the northern Lake District and the area around San Pedro de Atacama. Christian Martínez of Copenhagen (Denmark) updated the Easter Island section. See also below for Ben Box's personal thanks.

Colombia: many thanks to Jo Williams, who updated the chapter.

In Ecuador: Robert and Daisy Kunstaetter updated the chapter and would like to thank:

Jeaneth Barrionuevo, Jean Brown, Harry Jonitz, Patrick and Baiba Morrow, Popkje van der Ploeg, Michael Resch, Peter Schramm, Iván Suárez and RhoAnn Wallace.

The Paraguay chapter was updated by Geoffrey Groesbeck, author of the latest edition of Footprint's *Paraguay Focus Guide*.

Peru was updated jointly by Ben Box (see below) and Robert and Daisy Kunstaetter, who wish to thank: Chris Benway, Alberto and Ayde Cafferata, Rob Dover and Ricardo Espinosa. We should also like to thank Fiona Cameron and Armando Polanco, who updated the Cuzco section this year. Christian Martínez also provided much useful information for the Lima gastronomy section and other details on Peru. In addition, we are most grateful to John and Julia Forrest (UK), Michael White (UK), Jaime García Heras (USA), and Heather MacBrayne and Aaron Zarate of **Discover South America**.

Uruguay was updated by Anna Maria Espsäter, author of the latest edition of *Footprint Colombia* and *Uruguay Focus Guide*. Anna Maria wishes to thank: Diana Valente; Steven Chew; Inés Gamarra from **Branding Latin America**; Julia Parapugna from **VIK Retreats**; Paola Pirelli from **Lares Tours**; and Cecilia Ribó from **Posada Valizas**. In addition Anna Maria wishes to thank Bryony Addis-Jones and Caroline Maughan for support and inspiration, and all at Footprint.

Venezuela: warmest thanks to Richard Arghiris for updating the chapter in challenging circumstances. He would like to thank: in Caracas, Nelson Agelvis, Juan Carlos Ramírez and José Ernesto Bravo; in Santa Elena de Uairén, Francisco Alvarez and Roberto Marrero; in Mérida, Adelis Partida.

Guyana: once again we are grateful to Tony Thorne and Kenneth Shivdyal of **Wilderness Explorers** for updating the chapter.

In January and February 2014, Ben Box visited Lima and Chile. For their help and hospitality in Lima he would like to thank: Claudia Miranda (of **GHL Hoteles** and **Sonesta Collection, Peru**), Verónica Dupuy (**GHL**) and Ricardo Villanueva Wu (**Sonesta**); Miles Buesst (**Rainforest Cruises** and **Cricket Peru**); Mónica Moreno and staff at **Posada del Parque**; Carlos Jiménez of **The Andean Experience Co.** and the staff at **Hotel B**; Cecilia Kamiche; Maestro Máximo Laura and Sasha McInnes of **Puchka Perú**; Eduardo Arambarú (**Lima 27**); Joaquín de la Piedra (**Saqra**); Lic Arql Ignacio Alva Meneses of the **Proyecto arqueológico Ventarrón**; and Kieron Heath of **Proyectos Inca**.

In Santiago de Chile, Ben would like to thank Marilú Cerda of **Marilú's B&B**; in Valparaíso, Janak Jani of **Luna Sonrisa**; and in Viña del Mar, Adrian Turner. Ben would also like to thank Chris Rendell-Dunn and Tom Carroll at **Journey Latin America**.

Last but not least we should like to acknowledge the contributions from the travellers whose emails and letters have been used in part or in full this year: Daniel Albuquerque (Bra); Gwen von Bargen (Arg, Bol, Chi, Col, Ecu); Marieke Behrens, Germany (Per); Atli Bollason (Arg); Sarah Byttebier, Belgium (Arg); Amandine Canonne (Chi); Lucian Caspar (Per); F Jay Christian (Per); Peter Cleary (Arg, Bol); Paul Cripps, Peru (Chi); Keven Durand (Per); Axel Ebert, Switzerland (Per); Matt Elliott (Per); Michael Falk (Arg); Kate Follington (Col); Guy Geudens, Belgium (Arg, Chi, Par); Jochim Gockel, Germany (Per); Nigel Hawkes, UK (Bra, Par); Al Hill (Bol, Bra, Ecu, Per); Julia Hofer and Fortunato (Per); Graham House, UK (Chi); D Johnson (Bra); José Miguel (Chi); Kiran (Per); Patricia Laborie, France (Bol); Madeline Lamb (Arg); Wessel van Leeuwen, The Netherlands (Bra); Richard Leonardi, Nicaragua (Per); Herbert Levi, Argentina (Arg, Uru); Christoph Ley, Germany (Col); Lukas Rohrbach (Chi, Per); Asaf Manor (Per); Friedrich Martin, Germany (Chi); Tony and Marion Morrison, UK (Bol, Per); Lut de Naeyer, Belgium (Col); Flavia RF Neves (Per); Henrike Niebaum (Chi); Felice Pace, US (Bol); Chris Paine (Ecu); Joe Perri; Hilary Prowse (Bol, Per); Lukas Rohrbach (Chi, Per); Jost-Ullrich Schmidt, Germany (Chi); Hendrik Schulz, Germany (Arg); Natascha Scott-Stokes, Chile (Chi); Ella Smyth, UK (Per); Fábio Sombra, Brazil (Bra); John Thirtle, UK (Per); Henry Twinch (Chi); Laura Venturato, Italy (Col); Virgi (Col); Dorothea W, The Netherlands (Bra); Thomas van Walsem (Ven); Eliane Wiedmer (Per); Therese Wyder, Switzerland (Par).

Specialist contributors: Ashley Rawlings, Motorcycling; Hallam Murray, Cycling; Hilary Bradt, Hiking and trekking; Richard Robinson, Worldwide radio information.

Footprint Mini Atlas
South America

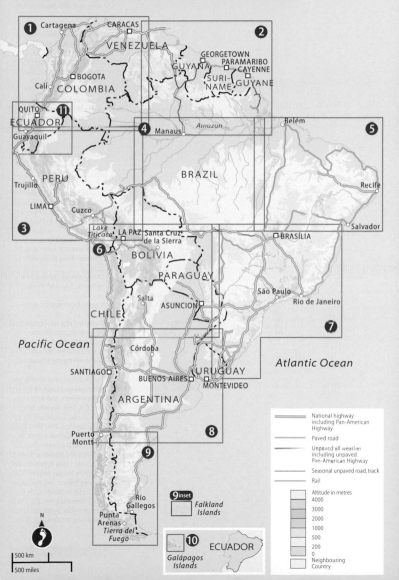

Cartagena · CARACAS · VENEZUELA

GEORGETOWN · PARAMARIBO · CAYENNE · GUYANA · SURI-NAME · GUYANE

Cali · BOGOTA · COLOMBIA

QUITO · ECUADOR · Guayaquil

Manaus · *Amazon* · Belém

BRAZIL

Recife

Trujillo · PERU

LIMA · Cuzco

Salvador

Lake Titicaca · LA PAZ · Santa Cruz de la Sierra · BRASÍLIA

BOLIVIA · PARAGUAY

Salta · ASUNCION

São Paulo · Rio de Janeiro

CHILE

Córdoba

Pacific Ocean

SANTIAGO · BUENOS AIRES · URUGUAY · MONTEVIDEO

Atlantic Ocean

ARGENTINA

Puerto Montt

Río Gallegos

Punta Arenas · *Tierra del Fuego*

9 inset · Falkland Islands

10 ECUADOR · *Galápagos Islands*

	National highway including Pan-American Highway
	Paved road
	Unpaved all weather including unpaved Pan-American Highway
	Seasonal unpaved road, track
	Rail

Altitude in metres
4000
3000
2000
1000
500
200
0
Neighbouring Country

N

500 km
500 miles

Map 1

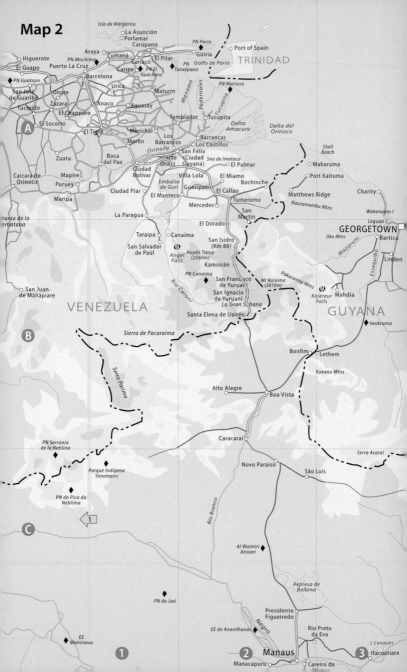

Map 2

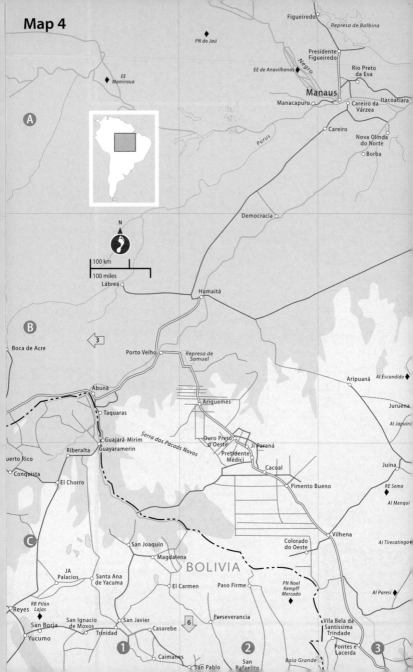

Map 5

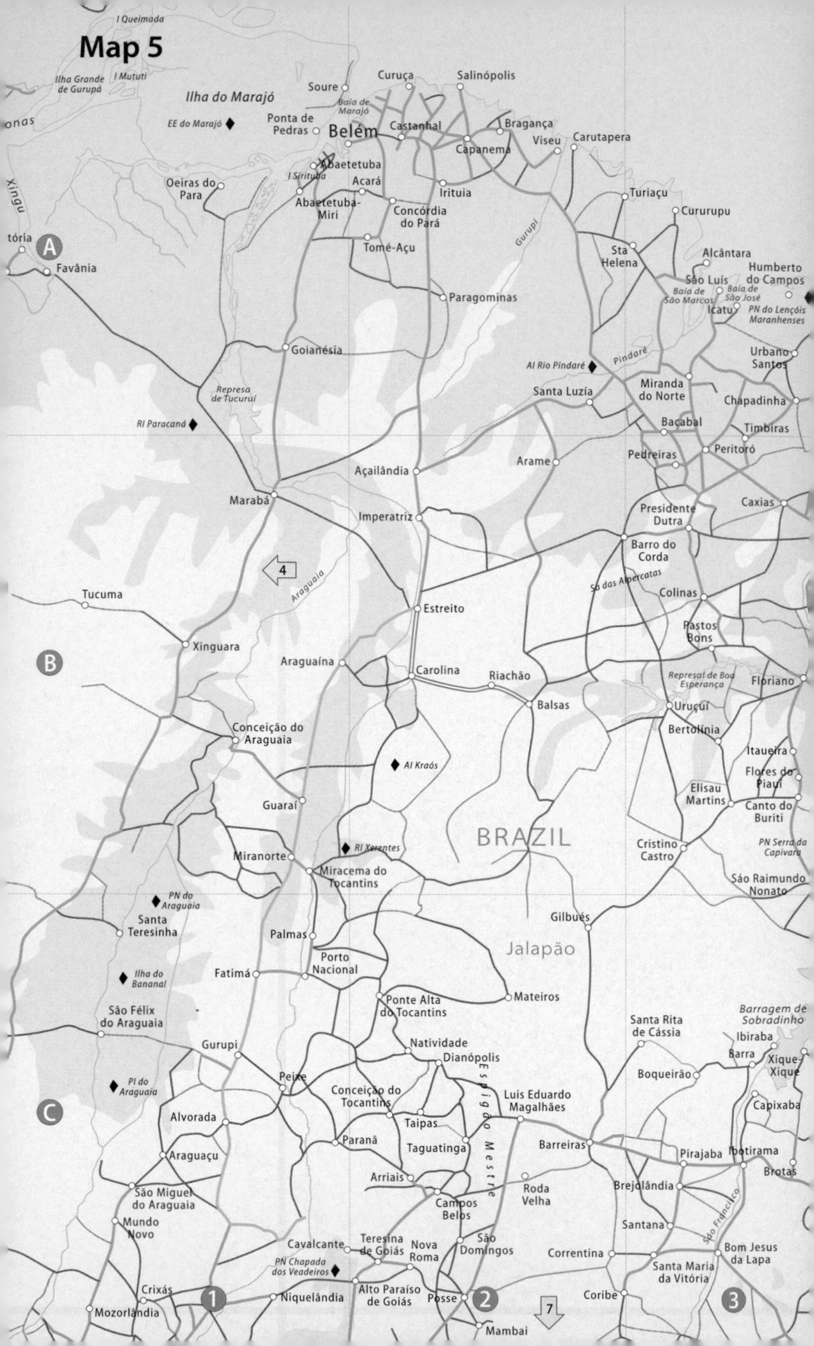

I Queimada

Ilha Grande de Gurupá · I Mututi

Ilha do Marajó

Soure · Curuçá · Salinópolis

Baía de Marajó

EE do Marajó ◆ · Ponta de Pedras · Belém · Castanhal · Bragança · Viseu · Carutapera

I Sirituba · Abaetetuba · Acará · Capanema · Turiaçu · Cururupu

Oeiras do Para · Abaetetuba-Miri · Irituia · Concórdia do Pará · Sta Helena · Alcântara · Humberto do Campos

tória · Favânia · Tomé-Açu · São Luís · Baía de São Marcos · Baía de São José · Icatu · PN do Lençóis Maranhenses

A

Paragominas · Gurupi · Pindaré · Urbano Santos

Goianésia · AI Rio Pindaré ◆ · Pindaré · Miranda do Norte · Chapadinha

Represa de Tucuruí · Santa Luzia · Bacabal · Timbiras

RI Paracaná ◆ · Pedreiras · Peritoró

Açailândia · Arame · Presidente Dutra · Caxias

Marabá · Imperatriz · Barro do Corda

Sa das Alpercatas · Colinas

Tucuma · Araguaia · 4 · Estreito · Pastos Bons

Xinguara · Araguaína · Carolina · Riachão · Represa de Boa Esperança · Floriano

B

Balsas · Uruçuí · Bertolínia

Conceição do Araguaia · Itaueira · Flores do Piauí

Guaraí · AI Kraós ◆ · Elisau Martins · Canto do Buriti

Miranorte · RI Xerentes · BRAZIL · Cristino Castro · PN Serra do Capivara

PN do Araguaia ◆ · Miracema do Tocantins · São Raimundo Nonato

Santa Teresinha · Palmas · Gilbués · Jalapão

Ilha do Bananal ◆ · Fatimá · Porto Nacional

São Félix do Araguaia · Ponte Alta do Tocantins · Mateiros · Santa Rita de Cássia · Barragem de Sobradinho

Gurupi · Natividade · Ibiraba · Barra · Xique-Xique

PI do Araguaia ◆ · Peixe · Dianópolis · Luis Eduardo Magalhães · Boqueirão

C

Alvorada · Conceição do Tocantins · Espigão Mestre · Capixaba

Araguaçu · Paranã · Taipas · Barreiras · Pirajaba · Ibotirama · Brotás

São Miguel do Araguaia · Taguatinga · Roda Velha · Brejolândia

Mundo Novo · Arraias · Santana

Cavalcante · Campos Belos · Correntina · São Francisco · Bom Jesus da Lapa

Crixás · Teresina de Goiás · Nova Roma · São Domingos · Santa Maria da Vitória

PN Chapada dos Veadeiros ◆ · Alto Paraíso de Goiás · Posse · Coribé

Mozorlândia · Niquelândia · Mambaí

1 · 2 · 7 · 3

Atlantic Ocean

N

100 km
100 miles

A

B

C

Barreirinhas
Tutóia
Parnaíba
Jericoacoara
Acaraú
Camocim
Parnaíba
Icaraí
Trairi
Paracuru
Brejo
Piracuruca
Tianguá
Itapipoca
PN de Sete Cidades
Sobral
PN de Ubajara
Caucaia
Fortaleza
Barras
Piripiri
Açude Araras
Sta Quitéria
Canindé
Parangaba
Messejana
Altos
Campo Maior
Poranga
Cascavel
Teresina
Tamboril
Chorozinho
Canoa Quebrada
Aracati
Beneditos
Crateús
Boa Viagem
Quixadá
Ibicuitaba
Grossos
Barro Duro
Alto Longá
Açude Banabuiú
Macau
Guamaré
São Pedro de Piauí
Minerilândia
Sobmupole
Jaguariburu
Mossoró
Touros
João Câmara
Várzea Grande
Parambu
Catarina
Acopiara
Apodi
Angicos
Riachuelo
Natal
Nazaré do Piauí
Pimenteiras
Iguatu
Açude Orós
Orós
Ico
Patu
Currais Novos
Tangará
Búzios
Oeiras
Picos
Campos Sales
Novo Oliinda
Alexandria
Sousa
Brejo da Cruz
Cuité
Tibau do Sul
Pipa
Araripina
Chapada do Araripe
Cajazeiros
FE de Crism
Arara
Guarabira
Itaínópolis
Juazeiro do Norte
Patos
Teixeira
Campina Grande
Juão Pessoa
Paulistana
Ouricuri
Salgueiro
Sumé
Boqueirão
Caraúbas
Itambé
PN da Serra da Capivara
Serra dos Irmãos
Serra Talhada
Floresta
Fazenda Nova
Igarassu
Isla de Itamaracá
Rajada
São Francisco
Arcoverde
Caruaru
Jaboatão
Olinda
Casa Nova
RB de Serra Negra
Pesquera
Vitória de Santo Antão
Recife
Muribeca dos Guararapes
Remanso
Sento Sé
Petrolina
Juazeiro
Petrolândia
Garanhuns
Porto de Galinhas
Amaniú
EE do Raso do Catarina
Paulo Afonso
RB da Pedra Talhada
Palmeira dos Índios
União dos Palmares
RB de Saltinho
Uauá
Canudos
Arapiraca
Maceió
Juçara
Senhor do Bonfim
Monte Santo
Euclides da Cunha
Cansanção
Carira
Traipu
Penedo
Marechal Deodoro
Irecê
Carnaíba
Tucano
Olindina
São Cristóvão
EE Foz de São Francisco
RB de Santa Isabel
Aracaju
Mundo Novo
Várzea de Poço
Serrinha
Estância
Barra de Estância
Indiaroba
Inhambupe
Lençóis
Itaberaba
Feira de Santana
Alagoinhas
Chapada Diamantina
Cachoeira
São Félix
Catu
Iramaia
San Antônio de Jesus
Camaçari
Praia do Forte
Itaparica
Salvador
Valença
Nazaré
Morro de São Paulo
Ilha de Tinharé

4
5
6

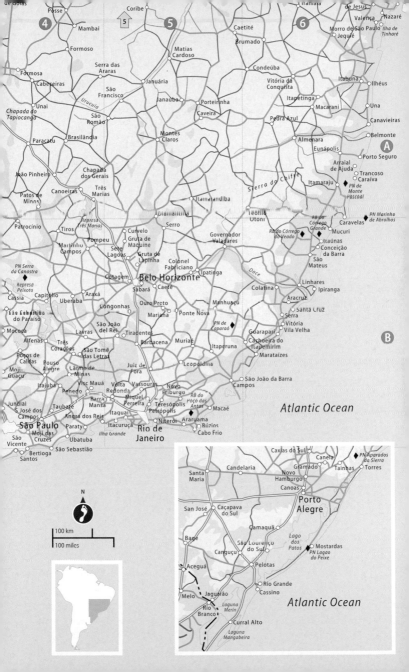

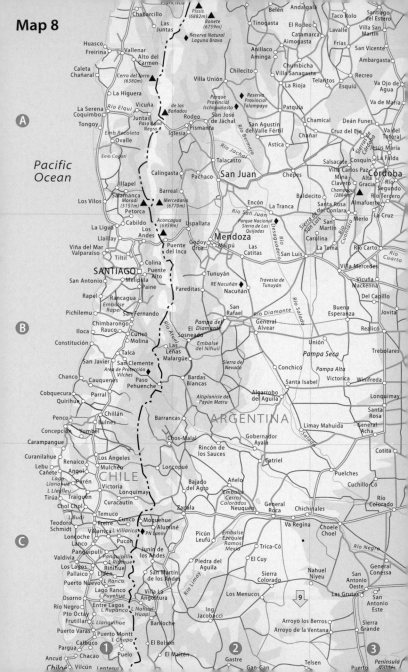

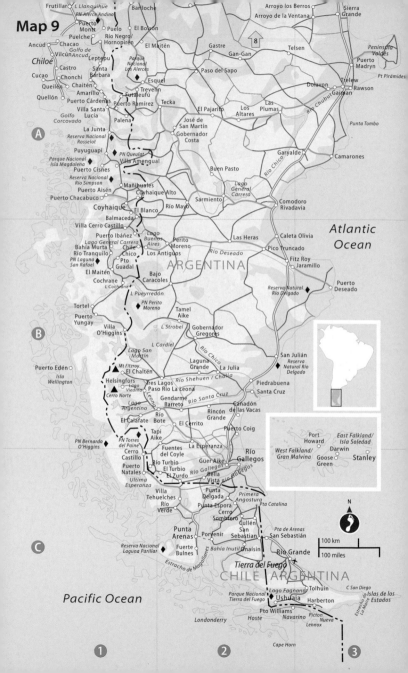

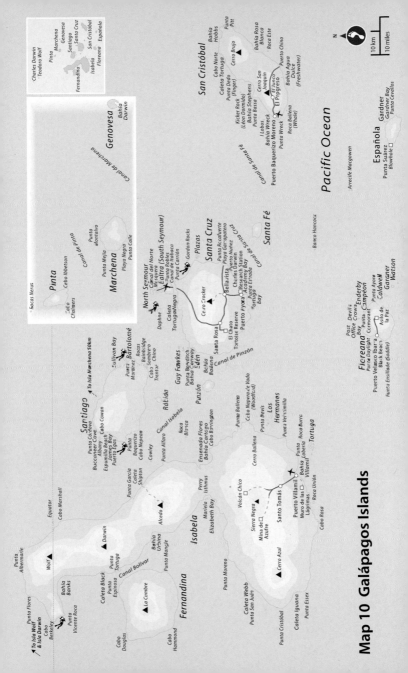

Map 10 Galápagos Islands

Driving distances

Cartagena – Medellín	652
Medellín – Bogotá	440
Bogotá – Ipiales	948
Ipiales/Tulcán – Quito	240
Quito – Guayaquil	420
Guayaquil – Tumbes	280
Tumbes – Lima	1320
Lima - Arequipa	1011
Lima – Cuzco	1105
Arequipa – Cuzco	521
Cuzco - La Paz	651
Lima – Arica	1348
La Paz – Arica	503
Arica – Santiago	2062
Santiago – Puerto Montt	1016
Santiago – Buenos Aires	1129
Buenos Aires – Ushuaia	3070
Buenos Aires - Asunción	1325
Asunción – Foz do Iguaçu	350
Buenos Aires – Montevideo	577
Montevideo - Porto Alegre	867
Porto Alegre - São Paulo	1123
Foz do Iguaçu - São Paulo	1045
São Paulo – Rio de Janeiro	429
Rio de Janeiro – Salvador	1726
Salvador – Belém	2149
Caracas – Manaus	2399
Caracas – Bogotá	1528

Driving distances in kms 1km = 0.62 miles

Map symbols

□	Capital city
○	Other city, town
≈	International border
≈	Regional border
⊖	Customs
◯	Contours (approx)
▲	Mountain, volcano
≒	Mountain pass
⊥⊥	Escarpment
⌣	Glacier
⣿	Salt flat
⣿	Rocks
ᵛᵛᵛ	Seasonal marshland
⣿	Beach, sandbank
⑄	Waterfall
⌒	Reef
▬	Motorway
▬	Main road
▬	Minor road
⁝⁝⁝	Track
⁝⁝⁝⁝	Footpath
▬	Railway
▬■	Railway with station
✈	Airport
🚌	Bus station
Ⓜ	Metro station

- - - -	Cable car
┼┼┼┼	Funicular
⛴	Ferry
▤	Pedestrianized street
⊃⊂	Tunnel
→	One way-street
⣿	Steps
⇌	Bridge
▬▬	Fortified wall
▦	Park, garden, stadium
🛏	Sleeping
❶	Eating
❶	Bars & clubs
▭	Building
†	Sight
⛪	Cathedral, church
⛩	Chinese temple
🛕	Hindu temple
🕉	Meru
🕌	Mosque
△	Stupa
✡	Synagogue
❢	Tourist office
🏛	Museum
✉	Post office
Ⓟᵒ	Police

⑤	Bank
@	Internet
♩	Telephone
🎪	Market
➕	Medical services
Ⓟ	Parking
⛽	Petrol
⛳	Golf
⁂	Archaeological site
♦	National park, wildlife reserve
⚜	Viewing point
Λ	Campsite
⌂	Refuge, lodge
🏯	Castle, fort
🐟	Diving
🌴	Deciduous, coniferous, palm trees
🌿	Mangrove
⌂	Hide
⚑	Vineyard, winery
△	Distillery
⛵	Shipwreck
✕	Historic battlefield
⇨	Related map

Index

Credits

Footprint credits
Editor: Nicola Gibbs
Production and layout: Emma Bryers
Maps: Kevin Feeney
Colour section: Angus Dawson

Publisher: Patrick Dawson
Managing Editor: Felicity Laughton
Advertising: Elizabeth Taylor
Sales and marketing: Kirsty Holmes

Photography credits
Front cover: Photononstop/SuperStock
Back cover: Eye Ubiquitous/SuperStock

Colour section
Page i: Superstock: Minden Pictures/
Minden Pictures
Page ii: Dreamstime: Bevanward/
Dreamstime.com
Page v: Superstock: Minden Pictures/
Minden Pictures
Page vi: Dreamstime: Attila Jandi/
Dreamstime.com; Superstock: imagebroker.
net/Imagebroker.net
Page vii: Superstock: Lazyllama/
Dreamstime.com
Page viii: Superstock: Fabian Michelangeli/
age fotostock
Page ix: Superstock: Jan Sochor/age fotostock
Page x: Superstock: Prisma/Prisma;
Dmitry Pichugin/Dreamstime.com
Page xi: Superstock: Tips Images/
Tips Images; Ian Trower/Robert Harding
Picture Library

Printed in India by Thomson Press Ltd,
Faridabad, Haryana

Publishing information
Footprint South American Handbook
91st edition
© Footprint Handbooks Ltd
October 2014

ISBN: 978 1 910120 026
CIP DATA: A catalogue record for this book
is available from the British Library

® Footprint Handbooks and the Footprint
mark are a registered trademark of
Footprint Handbooks Ltd

Published by Footprint
6 Riverside Court
Lower Bristol Road
Bath BA2 3DZ, UK
T +44 (0)1225 469141
F +44 (0)1225 469461
footprinttravelguides.com

Distributed in the USA by
National Book Network, Inc.

THE GUIDE TO LATIN AMERICA

LATA
LATIN AMERICAN
TRAVEL ASSOCIATION

For a free copy of the LATA Guide
please go to: **WWW.LATA.ORG**

You can also follow us on Twitter: Twitter @latauk